Roget's

INTERNATIONAL

THESAURUS®

Roget's

INTERNATIONAL

THESAURUS®

6

SIXTH EDITION

Edited by Barbara Ann Kipfer, Ph.D.

Robert L. Chapman, Ph.D., Consulting Editor

HarperResource

An Imprint of HarperCollinsPublishers

Lithograph of Peter Mark Roget:
Edward Mansfield Burbank, *Sketches of the Lives & Work of the Honorary Medical
Staff of the Manchester Infirmary, from 1752 to 1830*, Volume 1, 1904. Courtesy of
the New York Public Library.

HarperCollins books may be purchased for educational, business, or sales promotional use. For information please write: Special Markets Department, Harper-
Collins Publishers, Inc., 10 East 53rd Street, New York, NY 10022.

Designed by C. Linda Dingler

Library of Congress Cataloging-in-Publication Data has been applied for.

ISBN 0-06-273693-0 (plain)
0-06-018575-9 (thumb indexed)

01 02 03 04 05 QW 10 9 8 7 6 5 4 3 2 1

Contents

P. M. Roget

Peter Mark Roget

1779–1869

The author of the "Treasury of Words" could hardly have thought that his name would become forever associated with a particular book, even though he hoped that he was suggesting a unique way of utilizing the richness and flexibility of the English language. But for more than 150 years Roget's work has been the constant companion of all those who aspire to use the language most effectively.

The career of Peter Mark Roget prior to the publication of his *Thesaurus* in 1852, when he was seventy-three years old, while largely devoted to science and to medicine, required of him a facility with words in the delivery of ideas and concepts. A lifetime of secretaryships for several learned societies had thoroughly familiarized him with the need for clarity and forcefulness of expression. That he was justified in his concept is made obvious by the universal acceptance of his thesaurus as an indispensable tool for all those who wish to write and speak with eloquence.

Born in London the son of a Protestant pastor who died at an early age, Roget was raised by his mother. He studied at the University of Edinburgh from 1793 to 1798 and received an M.D. after his successful defense of his Latin thesis dealing with the laws of chemical affinity. He was, however, too late to share in that institution's happy days as a stunning example of the Scottish Enlightenment. He was not to know William Cullen, the great nosologist, nor Alexander Monro primus, who brought Hermann Boerhaave's ethos of a medical school from Leyden; but he did learn anatomy from Monro secundus and medicine from John Gregory. The bright stars of David Hume, denied professorship at the university for his radical thinking, and of Adam Smith had long since blazed across the Scottish intellectual world. Moreover, Roget was too early for Sir James Young Simpson and chloroform, or for the dexterous Syme, who was mentor and father-in-law to the great Lord Lister. While Roget was in Edinburgh, the soil was being prepared for the phenomenon of Paris Medicine, the next wave of medical advance, which would be built on the ruins of the French Revolution.

After his graduation, the young physician looked about for the connections he would need to launch a medical career. In this he was fortunate in having the concerned attention of his uncle, Sir Samuel Romilly, whose own promising political potential, shortened by his suicide, provided an entrée to certain segments of English scientific and intellectual life. Through his uncle, Roget was introduced to Lord Lansdowne, for whom he served briefly as personal physician, and to Jeremy Bentham. On his own initiative, Roget spent some time in Bristol in Thomas Beddoes's Pneumatic Institute, devoted to the treatment of human illness using various gases. There he may have met illustrious figures Humphry Davy, James Watt, Samuel Taylor Coleridge, William Wordsworth, and Robert Southey.

In the midst of his desultory round of attendance at lectures and dispensary duties, Roget learned that his uncle had maneuvered for him an opportunity to tutor two scions of a wealthy Manchester manufacturer on a grand tour of Europe. The Peace of Amiens had been signed in 1802, and Continental travel was once again open to English families anxious to provide their children with the advantages of foreign scenes.

Roget was twenty-three when he shepherded his charges across the English Channel and on to Paris, where they entered into the round of parties and dinners opened to them through letters from Sir Samuel and from the boys' family. But there was more than that. Roget hired a French tutor and supervised his charges' studies in mathematics, chemistry, and geology. He also saw to it that there were the obligatory trips to museums as well as to the theater and that the boys wrote their impressions and comments after each visit.

The little party pushed on to Geneva, not without encountering obstructions, delays, and disappointments injected by the French bureaucracy. In Geneva, although the city had recently been annexed by Napoleon, the group felt secure enough to settle down to a life of studies, parties, and local sight-seeing. The respite was short-lived, however. The Peace of Amiens was abrogated by Napoleon in 1803, and the position of any Englishman in French territory was in doubt. Warned by Madame de Staël that he faced internment, Roget undertook to establish for himself Genevan citizenship on the basis of his father's birth in that city. Through prodigious effort and resourcefulness remarkable in so young a man, Roget sneaked the party, dressed as peasants, into Germany. He was successful in making his way to Denmark and thence to England, delivering his charges back to their family.

Manchester now offered the best opportunity to establish a medical practice, since Roget could count on the support of the wealthy Philips family, whose sons had shared his French experience. He quickly became associated with the local infirmary and with the Manchester Literary and Philosophical Society, before which body he gave a series of lectures on physiology that historians credit as forming the basis of what became the School of Medicine in that city. As D. L. Emblen points out in his biography of Roget, "[he] showed that his chief interest in the new science of physiology lay in the organization and order of several aspects of that subject and in the relationship of the subject to such kindred fields as anatomy" (D. L. Emblen, *Peter Mark Roget: The Word and the Man*, New York: Thomas Crowell, 1970, p. 96). It was Roget's meticulous, precise way of looking at order, at plan, and at interdependence in animal economy that would eventually find expression in his unique and practical lexicographic experiment.

But the great metropolis beckoned, and the young physician finally decided on a London career. Roget was never outstandingly successful as a medical practitioner. He had, however, become associated with the establishment of the Northern Dispensary, the quintessential Victorian expression of medical charity, to which he devoted a lifetime of practice. Roget's métier was teaching and institutional activities. He lectured in the Theory and Practice of Physic at the Great Windmill Street School, which served as the school of anatomy of Middlesex Hospital before that institution was eclipsed by the new University College on Gower Street. The Medical and Chirurgical Society, founded to bridge the gap between medicine and surgery, commanded much of Roget's attention during his London days. He served as the society's secretary for twelve years and contributed to its journal, *Transactions*. In 1814 he became a fellow in the Royal Society on the basis of a paper he wrote describing a forerunner of the slide rule. He contributed many articles to the *Encyclopaedia Britannica* that were carried through several editions. In those pages he crossed swords with George Combe, the ardent promoter of phrenology, a discipline which Roget could not support. While serving as secretary of the Royal Society he wrote the Bridgewater Treatise of Physiology, which demonstrated anew Roget's ability to organize and classify the essentials of a rapidly developing science.

Although extremely occupied during these years, as a list of his extensive memberships in scientific and cultural organizations shows, Roget seems never to have captured the attention of his peers to the extent that many of his contemporaries enjoyed. There is a hint that he was always just below the top rank, never in the front. It was, after all, an age of giants, and to be even in the midst of all that ferment was remarkable enough. His active public life came to an end when he was eased out of the secretaryship of the Royal Society after a conflict over the operation of the library, and was literally forced into retirement.

An inactive retirement was not compatible with Roget's lifestyle. Since childhood, putting ideas and concepts in writing had been second nature to him. He dwelt in a world of language, and his orderly, systematic mind lent itself to classification. More than a list of synonyms, more than a dictionary, the thesaurus Roget devised and constantly improved upon during this time was a unique ordering of the English language to be used by those desiring to impart an exacting and felicitous tone to written or spoken material. Grouped by ideas rather than by a mere alphabetical listing, the thesaurus enabled the user to find the exact word or phrase needed for a specific purpose. Roget had been keeping such a word list for many years. He now proposed to enlarge it and present it to the world of users of the English language.

The success of this venture was never in doubt. Roget supervised some twenty-five editions and printings of the thesaurus and was actively at work on his masterpiece when he died in 1869 at the age of ninety. *Roget's International Thesaurus*® continues to be issued. For all those who deal with words and with ideas as expressed in words it has become indispensable. It remains a monument of scholarship and a tribute to the industry and breadth of knowledge of one of the lesser-known Victorian greats.

DONALD F. KENT, M.D.

How to Use This Book

Like other great reference books, *Roget's International Thesaurus*® is the product of continuous improvement and long-term investment by its editors. The process began almost two centuries ago, in 1805, when Dr. Peter Mark Roget began compiling a list of useful words for his own convenience.

The revolutionary achievement of Dr. Roget was his development of a brand-new principle: *the grouping of words according to ideas*. If the user cannot find something in a reference book, it is often because of the restriction of searching alphabetically by "known" headwords. Dr. Roget's thesaurus reversed the access to allow the user to find a word from another word, or a concept or idea. When in 1852 Roget published the first book ever to realize this concept with thoroughness and precision, he called it a *thesaurus* (from the Greek and Latin, meaning "treasury" or "storehouse"). And *thesaurus* it has remained to this day.

So successful was Roget's *Thesaurus of English Words and Phrases, Classified and Arranged so as to Facilitate the Expression of Ideas and Assist in Literary Composition* that a second edition followed one year later in 1853. By Dr. Roget's death in 1869 there had been no fewer than twenty-eight editions and printings.

Each subsequent edition introduced more efficient and useful features, all of which have contributed to the quality of the present edition. Over the years, tens of thousands of new words and phrases were added, the coverage of foreign expressions increased, and the scope of the book expanded to include slang and useful quotations: a recent innovation was the numbering of the paragraphs for the user's convenience. By 1992, when the fifth edition was published by HarperCollins, *Roget's International Thesaurus*® had become a greatly expanded and improved book, yet one which still retained Roget's brilliant organization.

The sixth edition of *Roget's International Thesaurus®*, prepared by Barbara Ann Kipfer, Ph.D., along with consulting editor Robert L. Chapman, has a text of about 330,000 words and phrases, arranged in categories by their meanings, and a comprehensive index.

The search for a word that you need is a simple, two-step process that begins in the index. Suppose that you want a word to describe something that first occurred in the past:

Step 1. In the index, look up the word *first* and pick the subentry closest to the meaning you want, which would likely be "previous."

Step 2. Follow its number (834.4) into the text of the thesaurus and you will find a whole paragraph of adjectives starting with **previous, prior, early.**

firmament 1072.2

first
  n baseball 745.1
  first ever 818.3
  adj leading 165.3
  front 216.10
  chief 249.14
  preceding 814.4
  beginning 818
  foremost 818.17
  previous 834.4
  novel 841.11
  adv before 216.12
  preferably 371.28
  firstly 818.18
first aid 91.14
first base 745.1
first-born
  n senior 304.5
  adj older 842.19
first-class
  superlative 249.13
  first-rate 999.17

834 PREVIOUSNESS
NOUNS **1 previousness, earliness 845, antecedence** *or* antecedency, priority, anteriority, precedence *or* precedency 814, precession; *status quo ante* <L>, previous *or* prior state, earlier state; preexistence; **anticipation,** predating, antedating; antedate; **past time 837.1**
  2 antecedent, precedent, premise; forerunner, **precursor 816,** ancestor
VERBS **3 be prior,** be before *or* early *or* earlier, come on the scene *or* appear earlier, **precede, antecede, forerun,** come *or* go before, set a precedent; **herald,** usher in, proclaim, announce; **anticipate,** antedate, predate; **preexist**

ADJS **4 previous, prior, early 845.7, earlier,** *ci-devant or ci-dessus* <Fr>, **former,** fore, prime, first, **preceding 165.3,** foregoing, above, anterior, **anticipatory,** antecedent; **preexistent;** older, elder, senior

Tracking down words in this way is the most obvious and direct use of the thesaurus. However, there are other ways in which the unique features of *Roget's International Thesaurus®* will help you solve word problems.

The thesaurus is a device for finding specific words or phrases for general ideas. A dictionary will tell you many things about a word—spelling, pronunciation, meaning, and origins. You use a thesaurus when you have an idea but do not know, or cannot remember, the word or phrase that expresses it best or when you want a more accurate or effective way of saying what you mean. A thesaurus gives you possibilities, and you choose the one that you think is best within your particular context. The range of possibilities includes not only meaning as we usually think of it, but the special sense and force given by nonformal words and phrases (slang and informal), of which many are included and labeled.

Roget's International Thesaurus® is an efficient word-finder because it has a structure especially designed to stimulate thought and help you organize your ideas. The backbone of this structure is the ingenious overall arrangement of the main categories. The plan is outlined in the "Synopsis of Categories," which begins on page xix. To make good use of the thesaurus's structure all you need to remember is that it contains many sequences of closely related categories. Beginning at 48, for example, you will see **HEARING, DEAFNESS, SOUND, SILENCE, FAINTNESS OF SOUND, LOUDNESS,** etc., a procession of similar, contrasting, and opposing concepts, all dealing with the perception and quality of sounds. So when you are not quite satisfied with what you find in one place, glance at nearby categories too; it may be that your original intention was not the best. If you are having trouble framing a thought in a positive way, you may find that it can be more effectively expressed negatively. Seeing related terms, and antonyms, often opens up lines of thought and chains of association that had not occurred to you.

You will already have noticed that the large categories of ideas are numbered in sequence; there are 1,075 of them in this edition of *Roget's International Thesaurus*®. Within each category the terms are presented in short paragraphs by basic meaning, and these are also numbered. References from the index to the text are made with two-part numbers such as 247.4, the first part being the number of the main category, the second the number of the paragraph within that category. This system, unique to this book, makes for quick and easy pinpointing of the place where you will find the words you need.

The terms within a category are organized also by part of speech, in this order: nouns, verbs, adjectives, adverbs, prepositions, conjunctions, and interjections. When you are casting about for a way of saying something, rather than looking for a specific word, do not limit your search to the narrow area of the category suggested by the index reference, but examine the offerings in all parts of speech.

There is a further refinement of word arrangement. The sequence of terms within a paragraph, far from being random, is determined by close, semantic relationships. The words closest in meaning are offered in clusters that are set off with semicolons; the semicolon signals a slight change in sense or application. A close examination of the clusters will make you aware of the fine distinctions between synonyms, and you will soon recognize that few words are exactly interchangeable. As an aid in focusing on the *right* word, terms with special uses are identified by labels in angle brackets—such as the label <nf> for nonformal terms, <Fr> for French terms, or <pl> for plural. A full list of the abbreviations often used within brackets can be found on page xxvi.

The connector "and" is used to group things so as to avoid using a label (say, <nf>) for each individual item. The connector "or" is used similarly to avoid needless repetition of a term that can be used with several modifiers.

Cross references also are an important feature of the text. They suggest additional meanings of the words you are examining. Notice, too, that the paragraphs of text are highlighted with terms in boldface type. The boldfaced words are those most commonly used for the idea at hand.

"Word elements," such as prefixes, suffixes, and combining forms, are listed when helpful after the final text paragraph of the category, and before any word lists.

The use of an appropriate quotation often enlivens one's prose. Here, again, *Roget's International Thesaurus*® can help you, for it contains hundreds of such quotes on scores of subjects. Another useful feature of the thesaurus is its word lists. These contain the names of specific things—animals, plants, measurements, and many other entities—few of which have synonyms. The lists can save you many excursions to specialized reference books.

Thus, *Roget's International Thesaurus*® can help you in countless ways to improve your writing and speech and to enrich your active vocabulary. But you should remember the caution that very few words are true synonyms: use the thesaurus in conjunction with a good dictionary whenever a selected word or phrase is unfamiliar to you.

Peter Roget's Preface
to the First Edition
(1852)

It is now nearly fifty years since I first projected a system of verbal classification similar to that on which the present work is founded. Conceiving that such a compilation might help to supply my own deficiencies, I had, in the year 1805, completed a classed catalog of words on a small scale, but on the same principle, and nearly in the same form, as the Thesaurus now published. I had often during that long interval found this little collection, scanty and imperfect as it was, of much use to me in literary composition, and often contemplated its extension and improvement; but a sense of the magnitude of the task, amidst a multitude of other avocations, deterred me from the attempt. Since my retirement from the duties of Secretary of the Royal Society, however, finding myself possessed of more leisure, and believing that a repertory of which I had myself experienced the advantage might, when amplified, prove useful to others, I resolved to embark in an undertaking which, for the last three or four years, has given me incessant occupation, and has, indeed, imposed upon me an amount of labor very much greater than I had anticipated. Notwithstanding all the pains I have bestowed on its execution, I am fully aware of its numerous deficiencies and imperfections, and of its falling far short of the degree of excellence that might be attained. But, in a work of this nature, where perfection is placed at so great a distance, I have thought it best to limit my ambition to that moderate share of merit which it may claim in its present form; trusting to the indulgence of those for whose benefit it is intended, and to the candor of critics who, while they find it easy to detect faults, can at the same time duly appreciate difficulties.

P. M. ROGET

April 29, 1852

Foreword

by Barbara Ann Kipfer, Ph.D.

In developing this new edition, I chose to focus on the modernity and scope of the language coverage. We live in the Internet age, making *Roget's International Thesaurus®* ever more valuable. It can now be used in the wording of queries for search engines accessing the World Wide Web. To this end, I have included as many new words and phrases as possible, from general vocabulary to scientific and technological terms.

The lists have been revised to add new terms, delete obsolete ones, and expand treatment. Quotations were retained if they could conceivably be valuable in a user's writings. Otherwise, unuseful quotations and outdated terms were set aside to make room for new synonyms, additional synonyms, and new lists.

I wish to acknowledge the help, support, and guidance of Dr. Robert L. Chapman. I am honored to have been his choice of successor.

I also thank John Atkins for his work in preparing the computerized manuscript. My editor, Greg Chaput, has worked hard to bring the project to fruition—and a successful publication. George Alexander and Donna Ruvituso have done a wonderful job putting this all together technologically and typographically. There was also a helpful list of errors in the previous edition, contributed by Dr. Tracy Mansfield of International Neural Machines.

No one is luckier than I to have the time and the environment I need to complete such a massive undertaking. To that I owe gratitude to my husband and frequent collaborator, Paul Magoulas. To him and to my sons, Kyle and Keir, I would like to repay their love and encouragement.

BARBARA ANN KIPFER, PH.D.

June 1, 2001

Synopsis of Categories

Abbreviations Used in This Book

ADJS	adjectives		Ital	Italy, Italian
ADVS	adverbs		L	Latin
Anon	anonymous		masc	masculine
Arab	Arabic		N	North, Northern
Austral	Australia, Australian		nf	nonformal usage
Brazil Pg	Brazilian Portuguese		Norw	Norway, Norwegian
Brit	British		old	older usage
Can	Canada, Canadian		Pg	Portugal, Portuguese
Can Fr	Canadian French		PHRS	phrases
Chin	China, Chinese		pl	plural
CONJ	conjunction		Pol	Poland, Polish
Cz	Czechoslovakian		PREP	preposition
Dan	Danish		Russ	Russia, Russian
E	East, Eastern		S	South, Southern
Eng	England, English		Scot	Scotland, Scottish
etc	et cetera		sing	singular
fem	feminine		Skt	Sanskrit
Fr	France, French		Sp	Spanish
Ger	Germany, German		Sp Amer	Spanish American
Gk	Greece, Greek		Swah	Swahili
gram	grammar		Swed	Sweden, Swedish
Heb	Hebrew		Turk	Turkey, Turkish
Hindu	Hinduism		UN	United Nations
Hung	Hungary, Hungarian		US	United States
INTERJS	interjections		W	West, Western
Ir	Ireland, Irish			

1 BIRTH

NOUNS **1 birth,** genesis, **nativity,** nascency, **childbirth, childbearing, having a baby, giving birth, birthing,** parturition, biogenesis, blessed event, the stork <nf>; **confinement,** lying-in, being brought to bed, **childbed,** *accouchement* <Fr>; **labor,** travail, birth throes *or* pangs; **delivery,** blessed event <nf>; the Nativity; multiparity; **hatching;** littering, whelping, farrowing; active birth, alternative birth

VERBS **2 be born,** have birth, come forth, issue forth, see the light of day, come into the world; **hatch;** be illegitimate *or* born out of wedlock, have the bar sinister; be born on the wrong side of the blanket, come in through a side door <nf>

3 give birth, bear, bear *or* have young, **have; have a baby,** bear a child, have children; drop, cast, throw, pup, whelp, kitten, foal, calve, fawn, lamb, cub, yean, farrow, litter, spawn, lay eggs; lie in, be confined, labor, travail

ADJS **4 born,** given birth; **hatched;** bred, begotten, cast, dropped, whelped, foaled, calved, etc; "cast naked upon the naked earth"—Pliny the Elder; née; newborn; stillborn; **bearing,** giving birth

2 THE BODY

NOUNS **1 body,** the person, carcass, anatomy, frame, bodily *or* corporal *or* corporeal entity, physical self, physical *or* bodily structure, physique, soma, somatotype, bod <nf>; organism, organic complex, flesh and blood <nf>; the material *or* physical part

2 the skeleton, the bones, one's bones, framework, frame, structure, bony framework, endoskeleton; axial skeleton, appendicular skeleton, visceral skeleton; rib cage; skeletology; **bone** <see list>; cartilage

3 the muscles <see list>, myon, voluntary muscle, involuntary muscle; **musculature,** physique; **connective tissue,** connectivum; sinew, tendon, ligament, cartilage

4 the skin, skin, dermis, integument, **epidermis,** scarfskin, ecderon; hypodermis, hypoderma; dermis, derma, corium, true skin, cutis, *cutis vera* <L>; epithelium, pavement epithelium; endothelium; mesoderm; endoderm, entoderm; blastoderm; ectoderm, epiblast, ectoblast; enderon; connective tissue

5 <castoff skin> slough, cast, desquamation, exuviae, molt

6 membrane, membrana, pellicle, chorion; basement membrane, membrana propria; allantoic membrane; amnion, amniotic sac, arachnoid membrane; serous membrane, serosa, membrana serosa; **eardrum,** tympanic membrane, tympanum, membrana tympana; **mucous membrane; velum; peritoneum;** periosteum; pleura; pericardium; meninx, **meninges;** perineurium, neurilemma; conjunctiva; **hymen** *or* maidenhead

7 member, appendage, external organ; head, noggin *and* noodle <nf>; **arm;** forearm; wrist; elbow; upper arm, biceps; **leg,** limb, shank, gam *and* pin <nf>, legs, wheels <nf>; shin, cnemis; ankle, tarsus; calf; knee; thigh, ham; popliteal space; **hand,** paw <nf>, finger; **foot,** dog *and* puppy <nf>, toe

8 teeth, dentition, ivories *and* choppers <nf>, pearly whites; periodontal tissue, alveolar ridge, alveolus; **tooth,** fang, tusk; snag, snaggletooth, peg; bucktooth, gagtooth *or* gang tooth <nf>; pivot tooth; cuspid, bicuspid; canine tooth, canine, dogtooth, eyetooth, carnassial, tush <nf>; molar, grinder; premolar; incisor, cutter, fore-tooth; wisdom tooth; milk tooth, baby tooth, deciduous tooth; permanent tooth; crown, cusp, dentine, enamel

9 eye, visual organ, organ of vision, oculus, optic, **orb,** peeper <nf>; clear eyes, bright eyes, starry orbs; saucer eyes, banjo eyes <nf>, popeyes, goggle eyes; naked eye, unassisted *or* unaided eye; corner of the eye; epicanthus, epicanthic fold; eyeball; retina; lens; cornea; sclera; optic nerve; iris; pupil; eyelid, lid, nictitating membrane; choroid coat, aqueous humor, vitreous humor

10 ear, auditory apparatus, hearing organ, lug <Scot>; external ear, **outer ear;** auricle, pinna; tragus; cauliflower ear; concha, conch, shell; ear lobe, lobe, lobule; auditory canal, acoustic *or* auditory meatus; helix; **middle ear,** tympanic cavity, tympanum; eardrum, drumhead, tympanic membrane; auditory ossicles; malleus, hammer, incus, anvil; stapes, stirrup; mastoid process; eustachian *or* auditory tube; **inner ear;** round window, secondary eardrum; oval window; bony labyrinth, membraneous labyrinth, utricle; perilymph, endolymph; vestibule; semicircular canals; cochlea; basilar membrane, organ of Corti; auditory *or* acoustic nerve

11 nose, nasal organ, snout, smeller, proboscis, beak, schnoz <nf>; nostril, naris, nasal cavity; olfactory nerve

12 mouth, oral cavity; lips, tongue, taste buds; mandible, jaw; gums, periodontal tissue; uvula; teeth

13 genitals, genitalia, sex organs, reproductive organs, pudenda, private parts, privy parts, privates *or* meat <nf>; **crotch,** crutch <Brit>, pubic region, perineum, pelvis; **male organs; penis, phallus,** *lingam* <Skt>, glans penis; gonads;

testes, testicles, balls *and* nuts *and* rocks *and* ballocks *and* family jewels <nf>, cullions <old>; spermary; scrotum, bag *and* basket <nf>, cod <old>; vas deferens; **female organs; vulva,** *yoni* <Skt>, cunt <nf>; **vagina;** clitoris, glans clitoridis; labia, labia majora, labia minora, lips, nymphae; cervix; ovary; uterus, womb, fallopian tubes; secondary sex characteristic, mons pubis, mons veneris, pubic hair, beard, breasts

14 **nervous system, nerves,** central nervous system, peripheral nervous system; autonomic nervous system; sympathetic *or* thoracolumbar nervous system, parasympathetic *or* craniosacral nervous system; **nerve; neuron;** nerve cell, sensory *or* afferent neuron, sensory cell; motor *or* afferent neuron; association *or* internuncial neuron; axon, dendrite, myelin *or* medullary sheath; **synapse;** effector organ; nerve trunk; **ganglion;** plexus, solar plexus; **spinal cord**

15 **brain,** encephalon; cerebrum, cerebellum

16 **viscera, vitals, internal organs, insides, innards** <nf>, entrails, inwards, internals, thoracic viscera, abdominal viscera; inner mechanism, works <nf>; peritoneum, peritoneal cavity; **guts** *and* kishkes *and* giblets <nf>; **heart,** ticker *and* pump <nf>, endocardium, atria, ventricles, aorta; **lung, lungs; liver;** gallbladder; spleen; pancreas; **kidney, kidneys;** urethra

17 **digestion,** ingestion, assimilation, absorption; primary digestion, secondary digestion, peristalsis; predigestion; salivary digestion, gastric *or* peptic digestion, pancreatic digestion, intestinal digestion; digestive system, alimentary canal, gastrointestinal tract; salivary glands, gastric glands, liver, pancreas; digestive secretions, saliva, gastric juice, pancreatic juice, intestinal juice, bile

18 <digestive system> mouth, maw, salivary glands; gullet, crop, craw, **throat,** pharynx; esophagus, gorge, weasand <old>, wizen <Brit nf>; fauces, isthmus of the fauces; **abdomen; stomach, belly** <nf>, **midriff,** diaphragm; swollen *or* distended *or* protruding *or* prominent belly, *embonpoint* <Fr>, **paunch,** ventripotence; underbelly; pylorus; **intestine, intestines,** entrails, **bowels;** small intestine, villus, odenum, jejunum, ileum; blind gut, cecum; foregut, hindgut; midgut, mesogaster; **appendix,** vermiform appendix *or* process; large intestine, colon, sigmoid flexure, rectum; anus

19 <nf terms> goozle, guzzle; tum, tummy, tum-tum, breadbasket, **gut,** bulge, fallen chest, corporation, spare tire, bay window, **pot,** potbelly, potgut, beerbelly, German *or* Milwaukee goiter, pusgut, swagbelly; **guts,** tripes, stuffings

20 **metabolism,** metabolic process; basal metabolism, acid-base metabolism, energy metabolism;

anabolism, substance metabolism, constructive metabolism, assimilation; **catabolism,** destructive metabolism, disassimilation; endogenous metabolism, exogenous metabolism; pharmacokinetic metabolism; uricotelic metabolism; metabolic rate

21 **breathing, respiration,** aspiration, **inspiration, inhalation; expiration, exhalation;** insufflation, exsufflation; **breath,** wind, breath of air; pant, puff; wheeze, asthmatic wheeze; broken wind; gasp, gulp; snoring, snore, stertor; sniff, sniffle, snuff, snuffle; sigh, suspiration; sneeze, sternutation; cough, hack; hiccup; **artificial respiration,** kiss of life, mouth-to-mouth resuscitation

22 <respiratory system> **lungs,** bellows <nf>, lights <old>; diaphragm; **windpipe, trachea,** weasand <old>, wizen <Brit nf>; bronchus, bronchi <pl>, bronchial tube; epiglottis

23 **duct, vessel,** canal, passage; gland; vasculature, vascularity, vascularization; vas, meatus; thoracic duct, lymphatic; emunctory <old>; pore; urethra, urete; vagina; oviduct, fallopian tube; salpinx; eustachian tube; ostium; fistula; **blood vessel; artery,** aorta, pulmonary artery, carotid; **vein,** jugular vein, vena cava, pulmonary vein; portal vein, varicose vein; venation; **capillary;** arteriole, veinlet, veinule, venule

24 <body fluids> humor, **lymph,** chyle, choler, yellow bile, black bile; rheum; serous fluid, serum; plasma; **pus, matter,** purulence, peccant humor <old>; suppuration; ichor, sanies; discharge; gleet, leukorrhea, the whites; mucus; **phlegm,** snot <nf>; **saliva, spit** <nf>; **urine, piss** <nf>; **perspiration, sweat** <nf>; **tear,** teardrop, lachryma; **milk,** mother's milk, colostrum, lactation; **semen;** cerumen, earwax

25 **blood,** whole blood, lifeblood, venous blood, arterial blood, **gore;** ichor, humor; grume; **serum,** blood serum; blood substitute; **plasma,** synthetic plasma, plasma substitute, dextran, clinical dextran; **blood cell** *or* **corpuscle,** hemocyte; **red corpuscle** *or* **blood cell,** erythrocyte; **white corpuscle** *or* **blood cell,** leukocyte, blood platelet; **hemoglobin;** blood pressure; circulation; **blood group** *or* **type,** type O *or* A *or* B *or* AB; Rh-type, Rh-positive, Rh-negative; **Rh factor** *or* Rhesus factor; antigen, antibody, isoantibody, globulin; opsonin; blood grouping; blood count; hematoscope, hematoscopy, hemometer; bloodstream

ADJS 26 **skeleton, skeletal; bone,** osteal; **bony,** osseous, ossiferous; ossicular; ossified; **spinal,** myelic; **muscle, muscular,** myoid; cartilage, cartilaginous

27 **cutaneous,** cuticular; skinlike, skinny; skin-deep; **epidermal,** epidermic, ecderonic; hypodermic,

hypodermal, subcutaneous; dermal, dermic; ectodermal, ectodermic; endermic, endermatic; cortical; epicarpal; testaceous; membranous

28 eye, optic, ophthalmic; visual; **ear,** otic; aural

29 genital; phallic, penile, penial; testicular; scrotal; spermatic, seminal; vulvar, vulval; vaginal; clitoral; cervical; ovarian; uterine; reproductive, generative, hormonal

30 nerve, neural; brain, cerebral, cerebellar, nervous, synaptic

31 digestive; stomachal, stomachic, abdominal; ventral, celiac, **gastric,** ventricular; big-bellied 257.18; **metabolic,** basal metabolic, anabolic, catabolic; assimilative, dissimilative

32 respiratory, breathing; inspiratory, expiratory; nasal, rhinal; bronchial, tracheal; **lung,** pulmonary, pulmonic, pneumonic; puffing, huffing, snorting, wheezing, wheezy, asthmatic, stertorous, snoring, panting, heaving; sniffy, sniffly, sniffling, snuffy, snuffly, snuffling; sneezy, sternutative, sternutatory, errhine

33 circulatory, vascular, vascularized, circulating; vasiform; venous, veinal, venose; capillary; arterial, aortic; **blood,** hematal, hematic; bloody, gory, sanguinary; lymphatic, rheumy, humoral, phlegmy, ichorous, serous, sanious; chylific, chylifactive, chylifactory; **pussy,** purulent, suppurated or suppurating, suppurative; teary, tearing, tearlike, **lachrymal,** lacrimal, lacrimatory; mucous; sweaty, perspiring; urinary

34 bones

acetabelum
aitchbone
alveolar bone
anklebone
anvil
astragalus or anklebone
backbone or spine or spinal
  column or myel
basilar or basioccipital
  bone
breastbone or sternum
calcaneus
calf bone or fibula
cannon bone
carpal or carpus
cheekbone
chin
clavicle
coccyx
collarbone
costa
cranial bones
cranium
cuboid
edgebone
ethmoid bone

femur
fibula
floating rib
frontal bone
funny or crazy bone
gladiolus
hallux
hammer
haunch bone
heel bone
hipbone
humerus
hyoid or lingual bone
ilium
incus
inferior maxillary
innominate bone
intermaxillary or
  premaxillary or incisive
  bone
interparietal or incarial
  bone
ischium
kneecap or patella or whirl
  bone
lacrimal bone

lenticular bone or os
  orbiculare
lentiform or pisiform or
  postular bone
malar or zygomatic bone
malleus
mandible and maxilla or
  jawbones
mastoid
maxillary
metacarpal or metacarpus
metatarsal or metatarsus
multangular bone large or
  trapezium
multangular bone small or
  trapezoid
nasal bone
occipital bone
palate bone
parietal bone
patella
pelvis
periotic bone or otocrane
petrosal or petrous bone
phalanx or phalanges <pl>
pterygoid bone
pubis
pyramidal bone or os
  triquetrum

rachidial
rachis or vertebral
  column
radius
rib
sacrum or resurrection
  bone
scaphoid bone
scapula
semilunar bone
sesamoid bones
shinbone
shoulder blade
skull
sphenoid bone
stapes
sternum
stirrup
sutural or wormian bone
talus
tarsal or tarsus
temporal bone
thighbone or femur
tibia
ulna
vertebra
vomer
wristbone
zygomatic

35 muscles

abdominal
anterior tibial
biceps brachii
biceps femoris
crural ligaments
  soleus
deltoid
erector
external oblique
extensor
fascia lata
flexor
gastrocnemius
gluteus maximus

gracilis
hamstring
latissimus dorsi
pectoralis major
pectoralis minor
quadriceps
rectus abdominis
rectus femoris
rotator cuff
sartorius
sternomastoid
tendon of Achilles
trapezius
triceps brachii

3 HAIR

NOUNS **1 hairiness, shagginess,** hirsuteness, pilosity, fuzziness, frizziness, **furriness,** downiness, fluffiness, woolliness, fleeciness, bristliness, stubbliness, burrheadedness, mopheadedness, shockheadedness; crinosity, hispidity, villosity; hypertrichosis, pilosis, pilosism, pilosity

2 hair, pile, **fur** 4.2, coat, pelt, **fleece,** wool, camel's hair, horsehair; **mane;** shag, tousled or matted hair, **mat of hair;** pubescence, pubes, pubic hair; hairlet, villus, capillament, cilium, ciliolum 271.1; seta, setula; bristle 288.3

3 gray hair, grizzle, silver *or* silvery hair, white hair, salt-and-pepper hair *or* beard, graying temples, "hoary hair"—Thomas Gray, "the silver livery of advised age"—Shakespeare, "a crown of glory"—Bible

4 **head of hair,** head, crine; **crop,** crop of hair, mat, elflock, **thatch,** mop, **shock,** shag, fleece, **mane; locks, tresses,** crowning glory, helmet of hair; "her native ornament of hair"—Ovid

5 **lock, tress;** flowing locks, flowing tresses; **curl, ringlet,** "wanton ringlets wav'd"—Milton; earlock, *payess* <Yiddish>; lovelock; frizz, frizzle; crimp; ponytail

6 **tuft, flock,** fleck; forelock, widow's peak, quiff <Brit>, fetlock, cowlick; **bang, bangs,** fringe

7 **braid,** plait, twist; **pigtail,** rat's-tail *or* rat-tail, tail; **queue,** cue; coil, knot; topknot, scalplock, pigtail, bunches; bun, chignon; widow's peak

8 **beard, whiskers;** beaver <nf>; full beard, chin whiskers, side whiskers; **sideburns,** burnsides, **muttonchops; goatee,** tuft; imperial, **Vandyke,** spade beard; adolescent beard, pappus, down, peach fuzz, "the soft down of manhood"—Callimachus, "his phoenix down"—Shakespeare; **stubble,** bristles, five o'clock shadow

9 <plant beard> awn, brush, arista, pile, pappus

10 <animal and insect whiskers> tactile process, tactile hair, **feeler, antenna,** vibrissa; barb, barbel, barbule; cat whisker

11 **mustache,** mustachio, soup-strainer <nf>, toothbrush, handle bars *or* handlebar mustache, Fu Manchu mustache, Zapata mustache, walrus mustache, tash <nf>

12 **eyelashes, lashes,** cilia; **eyebrows,** brows

13 false hair, hair extensions, switch, fall, chignon, rat <nf>

14 **wig, peruke, toupee,** hairpiece, rug *and* divot *and* doormat <nf>; **periwig**

15 **hairdo, hairstyle, haircut, coiffure,** coif, headdress; wave; marcel, marcel wave; **permanent,** permanent wave; home permanent; cold wave; blow-drying, finger-drying; hair dryer

16 **feather, plume,** pinion; **quill;** pinfeather; contour feather, penna, down feather, plume feather, plumule; filoplume; hackle; scapular; **crest,** tuft, topknot; panache

17 <parts of feathers> quill, calamus, barrel; barb, shaft, barbule, barbicel, cilium, filament, filamentule

18 **plumage, feathers,** feather, feathering; contour feathers; breast feathers, mail <of a hawk>; hackle; flight feathers; remiges, primaries, secondaries, tertiaries; covert, tectrices; speculum, wing bay

19 **down, fluff,** flue, floss, **fuzz, fur,** pile; eiderdown, eider; swansdown; thistledown; lint

VERBS 20 grow *or* sprout hair; whisker, **bewhisker**

21 **feather, fledge,** feather out; sprout wings

22 cut *or* dress the hair, trim, **barber, coiffure,** coif, style *or* shape the hair; pompadour, wave, marcel; process, conk; **bob, shingle**

ADJS 23 **hairlike,** trichoid, capillary; filamentous, filamentary, filiform; bristlelike 288.10

24 **hairy, hirsute,** barbigerous, crinose, crinite, pubescent; pilose, pilous, pileous, **furry,** furred; villous; villose; ciliate, cirrose; hispid, hispidulous, setal; **woolly, fleecy,** lanate, lanated, flocky, flocculent, floccose; woolly-headed, woolly-haired, ulotrichous; bushy, tufty, **shaggy,** shagged; matted, tomentose; mopheaded, burrheaded, shockheaded, unshorn; **bristly** 288.9; fuzzy

25 **bearded,** whiskered, whiskery, **bewhiskered,** barbate, barbigerous; mustached *or* mustachioed; awned, awny, pappose; goateed; unshaved, **unshaven;** stubbled, stubbly

26 **wigged,** periwigged, peruked, toupeed

27 **feathery, plumy;** hirsute; featherlike, plumelike, pinnate, pennate; **downy,** fluffy, nappy, velvety, peachy, fuzzy, flossy, furry

28 **feathered, plumaged,** flighted, **pinioned, plumed,** pennate, plumate, plumose

29 **tufted, crested,** topknotted

4 CLOTHING MATERIALS

NOUNS 1 **material, fabric** <see list>, **cloth, textile,** textile fabric, texture, tissue, stuff, weave, weft, woof, web, **goods,** drapery, *étoffe* or *tissu* <Fr>; thread, yarn, rope; napery, table linen, felt; silk; lace; cotton; wool; polyester; nylon; rag, rags

2 **fur, pelt, hide,** fell, fleece, vair <heraldry>; imitation fur, fake fur, synthetic fur; furring; peltry, skins; **leather** <see list>, rawhide; imitation leather, leather paper, leatherette

3 **leather**

alligator	levant morocco
buckskin	mocha
buff	morocco
cabretta	nappa
calf leather	oxhide
capeskin	patent leather
chamois *or* chammy	pebble leather
chamois skin	pigskin
chevrette	pig suede
Cordovan	rawhide
cowhide	Russian leather
deerskin	saddle leather
goatskin	shagreen
grain leather	sheepskin
horsehide	snakeskin
kid	sole-leather *or* shoe-leather
lambskin	stirrup leather

suede
tawed leather

whitleather *or* white
   leather

4 fabrics, fibers

acetate
acrylic
alpaca
angora
astrakhan
baize
balbriggan
baldachin
barathea
batik
batiste
bayadere
bengaline
bombazine
boucle
brilliantine
broadcloth
brocade
brocatel *or* brocatelle
buckram
bunting
burlap
byssus
calico
cambric
camel hair *or* camel's hair
candlewick
Canton crepe
canvas
cashmere
castor
challis
chambray
charmeuse
cheesecloth
chenille
cheviot
chiffon
chinchilla
chino
chintz
cire
cloque
cloth
combing wool
cord
corduroy
cotton
Courtelle
crash
crepe de Chine
cretonne
Crimplene
crinoline
Dacron

damask
denim
dimity
doeskin
Donegal tweed
drill
drugget
duck
duffel *or* duffle
dungaree
duetyn *or* duvetyne
ecru
faille
felt
flannel
flannelette
fleece
foulard
frieze
fustian
gabardine
galatea
gauze
Georgette
gingham
gossamer
grenadine
grogram
grosgrain
gunny
haircloth
Harris tweed
herringbone
homespun
honan
hopsack
horsehair
huckaback
jaconet
jacquard
jardiniere
jean
jersey
jute
Kendal green
kersey
khaki
lace
lamé
lawn
leatherette
leno
linen
linsey-woolsey
lisle

lisse
loden
Lurex
mackinaw
mackintosh *or*
   macintosh
madras
maline
marocain
marquisette
marseille *or* marseilles
mat
melton
merino
mesh
messaline
mohair
moire
moleskin
monk's cloth
moquette
mousseline
muslin
nainsook
nankeen
net or netting
ninon
nylon
oilcloth
oilskin
organdy
organza
organzine
paisley
panne
paramatta
percale
percaline
petersham
Pima
pique
plaid
plush
polyester
pongee
poplin
prunella
ragg
ratine
rayon
rep

russet
sackcloth
sacking
sailcloth
samite
sarcenet
sateen
satin
scrim
seersucker
serge
shalloon
shantung
sharkskin
Shetland wool
sheer
shoddy
shot silk
silk
spandex
stockinette
suede
surah
swansdown
swanskin
tabaret
tabby
taffeta
tapestry
terry cloth
ticking
tiffany
toile
toweling
tricot
tricotine
tulle
tussah
tweed
twill
velour
velvet
velveteen
Venetian cloth
vicuna
voile
webbing
whipcord
wool
worsted

5 CLOTHING

NOUNS **1 clothing, clothes, apparel, wear, wearing apparel, daywear, dress,** dressing, **raiment,** garmenture, **garb, attire, array,** habit, habiliment, fashion, style 578.1, guise, **costume,** costumery, gear, toilette, trim, bedizenment; **vestment,** vesture, investment, investiture, canonicals, liturgical garment; **garments,** robes, robing, rags <nf>, drapery, finery, feathers; toggery *or* togs *or* duds *or* threads <nf>, sportswear; work clothes, fatigues; linen; menswear, men's clothing, womenswear, women's clothing; unisex clothing, uniwear, gender-crossing clothing; gender bender; latest fashion

2 **wardrobe,** furnishings, things, accouterments, trappings; **outfit,** livery, harness, caparison; turnout *and* getup *and* rig *and* rig-out <nf>; wedding clothes, bridal outfit, trousseau; maternity clothes

3 **garment,** vestment, vesture, robe, frock, gown, rag <nf>, togs *and* duds <nf>

4 **ready-mades,** ready-to-wear, off-the-rack clothes, store *or* store-bought clothes, wash-and-wear, dry goods

5 **rags, tatters,** secondhand clothes, seconds, old clothes, consignment clothes, Goodwill clothes; worn clothes, **hand-me-downs** *and* reach-me-downs <nf>, castoffs; slops; consignment clothes

6 **suit** <see list>, suit of clothes, **frock,** dress, rig <nf>, **costume, habit,** bib and tucker <nf>

7 **uniform** <see list>, **livery,** monkey suit <nf>; nurse's uniform, police officer's uniform, etc; athletic team uniform, baseball uniform, etc

8 **mufti,** civilian dress *or* clothes, **civvies** *and* cits <nf>, plain clothes

9 **costume,** costumery, character dress; outfit *and* getup *and* rig <nf>; masquerade, disguise, mask; tights, leotards; ballet skirt, tutu, bodysuit; motley, cap and bells; silks; buskin, sock

10 **finery, frippery, fancy dress,** fine *or* full feather <nf>, investiture, regalia, caparison, fig *or* full fig <Brit nf>; **best clothes,** best bib and tucker <nf>; **Sunday best** *and* Sunday clothes *and* Sunday-go-to-meeting clothes *and* Sunday-go-to-meetings <nf>, **glad rags** <nf>, ostrich feathers <nf>, party dress, dressy clothes

11 **formal dress,** formals, **evening dress, full dress,** dress clothes, evening wear, white tie and tails, **soup-and-fish** <nf>; dinner clothes; dress suit, full-dress suit, tail coat, tails <nf>; tuxedo, tux <nf>, dinner jacket; **regalia,** court dress; dress uniform, full-dress uniform, special full-dress uniform, social full-dress uniform; whites <nf>, dress whites; evening gown *or* dress, dinner dress *or* gown; morning dress, morning coat; semiformal dress; black tie, bow tie, cummerbund

12 **cloak,** overgarment <see list>

13 **outerwear; coat, jacket** <see list>; **overcoat,** overgarment <see list>, great-coat, **topcoat,** surcoat; **rainwear;** rain gear, raincoat, slicker, rainsuit, foul weather gear

14 **waistcoat,** weskit <nf>, **vest;** down vest

15 **shirt** <see list>, waist, **shirtwaist,** linen, sark *and* shift <nf>; **blouse,** bodice; pullover, shell, T-shirt; dickey; sweater <see list>

16 **dress** <see list>, **gown, frock; skirt** <see list>

17 **apron,** *tablier* <Fr>; pinafore, bib, tucker; smock

18 **pants, trousers** <see list>, pair of trousers *or* pants, **breeches,** britches <nf>, **pantaloons;** jeans, designer jeans, blue jeans, dungarees; **slacks;** khakis, chinos; corduroys *or* cords, flannels, ducks, pinstripes, bell-bottoms, hiphuggers, Capri pants *or* Capris, pegged pants, pedal pushers, leggings, overalls, knickers, breeches, jodhpurs, sweatpants; shorts, short pants, Bermuda shorts, hot pants, Jamaica shorts, surfer shorts, short shorts, cycling shorts, gym shorts

19 **waistband,** belt 280.3; **sash,** cummerbund; **loincloth,** breechcloth *or* breechclout, waistcloth, **G-string,** loinguard, dhoti, moocha; **diaper,** dydee <nf>, napkins <Brit>, nappies <Brit nf>

20 **dishabille,** *déshabillé* <Fr>, **undress,** something more comfortable; **negligee,** *négligé* <Fr>; **wrap,** wrapper; sport clothes, playwear, activewear, sportswear, casual wear, leisurewear, **casual clothes** *or* **dress,** fling-on clothes, loungewear, plain clothes, dress-down clothes, knock-around clothes, grubbies <nf>; dress-down day, casual day

21 **nightwear,** nightclothes <see list>, sleepwear; **nightdress, nightgown, nightie** *and* shortie nightie <nf>, negligee, nightshirt; **pajamas,** pyjamas <Brit>, pj's <nf>, baby doll pajamas; sleepers; robe, bathrobe, dressing gown, housecoat, caftan, bed jacket

22 **underclothes,** underclothing, undergarments <see list>, bodywear, **underwear, undies** <nf>, skivvies, body clothes, smallclothes, unmentionables <nf>, intimate apparel, **lingerie, linen,** underlinen; flannels, woolens

23 **corset,** stays, foundation garment, corselet; **girdle,** undergirdle, panty girdle; garter belt

24 **brassiere, bra** <nf>, bandeau, underbodice, *soutien-gorge* <Fr>, uplift brassiere; falsies <nf>

25 **headdress,** headgear, headwear, headclothes; **millinery;** headpiece, **chapeau, cap, hat,** helmet; bonnet, stocking cap, cowboy hat, visor, baseball cap; lid <nf>; headcloth, **kerchief,** bandanna, coverchief; **handkerchief**

26 **veil,** veiling, veiler; *yashmak* <Turk>, *chador* <Iran>; mantilla

27 **footwear,** footgear, *chaussure* <Fr>; **shoes, boots;** clodhoppers *and* gunboats *and* waffle-stompers *and* shitkickers <nf>; oxfords, saddle shoes, pumps, espadrilles, high heels, platform shoes, penny loafers; sandals, flip-flops, zoris, jellies; athletic shoes, tennis shoes, sneakers; wooden shoes, clogs; slippers, moccasins

28 hosiery <see list>, legwear, **hose, stockings; socks**

29 swimwear; bathing suit, swimsuit, swimming suit, tank suit, tank top, *maillot* or *maillot de bain* <Fr>, one-piece suit, two-piece suit; **trunks;** bikini, string bikini or string, thong; trunks, swimming trunks; wet suit; coverup

30 children's wear; rompers, jumpers; creepers; layette, baby clothes, infantwear, infants' wear, baby linen; swaddling clothes, swaddle

31 <clothing accessory> scarf, shoulder pads, belt, glove, mitten, handkerchief, sunglasses, jewelry; neckwear, tie, necktie; collar, dickey

32 garment making, **tailoring; dressmaking, the rag trade** <nf>, fashion design, haute couture, **Seventh Avenue, the garment industry**, Garment District; **millinery,** hatmaking, hatting; hosiery; **shoemaking,** bootmaking, **cobbling;** habilimentation

33 clothier, haberdasher, draper <Brit>, outfitter; costumier, costumer; glover; hosier; furrier; dry goods dealer, mercer <Brit>

34 garmentmaker, garmentworker, needleworker; cutter, stitcher, finisher

35 tailor, tailoress, *tailleur* <Fr>, sartor; fitter; busheler, bushelman; furrier, cloakmaker

36 dressmaker, modiste, *couturière* or *couturier* <Fr>; fashion designer; seamstress 741.2

37 hatter, hatmaker, **milliner**

38 shoemaker, bootmaker, booter, **cobbler**

VERBS **39 clothe,** enclothe, **dress, garb, attire,** tire, array, **apparel,** raiment, garment, habilitate, **tog** *and* tog out <nf>, dud <nf>, robe, enrobe, invest, endue, **deck,** bedeck, dight, rag out or up <nf>; drape, bedrape; wrap, enwrap, lap, envelop, sheathe, shroud, enshroud, invest; wrap or bundle or muffle up; swathe, swaddle

40 cloak, mantle; coat, jacket; gown, frock; breech; shirt; **hat,** coif, bonnet, cap, hood; boot, shoe; stocking, sock

41 outfit; equip, **accouter,** uniform, caparison, rig, rig out or up, fit, **fit out,** turn out, **costume,** habit, suit; design; **tailor,** tailor-make, custom-make, make to order

42 dress up, get up, doll or **spruce up** <nf>, **primp** *and* prink *and* prank <nf>, gussy up <nf>, spiff or fancy or slick up <nf>, pretty up <nf>, deck out or up, trick out or up, tog out or up <nf>, rag out or up <nf>, fig out or up <nf>; dress to kill, titivate, bedeck, dizen, bedizen; overdress; put on the dog or style <nf>; **dress down,** underdress

43 don, put on, slip on or into, get on or into, try on, assume, dress in, adorn, dight <old>; change; suit up

44 wear, have on, dress in, be dressed in, put on, slip on, affect, sport <nf>; change into; try on

ADJS **45 clothing; dress,** vestiary, sartorial; **clothed, clad, dressed, attired, togged** <nf>, tired, arrayed, **garbed,** garmented, habited, habilimented, decked, bedecked, decked-out, turned-out, tricked-out, rigged-out, vested, vestmented, robed, gowned, raimented, **appareled,** invested, endued, liveried, uniformed; **costumed,** in costume, cloaked, mantled, disguised; breeched, trousered, pantalooned; coifed, capped, bonneted, hatted, hooded; **shod,** shoed, booted, *chaussé* <Fr>

46 dressed up, dolled or **spruced up** <nf>; spiffed or fancied or slicked up <nf>, gussied up <nf>; spruce, dressed to advantage, dressed to the nines, dressed or fit to kill <nf>; in Sunday best, *endimanché* <Fr>, in one's best bib and tucker <nf>, in fine or high feather; *en grande tenue* <Fr>, *en grande toilette* <Fr>, in full dress, in full feather, in white tie and tails, in tails; **well-dressed, chic,** *soigné* <Fr>, stylish, modish, well-turned, well turned-out; **dressy; overdressed**

47 in dishabille, *en déshabillé* <Fr>, **in negligee; casual,** nonformal, sporty, in one's shirtsleeves; baggy, sloppy; skintight, decollete, low-necked, low-cut; underdressed, half-dressed

48 tailored, custom-made, tailor-made, made-to-order, bespoke <Brit>; ready-made, store-bought *and* off-the-rack <nf>, ready-to-wear; vestmental; sartorial

49 suits

bodysuit	romper suit or
boiler suit	rompers
business suit	sack suit
camouflage suit or camo	separates
casual suit	single-breasted suit
cat suit	ski suit
coordinates	slack suit
coveralls	snowsuit
double-breasted suit	space suit
dress suit	sports suit
ensemble	summer suit
flight suit	sun suit
jogging suit or track suit	sweat suit
jumpsuit	swimsuit
leisure suit	tailored suit
livery	tank suit
lounge suit	three-piece suit
monkey suit	track suit
one-piece suit	tropical suit
pants suit or pantsuit	trouser suit
pinstripe suit	tuxedo
playsuit	two-piece suit
rain suit	wet suit
riding habit	zoot suit

50 uniforms

blues	dress blues
continentals	dress whites

fatigues
full dress
khaki
livery
nauticals
olive-drab *or* OD

regimentals
sailor suit
soldier suit
stripes
undress
whites

51 cloaks, overgarments

academic gown
academic hood
academic robe
afghan
bachelor's gown
burnoose
caftan
cap and gown
cape
capelet
capote
capuchin
cardinal
cashmere *or* cashmere
   shawl
cassock
chlamys
cowl
doctor's gown
domino
duster
frock
gaberdine
haik
houppelande
Inverness cape
judge's robe *or* gown
kaftan
kimono
kirtle
manta
manteau
mantelet
mantelletta
mantellone

mantilla
mantle
mantua
master's gown
military cloak
monk's robe
opera cloak *or* cape
pallium
pelerine
pelisse
peplos
peplum
plaid
poncho
robe
roquelaure
sagum
serape
shador
shawl
shoulderette
slop
smock
soutane
stole
tabard
talma
tippet
toga
toga virilis
tunic
wrap-around
wrapover
wrapper
wrap-up

52 coats, jackets, overcoats

anorak
balmacaan
benjamin
blazer
blouse
body-coat
bolero
bomber jacket
box coat
Burberry <trademark>
bush jacket
camelhair coat
capote

capuchin
car coat
chaqueta <Sp>
chesterfield
claw-hammer coat *or* claw
   hammer
cloth coat
coach coat
coatee
coolie jacket *or* coat
cutaway coat *or* cutaway
denim jacket *or* jean jacket
dinner coat *or* jacket

dolman
double-breasted jacket
doublet
down jacket
dreadnought
dress coat
dressing jacket
duffle coat
duster
Eton jacket
fearnought
fingertip coat
fitted coat
flack jacket
fleece jacket
frock coat *or* frock
fur coat
fur-lined coat
fur-trimmed coat
greatcoat
hacking jacket
happi coat
Inverness
jerkin
jumper
leather coat
loden coat
London Fog
   <trademark>
long coat
lounging jacket
mackinaw *or* mackinaw
   coat
mackintosh *or* mac
macfarlane
Mao jacket
maxicoat
mess jacket
midicoat
monkey jacket
morning coat
Nehru jacket
Newmarket *or* Newmarket
   coat
Norfolk jacket
oilskins
paletot
parka

peacoat *or* pea jacket
pilot jacket
Prince Albert *or* Prince
   Albert coat
raglan
raincoat
redingote
reefer *or* reefer jacket
sack *or* sack coat
safari jacket
sanbenito
shawl
shell jacket
shirtjac *or* shirt jacket
shooting jacket
single-breasted jacket
ski jacket
sleeve waistcoat
slicker
slip-on
smoking jacket
sou'wester
spencer
spiketail
sport coat *or* jacket
sports jacket
suit coat
surtout
swagger coat
swallow-tailed coat *or*
   swallowtail
sweater coat
swing coat
tabard
tail coat *or* tails
topcoat
topper
trench coat
tuxedo coat *or* jacket
ulster
watch coat
waterproof
Windbreaker
   <trademark>
winter coat
woolly
wrap-around *or* wrap
wraprascal

53 sweaters

bolero
boucle
bulky
cable-knit sweater
cardigan *or* cardigan jacket
cashmere sweater
crewneck sweater
Fair Isle sweater
fisherman's sweater

Guernsey
hand-knit
jersey
mohair sweater
polo sweater
poor boy sweater
pull-on sweater
pullover
rollneck sweater

shell
shoulderette
ski sweater
slip-on
slipover
sloppy Joe

sweatshirt
sweater vest
turtleneck sweater
twin sweater set *or* twin set
V-neck sweater
woolly

54 trousers and pants

bell-bottoms
Bermuda shorts
bloomers
blue jeans
breeches
buckskins
Capri pants
chaps
chinos
clam diggers
corduroys *or* cords
cutoffs
ducks
dungarees
gaiters
high-waters
hiphuggers
hot pants
jeans

jodhpurs
knee breeches
knickers *or* knickerbockers
lederhosen
Levi's <trademark>
loincloth
matador *or* toreador pants
moleskins
overalls
pantaloons
pedal pushers
pegleg trousers
plus fours
shorts
short shorts
slacks
stretch pants
trunk hose
waders

55 shirts

aloha *or* Hawaiian shirt
basque
benjamin
blouse
blouson
body shirt
body suit
bush shirt
bustier
button down
camp shirt
chambray shirt
coat shirt
crop top
denim shirt
dickey
doublet
dress shirt
evening shirt
flannel shirt
gipon
habit shirt
hair shirt
halter *or* halter top

hickory shirt
long-sleeved shirt
middy blouse
olive-drab *or* OD shirt
overblouse
oxford shirt
polo shirt
pourpoint
pullover
rugby shirt
sark
shell
shirt-jacket *or* shirt-jac
shirtwaist
short-sleeved shirt
sleeveless shirt
sport shirt
sweatshirt
tank top
tee-shirt *or* T-shirt
top
tube top
turtleneck
workshirt

56 dresses, skirts

A-line skirt
ballet skirt
backwrap

ball-gown
body dress
cheongsam

chiton
coat dress
cocktail dress
crinoline
culottes
dinner dress *or* gown
dirndl
divided skirt
evening dress
evening gown
farthingale
formal
full skirt
gown *or* evening gown
granny dress
grass skirt
harem skirt
hobble skirt
hoop skirt
housedress
hula skirt
jumper
kilt *or* filibeg *or* tartan
kirtle
little black dress
mantua
maternity dress
maxiskirt
microskirt *or* microminiskirt
midiskirt

miniskirt
Mother Hubbard
muu-muu
overdress
overskirt
pannier
pantdress
pantskirt
peplum
petticoat
pinafore
pleated skirt
sack
sari
sarong
sheath
shift
shirtdress *or* shirtwaist dress
skort
slit skirt
sundress
sweater dress
tank dress
T-dress
tea gown
tent dress
tube dress
tunic dress
tutu
wrap dress
wrap skirt

57 nightclothes

baby doll pajamas
bathrobe
bed gown
bed jacket
dishabille
dressing gown
dressing jacket
housecoat
jammies *or* p.j.'s <nf>
kimono
morning dress

negligee
nightgown
nightie <nf>
nightshirt
pajamas
peignor
robe
robe de chambre
romper
sleeper
smoking jacket

58 undergarments

all-in-one
athletic supporter *or* jockstrap
Balmoral
bloomers
bikini
bodice
body stocking
body suit
boxer shorts
brassiere *or* bra
breechclout *or* loin-cloth
briefs

bustle
BVD's <trademark>
cami-knickers
camisole
chemise
corselet
corset
crinoline
diapers
drawers
foundation garment
full slip
garter

garter belt
girdle
G-string
half-slip
Jockey <trademark>
  shorts
knickers <Brit>
leggings
leotard
lingerie
long underwear *or* long
  johns
napkins *or* nappies <Brit>
pannier
panties
pants
panty girdle
pantyhose
petticoat
push-up bra
scanties
shift
shorts
singlet <Brit>
skivvies

slip
smock
soakers
sport bra *or* sports bra
step-ins
string vest
support garment
tap pants
teddy
tee-shirt *or* T-shirt
thermal underwear *or*
  thermals
tournure <Fr>
underdrawers
underpants
undershirt
undershorts
underskirt
undervest
underwire bra
undies
union suit
unitard
unmentionables
woolens

59 hosiery

anklets *or* ankle socks
argyles
athletic socks
bobbysocks
boothose
boot socks
crew socks
dress sheers
fishnet stockings
footlets
full-fashioned stockings
garter stockings
hose
body stocking
knee-highs
knee-socks
leg-warmers
lisle hose

nylons
panty-hose *and* pantyhose
Peds <trademark>
rayon stockings
seamless stockings
sheer stockings *or* sheers
silk stockings
slouch socks
socks
stocking hose
stretch stockings
support hose
sweat socks
tights
tube socks
varsity socks
wigglers *or* toe socks
work socks

6 UNCLOTHING

NOUNS **1 unclothing,** divestment, divestiture,
divesture; **removal; stripping,** denudement,
denudation; baring, stripping *or* laying bare,
uncovering, **exposure,** exposing; indecent
exposure, exhibitionism, flashing <nf>;
decortication, excoriation; desquamation,
exfoliation; exuviation, ecdysis

2 disrobing, undressing, undress, disrobement,
unclothing; uncasing, discasing; shedding,
molting, peeling; striptease, stripping; skinny-
dipping <nf>, mooning <nf>, flashing <nf>

3 nudity, nakedness, bareness; **the nude, the
altogether** *and* **the buff** <nf>, **the raw** <nf>; state
of nature, **birthday suit** <nf>; not a stitch, not a
stitch to one's name, not a stitch on one's back;
full-frontal nudity; décolleté, décolletage,
toplessness; nudism, naturism, gymnosophy;
nudist, naturist, gymnosophist, exhibitionist;
stripper, stripteaser, ecdysiast, topless dancer

4 hairlessness, baldness, acomia, alopecia; calvities;
hair loss; beardlessness, bald-headedness *or*
-patedness; baldhead, baldpate, baldy <nf>,
skinhead; shaving, tonsure, depilation; hair
remover, depilatory

VERBS **5 divest, strip, strip away, remove; uncover,**
uncloak, unveil, **expose,** lay open, bare, lay *or* strip
bare, **denude,** denudate; fleece, shear; pluck; strip-
search

6 take off, remove, doff, off with, put off, slip *or* step
out of, slip off, slough off, cast off, throw off, drop;
unwrap, undo

7 undress, unclothe, undrape, ungarment,
unapparel, unarray, disarray; **disrobe;** unsheathe,
discase, uncase; **strip,** strip to the buff <nf>, do a
strip-tease; skinny-dip, flash <nf>, moon <nf>

8 peel, pare, skin, strip, flay, excoriate, decorticate,
bark; scalp; depilate, shave

9 husk, hull, pod, **shell,** shuck

10 shed, cast, throw off, **slough, molt,** slough off,
exuviate

11 scale, flake, scale *or* flake off, desquamate, exfoliate

ADJS **12 divested, stripped, bared,** denuded,
denudated, **exposed, uncovered,** stripped *or* laid
bare, unveiled, showing; unsheathed, discased,
uncased

**13 unclad, undressed, unclothed, unattired,
disrobed,** ungarmented, undraped, ungarbed,
unrobed, unappareled, uncased; **clothesless,**
garbless, garmentless, raimentless; half-clothed,
underclothed, *en déshabillé* <Fr>, in dishabille,
nudish; low-necked, low-cut, décolleté, strapless,
topless; **seminude,** scantily clad

14 naked, nude; bare, peeled, raw <nf>, **in the raw**
<nf>, *in puris naturalibus* <L>, in a state of
nature, in nature's garb; in one's birthday suit, **in
the buff** *and* in native buff *and* stripped to the buff
and **in the altogether** <nf>, with nothing on,
without a stitch, without a stitch to one's name *or*
on one's back; **stark-naked,** bare-ass <nf>, bare as
the back of one's hand, naked as the day one was
born, naked as a jaybird <nf>, starkers <Brit nf>;
topless, bare-breasted, bottomless, bare-bottomed,
"naked as a worm"—Chaucer; nudist, naturistic,
gymnosophical

15 barefoot, barefooted, unshod; discalced,
discalceate

16 bare-ankled, bare-armed, bare-backed, bare-breasted, topless, bare-chested, bare-faced, bare-handed, bare-headed, bare-kneed, bare-legged, bare-necked, bare-throated

17 hairless, depilous; **bald,** acomous; bald as a coot, bald as an egg; **bald-headed,** bald-pated, tonsured; **beardless,** whiskerless, shaven, clean-shaven, smooth-shaven, smooth-faced; smooth, glabrous

18 exuvial, sloughy; desquamative, exfoliatory; denudant or denudatory; peeling, shedding

ADVS **19** nakedly, barely, baldly

WORD ELEMENTS **20** de-, dis-, un-

7 NUTRITION

NOUNS **1 nutrition, nourishment,** nourishing, feeding, nurture; alimentation; **food** or **nutritive value, food intake;** food chain or cycle; food pyramid, recommended daily vitamins and minerals

2 nutritiousness, nutritiveness, **digestibility,** assimilability; healthfulness

3 nutrient, nutritive, **nutriment** 10.3, food; nutrilite, growth factor, growth regulator; **natural food,** health food <see list>; roughage, fiber, dietary fiber

4 vitamin <see list>, vitamin complex; provitamin, provitamin A or carotene

5 carbohydrate, carbo or carbs <nf>, simple carbohydrate, complex carbohydrate; hydroxy aldehyde, hydroxy ketone, glycogen, cellulose, ketone, saccharide, monosaccharide, disaccharide, trisaccharide, polysaccharide or polysaccharose; **sugar; starch**

6 protein or proteid, simple protein, conjugated protein, protein structure; **amino acid,** essential amino acid; peptide, dipeptide, polypeptide, etc; globulin, collagen, gluten, immunoglobulin, hemoglobin

7 fat, glyceride, **lipid,** lipoid; lecithin; fatty acid; steroid, sterol; **cholesterol,** glycerol-cholesterol, cephalin-cholesterol; triglyceride; **lipoprotein,** high-density lipoprotein or HDL, low-density lipoprotein or LDL; polyunsaturated fat; saturated fat; unsaturated fat

8 digestion, ingestion, assimilation, absorption; primary digestion, secondary digestion; predigestion; salivary digestion, gastric or peptic digestion, pancreatic digestion, intestinal digestion; digestive system, alimentary canal, gastrointestinal tract; salivary glands, gastric glands, liver, pancreas; digestive secretions, saliva, gastric juice, pancreatic juice, intestinal juice, bile

9 digestant, digester, digestive; pepsin; **enzyme,** proteolytic enzyme

10 enzyme, apoenzyme, coenzyme, isoenzyme;

transferase, hydrolase, lyase, isomerase, polymerase, amylase, diastase; pepsin, rennin; proenzyme, zymogen

11 essential element, macronutrient; carbon, hydrogen, oxygen, nitrogen, calcium, phosphorus, potassium, sodium, chlorine, sulfur, magnesium; trace element, micronutrient; iron, manganese, zinc, copper, iodine, cobalt, selenium, molybdenum, chromium, silicon

12 metabolism, basal metabolism, acid-base metabolism, energy metabolism; **anabolism,** assimilation; **catabolism,** disassimilation

13 diet, dieting, dietary; dietetics; **regimen,** regime; bland diet; soft diet, pap, spoon food or meat, spoon victuals <nf>; balanced diet; diabetic diet, allergy diet, reducing diet, weight-loss diet, obesity diet; high-calorie diet, low-calorie diet, watching one's weight or calories, calorie-counting; liquid diet; high-protein diet, low-carbohydrate diet; low-salt diet, low-sodium diet, salt-free diet; low-fat diet, fat-free diet; low-cholesterol diet; sugar-free diet; vegetarianism, lactovegetarianism, vegan diet; macrobiotic diet; crash diet, fad diet; diet book, calorie counter

14 vitaminization, **fortification, enrichment,** restoration; food additive

15 nutritionist, dietitian, vitaminologist, enzymologist

16 <science of nutrition> **dietetics,** dietotherapeutics, dietotherapy; vitaminology; enzymology

VERBS **17 nourish,** feed, sustain, aliment, nutrify <old>, nurture, fatten up; **sustain,** strengthen; cook for, wine and dine, regale; force-feed

18 digest, assimilate, absorb; metabolize; predigest

19 diet, go on a diet; watch one's weight or calories, count calories

20 vitaminize, **fortify, enrich,** restore

ADJS **21 nutritious,** nutritive, nutrient, **nourishing;** alimentary, alimental; digestible, assimilable

22 digestive, assimilative; peptic

23 dietary, dietetic, dietic <old>; regiminal

24 health foods

bran	nonfat or low-fat food
brown rice	nuts
buckwheat flour	soybeans
fiber	unrefined flour
fruits	vegetables
light or lite or low-calorie food	wheat germ
	yogurt

25 vitamins

vitamin A	vitamin A_2
vitamin A_1 or	biotin
antiophthalmic factor or	carotene
axerophthol, retinol	choline

cryptoxanthin
vitamin B
vitamin B complex
vitamin B$_1$ *or* thiamine *or* aneurin *or* anti-beriberi factor
vitamin B$_2$ *or* vitamin G *or* riboflavin *or* lactoflavin *or* ovoflavin *or* hepatoflavin
vitamin M *or* vitamin Bc
vitamin B$_6$ *or* pyridoxine *or* adermin
vitamin B$_{12}$ *or* cobalamin *or* cyanocobalamin *or* extrinsic factor *or* pentothenic acid *or* lipoid acid

biotin *or* vitamin H
choline
folic acid *or* pteroylglutamic acid *or* para-aminobenzoic acid *or* PABA
inositol
niacin *or* nicotinic acid
vitamin C *or* ascorbic acid
vitamin D$_2$ *or* calciferol
ergocalciferol
cholecalciferol *or* vitamin D$_3$
vitamin E *or* tocopherol
vitamin K *or* naphthoquinone menadione
vitamin P *or* bioflavinoid

8 EATING

NOUNS **1 eating, feeding, dining,** messing; the nosebag <nf>; ingestion, consumption, consuming, deglutition; **tasting,** relishing, savoring; **gourmet eating** *or* **dining,** fine dining, gourmandise, gastronomy; nibbling, pecking, licking, **munching;** snacking; **devouring,** gobbling, wolfing, downing, gulping; **gorging, overeating,** gluttony, overconsumption; **chewing,** mastication, manducation, rumination; **feasting, regaling,** regalement; **appetite,** hunger 100.7; nutrition 7; **dieting** 7.11; gluttony 672; carnivorism, carnivorousness, carnivority; herbivorism, herbivority, herbivorousness, grazing, browsing, cropping, pasturing, pasture; vegetarianism, phytophagy; omnivorism, omnivorousness, pantophagy; cannibalism, anthropophagy; omophagia *or* omophagy

2 bite, morsel, taste, swallow; mouthful, gob <nf>, piece, slice, tidbit; nibble, munchies; cud, quid; bolus, gobbet; **chew,** chaw <nf>; nip; munch; gnash; champ, chomp <nf>; appetizer, hors d'oeuvre

3 drinking, imbibing, imbibition, potation; lapping, sipping, tasting, nipping; quaffing, gulping, swigging <nf>, swilling *and* guzzling <nf>, pulling <nf>; winebibbing; compotation, symposium; drunkenness 88.1,3

4 drink, potation, beverage, potion, libation, oblation, thirst-quencher; draft, dram, drench, **swig** <nf>, swill *and* guzzle <nf>, quaff, **sip,** sup, suck, tot, bumper, snort *and* slug <nf>, pull <nf>, lap, gulp, slurp <nf>; nip, peg; toast, health; mixed drink, cocktail; nightcap <nf>

5 meal, repast, feed *and* sit-down <nf>, mess, spread <nf>, table, board, meat, *repas* <Fr>; **refreshment,** refection, regalement, collation, entertainment, treat; frozen meal

6 <meals> **breakfast,** *petit déjeuner* <Fr>, continental breakfast, English breakfast, American breakfast; meat breakfast, *déjeuner à la fourchette* <Fr>; **brunch** <nf>, Sunday brunch, elevenses <Brit nf>; **lunch, luncheon,** tiffin, hot lunch, light lunch, box lunch, brown-bag lunch; **tea,** teatime, high tea, afternoon tea, cream tea; **dinner,** *diner* <Fr>, evening meal; **supper,** *souper* <Fr>; buffet supper *or* lunch; box lunch, packed lunch <Brit>; takeout; precooked frozen meal, TV dinner; **picnic, cookout,** alfresco meal, fête champêtre, tailgate picnic, **barbecue,** fish fry, clambake, wiener roast *or* wienie roast; pot luck; midnight supper *or* snack

7 light meal, refreshments, light repast, light lunch, spot of lunch <nf>, collation, **snack** *and* nosh <nf>, **bite** <nf>, bite to eat <nf>, *casse-croûte* <Fr>; informal meal; coffee break, tea break

8 hearty meal, full meal, healthy meal, large *or* substantial meal, heavy meal, **square meal,** man-sized meal, large order; three squares; formal meal, sit-down meal

9 feast, banquet, regale, buffet, smorgasbord, festal board, groaning board, spread; Lucullan banquet, bacchanalia; blow *or* blowout <nf>, feeding frenzy <nf>; dinner party

10 serving, service; **portion, helping,** help; second helping, seconds; **course;** dish, plate; *plat du jour* <Fr>; antepast <old>; first course, starter, soup, entree, *entrée* <Fr>, main course, entremets, side dish; dessert

11 <manner of service> service, table service, counter service, self-service, curb service, take-out service; table d'hôte, ordinary; à la carte; cover, *couvert* <Fr>; cover charge; American plan, European plan

12 tableware, dining utensils; **silverware,** silver, silver plate, stainless-steel ware; **flatware,** flat silver; hollow ware; **cutlery,** knives, fish knife, carving knife, fruit knife, steak knife, butter knife; forks, fisk fork, salad fork, fondue fork; spoons, tablespoon, teaspoon, soup spoon, dessert spoon, coffee spoon, serving spoon; chopsticks; **dishware, china, dishes,** plates, cups, saucers, bowls, fingerbowls; glasses, glassware, tumbler, goblet, wineglass, flute; **dish,** salad dish, fruit dish, dessert dish; **bowl,** cereal bowl, fruit bowl, punchbowl; **tea service, tea set,** tea things, tea strainer, tea-caddy, tea-cozy

13 table linen, napery, tablecloth, table cover, table-mat, table pad, place mat; **napkin, table napkin,** serviette <Brit>

14 menu, bill of fare, carte

15 gastronomy, gastronomics, gastrology, **epicurism,** epicureanism

16 eater, feeder, consumer, devourer, partaker; **diner,** luncher; picnicker; mouth, hungry mouth, big eater; diner-out, eater-out; boarder, board-and-roomer; **gourmet,** gastronome, epicure, gourmand, connoisseur of food *or* wine, bon vivant, Lucullus, foodie; **glutton,** overeater, pig *and* wolf <nf>, trencherman, **glutton** 672.3; light eater, nibbler, picky eater, fussy eater; omnivore, pantophagist; **flesh-eater, meat-eater, carnivore,** omophagist, predacean; **man-eater, cannibal; vegetarian,** lactovegetarian, vegan, fruitarian, plant-eater, **herbivore,** phytophagan, phytophage; grass-eater, graminivore; grain-eater, granivore

17 **restaurant,** eating place, eating house, dining room; eatery *and* beanery *and* hashery *and* hash house *and* greasy spoon <nf>; **fast-food restaurant,** takeout, hamburger joint <nf>; *trattoria* <Ital>; **lunchroom,** luncheonette; **café,** *caffè* <Ital>, roadside café; **tearoom,** *bistro* <Fr>; **coffeehouse,** coffeeroom, **coffee shop,** coffee bar; **tea shop,** tea-garden, teahouse; pub, tavern; chophouse; **grill,** grillroom, steakhouse; brasserie; pancake house, waffle house; cookshop; buffet, smorgasbord, self-service restaurant; **lunch counter,** quick-lunch counter; salad bar; hot-dog stand, hamburger stand, drive-in restaurant, drive-in; **snack bar,** sandwich bar, *buvette* <Fr>, *cantina* <Sp>; milk bar; sushi bar; juice bar; raw bar; pizzeria; **cafeteria,** automat; mess hall, dining hall, refectory; canteen; cookhouse, cookshack, lunch wagon, chuck wagon; **diner,** dog wagon <nf>; delicatessen, deli; ice-cream parlor, soda fountain; dining car; vending machine; **kitchen** 11.3, breakfast nook, dining room, dinette

VERBS 18 **feed, dine,** wine and dine, mess; nibble, snack, graze <nf>; satisfy, gratify; regale; bread, meat; board, sustain; pasture, put out to pasture, graze, browse; forage, fodder; provision 385.9

19 **nourish, nurture,** nutrify, aliment, foster; **nurse, suckle,** lactate, breast-feed, wet-nurse, dry-nurse; fatten, fatten up, stuff, force-feed

20 **eat, feed,** fare, take, partake, partake of, *mange* <Fr>, take nourishment, subsist, break bread, break one's fast; refresh *or* entertain the inner man, feed one's face *and* put on the feed bag <nf>, fall to, pitch in <nf>; **taste,** relish, savor; hunger 100.19; get *or* have the munchies, **diet,** go on a diet, watch one's weight, count calories

21 **dine,** dinner; **sup,** breakfast; lunch; picnic, cook out; **eat out, dine out;** board; mess with, break bread with

22 **devour, swallow,** ingest, **consume,** take in, tuck in *or* away *and* tuck into *and* chow down <nf>, down, take down, get down, put away <nf>; **eat up;** dispatch *or* dispose of <nf>

23 **gobble, gulp, bolt,** wolf, gobble *or* gulp *or* bolt *or* wolf down

24 **feast, banquet,** regale; eat heartily, have a good appetite, eat up, lick the platter *or* plate, do oneself proud <nf>, do one's duty, do justice to, clean one's plate, polish the platter, put it away <nf>

25 **stuff,** gorge 672.4, pig out <nf>, engorge, glut, guttle, binge, cram, eat one's fill, stuff *or* gorge oneself, gluttonize, eat everything in sight

26 **pick, peck** <nf>, **nibble; snack** <nf>, nosh <nf>; pick at, peck at <nf>, eat like a bird, show no appetite

27 **chew,** chew up, chaw <nf>, bite into; **masticate,** manducate; ruminate, chew the cud; **bite,** grind, champ, chomp <nf>; **munch,** crunch; gnash; **gnaw;** mouth, mumble; gum

28 **feed on** *or* **upon, feast on** *or* **upon,** batten upon, fatten on *or* upon; prey on *or* upon, live on *or* upon, pasture on, browse, graze, crop

29 **drink,** drink in, **imbibe,** wet one's whistle <nf>; **quaff, sip, sup,** bib, swig *and* swill *and* guzzle *and* pull <nf>; **suck,** suckle, suck in *or* up; drink off *or* up, toss off *or* down, drain the cup; wash down; **toast,** drink to, pledge; tipple; **booze** 88.23

30 **lap up,** sponge *or* soak up, lick, lap, slurp <nf>

ADJS 31 **eating, feeding, gastronomical, dining,** mensal, commensal, prandial, postprandial, preprandial; **nourishing,** nutritious 7.19; empty-calorie; **dietetic; omnivorous,** pantophagous, **gluttonous** 672.6; **flesh-eating, meat-eating, carnivorous,** omophagic, omophagous, predacious; **man-eating, cannibal,** cannibalistic; insect-eating, insectivorous; vegetable-eating, **vegetarian,** lactovegetarian, vegan, fruitarian; plant-eating, **herbivorous,** phytivorous, phytophagous; grass-eating, graminivorous; grain-eating, granivorous

32 chewing, masticatory, masticating, manducatory; ruminant, ruminating, cud-chewing; tasting, nibbling

33 **edible, eatable,** comestible, consumable, esculent, digestible, gustable, esculent; kosher; **palatable,** succulent, mouth-watering, **delicious,** dainty, savory; **fine, fancy, gourmet;** calorific, fattening, rich

34 **drinkable,** potable, quaffable

INTERJS 35 chow down!, soup's on!, grub's on!, come and get it!; *bon appétit!* <Fr>, eat hearty!, eat up!

WORD ELEMENTS 36 phag-, phago-, -phagia, -phagy; -phage, -vore, -vora

9 REFRESHMENT

NOUNS 1 **refreshment,** refection, refreshing, freshening up, **bracing, exhilaration, stimulation,** enlivenment, vivification, **invigoration,** reinvigoration, reanimation, revival, revivification, revivescence *or* revivescency, renewal, recreation, rest and recreation, R and R; regalement, regale; **tonic,** bracer, breath of fresh air, pick-me-up *and* a shot in the arm *and* an upper <nf>; cordial

VERBS **2 refresh, freshen,** refreshen, freshen up, fresh up <nf>; **revive,** revivify, **reinvigorate,** reanimate; **exhilarate, stimulate, invigorate,** fortify, enliven, liven up, animate, vivify, quicken, brisk, brisken; brace, **brace up,** buck up *and* pick up <nf>, perk up *and* chirk up <nf>, set up, set on one's legs *or* feet <nf>; renew one's strength, put *or* breathe new life into, give a breath of fresh air, give a shot in the arm <nf>; renew, recreate, charge *or* recharge one's batteries <nf>, give a break, give a breather; **regale, cheer,** refresh the inner man

ADJS **3 refreshing,** refreshful, **fresh,** brisk, crisp, crispy, zesty, zestful, **bracing, tonic,** cordial; analeptic; **exhilarating, stimulating, stimulative, stimulatory, invigorating,** rousing, energizing; regaling, cheering; rejuvenating; recreative, recreational

4 refreshed, restored, invigorated, exhilarated, freshened up, enlivened, stimulated, energized, recharged, animated, reanimated, **revived,** renewed, recreated, ready for more, ready for another round

5 unwearied, untired, unfatigued, unexhausted

10 FOOD

NOUNS **1 food,** foodstuff, food and drink, sustenance, kitchen stuff, victualage, **comestibles, edibles,** eatables, viands, **cuisine,** tucker <Austral>, ingesta <pl>; soul food; fast food, junk food; **fare,** cheer, creature comfort; provision, provender; meat <old>, bread <see list>, daily bread, bread and butter, staff of life; health food; board, table, feast 8.9, spread <nf>; nouvelle cuisine, designer food

2 <nf terms> **grub,** grubbery, **eats, chow,** chuck, grits, groceries, nosh, the nosebag, scarf *or* scoff, tuck <Brit>, victuals *or* vittles; fast food

3 nutriment, nourishment, nurture; pabulum, pap; aliment, alimentation; **refreshment,** refection; **sustenance,** support, keep

4 feed, fodder, provender, animal food; forage, pasture, eatage, pasturage; grain; corn, oats, barley, wheat; meal, bran, chop; **hay,** timothy, clover, straw; ensilage, silage; chicken feed, scratch, scratch feed, mash; slops, swill; pet food, dog food, cat food; bird seed

5 provisions, groceries, provender, supplies, stores, larder, food supply, victuals; fresh foods, canned foods, frozen foods, dehydrated foods, precooked foods, convenience foods; commissariat, commissary, grocery

6 rations, board, meals, commons <chiefly Brit>, mess, allowance, allotment, food allotment, tucker <Austral>; short commons <chiefly Brit>; emergency rations; K ration, C ration, garrison *or* field rations

7 dish 11.1, culinary preparation *or* concoction; cover, **course** 8.10; casserole; grill, broil, boil, roast, fry; **main dish, entree,** main course, *pièce de résistance* <Fr>, culinary masterpiece, dish fit for a king; hors d'oeuvre, starter; side dish, salad, vegetables; dessert; dish of the day, soup of the day, specialty

8 delicacy, dainty, goody <nf>, treat, kickshaw, **tidbit,** titbit; **morsel,** choice morsel, *bonne bouche* <Fr>; savory; dessert <see list>; ambrosia, nectar, cate, manna

9 appetizer, whet, *apéritif* <Fr>; foretaste, antepast <old>, *antipasto* <Ital>, *Vorspeise* <Ger>; **hors d'oeuvre;** *crostato* <Ital>, starter, nibbles, tidbits; smorgasbord; crackers and cheese, crudites, **dip,** guacamole, salsa, pâté, cheese dip, nachos, potato skins, hummus; falafel; rumaki; **pickle,** dill pickle

10 soup, *potage* <Fr>, *zuppa or minestra* <Ital>, cream soup, clear soup, consommé, stock, bouillon, potage, bisque, borscht, gumbo, chowder, bouillabaisse

11 stew, olla, olio, *olla podrida* <Sp>; meat stew, *étuvée* <Fr>; Irish stew, mulligan stew *or* mulligan <nf>; goulash, Hungarian goulash; ragout; salmi; bouillabaisse, *paella* <Catalan>, oyster stew; fricassee; curry

12 sauce; tomato sauce, ketchup *or* catsup; brown sauce, Worcestershire sauce, soy sauce, Bordelaise; Tabasco sauce <trademark>, barbecue sauce; tartar sauce, horseradish; salsa, guacamole, pesto; applesauce; mayonnaise, salad dressing, vinaigrette; white sauce, veloute, Bearnaise, hollandaise, bechamel

13 meat, flesh, red meat, *viande* <Fr>, white meat; butcher's meat, *viande de boucherie* <Fr>; **cut of meat;** game, *menue viande* <Fr>; venison; **roast,** joint, *rôti* <Fr>; pot roast; chop, cutlet, grill; barbecue, boiled meat, *bouilli* <Fr>; forcemeat; mincemeat, mince, hash, *hachis* <Fr>; *civet* <Fr>; pemmican, jerky; sausage meat, scrapple; aspic; meat substitute, tofu, bean curd

14 beef, *bœuf* <Fr>; roast beef, *rosbif* <Fr>; chuck, rib roast, tenderloin, sirloin, steak, round, boneless rump, shank, brisket; hamburger, ground beef; corned beef; dried beef; chipped beef; jerky, charqui; pastrami; beef extract, bouillon; suet

15 veal, *vitello* <Ital>, *veau* <Fr>; veal cutlet, *côtelette de veau* <Fr>; shoulder, rib roast, chops, loin, rump, shank, leg, cutlet, escallop, breast, neck; *poitrine de veau* <Fr>; fricandeau; calf's head, *tête de veau* <Fr>; calf's liver, *foie de veau* <Fr>; sweetbread, *ris de veau* <Fr>; calf's brains

16 mutton, *mouton* <Fr>; muttonchop; **lamb,** *agneau* <Fr>; breast of lamb, *poitrine d'agneau* <Fr>; leg of lamb, leg of mutton, *gigot* <Fr>, *jambe de mouton* <Fr>; saddle of mutton

17 pork, *porc* <Fr>, pig, pigmeat <nf>

18 steak, *tranche* <Fr>, **beefsteak,** *bifteck* <Fr>, *tranche de bœuf* <Fr>, *bistecca* <Ital>

19 chop, cutlet, *côtelette* <Fr>; pork chop, *côtelette de porc frais* <Fr>; mutton chop, *côtelette de mouton* <Fr>, Saratoga chop; veal cutlet, veal chop, *côtelette de veau* <Fr>, *Wiener Schnitzel* <Ger>

20 <variety meats> kidneys; heart; brains; liver; gizzard; tongue; sweetbread <thymus>; beef bread <pancreas>; tripe <stomach>; marrow; cockscomb; chitterlings *or* chitlins <intestines>; prairie *or* mountain oyster <testis>; haslet, giblets, *abattis* <Fr>

21 sausage, *saucisse* <Fr>, *saucisson* <Fr>, *salsiccia* <Ital>, *Wurst* <Ger>; **pâté**

22 poultry, fowl, bird, edible bird, *volaille* <Fr>

23 <parts of poultry> leg, drumstick, thigh, wing, wishbone, breast; white meat, dark meat, giblets, pope's *or* parson's nose <nf>

24 fish, *poisson* <Fr>; seafood; fried fish, broiled fish, boiled fish, poached fish, smoked fish, fish cake *or* fish ball, fish stick, fish pie; fish and chips; food fish; finnan haddie; kipper, kippered salmon *or* herring, gravlax; smoked salmon, lox; smoked herring, red herring; eel, *anguille* <Fr>; fish eggs, roe, caviar; ceviche, sushi; squid, calamari; flatfish, sole, lemon sole, Dover sole, flounder, fluke, dab, sanddab

25 shellfish, *coquillage* <Fr>; **mollusc,** snail, *escargot* <Fr>

26 eggs, *œufs* <Fr>; fried eggs, *œufs sur le plat* <Fr>; hard- and soft-boiled eggs, *œufs à la coque* <Fr>, coddled eggs; poached eggs, *œufs pochés* <Fr>; scrambled eggs, buttered eggs, *œufs brouillés* <Fr>; dropped eggs, shirred eggs, stuffed eggs, deviled eggs; omelet *or* omelette; soufflé; Scotch egg, eggs Benedict; egg salad

27 stuffing, dressing, forcemeat *or* farce

28 bread, *pain* <Fr>, *pane* <Ital>, the staff of life; French bread, Italian bread, sourdough bread, ciabatta; loaf of bread; crust, breadcrust, crust of bread; breadstuff; **leaven,** leavening, ferment

29 corn bread; pone, ash pone, corn pone, corn tash, ash cake, hoecake, johnnycake; dodger, corn dodger, corn dab, hush puppy; cracklin' bread <nf>; *tortilla* <Sp>

30 biscuit, sinker <nf>; hardtack, sea biscuit, ship biscuit, pilot biscuit *or* bread; **cracker,** soda cracker *or* saltine, graham cracker, *biscotto* <Ital>, cream cracker, nacho, potato chip, potato crisp <Brit>, sultana, water biscuit, butter cracker, oyster cracker, pilot biscuit; wafer; rusk, zwieback, melba toast, Brussels biscuit; pretzel

31 roll, bun, muffin; bagel, bialy *or* bialystoker; brioche, croissant; English muffin; popover; scone; hard roll, kaiser roll, dinner roll, Parker House roll, Portuguese roll

32 sandwich, *canapé* <Fr>, *smörgåsbord* <Swed>; club sandwich, dagwood; hamburger, burger; submarine *or* sub *or* hero *or* grinder *or* hoagy *or* poorboy; veggieburger *or* vegeburger *or* gardenburger

33 noodles, pasta, Italian paste, paste; **spaghetti,** spaghettini, ziti, fettuccine, radiattore, vermicelli, **macaroni,** lasagne; ravioli, *kreplach* <Yiddish pl>, won ton; **dumpling;** spaetzle, dim sum, gnocchi, linguine; matzo balls, *knaydlach* <Yiddish>

34 cereal, breakfast food, dry cereal, hot cereal; **flour,** meal

35 vegetables, produce, *légumes* <Fr>, veg *and* veggies <nf>; **greens;** potherbs; **beans,** *frijoles* <Sp>, *haricots* <Fr>; leafy vegetable, stem vegetable, root vegetable, tuber, flower vegetable, seed vegetable, pulse; **potato,** spud <nf>, tater <nf>, *pomme de terre* <Fr>, Irish potato, pratie <nf>, white potato; **tomato,** love apple; mushroom; eggplant, *aubergine* <Fr>, mad apple; rhubarb, pieplant; cabbage, *Kraut* <Ger>; ratatouille, mixed vegetables

36 rice, white rice, long-grain rice, brown rice, wild rice, pilaf, orzo, risotto

37 salad, *salade* <Fr>; **greens,** *crudités* <Fr>, tossed salad, chef's salad, Caesar salad; fruit salad, pasta salad, potato salad

38 fruit; produce; stone fruit, drupe, berry, pome, pepo, sorosis, syconium, hesperidium; simple fruit, true fruit, composite fruit, aggregate fruit, multiple fruit, false fruit, succulent fruit; citrus fruit; dry fruit, dehiscent fruit, indehiscent fruit, fruiting body; fruit compote, fruit soup, fruit cup, fruit cocktail, fruit salad, stewed fruit

39 nut, *noix* <Fr>, *noisette* <Fr>; kernel, meat

40 sweets, sweet stuff, **confectionery; sweet, sweetmeat; confection; candy;** bonbon, comfit, confiture; **jelly, jam;** preserve, conserve; marmalade; toffee, butterscotch, caramel, chocolate, fudge; gelatin, Jell-O <trademark>; compote; pudding, custard, mousse; tutti-frutti; maraschino cherries; honey; icing, frosting, glaze; meringue; whipped cream

41 pastry, *patisserie* <Fr>; French pastry, Danish pastry; **tart;** turnover; timbale; **pie,** *tarte* <Fr>, fruit pie, tart, single-crust pie, double-crust pie, deep-dish pie, fruit pie, custard pie, meringue pie; *quiche* *or* *quiche Lorraine* <Fr>; cobbler, crisp, bread pudding; patty, patty cake; patty shell, *vol-au-vent* <Fr>; rosette; dowdy, pandowdy; phyllo *or* filo, strudel, baklava; puff pastry, flake pastry; puff, cream puff, croquembouche, profiterole; cannoli, cream horn; éclair; tiramisu; croissant, scone, shortbread, brioche

42 cake, *gâteau* <Fr>, *torte* <Ger>; *petit-four* <Fr>; layer cake, Bundt cake, pound cake, sponge cake, upside-down cake, fruitcake, gingerbread, cheesecake, shortcake, cupcake, tiramisu, brownie; petit four, madeleine; doughnut

43 cookie, biscuit <Brit>, biscotti

44 doughnut, friedcake, sinker <nf>, cymbal <old>, olykoek <nf>; French doughnut, raised doughnut; glazed doughnut; fastnacht; **cruller,** twister; jelly doughnut, bismarck; fritter, *beignet* <Fr>; apple fritter, *beignet aux pommes* <Fr>

45 pancake, griddlecake, **hot cake,** battercake, flapcake, **flapjack,** flannel cake; buckwheat cake; *chapatty* <India>; **waffle;** blintz, cheese blintz, *crêpe* and *crêpe suzette* <Fr>, *palacsinta* <Hung>, *Pfannkuchen* <Ger>, Swedish pancake

46 pudding, custard, mousse, flan

47 ice, *glace* <Fr>, frozen dessert; **ice cream,** ice milk, French ice-cream; **sherbet,** water ice <Brit>, Italian ice, sorbet, bombe; gelato; tortoni; parfait; sundae, ice-cream sundae, banana split; ice-cream soda; frappé; ice-cream cone; frozen pudding; frozen custard, soft ice cream; frozen yogurt

48 dairy products, milk products; **cheese; tofu,** bean curd

49 beverage, drink, thirst quencher, potation, potable, drinkable <nf>, **liquor,** liquid, hard liquor, alcoholic drink, liqueur, mixed drink, cocktail <see list>, beer <see list>, wine <see list>; **soft drink,** nonalcoholic beverage; cold drink; carbonated water, soda water, sparkling water, tap water, spring water, mineral water, seltzer water; **soda,** pop, soda pop, tonic; milk shake *or* milkshake, shake *and* frosted <nf>; malted milk, malt <nf>, hot chocolate, cocoa; smoothie; **milk,** pasteurized milk, homogenized milk, skim milk, condensed milk, evaporated milk, low-fat milk, chocolate milk; **coffee,** cappuccino, espresso, decaffeinated coffee *or* decaf, latte, café au lait, java *and* joe <nf>; **tea,** iced tea; **fruit juice,** lemonade, vegetable juice, tomato juice; juice box

50 <food packaging terms> use-by date, best-before date

51 breads

bagel	dinner roll
brioche	egg bread
brown bread	English muffin
challah	flatbread
corn bread	French bread
croissant	Irish soda bread

matzo	raisin bread
nut bread	roll
oatmeal bread	rye bread
plain white roll	sourdough bread
poppy-seed plait	Vienna bread
potato bread	white bread
pumpernickel bread	whole-wheat bread

52 cheeses

American	Lancashire
Banon	Leicester
Bel paese	Liederkranz
bleu cheese	Limburger
Bleu de Bresse	Liptauer
blue cheese	Livarot
Blue Cheshire	Maroilles
Boursin	Mimolette
Brick	Monterey Jack
Brie	mozzarella
Caciocavallo	Muenster
Caerphilly	Neufchatel
Camembert	New England Sage
Cheddar	Parmesan
Cheshire	pecorino
chevre	Pont l'Eveque
Chevret	Port Salut
cottage cheese	pot cheese
cream cheese	provolone
Danish blue	Quargel
Dolcelatte	rat cheese
Dunlop	red Windsor
Edam	ricotta
Edelpilzkase	Romano
Emmenthaler	Roquefort
Epoisses	Samsoe
Feta	sapsago
Fontina	smoked cheese
Fromage	St. Marcellin
Gloucester	St. Nectaire
goat cheese	Stilton
Gorgonzola	string cheese
Gouda	Swiss
Gruyere	Teleme
Havarti	Tillamook
hoop cheese	Tilsiter
Jaalsberg	Tome au raisin
jack cheese	Vacherin
Jarlsberg	White Wensleydale

53 desserts

angel food cake	Boston cream pie
apple pandowdy	brandy snap
apple pie	bread pudding
baked Alaska	brownie
baklava	cake
banana split	cannoli
Bavarian cream	charlotte
blancmange	charlotte russe
bombe	cheesecake

17

chocolate chip cookie
clafouti
cobbler
coffeecake
compote
cookie
coupe
cream puff
crème brulee
crème caramel
crepe suzette
crisp
cruller
cupcake
custard
Danish
deep dish pie
devil's food cake
doughnut
eclair
egg cream
Eskimo pie
fig bar
flan
floating island
flummery
frappe
frozen custard
frozen yogurt
fruitcake
fruit cup
fruit pie
frumenty
galatoboureko
gateau
gelatin
gelato
gingerbread
gingersnap
granita
halvah
ice cream
ice cream bar
ice cream cake
ice cream float
ice cream sandwich
ice cream soda
Indian pudding
Italian ice
Jell-O
jelly roll
junket
key lime pie
kuchen

lady finger
layer cake
lemon meringue pie
macaroon
marble cake
marshmallow
mela stregata
milkshake
mousse
mud pie
napoleon
Nesselrode
pandowdy
parfait
pastry
peach Melba
pie
pound cake
profiteroles
pudding
rice pudding
sacher torte
scone
sherbert
shortbread
shortcake
s'mores
snow cone
snow pudding
sorbet
souffle
spice cake
sponge cake
strawberry
   shortcake
streusel
strudel
sugar cookie
sundae
sweet potato pie
sweet roll
tapioca
tart
tiramisu
Toll House cookie
torte
trifle
turnover
upside-down cake
vacherin
wafer
wedding cake
zabaglione
zuppa inglese

54 beers

abbey ale
ale
altbier

amber ale
barley wine
Berliner weisse

Biere de Garde
bitter
bitter stout
bittersweet
bock beer
brown ale
bruised beer
caramel malt
cask-conditioned ale
chicha
copper ale
craft-brewed beer
cream ale
crystal malt
dark beer
diat pils
doppelbock
dort
dortmunder
draft beer
draught beer
dry beer
dunkel beer
dunkel weissbier
eisbock
faro
festbier
fire-brewed beer
framboise
gueuze
hefe weizen
home brew
ice beer
India pale ale
kellerbier
kolsch
krausen
kriek
kristall weizen
kruidenbier
Kulmbacher beer
kumiss

kvass
lager
lambic beer
light beer
loster bier
maibock
malt liquor
marzen
mead
melomel
Munchener
near beer
needled beer
nonalcoholic beer
nut brown ale
oatmeal stout
obergarig
old ale
oscura
pale ale
pilsener
poker beer
porter
rauchbier
saison
Scotch ale
schwarzbier
specialty malt
spruce beer
starkbier
steam beer
stout
Trappist
tripel beer
ur-bock
Vienna beer
weiss
weizenbier
wheat beer
white beer
witbier
zwickelbier

55 cocktails, mixed drinks

Adam and Eve
after-dinner cocktail
Alabama slammer
Alaska cocktail
alexander
Allegheny
Americana
angel's kiss
Bacardi cocktail
B & B
Bahama mama
banshee
Basin street
bay breeze
beachcomber

bee stinger
Bellini
Bermuda Rose
Betsy Ross
B-52
bijou cocktail
black Maria
Black Russian
black velvet
bloody Caesar
Bloody Mary
blue Hawaiian
blue lagoon
blue margarite
blue whale

bocce ball
Bombay cocktail
Boston cocktail
bourbon on the rocks
brandy alexander
brandy fizz
brandy smash
Bronx cocktail
buck's fizz
bull and bear
bull's eye
bull's milk
bullshot
buttered rum
Cape Codder
caudle
cement mixer
champagne cocktail
champagne cooler
Chapel Hill
cherry blossom
chi-chi
clamato cocktail
cobbler
coffee grasshopper
cooler
Cooperstown cocktail
Cuba libre
daiquiri
Daisy Dueller
depth charge
dingo
dirty banana
dixie julep
dream cocktail
dry martini
eggnog
English highball
Fifth Avenue
firefly
fizz
flip
foxy lady
frappe
French connection
frozen daiquiri
frozen Margarita
fuzzy navel
gentleman's cocktail
Georgia mint julep
Georgia peach
Gibson
gimlet
gin and bitters
gin and sin
gin and tonic
gin fizz
gin highball
gin rickey
gin sling

gin sour
gluhwein
godfather
godmother
golden Cadillac
grasshopper
greyhound
grog
Harvard cocktail
Harvard cooler
Harvey Wallbanger
highball
hole-in-one
Hollywood
Honolulu cocktail
hot buttered rum
hot toddy
hurricane
income tax cocktail
Indian Summer
Irish coffee
Jack Rose
kamikaze
Kentucky blizzard
Kentucky cocktail
King Alphonse
Kir
Kir royale
liberty cocktail
Long Island iced tea
Louisville lady
lover's kiss
madras
mai-tai
Manhattan
Margarita
martini
Mary Pickford cocktail
melon ball
merry widow
Mexican coffee
mimosa
mind eraser
mint julep
morning cocktail
Moscow mule
mudslide
Narragansett
New York cocktail
nutcracker
nutty professor
old-fashioned
orange blossom
orgeat
passion mimosa
peach sangaree
peppermint pattie
Peter Pan cocktail
Pimm's cup
pina colada

pink lady
pink squirrel
planter's punch
posset
pousse cafa
prairie oyster
presbyterian
Princeton cocktail
punch
Ramos gin fizz
red death
rickey
Rob Roy
rum and coke
rum cooler
rusty nail
salty dog
sangria
San Juan cooler
Scarlett O'Hara
Scotch and Soda
scotch on the rocks
screwdriver
seabreeze
Seven and Seven
shandy
shrub
sidecar cocktail
Singapore sling
slam dunk
sloe gin fizz
smash
snake bite

snowball
sombrero
soother cocktail
southern lady
southern peach
spritzer
stinger
syllabub
tequila sunrise
Thanksgiving special
thoroughbred cooler
toasted almond
toddy
Tom and Jerry
Tom Collins
to the moon
tropical special
velvet hammer
virgin Mary
vodka and tonic
vodka gimlet
vodka martini
Wassail
whiskey sour
white lady
White Russian
white satin
white spider
wild thing
wine cooler
wu-wu
Yale cocktail
zombie

56 wines

Alsace
amontillado
amoroso
apple wine
Asti spumante
Aveleda
Barbera
Bardolino
Barolo
Beaujolais
Bergerac
blanc de noir
blush
Bordeaux
Bordeaux Blanc
Burgundy
Cabernet Sauvignon
California wine
Chablis
Champagne
Chardonnay
Chateauneuf-du-Pape
Chenin blanc
Chianti
Christi

claret
cold duck
Condrieu
Cote Rotie
Cotes de Nuit
Cotes du Rhone
dandelion wine
Dao
dessert wine
DolcettoFrascati
Douro
dry wine
Entre-deux-Mers
fortified wine
Frascati
Fume Blanc
German wine
Gewurztraminer
Graves
Grenache
Hermitage
hock
Johannisberg Riesling
jug wine
Lacrima

Lambrusco
Liebfraumilch
Macon
Madeira
Malaga
Marsala
Mateus Rose
Medoc
Merlot
Mosel
Moselle
Muscadet
Muscat
Muscatel
Napa Valley wine
Navarra
Nierstein
noble wine
Oporto
Orvieto
Pauillac
Pinot Blanc
Pinot Grigio
Pinot Gris
Pinot Noir
Pomerol
Pommard
port
Pouilly-Fuisse
Pouilly-Fume
red wine
retsina
Rhine

Rhone
Riesling
Rioja
rose
ruby port
sake
Sancerre
Sangiovese
Sauternes
Sauvignon Blanc
Sekt
sherry
Shiraz
Soave
sparkling wine
St. Estephe
St. Julien
sweet wine
Sylvaner
Syrah
table wine
tawny port
Tokay-Pinot Gris
Valdepenas
Valpolicella
vermouth
vinho verde
vintage wine
Vouvray
white cabernet
white wine
white zinfandel
zinfandel

11 COOKING

NOUNS **1 cooking, cookery, cuisine, culinary art;** food preparation, food processing; home economics, domestic science, home management, culinary science; haute cuisine, *nouvelle cuisine* <Fr>; gastronomy; catering; nutrition 7

2 <cooking technique> manner of preparation, style of recipe; baking, toasting, roasting, oven-roasting, frying, deep-frying, pan-frying, stir-frying, searing, blackening, smoking, curing, sautéing, boiling, parboiling, simmering, steaming, stewing, basting, braising, poaching, shirring, barbecuing, steeping, brewing, grilling, broiling, pan-broiling, charbroiling, microwaving, pressure-cooking; canning, pickling, preserving

3 cook, chef, *cuisinier* or *cuisinière* <Fr>, kitchener, culinarian, culinary artist; **chief cook, head chef,** *chef de cuisine* <Fr>; sous chef, apprentice chef, fry cook or grease-burner <nf>, short-order cook; **baker,** *boulanger* <Fr>, pastry cook, pastry chef, *patissier* <Fr>; caterer

4 kitchen, cookroom, cookery, **scullery,** cuisine; kitchenette; **galley,** caboose or camboose;

cookhouse; **bakery,** bakehouse; barbecue; **cookware, kitchen ware,** cooker <see list>; pots and pans; refrigerator, fridge <nf>, freezer; bowl, bin, cabinet, tin, jar; cookbook, recipe, receipt

VERBS **5 cook,** prepare food, prepare, prepare a meal, do, cook up, fry up, boil up, rustle up <nf>; precook; boil, heat, heat up, stew, simmer, parboil, blanch; brew; poach, coddle; bake, fire, ovenbake; **microwave,** micro-cook, nuke <nf>; scallop; shirr; roast; toast; fry, deep-fry or deep-fat fry, griddle, pan, pan-fry; sauté, stir-fry; frizz, frizzle; sear, blacken, braise, brown; broil, grill, pan-broil; barbecue; fricassee; steam; devil; curry; baste; **do to a turn,** do to perfection, whip something up *and* throw something together <nf>

ADJS **6 cooking, culinary,** kitchen, gastronomic, epicurean; mealtime, mensal; preprandial, postprandial, after-dinner; au naturel, a la mode, a la carte, table d'hote

7 cooked, heated, stewed, fried, barbecued, curried, fricasseed, deviled, sautéed, shirred, toasted; roasted, roast; fired, pan-fried, deep-fried or deep-fat fried, stir-fried; broiled, grilled, pan-broiled; seared, blackened, braised, browned; boiled, simmered, parboiled; steamed; poached, coddled; baked, fired, oven-baked; scalloped

8 done, well-done, well-cooked; *bien cuit* <Fr>, done to a turn or to perfection; overcooked, **overdone,** burned; medium, medium-rare, al dente; doneness

9 underdone, undercooked, not done, **rare,** red, raw, *saignant* <Fr>; sodden, fallen

10 cookers

baker	galley stove
barbecue	griddle
boiler	grill
brazier	hibachi
broiler	hot plate
camp stove	infrared broiler
chafer	infrared cooker
chafing dish *or* pan	microwave oven
coffee maker	oven
convection oven	percolator
cook stove	pots and pans
cooktop	pressure cooker *or* autoclave
corn popper	range
Crockpot <trademark>	roaster
deep fat fryer	rotisserie
double boiler	samovar
Dutch oven	slow cooker
electric cooker	smoker
electric frying pan	steamer
electric roaster	stove
electric toaster	toaster
field range	toaster oven
fireless cooker	waffle iron
fry-cooker	waterless cooker

12 EXCRETION
<bodily discharge>

NOUNS **1 excretion,** egestion, extrusion, **elimination, discharge,** expulsion, call of nature <nf>; **emission;** eccrisis; **exudation,** transudation; extravasation, effusion, flux, flow; ejaculation, ejection 909; **secretion** 13

2 defecation, dejection, **evacuation,** voidance; movement, **bowel movement** *or* BM, number two <nf>, **stool,** shit *and* crap <nf>; **diarrhea,** loose bowels, flux; trots *and* runs *and* shits *and* GI's *and* GI shits <nf>; turistas *or* tourista *and* Montezuma's revenge *and* Aztec two-step <nf>; lientery; **dysentery,** bloody flux; catharsis, purgation, purge

3 excrement, dejection, dejecta, dejecture, **discharge,** ejection; matter; **waste,** waste matter; **excreta,** egesta, ejecta, ejectamenta; exudation, exudate; transudation, transudate; extravasation, extravasate; effluent; sewage, sewerage

4 feces, feculence; defecation, movement, bowel movement *or* **BM; stool, shit** <nf>, **ordure,** night soil, jakes <Brit nf>, crap *and* ca-ca *and* doo-doo *and* number two *and* poo-poo *and* poop <nf>; turd <nf>; dingleberry <nf>; **manure, dung, droppings;** cow pats, cow flops <nf>; cow chips, buffalo chips; guano; coprolite, coprolith; sewage, sewerage

5 urine, water, **piss** <nf>, number one, *pish* <Yiddish>, pee *and* pee-pee *and* wee-wee *and* whizz <nf>, piddle, leak, stale; **urination,** micturition, emiction, a piss *and* a pee *and* a whizz <nf>; urea, uric acid

6 pus; matter, purulence, peccant humor <old>, discharge, ichor, sanies; pussiness; **suppuration, festering,** rankling, mattering, running, weeping; gleet, leukorrhea

7 sweat, perspiration, perspiring, sweating, water; exudation, exudate; diaphoresis, sudor, sudation, sudoresis; honest sweat, the sweat of one's brow; beads of sweat, beaded brow; cold sweat; **lather,** swelter, streams of sweat; sudoresis; body odor *or* **BO,** perspiration odor

8 hemorrhage, hemorrhea, **bleeding;** nosebleed; ecchymosis, petechia

9 menstruation, menstrual discharge *or* flow *or* flux, catamenia, catamenial discharge, flowers <old>, **the curse** <nf>, the curse of Eve; **menses, monthlies,** courses, period, one's friend, time of the month, that time

10 latrine, convenience, **toilet,** toilet room, water closet *or* WC <nf>; **john** *and* johnny *and* **can** *and* crapper <nf>; loo <Brit nf>; **lavatory,** washroom, public convenience; **bathroom,** basement; **rest room,** comfort station *or* room; ladies' *or* women's *or* girls' *or* little girls' *or* powder room <nf>; men's *or* boys' *or* little boys' room <nf>, the ladies', the gents'; head; privy, outhouse, backhouse, shithouse <nf>, johnny house <nf>, earth closet <Brit>, closet *and* necessary <nf>; bog <Brit>; urinal

11 toilet, stool, **water closet; john** *and* johnny *and* **can** *and* crapper *and* thunderbox <nf>; latrine; commode, closetstool, potty-chair <nf>; **chamber pot,** chamber, pisspot, potty <nf>, jerry <Brit nf>, jordan <Brit nf>, thunder mug <nf>; throne <nf>; potty-chair; chemical toilet, chemical closet; urinal; bedpan

VERBS **12 excrete,** egest, **eliminate, discharge,** emit, give off, pass, expel; ease *or* relieve oneself, go to the bathroom *or* toilet <nf>; **exude,** exudate, transude; weep; effuse, extravasate; answer the call of nature, pay a call, make a pit stop; **secrete** 13.5

13 defecate, shit *and* crap <nf>, **evacuate,** void, **stool,** dung, have a bowel movement *or* BM, move one's bowels, soil, take a shit *or* crap <nf>, ca-ca *or* number two <nf>; have the runs *or* trots *or* shits <nf>

14 urinate, pass *or* **make water, wet,** stale, **piss** <nf>, piddle, pee, tinkle; pee-pee *and* wee-wee *and* whizz *and* take a whizz *and* take a leak <nf>, spend a penny, pump bilge, do number one

15 fester, suppurate, matter, rankle, run, weep; ripen, come *or* draw to a head

16 sweat, perspire, exude; break out in a sweat, **get all in a lather** <nf>; sweat like a trooper *or* horse *or* pig, swelter, wilt, steam

17 bleed, hemorrhage, lose blood, **shed blood,** spill blood; bloody; ecchymose, extravasate

18 menstruate, come sick, bleed, come around, have one's period, have the curse, have one's friend, be on the rag <nf>

ADJS **19 excretory,** excretive, excretionary; eliminative, eliminant, egestive; exudative, transudative; **secretory** 13.7

20 excremental, excrementary; **fecal,** feculent, shitty *and* crappy <nf>, scatologic *or* scatological, stercoral, stercorous, stercoraceous, dungy; **urinary,** urinative

21 festering, suppurative, rankling, mattering; pussy, purulent

22 sweaty, perspiry <nf>; sweating, perspiring; wet with sweat, beaded with sweat, **sticky** <nf>, **clammy;** bathed in sweat, drenched with sweat, wilted; in a sweat; sudatory, sudoric, sudorific, diaphoretic

23 bleeding, bloody, hemorrhaging; ecchymosed

24 menstrual, catamenial, menstruating; on the rag <nf>

13 SECRETION

NOUNS **1 secretion,** secreta, secernment; **excretion**
12; external secretion, internal secretion;
exudation, transudation; lactation; weeping,
lacrimation

  2 digestive secretion *or* juice, salivary secretion,
gastric juice, digestive juice, pancreatic juice,
intestinal juice; bile, gall; endocrine; prostatic
fluid, seminal fluid, semen, sperm; thyroxin;
autacoid, **hormone,** chalone; mucus; tears; rheum;
sebum, musk, pheromone; milk, colostrum; gland

  3 **saliva, spittle, sputum, spit, expectoration,**
spitting; phlegm, sputum; salivation, ptyalism,
sialorrhea, sialagogue, **slobber,** slabber, slaver,
drivel, dribble, **drool;** froth, foam; mouth-watering

  4 endocrinology, eccrinology, hormonology

VERBS **5 secrete,** produce, give out *or* off, exude,
transude, release, emit, discharge, eject; **excrete**
12.12; water; lactate; weep, tear, cry, lacrimate;
sweat, perspire

  6 **salivate,** ptyalize; **slobber,** slabber, slaver, **drool,**
drivel, dribble; **expectorate, spit,** spit up; spew;
hawk, clear the throat

ADJS **7 secretory,** secretive, secretional, secretionary,
secreting; **excretory** 12.19; exudative, transudatory,
emanative, emanatory, emanational; lymphatic,
serous; seminal, spermatic; watery, watering;
lactational; lacteal, lacteous, lactating; lachrymal,
lacrimatory, lachrymose; rheumy; salivary,
salivant, salivous, salivating, sialoid, sialagogic;
sebaceous, sebiferous; sweating, sweaty, sudatory

  8 **glandular,** glandulous; **endocrine,** humoral,
exocrine, eccrine, apocrine, holocrine, merocrine;
hormonal *or* hormonic; adrenal, pancreatic,
gonadal; ovarian; luteal; prostatic; splenetic;
thymic; thyroidal

14 BODILY DEVELOPMENT

NOUNS **1 bodily** *or* **physical development,** growth,
development 861.1, maturation, maturing,
maturescence, coming of age, growing up,
reaching one's full growth, upgrowth; growing like
a weed <nf>; plant growth, vegetation 310.32,
germination, pullulation; sexual maturity,
pubescence, puberty; nubility, marriageability,
marriageableness; adulthood, manhood,
womanhood; reproduction, procreation 78,
burgeoning, sprouting; budding, gemmation;
outgrowth, excrescence; overgrowth 257.5

VERBS **2 grow, develop,** wax, **increase** 251; gather,
brew; **grow up,** mature, maturate, spring up, ripen,
come of age, **shoot up,** sprout up, upshoot,
upspring, upsprout, upspear, overtop, tower; grow

like a weed <nf>; burgeon, **sprout** 310.34,
blossom 310.32, reproduce 78.7, procreate 78.8,
grow out of, germinate, pullulate; vegetate 310.34;
flourish, thrive; mushroom, balloon; outgrow;
overgrow, hypertrophy, overdevelop, grow
uncontrollably

ADJS **3 grown, full-grown, grown-up,** developed,
well-developed, fully developed, **mature, adult,**
full-fledged; growing, adolescent, maturescent,
pubescent; nubile, marriageable; **sprouting,**
crescent, budding, flowering 310.38, florescent,
flourishing, blossoming, blooming, burgeoning,
fast-growing, thriving; overgrown, hypertrophied,
overdeveloped

15 STRENGTH
  <inherent power>

NOUNS **1 strength, might,** mightiness, powerfulness,
stamina; **force, potency,** power 18; **energy** 17;
vigor, vitality, vigorousness, heartiness, lustiness,
lustihood; **stoutness, sturdiness,** stalwartness,
robustness, hardiness, ruggedness; **guts** *and*
gutsiness <nf>, fortitude, intestinal fortitude
<nf>, **toughness** 1049, **endurance, stamina,**
staying *or* sticking power, stick-to-it-iveness <nf>;
strength of will, decisiveness, obstinacy 361

  2 **muscularity,** brawniness; beefiness *and* huskiness
and heftiness *and* burliness <nf>, thewiness,
sinewiness; **brawn,** beef <nf>; **muscle,** brawn,
sinew, sinews, thew, thews; musculature, build,
physique; tone, elasticity 1048; brute strength

  3 **firmness, soundness,** staunchness, stoutness,
sturdiness, stability, solidity, **hardness** 1046, temper

  4 **impregnability,** impenetrability, **invulnerability,**
inexpugnability, inviolability; **unassailability,**
unattackableness; resistlessness, **irresistibility;**
invincibility, indomitability, insuperability,
unconquerableness, unbeatableness; invincibility

  5 **strengthening, invigoration,** fortification;
hardening, toughening, firming; case hardening,
tempering; **restrengthening,** reinforcement;
reinvigoration, refreshment, revivification;
fortifying

  6 **strong man, stalwart, tower of strength,** muscle
man, piledriver, bulldozer, hunk <nf>; **giant,**
Samson, Goliath; Charles Atlas, Mr Universe;
superhero, Hercules, Atlas, Antaeus, Cyclops,
Briareus, colossus, Polyphemus, Titan,
Brobdingnagian, Tarzan, Superman; the strong,
the mighty; bouncer

  7 <nf terms> **hunk, powerhouse, muscle man,** man
mountain, big bruiser, strong-arm man, bully,
bullyboy, ape, tough, toughie, tough guy, bozo,
goon 671.10, gorilla, meat-eater

8 <comparisons> horse, ox, lion; oak, heart of oak; rock, Gibraltar; iron, steel, nails

VERBS 9 **be strong,** overpower, overwhelm; have what it takes, pack a punch

10 **not weaken,** not flag; **bear up, hold up,** keep up, stand up; **hold out,** stay *or* see it out, not give up, **never say die,** not let it get one down, gird up one's loins

11 <nf terms> **tough it out, hang tough, hang in,** stick *or* take it, take it on the chin, sweat it out, go *or* stay the distance

12 **exert strength,** put beef *or* one's back into it <nf>; use force, get tough <nf>, muscle *and* manhandle *and* strong-arm <nf>

13 **strengthen, invigorate, fortify,** beef up <nf>, brace, buttress, prop, shore up, support, undergird, brace up; gird, gird up one's loins; steel, harden, case harden, anneal, stiffen, **toughen,** temper, nerve; confirm, sustain; **restrengthen, reinforce; reinvigorate,** refresh, revive, recruit one's strength; soup up, beef up

14 **proof,** insulate, weatherproof, soundproof, muffle, quietize, fireproof, waterproof, goofproof <nf>, etc

ADJS 15 **strong, forceful,** forcible, **mighty, powerful,** puissant <nf>, **potent** 18.12; **stout, sturdy, stalwart, rugged,** hale; hunky *and* husky *and* hefty *and* beefy <nf>, strapping, durable, doughty <nf>, **hardy,** hard, hard as nails, cast-iron, iron-hard, steely; **robust,** robustious, gutty *and* gutsy <nf>; strong-willed, obstinate 361.8; **vigorous, hearty,** nervy, **lusty,** bouncing, full- *or* red-blooded; bionic, sturdy as an ox, strong as a lion *or* an ox *or* a horse, strong as brandy, strong as strong; full-strength, double-strength, industrial-strength <nf>

16 **able-bodied, well-built,** well-set, well-set-up <nf>, well-knit, of good *or* powerful physique, broad-shouldered, barrel-chested, **athletic; muscular,** well-muscled, heavily muscled, thickset, burly, **brawny;** thewy, sinewy, **wiry;** muscle-bound, all muscle; strapping

17 **herculean,** Briarean, Antaean, Cyclopean, Atlantean, gigantic, gigantesque, Brobdingnagian, huge 257.20; amazonian

18 **firm, sound, stout,** sturdy, tough, hard-boiled <nf>, **staunch, stable,** solid; sound as a dollar, solid as a rock, firm as Gibraltar, made of iron; rigid, unbreakable, infrangible; braced, buttressed

19 **impregnable,** impenetrable, **invulnerable,** inviolable, inexpugnable; **unassailable,** unattackable, insuperable, unsurmountable; resistless, **irresistible; invincible,** indomitable, **unconquerable,** unsubduable, unyielding 361.9, incontestable, unbeatable, more than a match for; overpowering, overwhelming, avalanchine

20 **resistant, proof, tight;** impervious; foolproof; shatterproof; weatherproof, dampproof, watertight, leakproof; hermetic, airtight; soundproof, noiseproof; puncture proof, holeproof; bulletproof, ballproof, shellproof, bombproof; rustproof, corrosionproof; fireproof, flameproof, fire-resisting; burglarproof

21 **unweakened, undiminished,** unallayed, unbated, unabated, unfaded, unwithered, unshaken, unworn, unexhausted; **unweakening, unflagging, unbowed;** in full force *or* swing, **going strong** <nf>; in the plenitude of power

22 <of sounds and odors> **intense, penetrating,** piercing; **loud,** deafening, thundering 56.12; **pungent,** reeking 69.10

ADVS 23 **strongly, stoutly, sturdily,** stalwartly, robustly, ruggedly; **mightily, powerfully, forcefully,** forcibly; **vigorously, heartily,** lustily; **soundly, firmly,** staunchly; impregnably, invulnerably, **invincibly, irresistibly,** unyieldingly; resistantly, imperviously; **intensely; loudly,** at the top of one's lungs, clamorously, deafeningly; **pungently**

WORD ELEMENTS 24 muscul-, musculo-, my-, myo-; -eus

16 WEAKNESS

NOUNS 1 **weakness,** weakliness, **feebleness,** strengthlessness; **flabbiness, flaccidity,** softness; **impotence** *or* impotency 19; **debility,** debilitation, prostration, invalidism, collapse; **faintness,** faintishness, dizziness, lightheadedness, shakiness, gone *or* blah feeling <nf>; **fatigue** 21, exhaustion, weariness, dullness, sluggishness, languor, lassitude, **listlessness,** tiredness, languishment, atony, burn-out *or* burnout; anemia, bloodlessness, etiolation, asthenia, adynamia, cachexia *or* cachexy

2 **frailty,** slightness, **delicacy, daintiness,** lightness; **flimsiness, unsubstantiality,** wispiness, sleaziness, shoddiness; **fragility,** frangibility *or* frangibleness, brittleness, breakableness, destructibility; disintegration 806; **human frailty,** "amiable weakness"—Henry Fielding; gutlessness <nf>, cowardice 491; moral weakness, irresolution, **indecisiveness,** infirmity of will, velleity, changeableness 854; inherent vice

3 **infirmity, unsoundness,** incapacity, unfirmness, unsturdiness, **instability, unsubstantiality;** decrepitude; **unsteadiness, shakiness,** ricketiness, wobbliness, wonkiness <Brit nf>, caducity, senility, invalidism; wishy-washiness, insipidity, vapidity, wateriness

4 **weak point, weakness,** weak place, **weak side,** weak link, vulnerable point, chink in one's armor, Achilles' heel *or* heel of Achilles; feet of clay

5 weakening, enfeeblement, debilitation,
exhaustion, inanition, attrition; languishment;
devitalization, enervation, evisceration; fatigue;
attenuation, extenuation; softening, mitigation,
damping, abatement, slackening, relaxing,
relaxation, blunting, deadening, dulling; **dilution,**
watering, watering-down, attenuation, thinning,
reduction

6 weakling, weak *or* meek soul, weak sister <nf>,
hothouse plant, softy <nf>, softling, **jellyfish,**
invertebrate, gutless wonder <nf>, **baby,** big baby,
crybaby, chicken <nf>, Milquetoast, sop, **milksop,**
namby-pamby, mollycoddle, mama's boy, mother's
boy, mother's darling, teacher's pet; sissy *and* pansy
and pantywaist <nf>, pushover <nf>, lightweight;
wimp, poor *or* weak *or* dull tool <nf>; **nonentity,**
hollow man, doormat *and* empty suit *and* nebbish
and sad sack <nf>

7 <comparisons> kitten, reed, thread, matchwood,
rope of sand; house of cards, eggshell, glass, house
built on sand, sand castle, cobweb; water, milk and
water, gruel, dishwater, cambric tea

VERBS **8** <be weak> **shake,** tremble, quiver, quaver,
cringe, cower 491.9, totter, teeter, dodder; halt,
limp; be on one's last leg, have one foot in the grave

9 <become weak> **weaken,** grow weak *or* weaker, go
soft <nf>; **languish, wilt,** faint, **droop,** drop,
dwindle, **sink, decline, flag, pine, fade, tail away** *or*
off, fail, fall *or* drop by the wayside; crumble, go to
pieces, disintegrate 806.3; go downhill, hit the
skids <nf>, give way, break, collapse, cave in <nf>,
surrender, cry uncle <nf>; give out, have no staying
power, run out of gas <nf>, conk *or* peter *or* poop
or peg *or* fizzle out <nf>; come apart, come apart
at the seams, come unstuck *or* unglued <nf>;
yield; die on the vine <nf>; wear thin *or* away

10 <make weak> **weaken, enfeeble, debilitate,**
unstrengthen, unsinew, undermine, soften up
<nf>, unbrace, unman, unnerve, rattle, shake up
<nf>, **devitalize, enervate,** eviscerate; **sap,** sap the
strength of, exhaust, gruel, take it out of <nf>;
shake, unstring; reduce, lay low; attenuate,
extenuate, mitigate, abate; blunt, deaden, dull,
damp *or* dampen, take the edge off; draw the
teeth, defang; cramp, cripple

11 dilute, cut <nf>, **reduce, thin,** thin out, attenuate,
rarefy; **water,** water down, adulterate, irrigate *and*
baptize <nf>; soften, muffle, mute

ADJS **12 weak,** weakly, **feeble,** debilitated, imbecile;
strengthless, sapless, marrowless, pithless,
sinewless, listless, out of gas <nf>, nerveless,
lustless; **impotent,** powerless 19.13; spineless, lily-
livered, whitelivered, wimpy *and* wimpish *and*
chicken *and* gutless <nf>, cowardly 491.10;
unnerved, shookup <nf>, unstrung, faint, faintish,

lightheaded, dizzy, gone; dull, slack; **soft, flabby,**
flaccid, unhardened; **limp,** limber, limp *or* limber
as a dishrag, floppy, rubbery; **languorous,** languid,
drooping, droopy, pooped <nf>; asthenic, anemic,
bloodless, effete, etiolated; not what one used to be

13 "weak as water"—Bible, weak as milk and water,
weak as a drink of water, weak as a child *or* baby,
weak as a chicken, weak as a kitten, weak as a
mouse, "weak as a rained-on bee"—F R Torrence

14 frail, slight, delicate, dainty; puny; light,
lightweight; effeminate; namby-pamby, sissified,
pansyish; **fragile,** frangible, **breakable,**
destructible, shattery, crumbly, brittle,
fragmentable, fracturable; **unsubstantial, flimsy,**
sleazy, tacky <nf>, wispy, cobwebby, gossamery,
papery; gimcrack *and* gimcracky *and* cheap-jack
and ticky-tacky <nf>; jerry-built, jerry; gimpy

15 unsound, infirm, unfirm, **unstable, unsubstantial,**
unsturdy, unsolid, decrepit, crumbling,
fragmented, fragmentary, disintegrating 806.5;
poor, poorish; rotten, rotten to the core

16 unsteady, shaky, rickety, ricketish, wonky <Brit
nf>, spindly, spidery, teetering, teetery, tottery,
tottering, doddering, tumbledown, ramshackle,
dilapidated, rocky <nf>; groggy, wobbly, staggery

17 wishy-washy, tasteless, bland, **insipid,** vapid,
neutral, watery, milky, milk-and-water, mushy;
halfhearted, infirm of will *or* purpose, **indecisive,**
irresolute, changeable 853.7; limp-wristed, gutless

18 weakened, enfeebled, disabled, incapacitated,
challenged <nf>; **devitalized,** drained, exhausted,
sapped, burned-out, used up, played out, spent,
ausgespielt <Ger>, effete, etiolated; **fatigued,**
enervated, eviscerated; **wasted, rundown,** worn,
worn-out, worn to a frazzle <nf>, worn to a
shadow, reduced to a skeleton; stressed out; on
one's last legs

19 diluted, cut <nf>, **reduced, thinned,** rarefied,
attenuated; adulterated; watered, watered-down

20 weakening, debilitating, enfeebling; devitalizing,
enervating, sapping, exhausting, fatiguing,
grueling, trying, draining, unnerving

21 languishing, drooping, sinking, declining, flagging,
pining, fading, failing; on the wane

ADVS **22 weakly, feebly,** strengthlessly, languorously,
listlessly; faintly; delicately, effeminately, daintily;
infirmly, unsoundly, unstably, unsubstantially,
unsturdily, flimsily; shakily, unsteadily, teeteringly,
totteringly

17 ENERGY

NOUNS **1 energy, vigor, force, power, vitality,**
strenuousness, **intensity, dynamism,** demonic
energy; **potency** 18; **strength** 15; actual *or* kinetic

energy; dynamic energy; potential energy; energy source 1021.1, electrical energy, hydroelectric energy, water power, nuclear energy, solar energy, wind energy, alternative energy

2 **vim, verve,** fire, adrenalin, **dash, drive; aggressiveness, enterprise,** initiative, proactiveness, thrust, spunk; **eagerness** 101, zeal, heartiness, keenness, gusto

3 <nf terms> **pep,** bang, biff, get-up-and-go, ginger, gism, jazz, sizzle, kick, moxie, oomph, pepper, piss and vinegar, **pizzazz,** poop, punch, push, snap, spizzerinctum, starch, steam, zing, zip, zizz, sparkle, wallop, balls

4 **animation, vivacity,** liveliness, energy, **ardor,** vitality, glow, warmth, enthusiasm, lustiness, robustness, mettle, **zest,** zestfulness, **gusto, élan,** éclat, impetus, impetuosity, *joie de vivre* <Fr>, *brio* <Ital>, spiritedness, **briskness,** perkiness, sprightliness, pertness, sensibility, **life, spirit,** life force, vital force *or* principle, *élan vital* <Fr>; activity 330

5 <energetic disapproval or criticism> **acrimony,** acridity, acerbity, acidity, **bitterness,** tartness, **causticity,** mordancy *or* mordacity, **virulence; harshness,** fierceness, **rigor,** roughness, **severity, vehemence,** violence 671, stringency, astringency, stridency 58.1, **sharpness, keenness, poignancy,** trenchancy; edge, point; bite, teeth, grip, sting

6 **energizer, stimulus,** stimulator, vitalizer, arouser, needle <nf>, restorative; **stimulant,** tonic 86.8; **activator,** motivator, motivating force, motive power; **animator,** spark plug *and* human dynamo *and* ball of fire <nf>; life, life of the party

7 <units of energy> atomerg, dinamode, dyne, erg, energid, foot-pound, horsepower-hour, horsepower-year, joule, calorie 1019.19, kilogram-meter, kilowatt-hour, photon, quantum

8 **energizing, invigoration, animation, enlivenment,** quickening, **vitalization,** revival, revitalization; **exhilaration, stimulation**

9 **activation,** reactivation; viability

VERBS 10 **energize,** dynamize; **invigorate, animate, enliven, liven, liven up,** vitalize, quicken, goose *or* jazz up <nf>; **exhilarate, stimulate,** hearten, galvanize, enthuse, electrify, fire, build a fire under, inflame, warm, kindle, charge, charge up, psych *or* pump up <nf>, rouse, arouse, act like a tonic, be a shot in the arm <nf>, **pep** *or* snap *or* jazz *or* zip *or* perk up <nf>, put pep *or* zip into it <nf>

11 **have energy,** be energetic, be vigorous, **thrive,** burst *or* overflow with energy, flourish, tingle, feel one's oats, be up and doing, be full of beans *or* pep *or* ginger *or* zip <nf>, be full of piss and vinegar <nf>, champ at the bit <nf>; come on like gangbusters <nf>

12 **activate,** reactivate, recharge; step on the gas <nf>

ADJS 13 **energetic, vigorous, strenuous, forceful, forcible, strong, dynamic,** kinetic, intense, acute, keen, incisive, trenchant, vivid, vibrant; **enterprising, aggressive,** proactive, activist, can-do *and* gung ho *and* take-over *and* take-charge <nf>, go-getting; **active, lively,** living, **animated, spirited,** go-go <nf>, **vivacious,** brisk, bright-eyed and bushy-tailed <nf>, feisty, lusty, **robust,** hearty, enthusiastic, mettlesome, zesty, zestful, impetuous, spanking, smacking; pumped *and* pumped up *and* jazzed-up *and* charged up *and* switched on <nf>, snappy *and* zingy *and* zippy *and* peppy <nf>, full of pep *or* pizzazz *or* piss and vinegar <nf>, full of beans <nf>

14 **acrimonious, acrid,** acidulous, acid, **bitter,** tart, **caustic,** escharotic <med>, mordant *or* mordacious, **virulent, violent, vehement,** vitriolic; **harsh,** fierce, **rigorous,** severe, rough, stringent, astringent, strident 58.12, **sharp, keen,** sharpish, incisive, trenchant, **cutting,** biting, stinging, **scathing,** stabbing, **piercing, poignant,** penetrating, edged, double-edged

15 **energizing, vitalizing, enlivening,** quickening; tonic, bracing, rousing; **invigorating,** invigorative; **animating,** animative; **exhilarating,** exhilarative; **stimulating,** stimulative, stimulatory, vivifying; activating; viable

ADVS 16 **energetically, vigorously, strenuously, forcefully,** forcibly, intensely, like a house afire *and* like gangbusters <nf>, zestfully, lustily, heartily, keenly; **actively,** briskly; **animatedly, spiritedly,** vivaciously, with pep <nf>, *con brio* <Ital>

18 POWER, POTENCY
<effective force>

NOUNS 1 **power, potency** *or* potence, prepotency, **force, might,** mightiness, **vigor,** vitality, vim, push, drive, charge, puissance <old>; dint, virtue; moxie *and* oomph *and* pizzazz *and* poop *and* punch *and* bang *and* clout *and* steam <nf>; powerfulness, forcefulness; virulence, vehemence; **strength** 15; **energy** 17; **virility** 76.2, Viagra; cogence *or* cogency, validity, effect, impact, **effectiveness,** effectivity, effectuality, competence *or* competency; productivity, productiveness; power structure, corridors of power; **influence** 894, pull; **authority** 417, weight; **superiority** 249; power pack, amperage, wattage; main force, *force majeure* <Fr>, main strength, brute force *or* strength, compulsion, duress; muscle power, sinew, might and main, beef <nf>, strong arm; full force, full blast; power struggle; black power; flower power; mana; charisma

2 ability, capability, capacity, potentiality, faculty, facility, fitness, qualification, talent, flair, genius, caliber, **competence,** competency, adequacy, sufficiency, **efficiency,** efficacy; **proficiency** 413.1; the stuff *and* the goods *and* what it takes <nf>; susceptibility

3 omnipotence, almightiness, all-powerfulness; omnicompetence

4 manpower; horsepower, brake horsepower *or* bhp, electric power, electropower, hydroelectric power; hydraulic power, water power; steam power; geothermal power; solar power; atomic power, nuclear power, thermonuclear power; rocket power, jet power; **propulsion, thrust,** impulse

5 force of inertia, *vis inertiae* <L>; dead force, *vis mortua* <L>; living force, *vis viva* <L>; force of life, *vis vitae* <L>

6 centrifugal force *or* action, centripetal force *or* action, force of gravity

7 <science of forces> dynamics, statics

8 empowerment, enablement; investment, endowment, enfranchisement

9 work force, hands, men, manpower; **fighting force,** troops, units, the big battalions, firepower; **personnel** 577.11, human resources; **forces**

VERBS **10 empower, enable;** invest, clothe, invest *or* clothe with power, deputize; enfranchise; endue, endow, **authorize;** arm; strengthen

11 be able, be up to, up to, **lie in one's power; can,** may, can do; make it *or* make the grade <nf>; hack it *and* cut it *and* cut the mustard <nf>; charismatize; **wield power,** possess authority 417.13; take charge 417.14, get something under one's control *or* under one's thumb, hold all the aces *and* have the say-so <nf>

ADJS **12 powerful, potent,** prepotent, powerpacked, **mighty,** irresistible, avalanchine, **forceful,** forcible, dynamic; **vigorous,** vital, **energetic,** puissant, ruling, in power; **cogent,** striking, telling, effective, impactful, valid, operative, in force; **strong;** high-powered, high-tension, high-pressure, high-performance, high-potency, bionic; **authoritative;** armipotent, mighty in battle

13 omnipotent, almighty, all-powerful; plenipotentiary, absolute, unlimited, **sovereign** 417.17; **supreme** 249.13; omnicompetent

14 able, capable, equal to, up to, **competent,** adequate, effective, effectual, efficient, efficacious; productive; **proficient** 413.22

ADVS **15 powerfully, potently, forcefully,** forcibly, mightily, with might and main, **vigorously, energetically,** dynamically; **cogently,** strikingly, tellingly, impactfully; **effectively,** effectually; productively; with telling effect, to good account, to good purpose, with a vengeance

16 ably, capably, competently, adequately, effectively, effectually, **efficiently, well; to the best of one's ability,** as lies in one's power, so far as one can, as best one can; with all one's might, with everything that is in one

17 by force, by main *or* brute force, by force majeure, with the strong arm, with a high hand, high-handedly; **forcibly,** amain, with might and main; by force of arms, at the point of the sword, by storm

PREPS **18** by dint of, by virtue of

WORD ELEMENTS **19** dynam-, dynamo-; -dynamia

19 IMPOTENCE

NOUNS **1 impotence** *or* impotency, **powerlessness,** impuissance <old>, forcelessness, feebleness, softness, flabbiness, wimpiness *or* wimpishness <nf>, **weakness** 16; power vacuum

2 inability, incapability, incapacity, incapacitation, **incompetence** *or* incompetency, inadequacy, insufficiency, ineptitude, **inferiority** 250, inefficiency, unfitness, imbecility; disability, disablement, disqualification; legal incapacity, wardship, minority, infancy

3 ineffectiveness, ineffectualness, ineffectuality, inefficaciousness, **inefficacy,** counterproductiveness *or* counterproductivity, invalidity, **futility, uselessness,** inutility, bootlessness, failure 410; fatuity, inanity

4 helplessness, defenselessness, unprotectedness, vulnerability; **debilitation,** invalidism, effeteness, etiolation, enervation; wimpiness <nf>

5 emasculation, demasculinization, defeminization, effeminization, neutering, maiming, castration 255.4

6 impotent, weakling 16.6, invalid, incompetent; flash in the pan, blank cartridge, wimp *and* dud <nf>; eunuch, *castrato* <Ital>, gelding; pushover, easy mark <nf>

VERBS **7 be impotent,** lack force; be ineffective, avail nothing, not work *or* do not take <nf>; **waste one's effort,** bang one's head against a brick wall, have one's hands tied, spin one's wheels, tilt at windmills, run in circles, get nowhere

8 cannot, not be able, not have it *and* not hack it *and* not cut it *and* not cut the mustard <nf>, not make it *and* not make the grade *and* not make the cut <nf>

9 disable, disenable, unfit, **incapacitate,** drain, de-energize; enfeeble, debilitate, **weaken** 16.9,10; cripple, maim, lame, hamstring, knee-cap, defang, pull the teeth of <nf>; wing, clip the wings of; **inactivate,** disarm, unarm, put out of action, put *hors de combat;* **put out of order,** put out of commission <nf>, throw out of gear; bugger *and* bugger up *and* queer *and* queer the works *and* gum up *or* screw up <nf>, throw a wrench *or* monkey wrench in the machinery <nf>, sabotage, wreck; kibosh *and* put the kibosh on <nf>; spike, spike one's guns, put a spoke in one's wheels

10 <put out of action> **paralyze,** prostrate, shoot down in flames <nf>, put *hors de combat* <Fr>, knock out <nf>, break the neck *or* back of; hamstring; handcuff, tie the hands of, hobble, enchain, manacle, hog-tie <nf>, **tie hand and foot,** truss up; throttle, strangle, get a stranglehold on; muzzle, gag, silence; **take the wind out of one's sails,** deflate, knock the props out from under, undermine, cut the ground from under, not leave a leg to stand on

11 **disqualify; invalidate,** knock the bottom out of <nf>

12 **unman, unnerve, enervate,** exhaust, etiolate, **devitalize; emasculate,** cut the balls off <nf>, demasculinize, effeminize; desex, desexualize; sterilize; castrate 255.11, neuter

ADJS 13 **impotent, powerless, forceless, out of gas** <nf>; feeble, soft, flabby, **weak** 16.12, weak as a kitten, wimpy *or* wimpish <nf>

14 **unable, incapable, incompetent,** inefficient, ineffective, **unqualified,** inept, unendowed, ungifted, untalented, **unfit,** unfitted; **outmatched,** out of one's depth, in over one's head, outgunned; **inferior** 250.6

15 **ineffective, ineffectual, inefficacious,** counterproductive, feckless, not up to scratch *or* up to snuff <nf>, **inadequate** 250.7; **invalid, inoperative,** of no force; nugatory, nugacious; fatuous, fatuitous; **vain, futile, inutile, useless,** unavailing, bootless, fruitless; all talk and no action, all wind; **empty,** inane; **debilitated,** effete, enervated, etiolated, barren, sterile, washed-out <nf>

16 **disabled, incapacitated; crippled,** hamstrung; disqualified, invalidated; disarmed; paralyzed; hog-tied <nf>; prostrate, **on one's back,** on one's beam-ends; challenged

17 **out of action, out of commission** *and* out of it <nf>, out of gear; *hors de combat* <Fr>, out of the battle, off the field, out of the running; laid on the shelf, obsolete, life-expired

18 **helpless, defenseless, unprotected;** vulnerable, like a sitting duck <nf>, aidless, friendless, unfriended; fatherless, motherless; leaderless, guideless; **untenable,** pregnable, vulnerable; disenfranchised

19 **unmanned, unnerved, enervated,** debilitated, **devitalized;** nerveless, sinewless, marrowless, pithless, lustless; **castrated,** emasculate, emasculated, gelded, eunuchized, unsexed, deballed <nf>, demasculinized, effeminized

ADVS 20 **beyond one,** beyond one's power *or* capacity *or* ability, beyond one's depth, out of one's league <nf>, above one's head, too much for

INTERJ 21 no can do!

20 REST, REPOSE

NOUNS 1 **rest, repose, ease, relaxation,** slippered *or* unbuttoned ease, decompression <nf>; **comfort** 121; restfulness, quiet, tranquility; inactivity 331; sleep 22

2 **respite, recess, rest, pause,** halt, stay, lull, **break,** surcease, suspension, interlude, **intermission,** spell <Austral>, letup <nf>, **time out** <nf>, time to catch one's breath; **breathing spell,** breathing time, breathing place, breathing space, breath; **breather;** coffee break, tea break, cigarette break; cocktail hour, happy hour <nf>; enforced respite, downtime; R and R *or* rest and recreation

3 **vacation,** holiday <Brit>; **time off;** day off, week off, month off, etc; paid vacation, paid holiday <Brit>; weekend; **leave, leave of absence, furlough; liberty,** shore leave; **sabbatical,** sabbatical leave *or* year; **weekend; busman's holiday;** package tour *or* holiday

4 **holiday, day off; red-letter day,** gala day, fete day, festival day, day of festivities; national holiday, legal holiday, bank holiday <Brit>; High Holiday, High Holy Day; holy day; feast, feast day, high day, church feast, fixed feast, movable feast; half-holiday

5 **day of rest,** *dies non* <L>; **Sabbath,** Sunday, Lord's day, First day

VERBS 6 **rest, repose,** take rest, take one's ease, **take it easy** <nf>, lay down one's tools, rest from one's labors, rest on one's oars, take life easy; go to rest, settle to rest; lie down, have a lie-down, go to bed, snuggle down, curl up, tuck up, bed, bed down, couch, recline, lounge, drape oneself, sprawl, loll; take off one's shoes, unbuckle one's belt, get *or* take a load off one's feet, put one's feet up

7 **relax,** unlax <nf>, unbend, unwind, slack, slacken, **ease; ease up, let up,** slack up, slack off, **ease off,** let down, **slow down,** take it slow, take time to catch one's breath; mellow out, lay back *and* kick back *and* decompress <nf>

8 **take a rest, take a break, break, take time out** *and* grab some R and R <nf>, pause, lay off, **knock off** <nf>, recess, **take a recess,** take ten *and* take five <nf>; stop for breath, catch one's breath, breathe; stop work, suspend operations, call it a day; go to bed with the chickens, sleep in; take a nap, catch some Zs <nf>

9 **vacation, get away from it all,** holiday, take a holiday, make holiday; **take a leave of absence,**

take leave, go on leave, go on furlough, take one's sabbatical; weekend; Sunday, Christmas, etc

ADJS **10 vacational, holiday,** ferial <old>, festal; sabbatical; **comfortable** 121.11; **restful,** quiet 173.12

ADVS **11 at rest, at ease,** at one's ease; abed, in bed

12 on vacation, on leave, on furlough; off duty, on one's own time

21 FATIGUE

NOUNS **1 fatigue, tiredness, weariness,** wearifulness; **burnout,** end of one's tether, overtiredness, overstrain; faintness, goneness, weakness, enfeeblement, lack of staying power, enervation, debility, debilitation 16.1; jadedness; lassitude, languor; tension fatigue, stance fatigue, stimulation fatigue; fatigue disease, fatigue syndrome *or* post-viral fatigue syndrome, chronic fatigue syndrome; combat fatigue; mental fatigue, brain fag <nf>; strain, mental strain, heart strain, eyestrain; sleepiness 22.1

2 exhaustion, exhaustedness, draining; **collapse, prostration,** breakdown, crack-up <nf>, nervous exhaustion *or* prostration, burn-out *or* burnout; blackout

3 breathlessness, shortness of breath, windedness, short-windedness; panting, gasping; dyspnea, labored breathing

VERBS **4 fatigue, tire, weary, exhaust,** wilt, flag, jade, harass; **wear,** wear on *or* upon, **wear down; tire out, wear out, burn out; use up; do in; wind,** put out of breath; overtire, overweary, overfatigue, overstrain; weaken, enervate, debilitate 16.10; weary *or* tire to death, take it out of; prostrate; deprive of sleep

5 burn out, get tired, grow weary, tire, weary, fatigue, jade; **flag, droop,** faint, sink, feel dragged out, wilt; **play out,** run out, run down, burn out; gasp, wheeze, pant, puff, blow, puff and blow, puff like a grampus; collapse, break down, crack up <nf>, give out, drop, fall *or* drop by the wayside, drop in one's tracks, succumb; need a break

6 <nf terms> beat, poop, frazzle, fag, tucker; fag out, tucker out, knock out, do in, do up; **poop out,** peter out

ADJS **7 tired, weary, fatigued,** wearied, weariful, jaded, run-down, good and tired; unrefreshed, unrestored, in need of rest, ready to drop; **faint,** fainting, feeling faint, **weak,** rocky <nf>, enfeebled, enervated, debilitated, seedy <nf>, weakened 16.13,18; drooping, droopy, wilting, flagging, sagging; languid; worn, worn-down, **worn to a frazzle** *or* shadow, toilworn, weary-worn; wayworn, way-weary; foot-weary, weary-footed,

footsore; tired-armed; tired-winged, weary-winged; weary-laden

8 <nf terms> **beat, pooped, bushed,** poohed, paled, frazzled, bagged, fagged, tuckered, plumb tuckered, done, done in, all in, dead, dead beat, dead on one's feet, gone; **pooped out,** knocked out, wiped out, tuckered out, played out, fagged out; run ragged; used up, done up, beat up, washed-up, whacked out

9 tired-looking, weary-looking, tired-eyed, tired-faced, haggard, hollow-eyed, ravaged, drawn, cadaverous, worn, wan, zombiish

10 burnt-out, burned-out, **exhausted,** drained, **spent,** unable to go on, gone; **tired out, worn-out,** beaten; bone-tired, bone-weary; **dog-tired,** dog-weary; **dead-tired, tired to death,** weary unto death, dead-alive *or* dead-and-alive, more dead than alive, ready to drop, on one's last legs; prostrate

11 burnt-out, overtired, overweary, overwrought, overwearied, overstrained, overdriven, overfatigued, overspent

12 breathless, winded; wheezing, puffing, panting, **out of breath,** short of breath *or* wind, gasping for breath; short-winded, short-breathed, dyspneic

13 fatiguing, wearying, wearing, **tiring,** straining, stressful, trying, **exhausting,** draining, **grueling,** punishing, killing, demanding; **tiresome,** fatiguesome, **wearisome,** weariful; toilsome 725.18

ADVS **14 out,** to the point of exhaustion

22 SLEEP

NOUNS **1 sleepiness, drowsiness,** doziness, heaviness, lethargy, oscitation, somnolence *or* somnolency, yawning, stretching, oscitancy, pandiculation; languor 331.6; sand in the eyes, heavy eyelids; REM sleep *or* rapid-eye-movement sleep *or* dreaming sleep

2 sleep, slumber; repose, silken repose, *somnus* <L>, the arms of Morpheus; bye-bye *or* beddy-bye <nf>; doss <Brit nf>, blanket drill *and* shut eye <nf>; light sleep, fitful sleep, **doze, drowse,** snoozle <nf>; beauty sleep <nf>; sleepwalking, somnambulism; somniloquy; **land of Nod,** slumberland, sleepland, dreamland; hibernation, winter sleep, aestivation; bedtime, sack time <nf>; unconsciousness 25.2

3 nap, snooze <nf>, **catnap,** wink, **forty winks** *and* some Zs <nf>, zizz <Brit nf>, wink of sleep, spot of sleep; **siesta,** blanket drill *and* sack *or* rack time <nf>; power nap

4 sweet sleep, balmy sleep, downy sleep, soft sleep, gentle sleep, smiling sleep, golden slumbers; "folded sleep"—Tennyson, "the honey-heavy dew of slumber"—Shakespeare; peaceful sleep, sleep of the just; restful sleep, good night's sleep, "sleep that knits up the ravell'd sleave of care"—Shakespeare

5 **deep sleep,** profound sleep, heavy sleep, **sound sleep,** unbroken sleep, wakeless sleep, drugged sleep, dreamless sleep, the sleep of the dead, "sleep such as makes the darkness brief"—Martial; paradoxical *or* orthodox *or* dreaming *or* REM sleep, synchronized *or* S *or* NREM sleep

6 **stupor,** sopor, **coma, swoon,** lethargy <old>; **trance;** narcosis, narcohypnosis, narcoma, narcotization, narcotic stupor *or* trance; sedation; high <nf>; nod <nf>; narcolepsy; catalepsy; thanatosis, shock; sleeping sickness, encephalitis lethargica

7 **hypnosis,** mesmeric *or* **hypnotic sleep, trance,** somnipathy, hypnotic somnolence; lethargic hypnosis, somnambulistic hypnosis, cataleptic hypnosis, animal hypnosis; narcohypnosis; autohypnosis, self-hypnosis; hypnotherapy

8 **hypnotism, mesmerism;** hypnology; hypnotization, mesmerization; **animal magnetism,** od, odyl, odylic force; hypnotic suggestion, posthypnotic suggestion, autosuggestion

9 **hypnotist, mesmerist,** hypnotizer, mesmerizer; Svengali, Mesmer

10 **sleep-inducer,** sleep-producer, sleep-provoker, sleep-bringer, hypnotic, soporific, somnifacient; poppy, mandrake, mandragora, opium, opiate, morphine, morphia; nightcap; sedative 86.12; anesthetic; lullaby

11 **Morpheus,** Somnus, Hypnos; sandman, dustman <Brit>

12 **sleeper, slumberer;** sleeping beauty; **sleepyhead,** lie-abed, slugabed, sleepwalker, somnambulist; somniloquist

VERBS 13 **sleep, slumber,** rest in the arms of Morpheus, go to bed; **doze, drowse; nap, catnap,** take a nap, catch a wink, sleep soundly, **sleep like a top** *or* **log,** sleep like the dead; *dormir sur les deux oreilles* <Fr>; snore, saw wood *and* saw logs <nf>; have an early night, go to bed betimes; sleep in; oversleep

14 <nf terms> **snooze,** get some shut-eye, get some sack time, flake *or* sack out, crash, catch forty winks *or* some Zs, have a zizz <Brit>; pound the ear, kip *or* doss <Brit>

15 **hibernate,** aestivate, lie dormant

16 **go to sleep,** settle to sleep, go off to sleep, **fall asleep,** drop asleep, **drop off,** drift off, drift off to sleep; **doze off, drowse off,** nod off, dope off <nf>; close one's eyes, "let fall the shadow of mine eyes"—Shakespeare

17 **go to bed, retire;** lay me down to sleep; bed, bed down; go night-night *and* go bye-bye *and* go beddy-bye <nf>

18 <nf terms> **hit the hay, hit the sack,** crash, turn in, crawl in, flop, sack out, sack up, kip down *or* doss down <Brit>

19 **put to bed,** bed; nestle, cradle; **tuck in**

20 **put to sleep; lull to sleep,** rock to sleep; **hypnotize, mesmerize,** magnetize; **entrance,** trance, put in a trance; narcotize, drug, dope <nf>; anesthetize, put under; sedate

ADJS 21 **sleepy, drowsy,** dozy, snoozy <nf>, **slumberous,** slumbery, dreamy; **half asleep,** asleep on one's feet; sleepful, sleep-filled; yawny, stretchy <nf>, oscitant, yawning, napping, **nodding,** ready for bed; heavy, **heavy-eyed, heavy with sleep,** sleep-swollen, sleep-drowned, sleep-drunk, drugged with sleep; **somnolent,** soporific; **lethargic,** comatose, narcose *or* narcous, stuporose *or* **stuporous, in a stupor,** out of it <nf>; narcoleptic; cataleptic; narcotized, drugged, doped <nf>; sedated; anesthetized; **languid**

22 **asleep, sleeping, slumbering,** in the arms *or* lap of Morpheus, in the land of Nod; **sound asleep, fast asleep,** dead asleep, deep asleep, in a sound sleep, flaked-out <nf>; **unconscious, oblivious, out,** out like a light, out cold; comatose; dormant; dead, **dead to the world;** unwakened, unawakened

23 **sleep-inducing,** sleep-producing, sleep-bringing, sleep-causing, sleep-compelling, sleep-inviting, sleep-provoking, sleep-tempting; **narcotic,** hypnotic, **soporific, somniferous,** somnifacient; sedative 86.45

24 **hypnotic,** hypnoid, hypnoidal, **mesmeric;** odylic; narcohypnotic

23 WAKEFULNESS

NOUNS 1 **wakefulness,** wake; **sleeplessness,** restlessness, tossing and turning; **insomnia,** insomnolence *or* insomnolency, white night; vigil, all-night vigil, lidless vigil, *per vigilium* <L>; insomniac; consciousness, sentience; alertness 339.5

2 **awakening, wakening,** rousing, **arousal;** rude awakening, rousting out <nf>; reveille

VERBS 3 **keep awake,** keep one's eyes open; keep alert, be vigilant 339.8; stay awake, **toss and turn, not sleep a wink,** not shut one's eyes, count sheep; have a white night

4 **awake, awaken, wake, wake up, get up,** rouse, come alive <nf>; open one's eyes, stir <nf>

5 <wake someone up> **awaken, waken, rouse, arouse,** awake, wake, **wake up,** shake up, knock up <Brit>, roust out <nf>

6 **get up, get out of bed, arise,** rise, **rise and shine** <nf>, greet the day, **turn out** <nf>; roll out *and* pile out *and* **show a leg** *and* hit the deck <nf>

ADJS **7 wakeful, sleepless,** slumberless, **unsleeping,** insomniac, insomnious; restless; watchful, vigilant, lidless

8 awake, conscious, **up; wide-awake,** broad awake; alert 339.14

ADVS **9 sleeplessly, unsleepingly; wakefully,** with one's eyes open; alertly 339.17

24 SENSATION
<physical sensibility>

NOUNS **1 sensation, sense, feeling;** sense impression, sense-datum *or* -data, percept, perception, sense perception; experience, sensory experience; **sensuousness,** sensuosity, sensuality; **consciousness,** awareness, apperception; response, response to stimuli

2 sensibility, sensibleness, physical sensibility, sentience *or* sentiency; openness to sensation, readiness of feeling, receptiveness, receptivity; sensation level, threshold of sensation, limen; impressionability, impressibility, affectibility; **susceptibility,** susceptivity, perceptibility; esthesia, aesthesia, esthesis

3 sensitivity, sensitiveness; perceptivity, perceptiveness, feelings; responsiveness; **tact, tactfulness, considerateness,** courtesy, politeness; **compassion, sympathy;** empathy, identification; **concern,** solicitousness, solicitude; capability of feeling, passibility; **delicacy, exquisiteness,** tenderness, fineness; **oversensitiveness,** oversensibility, hypersensitivity, **thin skin,** hyperesthesia, hyperpathia, supersensitivity, overtenderness; **irritability,** prickliness, soreness, **touchiness,** tetchiness; ticklishness, nervousness 128; allergy, anaphylaxis; sensitization; photophobia

4 sore spot, sore point, soft spot, raw, exposed nerve, raw nerve, nerve ending, tender spot, the quick, where the shoe pinches, where one lives *and* in the gut <nf>; agitation

5 senses, five senses, sensorium; touch 74, taste 62, smell 69, sight 27, hearing 48; sixth sense, second sight, extrasensory perception *or* ESP; sense *or* sensory organ, sensillum, receptor; synesthesia, chromesthesia, color hearing; phonism, photism; kinesthesia, muscle sense, sense of motion; sense organ

VERBS **6 sense, feel,** experience, **perceive,** apprehend, be sensible of, be conscious *or* aware of, apperceive; taste 62.7, smell 69.8, see 27.12, hear 48.11,12, touch 73.6; respond, respond to stimuli; be sensitive to, have a thing about <nf>; overreact

7 sensitize, make sensitive; sensibilize, sensify;

sharpen, whet, quicken, stimulate, excite, stir, cultivate, refine

8 touch a sore spot, touch a soft spot, touch on the raw, touch a raw spot, touch to the quick, hit *or* touch a nerve *or* nerve ending, touch where it hurts, hit one where he lives <nf>, strike home

ADJS **9 sensory,** sensorial; **sensitive,** receptive, responsive; **sensuous;** sensorimotor, sensimotor; kinesthetic, somatosensory; feeling, percipient

10 neural, nervous, nerval; neurologic, neurological

11 sensible, sentient, sensile; **susceptible,** susceptive; **receptive,** impressionable, impressive <old>, impressible; **perceptive; conscious,** cognizant, **aware,** sensitive to, alive to, clued in, sussed <nf>

12 sensitive, responsive, sympathetic, compassionate; empathic, empathetic; passible; delicate, tactful, considerate, courteous, solicitous, tender, refined; **oversensitive, thin-skinned;** oversensible, hyperesthetic, hyperpathic, hypersensitive, supersensitive, overtender, overrefined, overwhelmed; **irritable, touchy,** irascible, tetchy <nf>, quick on the draw *or* trigger *or* uptake, itchy, ticklish, prickly; goosy <nf>, skittish; nervous; allergic, anaphylactic

13 <keenly sensitive> **exquisite,** poignant, **acute,** sharp, **keen,** vivid, intense, extreme, excruciating

14 sensate, perceptible, audible, visible, tactile, palpable, tangible, noticeable

25 INSENSIBILITY
<physical unfeeling>

NOUNS **1 insensibility,** insensibleness, **insensitivity,** insensitiveness, insentience, impassibility, lack of feeling; **unperceptiveness,** imperceptiveness, imperception, imperceptivity, impercipience, blindness, lack of concern, obtuseness; inconsiderateness; unsolicitousness; tactlessness; discourtesy, boorishness; philistinism; **unfeeling,** unfeelingness, **apathy,** affectlessness, lack of affect; thick skin *or* hide, callousness 94.3; **numbness,** dullness, hypothymia, **deadness;** pins and needles; hypesthesia; anesthesia, analgesia; narcosis, electronarcosis; narcotization; lack of awareness

2 unconsciousness, senselessness; nothingness, oblivion, obliviousness, indifference, heedlessness, nirvana; nirvana principle; **faint, swoon, blackout,** syncope, athymia, lipothymy *or* lipothymia; **coma; torpor, stupor;** trance; catalepsy, catatony *or* catatonia, sleep 22; knockout *or* KO *or* kayo <nf>; semiconsciousness, grayout; suspended animation

3 anesthetic, general anesthetic, local anesthetic, analgesic, anodyne, balm, ointment, **pain killer,** pain-reliever, antiodontalgic; tranquilizer, **sedative,** sleeping pill *or* tablet, somnifacient, knockout drops *and* Mickey Finn *and* Mickey <nf>; drug, dope <nf>, narcotic, opiate; acupuncture; desensitization

VERBS **4 deaden, numb,** benumb, blunt, dull, obtund, **desensitize;** paralyze, palsy; **anesthetize, put to sleep,** slip one a Mickey *or* Mickey Finn <nf>, chloroform, etherize; narcotize, drug, dope <nf>; freeze, **stupefy, stun,** bedaze, besot; knock unconscious, knock senseless, **knock out, KO** *and* kayo *and* lay out *and* coldcock *and* knock stiff *and* brain <nf>; concuss

5 faint, swoon, drop, succumb, keel over <nf>, fall in a faint, fall senseless, **pass** *or* **zonk out** <nf>, **black out,** go out like a light; gray out

ADJS **6 insensible, unfeeling, insensitive,** insentient, insensate, impassible; nerveless, senseless, unemotional; unsympathetic, uncompassionate; unconcerned, unsolicitous, non-caring, uncaring, impassive, cold-blooded, apathetic; tactless, boorish, heavy-handed; **unperceptive,** imperceptive, impercipient, blind, unmindful; thick-skinned, hardened, **dull,** obtuse, obdurate; **numb,** numbed, benumbed, dead, **deadened,** asleep, unfelt; **unfeeling, apathetic,** affectless; stoic; deaf; callous 94.12; anesthetized, narcotized, hypnotized

7 stupefied, stunned, dazed, bedazed

8 unconscious, senseless, oblivious, unaware, comatose, asleep, dead, **dead to the world,** cold, out, **out cold;** heedless, unmindful; nirvanic; half-conscious, semiconscious; drugged, narcotized; doped *and* stoned *and* spaced out *and* strung out *and* zonked *and* zonked out *and* out of it <nf>; catatonic, cataleptic; stunned, concussed, knocked out; desensitized; out for the count <nf>

9 deadening, numbing, dulling; **anesthetic,** analgesic, narcotic; stupefying, stunning, numbing, mind-boggling *or* -numbing; anesthetizing, narcotizing

26 PAIN
<physical suffering>

NOUNS **1 pain; suffering, hurt, hurting,** painfulness, misery <nf>, **distress,** *Schmerz* <Ger>, dolor <old>; **discomfort,** malaise; aches and pains

2 pang, pangs, throe, throes; seizure, spasm, paroxysm; ouch <nf>; **twinge,** twitch, wrench, jumping pain; crick, kink, hitch, cramp *or* cramps; **nip,** thrill, pinch, tweak, bite, prick, pinprick, **stab,** stitch, sharp *or* piercing *or* stabbing pain, acute pain, **shooting pain,** darting pain, fulgurant pain, lancinating pain, shooting, shoot; boring *or* terebrant *or* terebrating pain; gnawing, gnawing *or* grinding pain; griping *and* torment <old>; girdle pain; stitch in the side; charley horse <nf>; phantom limb pain; hunger pang *or* pain; wandering pain; psychalgia, psychosomatic pain, soul pain, mind pain

3 smart, smarting, **sting,** stinging, urtication, **tingle,** tingling; **burn,** burning, burning pain, fire; pins and needles

4 soreness, irritation, inflammation, tenderness, sensitiveness; algesia; rankling <old>, festering; sore; sore spot 24.4

5 ache, aching, throbbing, throbbing ache *or* pain, throb; **headache,** cephalalgia, misery in the head <nf>; splitting headache, **sick headache, migraine,** megrim, hemicrania; **backache; earache,** otalgia; **toothache,** odontalgia; **stomachache,** tummyache <nf>, bellyache *or* gut-ache <nf>; **colic,** collywobbles, gripes, gripe, gnawing, gnawing of the bowels, fret <nf>; **heartburn,** pyrosis; **angina**

6 agony, anguish, torment, torture, ordeal, exquisite torment *or* torture, the rack, excruciation, crucifixion, martyrdom, martyrization, excruciating *or* agonizing *or* atrocious pain, hell on earth, punishment

VERBS **7 pain,** give *or* inflict pain, **hurt, wound, afflict, distress,** injure; **burn;** sting; nip, bite, tweak, pinch; pierce, prick, stab, cut, lacerate, thrash; **irritate, inflame,** sear, harshen, exacerbate, intensify; chafe, gall, fret, rasp, rub, grate; gnaw, grind; gripe; fester, rankle <old>; **torture, torment,** rack, put to torture, put *or* lay on the rack, **agonize, harrow,** crucify, martyr, martyrize, traumatize, excruciate, wring, twist, contort, convulse; wrench, tear, rend; prolong the agony, kill by inches

8 suffer, feel pain, feel the pangs, anguish 96.19; **hurt, ache,** have a misery <nf>, ail, be afflicted; **smart,** tingle; throb, pound; shoot; twinge, thrill, twitch; **wince,** blanch, shrink, make a wry face, grimace; **agonize,** writhe

ADJS **9 pained,** in pain, **hurt,** hurting, **suffering,** afflicted, wounded, distressed, in distress; **tortured, tormented, racked, agonized, harrowed,** lacerated, crucified, martyred, martyrized, wrung, twisted, convulsed, anguished; on the rack, under the harrow; traumatized; stressed out

10 painful; hurtful, **hurting,** distressing, afflictive, miserable; **acute, sharp,** piercing, stabbing, shooting, stinging, biting, gnawing; **poignant,** pungent, burning, searing, **severe,** cruel, harsh, grave, hard; griping, cramping, spasmic, spasmatic, spasmodic, paroxysmal; **agonizing, excruciating,** exquisite, atrocious, torturous, tormenting, martyrizing, racking, **harrowing,** unbearable, intolerable

11 sore, raw; pained; smarting, tingling, **burning;**

irritated, inflamed, tender, sensitive, fiery, angry, red; algetic; chafed, galled; festering, rankling <old>; black-and-blue

12 aching, achy, throbbing; headachy, migrainous, backachy, toothachy, stomachachy, colicky, griping

13 irritating, irritative, irritant; chafing, galling, fretting, rasping, boring, grating, grinding, stinging, scratchy

27 VISION

NOUNS 1 vision, sight, eyesight, seeing; sightedness; eye, power of sight, sense of sight, visual sense; perception, discernment; perspicacity, perspicuity, sharp or acute or keen sight, visual acuity, quick sight, 20/20 vision; farsight, farsightedness; nearsightedness; astigmatism; clear sight, unobstructed vision; rod vision, scotopia; cone vision, photopia; color vision, twilight vision, daylight vision, day vision, night vision; eye-mindedness; field of vision, visual field, scope, ken, purview, horizon, sweep, range; line of vision, line of sight, sight-line; peripheral vision, peripheral field; field of view 31.3; sensitivity to light, phototonus

2 observation, observance; looking, watching, viewing, seeing, witnessing, espial; notice, note, respect, regard; watch, lookout; spying, espionage

3 look, sight, the eye and a look-see and a gander <nf>, glad eye <nf>, dekko <Brit nf>, eye, view, regard; sidelong look; leer, leering look, lustful leer; sly look; look-in; preview; scene, prospect 33.6

4 glance, glance or flick of the eye, squiz <Austral>, slant <nf>, rapid glance, cast, side-glance; glimpse, flash, quick sight; peek, peep; wink, blink, flicker or twinkle of an eye; casual glance, half an eye; coup d'œil <Fr>

5 gaze, stare, gape, goggle; sharp or piercing or penetrating look; ogle, glad eye, come-hither look <nf>, bedroom eyes <nf>; glare, glower, glaring or glowering look, black look, dirty look; evil eye, malocchio <Ital>, whammy <nf>; withering look, hostile look, chilly look, the fisheye <nf>

6 scrutiny, overview, survey, contemplation; examination, inspection 938.3, scrutiny, the once-over <nf>, visual examination, a vetting <Brit nf>, ocular inspection, eyeball inspection <nf>

7 viewpoint, standpoint, point of view, vantage, vantage point, perspective, point or coign of vantage, where one stands; bird's-eye view, worm's-eye view, fly on the wall; outlook, angle, angle or field of vision, optique <Fr>, eyeshot; mental outlook 978.2

8 observation post or point; observatory; lookout, outlook, overlook, scenic overlook; planetarium; watchtower, tower; Texas tower; beacon,

lighthouse, pharos; gazebo, belvedere; bridge, conning tower, crow's nest; peephole, sighthole, spyhole, loophole; ringside, ringside seat; grandstand, bleachers, stands; gallery, top gallery; paradise and peanut gallery <nf>; window

9 eye, visual organ, organ of vision, oculus, optic, orb, peeper <nf>, baby blues <nf>; clear eyes, bright eyes, starry orbs; saucer eyes, popeyes and goggle eyes and banjo eyes and googly eyes and sparklers <nf>; naked eye, unassisted or unaided eye; corner of the eye; eyeball; iris; pupil; eyelid, lid, nictitating membrane; eyeglasses

10 sharp eye, keen eye, piercing or penetrating eye, gimlet eye, X-ray eye; eagle eye, hawkeye, peeled eye <nf>, watchful eye; weather eye

11 <comparisons> eagle, hawk, cat, lynx, ferret, weasel; Argus

VERBS 12 see, behold, observe, view, witness, perceive, discern, spy, espy, sight, have in sight, make out, pick out, descry, spot <nf>, twig <Brit nf>, discover, notice, take notice of, have one's eye on, distinguish, recognize, ken <nf>, catch sight of, get a load of <nf>, take in, get an eyeful of <nf>, look on or upon, cast the eyes on or upon, set or lay eyes on, clap eyes on <nf>; glimpse, get or catch a glimpse of; see at a glance, see with half an eye; see with one's own eyes

13 look, peer, have a look, take a gander and take a look <nf>, direct the eyes, turn or bend the eyes, cast one's eye, lift up the eyes; look at, take a look at, eye, eyeball <nf>, have a look-see <nf>, have a dekko <Brit nf>, look on or upon, gaze at or upon; watch, observe, view, regard; keep one's eyes peeled or skinned, be watchful or observant or vigilant, keep one's eyes open; keep in sight or view, hold in view; look after; check and check out <nf>, scope <nf>, scope on or out <nf>; keep under observation, spy on, have an eye out, keep an eye out, keep an eye on, keep a weather eye on, follow, tail and shadow <nf>, stake out; reconnoiter, scout, get the lay of the land; peek, peep, pry, take a peep or peek; play peekaboo

14 scrutinize, survey, eye, contemplate, look over, give the eye or the once-over <nf>; ogle, ogle at, leer, leer at, give one the glad eye; examine, vet <Brit nf>, inspect 937.23; pore, pore over, peruse; take a close or careful look; take a long, hard look; size up <nf>; take stock of; have eyes in the back of one's head

15 gaze, gloat <old>, fix one's gaze, fix or fasten or rivet one's eyes upon, keep one's eyes upon, feast one's eyes on; eye, ogle; stare, stare at, stare hard, look, goggle, gape, gawk or gawp <nf>, gaze open-mouthed; crane, crane the neck, stand on tiptoe, rubberneck <nf>; strain one's eyes; look

straight in the eye, look full in the face, hold one's eye *or* gaze, stare down

16 glare, glower, look daggers, look black; give one the evil eye, give one a whammy <nf>; give one the fish eye <nf>, give one a dirty look

17 glance, glimpse, glint, cast a glance, glance at *or* upon, give a *coup d'œil* <Fr>, take a glance at, take a squint at <nf>

18 look askance *or* askant, give a sidelong look; squint, look asquint; cock the eye; **look down one's nose** <nf>

19 look away, look aside, **avert the eyes,** look another way, break one's eyes away, stop looking, turn away from, turn the back upon; drop one's eyes *or* gaze, cast one's eyes down; avoid one's gaze

ADJS **20 visual, ocular,** eye, eyeball <nf>; **sighted,** seeing, having sight *or* vision; **optic, optical;** ophthalmic; retinal; visible 31.6

21 clear-sighted, clear-eyed; twenty-twenty; **farsighted,** farseeing, telescopic; **sharp-sighted,** keen-sighted, sharp-eyed, **eagle-eyed,** hawk-eyed, ferret-eyed, lynx-eyed, cat-eyed, Argus-eyed; eye-minded, perceptive, aware

ADVS **22 at sight,** as seen, visibly, at a glance; by sight, by eyeball <nf>, visually; at first sight, **at the first blush,** *prima facie* <L>; out of the corner of one's eye; from where one stands, from one's viewpoint *or* standpoint

WORD ELEMENTS **23** opto-, -opsia, -opsy, -opsis; -opy, -opia; -scopy; ocul-, oculo-, ophthalm-, ophthalmo-

28 DEFECTIVE VISION

NOUNS **1** faulty eyesight, bad eyesight, visual handicap, defect of vision *or* sight, poor sight, impaired vision, imperfect vision, blurred vision, reduced sight, partial sightedness, partial blindness; legal blindness; **astigmatism,** astigmia; nystagmus; albinism; double vision, double sight, diplopia; tunnel vision; photophobia; **blindness** 30

2 dim-sightedness, dull-sightedness, near-blindness, amblyopia, gravel-blindness, sand-blindness, **purblindness,** dim eyes; blurredness, blearedness, bleariness, lippitude <old>; eyestrain, bloodshot eyes, redness, red eyes

3 nearsightedness, myopia, shortsightedness, short sight

4 farsightedness, hyperopia, longsightedness, long sight; presbyopia

5 strabismus, heterotropia; cast, cast in the eye; **squint,** squinch <nf>; **cross-eye, cross-eyedness;** convergent strabismus, esotropia; upward strabismus, anoöpsia; walleye, exotropia; detached retina; tic

6 <defective eyes> cross-eyes, cockeyes, squint eyes, lazy eye, swivel eyes <nf>, goggle eyes, walleyes, bug-eyes *and* popeyes <nf>, saucer eyes <nf>

7 winking, blinking, fluttering the eyelids, nictitation; winker, blinkard <old>; tic

VERBS **8** see badly *or* poorly, barely see, be half-blind; have a mote in the eye; see double

9 squint, squinch <nf>, squint the eye, look asquint, screw up the eyes, skew, goggle <old>

10 wink, blink, nictitate, bat the eyes <nf>

ADJS **11** poor-sighted; visually impaired, visually handicapped, sight-impaired; legally blind; **blind** 30.9; **astigmatic, astigmatical;** nystagmic; **nearsighted, shortsighted, myopic,** mope-eyed <old>; **farsighted,** longsighted, presbyopic; dayblind, hereralopic; nightblind, nyctalopic; colorblind; **squinting,** squinty, asquint, squint-eyed, squinch-eyed <nf>, strabismal, strabismic; winking, **blinking,** blinky, blink-eyed; blinkered; photophobic

12 cross-eyed, cockeyed, swivel-eyed <nf>, goggle-eyed, bug-eyed *and* popeyed <nf>, **walleyed,** saucer-eyed, glare-eyed; one-eyed, monocular, cyclopean; moon-eyed

13 dim-sighted, dim, dull-sighted, dim-eyed, weak-eyed, feeble-eyed, mole-eyed; **purblind,** half-blind, gravel-blind, sand-blind; bleary-eyed, blear-eyed; filmy-eyed, film-eyed; snow-blind; bloodshot, red-eyed; dry-eyed

29 OPTICAL INSTRUMENTS

NOUNS **1 optical instrument** <see list>, optical device, viewer; **microscope** <see list>; **spectroscope,** spectrometer <see list>

2 lens, glass; prism, objective prism; eyepiece, objective, condenser; mirror system, catadioptric system, telecentric system; **camera** 714.11

3 spectacles, specs <nf>, **glasses, eyeglasses,** pair of glasses *or* spectacles, barnacles <Brit nf>, cheaters *and* peepers <nf>; reading glasses, readers; bifocals, divided spectacles, trifocals, pince-nez, nippers <nf>; lorgnette, *lorgnon* <Fr>; horn-rimmed glasses; harlequin glasses; granny glasses; mini-specs <nf>; colored glasses, sunglasses, sun-specs <nf>, dark glasses, Polaroid <trademark> glasses, shades <nf>; goggles, blinkers; eyeglass, monocle, quizzing glass; thick glasses, thick-lensed glasses, thick lenses, Coke-bottle glasses <nf>; **contacts,** contact lenses, hard lenses, soft lenses, extended-wear lenses

4 telescope <see list>, scope, **spy glass,** terrestrial telescope, glass, **field glass; binoculars,** zoom binoculars, opera glasses

5 sight; sighthole; finder, viewfinder; panoramic sight; bombsight; peep sight, open sight, leaf sight

6 **mirror,** glass, **looking glass,** seeing glass <Brit nf>, reflector, speculum; hand mirror, window mirror, rear-view mirror, cheval glass, pier glass, shaving mirror; steel mirror; convex mirror, concave mirror, distorting mirror

7 **optics,** optical physics; **optometry;** microscopy, microscopics; telescopy; stereoscopy; spectroscopy, spectrometry; infrared spectroscopy; spectrophotometry; electron optics; fiber optics; **photography** 714

8 **oculist,** ophthalmologist, **optometrist;** microscopist, telescopist; optician

ADJS 9 **optic, optical,** ophthalmic, ophthalmologic, ophthalmological, optometrical; acousto-optic, acousto-optical; ocular, binocular, monocular

10 microscopic, telescopic, etc; stereoscopic, three-dimensional, 3-D

11 **spectacled, bespectacled,** four-eyed <nf>; goggled; monocled

12 **optical instruments and viewers**

abdominoscope	oscilloscope
amblyoscope	periscope
blink comparator	pharyngoscope
bronchoscope	photometer
camera lucida	photomultiplier
chromatoscope	photoscope
chromoscope	polariscope
cystoscope	polemoscope
diaphanoscope	prism
diffractometer	pseudoscope
endoscope	radarscope
epidiascope	radioscope
eriometer	rangefinder
fiberscope	retinoscope
gastroscope	saccarimeter
goniometer *or* gonioscope	sniperscope
image orthicon	snooperscope
kaleidoscope	spectroscope
laser	stereopticon
microfilm viewer *or*	stereoscope
reader	stroboscope
ophthalmoscope	telestereoscope
optometer	thaumatrope

13 **microscopes**

acoustic microscope	gravure microscope
binocular microscope	high-powered microscope
blink microscope	interference microscope
comparison microscope	laboratory microscope
compound microscope	light microscope
conoscope	metallograph
dark-field microscope	metallurgical microscope
dissecting microscope	microprojector
electron microscope	optical microscope
field-emission	oxyhydrogen microscope
microscope	phase contrast microscope
field-ion microscope	*or* phase microscope
fluorescence microscope	photomicroscope

pinion focusing	simple *or* single microscope
microscope	spectromicroscope
polarizing microscope	stereomicroscope *or*
power microscope	stereoscopic microscope
projecting microscope	surface microscope
scanning electron	transmission electron
microscope	microscope
scanning microscope	ultramicroscope
scanning tunneling	ultraviolet microscope
microscope	X-ray microscope

14 **spectroscopes, spectrometers**

analytical spectrometer	microwave
diffraction spectroscope	spectroscope
direct-reading	monochromator
spectrometer	ocular spectroscope
direct-reading spectroscope	prism spectroscope
direct-vision spectroscope	reversion spectroscope
mass spectrograph	spectrograph
mass spectroscope	spectrophotometer
microspectrophotometer	spectroradiometer
microspectroscope	star spectroscope

15 **telescopes**

astronomical telescope *or*	Mills cross
Kepler telescope	Multiple Mirror Telescope
Cassegrain telescope	*or* MMT
collimator	Newtonian telescope
coudé telescope	optical telescope
Dobsonian telescope	panoramic telescope
double-image telescope	prism *or* prismatic
elbow telescope	telescope
electron telescope	radio telescope
equatorial telescope	reflecting telescope
finder telescope	refracting telescope
Galilean telescope	Schmidt telescope
Gregorian telescope	spotting scope
guiding telescope	telescopic sight
Hale telescope	terrestrial telescope
heliometer	tower telescope
Hubble Space Telescope	twin telescope
inverting telescope	vernier telescope
Maksutov telescope	water telescope
mercurial telescope	zenith telescope *or* tube

30 BLINDNESS

NOUNS 1 **blindness, sightlessness,** cecity, ablepsia, unseeingness, sightless eyes, lack of vision, eyelessness; stone-blindness, total blindness; darkness, "total eclipse without all hope of day"— Milton; legal blindness; partial blindness, reduced sight, **blind side; blind spot;** dimsightedness; snow blindness, niphablepsia; amaurosis, *gutta serena* <L>, drop serene; cataract; glaucoma; trachoma; mental *or* psychic blindness, mind-blindness, soul-blindness, benightedness, unenlightenment, spiritual blindness; **blinding,** making blind, depriving of sight, putting out the eyes, excecation <old>;

blurring the eyes, blindfolding, hoodwinking, blinkering

2 day blindness, hemeralopia; **night blindness,** nyctalopia; moon blindness, moon-blind

3 color blindness; dichromatism; monochromatism, achromatopsia; red blindness, protanopia, green blindness, deuteranopia, red-green blindness, Daltonism; yellow blindness, xanthocyanopia; blue-yellow blindness, tritanopia; violet-blindness

4 the blind, the sightless, the unseeing; blind man; bat, mole; "blind leaders of the blind"—Bible

5 blindfold; eye patch; blinkers, blinds, blinders, rogue's badge

6 <aids for the blind> sensory aid, **Braille,** New York point, Gall's serrated type, Boston type, Howe's American type, Moon or Moon's type, Alston's Glasgow type, Lucas's type, sight-saver type, Frere's type; line letter, string alphabet, writing stamps; noctograph, writing frame, embosser, high-speed embosser; visagraph; talking book; optophone, Visotoner, Optacon; personal sonar, Pathsounder; ultrasonic spectacles; cane; Seeing Eye dog, guide dog; white stick or cane

VERBS **7 blind,** blind the eyes, deprive of sight, **strike blind,** render or make blind, excecate <old>; darken, dim, obscure, eclipse; **put one's eyes out,** gouge; **blindfold,** blinker, hoodwink, bandage; throw dust in one's eyes, benight; **dazzle,** bedazzle, daze; glare; snow-blind

8 be blind, not see, walk in darkness, grope in the dark, feel one's way; go blind, lose one's sight or vision, black out; be blind to, close or shut one's eyes to, wink or blink at, look the other way, blind oneself to, wear blinkers or have blinders on, avert one's eyes; have a blind spot or side

ADJS **9 blind, sightless, unsighted,** ableptical, eyeless, visionless, **unseeing,** undiscerning, unobserving, unperceiving; in darkness, rayless, bereft of light, dark <nf>, "dark, dark, dark, amid the blaze of noon"—Milton; **stone-blind,** stark blind, **blind as a bat,** blind as a mole or an owl; amaurotic; dim-sighted 28.13; hemeralopic; nyctalopic; color-blind; glaucomatous; legally blind; mind-blind, soul-blind, mentally or psychically or spiritually blind, benighted, unenlightened

10 blinded, excecate <old>, darkened, obscured; **blindfolded,** blindfold, hoodwinked, blinkered; **dazzled,** bedazzled, dazed; snow-blind, snow-blinded; sand-blind

11 blinding, obscuring; **dazzling,** bedazzling, stunning

31 VISIBILITY

NOUNS **1 visibility,** visibleness, perceptibility, discernibleness, observability, detectability,

visuality, seeableness; exposure; manifestation; outcrop, outcropping; the visible, the seen, what is revealed, what can be seen; revelation, epiphany

2 distinctness, plainness, evidence <old>, evidentness, obviousness, patentness, manifestness, recognizability; **clearness, clarity,** crystal-clearness, lucidity, limpidity; **definiteness,** definition, sharpness, microscopical distinctness; resolution, high resolution, low resolution; **prominence, conspicuousness,** conspicuity; **exposure,** public exposure, high profile, low profile; high or low visibility; atmospheric visibility, seeing, ceiling, ceiling unlimited, visibility unlimited, CAVU or ceiling and visibility unlimited, severe clear <nf>, visibility zero

3 field of view, field of vision, range or scope of vision, **sight,** limit of vision, eyereach, **eyesight,** eyeshot, ken; **vista, view, horizon, prospect, perspective, outlook,** survey, visible horizon; range, scan, scope; line of sight, sightline, line of vision; naked eye; command, domination, outlook over; **viewpoint, observation** point 27.8

VERBS **4 show,** show up, show through, shine out or through, **surface,** appear 33.8, **be visible,** be seen, be revealed, be evident, be noticeable, be obvious, meet the gaze, impinge on the eye, present to the eye, meet or catch or hit or strike the eye; **stand out,** stand forth, loom large, glare, **stare one in the face,** hit one in the eye, **stick out like a sore thumb;** dominate; emerge, come into view, materialize

5 be exposed, be conspicuous, have high visibility, stick out, hang out <nf>, crop out; live in a glass house; have or keep a high profile

ADJS **6 visible,** visual, **perceptible,** perceivable, **discernible, seeable,** viewable, witnessable, beholdable, observable, detectable, noticeable, recognizable, to be seen; **in sight,** in view, in plain sight, in full view, present to the eyes, before one's eyes, under one's eyes, open, naked, outcropping, hanging out <nf>, exposed, showing, open or exposed to view; **evident,** in evidence, **manifest, apparent;** revealed, disclosed, unhidden, unconcealed, unclouded, undisguised

7 distinct, plain, clear, obvious, evident, patent, unmistakable, unmissable, not to be mistaken, much in evidence, plain to be seen, for all to see, showing for all to see, plain as a pikestaff, plain as the nose on one's face, plain as day, clear as day, plain as plain can be, big as life and twice as ugly; **definite, defined, well-defined,** well-marked, well-resolved, in focus; **clear-cut,** clean-cut; crystal-clear, clear as crystal; **conspicuous,** glaring, staring, **prominent,** pronounced, well-pronounced,

in bold or strong or high relief, high-profile;
identifiable, recognizable

ADVS 8 **visibly, perceptibly,** perceivably, discernibly,
seeably, recognizably, observably, markedly,
noticeably; **manifestly, apparently,** evidently;
distinctly, clearly, with clarity or crystal clarity,
plainly, obviously, patently, definitely,
unmistakably; conspicuously, undisguisedly,
unconcealedly, prominently, pronouncedly,
glaringly, starkly, staringly

32 INVISIBILITY

NOUNS 1 **invisibility,** imperceptibility,
unperceivability, undetectability, indiscernibility,
unseeableness, viewlessness; nonappearance;
disappearance 34; the invisible, the unseen; more
than meets the eye; unsubstantiality 764,
immateriality 1053, **secrecy** 345, **concealment** 346;
hidden depths, tip of the iceberg; zero visibility

2 **inconspicuousness,** half-visibility, semivisibility,
low profile, latency; **indistinctness, unclearness,**
unplainness, **faintness,** paleness, feebleness,
weakness, **dimness,** bedimming, bleariness,
darkness, shadowiness, **vagueness,** vague
appearance, indefiniteness, obscurity, uncertainty,
indistinguishability; **blurriness,** blur, soft focus,
defocus, **fuzziness, haziness,** mistiness, filminess,
fogginess

VERBS 3 be invisible or unseen, escape notice; lie hid
346.8, **blush unseen;** disappear 34.2; white out,
black out

4 **blur, dim, pale,** soften, film, mist, fog; defocus, lose
resolution or sharpness or distinctness, go soft at
the edges

ADJS 5 **invisible; imperceptible,** unperceivable,
indiscernible, undiscernible, undetectable,
unseeable, viewless, unbeholdable, unapparent,
insensible; **out of sight,** à perte de vue <Fr>, out of
range; **secret** 345.11,15; **unseen,** sightless,
unbeheld, unviewed, unwitnessed, unobserved,
unnoticed, unperceived; unsubstantial,
transparent; behind the curtain or scenes;
disguised, camouflaged, hidden, **concealed**
346.11,14; undisclosed, unrevealed, in petto <L>;
latent, unrealized, submerged

6 **inconspicuous,** half-visible, semivisible, low-
profile; **indistinct, unclear,** unplain, **indefinite,**
undefined, ill-defined, ill-marked, **faint,** pale,
feeble, weak, **dim,** dark, **shadowy, vague, obscure,**
indistinguishable, unrecognizable; half-seen,
merely glimpsed; low-profile, half-seen, low-
definition; uncertain, confused, out of focus,
blurred, blurry, bleared, bleary, blear, **fuzzy, hazy,**
misty, filmy, foggy

33 APPEARANCE

NOUNS 1 **appearance, appearing,** apparition,
coming, forthcoming, showing-up, coming forth,
coming on the scene, making the scene <nf>,
putting in an appearance, arrival; **emergence,**
issuing, issuance; **arising,** rise, rising, occurrence;
materialization, materializing, coming into being;
manifestation, realization, incarnation, revelation,
showing-forth; epiphany, theophany, avatar, ostent
<old>; **presentation, disclosure, exposure,**
opening, unfolding, unfoldment, showing; rising of
the curtain

2 **appearance,** exterior, externals, **mere externals,**
facade, outside, **show, outward show, image,**
display, front <nf>, outward or external
appearance, surface appearance, surface show,
vain show, apparent character, public image,
window dressing, cosmetics; whitewash; whited
sepulcher; **glitz** and tinsel <nf>, gaudiness,
speciousness, meretriciousness, superficies,
superficiality; PR and flack <nf>; pretense

3 aspect, look, view; feature, lineaments; **seeming,**
semblance, image, imago, icon, eidolon, likeness,
simulacrum; effect, impression, total effect or
impression; **form, shape,** figure, configuration,
gestalt; **manner,** fashion, wise, guise, style; **respect,**
regard, reference, light; **phase; facet, side,** angle,
viewpoint 27.7, slant and twist and spin <nf>

4 **looks, features, lineaments,** traits, lines;
countenance, face, visage, feature, favor, brow,
physiognomy; cast of countenance, **cut of one's jib**
<nf>, facial appearance or expression, cast, turn;
look, air, mien, demeanor, carriage, bearing, port,
deportment, posture, stance, poise, presence;
guise, garb, dress, complexion, color

5 <thing appearing> apparition, appearance,
phenomenon; **vision, image, shape, form,** figure,
presence; false image, mirage, phasm <old>,
specter, **phantom** 987.1

6 **view, scene, sight;** prospect, outlook, lookout,
vista, perspective; scenery, scenic view; panorama,
sweep; scape, **landscape,** seascape, riverscape,
waterscape, airscape, skyscape, cloudscape,
cityscape, townscape; bird's-eye view, worm's-eye
view

7 **spectacle, sight;** exhibit, **exhibition,** exposition,
show, stage show 704.4, **display, presentation,**
representation; tableau, tableau vivant; panorama,
diorama, cosmorama, myriorama, cyclorama,
georama; son et lumière <Fr>, sound-and-light
show; phantasmagoria, shifting scene, light show;
psychedelic show; **pageant,** pageantry; parade,
pomp

VERBS 8 **appear,** become visible; **arrive, make one's**

appearance, make *or* put in an appearance, appear on the scene, make the scene *and* weigh in <nf>, appear to one's eyes, meet *or* catch *or* strike the eye, **come in sight** *or* **view, show,** show oneself, show one's face, nip in <nf>, **show up** <nf>, **turn up,** come, **materialize,** pop up, present oneself, present oneself to view, **manifest oneself,** become manifest, **reveal oneself,** discover oneself, uncover oneself, declare oneself, expose *or* betray oneself, flash; **come to light,** see the light, see the light of day; **emerge,** issue, issue forth, stream forth, come forth, come to the fore, present itself, come out, come forward, come to the surface, come one's way, come to hand, come into the picture; enter 189.7, come upon the stage; **rise, arise,** rear its head; look forth, peer *or* peep out; crop out, outcrop; loom, heave in sight, appear on the horizon; crawl out of the woodwork; fade in, wax

9 **burst forth,** break forth, debouch, erupt, irrupt, explode; **pop up, bob up** <nf>, start up, spring up, burst upon the view; flare up, flash, gleam

10 appear to be, seem to be, **appear, seem, look,** feel, sound, look to be, appear to one's eyes, have *or* present the appearance of, give the feeling of, strike one as, come on as <nf>; **appear like, seem like, look like,** have *or* wear the look of, **sound like; have every appearance of,** have all the earmarks of, have all the features of, show signs of, have every sign *or* indication of; assume the guise of, take the shape of, exhibit the form of

ADJS 11 **apparent,** appearing, **seeming, ostensible;** outward, surface, superficial; material, incarnate; **visible** 31.6

ADVS 12 **apparently, seemingly, ostensibly,** to *or* by all appearances, to *or* by all accounts, to all seeming, as it seems, to the eye; on the face of it, *prima facie* <L>; on the surface, outwardly, superficially; at first sight *or* view, at the first blush

34 DISAPPEARANCE

NOUNS 1 **disappearance,** disappearing, **vanishing,** vanishment; **going, passing, departure, loss;** dissipation, dispersion; dissolution, dissolving, melting, evaporation, evanescence, dematerialization 1053.5; fadeout, fading, fadeaway, blackout; wane, ebb; wipe, wipeout, wipeoff, erasure; eclipse, occultation, blocking; vanishing point; elimination 773.2; extinction 395.6; disappearing act

VERBS 2 **disappear, vanish,** vanish from sight, do a vanishing act <nf>, depart, fly, **flee** 368.10, go, be gone, **go away,** pass, pass out *or* away, pass out of sight, exit, pull up stakes <nf>, leave the scene *or* stage, clear out, pass out of the picture, pass *or*

retire from sight, become lost to sight, be seen no more; **perish, die,** die off; die out *or* away, dwindle, wane, fade, **fade out** *or* **away,** do a fade-out <nf>; sink, sink away, dissolve, melt, melt away, "melt, thaw, and dissolve itself"—Shakespeare, dematerialize 1053.6, evaporate, evanesce, **vanish** *or* **disappear into thin air,** go up in smoke; disperse, dispel, dissipate; cease, cease to exist, **cease to be;** cease publication, go out of print, go off the air, become obsolete, close down; leave no trace; waste, waste away, erode, be consumed, wear away; undergo *or* suffer an eclipse; **hide** 346.8; blend into the background

ADJS 3 **vanishing, disappearing,** passing, fleeting, fugitive, transient, flying, fading, dissolving, melting, evaporating, evanescent, waning, here today gone tomorrow

4 **gone,** away, gone away, past and gone, extinct, missing, no more, lost, lost to sight *or* view, long-lost, **out of sight; unaccounted for;** nonexistent; out of the picture

35 COLOR

NOUNS 1 **color, hue; tint,** tinct, tincture, **tinge, shade, tone,** cast; key; **coloring, coloration;** color harmony, color balance, color scheme; decorator color; **complexion,** skin color *or* coloring *or* tone, pigmentation; chromatism, chromaticism, chromism; achromatism 36.1; natural color; undercolor; pallor 36.2; color perception, color vision, color blindness

2 **warmth,** warmth of color, warm color; **blush, flush, glow,** healthy glow *or* hue

3 **softness,** soft color, subtle color, pale color, pastel, pastel color, pastel shade

4 **colorfulness,** color, bright color, pure color, **brightness, brilliance, vividness,** intensity, saturation; **richness,** gorgeousness, gaiety; riot *or* splash of color; Technicolor <trademark>; Day-Glo <trademark>; variegation, multicolor, polychrome; color scheme, color coordination

5 **garishness,** loudness, luridness, glitz <nf>, gaudiness 501.3; loud *or* screaming color <nf>; shocking pink, jaundiced yellow, arsenic green; clashing colors, color clash

6 **color quality;** chroma, Munsell chroma, brightness, purity, saturation; **hue,** value, lightness; colorimetric quality, chromaticity, chromaticness; tint, **tone;** chromatic color, achromatic *or* neutral color; warm color; cool color; tinge, shade

7 **color system,** chromaticity diagram, color triangle, Maxwell triangle; hue cycle, color disk, color wheel, color circle, chromatic circle, color cycle *or* gamut, color chart; Munsell scale; color solid;

fundamental colors; **primary color,** primary pigment, primary; secondary color, secondary; tertiary color, tertiary; complementary color; chromaticity coordinate; color mixture curve *or* function; spectral color, spectrum color, pure *or* full color; metamer; **spectrum,** solar spectrum, color spectrum, chromatic spectrum, color index; monochrome; demitint, half tint, halftone, mezzotint, half-light, patina; chromatic aberration

8 <coloring matter> **color, coloring, colorant,** tinction, tincture, **pigment, stain;** chromogen; **dye,** dyestuff, artificial coloring, color filter, color gelatin; paint, distemper, tempera, enamel, glaze; coat, coating, **coat of paint; undercoat,** undercoating, **primer,** priming, prime coat, **ground, flat coat,** dead-color; interior paint, exterior paint, floor enamel; wash, wash coat, flat wash, colorwash, whitewash; opaque color, transparent color; medium, vehicle; drier; thinner; turpentine, turps <nf>; additive color, subtractive color; artist's colors, colored pencils, crayons, chalk

9 <persons according to hair color> **brunet; blond,** Goldilocks; bleached blond, peroxide blond; ash blond, platinum blond, strawberry blond, honey blond; **towhead; redhead,** carrottop <nf>

10 <science of colors> chromatology; chromatics, chromatography, chromatoscopy, colorimetry; spectrum analysis, spectroscopy, spectrometry, spectrography; color theory

11 <applying color> **coloring,** coloration; **staining, dyeing; tie-dyeing; tinting,** tinging, tinction; pigmentation; illumination, emblazonry; color printing; lithography

12 **painting,** paint-work, coating, covering; **enameling,** glossing, glazing; **varnishing,** japanning, lacquering, shellacking; staining; **calcimining, whitewashing;** gilding; stippling; frescoing, fresco; undercoating, priming; watercoloring, pencilling, crayoning

13 spectrum, rainbow; red, orange, yellow, green, blue, indigo, violet

VERBS 14 **color,** hue, lay on color; **tinge, tint,** tinct, **tincture,** tone, complexion; pigment; bedizen; variegate, colorize; **stain, dye,** dip, tie-dye; imbue; deep-dye, fast-dye, double-dye, dye in the wool, yarn-dye; ingrain, grain; shade, shadow; illuminate, emblazon; **paint,** apply paint, paint up, **coat,** cover, face, watercolor, crayon; dab, **daub,** dedaub, smear, besmear, brush on paint, slap *or* slop on paint; **enamel,** gloss, glaze; **varnish,** japan, **lacquer, shellac; white out; calcimine, whitewash,** parget; wash; **gild,** begild, engild; stipple; fresco; distemper; undercoat, prime; emblazon; color-code

15 <be inharmonious> **clash,** conflict, collide, fight

ADJS 16 **chromatic,** colorational; **coloring,** colorific,

colorative, tinctorial, tingent; pigmental, pigmentary; monochrome, monochromic, monochromatic; dichromatic; many-colored, particolored, medley *or* motley <old>, rainbow, **variegated** 47.9, polychromatic, multicolored, kaleidoscopic, technicolored; prismatic, spectral; matching, toning, harmonious; warm, glowing; cool, cold

17 **colored,** hued, in color, colorized, in Technicolor <trademark>; **tinged, tinted,** tinctured, tinct, toned; **painted, enameled; stained, dyed;** tie-dyed; imbued; complexioned, complected <nf>; fullcolored, full; deep, deep-colored; wash-colored; washed

18 **deep-dyed, fast-dyed,** double-dyed, **dyed-in-thewool;** ingrained, ingrain; colorfast, fast, fadeless, unfading, indelible, constant

19 **colorful,** colory; **bright, vivid,** intense, **rich,** exotic, **brilliant,** burning, **gorgeous, gay,** bright-hued, bright-colored, rich-colored, gay-colored, highcolored, deep-colored

20 garish, lurid, loud, screaming, shrieking, glaring, flaring, flashy, glitzy <nf>, flaunting, crude, blinding, overbright, raw, gaudy 501.20; Day-Glo <trademark>

21 **off-color,** off-tone; **inharmonious, discordant,** incongruous, **harsh,** clashing, conflicting, colliding

22 soft-colored, soft-hued, **soft,** softened, **subdued,** understated, muted, delicate, light, creamy, peaches-and-cream, **pastel, pale,** palish, subtle, mellow, delicate, quiet, tender, sweet; pearly, nacreous, mother-of-pearl, iridescent, opalescent; patinaed; somber, simple, sober, sad; flat, eggshell, semigloss, gloss; weathered, heathered

WORD ELEMENTS 23 -chroia, -chromasia, chrom-, chromo-, chromat-, chromato-; -phyll; pigmento-; -chrome, -chromia, -chromy; pallidi-; -chroic, -chroous

36 COLORLESSNESS

NOUNS 1 **colorlessness,** lack *or* absence of color, huelessness, tonelessness, achromatism, achromaticity; dullness, lackluster 1027.5; neutral hue *or* tint

2 **paleness, dimness,** weakness, **faintness,** fadedness; lightness, fairness; **pallor,** pallidity, pallidness, prison pallor; **wanness, sallowness,** pastiness, ashiness; wheyface; muddiness, dullness, grayness, griseousness; **anemia,** hypochromic anemia, hypochromia, chloranemia; bloodlessness, exsanguination; **ghastliness, haggardness,** lividness, sickly hue, sickliness, deadly *or* deathly pallor, deathly hue, cadaverousness

3 **decoloration,** decolorizing, decolorization,

discoloration, achromatization, lightening; **fading, paling; dimming, bedimming; whitening,** blanching, etiolation, whiteness, albinism, pigment deficiency; bleeding, bleeding white; **bleaching,** bleach; market bleach, madder bleach; weathering

4 **bleach,** bleacher, bleaching agent *or* substance; color remover, decolorant, decolorizer, achromatizer; whitener

VERBS 5 decolor, decolorize, discolor, achromatize, etiolate; **fade, wash out; dim, dull, tarnish,** tone down; **pale, whiten,** blanch, drain, drain of color; **bleach,** peroxide, fume

6 **lose color, fade,** fade out; **bleach,** bleach out; **pale, turn pale,** grow pale, **change color,** change countenance, turn white, **whiten, blanch,** wan; come out in the wash; discolor

ADJS 7 **colorless, hueless,** toneless, uncolored, achromic, achromatic, achromatous, unpigmented; neutral; dull, flat, mat, dead, dingy, muddy, leaden, lusterless, lackluster 1027.17; **faded, washed-out,** dimmed, discolored, decolored, etiolated, weathered; **pale, dim,** weak, **faint; pallid, wan, sallow,** fallow; pale *or* blue *or* green around the gills, drained of color; **white,** white as a sheet; **pasty,** mealy, waxen; **ashen,** ashy, ashen-hued, cinereous, cineritious, gray, griseous, mousy, dingy; **anemic,** hypochromic, chloranemic; bloodless, exsanguine, exsanguinated, exsanguineous, bled white; **ghastly,** livid, lurid, **haggard,** cadaverous, unhealthy, sickly, deadly *or* deathly pale; pale as death *or* a ghost *or* a corpse; pale-faced, tallow-faced, wheyfaced, white-skinned

8 **bleached,** decolored, decolorized, achromatized, whitened, blanched, lightened, bleached out, bleached white; drained, drained of color

9 **light, fair,** light-colored, light-hued; pastel; whitish 37.8

WORD ELEMENTS 10 achromat-, achromato-, achro-, achroö-

37 WHITENESS

NOUNS 1 **whiteness, white, whitishness;** albescence; **lightness, fairness;** paleness 36.2; silveriness; snowiness, frostiness; chalkiness; pearliness; **creaminess,** off-whiteness, chalkiness; blondness; hoariness, grizzliness, canescence; milkiness, lactescence; glaucousness; glaucescence; silver; albinism, achroma, achromasia, achromatosis; albino; leukoderma, vitiligo; wheyface; white race 312.2,3

2 <comparisons> alabaster, bone, chalk, cream, ivory, lily, lime, milk, pearl, sheet, swan, sheep, fleece, flour, foam, paper, phantom, silver, snow, driven snow, tallow, teeth, wax, wool

3 **whitening,** albification, blanching; etiolation; **whitewashing;** bleaching 36.3; silvering, frosting, grizzling

4 whitening agent, whitener, whiting, whitening, **whitewash,** calcimine; pipe clay; correction fluid, Wite-Out <trademark>; bleach

VERBS 5 **whiten,** white, etiolate, **blanch;** bleach 36.5; pale, blench; decolorize; fade; silver, grizzle, frost, besnow; chalk

6 **whitewash,** white <old>, calcimine; pipe-clay, Blanco <Brit>, clean

ADJS 7 **white,** pure white, white as alabaster *or* bone *or* chalk *or* snow, etc 37.2, **snow-white,** snowy, niveous, "whiter than new snow on a raven's back"—Shakespeare, frosty, frosted; **hoary,** hoar, **grizzled,** grizzly, griseous, canescent; silver, **silvery,** silvered, argent <heraldry>, argentine; platinum; chalky, cretaceous; fleece- *or* fleecy-white; swan-white; foam-white; **milk-white,** milky, lactescent; marble, marmoreal; lily-white, white as a lily; white as a sheet, wheyfaced, ghastly; albescent; whitened, bleached, blanched, achromatic

8 **whitish,** whity, albescent; **light, fair;** pale 36.7; off-white; eggshell; glaucous, glaucescent; pearl, pearly, pearly-white, pearl-white; alabaster, alabastrine; cream, **creamy;** ivory, ivory-white; gray-white; dun-white; lint-white

9 **blond** *or* blonde; flaxen-haired, fair-haired; artificial blond, bleached-blond, peroxide-blond; ash-blond, platinum-blond, strawberry-blond, honey-blond, blond-headed, blond-haired; **towheaded,** tow-haired; golden-haired 43.5; white-haired

10 **albino,** albinic, albinistic, albinal

WORD ELEMENTS 11 alb-, albo-, leuc-, leuco-, leuk-, leuko-

38 BLACKNESS

NOUNS 1 **blackness,** nigritude, nigrescence; inkiness; **black, sable, ebony;** melanism; black race 312.2,3; darkness 1027

2 **darkness, darkishness,** darksomeness, blackishness; **swarthiness,** swartness, swarth; **duskiness,** duskness; soberness, sobriety; **somberness,** graveness, sadness, funereality; hostility, sullenness, anger, black mood, black looks, black words

3 **dinginess, griminess, smokiness,** sootiness, fuliginousness, fuliginosity, smudginess, smuttiness, blotchiness, dirtiness, **muddiness,** murkiness

4 <comparisons> ebony *or* ebon <old>, jet, ink, sloe, pitch, tar, coal, charcoal, smoke, soot, smut,

raven, obsidian, sable, crow, night, hell, sin, one's hat <Brit>

5 blackening, darkening, nigrification, melanization, melanism, melanosis, denigration; shading; **smudging,** smutching, **smirching;** smudge, smutch, smirch, smut

6 blacking, blackening, blackening agent, blackwash; charcoal, burnt cork, black ink; lampblack, carbon black, stove black, gas black, soot; japan; melanin

VERBS **7 blacken,** black, nigrify, melanize, denigrate; **darken,** bedarken; shade, shadow; blackwash, ink, charcoal, cork; **smudge,** smutch, **smirch,** besmirch, murk, blotch, blot, dinge, dirty; smut, soot; smoke, oversmoke, singe, char; ebonize; **smear** 661.9, 512.10, **blacken one's name** or **reputation,** give one a black eye, tear down; japan, niello

ADJS **8 black,** black as ink or pitch or tar or coal, etc 38.4; **sable** <heraldry>, nigrous, nigrescent; **ebony,** ebon; deep black, of the deepest dye; **pitch-black, pitch-dark,** pitchy, black or dark as pitch, tar-black, tarry; night-black, night-dark, black or dark as night; midnight, black as midnight; **inky,** inky-black, atramentous, ink-black, black as ink; **jet-black,** jet, jetty; **coal-black,** coaly, black as coal, coal-black; sloe, sloe-black, sloe-colored; raven, **raven-black,** black as a crow; blue-black, brown-black; **dark** 1026.13–16

9 dark, dark-colored, **darkish,** darksome, blackish; nigrescent; **swarthy,** swart; **dusky,** dusk; **somber,** sombrous, **sober, grave,** sad, funereal; hostile, sullen, angry; achromatic

10 dark-skinned, black-skinned, **dark-complexioned; black, colored;** swarthy, swart; melanian, melanic, melanotic, melanistic, melanous

11 dingy, grimy, smoky, sooty, fuliginous, **smudgy,** smutty, blotchy, dirty, **muddy,** murky, smirched, besmirched, dusky; blackened, singed, charred

12 livid, black-and-blue

13 black-haired, raven-haired, raven-tressed, black-locked, dark-haired; brunet or brunette

WORD ELEMENTS **14** atro-, mel-, mela-, melo-, melano-, melam-

39 GRAYNESS

NOUNS **1 grayness, gray,** grayishness, canescence; glaucousness, glaucescence; silveriness; ashiness; neutral tint; smokiness; mousiness; slatiness; leadenness; lividness, lividity; dullness, drabness, soberness, somberness; grisaille; oyster, taupe, greige; gunmetal, iron, lead, pewter, silver, slate, steel

2 gray-haired or **gray-headed person,** gray-hair, graybeard, grisard, salt-and-pepper, hoariness

VERBS **3 gray, grizzle,** silver, frost

ADJS **4 gray, grayish,** gray-colored, gray-hued, gray-toned, grayed, griseous; canescent; iron-gray, steely, steel-gray; Quaker-gray, Quaker-colored, acier, gray-drab; dove-gray, dove-colored; pearl-gray, pearl, pearly; silver-gray, silver, silvery, silvered; **grizzly,** grizzled, grizzle; ash-gray, ashen, ashy, cinerous, cinereous, cineritious, cinereal; dusty, dust-gray; smoky, smoke-gray; charcoal-gray; slaty, slate-colored; leaden, livid, lead-gray; glaucous, glaucescent; wolf-gray; mousy, mouse-gray, mouse-colored; taupe; dapple-gray, dappled-gray; gray-spotted, gray-speckled, salt-and-pepper; gray-black, gray-brown, etc; taupe, ecru, greige; neutral; **dull, dingy,** dismal, **somber, sober, sad, dreary;** winter-gray, hoar, hoary, frost-gray, rime-gray

5 gray-haired, gray-headed, silver-headed; hoar, hoary, hoary-haired, grizzled; gray-bearded, silver-bearded, salt-and-pepper or pepper-and-salt

40 BROWNNESS

NOUNS **1 brownness, brownishness, brown,** browning, infuscation; brown race 312.2; ochre, sepia, raw sienna, burnt sienna, raw umber, burnt umber; caramel, pumpernickel, coffee, chocolate, paper bag

VERBS **2 brown,** embrown, infuscate; rust; **tan, bronze,** suntan; sunburn, burn; fry, sauté, scorch, braise; toast

ADJS **3 brown, brownish;** cinnamon, hazel; fuscous; **brunet,** brune; tawny, fulvous; tan, tan-colored; tan-faced, tan-skinned, tanned, sun-tanned; khaki, khaki-colored; drab, olive-drab; **dun,** dun-brown, dun-drab, dun-olive; beige, grege, buff, biscuit, mushroom; **chocolate,** chocolate-colored, chocolate-brown; cocoa, cocoa-colored, cocoa-brown; coffee, coffee-colored, coffee-brown; toast, toast-brown; nut-brown; oatmeal; walnut, walnut-brown; seal, seal-brown; fawn, fawn-colored; grayish-brown; brownish-gray, fuscous, taupe, mouse-dun, mouse-brown; snuff-colored, snuff-brown, mummy-brown; umber, umber-colored, umber-brown; olive-brown; **sepia;** sorrel; yellowish-brown, brownish-yellow; lurid <old>; brown as a berry, berry-brown

4 reddish-brown, rufous-brown, brownish-red; roan; henna; terra-cotta; rufous, foxy; livid-brown; **mahogany,** mahogany-brown; auburn, Titian; **russet,** russety; rust, rust-colored, rusty, ferruginous, rubiginous; liver-colored, liver-brown; **bronze,** bronze-brown, bronze-colored, bronzed, brazen; copper, coppery, copperish, cupreous, copper-colored; **chestnut,** chestnut-brown, castaneous; bay, bay-colored; bayard <old>; sunburned, adust <old>

5 **brunet** *or* brunette; brown-haired; auburn-haired; xanthous

41 REDNESS

NOUNS 1 **redness, reddishness,** rufosity, rubricity; **red,** *rouge* <Fr>, gules <heraldry>; rubicundity, **ruddiness,** color, high color, floridness, floridity; rubor, erythema, erythroderma, "a fire-red cherubim's face"—Chaucer; erythrism; reddish brown; red race 312.3; "any color, so long as it's red"—Eugene Field; carmine, crimson, henna, rouge; cherry, ruby, fire engine

2 **pinkness, pinkishness; rosiness; pink,** rose

3 **reddening,** rubefaction, rubification, rubescence, erubescence, rufescence; **coloring,** mantling, crimsoning, **blushing, flushing; blush,** flush, glow, bloom, rosiness; hectic, hectic flush; rubefacient

VERBS 4 <make red> **redden, rouge,** ruddle, rubefy, raddle, rubric; warm, inflame; crimson, encrimson; vermilion, madder, miniate, henna, rust, carmine; incarnadine, pinkify; red-ink, red-pencil, lipstick

5 **redden,** turn *or* grow red, **color,** color up, **mantle, blush, flush, crimson;** flame, glow

ADJS 6 **red, reddish,** gules <heraldry>, red-colored, red-hued, red-dyed, red-looking; **ruddy,** ruddied, rubicund; rubric *or* rubrical, rubricate, rubricose; rufescent, rufous, rufulous; warm, hot, glowing; bright-red; fiery, flaming, flame-colored, flame-red, fire-red, red as fire, lurid, red as a hot *or* live coal; reddened, inflamed; **scarlet, vermilion, vermeil; crimson;** rubiate; maroon; damask; puce; stammel; cerise; iron-red; cardinal, cardinal-red; cherry, cherry-colored, cherry-red; carmine, incarmined; **ruby,** ruby-colored, ruby-red; wine, port-wine, wine-colored, wine-red, vinaceous; carnation, carnation-red; brick-red, bricky, tile-red, lateritious; rust, rust-red, rusty, ferruginous, rubiginous; lake-colored, laky; beet-red, red as a beet; lobster-red, red as a lobster; red as a turkey-cock; copper-red, carnelian; russet; Titian, Titian-red; infrared; reddish-amber, reddish-gray, etc; reddish-brown 40.4

7 **sanguine,** sanguineous, **blood-red,** blood-colored, bloody-red, bloody, gory, red as blood

8 **pink, pinkish,** pinky; **rose, rosy,** rose-colored, rose-hued, rose-red, roseate; primrose; flesh-colored, flesh-pink, incarnadine; coral, coral-colored, coral-red, coralline; salmon, salmon-colored, salmon-pink; damask, carnation; fuchsia

9 **red-complexioned,** ruddy-complexioned, warm-complexioned, red-fleshed, red-faced, ruddy-faced,

apple-cheeked, **ruddy,** rubicund, **florid,** sanguine, full-blooded; blowzy, blowzed; rosy, **rosy-cheeked;** glowing, blooming; hectic, blushing, rouged, flushed, flush; burnt, sunburned; erythematous

10 **redheaded,** red-haired, red-polled, red-bearded; erythristic; red-crested, red-crowned, red-tufted; ginger-haired, carroty, chestnut, auburn, Titian, xanthous

11 reddening, blushing, flushing, coloring; rubescent, erubescent; rubificative, rubrific; rubefacient

42 ORANGENESS

NOUNS 1 **orangeness,** oranginess; **orange;** cadmium orange, carotene

ADJS 2 **orange, orangeish,** orangey, orange-hued, reddish-yellow; ocherous *or* ochery, ochreous, ochroid, ocherish; old gold; saffron; pumpkin, pumpkin-colored; tangerine, tangerine-colored; apricot, peach, cantaloupe; carroty, carrot-colored; orange-red, orange-yellow, red-orange, reddish-orange, yellow-orange

43 YELLOWNESS

NOUNS 1 **yellowness, yellowishness;** goldenness, aureateness; **yellow,** gold, or <heraldry>; gildedness; fallowness; cadmium yellow, cadmium lemon, lemon, banana

2 yellow skin, yellow complexion, sallowness; biliousness; xanthochroism; **jaundice,** yellow jaundice, icterus, xanthoderma, xanthism; yellow race 312.2,3

VERBS 3 **yellow,** turn yellow; **gild,** begild, engild; aurify; sallow; **jaundice**

ADJS 4 **yellow, yellowish,** yellowy; lutescent, luteous, luteolous; xanthic, xanthous; flavescent; **gold, golden,** gold-colored, golden-yellow, gilt, gilded, auric, aureate; sunshine-yellow; **canary,** canary-yellow; citron, citron-yellow, citreous; **lemon,** lemon-colored, lemon-yellow; sulfur-colored, sulfur-yellow; mustard, mustard-yellow; pale-yellow, **sallow,** fallow; cream, creamy, cream-colored; straw, straw-colored, tow-colored; flaxen, flaxen-colored, flax-colored; sandy, sand-colored; ocherous *or* ochery, ochreous, ochroid, ocherish; buff, buff-colored, buff-yellow; honey-colored; saffron, saffron-colored, saffron-yellow; primrose, primrose-colored, primrose-yellow; topaz-yellow; greenish-yellow, chartreuse

5 **yellow-haired, golden-haired,** tow-headed, tow-haired, auricomous, xanthous; blond 37.9

6 yellow-faced, yellow-complexioned, sallow, yellow-cheeked; **jaundiced,** xanthodermatous, icteric, icterical, bilious

44 GREENNESS

NOUNS **1 greenness,** viridity; greenishness, virescence, viridescence; verdantness, verdancy, **verdure,** glaucousness, glaucescence; **green,** greensickness, chlorosis, chloremia, chloranemia; chlorophyll; grass, emerald
 2 verdigris, patina, aerugo; patination
VERBS **3 green;** verdigris, patinate, patinize
ADJS **4 green,** virid; **verdant,** verdurous, vert <heraldry>; grassy, leafy, leaved, foliaged; springlike, summerlike, summery, vernal, vernant, aestival; **greenish,** viridescent, virescent; **grass-green,** green as grass; citrine, citrinous; **olive,** olive-green, olivaceous; pea-green; avocado; jade; loden green; bottle-green; forest-green; sea-green; beryl-green, berylline; leek-green, porraceous <old>; holly, holly-green; ivy, ivy-green; emerald, emerald-green, smaragdine; chartreuse, yellow-green, yellowish-green, greenish-yellow; glaucous, glaucescent, glaucous-green; blue-green, bluish-green, green-blue, greenish-blue; greensick, chlorotic, chloremic, chloranemic
 5 verdigrisy, verdigrised, patinous, patinaed, patinated *or* patinized, aeruginous

45 BLUENESS

NOUNS **1 blueness, bluishness;** azureness; **blue, azure,** cyan, indigo; lividness, lividity; cyanosis
VERBS **2 blue,** azure
ADJS **3 blue, bluish,** cerulescent; cyanic, cyaneous, cyanean; cerulean, ceruleous; **azure** <heraldry>, azurine, azurean, azureous, azured, azure-blue, azure-colored, azure-tinted; sky-blue, sky-colored, sky-dyed; ice-blue; light-blue, lightish-blue, pale-blue, Oxford blue; dark-blue, deep-blue, midnight-blue, navy-blue; peacock-blue, pavonine, pavonian; beryl-blue, berylline; turquoise, turquoise-blue; aquamarine; electric-blue; ultramarine; royal-blue; indigo; sapphire, sapphire-blue, sapphirine; Wedgwood-blue, robin's-egg blue; livid; cyanotic

46 PURPLENESS

NOUNS **1 purpleness, purplishness,** purpliness; **purple; violet,** lavender, lilac, magenta, mauve; lividness, lividity, bruise
VERBS **2 purple,** empurple, purpurate <old>
ADJS **3 purple,** purpure <heraldry>, purpureal, purpureous, purpurean, purpurate <old>; **purplish,** purply, purplescent; **violet,** violaceous; plum-colored, plum-purple; amethystine; **lavender,** lavender-blue; lilac; magenta; mauve; mulberry; orchid; pansy-purple, pansy-violet;

raisin-colored; fuchsia, puce, aubergine, orchid; purple-blue; livid

47 VARIEGATION
<diversity of colors>

NOUNS **1 variegation, multicolor;** parti-color; medley *or* mixture of colors, spectrum, rainbow of colors, riot of color; polychrome, polychromatism; dichromatism, trichromatism, etc; dichroism, trichroism, etc
 2 iridescence, iridization, irisation, **opalescence,** nacreousness, pearliness, chatoyancy, **play of colors** *or* **light;** light show; moiré pattern, tabby; burelé *or* burelage
 3 spottiness, maculation, freckliness, speckliness, mottledness, mottlement, dappleness, dappledness, stippledness, spottedness, dottedness; **fleck, speck, speckle;** freckle; **spot,** dot, polka dot, macula, macule, blotch, splotch, patch, splash; **mottle, dapple;** brindle; **stipple,** stippling, pointillism, pointillage
 4 check, checker, checks, checking, checkerboard, chessboard; **plaid,** tartan; checker-work, variegated pattern, harlequin, colors in patches, crazy-work, patchwork; parquet, parquetry, marquetry, mosaic, tesserae, tessellation; crazy-paving <Brit>; hound's tooth; inlay, damascene
 5 stripe, striping, candy-stripe, pinstripe; barber pole; **streak, streaking;** striation, striature, stria; striola, striga; crack, craze, crackle, reticulation; bar, band, belt, list
 6 <comparisons> spectrum, rainbow, iris, chameleon, leopard, jaguar, cheetah, ocelot, zebra, barber pole, candy cane, Dalmatian, firedog, peacock, butterfly, mother-of-pearl, nacre, tortoise shell, opal, kaleidoscope, stained glass, serpentine, calico cat, marble, mackerel sky, confetti, crazy quilt, patchwork quilt, shot silk, moiré, watered silk, marbled paper, Joseph's coat, harlequin, tapestry; bar code, checkerboard
VERBS **7 variegate,** motley; parti-color; polychrome, polychromize; pattern; harlequin; **mottle, dapple,** stipple, **fleck,** flake, **speck, speckle,** bespeckle, freckle, **spot,** bespot, dot, sprinkle, blot, spangle, bespangle, pepper, stud, maculate; blotch, splotch; tattoo, stigmatize <old>; **check, checker;** tessellate; **stripe, streak,** striate, band, bar, vein, craze; marble, marbleize; tabby
 8 opalesce, opalize; iridesce
ADJS **9 variegated, many-colored,** many-hued, diverse-colored, **multicolored,** multicolor, multicolorous, **varicolored,** varicolorous, polychrome, polychromic, polychromatic; parti-colored, parti-color; of all manner of colors, of all

the colors of the rainbow; versicolor, versicolored, versicolorate, versicolorous; motley, medley <old>, harlequin; colorful, colory; daedal; crazy; thunder and lightning; kaleidoscopic, kaleidoscopical; prismatic, prismatical, prismal, spectral; shot, shot through; bicolored, bicolor, dichromic, dichromatic; tricolored, tricolor, trichromic, trichromatic; two-color or -colored, three-color or -colored, two-tone or -toned, etc

10 **iridescent,** iridal, iridial, iridine, iridian; irised, irisated, **rainbowy,** rainbowlike, rainbowed; **opalescent,** opaline, opaloid; nacreous, nacry, *nacré* <Fr>, nacred, **pearly,** pearlish, mother-of-pearl; tortoise-shell; peacock-like, pavonine, pavonian; chatoyant; moiré, burelé; watered

11 **chameleonlike,** chameleonic, changeable

12 **mottled, motley; pied, piebald,** skewbald, pinto; **dappled,** dapple; calico; marbled; clouded; salt-and-pepper

13 **spotted, dotted,** polka-dot, sprinkled, peppered, studded, pocked, pockmarked; **spotty,** dotty, patchy, pocky; **speckled, specked,** speckledy, speckly, specky; **stippled,** pointillé, pointillistic; **flecked,** fleckered; spangled, bespangled; maculate, maculated, macular; punctate, punctated; freckled, frecked, freckly; blotched, blotchy, splotched, splotchy; flea-bitten; tortoiseshell; foxed

14 **checked, checkered,** checkedy, check, **plaid,** plaided; tessellated, tessellate, mosaic

15 **striped,** stripy, candy-stripe, pinstripe; **streaked,** streaky; **striated,** striate, striatal, striolate, strigate or strigose; barred, banded, listed; veined; **brindle,** brindled, brinded; marbled, marbleized; reticulate; tabby

48 HEARING

NOUNS 1 **hearing,** audition; sense of hearing, auditory or aural sense, ear; listening, heeding, attention, hushed attention, rapt attention, eager attention, mind; auscultation, aural examination, examination by ear; audibility

2 **audition,** hearing, tryout, call <nf>, **audience, interview,** conference; attention, favorable attention, ear; **listening,** listening in; **eavesdropping,** overhearing, wiretapping, electronic surveillance, bugging <nf>

3 good hearing, refined or acute sense of hearing, sensitive ear, nice or quick or sharp or correct ear; **an ear for;** musical ear, ear for music, musicality; ear-mindedness; bad or poor ear, no ear, tin ear <nf>

4 **earshot,** earreach, **hearing,** range, auditory range, reach, carrying distance, **sound of one's voice**

5 **listener,** hearer, auditor, audient, hearkener, auditioner, earwitness; **eavesdropper,** overhearer, monitor; little pitcher with big ears, snoop <nf>, listener-in; fly on the wall <nf>

6 **audience,** auditory <old>, **house, congregation;** studio audience, live audience, captive audience, theatregoers, gallery, crowd, house; orchestra, pit; groundling, boo-bird <nf>, spectator 917

7 **ear** 2.10, auditory apparatus, hearing organ; external ear, **outer ear;** cauliflower ear, jug ear, bat ear

8 listening device; **hearing aid,** hard-of-hearing aid; electronic hearing aid, transistor hearing aid; vacuum-tube hearing aid; ear trumpet; amplifier, speaking trumpet, megaphone; stethoscope

9 <science of hearing> otology; otoscopy, auriscopy; otoneurology, otopathy, otography, otoplasty, otolaryngology, otorhinolaryngology; ear, nose, and throat or ENT; audiology; acoustic phonetics, phonetics 524.13; auriscope, otoscope, auscultator, stethoscope; audiometer

VERBS 10 **listen,** hark, **hearken, heed, hear, attend,** give attention, **give ear,** give or lend an ear, bend an ear; **listen to,** listen at <nf>, attend to, give a hearing to, give audience to, sit in on; **listen in; eavesdrop,** wiretap, tap, intercept, bug <nf>; **keep one's ears open,** be all ears <nf>, listen with both ears, strain one's ears; prick up the ears, cock the ears, keep one's ear to the ground, have long ears; hang on the lips of, hang on every word; hear out; auscultate, examine by ear

11 **hear,** catch, get <nf>, take in, hear from; **overhear; hear of,** hear tell of <nf>, pick up; get an earful <nf>, get wind of; have an ear for, have perfect pitch

12 be heard, **fall on the ear,** sound in the ear, catch or reach the ear, carry, sound, resound, echo, reverberate, come within earshot, come to one's ear, register, make an impression, get across <nf>; **have one's ear,** reach, contact, get to; make oneself heard, get through to, gain a hearing, reach the ear of; ring in the ear; caress the ear; assault or split or assail the ear

ADJS 13 **auditory,** audio, audile, **hearing, aural,** auricular, otic, audial, auditive; audio-visual; audible; otological, otoscopic, otopathic, etc; acoustic, acoustical, phonic

14 **listening, attentive,** open-eared, **all ears** <nf>, hearing

15 **eared,** auriculate; big-eared, cauliflower-eared, crop-eared, dog-eared, droop-eared, flap-eared, flop-eared, jug-eared, lop-eared, long-eared, mouse-eared, prick-eared; **sharp-eared;** tin-eared; ear-minded; ear-shaped, earlike, auriform

INTERJS 16 **hark!,** hark ye!, hear ye!, hearken!, hear!, oyez!, hear ye, hear ye!, now hear this!, list!,

listen!, listen up!, attend!, attention!, hist!, whisht!, psst!, yo!

49 DEAFNESS

NOUNS **1 deafness, hardness of hearing,** dull hearing, deaf ears; **stone-deafness;** nerve-deafness; mind deafness, word deafness; **tone deafness,** unmusicalness; impaired hearing, hearing *or* auditory impairment; loss of hearing, **hearing loss; deaf-muteness,** deaf-mutism, surdimutism <old>

2 the deaf, the hard-of-hearing; **deaf-mute,** surdo-mute <old>, deaf-and-dumb person; lip reader

3 deaf-and-dumb alphabet, manual alphabet, finger alphabet; dactylology, sign language, American Sign Language; lip reading, oral method; hearing aid

VERBS **4 be deaf;** have no ears, be earless; lose one's hearing, suffer hearing loss *or* impairment, go deaf; shut *or* stop *or* close one's ears, **turn a deaf ear;** fall on deaf ears; lipread, use sign language, sign

5 deafen, stun, split the ears *or* eardrums

ADJS **6 deaf, hard-of-hearing,** hearing-impaired, dull *or* thick of hearing, deaf-eared, dull-eared; surd <old>; deafened, stunned; **stone-deaf,** deaf as a stone, deaf as a door *or* a doorknob *or* doornail, **deaf as a post,** deaf as an adder; **unhearing;** earless; word-deaf; tone-deaf, unmusical; half-deaf, quasi-deaf; **deaf and dumb,** deaf-mute

50 SOUND

NOUNS **1 sound,** sonance, acoustic, acoustical *or* acoustic phenomenon; auditory phenomenon *or* stimulus, auditory effect; noise; ultrasound; sound wave, sound propagation; sound intensity, sound intensity level, amplitude, loudness 53; phone, speech sound 524.12; resonance

2 tone, pitch, frequency, audio frequency *or* AF; monotone, monotony, tonelessness; overtone, harmonic, partial, partial tone; undertone; fundamental tone, fundamental; intonation 524.7

3 timbre, tonality, **tone quality,** tone color, color, coloring, clang color *or* tint, *Klangfarbe* <Ger>

4 sounding, sonation, sonification

5 acoustics, phonics, radioacoustics; acoustical engineer, acoustician; radiophonics

6 sonics; subsonics, **supersonics,** ultrasonics; speed of sound 174.2; sound barrier, transonic barrier, sonic barrier *or* wall; sonic boom; ultrasonic frequency, infrasonic frequency

7 <sound unit> **decibel,** bel, phon

8 loudspeaker, speaker, dynamic speaker; speaker unit, speaker system; crossover network; voice coil; cone, diaphragm; acoustical network; horn <nf>; **headphone, earphone,** stereo headset, headset

9 microphone, mike <nf>; radiomicrophone; concealed microphone, **bug** <nf>

10 audio amplifier, amplifier, amp <nf>; **preamplifier,** preamp <nf>

11 sound reproduction system, audio sound system; **high-fidelity** system *or* **hi-fi** <nf>; **record player, phonograph,** gramophone, Victrola; **jukebox,** nickelodeon; radio-phonograph combination; monophonic *or* monaural system, **mono** <nf>, stereophonic *or* binaural system, stereo <nf>; four-channel stereo system, discrete four-channel system, derived four-channel system, quadraphonic sound system; multitrack player *or* recorder *or* sound system; **pickup** *or* cartridge, magnetic pickup *or* cartridge, ceramic pickup *or* cartridge, crystal pickup, photoelectric pickup; stylus, needle; tone arm; turntable, transcription turntable, record changer, changer; **public-address system** *or* PA *or* PA system; sound truck; loud-hailer, bullhorn; intercommunication system, **intercom** <nf>, squawk box <nf>; **tape recorder,** tape deck, cassette *or* audio-cassette player, cassette *or* audio-cassette recorder; boom box, ghetto blaster; compact disc *or* CD player; hi-fi fan *or* freak <nf>, audiophile

12 record, phonograph record, disc, wax, long-playing record *or* LP; transcription, electrical transcription, digital transcription, digital recording; **recording,** wire recording, tape recording; digital stereo; digital disc; tape, tape cassette, cassette; tape cartridge, cartridge; digital audio tape *or* DAT, DVD; compact disk *or* CD; video-cassette recorder *or* VCR

13 audio distortion, distortion; scratching, shredding, hum, 60-cycle hum, rumble, hissing, howling, blurping, blooping, woomping, fluttering, flutter, wow, wow-wows, squeals, whistles, birdies, motorboating; feedback; static 1034.21

VERBS **14 sound,** make a sound *or* noise, give forth *or* emit a sound; noise; speak 524.19; resound, reverberate, echo; **record,** tape, tape-record; prerecord; play back; broadcast, amplify

ADJS **15 sounding,** sonorous, soniferous; **sounded;** tonal; monotone, monotonic, toneless, droning; voiced

16 audible, hearable, heard; **distinct, clear,** plain, definite, articulate; distinctive, contrastive; high-fidelity, hi-fi <nf>, stereophonic

17 acoustic, acoustical, phonic, **sonic;** subsonic, supersonic, ultrasonic, hypersonic; transonic *or* transsonic, faster than sound

ADVS **18 audibly, aloud,** out, **out loud;** distinctly, clearly, plainly

51 SILENCE

NOUNS 1 silence, silentness, **soundlessness,** noiselessness, **stillness,** "lucid stillness"—T S Eliot, **quietness,** quietude, quiescence 173, **quiet, still,** peace, whisht <Scot & Ir>, **hush,** mum; lull, rest, calm; golden silence; total silence, deathlike or tomblike silence, dead silence, perfect silence, solemn or awful silence, the quiet or silence of the grave or the tomb; hush or dead of night, dead; tacitness, taciturnity, reticence, reserve; inaudibility; tranquillity; not a sound

2 muteness, mutism, **dumbness,** voicelessness, tonguelessness; speechlessness, wordlessness; inarticulateness; anaudia, aphasia, aphonia; hysterical mutism; deaf-muteness 49.1; standing mute, refusal to speak, stonewalling <nf>, the code of silence or omertà <Ital>, keeping one's lip buttoned <nf>; laryngitis

3 mute, dummy; deaf-mute 49.2

4 silencer, muffler, muffle, **mute,** baffle or baffler, quietener, cushion; **damper,** damp; dampener; **soft pedal,** sordine, sourdine, sordino <Ital>; hushcloth, silence cloth; **gag, muzzle;** antiknock; **soundproofing,** acoustic tile, sound-absorbing material, sound-proofing insulation

VERBS 5 be silent, keep silent or silence, **keep still or quiet; keep one's mouth shut, hold one's tongue,** keep one's tongue between one's teeth, bite one's tongue, put a bridle on one's tongue, seal one's lips, shut or close one's mouth, hold one's breath, muzzle oneself, **not breathe a word,** not speak, forswear speech or speaking, **keep mum, hold one's peace,** not let a word escape one, not utter a word, not open one's mouth, not make a sound, not make a peep; make no sign, keep to oneself; not have a word to say, be mute, stand mute; choke up, have one's words stick in one's throat; be taciturn, spare one's words, have little to say, keep one's counsel

6 <nf terms> **shut up,** keep one's trap or yap shut, button up, button one's lip, save one's breath, shut one's bazoo, can it, dummy up, clam up, close up like a clam, knock it off, not let out a peep, say nothing, not say 'boo', play dumb, stonewall

7 fall silent, hush, quiet, quieten, quiesce, **quiet down,** pipe down <nf>, check one's speech, stop talking; lose one's voice, get laryngitis

8 silence, put to silence, hush, hush one up, hush-hush, **shush,** quiet, quieten, **still; soft-pedal,** put on the soft pedal, play down; squash, squelch <nf>, stifle, choke, choke off, throttle, put the kibosh on <nf>, put the lid on and shut down on <nf>, put the damper on <nf>, **gag, muzzle,** muffle, stifle, stop one's mouth, cut one short; strike dumb or mute, dumbfound; tonguetie

9 muffle, mute, dull, soften, deaden, quietize, cushion, baffle, damp, **dampen,** deafen; subdue, stop, tone down, **soft-pedal,** put on the soft pedal

ADJS 10 silent, still, stilly, **quiet,** quiescent 173.12, **hushed, soundless,** noiseless; taciturn, uncommunicative, tight-lipped, clammed up <nf>; echoless; **inaudible,** subaudible, below the limen or threshold of hearing, unhearable; quiet as a mouse or lamb, mousy; silent as a post or stone, "noiseless as fear in a wide wilderness"—Keats, "silent as the shadows"—Coleridge, so quiet that one might hear a feather or pin drop; silent as the grave or tomb, still as death, "hush as death"—Shakespeare; **unsounded, unvoiced,** unpronounced

11 tacit, wordless, unspoken, unuttered, unexpressed, unsaid, unarticulated, unvocalized; **implicit** 519.8

12 mute, mum, dumb, voiceless, tongueless, **speechless,** wordless, breathless, at a loss for words, choked up; inarticulate; **tongue-tied,** dumbstruck, dumbstricken, stricken dumb, **dumbfounded;** anaudic, aphasic, aphonic

ADVS 13 silently, in silence, **quietly, soundlessly,** noiselessly; inaudibly

INTERJS 14 silence!, hush!, shush!, sh!, sh-sh!, whist! or whish! <Brit nf>, whisht! <Scot & Ir>, peace!, pax!, tais toi! <Fr>, **be quiet!,** be silent!, be still!, **keep still!,** keep quiet!, quiet!, quiet please!, soft!, belay that! or there!, stow it!; **hold your tongue!,** hold your jaw! or lip!, **shut up!** <nf>, **shut your mouth!** <nf>, save your breath!, not another word!, not another peep out of you!, mum!, mum's the word!; hush your mouth!, shut your trap!, shut your face!, button your lip!, pipe down!, clam up!, dry up!, can it!, that's enough!, knock it off!

52 FAINTNESS OF SOUND

NOUNS 1 faintness, lowness, softness, gentleness, subduedness, dimness, feebleness, weakness; indistinctness, unclearness, flatness; subaudibility, inaudibility; decrescendo; distant sound

2 muffled tone, veiled voice, voce velata <Ital>, covered tone; **mutedness; dullness, deadness,** flatness; noise abatement, sound reduction, soundproofing

3 thud, dull thud; **thump,** flump, crump, clop, clump, clunk, plunk, tunk, plump, bump; pad, pat; **patter,** pitter-patter, pit-a-pat; **tap,** rap, **click,** tick, flick, pop; tinkle, clink, chink, tingaling

4 murmur, murmuring, murmuration; **mutter,** muttering; **mumble,** mumbling; soft voice, low voice, small or little voice; **undertone,** underbreath, bated breath; susurration, susurrus, undercurrent; **whisper,** whispering, stage whisper, breathy voice; breath, sigh, sough, exhalation, aspiration; purl, hum, moan, white noise *or* sound; nonresonance

5 **ripple, splash,** ripple of laughter, ripple of applause; titter, chuckle

6 **rustle,** rustling, froufrou, swoosh, "a little noiseless noise among the leaves"—Keats

7 **hum, humming,** thrumming, low rumbling, booming, bombilation, bombination, **droning, buzzing,** whizzing, whirring, purring

8 **sigh, sighing, moaning,** sobbing, whining, soughing

VERBS 9 **steal** *or* **waft on the ear,** melt in the air, float in the air

10 **murmur, mutter, mumble,** mussitate <old>, maffle <Brit nf>; coo; susurrate; **lower one's voice, speak under one's breath; whisper,** whisper in the ear; breathe, sigh, aspirate

11 **ripple, babble, burble,** bubble, **gurgle,** guggle, **purl, trill;** lap, plash, **splash,** swish, swash, slosh, wash

12 **rustle,** crinkle; **swish,** whish

13 **hum,** thrum, bum <Brit nf>, boom, bombilate, bombinate, **drone, buzz,** whiz, whir, burr, birr <Scot>, purr

14 **sigh, moan, sob, whine,** sough; **whimper**

15 **thud, thump, patter,** clop, clump, clunk, plunk, flump, crump; pad, pat; **tap,** rap, **click,** tick, tick away; pop; tinkle, clink, chink

ADJS 16 **faint, low, soft, gentle, subdued, dim, feeble, weak,** faint-sounding, low-sounding, soft-sounding; soft-voiced, low-voiced, faint-voiced, weak-voiced; murmured, whispered, hushed; half-heard, barely heard, scarcely heard; distant, dying away; indistinct, unclear; barely audible, subaudible, near the limit *or* threshold of hearing; soft-pedaled, piano, pianissimo; decrescendo; unstressed, unaccented

17 **muffled, muted, softened, dampened,** damped, **smothered,** stifled, bated, dulled, deadened, subdued; **dull, dead, flat,** *sordo* <Ital>; nonresonant

18 **murmuring,** murmurous, murmurish, **muttering, mumbling;** susurrous, susurrant; **whispering,** whisper, whispery; **rustling**

19 **rippling, babbling, burbling,** bubbling, **gurgling,** guggling, **purling, trilling;** lapping, splashing, plashing, sloshing, swishing

20 **humming,** thrumming, **droning,** booming, bombinating, **buzzing,** whizzing, whirring, purring, burring

ADVS 21 **faintly, softly,** gently, subduedly, hushedly, dimly, feebly, weakly, low; piano, pianissimo; *sordo* and *sordamente* <Ital>, *à la sourdine* <Fr>

22 **in an undertone,** *sotto voce* <Ital>, **under one's breath,** with bated breath, in a whisper, in a stage whisper, between the teeth; aside, in an aside; out of earshot

53 LOUDNESS

NOUNS 1 **loudness,** intensity, volume, amplitude, fullness; sonorousness, sonority; surge of sound, surge, crescendo, swell, swelling; loudishness, high volume

2 **noisiness,** noisefulness, **uproariousness,** racketiness, tumultuousness, thunderousness, clamorousness, clangorousness, boisterousness, obstreperousness; vociferousness 59.5; stridency, stridor

3 **noise,** loud noise, **blast** 56.3, tintamarre, **racket, din, clamor;** outcry, **uproar,** hue and cry, noise and shouting; howl; clangor, clang, clatter, clap, jangle, rattle; roar, rumble, thunder, thunderclap 56.5; **crash, boom,** sonic boom; **bang,** percussion; brouhaha, **tumult, hubbub,** bobbery <India>, vociferation, ululation; fracas, **brawl,** commotion, drunken brawl; **pandemonium,** bedlam, hell *or* bedlam let loose; charivari, shivaree <nf>; discord 61; shattered silence; cachinnation, stertor; explosion, bombardment; crescendo, forte, fortissimo, tutti

4 <nf terms> row, flap, hullabaloo, brannigan, shindy, donnybrook, free-for-all, shemozzle, rumble, rhubarb, dustup, rumpus, ruckus, ruction, rowdydow, hell broke loose, foofooraw, hoo-ha, Katy-bar-the-door, tzimmes

5 **blare, blast,** shriek 58.4, peal; **toot,** tootle, **honk,** beep, blat, trumpet, report; bay, bray; **whistle,** tweedle, squeal; trumpet call, trumpet blast *or* blare, sound *or* flourish of trumpets, Gabriel's trumpet *or* horn, **fanfare,** tarantara, tantara, tantarara, clarion call; tattoo; taps; full blast

6 **noisemaker;** ticktack, bull-roarer, catcall, whizzer, whizgig, snapper, cricket, clapper, clack, clacker, cracker; firecracker, cherry bomb; rattle, rattlebox; horn, Klaxon <trademark>; whistle, steam whistle, siren; boiler room, boiler factory; loud-hailer, bullhorn <nf>

VERBS 7 **din; boom,** thunder 56.9; **resound,** ring, peal, ring *or* resound in the ears, din in the ear, **blast the ear,** pierce *or* split *or* rend the ears, rend *or* split the eardrums, split one's head; **deafen,** stun; blast 56.8, **bang,** crash 56.6; **rend the air** *or* skies *or* firmament, rock the sky, fill the air, make the welkin ring; shake *or* rattle the windows; awake *or* startle the echoes, set the echoes ringing, awake the dead, shatter the peace; surge, swell, rise, crescendo; **shout** 59.6

8 **drown out,** outshout, outroar, shout down, overpower, overwhelm; jam

9 **be noisy, make a noise** or **racket,** raise a clamor or din or hue and cry, noise, racket, **clamor,** roar, clangor; brawl, row, rumpus; **make an uproar,** kick up a dust or racket, kick up or raise a hullaballoo, raise the roof, raise Cain or Ned, howl like all the devils of hell, raise the devil, raise hell, whoop it up, maffick <Brit>; not be able to hear oneself think

10 **blare,** blast; shriek 58.8; **toot,** tootle, sound, peal, wind, blow, blat; pipe, trumpet, bugle, clarion; bay, bell, bray; **whistle,** tweedle, squeal; **honk,** honk or sound or blow the horn, beep; sound taps, sound a tattoo; go off

ADJS 11 **loud,** loud-sounding, forte, fortissimo; loudish; **resounding,** ringing, plangent, pealing; full, sonorous; **deafening,** ear-deafening, **ear-splitting,** head-splitting, ear-rending, ear-piercing, piercing; **thunderous,** thundering, tonitruous, tonitruant; **crashing,** booming 56.12; window-rattling, earthshaking, enough to wake the dead or the seven sleepers; crescendo, forte, fortissimo

12 **loud-voiced, loudmouthed,** fullmouthed, full-throated, big-voiced, clarion-voiced, trumpet-voiced, trumpet-tongued, brazen-mouthed, **stentorian,** stentorious, stentorophonic, like Stentor, booming

13 **noisy,** noiseful, rackety, clattery, clangorous, clanging, **clamorous,** clamoursome <Brit nf>, clamant, blatant, blaring, brassy, brazen, blatting; uproarious, **tumultuous,** turbulent, blustering, brawling, **boisterous,** rip-roaring, rowdy, mafficking <Brit>, strepitous, strepitant, obstreperous; vociferous 59.10

ADVS 14 **loudly, aloud,** loud, lustily; **boomingly, thunderously, thunderingly; noisily,** uproariously; ringingly, resoundingly; with a loud voice, at the top of one's voice, at the pitch of one's breath, in full cry, with one wild yell, with a whoop and a hurrah; forte, fortemente <Ital>, fortissimo

54 RESONANCE

NOUNS 1 **resonance, resoundingness, sonorousness,** sonority, plangency, **vibrancy;** mellowness, richness, fullness; deepness, lowness, bassness; hollowness; **snore,** snoring

2 **reverberation, resounding; rumble,** rumbling, thunder, thundering, boom, booming, growl, growling, grumble, grumbling, reboation; rebound, resound, **echo,** reecho

3 **ringing,** tintinnabulation, **pealing, chiming, tinkling,** tingling, **jingling,** dinging, donging; **tolling,** knelling; clangor, clanking, clanging; **ring, peal, chime; toll,** knell; **tinkle,** tingle, **jingle,** dingle, ding, dingdong, ding-a-ling, ting-a-ling; clink, tink, ting, ping, chink; clank, clang; jangle, jingle-jangle; campanology, bell ringing, change ringing, peal ringing; tinnitis, ringing of or in the ear

4 **bell** <see list>, tintinnabulum; **gong,** triangle, **chimes,** door chimes, clock chimes, Westminster chimes; clapper, tongue; carillon, set of bells

5 **resonator,** resounder, reverberator; **sounding board,** sound box; resonant chamber or cavity; echo chamber; loud pedal, damper pedal, sustaining pedal

VERBS 6 **resonate, vibrate,** pulse, throb; snore

7 **reverberate, resound,** sound, **rumble,** roll, boom, echo, reecho, rebound, bounce back, be reflected, be sent back, echo back, send back, return

8 **ring,** tintinnabulate, **peal,** sound; **toll,** knell, sound a knell; **chime;** gong; **tinkle,** tingle, **jingle,** ding, dingdong, dong; clink, tink, ting, chink; clank, clang, clangor; jangle, jinglejangle; ring on the air; ring changes or peals; ring in the ear

9 <deep voices> bass, basso, basso profundo, baritone, bass-baritone, contralto

ADJS 10 **resonant, reverberant, vibrant, sonorous,** plangent, rolling; mellow, rich, full; resonating, reverberating, echoing, reechoing, vibrating, pulsing, throbbing

11 **deep,** deep-toned, deep-pitched, deep-sounding, deepmouthed, deep-echoing; **hollow, sepulchral; low,** low-pitched, low-toned, grave, heavy; **bass;** baritone; contralto

12 **reverberating,** reverberant, reverberatory, reboant, **resounding,** rebounding, repercussive, sounding; **rumbling,** thundering, booming, growling; echoing, reechoing, echoic; undamped; persistent, lingering

13 **ringing, pealing, tolling,** belling, sounding, chiming; **tinkling,** tinkly, tingling, **jingling,** dinging; tintinnabular or tintinnabulary or tintinnabulous; campanological

14 **bells**

air bell	fog bell
alarm bell	gong bell
anchor bell	hand bell
angelus bell	harness bell
Big Ben	hour bell
bourdon	jingle bell
breakfast bell	Liberty Bell
call bell	minute bell
chiming bell	news bell
church bell	night bell
clinkum bell	pancake bell
computer bell	passing bell or death bell
cowbell	or end bell or mortbell
dinner bell or gong or	Sanctus bell or sacring bell
chimes	or saunce or saucing
doorbell	bell
fire bell	school bell

sheepbell
shop bell
signal bell
sleigh bell
tap bell

telephone bell
tocsin
vesper bell
watch bell
wind-bell

55 REPEATED SOUNDS

NOUNS 1 **staccato; drum, thrum, beat, pound, roll;**
drumming, tom-tom, beating, pounding,
thumping; **throb,** throbbing, pulsation 916.3;
palpitation, flutter; sputter, spatter, splutter; **patter,**
pitter-patter, pit-a-pat; rub-a-dub, rattattoo,
rataplan, rat-a-tat, rat-tat, rat-tat-tat, tat-tat, tat-tat-
tat; **tattoo,** devil's tattoo, ruff, ruffle, paradiddle;
drumbeat, drum music; drumfire, barrage
 2 **clicking, ticking, tick, ticktock,** ticktack, ticktick
 3 **rattle,** rattling, brattle <Scot>, ruckle <Brit nf>,
rattletybang; **clatter,** clitter, clunter <Brit nf>,
clitterclatter, chatter, clack, clacket <nf>; racket
53.3
VERBS 4 **drum, thrum, beat, pound, thump, thump**
out, roll; palpitate, flutter; sputter, splatter,
splutter; patter, pitter-patter, go pit-a-pat *or* pitter-
patter; **throb,** pulsate 916.12; beat *or* sound a
tattoo, beat a devil's tattoo, ruffle, beat a ruffle
 5 **tick, ticktock,** ticktack, tick away
 6 **rattle,** ruckle <Brit nf>, brattle <Scot>; **clatter,**
clitter, **chatter,** clack; rattle around, clatter about
ADJS 7 **staccato; drumming, thrumming, beating,**
pounding, thumping; throbbing; palpitant,
fluttering; sputtering, spattering, spluttering;
clicking, ticking
 8 **rattly,** rattling, chattering, **clattery,** clattering

56 EXPLOSIVE NOISE

NOUNS 1 **report, crash, crack, clap, bang,** wham,
slam, clash, burst; **knock, rap, tap,** smack, whack,
thwack, whop, whap, swap <nf>, whomp, splat,
crump <Brit nf>, bump, slap, slat <Brit nf>, flap,
flop
 2 **snap, crack;** click, clack; **crackle,** snapping,
cracking, crackling, crepitation, decrepitation,
sizzling, spitting; rale
 3 **detonation, blast, explosion,** fulmination,
discharge, burst, bang, pop, crack, bark; **shot,**
gunshot; volley, salvo, fusillade
 4 **boom,** booming, cannonade, **peal, rumble,**
grumble, growl, **roll, roar**
 5 **thunder,** thundering, clap *or* crash *or* peal of
thunder, **thunderclap,** thunderpeal, thundercrack,
thunderstroke; "heaven's artillery"—Shakespeare,
"the crashing of the chariot of God"—William
Cullen Bryant; thunderstorm 316.3; Thor *or* Donar,
Jupiter Tonans, Indra

VERBS 6 **crack, clap, crash,** wham, slam, **bang,**
clash; **knock, rap, tap,** smack, whack, thwack,
whop, whap, swap <nf>, whomp, splat, crump
<Brit nf>, bump, slat <Brit nf>, slap, flap
 7 **snap, crack;** click, clack; **crackle,** crepitate,
decrepitate; spit
 8 **blast, detonate, explode, discharge, burst,** go off,
bang, pop, crack, bark, fulminate; burst on the ear
 9 **boom, thunder, peal, rumble,** grumble, growl, **roll,**
roar
ADJS 10 **snapping, cracking, crackling,** crackly,
crepitant
 11 **banging,** crashing, bursting, exploding, explosive,
blasting, cracking, popping; knocking, rapping,
tapping; slapping, flapping, slatting <Brit nf>
 12 **thundering, thunderous,** thundery, fulminating,
tonitruous, tonitruant, thunderlike; **booming,**
pealing, rumbling, rolling, roaring; cannonading,
volleying
INTERJS 13 bang!, boom!, wham!, whammo!, blam!,
kerboom!, kerblam!

57 SIBILATION
   <hissing sounds>

NOUNS 1 sibilation, sibilance *or* sibilancy; **hiss,**
hissing, siss, sissing, white noise; hush, hushing,
shush, shushing; sizz, sizzle, sizzling; fizz, fizzle,
fizzling, effervescing, effervescence; swish, whish,
whoosh; whiz, buzz, zip; siffle; wheeze, *râle* <Fr>,
rhonchus; whistle, whistling; sneeze, sneezing,
sternutation; snort; snore, stertor; **sniff,** sniffle,
snuff, snuffle; spit, sputter, splutter; squash,
squish, squelch; sigmatism, lisp; assibilation;
frication, frictional rustling
VERBS 2 sibilate; **hiss,** siss; hush, shush; sizzle, sizz;
fizzle, fizz, effervesce; whiz, buzz, zip; swish,
whish, whoosh; whistle; wheeze; sneeze; snort;
snore; sniff, sniffle, snuff, snuffle; spit, sputter,
splutter; squash, squish, squelch; lisp; assibilate
ADJS 3 **sibilant; hissing,** hushing, sissing; sizzling,
fizzling, effervescent; **sniffing,** sniffling, snuffling;
snoring; wheezing, wheezy

58 STRIDENCY
   <harsh and shrill sounds>

NOUNS 1 **stridency,** stridence, stridor, stridulousness,
stridulation; **shrillness,** highness, sharpness,
acuteness, arguteness; **screechiness, squeakiness,**
creakiness, reediness, pipingness
 2 **raucousness, harshness,** raucity; discord,
cacophony 61.1; coarseness, rudeness, ugliness,
roughness, gruffness; **raspiness,** scratchiness,
scrapiness, **hoarseness,** huskiness, dryness;

stertorousness; roupiness <Scot>; gutturalness, gutturalism, gutturality, thickness, throatiness; cracked voice

3 rasp, scratch, scrape, grind; crunch, craunch, scranch <old>, scrunch, crump; burr, chirr, buzz; snore, snort, stertor; **jangle, clash, jar;** clank, clang, clangor, twang, twanging; blare, blat, bray; croak, caw, cackle; belch; growl, snarl; grumble, groan

4 screech, shriek, scream, squeal, shrill, keen, squeak, squawk, skirl, screak, skreak <nf>, skriech *or* skreigh <Scot>, creak; bleep; **whistle,** wolf-whistle; pipe; **whine, wail, howl,** ululation, yammer; vibrato; waul, caterwaul

5 <insect sounds> **stridulation,** cricking, creaking, chirking <Scot>; crick, creak, chirk, chirp, chirping, chirrup

6 <high voices> soprano, mezzo-soprano, treble; tenor, alto; male alto, countertenor; head register, head voice, head tone, falsetto

VERBS **7 stridulate,** crick, creak, chirk, chirp, chirrup

8 screech, shriek, screak, skreak <nf>, creak, squeak, squawk, **scream, squeal,** shrill, keen; **whistle,** wolf-whistle; pipe, skirl; **whine,** wail, howl, wrawl <Brit nf>, yammer, ululate; waul, caterwaul; raise the roof <nf>

9 <sound harshly> **jangle, clash, jar;** blare, blat, bray; croak, caw, cackle; belch; burr, chirr, buzz; snore; growl, snarl; grumble, groan; clank, clang, clangor; twang

10 grate, rasp, scratch, scrape, grind; crunch, craunch, scranch <old>, scrunch, crump

11 grate on, jar on, grate upon the ear, jar upon the ear, offend the ear, pierce *or* split *or* rend the ears, harrow *or* lacerate the ear, **set the teeth on edge, get on one's nerves,** jangle *or* wrack the nerves, make one's skin crawl

ADJS **12 strident,** stridulant, stridulous; strident-voiced

13 high, high-pitched, high-toned, high-sounding; treble, soprano, mezzo-soprano, tenor, alto, falsetto, countertenor

14 shrill, thin, sharp, acute, argute, keen, keening, **piercing,** penetrating, ear-piercing, ear-splitting; **screechy,** screeching, shrieky, shrieking, **squeaky,** squeaking, screaky, creaky, creaking; whistling, piping, skirling, reedy; whining, wailing, howling, ululating, ululant; vibrato

15 raucous, raucid, **harsh,** harsh-sounding; coarse, rude, rough, gruff, ragged; **hoarse, husky,** roupy <Scot>, cracked, dry; **guttural,** thick, throaty, croaky, croaking; choked, strangled; squawky, **squawking;** brassy, brazen, tinny, metallic; stertorous

16 grating, jarring, grinding; **jangling,** jangly; **rasping,** raspy; scratching, scratchy; scraping, scrapy

59 CRY, CALL

NOUNS **1 cry, call, shout, yell,** hoot; halloo, hollo, yo-ho, hello, hi, yo, hail; **whoop, holler** <nf>; **cheer, hurrah,** huzzah, hooray; **howl,** yowl, yawl <Brit nf>; bawl, bellow, roar; **scream, shriek,** screech, squeal, squall, caterwaul; yelp, yap, yammer, yawp, bark; war cry, battle cry, war whoop, rallying cry; jeer, boo, hiss, razz; guffah, cachinnation

2 exclamation, ejaculation, outburst, blurt, ecphonesis; expletive

3 hunting cry; tallyho, yoicks <old>, view halloo

4 outcry, vociferation, clamor; hullabaloo, hubbub, brouhaha, **uproar** 53.3; **hue and cry**

5 vociferousness, vociferance, clamorousness, clamoursomeness <Brit nf>, blatancy; noisiness 53.2

VERBS **6 cry, call, shout, yell, holler** <nf>, hoot; hail, halloo, hollo; **whoop;** cheer 116.6; **howl,** yowl, yammer, yawl <Brit nf>; squawk, yawp; **bawl, bellow,** roar, roar *or* bellow like a bull; cry *or* yell *or* scream bloody murder *or* blue murder; **scream, shriek,** screech, squeal, squall, waul, caterwaul; yelp, yap, bark

7 exclaim, give an exclamation, ejaculate, burst out, blurt, blurt out, jerk out, spout out; stammer out

8 vociferate, outcry, **cry out,** call out, bellow out, yell out, holler out <nf>, shout out, sing out; sound off <nf>, pipe up, **clamor,** make *or* raise a clamor; make an outcry, **raise a hue and cry,** make an uproar

9 cry aloud, raise *or* lift up the voice, give voice *or* tongue, shout *or* cry *or* thunder at the top of one's voice, split the throat *or* lungs, strain the voice *or* throat *or* vocal cords, rend the air

ADJS **10 vociferous,** vociferant, vociferating; **clamorous,** clamoursome <Brit nf>; **blatant;** obstreperous, brawling; **noisy;** crying, shouting, **yelling, hollering** <nf>, **bawling,** screaming; yelping, yapping, yappy, yammering; loud-voiced, loudmouthed, openmouthed, stentorian, Boanergean; booming

11 exclamatory, ejaculatory, blurting

60 ANIMAL SOUNDS

NOUNS **1** animal noise; **call, cry;** mating call *or* cry; grunt, howl, bark, howling, waul, caterwaul, ululation, barking; bird song, birdcall, note, woodnote, clang; stridulation 58.5; dawn chorus; warning cry

VERBS **2** cry, call; **howl,** yowl, yawp, yawl <nf>,

ululate; wail, whine, pule; **squeal,** squall, scream,
screech, screak, squeak; troat; **roar; bellow,** blare,
bawl; moo, low; **bleat,** blate, blat; **bray; whinny,
neigh,** whicker, nicker, bray; **bay,** bay at the moon,
bell; **bark,** latrate <old>, give voice *or* tongue;
yelp, yap, yip; **mew,** mewl, **meow,** miaow, waul,
caterwaul

3 **grunt,** gruntle <Brit nf>, oink; **snort**

4 **growl, snarl,** grumble, gnarl, snap; hiss, spit

5 <birds> **warble, sing,** carol, call; pipe, whistle;
trill, chirr, roll; **twitter,** tweet, twit, chatter,
chitter; **chirp,** chirrup, chirk, **cheep,** peep, pip;
quack, honk, cronk; **croak, caw; squawk,** scold,
screech; **crow,** cock-a-doodle-doo; **cackle,**
gaggle, gabble, guggle, **cluck,** clack, chuck; **gobble;
hoot,** hoo; **coo; cuckoo;** drum; tu-whit tu-whoo;
whoop

ADJS 6 **howling,** yowling, crying, wailing, whining,
puling, bawling, ululant, blatant; lowing, mugient,
snarling, growling; singing, humming

61 DISCORD
<dissonant sounds>

NOUNS 1 **discord,** discordance *or* discordancy,
dissonance *or* dissonancy, diaphony, **cacophony;**
stridor, stridency; **inharmoniousness,**
unharmoniousness, disharmony, inharmony;
unmelodiousness, unmusicalness, unmusicality,
untunefulness, tunelessness; atonality, atonalism;
flatness, sharpness, sourness <nf>; dissonant
chord, wolf; false note, sour note *and* clinker *and*
clam <nf>, off note; cipher; wolf-tone;
dodecaphonism *or* dodecaphony

2 **clash, jangle, jar; noise,** mere noise, confusion *or*
conflict *or* jarring *or* jostling of sounds; Babel,
witches' *or* devils' chorus; harshness 58.2; clamor
53.3

VERBS 3 sound *or* strike *or* hit a sour note <nf>, hit
a clinker *or* a clam <nf>; not carry a tune; **clash,
jar, jangle,** conflict, jostle; grate 58.10,11; untune,
unstring; hurt the ears

ADJS 4 **dissonant, discordant, cacophonous,**
absonant <old>, disconsonant, diaphonic;
strident, shrill, harsh, raucous, grating 58.16;
inharmonious, unharmonious, disharmonious,
disharmonic, inharmonic; **unmelodious,**
immelodious, nonmelodious; **unmusical,**
musicless, untuneful, tuneless; untunable,
untuned, atonal, toneless; droning, singsong;
cracked, **out of tune,** out of tone, out of pitch; **off-
key, off-tone, off-pitch,** off; flat, sharp, **sour** <nf>;
"above the pitch, out of tune, and off the hinges"—
Rabelais, "like sweet bells jangled, out of tune and
harsh"—Shakespeare

5 **clashing, jarring, jangling,** jangly, confused,
conflicting, jostling, warring, ajar; **harsh,** hoarse,
grating 58.16

62 TASTE
<sense of taste>

NOUNS 1 **taste,** gust <old>, *goût* <Fr>; sense of
taste; **flavor,** sapor; **smack, tang; savor, relish,**
sapidity, deliciousness; palate, tongue, tooth,
stomach; taste in the mouth; sweetness, sourness,
bitterness, bittersweetness, saltiness; sharp taste,
acid taste, tart taste, salty taste, spicy taste, sweet
taste, sour taste, bitter taste, pungent taste;
aftertaste; savoriness 63

2 **sip, sup, lick, bite**

3 tinge, soupçon, hint 248.4

4 **sample, specimen, taste,** taste test, taster, little
bite, little smack, taste treat; tidbit, sampler;
example 786.2; appetizer, hors d'oeuvre, canape,
aperitif, starter <Brit>

5 taste bud *or* bulb *or* goblet, taste *or* gustatory cell,
taste hair; **tongue,** lingua; **palate**

6 **tasting, savoring,** gustation, nibble, nip, sampling

VERBS 7 **taste,** taste of, sample, degust; **savor,** savor
of, relish; sip, sup <nf>, roll on the tongue, test;
lick; smack

ADJS 8 **gustatory,** gustative; tastable, gustable <old>

9 **flavored,** flavorous, flavory, sapid, saporous,
saporific; tasty, savory, flavorful 63.9; sweet, sour,
bitter, bittersweet, salt

10 **lingual,** glossal; **tonguelike,** linguiform, lingulate

63 SAVORINESS

NOUNS 1 **savoriness, palatableness,** palatability,
tastiness, toothsomeness, goodness, good taste,
right taste, **deliciousness,** gustatory delightfulness,
scrumptiousness *and* yumminess <nf>,
lusciousness, delectability, **flavorfulness,**
flavorsomeness, flavorousness, flavoriness, good
flavor, fine flavor, sapidity; full flavor, full-bodied
flavor; gourmet quality; succulence, juiciness

2 **savor, relish, zest, gusto,** *goût* <Fr>; richness

3 **flavoring, flavor,** flavorer; **seasoning,** seasoner,
relish, condiment, spice; flavor enhancer

VERBS 4 **taste good,** tickle *or* flatter *or* delight the
palate, tempt *or* whet the appetite, make one's
mouth water, melt in one's mouth

5 **savor, relish,** like, love, be fond of, be partial to,
enjoy, delight in, have a soft spot for, appreciate;
smack the lips; do justice to; taste 62.7

6 **savor of, taste of, smack of,** have a relish of, have
the flavor of, taste like

7 **flavor,** savor; **season,** salt, pepper, **spice,** sauce

ADJS **8 tasty,** fit to eat *and* finger-lickin' good <nf>, good-tasting, **savory,** savorous, **palatable, toothsome,** gustable <old>, sapid, **good,** good to eat, nice, agreeable, likable, pleasing, to one's taste, **delicious,** delightful, delectable, exquisite; delicate, dainty; juicy, succulent, **luscious,** lush; for the gods, ambrosial, nectarous, nectareous; fit for a king, gourmet, fit for a gourmet, of gourmet quality, epicurean; scrumptious *and* yummy <nf>

9 flavorful, flavorsome, flavorous, flavory, well-flavored; full-flavored, full-bodied; nutty, fruity; **rich,** rich-flavored

10 appetizing, mouth-watering, tempting, tantalizing, provocative, piquant

64 UNSAVORINESS

NOUNS **1 unsavoriness, unpalatableness,** unpalatability, **distastefulness,** untastefulness; bad taste, bad taste in the mouth

2 acridness, acridity, tartness, sharpness, causticity, astringence *or* astringency, acerbity, **sourness** 67; pungency 68; **bitterness,** bitter taste; gall, gall and wormwood, wormwood, bitter pill

3 nastiness, foulness, vileness, loathsomeness, repulsiveness, obnoxiousness, odiousness, offensiveness, disgustingness, nauseousness; **rankness,** rancidity, rancidness, overripeness, rottenness, malodorousness, fetor, fetidness; yuckiness <nf>; repugnance 99.2; nauseant, emetic, sickener

VERBS **4 disgust, repel,** turn one's stomach, nauseate; make one's gorge rise; gross one out <nf>

ADJS **5 unsavory, unpalatable, unappetizing,** untasteful, untasty, ill-flavored, foul-tasting, **distasteful,** dislikable, unlikable, uninviting, unpleasant, unpleasing, displeasing, disagreeable

6 bitter, bitter as gall *or* wormwood, amaroidal; **acrid,** sharp, caustic, tart, astringent; hard, harsh, rough, coarse; acerb, acerbic, sour; pungent

7 nasty, offensive 98.18, fulsome, noisome, noxious, rebarbative, mawkish, cloying, brackish, **foul, vile,** bad; gross *and* icky *and* yucky <nf>, **sickening, nauseating,** nauseous, nauseant, vomity *and* barfy <nf>; poisonous, toxic, rank, rancid, maggoty, weevily, spoiled, overripe, high, rotten, stinking, putrid, malodorous, fetid

8 inedible, uneatable, not fit to eat *or* drink, undrinkable, impotable; unfit for human consumption

65 INSIPIDNESS

NOUNS **1 insipidness,** insipidity, **tastelessness, flavorlessness,** blandness, savorlessness, saplessness, unsavoriness, dullness; **weakness, thinness,** mildness, **wishy-washiness; flatness, staleness,** lifelessness, deadness; vapidity, inanity, jejunity, jejuneness; adulteration, dilution

ADJS **2 insipid, tasteless, flavorless,** bland, nondescript, unexciting, plain, spiceless, **savorless,** sapless, unsavory, unflavored, unseasoned; pulpy, pappy, gruelly; **weak, thin,** mild, **wishy-washy,** milktoast, washy, watery, watered, watered-down, diluted, dilute, milk-and-water, dishwater; **flat, stale,** dead, *fade* <Fr>; vapid, inane, jejune; "weary, flat, stale, and unprofitable"—Shakespeare; unappetizing; indifferent, characterless, neither one thing nor the other

66 SWEETNESS

NOUNS **1 sweetness,** sweet, sweetishness, saccharinity, dulcitude <old>; **sugariness,** syrupiness; oversweetness, mawkishness, cloyingness, sickly-sweetness; sweet tooth; confectionery, sweet-shop <Brit>, candy store, bakery

2 sweetening, edulcoration <old>; sweetener; sugar, cane sugar, beet sugar, sugar lump, sugar loaf, caster sugar, granulated sugar, powdered sugar, brown sugar, raw sugar; sweetening agent, sugar-substitute, artificial sweetener, saccharin, aspartame, NutraSweet <trademark>, cyclamates, sodium cyclamate, calcium cyclamate; molasses, blackstrap, treacle <Brit>; syrup, maple syrup, cane syrup, corn syrup, sorghum, golden syrup *or* treacle <Brit>; **honey,** honeycomb, honeypot, comb honey, clover honey; honeydew; **nectar, ambrosia;** sugarcoating; sweets; sugar-making; sugaring off; saccharification; candy, sweets, dessert

VERBS **3 sweeten,** dulcify, edulcorate *or* dulcorate <old>; **sugar,** honey; sugarcoat, glaze, candy; ice, frost, glaze; mull; saccharify; sugar off

ADJS **4 sweet,** sweetish, sweetened; sacchariferous, saccharine; **sugary,** sugared, candied, **honeyed,** syrupy; mellifluous, mellifluent <old>; melliferous, nectarous, nectareous, ambrosial; sugarsweet, honeysweet, sweet as sugar *or* honey, sweet as a nut; sugar-coated; bittersweet; sour-sweet, sweet-sour, sweet and sour, sweet and pungent

5 oversweet, saccharine, rich, **cloying,** mawkish, luscious <old>, sickly-sweet

67 SOURNESS

NOUNS **1 sourness,** sour, sourishness, **tartness,** tartishness, acerbity, astringency, verjuice; acescency; acidity, acidulousness; hyperacidity, subacidity; vinegariness; unsweetness, **dryness;**

pungency 68; greenness, unripeness; bitterness, sharpness

2 **sour; vinegar,** acidulant; **pickle,** sour pickle, dill pickle, bread-and-butter pickle; verjuice; lemon, lime, crab apple, green apple, sour cherry; aloe; sourgrass; sour balls; sourdough; sour cream, sour milk; bitters; wormwood; **acid**

3 **souring,** acidification, acidulation, acetification, acescence; fermentation

VERBS 4 **sour,** turn sour *or* acid, go sour, sharpen, **acidify,** acidulate, acetify; ferment; set one's teeth on edge; curdle, spoil, turn, ferment, go off, go bad, molder

ADJS 5 **sour,** soured, sourish; **tart,** tartish; tangy, pungent; crab, **crabbed;** acerb, acerbic, acerbate; acescent; **vinegarish,** vinegary, sour as vinegar; pickled; lemony; **pungent** 68.6; unsweet, unsweetened, **dry,** sec; green, unripe

6 **acid,** acidulous, acidulent, acidulated; acetic, acetous, acetose; hyperacid; subacid, subacidulous

68 PUNGENCY

NOUNS 1 **pungency, piquancy, poignancy,** spiciness; strong flavor; **sharpness, keenness,** edge, **causticity,** astringency, mordancy, severity, asperity, trenchancy, cuttingness, bitingness, penetratingness, harshness, roughness, **acridity;** bitterness 64.2; acerbity, acidulousness, acidity, **sourness** 67; aroma

2 **zest,** zestfulness, zestiness, **briskness,** liveliness, raciness; **nippiness, tanginess,** snappiness; **spiciness,** pepperiness, hotness, fieriness; **tang, spice,** relish; **nip, bite,** kick; sting, punch, snap, zip, ginger, sharpness; **kick,** guts <nf>

3 **strength,** strongness; high flavor, highness, rankness, gaminess

4 **saltiness, salinity,** brininess; brackishness; **salt; brine;** pepperiness

VERBS 5 **bite, nip,** cut, penetrate, bite the tongue, sting, kick, make the eyes water, go up the nose

ADJS 6 **pungent, piquant, poignant; sharp, keen,** piercing, penetrating, nose-tickling, aromatic, stinging, **biting, acrid,** astringent, irritating, harsh, rough, severe, asperous, cutting, trenchant; **caustic,** vitriolic, mordant, escharotic; **bitter** 64.6; acerbic, acid, **sour,** tart, sharp

7 **zestful,** zesty, **brisk,** lively, racy, zippy, **nippy,** snappy, **tangy,** with a kick, strong; spiced, seasoned, high-seasoned, savory; **spicy,** curried, **peppery,** hot, burning, hot as pepper; mustardy; like horseradish, like Chinese mustard

8 **strong,** strong-flavored, strong-tasting; **high,** highly flavored, highy seasoned, high-tasted; **rank, gamy,** racy

9 **salty,** salt, salted, saltish, **saline, briny; brackish;** pickled

69 ODOR

NOUNS 1 **odor, smell, scent,** aroma, flavor <old>, savor; **essence,** definite odor, redolence, effluvium, emanation, exhalation, fume, breath, subtle odor, whiff, trace, detectable odor; trail, spoor; **fragrance** 70; **stink,** stench 71

2 **odorousness, smelliness,** headiness, pungency 68; aromatherapy

3 smelling, olfaction, nosing, scenting; sniffing, snuffing, snuffling, whiffing, odorizing, odorization

4 **sense of smell,** smell, smelling, scent, olfaction, olfactory sense

5 olfactory organ; olfactory pit, olfactory cell, olfactory area, **nose; nostrils,** noseholes <nf>, nares, naris, nasal cavity; olfactory nerves; **olfactories;** scent gland, pheromone

VERBS 6 <have an odor> **smell,** be aromatic, smell of, be redolent of; emit *or* emanate *or* give out a smell, reach one's nostrils, yield an odor *or* aroma, breathe, exhale; reek, **stink** 71.4; pong <Brit nf>

7 odorize; scent, aromatize, perfume 70.8

8 **smell, scent,** nose; **sniff,** snuff, snuffle, inhale, breathe, breathe in; get a noseful of, smell of, catch a smell of, get *or* take a whiff of, whiff, get wind of, follow one's nose

ADJS 9 **odorous,** odoriferous, odored, odorant, **smelling, smelly,** smellful <Austral>, smellsome, olent, **redolent, aromatic;** effluvious; **fragrant** 70.9; **stinking,** malodorous 71.5; emanative, pheromonal

10 **strong,** strong-smelling, strong-scented; **pungent,** penetrating, nose-piercing, sharp, heady; reeking, reeky; suffocating, stifling; noisome, noxious

11 **smellable,** sniffable, whiffable

12 **olfactory,** olfactive

13 keen-scented, quick-scented, sharp- *or* keen-nosed, **with a nose for**

70 FRAGRANCE

NOUNS 1 **fragrance,** fragrancy <old>, **perfume, aroma,** scent, redolence, balminess, **incense, bouquet,** nosegay <old>, sweet smell, sweet savor; **odor** 69; spice, spiciness; muskiness; fruitiness; perfume dynamics, aromatherapy

2 perfumery, *parfumerie* <Fr>; **perfume,** *parfum* <Fr>, **scent, essence,** extract; aromatic, ambrosia; attar, essential *or* volatile oil; aromatic water; balsam, **balm,** aromatic gum; balm of Gilead, balsam of Mecca; myrrh; bay oil, myrcia oil; champaca oil; rose oil, attar of roses, "the perfumed tincture of the roses"—Shakespeare;

lavender oil, heliotrope, jasmine oil, bergamot oil; fixative, musk, civet, ambergris

3 **toilet water,** Florida water; rose water, *eau de rose* <Fr>; lavender water, *eau de lavande* <Fr>; *eau de jasmin* <Fr>; cologne, cologne water, eau de Cologne; bay rum; **lotion,** after-shave lotion

4 **incense;** joss stick; pastille; frankincense *or* olibanum; agalloch *or* aloeswood, calambac, lignaloes *or* linaloa, sandalwood, frangipani, resin, myrrh, eucalyptus, attar, ambergris, patchouli

5 **perfumer,** *parfumeur* <Fr>; thurifer, censer bearer, censer, thurible; **perfuming,** censing, thurification, odorizing

6 <articles> perfumer, *parfumoir* <Fr>, fumigator, scenter, odorator, odorizer; atomizer, purse atomizer, spray; censer, thurible, incensory, incense burner; vinaigrette, scent bottle, smelling bottle, scent box, scent ball; scent strip; scent bag, sachet; pomander, pouncet-box <old>; potpourri; magazine scent strip

VERBS 7 **be fragrant,** smell sweet, **smell good,** please the nostrils, smell like a rose

8 **perfume, scent,** cense, incense, thurify, aromatize, odorize, fumigate, embalm, lay up in lavender

ADJS 9 **fragrant, aromatic,** odoriferous, redolent, perfumy, **perfumed, scented,** odorate *or* essenced <old>, **sweet, sweet-smelling,** sweet-scented, savory, balmy, ambrosial, incense-breathing; thuriferous; **odorous** 69.9; sweet as a rose, fragrant as new-mown hay; pungent, heady; flowery; fruity; musky; spicy; aromatherapeutic

71 STENCH

NOUNS 1 **stench, stink,** funk, malodor, fetidness, fetidity, fetor, foul *or* bad odor, offensive odor, unpleasant smell, offense to the nostrils, bad smell, niff *and* pong <Brit nf>, rotten smell, noxious stench, "the rankest compound of villainous smell that ever offended nostril"—Shakespeare, smell *or* stench of decay, **reek,** reeking, nidor; fug *and* frowst <Brit nf>; mephitis, miasma, graveolence <old>, effluvium, osmidrosis; body odor *or* BO; halitosis, **bad breath,** foul breath

2 **fetidness,** fetidity, malodourousness, **smelliness,** stinkingness, **odorousness,** noisomeness, **rankness, foulness,** putridness, offensiveness; repulsiveness; **mustiness,** funkiness, must, frowst *or* frowstiness <Brit nf>, moldiness, mildew, fustiness, frowziness, stuffiness; staleness; **rancidness,** rancidity, reastiness <Brit nf>; rottenness 393.7; putrefaction, putrescence, decay, gaminess

3 **stinker,** stinkard; skunk *or* polecat *or* rotten egg; stink ball, stinkpot, stink bomb; flatus, fart, cesspool, hydrogen sulfide, sulfur dioxide

VERBS 4 **stink,** smell, **smell bad,** niffy *and* pong <Brit nf>, assail *or* offend the nostrils, stink in the nostrils, stink to heaven *or* high heaven, smell of rotten eggs; **reek;** smell up, stink up; stink out

ADJS 5 **malodorous, fetid,** olid, **odorous, stinking, reeking,** reeky, nidorous, smelling, bad-smelling, **evil-smelling,** foul-smelling, ill-smelling, heavy-smelling, **smelly,** smellful <Austral>, niffy *and* pongy <Brit nf>, stenchy; **foul,** vile, putrid, bad, fulsome, noisome, fecal, feculent, excremental, offensive, repulsive, noxious, sulfurous, graveolent <old>; rotten; **rank,** strong, high, gamy; **rancid,** reasty *or* reasy <Brit nf>, reechy <old>; **musty,** funky, fusty, frowy <nf>, frowzy, frowsty <Brit>, stuffy, moldy, mildewed, mildewy; mephitic, miasmic, miasmal; asphyxiating

72 ODORLESSNESS

NOUNS 1 **odorlessness, inodorousness,** lack of smell, scentlessness, smell-lessness; inoffensiveness; anosmia

2 **deodorizing,** deodorization, fumigation, ventilation; freshness, fresh air; smoke-free area, no-smoking area

3 **deodorant,** deodorizer; antiperspirant; fumigant, fumigator; mouthwash, breath freshener; ventilator, air filter, air purifier

VERBS 4 **deodorize,** fumigate; ventilate, freshen the air; cleanse

ADJS 5 **odorless,** inodorous, nonodorous, smell-less, **scentless,** unscented; fragrance-free; smoke-free, smokeless; fumigated; neutral-smelling; inoffensive; in the fresh air

6 **deodorant,** deodorizing, freshening

73 TOUCH

NOUNS 1 **touch;** sense of touch, tactile sense, cutaneous sense; taction, **contact** 223.5; **feel,** feeling; hand-mindedness; light touch, lambency, whisper, breath, **kiss, caress,** fondling; loving touch; lick, lap; **brush,** graze, grazing, glance, glancing; stroke, rub; tap, flick; fingertip caress; tentative poke

2 **touching, feeling, fingering,** palpation, palpating; **handling,** manipulation, manipulating; petting, caressing, stroking, massaging, rubbing, frottage, frication, friction 1042; laying on of hands, fondling; pressure 902.2; feeling up <nf>; osteopathy, chiropractic

3 touchableness, **tangibility, palpability,** tactility, sensitivity, feel

4 **feeler,** tactile organ, tactor; tactile cell; tactile process, tactile corpuscle, **antenna;** tactile hair,

vibrissa; cat whisker; barbel, barbule; palp, palpus

5 **finger, digit;** forefinger, index finger, index; ring finger, annulary; middle finger, medius, dactylion; little finger, pinkie <nf>, minimus; thumb, pollex

VERBS 6 **touch, feel,** feel of, palpate; **finger,** pass *or* run the fingers over, feel with the fingertips, thumb; **handle,** palm, paw; **manipulate,** wield, ply; twiddle; poke at, prod, paw; tap, flick; come in contact 223.10

7 **touch lightly,** touch upon; kiss, **brush,** sweep, graze, brush by, glance, scrape, skim

8 **stroke, pet, caress,** fondle; **nuzzle,** nose, rub noses; feel up <nf>; rub, rub against, massage, knead 1044.6

9 **lick, lap,** tongue, mouth

ADJS 10 **tactile,** tactual; hand-minded

11 touchable, **palpable, tangible,** tactile, tactual; touchy-feely

12 lightly touching, lambent, playing lightly over, barely touching, grazing, skimming, tickling

74 SENSATIONS OF TOUCH

NOUNS 1 **tingle,** tingling, thrill, buzz; **prickle,** prickles, prickling, pins and needles; **sting,** stinging, urtication; paresthesia

2 **tickle,** tickling, **titillation,** pleasant stimulation, **ticklishness,** tickliness

3 **itch, itching,** itchiness; pruritus; prurigo

4 **creeps** *and* **cold creeps** *and* shivers *and* **cold shivers** <nf>, creeping of the flesh; gooseflesh, goose bumps, goose pimples; formication

VERBS 5 **tingle,** thrill; **itch;** scratch; **prickle,** prick, sting

6 **tickle, titillate**

7 **feel creepy,** feel funny, creep, crawl, **have the creeps** *or* **cold creeps** *or* the heebie-jeebies <nf>; have gooseflesh *or* goose bumps; give one the creeps *or* the willies <nf>

ADJS 8 **tingly,** tingling, atingle; **prickly,** prickling

9 **ticklish,** tickling, tickly, **titillative**

10 **itchy,** itching; pruriginous

11 **creepy, crawly,** creepy-crawly, formicative

75 SEX

NOUNS 1 **sex,** gender; male, maleness, masculinity 76, female, femaleness, femininity 77; **genitals, genitalia**

2 **sexuality,** sexual nature, sexualism, sex life, love life; **love** 104, sexual activity, lovemaking 562, marriage 563; heterosexuality; homosexuality; bisexuality, ambisexuality; **carnality,** sensuality 663; sexiness, voluptuousness, flesh, fleshiness;

libido, sex drive, sexual instinct *or* urge; **potency** 76.2; impotence; frigidity, coldness

3 **sex appeal,** sexual attraction *or* attractiveness *or* magnetism, sexiness, animal magnetism

4 **sex object;** piece *and* meat *and* piece of meat *and* ass *and* piece of ass *and* hot number <nf>; nooky *or* nookie; sex queen, sex goddess, sex kitten; skirt <nf>; hunk, sex god; beefcake *or* stud <nf>

5 **sexual desire,** sensuous *or* carnal desire, bodily appetite, **biological urge,** venereal appetite *or* desire, sexual longing, **lust,** desire, lusts *or* desires of the flesh, itch, lech <nf>, chemistry; **erection,** penile erection, hard-on <nf>; **passion,** carnal *or* sexual passion, fleshly lust, prurience *or* pruriency, concupiscence, hot blood, aphrodisia, the hots *and* hot pants *and* hot rocks *and* hot nuts <nf>, G-spot; lustfulness, goatishness, horniness, libidinousness; lasciviousness 665.5; **eroticism,** erotism; indecency 666; erotomania, eromania, *hysteria libidinosa* <L>; nymphomania, andromania, *furor uterinus* <L>; satyrism, satyriasis, gynecomania; infantile sexuality, polymorphous perversity; **heat,** rut, mating instinct; frenzy *or* fury of lust; estrus, estrum, estrous cycle, estral cycle

6 **aphrodisiac, love potion, philter,** love philter; cantharis, blister beetle, Spanish fly

7 **copulation, sex act,** having sex, having intercourse, *le sport* <Fr>, "making the beast with two backs"—Shakespeare, coupling, mating, pairing, intimacy, coition, **coitus,** pareunia, venery <old>, copula <law>, **sex, intercourse, sexual intercourse,** cohabitation, commerce, sexual commerce, congress, sexual congress, sexual union, sexual relations, relations, marital relations, marriage act, consummation, act of love, making love, sleeping together *or* with, going to bed with, going all the way <nf>; screwing *and* balling *and* nookie *and* diddling *and* making it with <nf>; meat *and* ass <nf>, intimacy, connection, carnal knowledge, aphrodisia, foreplay; **oral sex,** oral-genital stimulation, fellatio, fellation, blow job <nf>, cunnilingus, sixty-nine <nf>; **anal sex,** anal intercourse, sodomy, buggery <nf>; **orgasm,** climax, sexual climax; unlawful sexual intercourse, adultery, hanky-panky, fornication 665.7; coitus interruptus, onanism; group sex, group grope <nf>; serial sex, gang bang <nf>; spouse swapping, wife swapping, husband swapping; casual sex, one-night stand *or* quickie; phone sex; safe sex; sex shop; **lovemaking** 562; **procreation** 78; germ cell, sperm, ovum 305.12

8 **masturbation,** autoeroticism, self-abuse, onanism, manipulation, playing with oneself, jacking off *and*

jerking off *and* pulling off *and* hand job <nf>; sexual fantasy; wet dream

9 **sexlessness,** asexuality, neuterness; **impotence** 19; frigidity; eunuch, *castrato* <Ital>, spado, neuter, gelding; steer

10 **sexual preference; sexual orientation;** sexual normality, sexual nature; **heterosexuality; homosexuality,** homosexualism, homoeroticism, homophilia, *l'amour bleu* <Fr>, the love that dare not speak its name, sexual inversion, lesbianism, sapphism, tribadism; autoeroticism; transsexuality; **bisexuality,** bisexualism, ambisexuality, ambisextrousness, amphierotism, swinging *or* going both ways <nf>; **lesbianism,** sapphism, tribadism *or* tribady; **sexual prejudice,** sexism, genderism, phallicism, heterosexism, homosexism; coming out of the closet <nf>

11 **perversion,** sexual deviation, sexual deviance, sexual perversion, sexual abnormality; sexual pathology; psychosexual disorder; sexual psychopathy, *psychopathia sexualis* <L>; paraphilia; zoophilia, zooerastia, bestiality; pedophilia; algolagnia, algolagny, **sadomasochism** *or* s and m; active algolagnia, **sadism;** passive algolagnia, **masochism;** satyrism; fetishism; narcissism; pederasty, pedophilia; exhibitionism; nymphomania; necrophilia; coprophilia; scotophilia, voyeurism; transvestitism, cross-dressing; **incest,** incestuousness, **sex crime,** sexual offense; **sexual abuse,** carnal abuse, molestation; sexual harassment; unlawful sexual intercourse, rape; cybersex

12 **intersexuality,** intersexualism, epicenism, epicenity; hermaphroditism, pseudohermaphroditism; androgynism, androgyny, gynandry, gynandrism; transsexuality, transsexualism

13 **heterosexual, straight** <nf>, breeder <nf>

14 **homosexual,** gay person, homosexualist, homophile, invert; catamite, *mignon* <Fr>, Ganymede, chicken *and* punk *and* gunsel <nf>; **bisexual,** bi-guy <nf>; **lesbian,** sapphist, tribade, fricatrice <old>

15 <nf terms for male homosexuals> homo, queer, faggot, fag, fruit, flit, fairy, pansy, nance, auntie, queen, drag queen, closet queen, fruitcake, poof *and* poofter *and* poove <Brit>; <nf terms for female homosexuals> dyke, bull dyke, butchfemme, boondagger, diesel-dyke, lesbo, lez

16 sexual pervert; **pervert, deviant,** deviate, sex pervert, sex fiend, sex criminal, sexual psychopath; sodomist, sodomite, sob <Brit nf>, bugger; pederast; paraphiliac; zoophiliac; pedophiliac; sadist; masochist; sadomasochist,

algolagniac; fetishist; transvestite *or* TV, cross-dresser; narcissist; exhibitionist; necrophiliac; coprophiliac; scotophiliac, voyeur; erotomaniac, nymphomaniac, satyr; rapist 665.12

17 **intersex,** sex-intergrade, epicence; hermaphrodite, pseudohermaphrodite; androgyne, gynandroid; transsexual

18 **sexology,** sex study, sexologist; sexual counselor; sexual surrogate; sexual customs *or* mores *or* practices; sexual morality; new morality, sexual revolution; sexual freedom *or* liberation, free love; trial marriage

VERBS 19 sex, sexualize; genderize

20 lust, **lust after,** itch for, have a lech *and* have hot pants for <nf>, **desire; be in heat** *or* **rut,** rut, come in; get physical <nf>; get an erection, get a hard-on <nf>, tumesce

21 **copulate,** couple, **mate,** have intercourse, unite in sexual intercourse, **have sexual relations, have sex,** pair, make out <nf>, perform the act of love *or* marriage act, come together, cohabit, shack up <nf>, be intimate; sleep with *or* together, lie with, go to bed with, bonk; fuck *and* screw *and* lay *and* ball *and* frig *and* diddle *and* do it *and* **make it with** <nf>, go all the way, go to bed with, lie together, get laid <nf>; cover, mount, serve *or* service <of animals>; commit adultery, fornicate 665.19; **make love**

22 **masturbate,** play with *or* abuse oneself, jack off *and* whack off <nf>; fellate, suck *and* suck off <nf>; sodomize, bugger *and* ream <nf>

23 **stimulate,** have foreplay; go down on, give head, suck *or* suck off

24 **climax, come,** achieve satisfaction, achieve *or* reach orgasm; **ejaculate,** get off <nf>

ADJS 25 **sexual,** sex, sexlike, gamic, coital, libidinal; **erotic,** appealing, amorous, magnetic; nuptial; venereal; **carnal,** sensual 663.5, voluptuous, fleshly; desirable, baddable; **sexy;** erogenous, erogenic, erotogenic; sexed, oversexed, hypersexual, undersexed; procreative 78.15; potent 76.12

26 **aphrodisiac,** aphroditous, **arousing,** stimulating, eroticizing, venereal

27 **lustful, prurient, hot,** steamy, sexy, concupiscent, lickerish, libidinous, **salacious** 666.9, **passionate,** hot-blooded, itching, **horny** *and* hot to trot *and* sexed-up *and* hot and bothered <nf>, excited, aroused, randy, goatish, sexed-up; sex-starved, unsatisfied; lascivious 665.29; **orgasmic,** orgastic, **ejaculatory**

28 **in heat, burning, hot; in rut,** rutting, rutty, ruttish; in must, must, musty; estrous, estral, estrual

29 **unsexual,** unsexed; **sexless,** asexual, **neuter,** neutral; castrated, emasculated, eunuchized; **cold, frigid; impotent;** frustrated

30 homosexual, homoerotic, gay, queer *and* limp-
wristed *and* faggoty <nf>; **bisexual,** bisexed,
ambisexual, ambisextrous, amphierotic, AC-DC
<nf>, autoerotic; lesbian, sapphic, tribadistic;
butch *and* dykey <nf>; effeminate 77.15;
transvestite; outed
31 hermaphrodite, hermaphroditic,
pseudohermaphrodite, pseudohermaphroditic,
epicene, monoclinous; androgynous, androgynal,
gynandrous, gynandrian

76 MASCULINITY

NOUNS **1 masculinity,** masculineness, maleness;
manliness, manlihood, **manhood,** manfulness,
manlikeness; mannishness; gentlemanliness,
gentlemanlikeness
2 male sex, male sexuality, virility, virileness,
virilism, potence *or* **potency,** sexual power, manly
vigor, **machismo;** ultramasculinity; phallicism;
male superiority, patriarchy
3 mankind, man, men, manhood, menfolk *or*
menfolks <nf>, the sword side
4 male, male being, masculine; he, him, his, himself;
man, male person, *homme* <Fr>, *hombre* <Sp>;
gentleman, gent <nf>
5 <nf terms> **guy,** fellow, feller, lad, blade, chap, cat,
bird, duck, stud, joker, jasper, bugger, bastard,
bloke *and* cove *and* johnny *and* bod <Brit nf>,
customer, party, character, warm, body, bean,
cookie, dude, gent, Joe, Adam
6 real man, he-man, *and* two-fisted man <nf>, hunk
and jockstrap *and* jock <nf>, man with hair on his
chest; caveman *and* bucko <nf>
7 <forms of address> **Mister, Mr,** Messrs <pl>,
Master; **sir,** my good man, gentleman, my dear sir
or man; esquire; *monsieur or M* <Fr>, *messieurs*
or MM <Fr pl>; *signor and signore and signorino*
<Ital>; *señor and Sr and don* <Sp>, *Dom, senhor*
<Pg>; *Herr and mein Herr* <Ger>; *mijnheer*
<Dutch>, *sahib* <India>, *sri or babu* <Hindu>;
bwana <Swah>
8 <male animals> cock, rooster, chanticleer;
cockerel; drake; gander; peacock; tom turkey, tom,
turkey-cock, gobbler, turkey gobbler; dog; boar;
stag, hart, buck; stallion, studhorse, stud, top
horse <nf>, entire horse, entire, colt; tomcat, tom;
he-goat, billy goat, billy; boar, hog; ram, tup
<Brit>; wether; bull, bullock, top cow <nf>; steer,
stot <Brit nf>; drone
9 <mannish female> **amazon,** virago, androgyne;
lesbian, butch *and* dyke <nf>; **tomboy,** hoyden,
romp
10 man of the family, family man, married man,
husband, widower, househusband, patriarch,

paterfamilias, father, papa <nf>; son, brother,
uncle, nephew, godfather, godson, grandfather,
grandson, grandpa
VERBS **11** masculinize, virilize
ADJS **12 masculine, male,** bull, he-; **manly, manlike,**
mannish, manful, andric; uneffeminate;
gentlemanly, gentlemanlike
13 virile, potent, viripotent; ultramasculine, **macho,**
he-mannish *and* hunky <nf>, two-fisted <nf>,
broad-shouldered, hairy-chested
14 mannish, mannified; unwomanly, unfeminine,
uneffeminate, viraginous; **tomboyish,** hoyden,
rompish

77 FEMININITY

NOUNS **1 femininity,** feminality, feminacy,
feminineness, femaleness, femineity, feminism;
womanliness, womanlikeness, womanishness,
womanhood, womanity, muliebrity; girlishness,
little-girlishness; maidenhood, maidenliness;
ladylikeness, gentlewomanliness; **matronliness,**
matriarchy, matronage, matronhood, matronship;
the eternal feminine, *"das Ewig-Weibliche"*
<Ger>—Goethe
2 effeminacy, unmanliness, effeminateness, epicenity,
epicenism, **womanishness,** muliebrity, **sissiness**
<nf>, prissiness <nf>; androgyny; feminism
3 womankind, woman, women, femininity,
womanhood, womenfolk *or* womenfolks <nf>, the
distaff side; **the female sex;** the second sex, **the fair**
sex, the gentle sex, the softer sex, **the weaker sex,**
the weaker vessel
4 female, female being; she, her, herself
5 woman, Eve, daughter of Eve, Adam's rib, *femme*
<Fr>, distaff <old>, weaker vessel; frow, *Frau*
<Ger>, *vrouw* <Dutch>, *donna* <Ital>, wahine
<Hawaii>; **lady,** milady, gentlewoman, *domina*
<L>; feme sole *and* feme covert <law>; married
woman, wife; **matron,** dame, **dowager;** squaw;
unmarried woman, bachelor girl <nf>, single
woman, spinster, maiden; old maid; lass, lassie,
girl 302.6; career woman, businesswoman,
working woman, working wife *or* mother;
superwoman; liberated woman, feminist,
suffragette, women's libber <nf>
6 <nf terms> **gal, dame,** hen, biddy, skirt, missy,
toots, jane, broad, doll, damsel, babe, chick,
wench, bird <Brit>, tomato, bitch, minx, momma,
mouse, sister, squaw
7 woman of the family, married woman, wife,
widow, housewife, mother, matriarch,
materfamilias; daughter, sister, aunt, niece,
godmother, goddaughter, grandmother,
granddaughter

8 "O fairest of creation! last and best of all God's works"—Milton, "a temple sacred by birth, and built by hands divine"—Dryden, "one of Nature's agreeable blunders"—Hannah Cowley

9 <forms of address> **Ms;** Miss *or* miss; Mistress <old>, **Mrs;** **madam** *or* ma'am; missus; my good lady, my dear woman *or* lady, lady; *madame or Mme* <Fr>; *mesdames or Mmes* <Fr pl>; *Frau and Fraulein* <Ger>, *vrouw* <Dutch>, *signora* <Ital>, *señora* <Sp>, *senhora* <Pg>, *mem-sahib* <Hindu>; *donna* <Ital>, *doña* <Sp>, *dona* <Pg>, *mademoiselle or Mlle* <Fr>; *Fraülein* <Ger>; *signorina* <Ital>, *señorita* <Sp>, *senhorita* <Pg>, Dame *and* Lady <Brit>

10 <female animals> hen, biddy; guinea hen; peahen; bitch, slut, gyp; sow, gilt; ewe, ewe lamb; she-goat, nanny goat *or* nanny; doe, hind, roe; jenny; mare; brood mare; filly; cow, bossy; heifer; vixen; tigress; lioness; she-bear, she-lion, queen bee, etc

11 <effeminate male> **mollycoddle,** effeminate; **mother's darling, mother's boy, mama's boy,** Lord Fauntleroy, sissy, Percy, goody-goody; **pantywaist,** nancy *or* nance, chicken, lily; cream puff, weak sister, milksop; old woman

12 feminization, womanization, effemination, effeminization, sissification <nf>

VERBS **13** feminize; womanize, demasculinize, effeminize, effeminatize, effeminate, soften, sissify <nf>; emasculate, castrate, geld

ADJS **14 feminine, female;** gynic, gynecic, gynecoid; muliebral, distaff, **womanly, womanish, womanlike,** petticoat; **ladylike,** gentlewomanlike, gentlewomanly; **matronly,** matronal, matronlike; **girlish,** little-girlish, kittenish; maidenly 301.11

15 effeminate, womanish, fem <nf>, old-womanish, **unmanly,** muliebrous, soft, chicken, prissy, **sissified,** sissy, **sissyish**

78 REPRODUCTION, PROCREATION

NOUNS **1 reproduction, making, re-creation,** remaking, refashioning, reshaping, redoing, re-formation, reworking, rejiggering <nf>; **reconstruction,** rebuilding, redesign, restructuring, *perestroika* <Russ>; **revision;** reedition, reissue, reprinting; reestablishment, **reorganization,** reinstitution, reconstitution; redevelopment; **rebirth,** renascence, resurrection, revival; regeneration, regenesis, palingenesis; **duplication** 874, **imitation** 336, **copy** 784, **repetition** 849; **restoration** 396, renovation; producing *or* making *or* creating anew *or* over *or* again *or* once more; **birth rate,** fertility rate; baby boom *or* boomlet <nf>; baby bust <nf>

2 procreation, reproduction, generation, begetting, breeding, engenderment, engendering, fathering, siring, spawning; **propagation, multiplication,** proliferation; linebreeding; inbreeding, endogamy; outbreeding, xenogamy; dissogeny; crossbreeding 797.4

3 fertilization, fecundation; **impregnation,** insemination, begetting, getting with child, knocking up <nf>, mating, servicing; **pollination,** pollinization; germination; cross-fertilization, cross-pollination; self-fertilization, heterogamy, orthogamy; isogamy, artificial insemination; conjugation, zygosis; in vitro fertilization, test-tube baby technique

4 conception, conceiving, inception of pregnancy; superfetation, superimpregnation

5 pregnancy, gestation, incubation, parturiency, gravidness *or* gravidity, heaviness, greatness, bigness, the family way <nf>; brooding, sitting, covering

6 birth, generation, genesis; development; procreation; abiogenesis, archigenesis, biogenesis, blastogenesis, digenesis, dysmerogenesis, epigenesis, eumerogenesis, heterogenesis, histogenesis, homogenesis, isogenesis, merogenesis, metagenesis, monogenesis, oögenesis, orthogenesis, pangenesis, parthenogenesis, phytogenesis, sporogenesis, xenogenesis; spontaneous generation

VERBS **7 reproduce, remake,** make *or* do over, **re-create,** regenerate, resurrect, revive, re-form, refashion, **reshape,** remold, recast, rework, rejigger <nf>, redo, **reconstruct,** rebuild, redesign, restructure, **revise;** reprint, reissue; reestablish, reinstitute, reconstitute, refound, **reorganize; redevelop;** duplicate 873.3, **copy** 336.5, **repeat** 849.7, **restore** 396.11, **renovate**

8 procreate, generate, breed, beget, get, **engender; propagate, multiply;** proliferate; mother; father, sire; reproduce in kind, reproduce after one's kind, "multiply and replenish the earth"—Bible; breed true; inbreed, breed in and in; outbreed; cross-pollinate, crossbreed; linebreed; copulate, make love

9 lay <eggs>, deposit, drop, spawn

10 fertilize, fructify, fecundate, fecundify; **impregnate, inseminate,** spermatize, knock up <nf>, **get with child** *or* **young; pollinate** *or* pollinize, pollen; cross-fertilize, cross-pollinate *or* cross-pollinize

11 conceive, get in the family way <nf>; superfetate

12 be pregnant, be gravid, be great with child, **be with child** *or* **young;** be in the family way *and* have a bun in the oven *and* be expecting *and* anticipate a blessed event <nf>, be infanticipating *and* be knocked up <nf>, be blessed-eventing <nf>;

gestate, breed, carry, carry young; **incubate, hatch; brood,** sit, set, cover

13 give birth 1.3

ADJS **14 reproductive, re-creative, reconstructive,** re-formative; renascent, regenerative, resurgent, reappearing; reorganizational; revisional; **restorative** 396.22; Hydraheaded, phoenixlike

15 reproductive, procreative, procreant, **propagative,** life-giving; spermatic, spermatozoic, seminal, germinal, fertilizing, fecundative; multiparous

16 genetic, generative, genial, gametic; genital, genitive; abiogenetic, biogenetic, blastogenetic, digenetic, dysmerogenetic, epigenetic, eumerogenetic, heterogenetic, histogenetic, homogenetic, isogenetic, merogenetic, metagenetic, monogenetic, oögenetic, orthogenetic, pangenetic, parthenogenetic, phytogenetic, sporogenous, xenogenetic

17 bred, impregnated, inseminated; inbred, endogamic, endogamous; outbred, exogamic, exogamous; crossbred; linebred

18 pregnant, *enceinte* <Fr>, preggers *and* knocked-up <nf>, **with child** *or* **young, in the family way** <nf>, gestating, breeding, teeming, parturient; heavy with child *or* young, great *or* big with child *or* young, wearing her apron high, in a delicate condition, gravid, heavy, great, big-laden; carrying, carrying a fetus *or* an embryo; **expecting** <nf>, anticipating *and* anticipating a blessed event <nf>, infanticipating <nf>; superfetate, superimpregnated

79 CLEANNESS

NOUNS **1 cleanness, cleanliness; purity,** squeaky-cleanness <nf>, pureness; **immaculateness,** immaculacy; **spotlessness,** unspottedness, stainlessness, whiteness; freshness; fastidiousness, daintiness, cleanly habits, spit and polish; asepsis, sterility, hospital cleanliness; tidiness 807.3

2 cleansing, cleaning, cleaning up, detersion <old>; **purge,** purging, purgation, cleanout, cleaning out, purging, purgation, catharsis, abstersion <old>; **purification,** purifying, lustration; expurgation, bowdlerization; housecleaning, spring-cleaning, cleanup

3 sanitation, hygiene, hygenics; **disinfection, decontamination, sterilization,** antisepsis, asepsis; pasteurization; deodorization, fumigation, disinfestation, delousing; chlorination

4 refinement, clarification, purification, depuration; **straining,** colature; elution, elutriation; extraction 192.8; **filtering,** filtration; **percolation,** leaching, edulcoration <old>, lixiviation; **sifting,** separation, **screening,** sieving, bolting, riddling, winnowing;

essentialization; sublimation; **distillation,** destructive distillation, spiritualization <old>

5 washing, ablution; lavation, laving, lavage; lavabo; **wash, washup;** soaking, soaping, lathering; dip, dipping; rinse, rinsing; sponge, sponging; shampoo; washout, elution, elutriation; irrigation, flush, flushing, flushing out; douche, douching; enema; **scrub,** scrubbing, swabbing, mopping, scouring; **cleaning up** *or* **out,** washing up, scrubbing up *or* out, mopping up *or* down, wiping up *or* down

6 laundering, laundry, tubbing; **wash, washing;** washday

7 bathing, balneation

8 bath, bathe <Brit>, tub <nf>; **shower,** shower bath, needle bath, hot *or* cold shower; douche; sponge bath, sponge; hip bath, sitz bath; footbath; sweat bath, Turkish bath, hummum, Russian bath, Swedish bath, Finnish bath, sauna *or* sauna bath, steam bath, Japanese bath, hot tub, whirlpool bath, Jacuzzi <trademark>, plunge bath

9 dip, bath; acid bath, mercury bath, fixing bath; sheepdip

10 bathing place, bath, baths, public baths, **bathhouse,** bagnio <old>, sauna, Turkish baths; *balneum* and *balneae* and *thermae* <L>; mikvah <Judaism>; watering place, spa; lavatory, washroom, bathroom; steam room, sweat room, sudatorium, sudarium, sudatory, caldarium, tepidarium; rest room

11 washery, laundry; washhouse, washshed; **coin laundry, Laundromat** <trademark>, **launderette,** coin-operated laundry, laundrette <Brit>, washateria; automatic laundry; hand laundry; car wash

12 washbasin, washbowl, washdish, basin; **lavatory, washstand; bathtub,** tub, bath; bidet; basin and pitcher, basin and ewer; **shower,** showers, shower room, shower bath, shower stall, shower head, shower curtain; **sink,** kitchen sink; dishwasher; washing machine, washer; piscina, lavabo, ewer, aquamanile; washtub, washboard, washpot, washing pot, wash boiler, dishpan; finger bowl; wash barrel

13 refinery; refiner, purifier, clarifier; **filter; strainer,** colander; **percolator,** lixiviator; **sifter, sieve, screen,** riddle, cribble; winnow, winnower, winnowing machine, winnowing basket *or* fan; cradle, rocker

14 cleaner, cleaner-up, cleaner-off, cleaner-out; **janitor,** janitress, custodian; cleaning woman *or* lady *or* man, housecleaner, housemaid, maid, daily *or* daily woman *and* charwoman *or* char <Brit>; window cleaner, squeegee <nf>; scrubber, swabber; shoeshiner, bootblack

15 washer, launderer; **laundress,** laundrywoman, **washerwoman,** washwoman; **laundryman,** washerman, washman; dry cleaner; **dishwasher,** pot-walloper *and* pearl-diver <nf>, scullion, scullery maid; dishwiper

16 sweeper; street sweeper, crossing sweeper, whitewing, cleanser *or* scavenger <Brit>; **chimney sweep** *or* sweeper, sweep, flue cleaner; scavenger, beachcomber; garbage collector, trash collector, sanitary engineer

17 cleanser, cleaner; cleaning agent; antiseptic, disinfectant; cold cream, cleansing cream, **soap, detergent,** washing powder, soap flakes, abstergent; dishwashing liquid *or* powder; shampoo; rinse; bubble bath, shower gel; **solvent;** cleaning solvent; water softener; purifier, depurant; mouthwash, gargle; dentifrice, **toothpaste, tooth powder;** abrasive, pumice, pumice stone, holystone, hearthstone, scouring powder, scouring pad; polish, varnish, wax, whitewash; purge, purgative, cathartic, enema, diuretic, emetic, nauseant, laxative; **cleaning device,** cleaning tool, cleaning cloth

VERBS 18 clean, cleanse, purge, deterge, depurate; **purify,** lustrate, disinfect; sweeten, **freshen;** whiten, bleach; clean up *or* out, clear out, sweep out, clean up after; houseclean, clean house, spring-clean; spruce, **tidy** 808.12; scavenge; **wipe,** wipe up *or* out, wipe off, mop *or* mop up, swab, scrub, scour; dust, dust off; steam-clean, **dry-clean;** expurgate, bowdlerize

19 wash, bathe, bath <Brit>, shower, lave, have *or* take a bath; **launder,** tub; wash up *or* out *or* away; **rinse,** rinse out, dip, dunk, flush, flush out, irrigate, sluice, sluice out; ritually immerse, baptize, *toivel* <Yiddish>; sponge, sponge down *or* off; **scrub,** scrub up *or* out, **swab, mop,** mop up; **scour,** holystone; hose out *or* down; rinse off *or* out; soak out *or* away; soap, lather; shampoo; syringe, douche; gargle

20 groom, dress, fettle <Brit nf>, **brush up; preen,** plume, titivate; manicure

21 comb, curry, card, hackle *or* hatchel, heckle <nf>, rake

22 refine, clarify, clear, purify, rectify, depurate, decrassify; try; **strain;** elute, elutriate; **extract** 192.10; **filter,** filtrate; **percolate,** leach, lixiviate, edulcorate <old>; **sift,** separate, sieve, **screen,** decant, bolt, winnow; sublimate, sublime; **distill,** spiritualize <old>, essentialize

23 sweep, sweep up *or* out, **brush,** brush off, whisk, broom; vacuum <nf>, vacuum-clean

24 sanitize, sanitate, hygienize; **disinfect, decontaminate, sterilize,** antisepticize, radiosterilize; autoclave, boil; pasteurize, flash-

pasteurize; disinfest, fumigate, deodorize, delouse, chlorinate

ADJS 25 clean, pure; immaculate, spotless, stainless, white, fair, dirt-free, soil-free; **unsoiled, unsullied,** unmuddied, unsmirched, unbesmirched, unblotted, unsmudged, unstained, untarnished, **unspotted,** unblemished; smutless, smut-free; bleached, whitened; bright, shiny 1025.33; **unpolluted,** nonpolluted, untainted, unadulterated, **undefiled;** kosher, *tahar* <Heb>, ritually pure *or* clean; **squeaky-clean** *and* clean as a whistle *or* a new penny *or* a hound's tooth <nf>; **sweet, fresh,** fresh as a daisy; **cleanly,** fastidious, dainty, of cleanly habits; well-washed, well-scrubbed, tubbed <nf>

26 cleaned, cleansed, cleaned up, cleaned out; purged, purified; expurgated, bowdlerized; refined, filtered; spruce, spick and span, **tidy** 807.8

27 sanitary, hygienic, prophylactic; sterile, aseptic, antiseptic, **uninfected;** disinfected, decontaminated, sterilized; autoclaved, boiled; pasteurized

28 cleansing, cleaning; detergent, detersive; disinfectant, antibacterial; abstergent, abstersive, depurative; **purifying,** purificatory, lustral; expurgatory; purgative, purging, cathartic, diuretic, emetic; balneal, ablutionary

ADVS 29 cleanly, clean; **purely, immaculately, spotlessly**

80 UNCLEANNESS

NOUNS 1 uncleanness, immundity; **impurity,** unpureness; **dirtiness,** grubbiness, dinginess, griminess, messiness *and* grunginess *and* scuzziness <nf>, scruffiness, slovenliness, sluttishness, untidiness 810.6; miriness, muddiness 1062.4; uncleanliness

2 filthiness, foulness, vileness, scumminess <nf>, feculence, shittiness <nf>, muckiness, ordurousness, nastiness, grossness *and* yuckiness *and* ickiness <nf>; scurfiness, scabbiness; rottenness, putridness 393.7; rankness, fetidness 71.2; odiousness, repulsiveness 98.2; nauseousness, disgustingness 64.3; hoggishness, piggishness, swinishness, beastliness

3 squalor, squalidness, squalidity, **sordidness,** slum; slumminess <nf>; insanitation, lack of sanitation; unhealthy conditions

4 defilement, befoulment, dirtying, soiling, besmirchment; **pollution, contamination, infection;** abomination; ritual uncleanness *or* impurity *or* contamination

5 soil, soilure, soilage, smut; **smirch, smudge,** smutch, smear, **spot,** blot, blotch, **stain** 1004.3

6 dirt, grime; dust; soot, smut; **mud** 1062.8

7 filth, muck, slime, mess, sordes, foul matter; ordure, **excrement** 12.3; mucus, snot <nf>; scurf, furfur, dandruff; scuzz *and* mung <nf>; putrid matter, pus, corruption, gangrene, decay, carrion, **rot** 393.7; **obscenity,** smut <nf> 666.4

8 slime, slop, scum, sludge, slush; glop *and* gunk <nf>, **muck, mire,** ooze

9 offal, slough, **offscourings,** scurf, scum, riffraff, scum of the earth; residue; **carrion; garbage, swill,** slop, slops; dishwater, ditchwater, bilgewater, bilge; **sewage,** sewerage; rubbish, trash, **waste,** refuse 391.4

10 dunghill, manure pile, midden, mixen <Brit nf>, colluvies; compost heap; kitchen midden, refuse heap

11 sty, pigsty, pigpen; stable, Augean stables; dump *and* hole *and* shithole <nf>, rathole; tenement; warren, **slum,** rookery; the inner city, the ghetto, the slums; plague spot, pesthole; hovel

12 <receptacle of filth> **sink;** sump, **cesspool,** cesspit, septic tank; catchbasin; bilge *or* bilges; **sewer,** drain, *cloaca* and *cloaca maxima* <L>; sewage farm, purification plant; **dump,** garbage dump, dumpsite, sanitary landfill, landfill; **swamp,** bog, mire, quagmire, marsh

13 pig, swine, hog, slut, sloven, slattern 810.7

VERBS **14** wallow in the mire, live like a pig, roll in the dirt *or* mud

15 dirty, dirty up, dirt <old>, grime, **begrime;** muck, muck up <nf>; **muddy,** bemud <old>; mire, bemire; slime; dust; soot, smoke, besmoke

16 soil, besoil; black, **blacken; smirch,** besmirch, sully, slubber <Brit nf>, smutch *or* smouch, besmutch, smut, **smudge, smear,** besmear, daub, bedaub; **spot,** stain 1003.6; get one's hands dirty, dirty *or* soil one's hands

17 defile, foul, befoul; sully; foul one's own nest, shit where one eats <nf>, nasty *or* benasty <nf>, mess *and* mess up <nf>, make a mess of; **pollute, corrupt, contaminate, infect; taint,** tarnish, poison; profane, desecrate, unhallow

18 spatter, splatter, splash, **bespatter,** dabble, bedabble, spot, splotch

19 draggle, bedraggle, **drabble,** bedrabble, daggle <old>, drabble in the mud

ADJS **20 unclean, unwashed,** unbathed, unscrubbed, unscoured, unswept, unwiped; **impure,** unpure; **polluted, contaminated, infected, corrupted;** ritually unclean *or* impure *or* contaminated, *tref* <Yiddish>, *terefah* <Heb>, nonkosher; not to be handled without gloves; **uncleanly;** septic, unhygienic, contaminated, polluted, toxic

21 soiled, sullied, dirtied, smirched, besmirched, smudged, spotted, **tarnished,** tainted, **stained;**

defiled, fouled, **befouled;** draggled, drabbled, bedraggled

22 dirty, dirt-encrusted, **grimy, grubby,** grungy <nf>, scummy <nf>, smirchy, dingy, messy <nf>; scruffy, slovenly, untidy 810.15; miry, **muddy** 1062.14; **dusty;** smutty, smutchy, smudgy; sooty, smoky; snuffy

23 filthy, foul, vile, mucky, **nasty,** icky *and* yecchy *and* yucky *and* gross *and* grungy *and* scuzzy *and* grotty <nf>; malodorous, mephitic, rank, **fetid** 71.5; **putrid, rotten;** pollutive; nauseating, disgusting; **odious,** repulsive 98.18; **slimy;** barfy *and* vomity *and* puky <nf>; sloppy, sludgy; gloppy *and* gunky <nf>, scurfy, scabby; wormy, maggoty, flyblown; feculent, ordurous, crappy *and* shitty <nf>, excremental, excrementitious, fecal 12.20

24 hoggish, piggish, swinish, beastly

25 squalid, sordid, wretched, shabby; slumlike, slummy

ADVS **26 uncleanly, impurely,** unpurely; **dirtily,** grimily; **filthily, foully,** nastily, vilely

81 HEALTHFULNESS

NOUNS **1 healthfulness, healthiness, salubrity,** salubriousness, salutariness, **wholesomeness,** beneficialness, goodness

2 hygiene, hygienics; sanitation 79.3; public health, epidemiology; health physics; **preventive medicine,** prophylaxis, preventive dentistry, prophylactodontia; prophylactic psychology, mental hygiene; **fitness and exercise** 84; cleanliness

3 hygienist, hygeist, sanitarian; public health doctor *or* physician, epidemiologist; health physicist; preventive dentist, prophylactodontist; dental hygienist

VERBS **4 make for health,** conduce to health, **be good for,** agree with

ADJS **5 healthful, healthy, salubrious, salutary, wholesome,** health-preserving, health-enhancing, health-giving, life-promoting, **beneficial,** benign, good, **good for;** nutritious, nourishing; **hygienic, hygienical,** hygeian, sanitary; constitutional, for one's health; conditioning; bracing, refreshing, invigorating, tonic; what the doctor ordered

82 UNHEALTHFULNESS

NOUNS **1 unhealthfulness, unhealthiness, insalubrity,** insalubriousness, unsalutariness, ill health, poor health, **unwholesomeness,** badness; noxiousness, noisomeness, injuriousness, harmfulness 1000.5; pathenogenicity; chronic ill health, valetudinarianism; health hazard, threat *or* danger *or* menace to health; contamination, pollution, environmental pollution, air *or* water *or* noise pollution

2 innutritiousness, indigestibility

3 poisonousness, toxicity, venomousness; virulence *or* virulency, malignancy, noxiousness, destructiveness, deadliness; **infectiousness,** infectivity, contagiousness, communicability; poison, venom 1001.3

VERBS **4 disagree with,** not be good for, sicken

ADJS **5 unhealthful, unhealthy, insalubrious, unsalutary, unwholesome,** peccant, bad, **bad for;** noxious, noisome, injurious, baneful, harmful 999.12; **polluted,** contaminated, tainted, foul, septic; unhygienic, unsanitary, insanitary; morbific, pathogenic, pestiferous

6 innutritious, indigestible, unassimilable

7 poisonous, toxic, toxicant; **venomous,** envenomed, venenate, venenous; veneniferous, toxiferous; pollutive; **virulent, noxious, malignant,** malign, destructive, deadly; pestiferous, pestilential, pestilent; mephitic, miasmal, miasmic, miasmatic; **infectious,** infective, contagious, communicable, catching, germ-laden; mephitic; lethal, deadly

83 HEALTH

NOUNS **1 health, well-being; fitness,** health and fitness, physical fitness 84; bloom, flush, pink, glow, rosiness; mental health, emotional health; physical condition; Hygeia

2 healthiness, healthfulness, **soundness,** wholesomeness; healthy body, good *or* healthy constitution; **good health,** good state of health, "good estate of body"—Bible, "*mens sana in corpore sano*"—Juvenal <L, a sound mind in a sound body>; **robust health,** rugged health, rude health, glowing health, picture of health; **fine fettle,** fine whack <nf>, fine *or* high feather <nf>, **good shape,** good trim, fine shape, top shape <nf>, good condition, mint condition; eupepsia, good digestion; clean bill of health

3 haleness, heartiness, robustness, vigorousness, ruggedness, **vitality,** lustiness, hardiness, strength, vigor; longevity

4 immunity, resistance, nonproneness *or* nonsusceptibility to disease; **immunization;** antibody, antigen 86.27

5 health care, health protection, health *or* **medical management, health maintenance,** medical care 91.1; **wellness,** wellness program, disease prevention, preventive medicine; health awareness program; health policy, health-care policy; **health plan, health** *or* **medical insurance,** health service, health-care delivery service *or* plan, health maintenance organization *or* HMO, Medicare,

Medicaid; National Health Service *or* NHS *or* National Health <Brit>; socialized medicine; health department, health commissioner; health club, health spa

VERBS **6 enjoy good health,** have a clean bill of health, be in the pink; be in the best of health; **feel good,** feel fine, feel fit, feel like a million dollars *or* like a million <nf>, never feel better; feel one's oats, be full of pep; burst with health, bloom, glow, flourish; keep fit, stay in shape; wear well, stay young, be well-preserved

7 get well, recover 396.20, mend, get healthy, be oneself again, feel like a new person, get back on one's feet, bounce back, get over it, get the color back in one's cheeks; recuperate 396.19

ADJS **8 healthy, healthful,** enjoying health, **fine,** in health, in shape, in condition, **fit,** fit and fine; **in good health,** in the pink of condition, in mint condition, in good case, **in good** *or* **fine shape, in fine fettle,** in A1 condition, bursting with health, full of life and vigor, feeling one's oats; eupeptic

9 <nf terms> **in the pink,** in fine whack, in fine *or* high feather, chipper, **fit as a fiddle;** alive and kicking, bright-eyed and bushy-tailed; full of beans *or* of piss and vinegar

10 well, unailing, unsick, unsickly, unfrail; all right, doing nicely, up and about, sitting up and taking nourishment, alive and well

11 sound, whole, wholesome; unimpaired 1002.8; sound of mind and body, sound in wind and limb, sound as a dollar <nf>

12 hale, hearty, hale and hearty, **robust,** robustious, robustuous, vital, **vigorous, strong,** strong as a horse *or* an ox, bionic <nf>, stalwart, stout, sturdy, **rugged,** rude, hardy, lusty, bouncing, well-knit, flush <old>; **fit,** in condition *or* shape; of good constitution

13 fresh, green, youthful, **blooming;** flush, flushed, **rosy,** rosy-cheeked, apple-cheeked, ruddy, pink, pink-cheeked; fresh-faced, fresh as a daisy *or* rose, fresh as April

14 immune, resistant, nonprone *or* nonsusceptible to disease; health-conscious, health-protecting; immune response

84 FITNESS, EXERCISE

NOUNS **1 fitness, physical fitness, physical conditioning, condition, shape,** trim, tone, fettle, aerobic fitness, anaerobic fitness, cardiovascular fitness, cardiorespiratory fitness; **gymnasium, gym** <nf>, **fitness center, health club,** health spa, work-out room, weight room, exercise track *or* trail, trim trail <Brit>, *parcourse or parcours* <Fr>; **weight, barbell,** dumbbell, free weights, exercise machine, Nautilus <trademark>, bench, exercise bike, rowing machine, stair-climbing machine, treadmill, Nordic Trak <trademark>; whirlpool bath, Jacuzzi <trademark>, hot tub, spa

2 **exercise,** motion, movement, maneuver; **program,** routine, drill, work-out; **exercise systems; warm-up, stretching,** warm-down; **calisthenics,** free exercise, setting-up exercise *or* set-ups, physical jerks <Brit>, daily dozen <nf>, constitutional; **parcourse exercise; gymnastic exercise, gymnastics;** slimnastics; **isometrics,** isometric *or* no-movement exercise; **violent exercise,** breather, wind sprint; **aerobic exercise, aerobics,** aerobic dancing *or* dance, step aerobics, dancercize *or* dancercizing, fitaerobics, jazz ballet *or* Jazzercise; Callanetics; **bodybuilding,** weightlifting, weight training, pumping iron <nf>, bench press, arm raise, curl, wrist curl; **running, jogging,** roadwork, distance running; obligate running; cross-training, interval training, *fartlek* <Swed>; **walking,** fitness walking, healthwalking, aerobic walking, racewalking, powerwalking, powerstriding; **swimming,** swimnastics, water exercise, aquarobics *or* aquaerob *or* hydro-robics, aqua dynamics; tub toner

3 **physical fitness test;** stress test, treadmill test; cardiovascular text

VERBS 4 **exercise, work out,** warm up, train, aerobicize, stretch, lift weights, pump iron <nf>, jog, run, bicycle, walk, fitness-walk, power-walk, race-walk

85 DISEASE

NOUNS 1 **disease** <see list>, **illness, sickness, malady, ailment, indisposition, disorder,** complaint, morbidity, *morbus* <L>, **affliction,** affection, distemper <old>, **infirmity; disability,** defect, handicap; deformity 265.3; **birth defect,** congenital defect; abnormality, condition, pathological condition; **signs, symptoms, pathology,** symptomatology, symptomology, syndrome; **sickishness,** malaise, seediness *and* rockiness *and* the pip *and* the crud *and* the creeping crud <nf>; complication, secondary disease *or* condition; plant disease, blight 1001.2

2 **fatal disease,** deadly disease, terminal disease *or* illness, hopeless condition; **death** 307, clinical death, loss of vital signs; apparent death; **brain death,** local death, somatic death; sudden death, unexplained death; liver death; serum death; thymic death *or* mors thymica; cell death, molecular death; cot death *or* crib death *or* sudden infant death syndrome *or* SIDS

3 **unhealthiness,** healthlessness; **ill health,** poor health, delicate *or* shaky *or* frail *or* fragile health; **sickliness,** peakedness <nf>, **feebleness,** delicacy, weakliness, fragility, **frailty** 16.2; **infirmity, unsoundness,** debility, debilitation, enervation, exhaustion, decrepitude; wasting, languishing, languishment <old>, cachexia *or* cachexy; chronic ill health, invalidity, **invalidism;** unwholesomeness, morbidity, morbidness; hypochondria, hypochondriasis, valetudinarianism, history of illness

4 **infection, contagion,** contamination, taint, virus, affliction; **contagiousness, infectiousness, communicability;** pestiferousness, epidemicity, inoculability; carrier, vector; **epidemiology**

5 **epidemic, plague, pestilence,** pest, pandemic, pandemia, scourge, bane; white plague, tuberculosis; pesthole, plague spot

6 **seizure, attack,** access, visitation; arrest; blockage, stoppage, occlusion, thrombosis, thromboembolism; **stroke,** ictus, apoplexy; **spasm, throes, fit, paroxysm, convulsion,** eclampsia, frenzy; **epilepsy,** falling sickness; tonic spasm, tetany, lockjaw, trismus, tetanus; laryngospasm, laryngismus; clonic spasm, clonus; cramp; vaginismus

7 **fever, feverishness,** febrility, febricity, pyrexia; hyperpyrexia, hyperthermia; **heat, fire, fever heat;** flush, hectic flush; calenture; delirium 926.8, ague; chill, hypothermia, shivers, shakes

8 **collapse, breakdown, crackup** <nf>, **prostration,** exhaustion, burn-out *or* burnout; nervous prostration *or* breakdown *or* exhaustion, neurasthenia; circulatory collapse

9 <disease symptoms> indication, **syndrome;** anemia; ankylosis; asphyxiation, anoxia, cyanosis; ataxia; bleeding, hemorrhage; colic; dizziness, vertigo; ague, chill, chills; hot flash, hot flush; dropsy, hydrops, edema; morning sickness; fainting; fatigue 21; headache, migraine; fever; constipation; diarrhea, flux, dysentery; indigestion, upset stomach, dyspepsia; inflammation 85.9; necrosis; insomnia; malaise; itching, pruritus; jaundice, icterus; backache, lumbago; vomiting, nausea; paralysis; skin eruption, rash; sore, abscess, discharge; hypertension, high blood pressure; hypotension, low blood pressure; tumor, growth; shock; convulsion, seizure, spasm; pain 26; fibrillation, tachycardia; shortness of breath, labored breathing, apnea, dyspnea, asthma; blennorrhea; congestion, nasal discharge, rheum, sore throat, coughing, sneezing; wasting, cachexia *or* cachexy, tabes, marasmus, emaciation, atrophy; sclerosis

10 **inflammation,** inflammatory disease, -itis; muscle *or* muscular disease *or* disorder, myopathy; collagen disease, connective-tissue disease

11 deficiency diseases <see list>, nutritional disease, vitamin-deficiency disease, acquired immune deficiency syndrome *or* AIDS

12 genetic disease <see list>, gene disease, gene-transmitted disease, hereditary *or* congenital disease

13 infectious disease <see list>, infection

14 eye disease, ophthalmic disease, disease of the eye *or* of vision; cataract; conjunctivitis *or* pink eye; glaucoma; sty; eye *or* visual defect, defective vision 28

15 ear disease, otic disease *or* disorder; **deafness; earache,** otalgia; tympanitis; otosclerosis; **vertigo,** dizziness, loss of balance; Ménière's syndrome *or* disease *or* apoplectical deafness

16 respiratory disease, upper respiratory disease; lung disease; cold, sinusitis; influenza, flu; bronchitis, pneumonia

17 tuberculosis *or* **TB,** white plague, phthisis, consumption

18 venereal disease *or* **VD,** sexually transmitted disease *or* STD, social disease, Cupid's itch *or* Venus's curse, dose <nf>; chancre, chancroid; gonorrhea *or* clap *or* the clap *or* claps <nf>; syphilis *or* syph *or* the syph *or* the pox <nf>; herpes, crabs; acquired immune deficiency syndrome *or* AIDS

19 cardiovascular disease; heart disease, heart condition, heart trouble; vascular disease; hypertension *or* high blood pressure; angina *or* angina pectoris; cardiac *or* myocardial infarction; cardiac arrest; congenital heart disease; congestive heart failure; coronary *or* ischemic heart disease; coronary thrombosis; heart attack, coronary, heart failure; tachycardia; heart surgery, bypass surgery, angioplasty

20 blood disease, hemic *or* hematic disease, hematopathology, anemia, leukemia, lymphoma, Hodgkin's disease; blood poisoning, toxemia, septicemia; hemophilia

21 endocrine disease, gland *or* glandular disease, endocrinism, endocrinopathy; diabetes; goiter; hyper- *or* hypoglycemia; hyper- *or* hypothyroidism

22 metabolic disease; acidosis, alkalosis, ketosis; gout, podagra; galactosemia, lactose intolerance, fructose intolerance; phenylketonuria *or* PKU, maple syrup urine disease, congenital hypophosphatasia

23 liver disease, hepatic disease; gallbladder disease; jaundice *or* icterus

24 kidney disease, renal disease; nephritis

25 neural *or* **nerve disease,** neurological disease, neuropathy; brain disease; amyotrophic lateral sclerosis *or* Lou Gehrig's disease; palsy, cerebral palsy, Bell's palsy; chorea *or* St Vitus's dance *or* the jerks <nf>; Huntington's chorea; headache,

migraine; multiple sclerosis *or* MS; muscular dystrophy; Parkinson's disease *or* Parkinsonism; Alzheimer's disease; neuralgia; sciatica *or* sciatic neuritis; shingles *or* herpes zoster; spina bifida; meningitis; emotional trauma 92.17

26 shock, trauma; traumatism

27 paralysis, paralyzation, palsy, impairment of motor function; **stroke,** apoplexy; paresis; motor paralysis, sensory paralysis; hemiplegia, paraplegia, diplegia, quadriplegia; cataplexy, catalepsy; infantile paralysis, poliomyelitis, polio <nf>; atrophy, numbness

28 heatstroke; heat prostration *or* exhaustion; sunstroke, *coup de soleil* <Fr>, siriasis, insolation; calenture, thermic fever

29 gastrointestinal disease, disease of the digestive tract; stomach condition; colic; colitis; constipation *or* irregularity; diarrhea *or* dysentery *or* looseness of the bowels *or* flux, the trots *or* the shits *or* the runs <nf>, Montezuma's revenge; gastritis; gastroenteritis; indigestion *or* dyspepsia; stomachache, bellyache; cramps; heartburn, stomach flu; ulcer, peptic ulcer, stomach cancer

30 nausea, nauseation, queasiness, squeamishness, qualmishness; qualm, pukes <nf>; motion sickness, travel sickness, **seasickness,** *mal de mer* <Fr>, airsickness, car sickness; vomiting 908.8

31 poisoning, intoxication, venenation; septic poisoning, blood poisoning, sepsis, septicemia, toxemia, pyemia, septicopyemia; autointoxication; food poisoning, ptomaine poisoning, botulism, salmonellosis, listeriosis; milk sickness; ergotism, St Anthony's fire

32 environmental disease, occupational disease <see list>, disease of the workplace, environmental *or* occupational hazard, biohazard; tropical disease

33 vitamin deficiency disease, avitaminosis; night blindness, xerophthalmia, beriberi, pellagra, pernicious anemia, scurvy, rickets, osteomalacia

34 allergy, allergic disorder; allergic rhinitis, **hay fever,** rose cold, pollinosis; **asthma,** bronchial asthma; **hives,** urticaria; eczema; conjunctivitis; cold sore; allergic gastritis; cosmetic dermatitis; Chinese restaurant syndrome *or* Kwok's disease; allergen

35 skin diseases; acne, sebaceous gland disorder; dermatitis; eczema; herpes; hives; itch; psoriasis; scabies; athlete's foot; melanoma, skin cancer

36 skin eruption, eruption, **rash,** efflorescence, breaking out, acne, pimple; diaper rash; drug rash, vaccine rash; prickly heat, heat rash; hives, urticaria, nettle rash; papular rash; rupia

37 sore, lesion; pustule, papule, papula, fester, **pimple,** hickey *and* zit <nf>; pock; ulcer, ulceration; bedsore; tubercle; blister, bleb, bulla, blain; whelk, wheal, welt, wale; **boil,** furuncle, furunculus; carbuncle; canker; canker sore; cold sore, fever blister; sty; abscess, gathering, aposteme <old>; gumboil, parulis; whitlow, felon, paronychia; bubo; chancre; soft chancre, chancroid; hemorrhoids, piles; bunion; chilblain, kibe; polyp; stigma, petechia; scab, eschar; fistula; suppuration, festering; swelling, rising 283.4

38 trauma, wound, injury, hurt, lesion; **cut,** incision, scratch, gash; puncture, stab, stab wound; flesh wound; **laceration,** mutilation; abrasion, scuff, scrape, chafe, gall; frazzle, fray; run, **rip,** rent, slash, **tear; burn,** scald, scorch, first- *or* second- *or* third-degree burn; flash burn; **break, fracture,** bone-fracture, comminuted fracture, compound *or* open fracture, greenstick fracture, spiral *or* torsion fracture; rupture; crack, chip, craze, check, crackle; wrench; whiplash injury *or* whiplash; concussion; **bruise, contusion,** ecchymosis, **black-and-blue mark; black eye,** shiner *and* mouse <nf>; **battering;** battered child syndrome; sprain, strain, repetitive strain injury

39 growth, neoplasm; **tumor,** intumescence; benign tumor, nonmalignant tumor, innocent tumor; malignant tumor, malignant growth, metastatic tumor, **cancer,** sarcoma, carcinoma; morbid growth; excrescence, outgrowth; proud flesh; exostosis; cyst, wen; fungus, fungosity; callus, callosity, **corn,** clavus; **wart,** verruca; **mole,** nevus

40 gangrene, mortification, necrosis, sphacelus, sphacelation; noma; moist gangrene, dry gangrene, gas gangrene, hospital gangrene; caries, cariosity, tooth decay; slough; necrotic tissue

41 <animal diseases> anthrax, splenic fever, charbon, milzbrand, malignant pustule; malignant catarrh *or* malignant catarrhal fever; bighead; blackleg, black quarter, quarter evil *or* ill; cattle plague, rinderpest; glanders; foot-and-mouth disease, hoof-and-mouth disease, aphthous fever; distemper; gapes; heaves, broken wind; hog cholera; mad cow disease; loco, loco disease, locoism; mange, scabies; pip; rot, liver rot, sheep rot; staggers, megrims, blind staggers, mad staggers; swine dysentery, bloody flux; stringhalt; Texas fever, blackwater; John's disease, paratuberculosis, pseudotuberculosis; rabies, hydrophobia; myxomatosis

42 germ, pathogen, contagium, bug <nf>, disease-causing agent, disease-producing microorganism; **microbe,** microorganism; **virus,** filterable virus, nonfilterable virus, adenovirus, echovirus, reovirus, rhinovirus, enterovirus, picornavirus, retrovirus, virion, bacteriophage, phage; HIV *or* human immunodeficiency virus; rickettsia; bacterium, **bacteria,** germ, coccus, streptococcus,

staphylococcus, bacillus, spirillum, vibrio, spirochete, gram-positive bacteria, gram-negative bacteria, aerobe, aerobic bacteria, anaerobe, anaerobic bacteria; protozoon, amoeba, trypanosome; fungus, mold, spore; **carcinogen,** cancer-causing agent

43 sick person, ill person, sufferer, victim; valetudinarian, **invalid, shut-in;** incurable, terminal case; **patient, case;** inpatient, outpatient; apoplectic, bleeder, consumptive, dyspeptic, epileptic, rheumatic, arthritic, spastic; addict; **the sick, the infirm;** hypochondriac

44 carrier, vector, biological vector, mechanical vector; Typhoid Mary

45 cripple, defective, **handicapped person,** disabled person, physically challenged, incapable; amputee; paraplegic, quadriplegic, paralytic; deformity 265.3; the crippled, the handicapped, "the halt, the lame, and the blind"—Bible

VERBS **46 ail, suffer,** labor under, be affected with, complain of; **feel ill,** feel under the weather, feel awful *or* feel like hell <nf>, feel something terrible, not feel like anything <nf>, feel like the walking dead; look green about the gills <nf>

47 take sick *or* **ill, sicken; catch, contract, get,** take, sicken for <Brit>, **come down with** <nf>, be stricken *or* seized by, fall a victim to; catch cold; take one's death <nf>; **break out,** break out with, break out in a rash, erupt; run a temperature, fever; be laid by the heels, be struck down, be brought down, be felled; drop in one's tracks, **collapse;** overdose *or* **OD** <nf>; go into shock, be traumatized

48 fail, weaken, sink, decline, run down, lose strength, lose one's grip, dwindle, droop, flag, wilt, wither, wither away, fade, **languish,** waste, waste away, pine, peak

49 go lame, founder

50 afflict, disorder, derange; sicken, indispose; weaken, enfeeble, enervate, reduce, debilitate, devitalize; **invalid,** incapacitate, **disable;** lay up, hospitalize

51 infect, disease, contaminate, taint

52 poison, empoison <old>, envenom

ADJS **53 disease-causing, disease-producing, pathogenic;** threatening, life-threatening; unhealthful 82.5

54 unhealthy, healthless, in poor health; **infirm, unsound,** unfit, invalid, valetudinary, valetudinarian, debilitated, cachectic, enervated, exhausted, drained; shut-in, housebound, homebound, wheelchair-bound; **sickly,** peaky *or* peaked <nf>; **weakly, feeble,** frail 16.12–21; weakened, decrepit, with low resistance, **run-down,** reduced, reduced in health; **dying** 307.33,

terminal, moribund, languishing, failing 16.21; pale 36.7

55 **unwholesome, unhealthy,** unsound, morbid, diseased, pathological

56 **ill, ailing, sick, unwell, indisposed,** taken ill, down, bad, on the sick list; **sickish, seedy** *and* rocky <nf>, **under the weather, out of sorts** <nf>, below par <nf>, white as a sheet, off-color, off one's feed <nf>; not quite right, not oneself; faint, faintish, feeling faint; feeling awful *and* feeling something terrible <nf>, feel crummy *and* feel shitty <nf>; sick as a dog *or* a pig <nf>, laid low; in a bad way, critically ill, in danger, on the critical list, on the guarded list, in intensive care; terminal, inoperable, mortally ill, sick unto death, near death

57 **nauseated,** nauseous, **queasy, squeamish, qualmish,** qualmy; **sick to one's stomach;** pukish *and* puky *and* barfy <nf>; seasick, carsick, airsick, green around the gills

58 **feverish,** fevered, feverous, in a fever, febrile, pyretic; **flushed,** inflamed, **hot, burning,** fiery, hectic; hyperpyretic, hyperthermic; delirious 926.31

59 **laid up, invalided,** hospitalized, in hospital <Brit>; **bedridden, bedfast, sick abed; down,** prostrate, flat on one's back; in childbed, confined

60 **diseased, morbid, pathological,** bad, **infected, contaminated,** tainted, peccant, **poisoned,** septic; cankerous, cankered, ulcerous, ulcerated, ulcerative, gangrenous, gangrened, mortified, sphacelated; **inflamed;** congested; **swollen,** edematous

61 anemic, chlorotic; bilious; dyspeptic, liverish, colicky; dropsical, edematous, hydropic; gouty, podagric; neuritic, neuralgic; palsied, paralytic; pneumonic, pleuritic, tubercular, tuberculous, phthisic, consumptive; rheumatic, arthritic; rickety, rachitic; syphilitic, pocky, luetic; tabetic, tabid <old>; allergic; allergenic; apoplectic; hypertensive; diabetic; encephalitic; epileptic; laryngitic; leprous; malarial; measly; nephritic; scabietic, scorbutic, scrofulous; variolous, variolar; tumorous; cancerous, malignant; **carcinogenic,** tumorigenic

62 **contagious, infectious,** infective, **catching,** taking, spreading, **communicable,** zymotic, inoculable; pathogenic, germ-carrying; pestiferous, pestilent, pestilential, **epidemic,** epidemial, pandemic; epizootic, epiphytotic; endemic; sporadic; septic

63 **kinds of disease**

acute disease *or* condition
allergy *or* allergic disease
atrophy
autoimmune disease
bacterial disease
blood disease
bone disease
cancer
cardiovascular disease
childhood *or* pediatric disease
chronic disease *or* condition
chronic fatigue syndrome
circulatory disease
collagen disease
congenital disease
connective-tissue disease
contagious *or* infectious disease
deficiency disease
degenerative disease
digestive disease
endemic disease
endocrine disease
endocrine gland disease
epidemic disease
functional disease
fungus *or* fungal disease
gastric *or* stomach disease
gastroenterological disease
gastrointestinal disease
genetic disease
geriatric disease
glandular disease
hepatic *or* liver disease
hereditary disease
hypertrophy
iatrogenic disease
intestinal disease
joint disease
muscular disease
neurological disease
nutritional disease
occupational disease
ophthalmic disease
organic disease
pandemic disease
parasitic disease
protozoan disease
psychiatric disease
psychogenic *or* psychosomatic disease
pulmonary disease
radiation disease
renal *or* kidney disease
respiratory disease
skin disease
sexually transmitted disease *or* STD *and* venereal disease
tropical disease
ulcer
urinogenital *or* urogenital disease
venereal *or* sexually transmitted disease *or* STD
virus *or* viral disease
wasting disease
worm disease

64 **deficiency diseases and disorders**

acquired immune deficiency syndrome *or* AIDS
anemia
anhidrosis
anoxemia
ariboflavinosis
beriberi
cachexia
chlorosis
cretinism
cytopenia
deficiency anemia
dermatitis
goiter
greensickness
hypoadenia
hypochromia
hypothyroidism
immunodeficiency
ischemia
Italian *or* Lombardy leprosy
keratomalacia
kwashiorkor
leukopenia *or* leucopenia
lymphopenia
maidism
malnutrition
night blindness
osteomalacia
osteoporosis
pellagra
pernicious anemia
protein deficiency
rickets *or* rachitis
scurvy
severe combined immune deficiency
struma
thrombocytopenia
undernutrition
vitamin deficiency
Wernicke-Korsakoff syndrome
xerophthalmia

65 **genetic diseases and disorders**

achromatic vision
adenosine deaminase deficiency *or* ADA deficiency
albinism
Christmas disease
color blindness
cystic fibrosis

dichromatic vision
Down or Down's
  syndrome
dysautonomia
Hartnup's disease
hemophilia
hip dysplasia
Huntington's chorea
ichthyosis
lipid histiocytosis
maple syrup urine
  disease
Milroy's disease

mongolism or
  mongolianism <old>
mucoviscidosis
muscular dystrophy
neurofibromatosis
Niemann-Pick disease
pancreatic fibrosis
sickle-cell anemia or
  disease
Tay-Sachs disease
thalassemia
Turner's syndrome
Werdnig-Hoffmann disease

66 infectious diseases

acquired immune
  deficiency syndrome or
  AIDS
acute articular rheumatism
African lethargy or
  encephalitis lethargica
ague
AIDS-related complex or
  ARC or pre-AIDS
alkali disease
amebiasis
amebic dysentery
anthrax or pulmonary
  anthrax or woolsorter's
  disease
bacillary dysentery
bastard measles
black death
black fever
blackwater fever
breakbone fever
brucellosis
bubonic plague
cachectic fever
cerebral rheumatism
Chagas disease or
  American
  trypanosomiasis
Chagres fever
chicken pox or varicella
cholera or Asiatic cholera
cowpox
dandy fever
dengue or dengue fever
diphtheria
dumdum fever
dysentery
elephantiasis
enteric fever
erysipelas
famine fever
five-day fever
frambesia
German measles
glandular fever

grippe
Hansen's disease or leprosy
Haverhill fever
hepatitis
herpangina
herpes
histoplasmosis
hookworm
infectious hepatitis
inflammatory rheumatism
influenza or flu <nf>
jail fever
jungle rot
kala azar
Kew Gardens spotted fever
legionnaires' disease
lepra
leprosy
leptospirosis
loaiasis or loa loa
Lyme disease
lyssa
malaria or malarial fever
marsh fever
measles or rubeola
meningitis
milzbrand
mononucleosis or
  infectious
  mononucleosis or kissing
  disease or mono <nf>
mumps
ornithosis
osteomyelitis
paratyphoid fever
parotitis
pneumonia
poliomyelitis or infantile
  paralysis or polio <nf>
psittacosis or parrot fever
polyarthritis rheumatism
ponos
psittacosis or parrot fever
rabies or hydrophobia
rat-bite fever
relapsing fever

rheumatic fever
rickettsial pox
ringworm or tinea
Rocky Mountain spotted
  fever
rubella
scarlatina
scarlet fever
schistosomiasis
scrub typhus or
  tsutsugamushi disease
septic sore throat
shigellosis
sleeping sickness or sleepy
  sickness <Brit>
smallpox or variola
snail fever
splenic fever
sporotrichosis
spotted fever
St Anthony's fire
strep throat
streptococcus tonsilitis
swamp fever
syphilis
tetanus or lockjaw

thrush
tick-borne typhus
tick fever
toxic shock syndrome
tracheitis
trench fever
trench mouth or Vincent's
  infection or Vincent's
  angina
trypanosomiasis
tuberculosis
tularemia or deer fly fever
  or rabbit fever
typhoid fever or typhoid
typhus or typhus fever
undulant fever
vaccinia
venereal disease or VD
viral dysentery
viral pneumonia
whooping cough or
  pertussis
yaws
yellow fever or yellow
  jack
zoster or shingles or zona

67 environmental and occupational diseases and disorders

aeroembolism or caisson
  disease or
  decompression sickness
  or tunnel disease or
  diver's palsy or the bends
  <nf>
altitude sickness
anoxemia
anoxia
anoxic anoxia
anthrax or pulmonary
  anthrax or woolsorter's
  disease
cadmium poisoning
carpal tunnel
  syndrome
chilblain
frostbite

housemaid's knee
immersion foot
jet lag
lead poisoning
mercury poisoning
Minamata disease
motion sickness
pneumoconiosis or black
  lung <nf>
radiation sickness
radionecrosis
reactive schizophrenia
red-out
repetitive strain injury
sunstroke
trench foot
writer's cramp or palsy or
  spasm

86 REMEDY

NOUNS 1 remedy, cure, corrective, alterative,
remedial measure, sovereign remedy; **relief, help,
aid, assistance,** succor; balm, balsam; healing
agent; restorative, analeptic; healing quality or
virtue; oil on troubled waters; specific, specific
remedy; **prescription,** recipe, receipt
2 nostrum, patent medicine, quack remedy; snake oil
3 panacea, cure-all, universal remedy, theriac,
catholicon, philosophers' stone; polychrest, broad-

spectrum drug *or* antibiotic; elixir, elixir of life, *elixir vitae* <L>

4 medicine, medicament, medication, medicinal, theraputant, pharmaceutical, **drug, physic,** preparation, mixture; herbs, medicinal herbs, simples, vegetable remedies, "the physic of the field"—Pope; wonder drug, miracle drug; balsam, balm; tisane, ptisan; drops; powder; inhalant; electuary, elixir, syrup, lincture, linctus; officinal; specialized drug, orphan drug; **prescription drug,** ethical drug; over-the-counter *or* OTC drug, counter drug, **nonprescription drug;** proprietary medicine *or* drug, proprietary, patent medicine; proprietary name, generic name; materia medica; pharmacognosy; **placebo,** placebo effect

5 drug, narcotic drug, controlled substance, designer drug, illegal drug, dope <nf>

6 dose, dosage, draft, potion, portion, **shot,** injection; broken dose; booster, booster dose, recall dose, booster shot; drops; inhalant

7 pill, bolus, **tablet, capsule,** time-release capsule, lozenge, dragée, troche, pastille

8 tonic, bracer, cordial, restorative, analeptic, roborant, **pick-me-up** <nf>; **shot in the arm** <nf>; stimulant; vitamin shot, herb tea, ginseng, iron

9 stimulant; Adrenalin <trademark> *or* adrenaline <Brit> *or* epinephrine <US>, aloes; amphetamine sulphate, aromatic spirits of ammonia, caffeine, dextroamphetamine sulfate *or* Dexedrine <trademark>, digitalin *or* digitalis, methamphetamine hydrochloride *or* Methedrine <trademark>, smelling salts *or* salts; pep pill

10 palliative, alleviative, alleviatory, lenitive, assuasive, assuager; soothing, abirritant

11 balm, lotion, salve, ointment, unguent, *unguentum* <L>, cream, balm, cerate, unction, balsam, oil, emollient, demulcent; **liniment,** embrocation; vulnerary; collyrium, eyesalve, eyebath, eyewater <old>, eyewash; ear-drops

12 sedative, sedative hypnotic, depressant, amobarbital and secobarbital *or* Tuinal <trademark>, amobarbital sodium *or* Amytal <trademark>, atropine, barbital *or* barbitone <Brit>, barbituric acid, belladonna, chloral hydrate *or* chloral, laudanum, meperidine *or* Demerol <trademark>, morphine, pentobarbital *or* Nembutal <trademark>, phenobarbital *or* Luminal <trademark>, Quaalude <trademark>, reserpine, scopolamine, secobarbital *or* Seconal <trademark>; **sleeping pill** *or* **tablet** *or* potion; **calmative, tranquilizer,** chlorpromazine, Equanil <trademark>, Librium <trademark>, meprobamate, rauwolfia, reserpine, Thorazine <trademark>, Triavil <trademark>, Valium <trademark>; abirritant, soother, soothing syrup,

quietener, pacifier; **analgesic,** acetaminophen *or* Datril <trademark> *or* Tylenol <trademark>, acetanilide, acetophenetidin, aspirin *or* acetylsalicylic acid *or* Bayer <trademark>, buffered aspirin *or* Bufferin <trademark>, headache *or* aspirin powder, ibuprofen *or* Advil <trademark> *or* Motrin <trademark> *or* Nuprin <trademark>, phenacetin, propoxyphene *or* Darvon <trademark>, sodium salicylate; **anodyne,** paregoric <old>; **pain killer** *and* pain pill <nf>; alcohol, liquor 88.13,14

13 psychoactive drug, hallucinogen, psychedelic, psychedelic drug

14 antipyretic, febrifuge, fever-reducer, fever pill <nf>

15 anesthetic; local *or* topical *or* general anesthetic; differential anesthetic; chloroform, ether, ethyl chloride, gas, laughing gas, nitrous oxide, novocaine *or* Novocain <trademark>, thiopental sodium *or* Pentothal <trademark> *or* truth serum

16 cough medicine, cough syrup, cough drops; horehound

17 laxative, cathartic, physic, purge, purgative, aperient, carminative, diuretic; stool softener; milk of magnesia, castor oil, Epsom salts; nauseant, emetic; douche, enema

18 emetic, vomitive *or* vomit <old>, nauseant

19 enema, clyster, clysma, lavage, lavement <old>

20 prophylactic, prophylaxis, **preventive,** preventative, protective

21 antiseptic, disinfectant, fumigant, fumigator, **germicide,** bactericide, microbicide; alcohol, carbolic acid, hydrogen peroxide, merbromin *or* Mercurochrome <trademark>, tincture of iodine

22 dentifrice, toothpaste, tooth powder; mouthwash, gargle, fluoride, dental floss

23 contraceptive, birth control device, prophylactic, contraception; condom; **rubber** *and* skin *and* bag <nf>; oral contraceptive, **birth control pill, the pill** <nf>, Brompton *or* Brompton's mixture *or* cocktail, morning-after pill, abortion pill, RU-486; diaphragm, pessary; spermicide, spermicidal jelly, contraceptive foam; intrauterine device *or* IUD, Dalkon shield <trademark>, Lippes loop; abortion issue, anti-choice, pro-choice, pro-life, right-to-life

24 vermifuge, vermicide, worm medicine, anthelminthic

25 antacid, gastric antacid, alkalizer, Tums <trademark>

26 antidote, countermeasure, counterpoison, alexipharmic, antitoxin, counterirritant, theriaca *or* theriac

27 antitoxin, antitoxic serum; **antivenin; serum,** antiserum; interferon; **antibody,** antigen-antibody product, anaphylactic antibody, incomplete antibody, inhibiting antibody, sensitizing antibody;

gamma globulin, serum gamma globulin, immune globulin, antitoxic globulin; lysin, precipitin, agglutinin, anaphylactin, bactericidin; antiantibody; antigen, Rh antigen, Rh factor; allergen; **immunosuppressive drug**

28 vaccination, inoculation; vaccine

29 antibiotic, ampicillin, bacitracin, erythromycin, gramicidin, neomycin, nystatin, penicillin, polymyxin, streptomycin, tetracycline *or* Terramycin <trademark>; **miracle drug, wonder drug,** magic bullets; bacteriostat; **sulfa drug,** sulfa, sulfanilamide, sulfonamide, sulfathiazole

30 diaphoretic, sudorific

31 vesicant, vesicatory, epispastic

32 miscellaneous drugs, anabolic steroid *or* muscle pill, antihistamine, antispasmodic, beta blocker, counterirritant, decongestant, expectorant, fertility drug *or* pill, hormone, vasoconstrictor, vasodilator, AZT, hormone replacement therapy

33 dressing, application, epithem <old>; plaster, court plaster, mustard plaster, sinapism; **poultice,** cataplasm; formentation; **compress,** pledget; stupe; tent; tampon; **bandage, bandaging,** band <old>, binder, cravat, triangular bandage, roller *or* roller bandage, four-tailed bandage; bandage compress, adhesive compress, Band-Aid <trademark>; butterfly dressing; elastic bandage, Ace elastic bandage *and* Ace bandage <trademark>; rubber bandage; plastic bandage *or* strip; **tourniquet;** sling; splint, brace; cast, plaster cast; tape, **adhesive tape;** lint, cotton, gauze, sponge; patch, nicotine patch

34 pharmacology, pharmacy, pharmaceutics; posology; materia medica

35 pharmacist, pharmaceutist, pharmacopolist, **druggist, chemist** <Brit>, **apothecary,** dispenser, gallipot; pharmacologist, pharmaceutical chemist, posologist

36 drugstore, pharmacy, chemist *and* chemist's shop <Brit>, apothecary's shop, dispensary, dispensatory

37 pharmacopoeia, pharmacopedia, dispensatory

VERBS **38** remedy, help, relieve, cure 396.15; medicate; prescribe; treat

ADJS **39 remedial, curative, therapeutic, healing, corrective,** disease-fighting, alterative, restorative, curing, analeptic, sanative, sanatory; salubrious, salutiferous; all-healing, panacean; adjuvant; **medicinal,** medicative, theriac, theriacal, iatric; anticancer; first-aid

40 palliative, lenitive, alleviative, assuasive, soothing, balmy, balsamic, demulcent, emollient, pain-relieving, analgesic, anodyne

41 antidotal, alexipharmic, counteractant; **antitoxic; antibiotic,** synthetic antibiotic, semisynthetic antibiotic, bacteriostatic, antimicrobial; antiluetic,

antisyphilitic; antiscorbutic; antiperiodic; antipyretic, febrifugal; vermifugal, anthelmintic; **antacid**

42 prophylactic, preventive, protective

43 antiseptic, disinfectant, germicidal, bactericidal

44 tonic, stimulating, bracing, invigorating, stimulative, reviving, refreshing, restorative, analeptic, strengthening, roborant, corroborant

45 sedative, calmative, calmant, depressant, **soothing, tranquilizing, quietening; narcotic,** opiatic; **analgesic,** anodyne, paregoric <old>; anti-inflammatory; muscle relaxant; hypnotic, soporific, somniferous, somnifacient, sleep-inducing

46 psychochemical, psychoactive; ataractic; antidepressant, mood drug; hallucinogenic, **psychedelic,** mind-expanding, psychotomimetic

47 anesthetic, deadening, numbing

48 cathartic, laxative, purgative, aperient; carminative; diuretic

49 emetic, vomitive, vomitory <old>

87 SUBSTANCE ABUSE

NOUNS **1 substance abuse, drug abuse,** narcotics abuse, drug use, glue-sniffing, solvent abuse; **addiction, addictedness, drug addiction,** narcotic addiction, opium addiction *or* habit, opiumism, morphine addiction *or* habit, morphinism, heroin addiction *or* habit, cocaine addiction, cocainism, coke habit <nf>, crack habit, barbiturate addiction, amphetamine addiction; **habit,** drug habit, jones <nf>, drug habituation, drug dependence, physical addiction *or* dependence, psychological addiction *or* dependence, jones *and* monkey on one's back *and* Mighty Joe Young <nf>; **drug experience, drug intoxication,** high *and* buzz *and* rush <nf>; frightening drug experience, bad trip *and* bum trip *and* bummer *and* drag <nf>; **alcoholism** 88.3, alcohol abuse, drinking habit, acute alcoholism, chronic alcoholism, dipsomania, hitting the bottle <nf>, Dutch courage, hard drinking; **smoking,** smoking habit, one- *or* two- *or* three-pack-a-day habit, nicotine addiction 89.10, chain smoking; **tolerance,** acquired tolerance; **withdrawal, withdrawal sickness,** withdrawal syndrome, withdrawal symptoms, bogue *and* coming down *and* crash <nf>, abrupt withdrawal *and* cold turkey <nf>; **detoxification** *or* detox <nf>, drying out, taking the cure; Alcoholics Anonymous *or* AA

2 <drug use> smoking, sniffing, injecting, snorting, freebasing, hitting up, shooting up, skin-popping, mainlining, pill-popping, banging, blowing, cocktailing; buzz, trip, acid trip, bad trip; drug pushing, drug trafficking, holding <nf>; Narcotics Anonymous

3 drug, narcotic, dope <nf>, dangerous drug, controlled substance, abused substance, illegal drug, addictive drug, **hard drug;** soft drug, gateway drug; **opiate; sedative, depressant,** sedative hypnotic, **antipsychotic tranquilizer,** trank <nf>; **hallucinogen,** hallucinogenic drug, psychedelic, psychedelic drug, psychoactive drug, psychoactive chemical *or* psychochemical, psychotropic drug, psychotomimetic drug, mind-altering drug, mind-expanding drug, mind-blowing drug; designer drug; street drug; recreational drug; **stimulant; antidepressant,** Prozac, Valium; **inhalant,** volatile inhalant

4 <nf terms for amphetamines> bennies, benz, black mollies, brain ticklers, crank, crystal, dexies, diet pills, dolls, ecstasy, footballs, greenie, hearts, ice, jelly beans, lid poppers, meth, pep pills, purple hearts, speed, uppers, ups, white crosses

5 <nf terms for amyl nitrate> amies, blue angels, blue devils, blue dolls, blue heavens, poppers, snappers; **barbiturates,** barbs, black beauties, candy, dolls, downers, downs, goofballs, gorilla pills, nebbies, nimbies, phennies, phenos, pink ladies, purple hearts, yellow jackets

6 <nf terms for chloral hydrate> joy juice, knockout drops, mickey, Mickey Finn, peter

7 <nf terms for cocaine> basuco, bernice, big C, blow, C, charlie, coke, crack, crack cocaine, jumps, dust, flake, girl, gold dust, her, jay, joy powder, lady, lady snow, nose candy, Peruvian marching powder, rock, snow, star dust, toot, white, white girl, white lady, white stuff

8 <nf terms for hashish> black hash, black Russian, hash

9 <nf terms for heroin> big H, boy, brown, caballo, crap, doojee, flea powder, garbage, H, hard stuff, henry, him, his, horse, hombre, jones, junk, mojo, P-funk, scag, schmeck, smack, white stuff

10 <nf terms for LSD> acid, big D, blotter, blue acid, blue cheer, blue heaven, California sunshine, cap, cubes, D, deeda, dots, electric Kool-Aid, haze, L, mellow yellows, orange cubes, pearly gates, pink owsley, strawberry fields, sugar, sunshine, tabs, yellow, yellow sunshine, orange sunshine

11 <nf terms for marijuana> Acapulco gold, aunt mary, bomb, boo, bush, doobie, gage, ganja, grass, grefa, hay, hemp, herb, Indian hay, J, jane, kif, mary, maryjane, mary warner, meserole, mighty mezz, moota, muggles, pod, pot, smoke, snop, tea, Texas tea, weed, yerba

12 <nf terms for marijuana cigarette> joint, joy stick, kick stick, reefer, roach, stick, twist

13 <nf terms for mescaline> beans, big chief, buttons, cactus, mesc

14 <nf terms for morphine> big M, emm, hocus, M, miss emma, miss morph, morph, moocah, white stuff

15 <nf terms for pentobarbital> nebbies, nemmies, nimby, yellow dolls, yellows

16 <nf terms for opium> black pills, brown stuff, hop, O, tar

17 <nf terms for peyote> bad seed, big chief, buttons, cactus, P, topi

18 <nf terms for phencyclidine> angel dust, animal trank, DOA, dust, elephant, hog, PCP, peace, rocket fuel, supergrass, superweed

19 <nf terms for psilocybin> magic mushroom, mushroom, shroom, STP

20 dose, hit *and* fix *and* toke *and* rock <nf>; **shot, injection,** bang *or* bhang <nf>; **portion, packet,** spliff *and* snort *and* blockbuster *and* toke and blast <nf>, shoot-up *and* hype <nf>, bag *and* deck <nf>, dime bag; drug house, shooting gallery *and* needle park <nf>, crack house, opium den, balloon room *and* pot party *and* dope den <nf>

21 addict, drug addict, narcotics addict, user, drug user, drug abuser, junkie *and* head *and* druggy *and* doper *and* toker *and* fiend *and* freak *and* space cadet <nf>; cocaine user, cokie *and* coke head *and* crackhead *and* sniffer *and* snow drifter *and* flaky <nf>; opium user, opium addict, hophead *and* hopdog *and* tar distiller <nf>; heroin user *or* addict, smackhead *and* smack-sack *and* schmecker <nf>; methedrine user *or* methhead <nf>; amphetamine user, pillhead *and* pill popper *and* speed freak <nf>; LSD user, acidhead *and* acid freak *and* tripper *and* cubehead <nf>; marijuana smoker *and* pothead <nf>; **drug seller** *or* **dealer,** pusher, contact, connection; **alcoholic,** alcohol abuser 88; **smoker,** heavy smoker, chain smoker, nicotine addict

VERBS **22 use, be on,** get on; use occasionally *or* irregularly, have a cotton habit *and* chip *and* chippy *and* joy pop <nf>; **get a rush** *or* flush, go over the hump <nf>; **sniff,** snort, blow, toot, one and one <nf>; **smoke marijuana,** take on a number *and* blow a stick *and* toke *and* blast *and* weed out <nf>; **smoke opium,** blow a fill; freebase; **inject,** mainline, shoot *and* shoot up *and* jab *and* get down *and* get off <nf>, pop *and* skin pop <nf>; **take pills,** pop pills <nf>; **withdraw,** crash *and* come down <nf>, kick *or* go cold turkey *and* go a la canona *and* hang tough *and* water out <nf>, detoxify, disintoxicate, detoxicate, dry out, kick *and* kick the habit <nf>; **trip,** blow one's mind *and* wig out <nf>; **sell drugs,** deal *and* push <nf>; **buy drugs,** score *and* make *and* connect <nf>; **have drugs,** be heeled *and* carry *and* hold *and* sizzle <nf>; **drink** *or* **booze** 88.24–25; **smoke, smoke tobacco,** puff,

puff away, drag, chain-smoke, smoke like a chimney
ADJS **23 intoxicated,** under the influence, nodding, narcotized, poppied
24 <nf terms> **high,** bent, blasted, blind, bombed out, bonged out, buzzed, coked, coked out, flying, fried, geared, geared up, geezed, gonged, gorked, hopped-up, in a zone, junked, luded out, maxed, noddy, ripped, smashed, snowed, spaced, space out, spacey, stoned, strung out, switched on, tanked, totaled, tranqued, tripping, trippy, wired, zoned, zoned out, zonked, zonked out
25 addicted, hooked *and* zunked *and* on the needle <nf>; dependency-prone; **supplied with drugs,** holding *and* heeled *and* carrying *and* anywhere <nf>; using, on, behind acid <nf>

88 INTOXICATION, ALCOHOLIC DRINK

NOUNS **1 intoxication, inebriation, inebriety,** insobriety, besottedness, sottedness, **drunkenness, tipsiness,** befuddlement, fuddle, fuddlement, fuddledness, tipsification *and* tiddliness <nf>; a high, soaking <nf>; Dutch courage, pot-valiance *or* pot-valiancy, pot-valor; hangover, katzenjammer, morning after <nf>
2 bibulousness, bibacity, bibaciousness, bibulosity, sottishness; serious drinking; crapulence, crapulousness; **intemperance** 669; bacchanalianism; Bacchus, Dionysus, fondness for the bottle
3 alcoholism, dipsomania, oenomania, alcoholic psychosis *or* addiction, pathological drunkenness, problem drinking, heavy drinking, habitual drunkenness, ebriosity; delirium tremens 925.9,10; grog blossom *and* bottle nose <nf>; gin drinker's liver, cirrhosis of the liver
4 drinking, imbibing; social drinking; tippling, guzzling, gargling, bibing; winebibbing, winebibbery; toping; hard drinking, serious drinking <nf>; **boozing** *and* swilling <nf>, **hitting the booze** *or* **bottle** *or* **sauce** <nf>; alcoholism, Alcoholics Anonymous
5 spree, drinking bout, bout, **celebration,** potation, compotation, symposium, wassail, **carouse, carousal,** drunken carousal *or* revelry, revel; bacchanal, bacchanalia, bacchanalian; **debauch, orgy**
6 <nf terms> **binge, drunk,** bust, tear, **bender, toot, bat,** pub-crawl <Brit>, jag, booze-up <chiefly Brit>, brannigan, guzzle, randan, rip
7 drink, dram, potation, potion, libation, **nip,** draft, drop, spot, finger or two, sip, sup, suck, drench, guzzle, gargle, jigger; peg, swig, swill, pull; **snort,** jolt, **shot,** snifter, wet; quickie; round, round of drinks

8 bracer, refresher, reviver, pickup *and* **pick-me-up** <nf>, tonic, hair of the dog *or* hair of the dog that bit one <nf>
9 drink, cocktail, highball, long drink, mixed drink; liquor, spirits; **punch; eye-opener** <nf>, **nightcap** <nf>, sundowner <Brit nf>; **chaser** <nf>, *poussecafé* <Fr>, *apéritif* <Fr>; parting cup, stirrup cup, one for the road; hair of the dog; Mickey Finn *or* Mickey *and* knockout drops <nf>; mixer, chaser
10 toast, pledge, health
11 drinker, imbiber, **social drinker,** tippler, bibber; winebibber, oenophilist; **drunkard, drunk, inebriate, sot,** toper, guzzler, swiller, soaker, lovepot, tosspot, barfly, thirsty soul, **serious drinker,** devotee of Bacchus; swigger; hard drinker, heavy drinker, **alcoholic, dipsomaniac, problem drinker,** chronic alcoholic, chronic drunk, pathological drinker; carouser, reveler, wassailer; bacchanal, bacchanalian; pot companion
12 <nf terms> **drunk, lush,** lusher, **soak,** sponge, hooch hound, **boozer, boozehound,** booze fighter, booze freak, dipso, juicehead, loadie, ginhound, elbow bender *or* crooker, shikker, bottle sucker, swillbelly, swillpot, swillbowl; **souse, stew,** bum, rummy, rumhound, stewbum; wino
13 spirits, liquor, intoxicating liquor, adult beverage, **hard liquor,** hard stuff <nf>, **whiskey,** firewater, spiritus frumenti, usquebaugh <Scot>, schnapps, ardent spirits, strong waters, **intoxicant,** toxicant, inebriant, **potable,** potation, **beverage, drink, strong drink,** strong liquor, alcoholic drink *or* beverage, **alcohol,** aqua vitae, water of life, brew, **grog,** social lubricant, nectar of the gods; **booze** <nf>; **rum,** the Demon Rum, John Barleycorn; the bottle, the cup, the cup that cheers, "the ruddy cup"—Sir Walter Scott, little brown jug; punch bowl, the flowing bowl
14 <nf terms> **likker, hooch, juice, sauce,** tiger milk, pig *or* tiger sweat, sheepdip, moonshine, white lightning; **medicine,** snake medicine, corpse reviver; **rotgut, poison,** rat poison, formaldehyde, embalming fluid, shellac, **panther piss**
15 liqueur, cordial; brandy, flavored brandy
16 beer, brew *and* brewskie *and* suds <nf>, swipes <Brit nf>, "barmy beer"—Dryden; small beer; nonalcoholic beer, alcohol-free beer; draft beer, home-brew, microbrew
17 wine, vin <Fr>, *vino* <Sp & Ital>; vintage wine, nonvintage wine; the grape; red wine, white wine, rosé wine, pink wine, blush wine; dry *or* sweet wine, heavy *or* light wine, full *or* thin wine, rough *or* smooth wine, still wine, sparkling wine; extra sec *or* demi-sec *or* sec *or* brut champagne, bubbly; new wine, must; imported wine, domestic wine; fortified wine; wine of the country, *vin du*

campagne <Fr>; jug wine, plonk <Brit>;
Beaujolais wine

18 **bootleg liquor, moonshine** <nf>; hooch *and* shine
and mountain dew <nf>, white lightning *or* mule
<nf>; bathtub gin; home brew

19 **liquor dealer,** liquor store owner; **vintner,** wine
merchant; winegrower, winemaker, wine expert,
oenologist; **bartender,** mixologist, barkeeper,
barkeep, barman <Brit>, tapster, publican
<Brit>; barmaid, tapstress; **brewer,** brewmaster;
distiller; bootlegger, moonshiner <nf>

20 **bar,** barroom, *bistro* <Fr>, cocktail lounge;
taproom; **tavern, pub,** pothouse, alehouse,
rumshop, grogshop, dramshop, groggery, gin mill
<nf>, **saloon,** drinking saloon, saloon bar <Brit>;
lounge bar, piano bar, sports bar, singles bar, gay
bar; waterhole *or* watering hole <nf>; wine bar;
public house <Brit>; public *or* local <Brit nf>;
beer parlor, beer garden, rathskeller; **nightclub,
cabaret;** café, wine shop; barrel house *and* honky-
tonk *and* dive <nf>; **speakeasy** *and* blind tiger *and*
blind pig *and* after-hours joint <nf>

21 **distillery, still,** distiller; **brewery,** brewhouse;
winery, wine press; bottling works

VERBS 22 **intoxicate, inebriate, addle, befuddle,**
bemuse, besot, go to one's head, make one see
double, make one tiddly

23 <nf terms> **plaster,** pickle, swack, crock, stew,
souse, stone, pollute, tipsify, booze up, boozify,
fuddle, overtake

24 **tipple, drink,** dram <Brit>, nip; grog, **guzzle,**
gargle; **imbibe,** have a drink *or* nip *or* dram *or*
guzzle *or* gargle, soak, bib, quaff, sip, sup, lap, lap
up, take a drop, slake one's thirst, cheer *or* refresh
the inner man, drown one's troubles *or* sorrows,
commune with the spirits; **down,** toss off *or* down,
toss one's drink, knock back, throw one back,
drink off *or* up, drain the cup, drink bottoms-up,
drink deep; **drink hard,** drink like a fish, drink
seriously, **tope;** take to drink *or* drinking, drink
one's fill, "follow strong drink"—Bible

25 <nf terms> **booze,** swig, swill, moisten *or* wet
one's whistle; **liquor, liquor up,** lush, souse, tank
up, **hit the booze** *or* **bottle** *or* **sauce,** exercise *or*
bend *or* crook *or* raise the elbow, dip the beak,
splice the main brace; chug-a-lug, chug

26 **get drunk,** be stricken drunk, get high, put on a
high, take a drop too much; **get plastered** *or*
pickled, etc <nf>, tie one on *and* get a bun on
<nf>

27 **be drunk,** be intoxicated, have a drop too much,
have more than one can hold, have a jag on <nf>,
see double, be feeling no pain; **stagger, reel; pass
out** <nf>

28 go on a spree; go on a binge *or* **drunk** *or* **toot** *or*
bat *or* **bender** <nf>, **carouse, spree, revel,** wassail,
debauch, "eat, drink, and be merry"—Bible, paint
the town red <nf>, pub-crawl <Brit nf>

29 **drink to, toast, pledge,** drink a toast to, drink *or*
pledge the health of, give you

30 **distill; brew;** bootleg, moonshine <nf>, moonlight
<nf>

ADJS 31 **intoxicated, inebriated,** inebriate, inebrious,
drunk, drunken, *shikker* <Yiddish>, **tipsy,** in
liquor, **in one's cups, under the influence,** the
worse for liquor, having had one too many; nappy,
beery; **tiddly, giddy, dizzy,** muddled, addled,
flustered, bemused, reeling, seeing double; **mellow,
merry,** jolly, happy, gay, glorious; **full; besotted,**
sotted, sodden, drenched, far-gone; drunk as a
lord, drunk as a fiddler *or* piper, drunk as a skunk,
drunk as an owl; staggering drunk, drunk and
disorderly; crapulent, crapulous; **maudlin**

32 **dead-drunk,** blind drunk, overcome, out *and* out
cold *and* passed out <nf>, helpless, under the
table

33 <nf terms> **fuddled,** muzzy, **boozy,** overtaken;
swacked, plastered, shnockered, stewed, **pickled,**
pissed, **soused,** soaked, boiled, fried, canned,
tanked, potted, corned, bombed, ripped, smashed;
bent, **crocked,** crocko, shellacked, sloshed,
sozzled, zonked, tight, lushy, squiffy, afflicted, jug-
bitten, oiled, lubricated, feeling no pain, polluted,
raddled, organized, **high,** elevated, high as a kite,
lit, **lit up,** lit to the gills, illuminated, **loaded,
stinko,** tanked, tanked-up, stinking drunk, pie-
eyed, pissy-eyed, shitfaced, cockeyed, cockeyed
drunk, roaring *or* rip-roaring drunk, skunk-drunk;
half-seas over, three sheets to the wind, well-oiled,
blotto, stiff, blind, paralyzed, **stoned**

34 **full of Dutch courage, pot-valiant,** pot-valorous

35 **bibulous,** bibacious, drunken, sottish, liquorish,
given *or* addicted to drink, **liquor-loving,** liquor-
drinking, drinking, hard-drinking, swilling <nf>,
toping, tippling, winebibbing

36 **intoxicating,** intoxicative, **inebriating,** inebriative,
inebriant, heady

37 **alcoholic, spirituous, ardent, strong, hard,** with a
kick <nf>; winy, vinous

INTERJS 38 <toasts> skoal!, *skål!* <Norw>, prosit!
or prost!, *à votre santé!* <Fr>, *¡salud!* <Sp>,
l'chaim! <Heb>, *sláinte!* <Ir>, salute! <Ital>, *na
zdorovye!* <Russ>, *nazdrowie!* <Pol>, to your
health!, long life!, to life!, cheerio!, cheers!, to us!,
down the hatch!, bottoms up!, here's how!, here's
to you!, here's looking at you!, here's mud in your
eye!, here's good luck!, here's to absent friends!,
confusion to our enemies!

89 TOBACCO

NOUNS **1 tobacco,** *tabac* <Fr>, nicotine, nicotia *or* nicotian <old>; **the weed** <nf>, fragrant weed, Indian weed *or* drug, filthy weed, sot-weed <old>, "pernicious weed"—Cowper, "thou weed, who art so lovely fair and smell'st so sweet"—Shakespeare; carcinogenic substance; smoke, tobacco smoke, cigarette smoke, cigar smoke, pipe smoke; secondary smoke, secondhand smoke

2 <tobaccos> flue-cured *or* bright, fire-cured, air-cured; Broadleaf, Burley, Cuban, Havana, Havana seed, Latakia, Turkish, Russian, Maryland, Virginia; plug tobacco, bird's-eye, canaster, leaf, lugs, seconds, shag; pipe tobacco

3 smoking tobacco, smokings <nf>, smoke *and* smokes <nf>

4 cigar, seegar <nf>; rope *and* stinker <nf>; **cheroot, stogie,** corona, belvedere, Havana, panatella, colorado, trichinopoly; cigarillo; box of cigars, cigar box, cigar case, humidor; cigar cutter

5 cigarette; butt *and* cig *and* **fag** *and* coffin nail *and* cancer stick <nf>; filter tip, high tar, low tar, methol; cigarette butt, **butt,** stub; snipe <nf>; pack *or* deck of cigarettes, box *or* carton of cigarettes, cigarette case, cigarette paper

6 pipe, tobacco pipe; corncob, corncob pipe, Missouri meerschaum; briar pipe, briar; clay pipe, clay, churchwarden <Brit>; meerschaum; water pipe, hookah, nargileh, kalian, hubble-bubble; peace pipe, calumet; pipe rack, pipe cleaner, tobacco pouch

7 chewing tobacco, eating tobacco <nf>, oral tobacco; navy *or* navy plug, cavendish, twist, pigtail, plug, cut plug; **quid,** cud, fid <Brit nf>, **chew,** chaw <nf>; tobacco juice

8 snuff, snoose <nf>; rappee; pinch of snuff; snuff bottle, snuffbox, snuff mill <Scot>

9 nicotine, nicotia <old>

10 smoking, smoking habit, habitual smoking; chain-smoking; smoke, puff, drag <nf>; **chewing;** tobacco *or* nicotine addiction, tobaccoism, tabacosis, tabacism, tabagism, nicotinism; passive smoking

11 tobacco user, smoker, cigarette *or* pipe *or* cigar smoker, chewer, snuffer, snuff dipper

12 tobacconist; snuffman; tobacco store *or* shop, cigar store

13 smoking room, smoking car, **smoker;** smoke-free area, non-smoking section

VERBS **14** <use tobacco> **smoke;** inhale, puff, draw, drag <nf>, pull; smoke like a furnace *or* chimney; chain-smoke; **chew,** chaw <nf>; roll; **take snuff,** dip *or* inhale snuff

ADJS **15 tobacco,** tobaccoy *or* tobaccoey, tobaccolike; **nicotinic;** smoking, chewing; snuffy; smoke-free, non-smoking

90 HEALTH CARE

NOUNS **1 medicine, medical practice,** medical profession, medical care, **health care,** health-care industry, health-care delivery, primary care; **medical specialty** *or* **branch** <see list>; **treatment,** therapy 91; health insurance 83.5, Medicare, Medicaid; **care,** nursing care, home care, outpatient care, life care

2 surgery; operation; cosmetic surgery, plastic surgery, facelift, liposuction, nose job <nf>, tuck <nf>

3 dentistry <see list>, dental medicine, dental care

4 doctor, doc <nf>, **physician,** Doctor of Medicine *or* **MD** *or* medical doctor, **medical practitioner, medical man, medico** <nf>, leech <old>, croaker *and* sawbones <nf>; **general practitioner** *or* **GP;** family doctor; country doctor; **intern; resident,** house physician, resident physician; fellow; physician in ordinary; medical attendant, attending physician; **specialist,** board-certified physician *or* specialist; **medical examiner,** coroner; oculist, **optometrist,** radiologist, anesthesiologist; health maintenance organization *or* HMO

5 surgeon, sawbones <nf>; operator, operative surgeon

6 dentist, tooth doctor, toothdrawer; **dental surgeon,** oral surgeon, operative dentist; Doctor of Dental Surgery *or* DDS; Doctor of Dental Science *or* DDSc; Doctor of Dental Medicine *or* DMD; orthodondist, periodontist, exodontist, endodontist, prosthodontist

7 veterinary, veterinarian, vet <nf>, veterinary surgeon, horse doctor, animal doctor

8 health-care professional, health-care provider, physician, nurse, midwife, therapist, therapeutist, practitioner; physical therapist, physiotherapist, speech therapist, occupational therapist

9 healer, nonmedical therapist; theotherapist; Christian *or* spiritual *or* divine healer; **Christian Science practitioner; faith healer,** witch doctor <nf>, alternative practitioner, **osteopath, chiropractor,** podiatrist, acupuncturist, etc

10 nurse, sister *or* nursing sister <Brit>; **probationer,** probationist, probe <nf>; caregiver, hospice caregiver; practical nurse; registered nurse *or* RN, nurse practitioner

11 <hospital staff> paramedic, emergency medical technician *or* EMT; medevac; physician's assistant *or* PA; orderly, attendant, nurse's aide; audiologist; anesthetist; dietician, nutritionist; radiographer, X-ray technician; laboratory technician;

radiotherapist; dietitian; hospital administrator; ambulance driver; custodian

12 Hippocrates, Galen; Aesculapius, Asclepius

13 practice of medicine, medical practice; general practice, restricted *or* limited practice; group practice; professional association *or* PA; family practice, private practice, health maintenance organization *or* HMO; orthodox medicine, conventional medicine, general medicine, preventive medicine, internal medicine, occupational medicine, public-health medicine, community medicine; unorthodox medicine, alternative medicine, acupuncture, faith healing, homeopathy, naturopathy, etc

VERBS **14 practice medicine,** doctor <nf>; examine, diagnose, screen; treat; prescribe, medicate, administer, inject; make a house call, be on call; intern; practice surgery, operate; practice dentistry

ADJS **15 medical,** iatric, health, Hippocratic; surgical; chiropodic, pediatric, orthopedic, obstetric, obstetrical, neurological; dental; orthodontic, periodontic, prosthodontic, exodontic; osteopathic, chiropractic, naturopathic, hydropathic, allopathic, homeopathic; gynecological, internal, pathological, forensic; clinical; diagnostic; therapeutic; veterinary

16 branches of medicine

adolescence medicine	hygiene
anatomy	immunochemistry
anesthesiology	immunology
audiology	internal medicine
aviation medicine	materia medica
bacteriology	mental hygiene
cardiography	midwifery
cardiology	mycology
chemotherapy	neonatology
chiropody	nephrology
critical care medicine	neurology
dental surgery	neurosurgery
dentistry	nosology
dermatology	nutrition
diagnostics	obstetrics
dolorology	oncology
embryology	ophthalmology
endocrinology	optometry
epidemiology	orthopedics
etiology	orthotics
family practice	osteopathy
fetology	otolaryngology
fluoroscopy	otology
gastroenterology	parasitology
general medicine	pathology
geriatrics *or*	pediatrics
gerontology	pharmacology
gynecology	physical medicine
hematology	physiopathology
physiotherapy	space medicine
plastic surgery	surgery
podiatry	surgical anatomy
psychiatry	symptomatology *or*
psychology	semeiology
psychoneuroimmunology	teratology
pulmonology	therapeutics
radiology	tocology
rheumatology	toxicology
serology	virology

17 kinds and specialties of dentistry

endodontics *or* endodontia	orthodontics *or* orthodontia
exodontics *or* exodontia	
family dentistry	pedodontics *or* pedodontia
general dentistry	periodontics *or* periodontia
gerodontics	prosthetic dentistry *or*
implantology	prosthodontics *or*
operative dentistry	prosthodontia
oral surgery *or* surgical	radiodontics *or*
dentistry	radiodontia

18 types of surgery

apicectomy	labioplasty
appendectomy *or*	laparotomy
appendicectomy	laryngectomy
arterioplasty	lobotomy *or* leukotomy
autograft *or* autoplasty	lithonephrotomy *or*
cesarean section	nephrolithotomy
cholecystectomy	mastectomy
cholelithotomy	necrotomy
colostomy	nephrectomy
cordotomy	neurotomy
craniotomy	oophorectomy *or*
cryosurgery	ovariectomy
cystectomy	orchidectomy *or*
D & C *or* dilatation and	orchiectomy *or*
curettage	testectomy
debridement	ostectomy
episiotomy	otoplasty
fenestration	phlebotomy *or* venesection
gastrectomy	pneumonectomy
goniopuncture	rhinoplasty
hepatectomy	rhizotomy
homograft *or* allograft *or*	salpingectomy
homoplasty	thoracotomy
hysterectomy	tracheostomy *or*
ileostomy	tracheotomy
iridectomy	vasectomy

91 THERAPY, MEDICAL TREATMENT

NOUNS **1 therapy, therapeutics,** therapeusis, **treatment, medical care** *or* **treatment,** medication; noninvasive *or* nonsurgical therapy *or* treatment; disease-fighting, healing; healing arts; physical therapy, psychotherapy 92; medicines 86

2 nonmedical therapy; theotherapy; **healing;** Christian *or* spiritual *or* divine healing; **faith healing**

3 hydrotherapy, hydrotherapeutics; hydropathy, water cure; cold-water cure; contrast bath, whirlpool bath

4 heat therapy, thermotherapy; heliotherapy, solar therapy; fangotherapy; hot bath, sweat bath, sunbath

5 diathermy, medical diathermy; electrotherapy, electrotherapeutics; **radiothermy,** high-frequency treatment; shortwave diathermy, ultrashortwave diathermy, microwave diathermy; ultrasonic diathermy; surgical diathermy, radiosurgery, electrosurgery, electrosection, electrocautery, electrocoagulation

6 radiotherapy, radiation therapy, radiotherapeutics; adjuvant therapy

7 radiology, radiography, radioscopy, fluoroscopy, etc 1037.8; diagnostic radiology, scanning, magnetic resonance imaging *or* MRI

8 <radiotherapeutic substances> radium; cobalt; radioisotope, tracer, labeled *or* tagged element, radioelement; radiocarbon, carbon 14, radiocalcium, radiopotassium, radiosodium, radioiodine; atomic cocktail

9 <diagnostic pictures and graphs> **X ray,** scan, radiograph, radiogram, roentgenogram *or* roentgenograph; photofluorograph; X-ray movie; chest X-ray; pyelogram; orthodiagram; encephalograph, encephalogram; electroencephalograph, electroencephalogram *or* EEG; electrocorticogram; electrocardiogram *or* ECG *or* EKG; electromyogram; computer-assisted tomography *or* CAT, computerized axial tomography *or* computed tomography *or* computer-assisted tomography *or* computerized tomography *or* CAT; CAT scan; magnetic resonance imaging *or* MRI; MRI scan; positron emission tomography *or* PET; PET scan; ultrasound, ultrasonography; sonogram

10 case history, medical history, anamnesis; associative anamnesis; catamnesis, follow-up

11 diagnostics, prognostics; symptomatology, semeiology, semeiotics

12 diagnosis; examination, physical examination; study, test, workup <nf>; medical test, laboratory test, screening, diagnostic procedure; blood test, blood work <nf>, blood count, urinalysis, uroscopy; biopsy; Pap test *or* smear; stress test; electrocardiography, electroencephalography, electromyography; mammography; pregnancy test, amniocentesis *or* amnio, ultrasound

13 prognosis, prognostication; prognostic, **symptom, sign**

14 treatment, medical treatment *or* attention *or* care; **cure,** curative measures; **medication,** medicamentation; **regimen,** regime, protocol; first aid; hospitalization; physical therapy, acupressure, shiatsu

15 immunization; immunization therapy, immunotherapy; vaccine therapy, vaccinotherapy; toxin-antitoxin immunization; serum therapy, serotherapy, serotherapeutics; tuberculin test, scratch test, patch test; **immunology,** immunochemistry; immunity theory, side-chain theory; immunity; immunodeficiency

16 inoculation, vaccination; injection, hypodermic, hypodermic injection, shot *and* bing <nf>, hypospray *or* jet injection; booster, booster shot <nf>; antitoxin, vaccine 86.28

17 <methods of injection> cutaneous, percutaneous, subcutaneous, intradermal, intramuscular, intravenous, intramedullary, intracardiac, intrathecal, intraspinal

18 transfusion, blood transfusion; serum; blood bank, blood donor center, bloodmobile; blood donor

19 surgery, surgical treatment, **operation,** surgical operation, surgical intervention, surgical technique *or* measure, the knife <nf>; **instrument,** device; respirator; unnecessary surgery, *cacoëthes operandi* <L>, tomomania; major surgery, minor surgery, laser surgery, plastic surgery

20 bloodletting, bleeding, venesection, phlebotomy; leeching; cupping

21 hospital, clinic, *hôpital* <Fr>, treatment center; general hospital, teaching hospital, university hospital, health center; hospice, infirmary; nursing home, rest home, convalescent home, sanitarium; sick bay *or* berth; trauma center; wellness center

22 pesthouse, lazar house, lazaretto *or* lazaret <old>

23 health resort, spa, watering place, baths; mineral spring, warm *or* hot spring; pump room, pump house

VERBS **24 treat, doctor,** minister to, care for, give care to, physic; **diagnose;** nurse; **cure, remedy, heal;** dress the wounds, bandage, poultice, plaster, strap, splint; bathe; massage, rub; operate on; physic, purge, flux <old>; **operate,** perform a procedure; transplant, replant

25 medicate, medicine, drug, dope <nf>, dose; salve, oil, anoint, embrocate

26 irradiate, radiumize, **X-ray,** roentgenize

27 bleed, let blood, leech, phlebotomize; cup; **transfuse,** give a transfusion; perfuse

28 immunize, inoculate, vaccinate, shoot <nf>

29 undergo treatment, take the cure, doctor <nf>, take medicine; go under the knife <nf>

92 PSYCHOLOGY, PSYCHOTHERAPY

NOUNS **1 psychology** <see list>, science of the mind, science of human behavior, mental philosophy;

psychologism, pop psychology *and* psychobabble <nf>; mental states, mental processes

2 psychological school, school *or* system of psychology, psychological theory; Adlerian psychology; behaviorism *or* behavior *or* behavioristic psychology *or* stimulus-response psychology; Freudian psychology *or* Freudianism; Gestalt psychology *or* configurationism; Horneyan psychology; Jungian *or* analytical psychology; Pavlovian psychology; Reichian psychology *or* orgone theory; Skinnerian psychology; Sullivanian psychology

3 **psychiatry,** psychological medicine; neuropsychiatry; social psychiatry; prophylactic psychiatry

4 **psychosomatic medicine,** psychological medicine, medicopsychology; psychosocial medicine

5 **psychotherapy,** psychotherapeutics, mind cure

6 **psychoanalysis, analysis,** the couch <nf>, counseling, behavior therapy, behavior modification; psychoanalytic therapy, psychoanalytic method; **depth psychology,** psychology of depths; group analysis *or* psychology, family therapy; transactional analysis; psychognosis, psychognosy; dream analysis, interpretation of dreams, dream symbolism; depth interview; hypnotherapy; transcendental meditation

7 **psychodiagnostics,** psychodiagnosis, psychological *or* psychiatric evaluation

8 **psychometrics,** psychometry, psychological measurement; **intelligence testing;** mental test, psychological screening; psychography; psychogram, psychograph, psychological profile; psychometer, IQ meter <nf>; lie detector, polygraph, psychogalvanometer, psychogalvanic skin response

9 **psychological test** <see list>, mental test; standardized test; developmental test, achievement test

10 **psychologist; psychotherapist, therapist,** psychotherapeutist; clinical psychologist; licensed psychologist, psychological practitioner; child psychologist; **psychiatrist,** alienist, somatist; neuropsychiatrist; psychopathist, psychopathologist; psychotechnologist, industrial psychologist; hypnotherapist; behavior therapist; psychobiologist, psychochemist, psychophysiologist, psychophysicist; psychographer; psychiatric social worker; **psychoanalyst, analyst; shrink** *and* headshrinker *and* shrinker <nf>; **counselor,** psychological counselor; counseling service

11 **personality tendency,** complexion <old>, humor; somatotype; **introversion,** introvertedness, ingoingness; inner-directedness; **extroversion,** extrovertedness, outgoingness; other-directedness; syntony, ambiversion; schizothymia, schizothymic *or* schizoid personality; cyclothymia, cyclothymic *or* cycloid personality; mesomorphism, mesomorphy; endomorphism, endomorphy; ectomorphism, ectomorphy

12 <personality type> **introvert, extrovert,** syntone, ambivert; schizothyme, schizoid; cyclothymic, cyclothyme, cycloid; choleric, melancholic, sanguine, phlegmatic; endomorph, mesomorph, ectomorph

13 **pathological personality,** psychopathological personality, sick personality

14 **mental disorder, emotional disorder,** neurosis; psychonosema, psychopathyfunctional nervous disorder; reaction; emotional instability; **maladjustment,** social maladjustment; nervous *or* mental breakdown, crack-up <nf>; problems in living; brainstorm; **insanity,** mental illness 926.1; **psychosis** 926.3; **schizophrenia;** paranoia 926.4; **manic-depressive psychosis, depression,** melancholia 926.5; seasonal affective disorder *or* SAD, post-partum depression; melancholia *or* endogenous depression; pre-menstrual syndrome *or* PMS; **neurosis, psychoneurosis,** neuroticism, neurotic *or* psychoneurotic disorder; brain disease, nervous disorder; cognitive disorder, eating disorder, sleep disorder, somatoform disorder, dissociative disorder, mood disorder, anxiety disorder, sexual disorder, impulse-control disorder, conversion disorder; battle fatigue

15 **personality disorder, character disorder,** moral insanity, sociopathy, **psychopathy; psychopathic personality;** sexual pathology, sexual psychopathy 75.18; compulsion, fixation, complex; obsessive-compulsive disorder

16 **neurotic reaction,** overreaction, disproportionate reaction, depression, mania

17 **psychological stress, stress; frustration,** external frustration, internal frustration; conflict, ambivalence, ambivalence of impulse; **trauma,** psychological *or* emotional trauma, traumatism, mental *or* emotional shock, decompensation; rape trauma syndrome; post-traumatic stress disorder

18 **psychosomatic symptom; symptom of emotional disorder,** emotional symptom, psychological symptom; **thought disturbance,** thought disorder *or* disturbances, dissociative disorder, delirium, delusion, disorientation, hallucination; **speech abnormality**

19 **trance,** daze, stupor; catatonic stupor, catalepsy; cataplexy; dream state, reverie, daydreaming 985.2; somnambulism, sleepwalking; hypnotic trance; fugue, fugue state; **amnesia** 990.2; meditation

20 dissociation, mental *or* emotional dissociation, disconnection, dissociative disorder; dissociation of personality, personality disorganization *or* disintegration; **schizoid personality;** double *or* dual personality; multiple personality, split personality, alternating personality; schizoidism, schizothymia, **schizophrenia** 926.4; depersonalization; **paranoid personality;** paranoia 926.4

21 fixation, libido fixation *or* arrest, **arrested development;** infantile fixation, pregenital fixation, father fixation, Freudian fixation, mother fixation, parent fixation; **regression,** retreat to immaturity

22 complex, inferiority complex, superiority complex, parent complex, Oedipus complex, mother complex, Electra complex, father complex, Diana complex, persecution complex; castration complex; compulsion complex

23 defense mechanism, defense reaction; ego defense, psychotaxis; biological *or* psychological *or* sociological adjustive reactions; resistance; dissociation; **negativism, alienation; escapism,** escape mechanism, avoidance mechanism; escape, flight, **withdrawal; isolation,** emotional insulation; **fantasy,** fantasizing, escape into fantasy, dreamlike thinking, autistic *or* dereistic thinking, wishful thinking, autism, dereism; wish-fulfillment, wish-fulfillment fantasy; sexual fantasy; **compensation,** overcompensation, decompensation; substitution; **sublimation;** regression, reversion; **projection,** identification, blame-shifting; displacement; **rationalization**

24 suppression, repression, inhibition, resistance, restraint, censorship, censor; block, psychological block, blockage, blocking; denial, negation, rejection; reaction formation; rigid control; **suppressed desire**

25 catharsis, purgation, abreaction, motor abreaction, psychocatharsis, **emotional release,** relief of tension, outlet; release therapy, acting-out, psychodrama; imaging

26 conditioning, classical *or* Pavlovian conditioning; instrumental conditioning; operant conditioning; psychagogy, reeducation, reorientation; conditioned reflex, conditioned stimulus, conditioned response; reinforcement, positive reinforcement, negative reinforcement; simple reflex, unconditioned reflex, **reflex** 903.1; **behavior** 321; suggestion

27 adjustment, adjustive reaction; **readjustment, rehabilitation;** psychosynthesis, integration of personality; fulfillment, self-fulfillment; self-actualization, peak experience; integrated personality, syntonic personality

28 psyche, psychic apparatus, **personality, self,** personhood; **mind** 919.1,3,4, pneuma, soul; preconscious, foreconscious, coconscious; **subconscious, unconscious,** stream of consciousness, subconscious *or* unconscious mind, submerged mind, subliminal, subliminal self; **libido,** psychic *or* libidinal energy, motive force, vital impulse, ego-libido, object libido; **id,** primitive self, pleasure principle, life instinct, death instinct; **ego,** conscious self; **superego,** ethical self, conscience; ego ideal; ego-id conflict; anima, animus, persona; collective unconscious, racial unconscious; psychological me

29 engram, memory trace, traumatic trace *or* memory; unconscious memory; archetype, archetypal pattern *or* image *or* symbol; imago, image, father image, etc; race *or* racial memory; cultural memory; **memory** 989

30 symbol, universal symbol, father symbol, mother symbol, phallic symbol, fertility symbol, etc; symbolism, symbolization

31 surrogate, substitute; father surrogate, father figure, father image; mother surrogate, mother figure, mother image

32 gestalt, pattern, figure, configuration, form, sensory pattern; figure-ground

33 association, association of ideas, chain of ideas, concatenation, mental linking; controlled association, free association, association by contiguity, association by similarity; association by sound, clang association; stream of consciousness; transference, identification, positive transference, negative transference; synesthesia 24.5

34 cathexis, cathection, desire concentration; charge, energy charge, cathectic energy; anticathexis, countercathexis, counterinvestment; hypercathexis, overcharge

35 psychiatric treatment, psychiatric care; psychosurgery, shock treatment, shock therapy, convulsive therapy, electroconvulsive therapy

VERBS **36 psychologize, psychoanalyze,** analyze, counsel; abreact; fixate, obsess on <nf>

ADJS **37 psychological; psychiatric,** neuropsychiatric; psychometric; **psychopathic,** psychopathological; **psychosomatic,** somatopsychic, psychophysical, psychophysiological, psychobiological; psychogenic, psychogenetic, functional; psychodynamic, psychoneurological, psychosexual, psychosocial, psychotechnical; **psychotic**

38 psychotherapeutic; psychiatric, psychoanalytic, psychoanalytical; psychodiagnostic; hypnotherapeutic

39 neurotic, psychoneurotic, disturbed, disordered; neurasthenic, psychasthenic; hysteric *or* hysterical, hypochondriac, phobic; deluded; dissociated; depressed; stressed

40 introverted, introvert, introversive, **subjective, ingoing,** inner-directed; withdrawn, isolated

41 extroverted, extrovert, extroversive, **outgoing,** extrospective; other-directed

42 subconscious, unconscious; subliminal, extramarginal; preconscious, foreconscious, coconscious

43 kinds and branches of psychology

abnormal psychology
academic psychology
act psychology
analytic *or* introspective psychology
animal psychology
applied psychology
association psychology
behavioral psychology *or* behaviorism
biopsychology
child psychology
clinical psychology
cognitive psychology
comparative psychology
constitutional psychology
criminal psychology
depth psychology
developmental psychology
differential psychology
dynamic *or* functional psychology
ecological psychology
educational psychology
ego psychology
empirical psychology
existential psychology
experimental psychology
faculty psychology
folk *or* ethnic psychology
genetic psychology
Gestalt psychology *or* configurationism
group psychology
haptics
hedonics
holistic psychology
hormic psychology
individual psychology
industrial psychology
introspection psychology
Jungian psychology
mass psychology
medical psychology
morbid psychology
neuropsychology
objective psychology
ontogenetic psychology
parapsychology
phenomenological psychology
phylogenetic psychology
physiologic *or* physiological psychology
polygenetic psychology
popular psychology
psychoacoustics
psychoasthenics
psychobiochemistry
psychobiology
psychochemistry
psychodiagnostics
psychodynamics
psychoendocrinology
psychogenetics
psychogeriatrics
psychographics
psychohistory
psycholinguistics
psychological medicine
psychological warfare
psychomathematics
psychometrics *or* psychometry
psychonomy *or* psychonomics
psychopathology
psychopharmacology
psychophysics
psychophysiology
psychosociology
psychosomatics
psychotechnics *or* psychotechnology
psychotherapy *or* psychotherapeutics
race *or* racial psychology
rational psychology
reactology
reflexology
self psychology
social psychology
structural psychology
transpersonal psychology
voluntaristic psychology

44 psychological and mental tests

alpha test
apperception test
aptitude test
association test
Babcock-Levy test
Bernreuter personality inventory
beta test
Binet *or* Binet-Simon test
Brown personality inventory
Cattell's infant intelligence scale
CAVD test
controlled association test
free association test
frustration test
Gesell's development schedule
Goldstein-Sheerer test
inkblot test
intelligence quotient *or* IQ
intelligence test
interest inventory
IQ test
Kent mental test
Minnesota Multiphasic Personality Inventory
Minnesota Preschool Scale
Oseretsky test
personality test
Rogers's process scale
Rorschach test
Rotter incomplete sentences blank
Stanford revision
Stanford scientific aptitude test
Stanford-Binet test
Szondi test
thematic apperception test *or* TAT
Wechsler Adult Intelligence Scale
Wechsler-Bellevue intelligence scale
Wechsler Intelligence Scale for Children
word association test

93 FEELING

NOUNS **1 feeling, emotion, affect, sentiment,** affection, affections, sympathies, beliefs; affective faculty, affectivity; emotional charge, cathexis; **feelings, sensitiveness, sensibility,** susceptibility, thin skin; emotional life; the logic of the heart; **sense,** deep *or* profound sense, gut sense *or* sensation <nf>; **sensation** 24; **impression,** undercurrent, perception; hunch, intuition, feeling in one's bones, vibes <nf>, presentiment 934.3; foreboding; **reaction, response,** gut reaction <nf>; **instinct** 365.1; emotional coloring *or* shade *or* nuance, **tone**

2 passion, passionateness, strong feeling, powerful emotion; **fervor, fervency,** fervidness, impassionedness, **ardor, ardency,** *empressement* <Fr>, warmth of feeling, **warmth, heat, fire,** verve, furor, **fury,** vehemence; heartiness, gusto, relish, savor; spirit, heart, soul; **liveliness** 330.2; **zeal** 101.2; **excitement** 105; **ecstasy**

3 heart, soul, spirit, *esprit* <Fr>, **breast, bosom,** inmost heart *or* soul, heart of hearts, secret *or* inner recesses of the heart, secret places, heart's core, heartstrings, cockles of the heart, bottom of the heart, being, innermost being, core of one's being; viscera, pit of one's stomach, **gut** *or* guts <nf>; bones

4 sensibility, sensitivity, sensitiveness, delicacy, fineness of feeling, tenderness, affectivity, susceptibility, impressionability 24.2

5 sympathy, fellow feeling, sympathetic response, good feeling, responsiveness, relating, warmth, cordiality, **caring,** concern; response, echo, chord, sympathetic chord, vibrations, vibes <nf>; **empathy,** identification; involvement, sharing; pathos

6 tenderness, tender feeling, softness, gentleness, delicacy; **tenderheartedness,** softheartedness, warmheartedness, tender *or* sensitive *or* warm heart, soft place *or* spot in one's heart; warmth, **fondness,** weakness 100.2

7 bad feeling, hard feelings; immediate dislike, disaffinity, personality conflict, bad vibes *or* chemistry <nf>, bad blood, **hostility,** scunner, animosity 589.4; resentment, bitterness, ill will, intolerance; **hard-heartedness** 94.3

8 sentimentality, sentiment, sentimentalism, oversentimentality, oversentimentalism, bathos; nostalgia, nostomania; romanticism; sweetness and light, hearts-and-flowers; bleeding heart; mawkishness, cloyingness, maudlinness, namby-pamby, namby-pambyness, namby-pambyism; mushiness *or* sloppiness <nf>; **mush** *and* slush *and* slop *and* goo *and* schmaltz <nf>; sob story *and* tearjerker <nf>, soap opera

9 emotionalism, emotionality, lump in one's throat; emotionalizing, emotionalization; emotiveness, emotivity; visceralness; nonrationalness, unreasoningness; demonstrativeness, making scenes, excitability; **theatrics, theatricality, histrionics, dramatics,** hamminess *and* chewing up the scenery <nf>; **sensationalism, melodrama,** melodramatics, blood and thunder; yellow journalism; emotional appeal, human interest, love interest; **overemotionalism,** hyperthymia, excess of feeling, emotional instability

VERBS **10 feel,** entertain *or* harbor *or* cherish *or* nurture a feeling; feel deeply, feel in one's viscera *or* bones, feel in one's gut *or* guts <nf>; experience 831.8; have a sensation, get *or* receive an impression, **sense, perceive;** intuit, have a hunch

11 respond, react, be moved, be affected *or* touched, be inspired, echo, catch the flame *or* infection, be in tune; **respond to,** warm up to, take *or* lay to heart, open one's heart to, be turned on to <nf>, nourish in one's bosom, feel in one's breast, cherish at the heart's core, treasure up in the heart; enter into the spirit of, be imbued with the spirit of; care about, feel for, sympathize with, empathize with, identify with, relate to emotionally, dig *and* be turned on by <nf>, be involved, share; color with emotion

12 have deep feelings, be all heart, have a tender heart, take to heart, be a person of heart *or* sentiment; have a soft place *or* spot in one's heart;

be a prey to one's feelings; love 104.18–20; hate 103.5

13 emotionalize, emote <nf>, give free play to the emotions, make a scene; be theatrical, theatricalize, ham it up *and* chew up the scenery <nf>; **sentimentalize,** gush *and* slobber over <nf>

14 affect, touch, move, stir; melt, soften, melt the heart, choke one up, give one a lump in the throat; **penetrate,** pierce, go through one, go deep; touch a chord, **touch a sympathetic chord, touch one's heart,** tug at the heart *or* heartstrings, go to one's heart, get under one's skin; come home to; **touch to the quick,** touch on the raw, flick one on the raw, smart, sting

15 impress, affect, strike, hit, smite, rock; **make an impression, get to one** <nf>; make a dent in, make an impact upon, sink in <nf>, strike home, come home to, hit the mark <nf>; tell, have a strong effect, traumatize, strike hard, impress forcibly

16 impress upon, bring home to, make it felt; stamp, stamp on, etch, engrave, engrave on

ADJS **17 emotional, affective,** emotive, affectional, **feeling,** sentient; soulful, of soul, of heart, of feeling, of sentiment; visceral, gut <nf>; glandular; emotiometabolic, emotiomotor, emotiomuscular, emotiovascular; demonstrative, overdemonstrative

18 fervent, fervid, passionate, impassioned, intense, **ardent; hearty, cordial,** enthusiastic, exuberant, unrestrained, vigorous; keen, breathless, **excited** 105.18,20,22; **lively** 330.17; zealous; **warm, burning, heated, hot, volcanic,** red-hot, fiery, flaming, glowing, ablaze, afire, on fire, boiling over, steaming, steamy; delirious, fevered, feverish, febrile, flushed; intoxicated, drunk; obsessed

19 emotionalistic, emotive, overemotional, hysteric, hysterical, sensational, sensationalistic, melodramatic, theatric, theatrical, histrionic, dramatic, overdramatic, hammy <nf>, nonrational, unreasoning; overemotional, hyperthymic

20 sensitive, sensible, emotionable, passible <old>, delicate; responsive, sympathetic, receptive, empathetic, caring; susceptible, impressionable; **tender, soft, tenderhearted, softhearted,** warmhearted

21 sentimental, sentimentalized, soft, **mawkish, maudlin,** cloying; sticky *and* gooey *and* schmaltzy *and* sappy *and* soppy <nf>, oversentimental, oversentimentalized, bathetic; **mushy** *or* sloppy *or* gushing *or* teary *or* beery <nf>, treacly <Brit nf>; tearjerking <nf>; namby-pamby, romantic; nostalgic, nostomanic

22 affecting, touching, moving, emotive, pathetic

23 affected, moved, touched, impressed; impressed with *or* by, penetrated with, seized with, imbued with, devoured by, obsessed, obsessed with *or* by; wrought up by; stricken, wracked, racked, torn, agonized, tortured; worked up, all worked up, **excited** 105.18

24 **deep-felt,** deepgoing, from the heart, heartfelt, homefelt <old>; **deep, profound;** indelible; pervasive, pervading, absorbing; penetrating, penetrant, piercing; **poignant,** keen, sharp, acute

ADVS 25 **feelingly, emotionally,** affectively; affectingly, touchingly, movingly, **with feeling,** poignantly

26 **fervently, fervidly, passionately, impassionedly,** intensely, **ardently,** zealously; keenly, breathlessly, excitedly; warmly, heatedly, glowingly; heartily, cordially; enthusiastically, exuberantly, vigorously; kindly, heart and soul, with all one's heart, from the heart, from the bottom of one's heart

27 **sentimentally,** mawkishly, maudlinly, cloyingly; mushily *and* sloppily *and* gushingly <nf>

94 LACK OF FEELING

NOUNS 1 **unfeeling,** unfeelingness, affectlessness, lack of affect, lack of feeling *or* feeling tone, emotional deadness *or* numbness *or* paralysis, **anesthesia, emotionlessness,** unemotionalism, unexcitability; **dispassion,** dispassionateness, unpassionateness, **objectivity;** passionlessness, **spiritlessness, heartlessness,** soullessness; **coldness, coolness, frigidity,** chill, chilliness, frostiness, iciness; coldheartedness, cold-bloodedness; cold heart, cold blood; cold fish; **unresponsiveness,** unsympatheticness; lack of touch *or* contact, autism, self-absorption, withdrawal, catatonia; unimpressionableness, unimpressibility; insusceptibility, unsusceptibility; **impassiveness,** impassibility, impassivity; straight face *and* poker face <nf>, deadpan <nf>; immovability, untouchability; **dullness, obtuseness;** inexcitability 106

2 **insensibility,** insensibleness, **unconsciousness,** unawareness, **obliviousness,** oblivion; anesthesia, narcosis

3 **callousness, insensitivity,** insensitiveness, philistinism; **coarseness, brutalization, hardness,** hardenedness, **hard-heartedness, hardness of heart,** hard heart, stony-heartedness, heart of stone, stoniness, marbleheartedness, flintheartedness, flintiness; **obduracy,** obdurateness, induration, inuredness; imperviousness, **thick skin,** rhinoceros hide, thick *or* hard-shell, armor, formidable defenses

4 **apathy, indifference, unconcern,** lack of caring, disinterest; withdrawnness, **aloofness, detachment,** ataraxy *or* ataraxia, **dispassion; passiveness,**

passivity, supineness, insouciance, nonchalance; inappetence, lack of appetite; **listlessness, spiritlessness,** burnout, blah *or* blahs <nf>, heartlessness, plucklessness, spunklessness; **lethargy, phlegm,** lethargicalness, phlegmaticalness, phlegmaticness, hebetude, **dullness,** sluggishness, languor, languidness; soporifousness, sopor, coma, comatoseness, torpidness, torpor, torpidity, **stupor,** stupefaction, narcosis; acedia, sloth; **resignation,** resignedness, stoicism; **numbness,** benumbedness; hopelessness 125

VERBS 5 not be affected by, remain unmoved, not turn a hair, not care less <nf>; have a thick skin, have a heart of stone; be cold as ice, be a cold fish, be an icicle; not affect, leave one cold *or* unmoved, unimpress, underwhelm <nf>

6 **callous, harden,** case harden, **harden one's heart,** ossify, steel, indurate, inure; brutalize

7 **dull, blunt,** desensitize, obtund, hebetate

8 **numb, benumb,** paralyze, **deaden,** anesthetize, freeze, **stun, stupefy,** drug, narcotize

ADJS 9 **unfeeling, unemotional,** nonemotional, emotionless, affectless, emotionally dead *or* numb *or* paralyzed, anesthetized, drugged, narcotized; **unpassionate, dispassionate,** unimpassioned, **objective;** passionless, **spiritless, heartless,** soulless; lukewarm, Laodicean; **cold, cool, frigid,** frozen, chill, chilly, arctic, frosty, frosted, icy, **coldhearted, cold-blooded,** cold as charity; **unaffectionate,** unloving; **unresponsive,** unresponding, **unsympathetic;** out of touch *or* contact; in one's shell *or* armor, behind one's defenses; autistic, self-absorbed, self-centered, egocentric, catatonic; unimpressionable, unimpressible, insusceptible, unsusceptible, unperturbed, imperturbable, undisturbed; **impassive,** impassible; immovable, untouchable; dull, obtuse, blunt; **inexcitable** 106.10

10 **insensible, unconscious,** unaware, **oblivious,** blind to, deaf to, dead to, lost to

11 **unaffected, unmoved, untouched,** dry-eyed, unimpressed, unshaken, unstruck, **unstirred,** unruffled, unanimated, uninspired

12 **callous, calloused, insensitive,** Philistine; **thick-skinned,** pachydermatous; **hard, hard-hearted, hardened,** case-hardened, coarsened, brutalized, indurated, stony, stony-hearted, marblehearted, flinthearted, flinty, steely, impervious, inured, armored *or* steeled against, proof against, as hard as nails

13 **apathetic, indifferent, unconcerned,** uncaring, **disinterested, uninterested; withdrawn, aloof, detached,** Olympian, above it all; **passive,** supine; stoic, stoical; insouciant, nonchalant, blasé,

listless, spiritless, burned-out, blah <nf>, heartless, pluckless, spunkless; **lethargic, phlegmatic,** hebetudinous, **dull,** desensitized, sluggish, torpid, languid, slack, soporific, comatose, **stupefied,** in a stupor, **numb,** numbed, benumbed; resigned; hopeless 125.12

ADVS **14 unfeelingly, unemotionally,** emotionlessly; with a straight or poker face <nf>, deadpan <nf>; **dispassionately,** unpassionately; **spiritlessly, heartlessly,** coldly, coldheartedly, cold-bloodedly, **in cold blood;** with dry eyes

15 apathetically, indifferently, unconcernedly, disinterestedly, uninterestedly, uncaringly, impassively; **listlessly, spiritlessly,** heartlessly, plucklessly, spunklessly; **lethargically, phlegmatically,** dully, numbly

95 PLEASURE

NOUNS **1 pleasure, enjoyment;** quiet pleasure, euphoria, well-being, good feeling, **contentment, content, ease,** comfort 121; coziness, warmth; **gratification, satisfaction,** great satisfaction, hearty enjoyment, keen pleasure or satisfaction; **self-gratification,** self-indulgence; instant gratification; luxury; **relish, zest, gusto,** joie de vivre <Fr>; sweetness of life, douceur de vivre <Fr>; kicks <nf>, **fun,** entertainment, amusement 743; intellectual pleasure, pleasures of the mind; **strokes** and stroking and ego massage <nf>; physical pleasure, creature comforts, bodily pleasure, sense or sensuous pleasure; sexual pleasure, voluptuousness, sensual pleasure, volupté <Fr>, animal pleasure, animal comfort, bodily comfort, fleshly or carnal delight; forepleasure, titillation, endpleasure, fruition; sensualism, hedonism

2 happiness, felicity, gladness, delight, delectation; **joy, joyfulness,** joyance <old>; **cheer,** cheerfulness, exhilaration, **exuberance, high spirits, glee,** sunshine; gaiety 109.4, overjoyfulness, overhappiness; intoxication; **rapture,** ravishment, bewitchment, **enchantment,** unalloyed happiness; elation, exaltation; **ecstasy,** ecstasies, transport; **bliss,** blissfulness; beatitude, beatification, blessedness; paradise, heaven, seventh heaven, cloud nine; smiley face

3 treat, regalement, regale; **feast, banquet,** revelment, regale, Lucullan feast; feast or banquet of the soul; round of pleasures, mad round; **festivity,** fete, fiesta, festive occasion, celebration, merrymaking, revel, revelry, jubilation, joyance; carnival, Mardi Gras

4 pleasure-loving, pleasure principle, hedonism, hedonics; epicureanism, Cyrenaicism, eudaemonism

5 <period of pleasure> good time, fun time, happy hour, bread and circuses, la dolce vita <Ital>, life of Riley, easy street, bed of roses, Elysium, Elysian fields, land of milk and honey

VERBS **6 please, pleasure, give pleasure,** afford one pleasure, be to one's liking, sit well with one, meet one's wishes, take or strike one's fancy, feel good or right, strike one right; do one's heart good, warm the cockles of one's heart, tickle pink <nf>; **suit,** suit one down to the ground

7 <nf terms> **hit the spot,** be just the ticket, be just what the doctor ordered, **make a hit,** go over big, go over with a bang

8 gratify, satisfy, sate, satiate; slake, appease, allay, assuage, quench; regale, feed, feast; do one's heart good, warm the cockles of the heart

9 gladden, make happy, happify; bless, beatify; cheer 109.7

10 delight, delectate, **tickle, titillate, thrill, enrapture, enthrall, enchant,** entrance, fascinate, captivate, bewitch, **charm,** becharm; enravish, ravish, imparadise; ecstasiate, transport, carry away

11 <nf terms> **give one a bang** or kick or charge or rush, knock out, knock off one's feet or dead or for a loop, knock one's socks off, thrill to death or to pieces, tickle to death, tickle pink, **wow,** slay, send, freak out; **stroke,** massage one's ego

12 be pleased, feel happy, feel good, sing, purr, smile, laugh, be wreathed in smiles, beam; **delight,** joy, take great satisfaction; look like the cat that swallowed the canary; brim or burst with joy, walk or tread on air, have stars in one's eyes, be in heaven or seventh heaven or paradise, be on cloud nine; fall or go into raptures; die with delight or pleasure

13 enjoy, pleasure in, be pleased with, receive or derive pleasure from, take delight or pleasure in, get a kick or boot or bang or charge or lift or rush out of <nf>; **like, love,** adore <nf>; **delight in, rejoice in,** indulge in, luxuriate in, revel in, riot in, bask in, wallow in, swim in; groove on and get high on and freak out on <nf>; feast on, gloat over or on; **relish, appreciate,** roll under the tongue, do justice to, savor, smack the lips; devour, eat up

14 enjoy oneself, have a good time, party, live it up <nf>, have the time of one's life, have a ball or blast <nf>

ADJS **15 pleased, delighted; glad,** gladsome; **charmed,** intrigued <nf>; **thrilled; tickled,** tickled to death and tickled pink <nf>, exhilarated; **gratified, satisfied;** pleased with, taken with, favorably impressed with, sold on <nf>, turned-on; pleased as Punch, pleased as a child with a new toy; euphoric, eupeptic; **content, contented,** easy, **comfortable** 121.11, cozy, in clover, snug as a bug in a rug <nf>

16 **happy, glad, joyful, joyous,** flushed with joy, radiant, beaming, glowing, starry-eyed, sparkling, laughing, smiling, smirking, smirky, chirping, purring, singing, dancing, leaping, capering, **cheerful,** gay 109.14; **blissful,** "throned on highest bliss"—Milton; blessed; beatified, beatific; thrice happy, "thrice and four times blessed"—Vergil; happy as a lark, happy as a king, happy as the day is long, happy as a clam at high water, happy as a pig in shit <nf>, happy as a sand boy <Brit>

17 **overjoyed,** overjoyful, overhappy, brimming *or* bursting with happiness, on top of the world; **rapturous,** raptured, **enraptured, enchanted,** entranced, enravished, ravished, rapt, possessed; sent *and* high *and* freaked-out <nf>, **in raptures,** transported, in a transport of delight, **carried away,** rapt *or* ravished away, beside oneself, beside oneself with joy, all over oneself <nf>; **ecstatic,** in ecstasies, ecstasiating; rhapsodic, rhapsodical; imparadised, **in paradise,** in heaven, in seventh heaven, on cloud nine <nf>; **elated,** elate, exalted, jubilant, exultant, flushed

18 **pleasure-loving,** pleasure-seeking, fun-loving, hedonic, hedonistic; Lucullan; epicurean, Cyrenaic, eudaemonic

ADVS 19 **happily, gladly, joyfully, joyously, delightedly,** with pleasure, to one's delight; blissfully, blessedly; **ecstatically,** rhapsodically, **rapturously; elatedly,** jubilantly, exultantly

20 **for fun,** for the hell *or* heck *or* devil of it <nf>

INTERJS 21 **goody!,** goody, goody!, goody gumdrops!, good-o! <Brit>; whee!, **wow!,** u-mm!, mmmm!, oooo!, oo-la-la!; oh boy!, boy oh boy!, boy!, man!, hot dog!, hot ziggety!, hot diggety!, whoopee!, wowie zowie!, out of sight! *or* outa sight!, groovy!, keen-o!, keen-o-peachy!

96 UNPLEASURE

NOUNS 1 **unpleasure,** unpleasantness 98, **lack of pleasure,** joylessness, cheerlessness; unsatisfaction, nonsatisfaction, ungratification, nongratification; grimness; discontent 108; displeasure, dissatisfaction, **discomfort,** uncomfortableness, misease <old>, malaise, **painfulness; disquiet,** inquietude, **uneasiness,** unease, discomposure, vexation of spirit, **anxiety;** angst, anguish, dread, nausea, existential woe, existential vacuum; the blahs <nf>; **dullness,** flatness, staleness, tastelessness, savorlessness; ashes in the mouth; **boredom,** ennui, tedium, tediousness, spleen; emptiness, spiritual void, death of the heart *or* soul; unhappiness 112.2; dislike 99

2 **annoyance, vexation,** bothersomeness, exasperation, *tracasserie* <Fr>, **aggravation; nuisance, pest, bother,** botheration <nf>, public nuisance, **trouble, problem,** pain <nf>, difficulty, hot potato <nf>; **trial; bore,** crashing bore <nf>; **drag** *and* downer <nf>; **worry,** worriment <nf>; downside *and* the bad news <nf>; stress, fear, pressure, anxiety, angst; **headache** <nf>; **pain in the neck** *or* **in the ass** <nf>; **harassment,** molestation, persecution, dogging, hounding, harrying; devilment, bedevilment; vexatiousness 98.7; bogey *or* bogy

3 **irritation, aggravation,** exacerbation, worsening, salt in the wound, twisting the knife in the wound, embitterment, **provocation;** fret, gall, chafe; irritant; pea in the shoe

4 **chagrin, distress; embarrassment, abashment, discomfiture,** egg on one's face <nf>, disconcertion, disconcertment, discountenance, discomposure, disturbance, confusion; **humiliation, shame,** shamefacedness, mortification, red face

5 **pain, distress, grief,** stress, stress of life, suffering, passion, dolor; ache, aching; pang, wrench, throes, cramp, spasm, twinge; wound, injury, hurt; **sore,** sore spot, soreness, tender spot, tenderness, lesion; strain, sprain; cut, stroke; shock, blow, hard *or* nasty blow; malady, illness, disease, plague; bane

6 **wretchedness, despair,** bitterness, infelicity, **misery, anguish, agony, woe,** woefulness, woesomeness <old>, bale, balefulness; **melancholy,** melancholia, **depression, sadness,** grief 112.10; **heartache,** aching heart, heavy heart, bleeding heart, broken heart, agony of mind *or* spirit; suicidal despair, black night of the soul, **despondency,** gloom and doom, despond, "Slough of Despond"—Bunyan; **desolation,** prostration, crushing; extremity, depth of misery; sloth, acedia

7 **torment, torture,** cruciation <old>, excruciation, crucifixion, passion, laceration, clawing, lancination, flaying, excoriation; the rack, the iron maiden, thumbscrews; **persecution; martyrdom; purgatory,** living death, hell, hell upon earth; holocaust; nightmare, horror

8 **affliction,** infliction; **curse, woe,** distress, grievance, **sorrow,** *tsures* <Yiddish>; **trouble,** peck *or* pack of troubles, "sea of troubles"—Shakespeare; **care,** burden of care; **burden,** adversity, **oppression, cross, cross to bear** *or* **be borne, load,** fardel <old>, imposition, encumbrance, weight, albatross around one's neck, millstone around one's neck; thorn, thorn in the side, crown of thorns; white elephant; bitter pill, bitter draft, bitter cup, cup *or* waters of bitterness; gall, gall and wormwood; "the thousand natural

shocks that flesh is heir to"—Shakespeare, "all the ills that men endure"—Abraham Cowley; Pandora's box

9 trial, tribulation, trials and tribulations; **ordeal,** fiery ordeal, the iron entering the soul

10 tormentor, torment; torturer; **nuisance, pest,** pesterer, pain *and* pain in the neck *or* ass <nf>, nag, nudzh <nf>, *nudnik* <Yiddish>, public nuisance; **tease,** teaser; annoyer, harasser, harrier, badgerer, **heckler,** plaguer, persecutor, sadist; molester, **bully**

11 sufferer, victim, prey; **wretch,** poor devil <nf>, object of compassion; martyr

VERBS **12** give no pleasure *or* joy *or* cheer *or* comfort, **disquiet,** discompose, leave unsatisfied; discontent; taste like ashes in the mouth; **bore,** be tedious, cheese off <Brit nf>

13 annoy, irk, vex, nettle, provoke, pique, miff *and* peeve <nf>, distemper, **ruffle, disturb,** discompose, **roil,** rile, **aggravate,** make a nuisance of oneself, **exasperate,** exercise, try one's patience, try the patience of a saint; **put one's back up,** make one bristle; **gripe;** give one a pain <nf>; get, get one down, **get one's goat,** get under one's skin, get in one's hair, tread on one's toes; burn up *and* brown off <nf>; **torment, molest, bother,** pother; **harass,** harry, drive up the wall <nf>, **hound,** dog, nag, nobble <Brit nf>, nudzh <nf>, **persecute; heckle,** pick *or* prod at, rub it in *and* rub one's nose in it <nf>, badger, hector, bait, bullyrag, worry, worry at, nip at the heels of, chivy, hardly give one time to breathe, make one's life miserable, keep on at; **bug** <nf>, be on the back of *and* be at *and* ride <nf>, **pester, tease, needle,** devil, get after *or* get on <nf>, **bedevil, pick on** <nf>, tweak the nose, pluck the beard, give a bad time to <nf>; **plague,** beset, beleaguer; catch in the crossfire *or* in the middle; catch one off balance, trip one up

14 irritate, aggravate, exacerbate, worsen, rub salt in the wound, twist the knife in the wound, step on one's corns, barb the dart; touch a soft spot *or* tender spot, touch a raw nerve, touch where it hurts; provoke, **gall, chafe, fret,** grate, grit *and* gravel <nf>, rasp; **get on one's nerves, grate on,** set on edge; **set one's teeth on edge,** go against the grain; **rub one** *or* **one's fur the wrong way**

15 chagrin, embarrass, abash, discomfit, disconcert, discompose, confuse, throw into confusion *or* a tizzy *or* a hissy-fit, **upset,** confound, cast down, mortify, put out, put out of face *or* countenance, put to the blush

16 distress, afflict, trouble, burden, give one a tough row to hoe, load with care, **bother, disturb,** perturb, disquiet, discomfort, agitate, upset, put to it; **worry,** give one gray hair

17 pain, grieve, aggrieve, anguish; **hurt, wound,** bruise, **hurt one's feelings;** pierce, prick, stab, cut, sting; **cut up** <nf>, **cut to the heart,** wound *or* sting *or* cut to the quick, hit one where one lives <nf>; be a thorn in one's side

18 torture, torment, agonize, harrow, savage, **rack,** scarify, crucify, impale, excruciate, lacerate, claw, rip, bloody, lancinate, macerate, convulse, wring; prolong the agony, kill by inches, make life miserable *or* not worth living; martyr, martyrize; **tyrannize,** push around <nf>; punish 604.10

19 suffer, hurt, ache, bleed; anguish, **suffer anguish; agonize,** writhe; go hard with, have a bad time of it, go through hell; quaff the bitter cup, drain the cup of misery to the dregs, be nailed to the cross

ADJS **20 pleasureless,** joyless, cheerless, depressed 112.22, grim; **sad,** unhappy 112.21; unsatisfied, unfulfilled, ungratified; **bored,** cheesed off <Brit nf>; anguished, anxious, suffering angst *or* dread *or* nausea, uneasy, unquiet, prey to malaise; **repelled,** revolted, **disgusted,** sickened, nauseated, nauseous

21 annoyed, irritated, bugged <nf>; galled, chafed; **bothered, troubled, disturbed, ruffled, roiled,** riled; **irked, vexed, piqued, nettled, provoked, peeved** *and* miffed <nf>, **griped, aggravated, exasperated;** burnt-up *and* browned-off <nf>, resentful, angry 152.28

22 distressed, afflicted, put-upon, beset, beleaguered; caught in the middle *or* in the crossfire; **troubled, bothered, disturbed, perturbed, disquieted,** discomforted, discomposed, agitated; hung up <nf>; **uncomfortable,** uneasy, ill at ease; **chagrined, embarrassed,** abashed, discomfited, **disconcerted, upset, confused,** mortified, **put-out,** out of countenance, cast down, chapfallen

23 pained, grieved, aggrieved; **wounded, hurt,** injured, **bruised,** mauled; **cut,** cut to the quick; **stung;** anguished, aching, bleeding

24 tormented, plagued, harassed, harried, dogged, **hounded, persecuted,** beset; nipped at, worried, chivied, **heckled,** badgered, hectored, baited, bullyragged, ragged, **pestered, teased, needled,** deviled, **bedeviled, picked on** <nf>, **bugged** <nf>

25 tortured, harrowed, savaged, **agonized,** convulsed, wrung, racked, crucified, impaled, lacerated, excoriated, clawed, ripped, bloodied, lancinated; on the rack, under the harrow

26 wretched, miserable; woeful, woebegone, woesome <old>; crushed, stricken, **cut up** <nf>, heartsick, heart-stricken, heart-struck; deep-troubled; desolate, disconsolate, suicidal

ADVS **27** to one's displeasure, to one's disgust

97 PLEASANTNESS

NOUNS **1 pleasantness,** pleasingness, pleasance, **pleasure** 95, pleasurefulness, **pleasurableness,** pleasurability, pleasantry <old>, felicitousness, **enjoyableness; bliss, blissfulness;** felicitousness; sweetness, mellifluousness, *douceur* <Fr>; mellowness; **agreeableness,** agreeability, complaisance, rapport, harmoniousness; compatibility; welcomeness; geniality, congeniality, cordiality, *Gemütlichkeit* <Ger>, affability, amicability, amiability; amenity, graciousness; goodness, goodliness, niceness; **fun** 743.2, 95.1; heaven

2 delightfulness, exquisiteness, loveliness; **charm,** winsomeness, grace, **attractiveness, appeal,** appealingness, winningness; sexiness <nf>; **glamour;** captivation, enchantment, entrancement, bewitchment, witchery, enravishment, **fascination** 377.1; invitingness, temptingness, tantalizingness; voluptuousness, sensuousness; luxury

3 delectability, delectableness, deliciousness, lusciousness; tastiness, flavorsomeness, savoriness; juiciness; succulence

4 cheerfulness; brightness, sunniness; sunny side, bright side; fair weather

VERBS **5** make pleasant, brighten, sweeten, gild, gild the lily *or* pill; sentimentalize, saccharinize; please, gratify, satisfy; brighten one's day, make one's day <nf>

ADJS **6 pleasant, pleasing, pleasureful, pleasurable;** fair, fair and pleasant, **enjoyable,** pleasure-giving; felicitous, felicific; **likable, desirable,** to one's liking, to one's taste, to *or* after one's fancy, after one's own heart; **agreeable,** complaisant, harmonious, *en rapport* <Fr>, compatible; **blissful;** sweet, mellifluous, honeyed, dulcet; mellow; **gratifying,** satisfying, rewarding, heartwarming, grateful; **welcome,** welcome as the roses in May; genial, congenial, cordial, *gemütlich* <Ger>, affable, amiable, amicable, gracious; good, goodly, nice, fine; cheerful 109.11

7 delightful, exquisite, lovely; thrilling, titillative; good-natured; **charming, attractive, endearing, engaging, appealing,** prepossessing, heartwarming, sexy <nf>, **enchanting,** bewitching, witching, entrancing, enthralling, intriguing, fascinating; **captivating, irresistible, ravishing,** enravishing; **winning,** winsome, taking, fetching, heart-robbing; inviting, tempting, tantalizing; voluptuous, zaftig <nf>, sensuous; luxurious, delicious

8 <nf terms> **fun, kicky,** chewy, dishy, drooly, sexy, toast, yummy

9 blissful, beatific, saintly, divine; sublime; **heavenly,** idyllic, paradisal, paradisiac, paradisiacal,

paradisic, paradisical, empyreal *or* empyrean, Elysian; out of sight *or* of this world <nf>

10 delectable, delicious, luscious; tasty, flavorsome, savory; juicy, succulent

11 bright, sunny, fair, mild, balmy; halcyon, Saturnian

ADVS **12 pleasantly, pleasingly, pleasurably,** fair, **enjoyably; blissfully; gratifyingly,** satisfyingly; agreeably, genially, affably, cordially, amiably, amicably, graciously, kindly; cheerfully 109.17

13 delightfully, exquisitely; charmingly, engagingly, appealingly, enchantingly, bewitchingly, entrancingly, intriguingly, fascinatingly; ravishingly, enravishingly; **winningly,** winsomely; invitingly, temptingly, tantalizingly, voluptuously, sensuously; luxuriously

14 delectably, deliciously, lusciously, tastily, succulently, savorously

98 UNPLEASANTNESS

NOUNS **1 unpleasantness,** unpleasingness, displeasingness, displeasure; **disagreeableness,** disagreeability, *désagrément* <Fr>; **abrasiveness,** woundingess, hostility, unfriendliness; **undesirability,** unappealingness, unattractiveness, unengagingness, uninvitingness, unprepossessingness; **distastefulness,** unsavoriness, unpalatability, nastiness, **undelectability;** ugliness 1014; discomfort, pain, annoyance

2 offensiveness, objectionability, objectionableness, unacceptability; repugnance, contrariety, **odiousness, repulsiveness,** repellence *or* repellency, rebarbativeness, disgustingness, offensiveness, nauseousness, grossness *and* yuckiness *and* grunginess *and* scuzziness <nf>; **loathsomeness, hatefulness,** beastliness <nf>; **vileness, foulness,** putridness, putridity, rottenness, noxiousness; **nastiness,** fulsomeness, noisomeness, **obnoxiousness,** abominableness, heinousness; **contemptibleness,** contemptibility, despicability, **despicableness,** baseness, ignobleness, ignobility; unspeakableness; coarseness, grossness, crudeness, rudeness, obscenity

3 dreadfulness, horribleness, horridness, atrociousness, atrocity, hideousness, terribleness, awfulness <nf>; grimness, direness, banefulness

4 harshness, agony, agonizingness, excruciation, excruciatingness, **torture,** torturesomeness, torturousness, **torment,** tormentingness; desolation, desolateness; heartbreak, heartsickness

5 distressfulness, distress, grievousness, grief; painfulness, pain 26; **harshness,** bitterness, sharpness; lamentability, lamentableness, deplorability, deplorableness, pitiableness, pitifulness, pitiability, regrettableness; **woe,**

sadness, sorrowfulness, mournfulness, lamentation, woefulness, woesomeness <old>, woebegoneness, pathos, poignancy; comfortlessness, discomfort, misease <old>; dreariness, cheerlessness, joylessness, dismalness, **depression,** bleakness

6 **mortification,** humiliation, embarrassment, egg on one's face <nf>; disconcertedness, awkwardness

7 **vexatiousness, irksomeness, annoyance,** annoyingness, aggravation, exasperation, provocation, provokingness, tiresomeness, wearisomeness; **troublesomeness, bothersomeness,** harassment; worrisomeness, plaguesomeness, peskiness *and* pestiferousness <nf>

8 **harshness, oppressiveness, burdensomeness,** onerousness, weightiness, heaviness

9 **intolerability,** intolerableness, unbearableness, insupportableness, insufferableness, **unendurability**

VERBS 10 **be unpleasant; displease,** make unpleasant; be disagreeable *or* undesirable *or* distasteful *or* abrasive

11 **offend,** give offense, **repel,** put off, turn off <nf>, **revolt, disgust,** nauseate, sicken, make one sick, make one sick to *or* in the stomach, make one vomit *or* puke *or* retch, turn the stomach, gross out <nf>; stink in the nostrils; stick in one's throat, stick in one's crop *or* craw *or* gizzard <nf>; **horrify, appall,** shock; make the flesh creep *or* crawl, make one shudder

12 **agonize,** excruciate, **torture, torment,** desolate

13 **mortify,** humiliate, embarrass, disconcert, disturb

14 **distress, dismay,** grieve, mourn, lament, sorrow; pain, discomfort, misease <old>; get in one's hair, try one's patience, give one a hard time *or* a pain *or* a pain in the neck *or* ass *or* butt <nf>, disturb, put off

15 **vex, irk, annoy, aggravate,** exasperate, provoke; **trouble, worry,** give one gray hair, plague, harass, bother, hassle

16 **oppress, burden,** weigh upon, weight down, wear one down, be heavy on one, crush one; **tire, exhaust,** weary, wear out, wear upon one; prey on the mind, prey on *or* upon; **haunt,** haunt the memory, obsess

ADJS 17 **unpleasant, unpleasing, unenjoyable; displeasing, disagreeable; unlikable,** dislikable; **abrasive,** wounding, hostile, unfriendly; **undesirable,** unattractive, unappealing, unengaging, uninviting, unalluring; tacky *and* low rent *and* low ride <nf>; unwelcome, thankless; **distasteful,** untasteful, **unpalatable,** unsavory, unappetizing, undelicious, **undelectable;** ugly 1015.6; sour, **bitter**

18 **offensive, objectionable, odious, repulsive,** repellent, rebarbative, **repugnant, revolting,** forbidding; **disgusting, sickening, loathsome,** gross *and* yucky *and* grungy *and* scuzzy <nf>, beastly <nf>, **vile, foul, nasty,** nauseating 64.7; grody <nf>; fulsome, mephitic, miasmal, miasmic, malodorous, stinking, fetid, noisome, noxious; coarse, gross, crude, rude, obscene; **obnoxious, abhorrent, hateful, abominable,** heinous, **contemptible, despicable,** detestable, execrable, beneath *or* below contempt, **base,** ignoble, uncouth

19 **horrid, horrible,** horrific, **horrifying,** horrendous, unspeakable, beyond words; **dreadful, atrocious, terrible, rotten,** awful *and* beastly <nf>, **hideous; tragic;** dire, grim, baneful; appalling, shocking, disgusting

20 **distressing,** distressful, dismaying; from hell <nf>; afflicting, afflictive; **painful,** sore, **harsh, bitter,** sharp; **grievous,** dolorous, dolorific, dolorogenic; **lamentable, deplorable,** regrettable, pitiable, piteous, rueful, woeful, woesome <old>, woebegone, **sad,** sorrowful, wretched, mournful, **depressing,** depressive; **pathetic,** affecting, touching, moving, saddening, poignant; comfortless, discomforting, uncomfortable; **desolate,** dreary, cheerless, joyless, dismal, bleak

21 **mortifying,** humiliating, **embarrassing,** crushing, disconcerting, awkward, disturbing

22 **annoying, irritating,** galling, **provoking, aggravating** <nf>, **exasperating; vexatious,** vexing, irking, **irksome,** tiresome, wearisome; **troublesome, bothersome, worrisome,** bothering, troubling, disturbing, plaguing, plaguesome, plaguey <nf>, pestilent, pestilential, **pesky** *and* pesty *and* pestiferous <nf>; tormenting, harassing, worrying; pestering, teasing; importunate, importune; distasteful

23 **agonizing, excruciating, harrowing,** racking, rending, **desolating,** consuming; **tormenting,** torturous; **heartbreaking,** heartrending, **heartsickening,** heartwounding

24 **oppressive, burdensome, crushing,** trying, onerous, heavy, weighty; **harsh,** wearing, wearying, exhausting; overburdensome, tyrannous, grinding

25 **insufferable, intolerable, insupportable, unendurable, unbearable,** past bearing, not to be borne *or* endured, for the birds <nf>, **too much** *or* a bit much <nf>, more than flesh and blood can bear, enough to drive one mad, enough to provoke a saint, enough to make a preacher swear <nf>, enough to try the patience of Job

ADVS 26 **unpleasantly, distastefully** unpleasingly; **displeasingly, offensively, objectionably,** odiously, **repulsively,** repellently, rebarbatively, repugnantly,

revoltingly, disgustingly, sickeningly, loathsomely, vilely, foully, nastily, fulsomely, mephitically, malodorously, fetidly, noisomely, noxiously, obnoxiously, **abhorrently, hatefully, abominably,** contemptibly, **despicably, detestably,** execrably, nauseatingly

27 **horridly, horribly, dreadfully, terribly,** hideously; **tragically;** grimly, direly, banefully; appallingly, shockingly

28 **distressingly,** distressfully; **painfully,** sorely, **grievously,** lamentably, deplorably, pitiably, ruefully, woefully, woesomely <old>, sadly, pathetically; **agonizingly, excruciatingly,** harrowingly, heartbreakingly

29 **annoyingly, irritatingly, aggravatingly, provokingly, exasperatingly;** vexatiously, **irksomely,** tiresomely, wearisomely; **troublesomely, bothersomely,** worrisomely, regrettably

30 **insufferably, intolerably, unbearably, unendurably, insupportably**

INTERJS 31 yuck or eeyuck! or yeeuch! or yeeuch!, phew! or pugh!, ugh!; _feh!_ <Yiddish>; alas, alack

99 DISLIKE

NOUNS 1 **dislike, distaste,** disrelish, scunner; disaffection, **disfavor,** disinclination; disaffinity; **displeasure, disapproval,** disapprobation; instant dislike; rejection

2 **hostility,** antagonism, **enmity** 589; **hatred,** hate 103; **aversion, repugnance,** repulsion, **antipathy,** allergy <nf>, grudge, abomination, **abhorrence, horror,** mortal horror; **disgust, loathing;** nausea; shuddering, cold sweat, creeping flesh

VERBS 3 **dislike,** mislike, disfavor, not like, have no liking for, be no love lost between, **have no use for** <nf>, **not care for,** have no time for, have a disaffinity for, have an aversion to, want nothing to do with, not think much of, entertain or conceive or take a dislike to, take a scunner to, not be able to bear or endure or abide, not give the time of day to <nf>, **disapprove of; disrelish,** have no taste for, not stomach, not have the stomach for, not be one's cup of tea; be hostile to, have it in for <nf>; **hate, abhor, detest,** loathe 103.5

4 **feel disgust,** be nauseated, **sicken at,** choke on, have a bellyful of <nf>; **gag, retch,** keck, heave, vomit, puke, hurl and upchuck and barf <nf>

5 **shudder at,** have one's flesh creep or crawl at the thought of; shrink from, **recoil, revolt at; grimace,** make a face, make a wry face or mouth, turn up one's nose, look down one's nose, look askance, raise one's eyebrows, take a dim view of, show distaste for, disapprove of

6 **repel,** disgust 98.11, gross out <nf>; leave a bad taste in one's mouth, rub the wrong way, antagonize

ADJS 7 **unlikable, distasteful,** mislikable, dislikable, **uncongenial, displeasing,** unpleasant 98.17; **not to one's taste,** not one's sort, not one's cup of tea, counter to one's preferences, offering no delight, against the grain, uninviting; yucky <nf>, unlovable; **abhorrent,** odious 98.18; **intolerable** 98.25

8 **averse, allergic** <nf>, undelighted, out of sympathy, disaffected, disenchanted, **disinclined, displeased,** put off <nf>, not charmed, less than pleased; **disapproving, censorious, judgmental,** pofaced <Brit nf>; unamiable, **unfriendly,** hostile 589.10; death on, down on

9 **disliked, uncared-for, unvalued,** unprized, misprized, undervalued; **despised,** detested, lowly, spat-upon, untouchable; **unpopular, out of favor,** gone begging; **unappreciated,** misunderstood; unsung, thankless; unwept, unlamented, unmourned, undeplored, unmissed, unregretted

10 **unloved,** unbeloved, uncherished, loveless; **lovelorn,** forsaken, **rejected,** jilted, thrown over <nf>, spurned, crossed in love

11 **unwanted,** unwished, undesired; **unwelcome,** undesirous, unasked, unbidden, uninvited, uncalled-for, unasked-for

100 DESIRE

NOUNS 1 **desire, wish,** wanting, **want, need,** desideration; **hope; fancy; will, mind, pleasure,** will and pleasure; heart's desire; **urge,** drive, libido, pleasure principle; concupiscence; horme; wish fulfillment, fantasy; passion, ardor, sexual desire 75.5; **curiosity,** intellectual curiosity, thirst for knowledge, lust for learning; **eagerness** 101

2 **liking, love, fondness;** infatuation, crush; **affection; relish, taste,** gusto, gust <Scot>; **passion, weakness** <nf>

3 **inclination, penchant, partiality, fancy, favor, predilection, preference,** propensity, proclivity, **leaning, bent,** turn, tilt, bias, **affinity;** mutual affinity or attraction; **sympathy,** fascination

4 **wistfulness,** wishfulness, yearnfulness, **nostalgia;** wishful thinking; sheep's eyes, longing or wistful eye; daydream, daydreaming

5 **yearning, yen** <nf>; **longing,** desiderium, **hankering** <nf>, **pining,** honing <nf>, aching; languishment, languishing; **nostalgia, homesickness,** _Heimweh_ <Ger>, _mal du pays_ and _maladie du pays_ <Fr>; nostomania

6 **craving, coveting, lust; hunger, thirst, appetite,** "appetite, an universal wolf"—Shakespeare, appetition, appetency or appetence; aching void;

itch, itching, prurience *or* pruriency; lech <nf>, **sexual** desire 75.5; *cacoëthes* <L>, **mania** 926.12

7 **appetite,** stomach, relish, taste; **hunger, hungriness;** the munchies <nf>, peckishness <Brit nf>; tapeworm <nf>, eyes bigger than one's stomach, wolf in one's stomach, canine appetite; empty stomach, emptiness <nf>, hollow hunger; **thirst,** thirstiness, drought <nf>, dryness; polydipsia; torment of Tantalus; sweet tooth <nf>

8 **greed,** greediness, graspingness, **avarice, cupidity, avidity, voracity, rapacity, lust,** avariciousness, *avaritia and cupiditas* <L>; money-grubbing; avidness, esurience, wolfishness; voraciousness, ravenousness, rapaciousness, sordidness, **covetousness,** acquisitiveness; itching palm; grasping; **piggishness, hoggishness,** swinishness; **gluttony** 672, *gula* <L>; inordinate desire, furor, craze, fury *or* frenzy of desire, overgreediness; insatiable desire, insatiability; incontinence, intemperateness 669.1

9 **aspiration,** reaching high, upward looking; "the desire of the moth for the star"—Shelley; high goal *or* aim *or* purpose, dream, ideals; **idealism** 986.7

10 **ambition,** ambitiousness, vaulting ambition; aim; climbing, status-seeking, social climbing, careerism; opportunism; power-hunger; "the mind's immodesty"—d'Avenant, "the evil shadow of aspiration"—George Macdonald, "the avarice of power"—G G Coulton; noble *or* lofty ambition, magnanimity <old>; "the spur that makes man struggle with destiny"—Donald G Mitchell

11 <object of desire> **desire,** heart's desire, desideration, *desideratum* <L>; wish; **hope;** catch, quarry, prey, game, plum, prize, trophy, brass ring <nf>; status symbol; collectable, collectible; forbidden fruit, ideal, weakness, temptation; lodestone, magnet; golden vision, mecca, glimmering goal; land of heart's desire 986.11; something to be desired, "a consummation devoutly to be wish'd"—Shakespeare; dearest wish, ambition, the height of one's ambition; a sight for sore eyes, a welcome sight; the light at the end of the tunnel

12 **desirer,** wisher, wanter, hankerer <nf>, yearner, coveter; fancier, collector; addict, freak <nf>, glutton, greedy pig, devotee, votary; **aspirant,** aspirer, solicitant, wannabee *and* hopeful *and* would-be <nf>, candidate; **lover,** swain, suitor, squeeze <nf>

13 **desirability; agreeability,** acceptability, unobjectionableness; **attractiveness,** attraction, magnetism, **appeal,** seductiveness, provocativeness, pleasingness; likability, lovability 104.7

VERBS 14 **desire,** desiderate, be desirous of, **wish,** lust after, bay after, kill for *and* give one's right arm for <nf>, die for <nf>, **want,** have a mind to, choose <nf>; would fain do *or* have <old>, would be glad of; **like,** have *or* acquire a taste for, fancy, take to, **take a fancy** *or* a shine to, have a fancy for; have an eye to, have one's eye on; lean toward, tilt toward, have a penchant for, have a weakness *or* soft spot in one's heart for; aim at, set one's cap for, have designs on; wish very much, wish to goodness; **love** 104.18; lust; prefer, favor 371.17

15 **want to, wish to, like to,** love to, choose to; **itch to,** burn to; ache to, long to

16 **wish for, hope for, yearn for,** yen for *and* have a yen for <nf>, **itch for,** lust for, pant for, **long for, pine for,** hone for <nf>, ache for, be hurting for <nf>, weary for, languish for, **be dying for,** thirst for, sigh for, gape for <old>; cry for, clamor for; spoil for <nf>

17 **want with all one's heart, want in the worst way; set one's heart on, have one's heart set on,** give one's kingdom in hell for *or* one's eyeteeth for <nf>

18 **crave, covet, hunger after,** thirst after, crave after, **lust after,** have a lech for <nf>, pant after, run mad after, **hanker for** *or* **after** <nf>; crawl after; aspire after, be consumed with desire; have an itchy *or* itching palm *and* have sticky fingers <nf>

19 **hunger,** hunger for, feel hungry, be peckish <Brit nf>; starve <nf>, be ravenous, raven; **have a good appetite,** be a good trencherman, have a tapeworm <nf>, have a wolf in one's stomach; eye hungrily, lick one's chops <nf>; **thirst,** thirst for; lick one's lips

20 **aspire, be ambitious;** aspire to, try to reach; aim high, keep one's eyes on the stars, raise one's sights, set one's sights, reach for the sky, dream of, "hitch one's wagon to a star"—Emerson

ADJS 21 **desirous,** desiring, desireful <old>, lickerish, **wanting, wishing,** needing, hoping; dying to <nf>; tempted; appetitive, desiderative, optative, libidinous, libidinal; orectic; hormic; **eager;** lascivious, **lustful**

22 **desirous of** *or* **to,** keen on, set on <nf>, bent on; fond of, with a liking for, partial to <nf>; fain of *or* to <old>; inclined toward, leaning toward; **itching for** *or* **to,** aching for *or* to, **dying for** *or* **to;** spoiling for <nf>; mad on *or* for, wild to *or* for <nf>, crazy to *or* for <nf>

23 **wistful,** wishful; **longing, yearning,** yearnful, **hankering** <nf>, **languishing, pining,** honing <nf>; **nostalgic, homesick**

24 **craving,** coveting; **hungering,** hungry, thirsting, thirsty, athirst; **itching,** prurient; fervid; **devoured by desire,** in a frenzy *or* fury of desire, mad with lust, consumed with desire

25 **hungry,** hungering, peckish <Brit nf>; empty <nf>,

unfilled; ravening, **ravenous,** voracious, sharp-set, **wolfish,** dog-hungry <nf>, hungry as a bear; **starved, famished,** starving, famishing, perishing *or* pinched with hunger; fasting, off food, unfed; keeping Lent, Lenten; underfed; half-starved, half-famished

26 **thirsty,** thirsting, athirst; **dry,** parched, droughty <nf>

27 **greedy, avaricious, avid, voracious, rapacious,** cupidinous, esurient, **ravening, grasping, grabby** <nf>, graspy, acquisitive, mercenary, sordid, overgreedy; ravenous, gobbling, devouring; miserly, money-hungry, money-grubbing, money-mad, venal; **covetous,** coveting; **piggish, hoggish,** swinish, a hog for, greedy as a hog; **gluttonous** 672.6; omnivorous, all-devouring; insatiable, insatiate, unsatisfied, unsated, unappeased, unappeasable, limitless, bottomless, unquenchable, quenchless, unslaked, unslakeable, slakeless

28 **aspiring, ambitious,** sky-aspiring, upward-looking, high-reaching; high-flying, social-climbing, careerist, careeristic, fast-track, fast-lane, on the make <nf>; power-hungry; would-be

29 **desired, wanted,** coveted; **wished-for,** hoped-for, longed-for; sought after, in demand, popular

30 **desirable,** sought-after, much sought-after, to be desired, to die for <nf>, **much to be desired; enviable,** worth having; **likable, pleasing,** after one's own heart; **agreeable,** acceptable, unobjectionable; palatable; **attractive,** taking, winning, sexy <nf>, dishy <Brit nf>, **seductive, provocative,** tantalizing, exciting; appetizing, tempting, toothsome, mouth-watering; **lovable,** adorable

ADVS 31 **desirously, wistfully,** wishfully, **longingly, yearningly,** piningly, languishingly; cravingly, itchingly; hungrily, thirstily; aspiringly, ambitiously

32 **greedily, avariciously,** avidly, ravenously, raveningly, voraciously, rapaciously, **covetously,** graspingly, devouringly; wolfishly, **piggishly, hoggishly,** swinishly

101 EAGERNESS

NOUNS 1 **eagerness, enthusiasm, avidity,** avidness, keenness <chiefly Brit>, forwardness, prothymia, **readiness,** promptness, quickness, **alacrity,** cheerful readiness, *empressement* <Fr>; keen desire, **appetite** 100.7; anxiousness, anxiety; **zest,** zestfulness, gusto, verve, **liveliness,** life, **vitality,** vivacity, élan, spirit, animation; **impatience,** breathless impatience 135.1; keen interest, fascination; **craze** 926.12

2 **zeal, ardor, ardency, fervor, fervency, fervidness,**

spirit, warmth, fire, heat, heatedness, **passion,** passionateness, impassionedness, heartiness, intensity, **abandon,** vehemence; intentness, resolution 359; **devotion,** devoutness, devotedness, dedication, commitment, committedness; **earnestness, seriousness,** sincerity; loyalty, faithfulness, faith, fidelity 644.7; discipleship, followership

3 **overzealousness, overeagerness,** overanxiousness, overanxiety; unchecked enthusiasm, **overenthusiasm, infatuation; overambitiousness; frenzy, fury; zealotry,** zealotism; mania, **fanaticism** 925.11

4 **enthusiast, zealot,** infatuate, energumen, rhapsodist; addict; faddist; pursuer; hobbyist, collector; **fanatic,** trainspotter <Brit nf>; visionary 986.13; **devotee,** votary, aficionada, aficionado, **fancier,** admirer, **follower; disciple,** worshiper, idolizer, idolater; amateur, dilettante

5 <nf terms> **fan, buff, freak,** hound, fiend, demon, nut, bug, head, junkie, groupie, rooter, booster, great one for, sucker for; fan club, fanzine; eager beaver, -aholic

VERBS 6 **jump at,** catch, grab, grab at, snatch, snatch at, fall all over oneself, get excited about, go at hammer and tongs *or* tooth and nail, go hog wild <nf>; go to great lengths, lean *or* bend *or* fall over backwards; **desire** 100.14,18

7 **be enthusiastic, rave, enthuse** *and* be big for <nf>; get stars in one's eyes, **rhapsodize, carry on over** *and* rave on <nf>, make much of, **make a fuss over,** make an ado *or* much ado about, make a to-do over *and* take on over <nf>, be *or* go on over *or* about <nf>, rave about *and* whoop it up about <nf>; go nuts *or* gaga *or* ape over <nf>; gush, gush over; effervesce, bubble over

ADJS 8 **eager, anxious,** agog, all agog; **avid, keen,** forward, prompt, quick, ready, ready and willing, alacritous, bursting to, dying to, raring to; **zestful, lively,** full of life, vital, vivacious, vivid, spirited, **animated;** impatient 135.6; breathless, panting, champing at the bit; **desirous** 100.21

9 **zealous, ardent, fervent, fervid,** perfervid, **spirited, intense,** hearty, vehement, abandoned, **passionate,** impassioned, **warm,** heated, hot, hot-blooded, red-hot, fiery, white-hot, flaming, burning, afire, aflame, on fire, like a house afire <nf>; **devout, devoted;** dedicated, committed; **earnest, sincere, serious,** in earnest; loyal, faithful 644.20; intent, intent on, resolute 359.11

10 **enthusiastic, enthused** *and* big <nf>, **gung ho** <nf>, glowing, full of enthusiasm; enthusiastic about, infatuated with

11 <nf terms> **wild about, crazy about, mad about,** ape about *or* over, gone on, all in a dither over,

gaga over, starry-eyed over, all hopped up about, hepped up over, hot about *or* for *or* on, steamed up about, **turned-on, switched-on;** hipped on, **cracked on,** bugs on, freaked-out, **nuts on** *or* **over** *or* **about, keen on** *or* **about,** crazy *or* mad about

12 **overzealous,** ultrazealous, **overeager,** over-anxious; **overambitious;** overdesirous; **overenthusiastic, infatuated;** feverish, perfervid, febrile, at fever *or* fevered pitch; hectic, frenetic, furious, **frenzied,** frantic, **wild,** hysteric, hysterical, delirious; **insane** 926.26; **fanatical** 926.32

ADVS 13 **eagerly, anxiously; impatiently,** breathlessly; **avidly,** promptly, quickly, keenly, readily; zestfully, vivaciously, animatedly; **enthusiastically,** with enthusiasm; **with alacrity,** with zest, with gusto, with relish, with open arms

14 **zealously, ardently, fervently, fervidly,** perfervidly, heatedly, heartily, vehemently, **passionately,** impassionedly; intently, intensely; **devoutly, devotedly;** earnestly, sincerely, seriously

102 INDIFFERENCE

NOUNS 1 **indifference,** indifferentness; indifferentism; halfheartedness, zeallessness, perfunctoriness, fervorlessness; **coolness,** coldness, chilliness, chill, iciness, frostiness; tepidness, **lukewarmness,** Laodiceanism; **neutrality,** neutralness, neuterness; insipidity, vapidity; adiaphorism

2 **unconcern, disinterest, detachment; disregard, dispassion,** insouciance, **carelessness,** regardlessness; easygoingness; **heedlessness,** mindlessness, inattention 983; **unmindfulness,** incuriosity 982; **insensitivity;** disregardfulness, recklessness, negligence 340.1; *je-m'en-foutisme* or *je-m'en-fichisme* <Fr>; unsolicitousness, unanxiousness; pococurantism; **nonchalance,** inexcitability 106, ataraxy *or* ataraxia, samadhi; indiscrimination, casualness 945.1; **listlessness,** lackadaisicalness, lack of feeling *or* affect, **apathy** 94.4; sloth, acedia, phlegm, lethargy

3 **undesirousness,** desirelessness; nirvana; lovelessness, passionlessness; uneagerness, **unambitiousness;** lack of appetite, inappetence

VERBS 4 **not care, not mind, not give** *or* **care a damn,** not give a hoot *or* shit <nf>, not care less *or* two hoots <nf>, care nothing for *or* about, not care a straw about; shrug off, dismiss; **take no interest in,** have no desire for, not think twice about, have no taste *or* relish for; hold no brief for; be half-hearted, temper one's zeal; lose interest

5 **not matter to,** be all one to, take it or leave it; make no difference, make no never-mind <nf>; sit on the fence, remain neutral

ADJS 6 **indifferent, halfhearted,** zealless, perfunctory, fervorless; **cool,** cold 589.9; tepid, **lukewarm,** Laodicean; neither hot nor cold, neither one thing nor the other, "neither fish, nor flesh, nor good red herring"—John Heywood; unmoved; blah, **neuter, neutral**

7 **unconcerned, uninterested, disinterested,** turned-off, **dispassionate,** insouciant, **careless,** regardless; easygoing; incurious 982.3; mindless, **unmindful, heedless,** inattentive 984.6, disregardful; **devil-may-care,** reckless, negligent 340.10; unsolicitous, unanxious; pococurante, **nonchalant,** inexcitable 106.10; ataractic; **blasé,** undiscriminating, casual 945.5; **listless,** lackadaisical, sluggish; bovine; numb, **apathetic** 94.13

8 **undesirous,** unattracted, desireless; loveless, passionless; inappetent; nirvanic; **unenthusiastic,** uneager; **unambitious,** unaspiring

ADVS 9 **indifferently, with indifference,** with utter indifference; coolly, coldly; lukewarmly, halfheartedly; perfunctorily; for all *or* aught one cares

10 **unconcernedly, uninterestedly, disinterestedly,** dispassionately, insouciantly, **carelessly,** regardlessly; mindlessly; **unmindfully, heedlessly,** recklessly, negligently 340.17; **nonchalantly;** listlessly, lackadaisically; numbly, **apathetically** 94.15

PHRS 11 **who cares?,** I don't care, I couldn't care less <nf>; it's a matter of sublime indifference; never mind!, **what does it matter?,** what's the difference?, what's the diff? <nf>, what are the odds?, what of it?, what boots it?, **so what?,** what the hell <nf>, it's all one to me, it's all the same to me, it's no skin off one's nose *or* ass <nf>; like it or lump it; forget it!

12 **I should worry?,** I should fret?, that's your lookout, that's your problem, I feel for you but I can't reach you; that's your pigeon <nf>, that's your tough luck, tough titty *and* shit <nf>

103 HATE

NOUNS 1 **hate, hatred;** dislike 99; **detestation, abhorrence, aversion, antipathy,** repugnance, **loathing,** execration, **abomination,** odium; **spite,** spitefulness, despite, despitefulness, **malice, malevolence,** malignity; vials of hate *or* wrath; rancor, venom; misanthropy, misanthropism; misandry, misogyny; misogamy; misopedia; anti-Semitism; race hatred, racism, racialism; bigotry; phobia, Anglophobia, Russophobia, xenophobia, etc; grudge; scorn, despising, **contempt** 157

2 **enmity** 589; bitterness, **animosity** 589.4; hatefulness

3 <hated thing> **anathema, abomination,**

detestation, aversion, abhorrence, antipathy, execration, hate; peeve, pet peeve; phobia; bugbear, bête noire, bane, bitter pill; fear; dislike

4 hater, man-hater, woman-hater, misanthropist, misanthrope, misogynist, anti-Semite, racist, racialist, white supremacist, bigot, redneck <nf>; phobic, Anglophobe, Russophobe, xenophobe, etc; detester, loather

VERBS **5 hate, detest, loathe, abhor,** execrate, **abominate,** hold in abomination, take an aversion to, shudder at, utterly detest, be death on, not stand, not stand the sight of, not stomach; scorn, **despise** 157.3; hate someone's guts <nf>

6 dislike, have it in for <nf>, disrelish 99.3

ADJS **7 hating, abhorrent,** loathing, despising, venomous, death on; averse to 99.8; disgusted 96.20; scornful, **contemptuous** 157.8; antagonistic; execrative

8 hateful, loathsome, aversive, odious, detestable 98.18; despiteful; unlikable 99.7; **contemptible** 661.12, 98.18

WORD ELEMENTS **9** mis-, miso-; -phobia, -phobiac, -phobe

104 LOVE

NOUNS **1 love, affection, attachment, devotion, fondness,** sentiment, warm feeling, soft spot in one's heart, weakness <nf>, like, **liking,** fancy, shine <nf>; **partiality, predilection;** intimacy; **passion,** tender feeling or passion, **ardor,** ardency, fervor, heart, flame, the real thing <nf>; physical love, Amor, Eros, bodily love, libido, sexual love, sex 75; desire, yearning 100.5; lasciviousness 665.5; charity, *caritas* <L>, brotherly love, Christian love, agape, loving concern, fellow feeling, **caring;** sentimental attachment; spiritual love, platonic love; **adoration,** worship, hero worship; **regard,** admiration; idolization, idolism, idolatry; popular regard, popularity; faithful love, truelove; married love, conjugal love, uxoriousness; free love, free-lovism; **lovemaking** 562; self-love, narcissism, egotism; patriotism, love of one's country

2 "an insatiate thirst of enjoying a greedily desired object"—Montaigne, "the heart's immortal thirst to be completely known and all forgiven"—Henry Van Dyke, "the blood of life, the power of reunion of the separated"—Tillich, "the reflection of a man's own worthiness from other men"—Emerson, "a spiritual coupling of two souls"—Ben Jonson

3 amorousness, amativeness, lovingness, meltingness, **affection, affectionateness,** demonstrativeness; mating instinct, reproductive or procreative drive, libido; carnality, sexiness,

goatishness, hot pants *and* horniness <nf>; romantic love, romanticism, **sentimentality,** susceptibility; lovesickness, lovelornness; ecstasy, rapture; enchantment 95.2

4 infatuation, infatuatedness, passing fancy; **crush** *and* mash *and* pash *and* case <nf>; **puppy love** *and* young love *and* calf love <nf>; love at first sight; falling in love

5 parental love, natural affection, mother or maternal love, father or paternal love; filial love; parental instinct

6 love affair, affair, affair of the heart, **amour, romance,** *affaire d'amour* <Fr>, romantic tie or bond, something between, thing <nf>, relationship, liaison, entanglement, involvement, intrigue; **dalliance,** amorous play, the love game, flirtation, hanky-panky, lollygagging <nf>; triangle, eternal triangle; illicit or unlawful love, forbidden or unsanctified love, adulterous affair, adultery, unfaithfulness, infidelity, cuckoldry; courtship, courting, wooing, pursuit, dating, dallying, betrothal, engagement, going together *and* going out with <nf>, going steady <nf>

7 loveableness, likeableness, lovability, likability, adoreableness, adorability, sweetness, loveliness, lovesomeness; cuddliness, cuddlesomeness; amiability, attractiveness 97.2, desirability, agreeability, amiability; **charm, appeal,** allurement 377; winsomeness, winning ways

8 Love, Cupid, Amor, Eros, Kama; Venus, Aphrodite, Astarte, Freya

9 <symbols> **cupid,** cupidon, amor, amourette, amoretto, *amorino* <Ital>; love-knot

10 sweetheart, loved one, love, beloved, darling, dear, dear one, dearly beloved, well-beloved, truelove, beloved object, **object of one's affections,** light of one's eye or life, light of love; sex object, prey, quarry, game; valentine

11 <nf terms> **sweetie, honey,** honeybunch, honey-bunny, honey bun, honeypie, hon, main squeeze, sweetie-pie, sweet patootie, tootsie, tootsie-pie, tootsy-wootsy, dearie, baby, dreamboat, heartthrob, poopsy, poopsy-woopsy, sugar, sugar-bun, sweets, cookie

12 lover, admirer, adorer, amorist; infatuate, paramour, **suitor, wooer,** pursuer, follower; **flirt,** coquette; vampire, vamp; conquest, catch; devotee; escort, companion, date *and* steady <nf>; significant other, soul mate; squeeze <nf>; old flame <nf>, new flame <nf>

13 beau, inamorato, swain, suitor, escort, man, gallant, cavalier, squire, esquire, *caballero* <Sp>; *amoroso* and *cavaliere servente* <Ital>; sugar daddy <nf>; gigolo; **boyfriend** *and* **fellow** *and* young man *and* flame <nf>; old man <nf>; love-

maker, lover-boy <nf>; **seducer, lady-killer,** ladies'
man, sheik, philanderer, cocksman <nf>; Prince
Charming, Lothario, Romeo; Casanova, Don Juan

14 **ladylove, inamorata,** *amorosa* <Ital>, lady,
mistress, ladyfriend; lass, lassie, jo <Scot>, gill,
jill, Dulcinea

15 <nf terms> **doll, angel,** baby, baby-doll, doll-baby,
buttercup, ducks, ducky, pet, snookums, snooky,
girl, girlfriend, sweetheart, best girl, dream girl;
old lady

16 **favorite,** preference; **darling,** idol, jewel, apple of
one's eye, fair-haired boy, man after one's own
heart; **pet,** fondling, cosset, minion; spoiled child
or darling, *enfant gâté* <Fr>, lap dog; teacher's pet;
matinee idol; tin god, little tin god

17 **fiancé, fiancée,** bride-to-be, affianced, betrothed,
future, intended <nf>

18 **loving couple,** soul mates, lovebirds, turtledoves,
bill-and-cooers; newlyweds, honeymooners; star-
crossed lovers; Romeo and Juliet, Anthony and
Cleopatra, Tristan and Isolde, Pelléas and
Mélisande, Abélard and Héloïse, Daphnis and
Chloë, Aucassin and Nicolette; item <nf>

VERBS 19 **love, be fond of,** be in love with, **care for,**
like, fancy, have a fancy for, take an interest in, **dote**
on *or* **upon,** be desperately in love, burn with love;
be partial to, have a soft spot in one's heart for, have
a weakness *or* fondness for; court, woo, romance

20 <nf terms> **go for,** have an eye *or* eyes for, only
have eyes for, be sweet on, have a crush *or* mash
or case on; have it bad, carry a torch *or* the torch
for, have designs on

21 **cherish, hold dear,** hold in one's heart *or*
affections, think much *or* the world of, prize,
treasure; **admire, regard,** esteem, revere; **adore,**
idolize, worship, dearly love, think worlds *or* the
world of, love to distraction

22 **fall in love, lose one's heart, become enamored,** be
smitten; take to, **take a liking** *or* **fancy to,** take a
shine to *and* fall for <nf>, become attached to,
bestow one's affections on; fall head and ears *or*
head over heels in love, be swept off one's feet;
cotton to <nf>

23 **enamor, endear;** win one's heart, win the love *or*
affections of, take the fancy of, make a hit with
<nf>; **charm,** becharm, **infatuate,** hold in thrall,
command one's affection, **fascinate,** attract, allure,
grow on one, strike *or* tickle one's fancy, **captivate,**
bewitch, enrapture, carry away, sweep off one's
feet, turn one's head, inflame with love; **seduce,**
vamp <nf>, draw on, tempt, tantalize

ADJS 24 **beloved, loved, dear, darling, precious;** pet,
favorite; **adored, admired,** esteemed, revered;
cherished, prized, treasured, held dear; **well-liked,**
popular; **well-beloved,** dearly beloved, dear to one's

heart, after one's heart *or* own heart, dear as the
apple of one's eye

25 **endearing, lovable, likable, adorable,** admirable,
lovely, lovesome, sweet, winning, winsome;
charming; angelic, seraphic; caressable, kissable;
cuddlesome, cuddly

26 **amorous,** amatory, amative, erotic; **sexual**
75.28,29; loverly, loverlike; **passionate, ardent,**
impassioned; desirous 100.21,22; lascivious 665.29

27 **loving,** lovesome, **fond, adoring, devoted,**
affectionate, demonstrative, **romantic,**
sentimental, tender, soft <nf>, melting; lovelorn,
lovesick, languishing; wifely, husbandly, conjugal,
uxorious, faithful; parental, paternal, maternal,
filial; charitable, caritative; self-loving, narcissistic

28 **enamored, charmed,** becharmed, **fascinated,**
captivated, bewitched, enraptured, enchanted;
infatuated, infatuate; **smitten,** heartsmitten,
heartstruck, lovestruck, besotted with

29 **in love,** head over heels in love, over head and ears
in love

30 **fond of, enamored of,** partial to, **in love with,**
attached to, wedded to, devoted to, wrapped up in;
taken with, smitten with, struck with

31 <nf terms> **crazy about,** mad *or* nuts *or* nutty *or*
wild about, swacked on, sweet on, stuck on, gone
on

ADVS 32 **lovingly, fondly, affectionately, tenderly,**
dearly, **adoringly,** devotedly; amorously, ardently,
passionately; with love, with affection, with all
one's love

WORD ELEMENTS 33 phil-, philo-, -phily; -phile;
-philic, -philous

105 EXCITEMENT

NOUNS 1 **excitement,** emotion, excitedness, **arousal,**
stimulation, exhilaration; a high <nf>, manic
state *or* condition

2 **thrill, sensation,** titillation; **tingle,** tingling; quiver,
shiver, shudder, tremor, **tremor of excitement,** rush
<nf>; flush, rush of emotion, surge of emotion

3 <nf terms> **kick, charge,** boot, bang, belt, blast,
flash, hit, jolt, large charge, rush, upper, lift; jollies

4 **agitation, perturbation,** ferment, **turbulence,**
turmoil, tumult, embroilment, uproar, **commotion,**
disturbance, ado, *brouhaha* <Fr>, to-do <nf>;
pell-mell, **flurry,** ruffle, bustle, stir, swirl, swirling,
whirl, vortex, eddy, hurry, hurry-scurry, hurly-
burly; fermentation, yeastiness, effervescence,
ebullience, ebullition; fume

5 **trepidation,** trepidity; **disquiet,** disquietude,
inquietude, **unrest, restlessness,** fidgetiness; **fidgets**
or **shakes** *and* shivers *and* dithers *and* antsyness
<nf>; **quivering, quavering, quaking, shaking,**

trembling; **quiver,** quaver, shiver, shudder, didder <Brit nf>, twitter, **tremor,** tremble, flutter; palpitation, pitapatation <nf>, pit-a-pat, pitter-patter; **throb,** throbbing; panting, heaving

6 **dither, tizzy** <nf>, swivet, foofaraw, **pucker** <nf>, **twitter,** twitteration <nf>, **flutter, fluster,** flusteration *and* flustration <nf>, **fret, fuss,** pother, bother, lather *and* stew *and* snit <nf>, flap; emotional crisis, *crise* <Fr>

7 **fever of excitement, fever pitch,** fever, heat, fever heat, fire; sexual excitement, rut

8 **fury, furor,** furore <Brit>, fire and fury; **ecstasy,** transport, **rapture,** ravishment; intoxication, abandon; **passion, rage,** raging *or* tearing passion, towering rage *or* passion; **frenzy,** orgy, orgasm; madness, craze, **delirium,** hysteria

9 **outburst,** outbreak, **burst, flare-up,** blaze, **explosion,** eruption, irruption, upheaval, convulsion, spasm, seizure, fit, paroxysm; storm, tornado, whirlwind, cyclone, hurricane, gale, tempest, gust; steroid rage, roid rage <nf>; road rage <nf>

10 **excitability,** excitableness, perturbability, agitability; emotional instability, explosiveness, eruptiveness, inflammability, combustibility, tempestuousness, violence, latent violence; **irascibility** 110.2; irritability, edginess, touchiness, prickliness, **sensitivity** 24.3; skittishness, **nervousness** 128; excessive emotion, hyperthymia, **emotionalism** 93.9

11 **excitation, excitement, arousal,** arousing, **stirring,** stirring up, working up, working into a lather <nf>, lathering up, whipping up, steaming up, **agitation, perturbation; stimulation, stimulus, exhilaration,** animation; electrification, galvanization; **provocation, irritation,** aggravation, exasperation, exacerbation, fomentation, inflammation, infuriation, **incitement** 375.4

VERBS 12 **excite, impassion, arouse, rouse,** blow up <old>, **stir, stir up,** set astir, stir the feelings, stir the blood, cause a stir *or* commotion, play on the feelings; **work up,** work into, work up into a lather <nf>, lather up, whip up, **key up,** steam up; **move** 375.12; **foment,** incite 375.17; turn on <nf>; **awaken,** awake, wake, waken, wake up; call up, summon up, call forth; **kindle,** enkindle, light up, light the fuse, **fire, inflame,** heat, warm, set fire to, set on fire, fire *or* warm the blood; fan, fan the fire *or* flame, blow the coals, stir the embers, feed the fire, add fuel to the fire *or* flame, pour oil on the fire; raise to a fever heat *or* pitch, bring to the boiling point; overexcite; **annoy, incense; enrage, infuriate;** frenzy, madden

13 **stimulate, whet, sharpen,** pique, provoke, quicken, enliven, liven up, pick up, jazz up <nf>, animate,

exhilarate, invigorate, galvanize, fillip, give a fillip to; infuse life into, give new life to, revive, renew, resuscitate

14 **agitate, perturb, disturb, trouble, disquiet, discompose,** discombobulate <nf>, unsettle, **stir, ruffle, shake, shake up, shock, upset,** make waves, jolt, jar, rock, stagger, electrify, bring *or* pull one up short, give one a turn <nf>; fuss <nf>, flutter, flurry, rattle, disconcert, **fluster**

15 **thrill, tickle,** thrill to death *or* to pieces, give a thrill, **give one a kick** *or* boot *or* charge *or* bang *or* lift <nf>; intoxicate, fascinate, titillate, take one's breath away

16 **be excitable,** excite easily; **get excited, have a fit;** catch the infection; **explode, flare up,** flash up, flame up, fire up, catch fire, take fire; **fly into a passion,** go into hysterics, have a tantrum *or* temper tantrum, come apart; ride off in all directions at once, run around like a chicken with its head cut off; **rage, rave, rant,** rant and rave, rave on, bellow, **storm,** ramp; be angry, smolder, **seethe** 152.15

17 <nf terms> **work oneself up,** work oneself into a sweat, lather, have a short fuse, get hot under the collar, run a temperature, race one's motor, get into a dither *or* tizzy *or* swivet *or* pucker *or* stew; blow up, **blow one's top** *or* stack *or* cool, **flip,** flip out, flip one's lid *or* wig, pop one's cork, wig out, blow a gasket, fly off the handle, **hit the ceiling,** go ape, go hog wild, go bananas, lose one's cool, go off the deep end

18 <be excited> **thrill,** tingle, **tingle with excitement,** glow; swell, swell with emotion, be full of emotion; thrill to; turn on to *and* get high on *and* freak out on <nf>; heave, pant; **throb,** palpitate, go pit-a-pat; **tremble, shiver, quiver, quaver, quake,** flutter, twitter, **shake,** shake like an aspen leaf, have the shakes <nf>; **fidget,** have the fidgets *and* have ants in one's pants <nf>; toss and turn, toss, tumble, twist and turn, wriggle, wiggle, writhe, squirm; twitch, jerk

19 **change color,** turn color, go all colors; **pale,** whiten, blanch, turn pale; darken, look black; turn blue in the face; **flush, blush,** crimson, glow, mantle, color, redden, turn *or* get red

ADJS 20 **excited,** impassioned, **thrilled,** agog, tingling, tingly, atingle, aquiver, atwitter; **stimulated, exhilarated, high** <nf>; manic; **moved, stirred,** stirred up, **aroused, roused,** switched *or* turned on <nf>, on one's mettle, fired, inflamed, wrought up, **worked up,** all worked up, worked up into a lather <nf>, lathered up, whipped up, steamed up, keyed up, hopped up <nf>; turned-on <nf>; carried away; bursting, ready to burst; effervescent, yeasty, ebullient

21 in a dither, in a tizzy <nf>, in a swivet, in a foofaraw, **in a pucker** <nf>, in a quiver, **in a twitter,** in a flutter, all of a twitter *or* flutter, in a fluster, in a flurry, in a pother, in a bother, in a ferment, in a turmoil, in an uproar, in a stew *and* in a sweat <nf>, in a lather <nf>

22 heated, passionate, warm, hot, red-hot, flaming, **burning, fiery, glowing, fervent, fervid; feverish,** febrile, hectic, flushed; sexually excited, in rut 75.20; burning with excitement, het up <nf>, hot under the collar <nf>; seething, boiling, boiling over, steamy, steaming

23 agitated, perturbed, disturbed, troubled, disquieted, upset, antsy <nf>, unsettled, **discomposed, flustered,** ruffled, **shaken**

24 turbulent, tumultuous, tempestuous, boisterous, clamorous, uproarious

25 frenzied, frantic; ecstatic, transported, enraptured, ravished, in a transport *or* ecstasy; intoxicated, abandoned; orgiastic, orgasmic; raging, raving, roaring, bellowing, ramping, storming, howling, ranting, fulminating, frothing *or* foaming at the mouth; **wild,** hog-wild <nf>; **violent,** fierce, ferocious, feral, **furious; mad,** madding, **rabid,** maniac, maniacal, demonic, demoniacal, possessed; carried away, **distracted, delirious, beside oneself,** out of one's wits; uncontrollable, running mad, amok, berserk, hog-wild <nf>; **hysterical,** in hysterics; wild-eyed, wild-looking, haggard; blue in the face

26 overwrought, overexcited, overstimulated, hyper <nf>; **overcome,** overwhelmed, overpowered, overmastered; **upset,** *bouleversé* <Fr>

27 restless, restive, **uneasy,** unquiet, unsettled, unrestful, tense; **fidgety,** antsy <nf>, fussy, fluttery

28 excitable, emotional, highly emotional, overemotional, hyperthymic, perturbable, flappable <nf>, agitable; emotionally unstable; explosive, volcanic, eruptive, inflammable; irascible 110.19; irritable, edgy, touchy, wired <nf>, prickly, **sensitive 24.13; skittish,** startlish; **high-strung,** highly strung, high-spirited, mettlesome, high-mettled; **nervous**

29 passionate, fiery, vehement, hotheaded, **impetuous,** violent, volcanic, furious, fierce, **wild;** tempestuous, stormy, tornadic; simmering, volcanic, ready to burst forth *or* explode

30 exciting, thrilling, thrilly <nf>, **stirring, moving, breathtaking,** eye-popping <nf>; agitating, agitative, perturbing, disturbing, upsetting, troubling, disquieting, unsettling, distracting, jolting, jarring; heart-stirring, heart-thrilling, heart-swelling, heart-expanding, soul-stirring, spirit-stirring, deep-thrilling, mind-blowing <nf>;

impressive, striking, telling; **provocative** 375.27, provoking, piquant, tantalizing; **inflammatory** 375.28; **stimulating,** stimulative, stimulatory; exhilarating, heady, intoxicating, maddening, ravishing; **electric,** galvanic, charged, overcharged; **overwhelming,** overpowering, overcoming, overmastering, more than flesh and blood can bear; suspensive, **suspenseful,** cliff-hanging <nf>

31 penetrating, piercing, stabbing, cutting, stinging, biting, keen, brisk, sharp, caustic, astringent

32 sensational, lurid, yellow, **melodramatic,** Barnumesque; spine-chilling, eye-popping <nf>; blood-and-thunder, cloak-and-dagger

ADVS **33 excitedly, agitatedly,** perturbedly; with beating *or* leaping heart, with heart beating high, with heart going pitapat *or* pitter-patter <nf>, thrilling all over, with heart in mouth; with glistening eyes, all agog, all aquiver *or* atwitter *or* atingle; in a sweat *or* stew *or* dither *or* tizzy <nf>

34 heatedly, passionately, warmly, hotly, glowingly, fervently, fervidly, **feverishly**

35 frenziedly, frantically, wildly, furiously, violently, fiercely, madly, rabidly, distractedly, deliriously, till one is blue in the face <nf>

36 excitingly, thrillingly, stirringly, movingly; **provocatively,** provokingly; stimulatingly, exhilaratingly

106 INEXCITABILITY

NOUNS **1 inexcitability,** inexcitableness, unexcitableness, **imperturbability,** imperturbableness, unflappability <nf>; steadiness, evenness; inirritability, unirritableness; **dispassion,** dispassionateness, unpassionateness, ataraxy *or* ataraxia; quietism; stoicism; **even temper,** steady *or* smooth temper, good *or* easy temper; unnervousness 129; **patience** 134; **impassiveness,** impassivity, stolidity; bovinity, dullness

2 composure, countenance; **calm, calmness,** calm disposition, **placidity, serenity,** tranquility, soothingness, peacefulness; mental composure, peace *or* calm of mind; calm *or* quiet mind, easy mind; resignation, resignedness, acceptance, fatalism, stoic calm; philosophicalness, philosophy, philosophic composure; **quiet,** quietness of mind *or* soul, quietude; decompression, imperturbation, indisturbance, unruffledness; **coolness,** coolheadedness, cool <nf>, sangfroid; icy calm; Oriental calm, Buddha-like composure; shantih, "the peace that passeth all understanding"—Bible

3 equanimity, equilibrium, equability, balance; **levelheadedness,** level head, well-balanced *or* well-regulated mind; **poise,** aplomb, **self-possession,**

self-control, self-command, self-restraint, restraint, possession, **presence of mind;** confidence, assurance, **self-confidence, self-assurance,** centered

4 **sedateness, staidness,** soberness, sobriety, sober-mindedness, **seriousness,** gravity, solemnity, sobersidedness; temperance, moderation; sobersides

5 **nonchalance,** casualness, offhandedness; easygoingness, lackadaisicalness; **indifference,** unconcern 102.2

VERBS 6 **be cool** or **composed,** not turn a hair, not have a hair out of place, keep one's cool <nf>, look as if butter wouldn't melt in one's mouth; **tranquilize,** calm 670.7; **set one's mind at ease** or **rest,** make one easy

7 **compose oneself, control oneself,** restrain oneself, collect oneself, **get hold of oneself,** get a grip on oneself <nf>, get organized, master one's feelings, regain one's composure; **calm down, cool off,** cool down, sober down, hold or keep one's temper, simmer down and cool it <nf>; **relax,** decompress, unwind, take it easy, lay or kick back <nf>; **forget it,** get it out of one's mind or head, drop it

8 <control one's feelings> **suppress, repress,** keep under, smother, stifle, choke or hold back, fight down or back, inhibit; sublimate

9 **keep cool,** keep one's cool <nf>, **keep calm,** keep one's head, keep one's shirt on and hang loose <nf>, not turn a hair; take things as they come, roll with the punches <nf>; keep a stiff upper lip

ADJS 10 **inexcitable, imperturbable,** undisturbable, unflappable <nf>; **unirritable,** inirritable; **dispassionate,** unpassionate; **steady;** stoic, stoical; **even-tempered; impassive,** stolid; bovine, dull; unnervous 129.2; **patient**

11 **unexcited, unperturbed,** undisturbed, untroubled, unagitated, **unruffled,** unflustered, unstirred, unimpassioned

12 **calm, placid,** quiet, **tranquil, serene,** peaceful; **cool, coolheaded,** cool as a cucumber <nf>; philosophical

13 **composed, collected,** recollected, **levelheaded; poised,** together <nf>, in equipoise, equanimous, equilibrious, **balanced,** well-balanced; **self-possessed,** self-controlled, controlled, self-restrained; confident, assured, **self-confident, self-assured;** temperate, pacific

14 **sedate, staid,** sober, sober-minded, **serious,** grave, solemn, sobersided; temperate, moderate

15 **nonchalant, blasé, indifferent,** unconcerned 102.7; **casual, offhand, relaxed, laid-back** and throwaway <nf>; **easygoing,** easy, free and easy, devil-may-care, lackadaisical, *dégagé* <Fr>

ADVS 16 inexcitably, **imperturbably,** inirritably,

dispassionately; steadily; stoically; **calmly, placidly,** quietly, **tranquilly, serenely; coolly, composedly,** levelheadedly; impassively, stolidly, stodgily, stuffily

17 **sedately, staidly, soberly, seriously,** sobersiddedly

18 **nonchalantly, casually, relaxedly,** offhandedly, easygoingly, lackadaisically

107 CONTENTMENT

NOUNS 1 **contentment, content,** contentedness, satisfiedness; **satisfaction,** entire satisfaction, fulfillment, gratification; ease, peace of mind, composure 106.2; comfort 121; **quality of life; well-being,** euphoria; **happiness** 95.2; **acceptance,** resignation, reconcilement, reconciliation; clear or clean conscience, dreamless sleep; serenity; satiety

2 **complacency,** complacence; **smugness, self-complacence** or self-complacency, self-approval, self-approbation, **self-satisfaction, self-content,** self-contentedness self-contentness; bovinity

3 **satisfactoriness, adequacy,** sufficiency 991; **acceptability,** admissibility, **tolerability,** agreeability, unobjectionability, unexceptionability, tenability, viability; competency

VERBS 4 **content, satisfy;** gratify; put or set at ease, set one's mind at ease or rest, achieve inner harmony; indulge, satiate

5 **be content, rest satisfied, rest easy,** rest and be thankful, be of good cheer, be reconciled to, take the good the gods provide, accept one's lot, rest on one's laurels, let well enough alone, let sleeping dogs lie, take the bitter with the sweet; come to terms with oneself, learn to live in one's own skin; have no kick coming <nf>, not complain, not worry, have nothing to complain about, not sweat it and cool it and go with the flow <nf>; content oneself with, settle for; settle for less, take half a loaf, lower one's sights, cut one's losses; be pleased 95.12; have one's heart's desire

6 **be satisfactory, do,** suffice 991.4; **suit,** suit one down to the ground, serve, meet the needs of

ADJS 7 **content, contented, satisfied;** pleased 95.13; happy; **easy, at ease,** at one's ease, easygoing; composed 106.13; **comfortable** 121.11, of good comfort; fulfilled, gratified; euphoric, eupeptic; carefree, without care, *sans souci* <Fr>; accepting, resigned, reconciled; uncomplaining, unrepining

8 **untroubled, unbothered, undisturbed,** unperturbed 106.11, unworried, unvexed, unplagued, untormented

9 **well-content, well-pleased,** well-contented, **well-satisfied,** highly satisfied, satiated, full, full-up

10 **complacent,** bovine; **smug, self-complacent, self-satisfied,** self-content, **self-contented**

11 **satisfactory, satisfying;** sufficient 991.6, sufficing, **adequate, enough,** commensurate, proportionate, proportionable, ample, equal to, competent

12 **acceptable,** admissible, **agreeable,** unobjectionable, unexceptionable, tenable, viable; **OK** *and* okay *and* all right *and* alright <nf>; **passable,** good enough, not bad, so-so

13 **tolerable, bearable, endurable, supportable, sufferable**

ADVS 14 **contentedly,** to one's heart's content; **satisfiedly,** with satisfaction; **complacently, smugly,** self-complacently, self-satisfiedly, self-contentedly

15 **satisfactorily,** satisfyingly; **acceptably, agreeably,** admissibly; sufficiently, adequately, commensurately, amply, enough; **tolerably, passably**

16 **to one's satisfaction,** to one's delight, to one's great glee; to one's taste, to the king's *or* queen's taste

108 DISCONTENT

NOUNS 1 **discontent,** discontentment, discontentedness; **dissatisfaction,** unsatisfaction, dissatisfiedness, unfulfillment; **resentment,** envy 154; **restlessness, restiveness, uneasiness,** unease; malaise; rebelliousness 327.3; disappointment 132; unpleasure 96; unhappiness 112.2; ill humor 110; **disgruntlement,** sulkiness, sourness, petulance, peevishness, querulousness; vexation of spirit; cold comfort; divine discontent; Faustianism

2 **unsatisfactoriness,** dissatisfactoriness; **inadequacy,** insufficiency 992; **unacceptability,** inadmissibility, unsuitability, undesirability, objectionability, untenability, indefensibility; **intolerability** 98.9

3 **malcontent,** *frondeur* <Fr>; **complainer,** complainant, **faultfinder, grumbler,** growler, smellfungus, griper, grouser, croaker, carper, peevish *or* petulant *or* querulous person, whiner; reactionary, reactionist; rebel 327.5; spoilsport; dissatisfied customer, angry young man

4 <nf terms> **grouch, kvetch,** kicker, griper, moaner, moaning Minnie <Brit>, crank, crab, grump, beefer, bellyacher, bitcher, sorehead, picklepuss, sourpuss

VERBS 5 **dissatisfy, discontent, disgruntle, displease,** fail to satisfy, be inadequate, not fill the bill, disappoint, leave much *or* a lot to be desired, dishearten, disillusion, put out <nf>; **be discontented, complain**

6 <nf terms> **beef, bitch, kvetch,** bellyache, boo, hiss, carp, crab, gripe, grouch, grouse, grump, have an attitude, kick, moan, piss, make a stink, squawk

ADJS 7 **discontented, dissatisfied, disgruntled,** unaccepting, unaccommodating, **displeased,** less than pleased, let down, disappointed; **unsatisfied,**

ungratified, unfulfilled; resentful, dog-in-the-manger; envious 154.4; restless, restive, uneasy; rebellious 327.11; malcontent, malcontented, **complaining,** complaintful, critical of, pejorative, sour, **faultfinding,** grumbling, growling, murmuring, muttering, griping, croaking, **peevish, petulant,** sulky, brooding, **querulous,** querulant, whiny; unhappy 112.21; out of humor 110.17

8 <nf terms> **grouchy, kvetchy,** cranky, beefing, crabby, crabbing, grousing, griping, bellyaching, bitching

9 **unsatisfactory,** dissatisfactory; **unsatisfying, ungratifying,** unfulfilling; **displeasing** 98.17; disappointing, disheartening, not up to expectation, not good enough, substandard; **inadequate,** incommensurate, **insufficient** 992.9; unpopular, not up to snuff <nf>

10 **unacceptable,** inadmissible, unsuitable, undesirable, **objectionable,** exceptionable, impossible, untenable, indefensible; **intolerable** 98.25; rejected

ADVS 11 **discontentedly, dissatisfiedly**

12 **unsatisfactorily,** dissatisfactorily; **unsatisfyingly, ungratifyingly; inadequately, insufficiently; unacceptably,** inadmissibly, unsuitably, undesirably, objectionably; intolerably 98.30

109 CHEERFULNESS

NOUNS 1 **cheerfulness,** cheeriness, **good cheer, cheer,** cheery vein *or* mood; blitheness, blithesomeness; **gladness,** felicity, gladsomeness; **happiness** 95.2; **pleasantness,** winsomeness, geniality, conviviality; brightness, radiance, **sunniness;** sanguineness, sanguinity, sanguine humor, euphoric *or* eupeptic mein; optimism, rosy expectation, hopefulness; **irrepressibility,** irrepressibleness

2 **good humor, good spirits,** good cheer; **high spirits, exhilaration,** rare good humor; *joie de vivre* <Fr>

3 **lightheartedness,** lightsomeness, lightness, levity; **buoyancy,** buoyance, resilience, resiliency, bounce <nf>, springiness; springy step; **jauntiness,** perkiness, debonairness, carefreeness; **breeziness,** airiness, pertness, chirpiness, light heart

4 **gaiety,** gayness, *allégresse* <Fr>; **liveliness, vivacity, vitality,** life, **animation, spiritedness, spirit,** esprit, élan, **sprightliness,** high spirits, zestfulness, zest, vim, zip <nf>, vigor, verve, gusto, **exuberance,** heartiness; **spirits,** animal spirits; piss and vinegar <nf>; **friskiness,** skittishness, coltishness, rompishness, rollicksomeness, capersomeness; **sportiveness, playfulness, frolicsomeness,** gamesomeness, kittenishness

5 **merriment,** merriness; **hilarity,** hilariousness; **joy,**

joyfulness, joyousness; **glee,** gleefulness, high glee; **jollity,** jolliness, **joviality,** jocularity, jocundity; frivolity, **levity; mirth,** mirthfulness, **amusement** 743; **fun,** good time; laughter 116.4

VERBS **6** exude cheerfulness, radiate cheer, not have a care in the world, **beam,** burst *or* brim with cheer, glow, radiate, sparkle, sing, lilt, whistle, **chirp,** chirrup, chirp like a cricket; walk on air, dance, skip, caper, frolic, gambol, romp, caracole; **smile,** laugh 116.8

7 cheer, gladden, brighten, put in good humor; **encourage, hearten,** pick up <nf>; **inspire,** inspirit, warm the spirits, **raise the spirits,** elevate one's mood, buoy up, boost, give a lift <nf>, put one on top of the world *and* on cloud nine <nf>; **exhilarate,** animate, invigorate, liven, enliven, vitalize; **rejoice,** rejoice the heart, do the heart good

8 elate, exalt, elevate, lift, uplift, flush

9 cheer up, take heart, drive dull care away; **brighten up,** light up, **perk up; buck up** *and* brace up *and* chirk up <nf>; come out of it, snap out of it <nf>, revive

10 be of good cheer, bear up, **keep one's spirits up,** keep one's chin up <nf>, keep one's pecker up <Brit nf>, keep a stiff upper lip <nf>, grin and bear it

ADJS **11 cheerful, cheery,** of good cheer, in good spirits; in high spirits, exalted, elated, exhilarated, high <nf>; irrepressible; **blithe,** blithesome; **glad, gladsome; happy,** happy as a clam *or* a sand boy *or* a lark, on top of the world, sitting on top of the world, sitting pretty, on cloud nine, over the moon <nf>; **pleasant, genial,** winsome; **bright, sunny,** bright and sunny, **radiant,** riant, sparkling, beaming, glowing, flushed, perky, rosy, smiling, laughing; sanguine, sanguineous, euphoric, eupeptic, ebullient, exhilarated; optimistic, hopeful; **irrepressible;** up <nf>

12 lighthearted, light, lightsome; **buoyant,** corky <nf>, resilient; **jaunty,** perky, **debonair, carefree,** free and easy; **breezy,** airy

13 pert, chirk <nf>, chirrupy, **chirpy, chipper** <nf>

14 gay, gay as a lark; **spirited,** sprightly, **lively, animated, vivacious,** vital, zestful, zippy <nf>, **exuberant,** hearty; **frisky,** antic, skittish, coltish, rompish, capersome; **full of beans** *and* **feeling one's oats** <nf>, full of piss and vinegar <nf>; **sportive, playful,** playful as a kitten, kittenish, **frolicsome,** gamesome; rollicking, rollicky, rollicksome

15 merry, mirthful, hilarious; joyful, joyous, rejoicing; **gleeful,** gleesome; **jolly,** buxom; **jovial,** jocund, jocular; **frivolous;** laughter-loving, mirth-loving, risible; merry as a cricket *or* grig, "as merry as the day is long"—Shakespeare; tickled to death <nf>, tickled pink <nf>, high as a kite <nf>

16 cheering, gladdening; encouraging, heartening, heartwarming, uplifting; **inspiring,** inspiriting; **exhilarating,** animating, enlivening, invigorating; cheerful, cheery, glad, joyful

ADVS **17 cheerfully,** cheerily, with good cheer, with a cheerful heart; irrepressibly; **lightheartedly,** lightly; jauntily, perkily, airily; **pleasantly,** genially, blithely; **gladly, happily, joyfully,** smilingly; optimistically, hopefully

18 gaily, exuberantly, heartily, spiritedly, animatedly, vivaciously, zestfully, with zest, with vim, with élan, with zip <nf>, with verve, with gusto

19 merrily, gleefully, hilariously; jovially, jocundly, jocularly; frivolously; **mirthfully,** laughingly

PHRS **20** cheer up!, every cloud has a silver lining; don't let it get you down, *illegitimati non carborundum* <L, don't let the bastards grind you down>; chin up!, keep your pecker up! <Brit>; it's always darkest before the dawn

110 ILL HUMOR

NOUNS **1 ill humor,** bad humor, **bad temper,** rotten *or* ill *or* evil temper, **ill nature,** filthy *or* rotten *or* evil humor; **sourness,** biliousness, liverishness; choler, bile, gall, spleen; **abrasiveness,** causticity, corrosiveness, asperity 144.8; **anger** 152.5; discontent 108

2 irascibility, irritability, excitability, short *or* quick temper, short fuse <nf>; **crossness,** disagreeableness, disagreeability, gruffness, shortness, peevishness, querulousness, fretfulness, crabbedness, **crankiness, testiness,** crustiness, huffiness, huffishness, churlishness, bearishness, snappishness, waspishness; **perversity,** cross-grainedness, fractiousness

3 <nf terms> **crabbiness, grouchiness,** cantankerousness, crustiness, grumpiness *or* grumpishness, cussedness, huffiness *or* huffishness, **meanness, orneriness,** bitchiness, cussedness, feistiness, ugliness, miffiness, saltiness, scrappiness, shirtiness <Brit>, soreheadedness

4 hot temper, temper, quick *or* short temper, irritable temper, warm temper, fiery temper, fierce temper, short fuse <nf>, pepperiness, feistiness *and* spunkiness <nf>, **hotheadedness,** hot blood; sharp tongue

5 touchiness, tetchiness, ticklishness, prickliness, quickness to take offense, miffiness <nf>, **sensitiveness,** oversensitiveness, hypersensitiveness, sensitivity, oversensitivity, hypersensitivity, thin skin; temperamentalness

6 petulance *or* petulancy, **peevishness,** pettishness, **querulousness, fretfulness,** resentfulness; shrewishness, vixenishness

7 contentiousness, quarrelsomeness 456.3; **disputatiousness, argumentativeness,** litigiousness; **belligerence**

8 sullenness, sulkiness, surliness, moroseness, glumness, grumness, grimness, mumpishness, dumpishness, dourness, *bouderie* <Fr>; **moodiness,** moodishness; mopishness, mopiness <nf>; dejection, melancholy 112.5

9 scowl, frown, lower, **glower, pout,** moue, mow, grimace, wry face; sullen looks, black looks, hangdog look, **long face**

10 sulks, sullens, **mopes,** mumps, dumps, grumps <nf>, frumps <Brit nf>, **blues,** blue devils, mulligrubs, **pouts**

11 <ill-humored person> **sorehead, grouch, curmudgeon, grump, crank,** crab, **crosspatch,** feist *or* fice <nf>, wasp, **bear,** grizzly bear, pit bull, junkyard dog <nf>; fury, Tartar, dragon, ugly customer <nf>; **hothead,** hotspur; fire-eater; sulker, churl, bellyacher

12 bitch <nf>, **shrew, vixen,** virago, termagant, brimstone, fury, witch, beldam, cat, tigress, she-wolf, she-devil, spitfire; fishwife; **scold,** common scold, harpy, nag, Xanthippe; old bag; battle-ax <nf>

VERBS **13** have a temper, have a short fuse <nf>, have a devil in one, be possessed of the devil; be cross, get out on the wrong side of the bed

14 sulk, mope, mope around; grizzle <chiefly Brit nf>, grump *and* **grouch** *and* **bitch** <nf>, **fret;** get oneself in a sulk; have the blues, be down in the dumps

15 look sullen, look black, look black as thunder, gloom, pull *or* make *or* have a long face; **frown, scowl,** knit the brow, lower, **glower, pout,** make a moue *or* mow, grimace, make a wry face, make a lip, hang one's lip, thrust out one's lower lip

16 sour, acerbate, exacerbate; **embitter,** bitter, envenom

ADJS **17 out of humor,** out of temper, out of sorts, **in a bad humor,** in a shocking humor, feeling evil <nf>; **abrasive,** caustic, corrosive, acid; angry; discontented 108.5

18 ill-humored, bad-tempered, ill-tempered, evil-humored, evil-tempered, **ill-natured,** ill-affected, ill-disposed

19 irascible, irritable, excitable, flappable <nf>; **cross, cranky, testy;** cankered, crabbed, spiteful, spleeny, splenetic, churlish, bearish, snappish, waspish; **gruff,** grumbly, grumbling, growling; **disagreeable; perverse,** fractious, cross-grained

20 <nf terms> **crabby, grouchy,** cantankerous, crusty, grumpy *or* grumpish, cussed, huffy *or* huffish, mean, mean as a junkyard dog, ornery, bitchy,

feisty, ugly, miffy, salty, scrappy, shirty <Brit>, soreheaded

21 touchy, tetchy, miffy <nf>, ticklish, prickly, quick to take offense, **thin-skinned, sensitive,** oversensitive, hypersensitive, high-strung, highly strung, temperamental, prima-donnaish

22 peevish, petulant, pettish, **querulous, fretful,** resentful; catty; shrewish, vixenish, vixenly; nagging, naggy

23 sour, soured, **sour-tempered,** vinegarish; prune-faced <nf>; **choleric, dyspeptic, bilious,** liverish, jaundiced; **bitter,** embittered

24 sullen, sulky, surly, morose, dour, mumpish, dumpish, **glum,** grum, grim; **moody,** moodish; **mopish,** mopey <nf>, moping; **glowering,** lowering, **scowling, frowning;** dark, black; black-browed, beetle-browed; dejected, melancholy 112.23; somber

25 hot-tempered, hotheaded, passionate, hot, fiery, peppery, feisty, spunky <nf>, **quick-tempered, short-tempered;** hasty, quick, explosive, volcanic, combustible

26 contentious, quarrelsome 456.17; **disputatious,** controversial, litigious, polemic, polemical; **argumentative,** argumental; on the warpath, looking for trouble; scrappy <nf>; cat-and-doggish, cat-and-dog; **bellicose, belligerent**

ADVS **27 ill-humoredly, ill-naturedly; irascibly, irritably, crossly, crankily, testily,** huffily, cantankerously <nf>, crabbedly, sourly, churlishly, crustily, bearishly, snappily; perversely, fractiously, cross-grainedly

28 peevishly, petulantly, pettishly, **querulously, fretfully**

29 grouchily *and* **crabbily** *and* grumpily <nf>, grumblingly

30 sullenly, sulkily, surlily, morosely, mumpishly, glumly, grumly, grimly; moodily, mopingly; gloweringly, loweringly, scowlingly, frowningly

111 SOLEMNITY

NOUNS **1 solemnity, solemness, dignity, soberness, sobriety, gravity,** *gravitas* <L>, weightiness, **somberness, grimness; sedateness, staidness;** demureness, decorousness; **seriousness, earnestness, thoughtfulness, sober-mindedness,** sobersidedness; sobersides, humorlessness; long face, straight face; **formality** 580

VERBS **2** honor the occasion, keep a straight face, look serious, compose one's features, wear an earnest frown; repress a smile, not crack a smile <nf>, wipe the smile off one's face, keep from laughing, make a long face

ADJS **3 solemn, dignified, sober, grave,** unsmiling,

weighty, **somber**, frowning, **grim; sedate, staid;** demure, decorous; **serious, earnest, thoughtful,** pensive; **sober-minded,** sober-sided; straight-faced, long-faced, grim-faced, grim-visaged, stone-faced, stony-faced; sober as a judge, grave as an undertaker; **formal** 580.7

ADVS **4 solemnly, soberly,** gravely, somberly, grimly; **sedately, staidly,** demurely, decorously; with dignity, **seriously, earnestly,** thoughtfully, sober-mindedly, sobersidedly; with a straight face; formally 580.11

112 SADNESS

NOUNS **1 sadness,** sadheartedness, weight *or* burden of sorrow; heaviness, **heavyheartedness,** heavy heart, **heaviness of heart;** pathos, bathos

2 unhappiness, infelicity; displeasure 96.1; discontent 108; **uncheerfulness,** cheerlessness; **joylessness,** unjoyfulness; mirthlessness, unmirthfulness, humorlessness, infestivity; **grimness; wretchedness, misery**

3 dejection, depression, oppression, dejectedness, **downheartedness,** downcastness; **discouragement, disheartenment,** dispiritedness; *Schmerz* and *Weltschmerz* <Ger>; malaise 96.1; lowness, lowness *or* depression *or* oppression of spirit, downer *and* down trip <nf>; chill, chilling effect; **low spirits,** drooping spirits, sinking heart, funk; despondence *or* **despondency,** spiritlessness, heartlessness; black *or* blank despondency, "Slough of Despond"—Bunyan; demotivation, hopelessness 125, **despair** 125.2, pessimism 125.6, gloom and doom, suicidal despair, death wish, self-destructive urge; weariness of life, *taedium vitae* <L>; sloth, acedia, noonday demon

4 hypochondria, hypochondriasis, morbid anxiety

5 melancholy, melancholia, melancholiness, spleen <old>; gentle melancholy, romantic melancholy; **pensiveness, wistfulness,** tristfulness; **nostalgia,** homesickness, nostalgy <old>, *mal du pays* <Fr>

6 blues and blue devils *and* mulligrubs <nf>, mumps, **dumps** <nf>, **doldrums,** dismals, dolefuls <nf>, blahs *and* mopes *and* megrims *and* sulks <nf>

7 gloom, gloominess, darkness, murk, murkiness, **dismalness, bleakness, grimness, somberness, gravity, solemnity; dreariness,** drearisomeness; wearifulness, wearisomeness

8 glumness, grumness, **moroseness, sullenness,** sulkiness, **moodiness,** mumpishness, dumpishness; mopishness, mopiness <nf>

9 heartache, aching heart, bleeding heart, grieving heart; heartsickness, heartsoreness; **heartbreak, broken heart,** brokenheartedness, heartbrokenness

10 sorrow, sorrowing, **grief, care,** carking care, **woe;**

heartgrief, heartfelt grief; languishment, pining; **anguish, misery, agony;** prostrating grief, prostration; **lamentation** 115

11 sorrowfulness, mournfulness, ruefulness, **woefulness, dolefulness,** woesomeness <old>, dolorousness, **plaintiveness,** plangency, grievousness, aggrievedness, lugubriousness, funerealness; weeping and wailing and gnashing of teeth; *lacrimae rerum* <L>, **tearfulness** 115.2

12 disconsolateness, disconsolation, **inconsolability,** inconsolableness, unconsolability, comfortlessness; **desolation,** desolateness; forlornness

13 sourpuss and picklepuss *and* gloomy Gus <nf>, moaning Minnie <Brit nf>; mope, brooder; **melancholic,** melancholiac; depressive; Eeyore

14 killjoy, spoilsport, grinch *and* crepehanger *and* drag <nf>; damp, damper, **wet blanket,** party pooper; gloomster *and* doomster <nf>, doomsdayer, apocalypticist, apocalyptician, awfulizer <nf>, crapehanger; skeleton at the feast; pessimist 125.7

VERBS **15** hang one's head, pull *or* make a long face, look blue, sing *or* get *or* have the blues <nf>; drag one down; carry the weight *or* woe of the world on one's shoulders; hang crape <nf>, apocalypticize, catastrophize, awfulize <nf>

16 lose heart, despond, give way, give oneself up *or* over to; despondency; **despair** 125.10, sink into despair, throw up one's hands in despair, be *or* become suicidal, lose the will to live; **droop,** sink, languish, mope; reach *or* plumb the depths, touch *or* hit bottom, hit rock bottom

17 grieve, sorrow; weep, mourn 115.8,10; be dumb with grief; **pine,** pine away; **brood over, mope, fret,** take on <nf>; **eat one's heart out,** break one's heart over; **agonize,** ache, bleed

18 sadden, darken, cast a pall *or* gloom upon, weigh *or* weigh heavy upon; **deject, depress, oppress, crush,** press down, hit one like a ton of bricks <nf>, **cast down,** lower, lower the spirits, get one down <nf>, take the wind out of one's sails, rain on one's parade, burst one's bubble, **discourage, dishearten,** take the heart out of, **dispirit;** damp, dampen, damp *or* dampen the spirits; dash, knock down, beat down; sink, sink one's soul, plunge one into despair

19 aggrieve, oppress, **grieve, sorrow,** plunge one into sorrow, embitter; draw tears, bring to tears; **anguish, tear up** and **cut up** <nf>, wring *or* pierce *or* lacerate *or* rend the heart, pull at the heartstrings; be cut up; afflict 96.16, torment 96.18; **break one's heart, make one's heart bleed;** desolate, leave an aching void; prostrate, break down, crush, bear down, inundate, overwhelm

ADJS **20 sad,** saddened; sadhearted, **sad of heart;**

heavyhearted, heavy; oppressed, weighed upon, weighed *or* weighted down, bearing the woe of the world, burdened *or* laden with sorrow; sad-faced, long-faced; sad-eyed; sad-voiced

21 **unhappy, uncheerful,** uncheery, **cheerless, joyless, unjoyful,** unsmiling; mirthless, unmirthful, humorless, infestive; funny as a crutch <nf>; **grim; out of humor,** out of sorts, in bad humor *or* spirits; **sorry,** sorryish; discontented 108.5; **wretched, miserable;** pleasureless 96.20

22 **dejected, depressed, downhearted, down, downcast, cast down,** bowed down, subdued; **discouraged, disheartened, dispirited,** dashed; **low, feeling low,** low-spirited, **in low spirits; down in the mouth** <nf>, **in the doldrums, down in the dumps** *and* **in the dumps** *and* in the doleful dumps <nf>, in the depths; **despondent,** desponding; **despairing** 125.12, weary of life, suicidal, world-weary; pessimistic 125.16; spiritless, heartless, **woebegone; drooping,** droopy, languishing, pining, haggard; hypochondriac *or* hypochondriacal

23 **melancholy,** melancholic, splenetic <old>, **blue** <nf>, funky <nf>; atrabilious, atrabiliar; **pensive, wistful,** tristful; **nostalgic,** homesick

24 **gloomy, dismal, murky, bleak, grim, somber,** sombrous, **solemn, grave;** sad, *triste* <Fr>, **funereal,** funebrial, crepehanging <nf>, saturnine; **dark,** black, gray; **dreary,** drear, drearisome; weary, weariful, wearisome

25 **glum,** grum, **morose, sullen,** sulky, mumpish, dumpish, long-faced, crestfallen, chapfallen; **moody,** moodish, **brooding,** broody; mopish, mopey <nf>, **moping**

26 **sorrowful, sorrowing,** sorrowed, **mournful, rueful, woeful, woesome** <old>, **doleful, plaintive,** plangent; anguished; dolorous, **grievous, lamentable,** lugubrious; **tearful; care-worn;** grieved, **grief-stricken,** griefful, aggrieved, in grief, plunged in grief, dumb with grief, prostrated by grief, cut-up *and* torn-up <nf>, **inconsolable**

27 **sorrow-stricken,** sorrow-wounded, sorrow-struck, sorrow-torn, sorrow-worn, sorrow-wasted, sorrow-beaten, sorrow-blinded, sorrow-clouded, sorrow-shot, sorrow-burdened, sorrow-laden, sorrow-sighing, sorrow-sobbing, sorrow-sick

28 **disconsolate, inconsolable,** unconsolable, comfortless, prostrate *or* prostrated, **forlorn; desolate,** *désolé* <Fr>; sick, **sick at heart, heartsick,** soul-sick, heartsore

29 **overcome,** crushed, borne-down, overwhelmed, inundated, spazzed-out, **stricken, cut up** <nf>, **desolated,** prostrate *or* prostrated, broken-down, undone; **heart-stricken,** heart-struck; **brokenhearted,** heartbroken

30 **depressing,** depressive, depressant, **oppressive;**

discouraging, disheartening, dispiriting; morale-sapping, worst-case, downbeat <nf>

ADVS 31 **sadly, gloomily, dismally, drearily,** heavily, bleakly, grimly, somberly, sombrously, solemnly, funereally, gravely, with a long face; **depressingly**

32 **unhappily, uncheerfully,** cheerlessly, joylessly, unjoyfully

33 **dejectedly, downheartedly; discouragedly, disheartenedly, dispiritedly; despondently,** despairingly, spiritlessly, heartlessly; **disconsolately,** inconsolably, unconsolably, forlornly

34 **melancholily, pensively,** wistfully, tristfully; nostalgically

35 **glumly,** grumly, **morosely, sullenly; moodily,** moodishly, broodingly, broodily; mopishly, mopily <nf>, mopingly

36 **sorrowfully, mournfully, ruefully, woefully, woesomely** <old>, **dolefully, dolorously, plaintively, grievously,** grieffully, lugubriously; with a broken voice; **heartbrokenly,** brokenheartedly; **tearfully,** with tears in one's eyes

113 REGRET

NOUNS 1 **regret, regrets,** regretting, regretfulness; **remorse,** remorsefulness, remorse of conscience, ayenbite of inwit <old>; **shame,** shamefulness, shamefacedness, shamefastness; **sorrow, grief, sorriness,** repining; **contrition,** contriteness, attrition; bitterness; apologies; wistfulness 100.4

2 **compunction, qualm, qualms,** qualmishness, scruples, scrupulosity, scrupulousness, pang, pangs, **pangs of conscience,** throes, sting *or* pricking *or* twinge *or* twitch of conscience, touch of conscience, **voice of conscience,** pricking of heart, better self

3 **self-reproach,** self-reproachfulness, **self-accusation, self-condemnation,** self-conviction, self-punishment, self-humiliation, self-debasement, **self-hatred,** self-flagellation; hair shirt; self-analysis, soul-searching, examination of conscience

4 **penitence, repentance, change of heart; apology,** humble *or* heartfelt apology, abject apology; better nature, good angel, guardian angel; reformation 858.2; deathbed repentance; mea culpa; **penance** 658.3; wearing a hairshirt *or* sackcloth *or* sackcloth and ashes, mortification of the flesh

5 **penitent,** confessor, "a sadder and a wiser man"—Coleridge; **prodigal son,** prodigal returned; Magdalen

VERBS 6 **regret, deplore, repine, be sorry for; rue,** rue the day; **bemoan, bewail;** curse one's folly, **reproach oneself,** kick oneself <nf>, bite one's tongue, accuse *or* condemn *or* blame *or* convict *or* punish oneself, flagellate oneself, wear a hair shirt, make oneself miserable, humiliate *or* debase oneself, hate oneself for one's actions, hide one's face in shame; examine one's conscience, search one's soul, consult *or* heed one's better self, analyze *or* search one's motives; cry over spilled milk, waste time in regret

7 **repent, think better of,** change one's mind, have second thoughts; laugh out of the other side of one's mouth; **plead guilty,** own oneself in the wrong, humble oneself, **apologize** 658.5, beg pardon *or* forgiveness, throw oneself on the mercy of the court; do penance 658.6; reform

ADJS 8 **regretful, remorseful,** full of remorse, **ashamed,** shameful, shamefaced, shamefast, **sorry, rueful, repining,** unhappy about; **conscience-stricken,** conscience-smitten; **self-reproachful,** self-reproaching, self-accusing, self-condemning, self-convicting, self-punishing, self-flagellating, self-humiliating, self-debasing, self-hating; wistful 100.23

9 **penitent, repentant; penitential,** penitentiary; **contrite,** abject, humble, humbled, **sheepish, apologetic,** touched, softened, melted

10 **regrettable,** much to be regretted; **deplorable** 1000.9

ADVS 11 **regretfully, remorsefully,** sorrily, ruefully, unhappily

12 **penitently,** repentantly, penitentially; **contritely,** abjectly, **humbly, sheepishly, apologetically**

114 UNREGRETFULNESS

NOUNS 1 **unregretfulness, unremorsefulness, unsorriness,** unruefulness; **remorselessness,** regretlessness, sorrowlessness; **shamelessness,** unashamedness

2 **impenitence,** impenitentness; nonrepentance, irrepentance; **uncontriteness,** unabjectness; seared conscience, heart of stone, callousness 94.3; **hardness of heart,** hardness, induration, obduracy; **defiance** 327.454,2; **insolence** 142; no regrets, no remorse

VERBS 3 **harden one's heart,** steel oneself; **have no regrets,** not look backward, not cry over spilled milk; have no shame, have no remorse; feel nothing

ADJS 4 **unregretful,** unregretting, **unremorseful, unsorry, unsorrowful,** unrueful; **remorseless,** regretless, sorrowless, griefless; unsorrowing, ungrieving, unrepining; **shameless,** unashamed

5 **impenitent, unrepentant,** unrepenting, unrecanting; **uncontrite,** unabject; untouched, unsoftened, unmelted, callous 94.12; hard, hardened, obdurate; **defiant** 453.8,454.7; **insolent** 142.9

6 **unregretted, unrepented,** unatoned

ADVS 7 **unregretfully, unremorsefully,** unruefully; **remorselessly,** sorrowlessly, impenitently, shamelessly, unashamedly; **without regret,** without looking back, **without remorse,** without compunction, without any qualms *or* scruples

115 LAMENTATION

NOUNS 1 **lamentation,** lamenting, **mourning, moaning, grieving, sorrowing, wailing, bewailing, bemoaning,** keening, howling, ululation; **sorrow** 112.10; woe, misery

2 **weeping, sobbing, crying,** bawling; blubbering, whimpering, sniveling; **tears,** flood of tears, fit of crying; cry *and* good cry <nf>; **tearfulness, weepiness** <nf>, lachrymosity, melting mood; tearful eyes, swimming *or* brimming *or* overflowing eyes; **tear,** teardrop, lachryma; lacrimatory, tear bottle

3 **lament, plaint,** *planctus* <L>; **murmur,** mutter; **moan, groan; whine, whimper; wail,** wail of woe; **sob,** *cri du coeur* <Fr>, **cry,** outcry, scream, **howl,** yowl, bawl, yawp, keen, ululation; jeremiad, tirade, dolorous tirade

4 **complaint, grievance, peeve,** pet peeve, **groan; dissent,** protest 333.2; hard luck story <nf>, sob story, tale of woe; **complaining,** scolding, groaning, **faultfinding** 510.4, sniping, destructive criticism, **grumbling, murmuring;** whining, petulance, peevishness, querulousness

5 <nf terms> **beef, kick, gripe,** kvetch, grouse, bellyache, howl, holler, **squawk,** bitch; **beefing, grousing, kicking, griping,** kvetching, **bellyaching,** squawking, **bitching,** yapping

6 **dirge, funeral** *or* **death song,** coronach, keen, elegy, epicedium, requiem, monody, threnody, threnode, coronach <Ir>, knell, death knell, passing bell, funeral *or* dead march, muffled drums; eulogy, funeral *or* graveside oration

7 <mourning garments> **mourning, weeds,** widow's weeds, crape, black; deep mourning; sackcloth, sackcloth and ashes; cypress, cypress lawn, yew; mourning band; mourning ring

8 **lamenter, griever,** mourner 309.7; moaner, weeper, sniveler; **complainer,** faultfinder, smellfungus, malcontent 108.3

9 <nf terms> **grouch, kvetch,** kicker, griper, moaner, moaning Minnie <Brit>, crank, crab, crybaby, blubberer, grouser, beefer, bellyacher, bitcher, sorehead, picklepuss, sourpuss

VERBS 10 **lament, mourn, moan, grieve, sorrow,** keen, weep over *or* for, **bewail, bemoan, deplore, repine, sigh,** rue, give sorrow words; sing the blues <nf>, elegize, dirge, knell, toll the knell; pay one's last respects; wake, hold a wake, go to a funeral, sound the last post

11 wring one's hands, tear one's hair, gnash one's teeth, beat one's breast, sing the blues

12 **weep, sob, cry, bawl,** boo-hoo; **blubber,** ululate, **whimper, snivel; shed tears,** drop a tear; **burst into tears,** burst out crying, give way to tears, melt *or* dissolve in tears, break down, break down and cry, turn on the waterworks <nf>; cry one's eyes out, cry oneself blind; cry before one is hurt

13 **wail,** ululate; **moan, groan; howl,** yowl, yawl <Brit nf>; **cry, squall, bawl,** yawp, **yell, scream,** shriek; cry out, make an outcry; bay at the moon; tirade

14 **whine, whimper,** yammer <nf>, pule, grizzle <chiefly Brit nf>

15 **complain, groan; grumble, murmur, mutter,** growl, clamor, croak, grunt, yelp; **fret,** fuss, make a fuss about, fret and fume; air a grievance, lodge *or* register a complaint; fault, find fault

16 <nf terms> **beef, bitch, kick, kvetch,** bellyache, crab, gripe, grouch, grouse, grump, have an attitude, holler, howl, moan, piss, make a stink, squawk, yap; raise a howl, put up a squawk *or* howl, take on, cry *or* yell *or* scream bloody murder, give one a hard time, piss *or* kick up a storm *or* row *or* fuss, make *or* raise a stink

17 **go into mourning;** put on mourning, wear mourning

ADJS 18 **lamenting, grieving, mourning, moaning, sorrowing;** wailing, bewailing, bemoaning; **in mourning,** in sackcloth and ashes; depressed, down <nf>

19 **plaintive,** plangent, **mournful,** moanful, wailful, lamentive, ululant; woebegone, disconsolate; **sorrowful** 112.26; **howling,** Jeremianic; whining, whiny, whimpering, puling; **querulous, fretful,** petulant, peevish; **complaining,** faultfinding 510.24

20 <nf terms> **grouchy, kvetchy,** cranky, beefing, crabby, crabbing, grousing, griping, bellyaching, bitching

21 **tearful,** teary, **weepy** <nf>; lachrymal, lachrymose, lacrimatory; in the melting mood, on the edge of tears, ready to cry; **weeping, sobbing, crying;** blubbering, whimpering, sniveling; red-eyed; **in tears,** with tears in one's eyes, with tearful *or* watery eyes, with swimming *or* brimming *or* overflowing eyes, with eyes suffused *or* bathed *or* dissolved in tears

22 dirgelike, knell-like, elegiac, elegiacal, epicedial, threnodic, plaintive, plangent

ADVS 23 **lamentingly, plaintively, mournfully,** moanfully, wailfully; **sorrowfully** 112.36; complainingly, groaningly, querulously, fretfully, petulantly, peevishly

116 REJOICING

NOUNS 1 **rejoicing, jubilation,** jubilance, jubilant display, jubilee, show of joy, raucous happiness; **exultation,** elation, triumph; the time of one's life, special day; whoopee *and* hoopla <nf>, festivity 743.3,4, merriment 109.5; celebration 487

2 **cheer, hurrah, huzzah,** hurray, hooray, yippee, rah; **cry, shout, yell;** hosanna, hallelujah, alleluia, paean, paean *or* chorus of cheers, three cheers; **applause** 509.2, fanfare; high-five <nf>

3 **smile,** smiling; bright smile, gleaming *or* glowing smile, beam; silly smile *or* grin; **grin,** grinning; broad grin, ear-to-ear grin, toothful grin; stupid grin, idiotic grin; sardonic grin, **smirk, simper**

4 **laughter, laughing,** hilarity 109.5, risibility; **laugh;** boff *and* boffola *and* yuck <nf>; **titter; giggle; chuckle, chortle;** cackle, crow; **snicker,** snigger, snort; ha-ha, hee-haw, hee-hee, ho-ho, tee-hee, yuk-yuk; guffaw, **horselaugh; hearty laugh, belly laugh** <nf>, Homeric laughter, cachinnation; **shout, shriek,** shout of laughter, burst *or* outburst of laughter, peal *or* roar of laughter, gales of laughter; fit of laughter, convulsion, "laughter holding both his sides"—Milton

VERBS 5 **rejoice,** jubilate, **exult, glory, joy, delight,** bless *or* thank one's stars *or* lucky stars, congratulate oneself, hug oneself, rub one's hands, clap hands; dance *or* skip *or* jump for joy, dance, skip, frisk, rollick, revel, frolic, caper, gambol, caracole, romp; sing, carol, chirp, chirrup, chirp like a cricket, whistle, lilt; make merry

6 **cheer,** give a cheer, give three cheers, **cry, shout, yell,** cry for joy, yell oneself hoarse; huzzah, hurrah, hurray, hooray; shout hosanna *or* hallelujah, "make a joyful noise unto the Lord"—Bible; **applaud** 509.10; high-five <nf>

7 **smile,** crack a smile <nf>, break into a smile; **beam,** smile brightly; **grin,** grin like a Cheshire cat *or* chessy-cat <nf>; **smirk, simper**

8 **laugh,** burst out laughing, burst into laughter, burst out, laugh outright; laugh it up <nf>; **titter; giggle; chuckle, chortle;** cackle, crow; **snicker,** snigger, snort; ha-ha, hee-haw, hee-hee, ho-ho, tee-hee, yuk-yuk; **guffaw,** belly laugh, horselaugh; **shout, shriek,** give a shout *or* shriek of laughter; **roar,** cachinnate, roar with laughter; shake with laughter, shake like jelly; be convulsed with laughter, go into convulsions, fall about <Brit nf>; burst *or* split with laughter, break up *and* crack up <nf>, split <nf>, **split one's sides,** laugh fit to burst *or* bust <nf>, bust a gut *and* pee in *or* wet one's pants laughing <nf>, **be in stitches** <nf>, hold one's sides, roll in the aisles <nf>; laugh oneself sick *or* silly *or* limp, die *or* nearly die

laughing; laugh in one's sleeve, laugh up one's sleeve, laugh in one's beard

9 **make laugh, kill** *and* **slay** <nf>, "set the table on a roar"—Shakespeare, break *or* crack one up <nf>, get a laugh

ADJS 10 **rejoicing,** delighting, exulting; **jubilant, exultant, elated,** elate, flushed, euphoric, ecstatic

ADVS 11 **rejoicingly,** delightingly, exultingly; **jubilantly, exultantly, elatedly**

117 DULLNESS

<being uninteresting>

NOUNS 1 **dullness, dryness,** dustiness, uninterestingness; **stuffiness, stodginess,** woodenness, stiffness; barrenness, sterility, aridity, jejunity; **insipidness,** insipidity, vapidness, vapidity, inanity, hollowness, emptiness, superficiality, **staleness, flatness,** tastelessness; characterlessness, colorlessness, pointlessness; **deadness,** lifelessness, spiritlessness, bloodlessness, paleness, pallor, etiolation, effeteness; **slowness,** pokiness, dragginess <nf>, unliveliness; **tediousness** 118.2; **dreariness,** drearisomeness, dismalness; **heaviness,** leadenness, ponderousness; inexcitability 106; solemnity 111; lowness of spirit 112.3

2 **prosaicness,** prosiness; prosaism, prosaicism, prose, plainness; **matter-of-factness,** unimaginativeness; matter of fact; **simplicity** 798, **plainness** 499

3 **triteness,** corniness *and* squareness <nf>, **banality,** banalness, unoriginality, sameness, **hackneyedness, commonplaceness,** commonness, familiarness, platitudinousness; a familiar ring; redundancy, repetition, **staleness,** mustiness, fustiness; cliché 974.3

VERBS 4 **fall flat,** fall flat as a pancake; leave one cold *or* unmoved, go over like a lead balloon <nf>, lay an egg *and* bomb <nf>, **wear thin**

5 prose, platitudinize, sing a familiar tune; pedestrianize; warm over; banalize

ADJS 6 **dull, dry,** dusty, dry as dust; **stuffy, stodgy,** wooden, stiff; arid, barren, blank, sterile, jejune; **insipid,** vapid, inane, hollow, empty, superficial; ho-hum *and* blah <nf>, **flat,** tasteless; characterless, colorless, pointless; **dead,** lifeless, spiritless, bloodless, pale, pallid, etiolated, effete; cold; **slow,** poky, draggy <nf>, pedestrian, plodding, unlively; **tedious; dreary,** drearisome, dismal; **heavy,** leaden, ponderous, elephantine; dull as dish water, "weary, stale, flat and unprofitable"—Shakespeare; inexcitable 106.10; solemn 111.3; low-spirited 112.22

7 **uninteresting,** uneventful, **unexciting; uninspiring; unentertaining,** unenjoyable, **unamusing,** unfunny, unwitty

8 **prosaic,** prose, prosy, prosing, plain; **matter-of-fact,** unimaginative, unimpassioned

9 **trite;** corny *and* square *and* square-John *and* Clyde <nf>, fade, **banal,** unoriginal, platitudinous, **stereotyped,** stock, set, **commonplace, common,** truistic, twice-told, **familiar,** bromidic <nf>, old hat <nf>, back-number, bewhiskered, warmed-over, **cut-and-dried; hackneyed,** hackney; well-known 928.27; **stale,** musty, fusty; **worn,** timeworn, well-worn, moth-eaten, threadbare, **worn thin**

ADVS 10 **dully, dryly,** dustily, **uninterestingly;** stuffily, stodgily; aridly, barrenly, jejunely, **insipidly, vapidly,** inanely, hollowly, emptily, superficially, tastelessly, **colorlessly,** pointlessly; lifelessly, spiritlessly, bloodlessly, pallidly, effetely; slowly, draggily <nf>, ploddingly; **tediously;** drearily, drearisomely, dismally; heavily, ponderously

11 **tritely,** cornily <nf>, **banally,** commonplacely, commonly, familiarly, hackneyedly, unoriginally, truistically, stalely

118 TEDIUM

NOUNS 1 **tedium, monotony, humdrum,** irksomeness, irk; **sameness,** sameliness, samesomeness <nf>, wearisome sameness, more of the same, the same old thing *or* story, the same damn thing <nf>; broken record, parrot; platitude, chestnut; undeviation, unvariation, invariability; the round, the daily round *or* grind, the weary round, the treadmill, the squirrel cage, the rat race <nf>, the beaten track *or* path, drag <nf>; time on one's hands, time hanging heavily on one's hands; **protraction,** prolongation 827.2

2 **tediousness, monotonousness, unrelievedness; humdrumness,** humdrumminess; **dullness** 117; **wearisomeness,** wearifulness; **tiresomeness, irksomeness,** drearisomeness; **boresomeness,** boringness; prolixity, **long-windedness** 538.2; redundancy, repetition, repetitiveness, tick-tock

3 **weariness, tiredness,** wearifulness; jadedness, fed-upness, satiation, satiety; **boredom,** boredness; **ennui,** spleen <old>, melancholy, life-weariness, *taedium vitae* <L>, world-weariness, *Weltschmerz* <Ger>, jadedness; languor, **listlessness** 94.4, **dispiritedness** 112.3

4 **bore,** crashing bore <nf>, frightful bore; **pest, nuisance;** dryasdust; proser, twaddler, **wet blanket;** buttonholer; bromide; egoist

5 <nf terms> **drag, drip, pill,** flat tire, deadass, deadfanny, dull tool; **headache,** pain, pain in the neck *or* ass; broken record

VERBS 6 **be tedious, drag on,** go on forever; have a certain sameness, be infinitely repetitive, do the same old thing; **weary, tire, irk,** wear, wear on *or* upon,

make one tired, fatigue, weary *or* tire to death, jade; give one a swift pain in the ass *and* give one a bellyful *and* make one fed-up <nf>, **pall, satiate,** glut

7 **bore,** leave one cold, set *or* send to sleep; **bore stiff** *or* to tears *or* to death *or* to extinction <nf>, bore to distraction, bore out of one's life, bore out of all patience; buttonhole; wear out one's welcome

8 **harp on** *or* **upon, dwell on** *or* **upon,** harp upon one *or* the same string, play *or* sing the same old song *or* tune, play the same broken record

ADJS 9 **tedious, monotonous, humdrum,** singsong, jog-trot, treadmill, unvarying, invariable, uneventful, broken-record, parrotlike, harping, everlasting, too much with us <nf>; blah <nf>, flat, **dreary,** drearisome, dry, dry-as-dust, dusty, **dull** 117.6; protracted, prolonged 827.11; prolix, **long-winded** 538.12; pedestrian, commonplace

10 **wearying,** wearing, **tiring; wearisome,** weariful, fatiguing, **tiresome, irksome; boring, boresome,** stupefyingly boring, stuporific, yawny <nf>

11 **weary,** weariful; **tired,** wearied, irked; good and tired, tired to death, weary unto death; sick, **sick of, tired of, sick and tired of;** jaded, satiated, palled, fed up <nf>, brassed off <Brit nf>; **blasé;** splenetic <old>, melancholy, melancholic, life-weary, world-weary, tired of living; **listless** 94.13, **dispirited** 112.22

12 **bored, uninterested;** bored stiff *or* to death *or* to extinction *or* to tears <nf>, stupefied *or* stuporous with boredom

ADVS 13 **tediously, monotonously,** harpingly, everlastingly, unvaryingly, endlessly; long-windedly; **boringly,** boresomely; **wearisomely,** fatiguingly, wearyingly, **tiresomely, irksomely,** drearisomely; dully 117.10

14 on a treadmill, in a squirrel cage, on the beaten track, on the same old round; without a change of menu *or* scenery *or* pace

PHRS 15 ho hum!, heigh ho!, what a life!, que sera sera; *plus ça change, plus c'est la même chose* <Fr, the more things change, the more they stay the same>; so what else is new?, go figure; MEGO *or* mine eyes glaze over

119 AGGRAVATION

NOUNS 1 **aggravation, worsening; exacerbation,** embittering, embitterment, souring, deterioration; **intensification, heightening,** stepping-up, sharpening, deepening, **increase,** enhancement, amplification, enlargement, magnification, augmentation, exaggeration; **exasperation, annoyance,** irritation 96.3; hassle <nf>, aggro <chiefly Brit>; deliberate aggravation, provocation; contentiousness

VERBS 2 **aggravate, worsen,** make worse; **exacerbate,** embitter, sour; deteriorate; **intensify, heighten,** step up, sharpen, make acute *or* more acute, bring to a head, deepen, **increase,** enhance, amplify, enlarge, magnify, build up, exaggerate; augment; rub salt in the wound, twist the knife, add insult to injury, inflame, pour oil on the fire, add fuel to the fire *or* flame, heat up *and* hot up <nf>; increase pressure *or* tension, tighten, tighten up, tighten the screws, put the squeeze on <nf>; bring to a head; **exasperate, annoy,** irritate 96.14; rub it in <nf>; provoke, antagonize, hassle <nf>, be an *agent provocateur*

3 **worsen,** get *or* grow worse, take a turn for the worse, deteriorate, degenerate; go from push to shove, **go from bad to worse; jump out of the frying pan and into the fire,** avoid Scylla and fall into Charybdis

ADJS 4 **aggravated, worsened, worse,** worse and worse, exacerbated, embittered, soured, deteriorated; **intensified, heightened,** stepped-up, **increased,** deepened, enhanced, amplified, magnified, enlarged, augmented, heated *or* hotted up <nf>; **exasperated, irritated,** annoyed 96.21; provoked, deliberately provoked; worse-off, out of the frying pan and into the fire

5 **aggravating,** aggravative; **exasperating,** exasperative; **annoying,** irritating 98.22; provocative; vexing, vexatious; contentious

ADVS 6 from bad to worse; aggravatingly, exasperatingly; annoyingly 98.29

120 RELIEF

NOUNS 1 **relief, easement, easing,** ease; **relaxation,** relaxing, relaxation *or* easing of tension, decompression, slackening, respite; **reduction,** diminishment, diminution, lessening, abatement, remission; **remedy** 86; **alleviation, mitigation, palliation,** softening, assuagement, allayment, defusing, appeasement, mollification, subduement; soothing, salving, anodyne; lulling; dulling, deadening, numbing, narcotizing, anesthesia, anesthetizing, analgesia; sedating, sedation; doping *or* doping up <nf>; comfort, solace, consolation; charity, benefaction

2 **release, deliverance, freeing,** removal; suspension, intermission, respite, surcease, reprieve; discharge; catharsis, purging, purgation, purge, cleansing, cleansing away, emotional release

3 **lightening, disburdening,** unburdening, unweighting, unloading, disencumbrance, disembarrassment, easing of the load, a load off one's mind, something out of one's system

4 sense *or* **feeling of relief,** sigh of relief
VERBS **5 relieve,** give relief; **ease,** ease matters; **relax,** slacken; **reduce,** diminish, lessen, abate, remit; **alleviate, mitigate, palliate,** soften, pad, cushion, assuage, allay, defuse, lay, appease, mollify, subdue, soothe; salve, pour balm into, pour oil on; poultice, foment, stupe; slake; lull; **dull, deaden,** dull *or* deaden the pain, numb, benumb, anesthetize, tranquilize; sedate, narcotize, dope *or* dope up <nf>; temper the wind to the shorn lamb, lay the flattering unction to one's soul; take the sting out of; comfort, solace, pacify

6 release, free, deliver, reprieve, remove, free from, liberate; suspend, intermit, give respite *or* surcease; **relax,** decompress, ease, destress; act as a cathartic, **purge, purge away, cleanse,** cleanse away; give release, cut loose

7 lighten, disburden, unburden, unweight, unload, unfreight, disencumber, disembarrass, ease one's load; **set one's mind at ease** *or* **rest,** set at ease, **take a load off one's mind,** smooth the ruffled brow of care; relieve oneself, let one's hair down, pour one's heart out, talk it out, let it all hang out *and* go public <nf>, get it off one's chest

8 be relieved, feel relief, feel better about, get something out of one's system, feel *or* be oneself again; get out from under <nf>; **breathe easy** *or* **easier,** breathe more freely, breathe again, rest easier; **heave a sigh of relief,** draw a long *or* deep breath

ADJS **9 relieving, easing, alleviative,** alleviating, alleviatory, **mitigative,** mitigating, **palliative,** assuaging, lenitive, assuasive, softening, subduing, soothing, demulcent, emollient, balmy, balsamic; **remedial** 86.39; dulling, deadening, numbing, benumbing, anesthetic, analgesic, anodyne, pain killing, sedative, hypnotic; cathartic, purgative, cleansing; **relaxing**

10 relieved, breathing easy *or* easier *or* freely, able to breathe again, out from under *and* out of the woods <nf>; **relaxed;** calmed, restored

121 COMFORT

NOUNS **1 comfort, ease, well-being;** contentment 107; clover, velvet <nf>, bed of roses; life of ease 1009.1; solid comfort

2 comfortableness, easiness; restfulness, reposefulness, peace, peacefulness; softness, cushiness <nf>, cushioniness; **coziness, snugness;** friendliness, warmness; **homelikeness,** homeyness <nf>, homeliness; **commodiousness,** roominess, convenience; luxuriousness 501.5; hospitality 585

3 creature comforts, comforts, conveniences, excellent accommodations, amenities, good things of life, cakes and ale, egg in one's beer <nf>, all the comforts of home; all the heart can desire, luxuries, the best

4 consolation, solace, solacement, easement, heart's ease, "surcease of sorrow"—Poe; **encouragement,** aid and comfort, **assurance, reassurance,** support, **comfort,** crumb *or* shred of comfort; condolence 147, sympathy; **relief** 120

5 comforter, consoler, solacer, encourager; the Holy Spirit *or* Ghost, the Comforter, the Paraclete
VERBS **6 comfort, console, solace,** give *or* bring comfort, bear up; condole with, sympathize with, extend sympathy; ease, **put** *or* **set at ease;** bolster, support; relieve 120.5; **assure, reassure; encourage, hearten,** pat on the back; **cheer** 109.7; wipe away the tears

7 be comforted, take comfort, take heart; take hope, lift up one's heart, pull oneself together, pluck up one's spirits; *sursum corda* <L>

8 be at ease, be *or* feel easy, stand easy <Brit>; **make oneself comfortable,** make oneself at home, feel at home, put one's feet up, take a load off <nf>; **relax,** be relaxed; live a life of ease 1010.10

9 snug, snug down *or* up; tuck in

10 snuggle, nestle, cuddle, cuddle up, curl up; nest; bundle; snuggle up to, snug up *or* together <old>
ADJS **11 comfortable,** comfy <nf>; contented 107.7,9,10; **easy,** easeful; **restful,** reposeful, peaceful, **relaxing;** soft, cushioned, cushy <nf>, cushiony; comfortable as an old shoe; **cozy, snug,** snug as a bug in a rug; friendly, warm; **homelike,** homey *and* down-home <nf>, homely, lived-in; **commodious,** roomy, convenient; luxurious 501.21

12 at ease, at one's ease, easy, relaxed, laid-back <nf>; at rest, resting easy; **at home,** in one's element

13 comforting, consoling, consolatory, of good comfort; condoling, condolent, condolatory, sympathetic; **assuring, reassuring,** supportive; **encouraging, heartening;** cheering 109.16; relieving 120.9; hospitable 585.11
ADVS **14 comfortably, easily,** with ease; **restfully,** reposefully, peacefully; **cozily, snugly; commodiously,** roomily, conveniently; luxuriously, voluptuously

15 in comfort, in ease, **in clover, on** *or* **in velvet** <nf>, on *or* in a bed of roses

16 comfortingly, consolingly, assuringly, reassuringly, supportively, encouragingly, hearteningly; hospitably

122 WONDER

NOUNS **1 wonder,** wonderment, sense of wonder, marveling, marvel, **astonishment, amazement,** amaze, **astoundment;** dumbfoundment, stupefaction; **surprise; awe,** breathless wonder *or* awe, sense of mystery, admiration; beguilement, fascination 377.1; bewilderment, puzzlement 971.3

2 **marvel, wonder, prodigy, miracle, phenomenon,** phenom <nf>; astonishment, amazement, marvelment, wonderment, wonderful thing, nine days' wonder, *annus mirabilis* <L>, amazing *or* astonishing thing, quite a thing, really something, **sensation,** rocker *and* stunner <nf>; one for the books *and* something to brag about *and* something to shout about *and* something to write home about *and* something else <nf>; **rarity,** nonesuch, nonpareil, exception, one in a thousand, one in a way, oner <Brit nf>; **curiosity,** gazingstock <old>, **sight, spectacle,** eye-popper <nf>; wonders of the world; masterpiece, chef d'oeuvre, masterstroke

3 **wonderfulness,** wondrousness, **marvelousness,** miraculousness, phenomenalness, **prodigiousness, stupendousness, remarkableness,** extraordinariness; beguilingness, fascination, enchantingness, enticingness, seductiveness, **glamorousness; awesomeness, mysteriousness,** mystery, numinousness; **transcendence,** transcendentness, surpassingness

4 **inexpressibility, ineffability,** ineffableness, inenarrability, noncommunicability, noncommunicableness, incommunicability, incommunicableness, indescribability, indefinableness, **unutterability, unspeakability,** unnameableness, innominability, unmentionability

VERBS 5 **wonder, marvel,** be astonished *or* amazed *or* astounded, be seized with wonder; **gaze, gape,** drop one's jaw, look *or* stand aghast *or* agog, gawk, **stare,** stare openmouthed, open one's eyes, rub one's eyes, hold one's breath; not know what to say, not know what to make of, not believe one's eyes *or* ears *or* senses

6 **astonish, amaze, astound, surprise,** startle, stagger, **bewilder,** perplex 971.13, flabbergast <nf>, confound, overwhelm, **boggle, boggle the mind; awe,** strike with wonder *or* awe; **dumbfound** *or* dumbfounder, strike dumb, strike dead; strike all of a heap *and* throw on one's beam ends *and* knock one's socks off *and* bowl down *or* over <nf>, dazzle, bedazzle, daze, bedaze; **stun, stupefy,** petrify, paralyze

7 take one's breath away, turn one's head, make one's head swim, make one's hair stand on end, make one's tongue cleave to the roof of one's mouth, make one stare, make one sit up and take notice, sweep *or* carry off one's feet; blow one's mind

8 beggar *or* baffle description, stagger belief

ADJS 9 **wondering,** wrapped *or* rapt in wonder, marveling, **astonished, amazed, surprised,**

astounded, flabbergasted <nf>, **bewildered,** puzzled, confounded, **dumbfounded,** dumbstruck, staggered, overwhelmed, unable to believe one's senses *or* eyes; **aghast,** agape, agog, all agog, gazing, gaping, at gaze staring, gauping, wide-eyed, popeyed, open-eyed, openmouthed, **breathless; thunderstruck,** wonder-struck, wonder-stricken, awestricken, awestruck, struck all of a heap <nf>; **awed, in awe,** in awe of; spellbound, fascinated, captivated, under a charm, beguiled, enthralled, enraptured, enravished, enchanted, entranced, bewitched, hypnotized, mesmerized, stupefied, lost in wonder *or* amazement; transfixed, rooted to the spot

10 **wonderful, wondrous, marvelous,** awesome, **miraculous,** fantastic, fabulous, ace, cool, rad *or* wicked <nf>, phenomenal, brilliant, **prodigious, stupendous,** unheard-of, unprecedented, extraordinary, exceptional, rare, unique, singular, **remarkable,** striking, **sensational; strange,** passing strange, "wondrous strange"—Shakespeare; **beguiling, fascinating;** incredible, inconceivable, outlandish, unimaginable, incomprehensible; . **bewildering, puzzling,** enigmatic

11 **awesome,** awful, awing, awe-inspiring; **transcendent,** transcending, surpassing; **mysterious,** numinous; weird, eerie, uncanny, bizarre; exotic

12 **astonishing, amazing, surprising,** startling, **astounding,** confounding, staggering, stunning <nf>, eye-opening, breathtaking, overwhelming, mind-boggling *or* -numbing, mind-blowing; **spectacular,** electrifying

13 **indescribable, ineffable,** inenarrable, inexpressible, unutterable, unspeakable, noncommunicable, incommunicable, indefinable, undefinable, unnameable, innominable, unwhisperable, unmentionable

ADVS 14 **wonderfully,** wondrously, **marvelously, miraculously,** fantastically, fabulously, phenomenally, prodigiously, stupendously, extraordinarily, exceptionally, remarkably, strikingly, **sensationally;** strangely, outlandishly, incredibly, inconceivably, unimaginably, incomprehensibly, **bewilderingly, puzzlingly,** enigmatically; **beguilingly,** fascinatingly

15 **awesomely,** awfully, awingly, awe-inspiringly; **mysteriously,** numinously, weirdly, eerily, uncannily, bizarrely; **transcendently,** surpassingly, surpassing, passing <old>

16 **astonishingly, amazingly, astoundingly,** staggeringly, confoundingly; **surprisingly,** startlingly, to one's surprise *or* great surprise, to one's astonishment *or* amazement; for a wonder, strange to say

17 **indescribably, ineffably,** inexpressibly, unutterably, **unspeakably,** inenarrably, indefinably, unnameably, unmentionably

18 in wonder, in astonishment, in amazement, in bewilderment, in awe, in admiration, with gaping mouth

INTERJS 19 <astonishment or surprise> my word!, I declare!, well I never!, of all things!, as I live and breathe!, what!, indeed!, really!, surely!, how now!, what on earth!, what in the world!, I'll be jiggered!, holy moly!, holy Christmas!, holy cow!, holy mackerel!, holy Moses!, holy smoke!, holy shit! <nf>, hush or shut my mouth!, blow me down!, strike me dead!, shiver my timbers!

20 oh!, O!, ah!, la!, lo!, lo and behold!, hello!, halloo!, hey!, whew!, phew!, wow!, yipes!, yike!

21 my!, oh, my!, dear!, dear me!, goodness!, gracious!, goodness gracious!, gee!, my goodness!, my stars!, good gracious!, good heavens!, good lack!, lackadaisy!, my gosh!, welladay!, hoity-toity!, zounds!, 'sdeath!, gadzooks!, gad so!, bless my heart!, God bless me!, heavens and earth!, for crying out loud! <nf>

22 imagine!, fancy!, fancy that!, just imagine!, only think!, well!, I never!, can you feature that!, can you beat that!, it beats the Dutch!, do tell!, you don't say!, the devil or deuce you say!, I'll be!, what do you know!, what do you know about that!, how about that!, who would have thought it!, did you ever!, can it be!, can such things be!, will wonders never cease!, go on!

23 **Seven Wonders of the Ancient World**

The Great Pyramids of Egypt at Giza	The Mausoleum of King Mausolus at Halicarnassus
The Hanging Gardens of Babylon	The Colossus of Rhodes
The Statue of Zeus at Olympia	The Lighthouse of Alexandria
The Temple of Artemis (Diana) at Ephesus	

123 UNASTONISHMENT

NOUNS 1 **unastonishment, unamazement,** unamazedness, nonastonishment, nonamazement, nonamazedness, nonwonder, nonwondering, nonmarveling, unsurprise, unsurprisedness, awelessness, wonderlessness; phlegmaticness, apathy, passivity; **calm,** calmness, coolness, **cool** <nf>, cool or calm or nodding acceptance, composure, composedness, sangfroid, inexcitability 106, expectation 130, unimpressibleness, refusal to be impressed or awed or amazed; poker face, straight face; predictability

VERBS 2 **accept, take for granted** or as a matter of course or in stride or as it comes, treat as routine, show no amazement, refuse to be impressed, not blink an eye, not turn a hair, keep one's cool <nf>; see it coming

ADJS 3 **unastonished, unsurprised, unamazed,** unmarveling, unwondering, unastounded, undumbfounded, unbewildered; undazzled, undazed; unawed, aweless, wonderless, blasé; **unimpressed,** unmoved; calm, **cool,** cool as a cucumber, composed, nonchalant, inexcitable 106.10; expecting, expected 130.13,14; phlegmatic

124 HOPE

NOUNS 1 **hope, hopefulness,** hoping, **hopes,** fond or fervent hope, good hope, good cheer; aspiration, **desire** 100; prospect, **expectation** 130; sanguine expectation, happy or cheerful expectation; **trust, confidence, faith,** assured faith, **reliance,** dependence; conviction, assurance, security, well-grounded hope; assumption, presumption; auspiciousness; **promise, prospect,** good or bright or fair prospect, good or hopeful prognosis, best case; great expectations, good prospects, high hopes; hoping against hope, prayerful hope; doomed hope or hopes

2 "the thing with feathers that perches in the soul"—Emily Dickinson, "the worst of all evils, because it prolongs the torments of man"—Nietzsche

3 **optimism,** optimisticalness, Pollyannaism, cheerful or bright or rosy outlook, rose-colored glasses; **cheerfulness** 109; bright side, silver lining; "the noble temptation to see too much in everything"—Chesterton; wishful thinking; philosophical optimism, Leibnizian or Rousseauistic optimism, utopianism, perfectionism, perfectibilism; millenarianism, chiliasm, millennialism

4 **ray of hope,** gleam or glimmer of hope; faint hope, last hope

5 **airy hope,** unreal hope, dream, false hope, golden dream, pipe dream <nf>, bubble, chimera, fool's paradise, quixotic ideal, utopia 986.11; vision, castles in the air, cloud-cuckoo-land

6 **optimist,** hoper, Pollyanna, ray of sunshine <nf>, irrepressible optimist, Dr Pangloss, idealist; "a proponent of the doctrine that black is white"—Ambrose Bierce, "one who makes the best of it when he gets the worst of it"—Anon, "one who makes the most of all that comes and the least of all that goes"—Sara Teasdale, Leibnizian optimist, philosophical optimist, utopian, perfectionist, perfectibilist, perfectibilitarian; millenarian, chiliast, millennialist, millennian; aspirer, aspirant, hopeful <nf>, dreamer, visionary

VERBS 7 **hope,** be or live in hopes, have reason to hope, entertain or harbor the hope, cling to the hope, cherish *or* foster *or* nurture the hope; look for, prognosticate, **expect** 130.5; **trust,** confide, presume, feel confident, rest assured; pin one's hope upon, put one's trust in, hope in, rely on, count on, lean upon, bank on, set great store on; hope for, **aspire to,** desire 100.14; **hope against hope,** hope and pray, hope to God <nf>

8 **be hopeful, get one's hopes up,** keep one's spirits up, never say die, take heart, cheer up, buck up, be of good hope, be of good cheer, keep hoping, keep hope alive, keep the faith <nf>, keep smiling, cling to hope; **hope for the best,** knock on wood, touch wood <Brit>, cross one's fingers, keep one's fingers crossed, allow oneself to hope; clutch *or* catch at straws

9 **be optimistic, look on the bright side; look through** *or* **wear rose-colored glasses,** *voir en couleur de rose* <Fr>; call the glass half full, look on the bright side, think positively *or* affirmatively, be upbeat <nf>, think the best of, **make the best of it,** say that all is for the best, put a good *or* bold face upon, put the best face upon; see the light at the end of the tunnel; count one's chickens before they are hatched, count one's bridges before they are crossed

10 **give hope, raise hope,** yield *or* afford hope, hold out hope, justify hope, inspire hope, **raise one's hopes,** raise expectations, **lead one to expect;** cheer 109.7; inspire, inspirit; **assure, reassure,** support; **promise,** hold out promise, augur well, bid fair *or* well, make fair promise, have good prospects

ADJS 11 **hopeful, hoping, in hopes,** full of hope, in good heart, of good hope, of good cheer; **aspiring** 100.28; **expectant** 130.11; **sanguine,** fond; **confident,** assured; undespairing

12 **optimistic,** upbeat *and* up <nf>, bright, sunny; bullish; **cheerful** 109.11; **rosy,** roseate, rose-colored, *couleur de rose* <Fr>; pollyannaish, Leibnizian, Rousseauistic, Panglossian; utopian 986.23, idealistic, perfectionist, perfectibilitarian, millenarian, chiliastic, millennialistic, visionary

13 **promising,** of promise, full of promise, bright with promise, pregnant of good, best-case, **favorable,** looking up; aspiring, aspirant; **auspicious,** propitious 133.18; heartening; inspiring, inspiriting, **encouraging,** cheering, reassuring, supportive

ADVS 14 **hopefully,** hopingly; **expectantly** 130.15; **optimistically;** cheerfully 109.17; sanguinely, fondly; confidently

125 HOPELESSNESS

NOUNS 1 **hopelessness,** unhopefulness, no hope, not a prayer *and* not a hope in hell <nf>, not the ghost of a chance; small hope, bleak outlook *or* prospect *or* prognosis, worst case, blank future, no future; inexpectation 131; futility 391.2; impossibility 967

2 **despair, desperation,** desperateness, loss of hope; no way <nf>, no way out, no exit, despondency 112.3; disconsolateness 112.12; forlornness; letdown; cave of despair, cave of Trophonius; gloom and doom; acedia, sloth; apathy 94.4; downer <nf>

3 **irreclaimability, irretrievability,** irredeemability, irrecoverableness, unsalvageability, unsalvability; incorrigibility, irreformability; irrevocability, **irreversibility; irreparability, incurability,** irremediableness, curelessness, remedilessness, immedicableness; unrelievability, unmitigability

4 **forlorn hope,** vain expectation, doomed *or* foredoomed hope, fond *or* foolish hope, futility; counsel of perfection

5 **dashed hopes,** blighted hope, hope deferred; disappointment 132

6 **pessimism, cynicism,** malism, nihilism; uncheerfulness 112.2; **gloominess,** dismalness, gloomy outlook; negativism; defeatism; retreatism

7 **pessimist, cynic,** malist, nihilist; killjoy 112.14, gloomy Gus *and* calamity howler *and* worrywart <nf>, seek-sorrow, Job's comforter, prophet of doom, Cassandra, Eeyore; negativist; defeatist; retreatist; loser, born loser; drag <nf>, "one who is not happy except when he is miserable"—Anon, "a man who feels bad when he feels good for fear he'll feel worse when he feels better"—George Burns, "one who is always building dungeons in the air"—John Galsworthy

8 **lost cause, fool's errand, wild-goose chase; hopeless case,** hopeless situation; **goner** *and* gone goose *or* gosling *and* dead duck <nf>; terminal case

VERBS 9 **be hopeless,** have not a hope *or* prayer, have no remedy, look bleak *or* dark; **be pessimistic, look on the dark side,** be *or* think downbeat <nf>, think negatively, think *or* make the worst of, put the worst face upon, call the glass half empty; not hold one's breath

10 **despair,** despair of, **despond** 112.16, falter, lose hope, **lose heart, abandon hope,** give up hope, **give up,** give up all hope *or* expectation, give way *or* over, fall *or* sink into despair, give oneself up *or* yield to despair, throw up one's hands in despair, turn one's face to the wall; curse God and die, write off

11 **shatter one's hopes,** dash *or* crush *or* blight *or* shatter one's hope, burst one's bubble <nf>, bring crashing down around one's head, dash the cup from one's lips, disappoint 132.2, drive to despair *or* desperation

ADJS 12 hopeless, unhopeful, without hope, affording no hope, worst-case, bleak, grim, dismal, cheerless, comfortless, down in the mouth; **desperate, despairing, in despair;** despondent 112.22; disconsolate 112.28; forlorn; apathetic 94.13

13 futile, vain 391.13; doomed, foredoomed, pointless

14 impossible, out of the question, not to be thought of, no-go *and* no-win *and* lose-lose <nf>

15 past hope, beyond recall, past praying for, beyond hope, abject; **irretrievable, irrecoverable, irreclaimable,** irredeemable, unsalvageable, unsalvable; incorrigible, irreformable; irrevocable, **irreversible; irremediable, irreparable,** inoperable, **incurable,** cureless, remediless, immedicable, beyond remedy, terminal; unrelievable, unmitigable; **ruined,** undone, kaput <nf>; lost, gone, gone to hell *and* gone to hell in a handbasket <nf>

16 pessimistic, pessimist, downbeat <nf>, **cynical,** nihilistic; uncheerful 112.21; **gloomy,** dismal, crepehanging, funereal, lugubrious; negative, negativistic; defeatist; Cassandran *or* Cassandrian, Cassandra-like

ADVS 17 hopelessly, desperately, forlornly; impossibly

18 irreclaimably, irretrievably, irrecoverably, irredeemably, unsalvageably, unsalvably; irrevocably, **irreversibly; irremediably, incurably, irreparably**

126 ANXIETY
<troubled thought>

NOUNS 1 anxiety, anxiousness; apprehension, apprehensiveness, antsyness <nf>, misgiving, foreboding, forebodingness, suspense, strain, tension, stress, nervous strain *or* tension; **dread,** fear 127; **concern,** concernment, anxious concern, **solicitude,** zeal 101.2; **care,** cankerworm of care; **distress,** trouble, vexation, unease; **uneasiness, perturbation, disturbance,** upset, **agitation, disquiet,** disquietude, inquietude, unquietness; **nervousness** 128; malaise, angst 96.1; pucker *and* yips *and* stew *and* all-overs <nf>, pins and needles, tenterhooks, shpilkes <nf>; overanxiety; anxious seat *or* bench; anxiety neurosis *or* hysteria

2 worry, worriment <nf>, worriedness; **worries,** worries and cares, troubles, concerns; worrying, fretting; harassment, torment

3 worrier, worrywart *and* nervous Nellie <nf>

VERBS 4 concern, give concern, **trouble, bother, distress, disturb, upset,** frazzle, **disquiet, agitate;** rob one of ease *or* sleep *or* rest, keep one on edge *or* on tenterhooks *or* on pins and needles *or* on shpilkes <nf>

5 <make anxious> **worry, upset, vex,** fret, agitate, get to <nf>, **harass,** harry **torment,** dog, hound, plague, persecute, haunt, beset

6 <feel anxious> **worry,** worry oneself, worry one's head about, worry oneself sick, trouble one's head *or* oneself, be a prey to anxiety, lose sleep; have one's heart in one's mouth, have one's heart miss *or* skip a beat, have one's heart stand still, get butterflies in one's stomach; **fret, fuss, chafe,** stew *and* take on <nf>, fret and fume; tense up, bite one's nails, walk the floor, go up the wall <nf>, be on tenterhooks *or* pins and needles *or* shpilkes <nf>

ADJS 7 anxious, concerned, apprehensive, foreboding, misgiving, suspenseful, strained, tense, tensed up <nf>, nail-biting, white-knuckle <nf>; **fearful** 127.32; **solicitous,** zealous 101.9; **troubled, bothered; uneasy, perturbed, disturbed, disquieted, agitated;** nervous 128.11; **on pins and needles,** on tenterhooks, on shpilkes <nf>, on the anxious seat *or* bench; all hot and bothered *and* in a pucker *and* in a stew <nf>; over-anxious, overapprehensive

8 worried, vexed, fretted; **harassed,** harried, tormented, dogged, hounded, persecuted, haunted, beset, plagued; worried sick, worried to a frazzle, worried stiff <nf>

9 careworn, heavy-laden, overburdened

10 troublesome, bothersome, **distressing,** distressful, **disturbing, upsetting, disquieting; worrisome,** worrying; fretting, chafing; **harassing,** tormenting, plaguing; **annoying** 98.22

ADVS 11 anxiously, concernedly, apprehensively, misgivingly, **uneasily;** worriedly; solicitously, zealously 101.14

127 FEAR, FEARFULNESS

NOUNS 1 fear, fright, affright; **scare, alarm, consternation, dismay; dread,** unholy dread, **awe; terror, horror,** horrification, mortal *or* abject fear; **phobia** <see list>, funk *or* blue funk <nf>; **panic,** panic fear *or* terror, blind panic; stampede; **cowardice** 491

2 fearfulness, frighteningness, frightfulness, awfulness, scariness, fearsomeness, alarmingness, dismayingness, disquietingness, startlingness, disconcertingness, terribleness, **dreadfulness, horror,** horribleness, **hideousness,** appallingness, direness, **ghastliness,** grimness, grisliness, **gruesomeness,** ghoulishness; **creepiness, spookiness,** eeriness, weirdness, uncanniness

3 fearfulness, afraidness; **timidity, timorousness, hyness;** shrinkingness, bashfulness, diffidence, stage fright, mike fright *and* flop sweat <nf>;

skittishness, startlishness, jumpiness, goosiness <nf>

4 apprehension, apprehensiveness, **misgiving, qualm,** qualmishness, funny feeling; **anxiety** 126, angst; worry; doubt 954.2; foreboding

5 trepidation, trepidity, perturbation, **fear and trembling; quaking,** agitation 105.4; **uneasiness, disquiet,** disquietude, inquietude; nervousness 128; palpitation, heartquake; shivers or cold shivers <nf>, creeps or cold creeps <nf>, heebie-jeebies <nf>, chills of fear or terror, icy fingers or icy clutch of dread, jimjams <nf>; horripilation, gooseflesh, goose bumps <nf>; sweat, cold sweat; thrill of fear, spasm or quiver of terror; sinking stomach; blood running cold, knocking knees, chattering teeth

6 frightening, intimidation, bullying, browbeating, cowing, bulldozing <nf>, hectoring; **demoralization,** psychological warfare, war of nerves

7 terrorization, terrorizing, horrification, scaremongering, panic-mongering, scare tactics; **terrorism,** terror or terroristic tactics, *Schrecklichkeit* <Ger>, rule by terror, reign of terror, sword of Damocles

8 alarmist, scaremonger, panic-monger; **terrorist,** bomber, assassin

9 frightener, scarer, hair-raiser; alarmist; scarebabe, **bogey,** bogeyman, **bugaboo,** bugbear; hobgoblin; **scarecrow; horror, terror,** holy terror; **ogre,** ogress, **monster,** vampire, werewolf, ghoul, bête noire, fee-faw-fum; incubus, succubus, nightmare; witch, goblin; **ghost,** specter, phantom, revenant; Frankenstein, Dracula, Wolf-man; mythical monsters

VERBS **10 fear, be afraid; apprehend,** have qualms, misgive, eye askance; **dread,** stand in dread of, be in mortal dread or terror of, stand in awe of, stand aghast; be on pins and needles, sit upon thorns; have one's heart in one's mouth, have one's heart stand still, have one's heart skip or miss a beat; quake in one's boots; **sweat,** break out in a cold sweat, sweat bullets <nf>

11 take fright, take alarm, push or press or hit the panic button <nf>; funk *and* go into a funk <nf>; get the wind up <Brit nf>; lose courage 491.8; pale, grow or turn pale, change or turn color; look as if one had seen a ghost; freeze, be paralyzed with fear, throw up one's hands in horror, jump out of one's skin; shit in one's pants *and* shit green <nf>

12 start, startle, **jump,** jump out of one's skin, jump a mile, leap like a startled gazelle; **shy,** fight shy, start aside, boggle, jib; **panic,** stampede, skedaddle <nf>

13 flinch, shrink, shy, shy away from, draw back, recoil, funk <nf>, **quail, cringe, wince, blench, blink,** say or cry uncle; put one's tail between one's legs

14 tremble, shake, quake, shiver, quiver, quaver; tremble or **quake** or **shake** in one's boots or **shoes,** tremble like an aspen leaf, quiver like a rabbit, shake all over

15 frighten, fright, affright, funk <nf>, frighten or scare out of one's wits; **scare,** spook <nf>, scare one stiff or shitless or spitless <nf>, scare the life out of, scare the pants off of *and* scare hell out of *and* scare the shit out of <nf>; scare one to death, scare the daylights or the living daylights or the wits or the shit out of <nf>; give one a fright or scare or turn; **alarm,** disquiet, raise apprehensions; shake, stagger; **startle** 131.8; **unnerve, unman,** unstring; give one goose-flesh, horripilate, give one the creeps or the willies <nf>, make one's flesh creep, chill one's spine, make one's nerves tingle, curl one's hair <nf>, make one's hair stand on end, make one's blood run cold, freeze or curdle the blood, make one's teeth chatter, make one tremble, take one's breath away, make one shit one's pants or shit green <nf>

16 put in fear, put the fear of God into, **throw a scare into** <nf>; **panic,** stampede, send scuttling, throw blind fear into

17 terrify, awe, strike terror into; **horrify, appall, shock,** make one's flesh creep; **frighten out of one's wits** or **senses;** strike dumb, **stun, stupefy, paralyze, petrify,** freeze

18 daunt, deter, shake, stop, stop in one's tracks, set back; **discourage, dishearten;** faze <nf>; **awe, overawe**

19 dismay, disconcert, appall, astound, confound, abash, discomfit, put out, take aback

20 intimidate, cow, browbeat, bulldoze <nf>, bludgeon, dragoon; **bully, hector, harass,** huff; bluster, bluster out of or into; **terrorize,** put in bodily fear, use terror or terrorist tactics, pursue a policy of *Schrecklichkeit*, systematically terrorize; threaten 514.2; **demoralize**

21 frighten off, scare away, bluff off, put to flight

ADJS **22 afraid, scared,** scared to death <nf>, spooked <nf>; feared or afeared <nf>; fear-stricken, fear-struck; haunted with fear, phobic

23 fearful, fearing, fearsome, **in fear;** cowardly 491.10; **timorous, timid, shy,** rabbity *and* mousy <nf>, afraid of one's own shadow; **shrinking,** bashful, diffident; scary; **skittish,** skittery <nf>, startlish, gun-shy, jumpy, goosy <nf>; **tremulous,** trembling, trepidant, shaky, shivery; **nervous;** waiting for the bomb to drop

24 apprehensive, misgiving, antsy <nf>, **qualmish,** qualmy; anxious 126.6

25 frightened, frightened to death, affrighted, in a fright, frit <Brit nf>, in a funk *or* blue funk <nf>; **alarmed,** disquieted; consternated, **dismayed,** daunted; **startled** 131.13; more frightened than hurt

26 terrified, terror-stricken, terror-struck, terror-smitten, terror-shaken, terror-troubled, terror-riven, terror-ridden, terror-driven, terror-crazed, terror-haunted; awestricken, awestruck; **horrified,** horror-stricken, horror-struck; **appalled, astounded, aghast;** frightened out of one's wits *or* mind, **scared to death, scared stiff** *or* **shitless** *or* spitless <nf>; unnerved, unstrung, unmanned, undone, **cowed,** awed, **intimidated; stunned, petrified, stupefied,** paralyzed, frozen; white as a sheet, pale as death *or* a ghost, deadly pale, ashen, blanched, pallid, gray with fear

27 panicky, panic-prone, panicked, in a panic, panic-stricken, panic-struck, terror-stricken, out of one's mind with fear, prey to blind fear

28 frightening, frightful; fearful, fearsome, fear-inspiring, nightmarish, hellish; **scary,** scaring, chilling; **alarming, startling,** disquieting, dismaying, disconcerting; **unnerving, daunting,** deterring, **deterrent,** discouraging, disheartening, fazing, awing, overawing; stunning, stupefying, mind-boggling *or* -numbing, hair-raising

29 terrifying, terrorful, terror-striking, terror-inspiring, terror-bringing, terror-giving, terror-breeding, terror-breathing, terror-bearing, terror-fraught; **bloodcurdling, hair-raising** <nf>; petrifying, paralyzing, stunning, stupefying; **terrorizing, terror, terroristic;** *schrecklich* <Ger>

30 terrible, terrific, tremendous; **horrid, horrible, horrifying,** horrific, horrendous; **dreadful, dread,** dreaded; **awful;** awesome, awe-inspiring; **shocking, appalling,** astounding; **dire,** direful, fell; formidable, redoubtable; **hideous, ghastly,** morbid, grim, grisly, gruesome, ghoulish, macabre

31 creepy, spooky, eerie, weird, uncanny

ADVS **32 fearfully, apprehensively, diffidently,** for fear of; **timorously, timidly, shyly,** mousily <nf>, bashfully, shrinkingly; tremulously, tremblingly, quakingly, **with** *or* **in fear and trembling;** with heart in mouth, with bated breath

33 in fear, in terror, in awe, in alarm, in consternation; in mortal fear, in fear of one's life

34 frightfully, fearfully; alarmingly, startlingly, disquietingly, dismayingly, disconcertingly; **shockingly, appallingly,** astoundingly; **terribly,** terrifically, tremendously; **dreadfully, awfully; horridly, horribly,** horrifyingly, horrifically, horrendously

35 phobias by subject

<accidents> dystychiphobia
<anemia> anemophobia
<animals> zoophobia
<ants> myrmecophobia
<bacteria> bacteriophobia
<baldness> phalacrophobia
<beards> pogonophobia
<bears> ursaphobia
<bees> apiphobia
<being alone> autophobia *or* monophobia *or* eremiophobia *or* eremophobia
<being dirty> automysophobia
<being idle> thaasophobia
<being whipped> mastigophobia
<birds> ornithophobia
<blood> hemaphobia *or* hematophobia *or* hemophobia
<blushing> erythrophobia
<body odor> bromidrophobia *or* bromidrosiphobia
<bridges> gephyrophobia
<bullets> ballistophobia
<bulls> taurophobia
<cancer> cancerphobia *or* cancerophobia *or* carcinophobia
<cats> ailurophobia
<cemeteries> coimetrophobia
<certain places> topophobia
<childbirth> tocophobia
<children> pedophobia
<Chinese> Sinophobia
<cholera> cholerophobia
<church> ecclesiophobia
<clouds> nephelophobia
<coitus> coitophobia
<cold> cheimaphobia *or* cheimatophobia
<color> chromophobia *or* chromatophobia
<comets> cometophobia
<computers> cyberphobia
<constipation> coprostasophobia
<corpses> necrophobia
<crossing a bridge> gephyrophobia
<crossing a street> agyrophobia

<crowds> demophobia
<crystals> crystallophobia
<dampness> hygrophobia
<dancing> chorophobia
<darkness> scotophobia *or* achluophobia *or* nyctophobia
<dawn> eosophobia
<daylight, sunlight> phengophobia
<death> thanatophobia
<decisions> decidophobia
<demons> demonophobia
<dentists> dentophobia
<depth> bathophobia
<diabetes> diabetophobia
<dirt> mysophobia
<disease> pathophobia
<doctors, hospitals> iatrophobia
<dogs> cynophobia
<double vision> diplopiaphobia
<draft> aerophobia
<dreams> oneirophobia
<drink> potophobia
<drugs> pharmacophobia
<duration> chronophobia
<dust> koniophobia *or* amathophobia
<electricity> electrophobia
<enclosed places> claustrophobia
<English> Anglophobia
<everything> panphobia *or* pantophobia
<eyes> ommataphobia
<failure> kakorraphiaphobia
<fatigue> kopophobia
<fear> phobophobia
<feathers> pteronophobia
<feces> coprophobia *or* scatophobia
<fever> febriphobia
<fire> pyrophobia
<fish> ichthyophobia
<floods> antlophobia
<flowers> anthophobia
<flutes> aulophobia
<flying> aviatophobia
<fog> homichlophobia
<food> cibophobia *or* sitophobia *or* sitiophobia
<foreigners> xenophobia
<forests> xylophobia

<freedom>
eleutherophobia
<French> Francophobia
or Gallophobia
<frogs, reptiles>
batrachophobia
<fur> doraphobia
<gaining weight>
obesophobia or
pocrescophobia
<Germans>
Germanophobia or
Teutonophobia
<germs> spermophobia or
spermatophobia
<ghosts> phasmophobia
<God> theophobia
<going to bed>
clinophobia
<gold> aurophobia
<gravity> barophobia
<growing old>
gerascophobia
<hair> chaetophobia or
trichophobia
<hair disease>
trichopathophobia
<heart disease>
cardiophobia
<heat> thermophobia
<heaven> uranophobia or
ouranophobia
<hell> hadephobia or
stygiophobia
<heredity>
patroiophobia
<high places> acrophobia
or altophobia or
batophobia or
hypsophobia or
hypsiphobia
<home> ecophobia or
oecophobia or
oikophobia
<homosexuality>
homophobia
<horses> hippophobia
<hospitals>
nosocomephobia
<hurricanes>
lilapsophobia
<ice, frost> cryophobia
<ideas> ideophobia
<illness> nosemaphobia
or nosophobia
<imperfection>
atelophobia
<infinity> apeirophobia
<injury> traumatophobia

<inoculation>
trypanophobia or
vaccinophobia
<insanity> lyssophobia or
maniaphobia
<insects> entomophobia
<insect stings>
cnidophobia
<itching> acarophobia
<Japanese> Japanophobia
<jealousy> zelophobia
<Jews> Judeophobia
<justice> dikephobia
<kissing> philemaphobia
or philematophobia
<lakes> limnophobia
<learning> sophophobia
<lice, parasites>
pediculophobia or
phthiriophobia
<light> photophobia
<light flashes> selaphobia
<lightning> astraphobia
or astrapophobia
<loneliness> autophobia
or monophobia or
eremitophobia
<love> philophobia
<machinery>
mechanophobia
<magic> rhabdophobia
<marriage> gametophobia
or gamophobia
<meat> carnophobia
<men> androphobia
<meningitis>
meningitophobia
<menstruation>
menophobia
<metal> metallophobia
<mice> musophobia or
murophobia
<microbes> bacillophobia
or microbiophobia
<mirrors> eisoptrophobia
or catoptrophobia
<mites> acarophobia
<mobs> ochlophobia
<money> chrometophobia
<monsters> teratophobia
<moon> selenophobia
<mother-in-law>
pentheraphobia
<motion> dromophobia or
kinetophobia
<moving vehicles>
ochophobia
<music> musicophobia
<names> onomatophobia

<narrowness>
anginophobia
<needles> belonephobia
<newness> cainophobia or
cainotophobia or
centophobia
<new things> neophobia
<night> nyctophobia
<noise> ligyrophobia
<nuclear weapons>
nucleomitophobia
<nudity> gymnophobia or
nudophobia
<numbers> arithmophobia
or numerophobia
<old people>
gerontophobia
<one thing> monophobia
<open places>
agoraphobia
<opposite sex> sexophobia
or heterophobia
<pain> algophobia or
odynesphobia
<parasites> parasitophobia
<passing high buildings>
batophobia
<people> anthropophobia
<philosophy>
philosophobia
<pins> enetophobia
<pleasure> hedonophobia
<poison> toxiphobia or
toxophobia or
toxicophobia
<politics> politicophobia
<the Pope> papaphobia
<poverty> peniaphobia
<precipices>
cremnophobia
<priests> hierophobia
<protein> proteinphobia
<punishment>
poinephobia
<rabies>
hydrophobophobia
<radiation> radiophobia
<rectum, rectal disease>
rectophobia or
proctophobia
<relatives>
syngenesophobia
<reptiles> batrachophobia
or herpetophobia
<responsibility>
hypegiaphobia
<ridicule> katagelophobia
<rivers> potamophobia
<robbers> harpaxophobia
<ruin> atephobia

<Russians> Russophobia
<saints> hagiophobia
<Satan> Satanophobia
<school>
didaskaleinophobia or
scolionophobia
<sea> thalassophobia
<sex> erotophobia or
genophobia
<shadows> sciophobia or
sciaphobia
<sharpness> acrophobia
or aichurophobia
<shock> hormephobia
<sin> hamartophobia or
peccatiphobia
<skin> dermatosiophobia
<skin disease>
dermatopathophobia
<sleep> hypnophobia
<slime> blennophobia or
myxophobia
<small things>
microphobia
<smell> olfactophobia or
osmophobia or
ophresiophobia
<smothering>
pnigophobia or
pnigerophobia
<snakes> ophiciophobia
or ophiophobia or
snakephobia
<snow> chionophobia
<soiling> rypophobia
<solitude> isolophobia
<sound> acousticophobia
<sourness> acerophobia
or acerbophobia
<speech> lalophobia or
laliophobia or
glossophobia or
phonophobia
<speed> tachophobia
<spiders> arachnophobia
<spirits> pneumatophobia
<stairs> climacophobia
<standing> stasophobia
<stars> siderophobia
<stealing> kleptophobia
<string> linonophobia
<sun> heliophobia
<surgery> tomophobia
<swallowing> phagophobia
<symmetry>
symmetrophobia
<syphilis> syphilophobia
<taste> geumatophobia
<technology>
technophobia

<teeth> odontophobia
<telephone> telephonophobia
<termites> isopterophobia
phronemophobia
<thirteen> tredecaphobia or triskaidekaphobia
<thunder> brontophobia or tonitrophobia or keraunophobia
<thunder and lightning> astraphobia or astrapophobia
<touch> haptophobia or haphophobia or thixophobia
<travel> hodophobia
<trees> dendrophobia
<trembling> tremophobia
<trichinosis> trichinophobia
<tuberculosis> tuberculophobia or phthisiophobia
<tyrants> tyrannophobia
<urine> urophobia

<vegetables> lachanophobia
<vehicles> ochophobia
<venereal disease> venereophobia or cypridophobia
<void> kenophobia
<vomiting> emetophobia
<washing, bathing> ablutophobia
<wasps> spheksophobia
<water> hydrophobia or aquaphobia
<waves> cymophobia
<weakness> asthenophobia
<wind> ancraophobia
<women> gynephobia or feminophobia
<words> logophobia
<work> ergophobia
<worms> vermiphobia or helminthophobia
<wound, injury> traumatophobia
<wrinkles> rhytiphobia
<writing> graphophobia
<young girls> parthenophobia

36 phobias by name

ablutophobia <washing, bathing>
acrophobia or altophobia or batophobia or hypsophobia <high places>
acrophobia <sharpness>
aerophobia <draft>
agoraphobia <open places>
agyrophobia <crossing a street>
ailurophobia <cats>
algophobia <pain>
ancraophobia <wind>
androphobia <men>
anemophobia <anemia>
anginophobia <narrowness>
Anglophobia <English>
anthophobia <flowers>
anthropophobia <people>
antlophobia <floods>
apeirophobia <infinity>
apiphobia <bees>
arachnophobia <spiders>
arithmophobia or numerophobia <numbers>
asthenophobia <weakness>

astraphobia or astrapophobia <lightning>
atelophobia <imperfection>
atephobia <ruin>
aulophobia <flutes>
aurophobia <gold>
automysophobia <being dirty>
autophobia or monophobia or ermitophobia <being alone, loneliness>
aviatophobia <flying>
bacillophobia or microbiophobia <microbes>
bacteriophobia <bacteria>
ballistophobia <bullets>
barophobia <gravity>
bathophobia <depth>
batophobia <passing high buildings>
batrachophobia or herpetophobia <reptiles, frogs>
belonephobia <needles>
blennophobia or myxophobia <slime>

bromidrosiphobia or bromidrophobia <body odor>
brontophobia or tonitrophobia or keraunophobia <thunder>
cancerphobia or cancerophobia or carcinophobia <cancer>
cainophobia or cainotophobia <newness>
cardiophobia <heart disease>
carnophobia <meat>
chaetophobia or trichophobia <hair>
cheimaphobia or cheimatophobia <cold>
chionophobia <snow>
cholerophobia <cholera>
chrometophobia <money>
chromophobia <color>
chronophobia <duration>
cibophobia or sitophobia or sitiophobia <food>
claustrophobia <enclosed places>
climacophobia <stairs>
clinophobia <going to bed>
cnidophobia <insect stings>
coimetrophobia <cemeteries>
coitophobia <coitus>
cometophobia <comets>
coprophobia <feces>
coprostasophobia <constipation>
cremnophobia <precipices>
cryophobia <ice>
crystallophobia <crystals>
cyberphobia <computers>
cymophobia <waves>
cynophobia <dogs>
decidophobia <decisions>
demonophobia <demons>
demophobia <crowds>
dendrophobia <trees>
dentophobia <dentists>
dermatopathophobia <skin disease>
dermatosiophobia <skin>
diabetophobia <diabetes>
didaskaleinophobia or scolionophobia <school>

dikephobia <justice>
diplopiaphobia <double vision>
doraphobia <fur>
dromophobia or kinetophobia <motion>
dystychiphobia <accidents>
ecclesiophobia <church>
ecophobia or oecophobia or oikophobia <home>
eisoptrophobia <mirrors>
electrophobia <electricity>
eleutherophobia <freedom>
emetophobia <vomiting>
enetophobia <pins>
entomophobia <insects>
eosophobia <dawn>
ergophobia <work>
erotophobia or genophobia <sex>
erythrophobia <blushing>
febriphobia <fever>
Francophobia or Gallophobia <French>
gametophobia <marriage>
gephyrophobia <crossing a bridge>
gerascophobia <growing old>
gerontophobia <old people>
Germanophobia or Teutonophobia <Germans>
geumatophobia <taste>
graphophobia <writing>
gymnophobia or nudophobia <nudity>
gynephobia <women>
hadephobia or stygiophobia <hell>
hagiophobia <saints>
hamartophobia or peccatiphobia <sin>
haptophobia or haphophobia or thixophobia <touch>
harpaxophobia <robbers>
hedonophobia <pleasure>
heliophobia <sun>
helminthophobia <worms>
hemaphobia or hematophobia or hemophobia <blood>
hierophobia <priests>
hippophobia <horses>

hodophobia <travel>
homichlophobia <fog>
homophobia <homosexuality>
hormephobia <shock>
hydrophobia <water>
hydrophobophobia <rabies>
hygrophobia <dampness>
hypegiaphobia <responsibility>
hypnophobia <sleep>
iatrophobia <doctors, hospitals>
ichthyophobia <fish>
ideophobia <ideas>
isolophobia <solitude>
isopterophobia <termites>
Japanophobia <Japanese>
Judeophobia <Jews>
kakorraphiaphobia <failure>
katagelophobia <ridicule>
kenophobia <void>
kleptophobia <stealing>
koniophobia or amathophobia <dust>
kopophobia <fatigue>
lachanophobia <vegetables>
lalophobia or laliophobia or glossophobia or phonophobia <speech>
ligyrophobia <noise>
lilapsophobia <hurricanes>
limnophobia <lakes>
linonophobia <string>
logophobia <words>
lyssophobia or maniaphobia <insanity>
mastigophobia <beating>
mechanophobia <machinery>
meningitophobia <meningitis>
menophobia <menstruation>
metallophobia <metal>
microphobia <small things>
monophobia <one thing>
musicophobia <music>
musophobia <mice>
myrmecophobia <ants>
mysophobia <dirt>
necrophobia <corpses>
neophobia <new things>
nephophobia <clouds>

nosemaphobia or nosophobia <illness>
nosocomephobia <hospitals>
nucleomitophobia <nuclear weapons>
nyctophobia <night>
obesophobia or pocrescophobia <gaining weight>
ochlophobia <mobs>
ochophobia <vehicles>
odontophobia <teeth>
olfactophobia or osmophobia or ophresiophobia <smell>
ommataphobia <eyes>
oneirophobia <dreams>
onomatophobia <names>
ophiciophobia or ophiophobia or snakephobia <snakes>
ornithophobia <birds>
panphobia or pantophobia <everything>
papaphobia <the Pope>
parasitophobia <parasites>
parthenophobia <young girls>
pathophobia <disease>
patroiophobia <heredity>
pediculophobia <lice, parasites>
pedophobia <children>
peniaphobia <poverty>
pentheraphobia <mother-in-law>
phagophobia <swallowing>
phalacrophobia <baldness>
pharmacophobia <drugs>
phasmophobia <ghosts>
phengophobia <daylight, sunlight>
philemaphobia or philematophobia <kissing>
philophobia <love>
philosophobia <philosophy>
phobophobia <fear>
photophobia <light>
phronemophobia <thinking>
pneumatophobia <spirits>
pnigophobia or pnigerophobia <smothering>

pogonophobia <beards>
poinephobia <punishment>
politicophobia <politics>
potamophobia <rivers>
potophobia <drink>
proteinphobia <protein>
pteronophobia <feathers>
pyrophobia <fire>
radiophobia <radiation>
rectophobia <rectum>
rhabdophobia <magic>
rhytiphobia <wrinkles>
Russophobia <Russians>
rypophobia <soiling>
Satanophobia <Satan>
scabiophobia <scabies>
sciophobia <shadows>
selaphobia <light flashes>
selenophobia <moon>
sexophobia or heterophobia <opposite sex>
siderophobia <stars>
Sinophobia <Chinese>
sophophobia <learning>
spermophobia or spermatophobia <germs>
spheksophobia <wasps>
stasophobia <standing>
symmetrophobia <symmetry>
syngenesophobia <relatives>
syphilophobia <syphilis>
tachophobia <speed>
taurophobia <bulls>
technophobia <technology>
telephonophobia <telephone>
teratophobia <monsters>

thaasophobia <being idle>
thalassophobia <sea>
thanatophobia <death>
theophobia <God>
thermophobia <heat>
tocophobia <childbirth>
tomophobia <surgery>
topophobia <certain places>
toxiphobia or toxophobia or toxicophobia <poison>
traumatophobia <wound, injury>
tredecaphobia or triskaidekaphobia <the number thirteen>
tremophobia <trembling>
trichinophobia <trichinosis>
trichopathophobia <hair disease>
trypanophobia or vaccinophobia <inoculation>
tuberculophobia or phthisiophobia <tuberculosis>
tyrannophobia <tyrants>
uranophobia or ouranophobia <heaven>
urophobia <urine>
ursaphobia <bears>
venereophobia <venereal disease>
vermiphobia or helminthophobia <worms>
xenophobia <foreigners>
xylophobia <forests>
zelophobia <jealousy>
zoophobia <animals>

128 NERVOUSNESS

NOUNS 1 **nervousness, nerves,** nervosity, **disquiet, uneasiness, apprehensiveness,** disquietude, qualmishness, malaise, funny or creepy feeling, **qualm, qualms, misgiving;** undue or morbid excitability, excessive irritability, state of nerves, case of nerves, spell of nerves, attack of nerves; **agitation, trepidation;** fear 127; panic; **fidgets,** fidgetiness, jitteriness, jumpiness; nail-biting; twitching, tic, vellication; stage fright, buck fever <nf>; nervous stomach, butterflies in one's stomach <nf>

2 <nf terms> **jitters,** willies, **heebie-jeebies,**

jimjams, **jumps, shakes,** quivers, trembles, dithers, collywobbles, butterflies, shivers, cold shivers, creeps, sweat, cold sweat; antsyness, ants in one's pants, yips

3 **tension,** tenseness, tautness, **strain, stress,** stress and strain, mental strain, nervous tension *or* strain, pressure

4 frayed nerves, frazzled nerves, jangled nerves, shattered nerves, raw nerves *or* nerve endings, twanging *or* tingling nerves; neurosis; neurasthenia, nervous prostration, crackup, **nervous breakdown**

5 **nervous wreck,** wreck, a bundle of nerves

VERBS 6 **fidget,** have the fidgets; jitter, have the jitters, etc; **tense up; tremble**

7 lose self-control, go into hysterics; lose courage 491.8; **go to pieces,** have a nervous breakdown, fall apart *or* to pieces, come apart, fall *or* come apart at the seams, spazz out <nf>

8 <nf terms> **crack, crack up,** go haywire, **blow one's cork** *or* mind *or* stack, **flip,** flip one's lid *or* wig, wig out, freak out, go out of one's skull; come unglued *or* unstuck, go up the wall

9 **get on one's nerves,** jangle the nerves, **grate on, jar on,** put on edge, **set one's teeth on edge, go against the grain, send one up the wall** <nf>, drive one crazy; **irritate** 96.14

10 **unnerve, unman, undo, unstring,** unbrace, reduce to jelly, **demoralize, shake, upset,** psych out <nf>, dash, knock down *or* flat, **crush,** overcome, prostrate

ADJS 11 **nervous,** nervy <Brit nf>; **high-strung,** overstrung, highly strung, all nerves; **uneasy, apprehensive,** qualmish, nail-biting, white-knuckle <nf>, frit <Brit nf>; nervous as a cat; **excitable; irritable,** edgy, **on edge,** nerves on edge, on the ragged edge <nf>, wired <nf>, panicky, **fearful, frightened**

12 **jittery** <nf>, **jumpy,** twittery, skittish, skittery, trigger-happy <nf>, gun-shy; **shaky,** shivery, quivery, in a quiver; tremulous, tremulant, trembly; jumpy as a cat on a hot tin roof; **fidgety,** fidgeting; fluttery, all of a flutter *or* twitter; twitchy; **agitated;** shaking, trembling, quivering, shivering; shook up *and* all shook up <nf>

13 **tense,** tensed-up, uptight <nf>, **strained,** stretched tight, taut, unrelaxed, **under a strain**

14 **unnerved, unmanned, unstrung, undone,** reduced to jelly, unglued <nf>, **demoralized, shaken, upset,** dashed, stricken, **crushed; shot,** shot to pieces; neurasthenic, prostrate, prostrated, overcome

15 **unnerving, nerve-racking,** nerve-rending, nerve-shaking, nerve-jangling, nerve-trying, nerve-stretching; jarring, grating

ADVS 16 **nervously, shakily,** shakingly, tremulously, tremblingly, quiveringly

129 UNNERVOUSNESS

NOUNS 1 **unnervousness, nervelessness; sangfroid, calmness,** inexcitability 106; unshakiness, untremulousness; **steadiness,** steady-handedness, steady nerves; no nerves, strong nerves, iron nerves, nerves of steel, icy nerves; cool head

ADJS 2 **unnervous, nerveless,** without a nerve in one's body; strong-nerved, iron-nerved, steel-nerved; coolheaded, **calm,** inexcitable 106.10; calm, cool, and collected; cool as a cucumber <nf>; **steady,** steady as a rock, rock-steady, steady-nerved, steady-handed; unshaky, unshaken, unquivering, untremulous, without a tremor; unflinching, unfaltering, unwavering, unshrinking, unblenching, unblinking; **relaxed,** unstrained

130 EXPECTATION

NOUNS 1 **expectation,** expectance *or* **expectancy,** state of expectancy; **predictability,** predictableness; **anticipation, prospect,** thought; contemplation; likelihood, probability 968; confidence, presumption, reliance 953.1, overreliance; certainty 970; imminence 840; unastonishment 123

2 sanguine *or* cheerful expectation, optimism, eager expectation, **hope** 124; the light at the end of the tunnel

3 **suspense,** state of suspense, cliff-hanging *and* nail-biting <nf>; **waiting,** expectant waiting, hushed expectancy; uncertainty 971, nervous expectation; **anxiety, dread, pessimism,** apprehension 126.1

4 **expectations,** prospects, outlook, hopes, apparent destiny *or* fate, future prospects; likelihoods, probabilities; prognosis; accountability, responsibility

VERBS 5 **expect,** be expectant, **anticipate, have in prospect,** face, think, **contemplate,** have in contemplation *or* mind, envision, envisage; **hope** 124.7; presume 951.10; dread; **take for granted;** not be surprised *or* a bit surprised; foresee 961.5

6 **look forward to,** reckon *or* calculate *or* count on, predict, foresee; look to, **look for, watch for,** look out for, watch out for, be on the watch *or* lookout for, keep a good *or* sharp lookout for; be ready for; forestall

7 **be expected,** be one's probable fate *or* destiny, be one's outlook *or* prospect, be in store

8 **await,** wait, wait for, wait on *or* upon, stay *or* tarry for; have *or* keep an eye out for, lie in wait for, line up for; wait around *or* about, watch, watch and wait; **bide one's time,** bide, abide, **mark time;** cool

one's heels <nf>; be in suspense, be on tenterhooks, be on pins and needles, hold one's breath, bite one's nails, sweat *or* sweat out *or* sweat it *or* sweat it out <nf>; **wait up for,** stay up for, sit up for; cross one's fingers; be on the waiting list; be on standby, be on call

9 **expect to,** intend, plan on 380.4,6,7

10 **be as expected,** be as one thought *or* looked for, turn out that way, come as no surprise; **be just like one,** be one all over <nf>; **expect it of,** think that way about, **not put it past** <nf>; **impend,** be imminent 840.2; lead one to expect 133.13

ADJS 11 **expectant,** expecting, in expectation *or* anticipation; **anticipative,** anticipant, anticipating, anticipatory; **holding one's breath; waiting,** awaiting, waiting for; forewarned, forearmed, forestalling, ready, prepared, on standby; **looking forward to,** looking for, watching for, on the watch *or* lookout for; gaping, agape, agog, all agog, atiptoe, atingle, **eager;** sanguine, optimistic, hopeful 124.11; sure, confident 953.21,969.21; certain 970.13; unsurprised, not surprised

12 **in suspense, on tenterhooks,** on pins and needles, on tiptoe, **on edge, with bated breath,** tense, taut, with muscles tense, quivering, keyed-up, biting one's nails; anxious, **apprehensive;** dreading; **suspenseful,** cliff-hanging <nf>

13 **expected, anticipated, awaited, predicted, foreseen;** presumed 951.14; probable 968.6; **looked-for,** hoped-for; **due, promised;** long-expected, long-awaited, overdue; **in prospect, prospective;** in the cards; **in view,** in one's eye, on the horizon; imminent 840.3

14 **to be expected,** as expected, up to *or* according to expectation, just as one thought, just as predicted, on schedule, **as one may have suspected,** as one might think *or* suppose; **expected of,** counted on, **taken for granted;** just like one, one all over <nf>, in character

ADVS 15 **expectantly,** expectingly; anticipatively, **anticipatingly,** anticipatorily; hopefully 124.14; **with bated breath,** in hushed expectancy, with breathless expectation; with ears pricked up, with eyes *or* ears strained

131 INEXPECTATION

NOUNS 1 **inexpectation,** nonexpectation, inexpectance *or* inexpectancy, no expectation, **unanticipation; unexpectedness;** unforeseeableness, unpredictableness, unpredictability; unreadiness, unpreparedness; the unforeseen, the unlooked-for, the last thing one expects; **improbability** 969

2 **surprise,** surprisal; **astonishment** 122.1-2;

surpriser, startler, shocker, **blow,** staggerer <nf>, **eye-opener,** revelation; **bolt out of *or* from the blue,** thunderbolt, thunderclap; **bombshell,** bomb; blockbuster, earthshaker; sudden turn *or* development, *peripeteia* <Gk>, switch; surprise ending, kicker *or* joker *or* catch <nf>; surprise package; surprise party

3 **start, shock, jar, jolt, turn,** fright

VERBS 4 **not expect,** hardly expect, **not anticipate, not look for,** not bargain for, **not foresee,** not think of, have no thought of, have no expectation, think unlikely *or* improbable

5 **be startled, be taken by surprise,** be taken aback, be given a start, be given a turn *or* jar *or* jolt; **start,** startle, **jump,** jump a mile <nf>, jump out of one's skin; **shy,** start aside, flinch

6 **be unexpected, come unawares,** come as a surprise *or* shock, come out of left field <nf>, come out of nowhere, appear unexpectedly, turn up, pop up *and* bob up <nf>, drop from the clouds, appear like a bolt out of the blue, come *or* burst like a thunderclap *or* thunderbolt, burst *or* flash upon one, come *or* fall *or* pounce upon, steal *or* creep up on

7 **surprise, take by surprise,** do the unexpected, spring a surprise <nf>, **open one's eyes,** give one a revelation; **catch *or* take unawares,** catch *or* take short, take aback, pull up short, raise some eyebrows, catch off-guard 941.7, cross one up <nf>; throw a curve <nf>, come from behind, come from an unexpected quarter, come out of the blue, come upon unexpectedly *or* without warning, spring *or* pounce upon; drop a bombshell, drop a brick <nf>; throw *or* knock for a loop <nf>; **blindside** <nf>, spring a mine under, ambush, bushwhack; drop in on <nf>; give a surprise party; **astonish** 122.6

8 **startle, shock, electrify, jar, jolt, shake,** stun, **stagger, give one a turn** <nf>, give the shock of one's life, make one jump out of his skin, take aback, take one's breath away, throw on one's beam ends, bowl down *or* over <nf>, strike all of a heap <nf>; frighten

ADJS 9 **inexpectant,** nonexpectant, unexpecting; **unanticipative,** unanticipating; **unsuspecting, unaware,** unguessing; uninformed, unwarned, unforewarned, unadvised, unadmonished; unready, unprepared; off one's guard 984.8

10 **unexpected, unanticipated, unlooked for,** unhoped for, unprepared for, undivined, unguessed, unpredicted, **unforeseen;** unforeseeable, unpredictable, off-the-wall <nf>; **improbable** 968.3; contrary to expectation, beyond *or* past expectation, out of one's reckoning, more than expected, more than one bargained for; out of the

blue, dropped from the clouds, out of left field *and* from out in left field <nf>; without warning, unheralded, unannounced; sudden 830.5; out-of-the-way, **extraordinary**

11 **surprising,** astonishing 122.12; eye-opening, eye-popping <nf>; **startling, shocking,** electrifying, boggling, staggering, stunning, jarring, jolting

12 **surprised,** struck with surprise, openmouthed; **astonished** 122.9; **taken by surprise,** taken unawares, caught short; blindsided <nf>

13 **startled, shocked, electrified,** jarred, jolted, shaken, shook <nf>, staggered, **given a turn** *or* **jar** *or* **jolt,** taken aback, bowled down *or* over <nf>, struck all of a heap <nf>, able to be knocked down with a feather; speechless, flabbergasted

ADVS 14 **unexpectedly,** unanticipatedly, improbably, implausibly, unpredictably, **unforseeably,** *à l'improviste* <Fr>, **by surprise, unawares,** against *or* contrary to all expectation, when least expected, as no one would have predicted, without notice *or* warning, in an unguarded moment, like a thief in the night; **out of a clear sky, out of the blue, like a bolt from the blue;** suddenly 830.9

15 **surprisingly, startlingly, to one's surprise,** to one's great surprise; shockingly, staggeringly, stunningly, **astonishingly** 122.16

132 DISAPPOINTMENT

NOUNS 1 **disappointment,** sad *or* sore disappointment, bitter *or* cruel disappointment, failed *or* blasted expectation; **dashed hope, blighted hope,** betrayed hope, hope deferred, forlorn hope; **dash** <old>, dash to one's hopes; blow, buffet; **frustration,** discomfiture, bafflement, defeat, balk, foiling; **comedown,** setback, **letdown** <nf>; failure, fizzle <nf>, fiasco; **disillusionment** 977; tantalization, mirage, tease; dissatisfaction 108.1; fallen countenance; bad news, bummer <nf>

VERBS 2 **disappoint,** defeat expectation *or* hope; **dash,** dash *or* blight *or* blast *or* crush one's hope; **balk,** bilk, **thwart, frustrate, baffle, defeat,** foil, cross; put one's nose out of joint; **let down,** cast down; **disillusion** 977.2; tantalize, tease; dissatisfy; leave in the lurch; burst someone's bubble

3 **be disappointing, let one down** <nf>, **not come up to expectation,** come to nothing, not live *or* measure up to expectation, go wrong, turn sour, disappoint one's expectations, come *or* fall short; peter out *or* fizzle *or* fizzle out <nf>, not make it *and* not hack it <nf>

4 **be disappointed,** have hoped for better, not realize one's expectations, fail of one's hopes *or* ambitions, run into a stone wall, be let down; look blue, laugh

on the wrong side of one's mouth <nf>; be crestfallen *or* chapfallen

ADJS 5 **disappointed,** bitterly *or* sorely disappointed; **let down,** betrayed, ill-served, ill done-by; **dashed,** blighted, blasted, crushed; **balked,** bilked, **thwarted, frustrated,** baffled, crossed, dished <Brit>, defeated, foiled; caught in one's own trap; disillusioned 977.5; disenchanted, crestfallen, chapfallen, out of countenance; soured; dissatisfied; regretful 113.8

6 **disappointing,** not up to expectation, falling short, out of the running, not up to one's hopes, second- *or* third-best; tantalizing, teasing; **unsatisfactory;** disheartening

133 PREMONITION

NOUNS 1 **premonition, presentiment,** preapprehension, forefeeling, presage, presagement; **hunch** 934.3, **feeling in one's bones;** prediction 962

2 foreboding, boding; **apprehension, misgiving,** chill *or* quiver along the spine, creeping *or* shudder of the flesh; wind of change

3 **omen, portent; augury,** auspice, soothsay, prognostic, prognostication; **premonitory sign** *or* **symptom,** premonitory shiver *or* chill, **foretoken,** foretokening, tokening, betokening, betokenment, foreshowing, prefiguration, presigning <old>, presignifying, presignification, **preindication,** indicant, indication, **sign, token,** type, **promise,** sign of the times; **foreshadowing, adumbration,** foreshadow, shadow

4 **warning, forewarning,** "warnings, and portents and evils imminent," "the baby figure of the giant mass of things to come"—Shakespeare, handwriting on the wall, *"mene, mene, tekel, upharsin"*—Bible <Aramaic>

5 **harbinger, forerunner, precursor,** messenger <old>, **herald,** announcer, *buccinator novi temporis* <L>; presager, premonitor, foreshadower

6 <omens> bird of ill omen, owl, raven, stormy petrel, Mother Carey's chicken; gathering clouds, clouds on the horizon, dark *or* black clouds, angry clouds, storm clouds, thundercloud, thunderhead; black cat; broken mirror; rainbow; ring around the moon; shooting star; halcyon bird; woolly bear, groundhog

7 **ominousness, portentousness, portent,** bodefulness, presagefulness, suggestiveness, significance, **meaning** 518, meaningfulness; fatefulness, fatality, doomfulness, sinisterness, banefulness, balefulness, direness

8 **inauspiciousness, unpropitiousness, unfavorableness, unfortunateness, unluckiness,** ill-fatedness, ill-omenedness; fatality

9 **auspiciousness, propitiousness, favorableness;**
luckiness, fortunateness, prosperousness,
beneficence, benignity, benignancy, benevolence;
brightness, cheerfulness, cheeriness; good omen,
good auspices, *auspicium melioris aevi* <L>

VERBS 10 **foreshow, presage;** omen, be the omen of,
auspicate <old>; **foreshadow, adumbrate,** shadow,
shadow forth, cast their shadows before; **predict**
961.9; have an intimation, have a hunch <nf>, feel
or know in one's bones, feel the wind of change

11 **forebode, bode,** portend, croak; **threaten, menace,**
lower, look black, spell trouble; **warn, forewarn,**
raise a warning flag, give pause; have a
premonition *or* presentiment, apprehend,
preapprehend, fear for

12 **augur,** hint, divine <old>; **foretoken, preindicate,**
presignify, presign, presignal, pretypify, **prefigure,**
betoken, token, typify, **signify,** mean 518.8, spell,
indicate, point to, look like, **be a sign of,** show
signs of

13 **promise, suggest, hint, imply,** give prospect of,
make likely, give ground for expecting, raise
expectation, **lead one to expect,** hold out hope,
make fair promise, have a lot going for, have *or*
show promise, **bid fair, stand fair to**

14 **herald, harbinger, forerun,** run before; **speak of,**
announce, proclaim, preannounce; give notice,
notify, talk about

ADJS 15 augured, **foreshadowed, adumbrated,**
foreshown; indicated, signified; preindicated,
prognosticated, **foretokened,** prefigured,
pretypified, presignified, presigned <old>;
presignaled; **presaged; promised, threatened;**
predicted 962.14

16 **premonitory, forewarning,** augural, monitory,
warning, presageful, presaging, **foretokening,**
preindicative, indicative, prognostic,
prognosticative, presignificant, prefigurative;
significant, meaningful 518.10, speaking;
foreshowing, foreshadowing; big *or* pregnant *or*
heavy with meaning; forerunning, precursory,
precursive; intuitive 933.5; predictive 962.11

17 **ominous, portentous,** portending; **foreboding,**
boding, **bodeful; inauspicious, ill-omened,** ill-
boding, of ill *or* fatal omen, of evil portent, loaded
or laden *or* freighted *or* fraught with doom,
looming, looming over; fateful, doomful;
apocalyptic; **unpropitious, unpromising,**
unfavorable, unfortunate, unlucky; sinister, dark,
black, gloomy, somber, dreary; **threatening,**
menacing, lowering; bad, evil, ill, untoward; dire,
baleful, baneful, **ill-fated,** ill-starred, evil-starred,
star-crossed

18 **auspicious,** of good omen, of happy portent;
propitious, favorable, favoring, fair, good;

promising, of promise, full of promise; **fortunate,**
lucky, prosperous; benign, benignant, bright,
happy, golden

ADVS 19 **ominously, portentously, bodefully,**
forebodingly; significantly, meaningly,
meaningfully, speakingly, sinisterly; **threateningly,**
menacingly, loweringly

20 **inauspiciously, unpropitiously, unpromisingly,**
unfavorably, unfortunately, unluckily

21 **auspiciously, propitiously, promisingly, favorably;**
fortunately, luckily, happily; brightly

134 PATIENCE

NOUNS 1 **patience,** patientness; **tolerance,** toleration,
acceptance; indulgence, lenience, leniency 427;
sweet reasonableness; **forbearance,** forbearing,
forbearingness; **sufferance, endurance; long-**
suffering, long-sufferance, longanimity; **stoicism,**
fortitude, self-control; patience of Job; "the art of
hoping"—Vauvenargues, "a minor form of despair,
disguised as a virtue"—Ambrose Bierce; waiting
game, waiting it out; **perseverance** 360

2 **resignation, meekness,** humility, humbleness;
obedience; amenability; submission,
submissiveness 433.3; acquiescence, compliance,
uncomplainingness; **fatalism,** submission to fate *or*
the inevitable *or* necessity; quietude, quietism,
passivity, **passiveness** 329.1; *zitzflaysh* <Yiddish>;
passive resistance, nonviolent resistance,
nonresistance; Quakerism

3 **stoic,** Spartan, man of iron; Job, Griselda

VERBS 4 **be patient,** forbear, bear with composure,
wait, wait it out, play a waiting game, wait around,
wait one's turn, watch for one's moment, keep
one's shirt *or* pants on <nf>, not hold one's breath
<nf>; contain oneself, possess oneself, possess
one's soul in patience; carry on, carry through;
"have patience and endure"—Ovid

5 **endure, bear, stand,** support, sustain, **suffer,**
tolerate, abide, bide, live with; persevere; **bear up**
under, bear the brunt, bear with, put up with,
stand for, tolerate, carry *or* bear one's cross, take
what comes, take the bitter with the sweet, abide
with, brook, brave, brave out, hang in there, keep
it up

6 <nf terms> **take it,** take it on the chin, take it like
a man, not let it get one down, stand the gaff; bite
the bullet; hold still *or* stand still for, swallow,
stick, **hang in, hang in there, hang tough,** tough *or*
stick it out; lump it

7 **accept, condone, countenance;** overlook, not make
an issue of, let go by, let pass; **reconcile oneself to,**
resign oneself to, yield *or* submit to, obey;
accustom *or* accommodate *or* adjust oneself to, sit

through; accept one's fate, lay in the lap of the gods, take things as they come, roll with the punches <nf>; **make the best of it,** make the most of it, make the best of a bad bargain, make a virtue of necessity; submit with a good grace, **grin and bear it,** grin and abide, shrug, shrug it off, slough off, not let it bother one; take in good part, take in stride; rise above

8 take, pocket, swallow, down, stomach, eat, digest, disregard, turn a blind eye, ignore; swallow an insult, pocket the affront, turn the other cheek, take it lying down, turn aside provocation

ADJS **9 patient,** armed with patience, with a soul possessed in patience, patient as Job, Job-like, Griselda-like, "like patience on a monument smiling at grief"—Shakespeare; **tolerant,** tolerative, tolerating, accepting; understanding, **indulgent,** lenient; **forbearing;** philosophical; **long-suffering,** longanimous; **enduring,** endurant; stoic, stoical, Spartan; disciplined, self-controlled; **persevering**

10 resigned, reconciled; wait-and-see; **meek,** humble; obedient, amenable, **submissive** 433.12; acquiescent, compliant; accommodating, adjusting, adapting, adaptive; unresisting, **passive** 329.6; **uncomplaining**

ADVS **11 patiently,** enduringly, stoically; **tolerantly, indulgently,** longanimously, leniently, forbearantly, forbearingly, philosophically, more in sorrow than in anger; perseveringly

12 resignedly, meekly, submissively, passively, acquiescently, compliantly, uncomplainingly

PHRS **13** Rome wasn't built in a day; all in good time; all things come to him who waits; don't hold your breath; time will tell

135 IMPATIENCE

NOUNS **1 impatience,** impatientness, unpatientness, breathless impatience; **anxiety,** eagerness 101; tense readiness, **restlessness,** restiveness, ants in one's pants <nf>, prothymia; **disquiet,** disquietude, unquietness, uneasiness, **nervousness** 128; sweat *and* lather *and* stew <nf>, **fretfulness,** fretting, chafing; **impetuousness** 365.2; **haste** 401; excitement 105

2 intolerance, intoleration, unforbearance, nonendurance

3 the last straw, the straw that breaks the camel's back, the limit, the limit of one's patience, all one can bear *or* stand

VERBS **4 be impatient,** hardly wait; hasten 401.4,5; itch to, burn to; **champ at the bit, pull at the leash,** not be able to sit down *or* stand still; **chafe, fret, fuss,** squirm; **stew,** sweat, sweat and stew, get into a dither, get into a stew <nf>, work oneself

into a lather *or* sweat <nf>, get excited; wait impatiently, sweat it out <nf>, pace the floor; beat the gun, jump the gun <nf>, go off half-cocked, shoot from the hip

5 have no patience with, be out of all patience; **lose patience,** run out of patience, call a halt, have had it <nf>, blow the whistle <nf>

ADJS **6 impatient,** unpatient; breathless; champing at the bit, rarin' to go <nf>; dying, **anxious, eager;** hopped-up *and* in a lather *and* in a sweat *or* stew <nf>, excited 105.18; edgy, **on edge; restless,** restive, unquiet, uneasy, on *shpilkes* <Yiddish>; **fretful,** fretting, chafing, antsy-pantsy *and* antsy <nf>, squirming, squirmy, about to pee *or* piss one's pants <nf>; **impetuous** 365.9; **hasty** 401.9

7 intolerant, unforbearing, unindulgent

ADVS **8 impatiently,** breathlessly; **anxiously;** fretfully; restlessly, restively, uneasily; intolerantly

136 PRIDE

NOUNS **1 pride,** proudness, pridefulness; **self-esteem, self-respect,** self-confidence, self-reliance, self-consequence, face, independence, self-sufficiency; pardonable pride; obstinate *or* stiff-necked pride, stiff-neckedness; **vanity,** conceit 140.4; haughtiness, **arrogance** 141, hubris; boastfulness 502.1; purse-pride

2 proud bearing, pride of bearing, military *or* erect bearing, stiff *or* straight backbone, **dignity,** dignifiedness, **stateliness,** courtliness, grandeur, **loftiness;** pride of place; **nobility,** lordliness, princeliness; **majesty,** regality, kingliness, queenliness; distinction, worthiness, augustness, venerability; **sedateness,** solemnity 111, gravity, *gravitas* <L>, sobriety

3 proudling; stiff neck; egoist 140.5; boaster 502.5, peacock; the proud

VERBS **4 be proud,** hold up one's head, hold one's head high, stand up straight, hold oneself erect, never stoop; look one in the face *or* eye; stand on one's own two feet, pay one's own way; have one's pride

5 take pride, pride oneself, preen oneself, plume oneself on, pique oneself, **congratulate oneself,** hug oneself; **be proud of,** glory in, exult in, **burst with pride**

6 make proud, do one's heart good, do one proud <nf>, **gratify, elate,** flush, turn one's head

7 save face, save one's face, preserve one's dignity, guard *or* preserve one's honor, be jealous of one's repute *or* good name

ADJS **8 proud, prideful,** proudful <nf>; **self-esteeming, self-respecting;** self-confident, self-reliant, **independent, self-sufficient;** proudhearted, proud-minded, proud-spirited, proud-blooded; proud-looking; proud as Punch, proud as Lucifer, proud as a peacock; erect, stiff-backed, **stiff-necked;** purse-proud, house-proud

9 **vain,** conceited 140.11; haughty, **arrogant** 141.9; boastful 502.10

10 **puffed up,** swollen, bloated, swollen *or* bloated *or* puffed-up with pride; elated, flushed, flushed with pride; bigheaded, swellheaded

11 **lofty, elevated,** triumphal, high, high-flown, highfalutin *and* highfaluting <nf>, high-toned <nf>; high-minded, lofty-minded; high-headed, high-nosed <nf>

12 **dignified, stately, imposing, grand, courtly,** magisterial, aristocratic; **noble,** lordly, princely; **majestic,** regal, royal, kingly, queenly; worthy, **august, venerable;** statuesque; **sedate,** solemn 111.3, sober, grave

ADVS 13 **proudly,** pridefully, **with pride;** self-esteemingly, self-respectingly, self-confidently, self-reliantly, independently, self-sufficiently; erectly, with head erect, with head held high, with nose in air; stiff-neckedly; like a lord, *en grand seigneur* <Fr>

14 **dignifiedly, with dignity;** nobly, stately, imposingly, loftily, grandly, magisterially; majestically, regally, royally; worthily, augustly, venerably; sedately, solemnly, soberly, gravely

137 HUMILITY

NOUNS 1 **humility, humbleness, meekness; lowliness,** lowlihood, poorness, meanness, smallness, ingloriousness, undistinguishedness; unimportance 997; innocuousness 999.9; teachableness 570.5; submissiveness 433.3; **modesty,** unpretentiousness 139.1; plainness, simpleness, homeliness

2 **humiliation,** mortification <old>, egg on one's face <nf>, **chagrin,** embarrassment 96.4; **abasement,** debasement, letdown, setdown, put-down *and* dump <nf>; **comedown,** descent, deflation, climb-down, wounded *or* injured pride; self-diminishment, **self-abasement,** self-abnegation 652.1; **shame, disgrace;** shamefacedness, shamefastness, hangdog look

3 **condescension,** condescendence, deigning, lowering oneself, stooping from one's high place

VERBS 4 **humiliate, humble;** mortify <old>, **embarrass** 96.15; put out, put out of face *or* countenance; **shame, disgrace,** put to shame, put to the blush, give one a red face; **deflate,** prick one's balloon; take it out of; marginalize; make one feel small *or* this high

5 **abase, debase, crush,** abash, **degrade, reduce,** diminish, **demean,** lower, **bring low,** bring down, trip up, take down, set down, put in one's place, put down, diss <nf>, dump *and* dump on <nf>, knock one off his perch; take down a peg *or* notch *or* two <nf>, make a fool *or* an ass *or* a monkey of one; put down <nf>

6 <nf terms> beat *or* knock *or* **cut one down to size,** take the shine *or* starch out of, take the wind out of one's sails; put one's nose out of joint, put a tuck in one's tail, make one sing small

7 **humble oneself, demean oneself,** abase oneself, climb down *and* get down from one's high horse <nf>; put one's pride in one's pocket; **eat humble pie,** eat crow *or* dirt, eat one's words, swallow one's pride, lick the dust, take *or* eat shit <nf>; come on bended knee, come hat in hand; go down on one's knees; pull *or* draw in one's horns *and* sing small <nf>, lower one's note *or* tone, tuck one's tail; come down a peg *or* a peg *or* two; **deprecate** *or* **depreciate oneself,** diminish oneself, discount oneself, belittle oneself; kiss one's ass <nf> 138.7

8 **condescend, deign, vouchsafe; stoop, descend,** lower *or* demean oneself, trouble oneself, set one's dignity aside *or* to one side; **patronize;** be so good as to, so forget oneself, dirty *or* soil one's hands; talk down to, talk *de haut en bas* <Fr, from high to low>

9 **be humiliated,** be put out of countenance; **be crushed, feel small, feel cheap,** look foolish *or* silly, be ready to sink through the floor; **take shame, be ashamed, feel ashamed of oneself,** be put to the blush, have a very red face; bite one's tongue; hang one's head, hide one's face, not dare to show one's face, not have a word to say for oneself; drink the cup of humiliation to the dregs

ADJS 10 **humble, lowly, low, poor, mean,** small, inglorious, undistinguished; unimportant 998.16; innocuous; biddable, teachable 570.18; **modest,** unpretentious 139.9, without airs; **plain, simple,** homely; humble-looking, humble-visaged; humblest, lowliest, lowest, least

11 **humble-hearted, humble-minded, humble-spirited,** poor in spirit; **meek,** meek-hearted, meek-minded, meek-spirited, lamblike, Christlike; **abject,** submissive 433.12

12 **self-abasing, self-abnegating, self-deprecating,** self-depreciating 139.10, self-doubting

13 **humbled,** reduced, diminished, lowered, brought down *or* low, set down, bowed down, in the dust, cut down to size; on one's knees, on one's marrowbones <nf>

14 **humiliated,** humbled, mortified <old>, **embarrassed, chagrined, abashed, crushed,** out of countenance; blushing, ablush, **red-faced,**

ashamed, shamed, ashamed of oneself, shamefaced, shamefast; crestfallen, chapfallen, hangdog

15 **humiliating,** humiliative, humbling, chastening, mortifying, **embarrassing,** crushing

ADVS 16 **humbly, meekly;** modestly 139.14; with due deference, with bated breath, "with bated breath and whispering humbleness"—Shakespeare; submissively 433.17; **abjectly,** on bended knee, **on one's knees,** on one's marrowbones <nf>, on all fours, with one's tail between one's legs, hat-in-hand

138 SERVILITY

NOUNS 1 **servility, slavishness,** subservience *or* subserviency, menialness, abjectness, **baseness,** meanness; **submissiveness** 433.3; slavery, helotry, helotism, serfdom, peonage

2 **obsequiousness, sycophancy,** fawningness, fawnery, **toadyism,** flunkyism; parasitism, sponging; **ingratiation,** insinuation; **truckling, fawning, toadying,** toadeating, groveling, cringing, **bootlicking** <nf>, back scratching, tufthunting <chiefly Brit old>, flattery; **apple-polishing** <nf>; ass-licking *and* ass-kissing *and* brown-nosing *and* sucking up <nf>; timeserving; obeisance, prostration; mealymouthedness

3 **sycophant, flatterer, toady,** toad, toadeater, lickspit, lickspittle, **truckler, fawner,** courtier, led captain *and* tufthunter <chiefly Brit old>, kowtower, groveler, cringer, spaniel; flunky, lackey, jackal; timeserver; creature, **puppet,** minion, lap dog, **tool,** cat's-paw, dupe, instrument, faithful servant, slave, helot, serf, peon; mealymouth

4 <nf terms> **apple-polisher, ass-kisser, brown-nose,** brown-noser, brownie, ass-licker, ass-wiper, suck-ass; **backslapper,** backscratcher, clawback, back-patter; **bootlicker,** bootlick; **handshaker; yes-man, stooge;** doormat

5 **parasite,** barnacle, leech; **sponger,** sponge <nf>, freeloader <nf>, gigolo, smell-feast; beat *and* deadbeat <nf>

6 **hanger-on, adherent,** dangler, appendage, **dependent, satellite, follower,** cohort, retainer, servant, man, shadow, tagtail, **henchman,** heeler <nf>

VERBS 7 **fawn, truckle; flatter; toady,** toadeat; **bootlick** <nf>, lickspittle, lick one's shoes, lick the feet of; **grovel,** crawl, creep, cower, cringe, crouch, stoop, kneel, bend the knee, fall on one's knees, prostrate oneself, throw oneself at the feet of, fall at one's feet, kiss *or* lick *or* suck one's ass *and* brown-nose <nf>, kiss one's feet, kiss the hem of one's garment, lick the dust, make a doormat of oneself; **kowtow,** bow, **bow and scrape**

8 **toady to, truckle to, pander to, cater to,** cater for <Brit>; **wait on** *or* **upon,** wait on hand and foot, dance attendance, do service, fetch and carry, do the dirty work of, do *or* jump at the bidding of, run after

9 **curry favor, court, pay court to,** make court to, run after <nf>, dance attendance on; **shine up to,** make up to <nf>; **suck up to** *and* **play up to** *and* act up to <nf>; be a yes-man <nf>, agree to anything; fawn upon, fall over *or* all over <nf>; **handshake** *and* back-scratch *and* **polish the apple** <nf>

10 **ingratiate oneself,** insinuate oneself, worm oneself in, get into the good graces of, get in with *or* next to <nf>, **get on the good** *or* **right side of,** rub the right way <nf>

11 **attach oneself to,** pin *or* fasten oneself upon, hang about *or* around, dangle, hang on the skirts of, hang on the sleeve of, become an appendage of, **follow,** follow at heel; follow the crowd, get on the bandwagon, go with the stream, hold with the hare and run with the hounds; latch onto <nf>

12 **sponge** *and* **sponge on** *and* **sponge off of** <nf>; feed on, fatten on, batten on, live off of, use as a meal ticket; parasitize

ADJS 13 **servile, slavish,** subservient, **menial, base,** mean; **submissive** 433.12; under one's thumb

14 **obsequious, flattering,** sycophantic, sycophantical, toadyish, fawning, truckling, ingratiating, smarmy <nf>, toadying, toadeating, **bootlicking** *and* back scratching *and* backslapping *and* ass-licking *and* brown-nosing <nf>; **groveling,** sniveling, cringing, cowering, crouching, crawling; **parasitic,** leechlike, sponging <nf>; timeserving; **abject,** beggarly, hangdog; obeisant, prostrate, on one's knees, on one's marrowbones <nf>, on bended knee; mealymouthed; overattentive

ADVS 15 **servilely, slavishly,** subserviently, menially; **submissively** 433.17

16 **obsequiously, sycophantically, ingratiatingly, fawningly, trucklingly;** hat-in-hand, cap-in-hand; **abjectly,** obeisantly, grovelingly, on one's knees; parasitically

139 MODESTY

NOUNS 1 **modesty, meekness;** humility 137; **unpretentiousness,** unassumingness, unpresumptuousness, **unostentatiousness,** unambitiousness, unobtrusiveness, unboastfulness

2 **self-effacement, self-depreciation,** self-deprecation, self-detraction, undervaluing of self, self-doubt, **diffidence;** hiding one's light under a bushel; low self-esteem, weak ego, lack of self-

confidence or self-reliance, self-distrust; inferiority complex

3 reserve, restraint, constraint, backwardness, retiring disposition; low key, low visibility, low profile; reticence, reluctance

4 shyness, timidity, timidness, timorousness, **bashfulness,** shamefacedness, shamefastness, pudicity, pudency, pudibundity *and* pudibundness *and* verecundity <old>; **coyness, demureness,** demurity, skittishness, mousiness; self-consciousness, embarrassment; stammering, confusion; stagefright, mike fright *and* flop sweat <nf>

5 blushing, flushing, coloring, mantling, reddening, crimsoning; **blush, flush,** suffusion, red face

6 shrinking violet, modest violet, mouse

VERBS **7 efface oneself,** depreciate *or* deprecate *or* doubt *or* distrust oneself; have low self-esteem; reserve oneself, retire, shrink, **retire into one's shell, keep in the background,** not thrust oneself forward, **keep a low profile,** keep oneself to oneself, keep one's distance, remain in the shade, take a back seat *and* play second fiddle <nf>, know one's place, hide one's face, hide one's light under a bushel, avoid the limelight, eschew self-advertisement; pursue the noiseless tenor of one's way

8 blush, flush, mantle, **color,** change color, color up, redden, crimson, turn red, have a red face, get red in the face, blush up to the eyes; stammer; squirm; die of embarrassment

ADJS **9 modest, meek;** humble; **unpretentious,** unpretending, **unassuming,** unpresuming, unpresumptuous, **unostentatious,** unassuming, unobtrusive, unimposing, unboastful; unambitious, unaspiring

10 self-effacing, self-depreciative, self-depreciating, self-deprecating; **diffident,** deprecatory, deprecative, self-doubting, unself-confident, unsure of oneself, unself-reliant, self-distrustful, self-mistrustful; low in self-esteem

11 reserved, restrained, constrained; quiet; low-keyed, keeping low visibility *or* a low profile; **backward, retiring, shrinking**

12 shy, timid, timorous, **bashful,** shamefaced, shamefast, pudibund *and* verecund *and* verecundious <old>; **coy, demure,** skittish, mousy; self-conscious, conscious, confused; stammering, inarticulate

13 blushing, blushful; **flushed,** red, ruddy, red-faced, red in the face; **sheepish; embarrassed**

ADVS **14 modestly, meekly;** humbly; **unpretentiously,** unpretendingly, **unassumingly,** unpresumptuously, **unostentatiously,** unobtrusively; quietly, without ceremony, *sans façon* <Fr>

15 shyly, timidly, timorously, **bashfully, coyly, demurely,** diffidently; **shamefacedly,** shamefastly, **sheepishly,** blushingly, with downcast eyes

140 VANITY

NOUNS **1 vanity, vainness;** overproudness, overweening pride; **self-importance,** consequentiality, consequentialness, **self-esteem,** high self-esteem *or* self-valuation, positive self-image, self-respect, self-assumption; **self-admiration,** self-delight, self-worship, self-endearment, **self-love,** *amour propre* <Fr>, self-infatuation, narcissism, narcism; autoeroticism, autoerotism, self-gratification; **self-satisfaction, self-content,** ego trip <nf>, self-approbation, self-congratulation, self-gratulation, self-complacency, **smugness,** complacency, self-sufficiency; vainglory, vaingloriousness; "an itch for the praise of fools"— Robert Browning

2 pride 136; **arrogance** 141; **boastfulness** 502.1

3 egotism, egoism, egoisticalness, egotisticalness, **ego** <nf>, self-interest, individualism; **egocentricity,** egocentrism, self-centeredness, self-centerment, self-obsession; selfishness 651

4 conceit, conceitedness, self-conceit, self-conceitedness, immodesty, side, self-assertiveness; **stuck-upness** <nf>, chestiness <nf>, swelled-headedness, swelled head, swollen head, big head, large hat size; **cockiness** <nf>, pertness, perkiness; pomposity; obtrusiveness, bumptiousness; egomania, megalomania

5 egotist, egoist, egocentric, individualist; show-off, peacock; narcissist, narcist, Narcissus; **swellhead** <nf>, **braggart** 502.5, know-it-all *or* know-all, smart-ass *and* wise-ass <nf>, smart aleck, no modest violet, "a person of low taste, more interested in himself than in me"—Ambrose Bierce

VERBS **6 be stuck on oneself** <nf>, be impressed *or* overly impressed with oneself; ego-trip *and* be *or* go on an ego trip <nf>; think well of oneself, think one is it *or* one's shit doesn't stink <nf>, get too big for one's breeches, have a swelled head, know it all, have no false modesty, have no self-doubt, love the sound of one's own voice, be blinded by one's own glory, lay the flattering unction to one's soul; fish for compliments; toot one's own horn, **boast** 502.6,7; be vain as a peacock, give oneself airs 501.14

7 puff up, inflate, swell; go to one's head, turn one's head

ADJS **8 vain, vainglorious,** overproud, overweening; **self-important, self-esteeming,** having high self-esteem *or* self-valuation, self-respecting, self-assuming, consequential; **self-admiring,** self-

delighting, self-worshiping, self-loving, self-
endeared, self-infatuated, narcissistic, narcistic;
autoerotic, masturbatory; **self-satisfied, self-
content,** self-contented, self-approving, self-
gratulating, self-gratulatory, self-congratulating,
self-congratulatory, self-complacent, **smug,**
complacent, self-sufficient

9 **proud** 136.8; arrogant 141.9; boastful 502.10

10 **egotistic, egotistical,** egoistic, egoistical, self-
interested; **egocentric,** egocentristic, self-centered,
self-obsessed, narcissistic, narcistic; selfish 651.5;
egomaniac

11 **conceited, self-conceited, immodest,** self-
opinionated; **stuck-up** <nf>, **puffed up**; swollen-
headed, **swelled-headed, big-headed** *and* too big
for one's shoes *or* britches *and* biggety *and* **cocky**
<nf>, jumped-up <chiefly Brit nf>; pert, perk,
perky; peacockish, peacocky; know-all *or* know-it-
all, smart-ass *and* wise-ass <nf>, smarty, smart-
alecky, smart-ass <nf>, overwise, wise in one's
own conceit; aggressively self-confident, obtrusive,
bumptious

12 **stuck on oneself** <nf>, impressed with oneself,
pleased with oneself, full of oneself, all wrapped
up in oneself

ADVS 13 **vainly,** self-importantly; **egotistically,**
egoistically; **conceitedly,** self-conceitedly,
immodestly; cockily <nf>, pertly, perkily

141 ARROGANCE

NOUNS 1 **arrogance,** arrogantness; overbearingness,
overbearing pride, overweening pride, stiff-necked
pride, assumption of superiority, domineering,
domineeringness; **pride,** proudness; superbia, sin
of pride, chief of the deadly sins; **haughtiness,
hauteur; loftiness,** Olympian loftiness *or*
detachment; **toploftiness** *and* stuckupness *and*
uppishness *and* uppityness <nf>, hoity-toitiness,
hoity-toity; haughty airs, airs of *de haut en bas*;
cornstarchy airs <nf>; high horse <nf>;
condescension, condescendence, patronizing,
patronization, patronizing attitude; purse-pride

2 **presumptuousness,** presumption, overweening,
overweeningness, assumption, total self-assurance;
hubris; **insolence** 142

3 **lordliness, imperiousness,** masterfulness,
magisterialness, **high-and-mightiness,** aristocratic
presumption; elitism

4 **aloofness, standoffishness,** offishness <nf>,
chilliness, coolness, distantness, remoteness

5 **disdainfulness, disdain,** aristocratic disdain,
contemptuousness, superciliousness,
contumeliousness, cavalierness, you-be-
damnedness <nf>

6 **snobbery, snobbishness,** snobbiness, snobbism;
priggishness, priggery, priggism; snootiness *and*
snottiness *and* sniffiness *and* high-hattedness *and*
high-hattiness <nf>; tufthunting

7 **snob, prig; elitist; highbrow** *and* egghead <nf>,
Brahmin, mandarin; name-dropper, tufthunter
<chiefly Brit old>

VERBS 8 give oneself airs 501.14; **hold one's nose in
the air, look down one's nose,** toss the head,
bridle; mount *or* get on one's high horse *and* ride
the high horse <nf>; **condescend, patronize,
deign,** vouchsafe, stoop, descend, lower *or* demean
oneself, trouble oneself, set one's dignity aside *or*
to one side, be so good as to, so forget oneself,
dirty *or* soil one's hands; deal with *or* treat *de haut
en bas* <Fr, from high to low> *or* *en grand seigneur*
<Fr, like a great lord>, talk down to, talk *de haut
en bas*

ADJS 9 **arrogant, overbearing, superior,** domineering,
proud, haughty; lofty, top-lofty <nf>; high-flown,
high-falutin *and* high-faluting <nf>; high-headed;
high-nosed *and* **stuck-up** *and* **uppish** *and* uppity
and **upstage** <nf>; **hoity-toity,** big, big as you
please, six feet above contradiction; on one's high
horse; **condescending, patronizing,** *de haut en bas*
<Fr>; purse-proud

10 **presumptuous,** presuming, assuming,
overweening, would-be, self-elect, self-elected, self-
appointed, self-proclaimed, *soi-disant* <Fr>;
insolent

11 **lordly, imperious,** aristocratic, totally self-assured,
noble; hubristic; masterful, magisterial, magistral,
high-and-mighty; elitist; U <Brit nf>; dictatorial
417.16

12 **aloof, standoffish,** standoff, offish <nf>, chilly,
cool, distant, remote, above all that; Olympian

13 **disdainful,** dismissive, **contemptuous,
supercilious,** contumelious, cavalier, you-be-
damned <nf>

14 **snobbish,** snobby, toffee-nosed <Brit nf>,
priggish, snippy <nf>; **snooty** *and* **snotty** *and*
sniffy <nf>; **high-hat** *and* high-hatted *and* high-
hatty <nf>

ADVS 15 **arrogantly, haughtily, proudly,** aloofly;
condescendingly, patronizingly, *de haut en bas* *and*
en grand seigneur <Fr>; loftily, toploftily <nf>;
imperiously, magisterially; Olympianly;
disdainfully, contemptuously, superciliously,
contumeliously; with nose in air, with nose
turned up, with head held high, with arms
akimbo

16 **presumptuously,** overweeningly, aristocratically;
hubristically; **insolently**

17 **snobbishly,** snobbily, **priggishly;** snootily *and*
snottily <nf>

142 INSOLENCE

NOUNS **1** **insolence; presumption,**
presumptuousness; **audacity, effrontery,** boldness,
assurance, hardihood, bumptiousness; hubris;
overweening, overweeningness; **contempt** 157,
contemptuousness, contumely; **disdain** 141.5,
sprezzatura <Ital>; **arrogance** 141, uppishness *and*
uppityness <nf>; obtrusiveness, pushiness <nf>

2 **impudence, impertinence,** flippancy, procacity *and*
malapertness <old>, pertness, **sauciness,** sassiness
<nf>, **cockiness** *and* cheekiness <nf>, freshness
<nf>, chutzpa *or* hutzpa, **brazenness,**
brazenfacedness, brassiness <nf>, face of brass,
shamelessness, **rudeness** 505.1, **brashness,**
disrespect, disrespectfulness, derision, ridicule 508

3 <nf terms> **cheek,** face, brass, **nerve, gall,**
chutzpah, crust

4 **sauce** *and* sass *and* lip <nf>, **back talk,** backchat
<nf>, mouth

5 <impudent person> malapert <old>; minx, hussy;
whippersnapper, puppy, pup, upstart; boldface,
brazenface; *chutzpadik* <Yiddish>; swaggerer 503.2

6 <nf terms> **smart aleck,** smarty, smart guy,
smartmouth, smart-ass, wise-ass, smarty-pants,
ho-dad, wisenheimer, wise guy, know-it-all,
saucebox

VERBS **7** **have the audacity, have the cheek; have the**
gall *or* a nerve *or* one's nerve <nf>; **get fresh**
<nf>, get smart <nf>, forget one's place, **dare,**
presume, take liberties, make bold *or* free; hold in
contempt 157.3, ridicule, taunt, deride 508.8

8 **sauce** *and* sass <nf>, **talk back,** answer back, lip
and give one the lip <nf>, mouth off <nf>,
provoke

ADJS **9** **insolent,** insulting; **presumptuous,**
presuming, overpresumptuous, overweening;
audacious, bold, assured, hardy, bumptious;
contemptuous 157.8, contumelious; **disdainful**
141.13, **arrogant** 141.9, uppish *and* uppity <nf>;
hubristic; forward, pushy <nf>, obtrusive,
familiar; cool, cold

10 **impudent, impertinent, pert,** malapert *and*
procacious <old>, flip <nf>, flippant, **cocky** *and*
cheeky *and* **fresh** *and* facy *and* crusty *and* nervy
<nf>, *chutzpadik* <Yiddish>; uncalled-for,
gratuitous, biggety <nf>; **rude** 505.4,6,
disrespectful, derisive 508.12, brash, bluff; **saucy,**
sassy <nf>; smart *or* smart-alecky <nf>, smart-ass
or wise-ass <nf>

11 **brazen,** brazenfaced, boldfaced, barefaced, brassy
<nf>, **bold,** bold as brass <nf>, unblushing,
unabashed, aweless, **shameless,** dead *or* lost to
shame; swaggering 503.4

ADVS **12** **insolently, audaciously,** bumptiously,
contumeliously; **arrogantly** 141.15;
presumptuously, obtrusively, pushily <nf>;
disdainfully 141.15

13 **impudently, impertinently,** pertly, procaciously *and*
malapertly <old>, flippantly, **cockily** *and* cheekily
<nf>, saucily; **rudely** 505.8, brashly,
disrespectfully, contemptuously 157.9, derisively
508.15, in a smart-alecky way <nf>, in a smart-ass
fashion <nf>

14 **brazenly,** brazenfacedly, **boldly,** boldfacedly,
shamelessly, unblushingly

143 KINDNESS, BENEVOLENCE

NOUNS **1** **kindness, kindliness,** kindly disposition;
benignity, benignancy; **goodness, decency,**
niceness; **graciousness; kindheartedness,**
goodheartedness, warmheartedness,
softheartedness, tenderheartedness, kindness *or*
goodness *or* warmth *or* softness *or* tenderness of
heart, affectionateness, warmth, **loving kindness,**
"milk of human kindness"—Shakespeare; soul of
kindness, kind heart, heart of gold; **brotherhood,**
fellow feeling, **sympathy,** fraternal feeling, feeling
of kinship; **pity** 145, **mercy, compassion;**
humaneness, humanity; charitableness

2 **good nature, good humor,** good disposition,
benevolent disposition, good temper, sweetness,
sweet temper *or* nature, good-naturedness, good-
humoredness, good-temperedness, bonhomie;
amiability, affability, geniality, cordiality;
gentleness, mildness, lenity

3 **considerateness, consideration, thoughtfulness,**
courteousness, mindfulness, heedfulness,
regardfulness, attentiveness, **solicitousness,**
solicitude, thought, regard, concern, delicacy,
sensitivity, tact, tactfulness; indulgence, toleration,
leniency 427; complaisance, accommodatingness,
helpfulness, obligingness, agreeableness

4 **benevolence,** benevolentness, benevolent
disposition, well-disposedness, **beneficence,**
charity, charitableness, **philanthropy; altruism,**
philanthropism, **humanitarianism,** welfarism, do-
goodism; utilitarianism, Benthamism, greatest
good of the greatest number; **goodwill,** grace,
brotherly *or* sisterly love, charity, Christian charity
or love, *caritas* <L>, love of mankind, love of man
or humankind, good will to *or* toward man, love,
agape <Gk>, flower power; BOMFOG *or*
brotherhood of man and fatherhood of God;
bigheartedness, largeheartedness,
greatheartedness; hospitality; **generosity** 485;
giving 478

5 **welfare; welfare work, social service,** social
welfare, social work; child welfare, etc;

commonweal, public welfare; welfare state, welfare statism, welfarism; relief, the dole, social security <Brit>

6 benevolences, philanthropies, charities; works, **good works,** public service

7 act of kindness, kindness, favor, mercy, **benefit,** benefaction, benevolence, benignity, blessing, **service,** turn, break <nf>, **good turn, good** *or* **kind deed,** *mitzvah* <Heb>, office, good *or* kind offices, obligation, grace, act of grace, courtesy, kindly act, labor of love, good work; rescue, relief, largess, donation, alms

8 philanthropist, altruist, benevolist, **humanitarian,** man of good will, **do-gooder,** goo-goo *and* bleeding heart <nf>, well-doer, power for good; good Samaritan; well-wisher; welfare worker, social worker, caseworker; welfare statist; almsgiver, almoner; Robin Hood, Lady Bountiful

VERBS **9 be kind,** be good *or* nice, show kindness; treat well, do right by; favor, oblige, accommodate

10 be considerate, consider, respect, regard, think of, **be thoughtful of,** have consideration *or* regard for; remember; be at one's service, fuss over one, spoil one <nf>

11 be benevolent, bear good will, wish well, give one's blessing, have one's heart in the right place, have a heart of gold; practice *or* follow the golden rule, do as you would be done by, do unto others as you would have others do unto you; make love not war

12 do a favor, do good, do a kindness, do a good turn, do a good *or* kind deed, do good works, do a *mitzvah* <Heb>, use one's good offices, render a service, confer a benefit; benefit, help 449.11; mean well

ADJS **13 kind, kindly,** kindly-disposed; **benign,** benignant; good as gold, **good, nice, decent; gracious; kindhearted, warm, warmhearted,** softhearted, tenderhearted, tender, loving, affectionate; **sympathetic,** sympathizing, **compassionate** 145.7, tolerant, merciful; brotherly, fraternal, sisterly; humane, human; charitable, caritative; Christian, Christly, Christlike

14 good-natured, well-natured, **good-humored, good-tempered,** bonhomous, **sweet, sweet-tempered; amiable, affable, genial, cordial,** congenial; **gentle,** mild, mild-mannered; easy, easy-natured, easy to get along with, able to take a joke, **agreeable**

15 benevolent, charitable, beneficent, philanthropic, altruistic, humanitarian; **bighearted,** largehearted, greathearted, freehearted; hospitable; **generous** 485.4; openhanded; almsgiving, eleemosynary; **welfare,** welfarist, welfaristic, welfare statist

16 considerate, thoughtful, mindful, heedful, regardful, solicitous, attentive, delicate, tactful, mindful of others; complaisant, **accommodating,**

accommodative, at one's service, **helpful,** agreeable, **obliging,** indulgent, tolerant, lenient 427.7

17 well-meaning, well-meant, well-affected, well-disposed, **well-intentioned**

ADVS **18 kindly,** benignly, benignantly; **good,** nicely, well, favorably; **kindheartedly, warmly,** warmheartedly, softheartedly, tenderheartedly; humanely, humanly

19 good-naturedly, good-humoredly, bonhomously; **sweetly; amiably,** affably, genially, cordially; graciously, in good part

20 benevolently, beneficently, charitably, philanthropically, altruistically, bigheartedly, with good will

21 considerately, thoughtfully, mindfully, heedfully, regardfully, tactfully, **sensitively,** solicitously, attentively; well-meaningly, well-disposedly; out of consideration *or* courtesy

144 UNKINDNESS, MALEVOLENCE

NOUNS **1 unkindness, unkindliness;** unbenignity, unbenignness; **unamiability,** uncordiality, ungraciousness, inhospitality, inhospitableness, ungeniality, unaffectionateness; unsympatheticness, uncompassionateness; disagreeableness

2 unbenevolentness, uncharitableness, ungenerousness

3 inconsiderateness, inconsideration, unthoughtfulness, unmindfulness, unheedfulness, **thoughtlessness,** heedlessness, respectlessness, disregardfulness, forgetfulness; **unhelpfulness,** unobligingness, unaccommodatingness

4 malevolence, ill will, bad will, bad blood, bad temper, ill nature, ill-disposedness, ill *or* evil disposition; evil eye, *malocchio* <Ital>, whammy <nf>, blighting glance

5 malice, maliciousness, maleficence; malignance *or* **malignancy,** malignity; **meanness** *and* orneriness *and* cussedness *and* bitchiness <nf>, hatefulness, nastiness, invidiousness; **wickedness,** iniquitousness 654.4; deviltry, devilry, devilment; malice prepense *or* aforethought, evil intent; **harmfulness,** noxiousness 1000.5

6 spite, despite; **spitefulness,** cattiness; gloating, unwholesome *or* unholy joy, *Schadenfreude* <Ger>

7 rancor, virulence, venomousness, **venom,** vitriol, gall, spleen, bile; sharp tongue; loathing

8 causticity, causticness, corrosiveness, mordancy, mordacity, bitingness; **acrimony, asperity,** acidity, acidness, acidulousness, acridity, acerbity, **bitterness,** tartness; sharpness, keenness, incisiveness, piercingness, stabbingness,

trenchancy; "sharp-toothed unkindness"—
Shakespeare

9 harshness, roughness, ungentleness; **severity,**
austerity, hardness, sternness, grimness,
inclemency; stringency, astringency

10 heartlessness, unfeeling, unnaturalness,
unresponsiveness, insensitivity, coldness, **coldheartedness,** cold-bloodedness; **hard-heartedness,**
hardness, hardness of heart, heart of stone;
callousness, callosity; obduracy, induration;
pitilessness, unmercifulness 146.1

11 cruelty, cruelness, sadistic *or* insensate cruelty,
sadism, wanton cruelty; **ruthlessness** 146.1;
inhumaneness, **inhumanity,** atrociousness; **brutality,**
mindless *or* senseless brutality, brutalness,
brutishness, bestiality, animality, beastliness;
barbarity, barbarousness, vandalism; **savagery,
viciousness, violence,** fiendishness, heinousness;
child abuse 389.2; truculence, fierceness,
ferociousness, **ferocity;** excessive force, piling on
<nf>; bloodthirst, bloodthirstiness, bloodlust,
bloodiness, bloody-mindedness, sanguineousness;
cannibalism; crime against humanity

12 act of cruelty, atrocity, cruelty, brutality, bestiality,
barbarity, inhumanity

13 bad deed, disservice, ill service, **ill turn,** bad turn

14 beast, animal, brute, monster, monster of cruelty,
devil, devil incarnate; **sadist,** torturer, tormenter;
Attila, Torquemada, the Marquis de Sade;
malefactor, malfeasor, malfeasant, evildoer,
miscreant

VERBS 15 bear malice *or* ill will, malign; do a bad
turn; **harshen, dehumanize,** brutalize, bestialize;
torture, torment; **have a cruel streak,** go for the
jugular, have the killer instinct; have it in for <nf>

ADJS 16 unkind, unkindly, ill; **unbenign,**
unbenignant; **unamiable,** disagreeable, **uncordial,
ungracious,** inhospitable, **ungenial,** unaffectionate,
unloving; **unsympathetic,** unsympathizing,
uncompassionate, uncompassioned

17 unbenevolent, unbeneficent, **uncharitable,**
unphilanthropic, unaltruistic, ungenerous

18 inconsiderate, unthoughtful, unmindful,
unheedful, disregardful, **thoughtless,** heedless,
respectless, mindless, unthinking, forgetful;
tactless, insensitive; uncomplaisant; **unhelpful,
unaccommodating, unobliging,** disobliging,
uncooperative

19 malevolent, ill-disposed, evil-disposed, **ill-natured,**
ill-affected, ill-conditioned, ill-intentioned,
loathing

20 malicious, maleficent, malefic; **malignant,** malign;
mean *and* **ornery** *and* **cussed** *and* **bitchy** <nf>,
hateful, nasty, baleful, baneful, invidious; **wicked,**
iniquitous 654.16; **harmful,** noxious 1000.12

21 spiteful, despiteful; **catty,** cattish, bitchy <nf>;
snide; despiteful

22 rancorous, virulent, vitriolic; **venomous,** venenate,
envenomed

23 caustic, mordant, mordacious, corrosive,
corroding; **acrimonious,** acrid, acid, acidic,
acidulous, acidulent, acerb, acerbate, acerbic,
bitter, tart; **sharp,** sharpish, keen, incisive,
trenchant, **cutting,** penetrating, piercing, biting,
stinging, stabbing, **scathing, scorching,** withering,
scurrilous, abusive, thersitical, foulmouthed,
harsh-tongued

24 harsh, rough, rugged, ungentle; **severe,** austere,
stringent, astringent, hard, stern, dour, grim,
inclement, unsparing

25 heartless, unfeeling, unnatural, unresponsive,
insensitive, **cold,** cold of heart, coldhearted, **cold-
blooded; hard, hardened,** hard of heart, **hard-
hearted,** stony-hearted, marble-hearted, flinthearted; **callous,** calloused; obdurate, indurated;
unmerciful 146.3

26 cruel, cruel-hearted, sadistic; **ruthless** 146.3;
brutal, brutish, brute, bestial, beastly, animal,
animalistic; **mindless, soulless,** insensate,
senseless, subhuman, dehumanized, brutalized;
sharkish, wolfish, slavering; **barbarous,** barbaric,
uncivilized, unchristian; **savage, ferocious,** feral,
mean *and* mean as a junkyard dog <nf>, **vicious,**
fierce, **atrocious,** truculent, fell; **inhuman,**
inhumane, unhuman; fiendish, fiendlike; demoniac
or demoniacal, diabolic, diabolical, devilish,
satanic, hellish, infernal; **bloodthirsty,** bloody-
minded, bloody, sanguineous, sanguinary;
cannibalistic, anthropophagous; murderous;
Draconian, Tartarean

ADVS 27 unkindly, ill; **unbenignly,** unbenignantly;
unamiably, disagreeably, uncordially, ungraciously,
inhospitably, ungenially, unaffectionately,
unlovingly; unsympathetically, uncompassionately

28 unbenevolently, unbeneficently, **uncharitably,**
unphilanthropically, unaltruistically, ungenerously

29 inconsiderately, unthoughtfully, thoughtlessly,
heedlessly, unthinkingly; unhelpfully,
uncooperatively

30 malevolently, maliciously, maleficently,
malignantly; meanly *and* ornerily *and* cussedly *and*
bitchily *and* cattily <nf>, hatefully, nastily,
invidiously, balefully; **wickedly,** iniquitously
654.19; **harmfully,** noxiously 1000.15, **spitefully,** in
spite; with bad intent, with malice prepense *or*
aforethought

31 rancorously, virulently, vitriolically; venomously,
venenately

32 caustically, mordantly, mordaciously, corrosively,
corrodingly; **acrimoniously,** acridly, acidly, acerbly,

acerbically, **bitterly,** tartly; **sharply,** keenly, incisively, trenchantly, **cuttingly,** penetratingly, piercingly, bitingly, **stingingly,** stabbingly, **scathingly,** scorchingly, witheringly, thersitically, scurrilously, abusively

33 harshly, roughly; severely, austerely, stringently, sternly, grimly, inclemently, unsparingly

34 heartlessly, soullessly, unfeelingly, callously, cold-heartedly; cold-bloodedly, **in cold blood**

35 cruelly, brutally, brutishly, bestially, animalistically, subhumanly, sharkishly, wolfishly, slaveringly; **barbarously, savagely, ferociously,** ferally, **viciously,** fiercely, **atrociously,** truculently; **ruthlessly** 146.4; **inhumanely,** inhumanly, unhumanly; fiendishly, diabolically, devilishly

145 PITY

NOUNS **1 pity, sympathy,** feeling, fellow feeling, **commiseration,** condolence, condolences; **compassion, mercy,** empathy, ruth, rue, humanity; **sensitivity; clemency,** quarter, reprieve, mitigation, relief 120, favor, grace; **leniency,** lenity, gentleness; forbearance; **kindness,** benevolence 143; pardon, **forgiveness** 601.1; self-pity; **pathos**

2 compassionateness, mercifulness, ruthfulness, ruefulness, softheartedness, tenderness, tenderheartedness, lenity, gentleness; bowels of compassion *or* mercy; bleeding heart

VERBS **3 pity, be** *or* **feel sorry for,** feel sorrow for; **commiserate,** compassionate; open one's heart; **sympathize, sympathize with,** feel for, weep for, lament for, bleed, bleed for, have one's heart bleed for *or* go out to, condole with 147.2

4 have pity, have mercy upon, take pity on *or* **upon;** melt, thaw; relent, forbear, relax, give quarter, spare, temper the wind to the shorn lamb, go easy on *and* let up *or* ease up on <nf>, soften, mitigate, unsteel; **reprieve, pardon,** remit, **forgive** 601.4; put out of one's misery; be cruel to be kind; give a second chance, give a break <nf>

5 <excite pity> **move, touch,** affect, reach, **soften,** unsteel, melt, melt the heart, appeal to one's better feelings; move to tears, sadden, grieve 112.17

6 beg for mercy, ask for pity, cry for quarter, beg for one's life; fall on one's knees, throw oneself at the feet of, throw oneself at someone's mercy

ADJS **7 pitying, sympathetic,** sympathizing, commiserative, condolent, understanding; **compassionate, merciful,** ruthful, rueful, **clement,** gentle, soft, melting, bleeding, tender, **tenderhearted,** softhearted, warmhearted; **humane,** human; lenient, forbearant 427.7; charitable 143.15

8 pitiful, pitiable, pathetic, piteous, touching, moving, affecting, heartrending, grievous, doleful 112.26, sad, heartbreaking, tearjerking <nf>

9 self-pitying, self-pitiful, sorry for oneself

ADVS **10 pitifully,** sympathetically; **compassionately, mercifully,** ruthfully, ruefully, clemently, humanely

146 PITILESSNESS

NOUNS **1 pitilessness, unmercifulness, uncompassionateness,** unsympatheticness, mercilessness, **ruthlessness,** unfeelingness, inclemency, relentlessness, inexorableness, unyieldingness 361.2, unforgivingness; **heartlessness,** heart of stone, hardness, steeliness, flintiness, harshness, induration, vindictiveness, **cruelty** 144.11; remorselessness, unremorsefulness; short shrift, tender mercies

VERBS **2 show no mercy,** give no quarter, turn a deaf ear, be unmoved, claim one's pound of flesh, harden *or* steel one's heart, go by the rule book

ADJS **3 pitiless,** unpitying, unpitiful; blind *or* deaf to pity; **unsympathetic,** unsympathizing; **uncompassionate,** uncompassioned; **merciless, unmerciful,** without mercy, unruing, **ruthless,** dog-eat-dog, vindictive; unfeeling, bowelless, inclement, relentless, inexorable, unyielding 361.9, unforgiving; **heartless,** coldhearted, hard, hard as nails, callous, steely, flinty, harsh, savage, **cruel;** remorseless, unremorseful

ADVS **4 pitilessly,** unsympathetically; mercilessly, **unmercifully, ruthlessly,** uncompassionately, inclemently, relentlessly, inexorably, unyieldingly, unforgivingly; heartlessly, harshly, savagely, cruelly; remorselessly, unremorsefully

147 CONDOLENCE

NOUNS **1 condolence, condolences,** condolement, **consolation,** comfort, balm, soothing words, **commiseration, sympathy,** sharing of grief *or* sorrow

VERBS **2 condole with, commiserate, sympathize with,** feel with, empathize with, express sympathy for, send one's condolences; pity 145.3; **console,** wipe away one's tears, comfort, speak soothing words, bring balm to one's sorrow; sorrow with, share *or* help bear one's grief, grieve *or* weep with, grieve *or* weep for, share one's sorrow, "weep with them that weep"—Bible

ADJS **3** condoling, condolent, consolatory, comforting, commiserating, commiserative, **sympathetic,** empathic, empathetic; pitying 145.7

148 FORGIVENESS

NOUNS **1 forgiveness,** forgivingness; unresentfulness, unrevengefulness; **condoning,** condonation, condonance, overlooking, disregard; **patience** 134; **indulgence, forbearance,** longanimity, long-suffering; **kindness,** benevolence 143; **magnanimity** 652.2; brooking, **tolerance** 979.4

2 pardon, excuse, sparing, **amnesty,** indemnity, exemption, immunity, reprieve, grace; **absolution,** shrift, remission, remission *or* forgiveness of sin; redemption, deliverance; **exoneration,** exculpation 601.1

VERBS **3 forgive, pardon, excuse,** give *or* grant forgiveness, spare; amnesty, grant amnesty to, grant immunity *or* exemption; hear confession, **absolve,** remit, acquit, give *or* grant absolution, shrive, grant remission; **exonerate,** exculpate 601.4; blot out one's sins, wipe the slate clean, expunge from the record

4 condone 134.7, **overlook, disregard, ignore,** accept, take *and* swallow *and* let go <nf>, pass over, give one another chance, let one off this time *and* let one off easy <nf>, close *or* shut one's eyes to, turn a blind eye to, **blink** *or* **wink at,** connive at; show mercy; allow for, make allowances for; bear with, endure, regard with indulgence; pocket the affront, leave unavenged, turn the other cheek, bury *or* hide one's head in the sand

5 forget, forgive and forget, dismiss from one's thoughts, think no more of, not give it another *or* a second thought, let it go <nf>, let it pass, **let bygones be bygones;** write off, charge off, charge to experience; bury the hatchet; make peace, make up, shake hands

ADJS **6 forgiving,** sparing, placable, conciliatory; **kind,** benevolent 143.15; **magnanimous,** generous 652.6; **patient** 134.9; **forbearing,** longanimous, long-suffering, stoic; unresentful, unrevengeful; **tolerant** 978.11, more in sorrow than in anger

7 forgiven, pardoned, excused, spared, amnestied, reprieved, remitted; overlooked, disregarded, forgotten, not held against one, wiped away, removed from the record, blotted, canceled, **condoned,** indulged; **absolved,** shriven; redeemed, delivered; exonerated, exculpated, acquitted, not guilty, innocent, cleared, absolved, vindicated, off the hook; unresented; unavenged, unrevenged; uncondemned; wiped away, swept clean

149 CONGRATULATION

NOUNS **1 congratulation, congratulations,** congrats <nf>, gratulation, **felicitation,** blessing, compliment, pat on the back; good wishes, best wishes; **applause** 509.2, **praise** 509.5, flattery 511

VERBS **2 congratulate,** gratulate, **felicitate,** bless, **compliment,** tender *or* offer one's congratulations *or* felicitations *or* compliments; shake one's hand, pat one on the back; **rejoice with one,** wish one joy; **applaud** 509.10, **praise** 509.12, flatter 511.5

ADJS **3 congratulatory,** congratulant, congratulational; gratulatory, gratulant; **complimentary** 509.16, flattering 511.8

INTERJS **4 congratulations!,** take a bow!, nice going!, **bravo!, well done!,** good show! <Brit>

5 <nf terms> **congrats!, all right!, aw right!, right on!,** way to go!, attaboy!, attagirl!, good deal!, looking good!, nice going!, that's my boy!, that's my girl!

150 GRATITUDE

NOUNS **1 gratitude, gratefulness, thankfulness, appreciation, appreciativeness;** obligation, sense of obligation *or* indebtedness

2 thanks, thanksgiving, praise, laud, hymn, paean, benediction, eucharist, grace, prayer of thanks; **thank-you;** sincere thanks; **acknowledgment,** cognizance, **credit,** crediting, recognition; bonus, gratuity, tip; thank offering, votary offering

VERBS **3 be grateful, be obliged,** feel *or* be *or* lie under an obligation, be obligated *or* indebted, be in the debt of, give credit *or* due credit; **be thankful,** thank God, thank one's lucky stars, thank *or* bless one's stars; **appreciate,** be appreciative of; never forget; overflow with gratitude; not look a gift horse in the mouth

4 thank, extend gratitude *or* **thanks,** bless; give one's thanks, **express one's appreciation; offer** *or* **give thanks,** tender *or* render thanks, return thanks; acknowledge, make acknowledgments of, credit, recognize, give *or* render credit *or* recognition, give a big hand; fall all over one with gratitude; fall on one's knees; pay tribute

ADJS **5 grateful, thankful; appreciative,** appreciatory, sensible; **obliged, much obliged,** beholden, indebted to, crediting, under obligation, acknowledging, cognizant of

INTERJS **6 thanks!, thank you!,** I thank you!, *merci!* <Fr>, *¡gracias!* <Sp>, *grazie!* <Ital>, *danke!* and *danke schön!* <Ger>, gramercy!, *domo* and *domo arrigato* <Japanese>, **much obliged!,** many thanks!, thank you kindly!; thank you very much!, *merci beaucoup!* and *je vous remercie beaucoup!* <Fr>; thanks a lot! *or* a bunch! *or* a heap! <nf>, ta! <Brit>

151 INGRATITUDE

NOUNS **1 ingratitude, ungratefulness, unthankfulness,** thanklessness, unappreciation, **unappreciativeness;** nonacknowledgment, nonrecognition, denial of due *or* proper credit; "benefits forgot"—Shakespeare; grudging *or* halfhearted thanks

2 ingrate, ungrateful wretch

VERBS **3 be ungrateful,** feel no obligation, **not appreciate,** owe one no thanks; look a gift horse in the mouth; bite the hand that feeds one

ADJS **4 ungrateful, unthankful,** unthanking, thankless, unappreciative, unappreciatory, unmindful, nonrecognitive, unrecognizing, ungracious, discourteous

5 unthanked, unacknowledged, unrecognized, nonrecognized, uncredited, denied due *or* proper credit, unrequited, unrewarded, forgotten, neglected, unduly *or* unfairly neglected, ignored, blanked, cold-shouldered; ill-requited, ill-rewarded

152 RESENTMENT, ANGER

NOUNS **1 resentment,** resentfulness; **displeasure,** disapproval, disapprobation, dissatisfaction, **discontent; vexation,** irritation, **annoyance,** aggravation <nf>, exasperation; slow burn <nf>

2 offense, umbrage, pique; glower, scowl, angry look, dirty look <nf>, glare, frown

3 bitterness, bitter resentment, bitterness of spirit, heartburning; **rancor,** virulence, **acrimony,** acerbity, asperity; causticity 144.8; **choler,** gall, bile, spleen, acid, acidity, acidulousness; hard feelings, **animosity** 589.4; soreness, rankling, slow burn <nf>; gnashing of teeth

4 indignation, indignant displeasure, righteous indignation

5 anger, wrath, ire, *saeva indignatio* <L>, mad <nf>; angriness, irateness, wrathfulness, soreness <nf>, "a transient madness"—Horace; infuriation, enragement; vials of wrath, grapes of wrath; **heat,** more heat than light <nf>; pugnacity, aggro <Brit nf>, dancer <nf>

6 temper, dander *and* Irish <nf>, monkey <Brit nf>; bad temper 110.1

7 dudgeon, high dudgeon; **huff,** pique, pet, tiff, miff *and* stew <nf>, fret, **fume,** ferment

8 fit, fit of anger, fit of temper, rage, wax <Brit nf>, **tantrum,** temper tantrum; duck *or* cat fit *and* **conniption** *or* conniption fit *and* snit <nf>, paroxysm, convulsion; agriothymia; stamping one's foot

9 outburst, outburst of anger, burst, **explosion,** eruption, blowup *and* **flare-up** <nf>, access, blaze of temper; **storm, scene,** high words

10 rage, passion; fury, furor; livid *or* towering rage *or* passion, blind *or* burning rage, raging *or* tearing passion, furious rage; vehemence, violence; the Furies, the Eumenides, the Erinyes; Nemesis; Alecto, Tisiphone, Megaera; steroid rage, road rage <nf>

11 provocation, affront, offense, "head and front of one's offending"—Shakespeare; *casus belli* <L>, red rag, red rag to a bull, red flag, sore point, sore spot, tender spot, delicate subject, raw nerve, the quick, where one lives; slap in the face; last straw

VERBS **12 resent,** be resentful, feel *or* harbor *or* nurse resentment, feel hurt, smart, feel sore *and* have one's nose out of joint <nf>; bear *or* hold *or* have a grudge, bear malice

13 take amiss, take ill, **take in bad part,** take to heart, not take it as a joke, **mind; take offense, take umbrage,** get miffed *or* huffy <nf>; be cut *or* cut to the quick, get one's back up <nf>

14 <show resentment> redden, color, flush, mantle; **growl, snarl,** gnarl, **snap,** show one's teeth, spit; gnash *or* grind one's teeth; **glower,** lower, scowl, **glare, frown,** give a dirty look <nf>, look daggers; **stew,** stew in one's own juice

15 <be angry> **burn, seethe, simmer,** sizzle, smoke, smolder, steam; be pissed *or* pissed off *or* browned off <nf>, be livid, be beside oneself, **fume,** stew <nf>, boil, fret, chafe; foam at the mouth; breathe fire and fury; **rage, storm, rave,** rant, bluster; take on *and* go on *and* carry on <nf>, rant and rave, kick up a row *or* dust *or* a shindy <nf>; raise Cain *or* raise hell *or* raise the devil *or* raise the roof <nf>, tear up the earth; throw a fit, have a conniption *or* conniption fit *or* duck fit *or* cat fit <nf>, go into a tantrum; stamp one's foot

16 vent one's anger, vent one's rancor *or* choler *or* spleen, pour out the vials of one's wrath; **snap at, bite** *or* **snap one's nose off, bite** *or* **take one's head off, jump down one's throat;** expend one's anger on, take it out on <nf>

17 <become angry> **anger, lose one's temper,** become irate, forget oneself, let one's angry passions rise; **get one's gorge up,** get one's blood up, **bridle,** bridle up, **bristle,** bristle up, raise one's hackles, get one's back up; reach boiling point, boil over, climb the wall, go through *or* hit the roof

18 <nf terms> **get mad** *or* **sore,** get one's Irish *or* dander *or* hackles up, get one's monkey up <Brit>; **see red, get hot under the collar,** flip out, work oneself into a lather *or* sweat *or* stew, get oneself in a tizzy, do a slow burn, blow one's cool

19 flare up, blaze up, fire up, flame up, spunk up, ignite, kindle, take fire

20 fly into a rage *or* **passion** *or* **temper,** fly out, fly off at a tangent; **fly off the handle** *and* **hit the ceiling** *and* go into a tailspin *and* have a hemorrhage <nf>; **explode, blow up** <nf>; blow one's top *or* stack <nf>, blow a fuse *or* gasket <nf>, flip one's lid *or* wig <nf>, wig out <nf>; kick *or* piss up a fuss *or* a row *or* a storm <nf>; jump down someone's throat <nf>, take it out on someone <nf>

21 **offend, give offense, give umbrage,** affront, outrage; grieve, aggrieve; wound, hurt, cut, cut to the quick, hit one where one lives <nf>, **sting,** hurt one's feelings; step *or* tread on one's toes

22 **anger, make angry, make mad,** raise one's gorge *or* choler; make one's blood boil

23 <nf terms> **piss** *or* tee off, tick off, piss, **get one's goat, get one's Irish** *or* back *or* dander *or* hackles up, **make sore,** make one hot under the collar, put one's nose out of joint, burn one up, burn one's ass *or* butt, steam

24 **provoke, incense,** arouse, inflame, embitter; **vex, irritate, annoy, aggravate** <nf>, **exasperate, nettle,** fret, chafe; **pique, peeve** *and* miff <nf>, huff; **ruffle, roil, rile** <nf>, ruffle one's feathers, **rankle;** bristle, put *or* get one's back up, set up, put one's hair *or* fur *or* bristles up; stick in one's craw <nf>; **stir up, work up,** stir one's bile, stir the blood; wave the bloody shirt

25 **enrage, infuriate, madden,** drive one mad, frenzy, lash into fury, work up into a passion, **make one's blood boil**

ADJS 26 **resentful,** resenting; **bitter,** embittered, rancorous, virulent, **acrimonious,** acerb, acerbic, acerbate; caustic; **choleric,** splenetic, acid, acidic, acidulous, acidulent; **sore** <nf>, rankled, burning *and* stewing <nf>

27 **provoked, vexed, piqued; peeved** *and* miffed *and* huffy <nf>, riled, **nettled, irritated, annoyed,** aggravated <nf>, exasperated, put-out; huffed, miffed, peeved, in a snit

28 **angry,** angered, **incensed, indignant, irate,** ireful; **livid,** livid with rage, beside oneself, **wroth, wrathful,** wrathy, **cross,** wrought-up, worked up, riled up <nf>

29 **burning, seething,** simmering, smoldering, sizzling, boiling, **steaming;** flushed with anger

30 <nf terms> **mad, sore,** mad as a hornet *or* as a wet hen *or* as hell, sore as a boil, pissed; **pissed-off** *or* PO'd; teed off *or* TO'd; ticked *or* ticked off, browned-off, waxy *and* stroppy <Brit>, **hot,** het up, **hot under the collar,** burned up, hot and bothered, boiling, boiling *or* hopping *or* fighting *or* roaring mad, fit to be tied, good and mad, steamed, hacked, bent out of shape, in a lather *or* lava *or* pucker, red-assed

31 **in a temper, in a huff, in a pet,** in a snit *or* a stew <nf>; in a wax <Brit nf>, **in high dudgeon**

32 **infuriated,** infuriate, in a rage *or* passion *or* fury; **furious,** fierce, wild, savage; raving mad <nf>, **rabid,** foaming *or* frothing at the mouth; **fuming,** in a fume; **enraged, raging, raving, ranting, storming**

ADVS 33 **angrily, indignantly, irately,** wrathfully, infuriatedly, infuriately, furiously, heatedly; **in anger,** in hot blood, in the heat of passion

153 JEALOUSY

NOUNS 1 **jealousy,** *jalousie* <Fr>, jealousness, heartburning, heartburn, **jaundice,** jaundiced eye, green in the eye <nf>, "the jaundice of the soul"—Dryden; "green-eyed jealousy," "green-eyed monster," "a monster begot upon itself, born on itself"—all Shakespeare; Othello's flaw, horn-madness; **envy** 154

2 **suspiciousness,** suspicion, doubt, misdoubt, mistrust, distrust, distrustfulness

VERBS 3 suffer pangs of jealousy, have green in the eye <nf>, be possessive *or* overpossessive, view with a jaundiced eye; **suspect,** distrust, mistrust, doubt, misdoubt

4 make one jealous, put someone's nose out of joint

ADJS 5 **jealous, jaundiced,** jaundice-eyed, yellow-eyed, green-eyed, yellow, green, green with jealousy; horn-mad; invidious, **envious** 154.4; **suspicious,** distrustful

154 ENVY

NOUNS 1 **envy,** enviousness, **covetousness;** emulousness <old>; invidia, deadly sin of envy, **invidiousness;** grudging, grudgingness; resentment, resentfulness; **jealousy** 153; rivalry, competitiveness; meanness, meanspiritedness, ungenerousness

2 "emulation adapted to the meanest capacity"—Ambrose Bierce, "a kind of praise"—John Gay

VERBS 3 **envy,** be envious *or* covetous of, **covet,** cast envious eyes, desire for oneself; resent; **grudge, begrudge;** turn green with envy, be jealous, eat one's heart out

ADJS 4 **envious,** envying, **invidious,** green with envy, green-eyed; **jealous** 153.4; **covetous,** desirous of; resentful; **grudging, begrudging;** mean, mean-spirited, ungenerous

155 RESPECT

NOUNS 1 **respect, regard,** consideration, appreciation, favor; approbation, approval; **esteem,** estimation, prestige; **reverence,** veneration, awe; **deference,** deferential *or* reverential regard; **honor, homage,** duty; great respect, high regard, high opinion, **admiration;** adoration, breathless adoration, exaggerated respect, worship, hero worship, **idolization;** idolatry, deification, apotheosis; courtesy 504

2 **obeisance,** reverence, homage; **bow, nod, bob,** bend, inclination, inclination of the head, **curtsy, salaam, kowtow,** scrape, bowing and scraping, making a leg; **genuflection,** kneeling, bending the knee; prostration; salute, salutation, namaste; salaam, kowtow; presenting arms, dipping the colors *or* ensign, standing at attention; red carpet; **submissiveness,** submission 433; **obsequiousness,** servility 138

3 **respects, regards,** *égards* <Fr>; duties, *devoirs* <Fr>; attentions

VERBS 4 **respect,** entertain respect for, accord respect to, **regard, esteem,** hold in esteem *or* consideration, favor, **admire,** think much of, think well of, think highly of, have *or* hold a high opinion of; **appreciate, value,** prize, treasure; **revere, reverence,** hold in reverence, **venerate, honor, look up to, defer to, bow to,** exalt, put on a pedestal, **worship,** hero-worship, deify, apotheosize, **idolize, adore,** worship the ground one walks on, stand in awe of; hold dear

5 **do** *or* **pay homage to,** show *or* demonstrate respect for, pay respect to, pay tribute to, **do** *or* **render honor to, do the honors for; doff one's cap to, take off one's hat to;** salute, present arms, dip the colors *or* ensign, stand at *or* to attention; give the red-carpet treatment, roll out the red carpet; fire a salute

6 **bow, make obeisance, salaam, kowtow,** make one's bow, bow down, **nod,** incline *or* bend *or* bow the head, bend the neck, **bob,** bob down, **curtsy,** bob a curtsy, bend, make a leg, scrape, **bow and scrape; genuflect, kneel,** bend the knee, get down on one's knees, throw oneself on one's knees, fall on one's knees, fall down before, fall at the feet of, prostrate oneself, kiss the hem of one's garment

7 **command respect,** inspire respect, stand high, impress, have prestige, rank high, be widely reputed, be up there *or* way up there <nf>; awe 122.6, overawe

ADJS 8 **respectful, regardful,** attentive; **deferential,** conscious of one's place, dutiful, honorific, ceremonious, appreciative, cap in hand; **courteous** 504.14

9 **reverent,** reverential; admiring, **adoring, worshiping,** worshipful, hero-worshiping, **idolizing,** idolatrous, deifying, apotheosizing; **venerative,** venerational; awestruck, awestricken, awed, in awe; on bended knee; solemn 111.3

10 **obeisant,** prostrate, on one's knees, on bended knee; **submissive** 433.12; **obsequious;** knowing one's place

11 **respected, esteemed, revered,** reverenced, adored, worshiped, **venerated, honored,** well-thought-of, admired, much-admired, appreciated, valued, prized, in high esteem *or* estimation, highly considered, well-considered, held in respect *or* regard *or* favor *or* consideration, time-honored, prestigious

12 **venerable, reverend, estimable, honorable,** worshipful, august, awe-inspiring, awesome, awful, dreadful; time-honored

ADVS 13 **respectfully,** regardfully, deferentially, reverentially; dutifully

ADVS, PREPS 14 **in deference to,** with due respect, with all respect, **with all due respect** *or* **for,** saving, excusing the liberty, saving your reverence, sir-reverence; out of respect *or* consideration for, out of courtesy to

156 DISRESPECT

NOUNS 1 **disrespect, disrespectfulness,** lack of respect, low estimate *or* esteem, **disesteem,** dishonor, **irreverence;** ridicule 508; **disparagement** 512; **discourtesy** 505; **impudence,** insolence 142; opprobrium

2 **indignity, affront, offense, injury,** humiliation; scurrility, contempt 157, contumely, despite, flout, flouting, mockery, jeering, jeer, mock, scoff, gibe, taunt, brickbat <nf>; **insult, aspersion,** uncomplimentary remark, snub, slight, slap *or* kick in the face, left-handed *or* backhanded compliment, damning with faint praise; cut, "most unkindest cut of all"—Shakespeare; **outrage, atrocity,** enormity

3 <nf terms> **put-down,** dump, bringdown, brickbat, **dig,** dirty dig, ding, rank-out, rip, shot, slam, go-by

VERBS 4 **disrespect,** not respect, disesteem, hold a low opinion of, rate *or* rank low, hold in low esteem, not care much for, pay a lefthanded *or* backhanded compliment, damn with faint praise, hold in contempt, have no time for; **show disrespect for,** show a lack of respect for, **be disrespectful,** treat with disrespect, turn one's back on, be overfamiliar with; trifle with, make bold *or* free with, take a liberty, take liberties with, play fast and loose with; **ridicule** 508.8; **disparage** 512.8

5 **offend, affront,** give offense to, snub, slight, disoblige, outrage, step *or* tread on one's toes; dishonor, humiliate, treat with indignity; flout, mock, jeer at, scoff at, fleer at, gibe at, taunt; **insult,** call names, kick *or* slap in the face, take *or*

pluck by the beard; **add insult to injury;** give the cold shoulder, cut dead, spurn

6 <nf terms> **bad-mouth, put down, trash,** give the go-by, rubbish, dump on, dig at, dis *or* diss, rank out, rip *or* rip on, ride, roast, slam, hurl a brickbat

ADJS 7 **disrespectful, irreverent,** aweless; **discourteous** 505.4; **insolent, impudent;** ridiculing, **derisive** 508.12; **disparaging** 512.13

8 **insulting, insolent, abusive, offensive,** humiliating, degrading, pejorative, contemptuous 157.8, contumelious, calumnious; blasphemous; scurrilous, scurrile; backhand, backhanded, left-handed, cutting; contumacious, outrageous, atrocious, unspeakable

9 **unrespected,** disrespected, **unregarded, unrevered,** unvenerated, unhonored, unenvied; trivialized

157 CONTEMPT

NOUNS 1 **contempt, disdain, scorn,** contemptuousness, disdainfulness, superciliousness, snootiness, snottiness, sniffiness, toploftiness, scornfulness, despite, contumely, sovereign contempt; snobbishness; clannishness, cliquishness, exclusiveness, exclusivity; hauteur, airs, arrogance 141; **ridicule** 508; **insult** 156.2; **disparagement** 512

2 **snub, rebuff,** repulse; **slight,** humiliation, spurning, spurn, disregard, the go-by <nf>; cut, cut direct, **the cold shoulder** <nf>; sneer, snort, sniff; contemptuous dismissal, **dismissal** 908.2, kiss-off <nf>; **rejection** 372

VERBS 3 **disdain, scorn, despise,** contemn, vilipend, disprize, misprize, rate *or* rank low, be contemptuous of, feel contempt for, **hold in contempt,** hold cheap, look down upon, think little *or* nothing of, feel superior to, be above, hold beneath one *or* beneath contempt, look with scorn upon, view with a scornful eye, give one the fish-eye *or* the beady eye *or* the hairy eyeball <nf>; **put down** *or* dump on <nf>; deride, **ridicule** 508.8; **insult;** disparage 512.8; thumb one's nose at, sniff at, sneeze at, snap one's fingers at, sneer at, snort at, curl one's lip at, shrug one's shoulders at; care nothing for, couldn't care less about, think nothing of, set at naught

4 **spurn, scout, turn up one's nose at,** scorn to receive *or* accept, not want any part of; spit upon

5 **snub, rebuff,** cut *or* cut dead <nf>, drop, repulse; **high-hat** *and* upstage <nf>; **look down one's nose at,** look cool *or* coldly upon; cold-shoulder *or* turn a cold shoulder upon *or* **give the cold shoulder** <nf>, give *or* turn the shoulder <nf>, give the go-by *or* the kiss-off <nf>; turn one's back upon, turn away from, turn on one's heel, set one's face

against, slam the door in one's face, show one his place, put one in his place, wave one aside; not be at home to, not receive

6 **slight, ignore,** pooh-pooh <nf>, make little of, dismiss, pretend not to see, disregard, overlook, neglect, pass by, pass up *and* give the go-by <nf>, leave out in the cold <nf>, take no note *or* notice of, look right through <nf>, pay no attention *or* regard to, refuse to acknowledge *or* recognize

7 **avoid** 368.6, avoid like the plague, go out of one's way to avoid, shun, dodge, steer clear of *and* have no truck with <nf>; **keep one's distance,** keep at a respectful distance, **keep** *or* **stand** *or* **hold aloof;** keep at a distance, hold *or* keep at arm's length; **be stuck-up** <nf>, act holier than thou, give oneself airs

ADJS 8 **contemptuous, disdainful,** supercilious, snooty, snotty, sniffy, toplofty, toploftical, **scornful,** sneering, withering, contumelious; snobbish, snobby; clannish, cliquish, exclusive; stuck-up <nf>, **conceited** 140.11; haughty, **arrogant** 141.9

ADVS 9 **contemptuously, scornfully, disdainfully;** in *or* with contempt, in disdain, in scorn; sneeringly, with a sneer, with curling lip

INTERJS 10 **bah!,** pah!, phooey!, boo!, phoo!, pish!, ecch!, yeech!, eeyuck!, eeyuch!, yeeuck!, *feh!* <Yiddish>

158 SPACE

<indefinite space>

NOUNS 1 **space, extent,** extension, spatial extension, uninterrupted extension, space continuum, continuum; **expanse,** expansion; spread, breadth; depth, deeps; height, vertical space, air space; length; width; **measure,** volume; **dimension,** proportion, size; **area,** expanse tract, surface, surface *or* superficial extension; diameter, circumference; **field,** arena, sphere; capacity; acreage; **void,** empty space, emptiness, nothingness; infinite space, infinity, outer space, wastes of outer space, deep space, depths of outer space, interplanetary *or* interstellar *or* intergalactic space

2 **range, scope, compass, reach, stretch, expanse;** radius, sweep, carry, fetch, grasp; **gamut, scale,** register, diapason; **spectrum,** array; tract

3 **room, latitude,** swing, play, way; spare room, room to spare, room to swing a cat <nf>, **elbowroom,** legroom; **margin, leeway;** breathing space; sea room; headroom, clearance; windage; amplitude; headway; living space

4 **open space,** clear space; **clearing,** clearance, glade; open country, wide-open spaces, **terrain,** prairie, steppe, plain 236; field, glade; wilderness, back

country, boonies *and* boondocks <nf>, outback <Austral>, desert, back o' beyond <Austral nf>; distant prospect *or* perspective, empty view, far horizon; **territory;** living space, *Lebensraum* <Ger>; national territory, air space

5 **spaciousness, roominess, size** commodiousness, capacity, capaciousness, amplitude, extensiveness, extent, expanse; stowage, storage; seating capacity, seating

6 **fourth dimension, space-time,** time-space, space-time continuum, continuum, four-dimensional space; four-dimensional geometry, Minkowski world *or* universe; spaceworld; other continuums; **relativity,** theory of relativity, Einstein theory, principle of relativity, principle of equivalence, general theory of relativity, special *or* restricted theory of relativity, continuum theory; time warp; cosmic constant

7 **inner space,** psychological space, the realm of the mind; personal space, room to be, individual *or* private space, space <nf>; semantic space

8 intervening space; distance, interval, gap, remove; break, hiatus, lacuna, pause, interruption, intermission, lapse, blank; duration, period, span, spell, stretch, turn, while

VERBS 9 **extend, reach, stretch,** expand, sweep, spread, run, **go** *or* **go out,** cover, carry, **range,** lie; **reach** *or* stretch *or* thrust out; span, straddle, take in, hold, enclose, encompass, surround, environ, contain, hold; lengthen, widen, deepen, raise

ADJS 10 **spatial,** space, spacial; **dimensional,** proportional; two-dimensional, flat, surface *or* superficial, radial, three-dimensional *or* 3-D, spherical, cubic, volumetric; galactic, intergalactic, interstellar; stereoscopic; fourth-dimensional; space-time, spatiotemporal

11 **spacious, sizeable, roomy, commodious, capacious,** ample; **extensive,** expansive, extended, wide-ranging; far-reaching, extending, spreading, **vast,** vasty, broad, **wide,** deep, high, voluminous, cavernous; airy, lofty; oversized; amplitudinous; widespread 864.13; **infinite** 823.3

ADVS 12 **extensively, widely,** broadly, vastly, abroad; **far and wide,** far and near; **right and left,** on all sides, on every side; infinitely

13 **everywhere,** everywheres <nf>, **here, there, and everywhere;** in every place, in every clime *or* region, in all places, in every quarter, in all quarters; **all over,** all round, all over hell *and* all over the map *and* all over the place *and* all over the ballpark *and* all over town <nf>, all over the world, the world over, on the face of the earth, under the sun, throughout the world, throughout the length and breadth of the land; from end to

end, from pole to pole, from here to the back of beyond <Brit nf>, "from Dan to Beersheba"—Bible, from hell to breakfast <nf>; **high and low,** upstairs and downstairs, inside and out, in every nook and cranny *or* hole and corner; **universally,** in all creation

14 **from everywhere,** everywhence, "from the four corners of the earth"—Shakespeare, from all points of the compass, from every quarter *or* all quarters; everywhere, everywhither, to the four winds, to the uttermost parts of the earth, "unto the ends of the earth"—Bible, to hell and back <nf>

159 LOCATION

NOUNS 1 **location, situation, place, position,** spot, *lieu* <Fr>, placement, emplacement, stead; **whereabouts,** whereabout, ubicity; **area, district,** region 231; **locality, locale,** locus; venue; **abode** 228; **site,** situs; **spot, point,** pinpoint, exact spot *or* point, very spot *or* point, dot; benchmark; *locus classicus* <L>; bearings, coordinates, latitude and longitude, direction; setting, environs, environment; habitat, address

2 **station,** status, **stand, standing,** standpoint, pou sto; **viewpoint,** *optique* <Fr>, point of reference, reference-point, angle, perspective, distance; coign of vantage; **seat, post,** base, footing, ground, venue

3 **navigation,** guidance; dead reckoning, pilotage; coastal navigation; celestial guidance *or* astro-inertial guidance, celestial navigation *or* celo-navigation *or* astronavigation; consolan; loran; radar navigation; radio navigation; orienteering; **position, orientation,** lay, lie, set, **attitude,** aspect, exposure, frontage, **bearing** *or* **bearings,** radio bearing, azimuth; position line *or* line of position; **fix**

4 **place,** stead, lieu

5 **map, chart;** hachure, contour line, isoline, layer tint; **scale,** graphic scale, representative fraction; **legend;** grid line, meridian, parallel, latitude, longitude; inset; index; **projection,** map projection, azimuthal equidistant projection *or* azimuthal projection, conic projection, Mercator projection; **cartography, mapmaking;** chorography, topography, photogrammetry, phototopography; **cartographer, mapmaker, mapper;** chorographer, topographer, photogrammetrist

6 <act of placing> **placement, positioning, emplacement, situation, location, siting,** localization, **locating, placing,** putting; establishment, installation; **allocation,** collocation, **disposition,** assignment, **deployment,** posting, **stationing,** spotting; fixing, fixation, settling;

deposition, reposition, **deposit,** disposal, dumping; **stowage,** storage, warehousing; loading, lading, packing

7 **establishment, foundation,** settlement, settling, colonization, population, peopling, plantation; lodgment, fixation; anchorage, mooring; **installation,** installment, inauguration, investiture, placing in office, initiation

8 topography, geography; cartography, chorography; surveying, triangulation, navigation, geodesy; geodetic satellite, orbiting geophysical observatory *or* OGO; global positioning system *or* GPS

VERBS **9** **have place,** be there; have its place *or* slot, **belong, go, fit,** fit in

10 **be located** *or* **situated, lie, be found,** stand, rest, repose; lie in, have its seat in

11 **locate, situate, site, place, position;** emplace, spot <nf>, **install,** put in place; **allocate,** collocate, **dispose, deploy,** assign; **localize,** narrow *or* pin down; **map, chart,** put on the map *or* chart; put one's finger on, **fix,** assign *or* consign *or* relegate to a place; **pinpoint,** zero in on, home in on, find the spot; find *or* fix *or* calculate one's position, triangulate, survey, find a line of position, **get a fix on** *or* navigational fix, get a bearing, navigate; turn up, track down

12 **place, put, set, lay,** pose, posit, site, seat, stick <nf>, **station, post;** billet, quarter; **park,** plump down <nf>; **dump**

13 <place violently> **clap,** slap, **thrust, fling, hurl,** throw, cast, chuck, toss; **plump;** plunk *and* plank *and* plop <nf>

14 **deposit,** repose, reposit, rest, lay, lodge; **put down,** set down, lay down

15 **load, lade,** freight, burden; fill 794.7; **stow,** store, put in storage, warehouse; **pack,** pack away; pile, dump, heap, heap up, stack, mass; bag, sack, pocket

16 **establish, fix, plant,** ensconce, **site,** pitch, seat, **set,** spot; **found, base,** ground, lay the foundation; **build,** put up, set up; build in; **install, invest,** vest, place in office, put in

17 **settle, settle down,** sit down, locate, park <nf>, ensconce, ensconce oneself; take up one's abode *or* quarters, make one's home, **reside,** inhabit 225.7; **move,** relocate, change address, establish residence, make one's home, **take up residence,** take residence at, put up *or* live *or* stay at, quarter *or* billet at, move in, hang up one's hat <nf>; take *or* strike root, put down roots, place oneself, plant oneself, get a footing, stand, take one's stand *or* position; **anchor,** drop anchor, come to anchor, moor; **squat;** camp, bivouac; perch, roost, nest,

hive, burrow; domesticate, **set up housekeeping,** keep house; **colonize,** populate, people; **set up in business,** go in business for oneself, set up shop, hang up one's shingle <nf>

ADJS **18** **located, placed, sited, situated,** situate, **positioned,** installed, emplaced, spotted <nf>, **set,** seated; **stationed, posted,** deployed, assigned, positioned, prepositioned, oriented; **established,** fixed, in place, **settled,** planted, ensconced, embosomed

19 locational, positional, situational, situal, directional; **cartographic;** topographic, geographic, chorographic, geodetic; navigational; **regional** 231.8

ADVS **20** **in place,** in position, in situ, in loco

21 **where,** whereabouts, in what place, in which place; **whither,** to what *or* which place

22 **wherever,** where'er, **wheresoever,** wheresoe'er, wheresomever <nf>, whithersoever, wherever it may be; **anywhere,** anyplace <nf>

23 **here,** hereat, in this place, just here, on the spot; **hereabouts,** hereabout, in this vicinity, near here; somewhere about *or* near; aboard, on board, with *or* among us; **hither,** hitherward, hitherwards, hereto, hereunto, hereinto, to this place

24 **there,** thereat, in that place, in those parts; thereabout, **thereabouts,** in that vicinity *or* neighborhood; **thither,** thitherward, thitherwards, to that place

25 **here and there, in places,** in various places, in spots, *passim* <L>

26 **somewhere, someplace,** in some place, someplace or other

PREPS **27** **at, in, on, by; near, next to; with, among,** in the midst of; to, toward; from

28 over, all over, here and there, on *or* in, at about, round about; through, **all through,** throughout 794.17

PHR **29** X marks the spot

160 DISPLACEMENT

NOUNS **1** **dislocation, displacement;** disjointing 802.1, disarticulation, unjointing, unhinging, luxation; heterotopia; **shift, removal,** forcible shift *or* removal; knocking off course; eviction; **uprooting,** ripping out, deracination; rootlessness; **disarrangement** 811; incoherence 803.1; discontinuity 813; Doppler effect *and* red shift *and* violet shift <physics>

2 **dislodgment;** unplacement, **unseating,** upset, unsaddling, unhorsing, unsettling; **deposal** 447; relocation, translocation, transference, transshipment

3 misplacement, mislaying, misputting, mislocation, losing

4 displaced person *or* DP, stateless person, homeless person, bag person, Wandering Jew, man without a country, exile, drifter, vagabond, deportee, repatriate; displaced *or* deported population; *déraciné* <Fr>; refugee, evacuee; outcast; waif, stray

VERBS **5 dislocate, displace, disjoint,** disarticulate, unjoint, luxate, unhinge, put *or* force *or* push out of place, **put** *or* **throw out of joint,** throw out of gear, knock *or* throw off course; **disarrange** 811.2

6 dislodge, unplace; evict; **uproot,** root up *or* out, deracinate; relocate; depose 447.4, **unseat,** unsaddle, unsettle; **unhorse,** dismount; throw off, buck off

7 misplace, mislay, misput, lose, lose track of

ADJS **8** dislocatory, dislocating, heterotopic

9 dislocated, displaced; disjointed, unjointed, unhinged; dislodged; out, **out of joint,** out of gear; **disarranged** 810.13

10 unplaced, unestablished, unsettled; **uprooted,** deracinated; unhoused, evicted, unharbored, houseless, made homeless, homeless, stateless, exiled, outcast, expatriated

11 misplaced, mislaid, misput, gone missing *or* astray; **out of place,** out of one's element, like a fish out of water, in the wrong place, in the wrong box *or* pew *and* in the right church but the wrong pew <nf>

12 eccentric, off-center, off-balance, unbalanced, uncentered

161 DIRECTION
<compass direction or course>

NOUNS **1 direction,** directionality; **line,** direction line, line of direction, point, quarter, **aim, way,** track, range, **bearing,** azimuth, compass reading, **heading, course;** current, set; tendency, trend, inclination, bent, tenor, run, drift; **orientation,** lay, lie, lay of the land; steering, helmsmanship, piloting; navigation 182.1,2; line of march

2 <nautical & aviation terms> vector, tack; compass direction, azimuth, compass bearing *or* heading, magnetic bearing *or* heading, relative bearing *or* heading, true bearing *or* heading *or* course; lee side, weather side 218.3

3 points of the compass, cardinal points, half points, quarter points, degrees, compass rose; compass card, lubber line; rhumb, loxodrome; magnetic north, true north, magnetic *or* compass directions, true directions; **north,** northward, nor'; **south,** southward; **east,** eastward, orient, sunrise; **west,** westward, occident, sunset; southeast, southwest,

northeast, northwest; northing, southing, easting, westing

4 orientation, bearings; adaptation, adjustment, accommodation, alignment, collimation; disorientation; deviation

VERBS **5 direct, point, aim, turn, bend, train,** fix, set, determine; point to *or* at, hold on, fix on, sight on; take aim, aim at, turn *or* train upon; directionize, give a push in the right direction; guide, signpost, indicate

6 direct to, give directions to, lead *or* conduct to, point out to, show, **show** *or* **point the way,** steer, put on the track, put on the right track, set straight, set *or* put right

7 <have or take a direction> **bear, head, turn, point, aim,** take *or* hold a heading, lead, go, steer, direct oneself, align oneself; **incline, tend, trend,** set, dispose, verge, tend to go, pilot, navigate

8 go west, wester, go east, easter, go north, go south

9 head for, bear for, **go for, make for,** hit *or* hit out for <nf>, **steer for,** hold for, put for, **set out** *or* **off for,** strike out for, take off for <nf>, bend one's steps for, lay for, bear up for, bear up to, make up to, set in towards; set *or* direct *or* shape one's course for, set one's compass for, sail for 182.35; align one's march; **break for,** make a break for <nf>, run *or* dash for, make a run *or* dash for

10 go directly, go straight, follow one's nose, go straight on, **head straight for,** vector for, go straight to the point, steer a straight course, follow a course, keep *or* hold one's course, hold steady for, arrow for, cleave to the line, keep pointed; **make a beeline,** go as the crow flies; take the air line, stay on the beam

11 orient, orientate, orient *or* orientate oneself, orient the map *or* chart, **take** *or* **get one's bearings,** get the lay *or* lie of the land, see which way the land lies, see which way the wind blows; adapt, adjust, accommodate

ADJS **12 directional,** azimuthal; **direct, straight,** arrow-straight, ruler-straight, straight-ahead, straightforward, straightaway, straightway; **undeviating,** unswerving, unveering; uninterrupted, unbroken; one-way, unidirectional, irreversible

13 directable, aimable, pointable, trainable; **steerable,** dirigible, guidable, leadable; **directed,** guided, aimed; well-aimed *or* -directed *or* -placed, on the mark, on the nose *or* money <nf>; **directional,** directive

14 northern, north, northernmost, northerly, northbound, **arctic,** boreal, hyperborean; **southern,** south, southernmost, southerly, southbound, meridional, **antarctic,** austral;

eastern, east, easternmost or eastermost, easterly, eastbound, **oriental; western,** west, westernmost, westerly, westbound, **occidental; northeastern,** northeast, northeasterly; **southeastern,** southeast, southeasterly; **southwestern,** southwest, southwesterly; **northwestern,** northwest, northwesterly; cross-country, downwind, upwind; oblique, axial, parallel

ADVS **15 north,** N, nor', northerly, northward, north'ard, norward, northwards, northwardly; north about

16 south, S, southerly, southward, south'ard, southwards, southwardly; south about

17 east, E, easterly, eastward, eastwards, eastwardly, where the sun rises; eastabout

18 west, W, westerly, westernly, westward, westwards, westwardly, where the sun sets; westabout

19 northeast or NE, nor'east, northeasterly, northeastward, northeastwards, northeastwardly; north-northeast or NNE; northeast by east or NE by E; northeast by north or NE by N

20 northwest or NW, nor'west, northwesterly, northwestward, northwestwards, northwestwardly; north-northwest or NNW; northwest by west or NW by W; northwest by north or NW by N

21 southeast or SE, southeasterly, southeastward, southeastwards, southeastwardly; south-southeast or SSE; southeast by east or SE by E; southeast by south or SE by S

22 southwest or SW, southwesterly, southwestward, southwestwards, southwestwardly; south-southwest or SSW; southwest by south or SW by S

23 directly, direct, straight, straightly, **straightforward,** straightforwards, **undeviatingly,** unswervingly, unveeringly; **straight ahead,** dead ahead; due, dead, due north, etc; right, forthright; in a direct or straight line, in line with, in a line for, **in a beeline, as the crow flies,** straight across; straight as an arrow

24 clockwise, rightward 219.7; **counterclockwise,** anticlockwise, widdershins, leftward 220.6; homeward; landward; seaward; earthward; heavenward; leeward, windward 218.9

25 in every direction, in all directions, in all manner of ways, every which way <nf>, everywhither, **everyway, everywhere,** at every turn, in all directions at once, in every quarter, on every side, all over the place or the ballpark or the map <nf>; around, all round, round about; forty ways or six ways from Sunday <nf>; from every quarter, everywhere; from or to the four corners of the earth, from or to the four winds

PREPS **26 toward,** towards, **in the direction of, to,** up, on, upon; against, over against, versus; headed for, bound for, on the way to, on the road or high road to, in transit to, en route to, on route to, in passage to

27 through, by, passing by or through, **by way of,** by the way of, **via;** over, around, round about, here and there in, all through

162 PROGRESSION
<motion forwards>

NOUNS **1 progression, progress,** going, going forward; **ongoing,** on-go, go-ahead <nf>, onward course, rolling, rolling on; **advance,** advancing, **advancement, promotion, furtherance,** furthering, preferment; forward motion, forwarding, forwardal; **headway,** way; **leap, jump,** forward leap or jump, quantum jump or leap, leaps and bounds, spring, forward spring; progressiveness, progressivity; **passage,** course, march, career, full career; midpassage, midcourse, midcareer; travel 177; improvement 392

VERBS **2 progress, advance, proceed, go,** go or move forward, step forward, go on, **go ahead,** go along, push ahead, press on, pass on or along, roll on; move, travel; go fast 174.8; **make progress,** come on, **get along,** come along <nf>, **get ahead;** further oneself; **make headway, roll,** gather head, gather way; make strides or rapid strides, cover ground, get over the ground, make good time, make the best of one's way, leap or jump or spring forward, catapult oneself forward; make up for lost time, gain ground, make up leeway, make progress against, stem

3 march on, run on, rub on, **jog on, roll on,** flow on; drift along, go with the stream

4 make or **wend one's way, work** or weave one's way, worm or thread one's way, inch forward, feel one's way, muddle along or through; go slow 175.6; carve one's way; push or force one's way, fight one's way, go or swim against the current, swim upstream; come a long way, move up in the world; **forge ahead,** drive on or ahead, **push** or **press on** or **onward,** push or press forward, push, crowd; get somewhere, reach toward, raise one's sights

5 advance, further, promote, forward, hasten, contribute to, foster, aid, facilitate, expedite, abet

ADJS **6 progressive,** progressing, advancing, proceeding, **ongoing,** proceeding, oncoming, onward, forward, **forward-looking,** go-ahead <nf>; moving; go-getting <nf>

ADVS **7 in progress,** in mid-progress, in midcourse, in midcareer, in full career; **going on;** by leaps and bounds

8 forward, forwards, onward, onwards, forth, on, along, **ahead;** on the way to, on the road or high road to, en route to or for

163 REGRESSION
<motion backwards>

NOUNS **1 regression,** regress; recession 168; **retrogression,** retrocession, retroflexion, retroflection, reflux, refluence, retrogradation, retroaction, retrusion, reaction; return, reentry; **setback,** backset <nf>, throwback, **rollback;** back-pedalling, backward motion, backward step; sternway; **backsliding,** lapse, relapse, recidivism, recidivation

2 retreat, *reculade* <Fr>, motion from, **withdrawal,** withdrawment, strategic withdrawal, exfiltration; **retirement, fallback,** pullout, pullback; advance to the rear; rout; disengagement; **backing down** *or* **off** *or* **out** <nf>; reneging, copping *or* weaseling out <nf>, resigning, resignation

3 reverse, reversal, reversing, reversion, inversion; **backing,** backing up, backup, backflow; **about-face,** *volte-face* <Fr>, about-turn, right-about, right-about-face, turn to the right-about, U-turn, turnaround, turnabout, swingaround; back track, back trail; turn of the tide, reflux, refluence

4 countermotion, countermovement, counteraction; recoil, rebound; countermarching

VERBS **5 regress,** go backwards, **recede,** return, revert; **retrogress,** retrograde, retroflex, retrocede; pull back, jerk back, reach back, cock <the arm, fist, etc>; *reculer pour mieux sauter* <Fr>; fall *or* get *or* go behind, fall astern, lose ground, slip back; **backslide,** lapse, relapse, recidivate; go down the tubes *or* drain <nf>

6 retreat, sound *or* beat a retreat, beat a hasty retreat, **withdraw, retire,** pull out *or* back, exfiltrate, advance to the rear, disengage; **fall back,** move back, go back, stand back; run back; **draw back,** draw off; **back out** *or* **out of** *and* back off *and* back down <nf>; defer, give ground, give place, take a back seat, play second fiddle; resign; crawfish <nf>

7 reverse, go into reverse; **back, back up,** backpedal, back off *or* away, go into reverse; **backwater,** make sternway; **backtrack,** backtrail, take the back track; countermarch; reverse one's field; take the reciprocal course; have second thoughts, think better of it, cut one's losses, go back to the drawing board

8 turn back, put back; double, double back, retrace one's steps; turn one's back upon; **return,** go *or* come back, go *or* come home

9 turn round *or* **around** *or* **about,** turn, make a U-turn, turn on a dime, turn tail, **come** *or* **go about,** put about, fetch about; veer, veer around; **swivel,** pivot, pivot about, swing, round, swing round; wheel, wheel about, double wheel, whirl, spin; heel, turn upon one's heel; recoil, rebound, quail

10 about-face, *volte-face* <Fr>, right-about-face, **do an about-face** *or* a right-about-face *or* an about-turn, perform a *volte-face,* **face about,** turn *or* face to the right-about, do a turn to the right-about

ADJS **11 regressive,** recessive; **retrogressive,** retrocessive, retrograde, retral; retroactive; reactionary

12 backward, reversed, reflex, **turned around,** back; wrong-way, wrong-way around, counter, ass-backwards *and* bassackwards <nf>

ADVS **13 backwards,** backward, retrally, **hindwards,** hindward, **rearwards,** rearward, arear, astern; **back,** away, fro, *à reculons* <Fr>; **in reverse,** ass-backwards <nf>; against the grain, *à rebours* <Fr>; counterclockwise, anticlockwise, widdershins

WORD ELEMENTS **14** an-, ana-, re-, retro-

164 DEVIATION
<indirect course>

NOUNS **1 deviation,** deviance *or* deviancy, deviousness, **departure, digression,** diversion, **divergence,** divarication, branching off, divagation, declination, aberration, aberrancy, **variation,** indirection, exorbitation; tangent, parenthesis; detour, excursion, excursus, discursion; obliquity, bias, skew, slant; **circuitousness** 913; **wandering,** rambling, **straying,** errantry, pererration; drift, drifting; turning, shifting, swerving, swinging; **turn, corner, bend, curve,** dogleg, crook, hairpin, zigzag, twist, warp, swerve, **veer,** sheer, sweep; shift, double; tack, yaw; wandering *or* twisting *or* zigzag *or* shifting course *or* path, slalom course; long way around

2 deflection, bending, deflexure, flection, flexure; torsion, distortion, contortion, torture *or* torturing, twisting, warping; skewness; **refraction, diffraction, scatter,** diffusion, dispersion; side step, crabwalk

VERBS **3 deviate, depart from, vary, diverge,** divaricate, branch off, angle, angle off; **digress,** divagate, turn aside, go out of the way, detour, take a side road; **swerve, veer,** sheer, curve, **shift, turn,** trend, bend, heel, bear off; turn right, turn left, hang a right *or* left <nf>; alter one's course, make a course correction, change the bearing; tack 182.30

4 stray, go astray, lose one's way, err; go off on a tangent; take a wrong turn *or* turning; drift, go adrift; **wander,** wander off, ramble, rove, straggle, divagate, excurse, pererrate; meander, wind, twist, snake, twist and turn; lose one's bearings

5 deflect, deviate, divert, diverge, **bend,** curve, pull, crook, dogleg, hairpin, zigzag; **warp,** bias, twist, distort, contort, torture, skew; refract, diffract, **scatter, diffuse, disperse;** put rudder on

6 avoid, evade, dodge, duck <nf>, turn aside *or* to the side, draw aside, **turn away,** jib, shy, shy off; gee, haw; **sidetrack,** shove aside, shunt, switch; **avert; head off,** turn back 908.3; **step aside,** sidestep, move aside *or* to the side, sidle; **steer clear of,** make way for, get out of the way of; go off, bear off, sheer off, veer off, ease off, edge off; fly off, go *or* fly off at a tangent; glance, glance off

ADJS **7 deviative,** deviatory, deviating, **deviant,** departing, aberrant, aberrational, aberrative, shifting, turning, swerving, veering; **digressive,** discursive, excursive, **circuitous; devious,** indirect, out-of-the-way; errant, erratic, zigzag, doglegged, **wandering,** rambling, roving, winding, twisting, meandering, snaky, serpentine, mazy, labyrinthine, vagrant, stray, desultory, planetary, undirected; out of sync <nf>

8 deflective, inflective, flectional, diffractive, refractive; refractile, refrangible; deflected, flexed, refracted, diffracted, scattered, diffuse, diffused, dispersed; distorted, skewed, skew; off-course, off-target, wide of the mark

9 avertive, evasive, dodging, dodgy

165 LEADING
<going ahead>

NOUNS **1 leading, heading,** foregoing; anteposition, the lead, *le pas* <Fr>; **preceding,** precedence 814; priority 834.1; front, point, leading edge, cutting edge, forefront, vanguard, van 216.2; vaunt-courier <old>, herald, precursor 816

VERBS **2 lead, head,** spearhead, stand at the head, stand first, be way ahead <nf>, head the line; take the lead, go in the lead, **lead the way,** break the trail, be the bellwether, lead the pack; be the point *or* point man; lead the dance; **light the way,** show the way, beacon, guide; get before, get ahead *or* in front of, come to the front, come to the fore, lap, outstrip, pace, set the pace; not look back; get *or* have the start, get a head start, steal a march upon; **precede** 814.2, go before 815.3

ADJS **3 leading, heading,** precessional, precedent, precursory, foregoing; **first, foremost,** headmost; **preceding,** antecedent 814.4; **prior** 834.4; **chief** 249.14

ADVS **4 before** 814.6, in front, out in front, outfront, foremost, headmost, in the van, in the forefront, in advance 216.12

166 FOLLOWING
<going behind>

NOUNS **1 following,** heeling, **trailing,** tailing <nf>, shadowing; **hounding, dogging,** chasing, **pursuit,** pursual, pursuance; sequence 814; sequel 817; series 812.2

2 follower, successor; shadow *and* tail <nf>; **pursuer,** pursuivant; **attendant** 769.4, **satellite, hanger-on,** dangler, adherent, appendage, dependent, parasite, stooge <nf>, flunky; **henchman,** ward heeler, partisan, supporter, votary, sectary; camp follower, groupy <nf>; fan *and* buff <nf>; courtier, *homme de cour* <Fr>, *cavaliere servente* <Ital>; trainbearer; **public; entourage,** following 769.6; disciple 572.2, discipleship

VERBS **3 follow,** go after *or* behind, come after *or* behind, move behind; **pursue, shadow** *and* **tail** <nf>, **trail,** trail after, follow in the trail of, camp on the trail of, **heel,** follow *or* tread *or* step on the heels of, follow in the steps *or* footsteps *or* footprints of, tread close upon, breathe down the neck of, follow in the wake of, hang on the skirts of, stick like the shadow of, sit on the tail of, tailgate <nf>, go in the rear of, bring up the rear, eat the dust of, take *or* swallow one's dust; tag *and* **tag after** *and* tag along <nf>; string along <nf>; **dog,** bedog, **hound,** chase, get after, take out *or* take off after, **pursue**

4 lag, lag behind, straggle, lag back, drag, trail, **trail behind,** hang back *or* behind, loiter, linger, **loiter** *or* **linger behind,** dawdle, get behind, fall behind *or* behindhand, let grass grow under one's feet

ADJS **5 following,** trailing, on the track *or* trail; succeeding 815.4; back-to-back <nf>, consecutive 811.9

ADVS **6 behind, after,** in the rear, in the train *or* wake of; in back of 217.13

167 APPROACH
<motion towards>

NOUNS **1 approach,** approaching, coming *or* going toward, coming *or* going near, proximation, appropinquation <old>, **access,** accession, nearing; advance, oncoming; **advent, coming,** forthcoming; flowing toward, afflux, affluxion; appulse; nearness 223; imminence 840; approximation 223.1

2 approachability, accessibility, access, getatableness *and* come-at-ableness <nf>, attainability, openness

VERBS **3 approach, near, draw near** *or* nigh, go *or* come near, go *or* come toward, come closer *or* nearer, come to close quarters; **close,** close in, close in on, close with; zoom in on; **accost,** encounter, confront; proximate, appropinquate <old>; **advance,** come, **come forward,** come on, come up, bear up, step up; ease *or* edge *or* sidle up to; bear down on *or* upon, be on a collision course with; gain upon, narrow the gap; approximate 784.7, 223.8

ADJS 4 approaching, nearing, advancing; attracted to, drawn to; **coming, oncoming, forthcoming,** upcoming, to come; approximate, proximate, approximative; near 223.14; imminent 840.3

5 approachable, accessible, getatable *and* come-at-able <nf>, attainable, open, easy to find, meet, etc

168 RECESSION
<motion from>

NOUNS 1 recession, recedence, receding, retrocedence; **retreat, retirement, withdrawing, withdrawal;** retraction, retractation, retractility; fleetingness, fugitiveness, fugitivity, evanescence

VERBS 2 recede, retrocede; **retreat, retire, withdraw;** move off *or* away, stand off *or* away, stand out from the shore; go, **go away; die away,** fade away, drift away; erode, wash away; **diminish,** decline, sink, shrink, dwindle, **fade, ebb,** wane; shy away, tail away, tail off; go out with the tide, fade into the distance; pull away, widen the distance

3 retract, withdraw, **draw** *or* **pull back,** pull out, draw *or* pull in; draw in one's claws *or* horns; defer, take a back seat, play second fiddle; **shrink,** wince, cringe, flinch, shy, fight shy, duck

ADJS 4 recessive, recessional, recessionary; recedent, retrocedent

5 receding, retreating, retiring, withdrawing; shy; **diminishing, declining,** sinking, shrinking, eroding, dwindling, **ebbing,** waning; **fading,** dying; fleeting, fugitive, evanescent

6 retractile, retractable, retrahent

169 CONVERGENCE
<coming together>

NOUNS 1 convergence, converging, confluence, concourse, conflux; mutual approach, approach 167; **meeting,** congress, concurrence, coming together; **concentration,** concentralization, focalization 208.8, focus 208.4; meeting point, point of convergence, vanishing point; union, merger; crossing point, crossroads, crossing 170; collision course, narrowing gap; funnel, bottleneck; hub, spokes; asymptote; radius; tangent

VERBS 2 converge, come together, approach 167.3, run together, **meet,** unite, connect, merge; **cross,** intersect 170.6; fall in with, link up with; be on a collision course; go toward, narrow the gap, close with, close, close up, close in; funnel; taper, pinch, nip; centralize, center, **come to a center;** center on *or* around, concentralize, concenter, **concentrate,** come *or* tend to a point; come to a focus 208.10

ADJS 3 converging, convergent; **meeting,** uniting, merging; concurrent, confluent, mutually approaching, approaching; **crossing,** intersecting 170.8; connivent; **focal,** confocal, focusing, focused; centrolineal, centripetal; asymptotic, asymptotical; tangent, tangential, radial, radiating

170 CROSSING

NOUNS 1 crossing, intercrossing, intersecting, **intersection;** decussation, chiasma; traversal, transversion; cross section, transection; cruciation; **transit,** transiting

2 crossing, crossway, **crosswalk, crossroad,** pedestrian crosswalk, zebra *or* zebra crossing <Brit>; *carrefour* <Fr>; **intersection,** intercrossing; level crossing, grade crossing; crossover, overpass, flyover <Brit>, viaduct, undercrossing; traffic circle, rotary, roundabout <Brit>; highway interchange, **interchange,** cloverleaf, spaghetti junction <Brit>

3 network, webwork, weaving 740, **meshwork,** tissue, crossing over and under, interlacement, intertwinement, intertexture, texture, reticulum, reticulation; "Any thing reticulated or decussated, at equal distances, with interstices between the intersections"—Samuel Johnson; crossing-out, cancellation, scrubbing <nf>; **net,** netting; **mesh,** meshes; **web,** webbing; weave, weft; lace, lacery, lacing, lacework; screen, screening; sieve, riddle, raddle; wicker, wickerwork; basketwork, basketry; lattice, latticework; hachure *or* hatchure, hatching, cross-hatching; trellis, trelliswork, treillage; grate, grating; grille, grillwork; **grid,** gridiron; tracery, fretwork, fret, arabesque, filigree; plexus, plexure; reticle, reticule; wattle, wattle and daub

4 cross, crux, cruciform; **crucifix,** rood, tree *or* rood tree <old>; X *or* ex, exing, T, Y; **swastika,** gammadion, fylfot, *Hakenkreuz* <Ger>; crossbones; dagger

5 crosspiece, traverse, transverse, transversal, transept, transom, cross bitt; diagonal; **crossbar,** crossarm; swingletree, singletree, whiffletree, whippletree; doubletree

VERBS 6 cross, crisscross, cruciate; **intersect,** intercross, decussate; **cut across,** crosscut; **traverse,** transverse, lie across; bar, crossbar

7 net, web, mesh; lattice, trellis; grate, grid

ADJS 8 cross, crossing, crossed; crisscross, crisscrossed; intersecting, intersected, intersectional; crosscut, cut across; decussate, decussated; chiasmal *or* chiasmic *or* chiastic; secant

9 transverse, transversal, traverse; **across,** cross, crossway, **crosswise** *or* crossways, thwart, athwart, overthwart; oblique 204.13

10 cruciform, crosslike, cross-shaped, cruciate, X-shaped, cross, crossed; cruciferous

11 netlike, retiform, plexiform; **reticulated,** reticular, reticulate; cancellate, cancelled; **netted,** netty; **meshed,** meshy; laced, lacy, lacelike; filigreed; latticed, latticelike; grated, gridded; barred, crossbarred, mullioned; streaked, striped

12 webbed, webby, weblike, woven, interwoven, interlaced, intertwined; web-footed, palmiped

ADVS **13 crosswise** or crossways or crossway, decussatively; **cross, crisscross, across,** thwart, thwartly, thwartways, **athwart,** athwartwise, overthwart; **traverse,** traversely; **transverse,** transversely, transversally; obliquely 204.21; **sideways** or sidewise; contrariwise, contrawise; crossgrained, across the grain, against the grain; athwartship, athwartships

171 DIVERGENCE
<recession from one another>

NOUNS **1 divergence** or divergency, divarication; aberration, deviation 164; **separation,** division, decentralization; centrifugence; **radial, radiating,** radiating out, raying out, beaming out; **spread,** spreading, spreading out, splaying, fanning, fanning out, deployment; ripple effect

2 radiation, ray, sunray, radius, spoke; radiance, diffusion, scattering, dispersion, emanation; halo, aureole, glory, corona; ripple effect

3 forking, furcation, bifurcation, biforking, trifurcation, divarication, triforking; **branching,** branching off or out, **ramification;** arborescence, arborization

4 fork, prong, trident; Y, V; **branch, ramification,** stem, offshoot; **crotch,** crutch; **fan, delta; groin,** inguen; furcula, furculum, **wishbone**

VERBS **5 diverge,** divaricate; aberrate; **separate,** divide, separate off, split off; spread, **spread out,** outspread, splay, fan out, deploy; go off or away, **fly** or **go off at a tangent;** part company

6 radiate, radiate out, ray, ray out, beam out, diffuse, emanate, spread, disperse, scatter

7 fork, furcate, bifurcate, trifurcate, divaricate; **branch,** stem, ramify, branch off or out, spread-eagle

ADJS **8 diverging,** divergent; divaricate, divaricating; palmate, palmated; fanlike, fan-shaped; deltoid, deltoidal, deltalike, delta-shaped; splayed; centrifugal

9 radiating, radial, radiate, radiated; rayed, spoked; radiative

10 forked, forking, furcate, biforked, bifurcate, bifurcated, forklike, trifurcate, trifurcated; tridentlike, pronged; **crotched,** Y-shaped,

V-shaped; **branched, branching;** arborescent, arboreal, arboriform, treelike, tree-shaped, dendriform, dendritic; branchlike, ramous

172 MOTION
<motion in general>

NOUNS **1 motion; movement,** moving, **momentum; stir,** unrest, restlessness; **going,** running, stirring; **operation,** operating, **working,** ticking; **activity** 330; kinesis, kinetics, kinematics; dynamics; kinesiatrics, kinesipathy, kinesitherapy, kinesiology; **actuation,** motivation; mobilization

2 course, career, set, midcareer, **passage, progress,** trend, **advance,** forward motion, going or moving on, momentum; **travel** 177; **flow,** flux, flight, **trajectory; stream, current,** run, rush, onrush, ongoing; drift, driftage; backward motion, **regression,** retrogression, sternway, backing, going or moving backwards; backflowing, reflowing, refluence, reflux, ebbing, subsiding, withdrawing; downward motion, **descent,** descending, sinking, plunging; upward motion, mounting, climbing, rising, **ascent,** ascending, **soaring,** mounting; oblique or crosswise motion; sideward or sidewise or sideways motion; radial motion, angular motion, axial motion; random motion, Brownian movement; perpetual motion

3 mobility, motivity, motility, movableness, movability; **locomotion;** motive power

4 velocity 174.1,2, rate, gait, pace, tread, step, stride, clip and lick <nf>

VERBS **5 move, budge, stir;** go, run, flow, stream; **progress,** advance; wend, wend one's way; **back,** back up, regress, retrogress; ebb, subside, wane; **descend,** sink, plunge; **ascend,** mount, rise, climb, soar; go sideways, go crabwise; go round or around, circle, rotate, gyrate, spin, whirl; travel; move over, get over; shift, change, shift or change place; **speed** 174.8; **hurry** 401.5, do on the fly or run

6 set in motion, move, actuate, motivate, push, shove, nudge, **drive,** impel, propel; mobilize; dispatch

ADJS **7 moving, stirring, in motion;** transitional; **mobile,** motive, motile, motor, motorial, motoric; motivational, impelling, propelling, propellant, driving, self-propelled; traveling; **active** 330.17

8 flowing, fluent, passing, streaming, flying, **running, going, progressive,** rushing, onrushing; drifting; **regressive,** retrogressive, back, **backward;** backflowing, refluent, reflowing; descending, sinking, plunging, **downward,** down-trending; ascending, mounting, rising, soaring, **upward,** up-trending; sideward, sidewise, sideways; **rotary,** rotatory, rotational, round-and-round; axial, gyrational, gyratory

ADVS **9 under way,** under sail, on one's way, on the go *or* move *or* fly *or* run *or* march, **in motion, astir;** from pillar to post

WORD ELEMENTS **10** moto-; -kinesia, kin-, kine-, kino-, kinesi-, kinesio-, kinet-, kineto-

173 QUIESCENCE
<being at rest; absence of motion>

NOUNS **1 quiescence,** *or* quiescency, **stillness,** silence 51, quietness, **quiet,** quietude, "lucid stillness" —T S Eliot; **calmness,** restfulness, **peacefulness,** imperturbability, passiveness, passivity, "wise passiveness"—Wordsworth, placidness, **placidity, tranquillity, serenity, peace, composure;** quietism, contemplation, satori, nirvana, samadhi, ataraxy *or* ataraxia; **rest, repose,** silken repose, statuelike *or* marmoreal repose; sleep, slumber 22.2

2 motionlessness, immobility; inactivity, inaction; fixity, fixation 855.2

3 standstill, stand, stillstand; **stop, halt,** cessation 857; dead stop, dead stand, full stop; deadlock, lock, dead set; gridlock, stalemate, stoppage; freeze, strike; running *or* dying down, subsidence, waning, ebbing, wane, ebb

4 inertness, dormancy; inertia, *vis inertiae* <L>; passiveness, passivity; suspense, abeyance, latency; torpor, apathy, indifference, indolence, lotus-eating, languor; **stagnation,** stagnancy, **vegetation;** stasis; sloth; deathliness, deadliness; catalepsy, catatonia; entropy

5 calm, lull, lull *or* calm before the storm; dead calm, flat calm, oily calm, windlessness, deathlike calm; doldrums, horse latitudes; anticyclone, eye of the hurricane

6 stuffiness, airlessness, closeness, oppressiveness, stirlessness, oppression

VERBS **7 be still, keep quiet,** lie still; **stop moving,** cease motion, freeze *or* seize up, come to a standstill; **rest, repose; remain, stay,** tarry; remain motionless, freeze <nf>; stand, **stand still,** be at a standstill; stand *or* stick fast, stick, stand firm, stay put <nf>; stand like a post; **not stir,** not stir a step, not move a muscle; not breathe, hold one's breath; bide, bide one's time, mark time, tread water, coast; rest on one's oars, put one's feet up, rest and be thankful

8 quiet, quieten, **lull, soothe,** quiesce, **calm,** calm down, tranquilize 670.7, pacify, passivize, assuage, pour oil on troubled waters; **stop** 857.7, halt, bring to a standstill; **cease** 857.6, wane, subside, ebb, run *or* die down, die off, dwindle, molder

9 stagnate, vegetate, fust <old>; sleep, slumber; smolder, hang fire; **idle**

10 sit, set <nf>, **sit down, be seated,** remain seated, remain in situ; perch, roost

11 becalm, take the wind out of one's sails

ADJS **12 quiescent, quiet, still,** stilly <old>, stillish, hushed; quiet as a mouse; waning, subsiding, ebbing, dwindling, moldering; **at rest,** resting, reposing; restful, reposeful, relaxed; cloistered, sequestered, sequestrated, isolated, secluded, sheltered; **calm, tranquil, peaceful,** peaceable, pacific, halcyon; **placid, smooth; unruffled, untroubled,** cool, undisturbed, unperturbed, unagitated, unmoved, unstirring, laid-back <nf>; stolid, stoic, stoical, impassive; even-tenored; calm as a mill pond; still as death, "quiet as a street at night"—Rupert Brooke

13 motionless, unmoving, unmoved, moveless, **immobile,** immotive; **still, fixed, stationary, static,** at a standstill; **stock-still,** dead-still; still as a statue, statuelike; still as a mouse; at anchor, riding at anchor; **idle,** unemployed; out of commission, down

14 inert, inactive, static, dormant, passive, sedentary; **latent,** unaroused, suspended, abeyant, in suspense *or* abeyance; sleeping, slumbering, smoldering; **stagnant,** standing, foul; **torpid, languorous, languid,** apathetic, phlegmatic, **sluggish,** logy, dopey <nf>, groggy, heavy, leaden, **dull,** flat, slack, tame, **dead,** lifeless; catatonic, cataleptic

15 untraveled, stay-at-home, stick-in-the-mud <nf>, home-keeping

16 stuffy, airless, breathless, breezeless, windless; **close, oppressive, stifling, suffocating;** stirless, unstirring, not a breath of air, not a leaf stirring, "not wind enough to twirl the one red leaf"—Coleridge; ill-ventilated, unventilated, unvented

17 becalmed, in a dead calm

ADVS **18** quiescently, **quietly,** stilly, still; **calmly, tranquilly, peacefully,** serenely; **placidly,** smoothly, unperturbedly, **coolly**

19 motionlessly, movelessly, stationarily, fixedly

20 inertly, inactively, statically, dormantly, passively, latently; stagnantly; **torpidly, languorously, languidly; like a bump on a log; sluggishly,** heavily, dully, coldly, lifelessly, apathetically, phlegmatically; stoically, stolidly, impassively

174 SWIFTNESS

NOUNS **1 velocity, speed; rapidity,** celerity, **swiftness,** fastness, **quickness,** snappiness <nf>, **speediness;** haste 401.1, hurry, flurry, rush, precipitation;

dispatch, **expedition, promptness,** promptitude, instantaneousness; flight, flit; lightning speed; fast *or* swift rate, smart *or* rattling *or* spanking *or* lively *or* snappy pace, round pace; relative velocity, angular velocity; air speed, ground speed, speed over the bottom; miles per hour, knots; rpm 915.3

2 **speed of sound, sonic speed,** Mach, Mach number, Mach one, Mach two, etc; subsonic speed; supersonic *or* ultrasonic *or* hypersonic *or* transsonic speed; transsonic barrier, sound barrier; escape velocity; speed of light, terminal velocity; warp speed, lightning speed

3 **run, sprint; dash, rush,** plunge, headlong rush *or* plunge, **race, scurry, scamper,** scud, scuttle, **spurt,** burst, **burst of speed;** canter, **gallop,** lope; high lope, hand gallop, full gallop; dead run; **trot,** extended trot, dogtrot, jog trot; **full speed,** open throttle, flat-out speed <Brit>, wide-open speed, heavy right foot, maximum speed; **fast-forward;** fast track *or* lane; forced draft *and* flank speed <nautical>

4 **acceleration, quickening; pickup,** getaway; burst of speed; step-up, speedup; thrust, drive, impetus, kick-start; free fall; flying start; headlong plunge; overtaking; zip *or* zing <nf>

5 **speeder,** scorcher *and* hell-driver <nf>, **sprinter,** harrier; flier, goer, stepper; hummer *and* hustler *and* sizzler <nf>; **speed demon** *or* maniac <nf>; **racer, runner;** horse racer, turfman, jockey; Jehu; express messenger, courier

6 <comparisons> lightning, greased lightning <nf>, thunderbolt, flash, streak of lightning, streak, blue streak <nf>, bat out of hell <nf>, light, electricity, thought, wind, shot, bullet, cannonball, rocket, arrow, dart, quicksilver, mercury, express train, jet plane, torrent, eagle, swallow, antelope, courser, gazelle, greyhound, hare, blue darter, striped snake, scared rabbit

7 **speedometer,** accelerometer; cyclometer; tachometer; Mach meter; knotmeter, log, log line, patent log, taffrail log, harpoon log, ground log; windsock; wind gauge, anemometer

VERBS 8 **speed, go fast,** skim, **fly,** flit, fleet, wing one's way, outstrip the wind; **zoom;** make knots, foot; break the sound barrier, go at warp speed; go like the wind, go like a shot *or* flash, go like lightning *or* a streak of lightning, go like greased lightning; **rush, tear,** dash, dart, shoot, hurtle, bolt, fling, **scamper, scurry,** scour, scud, scuttle, scramble, **race,** careen; **hasten,** haste, make haste, **hurry** 401.4, hie, post, kick-start; march in quick *or* double-quick time; **run, sprint, trip,** spring, **bound,** leap; gallop, lope, canter, trot; **make time,** make good time, **cover ground,** get over the ground,

make strides *or* **rapid strides,** make the best of one's way

9 <nf terms> **barrel,** clip, spank *or* cut along, tear *or* tear along *or* off, bowl along, thunder along, storm along, breeze *or* breeze along, tear up the track *or* road, eat up the track *or* road, scorch, sizzle, rip, zip, whiz, whisk, sweep, brush, nip, zing, fly low, highball, ball the jack, pour it on, boom, shake *or* get the lead out, lollop <Brit>, give it the gun, skedaddle, scoot, step on it, step on the gas, hump *or* hump it, stir one's stumps, hotfoot, hightail, make tracks, step lively, step, step along, carry the mail, hop, hop along, hop it, get, git, go like a bat out of hell, run like a scared rabbit, run like mad, go at full blast, go all out, go flat out, run wide open, go at full tilt *or* steam, let her out, open her up, go hell-bent for election *or* leather, get a move on, give it the gas, go like blazes *or* blue blazes, floor it, let her rip, put the pedal to the metal, tool

10 **accelerate, speed up, step up** <nf>, **hurry up, quicken;** hasten 401.4; crack on, put on, put on steam, pour on the coal, put on more speed, open the throttle; quicken one's pace; pick up speed, gain ground; race <a motor>, rev <nf>

11 <naut terms> put on sail, crack *or* pack on sail, crowd sail, press her

12 **spurt,** make a spurt *or* dash, **dash** *or* dart *or* shoot ahead, rush ahead, put on *or* make a burst of speed; make one's move

13 **overtake, outstrip, overhaul,** catch up, **catch up with,** come up with *or* to, gain on *or* upon, pass, lap; outpace, outrun, outsail; leave behind, leave standing *or* looking *or* flatfooted

14 **keep up with,** keep pace with, run neck and neck

ADJS 15 **fast, swift, speedy, rapid; quick,** double-quick, express, **fleet, hasty, expeditious,** hustling, snappy <nf>, rushing, onrushing, dashing, flying, galloping, running, **agile, nimble,** lively, nimble-footed, light-footed, light-legged, light of heel; winged, eagle-winged; mercurial; quick as lightning, quick as thought, swift as an arrow, "swifter than arrow from the Tartar's bow"— Shakespeare; **breakneck,** reckless, headlong, precipitate; quick as a wink, quick on the trigger <nf>, hair-trigger <nf>; **prompt** 845.9

16 **supersonic,** transsonic, ultrasonic, hypersonic, faster than sound; warp; **high-speed,** high-velocity, high-geared

ADVS 17 **swiftly, rapidly, quickly,** snappily <nf>, **speedily,** with speed, **fast, quick,** apace, amain, on eagle's wings, *ventre à terre* <Fr>; at a great rate, at a good clip <nf>, with rapid strides, with giant strides, *à pas de géant* <Fr>, in seven-league boots, **by leaps and bounds,** trippingly; **lickety-split** *and* lickety-cut <nf>; hell-bent *and* hell-bent for election *and* hell-bent for leather <nf>; **posthaste, post, hastily,** expeditiously, promptly, with great *or* all haste, whip and spur, **hand over hand** *or* **fist;** double-quick, in double time, in double-quick time, on the double *or* the double-quick <nf>; in high gear, in high; under press of sail, all sails set, under crowded sails, under press of sail and steam, under forced draft, at flank speed <all nautical>

18 <nf terms> **like a shot, as if shot out of a cannon, like a flash,** like a streak, like a blue streak, like a streak of lightning, like lightning, like greased lightning, **like a bat out of hell, like a scared rabbit,** like a house afire, like sixty, like mad *and* **crazy** *and* fury, like sin, to beat the band *or* the Dutch *or* the deuce *or* the devil

19 **in short order, in no time,** instantaneously, immediately if not sooner, in less than no time, in nothing flat <nf>; in a jiff *or* jiffy <nf>, before you can say Jack Robinson, **in a flash,** in a twink, **in a twinkling,** "in the twinkling of an eye"—Bible, *tout de suite* <Fr>, pronto <nf>, PDQ *or* pretty damn quick <nf>

20 **at full speed,** with all speed, at full throttle, **at the top of one's bent, for all one is worth** <nf>, hit the ground running <nf>, as fast as one's legs will carry one, as fast as one can lay feet to the ground; **at full blast,** at full drive *or* pelt; under full steam, in full sail; **all out** <nf>, flat out <Brit>, **wide open;** full speed ahead

175 SLOWNESS

NOUNS 1 **slowness, leisureliness,** pokiness, slackness, creeping, no hurry; **sluggishness,** sloth, laziness, idleness, indolence, sluggardy, languor, inertia, inertness, lentitude *or* lentor <old>; deliberateness, deliberation, circumspection, tentativeness, cautiousness, reluctance, foot-dragging <nf>; drawl; gradualism; hesitation, slow start

2 **slow motion, leisurely gait,** snail's *or* tortoise's pace; **creep, crawl; walk,** footpace, dragging *or* lumbering pace, trudge, waddle, saunter, stroll; slouch, shuffle, plod, shamble; limp, claudication, hobble; dogtrot, jog trot; jog, rack; mincing steps; slow march, dead *or* funeral march, largo, andante

3 **dawdling, lingering, loitering, tarrying,** dalliance, **dallying,** dillydallying, shillyshallying, lollygagging, dilatoriness, delaying tactic, delayed action, procrastination 845.5, lag, **lagging,** goofing off <nf>

4 **slowing, retardation,** retardment, **slackening,** flagging, slowing down *or* up; **slowdown,** slowup,

letup, letdown, slack-up, slack-off, ease-off, ease-up; **deceleration,** negative *or* minus acceleration; **delay** 846.2, **detention, setback, holdup** <nf>, check, arrest, brake, obstruction; lag, drag

5 **slowpoke** *and* slowcoach <nf>, plodder, slow goer, slow-foot, **lingerer, loiterer, dawdler,** dawdle, **laggard,** procrastinator, foot-dragger, stick-in-the-mud <nf>, drone, slug, sluggard, lie-abed, sleepy-head, slow starter, goof-off <nf>, goldbrick <nf>; tortoise, snail

VERBS 6 **go slow** *or* **slowly,** go at a snail's pace, take it slow, get no place fast <nf>; **drag,** drag out; **creep, crawl;** laze, idle; go dead slow, get nowhere fast; inch, inch along; worm, worm along; poke, **poke along;** shuffle *or* stagger *or* totter *or* toddle along; drag along, drag one's feet, walk, traipse *and* **mosey** <nf>; **saunter, stroll, amble,** waddle, toddle <nf>; jogtrot, dogtrot; limp, hobble, claudicate; *festina lente* <L>

7 **plod,** plug <nf>, peg, shamble, **trudge,** tramp, stump, lumber; plod along, plug along <nf>, schlep <nf>; rub on, jog on, chug on

8 **dawdle, linger, loiter, tarry, delay, dally, dillydally,** shilly-shally, lollygag, waste time, **take one's time,** take one's own sweet time; goof off *or* around <nf>; lag, drag, trail; flag, falter, halt, not get started

9 **slow, slow down** *or* **up, let down** *or* **up, ease off** *or* **up, slack off** *or* **up, slacken,** relax, moderate, taper off, lose speed *or* momentum; **decelerate, retard,** delay 846.8, **detain,** impede, obstruct, arrest, stay, **check,** curb, **hold up, hold back,** keep back, set back, hold in check; draw rein, rein in; throttle down, take one's foot off the gas; idle, barely tick over; brake, **put on the brakes,** put on the drag; reef, take in sail; backwater, backpedal; lose ground; clip the wings; regress

ADJS 10 **slow, leisurely,** slack, moderate, gentle, **easy,** deliberate, go-slow, unhurried, relaxed, gradual, circumspect, tentative, cautious, reluctant, foot-dragging <nf>; **creeping, crawling; poking,** poky, slow-poky <nf>; tottering, staggering, toddling, trudging, **lumbering,** ambling, waddling, shuffling, **sauntering,** strolling; **sluggish,** languid, languorous, lazy, slothful, indolent, idle, slouchy; **slow-going, slow-moving,** slow-creeping, slow-crawling, slow-running, slow-sailing, **slow-footed,** slow-foot, slow-legged, slow-gaited, slow-paced, slow-stepped, easy-paced, slow-winged; snail-paced, snail-like, tortoiselike, turtlelike, "creeping like snail"—Shakespeare; limping, hobbling, hobbled; halting, claudicant; faltering, flagging; slow as slow, slow as molasses *or* molasses in January, slow as death, slower than the seven-year itch <nf>

11 dawdling, lingering, loitering, tarrying, dallying, dillydallying, shilly-shallying, lollygagging, procrastinatory *or* procrastinative, dilatory, delaying 846.17, **lagging,** dragging

12 retarded, slowed-down, eased, slackened; **delayed, detained,** checked, **arrested,** impeded, set back, backward, behind; late, **tardy** 846.16

ADVS **13 slowly,** slow, **leisurely,** unhurriedly, relaxedly, easily, moderately, gently; creepingly, crawlingly, pokingly, pokily; **sluggishly,** languidly, languorously, lazily, indolently, idly, deliberately, with deliberation, circumspectly, tentatively, cautiously, reluctantly; **lingeringly,** loiteringly, tarryingly, dilatorily; limpingly, haltingly, falteringly; **in slow motion,** at a funeral pace, with faltering *or* halting steps; at a snail's *or* turtle's pace, "in haste like a snail"—John Heywood; in slow tempo, in march time; with agonizing slowness; in low gear; under easy sail

14 gradually, little by little 245.6

PHRS **15 easy does it,** take it easy, go easy, slack off, slow down

176 TRANSFERAL, TRANSPORTATION

1 transferal, transfer; transmission, transference, transmittal, transmittance; **transposition,** transposal, transplacement; mutual transfer, interchange, metathesis; translocation, **transplantation,** translation; migration, transmigration; **import, importation; export, exportation;** deportation, extradition, expulsion, **transit,** transition, **passage; communication,** spread, spreading, dissemination, diffusion, contagion, ripple effect; metastasis; transmigration of souls, metempsychosis; passing over; osmosis, diapedesis; transduction, conduction, convection; transfusion, perfusion; transfer of property *or* right 629

2 transferability, conveyability; transmissibility, transmittability; movability, removability; **portability,** transportability; communicability, impartability; deliverability

3 transportation, conveyance, transport, carrying, bearing, packing, toting *and* lugging <nf>; **carriage,** carry, **hauling,** haulage, portage, porterage, waft, waftage; **cartage, truckage,** drayage, wagonage; ferriage, lighterage; telpherage; **freightage,** freight, expressage, railway express; **airfreight, air express,** airlift; **package freight,** package service; **shipment, shipping,** transshipment; containerization, cargo-handling; delivery 478.1; travel 177; expressage

4 moving, removal, movement, relocation, shift, removement, remotion; **displacement,** delocalization

5 people mover, moving sidewalk, automated monorail; conveyor belt; elevator, lift <Brit>, escalator 912.4

6 freight, freightage; **shipment, consignment,** goods <Brit>; **cargo,** payload; lading, load, pack; **baggage, luggage,** impedimenta

7 carrier, conveyer; transporter, hauler, carter, wagoner, drayman, shipper, trucker, common carrier, truck driver, driver; freighter; containerizer; stevedore, cargo handler; expressman, express, messenger, courier; importer, exporter; **bearer, porter,** redcap, skycap, bell boy; bus boy; coolie; litter-bearer, stretcher-bearer; caddie; shield-bearer, gun bearer; water carrier *or* bearer, water boy, bheesty <India>; the Water Bearer, Aquarius; letter carrier 353.5; cupbearer, Ganymede, Hebe; carrier pigeon, homing pigeon

8 beast of burden; pack *or* **draft animal,** pack horse *or* mule, sumpter, sumpter horse *or* mule; **horse** 311.10–15, ass, mule; ox; camel, ship of the desert, dromedary, llama; reindeer; elephant; sledge dog, husky, malamute, Siberian husky

9 <geological terms> **deposit,** sediment; drift, silt, loess, moraine, scree, sinter; alluvium, alluvion, diluvium; detritus, debris

VERBS **10 transfer, transmit, transpose,** translocate, transplace, metathesize, switch; **transplant,** translate; **pass,** pass over, **hand over,** turn over, carry over, make over, consign, assign; **deliver** 478.13; pass on, pass the buck <nf>, hand forward, hand on, relay; **import, export;** deport, extradite, expel; communicate, diffuse, disseminate, spread, impart; expedite; transfuse, perfuse, transfer property *or* right 629.3

11 remove, move, relocate, shift, send, shunt; displace, delocalize, dislodge; **take away,** cart off *or* away, carry off *or* away; manhandle; set *or* lay *or* put aside, put *or* set to one side, side

12 transport, convey, freight, conduct, **take; carry, bear,** pack, tote *and* lug <nf>, manhandle; lift, waft, whisk, wing, fly; schlep <nf>

13 haul, cart, truck, bus; **ship,** barge, lighter, ferry; raft, float

14 channel, put through channels; **pipe,** tube, pipeline, flume, **siphon, funnel,** tap

15 send, send off *or* away, send forth; **dispatch,** transmit, remit, consign, forward; expedite; **ship,** ship off, freight, airfreight, embark, containerize, **transship,** pass along, send on; **express,** air-express; express-mail; package-express; **post, mail,** airmail, drop a letter; messenger; export; e-mail

16 fetch, bring, go get, go and get, go to get, **go after,** go fetch, **go for,** call for, pick up; **get,** obtain, procure, secure; **bring back, retrieve;** chase after, run after, shag, fetch and carry

17 ladle, dip, scoop; bail, bucket; **dish,** dish out *or* up; cup; **shovel,** spade, fork; spoon; **pour,** decant

ADJS **18 transferable, conveyable; transmittable,** transmissible, transmissive, consignable, deliverable; **movable,** removable; **portable,** portative; transportable, transportative, transportive, carriageable; roadworthy, seaworthy, airworthy; importable, exportable; conductive, conductional; transposable, interchangeable; **communicable,** contagious, impartable; transfusable; metastatic *or* metastatical, metathetic *or* metathetical; mailable, expressable; assignable 629.5

ADVS **19** by transfer, from hand to hand, from door to door; by freight, by express, by rail, by trolley, by bus, by steamer, by airplane, by mail, by special delivery, by package express, by messenger, by hand; by e-mail

20 on the way, along the way, on the road *or* high road, **en route, in transit,** *in transitu* <L>, on the wing, as one goes; in passing, *en passant* <Fr>; in mid-progress

177 TRAVEL

NOUNS **1 travel,** traveling, going, journeying, touring, moving, **movement, motion, locomotion, transit, progress, passage,** course, crossing; commutation, straphanging; world travel, globe-trotting <nf>; junketing; **tourism,** touristry

2 travels, journeys, **journeyings, wanderings,** voyagings, transits, peregrinations, peripatetics, migrations, transmigrations; odyssey

3 wandering, roving, roaming, rambling, gadding, traipsing <nf>, wayfaring, flitting, straying, drifting, gallivanting, peregrination, peregrinity, pilgrimage, errantry, divagation; roam, rove, ramble; **itinerancy,** itineracy; **nomadism,** nomadization, gypsydom; vagabonding, vagabondism, vagabondage; **vagrancy,** hoboism, waltzing Matilda <Austral>; bumming <nf>; the open road; wanderyear, *Wanderjahr* <Ger>; **wanderlust;** "afoot and lighthearted"—Whitman

4 migration, transmigration, passage, trek; run <of fish>, flight <of birds and insects>; swarm, swarming <of bees>; **immigration,** in-migration; **emigration,** out-migration, expatriation; remigration; intermigration

5 journey, trip, *jornada* <Sp>, peregrination, sally, **trek;** progress, course, run; **tour,** grand tour; tourist season, low season, high season; tourist class; travel agency *or* bureau, holiday company <chiefly Brit>; **conducted tour,** package tour *or* holiday; **excursion, jaunt, junket, outing,** pleasure trip; sight-seeing trip *or* tour, rubberneck tour

<nf>; day-trip; round trip, circuit, turn; **cruise,** package cruise, cruise to nowhere; **expedition,** campaign; safari, hunting expedition, hunting trip, stalk, shoot, photography safari; **pilgrimage,** hajj; **voyage** 182.6

6 riding, driving; motoring, automobiling; busing; motorcycling, bicycling, cycling, pedaling, biking <nf>; **horseback riding,** horse-riding, equitation; horsemanship, manège; pony-trekking

7 ride, drive; spin *and* whirl <nf>; joyride <nf>; Sunday drive; airing; lift <nf>, pickup <nf>

8 walking, ambulation, perambulation, pedestrianism, shank's mare *or* pony <nf>, going on foot *or* afoot, footing *or* hoofing, footing it *or* hoofing it; strolling, sauntering, ambling, *flânerie* <Fr>; **tramping, marching, hiking,** backpacking, trail-hiking, footslogging, trudging, treading; lumbering, waddling; toddling, staggering, tottering; **hitchhiking** *and* hitching <nf>, thumbing *and* thumbing a ride <nf>; jaywalking

9 nightwalking, noctambulation, noctambulism; night-wandering, noctivagation; **sleepwalking,** somnambulation, somnambulism; sleepwalk

10 walk, ramble, amble, **hike, tramp,** traipse <nf>; slog, trudge, schlep <nf>; **stroll,** saunter; **promenade;** *passeggiata* <Ital>; jaunt, airing; **constitutional** <nf>, stretch; turn; peripatetic journey *or* exercise, peripateticism; walking tour *or* excursion; **march,** forced march, route march; parade

11 step, pace, stride; footstep, footfall, tread; hoofbeat, clop; hop, jump; skip, hippety-hop <nf>

12 gait, pace, walk, step, stride, tread; saunter, stroll, strolling gait; shuffle, shamble, hobble, limp, hitch, waddle; totter, stagger, lurch; toddle, paddle; slouch, droop, drag; mince, mincing steps, scuttle, prance, flounce, stalk, strut, swagger; slink, slither, sidle; jog; swing, roll; amble, single-foot, rack, piaffer; trot, gallop 174.3; lock step; velocity 174.1,2; slowness 175

13 march; quick *or* quickstep march, quickstep, quick time; lockstep; double march, double-quick, double time; slow march, slow time; half step; goose step

14 leg, limb, shank; hind leg, foreleg; gamb, jamb <heraldry>; shin, cnemis; ankle, tarsus; hock, gambrel; calf; knee; thigh; popliteal space, ham, drumstick; gigot

15 <nf terms> gams, stems, trotters, hind legs, underpinnings, wheels, shanks, sticks, pins, stumps

16 gliding, sliding, slipping, slithering, coasting, sweeping, flowing, sailing; **skating, skiing, tobogganing, sledding;** glide, slide, slither, sweep, skim, flow

17 creeping, crawling, going on all fours; sneaking, stealing, slinking, sidling, gumshoeing *and* pussyfooting <nf>, walking on eggs, padding, prowling, nightwalking; worming, snaking; tiptoeing, tiptoe, tippytoe; creep, crawl, scramble, scrabble; all fours

VERBS **18 travel, go, move, pass,** fare, wayfare, fare forth, fetch, flit, hie, sashay <nf>, cover ground; **progress** 162.2; move on *or* along, go along; wend, **wend one's way;** betake oneself, direct one's course, bend one's course; course, run, flow, stream; roll, roll on; commute, straphang

19 <go at a given speed> **go, go at,** reach, **make, do,** hit <nf>, clip off <nf>

20 traverse, cross, travel over *or* through, pass through, **go** *or* **pass over, cover,** measure, transit, track, range, range over *or* through, course, do, perambulate, peregrinate, overpass, go over the ground; patrol, reconnoiter, scout; sweep, go *or* make one's rounds, scour, scour the country; ply, voyage 182.13

21 journey, travel, make *or* take *or* go *or* go on a journey, **take** *or* **make a trip,** fare, **wayfare, gad around** *or* **about,** get around *or* about, navigate, trek, jaunt, peregrinate; junket, go on a junket; **tour;** hit the trail <nf>, take the road, go on the road; **cruise, go on a cruise,** voyage 182.13; go abroad, go to foreign places *or* shores, range the world, globe-trot <nf>; travel light, live out of a suitcase; pilgrimage, pilgrim, go on *or* make a pilgrimage; campaign, go overseas, go on an expedition, go on safari; go on a sight-seeing trip, sight-see, rubberneck <nf>

22 migrate, transmigrate, trek; flit, take wing; run <of fish>, swarm <of bees>; **emigrate,** out-migrate, expatriate; **immigrate,** in-migrate; remigrate; intermigrate

23 wander, roam, rove, range, nomadize, **gad,** gad around *or* about, follow the seasons, wayfare, flit, traipse <nf>, gallivant, knock around *or* about *and* bat around *or* about <nf>, prowl, **drift, stray,** float around, straggle, **meander, ramble,** stroll, saunter, jaunt, peregrinate, pererrate, divagate, go *or* run about, go the rounds; **tramp,** hobo, bum *or* go on the bum <nf>, vagabond, vagabondize, take to the road, "travel the open road"—Whitman, beat one's way; **hit the road** *or* **trail** <nf>, walk the tracks *and* count ties <nf>, pound the pavement

24 go for an outing *or* **airing,** take the air, get some air; go for a walk; go for a ride

25 go to, repair to, resort to, hie to, hie oneself to, arise and go to, direct one's course to, turn one's tracks to, make one's way to, set foot in, bend one's steps to, betake oneself to, **visit,** drop in *or* around *or* by, make the scene <nf>

26 creep, crawl, scramble, scrabble, grovel, **go on hands and knees,** go on all fours; worm, worm along, worm one's way, snake; inch, inch along; **sneak, steal,** steal along; pussyfoot *and* gumshoe <nf>, slink, sidle, pad, prowl, nightwalk; **tiptoe,** tippytoe, go on tiptoe

27 walk, ambulate, peripateticate, pedestrianize, traipse <nf>; **step, tread, pace, stride,** pad; foot, foot it; leg, leg it; hoof it, ankle, go on the heel and toe, ride shank's mare *or* pony <nf>, ride the shoeleather *or* hobnail express, stump it <nf>; peg *or* jog *or* shuffle on *or* along; perambulate; circumambulate; jaywalk; power walk, exercise walk, speed walk, race walk

28 <ways of walking> **stroll,** saunter, *flâner* <Fr>; shuffle, scuff, scuffle, straggle, shamble, slouch; stride, straddle; **trudge, plod,** peg, traipse <nf>, clump, stump, slog, footslog, drag, **lumber, barge;** stamp, stomp <nf>; swing, roll, lunge; hobble, halt, limp, hitch, lurch; totter, stagger; toddle, paddle; waddle, wobble, wamble, wiggle; link, slither, sidle, stalk; **strut, swagger;** mince, sashay <nf>, scuttle, prance, tittup, flounce, trip, skip, foot; hop, jump, hippety-hop <nf>; jog, jolt; bundle, bowl along; **amble,** pace; singlefoot, rack; piaffe, piaffer

29 go for a walk, perambulate, take a walk, take one's constitutional <nf>, take a stretch, stretch the legs; **promenade,** *passeggiare* <Ital>, parade

30 march, mush, footslog, **tramp, hike,** backpack, trail-hike; route-march; file, defile, file off; **parade,** go on parade; goose-step, do the goose step; do the lock step

31 hitchhike *or* **hitch** <nf>, beat one's way, **thumb** *or* **thumb one's way** <nf>, **catch a ride;** hitch *or* hook *or* bum *or* cadge *or* thumb a ride <nf>

32 nightwalk, noctambulate; **sleepwalk,** somnambulate, walk in one's sleep

33 ride, go for a ride *or* **drive;** go for a spin <nf>, take *or* go for a Sunday drive; **drive, chauffeur; motor,** taxi; bus; bike *and* cycle *and* wheel *and* pedal <nf>; **motorcycle, bicycle,** mountain bike; BMX, bicycle moto-cross; go by rail, entrain; joyride *or* take a joyride <nf>; catch *or* make a train <nf>

34 go on horseback, ride, horse-ride, pony-trek; ride bareback; mount, take horse; hack; ride hard, clap spurs to one's horse; trot, amble, pace, canter, gallop, tittup, lope; prance, frisk, curvet, piaffe, caracole

35 glide, coast, skim, sweep, flow; **sail, fly,** flit; **slide,** slip, skid, skitter, sideslip, slither, glissade; skate, ice-skate, roller-skate, rollerblade, skateboard; ski; toboggan, sled, sleigh; bellywhop <nf>

ADJS **36 traveling, going, moving,** trekking, passing;

progressing; itinerant, itinerary, circuit-riding; **journeying, wayfaring,** strolling; **peripatetic;** ambulant, ambulatory; ambulative; perambulating, perambulatory; peregrine, peregrinative, pilgrimlike; locomotive; **walking, pedestrian, touring,** on tour, globe-trotting <nf>, globe-girdling, mundivagant <old>; touristic, touristical, touristy <nf>; expeditionary

37 **wandering, roving, roaming,** ranging, **rambling, meandering,** strolling, **straying,** straggling, shifting, flitting, landloping, errant, divagatory, discursive, circumforaneous; **gadding,** traipsing <nf>, gallivanting; **nomad,** nomadic, floating, drifting, gypsyish or gypsylike; **transient,** transitory, fugitive; **vagrant,** vagabond, vagabondish; **footloose,** footloose and fancy-free; **migratory,** migrational, transmigrant, transmigratory

38 **nightwalking,** noctambulant, noctambulous; night-wandering, noctivagant; **sleepwalking,** somnambulant, somnambular

39 **creeping, crawling, on hands and knees, on all fours;** reptant, repent, reptile, reptatorial; **on tiptoe,** on tippytoe, atiptoe, tiptoeing, tiptoe, tippytoe

40 **traveled,** well-traveled, cosmopolitan

41 **wayworn,** way-weary, road-weary, leg-weary, **travel-worn,** travel-weary, travel-tired; travel-sated, travel-jaded; travel-soiled, travel-stained, dusty

ADVS 42 **on the move** or go, en route, in transit, on the wing or fly; on the run, on the jump <nf>, on the road, on the tramp or march; on the gad <nf>, on the bum <nf>

43 **on foot, afoot,** by foot, footback or on footback <nf>; on the heel and toe, on or by shank's mare or pony <nf>

44 **on horseback,** horseback, by horse, mounted

178 TRAVELER

NOUNS 1 **traveler, goer,** viator, comer and goer; **wayfarer, journeyer,** trekker; **tourist,** tourer; **tripper** <Brit>, day-tripper; cicerone, travel or tourist guide; **visitor,** visiting fireman <nf>; **excursionist, sightseer,** rubberneck or rubbernecker <nf>; **voyager,** cruise-goer, cruiser, sailor, mariner 183; **globe-trotter** <nf>, globe-girdler, world-traveler, cosmopolite; jet set, jet-setter; **pilgrim,** palmer, hajji; **passenger,** fare; **commuter,** straphanger <nf>; transient; passerby; adventurer, alpinist, climber, mountaineer, ecotourist; explorer, forty-niner, pioneer, pathfinder, voortrekker, trailblazer, trailbreaker; camper; astronaut 1075.8

2 **wanderer, rover, roamer,** rambler, stroller, straggler, mover; **gad, gadabout** <nf>, runabout, go-about <nf>; **itinerant,** peripatetic, rolling stone, peregrine, peregrinator, bird of passage, visitant; **drifter** and **floater** <nf>; Wandering Jew, Ahasuerus, Ancient Mariner <Coleridge>, Argonaut, Flying Dutchman, Oisin, Ossian, Gulliver <Swift>, Ulysses, Odysseus <Homer>; wandering scholar, Goliard, vaganti <L>; strolling player, wandering minstrel, troubadour

3 **vagabond, vagrant,** vag <nf>; **bum** or bummer <nf>, loafer, wastrel, losel <old>, lazzarone <Ital>; **tramp,** turnpiker, piker, knight of the road, easy rider, **hobo** or bo <nf>, rounder <nf>, stiff or bindlestiff <nf>; landloper, sundowner or swagman or swagsman <Austral nf>; beggar 440.8; **waif,** homeless waif, bag person, dogie, stray, waifs and strays; ragamuffin, tatterdemalion; **gamin,** gamine, urchin, street urchin, dead-end kid <nf>, mudlark, guttersnipe <nf>; beachcomber, loafer, idler; ski bum, beach bum, surf bum, tennis bum; ragman, ragpicker

4 **nomad,** Bedouin, Arab; gypsy, Bohemian, Romany, zingaro <Ital>, Zigeuner <Ger>, tzigane <Fr>

5 **migrant,** migrator, trekker; **immigrant,** in-migrant; migrant or migratory worker; **emigrant,** out-migrant, émigré <Fr>; expatriate; **evacuee,** évacué <Fr>; displaced person or DP, stateless person, exile; wetback <nf>

6 **pedestrian, walker,** walkist; foot traveler, foot passenger, hoofer <nf>, footbacker <nf>, ambulator, peripatetic; **hiker,** backpacker, trailsman, tramper; marcher, footslogger, foot soldier, infantryman, paddlefoot <nf>; **hitchhiker** <nf>; jaywalker; power walker, exercise walker, speed walker, race walker

7 **nightwalker,** noctambulist, noctambule, **sleepwalker,** somnambulist, somnambulator, somnambule

8 **rider, equestrian, horseman,** horserider, horseback rider, horsebacker, caballero <Sp>, cavalier, knight, chevalier; horse soldier, cavalryman, mounted policeman; horsewoman, equestrienne; cowboy, cowgirl, puncher or cowpuncher or cowpoke <nf>, vaquero and gaucho <Sp>; broncobuster <nf>, buckaroo; postilion, postboy; roughrider; **jockey;** steeplechaser; circus rider, trick rider

9 **driver,** reinsman, whip, Jehu, skinner <nf>; **coachman,** coachy <nf>, cocher <Fr>, cochero <Sp>, voiturier <Fr>, vetturino <Ital>, gharry-wallah <India>; stage coachman; charioteer; harness racer; **cabdriver,** cabman, cabby <nf>, hackman, hack or hacky <nf>, jarvey <Brit nf>; wagoner, wagonman, drayman, truckman; **carter,** cartman, carman; **teamster;** muleteer, mule

skinner <nf>; bullwhacker; elephant driver, mahout; cameleer

10 **driver, motorist,** automobilist; **chauffeur; taxidriver,** cabdriver, cabby <nf>, hackman, **hack** *or* hacky <nf>, hackdriver; jitney driver; **truck driver, teamster,** truckman, **trucker; bus driver,** busman, bus jockey <nf>; speeder 174.5, road hog <nf>, Sunday driver, joyrider <nf>; hit-and-run driver; backseat driver

11 **cyclist,** cycler; **bicyclist,** bicycler, mountain biker, biker; **motorcyclist,** motorcycler, biker <nf>

12 **engineer,** engineman, engine driver <Brit>; hogger *or* hoghead <nf>; Casey Jones; **motorman;** gripman

13 **trainman,** railroad man, **railroader;** conductor, guard <Brit>; brakeman, brakie <nf>; fireman, footplate man <Brit>, stoker; smoke agent *and* bakehead <nf>; switchman; yardman; yardmaster; trainmaster, dispatcher; stationmaster; lineman; baggage man, baggagesmasher <nf>; porter, redcap; trainboy, butcher <nf>

179 VEHICLE
<means of conveyance>

NOUNS 1 **vehicle, conveyance,** carrier, means of carrying *or* transporting, means of transport, medium of transportation, carriage; watercraft 180.1, aircraft 181

2 **wagon,** waggon <Brit>, wain; haywagon, milkwagon; dray, van, caravan; covered wagon, prairie schooner, Conestoga wagon, stagecoach

3 **cart,** two-wheeler; oxcart, horsecart, ponycart, dogcart; dumpcart; **handcart,** barrow, wheelbarrow, handbarrow; jinrikisha, ricksha; pushcart

4 **carriage,** four-wheeler, *voiture* <Fr>, gharry <India>; **chaise,** shay <nf>

5 **rig, equipage,** turnout <nf>, coach-and-four; team, pair, span; tandem, random; spike, spike team, unicorn; three-in-hand, four-in-hand, etc; three-up, four-up, etc

6 **baby carriage,** baby buggy <nf>, perambulator, pram <Brit>; go-cart; **stroller,** walker

7 **wheel chair,** Bath chair, push chair

8 **cycle,** wheel <nf>; **bicycle,** bike <nf>, mountain bike, all-terrain bike, touring bike, racing bike, hybrid bike, velocipede; tandem bicycle; **tricycle,** three-wheeler, trike <nf>; BMX; **motorcycle,** motocycle, motorbike, bike *and* iron <nf>; pig <nf>, chopper <nf>, motorscooter, minibike, moped, dirt *or* trail bike; pedicab

9 **automobile** <see list>, **car, auto,** motorcar, motocar, autocar, **machine,** motor, motor vehicle, motorized vehicle, *voiture* <Fr>

10 <nf terms> **jalopy,** banger, bus, buggy, wheels, tub, tuna wagon, heap, boat, short, crate, wreck, bomb, clunker, junker, junkheap, junkpile

11 **police car, patrol car; prowl car,** squad car, cruiser; **police van,** patrol wagon; wagon *and* paddy wagon *and* Black Maria <nf>, panda car <Brit>

12 **truck** <see list>, lorry <Brit>, *camion* <Fr>; trailer truck, truck trailer, tractor trailer, semitrailer, rig *and* semi <nf>; eighteen-wheeler <nf>

13 <public vehicles> **commercial vehicle; bus,** omnibus, chartered bus, autobus, motorbus, motor coach, articulated bus, jitney <nf>; express bus, local bus; schoolbus; **cab, taxicab, taxi,** hack <nf>, gypsy cab <nf>; rental car; hired car, limousine, limo *and* stretch limo <nf>

14 **train,** railroad train; choo-choo *and* choo-choo train <nf>; passenger train, Amtrak; aerotrain, bullet train, *train de haute vitesse* <Fr>; local, way train, milk train, accommodation train; shuttle train, shuttle; express train, express; lightning express, flier, cannonball express <nf>; local express; special, limited; parliamentary train *or* parliamentary <Brit>; freight train, goods train <Brit>, freight, freighter, rattler <nf>; baggage train, luggage train; electric train; cable railroad; funicular; cog railroad *or* railway, rack-and-pinion railroad; subway, *métro* <Fr>, tube, underground <Brit>; elevated, el <nf>; monorail; streamliner; rolling stock

15 **railway car,** car, waggon <Brit>; baggage car, boxcar, caboose, coach, gondola; diner, dining car *or* compartment; drawing room; freight car; hopper car; flatcar; parlor car; Pullman *or* Pullman car; refrigerator car *or* reefer <nf>; roomette, sleeper *or* sleeping car or *wagon-lit* <Fr>; smoker *or* smoking car *or* compartment

16 **handcar,** go-devil; push car, trolley, truck car, rubble car

17 **streetcar, trolley** *or* trolley car, **tram** *or* tramcar; electric car, electric <nf>; trolley bus, trackless trolley; horsecar, horse box <Brit>; cable car, grip car

18 **tractor,** traction engine; Caterpillar <trademark>, Cat <nf>, tracked vehicle; bulldozer, dozer <nf>

19 **trailer,** trail car; house trailer, mobile home; recreation vehicle *or* RV; truck trailer, **semitrailer,** highway trailer; camp *or* camping trailer, caravan <Brit>; **camper,** camping bus

20 **sled, sleigh,** *traîneau* <Fr>, sledge, dogsled, troika; snowmobile, weasel, skimobile, bombardier <Can>; runner, blade; toboggan

21 **skates,** ice skates, hockey skates, figure skates; roller skates, skateboard, bob skates; **skis, snowshoes**

22 Hovercraft <trademark>, hovercar, air-cushion vehicle *or* ACV, cushioncraft, ground-effect machine *or* GEM, captured-air vehicle *or* CAV, captured-air bubble *or* CAB, surface-effect ship

ADJS **23 vehicular,** transportational; automotive, locomotive

24 automobiles

brougham	race car *or* racer *or* racing
cabriolet	car
compact car	roadster
convertible	runabout
coupe	saloon <Brit>
estate car <Brit>	sedan
four-door	sedan limousine
hardtop	sports car
hatchback	station wagon
jeep	stock car
limousine *or* limo	stretch limousine *or* limo
luxury	tourer <Brit>
mid-size	touring car
mini-bus	two-door
minicar	two-seater <Brit>

25 trucks

articulated vehicle	recreational vehicle *or*
duck *or* DUKW	RV
dump truck	semitrailer *or* semi
fork *or* forklift truck	six-by-six
four-by-four *or* 4x4	tank truck
lorry <Brit>	tractor *or* tractor-trailer *or*
minivan	tractor truck *or* truck
panel truck	tractor
pick-up truck *or* pickup	van

180 SHIP, BOAT

NOUNS **1 ship,** argosy, cargo ship, container ship, cruise ship, dredge, freighter, liner, merchant ship *or* merchantman, motorship, oceanographic research ship, paddle boat *or* steamer, refrigeration ship, roll-on roll-off ship *or* ro-ro, side-wheeler, supertanker, tanker, trawler, ULCC *or* ultra-large crude carrier, VLCC *or* very large crude carrier, whaler; **boat,** ark, canoe, gondola, kayak, lifeboat, motorboat, shell, skiff, whaleboat, workboat; vessel, craft, bottom, bark, argosy, hull, hulk, keel, watercraft; tub *and* bucket *and* rustbucket *and* hooker <nf>, packet; leviathan; "that packet of assorted miseries which we call a ship"—Kipling

2 steamer, steamboat, steamship; motor ship

3 sailboat, sailing vessel, sailing boat, wind boat, ragboat <nf>, sailing yacht, sailing cruiser, sailing ship, tall *or* taunt ship, sail, sailer, **windjammer** <nf>, windship, windboat; **galley; yacht,** pleasure boat, a hole in the water into which one pours money <nf>

4 motorboat, powerboat, speedboat, stinkpot <nf>; **launch,** motor launch, steam launch, naphtha launch; **cruiser,** power cruiser, **cabin cruiser,** sedan cruiser, outboard cruiser

5 liner, ocean liner, ocean greyhound <nf>, passenger steamer, floating hotel *or* palace, luxury liner; **cruise ship**

6 warship, war vessel, naval vessel; warship; **man-of-war,** man-o'-war, ship of war, armored vessel; USS *or* United States Ship; HMS *or* His *or* Her Majesty's Ship; line-of-battle ship, ship of the line; aircraft carrier *or* flattop <nf>, assault transport, battle cruiser, battleship, coast guard cutter, communications ship, cruiser, destroyer, destroyer escort, guided missile cruiser, heavy cruiser, patrol boat *or* PT boat, gunboat, hospital ship, minelayer, mine ship, minesweeper; icebreaker

7 battleship, battlewagon <nf>, capital ship; **cruiser,** battle-cruiser; **destroyer,** can *or* tin can <nf>

8 carrier, aircraft carrier, seaplane carrier, **flattop** <nf>

9 submarine, sub, submersible, underwater craft; **U-boat,** *U-boot or Unterseeboot* <Ger>, pigboat <nf>; nuclear *or* nuclear-powered submarine; Polaris submarine; Trident submarine; hunter-killer submarine

10 ships, shipping, merchant *or* mercantile marine, merchant navy *or* fleet, bottoms, tonnage; **fleet,** flotilla, argosy; line; fishing fleet, whaling fleet, etc; **navy** 461.26

11 float, raft; balsa, balsa raft, Kon Tiki; life raft, Carling float; boom; pontoon; buoy, life buoy; life preserver 397.5; surfboard; cork; bob

12 rigging, rig, tackle, tackling, **gear; ropework,** roping; service, serving, whipping; standing rigging, running rigging; boatswain's stores; ship chandlery

13 spar, timber; **mast,** pole, stick *and* tree <nf>; bare pole

14 sail, canvas, muslin, cloth, rag <nf>; **full *or* plain sail,** press *or* crowd of sail; reduced sail, reefed sail; square sail; fore-and-aft sail; luff, leech, foot, earing, reef point, boltrope, clew, cringle, head

15 oar; paddle, scull, sweep, pole; steering oar

16 anchor, mooring, hook *and* mudhook <nf>; **anchorage,** moorings; **berth,** slip; mooring buoy

ADJS **17 rigged,** decked, trimmed; square-rigged, fore-and-aft rigged, Marconi-rigged, gaff-rigged, lateen-rigged

18 seaworthy, sea-kindly, fit for sea, **snug, bold; watertight,** waterproof; **A1,** A1 at Lloyd's; stiff, tender; weatherly; yare

19 trim, in trim; apoise, on an even keel

20 shipshape, Bristol fashion, shipshape and Bristol fashion, trim, trig, neat, tight, taut, ataunt, all at\u00e0unto, bungup and bilge-free

181 AIRCRAFT

NOUNS **1** **aircraft, airplane,** aeroplane <Brit>, **plane, ship,** fixed-wing aircraft, flying machine <old>, *avion* <Fr>; aerodyne, heavier-than-air craft; kite <Brit nf>; **shuttle, space shuttle,** lifting body; **airplane part; flight instrument,** aircraft instrument; **aircraft engine; piston engine,** radial engine, rotary engine, pancake engine; **jet engine,** fan-jet engine, rocket motor, turbofan, turbojet, turboprop, pulse jet, ramjet, reaction engine *or* motor

2 **propeller plane,** single-prop, double-prop *or* twin-prop, multi-prop; piston plane; turbo-propeller plane, turbo-prop, prop-jet

3 **jet plane, jet; turbojet,** ramjet, pulse-jet, blowtorch <nf>; single-jet, twin-jet, multi-jet; jet liner, business jet; deltaplanform jet, tailless jet, twin-tailboom jet; jumbo jet; subsonic jet; supersonic jet, supersonic transport *or* SST, Concorde

4 **rocket plane,** repulsor; rocket ship, spaceship 1075.2; rocket 1074.2

5 **rotor plane,** rotary-wing aircraft, rotocraft, rotodyne; gyroplane, gyro, **autogiro,** windmill <nf>; **helicopter,** copter *and* whirlybird *and* chopper *and* eggbeater <nf>

6 **ornithopter,** orthopter, wind flapper, mechanical bird

7 **flying platform,** flying ring, Hiller-CNR machine, flying bedstead *or* bedspring; **Hovercraft** <trademark>, air car, ground-effect machine, air-cushion vehicle, hovercar, cushioncraft; flying crow's nest, flying motorcycle, flying bathtub

8 **seaplane,** waterplane, **hydroplane,** aerohydroplane, aeroboat, **floatplane,** float seaplane; **flying boat,** clipper, boat seaplane; **amphibian,** triphibian

9 **military aircraft, warplane,** battle plane, combat plane; carrier fighter, carrier-based plane, bomber, dive bomber, fighter, helicopter gunship, jet bomber, strategic bomber, jet fighter, jet tanker, night fighter, photo-reconnaissance plane, reconnaissance fighter, spy plane, airborne warning and control systems *or* AWACS plane, Stealth Bomber, Stealth Fighter, tactical support bomber, torpedo bomber, troop carrier *or* transport; amphibian, flying boat; helicopter; suicide plane, kamikaze; bogey, bandit, enemy aircraft; air fleet, air armada; air force 461.29

10 **trainer;** Link trainer; **flight simulator;** dual-control trainer; basic *or* primary trainer, intermediate trainer, advanced trainer; crew trainer, flying classroom; navigator-bombardier trainer, radio-navigational trainer, etc

11 **aerostat,** lighter-than-air craft; **airship,** ship, dirigible balloon, **blimp** <nf>; rigid airship, semirigid airship; **dirigible,** zeppelin, Graf Zeppelin; gasbag, ballonet; **balloon,** *ballon* <Fr>

12 **glider,** gliding machine; **sailplane,** soaring plane; rocket glider; student glider; air train, glider train

13 **parachute, chute** <nf>, umbrella <nf>, brolly <Brit nf>; pilot chute, drogue chute; rip cord, safety loop, shroud lines, harness, pack, vent; parachute jump, brolly-hop <Brit nf>; sky dive; brake *or* braking *or* deceleration parachute; parawing *or* paraglider *or* parafoil

14 **kite,** box kite, Eddy kite, Hargrave *or* cellular kite, tetrahedral kite

182 WATER TRAVEL

NOUNS **1** water travel, travel by water, marine *or* ocean *or* sea travel, **navigation,** navigating, **seafaring, sailing,** steaming, passage-making, voyaging, **cruising,** coasting, gunkholing <nf>; inland navigation; **boating, yachting,** motorboating, canoeing, rowing, sculling; circumnavigation, periplus; navigability

2 <methods> celestial navigation, astronavigation; radio navigation, radio beacon; loran; consolan, shoran; coastal *or* coastwise navigation; dead reckoning; point-to-point navigation; pilotage; sonar, radar, sofar; plane *or* traverse *or* spherical *or* parallel *or* middle *or* latitude *or* Mercator *or* great-circle *or* rhumbline *or* composite sailing; fix, line of position; sextant, chronometer, tables

3 **seamanship,** shipmanship; seamanliness, seamanlikeness; weather eye; sea legs

4 **pilotship,** pilotry, pilotage, **helmsmanship;** steerage; proper piloting

5 embarkation 188.3; disembarkation 186.2

6 **voyage,** ocean *or* sea trip, **cruise,** sail; course, **run, passage; crossing;** shakedown cruise; leg

7 **wake,** track; wash, backwash

8 <submarines> **surfacing,** breaking water; **submergence, dive;** stationary dive, running dive, crash dive

9 **way, progress; headway,** steerageway, sternway, leeway, driftway

10 **seaway, waterway,** fairway, road, channel, ocean *or* sea lane, ship route, steamer track *or* lane; crossing; approaches; navigable water

11 aquatics, **swimming, bathing,** natation, balneation, **swim, bathe;** crawl, freestyle, trudgen, Australian crawl, breaststroke, butterfly, sidestroke, dog *or* doggie paddle, backstroke; treading water; floating; diving 367.3; wading; fin; flipper, flapper; fishtail; waterskiing, aquaplaning, surfboarding; surfing; windsurfing, boardsailing

12 **swimmer, bather,** natator, merman; bathing girl, mermaid; bathing beauty; frogman; diver 367.4

VERBS 13 **navigate, sail, cruise,** steam, run, **seafare, voyage,** ply, go on shipboard, go by ship, go on *or* take a voyage; go to sea, sail the sea, sail the ocean blue; **boat, yacht,** motorboat, canoe, row, scull; surf, windsurf, boardsail; steamboat; bear *or* carry sail; cross, traverse, make a passage *or* run; sail round, circumnavigate; coast

14 **pilot,** helm, coxswain, **steer,** guide, be at the helm *or* tiller, direct, manage, handle, run, operate, **conn** *or* cond, be at *or* have the conn; **navigate,** shape *or* chart a course

15 **anchor,** come to anchor, lay anchor, **cast anchor,** let go the anchor, drop the hook; carry out the anchor; kedge, kedge off; **dock, tie up; moor,** pick up the mooring; run out a warp *or* rope; lash, lash and tie; foul the anchor; disembark 186.8

16 **ride at anchor,** ride, lie, rest; ride easy; ride hawse full; lie athwart; set an anchor watch

17 **lay** *or* **lie to,** lay *or* lie by; lie near *or* close to the wind, head to wind *or* windward, be under the sea; lie ahull; lie off, lie off the land; lay *or* lie up

18 **weigh anchor,** up-anchor, bring the anchor home, break out the anchor, cat the anchor, break ground, loose for sea; **unmoor,** drop the mooring, cast off *or* loose *or* away

19 **get under way,** put *or* have way upon, **put** *or* **push** *or* **shove off;** hoist the blue Peter; **put to sea,** put out to sea, go to sea, head for blue water, go off soundings; **sail,** sail away; embark

20 **set sail,** hoist sail, unfurl *or* spread sail, heave out a sail, **make sail,** trim sail; square away, square the yards; **crowd** *or* **clap** *or* **crack** *or* **pack on sail,** put on <more> sail; clap on, crack on, pack on; give her beans <nf>

21 **make way,** gather way, **make headway,** make sternway; make knots, foot; **go full speed ahead,** go full speed astern; go *or* run *or* steam at flank speed

22 run, **run** *or* **sail before the wind,** run *or* sail with the wind, run *or* sail down the wind, make a spinnaker run, sail off the wind, sail free, sail with the wind aft, sail with the wind abaft the beam; tack down wind; run *or* sail with the wind quartering

23 **bring off the wind, pay off,** bear off *or* away, put the helm to leeward, bear *or* head to leeward, pay off the head

24 **sail against the wind,** sail on *or* by the wind, sail to windward, bear *or* head to windward; **bring in** *or* **into the wind,** bring by *or* on the wind, haul the wind *or* one's wind; uphelm, put the helm up; haul, haul off, haul up; **haul to, bring to, heave to;** sail in *or* into the wind's eye *or* the teeth of the wind; sail to the windward of, weather

25 **sail near the wind,** sail close to the wind, lie near *or* close to the wind, sail full and by, hold a close wind, **sail close-hauled,** close-haul; work *or* go *or* beat *or* eat to windward, **beat, ply; luff,** luff up, sail closer to the wind; sail too close to the wind, sail fine, touch the wind, pinch

26 **gain to windward of,** eat *or* claw to windward of, eat the wind out of, have the wind of, be to windward of

27 **chart** *or* **plot** *or* **lay out a course;** shape a course, lay *or* lie a course

28 take *or* follow a course, **keep** *or* **hold the course** *or* **a course,** hold on the course *or* a course, stand on *or* upon a course, stand on a straight course, maintain *or* keep the heading, keep her steady, keep pointed

29 **drift off course, yaw,** yaw off, pay off, bear off, drift, sag; sag *or* bear *or* ride *or* drive to leeward, make leeway, drive, fetch away; be set by the current, drift with the current, fall down

30 **change course,** change the heading, bear off *or* away, bear to starboard *or* port; sheer, swerve; **tack,** cast, break, yaw, slew, shift, turn; **cant,** cant round *or* across; **beat, ply; veer, wear, wear ship; jibe** *or* gybe <Brit>, jibe all standing, make a North River jibe; **put about,** come *or* go *or* bring *or* fetch about, beat about, cast *or* throw about; bring *or* swing *or* heave *or* haul round; **about ship,** turn *or* put back, turn on her heel, wind; swing the stern; box off; back and fill; stand off and on; double *or* round a point; miss stays

31 put the rudder hard left *or* right, put the rudder *or* helm hard over, put the rudder amidships, ease the rudder *or* helm, give her more *or* less rudder

32 **veer** *or* **wear short,** bring by the lee, **broach to,** lie beam on to the seas

33 <come to a stop> **fetch up, heave to,** haul up, fetch up all standing

34 **backwater,** back, reverse, go astern; **go full speed astern;** make sternway

35 **sail for, put away for, make for** *or* toward, make at, **run for,** stand for, head *or* steer toward, lay for, **lay a** *or* **one's course for,** bear up for; bear up to, **bear down on** *or* **upon,** run *or* bear in with, **close with;** make, reach, fetch; heave *or* go alongside; lay *or* go aboard; lay *or* lie in; **put in** *or* into, put into port, approach anchorage

36 **sail away from,** head *or* steer away from, run from, **stand from,** lay away *or* off from; **stand off,** bear off, put off, shove off, haul off; stand off and on

37 **clear the land,** bear off the land, lay *or* settle the land, make *or* get sea room

38 **make land,** reach land; close with the land, stand in for the land; sight land; smell land; make a landfall

39 coast, sail coast-wise, stay in soundings, range the coast, skirt the shore, lie along the shore, **hug the shore** or **land** or **coast**

40 weather the storm, weather, ride, **ride out,** outride, ride or ride out a storm; make heavy or bad weather

41 sail into, run down, run in or into, **ram; come** or **run foul** or **afoul of, collide,** fall aboard; nose or head into, run prow or end or head on, run head and head; run broadside on

42 shipwreck, wreck, pile up <nf>, cast away; **go** or **run aground,** ground, take the ground, beach, strand, run on the rocks; ground hard and fast

43 careen, list, heel, tip, cant, heave or lay down, lie along; be on beam ends

44 capsize, upset, overset, **overturn,** turn over, turn turtle, upset the boat, keel, keel over or up; pitchpole, somersault; **sink, founder,** be lost, go down, go to the bottom, go to Davy Jones's locker; scuttle

45 go overboard, go by the board, go over the board or side

46 maneuver, execute a maneuver; heave in together, keep in formation, maintain position, **keep station,** keep pointed, steam in line, steam in line of bearing; convoy

47 <submarines> surface, break water; **submerge, dive,** crash-dive, go below; rig for diving; flood the tanks, flood negative

48 <activities aboard ship> lay, lay aloft, lay forward, etc; traverse a yard, brace a yard fore and aft; heave, haul; kedge; warp; boom; heave round, heave short, heave apeak; log, heave or stream the log; haul down, board; spar down; ratline down, clap on ratlines; batten down the hatches; unlash, cut or cast loose; clear hawse

49 trim ship, trim, trim up; trim by the head or stern, put in proper fore-and-aft trim, give greater draft fore and aft, **put on an even keel; ballast,** shift ballast, wing out ballast; break out ballast, break bulk, shoot ballast; **clear the decks,** clear for action, take action stations

50 reduce sail, shorten or take in sail, hand a sail, **reef,** reef one's sails; double-reef; lower sail, dowse sail; run under bare poles; snug down; **furl,** put on a harbor furl

51 take bearings, cast a traverse; correct distance and maintain the bearings; run down the latitude, **take a sight,** shoot the sun, bring down the sun; **box the compass;** take soundings 275.9

52 signal, make a signal, speak, hail and speak; dress ship; unfurl or hoist a banner, unfurl an ensign, **break out a flag;** hoist the blue Peter; show one's colors, **exchange colors;** salute, dip the ensign

53 row, paddle, ply the oar, **pull, scull, punt;** give way, row away; catch or cut a crab or lobster <nf>; feather, feather an oar; sky an oar <nf>; row dry <Brit nf>; pace, shoot; ship oars

54 float, ride, drift; **sail, scud, run,** shoot; skim, foot; ghost, glide, slip; ride the sea, plow the deep, walk the waters

55 pitch, toss, tumble, toss and tumble, pitch and toss, **plunge,** hobbyhorse, pound, **rear, rock, roll, reel, swing, sway, lurch, yaw, heave,** scend, **flounder, welter, wallow;** make heavy weather

56 swim, bathe, go in swimming or bathing; tread water; **float,** float on one's back, do the deadman's float; **wade,** go in wading; skinny-dip; dive 367.6

ADJS **57 nautical, marine, maritime, naval, navigational; seafaring, seagoing, oceangoing,** seaborne, water-borne; seamanly, seamanlike, **salty** <nf>; pelagic, oceanic 240.9

58 aquatic, water-dwelling, water-living, water-growing, water-loving; **swimming,** balneal, natant, natatory, natatorial; shore, seashore; tidal, estuarine, littoral, grallatorial; riverine; deep-sea 275.14

59 navigable, boatable

60 floating, afloat, awash; water-borne

61 adrift, afloat, unmoored, untied, loose, unanchored, aweigh; cast-off, started

ADVS **62 on board,** on shipboard, on board ship, **aboard,** all aboard, afloat; **on deck,** topside; aloft; in sail; before the mast; athwart the hawse, athwarthawse

63 under way, making way, with steerageway, with way on; **at sea,** on the high seas, off soundings, in blue water; **under sail** or **canvas,** with sails spread; under press of sail or canvas or steam; under steam or power; under bare poles; on or off the heading or course; in soundings, homeward bound

64 before the wind, with the wind, down the wind, running free; off the wind, with the wind aft, with the wind abaft the beam, wing and wing, under the wind, under the lee; on a reach, on a beam or broad reach, with wind abeam

65 against the wind, on the wind, in or into the wind, up the wind, by the wind, head to wind; in or into the wind's eye, in the teeth of the wind

66 near the wind, close to the wind, **close-hauled,** on a beat, full and by

67 coastward, landward, to landward; **coastwise,** coastways

68 leeward, to leeward, alee, downwind; **windward,** to windward, weatherward, aweather, upwind

69 aft, abaft, baft, **astern;** fore and aft

70 alongside, board and board, yardarm to yardarm

71 at anchor, riding at anchor; lying to, hove to; lying ahull

72 afoul, foul, in collision; head and head, head or end or prow on; broadside on

73 aground, on the rocks; hard and fast
74 overboard, over the board *or* side, by the board; aft the fantail

183 MARINER

NOUNS **1 mariner, seaman, sailor,** sailorman, **navigator, seafarer,** seafaring man, bluejacket, sea *or* water dog <nf>, Seabee, crewman, shipman, jack, jacky, jack afloat, jack-tar, **tar, salt** <nf>, gob, swabby, hearty, lobscouser <nf>, *matelot* <Fr>, windsailor, windjammer; limey *or* limejuicer <nf>, lascar <India>; common *or* ordinary seaman, OD; able *or* able-bodied seaman *or* AB; deep-sea man, saltwater *or* bluewater *or* deepwater sailor; fresh-water sailor; fair-weather sailor; whaler, fisherman, lobsterman; viking, sea rover, buccaneer, privateer, pirate; Jason, Argonaut, Ancient Mariner, Flying Dutchman; Neptune, Poseidon, Varuna, Dylan; **yachtsman, yachtswoman,** cruising sailor, racing sailor; submariner

2 <novice> **lubber, landlubber;** polliwog

3 <veteran> **old salt** *and* old sea dog *and* shellback *and* barnacle-back <nf>; **master mariner**

4 navy man, man-of-war's man, **bluejacket; gob** *and* swabbie *and* swabber <nf>; **marine, leatherneck** *and* gyrene *and* devil dog *or* jarhead <nf>, Royal Marine, jolly <Brit nf>; horse marine; boot <nf>; **midshipman,** midshipmate, middy <nf>; cadet, naval cadet; coastguardsman, Naval Reservist, Seabee, frogman

5 boatman, boatsman, boat-handler, **boater,** waterman; **oarsman,** oar, rower, sculler, punter; galley slave; **ferryman,** ferrier; **bargeman,** barger, bargee <Brit>, bargemaster; lighterman, wherryman; **gondolier,** *gondoliere* <Ital>

6 hand, **deckhand,** deckie <Brit>, roustabout <nf>; stoker, fireman, bakehead <nf>; black gang; wiper, oiler, boilerman; cabin boy; yeoman, ship's writer; purser; ship's carpenter, chips <nf>; ship's cooper, bungs *or* Jimmy Bungs <nf>; ship's tailor, snip *or* snips <nf>; steward, stewardess, commissary steward, mess steward, hospital steward; commissary clerk; mail orderly; navigator; radio operator, sparks <nf>; landing signalman; gunner, gun loader, torpedoman; afterguard; complement; watch

7 <ship's officers> **captain,** shipmaster, **master, skipper** <nf>, **commander,** the Old Man <nf>, *patron* <Fr>; navigator, navigating officer, sailing master; deck officer, officer of the deck *or* OD; watch officer, officer of the watch; **mate,** first *or* chief mate, second mate, third mate, boatswain's mate; **boatswain,** bos'n, pipes <nf>;

quartermaster; sergeant-at-arms; chief engineer, engine-room officer; naval officer 575.20

8 steersman, helmsman, wheelman, wheelsman, boatsteerer; quartermaster; **coxswain,** cox <nf>; **pilot,** conner, sailing master; harbor pilot, docking pilot

9 longshoreman, wharf hand, dockhand, docker, dockworker, dock-walloper <nf>; **stevedore,** loader; **roustabout** <nf>, lumper

184 AVIATION

NOUNS **1 aviation, aeronautics;** airplaning, skyriding, **flying, flight,** winging; volation, volitation; aeronautism, aerodromics; powered flight, jet flight, subsonic *or* supersonic flight; cruising, cross-country flying; bush flying; **gliding,** sail-planing, soaring, sailing; volplaning; ballooning, balloonery, lighter-than-air aviation; barnstorming <nf>; high-altitude flying; blind *or* instrument flight *or* flying, instrument flight rules *or* IFR; contact flying, visual flight *or* flying, visual flight rules *or* VFR, pilotage; skywriting; cloud-seeding; in-flight training, ground school; **air traffic,** airline traffic, air-traffic control, air-traffic controller; commercial aviation, general aviation, private aviation, private flying; astronautics 1073.1; air show, flying circus

2 air sciences <see list>, aeronautical sciences

3 airmanship, pilotship; **flight plan;** briefing, brief, rundown <nf>, debriefing; flight *or* pilot training, flying lessons; washout <nf>

4 air-mindedness, aerophilia; air legs

5 airsickness; aerophobia, aeropathy

6 navigation, avigation, aerial *or* air navigation; celestial navigation, astronavigation; electronic navigation, automatic electronic navigation, radio navigation, navar, radar, consolan, tacan, teleran, loran, shoran; omnidirectional range, omni-range, visual-aural range *or* VAR

7 <aeronautical organizations> Civil Aeronautics Administration *or* CAA; Federal Aviation Agency *or* FAA; Bureau of Aeronautics *or* BuAer; National Advisory Committee for Aeronautics *or* NACA; Office of Naval Research *or* ONR; Civil Air Patrol *or* CAP; Caterpillar Club; Airline Pilots Association; Air Force 461.29

8 takeoff, liftoff, hopoff <nf>; rollout, climb; taxiing, takeoff run, takeoff power, rotation; daisy-clipping *and* grass-cutting <nf>; ground loop; level-off; jet-assisted takeoff *or* JATO, booster rocket, takeoff rocket; catapult, electropult

9 flight, trip, run; hop *and* **jump** <nf>; powered flight; solo flight, **solo;** inverted flight; supersonic flight; test flight, **test hop** <nf>; **airlift;** airdrop;

scheduled flight; mercy flight; flying circus; crop-dusting; skywriting

10 **air travel,** air transport, air transportation; **airfreight, air cargo; airline travel, airline,** airline service, air service, feeder airline, commuter airline, scheduled airline, charter airline, nonscheduled airline *or* nonsked <nf>, short-hop airline; **shuttle,** air shuttle, shuttle service, shuttle trip; air taxi; red-eye

11 <Air Force> **mission,** flight operation; training mission; gunnery mission; combat rehearsal, **dry run** <nf>; transition mission; reconnaissance mission, reconnaissance, observation flight, search mission; **milk run** <nf>; box-top mission <nf>; combat flight; **sortie,** scramble <nf>; **air raid;** shuttle raid; bombing mission; bombing, strafing 459.7; **air support** <for ground troops>, **air cover,** cover, umbrella, air umbrella

12 flight formation, formation flying, formation; close formation, loose formation, wing formation; V formation, echelon

13 <maneuvers> acrobatic *or* tactical evolutions *or* maneuvers, acrobatics, **aerobatics;** stunting *and* **stunt flying** <nf>, rolling, crabbing, banking, porpoising, fishtailing, diving; **dive, nose dive, power dive; zoom,** chandelle; stall, whip stall; **glide,** volplane; spiral, split 'S', lazy eight, sideslip, pushdown, pull-up, pull-out; turn, vector in flight *or* VIF

14 **roll, barrel roll,** aileron roll, outside roll, **snap roll**

15 **spin,** autorotation, **tailspin,** flat spin, inverted spin, normal spin, power spin, uncontrolled spin, falling leaf; whipstall

16 **loop,** spiral loop, ground loop, normal loop, outside loop, inverted normal *or* outside loop, dead-stick loop, wingover, looping the loop; Immelmann turn, reverse turn, reversement; flipper turns

17 **buzzing,** flathatting *and* **hedgehopping** <nf>

18 **landing,** coming in <nf>, touching down, touchdown; arrival; landing run, landing pattern; approach, downwind leg, approach leg; holding pattern, stack up <nf>; ballooning in, parachute approach; blind *or* instrument landing, dead-stick landing, glide landing, stall landing, fishtail landing, sideslip landing, level *or* two-point landing, normal *or* three-point landing, Chinese landing <nf>, tail-high landing, tail-low landing, thumped-in landing <nf>, pancake landing, belly landing, crash landing, noseover, nose-up; overflight, overshoot, undershoot; practice landing, bounce drill

19 flying and landing guides marker, pylon; beacon; radio beacon, radio range station, radio marker; fan marker; radar beacon, racon; beam, radio beam; beacon lights; runway lights, high-intensity runway approach lights, sequence flashers, flare path; wind indicator, wind cone *or* sock, air sleeve; instrument landing system *or* ILS; touchdown rate of descent indicator *or* TRODI; ground-controlled approach *or* GCA; talking-down system, talking down

20 **crash, crack-up,** prang <Brit nf>; crash landing; collision, mid-air collision; near-miss, near collision

21 **blackout;** grayout; anoxia; useful consciousness; pressure suit, antiblackout suit

22 **airport, airfield, airdrome,** aerodrome <Brit>, drome, port, air harbor <Can>, aviation field, **landing field,** landing, field, airship station; **air terminal, jetport; air base,** air station, naval air station; airpark; **heliport,** helidrome; control tower, island; Air Route Traffic Control Center; baggage pickup, baggage carousel; airside, landside

23 **runway, taxiway,** strip, landing strip, **airstrip, flight strip,** take-off strip; fairway, launching way; stopway; clearway; transition strip; apron; **flight deck,** landing deck; helipad; ramp, apron

24 **hangar,** housing, dock, airdock, shed, airship shed; mooring mast

25 <propulsion> rocket propulsion, rocket power; **jet propulsion,** jet power; turbojet propulsion, pulse-jet propulsion, ram-jet propulsion, resojet propulsion; constant *or* ram pressure, air ram; reaction propulsion, reaction, action and reaction; aeromotor, aircraft engine, power plant

26 **lift,** lift ratio, lift force *or* component, lift direction; aerostatic lift, dynamic lift, gross lift, useful lift, margin of lift

27 **drag,** resistance; drag ratio, drag force *or* component, induced drag, wing drag, parasite *or* parasitic *or* structural drag, profile drag, head resistance, drag direction, cross-wind force

28 **drift,** drift angle; lateral drift, leeway

29 flow, air flow, laminar flow; **turbulence,** turbulent flow, burble, burble point, eddies

30 wash, wake, stream; downwash; backwash, **slipstream,** propeller race, propwash; **exhaust,** jet exhaust, blow wash; **vapor trail,** condensation trail, contrail, vortex

31 <speed> **air speed,** true air speed, operating *or* flying speed, cruising speed, knots, minimum flying speed, hump speed, peripheral speed, pitch speed, terminal speed, sinking speed, get-away *or* take-off speed, landing speed, ground speed, speed over the ground; speed of sound 174.2; zone of no signal, Mach cone; **sound barrier,** sonic barrier *or* wall; sonic boom, shock wave, Mach wave

32 <air, atmosphere> **airspace,** navigable airspace;

aerosphere; **aerospace;** space, empty space; **weather, weather conditions; ceiling,** ballonet ceiling, service ceiling, static ceiling, absolute ceiling; ceiling and visibility unlimited or CAVU; severe clear <nf>; cloud layer or cover, ceiling zero; visibility, visibility zero; **overcast,** undercast; fog, soup <nf>; high-pressure area, low-pressure area; trough, trough line; front; **air pocket** or **hole,** air bump, pocket, hole, bump; **turbulence;** clear-air turbulence or CAT; roughness; head wind, unfavorable wind; tail wind, favorable or favoring wind; cross wind; atmospheric tides; jetstream

33 airway, air lane, air line, air route, skyway, corridor, flight path, lane, path

34 course, heading, vector; compass heading or course, compass direction, magnetic heading, true heading or course

35 <altitude> altitude of flight, absolute altitude, critical altitude, density altitude, pressure altitude, sextant altitude; clearance; ground elevation

VERBS **36 fly,** be airborne, wing, take wing, wing one's way, take or make a flight, take to the air, take the air, volitate, be wafted; **jet;** aviate, airplane, aeroplane; travel by air, go or travel by airline, go by plane or air, take to the airways, ride the skies; hop <nf>; **soar,** drift, hover; **cruise; glide,** sailplane, sail, volplane; hydroplane, seaplane; balloon; ferry; airlift; break the sound barrier; navigate, avigate

37 pilot, control, be at the controls, **fly,** manipulate, drive <nf>, fly left seat; **copilot,** fly right seat; solo; **barnstorm** <nf>; fly blind, fly by the seat of one's pants <nf>; follow the beam, ride the beam, fly on instruments; fly in formation, take position; peel off

38 take off, hop or jump off <nf>, become airborne, get off or leave the ground, take to the air, go or fly aloft, clear; rotate, power off; **taxi**

39 ascend, climb, gain altitude, mount; **zoom,** hoick <nf>, chandelle

40 <maneuver> stunt <nf>, perform aerobatics; crab, fishtail; **spin,** go into a tailspin; **loop,** loop the loop; **roll,** wingover, spiral, undulate, porpoise, feather, yaw, sideslip, skid, bank, dip, crab, nose down, nose up, pull up, push down, pull out, plow, mush through

41 dive, nose-dive, power-dive, go for the deck; lose altitude, settle, dump altitude <nf>

42 buzz, flathat and **hedgehop** <nf>

43 land, set her down <nf>, **alight, light,** touch down; **descend,** come down, dump altitude <nf>, fly down; come in, come in for a landing; **level off,** flatten out; upwind, downwind; overshoot, undershoot; make a dead-stick landing; pancake, thump in <nf>; bellyland, settle down, balloon in;

fishtail down; **crash-land;** ditch <nf>; nose up, nose over; talk down

44 crash, crack up, prang <Brit nf>, spin in, fail to pull out

45 stall, lose power, conk out <nf>; flame out

46 black out, gray out

47 parachute, bail out, jump, make a parachute jump, hit the silk, make a brollyhop <Brit nf>, sky-dive

48 brief, give a briefing; debrief

ADJS **49 aviation, aeronautic, aeronautical,** aerial; **aviatorial,** aviational, aviatic; aerodontic, **aerospace,** aerotechnical, aerostatic, aerostatical, aeromechanic, aeromechanical, aerodynamic, aerodynamical, avionic, aeronomic, aerophysical; aeromarine; aerobatic; airworthy, air-minded, air-conscious, aeromedical; air-wise; airsick; air-traffic; subsonic, supersonic, hypersonic; propeller, prop, jet, turbojet

50 flying, airborne, winging, soaring; volant, volitant, volitational, hovering, fluttering; gliding; jet-propelled, rocket-propelled

ADVS **51 in flight, on the wing** or fly, while airborne

52 air or atmospheric sciences

acronomy	aerothermodynamics
aerial photography	aircraft design
aeroballistics	aircraft hydraulics
aerocartography	aviation medicine or
aerodontia	aeromedicine
aerodynamics	aviation technology
aerogeography	avionics
aerogeology	climatology
aerography	hydrostatics
aerology	jet engineering
aeromechanics	kinematics
aerometry	kinetics
aeronautical engineering	meteorology
aeronautical meteorology	micrometry
aerophotography	photometry
aerophysics	pneumatics
aeroscopy	rocket engineering
aerospace research	rocketry
aerostatics	supersonic
aerostation	aerodynamics
aerotechnics	supersonics

185 AVIATOR

NOUNS **1 aviator, airman, flier, pilot,** air pilot, licensed pilot, private pilot, airline pilot, commercial pilot, aeronaut, flyboy and airplane driver and birdman <nf>; aircrew member; captain, chief pilot; copilot, second officer; flight engineer, third officer; jet pilot, jet jockey <nf>; instructor; test pilot; bush pilot; astronaut 1075.8; cloud seeder, rainmaker; cropduster; barnstormer <nf>; stunt man, stunt flier

2 aviatrix, aviatress, **airwoman,** birdwoman <nf>; stuntwoman

3 military pilot, naval pilot, combat pilot; fighter pilot; bomber pilot; observer, reconnaissance pilot; radarman; **aviation cadet,** air *or* flying cadet, pilot trainee; flyboy <nf>; ace; air force 461.29

4 crew, aircrew, flight crew; crewman, crewmate, crewmember, aircrewman; **navigator,** avigator; **bombardier;** gunner, machine gunner, belly gunner, tail gunner; crew chief; aerial photographer; meteorologist; **flight attendant, steward, stewardess,** hostess, purser, stew <nf>

5 ground crew, landing crew, plane handlers; crew chief

6 aircraftsman, aeromechanic, aircraft mechanic, mechanic, grease monkey <nf>, ground engineer; rigger; aeronautical engineer, jet engineer, rocket engineer 1074.11; ground tester, flight tester; air-traffic controller

7 balloonist, ballooner, aeronaut

8 parachutist, chutist *or* chuter <nf>, parachute jumper, sports parachutist; sky diver; **paratrooper;** paradoctor, paramedic; jumpmaster

9 <mythological fliers> Daedalus, Icarus

186 ARRIVAL

NOUNS **1 arrival, coming, advent,** approach, appearance, **reaching; attainment, accomplishment, achievement**

2 landing, landfall; docking, mooring, tying up, dropping anchor; **getting off, disembarkation,** disembarkment, debarkation, coming *or* going ashore; **deplaning,** dropping *or* weighing anchor

3 return, homecoming, recursion; reentrance, **reentry;** remigration; prodigal's return

4 welcome, greetings 585.3

5 destination, goal, bourn <old>; port, haven, harbor, anchorage, **journey's end;** end of the line, terminus, **terminal,** terminal point, home plate; stop, stopping place, last stop; **airport,** air terminal 184.22

VERBS **6 arrive,** arrive at, arrive in, come, **come** *or* **get to,** approach, access, **reach, hit** <nf>; find, **gain,** attain, attain to, accomplish, achieve, make, **make it** <nf>, fetch, fetch up at, get there, reach one's destination, come to one's journey's end, end up; **come to rest,** settle, settle in; **make** *or* **put in an appearance, show up** <nf>, turn up, **surface,** pop *or* bob up *and* make the scene <nf>; **get in, come in,** blow in <nf>, pull in, roll in; **check in;** clock *or* punch *or* ring *or* time in <nf>, sign in; hit town <nf>; come to hand, be received

7 arrive at, come at, get at, **reach,** arrive upon, **come upon, hit upon,** strike upon, fall upon, light upon, pitch upon, stumble on *or* upon

8 land, come to land, make a landfall, set foot on dry land; reach *or* make land, make port; put in *or* into, put into port; dock, moor, tie up, anchor, drop anchor; go ashore, **disembark,** debark, unboat; **detrain,** debus, **deplane, disemplane;** alight

ADJS **9 arriving,** approaching, entering, **coming,** incoming; inbound, inwardbound; homeward, homeward-bound; immigrant

ADVS **10 arriving,** on arrival *or* arriving

187 RECEPTION

NOUNS **1 reception, taking in,** receipt, receiving; **welcome,** welcoming, cordial welcome, open *or* welcoming arms; refuge 1009

2 admission, admittance, acceptance; immission <old>, intromission 191.1; **installation,** installment, instatement, inauguration, initiation; baptism, investiture, ordination; enlistment, enrollment, induction

3 entree, entrée, in <nf>, entry, **entrance** 189, **access,** opening, **open door,** open arms; a foot in the door, opening wedge

4 ingestion; eating 8; **drinking** 8.3, imbibing, imbibition; engorgement, ingurgitation, engulfment; **swallowing,** gulping; swallow, gulp, slurp

5 <drawing in> **suction,** suck, sucking; **inhalation,** inhalement, inspiration, aspiration; snuff, snuffle, sniff, sniffle

6 sorption, **absorption,** adsorption, chemisorption *or* chemosorption, engrossment, digestion, **assimilation,** infiltration; **sponging, blotting; seepage,** percolation; **osmosis,** endosmosis, exosmosis, electroosmosis; absorbency; **absorbent,** adsorbent, **sponge, blotter,** blotting paper

7 <bringing in> **introduction; importing,** import, **importation,** investiture, naturalization

8 readmission; reabsorption, resorbence

9 receptivity, receptiveness, welcoming, welcome, invitingness, openness, hospitality, cordiality, recipience *or* recipiency; receptibility, admissibility

VERBS **10 receive, take in; admit, let in,** immit <old>, intromit, give entrance *or* admittance to; **welcome,** bid welcome, give a royal welcome, roll out the red carpet; give an entree, open the door to, give refuge *or* shelter *or* sanctuary to, throw open to; include

11 ingest, eat 8.18, tuck away, put away; imbibe, **drink; swallow, devour,** ingurgitate; **engulf,** engorge; **gulp,** gulp down, swill, swill down, wolf down, gobble

12 draw in, suck, suckle, suck in *or* up, aspirate; **inhale,** inspire, breathe in; snuff, snuffle, sniff, sniffle, snuff in *or* up, slurp

13 absorb, adsorb, chemisorb *or* chemosorb, **assimilate,** engross, digest, **drink,** imbibe, take up *or* in, drink up *or* in, slurp up, swill up; blot, **blot up, soak up,** sponge; osmose; infiltrate, filter in; **soak in, seep in,** percolate in; internalize

14 bring in, introduce, import

15 readmit; reabsorb, resorb

ADJS **16 receptive,** recipient; welcoming, open, hospitable, cordial, inviting, invitatory; introceptive; **admissive,** admissory; receivable, receptible, admissible; intromissive, intromittent; ingestive, imbibitory

17 sorbent, **absorbent,** adsorbent, chemisorptive *or* chemosorptive, **assimilative,** digestive; bibulous, imbibitory, thirsty, soaking, blotting; spongy, spongeous; osmotic, endosmotic, exosmotic; resorbent

18 introductory, introductive; **initiatory,** initiative, baptismal

188 DEPARTURE

NOUNS **1 departure, leaving, going,** passing, **parting; exit,** walkout <nf>; egress 190.2; **withdrawal,** removal, retreat 163.2, retirement; evacuation, abandonment, desertion; decampment; escape, flight, getaway <nf>, elopement; exodus, hegira; migration, mass migration; defection, voting with one's feet

2 start, starting, start-off, setoff, setout, takeoff *and* getaway <nf>, liftoff; the starting gun *or* pistol; break; the green light

3 embarkation, embarkment, boarding; entrainment; enplanement *or* emplanement

4 leave-taking, leave, parting, departure, congé; **send-off,** Godspeed; **adieu,** one's adieus, **farewell,** aloha, **good-bye;** valedictory address, valedictory, valediction, parting words; parting *or* Parthian shot; swan song; viaticum; stirrup cup, one for the road, nightcap <nf>

5 point of departure, starting place *or* **point,** takeoff, **start,** base, baseline, basis; line of departure; starting line *or* post *or* gate, starting blocks, springboard, jumping-off point; stakeboat; port of embarkation

VERBS **6 depart,** make off, begone, be off, take oneself off *or* away, take one's departure, take leave *or* take one's leave, **leave, go, go away, go off, get off** *or* **away,** get under way, come away, go one's way, go *or* get along, be getting along, go on, get on; move off *or* away, move out, march off *or* away; **pull out;** decamp; exit; take *or* break *or* tear oneself away, take oneself off, take wing *or* flight

7 <nf terms> **beat it, split,** scram, up and go, trot, toddle, stagger along, mosey *or* sashay along, buzz off, buzz along, bug out, bugger off <Brit>, beetle off, fuck off *or* f off, get rolling, hightail it, pull up stakes, check out, clear out, cut out, haul ass, hit the road *or* trail, piss off <chiefly Brit>, get lost, flake off, get going, shove off, push along, push off, get out, get *or* git, get the hell out, make oneself scarce, vamoose, take off, skip, skip out, lam, take it on the lam, powder, take a powder, take a runout powder, skedaddle, absquatulate <old>

8 set out, set forth, put forth, go forth, **sally forth,** sally, issue, issue forth, launch forth, set forward, **set off,** be off, be on one's way, outset, **start, start out** *or* **off, strike out,** get off, get away, get off the dime <nf>; get the green light, break; set sail

9 quit, vacate, evacuate, abandon, desert, turn one's back on, walk away from, leave to one's fate, leave flat *or* high and dry; leave *or* desert a sinking ship; **withdraw,** retreat, **beat a retreat,** retire, remove; walk away, abscond, disappear, vanish; **bow out** <nf>, make one's exit; jump ship

10 hasten off, hurry away; scamper off, dash off, whiz off, whip off *or* away, nip *and* nip off <nf>, tear off *or* out, **light out** <nf>, dig *or* skin out *and* burn rubber <nf>

11 fling out *or* **off,** flounce out *or* off

12 run off *or* **away,** run along, flee, take to flight, fly, take to one's heels, cut and run *and* hightail *and* make tracks *and* absquatulate <nf>, scarper <Brit nf>; run for one's life; beat a retreat *or* a hasty retreat; run away from 368.10

13 check out; clock *and* ring *and* punch out <nf>, sign out

14 decamp, break camp, strike camp *or* tent, **pull up stakes**

15 embark, go aboard, board, go on board; go on shipboard, take ship; hoist the blue Peter; **entrain,** enplane *or* emplane, embus; weigh anchor, up-anchor, put to sea 182.19

16 say *or* bid good-bye *or* farewell, take leave, make one's adieus; bid Godspeed; give one a send-off *or* a big send-off, see off *or* out, "speed the parting guest"—Pope; drink a stirrup cup, have one for the road

17 leave home, go from home; leave the country, emigrate, out-migrate, expatriate, defect; vote with one's feet; burn one's bridges

ADJS **18 departing, leaving; parting,** last, final, farewell; valedictory; outward-bound

19 departed, left, gone, gone off *or* away

ADVS **20 hence,** thence, whence; off, **away,** forth, out; therefrom, thereof

PREPS **21 from, away from;** out, out of

INTERJS **22 farewell!, good-bye!, adieu!, so long!, I'm outa here** <nf>, cheerio! <Brit>, *au revoir!* <Fr>, *¡adios!* <Sp>, *¡hasta la vista!* <Sp>, *¡hasta* *luego!* <Sp>, *¡vaya con Dios!* <Sp>, *auf Wiedersehen!* <Ger>, *addio!* <Ital>, *arrivederci!* and *arrivederla!* <Ital>, *ciao!* <Ital nf>, *do svidanye!* <Russ>, *shalom!* <Heb>, *sayonara!* <Japanese>, *vale!* and *vive valeque!* <L>, aloha!, **until we meet again!**, until tomorrow!, *à demain!* <Fr>, **see you later!**, see you!, tata!, toodleoo!, I'll be seeing you!, see you around!, we'll see you!, *à bientôt!* <Fr>, *à toute a l'heure!* <Fr>, *a domani* <Ital>; be good!, keep in touch!, come again!; *bon voyage!* <Fr>, pleasant journey!, have a nice trip!, *tsetchem leshalom!* <Heb>, *glückliche Reise!* <Ger>, happy landing!; Godspeed!, peace be with you!, *pax vobiscum!* <L>; all good go with you!, God bless you!

23 **good night!**, nighty-night! <nf>, *bonne nuit!* <Fr>, *gute Nacht!* <Ger>, *¡buenas noches!* <Sp>, *buona notte!* <Ital>

189 ENTRANCE

NOUNS 1 **entrance, entry,** access, entree, entrée; **ingress,** ingression; **admission,** reception 187; **ingoing, incoming,** income; **importation,** import, importing; **input, intake; penetration,** interpenetration, injection; infiltration, percolation, seepage, leakage; insinuation; intrusion 214; introduction, **insertion** 191

2 **influx, inflow,** inflooding, incursion, indraft, indrawing, inpour, inrun, inrush; afflux

3 **immigration,** in-migration, incoming population, foreign influx; border-crossing

4 **incomer, entrant,** comer, arrival; **visitor,** visitant; **immigrant,** in-migrant; newcomer 774.4, new girl, new boy; settler 227.9; **trespasser,** intruder 214.3

5 **entrance,** entry, gate, door, portal, **entranceway,** entryway; **inlet,** ingress, intake, adit, approach, **access,** means of access, in <nf>, way in; a foot in the door, an opening wedge, the camel's nose under the wall of the tent; **opening** 292; **passageway,** corridor, companionway, hall, hallway, passage, way; jetway, jet bridge; gangway, gangplank; **vestibule** 197.19; air lock

6 **porch,** propylaeum, portico, porte cochere; **portal, threshold,** doorjamb, gatepost, doorpost, lintel; **door, doorway,** French door; **gate, gateway; hatch,** hatchway, scuttle; turnstile

VERBS 7 **enter, go in** *or* **into,** access, cross the threshold, **come in,** find one's way into, put in *or* into; be admitted, gain admission *or* admittance, have an entree, have an in <nf>; **set foot in,** step in, walk in; **get in,** jump in, leap in, hop in; **drop in,** look in, visit, drop by, pop in <nf>; **breeze in,** come breezing in; break *or* burst in, bust *or* come busting in <nf>; **barge in** *or* come barging in *and*

wade in <nf>; thrust in, push *or* press in, crowd in, jam in, wedge in, pack in, squeeze in; slip *or* creep in, wriggle *or* worm oneself into, get one's foot in the door, edge in, work in, insinuate oneself, weigh in <nf>; irrupt, intrude 214.5; take in, admit 187.10; insert 191.3

8 **penetrate,** interpenetrate, **pierce,** pass *or* go through, get through, get into, make way into, make an entrance, gain entree; crash <nf>, gatecrash <nf>

9 **flow in,** inpour, **pour in,** inrush, inflow

10 **filter in, infiltrate, seep in,** percolate into, leak in, soak in, perfuse, worm one's way into, insinuate

11 **immigrate,** in-migrate; cross the border

ADJS 12 **entering,** ingressive, **incoming, ingoing;** in, inward; **inbound,** inward-bound; inflowing, influent, inflooding, inpouring, inrushing; invasive, intrusive, irruptive; ingrowing

ADVS 13 **in,** inward, inwards, inwardly; thereinto

PREPS 14 **into, in,** to

190 EMERGENCE

NOUNS 1 **emergence,** coming out, coming forth, coming into view, rising to the surface, surfacing, emerging; **issuing,** issuance, issue; extrusion; **emission,** emitting, giving forth, giving out; emanation; **vent,** venting, discharge; outbreak, breakout

2 **egress,** egression; **exit,** exodus; outgoing, outgo, going out; emersion <astronomy>; **departure** 188; evacuation; extraction 192; exfiltration

3 **outburst** 671.6, ejection 909

4 **outflow,** outflowing; discharge; **outpouring,** outpour; effluence, effusion, exhalation; **efflux,** effluxion, defluxion; **exhaust; runoff, flowoff;** outfall; drainage, drain; gush 238.4

5 **leakage,** leaking, weeping <nf>; **leak; dripping,** drippings, **drip,** dribble, drop, trickle; distillation

6 **exuding,** exudation, transudation; **filtration,** exfiltration, filtering; straining; **percolation,** percolating; leaching, lixiviation; effusion, extravasation; **seepage,** seep; perfusion; **oozing,** ooze; weeping, weep; **excretion** 12

7 **emigration,** out-migration, remigration; exile, expatriation, defection, deportation

8 **export,** exporting, exportation; outgoings

9 **outlet,** egress, **exit,** outgo, outcome, out <nf>, way out; loophole, escape; **opening** 292; outfall, estuary; chute, flume, sluice, weir, floodgate; **vent,** ventage, venthole, port; safety valve; avenue, channel; spout, tap; opening, orifice; debouch; **exhaust;** door 189.6; outgate, sally port; vomitory; emunctory; pore; blowhole, spiracle

10 **goer,** outgoer, leaver, departer; **emigrant, émigré,**

VERBS **11 emerge, come out, issue,** issue forth, come into view, extrude, **come forth; surface,** rise to the surface; sally, sally forth, come to the fore; emanate, effuse, arise, come; debouch, disembogue; jump out, leap out, hop out; bail out; **burst forth, break forth, erupt;** break cover, **come out in the open;** protrude

12 exit, make an exit, **make one's exit;** egress, **go out,** get out, walk out, march out, run out, pass out, bow out *and* include oneself out <nf>; walk out on, leave cold <nf>; **depart** 188.6

13 run out, empty, find vent; **exhaust, drain,** drain out; **flow out,** outflow, outpour, **pour out,** sluice out, well out, gush *or* spout out, spew, flow, pour, well, surge, gush, jet, spout, spurt, vomit forth, blow out, spew out

14 leak, leak out, drip, dribble, drop, trickle, trill, distill

15 exude, exudate, transude, transpire, reek; **emit, discharge,** give off; **filter,** filtrate, exfiltrate; strain; **percolate;** leach, lixiviate; effuse, extravasate; **seep, ooze;** bleed; weep; excrete 12.12

16 emigrate, out-migrate, remigrate; exile, expatriate, defect; deport

17 export, send abroad

ADJS **18 emerging,** emergent; **issuing,** arising, surfacing, coming, forthcoming; emanating, emanent, emanative, transeunt, transient

19 outgoing, outbound, outward-bound; **outflowing,** outpouring, effusive, effluent; effused, extravasated

20 exudative, exuding, transudative; percolative; porous, permeable, pervious, oozy, runny, weepy, leaky; excretory 12.19

ADVS **21 forth; out,** outward, outwards, outwardly

PREPS **22 out of,** ex; **from; out, forth**

191 INSERTION

<putting in>

NOUNS **1 insertion, introduction,** insinuation, injection, infusion, perfusion, inoculation, intromission; **entrance** 189; **penetration** 292.3; interjection, interpolation 213.2; graft, grafting, engrafting, transplant, transplantation; infixing, implantation, embedment, tessellation, impactment, impaction

2 insert, insertion; **inset, inlay;** gore, godet, gusset; **graft,** scion *or* cion; tessera; parentheses; filling, stuffing; inclusion, supplement; tampon

VERBS **3 insert, introduce,** insinuate, inject, infuse, perfuse, inoculate, intromit; **enter** 189.7; **penetrate; put in, stick in,** set in, throw in, pop in, tuck in, whip in; slip in, ease in; interject; pot, hole; import; inoculate, vaccinate

4 install, instate, inaugurate, initiate, invest, ordain; enlist, enroll, induct, sign up, sign on

5 inset, inlay; embed *or* bed, bed in; dovetail, mount

6 graft, engraft, ingraft, **implant,** imp <old>; bud; inarch

7 thrust in, drive in, run in, plunge in, force in, push in, **ram in,** press in, stuff in, crowd in, squeeze in, cram in, jam in, tamp in, pound in, pack in, poke in, knock in, wedge in, impact; shoot

8 implant, transplant, bed out; infix 855.9; fit in, **inlay;** tessellate

192 EXTRACTION

<taking or drawing out>

NOUNS **1 extraction, withdrawal,** removal; **drawing, pulling,** drawing out; ripping *or* tearing *or* wresting out; eradication, **uprooting,** unrooting, deracination; squeezing out, pressing out, expressing, expression; avulsion, evulsion, cutting out, exsection, extirpation, excision, enucleation; extrication, evolvement, disentanglement, unravelment; excavation, mining, quarrying, drilling; dredging; rooting out, uprooting

2 disinterment, exhumation, disentombment, **unearthing,** uncovering, digging out; graverobbing

3 drawing, drafting, sucking, **suction,** aspiration, pipetting; pumping, siphoning, tapping, broaching; milking; drainage, draining, emptying; cupping; bloodletting, bleeding, phlebotomy, venesection

4 evisceration, gutting, **disembowelment,** shelling

5 elicitation, eduction, drawing out *or* forth, bringing out *or* forth; **evocation,** calling forth; arousal, derivation

6 extortion, exaction, claim, demand; **wresting, wrenching, wringing, rending,** tearing, ripping; wrest, wrench, wring

7 <obtaining an extract> **squeezing, pressing,** expression; **distillation;** decoction; **rendering,** rendition; **steeping,** soaking, infusion, marinating; concentration

8 extract, extraction; **essence, quintessence, spirit, elixir;** decoction; **distillate,** distillation, sublimate; **concentrate,** concentration; infusion; refinement, purification

9 extractor, separator, excavator, digger, miner; siphon; aspirator, pipette; pump, vacuum pump; press, wringer; corkscrew; forceps, pliers, pincers, tweezers; crowbar; smelter; scoop

VERBS **10 extract, take out,** get out, **withdraw, remove;** pull, draw; **pull out, draw out,** tear out, rip out, wrest out, pluck out, pick out, weed out, rake out; **pry out,** prize out, winkle out <Brit>; **pull up,** pluck up; **root up** *or* **out, uproot,** unroot, eradicate, deracinate, pull *or* pluck out by the roots, pull *or* pluck up by the roots; cut out, excise, exsect; enucleate; gouge out, avulse, evulse; extricate, evolve, disentangle, unravel; free, liberate; **dig up** *or* **out,** grub up *or* out, excavate, **unearth,** mine, quarry; dredge, dredge up *or* out; smelt

11 **disinter, exhume,** disentomb, unbury, unsepulcher, dig up, excavate, uncover

12 **draw off, draft off,** draft, draw, draw from; **suck,** suck out *or* up, **siphon off;** pipette; vacuum; pump, pump out; tap, broach; let, let out; bleed; let blood, venesect, phlebotomize; milk; **drain,** decant; exhaust, empty

13 **eviscerate, disembowel, gut,** shell

14 **elicit,** educe, deduce, induce, derive, obtain, procure, secure; **get from,** get out of; **evoke, call up, summon up,** call *or* summon forth, call out; rouse, arouse, stimulate; **draw out** *or* **forth,** bring out *or* forth, pry *or* prize out, winkle out <Brit>, drag out, worm out, bring to light; wangle, wangle out of, worm out of

15 **extort, exact,** squeeze, claim, demand; **wrest, wring from, wrench from, rend from,** wrest *or* tear from, force out

16 <obtain an extract> **squeeze** *or* **press out,** express, wring, wring out; **distill,** distill out, elixirate <old>; **filter,** filter out; decoct; **render,** melt down; refine; **steep,** soak, infuse; **concentrate,** essentialize

ADJS 17 extractive, eductive; educible; eradicative, uprooting; elicitory, **evocative,** arousing; **exacting,** exactive; **extortionate,** extortionary, extortive

18 **essential,** quintessential, pure 798.6

193 ASCENT
<motion upward>

NOUNS 1 **ascent,** ascension, levitation, **rise, rising,** uprising, **uprise,** uprisal; **upgoing,** upgo, uphill, upslope, upping; upcoming; **taking off,** leaving the ground, takeoff; **soaring,** zooming, gaining altitude, leaving the earth behind; spiraling *or* gyring up; shooting *or* rocketing up; defying gravity; **jump,** vault, spring, saltation, **leap** 366; mount, **mounting; climb, climbing,** upclimb, anabasis, clamber, escalade; surge, upsurge, upsurgence, upleap, upshoot, uprush; **gush, jet,** spurt, spout, fountain; updraft; upswing, upsweep, bounce; upgrowth; upgrade 204.6; **uplift,** elevation 912; **uptick** <nf>, **increase** 251; surfacing, breaking the surface

2 **upturn, uptrend,** upcast, upsweep, upbend, upcurve, upsurge

3 **stairs, stairway, staircase,** *escalier* <Fr>, flight of stairs, pair of stairs; **steps,** treads and risers;

stepping-stones; spiral staircase, winding staircase, cockle stairs <nf>; companionway, companion; stile; back stairs; perron; fire escape; landing, landing stage; ramp, incline; escalator

4 **ladder,** scale; stepladder, folding ladder, rope ladder, fire ladder; hook ladder, extension ladder; Jacob's ladder, companion ladder, accommodation ladder, boarding ladder, loft ladder, side ladder, gangway ladder, quarter ladder, stern ladder

5 **step, stair, footstep,** rest, footrest, stepping-stone; **rung, round,** rundle, spoke, stave, scale; doorstep; tread; riser; bridgeboard, string; step stool

6 **climber,** ascender, upclimber, soarer; mountain climber, **mountaineer,** alpinist, rock climber, rock-jock <nf>, cragsman; steeplejack; stegophilist

7 <comparisons> rocket, skyrocket; lark, skylark, eagle

VERBS 8 **ascend, rise, mount,** arise, up, uprise, levitate, upgo, **go up,** rise up, come up; go onwards and upwards, go up and up; upsurge, **surge,** upstream, upheave; swarm up, upswarm, sweep up; upwind, upspin, spiral, spire, curl upwards; stand up, **rear,** rear up, **tower,** loom; upgrow, grow up

9 **shoot up, spring up,** jump up, **leap up,** vault up, start up, fly up, pop up, bob up; float up, surface, break water; **gush, jet,** spurt, fountain; upshoot, upstart, upspring, upleap, upspear, rocket, **skyrocket**

10 **take off,** leave the ground, leave the earth behind, gain altitude, claw skyward; become airborne; **soar,** zoom, fly, plane, kite, fly aloft; aspire; spire, spiral *or* gyre upward; **hover,** hang, poise, float, float in the air; rocket, skyrocket

11 **climb,** climb up, upclimb, **mount,** clamber, **clamber up,** scramble *or* scrabble up, claw one's way up, struggle up, inch up, shin, shinny *or* shin up <nf>, ramp <nf>, work *or* inch one's way up, climb the ladder; **scale,** escalade, scale the heights; climb over, surmount, go over the top

12 **mount, get on,** climb on, back; **bestride,** bestraddle; **board,** go aboard, go on board; **get in,** jump in, hop in, pile in <nf>

13 **upturn, turn up,** cock up; trend upwards, slope up; upcast, upsweep, upbend, upcurve

ADJS 14 **ascending,** in the ascendant, **mounting, rising,** uprising, upgoing, upcoming; ascendant, ascensional, ascensive, anabatic; **leaping,** springing, saltatory; spiraling, skyrocketing; **upward;** uphill, uphillward, upgrade, upsloping; uparching, rearing, rampant; climbing, scandent, scansorial; gravity-defying

15 **upturned, upcast,** uplifted, **turned-up,** retroussé

ADVS 16 **up, upward, upwards,** upwith <Scot>; skyward, heavenward; uplong, upalong; upstream, upstreamward; uphill; uphillward; upstairs; up attic *and* up steps <nf>; uptown; up north

INTERJS **17 alley-oop!, upsy-daisy!;** excelsior!, onward and upward!

194 DESCENT

<motion downward>

NOUNS **1 descent, descending,** descension *or* downcome <old>, **comedown,** down; **dropping, falling,** plummeting, **drop, fall, free-fall,** *chute* <Fr>, **downfall,** debacle, **collapse,** crash; **swoop,** stoop, pounce, downrush, downflow, cascade, waterfall, cataract, **downpour,** defluxion; downturn, downcurve, downbend, downward trend, downtrend; declension, declination, inclination; gravitation; abseil, rappel; downgrade 204.5; **down tick;** decrease 252

2 sinkage, lowering, **decline, slump,** subsidence, submergence, lapse, decurrence, downgrade; cadence; **droop, sag,** swag; catenary; downer <nf>

3 tumble, fall, *culbute* <Fr>, cropper *and* **spill** <nf>, **flop** <nf>; **header** <nf>; **sprawl; pratfall** <nf>; **stumble,** trip; **dive,** plunge 367, belly flop, nosedive; forced landing

4 slide; slip, slippage; **glide,** coast, glissade; glissando; **slither; skid,** sideslip; **landslide,** mudslide, landslip, subsidence, **snowslide,** snowslip <Brit>; **avalanche**

VERBS **5 descend, go** *or* **come down,** down, dip down, lose altitude, dump altitude <nf>; gravitate; **fall, drop,** precipitate, rain, rain *or* pour down, fall *or* drop down; **collapse,** crash; **swoop,** stoop, pounce; **pitch,** plunge 367.6, **plummet;** cascade, cataract; parachute; come down a peg <nf>; **fall off,** drop off; trend downward, down-tick, go downhill

6 sink, go down, sink down, submerge; **set, settle,** settle down; **decline,** lower, **subside,** give way, lapse, cave, cave in; **droop,** slouch, **sag,** swag; **slump,** slump down; flump, flump down; flop *and* flop down <nf>; plump, plop *or* plop down, plunk *or* plunk down <nf>; founder 367.8

7 get down, alight, touch down, **light; land,** settle, perch, come to rest; **dismount, get off,** uphorse; climb down; abseil, rappel

8 tumble, fall, fall down, come *or* fall *or* get a cropper <nf>, take a fall *or* tumble, take a flop *or* spill <nf>, precipitate oneself; fall over, tumble over, trip over; **sprawl,** sprawl out, take a pratfall <nf>, spread-eagle <nf>, measure one's length; fall headlong, **take a header** <nf>, nosedive; fall prostrate, fall flat, fall on one's face, fall flat on one's ass <nf>; **fall over,** topple down *or* over; capsize, turn turtle; **topple,** lurch, pitch,

stumble, stagger, totter, career, list, tilt, trip, flounder

9 slide, slip, slidder <nf>, slip *or* slide down; **glide,** skim, coast, glissade; **slither; skid,** sideslip; avalanche

10 light upon, alight upon, settle on; **descend upon, come down on, fall on,** drop on, hit *or* strike upon

ADJS **11 descending,** descendant, on the descendant; **down,** downward, declivitous; decurrent, deciduous; **downgoing,** downcoming; down-reaching; **dropping, falling, plunging, plummeting,** downfalling; **sinking,** downsinking, foundering, submerging, setting; declining, **subsiding;** collapsing, tumbledown, tottering; drooping, sagging; on the downgrade, downhill 204.16

12 downcast, downturned; hanging, down-hanging

ADVS **13 down, downward, downwards,** from the top down, *de haut en bas* <Fr>; adown, below; downright; downhill, downgrade; downstreet; downline; downstream; downstairs; downtown; south, down south

195 CONTAINER

NOUNS **1 container, receptacle;** receiver 479.3, holder, vessel, utensil; repository, depository, reservoir, store; basin, pot, pan, drinking vessel, cup, glass, bottle, crockery, ladle; cask; box, case, crate, carton; bucket; bottle, can; basket; luggage, suitcase, baggage, trunk; cabinet, cupboard; shelf, drawer, locker; frame; compartment; packet; cart, truck

2 bag, sack, sac, poke <nf>, bundle; **pocket,** fob; **balloon, bladder;** carryall, pouch; purse, handbag, tote, satchel

196 CONTENTS

NOUNS **1 contents, content,** what is contained *or* included *or* comprised; **insides** 207.4, innards <nf>, guts, inner workings; **components, constituents, ingredients,** elements, **items, parts, divisions,** subdivisions; **inventory,** index, census, list 871; part 792; whole 792; composition 796; constitution, makeup, embodiment

2 load, lading, cargo, freight, charge, burden; payload; boatload, busload, carload, cartload, containerload, shipload, trailerload, trainload, truckload, vanload, wagonload; shipment, stowage, tonnage

3 lining, liner; **interlining,** interlineation; inlayer, inside layer, **inlay,** inlaying; **filling,** filler; **packing,** padding, wadding, **stuffing;** facing; doubling, doublure; bushing, bush; wainscot; insole; facing

4 <contents of a container> cup, cupful, etc

5 <essential content> **substance, sum and substance, stuff, material, matter,** medium, building blocks, fabric; **gist, heart, soul, meat, nub;** the nitty-gritty *and* the bottom line *and* the name of the game <nf>, **core,** kernel, marrow, pith, sap, spirit, **essence,** quintessence, elixir, distillate, distillation, distilled essence; sine qua non, irreducible *or* indispensable content
6 **enclosure,** the enclosed
VERBS 7 **fill,** pack 794.7, **load; line,** interline, interlineate; inlay; face; wainscot, ceil; **pad,** wad, **stuff;** feather, fur; fill up, top up

197 ROOM
    <compartment>

NOUNS 1 **room, chamber,** *chambre* <Fr>, *salle* <Fr>, four walls
 2 **compartment,** chamber, space, enclosed space; **cavity,** hollow, hole, concavity; **cell,** cellule; booth, stall, crib, manger; box, pew; **crypt, vault**
 3 **nook, corner, cranny, niche, recess,** cove, bay, oriel, alcove; cubicle, roomlet, carrel, hole-in-the-wall <nf>, cubby, **cubbyhole,** snuggery, hidey-hole <nf>
 4 **hall;** assembly hall, exhibition hall, convention hall; gallery; meetinghouse, meeting room; **auditorium; concert hall; theater,** music hall; stadium, dome, sports dome, **arena** 463; lecture hall, lyceum, amphitheater; operating theater; dance hall; ballroom, grand ballroom; **chapel** 703.3
 5 **parlor, living room, sitting room, morning room, drawing** *or* **withdrawing room, front room,** best room <nf>, foreroom <nf>, **salon,** saloon <old>; sun parlor *or* sunroom, lounge, sun lounge, sunporch, solarium, conservatory
 6 **library,** stacks; **study,** studio, *atelier* <Fr>, workroom, den; **office,** workplace, home office; **loft,** sail loft
 7 **bedroom, boudoir,** chamber, sleeping chamber, **bedchamber,** master bedroom, guest room, sleeping room, cubicle, cubiculum; nursery; dormitory *or* dorm room
 8 <private chamber> **sanctum,** sanctum sanctorum, holy of holies, adytum; **den,** retreat, closet, cabinet
 9 <ships> cabin, stateroom; saloon; house, deckhouse, trunk cabin, cuddy, shelter cabin
10 <trains> drawing room, stateroom, parlor car, Pullman car, roomette
11 **dining room,** *salle à manger* <Fr>, dinette; breakfast room, breakfast nook, dining hall, refectory, mess *or* messroom *or* mess hall, commons, canteen; dining car *or* diner; **restaurant, cafeteria**
12 **playroom,** recreation room, rec room <nf>, family room, game room, **rumpus room** <nf>; **gymnasium**
13 **utility room,** laundry room, sewing room
14 **kitchen** 11.4, kitchenette, galley, pantry, larder, scullery; **storeroom** 386.6, smoking room 89.13
15 **closet,** clothes closet, wardrobe, cloakroom; checkroom; linen closet; dressing room, fitting room, pantry
16 **attic,** attic room, **garret, loft,** sky parlor; cockloft, hayloft; storeroom, junk room, lumber room <Brit>
17 **cellar,** cellarage, **basement;** subbasement; wine cellar, potato cellar, storm cellar, cyclone cellar; coal bin *or* hole, hold, hole, bunker; glory hole
18 **corridor, hall,** hallway; passage, **passageway; gallery,** loggia; arcade, colonnade, pergola, cloister, peristyle; areaway; breezeway
19 **vestibule,** portal, **portico,** entry, entryway, entrance, **entrance hall,** entranceway, **threshold; lobby, foyer;** propylaeum, stoa; narthex, galilee
20 **anteroom,** antechamber; side room, byroom; **waiting room,** *salle d'attente* <Fr>; **reception room,** presence chamber *or* room, audience chamber; throne room; lounge, greenroom, wardroom
21 **porch,** stoop, **veranda,** piazza <nf>, patio, lanai, gallery; sleeping porch
22 **balcony,** gallery, terrace
23 **floor, story,** level, flat; first floor *or* story, ground *or* street floor, *rez-de-chaussée* <Fr>; mezzanine, mezzanine floor, *entresol* <Fr>; clerestory
24 **showroom,** display room, exhibition room, gallery
25 **hospital room; ward,** maternity ward, fever ward, charity ward, prison ward, etc; private room, semi-private room; examining *or* examination room, consulting *or* consultation room, treatment room; **operating room** *or* OR, operating theater, surgery; labor room, delivery room; recovery room; emergency, emergency room; intensive care unit *or* ICU; pharmacy, dispensary; clinic, nursery; laboratory *or* blood bank; nurses' station
26 **bathroom, lavatory,** washroom 79.10, **water closet** *or* **WC,** closet, **rest room,** comfort station, **toilet** 12.10; ladies' room, men's room
27 <for vehicles> **garage,** carport; coach *or* carriage house; carbarn; roundhouse; hangar; boathouse

198 TOP

NOUNS 1 **top,** top side, upper side, upside; surface 206.2; superstratum; topside *or* topsides; upper story, top floor; clerestory; **roof,** ridgepole *or* roofpole; rooftop; ceiling
 2 **summit,** top; **tip-top,** peak 3.6, pinnacle; **crest, brow;** ridge, edge; **crown,** cap, **tip,** point, spire,

pitch; highest pitch, no place higher, **apex**, vertex, **acme**, *ne plus ultra* <Fr>, **zenith, climax**, apogee, pole; **culmination; extremity, maximum, limit,** upper extremity, highest point, very top, top of the world, extreme limit, utmost *or* upmost *or* uppermost height, "the very acme and pitch"—Pope; exosphere, **sky**, heaven *or* heavens, seventh heaven, cloud nine <nf>; meridian, noon, high noon; mountaintop

3 topping, icing, frosting; dressing

4 <top part> **head**, heading, **headpiece**, cap, *caput* <L>, capsheaf, **crown, crest**; topknot; pinhead, nailhead

5 architectural topping, capital <see list>, head, crown, cap; bracket capital; cornice; cymatium, clerestory

6 head, headpiece, **pate**, poll <nf>, crown, **sconce** *and* **noodle** *and* **noddle** *and* **noggin** *and* **bean** *and* dome <nf>; brow, ridge; "the dome of Thought, the palace of the Soul"—Byron

7 skull, cranium, pericranium, epicranium; brainpan, brain box *or* case

8 phrenology, craniology, metoposcopy, physiognomy; phrenologist, craniologist, metoposcopist, physiognomist

VERBS **9 top**, top off, **crown, cap**, crest, **head**, tip, peak, surmount; overtop *or* outtop, have the top place *or* spot, overarch; **culminate**, consummate, climax; ice, frost, dress; fill, top up

ADJS **10 top**, topmost, **uppermost**, upmost, overmost, **highest**; tip-top, tip-crowning, **maximum**, maximal, ultimate; summital, apical, vertical, zenithal, climactic, climactical, **consummate;** acmic, acmatic; meridian, meridional; **head**, headmost, capital, chief, paramount, supreme, preeminent; **top-level**, highest level, top-echelon, top-flight, top-ranking, top-drawer <nf>; peak, pitch, ultimate, maximum, crowning

11 topping, crowning, capping, heading, surmounting, overtopping *or* outtopping, overarching; **culminating**, consummating, perfecting, climaxing

12 topped, headed, **crowned, capped**, crested, plumed, tipped, peaked, roofed

13 topless, headless, crownless

14 cranial; cephalic, encephalic

ADVS **15 atop**, on top, at *or* on the top, topside <nf>; at the top of the tree *or* ladder, on top of the roost *or* heap; on the crest *or* crest of the wave; at the head, at the peak *or* pinnacle *or* summit

PREPS **16 atop, on, upon**, on top of, surmounting, topping

17 capital styles

baroque	composite
Byzantine	Corinthian
Doric	Moorish
Gothic	Roman Corinthian
Greek	Roman Doric
Greek Corinthian	Romanesque
Greek Ionic	Roman Ionic
Ionic	Tuscan

199 BOTTOM

NOUNS **1 bottom**, bottom side, **underside**, nether side, lower side, downside, **underneath**, fundament; belly, underbelly; buttocks 217.4, breech; **rock bottom, bedrock**, bed, hardpan; **grass roots;** substratum, underlayer, lowest level *or* layer *or* stratum, nethermost level *or* layer *or* stratum, basecoat; **nadir**, the pits <nf>

2 base, basement, **foot**, footing, sole, toe; **foundation** 901.6, underpinning, infrastructure; baseboard, mopboard, skirt; wainscot, dado; skeleton, bare bones, chassis, frame, undercarriage; keel, keelson

3 ground covering, ground, earth, *terra firma* <L>; **floor**, flooring; parquet; **deck; pavement**, *pavé* <Fr>, paving, surfacing, asphalt, blacktop, macadam, concrete; **cover**, carpet, floor covering; artificial turf, Astroturf <trademark>

4 bed, bottom, floor, ground, **basin, channel**, coulee; riverbed, seabed, ocean bottom 275.4

5 foot, extremity, pes, pedes, *pied* <Fr>, trotter, pedal extremity, dog, tootsy <nf>; **hoof**, ungula; **paw**, pad, pug, *patte* <Fr>; forefoot, forepaw; harefoot, splay-foot, clubfoot; **toe**, digit; **heel; sole**, pedi *or* pedio; instep, arch; pastern; fetlock

VERBS **6 base on, found on, ground on, build on**, bottom on, bed on, set on; root in; **underlie**, undergird; bottom, bottom out, hit bottom

ADJS **7 bottom**, bottommost, **undermost**, nethermost, lowermost, deepest, **lowest; rock-bottom**, bedrock; ground, ground-level

8 basic; basal, basilar; **underlying, fundamental**, foundational, essential, elementary, elemental, primary, primal, primitive, rudimentary, original, grass-roots; supporting; radical; nadiral

9 pedal; plantar; footed, hoofed, ungulate, clawed, taloned; toed

200 VERTICALNESS

NOUNS **1 verticalness**, verticality, verticalism; **erectness, uprightness;** stiffness *or* erectness of posture, position of attention, brace; straight up-and-downness, up-and-downness; steepness, sheerness, precipitousness, plungingness, **perpendicularity**, plumbness, aplomb; right-angledness *or* -angularity, squareness, orthogonality

2 vertical, upright, perpendicular, plumb, normal;

right angle, orthodiagonal; vertical circle, azimuth circle

3 precipice, cliff, sheer *or* yawning cliff *or* precipice *or* drop, steep, bluff, wall, face, scar; crag; scarp, **escarpment; palisade,** palisades

4 erection, erecting, **elevation; rearing,** raising; **uprearing,** upraising, lofting, uplifting, heaving up *or* aloft; standing on end *or* upright *or* on its feet *or* on its base *or* on its legs *or* on its bottom

5 rising, uprising, ascension, ascending, ascent; vertical height *or* dimension; **gradient,** rise, uprise

6 <instruments> square, T square, try square, set square, carpenter's square; plumb, plumb line, plumb rule, plummet, bob, plumb bob, lead

VERBS 7 stand, stand erect, stand up, stand upright, stand up straight, be erect, be on one's feet; hold oneself straight *or* stiff, stand ramrod-straight, have an upright carriage; stand at attention *and* brace *and* stand at parade rest <military>

8 rise, arise, ascend, mount, uprise, **rise up, get up,** get to one's feet; **stand up, stand on end; stick up,** cock up; bristle; **rear,** ramp, uprear, rear up, rise on the hind legs; upheave; sit up, sit bolt upright, straighten up; jump up, spring to one's feet

9 erect, elevate, rear, raise, pitch, **set up,** raise *or* lift *or* cast up; raise *or* heave *or* rear aloft; uprear, upraise, uplift, upheave; upright; **upend,** stand on end, stand upright *or* on end; set on its feet *or* legs *or* base *or* bottom

10 plumb, plumb-line, set *à plomb;* **square,** square up

ADJS 11 vertical, upright, bolt upright, ramrod straight, **erect,** upstanding, standing up, stand-up; rearing, rampant; **upended,** upraised, upreared; downright

12 perpendicular, plumb, straight-up-and-down, straight-up, **up-and-down;** sheer, steep, precipitous, plunging; **right-angled,** right-angle, right-angular, orthogonal, orthodiagonal

ADVS 13 vertically, erectly, upstandingly, uprightly, **upright,** up, stark *or* bolt upright; **on end,** up on end, right on end, endwise, endways; on one's feet *or* legs, on one's hind legs <nf>; at attention *and* braced *and* at parade rest <military>

14 perpendicularly, sheer, sheerly; up and down, **straight up and down; plumb,** *à plomb* <Fr>; **at right angles,** square

201 HORIZONTALNESS

NOUNS 1 horizontalness, horizontality; **levelness, flatness,** planeness, planarity, evenness, smoothness, flushness, alignment; unbrokenness, unrelievedness

2 recumbency, recumbence, decumbency *or* decumbence, accumbency; accubation; prostration, proneness; supineness, reclining, reclination; lying, lounging, **repose** 20; sprawl, loll

3 horizontal, plane, level, flat, dead level *or* flat, homaloid; **horizontal** *or* level plane; horizontal *or* level line; horizontal projection; horizontal surface, fascia; horizontal parallax; horizontal axis; horizontal fault; water level, sea level, mean sea level; ground, earth, steppe, **plain, flatland,** prairie, savanna, flats, sea of grass, bowling green, table, billiard table; floor, platform, ledge, terrace

4 horizon, skyline, rim of the horizon; sea line; apparent *or* local *or* visible horizon, sensible horizon, celestial *or* rational *or* geometrical *or* true horizon, artificial *or* false horizon; azimuth

VERBS 5 lie, lie down, lay <nf>, **recline, repose,** lounge, sprawl, loll, drape *or* spread oneself, spread-eagle, splay, lie limply; **lie flat** *or* prostrate *or* prone *or* supine, lie on one's face *or* back, lie on a level, hug the ground *or* deck; **grovel, crawl,** kowtow

6 level, flatten, even, equalize, align, smooth *or* smoothen, level out, smooth out, flush; grade, roll, roll flat, steamroller *or* steamroll; **lay,** lay down *or* out; **raze,** rase, lay level, lay level with the ground; lay low *or* flat; **fell** 913.5; deck <nf>

ADJS 7 horizontal, level, flat, flattened; **even,** smooth, smoothened, smoothed out; table-like, tabular; **flush;** homaloidal; **plane,** planar, plain; rolled, trodden, squashed, rolled *or* trodden *or* squashed flat, razed; flat as a pancake, "flat as a cake"— Erasmus, flat as a table *or* billiard table *or* bowling green *or* tennis court, flat as a board, "flat as a flounder"—John Fletcher, level as a plain

8 recumbent, accumbent, procumbent, decumbent; **prostrate, prone,** flat; **supine,** resupine; couchant, *couché* <Fr>; **lying, reclining, reposing,** flat on one's back; sprawling, lolling, lounging; sprawled, spread, splay, splayed, draped; groveling, crawling, flat on one's belly *or* nose

ADVS 9 horizontally, flat, flatly, flatways, flatwise; **evenly,** flush; **level, on a level;** lengthwise, lengthways, at full length, on one's back *or* belly *or* nose

202 PENDENCY

NOUNS 1 pendency, pendulousness *or* pendulosity, pensileness *or* pensility; **hanging, suspension,** dangling *or* danglement, suspense, dependence *or* dependency

2 hang, droop, dangle, swing, fall; **sag,** swag, bag

3 overhang, overhanging, impendence *or* impendency, **projection,** extension, protrusion, beetling, jutting; cantilever

4 pendant, hanger; **hanging,** drape; **lobe,** ear lobe, lobule, lobus, lobation, lappet, wattle; **uvula**

5 suspender, hanger, supporter; **suspenders,** pair of suspenders, braces <Brit>, galluses <nf>

VERBS **6 hang,** hang down, fall; **depend,** pend; **dangle,** swing, flap, flop <nf>; flow, drape, cascade; **droop,** lop; nod, weep; **sag,** swag, bag; **trail, drag, draggle,** drabble, daggle

7 overhang, hang over, hang out, **impend,** impend over, **project,** project over, beetle, **jut,** beetle *or* jut *or* thrust over, stick out over

8 suspend, hang, hang up, put up, fasten up; sling; oscillate, swing, sway, hover

ADJS **9 pendent,** pendulous, pendulant, pendular, penduline, pensile; **suspended,** hung; **hanging,** pending, depending, dependent; **falling; dangling,** swinging, oscillating, falling loosely; weeping; flowing, cascading

10 drooping, droopy, limp, loose, nodding, floppy <nf>, loppy, lop; **sagging,** saggy, swag, sagging in folds; **bagging,** baggy, ballooning; lop-eared

11 overhanging, overhung, lowering, **impending,** impendent, **pending;** incumbent, superincumbent; **projecting, jutting; beetling,** beetle; beetle-browed; cantilevered

12 lobular, lobar, lobed, lobate, lobated

203 PARALLELISM
<physically parallel direction or state>

NOUNS **1 parallelism,** coextension, nonconvergence, nondivergence, collaterality, concurrence, equidistance; collineation, collimation; alignment; parallelization; parallelotropism; **analogy** 943.1

2 parallel, paralleler; parallel line, parallel dash, parallel bar, parallel file, parallel series, parallel column, parallel trench, parallel vector; parallelogram, parallelepiped *or* parallelepipedon

3 <instruments> parallel rule *or* rules *or* ruler, parallelograph, parallelometer

VERBS **4 parallel,** be parallel, coextend; run parallel, go alongside, go beside, run abreast, run side by side; match, equal

5 parallelize, place parallel to, equidistance; line up, align, realign; collineate, collimate; match; correspond, follow, equate

ADJS **6 parallel,** paralleling, parallelistic; coextending, coextensive, nonconvergent, nondivergent, **equidistant,** equispaced, collateral, concurrent; lined up, aligned; equal, even; parallelogrammical, parallelogrammatical; parallelepipedal; parallelotropic; parallelodrome, parallelinervate; analogous 943.8

ADVS **7 in parallel,** parallelwise, parallelly; side by side, alongside, abreast; equidistantly, nonconvergently, nondivergently; collaterally, coextensively

204 OBLIQUITY

NOUNS **1 obliquity,** obliqueness; **deviation** 164, deviance, divergence, digression, divagation, vagary, excursion, skewness, aberration, squint, declination; deflection, deflexure; nonconformity 868; diagonality, crosswiseness, transverseness; indirection, indirectness, deviousness, circumlocution, circuitousness 914

2 inclination, leaning, lean, angularity; **slant,** slaunch <nf>, rake, **slope; tilt, tip,** pitch, **list, cant,** swag, sway; leaning tower, tower of Pisa

3 bias, bend, bent, **crook, warp, twist, turn, skew,** slue, **veer,** sheer, **swerve,** lurch; deflection

4 incline, inclination, **slope, grade,** gradient, pitch, **ramp,** launching ramp, bank, talus, gentle *or* easy slope, glacis; rapid *or* steep slope, stiff climb, scarp, chute; helicline, inclined plane <phys>; **bevel,** bezel, fleam; hillside, side; hanging gardens; shelving beach

5 declivity, descent, dip, drop, fall, falling-off *or* -away, **decline;** hang, hanging; **downgrade, downhill**

6 acclivity, ascent, climb, **rise,** rising, uprise, uprising, rising ground; **upgrade, uphill,** upgo, upclimb, uplift, steepness, precipitousness, abruptness, verticalness 200

7 diagonal, oblique, transverse, bias, bend <heraldry>, oblique line, slash, **slant,** virgule, scratch comma, separatrix, solidus, cant; oblique angle *or* figure, rhomboid, rhombus

8 zigzag, zig, zag; zigzaggery, flexuosity, **crookedness,** crankiness; switchback, hairpin, dogleg; chevron

VERBS **9 oblique, deviate, diverge,** deflect, divagate, **bear off,** digress; angle, **angle off, swerve,** shoot off at an angle, **veer,** sheer, sway, slue, **skew, twist, turn,** bend, bias, dogleg; crook; circumlocute

10 incline, lean; slope, slant, camber, slaunch <nf>, rake, pitch, grade, bank, shelve; **tilt, tip, list, cant,** bevel, careen, keel, sidle, swag, sway; **ascend, rise,** uprise, climb, **go uphill; descend, decline,** dip, drop, fall, fall off *or* away, **go downhill;** retreat

11 cut, cut *or* slant across, cut crosswise *or* transversely *or* diagonally, catercorner, diagonalize, slash, slash across

12 zigzag, zig, zag, **stagger,** crank *or* crankle <old>, wind in and out

ADJS **13 oblique,** obliquitous; **devious,** deviant, deviative, divergent, digressive, divagational, deflectional, excursive, off course; **indirect,** side, sidelong, roundabout; left-handed, sinister, sinistral; backhand, backhanded; circuitous 914.7

14 askew, skew, skewed; skew-jawed *and* skewgee *and* skew-whiff *and* askewgee *and* agee *and* agee-jawed <nf>; **awry,** wry; askance, askant, asquint,

squinting, **cockeyed** <nf>; **crooked** 265.10;
slaunchwise *or* slaunchways <nf>; wamperjawed
and catawampous *and* yaw-ways <nf>, wonky
<Brit nf>

15 inclining, inclined, inclinatory, inclinational;
leaning, recumbent; **sloping,** sloped, aslope;
raking, pitched; **slanting,** slanted, slant, aslant,
slantways, slantwise; bias, biased; shelving, shelvy;
tilting, tilted, atilt, tipped, **tipping,** tipsy, listing,
canting, careening; sideling, sidelong; out of the
perpendicular *or* square *or* plumb, bevel, beveled

16 <sloping downward> **downhill, downgrade;**
descending, falling, dropping, dipping; **declining,**
declined; declivous, declivitous, declivate

17 <sloping upward> **uphill, upgrade; rising,**
uprising, **ascending,** climbing; acclivous,
acclivitous, acclinate

18 steep, precipitous, bluff, plunging, abrupt, bold,
sheer, sharp, rapid; headlong, breakneck; vertical
200.11

19 transverse, crosswise *or* crossways, thwart,
athwart, across 170.9; **diagonal,** bendwise;
catercorner *or* **catercornered** *or* cattycorner *or*
cattycornered *or* kittycorner *or* kittycornered;
slant, bias, biased, biaswise *or* biasways

20 crooked, zigzag, zigzagged, zigzaggy, zigzagwise *or*
zigzagways, dogleg *or* doglegged; flexuous, twisty,
hairpin, bendy, curvy, meandering; staggered,
crankled <old>; chevrony, chevronwise *or*
chevronways <architecture>

ADVS **21 obliquely, deviously,** deviately, **indirectly,**
circuitously 914.9; divergently, digressively,
excursively, divagationally; **sideways** *or* sidewise,
sidelong, sideling, on *or* to one side; at an angle

22 askew, awry; askance, askant, asquint

23 slantingly, slopingly, aslant, aslope, atilt, rakingly,
tipsily, slopewise, slopeways, slantwise, slantways,
aslantwise, on *or* at a slant; slaunchwise *and*
slaunchways <nf>; off plumb *or* the vertical;
downhill, downgrade; uphill, upgrade

24 transversely, crosswise *or* crossways, athwart,
across 170.13

25 diagonally, diagonalwise; **on the bias,** bias,
biaswise; **cornerwise,** cornerways;
catercornerways *or* **catercorner** *or* cattycorner *or*
kittycorner

205 INVERSION

NOUNS **1 inversion,** turning over *or* around *or* upside
down, the other way round, inverted order;
eversion, turning inside out, invagination,
intussusception; introversion, turning inward;
reversing, reversal 859.1, turning front to back *or*
side to side; **reversion,** turning back *or* backwards,

retroversion, retroflexion, retroflection, revulsion;
devolution, atavism; recidivism; **transposition,**
transposal; topsy-turvydom *or* topsy-turviness; the
world turned upside-down, upside-downness, the
tail wagging the dog; pronation, supination,
resupination

2 overturn, upset, overset, **overthrow,** upturn,
turnover, spill <nf>; subversion; **revolution** 860;
capsizing, capsize, capsizal, turning turtle;
somersault, somerset, *culbute* <Fr>, cartwheel,
handspring; headstand, handstand; turning head
over heels

3 <grammatical and rhetorical terms> metastasis,
metathesis; anastrophe, chiasmus, hypallage,
hyperbaton, hysteron proteron, palindrome,
parenthesis, synchysis, tmesis

4 inverse, reverse, converse, opposite 215.5, other
side of the coin *or* picture, the flip side *and* B side
<nf>; counter, contrary

VERBS **5 invert,** inverse, turn over *or* around *or*
upside down; introvert, turn in *or* inward; **turn
down; turn inside out,** turn out, evert, invaginate,
intussuscept; **revert,** recidivate, relapse, lapse,
back-slide; **reverse** 859.4, **transpose,** convert; put
the cart before the horse, put in inverted order;
turn into the opposite, turn about, turn the tables,
turn the scale *or* balance; rotate, revolve, pronate,
supinate, resupinate

6 overturn, turn over, turn upside down, turn
bottom side up, upturn, **upset,** overset, **overthrow,**
subvert, *culbuter* <Fr>; go *or* turn ass over elbows
or ass over tincups <nf>, turn a somersault, go *or*
turn head over heels; **turn turtle, turn topsy-turvy,**
topsy-turvy, topsy-turvify; **tip over,** keel over, topple
over; **capsize;** careen, set on its beam ends, set on
its ears

ADJS **7 inverted,** inversed, back-to-front, **backwards,**
retroverted, **reversed, transposed, back side
forward, tail first; inside out,** outside in, everted,
invaginated, wrong side out, back-to-front;
reverted, lapsed, recidivist *or* recidivistic; atavistic;
devolutional; **upside-down, topsy-turvy,** ass over
elbows *and* ass over tincups *and* arsy-varsy <nf>,
bottom-up; **capsized,** head-over-heels; hyperbatic,
chiastic, palindromic; resupinate; introverted

ADVS **8 inversely, conversely,** contrarily, contrariwise,
vice versa, the other way around, **backwards,**
turned around; **upside down,** over, **topsy-turvy;**
bottom up, bottom side up; head over heels, heels
over head

206 EXTERIORITY

NOUNS **1 exteriority,** externalness, externality,
outwardness, outerness; appearance, outward

appearance, seeming, mien, **front,** manner; window-dressing, cosmetics; openness; extrinsicality 768; **superficiality,** shallowness 276; extraterritoriality, foreignness

2 **exterior,** external, **outside; surface,** superficies, covering 295, skin 2.4, outer skin *or* layer, epidermis, integument, envelope, crust, cortex, rind, shell 295.16; exoskeleton; cladding, plating; top, superstratum; **periphery, fringe,** circumference, outline, lineaments, border; **face,** outer face *or* side, facade, **front;** facet; extrados, back; store-front, shop-front, shop-window, street-front

3 **outdoors,** outside, **the out-of-doors,** the great out-of-doors, the open, **the open air;** outland, hinterland

4 **externalization,** exteriorization, bringing into the open, show, showing, display, displaying; projection; **objectification,** actualization, realization

VERBS 5 **externalize,** exteriorize, bring into the open, bring out, show, display, exhibit; **objectify,** actualize, project, realize; direct outward

6 <nf terms> **scratch the surface;** give a lick and a promise, do a cosmetic job, give a once-over-lightly, whitewash, give a nod

ADJS 7 **exterior, external;** extrinsic 768; **outer, outside, out, outward,** outward-facing, outlying, outstanding; **outermost,** outmost; front, facing; surface, superficial 276.5, epidermic, cortical, cuticular; exoskeletal; cosmetic, merely cosmetic; peripheral, **fringe,** roundabout; apparent, seeming; open 348.10, public 352.17; exomorphic

8 **outdoor, out-of-door,** out-of-doors, **outside, without-doors; open-air,** alfresco; out and about

9 extraterritorial, exterritorial; extraterrestrial, exterrestrial, extramundane; extragalactic, extralateral, extraliminal, extramural, extrapolar, extrasolar, extraprovincial, extratribal; foreign, outlandish, **alien**

ADVS 10 **externally, outwardly,** on the outside, exteriorly; **without, outside, outwards, out;** apparently, to all appearances; openly, publically, to judge by appearances; superficially, on the surface

11 **outdoors, out of doors, outside,** abroad; in the open, **in the open air,** alfresco, *en plein air* <Fr>

WORD ELEMENTS 12 e-, ec-, ect-, ecto-, ex-, ef-, epi-, eph-, extra-, hyper-, peripher-, periphero-

207 INTERIORITY

NOUNS 1 interiority, internalness, internality, **inwardness, innerness,** inness; introversion, internalization; **intrinsicality** 767; depth 275

2 **interior, inside,** inner, inward, internal, intern; inner recess, recesses, **innermost** *or* **deepest recesses,** penetralia, intimate places, secret place *or* places; bosom, secret heart, heart, heart of hearts, soul, vitals, vital center; inner self, inner life, inner landscape, inner *or* interior man, inner nature; intrados; core, center 208.2

3 **inland,** inlands, **interior,** up-country; **midland,** midlands; heartland; hinterland 233.2; Middle America

4 **insides, innards** <nf>, inwards, internals; inner mechanism, what makes it tick *and* works <nf>; **guts** <nf>, **vitals, viscera,** *kishkes* <Yiddish>, giblets; entrails, bowels, guts, enteron; tripes *and* stuffings <nf>

VERBS 5 internalize, put in, keep within; introvert, bottle up; enclose, embed, surround, contain, comprise, include, enfold, take to heart, assimilate; introspect; retreat into

ADJS 6 **interior, internal, inner, inside, inward;** intestine; **innermost,** inmost, **intimate,** private; visceral, gut <nf>; **intrinsic** 766.7; deep 275.10; central 208.11; indoor; live-in

7 **inland, interior,** up-country, up-river, landlocked; hinterland; **midland,** mediterranean; Middle American

8 intramarginal, intramural, intramundane, intramontane, intraterritorial, intracoastal, intragroupal

ADVS 9 **internally, inwardly,** interiorly, inly, **intimately,** deeply, profoundly, under the surface; **intrinsically** 767; centrally

10 **in, inside, within;** herein, therein, wherein

11 **inward, inwards, inwardly,** withinward, withinwards; inland, inshore

12 **indoors,** indoor, withindoors

PREPS 13 **in, into; within,** at, inside, **inside of,** in the limits of; to the heart *or* core of

WORD ELEMENTS 14 en-, em-, end-, endo-, ent-, ento-, eso-, infra-, in-, im-, il-, ir-, inter-, intra-, ob-

208 CENTRALITY

NOUNS 1 **centrality,** centralness, middleness, central *or* middle *or* mid position; equidistance; centricity, centricality; concentricity; centripetalism

2 **center,** centrum; **middle** 819, midpoint, **heart, core, nucleus; core of one's being, where one lives; kernel; pith,** marrow, medulla; **nub, hub,** nave, axis, pivot, fulcrum; **navel,** umbilicus, omphalos, belly button <nf>; bull's-eye; dead center; omphalos; "the still point of the turning world"— T S Eliot; storm center, eye of the storm

3 <biological terms> central body, centriole, centrosome, centrosphere

4 focus, focal point, prime focus, point of convergence; **center of interest** *or* attention, focus of attention; center of consciousness; **center of attraction, centerpiece,** clou, mecca, cynosure; star, key figure; polestar, lodestar; magnet; center of gravity

5 nerve center, ganglion, center of activity, hub, epicenter, hotbed, vital center; control center, guidance center

6 headquarters *or* **HQ,** central station, central office, main office, central administration, seat, base, **base of operations,** center of authority; general headquarters *or* **GHQ,** command post *or* **CP,** company headquarters; where the action is <nf>

7 metropolis, capital; art center, cultural center, medical center, shopping center, transportation center, trade center, manufacturing center, tourist center, community center, civic center, etc; capital city; holy place, place of pilgrimage

8 centralization, centering; nucleation; **focalization,** focus, focusing; convergence 169; **concentration,** concentralization, pooling; centralism

VERBS **9 centralize, center,** middle; center round; center on *or* in, pivot on, revolve around

10 focus, focalize, come to a point *or* focus, bring to *or* into focus; bring *or* come to a head, get to the heart of the matter, home in on; zero in on, pinpoint; draw a bead on *and* get a handle on <nf>; **concentrate,** concenter, get it together <nf>; **channel,** direct, canalize, channelize; converge 169.2

ADJS **11 central,** centric, **middle** 819; centermost, middlemost, **midmost; equidistant;** centralized, concentrated; umbilical, omphalic; axial, **pivotal,** key; centroidal; centrosymmetric; geocentric; epicentral; halfway

12 nuclear, nucleate, core

13 focal, confocal; converging; centrolineal, centripetal; cynosural; pivotal

14 concentric; homocentric, centric; **coaxial,** coaxal

ADVS **15 centrally,** in the center *or* middle of, at the heart of

209 ENVIRONMENT

NOUNS **1 environment, surroundings, environs,** surround, ambience, entourage, circle, circumjacencies, circumambiencies, **circumstances,** environing circumstances, *alentours* <Fr>; **precincts,** ambit, purlieus, **milieu; neighborhood, vicinity,** vicinage, area; **suburbs,** burbs <nf>; outskirts, outposts, borderlands; borders, boundaries, limits, periphery, perimeter, compass, circuit; **context, situation;** habitat 228; total environment, configuration, gestalt

2 setting, background, backdrop, ground, surround, field, scene, arena, theater, locale, confines; back, rear, hinterland, distance; stage, stage setting, stage set, *mise-en-scène* <Fr>

3 <surrounding influence or condition> **milieu, ambience, atmosphere, climate, air,** aura, spirit, feeling, feel, quality, color, local color, sense, sense of place, note, tone, overtone, undertone, vibrations *or* vibes <nf>

4 <natural or suitable environment> **element,** medium; **the environment**

5 surrounding, encompassment, environment, circumambience *or* circumambiency, circumjacence *or* circumjacency; containment, **enclosure** 212; **encirclement,** cincture, encincture, circumcincture, circling, girdling, girding; **envelopment,** enfoldment, encompassment, encompassing, compassing, embracement; circumposition; circumflexion; inclusion 771, involvement 898

VERBS **6 surround, environ,** compass, **encompass,** enclose, close; go round *or* around, compass about, outlie; **envelop,** enfold, lap, wrap, enwrap, embrace, enclasp, embosom, embay, involve, invest

7 encircle, circle, ensphere, belt, belt in, zone, cincture, encincture; **girdle,** gird, begird, engird; ring, band; loop; wreathe, wreathe *or* twine around

ADJS **8 environing, surrounding,** encompassing, enclosing; **enveloping,** wrapping, enwrapping, enfolding, embracing; **encircling,** circling; bordering, peripheral, perimetric; circumjacent, circumferential, circumambient, ambient; circumfluent, circumfluous; circumflex; **roundabout,** suburban, neighboring, neighbhorhood

9 environmental, environal; **ecological**

10 surrounded, environed, compassed, **encompassed,** enclosed, on all sides, hemmed-in; **enveloped,** wrapped, enfolded, lapped, wreathed

11 encircled, circled, ringed, cinctured, encinctured, belted, girdled, girt, begirt, zoned

ADVS **12 around,** round, **about,** round about, in the neighborhood *or* vicinity *or* vicinage; close, close about

13 all round, all about, on every side, on all sides, on all hands, right and left

WORD ELEMENTS **14** amph-, amphi-, circum-, peri-

210 CIRCUMSCRIPTION

NOUNS **1 circumscription, limiting,** circumscribing, **bounding, demarcation,** delimitation, definition, determination, specification; limit-setting, inclusion-exclusion, circling-in *or* -out, encincture, boundary-marking; containment

2 **limitation, limiting, restriction,** restricting, confinement 212.1, prescription, proscription, restraint, discipline, moderation, continence; qualification, **hedging;** bounds 211, boundary, cap, limit 211.3; time-limit, time constraint; quota; small space 258.3; proviso, condition

3 **patent, copyright,** certificate of invention, *brevet d'invention* <Fr>; **trademark, logo** or logotype, registered trademark, trade name, service mark

VERBS 4 **circumscribe, bound; mark off** or mark out, stake out, lay off, rope off; **demarcate,** delimit, delimitate, draw or mark or set or lay out boundaries, circle in or out, hedge in, set the limit, mark the periphery; **define,** determine, fix, specify; surround 209.6; enclose 212.5

5 **limit, restrict, restrain, bound, confine,** cap, ground <nf>; straiten, narrow, tighten; specialize; stint, scant; **condition,** qualify, hedge, hedge about; constrain; draw the line, set an end point or a stopping place; set a quota; discipline, moderate, contain; restrain oneself, pull one's punches <nf>; **patent, copyright,** register

ADJS 6 **circumscribed,** circumscript; ringed or circled or hedged about; **demarcated, delimited, defined,** definite, determined, determinate, specific, stated, set, fixed; surrounded 209.10, encircled 209.11

7 **limited, restricted,** bound, **bounded, finite;** confined 212.10, prescribed, proscribed, cramped, strait, straitened, narrow; conditioned, qualified, hedged, capped; disciplined, moderated; **deprived,** in straitened circumstances, pinched, inhibiting, on short commons, on short rations, strapped; patented, registered, protected, copyrighted

8 **restricted,** out of bounds, off-limits

9 **limiting, restricting,** defining, determining, determinative, confining; limitative, limitary, restrictive, definitive, exclusive; frozen, rationed

10 **terminal,** limital; limitable, terminable

211 BOUNDS

NOUNS 1 **bounds, limits,** boundaries, limitations, **confines, pale,** marches, bourns, verges, edges, outlines, outer markings, skirts, outskirts, **fringes,** metes, metes and bounds; periphery, **perimeter;** coordinates, parameters; **compass, circumference,** circumscription 210

2 **outline, contour,** delineation, lines, lineaments, shapes, figure, figuration, **configuration,** gestalt; **features,** main features; **profile, silhouette;** relief; skeleton, framework, frame, armature

3 **boundary, bound, limit,** limitation, extremity 794.5; **barrier,** block, claustrum; delimitation, hedge, break or breakoff point, cutoff, cutoff point,

terminus; time limit, time frame, term, deadline, target date, terminal date, time allotment; finish, **end** 820, tail end; **start,** starting line or point, mark; **limiting factor,** determinant, limit or boundary condition; bracket, brackets, **bookends** <nf>; threshold, limen; upper limit, ceiling, apogee, high-water mark; lower limit, floor, low-water mark, nadir; **confine,** march, mark, bourn, mete, compass, circumscription; **boundary line, line, border line,** frontier, division line, interface, break, boundary, line of demarcation or circumvallation

4 **border,** limbus, bordure <heraldry>, **edge,** limb, **verge, brink,** brow, **brim, rim, margin,** marge, **skirt, fringe, hem,** list, selvage or selvedge, side; **forefront, cutting edge,** front line, vanguard 216.2; sideline; shore, bank, coast; **lip,** labium, labrum, labellum; flange; ledge; frame, enframement, mat; featheredge; ragged edge

5 **frontier, border, borderland,** border ground, marchland, march, marches; outskirts, outpost; frontier post; iron curtain, bamboo curtain, Berlin wall; Pillars of Hercules; three-mile or twelve-mile limit

6 **curb,** kerb <Brit>, curbing; border stone, curbstone, kerbstone <Brit>, edgestone

7 **edging, bordering,** bordure <heraldry>, **trimming,** binding, skirting; fringe, fimbriation, fimbria; **hem,** selvage, list, welt; frill, frilling; beading, flounce, furbelow, galloon, motif, ruffle, valance

VERBS 8 **bound,** circumscribe 210.4, surround 209.6, limit 210.5, enclose 212.5, divide, separate

9 **outline,** contour; **delineate;** silhouette, profile, limn

10 **border, edge, bound, rim, skirt, hem, hem in, ringe,** befringe, lap, list, margin, marge, marginate, march, verge, line, side; **adjoin** 223.9; **frame,** enframe, set off; trim, bind; purl; purfle

ADJS 11 **bordering, fringing,** rimming, skirting; **bounding,** boundary, **limiting,** limit, determining or determinant or determinative; threshold, liminal, limbic; extreme, terminal; **marginal, borderline,** frontier; coastal, littoral

12 **bordered,** edged; margined, marged, marginate, marginated; **fringed,** befringed, trimmed, skirted, fimbriate, fimbriated

13 lipped, labial, labiate

14 outlining, delineatory; peripheral, perimetric, perimetrical, circumferential; outlined, **in outline**

ADVS 15 **on the verge, on the brink,** on the borderline, on the point, on the edge, on the ragged edge, at the threshold, at the limit or bound; **peripherally,** marginally, at the periphery

16 **thus far,** so far, thus far and no farther

212 ENCLOSURE

NOUNS **1 enclosure; confinement,** containing, containment, circumscription 210, immurement, walling- *or* hedging- *or* hemming- *or* boxing- *or* fencing-in, circumvallation; **imprisonment,** incarceration, jailing, locking-up, lockdown; **siege,** besieging, beleaguerment, blockade, blockading, cordoning, quarantine, besetment; inclusion 771; **envelopment** 209.5

2 packaging, packing, package; boxing, crating, encasement; canning, tinning <Brit>; bottling; **wrapping,** enwrapment, bundling; shrink-wrapping

3 <enclosed place> **enclosure,** close, **confine,** precinct, enclave, pale, paling, list, cincture; **cloister; pen, coop,** fold; **yard,** park, court, courtyard, curtilage, toft; square, quadrangle, quad <nf>; **field,** delimited field, **arena,** theater, ground; reserve, sanctuary; **container** 195

4 fence, wall, boundary 211.3, **barrier;** stone wall; paling, palisade; rail, railing; balustrade, balustrading; moat; arcade

VERBS **5 enclose,** close in, bound, include, **contain;** compass, encompass; **surround,** encircle 209.7; **shut** *or* **pen in,** coop in; **fence in,** wall in, wall up, rail in, rail off, screen off, curtain off; **hem** *or* **hedge in,** box in, pocket; shut *or* coop *or* mew up; pen, coop, corral, cage, impound, mew; **imprison,** incarcerate, jail, lock up, lock down; **besiege,** beset, beleaguer, leaguer, cordon, cordon off, quarantine, blockade; yard, yard up; house in; chamber; stable, kennel, shrine, enshrine; **wrap** 295.20

6 confine, immure; quarantine; cramp, straiten, encase; cloister, closet, cabin, crib; bury, entomb, coffin, casket; bottle up *or* in, box up *or* in

7 fence, wall, fence in, fence up; pale, rail, bar; pen up; hem, hem in, hedge, hedge in, hedge out; picket, palisade; bulkhead in

8 parenthesize, bracket, precede and follow, bookend

9 package, pack, parcel; box, box up, case, encase, crate, carton; can, tin <Brit>; bottle, jar, pot; barrel, cask, tank; sack, bag; basket, hamper; capsule, encyst; contain; **wrap,** enwrap, bundle; shrink-wrap; bandage

ADJS **10 enclosed,** closed-in; **confined,** bound, immured, cloistered, "cabined, cribbed, confined"—Shakespeare; **imprisoned,** incarcerated, jailed; caged, cramped, restrained, corralled; besieged, beleaguered, leaguered, beset, cordoned, cordoned off, quarantined, blockaded; **shut-in,** pent-up, penned, cooped, mewed, walled- *or* hedged- *or* hemmed- *or* boxed- *or* fenced-in, fenced, walled, paled, railed, barred; hemmed, hedged

11 enclosing, confining, **cloistered,** cloisterlike, claustral, parietal, surrounding 209.8; limiting 210.9

12 packed, packaged, boxed, crated, canned, tinned <Brit>, parceled, cased, encased; bottled; capsuled, encapsuled; **wrapped,** enwrapped, bundled; shrink-wrapped; prepacked; vacuum-packed; bandaged, sheathed

213 INTERPOSITION

<a putting or lying between>

NOUNS **1 interposition, interposing,** interposal, interlocation, intermediacy, interjacence; **intervention,** intervenience, intercurrence, slipping-in, sandwiching; leafing-in, interleaving, interfoliation, tipping-in; **intrusion** 214

2 interjection, interpolation, introduction, throwing- *or* tossing-in, **injection,** insinuation; intercalation, interlineation; **insertion** 191; interlocution, remark, parenthetical *or* side *or* incidental *or* casual remark, *obiter dictum* <L>, aside, parenthesis; episode; infix, insert

3 interspersion, interfusion, interlardment, interpenetration

4 intermediary, intermedium, mediary, medium; link, **connecting link,** tie, connection, **go-between,** liaison; middleman, broker, agent, wholesaler, jobber, distributor; **mediator** 466.3

5 partition, dividing wall, division, separation, *cloison* <Fr>; **wall, barrier;** panel; paries, parietes; brattice <mining>; bulkhead; diaphragm, midriff, midsection; septum, interseptum, septulum, dissepiment; **border** 211.4, **dividing line,** property line, party wall; **buffer, bumper,** mat, fender, cushion, pad, shock pad, collision mat; buffer state

VERBS **6 interpose, interject, interpolate,** intercalate, interjaculate; **mediate, go between,** liaise <Brit nf>; **intervene;** put between, sandwich; **insert in,** stick in, introduce in, insinuate in, sandwich in, slip in, inject in, implant in; leaf in, interleaf, tip in, interfoliate; **foist in,** fudge in, work in, drag in, lug in, drag *or* lug in by the heels, worm in, squeeze in, smuggle in, throw in, run in, thrust in, edge in, wedge in; **intrude** 214.5

7 intersperse, interfuse, interlard, interpenetrate; intersow, intersprinkle

8 partition, set apart, separate, divide; **wall off,** fence off, screen off, curtain off

ADJS **9** interjectional, interpolative, intercalary; parenthetical, episodic

10 intervening, intervenient, **interjacent,** intercurrent;

intermediate, intermediary, medial, mean, medium, mesne, median, **middle**

11 partitioned, walled; mural; septal, parietal

PREPS **12 between, betwixt,** 'twixt, betwixt and between <nf>; **among, amongst,** 'mongst; **amid, amidst,** mid, 'mid, midst, 'midst; in the midst of, in the thick of

WORD ELEMENTS **13** medi-, medio-, mes-, meso-; inter-, intra-

214 INTRUSION

NOUNS **1 intrusion,** obtrusion, **interloping;** interposition 213, interposal, imposition, insinuation, **interference,** intervention, interventionism, interruption, injection, interjection 213.2; **encroachment,** entrenchment, trespass, trespassing, unlawful entry; impingement, **infringement,** invasion, incursion, inroad, influx, irruption, infiltration; entrance 189

2 meddling, intermeddling; **butting-in** and kibitzing and sticking one's nose in<nf>; **meddlesomeness, intrusiveness, forwardness,** obtrusiveness; **officiousness,** impertinence, presumption, presumptuousness; inquisitiveness 981.1

3 intruder, interloper, trespasser; crasher and gate-crasher <nf>, unwelcome or uninvited guest; invader, encroacher, infiltrator

4 meddler, intermeddler; **busybody, pry,** Paul Pry, prier, Nosey Parker or nosey Parker or Nosy Parker <nf>, snoop or snooper, *yenta* <Yiddish>, **kibitzer** and backseat driver <nf>

VERBS **5 intrude,** obtrude, **interlope;** come between, **interpose** 213.6, insert oneself, **intervene, interfere,** insinuate, impose; **encroach, infringe,** impinge, **trespass,** trespass on or upon, trench, entrench, invade, infiltrate; **break in upon,** break in, burst in, charge in, crash in, smash in, storm in; **barge in** <nf>, irrupt, **cut in,** thrust in 191.7, push in, press in, rush in, throng in, crowd in, squeeze in, elbow in, muscle in <nf>; **butt in** and **horn in** and chisel in and muscle in <nf>; appoint oneself; crash and crash the gates <nf>; **get in,** get in on, creep in, steal in, sneak in, slink in, slip in; foist in, worm or work in, edge in, put in or shove in one's oar; **foist oneself upon,** thrust oneself upon; put on or upon, impose on or upon, put one's two cents in <nf>

6 interrupt, put in, cut in, break in; jump in, chime in and chip in and put in one's two-cents worth <nf>

7 meddle, intermeddle, busybody, not mind one's business; **meddle with, tamper with,** mix oneself up with, inject oneself into, monkey with, fool with or around with <nf>, mess with or around with <nf>; **pry,** Paul-Pry, snoop, nose, **stick or poke one's nose in,** stick one's long nose into; have a finger in, have a finger in the pie; kibitz <nf>

ADJS **8 intrusive,** obtrusive, **interfering,** intervenient, invasive, interruptive

9 meddlesome, meddling; **officious,** overofficious, self-appointed, impertinent, presumptuous; **busybody,** busy; pushing, pushy, forward; **prying,** nosy or nosey and snoopy <nf>; inquisitive 981.5

PHRS **10** <nf terms> **none of your business;** what's it to you?, **mind your own business,** keep your nose out of this, **butt out,** go soak your head, go sit on a tack, go roll your hoop, go peddle your fish, go fly a kite, go chase yourself, go jump in the lake; too many cooks spoil the broth

215 CONTRAPOSITION
<a placing over against>

NOUNS **1** contraposition, anteposition, posing against or over against; **opposition,** opposing, opposure; **antithesis,** contrast, ironic or contrastive juxtaposition; confrontment, **confrontation;** polarity, polar opposition, **polarization;** contrariety 779; contention 457; hostility 451.2

2 opposites, antipodes, polar opposites, contraries; **poles,** opposite poles, antipoles, counterpoles, North Pole, South Pole; antipodal points, antipoints; contrapositives <logic>; night and day, black and white

3 opposite side, other side, the other side of the picture or coin, other face; **reverse, inverse, obverse, converse;** heads, tails <of a coin>; flip side and B-side <nf>

VERBS **4** contrapose, **oppose,** contrast, match, **set over against,** pose against or over against, put in opposition, set or pit against one another; **confront,** face, front, stand or lie opposite, stand opposed or vis-à-vis; be at loggerheads, be eyeball to eyeball, bump heads, meet head-on; counteract 451.3; contend; subtend; **polarize;** contraposit <logic>

ADJS **5 contrapositive,** opposite, opposing, **facing,** confronting, confrontational, confrontive, eyeball-to-eyeball, one-on-one; **opposed,** on opposite sides, adversarial, at loggerheads, at daggers drawn, antithetic, antithetical; **reverse, inverse, obverse, converse; antipodal; polar,** polarized one-on-one, up against

ADVS **6 opposite,** poles apart, at opposite extremes; contrary, contrariwise, counter; just opposite, **face-to-face,** vis-à-vis, *front à front* <Fr>, nose to nose, one on one, eyeball-to-eyeball, back to back

PREPS **7 opposite to,** in opposition to, against, over against; versus, v *or* vs; **facing, across, fronting,** confronting, **in front of;** toward

WORD ELEMENTS **8** ant-, anti-, anth-, cat-, cata-, cath-, kat-, kata-, co-, contra-, counter-, enantio-, ob-

216 FRONT

NOUNS **1 front, fore,** forepart, forequarter, foreside, forefront, forehand; **priority,** anteriority; front office; **frontier** 211.5; foreland; **foreground;** proscenium; frontage; front page; frontispiece; **preface,** front matter, foreword; prefix; front view, front elevation, front seat, front yard; **head,** heading; **face,** façade, frontal; fascia; **false front,** window dressing, display, persona; front man; bold *or* brave front, brave face; facet; obverse <of a coin or medal>, head <of a coin>; lap

2 vanguard, van, point, point man; **spearhead,** advance guard, **forefront, cutting edge,** avant-garde, outguard; scout; **pioneer;** precursor 816; **front-runner,** leader, first in line; **front,** battlefront, line, front line, forward line, battle line, line of departure; front rank, first line, first line of battle; **outpost,** farthest outpost; **bridgehead,** beachhead, airhead, railhead; advanced base

3 prow, bow, stem, rostrum, figurehead, nose, beak; bowsprit, jib boom; forecastle, forepeak; foredeck; foremast

4 face, facies, **visage;** physiognomy, phiz *and* dial <nf>; **countenance,** features, lineaments, favor; mug *and* mush *and* pan *and* kisser *and* map *and* puss <nf>

5 forehead, brow, lofty brow

6 chin, point of the chin, button <nf>

VERBS **7** be *or* stand in front, **lead, head,** head up; **get ahead of,** steal a march on, take the lead, come to the front *or* fore, forge ahead; be the front-runner, lead, lead the pack *or* field, be first; **pioneer;** front, front for, represent, speak for; spearhead; push the envelope <nf>

8 confront, front, affront <old>, **face, meet, encounter,** breast, stem, brave, meet squarely, square up to, come to grips with, head *or* wade into, meet face to face *or* eyeball to eyeball *or* one-on-one, come face to face with, look in the face *or* eye, stare in the face, stand up to, stand fast, hold one's ground, hang tough *and* tough it out *and* gut it out <nf>; call someone's bluff, call *or* bring someone to account; **confront with, face with,** bring face to face with, tell one to one's face, cast *or* throw in one's teeth, present to, **put** *or* **bring before,** set *or* place before, lay before, put *or* lay it on the line; bring up, bring forward; put it to, put

it up to; **challenge,** dare, defy, fly in the teeth of, throw down the gauntlet, ask for trouble, start something, do something about it

9 front on, face upon, give upon, face *or* look toward, look out upon, look over, **overlook**

ADJS **10 front, frontal, anterior; full-face, full-frontal,** physiognomic; **fore, forward,** forehand; foremost, headmost; first, earliest, **pioneering, trail-blazing, advanced,** front-running; **leading,** up-front <nf>, first, chief, head, prime, primary; **confronting,** confrontational, head-on, one-on-one *and* eyeball-to-eyeball <nf>; **ahead, in front,** one-up, one jump *or* move ahead

11 fronting, facing, looking on *or* out on, opposite

ADVS **12 before, ahead,** out *or* up ahead, **in front,** in the front, in the lead, in the van, in advance, **in the forefront,** in the foreground; **to the fore,** to the front; foremost, headmost, first; before one's face *or* eyes, under one's nose

13 frontward, frontwards, **forward,** forwards, vanward, **headward,** headwards, **onward,** onwards; **facing** 215.7

217 REAR

NOUNS **1 rear, rear end, hind end,** hind part, hinder part, afterpart, rearward, **posterior, behind,** breech, stern, tail, tail end; **afterpiece,** tailpiece, heelpiece, heel; **back,** back side, reverse <of a coin or medal>, tail <of a coin>; back door, postern, postern door; back seat, rumble seat; hindhead, occiput; wake, train; back burner

2 rear guard, rear, rear area, backyard

3 back, dorsum, ridge; dorsal region, lumbar region, backbone; hindquarter; loin

4 buttocks, rump, bottom, posterior, derrière; croup, crupper; podex; haunches; gluteal region; nates

5 <nf terms> **ass,** arse *and* bum <chiefly Brit>, behind, backside, buns, **butt, can,** cheeks, hind end, nether cheeks, stern, tail, rusty-dusty, **fanny,** prat, keister, popo, rear, rear end, tuchis *or* tushy *or* tush

6 tail, cauda, caudation, caudal appendage; tailpiece, scut <of a hare, rabbit, or deer>, brush <of a fox>, fantail <of fowl>; rattail, rat's-tail; dock, stub; caudal fin; **queue,** cue, **pigtail**

7 stern, heel; poop, transom, counter, fantail; sternpost, rudderpost; after mast

VERBS **8** <be behind> **bring up the rear,** come last, **follow,** come after; trail, trail behind, lag behind, draggle, **straggle;** fall behind, fall back, fall astern; **back up, back,** go back, go backwards, regress 163.5, retrogress, get behind; revert 859.4

ADJS **9 rear,** rearward, **back,** backward, retrograde, **posterior,** postern, tail; after *or* aft; **hind, hinder;**

hindmost, hindermost, hindhand, posteriormost, **aftermost,** aftmost, rearmost; latter

10 <anatomy> posterial, dorsal, retral, tergal, lumbar, gluteal, sciatic, occipital

11 **tail,** caudal, caudate, caudated, tailed; taillike, caudiform

12 backswept, swept-back

ADVS 13 **behind, in the rear, in back of;** in the background; behind the scenes; behind one's back; back to back; tandem

14 **after;** aft, abaft, baft, astern; aback

15 **rearward,** rearwards, to the rear, **hindward,** hindwards, **backward,** backwards, posteriorly, retrad, tailward, tailwards

218 SIDE

NOUNS 1 **side, flank, hand;** laterality, sidedness, handedness; unilaterality, unilateralism, bilaterality, bilateralism, etc, multilaterality, many-sidedness; border 211.4; parallelism 203; bank, shore, coast; siding, planking; beam; broadside; quarter; hip, haunch; cheek, jowl, chop; temple; **profile,** side-view, half-face view; side entrance, side door

2 **lee side, lee,** leeward; lee shore; lee tide; lee wheel, lee helm, lee anchor, lee sheet, lee tack

3 **windward side, windward,** windwards, weather side, weather, weatherboard; weather wheel, weather helm, weather anchor, weather sheet, weather tack, weather rail, weather bow, weather deck; weather roll; windward tide, weather-going tide, windward ebb, windward flood

VERBS 4 **side, flank;** edge, skirt, border 211.10; stand side by side

5 **go sideways, sidle,** lateral, lateralize, **edge, veer, angle, slant, skew,** sidestep; go crabwise; **sideslip, skid;** make leeway

ADJS 6 **side, lateral;** flanking, skirting, facing, oblique; **beside,** to the side, off to one side; **alongside,** parallel 203.6; next-beside; **sidelong,** sideling, **sidewise,** sideway, **sideways,** sideward, **sidewards,** glancing; leeward, lee; windward, weather; side-by-side

7 **sided, flanked,** handed; lateral; **one-sided,** unilateral, unilateralist, **two-sided, bilateral,** bilateralist, etc; dihedral, bifacial; **three-sided, trilateral,** trihedral, triquetrous; **four-sided, quadrilateral,** tetrahedral, etc; **many-sided, multilateral,** multifaceted, polyhedral; left-hand, sinistral, right-hand, dextral

ADVS 8 **laterally,** laterad; **sideways,** sideway, **sidewise, sidewards,** sideward, sideling, sidling, sidelong, aside, crabwise; side-to-side; **edgeways,** edgeway, **edgewise; widthwise, widthways,**

thwartwise; askance, askant, asquint, glancingly; broadside, **broadside on,** on the beam; on its side, on its beam ends; on the other hand; right and left

9 **leeward,** to leeward, alee, downwind; **windward,** to windward, weatherward, aweather, upwind

10 **aside,** on one side, **to one side,** to the side, sidelong, on the side, on the one hand, on one hand, on the other hand; **alongside,** in parallel 203.7, side-by-side; nearby, in juxtaposition 223.21; away

PREPS 11 **beside, alongside, abreast,** abeam, by, on the flank of, along by, **by the side of,** along the side of

PHRS 12 **side by side,** cheek to cheek, cheek by cheek, cheek by jowl, shoulder to shoulder, yardarm to yardarm

219 RIGHT SIDE

NOUNS 1 **right side, right,** off side <of a horse or vehicle>, starboard; Epistle side, decanal side; recto <of a book>; right field; starboard tack; right wing; right-winger, conservative, reactionary

2 **rightness,** dextrality; dexterity, **right-handedness;** dextroversion, dextrocularity, dextroduction; dextrorotation, dextrogyration

3 right-hander; righty <nf>

ADJS 4 **right, right-hand,** dextral, dexter; off, **starboard;** rightmost; dextrorse; dextropedal; dextrocardial; dextrocerebral; dextrocular; **clockwise,** dextrorotary, dextrogyrate, dextrogyratory; right-wing, right-wingish, right-of-center, conservative, reactionary, dry <Brit nf>

5 **right-handed,** dextromanual, dexterous

6 **ambidextrous,** ambidextral, ambidexter; dextrosinistral, sinistrodextral

ADVS 7 **rightward,** rightwards, rightwardly, **right, to the right,** dextrally, dextrad; on the right, dexter; starboard, astarboard

220 LEFT SIDE

NOUNS 1 **left side, left, left hand,** left-hand side, wrong side <nf>, near or nigh side <of a horse or vehicle>, portside, port, larboard; Gospel side, cantorial side, verso <of a book>; left field; port tack; left wing, left-winger, radical, liberal, progressive

2 **leftness,** sinistrality, **left-handedness;** sinistration; levoversion, levoduction; levorotation, sinistrogyration

3 **left-hander, southpaw** and lefty and portsider <nf>

ADJS 4 **left, left-hand,** sinister, sinistral; near, nigh; **larboard, port;** sinistrorse; sinistrocerebral;

sinistrocular; counterclockwise, levorotatory, sinistrogyrate; left-wing, left-wingish, left-of-center, radical, liberal, progressive, wet <Brit nf>

5 left-handed, sinistromanual, sinistral, lefty *and* southpaw <nf>

ADVS **6 leftward,** leftwards, leftwardly, **left, to the left,** sinistrally, sinister, sinistrad; on the left; larboard, port, aport

221 PRESENCE

NOUNS **1 presence,** being here *or* there, hereness, thereness, physical *or* actual presence, spiritual presence; **immanence,** indwellingness, **inherence; whereness, immediacy;** ubiety; availability, accessibility; nearness 223; **occurrence** 831.2, existence 761; manifestness, materialness

2 omnipresence, all-presence, **ubiquity;** continuum, plenum; infinity

3 permeation, pervasion, penetration; **suffusion,** transfusion, perfusion, diffusion, imbuement; absorption; **overrunning,** overspreading, ripple effect, overswarming, whelming, overwhelming

4 attendance, frequenting, frequence; participation; number present; turnout *and* box office *and* draw <nf>

5 attender, visitor, churchgoer, moviegoer, etc; **patron; fan** *and* buff <nf>, aficionado, supporter; **frequenter,** habitué, haunter; spectator 918; theatergoer; audience 48.6; regular customer, regular

VERBS **6 be present,** be located *or* situated 159.10, be there, be found, be met with; **occur** 830.5, exist 761.8; lie, stand, remain; fall in the way of; dwell in, indwell, inhere

7 pervade, permeate, penetrate; **suffuse,** inform, transfuse, perfuse, diffuse, leaven, imbue; **fill,** extend throughout, leave no void, occupy; **overrun,** overswarm, overspread, bespread, run through, meet one at every turn, whelm, overwhelm; creep *or* crawl *or* swarm with, be lousy with <nf>, teem with; honeycomb

8 attend, be at, be present at, find oneself at, **go** *or* **come to;** appear 33.8, turn up, set foot in, show up <nf>, show one's face, make *or* put in an appearance, give the pleasure of one's company, make a personal appearance; materialize; **visit, take in** *and* do *and* catch <nf>; sit in *or* at; be on hand, be on deck <nf>; watch, see; witness, look on, *assister* <Fr>; participate, take part

9 revisit, return to, go back to, come again

10 frequent, haunt, resort to, hang *and* hang around *and* hang about *and* hang out <nf>

11 present oneself, report; report for duty

ADJS **12 present,** attendant; **on hand,** on deck <nf>,

on board, in attendance; **immediate,** immanent, indwelling, inherent, **available, accessible, at hand,** in view, within reach *or* sight *or* call, in place

13 omnipresent, all-present, ubiquitous, everywhere; continuous, uninterrupted, infinite

14 pervasive, pervading, suffusive, perfusive, diffusive, suffusing

15 permeated, saturated, shot through, filled with, perfused, suffused, imbued; honeycombed; crawling, creeping, swarming, teeming, lousy with <nf>

ADVS **16 here, there**

17 in person, personally, bodily, **in the flesh** <nf>, in one's own person, *in propria persona* <L>

PREPS **18 in the presence of,** in the face of, under the eyes *or* nose of, **before**

PHRS **19** all present and accounted for; standing room only *or* SRO

222 ABSENCE

NOUNS **1 absence,** nonpresence, awayness; nowhereness, **nonexistence** 762; want, **lack,** total lack, blank, deprivation; nonoccurrence, neverness; **subtraction** 255

2 vacancy, vacuity, voidness, **emptiness,** blankness, hollowness, inanition; **bareness,** barrenness, desolateness, bleakness, desertedness; **nonoccupancy,** nonoccupation, vacancy, noninhabitance, nonresidence; vacancy, job vacancy, opening, open place *or* post, vacant post

3 void, vacuum, blank, emptiness, empty space, inanity, vacuity; **nothingness;** *tabula rasa* <L>, clean *or* blank slate; **nothing** 762.2

4 absence, nonattendance, **absenting, leaving,** taking leave, **departure** 188; "to leave is to die a little"— French saying, "Say, is not absence death to those who love?"—Pope; running away, fleeing, decamping, bolting, skedaddling *and* absquatulating <old nf>, abscondence, scarpering <Brit nf>, desertion, defection; **disappearance** 34, escape 369; **absentation,** nonappearance, default, unauthorized *or* unexcused absence; **truancy, hooky** <nf>, French leave, **cut** <nf>; **absence without leave** *or* AWOL; **absenteeism,** truantism, absentation; **leave, leave of absence,** furlough; **vacation,** holiday, paid vacation, paid holiday, time off, day off, comp *or* compensation time; authorized *or* excused absence, sick leave; sabbatical

5 absentee, truant, no-show, missing person

6 nobody, no one, no man, no woman, not one, not a single one *or* person, **not a soul** *or* **blessed soul** *or* **living soul,** never a one, ne'er a one, nary one <nf>, nobody on earth *or* under the sun, nobody present; nonperson, unperson; nonentity

VERBS **7 be absent, stay away,** keep away, keep out of the way, not come, not show up <nf>, not turn up, turn up missing <nf>, stay away in droves <nf>, fail to appear, default, sit out, include oneself out <nf>

8 absent oneself, take leave or **leave of absence,** go on leave or furlough; **vacation,** go on vacation or holiday, take time off, take off from work; slip off or away, duck or sneak out <nf>, slip out, make oneself scarce <nf>, leave the scene, bow out, exit, vacate, **depart** 188.6, **disappear** 34.2, escape 369.6; defect, desert

9 play truant, go AWOL, take French leave; play hooky, cut or skip <nf>, cut classes; jump ship

10 <nf terms> **split,** bugger off, fuck off, f off, make tracks, pull up stakes, push along, scarper <Brit>, push off, skedaddle or absquatulate <old>, **haul ass,** bag ass, **beat it, blow,** boogie, bug out, cut, **cut out,** cut and run, peel out, bunk off or piss off <Brit>, scram, shove off, vamoose

ADJS **11 absent,** not present, nonattendant, **away, gone,** departed, disappeared, vanished, absconded, out of sight; **missing,** among the missing, wanting, **lacking,** not found, nowhere to be found, omitted, taken away, subtracted, deleted; no longer present or with us or among us; long-lost; **nonexistent;** conspicuous by its absence

12 nonresident, not in residence, from home, **away from home,** on leave or vacation or holiday, on sabbatical leave; on tour, on the road; abroad, overseas

13 truant, absent without leave or **AWOL**

14 vacant, empty, hollow, inane, **bare, vacuous, void,** without content, with nothing inside, devoid, null, null and void; **blank,** clear, white, bleached; featureless, unrelieved, characterless, bland, insipid; **barren** 891.4

15 available, open, free, **unoccupied,** unfilled, **uninhabited,** unpopulated, unpeopled, untaken, untenanted, tenantless, untended, unmanned, unstaffed; **deserted,** abandoned, forsaken, godforsaken <nf>

ADVS **16 absently; vacantly, emptily,** hollowly, vacuously, blankly

17 nowhere, in no place, neither here nor there; nowhither

18 away 188.21, **elsewhere,** somewhere else, not here; elsewhither

PREPS **19 absent,** lacking, sans; void of, empty of, free of, **without** 992.17

223 NEARNESS

NOUNS **1 nearness, closeness,** nighness, **proximity,** propinquity, intimacy, immediacy; approximation, approach, convergence; a rough idea <nf>; **vicinity,** vicinage, **neighborhood,** environs, surroundings, surround, setting, grounds, purlieus, confines, precinct; **foreground,** immediate foreground; convenience, handiness, accessibility

2 short distance, short way, little ways, **step,** short step, span, brief span, short piece <nf>, a little, intimate distance; shortcut; short range; close quarters or range or grips; middle distance; **stone's throw,** spitting distance <nf>, bowshot, gunshot, pistol shot; earshot, earreach, a whoop and a whoop and a holler and two whoops and a holler <nf>, ace, bit <nf>, **hair, hairbreadth** or **hairsbreadth,** finger's breadth or width, an inch; inch, millimeter, centimeter; near miss

3 juxtaposition, apposition, adjacency; **contiguity,** contiguousness, conterminousness or coterminousness; butting, abuttal, abutment; adjunction, junction 800.1, connection, union; **conjunction,** conjugation; appulse, syzygy; perigee, perihelion

4 meeting, meeting up, joining, joining up, **encounter;** juncture; confrontation; rencontre; near-miss, collision course, near thing, narrow squeak or brush

5 contact, touch, touching, attouchement <Fr>, taction, tangency, contingence; gentle or tentative contact, caress, brush, glance, nudge, kiss, rub, graze; impingement, impingence; osculation

6 neighbor, neighborer, next-door or immediate neighbor; borderer; abutter, adjoiner; bystander, onlooker, looker-on; tangent; buffer state; ringside seat

VERBS **7 near, come near,** nigh, draw near or nigh, **approach** 167.3, come within shouting distance; **converge,** shake hands <nf>; come within an ace or an inch

8 be near or **around,** be in the vicinity or neighborhood, **approximate, approach,** get warm <nf>, come near, have something at hand or at one's fingertips; give or get a rough idea <nf>

9 adjoin, join, conjoin, **connect,** butt, **abut,** abut on or upon, be contiguous, be in contact; **neighbor,** border, **border on** or **upon,** verge on or upon; lie by, stand by

10 contact, come in contact, touch, feel, impinge, bump up against, hit; osculate; **graze,** caress, kiss, nudge, rub, brush, glance, scrape, sideswipe, skim, skirt, shave; grope and feel up and cop a feel <nf>; have a near miss, brush or graze or squeak by

11 meet, encounter; come across, run across, meet up, fall across, cross the path of; **come upon,** run upon, fall upon, light or alight upon; come among, fall among; **meet with,** meet up with <nf>, come face to face with, **confront**, meet head-on *or* eyeball to eyeball; **run into, bump into** *and* run smack into <nf>, join up with, come *or* run up against <nf>, run *and* fall foul of; burst *or* pitch *or* pop *or* bounce *or* plump upon <nf>; be on a collision course

12 **stay near, keep close to;** stand by, lie by; go with, march with, follow close upon, breathe down one's neck, tread *or* stay on one's heels, stay on one's tail, tailgate <nf>; hang about *or* around, hang upon the skirts of, hover over; **cling to,** clasp, hug, huddle; hug the shore *or* land, keep hold of the land, stay inshore

13 **juxtapose,** appose, join 800, **adjoin, abut,** butt against, neighbor; bring near, put with, place *or* set side by side

ADJS **14** **near, close, nigh,** close-in, nearish, nighish, intimate, cheek-by-jowl, side-by-side, hand-in-hand, arm-in-arm, *bras-dessus-bras-dessous* <Fr>, shoulder-to-shoulder, neck and neck; **approaching,** nearing, approximate *or* approximating, proximate, proximal, propinque <old>; **short-range;** near the mark; warm *or* hot *or* burning <nf>

15 **nearby, handy, convenient,** neighboring, vicinal, propinquant *or* propinquous, ready at hand, easily reached *or* attained; accessible

16 **adjacent, next,** immediate, contiguous, **adjoining, abutting; neighboring,** neighbor; in the neighborhood, in the vicinity; **juxtaposed,** juxtapositional, tangential; **bordering,** conterminous *or* coterminous, connecting; **face-to-face** 215.6; end-to-end, endways, endwise; **joined**

17 **in contact,** contacting, **touching, meeting,** contingent; impinging, impingent; tangent, tangential; osculatory; grazing, kissing, glancing, brushing, rubbing, nudging; interfacing, linking

18 **nearer,** nigher, **closer**

19 **nearest,** nighest, **closest,** nearmost, next, immediate

ADVS **20** **near, nigh, close;** hard, at close quarters; **nearby, close by,** hard by, fast by, not far *or* far off, in the vicinity *or* **neighborhood of,** at hand, at close range, **near** *or* **close at hand;** thereabout *or* thereabouts, hereabout *or* hereabouts; nearabout *or* nearabouts *or* nigh about <dial>; **about, around** <nf>, close about, along toward <nf>; at no great distance, only a step; as near as no matter *or* makes no difference <nf>; **within reach** *or* **range,** within call *or* hearing, within earshot *or* earreach, within a whoop *or* two whoops and a holler <nf>, within a stone's throw, a stone's throw away, in spitting distance <nf>, at one's elbow, at one's feet, at one's fingertips, under one's nose, at one's side,

within one's grasp; just around the corner, just across the street, next-door, right next door, just next door

21 **in juxtaposition, in conjunction,** in apposition; beside 218.11

22 **nearly, near,** pretty near <nf>, close, **closely; almost,** all but, not quite, as good as, as near as makes no difference; **well-nigh, just about;** nigh, nigh hand

23 **approximately,** approximatively, practically <nf>, for practical purposes *or* all practical purposes, at a first approximation, give or take a little, **more or less; roughly,** roundly, in round numbers; **generally,** generally speaking, roughly speaking, say; in the ballpark <nf>

PREPS **24** **near, nigh,** near to, **close to,** near upon, close upon, hard on *or* upon, bordering on *or* upon, **verging on** *or* upon, on the confines of, at the threshold of, **on the brink** *or* **verge of,** on the edge of, at next hand, at *or* on the point of, on the skirts of; **not far from;** next door to, at one's door; nigh about *or* nearabout *or* nigh on *or* nigh onto <dial>

25 **against,** up against, on, upon, over against, opposite, nose to nose with, vis-à-vis, in contact with

26 **about, around,** just about, circa, c, somewhere about *or* near, near *or* close upon, give or take, near enough to, upwards of <nf>, -ish, -something; **in the neighborhood** *or* **vicinity of**

224 INTERVAL
<space between>

NOUNS **1** **interval, gap,** space 158, intervening *or* intermediate space, **interspace,** distance *or* space between, interstice; **clearance,** margin, leeway, headroom, **room** 158.3; discontinuity 813, jump, leap, interruption; daylight; hiatus, caesura, lacuna, intermission; half space, single space, double space, em space, en space, hair space; time interval, interim 826

2 **crack, cleft,** cranny, chink, check, craze, chap, **crevice,** fissure, scissure, incision, notch, score, cut, gash, slit, split, **rift,** rent; crack, hairline crack; **opening,** excavation, cavity, concavity, hole; **gap,** gape, **abyss,** abysm, **gulf, chasm,** void 222.3, canyon; **breach, break,** fracture, rupture; fault, flaw; slot, groove, furrow, moat, ditch, trench, dike, ha-ha; joint, seam; **valley**

VERBS **3** **interspace, space,** make a space, make room, set at intervals, dot, scatter 771.4, **space out, separate,** split off, part, dispart, set *or* keep apart

4 **cleave, crack,** check, incise, craze, **cut, cut apart,** gash, slit, **split,** rive, rent, rip open; **open; gap,**

breach, break, fracture, rupture; slot, groove, furrow, ditch, trench

ADJS **5** intervallic, intervallary, interspatial, interstitial, discontinuous

6 **interspaced, spaced,** intervaled, **spaced out,** set at intervals, with intervals *or* an interval, interspacial, interstitial; dotted, scattered 771.9, **separated, parted,** disparted, split-off

7 **cleft, cut,** cloven, **cracked,** sundered, rift, riven, rent, chinky, chapped, crazed; **slit, split;** gaping, gappy; hiatal, caesural, lacunar; fissured, fissural, fissile

225 HABITATION

<an inhabiting>

NOUNS **1** **habitation,** inhabiting, inhabitation, habitancy, inhabitancy, **tenancy, occupancy,** occupation, **residence** *or* **residency,** residing, abiding, **living,** nesting, **dwelling,** commorancy <law>, lodging, staying, stopping, sojourning, staying over; squatting; cohabitation, living together, sharing quarters; living in sin; **abode, habitat** 228

2 **peopling,** peoplement, empeoplement, **population,** inhabiting; **colonization, settlement,** plantation

3 **housing,** domiciliation; lodgment, **lodging,** transient lodging, doss <Brit>, **quartering,** billeting, hospitality; living quarters; **housing development,** subdivision, tract; housing problem, housing bill

4 **camping,** tenting, **encampment,** bivouacking; camp 228.29

5 **sojourn,** sojourning, sojournment, temporary stay; **stay,** stop; **stopover,** stopoff, stayover, layover

6 **habitability,** inhabitability, **livability**

VERBS **7** **inhabit, occupy,** tenant, move in *or* into, take up one's abode, make one's home; rent, lease; **reside, live, live in, dwell, lodge, stay,** remain, abide, hang *or* hang out <nf>, domicile, domiciliate; **room,** bunk, crash <nf>, berth, doss down <Brit>; perch *and* roost *and* squat <nf>; nest; room together; cohabit, live together; live in sin

8 **sojourn,** stop, stay, **stop over,** stay over, lay over

9 **people,** empeople, **populate, inhabit,** denizen; colonize, **settle,** settle in, plant

10 **house,** domicile, domiciliate; provide with a roof; have as a guest *or* lodger, shelter, harbor; **lodge, quarter, put up,** billet, room, bed, berth, bunk; stable

11 **camp, encamp,** tent; pitch, **pitch camp,** pitch one's tent, drive stakes <nf>; bivouac; go camping, camp out, sleep out, rough it

ADJS **12** **inhabited, occupied,** tenanted; **peopled,** empeopled, populated, colonized, settled; populous

13 **resident,** residentiary, **in residence; residing, living, dwelling,** commorant, lodging, **staying,** remaining, abiding, living in; cohabiting, live-in

14 **housed,** domiciled, domiciliated, **lodged,** quartered, billeted; stabled

15 **habitable,** inhabitable, occupiable, lodgeable, tenantable, **livable, fit to live in, fit for occupation;** homelike 228.33

ADVS **16** **at home,** in the bosom of one's family, *chez soi* <Fr>; in one's element; back home *and* down home <nf>

226 NATIVENESS

NOUNS **1** **nativeness,** nativity, native-bornness, indigenousness *or* indigenity, aboriginality, autochthonousness, **nationality;** nativism

2 **citizenship,** native-born citizenship, citizenship by birth, citizenhood, subjecthood; civism

3 **naturalization,** naturalized citizenship, citizenship by naturalization *or* adoption, nationalization, adoption, admission, affiliation, **assimilation;** indigenization; Americanization, Anglicization, etc; acculturation, enculturation; papers, citizenship papers; culture shock

VERBS **4** **naturalize,** grant *or* confer citizenship, adopt, admit, affiliate, **assimilate;** Americanize, Anglicize, etc; acculturate, acculturize; indigenize, go native <nf>

ADJS **5** **native,** natal, **indigenous,** endemic, autochthonous; mother, maternal, original, aboriginal, primitive; native-born, home-grown, homebred, native to the soil *or* place *or* heath

6 **naturalized,** adopted, **assimilated;** indoctrinated, Americanized, Anglicized, etc; acculturated, acculturized; indigenized

227 INHABITANT, NATIVE

NOUNS **1** **population, inhabitants,** habitancy, dwellers, **populace, people,** whole people, people at large, citizenry, folk, souls, living souls, body, whole body, warm bodies <nf>; **public,** general public; community, society, **nation,** commonwealth, constituency, body politic, electorate; speech *or* linguistic community, ethnic *or* cultural community; colony, commune, neighborhood; nationality; **census,** head count; population statistics, demography, demographics

2 **inhabitant,** inhabiter, habitant; **occupant,** occupier, **dweller, tenant, denizen,** inmate; **resident,** residencer, residentiary, resider; inpatient; resident *or* live-in maid; writer- *or* poet- *or* artist- *or*

composer-in-residence; house detective; incumbent, *locum tenens* <L>; sojourner; addressee; indweller, inmate

3 **native,** indigene, autochthon, earliest inhabitant, first comer, primitive settler; primitive; **aborigine,** aboriginal; local *and* local yokel <nf>; nativeness, indigenousness, indigeneity

4 **citizen, national,** subject; **naturalized citizen,** nonnative citizen, citizen by adoption, immigrant, metic; hyphenated American, hyphenate; **cosmopolitan,** cosmopolite, citizen of the world; active citizen; citizenship, dual citizenship

5 **fellow citizen,** fellow countryman *or* countrywoman, **compatriot,** congener, **countryman,** countrywoman, *landsman* <Yiddish>, *paesano* <Ital>, *paisano* <Sp>; fellow townsman, home boy *and* home girl *and* hometowner <nf>

6 **townsman, townswoman,** townsperson, towny *and* towner *and* townie <nf>, **villager,** oppidan, city dweller, city person; big-city person, **city slicker** <nf>; metropolitan, urbanite; suburbanite; exurbanite; burgher, burgess, *bourgeois* <Fr>; townspeople, townfolks, townfolk

7 **householder,** homeowner, house-owner, proprietor, freeholder, occupier, addressee; cottager, cotter, cottier, crofter; head of household

8 **lodger, roomer,** paying guest; **boarder,** board-and-roomer, **transient,** transient guest *or* boarder; **renter, tenant,** leaser *or* lessee, leaseholder, time-sharer, subleaser *or* sublessee; roommate, flatmate <Brit>; visitor, guest

9 **settler,** *habitant* <Canadian & Louisiana Fr>; **colonist,** colonizer, colonial, immigrant, incomer, planter; **homesteader; squatter,** nester; **pioneer;** sooner; precursor 815

10 wilderness settler *or* hinterlander; **frontiersman,** mountain man; **backwoodsman,** woodlander, woodsman, woodman, woodhick <nf>; **mountaineer, hillbilly** *and* ridge runner <nf>, brush ape *and* briar-hopper <nf>; cracker *and* redneck <nf>, desert rat <nf>, clam digger <nf>, piny <nf>; country gentleman, ruralist, provincial, rustic, peasant, hayseed, hick, cottager

11 <regional inhabitants> **Easterner,** eastlander; **Midwesterner; Westerner,** westlander; **Southerner,** southlander; **Northener,** northlander, Yankee; Northman; New Englander, Down-Easter Yankee; Maritimer <Can>

228 ABODE, HABITAT
<place of habitation or resort>

NOUNS 1 **abode, habitation, place, dwelling,** dwelling place, abiding place, place to live, where one lives *or* resides, where one is at home, roof, roof over one's head, **residence,** place of residence, **domicile,** *domus* <L>; **lodging,** lodgment, lodging place; seat, nest, living space, houseroom, sleeping place, place to rest one's head, crash pad <nf>; native heath, turf, home turf; **address,** permanent residence; **housing; affordable housing,** low-cost housing, low-and-middle-income housing, public housing, public-sector housing, scattersite housing; council house <Brit>; private housing, private-sector housing, market-rate housing

2 **home,** home sweet home, "the place where, when you go there, They have to take you in"—Robert Frost, "the place to do things you want to do"—Zelda Fitzgerald; **fireside, hearth,** hearth and home, hearthstone, fireplace, *foyer* <Fr>, chimney corner, ingle, ingleside *or* inglenook; base, nest; **household,** *ménage;* **homestead,** home place, home roof, roof, rooftree, toft <Brit old>; place where one hangs one's hat; paternal roof *or* domicile, family homestead, ancestral halls; hometown, birthplace, cradle; homeland, native land, motherland, fatherland; **hominess** *or* homeyness

3 **domesticity;** housewifery, **housekeeping, homemaking;** householding, householdry

4 **quarters, living quarters; lodgings,** lodging, lodgment; diggings *and* digs <Brit nf>, pad *and* crib <nf>; **room, rooms,** berth, roost, accommodations; **housing** 225.3, shelter, *gîte* <Fr>

5 **house,** dwelling, dwelling house, *casa* <Sp & Ital>; house and grounds, house and lot, homesite; **building, structure, edifice,** fabric, erection, **hall** 197.4; roof; lodge; manor house, hall; town house, *rus in urbe* <L>, semidetached house, duplex, row house; country house, *dacha* <Russ>, country seat; ranch house, farmhouse, farm, country house; prefabricated house, modular house; sod house, adobe house; lake dwelling 241.3; houseboat; cave *or* cliff dwelling; penthouse; split-level; parsonage 703.7, **rectory,** vicarage, deanery, manse; official residence, White House, 10 Downing Street, the Kremlin, governor's mansion; presidential palace; embassy, consulate

6 **farmstead; ranch,** *rancho and hacienda* <Sp>, toft *or* steading <Brit old>, grange, plantation

7 **estate; mansion,** palatial residence, stately home <Brit>, manor house; **villa, château,** *hôtel* <Fr>, **castle,** tower; **palace,** *palais* <Fr>, *palazzo* <Ital>, court; ancestral hall *or* seat

8 **cottage,** cot *or* cote, **bungalow,** box; **cabin,** log cabin; **second home, vacation home;** chalet, lodge, snuggery; home away from home, *pied-à-terre* <Fr>

9 **hut,** hutch, **shack, shanty,** crib, hole-in-the-wall <nf>, **shed; lean-to; booth,** stall; tollbooth *or* tollhouse, sentry box, gatehouse, porter's lodge;

outhouse, outbuilding; privy; **pavilion,** kiosk; Quonset hut *or* Nissen hut; hutment

10 <Native American houses> wigwam, tepee *or* tipi, hogan, wickiup, jacal, longhouse; tupik *and* igloo <Eskimo>; ajouba

11 **hovel, dump** <nf>, rathole, hole, sty, pigsty, pigpen, tumbledown shack; squat

12 **summerhouse,** arbor, bower, **gazebo,** pergola, kiosk, alcove, retreat; **conservatory, greenhouse,** glasshouse <Brit>, lathhouse

13 **apartment, flat,** tenement, chambers <Brit>, room *or* rooms; studio apartment *or* flat; bed-sitter <Brit>, granny flat, flatlet; **suite,** suite *or* set of rooms; walkup, cold-water flat; **penthouse;** garden apartment; duplex apartment; railroad *or* shotgun flat

14 **apartment house, flats, tenement;** duplex, duplex house; tower block; apartment complex; cooperative apartment house *or* co-op <nf>; condominium *or* condo <nf>; high-rise apartment building *or* high rise

15 **inn, hotel,** hostel, hostelry, **tavern,** *posada* <Sp>; tourist hotel, *parador* <Sp>; **roadhouse,** caravansary *or* caravanserai, guesthouse, bed and breakfast *or* B and B; youth hostel, hospice, elder hostel; **lodging house,** rooming house; **boardinghouse,** *pension* <Fr>, *pensione* <Ital>; **dormitory,** dorm <nf>, fraternity *or* sorority house; bunkhouse; **flophouse** *and* fleabag <nf>, dosshouse <Brit nf>

16 **motel,** motor court, motor inn *or* lodge, motor hotel, auto court; boatel

17 **trailer,** house *or* camp trailer, **mobile home,** motor home, recreational vehicle *or* RV, camper, caravan <Brit>; trailer court *or* camp *or* park, campground

18 **habitat,** home, **range,** environment, surroundings, stamping grounds, locality, native environment; microhabitat, ecosystem, terrain, purlieu

19 **zoo,** menagerie, *Tiergarten* <Ger>, zoological garden *or* park, marine park, sea zoo; animal shelter

20 **barn, stable,** stall; **cowbarn,** cowhouse, cowshed, cowbyre, byre; mews

21 **kennel, doghouse;** pound, dog pound; cattery

22 **coop, chicken house** *or* **coop,** henhouse, hencote, hencoop, hennery; brooder

23 **birdhouse, aviary,** bird cage; dovecote, pigeon house *or* loft, columbary; roost, perch, roosting place; rookery, heronry; eyrie

24 vivarium, terrarium, aquarium; fishpond

25 **nest,** nidus; **beehive, apiary,** hive, bee tree, hornet's nest, wasp's nest, vespiary

26 **lair, den,** cave, **hole,** covert, mew, form; **burrow,** tunnel, earth, run, couch, lodge

27 **resort, haunt,** purlieu, **hangout** <nf>, **stamping ground** <nf>; gathering place, rallying point, meeting place, clubhouse, club; casino, gambling house; health resort; **spa,** baths, springs, watering place

28 <disapproved place> **dive** <nf>, **den, lair,** den of thieves; hole *and* dump *and* **joint** <nf>; gyp *or* clip joint <nf>; **whorehouse,** cathouse <nf>, sporting house, brothel, bordello, stews, fleshpots

29 **camp, encampment,** *Lager* <Ger>; bivouac; barrack *or* **barracks,** casern, *caserne* <Fr>, cantonment, lines <Brit>; hobo jungle *or* camp; detention camp, concentration camp, *Konzentrationslager* <Ger>; campground *or* campsite

30 <deities of the household> lares and penates, Vesta, Hestia

VERBS 31 **keep house,** housekeep <nf>, practice domesticity, maintain *or* run a household

ADJS 32 **residential,** residentiary, residing, in residence; domestic, domiciliary, domal; **home, household,** at home; mansional, manorial, palatial

33 **homelike,** homish, **homey** <nf>, homely; comfortable, friendly, cheerful, peaceful, cozy, snug, intimate; simple, plain, unpretending

34 **domesticated, tame,** tamed, broken; housebroken

229 FURNITURE

NOUNS 1 **furniture,** furnishings, movables, home furnishings, house furnishings, household effects, household goods, office furniture, school furniture, church furniture, library furniture, furnishments <old>; **cabinetmaking,** cabinetwork, cabinetry; **furniture design, furniture style** <see list>; period furniture; **piece of furniture, furniture piece,** chair, couch, sofa, bed, table, desk, cabinet, mirror, clock, screen; **suite, set of furniture,** ensemble, decor

2 **furniture styles and periods**

Adam	Baroque
Adapted Colonial	Bauhaus
Adirondack	Biedermeier
American Chippendale *or*	Block-front
Pilgrim	Boston Chippendale
American Empire	boule *or* boulework
American Jacobean	Byzantine
American Moderne	Chinese Chippendale
American Queen Anne	Chinoiserie
American Regency *or*	Chippendale
Directory	Colonial *or* Campaign
American Restoration *or*	Contemporary
Pillar and Scroll	Cotswold School
Anglo-Dutch	Country Chippendale
Art Deco	Cromwellian *or*
Art Nouveau	Commonwealth
Arts and Crafts	Desornamentado

De Stijl
Directoire
Duncan Phyfe
Early American
Early Georgian
Eastlake
Egyptian
Elizabethan
Empire
Federal
French Provincial
French Renaissance
Georgian
Gothic
Gothic-Renaissance
Hepplewhite
International *or*
    International Gothic
Italian Renaissance
Jacobean
Japanese
Japonisme
Late Regency
Later Victorian
Louis XIII
Louis XIV
Louis XV
Louis XVI
Mannerist
Mission
Modern
Modernist
Morris
National Romanticism

Naturalistic
Neoclassical *or le style
    antique* <Fr>
Neo-Gothic *or* Cathédrale
Neo-Grec
Newport Chippendale
New York Chippendale
Palladian
Pennsylvania Dutch
Philadelphia Chippendale
Pop Art
Queen Anne
Regency
Renaissance Revival
Restoration *or* Carolean
Rococo
Rococo Revival *or* Louis
    Philippe *or* Louis XV
    Revival
Romano-Byzantine *or*
    Italo-Byzantine *or*
    Romanesque
Scandinavian Modern
Shaker
Sheraton
Spanish Renaissance
Stuart
Tudor
Turkish
Venetian
Victorian
Viking Revival *or*
    Dragonesque
William and Mary

230 TOWN, CITY

NOUNS **1 town,** township; **city, metropolis,** metro,
metropolitan area, greater city, megalopolis,
supercity, conurbation, urban complex, spread city,
urban sprawl *or* spread, Standard Metropolitan
Statistical Area *or* SMSA, urban corridor, strip city,
municipality, *urbs* <L>, *polis* <Gk>, city *or*
municipal government; *ville* <Fr>, *Stadt* <Ger>;
borough, burg <nf>, bourg, burgh <Scot>;
suburb, suburbia, burbs <nf>, slurb, stockbroker
belt <Brit nf>, garden suburb <Brit>, commuter
belt, outskirts, *faubourg* <Fr>, *banlieue* <Fr>;
exurb, exurbia, bedroom town, streetcar suburb;
market town <Brit>; small town; twin town; boom
town, ghost town; industrial city; sister city;
urbanization, citifying

2 village, hamlet; ham *and* thorp *and* wick <old>;
country town, crossroads; "a little one-eyed,
blinking sort o' place"—Thomas Hardy, "a hive of
glass, where nothing unobserved can pass"—C H
Spurgeon

3 <nf terms> **one-horse town,** jerkwater town, one-

gas-station town, **tank town** *or* station, **whistle-
stop,** jumping-off place; **hick town,** rube town,
Podunk; hoosier town; wide place in the road

4 capital, capital city, **seat,** seat of government;
county seat *or* county site, county town *or*
shiretown <Brit>

5 town hall, city hall, municipal building;
courthouse; police headquarters *or* station, station
house, precinct house; firehouse, fire station,
station house; county building, county courthouse;
community center; school

6 <city districts> East Side *or* End, West Side *or*
End; **downtown,** uptown, midtown; city center,
main street, city centre <Brit>, urban center,
central *or* center city, core, core city, inner city,
suburbs, suburbia, burbs <nf>, outskirts,
greenbelt, residential district, business district *or*
section, shopping center, financial district,
residential area; Chinatown, Little Italy, Little
Hungary, etc; **asphalt** *or* **concrete jungle,** mean
streets; **slum** *or* **slums,** the other side *or* the wrong
side of the tracks, blighted area *or* neighborhood
or section, run-down neighborhood, tenement
district, shanty-town, hell's kitchen *or* half-acre;
favela, tenderloin, red-light district, Bowery, **skid
row** *or* skid road <nf>; **ghetto, inner city,** urban
ghetto, barrio

7 block, city block, square

8 square, plaza, *place* <Fr>, *piazza* <Ital>, *campo*
<Ital>, **marketplace,** market, mart, rialto, forum,
agora

9 circle, circus <Brit>; crescent

10 city planning, urban planning; urban studies,
urbanology

ADJS **11 urban, metropolitan, municipal,** metro,
burghal, **civic,** oppidan; main-street; citywide; city,
town, village; citified; urbane; suburban;
interurban; downtown, uptown, midtown; **inner-
city,** core, core-city, ghetto; small-town; boom-town

231 REGION

NOUNS **1 region, area, zone,** belt, **territory,** terrain;
place 159.1; **space** 158; **country** 232, **land** 234,
ground, soil; territoriality; territorial waters,
twelve- *or* three-mile limit, continental shelf,
offshore rights; air space; heartland; hinterland;
district, quarter, section, sector, department,
division; salient, corridor; part, parts;
neighborhood, vicinity, vicinage, neck of the
woods <nf>, stamping ground, turf <nf>,
backyard <nf>, purlieu *or* purlieus; premises,
confines, precincts, environs, milieu

2 sphere, hemisphere, orb, **orbit,** ambit, circle;
circuit, judicial circuit, **beat, round,** walk; **realm,**

demesne, **domain,** dominion, jurisdiction, bailiwick, niche, forté; border, borderland, march; **province,** precinct, department; **field,** pale, arena

3 zone; climate *or* clime <old>; **longitude,** longitude in arc, longitude in time; meridian, prime meridian; **latitude,** parallel; equator, the line; tropic, Tropic of Cancer, Tropic of Capricorn; tropics, subtropics, Torrid Zone; Temperate *or* Variable Zones; Frigid Zones, Arctic Zone *or* Circle, Antarctic Zone *or* Circle; horse latitudes, roaring forties; doldrums

4 plot, plot of ground *or* land, parcel of land, plat, **patch, tract, field,** enclosure; lot; air space; block, square; section, forty <sixteenth of a section>; close, quadrangle, quad, enclave, pale, *clos* <Fr>, croft <Brit>, *kraal* <Africa>; real estate; allotment, holding, claim

5 <territorial divisions> **state, territory, province,** region, duchy, electorate, government, principality; **county,** shire, canton, *oblast* and *okrug* <Russ>, *département* <Fr>, *Kreis* or *Land* <Ger>; **borough, ward,** precinct, riding, *arrondissement* <Fr>; **township,** hundred, commune, wapentake; metropolis, metropolitan area, **city, town** 230; **village,** hamlet; **district,** congressional district, electoral district, precinct; magistracy, soke, bailiwick; shrievalty, sheriffalty, sheriffwick, constablewick <Brit>; archdiocese, archbishopric, stake; **diocese,** bishopric, parish; colony

6 <regions of the world> continent, landmass; **Old World,** the old country; **New World,** America; **Northern Hemisphere,** North America; Central America; **Southern Hemisphere,** South America; Latin America; **Western Hemisphere, Occident, West; Eastern Hemisphere, Orient,** Levant, East, eastland; Far East, Mideast *or* Middle East, Near East; Asia, Europe, Eurasia, Asia Major, Asia Minor, Africa; Antipodes, Australia, down under <nf>, Australasia, Oceania; Arctic, Antarctica; Third World

7 <regions of the US> West, westland, wild West, West Coast, Coast, left Coast <nf>; Northwest, Pacific Northwest; Silicon Valley; Sierras; Rockies; Sunbelt; Southwest; Middle West *or* Midwest, Middle America; Great Plains, heartlands, Plains states; North Central region; Rust Belt; East, eastland, East Coast, Eastern Seaboard; Middle Atlantic; Northeast, Southeast; North, northland, Snow Belt, Frost Belt; Appalachia; South, southland, Dixie, Dixieland; Deep South, Old South; Delta, bayous; Bible Belt; borscht belt; Gulf Coast; New England, Down East, Yankeeland <nf>

ADJS **8 regional, territorial, geographical,** areal, sectional, zonal, topographic *or* topographical

9 local, localized, of a place, geographically limited, topical, vernacular, parochial, provincial, insular, limited, confined

10 US state mottoes and nicknames

Alabama "We dare defend our rights"; Heart of Dixie *or* Camellia State

Alaska "North to the future"; The Last Frontier

Arizona "Diat Deus"; Grand Canyon State

Arkansas "Regnat populus"; Land of Opportunity

California "Eureka"; Golden State

Colorado "Nil sine numine"; Centennial State

Connecticut "Qui transtulit sustinet"; Constitution State; Nutmeg State

Delaware "Liberty and independence"; First State *or* Diamond State

District of Columbia "Justitia Omnibus"; Capital City

Florida "In God we trust"; Sunshine State

Georgia "Wisdom, justice, and moderation"; Empire State of the South; Peach State

Hawaii "The life of the land is perpetuated in righteousness"; Aloha State

Idaho "Esto perpetua"; Gem State

Illinois "State sovereignty—national union"; Prairie State

Indiana "Crossroads of America"; Hoosier State

Iowa "Our liberties we prize and our rights we will maintain"; Hawkeye State

Kansas "Ad astra per aspera"; Sunflower State

Kentucky "United we stand, divided we fall"; Bluegrass State

Louisiana "Union, justice and confidence"; Pelican State

Maine "Dirigo"; Pine Tree State

Maryland "Fatti maschii, parole femine"; Old Line State *or* Free State

Massachusetts "Ense petit placidam sub libertate"; Bay State; Colony State

Michigan "Si quaeris peninsulam amoenam"; Great Lake State *or* Wolverine State

Minnesota "L'Etoile du nord"; North Star State *or* Gopher State

Mississippi "Virtute et armis"; Magnolia State

Missouri "Salus populi suprema lex esto"; Show-Me State

Montana "Oro y plato"; Treasure State

Nebraska "Equality before the law"; Cornhusker State

Nevada "All for our country"; Sagebrush State *or* Battle-Born State

New Hampshire "Live free or die"; Granite State

New Jersey "Liberty and prosperity"; Garden State

New Mexico "Crescit eundo"; Land of Enchantment

New York "Excelsior"; Empire State

North Carolina "Esse quam videri"; Tar Heel State *or* Old North State

North Dakota "Liberty and union, now and forever, one and inseparable"; Peace Garden State

Ohio "With God, all things are possible"; Buckeye State

Oklahoma "Labor omnia vincit"; Sooner State

Oregon "The union"; Beaver State

Pennsylvania "Virtue, liberty and independence"; Keystone State

Rhode Island "Hope"; Little Rhody; Ocean State

South Carolina "Dum spiro spero"; Palmetto State

South Dakota "Under God, the people rule"; Coyote State *or* Sunshine State

Tennessee "Agriculture and commerce"; Volunteer State

Texas "Friendship"; Lone Star State

Utah "Industry"; Beehive State

Vermont "Freedom and unity"; Green Mountain State

Virginia "Sic semper tyrannis"; Old Dominion

Washington "Alki"; Evergreen State

West Virginia "Montani semper liberi"; Mountain State

Wisconsin "Forward"; Badger State

Wyoming "Equal rights"; Equality State

11 US territories and commonwealths; mottoes

American Samoa "Samoa Muamua le Atua"

Guam "Where America's day begins"

Commonwealth of the Northern Mariana Islands

Commonwealth of Puerto Rico "Joannes est nomen eius"

Virgin Islands

232 COUNTRY

NOUNS **1 country,** land; **nation,** nationality, **state,** nation-state, sovereign nation *or* state, self-governing state, polity, **body politic; power,** superpower, world power; microstate; **republic,** people's republic, **commonwealth,** commonweal; **kingdom,** sultanate; **empire,** empery; superpower, power; **realm,** dominion, domain; **principality,** principate; duchy, dukedom; grand duchy, archduchy, archdukedom, earldom, county, palatinate, seneschalty; chieftaincy, chieftainry; toparchy, *toparchia* <L>; city-state, *polis* <Gk>, free city; **province,** territory, possession; colony, settlement; protectorate, mandate, mandated territory, mandant, mandatee, mandatory; buffer state; **ally,** military ally, cobelligerent, treaty partner; satellite, puppet regime *or* government; free nation *or* country, captive nation, iron-curtain country; nonaligned *or* unaligned *or* neutralist nation; developed nation, industrial *or* industrialized nation; underdeveloped nation, third-world nation; federation, confederation, commonwealth, commonweal, bloc, comity; United Nations

2 fatherland, *Vaterland* <Ger>, *patria* <L>, *la patrie* <Fr>, land of our fathers, **motherland,** mother country, **native land,** native soil, one's native heath *or* ground *or* soil *or* place, the old country, country of origin, **birthplace,** cradle; **home, homeland,** home ground, "home is where one starts"—T S Eliot, God's country; the home front

3 United States, United States of America, US, USA, US of A <nf>, **America,** Columbia, the States,

Uncle Sugar *and* Yankeeland <nf>, Land of Liberty, the melting pot; stateside

4 Britain, Great Britain, United Kingdom, the UK, Britannia, Albion, Blighty <Brit nf>, Limeyland <US nf>, Tight Little Island, Land of the Rose, "This royal throne of kings, this scepter'd isle, This earth of majesty, this seat of Mars, This other Eden, demi-paradise"—Shakespeare, Sovereign of the Seas; British Empire, Commonwealth of Nations, British Commonwealth of Nations, the Commonwealth; perfidious Albion

5 <national personifications> Uncle Sam *or* Brother Jonathan <US>; John Bull <Eng>

6 nationhood, peoplehood, **nationality; statehood, nation-statehood, sovereignty,** sovereign nationhood *or* statehood, independence, self-government, self-determination; internationality, internationalism; **nationalism**

7 native, countryman, countrywoman, citizen, national; nationalist, ultranationalist; patriot

233 THE COUNTRY

NOUNS **1 the country,** agricultural region, farm country, farmland, arable land, grazing region *or* country, rural district, rustic region, province *or* **provinces,** countryside, woodland 310.13, grassland 310.8, woods and fields, meadows and pastures, the soil, grass roots; **the sticks** *and* the tall corn *and* yokeldom *and* hickdom <nf>; cotton belt, tobacco belt, black belt, farm belt, corn belt, fruit belt, wheat belt, citrus belt; dust bowl; highlands, moors, uplands, foothills; lowlands, veld *or* veldt, savanna *or* savannah, plains, prairies, steppes, wide-open spaces

2 hinterland, back country, outback <Austral>, up-country, boonies *and* boondocks <nf>; **the bush,** bush country, bushveld, **woods,** woodlands, **backwoods,** forests, timbers, the big sticks <nf>, brush; wilderness, wilds, uninhabited region, virgin land *or* territory; **wasteland** 891.2; **frontier,** borderland, outpost; wild West, cow country

3 rusticity, ruralism, inurbanity, agrarianism, bucolicism, **provincialism,** provinciality, simplicity, pastoral simplicity, unspoiledness; yokelism, hickishness, backwoodsiness; **boorishness,** churlishness, unrefinement, uncultivation

4 ruralization, countrification, rustication, pastoralization

VERBS **5 ruralize, countrify, rusticate,** pastoralize; farm 1069.16; return to the soil

ADJS **6 rustic, rural, country, provincial, farm, pastoral, bucolic,** Arcadian, **agrarian,** agrestic; **agricultural** 1069.20; lowland, low-lying, upland, highland, prairie, plains

7 countrified, inurbane; country-born, country-bred, up-country; farmerish, hobnailed, clodhopping, clodhopperish; **boorish,** clownish, loutish, lumpish, lumpen, cloddish, churlish; **uncouth,** unpolished, uncultivated, uncultured, unrefined; country-style, country-fashion

8 <nf terms> **hick,** hicky, hickified, from the sticks, rube, hayseed, yokel, yokelish, down-home, shit-kicking, hillbilly, redneck

9 hinterland, back, **back-country,** up-country, backroad, outback <Austral>, wild, wilderness, virgin; wild-West, cow-country; **waste** 891.4; backwood *or* **backwoods,** back of beyond, backwoodsy; woodland, sylvan

234 LAND

NOUNS **1 land, ground,** landmass, earth, glebe <old>, **sod,** clod, **soil, dirt,** dust, clay, marl, mold <Brit nf>; *terra* <L>, **terra firma;** terrain; **dry land;** arable land; marginal land; grassland 310.8, woodland 310.13; crust, earth's crust, lithosphere; regolith; topsoil, subsoil; alluvium, alluvion; eolian *or* subaerial deposit; **real estate,** real property, landholdings, acres, territory, freehold; region 231; the country 233; earth science 1071

2 shore, coast, *côte* <Fr>; **strand,** *playa* <Sp>, **beach,** beachfront, beachside shingle, plage, lido, riviera, sands, berm; waterside, **waterfront;** shoreline, coastline; foreshore; bank, embankment; riverside; lakefront, lakeshore; **seashore, coast, seacoast, seaside, seaboard,** seabeach, seacliff, seabank, sea margin, oceanfront, oceanside, seafront, shorefront, tidewater, tideland, coastland, littoral, littoral zone; sand dune, sand bar, sandbank, tombolo; wetland, wetlands; **bay,** bayfront, bayside; drowned *or* submerged coast; rockbound coast, ironbound coast; loom of the land

3 landsman, landman, **landlubber**

ADJS **4 terrestrial,** terrene <old>, **earth, earthly,** telluric, tellurian; earthbound; sublunar, subastral; geophilous; terraqueous; fluvioterrestrial

5 earthy, earthen, soily, loamy, marly, gumbo; clayey, clayish; adobe

6 alluvial, estuarine, fluviomarine

7 coastal, littoral, seaside, shore, shoreside; shoreward; riparian *or* riparial *or* riparious; riverain, riverine; riverside; lakefront, lakeshore; oceanfront, oceanside; seaside, seafront, shorefront, shoreline; beachfront, beachside; bayfront, bayside; tideland, tidal, wetland

ADVS **8 on land,** on dry land, on terra firma; onshore, ashore; alongshore; shoreward; by land, overland

9 on earth, on the face of the earth *or* globe, in the world, in the wide world, in the whole wide world; **under the sun,** under the stars, beneath the sky, under heaven, below, **here below**

235 BODY OF LAND

NOUNS **1 continent, mainland,** main <old>, landform, continental landform, landmass; North America, South America, Africa, Europe, Asia, Eurasia, Eurasian landmass, Australia, Antarctica; subcontinent, India, Greenland; peninsula; **plate,** crustal plate, crustal segment, Pacific plate, American plate, African plate, Eurasian plate, Antarctic plate, Indian plate; continental divide, continental drift; plate tectonics; Gondwana, Laurasia, Pangaea

2 island, isle; islet, holm, ait <Brit nf>; continental island; oceanic island; volcanic island; **key,** cay; sandbank, sandbar, bar; floating island; **reef,** coral reef, coral head; coral island, atoll; archipelago, island group *or* chain; insularity; islandology

3 continental, mainlander; continentalist

4 islander, islandman, island-dweller, islesman, insular; islandologist

VERBS **5** insulate, isolate, island, enisle; island-hop

ADJS **6 continental,** mainland

7 insular, insulated, isolated; island, islandy *or* islandish, islandlike; islanded, isleted, island-dotted; seagirt; archipelagic *or* archipelagian

236 PLAIN
<open country>

NOUNS **1 plain, plains,** flat country, flatland, **flats,** flat, level; champaign, champaign country, open country, **wide-open spaces; prairie,** grassland 310.8, sea of grass, **steppe, pampas,** *pampa* <Sp>, savanna, tundra, vega, campo, llano, sebkha; **veld,** grass veld, bushveld, tree veld; wold, weald; **moor,** moorland, down, **downs,** lande, **heath,** fell <Brit>; lowland, lowlands, bottomland; basin, playa; sand plain, sand flat, strand flat; tidal flat, salt marsh; salt pan; salt flat, alkali flat; **desert** 891.2 <see list>; **plateau,** upland, tableland, table, **mesa,** mesilla; peneplain; coastal plain, tidal plain, alluvial plain, delta, delta plain, flood plain; mare, lunar mare

ADJS **2** champaign, **plain, flat,** open; campestral *or* campestrian

3 major deserts

An Nafud <Saudi Arabia>	Chihuahuan <US, Mex>
	Colorado <US>
Arabian or Eastern <Egypt>	Dahna <Saudi Arabia>
	Dasht-e-Kavir <Iran>
Atacama <Chile>	Dasht-e-Lut <Iran>
Black Rock <US>	Death Valley <US>

Eastern or Arabian
<Egypt>
Gibson <Australia>
Gobi or Shamo
<Mongolia>
Great Arabian <Saudi
Arabia>
Great Australian
<Australia>
Great Basin <US>
Great Indian or Thar
<India, Pakistan>
Great Salt Lake <US>
Great Sandy <Australia>
Great Victoria <Australia>
Iranian <Iran>
Kalahari <South Africa,
Nambia, Botswana>
Kara Kum
<Turkmenistan>
Kyzyl Kum <Uzbekistan,
Kazakhstan>
Libyan <Libya, Egypt,
Sudan>
Lut <Iran>

Mojave <US>
Namib <Namibia>
Negev <Israel>
Nubian <Sudan>
Painted Desert <US>
Patagonian <Argentina>
Rub' al Khali <Saudi
Arabia, Oman, Yemen,
UAE>
Sahara <North Africa>
Shamo or Gobi
<Mongolia>
Simpson <Australia>
Sinai <Egypt>
Sonoran <US>
Sturt Stony <Australia>
Syrian <Syria, Iraq,
Jordan, Saudi
Arabia>
Takla Makan <China>
Thar or Great Indian
<India, Pakistan>
Turfan Depression
<China>
Yuma <US, Mex>

237 HIGHLANDS

NOUNS **1 highlands, uplands,** highland, upland, high
country, elevated land, dome, **plateau, tableland,**
mesa, upland area, downs, downland, piedmont,
moor, moorland, **hills, heights,** hill or hilly country,
downs, wold, foothills, rolling country, **mountains,**
mountain or mountainous country, high terrain,
peaks, range, *massif* <Fr>

2 slope, declivity, steep, versant, incline, rise, talus,
brae <Scot>, mountainside, hillside, bank, gentle
or easy slope, glacis, angle of repose, steep or rapid
slope, fall line, bluff, cliff, headland, ness, ben
<Scot, Ir>; precipice, wall, palisade, scar <Brit>,
escarpment, scarp, fault scarp, rim, face; upper
slopes, upper reaches, timberline or tree line

3 plateau, tableland, high plateau, table, mesa, table
mountain, butte, moor, fell <Brit>, hammada

4 hill, down <chiefly Brit>; brae *and* fell <Scot>;
hillock, knob, butte, kopje, kame, monticle,
monticule, monadnock, **knoll,** hummock,
hammock, eminence, rise, mound, swell, barrow,
tumulus, kop, tel, jebel; **dune,** sand dune; moraine,
drumlin; anthill, molehill; **dune,** sand dune,
sandhill

5 ridge, ridgeline, *arête* <Fr>, chine, spine, horst,
kame, comb <Brit>, esker, os, cuesta, serpent
kame, Indian ridge, moraine, terminal moraine;
saddle, hogback, hog's-back, saddleback,
horseback, col, watershed; **pass,** gap, notch, wind
gap, water gap

6 mountain <see list>, mount, alp, hump, tor,
height, dizzying height, nunatak, dome; **peak,
pinnacle, summit** 198.2, mountaintop, point,
topmost point or pinnacle, **crest,** spine, tor, pike
<Brit>, *pic* <Fr>, *pico* <Sp>; crag, spur, cloud-
capped or cloud-topped or snow-clad or snow-
capped peak, the roof of the world; needle,
aiguille, pyramidal peak, horn; fold mountain,
fold-belt mountain, alpine chain, fault-block
mountain, basin and range; oceanic ridge, oceanic
rise; **volcano,** volcanic mountain, volcanic spine,
volcanic neck; seamount, submarine mountain,
guyot; **mountain range,** range, massif; **mountain
system, chain,** mountain chain, cordillera, sierra,
cordilleran belt, fold belt; hill heaped upon hill;
divide, Continental Divide; mountain-building,
orogeny, orogenesis, epeirogeny, folding, faulting,
block-faulting, volcanism; isostasy; orography,
orology

7 valley, vale, glen, dale, dell, hollow, holler <nf>,
dip, flume, cleuch or corrie <Scot>, cwm
<Welsh>; **ravine, gorge, canyon,** box canyon,
arroyo <Sp>, barranca, bolson, coulee, gully,
gulch, combe or coomb or comb <Brit>, cirque,
dingle, rift, rift valley, kloof, donga, graben, draw,
wadi, basin, cirque, corrie, hanging valley;
crevasse; chimney, ditch, chine, clough <Brit>,
couloir; **defile,** pass, passage, col; **crater,** volcanic
crater, caldera, meteorite or meteoritic crater

ADJS **8 hilly, rolling,** undulating, upland;
mountainous, montane, alpine, alpestrine,
altitudinous; orogenic, orographic, orological,
orometric

9 famous and high mountains

Aconcagua <Argentina 22,834 feet>	Etna <Sicily 10,900 feet>
Annapurna I <Nepal 26,504 feet>	Everest <Nepal-Tibet 29,028 feet>
Annapurna II <Nepal 26,041 feet>	Fuji <Japan 12,388 feet>
Ararat <Turkey 16,804 feet>	Gannett Peak <Wyoming 13,804 feet>
Ben Nevis <Scotland 4,406 feet>	Grand Teton <Wyoming 13,766 feet>
Cho Oyu <Nepal-Tibet 26,750 feet>	Hood <Oregon 11,239 feet>
Communism Peak <Tajikistan 24,590 feet>	Jaya <New Guinea 16,500 feet>
Cook <New Zealand 12,349 feet>	Jungfrau <Switzerland 13,642 feet>
Dhaulagiri <Nepal 26,810 feet>	K2 or Godwin Austen <Kashmir 28,250 feet>
Elbert <Colorado 14,433 feet>	Kanchenjunga <Nepal-India 28,208 feet>
Elbrus <Russia 18,841 feet>	Kenya <Kenya 17,058 feet>
Erebus <Antarctica 12,450 feet>	Kilimanjaro <Tanzania 19,340 feet>
	Kosciusko <Australia 7,310 feet>

Lhotse I <Nepal-Tibet 27,923 feet>

Lhotse II <Nepal-Tibet 27,560 feet>

Logan <Yukon 19,850 feet>

Makalu I <Nepal-Tibet 27,824 feet>

Manaslu I <Nepal 26,760 feet>

Matterhorn <Switzerland-Italy 14,690 feet>

McKinley <Alaska 20,320 feet>

Mitchell <North Carolina 6,684 feet>

Mont Blanc <France-Italy 15,771 feet>

Monte Rosa <Switzerland 15,203 feet>

Mount Saint Helens <Washington 8,364 feet>

Ojos del Salado <Argentina-Chile 22,572 feet>

Olympus <Greece 9,570 feet>

Pico de Orizaba <Mexico 18,555 feet>

Pikes Peak <Colorado 14,110 feet>

Popocatépetl <Mexico 17,930 feet>

Rainier <Washington 14,410 feet>

Rushmore <South Dakota 6,050 feet>

St. Elias <Alaska-Yukon 18,008 feet>

Teide <Canary Islands 12,198 feet>

Toubaki <Morocco 13,661 feet>

Vesuvius <Italy 3,891 feet>

Vinson Massif <Antarctica 16,864 feet>

Washington <New Hampshire 6,288 feet>

Whitney <California 14,494 feet>

238 STREAM
<running water>

NOUNS 1 **stream, waterway, watercourse** 239.2, **channel** 239; meandering stream, flowing stream, lazy stream, racing stream, braided stream; spill stream; adolescent stream; mountain stream; **river;** navigable river, underground *or* subterranean river, "moving road"—Pascal; dry stream, stream bed, stream channel, stream course, winterbourne, wadi, *arroyo* <Sp>, *donga* <Africa>, *nullah* <India>; **brook,** branch; kill, bourn *or* bourne, run <Brit nf>, **creek,** crick <nf>; **rivulet,** rill, rillet, **streamlet,** brooklet, runlet, runnel, rundle <nf>, rindle <Brit nf>, beck <Brit>, gill <Brit>, burn <Scot>, sike <Brit nf>; **freshet,** fresh; millstream, race; midstream, midchannel; drainage pattern, watershed; stream action, fluviation

2 **headwaters, headstream,** headwater, head, riverhead; **source,** fountainhead 886.6

3 **tributary,** feeder, **branch, fork,** prong <nf>, confluent, confluent stream, affluent, distributary; effluent, anabranch, branch feeder; bayou; billabong <Austral>

4 **flow,** flowing, **flux,** fluency, profluence, fluid motion *or* movement; hydrodynamics; **stream, current,** set, trend, tide, water flow; drift, driftage; **course,** onward course, **surge, gush, rush,** onrush, spate, run, race; millrace, mill run; undercurrent, undertow; crosscurrent, crossflow; affluence, afflux, affluxion, confluence, convergence,

concourse, conflux; **downflow,** downpour; defluxion; inflow 189.2; outflow 190.4

5 **torrent, river, flood,** flash flood, wall of water, waterflood, **deluge;** spate, **pour,** freshet, fresh

6 **overflow,** spillage, spill, spillover, overflowing, overrunning, alluvion, alluvium, **inundation, flood, deluge,** whelming, overwhelming, flush, washout, engulfment, submersion 367.2, cataclysm; the Flood, the Deluge; washout

7 **trickle,** tricklet, **dribble, drip,** dripping, stillicide <old>, drop, spurtle; percolation, leaching, lixiviation; distillation, condensation, sweating; seeping, seepage

8 **lap, swash, wash, slosh, plash, splash;** lapping, washing, etc

9 **jet, spout, spurt,** spurtle, squirt, spit, spew, spray, spritz <nf>; rush, **gush,** flush; **fountain,** fount, font, *jet d'eau* <Fr>; geyser, spouter <nf>

10 **rapids, rapid,** white water, wild water; ripple, **riffle,** riff <nf>; chute, shoot, sault

11 **waterfall, cataract,** fall, **falls, Niagara, cascade,** force <Brit>, linn <Scot>, sault; nappe; watershoot

12 **eddy,** back stream, gurge, **swirl,** twirl, whirl; **whirlpool,** vortex, gulf, **maelstrom;** Maelstrom, Charybdis; countercurrent, counterflow, counterflux, backflow, reflux, refluence, regurgitation, ebb, backwash, backwater, snye <Can>

13 **tide,** tidal current *or* stream, tidal flow *or* flood, **tide race; tidewater;** tideway, tide gate; **riptide,** rip, tiderip, overfalls; direct tide, opposite tide; **spring tide; high tide,** high water, full tide; **low tide,** low water; **neap tide,** neap; lunar tide, solar tide; **flood tide, ebb tide;** rise of the tide, rising tide, flux, flow, flood; ebb, reflux, refluence; ebb and flow, flux and reflux; tidal amplitude, tidal range, intertidal zone, tidal flat, tidal pool; tideland; tide chart *or* table, tidal current chart; tide gauge, thalassometer

14 **wave, billow,** surge, **swell,** heave, undulation, lift, rise, send, scend; trough, peak; **sea,** heavy swell, ocean swell, ground swell; **roller,** roll; **comber,** comb; **surf, breakers,** spume; wavelet, **ripple,** riffle; **tidal wave,** tsunami, seismic sea wave, seiche, rogue wave; gravity wave, water wave; tide wave; bore, tidal bore, eagre, traveling wave; **whitecap,** white horse, white foam; rough *or* heavy sea, rough water, broken water, dirty water *or* sea, choppy *or* chopping sea, popple, lop, chop, choppiness, overfall, angry sea; standing wave

15 water gauge, fluviograph, fluviometer; marigraph; Nilometer

VERBS 16 **flow, stream, issue, pour, surge, run, course, rush, gush, flush, flood;** empty into, flow into, join, join with, mingle waters; set, make, trend; flow in 189.9; flow out 190.13; flow back, surge back, ebb, regurgitate; meander

17 overflow, flow over, wash over, **run over, well over, brim over,** lap, lap at, lap over, overbrim, overrun, pour out *or* over, **spill, slop, slosh,** spill out *or* over; **cataract, cascade; inundate,** engulf, swamp, sweep, whelm, overwhelm, **flood,** deluge, submerge 367.7

18 trickle, dribble, dripple, **drip,** drop, spurtle; **filter,** percolate, leach, lixiviate; distill, condense, sweat; seep, weep; **gurgle** 52.11, murmur

19 lap, plash, splash, wash, swash, slosh

20 jet, spout, spurt, spurtle, **squirt,** spit, spew, spray, spritz <nf>, play, **gush,** well, surge; vomit, vomit out *or* forth

21 eddy, gurge, **swirl,** whirl, purl, reel, spin

22 billow, surge, swell, heave, lift, rise, send, scend, toss, popple, **roll,** wave, **undulate; peak,** draw to a peak, be poised; comb, **break,** dash, crash, smash; rise and fall, ebb and flow

ADJS **23 streamy,** rivery, brooky, creeky; streamlike, riverine, riverlike; fluvial, fluviatile *or* fluviatic, fluviomarine

24 flowing, streaming, running, pouring, fluxive, fluxional, coursing, racing, gushing, rushing, onrushing, surging, surgy, torrential, rough, whitewater; **fluent,** profluent, affluent, defluent, decurrent, confluent, diffluent, refluent; tidal; gulfy, vortical; meandering, mazy, sluggish, serpentine

25 flooded, deluged, inundated, engulfed, swamped, swept, whelmed, drowned, overwhelmed, afloat, awash; washed, water-washed; in flood, at flood, in spate

26 major rivers

Nile <Africa>	Huang Ho or Yellow
Amazon <South America>	<China>
Mississippi <North	Congo <Africa>
America>	Amur <Russ>
Ob-Irtysh <Russ>	Lena <Russ>
Yangtze Kiang <China>	Mackenzie <Can>

239 CHANNEL

NOUNS **1 channel, conduit, duct,** canal, course; **way, passage, passageway;** trough, troughway, troughing; tunnel; ditch, trench 290.2; adit; ingress, entrance 189; egress, exit; **stream** 238

2 watercourse, waterway, aqueduct, water channel, water gate, water carrier, culvert, **canal;** side-channel, intrariverine channel, snye <Can>; streamway, riverway; **bed,** stream bed, river bed, creek bed, runnel; water gap; dry bed, *arroyo* <Sp>, wadi, winterbourne, *donga* <Africa>, *nullah* <India>, **gully,** gullyhole, gulch; swash,

swash channel; race, headrace, tailrace; flume; sluice; spillway; spillbox; irrigation ditch, water furrow; waterworks

3 gutter, trough, eave *or* eaves trough; **flume,** chute, shoot; pentrough, penstock; guide

4 <metal founding> gate, ingate, runner, sprue, tedge

5 drain, sough <Brit nf>, sluice, scupper; **sink,** sump; piscina; **gutter,** kennel; **sewer,** cloaca, headchute; cloaca maxima

6 tube; pipe; tubing, piping, tubulation; tubulure; nipple, pipette, tubulet, tubule; reed, stem, straw; **hose,** hosepipe <Brit>, garden hose, fire hose; pipeline; catheter; **siphon;** tap; efflux tube, adjutage; funnel; snorkel; siamese, siamese connection *or* joint

7 main, water main, gas main, fire main

8 spout, beak, waterspout, downspout; gargoyle

9 nozzle, bib nozzle, pressure nozzle, spray nozzle, nose, snout; rose, rosehead; shower head, sprinkler head

10 valve, gate; **faucet, spigot, tap;** cock, **petcock,** draw cock, stopcock, sea cock, drain cock, ball cock; bunghole; needle valve; valvule, valvula

11 floodgate, flood-hatch, gate, **head gate,** penstock, water gate, **sluice,** sluice gate; tide gate, aboiteau <Can>; weir; **lock,** lock gate, dock gate; air lock

12 hydrant, fire hydrant, **plug,** water plug, fireplug

13 air passage, air duct, airway, air shaft, shaft, **air hole,** air tube; speaking tube *or* pipe; **blowhole,** breathing hole, spiracle; nostril; touchhole; spilehole, **vent, venthole,** ventage, ventiduct; **ventilator,** ventilating shaft; transom, louver, louverwork; wind tunnel

14 chimney, flue, flue pipe, funnel, **stovepipe, stack, smokestack,** smoke pipe, smokeshaft; Charley Noble; fumarole

VERBS **15 channel,** channelize, canalize, **conduct, convey,** put through; pipe, funnel, siphon; trench 290.3; direct 573.8

ADJS **16 tubular,** tubate, tubiform, tubelike, pipelike; cylindrical; tubed, piped; cannular; tubal

17 valvular, valval, valvelike; valved

240 SEA, OCEAN

NOUNS **1 ocean, sea,** ocean sea, great *or* main sea, *thalassa* <Gk>, **main** *or* ocean main, the bounding main, tide, salt sea, salt water, blue water, ocean blue, deep water, open sea, **the brine,** the briny *and* the big pond <nf>, the briny deep, **the deep,** the deep sea, the deep blue sea, drink *and* big drink <nf>, the herring pond <Brit nf>; **high sea, high seas;** the seven seas; hydrosphere; **ocean depths,** ocean deeps and trenches 275.4,17

2 "great Neptune's ocean," "unpath'd waters," —both Shakespeare, "Uterine Sea of our dreams and Sea haunted by the true dream," "Sea of a thousand creases, like the infinitely pleated tunic of the god in the hands of women of the sanctuary"—both S J Perse, "the great naked sea shouldering a load of salt"—Sandburg, "old ocean's gray and melancholy waste"—William Cullen Bryant, "the world of waters wild"—James Thomson, "the rising world of waters dark and deep," "the clear hyaline, the glassy sea"—both Milton

3 **ocean** <see list>; **sea,** tributary sea <see list>, gulf, bay

4 spirit of the sea, "the old man of the sea"—Homer, sea devil, Davy, **Davy Jones;** sea god, **Neptune,** Poseidon, Oceanus, Triton, Nereus, Oceanid, Nereid, Thetis, Amphitrite, Calypso; Varuna, Dylan; **mermaid,** siren; merman, seaman, undine, sea nymph, water sprite, sea serpent

5 <ocean zones> pelagic zone, benthic zone, estuarine area, sublittoral, littoral, intertidal zone, splash zone, supralittoral

6 ocean floor, seabed, sea bottom, benthos, Davy Jones's locker; continental shelf, continental slope, submarine canyon, land bridge, abyssal plain, abyssal hill, midoceanic ridge, oceanic ridge, oceanic trench, volcanic island, seamount, guyot, atoll

7 oceanography, thalassography, hydrography, bathymetry; marine biology; aquaculture

8 oceanographer, thalassographer, hydrographer, marine biologist, deep-sea diver, underwater explorer

ADJS **9** **oceanic, marine, maritime,** pelagic, thalassic; ocean-going, sea-going, seafaring; undersea, underwater; nautical 182.57; oceanographic, oceanographical, hydrographic, hydrographical, bathymetric, bathymetrical, bathyorographical, thalassographic, thalassographical; terriginous; deep-sea 275.14

ADVS **10** **at sea,** on the high seas; afloat 182.62; by water, by sea

11 **oversea, overseas,** beyond seas, over the water, transmarine, across the sea

12 **oceanward,** oceanwards, **seaward,** seawards, off; offshore, off soundings, out of soundings, in blue water

WORD ELEMENTS **13** mari-, thalass-, thalasso-; oceano-; bathy-

14 **oceans**

Antarctic	South Atlantic
Arctic	North Pacific
Indian	Pacific
North Atlantic	South Pacific

15 **seas**

Adriatic Sea	Gulf of Saint
Aegean Sea	Lawrence
Amundsen Sea	Hudson Bay
Andaman Sea	Inland Sea
Arabian Sea	Ionian Sea
Arafura Sea	Irish Sea
Aral Sea	Kara Sea
Baffin Bay	Laptev Sea
Bali Sea	Ligurian Sea
Baltic Sea	Macassar Strait
Banda Sea	Mediterranean Sea
Barents Sea	Molukka Sea
Bay of Bengal	North Sea
Beaufort Sea	Norwegian Sea
Bellingshausen Sea	Persian Gulf
Bering Sea	Philippine Sea
Black Sea	Red Sea
Caribbean Sea	Ross Sea
Caspian Sea	Sargasso Sea
Celebes Sea	Savu Sea
Ceram Sea	Sea of Azov
China Sea	Sea of Galilee
Chukchi Sea	Sea of Japan
Coral Sea	Sea of Marmara
East China Sea	Sea of Okhotsk
East Siberian Sea	South China Sea
Flores Sea	Sulu Sea
Great Australian Bight	Tasman Sea
Greenland Sea	Timor Sea
Gulf of Alaska	Tyrrhenian Sea
Gulf of California	Weddell Sea
Gulf of Guinea	White Sea
Gulf of Mexico	Yellow Sea

241 LAKE, POOL

NOUNS **1** **lake,** landlocked water, loch <Scot>, lough <Ir>, *nyanza* <Africa>, mere, freshwater lake, natural lake; oxbow lake, bayou lake, glacial lake; volcanic lake; mountain lake; salt lake; tarn; inland sea; **pool,** lakelet, **pond,** pondlet, dew pond, linn <Scot>, dike <Brit nf>, *étang* <Fr>; standing water, still water, stagnant water, dead water, bayou; **water** or watering hole, water pocket, swimming hole; **oasis;** farm pond; fishpond; millpond, millpool; salt pond, salina, tidal pond or pool; backwater; **puddle,** plash, sump <nf>; **lagoon,** *laguna* <Sp>; **reservoir,** artificial or manmade lake; dam; **well, cistern,** tank, artesian well, flowing well, **spring**

2 **lake dweller,** lakeside dweller, lacustrian, lacustrine dweller or inhabitant, **pile dweller** or builder; laker

3 **lake dwelling,** lacustrine dwelling, **pile house** or **dwelling,** stilt house, palafitte; crannog <Scot, Ir>; lake house, lakeside home; lakeside village

4 limnology, limnologist; limnimeter, limnograph

ADJS **5** **lakish,** laky, lakelike; lacustrine, lacustral, lacustrian; pondy, pondlike, lacuscular; limnetic, limnologic, limnological, limnophilous; landlocked; lakeside, lake-dwelling

6 major lakes

Aral Sea <Kazakhstan, Uzbekistan>	Manzala <Egypt>
Athabaska <Can>	Maracaibo <Venezuela>
Baikal <Russia>	Mead <US>
Balkhash <Kazakhstan>	Michigan <US>
Bangweulu <Zambia>	Mobutu Sese Seko <Uganda>
Bear <US>	Moosehead <US>
Becharof <US>	Ness <Scot>
Biwa <Japan>	Nettilling <Can>
Caspian Sea <Azerbaijan, Kazakhstan, Turkmenistan, Iran, Russ>	Nicaragua
	Nipigon <Can>
	Nyasa <Malawi, Mozambique, Tanzania>
Chad <Chad, Niger, Nigeria>	Okeechobee <US>
Champlain <US, Can>	Onega <Russ>
Chapala <Mex>	Ontario <US, Can>
Derwent Water <Brit>	Patos <Brazil>
Edward <Uganda, Zaire>	Pontchartrain <US>
Erie <US, Can>	Reindeer <Can>
Eyre <Australia>	Rudolf <Kenya>
Finger Lakes <US>	St. Clair <US, Can>
Flathead <US>	Superior <US, Can>
Gairdner <Australia>	Tahoe <US>
Garda <Ital>	Tanganyika <Tanzania, Congo>
George <US>	Texcoco <Mex>
Great Bear <Can>	Titicaca <Bolivia, Peru>
Great Salt <US>	Torrens <Australia>
Great Slave <Can>	Trasimeno <Ital>
Huron <US, Can>	Tung-t'ing <China>
Issyk-Kul <Kyrgyzstan>	Turkana <Kenya, Ethiopia>
Katrine <Scot>	Urmia <Iran>
Kioga <Uganda>	Utah <US>
Kivu <Zaire, Rwanda>	Vanem <Swed>
Koko-Nor <China>	Victoria <Tanzania, Uganda>
Ladoga <Russ>	
Lake of the Woods <Can>	Volta <Ghana>
Lochy <Scot>	Winnebago <US>
Lomond or Loch <Scot>	Winnipeg <Can>
Maggiore <It, Switz>	Yellowstone <US>
Malawi <Malawi, Mozambique, Tanzania>	Zurich <Switz>
Manitoba <Can>	

WORD ELEMENTS **7** limn-, limno-, limni-, -limnion

242 INLET, GULF

NOUNS **1 inlet, cove,** creek <Brit>, arm of the sea, arm, armlet, canal, reach, loch <Scot>, **bay, fjord** *or* fiord, bight; cove; **gulf; estuary,** firth *or* frith, bayou, mouth, outlet, *boca* <Sp>; **harbor,** natural harbor; bay; road *or* roads, roadstead; **strait** *or* straits, kyle <Scot>, **narrow** *or* **narrows,** euripus, belt, gut, narrow seas; **sound**

ADJS **2** gulfy, gulflike; gulfed, bayed, embayed; estuarine, fluviomarine, tidewater; drowned

243 MARSH

NOUNS **1 marsh,** marshland, **swamp,** swampland, fen, fenland, **morass,** mere *or* marish <old>, *marais* <Fr>, *maremma* <Ital>, **bog, mire, quagmire,** sump <nf>, wash, baygall; glade, everglade; slough, swale, wallow, hog wallow, buffalo wallow, sough <Brit>; bottom, **bottoms,** bottomland, slob land, holm <Brit>, water meadow, meadow; **moor,** moorland, moss <Scot>, peat bog; salt marsh; quicksand; taiga; mud flat, **mud** 1062.8,9

VERBS **2 mire,** bemire, sink in, **bog,** mire *or* bog down, stick in the mud; stodge

ADJS **3 marshy, swampy,** swampish, **moory,** moorish, fenny, marish <old>, paludal *or* paludous; **boggy,** boggish, **miry,** mirish, quaggy, quagmiry, spouty, poachy; **muddy** 1062.14; swamp-growing, uliginous

244 QUANTITY

NOUNS **1 quantity,** quantum, amount, **whole** 792; mass, **bulk,** substance, matter, magnitude, amplitude, **extent, sum; measure,** measurement; strength, force, numbers

2 amount, quantity, large amount, small amount, **sum, number,** count, group, total, reckoning, **measure,** parcel, passel <nf>, **part** 793, **portion,** clutch, ration, share, issue, allotment, lot, deal; **batch,** bunch, heap <nf>, pack, mess <nf>, gob *and* chunk *and* hunk <nf>, budget <old>, dose

3 some, somewhat, something; **aught; any,** anything

VERBS **4 quantify,** quantize, **count, number off, enumerate, number** 1017.10, rate, fix; parcel, apportion, mete out, issue, allot, divide 802.18; **increase** 251.4,6, **decrease** 252.6, reduce 252.7; quantitate, **measure** 300.11; set a quota

ADJS **5 quantitative,** quantitive, quantified, quantized, measured; **some,** certain, one; a, an; **any**

ADVS **6 approximately,** nearly, some, about, circa; more or less, *plus ou moins* <Fr>, by and large, upwards of

PREPS **7 to the amount of,** to the tune of <nf>; as much as, all of <nf>, no less than, upwards of

8 indefinite quantities

armful *or* armload	basket *or* basketful
bag *or* bagful	bin *or* binful
bargeload	bottle *or* bottleful
barrel *or* barrelful	bowl *or* bowlful
basin *or* basinful	box *or* boxful

bucket *or* bucketful
bundle
can *or* canful
cap *or* capful
carton *or* cartonful
case *or* caseful
crate *or* crateful
cup *or* cupful
flask *or* flaskful
glass *or* glassful
handful
jar *or* jarful
keg *or* kegful
kettle *or* kettleful
lapful
mouthful
mug *or* mugful
pail *or* pailful
pitcher *or* pitcherful

planeful *or* planeload
plate *or* plateful
pocketful
pot *or* potful
roomful
sack *or* sackful *or*
    sackload
scoop *or* scoopful
shovel *or* shovelful
spoon *or* spoonful
tablespoon *or*
    tablespoonful
tank *or* tankful
tankerload
teacup *or* teacupful
teaspoon *or* teaspoonful
thimble *or* thimbleful
truckload
tub *or* tubful

245 DEGREE

NOUNS **1 degree, grade, step,** *pas* <Fr>, leap; round,
rung, tread, stair; **point,** mark, peg, tick; **notch,**
cut; **plane,** level, plateau; **period,** space, interval;
extent, measure, amount, ratio, proportion, stint,
standard, height, pitch, reach, remove, compass,
range, scale, scope, caliber; **shade,** shadow, nuance

2 rank, standing, level, footing, **status,** station;
position, place, sphere, orbit, echelon; **order,**
estate, precedence, condition; rate, rating; **class,**
caste; **hierarchy,** power structure

3 gradation, graduation, grading, staging, phasing,
tapering, shading; gradualism

VERBS **4 graduate, grade,** calibrate; phase in, phase
out, taper off, shade off, scale; **increase** 251,
decrease 252.6,7; change by degrees

ADJS **5 gradual,** gradational, calibrated, graduated,
phased, staged, tapered, scalar; regular,
progressive; hierarchic, hierarchical; in scale,
calibrated; proportional

ADVS **6 by degrees,** degreewise; **gradually,** gradatim;
step by step, grade by grade, *di grado in grado*
<Ital>, **bit by bit, little by little,** inch by inch,
inchmeal, drop by drop; a little, fractionally; a little
at a time, by slow degrees, by inches; slowly 175.13

7 to a degree, to some extent, in a way, in a
measure, in some measure; somewhat, kind of
<nf>, sort of <nf>, rather, pretty, quite, fairly; a
little, a bit; slightly, scarcely, to a small degree
248.9,10; very, extremely, to a great degree
247.19,22

246 MEAN

NOUNS **1 mean, median, middle** 819; **golden mean,**
juste milieu <Fr>; **medium,** happy medium;

middle of the road, middle course, *via media* <L>;
middle state *or* ground *or* position *or* echelon *or*
level *or* point, midpoint; **average,** balance, par,
normal, norm, rule, run, generality; **mediocrity,**
averageness, passableness, adequacy; averaging,
mediocritization; **center** 208.2

VERBS **2 average,** average out, **split the difference,**
take the average, strike a balance, pair off, split
down the middle; strike *or* hit a happy medium;
keep to the middle, avoid extremes; **do,** just do,
pass, barely pass; mediocritize

ADJS **3 medium,** mean, **intermediate,** intermediary,
median, medial, mesial, mid-level, middle-echelon;
average, normal, standard, par for the course;
middle-of-the-road, moderate, fence-sitting,
middle-ground; **middling, ordinary,** usual, routine,
common, mediocre, merely adequate, passing,
banal, so-so, vanilla <nf>; **central** 208.11

ADVS **4 mediumly,** medianly; medially, midway
819.5, intermediately, in the mean; **centrally**
208.15

**5 on the average, in the long run, over the long
haul; taking one thing with another,** taking all
things together, **all in all, on the whole,** all things
considered, on balance; **generally** 863.17

WORD ELEMENTS **6** medi-, mes-, mezzo-, semi-

247 GREATNESS

NOUNS **1 greatness, magnitude,** muchness;
amplitude, ampleness, fullness, plenitude, great
scope *or* compass *or* reach; **grandeur,** grandness;
immensity, enormousness *or* enormity, **vastness,**
vastitude, tremendousness, expanse,
boundlessness, infinity 823; stupendousness,
formidableness, prodigiousness, humongousness
<nf>; **might,** mightiness, strength, power,
intensity; **largeness** 257.6, **hugeness,** gigantism,
bulk; **superiority** 249

**2 glory, eminence, preeminence, majesty, loftiness,
prominence,** distinction, outstandingness,
consequence, notability; **magnanimity,** nobility,
sublimity; **fame,** renown, celebrity; heroism

3 quantity 244, **numerousness** 884; **quantities,
much, abundance,** copiousness, superabundance,
superfluity, profusion, plenty, plenitude; **volume,
mass,** mountain, load; peck, bushel; bag, barrel,
ton; world, acre, ocean, sea; flood, spate; **multitude**
884.3, countlessness 823.1

4 lot, lots, deal, no end of, **good** *or* **great deal,
considerable,** sight, **heap, pile, stack,** loads, **raft,
slew,** whole slew, spate, wad, **batch,** mess, mint,
peck, pack, pot, **tidy sum,** quite a little; **oodles,
gobs, scads,** bags *and* masses *and* lashings <Brit>

VERBS **5 loom, bulk,** loom large, bulk large, stand

out; **tower,** rear, soar, outsoar; **tower above,** rise above, overtop; **exceed, transcend,** outstrip

ADJS **6 great, grand, considerable,** consequential; **mighty,** powerful, strong, irresistible, intense; main, maximum, **total, full,** plenary, comprehensive, exhaustive; grave, **serious,** heavy, deep

7 large 257.16, **immense, enormous, huge** 257.20; **gigantic,** mountainous, titanic, colossal, mammoth, Gargantuan, gigantesque, monster, monstrous, outsize, sizable, larger-than-life, overgrown, king-size, monumental; **massive,** massy, weighty, bulky, voluminous; **vast,** vasty, boundless, **infinite** 822.3, immeasurable, cosmic, astronomical, galactic; **spacious,** amplitudinous, extensive; **tremendous,** stupendous, awesome, prodigious

8 much, many, beaucoup <nf>, ample, **abundant,** copious, generous, overflowing, superabundant, multitudinous, plentiful, **numerous** 884.6, countless 823.3

9 eminent, prominent, outstanding, standout, high, elevated, towering, soaring, overtopping, exalted, **lofty,** sublime; august, majestic, noble, distinguished; **magnificent,** magnanimous, heroic, godlike, superb; famous, renowned, lauded, glorious

10 remarkable, outstanding, extraordinary, **superior** 249.12, **marked,** of mark, signal, conspicuous, **striking; notable,** much in evidence, noticeable, noteworthy; **marvelous,** wonderful, formidable, exceptional, uncommon, astonishing, appalling, humongous <nf>, fabulous, fantastic, incredible, brilliant, egregious

11 <nf terms> **terrific,** terrible, horrible, **dreadful, awful,** fearful, frightful, deadly; **whacking, thumping, rousing,** howling

12 downright, outright, out-and-out; absolute, utter, perfect, consummate, superlative, surpassing, the veriest, positive, definitive, classical, pronounced, decided, regular <nf>, proper <Brit nf>, precious, profound, stark; **thorough,** thoroughgoing, **complete,** total; **unmitigated,** unqualified, unrelieved, unspoiled, undeniable, unquestionable, unequivocal; **flagrant,** arrant, shocking, shattering, egregious, intolerable, unbearable, unconscionable, glaring, stark-staring, **rank,** crass, gross

13 extreme, radical, out of this world, way or far out <nf>, too much <nf>; **greatest,** furthest, **most, utmost,** uttermost, the max <nf>; **ultra,** ultra-ultra; at the height or peak or limit or summit or zenith

14 undiminished, unabated, unreduced, unrestricted, unretarded, unmitigated

ADVS **15 greatly, largely,** to a large or great extent, in great measure, on a large scale; **much,** muchly <nf>, pretty much, very much, so, so very much, ever so much, ever so, never so; **considerably,** considerable <nf>; abundantly, plenty <nf>, no end of, no end, not a little, galore <nf>, **a lot,** a deal <nf>, **a great deal,** beaucoup <Fr>; **highly,** to the skies; like or as all creation <nf>, like or as all get-out <nf>, in spades and with bells on and with bells on one's toes <nf>; **undiminishedly,** unabatedly, unreducedly, unrestrictedly, unretardedly, unmitigatedly

16 vastly, immensely, enormously, hugely, tremendously, gigantically, colossally, titanically, prodigiously, stupendously, humongously <nf>

17 by far, far and away, far, far and wide, by a long way, by a great deal, by a long shot or long chalk <nf>, out and away, by all odds

18 very, exceedingly, awfully and terribly and terrifically <nf>, **quite,** just, so, **really,** real and right <nf>, **pretty,** only too, mightily, **mighty** and almighty and powerfully and powerful <nf>

19 <in a positive degree> **positively, decidedly, clearly,** manifestly, unambiguously, patently, **obviously,** visibly, unmistakably, unquestionably, observably, **noticeably,** demonstrably, sensibly, quite; **certainly,** actually, **really, truly,** basically, verily, **undeniably,** indubitably, without doubt, assuredly, **indeed,** for a certainty, for real <nf>, seriously, in all conscience

20 <in a marked degree> **intensely, acutely,** exquisitely, **exceptionally,** surpassingly, superlatively, eminently, preeminently; **remarkably, markedly, notably, strikingly,** signally, emphatically, pointedly, prominently, conspicuously, pronouncedly, impressively, famously, glaringly; **particularly, singularly,** peculiarly; uncommonly, extraordinarily, **unusually; wonderfully,** wondrous, amazingly, magically, surprisingly, astonishingly, marvelously, exuberantly, incredibly, awesomely; **abundantly,** richly, profusely, amply, **generously,** copiously; **magnificently,** splendidly, nobly, worthily, magnanimously

21 <in a distressing degree> **distressingly, sadly, sorely, bitterly,** piteously, grievously, miserably, **cruelly,** woefully, lamentably, balefully, dolorously, shockingly; **terribly, awfully, dreadfully, frightfully, horribly,** abominably, **painfully,** excruciatingly, torturously, **agonizingly,** deathly, deadly, something awful or fierce or terrible and in the worst way <nf>, within an inch of one's life; shatteringly, staggeringly; **excessively,** exorbitantly, extravagantly, **inordinately,** preposterously; **unduly, improperly,** intolerably, unbearably; **inexcusably,**

unpardonably, unconscionably; **flagrantly,**
blatantly, egregiously; **unashamedly,** unabashedly,
baldly, nakedly, brashly, openly; **cursedly,**
confoundedly, **damnably,** deucedly <nf>,
infernally, hellishly

22 <in an extreme degree> **extremely, utterly, totally,**
in the extreme, **most,** *à outrance* <Fr, to the
utmost>; mondo <nf>; **immeasurably,**
incalculably, indefinitely, **infinitely;** beyond
compare *or* comparison, **beyond measure,** beyond
all bounds, all out <nf>, flat out <Brit nf>;
perfectly, absolutely, essentially, fundamentally,
radically; **purely, totally,** completely, to the max;
unconditionally, with no strings attached,
unequivocally, downright, dead; with a vengeance

23 <in a violent degree> **violently,** furiously, hotly,
fiercely, severely, **desperately,** madly, **like mad**
<nf>; **wildly,** demonically, like one possessed,
frantically, frenetically, fanatically, uncontrollably

WORD ELEMENTS **24** meg-, mega-, multi-, super-

248 INSIGNIFICANCE

NOUNS **1 insignificance,** inconsiderableness,
unimportance 998, inconsequentialness,
inconsequentiality, lowness, pettiness, meanness,
triviality, nugacity, nugaciousness; **smallness,**
tininess, diminutiveness, minuteness, exiguity *or*
exiguousness; **slightness,** moderateness,
scantiness, puniness, picayunishness, meanness,
meagerness; daintiness, delicacy; **littleness** 258;
fewness 885; insufficiency 991

2 modicum, minim; **minimum; little, bit,** little *or*
wee *or* tiny bit <nf>, bite, **particle,** fragment, spot,
speck, flyspeck, fleck, point, dot, jot, tittle, **iota,**
ounce, **dab** <nf>, mote, **mite** <nf> 258.7; whit,
ace, **hair,** scruple, groat, farthing, pittance, dole,
trifling amount, **smidgen** *and* skosh *and* smitch
<nf>, pinch, gobbet, dribble, driblet, dram, drop,
drop in a bucket *or* in the ocean, tip of the iceberg;
grain, granule, pebble; molecule, **atom;** thimbleful,
spoonful, handful, nutshell; trivia, minutiae; dwarf

3 scrap, tatter, smithereen <nf>, patch, **stitch,**
shred, tag; snip, **snippet,** snick, chip, nip; splinter,
sliver, shiver; **morsel,** *morceau* <Fr>, **crumb**

4 hint, *soupçon* <Fr>, **suspicion, suggestion,**
intimation; tip of the iceberg; **trace, touch, dash,**
cast, **smattering,** sprinkling; tinge, tincture; **taste,**
lick, smack, sip, sup, **smell;** look, **thought,** idea;
shade, shadow; gleam, spark, scintilla

5 hardly anything, mere nothing, next to nothing,
less than nothing, **trifle,** bagatelle, **a drop in the**
bucket *or* **in the ocean;** the shadow of a shade, the
suspicion of a suspicion

ADJS **6 insignificant, small, inconsiderable,**

inconsequential, **negligible,** no great shakes,
footling, one-horse *and* pint-size *and* vest-pocket
<nf>; unimportant, no skin off one's nose *or* ass,
trivial, trifling, nugacious, nugatory, petty, mean,
niggling, picayune *or* picayunish, nickel-and-dime
and penny-ante *and* Mickey-Mouse *and*
chickenshit <nf>; shallow, depthless, cursory,
superficial, skin-deep; **little** 258.10, **tiny** 258.11,
weeny, miniature 258.12, **meager** 992.10, **few**
885.4; **short** 268.8; **low** 274.7

7 dainty, delicate, gossamer, diaphanous; subtle,
subtile, tenuous, thin 270.16, rarefied 299.4

8 mere, sheer, stark, bare, bare-bones, plain, simple,
unadorned, unenhanced

ADVS **9** <in a small degree> **scarcely, hardly,** not
hardly <nf>, **barely,** only just, by a hair, by an ace
or a jot *or* a whit *or* an iota, **slightly,** lightly,
exiguously, fractionally, scantily, inconsequentially,
insignificantly, negligibly, imperfectly, minimally,
inappreciably, **little; minutely,** meagerly, triflingly,
faintly, weakly, feebly; **a little, a bit,** just a bit, to a
small extent, on a small scale; ever so little, *tant*
soit peu <Fr>, as little as may be

10 <in a certain or limited degree> **to a degree, to a**
certain extent, to some degree, in some measure,
to such an extent, *pro tanto* <L>; **moderately,**
mildly, **somewhat,** detectably, just visibly, modestly,
appreciably, visibly, **fairly,** tolerably, **partially,**
partly, part, in part, incompletely, not exhaustively,
not comprehensively; **comparatively, relatively;**
merely, simply, purely, only; **at least,** at the least,
leastwise, at worst, at any rate; **at most,** at the
most, at best, at the outside <nf>; in a manner, in
a manner of speaking, **in a way,** after a fashion; so
far, thus far

11 <in no degree> **noway,** noways, **nowise,** in no
wise, in no case, in no respect, **by no means,** by no
manner of means, **on no account, not on any**
account, not for anything in the world, under no
circumstances, at no hand, nohow <nf>, **not in**
the least, not much, **not at all,** never, not by a
damn sight <nf>, not by a long shot <nf>; not
nearly, **nowhere near; not a bit,** not a bit of it, not
a whit, not a speck, not a jot, not an iota

249 SUPERIORITY

NOUNS **1 superiority, preeminence, greatness** 247,
lead, pride of place, transcendence *or*
transcendency, ascendancy *or* ascendance,
prestige, favor, prepotence *or* prepotency,
preponderance; predominance *or* predominancy,
hegemony; precedence 814, **priority,** prerogative,
privilege, right-of-way; **excellence** 999.1, virtuosity,
high caliber, inimitability, incomparability;

seniority, precedence, deanship; clout, pull <nf>; **success** 409, accomplishment 407, **skill** 413

2 **advantage,** vantage, odds, leg up *and* inside track *and* pole position <nf>; **upper hand,** whip hand, trump hand; start, head *or* flying *or* running start; **edge,** bulge *and* jump *and* drop <nf>; **card up one's sleeve** <nf>, ace in the hole <nf>, something extra *or* in reserve; vantage ground *or* point, coign of vantage, high ground; one-upmanship

3 **supremacy, primacy,** paramountcy, **first place,** height, acme, zenith, be-all and end-all, summit, top spot <nf>; **sovereignty, rule, hegemony, control** 417.5; kingship, **dominion** 417.6, lordship, imperium, world power; **command,** sway; **mastery,** mastership 417.7; **leadership,** headship, presidency; **authority** 417, directorship, management, jurisdiction, power, say *and* last word <nf>; influence 894; effectiveness; **maximum,** highest, most, *ne plus ultra* <Fr, no more beyond>, the max <nf>; **championship,** crown, laurels, palms, first prize, blue ribbon, new high, record

4 **superior, chief, head, boss** 575.1, employer, honcho <nf>, commander, **ruler, leader,** dean, *primus inter pares* <L, first among equals>, **master** 575; higher-up <nf>, senior, principal, big shot <nf>; superman, **genius** 413.12; prodigy, nonpareil, paragon, virtuoso, ace, **star, superstar,** champion, winner, top dog *and* top banana <nf>, one in a thousand, one in a million, etc, laureate, fugleman, Cadillac *and* Rolls-Royce <trademark>, A per se, A1, A number 1, standout, money-maker, record-breaker, the greatest *and* the most whiz *and* whizbang *and* world-beater *and* a tough act to follow <nf>; big fish in a small pond <nf>

5 **the best** 999.8, the top of the line <nf>; the best people, nobility 608; **aristocracy,** barons, top people <nf>, **elite,** cream, crème de la crème, top of the milk, upper crust, upper class, one's betters; **the brass** <nf>, the VIP's <nf>, higher-ups, movers and shakers, lords of creation, ruling circles, **establishment,** power elite, power structure, **ruling class,** bigwigs <nf>, big boys <nf>, authorities, powers that be, officialdom; fast track; happy few, chosen few

VERBS 6 **excel, surpass, exceed, transcend,** get *or* have the ascendancy, get *or* have the edge, have it all over <nf>, overcome, overpass, best, **better,** improve on, perfect, go one better <nf>; **cap,** trump; top, tower above *or* over, overtop; **predominate,** prevail, preponderate, carry the day; **outweigh,** overbalance, overbear

7 **best, beat, beat out, defeat** 412.6; beat all hollow <nf>, trounce, clobber *and* take to the cleaners *and* smoke *and* skin *and* skin alive <nf>, worst, whip *and* lick *and* have it all over *and* cut down to size <nf>; bear the palm, take the cake <nf>, bring home the bacon <nf>; **triumph; win** 411.4

8 **overshadow, eclipse, throw into the shade, top,** extinguish, take the shine out of <nf>; put to shame, show up <nf>, put one's nose out of joint, put down <nf>, fake out <nf>

9 **outdo, outrival,** outvie, outachieve, edge out, **outclass, outshine,** overmatch, outgun <nf>; **outstrip,** outgo, outrange, outreach, outpoint, **outperform;** outplay, overplay, outmaneuver, outwit; outrun, outstep, outpace, outmarch, run rings *or* circles around <nf>; outride, override; outjump, overjump; outleap, overleap

10 **outdistance, distance; pass, surpass,** overpass; **get ahead,** pull ahead, shoot ahead, walk away *or* off <nf>; **leave behind,** leave at the post, leave in the dust, leave in the lurch; **come to the front,** have a healthy lead <nf>, hold the field; steal a march

11 **rule, command, lead,** possess authority 417.13, have the authority, have the say *or* the last word, have the whip hand *and* hold all the aces <nf>; **take precedence, precede** 814.2; **come** *or* **rank first, outrank,** rank, rank out <nf>; **come to the fore,** come to the front, **lead** 165.2; play first fiddle, **star**

ADJS 12 **superior, greater,** better, finer; **higher,** upper, over, super, above; ascendant, in the ascendant, in ascendancy, coming <nf>; **eminent,** outstanding, rare, distinguished, marked, of choice, chosen; **surpassing, exceeding, excellent** 999.12, **excelling, rivaling, eclipsing,** capping, topping, **transcending,** transcendent *or* transcendental, bad <nf>; **ahead,** a cut *or* stroke above, one up on <nf>; more than a match for

13 **superlative, supreme, greatest, best, highest,** veriest, maximal, maximum, most, utmost, outstanding, stickout <nf>; top, topmost, **uppermost,** tip-top, top-level, top-echelon, top-notch *and* top-of-the-line <nf>, **first-rate,** first-class, of the first water, top of the line, highest-quality, best-quality, far and away the best, the best by a long shot *or* long chalk, head and shoulders above, of the highest type, A1, A number 1, drop-dead <nf>

14 **chief, main, principal,** paramount, **foremost,** headmost, **leading, dominant,** crowning, capital, **cardinal;** great, arch, banner, master, magisterial; central, focal, prime, **primary,** primal, first; **preeminent,** supereminent; **predominant,** preponderant, prevailing, hegemonic *or* hegemonical; ruling, overruling; **sovereign** 417.17; topflight, highest-ranking, ranking; **star,** superstar, stellar, world-class

15 **peerless, matchless, champion; unmatched,**
unmatchable, makeless <old>, unrivaled,
unparagoned, unparalleled, immortal, **unequaled,**
never-to-be-equaled, unpeered, unexampled,
unapproached, unapproachable, **unsurpassed,**
unexcelled; unsurpassable; inimitable,
incomparable, beyond compare *or* comparison,
unique; without equal *or* parallel, *sans pareil*
<Fr>; in a class by itself, *sui generis* <L>, easily
first, *facile princeps* <L>; second to none, *nulli*
secundus <L>; **unbeatable,** invincible

ADVS **16** **superlatively, exceedingly, surpassingly;**
eminently, egregiously, prominently; supremely,
paramountly, preeminently, **the most,**
transcendently, to crown all, *par excellence* <Fr>;
inimitably, incomparably; to *or* in the highest
degree, far and away

17 **chiefly, mainly, in the main,** in chief; dominantly,
predominantly; mostly, for the most part;
principally, especially, particularly, peculiarly;
primarily, in the first place, first of all, **above all;**
indeed, even, yea, still more, more than ever, all
the more, *a fortiori* <L>; ever so, never so, no end

18 **peerlessly, matchlessly,** unmatchably;
unsurpassedly, unsurpassably; inimitably,
incomparably; uniquely, second to none, *nulli*
secundus <L>; **unbeatably,** invincibly

19 **advantageously,** to *or* with advantage, favorably;
melioratively, amelioratively, improvingly

WORD ELEMENTS **20** preter-, super-, supra-, sur-,
trans-, ultra-, arch-, prot-

250 INFERIORITY

NOUNS **1** **inferiority, subordinacy,** subordination,
secondariness; **juniority,** minority; **subservience,**
subjection, servility, lowliness, humbleness,
humility; back seat *and* second fiddle <nf>,
second *or* third string <nf>; insignificance

2 **inferior, underling,** understrapper <Brit>,
subordinate, subaltern, **junior;** secondary, second
fiddle *and* second stringer *and* third stringer *and*
benchwarmer *and* low man on the totem pole
<nf>, loser *and* nonstarter <nf>; lightweight,
follower, pawn, cog, flunky, yes-man, creature;
lower class *or* orders *or* ranks, lowlife,
commonalty; infrastructure *or* commonality, *hoi*
polloi <Gk>, masses; satellite

3 **inadequacy, mediocrity** 1005, deficiency,
imperfection, insufficiency 992; **incompetence** *or*
incompetency, maladroitness, unskillfulness 414;
failure 410; smallness 248.1; littleness 258;
meanness, lowness, baseness, pettiness, triviality,
shabbiness, vulgarity 497; **fewness** 885;
subnormality

VERBS **4** **be inferior, not come up to, not measure**
up, fall *or* **come short, fail** 410.8, not make *or* hack
it *and* not cut the mustard *and* not make the cut
<nf>, not make the grade; want, leave much to be
desired, be found wanting; **not compare,** have
nothing on <nf>, **not hold a candle to** <nf>, not
approach, not come near; serve, subserve, rank
under *or* beneath, follow, play second fiddle *and*
take a back seat *and* sit on the bench <nf>

5 **bow to, hand it to** <nf>, tip the hat to <nf>, yield
the palm; retire into the shade; give in <nf>, lose
face; submit

ADJS **6** **inferior, subordinate,** subaltern, sub, small-
scale, **secondary; junior, minor;** second *or* third
string *and* one-horse *and* penny-ante *and* dinky
<nf>, second *or* third rank, low in the pecking
order, low-rent *and* downscale <nf>, below the
salt; **subservient,** subject, servile, low, **lowly,**
humble, modest; **lesser,** less, lower; in the shade,
thrown into the shade; **common,** vulgar, **ordinary;**
underprivileged, disadvantaged, nothing to write
home about; **beneath one's dignity** *or* station, infra
dig, demeaning

7 **inadequate, mediocre,** deficient, imperfect,
insufficient; incompetent, unskillful, maladroit;
small, small-time, little, mean, base, petty, trivial,
shabby; **not to be compared, not comparable, not**
a patch on <nf>; **outclassed,** outshone, not in it
and not in the same street *or* league with <nf>,
out of it *and* out of the picture *and* **out of the**
running *and* left a mile behind <nf>

8 **least, smallest,** littlest, slightest, **lowest,** shortest;
minimum, minimal, minim; few 885.4

ADVS **9** **poorly, incompetently, inadequately,** badly,
maladroitly; least of all, at the bottom of the scale,
at the nadir, at the bottom of the heap *and* in the
gutter <nf>; at a disadvantage

WORD ELEMENTS **10** sub-, hyp-, hypo-

251 INCREASE

NOUNS **1** **increase, gain,** augmentation, greatening,
enlargement, amplification, growth, development,
widening, spread, broadening, elevation,
extension, aggrandizement, access, accession,
increment, accretion; **addition** 253; **expansion** 259;
inflation, swelling, ballooning, edema, fattening,
tumescence, bloating, dilation; **multiduplication,**
proliferation, productiveness 890; accruement,
accrual, accumulation; **advance,** appreciation,
ascent, mounting, crescendo, waxing, snowballing,
rise *or* raise, fattening *and* boost *and* hike <nf>,
up *and* upping <nf>, buildup; **upturn,** uptick
<nf>, uptrend, upsurge, upswing; **leap,** jump;
flood, surge, gush

2 intensification, heightening, deepening; tightening, turn of the screw; **strengthening,** beefing-up <nf>, enhancement, **magnification,** blowup, blowing up, exaggeration; aggravation, exacerbation, heating-up; **concentration,** condensation, consolidation; **reinforcement,** redoubling; pickup *and* step-up <nf>, **acceleration,** speedup, accelerando, escalation, upsurge; **boom, explosion,** baby boom, population explosion, information explosion

3 gains, winnings, cut *and* take <nf>, increase <old>, **profits** 472.3

VERBS **4 increase, enlarge,** aggrandize, **amplify, augment, extend,** maximize, **add to; expand** 259.4, **inflate;** lengthen, broaden, fatten, fill out, thicken; **raise,** exalt, boost <nf>, hike *and* hike up *and* jack up *and* jump up <nf>, mark up, put up, **up** <nf>; **build, build up;** pyramid, parlay; progress

5 intensify, heighten, deepen, amplify, enhance, **strengthen,** beef up <nf>, aggravate, exacerbate; **exaggerate,** blow up *and* puff up <nf>, **magnify;** whet, sharpen; **reinforce,** double, redouble, triple; **concentrate,** condense, consolidate; **complicate,** ramify, make complex; give a boost to, **step up** <nf>, accelerate; key up, hop up *and* soup up *and* jazz up <nf>; add fuel to the flame *or* the fire, heat *or* hot up <nf>

6 grow, increase, advance, appreciate; **spread, widen,** broaden; **gain,** get ahead; wax, swell, balloon, bloat, mount, **rise,** go up, crescendo, snowball, skyrocket; **intensify, develop,** gain strength, strengthen; accrue, accumulate; **multiply, proliferate,** breed, teem; run *or* shoot up, **boom, explode**

ADJS **7 increased, heightened,** raised, elevated, stepped-up <nf>; **intensified,** deepened, reinforced, strengthened, fortified, beefed-up <nf>, tightened, stiffened; **enlarged, extended,** augmented, aggrandized, amplified, **enhanced,** boosted, hiked <nf>; broadened, widened, spread; **magnified, inflated, expanded,** swollen, bloated; **multiplied,** proliferated; **accelerated,** hopped-up *and* jazzed-up <nf>, hiked

8 increasing, rising, fast-rising, skyrocketing, meteoric; on the upswing, on the increase, on the rise; crescent, waxing, **growing,** fast-growing, flourishing, burgeoning, blossoming, waxing, swelling, lengthening, **multiplying,** proliferating; spreading, spreading like a cancer *or* like wildfire, expanding; tightening, intensifying; incremental; **on the increase,** crescendoing, snowballing, mushrooming, growing like a mushroom

ADVS **9 increasingly,** growingly, more, **more and more,** on and on, greater and greater, ever more; in a crescendo

252 DECREASE

NOUNS **1 decrease,** decrescence, decrement, **diminishment,** diminution, **reduction, lessening, lowering,** waning, shrinking *or* shrinkage, withering, withering away, scaling down, scaledown, downsizing, build-down; miniaturization; downplaying, underplaying; depression, damping, dampening; **letup** <nf>, abatement, easing, easing off, slackening; de-escalation; **alleviation,** relaxation, mitigation; attenuation, extenuation, weakening, sagging, dying, dying off *or* away, trailing off, tailing off, tapering off, fade-out, languishment; depreciation, **deflation; deduction** 255.1; subtraction, **abridgment** 268.3; **contraction** 260; simplicity 798

2 decline, declension, **subsidence,** slump <nf>, lapse, **drop,** downtick <nf>; **collapse,** crash; dwindling, wane, ebb; downturn, downtrend, downward trend *or* curve, retreat, remission; **fall, plunge,** dive, decline and fall; decrescendo, diminuendo; catabasis, deceleration, slowdown; leveling off, bottoming out

3 decrement, waste, loss, dissipation, wear and tear, erosion, ablation, wearing away, depletion, corrosion, attrition, consumption, shrinkage, exhaustion; deliquescence, dissolution; extinction, consumption

4 curtailment, retrenchment, cut, cutback, drawdown, rollback, scaleback, pullback; moderation, restraint; abridgment

5 minimization, minification, making light of, devaluing, undervaluing, **belittling,** belittlement, detraction; qualification 959

VERBS **6 decrease, diminish, lessen; let up,** bate, abate; **decline, subside,** shrink, wane, wither, ebb, ebb away, dwindle, languish, sink, sag, die down *or* away, wind down, taper off *and* trail off *or* away *and* tail off *or* away <nf>; **drop,** drop off, dive, take a nose dive, plummet, plunge, fall, fall off, fall away, fall to a low ebb, run low; **waste,** wear, waste *or* wear away, crumble, erode, ablate, corrode, consume, consume away, be eaten away; melt away, deliquesce; become extinct

7 reduce, decrease, diminish, lessen, take from; **lower, depress,** de-escalate, damp, dampen, **step down** *and* tune down *and* phase down *or* out *and* scale back *or* down *and* roll back *or* down <nf>; **downgrade;** depreciate, **deflate; curtail,** retrench; **cut,** cut down *or* back, cut down to size <nf>, trim away, chip away at, whittle away *or* down, pare, pare down, roll back <nf>; deduct 255.9; **shorten** 268.6, abridge; **compress** 260.7, shrink, retrench, downsize; **simplify** 798.4

8 abate, bate, ease; **weaken,** dilute, water, water

down, attenuate, extenuate; alleviate, mitigate, slacken, remit; enfeeble, debilitate

9 minimize, minify, **belittle,** detract from; dwarf, bedwarf; play down, underplay, downplay, de-emphasize, play down, tone down, moderate; hush

ADJS 10 reduced, decreased, diminished, lowered, dropped, fallen; bated, **abated; deflated,** contracted, shrunk, shrunken; **simplified** 797.9; back-to-basics, no-frills; dissipated, **eroded,** consumed, ablated, **worn;** curtailed, shorn, retrenched, cutback; weakened, attenuated, watered-down, diluted; scaled-down, miniaturized, pared down; minimized, belittled, on a downer <nf>; **lower,** less, lesser, smaller, shorter; off-peak; downplayed, underplayed, toned down, de-emphasized

11 decreasing, diminishing, lessening, subsiding, declining, languishing, dwindling, waning, on the wane, on the slide, wasting; decrescent, reductive, deliquescent, **contractive;** diminuendo, decrescendo

ADVS 12 decreasingly, diminishingly, less, **less and less,** ever less; decrescendo, diminuendo; on a declining scale, at a declining rate

253 ADDITION

NOUNS 1 addition, accession, annexation, affixation, suffixation, prefixation, agglutination, attachment, junction, **joining** 800, adjunction, uniting; **increase** 251; **augmentation, supplementation, complementation,** reinforcement; superaddition, admixture, superposition, superjunction, superfetation, suppletion; juxtaposition 223.3; adjunct 254, add-on, accessory

2 <math terms> plus sign, plus; addend; sum, summation, total, aggregate; subtotal

3 adding, totalizing or totalization, reckoning, computation, calculation, ringing up; **adding machine,** calculator

VERBS 4 add, plus <nf>, put with, **join** or **unite with, bring together, affix, attach,** annex, adjoin, append, conjoin, subjoin, prefix, suffix, infix, postfix, tag, tag on, **tack on** <nf>, slap on <nf>, hitch on <nf>, carry over; glue on, paste on, agglutinate; superpose, superadd; burden, encumber, saddle with; **complicate,** ornament, decorate

5 add to, augment, supplement; increase 251.4; **reinforce,** strengthen, fortify, beef up <nf>; recruit, swell the ranks of; superadd

6 compute, add up; sum, total, totalize, total up, tot and tot up and tote and tote up <nf>, tally, calculate

7 be added, advene, supervene

ADJS 8 additive, additional, additory; **cumulative,** accumulative; summative or summational; loaded

9 added, affixed, add-on, **attached,** annexed, appended, appendant; adjoined, adjunct, adjunctive, conjoined, subjoined; superadded, superposed, superjoined

10 additional, supplementary, supplemental; extra, plus, further, farther, fresh, **more,** new, **other,** another, ulterior; **auxiliary,** ancillary, supernumerary, contributory, **accessory,** collateral, supererogatory; **surplus,** spare, superfluous

ADVS 11 additionally, in addition, also, and then some, even more, more so, and also, and all <nf>, and so, **as well, too,** else, beside, **besides, to boot, not to mention, let alone, into the bargain;** on top of, over, above; **beyond, plus; extra,** on the side <nf>, for lagniappe; **more, moreover,** au reste <Fr>, en plus <Fr>, thereto, farther, further, **furthermore,** at the same time, then, again, yet; similarly, likewise, by the same token, by the same sign; item; therewith, withal <old>; all included, altogether; among other things, inter alia <L>

PREPS 12 with, plus, including, inclusive of, **along** or **together with,** coupled with, **in conjunction with; as well as,** to say nothing of, not to mention, let alone; over and above, **in addition to,** added to, linked to; with the addition of, attended by

CONJS 13 and, also, and also

PHRS 14 et cetera, etc, and so forth, and so on, und so weiter <Ger>; et al, et alii <L>, and all <nf>, and others, and other things, cum multis aliis <L, with many others>; and everything else, **and more of the same, and the rest, and the like;** blah blah blah blah and dah-dah dah-dah dah-dah and and suchlike or and all that sort of thing and and all that and and all like that and and stuff like that and and all that jazz <nf>; **and what not** and and what have you and and I don't know what and and God knows what and and then some and you name it <nf>; and the following, et sequens <L>, et seq

WORD ELEMENTS 15 super-, pleo-, pleio-

254 ADJUNCT

<thing added>

NOUNS 1 adjunct, addition, increase, **increment,** augmentation, supplementation, complementation, additum <L>, additament, additory, addendum, addenda <pl>, accession, fixture; **annex,** annexation; **appendage,** appendant, pendant, appanage, tailpiece, coda; undergirding, reinforcement; appurtenance, appurtenant; **accessory,** attachment; **supplement,** complement, continuation, extrapolation, extension; offshoot, side issue, corollary, sidebar <nf>, side effect, spin-off <nf>, aftereffect; **concomitant, accompaniment** 769, **additive,** adjuvant; leftover, carry-over

2 <written text> **postscript** or **P.S., appendix;** rider, allonge, codicil; **epilogue,** envoi, coda, tail, afterword; back matter, front matter; note, marginalia, scholia, commentary, annotation, footnote; **interpolation,** interlineation; affix, prefix, suffix, infix; subscript, superscript; enclitic, proclitic

3 <building> wing, **addition, annex,** extension, ell or L, outhouse, outbuilding

4 extra, bonus, premium, something extra, extra dash, little extra, extra added attraction, lagniappe, something into the bargain, something for good measure, baker's dozen; peripheral; **padding,** stuffing, filling; trimming, **frill,** flourish, filigree, decoration, ornament; bells and whistles <nf>; superaddition; fillip, wrinkle, twist; the works <nf>; benefit, perquisite, perk; freebie <nf>

255 SUBTRACTION

NOUNS **1 subtraction, deduction,** subduction, **removal,** taking away; abstraction, ablation, sublation; erosion, abrasion, wearing, wearing away; refinement, purification; detraction

2 reduction, diminution, decrease 252, build-down, phasedown, drawdown, decrement, impairment, **cut** or **cutting,** curtailment, shortening, truncation; **shrinkage,** depletion, **attrition,** remission; **depreciation,** detraction, disparagement, derogation; retraction, retrenchment; **extraction**

3 excision, abscission, rescission, extirpation; **elimination,** exclusion, extinction, eradication, destruction 395, annihilation; cancellation, write-off, erasure; circumcision; **amputation,** mutilation

4 castration, gelding, emasculation, deballing <nf>, altering and fixing <nf>, spaying

5 <written text> **deletion,** erasure, cancellation, omission; editing, blue-penciling, striking or striking out; expurgation, bowdlerization, censoring or censorship; abridgment, abbreviation

6 <math terms> difference; subtrahend, minuend; negative; minus sign, minus

7 <thing subtracted> **deduction,** decrement, minus; refund, rebate

8 <result> **difference, remainder** 256, epact <astronomy>, discrepancy, net, balance, surplus 993.5, deficit, credit

VERBS **9 subtract, deduct,** subduct, take away, take from, **remove,** withdraw, abstract; **reduce,** shorten, curtail, retrench, lessen, **diminish, decrease,** phase down, impair, bate, abate; **depreciate,** disparage,

detract, derogate; **erode,** abrade, eat or wear or rub or shave or file away; **extract,** leach, drain, wash away; thin, thin out, weed; **refine,** purify

10 excise, cut out, cut, extirpate, enucleate; **cancel,** write off; **eradicate,** root out, wipe or stamp out, **eliminate,** kill, kill off, liquidate, annihilate, destroy 395.10, extinguish; **exclude,** except, take out, cancel, cancel out, censor out, bleep out <nf>, rule out, bar, ban; set aside or apart, isolate, pick out, cull; **cut off** or **away,** shear or take or strike or knock or lop off, truncate; **amputate,** mutilate, abscind; **prune,** pare, peel, clip, crop, bob, dock, lop, nip, shear, shave, strip, strip off or away

11 castrate, geld, emasculate, eunuchize, neuter, spay, fix or alter <nf>, unsex, deball <nf>; geld, caponize; unman

12 <written text> **delete,** erase, expunge, **cancel,** omit; **edit,** edit out, blue-pencil; strike, strike out or off, rub or blot out, cross out or off, kill, cut; void, rescind; **censor,** bowdlerize, expurgate; abridge, abbreviate

ADJS **13 subtractive, reductive,** deductive, extirpative; ablative, erosive; censorial; removable, eradicable

PREPS **14 off, from; minus,** less, without, excluding, except or excepting, with the exception of, save, leaving out or aside, barring, exclusive of, not counting, exception taken of, discounting

256 REMAINDER

NOUNS **1 remainder, remains, remnant, relict, residue,** residuum, residual, **rest, balance;** holdover; **leavings, leftovers, oddments; refuse,** odds and ends, scraps, rags, **rubbish, waste,** litter, orts, candle ends; scourings, offscourings; parings, sweepings, filings, shavings, sawdust; chaff, straw, stubble, husks; **debris,** detritus, ruins; end, fag end; stump, butt or butt end, stub, roach <nf>, rump; survival, vestige, trace, hint, shadow, afterimage, afterglow; **fossil,** relics

2 dregs, grounds, lees, dross, slag, draff, scoria, feces; **sediment, settlings, deposits,** deposition; precipitate, precipitation, sublimate <chem>; alluvium, alluvion, diluvium; silt, loess, moraine; scum, off-scum, froth; ash, ember, cinder, sinter, clinker; soot, smut

3 survivor, heir, successor, inheritor; **widow,** widower, relict, war widow, **orphan**

4 excess 993, **surplus,** surplusage, overplus, overage; superfluity, redundancy, pleonasm; something for a rainy day

VERBS **5 remain, be left** or **left over, survive,** subsist, rest, stay

6 leave, leave over, leave behind, bequeath

ADJS **7 remaining, surviving, extant,** vestigial, over, left, **leftover, still around, remnant,** remanent, odd, on the shelf; **spare,** to spare; unused, unconsumed; **surplus,** superfluous; **outstanding,** unmet, unresolved; net

8 residual, residuary; sedimental, sedimentary

257 SIZE, LARGENESS

NOUNS **1 size, largeness, bigness, greatness** 247, vastness, vastitude, **magnitude,** order of magnitude, amplitude; mass, bulk, **volume,** body; **dimensions, proportions,** dimension, caliber, scantling, proportion; **measure,** measurement 300, gauge, **scale; extent,** extension, expansion, expanse, square footage *or* yardage etc, **scope,** reach, range, ballpark <nf>, spread, coverage, area, circumference, ambit, girth, diameter, radius, boundary, border, periphery; linear measure *or* dimension, length, height, procerity <depth>; depth, breadth, width; wheelbase, wingspan

2 capacity, volume, content, holding capacity, cubic footage *or* yardage etc, accommodation, room, space, measure, limit, burden; gallonage, tankage; poundage, tonnage, cordage; stowage; **quantity** 244

3 full size, full growth; life size

4 large size, economy size, family size, **king size,** queen size, giant size

5 oversize, outsize; overlargeness, overbigness; **overgrowth,** wild *or* uncontrolled growth, overdevelopment, sprawl; **overweight,** overheaviness; overstoutness, overfatness, overplumpness, bloat, bloatedness, obesity; gigantism, giantism, titanism; hyperplasia, hypertrophy, acromegalic gigantism, acromegaly, pituitary gigantism, normal gigantism

6 <large size> **sizableness, largeness, bigness,** greatness, grandness, grandeur, grandiosity; largishness, biggishness; voluminousness, capaciousness, generousness, copiousness, ampleness; tallness, toweringness; broadness, wideness; profundity; extensiveness, expansiveness, comprehensiveness; spaciousness 158.5; bagginess

7 <very large size> **hugeness, vastness,** vastitude; humongousness <nf>; **enormousness, immenseness, enormity, immensity,** tremendousness, **prodigiousness,** stupendousness, mountainousness; **gigantism,** giganticness, giantism, giantlikeness; monumentalism; **monstrousness, monstrosity**

8 corpulence, obesity, stoutness, largeness, bigness, *embonpoint* <Fr>; **fatness,** fattishness, adiposis *or* adiposity, endomorphy, fleshiness, beefiness, meatiness, heftiness, grossness; **plumpness,**

buxomness, rotundity, fubsiness <Brit>, tubbiness <nf>, roly-poliness; pudginess, podginess; chubbiness, chunkiness <nf>, stockiness, squattiness, squatness, dumpiness, portliness; paunchiness, bloatedness, puffiness, pursiness, blowziness; middle-age spread; weight problem; hippiness <nf>; steatopygia *or* steatopygy; bosominess, bustiness <nf>

9 bulkiness, bulk, hulkingness *or* hulkiness, **massiveness,** lumpishness, clumpishness; **ponderousness,** cumbrousness, cumbersomeness; clumsiness, awkwardness, unwieldiness, clunkiness <nf>

10 lump, clump, **hunk** *and* **chunk** <nf>, wodge <Brit nf>; **mass,** piece, **gob** *and* glob <nf>, gobbet, dollop, cluster, gobs <nf>; batch, **wad,** heap, block, loaf; pat <of butter>; clod; nugget; **quantity** 244

11 <something large> **whopper** *and* thumper *and* lunker *and* whale *and* jumbo <nf>; monster, hulk; large part, bulk, mass, lion's share, majority, better part

12 <corpulent person> **heavyweight, pig,** porker, heavy <nf>, human *or* man mountain <nf>; big *or* large person; **fat person, fatty** *and* **fatso** <nf>, roly-poly, **tub, tub of lard,** tun, tun of flesh, whale, blimp <nf>, hippo <nf>, **potbelly,** gorbelly <old *or* dial>, swagbelly, dumpling, lardass <nf>

13 giant <see list>, giantess, **amazon, colossus, titan,** titaness, *nephilim* <Heb pl>, hulk; long drink of water

14 behemoth, leviathan, monster; mammoth, mastodon; elephant, jumbo <nf>; whale; hippopotamus, hippo <nf>; **dinosaur**

VERBS **15 size, adjust, grade,** group, range, rank, graduate, sort, match; gauge, **measure** 300.11, proportion; **bulk** 247.5; **enlarge** 259.4,5; fatten

ADJS **16 large, sizable, big, great** 247.6, **grand,** tall <nf>, **considerable, goodly,** healthy, tidy <nf>, **substantial,** bumper; as big as all outdoors; numerous 884.6; largish, biggish; large-scale, larger than life; man-sized <nf>; large-size *or* -sized, man-sized, king-size, queen-size; economy-size, family-size; good-sized, life-size *or* -sized

17 voluminous, capacious, generous, ample, copious, broad, wide, extensive, expansive, comprehensive; **spacious**

18 corpulent, stout, fat, overweight, fattish, **obese,** adipose, gross, fleshy, beefy, meaty, hefty, porky, porcine; paunchy, paunched, bloated, puffy, blowzy, distended, swollen, pursy; abdominous, big-bellied, full-bellied, potbellied, gorbellied <old *or* dial>, swag-bellied, pot-gutted *and* pussle-gutted <nf>, **plump, buxom,** *zaftig* <Yiddish>, pleasantly plump, full, huggy <nf>, rotund,

fubsy <Brit>, **tubby** <nf>, roly-poly; **pudgy,**
podgy; thickbodied, thick-girthed, **heavyset,**
thickset, chubby, chunky <nf>, fubsy <Brit nf>,
stocky, squat, squatty, dumpy, square; pyknic,
endomorphic; **stalwart, brawny, burly;** lusty,
strapping <nf>; **portly,** imposing; well-fed, corn-
fed, grain-fed; chubby-faced, round-faced,
moonfaced; hippy <nf>, full-buttocked,
steatopygic *or* steatopygous, fat-assed *and* lard-
assed <nf>, broad in the beam <nf>, well-
upholstered <nf>; bosomy, full-bosomed, chesty,
busty <nf>, top-heavy; plump as a dumpling *or*
partridge, fat as a quail, fat as a pig *or* hog, fat as
brawn *or* bacon

19 bulky, hulky, hulking, lumpish, lumpy, lumping
<nf>, clumpish, lumbering, lubberly; **massive,**
massy; elephantine, hippopotamic; **ponderous,**
cumbrous, cumbersome; **clumsy,** awkward,
unwieldy; clunky <nf>

20 huge, immense, vast, enormous, astronomic,
astronomical, humongous *and* jumbo <nf>, king-
size, queen-size, tremendous, prodigious,
stupendous, macro, mega, giga; great big, larger
than life, Homeric, mighty, **titanic, colossal,**
monumental, heroic, heroical, epic, epical,
towering, mountainous; profound, abysmal, deep
as the ocean *or* as China; **monster,** monstrous;
mammoth, mastodonic; **gigantic, giant,** giantlike,
gigantesque, gigantean; Cyclopean,
Brobdingnagian, Gargantuan, Herculean,
Atlantean; elephantine, jumbo <nf>; dinosaurian,
dinotherian; **infinite** 823.3

21 <nf terms> **whopping, walloping, whaling,**
whacking, spanking, slapping, lolloping,
thumping, thundering, bumping, banging

22 full-sized, full-size, full-scale; **full-grown, full-**
fledged, full-blown; full-formed, **life-sized,** large as
life, larger than life

23 oversize, oversized; **outsize,** outsized; giant-
size, **king-size, queen-size,** record-size, extra-
large *or* XL, XXL, **overlarge,** overbig, too big;
overgrown, overdeveloped; **overweight,** overheavy;
overfleshed, overstout, overfat, overplump,
overfed, obese

24 this big, so big, yay big <nf>, this size, about this
size, of that order

ADVS **25** largely, on a large scale, in a big way; in the
large; as can be

WORD ELEMENTS **26** hyper-, macr-, macro-, maxi-,
meg-, mega-, megal-, megalo-, super-

27 giants

Abominable Snowman *or*	Antaeus
yeti	Ascapart
Aegir	Atlas
Alifanfaron	Balan
Bellerus	Goliath
Big Foot *or* Sasquatch *or*	Hercules *or* Heracles
Omah	Hymir
Blunderbore	Jötunn
Briareüs	King Kong
Brobdingnagian	Magog
Colossus	Mimir
Cormoran	Og
Cottus	Orion
Cyclops	Pantagruel
Enceladus	Patagonian
Ephialtes	Paul Bunyan
Ferragus	Polyphemus
Galligantus	Titan
Gargantua	Tityus
Godzilla	Typhon
Gog	Ymir

258 LITTLENESS

NOUNS **1 littleness, smallness,** smallishness,
diminutiveness, miniatureness, slightness,
exiguity; puniness, pokiness, dinkiness <nf>;
tininess, **minuteness;** undersize; petiteness;
dwarfishness, stuntedness, runtiness, shrimpiness;
shortness 268; **scantiness** 885.1; small scale;
compactness, portability; miniaturization,
microminiaturization, microscopy, micrography

2 infinitesimalness; undetectability, inappreciability,
evanescence; intangibility, impalpability,
tenuousness, imponderability; imperceptibility,
invisibility

3 <small space> **tight spot** *and* corner *and* squeeze
and **pinch** <nf>, not enough room to swing a cat
<nf>; hole, pigeonhole; hole-in-the-wall; cubby,
cubbyhole; dollhouse, playhouse, doghouse; no
room to swing a cat

4 <small person or creature> **runt, shrimp** <nf>,
wart <nf>, diminutive, wisp, chit, slip, snip,
snippet, minikin <old>, **peanut** *and* **peewee** <nf>,
pipsqueak, squirt, half pint, shorty, fingerling,
small fry <nf>, dandiprat *and* tiddler <Brit old>;
lightweight, featherweight; bantam, banty <nf>;
pony; minnow, mini *and* minny <nf>; mouse, tit,
titmouse, tomtit <nf>; nubbin, button

5 <creature small by species or birth> **dwarf,**
dwarfling, **midget,** midge, **pygmy,** manikin,
homunculus, atomy, micromorph, hop-o'-my-
thumb; elf, gnome, brownie, hobbit, leprechaun;
Lilliputian, Pigwiggen, Tom Thumb, Thumbelina,
Alberich, Alviss, Andvari, Nibelung, Regin

6 miniature, mini; scaled-down *or* miniaturized
version; microcosm, microcosmos; baby; doll,
puppet, toy; microvolume; Elzevir, Elzevir edition;
duodecimo, twelvemo, pocket edition

7 <minute thing> minutia, **minutiae** <pl>, minim,
drop, droplet, **mite** <nf>, **point,** vanishing point,

mathematical point, point of a pin, pinpoint, pinhead, **dot;** mote, fleck, **speck,** flyspeck, jot, tittle, jot nor tittle, iota, **trace,** trace amount, suspicion, *soupçon* <Fr>; **particle,** crumb, scrap, bite, snip, snippet; grain, grain of sand; barleycorn, millet seed, mustard seed; midge, gnat; microbe, **microorganism,** amoeba, bacillus, bacteria, diatom, germ, paramecium, protozoon, zoospore, animalcule, plankton, virus; cell; microchip; pixel

8 **atom,** atomy, monad; **molecule,** ion; nucleus; **electron,** proton, meson, neutrino, muon, quark, parton, subatomic *or* nuclear particle

VERBS 9 **make small, contract** 260.7; **shorten** 268.6; **miniaturize,** minify, minimize, scale down; **reduce** 252.7, scale back

ADJS 10 **little, small** 248.6, smallish; **slight,** exiguous; **puny, trifling,** poky, piffling *and* pindling *and* piddling *and* piddly <nf>, paltry, picayune, **dinky** <nf>, negligible; cramped, limited; one-horse, two-by-four <nf>; pintsized <nf>, half-pint; knee-high, knee-high to a grasshopper; petite; short 268.8

11 **tiny;** teeny *and* teeny-weeny *and* eentsy-weentsy <nf>, wee *and* peewee <nf>, bitty *and* bitsy *and* little-bitty *and* little-bitsy *and* itsy-bitsy *and* itsy-witsy <nf>, dinky <nf>; **minute,** fine

12 **miniature, diminutive, minuscule,** minuscular, mini, micro, miniaturized, subminiature, minikin <old>, **small-scale,** minimal; pony, bantam, banty <nf>; **baby,** baby-sized; pocket, pocketsized, pocket-size, **vest-pocket; toy;** handy, compact, portable; duodecimo, twelvemo

13 **dwarf,** dwarfed, dwarfish, **pygmy, midget,** nanoid, elfin; Lilliputian, Tom Thumb; **undersized,** undersize, squat, dumpy; **stunted,** undergrown, runty, pint-size *or* -sized *and* sawed-off <nf>; shrunk, shrunken, wizened, shriveled; meager, scrubby, scraggy; rudimentary, rudimental

14 **infinitesimal, microscopic,** ultramicroscopic; evanescent, thin, tenuous; inappreciable; impalpable, imponderable, intangible; imperceptible, indiscernible, invisible, unseeable; atomic, subatomic; molecular; granular, corpuscular, microcosmic *or* microcosmical; embryonic, germinal

15 **microbic,** microbial, **microorganic;** animalcular, bacterial; microzoic; protozoan, microzoan, amoebic *or* amoeboid

ADVS 16 **small,** little, **slightly** 248.9, fractionally; **on a small scale,** in a small compass, in a small way, on a minuscule *or* infinitesimal scale; **in miniature,** in the small; in a nutshell

WORD ELEMENTS 17 micr-, micro-, ultramicr-, ultramicro-; granul-, granulo-, granuli-, chondr-, chondro-; -cle, -ee, -een, -el, -ella, -illa, -et, -ette,

-idium, -idion, -ie, -y, -ey, -ium, -kin, -let, -ling, -ock, -sy, -ula, -ule, -ulum, -ulus

259 EXPANSION, GROWTH
<increase in size>

NOUNS 1 **expansion, extension, enlargement, increase** 251, uptick, crescendo, upping, raising, hiking, magnification, aggrandizement, amplification, ampliation <old>, broadening, widening; **spread,** spreading, creeping, fanning out, dispersion, ripple effect, sprawl; **flare,** splay, ramification; deployment; augmentation, **addition** 253; adjunct 254

2 **distension,** stretching; **inflation,** sufflation, blowing up; **dilation,** dilatation, dilating; diastole; **swelling,** swell 283.4; puffing, puff, puffiness, **bloating,** bloat, **flatulence** *or* flatulency, flatus, gassiness, windiness; **turgidity,** turgidness, turgescence; tumidness *or* tumidity, tumefaction; tumescence, intumescence; **swollenness,** bloatedness; dropsy, edema; tympanites, tympany, tympanism

3 **growth, development** 861.1; **bodily development** 14, **maturation,** maturing, coming of age, growing up, upgrowth; vegetation 310.32; reproduction, procreation 78, germination, pullulation; burgeoning, sprouting; budding, gemmation; outgrowth, excrescence; overgrowth 257.5

VERBS 4 <make larger> **enlarge, expand, extend, widen, broaden,** build, build up, aggrandize, **amplify,** crescendo, **magnify, increase** 251.4, augment, add to 253.5, raise, up, scale up, hike *or* hike up; develop, bulk *or* bulk up; **stretch, distend, dilate, swell, inflate,** sufflate, **blow up,** puff up, huff, puff, bloat; pump, pump up; rarefy

5 <become larger> **enlarge, expand, extend, increase,** greaten, crescendo, **develop, widen, broaden,** bulk; **stretch, distend, dilate, swell, swell up, swell out, puff up, puff out, pump up, bloat,** tumefy, balloon, fill out; snowball

6 **spread,** spread out, outspread, outstretch; **expand, extend,** widen; open, **open up,** unfold; **flare,** flare out, broaden out, splay; spraddle, sprangle, sprawl; branch, branch out, ramify; fan, fan out, disperse, deploy; spread like wildfire; overrun, overgrow

7 **grow, develop,** wax, **increase** 251; gather, brew; **grow up,** mature, spring up, ripen, come of age, **shoot up,** sprout up, upshoot, upspring, upsprout, upspear, overtop, tower; burgeon, **sprout** 310.34, blossom 310.35, reproduce 78.7, procreate 78.8, grow out of, germinate, pullulate; vegetate 310.34; **flourish, thrive,** grow like a weed; mushroom; outgrow; overgrow, hypertrophy, overdevelop, grow uncontrollably

8 **fatten,** fat, plump, pinguefy *and* engross <old>, fill

out; **gain weight,** gather flesh, take *or* put on weight, become overweight

ADJS **9 expansive, extensive;** expansional, extensional; **expansile, extensile,** elastic, stretchy; expansible, inflatable, augmentative; distensive, dilatant; inflationary; developable

10 expanded, extended, enlarged, increased 251.7, upped, raised, hiked, **amplified,** ampliate <old>, crescendoed, widened, broadened, built-up, beefed-up <nf>

11 spread, spreading; sprawling, sprawly; **outspread, outstretched,** spreadout, stretched-out, drawn-out; open, unfolded, gaping, patulous; widespread, wide-open; flared, spraddled, sprangled, splayed; flaring, flared, flared-out, spraddling, sprangling, splaying; splay; fanned, fanning; fanlike, fan-shaped, fan-shape, flabelliform, deltoid

12 grown, full-grown, grown-up, mature, developed, well-developed, fully developed, full-fledged, of age; growing, sprouting, crescent, budding, flowering 310.38, florescent, **flourishing,** blossoming, blooming, burgeoning, fast-growing, thriving; overgrown, hypertrophied, overdeveloped

13 distended, dilated, inflated, sufflated, **blown up, puffed up, swollen,** swelled, **bloated,** turgid, tumid, plethoric, incrassate; **puffy,** pursy; flatulent, gassy, windy, ventose; tumefacient; dropsical; edematous; enchymatous; fat; puffed out, bouffant, bouffed up *and* bouffy <nf>, stuffed

260 CONTRACTION
<decrease in size>

NOUNS **1 contraction,** contracture; systole, syneresis, synizesis; **compression,** compressure, pressurizing, pressurization; **compacting,** compaction, compactedness; **condensation, concentration,** consolidation, solidification; **circumscription, narrowing;** reduction, diminuendo, lessening, waning; miniaturization; **decrease** 252; abbreviation, curtailment, shortening 268.3; **constriction,** stricture *or* striction, astriction, strangulation, stenosis, **choking,** choking off, coarctation; bottleneck, chokepoint, hourglass, hourglass figure, nipped *or* wasp waist; neck, cervix, isthmus, narrow place; astringency, constringency; puckering, pursing; knitting, wrinkling

2 squeezing, compression, clamping *or* clamping down, tightening; **pressure,** press, crush; **pinch, squeeze, tweak, nip;** scrunch

3 shrinking, shrinkage, atrophy; **shriveling, withering;** searing, parching, drying *or* drying up; attenuation, thinning; wasting, consumption, emaciation, emaceration <old>; skin and bones;

preshrinking, preshrinkage, Sanforizing <trademark>

4 collapse, prostration, cave-in; implosion; **deflation**

5 contractibility, contractility, compactability, **compressibility,** condensability, reducibility; collapsibility; shrinkability

6 contractor, constrictor, clamp, compressor, compacter, condenser, vise, pincer, squeezer; thumbscrew; **astringent,** styptic; alum, astringent bitters, styptic pencil; tourniquet

VERBS **7 contract, compress,** cramp, compact, condense, concentrate, consolidate, solidify; **reduce, decrease** 252; abbreviate, curtail, **shorten** 268.6; miniaturize; **constrict,** constringe, circumscribe, coarct, **narrow,** draw, draw in *or* together; strangle, strangulate, choke, choke off; **pucker,** pucker up, **purse; knit, wrinkle**

8 squeeze, compress, clamp, cramp, cramp up, tighten; roll *or* wad up, roll up into a ball, scrunch, ensphere; **press,** pressurize, crush; **pinch, tweak, nip**

9 shrink, shrivel, wither, sear, parch, dry up; **wizen,** weazen; consume, waste, waste away, attenuate, thin, emaciate, macerate *or* emacerate <old>; preshrink, Sanforize <trademark>

10 collapse, cave, cave in, fall in; telescope; fold, fold up; implode; **deflate,** let the air out of, take the wind out of, flatten; puncture

ADJS **11 contractive,** contractional, contractible, contractile, compactable; **astringent,** constringent, styptic; **compressible,** condensable, reducible; shrinkable; **collapsible,** foldable; deflationary; consumptive; circumscribable

12 contracted, compressed, cramped, compact *or* compacted, concentrated, condensed, consolidated, solidified, boiled-down; **constricted,** strangled, strangulated, choked, choked off, coarcted, **squeezed,** clamped, nipped, pinched *or* pinched-in, wasp-waisted; puckered, pursed; knitted, wrinkled; miniaturized; scaled-down; shortened, abbreviated

13 shrunk, shrunken; **shriveled,** shriveled up; **withered,** sear, parched, corky, dried-up; **wasted,** wasted away, consumed, emaciated, emacerated, thin, attenuated; **wizened,** wizen, weazened; preshrunk, Sanforized <trademark>

14 deflated, punctured, flat, holed

261 DISTANCE, REMOTENESS

NOUNS **1 distance, remoteness,** farness, far-offness, longinquity; **separation,** separatedness, divergence, clearance, margin, leeway; **extent, length,** space 158, **reach,** stretch, range, compass, span, stride, haul, a way, ways *and* piece <nf>; perspective, aesthetic distance, distancing; astronomical *or* interstellar *or* galactic *or* intergalactic distance, deep space, depths of space, **infinity** 823; **mileage,** light-years, parsecs; aloofness, standoffishness

2 **long way,** good ways <nf>, **great distance, far cry,** far piece <nf>; long step, tidy step, giant step *or* stride; long run *or* haul, long road *or* trail, day's march, miles away; marathon; far cry, long shot; long range; apogee, aphelion

3 the distance, **remote distance, offing; horizon,** the far horizon, where the earth meets the sky, vanishing point, background

4 <remote region> jumping-off place *and* godforsaken place *and* God knows where *and* the middle of nowhere <nf>, the back of beyond, the end of the rainbow, Thule *or* Ultima Thule, Timbuktu, Siberia, Darkest Africa, the South Seas, Pago Pago, the Great Divide, China, Outer Mongolia, pole, antipodes, end of the earth, North Pole, South Pole, Tierra del Fuego, Greenland, Yukon, Pillars of Hercules, remotest corner of the world, four corners of the earth; outpost, outskirts; the sticks *and* the boondocks *and* the boonies <nf>; **nowhere;** frontier, outback <Austral>; the moon; outer space

VERBS 5 **reach out, stretch out,** extend, extend out, go *or* go out, range out, carry out; outstretch, outlie, outdistance, outrange

6 **extend to,** stretch to, stretch away to, **reach to,** lead to, go to, get to, come to, run to, carry to

7 **keep one's distance, distance oneself,** remain at a distance, maintain distance *or* clearance, keep at a respectful distance, separate oneself, **keep away,** stand off *or* away; keep away from, keep *or* stand clear of, **steer clear of** <nf>, hold away from, give a wide berth to, keep a good leeway *or* margin *or* offing, keep out of the way of, keep at arm's length, keep a safe distance from, not touch with a ten-foot pole <nf>, keep *or* stay *or* stand aloof; maintain one's perspective, keep one's esthetic distance

ADJS 8 **distant,** distal, **remote, removed, far, far-off,** away, **faraway,** way-off, far-flung, at a distance, exotic, separated, apart, asunder; long-distance, long-range

9 **out-of-the-way,** godforsaken, back of beyond, upcountry; **out of reach, inaccessible,** ungetatable, unapproachable, untouchable, hyperborean, antipodean

10 **thither,** ulterior; **yonder,** yon; **farther, further,** remoter, more distant; outlying

11 transoceanic, transmarine, ultramarine, oversea, overseas; transatlantic, transpacific; tramontane, transmontane, ultramontane, transalpine; transarctic, transcontinental, transequatorial, transpolar, transpontine, transmundane, ultramundane; offshore, overseas

12 **farthest, furthest,** farthermost, farthest off, furthermost, ultimate, extreme, remotest, most distant, terminal

ADVS 13 **yonder,** yon; **in the distance,** in the remote distance; **in the offing,** on the horizon, in the background

14 **at a distance, away, off,** aloof, at arm's length; distantly, remotely

15 **far, far off,** far away, **afar,** afar off, a long way off, a good ways off <nf>, a long cry to, "over the hills and far away"—John Gay, as far as the eye can see, out of sight; clear to hell and gone <nf>

16 **far and wide,** far and near, distantly and broadly, wide, widely, broadly, abroad

17 **apart, away, aside,** wide apart, wide away, "as wide asunder as pole and pole"—J A Froude, "as far as the east is from the west"—Bible

18 **out of reach,** beyond reach, **out of range,** beyond the bounds, out-of-the-way, out of the sphere of; out of sight, *à perte de vue* <Fr>; out of hearing, out of earshot *or* earreach

19 **wide, clear;** wide of the mark, abroad, all abroad, astray, afield, far afield

PREPS 20 **as far as, to, all the way to,** the whole way to

21 **beyond, past, over, across,** the other *or* far side of

262 FORM

NOUNS 1 **form, shape, figure;** figuration, **configuration;** formation, **conformation; structure** 266; **build,** make, frame; **arrangement** 808; makeup, format, layout; **composition** 796; cut, set, stamp, type, turn, cast, mold, impression, pattern, matrix, model, mode, modality; archetype, prototype 786.1, Platonic form *or* idea; style, fashion; aesthetic form, inner form, significant form; art form, genre

2 **contour,** *tournure* <Fr>, *galbe* <Fr>; broad lines, silhouette, profile, **outline** 211.2; organization 807.1

3 **appearance** 33, lineaments, features, physiognomy, cut of one's jib

4 <human form> **figure, form,** shape, frame, anatomy, **physique,** build, body-build, person; body 1052.3

5 **forming, shaping,** molding, modeling, fashioning, making, making up, formulation; **formation,** conformation, figuration, configuration; sculpture; morphogeny, morphogenesis; creation

6 <grammatical terms> form, morph, allomorph, morpheme; morphology, morphemics

VERBS 7 **form,** formalize, **shape, fashion,** tailor, frame, figure, **lick into shape** <nf>; work, knead; set, fix; **forge,** drop-forge; **mold,** model, sculpt *or* sculpture; cast, found; thermoform; stamp, mint; carve, whittle, cut, chisel, hew, hew out; roughhew, roughcast, rough out, block out, lay out, sketch out; hammer *or* knock out; whomp out *or* up <nf>, cobble up; create; organize 807.4, systematize

8 <be formed> **form,** take form, shape, **shape up, take shape;** materialize

ADJS 9 **formative,** formal, formational, plastic, morphotic; **formed, shaped,** patterned, fashioned, tailored, framed; **forged,** molded, modeled, sculpted; cast, founded; stamped, minted; carved, cut, whittled, chiseled, hewn; roughhewn, roughcast, roughed-out, blocked-out, laid-out, sketched-out; hammered-out, knocked-out, cobbled-up; **made, produced**

10 <biological terms> plasmatic, plasmic, protoplasmic, plastic, metabolic

11 <grammatical terms> morphologic, morphological, morphemic

WORD ELEMENTS 12 morph-, morpho-, -morph, -morphism, -morphy, -form, -iform, -morphic, -morphous

263 FORMLESSNESS

NOUNS 1 **formlessness, shapelessness;** unformedness, amorphousness, amorphism; misshapenness; lack of definition; **chaos** 810.2, confusion, messiness, mess, muddle 810.2, orderlessness, untidiness; **disorder** 810; entropy; anarchy 418.2; **indeterminateness, indefiniteness,** indecisiveness, vagueness, mistiness, haziness, fuzziness, blurriness, unclearness, obscurity; lumpiness, lumpishness

2 unlicked cub, diamond in the rough, raw material

VERBS 3 **deform, distort** 265.5; misshape; unform, unshape; disorder, jumble, mess up, muddle, confuse; obfuscate, obscure, fog up, blur

ADJS 4 **formless, shapeless,** featureless, characterless, nondescript, inchoate, lumpy, lumpish, blobby *and* baggy <nf>, inform; amorphous, **chaotic, orderless,** disorderly 810.13, unordered, unorganized, confused, anarchic 418.6; kaleidoscopic; **indeterminate, indefinite,** undefined, indecisive, vague, misty, hazy, fuzzy, blurred *or* blurry, unclear, obscure; obfuscatory; unfinished, undeveloped

5 **unformed, unshaped,** unshapen, unfashioned, unlicked; unstructured; uncut, unhewn

264 SYMMETRY

NOUNS 1 **symmetry,** symmetricalness, **proportion,** proportionality, **balance** 790.1, equilibrium;

regularity, uniformity 781, evenness; equality 790; finish; harmony, congruity, consistency, conformity 867, **correspondence,** keeping; eurythmy, eurythmics; dynamic symmetry; bilateral symmetry, trilateral symmetry, etc, multilateral symmetry; parallelism 203, polarity; shapeliness

2 symmetrization, regularization, balancing, harmonization; evening, equalization; coordination, integration; **compensation,** playing off, playing off against, posing against *or* over against; counterbalance

VERBS 3 symmetrize, regularize, **balance,** balance off, compensate; harmonize; **proportion,** proportionate; even, even up, equalize; coordinate, integrate; play off, play off against

ADJS 4 **symmetric, symmetrical, balanced,** balanced off, proportioned, eurythmic, harmonious; **regular,** uniform 781.5, even, even-steven <nf>, equal 790.7, equal on both sides, fifty-fifty <nf>, square, squared-off; coequal, coordinate, equilateral; **well-balanced,** well-set, well-set-up <nf>; finished; enantiomorphic

5 **shapely, well-shaped, well-proportioned,** well-made, **well-formed,** well-favored; comely; trim, trig <old>, neat, spruce, clean, clean-cut, clean-limbed

265 DISTORTION

NOUNS 1 **distortion,** torsion, twist, twistedness, **contortion, crookedness,** tortuosity; **asymmetry,** unsymmetry, disproportion, lopsidedness, imbalance, irregularity, skewness, **deviation; twist,** quirk, turn, screw, wring, wrench, wrest; **warp,** buckle; knot, gnarl; anamorphosis; anamorphism

2 **perversion, corruption,** misdirection, misrepresentation 350, misinterpretation, misconstruction; **falsification** 354.9; **twisting,** false coloring, bending the truth, **spin,** spin control, slanting, straining, torturing; misuse 389; falsehood, travesty

3 **deformity,** deformation, **malformation,** malconformation, monstrosity 870.6, teratology, freakishness, misproportion, **misshapenness,** misshape; **disfigurement, defacement;** mutilation, truncation; humpback, hunchback, crookback, camelback, kyphosis; swayback, lordosis; wryneck, torticollis; clubfoot, talipes, flatfoot, splayfoot; knock-knee; bowlegs; valgus; harelip; cleft palate; mutation

4 **grimace, wry face,** wry mouth, rictus, snarl; moue, mow, pout; scowl, frown; squint; tic

VERBS 5 **distort, contort,** turn awry; **twist,** turn, screw, wring, wrench, wrest; writhe; **warp,** buckle, crumple; knot, gnarl; **crook,** bend, spring; put out of kilter

6 **pervert, falsify, twist, garble, put a false construction upon, give a spin, give a false coloring,** color, varnish, slant, strain, torture; put words in someone's mouth; **bias;** misrepresent 350.3, misconstrue, misinterpret, misrender, misdirect; misuse 389.4; send *or* deliver the wrong signal *or* message, lead up *or* down the garden path; exaggerate

7 **deform,** malform, misshape, twist, torture, disproportion; **disfigure, deface;** mutilate, truncate; blemish, mar

8 **grimace, make a face,** make a wry face *or* mouth, pull a face, **screw up one's face,** mug <nf>, mouth, make a mouth, mop, mow, mop and mow; pout

ADJS **9** distortive, contortive, contortional, torsional

10 **distorted, contorted, warped, twisted, crooked;** tortuous, labyrinthine, buckled, sprung, bent, bowed; cockeyed <nf>, crazy; crunched, crumpled; unsymmetric, unsymmetrical, asymmetric, asymmetrical, nonsymmetric, nonsymmetrical; irregular, deviative, anamorphous; one-sided, lopsided; askew 204.14, off-center, left *or* right of center, off-target; cockeyed

11 **falsified, perverted, twisted, garbled,** slanted, doctored, biased, crooked; strained, tortured; misrepresented, misquoted; half-true, partially true, falsely colored; creative <nf>

12 **deformed, malformed, misshapen,** misbegotten, misproportioned, ill-proportioned, ill-made, ill-shaped, **out of shape;** dwarfed, stumpy; bloated; **disfigured,** defaced, blemished, marred; mutilated, truncated; grotesque, **monstrous** 870.13; sway-backed, round-shouldered; bowlegged, bandy-legged, bandy; knock-kneed; rickety, rachitic; club-footed, talipedic; flatfooted, splayfooted, pigeon-toed; pug-nosed, snub-nosed, simous

13 **humpbacked, hunchbacked,** bunchbacked, crookbacked, crookedbacked, camelback, humped, gibbous, kyphotic

266 STRUCTURE

NOUNS **1** **structure, construction,** architecture, tectonics, architectonics, **frame,** make, **build,** fabric, tissue, warp and woof *or* weft, web, weave, texture, contexture, mold, **shape, pattern, plan,** fashion, arrangement, **organization** 807.1; organism, organic structure, **constitution, composition; makeup,** getup <nf>, setup; **formation,** conformation, **format; arrangement** 808, configuration; **composition** 796; making, building, creation, production, forging, fashioning, molding, fabrication, manufacture, shaping,

structuring, patterning; anatomy, physique, organic structure; form 262; **morphology,** science of structure; anatomy, histology, zootomy

2 **structure, building, edifice, construction,** construct, erection, establishment, fabric; house; tower, pile, pyramid, skyscraper, ziggurat; prefabrication, prefab, packaged house; air structure, bubble <nf>, air hall <Brit>; superstructure, structural framework; flat-slab construction, post-and-beam construction, steel-cage construction, steel construction; complex

3 **understructure,** understruction, underbuilding, undercroft, crypt; **substructure,** substruction; infrastructure, underpinning; spread foundation, footing; fill, backfill

4 **frame,** framing; braced framing; **framework, skeleton,** fabric, cadre, chassis, shell, armature; lattice, latticework, scaffold; sash, casement, case, casing; window case *or* frame, doorframe; picture frame

VERBS **5** **construct, build; structure; organize** 807.4; **form** 262.7; erect, raise, put up

ADJS **6** **structural,** formal, morphological, edificial, tectonic, textural; **anatomic,** anatomical, **organic,** organismal, organismic; **structured, patterned,** shaped, formed; **architectural,** architectonic; constructional; superstructural, substructural, infrastructural; organizational

267 LENGTH

NOUNS **1** **length,** longness, lengthiness, overall length; wheelbase; **extent, extension, measure, span, reach, stretch; distance** 261; footage, yardage, mileage; infinity 823; perpetuity 829; long time 827.4; linear measures; oblongness; longitude

2 a length, **piece, portion,** part; coil, **strip,** bolt, roll; run

3 **line, strip,** bar, streak; stripe 517.6; string

4 **lengthening, prolongation, elongation,** production, protraction; prolixity, prolixness; **extension,** stretching, stretching *or* spinning *or* stringing out, dragging out

VERBS **5** **be long, be lengthy, extend,** be prolonged, **stretch,** span; **stretch out,** extend out, reach out; stretch oneself, crane, crane one's neck, rubberneck; stand on tiptoes; outstretch, outreach; sprawl, straggle; last, endure

6 **lengthen, prolong,** prolongate, **elongate, extend,** expand, produce, **protract,** continue; make prolix; lengthen out, let out, **draw** *or* drag *or* stretch *or* string *or* spin out; **stretch,** draw, pull

ADJS **7** **long, lengthy;** longish, longsome; tall; **extensive, far-reaching,** fargoing, far-flung; sesquipedalian, sesquipedal; unabridged, full-length; as long as one's arm, a mile long; **time-consuming,** interminable, without end, no end of *or* to, infinite; long-lasting, enduring, long-range

8 **lengthened, prolonged,** prolongated, **elongated, extended, protracted; prolix; long-winded; drawn-out,** dragged out, long-drawn-out, stretched *or* spun *or* strung out, straggling; **stretched,** drawn, pulled

9 **oblong,** oblongated, oblongitudinal, **elongated;** rectangular; elliptical; lengthwise, lengthways, longitudinal

ADVS 10 lengthily, extensively, at length, *in extenso* <L>, *ad infinitum* <L>, ad nauseam

11 **lengthwise** *or* lengthways, longwise *or* longways, longitudinally, along, in length, at length; **endwise** *or* endways, endlong; *in extenso* <L>

268 SHORTNESS

NOUNS 1 **shortness, briefness, brevity; succinctness,** curtness, terseness, summariness, compendiousness, compactness; **conciseness** 537; **littleness** 258; transience 828, short time 828.3, instantaneousness 829

2 **stubbiness,** stumpiness <nf>, **stockiness, fatness** 257.8, chubbiness, chunkiness <nf>, blockiness, squatness, squattiness, dumpiness; pudginess, podginess; snubbiness; **lowness** 274

3 **shortening, abbreviation; reduction; abridgment, condensation,** compression, conspectus, epitome, epitomization, summary, summation, précis, abstract, recapitulation, recap <nf>, wrapup, synopsis, encapsulation; **curtailment,** truncation, retrenchment; telescoping; elision, ellipsis, syncope, apocope; foreshortening; cutback; docking; contraction, syncope, apocope

4 shortener, cutter, abridger; abstracter, epitomizer *or* epitomist

5 **shortcut,** cut, cutoff; shortest way; **beeline,** air line

VERBS 6 **shorten, abbreviate, cut; reduce** 260.7; **abridge, condense,** compress, contract, **boil down,** abstract, sum up, summarize, recapitulate, recap <nf>, synopsize, epitomize, encapsulate, capsulize; **curtail,** truncate, retrench; bowdlerize; elide, **cut short,** cut down, cut off short, cut back, take in; **dock,** bob, shear, shave, trim, clip, snub, nip; hem; mow, reap, **crop; prune,** poll, pollard; stunt, check the growth of; telescope; foreshorten

7 **take a short cut,** short-cut; **cut across,** cut through; **cut a corner,** cut corners; **make a beeline,** take the air line, go as the crow flies

ADJS 8 **short, brief, abbreviated,** abbreviatory, "short and sweet"—Thomas Lodge; **concise** 537.6; **curt,** curtal <old>, curtate, decurtate; **succinct, summary,** synoptic, synoptical, compendious,

compact; **little** 258.10; **low** 274.7; transient 828.7, instantaneous 830.4

9 **shortened, abbreviated; abridged,** compressed, condensed, epitomized, digested, abstracted, capsule, capsulized, encapsulated; bowdlerized; nutshell, vest-pocket; **curtailed,** cut short, short-cut, **docked,** bobbed, sheared, shaved, trimmed, clipped, snub, snubbed, nipped; mowed, mown, reaped, **cropped; pruned,** polled, pollarded; elided, elliptic, elliptical; foreshortened

10 **stubby,** stubbed, stumpy <nf>, undergrown, **thickset, stocky,** blocky, **chunky** <nf>, **fat** 257.18, **chubby,** tubby <nf>, dumpy; **squat,** squatty, squattish; **pudgy,** podgy; pug, **pugged;** snub-nosed; turned-up, *retroussé* <Fr>

11 short-legged, breviped; short-winged, brevipennate

ADVS 12 **shortly, briefly,** summarily, *tout court* <Fr>, in brief compass, economically, sparely, curtly, succinctly, in a nutshell, in two *or* a few words; abbreviatedly, for short; **concisely** 537.7, compendiously, synoptically

13 **short, abruptly,** suddenly 830.9, all of a sudden

269 BREADTH, THICKNESS

NOUNS 1 **breadth, width,** broadness, wideness, fullness, amplitude, latitude, distance across *or* crosswise *or* crossways, extent, **span, expanse, spread;** beam

2 **thickness,** the third dimension, distance through, depth; **mass, bulk, body;** corpulence, fatness 257.8, bodily size; **coarseness,** grossness 294.2

3 **diameter, bore, caliber; radius,** semidiameter; handbreadth, beam

VERBS 4 **broaden, widen,** deepen; **expand,** extend, extend to the side *or* sides; **spread** 259.6, spread out *or* sidewise *or* sideways, outspread, outstretch; span

5 **thicken,** grow thick, thick; incrassate, inspissate; congeal, gel; fatten 259.8

ADJS 6 **broad, wide,** deep; broad-scale, wide-scale, wide-ranging, broad-based, exhaustive, comprehensive, in-depth, extensive; spread-out, **expansive;** spacious, **roomy;** ample, full; widespread 864.13; "broad as the world"—James Russell Lowell, "wide as a church door"—Shakespeare

7 broad of beam, broad-beamed, broad-sterned, beamy, wide-set; wide-angle, wide-screen; broad-ribbed, wide-ribbed, laticostate; broad-toothed, wide-toothed, latidentate; broad-gauge; broadloom

8 **thick,** three-dimensional; **thickset, heavyset,** thick-bodied, broad-bodied, thick-girthed; **massive,**

bulky 257.19, corpulent 257.18; coarse, heavy, gross, crass, fat; full-bodied, full, viscous; **dense** 1045.12; thicknecked, bullnecked

ADVS **9** breadthwise or breadthways, in breadth; widthwise or widthways; broadwise or broadways; broadside, broad side foremost; side-wise or -ways; through, depth-wise or -ways, in depth

270 NARROWNESS, THINNESS

NOUNS **1** **narrowness, slenderness; closeness,** nearness; **straitness,** restriction, restrictedness, limitation, strictness, confinement; circumscription; crowdedness, incapaciousness, incommodiousness, crampedness; **tightness,** tight squeeze; hair, hairbreadth or hairsbreadth; finger's breadth or width; narrow gauge

2 **narrowing, tapering,** taper; **contraction** 260, compression; stricture, constriction, strangulation, coarctation

3 <narrow place> narrow, **narrows, strait; bottleneck,** chokepoint; isthmus; channel 239, canal; pass, defile; neck, throat, craw; narrow gauge, single track

4 **thinness, slenderness, slimness, frailty,** slightness, gracility, lightness, airiness, delicacy, flimsiness, wispiness, laciness, paperiness, gauziness, gossameriness, diaphanousness, insubstantiality, ethereality, mistiness, vagueness; light or airy texture; **fineness** 294.3; **tenuity, rarity,** subtility, exility, exiguity; **attenuation;** dilution, dilutedness, wateriness 1061.1, weakness

5 **leanness, skinniness,** fleshlessness, slightness, frailness, twigginess, spareness, meagerness, **scrawniness, gauntness,** gangliness, lankness, **lankiness,** gawkiness, **boniness,** skin and bones; haggardness, poorness, paperiness, peakedness <nf>, puniness, "lean and hungry look"— Shakespeare; undernourishment, undernutrition, underweight; hatchet face, lantern jaw

6 **emaciation,** malnutrition, emaceration <old>, attenuation, atrophy, tabes, marasmus, anorexia nervosa

7 <comparisons> paper, wafer, lath, slat, **rail,** rake, splinter, slip, shaving, streak, vein; gruel, soup; shadow, mere shadow; **skeleton**

8 <thin person> **slim, lanky;** twiggy, **shadow, skeleton,** stick, walking skeleton, corpse, barebones, bag or stack of bones; rattlebones or **spindleshanks** or spindlelegs <nf>, gangleshanks and gammerstang <nf>, lathlegs and sticklegs <nf>, **beanpole,** beanstalk, broomstick, clothes pole, stilt; slip, sylph, ectomorph

9 **reducing, slenderizing, slimming down;** weight-watching, calorie-counting; fasting, dieting

10 **thinner,** solvent 1064.4

VERBS **11** **narrow,** constrict, diminish, draw in, go in; restrict, limit, straiten, confine; **taper; contract** 260.7, compress, zip <nf>

12 **thin,** thin down, thin away or off or out, down; **rarefy,** subtilize, **attenuate;** dilute, water, water down, weaken; undernourish; **emaciate,** emacerate <old>

13 **slenderize, reduce,** lose weight, reduce or lose or take off weight, watch one's weight, lose flesh, weight-watch, count calories, diet, crash-diet; slim, **slim down,** thin down

ADJS **14** **narrow, slender;** narrowish, narrowy; **close, near; tight, strait,** isthmic, isthmian; close-fitting; **restricted,** limited, circumscribed, **confined,** constricted; **cramped,** cramp; incapacious, incommodious, crowded; **meager,** scant, scanty; narrow-gauge or narrow-gauged, single-track; angustifoliate, angustirostrate, angustiseptal, angustisellate; stenopeic, isthmian

15 **tapered,** taper, tapering, cone- or wedge-shaped, attenuated, fusiform, stenosed

16 **thin, slender, slim,** gracile, "imperially slim"—E A Robinson; thin-bodied, thin-set, ectomorphic, narrow- or wasp-waisted; **svelte,** slinky, sylphlike, willowy; girlish, boyish; thinnish, slenderish, slimmish; **slight,** slight-made; **frail,** delicate, light, airy, wispy, lacy, gauzy, papery, gossamer, diaphanous, insubstantial, ethereal, misty, vague, flimsy, wafer-thin, **fine; finespun,** thin-spun, fine-drawn, wiredrawn; threadlike, slender as a thread; **tenuous,** subtle, rare, **rarefied;** attenuated, attenuate, **watery, weak,** diluted, watered or watered-down, small

17 **lean,** lean-looking, **skinny** <nf>, fleshless, lean-fleshed, thin-fleshed, **spare,** meager, **scrawny,** scraggy, thin-bellied, **gaunt, lank, lanky,** wiry; **gangling** and gangly <nf>, gawky, **spindling,** spindly; flat-chested, flat <nf>; **bony, rawboned,** bare-boned, rattleboned <nf>, skeletal, **mere skin and bones, all skin and bones, nothing but skin and bones;** twiggy; **underweight,** undersized, undernourished, spidery, thin or skinny as a lath or rail, "lean as a rake"—Chaucer

18 lean-limbed, thin-legged, lath- or stick-legged <nf>, spindle-legged or -shanked <nf>, gangle-shanked <nf>, stilt-legged

19 lean- or horse- or thin-faced, thin-featured, **hatchet-faced;** wizen- or weazen-faced; lean- or thin-cheeked; lean- or lantern-jawed

20 **haggard, poor,** puny, **peaked** and peaky <nf>, **pinched;** shriveled, withered; **wizened,** weazeny; emaciated, emaciate, emacerated, **wasted,** attenuated, corpselike, skeletal, hollow-eyed, wraithlike, cadaverous; tabetic, tabid, marantic, marasmic; **starved,** anorexic, anorectic, starveling, starved-looking; undernourished, underfed, jejune; worn to a shadow, "worn to the bones"— Shakespeare

21 slenderizing, reducing, slimming

ADVS **22 narrowly,** closely, nearly, **barely,** hardly, only just, **by the skin of one's teeth**

23 thinly, thin; meagerly, sparsely, sparingly, scantily

271 FILAMENT

NOUNS **1 filament; fiber; thread; strand,** suture; filature; **hair** 3; artificial fiber, natural fiber, animal fiber; fibril, fibrilla; cilium, ciliolum; **tendril,** cirrus; flagellum; **web,** cobweb, gossamer, spider *or* spider's web; denier

 2 cord, line, rope, wire, braided rope, twisted rope, flattened-strand rope, wire rope, locked-wire rope, **cable,** wire cable; **yarn,** spun yarn, skein, hank; **string, twine;** braid; **ligament,** ligature, ligation; **tendon**

 3 cordage, cording, **ropework,** roping; tackle, tack, gear, rigging; ship's ropes

 4 strip, strap, strop; **lace,** thong; **band,** bandage, fillet, fascia, taenia; **belt,** girdle; **ribbon,** ribband; **tape,** tapeline, tape measure; slat, lath, batten, spline, strake, plank; ligule, ligula

 5 spinner, spinster; silkworm, spider; spinning wheel, spinning jenny, jenny, mule, mule-jenny; spinning frame, bobbin and fly frame; spinneret; rope walk

VERBS **6 <make threads> spin; braid,** twist

ADJS **7 threadlike,** thready; **stringy,** ropy, wiry; **hairlike** 3.23, hairy 3.24; filamentary, filamentous, filiform; fibrous, fibered, fibroid, fibrilliform; ligamental; capillary, capilliform; cirrose, cirrous; funicular, funiculate; flagelliform; taeniate, taeniform; ligulate, ligular; gossamer, gossamery, flossy, silky

272 HEIGHT

NOUNS **1 height,** heighth <nf>, vertical *or* perpendicular distance; **highness, tallness,** procerity; **altitude, elevation,** ceiling; **loftiness,** sublimity, exaltation; hauteur, toploftiness 141.1; eminence, prominence; **stature**

 2 height, elevation, eminence, **rise,** raise, **uprise,** lift, rising ground, vantage point *or* ground; **heights,** soaring *or* towering *or* Olympian heights, aerial heights, dizzy *or* dizzying heights; upmost *or* uppermost *or* utmost *or* extreme height; sky, stratosphere, ether, heaven *or* heavens; **zenith, apex, acme**

3 highlands 237.1, highland, upland, uplands, moorland, moors, downs, wold, rolling country

4 plateau, tableland, table, mesa, table mountain, bench; **hill; ridge; mountain; peak; mountain range**

5 watershed, water parting, **divide;** Great Divide, Continental Divide

6 tower; turret, *tour* <Fr>; campanile, bell tower, belfry; **spire,** church spire; **lighthouse,** light tower; cupola, lantern; dome; martello, martello tower; barbican; **derrick,** pole; windmill tower, observation tower, fire tower; **mast,** radio *or* television mast, antenna tower; water tower, standpipe; **spire,** pinnacle; **steeple,** *flèche* <Fr>; minaret; stupa, tope, pagoda, pyramid; pylon; **shaft,** pillar, column; pilaster; obelisk; monument; colossus; skyscraper

7 <tall person> longlegs *and* longshanks *and* highpockets *and* long drink of water <nf>; beanpole 270.8; **giant** 257.13; six-footer, seven-footer, grenadier <Brit>

8 high tide, high water, mean high water, flood tide, spring tide, flood; storm surge

9 <measurement of height> altimetry, hypsometry, hypsography; altimeter, hypsometer

VERBS **10 tower, soar,** spire, "buss the clouds"— Shakespeare; **rise, uprise, ascend, mount, rear;** stand on tiptoe

11 rise above, tower above *or* **over,** clear, overtop, o'er top, outtop, **top, surmount; overlook,** look down upon *or* over; overhang, beetle; **command,** dominate, overarch, overshadow, command a view of; bestride, bestraddle

12 <become higher> grow, grow up, upgrow; uprise, **rise** *or* **shoot up,** mount, sprout

13 heighten, elevate 912.5

ADJS **14 high,** high-reaching, high-up, **lofty, elevated,** altitudinous, altitudinal, uplifted *or* upreared, uprearing, **eminent, exalted, prominent,** supernal, **superlative,** sublime; **towering,** towery, **soaring,** spiring, aspiring, mounting, ascending; towered, turreted, steepled; **topping,** outtopping *or* overtopping; overarching, **overlooking, dominating;** airy, aerial, ethereal; Olympian; monumental, colossal; high as a steeple; topless; high-set, high-pitched; high-rise, multistory; **haughty** 141.9,157.8, toplofty

15 skyscraping, sky-high, heaven-reaching *or* -aspiring, heaven-high, heaven-kissing, "as high as Heaven and as deep as Hell"—Beaumont and Fletcher; cloud-touching *or* -topped *or* -capped, supernal; **mid-air**

16 giant 257.20, gigantic, colossal, statuesque, amazonian; **tall, lengthy,** long 267.8; **rangy, lanky,** lank, tall as a maypole; **gangling** *and* gangly <nf>; **long-legged,** long-limbed, leggy

17 highland, upland; hill-dwelling, mountain-
dwelling
18 hilly, knobby, rolling; **mountainous,** mountained,
alpine, alpen, alpestrine, alpigene; subalpine;
monticuline, monticulous
19 higher, superior, greater; **over, above;** upper,
upmost *or* uppermost, outtopping, overtopping,
topmost; highest 198.10
20 altimetric, altimetrical, hypsometrical,
hypsographic
ADVS **21 on high,** high up, high; **aloft,** aloof; **up,**
upward, upwards, straight up, to the zenith; **above,
over,** o'er, **overhead;** above one's head, over head
and ears; skyward, airward, in the air, in the
clouds; on the peak *or* summit *or* crest *or* pinnacle;
upstairs, abovestairs; tiptoe, on tiptoe; on stilts; on
the shoulders of; supra, *ubi supra* <L>,
hereinabove, hereinbefore

273 SHAFT

NOUNS **1 shaft, pole, bar, rod, stick,** scape, scapi-;
stalk, stem; thill; tongue, wagon tongue; flagstaff;
totem pole; Maypole; utility *or* telephone *or*
telegraph pole; tent pole
2 staff, stave; **cane, stick, walking stick,** handstaff,
shillelagh; Malacca cane; baton, marshal's baton,
drum-major's baton, conductor's baton; swagger
stick, swanking stick; pilgrim's staff, pastoral staff,
shepherd's staff, crook; crosier, cross-staff, cross,
paterissa; pikestaff, alpenstock; quarterstaff; lituus,
thyrsus; **crutch,** crutch-stick
3 beam, timber, pole, spar
4 post, standard, upright; king post, queen post,
crown post; newel; banister, baluster; balustrade,
balustrading; gatepost, swinging *or* hinging post,
shutting post; doorpost, jamb, doorjamb; signpost,
milepost; stile, mullion; stanchion; hitching post,
snubbing post, Samson post
5 pillar, column, post, pier, pilaster; colonnette,
columella; caryatid; atlas, atlantes <pl>; telamon,
telamones; **colonnade, arcade,** pilastrade, portico,
peristyle
6 leg, shank; **stake,** peg; pile, spile, stud; picket, pale,
palisade

274 LOWNESS

NOUNS **1 lowness, shortness,** squatness, squattiness,
stumpiness, shallowness, stuntedness; **prostration,**
supineness, proneness, recumbency, reclination,
lying, lying down, reclining; depression,
debasement; subjacency
2 low tide, low water, mean low water, dead low
water *or* tide, ebb tide, neap tide, neap, low ebb

3 lowland, **lowlands,** bottomland, swale; water
meadow, piedmont, foothills, flats, depression
4 base, bottom 199, lowest point, nadir, depths; the
lowest of the low; lowest *or* underlying level, lower
strata, substratum, bedrock
VERBS **5 lie low, squat, crouch,** lay low <nf>, couch;
crawl, grovel, lie prone *or* supine *or* prostrate, hug
the earth, lie down; lie under, underlie
6 lower, debase, depress 913.4; flatten
ADJS **7 low, unelevated, flat, low-lying; short, squat,**
squatty, stumpy, runty 258.13; **lowered,** debased,
depressed 912.12; demoted; **reduced** 252.10;
prone, supine, prostrate *or* prostrated, couchant,
crouched, stooped, recumbent, bowed; laid low,
knocked flat, decked <nf>; low-set, low-hung; **low-
built,** low-rise, low-sized, low-statured, low-bodied;
low-level, low-leveled; neap, shallow, shoal; knee-
high, knee-high to a grasshopper <nf>; low-
necked, low-cut, décolleté
8 lower, inferior, **under, nether,** subjacent; down; less
advanced; earlier; substrative, rock-bottom; lowest
199.7
ADVS **9 low,** near the ground; at a low ebb
10 below, down below, **under;** infra, hereunder,
hereinafter, hereinbelow; thereunder; belowstairs,
downstairs, below deck; underfoot; below par,
below the mark
PREPS **11 below, under, underneath, beneath,** neath,
at the foot of, at the base of

275 DEPTH

NOUNS **1 depth, deepness,** profoundness, profundity;
deep-downness, extreme innerness, deep-
seatedness, deep-rootedness; bottomlessness,
plumblessness, fathomlessness; subterraneity,
undergroundness; interiority 207; extensiveness,
unfathomableness
2 pit, deep, depth, hole, hollow, **cavity,** shaft, well,
gulf, chasm, abyss, abysm, yawning abyss; crater;
crevasse; valley; underground, subterrane
3 depths, deeps, bowels, bowels of the earth, core;
bottomless pit; infernal pit, hell, nether world,
underworld; dark *or* unknown *or* yawning *or*
gaping depths, unfathomed deeps; outer *or* deep
space
4 ocean depths, the deep sea, the deep, trench,
deep-sea trench <see list>, hadal zone, **the deeps,
the depths,** bottomless depths, inner space, abyss;
bottom waters; abyssal zone, Bassalia *or* Bassalian
realm, bathyal zone, pelagic zone; **seabed,** seafloor,
bottom of the sea, ocean bottom *or* floor *or* bed,
ground, benthos, benthonic division, benthonic
zone; Davy Jones's locker <nf>; Mariana Trench
5 sounding *or* **soundings,** fathoming, depth

sounding, probing; **echo sounding,** echolocation; sonar; **depth indicator;** oceanography, bathometry, bathymetry; fathomage, water <depth of water>

6 **draft,** submergence, submersion, sinkage, **displacement**

7 **deepening, lowering, depression;** sinking, sinkage, descent; excavation, digging, mining, tunneling; drilling, probing

VERBS 8 **deepen, lower, depress, sink;** founder; countersink; **dig,** excavate, tunnel, mine, **drill;** pierce to the depths; **dive** 367.6

9 **sound, take soundings,** make a sounding, heave *or* cast *or* sling the lead, **fathom, plumb,** plumb-line, plumb the depths, probe

ADJS 10 **deep, profound,** deep-down, penetrating; deepish, deepsome; **deep-going,** deep-lying, deep-reaching; **deep-set,** deep-laid; deep-sunk, deep-sunken, deep-sinking; **deep-seated, deep-rooted,** deep-fixed, deep-settled; deep-cut, deep-engraven; knee-deep, ankle-deep, waist-deep

11 **abysmal,** abyssal, yawning, cavernous, gaping, plunging; **bottomless,** without bottom, soundless, unsounded, plumbless, **fathomless,** unfathomed, unfathomable, rock-bottom; deep as a well, deep as the sea *or* ocean, deep as hell

12 **underground, subterranean,** subterraneous, hypogeal, buried, deep-buried

13 **underwater,** subaqueous; **submarine, undersea;** submerged, submersed, immersed, buried, engulfed, inundated, flooded, drowned, sunken

14 **deep-sea,** deep-water, blue-water; oceanographic, bathyal; benthic, benthal, benthonic; abyssal, Bassalian; bathyorographic, bathyorographical, bathymetric, bathymetrical; benthopelagic, bathypelagic

15 **deepest, deepmost,** profoundest; bedrock, rock-bottom

ADVS 16 **deep; beyond one's depth,** out of one's depth; over one's head, over head and ears; at bottom, at the core, at rock bottom

17 **deep-sea trenches and deeps**

Aleutian Trench 25,194 feet	Java *or* Sunda Trench, Planet Deep 23,376 feet
Bonin Trench 32,788 feet	
Cayman Trench 24,721 feet	Kermandec Trench 32,963 feet
Diamantina Fracture, Ob' Trench 22,553 feet	Kuril Trench 31,988 feet
Eurasia Basin (Arctic Ocean) 17,881 feet	Mariana Trench, Challenger Deep 35,840 feet
Guatemala Trench 21,228 feet	North Ryukyu Trench 23,560 feet
Ionian Basin (Mediterranean) 16,896 feet	Peru-Chile *or* Atacama Trench, Bartholomew Deep 26,160 feet
Japan Trench, Ramapo Deep 27,599 feet	Philippine Trench, Galathea Deep 32,995 feet
Puerto Rico Trench, Milwaukee Deep 28,232 feet	South Sandwich Trench, Meteor Deep 27,313 feet
Romanche Trench 25,354 feet	Tonga Trench 35,433 feet
Solomon Trench 29,988 feet	Verna Trench 21,004 feet
	Yap Trench 27,976 feet

276 SHALLOWNESS

NOUNS 1 **shallowness, depthlessness;** shoalness, shoaliness, no water, no depth; **superficiality,** exteriority, triviality, **cursoriness,** slightness; insufficiency 991; a lick and a promise *and* once-over-lightly <nf>; **surface,** superficies, skin, rind, epidermis; veneer, gloss; pinprick, scratch, mere scratch

2 **shoal, shallow,** shallows, shallow *or* shoal water, flat, shelf; **bank, bar,** sandbank, sandbar, tombolo; **reef,** coral reef; ford; wetlands, tidal flats, flats, mud flat

VERBS 3 **shoal,** shallow; fill in *or* up, silt up

4 **scratch the surface, touch upon,** hardly touch, skim, skim over, skim *or* graze the surface, hit the high spots *and* give a lick and a promise *and* give it once over lightly <nf>, apply a Band-Aid <trademark> <nf>; trivialize, trifle

ADJS 5 **shallow,** shoal, **depthless,** not deep, unprofound; **surface,** on *or* near the surface, merely surface; **superficial, cursory,** slight, light, cosmetic, merely cosmetic, thin, jejune, trivial; **skin-deep,** epidermal; one-dimensional, trifling, trivial; ankle-deep, knee-deep; shallow-rooted, shallow-rooting; shallow-draft *or* -bottomed *or* -hulled

6 shoaly, shelfy; reefy; unnavigable; shallow-sea

277 STRAIGHTNESS

NOUNS 1 **straightness,** directness, unswervingness, lineality, **linearity,** rectilinearity; verticalness 200; flatness, horizontalness 201; perpendicularity

2 **straight line,** straight, right line, direct line; straight course *or* stretch, straightaway; **beeline,** air line; **shortcut** 268.5; great-circle course; streamline; edge, side, diagonal, secant, transversal, chord, tangent, perpendicular, normal, segment, directrix, diameter, axis, radius, vector, radius vector <all mathematics>; ray, beeline, plumb line, column

3 **straightedge, rule,** ruler; square, T square, triangle

VERBS 4 **be straight,** have no turning *or* turns; arrow; go straight, make a beeline

5 **straighten, set** *or* **put straight,** rectify, make right *or* good, square away; **unbend,** unkink, uncurl, unsnarl, disentangle 798.5; straighten up, square

up; straighten out, extend; flatten, smooth 201.6; iron, flatten

ADJS 6 straight; straight-lined, dead straight, straight as an edge *or* a ruler, ruler-straight, even, right, true, straight as an arrow, arrowlike; straightaway; **rectilinear,** rectilineal; **linear,** lineal, in a line; **direct, undeviating, unswerving,** unbending, undeflected; **unbent, unbowed,** unturned, uncurved, undistorted, uncurled; **uninterrupted, unbroken;** straight-side, straight-front, straight-cut; upright, vertical 200.11; flat, level, smooth, horizontal 201.7; plumb, true, right

ADVS 7 straight, straightly, on the straight, unswervingly, undeviatingly, **directly;** straight to the mark; down the alley *and* down the pipe *and* in the groove *and* on the beam *and* on the money <nf>

278 ANGULARITY

NOUNS 1 angularity, angularness, crookedness, hookedness; squareness, orthogonality, right-angledness, rectangularity; flection, flexure

2 **angle,** point, bight; vertex, apex 198.2; **corner,** quoin, coin, nook; **crook, hook,** crotchet; **bend,** curve, swerve, veer, inflection, deflection; ell, L; cant; furcation, bifurcation, fork 171.4; zigzag, zig, zag; chevron; elbow, knee, dogleg <nf>; crank; obtuse angle, oblique angle, acute angle, right angle, perpendicular

3 <angular measurement> goniometry; trigonometry; geometry

4 <instruments> goniometer, radiogoniometer; pantometer, clinometer, graphometer, astrolabe; azimuth compass, azimuth circle; theodolite, transit theodolite, transit, transit instrument, transit circle; sextant, quadrant; bevel, bevel square, set square, T square; protractor, bevel protractor

VERBS 5 angle, crook, hook, bend, elbow; crank; angle off *or* away, curve, swerve, veer, veer off, slant off, go off on a tangent; furcate, bifurcate, branch, fork 171.7; zigzag, zig, zag

ADJS 6 angular; cornered, **crooked, hooked, bent,** flexed, flexural; akimbo; knee-shaped, geniculate, geniculated, doglegged <nf>; crotched, Y-shaped, V-shaped; furcate, furcal, forked 171.10; sharp-cornered, **sharp, pointed;** zigzag, jagged, serrate, sawtooth *or* saw-toothed; mitered

7 **right-angled, rectangular,** right-angular, right-angle; **orthogonal,** orthodiagonal, orthometric; **perpendicular,** normal

8 **triangular, trilateral,** trigonal, oxygonal, deltoid; wedgeshaped, cuneiform, cuneate, cuneated

9 **quadrangular, quadrilateral,** quadrate, quadriform;

rectangular, square; foursquare, orthogonal; tetragonal, tetrahedral; **oblong;** trapezoid *or* trapezoidal, rhombic *or* rhombal, rhomboid *or* rhomboidal; **cubic** *or* **cubical,** cubiform, cuboid, cube-shaped, cubed, diced; rhombohedral, trapezohedral

10 pentagonal, hexagonal, heptagonal, octagonal, decagonal, dodecagonal, etc; pentahedral, hexahedral, octahedral, dodecahedral, icosahedral, etc

11 multilateral, multiangular, polygonal; polyhedral, pyramidal, pyramidic; prismatic, prismoid; diamond

279 CURVATURE

NOUNS 1 curvature, curving, curvation, arcing; incurvature, incurvation; excurvature, excurvation; decurvature, decurvation; recurvature, recurvity, recurvation; rondure; **arching, vaulting,** arcuation, concameration; aduncity, aquilinity, crookedness, hookedness; sinuosity, sinuousness, tortuosity, tortuousness; circularity 280; convolution 281; rotundity 282, roundness; convexity 283; concavity 284; curvaceousness

2 **curve,** sinus; **bow, arc; crook, hook;** parabola, hyperbola, witch of Agnesi; ellipse; caustic, catacaustic, diacaustic; catenary, festoon, swag; conchoid; lituus; tracery; circle 280.2; curl 281.2; coil, loop, spiral

3 **bend,** bending; **bow,** bowing, oxbow; Cupid's bow; **turn,** turning, sweep, meander, hairpin turn *or* bend, S-curve, U-turn; **flexure,** flex, **flection,** conflexure, inflection, deflection; reflection; geanticline, geosyncline; detour

4 **arch, span, vault,** vaulting, concameration, camber; ogive; apse; **dome,** cupola, geodesic dome, igloo, concha; cove; arched roof, ceilinged roof; **arcade, archway,** arcature; voussoir, keystone, skewback

5 **crescent, semicircle,** scythe, sickle, meniscus; crescent moon, half-moon; lunula, lunule; horseshoe; rainbow

VERBS 6 curve, turn, arc, sweep; **crook, hook,** loop; incurve, incurvate; recurve, decurve, bend back, retroflex, detour; sag, swag <nf>; **bend,** flex; deflect, inflect; reflect, reflex; **bow,** embow; **arch,** vault; dome; **hump,** hunch; wind, curl 281.5; round 282.6

ADJS 7 curved, curve, curvate, curvated, **curving,** curvy, curvaceous <nf>, curvesome, curviform; curvilinear, curvilineal; wavy, undulant, billowy, billowing; sinuous, tortuous, serpentine, mazy, labyrinthine, meandering; **bent,** flexed, flexural, flexuous; incurved, incurving, incurvate, incurvated; recurved, recurving, recurvate, recurvated; geosynclinal, geanticlinal

8 **hooked, crooked, aquiline,** aduncous; **hook-shaped,** hooklike, uncinate, unciform; hamulate, hamate, hamiform; claw-like, unguiform, down-curving; **hook-nosed,** beak-nosed, parrot-nosed, aquiline-nosed, Roman-nosed, crooknosed, crookbilled; **beaked,** billed; **beak-shaped,** beak-like; bill-shaped, bill-like; rostrate, rostriform, rhamphoid

9 turned-up, upcurving, upsweeping, *retroussé* <Fr>

10 **bowed,** embowed, bandy; bowlike, bow-shaped, oxbow, Cupid's-bow; **convex, concave** 284.16, convexoconcave; arcuate, arcuated, arcual, arciform, arclike; **arched,** vaulted; **humped,** hunched, humpy, hunchy; gibbous, gibbose; humpbacked 265.13

11 **crescent-shaped,** crescentlike, crescent, crescentic, crescentiform; meniscoid *or* meniscoidal, menisciform; S-shaped, ess, S, sigmoid; **semicircular,** semilunar; horn-shaped, hornlike, horned, corniform; bicorn, two-horned; sickle-shaped, sickle-like, falcate, falciform; moon-shaped, moonlike, lunar, lunate, lunular, luniform

12 lens-shaped, lenticular, lentiform

13 parabolic, parabolical, paraboloid, saucer-shaped; elliptic, elliptical, ellipsoid; bell-shaped, bell-like, campanular, campanulate, campaniform; hyperbolic, domical

14 pear-shaped, pearlike, pyriform

15 heart-shaped, heartlike; cordate, cardioid, cordiform

16 kidney-shaped, kidneylike, reniform

17 turnip-shaped, turniplike, napiform

18 shell-shaped, shell-like; conchate, conchiform

19 shield-shaped, shieldlike, peltate, scutate, scutiform; clypeate, clypeiform

20 helmet-shaped, helmetlike, galeiform, cassideous

280 CIRCULARITY

NOUNS 1 **circularity, roundness,** ring-shape, ringliness, annularity; annulation

2 **circle,** circus, rondure, **ring,** annulus, O, full circle; **circumference,** radius; **round,** roundel, rondelle; **cycle, circuit;** orbit 1072.16; closed circle *or* arc; vicious circle, eternal return; magic circle, charmed circle, fairy ring; logical circle, circular reasoning, petitio principii; **wheel** 915.4; **disk,** discus, saucer; **loop,** looplet; noose, lasso; crown, diadem, coronet, corona; garland, chaplet, wreath; halo, glory, areola, aureole; annular muscle, sphincter

3 <thing encircling> **band, belt, cincture,** cingulum, **girdle, girth,** girt, zone, fascia, fillet; collar,

collarband, neckband; necktie; necklace, bracelet, armlet, torque, wristlet, wristband, anklet; ring, earring, nose ring, finger ring; hoop; quoit; zodiac, ecliptic, equator, great circle; round trip

4 **rim,** felly; **tire**

5 circlet, **ringlet,** roundlet, annulet, eye, **eyelet,** grommet

6 **oval,** ovule, ovoid; ellipse

7 cycloid; epicycloid, epicycle; hypocycloid; lemniscate; cardioid; Lissajous figure

8 **semicircle,** half circle, hemicycle; crescent 279.5; quadrant, sextant, sector

9 <music and poetry> **round,** canon; rondo, rondino, rondeau, rondelet

VERBS 10 circle, round; orbit; **encircle** 209.7, surround, encompass, girdle; make a round trip, circumnavigate

ADJS 11 **circular, round,** rounded, circinate, annular, annulate, ring-shaped, ringlike; annulose; disklike, discoid; cyclic, cyclical, cycloid, cycloidal; epicyclic; planetary; coronal, crownlike; orbital; circulatory, circumferential

12 **oval,** ovate, ovoid, oviform, egg-shaped, obovate

281 CONVOLUTION
<complex curvature>

NOUNS 1 **convolution,** involution, circumvolution, **winding, twisting, turning; meander, meandering;** crinkle, crinkling; circuitousness, circumlocution, circumbendibus, circumambages, ambagiousness, ambages, convolutedness; Byzantinism; tortuousness, tortuosity; torsion, intorsion; sinuousness, **sinuosity,** sinuation, slinkiness; anfractuosity; snakiness; flexuousness, flexuosity; undulation, wave, waving; rivulation; **complexity** 799

2 **coil, whorl,** roll, **curl,** curlicue, ringlet, pigtail, **spiral,** helix, double helix, volute, volution, involute, evolute, gyre, scroll, turbination; **kink, twist, twirl;** screw, corkscrew, screw thread; tendril, cirrus; whirl, swirl, vortex; intricacy; squiggle

3 curler, curling iron; curlpaper, papillote; straightening iron; crimper, crimping iron

VERBS 4 convolve, convolute, **wind, twine,** twirl, **twist, turn, twist and turn, meander,** crinkle; serpentine, snake, slink, worm; screw, corkscrew; whirl, swirl; whorl; scallop; wring; intort; contort; undulate, squiggle, twist and turn

5 **curl, coil;** crisp, kink, crimp, wave

ADJS 6 **convolutional, convoluted, winding, twisting,** twisty, **turning; meandering,** meandrous, mazy, labyrinthine; **serpentine,** snaky, anfractuous; roundabout, circuitous, ambagious, circumlocutory; labyrinthine; Byzantine; **sinuous,** sinuose, sinuate; **tortuous,** torsional; tortile; flexular, flexuous, flexuose; involutional, involute, involuted; rivose, rivulose; sigmoidal; wreathy, wreathlike; ruffled, whorled, turbinate

7 **coiled,** tortile, **snakelike, snaky,** snake-shaped, **serpentine,** serpentlike, serpentiform; anguine <old>, anguiform; eellike, eelshaped, anguilliform; wormlike, vermiform, lumbricoid, lumbricine, lumbriciform

8 **spiral,** spiroid, volute, voluted; **helical,** helicoid, helicoidal; anfractuous; screw-shaped, corkscrew, corkscrewy; verticillate, whorled, scrolled; cochlear, cochleate; turbinal, turbinate

9 **curly, curled; kinky,** kinked; **frizzly,** frizzy, frizzled, frizzed; crisp, crispy, crisped

10 **wavy, undulant,** undulatory, undulative, undulating, undulate, undulated; **billowy,** billowing, surgy, rolling

ADVS 11 **windingly, twistingly,** sinuously, tortuously, serpentinely, meanderingly, meandrously; in waves; wavily; **in and out,** round and round

282 SPHERICITY, ROTUNDITY

NOUNS 1 **sphericity, rotundity, roundness,** ball-likeness, rotundness, orbicularness, orbicularity, orbiculation, orblikeness, **sphericalness,** sphericality, globularity, globularness, globosity, globoseness; spheroidity, spheroidicity; belly; cylindricality; convexity 283

2 **sphere; ball,** orb, orbit, **globe,** rondure; geoid; spheroid, globoid, ellipsoid, oblate spheroid, prolate spheroid; spherule, globule, globelet, orblet; glomerulus; **pellet;** boll; **bulb,** bulbil *or* bulbel, bulblet; knob, knot; **gob,** glob <nf>, blob, gobbet; pill, bolus; **balloon,** bladder, bubble; marble

3 **drop,** droplet; dewdrop, raindrop, teardrop; bead, pearl

4 **cylinder,** cylindroid, pillar, column; barrel, drum, cask; pipe, tube; roll, rouleau, roller, rolling pin; bole, trunk; rung

5 **cone,** conoid, conelet; complex cone, cone of a complex; funnel; ice-cream cone, cornet <Brit>; pine cone; cop; trumpet; top

VERBS 6 **round; round out, fill out; cone**

7 **ball, snowball;** sphere, spherify, globe, conglobulate; roll; bead; balloon, mushroom

ADJS 8 **rotund, round,** rounded, rounded out, round as a ball; bellied, bellylike; convex, bulging

9 **spherical,** sphereic, spheriform, spherelike, sphere-shaped; **globular, global,** globed, globose, globate, globelike, globe-shaped; orbicular, orbiculate, orbiculated, orbed, orb, orby <old>, orblike;

spheroid, spheroidal, globoid, ellipsoid, ellipsoidal; hemispheric, hemispherical; **bulbous,** bulblike, bulging; ovoid, obovoid

10 **beady,** beaded, bead-shaped, bead-like

11 **cylindric, cylindrical,** cylindroid, cylindroidal; **columnar,** columnal, columned, columelliform; **tubular,** tube-shaped; barrel-shaped, drum-shaped

12 **conical,** conic, coned, cone-shaped, conelike; conoid, conoidal; spheroconic; funnel-shaped, funnellike, funnelled, funnelform, infundibuliform, infundibular; bell-shaped

283 CONVEXITY, PROTUBERANCE

NOUNS 1 **convexity,** convexness, convexedness; excurvature, excurvation; camber; gibbousness, gibbosity; tuberousness, tuberosity; **bulging,** bulbousness, bellying, puffing, puffing out

2 **protuberance** *or* protuberancy, **projection, protrusion, extrusion;** prominence, eminence, salience, boldness, **bulging,** bellying; gibbousness, gibbosity; excrescence *or* excrescency; tuberousness, tuberosity, puffiness; salient; relief, high relief, *alto-rilievo* <Ital>, low relief, bas-relief, *basso-rilievo* <Ital>, embossment

3 **bulge,** bilge, bow, convex; **bump;** thank-you-ma'am *and* whoopdedoo <nf>, cahot <Can>; speed bump, sleeping policeman <Brit>; hill, mountain; **hump,** hunch; **lump,** clump, bunch, blob; nubbin, nubble, nub; **mole,** nevus; **wart,** papilloma, verruca; **knob,** boss, bulla, button, bulb; stud, jog, joggle, peg, dowel; flange, lip; tab, ear, flap, loop, ring, handle; knot, knur, knurl, gnarl, burl, gall; **ridge,** rib, cost- *or* costo- *or* costi-, chine, spine, shoulder; welt, wale; blister, bleb, vesicle <anat>, blain; bubble; condyle; bubo; tubercle *or* tubercule; beer belly

4 **swelling,** swollenness, edema; **rising, lump, bump,** pimple; pock, furuncle, boil, carbuncle; corn; pustule; dilation, dilatation; turgidity, turgescence *or* turgescency, tumescence, intumescence; tumor, tumidity, tumefaction; wen, cyst, sebaceous cyst; bunion; distension 259.2

5 **node,** nodule, nodulus, nodulation, nodosity

6 **breast, bosom, bust, chest,** crop, brisket; thorax; pigeon breast; **breasts,** dugs, teats; **nipple,** papilla, pap, mammilla, *mamelon and téton* <Fr>; mammillation, mamelonation; mammary gland, udder, bag; testicles

7 <nf terms> **tits,** titties, **boobs,** boobies, bubbies, jugs, headlights, **knockers,** knobs, *nénés* <Fr>, bazooms, bags, bazongas, coconuts, hooters; balls

8 **nose,** olfactory organ; **snout, snoot** <nf>, nozzle <nf>, **muzzle; proboscis,** antlia, **trunk; beak,** rostrum; **bill** *and* pecker <nf>; nib, neb; smeller

and beezer *and* bugle *and* schnozzle *and* schnoz *and* schnozzola *and* conk <nf>; muffle, rhinarium; nostrils, noseholes <Brit nf>, nares

9 <point of land> **point**, hook, spur, **cape**, tongue, bill; **promontory**, foreland, **headland**, head; naze, ness; **peninsula**, chersonese; **delta; spit**, sandspit; **reef**, coral reef; breakwater 901.4

VERBS 10 **protrude, protuberate, project, extrude; stick out**, jut out, poke out, stand out, shoot out; **stick up**, bristle up, start up, cock up, shoot up

11 **bulge**, bilge, bouge <nf>, **belly**, bag, balloon, **pouch**, pooch <nf>; pout; **goggle**, bug <nf>, pop; **swell, swell up, dilate, distend**, billow; swell out, **belly out**, round out

12 **emboss, boss**, chase, raise; ridge

ADJS 13 **convex**, convexed; excurved, excurvate, excurvated; **bowed**, bowed-out, out-bowed, arched 279.10; gibbous, gibbose; humped 279.10; rotund 282.8

14 **protruding, protrusive**, protrudent; protrusile, protrusible; **protuberant**, protuberating; **projecting, extruding**, jutting, outstanding; prominent, eminent, salient, bold; prognathous; excrescent, excrescential; protrusile, emissile; sticking out

15 **bulging, swelling**, distended, bloated, potbellied, bellying, pouching; bagging, baggy; rounded, hillocky, hummocky, moutonnée; billowing, billowy, bosomy, ballooning, pneumatic; **bumpy**, bumped; bunchy, bunched; **bulbous**, bulbose; warty, verrucose, verrucated; meniscoid

16 **bulged, bulgy**, bugged-out <nf>; swollen 259.13, turgid, tumid, turgescent, tumescent, tumorous; bellied, ventricose; pouched, pooched <nf>; goggled, goggle; exophthalmic, bug-eyed <nf>, popeyed <nf>

17 **studded, knobbed, knobby**, knoblike, nubbled, nubby, nubbly, torose; **knotty, knotted; gnarled**, knurled, knurly, burled, gnarly; noded, nodal, nodiform; noduled, nodular; nodulated; bubonic; tuberculous, tubercular; tuberous, tuberose

18 **in relief**, in bold *or* high relief, bold, raised, *repoussé* <Fr>; chased, bossed, embossed, bossy

19 **pectoral**, chest, thoracic; pigeon-breasted; mammary, mammillary, mammiform; mammalian, mammate; papillary, papillose, papulous; breasted, bosomed, chested; teated, titted <nf>, nippled; busty, bosomy, chesty

20 **peninsular;** deltaic, deltal

284 CONCAVITY

NOUNS 1 **concavity, hollowness;** incurvature, incurvation; depression, impression; emptiness 222.2

2 **cavity**, concavity, concave; **hollow**, hollow shell, shell; **hole, pit, depression, dip**, sink, fold <Brit>; scoop, pocket; **basin**, trough, **bowl**, punch bowl, cup, container 195; **crater;** antrum; lacuna; alveola, alveolus, alveolation; vug *or* vugg *or* vugh; crypt; armpit; socket; funnel chest *or* breast

3 **pothole, sinkhole**, pitchhole, chuckhole, **mudhole, rut** 290.1

4 **pit, well, shaft**, sump; **chasm, gulf, abyss**, abysm; **excavation**, dig, diggings, workings; mine, quarry

5 **cave, cavern**, cove <Scot>, **hole, grotto**, grot, antre, subterrane; lair 228.26; **tunnel, burrow**, warren; subway; bunker, foxhole, dugout, *abri* <Fr>; sewer

6 **indentation**, indent, indention, indenture, **dent**, dint; gouge, **furrow** 290; sunken part *or* place, **dimple; pit**, pock, pockmark; impression, impress; imprint, print; alveolus, alveolation; honeycomb, Swiss cheese; **notch** 289

7 **recess**, recession, **niche, nook**, inglenook, corner; cove, alcove; bay; pitchhole

8 <hollow in the side of a mountain> combe, cwm <Welsh>, cirque, corrie

9 **valley**, vale, dale, dell, dingle; **glen**, bottom, bottoms, bottom glade, intervale, strath <Scot>, gill <Brit>, cwm <Welsh>, wadi, grove; trench, trough, lunar rill; gap, pass, ravine

10 **excavator, digger;** sapper; **miner;** tunneler, sandhog *and* groundhog <nf>, burrower; gravedigger; dredger; quarryman; driller; steam shovel, navvy <Brit>; dredge, dredger

11 **excavation**, digging; mining; indentation, **engraving**

VERBS 12 <be concave> **sink, dish**, cup, bowl, hollow; retreat, retire; incurve, curve inward

13 **hollow**, hollow out, concave, **dish**, cup, bowl; cave, cave in

14 **indent, dent**, dint, **depress**, press in, stamp, tamp, punch, punch in, impress, imprint; **pit**; pock, pockmark; dimple; honeycomb; **recess**, set back; set in; **notch** 289.4; engrave

15 **excavate, dig**, dig out, **scoop**, scoop out, **gouge**, gouge out, grub, shovel, spade, trowel, dike, delve; scrape, scratch, scrabble; dredge; **trench**, trough, furrow, groove; **tunnel, burrow**; drive, sink, lower; **mine**, sap; quarry; drill, bore

ADJS 16 **concave**, concaved, **incurved**, incurving, incurvate; **sunk**, sunken; retreating, recessed, retiring; **hollow**, hollowed, empty; palm-shaped; dish-shaped, dished, dishing, dishlike, bowl-shaped; bowllike, crater-shaped, craterlike, saucer-shaped; spoon-like; **cupped**, cup-shaped, scyphate; funnel-shaped, infundibular, infundibuliform; funnel-chested, funnel-breasted; boat-shaped, boatlike, navicular, naviform, cymbiform, scaphoid; **cavernous**, cavelike

17 indented, dented, depressed; **dimpled; pitted;** cratered; pocked, pockmarked; honeycombed, alveolar, alveolate, faveolate; **notched** 289.5; **engraved**

285 SHARPNESS

NOUNS 1 **sharpness, keenness, edge;** acuteness, acuity; **pointedness,** acumination; thorniness, prickliness, spinosity, spininess, bristliness; mucronation; denticulation, dentition; serration; cornification; acridity 68.1

2 <sharp edge> **edge, cutting edge, honed edge, knife-edge, razor-edge,** saw-edge; jagged edge; featheredge, fine edge; edge tool; weapon 462.21–26

3 **point, tip,** cusp, vertex; acumination, mucro; **nib,** neb; needle; hypodermic needle, hypodermic syringe; **drill,** borer, auger, bit; prong, tine; **prick, prickle;** sting, acus or aculeus; **tooth** 2.8

4 <pointed projection> **projection,** spur, jag, **snag,** snaggle; **horn,** antler; cornicle; crag, peak, arête; spire, steeple, flèche; **cog, sprocket,** ratchet; sawtooth; harrow, rake; comb, pecten; nail, tack, pin; arrowhead; skewer, spit; tooth, snaggletooth, fang, denticle

5 **thorn, bramble, brier, nettle,** burr, awn, prickle, sticker <nf>; **spike,** spikelet, spicule, spiculum; **spine;** bristle; quill; **needle,** pine needle; **thistle,** catchweed, cleavers, goose grass, cactus; yucca, Adam's-needle, Spanish bayonet

VERBS 6 come or taper to a point, end in a point, acuminate; prick, prickle, sting, stick, bite; be keen, have an edge, cut, needle; bristle with

7 **sharpen, edge,** acuminate, aculeate, spiculate, taper; **whet, hone,** oilstone, file, grind; strop, strap; set, reset; **point;** barb, spur, point, file to a point

ADJS 8 **sharp, keen, edged, acute,** fine, **cutting,** knifelike, cultrate; sharp-edged, keen-edged, razor-edged, knife-edged, sharp as broken glass; featheredged, fine-edged; acrid 68.6; two-edged, double-edged; sharp-set, sharp as a razor or needle or tack, "sharp as a two-edged sword"—Bible, "sharper than a serpent's tooth"—Shakespeare; sharpened, set

9 **pointed,** pointy, acuminate, acuate, aculeate, aculeated, acute, unbated; tapered, tapering; cusped, cuspate, cuspated, cuspidal, cuspidate, cuspidated; **sharp-pointed; needlelike,** needle-sharp, needle-pointed, needly, acicular, aciculate, aculeiform; mucronate, mucronated; acuminate; toothed; **spiked,** spiky, spiculate; **barbed, tined, pronged; horned,** horny, cornuted, corniculate, cornified, ceratoid; **spined, spiny,** spinous, hispid, acanthoid, acanthous; "like quills upon the fretful porpentine"—Shakespeare

10 **prickly,** pricky <nf>, muricate, echinate, acanaceous, acanthous, aculeolate; pricking, stinging; **thorny,** brambly, briery, thistly, nettly, burry; bristly

11 **arrowlike,** arrowy, arrowheaded; sagittal, sagittate, sagittiform

12 **spearlike,** hastate; lancelike, lanciform, lanceolate, lanceolar; **spindle-shaped,** fusiform

13 **swordlike,** gladiate, ensate, ensiform

14 **toothlike,** dentiform, dentoid, odontoid; **toothed,** toothy, **fanged, tusked,** corniculate, denticulate, cuspidate, muricate; snaggle-toothed, snaggled, jagged; emarginate

15 **star-shaped, starlike,** star-pointed, stellate, stellular

286 BLUNTNESS

NOUNS 1 **bluntness, dullness,** unsharpness, obtuseness, obtundity; bluffness; abruptness; flatness, smoothness; toothlessness, lack of bite or incisiveness

VERBS 2 **blunt, dull,** disedge, retund, obtund, **take the edge off,** take the sting or bite out; turn, turn the edge or point of; weaken, repress; draw the teeth or fangs; bate; flatten, smooth

ADJS 3 **blunt, dull,** obtuse, obtundent; bluntish, dullish; **unsharp,** unsharpened, unwhetted; **unedged,** edgeless; rounded, faired, smoothed, streamlined; **unpointed,** pointless; blunted, dulled; blunt-edged, dull-edged; blunt-pointed, dull-pointed, blunt-ended; bluff, abrupt; flat

4 **toothless,** teethless, edentate, edental, edentulous, biteless

287 SMOOTHNESS

NOUNS 1 **smoothness, flatness, levelness,** evenness, uniformity, regularity; **sleekness,** glossiness; **slickness,** slipperiness, lubricity, oiliness, greasiness, frictionlessness; silkiness, satininess, velvetiness; glabrousness, glabriety; downiness; suavity 504.5; peacefulness, dead calm

2 **polish, gloss, glaze,** burnish, varnish, wax, enamel, **shine, luster,** finish; **patina**

3 <smooth surface> smooth, **plane, level, flat;** tennis court, bowling alley or green, billiard table or ball; slide; glass, ice; marble, alabaster, ivory; silk, satin, velvet, a baby's ass <nf>; mahogany

4 **smoother;** roller, lawn-roller; sleeker, slicker; **polish,** burnish; **abrasive,** abrader, abradant; lubricant; flattener, iron; buffer, sander, burnisher

VERBS 5 **smooth, flatten, plane,** planish, **level,** even, equalize; **dress,** dub, dab; smooth down or out, lay; plaster, plaster down; roll, roll smooth; harrow, drag; grade; mow, shave; lubricate, oil, grease

6 press, hot-press, **iron, mangle,** calender; roll

7 polish, shine, burnish, furbish, sleek, slick, slick
down, gloss, glaze, glance, luster; **rub,** scour, **buff;**
wax, varnish; finish

8 grind, file, sand, scrape, sandpaper, emery,
pumice; levigate; abrade; sandblast

9 move smoothly; glide, skate, roll, ski, float, slip,
slide, skid, coast

ADJS **10 smooth;** smooth-textured *or* -surfaced, **even,
level, plane, flat,** regular, uniform, **unbroken;**
peaceful, still; unrough, unroughened, unruffled,
unwrinkled, unrumpled; glabrous, glabrate,
glabrescent; downy, peachlike; silky, satiny, velvety,
smooth as silk *or* satin *or* velvet, smooth as a
billiard ball *or* baby's ass <nf>; leiotrichous,
lissotrichous; smooth-shaven 6.17; suave 504.18

11 sleek, slick, glossy, shiny, gleaming; silky, silken,
satiny, velvety; **polished,** burnished, furbished;
buffed, rubbed, finished; varnished, lacquered,
shellacked, glazed, *glacé* <Fr>; **glassy,** smooth as
glass

12 slippery, slippy, **slick,** slithery *and* sliddery <nf>,
slippery as an eel; lubricous, lubric, oily,
oleaginous, greasy, buttery, soaped, soapy;
lubricated, oiled, greased

ADVS **13 smoothly, evenly,** regularly, uniformly; **like
clockwork,** on wheels

288 ROUGHNESS

NOUNS **1 roughness, unsmoothness, unevenness,**
irregularity, ununiformity, nonuniformity 782,
inequality; **bumpiness,** pockedness, pockiness,
holeyness; **abrasiveness, abrasion,** harshness,
asperity; **ruggedness,** rugosity; **jaggedness,**
raggedness, cragginess, scraggliness; joltiness,
bumpiness; rough air, turbulence; choppiness;
tooth; granulation; hispidity, bristliness, spininess,
thorniness; nubbiness, nubbliness; scaliness,
scabrousness

2 <rough surface> **rough,** broken ground; broken
water, chop; **corrugation,** ripple, washboard;
serration; gooseflesh, goose bumps, goose pimples,
horripilation; tweed, corduroy, sackcloth; steel
wool; sandpaper; potholed road, dirt road

3 bristle, barb, barbel, striga, setule, setula, seta;
stubble; whiskers, five o'clock shadow

VERBS **4 roughen,** rough, rough up, harshen;
coarsen; granulate; gnarl, knob, stud, boss; pimple,
horripilate; roughcast, rough-hew

5 ruffle, wrinkle, corrugate, crinkle, crumple,
corrugate, **rumple; bristle; rub the wrong way, go
against the grain,** set on edge

ADJS **6 rough, unsmooth; uneven,** ununiform,
unlevel, inequal, **broken,** irregular, textured; jolty,

bumpy, rutty, rutted, pitted, pocky, potholed;
horripilant, pimply; **corrugated,** ripply, wimpled;
choppy; ruffled, unkempt; **shaggy,** shagged; **coarse,**
rank, unrefined; unpolished; rough-grained,
coarse-grained, cross-grained; grainy, granulated;
rough-hewn, rough-cast; homespun, linsey-
woolsey; bouclé, tweed, tweedy, corduroy

7 rugged, ragged, harsh; rugose, rugous, wrinkled,
crinkled, crumpled, corrugated; **scratchy, abrasive,**
rough as a cob <nf>; **jagged,** jaggy; **snaggy,**
snagged, snaggled; scraggy, scragged, scraggly;
sawtooth, sawtoothed, serrate, serrated; **craggy,**
cragged; **rocky,** gravelly, stony; rockbound,
ironbound

8 gnarled, gnarly; **knurled,** knurly; **knotted,** knotty,
knobbly, nodose, nodular, studded, lumpy

9 bristly, bristling, bristled, hispid, hirsute, whiskery;
barbellate, whiskered, glochidiate, setaceous,
setous, setose; strigal, strigose, strigate, studded;
stubbled, stubbly; hairy 3.24

10 bristlelike, setiform, aristate, setarious

ADVS **11 roughly,** rough, in the rough; **unsmoothly,**
brokenly, **unevenly,** irregularly, raggedly, choppily,
jaggedly; **abrasively**

12 cross-grained, **against the grain,** the wrong way

289 NOTCH

NOUNS **1 notch, nick,** nock, **cut,** cleft, **incision, gash,**
hack, blaze, scotch, **score,** kerf, crena, depression,
jag; jog; joggle; **indentation** 284.6

2 notching, serration, serrulation, saw, saw tooth *or*
teeth; denticulation, dentil, dentil band, dogtooth;
crenation, crenelation, crenature, crenulation;
scallop; rickrack; picot edge, Vandyke edge; deckle
edge; cockscomb, crest; pinking shears

3 battlement, crenel, merlon, embrasure, castellation,
machicolation; cog, zigzag

VERBS **4 notch, nick, cut, incise, gash,** nock, slash,
chop, crimp, scotch, **score,** blaze, jag, scarify; **indent**
284.14; **scallop,** crenelate, crenulate, machicolate;
serrate, pink, mill, knurl, tooth, picot, Vandyke

ADJS **5 notched, nicked,** incised, incisural, gashed,
scotched, scored, chopped, blazed; **indented**
284.17; serrate, serrated, serrulated, **saw-toothed,**
saw-edged, sawlike; crenate, crenated, crenulate,
crenellated, battlemented, embrasured; scalloped;
dentate, dentated, **toothed,** toothlike, tooth-
shaped; lacerate, lacerated; **jagged,** jaggy; erose;
serrated, serriform

290 FURROW

NOUNS **1 furrow, groove,** scratch, crack, fissure,
cranny, chase, chink, score, **cut,** gash, striation,

streak, stria, **gouge,** slit, incision; sulcus, sulcation; **rut,** ruck <nf>, wheeltrack, well-worn groove; wrinkle 291.3; **corrugation;** flute, fluting; rifling; chamfer, bezel, rabbet, dado; microgroove; **engraving** 713.2

2 **trench, trough, channel, ditch,** dike <old>, fosse, **canal,** cut, gutter, conduit, kennel <Brit>; moat; sunk fence, ha-ha; aqueduct 239.2; entrenchment 460.5; canalization; pleat, crimp, goffer

VERBS 3 **furrow, groove,** score, scratch, incise, cut, carve, chisel, gash, striate, streak, gouge, slit, crack; plow; rifle; **channel, trough, flute,** chamfer, rabbet, dado; **trench,** canal, canalize, **ditch,** dike <old>, gully, **rut; corrugate;** wrinkle 291.6; pleat, crimp, goffer; **engrave** 713.10

ADJS 4 **furrowed, grooved,** scratched, scored, incised, cut, gashed, gouged, slit, striated, slotted; **channeled, troughed,** trenched, ditched, plowed; fluted, chamfered, rabbeted, dadoed; rifled; sulcate, sulcated; canaliculate, canaliculated; **corrugated,** corrugate; corduroy, corduroyed, **rutted,** rutty, rimose; wrinkled 291.8, pleated, crimped, goffered; **engraved;** ribbed, costate

291 FOLD

NOUNS 1 **fold, double,** fold on itself, doubling, doubling over, duplicature; ply; plication, plica, plicature; flection, flexure; **crease,** creasing; crimp; **tuck, gather;** ruffle, frill, ruche, ruching; flounce; lappet; lapel; buckling, geological fold, anticline, syncline; dog-ear

2 **pleat,** pleating, plait *or* plat; accordion pleat, box pleat, knife pleat

3 **wrinkle, corrugation,** ridge, **furrow** 290, **crease, crimp,** ruck, **pucker,** cockle; **crinkle,** crankle, rimple, ripple, wimple; crumple, rumple; crow's-feet

4 **folding, creasing,** infolding, infoldment *or* enfoldment, envelopment; plication, plicature; paper-folding, origami

VERBS 5 **fold,** fold on itself, fold up; **double,** ply, plicate; fold over, double over *or* under, lap, turn over *or* under; **crease, crimp;** crisp; **pleat,** plait, plat <nf>; **tuck, gather,** tuck up, ruck, ruck up; ruffle, ruff, frill; flounce; twill, quill, flute; turn up *or* down, dog-ear; **fold in,** enfold *or* infold, wrap, lap; interfold

6 **wrinkle, corrugate,** shirr, ridge, **furrow, crease,** crimp, crimple, cockle, cocker, **pucker, purse; knit;** ruck, ruckle; **crumple,** rumple; **crinkle,** rimple, ripple, wimple

ADJS 7 **folded, doubled;** plicate, plicated, plical; **pleated,** plaited; **creased,** crimped; tucked, gathered; flounced, ruffled; twilled, quilled, fluted;

dog-eared; foldable, folding, flexural, flexible, flectional, pliable, pliant, willowy

8 **wrinkled, wrinkly; corrugated,** corrugate; **creased,** rucked, ruched, **furrowed** 290.4, ridged; cockled, cockly; puckered, puckery; pursed, pursy; knitted, knotted; rugged, rugose, rugous; **crinkled,** crinkly, cranklety <nf>, rimpled, rippled; crimped, crimpy; **crumpled,** rumpled

292 OPENING

NOUNS 1 **opening, aperture, hole,** hollow, **cavity** 284.2, **orifice; slot,** split, crack, check, leak, hairline crack; opening up, unstopping, uncorking, clearing, throwing open, laying open, broaching, cutting through; passageway; inlet 189.5; outlet 190.9; **gap,** gape, yawn, hiatus, lacuna, gat, space, interval; **chasm, gulf;** cleft 224.2; fontanel; foramen, fenestra; stoma; pore, porosity; fistula; **disclosure** 351; open space, clearing

2 **gaping, yawning,** oscitation, oscitancy, dehiscence, pandiculation; **gape, yawn;** the gapes

3 **hole, perforation, penetration, piercing,** empiercement, **puncture,** goring, boring, puncturing, punching, pricking, lancing, broach, transforation, terebration; acupuncture, acupunctuation; trephining, trepanning; **impalement,** skewering, fixing, transfixion, transfixation; bore, borehole, drill hole; ear piercing, body piercing

4 **mouth;** maw, oral cavity, gob <nf>, gab <Scot>; **muzzle,** jaw, lips, embouchure; bazoo *or* kisser *or* mug *or* mush *or* trap *or* yap <nf>; **jaws,** mandibles, chops, chaps, jowls; premaxilla

5 <other body orifices> pore, sweat gland; aural cavity, nasal cavity, nostril; stoma; **anus; asshole** *and* bumhole *and* bunghole <nf>; urethra; vagina

6 **door, doorway** 189.6; **entrance, entry** 189.5

7 **window,** casement; **windowpane,** window glass, pane, skylight; window frame, window ledge, window-sill, window bay

8 **porousness,** porosity; sievelikeness, cribriformity, cribrosity; screen, lattice, grate; sieve, strainer, colander; honeycomb; sponge; tea bag; filter, net

9 **permeability, perviousness**

10 **opener;** can opener, tin opener <Brit>; corkscrew, bottle screw, bottle opener, church key <nf>; **key,** clavis; latchkey; passkey, *passe-partout* <Fr>; master key, skeleton key; password, open sesame; key card, smart card

VERBS 11 **open,** ope <old>, **open up;** lay open, throw open; fly open, spring open, swing open; **tap, broach;** cut open, cut, cleave, split, slit, crack, chink, fissure, crevasse, incise; rift, rive; tear open, rent, tear, rip, rip open, part, dispart, separate, divide, divaricate; spread, spread out, open out, splay, splay out

12 unclose, unshut; **unfold,** unwrap, unroll; **unstop, unclog, unblock,** clear, unfoul, free, deobstruct; **unplug,** uncork, uncap; crack; **unlock,** unlatch, undo, unbolt; unseal, unclench, unclutch; **uncover,** uncase, unsheathe, unveil, undrape, uncurtain; **disclose** 351.4, expose, reveal, bare, take the lid off, manifest; gain access

13 make an opening, find an opening, make place *or* space, **make way, make room**

14 breach, rupture; **break open,** force *or* pry *or* prize open, crack *or* split open, rip *or* tear open; break into, break through; break in, burst in, bust in <nf>, stave *or* stove in, cave in; excavate, dig

15 perforate, pierce, empierce, **penetrate, puncture, punch, hole,** prick; **tap, broach; stab, stick,** pink, run through; **transfix,** transpierce, fix, **impale,** spit, skewer; gore, spear, lance, spike, needle; **bore, drill,** auger; **ream,** ream out, countersink, gouge, gouge out; trepan, trephine; punch full of holes, make look like Swiss cheese *or* a sieve, **riddle, honeycomb**

16 gape, gap <nf>, **yawn,** oscitate, dehisce, hang open

ADJS **17 open, unclosed,** uncovered; **unobstructed, unstopped, unclogged;** clear, cleared, free; wide-open, unrestricted; **disclosed** 348.10; bare, exposed, unhidden 348.11, naked, bald; accessible

18 gaping, yawning, agape, oscitant, slack-jawed, openmouthed; dehiscent, ringent; ajar, half-open, cracked

19 apertured, slotted, **holey;** pierced, **perforated,** perforate, holed; honeycombed, like Swiss cheese, riddled, *criblé* <Fr>, shot through, peppered; windowed, fenestrated; leaky

20 porous, porose; poriferous; like a sieve, sievelike, cribose, cribriform; spongy, spongelike; percolating, leachy

21 permeable, pervious, penetrable, openable, accessible

22 mouthlike, oral, orificial; mandibular, maxillary

INTERJS **23 open up!,** open sesame!, **gangway!,** passageway!, **make way!,** make a hole!, coming through!, heads up!

293 CLOSURE

NOUNS **1 closure, closing, shutting,** shutting up, occlusion; **shutdown,** shutting down, cloture; **exclusion** 773, shutting out, **ruling out;** blockade, embargo

2 imperviousness, impermeability, impenetrability, impassability; imperforation

3 obstruction, clog, block, blockade, sealing off,

blockage, strangulation, choking, choking off, **stoppage,** stop, **bar, barrier, obstacle,** impediment; occlusion; **bottleneck,** chokepoint; **congestion,** jam, traffic jam, gridlock, rush hour; gorge; constipation, obstipation, costiveness; infarct, infarction; embolism, embolus; **blind alley,** blank wall, **dead end,** cul-de-sac, dead-end street, impasse; cecum, blind gut; standstill, deadlock, stalemate

4 stopper, stop, **stopple,** stopgap; **plug, cork,** bung, spike, spill, spile, tap, faucet, spigot, valve, check valve, cock, sea cock, peg, pin; lid 295.5; tamper-resistant packaging

5 stopping, wadding, stuffing, padding, **packing,** pack, tampon; gland; gasket; bandage, tourniquet; wedge

VERBS **6 close, shut,** occlude; close up, shut up, contract, constrict, strangle, strangulate, choke, choke off, squeeze, squeeze shut; **exclude** 772.4, shut out, squeeze out; **rule out** 444.3; **fasten, secure; lock,** lock up, lock out, key, padlock, latch, bolt, bar, barricade; **seal,** seal up, seal in, seal off; button, button up; snap; zipper, zip up; batten, batten down the hatches; put *or* slap the lid on, **cover;** contain; **shut the door,** slam, clap, bang

7 stop, stop up; obstruct, bar, stay; **block,** block up; **clog,** clog up, foul; **choke,** choke up *or* off; **fill,** fill up; **stuff,** pack, jam; **congest,** stuff up; **plug,** plug up; stopper, stopple, **cork,** bung, spile; cover; **dam,** dam up; stanch; chink; caulk; blockade, barricade, embargo; constipate, obstipate, bind; occlude

8 close shop, close up *or* **down,** shut up, **shut down,** go out of business, fold *or* fold up *and* pull an el foldo <nf>, shutter, put up the shutters, discontinue; cease 857.6

ADJS **9 closed, shut, unopen,** unopened; unvented, unventilated; fastened, secured; **excluded** 773.7, shut-out; **ruled out, barred** 444.7; contracted, constricted, choked, choked off, choked up, squeezed shut, strangulated, occluded; blank; blind, cecal, dead; dead-end, blind-alley, closed-end, closed-ended; **exclusive,** exclusionary, closed-door, in-camera, private, closed to the public; tamper-resistant

10 unpierced, pierceless, **unperforated,** imperforate, intact; **untrodden,** pathless, wayless, trackless

11 stopped, stopped up; obstructed, infarcted, **blocked; plugged,** plugged up, bunged; **clogged,** clogged up; foul, fouled; **choked,** choked up, strangulated, strangled; **full, stuffed,** packed, jammed, bumper-to-bumper <nf>, jam-packed, like sardines; **congested,** stuffed up; constipated, obstipated, costive, bound

12 close, tight, compact, fast, shut fast, **snug,** staunch, firm; **sealed;** hermetic, hermetical, hermetically sealed; airtight, dusttight *or* dustproof, gastight *or* gasproof, lighttight *or* lightproof, oil-tight *or* oil-proof, raintight *or* rainproof, smoketight *or* smokeproof, stormtight *or* stormproof, watertight *or* waterproof, windtight *or* windproof; water-repellant *or* -resistant

13 **impervious, impenetrable, impermeable; impassable,** unpassable; unpierceable, unperforable; **punctureproof,** nonpuncturable, holeproof

294 TEXTURE
<surface quality>

NOUNS 1 **texture,** surface texture; **surface; finish,** feel, touch; intertexture, contexture, constitution, consistency; **grain,** granular texture, fineness *or* coarseness of grain; **weave,** woof 740.3, wale; **nap,** pile, shag, nub, knub, protuberance 283; **pit,** pock, indentation 284.6; structure 266

2 **roughness** 288; irregularity; bumpiness, lumpiness; **coarseness, grossness, unrefinement,** coarse-grainedness; cross-grainedness; **graininess,** granularity, granulation, grittiness, grit; pockiness; hardness 1046

3 **smoothness** 287, **fineness, refinement,** fine-grainedness; **delicacy, daintiness;** filminess, gossameriness 1029.1; down, **downiness,** fluff, fluffiness, velvet, velvetiness, fuzz, fuzziness, peach fuzz, peachiness; pubescence; satin, satininess; silk, silkiness; softness 1047

VERBS 4 **coarsen; grain,** granulate; tooth, **roughen** 288.4; gnarl, knob; rumple, wrinkle; smooth 287.5, flatten

ADJS 5 **textural, textured,** -surfaced

6 **rough** 288.6, **coarse, gross, unrefined, coarse-grained;** cross-grained; grained, **grainy,** granular, granulated, gritty, gravelly, gravelish

7 **nappy,** pily, **shaggy,** hairy, hirsute; nubby *or* nubbly; bumpy, lumpy; studded, knobbed; pocked, pitted 284.17; woven, matted, ribbed, twilled, tweedy, woolly; fibrous

8 **smooth** 287.10; **fine, refined,** attenuate, attenuated, **fine-grained; delicate, dainty; finespun,** thin-spun, fine-drawn, wiredrawn; gauzy, filmy, gossamer, gossamery 1029.4, **downy,** fluffy, velvety, velutinous, fuzzy, pubescent; satin, satiny, silky

295 COVERING

NOUNS 1 <act of covering> **covering,** coverage, obduction; **coating,** cloaking; **screening,** shielding, hiding, curtaining, **veiling,** clouding, obscuring, befogging, fogging, fuzzing, masking, mantling, shrouding, shadowing, blanketing; blocking, blotting out, eclipse, eclipsing, occultation; **wrapping,** enwrapping, enwrapment, sheathing, envelopment; **overlaying,** overspreading, laying on *or* over, superimposition, superposition; superincumbence; upholstering, upholstery; plasterwork, stuccowork, brickwork, cementwork, pargeting; incrustation

2 **cover, covering,** coverage, covert, coverture, housing, hood, cowl, cowling, **shelter; screen,** shroud, shield, veil, pall, mantle, curtain, hanging, drape, drapery; **coat,** cloak, mask, guise; vestment 5.1; camouflage, shroud

3 **skin,** dermis; **cuticle; rind; flesh;** bare skin *or* flesh, the buff; integument, tegument 206.2, tegmen, tegmentum, testa; scab; **pelt, hide, coat, jacket, fell, fleece, fur, hair,** vair <heraldry>; feathers, plumage; **peel, peeling, rind; skin,** epicarp; **bark;** cork, phellum; cortex, cortical tissue, epidermis; periderm, phelloderm; peridium; dermatogen; protective coloring

4 **overlayer,** overlay; appliqué, **lap, overlap,** overlapping, imbrication; **flap,** fly, tentfly; shutter

5 **cover, lid, top, cap, screw-top;** operculum; stopper 293.4

6 **roof,** roofing, roofage, top, **housetop,** rooftop; roof-deck, roof garden, penthouse; roofpole, ridgepole, rooftree; shingles, slates, tiles; eaves; **ceiling,** *plafond* <Fr>, overhead; skylight, lantern, cupola, dome; widow's walk *or* captain's walk; canopy, awning, marquee

7 **umbrella,** gamp *or* brolly <Brit nf>, bumbershoot <nf>; **sunshade, parasol,** beach umbrella

8 **tent,** canvas; top, whitetop, round top, big top; tentage; tepee, wigwam

9 **rug, carpet,** floor cover *or* covering; carpeting, wall-to-wall carpet *or* carpeting; mat; drop cloth, ground cloth, groundsheet; **flooring,** floorboards, duckboards; **tiling; pavement,** pavé; tarpaulin

10 **blanket, coverlet,** coverlid <nf>, space blanket, cover, covers, **spread,** robe, buffalo robe, **afghan,** rug <Brit>; lap robe; **bedspread; bedcover;** counterpane, counterpin <nf>; comfort, **comforter, down comforter, duvet, continental quilt** <Brit>, **quilt,** feather bed, eiderdown; patchwork quilt; **bedding, bedclothes,** clothes; **linen,** bed linen; **sheet,** sheeting, bedsheet, fitted sheet, contour sheet, dust ruffle; **pillowcase,** pillow slip, case, slip, sham; duvet cover

11 horsecloth, **horse blanket;** caparison, housing; **saddle blanket,** saddlecloth

12 **blanket, coating,** coat; **veneer, facing,** veneering, revetment; pellicle, **film, scum,** skin, scale; **slick,** oil slick; varnish, enamel, lacquer, paint 35.8

13 **plating,** plate, cladding; nickel plate, silver plate, gold plate, copperplate, chromium plate, anodized

aluminum; electroplate, electroplating, electrocoating

14 crust, incrustation *or* encrustation, shell; piecrust, pastry shell; stalactite, stalagmite; scale, scab, eschar

15 shell, seashell, lorication, lorica, conch; test, testa, episperm, pericarp, elytron, scute, scutum; operculum; **armor,** mail, **shield; carapace,** plate, chitin, scale, scute; **protective covering,** cortex, thick skin *or* hide, elephant skin

16 hull, shell, pod, capsule, case, **husk, shuck;** cornhusk, corn shuck; bark, jacket; chaff, bran, palea; seed coat

17 case, casing, encasement; **sheath,** sheathing

18 wrapper, wrapping, gift wrapping, gift wrap, wrap; wrapping paper, tissue paper, waxed paper, aluminum foil, tin foil, plastic wrap, clingfilm <Brit>, cellophane; **binder,** binding; **bandage,** bandaging; **envelope,** envelopment; **jacket,** jacketing; dust jacket *or* cover

VERBS 19 cover, cover up; apply to, **put on,** lay on; **superimpose,** superpose; **lay over,** overlay; **spread over,** overspread; **clothe, cloak,** mantle, muffle, blanket, canopy, cope, cowl, hood, **veil,** curtain, **screen, shield,** screen off, mask, cloud, obscure, fog, befog, fuzz; block, eclipse, occult; film, film over, scum

20 wrap, enwrap, wrap up, wrap about *or* around; **envelop, sheathe;** surround, encompass, lap, smother, enfold, embrace, invest; shroud, enshroud; swathe, swaddle; **box, case,** encase, **crate,** pack, embox; containerize; **package,** encapsulate

21 top, cap, tip, crown; put the lid on, cork, stopper, plug; hood, hat, coif, bonnet; roof, roof in *or* over; ceil; dome, endome

22 floor; carpet; pave, causeway, cobblestone, flag, pebble; cement, concrete; **pave, surface,** pave over, repave, resurface; blacktop, tar, asphalt, metal <old>, macadamize

23 face, veneer, revet; **sheathe;** board, plank, weatherboard, clapboard, lath; shingle, shake; tile, stone, brick, slate; thatch; glass, glaze, fiberglass; paper, wallpaper; wall in *or* up

24 coat, spread on, **spread with;** smear, **smear on,** besmear, slap on, dab, daub, bedaub, plaster, beplaster; flow on, pour on; lay on, lay it on thick, slather; undercoat, prime; enamel, gild, gloss, lacquer; butter; tar

25 plaster, parget, stucco, cement, concrete, mastic, grout, mortar; face, line; roughcast, pebble-dash, spatter-dash

26 plate, chromium-plate, copperplate, gold-plate, nickel-plate, silver-plate; **electroplate, galvanize,** anodize

27 crust, incrust, encrust; loricate; effloresce; scab, scab over

28 upholster, overstuff

29 re-cover, reupholster, recap

30 overlie, lie over; **overlap,** lap, **lap over,** override, imbricate, jut, shingle; **extend over,** span, bridge, bestride, bestraddle, arch over, overarch, hang over, overhang

ADJS 31 covered, covert, under cover; **cloaked,** mantled, blanketed, muffled, canopied, coped, cowled, hooded, **shrouded, veiled,** clouded, obscured, fogged, fogged in; eclipsed, occulted, curtained, **screened,** screened-in, screened-off; shielded, masked, **housed;** tented, under canvas; roofed, roofed-in *or* -over, domed; walled, walled-in; **wrapped,** enwrapped, jacketed, **enveloped,** sheathed, swathed; **boxed, cased,** encased, encapsuled *or* encapsulated, **packaged; coated,** filmed, filmed-over, scummed; shelled, loricate, loricated; armored; ceiled; **floored; paved, surfaced;** plastered, stuccoed

32 cutaneous, cuticular; skinlike, skinny; skin-deep; **epidermal,** epidermic, dermal, dermic; ectodermal, ectodermic; endermic, endermatic; cortical; epicarpal; testaceous; hairy, furry 3.24; integumental, integumentary, tegumentary, tegumental, tegmental; vaginal; thecal

33 plated, chromium-plated, copperplated, gold-plated, nickel-plated, silver-plated; electroplated, galvanized, anodized

34 upholstered, overstuffed

35 covering, coating; cloaking, blanketing, shrouding, obscuring, **veiling, screening,** shielding, sheltering; wrapping, **enveloping,** sheathing

36 overlying, incumbent, superincumbent, superimposed; **overlapping,** lapping, shingled, equitant; imbricate, imbricated; spanning, bridging; overarched, overarching

PREPS 37 on, upon, over, o'er, **above, on top of**

296 LAYER

NOUNS 1 layer, thickness; **level, tier,** stage, story, floor, gallery, step, ledge, deck, row, landing; **stratum,** seam, *couche* <Fr>, vein, lode, belt, band, **bed, course,** measures; zone; shelf; **overlayer, superstratum,** overstory, topsoil, topcoat; **underlayer, substratum,** understratum, understory, underlay, undercoat; bedding

2 lamina, lamella; **sheet,** leaf, *feuille* <Fr>, foil; wafer, disk; **plate,** plating, cladding; covering 295, **coat,** coating, veneer, film, patina, scum, membrane, pellicle, sheathe, peel, skin, rind, hide; slick, oil slick; **slice,** cut, rasher, collop, sliver; **slab,** plank, deal <Brit>, slat, tablet, table; panel, pane;

fold, lap, flap, **ply**, plait; laminate; laminated glass, safety glass; laminated wood, plywood, layered fiberglass; liner

3 **flake**, flock, floccule, flocculus; **scale, scurf,** dandruff, squama; chip; shaving, paring, swarf

4 **stratification, layering, lamination,** lamellation; foliation; delamination, exfoliation; desquamation, furfuration; flakiness, scaliness

VERBS 5 **layer**, lay down, lay up, **stratify**, arrange in layers *or* levels *or* strata *or* tiers, **laminate;** shingle, sandwich; flake, scale; delaminate, desquamate, exfoliate; interface

ADJS 6 **layered**, in layers; **laminated**, laminate, laminous; lamellated, lamellate, lamellar, lamelliform; plated, coated; veneered, faced; two-ply, three-ply, etc; two-level, bilevel, three-level, trilevel, etc; one-story, single story, two-story, double-story, etc; **stratified**, stratiform, staticulate; foliated, foliaceous, leaflike; terraced, multistage

7 **flaky**, flocculent, floccose; **scaly**, scurfy, squamous, lentiginous, furfuraceous, lepidote; scabby, scabious, scabrous

WORD ELEMENTS 8 strati-, lamin-, lamino-, lamini-, lamell-, lamelli-

297 WEIGHT

NOUNS 1 **weight, heaviness, weightiness, ponderousness**, ponderosity, ponderability, leadenness, heftiness *and* heft <nf>; body weight, avoirdupois <nf>, fatness 257.8, beef *and* beefiness <nf>, heft, chunk; poundage, tonnage; deadweight, live weight; gross weight, gr wt; **net weight**, neat weight, nt wt, net, nett <Brit>; short-weight; underweight; overweight; overbalance, overweightage; **solemnity, gravity** 111.1, 580.1

2 onerousness, **burdensomeness, oppressiveness, deadweight, overburden, cumbersomeness,** cumbrousness; massiveness, massiness <old>, bulkiness 257.9, lumpishness, unwieldiness

3 <sports> bantamweight, featherweight, flyweight, heavyweight, light heavyweight, lightweight, middleweight, cruiser weight, welterweight; catchweight; fighting weight; jockey weight

4 **counterbalance** 900.4; makeweight; **ballast,** ballasting

5 <physics terms> **gravity, gravitation,** G, supergravity; specific gravity; gravitational field, gravisphere; gravitational pull; graviton; geotropism, positive geotropism, apogeotropism, negative geotropism; G suit, anti-G suit; **mass;** atomic weight, molecular weight, molar weight; quagma

6 **weight,** paperweight, letterweight; sinker, lead, plumb, plummet, bob; sash weight; sandbag

7 **burden**, burthen <old>, pressure, **oppression, deadweight;** burdening, saddling, charging, taxing; overburden, overburdening, overtaxing, overweighting, weighing *or* weighting down; charge, **load,** loading, lading, freight, cargo, bale, ballast; cumber, cumbrance, **encumbrance;** incubus; incumbency *or* superincumbency <old>; handicap, drag, millstone; surcharge, overload

8 <systems of weight> avoirdupois weight, troy weight, apothecaries' weight; atomic weight, molecular weight; **pound, ounce, gram,** etc, **unit of weight,** <see list>

9 **weighing,** hefting <nf>, balancing; weighing-in, weigh-in, weighing-out, weigh-out; **scale,** weighing instrument

VERBS 10 **weigh,** weight; **heft** <nf>, **balance,** weigh in the balance, strike a balance, hold the scales, put on the scales, lay in the scales; **counterbalance; weigh in,** weigh out; be heavy, weigh heavy, lie heavy, have weight, carry weight; **tip the scales,** turn *or* depress *or* tilt the scales, tip the balance

11 **weigh on** *or* **upon,** rest on *or* upon, bear on *or* upon, lie on, press, press down, press to the ground

12 **weight, weigh** *or* **weight down;** hang like a millstone; **ballast;** lead, sandbag

13 **burden,** burthen <old>, **load,** load down *or* up, lade, cumber, **encumber, charge, freight,** tax, handicap, hamper, saddle; **oppress, weigh one down, weigh on** *or* **upon, weigh heavy on,** bear *or* rest hard upon, lie hard *or* heavy upon, press hard upon, be an incubus to; **overburden,** overweight, overtax, **overload** 993.15

14 **outweigh,** overweigh, overweight, overbalance, **outbalance,** outpoise, overpoise

15 **gravitate, descend** 194.5, drop, plunge 367.6, precipitate, sink, settle, subside; tend, tend to go, **incline,** point, head, lead, lean

ADJS 16 **heavy, ponderous, massive,** massy, weighty, hefty <nf>, bulky, fat 257.18; **leaden,** heavy as lead; deadweight; heavyweight; overweight; **solemn, grave** 111.3, 580.8

17 **onerous, oppressive, burdensome,** incumbent *or* superincumbent, **cumbersome,** cumbrous; massive; lumpish, **unwieldy;** ponderous

18 **weighted, weighed** *or* **weighted down; burdened, oppressed, laden, encumbered,** cumbered, fraught, freighted, taxed, saddled, hampered; **overburdened,** overloaded, overladen, overcharged, overfreighted, overfraught, overweighted, overtaxed; borne-down, sinking, foundering

19 **weighable,** ponderable; **appreciable,** palpable, sensible

20 gravitational, mass

ADVS **21 heavily,** heavy, weightily, leadenly; burdensomely, onerously, oppressively; **ponderously,** cumbersomely, cumbrously

22 units of weight *or* **force** *or* **mass**

assay ton	microgram *or* mcg
carat *or* c	milligram *or* mg
carat grain	mole *or* mol
centigram *or* cg	myriagram *or* myg
dead-weight ton	net ton
decagram *or* dkg	newton
decigram *or* dg	ounce *or* ounce
displacement ton	avoirdupois *or* oz *or*
dram *or* dram avoirdupois	oz av
or dr	ounce apothecaries' *or*
dram apothecaries' *or* dr ap	oz ap
dyne	ounce troy *or* oz t
grain *or* gr	pearl grain
gram *or* g	pennyweight *or* dwt *or* pwt
gram equivalent *or* gram	pound *or* pound
equivalent weight	avoirdupois *or* lb *or*
gram molecule *or* gram-	lb av
molecular weight	poundal
gross ton	pound apothecaries' *or*
hectogram *or* hg	lb ap
hundredweight *or* cwt	pound troy *or* lb t
international carat	quintal *or* q
kilogram *or* kilo *or* kg	scruple *or* s ap
kiloton	shipping ton
long hundredweight	short hundredweight
long ton *or* lt	short ton *or* st
measurement ton	slug
megaton	sthene
metric carat	stone *or* st
metric ton *or* MT *or* t	ton *or* tn

298 LIGHTNESS

NOUNS **1 lightness, levity,** unheaviness, lack of weight; **weightlessness; buoyancy,** buoyance, floatability; levitation, ascent 193; **volatility; airiness,** ethereality; foaminess, frothiness, bubbliness, yeastiness; downiness, fluffiness, gossameriness 1029.1; softness, gentleness, delicacy, daintiness, tenderness; light touch, gentle touch; frivolity 923.1, 109.5

2 <comparisons> air, ether, feather, down, thistledown, flue, fluff, fuzz, sponge, gossamer, cobweb, fairy, straw, chaff, dust, mote, cork, chip, bubble, froth, foam, spume

3 lightening, easing, **easement, alleviation, relief;** disburdening, **disencumberment,** unburdening, **unloading,** unlading, unsaddling, untaxing, unfreighting; unballasting

4 leavening, fermentation; leaven, ferment

5 <indeterminacy of weight> **imponderableness** *or* imponderability, unweighableness *or* unweighability; imponderables, imponderabilia

VERBS **6 lighten,** make light *or* lighter, reduce weight; unballast; **ease, alleviate, relieve; disburden, disencumber,** unburden, unload, unlade, off-load; **be light,** weigh lightly, have little weight, kick the beam; lose weight

7 leaven, raise, **ferment**

8 buoy, buoy up; float, float high, ride high, waft; **sustain, hold up,** bear up, uphold, upbear, uplift, upraise; refloat

9 levitate, rise, ascend 193.8; hover, **float**

ADJS **10 light,** unheavy, imponderous, lightweight; **weightless; airy, ethereal; volatile;** frothy, foamy, spumy, spumous, spumescent, bubbly, yeasty; downy, feathery, fluffy, gossamery 1029.4; *soufflé* *or* *moussé* *or* *léger* <Fr>; light as air *or* a feather *or* gossamer, etc 298.2; **frivolous** 922.20, 109.15; insubstantial

11 lightened, eased, unburdened, disburdened, disencumbered, unencumbered, relieved, alleviated, out from under, breathing easier; mitigated

12 light, gentle, soft, delicate, dainty, tender, **easy**

13 lightweight, bantamweight, featherweight; underweight

14 buoyant, floaty, floatable; floating, supernatant

15 levitative, levitational

16 lightening, easing, alleviating, alleviative, alleviatory, relieving, disburdening, unburdening, disencumbering

17 leavening, raising, **fermenting,** fermentative, working; yeasty, barmy; enzymic, diastatic

18 imponderable, unweighable

299 RARITY

<lack of density>

NOUNS **1 rarity,** rareness; **thinness, tenuousness,** tenuity; **subtlety,** subtility; **fineness,** slightness, flimsiness, **unsubstantiality** *or* **insubstantiality** 764; **ethereality,** airiness, immateriality, incorporeality, bodilessness, insolidity; **diffuseness,** dispersedness, scatter, scatteredness; "such stuff as dreams are made on"—Shakespeare

2 rarefaction, attenuation, subtilization, etherealization; **diffusion,** dispersion, scattering; **thinning,** thinning-out, dilution, adulteration, watering, watering-down; decompression

VERBS **3 rarefy, attenuate,** thin, thin out; dilute, adulterate, water, water down, cut; subtilize, **etherealize; diffuse,** disperse, scatter; expand 259.4; decompress

ADJS **4 rare,** rarefied; **subtle; thin,** thinned, dilute, attenuated, attenuate; thinned-out, diluted, adulterated, watered, watered-down, cut; **tenuous, fine,** flimsy, slight, **unsubstantial** *or* insubstantial 764; **airy, ethereal,** vaporous, gaseous, windy; **diffused,** diffuse, dispersed, scattered; uncompact, uncompressed, decompressed

5 **rarefactive, rarefactional**

300 MEASUREMENT

NOUNS 1 **measurement, measure;** mensuration, measuring, **gauging;** admeasurement; metage; **estimation,** estimate, rough measure, approximation, ballpark figure <nf>; **quantification,** quantitation, quantization; **appraisal,** appraisement, **stocktaking, assay,** assaying; **assessment,** determination, rating, valuation, evaluation; assizement, assize, sizing up <nf>; **survey,** surveying; triangulation; **instrumentation;** telemetry, telemetering; metric system; metrication; English system of measurement; calibration, correction, computation, calculation

2 **measure,** measuring instrument, **meter, instrument, gauge,** barometer, **rule, yardstick,** measuring rod or stick, **standard,** norm, canon, **criterion,** test, touchstone, check, benchmark; rule of thumb; **pattern,** model, type, prototype; **scale,** graduated or calibrated scale; meter-reading, reading, readout, value, degree, quantity; parameter

3 **extent,** quantity 244, degree 245, size 257, distance 261, length 267, breadth 269; **weight** 297

4 <measures> US liquid measure, British imperial liquid measure, US dry measure, British imperial dry measure, apothecaries' measure, linear measure <see list>, square measure, circular measure, cubic measure, volume measure <see list>, area measure <see list>, surface measure, surveyor's measure, land measure, board measure

5 coordinates, Cartesian coordinates, rectangular coordinates, polar coordinates, cylindrical coordinates, spherical coordinates, equator coordinates; latitude, longitude; altitude, azimuth; declination, right ascension; ordinate, abscissa

6 **waterline;** watermark, tidemark, floodmark, **high-water mark;** load waterline, load line mark, Plimsoll mark or line

7 **measurability,** mensurability, computability, determinability, quantifiability

8 science of measurement, **mensuration,** metrology

9 **measurer,** meter, gauger; **geodesist,** geodetic engineer; **surveyor,** land surveyor, quantity surveyor; topographer, cartographer, mapmaker, oceanographer, chorographer; **appraiser, assessor;** assayer; valuer, valuator, evaluator; estimator; quantifier, actuary; timekeeper

VERBS 10 **measure, gauge, quantify,** quantitate, quantize, mete <old>, take the measure of, mensurate, triangulate, apply the yardstick to; **estimate,** make an approximation; **assess, rate, appraise, valuate, value,** evaluate, appreciate, prize; **assay;** size or size up <nf>, take the dimensions of; **weigh,** weigh up 297.10; survey; plumb, probe, sound, fathom; span, pace, step; calibrate, graduate, grade; divide; caliper; meter; read the meter, take a reading, check a parameter; compute, calculate, reckon

11 **measure off, mark off, lay off,** set off, rule off; **step off,** pace off or out; **measure out,** mark out, lay out; put at

ADJS 12 **measuring, metric, metrical,** mensural, mensurative, mensurational; valuative, valuational; **quantitative,** numerative; approximative, estimative; geodetic, geodetical, geodesic, geodesical, hypsographic, hypsographical, hypsometric, hypsometrical; topographic, topographical, chorographic, chorographical, cartographic, cartographical, oceanographic, oceanographical

13 **measured, gauged,** metered, **quantified;** quantitated, quantized; **appraised, assessed, valuated,** valued, rated, ranked; **assayed; surveyed,** plotted, mapped, admeasured, triangulated; known by measurement

14 **measurable,** mensurable, **quantifiable,** numerable, meterable, gaugeable, fathomable, **determinable,** computable, calculable; quantifiable, quantitatable, quantizable; estimable; assessable, appraisable, ratable; appreciable, perceptible, noticeable

ADVS 15 **measurably, appreciably, perceptibly, noticeably**

16 **linear measures**

absolute angstrom	foot or ft
Admiralty mile	footstep
angstrom or angstrom unit	furlong or fur
or a or å or A or Å	hand
arpent	handbreadth or
astronomical unit	handsbreadth
block	hectometer or hm
board foot or bd ft	inch or in
cable length	international angstrom
centimeter or cm	kilometer or km
chain or Gunter's chain or	land mile
chn	league
cubit	light-year
decameter or dkm	line
decimeter or dm	link or li
ell	meter or m
em	micron or μ
en	mil
fathom or fthm	mile or mi
fingerbreadth or finger	millimeter or mm

millimicron *or*	pica
micromillimeter	point *or* pt
myriameter *or* mym	pole *or* p
nail	rod *or* r
nautical mile *or* naut mi	statute mile *or* stat mi
pace	step
palm	stride
parsec	wavelength
perch	yard *or* yd

17 volume measures

barrel	hectoliter *or* hl
bushel *or* bu	hogshead *or* hhd
centiliter *or* cl	jeroboam
cord *or* cd	jigger
cubic foot *or* yard *or* etc	kiloliter *or* kl
cubic meter	liquid pint *or* quart
cup	*or* etc
decaliter *or* dkl	liter *or* l
decastere *or* dks	magnum
deciliter *or* dl	milliliter *or* ml
drop	minim *or* min
dry pint *or* quart *or* etc	peck *or* pk
fifth	pint *or* pt
finger	pony
fluid ounce *or* fl oz	quart *or* qt
fluid dram *or* fl dr	stere *or* s
gallon *or* gal	tablespoon *or* tbs
gill *or* gi	teaspoon *or* tsp

18 area measures

acre *or* a *or* ac	rood
are *or* a	section *or* sec
arpent	square inch *or* foot *or* mile
centare *or* ca	*or* etc
hectare *or* ha	square meter *or*
perch	kilometer
pole *or* p	*or* etc

301 YOUTH

NOUNS **1 youth, youthfulness,** youngness, **juvenility,** juvenescence, tenderness, tender age, early years, school age, *jeunesse* <Fr>, prime of life, flower of life, salad days, springtime *or* springtide of life, seedtime of life, flowering time, bloom, florescence, budtime, younger days, school days "the very May-morn of his youth"—Shakespeare, "the summer of your youth"—Edward Moore, golden season of life, "the glad season of life"—Carlyle, heyday of youth *or* of the blood, young blood, "my green age"—Dylan Thomas

2 childhood; boyhood; girlhood, maidenhood *or* maidenhead; puppyhood, calfhood; subteens, pre-teens

3 immaturity, undevelopment, inexperience, **callowness, unripeness,** greenness, rawness,

naiveté, sappiness, freshness, juiciness, dewiness; **minority,** juniority, infancy, nonage

4 childishness, childlikeness, **puerility; boyishness,** boylikeness; **girlishness,** girl-likeness, maidenliness

5 infancy, babyhood, the cradle, the crib, the nursery

6 adolescence, maturation, maturement, pubescence, **puberty;** nubility

7 teens, teen years *or* age, **awkward age,** age of growing pains <nf>

VERBS **8** make young, youthen, **rejuvenate,** reinvigorate; turn back the clock

ADJS **9 young,** youngling, youngish, **juvenile,** juvenal, juvenescent, **youthful,** youthlike, in the flower *or* bloom of youth, blooming, florescent, flowering, dewy, fresh-faced; "towering in confidence of twenty-one"—Samuel Johnson; young-looking, well-preserved

10 immature, unadult; **inexperienced,** unseasoned, unfledged, new-fledged, fledgling, **callow, unripe,** ripening, unmellowed, **raw, green,** vernal, primaveral, dewy, juicy, sappy, budding, tender, virginal, intact, innocent, naive, ingenuous, **undeveloped,** growing, unformed, unlicked, wet *or* not dry behind the ears, unprepared; **minor,** underage, underaged

11 childish, childlike, kiddish <nf>, **puerile; boyish,** boylike, beardless; **girlish,** girl-like, maiden, maidenly; puppyish, puppylike, puplike, calflike, coltish, coltlike; knee-high

12 infant, infantile, infantine, **babyish,** baby; dollish, doll-like; kittenish, kittenlike; **newborn,** neonatal; in the cradle *or* crib *or* nursery, in swaddling clothes, in diapers, in nappies <Brit>, in arms, at the breast, tied to mother's apron strings

13 adolescent, pubescent, nubile, marriageable

14 teen-age, teen-aged, teenish, **in one's teens;** sweet sixteen <nf>

15 junior, Jr; **younger,** puisne

302 YOUNGSTER

NOUNS **1 youngster,** young person, **youth, juvenile,** youngling, young'un <nf>, juvenal <old>; **stripling,** slip, sprig, sapling; fledgling; hopeful, young hopeful; **minor,** infant; **adolescent,** pubescent; **teenager,** teener, teenybopper <nf>, young adult; junior, younger, youngest, baby

2 young people, youth, young, **younger generation,** rising *or* new generation, baby boomers *or* boomers, Generation X, young blood, young fry <nf>, *ragazze* <Ital>; **children,** tots, childkind; small fry *and* **kids** *and* **little kids** *and* little guys <nf>; boyhood, girlhood; babyhood

3 child; nipper, **kid** *and* kiddy *and* kiddo *and* kiddie <nf>, **little one,** little fellow *or* guy, little bugger <nf>, shaver *and* little shaver <nf>, little squirt <nf>, **tot, little tot,** wee tot, pee-wee, tad *or* little tad, tyke, mite, chit <nf>, innocent, little innocent, moppet, poppet; darling, cherub, lamb, lambkin, kitten, **offspring** 561.3

4 **brat, urchin; minx, imp,** puck, elf, gamin, little monkey, **whippersnapper,** young whippersnapper, *enfant terrible* <Fr>, little terror, holy terror; spoiled brat; snotnose kid <nf>; juvenile delinquent, JD <nf>, punk *and* punk kid <nf>

5 **boy, lad,** laddie, **youth,** manchild, manling, young man, *garçon* <Fr>, *muchacho* <Sp>, schoolboy, schoolkid <nf>, fledgling, hobbledehoy; fellow 76.5; pup, puppy, whelp, cub, colt; master; sonny, sonny boy; bud *and* buddy <nf>; bub *and* bubba <nf>; buck, young buck; schoolboy

6 **girl,** girlie <nf>, **maid, maiden, lass,** girlchild, **lassie,** young thing, young creature, young lady, damsel in distress, **damsel,** damoiselle, demoiselle, *jeune fille* <Fr>, *mademoiselle* <Fr>, *muchacha* <Sp>, miss, missy, little missy, slip, wench <dial *or* nf>, colleen <Ir>

7 <nf terms> **gal,** dame, **chick,** tomato, **babe** *or* baby, **broad,** frail, **doll,** skirt, jill, chit, cutie, filly, heifer; teenybopper *and* weenybopper <nf>

8 **schoolgirl,** schoolmaid, schoolmiss, junior miss, subteen, subteener; subdebutante, subdeb <nf>; bobbysoxer <nf>, **tomboy,** hoyden, romp; piece <nf>, nymphet; virgin, *virgo intacta* <L>

9 **infant, baby, babe,** babe in arms, little darling *or* angel *or* doll *or* cherub, bouncing baby, puling infant, mewling infant, babykins <nf>, baby bunting; papoose, *bambino* <Ital>; **toddler; suckling,** nursling, fosterling, weanling; neonate; yearling, yearold; premature baby, preemie <nf>, incubator baby; preschooler; crumbcrusher *and* - cruncher *and* -grinder *and* -snatcher; rug rat *and* carpet rat *and* rug ape *and* carpet ape *and* curtain-climber <nf>

10 <animals> yearling, **fledgling,** birdling, nestling; **chick,** chicky, chickling; **pullet,** fry, fryer; **duckling;** gosling, cygnet; **kitten,** kit, catling; **pup,** puppy, whelp; **cub; calf,** dogie, weaner; **colt,** foal, filly; piglet, pigling, shoat; **lamb,** lambkin; kid, yeanling; fawn; **tadpole,** polliwog; litter, nest, brood, clutch, spawn, farrow

11 <plants> **sprout, seedling,** set; sucker, shoot, slip, offshoot; **twig,** sprig, scion, sapling

12 <insects> **larva, chrysalis,** aurelia, **cocoon,** pupa, grub; nymph, nympha; wriggler, wiggler; caterpillar, maggot, grub

303 AGE
<time of life>

NOUNS 1 **age,** years, "the measure of my days"— Bible; time *or* stage of life; lifetime, lifespan, life expectancy, timespan, longevity; seven ages of man: infancy, childhood, youth, adolescence, adulthood, middle age, maturity, old age, senility

2 **maturity, adulthood, majority,** adultness, grown-upness, maturation, matureness, full growth, mature age, legal age, voting age, driving age, drinking age, *legalis homo* <L>; age of consent; ripeness, ripe age, riper years, full age *or* growth *or* bloom, flower of age, **prime, prime of life,** age of responsibility, age *or* years of discretion, age of matured powers; **manhood,** man's estate, virility, *toga virilis* <L>, masculinity, maleness, manliness; **womanhood,** womanness, femininity, femaleness, womanliness

3 **seniority, eldership,** deanship, primogeniture

4 **middle age,** middle life, meridian of life, the middle years, the wrong side of forty, the dangerous age, prime of life; change of life, menopause, climacteric, midlife crisis

5 **old age, oldness,** eld <old>, **elderliness,** senectitude, senescence, agedness, advanced age *or* years; superannuation, pensionable age, retirement age, age of retirement; **ripe old age,** the golden years, advanced years, senior citizenship, hoary age, hoariness, gray *or* white hairs, grayness; **decline of life,** declining years, youth deficiency, the vale of years, threescore years and ten, "an incurable disease," "the downward slope"—both Seneca, "slow-consuming age"—Thomas Gray, "a tyrant, which forbids the pleasures of youth on pain of death"—La Rochefoucauld, "old age is fifteen years older than I"—Bernard Baruch, "the arctic regions of our lives"—Longfellow, the shady side <nf>; "the silver livery of advised age"— Shakespeare, "a crown of glory"—Bible; sunset *or* twilight *or* evening *or* autumn *or* winter of one's days; **decrepitude,** ricketiness, infirm old age, infirmity of age, infirmity, debility, caducity, feebleness; dotage, anecdotage, second childhood; senility 922.10, anility; **longevity,** long life, length of years, green *or* hale old age

6 **maturation, development,** growth, ripening, blooming, blossoming, flourishing; **mellowing,** seasoning, tempering; **aging,** senescence

7 **change of life, menopause,** climacteric, grand climacteric

8 **geriatrics,** gerontology, geriatric medicine

VERBS 9 **mature, grow up,** grow, **develop, ripen,** flower, flourish, bloom, blossom; fledge, leave the nest, put up one's hair, not be in pigtails, put on long pants; **come of age,** come to maturity, attain majority, **reach one's majority,** reach twenty-one, reach voting age, reach the age of consent, reach manhood *or* womanhood, write oneself a man, come to *or* into man's estate, put on long trousers *or* pants, assume the toga virilis, come into years of discretion, be in the prime of life, cut one's wisdom teeth *or* eyeteeth <nf>, have sown one's wild oats, settle down; **mellow,** season, temper

10 **age, grow old,** senesce, get on *or* along, **get on** *or* **along in years,** grow *or* have whiskers, be over the hill <nf>, turn gray *or* white; **decline,** wane, fade, fail, sink, waste away; **dodder,** totter, shake; wither, wrinkle, shrivel, wizen; **live to a ripe old age,** cheat the undertaker <nf>; be in one's dotage *or* second childhood

11 **have had one's day,** have seen one's day *or* best days, **have seen better days; show one's age,** show marks of age, have one foot in the grave

ADJS 12 **adult, mature, of age,** out of one's teens, big, grown, **grown-up;** old enough to know better; **marriageable,** of marriageable age, marriable, nubile

13 **mature, ripe,** ripened, of full *or* ripe age, **developed,** fully developed, well-developed, **full-grown,** full-fledged, fully fledged, full-blown, in full bloom, in one's prime; **mellow** *or* mellowed, seasoned, tempered, aged

14 **middle-aged,** mid-life, *entre deux âges* <Fr>, fortyish, matronly

15 **past one's prime,** senescent, on the shady side <nf>, overblown, overripe, of a certain age, over the hill <nf>; "fall'n into the sere, the yellow leaf"—Shakespeare

16 **aged, elderly, old,** grown old in years, along *or* up *or* advanced *or* on in years, years old, advanced, advanced in life, **at an advanced age, ancient,** geriatric, gerontic; **venerable,** old as Methuselah *or* as God *or* as the hills; patriarchal; hoary, hoar, **gray,** white, gray- *or* white-headed, gray- *or* white-haired, gray- *or* white-crowned, gray- *or* white-bearded, gray *or* white with age; wrinkled, prune-faced <nf>; wrinkly, with crow's feet, marked with the crow's foot

17 **aging,** growing old, senescent, **getting on** *or* **along,** getting on *or* along *or* up in years, not as young as one used to be, long in the tooth; **declining,** sinking, waning, fading, wasting, doting

18 **stricken in years, decrepit, infirm,** weak, debilitated, feeble, geriatric, timeworn, the worse for wear, rusty, moth-eaten *or* mossbacked <nf>, fossilized, wracked *or* ravaged with age, run to seed; **doddering,** doddery, doddered, tottering,

tottery, rickety, shaky, palsied; on one's last legs, with one foot in the grave; **wizened,** crabbed, **withered,** shriveled, like a prune, mummylike, papery-skinned; **senile** 922.23, anile

304 ADULT OR OLD PERSON

NOUNS 1 **adult, grownup,** mature man *or* woman, grown man *or* woman, big boy *and* big girl <nf>; **man, woman;** major, *legalis homo* <L>; no chicken *and* no spring chicken <nf>

2 **old man, elder, oldster** <nf>; golden-ager, senior citizen, geriatric, patron; old chap, old party, **old gentleman,** old gent <nf>, old codger <nf>, geezer *and* old geezer <nf>, gramps <nf>, gaffer, old duffer <nf>, old dog *and* old-timer <nf>, dotard, veteran, pantaloon, man of the world; **patriarch,** graybeard *or* greybeard, reverend *or* venerable sir; grandfather, grandsire; Father Time, Methuselah, Nestor, Old Paar; sexagenarian, septuagenarian, octogenarian, nonagenarian, centenarian; "a paltry thing, a tattered coat upon a stick"—Yeats

3 **old woman, old lady,** dowager, granny, old granny, dame, **grandam,** matron, matriarch, trot *and* old trot <nf>; old dame *and* hen *and* girl <nf>; old bag *and* bat *and* battleax *and* witch <nf>; **crone,** hag, witch, beldam, frump <nf>, old wife; grandmother; woman of the world

4 <old people> the old, older generation, seniors, retirees, over-the-hill gang <nf>; Darby and Joan, Baucis and Philemon

5 **senior,** Sr, *senex* <L>, **elder,** older; dean, *doyen* <Fr>, *doyenne* <Fr>; father, sire; firstling, first-born, **eldest,** oldest

VERBS 6 **mature** 303.9; grow old 303.10

ADJS 7 **mature** 303.12; middle-aged 303.14; aged 303.16, older 842.19

305 ORGANIC MATTER

NOUNS 1 **organic matter,** animate *or* living matter, all that lives, living nature, organic nature, organized matter; **biology** 1068; **flesh, tissue,** fiber, brawn, plasm; **flora and fauna,** plant and animal life, animal and vegetable kingdom, biosphere, biota, ecosphere, noosphere

2 **organism,** organization, organic being, life-form, form of life, **living being** *or* **thing,** being, creature, created being, **individual,** genetic individual, physiological individual, morphological individual; zoon, zooid; virus; aerobic organism, anaerobic organism; heterotrophic organism, autotrophic organism; microbe, microorganism

3 biological classification, taxonomy, kingdom, phylum, etc

4 **cell,** bioplast, cellule; procaryotic cell, eucaryotic cell; plant cell, animal cell; germ cell, somatic cell; corpuscle; unicellularity, multicellularity; germ layer, ectoderm, endoderm, mesoderm; **protoplasm,** energid; trophoplasm; chromatoplasm; germ plasm; cytoplasm; ectoplasm, endoplasm; cellular tissue, reticulum; plasmodium, coenocyte, syncytium

5 organelle; plastid; chromoplast, plastosome, chloroplast; mitochondrion; Golgi apparatus; ribosome; spherosome, microbody; vacuole; central apparatus, cytocentrum; centroplasm; centra body, microcentrum; centrosome; centrosphere; centriole, basal body; pili, cilia, flagella, spindle fibers; aster; kinoplasm; plasmodesmata; cell membrane

6 metaplasm; cell wall, cell plate; structural polysaccharide; bast, phloem, xylem, xyl- or xylo-, cellulose, chitin

7 **nucleus,** cell nucleus; macronucleus, meganucleus; micronucleus; nucleolus; plasmosome; karyosome, chromatin strands; nuclear envelope; chromatin, karyotin; basichromatin, heterochromatin, oxychromatin

8 **chromosome;** allosome; heterochromosome, sex chromosome, idiochromosome; W chromosome; X chromosome, accessory chromosome, monosome; Y chromosome; Z chromosome; euchromosome, autosome; homologous chromosomes; univalent chromosome, chromatid; centromere; gene-string, chromonema; genome; chromosome complement; chromosome number, diploid number, haploid number; polyploidy

9 **genetic material, gene;** allele; operon; cistron, structural gene, regulator gene, operator gene; altered gene; deoxyribonucleic acid or **DNA;** DNA double helix, superhelix or supercoil; nucleotide, codon; ribonucleic acid or **RNA;** messenger RNA, mRNA; transfer RNA, tRNA; ribosomal RNA; anticodon; gene pool, gene complex, gene flow, genetic drift; genotype, biotype; **hereditary character,** heredity 560.6; genetic counseling; genetic screening; **recombinant DNA technology,** gene mapping, gene splicing; gene transplantation, gene transfer, germline insertion; intronizing, intron or intervening sequence; exonizing, exon; **genetic engineering,** genetic fingerprinting; designer gene

10 **gamete, germ cell,** reproductive cell; macrogamete, megagamete; microgamete; planogamete; genetoid; gamone; gametangium; gametophore; gametophyte; germ plasm, idioplasm

11 **sperm, spermatozoa, seed, semen,** jism or gism and come or cum and scum and spunk <nf>; seminal or spermatic fluid, milt; **sperm cell,** male gamete; spermatozoon, spermatozoid, antherozoid; antheridium; spermatium, spermatiophore or spermatophore, spermagonium; pollen; spermatogonium; androcyte, spermatid, spermatocyte

12 **ovum, egg, egg cell,** female gamete, oösphere; oöcyte; oögonium; ovicell, oöecium; ovule; stirp; ovulation; donor egg

13 **spore;** microspore; macrospore, megaspore; swarm spore, zoospore, planospore; spore mother cell, sporocyte; zygospore; sporocarp, cystocarp; basidium; sporangium, megasporangium; microsporangium; sporocyst; gonidangium; sporogonium, sporophyte; sporophore; sorus

14 **embryo,** zygote, oösperm, oöspore, blastula; *Anlage* <Ger>; **fetus,** germ, germen <old>, rudiment; **larva,** nymph

15 **egg;** ovule; bird's egg; **roe,** fish eggs, caviar, spawn; **yolk,** yellow, vitellus; white, **egg white,** albumen, glair; eggshell

16 **cell division; mitosis;** amitosis; metamitosis, eumitosis; endomitosis, promitosis; haplomitosis, mesomitosis; karyomitosis; karyokinesis; interphase, prophase, metaphase, anaphase, telophase, diaster, cytokinesis; **meiosis**

ADJS **17** **organic,** organismic; organized; **animate, living,** vital, zoetic; **biological,** biotic; physiological

18 **protoplasmic,** plasmic, plasmatic; **genetic,** genic, hereditary

19 **cellular,** cellulous; unicellular, multicellular; corpuscular

20 gametic, gamic, sexual; **spermatic,** spermic, **seminal,** spermatozoal, spermatozoan, spermatozoic; sporal, sporous, sporoid; sporogenous

21 **nuclear,** nucleal, nucleary, nucleate; multinucleate; nucleolar, nucleolate, nucleolated; **chromosomal;** chromatinic; haploid, diploid, polyploid

22 **embryonic, germinal,** germinant, germinative, germinational; larval; fetal; in the bud; germiparous

23 **egglike,** ovicular, eggy; ovular; albuminous, albuminoid; yolked, yolky; oviparous

306 LIFE

NOUNS **1** **life, living, vitality,** being alive, having life, animation, animate existence; breath; liveliness, animal spirits, vivacity, spriteliness; long life, longevity; life expectancy, life-span; viability; lifetime 827.5; immortality 828.3; birth 1; existence 761

2 "a little gleam of Time between two eternities"—

Carlyle, "a perpetual instruction in cause and effect"—Emerson, "a flame that is always burning itself out"—G B Shaw, "a long lesson in humility"—J M Barrie, "a play of passion"—Sir W Raleigh

3 life force, soul, spirit, indwelling spirit, force of life, living force, *vis vitae* or *vis vitalis* <L>, **vital force** or energy, animating force or power or principle, inspiriting force or power or principle, archeus, élan vital, impulse of life, vital principle, **vital spark** or **flame,** spark of life, divine spark, life principle, vital spirit, vital fluid, anima, consciousness; **breath,** life breath, **breath of life,** breath of one's nostrils, divine breath, life essence, essence of life, pneuma; prana, atman, jivatma, jiva; blood, **lifeblood,** heartblood, heart's blood; **heart,** heartbeat, beating heart; seat of life; growth force, bathmism; **life process;** biorhythm, biological clock, life cycle

4 the living, the living and breathing, all animate nature, the quick; the quick and the dead

5 living being, human being, living person, entity, living soul, living thing; life on earth; survivor; the quick

6 life cycle, lifetime, longevity, life expectancy

7 vivification, vitalization, animation, quickening

8 biosphere, ecosphere, noosphere; biochore, biotype, biocycle

VERBS **9 live,** be alive or animate or vital, have life, exist 761.8, be, breathe, respire, live and breathe, fetch or draw breath, draw the breath of life, walk the earth, subsist

10 come to life, come into existence or being, come into the world, see the light, be incarnated, **be born** or begotten or conceived; quicken; **revive, come to,** come alive, come around, regain consciousness, show signs of life; **awake, awaken;** rise again, live again, rise from the grave, resurge, resurrect, resuscitate, reanimate, return to life

11 vivify, vitalize, energize, animate, quicken, inspirit, invigorate, enliven, imbue or endow with life, give birth to, give life to, put life or new life into, breathe life into, give a new lease on life, bring to life, bring or call into existence or being; conceive; give birth, reproduce

12 keep alive, feed, nourish, provide for, keep body and soul together, endure, survive, persist, last, last out, hang on, hang in <nf>, be spared, come through, continue, carry on, have nine lives; support life; cheat death

ADJS **13 living, alive,** having life, live, very much alive, alive and well, alive and kicking <nf>, conscious, breathing, quick <old>, **animate,** animated, **vital,** viable, zoetic, instinct with life, imbued or endowed with life, vivified, enlivened,

inspirited; in the flesh, among the living, in the land of the living, on this side of the grave, still with us, still breathing, above-ground, incarnate; existent 761.13; long-lived, tenacious of life; capable of life or survival, viable

14 life-giving, animating, animative, quickening, vivifying, energizing

307 DEATH

NOUNS **1 death, dying,** somatic death, clinical death, biological death, abiosis, **decease, demise;** brain death; perishing, release, **passing away,** passing, passing over, "crossing the bar"—Tennyson, leaving life, making an end, departure, parting, going, going off or away, exit, ending, **end** 819, end of life, cessation of life, end of the road or line <nf>; **loss of life,** no life, ebb of life, expiration, expiry, **dissolution, extinction,** bane, annihilation, extinguishment, quietus; doom, crack of doom, summons of death, final summons, sentence of death, death knell, knell; **sleep, rest,** eternal rest or sleep, last sleep, last rest; **grave** 309.16; reward, debt of nature, last debt; last muster, last roundup, curtains <nf>; jaws of death, hand or finger of death, shadow or shades of death; rigor mortis; near-death experience or NDE; the beyond, the other side, the Great Divide

2 "the journey's end," "the undiscovered country from whose bourn no traveler returns,"—both Shakespeare, "that dreamless sleep"—Byron, "a debt we all must pay"—Euripides, "the sleeping partner of life"—Horace Smith, "kind Nature's signal of retreat"—Samuel Johnson, "a little sleep, a little slumber, a little folding of the hands to sleep"—Bible, "the big sleep"—Raymond Chandler

3 <personifications and symbols> **Death,** "Black Death"—Ovid, "Pale Death"—Horace, **Grim Reaper,** Reaper; pale horse, pale rider; angel of death, death's bright angel, Azrael; scythe or sickle of Death; **skull,** death's-head, grinning skull, crossbones, skull and crossbones; *memento mori* <L>; white cross; great leveler, thief in the night, Last Summoner; shadow of death, dance of death

4 river of death, Styx, Stygian shore, Acheron; Jordan, Jordan's bank; "valley of the shadow of death"—Bible; Heaven 681; Hell 682

5 early death, early grave, **untimely end,** premature death; sudden death; stroke of death, death stroke; deathblow

6 violent death; killing 308; suffocation, smothering, smotheration <nf>; asphyxiation; choking, choke, strangulation, strangling; drowning, watery grave; fatal accident, accidental death; starvation; liver death, serum death; megadeath; suicide, assisted suicide; murder, assassination; capital punishment, execution

7 **natural death;** easy *or* quiet *or* peaceful death *or* end, euthanasia, blessed *or* welcome release; stillbirth

8 dying day, deathday, "the supreme day and the inevitable hour"—Virgil; final *or* fatal *or* last hour, dying hour, running-out of the sands, deathtime

9 moribundity, extremity, last *or* final extremity; **deathbed;** deathwatch; death struggle, agony, last agony, death agony, death throes, throes of death; last breath *or* gasp, dying breath; **death rattle,** death groan; making an end, passing, passing away, crossing the Styx; extreme unction, last rites

10 **swan song,** *chant du cygne* <Fr>, death song, final words, last words

11 **bereavement** 473.1

12 **deathliness,** deathlikeness, deadliness; **weirdness, eeriness, uncanniness,** unearthliness; ghostliness, ghostlikeness; **ghastliness, grisliness, gruesomeness,** macabreness; paleness, haggardness, wanness, luridness, pallor; cadaverousness, corpselikeness; *facies Hippocratica* <L>, Hippocratic face *or* countenance, mask of death

13 **death rate,** death toll; **mortality,** mortalness, mortality rate; extinction, dissolution, abiosis; transience 828; mutability 853.1

14 **obituary,** obit <nf>, death notice, necrology, necrologue; register of deaths, roll of the dead, death roll, mortuary roll, bill of mortality; fatality list, casualty list; martyrology; death toll, body count

15 terminal case; **dying**

16 **corpse,** dead body, dead man *or* woman, dead person, **cadaver, carcass, body;** *corpus delicti* <L>; **stiff** <nf>; **the dead,** the defunct, **the deceased,** the departed, the loved one; **decedent,** the late lamented; **remains,** mortal *or* organic remains, carrion, bones, skeleton, dry bones, relics, reliquiae; dust, ashes, earth, clay, tenement of clay; **carrion,** crowbait, food for worms; **mummy,** mummification; embalmed corpse

17 **dead,** the majority, the great majority; one's fathers, one's ancestors; the choir invisible

18 **autopsy, postmortem, inquest,** postmortem examination, ex post facto examination, necropsy, necroscopy; medical examiner, coroner, pathologist, mortality committee

VERBS 19 **die, decease, succumb, expire, perish,** be taken by death, up and die <nf>, cease to be *or* live, part, depart, quit this world, make one's exit, go, go the way of all flesh, go out, pass, pass on *or* over, **pass away, meet one's death** *or* **end** *or* **fate,** end one's life *or* days, depart this life, "shuffle off this mortal coil"—Shakespeare, put off mortality, **lose one's life,** fall, be lost, relinquish *or* surrender one's life, resign one's life *or* being, **give up the ghost,** yield the ghost *or* spirit, yield one's breath, take one's last breath, breathe one's last, stop breathing, fall asleep, close one's eyes, take one's last sleep, pay the debt of *or* to nature, go out with the ebb, "go the way of all earth"—Bible, return to dust *or* the earth

20 <nf terms> **croak,** go west, kick the bucket, kick in, pop off, conk off, conk out, cop it, drop off, step off, go to the wall, go home feet first, knock off, pipe off, kick off, shove off, bow out, pass out, peg out, push up daisies, go for a burton <Brit>, belly up, go belly up, bite the dust, take the last count; flatline; check out, check in, cash in, hand *or* pass *or* cash in one's checks *or* chips; turn up one's toes; slip one's cable; buy the farm *or* the ranch, farm, have one's time *and* have it *and* buy it <Brit>

21 **meet one's Maker,** go to glory, go to kingdom come <nf>, go to the happy hunting grounds, go to *or* reach a better place *or* land *or* life *or* world, go to one's rest *or* reward, go home, go home feet first <nf>, go to one's last home, go to one's long account, go over to *or* join the majority *or* great majority, **be gathered to one's fathers,** join one's ancestors, join the angels, join the choir invisible, die in the Lord, go to Abraham's bosom, pass over Jordan, "walk through the valley of the shadow of death"—Bible, cross the Stygian ferry, give an obolus to Charon; awake to life immortal, "put on immortality"—Bible

22 **drop dead, fall dead,** fall down dead; come to an untimely end; predecease

23 die in harness, die with one's boots on, make a good end, die fighting, die in the last ditch, die like a man

24 die a natural death; die a violent death, be killed; **starve,** famish; smother, **suffocate;** asphyxiate; choke, strangle; **drown,** go to a watery grave, go to Davy Jones's locker <nf>; catch one's death, catch one's death of cold

25 **lay down** *or* **give one's life for one's country, die for one's country,** "*pro patria mori*"—Horace, make the supreme sacrifice, do one's bit

26 be dying, be moribund, be terminal; die out, become extinct

27 be dead, be no more, sleep *or* be asleep with the Lord, sleep with one's fathers *or* ancestors; lie in the grave, lie in Abraham's bosom <nf>

28 **bereave;** leave, leave behind; orphan, widow

ADJS 29 **deathly, deathlike,** deadly; **weird, eerie, uncanny,** unearthly; ghostly, ghostlike; **ghastly, grisly, gruesome, macabre;** pale, deathly pale, wan, lurid, blue, livid, haggard; **cadaverous,** corpselike; mortuary

30 **dead, lifeless,** breathless, without life, inanimate 1055.5, exanimate, without vital functions; **deceased, demised, defunct,** croaked <nf>, departed, departed this life, destitute of life, **gone, passed on,** passed away, gone the way of all flesh, gone west <nf>, extinct, gone before, long gone, dead and gone, done for <nf>, dead and done for <nf>, no more, finished <nf>, taken off *or* away, released, fallen, bereft of life, gone for a burton <Brit nf>; **at rest,** resting easy <nf>, still, out of one's misery; **asleep,** sleeping, reposing; asleep in Jesus, with the Lord, asleep *or* dead in the Lord; **called home,** out of the world, gone to a better world *or* place *or* land, gone but not forgotten, launched into eternity, gone to glory, taken *or* called by God, at the Pearly Gates, in Abraham's bosom, joined the choir invisible, gone to kingdom come <nf>, with the saints, sainted, numbered with the dead; in the grave, deep-sixed <nf>, six feet under *and* pushing up daisies <nf>; carrion, food for worms; martyred; death-struck, death-stricken, smitten with death; stillborn, dead on arrival, DOA; late, late lamented

31 **stone-dead;** dead as a doornail *and* dead as a dodo *and* dead as a herring *and* dead as mutton <nf>; cold, stone-cold, "as cold as any stone"— Shakespeare, stiff <nf>

32 **drowned,** in a watery grave *or* bier, in Davy Jones's locker

33 **dying, terminal,** expiring, going, slipping, slipping away, sinking, sinking fast, fading, low, despaired of, given up, given up for dead, not long for this world, hopeless, bad, **moribund,** near death, deathlike, perishing, doomed, near one's end, at the end of one's rope <nf>, hanging by a thread, done for <nf>, at the point of death, **at death's door,** at the portals of death, *in articulo mortis* <L>, *in extremis* <L>, in the jaws of death, facing *or* in the face of death; **on one's last legs** <nf>, half-dead, with one foot in the grave, tottering on the brink of the grave; on one's deathbed; at the last gasp; in critical condition, mortally ill, terminal; nonviable, unviable, incapable of life

34 **mortal, perishable,** subject to death, ephemeral, transient 828.7, mutable 854.6

35 **bereaved,** bereft, deprived; widowed; orphan, **orphaned,** parentless, fatherless, motherless

36 **postmortem,** postmortal, postmortuary, postmundane, post-obit, postobituary, **posthumous**

ADVS 37 **deathly, deadly;** to the death, *à la mort* <Fr>

PHRS 38 one's hour is come, one's days are numbered, one's race is run, one's doom is sealed, life hangs by a thread, one's number is up, Death knocks at the door, Death stares one in the face, the sands of life are running out

308 KILLING

NOUNS 1 **killing** <see list>, **slaying, slaughter, dispatch, extermination, destruction, murder,** destruction of life, taking of life, death-dealing, dealing of death, bane; kill; **bloodshed,** bloodletting, blood, gore, flow of blood; mercy killing, euthanasia, negative *or* passive euthanasia; ritual murder *or* killing, immolation, sacrifice, religious sacrifice, crucifixion, martyrdom; *auto-da-fé* <Sp, literally, act of faith>, martyrdom, martyrization; lynching; stoning, lapidation; defenestration; braining; shooting, drive-by shooting; poisoning; execution 604.7; mass killing, biocide, ecocide, genocide; Holocaust; mass murder

2 **homicide, manslaughter;** negligent homicide, **unlawful killing; murder,** bloody murder <nf>, first-degree murder, second-degree murder, capital murder; serial killing; hit *and* bump-off *and* bumping-off *and* rubbing out *and* blowing away *and* wasting <nf>, gangland-style execution, contract murder; kiss of death; foul play; **assassination;** terrorist killing; crime of passion; removal, elimination; liquidation, purge, purging; thuggery, thuggism, thuggee; justifiable homicide

3 **butchery,** butchering, **slaughter,** shambles, occision, slaughtering, hecatomb, holocaust

4 **carnage, massacre, bloodbath, decimation,** saturnalia of blood; **mass murder, mass destruction,** mass extermination, wholesale murder, pogrom, race-murder, genocide, race extermination, ethnic cleansing, **the Holocaust,** the final solution, Roman holiday

5 **suicide,** autocide, self-murder, self-homicide, self-destruction, self-slaughter, death by one's own hand, *felo-de-se* <L>, self-immolation, self-sacrifice; slashing one's wrists, **disembowelment,** ritual suicide, self-immolation, *hara-kiri* and *seppuku* <Japan>, suttee, sutteeism, kamikaze; car of Jagannath *or* Juggernaut; mass suicide, race suicide, suicide pact

6 **suffocation,** smothering, smotheration <nf>, **asphyxiation,** asphyxia; **strangulation,** strangling, burking, throttling, stifling, garrote, garroting; **choking,** choke; **drowning**

7 **execution,** capital punishment, death penalty, legalized killing, judicial murder, judicial execution

8 **fatality,** fatal accident, violent death, **casualty,** disaster, calamity; DOA *or* dead-on-arrival

9 **deadliness, lethality,** mortality, fatality; **malignance**

or malignancy, malignity, **virulence, perniciousness,** banefulness

10 **deathblow,** death stroke, final stroke, fatal *or* mortal *or* lethal blow, *coup de grâce* <Fr>

11 **killer, slayer, slaughterer, butcher,** bloodshedder; massacrer; **manslayer, homicide, murderer,** man-killer, bloodletter, man of blood, Cain; **assassin,** assassinator; **cutthroat,** thug, desperado, bravo, gorilla <nf>, apache, gunman; professional killer, contract killer, hired killer, hit man *or* button man *or* gun *or* trigger man *or* torpedo *or* gunsel <nf>; **hatchet man;** poisoner; strangler, hangman, garroter, burker; cannibal, maneater, anthropophagus; headhunter; mercy killer, euthanasiast; thrill killer, psychopath, homicidal maniac; serial killer; executioner 604.8; matador; exterminator, eradicator; death squad; terrorist, bomber; poison, pesticide 1001.3

12 <place of slaughter> aceldama, field of blood *or* bloodshed; **slaughterhouse,** butchery <Brit>, shambles, abattoir; bullring, arena, battleground, battlefield; stockyard; gas chamber, concentration camp, death camp, killing fields; Auschwitz, Belsen, etc

VERBS 13 **kill, slay, put to death,** deprive of life, bereave of life, **take life,** take the life of, take one's life away, **do away with,** make away with, **put out of the way,** put to sleep, end, **put an end to,** end the life of, hasten someone's end, **dispatch, do to death,** do for, finish, finish off, kill off, take off, **dispose of, exterminate, destroy,** annihilate; **liquidate,** purge; carry off *or* away, remove from life; put down, put away, put to sleep, put one out of one's misery; launch into eternity, send to glory, send to kingdom come <nf>, send to one's last account, send to one's Maker; **martyr,** martyrize; immolate, sacrifice; lynch; cut off, cut down, nip in the bud; poison; chloroform; starve; euthanatize; **execute**

14 <nf terms> **waste, zap,** nuke, rub out, croak, snuff, bump off, knock off, bushwhack, lay out, polish off, blow away, blot out, erase, wipe out, blast, do in, off, hit, ice, gun down, pick off, put to bed with a shovel, scrag, take care of, take out, take for a ride, give the business *or* works, deep-six, get, fix, settle

15 **shed blood,** spill blood, let blood, bloody one's hands with, dye one's hands in blood, have blood on one's hands, pour out blood like water, wade knee-deep in blood

16 **murder,** commit murder; **assassinate;** remove, **purge, liquidate,** eliminate, get rid of

17 **slaughter, butcher, massacre, decimate,** mow down, spare none, take no prisoners, wipe out, wipe off the face of the earth, annihilate, exterminate, liquidate, commit carnage, depopulate, murder *or* kill *or* slay en masse; purge, commit mass murder *or* destruction, murder wholesale, commit genocide

18 **strike dead,** fell, bring down, lay low; drop, drop *or* stop in one's tracks; **shoot,** shoot down, pistol, shotgun, machinegun, gun down, riddle, shoot to death; cut down, cut to pieces *or* ribbons, **put to the sword,** stab to death, jugulate, cut *or* slash the throat; **deal a deathblow,** give the quietus *or* coup de grâce <Fr>, silence; knock in *or* on the head; **brain,** blow *or* knock *or* dash one's brains out, poleax; **stone,** lapidate, stone to death; defenestrate; blow up, blow to bits *or* pieces *or* kingdom come, frag; disintegrate, vaporize; burn to death, incinerate, burn at the stake

19 **strangle,** garrote, **throttle, choke,** burke; **suffocate, stifle, smother, asphyxiate,** stop the breath; **drown**

20 **condemn to death,** sign one's death warrant, strike the death knell of, finger <nf>, give the kiss of death to

21 **be killed,** get killed, die a violent death, **come to a violent end,** meet with foul play; welter in one's own blood

22 **commit suicide, take one's own life, kill oneself,** die by one's own hand, do away with oneself, put an end to oneself; blow one's brains out, take an overdose <of a drug>, overdose *or* OD <nf>; commit hara-kiri *or* seppuku; sign one's own death warrant, doom oneself; jump overboard, do oneself in *or* off oneself <nf>

ADJS 23 **deadly, deathly,** deathful, **killing, destructive,** death-dealing, death-bringing, feral <old>, fell; savage, brutal; internecine; **fatal, mortal, lethal, malignant,** malign, **virulent, pernicious,** baneful; **life-threatening, terminal;** capital; incurable, terminal, inoperable

24 **murderous,** slaughterous; cutthroat; redhanded; **homicidal,** man-killing, death-dealing; biocidal, genocidal; suicidal, self-destructive; soul-destroying; cruel; **bloodthirsty,** bloody-minded; **bloody, gory,** sanguinary; psychopathic, pathological

25 **types of killing and killers**

aborticide *or* feticide <fetus>	fungicide <fungi>
amicicide <friend>	genocide <race or ethnic group>
avicide <birds>	giganticide <giant>
biocide <chemical>	gynecide *or* femicide <woman>
ceticide <whales>	herbicide <plants>
deicide <god>	homicide <person>
ecocide <large area>	infanticide <infant>
elephanticide <elephants>	insecticide <insects>
felicide <cats>	mariticide <spouse, especially husband>
formicicide <ants>	
fratricide <brother>	

matricide <mother>
microbicide *or* germicide
  <germs>
ovicide <egg cell>
parenticide <parent>
parricide <kinsman>
patricide <father>
pesticide <pest>
phytocide <plants>
prolicide <own child>
regicide <king>
rodenticide <rodent>
senicide <old person>
sororicide <sister>

spermicide *or*
  spermaticide *or*
  spermatozoicide
  <spermatozoa>
suicide *or* autocide <self>
tauricide <bulls>
tickicide <ticks>
tyrannicide <tyrant>
uxoricide <wife>
vaticide <prophet>
vermicide *or* filaricide
  <worms>
vespacide <wasps>
viricide <viruses>

309 INTERMENT

NOUNS 1 **interment, burial,** burying, inhumation, sepulture, **entombment;** encoffinment, inurning, inurnment, urn burial; primary burial; secondary burial, reburial; disposal of the dead; burial *or* funeral *or* funerary customs; mass burial, burial at sea, military burial, full military rites

2 **cremation, incineration, burning,** reduction to ashes, pyre, scattering of the ashes

3 **embalmment,** embalming; mummification

4 **last offices,** last honors, **last rites,** funeral rites, last duty *or* service, funeral service, funeral ceremony, burial service, graveside service, memorial service, exequies, **obsequies;** Office of the Dead, Memento of the Dead, requiem, requiem mass, dirge <old>; **extreme unction;** viaticum; funeral oration *or* sermon, eulogy; **wake,** deathwatch, Irish wake; lowering the body

5 **funeral, burial,** burying; funeral procession, cortege; dead march, muffled drum, last post <Brit>, taps; dirge; burial at sea, deep six <nf>

6 **knell,** passing bell, death bell, funeral ring, tolling, tolling of the knell, funeral hymn, dirge

7 **mourner, griever, lamenter,** keener; mute, professional mourner; **pallbearer,** bearer; eulogist, eulogizer, elegist, epitaphist, obituarist

8 **undertaker, mortician,** funeral director; embalmer; gravedigger; sexton

9 **mortuary, morgue,** deadhouse <old>, charnel house, lichhouse <Brit nf>; ossuary *or* ossuarium; **funeral home** *or* **parlor,** undertaker's establishment; **crematorium,** crematory, cinerarium; pyre, funeral pile; burning ghat

10 **hearse,** funeral car *or* coach; catafalque

11 **coffin, casket,** burial case, box, kist <Scot>; wooden kimono *or* overcoat <nf>; **sarcophagus;** mummy case

12 **urn,** cinerary urn, funerary *or* funeral urn *or* vessel, bone pot, ossuary *or* ossuarium, canopic urn *or* jar *or* vase

13 **bier,** litter

14 **graveclothes, shroud,** winding sheet, cerecloth, cerements; pall

15 **graveyard, cemetery, burial ground** *or* **place,** plot, family plot, burying place *or* ground, *campo santo* <Ital>, boneyard *and* bone orchard <nf>, burial yard, necropolis, polyandrium, **memorial park,** city *or* village of the dead; **churchyard,** God's acre, final resting place; garden of remembrance *or* rest; **potter's field;** Golgotha, Calvary; urnfield; lychgate; columbarium, cinerarium

16 **tomb, sepulcher; grave,** gravesite, burial, pit, deep six <nf>; resting place, "the lone couch of his everlasting sleep"—Shelley; last home, long home, narrow house, house of death, low house, low green tent; **crypt, vault,** burial chamber; ossuary *or* ossuarium; charnel house, bone house; **mausoleum; catacombs;** mastaba; cist grave, box grave, passage grave, shaft grave, beehive tomb; catafalque; **shrine,** reliquary, monstrance, tope, stupa; cenotaph; dokhma, tower of silence; pyramid, mummy chamber; burial mound, tumulus, barrow, cist, cromlech, dolmen, menhir, cairn, tower of silence; grave pit, common grave, mass grave, open grave

17 monument, gravestone 549.12

18 **epitaph,** inscription, *hic jacet* <L>, here lies, Rest in Peace, RIP; tombstone marking

VERBS 19 **inter,** inhume, **bury,** sepulture, inearth <old>, **lay to rest, consign to the grave,** consign to earth, lower the body, lay in the grave *or* earth, lay under the sod, put six feet under <nf>; plant <nf>; tomb, **entomb,** ensepulcher, hearse; enshrine; inurn; encoffin, coffin; hold *or* conduct a funeral

20 **cremate, incinerate, burn,** reduce to ashes, burn on the pyre

21 **lay out; embalm;** mummify; lie in state

ADJS 22 **funereal,** funeral, funerary, funebrial, funebrous *or* funebrious, *funèbre* <Fr>, feral <old>; burial, mortuary, exequial, obsequial; graveside; sepulchral, tomblike; cinerary; necrological, obituary, epitaphic; **dismal** 112.24; **mournful** 112.26; dirgelike; memorial, eulogistic, elegiac

ADVS 23 beneath the sod, underground, six feet under <nf>, "in the dark union of insensate dust"—Byron; at rest, resting in peace

PHRS 24 **RIP,** *requiescat in pace* <L singular>, *requiescant in pace* <L plural>, rest in peace; *hic jacet* <L>, *ci-gît* <Fr>, here lies; "ashes to ashes and dust to dust"—Book of Common Prayer

310 PLANTS

NOUNS 1 **plants, vegetation;** flora, **plant life,** vegetable life; **vegetable kingdom,** plant kingdom;

herbage, flowerage, verdure, greenery, greens, green plants; botany 1068.6; vegetation spirit 1069.4

2 **growth,** stand, crop; plantation, planting; **clump,** tuft, tussock, hassock

3 **plant,** green plant; **vegetable** <see list>; **weed;** seedling; cutting; vascular plant, herbaceous plant; seed plant, spermatophyte; gymnosperm; angiosperm, flowering plant; monocotyledon *or* monocot *or* monocotyl; dicotyledon *or* dicot *or* dicotyl; polycotyledon *or* polycot *or* polycotyl; thallophyte, fungus, gametophyte, sporophyte; exotic, hothouse plant, greenhouse plant; ephemeral, annual, biennial, triennial, perennial; evergreen, deciduous plant; cosmopolite; aquatic plant, hydrophyte, amphibian; cultivated plant, garden plant, houseplant, pot plant; food plant, cereal, vegetable, herb; medicinal plant

4 <varieties> **legume,** pulse, vetch, bean, pea, lentil; **herb** <see list>, pot-herb; succulent; **vine** <see list>, grapevine, creeper, ivy, climber, liana; **fern** <see list>, bracken; **moss; wort,** liverwort; **algae; seaweed,** kelp, sea moss, rockweed, gulfweed, sargasso *or* sargassum, sea lentil, wrack, sea wrack; **fungus** <see list>, mold, rust, smut, puffball, mushroom, toad-stool; lichen; parasitic plant, parasite, saprophyte, perthophyte, heterophyte, autophyte; plant families 1068.4; fruits and vegetables

5 **grass,** gramineous *or* graminaceous plant, pasture *or* forage grass, lawn grass, ornamental grass; aftergrass, fog <nf>; **cereal** <see list>, cereal plant, farinaceous plant, **grain,** corn <Brit>; sedge; rush, reed, cane, bamboo

6 **turf, sod, sward,** greensward; divot

7 **green, lawn;** artificial turf, Astroturf <trademark>; grassplot, greenyard; grounds; **common, park, village green;** golf course *or* links, fairway; bowling green, putting green; grass court

8 **grassland,** grass; parkland; **meadow,** meadow land, field, mead <old>, swale, lea *or* ley, haugh *or* haughland <Scot>, vega; bottomland, water meadow; **pasture,** pastureland, pasturage, pasture land, park <Brit nf>; **range,** grazing, grazing land; **prairie, savanna,** savannah, **steppe,** steppeland, **pampas,** pampa, campo, llano, **veld** *or* veldt, grass veld, plain, range, champaign, campagna; herbage, verdure; moor, moorland, common, heath, downs, downland, wold

9 **shrubbery; shrub, bush;** scrub, bramble, brier, brier bush; topiary

10 **tree** <see list>, timber; shade tree, fruit tree, timber tree; softwood tree, hardwood tree; sapling, seedling; conifer *or* coniferous tree,

evergreen; pollard, pollarded tree, standard; deciduous tree, borad-leaved tree; ornamental tree; Christmas tree

11 <tree parts> trunk, bole, gnarl, knot, burl, burr, crown, limb, branch, bough, twig, switch, sprig, spur, leader, leaf, needle, cone, root, tree *or* annual *or* growth ring

12 <tree groupings> forest, tree line *or* zone, timberline, jungle, gallery forest, fringing forest, virgin forest, primeval forest, coniferous forest; taiga, woodland, chaparral, plantation, stand, timberland, tree farm, tree nursery, orchard, orangery

13 **woodland, wood, woods, timberland; timber,** stand of timber, **forest,** forest land, forest cover, forest preserve, state *or* national forest; forestry, dendrology, silviculture; afforestation, reforestation; boondocks <nf>; wildwood, **bush,** scrub; bushveld, tree veld; shrubland, scrubland; pine barrens, palmetto barrens; hanger; **park,** parkland, chase <Brit>; park forest; arboretum; conservation land

14 **grove, woodlet;** holt <nf>, hurst, spinney <Brit>, *tope* <India>, shaw <nf>, bosk <old>; **orchard;** wood lot; coppice, copse; *bocage* <Fr>

15 **thicket,** thickset, **copse, coppice,** copsewood, frith <Brit nf>; bosket *or* bosquet <old>, boscage; covert; motte; **brake,** canebrake; chaparral; chamisal; ceja

16 **brush, scrub,** bush, **brushwood,** shrubwood, scrubwood, shrub

17 **undergrowth, underwood, underbrush,** copsewood, undershrubs, boscage, frith <Brit nf>; ground cover, tree litter, leaf litter, leaf mold, covert

18 **foliage, leafage,** leafiness, umbrage, foliation; frondage, frondescence; vernation; greenery

19 **leaf, frond;** leaflet, foliole; ligule; lamina, **blade,** leaf blade, spear, spire, pile, flag; **needle,** pine needle; floral leaf, **petal,** sepal; bract, bractlet, bracteole, spathe, involucre, involucrum, glume, lemma; cotyledon, seed leaf; stipule, stipula; scale leaf, modified leaf

20 **branch,** fork, **limb, bough;** deadwood; **twig, sprig,** switch; spray; **shoot,** offshoot, spear, frond; scion; **sprout,** sprit, slip, burgeon, thallus; sucker; **runner,** stolon, flagellum, sarmentum, sarment; bine; **tendril;** ramage; branchiness, branchedness, ramification

21 **stem, stalk, stock,** axis, *caulis* <L>; **trunk,** bole; spear, spire; straw; reed; cane; culm, haulm <Brit>; caudex; footstalk, pedicel, peduncle; leafstalk, petiole, petiolus, petiolule; seedstalk; caulicle; tigella; funicule, funiculus; stipe, anthrophore, carpophore, gynophore

22 root, radix, radicle; rootlet; **taproot,** tap; **rhizome,** rootstock; **tuber,** tubercle, tuberous root, root tuber; **bulb,** bulbil, corm, earthnut; lateral root, prop root, aerial root

23 bud, burgeon, gemma; leaf bud, foliage bud; apical bud, terminal bud, axillary bud, lateral bud, resting bud; gemmule, gemmula; plumule, acrospire; leaf bud, flower bud

24 flower <see list>, **posy, blossom, bloom,** blow <old>; floweret, floret, floscule; **wildflower;** garden flower, pot plant, cut flowers; **gardening,** horticulture, floriculture; hortorium

25 bouquet, nosegay, posy, boughpot, flower arrangement; **boutonniere,** buttonhole <Brit>; **corsage; spray; wreath;** festoon; **garland,** daisy chain, chaplet, lei; dried flower, pressed flower

26 flowering, florescence, efflorescence, flowerage, **blossoming, blooming;** inflorescence; **blossom, bloom,** blowing, blow, full blow; unfolding, unfoldment; anthesis, full bloom

27 <types of inflorescence> flower head; raceme, corymb, umbel, panicle, cyme, thyrse or thyrsus, verticillaster, spadix; head, capitulum; spike, spikelet; ament, catkin; strobile, cone, pine cone; ray flower, disk flower, cymose inflorescence

28 <flower parts> petal, perianth, floral envelope; calyx, epicalyx, sepal; nectary; corolla, corolla tube, corona; androecium, anther, stamen, microsporophyll; pistil, gynoecium, ovary, ovule, micrypyle; style; stigma, carpel, megasporophyll; receptacle, torus; involucre, bract, whorl, spathe; pollen, pollen grain, pollen sac, pollen tube

29 ear, spike; auricle; ear of corn, mealie; **cob,** corncob

30 seed vessel, seedcase, seedbox, pericarp; hull, husk; **capsule, pod,** cod <nf>, seed pod, seed coat; pease cod, legume, legumen, boll, burr, follicle, silique

31 seed; stone, pit, nut; pip; fruit <see list>; **grain, kernel, berry;** flaxseed, linseed; hayseed; bird seed

32 vegetation, growth; germination, pullulation; burgeoning, sprouting; budding, luxuriation

33 <garden plants> seedling, cutting, bulb, corm, rhizome, tuber; rock plant, alpine plant, bedding plant, creeper, ground cover, turf, climber or climbing plant, rambler; annual, biennial, perennial; herb, flower, woody plant, succulent

VERBS **34 vegetate, grow;** germinate, pullulate; root, take root, strike root; sprout up, shoot up, upsprout, upspear; **burgeon,** put forth, burst forth; **sprout,** shoot; **bud,** gemmate, put forth or put out buds; **leaf,** leave, leaf out, put out or put forth leaves; flourish, luxuriate, riot, grow rank or lush; overgrow, overrun; run to seed, dehisce; photosynthesize, change color

35 flower, be in flower, **blossom, bloom,** bud, be in bloom, blow, effloresce, floreate, burst into bloom, flourish, burgeon

ADJS **36 vegetable,** vegetal, vegetative, vegetational, vegetarian; **plantlike; herbaceous,** herbal, herbous, herbose, herby; leguminous, leguminose, leguminiform; cereal, farinaceous; weedy; fruity, fruitlike; tuberous, bulbous; rootlike, rhizoid, radicular, radicated, radiciform; botanic, botanical; green, grassy, leafy, verdant

37 algal, fucoid, confervoid; phytoplanktonic, diatomaceous; fungous, fungoid, fungiform

38 floral; flowery, florid <old>; **flowered,** floreate, floriate, floriated; **flowering, blossoming, blooming,** abloom, bloomy, florescent, inflorescent, efflorescent, in flower, in bloom, in blossom; uniflorous, multiflorous; radiciflorous, rhizanthous; **garden,** horticultural, hortulan, floricultural; flowerlike

39 arboreal, arborical, arboresque, arboreous, arborary, arboraceous; **treelike,** arboriform, arborescent, dendroid, dendroidal, dendriform, dendritic; deciduous, nondeciduous; evergreen; softwood, hardwood; piny or piney; coniferous; citrous; palmate, palmaceous; **bosky,** bushy, shrubby, scrubby, scrubbly; bushlike, shrublike, scrublike

40 sylvan, silvan, sylvatic, woodland, forest, forestal; dendrologic, dendrological, silvicultural, afforestational, reforestational, reforested; tree-covered; **wooded,** timbered, forested, afforested, timbered, arboreous; **woody,** woodsy, bosky, bushy, shrubby, scrubby; copsy, braky; ligneous, ligniform

41 leafy, leavy <old>, bowery; foliated, foliate, foliose, foliaged, leaved; **branched,** branchy, branching, ramified, ramate, ramous or ramose; twiggy

42 verdant, verdurous, verdured; **mossy,** moss-covered, moss-grown; **grassy,** grasslike, gramineous, graminaceous; turfy, swardy, turflike, caespitose, tufted; meadowy

43 luxuriant, flourishing, **rank, lush,** riotous, exuberant; dense, impenetrable, thick, heavy, gross; jungly, jungled; overgrown, overrun; **weedy,** unweeded, weed-choked, weed-ridden; gone to seed

44 perennial, ephemeral; hardy, half-hardy; **deciduous,** evergreen

45 herbs

angelica	borage
anise	calendula
balm	camomile
basil	caraway
belladonna	cardamom
bergamot	catnip or catmint

chervil
chicory
chive
cilantro
clover
coriander
cum(m)in
deadly nightshade
dill
fennel
feverroot
figwort
fraxinella *or* gas plant
garlic
ginseng
hemp
henbane
horehound
hyssop
licorice
liverwort
mandrake

marjoram
mint
monkshood
mullein
mustard
oregano *or* origanum
parsley
peppermint
rosemary
rue
sage
savory
sesame
sorrel
spearmint
sweet cicely
sweet woodruff
tansy
tarragon
thyme
wintergreen
yarrow

46 vines

air potato
bittersweet
Boston ivy
cissus
clematis
cypress vine
English ivy
grape
greenbrier
honeysuckle
hop
ivy
jasmine
liana

morning glory
paradise flower
poison ivy
stephanotis
sword bean
traveler's-joy
trumpet creeper
trumpet flower
trumpet honeysuckle
velvet bean
Virginia creeper
virgins-bower
wisteria
woodbine

47 ferns

adder's fern
asparagus fern
basket fern
beech fern
bladder fern
boulder fern
bracken
calamite
chain fern
Christmas fern
cliff brake
climbing fern
club moss
cycad
curly grass
grape fern
hart's tongue
holly fern
horsetail

interrupted fern
lady fern
lip fern
lycopod
maidenhair
marsh fern
moonwort
oak fern
osmunda
ostrich fern
polypody
rattlesnake fern
rock brake
seed fern
shield fern
silvery
  spleenwort
snuffbox fern
sword fern

tree fern
tropical fern
true fern
walking fern

wall fern
water clover
wood fern
woodsia

48 trees

abele
acacia
acajou
ailanthus *or* tree of heaven
alder
Aleppo pine
allspice
almond
apple
apricot
ash
aspen
avocado *or* alligator pear
bald cypress
balsa
balsam
banyan
basswood
bay
bayberry
bean
beech
betel palm
birch
bonsai
bo tree
boxwood
Brazil-nut
breadfruit
buckeye
buckthorn
butternut
buttonwood
cabbage tree
cacao
camphor tree
carnauba
carob
cashew
cassia
catalpa
cedar
cherimoya
cherry
chestnut
chinaberry tree *or* China
  tree
chinquapin
Christmas tree
cinnamon
citron
clove
coconut *or* coco
cork oak

cottonwood
cypress
date palm
devilwood
dogwood
dwarf
ebony
elder
elm
eucalyptus
evergreen
ficus
fig
filbert
fir
flame tree
fruit
ginkgo
grapefruit
guava
gum
hardwood
hawthorn
hazel *or* hazelnut
hemlock
henna
hickory
holly
hoptree
hornbeam
horse chestnut
horseradish tree
inkwood
juniper
kola
kumquat
laburnum
lancewood
larch
laurel
lemon
lignum vitae
lime
linden
litchi *or* litchi nut
locust
logwood
loquat *or* Japanese plum
macadamia
madroña *or* madrone
magnolia
mahogany
mango
mangrove

maple
medlar
mesquite
mimosa
monkey puzzle
mountain ash
mulberry
nutmeg
nux vomica
oak
olive
orange
osier
pagoda tree
palm
papaw
papaya
peach
pear
pecan
persimmon
pine
pistachio
pitch pine
plane
plum
poison sumac
pomegranate
pomelo
poplar
quince
raffia palm
rain tree
redwood
rice-paper tree
rosewood
rubber tree
sandalwood
sapodilla
sassafras
satinwood
senna
sequoia
serviceberry
shade tree

shortleaf pine
silver maple
sorrel tree
spruce
sugar maple
sycamore
tamarillo
tamarind
tamarugo
tangerine
teak
thorn tree
thuja
torchwood
tulip tree
tupelo
umbrella tree
upas
varnish tree
walnut
wandoo
wax palm
wax tree
wayfaring tree
weeping willow
western hemlock
whitebeam
white birch
white cedar
white oak
white pine
white poplar
white spruce
whitethorn
wicopy
willow
witch hazel
woollybutt
wychelm
yellow poplar
yellowwood *or* gopher
  wood
yew
ylang-ylang
zebrawood

cactus
calendula
calla lily
camellia
camomile
campanula
candytuft
carnation
cat's-paw
cattail
century plant
chamomile
Chinese lantern
Christmas cactus
Christmas rose
chrysanthemum
cineraria
clematis
clover
cockscomb
columbine
cornel
cornflower
cosmos
cowbell
cowslip
crocus
cyclamen
daffodil
dahlia
daisy
damask rose
dandelion
delphinium
dogtooth violet
Dutchman's-breeches
Easter lily
edelweiss
eglantine
elderflower
fireweed
flax
fleur-de-lis <Fr>
forget-me-not
forsythia
foxglove
foxtail
frangipani
freesia
fuchsia
gardenia
gentian
geranium
gladiolus
globeflower
goldenrod
groundsel
guelder rose
harebell
hawthorn

heather
hepatica
hibiscus
hollyhock
honeysuckle
horehound
hyacinth
hydrangea
hyssop
impatience *or* impatiens
Indian paintbrush
indigo
iris
jack-in-the-pulpit
japonica
jasmine
jonquil
kingcup
laburnum
lady's-slipper
larkspur
lavender
lilac
lily
lily of the valley
lobelia
lotus
love-lies-bleeding
lupine
magnolia
mallow
marguerite
marigold
marshmallow
marsh marigold
mayflower
meadow saffron
Michaelmas daisy
mignonette
milkwort
mimosa
moccasin flower
mock orange
monkshood
moonflower
morning glory
moss rose
motherwort
mullein
musk rose
myrtle
narcissus
nasturtium
oleander
opium poppy
orchid
oxalis
oxeye daisy
pansy
paper-white narcissus

49 flowers

acacia
acanthus
African violet
amaranthus
amaryllis
anemone *or* windflower
arbutus
arrowhead
asphodel
aster
autumn crocus
azalea
baby's breath

bachelor's button
begonia
belladonna
bitterroot
bittersweet
black-eyed Susan
bleeding heart
bluebell
bluet
bougainvillea
bridal wreath
broom
buttercup

passionflower
pennyroyal
peony
periwinkle
petunia
phlox
pink
plumbago
poinsettia
polyanthus
poppy
portulaca
pot marigold
primrose
primula
Queen Anne's lace
ragged robin
ragwort
rambler rose
ranunculus
resurrection plant
rhododendron
rose
safflower
shooting star
smilax
snapdragon
snowdrop
spiraea
St. John's wort
stock
strawflower
sunflower
sweet alyssum
sweetbrier
sweet pea

sweet william
tea rose
thistle
tiger lily
trailing arbutus
trillium
trumpet creeper
tulip
twinflower
umbrella plant
valerian
Venus's flytrap
verbena
veronica
viburnum
viola
violet
wake-robin
wallflower
water hyacinth
water lily
water milfoil
water pimpernel
wax flower
waxplant
white clover
wisteria
wolfsbane
wood anemone
wood hyacinth
woody nightshade
wood sorrel
yarrow
yellow water lily
yucca
zinnia

50 cereal grasses

barley
buckwheat
corn
maize
millet

oats
rice
rye
wheat

51 fruit

apple
apricot
atemoya
avocado
banana
berry
black currant
breadfruit
bullace plum
calmyrna
canistel
cantaloupe
carambola
cherimoya
cherry

citron
clementine
coconut
crabapple
currant
custard apple
damson
date
durian
fig
granadilla
grape
grapefruit
greengage
ground cherry

guava
haw
jackfruit
jujube
kiwi
kumquat
lemon
lime
longan
loquat
mandarin orange
mango
May apple
medlar
melon
muskmelon
navel orange
nectarine
olive
orange
papaya
passion fruit
pawpaw
peach
pear

pepino
Persian melon
persimmon
pineapple
plantain
plum
pomegranate
pomelo
prickly pear
prune
quince
quinoa
raisin
rambutan
sapodilla
sapote
satsuma
sea grape
soursop
tamarillo
tamarind
tangelo
tangerine
tomato
watermelon

52 apples

Anna
Arctic
Arkansas Black
Bailey Sweet
Baldwin
Belmont
Ben Davis
Blue Permain
Braeburn
Bramley
Buckingham
Collins
Cortland
Cox's Orange Pippin
Criterion
Delicious
Dorset Golden
Earliblaze
Early Harvest
Ein Shemer
Empire
English Sweet
Freedom
Gala
Gideon
Golden Delicious
Golden Harvest
Granny Smith
Gravenstein
Green Sweet
Grimes Golden
Hubbardston
Ingram

Jersey Black
Jerseymac
Jonared
Jonathan
Lady Sweet
Liberty
Lodi
Longfield
Macoun
McIntosh
McMahon
Missouri
Monroe
Mutsu
Newton
  Pippin
Northern Spy
Oldenburg
Ortley
Permain
Pippin
Porter
Prima
Priscilla
Rambo
Red Delicious
Redfree
Red Rome
Rhode Island
  Greening
Roman Stem
Rome
Rome Beauty

Roxbury Russet
Russet
Saint Lawrence
Sir Prize
Snowapple
Spartan
Starkrimson
Starr
Stayman

Twenty Ounce
Tydeman's Red
Virginia Beauty
Wealthy
Williams
Winesap
Winter Banana
Yellow Transparent
York Imperial

53 berries

bearberry
bilberry
blackberry
black raspberry
blueberry
boysenberry
buffalo berry
candleberry
checkerberry
cloudberry
cranberry
currant
dangleberry
dewberry

elderberry
gooseberry
huckleberry
Juneberry
lingonberry
loganberry
mulberry
partridgeberry
raspberry
sala berry
serviceberry
shadberry
strawberry
whortleberry

54 citrus fruit

citron
clementine
grapefruit
kumquat
lemon
lime
mandarin
naartje

orange
ortanique
pomelo
satsuma
shaddock
tangelo
tangerine

55 grapes

Alicante
Almeria
Cabernet Sauvignon
cardinal
Champion
Chardonnay
Chenin Blanc
Concord
Delaware
Franconian
Hamburgh
Isabella
Italia
Labrusca
Lady Finger

Malaga
Martha
Merlot
Muscadet
Muscat
Pinot Blanc
Pinot Noir
Riesling
seedless
Superb
Thompson seedless
Tokay
White Corinth
Woodbury
zinfandel

56 melons

cantaloupe
casaba
Crenshaw
honeydew

muskmelon
Persian
watermelon
winter melon

57 peaches

Clingstone
Elberta

Freestone
Greensboro

Heath
Late Crawford
Lovell
Mountain Rose
Muir

nectarine
Phillips
Susquehanna
Triumph
Yellow

58 pears

Anjou
Bartlett
Bosc
Clapp Favorite
Comice

Kieffer
Le Conte
Sheldon
Wilder Early
winter nellis

59 vegetables

alfalfa sprout
artichoke
arugula
asparagus
bamboo sprout or shoot
bean
bean sprout
beet
bell pepper
black-eyed pea
Boston lettuce
broad bean
broccoli
Brussels sprout
butter bean
cabbage
cardoon
carrot
cassava
cauliflower
celery
chard
chayote
chickpea
chicory
Chinese cabbage
chive
collard greens
corn
cress
cucumber
dandelion
eggplant
endive
escarole
fennel
garbanzo bean
garlic
glasswort
globe artichoke
gourd
green bean
green pepper
iceberg lettuce
jalapeno pepper
kale
kidney bean

kohlrabi
leek
lentil
lettuce
lima bean
mung bean
mushroom
muskmelon
mustard
navy bean
New Zealand spinach
okra
olive
onion
parsley
parsnip
pea
pepper
petsai
pinto bean
plantain
pokeweed
potato
pumpkin
radiccio
radish
rampion
red bean
red cabbage
red pepper
rhubarb
rice
romaine
rutabaga
sauerkraut
scallion
sea kale
seaweed
shallot
snap bean
snow pea
sorrel
soybean
spinach
squash
string bean
succotash

sugar pea
summer squash
sweet corn
sweet potato
tomato
truffle
turnip
water chestnut

watercress
watermelon
wax bean
white bean
yam
yellow pepper
yellow squash
zucchini

311 ANIMALS, INSECTS

NOUNS 1 **animal life, animal kingdom,** brute creation, **fauna,** Animalia <zoology>, animality; animal behavior, biology ; birds, beasts, and fish; the beasts of the field, the fowl of the air, and the fish of the sea; domestic animals, livestock, stock <nf>, cattle; wild animals *or* beasts, beasts of field, wildlife, denizens of the forest *or* jungle *or* wild, furry creatures; predators, beasts of prey; game, big game, small game; animal rights

2 **animal, creature,** critter <nf>, living being *or* thing, creeping thing; **brute, beast,** varmint <nf>, dumb animal *or* creature, dumb friend, furry friend, four-legged friend, critter <nf>

3 <varieties> **vertebrate; invertebrate; biped, quadruped; mammal,** mammalian, **primate** <see list>, warm-blooded animal; chordate; **marsupial,** marsupialian; canine; **feline; rodent,** gnawer; **ungulate; ruminant;** insectivore, herbivore, carnivore, omnivore; cannibal; scavenger; reptile; amphibian; fish; aquatic; bird; cosmopolite; vermin, varmint <nf>; zooid, protist, protozoan; worm, mollusk, gastropod, arthropod, insect, arachnid; parasite, scavenger, predator, grazer

4 **pachyderm; elephant,** Jumbo, *hathi* <India>, "heffalump"—A A Milne; mammoth, woolly mammoth; mastodon; **rhinoceros,** rhino; **hippopotamus,** hippo, river horse; subungulate, proboscidean, Proboscidea

5 <hoofed animals> ungulate, ungulant; odd-toed ungulate, perissodactyl; even-toed ungulate, artiodactyl; **deer, buck, doe, fawn;** red deer, **stag,** hart, hind; roe deer, roe, roebuck; musk deer; fallow deer; hogdeer; white-tailed *or* Virginia deer; mule deer; **elk,** wapiti; **moose; reindeer,** caribou; deerlet; **antelope;** gazelle, kaama, wildebeest *or* gnu, hartebeest, springbok, reebok, dik-dik, eland *or* Cape elk, koodoo; **camel,** dromedary, ship of the desert; **giraffe,** camelopard, okapi; equine, equid, horse; pig, hog, swine; camel, llama; goat, sheep

6 **cattle** <see list>, kine <old pl>, neat; beef cattle, beef, beeves <pl>; dairy cattle *or* cows; bovine animal, **bovine,** critter <nf>; **cow,** moo-cow *and* bossy <nf>; milk *or* milch cow, milker, milcher, dairy cow; **bull,** bullock, top cow <nf>; **steer,** stot <Brit nf>, **ox,** oxen <pl>; **calf, heifer,** yearling, fatling, stirk <Brit>; **dogie** *and* leppy <W US>; maverick <W US>; hornless cow, butthead *and* muley head <nf>, muley cow; zebu, Brahman; yak; musk-ox; **buffalo,** water buffalo, Indian buffalo, carabao; bison, aurochs, wisent

7 **sheep** <see list>, jumbuck <Austral>; **lamb,** lambkin, yeanling; teg <Brit>; **ewe,** yow <nf>; ewe lamb; **ram,** tup <Brit>, wether; bellwether; mutton

8 **goat;** he-goat, buck, **billy goat** *and* billy <nf>; she-goat, doe, **nanny goat** *and* nanny <nf>; **kid,** doeling; mountain goat

9 **swine** <see list>, **pig, hog,** porker; **shoat,** piggy, piglet, pigling; sucking *or* suckling pig; gilt; **boar, sow;** barrow; wild boar, tusker, razorback; warthog, babirusa

10 **horse;** horseflesh, hoss <nf>, critter <nf>; **equine,** mount, **nag** <nf>; **steed,** prancer, dobbin; charger, courser, war-horse, destrier <old>; Houyhnhnm <Jonathan Swift>; **colt,** foal, filly; **mare,** brood mare; **stallion, studhorse, stud,** top horse <nf>, entire horse, entire; gelding, purebred horse, thoroughbred, blood horse; wild horse, Przewalsky's horse, tarpan; **pony,** Shetland pony, Shetland, shelty, Iceland pony, Galloway, cob; **bronco,** bronc, range horse, Indian pony, cayuse, mustang; bucking bronco, buckjumper, sunfisher, broomtail; cowcutting horse, stock horse, roping horse, cow pony, circus horse

11 <colored horses> appaloosa, bay, blood bay, bayard, chestnut, liver chestnut, gray, dapple-gray, black, grizzle, roan, sorrel, dun, buckskin, pinto, paint, piebald, skewbald, palomino, seal brown, strawberry roan, calico pony, painted pony

12 <inferior horse> **nag, plug,** hack, jade, crock, garron <Scot & Ir>, crowbait <nf>, scalawag, rosinante; goat *and* stiff *and* dog <nf>; roarer, whistler; balky horse, balker, jughead; rogue; rackabones, scrag, stack of bones

13 **workhorse,** plow horse, beast of burden; **hunter;** stalking-horse, **saddle horse,** saddler, rouncy <old>, steed, **riding horse,** rider, palfrey, **mount;** remount; polo pony; post-horse; cavalry horse; **driving horse,** road horse, roadster, carriage horse, coach horse, gigster; hack, hackney; **draft horse,** dray horse, cart horse, shaft horse, pole horse, thill horse, thiller, fill horse *or* filler <nf>; wheelhorse, wheeler, lead, leader; pack horse, jument <old>, sumpter, sumpter horse, bidet; pit-pony; cow pony; war-horse

14 **race horse; show-horse, gaited horse,** racer, galloper, trotter, pacer, sidewheeler <nf>; stepper, high-stepper, cob, prancer, turf horse, sprinter; ambler, padnag, pad; racker; single-footer; steeplechaser; bangtail <nf>

15 <distinguished horses> Al Borak <Mohammed's winged horse of ascension>, Baiardo <Rinaldo's bay horse>, Black Beauty, Black Bess <Dick Turpin's horse>, Black Saladin <Warwick's horse>, Bucephalus <Alexander the Great's horse>, Buttermilk <Dale Evans' horse>, Champion <Gene Autry's horse>, Copenhagen <Wellington's horse at Waterloo>, Grani <Sigurd's magic horse>, Incitatus <Caligula's horse>, Marengo <Napoleon's white horse>, Pegasus <winged horse of the Muses>, Roan Barbary <favorite horse of Richard II>, Rosinante <Don Quixote's bony horse>, Scout <Tonto's horse>, Silver <the Lone Ranger's horse>, Sleipnir <Odin's eight-legged horse>, Tony <Tom Mix's horse>, Trigger <Roy Rogers' horse>, Topper <Hopalong Cassidy's horse>, Traveller <Robert E Lee's horse>, Vegliantino *or* Veillantif <Orlando's horse>, White Surrey <favorite horse of Richard III>; <race horses> Affirmed, Alydar, Assault, Citation, Dr Fager, Forego, John Henry, Kelso, Man O'War, Nashua, Native Dancer, Ruffian, Seabiscuit, Seattle Slew, Secretariat, Spectacular Bid, Swaps, Whirlaway

16 ass, donkey, burro, neddy *or* cuddy <Brit nf>, moke <Brit nf>, Rocky Mountain canary <W US>; **jackass,** jack, dickey <Brit nf>; jenny, jenny ass, jennet; **mule,** sumpter mule, sumpter; hinny, jennet

17 dog <see list>, **canine, pooch** *and* bow-wow <nf>; **pup, puppy,** puppy dog *and* perp <nf>, **whelp;** bitch, gyp <S US>, slut; toy dog, lap dog; working dog; ratter; watchdog, bandog; sheep dog, shepherd *or* shepherd's dog; hound; Seeing Eye dog, guide dog; guard dog, watchdog; police dog, sled dog; gazehound, sighthound; show dog, fancy dog, toy dog; man's best friend <nf>, bowwow, pooch; kennel, pack of dogs

18 sporting dog, **hunting dog,** hunter, field dog, bird dog, gundog, water dog, hound, courser, setter, pointer, spaniel, retriever

19 cur, mongrel, lurcher <Brit>, tyke, **mutt** <nf>; pariah dog

20 fox, reynard; **wolf,** timber wolf, lobo <W US>, **coyote,** brush wolf, prairie wolf, medicine wolf <W US>; dingo, jackal, **hyena;** Cape hunting dog, African hunting dog

21 cat <see list>, **feline,** pussy *and* **puss** *and* **pussycat** <nf>, domestic cat, house cat, tabby, grimalkin; house cat; **kitten, kitty** *and* kitty-cat <nf>; kit, kitling <Brit nf>; **tomcat,** tom; gib *or* gib-cat <Brit nf>; mouser; ratter; Cheshire cat, Chessycat <nf>; silver cat, Chinchilla cat; blue cat, Maltese cat; tiger cat, tabby cat; tortoise-shell cat, calico cat; alley cat

22 <wild cats> **big cat, jungle cat; lion,** Leo <nf>, *simba* <Swah>; **tiger,** Siberian tiger; **leopard,** panther, jaguar, cheetah; cougar, painter <S US>, puma, mountain lion, catamount *or* cat-a-mountain; lynx, ocelot; wildcat, bobcat, steppe cat, Pallas's cat

23 <wild animals> **bear,** bar <nf>; guinea pig, cavy; hedgehog, **porcupine,** quill pig <nf>; woodchuck, **groundhog, whistle-pig** <nf>; prairie dog, prairie squirrel; **raccoon,** coon; **opossum,** possum; **weasel,** mousehound <Brit>; **wolverine,** glutton; ferret, monk <nf>; **skunk,** polecat <nf>; zoril, stink cat <South Africa>, Cape polecat; foumart; **primate, simian; ape; monkey,** monk <nf>, chimpanzee, chimp

24 hare, leveret, jackrabbit; **rabbit, bunny** *and* bunny rabbit <nf>, lapin; cottontail; Belgian hare, leporide; buck, doe

25 reptile <see list>, reptilian; **lizard;** saurian, dinosaur; crocodile, crocodilian, alligator, gator <nf>; tortoise, turtle, terrapin; cold-blooded animal, poikilotherm, Reptilia, Squamata, Rhynchocephalia, Crocodilia

26 serpent, snake, ophidian; **viper,** pit viper; sea snake

27 amphibian <see list>, batrachian, croaker, paddock <nf>; **frog,** rani-, tree toad *or* frog, bullfrog; **toad,** hoptoad *or* hoppytoad; newt, salamander; **tadpole, polliwog;** caecilian, apodan, urodele, caudate, salientian, anuran

28 bird, fowl; dicky-bird *and* birdy *and* birdie <nf>; fowls of the air, birdlife, avifauna, Aves, feathered friends; baby bird, chick, nestling, fledgling; wildfowl, game bird; waterfowl, water bird, wading bird, diving bird; sea bird; shore bird; migratory bird, migrant, bird of passage; **songbird,** oscine bird, warbler, passerine bird, perching bird; cage bird; flightless bird, ratite; seed-eating bird, insect-eating bird, fruit-eating bird, fish-eating bird; **raptor,** bird of prey; **eagle,** bird of Jove, eaglet; **hawk, falcon; owl,** bird of Minerva, bird of night; peafowl, peahen, **peacock,** bird of Juno; **swan,** cygnet; **pigeon, dove,** squab; stormy *or* storm petrel, Mother Carey's chicken; fulmar, Mother Carey's goose

29 poultry, fowl, domestic fowl, barnyard fowl, barn-door fowl, dunghill fowl; **chicken** <see list>, chick, chicky *and* chickabiddy <nf>; **cock, rooster,** chanticleer; **hen,** biddy <nf>, partlet; cockerel, pullet; setting hen, brooder, broody hen; capon, poulard; broiler, fryer, spring chicken, roaster, stewing chicken; Bantam, banty <nf>; game fowl; guinea fowl, guinea cock, guinea hen; **goose,** gander, gosling; **duck,** drake, duckling; **turkey,** gobbler, turkey gobbler; turkey-cock, tom, tom turkey; hen turkey; poult

30 marine animal <see list>, denizen of the deep; **whale,** cetacean; **porpoise, dolphin,** sea pig; **sea serpent,** sea snake, Loch Ness monster, sea monster, Leviathan <Bible>; **fish** <see list>, game fish, tropical fish, panfish; **shark,** man-eating shark, man-eater; **salmon,** kipper, grilse, smolt, parr, alevin; **minnow** or minny <nf>, fry, fingerling; **sponge; plankton,** zooplankton, nekton, benthon, benthos, zoobenthos; **crustacean,** lobster, spiny lobster, **crab,** blueclaw, Dungeness crab, king crab, spider crab, land crab, stone crab, soft-shell crab; crayfish or crawfish or crawdaddy; **mollusc** <see list>, wentletrap, whelk, snail, cockle, mussel, **clam, oyster,** razor clam, quahog, steamer, toheroa, tridachna or giant clam

31 fish; saltwater fish, marine fish, freshwater fish; jawless fish, cyclostome, cartilaginous fish, elasmobranch, selachian, holocephalan, bony fish, lobe-finned fish, crossopterygian, dipnoan, ray-finned fish, teleost fish, flying fish, mouthbreeder, flatfish; food fish, game fish, aquarium fish, tropical fish, fossil fish; shoal, school

32 **invertebrate;** lower animal, protochordate, echinoderm, arthropod, arachnid, insect, crustacean <see list>, myriapod, mollusk, worm, coelenterate, sponge, protozoan or protozoon

33 **insect** <see list>, **bug; beetle;** arthropod; hexapod, myriapod; centipede, chilopod; millipede, diplopod; social insect; **mite; arachnid, spider,** tarantula, black widow spider, daddy longlegs or harvestman; **scorpion; tick;** larva, maggot, nymph, **caterpillar;** winged insect, **fly,** gnat, midge, mosquito, dragonfly, butterfly, moth, bee, wasp; creepy-crawly <nf>, pest

34 **ant,** emmet <nf>, pismire, pissant and antymire <nf>; red ant, black ant, fire ant, house ant, agricultural ant, carpenter ant, army ant; slave ant, slave-making ant; **termite,** white ant; queen, worker, soldier

35 **bee,** honeybee, bumblebee, carpenter bee; queen, queen bee, worker, drone, Africanized bee; **wasp; hornet,** yellow jacket

36 **locust,** acridian; **grasshopper,** hopper, hoppergrass <nf>; **cricket;** cicada, cicala, dog-day cicada, seventeen-year locust; stick insect, mantis

37 **vermin;** parasite; **louse,** head louse, body louse, grayback, cootie <nf>; crab, crab louse; weevil; nit; **flea,** sand flea, dog flea, cat flea, chigoe, chigger, jigger, red bug, mite, harvest mite; **roach, cockroach,** cucaracha <Sp>

38 bloodsucker, parasite; **leech; tick,** wood tick, deer tick; **mosquito,** skeeter <nf>, culex; bedbug, housebug <Brit>

39 **worm** <see list>; earthworm, angleworm, fishworm, night crawler, nightwalker <N US>;

measuring worm, inchworm; tapeworm, helminth

ADJS 40 **animal,** animalian, animalic, animalistic, animal-like, theriomorphic, zoic, zooidal; zoologic, zoological; **brutish, brutal,** brute, brutelike; **bestial, beastly,** beastlike; **wild,** feral; subhuman, soulless; dumb, "that wants discourse of reason"—Shakespeare; instinctual or instinctive, mindless, nonrational; half-animal, half-human, anthropomorphic, therianthropic

41 **vertebrate,** chordate, mammalian; viviparous; marsupial, cetacean

42 **canine,** doggish, doggy, doglike; vulpine, foxy, foxlike; lupine, wolfish, wolflike

43 **feline,** felid, cattish, catty, catlike; kittenish; leonine, lionlike; tigerish, tigerlike

44 ursine, bearish, bearlike

45 **rodent,** rodential; verminous; mousy, mouselike; ratty, ratlike

46 ungulate, hoofed, hooved; **equine,** hippic, horsy, horselike; **equestrian;** asinine, mulish; bovid, ruminant, "that chew the cud"—Bible; **bovine,** cowlike, cowish; bull-like, bullish, taurine; cervine, deerlike; caprine, caprid, hircine, goatish, goatlike; ovine, sheepish, sheeplike; porcine, swinish, piggish, hoggish

47 elephantlike, elephantine, pachydermous

48 **reptile,** reptilian, **reptilelike,** reptiloid, reptiliform; reptant, repent, creeping, crawling, slithering; **lizardlike,** saurian; crocodilian; **serpentine,** serpentile, serpentoid, serpentiform; **serpentlike;** snakish, **snaky, snakelike,** colubrine, ophidian, anguine <old>; viperish, viperous, vipery, viperine, viperoid, viperiform, viperlike; amphibian, batrachian, froggy, toadish, salamandrian

49 **birdlike,** birdy; avian, avicular; gallinaceous, rasorial; oscine, passerine, perching; columbine, columbaceous, dovelike; psittacine; aquiline, hawklike; anserine, anserous, goosy; nidificant, nesting, nest-building; nidicolous, altricial; nidifugous, precocial

50 **fishlike,** fishy; piscine, pisciform; piscatorial, piscatory; eellike; selachian, sharklike, sharkish

51 **invertebrate,** invertebral; protozoan, protozoal, protozoic; crustaceous, crustacean; molluscan, molluscoid

52 **insectile, insectlike,** buggy; verminous; lepidopterous, lepidopteran; weevily

53 **wormlike,** vermicular, vermiform; wormy

54 planktonic, nektonic, benthonic, zooplanktonic, zoobenthoic

55 **primates**

angwantibo	aye-aye
anthropoid ape	baboon
ape	Barbary ape

Bengal monkey
bonnet monkey *or*
  macaque
bush baby
capuchin
chacma
chimpanzee
colobus
drill
entellus
gibbon
gorilla
great ape
grivet
guenon
guereza
hanuman
howling monkey *or* howler
king monkey
langur
lemur

lion-tailed monkey *or*
  macaque
loris
macaque
man
mandrill
marmoset
mountain gorilla
orangutan *or* orang
owl monkey
pongid
proboscis monkey
rhesus
saki
siamang
sloth monkey
spider monkey
squirrel monkey
tamarin
tarsier
vervet

Romanov
Romney
Romney Marsh
Ryeland
Scottish blackface
Shetland
Shropshire

Southdown
Suffolk
Tajik
Targhee
Tibetan
Welsh Mountain
Wensleydale

58 breeds of swine

American Landrace
Berkshire
Cheshire
Chester White
Dorset
Duroc
Duroc Jersey
Hampshire
Hereford
Landrace
large black

large white
Mangalitsa
middle white
National Long White Lop-
  eared
Poland China
Romagna
Tamworth
Vietnamese Pot-bellied
Wessex saddleback
Yorkshire

56 breeds of cattle

Aberdeen Angus *or* Angus
  or black Angus
Africander
Alderney
Andalusian
Ayrshire
Beefalo
Belted Galloway
Black Angus
Brahman
Brown Swiss
Cattalo
Charolais
Dairy Shorthorn
Devon
Dexter
Durham
Dutch Belted
Egyptian
French Canadian
Fribourg
Galloway

Guernsey
Hereford
Holstein *or* Holstein-
  Friesian
Icelandic
Jersey
Lincoln Red
Longhorn
Norwegian Red
Polled Durham *or*
  Shorthorn
Polled Hereford
Red Poll *or* Red
  Polled
Red Sindhi
Santa Gertrudis
Shetland
Shorthorn
Sussex
Texas Longhorn
Welsh *or* Welsh Black
West Highland

59 breeds of dogs

affenpinscher
Afghan hound
Airedale *or* Airedale terrier
Akita
Alaskan malamute
Alsatian
American foxhound
American water spaniel
Australian cattle dog
Australian heeler
Australian terrier
Basenji
basset *or* basset hound
beagle
Bedlington terrier
Belgian sheepdog *or*
  shepherd
Bernese mountain dog
Bichon Frise
black Labrador
Blenheim spaniel
bloodhound *or* sleuth *or*
  sleuthhound
Border terrier
borzoi
Boston bull *or* terrier
Bouvier des Flandres
boxer
Briard
Brittany spaniel
Brussels griffon
bulldog *or* bull
bull mastiff
bull terrier
cairn terrier
carriage *or* coach dog
Chesapeake Bay retriever
Chihuahua

chow *or* chow chow
clumber spaniel
Clydesdale terrier
cocker spaniel
collie
coonhound
corgi
dachshund *or* sausage dog
  or sausage hound
Dalmatian
Dandie Dinmont
deerhound
Doberman pinscher
elkhound
English bulldog
English cocker spaniel
English foxhound
English setter
English springer spaniel
English toy spaniel
Eskimo dog *or* husky
field spaniel
foxhound
fox terrier
French bulldog
gazelle hound
German shepherd
German shorthaired
  pointer
German wirehaired pointer
giant schnauzer
golden retriever
Gordon setter
Great Dane
Great Pyrenees
greyhound
griffon
Groenendael

57 breeds of sheep

Abyssinian
American merino
American Rambouillet
American Tunis
Berber
Black-faced Highland
Blackhead Persian
broadtail
Cheviot
Columbia
Corriedale
Corsican
Cotswold

Dorset Down
Hampshire
Karakul
Kerry Hill
Leicester
Lincoln
Merino
Mongolian
Oxford *or* Oxford
  Down
Panama
Rambouillet
Romeldale

harrier
hound *or* hound-dog
   <S US>
husky
Irish setter
Irish terrier
Irish water spaniel
Irish wolfhound
Italian greyhound
Jack Russell terrier
Japanese spaniel *or*
   Japanese Chin
keeshond
kelpie
Kerry blue terrier
King Charles spaniel
Komondor
kuvasz
Labrador retriever
Lakeland terrier
Lhasa apso
malamute
Malinois
Maltese
Manchester terrier
mastiff
Mexican hairless
miniature pinscher
miniature poodle
miniature schnauzer
Newfoundland
Norfolk spaniel
Norwegian elkhound
Norwich terrier
Old English sheepdog
otterhound
papillon
Pekingese
pit bull terrier
pointer
police dog
Pomeranian
poodle
pug *or* pug dog *or*
   mops
puli

rat terrier
retriever
Rhodesian ridgeback
Rottweiler
Russian owtchar
Russian wolfhound
St. Bernard
Saluki
Samoyed
schipperke
schnauzer
Scottish deerhound
Scottish terrier
Sealyham terrier
setter
Shar-Pei
shepherd dog
Shetland sheepdog *or*
   sheltie
Shih Tzu
Siberian husky
silky terrier
Skye terrier
spaniel
spitz
springer spaniel
Staffordshire bull terrier
Sussex spaniel
terrier
toy poodle
toy spaniel
toy terrier
Vizsla
water spaniel
Weimaraner
Welsh collie
Welsh corgi
Welsh springer spaniel
Welsh terrier
West Highland white
   terrier
whippet
wirehaired terrier
wolfhound
yellow Labrador
Yorkshire terrier

60 breeds and varieties of domestic cats

Abyssinian cat
American shorthair
Angora cat
Balinese
blue-point Siamese
Burmese
calico *or* tortoiseshell
chartreuse cat
Chinese
chocolate-point
   Siamese
Cornish rex

domestic shorthair cat
Egyptian cat *or* mau
exotic shorthair
Havana brown
Himalayan
Kashmir
Maine coon
Malayan cat
Maltese
Manx
marmalade cat
Oriental Shorthair

Persian
rex
Russian blue
seal-point Siamese
Siamese

Singapura
sphynx
tabby *or* tabby-cat
tortoiseshell cat
Turkish cat

61 breeds of chickens

Ameraucana
Ancona
Andalusian
Araucana
Australorp
Bantam
Barred Plymouth Rock
Brahma
Buckeye
Buttercup
Campine
Cochin
Cornish
Crevecoeur
Delaware
Dorking
Faverolle
Frizzle
Hamburg
Holland
Houdan

Ixworth
Jersey black giant
Langshan
Leghorn
Minorca
New Hampshire *or* New
   Hampshire red
Orpington
Plymouth Rock
Rhode Island red
Rhode Island white
Rock
Rock Cornish
Silkie
Spanish
Sultan
Sumatra
Sussex
Turken
white Leghorn
Wyandotte

62 marine animals

cetacean
crustacean
dolphin
dugong
elephant seal
fur seal
harbor seal
manatee
octopus *or* octopod
phocid
pinniped
porpoise

sea calf
sea cow
sea dog
sea elephant
seal
sea lion
sea urchin
shellfish
sirenian
squid
walrus
whale

63 birds

albatross
auk
avocet
bald eagle
barn owl
bittern
blackbird
blue jay
bluebill
bluebird
bowerbird
bufflehead
bullfinch
bunting
buzzard
canary

cardinal
cassowary
catbird
chaffinch
chickadee
chicken
chicken hawk
chimney swift
cockatoo
condor
coot
cormorant
cowbird
crake
crane
crow

curlew
dipper
diver
dove
duck
dunlin
eagle
egret
emu
falcon
finch
flamingo
flycatcher
frigate bird
frogmouth
fulmar
gannet
gnatcatcher
goldfinch
gooney bird
goose
goshawk
grackle
grebe
greenfinch
grey heron
grouse
guinea fowl
gull
harrier
hawk
heron
honeycreeper
hummingbird
ibis
jackdaw
jaeger
jay
kestrel
king eider
kingfisher
kite
kiwi
lapwing
lark
loon
lovebird
magpie
mallard
man-o-war bird
meadowlark
merlin
mockingbird
mud hen
myna
nighthawk
nightingale
notornis
oriole
osprey

ostrich
ouzel
owl
oystercatcher
parakeet
parrot
partridge
peacock
pelican
penguin
petrel
pewit
pheasant
pigeon
pipit
plover
pochard
prairie chicken
puffin
purple martin
quail
raptor
ratite
raven
razorbill
redpoll
redwing
rhea
roadrunner
robin
rook
sandpiper
sapsucker
scissortail
seabird
seagull
shag
shama
shelduck
shrike
skua
snipe
snowbird
sparrow
song thrush
spoonbill
starling
stork
sunbird
surfbird
swallow
swan
takahe
tern
thrasher
thrush
tit
towhee
turkey
vulture

wader
wagtail
warble
waterfowl
weaverbird
whippoorwill
whitethroat

64 crustaceans
amphipod
barnacle
bass yabby
beach flea
branchiopod
brine shrimp
copepod
crab
crawdad
crawfish
crayfish
cumacean
daphnia
fiddler crab
hairy crab
hermit crab
horseshoe crab
isopod
king crab
krill
lobster
mantas shrimp

65 fish
albacore
alewife
alligator gar
amberjack
angelfish
arauana
archerfish
asp
balloonfish
barracuda
basking shark
bass
batfish
beluga
betta
blackfish
blindfish
blowfish
bluefish
bonefish
bowfin
boxfish
bream
brook trout
buffalofish
bullhead
butterfish

wigeon
woodcock
woodpecker
wren
yellow finch
yellowbird
yellowhammer

mussel shrimp
opossum shrimp
ostracod
pea crab
pebble crab
prawn
sailor shrimp
sand hopper
sand skater
sea centipede
sea flea
shellfish
shrimp
skeleton louse
soft-shell crab
spider crab
sponge crab
sponge shrimp
stenetrium
tadpole shrimp
water flea
weed shrimp

butterflyfish
candlefish
capelin
cardinalfish
carp
catfish
cavefish
char
chimaera
chub
cichlid
clingfish
clown anemone
clownfish
cod
codfish
cowfish
cutlassfish
damselfish
danios
darter
devilfish
devil ray
discus
doctorfish
dogfish
dolphin

dragonfish
eel
electric eel
electric ray
flatfish
flounder
flying fish
frogfish
garpike
giant bass
globefish
goatfish
goby
goldfish
gourami
grayling
grouper
gudgeon
guppy
haddock
hagfish
hake
halibut
hammerhead shark
hatchetfish
headstander
herring
hogfish
ide
kelpfish
killifish
kingfish
koi
lake trout
lanternfish
lionfish
loach
lumpfish
mackerel
manta
marlin
minnow
molly
mudfish
mudskipper
mullet
needlefish
northern pike
oarfish
oscar
paddlefish
paradise fish
parrotfish
perch
pickerel
pike

pikeperch
pipefish
piranha
platyfish
pollack
pompano
porgy
puffer
pupfish
rainbow trout
ray
redfin
redfish
red snapper
sailfish
salmon
salmon trout
sardine
sawfish
sea bass
sea horse
seaperch
sea trout
shad
shark
shiner
skate
smelt
snapper
snook
sole
spearfish
squawfish
stingray
striped bass
sturgeon
sucker
sunfish
surffish
swordfish
swordtail
tang
tarpon
tetra
tigerfish
tiger shark
triggerfish
trout
tuna
weakfish
whitefish
white shark
wimplefish
yellowtail
zander
zebrafish

66 fungi
agarics
ascomycetes

Ascomycota
aspergillus

basidiomycetes
Basidiomycota
bird's-nest fungus
black bread mold
black mold
blue mold
blue-green mold
boletus
bracket fungus
bread mold
brittlegill
cellular slime
  molds
chanterelle
club fungus
coral fungus
crumblecap
cup fungus
dead-man's fingers
deathcap
deuteromycetes
Deuteromycota
downy mildew
dung fungus
earth tongue
earthstar
Eumycota
false mildew
false morel
field mushroom
flask fungus
Fungi Imperfecti
gill fungus
green mold
groundwart
inky cap
jelly fungus
lorchel
Mastigomycotina
mildew
milkcap

67 insects
acarid
acarine
ant
ant lion
aphid
apple maggot
arachnid
Arachnida
armyworm
bagworm
bark beetle
bedbug
bee
beetle
billbug
black fly
black widow

mold
moniliales
morel
mushroom
mushroom pimple
myxomycetes
Myxomycota
oyster cap
penicillium
phycomycetes
pink gill
pore fungus
powdery mildew
puffball
read bread mold
ringstalk
ringworm fungus
roof mushroom
rust
sac fungus
scalecap
sheath mushroom
shell fungus
skin fungus
slime molds
slime mushroom
smoothcap
smut
stinkhorn
thrush fungus
toadstool
tooth fungus
tricholoma
truffle
verticillium
waxy cap
webcap
woodcrust
yeast
zygomycetes
Zygomycota

blackbeetle
bloodworm
boll weevil
bookworm
borer
bug
bumblebee
butterfly
carpet beetle
caterpillar
centipede
chafer
chigger
chinch bug
click beetle
cockroach
cootie

cricket
cutworm
daddy-longlegs
deer fly
doodlebug
dragonfly
drone
dung beetle
emperor butterfly
false scorpion
firefly
flea
fruit fly
gadfly
glowworm
gnat
grasshopper
grub
gypsy moth
harvestman
honeybee
hornet
horse fly
housefly
Japanese bettle
June bug
ladybug
leafhopper
locust
long-horned beetle
looper
louse
maggot
mayfly
mealworm
medfly
midge

mite
mosquito
moth
nit
nymph
opilionid
phalangid
pismire
praying mantis
pseudoscorpion
pupa
queen bee
roach
scale
scorpion
screwworm
silkworm
skipper
snapping beetle
soldier ant
spider
stag beetle
tarantula
tent fly
termite
tick
tiger beetle
tiger moth
wasp
water beetle
water bug
weevil
wireworm
woodworm
woolly bear
worker
yellow jacket

68 mollusks

amphineuran
bivalve
cephalopod
chambered nautilus
chiton
clam
conch
cone
cowry
cuttlefish
gastropod
lamellibranch
lampshell
limpet
murex

mussel
neopilina
octopod
octopus
oyster
rock shell
scallop
scaphopod
shellfish
slug
snail
spider conch
squid
tusk shell
volute

69 reptiles and amphibians

agama
alligator
anaconda
apodan
asp

auratus
basilisk
blindworm
boa
bog turtle

bullfrog
caecilian
caiman
chameleon
chelonid
chicken turtle
Chinese water dragon
cobra
congo snake
constrictor
cricket frog
crocodile
dinosaur
flying dragon
frog
galliwasp
gecko
Gila monster
glass snake
green frog
horned toad
iguana
Komodo dragon
lizard
loggerhead turtle

mamba
marine toad
monitor
mudpuppy
newt
pig frog
python
rainbow snake
rattlesnake
red-eyed tree frog
salamander
serpent
skink
slow worm
snake
snapping turtle
soft-shelled turtle
spring peeper
terrapin
toad
tortoise
tuatara
turtle
viper
waterdog

70 worms

angleworm
annelid
apple pomice
  worm
armyworm
arrowworm
bearded worm
bloodworm
bollworm
bookworm
cankerworm
clamworm
composting worm
cottonworm
cutworm
dung worm
earthworm
earworm
eelworm
fecal worm
fireworm
fish worm
flatworm
fluke
glowworm
grey worm
hairworm
heligrammite
hookworm
hornworm
horsehair worm
inchworm
leech

looper
lugworm
manure worm
measuringworm
nematode
night crawler
pinworm
platyhelminth
polychaete
red hybrid
redworm
red wiggler
ribbon worm
rotifer
roundworm
sandworm
sea mouse
sea worm
silkworm
stink worm
striped worm
tapeworm
threadworm
tiger worm
tobacco hornworm
tomato hornworm
tubeworm
vinegar eel
vinegar worm
webworm
whipworm
wireworm
woodworm

71 animal collective names

<antelopes> herd
<ants> colony
<apes> shrewdness
<asses> pace, herd, drove
<baboons> congress
<badgers> cete
<bass> shoal
<bears> sleuth, sloth
<beavers> colony
<bees> colony, grist, hive, hum, swarm
<birds> dissimulation, flight, volery
<bison> herd, troop
<boars> singular, sounder
<bovines> herd
<buffalo> herd
<camels> herd, flock
<caterpillars> army
<cats and dogs> rain
<cats> clowder, clutter
<cattle> herd, drove
<chickens> brood, clutch, flock, peep
<clams> bed
<colts> rag
<cows> flink, herd
<cranes> sedge, siege
<crickets> orchestra
<crows> murder
<deers> herd
<dogs> kennel, pack
<doves> dole, dule, flight
<ducks> brace, flock, gaggle, paddling, raft, team
<eagles> convocation
<eels> knot
<eggs> clutch
<elephants> herd, host, parade
<elks> gang, herd
<falcons> cast, passager
<ferrets> business
<finches> charm
<fishes> draught, school, shoal
<foxes> leash, skulk
<frogs> army, knot, colony
<geese> flock, gaggle, skein, wedge
<giraffes> herd
<gnats> cloud, horde
<goats> tribe, trip, herd
<goldfinches> charm
<gorillas> band
<grasshoppers> cluster

<grouses> covey
<hares> down, husk, leap
<hawks> cast, kettle
<hedgehogs> prickle
<hens> brood
<herons> siege
<hippopotami> huddle
<hogs> drift
<horses> harras, herd, pair, stable, team
<hounds> cry, mute, pack
<hummingbirds> hover
<jack rabbits> husk
<jays> band, party
<jellyfish> smack
<kangaroos> mob, troop
<kittens> kindle, kendle, litter
<lapwings> deceit
<larks> ascension, chattering, exaltation
<leopards> leap
<lions> pride
<locusts> host, plague
<magpies> tidings
<mallards> sord, sort
<mares> stud
<martens> richness
<mice> nest
<moles> labor, lobor
<monkeys> tribe, troop
<mules> barren, pack, rake, span
<nightingales> watch
<owls> parliament, wisdom
<oxen> team, yoke, drove, herd
<oysters> bed
<parrots> company
<partridges> covey
<peacocks> muster, ostentation
<penguins> colony
<pheasants> bouquet, covey, nest, nye, nide
<pigeons> flock
<pigs> drove, litter, herd
<plovers> congregation, wing
<polar bears> aurora
<ponies> string
<porpoises> school
<quails> bevy, covey
<rabbits> colony, nest
<racehorses> field
<ravens> conspiracy, unkindness

<reindeers> herd
<rhinoceroses> crash
<seals> pod, herd, school, trip, harem, rookery, spring
<sheeps> drove, flock, herd
<skunks> stench
<slugs> cornucopia
<snakes> bed, slither
<sparrows> host
<squirrels> dray
<starlings> murmuration
<storks> mustering
<swallows> flight
<swans> ballet, bevy, wedge
<swines> drift, sounder

72 animal young names

<antelope> calf
<bear> cub, whelp
<beaver> kit, kitten, pup
<bird> fledgling, nestling
<bison> calf
<bovine> calf
<cat> kit, kitten, kitty, puss, pussy
<cattle> calf, yearling
<chicken> chick, pullet, cockerel
<cow> calf, heifer
<deer> fawn
<dog> pup, whelp
<duck> duckling
<eagle> eaglet, fledgling
<elephant> calf
<elk> calf
<falcon> cast
<fish> fingerling, fry
<fox> cub, kit, pup, whelp
<frog> polliwog, tadpole
<giraffe> cub, whelp
<goat> kid
<goose> gosling
<grouse> cheeper, poult
<hare> leveret
<hawk> eyas
<hen> chick, pullet
<hippopotamus> calf

<teal> spring
<tigers> hide, streak
<toads> knot
<trout> hover
<turkeys> rafter
<turtledoves> pitying
<turtles> bale, bevy
<unicorns> blessing
<wasps> pail
<waterfowl> plump
<weasels> gam, sneak
<whales> gam, herd, pod, shoal, surfers
<wolves> pack, rout
<woodchucks> fall
<woodpeckers> descent
<worms> wriggle
<zebras> herd, stripe

<horse> colt, filly, filt, foal, yearling
<kangaroo> joey
<lion> cub, whelp
<monkey> baby
<moose> cub, calf
<owl> owlet
<oyster> spat
<partridge> cheeper
<pig> piglet, shoat, farrow, suckling
<pigeon> squab, squeaker
<quail> cheeper
<rabbit> bunny, kit, leveret
<reindeer> fawn
<rhinoceros> calf
<rooster> cockerel
<sea lion> pup
<seal> calf, pup
<shark> cub
<sheep> lamb, lambkin, cosset, hog, yearling
<swan> cygnet
<swine> piglet, shoat, farrow
<tiger> cub, whelp
<turkey> poult, chick)
<whale> calf
<wolf> cub, whelp
<zebra> colt, foal

312 HUMANKIND

NOUNS 1 **humankind, mankind, womankind, personkind, man,** human species, **human race,** race of man, human family, the family of man, **humanity,** human beings, mortals, earthlings, mortality, flesh, mortal flesh, clay; generation of man <old>, *le genre humain* <Fr>, "the plumeless genus of bipeds"—Plato, homo, genus Homo, **Homo sapiens,** Hominidae, hominids; archaic Homo; **race,** strain, stock, subrace, infrarace, subspecies; **culture** 373.2; ethnic group; ethnicity, ethnicism, roots <nf>; **society,** speech community, **ethnic group;** community, folk, persons, **the people, the populace,** world population; **nationality, nation**

2 <races of humankind> **Caucasoid** or **Caucasian** or **white race;** Nordic subrace, Alpine subrace, Mediterranean subrace; dolichocephalic people, brachycephalic people; xanthochroi, melanochroi; Archaic Caucasoid or archaic white or Australoid race; Polynesian race; **Negroid** or **black race;** Nilotic race, Melanesian race, Papuan race; Pygmoid race; Bushman race; **Mongoloid** or **Mongolian** or **yellow race;** Malayan or Malaysian or brown race; prehistoric races; majority, racial or ethnic majority; minority, racial or ethnic minority; persons of color

3 **Caucasian, white man** or **woman, white person,** paleface and ofay and the Man and Mister Charley and whitey and honky <nf>; Australian aborigine, blackfellow <Austral>; **Negro, black man** or **woman, black,** colored person, person of color, darky and spade and nigger <nf>; African-American; negritude, Afroism, blackness; pygmy, Negrito, Negrillo; Bushman; **Native American,** Indian, American Indian, Amerindian, Amerind, Red Indian <Brit>, red man or woman; injun and redskin <nf>; Latino; Mongolian, yellow man or woman, **Oriental,** Asian; gook and slant-eye <nf>; Malayan, brown man; mixed race, mulatto, quadroon, half-breed

4 **the people** 606, the populace, the population, the public, the world, everyone, everybody

5 **person, human, human being, man, woman, child,** member of the human race or family, Adamite, daughter of Eve; ethnic; **mortal,** life, **soul,** living soul; **being,** creature, fellow creature, clay, ordinary clay, flesh and blood, the naked ape, the noble animal; **individual;** personage, **personality, personhood,** individuality; **body;** somebody, one, someone; earthling, groundling, terran, worldling, tellurian; **ordinary person;** head, hand, nose; fellow <nf> 76.5; gal <nf> 77.6

6 **human nature, humanity;** frail or fallen humanity, Adam, the generation of Adam, Adam's seed or offspring

7 **God's image, lord of creation,** God's creation; homo faber, symbol-using animal; "the measure of all things"—Protagoras, "a reasoning animal"—Seneca, "the most intelligent of animals—and the most silly"—Diogenes, "a tool-using animal"—

Carlyle, "a tool-making animal"—Benjamin Franklin, "the only animal that blushes or needs to"—Mark Twain, "an intelligence served by organs"—Emerson, rational animal, animal capable of reason, "this quintessence of dust"—Shakespeare, "political animal"—Aristotle; "the naked ape"—Desmond Morris

8 **humanness, humanity,** mortality; **human nature,** the way you are; **frailty,** human frailty, human fallibility, weakness; **human weakness,** weakness of the flesh, flesh, "one touch of nature"—Shakespeare, the weaknesses human flesh is heir to; human equation

9 humanization, humanizing; **anthropomorphism,** pathetic fallacy, anthropopathism, anthropomorphology

10 **anthropology,** science of man; cultural anthropology, physical anthropology, anthropogeny, anthropography, anthropogeography, human geography, demography, human ecology, anthropometry, craniometry, craniology, ethnology, ethnography, paleoanthropology, paleoethnology; behavioral science, sociology, social anthropology, social psychology, psychology 92; anatomy; **anthropologist,** ethnologist, ethnographer; sociologist; demographics, population study, population statistics; demographer

11 **humanism;** naturalistic humanism, scientific humanism, secular humanism; religious humanism; Christian humanism, integral humanism; new humanism; anthroposophy

VERBS 12 **humanize,** anthropomorphize, make human, civilize

ADJS 13 **human;** hominal; creaturely, creatural; Adamite or Adamitic; **frail, weak,** fleshly, finite, **mortal; only human;** earthborn, of the earth, earthy, tellurian, unangelic; humanistic; man-centered, homocentric, anthropocentric; anthropological, ethnographic, ethnological; demographic, epigraphic; social, societal, sociological

14 **manlike, anthropoid,** humanoid, hominid; anthropomorphic, anthropopathic, therioanthropic

15 **personal, individual,** private, peculiar, idiosyncratic; person-to-person, one-to-one, one-on-one

16 **public, general, common; communal, societal, social;** civic, civil; **national,** state; international, cosmopolitan, supernatural, supranational

ADVS 17 **humanly,** mortally, after the manner of men

WORD ELEMENTS 18 anthrop-, anthropo-, homin-, homini-

313 SEASON

<time of year>

NOUNS **1 season,** time of year, season of the year, **period,** annual period; dry *or* rainy *or* cold season, monsoon; theatrical *or* opera *or* concert season; **social season,** the season; dead *or* off-season; baseball season, football season, basketball season, hunting season, etc; open season, closed season; seasonality, periodicity 850.2; **seasonableness** 843.1; seasonal affective disorder *or* SAD

2 spring, springtide, **springtime,** seedtime *or* budtime, Maytime, Eastertide; *primavera* <Ital>, prime, prime of the year, vernal equinox, "the boyhood of the year"—Tennyson, "Sweet Spring, full of sweet days and roses"—George Herbert, "the time of the singing of birds"—Bible

3 summer, summertide, **summertime,** good old summertime; growing season; midsummer; **dog days,** canicular days; the silly season, high summer; summer solstice; estivation

4 autumn, fall, fall of the year, fall of the leaf, harvest, harvest time, harvest home; autumnal equinox; "Season of mists and mellow fruitfulness!"—Keats

5 Indian summer, St Martin's summer, St Luke's summer, little summer of St Luke, St Austin's *or* St Augustine's summer, "the dead Summer's soul"—Mary Clemmer

6 winter, wintertide, **wintertime;** midwinter; Christmastime *or* Christmastide, Yule *or* Yuletide; winter solstice; hibernation

7 equinox, vernal equinox, autumnal equinox; **solstice,** summer solstice, winter solstice

VERBS **8** summer, winter, overwinter, spend *or* pass the spring, summer, etc; hibernate, estivate

ADJS **9 seasonal,** in *or* out of season, in season and out of season, off-season; early-season, mid-season, late-season; **spring,** springlike, vernal; **summer,** summery, summerly, summerlike, canicular, aestival; midsummer; **autumn,** autumnal; **winter,** wintry, wintery, hibernal, hiemal, brumal, boreal, arctic 1023.14, winterlike, snowy, icy; midwinter; equinoctial, solstitial, periodic

314 MORNING, NOON

NOUNS **1 morning,** morn, morningtide, morning time, morntime, matins, morrow <old>, waking time, reveille, get-up time <nf>, **forenoon;** *ante meridiem* <L> *or* **AM,** Ack Emma <Brit old>; "dewy morn"—Byron; this morning, this AM <nf>; early bird; breakfast time

2 Morning, Aurora, Eos; "daughter of the dawn"—

Homer, "meek-eyed Morn, mother of dews"—James Thomson

3 dawn, the dawn of day, dawning, **daybreak,** dayspring, day-peep, **sunrise, sunup** <nf>, cockcrowing *or* cocklight <Brit nf>, light 1025, first light, daylight, aurora; **break of day,** peep of day, **crack of dawn,** prime, prime of the morning, first blush *or* flush of the morning, brightening *or* first brightening; "the opening eyelids of the morn"—Milton, "vestibule of Day"—Bayard Taylor; chanticleer *or* chantecler

4 foredawn, twilight, morning twilight, half-light, glow, dawnlight, first light, "the dawn's early light"—Francis Scott Key, crepuscule, aurora; **the small hours;** alpenglow

5 noon, noonday, noontide, nooning <nf>, noontime, **high noon, midday,** meridian, *meridiem* <L>, twelve o'clock, 1200 hours, eight bells; noonlight, "the blaze of noon"—Milton; meridian devil *or* *daemonium meridianum* <L>; lunchtime; sext

ADJS **6 morning,** matin, matinal, matutinal, **antemeridian;** auroral, dawn, dawning; forenoon

7 noon, noonday, noonish, **midday,** meridian, twelve-o'clock, high-noon; noonlit

ADVS **8 in the morning,** before noon, mornings <nf>; at sunrise, at dawn, at dawn of day, at cockcrow, at first light, **at the crack** *or* **break of dawn;** with the sun, with the lark

9 at noon, at midday, at twelve-o'clock sharp

315 EVENING, NIGHT

NOUNS **1 afternoon,** *post meridiem* <L> *or* **PM;** this afternoon, this aft <nf>, this PM <nf>; matinee; siesta

2 evening, eve, even, evensong time *or* hour, **eventide,** vesper, crepuscle; **close of day,** decline *or* fall of day, shut of day, gray of the evening, grayness 39, evening's close, when day is done; **nightfall, sunset, sundown,** setting sun, going down of the sun, cockshut *and* cockshut time *and* cockshut light <nf>, retreat; shank of the afternoon *or* evening <nf>, the cool of the evening; "the expiring day"—Dante, "evening's calm and holy hour"—S G Bulfinch; cocktail hour, suppertime, dinnertime

3 dusk, dusking time *or* -tide, dusk-dark *and* dust-dark *and* dusty-dark <nf>, **twilight,** evening twilight, crepuscule, crepuscular light, gloam, **gloaming,** glooming; duskiness, duskishness, brown of dusk, brownness 40, candlelight, candlelighting, owllight *or* owl's light, cocklight <Brit nf>, "the pale dusk of the impending night"—Longfellow

4 night, nighttime, nighttide, lights-out, taps, bedtime, sleepy time <nf>, **darkness** 1027, blackness 38, "sable-vested Night, eldest of things"—Milton, "empress of silence, and the queen of sleep"—Christopher Marlowe; dark of night

5 eleventh hour, curfew

6 midnight, dead of night, hush of night, the witching hour; "the very witching time of night"—Shakespeare, "outpost of advancing day"—Longfellow; midnight hours, small *or* wee small hours; late-night *or* midnight supper *or* snack

ADJS **7 afternoon,** postmeridian

8 evening, evensong, vesper, vespertine *or* vespertinal, vesperal; **twilight,** twilighty, twilit, crepuscular; **dusk,** dusky, duskish

9 nocturnal, night, **nightly,** nighttime; nightlong, all-night; night-fallen; midnight

10 benighted, night-overtaken

ADVS **11 nightly,** nights <nf>, at *or* by night; **overnight,** through the night, all through the night, nightlong, the whole night, all night

WORD ELEMENTS **12** noc-, nocto-, nocti-, nyct-, nycto-, nycti-

316 RAIN

NOUNS **1 rain, rainfall,** fall, **precipitation,** moisture, wet, rainwater, raininess; **shower, sprinkle,** flurry, patter, pitter-patter, splatter, intermittent rain *or* showers; streams of rain, sheet of rain, splash *or* spurt of rain, fine rain, light rain, occasional rain *or* showers, April showers; **drizzle,** mizzle; **mist,** misty rain, Scotch mist; evening mist; fog drip; blood rain; raindrop, unfrozen hydrometeor; acid rain

2 rainstorm, brash *and* scud <Scot>; **cloudburst,** rainburst, burst of rain, torrent of rain, torrential rain *or* downpour; waterspout, spout, rainspout, **downpour,** downflow, downfall, pour, pouring *or* pelting *or* teeming *or* drowning rain, spate <Scot>, plash <nf>, **deluge, flood,** heavy rain, driving *or* gushing rain, drenching *or* soaking rain, drencher, soaker, gullywasher, pluviosity, goosedrownder <nf>, lovely weather for ducks

3 thunderstorm, thundersquall, thundergust, thundershower; electric storm

4 wet weather, raininess, rainy weather, stormy *or* dirty weather, rainy season, cat-and-dog weather <nf>, spell of rain, wet; rainy day; **rains,** rainy *or* wet season, spring rains, **monsoon;** predominance of Aquarius, reign of St Swithin; flood

5 rainmaking, seeding, cloud seeding, nucleation, artificial nucleation; **rainmaker,** rain doctor, cloud seeder; dry ice, silver iodide

6 Jupiter Pluvius, Zeus; Thor

7 rain gauge, pluviometer, pluvioscope, pluviograph; ombrometer, ombrograph; udometer, udomograph; hyetometer, hyetometrograph, hyetograph

8 rainbow, arc, double rainbow, primary rainbow, secondary rainbow, fogdog, fogbow *or* white rainbow, mistbow *or* seadog

9 <science of precipitation> hydrometeorology, hyetology, hyetography; pluviography, pluviometry, ombrology

VERBS **10 rain, precipitate,** rain down, fall; weep; **shower,** shower down; **sprinkle,** spit *and* spritz <nf>, spatter, patter, pitter-patter, plash; **drizzle,** mizzle; **pour,** stream, stream down, pour with rain, **pelt,** pelt down, drum, tattoo, come down in torrents *or* sheets *or* buckets *or* curtains, **rain cats and dogs** <nf>, rain tadpoles *or* bullfrogs *or* pitchforks <nf>, "rain daggers with their points downward"—Robert Burton; rainmake, seed clouds

ADJS **11 rainy, showery;** pluvious *or* pluviose *or* pluvial; **drizzly,** drizzling, mizzly, drippy; **misty,** misty-moisty; torrential, pouring, streaming, pelting, drumming, driving, blinding, cat-and-doggish <nf>; wet

12 pluviometric *or* pluvioscopic *or* pluviographic, ombrometric *or* ombrographic, udometric *or* udographic, hyetometric, hyetographic, hyetometrographic; hydrometeorological, hyetological

317 AIR, WEATHER

NOUNS **1 air;** ether; ozone <nf>; thin air, rarity

2 atmosphere; aerosphere, gaseous envelope *or* environment *or* medium *or* blanket, welkin, lift <nf>; biosphere, ecosphere, noosphere; air mass; atmospheric component, atmospheric gas; atmospheric layer *or* stratum *or* belt <see list>

3 weather, climate, clime; **the elements,** forces of nature; microclimate, macroclimate; weather situation, weather pattern, weather conditions; fair weather, calm weather, halcyon days, good weather; stormy weather 671.4; rainy weather 316.4; windiness 318.15; heat wave, hot weather 1019.7; cold wave, cold weather 1023.3

4 weather map; isobar, isobaric *or* isopiestic line; isotherm, isothermal line; isometric, isometric line; frontal system; high, high-pressure area, ridge; low, low-pressure area; front, wind-shift line, squall line; cold front, polar front, cold sector; warm front; occluded front, occlusion, stationary front; air mass; thermal, downdraft, updraft; cyclone, anticyclone; air pressure, air temperature, heat index, temperature-humidity index, dewpoint;

humidity, relative humidity; precipitation; wind speed, wind strength, chill factor, wind-chill factor

5 meteorology, weather science, aerology, aerography, air-mass analysis, weatherology, climatology, climatography, microclimatology, forecasting, long-range forecasting; barometry; pneumatics 1038.5; anemology 318.16; nephology 319.5 anemometry, anemology, hyetography, nephology, micrometeorology, macrometeorology, mesometeorology, agricultural meteorology, aviation meteorology, maritime meteorology, hydrometeorology, mountain meteorology, planetary meteorology, atmospheric physics

6 meteorologist, weather scientist, aerologist, aerographer, weatherologist; climatologist, microclimatologist; **weatherman, weather forecaster,** weather prophet; **weather report,** weather forecast; weather bureau; weather ship; weather station; weather-reporting network

7 weather forecast, forecast, weather report, regional forecast, local forecast, general outlook, travel report, boating report, small craft advisory, long-term forecast, 5-day forecast, storm watch *or* warning, tornado watch *or* warning, hurricane watch *or* warning

8 weather instrument, meteorological *or* aerological instrument; **barometer,** aneroid barometer, glass, weatherglass; barograph, barometrograph, recording barometer, mercury barometer; thermometer, thermograph; aneroidograph; vacuometer; hygrometer; wind gauge, anemometer, anemograph, wind sock, wind cone, wind sleeve, drogue, weathercock; rain gauge, pluviometer, udometer; weather balloon, radiosonde; weather satellite, weather radar; hurricane-hunter aircraft; weather vane 318.17

9 ventilation, cross-ventilation, **airing,** aerage, perflation, refreshment; fanning, **aeration; air conditioning,** air cooling; oxygenation, oxygenization

10 ventilator; aerator; air conditioner, air filter, air cooler, ventilating *or* cooling system; blower; heat pump; air passage; fan

VERBS **11 air,** air out, **ventilate,** cross-ventilate, wind, refresh, freshen; **air-condition,** air-cool; **fan,** winnow; **aerate,** airify, aerify; oxygenate, oxygenize

ADJS **12 airy,** aery, **aerial,** aeriform, airlike, aeriferous, **pneumatic,** ethereal; exposed, roomy, light; airish, breezy; open-air, alfresco; **atmospheric,** tropospheric, stratospheric

13 climatal, climatic, climatical, climatographical, **elemental;** meteorological, meteorologic, aerologic, aerological, aerographic, aerographical, climatologic, climatological; macroclimatic, microclimatic, microclimatologic; barometric,

barometrical, baric, barographic; isobaric, isopiestic, isometric; high-pressure, low-pressure; cyclonic, anti-cyclonic; seasonal

14 atmospheric layers

boundary layer	mesosphere
chemosphere	outer atmosphere
D layer *or* region	ozone layer *or*
E *or* Heaviside *or* Kennelly-	ozonosphere
Heaviside layer *or* region	stratopause
exosphere	stratosphere
F$_1$ layer *or* region	substratosphere
F$_2$ *or* Appleton layer *or*	thermosphere
region	tropopause
ionosphere	troposphere
isothermal region	upper atmosphere
lower atmosphere	Van Allen belt *or* radiation
magnetosphere	belt

318 WIND
<airflow>

NOUNS **1 wind,** current, **air current,** current of air, **draft,** movement of air, stream, stream of air, flow of air; updraft, uprush; downdraft, downrush; microburst; indraft, inflow, inrush; crosscurrent, crosswind, undercurrent; fall wind, gravity wind, katabatic wind, anabatic wind, head wind, tail wind, following wind; wind aloft; jet stream, upper-atmosphere *or* upper-atmospheric wind, high-altitude wind, gradient wind, geostrophic wind, prevailing wind; surface wind, mountain wind, valley wind; wind shift, wind shear

2 "scolding winds"—Shakespeare, "the wings of the wind"—Bible

3 <wind god; the wind personified> Aeolus, Boreas, Aquilo <north wind>; Eurus <east wind>; Zephyr *or* Zephyrus, Favonius <west wind>; Notus, Auster <south wind>; Caurus *or* Caecias <northwest wind>; Afer *or* Africus <southwest wind>; Argestes <northeast wind>

4 puff, puff of air *or* wind, breath, breath of air, flatus, waft, capful of wind, whiff, whiffet, stir of air

5 breeze, light *or* gentle wind *or* breeze, softblowing wind, **zephyr,** gale <old>, air, light air, moderate breeze; fresh *or* stiff breeze; cool *or* cooling breeze; land breeze; sea breeze, onshore breeze, ocean breeze, cat's-paw

6 gust, wind gust, **blast,** blow, flaw, **flurry,** scud <Scot>, squall

7 hot wind; snow eater, thawer; chinook, **chinook wind;** simoom, samiel; foehn *or* föhn; khamsin; harmattan; sirocco *or* yugo; solano; Santa Ana; volcanic wind

8 wintry wind, winter wind, raw wind, chilling *or* freezing wind, bone-chilling wind, sharp *or* piercing wind, cold *or* icy wind, biting wind, the hawk <nf>, nipping *or* nippy wind, "a nipping and an eager air"—Shakespeare, icy blasts; Arctic *or* boreal *or* hyperboreal *or* hyperborean blast; wind chill *or* wind chill factor

9 **north wind, norther,** mistral, bise, tramontane, Etesian winds, meltemi, vardarac, Papagayo wind; northeaster, **nor'easter,** Euroclydon *or* gregale *or* gregal *or* gregau, bura, Tehuantepec wind, Tehuantepecer; northwester, **nor'wester;** southeaster, **sou'easter;** southwester, **sou'wester,** kite-wind, libeccio; **east wind,** easter, easterly, levanter, sharav; **west wind,** wester, westerly; **south wind,** souther, southerly buster <Austral>

10 prevailing wind; polar easterlies; prevailing westerlies, prevailing southwesterlies, prevailing northwesterlies, antitrades; trade winds *or* trades; antitrade winds; doldrums, wind-equator; horse latitudes, roaring forties; intertropical convergence zone *or* ITCZ; equatorial low *or* doldrums

11 <naut terms> **head wind, beam wind, tail wind,** following wind, fair *or* favorable wind, apparent *or* relative wind, backing wind, veering wind, slant of wind; onshore wind, offshore wind, wind shear

12 **windstorm,** vortex, eddy, big *or* great *or* fresh *or* strong *or* stiff *or* high *or* howling *or* spanking wind, ill *or* dirty *or* ugly wind; storm, storm wind, stormy winds, **tempest,** tempestuous wind; williwaw; **blow,** violent *or* heavy blow; **squall,** thick squall, black squall, white squall; squall line, wind-shift line, line squall; line storm; equinoctial; **gale,** half a gale, whole gale; tropical cyclone, **hurricane,** typhoon, tropical storm, **blizzard** 1023.8; **thundersquall,** thundergust; wind shear

13 **dust storm, sandstorm,** shaitan, peesash, devil, khamsin, sirocco, simoom, samiel, harmattan

14 **whirlwind,** whirlblast, tourbillon, wind eddy; **cyclone, tornado, twister,** rotary storm, typhoon, *baguio* <Sp>; sandspout, sand column, dust devil; waterspout, rainspout

15 **windiness,** gustiness; airiness, **breeziness;** draftiness

16 **anemology,** anemometry; **wind direction; wind force, Beaufort scale,** half-Beaufort scale, International scale; wind rose, barometric wind rose, humidity wind rose, hyetal *or* rain wind rose, temperature wind rose, dynamic wind rose; wind arrow, wind marker

17 **weather vane, weathercock,** vane, cock, wind vane, wind indicator, wind cone *or* sleeve *or* sock, anemoscope; anemometer, wind-speed indicator, anemograph, anemometrograph

18 **blower,** bellows; blowpipe, blowtube, blowgun

19 **fan,** flabellum; punkah, thermantidote, electric fan, blower, window fan, attic fan, exhaust fan; ventilator; windsail, windscoop, windcatcher

VERBS 20 **blow, waft; puff,** huff, whiff; whiffle; **breeze;** breeze up, freshen; **gather, brew,** set in, blow up, pipe up, come up, **blow up a storm;** bluster, squall; **storm,** rage, blast, blow great guns, blow a hurricane; blow over

21 **sigh,** sough, whisper, mutter, murmur, **sob, moan,** groan, growl, snarl, **wail, howl,** scream, screech, shriek, **roar,** whistle, pipe, sing, sing in the shrouds

ADJS 22 **windy, blowy; breezy, drafty,** airy, airish; brisk, fresh; **gusty,** blasty, puffy, flawy; **squally;** prevailing; blustery, blustering, blusterous; aeolian, favonian, boreal; ventose

23 **stormy, tempestuous,** raging, storming, angry; turbulent; gale-force, storm-force, hurricane-force; dirty, foul; cyclonic, tornadic, typhonic, typhoonish; inclement; rainy 316.10; cloudy 319.8

24 **windblown,** blown; **windswept,** bleak, raw, exposed

25 anemological, anemographic, anemometric, anemometrical

319 CLOUD

NOUNS 1 **cloud,** high fog; "the clouds—the only birds that never sleep"—Victor Hugo, "islands on a dark-blue sea"—Shelley; fleecy cloud, cottony cloud, billowy cloud; **cloud bank,** cloud mass, cloud cover, cloud drift; cloudling, cloudlet; cloudscape, cloud band; cloudland, Cloudcuckooland *or* Nephelococcygia <Aristophanes>; mackerel sky, buttermilk sky

2 <cloud types> ice cloud, water cloud, storm cloud, thunderhead, thunder cloud; cirrus, cirrocumulus, altostratus, cirrostratus, altocumulus, nimbostratus, stratocumulus *or* cumulostratus, stratus, cumulus, cumulonimbus, nimbus

3 **fog,** pea soup *and* peasouper *and* pea-soup fog <nf>; ground fog, coastal fog, fog drip, dense fog; London fog, London special <Brit nf>, Scotch mist, brume; fog-bank; **smog** <smoke-fog>, smaze <smoke-haze>; frost smoke; mist, drizzling mist, drisk <nf>; haze, gauze, film; vapor 1067

4 **cloudiness,** cloud cover, **haziness, mistiness, fogginess,** nebulosity, nubilation, nimbosity, **overcast,** heavy sky, dirty sky, lowering *or* louring sky

5 nephology, nephelognosy; nephologist

6 nephelometer, nepheloscope

VERBS 7 **cloud,** becloud, encloud, cloud over, overcloud, cloud up, clabber up <nf>, **overcast,** overshadow, shadow, shade, **darken** 1026.9, darken over, nubilate, obnubilate, obscure; **smoke,** oversmoke; **fog,** befog; fog in; smog; **mist,** mist over, mist up, bemist, enmist; **haze**

ADJS **8 cloudy,** nebulous, nubilous, nimbose, nebulosus, nephological; **clouded,** overclouded, **overcast;** dirty, heavy, lowering *or* louring; dark 1026.13; **gloomy** 1027.14; cloud-flecked; cirrous, cirrose; cumulous, cumuliform, stratous, stratiform, cirrocumiliform, cirrocumuous, altocumuliform, altocumulous, altostratous, cirrostratous, nimbostratous, cumulonimbiform; lenticularis, mammatus, castellatus; thunderheaded, stormy, squally

9 cloud-covered, cloud-laden, cloud-curtained, cloud-crammed, cloud-crossed, cloud-decked, cloud-hidden, cloud-wrapped, cloud-enveloped, cloud-surrounded, cloud-girt, cloud-flecked, cloud-eclipsed, **cloud-capped,** cloud-topped

10 foggy, soupy *or* pea-soupy <nf>, nubilous; fog-bound, fogged-in; smoggy; hazy, misty; so foggy the seagulls are walking, so thick you can cut it with a knife

11 nephological

320 BUBBLE

NOUNS **1 bubble,** bleb, **globule;** vesicle, bulla, **blister,** blood blister, fever blister; balloon, bladder 195.2; air bubble, soap bubble

2 foam, froth; spume, sea foam, scud; **spray, surf,** breakers, white water, spoondrift *or* **spindrift; suds, lather,** soap-suds; beer-suds, head; **scum,** off-scum; head, collar; puff, mousse, soufflé, meringue

3 bubbling, bubbliness, **effervescence** *or* effervescency, **sparkle,** spumescence, frothiness, frothing, foaming; **fizz,** fizzle, carbonation; ebullience *or* ebulliency; **ebullition,** boiling; **fermentation,** ferment

VERBS **4 bubble,** bubble up, burble; **effervesce, fizz, fizzle;** hiss, **sparkle; ferment,** work; **foam, froth,** froth up; have a head, foam over; **boil,** seethe, simmer; plop, blubber; guggle, gurgle; bubble over, **boil over**

5 foam, froth, spume, cream; **lather,** suds, sud; scum, mantle; **aerate,** whip, beat, whisk

ADJS **6 bubbly,** burbly, **bubbling,** burbling; **effervescent,** spumescent, **fizzy, sparkling,** *mousseux* <Fr>, *spumante* <Ital>; carbonated; ebullient; puffed, soufflé *or* souffléed, beaten, whipped, chiffon; **blistered,** blistery, blebby, vesicated, vesicular; blistering, vesicant, vesicatory

7 foamy, foam-flecked, **frothy,** spumy, spumous *or* spumose; yeasty, barmy; **sudsy,** suddy, **lathery,** soapy, soapsudsy, soapsuddy; heady, with a head *or* collar on

321 BEHAVIOR

NOUNS **1 behavior, conduct, deportment, comportment, manner, manners, demeanor, mien,** *maintien* <Fr>, **carriage, bearing,** port, poise, posture, guise, **air,** address, presence; tone, style, lifestyle; way of life, habit of life, modus vivendi; **way, way of acting, ways; trait behavior,** behavior trait; methods, **method, methodology; practice,** praxis; procedure, proceeding; **actions,** acts, goings-on, doings, what one is up to, movements, moves, tactics; action, doing 328.1; activity 330; objective *or* observable behavior; motions, gestures, gesticulation; pose, affectation 500; pattern, behavior pattern; Type A behavior, Type B behavior; culture pattern, behavioral norm, folkway, **custom 373;** behavioral science, social science

2 good behavior, sanctioned behavior; good citizenship; good manners, correct deportment, **etiquette 580.3; courtesy 504;** social behavior, sociability 582; bad *or* poor behavior, **misbehavior 322; discourtesy 505**

3 behaviorism, behavioral science, behavior *or* behavioristic psychology, Watsonian psychology, Skinnerian psychology; behavior modification, behavior therapy ethology, animal behavior, human behavior, social behavior, ethology

VERBS **4 behave, act, do,** go on; **behave oneself, conduct oneself,** manage oneself, **handle oneself,** guide oneself, **comport oneself, deport oneself,** demean oneself, **bear oneself, carry oneself;** acquit oneself, quit oneself <old>; proceed, move, swing into action; **misbehave 322.4**

5 behave oneself, behave, act well, clean up one's act <nf>, act one's age, **be good,** be nice, **do right,** do what is right, do the right *or* proper thing, keep out of mischief, play the game *and* mind one's P's and Q's <nf>, be on one's good *or* best behavior, play one's cards right, set a good example

6 treat, use, do by, deal by, **act** *or* **behave toward,** conduct oneself toward, act with regard to, conduct oneself vis-à-vis *or* in the face of; **deal with,** cope with, **handle;** respond to

ADJS **7 behavioral;** behaviorist, behavioristic; ethological; **behaved,** behaviored, **mannered,** demeanored

322 MISBEHAVIOR

NOUNS **1 misbehavior, misconduct,** misdemeanor <old>; unsanctioned *or* nonsanctioned behavior; frowned-upon behavior; **naughtiness,** badness; impropriety; venial sin; **disorderly conduct,** disorder, disorderliness, disruptiveness, disruption,

rowdiness, rowdyism, riotousness, ruffianism, hooliganism, hoodlumism, aggro <Brit nf>; vandalism, trashing; roughhouse, horseplay; discourtesy 505; vice 654; misfeasance, malfeasance, misdoing, delinquency, **wrongdoing** 655

2 **mischief, mischievousness; devilment, deviltry,** devilry; **roguishness,** roguery, scampishness; **waggery,** waggishness; **impishness,** devilishness, puckishness, elfishness; **prankishness,** pranksomeness; sportiveness, playfulness, *espièglerie* <Fr>; high spirits, youthful spirits; foolishness 923

3 **mischief-maker,** mischief, **rogue, devil,** knave, **rascal,** rapscallion, scapegrace, **scamp; wag** 489.12; buffoon 707.10; funmaker, joker, jokester, practical joker, prankster, life of the party, **cutup** <nf>; **rowdy,** ruffian, hoodlum, hood <nf>, hooligan; **imp, elf, puck,** pixie, **minx,** bad boy, bugger *and* booger <nf>, little devil, little rascal, little monkey, *enfant terrible* <Fr>

VERBS 4 **misbehave,** misdemean <old>, **misbehave oneself, misconduct oneself,** misdemean oneself <old>, behave ill; get into mischief; **act up** *and* make waves *and* **carry on** *and* carry on something scandalous <nf>, sow one's wild oats; **cut up** <nf>, horse around <nf>, roughhouse *and* cut up rough <nf>; play the fool 923.6

ADJS 5 **misbehaving, unbehaving; naughty, bad;** improper, not respectable; out-of-order *and* off-base *and* out-of-line <nf>; **disorderly,** disruptive, **rowdy,** rowdyish, **ruffianly**

6 **mischievous,** mischief-loving, full of mischief, full of the devil *or* old nick; **roguish,** scampish, scapegrace, arch, knavish; **devilish; impish, puckish, elfish,** elvish; **waggish, prankish,** pranky, pranksome, trickish, tricksy; **playful,** sportive, high-spirited, *espiègle* <Fr>; foolish 923.8,9

ADVS 7 **mischievously, roguishly,** knavishly, scampishly, devilishly; impishly, puckishly, elfishly; waggishly; prankishly, playfully, sportively, in fun

323 WILL

NOUNS 1 **will, volition; choice,** determination, **decision** 371.1; **wish, mind, fancy,** discretion, pleasure, **inclination, disposition,** liking, appetence, appetency, **desire** 100; half a mind *or* notion, idle wish, velleity; **appetite, passion, lust, sexual desire** 75.5; animus, **objective, intention** 380; **command** 420; **free choice,** one's own will *or* choice *or* discretion *or* initiative, **free will** 430.6, free hand; conation, conatus; will power, **resolution** 359; final will *or* wishes

VERBS 2 **will, wish,** see *or* think fit, think good, think

proper, **choose to, have a mind to;** have half a mind *or* notion to; **choose,** determine, **decide** 371.14,16; **resolve** 359.7; command, decree; **desire** 100.14,18

3 have one's will, **have** *or* **get one's way, get one's wish, have one's druthers** <nf>, **write one's own ticket,** have it all one's way, do *or* go as one pleases, please oneself; assert oneself, take the bit in one's teeth, take charge of one's destiny; stand on one's rights; take the law into one's own hands; have the last word, impose one's will; know one's own mind

ADJS 4 **volitional, volitive; willing, voluntary;** conative; *ex gratia* <L>; intentional

ADVS 5 **at will,** at choice, at pleasure, *al piacere* <Ital>, **at one's pleasure,** *a beneplacito* <Ital>, at one's will and pleasure, at one's own sweet will, **at one's discretion,** *à discrétion* <Fr>, *ad arbitrium* <L>; *ad libitum* <L>, ad lib; as one wishes, as it pleases *or* suits oneself, **in one's own way,** in one's own sweet way *or* time <nf>, **as one thinks best,** as it seems good *or* best, as far as one desires; of one's own free will, of one's own accord, on one's own; without coercion, unforced

324 WILLINGNESS

NOUNS 1 **willingness, gameness** <nf>, readiness; **unreluctance,** unloathness, ungrudgingness; agreeableness, **agreeability,** favorableness; **acquiescence, consent** 441; **compliance,** cooperativeness; receptivity, receptiveness, responsiveness; amenability, tractableness, tractability, docility, biddability, biddableness, pliancy, pliability, malleability; **eagerness,** keenness, promptness, forwardness, alacrity, zeal, zealousness, ardor, enthusiasm, fervor; goodwill, cheerful consent; **willing heart** *or* **mind** *or* **humor, favorable disposition,** positive *or* right *or* receptive mood, willing ear

2 **voluntariness,** volunteering; **gratuitousness; spontaneity,** spontaneousness, unforcedness; **self-determination,** self-activity, self-action, autonomy, autonomousness, independence, free will 430.5–7; **volunteerism,** voluntaryism, voluntarism; volunteer; labor of love

VERBS 3 **be willing, be game** <nf>, be ready; be of favorable disposition, take the trouble, find it in one's heart, find one's heart <old>, have a willing heart; **incline, lean;** look kindly upon; be open to, bring oneself, **agree,** be agreeable to; **acquiesce, consent** 441.2; not hesitate to, would as lief, would as leave <nf>, would as lief as not, not care *or* mind if one does <nf>; **play** *or* **go along** <nf>, do one's part *or* bit, have a good mind to; be eager, be keen, be dying to, fall all over oneself, be spoiling for, be champing at the bit; be Johnny on the spot, step into the breach; **enter with a will,** lean or bend over backward, go into heart and soul, go the extra mile, plunge into; **cooperate,** collaborate 450.3; lend or give or turn a willing ear

4 **volunteer,** do voluntarily, do ex gratia, **do of one's own accord,** do of one's own volition, **do of one's own free will** or **choice;** do independently; put forward, sacrifice oneself

ADJS 5 **willing, willinghearted, ready, game** <nf>; **disposed, inclined, minded, willed,** fain and prone <old>; **well-disposed,** well-inclined, favorably inclined or disposed; predisposed; **favorable, agreeable, cooperative; compliant,** content <old>, acquiescent 332.13, **consenting** 441.4; **eager;** keen, prompt, quick, alacritous, forward, ready and willing, zealous, ardent, enthusiastic; in the mood or vein or humor or mind, in a good mood; receptive, responsive; amenable, tractable, docile, pliant, in favor

6 **ungrudging,** ungrumbling, **unreluctant,** unloath, **nothing loath,** unaverse, unshrinking

7 **voluntary, volunteer;** ex gratia <L>, **gratuitous; spontaneous, free, freewill;** offered, proffered; **discretionary,** discretional, nonmandatory, **optional,** elective; arbitrary; **self-determined,** self-determining, autonomous, independent, self-active, self-acting; **unsought,** unbesought, **unasked,** unrequested, **unsolicited, uninvited,** unbidden, uncalled-for; **unforced,** uncoerced, unpressured, unrequired, uncompelled; unprompted, uninfluenced; spontaneous

ADVS 8 **willingly, with a will,** with good will, with right good will, de bonne volonté <Fr>; **eagerly,** with zest, with relish, with open arms, without question, zealously, ardently, enthusiastically; **readily,** promptly, at the drop of a hat <nf>

9 **agreeably, favorably, compliantly;** lief, lieve <nf>, fain, as lief, as lief as not; **ungrudgingly,** ungrumblingly, **unreluctantly, nothing loath,** without reluctance or demur or hesitation, unstintingly, unreservedly

10 **voluntarily, freely, gratuitously, spontaneously;** optionally, electively, by choice; **of one's own accord,** of one's own free will, of one's own volition, without reservation, of one's own choice, at one's own discretion; without coercion or pressure or compulsion or intimidation; independently

325 UNWILLINGNESS

NOUNS 1 **refusal** 442, **unwillingness, disinclination,** nolition, **indisposition,** indisposedness, **reluctance,** renitency, renitence, grudgingness, grudging consent; unenthusiasm, lack of enthusiasm or zeal or eagerness, slowness, backwardness, dragging of the feet and foot-dragging <nf>, apathy, indifference; sullenness, sulk, sulks, sulkiness; cursoriness, perfunctoriness; recalcitrance or recalcitrancy, disobedience, refractoriness, fractiousness, intractableness, indocility, mutinousness; averseness, aversion, repugnance, antipathy, distaste, disrelish, no stomach for; **obstinacy, stubbornness** 361.1; opposition 451; **resistance** 453; **disagreement,** dissent 456.3

2 **demur,** demurral, **scruple, qualm,** qualm of conscience, reservation, compunction; **hesitation,** hesitancy or hesitance, pause, boggle, **falter;** qualmishness, scrupulousness, scrupulosity; **stickling,** boggling; **faltering;** shrinking; shyness, **diffidence,** modesty, bashfulness, retiring disposition, restraint; recoil; **protest, objection** 333.2

VERBS 3 **refuse** 442.3, **be unwilling, would** or **had rather not, not care to,** not feel like <nf>, not find it in one's heart to, not have the heart or stomach to; **mind,** object to, draw the line at, be dead set against, **balk at;** grudge, begrudge

4 **demur, scruple,** have qualms or scruples; **stickle, stick at,** boggle, strain; falter, waver; **hesitate,** pause, be half-hearted, **hang back,** hang off, hold off; **fight shy of,** shy at, shy, crane, shrink, recoil, blench, flinch, wince, quail, pull back; make bones about or of

ADJS 5 **unwilling, disinclined, indisposed,** not in the mood, averse, not feeling like; **unconsenting** 442.6; dead set against, opposed 451.8; **resistant** 453.5; **disagreeing,** differing, at odds 456.16; disobedient, recalcitrant, refractory, fractious, sullen, sulky, indocile, mutinous; cursory, perfunctory; **involuntary, forced**

6 **reluctant,** renitent, **grudging, loath;** backward, laggard, dilatory, slow, slow to, foot-dragging; unenthusiastic, unzealous, indifferent, apathetic, perfunctory; balky, balking, restive

7 **demurring, qualmish,** boggling, stickling, hedging, squeamish, **scrupulous; diffident,** shy, modest, bashful; **hesitant,** hesitating, faltering; shrinking

ADVS 8 **unwillingly, involuntarily, against one's will,** à contre coeur <Fr>; under compulsion or coercion or pressure; in spite of oneself, malgré soi <Fr>

9 **reluctantly, grudgingly,** sullenly, sulkily; unenthusiastically, perfunctorily; with dragging feet, with a bad or an ill grace, **under protest;** with a heavy heart, with no heart or stomach; over one's dead body, not on one's life

326 OBEDIENCE

NOUNS **1 obedience** or **obediency, compliance;** acquiescence, consent 441; **deference** 155.1, self-abnegation, submission, submissiveness 433.3; servility 138; eagerness or readiness or willingness to serve, **dutifulness,** duteousness; **service,** servitium, homage, fealty, **allegiance, loyalty,** faithfulness, faith, suit and service or suit service, observance <old>; doglike devotion or obedience; **conformity** 867, lockstep; law-abidingness; obeisance

VERBS **2 obey, mind, heed, keep, observe,** listen or hearken to; **comply, conform** 867.3, walk in lockstep; stay in line and not get out of line and not get off base <nf>, **toe the line** or mark, come to heel, fall in, fall in line, obey the rules, follow the book, keep the law, **do what one is told;** do as one says, do the will of, defer to 155.4, do one's bidding, come at one's call, lie down and roll over for <nf>; take orders, attend to orders, do suit and service, follow the lead of; **submit** 433.6,9

ADJS **3 obedient, compliant,** complying, allegiant; **acquiescent,** consenting 441.4, **submissive** 433.12, deferential 155.8, self-abnegating; willing, **dutiful,** duteous; under control; loyal, faithful, devoted; uncritical, unshakeable, doglike; conforming, in conformity; law-abiding

4 at one's command, at one's whim or pleasure, at one's disposal, at one's nod, at one's call, **at one's beck and call**

5 henpecked, tied to one's apron strings, on a string, on a leash, in leading strings; wimpish <nf>; milktoast or milquetoast, Caspar Milquetoast; under one's thumb

ADVS **6 obediently, compliantly; acquiescently, submissively** 433.17; willingly, **dutifully,** duteously; loyally, faithfully, devotedly; in obedience to, in compliance or conformity with

7 at your service or command or orders, as you please, as you will, as thou wilt <old>

327 DISOBEDIENCE

NOUNS **1 disobedience,** nonobedience, **noncompliance; undutifulness,** unduteousness; willful disobedience; **insubordination,** indiscipline; **unsubmissiveness, intractability,** indocility 361.4, recusancy; **nonconformity** 868; **disrespect** 156; **lawlessness,** waywardness, frowardness, naughtiness; violation, transgression, infraction, infringement, lawbreaking; civil disobedience, passive resistance; uncooperativeness, noncooperation; **dereliction,** deliberate negligence, default, delinquency, nonfeasance

2 defiance, refractoriness, recalcitrance or recalcitrancy, recalcitration, defiance of authority, contumacy, **contumaciousness, obstreperousness, unruliness,** restiveness, fractiousness, orneriness and feistiness <nf>; wildness 430.3; **obstinacy, stubbornness** 361.1

3 rebelliousness, mutinousness; riotousness; insurrectionism, insurgentism; factiousness, **sedition,** seditiousness; treasonableness, traitorousness, subversiveness, subversion; extremism 611.4

4 revolt, rebellion, revolution, mutiny, insurrection, insurgence or insurgency, émeute <Fr>, **uprising,** rising, outbreak, general uprising, levée en masse <Fr>, **riot,** civil disorder; peasant revolt, jacquerie <Fr>; putsch, coup, coup d'état; **strike, general strike;** intifada; resistance movement, resistance; terrorism

5 rebel, revolter; **insurgent,** insurrectionary, insurrecto, **insurrectionist;** malcontent, frondeur <Fr>; **insubordinate; mutineer,** rioter, brawler; maverick <nf>, noncooperator, troublemaker, refusenik <nf>, agent provocateur; nonconformist 868.3; agitator 375.11; extremist 611.12; reactionary; revolutionary, revolutionist 860.3; traitor, subversive 357.11; freedom fighter; contra

VERBS **6 disobey,** not mind, not heed, not keep or observe, not listen or hearken, pay no attention to, **ignore, disregard, defy,** set at defiance, fly in the face of, snap one's fingers at, scoff at, flout, go counter to, set at naught, set naught by, care naught for; be a law unto oneself, step out of line, get off-base <nf>, refuse to cooperate; not conform 867.4, hear a different drummer; **violate,** transgress 435.4; break the law 674.5; thumb one's nose at

7 revolt, rebel, kick over the traces, reluct, reluctate; **rise up,** rise, arise, rise up in arms, mount the barricades; mount or make a coup d'état; **mutiny,** mutineer <old>; insurge and insurrect <old>, **riot,** run riot; revolutionize, revolution, revolute, subvert, overthrow 860.4; call a general strike, strike 727.8; secede, break away

ADJS **8 disobedient, transgressive,** uncomplying, violative, lawless, wayward, froward, naughty; recusant, nonconforming 868.5; **undutiful,** unduteous; self-willed, willful, obstinate 361.8; **defiant** 454.7; **undisciplined,** ill-disciplined, indisciplined

9 insubordinate, unsubmissive, indocile, **uncompliant, uncooperative,** noncooperative, noncooperating, **intractable** 361.12

10 defiant, refractory, recalcitrant, contumacious, obstreperous, unruly, restive, impatient of control or discipline; fractious, ornery and feisty <nf>; wild, untamed 430.29

11 rebellious, rebel, breakaway; **mutinous,** mutineering; **insurgent, insurrectionary,** riotous, turbulent; factious, **seditious,** seditionary; revolutionary, revolutional; traitorous, treasonable, subversive; extreme, extremistic 611.20

ADVS **12 disobediently,** uncompliantly, against *or* contrary to order and discipline; **insubordinately, unsubmissively,** indocilely, **uncooperatively;** unresignedly; disregardfully, floutingly, **defiantly;** intractably 361.17; obstreperously, contumaciously, restively, fractiously; **rebelliously,** mutinously; riotously

328 ACTION
<voluntary action>

NOUNS **1 action, activity** 330, act, willed action *or* activity; **acting, doing,** activism, direct action, not words but action, happening; **practice,** actual practice, praxis; **exercise,** drill; **operation,** working, function, functioning; play; **operations,** affairs, workings; **business,** employment, work, occupation; **behavior** 321

2 performance, execution, carrying out, enactment; **transaction; discharge, dispatch;** conduct, **handling,** management, administration; **achievement, accomplishment, effectuation, implementation; commission, perpetration;** completion 407.2

3 act, action, deed, doing, thing, thing done, overt act; **turn; feat, stunt** *and* **trick** <nf>; **master stroke,** *tour de force* <Fr>, **exploit,** adventure, **enterprise, initiative,** achievement, accomplishment, **performance,** production, track record <nf>; gesture; effort, endeavor, job, undertaking; **transaction;** dealing, deal <nf>; passage; **operation, proceeding,** process, **step, measure, maneuver, move, movement;** policy, tactics; *démarche* <Fr>, coup, stroke; blow, go <nf>; accomplished fact, *fait accompli* <Fr>, done deal <nf>; overt act <law>; acta, *res gestae* <L>, **doings, dealings,** affairs; **works;** work, handiwork, hand

VERBS **4 act, serve, function; operate, work, move,** practice, do one's stuff *or* one's thing <nf>; **move,** proceed; make, play, **behave** 321.4

5 take action, take steps *or* **measures; proceed,** proceed with, go ahead with, go with, go through with; do something, go *or* swing into action, **do something about, act on** *or* **upon,** take it on, run with it <nf>, get off the dime *or* one's ass *or* one's dead ass <nf>, get with it *or* the picture <nf>; fish or cut bait, shit or get off the pot *and* put up or shut up *and* put one's money where one's mouth is <nf>; **go,** have a go <chiefly Brit nf>, take a

whack *or* a cut <nf>, lift a finger, **take** *or* **bear a hand;** play a role *or* part in; stretch forth one's hand, strike a blow; **maneuver,** make moves <nf>; get a life <nf>

6 do, effect, effectuate, **make; bring about,** bring to pass, **bring off, produce, deliver** <nf>, **do the trick,** put across *or* through; swing *or* swing it *and* hack it *and* cut it *and* cut the mustard <nf>; **do one's part,** carry one's weight, carry the ball <nf>, hold up one's end *or* one's end of the bargain; tear off <nf>, **achieve, accomplish,** realize 407.4; **render, pay; inflict, wreak,** do to; **commit, perpetrate;** pull off <nf>; go and do, up and do *or* take and do <nf>

7 carry out, carry through, go through, fulfill, work out; **bring off,** carry off; **put through,** get through; **implement; put into effect, put in** *or* **into practice,** carry into effect, execute, carry into execution, **translate into action;** suit the action to the word; rise to the occasion, come through <nf>

8 practice, put into practice, exercise, employ, use; carry on, conduct, prosecute, wage; follow, pursue; engage in, work at, devote oneself to, **do,** turn to, apply oneself to, employ oneself in; play at; **take up,** take to, **undertake, tackle,** take on, address oneself to, have a go at, turn one's hand to, **go in** *or* **out for** <nf>, make it one's business, follow as an occupation, set up shop; specialize in 866.4

9 perform, execute, enact; transact; discharge, dispatch; conduct, **manage, handle;** legislate, commission; dispose of, take care of, **deal with,** cope with; **make, accomplish,** complete 407.6

ADJS **10 acting,** performing, practicing, serving, functioning, functional, operating, operative, operational, working, in harness; in action 889.11; behavioral 321.7

329 INACTION
<voluntary inaction>

NOUNS **1 inaction,** passiveness, **passivity,** passivism; passive resistance, nonviolent resistance; nonresistance, nonviolence; pacifism; neutrality, neutralness, neutralism, **nonparticipation, noninvolvement;** standpattism <nf>; **do-nothingism,** do-nothingness, do-nothing policy; **laissez-faireism,** *laissez-faire* and *laissez-aller* <Fr>; watching and waiting, watchful waiting, waiting game, a wait-and-see attitude, indecision; **inertia,** inertness, **immobility,** dormancy, stagnation, stagnancy, vegetation, stasis, paralysis, standstill; **procrastination; idleness,** indolence, torpor, torpidness, torpidity, sloth; stalemate, logjam; **immobility** 853.1; equilibrium, dead center; **inactivity** 331; **quietude, serenity, quiescence** 173;

quietism, contemplation, meditation, passive self-annihilation; leisure; contemplative life, *vita contemplativa* <L>

VERBS **2 do nothing,** not stir, not budge, **not lift a finger** or **hand,** not move a foot, **sit back, sit on one's hands** <nf>, sit on one's ass or dead ass or butt or duff <nf>, sit on the sidelines, be a sideliner, sit it out, take a raincheck <nf>, fold one's arms, twiddle one's thumbs; **cool one's heels** or **jets** <nf>; **bide one's time, delay,** watch and wait, wait and see, play a waiting game, lie low, tread water <nf>; hang fire, not go off half-cocked; lie or sit back, lie or rest upon one's oars, rest, put one's feet up and kick back <nf>, be still 173.7; repose on one's laurels; drift, coast; **stagnate,** vegetate, veg out <nf>, lie dormant, hibernate; lay down on the job <nf>, idle 331.11; not stir, freeze

3 refrain, abstain, hold, **spare, forbear, forgo,** keep from; hold or stay one's hand, sit by or idly by, sit on one's hands

4 let alone, leave alone, **leave** or **let well enough alone;** look the other way, not make waves, not look for trouble, not rock the boat; **let be,** leave be <nf>, let things take their course, let it have its way; leave things as they are; *laisser faire* or *laisser passer* or *laisser aller* <Fr>, live and let live; **take no part in,** not get involved in, **have nothing to do with,** have no hand in, stand or hold or remain aloof, keep out of; tolerate, sit on the fence

5 let go, let pass, **let slip, let slide** and **let ride** <nf>; procrastinate, sit tight, defer

ADJS **6 passive; neutral,** neuter; standpat <nf>, **do-nothing;** *laissez-faire* and *laissez-aller* <Fr>; **inert,** like a bump on a log <nf>, immobile, dormant, stagnant, stagnating, vegetative, vegetable, static, stationary, motionless, unmoving, paralyzed, paralytic; procrastinating; **inactive, idle** 331.16; quiescent 173.12; quietist, quietistic, contemplative, meditative

ADVS **7 at a stand** or **standstill,** at a halt; as a last resort

PHRS **8** if it ain't broke don't fix it, let sleeping dogs lie; *dolce far niente* <Ital>

330 ACTIVITY

NOUNS **1 activity, action,** activeness; **movement,** motion, **stir; proceedings, doings, goings-on; activism,** political activism, judicial activism, etc; **militancy;** business 724

2 liveliness, animation, vivacity, vivaciousness, **sprightliness, spiritedness,** bubbliness, ebullience, effervescence, **briskness, breeziness, peppiness** <nf>; **life, spirit, verve,** energy, adrenalin; pep and

moxie and oomph and pizzazz and piss and vinegar <nf>, **vim** 17.2

3 quickness, swiftness, speediness, alacrity, celerity, readiness, smartness, sharpness, briskness; **promptness,** promptitude; dispatch, expeditiousness, expedition; **agility, nimbleness, spryness,** springiness

4 bustle, fuss, flurry, flutter, fluster, scramble, ferment, stew, sweat, whirl, swirl, vortex, maelstrom, **stir,** hubbub, hullabaloo, hoo-ha and foofaraw and flap <nf>, schemozzle <Brit nf>, feery-fary <Scot>, ado, to-do <nf>, bother, botheration <nf>, pother; fussiness, flutteriness; tumult, commotion, **agitation; restlessness,** unquiet, fidgetiness; **spurt, burst,** fit, spasm

5 busyness, press of business, hive of activity; plenty to do, many irons in the fire, much on one's plate; the battle of life, rat race <nf>

6 industry, industriousness, assiduousness, **assiduity, diligence, application,** concentration, laboriousness, sedulity, **sedulousness,** unsparingness, relentlessness, zealousness, ardor, fervor, vehemence; **energy,** energeticalness, strenuousness, strenuosity, tirelessness, indefatigability

7 enterprise, enterprisingness, dynamism, **initiative,** aggression, **aggressiveness,** killer instinct, force, forcefulness, pushfulness, pushingness, **pushiness, push, drive, hustle, go,** getup, get-up-and-get or **get-up-and-go** <nf>, go-ahead, go-getting, go-to-itiveness <nf>, **up-and-comingness; adventurousness,** venturousness, venturesomeness, adventuresomeness; spirit, gumption and spunk <nf>; **ambitiousness** 100.10; "the strenuous life"— Theodore Roosevelt

8 man or **woman of action, doer,** man of deeds; **hustler** and self-starter <nf>, bustler; go-getter and ball of fire and live wire and powerhouse and human dynamo and spitfire <nf>; **workaholic,** overachiever; beaver, busy bee, **eager beaver** <nf>, no slouch <nf>; operator and big-time operator and wheeler-dealer <nf>; winner <nf>; **activist,** political activist, **militant;** enthusiast 101.4; new broom, take-charge guy <nf>

9 overactivity, hyperactivity; hyperkinesia or hyperkinesis; franticness, frenziedness; overexertion, overextension; officiousness 214.2; a finger in every pie

VERBS **10 be busy, have one's hands full,** have many irons in the fire, have a lot on one's plate; not have a moment to spare, not have a moment to call one's own, not be able to call one's time one's own; do it on the run; have other things to do, have other fish to fry; **work, labor, drudge** 725.14; **busy oneself** 724.10,11

11 **stir,** stir about, **bestir oneself,** stir one's stumps <nf>, get down to business, sink one's teeth into it, take hold, be up and doing

12 **bustle, fuss,** make a fuss, stir, stir about, rush around *or* about, tear around, hurry about, buzz *or* whiz about, dart to and fro, run *or* go around like a chicken with its head cut off, run around in circles

13 **hustle** <nf>, **drive,** drive oneself, **push, scramble,** go all out <nf>, **make things hum,** step lively <nf>, make the sparks *or* chips fly <nf>, do one's damnedest <nf>; make up for lost time; press on, drive on; go ahead, forge ahead, shoot ahead, go full steam ahead

14 <nf terms> **hump,** get cutting, break one's neck, bear down on it, put one's back into it, get off the dime, get off one's ass *or* duff *or* dead ass, **hit the ball,** pour it on, lean on it, shake a leg, go to town, get the lead out, floor it

15 **keep going, keep on,** keep on the go, keep on keeping on, keep on trucking <nf>, **carry on,** peg *or* plug away <nf>, **keep at it,** keep moving, keep driving, **keep the pot boiling,** keep the ball rolling; keep busy, **keep one's nose to the grindstone,** stay on the treadmill, burn the candle at both ends

16 make the most of one's time, improve the shining hour, make hay while the sun shines, not let the grass grow under one's feet; get up early

ADJS 17 **active, lively, animated, spirited,** bubbly, ebullient, effervescent, **vivacious, sprightly,** chipper *and* perky <nf>, pert; **spry, breezy, brisk, energetic,** eager, keen, can-do <nf>; smacking, spanking; alive, live, full of life, full of pep *or* go *and* pizzazz *or* moxie <nf>, alive and kicking; **peppy** *and* snappy *and* zingy <nf>; frisky, bouncing, bouncy; mercurial, quicksilver; **activist,** activistic, **militant**

18 **quick, swift, speedy, expeditious, snappy** <nf>, celeritous, alacritous, dispatchful <old>, **prompt,** ready, smart, sharp, quick on the draw *or* trigger *or* upswing <nf>; **agile, nimble, spry,** springy

19 **astir, stirring,** afoot, **on foot;** in full swing

20 **bustling,** fussing, fussy; **fidgety,** restless, fretful, jumpy, unquiet, unsettled 105.23; **agitated, turbulent**

21 **busy,** full of business; **occupied, engaged, employed, working;** at it; **at work,** on duty, on the job, in harness; involved, engagé; **hard at work, hard at it; on the move, on the go,** on the run, **on the hop** *or* **jump** <nf>, on the make <nf>; busy as a bee *or* beaver, busier than a one-armed paper hanger <nf>; up to one's ears *or* elbows *or* neck *or* eyeballs in <nf>; tied up

22 **industrious, assiduous, diligent, sedulous,** laborious, **hardworking,** workaholic; hard,

unremitting, unsparing, relentless, zealous, ardent, fervent, vehement; **energetic,** strenuous; never idle; unsleeping; tireless, unwearied, unflagging, indefatigable; stick-to-it-ive <nf>

23 **enterprising, aggressive, dynamic,** activist, proactive, driving, forceful, **pushing,** pushful, **pushy, up-and-coming, go-ahead** *and* **hustling** <nf>, go-getting <nf>; adventurous, venturous, venturesome, adventuresome; **ambitious** 100.28

24 **overactive,** hyperactive, hyper <nf>; hectic, frenzied, frantic, frenetic; hyperkinetic; intrusive, officious 214.9; full of beans <nf>

ADVS 25 **actively, busily; lively,** sprightly, **briskly, breezily, energetically, animatedly, vivaciously, spiritedly,** with life and spirit, with gusto; allegro, allegretto; full tilt, in full swing, all out <nf>; like a house afire

26 **quickly, swiftly, expeditiously,** with dispatch, readily, **promptly; agilely, nimbly, spryly**

27 **industriously, assiduously, diligently, sedulously,** laboriously; unsparingly, relentlessly, zealously, ardently, fervently, vehemently; **energetically,** strenuously, tirelessly, indefatigably

331 INACTIVITY

NOUNS 1 **inactivity, inaction** 329, inactiveness; lull, suspension; suspended animation; dormancy, hibernation; immobility, motionlessness, quiescence 173; **inertia** 329.1; underactivity

2 **idleness,** unemployment, nothing to do, otiosity, inoccupation; **leisure,** leisureliness, unhurried ease; idle hands, idle hours, time on one's hands; "a life of dignified otiosity"—Thackeray; **relaxation,** letting down, unwinding, putting one's feet up, slippered ease

3 **unemployment,** lack of work, joblessness, inoccupation; layoff, furlough; normal unemployment, seasonal unemployment, technological unemployment, cyclical unemployment; unemployment insurance; shutdown, recession, depression

4 **idling, loafing,** lazing, *flânerie* <Fr>, goofing off <nf>, slacking <nf>, goldbricking <nf>; *dolce far niente* <Ital>; trifling; dallying, dillydallying, mopery, dawdling; loitering, tarrying, lingering; lounging, **lolling**

5 **indolence, laziness, sloth,** slothfulness, bone-laziness; laggardness, slowness, dilatoriness, remissness, do-nothingness, faineancy, *fainéantise* <Fr>; inexertion, inertia, **shiftlessness,** do-lessness <nf>; hoboism, vagrancy; spring fever; ergophobia

6 **languor,** languidness, languorousness, languishment <old>, lackadaisicalness, lotus-eating; **listlessness,** lifelessness, inanimation,

enervation, slowness, lenitude *or* lentor <old>, **dullness, sluggishness,** heaviness, dopiness <nf>, hebetude, supineness, **lassitude, lethargy,** loginess; kef, nodding; phlegm, **apathy, indifference, passivity;** torpidness, torpor, torpidity; stupor, stuporousness, stupefaction; **sloth,** slothfulness, acedia; **sleepiness, somnolence, oscitancy, yawning, drowsiness** 22.1; **weariness, fatigue** 21; jadedness, satedness 994.2; world-weariness, ennui, boredom 118.3

7 **lazybones,** lazyboots, lazylegs, indolent, lie-abed, slugabed

8 **idler, loafer, lounger,** loller, layabout <Brit nf>, couch potato <nf>, lotus-eater, *flâneur* and *flânéuse* <Fr>, **do-nothing,** dolittle, *fainéant* <Fr>, goof-off *and* fuck-off *and* goldbrick *and* goldbricker <nf>, clock watcher; **sluggard,** slug, slouch, sloucher, lubber, stick-in-the-mud <nf>, gentleman of leisure; **time waster,** time killer; **dallier, dillydallier,** mope, moper, doodler, diddler <nf>, **dawdler,** dawdle, laggard, **loiterer,** lingerer; waiter on Providence; trifler, **putterer,** potterer

9 **bum,** stiff <nf>, derelict, skid-row bum, Bowery bum, *lazzarone* <Ital>; beachcomber; **good-for-nothing,** good-for-naught, **ne'er-do-well,** wastrel; drifter, vagrant, hobo, tramp 178.3; beggar 440.8

10 homeless person; street person; shopping-bag lady *or* woman, bag person

11 **nonworker, drone;** cadger, bummer *and* moocher <nf>, **sponger,** freeloader, lounge lizard <nf>, social parasite, parasite, spiv <Brit>; beggar, mendicant, panhandler <nf>; **the unemployed;** the unemployable; the chronically unemployed, discouraged workers, lumpen proletariat; leisure class, rentiers, coupon-clippers, idle rich

VERBS 12 **idle,** do nothing, **laze,** lazy <nf>, take one's ease *or* leisure, take one's time, **loaf, lounge; lie around,** lounge around, loll around, lollop about <Brit nf>, moon, moon around, sit around, sit on one's ass *or* butt *or* duff <nf>, stand *or* hang around, **loiter about** *or* **around,** slouch, slouch around, **bum around** *and* mooch around <nf>; **shirk,** avoid work, **goof off** *and* **lie down on the job** <nf>; sleep at one's post; let the grass grow under one's feet; twiddle one's thumbs, fold one's arms

13 **waste time,** consume time, **kill time,** idle *or* trifle *or* fritter *or* fool away time, loiter away *or* loiter out the time, beguile the time, **while away the time,** pass the time, lose time, waste the precious hours, burn daylight <old>; **trifle,** dabble, fribble, footle, putter, potter, piddle, diddle, doodle

14 **dally, dillydally,** piddle, diddle, diddle-daddle, doodle, **dawdle, loiter,** lollygag <nf>, linger, lag, poke, take one's time, hang around *or* about <nf>, kick around <nf>

15 **take it easy,** take things as they come, **drift,** drift with the current, go with the flow, swim with the stream, coast, lead an easy life, **live a life of ease,** eat the bread of idleness, lie *or* rest on one's oars; rest *or* repose on one's laurels, lie back on one's record

16 **lie idle, lie fallow;** aestivate, hibernate, lie dormant; lie *or* lay off, charge *or* recharge one's batteries <nf>; lie up, lie on the shelf; ride at anchor, lay *or* lie by, lay *or* lie to; have nothing to do, have nothing on <nf>

ADJS 17 **inactive,** unactive; stationary, static, at a standstill; sedentary; **quiescent,** motionless 173.13; inanimate

18 **idle,** fallow, otiose; **unemployed, unoccupied,** disengaged, *désœuvré* <Fr>, **jobless, out of work,** out of employ, out of a job, out of harness; free, available, at liberty, at leisure; at loose ends; unemployable, lumpen; leisure, leisured; off-duty, off-work, off; housebound, shut-in

19 **indolent, lazy,** bone-lazy, **slothful,** workshy, ergophobic; **do-nothing,** *fainéant* <Fr>, **laggard,** slow, **dilatory,** procrastinative, remiss, slack, slacking, lax; easy; **shiftless,** do-less <nf>; **unenterprising,** nonaggressive; good-for-nothing, ne'er-do-well; drony, dronish, spivvish <Brit>, parasitic, cadging, sponging, scrounging

20 **languid, languorous, listless,** lifeless, inanimate, enervated, debilitated, **pepless** <nf>, lackadaisical, slow, wan, **lethargic,** logy, hebetudinous, supine, lymphatic, apathetic, **sluggish,** dopey <nf>, drugged, nodding, droopy, **dull,** heavy, leaden, lumpish, **torpid,** stultified, stuporous, **inert,** stagnant, stagnating, vegetative, vegetable, dormant; phlegmatic, numb, benumbed; moribund, dead, exanimate, dead to the world; sleepy, somnolent 22.21; **pooped** <nf>, weary; jaded, sated 994.6; **blasé,** world-weary, bored; out cold, comatose

332 ASSENT

NOUNS 1 **assent, acquiescence, concurrence, concurring, concurrency, compliance, agreement, acceptance,** accession; eager *or* hearty *or* warm assent, welcome; assentation; agreement in principle, general agreement; support; **consent** 441

2 **affirmative; yes,** yea, aye, amen, OK, yeah <nf>; nod, nod of assent; thumbs-up; **affirmativeness,** affirmative attitude, yea-saying; **me-tooism;** toadying, automatic agreement, knee-jerk assent, subservience, ass-licking <nf>

3 **acknowledgment, recognition, acceptance;** appreciation; **admission,** confession, concession, allowance; avowal, profession, declaration

4 ratification, endorsement, acceptance, approval, approbation 509.1, subscription, subscribership, signing-off, imprimatur, **sanction, permission, the OK** *and* the okay *and* **the green light** *and* **the go-ahead** *and* the nod <nf>, **certification, confirmation, validation, authentication,** authorization, warrant; **affirmation,** affirmance; stamp, rubber stamp, seal *or* **stamp of approval;** seal, signet, sigil; **subscription, signature,** John Hancock <nf>; countersignature; visa, *visé* <Fr>; notarization

5 **unanimity,** unanimousness, universal *or* univocal *or* unambiguous assent; **like-mindedness, meeting of minds,** one *or* same mind; total agreement; **understanding,** mutual understanding; **concurrence, consent,** general consent, common assent *or* consent, consentaneity, **accord,** accordance, **concord,** concordance, **agreement,** general agreement; **consensus,** consensus of opinion <nf>; *consensus omnium* <L>, universal agreement *or* accord, *consensus gentium* <L>, agreement of all, shared sense, sense of the meeting; **acclamation,** general acclamation; unison, harmony, **chorus, concert,** one *or* single voice, one accord; general voice, vox pop, *vox populi* <L>

6 **assenter, consenter, accepter,** covenanter, covenantor; assentator, yea-sayer; **yes-man,** toady, creature, ass-licker *and* ass-kisser *and* brown-nose *and* boot-licker <nf>, fellow traveler, supporter

7 **endorser, subscriber, ratifier,** approver, upholder, certifier, confirmer; **signer,** signatory, the undersigned; seconder; cosigner, cosignatory, party; underwriter, guarantor, insurer; notary, notary public

VERBS **8** **assent,** give *or* yield assent, **acquiesce, consent** 441.2, **comply, accede, agree,** agree to *or* with, have no problem with; find it in one's heart; take kindly to *and* hold with <nf>; **accept,** receive, buy <nf>, take one up on <nf>; **subscribe to,** acquiesce in, abide by; yes, **say 'yes' to; nod,** nod assent, vote for, cast one's vote for, give one's voice for; welcome, hail, cheer, acclaim, applaud, accept in toto

9 **concur, accord,** coincide, **agree, agree with,** agree in opinion; enter into one's view, enter into the ideas *or* feelings of, **see eye to eye, be at one with,** be of one mind with, go with, **go along with,** fall *or* chime *or* strike in with, close with, meet, conform to, side with, join *or* identify oneself with; cast in one's lot, fall in *or* into line, lend oneself to, play *or* go along, take kindly to; **echo,** ditto <nf>, say 'ditto' to, say 'amen' to; join in the chorus, go along with the crowd <nf>, run with the pack, go *or* float *or* swim with the stream *or* current; get on the bandwagon <nf>; rubber-stamp

10 **come to an agreement, agree, concur on, settle on,** agree with, **agree on** *or* **upon, arrive at an agreement, come to an understanding, come to terms, reach an understanding** *or* **agreement** *or* **accord,** strike *or* hammer out a bargain, covenant, get together <nf>; **shake hands on,** shake on it <nf>; come around to

11 **acknowledge, admit, own, confess, allow,** avow, **grant,** warrant, **concede,** yield <old>, defer; **accept, recognize;** agree in principle, express general agreement, go along with, not oppose *or* deny, agree provisionally *or* for the sake of argument; bring oneself to agree, assent grudgingly *or* under protest; let the ayes have it

12 **ratify, endorse,** sign off on, second, support, **certify, confirm, validate, authenticate, accept,** give the nod *or* the green light *or* the go-ahead *or* the OK <nf>, give a nod of assent, give one's imprimatur, permit, give permission, **approve** 509.9; sanction, **authorize,** warrant, accredit; **pass,** pass on *or* upon, give thumbs up <nf>; amen, say amen to; visa, *visé* <Fr>; underwrite, subscribe to; **sign,** undersign, sign on the dotted line, put one's John Hancock on <nf>, initial, put one's mark *or* X *or* cross on; autograph; cosign, countersign; seal, sign and seal, set one's seal, **set one's hand and seal;** affirm, swear and affirm, take one's oath, swear to; rubber stamp <nf>; notarize

ADJS **13** **assenting, agreeing,** acquiescing, **acquiescent, compliant,** consenting, consentient, consensual, submissive, unmurmuring, conceding, concessive, assentatious, **agreed, content**

14 **accepted, approved,** received; acknowledged, admitted, allowed, granted, conceded, recognized, professed, confessed, avowed, warranted; self-confessed; **ratified, endorsed, certified,** confirmed, validated, authenticated; certificatory, confirmatory, validating, warranting; **signed,** sealed, signed and sealed, countersigned, underwritten; stamped; sworn to, notarized, affirmed, sworn and affirmed

15 **unanimous, solid,** consentaneous, **with one consent** *or* **voice;** uncontradicted, unchallenged, uncontroverted, uncontested, unopposed; **concurrent,** concordant, **of one accord; agreeing, in agreement, like-minded, of one mind,** of the same mind; of a piece, **at one,** at one with, agreed on all hands, carried by acclamation

ADVS **16** **affirmatively,** assentingly, in the affirmative

17 **unanimously,** concurrently, consentaneously, **by common** *or* **general consent,** with one consent, **with one accord,** with one voice, without contradiction, *nemine contradicente* <L>, nem con, without a dissenting voice, *nemine dissentiente* <L>, in chorus, in concert, in unison, in one voice, univocally, unambiguously, to a man, **together,** all together, all agreeing, **as one,** as one man, one and all, on all hands; by acclamation

INTERJS **18 yes, yea,** aye, *oui* <Fr>, *sí* <Sp>, *da* <Russ>, *ja* <Ger>; yes sir, yes ma'am; why yes, *mais oui* <Fr>; **indeed,** yes indeed; **surely, certainly,** assuredly, most assuredly, **right, right you are, exactly, precisely,** just so, absolutely, positively, really, truly, rather <Brit>, quite, to be sure; **all right, right, good,** well and good, good enough, **very well,** *très bien* <Fr>; naturally, *naturellement* <Fr>; **of course,** as you say, **by all means,** by all manner of means; **amen;** hear hear <Brit>

19 <nf terms> **yeah,** yep, yup, uh-huh; yes sirree, same here, likewise, indeedy, yes indeedy, sure, sure thing, sure enough, surest thing you know; right on!, righto!; OK, okay, Roger, Roger-dodger; fine; you bet!, bet your ass!, you can bet on it!, you can say that again!, you said it!, you better believe it

PHRS **20 so be it,** be it so, so mote it be <old>, so shall it be, *amen* <Heb>; so it is, so is it; agreed, done, that's about the size of it; *c'est bien* <Fr>; that takes care of that, that's that, that's right; that makes two of us

333 DISSENT

NOUNS **1 dissent, dissidence,** dissentience; nonassent, nonconsent, nonconcurrence, nonagreement, agreement to disagree; minority opinion *or* report *or* position; **disagreement, difference, variance,** diversity, disparity; **dissatisfaction, disapproval,** disapprobation, red light, thumbs down; repudiation, **rejection; refusal, opposition** 451; dissension, disaccord 456; **alienation,** withdrawal, dropping out, secession; recusance *or* recusancy, **nonconformity** 868; apostasy 363.2; counterculture, underground, alternative; raspberry *or* Bronx cheer <nf>

2 objection, protest; kick *and* **beef** *and* **bitch** *and* squawk *and* howl <nf>, protestation; **remonstrance, remonstration,** expostulation; **challenge; demur,** demurrer; **reservation, scruple,** compunction, qualm, twinge *or* qualm of conscience; **complaint, grievance; exception;** peaceful *or* nonviolent protest; **demonstration, demo** <nf>, protest demonstration, counterdemonstration, **rally,** march, sit-in, teach-in, boycott, strike, picketing, indignation meeting; grievance committee; **rebellion** 327.4

3 dissenter, dissident, dissentient, recusant; **objector,** demurrer; minority *or* opposition voice; **protester,** protestant, detractor; **separatist,** schismatic;

sectary, sectarian, opinionist; nonconformist 868.3, odd man out; apostate 363.5; conscientious objector, passive resister; dissatisfied customer, bellyacher <nf>

VERBS **4 dissent,** dissent from, be in dissent, say nay, **disagree,** discord with, **differ,** not agree, disagree with, agree to disagree *or* differ; divide on, be at variance; **take exception,** withhold assent, **take issue, beg to differ,** raise an objection, rise to a point of order; be in opposition to, oppose, be at odds with; refuse to conform, kick against the pricks, march to *or* hear a different drummer, swim against the tide *or* against the current *or* upstream; **split off, withdraw,** drop out, secede, separate *or* disjoin oneself, schismatize

5 object, protest, kick *and* **beef** <nf>, put up a struggle *or* fight; **bitch** *and* **beef** *and* **squawk** *and* howl *and* holler *and* put up a squawk *and* raise a howl <nf>; exclaim *or* cry out against, make *or* create *or* raise a stink about <nf>; yell bloody murder <nf>; **remonstrate,** expostulate; raise *or* press objections, raise one's voice against, enter a protest; **complain,** exclaim at, state a grievance, air one's grievances; **dispute, challenge,** call in question; **demur, scruple,** boggle, dig in one's heels; **demonstrate, demonstrate against,** rally, march, sit-in, teach-in, boycott, strike, picket; **rebel** 327.7

ADJS **6 dissenting, dissident,** dissentient, recusant; **disagreeing, differing; opposing** 451.8, in opposition; alienated; counterculture, antiestablishment, underground, alternative; breakaway <Brit>; at variance with, at odds with; schismatic, schismatical, sectarian, sectary; heterodox; nonconforming 868.5; rebellious 327.11; resistant 453.5

7 protesting, protestant; **objecting,** expostulative, expostulatory, remonstrative, remonstrant; under protest

334 AFFIRMATION

NOUNS **1 affirmation,** affirmance, **assertion, asseveration,** averment, **declaration,** vouch <old>, allegation; **avouchment, avowal; position, stand,** stance; profession, **statement, word,** say, saying, say-so <nf>, positive declaration *or* statement, affirmative; manifesto, position paper; statement of principles, **creed** 953.3; **pronouncement, proclamation,** announcement, annunciation, enunciation; proposition, conclusion; predication, predicate; protest, protestation; utterance, dictum, *ipse dixit* <L>; emphasis, stress; admission, confession, disclosure; mission statement

2 affirmativeness; assertiveness, positiveness,

absoluteness, speaking out, table-thumping <nf>; definiteness

3 deposition, sworn statement, affidavit, statement under oath, notarized statement, sworn testimony *or* statement, affirmation; **vouching, swearing; attestation;** certification; **testimony;** authentication, validation, verification, vouch <old>; substantiation, proof

4 oath, vow, avow <old>, **word, assurance, guarantee, warrant,** promise, solemn oath *or* affirmation *or* word *or* declaration, word of honor; **pledge** 436.1; Bible oath, ironclad oath; judicial oath, extrajudicial oath; oath of office, official oath; oath of allegiance, loyalty oath, test oath; commitment

VERBS **5 affirm, assert,** assever <old>, asseverate, **aver,** state positively, protest, lay down, avouch, avow, **declare,** say, say loud and clear, say out loud, sound off <nf>, have one's say, speak, speak one's piece *or* one's mind, speak up *or* out, **state,** set down, express, put, put it, put in one's two-cents worth <nf>; **allege,** profess; stand on *or* for; predicate; issue a manifesto *or* position paper, manifesto; announce, **pronounce,** annunciate, enunciate, **proclaim; maintain,** have, **contend,** argue, **insist, hold,** submit, maintain with one's last breath

6 depose, depone; **testify,** take the stand, witness; **warrant, attest,** certify, **guarantee, assure; vouch, vouch for, swear, swear to,** swear the truth, **assert under oath;** make *or* take one's oath, **vow;** swear by bell, book, and candle; call heaven to witness, declare *or* swear to God, swear on the Bible, kiss the book, swear to goodness, hope to die, cross one's heart *or* cross one's heart and hope to die; swear till one is black *or* blue in the face <nf>; corroborate, substantiate

7 administer an oath, **place** *or* **put under oath,** put to one's oath, put upon oath; **swear, swear in,** adjure <old>; charge

ADJS **8 affirmative,** affirming, affirmatory, certifying, certificatory; **assertive,** assertative, assertional; annunciative, annunciatory; enunciative, enunciatory; **declarative,** declaratory; predicative, predicational; **positive,** absolute, emphatic, decided, table-thumping <nf>, unambiguously, unmistakably, loud and clear; attested, corroboratory, substantiating

9 affirmed, asserted, asseverated, avouched, avowed, averred, **declared; alleged,** professed; **stated,** pronounced, announced, annunciated, enunciated; predicated; manifestoed; **deposed,** warranted, **attested, certified,** vouched, **vouched for,** vowed, pledged, **sworn, sworn to;** strongly worded, emphatic, underscored

ADVS **10 affirmatively,** assertively, assertorily, declaratively, predicatively; **positively,** absolutely, decidedly, loudly, loud and clear, at the top of one's voice *or* one's lungs; emphatically, with emphasis, pointedly; without fear of contradiction; under oath, on one's honor *or* one's word

335 NEGATION, DENIAL

NOUNS **1 negation,** negating, abnegation; negativeness, negativity, **negativism,** negative attitude, naysaying; **obtusenss,** perversity, orneriness <nf>, cross-grainedness; **negative, no,** nay, nix <nf>; defiance; refusal; unacceptance; pessimism, defeatism

2 denial, disavowal, disaffirmation, disaffirmance, disownment, disallowance; disclamation, disclaimer; **renunciation, retraction,** retractation, **repudiation,** recantation; revocation, nullification, annulment, abrogation; abjuration, abjurement, forswearing; **contradiction,** flat *or* absolute contradiction, contravention, contrary assertion, controversion, countering, crossing, gainsaying, impugnment; flat denial, emphatic denial, **refutation, disproof** 958; **apostasy, defection** 363.2; **about-face, reversal** 363.1

VERBS **3 negate,** abnegate, negative; **say 'no',** no, naysay; shake one's head, wag *or* waggle the beard, nix <nf>; refuse, reject

4 deny, not admit, not accept, refuse to admit *or* accept; **disclaim, disown, disaffirm, disavow, disallow,** abjure, forswear, **renounce, retract,** take back, recant; revoke, nullify, **repudiate; contradict,** fly in the face of, cross, assert the contrary, contravene, controvert, impugn, **dispute,** gainsay, **oppose, counter,** go counter to, go contra, contest, take issue with, join issue upon, run counter to; belie, give the lie to, give one the lie direct *or* in his throat; deprecate; **refute** 958.5, **disprove** 957.4; **reverse oneself** 363.6; **defect, apostatize** 363.7

ADJS **5 negative,** negatory, abnegative, negational; **denying, disclaiming,** disowning, disaffirming, disallowing, disavowing, renunciative, renunciatory, repudiative, recanting, abjuratory, revocative *or* revocatory; **contradictory,** contradicting, contradictive, **opposing, contrary,** contra, counter, opposite, nay-saying, refuting, adversative, repugnant; **obtuse,** perverse, ornery <nf>, crossgrained, contrarious <nf>

ADVS **6 negatively, in the negative;** in denial, in contradiction, in opposition; in no way

CONJS **7 neither,** not either, **nor,** nor yet, or not, and not, also not

INTERJS **8 no, nay,** negative, *non* <Fr>, *nein* <Ger>, *nyet* <Russ>; certainly not, absolutely no; no sir, no ma'am, no siree; **not,** not a bit *or* whit *or* jot, I think not, not really; to the contrary, *au contraire* <Fr>, quite the contrary, far from it; no such thing, nothing of the kind *or* sort, not so

9 **by no means, by no manner of means; on no account,** in no respect, **in no case, under no circumstances, on no condition,** no matter what; **not at all,** not in the least, **never;** in no wise, in no way, noways, noway, nohow <nf>; out of the question; **not for the world,** not for anything in the world, not if one can help it, not if I know it, not at any price, not for love or money, not for the life of me, over one's dead body; a thousand times no; to the contrary, *au contraire* <Fr>, quite the contrary, far from it; God forbid 510.27

10 <nf terms> nope, nix, no dice, unhunh, no sirree; no way, no way José, not on your life, not by a long chalk, not by a long shot *or* sight, not by a darn *or* damn sight, not a bit of it, not much, not a chance, fat chance, nothing doing, forget it, that'll be the day

336 IMITATION

NOUNS 1 **imitation, copying,** counterfeiting, repetition; **me-tooism** <nf>, emulation, the sincerest form of flattery, following, mirroring, reflection, echo; copycat crime <nf>; **simulation** 354.3, modeling; fakery, forgery, plagiarism, plagiarizing, plagiary; **imposture, impersonation, takeoff** *and* hit-off <nf>, **impression,** burlesque, pastiche, *pasticcio* <Ital>; mimesis; parody, onomatopoeia

2 **mimicry, mockery,** apery, parrotry, mimetism; protective coloration *or* mimicry, aggressive mimicry, aposematic *or* synaposematic mimicry *and* cryptic mimicry <biology>, playing possum

3 **reproduction, duplication, imitation** 785.1, **copy** 785.1, dummy, mock-up, **replica,** facsimile, representation, paraphrase, approximation, model, version, knockoff <nf>, recording, transcript; computer model *or* simulation; parody, burlesque, pastiche, *pasticcio* <Ital>, travesty 508.6

4 **imitator,** simulator, me-tooer <nf>, **impersonator, impostor** 357.6, **mimic,** mimicker, mimer, mime, **mocker;** ventriloquist; mockingbird, cuckoo; **parrot,** polly, poll-parrot *or* polly-parrot, **ape,** aper, monkey; **echo,** echoer, echoist; **copier,** copyist, **copycat** <nf>; **faker, imposter,** counterfeiter, forger, plagiarist; dissimulator, dissembler, deceiver, gay deceiver, hypocrite, phony <nf>, poseur; conformist, sheep, slave to fashion

VERBS 5 **imitate, copy, repeat,** ditto <nf>; do like <nf>, do <nf>, act *or* go *or* make like <nf>; **mirror, reflect; echo,** reecho, chorus; **borrow,** steal

one's stuff <nf>, take a leaf out of one's book; assume, **affect; simulate;** counterfeit, fake <nf>, hoke *and* hoke up <nf>, forge, plagiarize, crib, lift <nf>; **parody,** pastiche, travesty; **paraphrase,** approximate

6 **mimic, impersonate,** mime, **ape, parrot,** copycat <nf>; do an impression; take off, hit off, hit off on, take off on, send up

7 **emulate, follow,** follow in the steps *or* footsteps of, walk in the shoes of, put oneself in another's shoes, follow in the wake of, follow the example of, follow suit, follow like sheep, jump on the bandwagon, play follow the leader; **copy after,** model after, model on, pattern after, pattern on, shape after, take after, take a leaf out of one's book, take as a model

ADJS 8 **imitation, mock, sham,** copied, fake *and* phony <nf>, counterfeit, forged, plagiarized, unoriginal, ungenuine; **pseudo,** synthetic, synthetical, artificial, man-made, ersatz, hokey *and* hoked-up <nf>, quasi

9 **imitative,** simulative, me-too <nf>, derivative; **mimic,** mimetic, **apish,** parrotlike; **emulative;** echoic, onomatopoetic, onomatopoeic

10 imitable, copiable, duplicable, replicable

ADVS 11 imitatively, apishly, apewise, parrotwise; onomatopoetically; synthetically; quasi

PREPS 12 **like, in imitation of,** after, in the semblance of, on the model of, *à la* <Fr>

WORD ELEMENTS 13 quasi-, mim-, ne-, near-, semi-; -ish, -like

337 NONIMITATION

NOUNS 1 **nonimitation, originality, novelty,** newness, innovation, freshness, uniqueness; **authenticity;** inventiveness, creativity, creativeness 985.3; idiosyncrasy

2 **original, model** 786, archetype, prototype 786.1, **pattern, mold,** pilot model; **innovation,** new departure; original thought; precedent, invention

3 **autograph,** holograph, first edition; genuine article

VERBS 4 **originate, invent; innovate; create;** revolutionize; pioneer

ADJS 5 **original, novel, unprecedented; unique,** *sui generis* <L>; new, fresh 841.7; underived, **firsthand; authentic, imaginative, creative** 986.18; **avant-garde,** revolutionary; **pioneer,** bellwether, trail-blazing, first in the field; nouvelle

6 **unimitated,** uncopied, **unduplicated,** unreproduced, unprecedented, unexampled; **archetypal,** archetypical, archetypic, seminal, prototypal 786.9; **prime,** primary, primal, primitive, pristine

338 COMPENSATION

NOUNS 1 compensation, recompense, repayment, payback, indemnity, indemnification, measure for measure, rectification, restitution, **reparation; amends,** expiation, atonement, meed <old>; damage control; **redress,** satisfaction, remedy; commutation, substitution; **offsetting,** balancing, **counterbalancing,** counteraction; **retaliation** 506, revenge, *lex talionis* <L>

2 offset, setoff; **counterbalance,** counterpoise, equipoise, counterweight, makeweight; **balance,** ballast; **trade-off,** equivalent, consideration, something of value, *quid pro quo* <L, something for something>, tit for tat, give-and-take 863.1; retroaction

3 counterclaim, counterdemand

VERBS 4 compensate, make compensation, make good, set right, restitute, pay back, rectify, **make up for; make amends,** expiate, do penance, atone; **recompense,** pay back, repay, indemnify, cover; **trade off,** give and take; **retaliate** 506

5 offset 779.4, set off, **counteract,** countervail, **counterbalance,** counterweigh, counterpoise, **balance,** play off against, set against, set over against, equiponderate; **square,** square up, settle the score

ADJS 6 compensating, compensatory; recompensive, amendatory, indemnificatory, reparative, rectifying, retributive; **offsetting,** counteracting *or* counteractive, countervailing, balancing, **counterbalancing,** zero-sum; **expiatory,** penitential; **retaliatory** 506

ADVS 7 in compensation, in return, back; in consideration, for a consideration

ADVS, CONJS 8 notwithstanding, but, all the same <nf>, still, yet, even; **however, nevertheless,** nonetheless; **although,** when, though; howbeit, albeit; **at all events,** in any event, **in any case,** at any rate; **be that as it may,** for all that, even so, **on the other hand,** rather, again, at the same time, all the same, just the same, **however, that may be;** after all, after all is said and done

ADVS, PREPS 9 in spite of, spite of <nf>, **despite,** in despite of, with, even with; **regardless of,** regardless, irregardless <nf>, irrespective of, without respect *or* regard to; cost what it may, regardless of cost, at any cost, at all costs, whatever the cost

339 CAREFULNESS

<close or watchful attention>

NOUNS 1 carefulness, care, heed, concern, regard; attention 983; **heedfulness,** regardfulness, mindfulness, **thoughtfulness; consideration,** solicitude, caring, loving care, tender loving care, TLC <nf>, caregiving, compassion; circumspectness, circumspection; forethought, anticipation, preparedness; **caution** 494

2 painstakingness, painstaking, **pains; diligence,** assiduousness, assiduity, sedulousness, industriousness, industry; **thoroughness,** thoroughgoingness

3 meticulousness, exactingness, **scrupulousness,** scrupulosity, **conscientiousness,** punctiliousness, attention to detail, fine-tuning; **particularness,** particularity, circumstantiality; **fussiness, criticalness,** criticality; **finicalness,** finickingness, finickiness, finicality, persnicketiness <nf>; **exactness, exactitude, accuracy, preciseness, precision,** precisionism, precisianism, punctuality, correctness, prissiness; **strictness, rigor,** rigorousness, spit and polish; nicety, niceness, delicacy, detail, subtlety, refinement, minuteness, exquisiteness, elegance

4 vigilance, wariness, prudence, **watchfulness,** watching, observance, **surveillance; watch, vigil, lookout;** *qui vive* <Fr>; invigilation, proctoring, monitoring; inspection; watch and ward; custody, custodianship, guardianship, stewardship; **guard,** guardedness, guard duty; **sharp eye, weather eye,** peeled eye, watchful eye, eagle eye, lidless *or* sleepless *or* unblinking *or* unwinking eye

5 alertness, attentiveness; attention 983; **wakefulness,** sleeplessness; **readiness,** promptness, promptitude, punctuality; **quickness,** agility, nimbleness; **smartness,** brightness, keenness, sharpness, acuteness, acuity

VERBS 6 care, mind, heed, reck, think, consider, regard, pay heed to, take heed *or* thought of; **take an interest,** be concerned; **pay attention** 982.8

7 be careful, take care *or* **good care,** take heed, have a care, exercise care; **be cautious** 494.5; **take pains,** take trouble, **be painstaking,** go to great pains, go to great lengths, go out of one's way, go the extra mile <nf>, bend over backwards <nf>, use every trick in the book, not miss a trick; mind what one is doing *or* about, mind one's business, **mind one's P's and Q's** <nf>; **watch one's step** <nf>, pick one's steps, tread on eggs, tread warily, walk on eggshells, place one's feet carefully, feel one's way; treat gently, **handle with gloves** *or* **kid gloves**

8 be vigilant, be watchful, never nod *or* sleep, **be on the watch** *or* **lookout,** be on the *qui vive* <Fr>, keep a good *or* sharp lookout, keep in sight *or* view; **keep watch,** keep watch and ward, keep vigil; **watch, look sharp,** look about one, look with one's own eyes, **be on one's guard,** keep an eye out, sleep with one eye open, have all one's eyes *or* wits about one, keep one's eye on the ball <nf>, keep one's eyes open, keep a weather eye open *and* **keep one's eyes peeled** <nf>, keep the ear to the ground, keep a nose to the wind; keep alert, **be on the alert; look out, watch out;** look lively *or* alive; stop, look, and listen

9 look after, nurture, foster, **tend, take care of** 1008.19, care for, keep an eye on

ADJS 10 **careful, heedful, regardful, mindful, thoughtful, considerate, caring,** solicitous, loving, tender, curious <old>; circumspect; **attentive** 982.15; **cautious** 494.8

11 **painstaking, diligent, assiduous,** sedulous, **thorough, thoroughgoing,** operose, industrious, elaborate

12 **meticulous, exacting, scrupulous, conscientious,** religious, punctilious, punctual, **particular, fussy, critical, attentive,** scrutinizing; **thorough,** thoroughgoing, thoroughpaced; **finical,** finicking, finicky; **exact, precise,** precisionistic, precisianistic, persnickety, prissy, **accurate, correct;** close, narrow; **strict,** rigid, **rigorous,** spit-and-polish, exigent, demanding; nice, delicate, subtle, fine, refined, minute, detailed, exquisite

13 **vigilant, wary,** prudent, **watchful,** lidless, sleepless, observant, chary; **on the watch, on the lookout,** *aux aguets* <Fr>; **on guard,** on one's guard, guarded; with open eyes, with one's eyes open, with one's eyes peeled *or* with a weather eye open <nf>; open-eyed, sharp-eyed, keen-eyed, Argus-eyed, eagle-eyed, hawk-eyed; all eyes, all ears, **all eyes and ears;** custodial

14 **alert, on the alert,** on the *qui vive* <Fr>, **on one's toes, on top** *and* **on the job** *and* on the ball <nf>, **attentive; awake,** wakeful, **wide-awake,** sleepless, unsleeping, unblinking, unwinking, unnodding, alive, ready, prompt, quick, agile, nimble, quick on the trigger *or* draw *or* uptake <nf>; **smart, bright, keen, sharp**

ADVS 15 **carefully, heedfully,** regardfully, **mindfully,** thoughtfully, **considerately,** solicitously, tenderly, lovingly; circumspectly; **cautiously** 494.12; **with care,** with great care; **painstakingly, diligently,** assiduously, industriously, sedulously, thoroughly, thoroughgoingly, nine ways to Sunday *and* to a t *or* a turn *and* to a fare-thee-well <nf>

16 **meticulously, exactingly, scrupulously, conscientiously,** religiously, punctiliously, punctually, fussily; strictly, rigorously; exactly, **accurately, precisely, with exactitude, with precision;** nicely, with great nicety, refinedly, minutely, in detail, exquisitely

17 **vigilantly, warily,** prudently, **watchfully,** observantly; **alertly,** attentively; sleeplessly,

unsleepingly, unwinkingly, unblinkingly, lidlessly, unnoddingly

340 NEGLECT

NOUNS 1 **neglect,** neglectfulness, **negligence,** inadvertence *or* inadvertency, malperformance, dereliction, *culpa* <L>, culpable negligence, criminal negligence; **remissness,** laxity, laxness, slackness, looseness, laches; unrigorousness, permissiveness; noninterference, *laissez-faire* <Fr>, nonrestriction; **disregard,** airy disregard, slighting; **inattention** 983; **oversight,** overlooking; **omission,** nonfeasance, nonperformance, lapse, failure, **default;** poor stewardship *or* guardianship *or* custody; procrastination 845.5

2 **carelessness, heedlessness, unheedfulness,** disregardfulness, regardlessness; unperceptiveness, impercipience, blindness, deliberate blindness; uncaring, unsolicitude, unsolicitousness, **thoughtlessness,** tactlessness, inconsiderateness, **inconsideration;** unthinkingness, unmindfulness, oblivion, forgetfulness; **unpreparedness,** unreadiness, lack of foresight *or* forethought; **recklessness** 493.2; **indifference** 102, *je-m'en-fichisme* and *je-m'en-foutisme* <Fr>; **laziness** 331.5; perfunctoriness; cursoriness, hastiness, offhandedness, casualness; easiness; nonconcern, insouciance; abandon, careless abandon, *sprezzatura* <Ital>

3 **slipshodness,** slipshoddiness, **slovenliness,** slovenry, sluttishness, untidiness, **sloppiness** *and* **messiness** <nf>; haphazardness; slapdash, slapdashness, a lick and a promise <nf>, loose ends; bad job, sad work, botch, slovenly performance; bungling 414.4; procrastination, avoidance

4 **unmeticulousness,** unexactingness, **unscrupulousness,** unrigorousness, **unconscientiousness,** unpunctiliousness, unpunctuality, unparticularness, unfussiness, unfinicalness, **uncriticalness;** inexactness, **inexactitude,** inaccuracy, imprecision, unpreciseness

5 **neglecter,** negligent <old>, ignorer, disregarder; *je-m'en-fichiste* and *je-m'en-foutiste* <Fr>; **procrastinator,** waiter on Providence, Micawber <Dickens>; slacker, shirker, malingerer, dodger, goof-off *and* goldbrick <nf>, idler; skimper <nf>; trifler; sloven, slob; bungler 414.8

VERBS 6 **neglect, overlook, disregard,** not heed, not attend to, take for granted, **ignore;** not care for, not take care of; **pass over,** gloss over; **let slip, let slide** <nf>, let the chance slip by, **let go,** let ride <nf>, let take its course; let the grass grow under one's feet; put off till tomorrow; not think *or* consider, not give a thought to, take no thought *or* account of, blind oneself to, turn a blind eye to, leave out of one's calculation; lose sight of, lose track of; **be neglectful** *or* **negligent**, fail in one's duty, **fail**, lapse, **default**, let go by default; not get involved; nod, nod *or* sleep through, sleep <old>, be caught napping, be asleep at the switch <nf>

7 **leave undone**, leave, **let go**, leave half-done, pretermit, **skip**, jump, **miss**, **omit**, cut *and* blow off <nf>, let be *or* alone, pass over, pass up <nf>, abandon; leave a loose thread, leave loose ends, let dangle, give a lick and a promise; **slack**, **shirk**, malinger, goof off *and* goldbrick <nf>; trifle; **procrastinate** 846.11

8 **slight**; turn one's back on, turn a cold shoulder to, get *or* give the cold shoulder *and* get *or* give the go-by *and* cold-shoulder <nf>, leave out in the cold; not lift a finger, leave undone; scamp, skimp <nf>; slur, **slur over**, pass over, skate over <Brit>, slubber over, slip *or* **skip over**, dodge, waffle <Brit nf>, fudge, blink, carefully ignore; skim, **skim over**, skim the surface, **touch upon**, touch upon lightly *or* in passing, pass over lightly, go once over lightly, **hit the high spots** *and* **give a lick and a promise** <nf>; **cut corners**, cut a corner

9 **do carelessly**, do by halves, do in a half-assed way <nf>, do in a slip-shod fashion, do anyhow, do in any old way <nf>; botch, **bungle** 414.11; **trifle with**, play *or* play at fast and loose with, mess around *or* about with *and* muck around *or* about with *and* piss around *or* about with <nf>; **do offhand**, dash off, knock off *and* throw off <nf>, **toss off** *or* **out** <nf>; **roughhew**, roughcast, rough out; **knock out** <nf>, hammer *or* pound out, bat out <nf>; toss *or* slap *or* **throw together**, knock together, cobble up, patch together, patch, patch up, fudge up, fake up, whomp up <nf>, lash up <Brit nf>, slap up <nf>; jury-rig

ADJS 10 **negligent, neglectful,** neglecting, derelict, culpably negligent; inadvertent, uncircumspect; **inattentive** 984.6; unwary, unwatchful, asleep at the switch, off-guard, unguarded; **remiss**, slack, lax, relaxed, laid-back <nf>, loose, loosey-goosey <nf>, unrigorous, permissive, overly permissive; noninterfering, *laissez-faire* <Fr>, nonrestrictive; slighting; slurring, scamping, skimping <nf>; procrastinating 846.17

11 **careless, heedless, unheeding, unheedful, disregardful,** disregardant, regardless, **unsolicitous, uncaring;** tactless, respectless, **thoughtless, unthinking, inconsiderate,** untactful, undiplomatic, mindless of, **unmindful,** forgetful, oblivious; **unprepared,** unready; **reckless** 493.8; **indifferent** 102.6; lackadaisical; lazy, shirking;

perfunctory, cursory, casual, offhand; easygoing, *dégagé* <Fr>, airy, flippant, insouciant, free and easy, free as a bird

12 **slipshod,** slipshoddy, **slovenly,** sloppy *and* **messy** *and* half-assed <nf>, lax, slapdash, shoddy, sluttish, untidy, messy; **clumsy, bungling** 414.20; **haphazard, promiscuous, hit-or-miss,** hit-and-miss; deficient, half-assed <nf>, botched

13 **unmeticulous, unexacting, unpainstaking, unscrupulous,** unrigorous, **unconscientious,** unpunctilious, unpunctual, **unparticular, unfussy, unfinical, uncritical;** inexact, inaccurate, unprecise

14 **neglected,** unattended to, untended, unwatched, unchaperoned, uncared-for; **disregarded,** unconsidered, unregarded, **overlooked, missed,** omitted, passed by, passed over, passed up <nf>, gathering dust, **ignored, slighted,** blanked; unasked, unsolicited; half-done, undone, left undone; deserted, abandoned; in the cold *and* out in the cold <nf>; on the shelf, shelved, pigeonholed, on hold *and* on the back burner <nf>, **put** *or* **laid aside,** sidetracked *and* sidelined <nf>, shunted

15 **unheeded, unobserved, unnoticed, unnoted, unperceived, unseen,** undiscerned, undescried, unmarked, unremarked, unregarded, unminded, unconsidered, unthought-of, unmissed

16 **unexamined, unstudied,** unconsidered, unsearched, unscanned, unweighed, unsifted, unexplored, uninvestigated, unindagated, unconned

ADVS 17 **negligently, neglectfully,** inadvertently; **remissly,** laxly, slackly, loosely; **unrigorously,** permissively; nonrestrictively; **slightingly,** lightly, slurringly; scampingly, skimpingly <nf>

18 **carelessly, heedlessly,** unheedingly, unheedfully, disregardfully, regardlessly, **thoughtlessly, unthinkingly, unsolicitously,** tactlessly, **inconsiderately,** unmindfully, forgetfully; **inattentively, unwarily,** unvigilantly, unguardedly, unwatchfully; **recklessly** 493.11; perfunctorily; once over lightly, cursorily; casually, offhand, offhandedly, airily; clumsily, bunglingly 414.24; **sloppily** *and* **messily** <nf>, sluttishly, shoddily, shabbily; haphazardly, promiscuously, hit or miss *and* hit and miss *and* helter-skelter *and* slapdash *and* anyhow *and* any old way *and* any which way <nf>

19 **unmeticulously, unscrupulously, unconscientiously,** unfussily, **uncritically;** inexactly, inaccurately, unprecisely, imprecisely, unrigorously, unpunctually

341 INTERPRETATION

NOUNS 1 **interpretation, construction, reading,** way of seeing *or* understanding *or* putting;

constructionism, strict constructionism, loose constructionism; **diagnosis; definition,** description; **meaning** 518

2 **rendering, rendition; text,** edited text, diplomatic text, normalized text; **version;** reading, lection, variant, variant reading; **edition,** critical *or* scholarly edition; variorum edition *or* variorum; conflation, composite reading *or* text

3 **translation,** transcription, transliteration; Englishing; **paraphrase,** loose *or* free translation; decipherment, decoding, code cracking, unscrambling; amplification, restatement, rewording, simplification; metaphrase, literal *or* verbal *or* faithful *or* word-for-word translation; **pony** *and* trot *and* crib <nf>; interlinear, interlinear translation, bilingual text *or* edition; **gloss, glossary;** key, *clavis* <L>; lipreading

4 **explanation,** explication, unfolding, **elucidation,** illumination, enlightenment, light, **clarification,** *éclaircissement* <Fr>, simplification; take <nf>; **exposition,** expounding, exegesis; **illustration, demonstration,** exemplification; **reason,** rationale; euhemerism, demythologization, allegorization; decipherment, decoding, cracking, unlocking, **solution** 940; editing, emendation; critical revision, rescension, diaskeuasis

5 <explanatory remark> **comment, word of explanation, explanatory remark; annotation,** notation, **note,** note of explanation, footnote, gloss, scholium; exegesis; *apparatus criticus* <L>; commentary, commentation <old>; legend, appendix

6 **interpretability,** interpretableness, construability; **definability, describability;** translatability; **explicability,** explainableness, accountableness

7 **interpreter,** exegete, exegetist, exegesist, hermeneut; constructionist, strict constructionist, loose constructionist; **commentator,** annotator, scholiast; critic, textual critic, **editor,** diaskeuast, emender, emendator; cryptographer, cryptologist, decoder, decipherer, cryptanalyst, lipreader; **explainer,** lexicographer, definer, **explicator,** exponent, expositor, expounder, clarifier; demonstrator, euhemerist, demythologizer, allegorist; go-between 576.4; **translator,** metaphrast, paraphrast; oneirocritic; guide, *cicerone* <Ital>, dragoman

8 <science of interpretation> exegetics, hermeneutics; tropology; criticism, literary criticism, textual criticism; paleography, epigraphy; cryptology, cryptography, cryptanalysis; lexicography; diagnostics, symptomatology, semiology, semiotics; pathognomy; physiognomics, physiognomy; metoposcopy; oneirology, oneirocriticism

VERBS 9 **interpret, diagnose; construe,** put a construction on, **take;** understand, **understand by, take to mean,** take it that; **read; read into,** read between the lines; see in a special light, read in view of, take an approach to, **define, describe**

10 **explain, explicate, expound,** make of, exposit; **give the meaning,** tell the meaning of; **spell out,** unfold; **account for,** give reason for; **clarify, elucidate,** clear up, clear the air, **cover** *and* cover the waterfront *or* the territory <nf>, **make clear,** make plain; **simplify,** popularize; **illuminate,** enlighten, give insight, **shed** *or* **throw light upon;** rationalize, euhemerize, demythologize, allegorize; tell *or* show how, show the way; **demonstrate, show, illustrate,** exemplify; get to the bottom of *or* to the heart of, make sense of, make head or tails of; decipher, crack, unlock, find the key to, unravel, demystify, read between the lines, read into, **solve** 940.2; explain oneself; explain away; overinterpret

11 **comment upon,** commentate, remark upon; **annotate,** gloss; **edit,** make an edition

12 **translate, render,** transcribe, transliterate, put *or* turn into, transfuse the sense of; construe; disambiguate

13 **paraphrase, rephrase, reword, restate,** rehash; give a free *or* loose translation

ADJS 14 **interpretative,** interpretive, interpretational, exegetic, exegetical, hermeneutic, hermeneutical; constructive, constructional; **diagnostic;** symptomatological, semeiological; tropological; **definitional, descriptive**

15 **explanatory,** explaining, exegetic, exegetical, **explicative,** explicatory; **expository,** expositive; **clarifying, elucidative, elucidatory; illuminating,** illuminative, enlightening; **demonstrative, illustrative,** exemplificative; glossarial, annotative, critical, editorial, scholiastic; rationalizing, rationalistic, euhemeristic, demythologizing, allegorizing

16 **translational,** translative; paraphrastic, metaphrastic; literal, word-for-word, verbatim

17 **interpretable, construable; definable,** describable; translatable, renderable; Englishable <old>; explainable, explicable, accountable; diagnosable

ADVS 18 **by interpretation,** as here interpreted, as here defined, according to this reading; **in explanation, to explain; that is,** that is to say, as it were, *id est* <L>, i.e.; **to wit, namely,** *videlicet* <L>, *viz, scilicet* <L>, sc; **in other words,** in words to that effect

342 MISINTERPRETATION

NOUNS 1 **misinterpretation, misunderstanding,** *malentente* <Fr>, misintelligence, misapprehension, **misreading, misconstruction,** mistaking, malobservation, **misconception; misrendering,** mistranslation, translator's error, eisegesis; misexplanation, misexplication, misexposition; misreading; misapplication; gloss; **perversion, distortion,** wrenching, twisting, contorting, torturing, squeezing, garbling; reversal; abuse of terms, misuse of words, catachresis; misquotation, miscitation; "blunders round about a meaning"—Pope; misjudgment 948; **error** 975; misrepresentation

VERBS 2 **misinterpret, misunderstand,** misconceive, **mistake, misapprehend; misread, misconstrue,** put a false construction on, miss the point, **take wrong, get wrong,** get one wrong, take amiss, take the wrong way; **get backwards,** reverse, have the wrong way round, put the cart before the horse; misapply; misexplain, misexplicate, misexpound; **misrender,** mistranslate; quote out of context; misquote, miscite, give a false coloring, give a false impression *or* idea, gloss; misread; **garble, pervert, distort,** wrench, contort, torture, squeeze, twist the words *or* meaning, stretch *or* strain the sense *or* meaning, misdeem, **misjudge** 948.2; bark up the wrong tree; misrepresent

ADJS 3 **misinterpreted, misunderstood, mistaken, misapprehended, misread,** eisegetical, misconceived, **misconstrued; garbled,** misquoted, misrepresented, **perverted, distorted,** catachrestic, catechrestical; backwards, reversed, ass-backwards <nf>

4 **misinterpretable, misunderstandable,** mistakable

343 COMMUNICATION

NOUNS 1 **communication,** communion, congress, **commerce, intercourse;** means of communication, **speaking, speech** 524, utterance, speech act, talking, linguistic intercourse, speech situation, speech circuit, converse, **conversation** 541; signaling; **contact, touch, connection; interpersonal communication, intercommunication,** intercommunion, grokking <nf>, **interplay,** interaction; **exchange,** interchange; answer, response, reply; one-way communication, two-way communication; **dealings,** dealing, **traffic, truck** <nf>; information 551; message 552.4; ESP, telepathy 689.9; writing; correspondence 553; social intercourse 582.4; miscommunication

2 **informing, telling,** imparting, impartation, impartment, **conveyance, transmission,** transmittal, transfer, transference, sharing, giving, sending, signaling; notification, alerting, **announcement** 352.2, publication 352, **disclosure** 351

3 **communicativeness, talkativeness** 540, **sociability** 582; **unreserve,** unreservedness, **unreticence, unrestraint, unconstraint,** unrestriction; **unrepression,** unsuppression; **unsecretiveness,** untaciturnity; candor, **frankness** 644.4; **openness,** plainness, freeness, outspokenness, plainspokenness; **accessibility,** approachability, conversableness; **extroversion,** outgoingness; **uncommunicativeness** 344, reserve, taciturnity

4 **communicability, impartability, conveyability, transmittability,** transmissibility, transferability; contagiousness

5 **communications,** electronic communications, communications industry, media, communications medium *or* media, mass communications, communications network; telecommunication 347.1, long-distance communication, electronic communication; radio communication, wire communication, broadcasting; communication *or* information theory 551.7; signaling

VERBS 6 **communicate, be in touch** *or* **contact,** be in connection *or* intercourse, have intercourse, hold communication; **intercommunicate,** interchange, commune with; grok <nf>; commerce with, **deal with, traffic with, have dealings with, have truck with** <nf>; **speak, talk,** be in a speech situation, **converse** 541.9, pass the time of day

7 **communicate, impart, tell,** lay on one <nf>, **convey, transmit,** transfer, send, send word, deliver *or* send a signal *or* message, **disseminate,** broadcast, pass, **pass on** *or* **along, hand on; report, render, make known,** get across *or* over; give *or* send *or* leave word; **signal;** share, share with; **leak,** let slip out, **give** 478.12; tell 551.8

8 **communicate with, get in touch** *or* **contact with, contact** <nf>, **make contact with,** raise, reach, get to, get through to, get hold of, make *or* establish connection, get in connection with; **make advances,** make overtures, **approach,** make up to <nf>; relate to; keep in touch *or* contact with, maintain connection; **answer,** respond *or* reply to, get back to; **question,** interrogate; **correspond,** drop a line

ADJS 9 **communicational, communicating,** communional; transmissional; speech, **verbal,** linguistic, oral; **conversational** 541.13; **intercommunicational,** intercommunicative, intercommunional, interactional, interactive, interacting, interresponsive, responsive, answering; questioning, interrogative, interrogatory; telepathic

10 **communicative, talkative** 540.9, gossipy, newsy; **sociable; unreserved, unreticent,** unshrinking, **unrestrained, unconstrained,** unhampered, unrestricted; demonstrative, expansive, effusive; **unrepressed, unsuppressed; unsecretive,** unsilent,

untaciturn; candid, **frank** 644.17; self-revealing, self-revelatory; **open,** free, outspoken, free-speaking, free-spoken, free-tongued; **accessible, approachable,** conversable, easy to speak to; **extroverted,** outgoing; **uncommunicative** 344.8

11 **communicable, impartable, conveyable, transmittable,** transmissible, transferable; contagious

12 communicatively; verbally, talkatively, by word of mouth, orally, viva voce

344 UNCOMMUNICATIVENESS

NOUNS 1 **uncommunicativeness,** closeness, indisposition to speak, disinclination to communicate; unconversableness, **unsociability** 583; nondisclosure, **secretiveness** 345.1; lack of message *or* meaning, meaninglessness 520

2 **taciturnity, untalkativeness,** unloquaciousness; **silence** 51; **speechlessness,** wordlessness, dumbness, **muteness** 51.2; quietness, quietude; laconicalness, laconism, curtness, shortness, terseness; brusqueness, briefness, brevity, conciseness, economy *or* sparingness of words, pauciloquy <old>

3 **reticence** *or* reticency; **reserve,** reservedness, restraint, low key, **constraint;** guardedness, discreetness, discretion; suppression, repression; subduedness; backwardness, retirement, low profile; **aloofness, standoffishness,** distance, remoteness, **detachment,** withdrawal, withdrawnness, reclusiveness, solitariness; impersonality; **coolness,** coldness, frigidity, iciness, frostiness, chilliness; **inaccessibility, unapproachability; undemonstrativeness,** unexpansiveness, unaffability, uncongeniality; **introversion;** modesty, bashfulness 139.4, pudency; expressionlessness, blankness, impassiveness, impassivity; straight *or* poker face, mask

4 **prevarication, equivocation,** tergiversation, **evasion,** shuffle, fencing, dodging, parrying, waffling *and* tap-dancing <nf>; *suppressio veri* <L>; weasel words

5 **man of few words,** clam <nf>, strong silent type, laconic <old>; Spartan, Laconian; evader, weasel

VERBS 6 **keep to oneself,** keep one's own counsel; not open one's mouth, not say a word, not breathe a word, stand mute, **hold one's tongue** 51.5, clam up <nf>; bite one's tongue; have little to say, refuse comment, say neither yes nor no, waste no words, save one's breath; retire; **keep one's distance,** keep at a distance, keep oneself to oneself, **stand aloof,** hold oneself aloof; keep secret 345.7

7 **prevaricate, equivocate, waffle** <nf>, tergiversate, evade, dodge, sidestep, pussyfoot, say in a roundabout way, parry, duck, weasel *and* weasel out <nf>, palter; hum and haw, **hem and haw,** back and fill; **mince words,** mince the truth, euphemize

ADJS 8 **uncommunicative,** indisposed *or* disinclined to communicate; unconversational, unconversable <old>; **unsociable** 583.5; **secretive** 345.15; meaningless 520.6

9 **taciturn, untalkative,** unloquacious, indisposed to talk; **silent, speechless,** wordless, **mum; mute** 51.12, dumb, quiet; close, **closemouthed,** close-tongued, snug <nf>, **tight-lipped;** close-lipped, tongue-tied, word-bound; **laconic,** curt, brief, terse, brusque, short, concise, **sparing of words,** economical of words, of few words

10 **reticent, reserved,** restrained, nonassertive, low-key, low-keyed, constrained; **suppressed,** repressed; subdued; guarded, discreet; backward, **retiring,** shrinking; **aloof, standoffish,** offish <nf>, standoff, **distant,** remote, removed, **detached,** Olympian, withdrawn; impersonal; **cool,** cold, frigid, icy, frosty, chilled, chilly; **inaccessible, unapproachable,** forbidding; **undemonstrative,** unexpansive, unaffable, uncongenial, ungenial; **introverted;** modest, verecund, verecundious, *pudique* <Fr>, bashful 139.12; expressionless, blank, impassive

11 **prevaricating, equivocal,** tergiversating, tergiversant, waffling <nf>, **evasive,** weaselly, weasel-worded

345 SECRECY

NOUNS 1 **secrecy,** secretness, airtight secrecy, close secrecy; crypticness; the dark; hiddenness, hiding, **concealment** 346; **secretiveness,** closeness; discreetness, discretion, **uncommunicativeness** 344; **evasiveness,** evasion, subterfuge; hugger-mugger, hugger-muggery

2 **privacy,** retirement, isolation, sequestration, seclusion; incognito, anonymity; **confidentialness,** confidentiality; closed meeting *or* session, executive session, private conference, secret meeting

3 **veil of secrecy, veil,** curtain, pall, wraps; iron curtain, "curtains of fog and iron"—Churchill, bamboo curtain; wall *or* barrier of secrecy; **suppression,** repression, stifling, smothering; **censorship,** blackout <nf>, **hush-up, cover-up; seal of secrecy,** official secrecy, classification, official classification; security, ironbound security; pledge *or* oath of secrecy

4 **stealth,** stealthiness, **furtiveness, clandestineness,** clandestinity, clandestine behavior, **surreptitiousness, covertness,** slyness, shiftiness,

sneakiness, slinkiness, underhandedness, underhand dealing, undercover *or* underground activity, **covert activity** *or* **operation;** prowl, prowling; stalking; hugger-mugger; counterintelligence; conspiracy, cabal, intrigue; secret service, intelligence agency

5 **secret, confidence;** private *or* personal matter, privity <old>; trade secret; confidential *or* **privileged information** *or* **communication;** doctor-patient *or* lawyer-client confidentiality; seal *or* secret of the confessional; more than meets the eye; deep dark secret; solemn secret; guarded secret, hush-hush matter, classified information, eyes-only *or* top-secret information, restricted information; confession; inside information, inside skinny <nf>; **mystery, enigma** 522.8; the arcane, arcanum, *arcanum arcanorum* <L>; esoterica, cabala, the occult, occultism, hermetism, hermeticism, hermetics; deep *or* profound secret, sealed book, mystery of mysteries; skeleton in the closet *or* cupboard, family secret; sealed orders, state secret

6 **cryptography,** cryptoanalysis, cryptoanalytics; **code, cipher;** secret language; code book, code word, code name; **secret writing,** coded message, cryptogram, cryptograph; secret *or* invisible *or* sympathetic ink; cryptographer

VERBS 7 **keep secret, keep mum, veil,** keep dark; keep it a deep, dark secret; secrete, **conceal;** keep to oneself 344.6, keep *in petto* <Ital>, bosom, keep close, keep snug <nf>, keep back, keep from, **withhold,** hold out on <nf>; not let it go further, keep within these walls, keep within the bosom of the lodge, keep between us; **not tell,** hold one's tongue 51.5, never let on <nf>, make no sign, not breathe *or* whisper a word, clam up <nf>, be the soul of discretion; **not give away** <nf>, "tell it not in Gath"—Bible, **keep it under one's hat** <nf>, keep under wraps <nf>, keep a lid on, keep buttoned up <nf>, keep one's own counsel; play one's cards close to the chest *or* to one's vest; play dumb; clam up; not let the right hand know what the left is doing; keep in ignorance, keep *or* leave in the dark; classify; file and forget; **have secret** *or* **confidential information,** be in on the secret *and* know where the bodies are buried <nf>

8 **cover up,** muffle up; **hush up, hush,** hush-hush, shush, hugger-mugger; **suppress,** repress, **stifle,** muffle, **smother,** squash, quash, squelch, kill, sit on *or* upon, put the lid on <nf>; **censor,** black out <nf>

9 **tell confidentially,** tell for one's ears only, mention privately, **whisper, breathe, whisper in the ear;** tell one a secret; take aside, see one alone, talk to in private, speak in privacy; say under one's breath

10 code, encode, encipher, cipher

ADJS 11 **secret,** close, closed, closet; cryptic, dark; unuttered, unrevealed, undivulged, undisclosed, unspoken, untold; **hush-hush, top secret,** supersecret, eyes-only, classified, restricted, under wraps <nf>, under security *or* security restrictions; **censored,** suppressed, stifled, smothered, hushed-up, under the seal *or* ban of secrecy; **unrevealable, undivulgable, undisclosable, untellable,** unwhisperable, unbreatheable, unutterable; latent, ulterior, concealed, hidden 346.11; arcane, esoteric, occult, cabalistic, hermetic; enigmatic, mysterious 522.18

12 **covert, clandestine,** quiet, unobtrusive, hugger-mugger, **surreptitious, undercover,** underground, under-the-counter, under-the-table, **cloak-and-dagger** <nf>, backdoor, hole-and-corner <nf>, underhand, **underhanded; furtive, stealthy,** privy, backstairs, **sly, shifty, sneaky,** sneaking, skulking, slinking, slinky, feline

13 **private, privy, closed-door; intimate, inmost,** innermost, interior, inward, **personal; privileged,** protected; **secluded, sequestered,** isolated, withdrawn, retired; incognito, anonymous

14 **confidential,** auricular, **inside** <nf>, esoteric; *in petto* <Ital>, close to one's chest *or* vest <nf>, under one's hat <nf>; **off the record,** not for the record, not to be minuted, within these four walls, in the bosom of the lodge, for no other ears, eyes-only, between us; not to be quoted, not for publication *or* release; not for attribution; unquotable, unpublishable, sealed; sensitive, privileged, under privilege

15 **secretive,** close-lipped, secret, close, dark; discreet; evasive, shifty; **uncommunicative, close-mouthed**

16 coded, encoded; ciphered, enciphered; cryptographic, cryptographical; hieroglyphic

ADVS 17 **secretly, in secret,** in *or* up one's sleeve; in the closet; with nobody the wiser; **covertly,** stownlins *and* in hidlings <Scot>, **undercover,** *à couvert* <Fr>, under the cloak of; **behind the scenes,** in the background, in a corner, in the dark, in darkness, behind the veil *or* curtain, behind the veil of secrecy; *sub rosa* <L>, under the rose; underground; *sotto voce* <Ital>, under the breath, with bated breath, in a whisper; off the record

18 **surreptitiously, clandestinely, secretively, furtively, stealthily, slyly,** shiftily, sneakily, sneakingly, skulkingly, slinkingly, slinkily; by stealth, **on the sly** *and* **on the quiet** *and* on the qt <nf>, *à la dérobée* <Fr>, *en tapinois* <Fr>, behind one's back, by a side door, **like a thief in the night,** underhand, underhandedly, under the table, in holes and corners *and* in a hole-and-corner way <nf>

19 privately, privily, **in private,** in privacy, in privy; apart, aside; **behind closed doors,** *januis clausis* <L>, *à huis clos* <Fr>, *in camera* <L>, in chambers, in secret *or* closed meeting, in executive session, in private conference

20 confidentially, in confidence, in strict confidence, under the seal of secrecy, **off the record; between ourselves,** strictly between us, *entre nous* <Fr>, *inter nos* <L>, for your ears *or* eyes only, between you and me, from me to you, between you and me and the bedpost *or* lamppost <nf>

346 CONCEALMENT

NOUNS 1 concealment, hiding, secretion; burial, burying, interment, putting away; **cover, covering,** covering up, masking, screening 295.1; mystification, obscuration; darkening, obscurement, clouding 1027.6; hiddenness, concealedness, **covertness,** occultation; eclipse; disappearance; **secrecy** 345; uncommunicativeness 344; invisibility 32; **subterfuge, deception** 356

2 veil, curtain, **cover, screen** 295.2, mask; fig leaf; **wraps** <nf>; **cover, disguise**

3 ambush, ambushment, **ambuscade,** *guet-apens* <Fr>; surveillance, shadowing 938.9; lurking hole *or* place; blind, stalking-horse; booby trap, trap

4 hiding place, hideaway, hideout, hidey-hole <nf>, hiding, concealment, **cover,** secret place; safe house; drop, accommodation address <Brit>; **recess, corner,** dark corner, nook, cranny, niche; **hole,** bolt-hole, foxhole, trench, dugout, lair, den; bomb shelter, storm shelter; **asylum, sanctuary, retreat, refuge** 1009; covert, coverture, undercovert; **cache,** stash <nf>; safe-deposit box, bank vault, safe; cubbyhole, cubby, pigeonhole; secret compartment; mother's skirts

5 secret passage, covert way, secret exit; **back way, back door, side door;** bolt-hole, escape route, escape hatch, escapeway; secret staircase, *escalier dérobé* <Fr>, **back stairs; underground,** underground route, underground railroad

VERBS 6 conceal, hide, ensconce; **cover, cover up,** blind, **screen, cloak, veil,** screen off, curtain, blanket, shroud, enshroud, envelop; **disguise, camouflage, mask,** dissemble; plain-wrap, wrap in plain brown paper; whitewash <nf>; **paper over,** gloss over, varnish, slur over; distract attention from; **obscure,** obfuscate, cloud, becloud, befog, throw out a smoke screen, shade, throw into the shade; **eclipse,** occult; put out of sight, sweep under the rug *or* carpet, keep under cover, keep under wraps; cover up one's tracks, lay a false scent, hide one's trail; hide one's light under a bushel

7 secrete, hide away, keep hidden, put away, store away, stow away, file and forget, bottle up, lock up, seal up, put out of sight; **keep secret** 345.7; **cache,** stash <nf>, deposit, plant <nf>; **bury;** bosom, embosom <old>

8 <hide oneself> hide, conceal oneself, take cover, hide out <nf>, hide away, **go into hiding,** go to ground; stay in hiding, **lie hid** *or* **hidden,** lie *or* lay low <nf>, lie perdue, lie snug *or* close <nf>, lie doggo *and* sit tight <nf>, burrow <old>, **hole up** <nf>, **go underground;** play peekaboo *or* bopeep *or* hide and seek; keep out of sight, retire from sight, drop from sight, disappear 34.2, crawl *or* retreat into one's shell, keep *or* stay in the background, keep a low profile, stay in the shade; **disguise oneself,** masquerade, take an assumed name, assume a cover, change one's identity, go under an alias, remain anonymous, be incognito, go *or* sail under false colors, wear a mask; leave no address

9 lurk, couch; **lie in wait,** lay wait; **sneak, skulk, slink, prowl,** nightwalk, **steal, creep,** pussyfoot <nf>, gumshoe <nf>, tiptoe; stalk, shadow 938.34

10 ambush, ambuscade, **waylay; lie in ambush,** lay wait for, **lie in wait for,** lay for <nf>; stalk; set a trap for

ADJS 11 concealed, hidden, hid, occult, recondite <old>, blind; **covered** 295.31; **covert, under cover,** under wraps <nf>; code-named; **obscured,** obfuscated, clouded, clouded over, wrapped in clouds, in a cloud *or* fog *or* mist *or* haze, beclouded, befogged; eclipsed, in eclipse, under an eclipse; in the wings; buried; underground; close, secluded, secluse, sequestered; in purdah, under house arrest, incommunicado; **obscure,** abstruse, mysterious 522.18; **secret** 345.11; unknown 930.17, latent 519.5

12 unrevealed, undisclosed, undivulged, **unexposed;** unapparent, **invisible, unseen,** unperceived, unspied, undetected; undiscovered, unexplored, untraced, untracked; unaccounted for, unexplained, unsolved

13 disguised, camouflaged, in disguise; masked, masquerading; **incognito,** incog <nf>, anonymous, unrecognizable; in plain wrapping *or* plain brown paper <nf>; cryptic, coded, codified

14 in hiding, hidden out, **under cover,** in a dark corner, lying hid, doggo <nf>; in ambush *or* ambuscade; waiting concealed, lying in wait; in the wings; lurking, skulking, prowling, sneaking, stealing; pussyfooted, pussyfoot, on tiptoe; stealthy, furtive, surreptitious 345.12

15 concealing, hiding, obscuring, obfuscatory; covering; unrevealing, nonrevealing, undisclosing

347 COMMUNICATIONS

NOUNS 1 communications, signaling, telecommunication, comms <Brit nf>, transmission; electronic communication, electrical communication; satellite communication; wire communication, wireless communication; communications engineering, communications technology; communications engineer; media, communications medium *or* media; communication *or* information theory 551.7; communication *or* information explosion

2 telegraph, telegraph recorder, ticker; **telegraphy,** telegraphics, data transmission; **teleprinter,** Telex <trademark>, teletypewriter; teleprinter exchange *or* telex; wire service; code 345.6; electricity 1032; **key,** interrupter, transmitter, sender; receiver, **sounder**

3 radio 1034, **radiotelephony, radiotelegraphy,** wireless <Brit>, wireless telephony, wireless telegraphy; line radio, wire *or* wired radio, wired wireless <Brit>, wire wave communication; radiophotography; digital audio broadcasting *or* DAB; **television** 1035; electronics 1033

4 telephone, phone *and* horn <nf>, dog <Brit nf>, telephone set, handset; telephony, telephonics, telephone mechanics, telephone engineering; high-frequency telephony; receiver, telephone receiver, earpiece; mouthpiece, transmitter; telephone extension, extension; wall telephone, desk telephone; dial *or* rotary telephone, Touch-Tone telephone, push-button telephone, cordless phone; beeper; scrambler; telephone booth, telephone box, call box <Brit>, telephone kiosk <Brit>, public telephone, coin telephone, pay station, pay phone; mobile telephone *or* phone <nf>, cellular *or* cell telephone *or* phone <nf>, car phone, digital phone; speakerphone, videophone; speed calling, call forwarding, call waiting, redial, caller ID service; phone card; facsimile transmission, fax

5 radiophone, radiotelephone, wireless telephone, wireless; headset, headphone 50.8

6 intercom <nf>, Interphone, intercommunication system

7 telephone exchange, telephone office, central office, **central;** automatic exchange, machine-switching office; step-by-step switching, panel switching, crossbar switching, electronic switching

8 switchboard; PBX *or* private branch *or* business exchange, private exchange; in *or* A board, out *or* B board

9 telephone operator, operator, switchboard operator, telephonist, **central** <old>; long distance; **PBX operator**

10 telephone man; telephone mechanic; telephonic engineer; lineman *or* linewoman

11 telephoner, phoner <nf>, caller, **party,** calling party, subscriber

12 telephone number, **phone number** <nf>, unlisted number; telephone directory *or* book, phone book <nf>; telephone exchange, exchange; telephone area, area code; calling zone

13 telephone call, **phone call** <nf>, **call, ring** *and* buzz <nf>; local call, toll call, long-distance call; long distance, direct distance nondialing, DDD; trunk call; station-to-station call, person-to-person call; collect call; toll-free call; mobile call; dial tone, busy signal; crank call, nuisance call; conference call, video teleconference, teleconference; hot line; chat *or* talk *or* gab line, messagerie; voicemail, phonemail; electronic mail *or* e-mail *or* email; telemarketing; multilevel marketing, multilevel sales; cold call; ringy-dingy *or* jingle *or* tinkle <nf>

14 telegram, telegraph, wire <nf>, telex; **cablegram, cable; radiogram,** radiotelegram; **day letter, night letter;** fast telegram

15 Telephoto <trademark>, Wirephoto <trademark>, Telecopier <trademark>, **facsimile, fax** <nf>; telephotograph, radiophotograph

16 telegrapher, telegraphist, telegraph operator; **sparks** *and* brass pounder *and* dit-da artist <nf>; radiotelegrapher; wireman, wire chief

17 line, wire line, telegraph line, telephone line; private line, direct line; party line; hot line; trunk, trunk line; WATS *or* wide area telecommunications service, WATS line; cable, telegraph cable; transmission line, concentric cable, coaxial cable, co-ax <nf>, fiber cable, fiberoptic cable

18 computer networking, Internet, World Wide Web *or* WWW, electronic mail; modem; digital compression

VERBS 19 telephone, phone <nf>, call, call on the phone <nf>, put in *or* make a call, **call up, ring,** ring up, give a ring *or* buzz *or* call *or* tinkle *or* jingle <nf>, buzz <nf>; nonformal; listen in; hold the phone *or* wire; hang up, ring off <Brit>; cold call

20 telegraph, telegram, flash, **wire** *and* send a wire <nf>, telex; **cable;** Teletype; radio; sign on, sign off; fax

ADJS 21 communicational, telecommunicational, **communications,** communication, signal; **telephonic,** magnetotelephonic, microtelephonic, monotelephonic, thermotelephonic; **telegraphic; Teletype;** Wirephoto, facsimile, fax; phototelegraphic, telephotographic; **radio,** wireless <Brit>; radiotelegraphic

348 MANIFESTATION

NOUNS 1 manifestation, appearance; expression, evincement; **indication, evidence,** proof 957; embodiment, incarnation, bodying forth, materialization; epiphany, theophany, angelophany, Satanophany, Christophany, pneumatophany, avatar; **revelation, disclosure** 351, showing forth; dissemination, **publication** 352

2 display, demonstration, show, showing; presentation, showing forth, presentment, ostentation <old>, **exhibition, exhibit, exposition,** expo, retrospective; production, performance, representation, enactment, projection; opening, unfolding, unfoldment; **showcase,** showcasing, unveiling, exposure, varnishing day, *vernissage* <Fr>

3 manifestness, apparentness, obviousness, plainness, clearness, crystal-clearness, perspicuity, distinctness, microscopical distinctness, patency, patentness, palpability, tangibility; evidentness, evidence <old>, **self-evidence; openness,** openness to sight, overtness; visibility 31; unmistakableness, unquestionability 970.3

4 conspicuousness, prominence, salience or saliency, bold or high or strong relief, boldness, **noticeability,** pronouncedness, strikingness, demonstrativeness, outstandingness; highlighting, spotlighting, featuring; obtrusiveness; **flagrance** or flagrancy, arrantness, blatancy, notoriousness, notoriety; ostentation 501; dramatics, theatrics

VERBS 5 manifest, show, exhibit, demonstrate, display, breathe, unfold, develop; **present,** represent <old>, **evince, evidence; indicate,** give sign or token, token, betoken, mean 518.8; **express,** show forth, set forth; show off, showcase; **make plain, make clear;** produce, bring out, roll out, trot out <nf>, bring forth, bring forward or to the front, put forward, bring to notice, expose to view, bring to or into view; **reveal, divulge, disclose** 351.4; **illuminate, highlight, spotlight, feature,** bring to the fore, place in the foreground, bring out in bold or strong or high relief; **flaunt,** dangle, wave, **flourish,** brandish, parade; affect, make a show or a great show of; perform, enact, dramatize; **embody,** incarnate, body forth, **materialize**

6 <manifest oneself> come out, come into the open, come out of the closet <nf>, come forth, **surface; show one's colors** or true colors, wear one's heart upon one's sleeve; **speak up, speak out,** raise one's voice, **assert oneself,** let one's voice be heard, speak one's piece or one's mind, **stand up and be counted,** take a stand; open up, show one's mind, have no secrets; **appear, materialize**

7 be manifest, be there for all to see, make an appearance, be no secret or revelation, **surface,** lie on the surface, be seen with half an eye; need no explanation, **speak for itself,** tell its own story or tale; **go without saying,** *aller sans dire* <Fr>; **leap to the eye,** *sauter aux yeux* <Fr>, **stare one in the face,** hit one in the eye, strike the eye, glare, shout; come across, project; stand out, stick out, stick out a mile, stick out like a sore thumb, hang out <nf>

ADJS 8 manifest, apparent, evident, self-evident, axiomatic, indisputable, **obvious, plain, clear,** perspicuous, distinct, palpable, patent, tangible; **visible, perceptible, perceivable, discernible,** seeable, observable, **noticeable, much in evidence; to be seen,** easy to be seen, plain to be seen; plain as day, plain as the nose on one's face, plain as a pikestaff, big as life, big as life and twice as ugly; **crystal-clear,** clear as crystal; **express, explicit, unmistakable,** not to be mistaken, open-and-shut <nf>; self-explanatory, self-explaining; **indubitable** 969.15

9 manifesting, manifestative, showing, displaying, showcasing, demonstrating, **demonstrative,** presentational, expository, expositional, exhibitive, exhibitional, **expressive;** evincive, evidential; **indicative,** indicatory; appearing, incarnating, incarnational, materializing; epiphanic, theophanic, angelophanic, Satanophanic, Christophanic, pneumatophanic; **revelational,** revelatory, **disclosive** 351.10; promulgatory 352.18; histrionic

10 open, overt, open to all, open as day, out of the closet <nf>; unclassified; **revealed, disclosed, exposed;** made public; bare, bald, naked

11 unhidden, unconcealed, unscreened, uncurtained, unshaded, veilless; **unobscure,** unobscured, undarkened, unclouded; **undisguised,** uncamouflaged

12 conspicuous, noticeable, notable, ostensible, **prominent, bold, pronounced, salient,** in relief, in bold or high or strong relief, **striking, outstanding,** in the foreground, sticking or hanging out <nf>; highlighted, spotlighted, featured; obtrusive; **flagrant,** arrant, blatant, notorious; **glaring,** staring, stark-staring

13 manifested, demonstrated, exhibited, shown, displayed, showcased; **manifestable,** demonstrable, exhibitable, displayable

ADVS 14 manifestly, apparently, evidently, obviously, patently, plainly, clearly, distinctly, **unmistakably,** expressly, explicitly, palpably, tangibly; **visibly, perceptibly,** perceivably, discernibly, observably, **noticeably**

15 openly, overtly, before one, **before one's eyes** or very eyes, under one's nose <nf>; to one's face, face-to-face; **publicly,** in public; **in the open,** out in the open, in open court, **in plain sight,** in broad daylight, in the face of day *or* heaven, for all to see, in public view, in plain view, in the marketplace; aboveboard, on the table

16 **conspicuously, prominently, noticeably,** ostensibly, **notably, markedly, pronouncedly, saliently, strikingly, boldly, outstandingly;** obtrusively; arrantly, flagrantly, blatantly, notoriously; glaringly, staringly

349 REPRESENTATION, DESCRIPTION

NOUNS 1 **representation, delineation,** presentment, drawing, **portrayal, portraiture, depiction,** depictment, rendering, rendition, characterization, charactering <old>, picturization, figuration, limning, imaging; prefigurement; **illustration,** exemplification, demonstration; projection, **realization,** manifestation, presentment; imagery, iconography; **art 712; drama 704.1,4-6;** conventional representation, plan, diagram, schema, schematization, **blueprint, chart, map;** drawing, sketch; visual; **notation,** mathematical notation, musical notation, score, tablature; dance notation, Laban dance notation system *or* labanotation, choreography; symbolization; **writing,** script, written word, text; **writing system; alphabet,** syllabary; alphabetic symbol, syllabic symbol, letter, ideogram, pictogram, logogram, logograph, hieroglyphic *or* hieroglyph, rune; printing 548; **symbol**

2 **description, portrayal,** portraiture, **depiction,** rendering, rendition, **delineation,** limning, **representation 349;** imagery; stream of consciousness; **word painting** *or* **picture, picture, portrait, image,** photograph; evocation, impression; **sketch,** vignette, cameo; **characterization,** character, character sketch, profile; vivid description, exact description, realistic *or* naturalistic description, slice of life, *tranche de vie* <Fr>, graphic account; specification, particularization, particulars, details, itemization, catalog, cataloging; **narration;** version

3 **account, recounting,** statement, report, word, statement of fact; play-by-play description, blow-by-blow account *or* description; case study *or* history

4 **impersonation,** personation; mimicry, mimicking, mime, miming, pantomime, pantomiming, aping, dumb show; mimesis, **imitation 336;** personification, embodiment, incarnation, realization; **characterization,** portrayal; **acting,** playing, dramatization, enacting, enactment, performing, performance; **posing,** masquerade

5 **image, likeness; resemblance,** semblance, similitude, simulacrum; **effigy,** icon, idol; **copy 785,** fair copy; **picture; portrait,** likeness; **photograph 714.3,6; perfect** *or* **exact likeness, duplicate, double,** clone; replica, facsimile; match, fellow, mate, companion, **twin;** living image, very image, very picture, living picture, dead ringer <nf>, spitting image *or* spit and image <nf>, eidetic image; miniature, model; **reflection,** shadow, mirroring; trace, tracing; rubbing

6 **figure, figurine; doll,** dolly <nf>; teddy bear; **puppet, marionette,** *fantoche* <Fr>, *fantoccino* and *fantoccio* <Ital>, hand puppet, glove puppet; **mannequin** *or* manikin, model, dummy, working model, lay figure; wax figure, waxwork; scarecrow, corn dolly <Brit>, woman *or* man of straw, snowman, snowwoman, gingerbread woman *or* man, scarecrow, robot, automaton; **sculpture, bust, statue, statuette,** statuary, monument <old>; portrait bust *or* statue; death mask, life mask; carving, wood carving; figurehead

7 **representative,** representation, **type, specimen,** typification, embodiment, type specimen; **cross section;** exponent; **example 786.2,** exemplar; exemplification, typicality, typicalness, representativeness; epitome, quintessence, figuration

VERBS 8 **represent, delineate, depict,** render, characterize, hit off, character <old>, **portray, picture,** picturize, limn, draw, paint 712.20; **register,** convey an impression of; take *or* catch a likeness, capture; **notate, write,** print, map, chart, diagram, schematize; trace, trace out, trace over; rub, take a rubbing; record, photograph, film, shoot, scan; **symbolize 517.18**

9 **describe, portray, picture,** render, **depict, represent, delineate,** limn, **paint,** draw; evoke, bring to life, make one see; outline, sketch; **characterize,** character; **express,** set forth, give words to; **write 547.21**

10 **go for** *or* **as, pass for** *or* **as, count for** *or* **as,** answer for *or* as, stand in the place of, be taken as, be regarded as, be the equivalent of; **serve as,** be accepted for

11 **image, mirror,** hold the mirror up to nature, reflect, figure; **embody,** body forth, incarnate, **personify,** personate, impersonate; **illustrate,** demonstrate, exemplify; project, realize; shadow, shadow forth; **prefigure, pretypify,** foreshadow, adumbrate

12 **impersonate,** personate; **mimic,** mime, pantomime, take off, do *or* give an impression of, mock; ape, copy; **pose as, masquerade as,** affect

the manner *or* guise of, pass for, pretend to be, represent oneself to be; **act,** enact, perform, do; **play, act as,** act *or* play a part, act the part of, act out, role-play, portray

ADJS **13 representational, representative, depictive, delineatory, resemblant; illustrative,** illustrational; pictorial, graphic, vivid; ideographic, pictographic, figurative; **representing, portraying,** limning, illustrating; **typifying, symbolizing,** symbolic, personifying, incarnating, embodying; imitative, mimetic, simulative, apish, mimish; echoic, onomatopoeic

14 descriptive, depictive, expositive, **representative,** representational, **delineative; expressive, vivid, graphic,** well-drawn, detailed; realistic, naturalistic, true to life, lifelike, real-life, faithful; evocative

15 typical, typic, typal; exemplary, sample; **characteristic,** distinctive, distinguishing, quintessential; **realistic, naturalistic; natural, normal,** usual, regular, par for the course <nf>; **true to type, true to form,** the nature of the beast <nf>

ADVS **16 descriptively,** representatively; **expressively, vividly, graphically;** faithfully, realistically, naturalistically

350 MISREPRESENTATION

NOUNS **1 misrepresentation, perversion, distortion,** deformation, garbling, twisting, slanting; inaccuracy; **coloring,** miscoloring, **false coloring;** false pretenses; **falsification** 354.9, **spin,** spin control, disinformation; misteaching 569; injustice, unjust representation; misdrawing, mispainting; misstatement, misreport, misquotation, misinformation; misdirection, misguidance; nonrepresentationalism, nonrealism, abstractionism, expressionism, calculated distortion; overstatement, exaggeration, hyperbole, overdrawing; understatement, litotes, conservative estimate; adulteration, forgery, counterfeiting; cover-up, whitewash

2 bad *or* poor likeness, **daub,** botch; scribble, scratch, hen tracks *or* scratches <nf>; distortion, distorted image, false image, anamorphosis, astigmatism; **travesty,** parody, **caricature, burlesque,** gross exaggeration

VERBS **3 misrepresent, belie,** give a wrong idea, pass *or* pawn *or* foist *or* fob off as, send *or* deliver the wrong signal *or* message; put in a false light, **pervert, distort, garble, twist,** warp, deform, wrench, slant, put a spin on, twist the meaning of; **color,** miscolor, pervert, **give a false coloring,** put a false construction *or* appearance upon, slant,

falsify 354.18; misteach 569.3; **disguise,** camouflage; misstate, misreport, misquote, put words into one's mouth, quote out of context; overstate, exaggerate, overdraw, blow up, blow out of all proportion, overemphasize; understate; **travesty,** parody, **caricature, burlesque;** misinform, disinform

4 misdraw, mispaint; overdraw, daub, botch, butcher, scribble, scratch

351 DISCLOSURE

NOUNS **1 disclosure,** disclosing; **revelation,** revealment, revealing, making public, publicizing, broadcasting, announcement; apocalypse; discovery, discovering; manifestation 348; unfolding, unfoldment, **uncovering,** unwrapping, uncloaking, taking the wraps off, taking from under wraps, removing the veil, **unveiling, unmasking; exposure,** exposition, **exposé; baring,** stripping, stripping *or* laying bare; outing <nf>; **showing up**

2 divulgence, divulging, divulgement, divulgation, evulgation <old>, letting out, full report; **betrayal,** unwitting disclosure, indiscretion; leak, communication leak; **giveaway** *and* dead giveaway <nf>; telltale, telltale sign, obvious clue; **blabbing** *and* blabbering <nf>, babbling; **tattling;** state's evidence

3 confession, confessing, shrift, **acknowledgment, admission,** concession, avowal, self-admission, self-concession, self-avowal, owning, owning up *and* coming clean <nf>, unbosoming, unburdening oneself, getting a load off one's mind <nf>, fessing up <nf>, making a clean breast, baring one's breast; rite of confession

VERBS **4 disclose, reveal, let out, show,** impart, discover, develop <old>, **leak,** let slip out, let the cat out of the bag *and* spill the beans <nf>; manifest 348.5; unfold, unroll; **open,** open up, lay open, break the seal, bring into the open, get out in the open, bring out of the closet; **expose, show up; bare,** strip *or* lay bare, blow the lid off *and* blow wide open *and* rip open *and* crack wide open <nf>; take the lid off, **bring to light,** bring into the open, hold up to view; hold up the mirror to; **unmask,** dismask, tear off the mask, **uncover,** unveil, take the lid off <nf>, ventilate, take out from under wraps, take the wraps off, lift *or* draw the veil, raise the curtain, let daylight in, shine some light on, unscreen, uncloak, undrape, unshroud, unfurl, unsheathe, unwrap, unpack, unkennel; put one wise *and* clue one in *and* bring one up to speed <nf>, put one in the picture <chiefly Brit nf>, open one's eyes

5 divulge, divulgate, evulgate <old>; **reveal, make known, tell,** breathe, utter, vent, ventilate, air, give vent to, **give out, let out** <Brit>, let get around, out with <nf>, come out with; break it to, **break the news;** let in on *or* to, **confide,** confide to, let one's hair down <nf>, unbosom oneself, let into the secret; **publish** 352.10

6 betray, inform, **inform on** 551.12, talk *and* peach <nf>; rat *and* stool *and* sing *and* squeal <nf>, turn state's evidence; leak <nf>, spill <nf>, **spill the beans** <nf>; **let the cat out of the bag** <nf>, speak before one thinks, be unguarded *or* indiscreet, kiss and tell, **give away** *and* give the show away *and* give the game away <nf>, betray a confidence, tell secrets, reveal a secret; have a big mouth *or* bazoo <nf>, **blab** *or* blabber <nf>; babble, **tattle,** tell *or* tattle on, tell tales, **tell tales out of school;** talk out of turn, let slip, let fall *or* drop; **blurt, blurt out**

7 confess, break down and confess, **admit, acknowledge,** tell all, avow, concede, grant, **own, own up** <nf>, let on, implicate *or* incriminate oneself, come clean <nf>; spill *and* spill it *and* spill one's guts <nf>; **tell the truth,** tell all, admit everything, let it all hang out <nf>, throw off all disguise; **plead guilty,** own oneself in the wrong, cop a plea <nf>; **unbosom oneself, make a clean breast, get it off one's chest** <nf>, **get it out of one's system** <nf>, disburden *or* unburden one's mind *or* conscience *or* heart, **get a load off one's mind** <nf>, fess up <nf>; out with it *and* spit it out *and* open up <nf>; throw oneself on the mercy of the court; **reveal oneself,** show one's colors *or* true colors, come out of the closet <nf>, show one's hand *or* cards, put *or* lay one's cards on the table

8 be revealed, become known, surface, come to light, appear, manifest itself, come to one's ears, transpire, **leak out, get out, come out,** out, come home to roost, come out in the wash, break forth, show its face; show its colors, be seen in its true colors, stand revealed; blow one's cover <nf>

ADJS **9 revealed, disclosed** 348.10

10 disclosive, revealing, revelatory, revelational; **disclosing,** showing, exposing, betraying; kiss-and-tell; eye-opening; **talkative** 343.10,540.9; admitted, confessed, self-confessed

11 confessional, admissive

352 PUBLICATION

NOUNS **1 publication, publishing, promulgation,** evulgation, **propagation, dissemination, diffusion, broadcast, broadcasting, spread, spreading,** spreading abroad, divulgence, disclosure, **circulation,** ventilation, airing, noising, bandying, bruiting, bruiting about, spreading the word; **display;** issue, issuance; telecasting, videocasting; printing 548; book, periodical 555

2 announcement, annunciation, enunciation; **proclamation,** pronouncement, pronunciamento; edict, decree; **report,** communiqué, **declaration, statement;** public declaration *or* statement, program, programma, **notice, notification,** public notice; speech; circular, encyclical, encyclical letter; manifesto, position paper; broadside; rationale; white paper, white book; ukase, edict 420.4; bulletin board, notice board

3 press release, release, handout, bulletin, official bulletin, notice

4 publicity, publicness, **notoriety, fame,** famousness, renown, notoriousness, infamy, notice, public notice *or* recognition, **celebrity,** *réclame* and *éclat* <Fr>; **limelight** *and* **spotlight** <nf>, daylight, bright light, glare, public eye *or* consciousness, **exposure, currency,** common *or* public knowledge, widest *or* maximum dissemination, public forum; **ballyhoo** *and* hoopla <nf>; report, public report; cry, hue and cry; **public relations** *or* PR, flackery <nf>; **publicity story,** press notice; propaganda; **writeup, puff** <nf>, **plug** <nf>, **blurb** <nf>, hype <nf>; photo opportunity, photo op <nf>; name in bright lights <nf>

5 promotion, buildup *and* promo <nf>, flack <nf>, publicization, publicizing, promoting, advocating, advocacy, bruiting, drumbeating, tub-thumping, press-agentry; **advertising,** salesmanship 734.2, Madison Avenue, hucksterism <nf>; advertising campaign; advertising agency; advertising medium *or* media; advocacy, advocacy group

6 advertisement, ad <nf>, advert <Brit nf>, notice; **commercial,** message, important message, message *or* words from the sponsor; spot commercial *or* spot, network commercial; infomercial; reader, reading notice; display ad; want ad <nf>, classified ad; spread, two-page spread, testimonial; advertorial; trailer; teaser

7 poster, bill, placard, sign, show card, banner, *affiche* <Fr>; **signboard, billboard,** highway sign, hoarding <Brit>; sandwich board; marquee; bulletin board

8 advertising matter, promotional material, public relations handout *or* release, **literature** <nf>; **leaflet,** leaf, **folder, handbill, bill, flier, throwaway, handout, circular,** pamphlet, brochure, broadside, broadsheet; insert *or* insertion

9 publicist, publicizer, public relations person, public relations officer, PR person, flack *and* pitchman *or* pitchperson <nf>, public relations specialist, **publicity man** *or* agent, **press agent,** flack <nf>, imagemaker; **advertiser; adman** *and*

huckster *and* pitchman <nf>; ad writer <nf>, copywriter, blurb writer; **promoter, booster** <nf>, plugger <nf>; **ballyhooer** *or* **ballyhoo man** <nf>; **barker,** spieler <nf>, skywriter; billposter; sign-painter; sandwich boy *or* man; spin doctor

VERBS **10 publish, promulgate, propagate, circulate,** circularize, **diffuse, disseminate,** distribute, **broadcast,** televise, telecast, videocast, air, **spread,** spread around *or* about, spread far and wide, publish abroad, **pass the word around,** bruit, **bruit about, advertise,** repeat, retail, put about, **bandy about, noise about,** cry about *or* abroad, noise *or* sound abroad, bruit abroad, set news afloat, **spread a report; rumor,** launch a rumor, voice <old>, whisper, buzz, **rumor about,** whisper *or* buzz about

11 make public, go public with <nf>; bring *or* lay *or* drag before the public, **display,** take one's case to the public, **give** *or* **put out,** give to the world, **make known; divulge** 351.5; **ventilate,** air, give air to, bring into the open, get out in the open, open up, broach, give vent to

12 announce, annunciate, enunciate; **declare, state,** declare roundly, affirm, pronounce, give notice; **say,** make a statement, send a message *or* signal; **report,** make an announcement *or* a report, issue a statement, publish *or* issue a manifesto, present a position paper, issue a white paper, hold a press conference

13 proclaim, cry, cry out, **promulgate,** give voice to; **herald,** herald abroad; **blazon,** blaze, blaze *or* blazon about *or* abroad, blare, blare forth *or* abroad, thunder, declaim, shout, trumpet, trumpet *or* thunder forth, announce with flourish of trumpets *or* beat of drum; shout from the housetops, proclaim at the crossroads *or* market cross, proclaim at Charing Cross <Brit>

14 issue, bring out, put out, get out, launch, get off, emit, put *or* give *or* send forth, offer to the public, pass out

15 publicize, give publicity; go public with <nf>; bring *or* drag into the limelight, throw the spotlight on <nf>; **advertise, promote,** build up, cry up, sell, puff <nf>, **boost** <nf>, **plug** <nf>, **ballyhoo** <nf>; put on the map, make a household word of, establish; bark *and* spiel <nf>; make a pitch for *and* beat the drum for *and* thump the tub for <nf>; **write up,** give a write-up, press-agent <nf>; circularize; bulletin; bill; **post bills,** post, post up, placard; skywrite

16 <be published> **come out, appear,** break, hit the streets <nf>, **issue,** go *or* come forth, find vent, **see the light,** see the light of day, become public; **circulate, spread,** spread about, have currency, **get around** *or* about, get abroad, get afloat, get exposure, go *or* fly *or* buzz *or* blow about, **go the rounds,** pass from mouth to mouth, be on everyone's lips, go through the length and breadth of the land; spread like wildfire

ADJS **17 published, public,** made public, **circulated,** in circulation, promulgated, propagated, **disseminated,** issued, spread, diffused, distributed; in print; **broadcast,** telecast, televised; **announced,** proclaimed, declared, **stated,** affirmed; **reported,** brought to notice; common knowledge, common property, current; **open,** accessible, open to the public; hot off the press

18 publicational, promulgatory, propagatory; proclamatory, annunciatory, enunciative; declarative, declaratory; heraldic; promotional

ADVS **19 publicly, in public; openly** 348.15; in the public eye, in the glare of publicity, in the limelight *or* spotlight <nf>, reportedly

353 MESSENGER

NOUNS **1 messenger,** message-bearer, **dispatch-bearer,** commissionaire <Brit>, nuncio <old>, **courier,** diplomatic courier, carrier, **runner,** express <Brit>, dispatch-rider, pony-express rider, post <old>, postboy, postrider, *estafette* <Fr>; bicycle *or* motorcycle messenger; **go-between** 576.4; **emissary** 576.6; Mercury, Hermes, Iris, Pheidippides, Paul Revere; post office, courier service, package service, message service *or* center; answering service

2 herald, harbinger, forerunner, vaunt-courier; evangel, evangelist, bearer of glad tidings; herald angel, Gabriel, *buccinator* <L>

3 announcer, annunciator, enunciator; nunciate <old>; **proclaimer; crier, town crier,** bellman

4 errand boy, office boy, messenger-boy, copyboy; bellhop <nf>, bellboy, bellman, callboy, caller

5 postman, mailman, mail carrier, letter carrier; postmaster, postmistress; postal clerk

6 <mail carriers> carrier pigeon, carrier, homing pigeon, homer <nf>; pigeon post; post-horse, poster; post coach, mail coach; post boat, packet boat *or* ship, mail boat, mail packet, mailer <old>; mail train, mail car, post car, post-office car, railway mail car; mail truck; mailplane; electronic mail

354 FALSENESS

NOUNS **1 falseness, falsehood,** falsity, inveracity, untruth, **truthlessness, untrueness; fallaciousness,** fallacy, **erroneousness** 974.1

2 spuriousness, phoniness <nf>, bogusness, **ungenuineness, unauthenticity,** unrealness, artificiality, factitiousness, syntheticness

3 sham, fakery, faking, falsity, feigning, pretending; feint, pretext, **pretense,** hollow pretense, **pretension, false pretense** *or* **pretension;** humbug, humbuggery; **bluff,** bluffing, four-flushing <nf>; speciousness, meretriciousness; cheating, fraud; imposture; deception, delusion 356.1; acting, playacting; representation, **simulation,** simulacrum; dissembling, **dissemblance, dissimulation;** seeming, semblance, appearance, face, ostentation, **show, false show,** outward show, false air; window dressing, front, **false front, façade,** gloss, varnish; gilt; color, coloring, false color; masquerade, disguise; posture, pose, posing, attitudinizing; mannerism, affectation 500

4 falseheartedness, falseness, doubleheartedness, doubleness of heart, doubleness, **duplicity, two-facedness,** double-facedness, **double-dealing,** ambidexterity; double standard; **dishonesty,** improbity, lack of integrity, Machiavellianism, bad faith; low cunning, **cunning,** artifice, wile 415.1,3; **deceitfulness** 356.3; faithlessness, treachery 645.6

5 insincerity, uncandidness, uncandor, **unfrankness,** disingenuousness, indirectness; emptiness, hollowness; mockery, hollow mockery; crossed fingers, tongue in cheek, unseriousness; halfheartedness; sophistry, jesuitry, jesuitism, casuistry 936.1

6 hypocrisy, hypocriticalness; Tartuffery, Tartuffism, Pecksniffery, pharisaism, **sanctimony** 693, sanctimoniousness, religiosity, false piety, ostentatious devotion, pietism, Bible-thumping <nf>; **mealymouthedness, unctuousness,** oiliness, smarminess *or* smarm <nf>; cant, mummery, snuffling <old>, **mouthing; lip service;** tokenism; token gesture, empty gesture; smooth tongue, smooth talk, sweet talk *and* soft soap <nf>; crocodile tears

7 quackery, chicanery, quackishness, quackism, **mountebankery, charlatanry,** charlatanism; **imposture; humbug,** humbuggery

8 untruthfulness, dishonesty, falsehood, **unveracity,** unveraciousness, truthlessness, **mendaciousness, mendacity;** credibility gap; **lying, fibbing,** fibbery, pseudology; pathological lying, habitual lying, mythomania, *pseudologia phantastica* <L>

9 deliberate falsehood, disinformation, falsification, disinforming, falsifying; confabulation; **perversion, distortion,** straining, **bending; misrepresentation,** misconstruction, misstatement, coloring, false coloring, miscoloring, slanting, imparting a spin <nf>; tampering, cooking *and* fiddling <nf>; stretching, fictionalization, **exaggeration** 355; **prevarication,** equivocation 344.4; **perjury,** false swearing, oath breaking, false oath, false plea

10 fabrication, invention, concoction, disinformation; canard, base canard; **forgery; fiction,** figment, **myth,** legend, fable, story, romanticized version, extravaganza; old wives' tale, unfact

11 lie, falsehood, falsity, **untruth,** false statement, untruism, mendacity, **prevarication, fib,** taradiddle *or* tarradiddle <nf>, flimflam *or* flam, a crock *and* a crock of shit <nf>, *blague* <Fr>; **fiction,** pious fiction, legal fiction; **story** <nf>, **trumped-up story,** farrago; **yarn** <nf>, **tale,** fairy tale <nf>, ghost story; farfetched story, tall tale *and* **tall story** <nf>, **cock-and-bull story,** fish story <nf>, flight of fancy; exaggeration 355; half-truth, stretching of the truth, slight stretching, white lie, little white lie; *suggestio falsi* <L>; partial truth; propaganda, rumor, gossip, empty talk; a pack of lies

12 monstrous lie, consummate lie, deep-dyed falsehood, out-and-out lie, **whopper** <nf>, gross *or* flagrant *or* shameless falsehood, downright lie, **barefaced lie, dirty lie** <nf>, big lie; **slander, libel** 512.3; the big lie; bullshit *or* load of crap <nf>

13 fake, fakement *and* put-up job <nf>, **phony** <nf>, **rip-off** <nf>, **sham, mock, imitation,** simulacrum, dummy; paste, tinsel, *clinquant* <Fr>, pinchbeck, shoddy, junk; **counterfeit, forgery;** put-up job *and* frame-up <nf>, put-on <nf>; **hoax, cheat, fraud, swindle** 356.8; whited sepulcher, whitewash job <nf>; impostor 357.6

14 humbug, humbuggery; **bunk** <nf>, **bunkum;** hooey *and* hoke *and* **hokum** <nf>, **bosh** <nf>, bull *and* **bullshit** *and* crap <nf>, baloney <nf>, flimflam, flam, smoke and mirrors <nf>, claptrap, moonshine, eyewash, hogwash, gammon <Brit nf>, *blague* <Fr>, jiggery-pokery <Brit>

VERBS 15 ring false, **not ring true**

16 falsify, belie, misrepresent, miscolor; misstate, misquote, misreport, miscite; overstate, understate; **pervert, distort,** strain, warp, **slant, twist,** warp, stretch the truth, impart spin <nf>; garble; put a false appearance upon, give a false coloring, falsely color, give a color to, **color, gild,** gloss, gloss over, whitewash, varnish, paper over <nf>; fudge <nf>; dress up, titivate, embellish, embroider, trick *or* prink out; deodorize, make smell like roses; **disguise, camouflage, mask;** propagandize, gossip

17 tamper with, manipulate, fake, juggle, sophisticate, **doctor** *and* **cook** <nf>, rig, cook *or* juggle the books *or* the accounts <nf>; pack, stack; **adulterate;** retouch; **load; salt,** plant <nf>, salt a mine

18 fabricate, invent, manufacture, trump up, make up, hatch, concoct, cook up *and* make out of whole cloth <nf>, fictionalize, mythologize, fudge <nf>, fake, hoke up <nf>; **counterfeit, forge;** fantasize, fantasize about

19 lie, tell a lie, falsify, speak falsely, speak with forked tongue <nf>, be untruthful, trifle with the truth, deviate from the truth, **fib, story** <nf>; **stretch the truth,** strain *or* bend the truth; draw the longbow; **exaggerate** 355.3; lie flatly, lie in one's throat, lie through one's teeth, lie like a trooper, **prevaricate,** misstate, equivocate 344.7; **deceive, mislead,** tell a white lie; bullshit <nf>

20 swear falsely, forswear oneself <old>, perjure, **perjure oneself, bear false witness**

21 sham, fake <nf>, **feign, counterfeit, simulate,** put up <nf>, gammon <Brit nf>; **pretend,** make a pretense, **make believe, make a show of,** make like <nf>, make as if *or* as though; go through the motions <nf>; let on, let on like <nf>; **affect,** profess, **assume,** put on; **dissimulate, dissemble,** cover up; **act, play,** play-act, **put on an act** *or* a charade <nf>, act *or* play a part; **put up a front** <nf>, put on a front *or* false front <nf>; four-flush <nf>, **bluff,** pull *or* put up a bluff <nf>; **play possum** <nf>, roll over and play dead

22 pose as, masquerade as, impersonate, pass for, assume the guise *or* identity of, set up for, act the part of, represent oneself to be, claim *or* pretend to be, **make false pretenses,** go under false pretenses, **sail under false colors**

23 be hypocritical, act *or* **play the hypocrite;** cant, be holier than the Pope *or* thou, reek of piety; shed crocodile tears, snuffle <old>, snivel, mouth; give mouth honor, render *or* give lip service; sweet-talk, soft-soap, blandish 511.5

24 play a double game *or* **role, play both ends against the middle,** work both sides of the street, have it both ways at once, have one's cake and eat it too, run with the hare and hunt with the hounds <Brit>; two-time <nf>

ADJS **25 false, untrue, truthless, not true,** void *or* devoid of truth, contrary to fact, in error, **fallacious, erroneous** 974.16; unfounded 936.13; disinformative

26 spurious, ungenuine, unauthentic, supposititious, bastard, **pseudo, quasi,** apocryphal, **fake** <nf>, **phony** <nf>, **sham, mock, counterfeit,** colorable, **bogus,** queer <nf>, dummy, **make-believe,** so-called, **imitation** 336.8; not what it's cracked up to be <nf>; **falsified;** dressed up, titivated, embellished, embroidered; garbled; twisted, distorted, warped, perverted, slanted; half-true, falsely colored; **simulated, faked, feigned,** colored, fictitious, fictive, **counterfeited, pretended, affected, assumed, put-on; artificial, synthetic,** ersatz; unreal; factitious, unnatural, man-made; illegitimate; *soi-disant* <Fr>, self-styled; pinchbeck, brummagem <Brit>, tinsel, shoddy, tin, junky

27 specious, meretricious, gilded, tinsel, **seeming,** apparent, colored, colorable, plausible, **ostensible**

28 quack, quackish; charlatan, charlatanish, charlatanic

29 fabricated, invented, manufactured, **concocted, hatched, trumped-up, made-up,** put-up, cooked-up <nf>; **forged;** fictitious, fictional, fictionalized, figmental, **mythical,** fabulous, legendary; fantastic, fantasied, fancied, legendary

30 tampered with, manipulated, cooked *and* **doctored** <nf>, juggled, **rigged,** engineered; packed

31 falsehearted, false, false-principled, false-dealing; double, duplicitous, ambidextrous, **double-dealing,** doublehearted, double-minded, double-tongued, double-faced, **two-faced,** Janus-faced; Machiavellian, dishonest; **crooked, deceitful;** creative, artful, cunning, crafty 415.12; faithless, perfidious, treacherous 645.21

32 insincere, uncandid, unfrank, mealymouthed, unctuous, oily, disingenuous, ungenuine, pseudo, smarmy <nf>; dishonest; **empty, hollow;** tongue in cheek, unserious; sophistic *or* sophistical, jesuitic *or* jesuitical, casuistic 936.10

33 hypocritic *or* **hypocritical,** canting, Pecksniffian, pharisaic, pharisaical, pharisean, **sanctimonious, goody-goody** <nf>, holier-than-the-Pope, holier-than-thou, simon-pure; artificial, dissembling, phony

34 untruthful, dishonest, unveracious, unveridical, truthless, **lying, mendacious,** untrue; perjured, forsworn; prevaricating, equivocal 344.11

ADVS **35 falsely, untruly,** truthlessly; **erroneously** 975.20; **untruthfully,** unveraciously; mendaciously; **spuriously,** ungenuinely; artificially, synthetically; unnaturally, factitiously; speciously, seemingly, apparently, plausibly, ostensibly; nominally, in name only

36 insincerely, uncandidly, unfrankly; emptily, hollowly; unseriously; ambiguously; **hypocritically,** mealy-mouthedly, unctuously

355 EXAGGERATION

NOUNS **1 exaggeration,** exaggerating; **overstatement,** big *or* tall talk <nf>, **hyperbole,** hyperbolism; **superlative; extravagance,** profuseness, **prodigality** 486, overdoing it, going too far, overshooting; **magnification, enlargement,** amplification <old>, dilation, dilatation, **inflation,** expansion, blowing up, puffing up, aggrandizement, embellishment, elaboration, embroidery; **stretching, heightening,** enhancement; overemphasis, overstressing; overestimation 949; exaggerated lengths, **extreme,** extremism, stretch, exorbitance, inordinacy, **overkill, excess** 993; burlesque, travesty, caricature; crock <nf>, whopper, tall story; sensationalism, puffery *and* ballyhoo <nf>, touting, huckstering; grandiloquence 545; painting *or* gilding the lily; to-do *and* hype *and* hoopla <nf>

2 overreaction, much ado about nothing, fuss, uproar, commotion, storm *or* tempest in a teapot, making a mountain out of a molehill

VERBS **3 exaggerate,** hyperbolize; **overstate,** overspeak <old>, overreach, **overdraw,** overcharge; overstress, overemphasize; **overdo, carry too far, go to extremes;** push to the extreme, indulge in overkill, overestimate 949.2; gild the lily; overpraise, oversell, tout, puff *and* ballyhoo *and* hype <nf>; **stretch,** stretch the truth, stretch the point, draw the longbow, embellish; **magnify, inflate,** amplify <old>; aggrandize, build up; pile *or* lay it on *and* pour *or* spread *or* lay it on thick *and* lay it on with a trowel <nf>; pile Pelion on Ossa; talk big <nf>, talk in superlatives, deal in the marvelous, make much of; **overreact,** make a Federal case out of it <nf>, something out of nothing, make a mountain out of a molehill, create a tempest in a teapot *or* teacup, make too much of, cry over spilt milk; caricature, travesty, burlesque, ham, ham it up

ADJS **4 exaggerated,** hyperbolical, **magnified,** amplified <old>, **inflated,** aggrandized, stylized, embroidered, embellished, varnished; **stretched,** disproportionate, **blown up out of all proportion,** blown out of proportion, overblown; overpraised, oversold, overrated, touted, puffed *and* ballyhooed <nf>, hyped <nf>; overemphasized, **overemphatic, overstressed; overemphatic, overstressed; overstated, overdrawn; overdone,** overwrought, a bit thick; caricatural, melodramatic, farfetched, too much <nf>, over the top; overestimated 949.3; overlarge, overgreat; **extreme,** pushed to the extreme, exorbitant, inordinate, **excessive** 993.16; **superlative, extravagant,** profuse, **prodigal** 486.8; high-flown, grandiloquent 545.8; overexposed

5 exaggerating, exaggerative, hyperbolical

356 DECEPTION

NOUNS **1 deception,** calculated deception, **deceptiveness, subterfuge,** gimmickry *or* gimmickery, **trickiness; falseness** 354; fallaciousness, fallacy; self-deception, fond illusion, wishful thinking, willful misconception; vision, hallucination, phantasm, mirage, will-o'-the-wisp, **delusion,** delusiveness, illusion 975; deceiving, **victimization, dupery;** bamboozlement <nf>, hoodwinking; swindling, defrauding, conning, flimflam *or* flimflammery <nf>; **fooling,** befooling,

tricking, **kidding** *and* putting on <nf>; spoofing *and* spoofery <nf>; bluffing; circumvention, overreaching, outwitting; ensnarement, entrapment, enmeshment, entanglement; smoke and mirrors

2 misleading, misguidance, misdirection; bum steer <nf>; misinformation 569.1

3 deceit, deceitfulness, guile, falseness, insidiousness, **underhandedness; shiftiness, furtiveness,** surreptitiousness, indirection; **hypocrisy** 354.6; **falseheartedness, duplicity** 354.4; **treacherousness** 645.6; **artfulness,** craft, guile, **cunning** 415; sneakiness 345.4; sneak attack

4 chicanery, chicane, **skulduggery** <nf>, knavery, **trickery,** dodgery, pettifogging, pettifoggery, *supercherie* <Fr>, **artifice,** sleight, machination; **sharp practice, underhand dealing, foul play;** connivery, connivance, collusion, conspiracy, covin <law>; fakery, charlatanism, mountebankery, quackery

5 juggling, jugglery, **trickery,** dirty pool <nf>, *escamotage* <Fr>, prestidigitation, conjuration, **legerdemain, sleight of hand,** smoke and mirrors <nf>; mumbo jumbo, **hocus-pocus,** hanky-panky *and* monkey business *and* hokey-pokey <nf>, nobbling *and* jiggery-pokery <Brit nf>, shenanigans <nf>

6 trick, artifice, device, ploy, gambit, stratagem, scheme, **design,** *ficelle* <Fr>, **subterfuge,** blind, **ruse, wile,** chouse <nf>, shift, **dodge,** artful dodge, sleight, pass, feint, fetch, chicanery; **bluff;** gimmick, joker, catch; curve, curve-ball, googly *or* bosey *or* wrong'un <Brit nf>; **dirty trick,** dirty deal, fast deal, scurvy trick; sleight of hand, sleight-of-hand trick, hocus-pocus <old>; juggle, juggler's trick; **bag of tricks,** tricks of the trade

7 hoax, deception, spoof <nf>, **humbug,** flam, **fake** *and* fakement, **rip-off** <nf>, **sham;** mare's nest; put-on <nf>

8 fraud, fraudulence *or* fraudulency, **dishonesty; imposture; imposition, cheat, cheating,** cozenage, **swindle,** dodge, fishy transaction, piece of sharp practice; customer-gouging, insider-trading, short weight, chiseling; **gyp joint** <nf>; **racket** <nf>, illicit business 732; **graft** <nf>, grift <nf>; bunco; cardsharping; ballot-box stuffing, gerrymandering

9 <nf terms> **gyp,** diddle, diddling, scam, flimflam flam, ramp <Brit>, snow job, song and dance, number, bill of goods, burn, the business, dipsy-doodle, double cross, fiddle, hosing, the old army game, reaming, suckering, sting, con, ripoff

10 confidence game, con game <nf>, **skin game** <nf>, **bunco game; shell game,** thimblerig, thimblerigging; bucket shop, boiler room <nf>;

goldbrick; bait-and-switch, the wire, the pay-off, the rag, pastposting

11 cover, disguise, camouflage, protective coloration; **false colors, false front** 354.3; **incognito;** smoke screen; **masquerade,** masque, mummery; **mask,** visor, vizard, vizard mask <old>, false face, domino, domino mask; red herring, diversion

12 trap, gin; pitfall, trapfall, deadfall; flytrap, mousetrap, mole trap, rattrap, bear trap; deathtrap, firetrap; Venus's flytrap, Dionaea; Catch-22; spring gun, set gun; baited trap; **booby trap, mine; decoy** 357.5; hidden danger

13 snare, springe; noose, lasso, lariat; bola; **net,** trawl, dragnet, seine, purse seine, pound net, gill net; cobweb; **meshes, toils; fishhook, hook,** sniggle; **bait,** ground bait; lure, fly, jig, squid, plug, wobbler, spinner; lime, birdlime

VERBS **14 deceive, beguile, trick, hoax, dupe,** gammon, **gull,** pigeon, play one for a fool *or* sucker, **bamboozle** *and* snow *and* **hornswoggle** *and* diddle *and* scam <nf>, nobble <Brit nf>, **humbug, take in,** put on *and* hocus-pocus <nf>, string along, **put something over** *or* **across,** slip one over on <nf>, pull a fast one on; **play games** <nf>; **delude,** mock; **betray,** let down, leave in the lurch, leave holding the bag, play one false, **double-cross** <nf>, cheat on; two-time <nf>; juggle, conjure; **bluff;** cajole, **circumvent,** get around, forestall; **overreach,** outreach, outwit, outmaneuver, outsmart

15 fool, befool, make a fool of, practice on one's credulity, **pull one's leg,** make an ass of; **trick; spoof** *and* **kid** *and* put one on <nf>; **play a trick on,** play a practical joke upon, send on a fool's errand; fake one out <nf>; sell one a bill of goods, give one a snow job

16 mislead, misguide, misdirect, lead astray, lead up the garden path, **give a bum steer** <nf>; fake someone out, feed one a line <nf>, throw off the scent, throw off the track *or* trail, put on a false scent, drag *or* draw a red herring across the trail; throw one a curve *or* curve ball <nf>, bowl a googly *or* bosey *or* wrong 'un <Brit nf>; misinform 569.3

17 hoodwink, blindfold, blind, blind one's eyes, blear the eyes of <old>, throw dust in one's eyes, **pull the wool over one's eyes**

18 cheat, victimize, gull, pigeon, fudge, **swindle, defraud,** practice fraud upon, euchre, **con,** finagle, **fleece,** mulct, fob <old>, **bilk,** cozen, cog <old>, chouse, **cheat out of, do out of,** chouse out of, beguile of *or* out of; obtain under false pretenses; live by one's wits; bunco, play a bunco game; sell gold bricks <nf>; shortchange, shortweight, skim off the top; stack the cards *or* deck, pack the deal

<nf>, deal off the bottom of the deck, play with marked cards; cog the dice, load the dice; thimblerig; crib <nf>; throw a fight *or* game <nf>, take a dive <nf>

19 <nf terms> **gyp, clip, scam,** rope in, hose, shave, beat, rook, flam, flimflam, diddle, dipsy-doodle, do a number on, hustle, fuck, screw, have, pull something, pull a trick *or* stunt, give the business, ramp <Brit>, stick, sting, burn, gouge, chisel, hocus, hocus-pocus, play *or* take for a sucker, make a patsy of, do, run a game on, slicker, take for a ride

20 trap, entrap, gin, catch, catch out, catch in a trap; catch unawares, ambush; **ensnare, snare,** hook, **hook in,** sniggle, noose; inveigle; net, mesh, enmesh, snarl <old>, ensnarl, wind, tangle, entangle, entoil, enweb; trip, trip up; **set** *or* **lay a trap for,** bait the hook, spread the toils; lime, birdlime; **lure,** allure, **decoy** 377.3

ADJS **21 deceptive, deceiving, misleading,** beguiling, **false, fallacious,** delusive, delusory; hallucinatory, illusive, **illusory;** tricky, trickish, tricksy <old>, catchy; **fishy** <nf>, questionable, dubious; delusional

22 deceitful, false; fraudulent, sharp, guileful, **insidious,** slick, slippery, slippery as an eel, **shifty, tricky,** trickish, cute, finagling, chiseling <nf>; underhand, **underhanded, furtive, surreptitious,** indirect; collusive, covinous; **falsehearted, two-faced; treacherous** 645.21; sneaky 345.12; **cunning,** artful, gimmicky <nf>, **wily, crafty** 415.12; calculating, scheming, double-dealing

ADVS **23 deceptively,** beguilingly, **falsely,** fallaciously, delusively, **trickily, misleadingly,** with intent to deceive; under false colors, under cover of, under the garb of, in disguise

24 deceitfully, fraudulently, guilefully, insidiously, **shiftily, trickily; underhandedly,** furtively, surreptitiously, indirectly, like a thief in the night; **treacherously** 645.25

357 DECEIVER

NOUNS **1 deceiver, deluder,** duper, misleader, **beguiler, bamboozler** <nf>; actor, playactor <nf>, role-player; **dissembler,** dissimulator; confidence man; **double-dealer,** Machiavelli, Machiavel, Machiavellian; dodger, Artful Dodger <Charles Dickens>, **counterfeiter, forger, faker;** plagiarizer, plagiarist; entrancer, **enchanter,** charmer, befuddler, hypnotizer, mesmerizer; **seducer,** Don Juan, Casanova; tease, teaser; jilt, jilter; gay deceiver; **fooler, joker,** jokester, **hoaxer,** practical joker; spoofer *and* **kidder** *and* ragger *and* leg-puller <nf>

2 trickster, tricker; **juggler,** sleight-of-hand performer, magician, illusionist, conjurer, **prestidigitator,** *escamoteur* <Fr>, manipulator

3 cheat, cheater; two-timer <nf>; **swindler, defrauder,** cozener, juggler; **sharper, sharp,** spieler, pitchman, pitchperson; **confidence man, confidence trickster, horse trader,** horse coper <Brit>; **cardsharp,** cardsharper; thimblerigger; shortchanger; **shyster** *and* pettifogger <nf>; land shark, land pirate, land grabber, mortgage shark; carpetbagger; crimp

4 <nf terms> gyp, gypper, gyp artist, flimflammer, flimflam man, blackleg, chiseler, bilker, fleecer, diddler, crook, sharpie, shark, jackleg, slicker, con man, con artist, bunco, bunco artist, bunco steerer, scammer, clip artist, smoothie, dipsy-doodle, hustler, hoser

5 shill, decoy, **come-on man** <nf>, plant, capper, stool pigeon, stoolie <nf>; *agent provocateur* <Fr>

6 impostor, ringer; impersonator; pretender; sham, shammer, **humbug,** *blagueur* <Fr>, **fraud** <nf>, **fake** *and* **faker** *and* **phony** <nf>, **fourflusher** <nf>, bluff, bluffer; **charlatan, quack,** quacksalver, quackster, **mountebank,** saltimbanco; **wolf in sheep's clothing,** ass in lion's skin, jackdaw in peacock's feathers; poser, poseur; malingerer

7 masquerader, masker; **impersonator,** personator; mummer, guiser <Scot>, guisard; incognito, incognita

8 hypocrite, phony <nf>, sanctimonious fraud, pharisee, whited sepulcher, **canter,** snuffler, mealy-mouth, dissembler, dissimulator, pretender, poseur, poser, "a saint abroad and a devil at home"— Bunyan; Tartuffe <Molière>, Pecksniff *and* Uriah Heep <Charles Dickens>, Joseph Surface <Richard B Sheridan>; false friend, fair-weather friend; summer soldier; cupboard lover

9 liar, fibber, fibster, fabricator, fabulist, pseudologist; falsifier; **prevaricator,** equivocator, evader, mudger <Brit nf>, waffler <nf>, palterer; **storyteller;** yarner *and* yarn spinner *and* spinner of yarns <nf>, double-talker; Ananias; Satan, Father of Lies; Baron Münchausen; Sir John Mandeville; consummate liar, "liar of the first magnitude"— Congreve; *menteur à triple étage* <Fr>, dirty liar; pathological liar, mythomane, mythomaniac, pseudologue, confirmed *or* habitual liar, consummate liar; **perjurer,** false witness; slanderer, libeler, libelant; bullshitter <nf>

10 traitor, treasonist, **betrayer, quisling, rat** <nf>, serpent, snake, cockatrice, **snake in the grass, double-crosser** <nf>, double-dealer; double agent; trimmer, time-server; turncoat 363.5; informer 551.6; archtraitor; Judas, Judas Iscariot, Benedict Arnold, Quisling, Brutus; **schemer, plotter,**

intriguer, *intrigant* <Fr>, conspirer, **conspirator,** conniver, machinator; pseud <nf>, two-timer <nf>

11 subversive; saboteur, fifth columnist, crypto; security risk; **collaborationist,** collaborator, fraternizer; fifth column, underground; Trojan horse; renegade

358 DUPE

NOUNS **1 dupe, gull,** gudgeon, *gobe-mouches* <Fr>; **victim;** gullible *or* dupable *or* credulous person, trusting *or* simple soul, innocent, *naïf* <Fr>, babe, babe in the woods; greenhorn; toy, plaything; monkey; **fool** 924; stooge, **cat's-paw**

2 <nf terms> sucker, patsy, pigeon, chicken, fall guy, doormat, mug <Brit>, fish, jay <chiefly Brit>, easy mark, sitting duck, juggin <chiefly Brit>, pushover, cinch, mark, vic, easy pickings, greeny, greener, chump, boob, schlemiel, sap, saphead, prize sap, easy touch, soft touch

359 RESOLUTION

NOUNS **1 resolution,** resolve, resolvedness, **determination, decision,** fixed *or* firm resolve, will, purpose; **resoluteness, determinedness,** determinateness, decisiveness, decidedness, **purposefulness;** definiteness; **earnestness, seriousness,** sincerity, devotion, dedication, commitment, total commitment; "the native hue of resolution"—Shakespeare; single-mindedness, relentlessness, persistence, tenacity, perseverance 360; self-will, obstinacy 361

2 firmness, firmness of mind *or* spirit, fixity of purpose, **staunchness,** settledness, steadiness, constancy, steadfastness, fixedness, unshakableness; **stability** 854; concentration; flintiness, steeliness; inflexibility, rigidity, unyieldingness 361.2; trueness, loyalty 644.7

3 pluck, spunk <nf>, **mettle, backbone** <nf>, **grit,** true grit, spirit, **stamina, guts** *and* moxie <nf>, pith <old>, bottom, **toughness** <nf>; clenched teeth, gritted teeth; pluckiness, spunkiness <nf>, **gameness,** feistiness <nf>, mettlesomeness; courage 492

4 will power, will, power, **strong-mindedness,** strength of mind, strength *or* fixity of purpose, strength, fortitude, **moral fiber; iron will,** will of iron *or* steel; a will *or* mind of one's own, law unto oneself; the courage of one's convictions, moral courage

5 self-control, self-command, self-possession, strength of character, self-mastery, self-government, self-domination, **self-restraint,** self-conquest, self-discipline, **self-denial;** control, restraint, constraint, discipline; composure, possession, aplomb; **independence** 430.5

6 **self-assertion,** self-assertiveness, forwardness, **nerve** and pushiness <nf>, importunateness, importunacy; self-expression, self-expressiveness

VERBS 7 **resolve, determine, decide, will, purpose, make up one's mind,** make or take a resolution, make a point of; **settle,** settle on, fix, seal; conclude, come to a determination or conclusion or decision, determine once for all

8 **be determined,** be resolved; **have a mind or will of one's own,** know one's own mind; **be in earnest, mean business** <nf>, mean what one says; have blood in one's eyes and be out for blood <nf>, **set one's mind or heart upon;** put one's heart into, devote or commit or dedicate oneself to, give oneself up to; buckle oneself, buckle down, buckle to; steel oneself, brace oneself, grit one's teeth, set one's teeth or jaw; put or lay or set one's shoulder to the wheel; take the bull by the horns, take the plunge, cross the Rubicon; nail one's colors to the mast, burn one's bridges or boats, go for broke and shoot the works <nf>, kick down the ladder, throw away the scabbard; never say die, die hard, die fighting, die with one's boots on

9 **remain firm, stand fast or firm, hold out,** hold fast, get tough <nf>, **take one's stand,** set one's back against the wall, **stand or hold one's ground,** keep one's footing, hold one's own, hang in and hang in there and hang tough <nf>, dig in, dig one's heels in; **stick to one's guns,** stick, stick with it, stick fast, stick to one's colors, adhere to one's principles; not listen to the voice of the siren; take what comes, stand the gaff; **put one's foot down** <nf>, stand no nonsense

10 **not hesitate,** think nothing of, think little of, **make no bones about** <nf>, have or make no scruple of <old>, **stick at nothing,** stop at nothing; not look back; go the whole hog <nf>, carry through, face out; go the whole nine yards <nf>

ADJS 11 **resolute, resolved, determined,** bound and bound and determined <nf>, **decided,** decisive, **purposeful;** definite; **earnest, serious,** sincere; devoted, dedicated, committed, wholehearted; single-minded, relentless, persistent, tenacious, persevering; **obstinate** 361.8

12 **firm, staunch,** standup <nf>, fixed, settled, steady, steadfast, constant, set or sot <nf>, flinty, steely; unshaken, not to be shaken, unflappable <nf>; undeflectable, **unswerving,** not to be deflected; immovable, unbending, inflexible, **unyielding** 361.9; true, committed, loyal 644.20

13 **unhesitating,** unhesitant, **unfaltering,** unflinching, unshrinking; stick-at-nothing <nf>

14 **plucky, spunky** and feisty and gutty or gutsy <nf>, gritty, **mettlesome,** dauntless, **game,** game to the last or end; **courageous** 492.17

15 **strong-willed, strong-minded,** firm-minded; **self-controlled,** controlled, self-disciplined, self-restrained; **self-possessed; self-assertive,** self-asserting, forward, pushy <nf>, importunate; self-expressive; **independent**

16 **determined upon,** resolved upon, decided upon, intent upon, fixed upon, settled upon, **set on,** dead set on <nf>, sot on <nf>, **bent on,** hell-bent on <nf>; obsessed

ADVS 17 **resolutely, determinedly, decidedly,** decisively, resolvedly, **purposefully, with a will;** firmly, steadfastly, steadily, fixedly, with constancy, staunchly; **seriously,** in all seriousness, **earnestly,** in earnest, in good earnest, sincerely; devotedly, with total dedication, committedly; hammer and tongs, tooth and nail, *bec et ongles* <Fr>; heart and soul, with all one's heart or might, wholeheartedly; **unswervingly;** singlemindedly, relentlessly, persistently, tenaciously, like a bulldog, like a leech, perseveringly; **obstinately, unyieldingly, inflexibly** 361.15

18 **pluckily, spunkily** and feistily and gutsily <nf>, mettlesomely, **gamely,** dauntlessly, manfully, like a man; on one's mettle; **courageously, heroically** 492.23

19 **unhesitatingly,** unhesitantly, **unfalteringly,** unflinchingly, unshrinkingly

PHRS 20 **come what may,** *venga lo que venga* <Sp>, *vogue la galère* <Fr>, **cost what it may,** *coûte que coûte* <Fr>, whatever the cost, at any price or cost or sacrifice, at all risks or hazards, **whatever may happen,** *ruat caelum* <L>, though the heavens may fall, at all events, live or die, survive or perish, sink or swim, rain or shine, come hell or high water; in some way or other

360 PERSEVERANCE

NOUNS 1 **perseverance, persistence** or persistency, insistence or insistency, singleness of purpose; **resolution** 359; **steadfastness, steadiness,** stability 855; **constancy, permanence** 853.1; loyalty, fidelity 644.7; **single-mindedness,** concentration, undivided or unswerving attention, engrossment, preoccupation 983.3; **endurance, stick-to-itiveness** <nf>, staying power, bitterendism, **pertinacity,** pertinaciousness, **tenacity,** tenaciousness, **doggedness,** unremittingness, relentlessness, dogged perseverance, bulldog tenacity, unfailing or leechlike grip; plodding, plugging, slogging; **obstinacy, stubbornness** 361.1; **diligence,** application, sedulousness, sedulity, industry, industriousness, hard work, assiduousness, assiduity, unflagging efforts; **tirelessness, indefatigability, stamina; patience,** patience of Job 134.1

VERBS **2 persevere, persist, carry on,** go on, **keep on,** keep up, keep at, **keep at it,** keep going, keep driving, keep trying, try and try again, **keep the ball rolling,** keep the pot boiling, keep up the good work; not take 'no' for an answer; not accept compromise *or* defeat; **endure,** last, **continue** 827.6

3 keep doggedly at, **plod,** drudge, slog *or* slog away, soldier on, put one foot in front of the other, peg away *or* at *or* on; **plug,** plug at, plug away *or* along; pound *or* hammer away; **keep one's nose to the grindstone**

4 stay with it, hold on, hold fast, **hang on,** hang on like a bulldog *or* leech, **stick to one's guns;** not give up, **never say die,** not give up the ship, not strike one's colors; come up fighting, come up for more; **stay it out, stick out, hold out;** hold up, last out, **bear up,** stand up; **live with it,** live through it; stay the distance *or* the course; sit tight, be unmoved *or* unmoveable; brazen it out

5 prosecute to a conclusion, **go through with it, carry through, follow through, see it through,** see it out, follow out *or* up; go through with it, go to the bitter end, go the distance, go all the way, go to any length, go to any lengths; **leave no stone unturned,** leave no avenue unexplored, overlook nothing, exhaust every move; move heaven and earth, go through fire and water

6 die trying, die in the last ditch, die in harness, **die with one's boots on** *or* die in one's boots, die at one's post, die in the attempt, die game, die hard, **go down with flying colors**

7 <nf terms> **stick,** stick to it, stick with it, stick it, stick it out, hang on for dear life, hang in, hang in there, hang tough, tough it out, keep on trucking, keep on keeping on; **go the limit,** go the whole hog, go the whole nine yards, go all out, shoot the works, go for broke, go through hell and high water; work one's ass *or* butt *or* tail off

ADJS **8 persevering,** perseverant, **persistent,** persisting, insistent; **enduring,** permanent, **constant, lasting;** continuing 853.7; **stable, steady, steadfast** 855.12; immutable, inalterable; **resolute** 359.11; **diligent, assiduous, sedulous,** industrious; dogged, plodding, slogging, plugging; **pertinacious, tenacious, stick-to-itive** <nf>; loyal, faithful 644.20; **unswerving,** unremitting, unabating, unintermitting, uninterrupted; single-minded, utterly attentive; rapt, preoccupied 983.17; **unfaltering, unwavering,** unflinching; relentless, **unrelenting; obstinate, stubborn** 361.8; **unrelaxing,** unfailing, **untiring,** unwearying,

unflagging, never-tiring, **tireless,** weariless, **indefatigable,** unwearied, unsleeping, undrooping, unnodding, unwinking, sleepless; undiscouraged, undaunted, indomitable, unconquerable, invincible, game to the last *or* to the end, hanging in there; **patient,** patient as Job 134.9

ADVS **9 perseveringly, persistently,** persistingly, insistently; resolutely 359.17; loyally, faithfully, devotedly 644.25; **diligently,** industriously, assiduously, sedulously; **doggedly,** sloggingly, ploddingly; pertinaciously, tenaciously; unremittingly, unabatingly, unintermittingly, uninterruptedly; unswervingly, unwaveringly, unfalteringly, unflinchingly; relentlessly, unrelentingly; **indefatigably, tirelessly,** wearilessly, untiringly, unwearyingly, unflaggingly, unrestingly, unsleepingly; **patiently**

10 through thick and thin, through fire and water, come hell or high water, through evil report and good report, rain or shine, fair or foul, in sickness and in health; **come what may** 359.20, **all the way, down to the wire,** to the bitter end

361 OBSTINACY

NOUNS **1 obstinacy,** obstinateness, pertinacity, restiveness, **stubbornness, willfulness,** self-will, hardheadedness, **headstrongness,** strongheadness; mind *or* will of one's own, set *or* fixed mind, inflexible will; **perseverance** 360, **doggedness, determination,** tenaciousness, tenacity, bitterendism; **bullheadedness, pigheadedness, mulishness; obduracy,** unregenerateness; stiff neck, stiff-neckedness; sullenness, sulkiness; balkiness; uncooperativeness; dogmatism, opinionatedness 970.6; overzealousness, fanaticism 926.11; intolerance, bigotry 980.1; bloody-mindedness <Brit>

2 unyieldingness, unbendingness, stiff temper, **inflexibility,** inelasticity, impliability, ungivingness, **obduracy,** toughness, **firmness,** stiffness, adamantness, rigorism, **rigidity,** strait-lacedness *or* straight-lacedness, stuffiness; **hard line,** hard-bittenness, hard-nosedness <nf>; fixity; unalterability, unchangeability, immutability, immovability; irreconcilability, uncompromisingness, **intransigence** *or* intransigency, *intransigeance* <Fr>, intransigentism; **implacability,** inexorability, **relentlessness,** unrelentingness; sternness, grimness, dourness, flintiness, **steeliness**

3 perversity, perverseness, **contrariness, wrongheadedness, waywardness,** forwardness, difficultness, crossgrainedness, cantankerousness,

feistiness *and* orneriness *and* cussedness <nf>;
sullenness, sulkiness, dourness, stuffiness;
irascibility 110.2

4 ungovernability, unmanageability,
uncontrollability; indomitability, untamableness,
intractability, refractoriness, shrewishness;
incorrigibility; **unsubmissiveness,** unbiddability
<Brit>, **indocility;** irrepressibility,
insuppressibility; unmalleability, unmoldableness;
recidivism; **recalcitrance** *or* recalcitrancy,
contumacy, contumaciousness; **unruliness,**
obstreperousness, restiveness, fractiousness,
wildness; defiance 454; resistance 453

5 unpersuadableness, deafness, blindness; closed-
mindedness; positiveness, dogmatism 970.6

6 <obstinate person> **mule** *and* donkey <nf>, ass,
perverse fool; bullethead, pighead; hardnose <nf>,
hardhead, hammerhead <nf>, hard-liner; standpat
and **standpatter, stickler; intransigent,** maverick;
dogmatist, positivist, bigot, fanatic, purist;
diehard, bitter-ender, last-ditcher; conservative;
stick-in-the-mud

VERBS **7 balk, stickle;** hold one's ground, not budge,
dig one's heels in, **stand pat** <nf>, **not yield an
inch,** stick to one's guns; hold out; stand firm; take
no denial, not take 'no' for an answer; take the bit
in one's teeth; die hard; cut off one's nose to spite
one's face; **persevere** 360.2,7; turn a deaf ear

ADJS **8 obstinate, stubborn, pertinacious, restive;
willful, self-willed,** strong-willed, hardheaded,
headstrong, strongheaded, *entêté* <Fr>; **dogged,**
bulldogged, **tenacious, perserving; bullheaded,**
bulletheaded, **pigheaded, mulish** <nf>, stubborn
as a mule; set, **set in one's ways,** case-hardened,
stiff-necked; sullen, sulky; balky, balking;
unregenerate, uncooperative; bigoted, intolerant
980.11, overzealous, fanatic, fanatical 926.32;
dogmatic, opinionated 970.22

9 unyielding, unbending, inflexible, hard, hard-line,
inelastic, impliable, ungiving, **firm, stiff,** rigid,
rigorous, stuffy; rock-ribbed, rock-hard, rock-like;
adamant, adamantine; unmoved, unaffected;
immovable, not to be moved; **unalterable,**
unchangeable, immutable; **uncompromising,**
intransigent, irreconcilable, hard-shell *and* hard-
core <nf>; implacable, inexorable, **relentless,**
unrelenting; stern, grim, dour; iron, cast-iron,
flinty, steely

10 obdurate, tough, **hard,** hard-set, hard-mouthed,
hard-bitten, hard-nosed *and* hard-boiled <nf>

**11 perverse, contrary, wrongheaded, wayward,
froward, difficult,** cross-grained, cantankerous,
feisty, ornery <nf>; sullen, sulky, stuffy; irascible
110.19

12 ungovernable, unmanageable, uncontrollable,

indomitable, untamable, **intractable, refractory;**
shrewish; **incorrigible, unreconstructed;
unsubmissive,** unbiddable <Brit>, **indocile;**
irrepressible, insuppressible; unmalleable,
unmoldable; recidivist, recidivistic; **recalcitrant,**
contumacious; obstreperous, **unruly, restive,** wild,
fractious, breachy <nf>; beyond control, out of
hand; **resistant, resisting** 453.5; **defiant** 454.7;
irascible

13 unpersuadable, deaf, blind; closed-minded;
positive; dogmatic 970.22

ADVS **14 obstinately, stubbornly,** pertinaciously;
willfully, headstrongly; **doggedly,** tenaciously;
bullheadedly, pigheadedly, mulishly;
unregenerately; uncooperatively; with set jaw, with
sullen mouth, with a stiff neck

15 unyieldingly, unbendingly, inflexibly, adamantly,
obdurately, **firmly,** stiffly, rigidly, rigorously;
unalterably, unchangeably, immutably, immovably,
unregenerately; uncompromisingly, intransigently,
irreconcilably; implacably, inexorably, relentlessly,
unrelentingly; sternly, grimly, dourly

16 perversely, contrarily, contrariwise, waywardly,
wrongheadedly, frowardly, crossgrainedly,
cantankerously, feistily, sullenly, sulkily

17 ungovernably, unmanageably, uncontrollably,
indomitably, untamably, intractably; shrewishly;
incorrigibly; unsubmissively; irrepressibly,
insuppressibly; contumaciously; unrulily,
obstreperously, restively, fractiously

362 IRRESOLUTION

NOUNS **1 irresolution, indecision,** unsettlement,
unsettledness, irresoluteness, undeterminedness,
indecisiveness, undecidedness, infirmity of
purpose; mugwumpery, mugwumpism, fence-
sitting, fence-straddling; double-mindedness,
ambivalence, ambitendency; dubiety, dubiousness,
uncertainty 971; **instability, inconstancy,**
changeableness 854; capriciousness, mercuriality,
fickleness 364.3; change of mind, second thoughts,
tergiversation 363.1; fence-sitting

2 vacillation, fluctuation, oscillation, pendulation,
mood swing, **wavering,** wobbling, waffling <nf>,
shilly-shally, **shilly-shallying,** blowing hot and cold;
equivocation 344.4; second thoughts; back-
pedaling, reversal, about-face

3 hesitation, hesitance, **hesitancy,** hesitating, holding
back, dragging one's feet; falter, faltering, shilly-
shally, shilly-shallying; diffidence, tentativeness,
caution, cautiousness

4 weak will, weak-mindedness; feeblemindedness
<old>, **weakness,** feebleness, faintness,
faintheartedness, **frailty, infirmity; wimpiness** *or*

wimpishness <nf>, spinelessness, invertebracy; abulia; fear 127; cowardice 491; **pliability** 1047.2

5 **vacillator, shillyshallyer,** shilly-shally, **waverer,** wobbler, butterfly; mugwump, fence-sitter, fence-straddler; equivocator, tergiversator, prevaricator; ass between two bundles of hay; yo-yo <nf>; **wimp** <nf>, weakling, jellyfish, Milquetoast; quitter; don't know

VERBS 6 **not know one's own mind,** not know where one stands, **be of two minds,** have two minds, have mixed feelings, be in conflict, be conflicted <nf>; stagger, stumble, boggle

7 **hesitate, pause, falter, hang back,** hover; procrastinate; shilly-shally, hum and haw, **hem and haw;** wait to see how the cat jumps *or* the wind blows, scruple, jib, demur <old>, stick at, stickle, strain at; think twice about, stop to consider, ponder, wrinkle one's brow; debate, deliberate, see both sides of the question, balance, weigh one thing against another, consider both sides of the question, weigh the pros and cons; be divided, come down squarely in the middle, sit on *or* straddle the fence, fall between two stools; yield, back down 433.7; retreat, withdraw 163.6, wimp *or* chicken *or* cop out <nf>; pull back, drag one's feet; **flinch, shy away from, shy** 903.7, back off <nf>; fear; not face up to, hide one's head in the sand

8 **vacillate, waver, waffle** <nf>, **fluctuate,** pendulate, oscillate, wobble, wobble about, teeter, totter <old>, dither, swing from one thing to another, **shilly-shally,** back and fill, keep off and on, will and will not, keep *or* leave hanging in midair; blow hot and cold 364.4; **equivocate** 344.7, fudge and mudge <Brit nf>; change one's mind, tergiversate; vary, **alternate** 854.5; shift, change horses in midstream, **change** 852.5

ADJS 9 **irresolute,** irresolved, **unresolved; undecided, indecisive, undetermined,** unsettled, infirm of purpose; dubious, **uncertain** 970.15; at loose ends, at a loose end; **of two minds,** in conflict, double-minded, ambivalent, ambitendent; changeable, mutable 854.6; capricious, mercurial, fickle 364.6; mugwumpian, mugwumpish, fence-sitting, fence-straddling

10 **vacillating,** vacillatory, waffling <nf>, oscillatory, wobbly, **wavering, fluctuating,** pendulating, oscillating, **shilly-shallying,** shilly-shally; inconsistent

11 **hesitant,** hesitating, pikerish; faltering; shilly-shallying; diffident, tentative, timid, cautious; scrupling, jibbing, demurring <old>, sticking, straining, stickling

12 **weak-willed, weak-minded,** feebleminded <old>, weak-kneed, **weak,** wimpy *or* wimpish <nf>, feeble, fainthearted, **frail, faint, infirm; spineless,** invertebrate; without a will of one's own, unable to say 'no'; abulic; afraid, **chicken** *and* chicken-hearted *and* chicken-livered <nf>, cowardly 491.10; like putty, **pliable** 1045.9

ADVS 13 **irresolutely,** irresolvedly, **undecidedly, indecisively, undeterminedly; uncertainly;** hesitantly, hesitatingly, falteringly; waveringly, vacillatingly, shilly-shally, shilly-shallyingly

363 CHANGING OF MIND

NOUNS 1 **reverse, reversal,** flip *and* flip-flop *and* U-turn <nf>, turnabout, turnaround, **about-face,** about turn <Brit>, *volte-face* <Fr>, right-about-face, right-about turn <Brit>, right-about, a turn to the right-about; tergiversation, tergiversating; **change of mind;** second thoughts, better thoughts, afterthoughts, mature judgment

2 **apostasy,** recreancy; **treason,** misprision of treason, betrayal, turning traitor, turning one's coat, changing one's stripes, ratting <nf>, going over, joining *or* going over to the opposition, siding with the enemy; **defection;** bolt, bolting, secession, breakaway; **desertion** 370.2; **recidivism,** recidivation, relapse, backsliding 394.2; faithlessness, **disloyalty** 645.5

3 **recantation, withdrawal, disavowal, denial,** reneging, **unsaying, repudiation,** palinode, palinody, **retraction,** retractation; **disclaimer,** disclamation, **disownment,** disowning, abjurement, abjuration, **renunciation,** renouncement, forswearing; expatriation, self-exile

4 **timeserver,** timepleaser <old>, temporizer, opportunist, trimmer, weathercock; mugwump; chameleon, Vicar of Bray

5 **apostate, turncoat,** turnabout, **recreant, renegade,** renegado, renegate *or* runagate <old>, **defector,** tergiversator, tergiversant; **deserter,** turntail, quisling, fifth columnist, collaborationist, collaborator, **traitor** 357.10; strikebreaker; **bolter, seceder,** secessionist, **separatist,** schismatic; **backslider,** recidivist; reversionist; convert, proselyte

VERBS 6 **change one's mind** *or* **song** *or* **tune** *or* **note,** sing a different tune, dance to another tune; come round, wheel, do an about-face, reverse oneself, do a flip-flop *or* U-turn <nf>, go over, change sides; swing from one thing to another; think better of it, have second thoughts, be of another mind; bite one's tongue

7 **apostatize** *or* apostacize, go over, change sides, switch, switch over, change one's allegiance, **defect; turn one's coat,** turn cloak; desert *or* leave a sinking ship; secede, break away, bolt, fall off *or* away; desert

8 recant, retract, repudiate, withdraw, take back, unswear, renege, welsh <nf>, **abjure, disavow, disown; deny,** disclaim, unsay, unspeak; **renounce, forswear, eat one's words,** eat one's hat, swallow, eat crow, eat humble pie; **back down** or **out,** climb down, crawfish out <nf>, backwater, weasel

9 be a timeserver, trim, temporize, change with the times; sit on or straddle the fence

ADJS **10 timeserving, trimming, temporizing;** supple, neither fish nor fowl

11 apostate, recreant, renegade, tergiversating, tergiversant; **treasonous, treasonable, traitorous,** forsworn; collaborating; faithless, **disloyal** 645.20

12 repudiative, repudiatory; abjuratory, renunciative, renunciatory; schismatic; **separatist,** secessionist, breakaway <nf>; **opportunistic,** mugwumpian, mugwumpish, fence-straddling, fence-sitting

364 CAPRICE

NOUNS **1 caprice, whim,** *capriccio* <Ital>, *boutade* <Fr>, humor, **whimsy,** freak, whim-wham; **fancy,** fantasy, **conceit, notion,** flimflam, toy, freakish inspiration, crazy idea, fantastic notion, fool notion <nf>, harebrained idea, brainstorm, **vagary,** megrim; **fad, craze, passing fancy; quirk, crotchet,** crank, kink; maggot, maggot in the brain, bee in one's bonnet <nf>, flea in one's nose <nf>

2 capriciousness, caprice, **whimsicalness,** whimsy, whimsicality; humorsomeness, **fancifulness,** fantasticality, **freakishness;** crankiness, crotchetiness, quirkiness; **moodiness,** temperamentalness, prima-donnaism; petulance 110.6; **arbitrariness,** motivelessness

3 fickleness, flightiness, skittishness, inconstancy, **lightness, levity,** *légèreté* <Fr>; flakiness <nf>; volatility, mercurialness, mercuriality, erraticism; **mood swing;** faddishness, faddism; **changeableness** 854; unpredictability 971.1; unreliability, undependability 645.4; coquettishness; frivolousness 922.7; purposelessness, motivelessness

VERBS **4 blow hot and cold,** keep off and on, have as many phases as the moon, chop and change, **fluctuate** 854.5, vacillate 362.8, flip-flop <nf>; act on impulse

ADJS **5 capricious, whimsical,** freakish, humorsome, vagarious; **fanciful, notional,** fantasied <old>, fantastic or fantastical, maggoty, **crotchety,** kinky, harebrained, cranky, flaky <nf>, quirky; wanton, wayward, vagrant; **arbitrary, unreasonable,** motiveless; **moody, temperamental,** prima-donnaish; petulant 110.22; unrestrained

6 fickle, flighty, skittish, **light;** coquettish, flirtatious, toying; versatile; **inconstant,** erratic, **changeable**

854.7; vacillating 362.10; volatile, mercurial, quicksilver; faddish; **scatterbrained** 985.16, unpredictable; **impulsive;** idiosyncratic; unreliable, undependable 645.19

ADVS **7 capriciously, whimsically,** fancifully, at one's own sweet will <nf>; **flightily, lightly;** arbitrarily, unreasonably, without rhyme or reason

365 IMPULSE

NOUNS **1 impulse;** natural impulse, blind impulse, **instinct,** urge, drive; vagrant or fleeting impulse; involuntary impulse, reflex, knee jerk, automatic response; gut response or reaction <nf>; **notion, fancy; sudden thought,** flash, inspiration, brainstorm, brain wave, quick hunch

2 impulsiveness, impetuousness, impulsivity, impetuousity; **hastiness,** overhastiness, haste, quickness, suddenness; **precipitateness,** precipitance, precipitancy, precipitation; hair-trigger; **recklessness, rashness** 493; impatience 135

3 thoughtlessness, unthoughtfulness, **heedlessness** 984.1, **carelessness,** inconsideration, inconsiderateness; **negligence** 102.2, caprice 364

4 unpremeditation, indeliberation, **undeliberateness,** uncalculatedness, undesignedness, **spontaneity, spontaneousness,** unstudiedness; involuntariness 963.5; snap judgment or decision; snap shot, offhand shot

5 improvisation, extemporization, improvision, improvising, extempore <old>, **impromptu, ad-lib,** ad-libbing and playing by ear <nf>, **ad hoc measure** or solution, adhocracy <nf>, ad hockery or hocery or hocism <nf>; extemporaneousness, extemporariness; temporary measure or arrangement, pro tempore measure or arrangement, **stopgap, makeshift,** jury-rig; cannibalization; bricolage; jam session; thinking on one's feet

6 improviser, improvisator, *improvvisatore* and *improvvisatrice* <Ital>, **extemporizer,** ad-libber <nf>; cannibalizer; bricoleur; creature of impulse

VERBS **7 act on the spur of the moment,** obey one's impulse, let oneself go; shoot from the hip <nf>, be too quick on the trigger or the uptake or the draw; **blurt out,** come out with, let slip out, say what comes uppermost, say the first thing that comes into one's head or to one's mind; be unable to help oneself

8 improvise, extemporize, improvisate, improv and tapdance and talk off the top of one's head <nf>, speak off the cuff, think on one's feet, invent, make it up as one goes along, play it by ear <nf>, throw away or depart from the prepared text, throw away the speech, scrap the plan, **ad-lib** <nf>, **do**

offhand, wing it <nf>, vamp, fake <nf>, play by ear <nf>; **dash off, strike off,** knock off, throw off, toss off *or* out; make up, whip up, **cook up,** run up, rustle up *or* whomp up <nf>, slap up *or* together *and* throw together <nf>, lash up <Brit>, cobble up; jury-rig; rise to the occasion; cannibalize

ADJS **9 impulsive, impetuous, hasty,** overhasty, quick, sudden, snap; quick on the draw *or* trigger *or* uptake, hair-trigger; **precipitate,** headlong; **reckless, rash** 493.7; impatient 135.6

10 unthinking, unreasoning, unreflecting, uncalculating, unthoughtful, **thoughtless, inadvertent,** reasonless, **heedless, careless,** inconsiderate; unguarded; arbitrary, capricious 364.5

11 unpremeditated, unmeditated, **uncalculated,** undeliberated, **spontaneous, undesigned, unstudied;** unintentional, unintended, inadvertent, unwilled, **indeliberate,** undeliberate; **involuntary,** reflex, reflexive, knee-jerk <nf>, automatic, goose-step, lockstep; gut <nf>, unconscious; **unconsidered,** unadvised, snap, casual, offhand, throwaway <nf>; **ill-considered,** ill-advised, ill-devised; act-first-and-think-later

12 extemporaneous, extempory, extempore, **impromptu,** unrehearsed, **improvised,** improvisatory, improvisatorial, improviso, *improvisé* <Fr>; **ad-lib,** *ad libitum* <L>; **ad-hoc,** stopgap, makeshift, jury-rigged; **offhand,** off the top of one's head *and* off-the-cuff <nf>, **spur-of-the-moment, quick and dirty** <nf>; catch-as-catch-can; potluck

ADVS **13 impulsively, impetuously, hastily,** suddenly, quickly, **precipitately,** headlong; **recklessly, rashly** 493.10

14 on impulse, on a sudden impulse, **on the spur of the moment; without premeditation,** unpremeditatedly, uncalculatedly, undesignedly; unthinkingly, unreflectingly, unreasoningly, unthoughtfully, thoughtlessly, heedlessly, carelessly, inconsiderately, unadvisedly; unintentionally, inadvertently, without willing, indeliberately, involuntarily

15 extemporaneously, extemporarily, extempore, *à l'improviste* <Fr>, **impromptu, ad lib, offhand,** out of hand; at *or* on sight; by ear, off the hip *and* off the top of one's head *and* off the cuff <nf>; at short notice

366 LEAP

NOUNS **1 leap, jump, hop, spring, skip, bound,** bounce; **pounce;** upleap, upspring, jump-off; **hurdle; vault,** pole vault; demivolt, curvet, capriole;

jeté, grand jeté, tour jeté, saut de basque; jig, galliard, lavolta, Highland fling, morris; standing *or* running *or* flying jump; long jump, broad jump, standing *or* running broad jump; high jump, standing *or* running high jump; leapfrog; jump shot; handspring; buck, buckjump; ski jump, jump turn, geländesprung, gelände jump; steeplechase; hippety-hop <nf>; jump-hop; hop, skip, and jump

2 caper, dido <nf>, **gambol, frisk,** curvet, cavort, capriole; **prance,** caracole; *gambade* <Fr>, gambado; falcade

3 leaping, jumping, bouncing, bounding, hopping, capering, cavorting, prancing, skipping, **springing,** saltation; **vaulting,** pole vaulting; **hurdling,** the hurdles, hurdle race, timber topping <nf>, steeplechase; leapfrogging

4 jumper, leaper, hopper; broad jumper, high jumper; **vaulter,** pole vaulter; **hurdler,** hurdle racer, timber topper <nf>; jumping jack; bucking bronco, buckjumper, sunfisher <nf>; jumping bean; kangaroo, gazelle, stag, jackrabbit, goat, frog, grasshopper, flea; salmon

VERBS **5 leap, jump, vault, spring, skip, hop, bound,** bounce; upleap, upspring, updive; leap over, jump over, etc; overleap, overjump, overskip, leapfrog; **hurdle,** clear, negotiate; curvet, capriole; buck, buckjump; ski jump; steeplechase; start, start up, start aside; **pounce,** pounce on *or* upon; hippety-hop <nf>

6 caper, cut capers, cut a dido <nf>, curvet, cavort, capriole; **gambol,** gambado, **frisk,** flounce, **trip, skip,** bob, bounce, jump about; **romp,** ramp <nf>; **prance;** caracole

ADJS **7 leaping, jumping,** springing, hopping, skipping, prancing, bouncing, bounding; saltant, saltatory, saltatorial

367 PLUNGE

NOUNS **1 plunge, dive, pitch, drop, fall;** free-fall; header <nf>; **swoop, pounce,** stoop; swan dive, gainer, jackknife, cannonball; belly flop *and* belly buster *and* belly whopper <nf>; nose dive, power dive; parachute jump, sky dive; bungee jump; crash dive, stationary dive, running dive

2 submergence, submersion, immersion, immergence, engulfment, **inundation,** burial; **dipping, ducking,** dousing, sousing, dunking <nf>, sinking; **dip, duck, souse;** baptism

3 diving, plunging; skydiving; bungee jumping; fancy diving, high diving; scuba diving, snorkeling, skin diving, pearl diving, deep-sea diving

4 diver, plunger; high diver; bungee jumper; parachute jumper, jumper, sky diver, sport jumper, paratrooper, smoke jumper, paramedic; skin diver, snorkel diver, scuba diver, free diver, pearl diver, deep-sea diver, frogman

5 <diving equipment> diving bell, diving chamber, bathysphere, bathyscaphe, benthoscope, aquascope; submarine 180.9; diving boat; scuba *or* self-contained underwater breathing apparatus, Aqua-Lung <trademark>; Scuba; diving goggles, diving mask, swim fins; wet suit; air cylinder; diving suit; diving helmet, diving hood; snorkel, periscope

VERBS **6 plunge, dive, pitch, plummet, drop, fall;** skydive; bungee jump; free-fall; plump, plunk, plop; swoop, swoop down, stoop, **pounce,** pounce on *or* upon; nose-dive, make *or* take a nose dive; parachute, sky-dive; skin-dive; sound; take a header <nf>

7 submerge, submerse, **immerse,** immerge, merge, **sink,** bury, engulf, **inundate,** deluge, drown, overwhelm, whelm; **dip, duck, dunk** <nf>, douse, souse, plunge in water; baptize

8 sink, scuttle, send to the bottom, send to Davy Jones's locker; **founder, go down,** go to the bottom, sink like lead, go down like a stone; get out of one's depth

ADJS **9 submersible,** submergible, immersible, sinkable

368 AVOIDANCE

NOUNS **1 avoidance, shunning; forbearance,** refraining; hands-off policy, **nonintervention,** noninvolvement, neutrality; **evasion,** elusion; side-stepping, getting around <nf>, working around, **circumvention;** prevention, forestalling, forestallment; **escape** 369; evasive action, the runaround <nf>; zigzag, jink *and* juke <nf>, slip, dodge, duck, side step, shy; shunting off, sidetracking; bypassing; evasiveness, elusiveness; **equivocation** 344.4, waffle <nf>, fudging, fudge and mudge <Brit nf>; avoiding reaction, defense mechanism *or* reaction; safe distance, wide berth; cold shoulder, snub; abstinence; shyness

2 shirking, slacking, goldbricking <nf>, cop-out <nf>, soldiering, goofing *and* goofing off *and* fucking off <nf>; clock-watching; **malingering,** skulking <Brit>; passivity; **dodging,** ducking; welshing <nf>; truancy; tax evasion, tax dodging

3 shirker, shirk, **slacker,** eye-servant *or* eye-server <old>, goof-off <nf>, soldier *or* old soldier, **goldbricker,** goldbrick <nf>; clock watcher; **welsher** <nf>; **malingerer,** skulker *or* skulk <Brit>; truant; tax dodger *or* evader

4 flight, fugitation, exit, quick exit, making oneself scarce *and* getting the hell out <nf>, bolt, scarpering <Brit nf>, disappearing act <nf>, hasty retreat; **running away, decampment,** bugging out <nf>; skedaddle *and* skedaddling *and* scramming *and* absquatulation <old> <nf>; **elopement;** disappearance 34; French leave, absence without leave *or* AWOL; desertion 370.2; hegira; truancy, hooky *or* hookey

5 fugitive, fleer, person on the run, **runaway,** runagate, **bolter,** skedaddler <nf>; **absconder, eloper; refugee, evacuee,** boat person, *émigré* <Fr>; **displaced person** *or* DP, stateless person; **escapee** 369.5; illegal immigrant, wetback <nf>, day-crosser; draft dodger; truant, absentee; desserter

VERBS **6 avoid, shun, fight shy of, shy away from,** keep from, **keep away from, circumvent,** keep clear of, avoid like the plague, **steer clear of** <nf>, give a miss to <nf>, skate around <Brit nf>, keep *or* get out of the way of, **give a wide berth,** keep remote from, stay detached from; make way for, give place to; **keep one's distance,** keep at a respectful distance, keep *or* stand *or* hold aloof; give the cold shoulder to <nf>, have nothing to do with, have no association with, not give the time of day, **have no truck with** <nf>; not meddle with, let alone, let well enough alone, keep hands off, not touch, not touch with a ten-foot pole, back off; turn away from, turn one's back upon, slam the door in one's face

7 evade, elude, beg, **get out of,** shuffle out of, skirt, **get around** <nf>, circumvent; take evasive action; give one the run-around; ditch *and* shake *and* shake off <nf>, get away from, give the runaround *or* the slip <nf>; throw off the scent; play at hide and seek; lead one a chase *or* merry chase, lead one a dance *or* pretty dance; escape 369.6-8

8 dodge, duck; take evasive action, juke *and* jink <nf>, zig-zag; throw off the track *or* trail; shy, shy off *or* away; swerve, sheer off; pull away *or* clear; pull back, shrink, recoil 903.6,7; **sidestep,** step aside; parry, fence, ward off; have an out *or* escape hatch; shift, shift *or* put off; **hedge,** pussyfoot <nf>, be *or* sit on the fence, beat around *or* about the bush, hem and haw, beg the question, tapdance <nf>, dance around, equivocate 344.7, fudge and mudge <Brit nf>

9 shirk, slack, lie *or* **rest upon one's oars,** not pull fair, not pull one's weight; **lie down on the job** <nf>; soldier, duck duty, **goof off** *and* dog it <nf>, **goldbrick** <nf>; **malinger,** skulk <Brit>; **get out of,** sneak *or* slip out of, slide out of, pass the buck, cop out <nf>, dodge, duck; welsh <nf>

10 flee, fly, take flight, take to flight, take wing, fugitate, **run, cut and run** <nf>, make a precipitate departure, **run off** *or* **away,** run away from, bug out <nf>, **decamp,** pull up stakes, **take**

to one's heels, make off, **depart** 188.6, do the disappearing act, make a quick exit, **beat a retreat** *or* **a hasty retreat, turn tail,** show the heels, show a clean *or* light pair of heels; **run for it,** "show it a fair pair of heels and run for it"—Shakespeare, **bolt, run for one's life;** make a run for it; advance to the rear, make a strategic withdrawal; **take French leave,** go AWOL, slip the cable; **desert; abscond,** levant <Brit>, **elope,** run away with; skip *or* jump bail; play hooky *or* hookey

11 <nf terms> **beat it, blow, scram,** bug off, lam, book, air out, shemozzle *and* bugger off <Brit>, **take it on the lam,** take a powder *or* runout powder, make tracks, cut ass, cut and run, peel out, **split,** skin out, **skip,** skip out, duck out, duck and run, dog it, vamoose, absquatulate *and* skedaddle <old>, **clear out,** make oneself scarce, get the hell out, make a break for it, warp out, scram

12 **slip away, steal away, sneak off,** shuffle off, slink off, slide off, slither off, skulk away, mooch off *and* duck out <nf>, slip out of

13 **not face up to,** hide one's head in the sand, not come to grips with, put off, procrastinate, temporize, waffle <nf>

ADJS 14 **avoidable, escapable,** eludible; evadable; preventable

15 **evasive, elusive,** elusory; **shifty,** slippery, slippery as an eel; cagey <nf>; shirking, malingering

16 **fugitive, runaway,** in flight, on the lam <nf>, hot <nf>; disappearing 34.3

369 ESCAPE

NOUNS 1 **escape; getaway** *and* break *and* breakout <nf>; **deliverance; delivery,** riddance, **release,** setting-free, freeing, freedom, **liberation, extrication, rescue;** emergence, issuance, issue, outlet, vent; **leakage,** leak; jailbreak, prisonbreak, break, breakout; evasion 368.1; **flight** 368.4; retreat; French leave; hooky; elopement; escapology; escapism

2 **narrow escape,** hairbreadth escape, **close call** *or* **shave** <nf>, **near miss,** near go *or* thing <Brit nf>, near *or* narrow squeak <Brit nf>, close *or* tight squeeze <nf>, squeaker <nf>

3 bolt-hole, escape hatch, fire escape, life net, lifeboat, life raft, life buoy, lifeline, sally port, slide, inflatable slide, ejection *or* ejector seat, emergency exit, escapeway, back door, trapdoor, escape hatch, secret passage

4 **loophole, way out,** way of escape, hole to creep out of, escape hatch, escape clause, saving clause, technicality; pretext 376; **alternative,** choice 371

5 **escapee,** escaper, evader; escape artist;

escapologist; runaway, **fugitive** 368.5; escapist, Houdini

VERBS 6 **escape,** make *or* effect one's escape, make good one's escape; **get away, make a getaway** <nf>; **free oneself,** deliver oneself, gain one's liberty, **get free, get clear of,** bail out, **get out, get out of,** get well out of; **break loose,** cut loose, break away, break one's bonds *or* chains, slip the collar, shake off the yoke; **jump** *and* **skip** <nf>; **break jail** *or* **prison,** escape prison, fly the coop <nf>; leap over the wall; evade 368.7; flee 368.10; vamoose, take it on the lam

7 **get off, go free,** win freedom, go at liberty, **go scot free,** escape with a whole skin, escape without penalty, walk *and* beat the rap <nf>; **get away with** <nf>, get by, get by with, get off easy *or* lightly, get away with murder <nf>, **get off cheap;** cop a plea *and* cop out <nf>, get off on a technicality

8 scrape *or* squeak through, squeak by, escape with *or* by the skin of one's teeth, have a close call *or* close shave <nf>

9 **slip away, give one the slip,** slip through one's hands *or* fingers; slip *or* sneak through; **slip out of,** slide out of, crawl *or* creep out of, sneak out of, wiggle *or* squirm *or* shuffle *or* wriggle *or* worm out of, find a loophole, elude

10 **find vent,** issue forth, come forth, exit, **emerge, issue,** debouch, erupt, break out, break through, come out, run out, **leak out,** ooze out

ADJS 11 **escaped, loose,** on the loose, disengaged, out of, well out of; fled, flown; fugitive, runaway; free as a bird, scot-free, at large, **free**

370 ABANDONMENT

NOUNS 1 **abandonment, forsaking, leaving;** jettison, jettisoning, throwing overboard *or* away *or* aside, casting away *or* aside; **withdrawal,** evacuation, pulling out, absentation; cessation 857; disuse, desuetude

2 **desertion, defection,** ratting <nf>; dereliction; **secession,** bolt, breakaway, walkout; betrayal 645.8; schism, apostasy 363.2; deserter 363.5

3 <giving up> **relinquishment, surrender, resignation, renouncement,** renunciation, abdication, waiver, abjurement, abjuration, ceding, cession, handing over, standing *or* stepping down, **yielding, forswearing; withdrawing, dropping out** <nf>

4 **derelict,** castoff; jetsam, flotsam, lagan, **flotsam and jetsam;** waifs and strays; **rubbish, junk,** trash, refuse, waste, waste product, solid waste; liquid waste, wastewater; **dump,** dumpsite, garbage dump, landfill, sanitary landfill, junkheap, junkpile, scrap heap, midden; abandonee, waif, throwaway,

orphan, dogie <nf>; **castaway;** foundling; wastrel, reject, deselect, **discard** 390.3

VERBS **5 abandon, desert, forsake; quit, leave,** leave behind, take leave of, depart from, absent oneself from, turn one's back upon, turn one's tail upon, say goodbye to, bid a long farewell to, walk away, **walk** or **run out on** <nf>, **leave flat** and leave high and dry or holding the bag or in the lurch <nf>, leave one to one's fate, throw to the wolves <nf>; **withdraw, back out, drop out** <nf>, pull out, stand down <nf>; **go back on, go back on one's word;** cry off <Brit>, beg off, renege; **vacate,** evacuate; quit cold and leave flat <nf>, toss aside; jilt, throw over <nf>; maroon; **jettison; junk,** deep-six <nf>, **discard** 390.7; let fall into disuse or desuetude

6 defect, secede, bolt, break away; pull out <nf>, withdraw one's support; sell out and sell down the river <nf>, **betray** 645.14; turn one's back on; apostatize

7 give up, relinquish, surrender, yield, yield up, waive, **forgo, resign, renounce,** throw up, abdicate, **abjure, forswear, give up on, have done with,** give up as a bad job, cede, hand over, lay down, wash one's hands of, **write off,** drop, drop all idea of, drop like a hot potato; **cease** 857.6, **desist from,** leave off, give over; hold or stay one's hand, cry quits, acknowledge defeat, **throw in the towel** or **sponge** 433.8

ADJS **8 abandoned, forsaken, deserted,** left; disused; **derelict,** castaway, jettisoned; marooned; junk, junked, discarded 390.11

371 CHOICE

NOUNS **1 choice, selection, election,** preference, decision, **pick, choosing,** free choice; alternativity; co-option, co-optation; **will,** volition, free will 430.6,7; preoption, first choice; the pick 999.7

2 option, discretion, pleasure, will and pleasure; optionality; possible choice, alternative, alternate choice

3 dilemma, Scylla and Charybdis, the devil and the deep blue sea; *embarras de choix* <Fr>; choice of Hercules; Hobson's choice, **no choice,** only choice, zero option; limited choice, positive discrimination <Brit>, affirmative action; lesser of two evils

4 adoption, embracement, acceptance, espousal; affiliation

5 preference, predilection, proclivity, bent, affinity, prepossession, predisposition, partiality, inclination, leaning, tilt, penchant, bias, tendency, taste, favoritism; favor, fancy; prejudice; personal choice, particular choice <old>, druthers <nf>; chosen kind or sort, style, one's cup of tea <nf>, type, bag and thing <nf>; way of life, lifestyle

6 vote, voting, **suffrage,** franchise, enfranchisement, voting right, right to vote; **voice, say;** representation; **poll,** polling, canvass, canvassing, division <Brit>, counting heads or noses or hands, exit poll; **ballot,** balloting, secret ballot, absentee ballot; ballot-box, voting machine; **plebiscite,** plebiscitum, **referendum;** yeas and nays, yea, aye, yes, nay, no; voice vote, *viva voce* vote; rising vote; hand vote, show of hands; absentee vote, proxy; casting vote, deciding vote; write-in vote, write-in; faggot vote <Brit old>; graveyard vote; single vote, plural vote; transferable vote, nontransferable vote; direct vote; Hare system, list system, cumulative voting, preferential voting, proportional representation; **straw vote** or **poll;** record vote, snap vote

7 selector, chooser, optant, elector, balloter, **voter; electorate;** electoral college

8 nomination, designation, naming, proposal

9 election, appointment; political election; caucus; primary

10 selectivity, selectiveness, picking and choosing; **choosiness** 495.1; eclecticism; discretion, **discrimination** 943

11 eligibility, qualification, fitness, fittedness, **suitability,** acceptability, worthiness, desirability; eligible

12 elect, elite, the chosen, the cream, crème de la crème

VERBS **13 choose,** elect, pick, go with <nf>, opt, opt for, co-opt, make or take one's choice, make choice of, have one's druthers <nf>, use or take up or exercise one's option, exercise one's discretion; **shop around** <nf>, pick and choose

14 select, make a selection; **pick,** handpick, **pick out, single out,** choose out, smile on, give the nod <nf>, jump at, seize on; extract, excerpt; **decide between, choose up sides** <nf>, cull, glean, winnow, sift; side with; cherry-pick, separate the wheat from the chaff or tares, separate the sheep from the goats

15 adopt; approve, ratify, pass, carry, endorse, sign off on <nf>; **take up, go in for** <nf>; accept, take on up on <nf>, **embrace,** espouse; affiliate

16 decide upon, determine upon, settle upon, fix upon, resolve upon; make or take a decision, **make up one's mind**

17 prefer, have preference, **favor, like better** or **best,** prefer to, set before or above, regard or honor before; rather <nf>, **had** or **have rather,** would rather, choose rather, had sooner, had or would as soon; think proper, see or think fit, think best, please; tilt or incline or lean or tend toward, have a bias or partiality or penchant

18 vote, cast one's vote, ballot, cast a ballot; go to the polls; have a say *or* a voice; hold up one's hand, exercise one's suffrage *or* franchise, stand up and be counted; plump *or* plump for <Brit>; divide <Brit>; **poll,** canvass

19 **nominate, name, designate;** put up, propose, submit, name for office; run, run for office

20 **elect, vote in,** place in office; **appoint**

21 **put to choice,** offer, present, set before; put to vote, have a show of hands

ADJS 22 **elective;** volitional, voluntary, volitive; **optional,** discretional; **alternative,** disjunctive

23 **selective,** selecting, choosing; eclectic *or* eclectical; elective, electoral; appointing, appointive, constituent; adoptive; exclusive, discriminating 944.7; **choosy** <nf>, particular 495.9

24 **eligible, qualified, fit,** fitted, **suitable,** acceptable, admissible, worthy, desirable; with voice, with vote, with voice and vote, enfranchised

25 **preferable,** of choice *or* preference, **better,** preferred, **to be preferred,** more desirable, favored; handpicked; preferential, preferring, favoring; not to be sniffed *or* sneezed at <nf>

26 **chosen, selected, picked;** select, elect; handpicked, singled-out; **adopted,** accepted, embraced, espoused, approved, ratified, passed, carried; **elected,** unanimously elected, elected by acclamation; appointed; **nominated,** designated, named

ADVS 27 **at choice, at will,** at one's will and pleasure, at one's pleasure, electively, at one's discretion, at the option of, if one wishes; on approval; **optionally;** alternatively

28 **preferably, by choice** *or* **preference,** in preference; by vote, by election *or* suffrage; **rather than,** sooner than, first, sooner, rather, before

CONJS 29 or, either/or; and/or

PHRS 30 one man's meat is another man's poison, there's no accounting for taste

372 REJECTION

NOUNS 1 **rejection, repudiation;** abjurement, abjuration, **renouncement** 370.3; disownment, disavowal, disclamation, **recantation** 363.3; **exclusion,** exception 773.1; **disapproval, nonacceptance,** nonapproval, declining, declination, veto, **refusal** 442; contradiction, **denial** 335.2; passing by *or* up <nf>, ignoring, nonconsideration, discounting, dismissal, disregard 983.1; throwing out *or* away, putting out *or* away, chucking *and* chucking out <nf>, heave-ho; discard 390.3; turning out *or* away, repulse, a flea in one's ear, rebuff 908.2; **spurning,** kiss-off *and* brush-off <nf>, cold shoulder, despising, despisal, contempt 157; scorn, disdain; bum's rush <nf>

VERBS 2 **reject, repudiate,** abjure, forswear, **renounce** 370.7, **disown, disclaim, recant;** vote out; except, **exclude** 773.4, deselect, include out <nf>, close out, close the door on, leave out in the cold, cut out, blackball, blacklist; **disapprove, decline, refuse** 442.3; contradict, **deny** 335.4; pass by *or* up <nf>, waive, ignore, not hear of, wave aside, brush away *or* aside, refuse to consider, discount, **dismiss,** dismiss out of hand; **disregard** 984.2; throw out *or* away, chuck *and* chuck out <nf>, **discard** 390.7; turn out *or* away, shove away, push aside, repulse, repel, slap *or* smack down <nf>, rebuff 908.2, send away with a flea in one's ear, show the door, send about one's business, send packing; turn one's back on; **spurn, disdain,** scorn, contemn, make a face at, turn up one's nose at, look down one's nose at, raise one's eyebrows at, **despise** 157.3

ADJS 3 **rejected, repudiated; renounced,** forsworn, **disowned; denied,** refused; excluded, excepted; **disapproved, declined;** ignored, blanked, discounted, not considered, **dismissed,** dismissed out of hand; **discarded;** repulsed, rebuffed; **spurned,** snubbed, **disdained, scorned,** contemned, **despised;** out of the question, not to be thought of, declined with thanks; discarded

4 rejective; renunciative, abjuratory; declinatory; dismissive; contemptuous, despising, **scornful,** disdainful

373 CUSTOM, HABIT

NOUNS 1 **custom, convention,** use, **usage,** standard usage, standard behavior, **wont,** wonting, **way,** established way, time-honored practice, **tradition,** standing custom, **folkway,** manner, **practice,** praxis, prescription, **observance,** ritual, rite, consuetude, **mores;** institution; unwritten law; proper thing, what is done, **social convention** 579; bon ton, **fashion** 578; manners, protocol, etiquette 580.3; way of life, lifestyle; conformity 867; **generalization** 864.1, labeling, stereotyping

2 **culture, society, civilization;** trait, culture trait; key trait; complex, culture complex, trait-complex; culture area; culture center; shame culture, memory culture; **folkways, mores,** system of values, **ethos, culture pattern;** cultural change; cultural lag; culture conflict; acculturation, enculturation; culture contact <Brit>, cultural drift; ancient wisdom

3 **habit,** habitude, **custom, second nature,** matter of course; use, **usage,** trick, wont, **way,** practice, praxis; bad habit; stereotype; "the petrifaction of feelings"—L E Landon; "a second nature, and no less powerful"—Montaigne; pattern, **habit pattern;**

stereotyped behavior; force of habit; creature of habit; knee-jerk reaction <nf>, automatism 963.5; peculiarity, characteristic 865.4

4 **rule, norm,** procedure, **common practice,** the way things are done, form, prescribed *or* set form; common *or* ordinary run of things, matter of course, par for the course <nf>; standard operating procedure *or* SOP, standard procedure, drill; standing orders

5 **routine,** run, ritual, round, beat, track, beaten path *or* track; pattern, custom; jog trot, **rut, groove,** well-worn groove; **treadmill,** squirrel cage; the working day, nine-to-five, the grind *or* the daily grind <nf>; **red tape,** redtapeism, **bureaucracy,** bureaucratism, *chinoiseries* <Fr>

6 **customariness,** accustomedness, wontedness, **habitualness; inveteracy,** inveterateness, confirmedness, settledness, fixedness; commonness, prevalence 864.2

7 **habituation, accustoming; conditioning,** seasoning, training; **familiarization,** naturalization <old>, breaking-in <nf>, orientation, adaptation; **domestication, taming,** breaking, housebreaking; acclimation, acclimatization; **inurement,** hardening, case hardening, seasoning; adaption, adjustment, accommodation 867.1

8 **addiction** 87.1; **addict** 87.3

VERBS 9 **accustom, habituate,** wont; **condition,** season, **train;** familiarize, naturalize <old>, break in <nf>, orient, orientate; **domesticate,** domesticize, **tame,** break, gentle, housebreak; put through the mill; acclimatize, acclimate; inure, harden, case harden; adapt, adjust, accommodate 788.7; confirm, fix, establish 855.9; acculturate, enculturate

10 **become a habit,** take root, become fixed, **grow on one,** take hold of one, take one over

11 **be used to, be wont,** wont, **make a practice of;** get used to, get into the way of, get the knack of, get the hang of <nf>, **take to,** accustom oneself to, make a practice of; catch oneself doing; contract *or* fall into a habit, addict oneself to

12 **get in a rut, be in a rut,** move *or* travel in a groove *or* rut, run on in a groove, follow the beaten path *or* track

ADJS 13 **customary, wonted,** consuetudinary; traditional, time-honored, immemorial; familiar, everyday, ordinary, **usual; established,** received, accepted, handed down, time-honored; set, prescribed, prescriptive; **normative, normal; standard,** regular, stock, regulation; prevalent, prevailing, widespread, obtaining, generally accepted, popular, **current** 863.12; **conventional** 579.5, orthodox; conformist, conformable 867.5

14 **habitual, regular,** frequent, constant, persistent; repetitive, recurring, recurrent; stereotyped; knee-jerk <nf>, goose-step, lockstep, automatic 963.14; **routine,** usual, nine-to-five, workaday, well-trodden, well-worn, beaten; trite, hackneyed 117.9; predictable

15 **accustomed, wont, wonted, used to; conditioned,** trained, seasoned; experienced, **familiarized,** naturalized <old>, broken-in, run-in <nf>, oriented, orientated; acclimated, acclimatized; inured, hardened, case-hardened; adapted, adjusted, accommodated; housebroken, potty-trained

16 **used to, familiar with,** conversant with, **at home in** *or* **with,** no stranger to, an old hand at, *au fait* <Fr>

17 **habituated,** *habitué* <Fr>; **in the habit of,** used to; never free from; **in a rut**

18 **confirmed, inveterate, chronic, established,** long-established, **fixed, settled, rooted,** thorough; incorrigible, irreversible; **deep-rooted,** deep-set, deep-settled, **deep-seated,** deep-fixed, deep-dyed; **infixed, ingrained,** fast, dyed-in-the-wool, inveterate; implanted, inculcated, instilled; set, **set in one's ways,** settled in habit; addicted, given

ADVS 19 **customarily,** conventionally, accustomedly, wontedly; normatively, normally, **usually; as is the custom;** as is usual, *comme d'habitude* <Fr>; as things go, as the world goes

20 **habitually, regularly,** routinely, frequently, persistently, repetitively, recurringly; **inverterately, chronically;** from habit, **by** *or* **from force of habit,** as is one's wont

374 UNACCUSTOMEDNESS

NOUNS 1 **unaccustomedness, newness,** unwontedness, disaccustomedness, unusedness, unhabituatedness; shakiness <nf>; **unfamiliarity,** unacquaintance, unconversance, unpracticedness, newness to; inexperience 414.2; ignorance 930

VERBS 2 **disaccustom, cure, break off,** stop, **wean**

3 **break the habit, cure oneself of,** disaccustom oneself, kick a habit <nf>, wean oneself from, break the pattern, break one's chains *or* fetters; **give up,** leave off, **abandon,** drop, stop, discontinue, kick *and* shake <nf>, throw off, rid oneself of; get on the wagon, swear off 668.8

ADJS 4 **unaccustomed, new,** disaccustomed, **unused, unwonted;** uninured, unseasoned, untrained, unhardened; shaky <nf>, tyronic; unhabituated, **not in the habit of;** out of the habit of, rusty; unweaned; **unused to, unfamiliar with,** not used to, unacquainted with, unconversant with, unpracticed, new to, a stranger to; cub, greenhorn; inexperienced 414.17; ignorant 930.12

375 MOTIVATION, INDUCEMENT

NOUNS **1 motive, reason, cause,** source, spring, mainspring; matter, score, consideration; **ground, basis** 886.1; sake; **aim, goal** 380.2, end, end in view, telos, final cause; **ideal,** principle, **ambition,** aspiration, inspiration, guiding light *or* star, lodestar; impetus; calling, vocation; intention 380; ulterior motive, hidden agenda; rationale, justification, driving force

2 motivation, moving, **actuation, prompting, stimulation,** animation, triggering, setting-off, setting in motion, getting under way; direction, inner-direction, other-direction; **influence** 893; hot button; carrot

3 inducement, enlistment, engagement, solicitation, **persuasion,** suasion; exhortation, hortation, preaching, preachment; **selling,** sales talk, salesmanship, hard sell, high pressure, hawking, huckstering, flogging <Brit>; jawboning *and* arm-twisting <nf>; **lobbying; coaxing,** wheedling, working on <nf>, cajolery, cajolement, conning, snow job *and* smoke and mirrors <nf>, nobbling <Brit nf>, blandishment, sweet talk *and* soft soap <nf>, soft sell <nf>; **allurement** 377

4 incitement, incitation, **instigation, stimulation, arousal, excitement, agitation, inflammation,** excitation, fomentation, firing, stirring, stirring-up, impassioning, whipping-up, rabble-rousing; waving the bloody shirt, rallying cry; **provocation,** irritation, exasperation; pep talk, pep rally

5 urging, pressure, pressing, pushing, entreaty, plea, advocacy; **encouragement,** abetment; **insistence,** instance; **goading, prodding,** goosing <nf>, spurring, pricking, needling

6 urge, urgency; impulse, impulsion, compulsion; press, **pressure, drive,** push; sudden *or* rash impulse; constraint, exigency, stress, pinch

7 incentive, inducement, encouragement, persuasive, **invitation, provocation, incitement; stimulus, stimulation,** stimulative, fillip, whet; carrot; reward, payment 624; **profit** 472.3; bait, **lure** 377.2; palm oil <nf>, greased palm <nf>, bribe 378.2; sweetening *and* sweetener <nf>, flattery, interest, percentage, what's in it for one <nf>; offer one cannot refuse; payola <nf>, pork barrel <nf>; perk <nf>

8 goad, spur, prod, prick <old>, sting, **gadfly;** oxgoad; rowel; whip, lash, gad <nf>, crack of the whip

9 inspiration, infusion, infection; fire, firing, spark, sparking; **animation, exhilaration,** enlivenment; afflatus, divine afflatus; genius, animus, moving *or* animating spirit; muse; the Muses

10 prompter, mover, prime mover, motivator, impeller, energizer, galvanizer, inducer, **actuator, animator,** moving spirit, mover and shaker <nf>; **encourager,** abettor, **inspirer,** firer, spark, sparker, spark plug <nf>; persuader, salesperson, brainwasher, spin doctor <nf>; **stimulator, gadfly; tempter** 377.3; coaxer, coax <nf>, wheedler, cajoler, pleader

11 instigator, inciter, exciter, urger, motivator; **provoker,** *provocateur* <Fr>, *agent provocateur* <Fr>, catalyst; **agitator, fomenter,** inflamer; agitprop; **rabble-rouser,** rouser, **demagogue; firebrand, incendiary; seditionist,** seditionary; lobbyist, activist; **troublemaker,** makebate <old>, mischief-maker, ringleader; tactician, strategist; pressure group, special-interest group

VERBS **12 motivate, move,** set in motion, **actuate,** move to action, **impel,** propel; **stimulate,** energize, galvanize, **animate, spark;** promote, foster; force, compel 424.4; ego-involve

13 prompt, provoke, evoke, elicit, call up, summon up, muster up, call forth, **inspire;** bring about, **cause**

14 urge, press, push, work on <nf>, twist one's arm <nf>; **sell,** flog <Brit>; **insist,** push for, not take no for an answer, **importune, nag, pressure, high-pressure,** browbeat, bring pressure to bear upon, throw one's weight around, throw one's weight into the scale, jawbone *and* build a fire under <nf>, talk round *or* around; grind in; **lobby,** pitch <nf>; hype <nf>; **coax,** wheedle, cajole, blandish, plead with, sweet-talk *and* soft-soap <nf>, **exhort,** call on *or* upon, advocate, recommend, put in a good word, buck for *and* hype <nf>; insist, insist upon

15 goad, prod, poke, nudge, prod at, goose <nf>, **spur,** prick, sting, needle; whip, lash; pick at *or* on, nibble at, nibble away at

16 urge on *or* **along, egg on** <nf>, hound on, hie on, hasten on, hurry on, speed on; **goad on, spur on,** drive on, whip on *or* along; cheer on, root on <nf>, root from the sidelines <nf>; aid and abet

17 incite, instigate, put up to <nf>; set on, sic on; **foment,** ferment, **agitate, arouse, excite, stir up,** work up, whip up, turn on; rally; **inflame,** incense, **fire,** heat, heat up, impassion; **provoke,** pique, whet, tickle; nettle; lash into a fury *or* frenzy; wave the bloody shirt; pour oil on the fire, feed the fire, add fuel to the flame, fan, fan the flame, blow the coals, stir the embers

18 kindle, enkindle, **fire, spark, spark off, trigger, trigger off, touch off,** set off, light the fuse, **enflame,** set afire *or* on fire, turn on <nf>

19 rouse, arouse, raise, raise up, **waken, awaken,** wake up, turn on <nf>, charge *or* psych *or* pump up <nf>, stir, **stir up,** set astir, **pique**

20 inspire, inspirit, spirit, spirit up; **fire, fire one's imagination; animate, exhilarate,** enliven; **infuse, infect,** inject, inoculate, imbue, inform

21 encourage, hearten, embolden, give encouragement, pat *or* clap on the back, stroke <nf>; **invite,** ask for; **abet,** aid and abet, countenance, keep in countenance; **foster, nurture,** nourish, feed

22 induce, prompt, move one to, influence, sway, incline, **dispose,** carry, bring, lead, **lead one to; lure; tempt;** determine, decide; enlist, procure, engage <old>, interest in, get to do

23 persuade, prevail on *or* **upon,** prevail with, **sway,** convince, lead to believe, **bring round,** bring to reason, bring to one's senses; **win, win over,** win around, bring over, draw over, gain, gain over; **talk over, talk into,** argue into, out-talk <nf>; wangle, wangle into; hook and hook in <nf>, con *and* do a snow job on <nf>, nobble <Brit nf>, sell *and* sell one on <nf>, **charm, captivate;** wear down, overcome one's resistance, arm-twist *and* twist one's arm <nf>, put the screws to; **bribe** 378.3, grease *or* oil *or* cross one's palm <nf>; brainwash

24 persuade oneself, make oneself easy about, make sure of, make up one's mind; follow one's conscience; be persuaded, rest easy, come around, buy <nf>

ADJS **25 motivating, motivational, motive, moving, animating, actuating, impelling, driving,** impulsive, inducive, directive; **urgent, pressing, driving;** compelling; causal, causative; goal-oriented

26 inspiring, inspirational, inspiriting; infusive; animating, exhilarating, enlivening

27 provocative, provoking, piquant, **exciting,** challenging, prompting, **rousing, stirring, stimulating,** stimulant, stimulative, stimulatory, energizing, electric, galvanizing, galvanic; **encouraging,** inviting, **alluring;** enticing; addictive

28 incitive, inciting, incentive; **instigative,** instigating; **agitative,** agitational; **inflammatory, incendiary,** fomenting, rabble-rousing

29 persuasive, suasive, persuading; wheedling, cajoling; hortative, hortatory; exhortative, exhortatory; hard-selling

30 moved, motivated, prompted, impelled, actuated; stimulated, animated; minded, inclined, of a mind to, with half a mind to; inner-directed, other-directed; soft <nf>

31 inspired, fired, afire, on fire

376 PRETEXT

NOUNS **1 pretext, pretense, pretension,** lying pretension, **show,** ostensible *or* announced *or* public *or* professed motive; **front,** facade, **sham** 354.3; **excuse,** apology, protestation, poor excuse, lame excuse; **occasion,** mere occasion; put-off <nf>; handle, peg to hang on, leg to stand on, *locus standi* <L>; **subterfuge,** refuge, device, stratagem, feint, dipsy-doodle <nf>, **trick** 356.6; dust thrown in the eye, smoke screen, **screen, cover,** stalking-horse, **blind;** guise, semblance; mask, cloak, veil; **cosmetics,** mere cosmetics, gloss, varnish, color, coat of paint, whitewash <nf>; spit and polish; **cover,** cover-up, cover story, alibi; band-aid

2 claim, profession, allegation

VERBS **3** pretext, make a pretext of, take as an excuse *or* reason *or* occasion, urge as a motive, **pretend,** make a pretense of; put up a front *or* false front; **allege, claim,** profess, purport, avow; protest too much

4 hide under, cover oneself with, shelter under, take cover under, wrap oneself in, cloak *or* mantle oneself with, take refuge in; conceal one's motive with; **cover,** cover up, gloss *or* varnish over, apply a coat of paint *or* whitewash, stick on a band-aid

ADJS **5 pretexted, pretended, alleged, claimed, professed, purported,** avowed; **ostensible,** hypocritical, **specious;** so-called, in name only

ADVS **6 ostensibly, allegedly,** purportedly, professedly, avowedly; for the record, for public consumption; under the pretext of, **as a pretext,** as an excuse, as a cover *or* a cover-up *or* an alibi

377 ALLUREMENT

NOUNS **1 allurement, allure, enticement, inveiglement,** invitation, come-hither <nf>, blandishment, cajolery; inducement 375.7; **temptation,** tantalization; **seduction,** seducement; **beguilement,** beguiling; **fascination, captivation,** enthrallment, entrapment, snaring; **enchantment,** witchery, bewitchery, bewitchment; **attraction, interest, charm, glamour, appeal,** magnetism; charisma; star quality; wooing; flirtation

2 attractiveness, allure, charmingness, bewitchingness, impressiveness, **seductiveness,** winsomeness, winning ways, winningness; **sexiness,** sex appeal *or* SA <nf>

3 lure, charm, **come-on** <nf>, attention-getter *or* -grabber, **attraction, draw** *or* drawer *or* crowd-drawer, crowd-pleaser, headliner; clou, hook *and* gimmick <nf>, drawing card, drawcard; **decoy,** decoy duck; **bait,** ground bait, baited trap, baited hook; **snare,** trap; **endearment** 562; the song of the Sirens, the voice of the tempter, honeyed words; forbidden fruit

4 tempter, seducer, enticer, inveigler, **charmer,**

enchanter, fascinator, tantalizer, teaser; coquette, flirt; Don Juan; Pied Piper of Hamelin; **temptress,** enchantress, seductress, **siren;** Siren, Circe, Lorelei, Parthenope; **vampire,** vamp <nf>, *femme fatale* <Fr>

VERBS **5 lure,** allure, **entice, seduce, inveigle, decoy,** draw, **draw on, lead on;** come on to *and* give the come-on *and* give a come-hither look *and* bat the eyes at *and* make goo-goo eyes at <nf>, flirt with, flirt; **woo;** coax, cajole, blandish; **ensnare;** draw in, suck in *and* rope in <nf>; bait, offer bait to, bait the hook, angle with a silver hook

6 attract, interest, appeal, engage, impress, charismatize, fetch <nf>, catch *or* get one's eye, command one's attention, rivet one, attract one's interest, be attractive, take *or* tickle one's fancy; **invite,** summon, beckon; **tempt, tantalize, titillate,** tickle, **tease,** whet the appetite, make one's mouth water, dangle before one

7 fascinate, captivate, charm, becharm, spell, spellbind, cast a spell, put under a spell, **beguile, intrigue, enthrall,** infatuate, **enrapture, transport, enravish, entrance, enchant,** witch, **bewitch;** carry away, sweep off one's feet, turn one's head, knock one's socks off <nf>; hypnotize, mesmerize; vamp <nf>; charismatize

ADJS **8 alluring, fascinating, captivating, riveting, charming, glamorous,** exotic, **enchanting,** spellful, spellbinding, **entrancing,** ravishing, **enravishing, intriguing, enthralling,** witching, **bewitching; attractive, interesting, appealing,** dishy <Brit nf>, sexy <nf>, engaging, taking, eye-catching, catching, fetching, winning, winsome, prepossessing; exciting; charismatic; **seductive,** seducing, **beguiling, enticing, inviting,** come-hither <nf>; flirtatious, coquettish; coaxing, cajoling, blandishing; **tempting, tantalizing,** teasing, titillating, titillative, tickling; **provocative,** *provoquant* <Fr>; appetizing, mouth-watering, piquant; **irresistible;** siren, sirenic; hypnotic, mesmeric

ADVS **9 alluringly, fascinatingly,** captivatingly, charmingly, enchantingly, entrancingly, enravishingly, intriguingly, beguilingly, glamorously, bewitchingly; attractively, appealingly, engagingly, winsomely; **enticingly, seductively,** with bedroom eyes <nf>; **temptingly,** provocatively; **tantalizingly,** teasingly; piquantly; appetizingly; irresistibly; hypnotically, mesmerically

378 BRIBERY

NOUNS **1 bribery,** bribing, subornation, **corruption, graft,** bribery and corruption

2 bribe, bribe money, sop, sop to Cerberus, gratuity, gratification <old>, payoff <nf>, boodle <nf>; hush money <nf>; payola <nf>; protection

VERBS **3 bribe,** throw a sop to; grease *and* **grease the palm** *or* **hand** *and* oil the palm *and* tickle the palm <nf>; **purchase;** buy *and* **buy off** *and* pay off <nf>; suborn, **corrupt,** tamper with; reach *and* get at *and* get to <nf>; approach, try to bribe; **fix, take care of**

ADJS **4 bribable,** corruptible, purchasable, buyable; approachable; fixable; on the take *and* on the pad <nf>; **venal, corrupt,** bought and paid for, in one's pocket

379 DISSUASION

NOUNS **1 dissuasion,** talking out of <nf>, remonstrance, expostulation, admonition, monition, **warning,** caveat, **caution,** cautioning; intimidation, **determent,** deterrence, scaring *or* frightening off, turning around; contraindication

2 deterrent, determent; **discouragement,** disincentive, chilling effect, demotivation; deflection, roadblock, red light, closed door; damp, damper, **wet blanket,** cold water, chill; alienation, disaffection

VERBS **3 dissuade,** convince to the contrary, convince otherwise, **talk out of** <nf>; contraindicate; unconvince, unpersuade; remonstrate, expostulate, admonish, cry out against; **warn, warn off** *or* **away, caution;** enter a caveat; **intimidate,** scare *or* frighten off, daunt, cow; turn around

4 disincline, indispose, disaffect, disinterest; **deter,** repel, turn from, turn away *or* aside; divert, deflect; distract, put off *and* turn off <nf>; wean from; **discourage; pour** *or* **dash** *or* **throw cold water on,** throw *or* lay a wet blanket on, be a wet blanket, damp, dampen, demotivate, **cool, chill,** quench, blunt; nip in the bud; take the starch out of, take the wind out of one's sails

ADJS **5 dissuasive,** dissuading, disinclining, **discouraging; deterrent,** off-putting, repellent, disenchanting; expostulatory, admonitory, monitory, cautionary; intimidating

380 INTENTION

NOUNS **1 intention, intent,** intendment, mindset, **aim,** effect, meaning, view, study, animus, **point, purpose,** function, set *or* settled *or* fixed purpose; sake; **design, plan, project,** idea, notion; **quest,** pursuit; **proposal,** prospectus; **resolve,** resolution, mind, will; **motive** 375.1; determination 359.1; desideratum, desideration, **ambition,** aspiration, **desire** 100; striving, nisus

2 objective, object, aim, end, goal, destination, mark, object in mind, **end in view,** telos, final cause, ultimate aim *or* purpose, mission; end in itself; **target,** butt, bull's-eye, quintain; quarry, prey, game; reason for being, *raison d'être* <Fr>; by-purpose, by-end; "the be-all and the end-all"— Shakespeare; teleology

3 intentionality, deliberation, deliberateness, directedness; express intention, expressness, **premeditation, predeliberation,** preconsideration, **calculation, calculatedness, predetermination,** preresolution, forethought, aforethought, calculated risk

VERBS **4 intend, purpose, plan,** purport, **mean,** think, **propose; resolve,** determine 359.7; project, **design,** destine; **aim,** aim at, take aim at, draw a bead on, set one's sights on, have designs on, go for, drive at, aspire to *or* after, be after, set before oneself, purpose to oneself, have every intention; harbor a design; **desire** 100.14,18

5 contemplate, meditate; envisage, envision, **have in mind, have in view;** have an eye to, have every intention, have a mind *or* notion, have half a mind *or* notion, have a good *or* great mind *or* notion

6 plan, plan on, figure on, plan for *or* out, count on, figure out, calculate, calculate on, reckon, reckon *or* bargain on, bargain for, bank on *or* upon, make book on <nf>, expect, foresee

7 premeditate, calculate, preresolve, predetermine, predeliberate, preconsider, direct oneself, forethink, work out beforehand; plan; plot, scheme

ADJS **8 intentional, intended,** proposed, purposed, telic, **projected, designed,** of design, aimed, aimed at, **meant, purposeful,** purposive, **willful, voluntary, deliberate;** deliberated; considered, studied, advised, **calculated, contemplated, envisaged,** envisioned, meditated, **conscious,** knowing, witting; planned; teleological

9 premeditated, predeliberated, preconsidered, predetermined, preresolved, prepense, aforethought

ADVS **10 intentionally, purposely,** purposefully, purposively, pointedly, **on purpose,** with purpose, with a view *or* an eye to, **deliberately, designedly, willfully, voluntarily,** of one's own accord *or* one's own free will; **wittingly, consciously, knowingly; advisedly, calculatedly,** contemplatedly, meditatedly, premeditatedly, **with premeditation, with intent,** with full intent, **by design,** with one's eyes open; with malice aforethought, in cold blood

PREPS, CONJS **11 for, to; in order to *or* that,** so, **so that, so as to; for the purpose of,** to the end that, with the intent that, with the view of, with a view to, with an eye to; in contemplation of, in consideration of; **for the sake of**

381 PLAN

NOUNS **1 plan, scheme, design,** method, **program,** device, contrivance, game, envisagement, conception, enterprise, **idea, notion;** organization, rationalization, systematization, schematization; charting, mapping, graphing, blueprinting; **planning,** calculation, figuring; planning function; long-range planning, long-range *or* long-term plan; **master plan,** the picture *and* the big picture <nf>; approach, attack, plan of attack; way, procedure; **arrangement,** prearrangement, system, disposition, layout, setup, lineup; **schedule,** timetable, time-scheme, time frame; agenda, order of the day; deadline; plan of work; **schema,** schematism, scheme of arrangement; blueprint, **guideline, guidelines,** program of action; methodology; working plan, ground plan, tactical plan, strategic plan; tactics, **strategy,** game plan <nf>; mission statement; contingency plan; operations research; **intention** 380; forethought, foresight 961; back room

2 project, projection, scheme; proposal, prospectus, proposition; scenario, **game plan** <nf>

3 diagram, plot, chart, blueprint, graph, bar graph, pie *or* circle graph *or* chart, area graph; flow diagram, flow chart; **table; design, pattern,** copy <old>, cartoon; **sketch, draft, drawing,** working drawing, rough; *brouillon* and *ébauche* and *esquisse* <Fr>; **outline, delineation,** skeleton, figure, profile; house plan, ground plan, ichnography; elevation, projection; **map, chart** 159.5

4 policy, polity, principles, guiding principles; **procedure,** course, line, plan of action; creed 953.3; **platform,** party line; position paper; formula; rule

5 intrigue, web of intrigue, **plot, scheme,** deep-laid plot *or* scheme, underplot, game *or* little game <nf>, secret plan, trick, stratagem, finesse, method; counterplot; **conspiracy,** confederacy, covin, complot <old>, cabal; **complicity, collusion, connivance; artifice** 415.3; **contrivance,** contriving; **scheming,** schemery, plotting; finagling <nf>, **machination,** manipulation, **maneuvering,** engineering, rigging; frame-up <nf>; wire-pulling <nf>; inside job; expedient, last resort, eleventh-hour rescue; way out, loophole

6 planner, designer, deviser, contriver, framer, projector; enterpriser, entrepreneur; intrapreneur; organizer, promoter, developer, engineer; expediter, facilitator, animator; **policymaker, decision-maker; architect, tactician, strategist, strategian,** mastermind, brains <nf>

7 schemer, plotter, counterplotter, finagler <nf>,

Machiavelli; **intriguer,** *intrigant* and *intrigante*
<Fr>, cabalist; **conspirer, conspirator,**
coconspirator, **conniver;** maneuverer, machinator,
operator <nf>, opportunist, pot-hunter, exploiter;
wire-puller <nf>

VERBS **8 plan, devise, contrive, design,** frame, shape,
cast, concert, lay plans; organize, rationalize,
systematize, schematize, methodize, configure,
pull together, sort out; **arrange,** prearrange, make
arrangements, set up, work up, work out;
schedule; lay down a plan, shape *or* mark out a
course; program; **calculate,** figure; **project,** cut out,
make a projection, forecast <old>, plan ahead;
intend 380.4

9 plot, scheme, intrigue, be up to something;
conspire, connive, collude, complot <old>, cabal;
hatch, hatch up, cook up <nf>, brew, concoct,
hatch *or* lay a plot; **maneuver,** machinate, finesse,
operate <nf>, engineer, rig, wangle <nf>, angle,
finagle <nf>; frame *or* frame up <nf>;
counterplot, countermine

10 plot; map, chart 159.11, **blueprint; diagram,**
graph; **sketch,** sketch in *or* out, draw up a plan;
map out, plot out, **lay out,** set out, mark out; lay
off, mark off; design a prototype

11 outline, line, **delineate,** chalk out, brief; **sketch,
draft,** trace; block in *or* out; rough in, rough out;
chalk out

ADJS **12 planned, devised, designed,** shaped, set,
blueprinted, charted, mapped, **contrived; plotted;**
premeditated; arranged; organized, rationalized,
systematized, schematized, methodized,
strategized; worked out, calculated, figured;
projected; scheduled, on the agenda, in the works,
in the pipeline <nf>, on the calendar, on the
docket, on the anvil, on the carpet, on the tapis
<old>, *sur le tapis* <Fr>; tactical, **strategic**

**13 scheming, calculating, designing, contriving,
plotting, intriguing;** resourceful; manipulatory,
manipulative; opportunist, **opportunistic;**
Machiavellian, Byzantine; **conniving,** connivent
<old>, conspiring, conspiratorial, collusive;
stratagemical

14 schematic, diagrammatic

382 PURSUIT

NOUNS **1 pursuit,** pursuing, pursuance, prosecution
<old>; **quest,** seeking, hunting, searching;
following, follow, follow-up; tracking, trailing,
tracking down, dogging, hounding, shadowing,
stalking, tailing <nf>; **chase,** hot pursuit; hue and
cry; all points bulletin *or* APB, dragnet, manhunt

2 hunting, gunning, shooting, venery, cynegetics,
sport, sporting; **hunt, chase,** chevy *or* chivy

<Brit>, *shikar* <India>, coursing; blood sport; fox
hunt, fox hunting; hawking, falconry; stalking, still
hunt

3 fishing, fishery; **angling,** piscatology <old>,
halieutics; fly-fishing, saltwater fishing, ice fishing,
competitive fishing

4 pursuer, pursuant, **chaser,** follower; hunter,
quester, **seeker,** tracker, trailer, tail <nf>

5 hunter, huntsman, sportsman, **Nimrod;** huntress,
sportswoman; stalker; courser; trapper; big game
hunter, *shikari* <India>, white hunter; jacklighter,
jacker; gamekeeper; beater, whipper-in; falconer;
gundog; poacher

6 fisher, fisherman, angler, *piscator* <L>,
piscatorian, piscatorialist; Waltonian; dibber,
dibbler, troller, trawler, trawlerman, dragger,
jacker, jigger, bobber, guddler, tickler, drifter, drift
netter, whaler, clam digger, lobsterman, etc

7 quarry, game, prey, venery, beasts of venery, victim,
the hunted; kill; big game, small game

VERBS **8 pursue,** prosecute <old>, **follow,** follow up,
go after, take out *or* off after <nf>, bay after, run
after, run in pursuit of, make after, go in pursuit
of; raise the hunt, raise the hue and cry, hollo
after; **chase, give chase,** chivy; hound, dog; **quest,**
quest after, **seek,** seek out, hunt, **search** 937.29,30,
send out a search party; trawl

9 hunt, go hunting, hunt down, chase, run, *shikar*
<India>, sport; engage in a blood sport; shoot,
gun; course; ride to hounds, follow the hounds;
track, trail; **stalk,** prowl after, still-hunt; poach;
hound, dog; hawk, falcon; fowl; flush, start; drive,
beat; jack, jacklight; trap, ensnare

10 fish, go fishing, **angle;** cast one's hook *or* net; bait
the hook; shrimp, whale, clam, grig, still-fish, fly-
fish, troll, bob, dap, dib *or* dibble, gig, jig, etc; reel
in

ADJS **11 pursuing,** pursuant, following; **questing,** in
quest of, **seeking, searching** 938.37; **in pursuit,** in
hot pursuit, in full cry, tailing, chasing, trailing;
hunting, cynegetic, fishing, piscatory, piscatorial,
halieutic, halieutical

PREPS **12 after, in pursuit** *or* **pursuance of,** in search
of, on the lookout for, in the market for, out for; on
the track *or* trail of, on the scent of

INTERJS **13** <hunting cries> view halloo!, yoicks!
<old>; so-ho!, tallyho!, tallyho over!, tallyho back!

383 ROUTE, PATH

NOUNS **1 route, path, way, itinerary, course,** track,
run, line, road; trajectory, traject, *trajet* <Fr>;
direction; circuit, tour, orbit; walk, beat, round;
trade route, traffic lane, **sea lane,** shipping lane, **air
lane,** flight path; path of least resistance, primrose

path, garden path; shortcut, detour; line of advance, line of retreat

2 **path, track, trail, pathway,** footpath, footway, *piste* <Fr>; walkway, catwalk, skybridge *or* skywalk *or* flying bridge *or* walkway; **sidewalk, walk,** fastwalk, *trottoir* <Fr>, foot pavement <Brit>; boardwalk; hiking trail; public walk, promenade, esplanade, alameda, parade, *prado* <Sp>, mall; towpath *or* towing path; bridle path *or* road *or* trail *or* way; bicycle path; berm; run, runway; beaten track *or* path, rut, groove; garden path

3 **passageway, pass, passage, defile; avenue, artery; corridor, aisle, alley, lane; channel, conduit** 239.1; ford, ferry, traject, *trajet* <Fr>; opening, aperture; access, right of way, approach, inlet 189.5; exit, outlet 190.9; connection, communication; covered way, gallery, arcade, portico, colonnade, cloister, ambulatory; underpass, overpass, flyover <Brit>; tunnel, railroad tunnel, vehicular tunnel; junction, interchange, **intersection** 170.2

4 **byway, bypath,** byroad, by-lane, bystreet, side road, side street; **bypass, detour,** roundabout way; bypaths and crooked ways, side path; back way, back stairs, back door, side door; back road, back street

5 **road** <see list>, highway, roadway, carriageway <Brit>, right-of-way; **street** <see list>

6 **pavement,** paving; macadam, blacktop, bitumen, asphalt, tarmacadam, tarmac, tarvia, bituminous macadam; cement, concrete; tile, brick, paving brick; stone, paving stone, pavestone, flag, flagstone, flagging; cobblestone, cobble; road metal <Brit>; gravel; washboard; curbstone, kerbstone <Brit>, edgestone; curb, kerb <Brit>, curbing; gutter, kennel <Brit>

7 **railway** <see list>, **railroad,** rail, line, track, trackage, railway *or* railroad *or* rail line; subway; junction; terminus, terminal, the end of the line; roadway, roadbed, embankment; bridge, trestle

8 **cableway,** ropeway, wireway, wire ropeway, cable *or* rope railway, funicular *or* funicular railway; monorail; *téléphérique* <Fr>, telpher, telpherway, telpher ropeway, telpher line *or* railway; ski lift, chair lift, gondola, aerial tramway, tram

9 **bridge, span, viaduct;** cantilever bridge, clapper bridge, drawbridge, footbridge, pontoon bridge, rope bridge, skybridge *or* skywalk *or* flying bridge *or* walkway, suspension bridge, toll bridge, floating bridge, covered bridge, aqueduct; overpass, overcrossing, overbridge *or* flyover <Brit>; stepping-stone, stepstone, catwalk; Bifrost

10 **roads, highways**

access road
arterial highway
artery
Autobahn <Ger>
autoroute <Fr>
autostrada <Ital>

beltway *or* circumferential *or* ring road *or* belt highway
big road <S US>
busway
camino real <Sp>
causeway
country road
dirt road
divided *or* dual highway
expressway
freeway
highroad <Brit>
interstate highway
king's *or* queen's highway
limited access highway
main road *or* main drag <nf>
motorway <Brit>
parkway
pavé <Fr>
pike
post road
private road
shunpike
skyway
speedway
superhighway
switchback
throughway *or* thruway
toll road
trunk road
turnpike

11 **streets, alleys**

alley *or* alleyway
avenue
blind alley
boulevard
close <Brit>
court
crescent
cul-de-sac
dead-end street
drive
lane
mews
one-way street
place
row
thoroughfare
vennel <Scot>
wynd <Scot>

12 **railways**

cable railway
cog railway
electric railway
elevated railway *or* elevated *or* el *or* L <nf>
funicular railway
gravity-operated railway *or* gravity railroad
inclined railroad
light-rail rapid-transit system
mainline
métro <Fr>
monorail
rack *or* rack-and-pinion railway
scenic railroad
subway
tram *or* tramline *or* tramway *or* tramroad <Brit>
trolley *or* streetcar line
trunk *or* trunk line
underground *or* tube <Brit>

384 MANNER, MEANS

NOUNS 1 **manner, way,** wise, **means, mode,** modality, form <old>, **fashion, style,** tone, guise <old>; **method,** methodology, **system;** algorithm <math>; **approach,** attack, tack; **technique, procedure, process,** proceeding, measures, steps, course, practice; order; lines, line, line of action; *modus operandi* <L>, mode of operation *or* MO, manner of working, mode of procedure; **routine;** the way of, the how, the how-to, the drill <Brit>

2 **means,** ways, **ways and means,** means to an end; **wherewithal,** wherewith; funds 728.14; **resources,** disposable resources, capital 728.15; bankroll <nf>; stock in trade, inventory, stock, supply 386;

power, capacity, ability 18.2; power base, constituency, backing, support; recourses, resorts, devices; tools of the trade, tricks of the trade, bag of tricks

3 **instrumentality, agency;** machinery, **mechanism,** modality; gadgetry <nf>; mediation, going between, intermediation, service; **expedient,** recourse, resort, device 994.2

4 **instrument, tool, implement, appliance,** device; contrivance, makeshift, lever, mechanism; **vehicle, organ; agent** 576; medium, mediator, intermedium, intermediary, intermediate, interagent, liaison, go-between 576.4; expediter, facilitator, animator; midwife, servant, slave, handmaid, handmaiden, *ancilla* <L>; **cat's-paw, puppet, dummy, pawn,** creature, minion, stooge <nf>; stalking horse; toy, plaything; gadget, contrivance; dupe 358

VERBS 5 **use, utilize,** adopt, effect; **approach, attack;** proceed, practice, go about; routinize

6 **find means, find a way,** provide *or* have the wherewithal, develop a method; enable, facilitate; get by hook or by crook, obtain by fair means or foul; beg, borrow, or steal; think laterally; network

7 be instrumental, **serve, subserve,** serve one's purpose, come in handy, stand in good stead, fill the bill; minister to, act for, act in the interests of, **promote, advance, forward, assist,** facilitate; mediate, go between; liaise

ADJS 8 modal; **instrumental, implemental;** agential, agentive, agentival; effective, efficacious; **useful,** utile, handy, employable, **serviceable; helpful,** conducive, forwarding, favoring, promoting, assisting, facilitating; subservient, ministering, ministerial; mediating, mediatorial, intermediary

ADVS 9 **how, in what way** *or* **manner,** by what mode *or* means; to what extent; in what condition; by what name; at what price; after this fashion, in this way, in such wise, along these lines; **thus, so,** just so, thus and so; as, like, on the lines of

10 **anyhow, anyway,** anywise, anyroad <Brit nf>, in any way, **by any means, by any manner of means;** in any event, at any rate, leastways <nf>, in any case; **nevertheless, nonetheless, however, regardless,** irregardless <nf>; at all, nohow <nf>

11 **somehow, in some way,** in some way or other, someway <nf>, by some means, **somehow or other,** somehow or another, in one way or another, in some such way, after a fashion; no matter how, **by hook or by crook,** by fair means or foul

12 herewith, therewith, wherewith, wherewithal; whereby, thereby, hereby

PREPS 13 **by means of, by** *or* **through the agency of,** by *or* through the good offices of, through the instrumentality of, by the aid of, thanks to, by use of, **by way of,** by dint of, by the act of, through the medium of, by *or* in virtue of, at the hand of, at the hands of; **with, through,** by, per

PHRS 14 it isn't what you do, it's how you do it; there's more than one way to skin a cat

385 PROVISION, EQUIPMENT

NOUNS 1 **provision,** providing; **equipment, accouterment,** fitting out, outfitting; **supply,** supplying, finding; **furnishing,** furnishment; chandlery, **retailing, selling** 734.2; **logistics;** procurement 472.1; investment, endowment, subvention, subsidy, subsidization; provisioning, victualing, purveyance, catering; armament; resupply, replenishment, reinforcement; supply line, line of supply; **preparation** 405

2 **provisions, supplies** 386.1; provender 10.5; **merchandise** 735; basics

3 **accommodations,** accommodation, facilities; **lodgings;** bed, board, full board; **room and board,** bed and board; **subsistence,** keep, fostering

4 **equipment,** matériel, equipage, munitions; **furniture, furnishings,** furnishments <old>; **fixtures, fittings, appointments, accouterments, appurtenances,** trappings, installations, plumbing; **appliances,** utensils, **conveniences; outfit, apparatus, rig,** machinery; stock-in-trade; **plant,** facility, facilities; paraphernalia, harness, things, **gear, stuff** <nf>, impedimenta <pl>, **tackle;** rigging; armament, munition; **kit,** duffel, effects, personal effects

5 **harness,** caparison, trappings, **tack,** tackle

6 **provider, supplier,** furnisher; donor 478.11; patron; **purveyor,** provisioner, **caterer,** victualer, sutler; *vivandier* or *vivandière* <Fr>; chandler, retailer, merchant 730.2; commissary, commissariat, quartermaster, shopkeeper, storekeeper, merchant, stock clerk, steward, manciple; grocer, vintner; procurer; megastore

VERBS 7 **provide, supply,** find, dish up *and* rustle up <nf>, **furnish;** accommodate; invest, endow, fund, subsidize; donate, give, afford, contribute, kick in <nf>, yield, present 478.12; make available; stock, store; provide for, make provision *or* due provision for; prepare 405.6; support, maintain, keep; fill, fill up; replenish, restock, recruit

8 **equip, furnish, outfit,** gear, **prepare, fit,** fit up *or* out, fix up <nf>, **rig,** rig up *or* out, **turn out,** appoint, accouter, clothe, dress; arm, heel <nf>, munition; man, staff

9 **provision,** provender, cater, victual, plenish <old>, serve, cook for; provide a grubstake <nf>; **board,** feed; forage; fuel, gas, gas up, fill up, top off, coal, oil, bunker; **purvey,** sell 734.8

10 **accommodate,** furnish accommodations; house, lodge 225.10; **put up,** board

11 **make a living,** earn a living *or* livelihood, **make *or* earn one's keep**

12 **support oneself,** make one's way; **make ends meet, keep body and soul together, keep the wolf from the door,** keep *or* hold one's head above water, keep afloat; **survive, subsist, cope, eke out,** make out, scrape along, manage, get by

ADJS 13 **provided, supplied, furnished,** provisioned, purveyed, catered; invested, endowed; **equipped, fitted,** fitted out, outfitted, rigged, accoutered; armed, heeled <nf>; staffed, manned; readied, in place, **prepared 405.16**

14 **well-provided, well-supplied, well-furnished,** well-stocked, well-found; **well-equipped, well-fitted,** well-appointed; well-armed

386 STORE, SUPPLY

NOUNS 1 **store, hoard, treasure,** treasury; plenty, plenitude, abundance, cornucopia; heap, mass, stack, pile, dump, rick; **collection, accumulation,** cumulation, **amassment,** budget, **stockpile; backlog;** repertory, repertoire; stock-in-trade; **inventory, stock,** supply on hand; lock, stock, and barrel; **stores, supplies, provisions,** provisionment, rations; larder, commissariat, commissary; munitions; matériel; material, materials 1054

2 **supply, fund, resource, resources; means, assets,** liquid assets, balance, pluses <nf>, black-ink items, financial resources, **capital,** capital goods, capitalization, available means *or* resources *or* funds, cash flow, stock in trade; venture capital; backing, support; grist, grist for the mill; holdings, property 471; labor resources

3 **reserve, reserves,** reservoir, resource; proved *or* proven reserve; **stockpile, cache,** backup, reserve supply, store, standby, safeguard, something in reserve *or* in hand, something to fall back on, reserve fund, emergency funds, **nest egg, savings,** sinking fund; proved reserves; backlog, unexpended balance; ace in the hole <nf>, a card *or* ace up one's sleeve; spare *or* replacement part

4 **source of supply,** source, staple, resource; well, fountain, fount, font <old>, spring, wellspring; mine, **gold mine, bonanza,** luau <nf>; quarry, lode, vein; oilfield, oil well, oil rig; cornucopia

5 **storage, stowage;** preservation, conservation, safekeeping, warehousing; cold storage, cold store, dry storage, dead storage; storage space, shelf-room; custody, guardianship 1007.2; sequestration, escrow

6 **storehouse, storeroom,** stockroom, box room <Brit>, lumber room, store, storage, **depository,**

repository, conservatory <old>, reservoir, repertory, depot, supply depot, supply base, magazine, *magasin* <Fr>, warehouse, megastore, godown; bonded warehouse, entrepôt; dock; hold, cargo dock; attic, loft, cellar, basement; closet, cupboard; wine cellar, larder; shed, stable, garage; **treasury,** treasure house, treasure room, exchequer, coffers; bank, vault 729.13, strongroom, strongbox; **archives, library,** stack room; armory, arsenal, dump; lumberyard; drawer, shelf; bin, bunker, bay, crib; rack, rick, vat, tank; elevator; crate, box; chest, **locker,** hutch; bookcase, stack; sail locker, chain locker, lazaret, lazaretto, glory hole

7 **garner, granary,** grain bin, elevator, grain elevator, **silo;** mow, haymow, hayloft, hayrick; crib, corncrib

8 **larder, pantry,** buttery <nf>; spence <Brit nf>, stillroom <Brit>; root cellar; dairy, dairy house *or* room

9 **museum; gallery,** art gallery, picture gallery, pinacotheca; salon; Metropolitan Museum, National Gallery, Museum of Modern Art, Guggenheim Museum, Tate Gallery, British Museum, Louvre, Hermitage, Prado, Uffizi, Rijksmuseum; museology, curatorship

VERBS 10 **store, stow,** lay in store; **lay in,** lay in a supply *or* stock *or* store, store away, stow away, **put away, lay away,** put *or* lay by, pack away, bundle away, lay down, stow down, salt down *or* away *and* sock away *and* squirrel away <nf>; **deposit,** reposit, lodge; **cache,** stash <nf>, bury away; **bank,** coffer, hutch <old>; warehouse, reservoir; file, file away

11 **store up, stock up, lay up,** put up, **save up,** hoard up, treasure up, garner up, **heap up,** pile up, build up a stock *or* an inventory, provision; **accumulate,** cumulate, **collect, amass, stockpile;** backlog; garner, gather into barns; **hoard,** treasure, save, keep, hold, squirrel, squirrel away; hide, secrete 346.7

12 **reserve, save, conserve, keep,** retain, husband, husband one's resources, keep *or* hold back, withhold; **keep in reserve,** keep in store, keep on hand, keep by one; sequester, put in escrow; **preserve 397.7; set *or* put aside,** set *or* put apart, put *or* lay *or* set by; save up, save to fall back upon, keep as a nest egg, **save for a rainy day,** provide for *or* against a rainy day

13 **have in store** *or* **reserve,** have to fall back upon, have something to draw on, have something laid by, have something laid by for a rainy day, have something up one's sleeve

ADJS 14 **stored, accumulated,** amassed, laid up, stocked; gathered, garnered, collected, heaped, piled; **stockpiled;** backlogged; **hoarded,** treasured

15 **reserved, preserved, saved,** conserved, put by *or*

aside, kept, retained, held, filed, withheld, held back, kept *or* held in reserve; in storage, warehoused, mothballed; bottled, pickled, canned, refrigerated, frozen; spare

ADVS **16 in store,** in stock, in supply, **on hand**

17 in reserve, back, aside, by

387 USE

NOUNS **1 use, employment,** utilization, employ <old>, **usage; exercise, exertion,** active use; good use; ill use, wrong use, misuse 389; hard use, hard *or* rough usage; hard wear, heavy duty; **application,** appliance, deployment; expenditure, expending, using up, exhausting, dissipation, dissipating, **consumption** 388

2 usage, treatment, handling, management; way *or* means of dealing; stewardship, custodianship, guardianship, care

3 utility, usefulness, usability, use, utilizability, avail, good, advantage, benefit, **serviceability,** service, **helpfulness,** functionality, profitability, applicability, availability, **practicability,** practicality, practical utility, operability, **effectiveness,** efficacy, efficiency; readiness, availability; instrumentality; ultimate purpose

4 benefit, use, service, avail, profit, advantage, point, percentage *and* mileage <nf>, what's in it for one <nf>, convenience; interest, behalf, behoof; **value, worth,** fruitfulness; commonweal, public good

5 function, use, purpose, role, part, point, end use, immediate purpose, ultimate purpose, operational purpose, operation; work, duty, office

6 functionalism, utilitarianism; pragmatism, pragmaticism; functional design, functional furniture *or* housing, etc

7 <law terms> usufruct, imperfect usufruct, perfect usufruct, right of use, user, enjoyment of property; *jus primae noctis* <L>, *droit du seigneur* <Fr>; disposal; possession

8 utilization, using, making use of, making instrumental, using as a means *or* tool; **employment,** employing; **management,** manipulation, handling, working, operation, **exploitation,** recruiting, recruitment, calling upon, calling into service; mobilization, mobilizing

9 user, employer; **consumer,** enjoyer, exploiter; customer, client

VERBS **10 use, utilize, make use of,** do with; **employ,** practice, ply, work, manage, handle, manipulate, operate, **wield,** play, exercise; **have** *or* **enjoy the use of;** exercise, **exert**

11 apply, put to use *or* **good use,** carry out, put into execution, **put into practice** *or* **operation,** put in force, enforce; bring to bear upon

12 treat, handle, manage, use, **deal with, cope with,** come to grips with, take on, tackle <nf>, contend with, do with; steward, care for

13 spend, consume, expend, **pass,** employ, **put in;** devote, bestow, give to *or* give over to, devote *or* consecrate *or* dedicate to; while, while away, wile; dissipate, **exhaust, use up**

14 avail oneself of, make use of, resort to, put to use *or* **good use,** have recourse to, **turn to,** look to, recur to, refer to, take to <nf>, betake oneself to; revert to, fall back on *or* upon, rely on; convert *or* turn to use, put in *or* into requisition, press *or* enlist into service, lay under contribution, impress, **call upon,** call *or* bring into play, draw on *or* upon, recruit, muster; pick someone's brains

15 take advantage of, avail oneself of, make the most of, use to the full, make good use of, maximize, improve, **turn to use** *or* **profit** *or* **account** *or* **good account,** turn to advantage *or* good advantage, use to advantage, put to advantage, find one's account *or* advantage in; improve the occasion 843.8; **profit by, benefit from,** reap the benefit of; **exploit, capitalize on, make capital of,** make a good thing of <nf>, make hay <nf>, **trade on,** cash in on <nf>, play on, play off against; make the best of, make a virtue of necessity, "make necessity a virtue"—Quintilian

16 <take unfair advantage of> **exploit, take advantage of, use,** make use of, **use for one's own ends;** make a paw *or* cat's-paw of, make a pawn of, sucker *and* play for a sucker <nf>; **manipulate,** work on, work upon, stroke, play on *or* upon; play both ends against the middle; **impose upon,** presume upon; use ill, ill-use, abuse, misuse 389.4; batten on; milk, bleed, bleed white <nf>; drain, suck the blood of *or* from, suck dry; exploit one's position, feather one's nest <nf>, **profiteer;** abuse

17 avail, be of use, be of service, serve, **suffice, do,** answer, **answer** *or* **serve one's purpose,** serve one's need, fill the bill *and* do the trick <nf>, suit one's purpose; bestead <old>, **stand one in stead** *or* **good stead,** be handy, come in handy, stand one in hand <nf>; advantage, be of advantage *or* service to; **profit, benefit,** pay *and* pay off <nf>, give good returns, yield a profit, bear fruit

ADJS **18 useful,** employable, of use, of service, **serviceable,** commodious <old>; good for; **helpful,** of help 449.21; **advantageous, to one's advantage** *or* **profit, profitable,** remunerary, bankable, beneficial 999.12; **practical,** banausic, pragmatical, **functional, utilitarian,** of general utility *or* application, commodious; fitting, proper, appropriate, expedient 995.5; well-used, well-thumbed; reusable, recyclable

19 using, exploitive, exploitative, manipulative, manipulatory

20 handy, convenient; available, accessible, **ready, at hand,** to hand, **on hand,** on tap, on deck <nf>, on call, at one's call or beck and call, at one's elbow, at one's fingertips, just around the corner, at one's disposal; versatile, adaptable, all-around <nf>, of all work; crude but effective, quick and dirty <nf>; to the purpose; fast-food, convenience

21 effectual, effective, active, efficient, efficacious, operative; instrumental; subsidiary, subservient

22 valuable, of value, all for the best, all to the good, **profitable,** bankable, yielding a return, well-spent, **worthwhile,** rewarding; gainful, remunerative, moneymaking, lucrative

23 usable, utilizable; applicable, appliable, employable, serviceable; practical, operable; **reusable,** recyclable; **exploitable;** manipulable, pliable, compliant 433.12; at one's service

24 used, employed, exercised, exerted, **applied;** previously owned or pre-owned, secondhand 842.18

25 in use, in practice, in force, in effect, in service, in operation, in commission

ADVS **26 usefully,** to good use; **profitably, advantageously, to advantage,** to profit, to good effect; effectually, effectively, efficiently; serviceably, functionally, **practically;** handily, conveniently; by use of, by dint of

388 CONSUMPTION

NOUNS **1 consumption, consuming, using** or **eating up;** burning up; absorption, assimilation, digestion, ingestion, **expenditure,** expending, spending; squandering, wastefulness 486.1; finishing; **depletion,** drain, exhausting, **exhaustion,** impoverishment; **waste,** wastage, wasting away, erosion, ablation, wearing down, wearing away, attrition; throwing away

2 consumable, consumable item or **goods;** nonrenewable or nonreusable or nonrecyclable item or resource; **throwaway,** throwaway item, disposable goods or item; throwaway culture or psychology, instant obsolescence

VERBS **3 consume, spend, expend, use up;** absorb, assimilate, digest, ingest, eat, **eat up,** swallow, swallow up, gobble, gobble up; burn up; **finish,** finish off; **exhaust, deplete,** impoverish, drain, drain of resources; suck dry, bleed white <nf>, suck one's blood; wear away, erode, erode away, ablate; waste away; **throw away, squander** 486.3

4 be consumed, be used up, waste; **run out, give out,** peter out <nf>; run dry, dry up

ADJS **5 used up, consumed,** eaten up, burnt up; finished, gone; unreclaimable, irreplaceable; nonrenewable, nonrecyclable, nonreusable; **spent,** exhausted, effete, dissipated, depleted, impoverished, drained, worn-out; worn away, eroded, ablated; **wasted** 486.9

6 consumable, expendable, spendable; exhaustible; replaceable; disposable, throwaway, no-deposit, no-deposit-no-return

389 MISUSE

NOUNS **1 misuse, misusage, abuse, wrong use; misemployment, misapplication; mishandling,** mismanagement, poor stewardship; corrupt administration, malversation, breach of public trust, maladministration; diversion, defalcation, misappropriation, conversion, **embezzlement,** peculation, pilfering, fraud; perversion, prostitution; profanation, violation, pollution, fouling, befoulment, desecration, defilement, debasement; malpractice, abuse of office, misconduct, malfeasance, misfeasance

2 mistreatment, ill-treatment, maltreatment, ill-use, ill-usage, **abuse,** verbal abuse; **molesting, molestation,** child abuse or molestation; **violation,** outrage, violence, injury, atrocity; cruel and unusual punishment; overuse

3 persecution, oppression, harrying, hounding, tormenting, bashing <nf>, harassment, nobbling <Brit nf>, victimization; **witch-hunting,** witch-hunt, red-baiting <nf>, McCarthyism; open season, piling on <nf>

VERBS **4 misuse, misemploy, abuse, misapply; mishandle,** mismanage, maladminister; divert, misappropriate, expropriate, convert, defalcate <old>, embezzle, defraud, pilfer, peculate, feather one's nest <nf>; pervert, prostitute; profane, violate, pollute, foul, foul one's own nest, spoil, befoul, desecrate, defile, debase; verbally abuse, bad-mouth; misuse or abuse power

5 mistreat, maltreat, ill-treat, ill-use, abuse, injure, **molest;** do wrong to, do wrong by; outrage, do violence to, do one's worst to; mishandle, manhandle; buffet, batter, bruise, **savage,** manhandle, maul, knock about, rough, rough up; pollute; overuse, overwork, overtax

6 <nf terms> screw, screw over, shaft, stiff, give the short or the shitty end of the stick, fuck, fuck over

7 persecute, oppress, **torment,** victimize, play cat and mouse with, **harass,** get or keep after, get or keep at, harry, hound, beset, nobble <Brit nf>; pursue, hunt

ADVS **8 on one's back** and **on one's case** and **in one's face** <nf>

390 DISUSE

NOUNS **1 disuse,** disusage, desuetude; **nonuse, nonemployment; abstinence, abstention;** nonprevalence, unprevalence; **obsolescence,** obsoleteness, obsoletism, obsoletion, planned obsolescence; superannuation, retirement, pensioning off; redundancy <Brit>

2 discontinuance, cessation, desisting, desistance; **abdication,** relinquishment, forebearance, resignation, renunciation, renouncement, abjurement, abjuration; waiver, nonexercise; abeyance, suspension, back burner *and* cold storage <nf>, limbo; **phaseout, abandonment** 370

3 discard, discarding, jettison, deep six <nf>, disposal, dumping, **waste disposal,** solid waste disposal, burning, incineration, ocean burning *or* incineration; compacting; **scrapping, junking** <nf>; removal, elimination 773.2; **rejection** 372; **reject,** throwaway, castaway, castoff, remains, rejectamenta <pl>; **refuse** 391.4

VERBS **4 cease to use; abdicate, relinquish; discontinue, disuse,** quit, stop, drop <nf>, give up, give over, lay off <nf>, **phase out,** phase down, put behind one, let go, leave off, come off <nf>, cut out, desist, desist from, have done with; waive <old>, resign, renounce, abjure; nol-pros, not pursue *or* proceed with; decommission, put out of commission

5 not use, do without, dispense with, **let alone,** not touch, hold off; **abstain, refrain,** forgo, forbear, spare, waive; keep *or* hold back, reserve, save, save up, sock *or* squirrel away, tuck away, put under the mattress, hoard; keep in hand, have up one's sleeve; see the last of

6 put away, lay away, **put aside,** lay *or* set *or* wave *or* cast *or* push aside, sideline <nf>, put *or* lay *or* set by; stow, store 386.10; **pigeonhole, shelve,** put on the shelf, put in mothballs; **table,** lay on the table; table the motion, pass to the order of the day; put on hold *or* on the back burner <nf>, postpone, delay 845.8

7 discard, reject, throw away, throw out, chuck *or* chuck away *and* shit-can *and* eighty-six <nf>, cast, cast off *or* away *or* aside; **get rid of,** get quit of, get shut *or* shet of <nf>, rid oneself of, shrug off, **dispose of,** slough, **dump, ditch** <nf>, **jettison, throw** *or* **heave** *or* **toss overboard,** deep-six <nf>, throw out the window, throw *or* cast to the dogs, cast to the winds; sell off *or* out; throw over, jilt; part with, give away; throw to the wolves, write off, walk away from, **abandon** 370.5; remove, **eliminate** 772.5

8 scrap, junk <nf>, consign to the scrap heap, throw on the junk heap <nf>; superannuate, retire, pension off, put out to pasture *or* grass

9 obsolesce, fall into disuse, go out, pass away; be superseded; superannuate

ADJS **10 disused, abandoned,** deserted, **discontinued,** done with, derelict; out, **out of use;** old; relinquished, resigned, renounced, abjured; decommissioned, out of commission; **outworn,** worn-out, past use, not worth saving; **obsolete,** obsolescent, life-expired, superannuated, superannuate; superseded, outdated, out-of-date, outmoded, desuete; retired, pensioned off; on the shelf; written off <nf>; antique, antiquated, old-fashioned, old

11 discarded, rejected, **castoff,** castaway, scrapped, junked

12 unused, unutilized, **unemployed,** unapplied, unexercised; in abeyance, suspended; waived; **unspent,** unexpended, unconsumed; held back, held out, put by, put aside, saved, held in reserve, in hand, spare, to spare, extra, reserve; stored 386.14; untouched, unhandled; untapped; untrodden, unbeaten; **new,** original, pristine, virgin, fresh, fresh off the assembly line, mint, in mint condition, factory-fresh; underused

391 USELESSNESS

NOUNS **1 uselessness,** inutility; **needlessness,** unnecessity; unserviceability, **unusability,** unemployability, inoperativeness, inoperability, disrepair; unhelpfulness; inapplicability, unsuitability, unfitness; functionlessness; otioseness, otiosity; **superfluousness** 993.4

2 futility, vanity, emptiness, hollowness; **fruitlessness,** bootlessness, unprofitableness, profitability, unprofitability, otiosity, worthlessness, valuelessness; triviality, nugacity, nugaciousness; unproductiveness 891; **ineffectuality,** ineffectiveness, inefficacy 19.3; **impotence** 19.1; effeteness; **pointlessness,** meaninglessness, purposelessness, aimlessness, fecklessness; the absurd, absurdity; inanity, fatuity; vicious circle *or* cycle; **rat race** <nf>

3 labor in vain, labor lost, labor for naught; labor of Sisyphus, work of Penelope, Penelope's web; **wild-goose chase,** snipe hunt, bootless errand; waste of labor, waste of breath, waste of time, wasted effort, wasted breath, wasted labor; red herring; fool's errand; blind alley

4 refuse, waste, wastage, waste matter, waste stream, waste product, solid waste, liquid waste, wastewater, effluent, sewage, sludge; incinerator ash; industrial waste, hazardous waste, toxic waste, atomic waste, dumping; medical waste;

offal; **leavings,** sweepings, dust <Brit>, **scraps,**
orts; **garbage,** gash <nf>, swill, pig-swill, slop,
slops, hogwash <nf>; bilgewater; draff, lees, **dregs**
256.2; **offscourings,** scourings, rinsings, dishwater;
parings, raspings, filings, shavings; **scum;** chaff,
stubble, husks; weeds, tares; deadwood; rags,
bones, wastepaper, shard, potsherd; scrap iron;
slag, culm, slack

5 **rubbish, rubble, trash, junk** <nf>, shoddy, riffraff,
raff <Brit nf>, **scrap,** dust <Brit>, **debris, litter,**
lumber, clamjamfry <Scot>, truck <nf>

6 **trash pile,** rubbish heap, junkheap *and* junkpile
<nf>, scrap heap, dustheap, midden, kitchen
midden; wasteyard, **junkyard** <nf>, scrapyard,
dump, dumpsite, garbage dump, landfill, sanitary
landfill, toxic waste dump, dumping

7 wastepaper basket, wastebasket, shitcan <nf>;
litter basket, litter bin; garbage bag, garbage can,
wastebin, dustbin <Brit>, trash can; Dumpster
<trademark>, skip <Brit>; waste disposal unit,
compactor, garbage grinder <nf>; compost,
compost heap

VERBS 8 **be useless, be futile, make no difference,
cut no ice; die aborning; labor in vain, go on a
wild-goose chase,** run in circles, go around in
circles, fall by the wayside, spin one's wheels *and*
bang one's head against a brick wall <nf>, beat
the air, lash the waves, tilt at windmills, sow the
sand, bay at the moon, waste one's effort *or* breath,
preach *or* speak to the winds, beat *or* flog a dead
horse, roll the stone of Sisyphus, carry coals to
Newcastle, milk the ram, milk a he-goat into a
sieve, pour water into a sieve, hold a farthing
candle to the sun, look for a needle in a haystack,
lock the barn door after the horse is stolen;
attempt the impossible, spin one's wheels

ADJS 9 **useless,** of no use, no go <nf>; **aimless,**
meaningless, **purposeless,** of no purpose,
pointless, feckless; **unavailing,** of no avail, failed;
ineffective, **ineffectual** 19.15; impotent 19.13;
superfluous 993.17; dud

10 **needless, unnecessary, unessential,** nonessential,
unneeded, uncalled-for, unrequired; unrecognized,
neglected, "born to blush unseen"—Thomas Gray;
redundant

11 **worthless, valueless, good-for-nothing,** good-for-
naught, no-good *or* NG <nf>, no-account <nf>,
dear at any price, worthless as tits on a boar <nf>,
not worth a dime *or* a red cent *or* a hill of beans *or*
shit *or* bubkes <nf>, not worth the paper it's
written on, not worthwhile, not worth having, not
worth mentioning *or* speaking of, not worth a
thought, not worth a rap *or* a continental *or* a
damn, not worth the powder to blow it to hell, not
worth the powder and shot, not worth the pains *or*

the trouble, of no earthly use, fit for the junkyard
<nf>; trivial, penny-ante <nf>, nugatory,
nugacious; **junk** *and* **junky** <nf>; **cheap,** shoddy,
trashy, **shabby**

12 **fruitless,** gainless, profitless, bootless, otiose,
unprofitable, unremunerative, nonremunerative;
uncommercial; **unrewarding,** rewardless; abortive;
barren, sterile, unproductive 890.4

13 **vain, futile,** hollow, empty, "weary, stale, flat, and
unprofitable"—Shakespeare, idle, unavailing;
absurd; inane, fatuous, fatuitous

14 **unserviceable, unusable,** unemployable,
inoperative, inoperable, unworkable; out of order,
out of whack *and* on the blink *and* on the fritz
<nf>, in disrepair; **unhelpful,** unconducive;
inapplicable; unsuitable, unfit; functionless,
nonfunctional, otiose, nonutilitarian; kaput

ADVS 15 **uselessly; needlessly,** unnecessarily;
bootlessly, fruitlessly; **futilely, vainly;** purposelessly,
to little purpose, to no purpose, **aimlessly,
pointlessly,** fecklessly

392 IMPROVEMENT

NOUNS 1 **improvement, betterment,** bettering,
change *or* turn for the better; melioration,
amelioration; sea change; **mend,** mending,
amendment; progress, progression, headway;
breakthrough, quantum jump *or* leap; **advance,**
advancement; upward mobility; **promotion,
furtherance,** preferment; **rise,** ascent, **lift, uplift,**
uptick <nf>, upswing, uptrend, upbeat; **increase**
251, upgrade, upping *and* boost *and* pickup <nf>;
gentrification; **enhancement, enrichment,** good
influence; euthenics, eugenics; **restoration,** revival,
retro, recovery

2 **development, refinement,** elaboration, **perfection;**
beautification, embellishment; maturation,
coming-of-age, ripening, evolution, seasoning

3 **cultivation, culture, refinement, polish,** civility;
cultivation of the mind; **civilization;** acculturation;
enculturation, socialization; enlightenment,
education 928.4

4 **revision,** revise, revisal; revised edition;
**emendation, amendment, correction, corrigenda,
rectification;** editing, redaction, recension,
revampment, blue-penciling; **rewrite,** rewriting,
rescript, rescription <old>; **polishing,** touching up,
putting on the finishing touches, putting the gloss
on, finishing, perfecting, tuning, fine-tuning;
retrofitting

5 **reform, reformation;** regeneration 858.2;
transformation; conversion 858; makeover;
reformism, meliorism; gradualism, Fabianism,
revisionism; utopianism; progressiveness,

progressivism, progressism; radical reform, extremism, radicalism 611.4; revolution 859; perestroika

6 **reformer,** reformist, meliorist; gradualist, Fabian, revisionist; utopian, utopist; progressive, progressivist, progressionist, progressist; radical, extremist 611.12; revolutionary 860.3

VERBS 7 <get better> **improve, grow better,** look better, show improvement, **mend,** amend <old>, meliorate, ameliorate; **look up** or **pick up** or **perk up** <nf>; **develop,** shape up; **advance, progress, make progress, make headway, gain,** gain ground, go forward, get or go ahead, come on, come along and come along nicely <nf>, get along; make strides or rapid strides, take off and skyrocket <nf>, make up for lost time; straighten up and fly right <nf>; make the grade, graduate

8 **rally,** come about or round, **take a favorable turn,** get over <nf>, take a turn for the better, gain strength; come a long way <nf>; **recuperate, recover** 396.20

9 **improve, better,** change for the better, make an improvement; transform, transfigure; vet; improve upon, refine upon, **mend, amend,** emend; meliorate, **ameliorate; advance, promote,** foster, favor, nurture, forward, bring forward; **lift,** elevate, **uplift,** raise, boost <nf>; upgrade; gentrify; **enhance, enrich,** fatten, lard <old>; make one's way, better oneself; be the making of; **reform,** put or set straight; reform oneself, turn over a new leaf, mend one's ways, straighten out, straighten oneself out, go straight <nf>; get it together and get one's ducks in a row <nf>; **civilize,** acculturate, socialize; enlighten, edify; **educate**

10 **develop,** elaborate; beautify, embellish; **cultivate;** come of age, come into its own, mature, ripen, evolve, season; gild the lily

11 **perfect, touch up,** finish, put on the finishing touches, polish or polish up, fine down, fine-tune <nf>, tone up, **brush up, furbish,** furbish up, spruce, **spruce up,** freshen, vamp, vamp up, rub up, brighten up, shine <nf>; retouch; **revive, renovate** 396.17; **repair, fix** 396.14; retrofit; streamline

12 **revise,** redact, recense, **revamp, rewrite,** redraft, **rework,** work over; **emend, amend,** emendate, **rectify,** correct; **edit,** blue-pencil; straighten out

ADJS 13 **improved, bettered;** changed for the better, advanced, ameliorated, enhanced, enriched, touched up; developed, perfected; beautified, embellished; upgraded; gentrified; **reformed; transformed,** transfigured, converted; **cultivated,** cultured, **refined,** polished, civilized; **educated** 927.18

14 **better,** better off, better for, all the better for; before-and-after

15 **improving, bettering;** meliorative, ameliorative, amelioratory, medial; progressive, progressing, advancing, ongoing; mending, **on the mend;** on the lift or rise or upswing or upbeat or upgrade <nf>, looking up <nf>

16 **emendatory, corrective;** revisory, revisional; reformatory, reformative, reformational; **reformist,** reformistic, progressive, progressivist, melioristic; gradualistic, Fabian, revisionist; utopian; radical 611.20; revolutionary 860.5

17 **improvable,** ameliorable, corrigible, revisable, perfectible; **emendable** 396.25; curable

393 IMPAIRMENT

NOUNS 1 **impairment, damage, injury, harm,** mischief, scathe, **hurt, detriment,** loss, weakening, sickening; **worsening,** disimprovement; disablement, incapacitation; encroachment, inroad, infringement 214.1; **disrepair, dilapidation,** ruinousness; breakage; **breakdown, collapse,** crash and crack-up <nf>; **malfunction,** glitch <nf>; bankruptcy; hurting, spoiling, ruination; sabotage, monkey-wrenching <nf>; mayhem, mutilation, crippling, hobbling, hamstringing, laming, maiming; destruction 395; the skids <nf>

2 **corruption, pollution, contamination,** vitiation, **defilement,** fouling, befouling; **poisoning,** envenoming; infection, festering, suppuration; **perversion,** prostitution, misuse 389; denaturing, adulteration

3 **deterioration, decadence** or decadency, **degradation, debasement,** derogation, deformation; **degeneration,** degeneracy, degenerateness, effeteness; etiolation, loss of tone, failure of nerve; depravation, depravedness; **retrogression,** retrogradation, retrocession, **regression;** devolution, involution; demotion 447; downward mobility; **decline,** declination, declension, comedown, **descent,** downtick <nf>, downtrend, downward trend, downturn, depreciation, **decrease** 252, **drop, fall, plunge,** free-fall, falling-off, lessening, slippage, slump, lapse, fading, dying, failing, failure, wane, ebb; loss of morale; shadow of one's former self

4 **waste,** wastage, **consumption;** withering, wasting, wasting away, atrophy, wilting, marcescence; emaciation 270.6

5 **wear,** use, hard wear; **wear and tear;** erosion, **weathering,** ablation, ravages of time

6 **decay, decomposition, disintegration, dissolution,** resolution, degradation, biodegradation, breakup, disorganization, **corruption, spoilage, dilapidation; corrosion,** oxidation, oxidization, rust; mildew, mold 1001.2; degradability, biodegradability

7 rot, rottenness, foulness, putridness, putridity, rancidness, rancidity, rankness, **putrefaction,** putrescence, spoilage, decay, decomposition; carrion; dry rot, wet rot

8 wreck, ruins, ruin, total loss; hulk, carcass, skeleton; mere wreck, wreck of one's former self, perfect wreck; nervous wreck; rattletrap

VERBS **9 impair, damage,** endamage, **injure, harm, hurt,** irritate; **worsen,** make worse, disimprove, deteriorate, put or set back, aggravate, exacerbate, embitter; **weaken; dilapidate;** add insult to injury, rub salt in the wound

10 spoil, mar, botch, **ruin,** wreck, blight, **play havoc with; destroy** 395.10; pollute

11 <nf terms> **screw up, foul up,** fuck up, bitch up, **blow,** louse up, queer, snafu, snarl up, balls up <Brit>, bugger, bugger up, gum up, ball up, bollix, bollix up, **mess up,** hash up, muck up; play hob with, play hell with, play merry hell with, play the devil with, rain on one's picnic or parade; upset the apple cart, cook, sink, shoot down in flames; **total;** pulverize

12 corrupt, debase, degrade, degenerate, **deprave, debauch, defile,** violate, desecrate, profane, deflower, ravish, ravage, despoil; **contaminate,** confound, **pollute, vitiate, poison, infect, taint;** canker, ulcerate; **pervert,** warp, twist, distort; prostitute, misuse 389.4; denature; **cheapen,** devalue; coarsen, vulgarize, drag in the mud; adulterate, alloy, water, water down

13 <inflict an injury> **injure, hurt;** draw blood, wound, scotch <old>; **traumatize;** stab, stick, pierce, puncture; cut, incise, slit, slash, gash, scratch; abrade, eat away at, scuff, scrape, chafe, fret, gall, bark, skin; break, fracture, rupture; crack, chip, craze, check; lacerate, claw, tear, rip, rend; run; frazzle, fray; burn, scorch, scald; mutilate, maim, rough up <nf>, make mincemeat of, maul, batter, savage; sprain, strain, wrench; bloody; **blemish** 1004.4; **bruise, contuse,** bung and bung up <nf>; **buffet,** batter, bash <nf>, maul, pound, beat, beat black and blue; give a black eye; play havoc with

14 cripple, lame, maim; **hamstring,** hobble; wing; emasculate, castrate; incapacitate, **disable** 19.9

15 undermine, sap, mine, sap the foundations of, honeycomb; sabotage, monkey-wrench and throw or toss a monkey-wrench in the works <nf>, subvert

16 deteriorate, sicken, worsen, get or grow worse, get no better fast <nf>, disimprove, **degenerate;** slip back, **retrogress,** retrograde, regress, relapse, fall back; jump the track; go to the bad 395.24; let oneself go, let down, slacken; be the worse for, be the worse for wear and have seen better days <nf>

17 decline, sink, fail, fall, slip, fade, die, wane, ebb, subside, lapse, **run down,** go down, **go downhill, fall away, fall off,** go off <nf>, slide, slump, hit a slump, take a nose dive <nf>, go into a tailspin, take a turn for the worse; hit the skids <nf>; reach the depths, hit or touch bottom, hit rock bottom, have no lower to go

18 languish, pine, droop, flag, wilt; fade, fade away; **wither, shrivel,** shrink, diminish, wither or die on the vine, **dry up,** desiccate, wizen, wrinkle, sear; retrograde, retrogress

19 waste, waste away, wither away, atrophy, consume, consume away, erode away, emaciate, pine away; trickle or dribble away; run to waste, run to seed

20 wear, wear away, wear down, wear off; abrade, fret, whittle away, rub off; fray, frazzle, tatter, wear ragged; **wear out;** weather, erode, ablate

21 corrode, erode, eat, gnaw, eat into, eat away, nibble away, gnaw at the root of; canker; **oxidize, rust**

22 decay, decompose, disintegrate; biodegrade; go or fall into decay, go or fall to pieces, break up, crumble, crumble into dust; **spoil,** corrupt, canker, **go bad; rot, putrefy,** putresce; fester, suppurate, rankle <nf>; **mortify,** necrose, gangrene, sphacelate; mold, molder, molder away, rot away, rust away, mildew; gangrene

23 break, break up, fracture, **come apart,** come unstuck, **come or fall to pieces, fall apart, disintegrate;** burst, rupture; crack, split, fissure; snap; break open, give way or away, start, spring a leak, come apart at the seams, come unstuck <nf>

24 break down, founder, collapse; crash <nf>, cave or fall in, come crashing or tumbling down, topple, topple down or over, tremble or nod or totter to one's fall; totter, sway

25 get out of order, malfunction, get out of gear; get out of joint; go wrong

26 <nf terms> **get out of whack,** get out of kilter, get out of commission, go kaput, **go on the blink or fritz, go haywire,** fritz out, go blooey or kerflooey, give out, **break down,** pack up <Brit>, conk out

ADJS **27 impaired, damaged, hurt, injured, harmed; deteriorated, worsened,** cut to the quick, aggravated, exacerbated, irritated, embittered; weakened; **worse,** worse off, the worse for, all the worse for; imperfect; lacerated, mangled, cut, split, rent, torn, slit, slashed, mutilated, chewed-up; **broken** 802.24, **shattered, smashed,** in bits, in pieces, in shards, burst, busted <nf>, ruptured, sprung; cracked, chipped, crazed, checked; burned, scorched, scalded; **damaging, injurious,** traumatic, degenerative

28 spoiled or spoilt, **marred,** botched, blighted, **ruined,** wrecked; **destroyed** 395.28

29 <nf terms> **queered, screwed up, fouled up,** loused up, snafued, buggered, buggered up, gummed up, snarled up, balled up, bollixed up, **messed up,** hashed up, mucked up, botched up; beat up, clapped-out <Brit>; **totaled,** kaput, finished, packed-up <Brit>, done for, done in, cooked, sunk, shot

30 **crippled,** game <nf>, bad, handicapped, maimed; **lame, halt,** halting, hobbling, limping; knee-sprung; hamstrung; spavined; **disabled, incapacitated,** challenged; emasculated, castrated

31 **worn,** well-worn, deep-worn, worn-down, the worse for wear, dog-eared; timeworn; shopworn, shopsoiled <Brit>, shelfworn; worn to the stump, worn to the bone; **worn ragged,** worn to rags, worn to threads; **threadbare,** bare, sere <old>

32 **shabby, shoddy, seedy,** scruffy, **tacky** <nf>, dowdy, tatty, ratty; holey, full of holes; raggedy, raggedy-ass <nf>, **ragged, tattered, torn;** patchy; **frayed, frazzled;** in rags, in tatters, in shreds; **out at the elbows,** out at the heels, **down-at-heel** or **-heels, down-at-the-heel** or **-heels**

33 **dilapidated, ramshackle,** decrepit, shacky, tottery, slummy <nf>, **tumbledown, broken-down, run-down,** in ruins, ruinous, ruined, derelict, gone to wrack and ruin, the worse for wear; **battered,** beaten up, **beat-up** <nf>

34 **weatherworn, weather-beaten, weathered,** weather-battered, weather-wasted, weather-eaten, weather-bitten, weather-scarred; eroded; **faded,** washed-out, bleached, blanched, etiolated

35 **wasted,** atrophied, shrunken; **withered,** sere, shriveled, wilted, wizened, dried-up, desiccated; wrinkled, wrinkled like a prune; brittle, papery, parchmenty; **emaciated** 270.20; starved, worn to a shadow, reduced to a skeleton, skin and bones, "worn to the bones"—Shakespeare

36 **worn-out, used up** <nf>, worn to a frazzle, frazzled, fit for the dust hole or wastepaper basket; **exhausted, tired,** fatigued, pooped <nf>, **spent,** effete, etiolated, played out, *ausgespielt* <Ger>, shotten <nf>, jaded, emptied, done *and* done up <nf>; **run-down,** dragged-out <nf>, laid low, at a low ebb, in a bad way, far-gone, on one's last legs

37 **in disrepair, out of order, malfunctioning,** out of working order, out of condition, out of repair, inoperative; out of tune, out of gear; out of joint; **broken** 802.24

38 <nf terms> **out of whack** or **kilter** or kelter or sync or commission, on the fritz, fritzed, on the blink, blooey, kerflooey, haywire, wonky <Brit>

39 **putrefactive,** putrefacient, rotting; **septic;** saprogenic, saprogenous; saprophilous, saprophytic, saprobic

40 **decayed, decomposed; spoiled, corrupt,** peccant, bad, **gone bad; rotten, rotting, putrid, putrefied, foul;** putrescent, **mortified,** necrosed, necrotic, sphacelated, gangrened, gangrenous; carious; cankered, ulcerated, festering, suppurating, suppurative; rotten at or to the core

41 **tainted, off,** blown, frowy <nf>; **stale; sour,** soured, turned; **rank,** reechy <old>, **rancid,** strong <nf>, **high,** gamy

42 **blighted, blasted, ravaged,** despoiled; blown, **flyblown,** wormy, weevily, maggoty; **moth-eaten, worm-eaten; moldy,** moldering, **mildewed,** smutty, smutted; **musty, fusty,** frowzy or frowsy, frowsty <Brit>

43 **corroded, eroded,** eaten; **rusty,** rust-eaten, rust-worn, rust-cankered

44 **corrupting, corruptive;** corrosive, corroding; erosive, eroding, **damaging, injurious** 1000.12; pollutive

45 **deteriorating, worsening,** disintegrating, coming apart or unstuck, crumbling, cracking, fragmenting, going to pieces; **decadent, degenerate,** effete; **retrogressive,** retrograde, regressive, from better to worse; **declining, sinking, failing,** falling, waning, subsiding, **slipping,** sliding, slumping; **languishing, pining,** drooping, flagging, wilting; ebbing, draining, dwindling; **wasting,** fading, fading fast, **withering,** shriveling; tabetic, marcescent

46 **on the wane, on the decline,** on the downgrade, on the downward track, on the skids <nf>; tottering, nodding to its fall, on the way out

47 degradable, biodegradable, decomposable, putrefiable, putrescible

ADVS **48** out of the frying pan into the fire, from better to worse; for the worse

394 RELAPSE

NOUNS **1** **relapse, lapse,** falling back; **reversion, regression** 859.1; **reverse, reversal,** backward deviation, devolution, **setback,** backset; **return,** recurrence, renewal, recrudescence; throwback, atavism

2 **backsliding,** backslide; **fall, fall from grace;** recidivism, recidivation; apostasy 363.2

3 backslider, recidivist, reversionist; apostate 363.5

VERBS **4** **relapse, lapse, backslide,** slide back, lapse back, **slip back,** sink back, **fall back,** have a relapse, devolve, **return to, revert to,** recur to, yield again to, fall again into, recidivate; revert, **regress** 859.4; **fall, fall from grace**

ADJS **5** **relapsing, lapsing, lapsarian, backsliding,** recidivous; recrudescent; **regressive** 859.7; apostate 363.11

395 DESTRUCTION

NOUNS 1 destruction, ruin, ruination, rack, **rack and ruin,** blue ruin <nf>; perdition, damnation, eternal damnation; universal ruin; **wreck;** devastation, ravage, havoc, holocaust, firestorm, hecatomb, carnage, shambles, slaughter, bloodbath, **desolation; waste, consumption;** decimation; **dissolution, disintegration,** breakup, disruption, disorganization, undoing, lysis; vandalism, depredation, spoliation, despoliation, despoilment; the road to ruin *or* wrack and ruin; iconoclasm

2 end, fate, doom, death, death knell, bane, deathblow, death warrant, *coup de grâce* <Fr>, final blow, quietus, cutoff, end of the world, apocalypse

3 fall, downfall, prostration; **overthrow, overturn, upset, upheaval,** *bouleversement* <Fr>; convulsion, **subversion,** sabotage, monkey-wrenching <nf>

4 debacle, disaster, cataclysm, catastrophe; breakup, breaking up; **breakdown, collapse; crash,** meltdown, smash, **smashup,** crack-up <nf>; **wreck,** wrack, shipwreck; cave-in, cave; washout; total loss

5 demolition, demolishment; wrecking, wreckage, leveling, razing, flattening, smashing, tearing down, bringing to the ground; **dismantlement,** disassembly, unmaking; hatchet job

6 extinction, extermination, elimination, eradication, extirpation; rooting out, deracination, uprooting, tearing up root and branch; **annihilation,** extinguishment, **snuffing out; abolition,** abolishment; annulment, **nullification,** voiding, **negation; liquidation, purge; suppression;** choking, choking off, suffocation, stifling, strangulation; silencing; nuclear winter

7 obliteration, erasure, effacement, deletion, expunction, blot <old>, blotting, **blotting out, wiping out;** washing out *and* scrubbing <nf>, cancellation, cancel; deletion; annulment, abrogation; palimpsest, clean slate, tabula rasa

8 destroyer, ruiner, wrecker, bane, wiper-out, demolisher; **vandal,** hun; exterminator, annihilator; **iconoclast,** idoloclast; biblioclast; nihilist; terrorist, syndicalist; **bomber,** dynamiter, dynamitard; burner, arsonist; loose cannon

9 eradicator, expunger; **eraser,** rubber, India rubber, sponge; extinguisher

VERBS 10 destroy, deal *or* unleash destruction, unleash the hurricane, nuke <nf>; **ruin,** ruinate <nf>, bring to ruin, lay in ruins, play *or* raise hob with; throw into disorder, turn upside-down, upheave; **wreck,** wrack, shipwreck; damn, seal the doom of, **condemn,** confound; **devastate, desolate,**

waste, **lay waste, ravage,** havoc, wreak havoc, despoil, depredate; vandalize; **decimate;** devour, consume, engorge, gobble, gobble up, swallow up; gut, gut with fire, incinerate, vaporize, ravage with fire and sword; dissolve, lyse

11 do for, fix <nf>, settle, sink, cook *and* cook one's goose *and* cut one down to size *and* cut one off at the knees *and* pull the plug on *and* pull the rug out from under <nf>, dish, scuttle, put the kibosh on *and* put the skids under <nf>, do in, **undo,** knock in *or* on the head, poleax, torpedo, knock out, clobber, KO *and* banjax <nf>, deal a knockout blow to, zap *and* shoot down *and* shoot down in flames <nf>; break the back of; make short work of; hamstring; **defeat 412.6**

12 put an end to, make an end of, **end, finish,** finish off <nf>, put paid to <Brit>, give the *coup de grâce* <Fr> to, give the quietus to, deal a deathblow to, dispose of, get rid of, do in, do away with; cut off, take off, be the death of, sound the death knell of; put out of the way, put out of existence, **slaughter,** make away with, off *and* waste *and* blow away <nf>, kill off, strike down, **kill 308.13**; nip, nip in the bud; cut short; scrub <nf>

13 abolish, nullify, void, abrogate, annihilate, annul, tear up, repeal, revoke, negate, negative, invalidate, **undo, cancel,** cancel out, bring to naught, put *or* lay to rest

14 exterminate, eliminate, eradicate, deracinate, **extirpate, annihilate; wipe out** <nf>; cut out, root up *or* out, uproot, pull *or* pluck up by the roots, cut up root and branch, strike at the root of, lay the ax to the root of; **liquidate,** vaporize, **purge;** remove, sweep away, wash away; wipe off the map <nf>, leave no trace

15 extinguish, quench, snuff out, put out, stamp *or* trample out, trample underfoot; **smother,** choke, stifle, strangle, suffocate; silence; **suppress, quash,** squash *and* squelch <nf>, **quell,** put down

16 obliterate, expunge, efface, erase, raze <old>, blot, sponge, **wipe out,** wipe off the map, rub out, **blot out,** sponge out, wash away; cancel, strike out, cross out, scratch, scratch out, rule out; blue-pencil; **delete** *or* dele, kill; leave on the cutting-room floor <nf>

17 demolish, wreck, total *and* rack up <nf>, undo, unbuild, unmake, **dismantle, disassemble; take apart, tear apart, tear asunder, rend, take** *or* **pull** *or* **pick** *or* **tear to pieces,** pull in pieces, tear to shreds *or* rags *or* tatters; sunder, cleave, **split; disintegrate, fragment,** break to pieces, make mincemeat of, reduce to rubble, atomize, pulverize, **smash,** shatter 801.13

18 blow up, blast, spring, explode, blow to pieces *or*

bits *or* smithereens *or* kingdom come, bomb, bombard, blitz; mine; self-destruct

19 raze, rase, **fell, level,** flatten, smash, prostrate, raze to the ground *or* dust; steamroller, bulldoze; **pull down, tear down, take down,** bring down, bring down about one's ears, bring tumbling *or* crashing down, break down, throw down, cast down, beat down, knock down *or* over; cut down, chop down, mow down; blow down; burn down

20 overthrow, overturn; upset, overset, upend, **subvert,** throw down *or* over; undermine, honeycomb, **sap,** sap the foundations, **weaken**

21 overwhelm, whelm, swamp, engulf; inundate

22 <be destroyed> fall, fall to the ground, tumble, come tumbling *or* crashing down, topple, tremble *or* nod to its fall, bite the dust <nf>; **break up,** crumble, crumble to dust, disintegrate, go *or* fall to pieces; go by the board, go out the window *or* up the spout <nf>, go down the tube *or* tubes <nf>; self-destruct

23 perish, expire, succumb, die, cease, end, come to an end, go, pass, **pass away, vanish, disappear,** fade away, run out, peg *or* conk out <nf>, come to nothing *or* naught, be no more, be done for; be all over with, be all up with <nf>

24 go to ruin, go to rack and ruin, go to rack and manger <old>, **go to the bad,** go wrong, **go to the dogs** *or* **pot** <nf>, go *or* run to seed, go to hell in a handbasket <nf>, go to the deuce *or* devil <nf>, go to hell <nf>, go to the wall, go to perdition *or* glory <nf>; go up <nf>, go under; **go to smash,** go to shivers, go to smithereens <nf>

25 drive to ruin, drive to the bad, **force to the wall,** drive to the dogs <nf>, hound *or* harry to destruction

ADJS **26 destructive,** destroying; **ruinous,** ruining; demolishing, demolitionary; **disastrous, calamitous, cataclysmic,** cataclysmal, **catastrophic;** fatal, fateful, doomful, baneful; bad news <nf>; **deadly;** consumptive, consuming, withering; **devastating, desolating,** ravaging, wasting, wasteful, spoliative, depredatory; vandalic, vandalish, vandalistic; subversive, subversionary; nihilist, nihilistic; suicidal, self-destructive; fratricidal, internecine, internecive

27 exterminative, exterminatory, **annihilative, eradicative,** extirpative, extirpatory; all-destroying, all-devouring, all-consuming

28 ruined, destroyed, wrecked, blasted, undone, down-and-out, broken, bankrupt; spoiled; irremediable 125.15; fallen, overthrown; **devastated, desolated, ravaged,** blighted, wasted; ruinous, in ruins, gutted; gone to rack and ruin; obliterated, annihilated, liquidated, vaporized; doomed, not long for this world

29 <nf terms> shot, done for, done in, finished, *ausgespielt* <Ger>, kaput; gone to pot, gone to the dogs, gone to hell in a handbasket, phut, belly up, blooey, kerflooey, dead in the water, washed up, all washed up, history, **dead meat, down the tube** *or* **tubes,** zapped, nuked, tapped out, wiped out, rubbed out, bust

396 RESTORATION

NOUNS **1 restoration, restitution, reestablishment, redintegration, reinstatement,** reinstation, reformation <old>, reinvestment, reinvestiture, instauration, reversion, reinstitution, reconstitution, recomposition; replacement; **rehabilitation,** redevelopment, reconversion, reactivation, reenactment; improvement 392; return to normal

2 reclamation, recovery, retrieval, salvage, salving; redemption, salvation

3 revival, revivification, revivescence *or* revivescency, **renewal,** resurrection, resuscitation, restimulation, reanimation, resurgence, recrudescence, comeback; retro; **refreshment** 9; second wind; renaissance, renascence, **rebirth,** new birth; **rejuvenation,** rejuvenescence, second youth, new lease on life; **regeneration,** regeneracy, regenerateness; regenesis, palingenesis, reanimation, reincarnation; new hope, second chance

4 renovation, renewal; refreshment; **redecorating; reconditioning,** furbishment, refurbishment, refurbishing; retread *and* retreading <nf>; face-lifting *or* face-lift; slum clearance, urban renewal; remodeling; overhauling

5 reconstruction, re-creation, remaking, recomposition, remodeling, **rebuilding,** refabrication, refashioning; reassembling, reassembly; reformation; restructuring, perestroika

6 reparation, repair, repairing, **fixing, mending,** making *or* setting right, repairwork; servicing, maintenance; **overhaul,** overhauling; troubleshooting <nf>; **rectification, correction, remedy;** damage control; **redress,** making *or* setting right, amends, satisfaction, compensation, **recompense;** emendation

7 cure, curing, healing, remedy 86; **therapy** 91

8 recovery, rally, comeback <nf>, return, upturn; **recuperation, convalescence**

9 restorability, reparability, curability, recoverability, reversibility, remediability, retrievability, redeemability, salvageability, corrigibility

10 mender, fixer, doctor <nf>, restorer, renovator, repairer, **repairman, repairwoman,** handyman, maintenance man *or* woman, **serviceman,**

servicewoman; trouble man *and* troubleshooter <nf>; Mr Fixit *and* little Miss Fixit <nf>; **mechanic** *or* mechanician; tinker, tinkerer; cobbler; salvor, salvager

VERBS **11 restore, put back, replace, return,** place in *status quo ante;* **reestablish,** redintegrate, reform <old>, reenact, **reinstate,** restitute; **reinstall,** reinvest, revest, reinstitute, reconstitute, recompose, recruit, **rehabilitate,** redevelop; reintegrate, reconvert, reactivate; make as good as new; refill, replenish; give back 481.4

12 redeem, reclaim, recover, retrieve; ransom; rescue; salvage, salve; recycle; win back, **recoup**

13 remedy, rectify, correct, right, patch up, emend, amend, **redress,** make good *or* right, **put right,** set right, put *or* set to rights, put *or* set straight, set up, heal up, knit up, make all square; pay reparations, give satisfaction, requite, restitute, recompense, compensate, remunerate

14 repair, mend, fix, fix up <nf>, do up, doctor <nf>, put in repair, put in shape, set to rights, put in order *or* condition; **condition, recondition,** commission, put in commission, ready; **service, overhaul;** patch, **patch up;** tinker, tinker up, fiddle, fiddle around; cobble; sew up, darn; recap, retread

15 cure, work a cure, recure <old>, **remedy, heal, restore to health,** heal up, knit up, bring round *or* around, pull round *or* around, give a new *or* fresh lease on life, make better, make well, fix up, pull through, set on one's feet *or* legs; snatch from the jaws of death

16 revive, revivify, **renew,** recruit; **reanimate,** reinspire, **regenerate, rejuvenate, revitalize,** put *or* breathe new life into, restimulate; **refresh** 9.2; **resuscitate,** bring to, bring round *or* around; recharge; **resurrect,** bring back, call back, recall to life, raise from the dead; rewarm, warm up *or* over; **rekindle,** relight, reheat the ashes, stir the embers; restore to health

17 renovate, renew; recondition, refit, revamp, furbish, refurbish; refresh, face-lift; fix up, upgrade

18 remake, reconstruct, remodel, recompose, reconstitute, re-create, **rebuild,** refabricate, re-form, refashion, reassemble

19 recuperate, recruit, **gain strength,** recruit *or* renew one's strength, catch one's breath, **get better; improve** 392.7; **rally, pick up,** perk up *and* brace up <nf>, bounce back, take a new *or* fresh lease on life; **take a favorable turn,** turn the corner, be out of the woods, take a turn for the better; **convalesce;** sleep it off

20 recover, rally, revive, get well, get over, pull through, pull round *or* around, come round *or* around <nf>, come back <nf>, make a comeback <nf>; get about, get back in shape <nf>, be

oneself again, feel like a new person; **survive,** weather the storm, live through; **come to,** come to oneself, show signs of life; come up smiling <nf>, get one's second wind; come *or* pull *or* snap out of it <nf>

21 heal, heal over, close up, scab over, cicatrize, granulate; heal *or* right itself; **knit, set**

ADJS **22 tonic, restorative, restitutive,** restitutory, restimulative; analeptic; **reparative,** reparatory; sanative; remedial, **curative** 86.39

23 recuperative, recuperatory; revivescent; **convalescent;** buoyant, resilient, elastic

24 renascent, redivivus, redux, resurrected, renewed, revived, reborn, resurgent, recrudescent, reappearing, phoenix-like; like new; oneself again

25 remediable, curable; medicable, treatable; emendable, amendable, **correctable,** rectifiable, corrigible; **improvable,** ameliorable; **reparable,** repairable, **mendable, fixable;** restorable, recoverable, salvageable, retrievable, reversible, reclaimable, recyclable, redeemable; renewable; sustainable

397 PRESERVATION

NOUNS **1 preservation,** preserval, **conservation, saving, salvation,** salvage, **keeping, safekeeping,** maintenance, upkeep, support, service; custody, custodianship, guardianship, curatorship; protectiveness, protection 1008; conservationism, environmental conservation, environmentalism, ecology; nature conservation *or* conservancy, soil conservation, forest conservation, forest management, wildlife conservation, stream conservation, water conservation, wetlands conservation; salvage; self-preservation

2 food preservation; storage, retention; **curing,** seasoning, salting, brining, pickling, marinating, corning; **drying,** dry-curing, jerking; dehydration, anhydration, evaporation, desiccation; **smoking,** fuming, smoke-curing, kippering; **refrigeration,** freezing, quick-freezing, blast-freezing, deep-freezing; freeze-drying, lyophilization; irradiation; **canning,** tinning <Brit>; bottling, processing, packaging; irradiation, sterilization

3 embalming, mummification; taxidermy, stuffing; tanning

4 preservative, preservative medium; salt, brine, vinegar, formaldehyde, formalin *or* formol, embalming fluid, food additive, MSG *or* monosodium glutamate

5 preserver, saver, conservator, keeper, safekeeper; taxidermist; lifesaver, rescuer, deliverer, savior; **conservationist,** preservationist; National Wildlife Service, Audubon Society, Sierra Club, Nature

Conservancy; **ranger, forest ranger,** Smoky the Bear, fire warden, game warden

6 **life preserver,** life jacket, life vest, life belt, cork jacket, Mae West <nf>; life buoy, life ring, buoy, floating cushion; man-overboard buoy; water wings; breeches buoy; lifeboat, life raft, rubber dinghy <Brit>; life net; lifeline; safety belt; **parachute;** ejection seat *or* ejector seat, ejection capsule

7 **preserve, reserve, reservation; park,** paradise; national park, state park; national seashore; forest preserve *or* reserve, arboretum; national *or* state forest; wilderness preserve; Indian reservation; **refuge, sanctuary** 1009.1, game preserve *or* reserve, bird sanctuary, wildlife sanctuary *or* preserve; museum, library 558, archives 549.2, bank, store 386; protected area

VERBS 8 **preserve, conserve, save,** spare; **keep,** keep safe, keep inviolate *or* intact; patent, copyright, register; not endanger, not destroy; not use up, not waste, not expend; **guard, protect** 1008.18; **maintain, sustain,** uphold, support, **keep up,** keep alive

9 **preserve, cure,** season, salt, brine, marinate *or* marinade, pickle, corn, **dry, dry-cure,** jerk, dry-salt; dehydrate, anhydrate, evaporate, desiccate; vacuum-pack; **smoke,** fume, **smoke-cure,** smoke-dry, kipper; **refrigerate,** freeze, quick-freeze, blast-freeze, keep on ice; freeze-dry, lyophilize; irradiate

10 **embalm,** mummify; stuff; tan

11 **put up,** do up; **can,** tin <Brit>, bottle

ADJS 12 **preservative,** preservatory, conservative, conservatory; custodial, curatorial; **conservational,** conservationist; preserving, conserving, saving, salubrious, keeping; **protective** 1008.23

13 **preserved,** conserved, **kept,** saved, spared; protected 1008.21; **untainted, unspoiled;** intact, all in one piece, undamaged 1001.8; **well-preserved,** well-conserved, **well-kept,** in a good state of preservation, none the worse for wear; embalmed, laid up in lavender, mummified, stuffed

398 RESCUE

NOUNS 1 **rescue, deliverance,** delivery, **saving;** lifesaving; **extrication, release, freeing, liberation** 431; **bailout; salvation,** salvage, **redemption,** ransom; **recovery, retrieval;** good riddance; 911

2 **rescuer,** lifesaver, lifeguard; coast guard, lifesaving service, air-sea rescue; emergency medical technician *or* EMT; savior 592.2; lifeboat; salvager, salvor; emancipator

VERBS 3 **rescue,** come to the rescue, **deliver, save,** be the saving of, save by the bell, **redeem,** ransom, **salvage; recover, retrieve** 481.6; **free,** set free,

release, extricate, extract, **liberate** 431.4; snatch from the jaws of death; save one's bacon *and* save one's neck *or* ass *and* bail one out <nf>

ADJS 4 **rescuable, savable;** redeemable; deliverable, extricable; salvageable; fit for release

399 WARNING

NOUNS 1 **warning, caution,** caveat, **admonition,** monition, admonishment; **notice,** notification; **word to the wise,** *verbum sapienti* <L>, verb sap, enough said; **hint,** broad hint, measured words, flea in one's ear <nf>, little birdy <nf>, kick under the table; tip-off <nf>; **lesson,** object lesson, **example,** deterrent example, warning piece; moral, moral of the story; **alarm** 400; final warning *or* notice, ultimatum; **threat** 514

2 **forewarning,** prewarning, **premonition,** precautioning; advance warning *or* notice, plenty of notice, prenotification; presentiment, hunch *and* funny feeling <nf>, **foreboding; portent;** evil portent

3 **warning sign, premonitory sign, danger sign;** preliminary sign *or* signal *or* token; **symptom,** early symptom, premonitory symptom, prodrome, prodroma, prodromata <pl>; **precursor** 815; **omen** 133.3,6; **handwriting on the wall,** "*mene, mene, tekel, upharsin*"—Bible <Aramaic>; straw in the wind; gathering clouds, clouds on the horizon; thundercloud, thunderhead; falling barometer *or* glass; storm *or* stormy petrel, **red light,** red flag, Very lights; quarantine flag, yellow flag, yellow jack; death's-head, skull *and* crossbones; **high sign** <nf>, **warning signal, alert,** red alert; siren, klaxon, tocsin, alarm bell; tattoo

4 **warner,** cautioner, admonisher, monitor; prophet *or* messenger of doom, Cassandra, Jeremiah, Nostradamus, Ezekiel; **lookout, lookout man; sentinel, sentry; signalman,** signaler, flagman; lighthouse keeper

VERBS 5 **warn, caution, advise, admonish; give warning,** give fair warning, utter a caveat, address a warning to, put a flea in one's ear <nf>, drop a hint, have a word with one, say a word to the wise; tip *and* tip off <nf>; notify, put on notice, give notice *or* advance notice *or* advance word; tell once *and* for all; issue an ultimatum; **threaten** 514.2; **alert,** warn against, put on one's guard, warn away *or* off; **give the high sign** <nf>; **put on alert,** cry havoc, sound the alarm 400.3

6 **forewarn,** prewarn, precaution, premonish; prenotify, tell in advance, give advance notice; **portend, forebode;** give a head's up

ADJS 7 **warning,** cautioning, **cautionary; monitory,** monitorial, admonitory, admonishing, minatory; notifying, notificational; exemplary, deterrent

8 forewarning, premonitory; portentous, foreboding 133.17; **precautionary,** precautional; precursive, precursory, forerunning, prodromal, prodromic

400 ALARM

NOUNS **1 alarm,** alarum, alarm signal *or* bell, **alert;** hue and cry; **red light,** danger signal, amber light, caution signal; **alarm button,** panic button <nf>, nurse's signal; **beeper,** buzzer; note of alarm; air-raid alarm; all clear; tocsin, alarm bell; signal of distress, SOS, Mayday, upside-down flag, flare; *sécurité* <Fr>, notice to mariners; storm warning, storm flag *or* pennant *or* cone, hurricane watch *or* warning *or* advisory, gale warning, small-craft warning *or* advisory, tornado watch *or* warning, winter-storm watch *or* advisory, severe thunderstorm watch *or* warning; fog signal *or* alarm, foghorn, fog bell; burglar alarm; fire alarm, fire bell, fire flag, still alarm; siren, whistle, horn, klaxon, hooter <Brit>; police whistle, watchman's rattle; alarm clock; five-minute gun, two-minute gun; lighthouse, beacon; blinking light, flashing light, occulting light

2 false alarm, cry of wolf; bugbear, bugaboo; bogy; flash in the pan *and* dud <nf>

VERBS **3 alarm, alert, arouse,** put on the alert; **warn** 399.5; fly storm warnings; **sound the alarm,** give *or* raise *or* beat *or* turn in an alarm, ring *or* sound the tocsin, cry havoc, raise a hue *and* cry; give a false alarm, cry before one is hurt, **cry wolf;** frighten *or* scare out of one's wits *or* to death, **frighten,** startle 131.8

ADJS **4 alarmed, aroused;** alerted; frit <Brit nf>, frightened to death *or* out of one's wits, **frightened; startled** 131.13

401 HASTE

<rapidity of action>

NOUNS **1 haste, hurry, scurry, rush, race,** speed, dash, drive, scuttle, scamper, **scramble,** hustle <nf>, **bustle,** flutter, **flurry,** hurry-scurry, helter-skelter; no time to be lost

2 hastiness, hurriedness, quickness, swiftness, expeditiousness, alacrity, promptness 330.3; **speed** 174.1,2; furiousness, feverishness; **precipitousness,** precipitance *or* precipitancy, precipitation; rapidity; suddenness, abruptness; **impetuousness** 365.2, impetuosity, **impulsiveness, rashness** 493, impulsivity; eagerness, zealousness, **overeagerness, overzealousness**

3 hastening, hurrying, festination, speeding, forwarding, quickening, **acceleration;** forced march, double time, double-quick time, double-quick; fast-forward; skedaddle <nf>

VERBS **4 hasten,** haste, **hurry, accelerate, speed,** speed up, **hurry up,** hustle up <nf>, **rush,** quicken, hustle <nf>, bustle, bundle, precipitate, forward; **dispatch, expedite; whip,** whip along, spur, **urge** 375.14,16; push, press; crowd, stampede; **hurry on,** hasten on, drive on, hie on, push on, press on; **hurry along,** lollop <chiefly Brit>, rush along, speed along, **speed on its way; push through,** railroad <nf>, steamroll

5 make haste, hasten, festinate, **hurry, hurry up, race, run,** post, **rush, chase, tear, dash,** spurt, leap, plunge, **scurry,** hurry-scurry, **scamper, scramble, scuttle, hustle** <nf>, bundle, **bustle;** bestir oneself, move quickly 174.9; hurry on, dash on, press *or* push on, crowd; double-time, go at the double; break one's neck *or* fall all over oneself <nf>; lose no time, not lose a moment; rush through, romp through, hurry through; dash off; make short *or* fast work of, make the best of one's time *or* way, think on one's feet, make up for lost time; do on the run *or* on the fly

6 <nf terms> step on it, snap to it, hop to it, hotfoot, bear down on it, shake it up, **get moving** *or* **going,** get a move on, get cracking <chiefly Brit>, get *or* shake the lead out, get the lead out of one's ass, get one's ass in gear, give it the gun, hump, hump it, hump oneself, shag ass, tear ass, **get a hustle** *or* wiggle on, stir one's stumps, not spare the horses, barrel along, tear off, make tracks

7 rush into, plunge into, dive into, plunge, plunge ahead *or* headlong; **not stop to think,** go off half-cocked *or* at half cock <nf>, leap before one looks, cross a bridge before one comes to it

8 be in a hurry, be under the gun <nf>, have no time to lose *or* spare, not have a moment to spare, hardly have time to breathe, work against time *or* the clock, work under pressure, have a deadline, do at the last moment

ADJS **9 hasty, hurried,** festinate, **quick,** flying, **expeditious,** prompt 330.18; quick-and-dirty <nf>, **immediate,** instant, on the spot, precipitant; onrushing, **swift, speedy; urgent;** furious, feverish; slap-bang, slapdash, **cursory,** passing, cosmetic, snap <nf>, superficial; spur-of-the-moment, last-minute

10 precipitate, precipitant, precipitous; **sudden,** abrupt; **impetuous, impulsive, rash;** headlong, breakneck; breathless, panting

11 hurried, rushed, pushed, pressed, railroaded, crowded, **pressed for time,** hard-pushed *or* -pressed, hard-run; double-time, double-quick, on *or* at the double

ADVS **12 hastily, hurriedly, quickly; expeditiously,** promptly, with dispatch; all in one breath, in one word, in two words; apace, amain, hand over fist, **immediately,** instantly, in a second *or* split second *or* jiffy, at once, as soon as possible *or* **ASAP; swiftly, speedily,** on *or* at fast-forward; with haste, with great *or* all haste, in *or* with a rush, in a mad rush, at fever pitch; furiously, feverishly, in a sweat *or* lather of haste, hotfoot; by forced marches; **helter-skelter, hurry-scurry,** pellmell; slapdash, cursorily, superficially, on the run *or* fly, in passing, on the spur of the moment

13 posthaste, in posthaste; post, express; by express, by airmail, by return mail; by cable, by telegraph, by fax

14 in a hurry, in haste, in hot haste, in all haste; in short order; against time, against the clock

15 precipitately, precipitantly, precipitously, slap-bang; **suddenly,** abruptly, **impetuously, impulsively, rashly; headlong,** headfirst, headforemost, head over heels, heels over head <old>, *à corps perdu* <Fr>

INTERJS **16 make haste!,** make it quick!, **hurry up!; now!; at once!,** rush!, immediate!, **urgent!,** instanter!; **step lively!,** look alive!, on the double!

17 <nf terms> **step on it!,** snap to it!, **make it snappy!, get a move on!,** get a wiggle on!, **chop-chop!, shake a leg!,** stir your stumps!, get the lead out!, **get moving!, get going!,** get cracking!, get with it!, hop to it!, move your tail!, move your fanny!, get on the ball!, don't spare the horses!

402 LEISURE

NOUNS **1 leisure, ease, convenience,** freedom; retirement, semiretirement; rest, repose 20; **free time, spare time,** goof-off time <nf>, downtime, odd moments, idle hours; time to spare *or* burn *or* kill, time on one's hands, time at one's disposal *or* command, time to oneself; time, one's own sweet time <nf>; breathing room; all the time in the world; time off, holiday, vacation, furlough, sabbatical, leave; break, recess, breather, coffee break; day of rest; letup <nf>

2 leisureliness, unhurriedness, unhastiness, hastelessness, relaxedness; *dolce far niente* <Ital>; **inactivity** 331; **slowness** 175; deliberateness, deliberation; contentment

VERBS **3 have time,** have time enough, have time to spare, have plenty of time, have nothing but time, be in no hurry; lounge, loll

4 take one's leisure, take one's ease, **take one's time, take one's own sweet time** <nf>, do at one's leisure *or* convenience *or* pleasure; go slow 175.6; ride the gravy train *and* lead the life of Riley <nf>, take time to smell the flowers *or* roses; put one's feet up

ADJS **5 leisure, leisured;** idle, unoccupied, free, open, spare; retired, semiretired, unemployed, in retirement; on vacation, on holiday; after-dinner

6 leisurely, unhurried, laid-back <nf>, unhasty, hasteless, easy, relaxed; sluggish, lazy; deliberate; inactive 331.17; **slow** 175.10

ADVS **7 at leisure, at one's leisure, at one's convenience,** at one's own sweet time <nf>, when one gets around to it, when it is handy, when one has the time, when one has a minute to spare, when one has a moment to call one's own

INTERJS **8** easy does it!, take it easy!

403 ENDEAVOR

NOUNS **1 endeavor,** effort, striving, struggle, strain; **all-out effort,** best effort, college try *or* old college try <nf>, valiant effort; **exertion** 725; determination, resolution 359; **enterprise** 330.7

2 attempt, trial, effort, essay, assay <old>, first attempt, *coup d'essai* <Fr>; **endeavor, undertaking;** approach, move; coup, stroke 328.3, step; gambit, offer, **bid,** strong bid; experiment, tentative; tentation, trial and error

3 <nf terms> **try, whack, fling, shot, crack,** bash, belt, go, stab, leap, lick, rip, ripple, cut, hack, smack; last shot, swan song

4 one's best, one's level best, one's utmost, one's damnedest *or* darndest <nf>, one's best effort *or* endeavor, the best one can, the best one knows how, all one can do, all one's got, all one's got in one, one's all <nf>, the top of one's bent, as much as in one lies

VERBS **5 endeavor, strive, struggle,** strain, sweat, sweat blood, labor, get one's teeth into, come to grips with, take it on, make an all-out effort, move heaven and earth, **exert oneself,** apply oneself, use some elbow grease <nf>; spend oneself; seek, study, aim; resolve, be determined 359.8

6 attempt, try, essay, assay, offer; try one's hand *or* wings, try it on <chiefly Brit>; **undertake** 404.3, **approach,** come to grips with, engage, take the bull by the horns; venture, venture on *or* upon, chance; **make an attempt** *or* **effort,** lift a finger *or* hand

7 <nf terms> **tackle, take on, make a try, give a try,** have a go <chiefly Brit>, take a shot *or* stab *or* crack *or* try *or* whack at; try on for size, **go for it,** go for the brass ring, **have a fling** *or* **go at,** give a fling *or* a go *or* a whirl, **make a stab at,** have a shot *or* stab *or* crack *or* try *or* whack at

8 try to, try and <nf>, **attempt to, endeavor to,** strive to, seek to, study to, aim to, venture to, dare to, pretend to

9 try for, strive for, strain for, struggle for, contend for, pull for <nf>, bid for, make a bid *or* strong bid for, make a play for <nf>

10 **see what one can do,** see what can be done, see if one can do, do what one can, use one's endeavor; try anything once; **try one's hand,** try one's luck, tempt fate; make a cautious *or* tentative move, experiment, feel one's way, test the waters, run it up the flagpole <nf>

11 **make a special effort, go out of the way,** go out of one's way, take special pains, **put oneself out,** put oneself out of the way, lay oneself out *and* fall *or* bend *or* lean over backward <nf>, fall all over oneself, trouble oneself, **go to the trouble,** take trouble, **take pains,** redouble one's efforts

12 **try hard, push** <nf>, make a bold push, **put one's back to** *or* **into,** put one's heart into, try until one is blue in the face, die trying, **try and try;** try, try again; exert oneself 725.9

13 **do one's best** *or* **level best, do one's utmost,** try one's best *or* utmost, **do all** *or* **everything one can,** do the best one can, **do the best one knows how,** do all in one's power, do as much as in one lies, do what lies in one's power, do one's damnedest <nf>; put all one's strength into, put one's whole soul in, **strain every nerve; give it one's all**, go flat out <nf>; go for broke; be on one's mettle, **die trying**

14 <nf terms> **knock oneself out, break one's neck,** break *or* bust one's balls, bust a gut, bust one's ass *or* hump, rupture oneself, do it *or* know why not, do it *or* break a leg, do it *or* bust a gut, do *or* try one's damndest *or* darndest, go all out, go the limit, go for broke, shoot the works, give it all one's got, give it one's best shot, go for it

15 **make every effort, spare no effort** *or* **pains, go all lengths, go to great lengths,** go the whole length, go through fire and water, not rest, not relax, not slacken, move heaven and earth, leave no stone unturned, leave no avenue unexplored

ADJS 16 trial, tentative, experimental; venturesome, willing; determined, resolute 359.11; utmost, damndest

ADVS 17 **out for,** out to, trying for, **on the make** <nf>

18 **at the top of one's bent,** to one's utmost, as far as possible

404 UNDERTAKING

NOUNS 1 **undertaking, enterprise, operation,** work, **venture, project,** proposition *and* deal <nf>; matter at hand; **program, plan** 381; **affair, business, matter, task** 724.2, concern, interest; **initiative,** effort, attempt 403.2; **action** 328.3; **engagement, contract, obligation, commitment** 436.2; *démarche* <Fr>

2 **adventure,** emprise, **mission;** quest, pilgrimage; expedition, exploration

VERBS 3 **undertake, assume,** accept, **take on, take upon oneself,** take in hand, take upon one's shoulders, take up, sign up, go with, **tackle,** attack; engage *or* contract *or* obligate *or* commit oneself; **put** *or* **set** *or* **turn one's hand to, engage in, devote oneself to, apply oneself to,** betake oneself to <old>, address oneself to, give oneself up to; join oneself to, associate oneself with, take in hand, **come aboard** <nf>; busy oneself with 724.11; **take up,** move into, go into, **go in** *or* **out for** <nf>, **enter on** *or* **upon,** proceed to, embark in *or* upon, **venture upon,** go upon, launch, set forward, get going, get under way, initiate; set about, go about, lay about, go to do; **go** *or* **swing into action, set to, turn to, buckle to, fall to; pitch into** <nf>, plunge into, fall into, **launch into** *or* **upon;** go at, set at, have at <nf>, knuckle *or* buckle down to; put one's hand to the plow, put *or* lay one's shoulder to the wheel; take the bull by the horns; **endeavor, attempt;** dare, take a shot at

4 **have in hand, have one's hands in,** have on one's hands *or* shoulders

5 **be in progress** *or* **process,** be on the anvil, be in the fire, be in the works *or* hopper *or* pipeline <nf>, **be under way**

6 **bite off more than one can chew** <nf>, take on too much, overextend *or* overreach oneself, have too many irons in the fire, have too much on one's plate

ADJS 7 **undertaken, assumed,** accepted, **taken on** <nf>; **ventured,** attempted, chanced; **in hand,** on the anvil, in the fire, **in progress** *or* process, on one's plate, in the works *or* hopper *or* pipeline <nf>, on the agenda, **under way;** contractual

8 **enterprising,** venturesome, adventurous, plucky, keen, eager; resourceful, ambitious; pioneering

405 PREPARATION

NOUNS 1 **preparation,** preparing, prep *and* prepping <nf>, **readying,** getting *or* making ready, makeready, taking measures; warm-up, getting in shape *or* condition; mobilization; walk-up, **run-up; prearrangement** 965, lead time, advance notice, warning, advance warning, alerting; **planning** 381.1; trial, dry run, **tryout** 942.3; **provision, arrangement;** preparatory *or* preliminary act *or* measure *or* step; **preliminary, preliminaries;** clearing the decks <nf>; **grounding,** propaedeutic, preparatory study *or* instruction; basic training, familiarization, briefing; prerequisite; processing, treatment, pretreatment; equipment 385; training 568.3; manufacture; **spadework,** groundwork, foundation 901.6; pioneering, trailblazing, pushing the envelope <nf>

2 fitting, checking the fit, fit, fitting out; **conditioning; adaptation, adjustment,** tuning; **qualification,** capacitation, enablement; **equipment,** furnishing 385.1

3 <a preparation> **concoction,** decoction, *decoctum* <L>, brew, **confection; composition, mixture** 797.5, combination 804

4 preparedness, readiness; fitness, fittedness, suitedness, suitableness, **suitability;** condition, trim; **qualification,** qualifiedness, credentials, record, track record <nf>; **competence** *or* competency, **ability, capability, proficiency,** mastery; ripeness, maturity, seasoning, fitness, tempering

5 preparer, preparator, preparationist; trainer, coach, instructor, mentor, teacher, tutor; **trailblazer, pathfinder; forerunner** 816.1; **paver of the way,** pioneer

VERBS **6 prepare, make** *or* **get ready,** prep <nf>, do the prep work, trim <old>, **ready, fix** <nf>; provide <old>, **arrange; make preparations** *or* **arrangements,** take measures, sound the note of preparation, clear the decks <nf>, clear for action, settle preliminaries, tee up <nf>; mobilize, marshal, deploy, marshal *or* deploy one's forces *or* resources; **prearrange; plan; try out** 942.8; fix *or* ready up <nf>, put in *or* into shape; dress; treat, pretreat, process; cure, tan, taw; map out, sketch out, outline

7 make up, get up, fix up *and* rustle up <nf>; **concoct,** decoct, brew; **compound, compose, put together, mix;** make

8 fit, condition, adapt, adjust, suit, tune, attune, put in tune *or* trim *or* working order; **qualify,** enable, capacitate; **equip,** fit out, supply, **furnish** 385.7,8

9 prime, load, charge, cock, set; wind, wind up; steam up, get up steam, warm up

10 prepare to, get ready to, get set for <nf>, fix to <nf>; be about to, be on the point of; ready oneself to, hold oneself in readiness

11 prepare for, provide for, arrange for, make arrangements *or* dispositions for, look to, look out for, see to, **make provision** *or* **due provision for;** provide against, make sure against, forearm, **provide for** *or* **against a rainy day,** prepare for the evil day; lay in provisions, lay up a store, keep as a nest egg, save to fall back upon, lay by, husband one's resources, salt *or* squirrel something away; set one's house in order

12 prepare the way, pave the way, smooth the path *or* road, **clear the way,** open the way, open the door to; build a bridge; **break the ice;** pioneer, go in advance, be the point, push the envelope, **blaze** the trail; **prepare the ground,** cultivate the soil, sow the seed; do the spadework, lay the groundwork *or* foundation, lay the first stone, provide the basis; lead up to

13 prepare oneself, brace oneself, **get ready, get set** <nf>, put one's house in order, strip for action, get into shape *or* condition, roll up one's sleeves, spit on one's hands, limber up, warm up, flex one's muscles, gird up one's loins, buckle on one's armor, get into harness, shoulder arms; sharpen one's tools, whet the knife *or* sword; psych oneself up <nf>; do one's homework; get one's house in order; **run up to,** build up to, gear up, tool up, rev up

14 be prepared, be ready, stand by, stand ready, hold oneself in readiness, "put your trust in God, my boys, and keep your powder dry"—Cromwell

15 <be fitted> **qualify, measure up,** meet the requirements, check out <nf>, have the credentials *or* qualifications *or* prerequisites; be up to *and* be just the ticket *and* fill the bill <nf>

ADJS **16 prepared, ready,** well-prepared, prepped <nf>, in readiness *or* ready state, all ready, good *and* ready, prepared *and* ready; psyched *or* pumped up <nf>, eager, keen, champing at the bit; alert, vigilant 339.13; **ripe, mature; set** and **all set** <nf>, on the mark *and* teed up <nf>; about to, fixing to <nf>; **prearranged; planned; primed,** loaded, cocked, **loaded for bear** <nf>; familiarized, briefed, informed, put into the picture <Brit nf>; groomed, coached; ready for anything; in the saddle, booted and spurred; armed and ready, in arms, up in arms, **armed** 460.14; in battle array, mobilized; **provided, equipped** 385.13; dressed; treated, pretreated, processed; cured, tanned, tawed; **readied,** available 221.12

17 fitted, adapted, adjusted, suited; qualified, fit, competent, able, capable, proficient; checked out <nf>; well-qualified, well-fitted, well-suited

18 prepared for, ready for, alert for, set *or* all set for <nf>; loaded for, primed for; up for <nf>; equal to, up to

19 ready-made, ready-formed, ready-mixed, ready-furnished, ready-dressed; ready-built, prefabricated, prefab <nf>, preformed; ready-to-wear, ready-for-wear, off-the-rack; ready-cut, cut-and-dried; convenient, convenience, fast-food; ready-to-cook, precooked, oven-ready; instant

20 preparatory, preparative; propaedeutic; prerequisite; provident, provisional

ADJS, ADVS **21 in readiness, in store, in reserve;** in anticipation

22 in preparation, in course of preparation, **in progress** *or* **process,** under way, **going on,** in embryo, **in production,** on stream, under construction, **in the works** *or* hopper *or* pipeline <nf>, on the way, **in the making, in hand,** on the anvil, on the fire, in the oven; under revision; brewing, forthcoming

23 afoot, on foot, afloat, astir

PREPS **24** in preparation for, against, for; in order to; ready for, set for *and* fixing to <nf>

406 UNPREPAREDNESS

NOUNS **1 unpreparedness, unreadiness,** unprovidedness, nonpreparedness, nonpreparation, lack of preparation; vulnerability 1006.4; extemporaneousness, improvisation, ad lib <nf>, planlessness, disorganization; **unfitness,** unfittedness, unsuitedness, unsuitableness, **unsuitability, unqualifiedness,** unqualification, lack of credentials, poor track record <nf>, **disqualification,** incompetence *or* incompetency, incapability; rustiness

2 improvidence, thriftlessness, unthriftiness, poor husbandry, lax stewardship; **shiftlessness,** fecklessness, thoughtlessness, heedlessness; happy-go-luckiness; hastiness 401.2; negligence 340.1

3 <raw or original condition> **naturalness,** inartificiality; **natural state,** nature, **state of nature,** nature in the raw; pristineness, intactness, virginity; natural man, "unaccommodated man"— Shakespeare; artlessness 416

4 undevelopment, nondevelopment; **immaturity,** immatureness, callowness, unfledgedness, cubbishness, **rawness, unripeness, greenness; unfinish,** unfinishedness, unpolishedness, **unrefinement, uncultivation; crudity,** crudeness, **rudeness, coarseness,** roughness, the rough; **oversimplification,** oversimplicity, simplism, reductionism

5 raw material; crude, crude stuff <nf>; ore, rich ore, rich vein; unsorted *or* unanalyzed mass; rough diamond, **diamond in the rough;** unlicked cub; **virgin soil,** untilled ground

VERBS **6 be unprepared** *or* **unready,** not be ready, lack preparation; go off half-cocked *or* at half cock <nf>; be taken unawares *or* aback, be blindsided <nf>, be caught napping, be caught with one's pants down <nf>, be surprised, drop one's guard; **extemporize,** improvise, ad-lib *and* play by ear <nf>; have no plan, be innocent of forethought; improvise

7 make no provision, take no thought of tomorrow *or* the morrow, seize the day, *carpe diem* <L, Horace>, let tomorrow take care of itself, live for the day, live like the grasshopper, live from hand to mouth; "eat, drink, and be merry"—Bible; make it up as one goes along

ADJS **8 unprepared, unready,** unprimed; surprised, caught short, caught napping, caught with one's pants down <nf>, taken by surprise, taken aback, taken unawares, blindsided <nf>, caught off balance, caught off base <nf>, tripped up; **unarranged,** unorganized, haphazard; makeshift, rough-and-ready, **extemporaneous,** extemporized, improvised, ad-lib *and* off the top of one's head <nf>; spontaneous, ad hoc; impromptu, snap <nf>; **unmade,** unmanufactured, unconcocted, unhatched, uncontrived, undevised, unplanned, unpremeditated, undeliberated, unstudied; hasty, precipitate 401.10; unbegun

9 unfitted, unfit, ill-fitted, unsuited, unadapted, unqualified, disqualified, incompetent, incapable; **unequipped, unfurnished,** unarmed, ill-equipped, ill-furnished, **unprovided,** ill-provided 992.12

10 raw, crude; uncooked, unbaked, unboiled; underdone, undercooked, rare, red; half-baked

11 immature, unripe, underripe, unripened, impubic, **raw, green,** callow, wet behind the ears, cub, cubbish, unfledged, fledgling, unseasoned, unmellowed, vulnerable; ungrown, half-grown, adolescent, juvenile, puerile, boyish, girlish, inchoate; undigested, ill-digested; half-baked <nf>; half-cocked *and* at half cock <nf>, wet behind the ears

12 undeveloped, unfinished, unlicked, unformed; unfashioned, unwrought, unlabored, unworked, unprocessed, untreated; unblown; uncut, unhewn; **underdeveloped;** backward, arrested, stunted; **crude, rude, coarse, unpolished, unrefined; uncultivated, uncultured; rough,** roughcast, roughhewn, **in the rough; rudimentary,** rudimental; embryonic, in embryo, fetal, *in ovo* <L>; **oversimple, simplistic,** reductive, reductionistic, unsophisticated; untrained; rusty, unpracticed; scratch <nf>

13 <in the raw or original state> **natural, native, in a state of nature,** in the raw; inartificial, artless 416.5; virgin, virginal, pristine, untouched, unsullied

14 fallow, untilled, uncultivated, unsown, unworked

15 improvident, prodigal, unproviding; **thriftless, unthrifty,** uneconomical; grasshopper; hand-to-mouth; **shiftless, feckless, thoughtless, heedless;** happy-go-lucky; negligent 340.10

407 ACCOMPLISHMENT
<act of accomplishing; entire performance>

NOUNS **1 accomplishment, achievement, fulfillment, performance, execution, effectuation,** implementation, carrying out *or* through, **discharge, dispatch, consummation, realization,**

attainment, production, fruition; **success** 409; track record *or* track <nf>; *fait accompli* <Fr>, accomplished fact, done deal <nf>; mission accomplished

2 completion, completing, **finish,** finishing, **conclusion, end,** ending, **termination,** terminus, **close, windup** <nf>, rounding off *or* out, topping off, wrapping up, wrap-up, finalization; **perfection,** culmination 1002.3; ripeness, maturity, maturation, full development

3 finishing touch, final touch, last touch, last stroke, final *or* finishing stroke, finisher <nf>, icing the cake, the icing on the cake; copestone, capstone, crown, crowning of the edifice; capper <nf>, climax 198.2

VERBS **4 accomplish, achieve, effect, effectuate, compass, consummate, do, execute, produce, deliver, make,** enact, **perform, discharge, fulfill, realize, attain,** run with *and* hack *and* swing <nf>; **work,** work out; **dispatch, dispose of,** knock off <nf>, polish off <nf>, take care of <nf>, **deal with,** put away, make short work of; succeed, manage 409.12; come through *and* do the job <nf>, **do** *or* turn the trick <nf>

5 bring about, bring to pass, bring to effect, **bring to a happy issue; implement, carry out, carry through,** carry into execution; **bring off, carry off, pull off** <nf>; **put through,** get through, **put over** *or* **across** <nf>; come through with <nf>

6 complete, perfect, finish, finish off, conclude, terminate, end, bring to a close, carry to completion, prosecute to a conclusion; **get through, get done;** come off of, get through with, get it over, get it over with, **finish up;** clean up *and* wind up *and* button up *and* sew up *and* wrap up *and* mop up <nf>, close up *or* out; put the lid on *and* call it a day <nf>; **round off** *or* **out, wind up** <nf>, **top off;** top out, crown, cap 198.9; climax, culminate; **give the finishing touches** *or* **strokes,** put the finishing touches *or* strokes on, lick *or* whip into shape, finalize, put the icing on the cake

7 do to perfection, do up brown <nf>, **do to a turn,** do to a T *or* to a frazzle *or* down to the ground <nf>, not do by halves, do oneself proud <nf>, use every trick in the book, leave no loose ends, leave nothing hanging; go all lengths, go to all lengths, go the whole length *or* way, go the limit *and* go whole hog *and* go all out *and* shoot the works *and* go for broke <nf>

8 ripen, ripe <nf>, **mature,** maturate; bloom, blow, blossom, flourish; come to fruition, bear fruit; **mellow;** grow up, reach maturity, reach its season; come *or* draw to a head; bring to maturity, bring to a head

ADJS **9 completing,** completive, completory,

finishing, consummative, culminating, terminative, conclusive, **concluding,** fulfilling, finalizing, crowning; ultimate, **last, final,** terminal

10 accomplished, achieved, effected, effectuated, implemented, **consummated, executed, discharged, fulfilled, realized,** compassed, **attained; dispatched, disposed of,** set at rest; wrought, wrought out

11 completed, done, finished, concluded, terminated, ended, finished up; signed, sealed, *and* delivered; cleaned up *and* wound up *and* sewed *or* sewn up *and* wrapped up *and* mopped up <nf>; washed up <nf>, **through,** done with; all over with, all said *and* done, all over but the shouting; perfective

12 complete, perfect, consummate, polished; exhaustive, thorough 794.10; fully realized

13 ripe, mature, matured, maturated, seasoned; blooming, abloom; **mellow,** full-grown, fully developed

ADVS **14 to completion,** to the end, to the full, to the limit; to a turn, to a T <nf>, to a finish, to a frazzle <nf>

INTERJS **15** so much for that!, that's that!, *voilà!* <Fr>

408 NONACCOMPLISHMENT

NOUNS **1 nonaccomplishment, nonachievement, nonperformance,** inexecution, nonexecution, nondischarging, **noncompletion,** nonconsummation, nonfulfillment, unfulfillment; nonfeasance, omission; **neglect** 340; loose ends, rough edges; endless task, work of Penelope, Sisyphean labor *or* toil *or* task; **disappointment** 132; **failure** 410

VERBS **2** neglect, leave undone 340.7, fail 410.8–10,13; be disappointed 132.4

ADJS **3 unaccomplished, unachieved, unperformed,** unexecuted, undischarged, unfulfilled, unconsummated, unrealized, unattained; **unfinished, uncompleted, undone;** open-ended; **neglected** 340.14; **disappointed** 132.5

409 SUCCESS

NOUNS **1 success, successfulness,** fortunate outcome, prosperous issue, favorable termination; **prosperity** 1010; accomplishment 407; **victory** 411; the big time

2 sure success, foregone conclusion, sure-fire proposition <nf>; **winner** *and* **natural** <nf>; shoo-in *and* **sure thing** *and* sure bet *and* **cinch** *and* lead-pipe cinch <nf>

3 great success, triumph, resounding triumph, brilliant success, striking success, **meteoric** success; **stardom; success story;** brief *or*

momentary success, nine days' wonder, flash in the pan, fad; best seller

4 <nf terms> **smash, hit,** smash hit, gas, gasser, blast, boffo, showstopper, barn-burner, howling or roaring success, one for the book, wow, wowser, sensation, overnight sensation, sensaysh, phenom, sockeroo

5 **score, hit, bull's-eye;** goal, touchdown; slam, grand slam; strike; hole, hole in one; home run, homer <nf>

6 <successful person> **winner,** star, star in the firmament, success, superstar and megastar <nf>; phenom and comer <nf>, whiz kid, VIP; **victor** 411.2

VERBS **7** **succeed, prevail,** be successful, be crowned with success, meet with success, do very well, do famously, deliver, come through and make a go of it <nf>; **go, come off,** go off; **prosper** 1010.7; fare well, work well, do or work wonders, go to town or go great guns <nf>; **make a hit** <nf>, click and connect <nf>, **catch on** and take <nf>, catch fire, have legs <nf>; **go over** and go over big or with a bang <nf>; pass, graduate, qualify, win one's spurs or wings, get one's credentials, be blooded; pass with flying colors

8 **achieve one's purpose, gain one's end** or **ends,** secure one's object, attain one's objective, do what one set out to do, reach one's goal, bring it off, pull it off and hack it and swing it <nf>; make one's point; play it or handle it just right <nf>, not put a foot wrong, play it like a master

9 **score a success,** score, notch one up <nf>, hit it, hit the mark, ring the bell <nf>, turn up trumps, break the bank or make a killing <nf>, hit the jackpot <nf>

10 **make good, come through, achieve success,** make a success, have a good thing going <nf>, **make it** <nf>, get into the zone or bubble <nf>, wing and cruise, <nf>, hit one's stride, **make one's mark, give a good account of oneself,** bear oneself with credit, do all right by oneself and **do oneself proud,** make out like a bandit <nf>; **advance, progress,** make one's way, make headway, **get on,** come on <nf>, **get ahead** <nf>; go places, **go far;** rise, **rise in the world,** work one's way up, step up, come or move up in the world, claw or scrabble one's way up, mount the ladder of success, pull oneself up by one's bootstraps; **arrive,** get there <nf>, make the scene <nf>; come out on top, come out on top of the heap <nf>; **be a success,** have it made or hacked or wrapped up <nf>, have the world at one's feet, eat or live high on the hog <nf>; **make a noise in the world** <nf>, cut a swath, set the world or river or Thames on fire; break through, score or make a breakthrough

11 **succeed with,** crown with success; **make a go of it; accomplish,** compass, **achieve** 407.4; **bring off, carry off, pull off** <nf>, turn or do the trick <nf>, **put through,** bring through; **put over** or **across** <nf>; get away with it and get by <nf>

12 **manage, contrive, succeed in; make out, get on** or **along** <nf>, come on or along <nf>, go on; **scrape along,** worry along, **muddle through** <Brit>, get by, **manage somehow; make it** <nf>, **make the grade,** cut the mustard and hack it <nf>; **clear,** clear the hurdle; **negotiate** <nf>, **engineer; swing** <nf>, put over <nf>, put through

13 **win through, win out** <nf>, come through <nf>, rise to the occasion, beat the game and beat the system <nf>; **triumph** 411.3; weather out, **weather the storm,** live through, keep one's head above water; come up fighting or smiling, not know when one is beaten, persevere 360.2

ADJS **14** **successful,** succeeding, crowned with success; **prosperous,** fortunate 1010.14; **triumphant;** ahead of the game, out in front, on top, sitting on top of the world and sitting pretty <nf>, on top of the heap <nf>; assured of success, surefire, made; coming and on the up-and-up <nf>

ADVS **15** **successfully,** swimmingly <nf>, well, to some purpose, to good purpose; beyond all expectation, beyond one's fondest dreams, from rags to riches, with flying colors

410 FAILURE

NOUNS **1** **failure, unsuccessfulness,** unsuccess, successlessness, nonsuccess; no go <nf>; ill success; futility, uselessness 391; **defeat** 412; losing game, **no-win situation;** nonaccomplishment 408; **bankruptcy** 625.3

2 <nf terms> **flop,** flopperoo, megaflop, gigaflop, **bust,** frost, **fizzle,** lemon, clinker, dud, non-starter, **loser, washout,** turkey, bomb, flat failure, dull thud, total loss; the pits

3 **collapse, crash,** smash, comedown, breakdown, derailment, **fall,** pratfall <nf>, stumble, tumble, **downfall,** cropper <chiefly Brit nf>; nose dive and tailspin <nf>; deflation, bursting of the bubble, letdown, **disappointment** 132

4 **miss,** near-miss; **slip, slipup** <nf>, slip 'twixt cup and lip; **error, mistake** 975.3

5 **abortion, miscarriage,** miscarrying, abortive attempt, vain attempt; wild-goose chase, merry chase; **misfire, flash in the pan,** wet squib, malfunction, glitch <nf>; **dud** <nf>; **flunk** <nf>, **washout** <nf>

6 **fiasco, botch,** botch-up, cock-up and balls-up <Brit nf>, bungle, hash, mess, muddle, foozle and bollix *and* bitch-up *and* screw-up *and* fuck-up <nf>

7 <unsuccessful person> **failure,** flash in the pan; bankrupt 625.4

8 <nf terms> **loser, non-starter,** born loser, **flop,** washout, false alarm, **dud,** also-ran, bum, dull tool, bust, schlemiel, turkey, hopeless case

VERBS **9 fail,** be unsuccessful, fail of success, not work *and* not come off <nf>, come to grief, **lose,** not make the grade, be found wanting, not come up to the mark; not pass, **flunk** *and* **flunk out** <nf>; go to the wall, **go on the rocks;** labor in vain 391.8; come away empty-handed; tap out <nf>, go bankrupt 625.7

10 <nf terms> **lose out,** get left, **not make it,** not hack it, not get to first base, drop the ball, go for a Burton *and* come a cropper <Brit>, **flop,** flummox, fall flat on one's ass, lay an egg, go over like a lead balloon, draw a blank, bomb, drop a bomb; fold, fold up; take it on the chin, take the count; crap out; strike out, fan, whiff

11 sink, founder, go down, go under <nf>; **slip,** go downhill, be on the skids <nf>

12 fall, fall down <nf>, fall *or* drop by the wayside, fall flat, fall flat on one's face; fall down on the job <nf>; **fall short, fall through,** fall to the ground; fall between two stools; **fall dead; collapse,** fall in; **crash,** go to smash <nf>

13 come to nothing, hang up *and* get nowhere <nf>; **poop out** *and* go phut <nf>; be all over *or* up with; fail miserably *or* ignominiously; fizz out *and* **fizzle** *and* **fizzle out** *and* peter out *and* poop out <nf>; **misfire,** flash in the pan, hang fire; **blow up, blow up in one's face, explode, end** *or* **go up in smoke,** go up like a rocket *and* come down like a stick <nf>

14 miss, miss the mark, miss one's aim; slip, slip up <nf>; goof <nf>, blunder, foozle <nf>, **err** 975.9; **botch, bungle** 414.11,12; waste one's effort, run around in circles, spin one's wheels

15 miscarry, abort, be stillborn, die aborning; **go amiss,** go astray, **go wrong,** go on a wrong tack, take a wrong turn, derail, go off the rails

16 stall, stick, die, go dead, **conk out** <nf>, sputter *and* stop, run out of gas *or* steam, come to a shuddering halt, come to a dead stop

17 flunk *or* **flunk out** <nf>; **fail,** pluck *and* plough <Brit nf>, bust *and* wash out <nf>

ADJS **18 unsuccessful,** successless, failing; failed, *manqué* <Fr>, stickit <Scot>; **unfortunate** 1011.14; **abortive,** miscarrying, miscarried, stillborn, died aborning; fruitless, bootless, no-win <nf>, futile, useless 391.9; lame, **ineffectual,** ineffective, inefficacious, of no effect; malfunctioning, glitchy <nf>

ADVS **19 unsuccessfully,** successlessly, **without success;** fruitlessly, bootlessly, ineffectually, ineffectively, inefficaciously, lamely; to little *or* no purpose, **in vain**

411 VICTORY

NOUNS **1 victory, triumph, conquest,** subduing, subdual; a feather in one's cap <nf>; total victory, grand slam; **championship,** crown, laurels, cup, trophy, belt, blue ribbon, first prize; V-for-victory sign *or* V-sign, raised arms; victory lap; **winning,** win <nf>; knockout *or* KO <nf>; easy victory, walkover *and* walkaway <nf>, pushover *and* picnic <nf>; runaway victory, laugher *and* romp *and* shellacking <nf>; landslide victory, landslide; Pyrrhic victory, Cadmean victory; moral victory; winning streak <nf>; winning ways, triumphalism; **success** 409; ascendancy 417.6; mastery 612.2

2 victor, winner, victress, victrix, triumpher; **conqueror,** defeater, **vanquisher,** subduer, subjugator, *conquistador* <Sp>; top dog <nf>; master, master of the situation; hero, conquering hero; champion, champ *and* number one <nf>; easy winner, sure winner, shoo-in <nf>; pancratiast; runner-up

VERBS **3 triumph, prevail, be victorious,** come out ahead, come out on top <nf>, clean up, chain victory to one's car; **win, gain, capture, carry;** win out <nf>, **win through,** carry it, carry off *or* away; **win** *or* **carry** *or* **gain the day,** win the battle, come out first, finish in front, make a killing <nf>, remain in possession of the field; get *or* have the last laugh; **win the prize,** win the palm *or* bays *or* laurels, bear the palm, take the cake <nf>, win one's spurs *or* wings; fluke *and* win by a fluke <nf>; **win by a nose** *and* nose out *and* edge out <nf>; **succeed;** break the record, set a new mark <nf>

4 win hands down *and* win going away <nf>, win in a canter *and* walk *and* waltz <nf>, romp *or* breeze *or* waltz home <nf>, **walk off** *or* **away with,** waltz off with <nf>, walk off with the game, **walk over** <nf>; have the game in one's own hands, have it all one's way; **take** *or* carry by storm, sweep aside all obstacles, carry all before one, make short work of

5 defeat 412.6, **triumph over, prevail over,** best, **beat** <nf>, **get the better** *or* **best of; surmount, overcome,** outmatch, rise above

6 gain the ascendancy, come out on top <nf>, **get the advantage, gain the upper** *or* whip hand, dominate the field, get the edge on *or* jump on *or* drop on <nf>, get a leg up on <nf>, get a stranglehold on

ADJS **7 victorious, triumphant,** triumphal, **winning,**

prevailing; conquering, vanquishing, defeating, overcoming; ahead of the game, ascendant, in the ascendant, in ascendancy, sitting on top of the world *and* sitting pretty <nf>, dominant 612.18; successful; flushed with success *or* victory

8 **undefeated, unbeaten, unvanquished, unconquered,** unsubdued, unquelled, unbowed

ADVS 9 **triumphantly,** victoriously, **in triumph;** by a mile

412 DEFEAT

NOUNS 1 **defeat; beating,** drubbing, thrashing; clobbering *and* hiding *and* lathering *and* whipping *and* lambasting *and* trimming *and* licking <nf>, trouncing; **vanquishment, conquest, conquering,** mastery, subjugation, subduing, subdual; **overthrow,** overturn, overcoming; **fall, downfall,** collapse, smash, crash, **undoing, ruin,** debacle, derailing, derailment; **destruction** 395; deathblow, quietus; Waterloo; failure 410

2 **discomfiture, rout, repulse,** rebuff; **frustration,** bafflement, confusion; **checkmate,** check, balk, foil <old>; **reverse,** reversal, **setback**

3 **utter defeat,** total defeat, overwhelming defeat, crushing defeat, smashing defeat, decisive defeat; no contest; **smearing** *and* **pasting** *and* creaming *and* **clobbering** *and* **shellacking** *and* whopping *and* whomping <nf>; whitewash *or* **whitewashing** <nf>, **shutout**

4 **ignominious defeat,** abject defeat, inglorious defeat, disastrous defeat, utter rout, bitter defeat, stinging defeat, embarrassing defeat

5 **loser,** defeatee <nf>; the vanquished; good loser, game loser, sport *or* **good sport** <nf>; poor sport, poor loser; **underdog, also-ran;** booby *and* duck <nf>; stooge *and* fall guy <nf>; victim 96.11

VERBS 6 **defeat, worst, best, get the better** *or* **best of,** be too good for, be too much for, be more than a match for; **outdo,** outgeneral, outmaneuver, outclass, outshine, outpoint, outsail, outrun, outfight, etc; **triumph over; knock on the head,** deal a deathblow to, put *hors de combat* <Fr>; undo, ruin, destroy 395.10; beat by a nose *and* nose out *and* edge out <nf>

7 **overcome,** surmount; **overpower, overmaster,** overmatch; **overthrow, overturn,** overset; put the skids to <nf>; **upset,** trip, trip up, lay by the heels, send flying *or* sprawling; silence, floor, deck, make bite the dust; overcome oneself, master oneself; kick the habit <nf>

8 **overwhelm,** whelm, snow under <nf>, overbear, defeat utterly, deal a crushing *or* smashing defeat; **discomfit, rout, put to rout,** put to flight, scatter, stampede, panic; confound; put out of court

9 <nf terms> **clobber, trim, skin alive, beat,** skunk, drub, massacre, marmelize <Brit>, lick, whip, thrash, knock off, trim, hide, cut to pieces, run rings *or* circles around, throw for a loss, lather, trounce, **lambaste,** skin alive; fix, settle, settle one's hash, make one say 'uncle,' do in, lick to a frazzle, beat all hollow, beat one's brains out, cook one's goose, make hamburger *or* mincemeat out of, mop up the floor with, sandbag, banjax, bulldoze, steamroller, **smear,** paste, cream, **shellac,** whup, whop, whomp, shut out

10 **conquer, vanquish,** quell, **suppress, put down, subdue, subjugate,** put under the yoke, master; **reduce,** prostrate, fell, **flatten, break, smash, crush, humble,** bend, **bring one to his knees;** roll *or* trample in the dust, tread *or* trample underfoot, trample down, ride down, ride *or* run roughshod over, override; have one's way with

11 **thwart, frustrate,** dash, check, deal a check to, checkmate 1012.15

12 **lose,** lose out <nf>, lose the day, come off second best, **get** *or* **have the worst of it, meet one's Waterloo; fall,** succumb, tumble, bow, go down, go under, **bite** *or* **lick the dust,** take the count <nf>; snatch defeat from the jaws of victory; throw in the towel, say 'uncle'; have enough

ADJS 13 **lost,** unwon

14 **defeated, worsted, bested, outdone; beaten, discomfited,** put to rout, **routed,** scattered, stampeded, panicked; confounded; **overcome, overthrown,** upset, overturned, overmatched, **overpowered, overwhelmed,** whelmed, **overmastered,** overborne, overridden; **fallen,** down; floored, silenced; **undone, done for** <nf>, **ruined,** kaput *and* on the skids <nf>, *hors de combat* <Fr>; all up with <nf>

15 <nf terms> **beat, clobbered, licked, whipped,** trimmed, sandbagged, banjaxed, done in, lathered, creamed, shellacked, trounced, lambasted, settled, fixed; skinned alive; thrown for a loss

16 **shut out,** skunked *and* blanked *and* whitewashed <nf>, scoreless, not on the scoreboard

17 **conquered, vanquished,** quelled, suppressed, put down, **subdued, subjugated,** mastered; **reduced,** prostrate *or* prostrated, felled, **flattened,** smashed, **crushed,** broken; **humbled,** brought to one's knees

18 **irresistible, overpowering, overcoming, overwhelming, overmastering,** overmatching, avalanchine

413 SKILL

NOUNS 1 **skill,** skillfulness, **expertness, expertise, proficiency,** callidity <old>, craft, moxie <nf>, **cleverness; dexterity,** dexterousness *or* dextrousness; **adroitness,** address, **adeptness,** deftness, handiness, hand, practical ability; coordination, timing; quickness, readiness; **competence,** capability, capacity, ability; efficiency; **facility, prowess;** grace, style, finesse; **tact, tactfulness, diplomacy;** *savoir-faire* <Fr>; **artistry;** artfulness; **craftsmanship,** workmanship, artisanship; **know-how** *and* savvy *and* bag of tricks <nf>; technical skill, **technique, touch,** technical brilliance, technical mastery, **virtuosity,** bravura, wizardry; brilliance 920.2; cunning 415; **ingenuity,** ingeniousness, resource, resourcefulness, wit; **mastery,** mastership, **command,** control, grip; steady hand; marksmanship, seamanship, airmanship, horsemanship, etc

2 **agility, nimbleness, spryness,** lightness, featliness

3 **versatility, ambidexterity,** many-sidedness, all-roundedness <nf>, Renaissance versatility; **adaptability,** adjustability, flexibility; broad-gauge, many hats; Renaissance man *or* woman

4 **talent, flair,** strong flair, **gift, endowment,** dowry, dower, natural gift *or* endowment, **genius,** instinct, **faculty,** bump <nf>; **power, ability, capability, capacity,** potential; caliber; **forte,** speciality, métier, long suit, strong point, strong suit, strength; **equipment, qualification;** talents, powers, naturals <old>, parts; the goods *and* the stuff *and* the right stuff *and* what it takes *and* the makings <nf>

5 **aptitude,** inborn *or* innate aptitude, innate ability, genius, aptness, felicity, flair; **bent, turn,** propensity, **leaning,** inclination, tendency; turn for, capacity for, gift for, genius for; feeling for, good head for, an eye for, an ear for, a hand for, a way with

6 **knack, art, hang, trick,** way; **touch,** feel

7 **art, science, craft; skill; technique,** technic, **technics,** technology, technical knowledge *or* skill, technical know-how <nf>; **mechanics,** mechanism; method

8 **accomplishment, acquirement, attainment;** finish; coup, feat, clincher, classic; hit, smash hit

9 **experience, practice,** practical knowledge *or* skill, hands-on experience <nf>, field-work; background, past experience, seasoning, tempering; **worldly wisdom,** knowledge of the world, **sophistication;** sagacity 920.4

10 **masterpiece, masterwork,** *chef d'œuvre* <Fr>; **master stroke,** *coup de maître* <Fr>; **feat,** *tour de force* <Fr>, *pièce de résistance* <Fr>, magnum opus, classic, treasure, work of art, epic, crème de la crème, artistry

11 **expert, adept,** proficient, genius; **artist, craftsman,** artisan, skilled workman, journeyman; technician; seasoned *or* experienced hand; shark *or* sharp *or* sharpy *and* no slouch *and* tough act to follow

<nf>; graduate; **professional, pro** <nf>; **jack-of-all-trades,** all-rounder, Renaissance man *or* woman, handy man, Admirable Crichton <J M Barrie>; **authority,** maven <nf>, know-it-all <nf>; professor; **consultant,** expert consultant, specialist, attaché, technical adviser; counselor, adviser, mentor; boffin <Brit nf>, pundit, savant 929.3; diplomatist, diplomat; politician, statesman, statesperson, elder statesman; connoisseur, cognoscente; *cordon bleu* <Fr>; marksman, crack shot, dead shot; walking encyclopedia <nf>, illuminati

12 **talented person, talent,** man *or* woman of parts, gifted person, prodigy, natural <nf>, **genius,** mental genius, intellectual genius, intellectual prodigy, mental giant; rocket scientist *and* brain surgeon <nf>; phenom <nf>; gifted child, **child prodigy,** wunderkind, whiz kid *and* boy wonder <nf>; polymath

13 **master, past master,** grand master; master hand, world-class performer, champion, **good hand,** dab hand <Brit nf>, skilled *or* practiced hand, practitioner, specialist; first chair; **prodigy; wizard,** magician; **virtuoso;** maestro; **genius,** man *or* woman of genius, paragon; mastermind; master spirit, mahatma, sage 921.1

14 <nf terms> **ace, star, superstar, crackerjack,** dab, great, all-time great, topnotcher, first-rater, whiz, flash, hot stuff, pisser, piss-cutter, pistol, no slouch, world-beater, hot rock, the one who wrote the book, right person for the job, smart cookie

15 **champion,** champ <nf>, victor, title-holder, world champion; **record holder,** world-record holder; laureate; medal winner, Olympic medal winner, medalist, award winner, prizeman, prizetaker, **prizewinner,** titleholder; most valuable player *or* MVP; hall of famer

16 **veteran,** vet <nf>, seasoned *or* grizzled veteran, **old pro** <nf>; **old hand, old-timer** <nf> one of the old guard, old stager <Brit>; old campaigner, war-horse *or* old war-horse <nf>; salt *and* old salt *and* old sea dog <nf>, shellback <nf>

17 **sophisticate,** man of experience, **man of the world;** slicker *and* city slicker <nf>; man-about-town; **cosmopolitan,** cosmopolite, citizen of the world

VERBS 18 **excel in** *or* **at, shine in** *or* **at** <nf>, be master of; write the book <nf>, have a good command of, feel comfortable with, be at home in; **have a gift** *or* **flair** *or* **talent** *or* **bent** *or* **faculty** *or* **turn for,** have a bump for <nf>, be a natural *and* be cut out *or* born to be <nf>, **have a good head for,** have an ear for, have an eye for, be born for, show aptitude *or* talent for, have something to spare; have the knack *or* touch, have a way with, have the right touch, have the hang of it, have a lot going for one <nf>, be able to do it blindfolded *or* standing on one's head <nf>; have something *or* plenty on the ball <nf>

19 **know backwards and forwards, know one's stuff** *or* **know one's onions** <nf>, **know the ropes** *and* **know all the ins** *and* **outs** <nf>, know from A to Z *or* alpha to omega, know like the back of one's hand *or* a book, know from the ground up, know all the tricks *or* moves, know all the tricks of the trade, know all the moves of the game; **know what's what, know a thing or two,** know what it's all about, know the score *and* know all the answers <nf>, "know a hawk from a handsaw"—Shakespeare; have savvy <nf>; **know one's way about,** know the ways of the world, have been around <nf>, have been around the block <nf>, have been through the mill <nf>, have cut one's wisdom teeth *or* eyeteeth <nf>, be long in the tooth, **not be born yesterday;** get around <nf>

20 **exercise skill,** handle oneself well, demonstrate one's ability, **strut one's stuff** *and* hotdog *and* grandstand *and* showboat <nf>, show expertise; cut one's coat according to one's cloth, play one's cards well

21 **be versatile,** double in brass *and* wear more than one hat <nf>

ADJS 22 **skillful, good,** goodish, excellent, **expert, proficient; dexterous,** callid <old>, good at, **adroit, deft, adept, coordinated,** well-coordinated, **apt,** no mean, **handy;** quick, ready; **clever,** cute *and* slick *and* slick as a whistle <nf>, neat, clean; fancy, graceful, stylish; some *or* quite some *or* quite a *or* every bit a <nf>; **masterly, masterful;** magistral, magisterial; authoritative, consummate, professional; the compleat *or* the complete; crack *or* crackerjack <nf>, ace, first-rate, supreme; whiz-kid <nf>; **virtuoso,** bravura, technically superb; **brilliant** 919.14; cunning 415.12; tactful, diplomatic, politic, statesmanlike; **ingenious,** resourceful, daedal, Daedalian; **artistic; workmanlike, well-done**

23 **agile, nimble, spry,** sprightly, fleet, featly, peart <nf>, light, graceful, nimble-footed, light-footed, sure-footed; nimble-fingered, neat-fingered, neat-handed

24 **competent, capable, able, efficient, qualified, fit, fitted, suited, worthy;** journeyman; fit *or* fitted for; **equal to, up to;** up to snuff <nf>, up to the mark <nf>, *au fait* <Fr>; well-qualified, well-fitted, well-suited

25 **versatile, ambidextrous,** two-handed, **all around** <nf>, broad-gauge, **well-rounded, many-sided,** generally capable; **adaptable,** adjustable, flexible, resourceful, supple, ready for anything; amphibious

26 **skilled, accomplished; practiced; professional,** career; trained, coached, prepared, primed, finished; at one's best, at concert pitch; initiated, initiate; technical; conversant

27 **skilled in,** proficient in, adept in, versed in, **good at,** expert at, **handy at, a hand** *or* **good hand at,** master of, strong in, at home in; **up on,** well up on, well-versed 928.20

28 **experienced, practiced,** mature, matured, ripe, ripened, **seasoned,** tried, well-tried, tried *and* true, **veteran,** old, an old dog at <nf>; sagacious 919.16; **worldly, worldly-wise,** world-wise, wise in the ways of the world, knowing, shrewd, **sophisticated,** cosmopolitan, cosmopolite, blasé, dry behind the ears, not born yesterday, long in the tooth; been there done that <nf>

29 **talented, gifted, endowed,** with a flair; born for, made for, cut out for <nf>, with an eye for, with an ear for, with a bump for <nf>

30 **well-laid, well-devised,** well-contrived, well-designed, well-planned, well-worked-out; well-invented, *ben trovato* <Ital>; **well-weighed, well-reasoned,** well-considered, well-thought-out; **cunning, clever**

ADVS 31 **skillfully, expertly, proficiently,** excellently, well; **cleverly,** neatly, ingeniously, resourcefully; cunningly 415.13; **dexterously, adroitly, deftly, adeptly,** aptly, handily; agilely, nimbly, featly, spryly; **competently, capably, ably,** efficiently; **masterfully;** brilliantly, superbly, with genius, with a touch of genius; **artistically,** artfully; with skill, with consummate skill, with finesse

414 UNSKILLFULNESS

NOUNS 1 **unskillfulness,** skill-lessness, **inexpertness, unproficiency, uncleverness;** unintelligence 922; inadeptness, **undexterousness,** indexterity, **undeftness;** inefficiency; **incompetence** *or* incompetency, **inability, incapability, incapacity,** inadequacy; ineffectiveness, **ineffectuality; mediocrity,** pedestrianism; **inaptitude,** inaptness, unaptness, ineptness, maladroitness; unfitness, unfittedness; untrainedness, unschooledness; thoughtlessness, inattentiveness; maladjustment; rustiness <nf>, nonuse

2 **inexperience,** unexperience, unexperiencedness, unpracticedness; **rawness, greenness,** unripeness, callowness, unfledgedness, unreadiness, immaturity; ignorance 930; **unfamiliarity,** unacquaintance, unacquaintedness, unaccustomedness; rawness, greenness, **amateurishness,** amateurism, unprofessionalness, unprofessionalism

3 **clumsiness, awkwardness,** bumblingness,

maladroitness, unhandiness, left-handedness, heavy-handedness, fumblitis *and* ham-handedness <nf>, ham-fistedness <Brit nf>; handful of thumbs; ungainliness, uncouthness, ungracefulness, gracelessness, inelegance; gawkiness, gawkishness; lubberliness, oafishness, loutishness, boorishness, clownishness, lumpishness; cumbersomeness, hulkiness, ponderousness; unwieldiness, unmanageability

4 bungling, blundering, boggling, fumbling, malperformance, muffing, botching, botchery, blunderheadedness; sloppiness, carelessness 340.2; too many cooks

5 bungle, blunder, botch, flub, boner *and* bonehead play <nf>, boggle, bobble *and* boo-boo *and* screw-up *and* ball-up *and* fuck-up <nf>, foozle <nf>, bevue; fumble, muff, fluff, flop, miscue <nf>, misfire, mishit; slip, trip, stumble; *gaucherie* and *étourderie* and *balourdise* <Fr>; hash *and* mess <nf>; bad job, sad work, clumsy performance, poor show *or* performance; off day; error, mistake 975.3

6 mismanagement, mishandling, misdirection, misguidance, misconduct, misgovernment, misrule; misadministration, maladministration; malfeasance, malpractice, misfeasance, wrongdoing 655; nonfeasance, omission, negligence, neglect 340.6; bad policy, impolicy, inexpedience *or* inexpediency 996

7 incompetent, incapable; dull tool, mediocrity, duffer *and* hacker <nf>, no great shakes, no prize, no prize package, no brain surgeon, no rocket scientist; no conjuror; one who will not set the Thames on fire <Brit>; greenhorn 930.8

8 bungler, blunderer, blunderhead, boggler, slubberer, bumbler, hack, fumbler, botcher; bull in a china shop, ox; lubber, lobby, lout, oaf, gawk, boor, clown, slouch; clodhopper, clodknocker, bumpkin, yokel; clod, clot <Brit>, dolt, blockhead 924.4; awkward squad; blind leading the blind

9 <nf terms> goof, goofer, goofball, goofus, foul-up, fuck-up, screw-up, bobbler, bonehead, dub, jerk, bozo, foozler, clumsy, fumble-fist, klutz, butterfingers, muff, muffer, stumblebum, stumblebunny, duffer, lummox, slob, lump; gowk <Brit>, rube, hick

VERBS 10 not know how, not have the knack, not have it in one <nf>; not be up to <nf>; not be versed; muddle along, pedestrianize; show one's ignorance, not have a clue <nf>

11 bungle, blunder, bumble, boggle, bobble, muff, muff one's cue *or* lines, fumble, be all thumbs, have a handful of thumbs; flounder, muddle, lumber; stumble, slip, trip, trip over one's own feet, get in one's own way, miss one's footing,

miscue; commit a faux pas, commit a gaffe; blunder on *or* upon *or* into; blunder away, be not one's day; botch, mar, spoil, butcher, murder, make sad work of; play havoc with, play mischief with

12 <nf terms> goof, pull a boner, bobble, lay an egg, put *or* stick one's foot in it, stub one's toe, step on one's schvantz *or* pecker, drop the ball, drop a pop-up, drop a brick, bonehead into it; blow, blow it, bitch, bitch up, hash up, mess up, flub, flub the dub, make a mess *or* hash of, make a faux pas, foul up, fuck up, goof up, bollix up, screw up, louse up, gum up, gum up the works, bugger, bugger up, play the deuce *or* devil *or* hell *or* merry hell with; go at it ass-backwards; put one's foot in one's mouth; self-destruct

13 mismanage, mishandle, misconduct, misdirect, misguide, misgovern, misrule; misadminister, maladminister; be negligent 340.6

14 not know what one is about, not know one's interest, lose one's touch, make an ass of oneself, make a fool of oneself, lose face, stultify oneself, have egg on one's face, put oneself out of court, stand in one's own light, not know on which side one's bread is buttered, not know one's ass from one's elbow *or* a hole in the ground, kill the goose that lays the golden egg, cut one's own throat, dig one's own grave, behave self-destructively, play with fire, burn one's fingers, jump out of the frying pan into the fire, lock the barn door after the horse is stolen, count one's chickens before they are hatched, buy a pig in a poke, aim at a pigeon and kill a crow, put the cart before the horse, put a square peg into a round hole, paint oneself into a corner, run before one can walk

ADJS 15 unskillful, skill-less, artless, inexpert, unproficient, unclever; inefficient; undexterous, undeft, inadept, unfacile; unapt, inapt, inept, hopeless, half-assed *and* clunky <nf>, poor; mediocre, pedestrian; thoughtless, inattentive; unintelligent 922.13

16 unskilled, unaccomplished, untrained, untaught, unschooled, untutored, uncoached, unimproved, uninitiated, unprepared, unprimed, unfinished, unpolished; untalented, ungifted, unendowed; amateurish, unprofessional, unbusinesslike, semiskilled

17 inexperienced, unexperienced, unversed, unconversant, unpracticed; undeveloped, unseasoned; raw, green, green as grass, unripe, callow, unfledged, immature, unmatured, fresh, wet behind the ears, not dry behind the ears, in training, untried; unskilled in, unpracticed in, unversed in, unconversant with, unaccustomed to, unused to, unfamiliar *or* unacquainted with, new

to, uninitiated in, a stranger to, a novice *or* tyro at; ignorant 930.12; semiskilled

18 out of practice, out of training *or* form, soft <nf>, out of shape *or* condition, stiff, **rusty;** gone *or* run to seed *and* over the hill *and* not what one used to be <nf>, losing one's touch, slipping, on the downgrade

19 incompetent, incapable, unable, inadequate, unequipped, unqualified, ill-qualified, out of one's depth, outmatched, **unfit, unfitted,** unadapted, not equal *or* up to, not cut out for <nf>; ineffective, **ineffectual;** unadjusted, maladjusted

20 bungling, blundering, blunderheaded, bumbling, fumbling, mistake-prone, accident-prone; **clumsy, awkward, uncoordinated,** maladroit, unhandy, left-hand, left-handed, heavy-handed, ham-handed <nf>, ham-fisted *and* cack-handed <Brit nf>, clumsy-fisted, butterfingered <nf>, **all thumbs,** fingers all thumbs, with a handful of thumbs; stiff; **ungainly,** uncouth, **ungraceful,** graceless, inelegant, *gauche* <Fr>; **gawky,** gawkish; **lubberly, loutish, oafish,** boorish, clownish, lumpish, slobbish <nf>; **sloppy, careless** 340.11; **ponderous, cumbersome,** lumbering, hulking, hulky; **unwieldy**

21 botched, bungled, fumbled, muffed, spoiled, **butchered,** murdered; **ill-managed,** ill-done, ill-conducted, ill-devised, ill-contrived, ill-executed; mismanaged, misconducted, **misdirected, misguided;** impolitic, ill-considered, ill-advised; negligent 340.10

22 <nf terms> **goofed-up, bobbled,** bitched, bitched-up, hashed-up, **messed-up, fouled-up, fucked-up, screwed-up, bollixed-up, loused-up,** gummed-up, buggered, buggered-up, snafued; clunky, half-assed; ass-backwards

ADVS **23 unskillfully, inexpertly, unproficiently, uncleverly;** inefficiently; **incompetently, incapably,** inadequately, unfitly; **undexterously, undeftly, inadeptly,** unfacilely; **unaptly, inaptly, ineptly,** poorly

24 clumsily, awkwardly; bunglingly, blunderingly; maladroitly, unhandily; ungracefully, gracelessly, inelegantly, uncouthly; **ponderously, cumbersomely,** lumberingly, hulkingly, hulkily; ass-backwards <nf>

415 CUNNING

NOUNS **1 cunning,** cunningness, **craft, craftiness,** callidity <old>, **artfulness, art, artifice, wiliness,** wiles, guile, **slyness,** insidiousness, suppleness <Scot>, **foxiness,** slipperiness, shiftiness, trickiness; low cunning, animal cunning; gamesmanship *and* one-upmanship <nf>; **canniness, shrewdness,** sharpness, acuteness,

astuteness, **cleverness** 413.1; **resourcefulness, ingeniousness, wit,** inventiveness, readiness; subtlety, subtleness, Italian hand, fine Italian hand, finesse, restraint; acuteness, cuteness *and* cutification <nf>; Jesuitism, Jesuitry, **sophistry** 936; satanic cunning, the cunning of the serpent; sneakiness, concealment, **stealthiness, stealth** 345.4; cageyness <nf>, wariness 494.2

2 Machiavellianism, Machiavellism; realpolitik; **politics, diplomacy,** diplomatics; jobbery, jobbing

3 stratagem, artifice, art <old>, **craft, wile,** strategy, maneuver, **device,** wily device, **contrivance, expedient, design, scheme, trick,** cute trick, fetch, fakement <nf>, gimmick <nf>, **ruse, red herring, shift,** tactic, **maneuver, stroke,** stroke of policy, master stroke, **move,** coup, gambit, **ploy, dodge,** artful dodge; **game,** little game, racket *and* grift <nf>; **plot,** conspiracy, **intrigue;** sleight, feint, jugglery; method in one's madness; **subterfuge,** blind, dust in the eyes; chicanery, knavery, deceit, trickery 356.4

4 machination, manipulation, wire-pulling <nf>; influence, political influence, behind-the-scenes influence *or* pressure; **maneuvering,** maneuvers, tactical maneuvers; **tactics,** devices, expedients, gimmickry <nf>; web of deceit

5 circumvention, getting round *or* around; **evasion,** elusion, the slip <nf>, pretext; the runaround *and* buck-passing *and* passing the buck <nf>; **frustration, foiling, thwarting** 1012.3; **outwitting,** outsmarting, outguessing, **outmaneuvering**

6 slyboots, sly dog <nf>, **fox,** reynard, dodger, Artful Dodger <Charles Dickens>, crafty rascal, smooth *or* slick citizen <nf>, smooth *or* cool customer <nf>, smoothy, glib tongue, smooth *or* sweet talker, smoothie <nf>, charmer; **trickster,** shyster <nf>, shady character, Philadelphia lawyer <nf>; horse trader, Yankee horse trader, wheeler-dealer; **swindler** 357.3

7 strategist, tactician; maneuverer, machinator, manipulator, wire-puller <nf>; calculator, schemer, **intriguer**

8 Machiavellian, Machiavel, Machiavellianist; **diplomat,** diplomatist, **politician** 610; political realist; influence peddler; powerbroker, kingmaker; power behind the throne, gray eminence, *éminence grise* <Fr>

VERBS **9 live by one's wits,** fly by the seat of one's pants, play a deep game; use one's fine Italian hand, finesse; shift, dodge, twist and turn, zig and zag; have something up one's sleeve, hide one's hand, cover one's path, have an out *or* a way out *or* an escape hatch; **trick,** deceive 356.14

10 maneuver, manipulate, pull strings *or* wires; **machinate, contrive,** angle <nf>, **jockey, engineer;**

play games <nf>; **plot, scheme, intrigue; finagle, wangle;** gerrymander; know a trick or two

11 **outwit, outfox, outsmart,** outguess, outfigure, **outmaneuver,** outgeneral, outflank, outplay, be one up on; get the better *or* best of, go one better, know a trick worth two of that; play one's trump card; **overreach,** outreach; **circumvent,** get round *or* around, **evade,** stonewall <nf>, **elude, frustrate, foil,** give the slip *or* runaround <nf>; pass the buck <nf>; pull a fast one <nf>, steal a march on; make a fool of, make a sucker *or* patsy of <nf>; be too much for, be too deep for; throw a curve <nf>, **deceive, victimize** 356.18

ADJS 12 **cunning, crafty, artful, wily,** callid <old>, guileful, **sly,** insidious, **shifty,** pawky <Brit>, arch, **smooth, slick** *and* slick as a whistle <nf>, **slippery,** snaky, serpentine, **foxy,** vulpine, feline, no flies on <nf>; **canny, shrewd,** knowing, sharp, razor-sharp, cute *or* cutesy *or* cutesy-poo <nf>, acute, astute, **clever;** resourceful, ingenious, inventive, ready; subtle; Jesuitical, **sophistical** 936.10; **tricky,** trickish, tricksy <old>, gimmicky <nf>; **Machiavellian,** Machiavellic, politic, diplomatic; strategic, tactical; deep, deep-laid; cunning as a fox *or* serpent, crazy like a fox <nf>, slippery as an eel, too clever by half; sneaky, clandestine, **stealthy** 345.12; cagey <nf>, wary 494.9; **scheming, designing; manipulative,** manipulatory; **deceitful**

ADVS 13 **cunningly, craftily, artfully,** wilily, guilefully, insidiously, shiftily, foxily, trickily, smoothly, slick <nf>; **slyly,** on the sly; **cannily, shrewdly,** knowingly, astutely, **cleverly;** subtly; cagily <nf>, warily 494.13; diplomatically

416 ARTLESSNESS

NOUNS 1 **artlessness, ingenuousness, guilelessness; simplicity,** simpleness, plainness; simpleheartedness, simplemindedness; **unsophistication,** unsophisticatedness; *naïveté* <Fr>, naivety, naiveness, childlikeness; **innocence;** trustfulness, trustingness, unguardedness, unwariness, unsuspiciousness; **openness,** openheartedness, sincerity, **candor** 644.4; **integrity,** single-heartedness, single-mindedness, singleness of heart; directness, bluffness, bluntness, outspokenness

2 **naturalness,** naturalism, nature; state of nature; unspoiledness; **unaffectedness,** unaffection, **unassumingness,** unpretendingness, unpretentiousness, undisguise; **inartificiality,** unartificialness, genuineness

3 **simple soul,** unsophisticate, naïf, **ingenue, innocent,** pure heart, **child,** mere child, infant, **babe,** baby, newborn babe, babe in the woods, lamb, dove; child of nature, noble savage; primitive; yokel, rube *and* hick <nf>; oaf, lout 924.5; dupe 358

VERBS 4 wear one's heart on one's sleeve, look one in the face, have no affectations

ADJS 5 **artless, simple,** plain, **guideless;** simplehearted, simpleminded; **ingenuous,** *ingénu* <Fr>; **unsophisticated, naive;** childlike, born yesterday; **innocent;** trustful, trusting, unguarded, unwary, unreserved, confiding, unsuspicious, on the up and up; **open,** openhearted, sincere, candid, **frank** 644.17; single-hearted, single-minded; direct, bluff, blunt, outspoken

6 **natural,** naturelike, native; in the state of nature; primitive, primal, pristine, unspoiled, untainted, uncontaminated; **unaffected, unassuming, unpretending,** unpretentious, unfeigning, undisguising, undissimulating, undissembling, undesigning; **genuine, inartificial,** unartificial, unadorned, unvarnished, unembellished, uncontrived; homespun; **pastoral, rural,** arcadian, bucolic

ADVS 7 **artlessly, ingenuously, guilelessly;** simply, plainly; naturally, genuinely; naïvely; openly, openheartedly

417 AUTHORITY

NOUNS 1 **authority, prerogative, right, power,** faculty, competence *or* competency; **mandate,** popular authority *or* mandate, people's mandate, electoral mandate; regality, royal prerogative, constituted authority, vested authority; inherent authority; legal *or* lawful *or* rightful authority, legitimacy, law, eminent domain, divine right; derived *or* delegated authority, vicarious authority, indirect authority, constituted *or* invested authority, inherent authority; **the say** *and* **the say-so** <nf>; rubber stamp; divine right, *jus divinum* <L>; absolute power, absolutism 612.9

2 **authoritativeness, authority, power,** powerfulness, magisterialness, **potency** *or* potence, puissance, **strength,** might, mightiness, string pulling, wire pulling, clout <nf>

3 **authoritativeness, masterfulness, lordliness,** magistrality, magisterialness; **arbitrariness,** peremptoriness, imperativeness, **imperiousness,** autocraticalness, high-handedness, dictatorialness, overbearingness, overbearance, overbearing, domineering, domineeringness, tyrannicalness, authoritarianism, bossism <nf>

4 **prestige, authority, influence,** influentialness; pressure, **weight,** weightiness, moment, **consequence;** eminence, **stature,** rank, seniority,

preeminence, priority, precedence; **greatness** 247; **importance, prominence** 997.2

5 **governance, authority, jurisdiction, control, command, power, rule, reign,** regnancy, **dominion, sovereignty,** empire, empery, *raj* <India>, imperium, **sway;** government 612; administration, disposition 573.3; **control, grip,** claws, **clutches,** hand, hands, iron hand, talons

6 **dominance** or dominancy, **dominion, domination; preeminence, supremacy, superiority** 249; **ascendance** or **ascendancy; upper** or **whip hand, sway; sovereignty,** suzerainty, suzerainship, **overlordship;** primacy, principality, **predominance** or predominancy, predomination, prepotence or prepotency, hegemony; preponderance; balance of power; eminent domain

7 **mastership,** masterhood, masterdom, **mastery; leadership, headship, lordship;** hegemony; supervisorship, directorship 573.4; hierarchy, nobility, aristocracy, **ruling class** 575.15; chair, chairmanship; chieftainship, chieftaincy, chieftainry, chiefery; presidentship, presidency; premiership, prime-ministership, prime-ministry; governorship; princeship, princedom, principality; rectorship, rectorate; suzerainty, suzerainship; regency, regentship; prefectship, prefecture; proconsulship, proconsulate; provostship, provostry; protectorship, protectorate; seneschalship, seneschalsy; pashadom, pashalic; sheikhdom; emirate, viziership, vizierate; magistrateship, magistrature, magistracy; mayorship, mayoralty; sheriffdom, sheriffcy, sheriffalty, shrievalty; consulship, consulate; chancellorship, chancellery, chancellorate; seigniory; tribunate, aedileship; deanship, decanal authority, deanery; patriarchate, patriarchy <old>; bishopric, episcopacy; archbishopric, archiepiscopacy, archiepiscopate; metropolitanship, metropolitanate; popedom, popeship, popehood, papacy, pontificate, pontificality; dictatorship, dictature

8 **sovereignty, royalty,** regnancy, **majesty,** empire, empery, imperialism, **emperorship; kingship,** kinghood; queenship, queenhood; kaisership, kaiserdom; czardom; rajaship; sultanship, sultanate; caliphate; the throne, the Crown, the purple; royal insignia 647.3

9 **scepter, rod, staff,** wand, staff or rod or wand of office, baton, mace, truncheon, fasces; crosier, crook, cross-staff; caduceus; gavel; mantle; chain of office; portfolio

10 <seat of authority> **saddle** <nf>, **helm, driver's seat** <nf>; office of power, high office; seat, **chair,** bench; woolsack <Brit>; seat of state, seat of power; curule chair; dais; chairmanship, directorship, chieftainship, presidency, premiership, secretariat, governorship, mayoralty; consulate, proconsulate, prefecture, magistry

11 **throne,** royal seat; *musnud* or *gaddi* <India>; Peacock throne

12 <acquisition of authority> **accession; succession,** rightful or legitimate succession; **usurpation,** arrogation, assumption, taking over, seizure, seizure of power, takeover, coup d'etat, coup, revolution, overthrowing; anointment, anointing, consecration, coronation; selection, **delegation,** deputation, devolution, devolvement, assignment, nomination, **appointment; election,** mandate; **authorization,** empowerment, permission, grant, sanction, warrant, license, charter; consignation; job sharing

VERBS 13 **possess** or **wield** or **have authority, have power,** have the power, have in one's hands, have the right, have the say or say-so <nf>, have the whip hand, wear the crown, hold the prerogative, have the mandate; exercise sovereignty; be vested or invested, carry authority, have clout <nf>, have what one says go, have one's own way; show one's authority, crack the whip, throw one's weight around and ride herd <nf>, have under one's thumb, wear the pants, have over a barrel <nf>; **rule** 612.14, **control,** govern; supervise 573.10

14 **take command, take charge, take over,** take the helm, take the reins of government, take the reins into one's hand, take office, gain authority, get the power into one's hands, gain or get the upper hand, lead, take the lead; ascend or mount or succeed or accede to the throne, call the shots <nf>; **assume command,** assume, **usurp,** arrogate, seize; usurp or seize the throne or crown or mantle, usurp the prerogatives of the crown; seize power, execute a *coup d'état*

ADJS 15 **authoritative,** clothed or vested or invested with authority, **commanding, imperative; governing, controlling, ruling** 612.18; **preeminent, supreme,** administrative, managerial, bureaucratic, ruling, leading, **superior** 249.12; **powerful, potent,** puissant, mighty; dominant, ascendant, hegemonic, hegemonistic; **influential, prestigious, weighty,** momentous, consequential, eminent, substantial, considerable; great 247.6; important, prominent; ranking, senior; authorized, empowered, duly constituted, competent; **official,** *ex officio* <L>; authoritarian; absolute, autocratic, monocratic; **totalitarian**

16 **imperious,** imperial, **masterful,** authoritative, feudal, aristocratic, **lordly,** magistral, **magisterial,** commanding; arrogant 141.9; **arbitrary, peremptory,** imperative; absolute, absolutist, absolutistic; **dictatorial, authoritarian; bossy** <nf>,

domineering, high-handed, overbearing,
overruling, imperious; autocratic, monocratic,
despotic, tyrannical; tyrannous, grinding,
oppressive 98.24; repressive, suppressive 428.11;
strict, severe 425.6

17 sovereign; regal, royal, majestic, purple; kinglike,
kingly, "every inch a king"—Shakespeare; imperial,
imperious or imperatorious <old>; imperatorial;
monarchic or monarchical, monarchal,
monarchial; tetrarchic; princely, princelike;
queenly, queenlike; dynastic

ADVS 18 authoritatively, with authority, by virtue of
office; commandingly, imperatively; powerfully,
potently, puissantly, mightily; influentially,
weightily, momentously, consequentially; officially,
ex cathedra <L>

19 imperiously, masterfully, magisterially; arbitrarily,
peremptorily; autocratically, dictatorially, high-
handedly, domineeringly, overbearingly,
despotically, tyrannically

20 by authority of, in the name of, in or by virtue of,
by the power vested in

21 in authority, in power, in charge, in control, in
command, at the reins, at the head, at the helm, at
the wheel, in the saddle or driver's seat <nf>, on
the throne

418 LAWLESSNESS
<absence of authority>

NOUNS 1 lawlessness; licentiousness, license,
uncontrol, anything goes, unrestraint 430.3;
indiscipline, insubordination, mutiny,
disobedience 327; permissiveness; irresponsibility,
unaccountability; willfulness, unchecked or
rampant will; interregnum, power vacuum;
defiance of authority, lack of authority, breakdown
of authority, breakdown of law and order;
overthrow, coup, coup d'état

2 anarchy, anarchism; disorderliness, unruliness,
misrule, disorder, disruption, disorganization,
confusion, arrogation, unruliness, riot, turmoil,
chaos, primal chaos, tohubohu; antinomianism;
nihilism; syndicalism and anarcho-syndicalism and
criminal syndicalism <old>, lynch law, mob rule
or law, mobocracy, ochlocracy; law of the jungle;
dog eat dog; subversion, sedition, unrestraint,
insubordination, disobedience, revolution 860;
rebellion 327.4

3 anarchist, anarch; antinomian; nihilist, syndicalist
and anarcho-syndicalist <old>; subversive,
seditionary; revolutionist 860.3; mutineer, rebel
327.5

VERBS 4 reject or defy authority, usurp power or
authority, enthrone one's own will; take the law in

one's own hands, act on one's own responsibility;
do or go as one pleases, indulge oneself; be a law
unto oneself, answer to no man, undermine,
arrogate; resist control; overthrow, depose, topple;
"swear allegiance to the words of no master"—
Horace

ADJS 5 lawless; licentious, ungoverned, undisciplined,
unrestrained; permissive; insubordinate, mutinous,
disobedient 327.8; uncontrolled, uncurbed,
unbridled, unchecked, rampant, untrammeled,
unreined, unrestrained, reinless, anything goes;
irresponsible, wildcat, unaccountable; selfwilled,
willful, headstrong, heady, defiant; rebellious,
riotous, seditious, insurgent

6 anarchic, anarchical, anarchial, anarchistic;
unruly, disorderly, disorganized, chaotic;
antinomian; nihilistic, syndicalistic, ochlocratic,
mobocratic; every man for himself, ungovernable

ADVS 7 lawlessly, licentiously; anarchically,
chaotically

419 PRECEPT

NOUNS 1 precept, prescript, prescription, teaching;
instruction, direction, charge, commission,
injunction, dictate; order, command 420

2 rule, law, canon, maxim, dictum, moral, moralism;
norm, standard; formula, form; rule of action or
conduct, moral precept; commandment, mitzvah
<Heb>; tradition; ordinance, imperative,
regulation, reg <nf>, règlement <Fr>; principle,
principium, settled principle, general principle or
truth, tenet, convention; guideline, ground rule,
rubric, protocol, working rule, working principle,
standard procedure; guiding principle, golden rule;
code; gold standard

3 formula, form <old>, recipe, receipt; prescription;
formulary

ADJS 4 preceptive, didactic, instructive, moralistic,
prescriptive; prescript, prescribed, mandatory,
hard-and-fast, binding, dictated; formulary,
standard, regulation, official, authoritative,
canonical, statutory, rubric, rubrical, protocolary,
protocolic; normative; conventional; traditional

420 COMMAND

NOUNS 1 command, commandment, order, direct
order, command decision, bidding, behest, hest
<old>, imperative, dictate, dictation, will,
pleasure, say-so <nf>, word, word of command,
mot d'ordre <Fr>; special order; authority 417

2 injunction, charge, commission, mandate

3 direction, directive, instruction, rule, regulation;
prescript, prescription, precept 419; general order

4 decree, decreement <old>, decretum, decretal, rescript, fiat, **edict,** *edictum* <L>; **law** 673.3; **rule, ruling,** dictum, ipse dixit; ordinance, *ordonnance* <Fr>, appointment <old>; **proclamation,** pronouncement, pronunciamento, **declaration,** ukase; bull, brevet <old>; decree-law, *décret-loi* <Fr>; *senatus consultum* <L>, senatus consult; diktat

5 summons, bidding, beck, call, calling, nod, **beck and call,** preconization; **convocation,** convoking; evocation, calling forth, invocation; requisition, indent <chiefly Brit>

6 court order, injunction, legal order, warrant, subpoena, citation, injunction, interdict *or* interdiction

7 process server, summoner

VERBS **8 command, order, dictate, direct, instruct,** mandate, **bid, enjoin, charge,** commission, call on *or* upon; issue a writ *or* an injunction; **decree, rule, ordain,** promulgate; give an order *or* a direct order, issue a command, say the word, give the word *or* word of command; call the shots *or* tune *or* signals *or* play <nf>; order about *or* around; **speak, proclaim, declare,** pronounce 352.12

9 prescribe, require, demand, dictate, impose, lay down, set, fix, appoint, make obligatory *or* mandatory; decide once and for all, carve in stone, set in concrete <nf>; authorize 443.11

10 lay down the law, put one's foot down <nf>, read the riot act, lower the boom <nf>, set the record straight

11 summon, call, demand, preconize; call for, send for *or* after, bid come; **cite, summons** <nf>, **subpoena,** serve; page; convoke, convene, call together; call away; muster, invoke, conjure; order up, summon up, muster up, call up, conjure up, magic *or* magic up <Brit>; evoke, call forth, summon forth, call out; recall, call back, call in; requisition, indent <chiefly Brit>

ADJS **12 mandatory,** mandated, **imperative, compulsory,** prescript, prescriptive, **obligatory,** must <nf>; dictated, imposed, required, entailed, decretory; decisive, final, peremptory, absolute, eternal, written, hard-and-fast, carved in stone, set in concrete <nf>, ultimate, conclusive, binding, irrevocable, without appeal

13 commanding, imperious, imperative, jussive, peremptory, abrupt; **directive, instructive; mandating,** dictating, compelling, obligating, **prescriptive,** preceptive; decretory, decretive, decretal; **authoritative** 417.15

ADVS **14 commandingly, imperatively,** peremptorily

15 by order *or* **command,** at the word of command, as ordered *or* required, to order; mandatorily, compulsorily, obligatorily

421 DEMAND

NOUNS **1 demand, claim, call; requisition,** requirement, stated requirement, order, rush order, indent <chiefly Brit>; seller's market, land-office business; strong *or* heavy demand, draft, drain, levy, tax, taxing; imposition, impost, tribute, duty, contribution; insistent demand, rush; exorbitant *or* extortionate demand, exaction, extortion, blackmail; **ultimatum,** nonnegotiable demand; notice, warning 399

2 stipulation, provision, proviso, condition; **terms;** exception, reservation; **qualification** 959

3 <nf terms> **catch, Catch-22,** kicker, zinger, snag, joker; strings, strings attached; ifs, ands, and buts; whereases, howevers, howsomevers

4 insistence, exigence, importunity, importunateness, importunacy, **demandingness,** pertinaciousness, pertinacity; pressure, pressingness, **urgency, exigency** 996.4; **persistence** 360.1

VERBS **5 demand, ask, ask for,** make a demand; **call for,** call on *or* upon one for, appeal to one for; call out for, cry *or* cry out for, clamor for; **claim,** challenge, **require;** levy, **impose,** impose on one for; **exact, extort,** squeeze, screw; blackmail; requisition, make *or* put in **requisition,** indent <chiefly Brit>, **confiscate; order,** put in *or* place an order, order up; deliver *or* issue an ultimatum; warn 399.5

6 claim, pretend to, lay claim to, stake a claim <nf>, put *or* have dibs on <nf>, assert *or* vindicate a claim *or* right *or* title to; have going for it *or* one <nf>; **challenge**

7 stipulate, stipulate for, specifically provide, set conditions *or* terms, make reservations; **qualify** 959.3

8 insist, insist on *or* **upon,** stick to <nf>, set one's heart *or* mind upon; **take one's stand upon,** stand on *or* upon, put *or* lay it on the line <nf>, make no bones about it; stand upon one's rights, **put one's foot down** <nf>; brook *or* take no denial, not take no for an answer; **maintain, contend,** assert; urge, press 375.14; **persist** 360.2

ADJS **9 demanding, exacting,** exigent; draining, taxing, exorbitant, extortionate, grasping; **insistent,** instant, **importunate,** urgent, pertinacious, pressing, loud, clamant, crying, clamorous; persistent

10 claimed, spoken for; requisitioned; requisitorial, requisitory

ADVS **11 demandingly, exactingly,** exigently; exorbitantly, extortionately; **insistently, importunately, urgently,** pressingly, clamorously, loudly, clamantly

12 on demand, at demand, **on call,** upon presentation

422 ADVICE

NOUNS 1 advice, counsel, recommendation, suggestion, rede <Brit>; proposition, proposal; advising, advocacy; **direction, instruction,** guidance, briefing; **exhortation,** hortation <old>, enjoinder, expostulation, remonstrance; **sermons,** sermonizing, preaching, preachiness; **admonition,** monition, monitory *or* monitory letter, caution, caveat, **warning** 399; **idea,** thought, opinion 953.6, precept; consultancy, consultantship, **consultation,** parley 541.6, advisement; council 423; **counseling;** guidance counseling, educational counseling, vocational guidance; constructive criticism

2 piece of advice, **word of advice, word to the wise,** words of wisdom, pearls of wisdom, *verbum sapienti* <L>, verb *or* verbum sap <nf>, word in the ear, maxim, **hint, broad hint, flea in the ear** <nf>, **tip** <nf>, one's two cents' worth <nf>, intimation, insinuation

3 adviser, counsel, counselor, consultant, professional consultant, expert, maven <nf>, boffin <Brit nf>; instructor, guide, **mentor,** nestor, orienter; confidant *or* confidante, personal adviser; admonisher, monitor, Dutch uncle; Polonius <Shakespeare>, preceptist; **teacher** 571; meddler, buttinsky *and* yenta *and* kibitzer *and* backseat driver <nf>; advocate

4 advisee, counselee; client

VERBS 5 advise, counsel, recommend, suggest, advocate, propose, submit, propound; instruct, coach, guide, direct, brief; prescribe; weigh in with advice <nf>, give a piece of advice, give a hint *or* broad hint, hint at, intimate, insinuate, put a flea in one's ear <nf>, have a word with one, speak words of wisdom; meddle, kibitz <nf>; confer, consult with 541.11

6 admonish, exhort, expostulate, remonstrate, preach; **enjoin, charge,** call upon one to; caution, issue a caveat, wag one's finger <nf>; advise against, warn away, warn off, **warn** 399.5,6, dissuade; move, prompt, **urge, incite, encourage, induce, persuade** 375.23; **implore** 440.11

7 take *or* **accept advice, follow advice,** follow, follow implicitly, go along with <nf>, buy *or* buy into <nf>; consult, confer; solicit advice, desire guidance, implore counsel; **be advised by;** refer to, have at one's elbow, take one's cue from; seek a second opinion; put heads together *or* have a powwow with <nf>, huddle

ADJS 8 advisory, recommendatory; **consultative,** consultatory; directive, instructive; **admonitory,** monitory, monitorial, cautionary, **warning** 399.7; **expostulative,** expostulatory, **remonstrative,** remonstratory, remonstrant; **exhortative,** exhortatory, hortative, hortatory, preachy <nf>, **didactic,** moralistic, sententious

PHRS 9 too many cooks spoil the broth, another country heard from

423 COUNCIL

NOUNS 1 council, conclave, *concilium* <L>, deliberative *or* advisory body, **assembly;** deliberative assembly, consultative assembly; chamber, house; **board,** court, bench; **full assembly,** plenum, plenary session; **congress,** diet, synod, senate, soviet; **legislature** 613; **cabinet,** divan, council of ministers, council of state, US Cabinet, British Cabinet; kitchen cabinet, camarilla; staff; junta, directory; Sanhedrin; privy council; common council, county council, parish council, borough *or* town council, city *or* municipal council, village council; brain trust <nf>, brains trust <Brit nf>, group *or* corps *or* body of advisers, inner circle; council of war; council fire; syndicate, **association** 617; **conference** 541.6; **assembly** 770.2; **tribunal** 595

2 committee, subcommittee, standing committee; select committee, special committee, ad hoc committee; committee of one

3 forum, conference, discussion group, buzz session <nf>, **round table, panel;** open forum, colloquium, symposium; town meeting; board meeting; **powwow** <nf>; working lunch, power lunch, power breakfast

4 ecclesiastical council, chapter, classis, conclave, conference, caucus, congregation, consistory, convention, convocation, presbytery, session, synod, vestry; parochial council, parochial church council; diocesan conference, diocesan court; provincial court, plenary council; ecumenical council; Council of Nicaea, Council of Trent, Lateran Council, Vatican Council, Vatican Two; conciliarism

ADJS 5 conciliar, council, councilmanic, aldermanic; **consultative, deliberative, advisory;** synodal, synodic, synodical

ADVS 6 in council, in conference, in consultation, in a huddle <nf>, in conclave; **in session,** sitting

424 COMPULSION

NOUNS 1 compulsion, obligation, obligement; **command** 420; **necessity** 963; **inevitability** 963.7; **irresistibility, compulsiveness; forcing,** enforcement; command performance; **constraint,** coaction; **restraint** 428; obsession

2 force, *ultima ratio* <L>; **brute force,** naked force, rule of might, big battalions, **main force,** physical force; the right of the strong, the law of the jungle; **tyranny** 612.10; steamroller <nf>, irresistible force

3 coercion, intimidation, scare tactics, headbanging *and* arm-twisting <nf>, **duress; the strong arm** *and* strong-arm tactics <nf>, a pistol *or* gun to one's head, the sword, the mailed fist, the bludgeon, the boot in the face, the jackboot, the big stick, the club, *argumentum baculinum* <L>; **pressure, high pressure,** high-pressure methods; **violence** 671; impressment

VERBS **4 compel, force, make;** have, cause, cause to; **constrain, bind,** tie, tie one's hands; **restrain** 428.7; enforce, **drive,** impel; dragoon, use force upon, force one's hand, hold a pistol *or* gun to one's head; browbeat

5 oblige, necessitate, require, exact, demand, **dictate,** impose, call for; take *or* brook no denial; leave no option *or* escape, admit of no option

6 press; bring pressure to bear upon, put pressure on, bear down on, bear against, bear hard upon, put under duress

7 coerce, use violence, ride roughshod, intimidate, bully, bludgeon, blackjack; hijack, shanghai, dragoon, carjack

8 <nf terms> twist one's arm, arm-twist, twist arms, knock *or* **bang heads,** knock *or* bang heads together, strong-arm, steamroller, bulldoze, **pressure,** high-pressure, lean on, squeeze; put the screws on *or* to, get one over a barrel *or* under one's thumb, hold one's feet to the fire, turn on the heat; pull rank; ram *or* cram down one's throat

9 be compelled, be coerced, have to 963.10; be stuck with <nf>, can't help but

ADJS **10 compulsory, compulsive,** compulsatory, **compelling; pressing, driving,** imperative, imperious; constraining, coactive; **restraining** 428.11; **irresistible**

11 obligatory, compulsory, imperative, mandatory, required, dictated, **binding;** involuntary; **necessary** 963.12; **inevitable** 962.15

12 coercive, forcible; steamroller *and* bulldozer *and* sledgehammer *and* strong-arm <nf>; violent

ADVS **13 compulsively,** compulsorily, **compellingly,** imperatively, imperiously

14 forcibly, by force, by main force, by *force majeure,* by a strong arm; by force of arms, *vi et armis* <L>, at gunpoint, with a pistol *or* gun to one's head, at the point of a gun, at the point of the sword *or* bayonet, at bayonet point

15 obligatorily, compulsorily, mandatorily, by stress of, under press of; under the lash *or* gun; of necessity

425 STRICTNESS

NOUNS **1 strictness, severity, harshness, stringency,** astringency, **hard line; discipline,** strict *or* tight *or* rigid discipline, regimentation, spit and polish; **austerity, sternness,** grimness, ruggedness, **toughness** <nf>; **belt-tightening;** Spartanism; authoritarianism; demandingness, exactingness; **meticulousness** 339.3

2 firmness, rigor, rigorousness, rigidness, rigidity, stiffness, **hardness,** obduracy, obdurateness, **inflexibility,** inexorability, unyieldingness, unbendingness, impliability, unrelentingness, **relentlessness; uncompromisingness;** stubbornness, obstinacy 361; purism; precisianism, puritanism, fundamentalism, orthodoxy

3 firm hand, iron hand, heavy hand, strong hand, tight hand, tight rein; tight *or* taut ship

VERBS **4 hold** *or* **keep a tight hand upon,** keep a firm hand on, keep a tight rein on, rule with an iron hand, rule with a rod of iron, knock *or* bang heads together <nf>; regiment, discipline; run a tight *or* taut ship, ride herd, keep one in line; maintain the highest standards, not spare oneself nor anyone else, go out of one's way, go the extra mile <nf>

5 deal hardly *or* **harshly with,** deal hard measure to, lay a heavy hand on, bear hard upon, **take a hard line,** not pull one's punches <nf>

ADJS **6 strict, exacting,** exigent, demanding, not to be trifled with, **stringent,** astringent; disciplined, spit-and-polish; **severe, harsh,** dour, unsparing; **stern, grim, austere,** rugged, **tough** <nf>; Spartan, Spartanic; **hard-line,** authoritarian 417.16; **meticulous** 339.12

7 firm, rigid, rigorous, rigorist, rigoristic, stiff, **hard,** iron, steel, steely, hard-shell, obdurate, **inflexible,** ironhanded, inexorable, dour, **unyielding,** unbending, impliable, **relentless,** unrelenting, procrustean; **uncompromising;** stubborn, obstinate 361.8; purist, puristic; puritan, puritanic, puritanical, fundamentalist, orthodox; ironbound, rockbound, musclebound, ironclad <nf>; straitlaced, hidebound

ADVS **8 strictly, severely, stringently, harshly;** sternly, grimly, **austerely,** ruggedly, toughly <nf>

9 firmly, rigidly, rigorously, stiffly, stiff, hardly, obdurately, **inflexibly,** impliably, inexorably, unyieldingly, unbendingly; **uncompromisingly, relentlessly,** unrelentingly; ironhandedly, with a firm *or* a strong *or* a heavy *or* a tight *or* an iron hand

426 LAXNESS

NOUNS **1 laxness, laxity, slackness, looseness,** relaxedness; loosening, relaxation; imprecision, sloppiness <nf>, carelessness, remissness, negligence 340.1; indifference 102; weakness 16; impotence 19; unrestraint 430.3

2 unstrictness, nonstrictness, undemandingness, unsevereness, unharshness; leniency 427; **permissiveness,** overpermissiveness, overindulgence, **softness;** unsternness, unaustereness; easygoingness, easiness; **flexibility,** pliancy

VERBS **3 hold a loose rein, give free rein to,** give the reins to, **give one his head,** give a free course to, give rope enough to; permit all *or* anything

ADJS **4 lax, slack, loose,** relaxed; imprecise, sloppy <nf>, careless, slipshod; remiss, negligent 340.10; indifferent 102.6; weak 16.12; impotent 19.13; untrammeled, unrestrained

5 unstrict, undemanding, **unexacting; unsevere, unharsh; unstern,** unaustere; lenient 427.7; **permissive,** overpermissive, overindulgent, **soft;** easy, easygoing, laid-back <nf>; **flexible,** pliant, yielding

427 LENIENCY

NOUNS **1 leniency** *or* lenience, lenientness, lenity; **clemency,** clementness, **mercifulness,** mercy, **humaneness,** humanity, pity, **compassion** 145.1; **mildness, gentleness,** tenderness, softness, moderateness; **easiness,** easygoingness; laxness 426; **forebearance,** forbearing, patience 134; acceptance, **tolerance** 979.4; kid gloves, kid-glove treatment, light hand *or* rein

2 compliance, complaisance, obligingness, accommodatingness, **agreeableness;** affability, graciosity, graciousness, generousness, decency, amiability; kindness, kindliness, benignity, **benevolence** 143

3 indulgence, humoring, obliging; favoring, gratification, pleasing; **pampering,** cosseting, **coddling,** mollycoddling, petting, **spoiling; permissiveness,** overpermissiveness, overindulgence; sparing the rod; laissez faire

4 spoiled child *or* **brat,** *enfant gâté* <Fr>, pampered darling, mama's boy, mollycoddle, sissy; *enfant terrible* <Fr>, naughty child

VERBS **5 be** *or* **go easy on,** ease up on, handle with kid *or* velvet gloves, use a light hand *or* rein, slap one's wrist, spare the rod, let off the hook; **tolerate,** bear with 134.5

6 indulge, humor, oblige; favor, please, gratify, satisfy, **cater to; give way to,** yield to, let one have his own way; **pamper,** cosset, **coddle,** mollycoddle, pet, make a lap dog of, **spoil;** spare the rod; make few demands

ADJS **7 lenient, mild, gentle,** mild-mannered, tender, humane, compassionate, **clement,** merciful 145.7; soft, moderate, **easy,** easygoing; lax 426.4; forgiving 148.6; **forebearing, forbearant,** patient 134.9; accepting, **tolerant** 979.11

8 indulgent, compliant, complaisant, **obliging, accommodating, agreeable,** amiable, gracious, generous, magnanimous, benignant, affable, decent, kind, kindly, benign, benevolent 143.15; **hands-off** <nf>, permissive, overpermissive, overindulgent, spoiling

9 indulged, pampered, coddled, spoiled, spoiled rotten <nf>

428 RESTRAINT

NOUNS **1 restraint, constraint; inhibition;** legal restraint, injunction, enjoining, enjoinder, interdict, veto; **control, curb, check,** rein, arrest, arrestation; **retardation,** deceleration, slowing down; cooling *and* cooling off *and* cooling down <nf>; retrenchment, curtailment; self-control 359.5; **hindrance** 1012; rationing; thought control; restraint of trade, monopoly, protection, protectionism, protective tariff, tariff wall; clampdown *and* crackdown <nf>, proscription, **prohibition** 444

2 suppression, repression, oppression; **subdual,** quelling, putting down, shutting *or* closing down, smashing, crushing; quashing, squashing *and* squelching <nf>; smothering, stifling, suffocating, strangling, throttling; extinguishment, quenching; **censorship,** censoring, bleeping *or* bleeping out <nf>, blue laws

3 restriction, limitation, confinement; Hobson's choice, no choice, zero option; circumscription 210; stint, cramping, cramp; qualification 958

4 shackle, restraint, **restraints, fetter, hamper,** trammel, trammels, **manacle,** gyves, bond, **bonds,** irons, chains, Oregon boat; stranglehold; **handcuffs,** cuffs, bracelets <nf>; stocks, bilbo, pillory; **tether,** spancel, leash, lead <chiefly Brit>, leading string; **rein;** hobble, hopple; strait-jacket, strait-waistcoat <Brit>, camisole; yoke, collar; bridle, halter; **muzzle, gag;** electronic ankle bracelet *and* offender's tag *and* monitor; iron rule, iron hand

5 lock, bolt, bar, padlock, catch, safety catch; barrier 1012.5

6 restrictionist, protectionist, monopolist; censor; screw <nf>

VERBS **7 restrain, constrain, control, govern,** guard,

contain, keep under control, put *or* lay under restraint; **inhibit,** straiten <old>; enjoin, clamp *or* crack down on <nf>, proscribe, prohibit 444.3; **curb, check, arrest, bridle,** get under control, rein, snub, snub in; **retard,** slow down, decelerate; **cool** *and* **cool off** *and* **cool down** <nf>; retrench, curtail; hold, **hold in,** keep, withhold, hold up <nf>, **keep from;** hinder 1012.10; **hold back, keep back,** pull, set back; **hold in, keep in,** pull in, rein in; **hold** *or* **keep in check, hold at bay,** hold in leash, tie one down, tie one's hands; hold fast, keep a tight hand on; restrain oneself, not go too far, not go off the deep end <nf>

8 **suppress, repress,** stultify; **keep down,** hold down, keep under; **close** *or* **shut down; subdue, quell, put down,** smash, **crush; quash, squash** *and* **squelch** <nf>; **extinguish,** quench, stanch, damp down, pour water on, dash *or* pour cold water on, drown, kill; **smother, stifle,** suffocate, asphyxiate, strangle, throttle, choke off, **muzzle, gag;** censor, bleep *or* bleep out <nf>, silence; sit on *and* sit down on *and* slap *or* smack down <nf>; jump on *and* crack down on *and* clamp down on <nf>, put *or* keep the lid on <nf>; bottle up, cork, cork up

9 **restrict, limit, narrow, confine,** tighten; ground, restrict to home, barracks, bedroom, quarters, etc; circumscribe 210.4; keep in *or* within bounds, keep from spreading, localize; **cage in,** hem, hem in, box, box in *or* up; **cramp,** stint, cramp one's style; qualify 959.3

10 **bind, restrain, tie,** tie up, put the clamps on, **strap,** lash, leash, pinion, fasten, secure, make fast; **hamper, trammel,** entrammel; rope; **chain,** enchain; **shackle, fetter, manacle,** gyve, **put in irons; handcuff, tie one's hands; tie hand and foot,** hog-tie <nf>; straitjacket; hobble, hopple, fetter, leash, put on a lead <chiefly Brit>, spancel; tether, picket, moor, anchor; tie down, pin down, peg down; get a stranglehold on, put a half nelson on <nf>; **bridle;** gag, muzzle

ADJS 11 **restraining, constraining; inhibiting,** inhibitive; **suppressive, repressive,** oppressive, stultifying; controlling, on top of <nf>, prohibitive

12 **restrictive,** limitative, restricting, **narrowing, limiting, confining,** cramping; censorial

13 **restrained, constrained, inhibited,** pent up; guarded; controlled, curbed, bridled; **under restraint,** under control, in check, under discipline; grounded, out of circulation; slowed down, retarded, arrested, in remission; in *or* on leash, in leading strings

14 **suppressed, repressed; subdued,** quelled, put down, smashed, crushed; quashed, squashed *and* squelched <nf>; smothered, stifled, suffocated; censored

15 **restricted, limited, confined;** circumscribed 210.6, "cabined, cribbed, confined"—Shakespeare, hemmed in, hedged in *or* about, boxed in; landlocked; **shut-in,** stormbound, weatherbound, windbound, icebound, snowbound; cramped, stinted; qualified 959.10; under arrest, up the river <nf>, doing time <nf>, in the big house <nf>

16 **bound, tied,** bound hand and foot, tied up, tied down, strapped, hampered, trammeled, shackled, handcuffed, fettered, manacled, tethered, leashed; **in bonds,** in irons *or* chains, ironbound

429 CONFINEMENT

NOUNS 1 **confinement,** locking-up, lockup, lockdown, caging, penning, putting behind barriers, impoundment, **restraint,** restriction; check, **restraint, constraint** 428.1

2 **quarantine, isolation,** cordoning off, segregation, separation, sequestration, seclusion; walling in *or* up *or* off; sanitary cordon, *cordon sanitaire* <Fr>, cordon; quarantine flag, yellow flag, yellow jack

3 **imprisonment, jailing,** incarceration, **internment,** immurement, immuration; **detention, captivity,** detainment, duress, durance, durance vile; close arrest, house arrest; term of imprisonment; preventive detention; minimum- *or* maximum-security imprisonment *or* detention; lockdown, solitary confinement

4 **commitment,** committal, consignment; recommitment, remand; mittimus <law>; institutionalization

5 **custody,** custodianship, keep <old>, **keeping, care, change, ward,** guarding, hold, protective *or* preventive custody; protection, safekeeping 1008.1

6 **arrest,** arrestment, arrestation, pinch *and* bust *and* collar <nf>; **capture, apprehension, seizure,** netting <nf>; house arrest, protective *or* preventive custody

7 **place of confinement,** close quarters, not enough room to swing a cat; limbo, hell, purgatory; pound, pinfold *or* penfold; **cage; enclosure,** pen, coop 212.3

8 **prison,** prison house, correctional *or* correction facility, minimum- *or* maximum-security facility, **penitentiary,** pen <nf>, keep, penal institution, bastille, state prison, federal prison; house of detention *or* correction, detention center, detention home; **jail, gaol** <Brit>, jailhouse, lockup, bridewell <Brit>, county jail, city jail; maximum- *or* minimum-security prison; **military prison, guardhouse, stockade, brig; dungeon,** oubliette, black hole; **reformatory,** house of correction, reform school, training school, industrial school, borstal *or* borstal institution <Brit>; debtor's

prison *and* sponging house <old>; **prison camp,** internment camp, detention camp, labor camp, forced-labor camp, gulag, **concentration camp;** prisoner-of-war camp *or* stockade, POW camp, prison farm; cell; bullpen; solitary confinement, the hole <nf>, solitary; **cell,** prison *or* jail cell; **detention cell,** holding cell, lockup; tank *and* drunk tank <nf>; cellblock, cellhouse; condemned cell, death cell, death house *or* row, jail cell; penal settlement *or* colony, Devil's Island, Alcatraz; halfway house, reformatory, reform school, detention home

9 <nf terms> **slammer, slam, jug,** can, coop, cooler, hoosegow, stir, clink, pokey *or* poky, nick *and* quod *and* chokey <Brit>, hoosegow; **joint,** big house, big school, big cage, big joint, brig, tank, icebox

10 **jailer, gaoler** <Brit>, correctional *or* correction *or* corrections officer; **keeper, warder,** prison guard, **turnkey,** bull *and* screw <nf>; **warden,** governor <Brit>, commandant, principal keeper; custodian, caretaker, guardian 1008.6; **guard** 1008.9

11 **prisoner, captive, inmate,** *détenu* <Fr>, cageling; arrestee; **convict,** con <nf>; **jailbird** <nf>, gaolbird <Brit nf>, stir bird <nf>, lifer, collar, yardbird, lag *or* lagger <Brit>; **detainee; internee; prisoner of war** *or* POW; enemy prisoner of war *or* EPWS; political prisoner, prisoner of conscience; lifer <nf>; trusty *or* trustee; condemned prisoner; parolee, ticket-of-leave man *or* ticket-of-leaver <Brit>; ex-convict; chain-gang member, hostage

VERBS 12 **confine, shut in,** shut away, coop in, hem in, fence in *or* up, wall in *or* up, rail in; **shut up, coop up, pen up,** box up, mew up, bottle up, cork up, seal up, **impound;** pen, coop, pound <old>, crib, mew, cloister, immure, cage, cage in, encage; **enclose** 212.5; **hold, keep in,** hold *or* keep in custody, **detain,** keep in detention, constrain, ground, **restrain,** hold in restraint; check, inhibit 428.7; restrict 428.9; shackle 428.10

13 **quarantine, isolate,** segregate, separate, seclude; **cordon, cordon off,** seal off, rope off; wall off, set up barriers, put behind barriers

14 **imprison, incarcerate, intern,** immure; **jail,** gaol <Brit>, jug <nf>, put under security, put behind bars, put away, put *or* throw into jail, throw under the jailhouse <nf>; throw *or* cast in prison, clap up, clap in jail *or* prison, send up the river <nf>, send to the big house <nf>; **lock up,** lock in, bolt in, put *or* keep under lock and key; hold captive, hold prisoner, hold in captivity; hold under close *or* house arrest, throw in the tank *or* cooler

15 **arrest,** make an arrest, put under arrest, pick up; catch flat-footed; catch with one's pants down *or* hand in the till <nf>, catch one in the act *or* red-handed *or* in flagrante delicto, catch *or* have one

dead to rights; run down, run to earth, **take captive, take prisoner, apprehend, capture,** seize, net <nf>, lay by the heels, **take into custody,** entrap

16 <nf terms> **bust, pinch,** make a pinch, nab, collar, nick, pull in, **run in,** collar

17 **commit,** consign, commit to prison, send to jail, send up *and* send up the river <nf>; commit to an institution, institutionalize; recommit, remit, remand

18 **be imprisoned, do** *or* **serve time** <nf>; pay one's debt to society, land in the cooler, lag <Brit>

ADJS 19 **confined,** in confinement, **shut-in,** pent, **pent-up,** penned in, kept in, under restraint, held, in detention; "cabined, cribbed, confined"— Shakespeare; impounded; grounded, out of circulation; **detained;** restricted 428.15; cloistered, enclosed 212.10

20 **quarantined,** isolated, segregated, separated; cordoned, cordoned *or* sealed *or* roped off

21 **jailed,** jugged <nf>, **imprisoned, incarcerated, interned,** immured; **in prison,** in stir <nf>, in captivity, captive, **behind bars,** locked up, under lock and key, in durance vile, serving a sentence; doing time, on the inside, on ice, in the cooler, up the river, in the big house

22 **under arrest, in custody,** in hold, in charge <Brit>, under *or* in detention; under close arrest, under house arrest

430 FREEDOM

NOUNS 1 **freedom, liberty; license,** loose <old>; run *and* the run of <nf>, "the right to live as we wish"—Epictetus, "the will to be responsible to ourselves"—Nietzsche, "the choice of working *or* starving"—Samuel Johnson; **civil liberty,** the Four Freedoms <F D Roosevelt>: freedom of speech *and* expression, freedom of worship, freedom from want, freedom from fear; freedom of movement; constitutional freedom; lack of censorship; academic freedom; artistic license, poetic license

2 **right, rights, civil rights,** civil liberties, constitutional rights, legal rights; Bill of Rights, Petition of Right, Declaration of Right, Declaration of the Rights of Man, Magna Charta *or* Carta; **unalienable rights, human rights,** natural rights, "life, liberty, and the pursuit of happiness"— Thomas Jefferson; diplomatic immunity

3 **unrestraint, unconstraint,** noncoercion, nonintimidation; **unreserve,** irrepressibleness, irrepressibility, uninhibitedness, exuberance 109.4; **immoderacy, intemperance,** incontinence, uncontrol, unruliness, indiscipline; **abandon,** abandonment, **licentiousness,** wantonness,

riotousness, wildness; permissiveness, unstrictness, **laxness** 426; one's own way, one's own devices

4 **latitude, scope, room,** range, way, field, maneuvering space *or* room, room to swing a cat <nf>; **margin,** clearance, **space,** open space *or* field, elbowroom, breathing space, **leeway** <nf>, sea room, wide berth; **tolerance; free scope,** full *or* ample scope, **free hand,** free play, free course; **carte blanche,** blank check; no holds barred; swing, play, full swing; rope, long rope *or* tether, rope enough to hang oneself

5 **independence, self-determination, self government,** self-direction, autonomy, home rule; autarky, autarchy, self-containment, self-sufficiency; **individualism,** rugged individualism, individual freedom; **self-reliance,** self-dependence; inner-direction; no allegiance; singleness, bachelorhood; independent means

6 **free will,** free choice, **discretion,** option, choice, say, say-so *and* druthers <nf>, free decision; **full consent;** absolute *or* unconditioned *or* noncontingent free will

7 **own free will, own account, own accord, own hook** *and* own say-so <nf>, own discretion, own choice, **own initiative,** personal initiative, own responsibility, personal *or* individual responsibility, own volition, own authority, own power; own way, own sweet way <nf>; law unto oneself

8 **exemption,** exception, **immunity; release,** discharge; **franchise, license,** charter, patent, liberty; diplomatic immunity, congressional *or* legislative immunity; special case *or* privilege; grandfather clause, grandfathering; privilege; permission 443

9 **noninterference, nonintervention; isolationism; laissez-faireism,** let-alone principle *or* doctrine *or* policy, deregulation; *laissez-faire* and *laissez-aller* <Fr>; liberalism, free enterprise, free competition, self-regulating market; open market; capitalism 611.8; free trade; noninvolvement, nonalignment, neutrality

10 **liberalism,** libertarianism, latitudinarianism; broad-mindedness, open-mindedness, toleration, tolerance; unbigotedness 979.1; libertinism, **freethinking,** free thought; liberalization, **liberation** 431; nonconformity

11 **freeman,** freewoman; citizen, free citizen, burgess, bourgeois; franklin; emancipated *or* manumitted slave, freedman, freedwoman; deditician

12 **free agent, independent, free lance; individualist,** rugged individualist; free spirit; **liberal,** libertarian, latitudinarian; libertine, freethinker; free trader; **nonpartisan,** neutral, undecided, mugwump; isolationist; nonaligned nation; third world, third force; indie <nf>; lone wolf <nf>, loner, nonconformist

VERBS 13 **liberalize,** ease; **free, liberate** 431.4

14 **exempt, free, release,** discharge, **let go** *and* **let off** <nf>, set at liberty, spring <nf>; **excuse,** spare, except, grant immunity, make a special case of; grandfather; **dispense,** dispense from, give dispensation from; dispense with, save the necessity; remit, remise; absolve 601.4

15 **give a free hand,** let one have his head, **give one his head; give the run of** <nf>, give the freedom of; give one leeway <nf>, give full play; give one scope *or* space *or* room; **give rein** *or* **free rein to,** give the reins to, give bridle to, give one line, give one rope; **give one carte blanche, give one a blank check;** let go one's own way, let one go at will

16 **not interfere, leave** *or* **let alone, let be,** leave *or* let well enough alone, let sleeping dogs lie; **keep hands off,** not tamper, not meddle, not involve oneself, not get involved, let it ride <nf>, let nature take its course; live and let live, leave one to oneself, leave one in peace; mind one's own business; tolerate; **decontrol, deregulate**

17 <nf terms> **get off one's back** *or* **one's case** *or* **one's tail,** get out of one's face *or* hair, **butt out, back off,** leave be, call off the dogs, keep one's nose out, get lost, take a walk, not cramp someone's style

18 **be free,** feel free, feel free as a bird, feel at liberty; **go at large,** breathe free, breathe the air of freedom; **have free scope,** have one's druthers <nf>, have a free hand, have the run of <nf>; be at home, feel at home; be freed, be released; be exonerated, go *or* get off scot-free, walk

19 **let oneself go,** let go, let loose *and* cut loose *and* let one's hair down <nf>, **give way to,** open up, let it all hang out <nf>; go all out, go flat out <Brit>, pull out all the stops; go unrestrained, run wild, have one's fling, sow one's wild oats

20 **stand on one's own two feet, shift for oneself, fend for oneself,** stand on one's own, strike out for oneself, trust one's good right arm, look out for number one <nf>; **go it alone, be one's own man,** pull a lone oar, play a lone hand <nf>, **paddle one's own canoe** <nf>; suffice to oneself, do for oneself, make *or* pay one's own way; ask no favors, ask no quarter; **be one's own boss** <nf>, call no man master, answer only to oneself, ask leave of no man; **go one's own way,** take one's own course; do on one's own, do one's own thing, do on one's own initiative, do on one's own hook *or* say-so <nf>, do in one's own sweet way <nf>; **have a will of one's own,** have one's own way, do what one likes *or* wishes *or* chooses, do as one pleases, **go as one pleases,** please oneself <nf>, **suit oneself;** have a free mind; free-lance, be a free agent

ADJS **21 free; at liberty, at large,** on the loose, **loose,** unengaged, disengaged, detached, unattached, uncommitted, uninvolved, clear, in the clear, go-as-you-please, easygoing, footloose, footloose and fancy-free, free *and* easy; free as air, free as a bird, free as the wind; scot-free; **freeborn; freed, liberated, emancipated,** manumitted, released, uncaged, sprung <nf>

22 independent, self-dependent; free-spirited, freewheeling, free-floating, free-standing; **self-determined,** self-directing, one's own man; freelance; inner-directed, **individualistic;** self-governed, **self-governing, autonomous,** sovereign; stand-alone, self-reliant, self-sufficient, self-subsistent, self-supporting, self-contained, autarkic, autarchic; nonpartisan, neutral, **nonaligned;** third-world, third-force

23 free-acting, free-going, free-moving, free-working; freehand, freehanded; **free-spoken,** outspoken, **plain-spoken, open, frank,** direct, candid, blunt 644.17

24 unrestrained, unconstrained, unforced, uncompelled, uncoerced; unmeasured, **uninhibited, unsuppressed, unrepressed, unreserved,** go-go <nf>, exuberant 109.14; **uncurbed, unchecked, unbridled,** unmuzzled; **unreined,** reinless; **uncontrolled,** unmastered, unsubdued, ungoverned, **unruly;** out of control, out of hand, out of one's power; **abandoned,** intemperate, immoderate, **incontinent, licentious,** loose, wanton, rampant, riotous, wild; irrepressible; lax 426.4

25 nonrestrictive, unrestrictive; **permissive,** hands-off <nf>; indulgent 427.8; lax 426.4; **liberal,** libertarian, latitudinarian; broad-minded, open-minded, tolerant; unbigoted 979.8; libertine; freethinking

26 unhampered, untrammeled, unhandicapped, unimpeded, unhindered, unprevented, unclogged, unobstructed; clear, unencumbered, unburdened, unladen, unembarrassed, disembarrassed; free-ranging, free-range

27 unrestricted, unconfined, uncircumscribed, unbound <old>, unbounded, unmeasured; **unlimited,** limitless, illimitable; unqualified, unconditioned, **unconditional,** without strings, no strings, no strings attached; **absolute,** perfect, unequivocal, full, plenary; open-ended, open, **wide-open** <nf>; permissive; decontrolled, deregulated

28 unbound, untied, **unfettered,** unshackled, unchained; unmuzzled, ungagged; uncensored; declassified

29 unsubject, ungoverned, unenslaved, **unenthralled;** unvanquished, unconquered, unsubdued, unquelled, **untamed,** unbroken, undomesticated, unreconstructed

30 exempt, immune; exempted, **released, excused,** excepted, let off <nf>, spared; grandfathered; **privileged, licensed,** favored, chartered; permitted; dispensed; **unliable,** unsubject, irresponsible, unaccountable, unanswerable

31 quit, clear, free, rid; free of, clear of, quit of, rid of, shut of, shed of <nf>

ADVS **32 freely,** free; **without restraint,** without stint, **unreservedly,** with abandon; outright

33 independently, alone, by oneself, all by one's lonesome <nf>, under one's own power *or* steam, **on one's own** *and* **on one's own hook** <nf>, on one's own initiative, on one's own bottom <old>; **on one's own account** *or* **responsibility,** on one's own say-so <nf>; **of one's own free will, of one's own accord,** of one's own volition, at one's own discretion

431 LIBERATION

NOUNS **1 liberation, freeing,** setting free, setting at liberty; **deliverance, delivery; rescue** 398; **emancipation,** disenthrallment, manumission; enfranchisement, affranchisement; Emancipation Proclamation; Nineteenth Amendment; Equal Rights Amendment; women's liberation; gay liberation; women's *or* gay *or* men's lib <nf>

2 release, freeing, unhanding, **loosing,** unloosing; unbinding, untying, unbuckling, unshackling, unfettering, unlashing, unstrapping, untrussing *and* unpinioning <old>, unmanacling, **unleashing,** unchaining, untethering, unhobbling, unharnessing, unyoking, unbridling; unmuzzling, ungagging; unlocking, unlatching, unbolting, unbarring; unpenning, uncaging; **discharge, dismissal;** parole, bail; convict release, springing <nf>; demobilization, separation from the service

3 extrication, freeing, releasing, clearing; **disengagement, disentanglement,** untangling, unsnarling, unraveling, disentwining, disinvolvement, unknotting, disembarrassment, disembroilment; dislodgment, breaking out *or* loose, busting out *or* loose <nf>

VERBS **4 liberate, free, deliver, set free,** set at liberty, set at large; **emancipate,** manumit, disenthrall; enfranchise, affranchise; **rescue** 398.3

5 release, unhand, let go, let loose, turn loose, cast loose, let out, let off, let go free, let off the hook; **discharge, dismiss;** let out on bail, grant bail to, go bail for <nf>; parole, put on parole; release from prison, spring <nf>; demobilize, separate from the service

6 loose, loosen, let loose, cut loose *or* free, unloose, unloosen; **unbind, untie,** unstrap, unbuckle, unlash, untruss *and* unpinion <old>; **unfetter, unshackle,** unmanacle, unchain, unhandcuff, untie one's hands; **unleash,** untether, unhobble; unharness, unyoke, unbridle; unmuzzle, ungag; unlock, unlatch, unbolt, unbar, unpen, uncage

7 **extricate, free, release, clear,** get out; **disengage,** disentangle, untangle, unsnarl, unravel, disentwine, disinvolve, unknot, disembarrass, disembroil; dislodge, break out *or* loose, cut loose, tear loose

8 **free oneself from,** deliver oneself from, **get free of,** get quit of, **get rid of,** get clear of, **get out of,** get well out of, get around, extricate oneself, get out of a jam <nf>; **throw off, shake off;** break out, bust out <nf>, go over the wall <nf>, **escape** 369.6; wriggle out of

9 **go free,** go scot free, go at liberty, **get off,** get off scot-free, get out of, beat the rap *and* walk <nf>

ADJS 10 **liberated, freed, emancipated, released;** delivered, rescued, ransomed, redeemed; extricated, unbound, untied, unshackled, etc; free 430.20; scot-free; on parole, out on bail

432 SUBJECTION

NOUNS 1 **subjection, subjugation; domination** 612.2; **restraint, control** 428.1; **bondage, captivity; thrall, thralldom,** enthrallment; **slavery,** enslavement, master-slave relationship; **servitude,** compulsory *or* involuntary servitude, servility, bond service, indentureship; **serfdom,** serfhood, villenage, **vassalage;** helotry, helotism; debt slavery, **peonage;** feudalism, feudality; absolutism, tyranny 612.9,10; deprivation of freedom, disenfranchisement, disfranchisement

2 **subservience** *or* subserviency, subjecthood, subordinacy, **subordination,** juniority, **inferiority;** lower status, subordinate role, satellite status; back seat *and* second fiddle *and* hind tit <nf>; **service,** servitorship 577.12

3 **dependence** *or* dependency, codependency, tutelage, chargeship, wardship; apprenticeship; clientship, clientage

4 **subdual, quelling,** crushing, trampling *or* treading down, reduction, **humbling, humiliation; breaking, taming,** domestication, gentling; conquering 412.1; **suppression** 428.2

5 **subordinate,** junior, secondary, second-in-command, lieutenant, **inferior; underling,** understrapper, low man on the totem pole <nf>, errand boy, flunky, gofer <nf>, grunt <nf>; assistant, personal assistant, helper 616.6; strong right arm, **right-hand man** 616.7; **servant, employee** 577

6 **dependent, charge, ward,** client, protégé, encumbrance; pensioner, pensionary; public charge, ward of the state; child; foster child; dependency *or* dependent state, client state, satellite *or* satellite state, puppet government, creature; hanger-on, parasite

7 **subject, vassal,** liege, liege man, liege subject, homager; **captive; slave,** servant, chattel, chattel slave, **bondsman,** bondman, **bondslave,** theow, thrall; indentured servant; laborer, esne; bondwoman, bondswoman, bondmaid; odalisque, concubine; galley slave; **serf,** helot, villein; churl; debt slave, **peon;** conscript

VERBS 8 **subjugate, subject, subordinate; dominate** 612.15; disfranchise, disenfranchise, divest *or* deprive of freedom; **enslave,** enthrall, hold in thrall, make a chattel of; take captive, lead captive *or* into captivity; **hold in subjection,** hold in bondage, **hold captive,** hold in captivity; **hold down,** keep down, keep under; **keep** *or* **have under one's thumb,** have tied to one's apron strings, hold in leash, hold in leading strings, hold in swaddling clothes, hold *or* keep at one's beck and call; vassalize, make dependent *or* tributary; peonize

9 **subdue, master,** overmaster, **quell, crush, reduce,** beat down, **break,** break down, overwhelm; tread underfoot, trample on *or* down, trample underfoot, roll in the dust, trample in the dust, drag at one's chariot wheel; oppress, **suppress** 428.8; make one give in *or* say 'uncle' <nf>, **conquer** 412.10; kick around <nf>, tyrannize 612.16; unman 19.12; bring low, **bring to terms, humble,** humiliate, take down a notch *or* peg, bend, **bring one to his knees, bend to one's will**

10 **have subject,** twist *or* turn *or* wind around one's little finger, make lie down and roll over, have eating out of one's hand, **lead by the nose,** make a puppet of, make putty of, make a sport *or* plaything of; use as a doormat, treat like dirt under one's feet, walk all over

11 **domesticate, tame, break,** bust *and* gentle <nf>, break in, break to harness; housebreak

12 **depend on,** be at the mercy of, be the sport *or* plaything *or* puppet of, be putty in the hands of; not dare to say one's soul is one's own; eat out of one's hands; play second fiddle, suck hind tit <nf>, take a back seat; pay tribute

ADJS 13 **subject, dependent,** tributary, client; **subservient, subordinate, inferior;** servile; liege, **vassal,** feudal, feudatory

14 **subjugated,** subjected, **enslaved, enthralled, in thrall, captive,** bond, unfree; disenfranchised, disfranchised, **oppressed, suppressed** 428.14; **in subjection, in bondage, in captivity,** in slavery, in bonds, in chains; under the lash, under the heel; **in**

one's power, in one's control, in one's hands *or* clutches, in one's pocket, **under one's thumb,** at one's mercy, under one's command *or* orders, at one's beck and call, at one's feet, at one's pleasure; **subordinated,** playing second fiddle; at the bottom of the ladder, sucking hind tit <nf>

15 **subdued, quelled,** crushed, broken, reduced, mastered, overmastered, humbled, humiliated, brought to one's knees, brought low, made to grovel; **tamed, domesticated,** broken to harness, gentled; housebroken *or* housebroke

16 **downtrodden,** downtrod <old>, kept down *or* under, ground down, overborne, trampled, **oppressed; abused,** misused; **henpecked, browbeaten,** led by the nose, in leading strings, tied to one's apron strings, ordered *or* kicked around <nf>, regimented, tyrannized; slavish, servile, submissive 433.12; unmanned 19.19; treated like dirt under one's feet, treated like shit <nf>

PREPS 17 **under, below, beneath,** underneath, subordinate to; at the feet of; under the heel of; at the beck and call of, at the whim *or* pleasure of

433 SUBMISSION

NOUNS 1 **submission,** submittal, **yielding; compliance,** complaisance, **acquiescence, acceptance;** going along with <nf>, **assent** 332; **consent** 441; **obedience** 326; subjection 432; **resignation,** resignedness, stoicism, philosophical attitude; **deference,** homage, kneeling, obeisance; **passivity, unassertiveness,** passiveness, supineness, longanimity, long-suffering, long-sufferance <old>, nonresistance, nonopposition, nonopposal, quietness, nondissent, quietude, quietism; **cowardice** 491

2 **surrender, capitulation;** renunciation, giving over, abandonment, relinquishment, **cession;** giving up *or* in, backing off *or* down <nf>, retreat, recession, recedence, caving in <nf>, giving up the fort, the white flag <nf>, throwing in the towel *or* sponge <nf>

3 **submissiveness, docility, tractability,** biddability, yieldingness, compliableness <old>, pliancy, pliability, flexibility, malleability, moldability, ductility, plasticity, facility; agreeableness, agreeability; subservience, **servility** 138

4 **manageability, governability, controllability,** manipulability, manipulatability, corrigibility, untroublesomeness; **tameness,** housebrokenness; tamableness, domesticability; milk-toast, milquetoast, Caspar Milquetoast

5 **meekness, gentleness, tameness, mildness,** mild-

manneredness, peaceableness, lamblikeness, dovelikeness; **self-abnegation, humility** 137

VERBS 6 **submit, comply, take, accept,** go along with <nf>, suffer, bear, brook, **acquiesce,** be agreeable, accede, **assent** 332.8; **consent** 441.2; relent, **succumb,** resign, resign oneself, give oneself up, not resist; take one's medicine, swallow the pill, face the music, face the facts; **bite the bullet; knuckle down** *or* **under,** knock under <old>, take it, swallow it; jump through a hoop, dance to another's tune; take it lying down; put up with it, grin and bear it, make the best of it, take the bitter with the sweet, shrug, shrug off, **live with it;** obey 326.2

7 **yield, cede, give way, give ground, back down, give up, give in,** cave in <nf>, withdraw from *or* quit the field, break off combat, cease resistance, have no fight left

8 **surrender, give up, capitulate,** acknowledge defeat, **cry quits,** cry pax <Brit>, **say 'uncle'** <nf>, beg a truce, pray for quarter, implore mercy, **throw in the towel** *or* **sponge** <nf>, show *or* wave the white flag, lower *or* haul down *or* strike one's flag *or* colors, throw down *or* lay down *or* deliver up one's arms, hand over one's sword, yield the palm, ask for mercy, pull in one's horns <nf>, come to terms; renounce, abandon, relinquish, **cede,** give over, hand over

9 **submit to, yield to, defer to,** bow to, give way to, knuckle under to, succumb to

10 **bow down,** bow, bend, stoop, crouch, **bow one's head,** bend the neck, bow submission; genuflect, curtsy; **bow to,** bend to, knuckle to <nf>, bend *or* bow to one's will, bend to one's yoke; kneel to, **bend the knee to, fall on one's knees before,** crouch before, **fall at one's feet,** throw oneself at the feet of, prostrate oneself before, **truckle to,** cringe to, cave in; **kowtow,** bow and scrape, grovel, do obeisance *or* homage; kiss ass <nf>; take the line of least resistance

11 **eat dirt, eat crow, eat humble pie,** lick the dust, kiss the rod, take it on the chin

ADJS 12 **submissive, compliant,** compliable <old>, complaisant, complying, **acquiescent,** consenting 441.4; **assenting,** accepting, agreeable; subservient, abject, **obedient** 326.3; servile; **resigned,** uncomplaining; unassertive; **passive,** supine, **unresisting,** nonresisting, unresistant, nonresistant, nonresistive, long-suffering, longanimous, nonopposing, nondissenting

13 **docile, tractable,** biddable, unmurmuring, **yielding,** pliant, pliable, flexible, malleable, moldable, ductile, plastic, facile <old>, like putty in one's hands

14 manageable, governable, controllable,
manipulable, manipulatable, handleable,
corrigible, restrainable, untroublesome; domitable,
tamable, domesticable; milk-toast *or* milquetoast

15 meek, gentle, mild, mild-mannered, peaceable,
pacific, quiet; **subdued, chastened, tame,** tamed,
broken, housebroken, domesticated; lamblike,
gentle as a lamb, dovelike; humble; soft, weak-
kneed

16 deferential, obeisant; subservient, obsequious,
servile 138.13; crouching, prostrate, prone, on
one's belly, on one's knees, on one's marrowbones
<nf>, on bended knee

ADVS **17 submissively, compliantly,** complaisantly,
acquiescently, agreeably; **obediently** 326.6;
resignedly, uncomplainingly, with resignation;
passively, supinely, unresistingly, unresistantly,
nonresistively

18 docilely, tractably, biddably, **yieldingly,** pliantly,
pliably, malleably, flexibly, plastically, facilely
<old>

19 meekly, gently, tamely, mildly, peaceably,
pacifically, quietly, like a lamb

434 OBSERVANCE

NOUNS **1 observance,** observation; **keeping,**
adherence, heeding; compliance, conformance,
conformity, accordance; **faith,** faithfulness, fidelity;
respect, deference 155.1; **performance, practice,**
execution, discharge, carrying out *or* through;
dutifulness 641.2, acquittal *or* acquittance <old>,
fulfillment, satisfaction; heed, care 339.1; obeying
the law

VERBS **2 observe, keep, heed, follow,** keep the faith;
regard, defer to, **respect** 155.4, attend to, **comply
with,** conform to; hold by, **abide by,** adhere to; **live
up to,** act up to, practice what one preaches, **be
faithful to,** keep faith with, do justice to, do the
right thing by; **fulfill,** fill, meet, satisfy; **make good,**
keep *or* make good one's word *or* promise, be as
good as one's word, redeem one's pledge, stand to
one's engagement; keep to the spirit of, keep faith
with; obey the law

3 perform, practice, do, execute, discharge, carry
out *or* through, carry into execution, do one's duty
641.10, do one's office, fulfill one's role, discharge
one's function; honor one's obligations

ADJS **4 observant,** respectful 155.8, regardful,
mindful; **faithful,** devout, devoted, true, loyal,
constant; dutiful 641.13, duteous; as good as one's
word; **practicing,** active; compliant, conforming;
punctual, punctilious, scrupulous, meticulous,
conscientious 339.12; obedient

435 NONOBSERVANCE

NOUNS **1 nonobservance,** inobservance,
unobservance, nonadherence; nonconformity,
disconformity, **nonconformance, noncompliance;**
apostasy; inattention, indifference, **disregard**
984.1; laxity 426.1; **nonfulfillment,
nonperformance,** nonfeasance, failure, **dereliction,
delinquency,** omission, default, slight, oversight;
negligence; neglect 340, laches; abandonment 370;
lack of ceremony

2 violation, infraction, breach, breaking;
infringement, transgression, trespass,
contravention; offense 674.4; breach of promise,
breach of contract, breach of trust *or* faith, bad
faith, breach of privilege; breach of the peace

VERBS **3 disregard,** lose sight of, pay no regard to;
neglect 340.6; renege, abandon 370.5; defect
858.13; do one's own thing <nf>

**4 violate, break, breach; infringe, transgress,
trespass,** contravene, trample on *or* upon, trample
underfoot, do violence to, make a mockery of,
outrage; **defy,** set at defiance, flout, set at naught,
set naught by; take the law into one's own hands;
break one's promise, break one's word

ADJS **5 nonobservant,** inobservant, unobservant,
nonadherent; nonconforming, unconforming,
noncompliant, uncompliant; inattentive,
disregardful 983.6; **negligent** 340.10; unfaithful,
untrue, unloyal, inconstant, lapsed, renegade
858.20,363.11; contemptuous

436 PROMISE

NOUNS **1 promise, pledge,** solemn promise, troth,
plight, faith, parole, **word, word of honor,** debt of
honor, solemn declaration *or* word; **oath, vow;**
avouch, avouchment; **assurance, guarantee,**
warranty; entitlement

2 obligation, commitment, agreement, engagement,
undertaking, recognizance; **understanding,**
gentlemen's agreement, unwritten agreement,
handshake; verbal agreement, nonformal
agreement, pactum <law>; tacit *or* unspoken
agreement; **contract** 437.1, covenant, bond;
designation, committal, earmarking

3 betrothal, betrothment, intention, espousal,
engagement, handfasting *and* affiance <old>,
troth, marriage contract *or* vow, plighted troth *or*
faith *or* love, exchange of vows; banns, banns of
matrimony; prenuptial agreement *or* contract,
prenup <nf>

VERBS **4 promise,** give *or* make a promise, hold out
an expectation; **pledge,** plight, troth, **vow; give**

one's word, pledge *or* pass one's word, give one's parole, **give one's word of honor,** plight one's troth *or* faith, pledge *or* plight one's honor; cross one's heart *and* cross one's heart and hope to die <nf>, **swear;** vouch, avouch, **warrant, guarantee, assure;** underwrite, countersign

5 **commit, engage,** undertake, obligate, bind, **agree to,** say yes, answer for, be answerable for, take on oneself, be responsible for, be security for, go bail for, accept obligation *or* responsibility, bind oneself to, put oneself down for; have an understanding; enter into a gentlemen's agreement; take the vows *or* marriage vows; shake hands on, shake on it; contract, sign on the dotted line; designate, commit, earmark

6 **be engaged, affiance, betroth,** troth, plight one's troth, say 'I do'; **contract,** contract an engagement, pledge *or* promise in marriage; read *or* publish the banns

ADJS 7 **promissory,** votive; under *or* upon oath, on one's word, on one's word of honor, on the Book, under hand and seal, avowed

8 **promised, pledged, bound, committed,** compromised, **obligated; sworn,** warranted, **guaranteed,** assured, underwritten, cosigned; contracted 437.12; **engaged, plighted, affianced, betrothed,** intended

ADVS 9 on one's honor *or* word *or* word of honor *or* parole; solemnly

437 COMPACT

NOUNS 1 **compact, pact, contract,** legal contract, valid contract, **covenant,** convention, transaction, paction <Scot>, accord, **agreement,** mutual agreement, agreement between *or* among parties, signed *or* written agreement, formal agreement, legal agreement, undertaking, stipulation; adjustment, accommodation; **understanding, arrangement, bargain,** dicker *and* **deal** <nf>, informal agreement; **settlement,** negotiated settlement; **labor contract, union contract** 727.3, wage contract, employment contract, collective agreement; deed; cartel, consortium; protocol; bond, binding agreement, ironclad agreement, covenant of salt; gentleman's *or* gentlemen's agreement; prenuptial agreement; promise 436

2 **treaty,** international agreement, *entente* or *entente cordiale* <Fr>, concord, concordat, cartel, convention, consortium, protocol, paction, capitulation; **alliance, league;** nonaggression pact, mutual-defense treaty; trade agreement; arms control agreement; NATO *or* North Atlantic Treaty Organization; SEATO *or* Southeast Asia Treaty Organization; Warsaw Pact

3 signing, signature, sealing, closing, conclusion, solemnization; handshake

4 **execution, completion; transaction; carrying out, discharge, fulfillment,** prosecution, effectuation; enforcement; observance 434

VERBS 5 **contract,** compact, **covenant, bargain, agree, engage,** undertake, commit, mutually commit, make a deal <nf>, do a deal <Brit nf>, stipulate, agree to, bargain for, contract for; preset, prearrange, **promise** 436.4; subcontract, outsource; cut a deal <nf>

6 **treat with, negotiate, bargain,** make terms, sit down with, sit down at the bargaining table

7 **sign, shake hands** *or* shake <nf>, affix one's John Hancock <nf>, seal, formalize, make legal and binding, solemnize; agree on terms, come to terms, come to an agreement 332.10; strike a bargain 731.19; plea-bargain

8 **arrange, settle; adjust,** fine-tune, accommodate, reshuffle, rejigger <nf>, **compose,** fix, make up, straighten out, put *or* set straight, work out, sort out *and* square away <nf>; **conclude,** close, **close with,** settle with

9 **execute, complete, transact,** promulgate, make; close a deal; make out, fill out; **discharge, fulfill,** render, administer; **carry out,** carry through, put through, prosecute; effect, effectuate, set in motion, implement; enforce, put in force; **abide by, honor, live up to,** adhere to, live by, **observe** 434.2

ADJS 10 contractual, covenantal, conventional, consensual

11 **contracted,** compacted, **covenanted, agreed upon, bargained for,** agreed <Brit>, stipulated; engaged, undertaken; **promised** 436.8; arranged, settled; under hand and seal, **signed,** sealed; signed sealed and delivered, ratified

ADVS 12 **contractually, as agreed upon, as promised,** as contracted for, by the terms of the contract, according to the contract *or* bargain *or* agreement

438 SECURITY
<thing given as a pledge>

NOUNS 1 **security, surety,** indemnity, **guaranty, guarantee, warranty, insurance,** warrant, assurance, underwriting; **obligation** 436.2, full faith *and* credit; **bond,** tie; stocks and bonds 738.1

2 **pledge, gage,** *pignus* or *vadium* <L>; undertaking; **earnest,** earnest money, god's penny, handsel; escrow; token payment; pawn, hock <nf>; **bail,** bond, vadimonium; replevin, replevy, recognizance; mainprise; hostage, surety

3 **collateral,** collateral security *or* warranty; deposit, stake, forfeit; indemnity, IOU; caution money, caution; margin; cosigned promissory note

4 mortgage, mortgage deed, deed of trust, lien, security agreement; vadium mortuum *or* mortuum vadium; dead pledge; vadium vivum, living pledge, antichresis; hypothec, hypothecation, bottomry, bottomry bond; adjustment mortgage, blanket mortgage, chattel mortgage, closed mortgage, participating mortgage, installment mortgage, leasehold mortgage, trust mortgage, reverse mortgage; first mortgage, second mortgage, third mortgage; adjustable-rate mortgage *or* ARM, variable-rate mortgage *or* VRM, fixed-rate mortgage; equity loan; reverse equity

5 lien, general lien, particular lien; pignus legale, common-law lien, statutory lien, judgment lien, pignus judiciale, tax lien, mechanic's lien; mortgage bond

6 guarantor, warrantor, guaranty, guarantee; mortgagor; insurer, underwriter; sponsor, surety; godparent, godfather, godmother; bondsman, bailsman, mainpernor

7 warrantee, mortgagee; insuree, policyholder; godchild, godson, goddaughter

8 guarantorship, **sponsorship,** sponsion

VERBS **9 secure, guarantee, guaranty, warrant, assure, insure,** ensure, bond, **certify;** countersecure; stand surety; **sponsor,** be sponsor for, sign for, sign one's note, **back,** stand behind *or* back of, stand up for; **endorse;** indemnify, countersign; sign, cosign, **underwrite,** undersign, subscribe to; confirm, attest

10 pledge, impignorate *and* handsel <old>, **deposit, stake,** post, put in escrow, **put up,** put up as collateral, lay out *or* down; **pawn,** put in pawn, spout *or* put up the spout <old>, **hock** *and* **put in hock** <nf>; mortgage, hypothecate, bottomry, bond; **put up** *or* **go bail,** bail out

ADJS **11 secured,** covered, **guaranteed, warranted,** certified, **insured,** ensured, **assured;** certain, sure 970.13

12 pledged, staked, posted, deposited, in escrow, **put up,** put up as collateral; on deposit, at stake; as earnest; **pawned,** in pawn, **in hock** <nf>, hocked, up the spout <old>

13 in trust, held in trust, held in pledge, fiduciary; in escrow; mortgaged

439 OFFER

NOUNS **1 offer,** offering, proffer, presentation, **bid,** submission; **advance, overture,** approach, invitation, come-on <nf>; hesitant *or* tentative *or* preliminary approach, feeling-out, **feeler** <nf>; asking price; **counteroffer, counterproposal**

2 proposal, proposition, suggestion, instance; **motion,** resolution; sexual advance *or* approach *or* invitation *or* overture, indecent proposal, pass <nf>, improper suggestion; request 440

3 ultimatum, last *or* final word *or* offer, firm bid *or* price, sticking point

VERBS **4 offer, proffer, present,** tender, offer up, **put up, submit, extend,** prefer <old>, **hold out,** hold forth, place in one's way, lay at one's feet, put *or* place at one's disposal, put one in the way of

5 propose, submit, prefer; **suggest,** recommend, **advance,** commend to attention, **propound, pose, put forward,** bring forward, put *or* set forth, put it to, put *or* set *or* lay *or* bring before, dish up *and* come out *or* up with <nf>; put a bee in one's bonnet, put ideas into one's head; **bring up, broach, moot,** introduce, open up, launch, start, kick off <nf>; **move, make a motion,** offer a resolution; postulate 951.12

6 bid, bid for, make a bid

7 make advances, approach, overture, **make an overture,** throw *or* fling oneself at one <nf>; **solicit, importune**

8 <nf terms> **proposition, come on to,** hit on, put *or* make a move on, jump one's bones, make *or* throw a pass, george, **make a play for,** play footsie with, pitch, mash <old>

9 urge upon, press upon, ply upon, push upon, force upon, thrust upon; **press, ply;** insist

10 volunteer, come *or* **step forward,** offer *or* **proffer** *or* **present oneself,** be at one's service, not wait to be asked, not wait for an invitation, need no prodding, step into the breach, be Johnny-on-the-spot <nf>

440 REQUEST

NOUNS **1 request,** asking; the touch <nf>; desire, wish, expressed desire; **petition,** petitioning, impetration, address; **application; requisition,** indent <Brit>; demand 421; special request

2 entreaty, appeal, plea, bid, suit, call, cry, clamor, *cri du cœur* <Fr>, beseeching, impetration, obtestation; **supplication, prayer,** rogation, **beseechment,** imploring, imploration, obsecration, obtestation, adjuration, imprecation; **invocation,** invocatory plea *or* prayer

3 importunity, importunateness, urgency, pressure, high pressure *and* hard sell <nf>; **urging, pressing, plying;** buttonholing; dunning; teasing, pestering, plaguing, nagging, nudging <nf>; **coaxing,** wheedling, cajolery, cajolement, blandishment

4 invitation, invite *and* **bid** <nf>, engraved invitation, bidding, biddance, **call,** calling, **summons**

5 solicitation, canvass, canvassing; suit, addresses; **courting, wooing;** fund-raising; the touch <nf>

6 beggary, mendicancy, mendicity; **begging**, cadging, scrounging; mooching *and* bumming *and* panhandling <nf>

7 petitioner, supplicant, suppliant, suitor; **solicitor** 730.7; **applicant,** solicitant, claimant; aspirant, seeker, wannabee <nf>; **candidate,** postulant; bidder

8 beggar, mendicant, scrounger, **cadger; bum** *and* bummer *and* **moocher** *and* **panhandler** *and* sponger <nf>; *schnorrer* <Yiddish>; hobo, tramp 178.3; loafer 331.8; mendicant friar; mendicant order

VERBS **9 request, ask,** make a request, **beg leave,** make bold to ask; **desire,** wish, wish for, express a wish for, crave; **ask for,** order, put in an order for, bespeak, call for, trouble one for; whistle for <nf>; **requisition,** make *or* put in a requisition, indent <Brit>; make application, **apply for,** file for, **put in for;** demand 421.4

10 petition, present *or* prefer a petition, sign a petition, circulate a petition; **pray,** sue; **apply to, call on** *or* **upon;** memorialize

11 entreat, implore, beseech, beg, crave, **plead, appeal, pray, supplicate,** impetrate, obtest; adjure, conjure; invoke, imprecate <old>, **call on** *or* **upon,** cry on *or* upon, **appeal to,** cry to, run to; go cap *or* hat in hand to; kneel to, go down on one's knees to, fall on one's knees to, go on bended knee to, throw oneself at the feet of, get *or* come down on one's marrow-bones <nf>; **plead for,** clamor for, cry for, cry out for; call for help

12 importune, urge, press, pressure <nf>, prod, prod at, apply *or* exert pressure, push, **ply;** dun; **beset, buttonhole,** besiege, take *or* grasp by the lapels; work on <nf>, **tease,** pester, plague, nag, nag at, make a pest *or* nuisance of oneself, try one's patience, bug <nf>, nudge; **coax,** wheedle, cajole, blandish, flatter, soft-soap <nf>

13 invite, ask, call, summon, call in, bid come, extend *or* issue an invitation, request the presence of, request the pleasure of one's company, send an engraved invitation

14 solicit, canvass; court, woo, address, sue, sue for, pop the question <nf>; **seek, bid for,** look for; **fish for,** angle for; pass the hat

15 beg, scrounge, cadge; mooch *and* **bum** *and* **panhandle** <nf>; **hit** *and* hit up *and* **touch** *and* put the touch on *and* make a touch <nf>; pass the hat <nf>

ADJS **16 supplicatory, suppliant,** supplicant, supplicating, **prayerful,** precative; **petitionary; begging,** mendicant, cadging, scrounging, mooching <nf>; on one's knees *or* bended knees, on one's marrow-bones <nf>; with joined *or* folded hands

17 imploring, entreating, beseeching, begging, pleading, appealing, precatory, precative, adjuratory

18 importunate; teasing, pesty, pesky <nf>, pestering, plaguing, nagging, dunning; **coaxing,** wheedling, cajoling, flattering, soft-soaping <nf>; **insistent, demanding, urgent**

19 invitational, inviting, invitatory

INTERJS **20 please,** prithee <old>, pray, do, **pray do;** be so good as to, be good enough, have the goodness; will you, may it please you; **if you please,** *s'il vous plaît* <Fr>; I beg you, *je vous en prie* <Fr>; for God's *or* goodness *or* heaven's *or* mercy's sake; be my guest, feel free; gimme a break!, cut me some slack!

441 CONSENT

NOUNS **1 consent, assent, agreement,** accord <old>, acceptance, approval, blessing, approbation, sanction, **endorsement,** ratification, backing; affirmation, affirmative, affirmative voice *or* vote, yea, aye, **nod** *and* **okay** *and* **OK** <nf>; **leave, permission** 443; **willingness,** readiness, promptness, promptitude, eagerness, unreluctance, unloathness, ungrudgingness, tacit *or* unspoken *or* silent *or* implicit consent, **connivance; acquiescence, compliance;** submission 433

VERBS **2 consent, assent,** give consent, yield assent, be willing, be amenable, be persuaded, accede to, accord to *and* grant <old>, say yes *or* aye *or* yea, vote affirmatively, vote aye, **nod, nod assent; accept, play** *or* **go along** <nf>, **agree to, sign off on** <nf>, go along with <nf>; be in accord with, be in favor of, take kindly to, **approve of,** hold with; **approve,** give one's blessing to, **okay** *or* **OK** <nf>; sanction, **endorse, ratify;** consent to silently *or* by implication *or* in petto <Ital>; **wink at, connive at; be willing,** turn a willing ear; deign, condescend; have no objection, not refuse; permit 443.9

3 acquiesce, comply, comply with, fall in with, take one up on <nf>, be persuaded, come round *or* around, come over, come to <nf>, see one's way clear to; **submit** 433.6,9

ADJS **4 consenting, assenting,** affirmative, amenable, persuaded, approving, agreeing, favorable, accordant, consentient, consentual; sanctioning, endorsing, ratifying; **acquiescent, compliant,** compliable <old>; submissive 433.12; **willing, agreeable,** content; ready, prompt, eager, unreluctant, unloath, nothing loath, unmurmuring, ungrudging, unrefusing; permissive 443.14

ADVS **5 consentingly, assentingly,** affirmatively,

approvingly, favorably, positively, agreeably, accordantly; acquiescently, compliantly; willingly 324.8; **yes** 332.18

442 REFUSAL

NOUNS **1 refusal, rejection,** turndown, turning down; thumbs-down <nf>, *pollice verso* <L>; nonconsent, nonacceptance; **declining,** declination, declension, declinature; **denial,** disclamation, disclaimer, disallowance; decertification, disaccreditation; **repudiation** 372.1; disagreement, dissent 333; recantation 363.3; contradiction 335.2; negation, abnegation, negative, negative answer, nay, no, nix <nf>; unwillingness 325; disobedience 327; noncompliance, noncooperation, nonobservance 435; withholding, holding back, retention, deprivation

2 repulse, rebuff, peremptory *or* flat *or* point-blank refusal, summary negative; a flea in one's ear; kiss-off *and* slap in the face *and* kick in the teeth <nf>; short shrift

VERBS **3 refuse, decline,** not consent, refuse consent, **reject, turn down** <nf>, decline to accept, **not have,** not buy <nf>; not hold with, not think *or* hear of; **say no,** say nay, vote nay, vote negatively *or* in the negative, side against, disagree, beg to disagree, dissent 333.4; shake one's head, negative, negate; vote down, **turn thumbs down on;** be unwilling 325.3; turn one's back on, turn a deaf ear to, set oneself against, set one's face against, be unmoved, harden one's heart, resist entreaty *or* persuasion; stand aloof, not lift a finger, have nothing to do with, wash one's hands of; hold out against; put *or* set one's foot down, refuse point-blank *or* summarily; decline politely *or* with thanks, beg off; **repudiate,** disallow, disclaim 372.2; decertify, disaccredit

4 deny, withhold, hold back; grudge, begrudge; close the hand *or* purse; deprive one of

5 repulse, rebuff, repel, kiss one off *and* slap one in the face *and* kick one in the teeth <nf>, send one away with a flea in one's ear, give one short shrift, shut *or* slam the door in one's face, turn one away; slap *or* smack one down <nf>; deny oneself to, refuse to receive, not be at home to, cut, **snub** 157.5; not want anything to do with

ADJS **6 unconsenting,** nonconsenting, **negative; unwilling** 325.5; **uncompliant,** uncomplying, uncomplaisant, inacquiescent, uncooperative; disobedient; rejective, declinatory; deaf to, not willing to hear of; dissenting

PHRS **7 I refuse, I won't,** I will not, I will do no such thing; over my dead body, far be it from me, not if I can help it, not likely, not on your life, count me out, include me out, I'm not taking any, I won't buy it, it's no go, like hell I will, I'll be hanged if I will, try and make me, you have another guess coming, you should live so long, I'll see you in hell first, nothing doing <nf>; out of the question, not to be thought of, impossible; **no,** by no means, **no way, no way José, there's no way;** in a pig's eye *or* ear *or* ass, my eye *or* ass

443 PERMISSION

NOUNS **1 permission, leave, allowance,** vouchsafement; **consent** 441; permission to enter, admission, ticket, ticket of admission; implied consent; approbation, blessing; **license,** liberty 430.1; **okay** *and* **OK** *and* **nod** *and* **go-ahead** *and* **green light** *and* **go sign** *and* **thumbs-up** <nf>; special permission, charter, patent, dispensation, release, waiver; zoning variance, variance

2 sufferance, tolerance, toleration, **indulgence;** leniency; winking, overlooking, connivance; permissiveness; dispensation, exemption

3 authorization, authority, sanction, licensing, countenance, **warrant,** warranty, fiat; empowerment, enabling, entitlement, enfranchisement, certification; clearance, security clearance; ratification 332.4; legalization, legitimation, decriminalization

4 carte blanche, blank check <nf>, freedom, **full authority,** full power, free hand, open mandate

5 grant, concession; charter, franchise, liberty, diploma, patent, letters patent, brevet; royal grant

6 permit, license, warrant; building permit, learner's permit, work permit; driver's license, marriage license, hunting license, fishing license, etc; nihil obstat, imprimatur; credentials

7 pass, passport, safe-conduct, safeguard, protection; visa, entry visa, exit visa; green card; **clearance,** clearance papers; bill of health, clean bill of health, pratique, full pratique

8 permissibility, permissibleness, **allowableness; admissibility,** admissibleness; justifiableness, warrantableness, sanctionableness; **validity,** legitimacy, lawfulness, licitness, legality

VERBS **9 permit, allow, admit, let,** leave <nf>, give permission, give leave, make possible; **allow** *or* **permit of;** give *or* leave room for, open the door to; consent 441.2; **grant,** accord, vouchsafe; **okay** *and* **OK** *and* **give the nod** *or* **go-ahead** *or* **green light** *or* **go sign** <nf>, say *or* give the word <nf>; dispense, release, waive

10 suffer, countenance, have, **tolerate, condone,** brook, endure, stomach, bear, bear with, put up with, stand for, hear of *and* go along with <nf>;

indulge 427.6; shut one's eyes to, **wink at,** blink at, overlook, connive at; leave the door *or* way open to

11 **authorize, sanction, warrant;** give official sanction *or* warrant, legitimize, validate, legalize; empower, give power, enable, entitle; **license; privilege;** charter, patent, enfranchise, franchise; accredit, certificate, certify; ratify 332.12; **legalize,** legitimate, legitimize, decriminalize

12 **give carte blanche,** issue *or* accord *or* give a blank check <nf>, give full power *or* authority, give an open mandate *or* invitation, give free rein, give a free hand, leave alone, leave it to one; permit all *or* anything, open the floodgates, remove all restrictions, let someone get away with murder <nf>

13 **may,** can, have permission, **be permitted** *or* **allowed**

ADJS 14 **permissive,** admissive, permitting, allowing; consenting 441.4; **unprohibitive,** nonprohibitive; tolerating, obliging, **tolerant;** suffering, **indulgent, lenient** 427.7; hands-off <nf>; lax 426.4; easy come easy go <nf>

15 **permissible, allowable, admissible;** justifiable, warrantable, sanctionable; licit, **lawful, legitimate, legal,** legitimized, legalized, legitimated, decriminalized, legit <nf>

16 **permitted, allowed,** admitted; tolerated, on sufferance; unprohibited, unforbidden, unregulated, unchecked; unconditional, without strings

17 **authorized,** empowered, entitled; **warranted, sanctioned; licensed, privileged;** chartered, patented; franchised, enfranchised; accredited, certificated

ADVS 18 **permissively,** admissively; **tolerantly, indulgently**

19 **permissibly, allowably,** admissibly; with permission, by one's leave; licitly, lawfully, legitimately, legally

PHRS 20 **by your leave,** with your permission, if you please, with respect, may I?

444 PROHIBITION

NOUNS 1 **prohibition, forbidding,** forbiddance; **ruling out, disallowance,** denial, rejection 372; refusal 442; **repression, suppression** 428.2; **ban, embargo, enjoinder, injunction,** prohibitory injunction, **proscription,** inhibition, **interdict,** *interdictum* <L>, interdiction; index, *Index Expurgatorius* and *Index Librorum Prohibitorum* <L>; gag order; **taboo;** thou-shalt-not *and* don't *and* no-no <nf>; law, statute 673.3; preclusion, exclusion, **prevention** 1012.2; forbidden fruit, contraband; sumptuary law *or* ordinance; zoning,

zoning law, restrictive convenant; **forbidden ground** *or* **territory,** no-man's land <nf>, no-fly zone; curfew; restriction, circumscription

2 **veto,** negative <old>; absolute veto, qualified *or* limited *or* negative veto, countermand, suspensive *or* suspensory veto, item veto, pocket veto; **thumbs-down** <nf>, red light <nf>, *pollice verso* <L>; blacklist

VERBS 3 **prohibit, forbid; disallow, rule out** *or* **against;** deny, **reject** 372.2; say no to, **refuse** 442.3; **bar,** debar, preclude, exclude, exclude from, shut out, shut *or* close the door on, **prevent** 1012.14; **ban,** put under the ban, **outlaw,** criminalize, proscribe; **repress, suppress** 428.8; **enjoin,** put under an injunction, issue an injunction against, issue a prohibitory injunction; **proscribe,** inhibit, **interdict,** put *or* lay under an interdict *or* interdiction; put on the Index; embargo, **lay** *or* **put an embargo on; taboo;** outlaw, criminalize

4 **not permit** *or* **allow, not have, not suffer** *or* **tolerate,** not endure, not stomach, not bear, not bear with, **not countenance,** not brook, brook no, not condone, not accept, not put up with, not go along with <nf>; not stand for *and* not hear of <nf>, put *or* set one's foot down on <nf>

5 **veto,** put one's veto upon, decide *or* rule against, **turn thumbs down on** <nf>, **negative,** kill, nix <nf>

ADJS 6 **prohibitive,** prohibitory, prohibiting, **forbidding;** inhibitive, inhibitory, **repressive, suppressive** 428.11; proscriptive, interdictive, interdictory; preclusive, exclusive, **preventive** 1012.19

7 **prohibited, forbidden,** forbade, forbid, *verboten* <Ger>, **barred; vetoed; unpermissible,** nonpermissible, not permitted *or* allowed, unchartered, **unallowed;** disallowed, ruled out, contraindicated; beyond the pale, off limits, out of bounds; unauthorized, **unsanctioned,** unlicensed; banned, under the ban, **outlawed,** contraband; taboo, untouchable; **illegal,** unlawful, illicit

445 REPEAL

NOUNS 1 **repeal, revocation,** revoke, revokement; reneging, renigging *and* going back on *and* welshing <nf>, **rescinding,** rescindment, rescission, **reversal, striking down, abrogation,** cassation; suspension; waiving, **waiver, setting aside; countermand,** counterorder; **annulment,** nullification, withdrawal, **invalidation,** voiding, voidance, vacation, vacatur, defeasance; **cancellation,** canceling, cancel, write-off; **abolition,** abolishment; **recall,** retraction, recantation 363.3

VERBS 2 **repeal, revoke, rescind, reverse, strike**

down, **abrogate**; renege, renig *and* go back on *and* welsh <nf>; suspend; **waive, set aside; countermand,** counterorder; **abolish,** do away with; **cancel,** write off; **annul,** nullify, disannul, withdraw, **invalidate,** void, vacate, make void, declare null and void; **overrule,** override; **recall,** retract, recant; unwish

ADJS **3 repealed, revoked, rescinded,** struck down, set aside; **invalid,** void, **null and void**

446 PROMOTION

NOUNS **1 promotion, preferment, advancement, advance,** step-up *and* upping <nf>, rise, elevation, upgrading, jump, step up, step up the ladder; **raise, boost** <nf>; kicking *or* bumping upstairs <nf>; exaltation, aggrandizement; ennoblement, knighting; graduation, passing; pay raise

VERBS **2 promote, advance,** prefer <old>, up *and* boost <nf>, elevate, upgrade, jump; kick *or* bump upstairs <nf>; **raise;** exalt, aggrandize; **ennoble,** knight; pass, graduate; raise one's pay, up *or* boost one's pay <nf>

447 DEMOTION, DEPOSAL

NOUNS **1 demotion,** degrading, degradation, disgrading, downgrading, debasement; abasement, humbling, humiliation, casting down; **reduction,** bump *and* bust <nf>; stripping of rank, depluming, displuming

2 deposal, deposition, removal, displacement, outplacement, supplanting, supplantation, replacement, deprivation, **ousting,** unseating; **cashiering, firing** <nf>, **dismissal** 908.5; reduction in forces *or* RIF; forced resignation; kicking upstairs <nf>; **superannuation,** pensioning off, putting out to pasture, **retirement,** the golden handshake *or* parachute <nf>; **suspension;** impeachment; purge, **liquidation; overthrow,** overthrowal; **dethronement,** disenthronement, discrownment; **disbarment,** disbarring; unfrocking, defrocking, unchurching; deconsecration, expulsion, excommunication 909.4

VERBS **3 demote, degrade,** disgrade, downgrade, debase, abase, humble, humiliate, **lower, reduce,** bump *and* bust <nf>; strip of rank, cut off one's spurs, deplume, displume

4 depose, remove from office, send to the showers *and* give the gate <nf>, divest *or* deprive *or* strip of office, **remove,** displace, outplace, supplant, replace; **oust; suspend; cashier,** drum out, strip of rank, **break,** bust <nf>; **dismiss** 909.19; **purge, liquidate; overthrow; retire,** superannuate, pension, pension off, put out to pasture, give the

golden handshake *or* parachute <nf>; kick upstairs <nf>; **unseat,** unsaddle; **dethrone,** disenthrone, unthrone, uncrown, discrown; **disbar; unfrock,** defrock, unchurch; strike off the roll, read out of; **expel,** excommunicate 909.17; deconsecrate

448 RESIGNATION, RETIREMENT

NOUNS **1 resignation,** demission, **withdrawal, retirement,** pensioning, pensioning off, golden handshake *or* parachute <nf>, superannuation, emeritus status; **abdication;** voluntary resignation; forced resignation, forced retirement, early retirement, deposal 447; relinquishment 370.3

VERBS **2 resign,** demit, **quit,** leave, **vacate,** withdraw from; **retire,** superannuate, be superannuated, be pensioned *or* pensioned off, be put out to pasture, get the golden handshake *or* parachute <nf>; relinquish, give up 370.7; retire from office, stand down, stand *or* step aside, give up one's post, hang up one's spurs <nf>; **tender** *or* **hand in one's resignation,** send in one's papers, turn in one's badge *or* uniform; **abdicate,** renounce the throne, give up the crown; pension off 447.4; be invalided out

ADJS **3 retired,** in retirement, superannuated, on pension, pensioned, pensioned off, emeritus, emerita <fem>

449 AID

NOUNS **1 aid, help, assistance, support, succor, relief, comfort,** ease, remedy; mutual help *or* assistance; **service, benefit** 387.4; ministry, ministration, office, offices, good offices; yeoman's service; therapy 91; protection 1008; **bailout** <nf>, **rescue** 398; means to an end

2 assist, helping hand, hand, lift; boost *and* leg up <nf>; help in time of need; **support group,** self-help group, Alcoholics Anonymous *or* AA, Gamblers Anonymous, etc, 12-step group; tough love; social assistance, counsel, guidance, moral support, constructive criticism, tender loving care *or* TLC

3 support, maintenance, sustainment, sustentation, **sustenance, subsistence,** provision, total support, meal ticket <nf>; **keep, upkeep; livelihood, living,** meat, bread, daily bread; **nurture, fostering,** nurturance, nourishment, nutriture <old>, mothering, parenting, rearing, fosterage, foster-care, **care, caring,** care-giving, tender loving care *or* TLC <nf>; manna, manna in the wilderness; economic support, price support, subsidy, subsidization, subvention, endowment; **support services, social services,** welfare, relief, succor

4 patronage, fosterage, tutelage, sponsorship, backing, auspices, aegis, coattails <nf>, care, guidance, **championing, championship,** seconding; interest, advocacy, encouragement, **backing, abetment;** countenance, **favor, goodwill,** charity, **sympathy,** handout <nf>

5 furtherance, helping along, advancement, advance, **promotion, forwarding,** facilitation, speeding, easing or smoothing of the way, clearing of the track, greasing of the wheels, expedition, expediting, rushing; preferment, special or preferential treatment; tailwind

6 self-help, self-helpfulness, **self-support,** self-sustainment, self-improvement; independence 430.5

7 helper, assistant 616.6; benefactor 592; facilitator, animator

8 reinforcements, support, relief, auxiliaries, reserves, reserve forces, staff

9 facility, accommodation, appliance, convenience, amenity, appurtenance; advantage; labor-saving device, time-saving device

10 helpfulness, aidfulness <old>, cooperation, goodwill; serviceability, utility, **usefulness** 387.3; **advantageousness,** profitability, favorableness, beneficialness 999.1

VERBS **11 aid, help, assist,** comfort, abet <old>, succor, relieve, **ease,** doctor, remedy; be of some help, put one's oar in <nf>; do good, do a world of good, **benefit, avail** 999.10; **favor, befriend; give help,** render assistance, offer or proffer aid, come to the aid of, rush or fly to the assistance of, lend aid, **give or lend or bear a hand** or helping hand, stretch forth or hold out a helping hand, cater for <chiefly Brit>; take by the hand, take in tow; **give an assist, give a leg up** or lift or boost <nf>, help a lame dog over a stile; **save,** redeem, bail out <nf>, **rescue** 398.3; protect 1008.18; set up, put on one's feet; give new life to, resuscitate, rally, reclaim, revive, **restore** 396.11,15; be the making of, set one up in business; see one through

12 support, lend support, give or furnish or afford support; **maintain, sustain, keep,** upkeep <Brit>; **uphold,** hold up, bear, upbear, **bear up,** bear out; reinforce, undergird, bolster, **bolster up,** buttress, shore, shore up, prop, prop up, crutch; **finance,** fund, subsidize, subvention, subventionize; comp and pick up the tab or check <nf>, give new life to

13 back, back up, stand behind, stand back of or in back of, get behind, get in behind, get in back of; **stand by,** stick by and **stick up for** <nf>, **champion; second, take the part of,** take up or adopt or espouse the cause of, take under one's wing, **go to bat for** <nf>, take up the cudgels for, run interference for <nf>, **side with,** take sides

with, associate oneself with, join oneself to, align oneself with, ally with, come down or range oneself on the side of, find time for

14 abet, aid and abet, encourage, hearten, embolden, comfort <old>; advocate, hold a brief for <nf>, countenance, keep in countenance, **endorse, lend oneself to,** lend one's countenance to, lend one's favor or support to, lend one's offices, put one's weight in the scale, plump for and thump the tub for <nf>, lend one's name to, give one's support or countenance to, give moral support to, hold one's hand, make one's cause one's own, weigh in for <nf>; subscribe <Brit>, **favor, go for** <nf>, smile upon, shine upon

15 patronize, sponsor, take up, endow, finance

16 foster, nurture, nourish, mother, care for, lavish care on, feed, parent, rear, sustain, cultivate, **cherish;** pamper, coddle, cosset, fondle <old>; **nurse,** suckle, cradle; dry-nurse, wet-nurse; spoon-feed; take in hand

17 be useful, further, forward, advance, promote, stand in good stead, encourage, **boost** <nf>, favor, advantage, **facilitate,** set or put or push forward, give an impulse to; speed, expedite, quicken, hasten, lend wings to; conduce to, make for, contribute to

18 serve, lend or **give oneself,** render service to, do service for, **work for, labor in behalf of; minister to,** cater to, do for <Brit>; attend 577.13; pander to

19 oblige, accommodate, favor, do a favor, do a service

ADJS **20 helping,** assisting, serving, promoting; **assistant, auxiliary,** adjuvant, subservient, subsidiary, ancillary, accessory; ministerial, ministering, ministrant; fostering, nurtural; care, caring, care-giving; instrumental

21 helpful, useful, utile, aidful <old>; **profitable, salutary,** good for, **beneficial** 999.12; remedial, therapeutic; **serviceable, useful** 387.18; **contributory,** contributing, conducive, **constructive, positive,** promotional, furthersome <old>; at one's service, at one's command, at one's beck and call

22 favorable, propitious; kind, kindly, kindly-disposed, all for <nf>, **well-disposed,** well-affected, well-intentioned, well-meant, **well-meaning;** benevolent, beneficent, benign, benignant; friendly, amicable, neighborly; cooperative

23 self-helpful, self-helping, self-improving; **self-supporting, self-sustaining;** self-supported, self-sustained; independent

ADVS **24 helpfully,** helpingly; **beneficially,** favorably, profitably, advantageously, to advantage, to the good; serviceably, **usefully**

PREPS **25** helped by, with the help *or* assistance of, by the aid of; **by means of**

26 for, on *or* **in behalf of,** in aid of <chiefly Brit>, in the name of, on account of, **for the sake of,** in the service of, in furtherance of, in favor of; remedial of

27 behind, back of <nf>, supporting, **in support of**

450 COOPERATION

NOUNS **1 cooperation, collaboration, coaction,** concurrence, synergy, synergism; support, backup; **consensus, commonality; community,** harmony, concordance, concord, fellowship, fellow feeling, solidarity, concert, united front, **teamwork;** pulling *or* working together, communal *or* community activity, joining of forces, pooling, pooling of resources, joining of hands; bipartisanship, **mutualism,** mutuality, mutual assistance, coadjuvancy; **reciprocity;** back-scratching, give and take; joint effort, common effort, combined *or* joint operation, common enterprise *or* endeavor, collective *or* united action, mass action; job-sharing; coagency; coadministration, cochairmanship, codirectorship; duet, duumvirate; trio, triumvirate, troika; quartet, quintet, sextet, septet, octet; government by committee; symbiosis, commensalism; **cooperativeness,** collaborativeness, team spirit, morale, esprit, *esprit de corps* <Fr>; communism, communalism, communitarianism, collectivism; ecumenism, ecumenicism, ecumenicalism; **collusion,** complicity; networking

2 affiliation, alliance, allying, alignment, association, consociation, combination, **union,** unification, **coalition,** fusion, merger, coalescence, coadunation, amalgamation, **league, federation, confederation,** confederacy, consolidation, incorporation, inclusion, integration; hookup *and* tie-up *and* tie-in <nf>; **partnership,** copartnership, copartnery <old>, cahoots <nf>; colleagueship, **collegialism, collegiality; fraternity,** confraternity, fraternization, fraternalism; sorority; **fellowship,** sodality; comradeship, camaraderie, freemasonry, communalism, ecumenicism

VERBS **3 cooperate, collaborate,** do business *and* **play ball** <nf>, coact, concur; concert, harmonize, concord; **join,** band, league, **associate, affiliate,** ally, **combine, unite,** fuse, merge, coalesce, amalgamate, federate, confederate, consolidate; hook up *and* tie up *and* tie in <nf>; partner, be in league, **go into partnership with,** go partners <nf>, go *or* be in cahoots with; **join together,** club together, league together, band together; **work together,** get together *and* team up *and* buddy up

<nf>, work as a team, act together, act in concert, **pull together; hold together, hang together,** keep together, **stand together,** stand shoulder to shoulder; lay *or* put *or* get heads together; **close ranks,** make common cause, throw in together <nf>, unite efforts, join in, pitch in; network; reciprocate; **conspire,** collude, aid and abet

4 side with, take sides with, **unite with; join, join with,** join up with *and* get together with *and* team up with <nf>, strike in with <old>; **throw in with** *and* string along with *and* swing in with <nf>, **go along with; line up with** <nf>, align with, align oneself with, range with, range oneself with, stand up with, stand in with; **join hands with,** be hand in glove with, go hand in hand with; act with, take part with, **go in with;** cast in one's lot with, join one's fortunes with, stand shoulder to shoulder with, be cheek by jowl with, sink or swim with, stand or fall with; **close ranks with,** fall in with, make common cause with, pool one's interests with; enlist under the banner of, rally round, flock to

ADJS **5 cooperative, cooperating,** cooperant, **hand in glove;** in cahoots <nf>; **collaborative,** coactive, coacting, coefficient, synergetic, synergic, synergical, synergistic *or* synergistical; **fellow;** concurrent, concurring, concerted, **in concert; consensus,** consensual, agreeing, in agreement, of like mind; harmonious, harmonized, concordant, **common, communal,** collective; **mutual,** reciprocal; **joint, combined** 805.5; coadjuvant, coadjutant; symbiotic, symbiotical, commensal; uncompetitive, noncompetitive, communalist, communalistic, communist, communistic, communitarian, collectivist, collectivistic; ecumenic *or* ecumenical; **conniving, collusive**

ADVS **6 cooperatively,** cooperatingly, coactively, coefficiently, concurrently; in consensus, consensually; **jointly,** combinedly, **conjointly,** concertedly, in concert with; harmoniously, concordantly; communally, collectively, **together;** as one, with one voice, unanimously, in chorus, in unison, as one man, en masse; **side by side, hand in hand, hand in glove, shoulder to shoulder, back to back,** "all for one, one for all"—Dumas père

7 in cooperation, in collaboration, in partnership, in cahoots <nf>, **in collusion,** in league

PREPS **8 with, in cooperation with,** etc

451 OPPOSITION

NOUNS **1 opposition,** opposing, opposure, crossing, oppugnancy, bucking <nf>, standing against; contraposition 779.1; **resistance** 453; **noncooperation; contention** 457; negation 335;

rejection 372, refusal; **counteraction, counterworking** 900.1; refusal 442; **contradiction,** challenge, contravention, contraversion, rebutment, rebuttal, denial, impugnation, impugnment; countercurrent, head wind; crosscurrent, undercurrent, undertow; unfriendliness, stiff opposition

2 **hostility, antagonism,** oppugnancy, oppugnance *and* oppugnation <old>, **antipathy,** enmity, bad blood, inimicalness; **contrariness, contrariety,** orneriness <nf>, repugnance *or* repugnancy, perverseness, **obstinacy** 361; fractiousness, refractoriness, recalcitrance 327.2; uncooperativeness, noncooperation, negativeness, **obstructionism,** traversal, bloody-mindedness <Brit>; **friction, conflict,** clashing, **collision,** cross-purposes, dissension, disaccord 456; rivalry, vying, competition 457.2; polarity

VERBS 3 **oppose, counter, cross,** go *or* act in opposition to, **go against,** run against, strive against, **run counter to,** fly in the face of, fly in the teeth of, conflict with; kick out against, make waves <nf>, **protest** 333.5; set oneself against, set one's face *or* heart against; be *or* play at cross-purposes, **obstruct,** traverse, sabotage; **take issue with, take one's stand against,** lift *or* raise a hand against, declare oneself against, stand and be counted against, side against, vote against, vote nay, veto; make a stand against, make a dead set against; join the opposition; not put up with, not abide, not be content with; counteract, counterwork, countervail 899.6; **resist,** withstand 453.3

4 **contend against,** militate against, **contest, combat, battle, clash with, clash, fight against, strive against,** struggle against, labor against, **take on** <nf>, grapple with, join battle with, close with, come to close quarters with, go the the mat with <nf>, antagonize <old>, **fight, buck** <nf>, **counter;** buffet, beat against, beat up against, breast, stem, breast *or* stem the tide *or* current *or* flood, breast the wave, buffet the waves; rival, compete with *or* against, vie with *or* against; fight back, **resist, offer resistance** 453.3

5 **confront, affront,** front, go eyeball-to-eyeball *or* one-on-one with <nf>, take on, **meet, face, meet head-on; encounter**

6 **contradict,** cross, traverse, contravene, controvert, rebut, deny, **gainsay;** challenge, contest; oppugn, call into question; **belie,** be contrary to, come in conflict with, negate 335.3; **reject** 372.2

7 **be against,** be agin <nf>, reject; discountenance 510.11; not hold with, not have anything to do with; have a crow to pluck *or* pick, have a bone to pick

ADJS 8 **oppositional, opponent, opposing, opposed; anti** <nf>, contra, confrontational, confrontive; at odds, at loggerheads; **adverse, adversary,** adversarial, adversative, oppugnant, antithetic, antithetical, repugnant, con <nf>, **set** *or* **dead set against; contrary, counter; negative; opposite,** oppositive, death on; overthwart <old>, cross; **contradictory;** unfavorable, unpropitious 133.17; **hostile, antagonistic,** unfriendly, enemy, inimical, alien, antipathetic, antipathetical, unsympathetic, averse; fractious, refractory, recalcitrant 327.10; uncooperative, noncooperative, **obstructive,** bloody-minded <Brit>; ornery <nf>, perverse, obstinate 361.8; **conflicting, clashing,** dissentient, disaccordant 456.15; rival, competitive

ADVS 9 **in opposition, in confrontation,** eyeball-to-eyeball *and* one-on-one <nf>, head-on, **at variance, at cross-purposes, at odds,** at issue, at war with, up in arms, with crossed bayonets, at daggers drawn, at daggers, in hostile array, poised against one another; contra, contrariwise, counter, cross, athwart; against the tide *or* wind *or* grain

PREPS 10 **opposed to, adverse to,** counter to, **in opposition to,** in conflict with, at cross-purposes with; **against,** agin <nf>, dead against, athwart; **versus,** vs; **con,** contra, face to face with, *vis-à-vis* <Fr>

452 OPPONENT

NOUNS 1 **opponent, adversary, antagonist, assailant, foe,** foeman, **enemy,** archenemy; adverse *or* opposing party, opposite camp, opposite *or* opposing side, **the opposition,** the loyal opposition, unfriendly <nf>; **combatant** 461

2 **competitor, contestant, contender,** corrival, vier, player, entrant; **rival,** arch-rival; emulator; the field; finalist, semifinalist, etc

3 **oppositionist,** opposer; obstructionist, obstructive, negativist, naysayer; contra; **objector, protester,** dissident, dissentient; **resister;** noncooperator; **disputant,** litigant, plaintiff, defendant; quarreler, irritable man, scrapper <nf>, wrangler, brawler; die-hard, bitter-ender, last-ditcher, intransigent, irreconcilable

453 RESISTANCE

NOUNS 1 **resistance,** withstanding, countering, renitence *or* renitency, repellence *or* repellency; **defiance** 454; **opposing, opposition** 451; **stand; repulsion,** repulse, rebuff; **objection, protest,** remonstrance, **dispute,** challenge, **demur; complaint;** dissentience, **dissent** 333; reaction, hostile *or* combative reaction, **counteraction** 900;

revolt 327.4; recalcitrance *or* recalcitrancy, recalcitration, fractiousness, refractoriness 327.2; **reluctance** 325.1; **obstinacy** 361; passive resistance, noncooperation; uncooperativeness, negativism; obstinacy; resistance movement, passive resistance, civil disobedience, mutiny, insurrection, insurgence

VERBS **2 resist, withstand; stand; endure** 134.5; **stand up, bear up, hold up, hold out; defy** 454.3, tell one where to get off <nf>, throw down the gauntlet; be obstinate; be proof against, bear up against; **repel, repulse,** rebuff

3 offer resistance, fight back, bite back, not turn the other cheek, show fight, lift *or* raise a hand, stand *or* hold one's ground, **withstand,** stand, **take one's stand,** make a stand, make a stand against, take one's stand against, square off *and* put up one's dukes <nf>, **stand up to,** stand up against, stand at bay; front, **confront,** meet head-on, fly in the teeth *or* face of, **face up to,** face down, face out; **object, protest,** remonstrate, **dispute,** challenge, **complain,** complain loudly, exclaim at; **dissent** 333.4; revolt, mutiny; make waves <nf>; make a determined resistance; kick against, kick out against, recalcitrate; put up a fight *or* struggle <nf>, not take lying down, hang tough *and* tough it out <nf>; **revolt** 327.7; **oppose** 451.3; **contend with** 457.18; **strive against** 451.4

4 stand fast, stand *or* **hold one's ground,** make a resolute stand, **hold one's own,** remain firm, stick *and* stuck fast <nf>, **stick to one's guns, stay it out, stick it out** <nf>, **hold out,** not back down, not give up, not submit, **never say die; fight to the last ditch,** die hard, sell one's life dearly, go down with flying colors, refuse to bow down

ADJS **5 resistant, resistive,** resisting, renitent, up against, **withstanding,** repellent; obstructive, retardant, retardative; **unyielding,** unsubmissive 361.12; hard-shell, hard-nosed; rebellious 327.11; **proof against; objecting, protesting,** disputing, disputatious, complaining, dissentient, dissenting 333.6; recalcitrant, fractious, obstinate, refractory 327.10; **reluctant** 325.6; noncooperative, uncooperative; up in arms, on the barricades, not lying down

454 DEFIANCE

NOUNS **1 defiance,** defying, defial <old>; **daring,** daringness, **audacity,** boldness, bold front, brash bearing, brashness, brassiness <nf>, brazenness, bravado, insolence; bearding, beard-tweaking, nose-tweaking; **arrogance** 141; **sauciness,** sauce, **cheekiness** *or* cheek <nf>, pertness, impudence, impertinence; bumptiousness, cockiness;

contempt, contemptuousness, derision, **disdain,** disregard, despite; **risk-taking,** tightrope walking, funambulism; disobedience, insubordination

2 challenge, dare, double dare, threat, taunt; fighting words; **defy** *or* defi; gage, gage of battle, gauntlet, glove, chip on one's shoulder, slap of the glove, invitation *or* bid to combat, call to arms; war cry, war whoop, battle cry, rebel yell; back talk, insult

VERBS **3 defy,** bid defiance, hurl defiance, snarl *or* shout *or* scream defiance; **dare,** double-dare, outdare; **challenge,** call out, throw *or* fling down the gauntlet *or* glove *or* gage, stand up to, knock the chip off one's shoulder, cross swords; oppose, protest; beard, beard the lion in his den, face, face out, look in the eye, stare down, stare out <Brit>, **confront, affront,** front, say right to one's face, square up to, go eyeball-to-eyeball *or* one-on-one with <nf>; tweak the nose, pluck by the beard, slap one's face, double *or* shake one's fist at; give one the finger; **ask for it** <nf>, ask *or* look for trouble, make something of it <nf>, show fight, show one's teeth, bare one's fangs; dance the war dance; **brave** 492.11; be insubordinate

4 flout, disregard, **slight,** slight over, treat with contempt, set at defiance, fly in the teeth *or* face of, **snap one's fingers at; thumb one's nose at,** cock a snook at, bite the thumb at; **disdain, despise, scorn** 157.3; laugh at, laugh to scorn, laugh out of court, laugh in one's face; hold in derision, scout, scoff at, **deride** 508.8; give someone lip <nf>, sass <nf>

5 show *or* **put up a bold front,** bluster, throw out one's chest, strut, crow, look big, stand with arms akimbo

6 take a dare, accept a challenge, **take one up on** *and* **call one's bluff** <nf>; **start something,** take up the gauntlet

ADJS **7 defiant,** defying, challenging; **daring, bold,** brash, brassy <nf>, brazen, **audacious,** insolent; arrogant 141.9; saucy, cheeky <nf>, pert, impudent, impertinent; stubborn, obstinate; bumptious, cocky, sassy; **contemptuous,** disdainful, derisive, disregardful, greatly daring, regardless of consequences

ADVS **8 in defiance of,** in the teeth of, in the face of, under one's very nose

455 ACCORD

<harmonious relationship>

NOUNS **1 accord,** accordance, **concord,** concordance, **harmony,** symphony, sync <nf>; **rapport;** good vibrations <nf>, good vibes <nf>, good karma; amity 587.1; frictionlessness; *rapprochement* <Fr>; **sympathy,** empathy, identity, feeling of identity, fellow feeling, **fellowship,** kinship, togetherness, **affinity; agreement, understanding, like-mindedness, congruence;** congeniality, **compatibility; oneness,** unity, unison, union; **community,** communion, community of interests; solidarity, team spirit, esprit, *esprit de corps* <Fr>; mutuality, sharing, reciprocity, mutual supportiveness; bonds of harmony, ties of affection, cement of friendship; happy family; peace 464; **love,** *agape* <Gk>, charity, *caritas* <L>, brotherly love; correspondence 788.1

VERBS **2 get along,** harmonize, **agree with, agree, get along with,** get on with, cotton to *or* hit it off with <nf>, harmonize with, **be in harmony with,** be in tune with, fall *or* chime in with, blend in with, go hand in hand with, **be at one with;** sing in chorus, be on the same wavelength <nf>, see eye to eye; **sympathize,** empathize, identify with, respond to, understand one another, enter into one's views, enter into the ideas *or* feelings of; **accord,** correspond 788.6; reciprocate, interchange 863.4

ADJS **3 in accord,** accordant <old>, **harmonious, in harmony,** congruous, congruent, in tune, attuned, agreeing, in concert, **in rapport,** *en rapport* <Fr>, amicable 587.15,18; frictionless; **sympathetic,** simpatico <nf>, empathic, empathetic, **understanding; like-minded,** akin, of the same mind, of one mind, at one, united, together; concordant, corresponding 788.9; agreeable, congenial, **compatible; peaceful** 464.9

456 DISACCORD
<unharmonious relationship>

NOUNS **1 disaccord, discord,** discordance *or* discordancy, asynchrony, **unharmoniousness,** inharmoniousness, disharmony, inharmony, incongruence, disaffinity, incompatibility, incompatibleness; culture gap, generation gap, gender gap; noncooperation; **conflict,** open conflict *or* war, **friction,** rub; **jarring,** jangle, clash, clashing; touchiness, strained relations, **tension;** bad blood; **unpleasantness;** mischief; **contention** 457; **enmity** 589; Eris, Discordia; the Apple of Discord

2 disagreement, difficulty, misunderstanding, difference, difference of opinion, agreement to disagree, **variance,** division, dividedness; cross-purposes; polarity of opinion, polarization; **disparity** 789.1

3 dissension, dissent, dissidence, flak <nf>; bickering, infighting, faction, factiousness, partisanship, partisan spirit; **divisiveness; quarrelsomeness;** litigiousness; pugnacity,

bellicosity, combativeness, **aggressiveness,** contentiousness, belligerence; feistiness <nf>, **touchiness, irritability,** shrewishness, irascibility 110.2

4 falling-out, breach of friendship, parting of the ways, bust-up <nf>; **alienation, estrangement, disaffection,** disfavor; **breach, break, rupture, schism, split, rift,** cleft, **disunity, disunion, disruption,** separation, cleavage, divergence, division, dividedness; division in the camp, house divided against itself; open rupture, breaking off of negotiations, recall of ambassadors

5 quarrel, open quarrel, dustup **dispute, argument,** polemic, argy-bargy *and* slanging match <Brit>, fliting <old>, lovers' quarrel, **controversy,** altercation, **fight, squabble, contention,** strife, **tussle,** bicker, wrangle, snarl, **tiff, spat,** fuss; **breach of the peace; fracas,** donnybrook *or* donnybrook fair; dissent; broil, embroilment, imbroglio; words, sharp words, war of words, logomachy; **feud,** blood feud, vendetta; brawl 457.5

6 <nf terms> row, rumpus, row-de-dow, ruckus, ruction, brannigan, shindy, foofooraw, hoo-ha, barney *and* shemozzle <Brit>, set-to, run-in, **scrap, hassle,** rhubarb; knock-down-and-drag-out, knock-down-and-drag-out quarrel *or* fight; the dozens

7 bone of contention, apple of discord, sore point, tender spot, delicate *or* ticklish issue, rub, beef <nf>; **bone to pick,** crow to pluck *or* pick *or* pull; *casus belli* <L>, grounds for war

VERBS **8 disagree, differ,** differ in opinion, hold opposite views, disaccord, **be at variance,** not get along, pull different ways, be at cross-purposes, have no measures with, misunderstand one another; **conflict, clash,** collide, jostle, jangle, jar; live like cat and dog, live a cat-and-dog life

9 have a bone to pick with, have a crow to pluck with *or* pick with *or* pull with, have a beef with <nf>

10 fall out, have a falling-out, **break with, split,** separate, **diverge,** divide, agree to disagree, **part company,** come to *or* reach a parting of the ways

11 quarrel, dispute, oppugn, flite <old>, altercate, **fight, squabble,** tiff, spat, **bicker, wrangle,** spar, broil, have words, set to, join issue, make the fur fly; cross swords, **feud, battle; brawl; be quarrelsome** *or* contentious, be thin-skinned, be touchy *or* sensitive, get up on the wrong side of the bed

12 <nf terms> row, scrap, hassle, make *or* kick up a row; mix it up, lock horns, bump heads

13 pick a quarrel, fasten a quarrel on, look for trouble, pick a bone with, pluck a crow with; have a chip on one's shoulder; add insult to injury

14 sow dissension, stir up trouble, make *or* borrow trouble; **alienate, estrange,** separate, **divide, disunite,** disaffect, **come between; irritate, provoke,** aggravate; **set at odds,** set at variance; **set against,** pit against, **sic on** *or* **at, set on,** set by the ears, set at one's throat; add fuel to the fire *or* flame, fan the flame, pour oil on the blaze, light the fuse, stir the pot <nf>

ADJS **15 disaccordant, unharmonious,** inharmonious, disharmonious, out of tune, asynchronous, unsynchronized, out of sync <nf>, **discordant,** out of accord, dissident, dissentient, **disagreeing, differing; conflicting,** clashing, colliding; like cats and dogs; **divided,** faction-ridden, fragmented

16 at odds, at variance, at loggerheads, at square <old>, at cross-purposes; at war, at strife, at feud, at swords' points, at daggers *or* at daggers drawn, up in arms

17 partisan, polarizing, **divisive,** factional, factious; **quarrelsome,** bickering, disputatious, wrangling, eristic, eristical, polemical; litigious, pugnacious, combative, **aggressive,** bellicose, belligerent; feisty <nf>, touchy, irritable, shrewish, **irascible** 110.19

457 CONTENTION

NOUNS **1 contention, contest,** contestation, combat, **fighting, conflict, strife, war, struggle,** blood on the floor, cut and thrust; fighting at close quarters, infighting; **warfare** 458; **hostility,** enmity 589; **quarrel, altercation, controversy,** dustup, polemic, debate, forensics, **argument, dispute, disputation;** litigation; words, war of words, paper war, logomachy; **fighting,** scrapping *and* hassling <nf>; **quarreling, bickering, wrangling, squabbling;** oppugnancy, contentiousness, disputatiousness, litigiousness, **quarrelsomeness** 456.3; cat-and-dog life; Kilkenny cats; **competitiveness,** vying, rivalrousness, competitorship; cold war

2 competition, rivalry, trying conclusions *or* the issue, vying, emulation, jockeying <nf>; cutthroat competition; run for one's money; **sportsmanship, gamesmanship,** lifemanship, one-upmanship, **competitive advantage;** rat race <nf>; feeding frenzy <nf>

3 contest, engagement, encounter, match, matching, meet, meeting, derby, pissing match <nf>, **trial, test,** *concours* and *rencontre* <Fr>; **close contest, hard contest,** closely fought contest, close *or* tight one, horse race *and* crapshoot <nf>; fight, bout, go <nf>, tussle; joust, tilt; tournament, tourney; rally; **game** 743.9; **games,** Olympic games, Olympics, gymkhana; cookoff, Bake-Off <trademark>

4 fight, battle, fray, affray, combat, action, conflict, embroilment; gun battle; **clash; brush, skirmish,** scrimmage; tussle, **scuffle, struggle,** scramble, shoving match; exchange of blows, *passage d'armes* <Fr>, passage at *or* of arms, clash of arms; **quarrel** 456.5; pitched battle; battle royal; unarmed combat; **fistfight,** punch-out *and* duke-out <nf>, punch-up <Brit nf>; **hand-to-hand fight,** stand-up fight <nf>, running fight *or* engagement; tug-of-war; bull-fight, tauromachy; dogfight, cockfight; street fight, rumble <nf>; air *or* aerial combat, sea *or* naval combat, ground combat, armored combat, infantry combat, fire fight, hand-to-hand combat, house-to-house combat; **internal struggle,** intestine *or* internecine struggle *or* combat; rhubarb <nf>

5 free-for-all, knock-down-and-drag-out <nf>, **brawl,** broil, melee, scrimmage, **fracas,** riot

6 death struggle, life-and-death *or* **life-or-death struggle, struggle** *or* **fight** *or* **duel to the death,** *guerre à mort* and *guerre à outrance* <Fr>, all-out war, total war, last-ditch fight, fight to the last ditch, fight with no quarter given

7 duel, single combat, monomachy, satisfaction, **affair of honor,** *affaire d'honneur* <Fr>

8 fencing, swordplay; swordsmanship, dueling

9 boxing 754, **fighting,** noble *or* manly art of self-defense, **fisticuffs, pugilism, prize-fighting,** the fights <nf>, the ring; **boxing match, prizefight,** spar, bout; shadowboxing; close fighting, infighting, the clinches <nf>; Chinese boxing; savate

10 wrestling, rassling <nf>, grappling, *sumo* <Japanese>; **martial arts;** catch-as-catch-can; wrestling match, wrestling meet; Greco-Roman wrestling, Cornish wrestling, Westmorland wrestling, Cumberland wrestling

11 racing, track, track sports; **horse racing** 757, the turf, the sport of kings; dog racing, automobile racing 756

12 race, contest of speed *or* fleetness; derby; **horse race; automobile race,** off-road race; **heat, lap,** bell lap, victory lap; footrace, run, running event; torch race; match race, obstacle race, three-legged race, sack race, potato race; walk; ride and tie; endurance race, motorcycle race, bicycle race; boat race, yacht race, regatta; air race; dog race

VERBS **13 contend, contest,** jostle; **fight, battle, combat, war, declare** *or* **go to war,** take *or* take up arms, put up a fight <nf>, open hostilities, call to arms; wage war; **strive, struggle,** scramble, go for the brass ring; make the fur *or* feathers fly, **tussle, scuffle;** quarrel 456.11,12; clash, collide; **wrestle,** rassle <nf>, grapple, grapple with, go to the mat with; **come to blows,** close, try conclusions, **mix it**

up *and* go toe-to-toe <nf>, exchange blows *or* fisticuffs, **box**, spar, give and take, give one a knuckle sandwich <nf>; cut and thrust, **cross swords, fence,** thrust and parry; **joust, tilt, tourney,** run a tilt *or* a tilt at, break a lance with; **duel**, fight a duel, give satisfaction; feud; skirmish; fight one's way; fight the good fight; **brawl**, broil; **riot**; do a job on <nf>

14 **lift** *or* **raise one's hand against;** make war on; draw the sword against, take up the cudgels, couch one's lance; square up *or* off <nf>, come to the scratch; have at, jump; lay on, lay about one; **pitch into** *and* **sail into** *and* light into *and* lay into *and* rip into <nf>, strike the first blow, draw first blood; **attack** 459.15

15 **encounter, come** *or* **go up against,** fall *or* run foul *or* afoul of; close with, come to close quarters, bring to bay, meet *or* fight hand-to-hand

16 **engage, take on** <nf>, go against *or* up against, close with, try conclusions with, enter the ring *or* arena with, put on the gloves with, match oneself against; **join issue** *or* **battle, do** *or* **give battle,** engage in battle *or* combat

17 **contend with, engage with,** cope with, **fight with, strive with, struggle with,** wrestle with, grapple with, bandy with <old>, try conclusions with, measure swords with, tilt with, **cross swords with;** exchange shots, shoot it out with <nf>; **lock horns** *and* **bump heads** <nf>, fall *or* go to loggerheads <old>; **tangle with** *and* **mix it up with** <nf>, have a brush with; have it out, fight *or* battle it out, settle it; **fight** *or* **go at it hammer and tongs** *or* tooth and nail, fight it out, duke it out <nf>, fight like devils, ask *and* give no quarter, make blood flow freely, battle *à outrance,* fight to the death, fight to the finish

18 **compete, contend, vie,** try conclusions *or* the issue, jockey <nf>; **compete with** *or* **against, vie with, challenge,** cope <old>, enter into competition with, give a run for one's money, **meet;** try *or* test one another; **rival,** emulate, outvie; keep up with the Joneses

19 **race,** race with, run a race; horse-race, boat-race

20 **contend for, strive for, struggle for, fight for,** vie for; stickle for, stipulate for, hold out for, make a point of

21 **dispute, contest,** oppugn, take issue with; **fight over, quarrel over, wrangle over, squabble over,** bicker over, strive *or* contend about

ADJS 22 **contending,** contesting; **contestant,** disputant; striving, struggling; fighting, battling, warring; **warlike; quarrelsome** 456.17

23 **competitive,** competitory, competing, **vying,** rivaling, **rival,** rivalrous, emulous, in competition, in rivalry; **cutthroat**

458 WARFARE

NOUNS 1 **war, warfare, warring, warmaking,** art of war, **combat, fighting,** *la guerre* <Fr>; armed conflict, armed combat, military operation, the sword, arbitrament of the sword, appeal to arms *or* the sword, resort to arms, force *or* might of arms, bloodshed; **state of war, hostilities,** belligerence *or* belligerency, open war *or* warfare *or* hostilities; **hot war, shooting war;** total war, **all-out war; wartime;** battle 457.4; attack 459; **war zone, theater of operations;** trouble spot; warpath; localized war, major war, world war, atomic war, nuclear war, civil war, chemical war, war of independence, naval war; offensive warfare, preventive warfare, psychological warfare; static warfare, trench warfare, guerrilla warfare; nuclear winter

2 "a brain-spattering, windpipe-slitting art," "the feast of vultures, and the waste of life"—both Byron, "the business of barbarians"—Napoleon, "politics with bloodshed"—Mao Tse-tung

3 **battle array,** order of battle, **disposition, deployment, marshaling;** open order; close formation; echelon

4 **campaign,** war, **drive, expedition,** battle plan, hostile expedition; **crusade,** holy war, jihad

5 **operation,** action; **movement; mission; operations,** military operations, land operations, naval *or* sea operations, air operations; combined operations, joint operations, coordinated operations; active operations, amphibious operations, airborne operations, fluid operations, major operations, minor operations, night operations, overseas operations; war plans, staff work; logistic; war game, dry run, kriegspiel, maneuver, maneuvers; **strategy, tactics; battle**

6 **military science,** art *or* rules *or* science of war, military affairs, military strategy, military tactics, military operations; siegecraft; warcraft, war, **arms,** profession of arms; **generalship,** soldiership; chivalry, knighthood, knightly skill

7 **declaration of war,** challenge; defiance 454

8 **call to arms, call-up,** call to the colors, **rally; mobilization; muster,** levy; conscription, recruitment; **rallying cry,** slogan, watchword, catchword, exhortation; **battle cry,** war cry, war whoop, rebel yell; banzai, gung ho, St George, Montjoie, Geronimo, go for broke; **bugle call,** trumpet call, clarion, clarion call; remember the Maine *or* the Alamo *or* Pearl Harbor; battle orders, military orders

9 **service, military service;** active service *or* duty; military duty, military obligation, compulsory service, conscription, draft, impressment; selective

service, national service <Brit>; reserve status; recruiting, recruitment; enlisting, volunteering

10 **militarization,** activation, **mobilization;** war *or* wartime footing, national emergency; **war effort, war economy;** martial law, suspension of civil rights; garrison state, military dictatorship; remilitarization, reactivation; arms race; war clouds, war scare

11 **warlikeness,** unpeacefulness, war *or* warlike spirit, ferocity, fierceness; **hard line; combativeness, contentiousness; hostility, antagonism;** unfriendliness 589.1; aggression, **aggressiveness;** aggro <Brit nf>; belligerence *or* belligerency, **pugnacity,** pugnaciousness, **bellicosity, bellicoseness, truculence,** fight <nf>; chip on one's shoulder <nf>; militancy, **militarism,** martialism, militaryism; saber rattling; **chauvinism, jingoism,** hawkishness <nf>, **warmongering;** waving of the bloody shirt; warpath; war fever; oppugnancy, **quarrelsomeness** 456.3

12 <rallying devices and themes> battle flag, banner, colors, gonfalon, bloody shirt, bluidy sark <Scot>, fiery cross *or* crostarie, atrocity story, enemy atrocities; martial music, war song, battle hymn, national anthem, military band; national honor, face; foreign threat, totalitarian threat, Communist threat, colonialist *or* neocolonialist *or* imperialist threat, Western imperialism, yellow peril; expansionism, manifest destiny; independence, self-determination

13 war-god, Mars, Ares, Odin *or* Woden *or* Wotan, Tyr *or* Tiu *or* Tiw; war-goddess, Athena, Minerva, Bellona, Enyo, Valkyrie

VERBS 14 **war, wage war, make war, carry on war** *or* **hostilities,** engage in hostilities, wield the sword; battle, **fight;** spill *or* shed blood

15 **make war on,** levy war on; **attack** 459.15,17; **declare war, challenge,** combat, attack, throw *or* fling down the gauntlet; defy 454.3; open hostilities, plunge the world into war; launch a holy war on, go on a crusade against

16 **go to war,** break *or* breach the peace, take up the gauntlet, **go on the warpath, rise up in arms, take** *or* **resort to arms,** take arms, take up arms, take up the cudgels *or* sword, fly *or* appeal to the sword, unsheathe one's weapon, come to cold steel; take the offensive, take the field

17 **campaign,** undertake operations, open a campaign, make an expedition, go on a crusade

18 **serve,** do duty; fulfill one's military obligation, wear the uniform; **soldier,** see *or* do active duty; **bear arms,** carry arms, shoulder arms, shoulder a gun, defend, protect; see action *or* combat, hear shots fired in anger

19 **call to arms, call up,** call to the colors, **rally; mobilize; muster,** levy; **conscript, recruit;** sound the call to arms, give the battle cry, wave the bloody shirt, beat the drums, blow the bugle *or* clarion

20 **militarize, activate, mobilize,** go on a wartime footing, put on a war footing, call to the colors, gird *or* gird up one's loins, muster one's resources; reactivate, remilitarize, take out of mothballs *and* retread <nf>

ADJS 21 **warlike, militant,** fighting, warring, battling; **martial, military,** soldierly, soldierlike; **combative, contentious,** gladiatorial; trigger-happy <nf>; **belligerent, pugnacious,** pugilistic, **truculent, bellicose,** scrappy <nf>, full of fight; **aggressive,** offensive; fierce, ferocious, savage, bloody, bloody-minded, bloodthirsty, sanguinary, sanguineous; **unpeaceful,** unpeaceable, unpacific; **hostile, antagonistic,** agonistic, **enemy,** inimical; unfriendly 589.9; **quarrelsome** 456.17; paramilitary, mercenary, soldierlike

22 **militaristic, warmongering,** war-loving, warlike, saber-rattling, battle-hungry; **chauvinistic,** chauvinist, **jingoistic,** jingoist, jingoish, jingo, crusading; **hard-line, hawkish** <nf>, of the war party

23 **embattled,** battled, **engaged,** at grips, in combat, on the warpath, on the offensive; **arrayed, deployed,** ranged, in battle array, in the field; **militarized; armed** 460.14; war-ravaged, war-torn

ADVS 24 **at war, up in arms;** in the midst of battle, in the thick of the fray *or* combat; in the cannon's mouth, at the point of the gun; at swords' points, at the point of the bayonet *or* sword

25 **wars**

American Civil War <1861–65>	French Revolution <1789–99>
American Revolution *or* War of Independence *or* Revolutionary War <1775–83>	Gallic War <58–50 BC>
	Greco-Persian Wars <492–449 BC>
Arab-Israeli War <1948–49, 1956, 1967, 1973–74, 1982>	Hundred Years' War <1337–1453>
	Indian Wars <1622–75, 1840–80s>
Balkan Wars <1912–13>	Iran-Iraq War <1980–90>
Boer Wars <1880–81, 1899–1902>	
Crimean War <1853–56>	Italian Wars of Independence <1848–49, 1859–60>
Crusades <11th–13th centuries>	
	Korean War <1950–53>
English Civil War <1642–46>	Kosovo Crisis <1998–99>
	Mexican Civil War <1910–20>
Franco-Prussian War <1870–71>	Mexican War <1846–48>
French and Indian War <1754–63>	Napoleonic Wars <1793–1815>

Norman Conquest <1066>
Opium Wars <1839–42, 1856–60>
Peloponnesian Wars <431–404 BC>
Persian Gulf War <1990–91>
Punic Wars <264–241 BC, 218–201 BC>
Russian Revolution *or* Russian Civil War <1918–20>
Russo-Finnish War *or* Winter War <1939–40>
Russo-Japanese War <1904–05>
Samnite Wars <343–341, 326–304, 298–290 BC>
Seven Weeks' War <1866>
Seven Years' War <1756–63>
Sino-Japanese Wars <1894–95, 1937–45>
Six-Day War <1967>
Spanish-American War <1898>
Spanish Civil War <1936–39>
Taiping Rebellion <1850–64>
Thirty Years' War <1618–48>
Vietnam War *or* War in Southeast Asia <1955–75>
War of 1812 <1812–14>
War of the Austrian Succession <1740–48>
War of the Polish Succession <1733–38>
War of the Spanish Succession <1701–14>
Wars of the Roses <1455–85>
World War I *or* Great War *or* War of the Nations <1914–18>
World War II <1939–45>
Yom Kippur War <1973>

459 ATTACK

NOUNS **1 attack, assault,** assailing, assailment; **offense, offensive; aggression; onset, onslaught; strike;** surgical strike, first strike, preventive war; descent on *or* upon; **charge,** rush, dead set at, run at *or* against; **drive, push** <nf>; **sally, sortie;** infiltration; *coup de main* <Fr>; frontal attack *or* assault, head-on attack, flank attack; mass attack, kamikaze attack; banzai attack *or* charge, suicide attack *or* charge; hit-and-run attack; breakthrough; **counterattack, counteroffensive;** amphibious attack; gas attack; diversionary attack, diversion; assault and battery, simple assault, mugging <nf>, aggravated assault, armed assault, unprovoked assault; **preemptive strike; blitzkrieg, blitz,** lightning attack, lightning war, panzer warfare, sudden *or* devastating *or* crippling attack, deep strike, shock tactics; atomic *or* thermonuclear attack, first-strike capacity, megadeath, overkill; nuclear winter; land attack, air attack, combined attack, terrorist attack; personal attack

2 surprise attack, surprise, surprisal, unforeseen attack, **sneak attack** <nf>; Pearl Harbor; stab in the back; shock tactics

3 thrust, pass, lunge, swing, cut, stab, jab; feint; home thrust

4 raid, foray, razzia; **invasion, incursion,** inroad, irruption; **air raid, air strike,** air attack, shuttle raid, fire raid, saturation raid; escalade, scaling, boarding, **tank** *or* **armored attack,** panzer attack

5 siege, besiegement, beleaguerment; encompassment, investment, encirclement, envelopment; blockading, blockade; cutting of supply lines; vertical envelopment; pincer movement

6 storm, storming, taking by storm, overrunning

7 bombardment, bombing, air bombing, strategic bombing, tactical bombing, saturation bombing; strafing

8 gunfire, fire, firing, musketry, **shooting,** fireworks *or* gunplay <nf>; gunfight, shoot-out; **firepower,** offensive capacity, bang <nf>

9 volley, salvo, burst, spray, strafe, **fusillade,** rapid fire; cross fire; drumfire, **cannonade,** cannonry, **broadside,** enfilade; **barrage, artillery barrage;** sharpshooting, sniping

10 stabbing, piercing, sticking <nf>; **knifing,** bayonetting; the sword; **impalement, transfixion**

11 stoning, lapidation

12 assailant, assailer, **attacker;** assaulter, mugger <nf>; **aggressor;** invader, raider; warrior; terrorist

13 zero hour, H-hour; D-day, target day

VERBS **14 attack, assault, assail,** harry, assume *or* take the offensive; commit an assault upon; **strike, hit, pound; go at, come at,** have at, **launch out against,** make a set *or* dead set at; **fall on** *or* **upon, set on** *or* **upon, descend on** *or* **upon,** come down on, swoop down on; pounce upon; **lift** *or* **raise a hand against,** draw the sword against, take up arms *or* the cudgels against; **lay hands on,** lay a hand on, bloody one's hands with; gang up on, surprise, **ambush; blitz,** attack *or* hit like lightning

15 <nf terms> **pitch into, light into, lambaste,** pile into, sail into, wade into, lay into, plow into, tie into, rip into; **let one have it,** let one have it with both barrels, kick ass; **land on,** land on like a ton of bricks, climb all over, crack down on, lower the boom on, tee off on; **mug,** jump, bushwhack, sandbag, scrag; swipe at, lay at, **go for, go at;** blindside, blind-pop, sucker-punch; **take a swing** *or* **crack** *or* **swipe** *or* **poke** *or* punch *or* **shot at**

16 lash out at, strike out at, hit out at, let drive at, let fly at; **strike at,** hit at, poke at, thrust at, **swing at,** swing on, make a thrust *or* pass at, lunge at, aim *or* deal a blow at, flail at, flail away at, take a fling *or* shy at; cut and thrust; feint

17 launch an attack, kick off an attack, mount an attack, **push, thrust,** mount *or* open an offensive, **drive; advance against** *or* **upon, march upon** *or* **against,** bear down upon; **infiltrate; strike;** flank; press the attack, follow up the attack; **counterattack,** retaliate, take on

18 charge, rush, **rush at, fly at,** run at, dash at, make a dash *or* rush at; tilt at, go full tilt at, make *or* run a tilt at, ride full tilt against; **jump off,** go over the top <nf>

19 **besiege, lay siege to,** encompass, surround, **encircle,** envelope, invest, hem in, set upon on all sides, get in a pincers, close the jaws of the pincers *or* trap; **blockade; beset, beleaguer, harry, harass,** drive *or* press one hard; soften up

20 **raid,** foray, make a raid; **invade,** inroad, make an inroad, make an irruption into; escalade, scale, scale the walls, board; storm, take by storm, overwhelm, inundate

21 **pull a gun on,** draw a gun on; **get the drop on** *and* **beat to the draw** <nf>

22 **pull the trigger, fire upon,** fire at, **shoot at,** pop at *and* take a pop at <nf>, take *or* fire *or* let off a shot at, blaze away at <nf>; **open fire,** commence firing, open up on <nf>; aim at, take aim at, level at <old>, zero in on, take dead aim at, draw a bead on; **snipe,** snipe at; **bombard, blast, strafe, shell,** cannonade, mortar, barrage, blitz; pepper, fusillade, fire a volley; rake, enfilade; pour a broadside into; cannon; **torpedo; shoot**

23 **bomb,** drop a bomb, lay an egg <nf>; dive-bomb, glide-bomb, skip-bomb, pattern-bomb, etc; atom-bomb, hydrogen-bomb; nuke <nf>, plaster <nf>

24 **mine,** plant a mine, trigger a mine

25 **stab, stick** <nf>, **pierce,** plunge in; **run through, impale,** spit, **transfix,** transpierce; **spear,** lance, poniard, bayonet, saber, sword, put to the sword; **knife,** dirk, dagger, stiletto; spike; cut down

26 **gore,** horn, tusk

27 **pelt, stone,** lapidate <old>, pellet; brickbat *or* egg <nf>, chuck

28 **hurl at, throw at, cast at,** heave at, fling at, sling at, toss at, shy at, fire at, let fly at; hurl against, hurl at the head of

ADJS 29 **attacking,** assailing, assaulting, charging, driving, thrusting, advancing; **invading,** invasive, invasionary, incursive, incursionary, irruptive, storming

30 **offensive, combative,** on the offensive *or* attack; **aggressive;** militant, hawkish, on the warpath

ADVS 31 **under attack, under fire;** under siege; counterattacking

INTERJS 32 **attack!,** advance!, **charge!,** over the top!, up and at 'em!, have at them!, give 'em hell!, let 'em have it!, fire!, open fire!; banzai!, Geronimo!

460 DEFENSE

NOUNS 1 **defense,** defence <Brit>, **guard,** ward; **protection** 1008; resistance 453; self-defense, self-protection, self-preservation; deterrent capacity; defense in depth; the defensive; covering one's ass *or* rear-end <nf>; defenses, psychological defenses, ego defenses, defense mechanism, escape mechanism, avoidance reaction, negative taxis *or* tropism; bunker atmosphere *or* mentality

2 **military defense, national defense,** defense capability; Air Defense Command; **civil defense;** CONELRAD *or* control of electromagnetic radiation for civil defense, Emergency Broadcast System *or* EBS, Civil Defense Warning System; radar defenses, distant early warning *or* DEW Line; antimissile missile, antiballistic-missile system *or* ABM; strategic defense initiative *or* Star Wars

3 **armor,** armature; armor plate; body armor, suit of armor, plate armor, panoply, harness; **mail,** chain mail, chain armor; bulletproof vest; **battlegear; protective covering,** cortex, **thick skin,** carapace, shell 295.15; spines, needles; human shield

4 **fortification,** work, defense work, **bulwark, rampart, fence,** earthwork, stockade, **barrier** 1012.5; **enclosure** 212.3

5 **entrenchment, trench,** ditch, fosse; **moat; dugout,** *abri* <Fr>; **bunker; foxhole,** slit trench; approach trench, communication trench, fire trench, gallery, parallel, coupure; tunnel, fortified tunnel; undermining, sap, single *or* double sap, flying sap; mine, countermine

6 **stronghold,** hold, safehold, fasthold, strong point, **fastness,** keep, ward, **bastion,** donjon, **citadel, castle,** tower, tower of strength; mote *or* motte; **fort, fortress,** post; **bunker, pillbox,** blockhouse, garrison *or* trenches *or* barricades; garrison house; acropolis; peel, peel tower; rath; martello tower, martello; **bridgehead, beachhead;** safeguard

7 **defender, champion, advocate; upholder; guardian angel,** angel <nf>; **supporter** 616.9; vindicator, apologist; **protector** 1007.5; **guard** 1008.9; henchman; paladin, knight, white knight; guard dog, attack dog, junkyard dog

VERBS 8 **defend, guard, shield,** screen, secure, guard against, ward; defend tooth and nail *or* to the death *or* to the last breath; **safeguard, protect** 1008.18; stand by the side of, flank; **advocate, champion** 600.10; **defend oneself,** cover one's ass *or* rear-end <nf>, CYA *or* cover your ass <nf>

9 **fortify,** embattle *or* battle <old>; **arm; armor,** armor-plate; **man;** garrison, man the garrison *or* trenches *or* barricades; **barricade, blockade;** bulwark, wall, palisade, fence; castellate, crenellate; bank; entrench, **dig in;** mine; beef up

10 **fend off, ward off, stave off, hold off, fight off,** keep off, beat off, parry, fend, counter, turn aside; **hold** *or* **keep at bay,** keep at arm's length; **hold the fort, hold the line,** stop, check, block, hinder, obstruct; **repel, repulse, rebuff, drive back,** put back, push back; avert; go on the defensive, fight a

holding *or* delaying action, fall back to prepared positions

ADJS **11 defensive,** defending, **guarding,** shielding, screening; **protective** 1008.23; self-defensive, self-protective, self-preservative

12 fortified, battlemented, embattled *or* battled <old>, entrenched; castellated, crenellated, casemated, machicolated; secured, protected

13 armored, armor-plated; in armor, panoplied, armed cap-a-pie, armed at all points, in harness, "in complete steel"—Shakespeare; mailed, mailclad, ironclad; loricate, loricated

14 armed, heeled *and* carrying *and* gun-toting <nf>; accoutered, **in arms,** bearing *or* wearing *or* carrying arms, under arms, sword in hand; **well-armed,** heavy-armed, full-armed, bristling with arms, **armed to the teeth;** light-armed; **garrisoned,** manned

15 defensible, defendable, tenable

ADVS **16 defensively, in defense,** in self-defense; **on the defensive,** on guard; **at bay,** *aux abois* <Fr>, with one's back to the wall

461 COMBATANT

NOUNS **1 combatant, fighter, battler,** scrapper <nf>; **contestant, contender, competitor, rival,** adversary, opponent, agonist; disputant, wrangler, squabbler, bickerer, quarreler; struggler, tussler, scuffler; brawler, rioter; feuder; **belligerent,** militant; gladiator; jouster, tilter; knight, belted **knight;** swordsman, blade, sword, *sabreur or beau sabreur* <Fr>; fencer, foilsman, swordplayer <old>; duelist, dueler; gamecock, fighting cock; **tough,** rough, rowdy, **ruffian,** thug, **hoodlum, hood** <nf>, hooligan, streetfighter, bully, bullyboy, bravo; gorilla *and* goon *and* plug-ugly *and* skinhead <nf>; hatchet man *and* enforcer <nf>, strong-arm man, strong arm, strong-armer; fire-eater, swaggerer, swashbuckler

2 boxer, pugilist, pug *or* palooka <nf>; **street fighter,** scrapper, pit bull

3 wrestler, rassler *and* grunt-and-groaner <nf>, grappler, scuffler, matman

4 bullfighter, toreador, *torero* <Sp>; banderillero, picador, matador

5 militarist, warmonger, war dog *or* hound, war hawk, **hawk** <nf>; **chauvinist, jingo,** jingoist, hard-liner; conquistador, privateer, pirate, buccaneer

6 military man or **woman, serviceman, servicewoman,** navy man *or* woman; air serviceman *or* servicewoman; **soldier, warrior,** brave, fighting man, legionary, hoplite, **man-at-arms,** rifleman, rifle; ninja; **cannon fodder,** food for powder, trooper, militiaman; warrioress, Amazon;

spearman, pikeman, halberdier; military training, boot camp

7 <common soldiers> **GI,** GI Joe, dough *and* doughfoot *and* Joe Tentpeg *and* John Dogface *and* grunt <nf>, **doughboy, Yank;** Tommy Atkins *or* **Tommy** *or* Johnny *or* swaddy <Brit>; redcoat; *poilu* <Fr>; Aussie *and* Anzac *and* digger <Austral>; jock <Scot>; Fritz, Jerry, Heinie, Hun, Boche, Kraut, krauthead <Ger soldier>; Janissary <Turkish soldier>; *sepoy* <India>; *askari* <Africa>; weekend warrior

8 enlisted man, noncommissioned officer 575.19; **common soldier, private, private soldier,** buck private <nf>; private first class *or* pfc

9 infantryman, foot soldier; light infantryman, chasseur, *Jäger* <Ger>, Zouave; **rifleman,** rifle, musketeer; fusileer, carabineer; **sharpshooter,** marksman, expert rifleman, *bersagliere* <Ital>; **sniper;** grenadier

10 <nf terms> **grunt, dogface,** footslogger, paddlefoot, doughfoot, blisterfoot, crunchie, line doggie, groundpounder

11 artilleryman, artillerist, **gunner,** guns <nf>, cannoneer, machine gunner; **bomber,** bomb thrower, bombardier

12 cavalryman, mounted infantryman, **trooper;** dragoon, light *or* heavy dragoon; lancer, lance, uhlan, hussar; cuirassier; spahi; cossack

13 tanker, tank corpsman, tank crewman

14 engineer, combat engineer, pioneer, Seabee; sapper, sapper and miner

15 elite troops, shock troops, storm troops; rapid deployment force *or* RDF; commandos, rangers, Special Forces, Green Berets, marines, paratroops; guardsmen, guards, household troops; Life Guards, Horse Guards, Foot Guards, Grenadier Guards, Coldstream Guards, Scot Guards, Irish Guards; Swiss Guards

16 irregular, casual; **guerrilla,** partisan, franctireur; **bushfighter,** bushwhacker <nf>; underground, resistance, maquis; Vietcong *or* VC, Charley <nf>; SWAPO *or* South West African People's Organization guerrilla; Shining Path Guerrilla; Contra; *maquisard* <Fr>, underground *or* resistance fighter, freedom fighter; terrorist

17 mercenary, hireling, *condottiere* <Ital>, free lance, free companion, **soldier of fortune,** adventurer; gunman, gun, hired gun, hired killer, professional killer

18 recruit, rookie <nf>, **conscript,** drafted man, **draftee, inductee, selectee, enlistee,** enrollee, trainee, boot <nf>; **raw recruit,** tenderfoot; awkward squad <nf>; draft, levy

19 veteran, vet <nf>, campaigner, old campaigner, old soldier, old trooper, war-horse <nf>, Veterans

of Foreign Wars *or* VFW member, American
Legion member

20 defense forces, services, the service, armed forces,
armed services, fighting machine; **the military,** the
military establishment; professional forces,
standing forces, regular forces, reserve forces,
volunteer forces; combat troops, support troops

21 branch, branch of the service, corps <see list>;
service, arm of the service, Air Force, Army, Navy,
Marine Corps, Coast Guard, Merchant Marine

22 <military units> **unit, organization,** tactical unit,
outfit <nf>; **army,** field army, army group, corps,
army corps, **division,** infantry division, armored
division, airborne division, triangular division,
pentomic division, Reorganization Objective Army
Division *or* ROAD; **regiment, battle group,**
battalion, garrison, **company,** troop, brigade,
legion, phalanx, cohort, **platoon,** section, **battery,**
maniple; **combat team,** combat command; **task
force;** commando unit, combat team; **squad,**
squadron; detachment, detail, section, posse, unit,
detachment; kitchen police *or* KP; column, flying
column; rank, file; train, field train; cadre

23 army, this man's army <nf>, **soldiery, forces,**
armed forces, **troops, host,** array, legions; ranks,
rank and file; **standing army, regular army,** active
forces, regulars, professional *or* career soldiers; the
line, troops of the line; line of defense, first *or*
second line of defense; ground forces, ground
troops; storm troops, assault troops; **airborne
troops,** paratroops; ski troops, mountain troops;
occupation force; elite troops

24 militia, organized militia, national militia, mobile
militia, territorial militia, reserve militia, citizen's
army; home reserve; **National Guard,** Air National
Guard, state guard; home guard <chiefly Brit>;
minutemen, trainband, yeomanry

25 reserves, auxiliaries, **second line of defense,**
reinforcements, ready reserves, landwehr, army
reserves, home reserves, territorial reserves,
territorial *or* home defense army <Brit>,
supplementary reserves, organized reserves; US
Army Reserve, US Naval Reserve, US Marine
Corps Reserve, US Air Force Reserve, US Coast
Guard Reserve, National Guard; ready reserves,
standby reserves, retired reserves

26 volunteers, enlistees, volunteer forces, volunteer
army, volunteer militia, volunteer navy

27 navy, naval forces, **first line of defense; fleet,**
flotilla, argosy, armada, squadron, escadrille,
division, task force, task group; amphibious force;
mosquito fleet; support fleet, destroyer fleet,
auxiliary fleet, reserve fleet, mothball fleet; United
States Navy *or* USN; Royal Navy *or* RN; marine,
mercantile *or* merchant marine, merchant navy,

merchant fleet; naval militia; naval reserve; coast
guard; Seabees, Naval Construction Battalion;
admiralty; gunboat diplomacy

28 marines, sea soldiers, Marine Corps, Royal
Marines; **leathernecks** *and* devil dogs *and* gyrenes
<nf>, jollies <Brit nf>

29 air force, air corps, air service, air arm; US Air
Force *or* USAF; strategic air force, tactical air
force; squadron, escadrille, flight, wing

30 war-horse, charger, courser, trooper

31 US Army branches and corps

Adjutant General Corps	Finance Corps
Air Defense Artillery	General Staff Corps
Armored Corps	Infantry Corps
Army Air Corps	Judge Advocate General
Army Digitization Office	Corps
Army Nurse Corps	Medical Service Corps
Army Research Laboratory	Military Police Corps
Army Service Corps	Ordnance Corps
Chemical Corps	Quartermaster Corps
Corps of Cadets <West	Signal Corps
Point>	Special Operations
Corps of Engineers	Command
Dental Command	Transportation Corps

32 US Air Force branches and corps

Air Combat Command	Reserve Command
Air Education and Training	Reserve Officer Training
Command	Corps
Air National Guard	Space Command
Materiel Command	Special Operations
Mobility Command	Command

462 ARMS

NOUNS **1 arms, weapons,** deadly weapons,
instruments of destruction, offensive weapons,
military hardware, matériel, **weaponry, armament,
munitions, ordnance,** munitions of war, *apparatus
belli* <L>; musketry; missilery; small arms; side
arms; stand of arms; conventional weapons,
nonnuclear weapons; **nuclear weapons,** atomic
weapons, thermonuclear weapons, A-weapons,
strategic nuclear weapon, tactical nuclear weapon;
bacteriological *or* biological weapons, chemical
weapon; weapons of mass destruction; arms
industry, arms maker, military-industrial complex;
natural weapon; secret weapon

2 armory, arsenal, magazine, dump; ammunition
depot, ammo dump <nf>, arms depot; park, gun
park, artillery park, park of artillery; atomic
arsenal, thermonuclear arsenal, gun room, powder
barrel *or* keg

3 ballistics, gunnery, musketry, artillery; rocketry,
missilery; archery

4 fist, clenched fist; brass knuckles; knucks *and*
brass knucks <nf>, knuckles, knuckle-dusters;

club, bludgeon, blackjack, truncheon, billy, blunt instrument, etc

5 **sword, blade,** cutlass, saber, rapier, foil, bayonet, machete; steel, **cold steel;** Excalibur; **knife,** switchblade; **dagger; axe**

6 **arrow, shaft, dart,** reed, **bolt;** quarrel; chested arrow, footed arrow, bobtailed arrow; arrowhead, barb; flight, volley

7 **bow,** longbow, carriage bow; **bow and arrow;** crossbow, arbalest

8 **spear,** throwing spear, javelin, lance, harpoon, sharp weapon

9 **sling, slingshot;** throwing-stick, throw stick, spear-thrower, atlatl, wommera; **catapult,** arbalest, ballista, trebuchet

10 **gun, firearm;** shooting iron *and* gat *and* rod *and* heater *and* piece <nf>; shoulder weapon *or* gun *or* arm; gun make; gun part; stun gun; automatic, BB gun, blunderbuss <old>, Bren, Browning automatic rifle, burp gun <nf>, carbine, derringer, flintlock, forty-five *or* .45, forty-four *or* .44, Gatling gun, handgun, machine gun, musket, pistol, piece *or* equalizer <nf>, automatic, semiautomatic, repeater, revolver, rifle, Saturday night special, sawed-off shotgun, shotgun, six-gun *or* six-shooter <nf>, submachine gun, thirty-eight *or* .38, thirty-thirty *or* .30-30, thirty-two *or* .32, Thompson submachine gun *or* tommy gun <nf>, twenty-two *or* .22, Uzi submachine gun, zip gun

11 **artillery, cannon,** guns, cannonry, ordnance, engines of war, Big Bertha, howitzer; field artillery; heavy artillery, heavy field artillery; self-propelled artillery; siege artillery, bombardment weapons; breakthrough weapons; siege engine; mountain artillery, coast artillery, trench artillery, anti-aircraft artillery, flak <nf>; battery

12 **antiaircraft gun** *or* AA gun, ack-ack <nf>, pom-pom <nf>, *Fliegerabwehrkanone* <Ger>, skysweeper, Bofors, Oerlikon

13 **ammunition, ammo** <nf>, **powder and shot,** iron rations <nf>, round, live ammunition

14 **explosive,** high explosive; cellulose nitrate, cordite, dynamite, gelignite, guncotton, gunpowder, nitroglycerin *or* nitroglycerine, plastic explosive *or* plastique, powder, trinitrotoluene *or* trinitrotoluol *or* TNT

15 **fuse, detonator,** exploder; **cap,** blasting cap, percussion cap, mercury fulminate, fulminating mercury; electric detonator *or* exploder; detonating powder; **primer,** priming; primacord

16 **charge, load;** blast; warhead, payload

17 **cartridge,** cartouche, **shell;** ball cartridge; clip, blank cartridge, dry ammunition

18 **missile, projectile,** bolt; brickbat, stone, rock, alley apple *and* Irish confetti <nf>; boomerang; bola; throwing-stick, throw stick, waddy <Austral>; **ballistic missile,** cruise missile, Exocet missile, surface-to-air missile *or* SAM, surface-to-surface missile, Tomahawk missile; **rocket** 1074.2–6,14; **torpedo**

19 **shot; ball,** cannonball, rifle ball, minié ball; **bullet,** slug, pellet; buckshot; dumdum bullet, expanding bullet, explosive bullet, manstopping bullet, manstopper, copkiller *or* Teflon bullet <trademark>; tracer bullet, tracer; **shell,** high-explosive shell, **shrapnel**

20 **bomb,** bombshell, device <nf>; antipersonnel bomb, atomic bomb *or* atom bomb *or* A-bomb, atomic warhead, hydrogen bomb *or* H-bomb, nuclear bomb, blockbuster, depth charge *or* depth bomb *or* ash can <nf>, fire bomb *or* incendiary bomb *or* incendiary, grenade, hand grenade, pineapple <nf>, letter bomb, Molotov cocktail, napalm bomb, neutron bomb, nuclear warhead, pipe bomb, plastic *or* plastique bomb, plutonium bomb, smart bomb, stench *or* stink bomb, time bomb; clean bomb, dirty bomb; **mine,** landmine; booby trap

21 **launcher,** projector, bazooka; rocket launcher, grenade launcher, hedgehog, mine thrower, *Minenwerfer* <Ger>, **mortar**

463 ARENA

NOUNS 1 arena, scene of action, site, scene, setting, background, **field, ground,** terrain, sphere, place, locale, milieu, precinct, purlieu; course, range, walk <old>; campus; **theater,** stage, stage set *or* setting, scenery; **platform; forum,** agora, marketplace, open forum, public square; **amphitheater,** circus, **hippodrome, coliseum,** colosseum, **stadium, bowl; hall, auditorium;** gymnasium, gym <nf>, palaestra; **lists,** tiltyard, tilting ground; floor, **pit,** cockpit; bear garden; **ring,** prize ring, boxing ring, canvas, squared circle <nf>, wrestling ring, mat, bull ring; parade ground; athletic field, field, playing field, sports venue; stamping ground, turf, bailiwick 894.4

2 **battlefield, battleground,** battle site, **field,** combat area, **field of battle;** field of slaughter, field of blood *or* bloodshed, aceldama, killing ground *or* field, shambles; **battlefront, the front,** front line, line, enemy line *or* lines, firing line, battle line, line of battle; battle zone, war zone, combat zone; **theater, theater of operations,** theater *or* seat of war; beachhead, bridgehead; communications zone, zone of communications; no-man's-land; demilitarized zone *or* DMZ; jump area *or* zone, landing beach

3 campground, camp, encampment, bivouac, tented field

464 PEACE

NOUNS **1 peace,** *pax* <L>; **peacetime,** state of peace, peaceable kingdom, the storm blown over; freedom from war, cessation of combat, exemption from hostilities, public tranquillity, peace movement; "liberty in tranquillity"—Cicero; **harmony,** concord, accord 455; universal peace, lasting peace, Pax Romana

2 peacefulness, tranquillity, serenity, calmness, quiet, peace and quiet, quietude, quietness, quiescence, quiet life, restfulness, rest, stillness; order, orderliness, law and order, imposed peace; no hassle <nf>

3 peace of mind, peace of heart, peace of soul *or* spirit, peace of God, "peace which passeth all understanding"—Bible; ataraxia, shanti

4 peaceableness, unpugnaciousness, uncontentiousness, nonaggression; irenicism, dovelikeness, dovishness <nf>, **pacifism,** pacificism; peaceful coexistence; **nonviolence,** ahimsa; line of least resistance; meekness, lamblikeness 433.5

5 noncombatant, nonbelligerent, nonresistant, nonresister; **civilian,** citizen

6 pacifist, pacificist, peacenik <nf>, **peace lover, dove,** *and* dove of peace <nf>; pacificator, peacemaker, bridgebuilder; peacemonger; **conscientious objector,** passive resister, conchie <nf>

7 peace treaty, peace agreement, nonaggression pact, disarmament treaty, arms reduction, arms control; test ban; deescalation; amnesty, pardon, forgiveness, burying the hatchet <nf>

VERBS **8 keep the peace,** remain at peace, wage peace; refuse to shed blood, keep one's sword in its sheath; forswear violence, beat one's swords into plowshares; pursue the arts of peace, pour oil on troubled waters; make love not war; defuse

ADJS **9 pacific, peaceful, peaceable; tranquil, serene;** idyllic, pastoral; halcyon, soft, piping, **calm, quiet,** quiet as a lamb, quiescent, still, restful, **untroubled,** orderly, **at peace;** concordant 455.3; bloodless; peacetime; postwar, postbellum

10 unbelligerent, unhostile, unbellicose, **unpugnacious, uncontentious,** unmilitant, unmilitary, nonaggressive, noncombative, nonmilitant; noncombatant, civilian; **antiwar, pacific, peaceable,** peace-loving, dovelike; meek, passive, lamblike 433.15; **pacifistic,** pacifist, irenic; nonviolent; conciliatory 465.12

INTERJS **11 peace!, peace be with you!,** peace to you!, *pax vobiscum!* and *pax tecum!* <L>; *shalom!* or *shalom aleichem!* <Heb>, *salaam aleikum!* <Arabic>; "peace be to this house!," "peace be within thy walls, and prosperity within thy palaces," "let the peace of God rule in your hearts," "be at peace among yourselves"—all Bible; go in peace!, *vade in pace!* <L>

465 PACIFICATION

NOUNS **1 pacification, peacemaking,** irenics, peacemongering, **conciliation, propitiation, placation, appeasement, mollification,** dulcification; **calming, soothing,** tranquilization; détente, relaxation of tension, easing of relations; mediation 466; placability; peacekeeping force, United Nations peacekeeping force

2 peace offer, offer of parley, parley, peace overture; peace feelers; **peace offering,** propitiatory gift; **olive branch; white flag,** truce flag, flag of truce; calumet, peace pipe, **pipe of peace;** downing of arms, hand of friendship, empty hands, outstretched hand; **cooling off, cooling-off period;** peace sign; compensation, reparation, atonement, restitution; amnesty, pardon, mercy, leniency, clemency; dove, lamb

3 reconciliation, reconcilement, *rapprochement* <Fr>, **reunion,** shaking of hands, making up *and* kissing and making up <nf>

4 adjustment, accommodation, resolution, composition *or* settlement of differences, compromise, arrangement, settlement, terms; consensus building, consensus seeking

5 truce, armistice, peace; pacification, treaty of peace, suspension *or* end of hostilities, **cease-fire,** cessation, stand-down, breathing spell, cooling-off period, lull in hostilities; Truce *or* Peace of God, Pax Dei, Pax Romana; temporary truce, temporary arrangement, *modus vivendi* <L>; hollow truce, *pax in bello* <L>; demilitarized zone, buffer zone, neutral territory; uneasy truce

6 disarmament, reduction of armaments; unilateral disarmament; **demilitarization,** deactivation, disbanding, disbandment, **demobilization,** mustering out, reconversion, decommissioning; civilian life, mufti *and* civvy street <Brit>; defense cuts, arms reduction, arms control; test ban

VERBS **7 pacify, conciliate, placate, propitiate, appease, mollify,** dulcify; **calm, settle, soothe,** tranquilize 670.7; smooth, smooth over *or* out, smooth down, smooth one's feathers; allay, lay, lay the dust; pour oil on troubled waters, pour balm on, take the edge off of, take the sting out of; cool <nf>, defuse; clear the air

8 reconcile, bring to terms, bring together, reunite,

heal the breach; bring about a détente; **harmonize, restore harmony,** put in tune; **iron** or **sort out,** adjust, settle, compose, accommodate, arrange matters, settle differences, resolve, compromise; **patch things up,** fix up <nf>, patch up a friendship or quarrel, smooth it over; weave peace between, mediate 466.6

9 **make peace,** cease hostilities, cease fire, stand down, raise a siege; **cool it** and **chill out** <nf>, **bury the hatchet, smoke the peace pipe;** negotiate a peace, dictate peace; make a peace offering, hold out the olive branch, hoist or show or wave the white flag; make the world a safer place, make the lion lie down with the lamb; turn the other cheek

10 **make up** and **kiss and make up** and make it up and make matters up <nf>, **shake hands,** come round, come together, come to an understanding, **come to terms,** let the wound heal, let bygones be bygones, forgive and forget, put it all behind one, settle or compose one's differences, meet halfway, compromise

11 **disarm, lay down one's arms,** unarm, turn in one's weapons, down or ground one's arms, put down one's gun, sheathe the sword, turn swords into plowshares; **demilitarize,** deactivate, **demobilize, disband,** reconvert, decommission

ADJS 12 **pacificatory, pacific,** irenic, **conciliatory,** reconciliatory, **propitiatory,** propitiative, **placative,** placatory, **mollifying, appeasing; pacifying,** soothing 670.15, appeasable

13 **pacifiable, placable, appeasable, propitiable**

ADVS 14 **pacifically, peaceably; with no hard feelings**

466 MEDIATION

NOUNS 1 **mediation,** mediating, intermediation, **intercession; intervention,** interposition, putting oneself between, moderation, stepping in, declaring oneself in, involvement, interagency; interventionism; diplomacy, statesmanship; troubleshooting, good offices

2 **arbitration,** arbitrament, compulsory arbitration, binding arbitration; nonbinding arbitration; umpirage, refereeship, mediatorship

3 **mediator,** intermediator, intermediate agent, intermediate, intermedium, **intermediary,** interagent, internuncio; **medium; intercessor,** interceder; ombudsman; intervener, **intervenor;** interventionist; **go-between,** liaison, **middleman** 576.4; connection <nf>; front and front man <nf>; deputy, agent 576; **spokesman, spokeswoman,** spokesperson, spokespeople; **mouthpiece; negotiator,** negotiant, negotiatress or negotiatrix; Little Miss Fixit; troubleshooter; spin doctor <nf>

4 **arbitrator,** arbiter, impartial arbitrator, third party, unbiased observer; **moderator,** moderating influence; **umpire, referee, judge;** magistrate 596.1

5 **peacemaker,** make-peace, reconciler, smoother-over, peace negotiator, mediator; **pacifier,** pacificator, peace lover, pacifist; peacekeeper, United Nations peacekeeping force; **conciliator,** propitiator, **appeaser;** marriage counselor, family counselor; guidance counselor; patcher-up

VERBS 6 **mediate,** intermediate, **intercede,** go between; **intervene,** interpose, step in, step into the breach, declare oneself a party, involve oneself, put oneself between disputants, use one's good offices, act between; butt in and put one's nose in <nf>; represent 576.14; **negotiate,** bargain, **treat with,** make terms, meet halfway; **arbitrate,** moderate; **umpire, referee,** judge, officiate

7 **settle, arrange,** compose, patch up, adjust, straighten out, bring to terms or an understanding; make peace 465.9; reconcile, conciliate

ADJS 8 **mediatory,** mediatorial, mediative, mediating, arbitral, going or coming between; intermediatory, intermediary, intermedial, intermediate, **middle,** intervening, mesne, interlocutory; interventional, arbitrational, arbitrative; **intercessory,** intercessional; diplomatic; pacificatory 465.12

467 NEUTRALITY

NOUNS 1 **neutrality, neutralism,** strict neutrality; noncommitment, noninvolvement; **independence, nonpartisanism, unalignment, nonalignment;** anythingarianism or nothingarianism <nf>; mugwumpery, mugwumpism, fence-sitting or -straddling, trimming; **evasion, cop-out** <nf>, abstention; **impartiality** 649.4, coexistence, avoidance; nonintervention, nonaggression

2 **indifference,** indifferentness, Laodiceanism; passiveness 329.1; apathy 94.4

3 **middle course** or **way,** via media <L>; **middle ground,** neutral ground or territory, center; meeting ground, interface; gray area, penumbra; **middle of the road,** sitting on or straddling the fence <nf>; medium, **happy medium;** mean, **golden mean;** moderation, moderateness 670.1; compromise 468; halfway measures, half measures, half-and-half measures

4 **neutral,** neuter; **independent, nonpartisan;** mugwump, fence-sitter or -straddler, trimmer; anythingarian and nothingarian <nf>; unaligned or nonaligned nation, third force, third world

VERBS 5 **remain neutral,** stand neuter, hold no brief, **keep in the middle of the road, straddle** or **sit on the fence** and sit out and sit on the sidelines <nf>, trim; **evade,** evade the issue, duck the issue *and* waffle *and* **cop out** <nf>, abstain

6 **steer a middle course,** hold *or* keep *or* preserve a middle course, walk a middle path, follow the via media, strike *or* preserve a balance, stay on an even keel, **strike** *or* **keep a happy medium,** keep the golden mean, steer between *or* avoid Scylla and Charybdis; be moderate 670.5

ADJS 7 **neutral,** neuter; noncommitted, uncommitted, noninvolved, uninvolved; anythingarian *and* nothingarian <nf>; **indifferent,** Laodicean; tolerant; passive 329.6; apathetic 94.13; neither one thing nor the other, neither hot nor cold; even, half-and-half, fifty-fifty <nf>; **on the fence** *or* **sidelines** <nf>, **middle-of-the-road,** centrist, center, moderate, midway; **independent, nonpartisan; unaligned, nonaligned,** third-force, third-world; **impartial** 649.10

468 COMPROMISE
<mutual concession>

NOUNS 1 **compromise,** composition, adjustment, accommodation, settlement, mutual concession, give-and-take; abatement of differences; bargain, deal <nf>, arrangement, understanding; **concession,** giving way, yielding; surrender, desertion of principle, evasion of responsibility, cop-out <nf>; middle ground, happy medium; meeting halfway

VERBS 2 **compromise,** make *or* reach a compromise, compound, compose, accommodate, adjust, settle, make an adjustment *or* arrangement, **make a deal** <nf>, do a deal <Brit nf>, come to an understanding, strike a bargain, do something mutually beneficial; plea-bargain; strike a balance, take the mean, **meet halfway,** split the difference, go fifty-fifty <nf>, give and take; play politics; steer a middle course 467.6; **make concessions,** give way, yield, wimp *or* chicken out <nf>; **surrender** 433.8, desert one's principles, evade responsibility, sidestep, duck responsibility *and* cop out *and* punt <nf>

PHRS 3 half a loaf is better than none; you can't win them all

469 POSSESSION

NOUNS 1 **possession,** possessing, outright possession, free-and-clear possession; **owning,** having title to; seisin, nine points of the law, *de facto* possession, *de jure* possession, lawful *or* legal possession; property rights, proprietary rights; **title,** absolute title, free-and-clear title, original title; derivative title; adverse possession, squatting,

squatterdom, **squatter's right; claim, legal claim,** lien; usucapion, usucaption <old>, prescription; **occupancy,** occupation; **hold, holding, tenure; tenancy,** tenantry, **lease,** leasehold, sublease, underlease, undertenancy; gavelkind; villenage, villein socage, villeinhold; socage, free socage; burgage; frankalmoign, lay fee; tenure in chivalry, knight service; fee fief, fiefdom, feud, feodum; freehold, alodium; fee simple, fee tail, fee simple absolute, fee simple conditional, fee simple defeasible *or* fee simple determinable; fee position; dependency, colony, mandate; prepossession <old>, preoccupation, preoccupancy; chose in possession, bird in hand, nine tenths of the law <nf>; **property** 471

2 **ownership, title,** possessorship, *dominium* <L>, **proprietorship,** proprietary, **property right** *or* rights; lordship, **overlordship,** seigniory; **dominion, sovereignty** 417.5; landownership, landowning, landholding, land tenure; nationalization, public domain, state ownership

3 **monopoly,** monopolization; **corner** *and* cornering *and* a corner on <nf>; exclusive possession; engrossment, forestallment

VERBS 4 **possess, have, hold,** have and hold, possess outright *or* free and clear, **occupy, fill, enjoy,** boast; be possessed of, have tenure of, have in hand, be seized of, have in one's grip *or* grasp, have in one's possession, be enfeoffed of; **command,** have at one's command *or* pleasure *or* disposition *or* disposal, have going for one <nf>; claim, usucapt; squat, squat on, claim squatter's rights

5 **own, have title to,** have for one's own *or* very own, have to one's name, call one's own, have the deed for, hold in fee simple, etc

6 **monopolize,** hog *and* grab all of *and* gobble up <nf>, call one's own, take it all, have all to oneself, have exclusive possession of *or* exclusive rights to; engross, forestall, tie up; **corner** *and* get a corner on *and* corner the market <nf>

7 **belong to,** pertain to, appertain to; vest in

ADJS 8 **possessed, owned,** held; in seisin, in fee, in fee simple, **free and clear; own,** of one's own, in one's name; **in one's possession, in hand,** in one's grip *or* grasp, at one's command *or* disposal; on hand, by one, in stock, in store

9 **possessing, having, holding,** having and holding, **occupying, owning; in possession of, possessed of,** seized of, master of; tenured; enfeoffed; endowed with, blessed with; worth; propertied, property-owning, landed, landowning, landholding

10 **possessive,** possessory, **proprietary**

11 **monopolistic,** monopolist, monopolizing, hogging *or* hoggish <nf>; exclusive

ADVS **12 free and clear, outright;** bag and baggage; by fee simple, etc

470 POSSESSOR

NOUNS **1 possessor, holder,** keeper, haver, enjoyer; a have <nf>

2 proprietor, proprietary, **owner;** *rentier* <Fr>; titleholder, deedholder; proprietress, proprietrix; **master, mistress, lord; landlord, landlady;** lord *or* lady of the manor <Brit>, man *or* lady of the house, mesne lord, mesne, feudatory, feoffee; squire, country gentleman; householder; beneficiary, cestui, cestui que trust, cestui que use

3 landowner, landholder, property owner, propertied *or* landed person, man of property, freeholder; landed interests, landed gentry, slumlord, rent gouger; absentee landlord

4 tenant, occupant, occupier, incumbent, **resident; lodger,** roomer, boarder, paying guest; **renter,** hirer <Brit>, rent-payer, **lessee,** leaseholder; subtenant, sublessee, underlessee, undertenant; tenant at sufferance, tenant at will; tenant from year to year, tenant for years, tenant for life; squatter; homesteader

5 trustee, fiduciary, holder of the legal estate; depository, depositary

471 PROPERTY

NOUNS **1 property, properties, possessions, holdings,** havings, goods, chattels, goods *and* chattels, **effects,** estate and effects, what one can call one's own, what one has to one's name, all one owns *or* has, all one can lay claim to, one's all; household possessions *or* effects, lares *and* penates; hereditament, corporeal hereditament, incorporeal hereditament; acquest; acquisitions, receipts 627; **inheritance** 479.2; public property, common property

2 belongings, appurtenances, trappings, paraphernalia, appointments, accessories, perquisites, appendages, appanages, choses local; **things,** material things, mere things; consumer goods; choses, choses in possession, choses in action; **personal effects,** personal property, chattels personal, movables, choses transitory; what one can call one's own, what has to one's name

3 impedimenta, luggage, dunnage, baggage, bag and baggage, traps, tackle, apparatus, truck, gear, kit, outfit, duffel

4 estate, interest, equity, stake, part, percentage; **right, title** 469.1, **claim,** holding; use, trust, benefit; absolute interest, vested interest, contingent interest, beneficial interest, equitable interest;

easement, right of common, common, right of entry; limitation; settlement, strict settlement; copyright, patent

5 freehold, estate of freehold; alodium, alod; frankalmoign, lay fee, tenure in *or* by free alms, appanage; mortmain, dead hand; leasehold

6 real estate, realty, real property, land *and* buildings, chattels real, tenements; immoveables; *praedium* <L>, landed property *or* estate, **land, lands,** property, grounds, acres; lot, lots, parcel, plot, plat, quadrat; demesne, domain <old>; messuage, manor, honor, toft <Brit>

7 assets, means, resources, total assets *or* resources; stock, stock-in-trade; **worth,** net worth, what one is **worth;** circumstances, funds 728.14; wealth 618; **material assets,** tangible assets, tangibles; intangible assets, intangibles; current assets, deferred assets, fixed assets, frozen assets, liquid assets, quick assets, assets *and* liabilities, net assets; assessed valuation

ADJS **8 propertied,** proprietary; **landed;** copyrighted, patented

9 real, praedial; manorial, seignioral, seigneurial; feudal, feudatory, feodal; patrimonial

10 freehold, leasehold, copyhold; allodial

472 ACQUISITION

NOUNS **1 acquisition,** gaining, getting, getting hold of <nf>, coming by, **acquirement, obtainment,** obtention, **attainment,** securement, winning, realization; trover; accession; addition 253; **procurement,** procural, procurance, procuration; **earnings,** making, pulling *or* dragging *or* knocking down <nf>, moneymaking, breadwinning, moneygetting, moneygrubbing

2 collection, gathering, gleaning, bringing together, assembling, putting *or* piecing together, **accumulation,** cumulation, **amassment,** accretion, heaping up, grubbing

3 gain, profit, percentage <nf>, get <Brit nf>, **take** *or* take-in *and* piece *and* slice *and* end *and* rakeoff *and* skimmings <nf>; **gains, profits, earnings, winnings, return, returns, proceeds, bottom line** <nf>, ettings, makings; **income** 624.4; **receipts** 627; **fruits,** pickings, gleanings; **booty,** spoils 482.11; pelf, lucre, filthy lucre; perquisite, perk *or* perks; **pile** *and* bundle *and* cleanup *and* killing *and* haul *and* mint <nf>; net *or* neat profit, clean *or* clear profit, net; gross profit, gross; paper profits; capital gains; interest, dividends; getting ahead; hoard, store 386; wealth 618

4 profitableness, profitability, gainfulness, remunerativeness, rewardingness, bang for the buck <nf>

5 **yield, output,** make, production; **proceeds,**
produce, product; **crop, harvest,** fruit, vintage,
bearing; second crop, aftermath; bumper crop

6 **find,** finding, **discovery; trove,** *trouvaille* <Fr>;
treasure trove, buried treasure; **windfall,** windfall
money, windfall profit, found money, easy money,
money in the bank, **bonus, gravy** <nf>, bunce
<Brit nf>

7 **godsend, boon, blessing;** manna, manna from
heaven, loaves and fishes, gift from on high; piece
of luck

VERBS 8 **acquire, get, gain, obtain, secure, procure;
win,** score; **earn,** make; **reap, harvest;** contract;
take, catch, capture; **net;** come *or* enter into
possession of, **come into, come by,** come in for, be
seized of; draw, derive

9 <nf terms> **grab, latch** *or* glom on to, corral, bag,
get *or* lay hold of, rake in *or* up *or* off, skim *or*
skim off, catch, collar, cop, dig up, grub up, round
up, drum up, get *or* lay one's hands, get *or* lay one's
mitts on, get one's fingers *or* hands on, get one's
hooks into, snag, snaffle, scratch together, hook,
land, throw together, nab, pick up, nail, scare *or*
scrape up; take home, pull *or* drag *or* knock down

10 **take possession, appropriate, take up,** take over,
make one's own, move in *or* move in on <nf>,
annex

11 **collect, gather, glean,** harvest, **pick, pluck,** cull,
take up, pick up, get *or* gather in, gather to
oneself, bring *or* get together, scrape together,
scare up <nf>; heap up, amass, assemble,
accumulate 386.11

12 **profit, make** *or* **draw** *or* **realize** *or* **reap profit,
come out ahead, make money;** rake it in *and* coin
money *and* make a bundle *or* pile *or* killing *or*
mint *and* clean up <nf>, laugh all the way to the
bank; gain by, **capitalize on,** commercialize, make
capital out of, **cash in on** *and* make a good thing
of <nf>, turn to profit *or* account, **realize on,**
make money by, obtain a return, turn a penny *or*
an honest penny; **gross, net; realize, clear;** kill two
birds with one stone, turn to one's advantage;
make a fast *or* quick buck <nf>; line one's
pockets

13 **be profitable,** pay, repay, pay off <nf>, yield a
profit, show a percentage, be gainful, be
worthwhile *or* worth one's while, be a good
investment, show a profit, pay interest; roll in <nf>

ADJS 14 **obtainable, attainable, available,** accessible,
to be had

15 **acquisitive,** acquiring; grasping, hoggy *and* grabby
<nf>; **greedy** 100.27

16 **gainful,** productive, **profitable, remunerative,
remuneratory, lucrative,** fat, **paying,** well-paying,
high-yield, high-yielding, bankable; advantageous,

worthwhile, rewarding; banausic, moneymaking,
breadwinning

ADVS 17 **profitably, gainfully,** remuneratively,
lucratively, **at a profit,** in the black; for money;
advantageously, to advantage, to profit, to the good

473 LOSS

NOUNS 1 **loss, losing, privation,** getting away, losing
hold of; **deprivation, bereavement,** taking away,
stripping, dispossession, despoilment,
despoliation, spoliation, robbery; setback, reversal;
divestment, denudation; **sacrifice, forfeit,
forfeiture,** giving up *or* over, denial;
nonrestoration; **expense, cost, debit;** detriment,
injury, damage; **destruction, ruin,** perdition, total
loss, dead loss; losing streak <nf>; **loser** 412.5

2 **waste,** wastage, **exhaustion, depletion,** sapping,
depreciation, dissipation, diffusion, **wearing,
wearing away, erosion,** ablation, leaching away;
molting, shedding, casting *or* sloughing off; **using,
using up, consumption, expenditure, drain;**
stripping, clear-cutting; impoverishment,
shrinkage; leakage, evaporation; decrement,
decrease 252

3 **losses,** losings; red ink; net loss, bottom line <nf>;
diminishing returns; going to the wall *or* going
belly up <nf>

VERBS 4 **lose,** incur loss, **suffer loss,** undergo
privation *or* deprivation, be bereaved *or* bereft of,
have no more, meet with a loss; drop *and* kiss
good-bye <nf>; let slip, let slip through one's
fingers; **forfeit,** default; **sacrifice; miss,** wander
from, go astray from; **mislay,** misplace; lose out;
lose everything, go broke *and* lose one's shirt *and*
take a bath *or* to the cleaners *and* tap out *and* go to
Tap City <nf>; have a setback *or* reversal

5 **waste, deplete, depreciate,** dissipate, wear, wear
away, erode, ablate, consume, drain, **shrink,**
dribble away; **molt, shed,** cast *or* slough off;
decrease 252.6; squander 486.3; labor in vain

6 **go to waste,** come to nothing, come to naught, go
up in smoke *and* go down the drain <nf>; run to
waste, go to pot <nf>, run *or* go to seed, go down
the tubes <nf>, go to the dogs <nf>; dissipate,
leak, leak away, scatter to the winds

ADJS 7 **lost, gone;** forfeited, forfeit; by the board, out
the window *and* down the drain *or* tube <nf>;
nonrenewable, irreclaimable; long-lost; lost to;
wasted, consumed, depleted, dissipated, diffused,
expended; worn away, eroded, ablated, used, used
up, shrunken; stripped, clear-cut; squandered
486.9; irretrievable 125.15; astray; the worse for
wear

8 **bereft, bereaved,** divested, denuded, **deprived of,**

shorn of, parted from, bereaved of, stripped of, dispossessed of, despoiled of, robbed of; **out of, minus** <nf>, wanting, lacking; cut off, cut off without a cent; out-of-pocket; **penniless, destitute, broke** and cleaned out and tapped out and wiped out and bust and belly up <nf>

ADVS **9 at a loss, unprofitably,** to the bad <nf>; in the red <nf>; out, out-of-pocket

474 RETENTION

NOUNS **1 retention,** retainment, **keeping, holding, maintenance, preservation;** prehension; keeping or holding in, **bottling** or corking up <nf>, locking in, suppression, repression, inhibition, retentiveness, retentivity; **tenacity** 803.3; adhesion; tenaciousness; detention

2 hold, purchase, grasp, grip, clutch, clamp, clinch, clench; seizure 480.2; bite, nip, toothhold; **cling,** clinging; toehold, foothold, footing; **clasp, hug, embrace,** bear hug, squeeze; grapple; handhold, firm hold, tight grip, iron grip, grip of iron or steel, death grip, stranglehold

3 <wrestling holds> half nelson, full nelson, quarter nelson, three-quarter nelson, stranglehold, toehold, flying mare, body slam, lock, hammerlock, headlock, scissors, bear hug, pin, fall

4 clutches, claws, talons, pounces, unguals; **nails,** fingernails; **pincers,** nippers, chelae; **tentacles; fingers,** digits, hooks <nf>; **hands,** paws and meathooks and mitts <nf>; palm; prehensile tail; **jaws,** mandibles, maxillae; **teeth,** fangs

VERBS **5 retain, keep, save,** save up, pocket and hip-pocket <nf>; **maintain, preserve;** keep or hold in, **bottle** or cork up <nf>, lock in, suppress, repress, inhibit, keep to oneself; persist in; hold one's own, hold one's ground; get a foothold

6 hold, grip, grasp, clutch, clip, **clinch, clench;** bite, nip; grapple; **clasp, hug, embrace; cling, cling to,** cleave to, stick to, adhere to, freeze to; **hold on to,** hold fast or tight, hang on to, keep a firm or tight hold on; **hold on, hang on** <nf>, hold on like a bulldog, stick like a leech, cling like a winkle, hang on for dear life; keep hold of, never let go, not part with; **seize** 480.14

7 hold, keep, harbor, bear, have, have and hold, hold on to; **cherish,** fondle, entertain, treasure, treasure up; **foster, nurture, nurse;** embrace, hug, clip <Brit nf>, cling to; bosom or embosom <old>, take to the bosom

ADJS **8 retentive,** retaining, keeping, holding, gripping, grasping; **tenacious,** clinging; viselike; anal

9 prehensile, raptorial; fingered, digitate or digitated, digital; clawed, taloned, jawed, toothed, dentate, fanged

ADVS **10 for keeps** <nf>, to keep, **for good,** for good and all, for always; forever 829.12

475 RELINQUISHMENT

NOUNS **1 relinquishment, release,** giving up, letting go, dispensation; **disposal,** disposition, riddance, getting rid of, dumping 390.3; **renunciation,** forgoing, forswearing, swearing off, abstinence, resignation, abjuration; **abandonment** 370; recantation, retraction 363.3; **surrender,** cession, handover, turning over, **yielding;** sacrifice; abdication

2 waiver, quitclaim, deed of release

VERBS **3 relinquish, give up,** render up, **surrender, yield,** cede, hand or turn over, cough up <nf>; take one's hands off, loose one's grip on; spare; resign, vacate; drop, **waive,** dispense with; **forgo,** do without, get along without, forswear, abjure, **renounce,** swear off; walk away from, **abandon** 370.5; recant, retract; disgorge, throw up; have done with, wash one's hands of, pack it in; **part with,** give away, dispose of, rid oneself of, get rid of, see the last of, dump 390.7; kiss goodbye or off <nf>; **sacrifice,** make a sacrifice, forfeit; quitclaim; sell off

4 release, let go, leave go <nf>, **let loose of,** unhand, unclutch, unclasp, relax one's grip or hold

ADJS **5 relinquished,** released, disposed of; waived, dispensed with; forgone, forsworn, renounced, abjured, **abandoned** 370.8; recanted, retracted; **surrendered,** ceded, yielded; sacrificed, forfeited

476 PARTICIPATION

NOUNS **1 participation, partaking, sharing,** having a part or share or voice, contribution, association; **involvement,** engagement; complicity; **voting** 609.18, **suffrage** 609.17; **power-sharing;** partnership, copartnership, copartnery, joint control, cochairmanship, joint chairmanship; joint tenancy, cotenancy; joint ownership, condominium or condo, cooperative or coop; communal ownership, commune

2 communion, community, communal effort or enterprise, **cooperation,** cooperative society; social life, socializing; **collectivity,** collectivism, collective enterprise, collective farm, kibbutz, kolkhoz; **democracy,** participatory democracy, town meeting, self-rule; collegiality; common ownership, public ownership, state ownership, communism, socialism 611.5,6; profit sharing; sharecropping

3 communization, communalization, **socialization, nationalization, collectivization**

4 participator, participant, partaker, player, sharer;

party, **a party to,** accomplice, accessory; partner, copartner; cotenant; shareholder

VERBS **5 participate, take part, partake, contribute,** chip in, involve *or* engage oneself, get involved; **have** *or* **take a hand in,** get in on, have a finger in, have a finger in the pie, have to do with, have a part in, be an accessory to, be implicated in, be a party to, be a player in; **participate in,** partake of *or* in, **take part in,** take an active part in, **join, join in,** figure in, make oneself part of, join oneself to, associate oneself with, play *or* perform a part in, play a role in, get in the act <nf>; **join up,** sign on, enlist, volunteer, answer the call; climb on the bandwagon; **have a voice in,** help decide, be in on the decisions, **vote,** have suffrage, be enfranchised; **enter into,** go into; make the scene <nf>; sit in, sit on; bear a hand, pull an oar; come out of one's shell

6 share, share in, come in for a share, **go shares,** be partners in, have a stake in, have a percentage *or* piece of <nf>, **divide with, divvy up with** <nf>, halve, go halves; go halvers *and* **go fifty-fifty** *and* go even stephen <nf>, split the difference, **share and share alike;** do one's share *or* part, pull one's weight; cooperate 450.3; apportion 477.6

7 communize, communalize, **socialize, collectivize, nationalize**

ADJS **8 participating, participative,** participant, participatory; hands-on, involved, engaged, **in** *or* **in on** <nf>; implicated, accessory; **partaking, sharing**

9 communal, common, general, public, collective, popular, social, societal; **mutual,** commutual <old>, reciprocal, associated, **joint,** conjoint, **in common,** share *and* share alike; **cooperative** 450.5; power-sharing, profit-sharing; collectivistic, **communistic,** socialistic 611.22

477 APPORTIONMENT

NOUNS **1 apportionment, apportioning, portioning, division,** divvy <nf>, **partition,** repartition, partitionment, partitioning, parceling, budgeting, rationing, **dividing, sharing,** share-out, sharing out, splitting, cutting, slicing, cutting the pie *and* divvying up <nf>; reapportionment

2 distribution, dispersion, **disposal,** disposition; dole, doling, doling *or* parceling out, giving out, passing around; **dispensation,** administration, issuance; disbursal, disbursement, paying out; redistribution; maldistribution; dealing, dispensing, divvying <nf>

3 allotment, assignment, appointment, setting aside, **earmarking,** tagging; underallotment, overallotment; appropriation; **allocation;** misallocation; reallocation

4 dedication, commitment, devoting, devotion, consecration

5 portion, share, interest, part, stake, stock, **piece,** bit, segment; **bite** *and* **cut** *and* **slice** *and* **chunk** *and* slice *and* piece of the pie *or* melon <nf>, piece of the action <nf>, **lot, allotment, end** <nf>, **proportion, percentage,** measure, quantum, **quota,** deal *or* dole <old>, ratio, meed, moiety, mess, helping; contingent; dividend; **commission,** rake-off <nf>; equal share, half; **lion's share,** bigger half, big end <nf>; small share, modicum; **allowance, ration, budget; load,** work load; fate, destiny 964.2

VERBS **6 apportion, portion, parcel, partition, part, divide,** share; share with, cut *or* deal one in <nf>, share *and* share alike, divide with, go halvers *or* fifty-fifty *or* even stephen with <nf>; divide into shares, **share out** *or* **around,** divide up, divvy *or* divvy up *or* out <nf>, **split,** split up, carve, cut, slice, carve up, slice up, cut up, cut *or* slice the pie *or* melon <nf>; divide *or* split fifty-fifty

7 proportion, proportionate, **prorate,** divide *pro rata*

8 parcel out, portion out, measure out, serve out, spoon *or* ladle *or* dish out, **deal out, dole out, hand out, mete out,** ration out, give out, hand around, pass around; mete, dole, deal; **distribute,** disperse; **dispense,** dispose <old>, issue, administer; disburse, pay out

9 allot, lot, **assign, appoint, set,** detail; **allocate,** make assignments *or* allocations, schedule; **set apart** *or* **aside, earmark,** tag, mark out for; demarcate, set off, mark off, portion off; assign to, appropriate to *or* for; reserve, restrict to, restrict 210.5; **ordain, destine, fate**

10 budget, ration; allowance, put on an allowance; divvy <nf>

11 dedicate, commit, devote, consecrate, set apart

ADJS **12 apportioned,** portioned out, parceled, allocated, etc; **apportionable,** allocable, divisible, divvied <nf>, distributable, committable, appropriable, dispensable, donable, severable

13 proportionate, proportional; prorated, *pro rata* <L>; half; halvers *or* fifty-fifty *or* even stephen <nf>, half-and-half, equal; **distributive,** distributional; **respective,** particular, per head, per capita, several

ADVS **14 proportionately, in proportion,** *pro rata* <L>; **distributively; respectively,** severally, each to each; share *and* share alike, in equal shares, half-and-half; fifty-fifty *and* even stephen <nf>

478 GIVING

NOUNS **1 giving, donation,** bestowal, bestowment; **endowment,** gifting <nf>, **presentation,** presentment; **award,** awarding; grant, granting; accordance, vouchsafement <old>; conferment, conferral; investiture; **delivery,** deliverance, surrender; **concession,** communication, impartation, impartment; **contribution,** subscription; tithing; accommodation, supplying, furnishment, provision 385; **offer** 439; **liberality** 485

2 **commitment, consignment,** assignment, **delegation,** relegation, commendation, remanding, **entrustment;** enfeoffment, infeudation *or* infeodation; labor of love

3 **charity,** almsgiving; **philanthropy** 143.4

4 **gift, present,** presentation, *cadeau* <Fr>, **offering,** fairing <Brit>; tribute, **award;** free gift, freebie *and* gimme <nf>; oblation 696.7; handsel; box <Brit>; Christmas present *or* gift, birthday present *or* gift; peace offering; a little something

5 **gratuity, largess, bounty,** liberality, donative, sportula; perquisite, perks <Brit nf>; consideration, fee <old>, **tip,** *pourboire* <Fr>, *Trinkgeld* <Ger>, sweetener, inducement; grease *and* salve *and* palm oil <nf>; **premium, bonus,** something extra, **gravy** <nf>, bunce <Brit nf>, lagniappe; baker's dozen; honorarium; incentive pay, time and a half, double time; bribe 378.2; slush fund

6 **donation,** donative; **contribution, subscription; alms,** pittance, **charity, dole, handout** <nf>, alms fee, widow's mite; Peter's pence; **offering,** offertory, votive offering, collection; tithe

7 **benefit,** benefaction, benevolence, **blessing, favor, boon,** grace; manna, manna from heaven

8 **subsidy,** subvention, subsidization, support, price support, depletion allowance, tax benefit *or* write-off; **grant,** grant-in-aid, bounty; **allowance, stipend,** allotment; **aid,** assistance, financial assistance, financial aid; **help,** pecuniary aid; scholarship, fellowship; honorarium; **welfare,** public welfare, public assistance, relief, relief *or* welfare payments, welfare aid, dole, aid to dependent children, bailout, food stamps, meal ticket; guaranteed annual income; alimony, palimony; annuity; pension, old-age insurance, retirement benefits, social security, remittance; unemployment insurance; golden handcuffs; handout <nf>

9 **endowment,** investment, **settlement,** foundation; fund; charitable foundation; **dowry,** *dot* <Fr>, portion, marriage portion; **dower,** widow's dower; jointure, legal jointure, thirds; appanage; community chest; charity event, fund-raiser, telethon

10 **bequest,** bequeathal, **legacy,** devise; inheritance 479.2; **will, testament,** last will and testament, living will; probate, attested copy; codicil

11 **giver, donor,** donator, gifter <nf>, presenter, bestower, conferrer, grantor, awarder, imparter, vouchsafer; fairy godmother, Lady Bountiful, Santa Claus, Robin Hood, sugar daddy <nf>; cheerful giver; **contributor, subscriber,** supporter, backer, financer, funder, angel <nf>; subsidizer; patron, patroness, Maecenas; tither; almsgiver, almoner; **philanthropist** 143.8, humanitarian; assignor, consignor; settler; testate, testator, testatrix; feoffor; good neighbor, good Samaritan

VERBS 12 **give, present, donate,** slip <nf>, let have; **bestow, confer, award, allot, render,** bestow on; impart, let one know, communicate; **grant,** accord, **allow,** vouchsafe, yield, afford, make available; **tender,** proffer, offer, extend, come up with <nf>; **issue, dispense,** administer; serve, help to; distribute; deal, dole, mete; **give out, deal out, dole out, mete out, hand** or dish *or* shell out <nf>, fork out *or* over *or* up <nf>; make a present of, gift *or* gift with <nf>, give as a gift; **give generously,** give the shirt off one's back; be generous *or* liberal with, give freely; pour, shower, rain, snow, heap, lavish 486.3; give in addition *or* as lagniappe, give into the bargain

13 **deliver, hand, pass,** reach, forward, render, put into the hands of; transfer; **hand over,** give over, deliver over, fork over <nf>, **pass over, turn over,** come across with <nf>; hand out, give out, pass out, distribute, circulate; hand in, give in; **surrender,** resign

14 **contribute, subscribe, chip in** *and* kick in *and* pony up *and* pay up <nf>, give one's share *or* fair share; put oneself down for, pledge; contribute to, give to, **donate to,** gift *and* gift with <nf>; put something in the pot, sweeten the kitty

15 **furnish, supply, provide, afford,** provide for; **make available to,** put one in the way of; **accommodate with,** favor with, indulge with; **heap upon,** pour on, shower down upon, **lavish upon**

16 **commit, consign, assign, delegate,** relegate, confide, commend, remit, remand, give in charge; **entrust,** trust, give in trust; enfeoff, infeudate

17 **endow,** invest, vest; endow with, favor with, bless with, grace with, vest with; **settle on** *or* **upon; dower;** philanthropize, aid, benefit, relieve

18 **bequeath, will,** will and bequeath, **leave, devise, will to,** hand down, hand on, pass on, transmit, provide for; **make a will,** draw up a will, execute a will, make a bequest, write one's last will and testament, write into one's will; add a codicil; entail

19 **subsidize, finance,** bankroll *and* greenback <nf>, fund; angel <nf>; **aid, assist, support, help,** pay the bills, pick up the check *or* tab *and* spring for *and* pop for <nf>; pension, pension off

20 thrust upon, force upon, press upon, push upon, obtrude on, ram *or* cram down one's throat
21 give away, dispose of, part with, sacrifice, spare
ADJS **22** philanthropic, philanthropical, eleemosynary, **charitable** 143.15; giving, generous to a fault, liberal, **generous** 485.4; openhanded
23 giveable, presentable, bestowable; impartable, communicable; bequeathable, devisable; allowable; committable; fundable
24 given, allowed, accorded, granted, vouchsafed, bestowed, etc; gratuitous 634.5; God-given, providential
25 donative, contributory; concessive; testate, testamentary; intestate
26 endowed, dowered, subsidized, invested; dower, dowry, dotal; subsidiary, stipendiary, pensionary
ADVS **27** as a gift, gratis, on one, on the house, free; to his heirs, to the heirs of his body, to his heirs and assigns, to his executors *or* administrators and assigns

479 RECEIVING

NOUNS **1 receiving, reception,** receival, **receipt, getting, taking; acquisition** 472; derivation; **assumption, acceptance;** admission, admittance; **reception** 187
2 inheritance, heritance <old>, **heritage, patrimony, birthright, legacy, bequest,** bequeathal; reversion; entail; heirship; **succession,** line of succession, mode of succession, law of succession; primogeniture, ultimogeniture, postremogeniture, borough-English, coheirship, coparcenary, gavelkind; hereditament, corporeal *or* incorporeal hereditament; **heritable; heirloom**
3 recipient, receiver, accepter, getter, taker, acquirer, obtainer, procurer; payee, endorsee; addressee, consignee; holder, trustee; **hearer,** viewer, beholder, audience, auditor, listener, looker, spectator; the receiving end; charity case; receiver of stolen property, fence <nf>
4 beneficiary, allottee, **donee, grantee,** patentee; **assignee, assign; devisee, legatee,** legatary <old>; trustee; feoffee; almsman, almswoman; stipendiary; pensioner, pensionary; annuitant
5 heir, heritor, inheritor, *heres* <L>; **heiress,** inheritress, inheritrix; coheir, joint heir, fellow heir, coparcener; heir expectant; **heir apparent,** apparent heir; **heir presumptive,** presumptive heir; statutory next of kin; legal heir, heir at law, heir general; heir by destination; heir of the body; heir in tail, heir of entail; fideicommissary heir, fiduciary heir; reversioner; remainderman; **successor,** next in line
VERBS **6 receive, get, gain, secure,** have, come by, be in receipt of, be on the receiving end; **obtain, acquire** 472.8,9; **admit, accept, take,** take off one's hands; **take in** 187.10; assume, take on, take over; **derive, draw,** draw *or* derive from; have an income of, drag down *and* pull down *and* rake in <nf>, have coming in, take home; accept stolen property, fence <nf>
7 inherit, be heir to, **come into,** come in for, come by, fall *or* step into; step into the shoes of, succeed to
8 be received, come in, come to hand, pass *or* fall into one's hands, go into one's pocket, come *or* fall to one, fall to one's share *or* lot; **accrue,** accrue to
ADJS **9 receiving,** on the receiving end; **receptive, recipient** 187.16
10 received, accepted, admitted, recognized, approved

480 TAKING

NOUNS **1 taking,** possession, taking possession, taking away; **claiming,** staking one's claim; **acquisition** 472; **reception** 479.1; **theft** 482; bumming *or* mooching <nf>
2 seizure, seizing, grab, grabbing, snatching, snatch; **kidnapping, abduction,** forcible seizure; power grab <nf>, coup, coup d'état, seizure of power; hold 474.2; **catch,** catching; **capture,** collaring <nf>, nabbing <nf>; **apprehension,** prehension; **arrest,** arrestation, taking into custody; picking up *and* taking in *and* running in <nf>; dragnet
3 sexual possession, taking; sexual assault, ravishment, **rape,** violation, indecent assault, date rape *or* acquaintance rape, serial rape *or* gang bang <nf>; statutory rape; defloration, deflowerment, devirgination
4 appropriation, taking over, takeover <nf>, **adoption, assumption, usurpation,** arrogation; requisition, indent <Brit>; preoccupation, prepossession, preemption; **conquest,** occupation, subjugation, enslavement, colonization; infringement of copyright, plagiarism
5 attachment, annexation, annexure <Brit>; **confiscation,** sequestration; impoundment; **commandeering, impressment;** expropriation, nationalization, socialization, communalization, communization, collectivization; levy; distraint, distress; garnishment; execution; eminent domain, angary, right of eminent domain, right of angary
6 deprivation, deprival, privation, divestment; bereavement; relieving, disburdening, disburdenment; curtailment, abridgment <old>; disentitlement
7 dispossession, disseisin, expropriation; reclaiming, repossessing, **repossession,** foreclosure; **eviction**

909.2; disendowment; **disinheritance,** disherison, disownment

8 **extortion, shakedown** <nf>, **blackmail,** bloodsucking, vampirism; protection racket; badger game

9 **rapacity,** rapaciousness, ravenousness, sharkishness, wolfishness, **predaciousness,** predacity; pillaging, looting

10 **take, catch, bag,** capture, seizure, **haul;** booty 482.11; hot property

11 **taker;** partaker; **catcher, captor,** capturer; appropriator, expropriator

12 **extortionist,** extortioner, **blackmailer,** racketeer, shakedown artist <nf>, **bloodsucker,** leech, **vampire; predator,** raptor, bird of prey, beast of prey; harpy; **vulture,** shark; profiteer; rack-renter; kidnapper, abductor

VERBS 13 **take,** possess, take possession; **get,** get into one's hold *or* possession; pocket, palm; draw off, drain off; skim *and* skim off *and* take up front <nf>; **claim,** stake one's claim, enforce one's claim; partake; **acquire** 472.8,9; **receive** 479.6; **steal** 482.13

14 **seize,** take *or* get hold of, **lay hold of,** catch *or* grab hold of, glom *or* latch on to <nf>, **get** *or* **lay hands on,** clap hands on <nf>, put one's hands on, get into one's grasp *or* clutches; get one's fingers *or* hands on, get between one's finger *and* thumb; **grab, grasp, grip,** gripe <old>, **grapple, snatch,** snatch up, nip, nail <nf>, **clutch,** claw, clinch, clench; **clasp, hug, embrace;** snap up, nip up, whip up, catch up; pillage, loot; take by assault *or* storm; **kidnap, abduct,** snatch <nf>, carry off; shanghai; take by the throat, throttle

15 **possess sexually,** take; **rape,** commit rape, commit date *or* acquaintance rape, ravish, violate, assault sexually, lay violent hands on, have one's will of; deflower, deflorate, devirginate

16 **seize on** *or* **upon,** fasten upon; spring *or* pounce upon, jump <nf>, swoop down upon; **catch at, snatch at,** snap at, jump at, make a grab for, scramble for

17 **catch, take,** catch flatfooted, land *and* nail <nf>, hook, **snag, snare,** sniggle, spear, harpoon; ensnare, enmesh, entangle, tangle, foul, tangle up with; **net,** mesh; **bag,** sack; **trap,** entrap; lasso, rope, noose

18 **capture, apprehend, collar** <nf>, run down, run to earth, **nab** <nf>, grab <nf>, lay by the heels, take prisoner; **arrest,** place *or* put under arrest, take into custody; pick up *or* take in *or* run in <nf>

19 **appropriate, adopt, assume, usurp,** arrogate, accroach; requisition, indent <Brit>; **take possession of,** possess oneself of, take for oneself, arrogate to oneself, take up, **take over, help oneself to,** make use of, make one's own, make free with, dip one's hands into; take it all, take all of, hog <nf>, monopolize, sit on; preoccupy, prepossess, preempt; jump a claim; **conquer,** overrun, occupy, subjugate, enslave, colonize; squat on; bum *or* mooch <nf>

20 **attach, annex; confiscate,** sequester, sequestrate, impound; **commandeer,** press, **impress;** expropriate, nationalize, socialize, communalize, communize, collectivize; exercise the right of eminent domain, exercise the right of angary; levy, distrain, replevy, replevin; garnishee, garnish

21 **take from,** take away from, **deprive of,** do out of <nf>, relieve of, disburden of, lighten of, ease of; **deprive, bereave, divest;** tap, milk, mine, drain, bleed, curtail, abridge <old>; cut off; disentitle

22 **wrest,** wring, wrench, **rend,** rip; **extort, exact,** squeeze, screw, **shake down** <nf>, **blackmail,** levy blackmail, badger *and* play the badger game <nf>; **force from, wrest from, wrench from, wring from, tear from, rip from, rend from,** snatch from, pry loose from

23 **dispossess,** disseise, expropriate, foreclose; evict 909.15; disendow; **disinherit,** disherison, **disown,** cut out of one's will, **cut off,** cut off with a shilling, cut off without a cent

24 **strip,** strip bare *or* clean, **fleece** <nf>, **shear,** denude, skin *and* pluck <nf>, flay, **despoil, divest,** pick clean, pick the bones of; deplume, displume; **milk; bleed, bleed white;** exhaust, drain, dry, suck dry; **impoverish,** beggar; clean out *and* take to the cleaners <nf>; eat out of house *and* home

ADJS 25 **taking, catching;** private, deprivative; confiscatory, annexational, expropriatory; **thievish** 482.21; ripoff <nf>

26 **rapacious, ravenous,** ravening, vulturous, vulturine, sharkish, **wolfish,** lupine, predacious, **predatory,** raptorial; vampirish, **bloodsucking,** parasitic; **extortionate; grasping,** graspy, grabby <nf>, **insatiable** 100.27; all-devouring, all-engulfing

481 RESTITUTION

NOUNS 1 **restitution, restoration,** restoring, giving back, sending back, remitting, remission, **return;** reddition <old>; extradition, rendition; repatriation; recommitment, remandment, remand

2 **reparation, recompense,** paying back, squaring <nf>, repayment, reimbursement, refund, remuneration, **compensation, indemnification;** retribution, **atonement,** redress, satisfaction, **amends,** making good, **requital;** conscience money

3 **recovery,** regaining; **retrieval,** retrieve;

recuperation, recoup, recoupment; **retake,** retaking, recapture; **repossession,** resumption, reoccupation; **reclamation,** reclaiming; **redemption,** ransom, salvage, trover; replevin, replevy; **revival, restoration** 396, retro

VERBS **4 restore, return, give back,** restitute, hand back, put back; take back, bring back; put the genie back into the bottle, put the toothpaste back into the tube; **remit,** send back; repatriate; extradite; recommit, remand; requite

5 make restitution, make reparation, **make amends,** make good, make up for, atone, give satisfaction, redress, **recompense,** pay back, square <nf>, repay, reimburse, refund, remunerate, **compensate, requite,** indemnify, make it up; pay damages, pay reparations; pay conscience money; overcompensate

6 recover, regain, retrieve, recuperate, **recoup, get back,** come by one's own; **redeem,** ransom; **reclaim; repossess,** resume, reoccupy; **retake,** recapture, take back; replevin, replevy; revive, renovate, **restore** 396.11,15

ADJS **7 restitutive,** restitutory, **restorative;** compensatory, indemnificatory, retributive, reparative, reparatory; reversionary, reversional, revertible; redeeming, redemptive, redemptional; reimbursable

ADVS **8 in restitution,** in reparation, in recompense, in compensation, to make up for, in return for, in retribution, in requital, in amends, in atonement, to atone for

482 THEFT

NOUNS **1 theft, thievery,** stealage, **stealing,** thieving, **purloining;** swiping *and* lifting *and* snatching *and* snitching *and* pinching <nf>; conveyance <old>, **appropriation,** conversion, liberation *and* annexation <nf>; **pilfering,** pilferage, **filching,** scrounging <nf>; abstraction; sneak thievery; shoplifting, boosting <nf>; poaching; **graft; embezzlement** 389.1; **fraud, swindle** 356.8

2 larceny, petit *or* petty larceny, petty theft, grand larceny, grand theft, simple larceny, mixed *or* aggravated larceny; automobile theft

3 theft, robbery, robbing; bank robbery; banditry, highway robbery; **armed robbery, holdup,** assault *and* robbery, **mugging,** push-in job *or* crime; purse snatching; **pocket picking** *or* pick-pocketing, jostling; **hijacking,** asportation <old>; carjacking; cattle stealing, **cattle rustling** *and* cattle lifting <nf>; **extortion** 480.8

4 <nf terms> **heist, stickup,** job, stickup job, bag job, boost, hustle, pinch, swipe, lift, burn, knockover, **ripoff;** sticky fingers

5 burglary, burglarizing, housebreaking, **breaking and entering,** break and entry, break-in, unlawful entry; second-story work <nf>; safebreaking, **safecracking, safeblowing**

6 plundering, pillaging, looting, sacking, freebooting, ransacking, rifling, spoiling, **despoliation,** despoilment, despoiling; rapine, spoliation, depredation, direption <old>, **raiding,** ravage, ravaging, ravagement, rape, ravishment; **pillage, plunder,** sack; brigandage, brigandism, banditry; **marauding,** foraging; raid, foray, razzia

7 piracy, buccaneering, privateering, freebooting; letters of marque, letters of marque and reprisal; **air piracy,** airplane hijacking, skyjacking; carjacking

8 plagiarism, plagiarizing, plagiary, **piracy,** literary piracy, appropriation, borrowing, cribbing; infringement; infringement of copyright; autoplagiarism; cribbing <nf>

9 abduction, kidnapping, snatching <nf>; **shanghaiing,** impressment, crimping

10 grave-robbing, body-snatching <nf>, resurrectionism

11 booty, spoil, **spoils, loot, swag** <nf>, ill-gotten gains, **plunder,** prize, haul, take, pickings, stealings, stolen goods, hot goods *or* items <nf>; **boodle** *and* squeeze *and* **graft** <nf>; perquisite, perks <Brit nf>, pork barrel, spoils of office, public trough; till, public till; blackmail; hot property

12 thievishness, larcenousness, taking ways <nf>, light fingers, sticky fingers; kleptomania, bibliokleptomania, etc

VERBS **13 steal, thieve, purloin, appropriate, take,** snatch, palm, **make off with,** walk off with, run off *or* away with, abstract, disregard the distinction between *meum* and *tuum*; have one's hand in the till; **pilfer, filch;** shoplift; poach; rustle; **embezzle** 389.4; defraud, swindle; **extort** 480.22

14 rob, commit robbery; pick pockets, jostle; hold up, stick someone up

15 burglarize, burgle <nf>, commit burglary, housebreak; crack *or* blow a safe

16 <nf terms> **swipe, pinch,** bag, **lift,** hook, crib, **cop,** nip, snitch, snare, boost, annex, borrow, burn, clip, **rip off,** nick *and* nobble <Brit>; **heist, knock off** *or* **over,** tip over; **stick up; mug;** roll, jackroll; do a job; cook the books

17 plunder, pillage, loot, sack, ransack, rifle, freeboot, spoil, spoliate, despoil, depredate, prey on *or* upon, **raid,** reive <Scot>, ravage, ravish, raven, sweep, gut; **fleece** 480.24; maraud, foray, forage

18 pirate, buccaneer, privateer, freeboot

19 plagiarize, pirate, borrow *and* crib <nf>, appropriate; **pick one's brains;** infringe a copyright

20 abduct, abduce, spirit away, **carry off** or **away,** magic away <Brit>, run off or away with; **kidnap,** snatch <nf>, hold for ransom; skyjack, hijack, carjack; **shanghai,** crimp, impress

ADJS **21 thievish, thieving, larcenous, light-fingered, sticky-fingered;** kleptomaniacal, burglarious; brigandish, piratical, piratelike; fraudulent

22 plunderous, plundering, looting, pillaging, ravaging, marauding, spoliatory; predatory, predacious

23 stolen, pilfered, purloined, ripped off; pirated, plagiarized; hot <nf>

483 THIEF

NOUNS **1 thief, robber,** stealer, purloiner, lifter <nf>, ganef <Yiddish>, **crook** <nf>; larcenist, larcener; **pilferer, filcher,** petty thief, chicken thief; sneak thief, prowler; shoplifter, booster <nf>; poacher; **grafter,** petty grafter; jewel thief; **swindler,** con man 357.3,4; land pirate, land shark, land-grabber; grave robber, body snatcher, resurrectionist, ghoul; embezzler, peculator, white-collar thief; den of thieves

2 pickpocket, cutpurse, fingersmith and dip <nf>; **purse snatcher;** light-fingered gentry

3 burglar, yegg and cracksman <nf>; housebreaker, cat burglar, cat man, second-story thief or worker; **safecracker,** safebreaker, safeblower; pete blower or pete man or peterman <nf>

4 bandit, brigand, dacoit; **gangster** and mobster <nf>, goodfella <nf>; racketeer; **thug, hoodlum** 593.4

5 robber, holdup man and stickup man <nf>; highwayman, highway robber, footpad, road agent, bushranger <Austral>; **mugger** <nf>, sandbagger; train robber; bank robber, **hijacker** <nf>

6 plunderer, pillager, looter, marauder, rifler, sacker, spoiler, despoiler, spoliator, depredator, **raider,** moss-trooper, free-booter rapparee, reiver <Scot>, forayer, forager, ravisher, ravager; wrecker

7 pirate, corsair, buccaneer, privateer, sea rover, rover, picaroon; viking, sea king; Blackbeard, Captain Kidd, Jean Lafitte, Henry Morgan; Captain Hook, Long John Silver; air pirate, airplane hijacker, skyjacker; hijacker, carjacker; record pirate, video pirate, bootlegger

8 cattle thief, abactor, rustler and cattle rustler <nf>; poacher

9 plagiarist, plagiarizer, cribber <nf>, **pirate,** literary pirate, copyright infringer

10 abductor, kidnapper; shanghaier, snatcher and baby-snatcher <nf>; crimp, crimper

11 <famous thieves> Barabbas, Robin Hood, Jesse James, Clyde Barrow, John Dillinger, Claude Duval, Jack Sheppard, Willie Sutton, Dick Turpin, Jonathan Wild; Autolycus, Macheath, Thief of Baghdad, Jean Valjean, Jimmy Valentine, Raffles, Bill Sikes

484 PARSIMONY

NOUNS **1 parsimony,** parsimoniousness; frugality 635.1; **stinting, pinching, scrimping,** skimping, cheeseparing; economy, economy of means, economy of assumption, law of parsimony, Ockham's razor, elegance

2 niggardliness, penuriousness, **meanness,** minginess, shabbiness, sordidness

3 stinginess, ungenerosity, illiberality, cheapness, chintziness and tightness and narrowness <nf>, tight purse strings, nearness, closeness, closefistedness, closehandedness <old>, tightfistedness, hardfistedness, **miserliness,** penny-pinching, hoarding; **avarice** 100.8

4 niggard, tightwad and **cheapskate** <nf>, **miser,** hard man with a buck <nf>, **skinflint,** scrooge, penny pincher, moneygrubber <nf>, pinchfist, pinchgut <old>, churl, curmudgeon <old>, muckworm, save-all <nf>, Harpagon, Silas Marner

VERBS **5 stint, scrimp, skimp, scamp,** scant, screw, **pinch,** starve, famish; **pinch pennies,** rub the print off a dollar bill, rub the picture off a nickel; live upon nothing; grudge, begrudge

6 withhold, hold back, hold out on <nf>

ADJS **7 parsimonious, sparing,** cheeseparing, **stinting, scamping, scrimping,** skimping; frugal 635.6; too frugal, overfrugal, frugal to excess; penny-wise, penny-wise and pound-foolish

8 niggardly, niggard, pinchpenny, penurious, **grudging, mean,** mingy, shabby, sordid

9 stingy, illiberal, ungenerous, chintzy, miserly, save-all, **cheap** and **tight** and narrow <nf>, **near, close, closefisted,** closehanded, tightfisted, pinchfisted, hardfisted; near as the bark on a tree; pinching, **penny-pinching; avaricious** 100.27

ADVS **10 parsimoniously,** stintingly, scrimpingly, skimpingly

11 niggardly, stingily, illiberally, ungenerously, closefistedly, tightfistedly; meanly, shabbily, sordidly

485 LIBERALITY

NOUNS **1 liberality,** liberalness, freeness, freedom; **generosity,** generousness, largeness, **unselfishness, munificence,** largess, charity; bountifulness, bounteousness, **bounty;** hospitality, welcome, graciousness; **openhandedness,** freehandedness, open *or* free hand, easy purse strings; **givingness;** open-heartedness, bigheartedness, largeheartedness, greatheartedness, freeheartedness; open heart, big *or* large *or* great heart, heart of gold; **magnanimity** 652.2

2 **cheerful giver,** free giver; contributor; Lady Bountiful; Santa Claus; philanthropist

VERBS 3 **give freely,** give cheerfully, give with an open hand, give with both hands, put one's hands in one's pockets, open the purse, loosen *or* untie the purse strings; **spare no expense,** spare nothing, not count the cost, let money be no object; **heap upon,** lavish upon, shower down upon; give the coat *or* shirt off one's back, give more than one's share, **give until it hurts;** give of oneself, give of one's substance, not hold back, offer oneself; tip well; keep the change!

ADJS 4 **liberal, free,** free with one's money, free-spending; **generous, munificent,** large, princely, handsome; **unselfish,** ungrudging; **unsparing, unstinting,** stintless, unstinted; **bountiful,** bounteous, **lavish,** profuse; hospitable, gracious; **openhanded,** freehanded, open; **giving;** openhearted, **bighearted,** largehearted, greathearted, freehearted; **magnanimous** 652.6

ADVS 5 **liberally, freely; generously, munificently,** handsomely; **unselfishly,** ungrudgingly; **unsparingly, unstintingly; bountifully,** bounteously, **lavishly,** profusely; hospitably, graciously; **openhandedly,** freehandedly; openheartedly, bigheartedly, largeheartedly, greatheartedly, freeheartedly; with open hands, with both hands, with an unsparing hand, without stint

486 PRODIGALITY

NOUNS 1 **prodigality, overliberality,** overgenerousness, overgenerosity; profligacy, **extravagance,** pound-foolishness, recklessness, reckless spending *or* expenditure, overspending, frittering away; incontinence, intemperance 669; lavishness, profuseness, profusion; **wastefulness, waste; dissipation, squandering,** squandermania; *carpe diem* <L>; slack *or* loose purse strings, leaking purse; conspicuous consumption *or* waste; splurge, spree

2 **prodigal, wastrel,** waster, **squanderer; spendthrift,** wastethrift, spender, spendall, big spender <nf>; Diamond Jim Brady; prodigal son; last of the big spenders

VERBS 3 **squander, lavish,** slather, blow <nf>, play ducks and drakes with; **dissipate,** scatter <old>, sow, broadcast, scatter to the winds, fritter away; **run through,** go through; **throw away,** throw one's money away, throw money around, **spend money**

like water, hang the expense, let slip *or* flow through one's fingers, spend as if money grew on trees, spend money as if it were going out of style, spend like a drunken sailor; gamble away; burn the candle at both ends; seize the day, live for the day, let tomorrow take care of itself

4 **waste, consume, spend, expend, use up, exhaust;** deplete, drain, suck dry, milk dry; misuse, abuse; lose; spill, pour down the drain *or* rathole; pour water into a sieve, cast pearls before swine, kill the goose that lays the golden egg, *manger son blé en herbe* <Fr>, throw out the baby with the bathwater; waste effort, labor in vain

5 **fritter away,** fool away, fribble away, dribble away, drivel away, **trifle away,** dally away, potter away, piss away <nf>, muddle away, diddle away <nf>, squander in dribs and drabs; idle away, while away

6 **misspend,** misapply, **throw good money after bad,** throw the helve after the hatchet, throw out the baby with the bathwater, cast pearls before swine

7 **overspend,** spend more than one has, spend what one hasn't got; overdraw, overdraw one's account, live beyond one's means, have champagne tastes on a beer budget

ADJS 8 **prodigal, extravagant, lavish,** profuse, **overliberal,** overgenerous, overlavish, **spendthrift, wasteful,** profligate, dissipative; incontinent, intemperate 669.7; pound-foolish, penny-wise and pound-foolish; easy come, easy go

9 **wasted, squandered, dissipated,** consumed, spent, used, lost; **gone to waste,** run *or* gone to seed; down the drain *or* spout *or* rathole <nf>; misspent

487 CELEBRATION

NOUNS 1 **celebration,** celebrating; **observance,** formal *or* solemn *or* ritual observance, **solemnization;** marking *or* honoring the occasion; **commemoration,** memorialization, remembrance, memory; jubilee; red-letter day, **holiday** 20.4; anniversaries; **festivity** 743.3,4; **revel** 743.6; rejoicing 116; **ceremony,** rite 580.4; religious rites 701; ovation, triumph; **tribute;** testimonial, testimonial banquet *or* dinner; toast; roast; **salute;** salvo; flourish of trumpets, fanfare, fanfaronade; dressing ship; high-five; binge *or* bender <nf>, blowout <nf>

VERBS 2 **celebrate, observe, keep, mark,** solemnly mark, **honor; commemorate,** memorialize; **solemnize,** signalize, hallow, mark with a red letter; hold jubilee, jubilize, jubilate, maffick <Brit nf>; **make merry;** binge <nf>; kill the fatted calf; sound a fanfare, blow the trumpet, beat the drum, fire a salute; dress ship; high-five

ADJS 3 **celebrative,** celebratory, celebrating;

commemorative, commemorating; memorial; solemn; festive, festal, gala

ADVS **4 in honor of, in commemoration of,** in memory *or* remembrance of, to the memory of

488 HUMOROUSNESS

NOUNS **1 humorousness, funniness,** amusingness, laughableness, laughability, hilarity, hilariousness; wittiness 489.2; **drollness,** drollery; **whimsicalness,** quizzicalness; **ludicrousness, ridiculousness, absurdity,** absurdness, quaintness, eccentricity, incongruity, bizarreness, bizarrerie; richness, pricelessness <nf>; the funny side

2 comicalness, comicality, funiosity; farcicalness, **farcicality,** slapstick quality, broadness

3 bathos; anticlimax, comedown

ADJS **4 humorous, funny, amusing;** witty 489.15; **droll, whimsical,** quizzical; **laughable,** risible, good for a laugh; **ludicrous, ridiculous, hilarious, absurd,** quaint, eccentric, incongruous, bizarre

5 <nf terms> **funny ha-ha,** priceless, too funny *or* too killing for words, hardy-har *or* hardy-har-har *or* har-har-har, rich, hysterical

6 comic *or* **comical; farcical,** slapstick, broad; **burlesque** 508.14; tragicomic, serio-comic, mock-heroic

ADVS **7 humorously, amusingly,** funnily, **laughably;** wittily 489.18; drolly, whimsically, quizzically; **comically,** farcically, broadly; **ludicrously, ridiculously, absurdly,** quaintly, eccentrically, incongruously, bizarrely

489 WIT, HUMOR

NOUNS **1 wit, humor,** pleasantry, *esprit* <Fr>, salt, spice *or* savor of wit; Attic wit *or* salt, Atticism; ready wit, quick wit, nimble wit, agile wit, pretty wit; dry wit, dry humor, subtle wit; **comedy** 704.6; black humor, sick humor, gallows humor; **satire,** sarcasm, irony; Varonnian satire, Menippean satire; **parody, lampoon,** lampoonery, travesty, **caricature, burlesque,** squib, takeoff, spoof; **farce,** mere farce; **slapstick,** slapstick humor, broad humor; visual humor, cartoon, comic strip, the funnies

2 wittiness, humorousness 488, **funniness; facetiousness,** pleasantry, **jocularity,** jocoseness, jocosity; **joking,** japery, joshing <nf>; smartness, cleverness, brilliance; pungency, saltiness; keenness, sharpness; keen-wittedness, quick-wittedness, nimble-wittedness

3 drollery, drollness; **whimsicality,** whimsicalness, humorsomeness, antic wit

4 waggishness, waggery; roguishness 322.2;

playfulness, sportiveness, **levity, frivolity,** flippancy, merriment 109.5; **prankishness,** pranksomeness; trickery, trickiness, tricksiness, trickishness

5 buffoonery, buffoonism, clownery, clowning, clowning around, harlequinade; **clownishness,** buffoonishness; **foolery,** fooling, **tomfoolery;** horseplay; shenanigans *and* monkey tricks *and* monkeyshines <nf>; **banter** 490

6 joke, jest, gag *and* one-liner <nf>, **wheeze,** jape; **fun, sport, play,** kidding; story, yarn, **funny story,** good story; dirty story *or* joke, blue story *or* joke, *double entendre* <Fr>; one-liner; shaggy-dog story; sick joke <nf>; ethnic joke; capital joke, good one, laugh, belly laugh, rib tickler, sidesplitter, thigh-slapper, howler, wow, hoot, scream, riot, panic; visual joke, sight gag <nf>; **point,** punch line, gag line, tag line; cream of the jest; jest-book

7 witticism, pleasantry, *plaisanterie* and *boutade* <Fr>; **play of wit,** *jeu d'esprit* <Fr>; **crack** *and* smart crack *and* **wisecrack** <nf>; **quip,** conceit, bright *or* happy thought, bright *or* brilliant idea; **mot, bon mot,** smart saying, stroke of wit, one-liner *and* zinger <nf>; epigram, turn of thought, aphorism, apothegm; flash of wit, scintillation; sound bite; **sally,** flight of wit; **repartee,** backchat, retort, riposte, snappy comeback <nf>; facetiae <pl>, quips *and* cranks; **gibe, dirty** *or* **nasty crack** <nf>; persiflage 490.1

8 wordplay, play on words, *jeu de mots* <Fr>, missaying, corruption, paronomasia, *calembour* <Fr>, abuse of terms; **pun,** punning; equivoque, equivocality; anagram, logogram, logogriph, metagram; acrostic, double acrostic; amphiboly, amphibologism; palindrome; spoonerism; malapropism

9 old joke, old wheeze *or* turkey, **trite joke,** hoary-headed joke, joke with whiskers; **chestnut** *and* corn *and* **corny joke** *and* oldie <nf>; Joe Miller, Joe Millerism; twice-told tale, retold story, warmed-over cabbage <nf>

10 prank, trick, practical joke, waggish trick, *espièglerie* <Fr>, antic, caper, frolic; **monkeyshines** *and* **shenanigans** <nf>, leg-pull

11 sense of humor, risibility, funny bone

12 humorist, wit, funnyman, comic, *bel-esprit* <Fr>, life of the party; **joker,** jokester, gagman <nf>, **jester, quipster, wisecracker** *and* gagster <nf>; wag, wagwit; zany, madcap, cutup <nf>; **prankster; comedian,** stand-up comic *or* comedian, banana <nf>, straight man; **clown** 707.10; punster, punner; epigrammatist; satirist, ironist; burlesquer, caricaturist, cartoonist, parodist, lampooner; reparteeist; witling; gag writer <nf>, jokesmith

VERBS 13 **joke, jest, wisecrack** *and* **crack wise** <nf>,
utter a mot, **quip,** jape, josh <nf>, fun <nf>, make
fun, **kid** *or* **kid around** <nf>; **make a funny** <nf>;
crack a joke, get off a joke, tell a good story; pun,
play on words; scintillate, sparkle; **make fun of,**
gibe at, fleer at, mock, scoff at, poke fun at, send
up, take off, lampoon, make the butt of one's
humor, be merry with; ridicule 508.8

14 **trick, play a practical joke,** play tricks *or* pranks,
play a joke *or* **trick on,** make merry with; **clown
around,** pull a stunt *or* trick; pull one's leg *and* put
one on <nf>

ADJS 15 **witty, amusing,** *spirituel* <Fr>; **humorous**
488.4,5, **comic, comical,** farcical 488.6; **funny;
jocular,** joky <nf>, **joking, jesting, jocose, tongue-
in-cheek; facetious,** joshing <nf>, **whimsical,
droll,** humorsome; smart, clever, brilliant,
scintillating, sparkling, sprightly; keen, sharp,
rapier-like, pungent, pointed, biting, mordant;
teasing; satiric, **satirical, sarcastic, ironic,** ironical;
salty, salt, Attic; **keen-witted, quick-witted, nimble-
witted,** dry-witted, smart

16 **clownish,** buffoonish

17 **waggish;** roguish 322.6; **playful, sportive;
prankish,** pranky, pranksome; tricky, trickish,
tricksy

ADVS 18 **wittily, humorously; jocularly, jocosely;
facetiously; whimsically, drolly**

19 **in fun, in sport, in play, in jest,** in joke, as a joke,
jokingly, jestingly, with tongue in cheek; for fun,
for sport

490 BANTER

NOUNS 1 **banter, badinage, persiflage, pleasantry,
fooling, fooling around, kidding** *and* **kidding
around** <nf>, **raillery,** rallying, **sport,** good-
natured banter, harmless teasing; ridicule 508;
exchange, give-and-take; side-talk, **byplay,** asides;
flyting, slanging, the dozens <nf>

2 **bantering, twitting, chaffing, joking, jesting,**
japing, **fooling, teasing,** hazing; playing the dozens
<nf>

3 <nf terms> **kidding,** joshing, jollying, jiving,
fooling around; **ribbing,** ragging, razzing, **roasting**

4 **banterer,** *persifleur* <Fr>, **chaffer, twitter; kidder**
and josher <nf>

VERBS 5 **banter, twit, chaff,** rally, **joke, jest,** jape,
tease, haze; have a slanging match, play the
dozens <nf>

6 <nf terms> **kid,** jolly, josh, fool around, jive, rub,
put on; **razz, roast,** ride, needle

ADJS 7 **bantering, chaffing, twitting; jollying** *and*
kidding *and* joshing, etc <nf>, **fooling, teasing,**
quizzical

491 COWARDICE

NOUNS 1 **cowardice, cowardliness; fear** 127;
faintheartedness, faintheart, weakheartedness,
chickenheartedness, henheartedness,
pigeonheartedness; **yellowness,** white-liveredness
and lily-liveredness *and* chicken-liveredness <nf>,
weak-kneedness; weakness, softness; unmanliness,
unmanfulness; timidness, **timidity,** timorousness,
milksoppiness, milksoppishness, milksopism

2 **uncourageousness, unvaliantness,** unvalorousness,
unheroicness, ungallantness, unintrepidness;
plucklessness, spunklessness *and* gritlessness *and*
gutlessness *and* spinelessness <nf>, spiritlessness,
heartlessness; defeatism

3 **dastardliness,** pusillanimousness, **pusillanimity,
poltroonery,** poltroonishness, poltroonism,
baseness, abjectness, **cravenness;** desertion under
fire, bugout *and* skedaddling <nf>, lack of moral
fiber

4 **cold feet** <nf>, weak knees, **faintheart,** chicken
heart, **yellow streak** <nf>, white feather;
gutlessness

5 **coward,** jellyfish, invertebrate, faintheart,
weakling, weak sister <nf>, milksop, milquetoast,
mouse, **sissy, wimp** <nf>, baby, **big baby, chicken**
<nf>; namby-pamby; **yellow-belly,** *and* white-liver
and lily-liver *and* chicken-liver <nf>, jellyfish,
white feather; fraid-cat *and* **fraidy-cat** *and* scaredy-
cat <nf>; funk *and* funker <nf>

6 **dastard, craven, poltroon,** recreant, caitiff, arrant
coward; **sneak;** deserter

VERBS 7 **dare not;** have a yellow streak <nf>, **have
cold feet** <nf>, be unable to say 'boo' to a goose

8 **lose one's nerve,** lose courage, **get cold feet** <nf>,
show the white feather; falter, boggle, funk <nf>,
chicken <nf>; put one's tail between one's legs,
back out, funk out <nf>, **wimp** *or* **chicken out**
<nf>, have no stomach for; desert under fire, turn
tail, bug out *and* skedaddle <nf>, **run scared**
<nf>, scuttle, retreat

9 **cower, quail, cringe, crouch, skulk, sneak, slink**

ADJS 10 **cowardly,** coward; **afraid, fearful** 127.32,34;
timid, timorous, overtimorous, overtimid, rabbity
and mousy <nf>; **fainthearted,** weakhearted,
chicken-hearted, henhearted, pigeonhearted;
white-livered *and* lily-livered *and* chicken-livered
and milk-livered <nf>; **yellow** *and* yellow-bellied
and with a yellow streak <nf>; **weak-kneed,
chicken** <nf>, afraid of one's shadow; weak, soft;
wimpy *or* wimpish <nf>, unmanly, unmanful,
sissy, sissified; milksoppy, milksoppish; panicky,
panic-prone, funking *and* funky <nf>; daunted,
dismayed, unmanned, cowed, intimidated

11 **uncourageous, unvaliant, unvalorous, unheroic,**

ungallant, **unintrepid, undaring,** unable to say
'boo' to a goose; unsoldierlike, unsoldierly;
pluckless, spunkless *and* gritless <nf>, gutless
<nf>, spiritless, heartless

12 **dastardly,** dastard; hit-and-run; **poltroonish,**
poltroon; **pusillanimous,** base, craven, recreant,
caitiff; dunghill, dunghilly

13 **cowering, quailing, cringing; skulking, sneaking,
slinking,** sneaky, slinky

ADVS 14 **cravenly,** poltroonishly, like a coward,
cowardly, uncourageously, unvaliantly,
unvalorously, unheroically, ungallantly,
unintrepidly, undaringly; plucklessly, spunklessly
and gritlessly <nf>, spiritlessly, heartlessly;
faintheartedly, weakheartedly, chickenheartedly;
wimpishly

492 COURAGE

NOUNS 1 **courage,** courageousness, **nerve,** pluck,
bravery, braveness, ballsiness *and* gutsiness *or*
guttiness <nf>, **boldness,** nerves of steel, **valor,**
valorousness, valiance, valiancy, **gallantry,**
conspicuous gallantry, gallantry under fire *or*
beyond the call of duty, gallantness, **intrepidity,**
intrepidness, **prowess,** virtue; doughtiness,
stalwartness, stoutness, stoutheartedness,
lionheartedness, greatheartedness; **heroism,**
heroicalness; chivalry, chivalrousness, knightliness;
military *or* martial spirit, fighting spirit, soldierly
quality *or* virtues; **manliness,** manfulness,
manhood, virility, machismo; Dutch courage <nf>,
pot-valor, bold front, bravado

2 "fear holding on a minute longer"—George Patton,
"taking hard knocks like a man when occasion
calls"—Plautus

3 **fearlessness,** dauntlessness, **undauntedness,
unfearfulness,** unfearingness, unafraidness,
unapprehensiveness; confidence 970.5;
untimidness, untimorousness, unshrinkingness,
unshyness, unbashfulness

4 <nf terms> **balls, guts,** intestinal fortitude, spunk,
brass balls, cojones, moxie, spizzerinctum,
backbone, chutzpah

5 **daring,** derring-do, deeds of derring-do; **bravado,**
bravura; **audacity,** audaciousness, overboldness;
venturousness, venturesomeness, risk-taking,
tightrope walking, funambulism; **adventurousness,**
adventuresomeness, enterprise; foolhardiness
493.3

6 **fortitude, hardihood,** hardiness; **pluckiness;
spunkiness** *and* grittiness *and* nerviness <nf>,
mettlesomeness; **gameness,** gaminess; grit,
stamina, toughness, pith <old>, **mettle,** bottom;
heart, spirit, stout heart, heart of oak; **resolution**

359, resoluteness, tenaciousness, tenacity,
pertinaciousness, pertinacity, bulldog courage, true
grit, stiff upper lip

7 **exploit, feat, deed, enterprise, achievement,
adventure,** act of courage, gest, **bold stroke,** heroic
act *or* deed; prowess; heroics; aristeia

8 <brave person> **hero, heroine;** brave, stalwart,
gallant, valiant, man *or* woman of courage *or*
mettle, a man, valiant knight, good soldier, warrior,
knight in shining armor; demigod, paladin;
demigoddess; the brave; decorated hero; Hector,
Achilles, Roland, David; lion, **tiger,** bulldog,
fighting cock, gamecock; he-man; daredevil, stunt
person

9 **encouragement, heartening, inspiration,**
inspiriting, inspiritment, emboldening, assurance,
reassurance, pat *or* clap on the back, bucking up

VERBS 10 **dare, venture, make bold to,** make so bold
as to, take risks, walk the tightrope, **have the
nerve, have the guts** *or* the balls <nf>, have the
courage of one's convictions, be a man; defy 454.3

11 **brave, face, confront,** affront, front, look one in
the eye, say to one's face, **face up to,** meet, **meet
head-on** *or* boldly, square up to, stand up to *or*
against, go eyeball-to-eyeball *or* one-on-one with
<nf>; set at defiance 454.4; speak up, speak out,
stand up and be counted; not flinch *or* shrink
from, bite the bullet <nf>, look full in the face,
put a bold face upon, show *or* present a bold front;
head into, face up, come to grips with, grapple
with; face the music <nf>; **brazen,** brazen out *or*
through; beard, "beard the lion in his den"—Sir
Walter Scott; put one's head in the lion's mouth, fly
into the face of danger, take the bull by the horns,
march up to the cannon's mouth, bell the cat, go
through fire and water, court disaster, go in harm's
way, throw caution to the wind, run the gauntlet,
take one's life in one's hands, put one's ass *or* life
on the line <nf>

12 **outbrave, outdare; outface,** face down, face out;
outbrazen, brazen out; **outlook, outstare,** stare
down, stare out <Brit>, stare out of countenance

13 **steel oneself, get up nerve,** nerve oneself, muster
or summon up *or* gather courage, pluck up heart,
screw up one's nerve *or* courage, stiffen one's
backbone <nf>

14 **take courage, take heart,** pluck up courage, take
heart of grace; **brace** *or* **buck up** <nf>

15 keep up one's courage, bear up, **keep one's chin up**
<nf>, keep one's pecker up <Brit nf>, **keep a stiff
upper lip** <nf>, hold up one's head, take what
comes; hang in *or* hang in there *or* hang tough *or*
stick it out <nf>, stick to one's guns, grin and bear
it

16 **encourage, hearten, embolden, nerve,** pat *or* clap

on the back, **assure, reassure,** bolster, support, cheer on, root for; **inspire,** inspirit; incite, exhort; buck *or* brace up <nf>; put upon one's mettle, make a man of; cheer 109.7

ADJS **17 courageous, plucky, brave, bold, valiant, valorous, gallant, intrepid,** doughty, **hardy,** stalwart, stout, stouthearted, ironhearted, lionhearted, greathearted, bold-spirited, bold as a lion; **heroic,** herolike; **chivalrous,** chivalric, knightly, knightlike, soldierly, soldierlike; **manly,** manful, virile, macho

18 resolute, tough, game; spirited, spiritful, red-blooded, **mettlesome;** bulldoggish, tenacious, pertinacious

19 <nf terms> **ballsy,** gutsy, gutty, nervy, stand-up, dead game, gritty, spunky, nervy

20 unafraid, unfearing, unfearful; unapprehensive, undiffident; **confident** 970.21; **fearless, dauntless,** aweless, dreadless; **unfrightened,** unscared, unalarmed, unterrified; **untimid,** untimorous, unshy, unbashful

21 undaunted, undismayed, uncowed, unintimidated, unappalled, unabashed, unawed; **unflinching, unshrinking,** unquailing, unbowed, uncringing, unwincing, unblenching, unblinking

22 daring, audacious, overbold; **adventurous, venturous, venturesome,** adventuresome, enterprising; foolhardy 493.9

ADVS **23 courageously, bravely, boldly, heroically, valiantly,** valorously, **gallantly, intrepidly,** doughtily, stoutly, hardily, stalwartly; **pluckily, spunkily** <nf>, gutsily <nf>, **resolutely, gamely,** tenaciously, pertinaciously, bulldoggishly, **fearlessly,** unfearingly, unfearfully; **daringly,** audaciously; chivalrously, knightly, yeomanly; like a man, like a soldier

493 RASHNESS

NOUNS **1 rashness, brashness,** brazen boldness, **incautiousness,** overboldness, **imprudence, indiscretion,** injudiciousness, improvidence; irresponsibility; **unwariness,** unchariness; overcarelessness; overconfidence, oversureness, overweeningness; **impudence,** insolence 142; **gall** *and* brass *and* cheek *and* chutzpah <nf>; hubris; **temerity,** temerariousness; heroics

2 recklessness, devil-may-careness; heedlessness, **carelessness** 340.2; **impetuousness** 365.2, impetuosity, hotheadedness; **haste** 401, **hastiness,** hurriedness, overeagerness, overzealousness, overenthusiasm; **furiousness,** desperateness, wantonness, wildness, wild oats; frivolity; **precipitateness,** precipitousness, precipitance, precipitancy, precipitation

3 foolhardiness, harebrainedness; **audacity,** audaciousness; more guts than brains <nf>, *courage fou* <Fr>; forwardness, boldness, **presumption,** presumptuousness; **daring,** daredeviltry, daredevilry, fire-eating; playing with fire, flirting with death, courting disaster, stretching one's luck, going for broke <nf>, brinkmanship, tightrope walking, funambulism; adventurousness

4 daredevil, devil, **madcap,** madbrain, wild man, hotspur, hellcat, rantipole, harumscarum *and* fire-eater <nf>; **adventurer,** adventuress, adventurist; brazen-face

VERBS **5** be rash, be reckless, carry too much sail, sail too near the wind, throw caution to the wind, go out of one's depth, go too far, go to sea in a sieve, take a leap in the dark, buy a pig in a poke, count one's chickens before they are hatched, catch at straws, lean on a broken reed, put all one's eggs in one basket, live in a glass house; go out on a limb <nf>, leave oneself wide open <nf>, drop one's guard, stick one's neck out *and* ask for it <nf>

6 court danger, ask for it, ask for trouble, mock *or* defy danger, go in harm's way, thumb one's nose at the consequences, **tempt fate** *or* **the gods** *or* **Providence,** tweak the devil's nose, bell the cat, play a desperate game, ride for a fall; play with fire, flirt with death, stretch one's luck, march up to the cannon's mouth, put one's head in a lion's mouth, beard the lion in his den, sit on a barrel of gunpowder, sleep on a volcano, play Russian roulette, playing with a loaded pistol *or* gun, working without a net; **risk all,** go for broke *and* shoot the works <nf>

ADJS **7 rash, brash, incautious,** overbold, **imprudent, indiscreet,** injudicious, improvident; ill-considered; irresponsible; **unwary, unchary;** overcareless; overconfident, oversure, overweening, **impudent,** insolent, brazenfaced, brazen; hubristic; temerarious

8 reckless, devil-may-care; careless 340.11; **impetuous,** hotheaded; **hasty** 401.9, hurried, overeager, overzealous, overenthusiastic; **furious,** desperate, mad, wild, wanton, harum-scarum <nf>; precipitate, **precipitous, precipitant; headlong, breakneck;** slapdash, slap-bang; accident-prone; asking for it

9 foolhardy, harebrained, madcap, **wild,** wild-ass <nf>, madbrain, madbrained; **audacious;** forward, bold, **presumptuous; daring,** daredevil, risk-taking, fire-eating, death-defying; adventurous; frivolous, flippant

ADVS **10 rashly, brashly, incautiously, imprudently, indiscreetly,** injudiciously, improvidently; **unwarily,** uncharily; overconfidently, overweeningly, impudently, insolently, **brazenly,** hubristically, temerariously

11 recklessly, happen what may; heedlessly, **carelessly** 340.18; **impetuously,** hotheadedly; **hastily,** hurriedly, overeagerly, overzealously, overenthusiastically; **furiously,** desperately, wildly, wantonly, **madly,** like mad *or* crazy *and* like there was no tomorrow <nf>; **precipitately,** precipitiously, precipitantly; **headlong,** headfirst, headforemost, **head over heels,** heels over head, *à corps perdu* <Fr>; slapdash, slap-bang *or* slam-bang <nf>; helter-skelter, ramble-scramble <nf>, hurry-scurry, holus-bolus

12 foolhardily, daringly, audaciously, presumptuously, harebrainedly

494 CAUTION

NOUNS 1 caution, cautiousness; slowness to act *or* commit oneself *or* make one's move; **care, heed, solicitude; carefulness, heedfulness,** mindfulness, regardfulness, thoroughness; paying mind *or* attention; **guardedness;** uncommunicativeness 344; **gingerliness, tentativeness,** hesitation, hesitancy, unprecipitateness; slow and careful steps, deliberate stages, wait-and-see attitude *or* policy; **prudence,** prudentialness, **circumspection, discretion,** canniness <Scot>; **coolness, judiciousness** 920.7; calculation, **deliberateness,** deliberation, careful consideration, prior consultation; **safeness,** safety first, no room for error; **hedge, hedging,** hedging one's bets, cutting one's losses

2 wariness, chariness, cageyness *and* **leeriness** <nf>; **suspicion,** suspiciousness; **distrust,** distrustfulness, mistrust, mistrustfulness; reticence, skepticism, second thoughts, reservation

3 precaution, precautiousness; **forethought, foresight,** foresightedness, forehandedness, forethoughtfulness; **providence,** provision, nest egg, forearming; precautions, steps, measures, steps and measures, preventive measure *or* step; **safeguard,** protection 1008, preventive measure, safety net, safety valve, sheet anchor; **insurance;** rainy-day policy; lemon law

4 overcaution, overcautiousness, overcarefulness, overwariness; unadventurousness

VERBS 5 be cautious, be careful; think twice, give it a second thought; make haste slowly, take it easy *or* slow <nf>; put the right foot forward, take one step at a time, pick one's steps, go step by step, feel one's ground *or* way; pussyfoot, tiptoe, go *or* walk on tiptoe, walk on eggs *or* eggshells *or* thin ice; pull *or* draw in one's horns; doubt, have second thoughts

6 take precautions, take steps *or* **measures,** take steps and measures; **prepare** *or* **provide for** *or* **against,** forearm; **guard against, make sure against,** make sure; **play safe** <nf>, anticipate; keep on the safe side; leave no stone unturned, forget *or* leave out nothing, overlook no possibility, leave no room *or* margin for error, leave nothing to chance, consider every angle; **look before one leaps;** see how the land lies *or* the wind blows, see how the cat jumps <nf>; clear the decks, batten down the hatches, shorten sail, reef down, tie in *or* tuck in *or* take in a reef, get out a sheet-anchor, have an anchor to windward; **hedge,** provide a hedge, hedge one's bets, cut one's losses; take out insurance; keep something for a rainy day; provide for

7 beware, take care, have a care, take heed, take heed at one's peril; keep at a respectful distance, keep out of harm's way; mind, mind one's business; **be on one's guard,** be on the watch *or* lookout, be on the *qui vive*; **look out, watch out** <nf>; **look sharp,** keep one's eyes open, keep a weather eye out *or* open <nf>, keep one's eye peeled <nf>, **watch one's step** <nf>, look about one, look over one's shoulder, keep tabs on <nf>; stop, look, and listen; not stick one's neck out <nf>, not go out on a limb <nf>, not expose oneself, not be too visible, **keep a low profile,** lie low, stay in the background, blend with the scenery; not blow one's cover <nf>; hold one's tongue 51.5

ADJS 8 cautious, careful, heedful, mindful, alert, regardful, **thorough; prudent, circumspect,** slow to act *or* commit oneself *or* make one's move, noncommittal, uncommitted; canny <Scot>; sly, crafty, scheming; **discreet, politic, judicious** 920.19, Polonian, Macchiavelian; unadventurous, unenterprising, undaring; **gingerly; guarded,** on guard, on one's guard; uncommunicative 344.8; **tentative,** hesitant, unprecipitate, cool; **deliberate;** safe, on the safe side, leaving no stone unturned, forgetting *or* leaving out nothing, overlooking no possibility, leaving no room *or* margin for error

9 wary, chary, cagey <nf>, **leery** <nf>, **suspicious,** suspecting, **distrustful,** mistrustful, shy; guarded, on guard

10 precautionary, precautious, precautional; **preventive,** preemptive, prophylactic; **forethoughtful,** forethoughted, **foresighted,** foreseeing, forehanded; **provident,** provisional; anticipatory

11 overcautious, overcareful, overwary, unadventurous

ADVS 12 cautiously, carefully, heedfully, mindfully, regardfully; **prudently, circumspectly,** cannily, pawkily <Brit>, **discreetly,** judiciously; **gingerly,** guardedly, easy <nf>, with caution, with care

13 **warily, charily,** cagily <nf>; **askance,** askant, suspiciously, leerily <nf>, distrustfully

INTERJS 14 careful!, be careful!, **take care!,** have a care!, **look out!, watch out!, watch your step!,** watch it!, take heed!, steady!, look sharp!, easy!, take it easy!, easy does it!, go easy!

495 FASTIDIOUSNESS

NOUNS 1 **fastidiousness, particularity,** particularness; **scrupulousness,** scrupulosity; punctiliousness, punctilio, spit and polish; preciseness, precision; **meticulousness, conscientiousness,** criticalness; taste 496; **sensitivity, discrimination** 944, discriminatingness, discriminativeness; **selectiveness,** selectivity, pickiness <nf>, choosiness; **strictness** 339.3, **perfectionism,** precisianism, **purism; puritanism, priggishness, prudishness, prissiness** <nf>, propriety, strait-lacedness, censoriousness, judgmentalness

2 **finicalness,** finickiness, finickingness, finicality; **fussiness,** pernicketiness or persnicketiness <nf>; squeamishness, queasiness

3 **nicety,** niceness, **delicacy,** delicateness, daintiness, exquisiteness, fineness, refinement, **subtlety**

4 overfastidiousness, **overscrupulousness, overparticularity, overconscientiousness,** overmeticulousness, overniceness, **overnicety; overcriticalness,** hypercriticism, hairsplitting; overrefinement, oversubtlety, supersubtlety; oversqueamishness, oversensitivity, hypersensitivity, morbid sensibility

5 **exclusiveness,** exclusivity, selectness, selectiveness, selectivity; **cliquishness,** clannishness; **snobbishness,** snobbery, snobbism

6 **perfectionist,** precisian, precisianist, stickler, nitpicker <nf>, captious critic 946.7

7 **fussbudget, fusspot** <nf>, fuss, fusser, **fuddy-duddy** <nf>, granny, old woman, old maid; Mrs Grundy

VERBS 8 **be hard to please,** want everything just so, **fuss,** fuss over; pick and choose; **turn up one's nose,** look down one's nose, disdain, scorn, spurn; not dirty or soil one's hands

ADJS 9 **fastidious, particular, scrupulous, meticulous, conscientious,** exacting, precise, punctilious, spit-and-polish; **sensitive, discriminating** 943.7, discriminative; **selective, picky** <nf>, choosy, choicy <nf>; critical; **strict** 339.12, perfectionistic, precisianistic, puristic; puritanic, puritanical, priggish, prudish, prissy, proper, strait-laced, censorious, judgmental

10 **finical, finicky,** finicking, finikin; **fussy,** fuss-budgety <nf>; **squeamish,** pernickety and persnickety <nf>, difficult, hard to please

11 **nice, dainty, delicate,** délicat <Fr>, fine, refined, exquisite, **subtle**

12 **overfastidious,** queasy, **overparticular, overscrupulous, overconscientious,** overmeticulous, **overnice,** overprecise; **overcritical,** hypercritical, ultracritical, hairsplitting; overrefined, oversubtle, supersubtle; oversqueamish, oversensitive, hypersensitive, morbidly sensitive; **compulsive,** anal, anal-compulsive

13 **exclusive,** selective, **select,** elect, elite; **cliquish,** clannish; **snobbish,** snobby

ADVS 14 **fastidiously, particularly, scrupulously, meticulously, conscientiously,** critically, punctiliously; discriminatingly, discriminatively, selectively; **finically,** finickily, finickingly; **fussily; squeamishly,** queasily; refinedly, subtly

496 TASTE, TASTEFULNESS

NOUNS 1 **taste, good taste,** sound critical judgment, discernment or appreciation of excellence, preference for the best, goût raffiné <Fr>; **tastefulness,** quality, excellence, choiceness; **elegance,** grace, gracefulness, gracility, graciousness, graciosity, gracious living; propriety; **refinement,** finesse, **polish, culture, cultivation,** civilizedness, refined or cultivated or civilized taste, finish; niceness, nicety, delicacy, daintiness, **subtlety, sophistication; discrimination** 944, fastidiousness 495; acquired taste, connoisseurship, "caviare to the general"—Shakespeare; etiquette

2 "good sense delicately put in force"—Chévier, "the microscope of the judgment"—Rousseau

3 **decorousness, decorum,** decency, properness, propriety, rightness, right thinking, **seemliness,** becomingness, fittingness, fitness, appropriateness, suitability, meetness, happiness, felicity; gentility, genteelness; civility, urbanity 504.1

4 **restraint,** restrainedness, **understatement,** unobtrusiveness, quietness, subduedness, quiet taste; simplicity 499.1; subtlety

5 **aesthetic** or **artistic taste,** virtuosity, virtu, **expertise,** expertism, connoisseurship; dilettantism; fine art of living; epicurism, epicureanism; gastronomy, friandise <Fr>; aesthetics

6 **aesthete,** person of taste, lover of beauty

7 **connoisseur,** connaisseur <Fr>, cognoscente <Ital>; **judge,** good judge, **critic, expert,** authority, maven <nf>, arbiter, arbiter of taste, arbiter

elegantiarum <L>, tastemaker, trend-setter; **epicure,** epicurean; **gourmet, gourmand,** *bon vivant* <Fr>, good *or* refined palate; virtuoso; dilettante, amateur; culture vulture <nf>; collector; gentleperson

ADJS **8 tasteful, in good taste,** in the best taste; excellent, of quality, of the best, of the first water; **aesthetic,** artistic, pleasing, well-chosen, choice, of choice; pure, chaste; classic *or* classical, Attic, restrained, understated, unobtrusive, conservative, quiet, subdued, simple, low-key, unaffected 499.7

9 elegant, graceful, gracile, gracious; **refined, polished, cultivated,** civilized, **cultured;** nice, fine, delicate, dainty, **subtle, sophisticated,** discriminating 943.7, fastidious 495.9, sensitive, U <nf>

10 decorous, decent, proper, right, right-thinking, **seemly, becoming,** fitting, appropriate, suitable, meet, happy, felicitous; genteel; civil, urbane 504.14

ADVS **11 tastefully, with taste,** in good taste, in the best taste; aesthetically, artistically; elegantly, gracefully; decorously, genteelly, decently, properly, seemly, becomingly; quietly, unobtrusively; simply 499.10

497 VULGARITY

NOUNS **1 vulgarity,** vulgarness, vulgarism, commonness, meanness; **inelegance** *or* inelegancy, **indelicacy, impropriety, indecency, indecorum,** indecorousness, unseemliness, unbecomingness, unfittingness, inappropriateness, unsuitableness, unsuitability; ungentility; **untastefulness,** tastelessness, unaestheticness, unaestheticism, tackiness; low *or* bad *or* poor taste, *mauvais goût* <Fr>; vulgar taste, bourgeois taste, Babbittry, philistinism; popular taste, pop culture *and* pop <nf>; campiness, camp, high *or* low camp; baseness, kitsch

2 coarseness, grossness, *grossièreté* <Fr>, **rudeness, crudeness,** crudity, **crassness,** rawness, roughness, **earthiness;** ribaldness, ribaldry; raunchiness <nf>, **obscenity** 666.4; meretriciousness, **loudness** <nf>, **gaudiness** 501.3

3 unrefinement, uncouthness, uncultivation, uncultivatedness, unculturedness; uncivilizedness, wildness; impoliteness, incivility, ill breeding 505.1; **barbarism,** barbarousness, barbarity, philistinism, Gothicism; **savagery,** savagism; **brutality,** brutishness, bestiality, animality, **mindlessness;** Neanderthalism, troglodytism

4 boorishness, churlishness, carlishness, **loutishness,** lubberliness, lumpishness, cloddishness, clownishness, yokelism; ruffianism,

rowdyism, hooliganism; parvenuism, arrivism, upstartness; roughness

5 commonness, commonplaceness, ordinariness, homeliness; **lowness, baseness, meanness; ignobility,** plebeianism

6 vulgarian, low *or* vulgar *or* ill-bred fellow, mucker <nf>, guttersnipe <nf>, *épicier* <Fr>; Babbitt, Philistine, bourgeois; *parvenu and arriviste and nouveau riche* <Fr>, upstart; bounder <nf>, cad, **boor,** churl, clown, **lout,** yahoo, redneck <nf>, looby, peasant, groundling, yokel; rough, **ruffian,** roughneck <nf>, **rowdy,** hooligan; vulgarist, ribald; rascal, rapscallion; vulgus, hoi polloi, rabble, riffraff, great unwashed, scum, huddled masses

7 barbarian, savage, Goth, animal, brute; Neanderthal, troglodyte

8 vulgarization, coarsening; popularization; *haute vulgarisation* <Fr>; dumbing down <nf>

VERBS **9 vulgarize,** coarsen; popularize; dumb down <nf>; pander; commercialize

ADJS **10 vulgar, inelegant, indelicate, indecorous, indecent, improper, unseemly,** unbeseeming, unbecoming, unfitting, inappropriate, unsuitable, **ungenteel,** undignified, discourteous; **untasteful,** tasteless, in bad *or* poor taste, tacky *and* chintzy *and* Mickey Mouse <nf>, gauche, garish; **offensive,** offensive to gentle ears

11 coarse, gross, rude, crude, crass, raw, rough, **earthy;** ribald; raunchy <nf>, **obscene** 666.9; meretricious, **loud** <nf>, **gaudy** 501.20; cacological, solecistic

12 unrefined, unpolished, uncouth, unkempt, uncombed, unlicked; **uncultivated, uncultured; uncivilized,** noncivilized; impolite, uncivil, ill-bred 505.6; **wild,** untamed; **barbarous,** barbaric, barbarian, infra dig; outlandish, Gothic; primitive; **savage, brutal,** brutish, bestial, animal, **mindless;** Neanderthal, troglodytic; wild-and-woolly, rough-and-ready

13 boorish, churlish, carlish, **loutish,** redneck <nf>, lubberly, lumpish, cloddish, clownish, loobyish, yokelish; rowdy, **rowdyish, ruffianly,** roughneck <nf>, hooliganish, raffish, raised in a barn

14 common, commonplace, ordinary; plebeian; homely, homespun; **general, public, popular,** pop <nf>; vernacular; Babbittish, Philistine, bourgeois; campy, high-camp, low-camp, kitschy

15 low, base, mean, ignoble, vile, scurvy, sorry, scrubby, beggarly; low-minded, base-minded

ADVS **16 vulgarly, uncouthly, inelegantly,** indelicately, indecorously, indecently, improperly, unseemly, untastefully, offensively; **coarsely, grossly, rudely, crudely,** crassly, roughly; ribaldly

498 ORNAMENTATION

NOUNS **1 ornamentation, ornament; decoration,** decor; **adornment, embellishment,** embroidery, elaboration; nonfunctional addition *or* adjunct; garnish, garnishment, garniture; trimming, trim; flourish; emblazonment, emblazonry; illumination; **color,** color scheme, color pattern, color compatibility, color design, color arrangement; **arrangement,** flower arrangement, floral decoration, furniture arrangement; table setting *or* decoration; window dressing; **interior decoration** *or* decorating, room decoration, interior design; feng shui; **redecoration, refurbishment 396.4,** redoing

2 ornateness, elegance, fanciness, fineness, **elaborateness; ostentation 501;** richness, luxuriousness, luxuriance; **floweriness,** floridness, floridity; dizenment <old>, **bedizenment; gaudiness, flashiness 501.3;** flamboyance *or* flamboyancy, chi-chi; **overelegance,** overelaborateness, overornamentation, busyness; clutteredness; baroqueness, baroque, rococo, arabesque, moresque, chinoiserie

3 finery, frippery, gaudery, gaiety, bravery, trumpery, folderol, trickery, chiffon, trappings, festoons, superfluity; **frills,** frills and furbelows, bells and whistles *and* gimmickry *and* Mickey Mouse *and* glitz <nf>, **frillery,** frilling, frilliness, foofaraw <nf>, fuss <nf>, froufrou; gingerbread; tinsel, clinquant, pinchbeck, paste; gilt, gilding

4 trinket, gewgaw, **knickknack** *or* nicknack, knack <old>, **gimcrack,** kickshaw, doodad, whim-wham, **bauble,** fribble, bibelot, toy, gaud; bric-a-brac; sequin

5 jewelry, bijouterie, ice <nf>; costume jewelry, glass, paste, junk jewelry <nf>

6 jewel, bijou, **gem,** stone, precious stone; rhinestone; pin, brooch, stickpin, breastpin, scatter pin, chatelaine; cuff-link, tie clasp *or* clip, tie bar, tiepin *or* scarfpin, tie tack *or* tie tac; **ring,** band, wedding band, engagement ring, mood ring, signet ring, school *or* class ring, circle, earring, nose ring; bracelet, wristlet, wristband, armlet, anklet; chain, necklace, torque; locket; beads, chaplet, wampum; bangle; charm; fob; crown, coronet, diadem, tiara; laurel

7 motif, ornamental motif, **figure, detail,** form, touch, repeated figure; **pattern, theme,** design, ornamental theme, ornamental *or* decorative composition; foreground detail, background detail; **background,** setting, foil, **style,** ornamental *or* decorative style, national style, **period style**

VERBS **8 ornament, decorate, adorn, dress, trim, garnish,** array, **deck,** bedeck, dizen <old>,

bedizen; prettify, **beautify; redecorate,** refurbish, redo; gimmick *or* glitz *or* sex up <nf>; **embellish, furbish,** embroider, enrich, grace, set off *or* out, paint, color, blazon, emblazon, paint in glowing colors; **dress up; spruce up** *and* gussy up *and* doll up *and* fix up <nf>, **primp up,** prink up, prank up, trick up *or* out, deck out, bedight <old>, fig out; primp, prink, prank, preen; smarten, smarten up, dandify, titivate, give a face lift

9 figure, filigree; **spangle, bespangle;** bead; tinsel; jewel, bejewel, gem, diamond; ribbon, beribbon; flounce; flower, garland, wreathe; feather, plume; flag; illuminate; paint 35.13; engrave

ADJS **10 ornamental, decorative,** adorning, embellishing

11 ornamented, adorned, decorated, embellished, bedecked, decked out, tricked out, garnished, trimmed, dizened <old>, bedizened; figured; flowered; festooned, befrilled, wreathed; spangled, bespangled, spangly; jeweled, bejeweled; beaded; studded; plumed, feathered; beribboned

12 ornate, elegant, fancy, fine, chichi, pretty-pretty; picturesque; **elaborate,** overornamented, overornate, overelegant; etc; labored, high-wrought; **ostentatious 501.18;** glitzy, flashy; **rich, luxurious,** luxuriant; **flowery,** florid; flamboyant, fussy, frilly, frilled, flouncy, gingerbread *or* gingerbready; **overelegant,** overelaborate, overlabored, overworked, overwrought, overornamented, busy; cluttered; **baroque,** rococo, arabesque, moresque, gilded; gimmicked- *or* glitzed- *or* sexed-up <nf>

499 PLAINNESS

<unaffectedness>

NOUNS **1 plainness, simplicity 798, simpleness, ordinariness, commonness, commonplaceness,** homeliness, prosaicness, prosiness, matter-of-factness; **purity,** chasteness, classic *or* classical purity, Attic simplicity

2 naturalness, inartificiality; **unaffectedness,** unassumingness, **unpretentiousness;** directness, straightforwardness; innocence, naïveté

3 unadornment, unembellishment, unadornedness, unornamentation; **no frills,** no nonsense, back-to-basics; **uncomplexity,** uncomplication, uncomplicatedness, **unsophistication,** unadulteration; bareness, baldness, nakedness, nudity, undress, beauty unadorned

4 inornateness, unelaborateness, unfanciness, unfussiness; **austerity,** severity, starkness, Spartan simplicity

VERBS **5 simplify 798.4;** chasten, restrain, purify; put in words of one syllable, spell out

ADJS **6 simple** 798.6, **plain, ordinary, nondescript, common, commonplace, prosaic,** prosy, **matter-of-fact, homely, homespun,** everyday, vanilla <nf>, conventional, workday, workaday, household, garden, common- *or* garden-variety; pure, **pure and simple,** chaste, classic *or* classical, Attic

7 natural, native; **inartificial,** unartificial; **unaffected, unpretentious,** unpretending, unassuming, unfeigning, direct, straightforward, honest, candid; innocent, naive

8 unadorned, undecorated, unornamented, unembellished, ungarnished, unfurbished, unvarnished, untrimmed; olde *and* olde-worlde <nf>; back-to-basics, no-frills, no-nonsense, vanilla *or* plain-vanilla *and* white-bread *or* white-bready <nf>; back-to-nature; **uncomplex,** uncomplicated, **unsophisticated,** unadulterated; **undressed,** undecked, unarrayed; bare, bald, blank, naked, nude

9 inornate, unornate, **unelaborate,** unfancy, unfussy; austere, monkish, cloistral, severe, stark, Spartan

ADVS **10 plainly, simply,** ordinarily, commonly, commonplacely, prosaically, matter-of-factly

11 unaffectedly, naturally, unpretentiously, unassumingly, directly, straightforwardly

500 AFFECTATION

NOUNS **1 affectation, affectedness; pretension, pretense, airs,** pretentiousness, putting on airs, put-on <nf>; **show, false show,** mere show; front, false front <nf>, **facade,** mere facade, **image,** public image; feigned belief, **hypocrisy** 354.6; phoniness <nf>, sham 354.3; artificiality, unnaturalness, insincerity; prunes and prisms, airs and graces; stylishness, mannerism

2 mannerism, *minauderie* <Fr>, **trick of behavior,** trick, **quirk,** habit, peculiarity, peculiar trait, idiosyncrasy, trademark

3 posing, pose, posturing, attitudinizing, attitudinarianism; peacockery, peacockishness; pompousness; putting on airs

4 foppery, foppishness, dandyism, coxcombry, puppyism, conceit

5 overniceness, overpreciseness, **overrefinement, elegance,** exquisiteness, preciousness, preciosity; goody-goodyism *and* goody-goodness <nf>; purism, formalism, formality, pedantry, precisionism, precisianism; euphuism; euphemism

6 prudery, prudishness, prissiness, priggishness, primness, smugness, stuffiness <nf>, old-maidishness, **straitlacedness,** stiff-neckedness, hidebound, narrowness, censoriousness, sanctimony, sanctimoniousness, **puritanism,** puritanicalness; **false modesty,** overmodesty, demureness, *mauvaise honte* <Fr>

7 phony *and* **fake** *and* **fraud** <nf> 354.13; affecter; mannerist; **pretender,** actor, playactor <nf>, performer; paper tiger, hollow man, straw man, man of straw, empty suit <nf>

8 poser, poseur, striker of poses, **posturer,** posturist, posture maker, attitudinarian, attitudinizer, bluffer

9 dandy, fop, coxcomb, macaroni, gallant, dude *and* swell *and* sport <nf>, ponce *and* toff <Brit nf>, exquisite, blood, fine gentleman, puppy, jackanapes, jack-a-dandy, fribble, clotheshorse, fashion plate; beau, Beau Brummel, spark, blade, ladies' man, lady-killer <nf>, masher, cocksman <nf>; man-about-town, boulevardier

10 fine lady, *grande dame* and *précieuse* <Fr>; belle, toast

11 prude, prig, priss, puritan, bluenose, goody-goody <nf>, wowser <Brit nf>, old maid; Victorian, mid-Victorian

VERBS **12 affect, assume, put on,** assume *or* put on airs, wear, **pretend, simulate, counterfeit, sham, fake** <nf>, **feign,** make out like <nf>, make a show of, play, playact <nf>, act *or* play a part, play a scene, do a bit <nf>, put up a front <nf>, dramatize, histrionize, show off, play to the gallery, lay it on thick <nf>, overact, ham *and* ham it up *and* chew up the scenery *and* emote <nf>, tug at the heartstrings

13 pose, posture, attitudinize, peacock, strike a pose, strike an attitude, pose for effect

14 mince, mince it, prink <Brit nf>; **simper,** smirk, bridle

ADJS **15 affected, pretentious,** la-di-da, posy <Brit nf>; mannered, *maniéré* <Fr>; **artificial, unnatural,** insincere; theatrical, stagy, histrionic; overdone, overacted, hammed up <nf>

16 assumed, put-on, pretended, simulated, **phony** *and* **fake** *and* **faked** <nf>, feigned, counterfeited; spurious, sham; deceptive, specious; hypocritical

17 foppish, dandified, dandy, coxcombical, conceited, chichi, pompous

18 <affectedly nice> overnice, overprecise, precious, *précieuse* <Fr>, exquisite, **overrefined, elegant,** mincing, simpering, namby-pamby; **goody-goody** *and* goody good-good <nf>; puristic, formalistic, pedantic, precisionistic, precisian, precisianistic, euphuistic, euphemistic

19 prudish, priggish, prim, prissy, smug, stuffy <nf>, old-maidish, **overmodest,** demure, **straitlaced,** stiff-necked, hide-bound, narrow, censorious, po-faced <Brit>, sanctimonious, **puritanical,** Victorian, mid-Victorian

ADVS **20 affectedly, pretentiously;** elegantly, mincingly; for effect, for show

21 prudishly, priggishly, primly, smugly, stuffily <nf>, straitlacedly, stiffneckedly, puritanically

501 OSTENTATION

NOUNS **1 ostentation,** ostentatiousness, ostent; **pretentiousness, pretension, pretense;** loftiness, lofty affectations, **triumphalism**

2 pretensions, vain pretensions; **airs,** lofty airs, airs and graces, vaporing, highfalutin *or* highfaluting ways <nf>, side, swank <nf>, delusions of grandeur

3 showiness, flashiness, flamboyance, panache, dash, jazziness <nf>, jauntiness, sportiness <nf>, gaiety, glitter, glare, dazzle, dazzlingness; extravaganza; **gaudiness,** gaudery, glitz *and* gimmickry *and* razzmatazz *and* razzledazzle <nf>, **tawdriness,** meretriciousness; gorgeousness, colorfulness; loudness <nf>, **blatancy,** flagrancy, shamelessness, brazenness, luridness, extravagance, sensationalism, obtrusiveness, vulgarness, crudeness, extravagation

4 display, show, demonstration, manifestation, **exhibition, parade,** *étalage* <Fr>; **pageantry,** pageant, **spectacle,** gala; vaunt, fanfaronade, blazon, flourish, flaunt, flaunting; daring, brilliancy, éclat, bravura, flair; dash *and* splash *and* splurge <nf>; figure; showmanship, **exhibitionism,** showing-off, fuss and feathers; theatrics, histrionics, dramatics, staginess, camp; false front, **sham** 354.3

5 grandeur, grandness, grandiosity, **magnificence,** gorgeousness, **splendor,** splendidness, splendiferousness, resplendence, brilliance, glory; nobility, proudness, **state, stateliness, majesty;** impressiveness, imposingness; **sumptuousness, elegance, elaborateness, lavishness, luxuriousness;** ritziness *or* poshness *or* plushness *or* swankness *or* swankiness <nf>; **luxury,** barbaric *or* Babylonian splendor

6 pomp, circumstance, pride, **state,** solemnity, formality; **pomp and circumstance,** "pride, pomp, and circumstance"—Shakespeare; heraldry

7 pompousness, pomposity, pontification, pontificality, **stuffiness** <nf>, **self-importance,** inflation; grandiloquence, bombast, turgidity, orotundity

8 swagger, strut, swank <nf>, bounce, brave show; swaggering, strutting; swash, **swashbucklery,** swashbuckling, swashbucklering; peacockishness, peacockery

9 stuffed shirt <nf>, blimp <nf>, Colonel Blimp; bloated aristocrat

10 strutter, swaggerer, swanker <Brit>, swash, swasher, **swashbuckler,** peacock, miles gloriosus

11 show-off <nf>, **exhibitionist,** flaunter; **grandstander** *or* grandstand player *or* hot dog *or* **hotshot** *or* showboat <nf>

VERBS **12 put** *or* **thrust oneself forward,** come forward, step to the front *or* fore, step into the limelight, take center stage, attract attention, make oneself conspicuous

13 cut a dash, make a show, put on a show, make one's mark, cut a swath, cut *or* **make a figure;** make a splash *or* a splurge <nf>; **splurge** *and* splash <nf>; shine, glitter, glare, dazzle

14 give oneself airs, put on airs, put on, put on side, put on the dog <nf>, put up a front <nf>, put on the ritz *and* ritz it <nf>, look big, **swank** <nf>, swell, swell it, act the grand seigneur; pontificate, play the pontiff

15 strut, swagger, swank <Brit>, prance, stalk, peacock, swash, swashbuckle

16 show off <nf>, **grandstand** *and* hotdog *and* showboat <nf>, play to the gallery *or* galleries <nf>, please the crowd, ham it up; exhibit *or* parade one's wares <nf>, strut one's stuff <nf>, go through one's paces, show what one has

17 flaunt, vaunt, **parade, display, demonstrate,** manifest, make a great show of, **exhibit,** air, put forward, put forth, hold up, flash *and* sport <nf>; advertise; **flourish,** brandish, wave; dangle, dangle before the eyes; emblazon, blazon forth; trumpet, trumpet forth

ADJS **18 ostentatious, pretentious,** posy <Brit nf>; **ambitious,** vaunting, **lofty, highfalutin** *and* highfaluting <nf>, **high-flown,** high-flying; **high-toned,** tony <nf>, **fancy,** classy *or* glitzy *or* flossy <nf>

19 showy, flaunting, flashy, snazzy, flashing, glittering, **jazzy** *and* **glitzy** *and* gimmicky *and* splashy *and* splurgy <nf>; camp; exhibitionistic, showoffy <nf>, bravura; **gay,** jaunty, rakish, **dashing;** gallant, brave, daring; **sporty** *or* dressy <nf>; **frilly, flouncy,** frothy, chichi

20 gaudy, tawdry; gorgeous, colorful; **garish, loud** <nf>, **blatant, flagrant,** shameless, **brazen,** brazenfaced, lurid, extravagant, sensational, **spectacular,** glaring, flaring, flaunting, screaming <nf>, obtrusive, vulgar, crude; meretricious, low-rent *and* low-ride *and* tacky <nf>

21 grandiose, grand, magnificent, splendid, splendiferous, splendacious <nf>, **glorious,** superb, fine, superfine, fancy, superfancy, swell <nf>; **imposing, impressive,** larger-than-life, awful, awe-inspiring, awesome; **noble, proud, stately, majestic,** princely; **sumptuous, elegant, elaborate, luxurious,** luxuriant, extravagant, deluxe; executive *and* plush *and* posh *and* ritzy *and* swank *and* swanky <nf>, Corinthian; palatial, Babylonian

22 pompous, stuffy <nf>, **self-important,** impressed with oneself, pontific, pontifical; **inflated, swollen,** bloated, tumid, turgid, flatulent, gassy <nf>, stilted; grandiloquent, **bombastic** 545.9; solemn 111.3, formal

23 strutting, swaggering; swashing, **swashbuckling,** swashbucklering; peacockish, peacocky; too big for one's britches

24 theatrical, theatric, stagy, dramatic, histrionic; spectacular

ADVS **25 ostentatiously, pretentiously, loftily;** with flourish of trumpet, with beat of drum, with flying colors

26 showily, flauntingly, flashily, with a flair, glitteringly; gaily, jauntily, **dashingly;** gallantly, bravely, daringly

27 gaudily, tawdrily; gorgeously, colorfully; **garishly, blatantly, flagrantly,** shamelessly, **brazenly,** brazenfacedly, luridly, sensationally, **spectacularly,** glaringly, flaringly, obtrusively

28 grandiosely, grandly, magnificently, splendidly, splendiferously, splendaciously <nf>, gloriously, superbly; nobly, proudly, majestically; imposingly, impressively; **sumptuously, elegantly,** elaborately, luxuriously, **extravagantly;** palatially

29 pompously, pontifically, stuffily <nf>, **self-importantly;** stiltedly; **bombastically** 545.12

502 BOASTING

NOUNS **1 boasting, bragging,** vaunting; **boastfulness, braggadocio, braggartism; boast, brag,** vaunt; side, bombast, bravado, vauntery, fanfaronade, blowing-off or blowing or tooting one's own horn <nf>, gasconade, gasconism, rodomontade; bluster, swagger 503.1; vanity, conceit 140.4; jactation, jactitation; heroics

2 <nf terms> **big talk,** fine talk, fancy talk, tall talk, highfalutin or highfaluting, **hot air,** gas, bunk, bunkum, **bullshit;** tall story, fish story

3 self-approbation, self-praise, self-laudation, self-gratulation, self-applause, self-boosting, self-puffery, self-vaunting, self-advertising, self-advertisement, self-adulation, self-glorification, self-dramatizing, self-dramatization, self-promoting, self-promotion; **vainglory,** vaingloriousness

4 crowing, exultation, elation, triumph, jubilation; **gloating**

5 braggart, boaster, brag, braggadocio, exaggerator, hector, fanfaron, Gascon, gasconader, miles gloriosus; **blowhard** and blower and big mouth and bullshitter and bullshit artist and hot-air artist and gasbag and windbag and big bag of wind and windjammer and windy <nf>; blusterer 503.2,

panjandrum; Texan, Fourth-of-July orator; Braggadocchio <Spenser>, Captain Bobadil <Ben Jonson>, Thraso <Terence>, Parolles <Shakespeare>

VERBS **6 boast, brag,** make a boast of, vaunt, flourish, gasconade, vapor, puff, draw the longbow, advertise oneself, **blow one's own trumpet, toot one's own horn,** sing one's own praises, exaggerate one's own merits; bluster, swagger 503.3; speak for Buncombe

7 <nf terms> **blow,** blow off, mouth off, **blow hard, talk big,** sound off, blow off and toot or blow one's own horn, **bullshit,** shoot the shit, spread oneself, lay it on thick, brag oneself up

8 flatter oneself, conceit oneself, **congratulate oneself,** hug oneself, shake hands with oneself, form a mutual admiration society with oneself, **pat oneself on the back,** take merit to oneself; think one's shit doesn't stink <nf>

9 exult, triumph, glory, delight, joy, jubilate; **crow** or crow over, crow like a rooster or cock; **gloat,** gloat over

ADJS **10 boastful, boasting, braggart, bragging,** thrasonical, thrasonic, big-mouthed <nf>, vaunting, vaporing, gasconading, Gascon, fanfaronading, fanfaron; vain, pompous, conceited 140.11; **vainglorious**

11 self-approving, self-approbatory, self-praising, self-gratulating, self-boosting, self-puffing, self-adulating, self-adulatory, self-glorifying, self-glorying, self-glorious, self-lauding, self-laudatory, self-congratulatory, self-applauding, self-flattering, self-vaunting, self-advertising, self-dramatizing, self-promoting

12 inflated, swollen, windy and gassy <nf>, **bombastic,** high-swelling, **high-flown, highfalutin** and highfaluting <nf>, **pretentious,** extravagant, big, tall <nf>, hyped <nf>

13 crowing, exultant, exulting, elated, elate, jubilant, **triumphant, flushed,** cock-a-hoop, in high feather; **gloating**

ADVS **14 boastfully,** boastingly, braggingly, vauntingly, vaingloriously; **self-approvingly,** self-praisingly, etc

15 exultantly, exultingly, elatedly, jubilantly, triumphantly, triumphally, in triumph; **gloatingly**

503 BLUSTER

NOUNS **1 bluster,** blustering, hectoring, bullying, **swagger,** swashbucklery, side; **bravado,** rant, rodomontade, fanfaronade; sputter, splutter; fuss, bustle, fluster, flurry; bluff, bluster and bluff; intimidation 127.6; **boastfulness** 502.1

2 blusterer, swaggerer, swasher, swashbuckler,

fanfaron, bravo, **bully,** bullyboy, bucko, roisterer, cock of the walk, vaporer, blatherskite <nf>; ranter, raver, hectorer, hector, Herod; slanger <Brit>; bluff, bluffer; **braggart** 502.5

VERBS **3 bluster,** hector; **swagger,** swashbuckle; bully; bounce, vapor, roister, rollick, gasconade, kick up a dust <nf>; sputter, splutter; rant, rage, rave, rave on, storm, "out-herod Herod"— Shakespeare; slang <Brit>; bluff, bluster and bluff, put up a bluff <nf>; intimidate; shoot off one's mouth, sound off, **brag** 502.6

ADJS **4 blustering,** blustery, blusterous, hectoring, **bullying, swaggering,** swashing, swashbuckling, boisterous, roisterous, roistering, rollicking; ranting, raging, raving, storming; tumultuous; noisy, "full of sound and fury"—Shakespeare

504 COURTESY

NOUNS **1 courtesy,** courteousness, common courtesy, **politeness, civility,** *politesse* <Fr>, amenity, agreeableness, urbanity, comity, affability; graciousness, **gracefulness;** complaisance; **thoughtfulness, considerateness** 143.3, **tactfulness,** tact, consideration, **solicitousness, solicitude; respect,** respectfulness, deference; civilization, quality of life

2 gallantry, gallantness, **chivalry,** chivalrousness, knightliness; courtliness, courtly behavior *or* politeness; *noblesse oblige* <Fr>

3 mannerliness, manners, good manners, excellent *or* exquisite manners, good *or* polite deportment, good *or* polite behavior, *bienséance* <Fr>; *savoir-faire* and *savoir-vivre* <Fr>; decency; correctness, correctitude, **etiquette** 580.3

4 good breeding, breeding; refinement, finish, polish, culture, cultivation; gentility, gentleness, genteelness, elegance; gentlemanliness, gentlemanlikeness, ladylikeness

5 suavity, suaveness, smoothness, smugness, blandness; **unctuousness,** oiliness, oleaginousness, smarm *or* smarminess <nf>; **glibness,** slickness <nf>, fulsomeness; sweet talk, fair words, soft words *or* tongue, sweet *or* honeyed words *or* tongue, incense; soft soap *and* butter <nf>

6 courtesy, civility, amenity, urbanity, attention, polite act, act of courtesy *or* politeness, graceful gesture, pleasantry; old-fashioned courtesy *or* civility, courtliness

7 amenities, courtesies, civilities, gentilities, graces, elegancies; dignities; formalities, ceremonies, rites, rituals, observances

8 regards, compliments, respects, *égards* and *devoirs* <Fr>; **best wishes,** one's best, good wishes, best regards, kind *or* kindest regards, love, best love;

greetings 585.3; remembrances, kind remembrances; compliments of the season

9 gallant, cavalier, chevalier, **knight**

10 "the very pink of courtesy"—Shakespeare, "the very pineapple of politeness"—R B Sheridan

VERBS **11 mind one's manners,** mind one's P's and Q's <nf>; keep a civil tongue in one's head; mend one's manners; observe etiquette, observe *or* follow protocol; be polite, be considerate

12 extend courtesy, do the honors, pay one's respects, make one's compliments, present oneself, pay attentions to, do service, wait on *or* upon

13 give one's regards *or* **compliments** *or* love, give one's best regards, give one's best, send one's regards *or* compliments *or* love; wish one joy, wish one luck, bid Godspeed

ADJS **14 courteous, polite, civil, urbane, gracious,** graceful, agreeable, affable, fair; complaisant; obliging, accommodating; **thoughtful, considerate,** tactful, solicitous; respectful, deferential, attentive

15 gallant, chivalrous, chivalric, knightly; **courtly; formal,** ceremonious; old-fashioned, old-world

16 mannerly, well-mannered, good-mannered, **well-behaved,** well- *or* fair-spoken; **correct,** correct in one's manners *or* behavior; housebroken <nf>

17 well-bred, highbred, **well-brought-up; cultivated, cultured, polished, refined, genteel,** gentle; gentlemanly, gentlemanlike, ladylike

18 suave, smooth, smug, bland, **glib, unctuous,** oily, oleaginous, smarmy <nf>, soapy *and* buttery <nf>, fulsome, ingratiating, disarming; suave-spoken, fine-spoken, fair-spoken, soft-spoken, smooth-spoken, smooth-tongued, oily-tongued, honey-tongued, honey-mouthed, sweet-talking

ADVS **19 courteously, politely, civilly,** urbanely, mannerly; **gallantly, chivalrously,** courtly, knightly; **graciously,** gracefully, with a good grace; complaisantly, complacently; out of consideration *or* courtesy; obligingly, accommodatingly; respectfully, attentively, deferentially

505 DISCOURTESY

NOUNS **1 discourtesy,** discourteousness; **impoliteness,** unpoliteness; **rudeness, incivility,** inurbanity, **ungraciousness, ungallantness,** uncourtesy, uncourtliness, ungentlemanliness, **unmannerliness,** mannerlessness, bad *or* ill manners, **ill breeding,** conduct unbecoming a gentleman, caddishness; inconsiderateness, inconsideration, unsolicitousness, unsolicitude, tactlessness, **insensitivity; grossness, crassness,** gross *or* crass behavior, **boorishness, vulgarity, coarseness, crudeness,** offensiveness, loutishness, nastiness

2 disrespect, disrespectfulness 156.1; **insolence** 142

3 **gruffness, brusqueness,** *brusquerie* <Fr>, **curtness,** shortness, sharpness, abruptness, bluntness, brashness; **harshness,** roughness, severity; truculence, aggressiveness; **surliness,** crustiness, bearishness, beastliness, churlishness

ADJS **4** **discourteous,** uncourteous; **impolite,** unpolite, inurbane; **rude, uncivil, ungracious, ungallant,** uncourtly, inaffable, uncomplaisant, unaccommodating; disrespectful; **insolent**

5 **unmannerly,** unmannered, mannerless, **ill-mannered, ill-behaved,** ill-conditioned, bad-mannered

6 **ill-bred, ungenteel,** ungentle, caddish; **ungentlemanly,** ungentlemanlike; **unladylike,** unfeminine; **vulgar, boorish, unrefined** 497.12, **inconsiderate, unsolicitous, tactless, insensitive; gross,** offensive, crass, **coarse, crude,** loutish, nasty

7 **gruff, brusque, curt,** short, sharp, snippy <nf>, abrupt, **blunt,** bluff, brash, cavalier; **harsh,** rough, severe; truculent, aggressive; **surly,** crusty, bearish, beastly, churlish; vituperative

ADVS **8** **discourteously, impolitely, rudely,** uncivilly, ungraciously, ungallantly, ungenteelly, caddishly; inconsiderately, unsolicitously, tactlessly, insensitively

9 **gruffly, brusquely, curtly,** shortly, sharply, snippily <nf>, abruptly, bluntly, bluffly, brashly, cavalierly; harshly, crustily, bearishly, churlishly, **boorishly,** nastily

506 RETALIATION

NOUNS **1** **retaliation, reciprocation,** exchange, interchange, give-and-take; **retort, reply,** return, comeback <nf>; counter, counterblow, counterstroke, counterblast, counterpunch, recoil, boomerang, backlash

2 **reprisal, requital, retribution; recompense, compensation** 338, **reward,** comeuppance <nf>, desert, deserts, **just deserts,** what is merited, what is due *or* condign, what's coming to one *and* a dose of one's own medicine <nf>; quittance, return of evil for evil; **revenge** 507; **punishment** 604

3 **tit for tat, measure for measure,** like for like, quid pro quo, something in return, blow for blow, a Roland for an Oliver, a game two can play, **an eye for an eye,** a tooth for a tooth, "eye for eye, tooth for tooth, hand for hand, foot for foot"—Bible, law of retaliation *or* equivalent retaliation, *lex talionis* <L>, talion; game at which two can play

VERBS **4** **retaliate, retort,** counter, **strike back,** hit back at <nf>, give in return; **reciprocate,** give in exchange, give and take; **get** *or* **come back at**

<nf>, turn the tables upon; fight fire with fire, return the compliment

5 **requite,** quit, make requital *or* reprisal *or* retribution, get satisfaction, recompense, compensate, make restitution, indemnify, reward, redress, make amends, **repay,** pay, **pay back,** pay off; **give one his comeuppance** <nf>, give one his desserts *or* just desserts, serve one right, give one what is coming to him <nf>

6 **give in kind,** cap, match, give as good as one gets *or* as was sent; repay in kind, **pay one in one's own coin** *or* **currency, give one a dose of one's own medicine** <nf>; return the like, return the compliment; return like for like, **return evil for evil;** return blow for blow, **give one tit for tat,** give a quid pro quo, give as good as one gets, give measure for measure, give *or* get an eye for an eye and a tooth for a tooth, follow *or* observe the *lex talionis* <L>

7 **get even with** <nf>, even the score, **settle** *or* **settle up with,** settle *or* **square accounts** *and* settle the score *and* fix <nf>, pay off old scores, pay back in full measure, be *or* make quits; fix one's wagon <nf>, **take revenge** 507.4; **punish** 604.10,11

ADJS **8** **retaliatory,** retaliative; **retributive,** retributory; reparative, compensatory, restitutive, recompensing, recompensive, reciprocal; punitive; recriminatory, like for like; revengeful, vindictive

ADVS **9** **in retaliation, in exchange,** in reciprocation; **in return,** in reply; **in requital, in reprisal,** in retribution, in reparation, in amends; **in revenge,** *en revanche* <Fr>

PHRS **10** what goes around comes around, one's chickens come home to roost; the shoe is on the other foot

507 REVENGE

NOUNS **1** **revenge, vengeance, avengement,** sweet revenge, getting even, evening of the score; **wrath;** revanche, revanchism; **retaliation, reprisal** 506.2; vendetta, feud, blood feud; the wrath of God

2 **revengefulness, vengefulness, vindictiveness,** rancor, grudgefulness, irreconcilableness, unappeasableness, implacableness, implacability

3 **avenger, vindicator;** revanchist; Nemesis, the Furies, the Erinyes, the Eumenides

VERBS **4** **revenge, avenge, take** *or* **exact revenge,** have one's revenge, wreak one's vengeance; **retaliate, even the score, get even with** 506.4–7; launch a vendetta

5 **harbor revenge,** breathe vengeance; have accounts to settle, have a crow to pick *or* pluck *or* pull with; nurse one's revenge, brood over, dwell on *or* upon, keep the wound open, wave the bloody shirt

6 reap *or* suffer *or* incur vengeance *or* revenge; sow the wind and reap the whirlwind; live by the sword and die by the sword

ADJS 7 **revengeful, vengeful,** avenging; **vindictive,** vindicatory; revanchist; **punitive,** punitory; **wrathful,** rancorous, grudgeful, irreconcilable, unappeasable, implacable, unwilling to forgive and forget, unwilling to let bygones be bygones; **retaliatory** 506.8

508 RIDICULE

NOUNS 1 **ridicule, derision, mockery, raillery,** rallying, chaffing; panning *and* razzing *and* roasting *and* ragging <nf>, **scoffing, jeering, sneering,** snickering, sniggering, smirking, grinning, leering, fleering, snorting, levity, flippancy, smartness, smart-aleckiness *and* joshing <nf>, fooling, japery, twitting, taunting, booing, hooting, catcalling, hissing; **banter** 490

2 **gibe, scoff, jeer,** fleer, flout, mock, barracking <Brit>, **taunt, twit,** quip, jest, jape, put-on *and* leg-pull <nf>, foolery; **insult** 156.2; scurrility, caustic remark; **cut,** cutting remark, verbal thrust; gibing retort, rude reproach, short answer, back answer, comeback <nf>, parting shot, Parthian shot

3 **boo,** booing, **hoot, catcall;** Bronx cheer *and* **raspberry** *and* razz <nf>; **hiss, hissing,** the bird <nf>

4 scornful laugh *or* smile, snicker, snigger, **smirk,** sardonic grin, leer, fleer, **sneer,** snort

5 **sarcasm, irony, cynicism, satire,** satiric wit *or* humor, invective, innuendo; **causticity** 144.8

6 **burlesque, lampoon,** squib, **parody, satire, farce,** mockery, imitation, wicked imitation *or* pastiche, takeoff <nf>, **travesty, caricature**

7 **laughingstock,** jestingstock, gazingstock, derision, mockery, **figure of fun,** byword, byword of reproach, jest, joke, **butt,** target, stock, **goat** <nf>, toy, game, **fair game,** victim, dupe, fool, everybody's fool, monkey, mug <Brit nf>

VERBS 8 **ridicule, deride,** ride <nf>, make a laughingstock *or* a mockery of; roast <nf>, **insult** 156.5; **make fun** *or* **game of, poke fun at,** make merry with, put one on *and* pull one's leg <nf>; **laugh at,** laugh in one's face, grin at, smile at, snicker *or* snigger at; **laugh to scorn,** hold in derision, laugh out of court, hoot down; point at, point the finger of scorn; pillory

9 **scoff, jeer,** gibe, barrack <Brit>, **mock, revile, rail at, rally,** chaff, **twit, taunt,** jape, flout, scout, have a fling at, cast in one's teeth; cut at; jab, jab at, dig at, take a dig at; pooh, **pooh-pooh;** sneer, **sneer at,** fleer, curl one's lip

10 **boo, hiss, hoot,** catcall, give the raspberry *or* Bronx cheer <nf>, give the bird <nf>, whistle at

11 **burlesque, lampoon, satirize, parody, caricature,** travesty, hit *or* take off on

ADJS 12 **ridiculing, derisive,** derisory; **mocking,** railing, rallying, chaffing; panning *and* razzing *and* roasting *and* ragging <nf>, **scoffing,** jeering, sneering, snickering, sniggering, smirky, smirking, grinning, leering, fleering, snorting, flippant, smart, smart-alecky *and* smart-ass *and* wise-ass <nf>; joshing *and* jiving <nf>, fooling, japing, twitting, taunting, booing, hooting, catcalling, hissing, bantering, kidding, teasing, quizzical

13 **satiric, satirical; sarcastic, ironic, ironical, sardonic, cynical,** Rabelaisian, dry; caustic

14 **burlesque, farcical, broad,** slapstick; parodic, caricatural, macaronic, doggerel

ADVS 15 **derisively, mockingly, scoffingly,** jeeringly, sneeringly, "with scoffs and scorns and contumelious taunts"—Shakespeare

509 APPROVAL

NOUNS 1 **approval, approbation;** "Our polite recognition of another's resemblance to ourselves"—Ambrose Bierce; **sanction,** acceptance, countenance, **favor; admiration, esteem, respect** 155; endorsement, support, backing, vote, favorable vote, yea vote, yea, voice, adherence, blessing, seal of approval, nod *or* nod of approval, wink, stamp of approval, **OK** 332.4, rubber stamp, green light, go-ahead, thumbs up

2 **applause,** plaudit, éclat, **acclaim, acclamation; popularity;** clap, handclap, **clapping,** handclapping, clapping of hands; **cheer** 116.2; burst of applause, peal *or* thunder of applause; **round of applause, hand, big hand; ovation,** standing ovation; encore

3 **commendation,** good word, acknowledgment, recognition, appreciation; boost *and* buildup <nf>; **puff,** promotion; citation, accolade, kudos; good review; **blurb** *and* **plug** *and* promo *and* hype <nf>; honorable mention

4 **recommendation,** recommend <Brit nf>, letter of recommendation; **advocacy,** advocating, advocation, patronage; **reference, credential,** letter of reference, voucher, **testimonial;** character reference, character, certificate of character, good character; letter of introduction

5 **praise,** bepraisement; **laudation,** laud; **glorification,** glory, exaltation, extolment, magnification, **honor; eulogy,** éloge *and* hommage <Fr>, eulogium; **encomium,** accolade, kudos, high marks, panegyric; paean; **tribute,** homage, meed of praise; congratulation 149.1; flattery 511; overpraise,

excessive praise, idolizing, idolatry, deification, apotheosis, adulation, lionizing, hero worship

6 compliment, polite commendation, complimentary *or* flattering remark, flattery, pat on the back, stroke <nf>; **bouquet** and posy <nf>, trade-last <old nf>

7 praiseworthiness, laudability, laudableness, commendableness, estimableness, meritoriousness, exemplariness, admirability

8 commender, eulogist, eulogizer; **praiser,** lauder, laudator, extoller, encomiast, panegyrist, **booster** <nf>, puffer, promoter, champion; plugger *and* tout *and* touter <nf>; **applauder,** *claqueur* <Fr>; claque; rooter *and* fan *and* buff <nf>, adherent; admirer; appreciator; **flatterer** 138.3, 511.4, fan club

VERBS **9 approve, approve of,** think well of, take kindly to; **sanction, accept; admire, esteem, respect** 155.4; endorse, bless, sign off on <nf>, OK 332.12; **countenance,** keep in countenance; hold with, uphold; **favor,** be in favor of, view with favor, take kindly to

10 applaud, acclaim, hail; clap, clap one's hands, give a hand *or* big hand, have *or* hear a hand *or* big hand for, hear it for <nf>; **cheer** 116.6; root for <nf>, cheer on; encore; cheer *or* applaud to the very echo; huzzah; raise the roof <nf>

11 commend, speak well *or* **highly of,** speak in high terms of, speak warmly of, have *or* say a good word for; boost *and* give a boost to <nf>, puff, promote, cry up; plug *and* tout *and* hype; pour *or* spread *or* lay it on thick <nf>; **recommend, advocate,** put in a word *or* good word for, support, back, lend one's name *or* support *or* backing to, make a pitch for <nf>; condone, bless

12 praise, bepraise, talk one up <nf>; **laud,** belaud; **eulogize,** panegyrize, pay tribute, salute, hand it to one <nf>; **extol, glorify,** magnify, exalt, bless; cry up, blow up, puff, puff up; boast of, brag about <nf>, make much of; celebrate, emblazon, sound *or* resound the praises of, ring one's praises, sing the praises of, trumpet, hype <nf>; praise to the skies, *porter aux nues* <Fr>; flatter 511.5; overpraise, praise to excess, idolize, deify, apotheosize, adulate, lionize, hero-worship; put on a pedestal

13 espouse, join *or* associate oneself with, take up, take for one's own; **campaign for, crusade for,** put on a drive for, take up the cudgels for, push for <nf>; carry the banner of, march under the banner of; beat the drum for, thump the tub for; lavish oneself on, fight the good fight for; devote *or* dedicate oneself to, spend *or* give *or* sacrifice oneself for

14 compliment, pay a compliment, make one a compliment, give a bouquet *or* posy <nf>, say something nice about; hand it to *and* have to hand it to <nf>, pat on the back, take off one's hat to, doff one's cap to, congratulate 149.2

15 meet with approval, find favor with, **pass muster,** recommend itself, do credit to; redound to the honor of; ring with the praises of

ADJS **16 approbatory, approbative, commendatory, complimentary, laudatory,** acclamatory, felicitous, eulogistic, panegyric, panegyrical, encomiastic, **appreciative, appreciatory; admiring, regardful, respectful** 155.8; flattering 511.8

17 approving, favorable, favoring, in favor of, **pro,** well-disposed, well-inclined, supporting, backing, **advocating;** promoting, promotional; touting *and* puffing *and* hyping <nf>; recommending

18 uncritical, uncriticizing, **uncensorious,** unreproachful; overpraising, overappreciative, unmeasured *or* excessive in one's praise, idolatrous, adulatory, lionizing, hero-worshiping, fulsome; knee-jerk <nf>

19 approved, favored, backed, advocated, supported; favorite; **accepted,** received, admitted; **recommended,** bearing the seal of approval, highly touted <nf>, **admired** 155.11, **applauded,** well-thought-of, in good odor, **acclaimed,** cried up; **popular;** given a blessing

20 praiseworthy, worthy, **commendable,** estimable, **laudable,** admirable, meritorious, creditable; exemplary, model, unexceptionable; deserving, well-deserving; beyond all praise, *sans peur et sans reproche* <Fr>; **good** 999.12,13

PREPS **21 in favor of, for, pro,** all for

INTERJS **22 bravo!,** bravissimo!, **well done!,** ¡ole! <Sp>, *bene!* <Ital>, hear, hear!, aha!; hurrah!; **good!,** fine!, excellent!, whizzo! <Brit>, great!, beautiful!, swell!, good for you!, good enough!, not bad!, now you're talking!; way to go, attaboy!, attababy!, attagirl!, attagal!, good boy!, good girl!; that's the idea!, that's the ticket!; encore!, bis!, take a bow!, three cheers!, one cheer more!, **congratulations!** 149.4

23 hail!, all hail!, *ave!* <L>, *vive!* <Fr>, *viva! or evviva!* <Ital>, live live!, long life to!, glory be to!, honor be to!

510 DISAPPROVAL

NOUNS **1 disapproval, disapprobation,** disfavor, disesteem, disrespect 156; dim view, poor *or* low opinion, low estimation, adverse judgment; **displeasure,** distaste, **dissatisfaction,** discontent, discontentment, discontentedness, disgruntlement, indignation, **unhappiness;** disillusion, disillusionment, disenchantment, disappointment;

disagreement, **opposition** 451, opposure; rejection, thumbs-down, exclusion, ostracism, blackballing, blackball, ban; **complaint, protest,** objection, **dissent** 333

2 **deprecation,** discommendation, dispraise, denigration, disvaluation; **ridicule** 508; depreciation, disparagement 512; **contempt** 157

3 **censure, reprehension,** stricture, reprobation, **blame, denunciation,** denouncement, decrying, decrial, bashing *and* trashing <nf>, impeachment, arraignment, indictment, **condemnation,** damnation, fulmination, anathema; castigation, flaying, skinning alive <nf>, fustigation, excoriation; pillorying

4 **criticism,** adverse criticism, harsh *or* hostile criticism, flak <nf>, bad notices, bad press, panning, brickbat, animadversion, imputation, reflection, **aspersion,** stricture, obloquy; **knock** *and* **swipe** *and* **slam** *and* **rap** *and* hit <nf>, roasting <nf>, home thrust; minor *or* petty criticism, niggle, cavil, quibble, exception, nit <nf>; **censoriousness,** reproachfulness, priggishness; **faultfinding,** taking exception, carping, caviling, pettifogging, quibbling, captiousness, niggling, nitpicking, pestering, nagging; hypercriticism, hypercriticalness, overcriticalness, hairsplitting, trichoschistism

5 **reproof,** reproval, reprobation, a flea in one's ear; **rebuke, reprimand, reproach,** reprehension, **scolding, chiding,** rating, **upbraiding,** objurgation; **admonishment, admonition; correction,** castigation, chastisement, spanking, rap on the knuckles; lecture, lesson, sermon; **discommendation,** low rating, adverse report, wolf ticket

6 <nf terms> **piece** *or* bit of one's mind, **talking-to,** speaking-to, roasting, raking-down, **raking-over,** raking over the coals, dressing, dressing-down, setdown; **bawling-out,** cussing-out, **calling-down,** jacking-up, going-over, chewing-out, chewing, reaming-out, reaming, ass-chewing, ass-reaming, what-for, ticking-off

7 **berating,** rating, tongue-lashing; **revilement, vilification,** blackening, **execration, abuse, vituperation,** invective, contumely, hard *or* cutting *or* bitter words; **tirade, diatribe,** jeremiad, screed, philippic; **attack, assault,** onslaught, assailing; **abusiveness; acrimony**

8 **reproving look,** dirty *or* nasty look <nf>, black look, frown, scowl, glare; hiss, boo; Bronx cheer *or* raspberry <nf>

9 **faultfinder,** disapprover, *frondeur* <Fr>, momus, basher *and* tracher *and* boo-bird <nf>; **critic** 946.7, criticizer, **nitpicker** <nf>, smellfungus, belittler, censor, censurer, castigator, carper, caviler,

quibbler, pettifogger; **scold,** common scold; kvetch, **complainer** 108.3

VERBS **10 disapprove, disapprove of,** not approve, raise an objection, go *or* side against, go contra; **disfavor, view with disfavor, raise one's eyebrows, frown at** *or* **on,** look black upon, look askance at, make a wry face at, grimace at, **turn up one's nose at,** shrug one's shoulders at; **take a dim view of** <nf>, not think much of, think ill of, think little of, have no respect for, have a low opinion of, not take kindly to, not hold with, hold no brief for *and* not sign off on <nf>; not hear of, not go for *and* not get all choked up over *and* be turned off by <nf>; not want *or* have any part of, wash one's hands of, dissociate oneself from; **object to,** take exception to; **oppose** 451.3, set oneself against, set one's face *or* heart against; **reject,** categorically reject, disallow, not hear of; **turn thumbs down on** *and* thumb down <nf>, vote down, veto, frown down, exclude, ostracize, blackball, ban; say no to, shake one's head at; **dissent from, protest, object** 333.4,5; turn over in one's grave

11 **discountenance,** not countenance, **not tolerate,** not brook, not condone, not suffer, not abide, not endure, not bear with, not put up with, **not stand for** <nf>

12 **deprecate,** discommend, dispraise, disvalue, not be able to say much for, denigrate, **fault,** faultfind, find fault with, put down <nf>, pick at *or* on, pick holes in, pick to pieces; **ridicule** 508.8; **depreciate, disparage** 512.8; **hold in contempt,** disdain, **despise** 157.3

13 **censure,** reprehend; **blame,** lay *or* cast blame upon; **bash** *and* trash *and* rubbish <nf>; **reproach,** impugn; **condemn,** damn, take out after; damn with faint praise; fulminate against, anathematize, anathemize, put on the Index; **denounce,** denunciate, **accuse** 599.7,9, **decry,** cry down, impeach, arraign, indict, call to account, exclaim *or* declaim *or* inveigh against, peg away at, cry out against, cry out on *or* upon, cry shame upon, raise one's voice against, raise a hue and cry against, shake up <old>; reprobate, hold up to reprobation; animadvert on *or* upon, reflect upon, cast reflection upon, cast a reproach *or* slur upon, complain against; throw a stone at, cast *or* throw the first stone

14 **criticize; pan** *and* **knock** *and* **slam** *and* hit *and* rap *and* take a rap *or* swipe at <nf>, snipe at, strike out at, tie into *and* tee off on *and* rip into *and* open up on *and* plow into <nf>; belittle

15 **find fault,** take exception, fault-find, pick holes, cut up, pick *or* pull *or* tear apart, **pick** *or* **pull** *or* **tear to pieces; tear down,** carp, cavil, quibble, **nitpick,** pick nits, pettifog, catch at straws

16 nag, niggle, **carp at, fuss at, fret at,** yap or **pick at** <nf>, peck at, nibble at, **pester, henpeck, pick on** <nf>, bug and hassle <nf>

17 reprove, rebuke, reprimand, reprehend, put a flea in one's ear, **scold, chide,** rate, **admonish, upbraid,** objurgate, have words with, take a hard line with; **lecture,** read a lesson or lecture to; **correct,** rap on the knuckles, **chastise,** spank, turn over one's knees; **take to task,** call to account, bring to book, call on the carpet, read the riot act, give one a tongue-lashing, tonguelash; take down, set down, set straight, straighten out

18 <nf terms> **call down** or **dress down, speak** or **talk to, tell off,** tell a thing or two, pin one's ears back, **give a piece** or **bit of one's mind, rake** or **haul over the coals,** rake up one side and down the other, give it to, let one have it, let one have it with both barrels, trim, come down on or down hard on, jump on or all over or down one's throat; give one a hard time or what for; **bawl out,** give a bawling out, chew, **chew out,** chew ass, ream, ream out, ream ass, cuss out, jack up, sit on or upon, lambaste, give a going-over, tell where to get off; give the deuce or devil, give hell, give hail Columbia

19 berate, rate, betongue, jaw <nf>, clapper-claw <nf>, **tongue-lash, rail at,** rag, thunder or fulminate against, rave against, yell at, bark or yelp at; **revile, vilify,** blacken, **execrate, abuse,** vituperate, load with reproaches

20 <criticize or reprove severely> **attack, assail; castigate, flay,** skin alive <nf>, lash, slash, **excoriate,** fustigate, scarify, scathe, **roast** <nf>, scorch, blister, trounce; lay into <nf>

ADJS **21 disapproving, disapprobatory,** unapproving, turned-off, **displeased, dissatisfied,** less than pleased, discontented, disgruntled, indignant, **unhappy;** disillusioned, disenchanted, disappointed; **unfavorable,** low, poor, **opposed** 451.8, **opposing, con,** against, agin <nf>, dead set against, death on, down on, **dissenting** 333.6; **uncomplimentary;** unappreciative

22 condemnatory, censorious, censorial, damnatory, **denunciatory, reproachful,** blameful, reprobative, objurgatory, po-faced <Brit>, priggish, judgmental; deprecative, deprecatory; **derisive, ridiculing, scoffing** 508.12; **depreciative, disparaging** 512.13; **contemptuous** 157.8; invective, inveighing; reviling, vilifying, blackening, execrating, execrative, execratory, abusive, vituperative

23 critical, faultfinding, carping, picky and nitpicky <nf>, caviling, quibbling, pettifogging, captious, cynical; nagging, niggling; hypercritical, ultracritical, overcritical, hairsplitting, trichoschistic; abusive

24 unpraiseworthy, illaudable; uncommendable, discommendable, not good enough; objectionable, exceptionable, unacceptable, not to be thought of, beyond the pale

25 blameworthy, blamable, to blame, at fault, much at fault; **reprehensible,** censurable, reproachable, reprovable, open to criticism or reproach; **culpable,** chargeable, impeachable, accusable, indictable, arraignable, imputable

ADVS **26 disapprovingly, askance,** askant, **unfavorably;** censoriously, critically, reproachfully, rebukingly; captiously

INTERJS **27 God forbid!,** Heaven forbid!, Heaven forfend!, forbid it Heaven!; by no means!, not for the world!, not on your life!, over my dead body!, not if I know it!, nothing doing!, no way! and no way José! <nf>, perish the thought!, I'll be hanged or damned if!, **shame!,** for shame!, tuttut!

511 FLATTERY

NOUNS **1 flattery, adulation; praise** 509.5; **blandishment,** palaver, **cajolery,** cajolement, wheedling, inveiglement; **blarney** and bunkum and **soft soap** and soap or butter salve <nf>, oil, grease, eyewash <nf>; strokes and stroking and ego massage <nf>, sweet talk, fair or sweet or honeyed words, soft or honeyed phrases, incense, pretty lies, sweet nothings; trade-last <old nf>, **compliment** 509.6; ass-kissing <nf>, ingratiation, **fawning, sycophancy** 138.2

2 unction, "that flattering unction"—Shakespeare; **unctuousness,** oiliness, sliminess; slobber, gush, smarm and smarminess <nf>; flattering tongue; insincerity 354.5

3 overpraise, overprizing, excessive praise, overcommendation, overlaudation, overestimation; idolatry 509.5

4 flatterer, flatteur <Fr>, adulator, courtier; **cajoler, wheedler; backslapper,** back-scratcher, yes-man, bootlicker; blarneyer and soft-soaper <nf>; asskisser <nf>, brown-noser, **sycophant** 138.3

VERBS **5 flatter,** adulate, conceit; **cajole, wheedle, blandish,** palaver; slaver or slobber over, beslobber, beslubber; oil the tongue, lay the flattering unction to one's soul, make fair weather; **praise, compliment** 509.14, praise to the skies; scratch one's back, kiss ass <nf>, fawn upon 138.9

6 <nf terms> **soft-soap,** butter, honey, **butter up,** soften up; stroke <nf>, massage the ego <nf>; **blarney,** jolly, pull one's leg; lay it on <nf>, pour or spread or lay it on thick or with a trowel <nf>, overdo it, soap, oil; string along, kid along; play up to, get around; suck up to

7 overpraise, overprize, overcommend, overlaud;

overesteem, overestimate, overdo it, protest too much; idolize 509.12, put on a pedestal; puff

ADJS **8 flattering, adulatory;** complimentary 509.16; **blandishing, cajoling, wheedling,** blarneying *and* soft-soaping <nf>; fair-spoken, fine-spoken, smooth-spoken, smooth-tongued, **mealymouthed,** honey-mouthed, honey-tongued, honeyed, oily-tongued; fulsome, slimy, slobbery, gushing, protesting too much, smarmy <nf>, insinuating, oily, buttery <nf>, soapy <nf>, soft-soaping <nf>, **unctuous,** smooth, bland; insincere, hypocritical, tongue-in-cheek; courtly, courtierly; **fawning, sycophantic, obsequious**

512 DISPARAGEMENT

NOUNS **1 disparagement, faultfinding, depreciation, detraction,** deprecation, derogation, bad-mouthing *and* running down *and* knocking *and* putting down <nf>, **belittling;** sour grapes; slighting, minimizing, faint praise, lukewarm support, discrediting, decrying, decrial; **disapproval** 510; **contempt** 157; indignity, disgrace, comedown <nf>

2 defamation, malicious defamation, defamation of character, smear campaign, injury of *or* to one's reputation; **vilification,** revilement, defilement, blackening, denigration; **smear,** character assassination, *ad hominem* <L> *or* personal attack, name-calling, smear word; **muckraking, mudslinging**

3 slander, scandal, libel, traducement; calumny, calumniation; backbiting, cattiness *and* bitchiness <nf>

4 aspersion, slur, **remark, reflection,** imputation, **insinuation,** suggestion, sly suggestion, innuendo, whispering campaign; disparaging *or* uncomplimentary remark; poison-pen letter, hatchet job

5 lampoon, send-up <nf>, take-off, pasquinade, ridicule, pasquin, pasquil, squib, lampoonery, **satire,** malicious parody, **burlesque** 508.6; caricature

6 disparager, depreciator, decrier, detractor, basher *and* trasher *and* boo-bird <nf>, belittler, debunker, deflater, slighter, derogator, **knocker** <nf>, hatchet man; **slanderer,** libeler, defamer, backbiter; calumniator, traducer; **muckraker, mudslinger,** social critic; **cynic,** railer, Thersites, "A man who knows the price of everything, and the value of nothing"—Oscar Wilde

7 lampooner, lampoonist, **satirist,** pasquinader; poison-pen writer

VERBS **8 disparage, depreciate, belittle,** slight, minimize, make little of, degrade, debase, **run** *or*

knock down <nf>, **put down** <nf>, sell short; **discredit,** bring into discredit, reflect discredit upon, disgrace; detract from, derogate from, cut down to size <nf>; **decry,** cry down; speak ill of; speak slightingly of, not speak well of; disapprove of 510.10; hold in contempt 157.3; submit to indignity *or* disgrace, bring down, bring low

9 defame, malign, bad-mouth *and* poor-mouth <nf>; **asperse, cast aspersions on,** cast reflections on, injure one's reputation, damage one's good name, give one a black eye <nf>; **slur,** cast a slur on, do a number *or* a job on <nf>, tear down

10 vilify, revile, defile, sully, soil, smear, smirch, besmirch, bespatter, tarnish, **blacken,** denigrate, blacken one's good name, give a black eye <nf>; **call names,** give a bad name, give a dog a bad name, stigmatize 661.9; **muckrake, throw mud at,** mudsling, heap dirt upon, drag through the mud *or* the gutter; engage in personalities

11 slander, libel; calumniate, traduce; stab in the back, backbite, speak ill of behind one's back

12 lampoon, satirize, pasquinade; parody, send up <nf>, take off; dip the pen in gall, **burlesque** 508.11

ADJS **13 disparaging, derogatory,** derogative, **depreciatory,** depreciative, deprecatory, slighting, **belittling,** minimizing, detractory, pejorative, back-biting, catty *and* bitchy <nf>, contumelious, contemptuous, derisive, derisory, ridiculing 508.12; **snide,** insinuating; censorious; **defamatory,** vilifying, **slanderous, scandalous, libelous;** calumnious, calumniatory; **abusive,** scurrilous, scurrile <old>

513 CURSE

NOUNS **1 curse, malediction,** malison, damnation, denunciation, commination, imprecation, execration; blasphemy; anathema, fulmination, thundering, excommunication; ban, proscription; hex, evil eye, *malocchio* <Ital>, jinx, whammy *or* double whammy <nf>; ill wishes

2 vilification, abuse, revilement, **vituperation, invective,** opprobrium, obloquy, contumely, calumny, scurrility, blackguardism; **disparagement** 512; slanging match <nf>

3 cursing, cussing <nf>, **swearing, profanity,** profane swearing, foul *or* profane *or* obscene *or* blue *or* bad *or* strong *or* unparliamentary *or* indelicate language, vulgar language, vile language, colorful language, unrepeatable expressions, dysphemism, billingsgate, ribaldry, evil speaking, **dirty language** *or* **talk** <nf>, **obscenity,** scatology, coprology, **filthy language, filth;** foul mouth, dirty mouth <nf>

4 oath, profane oath, curse; **cuss** *or* cuss word *and* dirty word *and* four-letter word *and* **swearword** <nf>, profanity, bad word, naughty word, no-no <nf>, foul invective, **expletive, epithet,** dirty name <nf>, dysphemism, obscenity, vulgarity

VERBS **5 curse,** accurse, **damn,** darn, **confound,** blast, anathematize, fulminate *or* thunder against, execrate, imprecate, proscribe; excommunicate; call down evil upon, call down curses on the head of; put a curse on; curse up hill *and* down dale; curse with bell, book, and candle; blaspheme; hex, give the evil eye, put a whammy on <nf>

6 curse, swear, cuss <nf>, curse and swear, execrate, rap out *or* rip out an oath, take the Lord's name in vain; swear like a trooper, cuss like a sailor, make the air blue, swear till one is blue in the face; **talk dirty** <nf>, scatologize, coprologize, dysphemize, use strong language; blaspheme, profane

7 vilify, abuse, revile, vituperate, blackguard, call names, epithet, epithetize; **swear at,** damn, cuss out <nf>

ADJS **8 cursing, maledictory,** imprecatory, **damnatory,** denunciatory, epithetic, epithetical; **abusive,** vituperative, contumelious; calumnious, calumniatory; execratory, comminatory, fulminatory, excommunicative, excommunicatory; **scurrilous,** scurrile <old>; blasphemous, **profane, foul, foulmouthed, vile,** thersitical, **dirty** <nf>, **obscene,** dysphemistic, scatologic, scatological, coprological, toilet, sewer, cloacal; ribald, Rabelaisian, raw, risqué

9 cursed, accursed, bloody <Brit nf>, **damned, damn, damnable,** goddamned, goddamn, **execrable**

10 <euphemisms> **darned,** danged, **confounded,** deuced, blessed, **blasted,** dashed, blamed, goshdarn, doggone *or* doggoned, goldarned, goldanged, dadburned; blankety-blank; ruddy <Brit>

INTERJS **11** damn!, damn it!, God damn it! *or* goddam it!, confound it!, hang it!, devil take!, a plague upon!, a pox upon!, *parbleu!* <Fr>, *verdammt!* <Ger>, go to hell!

12 <euphemistic oaths> darn!, dern!, dang!, dash!, drat!, blast!, doggone!, goldarn!, goldang!, golding!, gosh-darn!, cripes!, crikey! <Brit>, golly!, gosh!, heck!, bugger it! <Brit>, goodness!, goodness gracious!, jeepers!, gee whillikers!, gee whiz!

514 THREAT

NOUNS **1 threat, menace,** threateningness, threatfulness, promise of harm, knife poised at one's throat, arrow aimed at one's heart, sword of Damocles; imminent threat, powder keg, timebomb, imminence 840; **foreboding; warning** 399; saber-rattling, muscle-flexing, woofing <nf>, bulldozing, scare tactics, **intimidation** 127.6, arm-twisting <nf>; denunciation, commination; veiled *or* implied threat, idle *or* hollow *or* empty threat

VERBS **2 threaten, menace,** bludgeon, bulldoze, put the heat *or* screws *or* squeeze on <nf>, lean on <nf>; hold a pistol to one's head, terrorize, **intimidate,** twist one's arm *and* arm-twist <nf>; utter threats against, shake *or* double *or* clench one's fist at; hold over one's head; denounce, comminate; **lower,** spell *or* mean trouble, look threatening, loom, loom up; **be imminent** 840.2; **forebode** 133.11; **warn** 399.5

ADJS **3 threatening, menacing,** threatful, minatory, minacious; **lowering; imminent** 840.3; **ominous,** foreboding 133.17; denunciatory, comminatory, abusive; fear-inspiring, **intimidating,** bludgeoning, muscle-flexing, saber-rattling, bulldozing, browbeating, bullying, hectoring, blustering, terrorizing, terroristic

ADVS **4** under duress *or* threat, under the gun, at gunpoint *or* knifepoint

515 FASTING

NOUNS **1 fasting,** abstinence from food; abstemiousness, starvation; punishment of Tantalus; religious fasting; hunger strike; anorexia nervosa

2 fast, lack of food; spare *or* meager diet, Lenten diet, Lenten fare, "Lenten entertainment"—Shakespeare; prison fare; short commons *or* rations, military rations, K rations; starvation diet, water diet, crash diet, bread and water, bare subsistence, bare cupboard; xerophagy, xerophagia; Barmecide *or* Barmecidal feast

3 fast day, *jour maigre* <Fr>; **Lent,** Good Friday, Quadragesima; Yom Kippur, Tishah B'Av *or* Ninth of Av; Ramadan; meatless day, fish day, day of abstinence

VERBS **4 fast,** not eat, go hungry, eat nothing, eat like a bird, dine with Duke Humphrey; eat sparingly, eat less, count calories

ADJS **5 fasting,** uneating, unfed; abstinent, abstemious; keeping Lent, **Lenten,** quadragesimal; underfed

516 SOBRIETY

NOUNS **1 sobriety, soberness;** unintoxicatedness, uninebriatedness, undrunkenness; abstinence, abstemiousness; temperance 668; clear head; prohibition, temperance society; nondrinker, teetotaler

VERBS **2 sober up,** sober off; sleep it off; bring one
down, take off a high <nf>; dry out, clear one's
head, detoxify; give up alcohol, go on the wagon

ADJS **3 sober,** in one's sober senses, in one's right
mind, in possession of one's faculties; clearheaded;
unintoxicated, uninebriated, uninebriate,
uninebrious, not drunk, undrunk, undrunken,
untipsy, unfuddled; stone-cold sober <nf>, **sober
as a judge;** able to walk the chalk, able to walk the
chalk mark *or* line <nf>; nondrinking, off the
bottle, dry, straight, on the wagon <nf>, temperate
668.9, abstinent

4 unintoxicating, nonintoxicating, uninebriating;
nonalcoholic, soft

517 SIGNS, INDICATORS

NOUNS **1 sign,** telltale sign, sure sign, tip-off <nf>,
index, indicant, **indicator,** signal <old>, measure;
tip of the iceberg; **symptom;** note, keynote, **mark,
earmark,** hallmark, **badge,** device, banner, stamp,
signature, sigil, seal, trait, **characteristic,** character,
peculiarity, idiosyncrasy, **property,** differentia;
image, picture, **representation,** representative;
insignia 647; notation; reference sign

2 symbol, emblem, icon, token, cipher <old>, type;
allegory; symbolism, symbology, iconology,
iconography, charactery; conventional symbol;
symbolic system; **symbolization;** semiotics,
semiology; **ideogram,** logogram, pictogram; **logo**
<nf>, logotype; **totem,** totem pole; love knot;
symbol list

3 indication, signification, identification,
differentiation, denotation, **designation,**
denomination; characterization, highlighting;
specification, naming, pointing, pointing out *or* to,
fingering <nf>, picking out, selection;
symptomaticness, indicativeness; **meaning** 518;
hint, suggestion 551.4; **expression, manifestation**
348; show, showing, disclosure 351

4 pointer, index, **lead; direction, guide;** fist, index
finger *or* mark, finger, arm; **arrow;** hand, hour
hand, minute hand, gauge, **needle,** compass
needle, lubber line; **signpost,** guidepost, finger
post, direction post; milepost; blaze; guideboard,
signboard 352.7

5 mark, marking; watermark; **scratch,** scratching,
engraving, graving, **score,** scotch, cut, hack, gash,
blaze; bar code; nick, notch 289; **scar,** cicatrix,
scarification, cicatrization; **brand, earmark;
stigma; stain, discoloration** 1004.2; blemish,
macula, **spot,** blotch, splotch, flick, patch, splash;
mottle, dapple; **dot,** point; polka dot; tittle, jot;
speck, speckle, fleck; tick, **freckle,** lentigo, mole;
birthmark, strawberry mark, port-wine stain,

vascular nevus, nevus, hemangioma; beauty mark
or spot; caste mark; **check,** checkmark; prick,
puncture; tattoo, tattoo mark

6 line, score, **stroke,** slash, virgule, diagonal, **dash,
stripe, strip, streak, striation,** striping, streaking,
bar, band; squiggle; hairline; dotted line; lineation,
delineation; sublineation, **underline,** underlining,
underscore, underscoring; hatching, cross-
hatching, hachure

7 print, imprint, impress, impression; dint, dent,
indent, indentation, indention, concavity;
sitzmark; **stamp,** seal, sigil, signet; colophon;
fingerprint, finger mark, thumbprint, thumbmark,
dactylogram, dactylograph; **footprint,** footmark,
footstep, step, vestige; hoofprint, hoofmark; pad,
paw print, pawmark, pug, pugmark; claw mark;
fossil print *or* footprint, ichnite, ichnolite; **bump,**
boss, stud, pimple, lump, excrescence, convexity,
embossment; ecological footprint

8 track, trail, path, course, *piste* <Fr>, **line, wake;**
vapor trail, contrail, condensation trail; **spoor,**
signs, traces, **scent**

9 clue, cue, key, tip-off <nf>, telltale, smoking gun
<nf>, straw in the wind; **trace, vestige, spoor,**
scent, whiff; **lead** *and* hot lead <nf>; catchword,
cue word, key word; **evidence** 957; **hint,
intimation,** suggestion 551.4

10 marker, mark; bookmark; **landmark,** seamark;
bench mark; **milestone,** milepost; cairn, menhir,
catstone; **lighthouse,** lightship, tower, Texas tower;
platform, watchtower, pharos; buoy, aid to
navigation, bell, gong, lighted buoy, nun, can, spar
buoy, wreck buoy, junction buoy, special-purpose
buoy; seamark, watermark, tidemark; **monument**
549.12

11 identification, identification mark; **badge,**
identification badge, identification tag, dog tag
<military>, passport, personal identification
number *or* PIN number *or* PIN, **identity card** *or* **ID
card** *or* **ID;** Social Security number, driver's license
number; card, business card, calling card, visiting
card, *carte de visite* <Fr>, press card; letter of
introduction; signature, initials, monogram,
calligram; credentials; serial number; countersign,
countermark; theme, theme tune *or* song; **criminal
identification,** forensic tool, DNA print, genetic
fingerprint, voiceprint; fingerprint 517.7; dental
record

12 password, watchword, countersign; token; open
sesame; secret grip; shibboleth

13 label, tag; ticket, docket <Brit>, tally; **stamp,
sticker;** seal, sigil, signet; cachet; stub, counterfoil;
token, check; **brand, brand name, trade name,**
trademark name; **trademark,** registered
trademark; government mark, government stamp,

broad arrow <Brit>; **hallmark,** countermark; price tag; plate, bookplate, book stamp, colophon, *ex libris* <L>, logotype *or* logo; International Standard Book Number *or* ISBN; masthead, imprint, title page; letterhead, billhead; running head *or* title

14 **gesture, gesticulation; motion,** movement; carriage, bearing, posture, poise, pose, stance, way of holding oneself; body language, kinesics; beck, beckon; shrug; charade, dumb show, **pantomime;** sign language, signing, gesture language; dactylology, deaf-and-dumb alphabet; hand signal; chironomy

15 **signal, sign; high sign** *and* the wink *and* the nod <nf>; wink, flick of the eyelash, glance, leer; look in one's eyes, tone of one's voice; nod; nudge, elbow in the ribs, poke, kick, touch; **alarm** 400; **beacon,** signal beacon, marker beacon, radio beacon, lighthouse beacon; signal light, signal lamp *or* lantern *or* light; blinker; signal fire, beacon fire, watch fire, balefire, smoke signal; **flare,** parachute flare; rocket, signal rocket, Roman candle; signal gun, signal shot; signal siren *or* whistle, signal bell, bell, signal gong, **police whistle,** watchman's rattle; fog signal *or* alarm, fog bell, **foghorn,** diaphone, fog whistle; **traffic signal,** traffic light, red *or* stop light, amber *or* caution light, green *or* go light; heliograph; signal flag; **semaphore,** semaphore telegraph, semaphore flag; **wigwag,** wigwag flag; international alphabet flag, international numeral pennant; red flag; white flag; yellow flag, quarantine flag; blue peter; pilot flag *or* jack; signal post, signal mast, signal tower; telecommunications

16 call, summons; whistle; moose call, bird call, duck call, hog call, goose call, crow call, hawk call, dog whistle; **bugle call,** trumpet call, fanfare, flourish; **reveille, taps,** last post <Brit>; alarm, alarum; **battle cry,** war cry, war whoop, rebel yell, rallying cry; call to arms; Angelus, Angelus bell

VERBS 17 **signify, betoken,** stand for, identify, differentiate, note <old>, speak of, talk, **indicate,** be indicative of, be an indication of, be significant of, connote, denominate, argue, bespeak, be symptomatic *or* diagnostic of, symptomize, **characterize, mark,** highlight, be the mark *or* sign of, give token, **denote, mean** 518.8; testify, give evidence, bear witness to; **show, express, display, manifest** 348.5, **hint,** suggest 551.10, reveal, **disclose** 351.4; entail, involve 772.4

18 **designate, specify;** denominate, name, denote; stigmatize; **symbolize, stand for,** typify, be taken as, symbol, emblematize, figure <old>; **point to,** refer to, advert to, allude to, make an allusion to;

pick out, select; **point out,** point at, put *or* lay one's finger on, finger <nf>

19 **mark,** make a mark, put a mark on; pencil, chalk; mark out, demarcate, delimit, define; **mark off, check, check off,** tick, tick off, chalk up; punctuate, point; **dot, spot,** blotch, splotch, dash, **speck, speckle,** fleck, freckle; mottle, dapple; blemish; **brand,** stigmatize; **stain, discolor** 1004.6; stamp, seal, punch, impress, imprint, **print, engrave; score, scratch,** gash, scotch, scar, scarify, cicatrize; nick, notch 289.4; **blaze,** blaze a trail; **line, seam,** trace, **stripe, streak, striate;** hatch; **underline, underscore;** prick, puncture, tattoo, riddle, pepper

20 **label, tag,** tab, ticket; stamp, seal; **brand, earmark;** hallmark; bar-code

21 **gesture, gesticulate; motion,** motion to; use body language; beckon, wiggle the finger at; wave the arms, wig-wag, saw the air; shrug, shrug the shoulders; pantomime, mime, mimic, imitate, ape, take off

22 **signal,** signalize, sign, give a signal, make a sign; speak; flash; **give the high sign** *or* **the nod** *or* a high five <nf>; nod; nudge, poke, kick, dig one in the ribs, touch; wink, glance, raise one's eyebrows, leer; hold up the hand; wave, wave the hand, wave a flag, **flag,** flag down; **unfurl a flag,** hoist a banner, break out a flag; **show one's colors,** exchange colors; **salute,** dip; dip a flag, hail, hail *and* speak; half-mast; give *or* sound an alarm, raise a cry; beat the drum, sound the trumpet

ADJS 23 **indicative,** indicatory, signifying; connotative, indicating, signifying, signalizing; **significant,** significative, meaningful; symptomatic, symptomatologic, symptomatological, diagnostic, pathognomonic, pathognomonical; evidential, **designative,** denotative, denominative, naming; **suggestive,** implicative; **expressive,** demonstrative, exhibitive, telltale; representative; identifying, identificational; individual, peculiar, idiosyncratic; **emblematic, symbolic,** emblematical, symbolical; symbolistic, symbological, typical; figurative, figural, metaphorical; ideographic; semiotic, semantic; nominal, diagrammatic

24 **marked, designated,** flagged; signed, signposted; monogrammed, individualized, personal; own-brand, own-label; punctuated

25 **gestural,** gesticulative, gesticulatory; kinesic; pantomimic, **in pantomime,** in dumb show

518 MEANING

NOUNS 1 **meaning, significance, signification,** *significatum* <L>, *signifié* <Fr>, point, **sense,** idea, **purport, import,** where one is coming from <nf>;

reference, referent; intension, extension;
denotation; dictionary meaning, lexical meaning;
emotive *or* affective meaning, undertone, overtone,
coloring; relevance, bearing, relation, pertinence
or pertinency; substance, gist, pith, core, spirit,
essence, gravamen, last word, name of the game
and meat *and* potatoes *and* bottom line <nf>;
drift, tenor; sum, sum and substance; literal
meaning, true *or* real meaning, unadorned
meaning; secondary meaning, connotation 519.2;
more than meets the eye, what is read between the
lines; effect, force, impact, consequence, practical
consequence, response; shifted *or* displaced
meaning, implied meaning, implication 519.2;
Aesopian *or* Aesopic meaning, Aesopian *or* Aesopic
language; totality of associations *or* references *or*
relations, value; syntactic *or* structural meaning,
grammatical meaning; symbolic meaning;
metaphorical *or* transferred meaning; semantic
content, deep structure; semantic field, semantic
domain, semantic cluster; range *or* span of
meaning, scope; topic, subject matter

2 intent, intention, purpose, point, aim, object, end,
design, plan; value, worth, use

3 explanation, definition, construction, sense-
distinction, interpretation 341

4 acceptation, acception, accepted *or* received
meaning; usage, acceptance

5 meaningfulness, suggestiveness, expressiveness,
pregnancy; significance, significancy,
significantness; intelligibility, interpretability,
readability; pithiness, meatiness, sententiousness;
importance, import

6 <units> sign, symbol, significant, type, token,
icon, verbal icon, lexeme, sememe, morpheme,
glosseme, word, term, phrase, utterance, lexical
form *or* item, linguistic form, semantic *or* semiotic
or semasiological unit; text; synonym, antonym;
derivation, etymology

7 semantics, semiotic, semiotics, significs,
semasiology, semiology, linguistics; lexicology

VERBS 8 mean, signify, denote, connote, import,
spell, have the sense of, be construed as, have the
force of; be talking *and* be talking about <nf>;
stand for, symbolize; imply, suggest, argue,
breathe, bespeak, betoken, indicate; refer to; mean
something, mean a lot, have impact, come home,
hit one where one lives *and* hit one close to home
<nf>; get across, convey

9 intend, have in mind, seek to communicate

ADJS 10 meaningful, meaning, significant,
significative; literal, explicit; denotative,
connotative, denotational, connotational,
intensional, extensional, associational; referential;
symbolic, metaphorical, figurative, allegorical,

idiomatic; transferred, extended; intelligible,
interpretable, definable, readable; suggestive,
indicative, expressive; pregnant, full of meaning,
loaded *or* laden *or* fraught *or* freighted *or* heavy
with significance; pithy, meaty, sententious,
substantial, full of substance; pointed, full of
point

11 meant, implied 519.7, intended

12 semantic, semantological, semiotic,
semasiological, semiological; linguistic;
lexological; symbolic, signific, iconic, lexemic,
sememic, glossematic, morphemic, verbal,
phrasal, lexical, philological; structural

ADVS 13 meaningfully, meaningly, significantly;
suggestively, indicatively; expressively

519 LATENT MEANINGFULNESS

NOUNS 1 latent meaningfulness, latency, latentness,
delitescence, latent content; potentiality, virtuality,
possibility; dormancy 173.4

2 implication, connotation, import, latent *or*
underlying *or* implied meaning, ironic suggestion
or implication, more than meets the eye, what is
read between the lines; meaning 518; suggestion,
allusion; coloration, tinge, undertone, overtone,
undercurrent, more than meets the eye *or* ear,
something between the lines, intimation, touch,
nuance, innuendo; code word, weasel word; hint
551.4; inference, supposition, presupposition,
assumption, presumption; secondary *or*
transferred *or* metaphorical sense; undermeaning,
undermention, subsidiary sense, subsense, subtext;
Aesopian *or* Aesopic meaning, cryptic *or* hidden *or*
esoteric *or* arcane meaning, occult meaning;
symbolism, allegory

VERBS 3 be latent, underlie, lie under the surface,
lurk, lie hid *or* low, lie beneath, hibernate, lie
dormant, smolder; be read between the lines;
make no sign, escape notice

4 imply, implicate, involve, import, connote, entail
772.4; mean 518.8; suggest, lead one to believe,
bring to mind; hint, insinuate, infer, intimate
551.10; allude to, point to from afar, point
indirectly to; write between the lines; allegorize;
suppose, presuppose, assume, presume, take for
granted; mean to say *or* imply *or* suggest

ADJS 5 latent, lurking, lying low, delitescent, hidden
346.11, obscured, obfuscated, veiled, muffled,
covert, occult, mystic <old>, cryptic; esoteric;
underlying, under the surface, submerged;
between the lines; hibernating, sleeping, dormant
173.14; potential, unmanifested, virtual, possible

6 suggestive, allusive, allusory, indicative,
inferential; insinuating, insinuative, insinuatory;

ironic; **implicative,** implicatory, implicational; referential

7 **implied,** implicated, involved; **meant,** indicated; **suggested, intimated, insinuated, hinted; inferred, supposed,** assumed, presumed, presupposed; hidden, arcane, esoteric, **cryptic,** Aesopian *or* Aesopic

8 **tacit, implicit, implied, understood,** taken for granted

9 **unexpressed,** unpronounced, **unsaid, unspoken, unuttered,** undeclared, unbreathed, unvoiced, wordless, silent; **unmentioned,** untalked-of, **untold,** unsung, unproclaimed, unpublished; unwritten, unrecorded

10 **symbolic,** symbolical, allegoric, allegorical, figural, figurative, tropological, **metaphoric,** metaphorical, anagogic, anagogical

ADVS 11 **latently,** underlyingly; **potentially,** virtually

12 **suggestively, allusively, inferentially,** insinuatingly; impliedly; by suggestion, by allusion, etc

13 **tacitly, implicitly,** unspokenly, wordlessly, silently

520 MEANINGLESSNESS

NOUNS 1 **meaninglessness,** unmeaningness, **senselessness,** nonsensicality; **insignificance,** unsignificancy, irrelevance; **noise,** mere noise, static, empty sound, talking to hear oneself talk, phatic communion; inanity, emptiness, nullity; "a tale told by an idiot, full of sound and fury, signifying nothing"—Shakespeare; purposelessness, aimlessness, futility; dead letter; no bearing

2 **nonsense, stuff and nonsense,** pack of nonsense, **folderol, balderdash,** *niaiserie* <Fr>, flummery, trumpery, **rubbish,** trash, *narrishkeit* <Yiddish>, vaporing, fudge; **humbug,** gammon, hocus-pocus; rant, claptrap, fustian, rodomontade, bombast, absurdity 923.3; stultiloquence, **twaddle,** twiddle-twaddle, fiddle-faddle, fiddledeedee, fiddlesticks, **blather, babble,** babblement, bibble-babble, **gabble,** gibble-gabble, **blabber, gibber, jabber,** prate, prattle, palaver, rigmarole *or* rigamarole, galimatias, skimble-skamble, drivel, drool; **gibberish,** jargon, mumbo jumbo, **double-talk,** evasion, equivoke, ambiguity, amphigory, gobbledygook <nf>; glossolalia, speaking in tongues

3 <nf terms> **bullshit,** shit, crap *or* crapola, horseshit, horsefeathers, bull, poppycock, bosh, tosh <Brit>, applesauce, bunkum, bunk, garbage, guff, hogwash, jive, bilge, piffle, moonshine, flapdoodle, a crock *or* a crock of shit, claptrap, tommyrot, rot, hogwash, malarkey, double Dutch, hokum, hooey, bushwa, balls <Brit>, blah-blah-

blah, baloney, blarney, tripe, hot air, gas, wind, waffle <Brit>

VERBS 4 **be meaningless, mean nothing,** signify nothing, not mean a thing, not convey anything; not make sense, not figure <nf>, not compute; **not register,** not ring any bells

5 **talk nonsense, twaddle, piffle,** waffle <Brit>, **blather,** blether, **blabber, babble, gabble,** gibble-gabble, **jabber, gibber,** prate, **prattle,** rattle, spiel <nf>; talk through one's hat; gas *and* bull *and* **bullshit** *and* throw the bull *and* shoot off one's mouth *and* shoot the bull <nf>; **drivel,** vapor, drool, run off at the mouth <nf>; speak in tongues; not mean what one says

ADJS 6 **meaningless,** unmeaning, **senseless,** purportless, importless, nondenotative, nonconnotative; **insignificant,** unsignificant; empty, inane, null; phatic, garbled, scrambled; **purposeless, aimless,** designless, **without rhyme or reason**

7 **nonsensical,** silly, poppycockish <nf>; **foolish, absurd;** twaddling, twaddly; rubbishy, trashy; skimble-skamble; Pickwickian

ADVS 8 **meaninglessly,** unmeaningly, nondenotatively, nonconnotatively, **senselessly, nonsensically;** insignificantly, unsignificantly; **purposelessly,** aimlessly

521 INTELLIGIBILITY

NOUNS 1 **intelligibility, comprehensibility, apprehensibility,** prehensibility, graspability, **understandability,** knowability, cognizability, scrutability, penetrability, fathomableness, decipherability; recognizability, readability, interpretability; articulateness

2 **clearness, clarity; plainness, distinctness,** microscopical distinctness, explicitness, clear-cutness, definition; **lucidity,** limpidity, pellucidity, crystal *or* crystaline clarity, crystallinity, perspicuity, perspicuousness, transpicuity, transparency; **simplicity,** straightforwardness, directness, literalness; unmistakableness, unequivocalness, unambiguousness, unambiguity; **coherence,** connectedness, consistency, structure; plain language, plain style, plain English, plain speech, unadorned style; clear, plaintext, unencoded text; lowest common denominator

3 **legibility,** decipherability, **readability**

VERBS 4 **be understandable, make sense;** be plain *or* clear, be obvious, be self-evident, be self-explanatory; **speak for itself,** tell its own tale, speak volumes, have no secrets, put up no barriers; read easily

5 <be understood> **get over** *or* **across** <nf>, come

through, **register** <nf>, **penetrate, sink in,** soak in; dawn on, be glimpsed; become apparent

6 **make clear,** make it clear, **let it be understood,** make crystal-clear, make oneself understood, get *or* put over *or* across <nf>; **simplify,** put in plain words *or* plain English, put in words of one syllable, spell out <nf>; elucidate, **explain,** define, demonstrate, explicate, **clarify** 341.10; illuminate, enlighten; put one in the picture <Brit>; disambiguate; demystify, descramble; **decode, decipher;** make available to all, popularize, vulgarize

7 **understand, comprehend, apprehend,** have, **know, conceive, realize,** appreciate, have no problem with, ken <Scot>, savvy <nf>, sense, make sense out of, make something of, make out, make heads or tails of; **fathom, follow; grasp, seize,** get hold of, grasp *or* seize the meaning, be seized of, take, **take in,** catch, **catch on,** get the meaning of, latch onto; **master, learn** 570.6–551.15,14; **assimilate, absorb, digest**

8 <nf terms> **read one loud and clear,** read, read one, dig, get the idea, be with one, be with it, get the message, get the word, get the picture, get up to speed, get into *or* through one's head *or* thick head, get, get it, catch *or* get the drift, have it taped, have it down pat, see where one is coming from, hear loud and clear, hear what one is saying, grok, have hold of, get the hang of, get *or* have a fix on, know like the back *or* palm of one's hand, know inside out

9 **perceive, see, discern, make out,** descry; see the light, see daylight <nf>, wake up, wake up to, tumble to <nf>, come alive; **see through,** see to the bottom of, penetrate, see into, pierce, plumb; see at a glance, see with half an eye; get *or* have someone's number *and* read someone like a book <nf>

ADJS 10 **intelligible, comprehensible, apprehensible,** prehensible, graspable, **knowable,** cognizable, scrutable, **fathomable,** decipherable, plumbable, penetrable, interpretable; **understandable,** easily understood, easy to understand, exoteric; readable; articulate

11 **clear, crystal-clear,** clear as crystal, clear as day, clear as the nose on one's face; **plain, distinct,** microscopically distinct, plain as pikestaffs; **definite,** defined, well-defined, **clear-cut,** clean-cut, crisp, obvious, made easy; **direct, literal;** simple, **straightforward; explicit, express; unmistakable, unequivocal,** univocal, unambiguous, unconfused; **loud and clear** <nf>; **lucid,** pellucid, limpid, crystal-clear, crystalline, perspicuous, transpicuous, **transparent,** translucent, luminous; **coherent,** connected, consistent

12 **legible, decipherable, readable,** fair; uncoded, unenciphered, in the clear, clear, plaintext

ADVS 13 **intelligibly, understandably, comprehensibly,** apprehensibly; articulately; **clearly, lucidly,** limpidly, pellucidly, perspicuously, **simply, plainly, distinctly,** definitely; **coherently; explicitly, expressly; unmistakably, unequivocally,** unambiguously; in plain terms *or* words, in plain English, in no uncertain terms, in words of one syllable

14 **legibly,** decipherably, readably, fairly

522 UNINTELLIGIBILITY

NOUNS 1 **unintelligibility, incomprehensibility,** inapprehensibility, ungraspability, unseizability, **ununderstandability,** inconceivability, unknowability, incognizability, inscrutability, impenetrability, unfathomableness, unsearchableness, numinousness; **incoherence,** unconnectedness, ramblingness; inarticulateness; **ambiguity** 539, equivocation

2 **abstruseness,** reconditeness; crabbedness, crampedness, knottiness; **complexity,** intricacy, **complication** 799.1; **hardness, difficulty; profundity,** profoundness, deepness; esotericism, esotery

3 **obscurity,** obscuration, obscurantism, obfuscation, mumbo jumbo <nf>, mystification; perplexity; **unclearness,** unclarity, unplainness, opacity; **vagueness,** indistinctness, indeterminateness, fuzziness, shapelessness, amorphousness; murkiness, murk, mistiness, mist, fogginess, fog, darkness, dark

4 **illegibility,** unreadability; undecipherability, indecipherability; invisibility; scribble, scrawl, **hen track** <nf>

5 **unexpressiveness,** inexpressiveness, **expressionlessness,** impassivity; uncommunicativeness; straight face, deadpan <nf>, poker face <nf>

6 **inexplicability,** unexplainableness, uninterpretability, indefinability, undefinability, unaccountableness; insolvability, inextricability; **enigmaticalness,** mysteriousness, mystery, strangeness, weirdness

7 <something unintelligible> Greek, Choctaw, double Dutch; gibberish, babble, jargon, garbage, gubbish, gobbledygook, noise, Babel; scramble, jumble, garble, muddle; purple prose; argot, cant, slang, secret language, Aesopian *or* Aesopic language, code, cipher, cryptogram; glossolalia, gift of tongues; enigma, riddle; double meaning

8 **enigma, mystery, puzzle,** puzzlement; Chinese puzzle, crossword puzzle, jigsaw puzzle; **problem,**

puzzling *or* baffling problem, why; question, question mark, vexed *or* perplexed question, enigmatic question, sixty-four dollar question <nf>; **perplexity;** obscure point; knot, knotty point, crux, point to be solved; **puzzler,** poser, brain twister *or* teaser <nf>, sticker <nf>; mind-boggler, **floorer** *or* **stumper** <nf>; nut to crack, **hard** *or* **tough nut to crack;** tough proposition <nf>, "a riddle wrapped in a mystery inside an enigma"—Winston Churchill

9 **riddle, conundrum,** paradox, charade, rebus; brainteaser, Chinese puzzle, tangram, acrostic, logograph, anagram; riddle of the Sphinx, squaring of the circle

VERBS 10 **be incomprehensible, not make sense,** be too deep, go over one's head, defy comprehension, be beyond one, beat one <nf>, elude *or* escape one, lose one, need explanation *or* clarification *or* translation, be Greek to, pass comprehension *or* understanding, not penetrate, make one's head swim; **baffle, perplex** 971.13, riddle, be sphinxlike, speak in riddles; speak in tongues; talk double Dutch, babble, gibber, ramble, drivel, mean nothing

11 **not understand, be unable to comprehend,** not have the first idea, not get *or* not get it <nf>, be unable to get into *or* through one's head *or* thick skull; be out of one's depth, be at sea, be lost; **not know what to make of,** make nothing of, not have the slightest idea, not be able to account for, not make head or tail of, not register; be unable to see, not see the wood for the trees; go over one's head, escape one; give up, pass <nf>; rack one's brains

12 **make unintelligible, scramble,** jumble, garble, mix up; encode, encipher; **obscure,** obfuscate, mystify, shadow; **complicate** 799.3

ADJS 13 **unintelligible, incomprehensible,** inapprehensible, ungraspable, unseizable, **ununderstandable,** unknowable, incognizable; **unfathomable, inscrutable,** impenetrable, unsearchable, numinous; **ambiguous,** equivocal; **incoherent,** unconnected, rambling; **inarticulate; past comprehension,** beyond one's comprehension, beyond understanding; Greek to one

14 **hard to understand, difficult, hard,** tough <nf>, beyond one, **over one's head,** beyond *or* out of one's depth; knotty, cramp, crabbed; intricate, **complex,** overtechnical, perplexed, **complicated** 799.4; **scrambled,** jumbled, **garbled;** Johnsonian

15 **obscure,** obscured, obfuscated; **vague, indistinct,** indeterminate, undiscernible, fuzzy, shapeless, amorphous, obfuscatory; unclear, unplain, opaque, muddy, **clear as mud** *and* clear as ditch water <nf>; **dark, dim,** blind <old>, shadowy; **murky,** cloudy, foggy, fogbound, hazy, misty, nebulous

16 **recondite, abstruse,** abstract, transcendental; **profound, deep;** hidden 346.11; arcane, **esoteric,** occult; **secret** 345.11

17 **enigmatic,** enigmatical, cryptic, cryptical; sphinxlike; **perplexing, puzzling;** riddling; logogriphic, anagrammatic, mysterious

18 **inexplicable, unexplainable,** uninterpretable, undefinable, indefinable, funny, funny peculiar <nf>, **unaccountable; insolvable,** unsolvable, insoluble, inextricable; mysterious, mystic, mystical, shrouded *or* wrapped *or* enwrapped in mystery

19 **illegible, unreadable, unclear; undecipherable,** indecipherable

20 **inexpressive,** unexpressive, impassive, po-faced <Brit>; uncommunicative; **expressionless; vacant, empty, blank;** glassy, glazed, glazed-over, fishy, wooden; deadpan, poker-faced <nf>

ADVS 21 **unintelligibly, incomprehensibly,** inapprehensibly, ununderstandably

22 **obscurely, vaguely, indistinctly,** indeterminately; **unclearly,** unplainly; illegibly

23 reconditely, **abstrusely;** esoterically, occultly

24 **inexplicably, unexplainably,** undefinably, bafflingly, **unaccountably, enigmatically; mysteriously,** mystically

25 **expressionlessly, vacantly, blankly, emptily,** woodenly, glassily, fishily

PREPS 26 **beyond,** past, above; **too deep for**

PHRS 27 **I don't understand, I can't see,** I don't see how *or* why, **it beats me** <nf>, you've got me <nf>, **it's beyond me,** it's too deep for me, it has me guessing, I don't have the first *or* foggiest idea, it's Greek to me, I'm clueless <Brit>; **I give up,** I pass <nf>

523 LANGUAGE

NOUNS 1 **language** <see list>, speech, tongue, *lingua* <L>, spoken language, natural language; **talk, parlance, locution,** phraseology, **idiom, lingo** <nf>; dialect; idiolect, personal usage, individual speech habits *or* performance, parole; code *or* system of oral communication, individual speech, competence, langue; **usage,** use of words; **language type; language family, subfamily, language group;** area language, regional language; world language, universal language

2 **dead language,** ancient language, lost language; archaic language, archaism, archaic speech; parent language; classical language; living language, vernacular; sacred language *or* tongue

3 **mother tongue,** native language *or* tongue, natal tongue, native speech, vernacular, first language

4 **standard language,** standard *or* prestige dialect,

acrolect; national language, official language; educated speech *or* language; literary language, written language, formal written language; classical language; correct *or* good English, **Standard English, the King's** *or* **Queen's English,** Received Standard, Received Pronunciation

5 **nonformal language** *or* **speech,** nonformal standard speech, **spoken language, colloquial language** *or* **speech,** vernacular language *or* speech, vernacular; **slang;** colloquialism, colloquial usage, conversationalism, vernacularism; ordinary language *or* speech; nonformal English, conversational English, colloquial English, English as it is spoken

6 **substandard** *or* nonstandard language *or* **speech,** nonformal language *or* speech; vernacular language *or* speech, **vernacular,** demotic language *or* speech, vulgate, vulgar tongue, common speech, low language; uneducated speech, illiterate speech; substandard usage; basilect; **nonformal**

7 **dialect,** idiom; class dialect; regional *or* local dialect; idiolect; subdialect; folk speech *or* dialect, patois; **provincialism, localism, regionalism,** regional accent 524.9; Canadian French, French Canadian; Pennsylvania Dutch, Pennsylvania German; Yankee, New England dialect; Brooklynese; Southern dialect *or* twang; Black English, Afro-Americanese; Cockney; Yorkshire; Midland, Midland dialect; Anglo-Indian; Australian English; Gullah; Acadian, Cajun; dialect atlas, linguistic atlas; isogloss, bundle of isoglosses; speech community; linguistic community; linguistic ambience; speech *or* linguistic island, relic area

8 <idioms> Anglicism, Briticism, Englishism; Americanism, Yankeeism; Westernism, Southernism; Gallicism, Frenchism; Irishism, Hibernicism; Canadianism, Scotticism, Germanism, Russianism, Latinism, etc

9 **jargon, lingo** <nf>, **slang, cant, argot, patois, patter, vernacular;** vocabulary, terminology, nomenclature, phraseology; gobbledygook, mumbo jumbo, gibberish; **nonformal;** taboo language, vulgar language; obscene language, scatology; doublespeak, bizspeak, mediaspeak, policyspeak, technospeak, winespeak

10 <jargons> Academese, cinemese, collegese, constablese, ecobabble, economese, sociologese, legalese, pedagese, societyese, stagese, telegraphese, Varietyese, Wall Streetese, journalese, newspaperese, newspeak, officialese, federalese, Pentagonese, Washingtonese, medical Greek, medicalese, businessese *or* businessspeak, computerese, technobabble, technospeak, psychobabble; Yinglish, Franglais, Spanglish;

Eurojargon; man-talk, bloke-talk <Brit nf>, woman-talk, hen-talk <nf>; shoptalk; pig Latin; glossolalia

11 **lingua franca,** international language, jargon, **pidgin,** trade language; auxiliary language, interlanguage; creolized language, creole language, creole; koine; diplomatic language, business language, language *or* linguistic universal; pidgin English, talkee-talkee, Bêche-de-Mer, Beach-la-mar; Kitchen Kaffir; Chinook *or* Oregon Jargon; Sabir; Esperanto; artificial language, sign language, sign, American Sign Language *or* ASL *or* Ameslan; Morse code, cryptography, cryptanalysis; computer language; shorthand, stenography

12 language family; Indo-European, Indo-Iranian, Anatolian, Hellenic, Tocharian, Italic, Celtic, Germanic, Baltic, Slavic; Finno-Ugric; Afroasiatic *or* Hamito-Semitic; Sino-Tibetan; Austronesian

13 **linguistics,** linguistic science, science of language; glottology, glossology <old>; linguistic analysis; linguistic terminology, metalanguage; **philology;** paleography; speech origins, language origins, bowwow theory, dingdong theory, pooh-pooh theory; language study, foreign-language study, linguistic theory

14 language element, morpheme, phoneme, grapheme; letter, alphabet, word, phrase, sentence; grammar, syntax, part of speech

15 **linguist,** linguistic scientist, linguistician, linguistic scholar; philologist, philologer, philologian; philologaster; **grammarian,** grammatist; grammaticaster; **etymologist,** etymologer; **lexicologist; lexicographer,** glossographer, glossarist; phoneticist, phonetician, phonemicist, phonologist, orthoepist; dialectician, dialectologist; semanticist, semasiologist; paleographer; logophile; morphologist, orthographer

16 **polyglot,** linguist, **bilingual** *or* diglot, trilingual, multilingual

17 **colloquializer;** jargonist, jargoneer, jargonizer; slangster

VERBS 18 **speak, talk,** use language, communicate orally *or* verbally; use nonformal speech *or* style, colloquialize, vernacularize; jargon, jargonize, cant; patter; utter, verbalize, articulate

ADJS 19 **linguistic,** lingual, glottological, glossological <old>; descriptive, structural, glottochronological, lexicostatistical, psycholinguistic, sociolinguistic, metalinguistic; **philological;** lexicological, lexicographic, lexicographical; syntactic, syntactical, **grammatical;** grammatic, semantic 518.12; phonetic 524.30, phonemic, phonological; morphological; morphophonemic, graphemic, paleographic, paleographical

20 **vernacular, colloquial, conversational, unliterary,**

nonformal, informal, demotic, spoken, vulgar, vulgate; unstudied, familiar, common, everyday; jargonistic; **substandard,** nonformal, uneducated, low

21 **jargonish,** jargonal; **slang,** slangy; taboo, four-letter, obscene, vulgar; scatological; rhyming slang

22 **idiomatic; dialect,** dialectal, dialectological; provincial, regional, local

WORD ELEMENTS 23 lingu-, linguo-, lingui-, gloss-, glosso-, glott-, glotto-

24 **types of language**

affixing	monosyllabic
agglutinative	polysyllabic
analytic	polysynthetic
fusional	polytonic
incorporative	symbolic
inflectional	synthetic
isolating	tonal

524 SPEECH
<utterance>

NOUNS 1 **speech, talk,** the power *or* faculty of speech, the verbal *or* oral faculty, talking, speaking, **discourse,** colloquy, oral communication, vocal *or* voice *or* viva-voce communication, communication, verbal intercourse; **palaver, prattle, gab** and jaw-jaw <nf>; rapping *and* yakking *and* yakkety-yak <nf>; **words, accents;** chatter 540.3; conversation 541; elocution 543.1; **language** 523; "the mirror of the soul"—Publilius Syrus

2 **utterance, speaking,** *parole* <Fr>, spoken language, vocalization, locution <old>, phonation, phonetics; **speech act,** linguistic act *or* behavior; string, utterance string, sequence of phonemes, expression; **voice, tongue,** vocalism, parlance; word of mouth, parol, the spoken word; vocable, **word** 526

3 **remark, statement,** earful *and* crack *and* one's two cents' worth <nf>, **word,** say, **saying, utterance, observation, reflection, expression; note,** thought, **mention; assertion,** averment, allegation, affirmation, pronouncement, position, dictum; **declaration;** interjection, exclamation; question 938.10; answer 939; address, greeting, apostrophe; sentence, phrase; subjoinder, Parthian shot

4 **articulateness,** articulacy, oracy, readiness *or* facility of speech; **eloquence** 544; way with words, word power

5 **articulation,** uttering, phonation, voicing, giving voice, **vocalization; pronunciation, enunciation,** utterance; **delivery, attack**

6 **intonation, inflection, modulation;** intonation pattern *or* contour, intonation *or* inflection of voice, speech tune *or* melody; suprasegmental, suprasegmental phoneme; **tone, pitch;** pitch accent, tonic accent

7 manner of speaking, way of saying, mode of expression *or* speech; **tone of voice, voice,** *voce* <Ital>, **tone;** speaking voice, voice quality, vocal style, **timbre;** voice qualifier; paralinguistic communication

8 **accent,** regional accent, brogue, twang, burr, drawl, broad accent, trill, whine, nasality, stridor; **foreign accent;** guttural accent, clipped accent; broken English; speech impediment, speech defect; speech community, isogloss

9 pause, juncture, open juncture, close juncture; terminal, clause terminal, rising terminal, falling terminal; sandhi; word boundary, clause boundary; pause

10 **accent,** accentuation, stress accent; **emphasis, stress, word stress;** ictus, beat, rhythmical stress; rhythm, rhythmic pattern, **cadence;** prosody, prosodics, metrics; stress pattern; level of stress; primary stress, secondary stress, tertiary stress, weak stress

11 vowel quantity, **quantity,** mora; long vowel, short vowel, full vowel, reduced vowel

12 **speech sound,** phone, vocable, phonetic unit *or* entity; puff of air, aspiration; stream of air, airstream, glottalic airstream; articulation, manner of articulation; **stop,** plosive, explosive, mute, check, occlusive, **affricate,** continuant, **liquid,** lateral, **nasal;** point *or* place of articulation; voice, voicing; sonority; aspiration, palatalization, labialization, pharyngealization, glottalization; surd, voiceless sound; sonant, voiced sound; **consonant; semivowel,** glide, transition sound; velar, guttural, voiced consonant, frictionless continuant, labial, labio-dental, labio-nasal, spirant, sibilant, aspirate, glottal stop, fricative, sonant, polyphone; vocalic, syllabic nucleus, syllabic peak, peak; vocoid, **vowel;** monophthong, **diphthong,** triphthong; **syllable; phoneme,** segmental phoneme, morphophoneme, digraph; modification, assimilation, dissimilation; **allophone;** parasitic vowel, epenthetic vowel, svarabhakti vowel, prothetic vowel; vowel gradation, vowel mutation; doubletalk

13 **phonetics,** articulatory phonetics, acoustic phonetics; phonology; morphophonemics, morphophonology; orthoepy; sound *or* phonetic law; pronunciation; phonography; sound shift, *Lautverschiebung* <Ger>; umlaut, mutation, ablaut, gradation; rhotacism, betacism; Grimm's law, Verner's law, Grassmann's law

14 **phonetician,** phonetist, phoneticist; orthoepist

15 **ventriloquism,** ventriloquy; **ventriloquist**

16 talking machine, sonovox, voder, vocoder

17 **talker, speaker,** sayer, utterer, patterer; chatterbox 540.4; conversationalist 541.8

18 vocal *or* **speech organ,** articulator, voice, mouth; tongue, apex, tip, blade, dorsum, back; vocal cords *or* bands, vocal processes, vocal folds; voice box, larynx, Adam's apple; syrinx; arytenoid cartilages; glottis, vocal chink, epiglottis; lips, teeth, palate, hard palate, soft palate, velum, alveolus, teeth ridge, alveolar ridge, uvula; nasal cavity, oral cavity; pharynx, throat *or* pharyngeal cavity

VERBS **19 speak, talk; patter** *or* **gab** *or* wag the tongue <nf>; mouth; chatter 540.5; converse 541.9; declaim 543.10

20 <nf terms> **yak,** yap, yakkety-yak, gab, spiel, chin, jaw, shoot off one's face *or* mouth, shoot *or* bat the breeze, beat *or* bat one's gums, bend one's ear, make chin music, rattle away, talk a blue streak, talk someone's ear *or* head off, flap one's jaw, natter <Brit>, spout off, sound off

21 speak up, speak out, speak one's piece *or* **one's mind,** pipe up, open one's mouth, open one's lips, say out, say loud *and* clear, say out loud, sound off, lift *or* raise one's voice, break silence, find one's tongue; take the floor; put in a word, get in a word edgewise *or* edgeway; **have one's say,** put in one's two cents worth <nf>, relieve oneself, get a load off one's mind <nf>, give vent *or* voice to, pour one's heart out

22 say, utter, breathe, sound, **voice,** vocalize, phonate, **articulate, enunciate, pronounce,** lip, give voice, give tongue, give utterance; whisper; **express,** give expression, verbalize, put in words, find words to express; **word,** formulate, put into words, couch, phrase 532.4; **present,** deliver; **emit,** give, raise, **let out,** out with, come *or* give out with, put *or* set forth, pour forth; throw off, fling off; chorus, chime; **tell,** communicate 343.6,7; **convey, impart,** disclose 351.4

23 state, declare, assert, aver, affirm, asserverate, allege; **say,** make a statement, send a message; **announce,** tell the world; **relate, recite;** quote; proclaim, nuncupate

24 remark, comment, observe, note; mention, speak <old>, let drop *or* fall, say by the way, make mention of; refer to, allude to, touch on, make reference to, call attention to; muse, reflect; opine <nf>; interject; blurt, blurt out, exclaim

25 <utter in a certain way> murmur, mutter, mumble, whisper, breathe, buzz, sigh; gasp, pant; exclaim, yell 59.6,8; sing, lilt, warble, chant, coo, chirp; pipe, flute; squeak; cackle, crow; bark, yelp, yap; growl, snap, snarl; hiss, sibilate; grunt, snort; roar, bellow, blare, trumpet, bray, blat, bawl, thunder, rumble, boom; scream, shriek, screech, squeal, squawk, yawp, squall; whine, wail, keen, blubber, sob; drawl, twang

26 address, speak to, talk to, bespeak, beg the ear of;

appeal to, invoke; apostrophize; **approach; buttonhole,** take by the button *or* lapel; take aside, talk to in private, closet oneself with; **accost, call to, hail,** halloo, greet, salute, speak, speak fair

27 pass one's lips, escape one's lips, fall from the lips *or* mouth

28 inflect, modulate, intonate

ADJS **29 speech; language, linguistic,** lingual; **spoken, uttered, said,** vocalized, **voiced, verbalized, pronounced, sounded, articulated, enunciated;** vocal, voiceful; **oral, verbal, unwritten,** *viva voce* <L>, nuncupative, parol

30 phonetic, phonic; articulatory, acoustic; intonated; pitched, pitch, **tonal,** tonic, oxytone, oxytonic, paroxytonic, barytone; **accented, stressed,** strong, heavy; unaccented, unstressed, weak, light, pretonic, atonic, posttonic; articulated; stopped, muted, checked, occlusive, nasal, nasalized, twangy, continuant, liquid, lateral, affricated; alveolabial, alveolar, alveolingual, etc; low, high, mid, open, broad, close; front, back, central; wide, lax, tense, narrow; voiced, sonant, voiceless, surd; rounded, unrounded, flat; aspirated; labialized; palatalized, soft, *mouillé* <Fr>; unpalatalized, hard; pharyngealized, glottalized; velar, guttural; burring, frictionless, labial, spirant, sibilant, fricative, polyphonic, polyphonous, digraphic; **consonant,** consonantal, semivowel, glide, **vowel;** vowellike, vocoid, vocalic, syllabic; monophthongal, diphthongal, triphthongal; **phonemic,** allophonic; assimilated, dissimilated

31 speaking, talking; articulate, talkative 540.9; **eloquent** 544.8, well-spoken; true-speaking, clean-speaking, plain-speaking, plain-spoken, **outspoken,** free-speaking, free-spoken, loud-speaking, loud-spoken, soft-speaking, soft-spoken; English-speaking, etc

32 ventriloquial, ventriloquistic

ADVS **33 orally, vocally, verbally, by word of mouth,** *viva voce* <L>; from the lips of, from his own mouth

525 IMPERFECT SPEECH

NOUNS **1 speech defect,** speech impediment, speech difficulty, impairment of speech; dysarthria, dysphasia, dysphrasia; dyslalia, dyslogia; idioglossia, idiolalia; **broken speech,** cracked *or* broken voice, broken tones *or* accents; indistinct *or* blurred *or* muzzy speech; loss of voice, aphonia; **nasalization,** nasal tone *or* accent, **twang,** nasal twang, talking through one's nose; **falsetto,** childish treble, artificial voice; **shake, quaver,** tremor; **lisp,** lisping; hiss, sibilation, lallation; **croak,** choked voice, hawking voice; **crow;**

harshness, dysphonia, hoarseness 58.2;
voicelessness, loss of voice

2 **inarticulateness,** inarticulacy, inarticulation;
thickness of speech

3 **stammering, stuttering,** hesitation, faltering,
traulism, dysphemia, *balbuties* <L>; palilalia;
stammer, stutter

4 **mumbling, muttering,** maundering; unintelligible
speech; droning, drone; mumble, mutter; jabber,
jibber, gibber, gibbering, gabble; whispering,
whisper, susurration; mouthing; murmuring

5 **mispronunciation,** misspeaking, cacology, cacoepy;
lallation, lambdacism, paralambdacism;
rhotacism, pararhotacism; gammacism; mytacism;
corruption, language pollution

6 **aphasia, agraphia;** aphrasia, aphrasia paranoica;
aphonia, loss of speech, aphonia clericorum,
hysterical aphonia, stage fright, aphonia paralytica,
aphonia paranoica, spastic aphonia, mutism,
muteness 51.2; voiceless speech, sign language

VERBS 7 **speak poorly,** talk incoherently, be unable
to put two words together; have an impediment in
one's speech, have a bone in one's neck *or* throat;
speak thickly; **croak; lisp; shake, quaver; drawl;**
mince, clip one's words; lose one's voice, get stage
fright, clank *or* clank up *and* freeze <nf>, be
struck dumb

8 **stammer, stutter,** stammer out; hesitate, falter,
halt, mammer <Brit nf>, stumble; hem, haw,
hum, **hum and haw, hem and haw**

9 **mumble, mutter,** maunder; drone, drone on;
swallow one's words, speak drunkenly *or*
incoherently; jabber, gibber, gabble; splutter,
sputter; blubber, sob; whisper, susurrate; murmur;
babble; mouth

10 nasalize, whine, **speak through one's nose,** twang,
snuffle

11 **mispronounce,** misspeak, missay, **murder the
King's** *or* **Queen's English**

ADJS 12 <imperfectly spoken> inarticulate,
indistinct, blurred, muzzy, unintelligible;
mispronounced; shaky, shaking, **quavering,**
breaking, cracked, tremulous, titubant; **drawling,**
drawly; **lisping; throaty, guttural,** thick, velar;
stifled, choked, choking, strangled; **nasal, twangy,**
breathy, adenoidal, snuffling; croaking, hawking;
harsh, dysphonic, hoarse 58.15

13 **stammering, stuttering,** halting, hesitating,
faltering, stumbling, balbutient; **aphasic;** aphrasic;
aphonic, dumb, **mute** 51.12

526 WORD

NOUNS 1 **word,** free form, minimum free form,
semanteme, **term,** name, expression, locution,

linguistic form, lexeme; written unit; content
word, function word; *logos* <Gk>, *verbum* <L>;
verbalism, vocable, utterance, articulation; **usage;**
syllable, polysyllable; homonym, homophone,
homograph; monosyllable; synonym; metonym;
antonym; easy word, hard word

2 **root,** etymon, primitive; eponym; derivative,
derivation; cognate; doublet

3 **morphology,** morphemics; morphophonemics;
morpheme; morph, allomorph; bound morpheme
or form, free morpheme *or* form; difference of
form, formal contrast; accidence; **inflection,**
conjugation, declension; paradigm; derivation,
word-formation; formative; root, radical; theme,
stem; word element, combining form; **affix, suffix,
prefix,** infix; proclitic, enclitic; affixation,
infixation, suffixation, prefixation; morphemic
analysis, immediate constituent *or* IC analysis,
cutting; morphophonemic analysis

4 **word form,** formation, construction; back
formation; clipped word; spoonerism; **compound;**
*tatpurusha, dvandva, karmadharaya, dvigu,
avyayibhava, bahuvrihi* <all Skt>; endocentric
compound, exocentric compound; acronym,
acrostic; paronym, conjugate; proclitic, enclitic

5 **technical term,** technicality; jargon word; jargon
523.9,10

6 **barbarism, corruption, vulgarism, impropriety,**
taboo word, dirty word *and* four-letter word <nf>,
swearword, naughty word, bad word, obscenity,
expletive; **colloquialism, slang, localism** 526.6

7 **loan word,** borrowing, borrowed word, paronym;
loan translation, calque; foreignism

8 **neologism,** neology, neoterism, new word *or* term,
newfangled expression; **coinage;** new sense *or*
meaning; **nonce word;** ghost word *or* name

9 **catchword,** catch phrase, shibboleth, slogan, cry;
pet expression, byword, cliché; **buzzword,** vogue
word, fad word, in-word; euphemism, **code word;**
commonplace, hackneyed expression

10 long word, hard word, jawbreaker *or* jawtwister
and two-dollar *or* five-dollar word <nf>,
polysyllable; sesquipedalian, sesquipedalia <pl>;
lexiphanicism, grandiloquence 545

11 hybrid word, **hybrid;** macaronicism, macaronic;
hybridism, contamination; blendword, blend,
portmanteau word, portmanteau,
portmantologism, telescope word, **counterword;**
ghost word

12 **archaism,** archaicism, antiquated word *or*
expression; obsoletism, obsolete

13 **vocabulary, lexis, words, word stock,** wordhoard,
stock of words; phraseology; **thesaurus,** Roget's;
lexicon

14 **lexicology; lexicography,** lexigraphy, glossography;

onomastics 527.1, toponymics; **meaning** 518, semantics, semasiology; denotation, connotation

15 etymology, derivation, origin, word origin, word history, semantic history, etymon; historical linguistics, comparative linguistics; eponymy; folk etymology

16 echoic word, onomatopoeic word, onomatope; onomatopoeia; bowwow theory

17 neologist, word-coiner, neoterist; phraser, phrasemaker, phrasemonger

ADJS **18 verbal,** vocabular, vocabulary

19 lexical, lexicologic, lexicological; lexigraphic, lexigraphical, **lexicographical,** lexicographic; glossographic, glossographical; etymological, etymologic, derivational; onomastic, onomatologic; onomasiological; echoic, onomatopoeic; conjugate, paronymous, paronymic

20 neological, neoterical

21 morphological, morphemic; morphophonemic; inflective, inflectional, paradigmatic, derivational; affixal, prefixal, infixal, suffixal

WORD ELEMENTS **22** log-, logo-, onomato-, -onym, -onymy

527 NOMENCLATURE

NOUNS **1 nomenclature, terminology,** orismology, glossology <old>, vocabulary; onomatology, onomastics; toponymics, toponymy, place-names, place-naming; antonomasia; orismology; polyonymy; **taxonomy,** classification, systematics, cladistics, biosystematics, cytotaxonomy, binomial nomenclature, binomialism, Linnaean method, trinomialism; kingdom, phylum, class, order, family, genus, species

2 naming, calling, denomination, appellation, designation, designating, styling, terming, definition, identification; **christening,** baptism; dubbing; nicknaming

3 name, appellation, appellative, **denomination, designation, style,** heading, *nomen* <L>, cognomen, cognomination, full name; proper name *or* noun; moniker *and* handle <nf>; **title,** honorific; empty title *or* name; **label, tag; epithet,** byword; **scientific name,** trinomen, trinomial name, binomen, binomial name; *nomen nudum* <L>, hyponym; tautonym; typonym; middle name; eponym; namesake; secret name, cryptonym, euonym, password; professional title; title of respect *or* address; military title; place name, toponym; trade name, trademark

4 first name, forename, **Christian name, given name,** baptismal name; **middle name**

5 surname, last name, family name, cognomen, byname; **maiden name;** married name; patronymic, matronymic

6 <Latin terms> *praenomen, nomen, agnomen, cognomen*

7 nickname, sobriquet, byname, cognomen; epithet, agnomen; **pet name,** diminutive, hypocoristic, affectionate name

8 alias, pseudonym, anonym, **assumed name,** false *or* fictitious name, *nom de guerre* <Fr>; **pen name, nom de plume;** stage name, *nom de théâtre* <Fr>, professional name; John Doe, Jane Doe, Richard Roe

9 misnomer, wrong name

10 signature, sign manual, **autograph, hand,** John Hancock <nf>; mark, mark of signature, cross, christcross, X; initials; subscription; countersignature, countersign, countermark, counterstamp; endorsement; visa, *visé* <Fr>; monogram, cipher, device; seal, sigil, signet

VERBS **11 name, denominate,** nominate, **designate, call, term, style, dub,** color <nf>; specify; define, identify; title, entitle; **label, tag; nickname; christen,** baptize

12 misname, misnomer, **miscall,** misterm, misdesignate

13 be called, be known by *or* as, go by, go as, **go by the name of,** go *or* pass under the name of, bear the name of, rejoice in the name of; go under an assumed *or* a false name, have an alias

ADJS **14 named, called,** yclept <old>, **styled, titled,** denominated, denominate <old>, **known as,** known by the name of, designated, termed, dubbed, identified as; christened, baptized; what one may well *or* fairly *or* properly *or* fitly call

15 nominal, cognominal; **titular, in name only,** nominative, formal; **so-called,** quasi; would-be, *soi-disant* <Fr>; **self-called, self-styled,** self-christened; honorific; agnominal, epithetic, epithetical; hypocoristic, diminutive; by name, by whatever name, under any other name; **alias,** a k a *or* also known as

16 denominative, nominative, appellative; eponymous, eponymic

17 terminological, nomenclatural, orismological; onomastic; toponymic, toponymous; taxonomic, classificatory, binomial, Linnaean, trinomial

WORD ELEMENTS **18** onomato-, -onym, -onymy

528 ANONYMITY

NOUNS **1 anonymity, anonymousness, namelessness; incognito;** cover, cover name; code name; anonym; unknown quantity, no-name; Unknown Soldier; Anon.

2 what's-its-name *and* **what's-his-name** *and* what's-his-face *and* what's-her-name *and* **what-you-may-call-it** *and* whatchamacallit *and* what-you-may-call-'em *and* what-d'ye-call-'em *and* what-d'ye-call-it *and* whatzit <nf>; *je ne sais quoi* <Fr>, I don't know what; such-and-such; **so-and-so,** certain person, X *or* Mr X; you-know-who

ADJS **3 anonymous, anon; nameless, unnamed,** unidentified, undesignated, unspecified, innominate, without a name, **unknown;** undefined; unacknowledged; **incognito;** cryptonymous, cryptonymic

529 PHRASE

NOUNS **1 phrase, expression, locution, utterance,** usage, term, verbalism; **word-group,** fixed expression, construction, endocentric construction, headed group, syntagm; syntactic structure; noun phrase, verb phrase, verb complex, adverbial phrase, adjectival phrase, prepositional phrase; conditional phrase; **clause,** coordinate clause, subordinate clause, independent clause; **sentence,** period, periodic sentence; **paragraph; idiom,** idiotism, phrasal idiom; turn of phrase *or* expression, peculiar expression, manner *or* way of speaking; set phrase *or* term; conventional *or* common *or* standard phrase; phraseogram, phraseograph; maxim, adage, moral, proverb, slogan, motto, quotation, quote, sound bite

2 diction, phrasing; phraseology, choice of words, wording

3 phraser, phrasemaker, phrasemonger, phraseman

ADJS **4 phrasal,** phrase; phrasey

5 in set phrases *or* terms, in good set terms, in round terms

530 GRAMMAR

NOUNS **1 grammar,** rules of language, linguistic structure, syntactic structure, sentence structure; "the rule and pattern of speech"—Horace; grammaticalness, well-formedness, grammaticality, grammatical theory; **traditional grammar, school grammar;** descriptive grammar, **structural grammar;** case grammar; phrase-structure grammar; generative grammar, **transformational grammar, transformational generative grammar;** comparative grammar; tagmemic analysis; glossematics; stratificational grammar; **parsing,** construing, grammatical analysis; **morphology** 526.3; **phonology** 524.13, good grammar, good English, Standard English, correct grammar

2 syntax, structure, syntactic structure, word order, word arrangement; syntactics, syntactic analysis; immediate constituent analysis *or* IC analysis,

cutting; phrase structure; surface structure, shallow structure, deep structure, underlying structure; levels, ranks, strata; tagmeme, form-function unit, slot, filler, slot *and* filler; **function, subject, predicate, complement, object,** direct object, indirect object, **modifier,** qualifier, sentence *or* construction modifier, appositive, attribute, attributive; inflection, diminuitive, intensive, formative; asyndeton, syndeton, apposition, hypotaxis, parataxis

3 part of speech, form class, major form class, function class; function *or* empty *or* form word; **adjective,** adjectival, attributive; **adverb,** adverbial; **preposition;** verbal adjective, gerundive; **participle,** present participle, past participle, perfect participle; **conjunction,** subordinating conjunction, coordinating conjunction, conjunctive adverb, adversative conjunction, copula, copulative, copulative conjunction, correlative conjunction, disjunctive, disjunctive conjunction; **interjection,** exclamatory noun *or* adjective; **particle**

4 verb, transitive, transitive verb, intransitive, intransitive verb, impersonal verb, neuter verb, deponent verb, defective verb, reflexive verb; predicate; finite verb; linking verb, copula; verbal, verbid, nonfinite verb form; **infinitive; auxiliary verb,** auxiliary, modal auxiliary; phrasal verb; verb phrase; present participle, past participle, perfect participle

5 noun, pronoun, substantive, substantival, common noun, proper noun, concrete noun, abstract noun, collective noun, quotation noun, hypostasis, adherent noun, adverbial noun; verbal noun, gerund; nominal; noun phrase; mass noun, count noun

6 article, definite article, indefinite article; determiner, noun determiner, determinative, post-determiner

7 person; first person; second person, proximate; third person; fourth person, obviative

8 number; singular, dual, trial, plural

9 case; common case, subject case, nominative; object *or* objective case, accusative, dative, possessive case, genitive; local case, locative, essive, superessive, inessive, adessive, abessive, lative, allative, illative, sublative, elative, ablative, delative, terminative, approximative, prolative, perlative, translative; comitative, instrumental, prepositional, vocative; oblique case

10 gender, masculine, feminine, neuter, common gender; grammatical gender, natural gender; animate, inanimate

11 mood, mode; indicative, subjunctive, imperative, conditional, potential, obligative, permissive, optative, jussive

12 tense; present; historical present; **past,** preterit *or* preterite; aorist; imperfect; future; **perfect,** present perfect, future perfect; past perfect, **pluperfect;** progressive tense, durative; point tense

13 aspect; perfective, imperfective, inchoative, iterative, frequentative, desiderative

14 voice; active voice, active, passive voice, passive; middle voice, middle; medio-passive; reflexive

15 punctuation, punctuation marks <see list>; diacritical mark *or* sign <see list>, accent; reference mark <see list>, reference; point, tittle; stop, end stop

VERBS **16 grammaticize;** parse, analyze; inflect, **conjugate, decline; punctuate,** mark, point; parenthesize, hyphenate, bracket; diagram, notate

ADJS **17 grammatical, syntactical,** formal, structural; correct, well-formed; tagmemic, glossematic; **functional;** substantive, nominal, pronominal; verbal, transitive, intransitive; linking, copulative; attributive, adjectival, adverbal, participial; prepositional, post-positional; conjunctive

18 punctuation marks

ampersand <&>	interrobang <?>
angle brackets <<>>	parentheses *or* parens
apostrophe <'>	<nf> <()>
braces <{}>	period, full stop <Brit>,
brackets *or* square brackets	point, decimal point, dot
<[]>	<.>
colon <:>	question mark *or*
comma <,>	interrogation mark *or*
ellipsis, suspension periods	point <?>
<. . .> *or* <***>	quotation marks, quotes
em dash <—>	<"">
en dash <–>	semicolon <;>
exclamation mark *or* point	single quotation marks,
<!>	single quotes <''>
guillemets <<< >>>	virgule, diagonal, solidus,
hyphen <->	slash mark </>

19 diacritical marks

acute accent <´>	grave accent <`>
breve *or* caron <˘>	*haček* <Cz> *or* wedge <^>
cedilla <¸>	krozek <°>
circumflex accent	ligature <æ>
<^, *or* ~>	macron <¯>
diaeresis *or* umlaut <¨>	tilde <~>

20 reference marks

asterisk, star <*>	double prime <">
asterism <***>	index *or* fist <☞>
bullet *or* centered dot	leaders <......>
<·>	obelus <÷>
caret <>>	paragraph <¶>
dagger *or* obelisk <†>	parallels <‖>
ditto mark <">	prime <'>
double dagger *or* diesis	section <§>
<‡>	swung dash <~>

531 UNGRAMMATICALNESS

NOUNS **1 ungrammaticalness,** bad *or* faulty grammar, faulty syntax; lack of concord *or* agreement, incorrect usage, faulty reference, misplaced *or* dangling modifier, shift of tense, shift of structure, anacoluthon, faulty subordination, faulty comparison, faulty coordination, faulty punctuation, lack of parallelism, sentence fragment, comma fault, comma splice; abuse of terms, corruption of speech, broken speech

2 solecism, ungrammaticism, **misusage, missaying, misconstruction,** barbarism, infelicity; corruption; antiphrasis, spoonerism, malapropism 975.7

VERBS **3 solecize, commit a solecism, use faulty** *or* inadmissable *or* inappropriate grammar, ignore *or* disdain *or* violate grammar, murder the King's *or* Queen's English, break Priscian's head <old>

ADJS **4 ungrammatic, ungrammatical,** solecistic, solecistical, **incorrect,** barbarous; faulty, erroneous 975.16; infelicitous, improper 789.7; careless, slovenly, slipshod 810.15; loose, imprecise 975.17

532 DICTION

NOUNS **1 diction,** words, wordage, verbiage, word-usage, **usage,** *usus loquendi* <L>, use *or* choice of words, formulation, way of putting *or* couching, word garment, word dressing; **rhetoric,** speech, talk <nf>; **language,** dialect, parlance, locution, expression, **grammar** 530; **idiom;** composition

2 style; mode, manner, strain, vein; fashion, way; **rhetoric; manner of speaking,** mode of expression, literary style, style of writing, command of language *or* idiom, form of speech, expression of ideas; feeling for words *or* language, way with words, sense of language, *Sprachgefühl* <Ger>; gift of gab *or* of the gab <nf>, blarney *or* the blarney <nf>; the power *or* grace of expression; linguistic tact *or* finesse; personal style; mannerism, trick, pecularity; affectation; "the dress of thought"— Charles Dickens, "a certain absolute and unique manner of expressing a thing"—Walter Pater; editorial style; inflation, exaggeration, grandiloquence 545; the grand style, the sublime style, the sublime; the plain style; **stylistics,** stylistic analysis

3 stylist, master of style; rhetorician, rhetor, rhetorizer <old>; mannerist; wordsmith; phrasemonger

VERBS **4 phrase, express,** find a phrase for, give expression *or* words to, **word,** state, **frame,** conceive, style, couch, **put in** *or* **into words,** clothe *or* embody in words, couch in terms, express by *or* in words, find words to express, find words for;

put, present, set out; **formulate,** formularize; paragraph; rhetorize <old>

ADJS **5 phrased,** expressed, worded, formulated, styled, put, presented, couched; stylistic, overdone

533 ELEGANCE
<of language>

NOUNS **1 elegance,** elegancy; **grace,** gracefulness, gracility; **taste,** tastefulness, good taste; **correctness,** seemliness, comeliness, **propriety,** aptness, fittingness; **refinement,** precision, exactitude, lapidary quality, finish; **discrimination,** choice; **restraint; polish, finish,** terseness, neatness; smoothness, flow, **fluency; felicity,** felicitousness, **ease;** clarity, clearness, lucidity, limpidity, pellucidity, perspicuity; distinction, dignity; **purity,** chastity, chasteness; **plainness,** straightforwardness, directness, **simplicity,** naturalness, unaffectedness, Atticism, unadorned simplicity, gracility, Attic quality; classicism, classicalism; well-rounded *or* well-turned periods, flowing periods; the right word in the right place, right word at the right time, *mot juste* <Fr>; fittingness, appropriateness; classicism, Atticism

2 harmony, proportion, symmetry, **balance,** equilibrium, order, orderedness, measure, measuredness, concinnity; rhythm; **euphony,** sweetness, beauty

3 <affected elegance> **affectation,** affectedness, studiedness, **pretentiousness, mannerism,** posiness <Brit>, manneredness, artifice, artfulness, **artificiality,** unnaturalness; **euphuism,** Gongorism, Marinism; **preciousness,** preciosity; euphemism; purism; overelegance, overelaboration, overniceness, overrefinement, hyperelegance, etc

4 purist, classicist, Atticist, plain stylist

5 euphuist, Gongorist, Marinist, *précieux* and *précieuse* <Fr>; phrasemaker, phrasemonger

ADJS **6 elegant, tasteful, graceful, polished,** finished, round, terse; neat, trim, **refined, exact,** lapidary *or* lapidarian; **restrained; clear,** lucid, limpid, pellucid, perspicuous; **simple, unaffected, natural,** unlabored, fluent, flowing, **easy; pure,** chaste; **plain,** straightforward, direct, unadorned, gracile, no-frills *and* vanilla *and* plain vanilla <nf>; classic, classical; Attic, Ciceronian, Augustan

7 appropriate, fit, fitting, just <old>, **proper, correct, seemly,** comely; **felicitous,** happy, **apt, well-chosen; well-put,** well-expressed, inspired

8 harmonious, balanced, symmetrical, orderly, ordered, measured, concinnate, concinnous; **euphonious,** euphonic, euphonical <old>, sweet; **smooth,** tripping, smooth-sounding, fluent, flowing, fluid; classical

9 <affectedly elegant> **affected,** euphuistic, euphuistical; elaborate, elaborated; **pretentious, mannered, artificial, unnatural,** posy <Brit>, studied; precious, *précieux* or *précieuse* <Fr>, overnice, overrefined, overelegant, overelaborate, hyperelegant, etc; Gongoristic, Gongoresque, Marinistic

534 INELEGANCE
<of language>

NOUNS **1 inelegance,** inelegancy; inconcinnity <old>, infelicity; **clumsiness,** cumbrousness, clunkiness *and* klutziness <nf>, leadenness, heavy-handedness, ham-handedness, ham-fistedness <chiefly Brit>, heavy-footedness, heaviness, stiltedness, **ponderousness,** unwieldiness; sesquipedalianism, sesquipedality; turgidity, bombasticness, pompousness 545.1; **gracelessness,** ungracefulness; **tastelessness,** bad taste, impropriety, indecorousness, unseemliness; incorrectness, impurity; **vulgarity,** vulgarism, Gothicism <old>, barbarism, barbarousness, **coarseness, unrefinement,** roughness, grossness, rudeness, crudeness, uncouthness; turgidity; dysphemism; solecism; cacology, poor diction; cacophony, uneuphoniousness, harshness; loose *or* slipshod construction, ill-balanced sentences; lack of finish *or* polish

ADJS **2 inelegant, clumsy, clunky** *and* **klutzy** <nf>, heavy-handed, heavy-footed, ham-handed, ham-fisted <chiefly Brit>, graceless, ungraceful, inconcinnate *and* inconcinnous <old>, infelicitous, unfelicitous; **tasteless,** in bad taste, offensive to ears polite; **incorrect, improper; indecorous, unseemly,** uncourtly, undignified; **unpolished, unrefined;** impure, unclassical; **vulgar,** barbarous, barbaric, rude, **crude, uncouth,** Doric, outlandish; low, gross, **coarse,** dysphemistic, doggerel; cacologic, cacological, cacophonous, uneuphonious, harsh, ill-sounding; solecistic

3 stiff, stilted, formal, Latinate, *guindé* <Fr>, **labored,** ponderous, elephantine, lumbering, cumbrous, leaden, heavy, unwieldy, sesquipedalian, inkhorn, turgid, bombastic, pompous 545.8; **forced,** awkward, cramped, halting; crabbed

535 PLAIN SPEECH

NOUNS **1 plain speech,** plain speaking, plain-spokenness, plain style, unadorned style, gracility, **plain English,** plain words, common speech, vernacular, household words, words of one syllable; **plainness,** simpleness, simplicity; "more matter with less art"—Shakespeare; soberness, restrainedness; severity, austerity; spareness, leanness, baldness, bareness, starkness, unadornedness, naturalness, unaffectedness; **directness, straightforwardness,** calling a spade a spade, mincing no words, making no bones about it <nf>; unimaginativeness, prosaicness, matter-of-factness, prosiness, unpoeticalness; homespun, rustic style; **candor,** frankness, openness

VERBS **2 speak plainly,** waste no words, **call a spade a spade,** come to the point, lay it on the line, not beat about the bush, mince no words, make no bones about it *and* talk turkey <nf>

ADJS **3 plain-speaking,** simple-speaking; **plain,** common; **simple,** unadorned, unvarnished, pure, neat; sober, severe, austere, ascetic, spare, lean, bald, bare, stark, Spartan; **natural, unaffected;** direct, straightforward, woman-to-woman, man-to-man, one-on-one; commonplace, homely, homespun, rustic; **candid,** up-front <nf>, plain-spoken, frank, straight-out <nf>, open; **prosaic,** prosing, prosy; unpoetical, unimaginative, dull, dry, **matter-of-fact**

ADVS **4 plainly, simply,** naturally, unaffectedly, matter-of-factly; in plain words, plain-spokenly, **in plain English,** in words of one syllable; **directly,** point-blank, to the point; candidly, frankly

PHRS **5** read my lips, I'll spell it out

536 FIGURE OF SPEECH

NOUNS **1 figure of speech** <see list>, **figure, image,** trope, turn of expression, manner *or* way of speaking, ornament, device, flourish, flower; purple passage; imagery, nonliterality, nonliteralness, figurativeness, figurative language; figured *or* florid *or* flowery style, Gongorism, floridity, euphuism

VERBS **2** metaphorize, figure <old>; similize; personify, personalize; symbolize

ADJS **3 figurative,** tropologic, tropological; **metaphorical,** trolatitious; allusive, referential; mannered, figured, ornamented, **flowery** 545.11

ADVS **4 figuratively,** tropologically; **metaphorically;** symbolically; **figuratively speaking,** so to say *or* speak, in a manner of speaking, **as it were**

5 figures of speech (literary devices)

adynaton	antanaclasis
agnomination	anthimeria
alliteration	antimetabole
allusion	antiphrasis
anacoluthon	antisthecon
anadiplosis	antithesis
analogy	antonomasia
anaphora	aphaersis
anapodoton	apocope
anastrophe	apophasis
aporia	malapropism
aposiopesis	meiosis
apostrophe	metalepsis
auxesis	metaphor
catachresis	metathesis
chiasmus	metonymy
circumlocution	mixed metaphor
climax	occupatio
congeries	onomatopoeia, onomatopy
conversion	oxymoron
correctio	paradiastole
ecphonesis	paradox
ellipsis	paragoge
emphasis	paralepsis
enallage	paregmenon
epanalepsis	parenthesis
epanaphora	periphrasis
epanodos	personification
epanorthosis	pleonasm
epenthesis	ploce
epidiplosis	polyptoton
epiphora	polysyndeton
epistrophe	preterition
epizeuxis	prolepsis
eroteme	prosopopoeia
exclamation	prosthesis
gemination	regression
gradatio	repetition
hendiadys	rhetorical question
hypallage	sarcasm
hyperbaton	scesis onamaton
hyperbole	simile, similitude
hypozeugma	spoonerism
hypozeuxis	syllepsis
hysteron proteron	symploce
inversion	syncope
irony	synecdoche
isocolon	tautology
kenning	Wellerism
litotes	zeugma

537 CONCISENESS

NOUNS **1 conciseness,** concision, briefness, brachylogy, **brevity,** "the soul of wit"— Shakespeare; shortness, compactness; **curtness,** brusqueness, **crispness, terseness,** summariness; compression; taciturnity 344.2, reserve 344.3; **pithiness,** succinctness, pointedness, sententiousness; compendiousness; heart of the matter

2 laconicness, laconism, laconicism, economy of language *or* words; laconics

3 aphorism, epigram 974.1; **abridgment** 557

4 abbreviation, shortening, clipping, cutting, pruning, truncation; ellipsis, aposiopesis, contraction, syncope, apocope, elision, crasis, syneresis <all rhetoric>

VERBS **5 be brief, come to the point,** get to the

bottom line *or* the nitty-gritty <nf>, **make a long story short,** cut the matter short, cut the shit <nf>, be telegraphic, waste no words, put it in few words, give more matter and less art; shorten, condense, **abbreviate** 268.6

ADJS **6 concise, brief, short,** "short and sweet"— Thomas Lodge; **condensed, compressed,** tight, close, compact; compendious 268.8; **curt,** brusque, **crisp, terse,** summary; taciturn 344.9; reserved 344.10; **pithy, succinct; laconic,** Spartan; **abridged, abbreviated,** vest-pocket, synopsized, shortened, clipped, cut, pruned, contracted, truncated, docked; elliptic, syncopic, aposiopestic; telegraphic; sententious, epigrammatic, epigrammatical, gnomic, aphoristic *or* aphoristical, **pointed,** to the point; brachylogous

ADVS **7 concisely, briefly,** shortly, standing on one leg; laconically; **curtly,** brusquely, **crisply, tersely,** summarily; **pithily, succinctly,** pointedly; sententiously, aphoristically, epigrammatically

8 in brief, in short, for short, *tout court* <Fr>; in substance, in epitome, in outline; **in a nutshell,** in a capsule; **in a word,** in two words, in a few words, without wasting *or* mincing words; **to be brief,** to the point, to sum up, to come to the point, to cut the matter short, **to make a long story short**

538 DIFFUSENESS

NOUNS **1 diffuseness,** diffusiveness, diffusion; shapelessness, **formlessness** 263, amorphousness, blobbiness <nf>, unstructuredness; obscurity 522.3

2 wordiness, verbosity, verbiage, verbalism, verbality; **prolixity, long-windedness,** longiloquence, loquacity; flow *or* flux of words, cloud of words; profuseness, **profusiveness,** profusion; **effusiveness,** effusion, gush, gushing; outpour, tirade; logorrhea, verbal diarrhea, diarrhea of the mouth, **talkativeness** 540; **copiousness, exuberance,** rampancy, amplitude, extravagance, prodigality, fertility, fecundity, rankness, teemingness, prolificity, prolificacy, productivity, abundance, overflow, fluency <old>; superfluity, superflux, superabundance, overflow, inundation; **redundancy,** pleonasm, repetitiveness, reiterativeness, reiteration, iteration, tautology, macrology, double-talk; repetition for effect *or* emphasis, palilogy

3 discursiveness, desultoriness, digressiveness, aimlessness; rambling, maundering, meandering, wandering, roving

4 digression, departure, deviation, **discursion,** excursion, excursus, sidetrack, side path, side road, byway, bypath; episode; rambling

5 circumlocution, roundaboutness, circuitousness, ambages <old>; deviousness, obliqueness, **indirection;** periphrase, periphrasis; ambagiousness

6 amplification, expatiation, enlargement, expansion, dilation, dilatation, dilating; **elaboration, laboring; development,** explication, unfolding, working-out, fleshing-out, detailing, filling in the empty places, filler, padding

VERBS **7 amplify, expatiate, dilate, expand,** enlarge, **enlarge upon,** expand on, **elaborate;** relate *or* rehearse in extenso; detail, particularize; **develop,** open out, fill in, flesh out, evolve, unfold; work out, explicate; descant, relate at large

8 protract, extend, spin out, string out, draw out, stretch out, go on *or* be on about, **drag out,** run out, drive into the ground <nf>; pad, fill out; perorate; **speak at length,** spin a long yarn, never finish; verbify, chatter, talk one to death 540.5,6

9 digress, wander, **get off the subject, wander from the subject,** get sidetracked, excurse, ramble, maunder, stray, go astray; depart, **deviate,** turn aside, jump the track; **go off on a tangent,** go up blind alleys

10 circumlocute <nf>, say in a roundabout way, talk in circles, **go round about,** go around and around, **beat around *or* about the bush,** go round Robin Hood's barn; periphrase

ADJS **11 diffuse,** diffusive; **formless** 263.4, unstructured; **profuse,** profusive; **effusive,** gushing, gushy; copious, exuberant, extravagant, prodigal, fecund, teeming, prolific, productive, abundant, superabundant, overflowing; **redundant,** pleonastic, repetitive, reiterative, iterative, tautologous, parrotlike

12 wordy, verbose; talkative 540.9; **prolix,** windy <nf>, **long-winded,** longiloquent; **protracted,** extended, *de longue haleine* <Fr>, lengthy, long, **long-drawn-out,** long-spun, spun-out, endless, unrelenting; padded, filled out

13 discursive, aimless, loose; **rambling, maundering, wandering,** peripatetic, roving, deviating; excursive, discursive, **digressive,** deviative, **desultory,** episodic; by the way; sidetracked

14 circumlocutory, circumlocutional, **roundabout, circuitous,** ambagious <old>, oblique, indirect; periphrastic

15 expatiating, dilative, dilatative, enlarging, amplifying, expanding; **developmental**

ADVS **16 at length,** *ad nauseam* <L>, at large, in full, *in extenso* <L>, in detail, on and on

539 AMBIGUITY

NOUNS **1 ambiguity,** ambiguousness; **equivocalness,** equivocacy, equivocality; **double meaning,** amphibology, multivocality, polysemy, polysemousness; punning, paronomasia; double reference, double entendre; twilight zone, gray area; six of one and half dozen of the other; inexplicitness, uncertainty 971; irony, contradiction, oxymoron, enantiosis; levels of meaning, richness of meaning, complexity of meaning

2 <ambiguous word or expression> **ambiguity,** equivoque, equivocal, equivocality; equivocation, amphibology, double entendre; counterword, portmanteau word; polysemant; weasel word; squinting construction; pun 489.8

VERBS **3** equivocate, weasel; ironize; have mixed feelings, be uncertain 971.9

ADJS **4 ambiguous, equivocal,** equivocatory; multivocal, polysemous, polysemantic, amphibolous, amphibological; two-edged, two-sided, either-or, betwixt and between; bittersweet, mixed; inexplicit, uncertain 971.15; ironic; obscure, mysterious, funny, funny peculiar <nf>, enigmatic 522.17

540 TALKATIVENESS

NOUNS **1 talkativeness, loquacity,** loquaciousness; overtalkativeness, loose tongue, runaway tongue, big mouth <nf>; gabbiness *and* windiness *and* gassiness <nf>; **garrulousness,** garrulity; **long-windedness, prolixity, verbosity** 538.2; multiloquence, multiloquy; **volubility, fluency, glibness;** fluent tongue, flowing tongue, **gift of gab** <nf>; openness, candor, frankness 644.4; effusion, gush, slush; gushiness, **effusiveness,** communicativeness; flow *or* flux *or* spate of words; *flux de bouche, flux de mots,* and *flux de paroles* <Fr>; **communicativeness** 343.3; gregariousness, sociability, conversableness 582

2 logomania, logorrhea, diarrhea of the mouth, verbal diarrhea, *cacoëthes loquendi* and *furor loquendi* <L>, gift of gab

3 chatter, jabber, gibber, **babble,** babblement, prate, **prating, prattle, palaver,** small talk, chat, natter <Brit>, **gabble, gab** *and* jaw-jaw <nf>, blab, **blabber, blather,** blether, blethers <Scot>, clatter, clack, cackle, talkee-talkee; *caquet* and *caqueterie* and *bavardage* <Fr>, twaddle, twattle, **gibble-gabble, bibble-babble, chitter-chatter, prittle-prattle, tittle-tattle,** mere talk, idle talk *or* chatter; **guff** *and* **gas** *and* **hot air** *and* blah-blah *and* yak *and* yakkety-yak *and* blah-blah-blah <nf>; **gossip;** nonsense talk 520.2

4 chatterer, chatterbox, babbler, jabberer, prater, prattler, gabbler, gibble-gabbler, **gabber** <nf>, **blabberer, blabber,** blatherer, patterer, word-slinger, *moulin à paroles* <Fr>, blab, rattle, bigmouth; magpie, jay, informer; **windbag** *and* gasbag *and* windjammer *and* hot-air artist *and* motor-mouth *and* ratchet-jaw *and* blabbermouth<nf>; idle chatterer, talkative person, **big** *or* **great talker** <nf>, nonstop talker, spendthrift of one's tongue

VERBS **5 chatter, chat, prate, prattle, patter,** palaver, **babble, gab** <nf>, natter <Brit>, **gabble, gibble-gabble,** tittle-tattle, **jabber,** gibber, **blab, blabber, blather,** blether, clatter, twaddle, twattle, rattle, clack, haver <Brit>, dither, spout *or* **spout off** <nf>, hold forth, pour forth, spin out, **gush,** have a big mouth <nf>, love the sound of one's own voice, talk to hear one's head rattle <nf>; **jaw** *and* **gas** *and* yak *and* **yakkety-yak** *and* run off at the mouth *and* beat one's gums <nf>, **shoot off one's mouth** *or* **face** <nf>; reel off; **talk on,** talk away, **go on** <nf>, run on, rattle on, run on like a mill race; ramble on; talk oneself hoarse, talk till one is blue in the face, talk oneself out of breath; "varnish nonsense with the charms of sound"—Charles Churchill; **talk too much; gossip;** talk nonsense 520.5

6 <nf terms> **talk one to death, talk one's head** *or* **ear off,** talk one deaf *and* dumb, talk one into a fever, talk the hind leg off a mule, like the sound of one's own voice, oil one's tongue

7 outtalk, outspeak, talk down, outlast; filibuster

8 be loquacious *or* garrulous, be a windbag *or* gasbag <nf>; have a big mouth *or* bazoo <nf>

ADJS **9 talkative, loquacious, talky,** big-mouthed <nf>, overtalkative, garrulous, running on, chatty; gossipy, newsy; gabby *and* windy *and* gassy <nf>, all jaw <nf>; multiloquent, multiloquious; **longwinded, prolix, verbose** 538.12; **voluble, fluent; glib,** flip <nf>, smooth; candid, frank 644.17; **effusive,** gushy; expansive, **communicative;** conversational; gregarious, sociable

10 chattering, prattling, prating, gabbling, jabbering, gibbering, babbling, blabbing, blabbering, blathering

ADVS **11 talkatively, loquaciously,** garrulously; **volubly, fluently,** glibly; effusively, expansively, gushingly

541 CONVERSATION

NOUNS **1 conversation, converse,** conversing, rapping <nf>; interlocution, colloquy; **exchange;** verbal intercourse, conversational interchange, interchange of speech, give-and-take, cross-talk, rapping <nf>, **repartee,** backchat; **discourse,** colloquial discourse; **communion, intercourse,** social intercourse, **communication** 343

2 **the art of conversation,** "a game of circles," "our account of ourselves"—both Emerson; "the feast of reason and the flow of soul"—Pope

3 **talk, palaver, speech, words;** confabulation, **confab** <nf>, banter, repartee; **chinfest** and **chinwag** and **talkfest** and **bull session** <nf>; **dialogue,** duologue, trialogue; **interview,** question-and-answer session, audience, audition, interlocution; interrogation, examination

4 **chat,** cozy chat, friendly chat or talk, **little talk,** coze, causerie, **visit** <nf>, gam, *tête-à-tête* <Fr>, **heart-to-heart talk** or heart-to-heart; pillow-talk, intimate discourse, backchat

5 **chitchat,** chitter-chatter, tittle-tattle, **small talk,** by-talk, cocktail-party chitchat, beauty-parlor chitchat, tea-table talk, table talk, idle chat or talk, gossip, backchat

6 **conference, congress, convention, parley, palaver, confab** <nf>, confabulation, **conclave, powwow, huddle** <nf>, **consultation,** colloquium, *pourparler* <Fr>, **meeting;** session, sitting, sit-down <nf>, séance; exchange or interchange of views; **council,** council of war; **discussion; interview, audience; news conference,** press conference; photo opportunity, photo op <nf>; high-level talk, conference at the summit, summit, summit conference; summitry; negotiations, bargaining, bargaining session; confrontation, eyeball-to-eyeball encounter <nf>; teleconference; council fire; conference table, negotiating table

7 **discussion, debate,** debating, **deliberation, nonformalogue,** exchange of views, canvassing, ventilation, airing, review, **treatment, consideration,** investigation, **examination, study, analysis,** logical analysis; logical discussion, dialectic; buzz session <nf>, rap or rap session <nf>; **panel,** panel discussion, open discussion, joint discussion, symposium, colloquium, conference, seminar; **forum,** open forum, town meeting; polemics

8 **conversationalist,** converser, conversationist; talker, discourser, verbalist, confabulator; colloquist, colloquialist, collocutor; conversational partner; interlocutor, interlocutress or interlocutrice or interlocutrix; parleyer, palaverer; dialogist; Dr Johnson; interviewer, examiner, interrogator, cross-examiner; chatterer

VERBS 9 **converse, talk together, talk** or **speak with,** converse with, strike up a conversation, visit with <nf>, discourse with, **commune with,** communicate with, take counsel with, commerce with, **have a talk with,** have a word with, **chin** <nf>, **chew the rag** or **fat** <nf>, **shoot the breeze** <nf>, hold or carry on or join in or engage in a conversation, exchange words; confabulate, confab

<nf>, parley; colloque, colloquize; "inject a few raisins of conversation into the tasteless dough of existence"—O Henry; **bandy words; communicate** 343.6,7

10 **chat, visit** <nf>, gam, coze, pass the time of day, touch base with, have a friendly or cozy chat; **have a little talk,** have a heart-to-heart, let one's hair down; talk with one in private, talk tête-à-tête, be closeted with, make conversation or talk, engage in small talk; prattle, prittle-prattle, tittle-tattle; **gossip**

11 **confer,** hold a conference, parley, palaver, powwow, hold talks, hold a summit, sit down together, meet around the conference table, **go into a huddle** <nf>, deliberate, take counsel, counsel, **lay** or **put heads together;** collogue; **confer with,** sit down with, **consult with, advise with, discuss with, take up with,** reason with; **discuss,** talk over; **consult,** refer to, call in; **compare notes,** exchange observations or views; have conversations; negotiate, bargain

12 **discuss, debate, reason, deliberate,** deliberate upon, exchange views or opinions, talk, **talk over, hash over** <nf>, talk of or about, rap <nf>, exchange ideas, colloquize, comment upon, reason about, discourse about, **consider, treat,** dissertate on, handle, deal with, take up, **go into, examine,** investigate, talk out, brainstorm, **analyze,** sift, **study,** canvass, review, pass under review, controvert, ventilate, air, thrash or thresh out, reason the point, consider the pros and cons; **kick** or **knock around** <nf>

ADJS 13 conversational, colloquial, confabulatory, interlocutory; communicative; chatty, chitchatty, cozy

ADVS 14 conversationally, colloquially; *tête-à-tête* <Fr>

542 SOLILOQUY

NOUNS 1 **soliloquy,** monology, self-address; **monologue;** aside; solo; monodrama; monody; interior monologue, stream of consciousness, apostrophe, aside; one-man or -woman show

2 **soliloquist,** soliloquizer, Hamlet; monodist, **monologist**

VERBS 3 **soliloquize,** monologize; **talk to oneself,** say to oneself, tell oneself, think out loud or aloud; address the four walls, talk to the wall; have an audience of one; say aside, apostrophize; do all the talking, monopolize the conversation, hold forth without interruption

ADJS 4 soliloquizing, monologic, monological, self-addressing; apostrophic; soloistic; monodramatic; thinking aloud, talking to oneself

543 PUBLIC SPEAKING

NOUNS **1 public speaking, declamation, speechmaking, speaking,** speechification <nf>, lecturing, speeching; after-dinner speaking; **oratory,** platform oratory *or* speaking; campaign oratory, stump speaking, the stump, the hustings <Brit>; the soap box; **elocution; rhetoric,** art of public speaking; **eloquence** 544; forensics, **debating;** speechcraft, wordcraft; **preaching,** pulpit oratory, Bible-thumping <nf>, the pulpit, homiletics; demagogism, demagogy <chiefly Brit>, demagoguery, rabble-rousing; **pyrotechnics**

2 speech, speeching, speechification <nf>, **talk, oration, address,** declamation, harangue; public speech *or* address, formal speech, set speech, prepared speech *or* text; welcoming address, farewell address; campaign speech, stump speech, stump oratory; soapbox oratory, tub-thumping <nf>; say; **tirade,** screed, **diatribe,** jeremiad, philippic, invective; after-dinner speech; funeral oration, eulogy; allocution, exhortation, hortatory address, forensic, forensic address; **recitation,** recital, reading; salutatory, salutatory address; valediction, valedictory, valedictory address; inaugural address, inaugural; chalk talk <nf>; pep talk <nf>; pitch, sales talk 734.5; talkathon, filibuster; peroration; debate

3 lecture, prelection, **discourse; sermon,** sermonette, homily, religious *or* pulpit discourse; preachment, preaching, preachification <nf>; **evangelism,** televison *or* TV evangelism; travel talk, travelogue

4 speaker, talker, public speaker, speechmaker, speecher, speechifier <nf>, spieler *and* jawsmith <nf>; after-dinner speaker; **spokesperson,** spokesman, spokeswoman; **demagogue,** rabble-rouser; declaimer, ranter, tub-thumper <nf>, haranguer, spouter <nf>; valedictorian, salutatorian; panelist, debater

5 lecturer, praelector, discourser, reader; **preacher;** sermonizer, sermonist, sermoner, homilist <old>, pulpitarian, pulpiteer <nf>, Boanerges, hellfire preacher; **evangelist,** televison *or* TV evangelist, televangelist; **expositor,** expounder; chalk talker <nf>

6 orator, public speaker, platform orator *or* speaker; rhetorician, rhetor; silver-tongued orator, **spellbinder;** Demosthenes, Cicero, Franklin D Roosevelt, Winston Churchill, William Jennings Bryan, Martin Luther King Jr.; **soapbox orator,** soapboxer, stump orator

7 elocutionist, elocutioner; **recitationist,** reciter, diseur, diseuse; reader; improvisator, *improvvisatore* <Ital>

8 rhetorician, teacher of rhetoric, rhetor, elocutionist; speech-writer

VERBS **9 make a speech, give a talk, deliver an address,** speechify <nf>, **speak, talk, discourse; address;** stump <nf>, go on *or* take the stump; platform, soapbox; take the floor

10 declaim, hold forth, **orate,** elocute <nf>, spout <nf>, spiel <nf>, mouth; **harangue, rant,** "out-herod Herod"—Shakespeare, tub-thump, perorate, rodomontade; **recite,** read; debate; demagogue, rabble-rouse

11 lecture, prelect, read *or* deliver a lecture; **preach,** Bible-thump *and* preachify <nf>, **sermonize,** read a sermon

ADJS **12 declamatory, elocutionary, oratorical, rhetorical,** forensic; eloquent 544.8; demagogic, demagogical

544 ELOQUENCE

NOUNS **1 eloquence, rhetoric, silver tongue,** eloquent tongue, facundity; **articulateness;** gift of gab <nf>, **glibness,** smoothness, slickness; **felicitousness,** felicity; **oratory** 543.1; expression, **expressiveness,** command of words *or* language, gift of gab *or* of the gab <nf>, gift of expression, vividness, graphicness; pleasing *or* effective style; **meaningfulness** 518.5

2 fluency, flow; **smoothness, facility, ease; grace,** gracefulness, poetry; **elegance** 533

3 vigor, force, power, strength, vitality, drive, sinew, sinewiness, nervousness, nervosity, vigorousness, forcefulness, effectiveness, impressiveness, pizzazz *and* punch *and* clout <nf>; incisiveness, trenchancy, cuttingness, poignancy, bitingness, bite, mordancy; strong language, "thoughts that breathe and words that burn"—Thomas Gray

4 spirit, pep <nf>, liveliness, raciness, sparkle, vivacity, dash, verve, vividness; piquancy, poignancy, pungency

5 vehemence, passion, impassionedness, enthusiasm, **ardor,** ardency, **fervor,** fervency, fire, fieriness, glow, warmth

6 loftiness, elevation, sublimity; grandeur, **nobility,** stateliness, majesty, gravity, *gravitas* <L>, solemnity, **dignity**

VERBS **7 have the gift of gab** *or* **of the gab** <nf>, have a tongue in one's head; **spellbind;** shine

ADJS **8 eloquent, silver-tongued,** silver; well-speaking, well-spoken, **articulate,** facund; **glib, smooth,** smooth-spoken, smooth-tongued, **slick; felicitous;** facile, slick as a whistle <nf>, spellbinding; Demosthenic, Demosthenian; Ciceronian, Tullian

9 **fluent, flowing,** tripping; **smooth,** pleasing, facile, **easy, graceful, elegant** 533.6

10 **expressive, graphic, vivid,** suggestive, imaginative; well-turned; **meaningful** 518.10

11 **vigorous,** strong, **powerful,** imperative, **forceful,** forcible, vital, driving, sinewy, sinewed, punchy *and* full of piss and vinegar *and* zappy <nf>, **striking, telling, effective,** impressive; incisive, trenchant, cutting, biting, piercing, poignant, penetrating, slashing, mordant, acid, corrosive; sensational

12 **spirited, lively,** peppy *and* gingery <nf>, racy, sparkling, vivacious; piquant, poignant, pungent

13 **vehement,** emphatic, **passionate, impassioned,** enthusiastic, **ardent,** fiery, **fervent,** burning, glowing, warm; urgent, stirring, exciting, stimulating, provoking

14 **lofty, elevated, sublime, grand, majestic,** noble, stately, grave, solemn, dignified; serious, weighty; moving, inspiring

ADVS 15 **eloquently; fluently,** smoothly, glibly, trippingly on the tongue; **expressively,** vividly, graphically; **meaningfully** 518.13; **vigorously,** powerfully, forcefully, spiritedly; tellingly, strikingly, effectively, impressively; **vehemently, passionately,** ardently, fervently, warmly, glowingly, in glowing terms

545 GRANDILOQUENCE

NOUNS 1 **grandiloquence,** magniloquence, lexiphanicism, **pompousness,** pomposity, orotundity; **rhetoric,** mere rhetoric, rhetoricalness; high-flown diction, big *or* tall talk <nf>; grandioseness, grandiosity; loftiness, stiltedness; fulsomeness; **pretentiousness,** pretension, **affectation** 533.3; ostentation; **flamboyancy,** showiness, flashiness, gaudiness, meretriciousness, bedizenment, **glitz** <nf>, garishness; sensationalism, luridness, Barnumism; **inflation, inflatedness,** swollenness, turgidity, turgescence, flatulence *or* flatulency, tumidness, tumidity; sententiousness, pontification; swollen phrase *or* diction, swelling utterance; platitudinous ponderosity, polysyllabic profundity, pompous prolixity; Johnsonese; prose run mad; convolution, tortuosity, tortuousness, ostentatious complexity *or* profundity

2 **bombast,** bombastry, pomposity, **fustian,** highfalutin <nf>, **rant,** rodomontade; **hot air** <nf>; balderdash, gobbledygook <nf>, purple prose

3 high-sounding words, lexiphanicism, hard words; **sesquipedalian word,** big *or* long word, twodollar *or* five-dollar word <nf>, **jawbreaker,** jawtwister,

mouthful; antidisestablishmentarianism, honorificabilitudinitatibus <Shakespeare>, pneumonoultramicroscopicsilicovolcanoconiosis; polysyllabism, sesquipedalianism, sesquipedality; Latinate diction; academic Choctaw, technical jargon

4 **ornateness, floweriness,** floridness, floridity, lushness, luxuriance; flourish, flourish of rhetoric, flowers of speech *or* rhetoric, **purple patches** *or* **passages,** beauties, fine writing; **ornament,** ornamentation, **adornment, embellishment,** elegant variation, **embroidery, frill,** colors *or* colors of rhetoric <old>, figure, **figure of speech** 536

5 **phrasemonger,** rhetorician; phraseman, phrasemaker, fine writer, wordspinner; euphuist, Gongorist, Marinist; pedant

VERBS 6 **talk big** <nf>, talk highfalutin <nf>, phrasemake, **pontificate, blow** <nf>, **vapor,** Barnumize; inflate, bombast, lay *or* pile it on <nf>, lay it on thick *and* lay it on with a trowel <nf>; smell of the lamp

7 **ornament, decorate, adorn, embellish, embroider,** enrich; overcharge, overlay, overload, load with ornament, festoon, weight down with ornament, flourish <old>; **gild,** gild the lily, trick out, varnish; paint in glowing colors, tell in glowing terms; "to gild refined gold, to paint the lily, to throw a perfume on the violet"—Shakespeare; elaborate, convolute, involve

ADJS 8 **grandiloquent,** magniloquent, **pompous, orotund; grandiose;** fulsome; lofty, elevated, tall <nf>, **stilted; pretentious,** affected 533.9; overdone, overwrought; **showy, flashy, ostentatious,** gaudy, glitzy <nf>, meretricious, flamboyant, flaming, bedizened, flaunting, garish; lurid, sensational, sensationalistic; **high-flown, high-falutin** <nf>, high-flying; high-flowing, **high-sounding, big-sounding,** great-sounding, grandisonant <old>, sonorous; **rhetorical,** declamatory; **pedantic,** inkhorn, lexiphanic <old>; sententious, Johnsonian; convoluted, tortuous, labyrinthine, overelaborate, overinvolved; euphuistic, Gongoresque

9 **bombastic,** fustian, mouthy, **inflated, swollen,** swelling, turgid, turgescent, tumid, tumescent, flatulent, windy *and* gassy <nf>; overadorned, fulsome

10 sesquipedalian, sesquipedal, polysyllabic, jawbreaking *and* jawtwisting <nf>

11 **ornate,** purple <nf>, colored, **fancy;** adorned, **embellished, embroidered,** lavish, decorated, festooned, overcharged, overloaded, befrilled; **flowery, florid,** lush, luxuriant; figured, **figurative** 536.3

ADVS 12 **grandiloquently,** magniloquently,

pompously, grandiosely, fulsomely, loftily, stiltedly, pretentiously; **ostentatiously,** showily; **bombastically,** turgidly, tumidly, flatulently, windily <nf>

13 **ornately,** fancily; **flowerily,** floridly

546 LETTER

NOUNS 1 **letter, written character, character, sign, symbol,** graph, digraph, grapheme, allograph, alphabetic character *or* symbol, phonetic character *or* symbol; diacritic, diacritical mark, vowel point; logographic *or* lexigraphic character *or* symbol; ideographic *or* ideogrammic *or* ideogrammatic character *or* symbol; initial; syllabic character *or* symbol, syllabic, syllabogram; pictographic character *or* symbol; cipher, device; monogram; graphy, *mater lectionis* <L>; **writing** 547

2 <phonetic *and* ideographic symbols> **phonogram;** phonetic symbol; **logogram,** logograph, grammalogue; word letter; **ideogram,** ideograph, phonetic, radical, determinative; **pictograph,** pictogram; **hieroglyphic,** hieroglyph, hieratic symbol, demotic character; **rune,** runic character *or* symbol; **cuneiform, character;** wedge, arrowhead, ogham; kana, hiragana, katakana; kanji; **shorthand** 547.8; hieroglyphics

3 **writing system, script, letters; alphabet,** letters of the alphabet, **ABC's;** christcross-row; **phonetic alphabet,** International Phonetic Alphabet *or* IPA; Initial Teaching Alphabet *or* ITA; phonemic alphabet; runic alphabet, futhark *or* futharc; alphabetism; **syllabary;** alphabetics, alphabetology, graphemics; paleography; speech sound 524.12

4 **spelling,** orthography; phonetic spelling *or* respelling, phonetics, phonography; normalization; spelling reform; spelling match *or* bee, spelldown; bad spelling, cacography; spelling pronunciation

5 **lettering,** initialing; **inscription,** epigraph, graffito, printing; handwriting; alphabetization; transliteration, romanization, pin-yin *or* pinyin, Wade-Giles system; transcription; phonetic transcription, phonography, lexigraphy

VERBS 6 **letter, initial, inscribe,** character, sign, mark; **capitalize; alphabetize,** alphabet; transliterate, transcribe

7 **spell,** orthographize; spell *or* respell phonetically; spell out, write out, trace out; spell backward; outspell, spell down; syllabify, syllabize, syllable, syllabicate

ADJS 8 **literal, lettered; alphabetic, alphabetical;** abecedarian; graphemic, allographic; large-lettered, majuscule, majuscular, uncial; **capital,** capitalized, upper-case; small-lettered, minuscule, minuscular, lower-case; logographic,

logogrammatic, lexigraphic, ideographic, ideogrammic, ideogrammatic, pictographic; transliterated, transcribed; orthographic, spelled; symbolical, phonogramic, phonographic, cuneiform, cuneal, hieroglyphic, hieroglyphical

547 WRITING

NOUNS 1 **writing,** scrivening *or* scrivenery <old>, inscription, lettering; engrossment; pen, **pen-and-ink;** inkslinging *and* ink spilling <nf>, pen *or* pencil driving *or* pushing <nf>; **typing, typewriting;** macrography, micrography; stroke *or* dash of the pen, *coup de plume* <Fr>; secret writing, cryptography 345.6; **alphabet, writing system** 546.3

2 **authorship, writing,** authorcraft, pencraft, wordsmanship, **composition,** the art of composition, inditing, inditement; one's pen; **creative writing,** literary art, verbal art, literary composition, literary production, verse-writing, short-story writing, novel-writing, playwriting, drama-writing; essay-writing; **expository writing;** technical writing; journalism, newspaper writing, investigative reporting, editorial-writing, feature-writing, rewriting; magazine writing; songwriting, lyric-writing, libretto-writing; artistry, literary power, literary artistry, literary talent *or* flair, skill with words *or* language, facility in writing, ready pen; **writer's itch,** graphomania, scribblemania, graphorrhea, *cacoëthes scribendi* <L>; automatic writing; writer's cramp, graphospasm

3 **handwriting, hand, script,** fist <nf>, chirography, **calligraphy,** autography; **manuscript,** scrive <Scot>; **autograph,** holograph; **penmanship,** penscript, pencraft; stylography; graphology, graphanalysis, graphometry; paleography

4 handwriting style; **printing,** handprinting, block letter, **lettering; stationery; writing materials,** paper, foolscap, note paper, pad, papyrus, parchment, tracing paper, typing paper, vellum

5 <good writing> **calligraphy,** fine writing, elegant penmanship, **good hand,** fine hand, good fist <nf>, fair hand, copybook hand

6 <bad writing> **cacography, bad hand,** poor fist <nf>, cramped *or* crabbed hand, botched writing, childish scrawl, illegible handwriting, *griffonage* <Fr>

7 **scribbling,** scribblement; **scribble,** scrabble, **scrawl, scratch,** *barbouillage* <Fr>; *pattes de mouche* <Fr>, hen tracks *and* hen scratches <nf>, pothookery, pothooks, pothooks *and* hangers

8 **stenography, shorthand,** brachygraphy, tachygraphy; speedwriting; phonography, stenotype; contraction

9 **letter, written character** 546.1; **alphabet, writing system** 546.3; punctuation 530.15,18-20

10 <written matter> **writing, the written word; piece;** piece of writing, text, screed; **copy, matter;** printed matter, literature, reading matter; the written word, *literae scriptae* <L>; nonfiction; fiction 722; **composition, work,** opus, production, literary production, literary artefact *or* artifact, lucubration, brainchild; essay, article 556.1; poem; play 704.4; letter 553.2; **document** 549.5,8; **paper,** parchment, scroll; **script,** scrip, scrive <Scot>; **penscript, typescript; manuscript** *or* MS *or* Ms *or* ms, holograph, autograph; **draft,** first draft, second draft, etc, recension, **version;** edited version, finished version, final draft; transcription, transcript, fair copy, engrossment; flimsy; original, author's copy; camera-ready copy; printout, computer printout, hard copy

11 <ancient manuscript> **codex;** scroll; palimpsest, *codex rescriptus* <L>; papyrus, parchment

12 **literature, letters, belles lettres,** polite literature, humane letters, *litterae humaniores* <L>, republic of letters, writing; **work, literary work, text, literary text; works, complete works, oeuvre, canon, literary canon, author's canon;** serious literature; **classics,** ancient literature; medieval literature, Renaissance literature, etc; national literature, English literature, French literature, etc; contemporary literature; underground literature; pseudonymous literature; folk literature, oral history; travel literature; wisdom literature; erotic literature, erotica; pornographic literature, pornography, porn *and* hard porn *and* soft porn <nf>, obscene literature, scatological literature; popular literature, pop literature <nf>; kitsch

13 **writer, scribbler** <nf>, **penman,** pen, penner; pen *or* pencil driver *or* pusher <nf>, word-slinger, **inkslinger** *and* ink spiller <nf>, knight of the plume *or* pen *or* quill <nf>; **scribe, scrivener, amanuensis, secretary,** recording secretary, **clerk;** letterer; **copyist,** copier, transcriber; chirographer, calligrapher

14 **writing expert,** graphologist, handwriting expert, graphometrist; paleographer

15 **author, writer,** scribe <nf>, composer, inditer; authoress, penwoman; **creative writer,** *littérateur* <Fr>, literary artist, literary craftsman *or* artisan *or* journeyman, belletrist, man of letters, literary man; wordsmith, word painter; free lance, free-lance writer; ghostwriter, ghost <nf>; collaborator, coauthor; prose writer, logographer; fiction writer, fictioneer <nf>; story writer, **short story writer;** storyteller; **novelist;** novelettist; diarist; **newspaperman; annalist;** poet 720.13; **dramatist,** humorist 489.12; scriptwriter, scenario writer,

scenarist; nonfiction writer; article writer, magazine writer; **essayist;** monographer; reviewer, critic, literary critic, music critic, art critic, drama critic, dance critic; columnist; pamphleteer; technical writer; copywriter, advertising writer; compiler, encyclopedist, bibliographer

16 **hack writer,** hack, literary hack, Grub Street writer <Brit>, **penny-a-liner, scribbler** <nf>, **potboiler** <nf>

17 **stenographer,** brachygrapher, tachygrapher; phonographer, stenotypist

18 **typist,** keyboarder; printer

VERBS 19 **write, pen, pencil,** drive *or* push the pen *or* pencil <nf>; stain *or* spoil paper <nf>, shed *or* spill ink <nf>, **scribe,** scrive <Scot>; inscribe, scroll; superscribe; enface; take pen in hand; **put in writing,** put in black and white; **draw up, draft, write out,** make out; **write down, record** 549.16; take down in shorthand; **type; transcribe,** copy out, engross, make a fair copy, copy; trace; **rewrite, revise, edit,** recense, make a recension, make a critical revision; highlight

20 **scribble,** scrabble, **scratch, scrawl,** make hen tracks *or* hen *or* chicken scratches <nf>, doodle

21 **write,** author, **compose, indite,** formulate, produce, prepare; dash off, knock off *or* out <nf>, throw on paper, pound *or* crank *or* grind *or* churn out; free-lance; collaborate, coauthor; ghostwrite, ghost <nf>; novelize; scenarize; pamphleteer; editorialize

ADJS 22 **written,** penned, penciled, lettered, literal, graphical, typed; **inscribed;** engrossed; **in writing, in black and white,** on paper; scriptural, scriptorial, graphic; calligraphic, chirographic, chirographical; stylographic, stylographical; manuscript, autograph, autographic, holograph, holographic, holographical, in one's own hand, under one's hand; **longhand,** in longhand, in script, handwritten; **shorthand,** in shorthand; italic, italicized; cursive, running, flowing; graphologic, graphological, graphometric, graphometrical; graphoanalytic, graphoanalytical; typewritten; printed

23 **scribbled,** scrabbled, **scratched, scrawled; scribbly, scratchy, scrawly**

24 **literary,** belletristic, lettered; classical

25 auctorial, authorial; polygraphic; graphomaniac, graphomaniacal, scribblemaniac, scribblemaniacal, scripturient <old>

26 **alphabetic,** ideographic, etc 546.8

27 stenographic, stenographical; **shorthand,** in shorthand

28 **clerical, secretarial**

WORD ELEMENTS 29 grapho-, -graphy, -graphia; -graph, -gram; -grapher

548 PRINTING

NOUNS **1 printing,** publishing, publication, photographic reproduction, photochemical process, phototypography, phototypy; **photoengraving; letterpress,** relief printing, **typography,** letterpress photoengraving; zincography, photozincography; line engraving, halftone engraving; stereotypy; wood-block printing, xylotypography, chromoxylography; intaglio printing, **gravure;** rotogravure, rotary photogravure; planographic printing, planography, **lithography,** typolithography, photolithography, lithogravure, lithophotogravure; offset lithography, offset, dry offset, photo-offset; photogelatin process, albertype, collotype; electronography, electrostatic printing, onset, xerography, xeroprinting; stencil, mimeograph, silk-screen printing; color printing, chromotypography, chromotypy, two-color printing, three-color printing; book printing, job printing, sheetwork; history of printing, palaeotypography; photography 714; **graphic arts, printmaking** 713.1

2 composition, typesetting, setting, composing; hand composition, machine composition; hot-metal typesetting, cold-type typesetting, photosetting, photocomposition; imposition; justification; composing stick, galley chase, furniture, quoin; typesetting machine, phototypesetter, phototypesetting machine; computer composition, computerized typesetting; composition tape; line of type, slug; layout, dummy

3 print, imprint, stamp, impression, impress, letterpress; reprint, reissue; offprint; offcut; offset, setoff, mackle; duplicate, facsimile, carbon copy, repro <nf>

4 copy, printer's copy, manuscript, typescript; **camera-ready copy; matter;** composed matter, live matter, dead matter, standing matter

5 proof, proof sheet, pull <Brit>, trial impression; galley, **galley proof,** slip; page proof, foundry proof, plate proof, stone proof, press proof, cold-type proof, color proof, computer proof, engraver's proof, reproduction or repro proof, blueprint, blue <nf>, vandyke, progressive proof; author's proof; revise

6 type, print, stamp, letter; type size; type body or shank or stem, body, shank, stem, shoulder, belly, back, bevel, beard, feet, groove, nick, face, counter; ascender, descender, serif; lower case, minuscule; upper case, majuscule; capital, cap <nf>, small capital, small cap <nf>; ligature, logotype; bastard type, bottle-assed type, fat-faced type; **pi;** type lice; **font; face,** typeface; type class, roman, sans serif, script, italic, black letter; case, typecase; point, pica; en, em; typefounders, typefoundry

7 space, spacing, patent space, justifying space, justification space; spaceband, slug; quadrat, quad; em quad, en quad; em, en; three-em space, thick space; four-em space, five-em space, thin space; hair space

8 printing surface, plate, printing plate; typeform, locked-up page; duplicate plate, electrotype, stereotype, plastic plate, rubber plate; zincograph, zincotype; **printing equipment**

9 presswork, makeready; **press, printing press,** printing machine <Brit>; platen press, flatbed cylinder press, cylinder press, rotary press, web press, rotogravure press; bed, platen, web

10 printed matter; reading matter, text, letterpress <Brit>; advertising matter; advance sheets

11 press, printing office, print shop, printery, printers; publishers, **publishing house; pressroom,** composing room, proofroom

12 printer, printworker; **compositor, typesetter,** typographer, Linotyper; keyboarder; stoneman, makeup man; proofer; stereotyper, stereotypist, electrotyper; apprentice printer, devil, printer's devil; **pressman**

13 proofreader, reader, printer's reader <Brit>, copyholder; **copyreader,** copy editor

VERBS **14 print; imprint, impress, stamp,** enstamp <old>; engrave; run, run off, strike; **publish, issue, put in print, bring out, put out, get out;** put to press, put to bed, see through the press; prove, proof, prove up, make or pull a proof, pull; overprint; reprint, reissue; mimeograph, hectograph; multigraph

15 autotype, electrotype, Linotype <trademark>, monotype, palaeotype, stereotype; keyboard

16 compose, set, set in print; **make up,** impose; justify, overrun; pi, pi a form

17 copy-edit; proofread, read, read or correct copy

18 <be printed> go to press, come off press, come out, appear in print

ADJS **19 printed, in print;** typeset

20 typographic, typographical; phototypic, phototypographic; chromotypic, chromotypographic; stereotypic, palaeotypographical; **boldface,** bold-faced, blackface, black-faced, full-faced; **lightface,** light-faced; **upper-case, lower-case**

549 RECORD

NOUNS **1 record, recording,** documentation, written word; **chronicle, annals,** history, story; roll, **rolls,** pipe roll <Brit>; account; register, registry, rota, roster, scroll, catalog, inventory, table, list 871, dossier, portfolio; letters, correspondence; **vestige, trace,** memorial, token, relic, remains; herstory <nf>

2 **archives,** public records, government archives, government papers, presidential papers, historical documents, historical records, memorabilia; clipping; cartulary; biographical records, life records, biographical material, papers, ana; parish rolls *or* register *or* records

3 registry, registry office; archives, files; chancery; National Archives, Library of Congress; Somerset House <Brit>

4 **memorandum, memo** <nf>, memoir, *aide-mémoire* <Fr>, memorial; **reminder** 989.6; **note, notation,** annotation, jotting, docket, marginal note, marginalia, scholium, scholia, adversaria, footnote; jottings; **entry,** register, **registry,** item; **minutes;** inscription, personal note

5 **document,** official document, legal document, legal paper, legal instrument, **instrument,** writ, **paper,** parchment, scroll, roll, **writing,** script, scrip; holograph, chirograph; **papers,** ship's papers; docket, **file,** personal file, **dossier;** blank, form; deed, title deed, muniments; registration document, insurance papers

6 **certificate,** certification, **ticket; authority,** authorization; **credential, voucher, warrant,** warranty, testimonial, charter; note; **affidavit,** sworn statement, notarized statement, deposition, witness, attestation, *procès-verbal* <Fr>; **visa,** *visé* <Fr>; passport; **bill of health,** clean bill of health; navicert <Brit>; **diploma,** sheepskin <nf>; certificate of proficiency, testamur <Brit>; birth certificate, death certificate, marriage certificate

7 **report, bulletin, brief, statement, account,** accounting; account rendered, *compte rendu* <Fr>; **minutes,** the record, proceedings, transactions, acta; official report, annual report; report card, transcript; **yearbook,** annual; **returns,** census report *or* returns, election returns, tally; case history

8 <official documents> state paper, white paper; blue book, green book, Red Book <Brit>, white book, yellow book, *livre jaune* <Fr>; gazette, official journal, Congressional Record, Hansard

9 <registers> genealogy, pedigree, studbook; Social Register, blue book; directory; Who's Who; Almanach de Gotha; Burke's Peerage Baronetage *and* Knightage; Debrett's Peerage Baronetage Knightage *and* Companionage; Red Book, Royal Kalendar; Lloyd's Register

10 <recording media> bulletin board, notice board; scoresheet, scorecard, scoreboard; **tape,** magnetic tape, magnetic track, magnetic storage, cassette tape, videotape, ticker tape; **computer disk,**

magnetic disk, diskette, floppy disk *or* floppy, hard disk, disk cartridge, CD-ROM, laser disk, optical disk; memory; computer file, database; compact disk *or* CD, multimedia CD, laser disk, DVD; phonograph record, disc *or* disk, platter <nf>; film, motion-picture film; slip, card, index card, filing card; library catalog, catalog card; microcard, microfiche, microdot, microfilm; **file** 871.3; recording instrument, photocopier, camera, videocamera, camcorder, recorder, tape recorder, wiretap, bug <nf>, answering machine, videocassette recorder *or* VCR, flight recorder, black box

11 <record books> **notebook, pocketbook,** pocket notebook, blankbook; loose-leaf notebook, spiral notebook; **memorandum book,** memo book <nf>, commonplace book, adversaria; address book, directory; workbook; **blotter,** police blotter; docket, court calendar; **calendar,** desk calendar, appointment calendar, appointment schedule, engagement book, agenda, agenda book, Filofax <trademark>, datebook; **tablet,** table <old>, writing tablet; diptych, triptych; pad, **scratch pad,** notepad; Post-it Note <trademark>, sticky <nf>; **scrapbook,** memory book, **album; diary, journal,** daybook; **log,** ship's log, **logbook; account book, ledger,** daybook; **cashbook,** petty cashbook; checkbook; Domesday Book; catalog, classified catalog, index; yearbook, annual; guestbook, guest register, register, registry; cartulary *or* chartulary

12 **monument,** monumental *or* memorial record, **memorial;** necrology, obituary, **memento,** remembrance, testimonial; cup, trophy, prize, ribbon, plaque; **marker;** inscription; **tablet,** stone, hoarstone <Brit>, boundary stone, memorial stone; **pillar,** stele *or* stela, shaft, column, memorial column, rostral column, manubial column; cross; war memorial; arch, memorial arch, triumphal arch, victory arch; memorial statue, bust; monolith, obelisk, **pyramid; tomb,** grave 309.16; tomb of unknown soldier; **gravestone, tombstone;** memorial tablet, brass; headstone, footstone; mausoleum; cenotaph; cairn, mound, barrow, cromlech, dolmen, megalith, menhir, cyclolith, earthwork, mound; **shrine,** reliquary, tope, stupa

13 recorder, registrar 550.1

14 **registration, register, registry; recording,** record keeping, recordation; archiving; minuting, **enrollment,** matriculation, enlistment; impanelment; **listing, tabulation, cataloging,** inventorying, indexing; chronicling; **entry,** insertion, entering, posting; docketing, inscribing, **inscription; booking, logging;** recording instruments

VERBS **15 record,** put *or* place upon record; **inscribe,** enscroll; **register, enroll,** matriculate, check in; impanel; poll; **file,** index, catalog, calendar, **tabulate, list,** docket; **chronicle,** document; minute, put in the minutes *or* on the record, spread on the record; commit to *or* preserve in an archive, archive; **write,** commit *or* reduce to writing, put in writing, put in black and white, put on paper; **write out; make out,** fill out; **write up,** chalk, chalk up; **write down, mark down, jot down, put down, set down, take down; note,** note down, make a note, make a memorandum; **post,** post up; **enter,** make an entry, insert, write in; **book, log;** cut, carve, grave, engrave, incise; put on tape, tape, tape-record; capture on film; record, cut; videotape; keyboard, key

ADJS **16 recording,** recordative <old>, registrational; certificatory

17 recorded, registered; inscribed, written down, down; **filed,** indexed, enrolled, **entered,** logged, booked, posted; documented, chronicled; minuted; **on record,** on file, on the books; official, legal, of record; in black and white

18 documentary, documentational, documental, archival, archived; epigraphic, inscriptional; necrological, obituary; testimonial

550 RECORDER

NOUNS **1 recorder,** recordist, record keeper; **registrar,** register, prothonotary; archivist, documentalist; master of the rolls <Brit>, *custos rotulorum* <L>; librarian; **clerk,** record clerk, penpusher <nf>, filing clerk; town *or* municipal clerk, county clerk; bookkeeper, accountant; **scribe,** scrivener; **secretary,** amanuensis; **stenographer** 547.17; notary, notary public; marker; scorekeeper, scorer, official scorer, timekeeper; engraver, stonecutter; reporter

2 annalist, genealogist, chronicler; cliometrician; historian

551 INFORMATION

NOUNS **1 information,** info <nf>, gen <Brit nf>, **facts, data, knowledge** 928; public knowledge, open secret, common knowledge; general information; news, factual information, hard information; **evidence, proof** 957; **enlightenment,** light; incidental information, sidelight; **acquaintance,** familiarization, briefing; **instruction** 568.1; **intelligence; the dope** *and* the goods *and* **the scoop** *and* the skinny *and* the straight skinny *and* the inside skinny <nf>, the know <nf>, the gen <Brit>; transmission, **communication** 343; report,

word, message, presentation, account, **statement,** mention; white paper, white book, blue book, command paper <Brit>; dispatch, bulletin, communiqué, handout <nf>, fact sheet, release; publicity, promotional material, broadside; **notice,** notification; notice board, bulletin board; announcement, publication 352; directory, guidebook 574.10; trivia

2 inside information, private *or* confidential information; **the lowdown** *and* **inside dope** *and* inside wire *and* **hot tip** *and* dirt <nf>; insider; pipeline <nf>; privileged information, classified information

3 tip *and* tip-off *and* **pointer** <nf>, clue, cue; steer <nf>; **advice;** whisper, passing word, **word to the wise,** word in the ear, bug in the ear <nf>, bee in the bonnet <nf>; warning, caution, monition, alerting, sound bite; aside

4 hint, gentle hint, **intimation, indication, suggestion, mere** *or* **faint suggestion, suspicion, inkling,** whisper, **glimmer, glimmering; cue, clue,** index, **symptom, sign,** spoor, track, scent, sniff, whiff, telltale, tip-off <nf>; **implication, insinuation, innuendo;** broad hint, gesture, signal, nod, wink, look, nudge, kick, prompt; disguised message, backward masking; rumor, leak, gossip

5 informant, informer, source, teller, interviewee, enlightener; **adviser,** monitor; **reporter,** notifier, **announcer,** annunciator; spokesperson, spokespeople, spokeswoman, spokesman, press secretary, press officer, information officer, mouthpiece, messenger, correspondent; spin doctor <nf>; communicator, communicant, publisher; **authority,** witness, expert witness; **tipster** <nf>, **tout** <nf>; newsmonger, gossipmonger; **information medium** *or* **media, mass media,** print media, electronic media, the press, radio, television; channel, the grapevine; information network, network; information center; public relations officer

6 informer, betrayer, double-crosser <nf>, delator <old>; fifth columnist; **snitch** *and* snitcher <nf>; whistle-blower <nf>; **tattler, tattletale, telltale, talebearer; blab** *or* blabber *or* blabberer *or* blabbermouth <nf>; **squealer** *and* preacher *and* **stool pigeon** *and* stoolie *and* **fink** *and* rat <nf>, nark <Brit nf>; **spy** 576.9; grapevine, channel

7 information technology, information *or* communication theory; data storage *or* retrieval, information retrieval *or* IT, EDP *or* electronic data processing, data processing, information processing; signal, noise; encoding, decoding; bit; redundancy, entropy; channel; information *or* communication explosion

VERBS **8 inform, tell, speak on** *or* **for,** apprise,

advise, advertise, advertise of, **give word,** mention to, **acquaint, enlighten,** familiarize, brief, verse, give the facts, give an account of, give by way of information; **instruct,** educate; possess or seize one of the facts; **let know, have one to know, give** or **lead one to believe** or understand; tell once and for all; notify, give notice or notification, serve notice; **communicate** 343.6,7; bring or send or leave word; **report** 552.11; **disclose** 351.4; put in a new light, shed new or fresh light upon; announce, broadcast, convey, break the news

9 **post** and **keep posted** <nf>; wise up and clue or fill in and bring up to speed or date and put in the picture <nf>

10 **hint, intimate, suggest, insinuate, imply, indicate,** adumbrate, lead or leave one to gather, justify one in supposing, give or drop or throw out a hint, give an inkling of, signal, suggest, **hint at; leak,** let slip out; allude to, make an allusion to, glance at <old>; **prompt,** give the cue, put onto; put in or into one's head, put a bee in one's bonnet

11 **tip** and tip off and **give one a tip** <nf>, alert; **give a pointer to** <nf>; put hep or hip <nf>, **let in on,** let in on the know <nf>; let next to and put next to and **put on to** and put on to something hot <nf>; **confide,** confide to, entrust with information, give confidential information, mention privately or confidentially, whisper, buzz, breathe, whisper in the ear, **put a bug in one's ear** <nf>

12 **inform on** or **against, betray; tattle;** turn informer; testify against, **bear witness against;** turn state's evidence, turn king's or queen's evidence <Brit>

13 <nf terms> **sell one out** or **down the river,** tell on, blab, snitch, squeal, peach <old>, sell out, sing, rat, stool, fink, nark, finger, put the finger on, blow the whistle, shop <Brit>, dime, drop a dime, spill one's guts, spill the beans, squawk, weasel, let the cat out of the bag, sell down the river

14 **learn, come to know, be informed** or **apprised of,** have it reported, get the facts, **get wise to** <nf>, **get hep to** and **next to** and **on to** <nf>; become conscious or aware of, become alive or awake to, awaken to, tumble to <nf>, open one's eyes to; realize, get wind of; overhear

15 **know** 928.12, be informed or apprised, have the facts, be in the know <nf>, **come to one's knowledge,** come to or reach one's ears; be told, **hear, overhear,** hear tell of and hear say <nf>; get scent or wind of; **know well** 928.13; have inside information, know where the bodies are buried <nf>

16 **keep informed,** keep posted <nf>, stay briefed, **keep up on,** keep up to date or au courant, keep abreast of the times; **keep track of,** keep count or account of, keep watch on, keep tab or tabs on <nf>, keep a check on, keep an eye on

ADJS 17 **informed** 927.18-20; informed of, enlightened, briefed, in the know 928.16, clued-in or clued-up <nf>

18 **informative,** informing, informational, informatory; illuminating, **instructive, enlightening;** educative, educational; advisory, monitory; **communicative**

19 telltale, tattletale, kiss-and-tell

ADVS 20 from information received, according to reports or rumor, from notice given, as a matter of general information, by common report, from what one can gather, as far as anyone knows

552 NEWS

NOUNS 1 **news, tidings, intelligence, information, word,** advice; happenings, current affairs, hard news; newsiness <nf>; newsworthiness; a nose for news; **journalism,** reportage, coverage, news coverage, news gathering; **the press,** the fourth estate, the press corps, print journalism, electronic journalism, investigative journalism, broadcast journalism, broadcast news, radio journalism, television journalism; **news medium** or **media,** newspaper, newsletter, newsmagazine, radio, television, press association, news service, news agency, press agency, wire service, telegraph agency; press box, press gallery; yellow press, tabloid press; pack journalism; alternative press

2 **good news,** good word, **glad tidings;** gospel, evangel; bad news

3 **news item,** piece or budget of news; **article, story,** piece, account; copy; scoop and beat <nf>, exclusive; interview; breaking story, newsbreak; feature story; follow-up, sidebar; column, editorial; spot news; photo opportunity; outtake; sound bite; media hype <nf>

4 **message, dispatch, word, communication, communiqué,** advice, press or news release, release; press conference, news conference; express <Brit>; embassy, embassage <old>; **letter** 553.2; **telegram** 347.14; pneumatogram, petit bleu <Fr>

5 **bulletin,** news report, **flash,** brief, update

6 **report, rumor,** flying rumor, unverified or unconfirmed report, **hearsay,** on-dit <Fr>, **scuttlebutt** and latrine rumor <nf>; **talk, whisper, buzz, rumble,** bruit, cry; idea afloat, news stirring; **common talk,** town talk, **talk of the town,** topic of the day, cause célèbre <Fr>; **grapevine; canard,** roorback

7 **gossip,** gossiping, gossipry, gossipmongering, newsmongering, mongering, back-fence gossip <nf>; **talebearing,** taletelling; **tattle,** tittle-tattle,

chitchat, **talk,** idle talk, small talk, by-talk; "putting two and two together, and making it five"—Pascal; piece of gossip, groundless rumor, tale, story

8 **scandal, dirt** <nf>, **malicious gossip,** "gossip made tedious by morality"—Oscar Wilde; juicy morsel, tidbit, choice bit of dirt <nf>; **scandalmongering;** gossip column; character assassination, **slander** 512.3; whispering campaign

9 **newsmonger, rumormonger, scandalmonger, gossip,** gossipmonger, gossiper, *yenta* <Yiddish>, quidnunc, **busybody,** tabby <nf>; **talebearer,** taleteller, telltale, **tattletale** <nf>, tattler, tittle-tattler; gossip columnist; reporter, newspaperman

10 <secret news channel> **grapevine, grapevine telegraph,** channel, bush telegraph <Austral>; **pipeline;** a little bird *or* birdie; informer, leak; contact

VERBS 11 **report,** give a report, give an account of, tell, relate, rehearse <old>; write up, make out *or* write up a report, publicize; editorialize; gather the news, newsgather; dig *or* dig up dirt <nf>; bring word, tell the news, break the news, give tidings of; bring glad tidings, give the good word; announce 352.12; put around, spread, **rumor** 352.10; clue in *or* clue up <nf>, **inform** 551.8

12 **gossip,** talk over the back fence <nf>; **tattle,** tittle-tattle; clatter <Scot>, **talk;** retail gossip, **dish the dirt** <nf>, tell idle tales

ADJS 13 **newsworthy,** front-page, with news value, newsy, informative; reportorial

14 **gossipy,** gossiping, newsy; **talebearing,** taletelling

15 **reported, rumored,** whispered; rumored about, talked about, whispered about, bruited about, bandied about; **in the news, in circulation, in the air, going around,** going about, going the rounds, **current, rife,** afloat, in every one's mouth, on all tongues, on the street, all over the town, hot off the press; made public 352.17

ADVS 16 reportedly, allegedly, as they say, as it is said, **as the story goes** *or* runs, as the fellow says <nf>, it is said

553 CORRESPONDENCE

NOUNS 1 **correspondence, letter writing,** written communication, exchange of letters, epistolary intercourse *or* communication; personal correspondence, business correspondence; mailing, mass mailing, electronic mail

2 **letter** <see list>, **epistle, message, communication, dispatch, missive,** favor <old>; personal letter, business letter; **note, line,** chit, billet <old>; **reply, answer, acknowledgment,** rescript

3 **card, postcard, postal card,** lettercard <Brit>; picture postcard

4 **mail, post** <chiefly Brit>, **postal services,** letter bag; post day <Brit>; domestic mail, general delivery, snail mail <nf>, airmail, surface mail, express mail, priority mail, special handling, special delivery, first- *or* second- *or* third- *or* fourth-class mail, parcel post, registered mail, certified mail, insured mail, metered mail; mailing list; junk mail <nf>; direct mail, direct-mail advertising *or* selling, mail-order selling; mail solicitation; fan mail; electronic mail; Pony Express <old>

5 **postage;** stamp, postage stamp; frank; postmark, cancellation; postage meter

6 **mailbox,** postbox *and* letter box <chiefly Brit>, pillar box <Brit>; letter drop, mail drop; mailing machine *or* mailer; mailbag, postbag <Brit>; e-mail box

7 **postal service, postal system; post office** *or* **PO,** general post office *or* GPO, sorting office, dead-letter office, sea post office, mailboat; postmaster, **mailman, postman,** mail carrier, letter carrier; mail clerk, post-office *or* postal clerk; messenger, courier; postal union, Universal Postal Union; electronic mail service

8 **correspondent, letter writer,** writer, communicator; pen pal <nf>; addressee

9 **address,** name *and* address, direction <old>, **destination,** superscription; zone, zip code *or* zip, zip plus four, postal code <Can>, postal code *or* postcode <Brit>; letterhead, billhead; drop, accommodation address <Brit>

VERBS 10 **correspond,** correspond with, **communicate with, write, write to,** write a letter, send a letter to, send a note, **drop a line** <nf>; use the mails; keep up a correspondence, exchange letters

11 **reply, answer, acknowledge,** respond; reply by return mail

12 **mail, post,** dispatch, send, forward; airmail

13 **address, direct,** superscribe

ADJS 14 epistolary; **postal,** post; letter; mail-order, direct-mail; mail-in; mailable; send-in, sendable

PHRS 15 please reply, RSVP *or* répondez s'il vous plaît <Fr>

16 **kinds of letters**

aerogram	drop letter
air letter	encyclical
airgraph <Brit>	encyclical letter
apostolic *or* papal brief	epistle
bull	fan letter
chain letter	form letter
circular letter	invitation
cover letter	letter credential
dead letter	letter of condolence
Dear John	letter of credence
dimissory letter *or*	letter of credit
dimissorial	letter of delegation

letter of introduction
letter of marque
letter of recommendation
letter of request
letter of resignation
letter overt
letter patent
letter rogatory
letter testamentary
love letter *or*
   billet doux <Fr>
market letter

memorandum *or*
   memo
monitory *or* monitory
   letter
newsletter
open letter
paschal letter
pastoral letter
pink slip
poison-pen letter
round robin

554 BOOK

NOUNS **1 book, volume, tome;** publication, writing, **work, opus, production; title;** opusculum, opuscule; **trade book; textbook,** schoolbook, reader, grammar; **reference book,** playbook; songbook 708.28; notebook 549.11; storybook, **novel; best seller** *or* bestseller; coffee-table book; nonbook; **children's book,** juvenile book, juvenile; picture book; coloring book, sketchbook; prayer book, psalter, psalmbook; **classic,** the book, the bible, magnum opus, great work, standard work, definitive work

2 publisher, book publisher; publishing house, press, small press, vanity press; **editor,** trade editor, reference editor, juvenile editor, textbook editor, dictionary editor, college editor, line editor; acquisitions editor, executive editor, managing editor, editor-in-chief; picture editor; packager; copy editor *or* copyeditor, fact checker, proofreader; production editor, permissions editor; **printer,** book printer, typesetter, compositor; **bookbinder,** bibliopegist; **bookdealer, bookseller,** book agent, book salesman; book manufacturer, press

3 book, printed book, bound book, bound volume, cased book, casebound book, cloth-bound book, clothback, leather-bound book; manufactured book, finished book; packaged book; **hardcover,** hardcover book, hardbound, hardbound book, hard book; **paperback,** paper-bound book; pocket book, soft-cover, soft-bound book, limp-cover book

4 volume, tome; folio; quarto *or* 4to; octavo *or* 8vo; twelvemo *or* 12mo; sextodecimo *or* sixteenmo *or* 16mo; octodecimo *or* eighteenmo *or* 18mo; imperial, super, royal, medium, crown; trim size

5 edition, issue; volume, number; **printing,** impression, press order, print order, print run; copy; series, set, boxed set, collection, library; library edition; back number; **trade edition,** subscription edition, subscription book; school edition, text edition

6 rare book, early edition; first edition; signed edition; Elzevir, Elzevir book *or* edition; Aldine, Aldine book *or* edition; manuscript, scroll, codex; incunabulum, cradle book

7 compilation, omnibus; symposium; collection, collectanea, miscellany; collected works, selected works, complete works, corpus, *œuvres* <Fr>, canon; **miscellanea,** analects; ana; chrestomathy, delectus; compendium, **anthology,** composition, garland, florilegium; flowers, beauties; garden; *Festschrift* <Ger>; quotation book; album, photograph album; scrapbook; yearbook; display, exhibition; series, serialization

8 handbook, manual, enchiridion, vade mecum, gradus, how-to book <nf>; **cookbook,** cookery book <Brit>; nature book, field guide; travel book, **guidebook** 574.10; sports book

9 reference book, work of reference; **encyclopedia,** cyclopedia; **concordance; catalog;** calendar; index; classified catalog, *catalogue raisonné* <Fr>, dictionary catalog; **directory,** city directory; telephone directory, telephone book, phone book <nf>; **atlas, gazetteer;** studbook; source book, casebook; record book 549.11; **language reference book** <see list>; **dictionary,** lexicon, wordbook, Webster's; glossary, gloss, **vocabulary,** onomasticon, nomenclator; **thesaurus, Roget's,** storehouse *or* treasury of words; **almanac**

10 textbook, text, schoolbook, manual, manual of instruction; **primer,** alphabet book, abecedary, abecedarium; hornbook, battledore; gradus, exercise book, workbook; **grammar, reader;** spelling book, speller, casebook

11 booklet, pamphlet, brochure, chapbook, leaflet, folder, tract; circular 352.8; comic book

12 makeup, design; front matter, preliminaries, text, back matter; head, fore edge, back, tail; page, leaf, folio; type page; trim size; flyleaf, endpaper, endleaf, endsheet, signature; recto, verso *or* reverso; title page, half-title page; title, bastard title, binder's title, subtitle, running title; copyright page, imprint, printer's imprint, imprimatur, colophon; catchword, catch line; dedication, inscription; acknowledgments, preface, foreword, introduction; contents, contents page, table of contents; appendix, notes, glossary; errata; bibliography; index

13 part, section, book, volume; article; serial, installment, *livraison* <Fr>; fascicle; **passage,** phrase, clause, verse, paragraph, chapter, column

14 bookbinding, bibliopegy; **binding, cover, book cover,** case, bookcase, hard binding, soft binding, mechanical binding, spiral binding, comb binding, plastic binding; library binding; headband, footband, tailband; **jacket, book jacket, dust**

jacket, dust cover, wrapper; slipcase, slipcover; book cloth, binder's cloth, binder's board, binder board; folding, tipping, gathering, collating, sewing; **signature;** collating mark, niggerhead; Smyth sewing, side sewing, saddle stitching, wire stitching, stapling, perfect binding; smashing, gluing-off, trimming, rounding, backing, lining, lining-up; casemaking, stamping, casing-in

15 <bookbinding styles> Aldine, Arabesque, Byzantine, Canevari, cottage, dentelle, Etruscan, fanfare, Grolier, Harleian, Jansenist, Maioli, pointillé, Roxburgh

16 **bookstore, bookshop,** *librairie* <Fr>, bookseller, book dealer; **bookstall,** bookstand; **book club;** bibliopole

17 **bookholder, bookrest,** book support, **book end; bookcase,** revolving bookcase *or* bookstand, bookrack, bookstand, **bookshelf;** stack, bookstack; book table, book tray, book truck; folder, folio; **portfolio**

18 **booklover,** philobiblist, bibliophile, bibliolater, book collector, bibliomane, bibliomaniac, bibliotaph; **bookworm,** bibliophage; book-stealer, biblioklept

19 **bibliology,** bibliography; bookcraft, bookmaking, book printing, book production, book manufacturing, bibliogenesis, bibliogony; bookselling, bibliopolism

ADJS 20 **bibliological,** bibliographical; bibliothecal, bibliothecary; bibliopolic; bibliopegic

21 **reference books**

almanac	guidebook
atlas	handbook
bilingual dictionary	how-to book
biographical dictionary	idiom dictionary
children's dictionary	index
college dictionary	lexicon
concordance	manual
desk dictionary	reverse dictionary
dialect dictionary	rhyming dictionary
dictionary of	Roget's Thesaurus
quotations	school dictionary
directory	specialized *or* special-
encyclopedia	subject dictionary
etymological dictionary	synonym dictionary
or etymologicon	telephone directory *or*
foreign-language	book
dictionary	thesaurus
geographical dictionary	unabridged dictionary
or gazetteer	usage dictionary
glossary	vade mecum

555 PERIODICAL

NOUNS 1 **periodical, serial, journal,** gazette; ephemeris; **magazine,** book *and* zine <nf>; pictorial; review; organ, **house organ; trade**

journal, trade magazine; academic journal; daily, weekly, biweekly, bimonthly, fortnightly, monthly, quarterly, seasonal; annual, yearbook; newsletter; daybook, diary 549.11

2 **newspaper,** news, **paper,** sheet *or* rag <nf>, **gazette,** daily newspaper, daily, weekly newspaper, weekly, local paper, neighborhood newspaper, national newspaper; newspaper of record; **tabloid,** scandal sheet, extra, special, extra edition, special edition, Sunday paper, early edition, late edition; magazine section, comics, color supplement

3 **the press,** journalism, the public press, **the fourth estate;** print medium, the print media, print journalism, the print press, the public print; Fleet Street <Brit>; **wire service,** newswire, Associated Press, AP; United Press International, UPI; Reuters; **publishing, newspaper publishing, magazine publishing; the publishing industry, communications,** mass media, the communications industry, public communication; satellite publishing; reportage, coverage, legwork

4 **journalist, newspaperman, newspaperwoman, newsman, newswoman,** journo <Brit nf>, newspeople, inkstained wretch, pressman <Brit>, newswriter, gazetteer <old>, gentleman *or* representative of the press; **reporter,** newshawk *and* newshound <nf>; leg man <nf>; interviewer; investigative reporter *or* journalist; **cub reporter; correspondent, foreign correspondent,** war correspondent, special correspondent, stringer; publicist; rewriter, **rewrite man;** reviser, diaskeuast; **editor,** subeditor, managing editor, city editor, news editor, sports editor, woman's editor, feature editor, **copy editor,** copyman, copy chief, slotman; reader, **copyreader;** editorial writer, leader writer <Brit>; **columnist,** paragrapher, paragraphist; freelance reporter; **photographer, news photographer,** photojournalist; paparazzo; press baron; press corps

ADJS 5 **journalistic,** journalese <nf>; **periodical,** serial; magazinish, magaziny; newspaperish, newspapery; **editorial; reportorial**

556 TREATISE

NOUNS 1 **treatise,** piece, treatment, handling, tractate, tract; contribution; examination, survey, inquiry, **discourse, discussion,** disquisition, descant, exposition, screed; homily; memoir; **dissertation, thesis; essay,** theme; pandect; excursus; **study,** lucubration, étude; **paper,** research paper, term paper, position paper; **sketch,** outline, aperçu; causerie; **monograph,** research monograph; *morceau* <Fr>, paragraph, **note;** preliminary study, introductory study, first approach, prolegomenon; **article,** feature, special article

2 **commentary,** commentation <old>; **comment, remark; criticism,** critique, *compte-rendu critique* <Fr>, analysis; **review,** critical review, **report,** notice, **write-up** <nf>; **editorial,** leading article *or* leader <Brit>; gloss, running commentary, Op-Ed column

3 **discourser,** discusser, disquisitor, dissertator, doctoral candidate, expositor, descanter; symposiast, discussant; essayist; monographer, monographist; tractation, tractator <old>; **writer, author** 547.15; scholar

4 **commentator,** commenter; expositor, expounder, exponent; annotator, scholiast; glossarist, glossographer; **critic; reviewer,** book reviewer; **editor;** editorial writer, editorialist, leader writer <Brit>; news analyst; publicist

VERBS 5 **write upon,** touch upon, **discuss, treat, treat of, deal with,** take up, handle, go into, inquire into, survey; discourse, dissert, dissertate, descant, develop at thesis; **comment upon,** commentate, remark upon, annotate; expound; **criticize, review, write up**

ADJS 6 dissertational, disquisitional, discoursive, discursive; expository, expositorial, expositive, exegetical; essayistic; monographic, commentative, commentatorial, annotative; critical, interpretive *or* interpretative; editorial

557 ABRIDGMENT

NOUNS 1 **abridgment,** compendium, compend, *abrégé* <Fr>, **condensation,** short *or* shortened version, condensed version, potted version <Brit>, abbreviation, abbreviature, diminution, brief, digest, **abstract,** epitome, **précis, capsule,** nutshell *or* capsule version, capsulization, encapsulation, sketch, thumbnail sketch, **synopsis,** conspectus, syllabus, *aperçu* <Fr>, **survey, review,** overview, pandect, bird's-eye view; **outline,** skeleton, draft, blueprint, prospectus; topical outline; head, rubric

2 **summary, résumé,** curriculum vitae *or* CV, **recapitulation, recap** <nf>, rundown, run-through; **summation;** review; sum, substance, sum and substance, **wrapup** <nf>; pith, meat, gist, drift, core, essence, main point 997.6

3 **excerpt, extract, selection,** extraction, excerption, snippet; passage, selected passage; **clip** <nf>, film clip, outtake, sound bite <nf>

4 **excerpts,** *excerpta* <L>, **extracts, gleanings,** cuttings, clippings, snippets, selections; flowers, florilegium, **anthology;** compendium, treasury; ephemera; fragments; analects; **miscellany,** miscellanea; **collection,** collectanea; ana

VERBS 5 **abridge, shorten** 268.6, **condense, cut, clip; summarize,** synopsize, wrap up <nf>; **outline, sketch,** sketch out, hit the high spots; capsule, capsulize, encapsulate; **put in a nutshell**

ADJS 6 **abridged,** condensed; shortened, clipped, abstracted, abbreviated, truncated, compressed; nutshell, compendious, **brief** 268.8

ADVS 7 in brief, in summary, in sum, to the point, laconically, in a nutshell 537.8

558 LIBRARY

NOUNS 1 **library,** book depository; learning center; media center, media resource center, information center; **public library,** town *or* city *or* municipal library, county library, state library; school library, community college library, college library, university library; **special library,** medical library, law library, art library, etc; **circulating library, lending library** <Brit>; rental library; **book wagon, bookmobile;** bookroom, bookery <old>, *bibliothèque* <Fr>, *bibliotheca* <L>, athenaeum; reading room; **national library,** Bibliothèque Nationale, Bodleian Library, British Library, Deutsche Bücherei, Library of Congress, Vatican Library, Faculty of Advocates Library; American Library Association *or* ALA, Association of College and Research Libraries, Special Libraries Association, International Federation of Library Associations, American Society for Information Science, Association of Library and Information Service Educators, etc

2 **librarianship,** professional librarianship; **library science,** information science, library services, library and information services, library and information studies

3 **librarian,** professional librarian, library professional; **director, head librarian, chief librarian;** head of service; library services director

4 **bibliography** <see list>, Modern Language Association Bibliography; **index;** Books in Print, Paperbound Books in Print; **publisher's catalog,** publisher's list, backlist; National Union Catalog, Library of Congress Catalog, General Catalogue of Printed Books <Brit>, Union List of Serials; **library catalog,** computerized catalog, on-line catalog, integrated on-line system; CD-ROM workstation

5 **bibliographies**

annotated bibliography	cumulative bibliography
annual bibliography	national bibliography
bibliography of	period bibliography
bibliographies	subject bibliography
critical bibliography	trade bibliography

559 RELATIONSHIP BY BLOOD

NOUNS 1 blood relationship, blood, ties of blood, consanguinity, common descent *or* ancestry, biological *or* genetic relationship, **kinship,** kindred, **relation, relationship,** sibship; propinquity; cognation; agnation, enation; filiation, affiliation; alliance, connection, **family connection** *or* tie; motherhood, maternity; fatherhood, paternity; patrocliny, matrocliny; patrilineage, matrilineage; patriliny, matriliny; patrisib, matrisib; brotherhood, brothership, fraternity; sisterhood, sistership; cousinhood, cousinship; **ancestry** 560

  2 kinfolk *and* **kinfolks** <nf>, **kinsmen, kinsfolk, kindred,** kinnery <nf>, **kin,** kith and kin, **family, relatives, relations, people,** folks <nf>, connections; **blood relation** *or* **relative,** flesh, blood, flesh and blood, uterine kin, consanguinean; cognate; agnate, enate; kinsman, kinswoman, sib, sibling; german; near relation, distant relation; next of kin; collateral relative, collateral; distaff *or* spindle side, distaff *or* spindle kin; sword *or* spear side, sword *or* spear kin; **tribesman,** tribespeople, clansman *or* -woman; **ancestry** 560, **posterity** 561

  3 brother, bub *and* bubba *and* bro *and* bud *and* buddy <nf>, frater; brethren 700.1; **sister,** sis *and* sissy <nf>; sistern <nf>; kid brother *or* sister; blood brother *or* sister, uterine brother *or* sister, brother- *or* sister-german; half brother *or* sister, foster brother *or* sister, stepbrother *or* stepsister; **aunt,** auntie <nf>; **uncle,** unc *and* uncs *and* nunks *and* nunky *and* nuncle <nf>, **nephew, niece; cousin,** cousin-german; first cousin, second cousin, etc; cousin once removed, cousin twice removed, etc; country cousin; great-uncle, granduncle; great-granduncle; great-aunt, grandaunt; great-grandaunt; grandnephew, grandniece; **father, mother; son, daughter** 561.2

  4 race, people, folk, family, house, clan, tribe, nation; patriclan, matriclan, deme, sept, gens, phyle, phratry, totem; **lineage,** line, blood, strain, stock, stem, species, stirps, **breed,** brood, kind; plant *or* animal kingdom, class, order, etc 809.5; **ethnicity,** tribalism, clannishness, roots <nf>

  5 family, brood, nuclear family, binuclear family, extended family, one-parent *or* single-parent family; **house, household,** hearth, hearthside, ménage, people, **folk,** homefolk, folks *and* homefolks <nf>; kin, relatives, relations; **children,** issue, descendants, progeny, **offspring,** litter, get, kids <nf>

ADJS 6 related, kindred, akin; consanguineous *or* consanguinean *or* consanguineal, consanguine, by *or* of the blood; **biological,** genetic; **natural, birth,** by birth; cognate, uterine, agnate, enate; sib,

sibling; allied, affiliated, congeneric; german, germane; collateral; foster, novercal; patrilineal, matrilineal; patroclinous, matroclinous; patrilateral, matrilateral; avuncular; intimately *or* closely related, remotely *or* distantly related

  7 racial, ethnic, tribal, national, family, clannish, totemic, **lineal; ethnic;** phyletic, phylogenetic, genetic; gentile, gentilic

WORD ELEMENTS 8 adelpho-, phyl-

560 ANCESTRY

NOUNS 1 ancestry, progenitorship; parentage, parenthood; grandparentage, grandfatherhood, grandmotherhood

  2 paternity, fatherhood, fathership; natural *or* birth *or* biological fatherhood; fatherliness, paternalness; adoptive fatherhood

  3 maternity, motherhood, mothership; natural *or* birth *or* biological motherhood; motherliness, maternalness; adoptive motherhood; surrogate motherhood

  4 lineage, line, bloodline, descent, descendancy, line of descent, ancestral line, succession, **extraction,** derivation, birth, **blood,** breed, **family,** house, **strain,** sept, **stock,** race, stirps, seed; direct line, phylum; **branch,** stem; filiation, affiliation, apparentation; side, father's side, mother's side; enate, agnate, cognate; male line, spear *or* sword side; female line, distaff *or* spindle side; consanguinity, common ancestry 559.1

  5 genealogy, pedigree, stemma, *Stammbaum* <Ger>, genealogical tree, **family tree,** tree; genogram; descent, lineage, line, bloodline, ancestry

  6 heredity, heritage, inheritance, birth; patrocliny, matrocliny; endowment, inborn capacity *or* tendency *or* susceptibility *or* predisposition; diathesis; inheritability, heritability, hereditability; Mendel's law, Mendelism *or* Mendelianism; Weismann theory, Weismannism; Altmann theory, De Vries theory, Galtonian theory, Verworn theory, Wiesner theory; **genetics,** genetic engineering, genetic fingerprinting, pharmacogenetics, genesiology, eugenics; **gene,** factor, inheritance factor, determiner, determinant; **character,** dominant *or* recessive character, allele *or* allelomorph; germ cell, germ plasm; **chromosome;** sex chromosome, X chromosome, Y chromosome; chromatin, chromatid; genetic code; DNA, RNA, replication

  7 ancestors, antecedents, predecessors, ascendants, **fathers, forefathers, forebears,** progenitors, primogenitors; **grandparents,** grandfathers; patriarchs, elders

  8 parent, progenitor, ancestor, procreator, begetter;

natural *or* birth *or* biological parent; grandparent; ancestress, progenitress, progenitrix; stepparent; adoptive parent; surrogate parent

9 **father, sire,** genitor, paternal ancestor, pater <nf>, the old man <nf>, governor <nf>, *abba* <Heb>; patriarch, paterfamilias; stepfather; foster father, adoptive father; birth father

10 <nf terms> **papa,** pa, pap, pappy, **pop,** pops, **dad, daddy,** daddums, daddyo, big daddy, the old man, the governor, pater

11 **mother,** genetrix, dam, maternal ancestor, matriarch, materfamilias; stepmother; foster mother, adoptive mother; birth mother

12 <nf terms> **mama,** mater, the old woman, mammy, mam, **ma, mom, mommy,** mummy, mumsy, mimsy, motherkin, motherkins

13 **grandfather,** grandsire; old man 304.2; great-grandfather

14 <nf terms> **grandpa,** grampa, gramper, gramp, gramps, grandpapa, grandpap, grandpappy, **granddad,** granddaddy, granddada, granfer, gramfer, granther, pop, grandpop

15 **grandmother,** grandam; great-grandmother

16 <nf terms> **grandma,** granma, old woman 304.3; grandmamma, grandmammy, **granny,** grammy, gammy, grannam, gammer

ADJS 17 **ancestral,** ancestorial, patriarchal; **parental,** parent; **paternal,** fatherly, fatherlike; **maternal,** motherly, motherlike; grandparental; grandmotherly, grandmaternal; grandfatherly, grandpaternal

18 **lineal,** family, familial, genealogical; kindred, akin; enate *or* enatic, agnate *or* agnatic, cognate *or* cognatic; direct, in a direct line; phyletic, phylogenetic; diphyletic

19 **hereditary,** patrimonial, **inherited, innate;** genetic, genic; patroclinous, matroclinous

20 **inheritable,** heritable, hereditable

561 POSTERITY

NOUNS 1 **posterity, progeny, issue, offspring,** fruit, seed, brood, breed, family; **descent,** succession; lineage 560.4, blood, bloodline; **descendants,** heirs, inheritors, sons, **children, kids** <nf>, little ones, little people <nf>, treasures, hostages to fortune, youngsters, younglings; grandchildren, great-grandchildren; new *or* young *or* rising generation

2 <of animals> **young, brood,** get, **spawn,** spat, fry; **litter,** farrow <of pigs>; clutch, hatch

3 **descendant; offspring, child, scion; son,** son and heir, a chip of *or* off the old block, sonny; **daughter,** heiress; grandchild, grandson, granddaughter; stepchild, stepson, stepdaughter; foster child

4 <derived or collateral descendant> **offshoot,** offset, **branch,** sprout, shoot, filiation

5 **bastard,** illegitimate, illegitimate *or* bastard child, whoreson, by-blow, child born out of wedlock *or* without benefit of clergy *or* on the wrong side of the blanket, natural *or* love child, *nullius filius* <L>; illegitimacy, bastardy, bar *or* bend sinister; hellspawn

6 sonship, sonhood; daughtership, daughterhood

ADJS 7 **filial,** sonly, sonlike; **daughterly,** daughterlike

562 LOVEMAKING, ENDEARMENT

NOUNS 1 **lovemaking,** dalliance, amorous dalliance, billing and cooing; **fondling, caressing,** hugging, kissing; cuddling, snuggling, nestling, nuzzling; bundling; sexual intercourse 75.7

2 <nf terms> **making out, necking, petting,** spooning, smooching, lollygagging, canoodling, playing kissy-face *or* kissy-kissy *or* kissy-poo *or* kissy-huggy *or* lickey-face *or* smacky-lips, pitching *or* flinging woo, sucking face, swapping spit

3 **embrace, hug, squeeze,** fond embrace, embracement, clasp, enfoldment, bear hug <nf>

4 **kiss,** buss, smack, smooch <nf>, **osculation;** French kiss, soul kiss

5 **endearment; caress,** pat; sweet talk, soft words, honeyed words, sweet nothings; line <nf>, blandishments, artful endearments; love call, mating call, wolf whistle

6 <terms of endearment> **darling, dear,** deary, **sweetheart, sweetie, sweet,** sweets, sweetkins, **honey,** hon, honeybun, honey-bunny, honeybunch, honey child, sugar, love, lover, precious, precious heart, pet, petkins, babe, **baby, doll,** baby-doll, cherub, angel, chick, chickabiddy, buttercup, duck, duckling, ducks, lamb, lambkin, snookums, poppet <Brit>

7 **courtship, courting, wooing;** court, suit, suing, amorous pursuit, addresses; gallantry; serenade

8 **proposal,** marriage proposal, offer of marriage, popping of the question; engagement 436.3

9 **flirtation, flirtiness, coquetry,** dalliance; flirtatiousness, coquettishness, coyness; sheep's eyes, goo-goo eyes <nf>, amorous looks, coquettish glances, come-hither look; ogle, side-glance; bedroom eyes <nf>

10 **philandering,** philander, lady-killing <nf>; lechery, licentiousness, unchastity 665

11 **flirt, coquette,** gold digger *and* vamp <nf>; strumpet, whore 665.14,16

12 **philanderer,** philander, woman chaser, **ladies' man,** heartbreaker, rake, cad, man of the world; masher, lady-killer, wolf, skirt chaser, man on the make *and* make-out artist <nf>; libertine, lecher,

cocksman <nf>, seducer 665.12, gigolo, Casanova, Don Juan, Lothario; male prostitute, stud

13 love letter, billet-doux, mash note <nf>; valentine

VERBS **14 make love,** bill and coo; dally, toy, trifle, wanton, make time; sweet-talk <nf>, whisper sweet nothings; go steady, keep company; copulate

15 <nf terms> **make out, neck,** pet, spoon, smooch, lollygag, canoodle, pitch *or* fling woo, play kissy-face *or* kissy-kissy *or* kissy-huggy *or* kissy-poo *or* lickey-face *or* smacky-lips, suck face, swap spit

16 caress, pet, pat; feel *or* feel up <nf>, **fondle,** dandle, coddle, cocker, cosset; pat on the head *or* cheek, chuck under the chin

17 cuddle, snuggle, nestle, nuzzle; lap; bundle

18 embrace, hug, clasp, press, squeeze <nf>, fold, **enfold,** bosom, embosom, put *or* throw one's arms around, take to *or* in one's arms, fold to the heart, press to the bosom

19 kiss, osculate, buss, smack, smooch <nf>; blow a kiss

20 flirt, coquet; philander, gallivant, play the field <nf>, run *or* play around, sow one's oats; **make eyes at, ogle,** eye, cast coquettish glances, cast sheep's eyes at, make goo-goo eyes at <nf>, *faire les yeux doux* <Fr>, look sweet upon <nf>; play hard to get

21 court, woo, sue, press one's suit, **pay court** *or* **suit to,** make suit to, cozy up to <nf>, eye up *and* chat up <Brit nf>, pay one's court to, address, pay one's addresses to, pay attention to, lay siege to, fling oneself at, throw oneself at the head of; **pursue,** follow; chase <nf>; set one's cap at *or* for <nf>; serenade; spark <nf>, squire, esquire, beau, sweetheart <nf>, swain

22 propose, pop the question <nf>, ask for one's hand; become engaged

ADJS **23** amatory, amative; sexual 75.28,29; caressive; **flirtatious,** flirty; **coquettish,** coy, come-hither

563 MARRIAGE

NOUNS **1 marriage, matrimony, wedlock, married status,** holy matrimony, holy wedlock, match, matching, match-up, splicing <nf>, union, matrimonial union, alliance, marriage sacrament, sacrament of matrimony *or* marriage, bond *or* state of matrimony, wedding knot, conjugal bond *or* tie *or* knot, conjugality, nuptial bond *or* tie *or* knot, one flesh, alliance; married state *or* status, wedded state *or* status, wedded bliss, conjugal bliss, weddedness, wifehood, coverture, husbandhood, spousehood; coverture, cohabitation; bed, marriage bed, bridal bed, bridebed; cohabitation, living as man and wife, common-law marriage; tying the knot *and* getting

hitched *and* getting spliced <nf>; intermarriage, mixed marriage, interfaith marriage, interracial marriage; remarriage; arranged marriage; lesbian marriage, homosexual marriage; miscegenation; misalliance, *mésalliance* <Fr>, ill-assorted marriage

2 marriageability, marriageableness, nubility, ripeness; age of consent

3 wedding, marriage, marriage *or* wedding ceremony, nuptial mass; church wedding, civil wedding, civil ceremony, courthouse wedding; espousement, bridal; banns; **nuptials,** spousals, espousals, marriage vows, hymeneal rites, wedding service; *chuppah* <Heb>, wedding canopy; white wedding; wedding song, marriage song, nuptial song, prothalamium, epithalamium, epithalamy, hymen, hymeneal; wedding veil, saffron veil *or* robe; bridechamber, bridal suite, nuptial apartment; **honeymoon;** forced marriage, shotgun wedding; Gretna Green wedding, elopement

4 wedding party; wedding attendant, usher; **best man,** bridesman, groomsman; paranymph; **bridesmaid,** bridemaiden, maid *or* matron of honor; attendant, flower girl, train bearer, ring bearer

5 newlywed; bridegroom, groom; bride, plighted bride, blushing bride; war bride, GI bride <nf>; honeymooner

6 spouse, espouser, espoused, **mate,** yokemate, partner, consort, **better half** <nf>, one's promised, one's betrothed, soul mate, helpmate, helpmeet, "bone of my bones, and flesh of my flesh"—Bible

7 husband, married man, man, benedict, goodman <old>, old man <nf>, hubby <nf>

8 wife, married woman, wedded wife, goodwife *or* goody <old>, squaw, woman, lady, matron, old lady *and* old woman *and* little woman *and* ball and chain <nf>, feme, feme covert, **better half** <nf>, **helpmate,** helpmeet, rib, wife of one's bosom; wife in name only; wife in all but name, concubine, common-law wife; blushing bride, war bride, GI bride

9 married couple, wedded pair, bridal pair, happy couple, **man and wife,** husband and wife, man and woman, *vir et uxor* <L>, one flesh, Mr and Mrs; newlyweds, **bride and groom,** honeymooners

10 harem, seraglio, serai, gynaeceum; zenana, purdah

11 monogamist, monogynist; **bigamist;** digamist, deuterogamist; trigamist; **polygamist,** polygynist, polyandrist; Bluebeard

12 matchmaker, marriage broker, matrimonial agent, *shadchan* <Yiddish>; matrimonial agency *or* bureau; go-between; dating agency *or* service, lonely hearts club, computer dating

13 <god> Hymen; <goddesses> Hera, Teleia; Juno, Pronuba; Frigg

VERBS 14 <join in marriage> **marry,** wed, nuptial, **join, unite, hitch** *and* **splice** <nf>, couple, match, match up, make *or* arrange a match, join together, **unite in marriage,** join *or* unite in holy wedlock *or* matrimony, tie the knot, tie the nuptial *or* wedding knot, celebrate a marriage, make one, pronounce man and wife; give away, give in marriage; marry off, find a mate for, find a husband *or* wife for

15 <get married> **marry, wed,** contract matrimony, say "I do", mate, couple, espouse, wive, **take to wife,** take a wife *or* husband, **get hitched** *or* spliced <nf>, tie the knot, become one, be made one, pair off, give one's hand to, bestow one's hand upon, lead to the altar, take for better *or* for worse; make an honest man *or* woman of; remarry, rewed; intermarry, interwed, miscegenate

16 **honeymoon,** go on a honeymoon, consummate one's marriage

17 **cohabit,** live together, live as man and wife, share one's bed and board

ADJS 18 **matrimonial, marital, conjugal, connubial, nuptial,** wedded, married, hymeneal; epithalamic; **spousal;** husbandly, uxorious; bridal, wifely, uxorial; premarital, concubinal, concubinary

19 **monogamous,** monogynous, monandrous; **bigamous,** digamous; **polygamous,** polygynous, polyandrous; morganatic; miscegenetic

20 **marriageable,** nubile, eligible, ripe, of age, of marriageable age

21 **married, wedded,** newlywed, espoused, one, one bone and one flesh, mated, matched, coupled, partnered, paired, hitched *and* spliced *and* hooked <nf>

WORD ELEMENTS 22 -gamy; -gamous

564 RELATIONSHIP BY MARRIAGE

NOUNS 1 **marriage relationship,** affinity, marital affinity; connection, family connection, marriage connection, matrimonial connection

2 **in-laws** <nf>, **relatives-in-law;** brother-in-law, sister-in-law, father-in-law, mother-in-law, son-in-law, daughter-in-law

3 stepfather, stepmother; stepbrother, stepsister; stepchild, stepson, stepdaughter

ADJS 4 **affinal,** affined, by marriage

565 CELIBACY

NOUNS 1 **celibacy, singleness,** singlehood, single blessedness, single *or* unmarried *or* unwed state *or* condition; **bachelorhood,** bachelordom, bachelorism, bachelorship; **spinsterhood,** maidenhood, maidenhead, **virginity,** maiden *or* virgin state, chastity, chasteness; **monasticism,** monachism, spiritual marriage, holy orders, the veil; misogamy, misogyny; self-restraint, self-denial; sexual abstinence *or* abstention, continence 664.3

2 **celibate,** *célibataire* <Fr>; monk, monastic, priest, nun, cenobite, eremite; virgin, vestal; misogamist, misogynist; unmarried, single <nf>

3 **bachelor,** bach *and* old bach <nf>, single *or* unmarried man, confirmed bachelor, **single man,** unattached male; misogamist

4 **single** *or* unmarried woman, spinster, spinstress, **old maid,** maid, maiden, bachelor girl, single girl, lone woman, maiden lady, feme sole, unattached female; **virgin,** virgo intacta, cherry <nf>; vestal, vestal virgin

VERBS 5 **be unmarried, be single, live alone,** enjoy single blessedness, **bach** *and* bach it <nf>, keep bachelor quarters, keep one's freedom, sit on the shelf <nf>

ADJS 6 **celibate,** celibatic; **monastic,** monachal, **monkish,** cenobitic, nunnish; misogamic, misogynous; sexually abstinent *or* continent, abstinent, abstaining; self-restrained

7 **unmarried, unwedded, unwed, single,** sole, spouseless, wifeless, husbandless, unmated, mateless; **bachelorly,** bachelorlike; **spinsterly,** spinsterish, spinsterlike; **old-maidish,** old-maidenish; maiden, maidenly; virgin, virginal; independent, unattached, fancy-free; on the shelf <nf>

566 DIVORCE, WIDOWHOOD

NOUNS 1 **divorce,** divorcement, grasswidowhood, civil divorce, **separation,** legal *or* judicial separation, separate maintenance; interlocutory decree; dissolution of marriage; divorce decree, decree nisi, decree absolute; annulment, decree of nullity; nonconsummation of marriage, estrangement, living apart, desertion; broken marriage, broken home; breakup, split-up, split, marriage on the rocks <nf>

2 **divorcé,** divorced person, divorced man, divorced woman, *divorcée* <Fr>; divorcer; grass widow, grass widower

3 **widowhood,** viduity <old>; **widowerhood,** widowership; weeds, widow's weeds

4 **widow,** widow woman <nf>, relict; dowager, queen dowager *or* dowager queen, merry widow, war widow; **widower,** widowman <nf>

VERBS 5 **divorce, separate,** part, split up *and* split the sheets <nf>, unmarry, put away, obtain a divorce, dissolve one's marriage, come to a parting of the ways, untie the knot, sue for divorce, file for divorce; have one's marriage annulled; grant a divorce, grant a final decree; grant an annulment, grant a decree of nullity, annul a marriage, put asunder, regain one's freedom; break up, split up, split, sunder; separate, live apart, part, be estranged; desert, abandon, leave, walk out

6 **widow,** bereave, make a widow

ADJS 7 widowly, widowish, widowlike; **widowed,** widowered; **divorced;** separated, legally separated, split, estranged; on the rocks <nf>

567 SCHOOL

NOUNS 1 **school** <see list>, **educational institution,** teaching institution, academic *or* scholastic institution, teaching and research institution, **institute, academy,** seminary, *Schule* <Ger>, *école* <Fr>, *escuela* <Sp>; alternative school; magnet school

2 **preschool,** infant school <Brit>, nursery, **nursery school;** day nursery, **day-care center,** crèche; playschool; **kindergarten**

3 **elementary school, grade school** *or* graded school, the grades; **primary school;** junior school <Brit>; **grammar school;** folk school, *Volksschule* <Ger>, home schooling

4 **secondary school,** middle school, **academy,** *Gymnasium* <Ger>; *lycée* <Fr>, lyceum; **high school,** high <nf>; **junior high school,** junior high <nf>, intermediate school; **senior high school,** senior high <nf>; **preparatory school,** prep school <nf>, public school <Brit>, seminary; **grammar school** <Brit>, Latin school, *Progymnasium* <Ger>; *Realschule* <Ger>; *Realgymnasium* <Ger>

5 **college, university,** institution *or* institute of higher education *or* learning, degree-granting institution; tertiary school, graduate school, postgraduate school, coeducational school; academe, academia, the groves of Academe, **the campus,** the halls of learning or ivy, ivied halls; alma mater; women's college; polytechnic, adult education, correspondence course; distance learning

6 **service school, service academy** <see list>, military academy, naval academy

7 **art school, performing arts school,** music school, conservatory, arts conservatory, school of the arts, dance school

8 **religious school** <see list>, parochial school, church-related school, church school; Sunday school

9 **reform school, reformatory,** correctional institution, industrial school, training school; borstal *or* borstal school *or* remand school <Brit>

10 **schoolhouse,** school building; little red schoolhouse; classroom building; hall; campus

11 **schoolroom, classroom;** recitation room; lecture

room *or* hall; auditorium, assembly hall; theater, amphitheater

12 **governing board, board;** board of education, school board; college board, board of regents, board of trustees, board of visitors

ADJS 13 **scholastic, academic,** institutional, **school,** classroom; **collegiate; university;** preschool; interscholastic, intercollegiate, extramural; intramural

14 **schools**

academy	military school *or* academy
adult-education school	night school
alternate *or* alternative school	open-classroom school
boarding school	polytechnic school *or* polytechnic <chiefly Brit>
business college *or* school	preparatory school *or* prep school <nf>
charm school	preschool
community college	primary school
comprehensive school	private school
conservatory	public school
correspondence school	reformatory school
country day school	school of continuing education *or* continuation school
day school	
distance learning institution	
elementary *or* grade school	secondary school *or* high school *or* senior high school
extension school *or* program	
finishing school	secretarial school
graduate school	special needs school
gymnasium	state school
institute	summer school
junior college	technical school *or* tech <nf>
junior high school *or* junior school *or* middle school *or* intermediate school	
	university extension
law school	vocational *or* trade school
lyceum *or* lycée	women's college
medical school	

15 **service schools or academies**

command and general staff school	Royal Military College of Canada <Kingston>
École de l'Air <Salon-de-Provence>	Royal Naval College <Dartmouth>
École Navale <Brest>	US Air Force Academy <Colorado Springs>
École Spéciale Militaire Interarmes <St Cyr>	US Coast Guard Academy <New London>
officer candidate school *or* OCS	US Merchant Marine Academy <Kings Point>
Royal Air Force College <Cranwell>	US Military Academy <West Point>
Royal Military Academy <Woolwich>	US Naval Academy <Annapolis>
Royal Military College <Sandhurst>	

16 **religious schools**

Bible institute	Catholic school
Bible school	church school

convent school
denominational school
divinity school
Hebrew school *or heder*
  <Yiddish>
madrasah
mesivta
parish school
parochial school
religious *or parochial*
  school

Sabbath school
schola cantorum
scholasticate
seminary
Sunday school
Talmud Torah
theological seminary *or*
  school
vacation church school
yeshiva

568 TEACHING

NOUNS **1 teaching, instruction, education, schooling, tuition; edification, enlightenment,** illumination; tutelage, tutorage, tutorship; tutoring, coaching, direction, training, preparation, private teaching, teacher 571; spoon-feeding; direction, guidance; **pedagogy,** pedagogics, didactics, didacticism; scholarship; catechization; computer-aided instruction, programmed instruction; home schooling; self-teaching, self-instruction; information 551; reeducation 857.4; **school** 567; **formal education,** coursework, school-work

2 inculcation, indoctrination, catechization, inoculation, **implantation,** infixation, infixion, **impression, instillment,** instillation, impregnation, **infusion,** imbuement; absorption and regurgitation; dictation; conditioning, brainwashing; reindoctrination 858.5

3 training, preparation, readying <nf>, **conditioning, grooming,** cultivation, development, improvement; **discipline;** breaking, housebreaking; **upbringing, bringing-up,** fetching-up <nf>, **rearing, raising, breeding, nurture,** nurturing, fostering; **practice,** rehearsal, **exercise, drill,** drilling; **apprenticeship,** in-service training, on-the-job training; work-study; military training, basic training; manual training, sloyd; vocational training *or* education

4 preinstruction, pre-education; **priming,** cramming <nf>

5 elementary education, nursery school, preschool, primary education, home schooling; **initiation, introduction,** propaedeutic; **rudiments,** grounding, first steps, elements, **ABC's, basics;** reading, writing, and arithmetic, **three R's;** primer, hornbook, abecedarium, abecedary

6 instructions, directions, orders; briefing, final instructions

7 lesson, teaching, instruction, lecture, lecture-demonstration, harangue, **discourse,** disquisition, exposition, **talk,** homily, **sermon,** preachment; chalk talk <nf>; skull session <nf>; **recitation,** recital; **assignment, exercise,** task, set task,

homework; moral, morality, moralization, moral lesson; object lesson

8 study, branch of learning; **discipline,** subdiscipline; **field, specialty,** academic specialty, area; **course,** course of study, **curriculum,** syllabus, module, department; **subject;** major, minor; requirement *or* required course, elective course, core curriculum; refresher course; summer *or* summer-session course, intersession course; gut course <nf>; correspondence course; distance-learning course; **seminar,** proseminar

9 physical education, physical culture, gymnastics, calisthenics, eurythmics

VERBS **10 teach, instruct,** give instruction, give lessons in, **educate, school; edify, enlighten,** civilize, illumine; **direct, guide;** get across, **inform** 551.8; **show,** show how, show the ropes, demonstrate; give an idea of; put in the right, set right; improve one's mind, enlarge *or* broaden the mind; sharpen the wits, open the eyes *or* mind; teach a lesson, give a lesson to; **ground,** teach the rudiments *or* elements *or* basics; catechize; teach an old dog new tricks; reeducate 858.14

11 tutor, coach, direct; prime, cram <nf>, cram with facts, stuff with knowledge

12 inculcate, indoctrinate, catechize, inoculate, **instill, infuse,** imbue, impregnate, **implant,** infix, impress; **impress upon the mind** *or* **memory,** urge on the mind, beat into, beat *or* knock into one's head, grind in, drill into, drum into one's head *or* skull; **condition, brainwash, program**

13 train; drill, exercise; practice, rehearse; keep in practice, keep one's hand in; **prepare,** ready, **condition, groom,** fit, put in tune, form, **lick into shape** <nf>; **rear, raise, bring up,** fetch up <nf>, bring up by hand, **breed; cultivate,** develop, improve; **nurture, foster,** nurse; **discipline,** take in hand; put through the mill *or* grind <nf>; break, break in, housebreak, house-train <Brit>; put to school, send to school, apprentice

14 preinstruct, pre-educate; **initiate,** introduce

15 give instructions, give directions; **brief,** give a briefing

16 expound, exposit; explain 341.10; **lecture, discourse,** harangue, hold forth, give or read a lesson; **preach,** sermonize; **moralize,** point a moral

17 assign, give *or* make an assignment, give homework, set a task, set hurdles; lay out a course, make a syllabus

ADJS **18 educational,** educative, educating, educatory, teaching, **instructive,** instructional, **tuitional,** tuitionary; **cultural, edifying, enlightening,** illuminating; informative, informational; edifying; didactic, preceptive; self-instructional, self-teaching, autodidactic; lecturing, preaching, hortatory, exhortatory, homiletic, homiletical; initiatory, introductory, propaedeutic; **disciplinary;** coeducational; remedial

19 **scholastic, academic, schoolish, pedantic, donnish** <Brit>; **scholarly; pedagogical;** collegiate, graduate, professional, doctoral, graduate-professional, postgraduate; interdisciplinary, cross-disciplinary; curricular, intramural, extramural, varsity

20 extracurricular, extraclassroom; nonscholastic, noncollegiate

569 MISTEACHING

NOUNS 1 **misteaching,** misinstruction; **misguidance,** misdirection, misleading; sophistry 936; perversion, corruption; mystification, obscuration, obfuscation, obscurantism; **misinformation,** misknowledge; the blind leading the blind; college of Laputa

2 **propaganda;** propagandism, indoctrination; brainwashing; **propagandist,** agitprop; **disinformation**

VERBS 3 **misteach,** misinstruct, miseducate; **misinform;** misadvise, **misguide,** misdirect, **mislead;** pervert, corrupt; mystify, obscure, obfuscate

4 **propagandize,** carry on a propaganda; indoctrinate; **disinform,** brainwash

ADJS 5 **mistaught,** misinstructed; **misinformed;** misadvised, **misguided,** misdirected, **misled**

6 misteaching, misinstructive, miseducative, **misinforming; misleading,** misguiding, misdirecting; obscuring, mystifying, obfuscatory; propagandistic, indoctrinational; disinformational

570 LEARNING

NOUNS 1 **learning,** intellectual acquirement *or* acquisition *or* attainment, stocking *or* storing the mind, mental cultivation, mental culture, improving *or* broadening the mind, acquisition of knowledge, scholarship; **mastery,** mastery of skills; **self-education,** self-instruction; **knowledge, erudition** 928.5; education 568.1; memorization 989.4

2 **absorption,** ingestion, imbibing, assimilation, taking-in, getting, getting hold of, getting the hang of <nf>, soaking-up, digestion

3 **study, studying,** application, conning; **reading, perusal;** restudy, restudying, brushing up, boning up <nf>, **review; contemplation** 931.2; **inspection** 938.3; **engrossment; brainwork, headwork,** lucubration, mental labor; exercise, **practice, drill;** grind *and* grinding *and* boning <nf>, boning up

<nf>; **cramming** *and* cram <nf>, swotting <Brit nf>; extensive study, wide reading; subject 568.8

4 **studiousness, scholarliness,** scholarship; bookishness, diligence 330.6; learnedness, intellectuality, literacy, polymathy, erudition

5 **teachableness, teachability, educability,** trainableness; **aptness, aptitude,** quickness, **readiness; receptivity,** mind like a blotter, ready grasp, quick mind, quick study; **willingness, motivation,** hunger *or* thirst for learning, willingness to learn, curiosity, inquisitiveness; docility, **malleability,** moldability, pliability, facility, plasticity, **impressionability,** susceptibility, formability; brightness, cleverness, quickness, readiness, **intelligence** 920

VERBS 6 **learn,** get, get hold of <nf>, get into one's head, get through one's thick skull <nf>; **gain knowledge,** pick up information, gather *or* collect *or* glean knowledge *or* learning; stock *or* store the mind, improve *or* broaden the mind; stuff *or* cram the mind; burden *or* load the mind; **find out, ascertain, discover,** find, determine; **become informed,** gain knowledge *or* understanding of, acquire information *or* intelligence about, research, become aware of, **learn about, find out about;** acquaint oneself with, make oneself acquainted with, become acquainted with; be informed 551.14

7 **absorb, acquire, take in,** ingest, imbibe, get by osmosis, **assimilate, digest, soak up,** drink in; **soak in, seep in,** percolate in

8 **memorize** 989.17, get by rote; fix in the mind 989.18

9 **master,** attain mastery of, make oneself master of, **gain command of, become adept in,** become familiar *or* conversant with, become versed *or* well-versed in, **get up in** *or* **on,** gain a good *or* thorough knowledge of, **learn all about, get down pat** <nf>, get down cold <nf>, get taped <Brit nf>, get to the bottom *or* heart of; **get the hang** *or* **knack of; learn the ropes,** learn the ins and outs; know well 928.13

10 **learn by experience,** learn by doing, **live and learn,** go through the school of hard knocks, learn the hard way <nf>; teach *or* school oneself; **learn a lesson,** be taught a lesson

11 **be taught, receive instruction,** be tutored, be instructed, undergo schooling, pursue one's education, attend classes, go to *or* attend school, take lessons, matriculate, enroll, register; **train,** prepare oneself, ready oneself, go into training; serve an apprenticeship; apprentice, apprentice oneself to; **study with,** read with, sit at the feet of, learn from, have as one's master; monitor, audit

12 **study,** regard studiously, apply oneself to, con,

crack a book *and* hit the books <nf>; **read, peruse,** go over, read up *or* read up on, have one's nose in a book <nf>; restudy, **review; contemplate** 931.12; **examine** 938.23; give the mind to 983.5; **pore over,** vet <Brit nf>; be highly motivated, hunger *or* thirst for knowledge; bury oneself in, wade through, plunge into; **dig** *and* **grind** *and* **bone** *and* bone up on <nf>, swot <Brit nf>; lucubrate, elucubrate, **burn the midnight oil;** make a study of; **practice, drill**

13 **browse, scan, skim, dip into,** thumb over *or* through, run over *or* through, glance *or* run the eye over *or* through, turn over the leaves, have a look at, hit the high spots, graze

14 **study up, get up,** study up on, read up on, get up on; **review, brush up,** polish up <nf>, rub up, **cram** *or* cram up <nf>, **bone up** <nf>; pull an all-nighter

15 **study to be, study for, read for,** read law, etc; **specialize in, go in for,** make one's field; major in, minor in

ADJS 16 educated, **learned** 928.21,22; knowledgeable, erudite; literate, numerate; self-taught, self-instructed, autodidactic

17 **studious,** devoted to studies, **scholarly,** scholastic, academic, professorial, tweedy, donnish <Brit>; owlish; rabbinic, mandarin; pedantic, dryasdust; bookish 928.22; diligent 330.22

18 **teachable, instructable, educable,** schoolable, trainable; **apt,** quick, **ready,** ripe for instruction; **receptive, willing,** motivated; hungry *or* thirsty for knowledge; docile, **malleable, moldable,** pliable, facile, plastic, **impressionable,** susceptible, formable; bright, clever, **intelligent** 920.12

571 TEACHER

NOUNS 1 **teacher, instructor, educator,** preceptor, **mentor; master,** maestro; **pedagogue,** pedagogist, educationist, educationalist, tutor; schoolman; **schoolteacher, schoolmaster,** schoolkeeper; abecedarian <old>, certified *or* licensed teacher; **professor, academic,** member of academy; don <Brit>, fellow; guide 574.7, docent; rabbi, *melamed* <Heb>, pandit, pundit, guru, *mullah* <Persian>, *starets* <Russ>; home tutor, private tutor, mentor

2 <woman teachers> instructress, educatress, preceptress, **mistress; schoolmistress;** schoolma'am *or* **schoolmarm,** dame, schooldame; **governess,** duenna

3 <academic ranks> professor, associate professor, assistant professor, instructor, tutor, associate, assistant, lecturer, reader <Brit>; visiting professor; emeritus, professor emeritus, retired professor

4 teaching fellow, teaching assistant; teaching intern, fellow, intern; practice teacher, apprentice teacher, student *or* pupil teacher; teacher's aide, paraprofessional; monitor, proctor, prefect, praepostor <Brit>; student assistant, graduate assistant

5 **tutor,** tutorer; **coach,** coacher; **private instructor,** *Privatdocent* or *Privatdozent* <Ger>; crammer <Brit nf>

6 **trainer, handler, groomer;** driller, drillmaster; **coach,** athletic coach

7 **lecturer,** lector, **reader** <Brit>, praelector, **preacher,** homilist

8 **principal, headmaster,** headmistress, vice-principal; president, chancellor, vice-chancellor, rector, provost, master; **dean,** academic dean, dean of the faculty, dean of women, dean of men; administrator, educational administrator; administration; department head *or* chair

9 **faculty,** staff <Brit>, faculty members, professorate, professoriate, professors, professordom, teaching staff

10 **instructorship, teachership,** preceptorship, schoolmastery; **tutorship,** tutorhood, tutorage, tutelage; **professorship,** professorhood, professorate, professoriate; **chair,** endowed chair; lectureship, readership <Brit>; fellowship, research fellowship; assistantship

ADJS 11 **pedagogic, pedagogical,** preceptorial, tutorial; **teacherish,** teachery, teacherlike, teachy, **schoolteacherish,** schoolteachery, **schoolmasterish,** schoolmasterly, schoolmastering, schoolmasterlike; schoolmistressy, schoolmarmish <nf>; **professorial,** professorlike, academic, tweedy, donnish <Brit>; pedantic 928.22

572 STUDENT

NOUNS 1 **student, pupil, scholar,** learner, studier, educatee, **trainee,** *élève* <Fr>; tutee; inquirer; mature student, adult-education *or* continuing education student; self-taught person, autodidact; auditor; **reader,** reading enthusiast, great reader, printhead <nf>; bookworm, researcher

2 **disciple, follower,** apostle; convert, proselyte 858.7; **discipleship,** disciplehood, pupilage, tutelage, studentship, followership

3 **schoolchild,** school kid <nf>; **schoolboy,** school lad; **schoolgirl;** day-pupil, day boy, day girl; preschool child, preschooler, nursery school child, infant <Brit>; kindergartner, grade schooler, primary schooler, intermediate schooler; secondary schooler, prep schooler, preppie <nf>, high schooler; schoolmate, schoolfellow, fellow student, classmate

4 special *or* exceptional student, gifted student; special education *or* special ed <nf> student; learning disabled *or* LD student; learning impaired student; slow learner, underachiever; handicapped *or* retarded student; emotionally disturbed student; culturally disadvantaged student

5 **college student, collegian,** collegiate, university student, **varsity student** <Brit nf>, college boy *or* girl; co-ed <nf>; seminarian, seminarist; *bahur* <Heb>, *yeshiva bocher* <Yiddish>

6 **undergraduate,** undergrad <nf>, cadet, midshipman; underclassman, **freshman,** freshie <nf>, plebe, **sophomore,** soph <nf>; **upperclassman, junior, senior**

7 <Brit terms> commoner, pensioner, sizar, servitor <old>, exhibitioner, fellow commoner; sophister *and* questionist <old>; wrangler, optime; passman

8 **graduate,** grad <nf>; **alumnus,** alumni, alumna, alumnae; old boy <Brit>; **graduate student,** grad student <nf>, master's degree candidate, doctoral candidate; **postgraduate,** postgrad <nf>; degrees; college graduate, college man *or* woman, educated man *or* woman, educated class; meritocracy

9 **novice,** novitiate *or* noviciate, **tyro,** abecedarian, alphabetarian, **beginner** 818.2, entrant, **neophyte, tenderfoot** *and* **greenhorn** <nf>, freshman, **fledgling;** catechumen, initiate, debutant; new boy <Brit>, newcomer 774.4; ignoramus 930.8; **recruit, raw recruit,** inductee, **rookie** *and* yardbird <nf>, boot; **probationer,** probationist, postulant; **apprentice,** articled clerk

10 **nerd** *and* grind *or* greasy grind <nf>, swotter *or* mugger <Brit nf>; bookworm 929.4

11 **class, form** <Brit>, **grade;** track; year

ADJS **12** **studentlike,** schoolboyish, schoolgirlish; undergraduate, graduate, postgraduate; **collegiate,** college-bred; sophomoric; sophomorical; autodidactic; **studious** 570.17; **learned, bookish** 928.22; exceptional, gifted, special

13 **probationary,** probational, on probation; in detention

573 DIRECTION, MANAGEMENT

NOUNS **1** **direction, management, managing,** managery <old>, handling, **running** <nf>, **conduct;** governance, **command, control, chiefdom, government** 612, governance, controllership; **authority** 417; **regulation,** ordering, husbandry; manipulation, orchestration; **guidance, lead, leading; steering, navigation,** pilotage, conning, the conn, the helm, the wheel

2 **supervision, superintendence,** intendance *or* intendancy, heading, heading up *and* **bossing** *and* running <nf>; **surveillance,** oversight, eye; **charge,** care, auspices, jurisdiction; **responsibility,** accountability 641.2

3 **administration,** executive function *or* role, command function, say-so *and* last word <nf>; **decision-making; disposition,** disposal, **dispensation;** officiation; lawmaking, legislation, regulation

4 **directorship, leadership, managership,** directorate, headship, governorship, chairmanship, convenership <Brit>, presidency, premiership, generalship, captainship; mastership 417.7; dictatorship, sovereignty 417.8; superintendence *or* **superintendency,** intendancy, foremanship, overseership, supervisorship; stewardship, custody, guardianship, shepherding, proctorship; personnel management; collective leadership

5 **helm,** conn, rudder, tiller, wheel, steering wheel; **reins;** joystick; remote control *or* remote

6 **domestic management, housekeeping,** homemaking, housewifery, ménage, husbandry <old>; domestic economy, home economics

7 **efficiency engineering,** scientific management, bean-counting <nf>, industrial engineering, management engineering, management consulting; management theory; efficiency expert, management consultant; time and motion study, time-motion study, time study; therblig

VERBS **8** **direct, manage, regulate, conduct, carry on, handle, run** <nf>, be in charge; **control, command, head, govern** 612.12, rule, **boss** *and* head up *and* pull the strings *and* **mastermind** *and* quarterback *and* call the signals <nf>; **order, prescribe;** organize; lay down the law, make the rules, call the shots *or* tune <nf>; **head,** head up, office, captain, skipper <nf>; **lead,** take the lead, lead on; manipulate, maneuver, engineer; take command 417.14; be responsible for; hold the purse strings <nf>

9 **guide, steer, drive, run** <nf>; herd, counsel, advise, shepherd; channel; **pilot,** take the helm *or* wheel, be at the helm *or* wheel *or* tiller *or* rudder, hold the reins, **be in the driver's seat** <nf>; emcee

10 **supervise, superintend, boss, oversee,** overlook, ride herd on <nf>, crack the whip <nf>, stand over, keep an eye on *or* upon, keep in order; cut work out for; straw-boss <nf>; take care of 1007.19

11 **administer,** administrate; **officiate; preside,** preside over, preside at the board; chair, chairman, occupy the chair, take the chair

ADJS **12** **directing, directive,** directory, directorial; **managing, managerial; commanding, controlling, governing** 612.18; regulating, regulative, regulatory; **head, chief;** leading, guiding

13 supervising, supervisory, overseeing, **superintendent, boss; in charge** 417.21, in the driver's seat *and* holding the reins <nf>

14 administrative, administrating; ministerial, **executive; officiating, presiding**

ADVS **15 in the charge of,** in the hands of, in the care of; **under the auspices of,** under the aegis of; in one's charge, on one's hands, under one's care, under one's jurisdiction

574 DIRECTOR

NOUNS **1 director,** *directeur* <Fr>, director general, **governor,** rector, **manager, administrator,** intendant, **conductor;** person in charge, responsible person, key person; ship's husband, supercargo; impresario, producer; deputy, agent 576

2 superintendent; supervisor, foreman, monitor, **head,** headman, overman, **boss,** chief, gaffer *and* ganger <Brit nf>, taskmaster; *sirdar* <India>, **overseer,** overlooker; inspector, surveyor; proctor; subforeman, **straw boss** <nf>; slave driver; boatswain; floorman, floorwalker, floor manager; noncommissioned officer 575.19; controller, comptroller, auditor; department head

3 executive, officer, official, pinstriper <nf>, employer, company official; suit <nf>; **president,** prexy <nf>, chief executive officer *or* CEO, chief executive, chief operating officer *or* COO, managing director, director; provost, prefect, warden, archon; policy-maker, agenda-setter; magistrate; **chairman of the board; chancellor,** vice-chancellor; vice-president *or* VP *or* veep <nf>; secretary; treasurer; dean; executive officer, executive director, executive secretary; **management,** the administration 574.11

4 steward, bailiff <Brit>, reeve <old>, factor <Scot>, seneschal; majordomo, butler, housekeeper, *maître d'hôtel* <Fr>; master of ceremonies *or* MC *and* emcee <nf>, master of the revels; proctor, procurator, attorney; guardian, custodian 1008.6, executor; curator, librarian; croupier; factor

5 chairman, chairwoman, **chair,** chairperson, convener <Brit>, speaker, presiding officer; co-chairman, etc

6 leader, conductor <old>; file leader, fugleman; pacemaker, pacesetter; bellwether, bell mare, bell cow, Judas goat; standard-bearer, torchbearer; **leader of men,** born leader, charismatic leader *or* figure, inspired leader; messiah, Mahdi; führer, duce; forerunner 816.1; ringleader 375.11; precentor, coryphaeus, choragus, symphonic conductor, choirmaster 710.18

7 guide, guider; **shepherd,** herd, herdsman, drover, cowherd, goatherd, etc; tour guide, tour director *or* conductor, cicerone, mercury <old>, courier, dragoman; **pilot,** river pilot, navigator, **helmsman,** timoneer, steerman, steerer, coxswain, boatsteerer, boatheader; automatic pilot, Gyropilot; pointer, fingerpost <Brit>, guidepost 517.4; leader, motivator, pacesetter, standard-bearer

8 guiding star, cynosure <old>, **polestar,** polar star, lodestar, Polaris, **North Star**

9 compass, magnetic compass, gyrocompass, gyroscopic compass, gyrostatic compass, Gyrosin compass, surveyor's compass, mariner's compass; needle, magnetic needle; direction finder, radio compass, radio direction finder *or* RDF

10 directory, guidebook, handbook, Baedeker; city directory, business directory; telephone directory, telephone book, phone book <nf>, classified directory, Yellow Pages; **bibliography;** catalog, index, handlist, checklist, finding list; itinerary, road map, roadbook; gazetteer, reference book; portal, web directory

11 directorate, directory, **management, the administration,** the brass *and* top brass <nf>, the people upstairs *and* the people in the front office <nf>, executive hierarchy; the executive, executive arm *or* branch; middle management; **cabinet; board,** governing board *or* body, board of directors, board of trustees, board of regents; steering committee, executive committee, interlocking directorate; cadre, executive council; infrastructure; council 423

575 MASTER

NOUNS **1 master, lord, lord and master,** overlord, seigneur, paramount, lord paramount, liege, liege lord, lord of the manor, *padrone* <Ital>, *patron and chef* <Fr>, patroon; **chief, boss,** *sahib* <India>, *bwana* <Swah>; employer; husband, man of the house, master of the house, goodman <old nf>, paterfamilias; patriarch, elder; teacher, rabbi, guru, starets; church dignitary, ecclesiarch

2 mistress, governess, dame <old>, madam; **matron, housewife,** homemaker, goodwife <Scot>, mistress *or* lady of the house, chatelaine; housemistress, housemother; rectoress, abbess, mother superior; great lady, first lady; materfamilias, matriarch, dowager

3 chief, principal, headman; **master,** dean, doyen, doyenne; high priest <nf>, superior, senior; **leader** 574.6; important person, personage 996.8; owner, landowner

4 <nf terms> **top dog,** boss man, big boy, Big Daddy, big cheese, kingpin, kingfish, el supremo, honcho *or* head honcho, top banana, big enchilada, bigwig, big gun, big shot, big wheel, VIP, himself, herself, man *or* woman upstairs, cock of the walk; queen bee, heavy momma, Big Momma, old man, quarterback, ringmaster, skipper, high priest

5 figurehead, nominal head, dummy, lay figure, front man *and* front <nf>, stooge *and* Charlie McCarthy <nf>, puppet, creature

6 governor, ruler; captain, master, commander, commandant, commanding officer, intendant, castellan, chatelain, chatelaine; **director, manager, executive** 574.3

7 head of state, chief of state, leader; premier, prime minister, chancellor, grand vizier, *dewan* <India>; doge; **president,** chief executive, the man in the White House

8 potentate, sovereign, monarch, ruler, prince, dynast, **crowned head, emperor,** *imperator* <L>, king-emperor, **king,** anointed king, majesty, royalty, royal, royal personage, emperor, etc; petty king, tetrarch, kinglet; grand duke; paramount, lord paramount, suzerain, overlord, overking, high king; **chief, chieftain,** high chief; prince consort 608.7

9 <rulers> **caesar,** kaiser, **czar;** Holy Roman Emperor; Dalai Lama; **pharaoh;** pendragon, rig, ardri; **mikado,** tenno; shogun, tycoon; khan *or* cham; shah, padishah; negus; bey; **sheikh;** sachem, sagamore; Inca; cacique; kaid

10 <Muslim rulers> sultan, Grand Turk, grand seignior; caliph, imam; hakim; khan *or* cham; nizam, nabab; emir; Great Mogul, Mogul

11 sovereign queen, sovereign princess, princess, queen, queen regent, queen regnant, **empress,** czarina, *Kaiserin* <Ger>; *rani* and *maharani* <India>; grand duchess; queen consort

12 regent, protector, prince regent, queen regent

13 <regional governors> **governor,** governor-general, lieutenant governor; **viceroy,** vice-king, exarch, proconsul, khedive, stadtholder, vizier; *nabob* and *nabab* and *subahdar* <India>; gauleiter; eparch; palatine; tetrarch; burgrave; collector; hospodar, vaivode; dey, bey *or* beg, beglerbeg, wali *or* vali, satrap; provincial; warlord; military governor

14 tyrant, despot, warlord, **autocrat, autarch;** oligarch; absolute ruler *or* master *or* monarch, omnipotent *or* all-powerful ruler; **dictator,** duce, führer, commissar, pharaoh, caesar, czar; usurper, arrogator; **oppressor, hard master,** driver, **slave driver,** Simon Legree <Harriet B Stowe>; **martinet, disciplinarian,** stickler, tin god, petty tyrant

15 the authorities, the powers that be, ruling class *or* classes, the lords of creation, **the Establishment,** the interests, the power elite, **the power structure; they,** them; the inner circle; the ins *and* the in-group *and* those on the inside <nf>; **management, the administration;** higher echelons, top brass <nf>; higher-ups *and* the people upstairs *or* in the front office <nf>; **the top** <nf>, the corridors of power; prelacy, hierarchy; ministry; **bureaucracy, officialdom;** directorate 574.11

16 official, officer, officiary, functionary, *fonctionnaire* <Fr>, apparatchik; **public official,** public servant; officeholder, office-bearer *and* placeman <Brit>; government *or* public employee; **civil servant; bureaucrat,** politician, mandarin, red-tapist, *rond-de-cuir* <Fr>; petty tyrant, jack-in-office

17 <public officials> **minister,** secretary, secretary of state <Brit>, undersecretary, cabinet minister, cabinet member, minister of state <Brit>; chancellor; warden; archon; magistrate; syndic; commissioner; commissar; county commissioners; city manager, mayor, *maire* <Fr>, lord mayor, burgomaster; headman, *induna* <Africa>; **councilman,** councilwoman, councillor, city councilman, elder, city father, alderman, bailie <Scot>, selectman; supervisor, county supervisor; reeve, portreeve; legislator 610.3

18 commissioned officer, officer, military leader, military officer; top brass *and* the brass <nf>; **commander in chief,** generalissimo, captain general; hetman, sirdar, commanding officer, commandant; general of the army, general of the air force, five-star general <nf>, **marshal,** *maréchal* <Fr>, field marshal; general officer, **general,** four-star general <nf>; lieutenant general, three-star general <nf>; major general, two-star general <nf>, brigadier general, one-star general <nf>, brigadier <Brit>; field officer; **colonel,** chicken colonel <nf>; lieutenant colonel; **major;** company officer; **captain; lieutenant,** first lieutenant; second lieutenant, shavetail <nf>, subaltern *and* sublieutenant <Brit>; warrant officer, chief warrant officer; **commander,** commandant, the Old Man <nf>; **commanding officer** *or* CO; executive officer, exec <nf>; chief of staff; aide, aide-de-camp *or* ADC; officer of the day *or* OD, orderly officer <Brit>; staff officer; senior officer, junior officer; brass hat <nf>

19 Army noncommissioned officer, noncom *or* NCO <nf>; centurion; sergeant, sarge <nf>, *havildar* <India>; sergeant major of the Army, command sergeant major, sergeant major, first sergeant, top sergeant *and* topkick *and* first man <nf>, master sergeant, sergeant first class, technical sergeant, staff sergeant, sergeant, specialist seven, platoon sergeant, mess sergeant, color sergeant, acting sergeant, lance sergeant <Brit>; **corporal,** acting corporal, lance corporal <Brit>, lance-jack <Brit nf>; **Air Force noncommissioned officer,** chief master sergeant of the Air Force, chief master sergeant, senior master sergeant, master sergeant, technical sergeant, staff sergeant, sergeant, airman first class

20 **Navy** *or* **naval officer; fleet admiral,** navarch, **admiral,** vice admiral, rear admiral, **commodore, captain, commander,** lieutenant commander, **lieutenant,** lieutenant junior grade, ensign; warrant officer; Navy *or* naval noncommissioned officer, master chief petty officer of the Navy, master chief petty officer, senior chief petty officer, chief petty officer, petty officer first class, petty officer second class, petty officer third class; **Marine Corps noncommissioned officer,** sergeant major of the Marine Corps, sergeant major, master gunnery sergeant, first sergeant, master sergeant, gunnery sergeant, staff sergeant, sergeant, corporal, lance corporal

21 <heraldic officials> herald, king of arms, king at arms, earl marshal; Garter, Garter King of Arms, Clarenceux, Clarenceux King of Arms, Norroy and Ulster, Norroy and Ulster King of Arms, Norroy, Norroy King of Arms, Lyon, Lyon King of Arms; College of Arms

576 DEPUTY, AGENT

NOUNS 1 **deputy, proxy, representative, substitute,** sub <nf>, vice, vicegerent, **alternate,** backup *and* stand-in <nf>, body double, alternative, alter ego, **surrogate,** procurator, secondary, understudy, pinch hitter <nf>, utility man *or* woman, scrub <nf>, reserve, the bench <nf>; assistant, right hand, second in command, number two, executive officer; exponent, advocate, pleader, paranymph, attorney, champion; **lieutenant;** aide; vicar, vicar general; locum tenens *or* locum <chiefly Brit>; amicus curiae; **puppet,** dummy, creature, cat's-paw, figurehead; stunt man *or* woman; ghost writer

2 **delegate,** legate, appointee; **commissioner,** commissary, *commissionaire* <Fr>, commissar; **messenger,** herald, **emissary, envoy; minister,** secretary

3 **agent, instrument,** implement, implementer, trustee, broker; expediter, facilitator; **tool; steward** 574.4; **functionary; official** 575.16; clerk, **secretary;** amanuensis; factor, consignee; puppet, cat's-paw; dupe 358

4 **go-between, middleman, intermediary, medium,** intermedium, intermediate, interagent, **internuncio,** broker; connection <nf>, **contact; negotiator,** negotiant; interpleader; arbitrator, mediator 466.3

5 **spokesman, spokeswoman, spokesperson,** spokespeople, official spokesman *or* -woman *or* -person, press officer, speaker, voice, mouthpiece <nf>; spin doctor <nf>; herald; messenger; prolocutor, prolocutress *or* prolocutrix; reporter, rapporteur

6 **diplomat,** diplomatist, diplomatic agent, diplomatic <old>; **emissary, envoy, legate, minister,** foreign service officer; **ambassador,** ambassadress, ambassador-at-large; envoy extraordinary, plenipotentiary, **minister plenipotentiary;** nuncio, internuncio, apostolic delegate; vice-legate; resident, minister resident; chargé d'affaires, chargé, chargé d'affaires ad interim; secretary of legation, chancellor <Brit>; **attaché,** commercial attaché, military attaché, **consul,** consul general, vice-consul, consular agent; career diplomat

7 **foreign office, foreign service,** diplomatic service; diplomatic mission, diplomatic staff *or* corps, *corps diplomatique* <Fr>; **embassy, legation;** consular service

8 vice-president, vice-chairman, vice-governor, vice-director, vice-master, vice-chancellor, vice-premier, vice-warden, vice-consul, vice-legate; vice-regent, viceroy, vicegerent, vice-king, vice-queen, vice-reine, etc

9 **secret agent,** operative, cloak-and-dagger operative, **undercover man,** inside man <nf>; **spy,** espionage agent; counterspy, double agent; **spotter; scout,** reconnoiterer; **intelligence agent** *or* **officer;** CIA man, military-intelligence man, naval-intelligence man; spymaster; spy-catcher <nf>, counterintelligence agent

10 **detective, operative, investigator, sleuth,** Sherlock Holmes <A Conan Doyle>; police detective, Bow Street runner *or* officer <Brit old>, **plainclothesman;** private detective *or* dick, private investigator *or* PI, inquiry agent <Brit>; hotel detective, house detective, house dick <nf>, store detective; arson investigator; narcotics agent, narc <nf>; FBI agent *or* G-man <nf>; treasury agent *or* T-man <nf>; Federal *or* fed <nf>; Federal Bureau of Investigation *or* FBI; Secret Service

11 <nf terms> **dick,** gumshoe, gumshoe man, hawkshaw, sleuthhound, beagle, flatfoot, tec; eye, private eye; skip tracer, spotter

12 **secret service,** intelligence service, intelligence bureau *or* department; intelligence, military intelligence, naval intelligence; **counterintelligence**

13 <group of delegates> **delegation, deputation, commission, mission,** legation; committee, subcommittee

VERBS 14 **represent, act for,** act on behalf of, substitute for, appear for, answer for, speak for, be the voice of, give voice to, be the mouthpiece of <nf>, hold the proxy of, hold a brief for, act in the place of, stand in the stead of, serve in one's stead, pinch-hit for <nf>; understudy, double for *and* stand in for *and* back up <nf>, substitute for; front for <nf>; deputize, commission; ghostwrite *or* ghost

15 deputize, depute, authorize, empower, charge, designate, nominate

ADJS 16 **deputy,** deputative; **acting,** representative

17 diplomatic, ambassadorial, consular, ministerial, plenipotentiary

ADVS 18 by proxy, indirectly; in behalf of 862.12

577 SERVANT, EMPLOYEE

NOUNS 1 **retainer,** dependent, follower; myrmidon, yeoman; vassal, liege, liege man, henchman, feudatory, homager; inferior, **underling, subordinate,** understrapper; **minion,** creature, hanger-on, lackey, flunky, stooge <nf>, drudge; peon, serf, bond servant, thrall, vassal, slave 432.7

2 **servant,** servitor, help, paid helper; **domestic,** domestic help, domestic servant, house *or* household servant; live-in help, day help; **menial,** drudge, slavey <nf>; scullion, turnspit; humble servant

3 **employee;** pensioner, **hireling, mercenary,** myrmidon; wage earner, staff member; hired man, hired hand, man *or* girl Friday, right-hand man, assistant 616.6; worker 726, subordinate, subaltern; white-collar worker, nonmanual worker, skilled worker, semiskilled worker, unskilled worker, blue-collar worker, manual worker, laborer; part-time worker, freelance worker; hourly worker; officer worker, assistant, administrative assistant, secretary, clerk, messenger, runner, gofer

4 **man,** manservant, serving man, gillie <Scot>, **boy,** *garçon* <Fr>, houseboy, houseman; butler; valet, *valet de chambre* <Fr>, gentleman, gentleman's gentleman; driver, chauffeur, coachman; gardener; handyman, odd-job man; lord-in-waiting, lord of the bedchamber, equerry; bodyguard, chaperon

5 **attendant,** tender, usher, server, squire, yeoman; errand boy *or* girl, gofer <nf>, office boy *or* girl, copyboy; page, footboy; concierge; bellboy, bellman, bellhop; cabin boy, purser; porter, redcap; printer's devil; chore boy; caddie; bootblack, boots <Brit>, shoeshine boy, shoeblack; trainbearer; cupbearer, Ganymede, Hebe; orderly, batman <Brit>; **cabin** *or* **flight attendant, steward, stewardess, hostess,** airline stewardess *or* hostess, stew <nf>, cabin crew, skycap; hat-check girl, cloakroom attendant; salesclerk *or* clerk, salesperson, shop assistant <Brit>

6 **lackey, flunky,** livery *or* liveried servant; **footman,** *valet de pied* <Fr>

7 **waiter, waitress;** carhop; counterman, soda jerk <nf>; busboy; headwaiter, *maître d'hôtel* <Fr>, maître d' <nf>; hostess; wine steward, sommelier; bartender, barkeeper *or* barkeep, barman, barmaid

8 **maid, maidservant,** servitress, **girl,** servant girl, *bonne* <Fr>, serving girl, wench, biddy <nf>, hired girl; lady-help <Brit>, au pair girl, *ayah* <India>, *amah* <China>; live-in maid, live-out maid; **handmaid,** handmaiden; personal attendant; **lady's maid,** waiting maid *or* woman, gentlewoman, abigail, soubrette; lady-in-waiting, maid-in-waiting, lady of the bedchamber; companion; chaperon; betweenmaid *or* tweeny <Brit>; duenna; parlormaid; kitchenmaid, scullery maid; cook; housemaid, chambermaid, *femme de chambre* or *fille de chambre* <Fr>, upstairs maid; nursemaid 1008.8

9 **factotum, do-all** <old>, general servant <Brit>, man of all work; maid of all work, domestic drudge, slavey <nf>, Mister Fix-it

10 **major-domo, steward,** house steward, **butler,** chamberlain, *maître d'hôtel* <Fr>, seneschal; **housekeeper**

11 **staff, personnel, employees,** help, hired help, occasional help, the help, **crew, gang,** men, force, servantry, retinue 769.6

12 **service,** servanthood, servitude <old>, servitorship, *servitium* <L>; **employment, employ; ministry, ministration, attendance,** tendance; serfdom, peonage, thralldom, slavery 432.1

VERBS 13 **serve, work for,** be in service, serve one's every need; minister *or* administer to, pander to, do service; **help** 449.11; **care for,** do for <nf>, **look after,** wait on hand and foot, take care of; **wait, wait on** *or* **upon, attend,** tend, attend on *or* upon, dance attendance upon; make oneself useful; lackey, valet, maid, chore; drudge 725.14

ADJS 14 **serving,** servitorial, servitial, **ministering,** waiting, waiting on, **attending,** attendant; in the train of, in one's pay *or* employ; helping 449.20; **menial, servile**

578 FASHION

NOUNS 1 **fashion, style, mode, vogue,** trend, prevailing taste; proper thing, ton, bon ton; design; custom 373; convention 579.1,2; the swim <nf>, current *or* stream of fashion; height of fashion; the new look, the season's look; high fashion, *haute couture* <Fr>, designer label; flavor of the month, flavor of the week; personal style, signature

2 **fashionableness,** chic, ton, bon ton, fashionability, **stylishness, modishness,** voguishness; with-itness <nf>; **popularity,** prevalence, currency 864.2

3 **smartness, chic,** elegance; style-consciousness,

clothes-consciousness; **spruceness, nattiness,** neatness, trimness, sleekness, **dapperness,** jauntiness; sharpness *and* spiffiness *and* classiness *and* niftiness <nf>; swankness *and* **swankiness** <nf>; foppery, foppishness, coxcombry, dandyism; hipness <nf>

4 the rage, the thing, **the last word** <nf>, *le dernier cri* <Fr>, **the latest thing,** the in thing *and* the latest wrinkle <nf>

5 fad, craze, rage; wrinkle <nf>; new take <nf>; novelty 841.2; faddishness, faddiness <nf>, faddism; **faddist;** the bandwagon, me-tooism

6 society, *société* <Fr>, fashionable society, **polite society, high society,** high life, *beau monde* and *haut monde* <Fr>, good society; best people, people of fashion, right people; *monde* <Fr>, world of fashion, Vanity Fair; **smart set** <nf>; the Four Hundred, **upper crust** *and* upper cut <nf>; **cream of society,** *crème de la crème* <Fr>, cream of the crop, elite, carriage trade; café society, jet set, beautiful people, in-crowd, glitterati <nf>; *jeunesse dorée* <Fr>; drawing room, salon; social register; fast track

7 person of fashion, fashionable, man-about-town, man *or* woman of the world, nob, *mondain or mondaine* <Fr>; leader *or* arbiter of fashion, tastemaker, trendsetter, tonesetter, *arbiter elegantiae* <L>, arbiter of fashion; ten best-dressed, fashion plate, clotheshorse, sharpy <nf>, snappy dresser; Beau Brummel, fop, dandy 500.9; **socialite; clubwoman,** clubman; salonist, salonnard; jet setter; swinger <nf>; **debutante,** subdebutante, deb *and* subdeb <nf>, Sloane Ranger <Brit nf>; rag trade <nf>

VERBS 8 catch on, become popular, **become the rage,** catch *or* take fire

9 be fashionable, be the style, be the rage, be the thing; have a run; cut a figure in society <nf>, give a tone to society, set the fashion *or* style *or* tone; dress to kill

10 follow the fashion, get in the swim <nf>, get *or* climb *or* jump on the bandwagon <nf>, join the parade, follow the crowd, go with the stream *or* tide *or* current *or* flow; keep in step, do as others do; keep up, **keep up appearances,** keep up with the Joneses

ADJS 11 fashionable, in fashion, smart, in style, in vogue; all the rage, all the thing; **popular,** prevalent, current 863.12; **up-to-date,** up-to-datish, up-to-the-minute, happening <nf>, switched-on *and* hip *and* with-it *and* in <nf>, trendy <nf>, newfashioned, modern, mod <nf>, new 840.9,10,12–14; **in the swim;** sought-after, much sought-after

12 stylish, modish, voguish, vogue; dressy <nf>;

soigné or *soignée* <Fr>; *à la mode* <Fr>, in the mode

13 chic, smart, elegant; style-conscious, clothes-conscious; **well-dressed,** well-groomed, *soigné* or *soignée* <Fr>, dressed to advantage, all dressed up, dressed to kill, dressed to the teeth, dressed to the nines, well-turned-out; **spruce, natty,** neat, trim, sleek, smug, trig, tricksy <old>; **dapper,** dashing, jaunty, braw <Scot>; sharp *and* spiffy *and* classy *and* nifty *and* snazzy <nf>; **swank** *or* **swanky** <nf>, posh <nf>, ritzy <nf>, swell *and* nobby <nf>; genteel; exquisite, *recherché* <Fr>; cosmopolitan, sophisticated

14 ultrafashionable, ultrastylish, ultrasmart; chichi; foppish, dandified, dandyish, dandiacal

15 trendy <nf>, **faddish,** faddy <nf>, groovy

16 socially prominent, in society, high-society, elite; café-society, jet-set; lace-curtain, silk-stocking

ADVS 17 fashionably, stylishly, modishly, *à la mode* <Fr>, in the latest style *or* mode

18 smartly, dressily, chicly, elegantly, exquisitely; **sprucely, nattily,** neatly, trimly, sleekly; **dapperly,** jauntily, dashingly, swankly *or* swankily <nf>; foppishly, dandyishly

579 SOCIAL CONVENTION

NOUNS 1 social convention, convention, conventional usage, what is done, what one does, **social usage, form, formality; custom** 373; **conformism, conformity** 867; **propriety, decorum,** decorousness, correctness, *convenance* and *bienséance* <Fr>, decency, seemliness, civility <old>, good form, etiquette 580.3; **conventionalism, conventionality, Grundyism; Mrs Grundy**

2 the conventions, the proprieties, the mores, the right things, accepted *or* sanctioned conduct, what is done, civilized behavior; **dictates of society,** dictates of Mrs Grundy

3 conventionalist, Grundy, Mrs Grundy; conformist 867.2

VERBS 4 conform, observe the proprieties, play the game, follow the rules 867.4, fall in or into line

ADJS 5 conventional, decorous, orthodox, **correct,** right, **right-thinking, proper,** decent, seemly, meet; **accepted, recognized,** acknowledged, received, admitted, approved, being done; *comme il faut* and *de rigueur* <Fr>; **traditional, customary;** formal 580.7; conformable 867.5

ADVS 6 conventionally, decorously, orthodoxly; **customarily, traditionally;** correctly, properly, as is proper, as it should be, *comme il faut* <Fr>; according to use *or* custom, according to the dictates of society *or* Mrs Grundy

580 FORMALITY

NOUNS 1 formality, form, formalness; ceremony, ceremonial, **ceremoniousness; the red carpet; ritual,** rituality; extrinsicality, impersonality 767.1; formalization, stylization, conventionalization; **stiffness, stiltedness,** primness, prissiness, rigidness, starchiness, buckram <old>, **dignity,** gravity, weight, *gravitas* <L>, weighty dignity, staidness, reverend seriousness, **solemnity** 111; **pomp** 501.6; pomposity 501.7

 2 formalism, ceremonialism, ritualism; legalism; pedantry, pedantism, pedanticism; precisianism, preciseness, preciousness, preciosity, purism; punctiliousness, punctilio, scrupulousness; overrefinement

 3 etiquette, social code, rules *or* code of conduct; **formalities,** social procedures, social conduct *or* convention, what is done, what one does; **manners,** good manners, exquisite manners, quiet good manners, **politeness,** *politesse* <Fr>, natural politeness, comity, civility 504.1; **amenities,** decencies, civilities, elegancies, **social graces, mores, proprieties;** decorum, good form; **courtliness,** elegance 533; **protocol,** diplomatic code; punctilio, point of etiquette; convention, social usage; table manners

 4 <ceremonial function> ceremony, ceremonial; **rite, ritual, formality; solemnity, service, function,** office, **observance,** performance; **exercise,** exercises; **celebration,** solemnization; **liturgy,** religious ceremony; **rite of passage,** *rite de passage* <Fr>; convocation; commencement, commencement exercises; graduation, graduation exercises; baccalaureate service; inaugural, inauguration; initiation; formal, ball; wedding; funeral; set piece; empty formality or ceremony, mummery

VERBS 5 formalize, ritualize, solemnize, **celebrate,** dignify; **observe;** conventionalize, stylize

 6 stand on ceremony, observe the formalities, follow protocol, do things by the book

ADJS 7 formal, formulary; formalist, formalistic; legalistic; pedantic, pedantical; official, stylized, conventionalized; extrinsic, outward, impersonal 768.3; surface, **superficial, nominal** 527.15

 8 ceremonious, ceremonial; red-carpet; ritualistic, ritual; hieratic, hieratical, sacerdotal, liturgic; **grave, solemn** 111.3; **pompous** 501.22; **stately** 501.21; well-mannered 504.16; **conventional,** decorous 579.5

 9 stiff, stilted, prim, prissy, rigid, starch, starchy, starched; buckram *and* in buckram <old>

 10 punctilious, scrupulous, precise, precisian, precisionist, precious, puristic; by-the-book; exact, **meticulous** 339.12; **orderly, methodical** 807.6

ADVS 11 formally, in due form, in set form; **ceremoniously, ritually,** ritualistically; **solemnly** 111.4; for form's sake, *pro forma* <L>, **as a matter of form;** by the book

 12 stiffly, stiltedly, starchly, primly, rigidly

581 INFORMALITY

NOUNS 1 informality, informalness, unceremoniousness; casualness, offhandedness, **ease, easiness,** easygoingness; **relaxedness;** affability, graciousness, cordiality, sociability 582; Bohemianism, unconventionality 868.2; **familiarity; naturalness,** simplicity, plainness, homeliness, homeyness, folksiness <nf>, common touch, **unaffectedness,** unpretentiousness 499.2; unconstraint, unconstrainedness, looseness; irregularity; lack of convention, freedom, license

VERBS 2 not stand on ceremony, let one's hair down <nf>, be oneself, be at ease, feel at home, come as you are; relax

ADJS 3 informal, unceremonious; casual, offhand, offhanded, throwaway <nf>, unstudied, easy, easygoing, free and easy, loose; *dégagé* <Fr>; **relaxed;** affable, gracious, cordial, sociable; Bohemian, unconventional 868.6, nonconformist; **familiar; natural,** simple, plain, homely, homey, down-home *and* folksy <nf>, *haymish* <Yiddish>; **unaffected, unassuming** 499.7; unconstrained, loose; irregular; unofficial

ADVS 4 informally, unceremoniously, without ceremony, *sans cérémonie* and *sans façon* <Fr>; **casually,** offhand, offhandedly; relaxedly; familiarly; **naturally,** simply, plainly; **unaffectedly, unassumingly** 499.11; unconstrainedly, unofficially; *en famille* <Fr>

582 SOCIABILITY

NOUNS 1 sociability, sociality, sociableness, fitness *or* fondness for society, socialmindedness, **gregariousness, affability,** companionability, compatibility, geniality, *Gemütlichkeit* <Ger>, **congeniality;** hospitality 585; clubbability <nf>, clubbishness, clubbiness, clubbism; intimacy, familiarity; amiability, **friendliness** 587.1; **communicativeness** 343.3; social grace, civility, urbanity, courtesy 504

 2 camaraderie, comradery, comradeship, **fellowship, good-fellowship;** male bonding; consorting, hobnobbing, hanging *and* hanging out <nf>

 3 conviviality, joviality, jollity, gaiety, heartiness, cheer, good cheer, festivity, partying, merrymaking, merriment, revelry

 4 social life, social intercourse, social activity,

intercourse, **communication, communion,**
intercommunion, **fellowship,** intercommunication,
community, collegiality, commerce, congress,
converse, conversation, social relations

5 **social circle** *or* **set,** social class, one's crowd *or* set,
clique, coterie, crowd <nf>; **association** 617

6 **association,** consociation, affiliation, bonding,
social bonding, **fellowship, companionship,
company, society;** fraternity, **fraternization;**
membership, participation, partaking, sharing,
cooperation 450

7 **visit, social call,** call, drop-in; formal visit, duty
visit, required visit; exchange visit; flying visit,
look-in; visiting, visitation; round of visits; social
round, social whirl, mad round

8 **appointment, engagement, date** <nf>, double date
and blind date <nf>; arrangement, interview;
engagement book

9 **rendezvous, tryst, assignation, meeting;** trysting
place, meeting place, place of assignation;
assignation house; love nest <nf>

10 **social gathering, social,** sociable, social affair,
social hour, hospitality hour, affair, gathering, get-
together <nf>; function; ladies' night, **reception,**
at home, salon, levee, soiree; matinee; reunion,
family reunion; wake

11 **party** <see list>, **entertainment,** celebration, fete,
bash, party time, **festivity** 743.3,4

12 <nf terms> **brawl, bash,** blast, clambake,
wingding, hoodang, blowout, shindig, shindy, do
and bean-feast *and* knees-up *and* rave *and* rave-up
<Brit>

13 **tea,** afternoon tea, five-o'clock tea, high tea, cream
tea

14 bee, quilting bee, raising bee, husking bee,
cornhusking, corn shucking, husking

15 **debut, coming out** <nf>, presentation

16 <sociable person> joiner, mixer *and* good mixer
<nf>, good *or* pleasant company, excellent
companion, life of the party, social butterfly, bon
vivant; social chairman; man-about-town, playboy,
social lion, habitué; clubman, clubwoman;
salonnard, salonist

VERBS 17 **associate with,** assort with, sort with,
consort with, hobnob with, fall in with, socialize,
interact, go around with, **mingle with, mix with,
touch** *or* **rub elbows** *or* **shoulders with,** eat off the
same trencher; **fraternize,** fellowship, join in
fellowship; **keep company with,** bear one's
company, walk hand in hand with; **join; flock
together,** herd together, club together

18 <nf terms> **hang with,** hang out *or* around with,
clique, clique with, gang up with, run *or* run around
with, chum, chum together, pal, pal with, pal up *or*
around with; take *or* tie up with, hook up with

19 **visit,** make *or* pay a visit, **call on** *or* **upon, drop in,**
run *or* stop in, look in, look one up, see, stop off *or*
over <nf>, drop *or* run *or* stop by, drop around *or*
round; leave one's card; exchange visits

20 have *or* give a party, entertain

21 <nf terms> **throw a party; party,** have fun, live it
up, have a ball, ball, boogie, jam, kick up one's
heels, make whoopee, whoop it up

ADJS 22 **sociable, social,** social-minded, fit for
society, fond of society, **gregarious, affable;
companionable,** companionate, compatible, genial,
gemütlich <Ger>, **congenial;** hospitable 585.11;
neighborly; clubby, clubbable <nf>, clubbish;
communicative 343.10; amiable, **friendly;** civil,
urbane, courteous 504.14

23 **convivial,** boon, free and easy, hail-fellow-well-met;
jovial, jolly, hearty, festive, gay

24 **intimate, familiar,** cozy, chatty, *tête-à-tête* <Fr>;
man-to-man, woman-to-woman

ADVS 25 **sociably,** socially, gregariously, affably;
friendlily, companionably, arm in arm, hand in
hand, hand in glove

26 **types of parties**

at-home	masquerade party *or* mask
ball	*or* masque *or* masquerade
birthday party	open house
cocktail party	pajama party
coffee party *or* kaffee	rave
klatsch *or* coffee klatsch	shindig *or* shindy
dinner party	shower
fête champêtre <Fr>	smoker <nf>
garden party	social
hen party	soiree
housewarming	stag *or* stag party <nf>
ladies' *or* men's night out	surprise party
masked ball *or* bal	tea party
masqué <Fr>	*thé dansante* <Fr>

583 UNSOCIABILITY

NOUNS 1 **unsociability,** insociability, unsociableness,
dissociability, dissociableness; **ungregariousness,**
uncompanionability; unclubbableness *or*
unclubbability <nf>, ungeniality, **uncongeniality;**
incompatibility, social incompatibility;
unfriendliness 589.1; **uncommunicativeness** 344;
sullenness, mopishness, moroseness; self-
sufficiency, self-containment; autism, catatonia;
bashfulness 139.4

2 **aloofness, standoffishness,** offishness,
withdrawnness, **remoteness,** distance, detachment;
coolness, coldness, frigidity, chill, chilliness,
iciness, frostiness; cold shoulder; inaccessibility,
unapproachability; private world

3 seclusiveness, **seclusion** 584; exclusiveness,
exclusivity

VERBS **4 keep to oneself,** keep oneself to oneself, not mix *or* mingle, enjoy *or* prefer one's own company, stay at home, shun companionship, be a poor mixer, **stand aloof,** hold oneself aloof *or* apart, keep one's distance, keep at a distance, keep in the background, retire, retire into the shade, creep into a corner, seclude oneself, stay in one's shell; have nothing to do with 586.5, be unfriendly, not give one the time of day

ADJS **5 unsociable,** insociable, dissociable, unsocial; **ungregarious,** nongregarious; **uncompanionable,** ungenial, uncongenial; incompatible, socially incompatible; unclubbable <nf>; **unfriendly** 589.9; **uncommunicative** 344.8; sullen, mopish, mopey, morose; close, snug; self-sufficient, self-contained; autistic, catatonic; bashful 139.12

6 aloof, standoffish, offish, standoff, **distant, remote,** withdrawn, removed, detached, **cool,** cold, coldfish, frigid, chilly, icy, frosty; seclusive; exclusive; inaccessible, unapproachable; tight-assed <nf>

584 SECLUSION

NOUNS **1 seclusion,** reclusion, **retirement, withdrawal, retreat,** recess; renunciation *or* forsaking of the world; cocooning; **sequestration,** quarantine, separation, detachment, apartness; segregation, apartheid, Jim Crow; **isolation,** "splendid isolation"—Sir William Goschen; ivory tower, ivory-towerism, ivory-towerishness; **privacy,** privatism, **secrecy;** rustication; privatization; isolationism; opt-out

2 hermitism, hermitry, eremitism, anchoritism, anchoretism, cloistered monasticism

3 solitude, solitariness, **aloneness,** loneness, singleness; **loneliness, lonesomeness**

4 forlornness, desolation; friendlessness, kithlessness, fatherlessness, motherlessness, homelessness, rootlessness; helplessness, defenselessness; abandonment, desertion

5 recluse, loner, solitaire, solitary, solitudinarian; **shut-in,** invalid, bedridden invalid; cloistered monk *or* nun; **hermit,** eremite, anchorite, anchoret; marabout; hermitess, anchoress; **ascetic;** closet cynic; stylite, pillarist, pillar saint; Hieronymite, Hieronymian; Diogenes, Timon of Athens, St Simeon Stylites, St Anthony, desert saints, desert fathers; outcast, pariah 586.4; **stay-at-home, homebody; isolationist,** seclusionist; ivory-towerist, ivory-towerite

6 retreat 1009.5, **hideaway, cell, ivory tower,** hidey-hole <nf>, lair, sanctum, sanctum sanctorum, inner sanctum

VERBS **7 seclude oneself, go into seclusion, retire, go into retirement,** retire from the world, abandon *or* forsake the world, live in retirement, lead a retired life, lead a cloistered life, sequester *or* sequestrate oneself, be *or* remain incommunicado, shut oneself up, live alone, live apart, retreat to one's ivory tower; stay at home; rusticate; take the veil; cop out <nf>, opt out *or* drop out of society

ADJS **8 secluded, seclusive, retired, withdrawn;** isolated, shut off, insular, **separate,** separated, **apart,** detached, removed; segregated, quarantined; **remote, out-of-the-way,** up-country, in a backwater, out-of-the-world, out-back *and* back of beyond <Austral>; **unfrequented,** unvisited, off the beaten track; untraveled

9 private, privatistic, reclusive; ivory-towered, ivory-towerish

10 recluse, reclusive, sequestered, cloistered, sequestrated, shut up *or* in; hermitlike, hermitic, hermitical, eremitic, eremitical, hermitish; anchoritic, anchoritical; stay-at-home, domestic; homebound

11 solitary, alone; in solitude, by oneself, all alone; **lonely, lonesome, lone;** lonely-hearts

12 forlorn, lorn; **abandoned, forsaken, deserted, desolate,** godforsaken <nf>, friendless, unfriended, kithless, fatherless, motherless, homeless; helpless, defenseless; outcast 586.10

ADVS **13 in seclusion, in retirement,** in retreat, in solitude; in privacy, in secrecy; "far from the madding crowd's ignoble strife"—Thomas Gray

585 HOSPITALITY, WELCOME

NOUNS **1 hospitality,** hospitableness, receptiveness; honors *or* freedom of the house; **cordiality,** amiability, graciousness, **friendliness,** neighborliness, geniality, heartiness, bonhomie, **generosity,** liberality, openheartedness, warmth, warmness, warmheartedness; open door

2 welcome, welcoming, **reception,** *accueil* <Fr>; cordial *or* warm *or* hearty welcome, pleasant *or* smiling reception, the glad hand <nf>, **open arms; embrace, hug;** welcome mat

3 greetings, salutations, salaams; **regards,** best wishes 504.8

4 greeting, salutation, salute, salaam; **hail, hello,** how-do-you-do; accost, address; nod, bow, bob; curtsy 155.2; wave; handshake, handclasp; namaste; open arms, embrace, hug, kiss; smile, smile *or* nod of recognition, nod

5 host, mine host; hostess, receptionist, greeter; landlord 470.2

6 guest, visitor, visitant; **caller,** company; invited guest, invitee; frequenter, habitué, haunter; uninvited guest, gate-crasher <nf>; moocher *and* freeloader <nf>

VERBS **7 receive, admit,** accept, take in, let in, open
the door to; **be at home to,** have the latchstring
out, keep a light in the window, put out the
welcome mat, keep the door open, keep an open
house, keep the home fires burning

8 entertain, entertain guests, guest; host, preside, do
the honors <nf>; give a party, throw a party <nf>;
spread oneself <nf>

9 welcome, make welcome, bid one welcome, bid
one feel at home, make one feel welcome *or* at
home *or* like one of the family, do the honors of
the house, give one the freedom of the house, hold
out the hand, extend the right hand of friendship;
glad hand *and* give the glad hand *and* glad eye
<nf>; **embrace, hug, receive** *or* **welcome with
open arms;** give a warm reception to, "kill the
fatted calf"—Bible, roll out the red carpet, give the
red-carpet treatment, receive royally, make feel like
a king *or* queen

10 greet, hail, accost, address; **salute,** make one's
salutations; **bid** *or* **say hello,** bid good day *or* good
morning, etc; exchange greetings, **pass the time of
day; give one's regards** 504.13; shake hands, shake
and give one some skin *and* give a high *or* a low
five <nf>, press the flesh <nf>, press *or* squeeze
one's hand; nod to, bow to; curtsy 155.6; tip the
hat to, lift the hat, touch the hat *or* cap; take one's
hat off to, uncover; pull *or* tug at the forelock; kiss,
greet with a kiss, kiss hands *or* cheeks

ADJS **11 hospitable, receptive,** welcoming; **cordial,**
amiable, gracious, **friendly,** neighborly, genial,
hearty, open, openhearted, warm, warmhearted;
generous, liberal

12 welcome, welcome as the roses in May, wanted,
desired, wished-for; **agreeable,** desirable,
acceptable; **grateful,** gratifying, pleasing

ADVS **13 hospitably, with open arms;** friendlily

INTERJS **14 welcome!,** *soyez le bienvenu!* <Fr>, *¡bien
venido!* <Sp>, *benvenuto!* <Ital>, *Willkommen!*
<Ger>; glad to see you!

15 greetings!, salutations!, **hello!,** hullo!, hail!, hey! *or*
heigh!, **hi!,** aloha!, *¡hola!* <Sp>; **how do you do?,
how are you?,** *comment allez-vous?* and *comment
ça va?* <Fr>, *¿cómo está Usted?* <Sp>, *come sta?*
<Ital>, *wie geht's?* <Ger>; **good morning!,** *guten
Morgen!* <Ger>; good day!, *bon jour!* <Fr>,
¡buenos días! <Sp>, *buon giorno!* <Ital>, *guten
Tag!* <Ger>; **good afternoon!,** *¡buenas tardes!*
<Sp>; **good evening!,** *bon soir!* <Fr>, *buona sera!*
<Ital>, *guten Abend!* <Ger>

16 <nf terms> **howdy!,** howdy-do!, how-de-do!, how-
do-ye-do!, how-d'ye-do!, how you doin'?, hi ya!;
how's things?, how's tricks?, how goes it?, how's
every little thing?, how's the world treating you?,
yo!, ahoy!, hey!; long time no see!

586 INHOSPITALITY

NOUNS **1 inhospitality,** inhospitableness,
unhospitableness, unreceptiveness; **uncordialness,**
ungraciousness, **unfriendliness,** unneighborliness;
nonwelcome, nonwelcoming

2 unhabitability, uninhabitability, unlivability

3 ostracism, ostracization, thumbs down;
banishment 909.4; **proscription, ban; boycott,**
boycottage; **blackball,** blackballing, blacklist;
rejection 442.1

4 outcast, social outcast, outcast of society,
castaway, derelict, Ishmael; **pariah, untouchable,**
leper; outcaste; *déclassé* <Fr>; **outlaw; expellee,
evictee; displaced person** *or* **DP; exile, expatriate,**
man without a country; undesirable; *persona non
grata* <L>, unacceptable person

VERBS **5 have nothing to do with,** have no truck with
<nf>, refuse to associate with, steer clear of <nf>,
spurn, turn one's back upon, not give one the time
of day <nf>; deny oneself to, refuse to receive, not
be at home to; shut the door upon

6 ostracize, turn thumbs down, disfellowship; **reject**
442.3, **exile, banish** 909.17; **proscribe, ban, outlaw**
444.3, put under the ban, criminalize; **boycott,
blackball,** blacklist

ADJS **7 inhospitable,** unhospitable; **unreceptive,**
closed; **uncordial,** ungracious, **unfriendly,**
unneighborly

8 unhabitable, uninhabitable, nonhabitable,
unoccupiable, untenantable, **unlivable, unfit to live
in,** not fit for man or beast

9 unwelcome, unwanted; unagreeable, undesirable,
unacceptable; **uninvited,** unasked, unbidden

10 outcast, cast-off, castaway, derelict; outlawed
444.7, outside the pale, outside the gates; **rejected,
disowned; abandoned, forsaken**

587 FRIENDSHIP

NOUNS **1 friendship, friendliness; amicability,**
amicableness, amity, peaceableness, unhostility;
amiability, amiableness, **congeniality,** well-
affectedness; neighborliness, neighborlikeness;
peaceableness; sociability 582; **affection, love** 104;
loving kindness, kindness 143

2 fellowship, companionship, comradeship,
colleagueship, chumship <nf>, palship <nf>,
circle of friends, freemasonry, consortship,
boon companionship; comradery, camaraderie,
male bonding; **brotherhood, fraternity,**
fraternalism, fraternization, sodality, confraternity;
sisterhood, sorority; brotherliness, sisterliness;
community of interest, *esprit de corps* <Fr>;
chumminess <nf>

3 **good terms, good understanding,** good footing, friendly relations; **harmony,** compatibility, sympathy, fellow feeling, bonding, understanding, **rapport** 455.1, rapprochement; **favor, goodwill, good graces, regard,** respect, mutual regard *or* respect, favorable regard, the good *or* right side of <nf>, esprit de corps; an in <nf>; entente, entente cordiale, hands across the sea

4 **acquaintance,** acquaintedness, close acquaintance; **introduction,** presentation, knockdown <nf>

5 **familiarity, intimacy,** intimate acquaintance, closeness, nearness, inseparableness, inseparability; affinity, special affinity, mutual affinity; chumminess <nf>, palliness *or* palsiness *or* palsy-walsiness <nf>, mateyness <Brit nf>; togetherness

6 **cordiality, geniality,** heartiness, bonhomie, ardency, warmth, warmness, affability, warmheartedness; hospitality 585

7 **devotion, devotedness;** dedication, commitment; fastness, steadfastness, firmness, constancy, staunchness; triedness, trueness, true-blueness, tried-and-trueness

8 cordial friendship, warm *or* ardent friendship, close friendship, passionate friendship, devoted friendship, bosom friendship, intimate *or* familiar friendship, sincere friendship, beautiful friendship, fast *or* firm friendship, staunch friendship, loyal friendship, lasting friendship, undying friendship

VERBS 9 **be friends,** have the friendship of, have the ear of; be old friends *or* friends of long standing, be long acquainted, go way back; **know, be acquainted with;** associate with; cotton to *and* hit it off <nf>, get on well with, hobnob with, fraternize with, keep company with, go around with; be close friends with, be best friends, be inseparable; **be on good terms,** enjoy good *or* friendly relations with; keep on good terms, have an in with <nf>

10 **befriend, make** *or* **win friends,** gain the friendship of, **strike up a friendship,** get to know one another, take up with <nf>, shake hands with, **get acquainted,** make *or* scrape acquaintance with, pick up an acquaintance with; win friends, win friends and influence people; break the ice; warm to

11 <nf terms> **be buddy-buddy** *or* **palsy-walsy with,** click, have good *or* great chemistry, team up; **get next to, get palsy** *or* **palsy-walsy with,** get cozy with, cozy *or* snuggle up to, get close to, get chummy with, buddy *or* pal up with, play footsie with

12 **cultivate,** cultivate the friendship of, **court,** pay court to, pay addresses to, seek the company of, **run after** <nf>, **shine up to,** make up to <nf>,

play up to *and* suck up to <nf>, hold out *or* extend the right of friendship *or* fellowship; **make advances,** approach, break the ice

13 **get on good terms with, get into favor,** win the regard of, **get in the good graces of, get in good with,** get in with *or* on the in with *and* get next to <nf>, **get on the good** *or* **right side of** <nf>; stay friends with, keep in with <nf>

14 **introduce, present, acquaint,** make acquainted, give an introduction, give a knockdown <nf>, do the honors <nf>

ADJS 15 **friendly,** friendlike; **amicable, peaceable,** unhostile; **harmonious** 455.3; **amiable, congenial,** *simpático* <Sp>, *simpatico* <Ital>, *sympathique* <Fr>, pleasant, agreeable, favorable, well-affected, well-disposed, well-intentioned, well-meaning, well-meant, well-intended; brotherly, fraternal, confraternal; sisterly; neighborly, neighborlike; sociable; kind 143.13

16 **cordial, genial,** gracious, courteous, hearty, ardent, warm, warmhearted, affable; compatible, cooperative; welcoming, receptive, hospitable 585.11

17 **friends with,** friendly with, at home with; **acquainted**

18 **on good terms,** on a good footing, on friendly *or* amicable terms, **on speaking terms,** on a first-name basis, on visiting terms; **in good with,** in with *and* on the in with *and* in <nf>, **in favor, in one's good graces,** in one's good books, on the good *or* right side of <nf>, regarded highly by, on a first-name basis with, in with <nf>

19 **familiar, intimate, close,** near, inseparable, on familiar *or* intimate terms, favorite, affectionate; just between the two, one-on-one, man-to-man, woman-to-woman; hand-in-hand, hand and glove *or* hand in glove; **thick, thick as thieves** <nf>; demonstrative, backslapping, effusive

20 **chummy** <nf>, matey <Brit nf>; pally *and* palsy *and* palsy-walsy *and* buddy-buddy <nf>; companionable

21 **devoted,** dedicated, committed, **fast,** steadfast, supportive, constant, faithful, staunch, firm; tried, true, **tried and true,** true-blue, loyal, tested, trusty, trustful, trustworthy

ADVS 22 **amicably,** friendly, friendlily, friendliwise; **amiably, congenially,** pleasantly, agreeably, favorably; **cordially, genially,** heartily, ardently, warmly, with open arms; familiarly, intimately; arm in arm, hand in hand, hand in glove

588 FRIEND

NOUNS 1 **friend,** acquaintance, close acquaintance; confidant, confidante, repository; **intimate,** familiar, **close friend,** intimate *or* familiar friend; **bosom friend,** friend of one's bosom, inseparable friend, **best friend;** alter ego, other self, shadow; brother, fellow, fellowman, fellow creature, neighbor; mutual friend; **sympathizer,** well-wisher, partisan, advocate, favorer, backer, **supporter** 616.9; casual acquaintance; pickup <nf>; lover 104.12; girlfriend, boyfriend; live-in lover, POSSLQ *or* person of opposite sex sharing living quarters, significant other

2 **good friend, best friend,** great friend, **devoted friend,** warm *or* ardent friend, **faithful friend,** trusted *or* trusty friend, *fidus Achates* <L>, constant friend, staunch friend, fast friend; friend in need, friend indeed

3 **companion, fellow,** fellow companion, **comrade,** *camarade* <Fr>, amigo <nf>, mate <Brit>, comate, company, **associate** 616, peer, consociate, compeer, confrere, consort, **colleague, partner,** copartner, side partner, **crony,** old crony, gossip; girlfriend <nf>; **roommate,** chamberfellow; flatmate; bunkmate, bunkie <nf>; bedfellow, bedmate; **schoolmate,** schoolfellow, classmate, classfellow, school companion, school chum, fellow student *or* pupil; **playmate,** playfellow; **teammate,** yokefellow, yokemate; workmate, workfellow 616.5; shipmate; messmate; comrade in arms; homeboy <nf>

4 <nf terms> **pal, buddy,** bud, buddy-boy, bosom buddy, asshole buddy, main man, home boy, goombah, landsman, paesan, paesano, pally, palsy-walsy, road dog, walkboy, cobber <Austral>, pardner, pard, sidekick, tillicum, **chum,** ace, mate *and* butty <Brit>, my man

5 **boon companion,** boonfellow; **good fellow,** jolly fellow, hearty, *bon vivant* <Fr>; pot companion

6 <famous friendships> Achilles and Patroclus, Castor and Pollux, Damon and Pythias, David and Jonathan, Diomedes and Sthenelus, Epaminondas and Pelopidas, Hercules and Iolaus, Nisus and Euryalus, Pylades and Orestes, Theseus and Pirithoüs, Christ and the beloved disciple; the Three Musketeers

589 ENMITY

NOUNS 1 **enmity, unfriendliness,** inimicality; **uncordiality,** unamiability, ungeniality, disaffinity, incompatibility, incompatibleness; personal conflict, strain, **tension;** coolness, coldness, chilliness, chill, frost, frostiness, iciness, the freeze; inhospitality 586, unsociability 583

2 **disaccord** 456; ruffled feelings, strained relations, alienation, **disaffection, estrangement** 456.4

3 **hostility, antagonism, repugnance, antipathy,** spitefulness, spite, despitefulness, bellicosity, malice, malevolence, malignity, **hatred, hate** 103; dislike; **conflict, contention** 457, collision, clash, clashing, **friction;** quarrelsomeness 456.3; belligerence, intolerance

4 **animosity,** animus; **ill will,** ill feeling, bitter feeling, **hard feelings,** no love lost; **bad blood,** ill blood, feud, blood feud, vendetta; **bitterness,** sourness, soreness, **rancor,** resentment, acrimony, virulence, venom, vitriol

5 **grudge, spite,** crow to pick *or* pluck *or* pull, bone to pick; peeve *and* pet peeve <nf>; peevishness

6 **enemy, foe,** foeman, **adversary, antagonist,** unfriendly <nf>; bitter enemy; sworn enemy; open enemy; secret enemy; public enemy, public enemy number one; archenemy, devil; "my nearest and dearest enemy"—Thomas Middleton; the other side, the opposition, opponent, rival; **bane** 395.8, bête noire; no friend

VERBS 7 **antagonize,** set against, make enemies, set at odds, set at each other's throat, sick on each other <nf>; aggravate, exacerbate, heat up, **provoke,** envenom, **embitter,** infuriate, irritate, madden; divide, disunite, **alienate,** estrange 456.14; be alienated *or* estranged, draw *or* grow apart

8 **bear ill will,** bear malice, have it in for <nf>, hold it against, be down on <nf>; **bear** *or* **harbor** *or* **nurse a grudge,** owe a grudge, have a bone to pick with; no love is lost between; have a crow to pick *or* pluck *or* pull with; pick a quarrel; take offense, take umbrage; scorn, **hate** 103.5

ADJS 9 **unfriendly, inimical, unamicable; uncordial,** unamiable, ungenial, incompatible; strained, tense; discordant, unharmonious; cool, cold, chill, chilly, frosty, icy; inhospitable 586.7; unsociable 583.5

10 **hostile, antagonistic,** repugnant, antipathetic, set against, ill-disposed, acrimonious, snide, spiteful, despiteful, malicious, malevolent, malignant, hateful, full of hate *or* hatred; virulent, **bitter,** sore, sour, rancorous, acrid, caustic, venomous, vitriolic; conflicting, clashing, colliding; resentful, grudging, peevish; quarrelsome 456.17, contentious; **provocative,** off-putting; belligerent, bellicose

11 **alienated, estranged,** pffft <nf>, disaffected, separated, divided, disunited, torn, at variance; irreconcilable; distant; not on speaking terms

12 **at outs, on the outs** <nf>, at enmity, at variance, **at odds,** at loggerheads, at cross-purposes, at sixes and sevens, at each other's throats, at swords points, at daggers drawn, at war; on bad terms, in bad with <nf>

13 on bad terms, not on speaking terms; in bad with <nf>, in bad odor with, in one's bad or black book, on one's shitlist or drop-dead list <nf>

ADVS **14 unamicably,** inimically; **uncordially,** unamiably, ungenially; coolly, coldly, chillily, frostily; **hostilely, antagonistically**

590 MISANTHROPY

NOUNS **1 misanthropy,** misanthropism, people-hating, Timonism, cynicism, antisociality, antisocial sentiments or attitudes; unsociability 583; **man-hating,** misandry; **woman-hating,** misogyny; **sexism,** sex discrimination, sexual stereotyping, male or female chauvinism

2 misanthrope, misanthropist, people-hater, cynic, Timon, Timonist; **man-hater,** misandrist; **woman-hater,** misogynist; **sexist,** male or female chauvinist, chauvinist

ADJS **3 misanthropic,** people-hating, Timonist, Timonistic, cynical, **antisocial;** unsociable 583.5; **man-hating,** misandrist; **woman-hating,** misogynic, misogynistic, misogynous; **sexist,** male- or female-chauvinistic, chauvinistic

591 PUBLIC SPIRIT

NOUNS **1 public spirit,** social consciousness or responsibility; **citizenship, good citizenship,** citizenism, civism; altruism

2 patriotism, love of country; "the last refuge of a scoundrel"—Samuel Johnson; **nationalism,** nationality, ultranationalism; Americanism, Anglicism, Briticism, etc; **chauvinism, jingoism,** overpatriotism; patriotics, flag-waving; saber-rattling

3 patriot; nationalist; ultranationalist; **chauvinist,** chauvin, **jingo,** jingoist; patrioteer <nf>, flag waver, superpatriot, hard hat <nf>, hundred-percenter, hundred-percent American; hawk

ADJS **4 public-spirited, civic; patriotic; nationalistic;** ultranationalist, ultranationalistic; overpatriotic, superpatriotic, flagwaving, **chauvinist, chauvinistic,** jingoist, jingoistic; hawkish

592 BENEFACTOR

NOUNS **1 benefactor,** benefactress, philanthropist, **benefiter,** succorer, befriender; ministrant, ministering angel; Samaritan, **good Samaritan; helper,** aider, assister, help, aid, helping hand; Johnny-on-the-spot <nf>, jack-at-a-pinch <old Brit nf>; **patron, backer** 616.9, angel and cash cow <nf>; **good person** 659

2 savior, redeemer, deliverer, **liberator,** rescuer, freer, **emancipator,** manumitter

VERBS **3 benefit, aid,** assist, succor; befriend, take under one's wing; back, support; save the day, save one's neck or skin or bacon

ADJS **4** benefitting, aiding, befriending, assisting; backing, supporting; saving, salving, salvational, redemptive, redeeming; liberating, freeing, emancipative, emancipating, manumitting

ADVS **5** by one's aid or good offices, with one's support, on one's shoulders or coattails

PREPS **6** with or by benefit of, with or by the aid of

593 EVILDOER

NOUNS **1 evildoer, wrongdoer,** worker of ill or evil, **malefactor,** malfeasant, malfeasor, misfeasor, malevolent, public enemy, **sinner, villain,** villainess, transgressor, delinquent, culprit; bad or bad guy and baddy and meany and wrongo and black hat <nf>, wrong'un <Brit nf>, villain; **criminal,** outlaw, felon, **crook** <nf>, lawbreaker, perpetrator, perp <nf>, gangster and mobster <nf>; racketeer, thief, robber, burglar, rapist, murderer, con; terrorist; **bad person** 660; deceiver 357

2 troublemaker, mischief-maker; holy terror; agitator 375.11

3 ruffian, rough, bravo, **rowdy, thug,** desperado, cutthroat, kill-crazy animal, mad dog; gunman; bully, bullyboy, bucko; devil, hellcat, hell-raiser; killer; gang member, gangster

4 <nf terms> **roughneck, tough,** bruiser, mug, mugger, bimbo, bozo, ugly customer, **hoodlum, hood, hooligan,** gorilla, ape, plug-ugly, strong-arm man, muscle man, **goon;** gun, gunsel, trigger man, rodman, torpedo, hatchet man; hellion, terror, holy terror, shtarker, ugly customer

5 savage, barbarian, brute, beast, animal, tiger, shark, hyena; wild man; cannibal, man-eater, anthropophagite; **wrecker, vandal,** nihilist, destroyer

6 monster, fiend, fiend from hell, **demon, devil,** devil incarnate, hellhound, hellkite; **vampire,** lamia, **harpy, ghoul;** werewolf, ape-man; ogre, ogress; Frankenstein's monster

7 witch, hag, vixen, hellhag, hellcat, she-devil, virago, brimstone, termagant, grimalkin, Jezebel, beldam, she-wolf, tigress, wildcat, bitch-kitty <nf>, siren, fury

594 JURISDICTION
<administration of justice>

NOUNS **1 jurisdiction,** legal authority or power or right or sway, the confines of the law; original or appellate jurisdiction, exclusive *or* concurrent jurisdiction, civil *or* criminal jurisdiction, common-law *or* equitable jurisdiction, *in rem* jurisdiction, *in personam* jurisdiction, subject-matter jurisdiction, territorial jurisdiction; voluntary jurisdiction; mandate, cognizance

2 judiciary, judicial *or* legal *or* court system, judicature, judicatory, court, the courts; criminal-justice system; **justice,** the wheels of justice, judicial process; judgment 945

3 magistracy, magistrature, magistrateship; **judgeship,** justiceship; mayoralty, mayorship

4 bureau, office, department; secretariat, ministry, commissariat; municipality, bailiwick; constabulary, constablery, sheriffry, sheriffalty, shrievalty; constablewick, sheriffwick

VERBS **5 administer justice,** administer, administrate; preside, preside at the board; **sit in judgment** 598.18; **judge** 946.8

ADJS **6 jurisdictional,** jurisdictive; **judicatory,** judicatorial, judicative, **juridic *or* juridical**; jural, jurisprudential, **judicial, judiciary;** magisterial; forensic

595 TRIBUNAL

NOUNS **1 tribunal, forum, board,** curia, Areopagus; judicature, judicatory, judiciary 594.2; council 423; inquisition, the Inquisition

2 court, law court, court of law *or* justice, court of arbitration, legal tribunal, judicature; **United States court** <see list>, federal court; **British court** <see list>, Crown court; high court, trial court, court of record, superior court, inferior court; criminal court, civil court

3 <ecclesiastical courts> Papal Court, Curia, Rota, Sacra Romana Rota, Court of Arches *and* Court of Peculiars <Brit>

4 military court, court-martial, general *or* special *or* summary court-martial, drumhead court-martial; naval court, captain's mast

5 seat of justice, judgment seat, mercy seat, siege of justice <old>; **bench;** woolsack <Brit>

6 courthouse, court; county *or* town hall, town house; **courtroom;** jury box; bench, bar; witness stand *or* box, dock

ADJS **7 tribunal, judicial,** judiciary, court, curial; appellate

8 United States courts

Court of Private Land Claims	Territorial court
Federal Court of Claims	United States Circuit Court of Appeals
Supreme Court *or* United States Supreme Court	United States District Court

9 British courts

Board of Green Cloth Council	Court of the Duchy of Lancaster
court of admiralty	Green Cloth
Court of Appeal	High Court
court of attachments	High Court of Appeal
Court of Common	High *or* Supreme Court of Judicature
Court of Common Bank	
Court of Common Pleas	High Court of Justice
Court of Criminal Appeal	Judicial Committee of the Privy Council
Court of Divorce and Matrimonial Causes	Lords Justices' Court
	Palatine Court
Court of Exchequer	Rolls Court
Court of Exchequer Chamber	Stannary Court
	superior courts of Westminster
court of piepoudre *or* dustyfoot	Teind Court <Scot>
Court of Queen's *or* King's Bench	Vice Chancellor's Court
	Wardmote *or* Wardmote Court
Court of Session <Scot>	Woodmote

596 JUDGE, JURY

NOUNS **1 judge** <see list>, **magistrate, justice,** adjudicator, bencher, man *or* woman on the bench, presiding officer, beak <Brit nf>; **justice of the peace *or* JP;** arbiter, arbitrator, moderator; umpire, referee; his *or* her honor, your honor, his *or* her worship, his lordship; Mr Justice; critic 946.7; **special judge**

2 <historical> tribune, praetor, ephor, archon, syndic, podesta; Areopagite; justiciar, justiciary; dempster, deemster, doomster, doomsman

3 <Muslim> mullah, ulema, hakim, mufti, cadi

4 Chief Justice, Associate Justice, Justice of the Supreme Court; Lord Chief Justice, Lord Justice, Lord Chancellor, Master of the Rolls, Baron of the Exchequer; Judge Advocate General

5 Pontius Pilate, Solomon, Minos, Rhadamanthus, Aeacus

6 jury <see list>, **panel,** jury of one's peers, country, twelve men in a box, twelve good men and true; inquest; jury panel, jury list, venire facias; hung *or* deadlocked jury; grand jury, petit jury, common jury, special jury *or* blue-ribbon jury *or* struck jury

7 juror, juryman, jurywoman, venire-man *or* -woman, talesman; foreman of the jury, foreman *or* foreperson; grand-juror, grand-juryman; petit-juror, petit-juryman; recognitor

8 judges

amicus curiae	chancellor
assessor *or* legal assessor	chief justice
associate justice	circuit judge
bankruptcy judge	district judge
barmaster <Brit>	hearing officer

judge advocate general
  or JAG
judge *or* justice of assize
jurat
justice in eyre
justice of the peace
justiciar
lay judge
magistrate
master
military judge

ombudsman
ordinary *or* judge ordinary
police judge *or* justice *or*
  magistrate *or* PJ
presiding judge *or* officer
probate judge
puisne judge *or* justice
recorder
tax judge
trial judge
vice-chancellor

9 juries

blue-ribbon jury *or* panel
common jury
coroner's jury
elisor jury
grand jury
Jedburgh jury <Scot>
jury of inquest
jury of matrons *or*
  women

jury of the vicinage
petit jury *or* petty jury *or*
  traverse jury
police jury
pyx jury
sheriff's jury
special jury
struck jury
trial jury

597 LAWYER

NOUNS **1 lawyer, attorney, attorney-at-law,** barrister, barrister-at-law, **counselor,** counselor-at-law, **counsel,** legal counsel *or* counselor, legal adviser, law officer, legal expert, **solicitor, advocate, pleader;** member of the bar, legal practitioner, officer of the court; smart lawyer, pettifogger, Philadelphia lawyer; Juris Doctor *or* JurD, proctor, procurator; friend at *or* in court, amicus curiae; deputy, agent 576; intercessor 466.3; sea lawyer, latrine *or* guardhouse lawyer <nf>, self-styled lawyer, legalist; public prosecutor, judge advocate, district attorney *or* DA, attorney general

2 legist, jurist, jurisprudent, jurisconsult; law member of a court-martial

3 <nf terms> **shyster, mouthpiece, ambulance chaser,** lip, fixer, legal eagle

4 bar, legal profession, members of the bar; representation, counsel, pleading, attorneyship; **practice,** legal practice, criminal practice, corporate practice, etc; legal-aid *or* pro bono practice; **law firm,** legal firm, partnership

VERBS **5 practice law,** practice at the bar; be admitted to the bar; take silk <Brit>

ADJS **6 lawyerly,** lawyerlike, barristerial; representing, of counsel

598 LEGAL ACTION

NOUNS **1 lawsuit, suit,** suit in *or* at law; countersuit; **litigation, prosecution, action, legal action,** proceedings, legal proceedings, legal process, legal procedure, due process, course of law; legal

remedy; **case, court case,** cause, cause in court, legal case; **judicial process;** claim, counterclaim; test case; one's day in court

2 summons, subpoena, writ of summons; **writ, warrant**

3 arraignment, indictment, impeachment; complaint, charge 599.1; presentment; information; bill of indictment, true bill; **bail** 438.2

4 jury selection, impanelment, venire, venire facias, venire facias de novo, jury service, sequestration

5 trial, jury trial, trial by jury, trial at the bar, trial by law, **hearing, inquiry, inquisition,** inquest, assize; court-martial; **examination,** cross-examination; retrial; mistrial; change of venue; civil trial, criminal trial, bench trial

6 pleadings, arguments at the bar; **plea,** pleading, argument; **defense,** statement of defense; demurrer, general *or* special demurrer; refutation 958.2; rebuttal 939.2

7 declaration, statement, allegation, allegation *or* statement of facts, procès-verbal; **deposition,** affidavit; claim; complaint; bill, bill of complaint; libel, narratio; nolle prosequi, nol pros; nonsuit

8 testimony; evidence 957; cross-examination, direct examination; **argument,** presentation of the case; resting of the case; **summing up,** summation, closing arguments, jury instructions, charge to the jury, charging of the jury

9 judgment, decision, landmark decision; **verdict,** directed verdict, special verdict, sealed verdict, **sentence** 946.5; acquittal 601; condemnation 602, penalty 603

10 appeal, appeal motion, application for retrial, appeal to a higher court; writ of error; certiorari, writ of certiorari

11 litigant, litigator, litigationist; suitor, **party,** party to a suit, injured *or* aggrieved party, **plaintiff** 599.5; **defendant** 599.6; witness; accessory, accessory before *or* after the fact; panel, parties litigant

12 <legal terms> motion for summary judgment, search warrant, bench warrant, discovery, written interrogatories, witness list, plea bargaining, objection, perjury

VERBS **13 sue, litigate, prosecute,** go into litigation, **bring suit,** put in suit, sue *or* prosecute at law, **go to law,** seek in law, appeal to the law, seek justice *or* legal redress, implead, **bring action against,** bring legal action, start an action, prosecute a suit against, take *or* institute legal proceedings against; law *or* have the law in <nf>; take to court, bring into court, hale *or* haul *or* drag into court, bring a case before the court *or* bar, bring before a jury, bring to justice, bring to trial, **put on trial,** bring to the bar, take before the judge; set down for hearing; implead, seek legal protection

14 summons, issue a summons, subpoena
15 arraign, indict, impeach, cite, serve notice on, find an indictment against, present a true bill, claim, prefer *or* file a claim, have *or* pull up <nf>, bring up for investigation; press charges, **prefer charges** 599.7
16 select *or* **impanel a jury,** impanel, panel
17 call to witness, bring forward, put on the stand; swear in 334.7; take oath; take the stand, testify
18 try, try a case, conduct a trial, bring to trial, put on trial, **hear,** give a hearing to, sit on; charge the jury, deliver one's charge to the jury; **judge, sit in judgment**
19 plead, enter a plea *or* **pleading,** implead, conduct pleadings, argue at the bar; **plead** *or* **argue one's case,** stand trial, present one's case, make a plea, tell it to the judge <nf>; hang the jury <nf>; rest, rest one's case; sum up one's case; throw oneself on the mercy of the court
20 bring in a verdict, judge, **pass** *or* **pronounce sentence** 946.13; acquit 601.4; convict 602.3; penalize 603.4
ADJS **21** litigious, litigant, litigatory, litigating; causidical, lawyerly; litigable, actionable, justiciable, prosecutable; prosecutorial; moot, sub judice; unactionable, unprosecutable, unlitigable, frivolous, without merit
PHRS **22 in litigation,** in court, in chancery, in jeopardy, **at law,** litigated, coram judice, brought before the court *or* judge, at bar, at the bar, **on trial,** up for investigation *or* hearing, before the court *or* bar *or* judge

599 ACCUSATION

NOUNS **1 accusation,** accusal, finger-pointing <nf>, **charge, complaint,** plaint, count, **blame, imputation,** delation, reproach, taxing; **accusing, bringing of charges,** laying of charges, bringing to book; **denunciation,** denouncement; **impeachment, arraignment, indictment,** bill of indictment, true bill; **allegation,** allegement; **imputation,** ascription; **insinuation, implication, innuendo,** veiled accusation, unspoken accusation; information, information against, bill of particulars; charge sheet; specification; gravamen of a charge; prosecution, suit, lawsuit 598.1
2 incrimination, crimination, **inculpation,** implication, **citation,** involvement, impugnment; attack, assault; **censure** 510.3
3 recrimination, retort, countercharge
4 trumped-up charge, false witness; **put-up job** *and* **frame-up** *and* **frame** <nf>; false charge
5 accuser, accusant, accusatrix; incriminator, delator, allegator, impugner; informer 551.6; impeacher,

indictor; **plaintiff, complainant,** claimant, appellant, petitioner, libelant, suitor, **party,** party to a suit, pursuer; **prosecutor,** the prosecution; hostile witness
6 accused, defendant, respondent, codefendant, corespondent, libelee, appellee, suspect, culprit, prisoner, prisoner before the court, accused person
VERBS **7 accuse,** bring accusation; **charge, press charges, prefer** *or* **bring charges,** lay charges; complain, **lodge a complaint,** lodge a plaint; **impeach, arraign, indict,** bring in *or* hand up an indictment, return a true bill, article, **cite,** cite on several counts; book; **denounce,** denunciate; **finger** *and* point the finger at *and* put *or* lay the finger on <nf>, throw the book at <nf>, **inform on** *or* **against** 551.12,13; **impute,** ascribe; allege, insinuate, imply; bring to book; tax, task, take to task *or* account; **reproach,** twit, taunt with; report, put on report
8 blame, blame on *or* upon <nf>, lay on, hold against, **put** *or* **place** *or* **lay the blame on,** lay *or* cast blame upon, place *or* fix the blame *or* responsibility for; fasten on *or* upon, pin *or* hang on <nf>
9 accuse of, charge with, tax *or* task with, saddle with, lay to one's charge, place to one's account, lay at one's door, bring home to, cast *or* throw in one's teeth, throw up to one, throw *or* thrust in the face of
10 incriminate, criminate, **inculpate,** implicate, involve; cry out against, cry out on *or* upon, cry shame upon, raise one's voice against; attack, assail, impugn; **censure** 510.13; throw a stone at, cast *or* throw the first stone
11 recriminate, countercharge, retort an accusation
12 trump up a charge, bear false witness; **frame** *and* frame up *and* set up *and* put up a job on <nf>, plant evidence
ADJS **13 accusing, accusatory,** accusatorial, accusative, pointing to; imputative, denunciatory; recriminatory; prosecutorial; **condemnatory**
14 incriminating, incriminatory, criminatory; delatorian; inculpative, inculpatory
15 accused, charged, blamed, tasked, taxed, reproached, **denounced, impeached, indicted, arraigned; under a cloud** *or* a cloud of suspicion, under suspicion; incriminated, recriminated, inculpated, implicated, involved, in complicity; **cited,** impugned; under attack, under fire

600 JUSTIFICATION

NOUNS **1 justification, vindication; clearing,** clearing of one's name *or* one's good name, clearance, purging, purgation, destigmatizing, destigmatization, **exculpation** 601.1; no bill, failure to indict; explanation, rationalization; reinstatement, restitution, restoration, **rehabilitation**

2 **defense, plea,** pleading; argument, statement of defense; answer, reply, counterstatement, response, riposte; grounds; **refutation** 958.2, **rebuttal** 939.2; demurrer, general *or* special demurrer; denial, objection, exception; **special pleading;** self-defense, plea of self-defense, Nuremberg defense, the devil-made-me-do-it defense, blame-the-victim defense

3 **apology,** apologia, apologetic

4 **excuse, cop-out** *and* **alibi** *and* **out** <nf>; lame excuse, poor excuse, likely story; escape hatch, way out

5 **extenuation, mitigation, palliation,** softening; extenuative, palliative, saving grace; **whitewash, whitewashing,** decontamination; gilding, gloss, varnish, color, putting the best color on; qualification, allowance; extenuating circumstances, mitigating circumstances, diminished responsibility

6 **warrant, reason,** good reason, **cause,** call, **right, basis,** substantive *or* material basis, **ground, grounds,** foundation, substance

7 **justifiability, vindicability, defensibility;** explainability, explicability; **excusability,** pardonableness, forgivableness, remissibility, veniality; warrantableness, allowableness, admissibility, reasonableness, reasonability, legitimacy

8 **justifier, vindicator; defender,** pleader; **advocate,** successful advocate *or* defender, proponent, **champion; apologist,** apologizer, apologetic, excuser; whitewasher

VERBS 9 **justify, vindicate,** do justice to, make justice *or* right prevail; fail to indict, no-bill; **warrant,** account for, show sufficient grounds for, give good reasons for; **rationalize,** explain; cry sour grapes, "make a virtue of necessity"— Shakespeare; get off the hook <nf>, find an out, **exculpate** 601.4; **clear,** clear one's name *or* one's good name, purge, destigmatize, reinstate, restore, rehabilitate

10 **defend,** offer *or* say in defense, allege in support *or* vindication, **support, uphold, sustain, maintain,** assert, stick up for; **answer,** reply, respond, riposte, counter; refute 958.5, **rebut** 939.5; **plead for,** make a plea, offer as a plea, plead one's case *or* cause, put up a front *or* a brave front; **advocate,** champion, go to bat for <nf>, espouse, join *or* associate oneself with, stand *or* stick up for, speak up for, contend for, speak for, argue for, urge reasons for, put in a good word for

11 **excuse,** alibi <nf>, offer excuse for, give as an excuse, cover with excuses, **explain,** offer an explanation; plead ignorance *or* insanity *or* diminished responsibility; **apologize for,** make apology for; alibi out of <nf>, crawl *or* worm *or* squirm out of, lie out of, have an out *or* alibi *or* story <nf>

12 **extenuate, mitigate, palliate,** soften, lessen, diminish, **ease,** mince; **soft-pedal;** slur over, ignore, pass by in silence, give the benefit of the doubt, not hold it against one, **explain away, gloss** *or* **smooth over,** put a gloss upon, put a good face upon, varnish, **white-wash,** color, lend a color to, put the best color *or* face on, show in the best colors, show to best advantage; **allow for,** make allowance for; give the Devil his due

ADJS 13 **justifying,** justificatory; **vindicative,** vindicatory, rehabilitative; refuting 958.6; **excusing,** excusatory; **apologetic, apologetical; extenuating,** extenuative, **palliative**

14 **justifiable, vindicable, defensible; excusable, pardonable, forgivable,** expiable, remissible, exemptible, venial; **condonable,** dispensable; **warrantable,** allowable, admissible, reasonable, colorable, legitimate; innocuous, unobjectionable, inoffensive

601 ACQUITTAL

NOUNS 1 **acquittal,** acquittance; **exculpation,** disculpation, verdict of acquittal *or* not guilty; **exoneration, absolution, vindication, remission,** compurgation, purgation, purging; **clearing,** clearance, destigmatizing, destigmatization, quietus; **pardon, excuse, forgiveness, free pardon; discharge, release, dismissal,** setting free; quashing of the charge *or* indictment

2 **exemption, immunity,** impunity, nonliability; diplomatic immunity; **amnesty,** indemnity, nonprosecution, non prosequitur, nolle prosequi; stay; dispensation

3 **reprieve,** respite, grace

VERBS 4 **acquit, clear, exculpate, exonerate, absolve,** give *or* grant absolution, bring in *or* return a verdict of not guilty; **vindicate,** justify; **pardon, excuse, forgive,** show mercy; remit, grant remission, remit the penalty of; amnesty, grant *or* extend amnesty; **discharge, release, dismiss, free, set free,** let off <nf>, let go, let off scot-free, spare; quash the charge *or* indictment, withdraw the charge; **exempt,** grant immunity, exempt from, dispense from; clear the skirts of, shrive, purge; blot out one's sins, wipe the slate clean; **whitewash,** decontaminate; destigmatize; non-pros

5 **reprieve,** respite, give *or* grant a reprieve

602 CONDEMNATION

NOUNS 1 **condemnation, damnation, doom,** guilty verdict, verdict of guilty; proscription, excommunication, anathematizing; **denunciation,** denouncement; **censure** 510.3; **conviction; sentence, judgment,** rap <nf>; capital punishment, death penalty, death sentence, death warrant

2 attainder, attainture, attaintment; bill of attainder

VERBS 3 **condemn, damn, doom; denounce,** denunciate; **censure** 510.13; **convict,** find guilty, bring home to; proscribe, excommunicate, anathematize; blacklist, put on the Index; pronounce judgment 946.13; **sentence,** pronounce sentence, pass sentence on; penalize 603.4; attaint; sign one's death warrant

4 **stand condemned,** be convicted, be found guilty

ADJS 5 **condemnatory, damnatory,** denunciatory, proscriptive; **censorious**

6 convicted, condemned, guilty, blameworthy, liable, sentenced

603 PENALTY

NOUNS 1 **penalty,** penalization, penance, penal retribution; **sanctions,** penal or punitive measures; **punishment** 604; **reprisal** 506.2, retaliation 506, compensation, price; the devil to pay

2 **handicap,** disability, **disadvantage** 1012.6

3 **fine,** monetary or financial penalty, mulct, amercement, sconce, **damages,** punitive damages, compensatory damages; distress, distraint; forfeit, forfeiture; escheat, escheatment

VERBS 4 **penalize,** put or impose or inflict a penalty or sanctions on; **punish** 604.10; **handicap,** put at a disadvantage

5 **fine,** mulct, amerce, sconce, escheat; distrain, levy a distress; award damages

ADVS 6 **on pain of,** under or upon pain of, **on** or **under penalty of**

604 PUNISHMENT

NOUNS 1 **punishment,** punition, **chastisement, chastening, correction, discipline,** disciplinary measure or action, **castigation,** infliction, scourge, ferule, what-for <nf>; pains, pains and punishments; pay, payment; **retribution,** retributive justice, nemesis; judicial punishment; punishment that fits the crime, condign punishment, well-deserved punishment; **penalty,** penal retribution; penalization; penology; cruel and unusual punishment; judgment; what's coming to one, **just desserts, desserts**

2 <forms of punishment> penal servitude, jailing,

imprisonment, incarceration, confinement; hard labor, rock pile, chain gang, labor camp; galleys; torture, torment, martyrdom; the gantlet, keelhauling, tar-and-feathering, railriding, picketing, the rack, impalement, dismemberment; walking the plank; house arrest; exile

3 **slap,** smack, whack, whomp, **cuff, box,** buffet, belt; blow 902.4; **rap on the knuckles,** box on the ear, slap in the face; slap on the wrist, token punishment

4 **corporal punishment, whipping, beating, thrashing, spanking, flogging,** paddling, flagellation, scourging, flailing, trouncing, basting, drubbing, buffeting, belaboring; **lashing, lacing,** stripes; horse-whipping, strapping, belting, rawhiding, cowhiding; **switching; clubbing,** cudgeling, caning, truncheoning, fustigation, bastinado; pistol-whipping; battery; dusting

5 <nf terms> licking, larruping, walloping, whaling, lathering, leathering, **hiding, tanning, dressing-down,** chewing out; **paddling,** swingeing; grounding

6 <old nf terms> strap oil, hazel oil, hickory oil, birch oil; dose of strap oil, etc

7 **capital punishment, execution;** legal or judicial murder, extreme penalty, death sentence or penalty or warrant; **hanging,** the gallows, the rope or noose; summary execution; **lynching,** necktie party or sociable <nf>, vigilanteism, vigilante justice; the necklace; **crucifixion,** impalement; **electrocution,** the chair <nf>, the hot seat <nf>; gassing, the gas chamber; lethal injection; **decapitation,** decollation, beheading, the guillotine, the ax, the block; **strangling,** strangulation, garrote; **shooting,** fusillade, firing squad; **burning,** burning at the stake; **poisoning,** hemlock; stoning, lapidation; drowning; defenestration

8 **punisher,** discipliner, chastiser, chastener; **executioner,** executionist, deathsman <old>, Jack Ketch <Brit>; **hangman; lyncher;** electrocutioner; headsman, **beheader,** decapitator; strangler, garroter; sadist, torturer; hatchet man, hit man <nf>

9 **penologist;** jailer 429.10

VERBS 10 **punish, chastise, chasten, discipline, correct, castigate, penalize, reprimand; take to task,** bring to book, bring or call to account; deal with, settle with, settle or square accounts, **give one his desserts** or **just desserts,** serve one right; inflict upon, visit upon; teach or give one a lesson, make an example of; pillory; masthead; reduce to the ranks

11 <nf terms> **attend to,** do for, take care of, serve one out, **give it to,** take or have it out of; pay, pay

out, **fix, settle,** fix one's wagon, settle one's hash, settle the score, give one his gruel, make it hot for one, **give one his comeuppance;** lower the boom, put one through the wringer, come down on *or* down hard on, throw the book at, throw to the wolves; **give what-for,** give a going-over, climb one's frame, let one have it, tell off, light into, lay into, land on, mop *or* wipe up the floor with, skin live, have one's hide

12 **slap,** smack, whack, thwack, whomp, **cuff, box,** buffet; strike 902.13; slap the face, box the ears, give a rap on the knuckles

13 **whip,** give a whipping *or* beating *or* thrashing, **beat, thrash, spank, flog,** scourge, flagellate, flay, flail, whale; **smite,** thump, trounce, baste, **pummel,** pommel, **drub, buffet, belabor,** lay on; **lash, lace,** cut, stripe; horsewhip; knout; **strap,** belt, rawhide, cowhide; **switch,** birch, give the stick; **club, cudgel,** cane, truncheon, fustigate, bastinado; pistol-whip

14 **thrash soundly, batter,** bruise

15 <nf terms> **beat up,** rough up, clobber, marmelize <Brit>, work over, lick, larrup, wallop, whop, swinge, beat one's brains out, whale, whale the tar out of, beat *or* kick the shit out of, beat to a jelly, **beat black and blue, knock one's lights out, nail,** welt, trim, flax, lather, leather, **hide,** tan, **tan one's hide,** dress down, **kick ass,** give a dressing-down, knock head, knock heads together; **paddle; lambaste, clobber,** dust one's jacket, give a dose of birch oil *or* strap oil *or* hickory oil *or* hazel oil, take it out of one's hide *or* skin

16 **torture,** put to the question; rack, put on *or* to the rack; dismember, tear limb from limb; draw and quarter, break on the wheel, tar and feather, ride on a rail, picket, keelhaul, impale, grill, thumbscrew, persecute, work over

17 **execute, put to death,** inflict capital punishment; **electrocute,** burn *and* fry <nf>; send to the gas chamber; **behead, decapitate,** decollate, guillotine, bring to the block; **crucify; shoot,** execute by firing squad; burn, **burn at the stake; strangle,** garrote, bowstring; stone, lapidate; defenestrate; send to the hot seat <nf>

18 **hang,** hang by the neck; **string up** *and* scrag *and* stretch <nf>; gibbet, noose, neck, bring to the gallows; **lynch;** hang, draw, and quarter

19 **be hanged,** suffer hanging, **swing,** dance upon nothing, kick the air *or* wind *or* clouds

20 **be punished, suffer,** suffer for, **suffer the consequences** *or* **penalty,** get it *and* **catch it** <nf>, get *or* catch it in the neck <nf>, catch hell *or* the devil <nf>, get *or* take a licking *or* shellacking <nf>; **get one's desserts** *or* **just desserts** 639.6; get it coming and going <nf>, be doubly punished, sow the wind and reap the whirlwind; get hurt, get

one's fingers burned, have *or* get one's knuckles rapped

21 **take one's punishment,** bow one's neck, take the consequences, **take one's medicine** *or* what is coming to one, swallow the bitter pill *or* one's medicine, pay the piper, face the music <nf>, stand up to it, make one's bed and lie on it, get what one is asking for; take the rap <nf>, take the fall <nf>

22 **deserve punishment, have it coming** <nf>, be for it *or* in for it, be heading for a fall, be cruising for a bruising <nf>

ADJS 23 **punishing, chastising,** chastening, corrective, disciplinary, correctional; retributive; grueling <nf>; **penal, punitive,** punitory, inflictive; castigatory; baculine; penological; capital; corporal

605 INSTRUMENTS OF PUNISHMENT

NOUNS 1 **whip, lash, scourge,** flagellum, strap, thong, rawhide, cowhide, blacksnake, kurbash, sjambok, belt, razor strap; knout; bullwhip, bullwhack; horsewhip; crop; quirt; rope's end; cat, cat-o'-nine-tails; whiplash

2 **rod, stick, switch; paddle,** ruler, ferule, pandybat; birch, rattan; cane; club

3 <devices> **pillory, stocks,** finger pillory; cucking stool, ducking stool, trebuchet; whipping post, branks, triangle *or* triangles, wooden horse, treadmill, crank

4 <instruments of torture> **rack,** wheel, Iron Maiden of Nuremberg; screw, thumbscrew; boot, iron heel, scarpines; Procrustean bed *or* bed of Procrustes

5 <instruments of execution> **scaffold; block, guillotine,** ax, maiden; **stake; cross; gallows,** gallows-tree, gibbet, tree, drop; **hangman's rope, noose,** rope, halter, hemp, hempen collar *or* necktie *or* bridle <nf>; **electric chair,** death chair, the chair <nf>, hot seat <nf>; **gas chamber,** lethal chamber, death chamber; the necklace

606 THE PEOPLE

<the population>

NOUNS 1 **the people, the populace, the public,** the general public, people in general, everyone, everybody; **the population,** the citizenry, the whole people, the polity, the body politic; **the community, the commonwealth, society,** the society, the social order *or* fabric, the nation; the commonalty *or* commonality, commonage, commoners, commons, *demos* <Gk>; **common people, ordinary people** *or* **folk, persons, folk, folks,** gentry; the common sort, plain people *or* folks, the common run <nf>, the rank and file, the boy *or* girl next door, Brown Jones and Robinson, John Q Public, Middle America; Tom, Dick, and Harry; the salt of the earth, Everyman, Everywoman, the man *or* woman in the street, the common man, you and me, John Doe, Joe Sixpack <nf>, *vulgus* <L>, the third estate; **the upper class; the middle class; the lower class;** demography, demographics; social anthropology

2 the masses, the hoi polloi, *hoi polloi* <Gk>, the many, **the multitude,** the crowd, **the mob,** the horde, the million, "the booboisie"—H L Mencken, **the majority,** the mass of the people, the herd, the great unnumbered, the great unwashed, **the vulgar** *or* **common herd,** vulgar masses; *profanum vulgus* and *ignobile vulgus* and *mobile vulgus* <L>; "the beast with many heads," "the blunt monster with uncounted heads, the still-discordant wavering multitude"—both Shakespeare

3 rabble, rabblement, rout, ruck, common ruck, canaille, *racaille* <Fr>, ragtag <nf>, **ragtag and bobtail;** rag, tag, and bobtail; **riffraff, trash,** raff, chaff, **rubbish,** dregs, sordes, offscourings, off-scum, **scum, scum of the earth, dregs** *or* **scum** *or* **off-scum** *or* **offscourings of society,** swinish multitude, vermin, cattle

4 the underprivileged, the disadvantaged, the poor, ghetto-dwellers, slum-dwellers, welfare cases, chronic poor, underclass, depressed class, poverty subculture, the wretched of the earth, outcasts, the homeless, the dispossessed, bag people, the powerless, the unemployable, lumpen, lumpenproletariat *or* lumpenprole <nf>, lower orders, second-class citizens, the have-nots, small potatoes

5 common man, commoner, little man, **little fellow, average man,** ordinary man, typical man, **man in the street,** one of the people, man of the people, regular guy, Everyman; **plebeian,** pleb <slang>; **proletarian,** prole <Brit nf>, *roturier* <Fr>; ordinary *or* average Joe *and* Joe Doakes *and* Joe Sixpack <nf>, John Doe, Jane Doe, John Smith, Mr *or* Mrs Brown *or* Smith, Joe Blow, John Q Public, Mr Nobody; bourgeois

6 peasant, countryman, countrywoman, **provincial,** son of the soil, tiller of the soil; **peon,** hind, fellah, muzhik, serf, villein, churl; "hewers of wood and drawers of water"—Bible; **farmer** 1069.5, **hick** *and* yokel *and* rube *and* hayseed *and* shit-kicker <nf>, **bumpkin,** country bumpkin, rustic, clod, **clodhopper** <nf>, hillbilly *and* woodhick <nf>, **boor,** clown, lout, looby

7 upstart, parvenu, adventurer, sprout <nf>; *bourgeois gentilhomme* <Fr>, would-be gentleman; *nouveau riche* and *nouveau roturier* <Fr>, *arriviste*

<Fr>, **newly-rich,** pig in clover <nf>; **social climber,** climber, name-dropper, tufthunter, status seeker

ADJS 8 populational, population; **demographic,** demographical; national, societal; **popular,** public, mass, grass-roots, cultural, **common,** common as dirt, commonplace, communal, folk, tribal, **plain, ordinary, lowly,** low, mean, base; **humble,** homely; rank-and-file, provincial, of the people; second-class, **lowborn,** lowbred, baseborn, earthborn, earthy, of humble birth, plebeian; third-estate; ungenteel, shabby-genteel, uncultured; **vulgar, rude,** coarse, below the salt; **parvenu, upstart,** risen from the ranks, jumped-up <nf>; newly rich, *nouveau-riche* <Fr>; non-U <Brit>

607 SOCIAL CLASS AND STATUS

NOUNS 1 class, social class, economic class, social group *or* grouping, status group, accorded status, social category, order, grade, caste, estate, rank; **status, social status, economic status,** socioeconomic status *or* background, standing, footing, prestige, rank, ranking, place, station, position, level, degree, stratum; **social structure, hierarchy,** pecking order, social stratification, social system, social gamut, social differentiation, social pyramid, class structure, class distinction, status system, power structure, ranking, stratification, ordering, social scale, gradation, division, social inequality, inequality, haves and have-nots, "the classes and the masses"—William Ewart Gladstone; **social bias, class conflict,** class identity, class difference, class prejudice, class struggle, class politics; ageism; **mobility, social mobility,** upward mobility, downward mobility, vertical mobility, horizontal mobility

2 upper class, upper classes, aristocracy, patriciate, second estate, ruling class, ruling circles, elite, elect, the privileged, the classes, the quality, the better sort, upper circles, upper cut *and* upper crust *and* crust *and* cream <nf>, upper-income group *or* higher-income group, gentry, gentlefolk, lords of creation; **high society,** high life, the Four Hundred, bon ton, *haut monde* <Fr>, First Families of Virginia *or* FFV; Social Register, Bluebook; nobility, gentry 608; status symbol

3 aristocracy, aristocratic status, aristocraticalness, aristocraticness, high status, high rank, quality, high estate, gentility, social distinction, social prestige; **birth,** high birth, distinguished ancestry *or* descent *or* heritage *or* blood, blue blood

4 aristocrat, patrician, Brahmin, blue-blood, thoroughbred, member of the upper class, socialite, swell *and* upper-cruster <nf>, grandee, grand dame, dowager, magnifico, lord of creation; **gentleman, lady,** person of breeding; trophy wife <nf>

5 **middle class,** middle order *or* orders, lower middle class, upper middle class, bourgeoisie, educated class, professional class, middle-income group, white-collar workers, salaried workers; suburbia; Middle America, silent majority; white bread <nf>

6 **bourgeois,** member of the middle class, white-collar worker 726.2, salaried worker; pillar of society, solid citizen

7 **lower class, lower classes,** lower orders, plebeians, plebs, workers, working class, working people, proletariat, proles <Brit nf>, rank and file, grass roots, laboring class *or* classes, toilers, toiling class *or* classes, the other half, low-income group, wage-earners, hourly worker, blue-collar workers

8 **the underclass, the underprivileged**

9 **worker** 726.2, **workman, working man, working woman,** working girl, proletarian, laborer, laboring man, toiler, stiff *and* working stiff <nf>, artisan, mechanic, industrial worker, factory worker

ADJS 10 **upper-class, aristocratic, patrician, upscale;** gentle, genteel, of gentle blood; gentlemanly, gentlemanlike; ladylike, quite the lady; **wellborn, well-bred, blue-blooded,** of good breed; **thoroughbred,** purebred, pure-blooded, *pur sang* <Fr>, full-blooded; **highborn,** highbred; born to the purple, "to the manner born"—Shakespeare, born with a silver spoon in one's mouth; **high-society,** socialite, hoity-toity <nf>, posh; **middle-class, bourgeois,** *petit-bourgeois* <Fr>, petty-bourgeois, suburban, white-bread <nf>; **working class, blue collar,** proletarian, lower-class, born on the wrong side of the tracks; **class-conscious; mobile, socially mobile,** upwardly mobile, downwardly mobile, vertically mobile, horizontally mobile, déclassé

608 ARISTOCRACY, NOBILITY, GENTRY
<noble rank or birth>

NOUNS 1 **aristocracy, nobility,** titled aristocracy, hereditary nobility, noblesse; **royalty; elite,** upper class, elect, the classes, **upper classes** *or* circles, upper cut *and* **upper crust** <nf>, upper ten <Brit nf>, **upper ten thousand,** the Four Hundred, Social Register <trademark>, high society, high life, *haut monde* <Fr>; old nobility, *ancienne noblesse* <Fr>, *noblesse de robe* and *noblesse d'épée* <Fr>, *ancien régime* <Fr>; First Families of Virginia *or* FFV; **peerage,** baronage, lords temporal and spiritual; baronetage; knightage, chivalry; gentlefolk, beau monde, jet set

2 **nobility, nobleness, aristocracy,** aristocraticalness;

gentility, genteelness; quality, rank, virtue, distinction; birth, high *or* noble birth, ancestry, high *or* honorable descent; lineage, pedigree; blood, **blue blood;** royalty 417.8

3 **gentry,** gentlefolk, gentlefolks, gentlepeople, better sort; lesser nobility, *petite noblesse* <Fr>; *samurai* <Japanese>; landed gentry, squirearchy

4 **nobleman, noble, gentleman; peer; aristocrat, patrician,** Brahman, **blue blood,** titled person, thoroughbred, silk-stocking, lace-curtain, swell *and* upper-cruster <nf>, life peer; **grandee,** magnifico, magnate, optimate; **lord,** laird <Scot>, lordling; seignior, seigneur, *hidalgo* <Sp>; **duke,** grand duke, archduke, marquis, **earl, count,** viscount, **baron,** daimio, **baronet;** squire; esquire, armiger; palsgrave, waldgrave, margrave, landgrave; jet-setter, patrician

5 **knight, cavalier,** chevalier, *caballero* <Sp>, *Ritter* <Ger>; **knight-errant,** knight-adventurer; companion; bachelor, knight bachelor; baronet, knight baronet; banneret, knight banneret; Bayard, Gawain, Lancelot, Sidney, Sir Galahad, Don Quixote

6 **noblewoman, peeress, gentlewoman; lady,** dame, *doña* <Sp>, khanum; **duchess,** grand duchess, archduchess, marchioness, marquise, viscountess, **countess, baroness,** margravine

7 **prince,** *Prinz* and *Fürst* <Ger>, *knez, atheling, sheikh, sherif, mirza, khan, emir, shahzada* <India>; princeling, princelet; crown prince, heir apparent; heir presumptive; prince consort; prince regent; **king;** princes of India; Muslim rulers 575.10

8 **princess,** *princesse* <Fr>, *infanta* <Sp>, *rani* and *maharani* and *begum* and *shahzadi* and *kumari* or *kunwari* and *raj-kumari* and *malikzadi* <India>; crown princess; **queen** 575.11

9 **<rank or office>** lordship, ladyship; dukedom, marquisate, earldom, barony, baronetcy; viscountship, viscountcy, viscounty; knighthood, knight-errantship; seigniory, seigneury, seignioralty; pashaship, pashadom; peerage; princeship, princedom; kingship, queenship 417.8

ADJS 10 **noble,** ennobled, titled, of rank, high, exalted; **aristocratic, patrician; gentle,** genteel, of gentle blood; gentlemanly, gentlemanlike; ladylike, quite the lady; knightly, chivalrous; ducal, archducal; princely, princelike; **regal** 417.17, kingly, kinglike, "every inch a king"—Shakespeare; queenly, queenlike; titled

11 **wellborn, well-bred, blue-blooded,** well-connected, of good breed; **thoroughbred,** purebred, pure-blooded, *pur sang* <Fr>, full-blooded; **highborn,** highbred; born to the purple, high-caste, of good family; classy <nf>, U <Brit>

609 POLITICS

NOUNS 1 politics, polity, the art of the possible;
practical politics, *Realpolitik* <Ger>; empirical
politics; **party** or **partisan politics, partisanism;**
politicization; reform politics; multiparty politics;
power politics, *Machtpolitik* <Ger>; machine
politics, bossism <nf>, Tammany Hall,
Tammanism <nf>; confrontation or confrontational
or confro politics; **interest politics,** single-issue
politics, interest-group politics, pressure-group
politics, PAC or political action committee politics;
consensus politics; fusion politics; career politics;
petty politics, peanut politics <nf>; pork-barrel
politics; kid-glove politics <nf>; silk-stocking
politics <nf>; ward politics; electronic or
technological politics; public affairs, civic affairs

2 political science, poli-sci <nf>, **politics,**
government, civics; political philosophy, political
theory; political behavior; political economy,
comparative government, international relations,
public administration; political geography,
geopolitics, *Geopolitik* <Ger>

3 statesmanship, statecraft, political or
governmental leadership, national leadership;
transpartisan or suprapartisan leadership;
kingcraft, queencraft; senatorship

4 policy, polity, public policy; line, **party line,** party
principle or doctrine or philosophy, **position,**
bipartisan policy; noninterference,
nonintervention, *laissez-faire* <Fr>, laissez-
faireism; free enterprise; go-slow policy;
government control, governmentalism; planned
economy, managed currency, price supports,
pump-priming <nf>; autarky, economic self-
sufficiency; free trade; protection, protectionism;
bimetallism; strict constructionism; localism,
sectionalism, states' rights, nullification; political
correctness

5 foreign policy, foreign affairs; world politics;
diplomacy, diplomatic or diplomatics <old>; shirt-
sleeve diplomacy; shuttle diplomacy; dollar
diplomacy, dollar imperialism; gunboat diplomacy;
brinkmanship; **nationalism, internationalism;**
expansionism, imperialism, manifest destiny,
colonialism, neocolonialism; spheres of influence;
balance of power; containment; deterrence;
militarism, preparedness; tough policy, the big
stick <nf>, twisting the lion's tail; brinksmanship;
nonresistance, isolationism, neutralism,
coexistence, peaceful coexistence; détente;
compromise, appeasement; peace offensive; good-
neighbor policy; open-door policy, open door;
Monroe Doctrine; Truman Doctrine; Eisenhower
Doctrine; Nixon Doctrine

6 program; Square Deal <Theodore Roosevelt>,
New Deal <Franklin D Roosevelt>, Fair Deal
<Harry S Truman>, New Frontier <John F
Kennedy>, Great Society <Lyndon B Johnson>;
austerity program; Beveridge Plan <Brit>;
Thatcherism <Brit>

7 platform, party platform, **program,** declaration of
policy; **plank; issue;** keynote address, keynote
speech; position paper

8 political convention, convention; conclave,
powwow <nf>; national convention, quadrennial
circus <nf>; state convention, county convention,
preliminary convention, nominating convention;
constitutional convention

9 caucus, legislative or congressional caucus, packed
caucus; secret caucus

10 candidacy, candidature <chiefly Brit>, **running,**
running for office, throwing or tossing one's hat in
the ring <nf>, standing or standing for office
<Brit>

11 nomination, caucus nomination, direct
nomination, petition nomination; acceptance
speech

12 electioneering, campaigning, politicking <nf>,
stumping and **whistle-stopping** <nf>; **rally,**
clambake <nf>; campaign dinner, fund-raising
dinner

13 campaign, all-out campaign, hard-hitting
campaign, hoopla or hurrah campaign <nf>;
canvass, solicitation; front-porch campaign; grass-
roots campaign; stump excursion and stumping
tour and whistle-stop campaign <nf>; TV or
media campaign; campaign commitments or
promises; campaign fund, campaign contribution;
campaign button

14 smear campaign, mudslinging campaign, negative
campaign; **whispering campaign;** muckraking,
mudslinging and **dirty politics** and **dirty tricks** and
dirty pool <nf>, character assassination; political
canard, roorback; last-minute lie

15 election, general election, by-election;
congressional election, presidential election;
partisan election, nonpartisan election; **primary,**
primary election; direct primary, open primary,
closed primary, nonpartisan primary, mandatory
primary, optional primary, preference primary,
presidential primary, presidential preference
primary, runoff primary; caucus 609.9; runoff,
runoff election; disputed or contested election;
referendum; close election, horse race and
toss-up <nf>

16 election district, precinct, ward, borough;
congressional district; safe district; swing district
<nf>; close borough and pocket borough and
rotten borough <Brit>; gerrymander,

gerrymandered district, shoestring district; silk-stocking district *or* ward; single-member district *or* constituency; body politic

17 suffrage, franchise, the vote, right to vote; universal suffrage, manhood suffrage, woman *or* female suffrage; suffragism, suffragettism; suffragist, woman-suffragist, suffragette; household franchise; one man one vote

18 voting, going to the polls, casting one's ballot; preferential voting, preferential system, alternative vote; proportional representation *or* PR, cumulative system *or* voting, Hare system, list system; single system *or* voting, single transferrable vote; plural system *or* voting; single-member district 609.16; absentee voting; proxy voting, card voting; voting machine; election fraud, colonization, floating, repeating, ballot-box stuffing; **vote** 371.6

19 ballot, slate, ticket, proxy <nf>; straight ticket, split ticket; Australian ballot; office-block ballot; Indiana ballot, party-column ballot; absentee ballot; long ballot, blanket ballot, jungle ballot <nf>; short ballot; nonpartisan ballot; sample ballot; party emblem

20 polls, poll, polling place, polling station <Brit>, balloting place; voting booth, polling booth; ballot box; voting machine; pollbook

21 returns, election returns, **poll,** count, official count; **recount;** landslide, tidal wave

22 electorate, electors; **constituency,** constituents; electoral college

23 voter, elector, balloter; registered voter; fraudulent voter, floater, repeater, ballot-box stuffer; proxy

24 political party <see list>, **party,** major party, minor party, third party, splinter party; party in power, opposition party, loyal opposition; **faction, camp; machine,** political *or* party machine, Tammany Hall; city hall; one-party system, two-party system, multiple party system, multiparty system; right, left, center; popular front; bloc, coalition

25 partisanism, partisanship, partisanry; Republicanism; Conservatism, Toryism; Liberalism; Whiggism, Whiggery

26 nonpartisanism, independence, neutralism; mugwumpery, mugwumpism

27 partisan, party member, party man *or* woman; regular, stalwart, loyalist; wheelhorse, party wheelhorse; heeler, ward heeler, **party hack;** party faithful

28 nonpartisan, independent, neutral, mugwump, undecided *or* uncommitted voter, centrist; swing vote

29 political influence, wire-pulling <nf>; **social pressure, public opinion, special-interest**

pressure, group pressure; **influence peddling; lobbying,** lobbyism; **logrolling,** back scratching

30 wire-puller <nf>; **influence peddler,** four-percenter, power broker, fixer <nf>, five-percenter <nf>; logroller

31 pressure group, interest group, special-interest group, political action committee *or* PAC, single-issue group; **special interest;** vested interest; financial interests, farm interests, labor interests, etc; minority interests, ethnic vote, black vote, Jewish vote, Italian vote, etc; **Black Power,** White Power, Polish Power, etc

32 lobby, legislative lobby, special-interest lobby; **lobbyist,** registered lobbyist, lobbyer, parliamentary agent <Brit>

33 front, movement, coalition, political front; popular front, people's front, communist front, etc; grass-roots movement, ground swell, the silent majority

34 <political corruption> **graft,** boodling <nf>, jobbery; pork-barrel legislation *or* pork-barreling; political intrigue

35 spoils of office; graft, boodle <nf>; slush fund <nf>; campaign fund, campaign contribution; public tit *and* public trough <nf>; spoils system; cronyism, nepotism

36 political patronage, patronage, favors of office, pork *and* **pork barrel** <nf>, plum, melon <nf>

37 political *or* **official jargon; officialese** *and* federalese *and* Washingtonese *and* gobbledygook <nf>; bafflegab <nf>; political doubletalk, doublespeak, bunkum <nf>; pussyfooting; pointing with pride and viewing with alarm; new world order

VERBS **38 politick** <nf>, politicize; look after one's fences *and* mend one's fences <nf>; caucus; gerrymander, lobby

39 run for office, run; **throw** *or* **toss one's hat in the ring** <nf>, go into politics, announce for, enter the lists *or* arena, stand *and* stand for office <Brit>; contest a seat <Brit>

40 electioneer, campaign; stump *and* take the stump *and* take to the stump *and* stump the country *and* take to the hustings *and* hit the campaign trail *and* **whistle-stop** <nf>; **canvass,** go to the voters *or* electorate, solicit votes, ring doorbells; shake hands and kiss babies

41 support, back *and* **back up** <nf>, come out for, **endorse;** go with the party, follow the party line; **get on the bandwagon** <nf>; **nominate, elect, vote** 371.18,20

42 hold office, hold *or* occupy a post, fill an office, be the incumbent, be in office, be elected, be voted in

ADJS **43 political,** politic; governmental, civic; geopolitical; statesmanlike; diplomatic; suffragist; politico-commercial, politico-diplomatic, politico-ecclesiastical, politico-economic, politico-ethical, politico-geographical, politico-judicial, politico-military, politico-moral, politico-religious, politico-scientific, politico-social, politico-theological; politically correct

44 partisan, party; bipartisan, biparty, two-party
45 nonpartisan, independent, neutral, mugwumpian *and* mugwumpish <nf>, **on the fence**
WORD ELEMENT **46** politico-
47 political parties

American Labor Party	New Democratic Party
American Party *or* Know-	<Can>
Nothing Party	People's *or* Populist Party
Anti-Masonic Party	Plaid Cymru <Wales>
Anti-Monopoly Party	Populist/America First
Bull Moose Party	Party <US>
Citizens Party <US>	Progressive Party
Communist Party	Progressive Conservative
Conservative Party	Party <US>
Conservative Union Party	Progressive Democrat
<Can>	Party <Ir>
Constitutional Union	Prohibition Party
Party	Republican Party *or*
Democratic Party <US>	GOP *or* Grand Old
Democratic-Republican	Party <US>
Party	Scottish National Party
Farmer-Labor Party	Sinn Fein <N Ir>
Federalist Party <US>	Social and Liberal
Fianna Fail <Ir>	Democratic Party
Fine Gael <Ir>	<Brit>
Free Soil Party	Social Democratic and
Green Party	Labour Party <N Ir>
Greenback Party	Social Democratic Party *or*
Labour Party <Brit>	SDP <Brit>
Liberal Democrat Party	Socialist Labor Party <US>
<Brit>	Socialist Party
Liberal Party	Socialist Workers Party
Liberal Republican Party	States' Rights Democratic
Libertarian Party <US>	Party *or* Dixiecrats <US>
Militant Tendency <Brit>	Tory Party <Brit>
National Republican	Ulster Democratic Unionist
Party	Party <N Ir>
National Front <Brit>	US Labor Party
New Alliance Party <US>	Whig Party

610 POLITICIAN

NOUNS **1 politician,** politico, political leader, professional politician; party leader, party boss *and* party chieftain <nf>; machine *or* clubhouse politician, **political hack,** Tammany man <old>; **pol** <nf>; old campaigner, war-horse; wheelhorse; reform politician, reformer, advocate
2 statesman, stateswoman, statesperson, solon, public man *or* woman, national leader; elder statesman; ruler; governor, executive, administrator, leader; president, vice president; prime minister, premier

3 legislator, lawmaker, legislatrix, solon, lawgiver; **congressman,** congresswoman, Member of Congress; **senator; representative;** Speaker of the House; majority leader, minority leader; floor leader; whip, party whip; Member of Parliament *or* MP; state senator, assemblyman, assemblywoman, chosen, freeholder, councilman, alderman, city father
4 <petty politician> **two-bit** *or* **peanut politician** <nf>, politicaster, statemonger <old>, political dabbler; **hack, party hack**
5 <corrupt politician> **dirty** *or* **crooked politician** *and* jackleg politician <nf>; **grafter,** boodler <nf>; spoilsman, spoilsmonger; influence peddler 609.30
6 <political intriguer> strategist, machinator, gamesman, wheeler-dealer <nf>; operator *and* finagler *and* **wire-puller** <nf>; **logroller,** pork-barrel politician; Machiavellian; behind-the-scenes operator, gray eminence, *éminence grise* <Fr>, power behind the throne, kingmaker <nf>, **powerbroker** 894.6
7 <political leader> **boss** <nf>, higher-up *or* man higher up <nf>, cacique *and* sachem <old>; keynoter <nf>, policy maker; standard-bearer; ringleader 375.11; **big shot** <nf> 997.9
8 henchman, cohort, hanger-on, buddy *and* sidekick <nf>; heeler *and* **ward heeler** <nf>; hatchet man
9 candidate, aspirant, hopeful *and* political hopeful *and* wannabee <nf>, office seeker *or* hunter, baby kisser <nf>; running mate; leading candidate, head of the ticket *or* slate; **dark horse;** stalking-horse; favorite son; presidential timber; defeated candidate, also-ran *and* dud <nf>
10 campaigner, electioneer, **stumper** <nf>, whistle-stopper <nf>, stump speaker *or* orator <nf>
11 officeholder, office-bearer <Brit>, jack-in-office, elected official, public servant, public official, **incumbent;** holdover, lame duck; new broom <nf>; president-elect; ins, the powers that be
12 political worker, committeeman, committeewoman, precinct captain, precinct leader, district leader; party chairperson, state chairperson, national chairperson, chairperson of the national committee; political philosopher
VERBS **13** go into politics; **run,** get on the ticket; **campaign,** stump
ADJS **14 statesmanlike,** statesmanly

611 POLITICO-ECONOMIC PRINCIPLES

NOUNS **1 conservatism, conservativeness, rightism;** standpattism <nf>, unprogressiveness, backwardness; **ultraconservatism, reaction,** arch-conservative, reactionism, reactionarism, reactionaryism, reactionariness, die-hardism <nf>

2 moderatism, moderateness, middle-of-the-roadism; middle of the road, moderate position, via media, **center,** centrism; third force, nonalignment

3 liberalism, progressivism, leftism; left, left wing, progressiveness

4 radicalism, extremism, ultraism; radicalization; revolutionism; ultraconservatism 611.1; extreme left, extreme left wing, left-wing extremism, loony left <Brit nf>; New Left, Old Left; Jacobinism, sansculottism, *sans-culotterie* <Fr>; **anarchism, nihilism,** syndicalism *and* anarcho-syndicalism *and* criminal syndicalism <old>; extreme rightism, radical rightism, know-nothingism; extreme right, extreme right wing; social Darwinism; laissez-faireism 329.1; **royalism, monarchism;** Toryism, Bourbonism

5 communism, Bolshevism, Marxism, Marxism-Leninism, Leninism, Trotskyism, Stalinism, Maoism, Titoism, Castroism, revisionism; Marxian socialism; dialectical materialism; democratic centralism; dictatorship of the proletariat; **Communist Party;** Communist International, Comintern; Communist Information Bureau, Cominform; iron curtain 1012.5

6 socialism, collective ownership, collectivization, public ownership; **collectivism;** creeping socialism; state socialism, *Staatsozialismus* <Ger>; guild socialism; Fabian socialism, Fabianism; utopian socialism; Marxian socialism, Marxism 611.5; phalansterism; Owenism; Saint-Simonianism, Saint-Simonism; **nationalization**

7 welfarism, welfare statism; womb-to-tomb security, cradle-to-grave security; social welfare; social security, social insurance; old-age and survivors insurance; unemployment compensation, unemployment insurance; workmen's compensation, workmen's compensation insurance; health insurance, Medicare, Medicaid, state medicine, socialized medicine; sickness insurance; public assistance, **welfare, relief,** welfare payments, aid to dependent children *or* ADC, old-age assistance, aid to the blind, aid to the permanently and totally disabled; guaranteed income, guaranteed annual income; welfare state; welfare capitalism

8 capitalism, capitalistic system, **free enterprise,** private enterprise, free-enterprise economy, free-enterprise system, free economy; finance capitalism; *laissez-faire* <Fr>, laissez-faireism; private sector; private ownership; state capitalism; **individualism,** rugged individualism

9 conservative, conservatist, **rightist, rightwinger;** dry <Brit nf>, "the leftover progressive of an earlier generation" —Edmund Fuller; standpat *and* standpatter <nf>; hard hat; social Darwinist;

ultraconservative, arch-conservative, extreme right-winger, **reactionary,** reactionarist, reactionist, diehard; **royalist, monarchist,** Bourbon, Tory, imperialist; **right, right wing; radical right**

10 moderate, moderatist, moderationist, **centrist,** middle-of-the-roader <nf>; independent; center

11 liberal, liberalist, wet <Brit nf>, **progressive,** progressivist, **leftist, left-winger;** welfare stater; Lib-Lab <Brit nf>; **left**

12 radical, extremist, ultra, ultraist; **revolutionary,** revolutionist; subversive; extreme left-winger, left-wing extremist, **red** <nf>, Bolshevik; yippie; Jacobin, sansculotte; **anarchist,** nihilist; mild radical, parlor Bolshevik <nf>, pink *and* parlor pink *and* pinko <nf>; lunatic fringe

13 Communist, Bolshevist; Bolshevik, **Red** *and* commie *and* bolshie <nf>; Marxist, Leninist, Marxist-Leninist, Trotskyite *or* Trotskyist, Stalinist, Maoist, Titoist, Castroite, revisionist; card-carrying Communist, avowed Communist; fellow traveler, Communist sympathizer, comsymp <nf>

14 socialist, collectivist; social democrat; state socialist; Fabian, Fabian socialist; Marxist 611.13; utopian socialist; Fourierist, phalansterian; Saint-Simonian; Owenite

15 capitalist; coupon-clipper <nf>; rich man 618.7

VERBS **16 politicize;** democratize, republicanize, socialize, communize; nationalize 476.7; deregulate, privatize, denationalize; radicalize

ADJS **17 conservative, right-wing,** right of center, dry <Brit nf>; old-line, die-hard, unreconstructed, standpat <nf>, unprogressive, nonprogressive; ultraconservative, **reactionary,** reactionist

18 moderate, centrist, middle-of-the-road <nf>, independent

19 liberal, liberalistic, liberalist, wet <Brit nf>, bleeding-heart <nf>; **progressive,** progressivistic; **leftist, left-wing,** on the left, left of center

20 radical, extreme, extremist, extremistic, ultraist, ultraistic; revolutionary, revolutionist; subversive; ultraconservative 611.17; extreme left-wing, **red** <nf>; anarchistic, nihilistic, syndicalist *and* anarcho-syndicalist <old>; mildly radical, pink <nf>

21 Communist, communistic, Bolshevik, Bolshevist, commie *and* bolshie *and* Red <nf>; **Marxist,** Leninist, Marxist-Leninist, Trotskyite *or* Trotskyist, Stalinist, Maoist, Titoist, Castroite; revisionist

22 socialist, socialistic, collectivistic; social-democratic; Fabian; Fourieristic, phalansterian; Saint-Simonian

23 capitalist, capitalistic, bourgeois, individualistic, nonsocialistic, free-enterprise, private-enterprise

612 GOVERNMENT

NOUNS **1 government,** governance, **discipline, regulation; direction, management, administration,** dispensation, disposition, oversight, **supervision** 573.2; **regime,** regimen; **rule, sway, sovereignty, reign,** regnancy, regency; empire, empery, dominion, dynasty, regime, regimen; social order, civil government, political government, political system; form or system of government, political organization, polity, political party; local government, state government, national government, world government, international government

2 control, mastery, mastership, command, power, jurisdiction, dominion, domination; hold, grasp, grip, gripe, command; hand, hands, iron hand, clutches; talons, claws; helm, reins of government

3 the government, the authorities; the powers that be, national government, central government, the Establishment; the corridors of power, government circles; Uncle Sam, Washington; John Bull, the Crown, His or Her Majesty's Government, Whitehall

4 <kinds of government> **federal government,** federation, federalism; **constitutional government,** majority rule; **republic,** commonwealth; **democracy,** representative government, representative democracy, direct or pure democracy, town-meeting democracy; "government of the people, by the people, for the people"—Lincoln, "the worst form of government except all those other forms that have been tried from time to time"—Winston Churchill, "the recurrent suspicion that more than half of the people are right more than half of the time" —E B White; **parliamentary government;** social democracy, welfare state; mob rule, tyranny of the majority, mobocracy <nf>, ochlocracy; minority government; pantisocracy; aristocracy, hierarchy, oligarchy, elitism, plutocracy, minority rule; feudal system; monarchy, monarchical government, absolute monarchy, constitutional monarchy, limited monarchy, kingship, queenship; dictatorship, tyranny, autocracy, autarchy; dyarchy, duarchy, duumvirate; triarchy, triumvirate; **totalitarian government** or regime, totalitarianism, police state, despotism; **fascism, communism;** stratocracy, demagogy, **military government,** militarism, garrison state; martial law, rule of the sword; regency; hierocracy, theocracy, thearchy; patriarchy, patriarchate; gerontocracy; technocracy, meritocracy; **autonomy, self-government,** autarchy, self-rule, self-determination, home rule; heteronomy, dominion rule, colonial government, colonialism, neocolonialism;

provisional government; coalition government; tribalism, tribal system, clan system; isocracy, egalitarianism; caretaker government, interregnum, provisional government, coalition government

5 <government by women> matriarchy, matriarchate, gynarchy, gynocracy, gynecocracy; petticoat government

6 <nf terms> foolocracy, gunocracy, mediocracy, moneyocracy, landocracy, cottonocracy, beerocracy, oiligarchy, parsonarchy, pedantocracy, pornocracy, snobocracy, squirearchy

7 supranational government, supergovernment, **world government,** World Federalism; League of Nations, United Nations 614

8 <principles of government> democratism, power-sharing, republicanism; constitutionalism, rule of law, parliamentarism, parliamentarianism; monarchism, royalism; feudalism, feudality; imperialism; fascism, neofascism, Nazism, national socialism; statism, governmentalism; collectivism, communism 611.5, socialism 611.6; federalism; centralism; pluralism; political principles 611; glasnost

9 absolutism, dictatorship, despotism, tyranny, autocracy, autarchy, monarchy, absolute monarchy; **authoritarianism;** totalitarianism; one-man rule, one-party rule; Caesarism, Stalinism, kaiserism, czarism; benevolent despotism, paternalism

10 despotism, tyranny, fascism, domineering, domination, oppression; heavy hand, high hand, iron hand, iron heel or boot; big stick, *argumentum baculinum* <L>; **terrorism,** reign of terror; thought control

11 officialism, bureaucracy; beadledom, bumbledom; **red-tapeism** and red-tapery and **red tape** <nf>; federalese, official jargon 609.37

VERBS **12 govern, regulate; wield authority** 417.13; **command,** officer, captain, **head, lead,** be master, be at the head of, **preside over,** chair; **direct, manage, supervise, administer,** administrate 573.11; discipline; stand over

13 control, hold in hand, have in one's power, be in power, have power, gain a hold upon; hold the reins, hold the helm, call the shots or tune and be in the driver's seat or saddle <nf>; direct, have control of, **have under control, have in hand** or **well in hand;** be master of the situation, have it all one's own way, have the game in one's own hands, hold all the aces <nf>; pull the strings or wires

14 rule, sway, hold sway, **reign,** bear reign, have the sway, wield the scepter, wear the crown, sit on the throne; rule over, overrule

15 dominate, predominate, preponderate, prevail;

have the ascendancy, have the upper *or* whip hand, get under control, have on the hip <old>; **master,** have the mastery of; bestride; dictate, lay down the law; **rule the roost** *and* wear the pants *and* crack the whip *and* ride herd <nf>; take the lead, play first fiddle; **lead by the nose, twist** *or* **turn around one's little finger; keep under one's thumb,** bend to one's will

16 **domineer,** domineer over, **lord it over;** browbeat, order around, henpeck <nf>, intimidate, bully, cow, bulldoze <nf>, walk over, walk all over; castrate, unman; daunt, terrorize; **tyrannize,** tyrannize over, push *or* kick around <nf>, despotize; **grind,** grind down, break, **oppress,** suppress, repress, weigh *or* press heavy on; keep under, keep down, beat down, clamp down on <nf>; overbear, overmaster, overawe; override, ride over, trample *or* stamp *or* tread upon, trample *or* tread down, **trample** *or* **tread underfoot,** keep down, crush under an iron heel, **ride roughshod over;** hold *or* keep a tight hand upon, rule with a rod of iron, rule with an iron hand *or* fist; enslave, subjugate 432.8; compel, coerce 424.7

ADJS 17 **governmental,** gubernatorial; **political, civil,** civic; **official,** bureaucratic, administrative; democratic, republican, fascist, fascistic, oligarchal, oligarchic, oligarchical, aristocratic, aristocratical, theocratic, **federal,** federalist, federalistic, **constitutional,** parliamentary, parliamentarian; monarchic *or* monarchical, monarchial, monarchal <old>; autocratic, monocratic, absolute; **authoritarian;** despotic, **dictatorial; totalitarian;** pluralistic; paternalistic, patriarchal, patriarchic, patriarchical; matriarchal, matriarchic, matriarchical; heteronomous; autonomous, self-governing, self-ruling, autarchic; executive, presidential; gubernatorial

18 **governing, controlling, regulating,** regulative, regulatory, **commanding; ruling, reigning, sovereign,** regnant, regnal, titular; **master, chief,** general, **boss, head; dominant, predominant,** predominate, preponderant, preponderate, prepotent, prepollent, prevalent, **leading, paramount, supreme,** number one <nf>, hegemonic, hegemonistic; ascendant, in the ascendant, in ascendancy; at the head, in chief; in charge 417.21

19 **executive, administrative,** ministerial; official, bureaucratic; **supervisory, directing, managing** 573.12

ADVS 20 **under control, in hand,** well in hand; **in one's power,** under one's control

WORD ELEMENTS 21 -archy, -cracy, -ocracy

613 LEGISLATURE, GOVERNMENT ORGANIZATION

NOUNS 1 **legislature** <see list>, legislative body; **parliament, congress, assembly,** general assembly, house of assembly, legislative assembly, **national assembly, chamber of deputies,** federal assembly, diet, soviet, court; unicameral legislature, bicameral legislature; legislative chamber, **upper chamber** *or* **house** <see list>, **lower chamber** *or* **house** <see list>; state legislature, state assembly; provincial legislature, provincial parliament; city council, city board, board of aldermen, common council, commission; representative town meeting, town meeting

2 United States Government, Federal Government; Cabinet <see list>; Executive Department, executive branch; government agency; legislature; Congress, Senate, Upper House, Senate committee; House of Representatives, House, Lower House, House of Representatives committee; Supreme Court

3 **cabinet,** ministry, British cabinet <see list>, **council,** advisory council, council of state, privy council, divan; shadow cabinet; kitchen cabinet, camarilla

4 **capitol, statehouse; courthouse;** city hall

5 **legislation, lawmaking,** legislature <old>; **enactment,** enaction, constitution, passage, passing; **resolution,** concurrent resolution, joint resolution; act 673.3

6 <legislative procedure> introduction, first reading, committee consideration, tabling, filing, second reading, deliberation, debate, third reading, **vote,** division, roll call; **filibustering,** filibuster, talkathon <nf>; cloture 857.5; **logrolling;** steamroller methods; guillotine <Brit>

7 **veto,** executive veto, absolute veto, qualified *or* limited veto, suspensive *or* suspensory veto, item veto, pocket veto; veto power; veto message; senatorial courtesy

8 **referendum,** constitutional referendum, statutory referendum, optional *or* facultative referendum, compulsory *or* mandatory referendum; **mandate; plebiscite,** plebiscitum; initiative, direct initiative, indirect initiative; recall

9 **bill,** omnibus bill, hold-up bill, companion bills amendment; **clause, proviso;** enacting clause, dragnet clause, escalator clause, saving clause; **rider;** joker <nf>; **calendar, motion;** question, previous question, privileged question

VERBS 10 **legislate,** make *or* enact laws, **enact, pass,** constitute, ordain, put in force; **put through, jam** *or* **steamroller** *or* **railroad through** <nf>, lobby through; table, pigeonhole; take the floor, get the floor, have the floor; yield the floor; **filibuster; logroll,** roll logs; **veto, pocket, kill; decree** 420.8

ADJS **11 legislative,** legislatorial, lawmaking;
deliberative; **parliamentary, congressional;**
senatorial; bicameral, unicameral

12 legislatures

Althing <Iceland>
bicameral legislature
  <Bosnia and
  Herzegovina, Haiti,
  Kazakhstan, Russia>
Assembly of the Republic
  <Portugal>
Chamber of Deputies
  <Luxembourg>
Congress <Argentina,
  Colombia, Liberia,
  Mexico, Philippines,
  Uruguay, US,
  Venezuela>
Cortes <Spain>
Diet <Japan>
Eduskunta <Finland>
Federal Assembly
  <Switzerland,
  Yugoslavia>
Federal Parliament
  <Australia>
Folketing <Denmark>
Grand National Assembly
  <Turkey>
Great and General Council
  <San Marino>
Great People's Khural
  <Mongolia>
House of Assembly
  <Bahamas, Kiribati>
House of Representatives
  <Cyprus, Gambia,
  Malta, Sierra Leone>
Knesset <Israel>
Landtag
  <Liechtenstein>
Legislative Assembly
  <Costa Rica, Tonga>
National Assembly
  <Benin, Bhutan,
  Bulgaria, Cameroon,
  Cuba, El Salvador,
  Gabon, Guyana, Haiti,
  Hungary, Ivory Coast,
  Kenya, Kuwait,
  Macedonia, Malawi,
  Mauritius, Morocco,
  Nicaragua, Pakistan,
  Panama, Rwanda,
  Senegal, South Korea,
  Sri Lanka, Suriname,
  Tanzania, Tunisia,
  Uganda, Zambia>

National Congress
  <Bolivia, Brazil, Chile,
  Ecuador, Honduras,
  Micronesia>
National Council
  <Monaco>
Oireachtas <Ireland>
Parliament <Afghanistan,
  Algeria, Andorra,
  Austria, Azerbaijan,
  Barbados, Belgium,
  Botswana, Canada,
  Czech Republic, Estonia,
  Ethiopia, Fiji, France,
  Germany, Ghana,
  Greece, Guinea, India,
  Italy, Jamaica, Jordan,
  Malaysia, Maldives,
  Mali, Moldova, Nauru,
  Nepal, Netherlands, New
  Zealand, Palau, Papua
  New Guinea, Romania,
  Sierra Leone, Singapore,
  Slovakia, Slovenia,
  South Africa, Swaziland,
  Taiwan, Tajikistan,
  Trinidad and Tobago,
  Turkmenistan, Tuvalu,
  Ukraine, United
  Kingdom, Yemen,
  Zimbabwe>
People's Assembly
  <Albania, Egypt,
  Seychelles>
People's Consultative
  Assembly <Indonesia>
People's Council <Syria>
Riksdag <Sweden>
Sejm <Poland>
Storting <Norway>
Supreme Assembly
  <Uzbekistan>
Supreme Military Council
  <Equatorial Guinea>
Supreme People's
  Assembly <North
  Korea>
unicameral legislature
  <Comoros, Djibouti,
  Dominican Republic,
  Georgia, Guatemala,
  Guinea-Bissau, Namibia,
  Peru, United Arab
  Emirates, Vanuatu>

13 upper houses

Bundesrat <Austria,
  Germany>
Federation Council
  <Russia>
House of Councilors
  <Japan>
House of Lords <United
  Kingdom>
Lagting <Norway>
Rajya Sabha <India>
Standerat <Switzerland>
Senate <Australia,
  Barbados, Belgium,
  Brazil, Canada, Chile,
Colombia, Czech
  Republic, Dominican
  Republic, Ecuador,
  Ethiopia, Fiji, France,
  Iran, Ireland, Italy,
  Jamaica, Liberia,
  Malagasy Republic,
  Malaysia, Mexico,
  Nicaragua, Paraguay,
  Philippines, Rhodesia,
  South Africa, Swaziland,
  Trinidad and Tobago,
  US, Venezuela>

14 lower houses

Bundestag <Germany>
Chamber of Deputies
  <Brazil, Chile, Czech
  Republic, Dominican
  Republic, Ecuador,
  Ethiopia, Italy, Jordan,
  Mexico, Nicaragua,
  Paraguay, Venezuela>
Chamber of
  Representatives
  <Belgium, Colombia>
Dáil Eireann <Ireland>
House of Assembly
  <Barbados, Rhodesia,
  South Africa,
  Swaziland>

House of Commons
  <Canada, United
  Kingdom>
House of Representatives
  <Australia, Fiji, Jamaica,
  Japan, Liberia, Malaysia,
  Philippines, US>
Lok Sabha <India>
National Assembly
  <France, Laos, Malagasy
  Republic, Portugal,
  Turkey>
Nationalrat <Austria>
Odelsting <Norway>
State Duma <Russia>

15 US Cabinet

Attorney General
Secretary of
  Agriculture
Secretary of Commerce
Secretary of Defense
Secretary of Education
Secretary of Energy
Secretary of Health and
  Human Services

Secretary of Housing and
  Urban Development
Secretary of Labor
Secretary of State
Secretary of the Interior
Secretary of the Treasury
Secretary of Transportation
Secretary of Veterans'
  Affairs

16 British Cabinet and Ministries

Chancellor of the
  Exchequer
Chief Secretary to the
  Treasury
Deputy Prime Minister
Chancellor of the Duchy of
  Lancaster
First Lord of the Admiralty
First Lord of the Treasury
First Secretary of State
Home Secretary <Home
  Office>
Lord Chancellor

Lord President of the
  Council
Lord Privy Seal
Minister of Agriculture,
  Fisheries, and Food
Minister of Defence
Minister of Housing and
  Local Government
Minister of Public Service
  and Science
Minister of State <Cabinet
  Office>
Minister of Technology

Minister of Transport
Paymaster-General
President of the Board of
Education
President of the Board of
Trade
Prime Minister
Secretary of State for
Culture, Media and Sport
Secretary of State for
Defence
Secretary of State for
Economic Affairs
Secretary of State for
Education and Science
Secretary of State for
Education and
Employment
Secretary of State for
Environment

Secretary of State for
Foreign Affairs
Secretary of State for
Foreign and
Commonwealth Affairs
Secretary of State for
Health
Secretary of State for
National Heritage
Secretary of State for
Northern Ireland
Secretary of State for
Scotland
Secretary of State for
Social Security
Secretary of State for
Trade and Industry
Secretary of State for
Wales

614 UNITED NATIONS, INTERNATIONAL ORGANIZATIONS

NOUNS **1** United Nations *or* **UN;** League of Nations
2 <United Nations organs> Secretariat; General
Assembly; Security Council; Trusteeship Council;
International Court of Justice; United Nations
agency <see list>, Economic and Social Council
or ECOSOC, ECOSOC commission
3 international organization, non-UN international
organization
4 United Nations agencies

Food and Agricultural
Organization *or* FAO
General Agreement on
Tariffs and Trade *or*
GATT
Intergovernmental
Maritime Consultative
Organization *or* IMCO
International Atomic
Energy Agency *or* IAEA
International Bank for
Reconstruction and
Development *or* World
Bank
International Civil Aviation
Organization *or* ICAO
International Development
Association *or* IDA
International Finance
Corporation *or* IFO
International Labor
Organization *or* ILO

International Monetary
Fund *or* the Fund
International
Telecommunication
Union *or* ITU
United Nations Children's
Fund *or* UNICEF
United Nations
Educational, Scientific
and Cultural
Organization *or*
UNESCO
United Nations Relief and
Works Agency *or*
UNRWA
Universal Postal Union *or*
UPU
World Health Organization
or WHO
World Meteorological
Organization *or* WMO

615 COMMISSION

NOUNS **1 commission,** commissioning, **delegation,**
devolution, devolvement, vesting, investing,
investment, investiture; **deputation;** commitment,
entrusting, entrustment, **assignment,** consignment,
consignation; **errand, task, office; care,** cure,
responsibility, purview, jurisdiction; **mission,**
legation, embassy; **authority** 417; **authorization,**
empowerment, power to act, full power,
plenipotentiary power, vicarious *or* delegated
authority; **warrant,** license, **mandate, charge, trust,**
brevet, exequatur; **agency,** agentship, factorship;
regency, regentship; lieutenancy; trusteeship,
executorship; **proxy,** procuration, **power of
attorney**
2 appointment, assignment, designation,
nomination, naming, selection, tabbing <nf>;
ordainment, ordination; posting, transferral
3 installation, installment, **instatement,** induction,
placement, **inauguration,** investiture, taking office;
accession, accedence; coronation, crowning,
enthronement
4 engagement, employment, hiring, appointment,
taking on <nf>, recruitment, recruiting; executive
recruiting, executive search; retaining, retainment,
briefing <Brit>; preengagement, bespeaking;
reservation, booking; exercise, function
5 executive search agency *or* firm; executive
recruiter, executive recruitment consultant,
executive development specialist; **headhunter** *and*
body snatcher *and* flesh peddler *and* talent scout
<nf>
6 rental, rent; lease, let <Brit>; hire, hiring;
sublease, subrent; **charter,** bareboat charter;
lend-lease
**7 enlistment, enrollment; conscription, draft,
drafting, induction,** impressment, press; call, draft
call, call-up, summons, call to the colors, letter
from Uncle Sam <nf>; **recruitment,** recruiting;
muster, mustering, mustering in, levy, levying;
mobilization; selective service, compulsory
military service
8 indenture, binding over; **apprenticeship**
9 assignee, appointee, selectee, nominee, candidate;
licensee, licentiate; deputy, agent 576
VERBS **10 commission, authorize,** empower,
accredit; **delegate,** devolute, devolve, devolve upon,
vest, invest; depute, **deputize; assign,** consign,
commit, charge, entrust, give in charge; license,
charter, warrant; detail, detach, post, transfer, send
out, mission, send on a mission
11 appoint, assign, designate, **nominate,** name, select,
tab <nf>, elect; **ordain,** ordinate <old>
12 install, instate, induct, **inaugurate,** invest, put in,
place, **place in office;** chair; crown, throne,
enthrone, anoint
13 be instated, take office, accede; take *or* mount the
throne; attain to

14 employ, hire, give a job to, take into employment, take into one's service, take on <nf>, recruit, headhunt <nf>, **engage,** sign up *or* on <nf>; retain, brief <Brit>; bespeak, preengage; sign up for <nf>, **reserve,** book

15 rent, lease, let <Brit>, hire, job, **charter; sublease, sublet,** underlet

16 rent out, rent; lease, lease out; let *and* let off *and* let out <Brit>; **hire out,** hire; charter; **sublease, sublet,** underlet; lend-lease, lease-lend; lease-back; farm, farm out; job

17 enlist, list <old>, **enroll, sign up** *or* on <nf>; **conscript, draft, induct,** press, impress, commandeer; detach, detach for service; summon, call up, call to the colors; **mobilize,** call to active duty; **recruit, muster,** levy, raise, muster in; join 617.14

18 indenture, article, bind, bind over; **apprentice**

ADJS **19 commissioned, authorized, accredited;** delegated, deputized, appointed; devolutionary

20 employed, hired, hireling, paid, mercenary; rented, leased, let <Brit>; sublet, underlet, subleased; chartered

21 indentured, articled, bound over; **apprenticed, apprentice,** prentice *or* 'prentice

ADVS **22 for hire,** for rent, to let, to lease

616 ASSOCIATE

NOUNS **1 associate, confederate,** consociate, **colleague,** fellow member, **companion, fellow,** bedfellow, **crony,** consort, cohort, compeer, compatriot, confrere, brother, brother-in-arms, **ally,** adjunct, coadjutor; comrade in arms, **comrade** 588.3

2 partner, pardner *or* pard <nf>, copartner, side partner, buddy <nf>, **sidekick** *and* sidekicker <nf>; **mate; business partner,** nominal *or* holding-out *or* ostensible *or* quasi partner, general partner, special partner, silent partner, secret partner, dormant *or* sleeping partner

3 accomplice, cohort, confederate, fellow conspirator, coconspirator, partner *or* accomplice in crime; *particeps criminis* and *socius criminis* <L>; **accessory,** accessory before the fact, accessory after the fact; **abettor**

4 collaborator, cooperator; coauthor; **collaborationist**

5 co-worker, workfellow, workmate, fellow worker, buddy <nf>, butty <Brit nf>; **teammate, yokefellow,** yokemate; benchfellow, shopmate

6 assistant, helper, auxiliary, aider, **aid,** aide, paraprofessional; **help, helpmate, helpmeet;** deputy, **agent** 576; **attendant, second,** acolyte; best man, groomsman, paranymph; **servant, employee**

577; adjutant, aide-de-camp; lieutenant, executive officer; coadjutant, coadjutor; coadjutress, coadjutrix; sidesman <Brit>; supporting actor *or* player; supporting instrumentalist, sideman

7 right-hand man *or* **woman, right hand,** strong right hand *or* arm, **man** *or* **gal Friday,** fidus Achates, second self, alter ego, confidant

8 follower, disciple, adherent, votary; **man, henchman,** camp follower, hanger-on, satellite, creature, lackey, flunky, stooge <nf>, jackal, minion, myrmidon; yes-man <nf>, sycophant 138.3; goon <nf>, thug 593.3; puppet, cat's-paw; dummy, figurehead

9 supporter, upholder, maintainer, sustainer; support, **mainstay, standby** <nf>, stalwart, reliance, dependence; **abettor, seconder,** second; endorser, sponsor; **backer, promoter,** angel <nf>, rabbi <nf>; **patron,** Maecenas; friend at *or* in court; **champion,** defender, apologist, **advocate,** exponent, **protagonist; well-wisher,** favorer, encourager, sympathizer; **partisan,** sider <old>, sectary, votary; **fan** *and* buff <nf>, aficionado, **admirer,** lover

617 ASSOCIATION

NOUNS **1 association, society,** body, organization; **alliance, coalition, league, union;** council; **bloc,** axis; **partnership; federation, confederation,** confederacy; grouping, assemblage 770; **combination,** combine; *Bund* and *Verein* <Ger>; **unholy alliance, gang** *and* **ring** *and* mob <nf>; machine, **political machine;** economic community, common market, free trade area, customs union; credit union; cooperative, cooperative society, consumer cooperative, Rochdale cooperative; syndicate, guild; college, **group,** corps, band 770.3; labor union 727

2 community, society, commonwealth, social system; body; **kinship group, clan,** sept <Scot>, moiety, clan, tribe, totemic *or* totemistic group, phyle, phratry *or* phratria, gens, caste, subcaste, endogamous group; **family,** extended family, nuclear family, binuclear family; order, **class, social class** 607, economic class; colony, settlement; **commune,** ashram

3 fellowship, sodality; **society,** guild, order; **brotherhood, fraternity,** confraternity, confrerie, fraternal order *or* society; **sisterhood, sorority; club,** country club, lodge; peer group; secret society, **cabal**

4 party, interest, camp, side; interest group, lobby, pressure group, ethnic group; minority group, vocal minority; political action committee *or* PAC; silent majority; **faction,** division, **sect,** wing,

caucus, splinter, splinter group, breakaway group, offshoot; **political party** 609.24

5 **school, sect,** class, order; **denomination, communion,** confession, faith, church; **persuasion, ism; disciples, followers,** adherents

6 **clique, coterie, set, circle,** ring, junto, junta, cabal, camarilla, **clan,** group, grouping; **crew** *and* mob *and* **crowd** *and* **bunch** *and* outfit <nf>; cell; cadre, cohort, inner circle; closed *or* charmed circle; ingroup, in-crowd, popular crowd, we-group; elite, elite group; leadership group; **old-boy network;** peer group, age group

7 **team, outfit,** squad, string, corps; eleven, nine, eight, five, etc; **crew,** rowing crew; varsity, first team, first string; bench, reserves, second team, second string, third string; platoon, troupe; complement; **cast,** company

8 **organization,** establishment, **foundation, institution, institute**

9 **company, firm, business firm, concern, house,** *compagnie* <Fr>, *compañía* <Sp>, *Aktiengesellschaft* <Ger>, *aktiebolag* <Swed>; **business, industry, enterprise,** business establishment, commercial enterprise; **trust, syndicate, cartel,** combine, pool, consortium, plunderbund <nf>; combination in restraint of trade; chamber of commerce, junior chamber of commerce; trade association

10 **branch, organ, division,** wing, arm, offshoot, **affiliate; chapter,** lodge, post; chapel; **local;** branch office

11 **member,** affiliate, belonger, insider, initiate, one of us, cardholder, card-carrier, card-carrying member; **enrollee,** enlistee; **associate,** socius, **fellow;** brother, sister; comrade; honorary member; life member; member in good standing, dues-paying member; charter member; clubman, clubwoman, clubber <nf>; fraternity man, fraternity *or* frat brother, Greek <nf>, sorority woman; sorority sister, guildsman; committeeman; conventionist, conventioner, conventioneer; joiner <nf>; pledge

12 **membership,** members, associates, affiliates, body of affiliates, constituency

13 **partisanism,** partisanship, **partiality; factionalism, sectionalism,** faction; sectarianism, denominationalism; **cliquism,** cliquishness, cliqueyness; **clannishness,** clanship; exclusiveness, exclusivity; ethnocentricity; party spirit, *esprit de corps* <Fr>; the old college spirit

VERBS 14 **join,** join up <nf>, **enter, go into,** come into, get into, make oneself part of, swell the ranks of; **enlist, enroll, affiliate, sign up** *or* on <nf>, take up membership, take out membership; inscribe oneself, put oneself down; associate oneself with, affiliate with, league with, team *or* team up with; sneak in, creep in, insinuate oneself into; **combine, associate** 805.4

15 **belong,** hold membership, be a member, be on the rolls, be inscribed, subscribe, hold *or* carry a card, be in <nf>

ADJS 16 **associated, corporate,** incorporated; **combined** 805.5; non-profit-making, non-profit, not-for-profit

17 **associational, social, society, communal;** organizational; coalitional; sociable

18 **cliquish,** cliquey, **clannish;** ethnocentric; exclusive

19 **partisan,** party; **partial,** interested; **factional, sectional,** sectarian, sectary, denominational

ADVS 20 **in association, conjointly** 450.6

618 WEALTH

NOUNS 1 **wealth, riches, opulence** *or* opulency 991.2, **luxuriousness** 501.5; richness, wealthiness; **prosperity,** prosperousness, **affluence,** comfortable *or* easy circumstances, independence; **money,** lucre, pelf, gold, mammon; **substance, property, possessions,** material wealth; **assets** 728.14; **fortune, treasure,** handsome fortune; full *or* heavy *or* well-lined *or* bottomless *or* fat *or* bulging purse, deep pockets <nf>; *embarras de richesses* <Fr>, money to burn <nf>; high income, six-figure income; high tax bracket, upper bracket; old money, new money

2 **large sum,** good sum, tidy sum *and* **pretty penny, king's ransom;** heaps of gold; thousands, millions, cool million, billion, etc

3 <nf terms> **bundle, big bucks,** megabucks, gigabucks, big money, serious money, gobs, heaps, heavy lettuce, heavy jack, heavy money, important money, pot, potful, power, mint, barrel, raft, load, **loads,** pile, wad, wads, nice hunk of change, packet <Brit>, long green

4 <rich source> **mine,** mine of wealth, **gold mine,** bonanza, luau <nf>, lode, rich lode, mother lode, pot of gold, Eldorado, Golconda, Seven Cities of Cibola; gravy train <nf>; rich uncle; golden goose; cash cow <nf>

5 **the golden touch,** Midas touch; philosophers' stone; Pactolus

6 **the rich, the wealthy,** the well-to-do, the well-off, the haves <nf>, privileged class; jet set, glitterati, country-club set, beau monde; **plutocracy,** timocracy

7 **rich man** *or* **woman,** wealthy man *or* woman, warm man *or* woman <Brit nf>, **moneyed man** *or* **woman,** man *or* woman of wealth, **man** *or* **woman of means** *or* **substance,** fat cat <nf>, richling, deep pocket *and* moneybags *and* Mr Moneybags <nf>,

tycoon, magnate, baron, Daddy Warbucks <Harold Gray>, coupon-clipper, **nabob; capitalist, plutocrat,** bloated plutocrat; **millionaire,** multimillionaire, megamillionaire, millionairess, multibillionaire, multibillionairess, billionaire; parvenu

8 Croesus, Midas, Plutus, Dives, Timon of Athens, Danaë; Rockefeller, Vanderbilt, Whitney, DuPont, Ford, Getty, Rothschild, Onassis, Hughes, Hunt, Trump

VERBS 9 **enrich, richen;** endow

10 **grow rich, get rich,** fill *or* line one's pockets, feather one's nest, **make** *or* **coin money,** have a gold mine, have the golden touch, **make a fortune,** make one's pile <nf>; **strike it rich;** come into money; make good, get on in the world, do all right by oneself *and* rake it in <nf>; hit the jackpot, clean up <nf>

11 **have money,** command money, **be loaded** *and* have deep pockets <nf>, have the wherewithal, have means, have independent means; **afford,** well afford

12 **live well,** live high, live high on the hog <nf>, **live in clover,** live the life of Riley, roll *or* wallow in wealth, roll *or* live in the lap of luxury; have all the money in the world, have a mint, have money to burn <nf>

13 worship mammon, worship the golden calf, worship the almighty dollar

ADJS 14 **wealthy, rich, affluent, affluential, moneyed** *or* **monied,** in funds *or* cash, **well-to-do,** well-to-do in the world, **well-off, well-situated, prosperous,** comfortable, provided for, well provided for, fat, **flush,** flush with *or* of money, abounding in riches, worth a great deal, in clover, frightfully rich, rich as Croesus; independent, independently rich, independently wealthy; **luxurious** 501.21; **opulent** 990.7; privileged, born with a silver spoon in one's mouth; higher-income, upper-income, well-paid

15 <nf terms> **loaded, well-heeled, filthy rich,** warm <Brit>, in the money *or* dough *or* chips *or* gravy, well-fixed, worth a bundle, made of money, **rolling in money,** rolling *or* wallowing in it, disgustingly rich, big-rich, rich-rich, oofy, lousy rich, upscale

619 POVERTY

NOUNS 1 **poverty,** poorness, impecuniousness, impecuniosity; **straits,** dire straits, difficulties, **hardship** 1010.1; financial distress *or* embarrassment, **embarrassed** *or* **reduced** *or* **straitened circumstances,** tight squeeze, hard pinch, crunch <nf>, cash *or* credit crunch <nf>; cash-flow shortage, cash-flow blowout <nf>; slender *or* narrow means, insolvency, light purse; unprosperousness; broken fortune; genteel poverty; vows of poverty, voluntary poverty

2 **indigence, penury, pennilessness,** penuriousness, moneylessness; **pauperism,** pauperization, **impoverishment,** grinding *or* crushing poverty, chronic pauperism; subsistence level, poverty line; **beggary,** beggarliness, mendicancy; homelessness; **destitution, privation, deprivation; neediness, want,** need, lack, pinch, gripe, necessity, dire necessity, disadvantagedness, necessitousness, **homelessness; hand-to-mouth existence,** bare subsistence, wolf at the door, bare cupboard, empty purse *or* pocket

3 **the poor, the needy,** the have-nots <nf>, the down-and-out, the disadvantaged, the underprivileged, the distressed, the underclass; the urban poor, ghetto-dwellers, barrio-dwellers; welfare rolls, welfare clients, welfare families; the homeless, the ranks of the homeless, bag people; "wretched of the earth"—E Pottier; the other America; the forgotten man, "the forgotten man at the bottom of the economic pyramid"—F D Roosevelt; depressed population, depressed area, chronic poverty area; underdeveloped nation, Third World

4 **poor person,** poorling, poor devil, down-and-out *or* down-and-outer, **pauper,** indigent, penniless man, hard case, starveling; homeless person, bag woman *or* lady, bag person, shopping-bag lady, shopping-cart woman *or* lady, street person, skell <nf>; hobo, bum; **beggar** 440.8; welfare client, almsman, almswoman, charity case, casual; bankrupt 625.4

VERBS 5 **be poor,** be hard up <nf>, find it hard going, have seen better days, be on one's uppers, be pinched *or* strapped, **be in want,** want, need, lack; **starve,** not know where one's next meal is coming from, **live from hand to mouth,** eke out *or* squeeze out a living; **not have a penny** *or* **sou,** not have a penny to bless oneself with, not have one dollar to rub against another; sing for one's supper; go on welfare, use food stamps

6 **impoverish,** reduce, **pauperize, beggar;** eat out of house and home; cut off without a penny; **bankrupt** 625.8

ADJS 7 **poor, ill off,** badly *or* poorly off, hard up <nf>, downscale, impecunious, **unmoneyed; unprosperous;** reduced, in reduced circumstances; **straitened, in straitened circumstances,** narrow, in narrow circumstances, feeling the pinch, strapped, **financially embarrassed** *or* distressed, **pinched,** squeezed, put to one's shifts *or* last shifts, at the end of one's rope, on the edge *or* ragged edge <nf>, down to bedrock, in Queer Street; short, **short of money** *or* **funds** *or* **cash,** out-of-pocket; unable to make ends meet, unable to keep the wolf from the door; poor as a church mouse, "poor as Job"—John Gower; land-poor

8 **indigent, poverty-stricken; needy,** necessitous, **in need, in want,** disadvantaged, deprived, underprivileged; **beggared,** beggarly, mendicant; **impoverished, pauperized,** starveling; ghettoized; bereft, bereaved; stripped, fleeced; **down at heels,** down at the heel, on *or* down on one's uppers, out at the heels, out at elbows, in rags; on welfare, on relief, on the bread line, on the dole <Brit>

9 **destitute, down-and-out,** in the gutter; **penniless,** moneyless, fortuneless, out of funds, **without a sou,** without a penny to bless oneself with, without one dollar to rub against another; insolvent, in the red, **bankrupt** 625.11; homeless; propertyless, landless

10 <nf terms> **broke, dead broke,** bust, busted, **flat, flat broke,** flat on one's ass, flat-ass, down for the count, belly up, stone *or* stony broke, stony, **strapped,** skint <Brit>, hurting, beat, oofless; down to one's last penny *or* cent, cleaned out, tapped out, Tap City, oofless, wasted, wiped out, without a pot to piss in

620 LENDING

NOUNS 1 **lending, loaning;** moneylending, lending at interest; advance, advancing, advancement; **usury,** loan-sharking *and* shylocking <nf>; pawnbroking, hocking; **interest,** interest rate, lending rate, the price of money; points, mortgage points

2 **loan,** the lend <nf>, **advance,** accommodation; lending on security; lend-lease

3 **lender, loaner;** loan officer; commercial banker; **moneylender,** moneymonger; money broker; banker 729.11; **usurer,** shylock *and* loan shark <nf>; **pawnbroker;** uncle <nf>; mortgagee, mortgage holder; creditor; financier

4 **lending institution,** savings and loan association *or* thrift *or* thrift institution *or* savings institution; savings and loan *or* thrift industry; building society <Brit>; finance company *or* corporation, loan office, mortgage company; commercial bank, **bank** 729.14; **credit union; pawnshop, pawnbroker,** pawnbrokery, **hock shop** <nf>, *mont-de-piété* <Fr>, sign of the three balls; World Bank

VERBS 5 **lend, loan, advance,** accommodate with; loan-shark <nf>; float *or* negotiate a loan; lend-lease, lease-lend; give credit

ADJS 6 **loaned, lent,** on loan, on credit

ADVS 7 **on loan,** on security; in advance

621 BORROWING

NOUNS 1 **borrowing,** money-raising; touching *or* hitting *or* hitting up <nf>; financing, mortgaging;

installment buying, installment plan, hire purchase <Brit>; debt, debtor 623.4; debt counseling

2 **adoption, appropriation, taking,** deriving, **derivation, assumption; imitation,** simulation, copying, mocking; borrowed plumes; a leaf from someone else's book; adaptation; plagiarism, plagiary, pastiche, pasticcio; infringement, pirating; cribbing, lifting

VERBS 3 **borrow,** borrow the loan of, get on credit *or* trust, get on tick *and* get on the cuff <nf>; get a loan, float *or* negotiate a loan, go into the money market, **raise money; touch** *and* hit up *and* hit one for *and* put the arm *or* bite *or* touch on <nf>; run into debt 623.6; pawn 438.10

4 **adopt, appropriate,** take, take on, take over, assume, make use of, take a leaf from someone's book, derive from; **imitate,** simulate, copy, mock, steal one's stuff <nf>; plagiarize, steal; pirate, infringe, crib, lift; adapt, parody

622 FINANCIAL CREDIT

NOUNS 1 **credit, trust,** tick <nf>; borrowing power *or* capacity; commercial credit, cash credit, bank credit, book credit, tax credit, investment credit; credit line, line of credit; installment plan, installment credit, consumer credit, store credit, hire purchase plan <Brit>, never-never <Brit nf>; **credit standing,** standing, **credit rating,** rating, Dun and Bradstreet rating, solvency 729.7; credit squeeze, insolvency; credit risk; credit bureau *or* agency; credit insurance, credit life insurance; credit union, cooperative credit union

2 **account,** credit account, charge account; bank account, savings account, checking account; share account; bank balance; expense account; current *or* open account; installment plan

3 **credit instrument;** paper credit; **letter of credit,** *lettre de créance* <Fr>, circular note; credit slip, credit memorandum, deposit slip, certificate of deposit; share certificate; negotiable instruments 728.11; **credit card,** plastic, plastic money *or* credit, bank card, affinity card, custom credit card, gold card, platinum card, charge card, charge plate; debit card; smart card, supersmart card; phonecard; automated teller machine *or* ATM, cash machine

4 **creditor,** creditress; debtee; mortgagee, mortgage-holder; note-holder; credit man; bill collector, collection agent; loan shark; pawnbroker; dunner, dun

VERBS 5 **credit, credit with; credit to one's account,** place to one's credit *or* account

6 **give** *or* **extend credit** *or* a line of credit; sell on credit, trust, entrust; give tick <nf>; carry, carry on one's books

7 receive credit, take credit, **charge,** charge to one's account, keep an account with, go on tick <nf>, buy on credit, buy on the cuff <nf>, buy on the installment plan, buy on time, defer payment, put on layaway; go in hock for <nf>; have one's credit good for

ADJS **8 credited,** of good credit, **well-rated**

ADVS **9 to one's credit** or **account,** to the credit or account of, to the good

10 on credit, on account, on trust, on tick and **on the cuff** <nf>; on terms, on good terms, on easy terms, on budget terms, in installments, on time

623 DEBT

NOUNS **1 debt, indebtedness,** indebtment, **obligation, liability,** financial commitment, due, **dues,** score, pledge, unfulfilled pledge, amount due, outstanding debt; **bill, bills,** chits <nf>, **charges;** floating debt; funded debt, unfunded debt; accounts receivable; accounts payable; borrowing 621; maturity; bad debts, uncollectibles, frozen assets; **national debt,** public debt; deficit, national deficit; megadebt <nf>; debt explosion

2 arrears, arrear, arrearage, back debts, back payments; the red; **deficit,** default, deferred payments; cash or credit crunch <nf>; overdraft, bounced or bouncing check, rubber check <nf>; dollar gap, unfavorable trade balance or balance of payments; deficit financing

3 interest, premium, price, rate; interest rate, rate of interest, prime interest rate or **prime rate,** bank rate, lending rate, borrowing rate, the price of money; discount rate; annual percentage rate or APR; **usury** 620.1, excessive or exorbitant interest; points, mortgage points; simple interest, compound interest; net interest, gross interest; compensatory interest; lucrative interest; penal interest

4 debtor, borrower; mortgagor

VERBS **5 owe,** be indebted, be obliged or obligated for, be financially committed, lie under an obligation, be bound to pay, owe money

6 go in debt, get into debt, run into debt, plunge into debt, incur or contract a debt, go in hock <nf>, be overextended, **run up a bill** or a score or an account or a tab; run or show a deficit, operate at a loss; borrow; overspend, overdraw

7 mature, accrue, fall due

ADJS **8 indebted, in debt,** plunged in debt, in difficulties, embarrassed, in embarrassed circumstances, in the hole and in hock <nf>, in the red, in dire straits, encumbered, mortgaged, mortgaged to the hilt, tied up, involved; deep in debt, involved or deeply involved in debt, burdened with debt, head over heels or up to one's ears in debt <nf>; cash poor

9 chargeable, obligated, liable, pledged, responsible, answerable for

10 due, owed, owing, payable, receivable, redeemable, mature, **outstanding, unpaid,** in arrear or arrears, back

624 PAYMENT

NOUNS **1 payment, paying,** paying off, paying up <nf>, payoff; **defrayment,** defrayal; paying out, doling out, **disbursal** 626.1; **discharge, settlement, clearance, liquidation, amortization, amortizement,** retirement, satisfaction; quittance; acquittance or acquitment or acquittal <old>; **debt service, interest payment,** sinking-fund payment; **remittance;** installment, installment plan, lay-away plan; hire purchase or hire purchase plan or never-never <Brit>; regular payments, monthly payments, weekly payments, quarterly payments, etc; down payment, deposit, earnest, earnest money, binder; god's penny; the King's shilling <Brit>; **cash,** hard cash, spot cash, cash payment, cash on the nail and cash on the barrelhead <nf>; pay-as-you-go; prepayment; **postponed** or **deferred payment,** contango or carryover and continuation and backwardation <Brit>; payment in kind; accounts receivable, receivables

2 reimbursement, recoupment, recoup, return, restitution, settlement; payment in lieu; **refund,** refundment; kickback <nf>; payback, chargeback, **repayment** 481.2

3 recompense, remuneration, compensation; requital, requitement, quittance, **retribution, reparation, redress,** satisfaction, **atonement, amends,** return, restitution 481; blood money, wergild <old>; **indemnity,** indemnification; price, consideration; **reward,** meed, guerdon; honorarium; workmen's compensation or comp <nf>, solatium, damages, smart money; salvage

4 pay, payment, remuneration, compensation, total compensation, wages plus fringe benefits, financial package, pay and allowances, financial remuneration; rate of pay; **salary, wage, wages, income, earnings,** hire; real wages, purchasing power; payday, pay check, pay envelope, pay packet <Brit>; take-home pay or income, wages after taxes, pay or income or wages after deductions, net income or wages or pay or earnings, taxable income; gross income; living wage; minimum wage, base pay; portal-to-portal pay; severance pay, discontinuance or dismissal wage, golden parachute; wage scale; escalator plan, escalator clause, sliding scale; guaranteed income, guaranteed annual income, negative income tax; fixed income; wage freeze, wage rollback, wage reduction, wage control; guaranteed annual wage, guaranteed income plan; overtime pay; danger money, combat pay, flight pay; back pay; strike pay; **payroll;** golden handcuffs; royalty, advance

5 **fee, stipend, allowance,** emolument, tribute, honorarium; **reckoning,** account, bill; assessment, scot; initiation fee, footing <old>; retainer, retaining fee; hush money, blackmail; blood money; mileage

6 <extra pay or allowance> **bonus, premium, fringe benefit** or **benefits,** bounty, perquisite, perquisites, perks <nf>, gravy <nf>, lagniappe, solatium; **tip** 478.5; overtime pay; bonus system; health insurance, life insurance, disability insurance; profit-sharing; holidays, vacation time, flextime or flexitime; pension program

7 **dividend; royalty; commission,** rake-off and cut <nf>

8 <the bearing of another's expense> **treat,** standing treat, picking up the check or tab <nf>; paying the bills, maintenance, support 449.3; subsidy 478.8

9 **payer,** remunerator, compensator, recompenser; paymaster, purser, bursar, cashier, treasurer 729.12; defrayer; liquidator; **taxpayer, ratepayer** <Brit>

VERBS 10 **pay,** render, tender; **recompense, remunerate, compensate, reward,** guerdon, indemnify, satisfy; salary, fee; remit; prepay; pay by or in installments, pay on, pay in; make payments to or towards or on

11 **repay,** pay back, restitute, **reimburse,** recoup; **requite,** quit, **atone,** redress <old>, **make amends,** make good, make up for, make up to, make restitution, make reparation 481.5; pay in kind, pay one in his own coin, give tit for tat; **refund,** kick back <nf>

12 **settle with,** reckon with, account with <old>, pay out, **settle** or **square accounts with,** square oneself with, get square with, **get even with,** get quits with; even the score <nf>, wipe or clear off old scores, pay old debts, clear the board

13 **pay in full, pay off, pay up** <nf>, **discharge, settle,** square, **clear, liquidate, amortize,** retire, take up, lift, take up and pay off, honor, acquit oneself of <old>; satisfy; meet one's obligations or commitments, redeem, redeem one's pledge or pledges, tear up or burn one's mortgage, have a mortgage-burning party, settle or square accounts, make accounts square, strike a balance; pay the bill, pay the shot

14 **pay out, fork out** or **over** <nf>, **shell out** <nf>; expend 626.5

15 **pay over,** hand over; ante, **ante up,** put up; put down, lay down, lay one's money down, show the color of one's money

16 <nf terms> **kick in, fork over,** pony up, pay up, cough up, stump up <Brit>, come across, come through with, come across with, come down with, come down with the needful, plank down, plunk down, post, tickle or grease the palm, cross one's palm with, lay on one; pay to the tune of

17 **pay cash,** make a cash payment, cash, **pay spot cash, pay cash down,** pay cash on the barrelhead <nf>, plunk down the money and put one's money on the line <nf>, pay at sight; pay in advance; pay as you go; pay cash on delivery or pay COD

18 **pay for,** pay or stand the costs, **bear the expense** or **cost,** pay the piper <nf>; **finance, fund** 729.16; **defray,** defray expenses; pay the bill, **foot the bill** and pick up the check or tab and spring or pop for <nf>; honor a bill, acknowledge, redeem; pay one's way; pay one's share, chip in <nf>, go Dutch <nf>

19 **treat,** treat to, **stand treat,** go treat, stand to <nf>, pick up the check or tab <nf>, pay the bill, set up, blow to <nf>; stand drinks; maintain, support 449.12; subsidize 478.19

20 **be paid, draw wages,** be salaried, work for wages, be remunerated, collect for one's services, **earn,** get an income, pull down and drag down <nf>

ADJS 21 **paying, remunerative, remuneratory; compensating,** compensative, compensatory; disbursing; retributive, retributory; **rewarding,** rewardful; lucrative, moneymaking, profitable, gainful; repaying, satisfying, reparative; bankable

22 **paid, paid-up,** discharged, settled, liquidated, acquitted <old>, paid in full, receipted, remitted; **spent, expended;** salaried, waged, hired; prepaid, postpaid

23 **unindebted,** unowing, **out of debt,** above water, out of the hole or the red <nf>, **clear,** all clear, free and clear, all straight; solvent 729.18

ADVS 24 **in compensation,** as compensation, in recompense, for services rendered, for professional services, **in reward,** in requital, in reparation, in retribution, in restitution, in exchange for, **in amends,** in atonement, to atone for

25 **cash,** cash on the barrelhead <nf>, strictly cash; **cash down, money down,** down; cash on delivery or **COD;** on demand, on call; pay-as-you-go

625 NONPAYMENT

NOUNS 1 **nonpayment, default, delinquency,** delinquence <old>, nondischarge of debts, nonremittal, failure to pay; defection; protest, repudiation; dishonor, dishonoring; bad debt, uncollectible, dishonored *or* protested bill; tax evasion; creative accounting

2 **moratorium,** grace period; embargo, freeze; **write-off,** cancellation, obliteration 395.7

3 **insolvency, bankruptcy,** receivership, Chapter 11, **failure; crash,** collapse, bust <nf>, ruin; run on a bank; insufficient funds, overdraft, overdrawn account, not enough to cover, bounced *or* bouncing check, bad check, kited *or* rubber check

4 **insolvent,** insolvent debtor; **bankrupt,** failure; **loser,** heavy loser, lame duck <nf>

5 **defaulter,** delinquent, nonpayer; **welsher** <nf>; levanter; tax evader, tax dodger *or* cheat <nf>

VERBS 6 **not pay;** dishonor, repudiate, disallow, protest, stop payment, refuse to pay; **default, welsh** <nf>, levant; button up one's pockets, draw the purse strings; **underpay;** bounce *or* kite a check <nf>

7 **go bankrupt, go broke** <nf>, go into receivership, become insolvent *or* bankrupt, **fail,** break, bust <nf>, crash, collapse, **fold, fold up,** belly up *and* go up *and* go belly up *and* **go under** <nf>, shut down, shut one's doors, go out of business, **be ruined,** go to ruin, go on the rocks, go to the wall, go to pot <nf>, go to the dogs, go bust <nf>; take a bath *and* be taken to the cleaners *and* be cleaned out *and* lose one's shirt *and* tap out <nf>

8 **bankrupt, ruin, break,** bust *and* wipe out <nf>; put out of business, drive to the wall, scuttle, sink; impoverish 619.6

9 **declare a moratorium; write off, forgive,** absolve, **cancel,** nullify, wipe the slate clean; wipe out, obliterate 395.16

ADJS 10 defaulting, nonpaying, **delinquent;** behindhand, in arrear *or* arrears, in hock, in the red

11 **insolvent, bankrupt,** in receivership, in the hands of receivers, belly-up <nf>, broken, **broke** *and* busted <nf>, **ruined,** failed, out of business, unable to pay one's creditors, unable to meet one's obligations, on the rocks; destitute 619.9

12 **unpaid, unremunerated,** uncompensated, unrecompensed, **unrewarded,** unrequited; underpaid

13 **unpayable,** irredeemable, inconvertible

626 EXPENDITURE

NOUNS 1 **expenditure, spending,** expense, disbursal, **disbursement;** debit, debiting; budgeting, scheduling; costing, costing-out; **payment** 624; deficit spending; **use** 387; **consumption** 388

2 **spendings,** disbursements, payments, outgoings, outgo, outflow, **outlay,** money going out

3 **expenses, costs,** charges, disbursals, **liabilities,** damages <nf>; **expense, cost,** burden of expenditure; budget, budget item, budget line, line item; **overhead,** operating expense *or* expenses *or* costs *or* budget, general expenses; expense account, swindle sheet <nf>; business expenses, nonremunerated business expenses, out-of-pocket expenses; direct costs, indirect costs; distributed costs, undistributed costs; material costs; labor costs; carrying charge; unit cost; replacement cost; prime cost; cost of living, cost-of-living index, cost-of-living allowance *or* COLA, inflation

4 **spender,** expender, expenditor, disburser, buyer, purchaser

VERBS 5 **spend, expend, disburse, pay out,** fork out *or* over <nf>, shell out <nf>, **lay out,** outlay; go to the expense of; **pay** 624.10; put one's hands in one's pockets, open the purse, loosen *or* untie the purse strings *and* throw money around <nf>, go on a spending spree, splurge, spend money like a drunken sailor *and* spend money as if it were going out of style <nf>, go *or* run through, be out of pocket, **squander** 486.3; **invest,** sink money in <nf>, put out; throw money at the problem; **incur costs** *or* **expenses;** budget, schedule, cost, cost out; **use** 387.13; **consume**

6 **be spent,** burn in one's pocket, burn a hole in one's pocket

7 **afford,** well afford, spare, spare the price, bear, stand, support, endure, undergo, meet the expense of, swing

627 RECEIPTS

NOUNS 1 **receipts,** receipt, **income, revenue, profits, earnings, returns, proceeds,** avails <old>, **take,** takings, intake, take-in <nf>, get <Brit nf>; credit, credits; gains 472.3; gate receipts, gate, box office; net receipts, net; gross receipts, gross; national income; net income, gross income; earned income, unearned income; **dividend** 738.7, dividends, payout, payback; interest; royalties, commissions; receivables; disposable income; make, produce, **yield, output** 893.2, bang for the buck <nf>, fruits, first fruits; bonus, premium; income; legacy; winnings

2 <written acknowledgment> **receipt, acknowledgment, voucher,** warrant <Brit>; canceled check, bank statement; proof of purchase; **receipt in full,** receipt in full of all demands, release, acquittance, quittance, discharge

VERBS 3 **receive** 479.6, **pocket, acquire** 472.8,9; accrue; acknowledge receipt of, receipt, mark paid

4 **yield, bring in, afford, pay,** pay off <nf>, **return; gross, net**

628 ACCOUNTS

NOUNS 1 **accounts; outstanding accounts,** *uncollected or* unpaid accounts; **accounts receivable,** receipts, assets; **accounts payable,** expenditures, liabilities; **budget,** budgeting; costing out

2 **account, reckoning, tally, rendering-up, score;** account current; account rendered, *compte rendu* <Fr>, account stated; balance, trial balance

3 **statement, bill,** itemized bill, bill of account, **account, reckoning, check,** *l'addition* <Fr>, score *or* tab <nf>; **dun; invoice,** manifest, bill of lading

4 **account book, ledger, journal,** daybook; **register,** registry, **record book,** books; inventory, catalog; **log,** logbook; **cashbook; bankbook,** passbook; balance sheet; cost sheet, cost card

5 **entry,** item, line item, minute, note, notation; single entry, double entry; **credit, debit**

6 **accounting, accountancy, bookkeeping,** double-entry bookkeeping *or* accounting, single-entry bookkeeping *or* accounting; comptrollership *or* controllership; business *or* commercial *or* monetary arithmetic; cost accounting, costing <Brit>, cost system, cost-accounting system; **audit, auditing;** stocktaking, inspection of books

7 **accountant, bookkeeper; clerk,** actuary <old>, registrar, recorder, journalizer; calculator, reckoner; cost accountant, cost keeper; certified public accountant *or* CPA; chartered accountant *or* CA <Brit>; **auditor,** bank examiner; bank accountant; actuary; accountant general; comptroller *or* controller; statistician

VERBS 8 **keep accounts, keep books,** make up *or* cast up *or* render accounts; make an entry, enter, post, post up, journalize, book, docket, log, note, minute; **credit, debit;** charge off, write off; capitalize; carry, carry on one's books; carry over; **balance,** balance accounts, balance the books, strike a balance; close the books, close out

9 **take account of, take stock,** overhaul; **inventory; audit,** examine *or* inspect the books

10 **falsify accounts,** garble accounts, cook *or* doctor accounts <nf>, cook the books <nf>, salt, fudge; surcharge

11 **bill,** send a statement; **invoice;** call, call in, demand payment, **dun**

ADJS 12 accounting, bookkeeping; budget, budgetary

629 TRANSFER OF PROPERTY OR RIGHT

NOUNS 1 **transfer,** transference; **conveyance,** conveyancing; **giving** 478; **delivery,** deliverance; **assignment,** assignation; **consignment,** consignation; conferment, conferral, settling, settlement; vesting; bequeathal 478.10; **sale** 734; surrender, cession; transmission, transmittal; disposal, disposition, deaccession, deaccessioning; demise; alienation, abalienation; amortization, amortizement; enfeoffment; deeding; bargain and sale; lease and release; **exchange,** barter, trading; entailment

2 devolution, succession, reversion; shifting use, shifting trust

VERBS 3 **transfer, convey, deliver,** hand, pass, negotiate; **give** 478.12–14,16,21; **hand over, turn over, pass over; assign, consign,** confer, settle, settle on; cede, surrender; bequeath 478.18; entail; **sell** 734.8,11,12, sell off, deaccession; **make over, sign over,** sign away; transmit, **hand down, hand on, pass on,** devolve upon; demise; alienate, alien, abalienate, amortize; enfeoff; **deed,** deed over, give title to; **exchange,** barter, trade, trade away

4 **change hands,** change ownership; devolve, pass on, descend, succeed <old>

ADJS 5 **transferable, conveyable,** negotiable, alienable; **assignable,** consignable; devisable, bequeathable; heritable, inheritable

630 PRICE, FEE

NOUNS 1 **price, cost, expense,** expenditure, **charge,** damage *and* score *and* tab <nf>; rate, figure, amount; **quotation,** quoted price, price tag *and* ticket *and* sticker <nf>; **price list,** price range, prices current; stock market quotations; standard price, list price, sale price

2 **worth, value,** account, rate; face value, face; par value; market value; street value; fair value; net worth; conversion factor *or* value; monetary value; money's worth, pennyworth, value received; bang for the buck <nf>; going rate

3 **valuation, evaluation,** value-setting, value-fixing, pricing, price determination, **assessment, appraisal,** appraisement, estimation, rating; unit pricing, dual pricing

4 **price index,** business index; wholesale price index; consumer price *or* retail price index; cost-of-living index; price level; price ceiling, ceiling price, ceiling, top price; floor price, floor, bottom price; demand curve; rising prices, **inflation,** inflationary spiral

5 **price controls,** price-fixing, valorization; managed prices, fair-trading, fair trade, fair-trade agreement; **price supports,** rigid supports, flexible supports; price freeze; rent control; prix fixe

6 **fee, dues, toll, charge, charges, demand, exaction,** exactment, scot, shot, scot and lot; hire; **fare,**

carfare; user fee; airport fee *or* charge; license fee; entrance *or* entry *or* admission fee, admission; cover charge; portage, towage; wharfage, anchorage, dockage; pilotage; storage, cellarage; brokerage; salvage; service fee *or* charge; commission, cut

7 freightage, freight, haulage, carriage, cartage, drayage, expressage, lighterage; poundage, tonnage

8 **rent, rental;** rent-roll; rent charge; rack rent, quitrent; ground rent, wayleave rent

9 **tax, taxation, duty, tribute,** taxes, rates <Brit>, contribution, **assessment, revenue enhancement,** cess <Brit>, **levy, toll, impost,** imposition; tax code, tax law; **tithe;** indirect taxation, direct taxation; **tax burden,** overtaxation, undertaxation; bracket *or* tax-bracket creep; progressive taxation, graduated taxation; regressive taxation; tax withholding; tax return, separate returns, joint return; tax evasion *or* avoidance; tax haven *or* shelter; **tax deduction, deduction; tax write-off,** write-off, tax relief; tax exemption, tax-exempt status; tax structure, tax base; taxable income *or* goods *or* land *or* property, ratables

10 **tax collector,** taxer, taxman, publican; collector of internal revenue, internal revenue agent, revenuer; tax farmer, farmer; assessor, **tax assessor;** exciseman <Brit>, revenuer; Internal Revenue Service *or* IRS; Inland Revenue *or* IR <Brit>; **customs agent; customs,** US Customs Service, Bureau of Customs and Excise <Brit>; customhouse; taxpayer

VERBS 11 **price,** set *or* name a price, fix the price of; place a value on, **value, evaluate,** valuate, **appraise, assess, rate,** prize, apprize; quote a price; set an arbitrary price on, control *or* manage the price of, valorize; mark up, mark down, **discount;** fair-trade; reassess

12 **charge, demand, ask,** require; overcharge, undercharge; **exact, assess, levy, impose; tax,** assess a tax upon, slap a tax on <nf>, lay *or* put a duty on, make dutiable, subject to a tax *or* fee *or* duty, collect a tax *or* duty on; tithe; prorate, assess *pro rata;* charge for, stick for <nf>

13 **cost, sell for, fetch, bring,** bring in, stand one *and* set *or* move one back <nf>, knock one back <Brit nf>; **come to,** run to *or* into, **amount to,** mount up to, come up to, total up to

ADJS 14 **priced, valued,** evaluated, assessed, appraised, rated, prized; **worth,** valued at; good for; ad valorem, pro rata

15 **chargeable, taxable,** ratable <Brit>, assessable, dutiable, leviable, declarable; tithable

16 tax-free, nontaxable, nondutiable, tax-exempt; deductible, tax-deductible; duty-free

ADVS 17 **at a price,** for a consideration; to the amount of, to the tune of *and* in the neighborhood of <nf>

631 DISCOUNT

NOUNS 1 **discount, cut, deduction,** slash, abatement, reduction, price reduction, price-cutting, price-cut, rollback <nf>; underselling; **rebate,** rebatement; bank discount, cash discount, chain discount, time discount, trade discount; write-off, charge-off; **depreciation; allowance,** concession; setoff; drawback, **refund,** kickback <nf>; **premium,** percentage, agio; trading stamp

VERBS 2 **discount,** cut, deduct, bate, abate; **take off,** write off, charge off; knock down <nf>; **depreciate,** reduce; sell at a loss; **allow,** make allowance; rebate, **refund,** kick back <nf>; take a premium *or* percentage

ADVS 3 **at a discount,** at a reduction, at a reduced rate, below par, below *or* under cost

632 EXPENSIVENESS

NOUNS 1 **expensiveness, costliness, dearness,** high *or* great cost, highness, stiffness *or* **steepness** <nf>, priceyness; **richness, sumptuousness, luxuriousness;** pretty penny <nf>

2 **preciousness, dearness, value,** high *or* great value, **worth,** extraordinary worth, price *or* great price <old>, **valuableness; pricelessness, invaluableness**

3 **high price,** high *or* big price tag *and* big ticket *and* big sticker price <nf>, **fancy price,** good price, steep *or* stiff price <nf>, luxury price, a pretty penny *or* an arm and a leg <nf>, exorbitant *or* unconscionable *or* extortionate price; famine price, scarcity price; rack rent; inflationary prices, rising *or* soaring *or* spiraling prices, soaring costs; sellers' market; **inflation,** cost *or* cost-push inflation *or* cost-push, inflationary trend *or* pressure, hot economy, inflationary spiral, inflationary gap; reflation; stagflation, slumpflation

4 **exorbitance,** exorbitancy <old>, **extravagance,** excess, **excessiveness,** inordinateness, immoderateness, immoderation, undueness, unreasonableness, outrageousness, preposterousness; unconscionableness, extortionateness

5 **overcharge,** surcharge, overassessment; gouging *or* price-gouging; **extortion,** extortionate price; **holdup** *and* armed robbery *and* highway robbery <nf>; profiteering, rack-rent; ripoff <nf>

VERBS 6 **cost much,** cost money *and* cost you <nf>, be dear, cost a pretty penny *or* an arm and a leg *or* a packet <nf>, **run into money;** be overpriced, price out of the market

7 **overprice,** set the price tag too high; **overcharge,** surcharge, overtax; **hold up** and **soak** and **stick** and **sting** and **clip** <nf>, **make pay through the nose, gouge;** commit highway robbery; victimize, rip off, swindle 356.18; exploit, skin <nf>, **fleece,** screw and put the screws to <nf>, bleed, bleed white; profiteer; rack or rack up the rents, rack rent

8 **overpay,** overspend, pay too much, pay more than it's worth, **pay dearly,** pay exorbitantly, pay, **pay through the nose,** be had or taken <nf>

9 **inflate,** heat or heat up the economy; reflate

ADJS 10 **precious, dear, valuable,** worthy, rich, golden, of great price <old>, worth a pretty penny <nf>, worth a king's ransom, worth its weight in gold, good as gold, precious as the apple of one's eye; **priceless, invaluable,** inestimable, without or **beyond price,** not to be had for love or money, not for all the tea in China

11 **expensive, dear, costly,** of great cost, dear-bought, **high, high-priced,** premium, at a premium, top; big ticket <nf>, **fancy** and stiff and steep <nf>, pricey; beyond one's means, not affordable, more than one can afford, sky-high; unpayable; upmarket, upscale <nf> rich, sumptuous, executive and posh <nf>, **luxurious** 501.21, gold-plated

12 **overpriced,** grossly overpriced, **exorbitant, excessive, extravagant, inordinate, immoderate,** undue, unwarranted, unreasonable, fancy, unconscionable, outrageous, preposterous, out of bounds, out of sight <nf>, **prohibitive; extortionate,** cutthroat, **gouging, usurious,** exacting; **inflationary,** spiraling, skyrocketing, mounting; stagflationary, slumpflationary; reflationary

ADVS 13 **dear, dearly;** at a high price, at great cost, at a premium, at a great rate, at heavy cost, at great expense

14 **preciously, valuably,** worthily; pricelessly, invaluably, inestimably

15 **expensively,** richly, sumptuously, luxuriously

16 **exorbitantly, excessively,** grossly, **extravagantly, inordinately,** immoderately, unduly, unreasonably, unconscionably, outrageously, preposterously; **extortionately,** usuriously, gougingly

633 CHEAPNESS

NOUNS 1 **cheapness, inexpensiveness,** affordableness, affordability, reasonableness, modestness, moderateness, nominalness; drug or glut on the market; shabbiness, shoddiness 998.2

2 **low price, nominal price,** reasonable price, modest or manageable price, sensible price, moderate price; low or nominal or reasonable charge; bargain prices, budget prices, economy prices, easy prices or terms, popular prices, rock-bottom prices; buyers' market; low or small price tag and low sticker price and low tariff <nf>; **reduced price,** cut price, sale price; cheap or reduced rates

3 **bargain,** advantageous purchase, **buy** <nf>, **good buy, steal** <nf>; money's worth, pennyworth, good pennyworth; special offer; loss leader

4 **cheapening, depreciation, devaluation,** reduction, lowering; deflation, deflationary spiral, cooling or cooling off of the economy; **buyers' market; decline,** plummet, plummeting, plunge, dive, nose dive and slump and sag <nf>, free fall; price fall, break; **price cut** or **reduction,** cut, slash, **markdown;** oversupply

VERBS 5 **be cheap,** cost little, not cost anything and cost nothing and next to nothing <nf>; **go dirt cheap** or for a song or for nickels and dimes or for peanuts <nf>, buy at a bargain, buy for a mere nothing; get one's money's worth, get a good pennyworth; buy at wholesale prices or at cost

6 **cheapen, depreciate, devaluate,** lower, reduce, devalue, **mark down, cut prices, cut,** slash, shave, trim, pare, underprice, knock the bottom out of <nf>, knock down <nf>; deflate, cool or cool off the economy; beat down; come down or fall in price; **fall,** decline, plummet, dive, nose-dive <nf>, drop, crash, head for the bottom, plunge, sag, slump; break, give way; reach a new low; unload

ADJS 7 **cheap, inexpensive,** unexpensive, **low, low-priced,** frugal, reasonable, sensible, manageable, modest, moderate, affordable, to fit the pocketbook, budget, easy, economy, economic, economical; within means, within reach or easy reach; nominal, token; worth the money, well worth the money; cheap or good at the price, cheap at half the price; shabby, shoddy, cheapo <nf>; deflationary

8 **dirt cheap,** cheap as dirt, dog-cheap <nf>, **a dime a dozen,** bargain-basement, five-and-ten, dime-store

9 **reduced,** cut, cut-price, slashed, **marked down;** cut-rate; half-price; priced to go; giveaway, sacrificial; **lowest,** rock-bottom, bottom

ADVS 10 **cheaply, cheap,** on the cheap <Brit nf>; **inexpensively,** reasonably, moderately, nominally; **at a bargain,** à bon marché <Fr>, for a song or mere song <nf>, for pennies or nickels and dimes or peanuts <nf>, at small cost, at a low price, at budget prices, at piggy-bank prices, at a sacrifice; at cost or cost price, at prime cost, wholesale, at wholesale; at reduced rates

634 COSTLESSNESS
<absence of charge>

NOUNS **1 costlessness,** gratuitousness, gratuity, **freeness,** expenselessness, complimentariness, no charge; free ride <nf>; freebie *and* gimme <nf>; labor of love; **gift** 478.4

2 complimentary ticket, pass, comp <nf>, free pass *or* ticket, paper <nf>, free admission, guest pass *or* ticket, Annie Oakley <nf>; discount ticket, twofer <nf>

3 freeloader, free rider, pass holder, deadhead <nf>

VERBS **4 give, present** 478.12, comp <nf>; freeload, sponge

ADJS **5 gratuitous, gratis, free, free of charge,** for free, for nothing, free for nothing, free for the asking, free gratis *and* free gratis for nothing <nf>, for love, free as air; freebie *and* freebee *and* freeby <nf>; costless, expenseless, untaxed, without charge, free of cost *or* expense; no charge; unbought, unpaid-for; **complimentary, on the house, comp** <nf>, given 478.24; giftlike; eleemosynary, charitable 143.15

ADVS **6 gratuitously, gratis, free, free of charge,** for nothing, for the asking, at no charge, without charge, with the compliments of the management, as our guest, on the house

635 THRIFT

NOUNS **1 thrift, economy, thriftiness,** economicalness, savingness, sparingness, unwastefulness, **frugality,** frugalness; tight purse strings; parsimony, **parsimoniousness** 484.1; false economy; carefulness, care, chariness, canniness; **prudence,** providence, forehandedness; **husbandry,** management, good management *or* stewardship, custodianship, prudent *or* prudential administration; **austerity,** austerity program, belt-tightening; economic planning; economy of means 484.1

2 economizing, economization, reduction of spending or government spending; **cost-effectiveness; saving,** scrimping, skimping <nf>, scraping, sparing, cheeseparing; **retrenchment, curtailment,** reduction of expenses, cutback, rollback, slowdown, cooling, cooling off *or* down, low growth rate; reduction in forces *or* RIF; budget, spending plan

3 economizer, economist <old>, **saver,** string-saver

VERBS **4 economize, save,** make *or* enforce economies; **scrimp, skimp** <nf>, **scrape,** scrape and save; **manage, husband,** husband one's resources, conserve; budget; live frugally, get along on a shoestring, get by on little; keep within compass <old>, keep *or* stay within one's means *or* budget, balance income with outgo, live within one's

income, make ends meet, cut one's coat according to one's cloth, keep *or* stay ahead of the game; put something aside, **save up,** save for a rainy day, have a nest egg; supplement *or* eke out one's income

5 retrench, cut down, cut *or* pare down expenses, **curtail expenses; cut corners, tighten one's belt,** cut back, roll back, take a reef, slow down

ADJS **6 economical, thrifty, frugal,** economic, unwasteful, conserving, **saving,** economizing, spare, **sparing;** Scotch; **prudent,** prudential, provident, forehanded; careful, chary, canny; scrimping, skimping <nf>, cheeseparing, austere; penny-wise; **parsimonious** 484.7; **cost-effective, cost-efficient; efficient,** labor-saving, time-saving, money-saving

ADVS **7 economically, thriftily, frugally,** husbandly <old>; **cost-effectively, cost-efficiently;** prudently, providently; carefully, charily, cannily; sparingly, with a sparing hand

636 ETHICS

NOUNS **1 ethics, principles,** standards, norms, principles of conduct *or* behavior, principles of professional practice; **morals,** moral principles; code, ethical *or* moral code, **ethic,** code of morals *or* ethics, ethical system, value system, values, axiology; **norm,** behavioral norm, normative system; moral climate, **ethos,** *Zeitgeist* <Ger>; Ten Commandments, decalogue; social ethics, professional ethics, bioethics, medical ethics, legal ethics, business ethics, etc

2 ethical *or* moral philosophy, ethonomics, aretaics, eudaemonics, casuistry, deontology, empiricism, evolutionism, hedonism, ethical formalism, intuitionism, perfectionism, Stoicism, utilitarianism, categorical imperative, golden rule; egoistic ethics, altruistic ethics; Christian ethics; situation ethics; comparative ethics

3 morality, morals, morale; virtue 653; ethicality, ethicalness; scruples, good conscience, moral fiber

4 amorality, unmorality; amoralism; moral delinquency, moral turpitude

5 conscience, grace, **sense of right and wrong;** inward monitor, inner arbiter, moral censor, censor, ethical self, superego; **voice of conscience,** still small voice within, guardian *or* good angel; tender conscience; clear *or* clean conscience; social conscience; conscientiousness 644.2; twinge of conscience 113.2

ADJS **6 ethical, moral,** moralistic; ethological; axiological

637 RIGHT

NOUNS **1 right,** rightfulness, rightness; what is right *or* proper, what should be, what ought to be, the seemly, the thing, the right *or* proper thing, the right *or* proper thing to do, what is done

2 propriety, decorum, decency, good behavior *or* conduct, correctness, correctitude, rightness, properness, decorousness, goodness, goodliness, niceness, seemliness, cricket <Brit nf>; fitness, fittingness, appropriateness, suitability 995.1; normativeness, normality; proprieties, decencies; rightmindedness, **righteousness** 653.1

ADJS **3 right,** rightful; fit, suitable 995.5; **proper, correct, decorous,** good, nice, decent, seemly, **due, appropriate,** fitting, condign, **right and proper,** as it should be, as it ought to be, up to par, *comme il faut* <Fr>; kosher *and* according to Hoyle <nf>; in the right; normative, normal; rightminded, right-thinking, **righteous**

ADVS **4 rightly, rightfully,** right; **by rights,** by right, with good right, **as is right** *or* **only right; properly,** correctly, as is proper *or* fitting, **duly, appropriately,** fittingly, condignly, **in justice,** in equity; in reason, in all conscience

638 WRONG

NOUNS **1 wrong,** wrongfulness, wrongness; **impropriety, indecorum;** incorrectness, improperness, indecorousness, unseemliness; unfitness, unfittingness, inappropriateness, unsuitability 996.1; infraction, violation, delinquency, criminality, illegality, unlawfulness; abnormality, deviance *or* deviancy, aberrance *or* aberrancy; sinfulness, wickedness, unrighteousness; **dysfunction,** malfunction; maladaptation, maladjustment; malfeasance, malversation, malpractice; malformation

2 abomination, horror, terrible thing; **scandal, disgrace, shame, pity,** atrocity, profanation, desecration, violation, sacrilege, infamy, ignominy

ADJS **3 wrong, wrongful; improper, incorrect, indecorous,** undue, unseemly; unfit, unfitting, inappropriate, unsuitable 995.5; delinquent, criminal, illegal, unlawful; fraudulent, creative <nf>; abnormal, deviant, aberrant; **dysfunctional; evil, sinful, wicked, unrighteous;** not the thing, hardly the thing, not done, not cricket <Brit>; **off-base** *and* **out-of-line** *and* **off-color** *and* off the beam <nf>; abominable, terrible, scandalous, disgraceful, immoral, shameful, shameless, atrocious, sacrilegious, infamous, ignominious; maladapted, maladjusted

ADVS **4 wrongly, wrongfully,** wrong; **improperly,** incorrectly, indecorously

WORD ELEMENTS **5** mis-, dis-; dys-, caco-

639 DUENESS

NOUNS **1 dueness, entitlement,** entitledness, deservingness, deservedness, meritedness, expectation, just *or* justifiable expectation, expectations, outlook, prospect, prospects; **justice** 649

2 due, one's due, what one merits *or* is entitled to, what one has earned, what is owing, what one has coming, what is coming to one, acknowledgment, cognizance, recognition, credit, crediting; **right**

3 deserts, just deserts, deservings, merits, dues, due reward *or* punishment, **comeuppance** <nf>, all that is coming to one; the wrath of God; retaliation 506, vengeance 507.1

VERBS **4 be due,** be one's due, **be entitled to,** have a right or title to, have a rightful claim to *or* upon, claim as one's right, **have coming,** come by honestly

5 deserve, merit, earn, rate *and* be in line for <nf>, **be worthy of,** be deserving, richly deserve

6 get one's deserts, get one's dues, **get one's comeuppance** *and* get his *or* hers <nf>, get what is coming to one; get justice; serve one right, be rightly served; get for one's pains, reap the fruits *or* benefit of, reap where one has sown, come into one's own

ADJS **7 due, owed, owing,** payable, redeemable, coming, **coming to**

8 rightful, condign, appropriate, proper; fit, becoming 995.5; **fair, just** 649.8

9 warranted, justified, entitled, qualified, worthy; **deserved, merited,** richly deserved, earned, well-earned

10 due, entitled to, with a right to; **deserving, meriting, meritorious, worthy of;** attributable, ascribable

ADVS **11 duly,** rightfully, condignly, as is one's due *or* right

PHRS **12** what's sauce for the goose is sauce for the gander; give the devil his due; give credit where credit is due; he's made his bed let him lie in it; let the punishment fit the crime

640 UNDUENESS

NOUNS **1 undueness, undeservedness,** undeservingness, unentitledness, unentitlement, unmeritedness; disentitlement; lack of claim *or* title, false claim *or* title, invalid claim *or* title, no claim *or* title, empty claim *or* title; unearned increment; **inappropriateness** 996.1; **impropriety** 638.1; **excess** 993

2 presumption, assumption, **imposition; license,**
licentiousness, **undue liberty,** liberties, familiarity,
presumptuousness, freedom *or* liberty abused,
hubris; lawlessness 418; injustice 650

3 usurpation, arrogation, seizure, unlawful seizure,
appropriation, assumption, adoption,
infringement, encroachment, invasion, trespass,
trespassing; playing God

4 usurper, arrogator, pretender

VERBS **5 not be entitled to,** have no right *or* title to,
have no claim upon, not have a leg to stand on

6 presume, assume, venture, hazard, dare, pretend,
attempt, **make bold** *or* so bold, make free, **take the
liberty,** take upon oneself, go so far as to

7 presume on *or* **upon, impose on** *or* **upon,** encroach
upon, obtrude upon; **take liberties,** take a liberty,
overstep, overstep one's rights *or* bounds *or*
prerogatives, make free with *or* of, abuse one's
rights, abuse a privilege, give an inch and take an
ell; **inconvenience,** bother, trouble, cause to go out
of one's way

8 <take to oneself unduly> **usurp, arrogate,** seize,
grab *and* latch on to <nf>, **appropriate,** assume,
adopt, take over, arrogate *or* accroach to oneself,
pretend to, infringe, encroach, invade, trespass;
play God

ADJS **9 undue, unowed, unowing,** not coming, not
outstanding; **undeserved, unmerited,** unearned;
unwarranted, unjustified, unprovoked; unentitled,
undeserving, unmeriting, nonmeritorious,
unworthy; preposterous, outrageous

10 inappropriate 996.5; **improper** 638.3; **excessive**
993.16

11 presumptuous, presuming, licentious; hubristic
493.7

PHRS **12** give him an inch he'll take a mile;
let a camel get his nose under the tent and he'll
come in

641 DUTY
<moral obligation>

NOUNS **1 duty, obligation,** charge, **onus, burden,**
mission, devoir, must, ought, imperative, bounden
duty, proper *or* assigned task, what ought to be
done, what one is responsible for, where the buck
stops <nf>, deference, respect 155, fealty,
allegiance, loyalty, homage; devotion, dedication,
commitment; self-commitment, self-imposed duty;
business 724, function, province, place 724.3;
ethics 636; line of duty; call of duty; duties and
responsibilities, assignment, work-load

2 responsibility, incumbency; **liability,
accountability,** accountableness, answerability,
answerableness, amenability; product liability;

responsibleness, **dutifulness,** duteousness,
devotion *or* dedication to duty, sense of duty *or*
obligation, code of honor, inner voice

VERBS **3 should, ought to,** had best, had better, be
expedient

4 behoove, become, befit, beseem, be bound, be
obliged *or* obligated, be under an obligation; **owe it
to,** owe it to oneself; must

5 be the duty of, be incumbent on *or* **upon,** be his *or*
hers to, fall to, stand on *or* upon, be a must *or* an
imperative for, duty calls one to

6 be responsible for, answer for, stand responsible
for, **be liable for,** be answerable *or* accountable
for; be on the hook for *and* take the heat *or* rap
for <nf>

7 be one's responsibility, be one's office, be one's
charge *or* mission, be one's concern, **rest with,** lie
upon, devolve upon, rest on the shoulders of, lie
on one's head *or* one's door *or* one's doorstep, fall
to one *or* to one's lot

8 incur a responsibility, become bound to, become
sponsor for

9 take *or* **accept the responsibility, take upon
oneself,** take upon one's shoulders, commit
oneself; be where the buck stops <nf>; **answer for,**
respect *or* defer to one's duty; sponsor, be *or* stand
sponsor for; do at one's own risk *or* peril; **take the
blame,** be in the hot seat *or* on the spot *and* take
the heat *or* rap for <nf>

10 do one's duty, perform *or* fulfill *or* discharge one's
duty, do what one has to do, pay one's dues <nf>,
do what is expected, do the needful, do the right
thing, do justice to, **do** *or* **act one's part,** play one's
proper role; answer the call of duty, do one's bit *or*
part

11 meet an obligation, satisfy one's obligations, stand
to one's engagement, stand up to, **acquit oneself,
make good,** redeem one's pledge

12 obligate, oblige, require, make incumbent *or*
imperative, tie, **bind,** pledge, commit, saddle with,
put under an obligation; call to account, hold
responsible *or* accountable *or* answerable

ADJS **13 dutiful, duteous;** moral, ethical;
conscientious, scrupulous, observant; obedient
326.3; deferential, respectful 155.8

14 incumbent on *or* **upon,** chargeable to, behooving

15 obligatory, binding, imperative, imperious,
peremptory, mandatory, compulsory, must, *de
rigueur* <Fr>; **necessary,** required 963.13

16 obliged, obligated, obligate, **under obligation;
bound, duty-bound,** in duty bound, tied, pledged,
committed, saddled, beholden, bounden; **obliged
to,** beholden to, bound *or* bounden to, **indebted to**

17 responsible, answerable; liable, accountable,
incumbent, amenable, unexempt from, chargeable,

on one's head, at one's doorstep, on the hook
<nf>; responsible for, at the bottom of; to blame
ADVS **18 dutifully, duteously, in the line of duty,** as in
duty bound; beyond the call of duty

642 PREROGATIVE

NOUNS **1 prerogative, right, due,** droit; power,
authority, prerogative of office; faculty,
appurtenance; **claim,** proper claim, demand,
interest, title, pretension, pretense, prescription;
birthright; natural right, presumptive right,
inalienable right; divine right; vested right or
interest; property right; conjugal right

2 privilege, license, liberty, freedom, immunity;
franchise, patent, copyright, grant, warrant, blank
check, carte blanche; favor, indulgence, **special
favor,** dispensation

3 human rights, rights of man; constitutional rights,
rights of citizenship, **civil rights** 430.2, civil
liberties; rights of minorities, minority rights; gay
rights, gay liberation

4 women's rights, rights of women; **feminism,
women's liberation,** women's lib <nf>, womanism,
women's movement or liberation movement,
sisterhood

5 women's rightist, feminist, women's liberationist,
women's liberation advocate or adherent or
activist, womanist, women's libber and libber
<nf>; suffragette, suffragist

VERBS **6** have or claim or assert a right, exercise a
right; defend a right

643 IMPOSITION

<a putting or inflicting upon>

NOUNS **1 imposition, infliction,** laying on or upon,
charging, taxing, tasking; burdening, weighting or
weighting down, freighting, loading or loading
down, heaping on or upon, imposing an onus;
exaction, demand 421; unwarranted demand,
obtrusiveness, presumptuousness 142.1;
inconvenience, trouble, bother, pain <nf>;
inconsiderateness 144.3

2 administration, giving, bestowal; applying,
application, dosing, dosage, meting out,
prescribing; **forcing,** forcing on or upon, enforcing

3 charge, duty, tax, task; **burden,** weight, freight,
cargo, load, onus

VERBS **4 impose, impose on or upon, inflict on or
upon, put on or upon, lay on or upon,** enjoin; **put,
place, set, lay,** put down; **levy, exact, demand**
421.4; **tax,** task, **charge,** burden with, weight or
freight with, weight down with, yoke with, **fasten
upon,** saddle with, stick with <nf>; subject to

5 inflict, wreak, do to, bring, bring upon, bring down
upon, bring on or down on one's head, visit upon

6 administer, give, bestow; apply, put on or upon,
lay on or upon, dose, dose with, dish out <nf>,
mete out, prescribe; **force, force upon,** impose by
force or main force, strongarm <nf>, force down
one's throat, enforce upon

7 impose on or upon, take advantage of 387.16;
presume upon 640.7; **deceive,** play or work on, out
on or upon, put over or across <nf>; palm or pass
or fob off on, fob or foist on; shift the blame or
responsibility, **pass the buck** <nf>

ADJS **8 imposed, inflicted,** piled or heaped on;
burdened with, stuck with <nf>; self-inflicted;
exacted, demanded

644 PROBITY

NOUNS **1 probity,** truthfulness, assured probity,
honesty, integrity, rectitude, uprightness,
upstandingness, erectness, **virtue,** virtuousness,
righteousness, goodness; cleanness, **decency;
honor,** honorableness, worthiness, estimableness,
reputability, nobility; unimpeachableness,
unimpeachability, irreproachableness,
irreproachability, blamelessness; immaculacy,
unspottedness, stainlessness, pureness, purity;
respectability; principles, high principles, high
ideals, high-mindedness; **character,** good or sterling
character, moral strength, moral excellence;
fairness, justness, justice 649; gentrification

2 conscientiousness, scrupulousness, scrupulosity,
scruples, punctiliousness, meticulousness; scruple,
point of honor, punctilio; qualm 325.2; twinge of
conscience 113.2; overconscientiousness,
overscrupulousness; fastidiousness 495

3 honesty, veracity, veraciousness, verity,
truthfulness, truth, veridicality, truth-telling, truth-
speaking; truth-loving; credibility, absolute
credibility; objectivity

4 candor, candidness, frankness, plain dealing;
sincerity, genuineness, authenticity;
ingenuousness; artlessness 416; **openness,**
openheartedness; freedom, freeness; **unreserve,**
unrestraint, unconstraint; **forthrightness,
directness, straightforwardness; outspokenness,**
plainness, plainspokenness, plain speaking, plain
speech, roundness, broadness; **bluntness,**
bluffness, brusqueness

5 undeceptiveness, undeceitfulness, guilelessness

6 trustworthiness, faithworthiness, trustiness,
trustability, **reliability, dependability,**
dependableness, sureness; answerableness,
responsibility 641.2; unfalseness, unperfidiousness,
untreacherousness; incorruptibility, inviolability

7 fidelity, faithfulness, loyalty, faith; **constancy, steadfastness,** staunchness, firmness; trueness, troth, true blue; good faith, *bona fides* <L>, *bonne foi* <Fr>; **allegiance, fealty, homage;** bond, tie; attachment, adherence, adhesion; devotion, devotedness

8 person *or* **man** *or* **woman of honor,** man of his word, woman of her word; gentleman, *gentilhomme* <Fr>, *galantuomo* <Ital>; **honest man,** good man; **lady, real lady; honest woman, good woman;** salt of the earth; square *or* straight shooter *and* straight arrow <nf>; true blue, truepenny; trusty, faithful

VERBS **9 keep faith,** not fail, **keep one's word** *or* **promise,** keep troth, show good faith, be as good as one's word, one's word is one's bond, redeem one's pledge, play by the rules, acquit oneself, make good; practice what one preaches

10 shoot straight <nf>, draw a straight furrow, **put one's cards on the table,** level with one <nf>, play it straight <nf>, shoot from the hip <nf>

11 speak *or* **tell the truth,** speak *or* tell true, paint in its true colors, tell the truth and shame the devil; tell the truth, the whole truth, and nothing but the truth, stick to the facts

12 be frank, speak plainly, speak out, speak one's mind, say what one thinks, **call a spade a spade,** tell it like it is, make no bones about it, not mince words

ADJS **13 honest, upright,** uprighteous, **upstanding,** erect, right, **righteous, virtuous, good,** clean, squeaky-clean <nf>, **decent; honorable,** full of integrity, **reputable,** estimable, creditable, worthy, noble, sterling, manly, yeomanly; Christian <nf>; unimpeachable, beyond reproach, irreproachable, squeaky-clean <nf>, blameless, immaculate, spotless, stainless, unstained, unspotted, unblemished, untarnished, unsullied, undefiled, pure; **respectable,** highly respectable; **ethical, moral; principled, high-principled,** high-minded, right-minded; uncorrupt, uncorrupted, inviolate; truehearted, true-blue, true-souled, true-spirited; true-dealing, true-disposing, true-devoted; **law-abiding,** law-loving, law-revering; **fair, just** 649.8

14 straight, square, foursquare, straight-arrow <nf>, honest and aboveboard, right as rain; **fair and square; square-dealing,** square-shooting, straight-shooting, up-and-up, **on the up-and-up** *and* **on the level,** *and* on the square <nf>; **aboveboard, open and aboveboard;** bona fide, good-faith; authentic, all wool and a yard wide, veritable, genuine; single-hearted; honest as the day is long

15 conscientious, tender-conscienced; **scrupulous,** careful 339.10; punctilious, punctual, meticulous, religious, strict, nice; fastidious 495.9; overconscientious, overscrupulous

16 honest, veracious, truthful, true, true to one's word, veridical; truth-telling, truth-speaking, truth-declaring, truth-passing, truth-bearing, truth-loving, truth-seeking, truth-desiring, truth-guarding, truth-filled; true-speaking, true-meaning, true-tongued

17 candid, frank, sincere, genuine, ingenuous, frankhearted; **open,** openhearted, transparent, open-faced; artless 416.5; **straightforward, direct,** up-front *and* straight <nf>, **forthright,** downright, straight-out <nf>, straight-from-the-shoulder; plain, broad, round; **unreserved,** unrestrained, unconstrained, unchecked; unguarded, uncalculating; free; **outspoken, plain-spoken,** free-spoken, free-speaking, free-tongued; explicit, unequivocal; **blunt,** bluff, brusque; heart-to-heart

18 undeceptive, undeceitful, undissembling, undissimulating, undeceiving, undesigning, uncalculating; **guileless,** unbeguiling, unbeguileful; unassuming, unpretending, unfeigning, undisguising, unflattering; undissimulated, undissembled; unassumed, unaffected, unpretended, unfeigned, undisguised, unvarnished, untrimmed

19 trustworthy, trusty, trustable, faithworthy, **reliable, dependable, responsible,** straight <nf>, sure, to be trusted, **to be depended** *or* **relied upon,** to be counted *or* reckoned on, as good as one's word; tried, true, **tried and true,** tested, proven; unfalse, unperfidious, untreacherous; incorruptible, inviolable

20 faithful, loyal, devoted, allegiant; **true, true-blue,** true to one's colors; **constant, steadfast,** unswerving, steady, consistent, stable, unfailing, staunch, firm, solid

ADVS **21 honestly, uprightly, honorably,** upstandingly, erectly, **virtuously, righteously, decently,** worthily, reputably, nobly; unimpeachably, irreproachably, blamelessly, immaculately, unspottedly, stainlessly, purely; high-mindedly, morally; **conscientiously, scrupulously,** punctiliously, meticulously, fastidiously 495.14

22 truthfully, truly, veraciously; to tell the truth, to speak truthfully; in truth, in sooth <old>, of a truth, with truth, in good *or* very truth; objectively

23 candidly, frankly, sincerely, genuinely, in all seriousness *or* soberness, from the heart, in all conscience; in plain words *or* English, straight from the shoulder, not to mince the matter, not to mince words, without equivocation, with no nonsense, all joking aside *or* apart; **openly,** openheartedly, **unreservedly,** unrestrainedly, unconstrainedly, **forthrightly, directly,**

straightforwardly, **outspokenly, plainly,** plain-spokenly, uninhibitedly, broadly, roundly, **bluntly,** bluffy, brusquely

24 **trustworthily,** trustily, **reliably, dependably, responsibly;** undeceptively, undeceitfully, guilelessly; incorruptibly, inviolably

25 **faithfully, loyally,** devotedly; **constantly, steadfastly,** steadily, responsibly, consistently, unfailingly, unswervingly, staunchly, firmly; in or with good faith, *bona fide* <L>

645 IMPROBITY

NOUNS 1 **improbity, untruthfulness, dishonesty,** dishonor; **unscrupulousness,** unconscientiousness; **corruption,** corruptness, corruptedness; **crookedness,** criminality, feloniousness, **fraudulence** or fraudulency, underhandedness, unsavoriness, fishiness and shadiness <nf>, indirection, shiftiness, slipperiness, deviousness, evasiveness, unstraightforwardness, trickiness

2 **knavery, roguery, rascality,** rascalry, **villainy,** reprobacy, scoundrelism; chicanery 356.4; knavishness, roguishness, scampishness, villainousness; **baseness, vileness,** degradation, turpitude, moral turpitude

3 **deceitfulness; falseness** 354; perjury, forswearing, untruthfulness 354.8, credibility gap; inveracity; mendacity, mendaciousness; **insincerity,** unsincereness, uncandidness, uncandor, unfrankness, disingenuousness; hypocrisy; sharp practice 356.4; fraud 356.8; artfulness, craftiness 415.1; intrigue

4 **untrustworthiness,** unfaithworthiness, untrustiness, **unreliability, undependability,** irresponsibility

5 **infidelity, unfaithfulness,** unfaith, faithlessness, trothlessness; **inconstancy, unsteadfastness,** fickleness; **disloyalty,** unloyalty; **falsity,** falseness, untrueness; disaffection, recreancy, dereliction; bad faith, *mala fides* <L>, Punic faith; breach of promise, breach of trust or faith, barratry; breach of confidence

6 **treachery,** treacherousness; **perfidy,** perfidiousness, falseheartedness 354.4, two-facedness, doubleness, sycophancy, false face; **duplicity, double-dealing,** foul play, dirty work and dirty pool and dirty trick and dirty game <nf>; broken promise, breach of promise, breach of faith

7 **treason,** petty treason, misprision of treason, high treason; lese majesty, sedition; quislingism, fifth-column activity; collaboration, fraternization; subversion, subversiveness, subversivism

8 **betrayal,** betrayment, letting down <nf>, **double cross** and sellout <nf>, Judas kiss, kiss of death, stab in the back

9 **corruptibility, venality,** bribability, purchasability

10 criminal 660.9, perpetrator, perp <nf>, scoundrel 660.3, traitor 357.10, deceiver 357

VERBS 11 <be dishonest> live by one's wits; shift, shift about, evade; deceive; cheat; falsify; lie; sail under false colors, put on a false face, pass oneself off as

12 **be unfaithful,** not keep faith or troth, **go back on** <nf>, **fail,** break one's word or promise, renege, go back on one's word <nf>, break faith, betray, perjure or forswear oneself; forsake, desert 370.5; pass the buck <nf>; shift the responsibility or blame; cheat on and two-time <nf>

13 **play one false,** prove false; **stab one in the back,** knife one <nf>; bite the hand that feeds one; play dirty pool <nf>; shift or move the goalposts and change the rules <nf>

14 **betray, double-cross** and two-time <nf>, sell out and sell down the river <nf>, turn in; **mislead,** lead one down the garden path; let down and let down one's side <nf>; inform on 551.12

15 **act the traitor,** turn against, go over to the enemy, turn one's coat, sell oneself, sell out <nf>; collaborate, fraternize

ADJS 16 **dishonest, dishonorable;** unconscientious, unconscienced, conscienceless, unconscionable, shameless, without shame or remorse, **unscrupulous, unprincipled,** unethical, immoral, amoral; **corrupt,** corrupted, rotten; **crooked, criminal,** felonious, **fraudulent,** creative <nf>, underhand, underhanded; shady <nf>, up to no good, not kosher <nf>, unsavory, dark, sinister, insidious, indirect, slippery, devious, tricky, shifty, evasive, unstraightforward; fishy <nf>, questionable, suspicious, doubtful, dubious; ill-gotten, ill-got

17 **knavish, roguish, scampish, rascally, scoundrelly,** blackguardly, villainous, reprobate, recreant, **base, vile,** degraded; **infamous, notorious**

18 **deceitful;** falsehearted; perjured, forsworn, untruthful 354.34; **insincere,** unsincere, uncandid, unfrank, disingenuous; artful, crafty 415.12; calculating, scheming; **tricky,** cute and dodgy <nf>, slippery as an eel

19 **untrustworthy,** unfaithworthy, untrusty, trustless, **unreliable, undependable,** fly-by-night, irresponsible, unsure, not to be trusted, not to be depended or relied upon

20 **unfaithful,** faithless, of bad faith, trothless; **inconstant, unsteadfast,** fickle; **disloyal,** unloyal; false, **untrue,** not true to; disaffected, recreant, derelict, barratrous; two-timing <nf>

21 **treacherous, perfidious,** falsehearted; **shifty,** slippery, tricky; **double-dealing,** double, ambidextrous; **two-faced**

22 traitorous, turncoat, double-crossing *and* two-timing <nf>, betraying; Judas-like, Iscariotic; **treasonable,** treasonous; quisling, quislingistic, fifth-column, Trojan-horse; subversive, seditious

23 corruptible, venal, bribable, purchasable, on the pad <nf>, mercenary, hireling

ADVS **24 dishonestly, dishonorably; unscrupulously,** unconscientiously; **crookedly,** criminally, feloniously, **fraudulently,** underhandedly, like a thief in the night, insidiously, deviously, shiftily, evasively, fishily <nf>, suspiciously, dubiously, by fair means or foul; **deceitfully;** knavishly, roguishly, villainously; basely, vilely; infamously, notoriously

25 perfidiously, falseheartedly; **unfaithfully,** faithlessly; **treacherously;** traitorously, treasonably

646 HONOR
<token of esteem>

NOUNS **1 honor,** great honor, distinction, glory, credit, ornament

2 award, reward, prize; first prize, second prize, etc; blue ribbon; consolation prize; booby prize; Nobel Prize, Pulitzer Prize; sweepstakes; jackpot; Oscar, Academy Award, Emmy, Tony; Olympic Gold *or* Silver *or* Bronze medal

3 trophy, laurel, **laurels,** bays, palm, palms, crown, chaplet, wreath, garland, **feather in one's cap** <nf>; civic crown *or* garland *or* wreath; **cup,** loving cup, pot <nf>; America's Cup, Old Mug; **belt,** championship belt, black belt, brown belt, etc; banner, flag

4 citation, eulogy, mention, honorable mention, kudos, **accolade, tribute, praise** 511.1

5 decoration, decoration of honor, order, ornament; ribbon, riband; blue ribbon, *cordon bleu* <Fr>; red ribbon, red ribbon of the Legion of Honor; cordon, grand cordon; garter; star, gold star

6 medal, military honor <see list>, order, medallion; military medal, service medal, war medal, soldier's medal; lifesaving medal, Carnegie hero's medal; police citation, departmental citation; spurs, stripes, pips, star, gold star

7 scholarship, fellowship; grant

VERBS **8 honor, do honor,** pay regard to, give *or* pay *or* render honor to, **recognize; cite; decorate,** pin a medal on; crown, crown with laurel; hand it to *or* take off one's hat to one <nf>, pay tribute, praise 511.5; give credit where credit is due; give one the red carpet treatment, roll out the red carpet

ADJS **9 honored, distinguished;** laureate, crowned with laurel

10 honorary, honorific, honorable

ADVS **11 with honor,** with distinction; *cum laude,*

magna cum laude, summa cum laude, insigne cum laude, honoris causa <all L>

12 military honors

Air Medal	Distinguished Service
Bronze Star Medal	Order
Congressional Medal of	Distinguished Unit Citation
Honor	Médaille Militaire
Croix de Guerre <France>	<France>
Distinguished Conduct	Medal of Honor
Medal	Military Cross
Distinguished Flying Cross	Navy Cross
Distinguished Service	Order of the Purple Heart
Cross	Silver Star Medal
Distinguished Service	Unit Citation
Medal	Victoria Cross <Britain>

647 INSIGNIA

NOUNS **1 insignia, regalia,** ensign, **emblem, badge, symbol,** logo <nf>, marking, attribute; badge of office, mark of office, chain, chain of office, collar; wand, verge, *fasces* <L>, **mace, staff, baton;** livery, uniform, mantle, dress; tartan, tie, old school tie, regimental tie, club tie; ring, school ring, class ring; pin, button, lapel pin *or* button; cap and gown, mortarboard; cockade; brassard; figurehead, eagle; cross 170.4, skull and crossbones, swastika, hammer and sickle, rose, thistle, shamrock, fleur-de-lis; medal, **decoration** 646.5; **heraldry,** armory, blazonry, sigillography, sphragistics

2 <heraldry terms> heraldic device, achievement, bearings, coat of arms, arms, armorial bearings, armory, blazonry, blazon; hatchment; shield, escutcheon, scutcheon, lozenge; charge, field; crest, torse, wreath, garland, bandeau, chaplet, mantling, helmet; crown, coronet; device, motto; pheon, broad arrow; animal charge, lion, unicorn, griffin, yale, cockatrice, falcon, alerion, eagle, spread eagle; marshaling, quartering, impaling, impalement, dimidiating, differencing, difference; ordinary, bar, bend, bar sinister, bend sinister, baton, chevron, chief, cross, fess, pale, paly, saltire; subordinary, billet, bordure, canton, flanch, fret, fusil, gyron, inescutcheon, mascle, orle, quarter, rustre, tressure; fess point, nombril point, honor point; cadency mark, file, label, crescent, mullet, martlet, annulet, fleur-de-lis, rose, cross moline, octofoil; tincture, gules, azure, vert, sable, purpure, tenne; metal, or, argent; fur, ermine, ermines, erminites, erminois, pean, vair; heraldic officials 575.21; Hershey bar *or* pip *or* hash mark <nf>

3 <royal insignia> regalia; scepter, rod, rod of empire; orb; armilla; purple, ermine, robe of state *or* royalty, robes of office; purple pall; crown, royal crown, coronet, tiara, diadem; cap of maintenance *or* dignity *or* estate, triple plume, Prince of Wales's feathers; uraeus; seal, signet, great seal, privy seal; throne; badge of office

4 <ecclesiastical insignia> tiara, triple crown; ring, keys; miter, crosier, crook, pastoral staff; pallium; cardinal's hat, red hat

5 <military insignia> insignia of rank, grade insignia, chevron, stripe; star, bar, eagle, spread eagle, chicken <nf>, pip <Brit>, oak leaf; branch of service insignia, insignia of branch *or* arm; unit insignia, organization insignia, shoulder patch, patch; shoulder sleeve insignia, badge, aviation badge *or* wings; parachute badge, submarine badge; service stripe, hash mark <nf>, overseas bar, Hershey bar <nf>; epaulet

6 <national insignia> American eagle, British lion and unicorn, Canadian maple leaf, English rose, French fleur-de-lis, Irish shamrock, Japanese rising sun, Nazi swastika, Roman eagle, Russian bear, Scottish thistle, Soviet hammer and sickle, Swiss cross, Welsh leek *or* daffodil

7 flag, banner, oriflamme, **standard,** gonfalon *or* gonfanon, guidon, *vexillum* <L>, *labarum* <L>; **pennant,** pennon, pennoncel, banneret *or* bannerette, banderole, swallowtail, burgee, ensign, **streamer; bunting;** coachwhip, long pennant; **national flag, colors;** royal standard; **ensign,** merchant flag, jack, Jolly Roger, black flag; house flag; <US> Old Glory, Stars and Stripes, Star-Spangled Banner, red, white, and blue; <Confederacy> Stars and Bars; <France> tricolor, *le drapeau tricolore* <Fr>; <Britain> Union Jack, Union Flag, white *or* red *or* blue ensign; yellow flag, white flag; vexillology; signal, flag 517.15

648 TITLE
<appellation of dignity or distinction>

NOUNS **1 title, honorific, honor,** title of honor; **handle** *and* handle to one's name <nf>; courtesy title

2 <honorifics> Excellency, Eminence, Reverence, Grace, Honor, Worship, Your *or* His *or* Her Excellency; Lord, My Lord, milord, Lordship, Your *or* His Lordship; Lady, My Lady, milady, Ladyship, Your *or* Her Ladyship; Highness, Royal Highness, Imperial Highness, Serene Highness, Your *or* His *or* Her Highness; Majesty, Royal Majesty, Imperial Majesty, Serene Majesty, Your *or* His *or* Her Majesty

3 Sir, sire, sirrah; Esquire; Master, Mister 76.7; mirza, effendi, sirdar, emir, khan, sahib

4 Mistress, madame 77.9

5 <ecclesiastical titles> Reverend, His Reverence,

His Grace; Monsignor; Holiness, His Holiness; Dom, Brother, Sister, Father, Mother; Rabbi

6 degree, academic degree <see list>; **bachelor,** baccalaureate, *baccalaureus* <L>, bachelor's degree; **master,** master's degree; **doctor,** doctorate, doctor's degree

ADJS **7 titular,** titulary; honorific; honorary

8 the Noble, the Most Noble, the Most Excellent, the Most Worthy, the Most Worshipful; the Honorable, the Most Honorable, the Right Honorable; the Reverend, the Very Reverend, the Right Reverend, the Most Reverend

9 academic degrees

AA *or* Associate of Arts
AAS *or* Associate in Applied Science
AB *or* Bachelor of Arts <Artium Baccalaureus>
ABLS *or* Bachelor of Arts in Library Science
AdjA *or* Adjunct in Arts
AM *or* Master of Arts <Artium Magister>
AMusD *or* Doctor of Musical Arts
AN *or* Associate in Nursing
ArtsD *or* Doctor of Arts
AS *or* Associate of Science
BA *or* Bachelor of Arts
BAE *or* Bachelor of Arts in Education
BAN *or* Bachelor of Arts in Nursing
BBA *or* Bachelor of Business Administration
BCE *or* Bachelor of Chemical Engineering
BCL *or* Bachelor of Civil Law
BD *or* Bachelor of Divinity
BFA *or* Bachelor of Fine Arts
BLitt *or* Blit *or* Bachelor of Literature
BMus *or* Bachelor of Music
BNS *or* Bachelor of Naval Science
BPhil *or* Bachelor of Philosophy
BS *or* Bachelor of Science
BSArch *or* Bachelor of Science in Architecture
ChD *or* Doctor of Chemistry
DD *or* Doctor of Divinity
DDS *or* Doctor of Dental Surgery
DEd *or* Doctor of Education

DJ *or* Djur *or* Doctor of Jurisprudence
DJS *or* D.Jur.Sc. *or* Doctor of Juridical Science
DLit *or* Dlitt *or* Doctor of Letters
DMD *or* Doctor of Dental Medicine
DMin *or* Doctor of Ministry
DMus *or* Doctor of Music
DO *or* Doctor of Osteopathy
DPH *or* Doctor of Public Health
DPhil *or* Doctor of Philosophy <Brit>
DS *or* Doctor of Science
DSC *or* Doctor of Surgical Chiropody
EdD *or* Doctor of Education
EdS *or* Education Specialist
JCD *or* Doctor of Canon Law
JD *or* Doctor of Jurisprudence
LittD *or* Doctor of Letters
LLB *or* Bachelor of Laws
LLD *or* Doctor of Laws
LLM *or* Master of Laws
MA *or* Master of Arts
MALS *or* Master of Arts in Library Science
MArch *or* Master of Architecture
MAT *or* Master of Arts in Teaching
MB *or* Bachelor of Medicine <Brit>
MBA *or* Master in Business Administration
MD *or* Doctor of Medicine
MDiv *or* Master of Divinity

MEd *or* Master of
   Education
MFA *or* Master of Fine Arts
MLitt *or* Master of
   Literature
MLS *or* Master of Library
   Science
MPhil *or* Master of
   Philosophy
MRE *or* Master of
   Religious Education
MS *or* Master of Science
MSW *or* Master of Social
   Work
MusD *or* Doctor of Music
OD *or* Doctor of Optometry

PharD *or* PharmD *or*
   Doctor of Pharmacy
PhD *or* Doctor of
   Philosophy
SB *or* Bachelor of Science
ScD *or* SD *or* Doctor of
   Science
SM *or* Master of Science
STD *or* Doctor of Sacred
   Theology
ThB *or* Bachelor of
   Theology
ThD *or* Doctor of Theology
ThM *or* Master of Theology
VMD *or* Doctor of
   Veterinary Medicine

649 JUSTICE

NOUNS **1 justice, justness; equity,** equitableness,
level playing field <nf>; **evenhandedness,** measure
for measure, give-and-take; balance, equality 790;
right, rightness, rightfulness, meetness,
properness, propriety, what is right; dueness 639;
justification, **justifiableness,** justifiability,
warrantedness, warrantability, defensibility; poetic
justice; retributive justice, nemesis; summary
justice, drumhead justice, rude justice; scales of
justice; lawfulness, legality 673

2 "truth in action"—Disraeli, "the firm and
continuous desire to render to everyone that which
is his due"—Justinian, "the ligament which holds
civilized beings and civilized nations together"—
Daniel Webster

3 fairness, fair-mindedness, candor; the fair thing,
the right *or* proper thing, the handsome thing
<nf>; level playing field, **square deal** *and* **fair
shake** <nf>; **fair play,** cricket <nf>;
sportsmanship, good sportsmanship,
sportsmanliness, sportsmanlikeness

4 impartiality, detachment, **dispassion,** loftiness,
Olympian detachment, **dispassionateness,
disinterestedness,** disinterest, unbias,
unbiasedness, a fair field and no favor; **neutrality**
467; selflessness, unselfishness 652

5 <personifications> Justice, Justitia, blind *or*
blindfolded Justice; Rhadamanthus, Minos;
<deities> Jupiter Fidius, Deus Fidius; Fides, Fides
publica Romani, Fides populi Romani; Nemesis,
Dike, Themis; Astraea

VERBS **6 be just, be fair,** do the fair thing, do the
handsome thing <nf>, do right, be righteous, do it
fair and square, do the right thing by; **do justice
to,** see justice done, see one righted *or* redressed,
redress a wrong *or* an injustice, remedy an injustice,
serve one right, shoot straight with *and* **give a**

square deal *or* **fair shake** <nf>; give the Devil his
due; give and take; bend *or* lean over backwards,
go out of one's way, go the extra mile <nf>

7 play fair, play the game <nf>, be a good sport,
show a proper spirit; judge on its own merits, hold
no brief

ADJS **8 just, fair,** square, **fair and square; equitable,**
balanced, level <nf>, **even,** evenhanded; **right,
rightful;** justifiable, justified, warranted,
warrantable, defensible; **due** 639.7,10, deserved,
merited; meet, meet and right, right and proper,
fit, **proper, good,** as it should *or* ought to be;
lawful, legal 673.11

9 fair-minded; **sporting,** sportsmanly, sportsmanlike;
square-dealing *and* square-shooting <nf>

10 impartial, impersonal, evenhanded, equitable,
dispassionate, disinterested, detached, objective,
lofty, Olympian; **unbiased,** uninfluenced,
unswayed; **neutral** 467.7; selfless, unselfish 652.5

ADVS **11 justly, fairly,** fair, in a fair manner; rightfully,
rightly, duly, deservedly, meetly, properly;
equitably, equally, evenly, upon even terms;
justifiedly, justifiably, warrantably, warrantedly;
**impartially, impersonally, dispassionately,
disinterestedly,** without distinction, without regard
or respect to persons, without fear or favor

12 in justice, in equity, in reason, in all conscience, in
all fairness, **to be fair,** as is only fair *or* right, as is
right *or* just *or* fitting *or* proper

650 INJUSTICE

NOUNS **1 injustice, unjustness; inequity,** iniquity,
inequitableness, iniquitousness; inequality 791,
inequality of treatment *or* dealing; **wrong,
wrongness,** wrongfulness, unmeetness,
improperness, **impropriety;** undueness 640; what
should not be, what ought not *or* must not be;
unlawfulness, illegality 674

2 unfairness; unsportsmanliness,
unsportsmanlikeness; foul play, foul, a hit below
the belt, dirty pool <nf>

3 partiality, onesidedness; bias, leaning, inclination,
tendentiousness; undispassionateness,
undetachment, interest, involvement, **partisanism,**
partisanship, *parti pris* <Fr>, *Tendenz* <Ger>;
unneutrality; **slant,** angle, spin <nf>; **favoritism,**
preference, nepotism; unequal *or* preferential
treatment, discrimination, unjust legal disability,
inequality

4 injustice, wrong, injury, grievance, disservice; raw
or rotten deal *and* bad rap <nf>; imposition;
mockery *or* miscarriage of justice; great wrong,
grave *or* gross injustice; atrocity, outrage

5 unjustifiability, unwarrantability, indefensibility;

inexcusability, unconscionableness, **unpardonability,** unforgivableness, inexpiableness, irremissibility

VERBS **6** not play fair, hit below the belt, give a raw deal *or* rotten deal *or* bad rap <nf>

7 do one an injustice, wrong, do wrong, do wrong by, **do one a wrong,** do a disservice; do a great wrong, do a grave *or* gross injustice, commit an atrocity *or* outrage

8 favor, prefer, show preference, **play favorites,** treat unequally, discriminate; **slant,** angle, put on spin <nf>

ADJS **9 unjust, inequitable,** unequitable, iniquitous, **unbalanced, discriminatory, uneven, unequal** 791.4; **wrong, wrongful,** unrightful; **undue** 640.9, unmeet, undeserved, unmerited; unlawful, illegal 674.6

10 unfair, not fair; **unsporting,** unsportsmanly, **unsportsmanlike,** not done, not kosher <nf>, not cricket <Brit nf>; **dirty** <nf>, foul, below the belt; sexist

11 partial, interested, involved, **partisan,** unneutral, **one-sided,** all on *or* way over to one side, undetached, unobjective, **undispassionate, biased,** tendentious, tendential, warped, influenced, swayed, slanted

12 unjustifiable, unwarrantable, unallowable, unreasonable, indefensible; **inexcusable,** unconscionable, **unpardonable, unforgivable,** inexpiable, irremissible

ADVS **13 unjustly, unfairly;** wrongfully, wrongly, undeservedly; inequitably, iniquitously, unequally, unevenly; partially, interestedly, one-sidedly, undispassionately; **unjustifiably, unwarrantably,** unallowably, unreasonably, indefensibly; inexcusably, unconscionably, unpardonably, unforgivably, inexpiably, irremissibly

651 SELFISHNESS

NOUNS **1 selfishness,** selfism, **self-seeking,** self-serving, self-pleasing, **self-indulgence,** hedonism; self-advancement, self-promotion, self-advertisement; **careerism,** personal ambition; **narcissism, self-love,** self-devotion, self-jealousy, **self-consideration,** self-solicitude, self-sufficiency, self-absorption, ego trip, self-occupation; self-containment, self-isolation; autism, catatonia, remoteness 583.2; **self-interest,** self-concern, self-interestedness, interest; self-esteem, self-admiration 140.1; **self-centeredness, self-obsession, narcissism, egotism** 140.3; **avarice, greed,** graspingness, grabbiness <nf>, acquisitiveness, possessiveness, covetousness; **individualism** 430.5, personalism, privatism,

private *or* personal desires, private *or* personal aims; looking out for number one

2 ungenerousness, unmagnanimousness, illiberality, meanness, smallness, littleness, paltriness, minginess, pettiness; **niggardliness, stinginess** 484.3

3 self-seeker, self-pleaser, self-advancer; member of the me generation; **narcissist, egotist** 140.5; timepleaser, timeserver, temporizer; fortune hunter, moneygrubber, tufthunter, name-dropper; self-server, careerist; opportunist; monopolist, hog, road hog; dog in the manger; **individualist,** loner *and* lone wolf <nf>

VERBS **4 please oneself,** gratify oneself; ego-trip *and* be *or* go on an ego trip <nf>, be full of oneself; indulge *or* pamper *or* coddle oneself, consult one's own wishes, look after one's own interests, know which side one's bread is buttered on, take care of *or* look out for number one *or* numero uno <nf>, think only of oneself; want everything, have one's cake and eat it; covet; monopolize, hog

ADJS **5 selfish, self-seeking, self-serving,** self-advancing, self-promoting, self-advertising, careerist, opportunistic, ambitious for self, **self-indulgent,** self-pleasing, hedonistic, self-jealous, self-sufficient, **self-interested,** self-considerative, self-besot, self-devoted, self-occupied, self-absorbed, wrapped up in oneself, self-contained, autistic, remote 583.6; self-esteeming, self-admiring 140.8; **self-centered, self-obsessed, narcissistic, egotistical** 140.10; possessive; **avaricious, greedy,** covetous, grasping, graspy *and* grabby <nf>, acquisitive; **individualistic,** personalistic, privatistic

6 ungenerous, illiberal, unchivalrous, mean, small, little, paltry, mingy, petty; **niggardly, stingy** 484.9

ADVS **7 selfishly, for oneself,** in one's own interest, from selfish *or* interested motives, to gain some private ends

652 UNSELFISHNESS

NOUNS **1 unselfishness, selflessness;** self-subjection, self-subordination, self-suppression, self-abasement, self-effacement; **humility** 137; modesty 139; self-neglect, self-neglectfulness, self-forgetfulness; **self-renunciation,** self-renouncement; **self-denial,** self-abnegation, self-effacement; **self-sacrifice,** sacrifice, self-immolation, self-devotion, devotion, dedication, commitment, consecration; disinterest, disinterestedness; unpossessiveness, unacquisitiveness; **altruism** 143.4; martyrdom

2 magnanimity, magnanimousness, greatness of spirit *or* soul, **generosity,** generousness, openhandedness, **liberality,** liberalness; **bigness, bigheartedness,** greateartedness, largeheartedness, big *or* large *or* great heart, greatness of heart; noble-mindedness, **high-mindedness, idealism; benevolence** 143.4; **nobleness,** nobility, princeliness, greatness, **loftiness,** elevation, exaltation, sublimity; chivalry, chivalrousness, knightliness, errantry, knight-errantry; heroism; consideration, considerateness, compassion

VERBS 3 not have a selfish bone in one's body, think only of others; be generous to a fault; put oneself out, go out of the way, lean over backwards; sacrifice, make a sacrifice; subject oneself, subordinate oneself, abase oneself; show compassion; take a backseat

4 observe the golden rule, do as one would be done by, do unto others as you would have others do unto you

ADJS 5 **unselfish, selfless;** self-unconscious, self-forgetful, self-abasing, self-effacing; **altruistic** 143.15, **humble; unpretentious, modest** 139.9; self-neglectful, self-neglecting; **self-denying,** self-renouncing, self-abnegating, self-abnegatory, self-effacing; **self-sacrificing,** self-immolating, sacrificing, self-devotional, self-devoted, devoted, dedicated, committed, consecrated, unsparing of self, disinterested; unpossessive, unacquisitive; ready to die for, martyred

6 **magnanimous,** great-souled *or* -spirited; **generous,** generous to a fault, openhanded, **liberal; big, bighearted,** greathearted, largehearted, great of heart *or* soul; noble-minded, **high-minded, idealistic; benevolent** 143.15, **noble,** princely, handsome, great, high, elevated, **lofty,** exalted, sublime; chivalrous, knightly; heroic

ADVS 7 **unselfishly, altruistically,** forgetful of self; for others

8 **magnanimously, generously,** openhandedly, **liberally; bigheartedly,** greatheartedly, largeheartedly; **nobly,** handsomely; chivalrously, knightly

653 VIRTUE
<moral goodness>

NOUNS 1 **virtue, virtuousness, goodness, righteousness,** rectitude, right conduct *or* behavior, the straight and narrow, the right thing, integrity; probity 644; **morality,** moral fiber *or* rectitude *or* virtue *or* excellence, morale; **saintliness,** saintlikeness, angelicalness; **godliness** 692.2

2 "victorious resistance to one's vital desire to do this, that or the other"—James Branch Cabell, "to do unwitnessed what we should be capable of doing before all the world"—La Rochefoucauld

3 **purity,** immaculacy, immaculateness, spotlessness, unspottedness; upstandingness; **uncorruptness,** uncorruptedness, incorruptness; **unsinfulness, sinlessness,** unwickedness, uniniquitousness; undegenerateness, undepravedness, undissoluteness, undebauchedness; **chastity** 664; guiltlessness, innocence 657

4 **cardinal virtues,** natural virtues; prudence, justice, temperance, fortitude; theological virtues *or* supernatural virtues; faith, hope, charity *or* love

VERBS 5 **be good,** do no evil, do the right thing; keep in the right path, walk the straight path, follow the straight and narrow, keep on the straight and narrow way *or* path, fly right, resist temptation; fight the good fight

ADJS 6 **virtuous, good, moral; upright, honest** 644.13,14,16; **righteous,** just, straight, rightminded, right-thinking; **angelic,** seraphic; **saintly,** saintlike; **godly** 692.9; irreproachable

7 **chaste, immaculate, spotless, pure** 664.4; **clean,** squeaky-clean <nf>; guiltless, **innocent** 657.6; pure as the driven snow

8 **uncorrupt,** uncorrupted, incorrupt, incorrupted; **unsinful,** sinless; **unwicked,** uniniquitous, unerring, unfallen; undegenerate, undepraved, undemoralized, undissolute, undebauched

654 VICE
<moral badness>

NOUNS 1 **vice,** viciousness; criminality, **wrongdoing** 655; **immorality,** unmorality, **evil; amorality** 636.4; **unvirtuousness,** ungoodness; **unrighteousness, ungodliness,** unsaintliness, unangelicalness; **uncleanness, impurity, unchastity** 665, fallenness, fallen state, lapsedness; waywardness, wantonness, prodigality; delinquency, moral delinquency; peccability; backsliding, recidivism; **evil nature, carnality** 663.2

2 **vice, weakness,** weakness of the flesh, **flaw,** moral flaw *or* blemish, **frailty, infirmity; failing,** failure; weak point, weak side, foible; bad habit, besetting sin; **fault, imperfection** 1003; laxity, lack of principle

3 **iniquity, evil,** bad, wrong, error, obliquity, villainy, knavery, reprobacy, peccancy, **abomination, atrocity, infamy,** shame, disgrace, scandal, unforgivable *or* cardinal *or* mortal sin, **sin** 655.2; seven deadly sins, pride, covetousness *or* avarice, lust, anger, gluttony, envy, sloth

4 **wickedness, badness,** naughtiness, **evilness, viciousness, sinfulness, iniquitousness,** wicked ways; **baseness,** rankness, **vileness,** foulness, arrantness, nefariousness, **heinousness,**

infamousness, villainousness, flagitiousness; fiendishness, hellishness; devilishness, devilry, deviltry

5 **turpitude, moral turpitude; corruption,** corruptedness, corruptness, rottenness, moral pollution *or* pollutedness, lack *or* absence of moral fiber; **decadence** *or* decadency, debasement, **degradation,** demoralization, abjection; **degeneracy,** degenerateness, degeneration, reprobacy, **depravity,** depravedness, depravation, corruption, perversion; **dissoluteness, profligacy;** abandonment, abandon; notoriety

6 **obduracy, hardheartedness, hardness, callousness,** heartlessness, hardness of heart, heart of stone

7 **sewer, gutter, pit, sink, sink of corruption,** sinkhole; **den of iniquity,** den, **fleshpot,** hellhole; hole *and* joint *and* the pits <nf>; Sodom, Gomorrah, Babylon; **brothel** 665.9; road to hell; hellhole

VERBS 8 **do wrong, sin** 655.5; misbehave, misdemean *and* misdo <old>

9 **go wrong,** stray, go astray, **err,** deviate, deviate from the path of virtue, leave the straight and narrow, step out of line, get *or* go off base <nf>; **fall,** fall from grace, **lapse,** slip, trip; **degenerate; go to the bad** 395.24, go to the dogs; **relapse,** recidivate, backslide 394.4

10 **corrupt; sully, soil, defile;** demoralize, vitiate; mislead; seduce, tempt

ADJS 11 vice-prone, vice-laden, vicious, **steeped in vice; immoral,** unmoral; **amoral,** nonmoral; unethical

12 **unvirtuous,** virtueless, ungood; **unrighteous, ungodly,** unsaintly, unangelic; morally weak, lax; **unclean, impure,** spotted, flawed, blemished, maculate <old>, **unchaste** 665.23; fleshly, carnal 663.6, wayward, wanton, prodigal; erring, **fallen, lapsed,** postlapsarian; frail, weak, infirm; Adamic; peccable; **relapsing, backsliding,** recidivist, recidivistic; of easy virtue 665.26

13 **diabolic, diabolical, devilish,** demonic, demoniac, demoniacal, **satanic,** Mephistophelian; **fiendish,** fiendlike; **hellish,** hellborn, **infernal**

14 **corrupt,** corrupted, vice-corrupted, polluted, morally polluted, rotten, tainted, contaminated, vitiated; warped, perverted; **decadent,** debased, degraded, reprobate, **depraved, debauched, dissolute, degenerate,** profligate, abandoned, gone to the bad *or* dogs, sunk *or* steeped in iniquity, rotten at *or* to the core, in the sewer *or* gutter

15 **evil-minded,** evilhearted, **blackhearted; baseminded,** low-minded; low-thoughted, dirty *or* dirty-minded <nf>; crooked

16 **wicked, evil, vicious, bad, naughty, wrong, sinful, iniquitous,** peccant, reprobate; dark, black; **base,** low, vile, foul, rank, flagrant, arrant, nefarious, **heinous,** villainous, criminal, up to no good, knavish, flagitious; abominable, atrocious, monstrous, unspeakable, execrable, damnable; shameful, disgraceful, scandalous, **infamous, unpardonable,** unforgivable; **improper,** reprehensible, blamable, blameworthy, unworthy

17 **hardened, hard, case-hardened, obdurate,** inured, indurated; **callous,** calloused, **seared; hardhearted,** heartless; **shameless,** lost to shame, blind to virtue, lost to all sense of honor, conscienceless, unblushing, **brazen**

18 **irreclaimable,** irredeemable, unredeemable, unregenerate, **irreformable,** incorrigible, past praying for; shriftless, graceless; **lost**

ADVS 19 **wickedly, evilly, sinfully, iniquitously,** peccantly, **viciously;** basely, vilely, foully, rankly, arrantly, flagrantly, flagitiously

655 WRONGDOING

NOUNS 1 **wrongdoing, evildoing, wickedness,** misdoing <old>, wrong conduct, **misbehavior** 322, **misconduct,** misdemeaning, misfeasance, malfeasance, malversation, **malpractice,** evil courses, machinations of the devil; **sin,** "the transgression of the law"—Bible; **crime, criminality,** lawbreaking, feloniousness, trespass, offense, transgression, infringement, infraction, breach, encroachment; criminal tendency; habitual criminality, criminosis; viciousness, **vice** 654; misprision, negative *or* positive misprision, misprision of treason *or* felony

2 **misdeed, misdemeanor,** misfeasance, malfeasance, malefaction, criminal *or* guilty *or* sinful act, **offense,** injustice, injury, **wrong, iniquity, evil,** peccancy, *malum* <L>; tort; **error, fault,** breach; **impropriety,** slight *or* minor wrong, venial sin, **indiscretion,** peccadillo, misstep, trip, slip, lapse; **transgression,** trespass; **sin; cardinal** *or* **deadly** *or* **mortal sin,** grave *or* heavy sin, unutterable sin, unpardonable *or* unforgivable *or* inexpiable sin, original sin, capital sin, carnal sin; sin against the Holy Ghost; sin of commission; sin of omission, nonfeasance, omission, failure, dereliction, delinquency; **crime, felony;** capital crime; white-collar crime, execu-crime; computer crime; copycat crime <nf>; war crime, crime against humanity, genocide; **outrage, atrocity,** enormity

3 **original sin,** fall from grace, fall, fall of man, fall of Adam *or* Adam's fall, sin of Adam

VERBS 4 **do wrong,** do amiss, misdo <old>, misdemean oneself, **misbehave** 322.4, **err,** offend; **sin,** commit sin; **transgress,** trespass

ADJS 5 **wrongdoing, evildoing,** malefactory,

malfeasant; **wrong,** iniquitous, **sinful, wicked**
654.16; **criminal,** felonious, criminous <old>;
crime-infested, crime-ridden

656 GUILT

NOUNS **1 guilt, guiltiness; criminality,** peccancy;
guilty *or* wrongful *or* criminal involvement;
culpability, reprehensibility, blamability,
blameworthiness; chargeability, answerability,
much to answer for; censurability, censurableness,
reproachability, reproachableness, reprovability,
reprovableness, inculpation, implication,
involvement, complicity, impeachability,
impeachableness, indictability, indictableness,
arraignability, arraignableness; bloodguilt *or*
-guiltiness, red-handedness, dirty hands, red *or*
bloody hands, "hangman's hands"—Shakespeare;
much to answer for; **ruth,** ruefulness, remorse,
guilty conscience, guilt feelings; onus, burden

VERBS **2** be guilty, look guilty, have no alibi, look
like the cat that swallowed the canary, blush,
stammer; have on one's hands *or* to one's discredit,
have much to answer for; have a red face; be
caught in the act *or* flatfooted *or* redhanded, be
caught with one's pants down *or* with one's
hand in the till *or* with one's hand in the cookie
jar <nf>

ADJS **3 guilty,** guilty as hell, peccant, **criminal, to
blame, at fault,** faulty, in the wrong, on one's head;
culpable, reprehensible, censurable, reproachable,
reprovable, inculpated, implicated, involved,
impeachable, indictable, arraignable; red-handed,
bloodguilty; caught in the act *or* flatfooted *or* red-
handed, caught with one's pants down *or* with
one's hand in the till *or* with one's hand in the
cookie jar <nf>

ADVS **4 red-handed,** red-hand, **in the act,** in the very
act, *in flagrante delicto* <L>

5 guilty, shamefacedly, sheepishly, with a guilty
conscience

657 INNOCENCE

NOUNS **1 innocence,** innocency, innocentness;
unfallen *or* unlapsed *or* prelapsarian state, state of
grace; unguiltiness, **guiltlessness,** faultlessness,
blamelessness, reproachlessness, **sinlessness,**
offenselessness; **spotlessness,** stainlessness,
taintlessness, unblemishedness; **purity,** cleanness,
cleanliness, whiteness, immaculateness,
immaculacy, impeccability; clean hands, clean
slate, clear conscience, nothing to hide

2 childlikeness 416.1; lamblikeness, dove-likeness,
angelicness; unacquaintance with evil,

uncorruptedness, incorruptness, pristineness,
undefiledness; naiveté

3 inculpability, unblamability, unblamableness,
unblameworthiness, irreproachability,
irreproachableness, impeccability, impeccableness,
unexceptionability, unexceptionableness,
irreprehensibility, irreprehensibleness,
uncensurability, uncensurableness,
unimpeachability, unimpeachableness,
unindictableness, unarraignableness

4 innocent, baby, babe, babe in arms, newborn babe,
infant, babe in the woods, child, mere child, lamb,
dove, angel; virgin

VERBS **5** know no wrong, have clean hands, have a
clear conscience, look as if butter would not melt
in one's mouth; have nothing to hide

ADJS **6 innocent;** unfallen, unlapsed, prelapsarian;
unguilty, not guilty, **guiltless, faultless, blameless,**
reproachless, **sinless,** offenseless, with clean
hands, "blameless in life and pure of crime"—
Horace; clear, in the clear; without reproach, *sans
reproche* <Fr>; innocent as a lamb, lamblike,
dovelike, angelic, childlike 416.5; unacquainted
with *or* untouched by evil, uncorrupted, incorrupt,
pristine, undefiled; innocuous

7 spotless, stainless, taintless, unblemished,
unspotted, **untainted, unsoiled, unsullied,
undefiled; pure, clean, immaculate,** impeccable,
white, pure *or* white as driven snow, squeaky-
clean <nf>

8 inculpable, unblamable, unblameworthy,
irreproachable, beyond reproach, irreprovable,
irreprehensible, uncensurable, unimpeachable,
unindictable, unarraignable, unobjectionable,
unexceptionable, above suspicion, squeaky-
clean <nf>, with clean hands

ADVS **9 innocently, guiltlessly, unguiltily,** with a clear
conscience; **unknowingly,** unconsciously, unawares

658 ATONEMENT

NOUNS **1 atonement, reparation, amends,** making
amends, **restitution, propitiation, expiation,
redress, recompense,** compensation, setting right,
making right *or* good, making up, squaring,
redemption, reclamation, satisfaction, quittance;
making it quits; indemnity, indemnification;
compromise, composition; expiatory offering *or*
sacrifice, piaculum, peace offering; eye for an eye,
measure for measure; conciliation, propitiation

2 apology, excuse, regrets; acknowledgment,
penitence, contrition, breast-beating, *mea culpa*
<L>, confession 351.3; abject apology

3 penance, penitence, repentance; penitential act *or*
exercise, **mortification,** maceration, flagellation,

lustration; sacrifice, offering, peace offering; **asceticism** 667, **fasting** 515; **purgation,** purgatory; **sackcloth and ashes;** hair shirt; **Lent;** Day of Atonement, Yom Kippur

VERBS **4 atone, atone for, propitiate, expiate,** compensate, restitute, recompense, redress, redeem, repair, satisfy, give satisfaction, **make amends, make reparation** *or* **compensation** *or* **expiation** *or* **restitution,** make good *or* right, rectify, set right, **make up for,** make matters up, square, square things, make it quits, pay the forfeit *or* penalty, pay one's dues <nf>, pay back, wipe off old scores; wipe the slate clean; set one's house in order; live down, unlive; reconcile, propitiate

5 apologize, beg pardon, ask forgiveness, beg indulgence, express regret; take back; get *or* fall down on one's knees, get down on one's marrowbones <nf>, come hat in hand; confess, admit

6 do penance, flagellate oneself, mortify oneself, mortify one's flesh, make oneself miserable, shrive oneself, purge oneself, cleanse oneself of guilt, stand in a white sheet, repent in sackcloth and ashes, wear a hair shirt, wear sackcloth *or* sackcloth and ashes; receive absolution; regret, show remorse *or* compunction

ADJS **7 atoning, propitiatory, expiatory,** piacular, reparative, reparatory, restitutive, restitutory, restitutional, redressing, recompensing, compensatory, compensational, righting, squaring, conciliatory; redemptive, redeeming, reclamatory, satisfactional; **apologetic, apologetical;** repentant, repenting; **penitential,** purgative, purgatorial; lustral, lustrative, lustrational, cleansing, purifying; ascetic

659 GOOD PERSON

NOUNS **1** good person, fine person, good *or* fine man *or* woman *or* child, worthy, prince, nature's nobleman *or* -woman, man *or* woman after one's own heart; *persona grata* <L>, acceptable person; **good fellow,** capital fellow, **good sort,** right sort, a decent sort of fellow, good lot <Brit nf>, no end of a fellow; real person, real man *or* woman, mensch <nf>; **gentleman,** perfect gentleman, a gentleman and a scholar; **lady,** perfect lady; **gem,** jewel, pearl, diamond; rough diamond, diamond in the rough; honest man 644.8

2 <nf terms> **good guy,** crackerjack, brick, trump, good egg, stout fellow, nice guy, Mr Nice Guy, good Joe, likely lad, no slouch, doll, living doll, pussycat, **sweetheart, sweetie**

3 good *or* **respectable citizen,** excellent *or* exemplary citizen, good neighbor, burgher, taxpayer, **pillar of**

society, pillar of the church, salt of the earth; Christian *and* true Christian <nf>

4 paragon, ideal, beau ideal, nonpareil, person to look up to, *chevalier sans peur et sans reproche* <Fr>, **good example, role model,** shining example; exemplar, epitome; **model, pattern, standard,** norm, mirror; *Übermensch* <Ger; Nietzsche>; **standout,** one in a thousand *or* ten thousand, man of men, a man among men, woman of women, a woman among women

5 hero, god, demigod, phoenix; **heroine, goddess,** demigoddess; **idol**

6 holy man; great soul, mahatma; guru, *rishi* <Skt>; *starets* <Russ>; saint, angel 679

660 BAD PERSON

NOUNS **1** bad person, bad man *or* woman *or* child, unworthy *or* disreputable person, unworthy, disreputable, **undesirable,** *persona non grata* <L>, unacceptable *or* unwanted *or* objectionable person, baddy *and* wrongo *and* bad news <nf>; bad example

2 wretch, mean *or* miserable wretch, **beggarly fellow, beggar, blighter** <Brit nf>; **bum** *and* bummer *and* lowlifer *and* lowlife *and* **mucker** <nf>, caitiff, *budmash* <India>, pilgarlic; devil, **poor devil,** *pauvre diable* <Fr>, poor creature, *mauvais sujet* <Fr>; **sad case,** sad sack *and* sad sack of shit <nf>; **good-for-nothing, good-for-naught, no-good** <nf>, **ne'er-do-well,** wastrel, *vaurien* <Fr>, worthless fellow; **derelict,** skid-row bum, Bowery bum, tramp, hobo, beachcomber, **drifter,** drunkard, vagrant, vag <nf>, vagabond, truant, stiff *and* bindlestiff <nf>, swagman *or* sundowner <Austral>; human wreck

3 rascal, precious rascal, rogue, knave, **scoundrel,** villain, blackguard, **scamp, scalawag** <nf>, spalpeen <Ir>, rapscallion, **devil;** shyster; sneak

4 reprobate, recreant, **miscreant,** bad *or* sorry lot <Brit nf>, bad egg *and* wrongo *and* wrong number <nf>, bad'un *or* wrong'un <Brit nf>; scapegrace, black sheep; lost soul, lost sheep, *âme damnée* <Fr>, backslider, recidivist, fallen angel; degenerate, pervert; profligate, **lecher** 665.11; trollop, **whore** 665.14,16; **pimp** 665.18

5 <nf terms> **asshole, prick, bastard, son of a bitch** *or* **SOB, jerk, horse's ass,** creep, motherfucker, mother, dork, **shit,** turd, birdturd, shithead, shitface, cuntface, dickhead, fart, **louse, meanie, heel, shitheel, rat, stinker,** stinkard, pill, bugger, dirtbag, geek, dweeb, nerd, twerp, sleaze, sleazoid, sleazebag, bad lot <Brit>; **hood, hooligan** 593.4

6 beast, **animal; cur,** dog, hound, whelp, mongrel; **reptile,** viper, serpent, snake; vermin, varmint <nf>, hyena; **swine,** pig; **skunk,** polecat; insect, worm

7 cad, bounder *and* rotter <nf>

8 **wrongdoer, malefactor, sinner,** transgressor, delinquent; malfeasor, misfeasor, nonfeasor; misdemeanant, misdemeanist; **culprit, offender; evil person, evil man** *or* **woman** *or* **child, evildoer** 593

9 **criminal, felon, perpetrator, crook** *and* perp <nf>, public enemy, **lawbreaker,** scofflaw; **gangster** *and* mobster *and* wiseguy <nf>, **racketeer; swindler** 357.3; thief 483; thug 593.3; **desperado,** desperate criminal; **outlaw,** fugitive, **convict,** jailbird, gaolbird <Brit>; gallows bird <nf>; **traitor,** betrayer, quisling, Judas, double-dealer, two-timer <nf>, **deceiver** 357; stalker

10 **the underworld,** gangland, gangdom, **organized crime,** organized crime family, the rackets, the mob, the syndicate, the Mafia, Cosa Nostra, Black Hand; **gangsterism; gangster,** ganglord, gangleader, caporegime *or* capo, button man, soldier

11 **the wicked,** the bad, the evil, the unrighteous, the reprobate; sons of men, sons of Belial, sons *or* children of the devil, limbs *or* get *or* imps of Satan, children of darkness; **scum of the earth,** dregs of society

661 DISREPUTE

NOUNS 1 **disrepute, ill repute,** bad repute, bad *or* poor reputation, evil repute *or* reputation, ill fame, shady *or* unsavory reputation, **bad name,** bad odor, bad report, bad character; **disesteem, dishonor,** public dishonor, **discredit; disfavor,** ill-favor; disapprobation 510.1

2 **disreputability,** disreputableness, **notoriety;** discreditableness, dishonorableness, unsavoriness, **unrespectability;** disgracefulness, **shamefulness**

3 **baseness, lowness, meanness, crumminess** <nf>, poorness, pettiness, paltriness, smallness, littleness, pokiness, cheesiness <nf>, beggarliness, **shabbiness, shoddiness, squalor,** scrubbiness, scumminess, scabbiness, scurviness, scruffiness, shittiness <nf>; **abjectness, wretchedness,** miserableness, despicableness, contemptibleness, contemptibility, abominableness, execrableness, obnoxiousness; **vulgarity,** tastelessness, crudity, crudeness, tackiness *and* chintziness <nf>; **vileness** 98.2, foulness, rankness, fulsomeness, grossness, nefariousness, heinousness, **atrociousness,** monstrousness, enormity; degradation, debasement, depravity

4 **infamy,** infamousness; **ignominy,** ignominiousness; ingloriousness, **ignobility,** odium, obloquy, opprobrium, "a long farewell to all my greatness"—Shakespeare; depluming, displuming, loss of honor *or* name *or* repute *or* face; degradation, comedown <nf>, **demotion** 447

5 **disgrace, scandal, humiliation; shame,** dirty shame *and* low-down dirty shame <nf>, crying *or* burning shame; **reproach,** byword, byword of reproach, a disgrace to one's name

6 **stigma,** stigmatism, onus; **brand,** badge of infamy; **slur,** reproach, censure, reprimand, imputation, aspersion, reflection, stigmatization; pillorying; **black eye** <nf>, black mark; **disparagement** 512; **stain, taint,** attaint, **tarnish,** blur, **smirch,** smutch *or* smooch, smudge, **smear,** spot, blot, blot on *or* in one's escutcheon *or* scutcheon; bend *or* bar sinister <heraldry>; baton *and* champain *and* point champain <heraldry>; mark of Cain; broad arrow <Brit>; shady past

VERBS 7 **incur disgrace,** incur disesteem *or* dishonor *or* discredit, get a black eye <nf>, be shamed, earn a bad name *or* reproach *or* reproof, forfeit one's good opinion, fall into disrepute, seal one's infamy; lose one's good name, **lose face,** lose countenance, lose credit, **lose caste; disgrace oneself,** lower oneself, demean oneself, drag one's banner in the dust, degrade *or* debase oneself, act beneath oneself, dirty *or* soil one's hands, get one's hands dirty, sully *or* lower oneself, derogate, stoop, descend, ride to a fall, fall from one's high estate, fall from grace *or* favor, foul one's own nest; **scandalize,** make oneself notorious, put one's good name in jeopardy; compromise oneself; raise eyebrows, cause eyebrows to raise, cause tongues to wag

8 **disgrace, dishonor, discredit,** reflect discredit upon, bring into discredit, reproach, cast reproach upon, be a reproach to; **shame, put to shame,** impute shame to, hold up to shame; hold up to public shame *or* public scorn *or* public ridicule, pillory, bring shame upon, **humiliate** 137.4; **degrade, debase** 447.3, deplume, displume, defrock, unfrock, bring low

9 **stigmatize, brand; stain, besmirch,** smirch, tarnish, taint, attaint, blot, **blacken, smear,** bespatter, desecrate, **sully,** soil, defile, vilify, **slur,** cast a slur upon, blow upon; disapprove 510.10; **disparage, defame** 512.9; censure, reprimand, **give a black eye** <nf>, give a black mark, put in one's bad *or* black books; give a bad name, give a dog a bad name; expose, expose to infamy; pillory, gibbet; burn *or* hang in effigy; **skewer,** impale, crucify

ADJS 10 **disreputable, discreditable, dishonorable,** unsavory, shady, **seamy, sordid; unrespectable, ignoble, ignominious, infamous,** inglorious; notorious; unpraiseworthy; derogatory 512.13

11 **disgraceful, shameful,** pitiful, deplorable,

opprobrious, sad, sorry, too bad; degrading, debasing, demeaning, beneath one, beneath one's dignity, *infra indignitatem* <L>, infra dig <nf>, unbecoming, unworthy of one; cheap, gutter; **humiliating,** humiliative; **scandalous,** shocking, outrageous

12 **base, low,** low rent *and* low ride *and* low-down *and* cotton-picking <nf>, **mean,** crummy <nf>, poor, petty, paltry, small, little, **shabby, shoddy, squalid,** lumpen, scrubby, scummy, scabby, **scurvy,** scruffy, mangy <nf>, measly *and* cheesy <nf>, poky, beggarly, **wretched, miserable,** abject, **despicable, contemptible,** abominable, execrable, obnoxious, **vulgar,** tasteless, crude, **tacky** *and* chintzy <nf>; **disgusting, odious** 98.18, vile, foul, **dirty,** rank, fulsome, gross, flagrant, grave, arrant, nefarious, heinous, reptilian, **atrocious,** monstrous, unspeakable, unmentionable; degraded, debased, depraved

13 **in disrepute,** in bad repute, in bad odor; **in disfavor,** in discredit, **in bad** <nf>, in one's bad *or* black books, out of favor, out of countenance, at a discount; **in disgrace,** in Dutch *and* **in the doghouse** <nf>, under a cloud; scandal-plagued *or* -ridden; stripped of reputation, disgraced, discredited, dishonored, shamed, loaded with shame, unable to show one's face; **in trouble**

14 **unrenowned,** renownless, nameless, inglorious, **unnotable, unnoted,** unnoticed, unremarked, **undistinguished, unfamed,** uncelebrated, unsung, unhonored, unglorified, unpopular; no credit to; **unknown,** little known, obscure, unheard-of, *ignotus* <L>

ADVS 15 **disreputably, discreditably, dishonorably, unrespectably, ignobly, ignominiously, infamously,** ingloriously

16 **disgracefully, scandalously,** shockingly, deplorably, outrageously; **shamefully,** to one's shame, to one's shame be it spoken

17 **basely, meanly,** poorly, pettily, **shabbily, shoddily,** scurvily, **wretchedly, miserably,** abjectly, **despicably, contemptibly,** abominably, execrably, obnoxiously, **odiously** 98.26, **vilely,** foully, grossly, flagrantly, arrantly, nefariously, heinously, **atrociously,** monstrously

662 REPUTE

NOUNS 1 **repute, reputation; name,** character, figure; **fame,** famousness, **renown, kudos,** report, **glory;** éclat, **celebrity, popularity,** recognition, a place in the sun; popular acceptance *or* favor, vogue; **acclaim, public acclaim,** réclame, **publicity; notoriety,** notoriousness, talk of the town; **exposure;** play *and* air-play <nf>

2 **reputability,** reputableness; good reputation, good name, **good** *or* **high repute,** good report, good track record <nf>, good odor, face, fair name, name to conjure with; good reference; good color

3 **esteem,** estimation, **honor, regard, respect,** approval, approbation, account, favor, consideration, **credit,** credibility, points *and* Brownie points <nf>

4 **prestige, honor; dignity; rank, standing,** stature, high place, eminence, position, station, face, **status**

5 **distinction, mark, note; importance, consequence,** significance; **notability, prominence, eminence, preeminence, greatness,** conspicuousness, outstandingness; **stardom;** elevation, exaltation, exaltedness, loftiness, high and mightiness <nf>; nobility, grandeur, sublimity; excellence 999.1, supereminence 999.2

6 **illustriousness, luster,** brilliance *or* brilliancy, radiance, splendor, resplendence *or* resplendency, refulgence *or* refulgency, refulgentness, **glory,** blaze of glory, nimbus, halo, aura, envelope; charisma, mystique, glamour, numinousness, magic; cult of personality, personality cult; claim to fame

7 <posthumous fame> **memory, remembrance,** blessed *or* sacred memory, legend, heroic legend *or* myth; **immortality,** lasting *or* undying fame, niche in the hall of fame, secure place in history; immortal name

8 **glorification, ennoblement,** dignification, **exaltation,** elevation, enskying, enskyment, magnification, aggrandizement; enthronement; immortalization, enshrinement; beatification, canonization, sainting, sanctification; **deification, apotheosis;** lionization

9 **celebrity,** man *or* woman of mark *or* note, person of note *or* consequence, **notable, notability, luminary, great man** *or* **woman,** eminence, master spirit, worthy, name, **big name,** figure, public figure, **somebody; important person, VIP** *and* **standout** <nf>, personage 997.8, one in a hundred *or* thousand *or* million etc; cynosure, model, very model, ideal type, **idol,** popular idol, tin god *or* little tin god <nf>; lion, social lion, pillar of the community; hero, heroine, popular hero, pop hero <nf>, folk hero, superhero; **star, superstar,** megastar, hot stuff <nf>; cult figure *or* hero; **immortal;** luminaries, galaxy, pleiad, constellation; semicelebrity; favorite

VERBS 10 **be somebody,** be something, **impress,** charismatize; **figure,** make *or* cut a figure, cut a dash *and* make a splash <nf>, **make a noise in the world,** make *or* leave one's mark; live, **flourish; shine,** glitter, gleam, glow

11 **gain recognition,** be recognized, get a reputation,

make a name or make a name for oneself, make oneself known, come into one's own, come to the front or fore, come into vogue; **burst onto the scene,** become an overnight celebrity, come onto the scene <nf>, come out of the woods or out of nowhere or out of left field <nf>; make points or Brownie points <nf>

12 **honor,** confer or bestow honor upon; **dignify,** adorn, grace; **distinguish,** signalize, confer distinction on, give credit where credit is due

13 **glorify,** glamorize; **exalt,** elevate, ensky, raise, uplift, set up, **ennoble,** aggrandize, magnify, exalt to the skies; crown; throne, enthrone; immortalize, enshrine, hand one's name down to posterity, make legendary; beatify, canonize, saint, sanctify; **deify,** apotheosize, apotheose; **lionize**

14 **reflect honor,** lend credit or distinction, shed a luster, redound to one's honor, give one a reputation

ADJS 15 **reputable,** highly reputed, of repute, **estimable, esteemed,** much or highly esteemed, **honorable,** honored; **meritorious,** worth one's salt, noble, worthy, creditable; respected, respectable, highly respectable; revered, reverend, venerable, venerated, worshipful; **well-thought-of,** highly regarded, held in esteem, in good odor, in favor, in high favor; in one's good books; prestigious

16 **distinguished,** distingué; **noted, notable,** marked, of note, of mark; **famous,** famed, honored, **renowned, celebrated, popular,** in favor, acclaimed, much acclaimed, sought-after, hot and world-class <nf>, **notorious, well-known,** best-known, in everyone's mouth, on everyone's tongue or lips, talked-of, talked-about; far-famed, far-heard; fabled, legendary, mythical

17 **prominent, conspicuous, outstanding,** stickout <nf>, much in evidence, to the front, in the limelight <nf>; **important,** consequential, significant

18 **eminent, high, exalted,** elevated, enskyed, lofty, sublime, held in awe, awesome; immortal; **great,** big <nf>, **grand;** excellent 999.12,13,15, supereminent, mighty, high and mighty <nf>; glorified, ennobled, magnified, aggrandized; enthroned, throned; immortalized, shrined, enshrined; beatified, canonized, sainted, sanctified; **idolized, godlike, deified,** apotheosized

19 **illustrious,** lustrous, glorious, brilliant, radiant, splendid, splendorous, splendrous, splendent, resplendent, bright, shining; charismatic, glamorous, numinous, magic, magical

ADVS 20 **reputably, estimably, honorably,** nobly, respectably, worthily, creditably

21 **famously, notably, notedly, notoriously,** popularly, celebratedly; **prominently, eminently,** conspicuously, outstandingly; **illustriously,** gloriously

663 SENSUALITY

NOUNS 1 **sensuality,** sensualness, sensualism; appetitiveness, appetite; **voluptuousness,** luxuriousness, luxury; **unchastity** 665; **pleasure-seeking;** sybaritism; **self-indulgence, hedonism,** Cyrenaic hedonism, Cyrenaicism, ethical hedonism, psychological hedonism, hedonics, hedonic calculus; epicurism, epicureanism; pleasure principle, *Lustprinzip* <Ger>; **instant gratification;** sensuousness 24.1

2 **carnality,** carnal-mindedness; **fleshliness,** flesh; animal or carnal nature, the flesh, the beast, Adam, the Old Adam, the offending Adam, fallen state or nature, lapsed state or nature, postlapsarian state or nature; **animality, animalism, bestiality,** beastliness, brutishness, **brutality;** coarseness, grossness; swinishness; **earthiness,** unspirituality, nonspirituality, materialism

3 **sensualist, voluptuary, pleasure-seeker,** sybarite, Cyrenaic, Sardanapalus, Heliogabalus, **hedonist,** *bon vivant* <Fr>, carpet knight; epicure, epicurean; gourmet, gourmand; swine

VERBS 4 sensualize, carnalize, coarsen, brutify; *carpe diem* <L, seize the day>, live for the moment

ADJS 5 **sensual,** sensualist, sensualistic; appetitive; **voluptuous,** luxurious; **unchaste** 665.23, **hedonistic, pleasure-seeking,** pleasure-bent, bent on pleasure, luxury-loving, hedonic, epicurean, sybaritic; Cyrenaic; sensory, sensuous

6 **carnal,** carnal-minded, **fleshly,** bodily, physical; Adamic, fallen, lapsed, postlapsarian; animal, animalistic; **brutish, brutal,** brute; **bestial,** beastly, beastlike; Circean; coarse, gross; swinish; orgiastic; **earthy,** unspiritual, nonspiritual, material, materialistic

664 CHASTITY

NOUNS 1 **chastity, virtue,** virtuousness, honor; **purity,** cleanness, cleanliness; whiteness, snowiness; **immaculacy,** immaculateness, spotlessness, stainlessness, taintlessness, blotlessness, unspottedness, unstainedness, unblottedness, untaintedness, unblemishedness, unsoiledness, unsulliedness, undefiledness, untarnishedness; uncorruptness; sexual innocence, innocence 657

2 **decency, seemliness, propriety, decorum,** decorousness, elegance, delicacy; **modesty,** shame, pudicity, pudency

3 **continence** or continency; abstemiousness,

abstaining, abstinence 668.2; celibacy; **virginity,** intactness, maidenhood, maidenhead; Platonic love; marital fidelity *or* faithfulness

ADJS **4 chaste, virtuous; pure,** purehearted, pure in heart; **clean,** cleanly; **immaculate, spotless,** blotless, stainless, taintless, white, snowy, pure *or* white as driven snow; **unsoiled, unsullied, undefiled,** untarnished, unstained, unspotted, untainted, unblemished, unblotted, uncorrupt; sexually innocent, innocent 657.6,7

5 decent, modest, decorous, delicate, elegant, proper, becoming, seemly

6 continent; abstemious, abstinent 668.10; celibate; virginal, **virgin,** maidenly, vestal, intact; Platonic

7 undebauched, undissipated, undissolute, unwanton, unlicentious

665 UNCHASTITY

NOUNS **1 unchastity,** unchasteness; unvirtuousness; **impurity,** uncleanness, uncleanliness, taintedness, soiledness, sulliedness; **indecency** 666

2 incontinence, uncontinence; intemperance 669; unrestraint 430.3

3 profligacy, dissoluteness, licentiousness, license, unbridledness, wildness, fastness, rakishness, gallantry, **libertinism,** libertinage; **dissipation, debauchery,** debauchment; venery, wenching, whoring, womanizing

4 wantonness, waywardness; looseness, laxity, lightness, loose morals, easy virtue, whorishness, chambering, **promiscuity,** sleeping around *and* swinging <nf>

5 lasciviousness, lechery, lecherousness, lewdness, bawdiness, **dirtiness,** salacity, salaciousness, **carnality,** animality, fleshliness, **sexuality, sexiness, lust, lustfulness; obscenity** 666.4; **prurience** *or* pruriency, sexual itch, concupiscence, lickerishness, libidinousness, randiness, horniness <nf>, lubricity, lubriciousness, **sensuality,** eroticism, goatishness; satyrism, satyriasis, gynecomania; nymphomania, *furor uterinus* <L>, hysteromania, uteromania, clitoromania; erotomania, eroticomania, aphrodisiomania

6 seduction, seducement, **betrayal; violation,** abuse; **debauchment, defilement,** ravishment, ravage, despoilment, fate worse than death; priapism; defloration, deflowering; **rape,** sexual *or* criminal assault; date *or* acquaintance rape

7 <illicit sexual intercourse> **adultery,** criminal conversation *or* congress *or* cohabitation, extramarital *or* premarital sex, extramarital *or* premarital relations, extracurricular sex *or* relations <nf>, **fornication;** free love, free-lovism; **incest;** concubinage; cuckoldry

8 prostitution, harlotry, whoredom, **street-walking;** soliciting, solicitation; Mrs Warren's profession; whoremonging, whoremastery, pimping, pandering

9 brothel, house of prostitution, house of assignation, house of joy *or* ill repute *or* ill fame, **whorehouse,** bawdyhouse, massage parlor, sporting house, disorderly house, **cathouse, bordello,** bagnio, stew, dive, den of vice, den *or* sink of iniquity, crib, joint; panel house *or* den; red-light district, tenderloin, stews, street of fallen women

10 libertine, swinger <nf>, **profligate, rake,** rakehell, rip <nf>, **roué,** wanton, womanizer, cocksman <nf>, walking phallus, debauchee, rounder <old>, **wolf** <nf>, woman chaser, skirt chaser <nf>, gay dog, gay deceiver, gallant, philanderer, lover-boy <nf>, lady-killer, Lothario, Don Juan, Casanova

11 lecher, satyr, goat, old goat, **dirty old man;** whorer *or* whoremonger <old>, whoremaster, whorehound <nf>; Priapus; gynecomaniac; erotomaniac, eroticomaniac, aphrodisiomaniac

12 seducer, betrayer, deceiver; **debaucher, ravisher,** ravager, violator, despoiler, defiler; raper, **rapist**

13 adulterer, cheater, fornicator; adulteress, fornicatress, fornicatrix

14 strumpet, trollop, wench, hussy, slut, jade, baggage, bimbo, *cocotte* <Fr>, grisette; **tart** *and* **chippy** *and* **floozy** *and* broad <nf>, bitch, drab, trull, quean, harridan, Jezebel, harlot, wanton, whore <nf>, bad woman, **loose woman,** easy woman <nf>, easy lay <nf>, woman of easy virtue, frail sister; pickup; nymphomaniac, nymphet, nympho <nf>, hysteromaniac, uteromaniac, clitoromaniac; nymphet

15 demimonde, demimondaine, demirep; **courtesan,** adventuress, **seductress,** femme fatale, vampire, vamp, temptress; hetaera, houri, harem girl, odalisque; Jezebel, Messalina, Delilah, Thais, Phryne, Aspasia, Lais

16 prostitute, harlot, whore, *fille de joie* <Fr>, daughter of joy, lady of the evening, call girl *and* B-girl <nf>, **scarlet woman,** unfortunate woman, painted woman, fallen woman, erring sister, **streetwalker,** hustler *and* **hooker** <nf>, woman of the town, *poule* <Fr>, stew, meretrix, Cyprian, Paphian; white slave

17 mistress, woman, **kept woman,** kept mistress, **paramour,** concubine, doxy, playmate, spiritual *or* unofficial wife; live-in lover <nf>

18 procurer, pimp, pander *or* panderer, *maquereau* <Fr>, mack *or* mackman, ponce <Brit nf>; **bawd; gigolo,** fancy man; procuress, **madam** <nf>; white slaver

VERBS **19 be promiscuous,** sleep around *and*

swing <nf>; **debauch, wanton,** rake, chase women, womanize, whore, sow one's wild oats; **philander; dissipate** 669.6; fornicate, **cheat, commit adultery,** get a little on the side <nf>; grovel, wallow, wallow in the mire

20 **seduce, betray, deceive,** mislead, lead astray, lead down the garden *or* the primrose path; **debauch, ravish,** ravage, despoil, ruin; deflower, pop one's cherry <nf>; **defile,** soil, sully; **violate,** abuse; **rape,** force

21 **prostitute oneself,** sell *or* peddle one's ass <nf>, streetwalk; pimp, procure, pander

22 **cuckold;** wear horns, wear the horn

ADJS 23 **unchaste, unvirtuous,** unvirginal; **impure, unclean; indecent** 666.5; soiled, sullied, smirched, besmirched, defiled, tainted, maculate

24 **incontinent,** uncontinent; **orgiastic;** intemperate 669.7; unrestrained

25 **profligate, licentious,** unbridled, untrammeled, uninhibited, free; **dissolute, dissipated, debauched,** abandoned; **wild, fast,** gallant, gay, rakish; rakehell, rakehellish, rakehelly

26 **wanton, wayward,** Paphian; **loose,** lax, slack, loose-moraled, of loose morals, of easy virtue, easy <nf>, **light,** no better than she should be, whorish, chambering, **promiscuous**

27 freeloving; **adulterous,** illicit, extramarital, premarital; incestuous

28 **prostitute, prostituted, whorish, harlot,** scarlet, fallen, meretricious, streetwalking, hustling <nf>, on the town *or* streets, on the *pavé,* in the life

29 **lascivious, lecherous, sexy, salacious, carnal,** animal, **sexual, lustful,** ithyphallic, **hot,** horny *and* sexed-up *and* hot to trot <nf>; prurient, itching, itchy <nf>; concupiscent, lickerish, libidinous, randy, horny <nf>, lubricious; **lewd, bawdy,** adult, X-rated, hard, pornographic, porno <nf>, **dirty, obscene** 666.9; erotic, **sensual,** fleshly; goatish, satyric, priapic, gynecomaniacal; nymphomaniacal, hysteromaniacal, uteromaniacal, clitoromaniacal; erotomaniacal, eroticomaniacal, aphrodisiomaniacal

666 INDECENCY

NOUNS 1 **indecency, indelicacy,** inelegance *or* inelegancy, **indecorousness,** indecorum, **impropriety** 638.1, inappropriateness, unseemliness, indiscretion, indiscreetness; **unchastity** 665

2 **immodesty,** unmodestness, impudicity; exhibitionism; **shamelessness,** unembarrassedness; **brazenness** 142.2, brassiness, pertness, forwardness, boldness, procacity, bumptiousness; **flagrancy,** notoriousness, scandal, scandalousness

3 **vulgarity** 497, **uncouthness, coarseness, crudeness, grossness,** rankness, rawness, raunchiness <nf>; **earthiness,** frankness; **spiciness, raciness,** saltiness

4 **obscenity, dirtiness,** bawdry, raunch <nf>, **ribaldry, pornography,** porno *and* porn <nf>, hard *or* hard-core pornography, soft *or* soft-core pornography, salacity, **smut, dirt, filth; lewdness, bawdiness,** salaciousness, **smuttiness, foulness, filthiness,** nastiness, vileness, offensiveness; scurrility, fescenninity; Rabelaisianism; erotic art *or* literature, pornographic art or literature; sexploitation; blue movie *and* dirty movie *and* porno film *and* skin flick <nf>, adult movie, stag film <nf>, X-rated movie; pornographomania, erotographomania, iconolagny, erotology; **dirty talk, scatology** 523.9

ADJS 5 **indecent, indelicate, inelegant, indecorous, improper,** inappropriate, **unseemly, unbecoming,** indiscreet

6 **immodest,** unmodest; exhibitionistic; **shameless,** unashamed, unembarrassed, unabashed, unblushing, **brazen,** brazenfaced, brassy; **forward,** bold, pert, procacious <old>, bumptious; **flagrant,** notorious, scandalous

7 **risqué,** risky, **racy,** salty, spicy, **off-color,** suggestive, scabrous

8 **vulgar, uncouth, coarse, gross,** rank, raw, broad, low, foul, gutter; **earthy,** frank, pulling no punches

9 **obscene, lewd, adult, bawdy,** ithyphallic, **ribald, pornographic, salacious,** sultry <nf>, lurid, **dirty, smutty,** raunchy <nf>, blue, smoking-room, impure, unchaste, unclean, **foul, filthy, nasty,** vile, fulsome, offensive, unprintable, unrepeatable, not fit for mixed company; scurrilous, scurrile, Fescennine; **foulmouthed,** foul-tongued, foul-spoken; Rabelaisian

667 ASCETICISM

NOUNS 1 **asceticism, austerity, self-denial,** self-abnegation, **rigor; puritanism,** eremitism, anchoritism, anchorite *or* anchoritic monasticism, monasticism, monachism; Sabbatarianism; Albigensianism, Waldensianism, Catharism; Yoga; mortification, self-mortification, maceration, flagellation; **abstinence** 668.2; belt-tightening, fasting 515; voluntary poverty, mendicantism, Franciscanism; Trappism

2 **ascetic, puritan,** Sabbatarian; Albigensian, Waldensian, Catharist; **abstainer** 668.4; anchorite, **hermit** 584.5; yogi, yogin; sannyasi, bhikshu, dervish, fakir, flagellant, Penitente; mendicant, Franciscan, Discalced *or* barefooted Carmelite; Trappist

VERBS 3 deny oneself; abstain, tighten one's belt;

flagellate oneself, wear a hair shirt, make oneself miserable

ADJS **4** ascetic, austere, self-denying, self-abnegating, **rigorous, rigoristic; puritanical,** eremitic, anchoritic, Sabbatarian; **penitential;** Albigensian, Waldensian, Catharist; **abstinent** 668.10; mendicant, discalced, barefoot, wedded to poverty, Franciscan; Trappist; flagellant

668 TEMPERANCE

NOUNS **1** temperance, temperateness, **moderation,** moderateness, sophrosyne; golden mean, via media, *juste milieu* <Fr>; nothing in excess, sobriety, soberness, frugality, forbearance, abnegation; renunciation, renouncement, forgoing; denial, **self-denial;** restraint, constraint, **self-restraint; self-control,** self-reining, self-mastery, **discipline,** self-discipline

2 abstinence, abstention, abstainment, **abstemiousness,** refraining, refrainment, avoidance, eschewal, denying *or* refusing oneself, saying no to, passing up <nf>; **total abstinence, teetotalism,** nephalism, Rechabitism; the pledge; Encratism, Shakerism; Pythagorism, Pythagoreanism; sexual abstinence, celibacy 565; chastity 664; gymnosophy; Stoicism; vegetarianism, veganism, fruitarianism; plain living, spare diet, simple diet; Spartan fare, Lenten fare; fish day, Friday, banyan day; fast 515.2,3; **continence** 664.3; **asceticism** 667; smokeout

3 prohibition, prohibitionism; Eighteenth Amendment, Volstead Act

4 abstainer, abstinent; **teetotaler,** teetotalist, sobersides <nf>; nephalist, Rechabite, hydropot, water-drinker; vegetarian, vegan, fruitarian; banian, banya; gymnosophist; Pythagorean, Pythagorist; Encratite, Apostolici, Shaker; **ascetic** 667.2; nonsmoker, nondrinker, etc

5 prohibitionist, dry <nf>; Anti-Saloon League; Women's Christian Temperance Union *or* WCTU

VERBS **6** restrain oneself, constrain oneself, curb oneself, hold back, **avoid excess; limit oneself, restrict oneself; control oneself,** control one's appetites, repress *or* inhibit one's desires, contain oneself, discipline oneself, master oneself, exercise self-control *or* self-restraint, keep oneself under control, keep in *or* within bounds, keep within compass *or* limits, know when one has had enough, **deny** *or* refuse oneself, **say no** *or* just say no; live plainly *or* simply *or* frugally; mortify oneself, mortify the flesh, control the fleshy lusts, control the carnal man *or* the old Adam; eat to live, not live to eat; eat sparingly, diet; tighten one's belt

7 abstain, abstain from, refrain, **refrain from,** forbear, forgo, spare, withhold, hold back, **avoid, shun,** eschew, **pass up** <nf>, **keep from,** keep *or* stand *or* hold aloof from, have nothing to do with, take no part in, have no hand in, **let alone,** let well enough alone, let go by, **deny oneself,** do without, go without, make do without, not *or* never touch, keep hands off; fast

8 swear off, renounce, forswear, **give up,** abandon, stop, discontinue; take the pledge, get on the wagon *or* water wagon <nf>, go on the wagon <nf>; **kick** *and* kick the habit <nf>, dry out

ADJS **9** temperate, moderate, sober, frugal, restrained, **sparing,** stinting, measured

10 abstinent, abstentious, **abstemious;** teetotal, sworn off, on the wagon *or* water wagon <nf>; nephalistic, Rechabite; Encratic, Apostolic, Shaker; Pythagorean; sexually abstinent, celibate, chaste; Stoic; fasting; vegetarian, veganistic, vegan, fruitarian; Spartan, Lenten; maigre, meatless; **continent** 664.6; **ascetic**

11 **prohibitionist, antisaloon, dry** <nf>

ADVS **12** temperately, moderately, sparingly, stintingly, frugally, in moderation, within compass *or* bounds

669 INTEMPERANCE

NOUNS **1** intemperance, intemperateness, **indulgence, self-indulgence,** self-absorption; **overindulgence,** overdoing; **unrestraint,** unconstraint, indiscipline, uncontrol; **immoderation,** immoderacy, immoderateness; inordinacy, inordinateness; **excess, excessiveness,** too much, too-muchness <nf>; addiction; prodigality, extravagance; crapulence *or* crapulency, crapulousness; **incontinence** 665.2; **swinishness, gluttony** 672; **drunkenness** 88.1

2 dissipation, licentiousness; riotous living, free living, high living <nf>, fast *or* killing pace, fast lane <nf>, burning the candle at both ends; **debauchery,** debauchment; **carousal** 88.5, carousing, carouse; **debauch, orgy,** saturnalia; hedonism, sybaritism

3 dissipater, rounder <old>, free liver, high liver <nf>; nighthawk *and* nightowl <nf>; debauchee; **playboy,** partyer, partygoer, party girl; pleasure-seeker

VERBS **4** indulge, indulge oneself, indulge one's appetites, "indulge in easy vices"—Samuel Johnson, deny oneself nothing *or* not at all; **give oneself up to,** give free course to, give free rein to; live well *or* high, live high on the hog <nf>, live it up <nf>, live off the fat of the land; indulge in, luxuriate in, wallow in; roll in; look out for number one

5 **overindulge, overdo, carry to excess,** carry too far, go the limit, go whole hog <nf>, know no limits, not know when to stop, bite off more than one can chew, spread oneself too thin; dine not wisely but too well; live above *or* beyond one's means; binge <nf>

6 **dissipate,** plunge into dissipation, **debauch, wanton, carouse,** run riot, live hard *or* fast, squander one's money in riotous living, burn the candle at both ends, keep up a fast *or* killing pace, not know when to stop, sow one's wild oats, have one's fling, **party** <nf>, "eat, drink, and be merry"—Bible

ADJS 7 **intemperate, indulgent, self-indulgent; overindulgent,** overindulging, unthrifty, unfrugal, **immoderate,** inordinate, **excessive,** too much, prodigal, extravagant, extreme, unmeasured, unlimited; crapulous, crapulent; undisciplined, uncontrolled, unbridled, unconstrained, uninhibited, **unrestrained; incontinent** 665.24; **swinish, gluttonous** 672.6; bibulous

8 **licentious, dissipated, riotous, dissolute, debauched;** free-living, high-living <nf>

9 **orgiastic,** saturnalian, corybantic

ADVS 10 **intemperately,** prodigally, **immoderately,** inordinately, excessively, **in** *or* **to excess,** to extremes, beyond all bounds *or* limits, without restraint; high, high on the hog <nf>

670 MODERATION

NOUNS 1 **moderation,** moderateness; **restraint,** constraint, control; **judiciousness,** prudence; steadiness, evenness, balance, equilibrium, **stability** 855; **temperateness,** temperance, sobriety; self-abnegation, self-restraint, self-control, self-denial; abstinence, continence, abnegation; **mildness,** lenity, gentleness; calmness, serenity, tranquillity, repose, calm, cool <nf>; unexcessiveness, unextremeness, unextravagance, nothing in excess, *meden agan* <Gk>; **happy medium, golden mean,** *juste-milieu* <Fr>, middle way *or* path, *via media* <L>, balancing act <nf>; moderationism, **conservatism** 853.3; **nonviolence,** pacifism, pacification, peace movement, ahimsa; impartiality, neutrality, dispassion; irenics, ecumenism

2 modulation, **abatement,** remission, **mitigation,** diminution, defusing, de-escalation, **reduction,** lessening, falling-off; **relaxation,** relaxing, slackening, **easing,** loosening, letup *and* letdown <nf>; **alleviation,** assuagement, allayment, palliation, leniency, relenting, lightening, **tempering, softening,** subdual; **deadening, dulling,** damping, blunting; drugging, narcotizing, sedating, sedation; **pacification, tranquilization,**

tranquilizing, mollification, demulsion, dulcification, **quieting,** quietening, lulling, **soothing, calming,** hushing

3 **moderator, mitigator,** modulator, stabilizer, temperer, assuager; **mediator, bridge-builder,** calming *or* restraining hand, wiser head; **alleviator,** alleviative, palliative, lenitive; **pacifier, soother,** comforter, peacemaker, pacificator, dove of peace, mollifier; **drug,** anodyne, dolorifuge, soothing syrup, **tranquilizer,** calmative; **sedative** 86.12; balm, salve; cushion, shock absorber

4 **moderate,** moderatist, moderationist, middle-of-the-roader, **centrist,** neutral, compromiser; **conservative** 853.4

VERBS 5 **be moderate, keep within bounds,** keep within compass; practice self-control *or* self-denial, live within one's means, live temperately, do nothing in excess, strike a balance, strike *or* keep a happy medium, seek the golden mean, steer *or* preserve an even course, keep to the middle path *or* way, steer *or* be between Scylla and Charybdis; keep the peace, not resist, espouse *or* practice nonviolence, be pacifistic; not rock the boat *and* not make waves *or* static <nf>; cool it *and* keep one's cool <nf>, keep one's head *or* temper; sober down, settle down; remit, relent; take in sail; go out like a lamb; be conservative 853.6

6 **moderate, restrain,** constrain, control, **keep within bounds; modulate, mitigate,** defuse, abate, weaken, **diminish, reduce,** de-escalate, slacken, lessen, slow down; **alleviate,** assuage, allay, lay, lighten, palliate, extenuate, **temper,** attemper, lenify; **soften, subdue,** tame, hold in check, keep a tight rein, chasten, underplay, play down, downplay, de-emphasize, tone *or* tune down; turn down the volume, lower the voice; **drug,** narcotize, sedate, tranquilize, deaden, dull, blunt, obtund, take the edge off, take the sting *or* bite out; smother, suppress, stifle; **damp, dampen,** bank the fire, reduce the temperature, throw cold water on, throw a wet blanket on; sober, sober down *or* up; clear the air

7 **calm,** calm down, **stabilize, tranquilize, pacify,** mollify, appease, dulcify; **quiet,** hush, still, rest, compose, **lull, soothe,** gentle, rock, cradle, rock to sleep; cool, **subdue,** quell; ease, steady, smooth, smoothen, smooth over, smooth down, even out; keep the peace, be the dove of peace, pour oil on troubled waters, pour balm into

8 **cushion,** absorb the shock, **soften the blow,** break the fall, deaden, damp *or* dampen, soften, suppress, neutralize, offset; show pity *or* mercy *or* consideration *or* sensitivity, temper the wind to the shorn lamb

9 **relax,** unbend; ease, **ease up,** ease off, **let up,** let

down; abate, bate, remit, mitigate; **slacken,** slack, slake, slack off, slack up; loose, **loosen;** unbrace, unstrain, unstring

ADJS **10 moderate, temperate,** sober; **mild,** soft, bland, **gentle,** tame; mild as milk *or* mother's milk, mild as milk and water, gentle as a lamb; nonviolent, peaceable, peaceful, pacifistic; **judicious, prudent**

11 restrained, constrained, limited, controlled, **stable,** in control, in hand; tempered, **softened,** hushed, **subdued,** quelled, chastened

12 unexcessive, unextreme, unextravagant, **conservative;** reasonable

13 equable, even, low-key *or* low-keyed, **cool,** even-tempered, level-headed, dispassionate; tranquil, reposeful, serene, calm 173.12

14 mitigating, assuaging, abating, **diminishing, reducing,** lessening, allaying, **alleviating, relaxing, easing;** tempering, **softening,** chastening, **subduing;** deadening, dulling, blunting, damping, dampening, cushioning

15 tranquilizing, pacifying, mollifying, appeasing; cooling-off; **calming,** lulling, gentling, rocking, cradling, hushing, quietening, stilling; **soothing,** soothful, restful; dreamy, drowsy

16 palliative, alleviative, alleviatory, assuasive, lenitive, **calmative,** calmant, **narcotic, sedative,** demulcent, anodyne; antiorgastic, anaphrodisiac

ADVS **17 moderately, in moderation,** restrainedly, subduedly, in *or* within reason, within bounds *or* compass, in balance; **temperately,** soberly, prudently, judiciously, dispassionately; composedly, calmly, coolly, evenly, steadily, equably, tranquilly, serenely; soothingly, conservatively

671 VIOLENCE
<vehement action>

NOUNS **1 violence, vehemence, virulence, venom, furiousness, force, rigor,** roughness, harshness, ungentleness, extremity, impetuosity, inclemency, **severity, intensity,** acuteness, **sharpness; acrimony** 17.5; fierceness, ferociousness, ferocity, furiousness, viciousness, insensateness, savagery, destructiveness, **destruction, vandalism; terrorism, barbarity, brutality, atrocity,** inhumanity, bloodlust, killer instinct, murderousness, malignity, mercilessness, pitilessness, mindlessness, animality, brutishness; **rage,** raging, **anger** 152

2 turbulence, turmoil, chaos, upset, **fury, furor,** *furore* <Ital>, **rage, frenzy, passion,** fanaticism, zealousness, zeal, tempestuousness, storminess, wildness, tumultuousness, **tumult, uproar,** racket, cacophony, pandemonium, hubbub, **commotion, disturbance, agitation,** bluster, broil, brawl, embroilment, brouhaha, fuss, flap <Brit nf>, **row, rumpus,** ruckus <nf>, foofaraw <nf>, **ferment,** fume, boil, boiling, seething, ebullition, fomentation; all hell let loose

3 unruliness, disorderliness, obstreperousness, Katy-bar-the-door <nf>; **riot, rioting;** looting, pillaging, plundering, rapine; wilding <nf>; laying waste, sowing with salt, sacking; scorched earth; **attack** 459, **assault,** onslaught, battering; **rape, violation,** forcible seizure; **killing** 308, butchery, massacre, slaughter

4 storm, tempest, squall, line squall, **tornado, cyclone, hurricane,** tropical cyclone, typhoon, storm-center, tropical storm, eye of the storm *or* hurricane, war of the elements, "groans of roaring wind and rain"—Shakespeare; stormy weather, rough weather, foul weather, dirty weather; rainstorm 316.2; thunderstorm 316.3; windstorm 318.12; **snowstorm** 1023.8; **firestorm**

5 upheaval, convulsion, cataclysm, catastrophe, disaster; meltdown; **fit,** spasm, **paroxysm,** apoplexy, stroke; climax; **earthquake,** quake, temblor, diastrophism, epicentre, shock-wave; tidal wave, *tsunami* <Japanese>

6 outburst, outbreak, eruption, debouchment, eructation, belch, spew; **burst,** dissilience *or* dissiliency; meltdown, atomic meltdown; **torrent,** rush, gush, spate, cascade, spurt, jet, rapids, **volcano,** volcan, burning mountain

7 explosion, discharge, blowout, blowup, detonation, fulmination, **blast, burst, report** 56.1; flash, flash *or* flashing point, flare, flare-up, fulguration; bang, boom 56.4; backfire

8 concussion, shock, impact, crunch, smash; percussion, repercussion

9 <violent person> berserk *or* berserker; **hothead,** hotspur; **devil, demon, fiend, brute,** hellhound, hellcat, hellion, hell-raiser; **beast,** wild beast, tiger, dragon, mad dog, wolf, monster, mutant, savage; **rapist, mugger, killer;** Mafioso, hit man <nf>, contract killer, hired killer, hired gun; **fury,** virago, vixen, termagant, beldam, she-wolf, tigress, witch; firebrand, revolutionary 860.3, **terrorist,** incendiary, bomber, guerrilla

10 <nf terms> **goon, gorilla,** ape, knuckle dragger, muscle man, plug-ugly, shtarker, cowboy, bimbo, bozo, bruiser, hardnose, tough guy, tough, hoodlum, hood, meat-eater, gunsel, terror, holy terror, fire-eater, spitfire, tough *or* ugly customer

VERBS **11 rage, storm, rant, rave,** roar; **rampage,** ramp, **tear,** tear around; go *or* carry on <nf>; come in like a lion; **destroy, wreck,** wreak havoc, ruin; sow chaos *or* disorder; **terrorize,** sow terror, vandalize, barbarize, brutalize; **riot,** loot, burn, pillage, sack, lay waste; **slaughter, butcher; rape,** violate; **attack, assault,** batter, savage, mug, maul, hammer; go for the jugular

12 seethe, boil, fume, foam, simmer, stew, ferment, stir, churn, see red

13 erupt, burst forth or out, **break out, blow out** or **open,** eruct, belch, **vomit,** spout, spew, disgorge, **discharge,** eject, throw or hurl forth

14 explode, blow up, burst, go off, go up, blow out, blast, bust <nf>; **detonate,** fulminate; **touch off,** trigger, trip, set off, let off; **discharge,** fire, shoot; backfire; melt down

15 run amok, go berserk, go on a rampage, cut loose, run riot, run wild

ADJS **16 violent, vehement, virulent, venomous, severe, rigorous, furious, fierce, intense,** sharp, acute, keen, cutting, splitting, piercing; **destructive;** rough, bruising, tough <nf>; **drastic,** extreme, outrageous, excessive, exorbitant, unconscionable, intemperate, immoderate, extravagant; acrimonious 17.14; on the warpath

17 unmitigated, unsoftened, untempered, unallayed, unsubdued, unquelled; unquenched, unextinguished, unabated; unmixed, unalloyed; **total**

18 turbulent, tumultuous, raging, chaotic, hellish, anarchic, **storming,** stormy, **tempestuous,** troublous, **frenzied, wild, wild-eyed, frantic, furious,** infuriate, insensate, **mad,** demented, insane, enraged, ravening, raving, slavering; **angry; blustering,** blustery, blusterous; **uproarious,** rip-roaring <nf>; pandemoniac

19 unruly, disorderly, obstreperous; **unbridled; riotous,** wild, rampant; **terroristic,** anarchic, nihilistic, revolutionary 860.5

20 boisterous, rampageous, rambunctious <nf>, on the rampage, rumbustious, roisterous, wild, rollicking, **rowdy,** rough, hoody <nf>, harum-scarum <nf>; knockabout, rough-and-tumble, knock-down-and-drag-out <nf>

21 savage, fierce, ferocious, vicious, murderous, cruel, atrocious, mindless, brutal, brutish, **bestial,** insensate, monstrous, mutant, inhuman, pitiless, ruthless, merciless, bloody, sanguinary, kill-crazy <nf>; malign, malignant; feral, ferine; **wild,** untamed, tameless, undomesticated, ungentle; **barbarous,** barbaric; **uncivilized,** noncivilized

22 fiery, heated, inflamed, flaming, scorching, hot, red-hot, white-hot; **fanatic, zealous,** totally committed, hard-core, hard-line, ardent, passionate; **hotheaded**

23 convulsive, cataclysmic, disastrous, upheaving; seismic; **spasmodic,** paroxysmal, spastic, jerky, herky-jerky <nf>; orgasmic

24 explosive, bursting, detonating, explosible, explodable, fulminating, fulminant, fulminatory; cataclysmic; dissilient; **volcanic,** eruptive

ADVS **25 violently, vehemently, virulently, venomously, rigorously, severely, fiercely, drastically; furiously,** wildly, madly, **like mad,** like fury <nf>, like blazes; all to pieces, with a vengeance

26 turbulently, tumultuously, riotously, uproariously, stormily, tempestuously, troublously, **frenziedly, frantically, furiously, ragingly, enragedly, madly; angrily** 152.33

27 savagely, fiercely, ferociously, atrociously, viciously, murderously, brutally or brutishly, mindlessly, bestially, barbarously, inhumanly, insensately, ruthlessly, pitilessly, mercilessly; **tooth and nail,** tooth and claw, bec et ongles <Fr>

672 GLUTTONY

NOUNS **1 gluttony,** gluttonousness, **greed,** greediness, voraciousness, voracity, ravenousness, edacity, crapulence or crapulency, gulosity, rapacity, insatiability; omnivorousness; big appetite, **piggishness, hoggishness,** swinishness, "swinish gluttony"—Milton; **overindulgence, overeating;** eating disorder, polyphagia, hyperphagia, bulimia, bulimia nervosa, binge-purge syndrome, binging <nf>; **intemperance** 669

2 epicurism, epicureanism, gourmandise; gastronomy

3 glutton, greedy eater, big or hearty or good eater <nf>, trencherman, trencherwoman, belly-god, gobbler, greedygut or greedyguts <nf>, gorger, **gourmand,** gourmandizer, gormand, gormandizer, guttler, cormorant, bon vivant; animal, **hog** and **pig** and chow hound and khazer and gobbler and wolf <nf>; omnivore; binger

VERBS **4 gluttonize,** gormandize, **indulge one's appetite,** live to eat, love to eat; **gorge,** engorge, glut, cram, stuff, batten, guttle, guzzle, **devour,** raven, bolt, gobble, gulp, **wolf,** gobble or gulp or bolt or wolf down, eat like a horse, tuck into, stuff oneself and hog it down and eat one's head off and fork or shovel it in <nf>, eat one out of house and home, wipe the plate clean

5 overeat, overgorge, **overindulge, make a pig** or **hog of oneself, pig out** or pork out or scarf out <nf>; glut oneself, stuff oneself

ADJS **6 gluttonous, greedy,** voracious, ravenous, edacious, esurient, rapacious, insatiable, polyphagic, bulimic, hyperphagic, Apician; **piggish, hoggish,** swinish; crapulous, crapulent; intemperate 669.7; omnivorous, all-devouring; **gorging,** cramming, glutting, guttling, stuffing,

guzzling, wolfing, bolting, **gobbling, gulping,** gluttonizing; binging <nf>
7 overfed, overgorged, overindulged
ADVS **8 gluttonously, greedily,** voraciously, ravenously, edaciously; **piggishly, hoggishly, swinishly**

673 LEGALITY

NOUNS **1 legality, legitimacy, lawfulness, legitimateness, licitness,** rightfulness, validity, scope, applicability; **jurisdiction** 594; actionability, justiciability, **constitutionality,** constitutional validity; letter of the law; legal process, legal form, **due process;** legalism, constitutionalism; **justice** 649
2 legalization, legitimation, legitimatization, decriminalization; money-washing or -laundering; validation; authorization, sanction; legislation, enactment, authority, license, warrant
3 law, *lex* and *jus* <L>, **statute,** rubric, **canon,** institution; **ordinance; act, enactment, measure,** legislation; **rule, ruling; prescript,** prescription; **regulation,** *règlement* <Fr>, reg <nf>; **dictate,** dictation; form, formula, formulary, formality; standing order; bylaw; **edict, decree** 420.4; **bill;** manifesto, order, standing order, rescript, precept
4 law, legal system, system of laws, legal branch or specialty
5 code, digest, pandect, capitulary, **body of law,** corpus juris, legal code, code of laws, digest of law; **codification; civil code, penal code;** Justinian Code; Napoleonic code, *Code Napoléon* <Fr>; lawbook, statute book, compilation; Blackstone; Uniform Code of Military Justice; written law, unwritten law, statute law, common law, private law, international law, military law, commercial law, contracts law, criminal law, civil law, labor law, constitutional law; law of the land; canon
6 constitution, written constitution, unwritten constitution; law and equity; charter, codification, codified law; constitutional amendment; Bill of Rights, constitutional guarantees; constitutional interpretation
7 jurisprudence, law, legal science; nomology, nomography; **forensic science,** science of law, forensic or legal medicine, medical jurisprudence, medico-legal medicine; forensic psychiatry; forensic or legal chemistry; criminology; constitutionalism, penology
8 <codes of law> Constitution of the U.S., Bill of Rights; Corpus Juris Civilis, Codex Juris Canonici, Digest or Pandects of Justinian; Law of Moses, Ten Commandments, Pentateuch, Torah, Koran or

Qur'an, the Bible; Code of Hammurabi, Magna Carta, Napoleonic Code
VERBS **9 legalize, legitimize,** legitimatize, legitimate, make legal, declare lawful, **decriminalize;** wash or launder money; validate; **authorize, sanction,** license, warrant; constitute, ordain, establish, put in force; prescribe, formulate; regulate, make a regulation, bring within the law; **decree; legislate, enact; enforce; litigate** 598.12, take legal action
10 codify, digest; compile, publish
ADJS **11 legal, legitimate,** legit *and* kosher <nf>, competent, by right, de jure, **licit, lawful,** rightful, according to law, within the law; **actionable,** litigable, justiciable, within the scope of the law; **enforceable,** legally binding; **judicial,** juridical; **authorized, sanctioned,** valid, applicable, warranted; **constitutional;** statutory, statutable; legalized, legitimized, decriminalized; **legislative, lawmaking;** lawlike; **just** 649.8
12 jurisprudent, jurisprudential; **legalistic; forensic;** nomistic, nomothetic; criminological
ADVS **13 legally, legitimately, licitly, lawfully,** by law, *de jure* <L>, in the eyes of the law, within the law

674 ILLEGALITY

NOUNS **1 illegality, unlawfulness, illicitness, lawlessness,** wrongfulness; unauthorization, impermissibility, **unconstitutionality;** legal or technical flaw, legal irregularity; **outlawry; anarchy,** collapse or breakdown or paralysis of authority, anomie; illicit business 732
2 illegitimacy, illegitimateness, illegitimation; **bastardy,** bastardism; bend or bar sinister, baton
3 lawbreaking, violation, breach or violation of law, infringement, contravention, infraction, **transgression,** trespass, trespassing, offense, breach, nonfeasance, encroachment; vice, fraud; crime, **criminality,** criminalism, habitual criminality, delinquency; flouting or making a mockery of the law
4 offense, wrong, illegality; **violation** 435.2; **wrongdoing** 655; much to answer for; **crime, felony; misdemeanor;** tort; delict, delictum
VERBS **5 break** or **violate the law,** breach the law, infringe, contravene, infract, violate 435.4, **transgress, trespass,** disobey the law, offend against the law, flout the law, make a mockery of the law, fly in the face of the law, set the law at defiance, snap one's fingers at the law, set the law at naught, circumvent the law, disregard the law, **take the law into one's own hands,** twist or torture the law to one's own ends or purposes; commit a crime; have much to answer for; live outside the law

ADJS **6 illegal, unlawful, illegitimate, illicit,** nonlicit,
nonlegal, lawless, wrongful, fraudulent, creative
<nf>, **against the law; unauthorized,** unallowed,
impermissible, unwarranted, unwarrantable,
unofficial, unlicensed; unstatutory, instatutory,
injudicial, extrajudicial; **unconstitutional,**
nonconstitutional; flawed, irregular, contrary to
law; actionable, chargeable, justiciable, litigable;
triable, punishable; **criminal, felonious; outlaw,
outlawed; contraband,** bootleg, black-market;
under-the-table, under-the-counter; unregulated,
unchartered; anarchic, anarchistic, anomic

7 illegitimate, spurious, false; **bastard,** misbegot,
misbegotten, miscreated, gotten on the wrong side
of the blanket, baseborn, born out of wedlock,
without benefit of clergy

ADVS **8 illegally, unlawfully, illegitimately, illicitly;**
impermissibly; criminally, feloniously; contrary to
law, in violation of law, against the law

675 RELIGIONS, CULTS, SECTS

NOUNS **1 religion,** religious belief *or* faith, **belief,
faith,** teaching, doctrine, creed, credo, dogma,
theology 676, orthodoxy 687; system of beliefs;
persuasion, tradition

2 cult, ism; cultism; **mystique**

3 sect <see list>, sectarism, religious order,
denomination, persuasion, faction, **church,**
communion, community, group, fellowship,
affiliation, order, school, party, society, body,
organization; branch, variety, version, segment;
offshoot; **schism,** division

4 sectarianism, sectarism, **denominationalism,**
partisanism, the clash of creeds; schismatism;
syncretism, eclecticism

5 theism; monotheism; polytheism, multitheism,
myriotheism; **ditheism,** dyotheism, dualism;
tritheism; tetratheism; **pantheism,** cosmotheism,
theopantism, acosmism; physitheism,
psychotheism, animotheism; physicomorphism;
hylotheism; anthropotheism, anthropomorphism;
anthropolatry; allotheism; monolatry, henotheism;
autotheism; zootheism, theriotheism; **deism**

6 animism, animistic **religion** *or* cult; voodooism,
voodoo, hoodoo, wanga, juju, jujuism, obeah,
obeahism; shamanism; fetishism, totemism; nature
worship, naturism; primitive religion

7 Christianity <see list>, Christianism,
Christendom; Latin *or* Roman *or* Western
Christianity; Eastern *or* Orthodox Christianity;
Protestant Christianity; Judeo-Christian religion *or*
tradition *or* belief; fundamentalism, Christian
fundamentalism

8 Catholicism, Catholicity; **Roman Catholicism,**
Romanism, Rome; papalism; popery *and* popeism
and papism *and* papistry <nf>; ultramontanism;
Catholic Church, **Roman Catholic Church,** Church
of Rome; Eastern Rites, Uniate Rites, Uniatism;
Alexandrian *or* Antiochian *or* Byzantine Rite

9 Orthodoxy; Eastern Orthodox Church, Holy
Orthodox Catholic Apostolic Church, Greek
Orthodox Church, Russian Orthodox Church;
patriarchate of Constantinople, patriarchate of
Antioch, patriarchate of Alexandria, patriarchate
of Jerusalem

10 Protestantism, Reform, Reformationism;
Evangelicalism; Zwinglianism; dissent 333;
apostasy 363.2; new theology

11 Anglicanism; High-Churchism, Low-Churchism;
Anglo-Catholicism; Church of England,
Established Church; High Church, Low Church;
Broad Church, Free Church

12 Judaism; Hebraism, Hebrewism; Israelitism;
Orthodox Judaism, Conservative Judaism, Reform
Judaism, Reconstructionism; Hasidism;
rabbinism, Talmudism; Pharisaism; Sadduceeism;
Karaism *or* Karaitism

13 Islam, Muslimism, Islamism, Moslemism,
Muhammadanism, Mohammedanism; Sufism,
Wahabiism, Sunnism, Shiism, Druzism; Black
Muslimism; Muslim fundamentalism, militant
Muslimism

14 <other religions> Christian Science; Mormonism;
New Thought, Higher Thought, Practical
Christianity, Mental Science, Divine Science
Church; Buddhism, Zen Buddhism; Hinduism;
Sikhism; Shintoism; Jainism; Rastafarianism;
Zoroastrianism; Confucianism

15 religionist, religioner; zealot, iconoclast; **believer**
692.4; worshiper; cultist

16 theist; monotheist; polytheist, multitheist,
myriotheist; ditheist, dualist; tritheist; tetratheist;
pantheist, cosmotheist; psychotheist; physitheist;
hylotheist; anthropotheist; anthropolater;
allotheist; henotheist; autotheist; zootheist,
theriotheist; **deist**

17 Christian, Nazarene, Nazarite; practicing
Christian; Christian sectarian

18 sectarian, sectary, **denominationalist,** factionist,
schismatic

19 Catholic, Roman Catholic *or* RC <nf>, Romanist,
papist <nf>; ultramontane; Eastern-Rite
Christian, Uniate

20 Protestant, non-Catholic, Reformed believer,
Reformationist, Evangelical; Zwinglian; dissenter
333.3; apostate 363.5; Anglican, Episcopalian,
Unitarian, born-again Christian

21 Jew, Hebrew, Judaist, Israelite; Orthodox *or*
Conservative *or* Reform Jew, Reconstructionist;

Hasid; Zionist; Essene; Rabbinist, Talmudist; Pharisee; Sadducee; Karaite

22 Mormon, Latter-day Saint, Josephite <nf>

23 Muslim, Muhammadan *and* Mohammedan <nf>, Mussulman, Moslem, Islamite; Shiite, Shia, Sectary; Motazilite, Sunni, Sunnite, Wahhabi, Sufi, Druze; dervish; abdal; Black Muslim; Muslim fundamentalist *or* militant

24 Christian Scientist, Christian Science Practitioner

ADJS **25 religious, theistic; monotheistic; polytheistic,** ditheistic, tritheistic, **pantheistic,** cosmotheistic; physicomorphic; anthropomorphic, anthropotheistic; **deistic**

26 sectarian, sectary, **denominational,** schismatic, schismatical

27 nonsectarian, undenominational, nondenominational; interdenominational

28 Protestant, non-Catholic, Reformed, Reformationist, Evangelical; Lutheran, Calvinist, Calvinistic, Zwinglian; dissentient 333.6; apostate 363.11

29 Catholic; Roman Catholic *or* **RC** <nf>, Roman; Romish *and* popish *and* papish *and* papist *and* papistical <nf>; ultramontane

30 Jewish, Hebrew, Judaic, Judaical, Israelite, Israelitic, Israelitish; Orthodox, Conservative, Reform, Reconstructionist; Hasidic

31 Muslim, Islamic, Moslem, Islamitic, Islamistic, Muhammadan, Mohammedan; Shiite, Sunni, Sunnite

32 <Eastern> Buddhist, Buddhistic; Brahmanic, Brahmanistic; Vedic, Vedantic; Confucian, Confucianist; Taoist, Taoistic, Shintoist, Shintoistic; Zoroastrian, Zarathustrian, Parsee

33 religions and sects

anthroposophy	Jainism
Babism *or* Babi	Jodo Buddhism
Baha'i *or* Bahaism	Judaism
Brahmanism	Lamaism
Brahmoism	Lingayat Hinduism
Buddhism	Magianism
Ch'an Buddhism	Mahayana Buddhism
Chen Yen Buddhism	Mandaeism
Ching-t'u Buddhism	Mithraism
Christianity	Nichiren Buddhism
Confucianism	Orphism
Conservative Judaism	Orthodox Judaism
Dakshincharin Hinduism	Parsiism *or* Parsism
Eleusinianism	Rastafarianism
Ethical Culture	Reconstructionism
Gnosticism	Reform Judaism
gymnosophy	reincarnationism
Hare Krishna	Rosicrucianism
Hasidism	Sabaeanism
Hinduism	Saivism
Hinayana Buddhism	Shaivite Hinduism
Islam	Shamanism

Shiite Muslimism	Theravada Buddhism
Shin Buddhism	T'ien-t'ai Buddhism
Shingon Buddhism	Unitarianism
Shinto *or* Shintoism	Vaishnavite Hinduism
Sikhism	Vajrayana Buddhism
Soka Gakkai	Vamacharin Hinduism
Buddhism	Vedanta *or* Vedantism
Sufism	Wahabiism
Sunni Muslimism	Yoga *or* Yogism
Taoism	Zen *or* Zen Buddhism
Tendai Buddhism	Zoroastrianism *or*
Theosophy	Zoroastrism

34 Christian denominations

Adventism *or* Second	latitudinarianism
Adventism	Laudism *or* Laudianism
African Methodist	Liberal Catholicism
Episcopal church	Lutheranism
African Methodist	Mennonitism
Episcopal Zion church	Methodism
Amish	Moral Rearmament
Anabaptism	Mormonism
Anglicanism	New Thought
Anglo-Catholicism	Origenism
antinomianism	Orthodox Christianity
Arianism	Oxford Movement
Assemblies of God	Pentecostal church
Athanasianism	Practical Christianity
Baptist church	Presbyterianism
Boehmenism	Puritanism
Calvinism	Puseyism
Catholicism	Quakerism *or* Society
Christadelphian	of Friends
Christian Science *or*	quietism
Church of Christ,	Roman Catholicism
Scientist	Rosicrucianism
Churches of Christ	Russian Orthodox
Churches of God	Sabellianism
Churches of the Brethren	Salvation Army
Churches of the Nazarene	Seventh-Day Adventist
Congregationalism	Socinianism
Coptic Church	Stundism
Eastern Orthodox	Swedenborgianism
Episcopalianism	Tractarianism
Erastianism	Trinitarianism
Evangelicanism	Ubiquitarianism
Greek Orthodox	Uniatism
homoiousianism	Unification church
homoousianism	Universalism
Jansenism	Wesleyanism *or*
Jehovah's Witness	Wesleyism

676 THEOLOGY

NOUNS **1 theology** <see list>, **religion, divinity;** theologism; doctrinism, doctrinalism; religious studies, religious education

2 doctrine, dogma 953.2; **creed,** credo; credenda, articles of religion *or* faith; Apostles' Creed, Nicene Creed, Athanasian Creed; Catechism

3 theologian, theologist, theologizer, theologer, theologician, theologue; **divine;** scholastic, schoolman; theological *or* divinity student, theological, theologue; canonist

ADJS **4 theological, religious; divine;** doctrinal, doctrinary, ecclesiological; canonic *or* canonical; physicotheological

5 kinds and branches of theology

angelology	Mercersburg theology
apologetics	natural *or* rational theology
Buddhist theology	neoorthodoxy *or*
canonics	neoorthodox theology
Christian theology	nonformalogical theology
Christology	patristics *or* patristic
covenant theology	theology
crisis theology	phenomenological
demonology	theology
doctrinal theology	philosophical theology
dogmatics *or* dogmatic	physicotheology
theology	rationalism
eschatology	sacerdotalism
existential theology	school theology *or*
feminist theology	scholastic theology
fideism	secularism
hagiology	sophiology
hierography *or*	soteriology *or* Christology
hagiography	*or* logos theology *or*
hierology	logos Christology
Islamic theology	systematics *or* systematic
Judaism theology	theology
liberation theology	theological hermeneutics

677 DEITY

NOUNS **1 deity, divinity,** divineness, supernatural being, immortal; **godliness,** godlikeness; **godhood,** godhead, godship, Fatherhood; heavenliness; divine essence; **transcendence;** god, goddess

2 God; Lord, Maker, Creator, Supreme Being, Almighty, King of Kings, Lord of Lords; Jehovah; *Yahweh, Adonai, Elohim* <all Heb>; **Allah;** the Great Spirit, Manitou, Prime Mover

3 <Hinduism> **Brahma,** the Supreme Soul, the Essence of the Universe; **Atman,** the Universal Ego *or* Self; **Vishnu,** the Preserver; **Siva,** the Destroyer, the Regenerator

4 <Buddhism> **Buddha,** the Blessed One, the Teacher, **the Lord Buddha,** bodhisattva

5 <Zoroastrianism> **Ahura Mazda,** Ormazd, Mazda, the Lord of Wisdom, the Wise Lord, the Wise One, the King of Light, the Guardian of Mankind

6 <Christian Science> **Mind, Divine Mind,** Spirit, Soul Principle, Life, Truth, Love

7 world spirit *or* **soul,** *anima mundi* <L>, universal life force, world principle, **world-self,** universal ego *or* self, infinite spirit, supreme soul *or* principle, **oversoul, nous, Logos,** World Reason

8 Nature, Mother Nature, Dame Nature, Natura, Great Mother

9 Godhead, Trinity; Trimurti, Hindu trinity *or* triad

10 Christ, Jesus Christ, Son of God, Emmanuel, Redeemer, Messiah; the Way, the Truth, and the Life; Light of the World

11 the Word, Logos, the Word Made Flesh, **the Incarnation,** God Incarnate, the Hypostatic Union

12 God the Holy Ghost, **the Holy Ghost, the Holy Spirit,** the Spirit of God, the Spirit of Truth, the Paraclete, the Comforter, the Intercessor, the Dove

13 <divine functions> creation, preservation, dispensation; **providence, divine providence,** dealings *or* dispensations *or* visitations of providence

14 <functions of Christ> salvation, redemption; atonement, propitiation; mediation, intercession; judgment

15 <functions of the Holy Ghost> inspiration, unction, regeneration, sanctification, comfort, consolation, grace, witness

ADJS **16 divine,** heavenly, celestial, empyrean; **godly, godlike** 692.9; **transcendent,** superhuman, supernatural; self-existent; Christly, Christlike, redemptive, salvational, propitiative, propitiatory, mediative, mediatory, intercessive, intercessional; incarnate, incarnated, made flesh; messianic

17 almighty, omnipotent, all-powerful; creating, creative, making, shaping; **omniscient,** providential, all-wise, all-knowing, all-seeing; **infinite,** boundless, limitless, unbounded, unlimited, undefined, omnipresent, ubiquitous; perfect, sublime; eternal, everlasting, timeless, perpetual, immortal, permanent; one; immutable, unchanging, changeless, eternally the same; supreme, sovereign, highest; holy, hallowed, sacred, numinous; glorious, radiant, luminous; majestic; good, just, loving, merciful; triune, tripersonal, three-personed, three-in-one

678 MYTHICAL AND POLYTHEISTIC GODS AND SPIRITS

NOUNS **1 the gods,** the immortals; the major deities, the greater gods, *di majores* <L>; the minor deities, the lesser gods, *di minores* <L>; pantheon; theogony; **spirits,** animistic spirit *or* powers, manitou, huaca, nagual, mana, pokunt, tamanoas, wakan, zemi

2 god, *deus* <L>; **deity, divinity,** immortal, heathen god, pagan deity *or* divinity; **goddess,** *dea* <L>; deva, devi, the shining ones; **idol,** false god, devil-god

3 godling, godlet, godkin; **demigod,** half-god, hero; cult figure; demigoddess, heroine

4 god, goddesses; Greek and Roman deities <see list>; **Norse and Germanic deities** <see list>; **Celtic deities** <see list>; **Hindu deities** <see list>; **avatars of Vishnu; Egyptian deities** <see list>; **Semitic deities; Chinese deities; Japanese deities; specialized** *or* **tutelary deities** <see list>

5 spirit, intelligence, supernatural being; **genius,** daemon, demon; atua; **specter** 988; **evil spirits** 680

6 elemental, elemental spirit; sylph, spirit of the air; gnome, spirit of the earth, earth-spirit; salamander, fire-spirit; undine, water spirit, water-sprite

7 fairyfolk, elfenfolk, shee *or* sidhe <Ir>, **the little people** *or* **men,** the good folk *or* people, denizens of the air; **fairyland,** faerie

8 fairy, sprite, fay, fairy man *or* woman; **elf, brownie, pixie, gremlin,** ouphe, hob, cluricaune, puca *or* pooka *or* pwca, kobold, nisse, peri; **imp, goblin** 680.8; **gnome,** dwarf; **sylph,** sylphid; **banshee; leprechaun;** fairy queen; Ariel, Mab, Oberon, Puck, Titania, Béfind, Corrigan, Finnbeara; little green men

9 nymph; nymphet, nymphlin; **dryad,** hamadryad, wood nymph; vila *or* willi; tree nymph; oread, mountain nymph; limoniad, meadow *or* flower nymph; Napaea, glen nymph; Hyades; Pleiades, Atlantides

10 water god, water spirit *or* **sprite** *or* **nymph;** undine, nix, nixie, kelpie; **naiad,** limniad, fresh-water nymph; Oceanid, Nereid, sea nymph, ocean nymph, **mermaid,** sea-maid, sea-maiden, siren; Thetis; **merman,** man fish; **Neptune,** "the old man of the sea"—Homer; Oceanus, Poseidon, Triton; Davy Jones, Davy

11 forest god, sylvan deity, vegetation spirit *or* daemon, field spirit, fertility god, corn spirit, **faun, satyr,** silenus, panisc, paniscus, panisca; **Pan,** Faunus; Cailleac; Priapus; Vitharr *or* Vidar, the goat god; Jack-in-the-green, Green Man

12 familiar spirit, familiar; **genius, good genius,** daemon, demon, *numen* <L>, totem; **guardian, guardian spirit, guardian angel,** angel, good angel, ministering angel, **fairy godmother;** guide, control, attendant godling *or* spirit, invisible helper, special providence; **tutelary** *or* **tutelar god** *or* **genius** *or* **spirit;** *genius tutelae, genius loci, genius domus, genius familiae* <all L>; **household gods;** *lares familiaris, lares praestites, lares compitales, lares viales, lares permarini* <all L>; penates, lares and penates; ancestral spirits; manes, pitris

13 Santa Claus, Santa, Saint Nicholas, Saint Nick, Kriss Kringle, Father Christmas

14 mythology, mythicism; **legend, lore, folklore,** mythical lore; fairy lore, fairyism; mythologist; urban legend

ADJS 15 mythic, mythical, mythological; fabulous, legendary; folkloric

16 divine, godlike

17 fairy, faery, **fairylike,** fairyish, fay; sylphine, sylphish, sylphy, sylphidine, sylphlike; **elfin,** elfish, elflike; gnomish, gnomelike; pixieish

18 nymphic, nymphal, nymphean, nymphlike

19 Greek and Roman deities

Aeolus	Neptune *or* Poseidon <Gk>
Apollo *or* Apollon *or* Phoebus *or* Phoebus Apollo	Nike
	Nyx
	Olympic gods *or* Olympians
Athena *or* Pallas Athena *or* Minerva <Rom>	Persephone <Gk> *or* Proserpina *or* Proserpine
Bacchus *or* Dionysus	
Chaos	Pluto <Rom> *or* Hades *or* Dis *or* Orcus
Cupid *or* Amor *or* Eros <Gk>	
	Rhea *or* Ops
Demeter *or* Ceres <Rom>	Saturn *or* Kronus <Gk>
Diana *or* Artemis <Gk>	Venus *or* Aphrodite <Gk>
Erebus	Vesta *or* Hestia <Gk>
Ge *or* Gaea *or* Gaia *or* Tellus <Rom>	Vulcan *or* Hephaestus <Gk>
Helios *or* Hyperion *or* Phaëthon	Zeus <Gk> *or* Jupiter <Rom> *or* Jove *or* Jupiter Fulgur *or* Fulminator *or* Jupiter Tonans *or* Jupiter Pluvius *or* Jupiter Optimus Maximus *or* Jupiter Fidius
Hymen	
Juno *or* Hera <Gk>	
Lares and Penates	
Mars *or* Ares <Gk>	
Mercury *or* Hermes <Gk>	
Mithras	
Momus	

20 Norse and Germanic deities

Aesir	Nanna
Asgard	Nerthus *or* Hertha
Balder	Njorth *or* Njord
Bor	Odin *or* Woden *or* Wotan
Bori	Reimthursen
Bragi	Sif
Forseti	Sigyn
Frey *or* Freyr	Thor *or* Donar
Freya *or* Freyja	Tyr *or* Tiu
Frigg *or* Frigga	Ull *or* Ullr
Heimdall	Vali
Hel	Vanir
Hermoder	Vitharr *or* Vidar
Höder *or* Hödr	Völund
Hoenir	Wayland
Ing	Weland
Ithunn *or* Idun	Wyrd
Loki	Ymir

21 Celtic deities

Aine	Blodenwedd
Amaethon	Bóann
Angus Og	Bodb
Arawn	Bran
Arianrhod	Brigit

Cernunnos	Llew Llaw Gyffes *or*
Dagda	Lleu
Danu	Lug *or* Lugh
Dewi	Macha
Dôn	Morrigan
Dylan	Neman
Epona	Ogma
Fomorians	Ogmios
Goibniu	Rhiannon
Gwydion	Shannon
Lir	Teutates

22 Hindu deities

Aditi	Jaganmati
Agni	Ka
Abhijit	Kala
Ardra	Kali
Aryaman	Kama
Asapurna	Kamsa
Asvins	Karttikeya
Avalokita *or* Avalokitesvara	Kaumudi
Bhaga	Krishna
Bhairava	Lakshmi
Bhairavi	Malhal Mata
Brahma	Manasa
Bhudevi	Marut
Brahma	Mitra
Brihaspati	Narada
Candika	Parjanya
Candra	Parvati
Chandi	Pushan *or* Pusan
Chitragupta	Rahu
Daksha	Rhibhus
Devaki	Rudra
Devi	Sarasvati
Dhara	Savitar
Dharma	Siddhi
Dhatar	Sita
Dharti Mai	Siva *or* Shiva
Didi Thakrun	Soma
Dipti	Surya
Durga	Uma
Dyaus	Ushas
Ganesa *or* Ganesh *or* Ganesha *or* Ganapati	Vaja
Garuda	Varuna
Gauri	Varuni
Hanuman	Vayu
Hardaul	Vibhu
Himavat	Vijaya
Hiranyagarbha	Vishnu
Hotra	Vivasvan
Indra *or* Indrani	Vrta
	Yama

23 Egyptian deities

Amon	Bastet
Ammut	Bes
Anubis	Buto
Aten	Geb
Bast	Hapi
Horus	Osiris
Imhotep	Ptah
Isis	Qebehsenuef
Khem	Ra *or* Amen-Ra
Khensu	*or* Re
Ma'at	Satet
Min	Sekhmet
Mut	Selket
Neph	Seth *or* Set
Nephthys	Tefnut
Nut	Thoth

24 specialized or tutelary deities

agricultural deities 1069.4	gods of lightning 1025.17
deities of fertility 890.5	gods of marriage 563.13
deities of justice 649.5	love deities 104.8
deities of the household 228.30	moon goddesses 1072.12
	Muses 986.2
deities of the nether world 682.5	music Muses 710.22
	poetry Muses 720.10
earth goddesses 1072.10	rain gods 316.6
Fates 964.3	sea gods 240.4
forest gods 678.11	sun gods 1072.14
goddesses of discord 456.1	thunder gods 56.5
	war gods 458.13
gods of commerce 731.11	water gods 678.10
gods of evil 680.5	wind gods 318.3

679 ANGEL, SAINT

NOUNS 1 angel, celestial, celestial *or* heavenly being; messenger of God; **seraph,** seraphim <pl>, angel of love; **cherub, cherubim** <pl>, angel of light; principality, archangel; recording angel; **saint,** beatified soul, canonized mortal; patron saint; martyr; redeemed *or* saved soul, soul in glory

2 heavenly host, host of heaven, choir invisible, angelic host, heavenly hierarchy, Sons of God, ministering spirits; Amesha Spentas

3 <celestial hierarchy of Pseudo-Dionysius> seraphim, cherubim, thrones; dominations *or* dominions, virtues, powers; principalities, archangels, angels; angelology

4 Azrael, angel of death, death's bright angel; Abdiel, Chamuel, Gabriel, Jophiel, Michael, Raphael, Uriel, Zadkiel

5 the Madonna; the Immaculate Conception; Mariology; Mariolatry

ADJS 6 angelic, angelical, seraphic, cherubic; heavenly, celestial; archangelic; **saintly, sainted,** full of grace, beatified, canonized; martyred; saved, redeemed, glorified, in glory

680 EVIL SPIRITS

NOUNS 1 evil spirits, demons, demonkind, powers of darkness, spirits of the air, host of hell, hellish host, hellspawn, denizens of hell, inhabitants of Pandemonium, souls in hell, damned spirits, lost souls, the lost, the damned

2 **devil,** *diable* <Fr>, *diablo* <Sp>, *diabolus* <L>, deil <Scot>, *Teufel* <Ger>, *diavolo* <Ital>

3 **Satan** <see list>, Satanas

4 Beelzebub, Belial, Eblis, Azazel, Ahriman *or* Angra Mainyu; Mephistopheles, Mephisto; Shaitan, Sammael, Asmodeus; Abaddon, Apollyon; Lilith; Aeshma, Pisacha, Putana, Ravana

5 <gods of evil> Set, Typhon, Loki; Nemesis; gods of the nether world; Namtar, Azazel, Asmodeus, Baba Yaga

6 **demon, fiend,** fiend from hell, **devil,** Satan, daeva, rakshasa, dybbuk, shedu, gyre <Scot>, bad *or* evil *or* unclean spirit; **hellion** <nf>, hellhound, hellkite <old>, she-devil; cacodemon, incubus, succubus; **jinni,** genie, genius, jinniyeh, afreet *or* afrit; evil genius; barghest; **ghoul,** lamia, Lilith, yogini, Baba Yaga, **vampire,** the undead

7 **imp, pixie, sprite, elf, puck,** kobold, *diablotin* <Fr>, tokoloshe, poltergeist, **gremlin,** Dingbelle, Fifinella, **bad fairy,** bad peri; little *or* young devil, devilkin, deviling; erlking; Puck, Robin Goodfellow, Hob, Hobgoblin

8 **goblin, hobgoblin,** hob, ouphe

9 **bugbear, bugaboo, bogey,** bogle, boggart; **booger, bugger,** bug <old>, **booger-man, bogeyman, boogeyman;** bête noire, fee-faw-fum, Mumbo Jumbo

10 **Fury,** avenging spirit; the Furies, the Erinyes, the Eumenides, the Dirae; Alecto, Megaera, Tisiphone

11 **changeling,** elf child; shape-shifter

12 **werefolk, were-animals; werewolf,** lycanthrope, *loup-garou* <Fr>; werejaguar, jaguar-man, uturuncu; wereass, werebear, werecalf, werefox, werehyena, wereleopard, weretiger, werelion, wereboar, werecrocodile, werecat, werehare

13 **devilishness,** demonishness, **fiendishness;** devilship, devildom; horns, the cloven hoof, the Devil's pitchfork

14 **Satanism,** diabolism, devil-worship, **demonism, devilry, diablerie, demonry;** demonomy, demonianism; black magic; Black Mass; sorcery 690; demonolatry, demon *or* devil *or* chthonian worship; demonomancy; demonology, diabolology *or* diabology, demonography, devil lore

15 **Satanist,** Satan-worshiper, diabolist, devil-worshiper, demonist; **demonomist,** demoniast; demonologist, demonologer; demonolater, chthonian, demon worshiper; sorcerer 690.5

VERBS 16 **demonize, devilize,** diabolize; possess, **obsess; bewitch,** bedevil

ADJS 17 **demoniac** *or* **demoniacal,** demonic *or* demonical, demonish, demonlike; **devilish,** devil-like; **satanic, diabolic, diabolical; hellish** 682.8;

fiendish, fiendlike; ghoulish, ogreish; foul, unclean, damned; inhuman

18 **impish, puckish,** elfish, elvish; mischievous 322.6

19 **designations of Satan**

Adversary	Mastema
Angel of the bottomless pit	Old Bendy <nf>
Angel *or* Prince of darkness	Old Enemy
Antichrist	Old Gentleman <nf>
Archfiend	Old Gooseberry <nf>
Apollyon	Old Harry <nf>
Author *or* Father of Evil	Old Ned <nf>
Beelzebub	Old Nick <nf>
Common Enemy	Old *or* Auld Clootie
Demon	<Scot nf>
Deuce <nf>	Old Poker <nf>
Devil Incarnate	Old Scratch <nf>
Dickens <nf>	Old Serpent
Eblis	O-Yama
Evil One	Prince of Darkness
Evil Spirit	Prince of the Devils
Father of Lies	Prince of the power of
Fiend	the air
Foul Fiend	Prince of this world
Haborym	Shaitan
His Satanic Majesty	Tempter
Lord of the Flies	Typhon
Lucifer	Wicked One

681 HEAVEN
<abode of the deity and blessed dead>

NOUNS 1 **Heaven** <see list>; "my Father's house"— Bible, "God's residence"—Emily Dickinson, "the great world of light, that lies behind all human destinies"—Longfellow

2 **the hereafter,** the afterworld, immortal life, life to come, immortality, eternal life, the afterlife 839.2, life after death

3 Holy City, **Zion,** New Jerusalem, Heavenly *or* Celestial City, Kingdom of God, City Celestial, Heavenly City of God, City of God, *Civitas Dei* <L>, "heaven's high city"—Francis Quarles

4 **heaven of heavens, seventh heaven,** the empyrean, throne of God, God's throne, celestial throne, the great white throne

5 <Christian Science> bliss, harmony, spirituality, the reign of Spirit, the atmosphere of Soul

6 <Mormon> celestial kingdom, terrestrial kingdom, telestial kingdom

7 <Muslim> Alfardaws, Assama *or* Assuma; Falak al Aflak

8 <Hindu, Buddhist, and Theosophical> nirvana; Buddha-field; devaloka, land of the gods; kamavachara, kamaloka; devachan; samadhi

9 <mythological> Olympus, Mount Olympus; Elysium, Elysian fields; fields of Aalu; Islands *or* Isles of the Blessed, Happy Isles, Fortunate Isles *or*

Islands; Avalon; garden *or* abode of the Gods, garden of the Hesperides, Bower of Bliss; Tir-na-n'Og, Annwfn

10 <Norse> Valhalla, Asgard, Fensalir, Glathsheim, Vingolf, Valaskjalf, Hlithskjalf, Thruthvang *or* Thruthheim, Bilskirnir, Ydalir, Sökkvabekk, Breithablik, Folkvang, Sessrymnir, Noatun, Thrymheim, Glitnir, Himinbjorg, Vithi

11 <removal to heaven> **apotheosis, resurrection, translation,** gathering, **ascension,** the Ascension; **assumption,** the Assumption; removal to Abraham's bosom

ADJS 12 **heavenly,** heavenish; **paradisal, paradisaic, paradisaical,** paradisiac, paradisiacal, paradisic, paradisical; **celestial,** supernal, ethereal; empyrean, empyreal; **unearthly,** unworldly; **otherworldly,** extraterrestrial, extramundane, transmundane, transcendental; Elysian, Olympian; blessed, beatified, beatific *or* beatifical, glorified, in glory; from on high

ADVS 13 **celestially,** paradisally, supernally, ethereally; in heaven, in Abraham's bosom, *in sinu Abraham* <L>, on high, among the blest, in glory

14 **designations of Heaven**

a better place	kingdom come <nf>
abode of the blessed	Land o' the Leal <Scot>
Abraham's bosom	my Father's house
better world	Olympus
Beulah	Paradise
Beulah Land	Svarga *or* Swarga *or* Swerga
eternal home	the happy land
eternity	the heavenly kingdom
Fiddler's Green	the kingdom of glory
firmament	the kingdom of God
glory	the kingdom of heaven
God's kingdom	the otherworld
God's presence	the place up there
happy hunting ground	the presence of God
heaven above	the Promised Land
high heaven	the realm of light
inheritance of the saints in light	the world above
	Zion

682 HELL

NOUNS 1 **hell, Hades,** Sheol, Gehenna, Tophet, Abaddon, Naraka, jahannan, avichi, **perdition, Pandemonium, inferno,** the pit, **the bottomless pit,** the abyss, "a vast, unbottom'd, boundless pit"— Robert Burns, **nether world,** lower world, underworld, infernal regions, abode *or* world of the dead, abode of the damned, eternal damnation, place of torment, the grave, shades below; **purgatory; limbo**

2 **hellfire,** fire and brimstone, lake of fire and brimstone, everlasting fire *or* torment, "the fire that never shall be quenched"—Bible

3 <mythological> **Hades,** Orcus, Tartarus, Avernus, Acheron, pit of Acheron; Amenti, Aralu; Hel, Niflhel, Niflheim, Naströnd

4 <rivers of Hades> Styx, Stygian creek; Acheron, River of Woe; Cocytus, River of Wailing; Phlegethon, Pyriphlegethon, River of Fire; Lethe, River of Forgetfulness

5 <deities of the nether world> Pluto, Orcus, Hades *or* Aides *or* Aidoneus, Dis *or* Dis pater, Rhadamanthus, Erebus, Charon, Cerberus, Minos; Osiris; Persephone, Proserpine, Proserpina, Persephassa, Despoina, Kore *or* Cora; Hel, Loki; Satan 680.3

VERBS 6 **damn,** doom, send *or* consign to hell, cast into hell, doom to perdition, condemn to hell *or* eternal punishment

7 go to hell *or* to the devil, be damned, go the other way *or* to the other place <nf>

ADJS 8 **hellish, infernal,** sulfurous, brimstone, fire-and-brimstone; chthonic, chthonian; pandemonic, pandemoniac; devilish; Plutonic, Plutonian; Tartarean; Stygian; Lethean; Acherontic; purgatorial, hellborn

ADVS 9 **hellishly, infernally,** in hell, in hellfire, below, in torment

683 SCRIPTURE

NOUNS 1 **scripture, scriptures, sacred writings** *or* **texts, bible;** canonical writings *or* books, sacred canon

2 **Bible, Holy Bible, Scripture, the Scriptures, Holy Scripture,** Holy Writ, the Book, the Good Book, the Book of Books, the Word, the Word of God; Vulgate, Septuagint, Douay Bible, Authorized *or* King James Version, Revised Version, American Revised Version; Revised Standard Version; Jerusalem Bible; Testament; canon

3 **Old Testament,** Tenach; Hexateuch, Octateuch; Pentateuch, Chumash, Five Books of Moses, **Torah,** the Law, the Jewish *or* Mosaic Law, Law of Moses; the Prophets, Nebiim, Major *or* Minor Prophets; the Writings, Hagiographa, Ketubim; Apocrypha, noncanonical writings

4 **New Testament; Gospels,** Evangels, the Gospel, Good News, Good *or* Glad Tidings; Synoptic Gospels, Epistles, Pauline Epistles, Catholic Epistles, Johannine Epistles; Acts, Acts of the Apostles; Apocalypse, Revelation

5 <Jewish> Torah, **Talmud,** Targum, Mishnah, Gemara; Masorah, Bahir, Midrash

6 <Islamic> **Koran, Qur'an,** Hadith, Sunna

7 <other text> sacred text, scripture, sacred writings, canonical writings, canon; Avesta, Zend-Avesta; Granth, Adigranth; Tao Té Ching; Analects of

Confucius; the Eddas; Arcana Caelestia; **Book of Mormon;** Science and Health with Key to the Scriptures

8 <Hindu> **the Vedas, Veda,** Rig-Veda, Yajur-Veda, Sama-Veda, Atharva-Veda, sruti; Brahmana, Upanishad, Aranyaka; Samhita; shastra, Smriti, Purana, Tantra, Agama; Bhagavad-Gita

9 <Buddhist> Pali Canon, Tripitaka; Vinaya Pitaka, Sutta Pitaka, Abhidamma Pitaka; Dhammapada, Jataka; The Diamond-Cutter, The Lotus of the True Law, Prajna-Paramita Sutra, Pure Land Sutras

10 **revelation, divine revelation; inspiration,** afflatus, divine inspiration; theopneusty, theopneustia; theophany, theophania, epiphany; **mysticism,** direct *or* immediate intuition *or* communication, mystical experience, mystical intuition, contemplation, ecstasy; **prophecy,** prophetic revelation, apocalypse

ADJS 11 **scriptural, Biblical,** Old-Testament, New-Testament, Gospel, Mosaic, Yahwist, Yahwistic, Elohist; **revealed, revelational;** prophetic, apocalyptic, apocalyptical; **inspired,** theopneustic; evangelic, evangelical, evangelistic, gospel; apostolic, apostolical; textual, textuary; canonical

12 Talmudic, Mishnaic, Gemaric, Masoretic; rabbinic

13 epiphanic, mystic, mystical

14 Koranic; Avestan; Eddic; Mormon

15 Vedic; tantrist

684 PROPHETS, RELIGIOUS FOUNDERS

NOUNS 1 **prophet** 962.4, *vates sacer* <L>; Old Testament prophets <see list>

2 <Christian founders> **evangelist, apostle, disciple, saint;** Matthew, Mark, Luke, John; Paul; Peter; **the Fathers, fathers of the church**

3 Martin Luther, John Calvin, John Wycliffe, Jan Hus, John Wesley, John Knox, George Fox <Protestant reformers>; Emanuel Swedenborg <Church of the New Jerusalem>; Mary Baker Eddy <Christian Science>; Joseph Smith <Church of Jesus Christ of Latter-day Saints>

4 Buddha, Gautama Buddha, Siddhartha Gautama <Buddhism>; Mahavira *or* Vardhamana *or* Jina <Jainism>; Mirza Ali Muhammad of Shiraz *or* the Bab <Babism>; Muhammad *or* Mohammed <Islam>; Confucius <Confucianism>; Lao-tzu <Taoism>; Zoroaster *or* Zarathustra <Zoroastrianism>; Nanak <Sikhism>; Ram Mohan Roy <Brahmo-Samaj>

5 **Old Testament prophets**

Abraham	Habakkuk
Amos	Haggai
Daniel	Hosea
Ezekiel	Isaac
Isaiah	Micah
Jacob	Moses
Jeremiah	Nahum
Joel	Obadiah
Jonah	Samuel
Joseph	Zechariah
Joshua	Zephaniah
Malachi	

685 SANCTITY

<sacred quality>

NOUNS 1 **sanctity,** sanctitude; **sacredness, holiness,** hallowedness, numinousness; sacrosanctness, sacrosanctity; heavenliness, transcendence, divinity, divineness 677.1; venerableness, **venerability, blessedness;** awesomeness, awfulness; inviolableness, **inviolability;** ineffability, unutterability, unspeakability, inexpressibility, inenarrableness; godliness 692.2; odor of sanctity

2 **the sacred,** the holy, the holy of holies, the numinous, the ineffable, the unutterable, the unspeakable, the inexpressible, the inenarrable, the transcendent

3 **sanctification, hallowing; purification;** beatitude, blessing; **glorification,** exaltation, enskying; **consecration,** dedication, devotion, setting apart; sainting, canonization, enshrinement; **sainthood, beatification; blessedness; grace,** state of grace; justification, justification by faith, justification by works

4 **redemption,** redeemedness, **salvation,** conversion, regeneration, new life, reformation, adoption; **rebirth, new birth, second birth;** circumcision, spiritual purification *or* cleansing

VERBS 5 **sanctify, hallow; purify,** cleanse, wash one's sins away; **bless,** beatify; **glorify,** exalt, ensky; **consecrate,** dedicate, devote, set apart; **beatify, saint, canonize;** enshrine

6 **redeem,** regenerate, reform, convert, save, give salvation

ADJS 7 **sacred, holy,** numinous, **sacrosanct, religious, spiritual,** heavenly, divine; **venerable,** awesome, awful; inviolable, **inviolate,** untouchable; **ineffable,** unutterable, unspeakable, inexpressible, inenarrable

8 **sanctified, hallowed; blessed,** consecrated, devoted, dedicated, set apart; **glorified, exalted,** enskied; **saintly,** sainted, beatified, canonized

9 **redeemed, saved,** converted, regenerated, regenerate, justified, reborn, born-again, renewed; circumcised, spiritually purified *or* cleansed

WORD ELEMENTS 10 sacr-, sacro-, hier-, hiero-, hagi-, hagio-

686 UNSANCTITY

NOUNS **1 unsanctity,** unsanctitude; **unsacredness, unholiness,** unhallowedness, unblessedness; profanity, profaneness; unregenerateness, reprobation; **worldliness,** secularity, secularism; secular humanism

2 the profane, the unholy; the temporal, the secular, **the worldly,** the fleshly, the mundane; the world, the flesh, and the devil

ADJS **3 unsacred,** nonsacred, **unholy,** unhallowed, unsanctified, unblessed; profane, **secular, temporal, worldly,** fleshly, mundane; unsaved, unredeemed, unregenerate, reprobate

687 ORTHODOXY

NOUNS **1 orthodoxy,** orthodoxness, orthodoxism; **soundness,** soundness of doctrine, rightness, right belief or doctrine; **authoritativeness,** authenticity, canonicalness, canonicity; traditionalism; the truth, religious truth, gospel truth

2 the faith, true faith, apostolic faith, primitive faith; old-time religion, faith of our fathers

3 the Church, the true church, Holy Church, Church of Christ, the Bride of the Lamb, body of Christ, temple of the Holy Ghost, body of Christians, members in Christ, disciples or followers of Christ; apostolic church; universal church, the church universal; church visible, church invisible; church militant, church triumphant

4 true believer, orthodox Christian; Sunni Muslim; Orthodox Jew; orthodox, orthodoxian, orthodoxist; textualist, textuary; canonist; fundamentalist; the orthodox

5 strictness, strict interpretation, scripturalism, evangelicalism; hyperorthodoxy, puritanism, puritanicalness, purism; staunchness; straitlacedness, stiff-neckedness, hideboundness; hard line <nf>; **bigotry** 980.1; **dogmatism** 970.6; **fundamentalism,** literalism, precisianism; bibliolatry; Sabbatarianism; sabbatism

6 bigot 980.5; **dogmatist** 970.7

ADJS **7 orthodox,** orthodoxical; of the faith, of the true faith; **sound,** firm, faithful, true, true-blue, right-thinking; Christian; **evangelical; scriptural,** canonical; traditional, traditionalistic; literal, textual; standard, customary, conventional; **authoritative,** authentic, accepted, received, approved; correct, right, proper

8 strict, scripturalistic, evangelical; hyperorthodox, puritanical, purist or puristic, straitlaced; staunch; hidebound, hardline <nf>, creedbound; **bigoted** 979.10; **dogmatic** 970.22; **fundamentalist,**

precisianist or precisianistic, literalist or literalistic; Sabbatarian

688 UNORTHODOXY

NOUNS **1 unorthodoxy, heterodoxy;** unorthodoxness, **unsoundness,** un-Scripturality; **unauthoritativeness,** unauthenticity, uncanonicalness, uncanonicity; **nonconformity** 868

2 heresy, false doctrine, **misbelief; fallacy, error** 975

3 infidelity, infidelism; unchristianity; gentilism; **atheism, unbelief** 695.5

4 paganism, heathenism; paganry, heathenry; pagandom, heathendom; pagano-Christianism; allotheism; animism, animatism; idolatry 697

5 heretic, misbeliever; heresiarch; nonconformist 868.3; antinomian, Albigensian, Arian, Donatist, etc

6 gentile; non-Christian; **non-Jew,** goy, goyim, non-Jewish man or shegets <Yiddish>, non-Jewish woman or shiksa <Yiddish>; non-Muslim, non-Moslem, non-Muhammadan, non-Mohammedan, giaour <Turk>, kaffir; zendik, zendician, zendikite; non-Mormon; infidel; unbeliever 695.11

7 pagan, heathen; allotheist; animist; idolater 697.4

VERBS **8 misbelieve, err,** stray, deviate, wander, go astray, stray from the path, step out of line <nf>, go wrong, fall into error; be wrong, be mistaken, be in error; serve Mammon

ADJS **9 unorthodox,** nonorthodox, **heterodox, heretical; unsound; unscriptural,** uncanonical, apocryphal; **unauthoritative,** unauthentic, unaccepted, unreceived, unapproved; **fallacious,** erroneous 975.16; antinomian, Albigensian, Arian, Donatist, etc

10 infidel, infidelic, misbelieving; **atheistic,** unbelieving 695.19; **unchristian,** non-Christian; gentile, non-Jewish, goyish, uncircumcised; non-Muslim, non-Muham-madan, non-Mohammedan, non-Moslem, non-Islamic; non-Mormon

11 pagan, paganish, paganistic; **heathen, heathenish;** pagano-Christian; allotheistic; animist, animistic; idolatrous 697.7

689 OCCULTISM

NOUNS **1 occultism, esoterics,** esotericism, esoterica, esoterism, esotery; cabalism, cabala or kabala or kabbala; yoga, yogism, yogeeism; **theosophy,** anthroposophy; symbolics, symbolism; anagogics; anagoge; hermetics; shamanism, spiritism, animism; mystery, mystification; hocus-pocus, mumbo jumbo; mysticism 683.10

2 supernaturalism, supranaturalism,

preternaturalism, **transcendentalism; the supernatural,** the supersensible, the paranormal

3 **metaphysics,** hyperphysics, transphysical science, the first philosophy *or* theology

4 **psychics,** psychism, psychicism; **parapsychology, psychical** *or* **psychic research;** metapsychics, metapsychism, metapsychology; psychosophy; panpsychism; psychic monism

5 **spiritualism,** spiritism; mediumism; necromancy; séance, sitting; spirit 988.1

6 psychic *or* psychical phenomena, spirit manifestation; materialization; spirit rapping, table tipping *or* turning; poltergeistism, poltergeist; telekinesis, psychokinesis, power of mind over matter, telesthesia, teleportation; levitation; trance speaking, glossolalia; psychorrhagy; hallucination, déjà vu; séance; automatism, psychography, automatic *or* trance *or* spirit writing; Ouija board, Ouija; planchette; out-of-body experience; cosmic vibration, synchronicity; UFO sighting, alien encounter

7 **ectoplasm,** exteriorized protoplasm; aura, emanation, effluvium; ectoplasy; bioplasma

8 **extrasensory perception** *or* **ESP; clairvoyance,** lucidity, second sight, insight, sixth sense, inner sense, third eye, the force <nf>; intuition 934; foresight 961; premonition 133.1; clairsentience, clairaudience, crystal vision, psychometry, metapsychosis, feyness

9 **telepathy, mental telepathy, mind reading,** thought transference, telepathic transmission; telergy, telesthesia; telepathic dream, telepathic hallucination, cosmic consciousness

10 **divination** 962.2; **sorcery** 690

11 **occultist,** esoteric, mystic, mystagogue, cabalist, supernaturalist, transcendentalist; adept, mahatma; yogi, yogin, yogist; theosophist, anthroposophist; fork bender, unspeller

12 **parapsychologist;** psychist, psychicist; **metapsychist;** panpsychist; **metaphysician,** metaphysicist

13 **psychic; spiritualist,** spiritist, **medium,** ecstatic, spirit rapper, automatist, psychographist; necromancer

14 **clairvoyant;** clairaudient, clairsentient; seer, prophet; psychometer, psychometrist

15 **telepathist, mental telepathist, mind reader,** thought reader

16 **diviner** 962.4; **sorcerer** 690.5

17 **astral body,** astral, linga sharira, design body, subtle body, vital body, etheric body, bliss body, Buddhic body, spiritual body, soul body; kamarupa, desire *or* kamic body; causal body; mental *or* mind body

18 <seven principles of man, theosophy> spirit, atman; mind, manas; soul, buddhi; life principle, vital force, prana; astral body, linga sharira; physical *or* dense *or* gross body, sthula sharira; principle of desire, kama

19 **spiritualization,** etherealization, idealization; **dematerialization,** immaterialization, unsubstantialization; **disembodiment,** disincarnation

VERBS 20 **spiritualize,** spiritize; etherealize; idealize; **dematerialize,** immaterialize, unsubstantialize; **disembody,** disincarnate

21 practice spiritualism, hold a séance *or* sitting; call up spirits 690.11

22 **telepathize, read one's mind**

ADJS 23 **occult, esoteric, esoterical, mysterious,** mystic, mystical, recondite, obscure, arcane; anagogic, anagogical; metaphysic, metaphysical; cabalic, cabalistic; **paranormal, supernatural** 870.15; theosophical, theosophist, anthroposophical

24 **psychic, psychical, spiritual; spiritualistic,** spiritistic; mediumistic; **clairvoyant,** second-sighted, clairaudient, clairsentient; **telepathic; extrasensory,** psychosensory; supersensible, supersensual, pretersensual; telekinetic, psychokinetic; automatist; unconscious, subconscious; transphysical

690 SORCERY

NOUNS 1 **sorcery, necromancy, magic,** sortilege, **wizardry,** theurgy, gramarye <old>, rune, glamour; **witchcraft,** spellcraft, spellbinding, spellcasting; **witchery,** witchwork, bewitchery, enchantment; possession; **voodooism, voodoo,** hoodoo, wanga, juju, jujuism, obeah, obeahism; shamanism; magism, magianism; fetishism; totemism; vampirism; thaumaturgy, thaumaturgia, thaumaturgics, thaumaturgism; theurgy; alchemy; white *or* natural magic; sympathetic magic, chaos magic; **divination** 962.2; spell, charm 691

2 **black magic,** the black art; **diabolism, demonism,** diablerie, demonology, Satanism

3 <practices> magic circle; ghost dance; Sabbath, coven, witches' Sabbath *or* Sabbat; ordeal, ordeal by battle *or* fire *or* water *or* lots; Halloween, Walpurgis Night, witching hour, black mass

4 **conjuration,** conjurement, evocation, invocation; **exorcism,** exorcisation; exsufflation; **incantation** 691.4

5 **sorcerer, necromancer, wizard, wonder-worker,** warlock, theurgist; warlock, male witch; thaumaturge, thaumaturgist, miracle- *or* wonder-worker; alchemist; **conjurer; diviner** 961.4; dowser, water witch *or* diviner; diabolist; Faust, Comus

6 **magician,** mage, magus; Merlin; prestidigitator, illusionist 357.2

7 **shaman,** shamanist; **voodoo,** voodooist, wangateur, **witch doctor,** obeah doctor, **medicine man,** mundunugu, isangoma; witch-hunter, witch-finder; exorcist, exorciser; unspeller

8 **sorceress,** shamaness; **witch,** witchwoman <nf>, witchwife <Scot>, **hex, hag,** lamia; witch of Endor; coven, witches' coven, Weird Sisters <Shakespeare>

9 **bewitcher, enchanter, charmer, spellbinder; enchantress, siren,** vampire; Circe; Medusa, Medea, Gorgon, Stheno, Euryale

VERBS 10 **sorcerize, shamanize; make** *or* **work magic,** wave a wand, rub the ring *or* lamp; ride a broomstick; alchemize

11 **conjure, conjure up,** evoke, invoke, raise, summon, call up; **call up spirits,** conjure *or* conjure up spirits, summon spirits, raise ghosts, evoke from the dead, "call spirits from the vasty deep"—Shakespeare

12 **exorcise,** lay; lay ghosts, **cast out devils;** unspell

13 cast a spell, wave a wand, bewitch 691.9

ADJS 14 sorcerous, necromantic, **magic, magical,** magian, numinous, thaumaturgic, thaumaturgical, miraculous, wizardlike, wizardly; alchemical, alchemistic, alchemistical; shaman, shamanic, shamanist *or* shamanistic; witchlike, witchy, witch; necromantic; voodoo, hoodoo <nf>, voodooistic; incantatory, incantational, spellbinding, hypnotic, autohypnotic; talismanic, fetishistic

691 SPELL, CHARM

NOUNS 1 **spell,** magic spell, **charm,** glamour, weird *or* cantrip <Scot>, wanga; hand of glory; evil eye, *malocchio* <Ital>, whammy <nf>; **hex, jinx, curse; exorcism**

2 **bewitchment, witchery, bewitchery; enchantment, entrancement,** fascination, captivation; illusion, maya; bedevilment; **possession, obsession**

3 **trance, ecstasy,** ecstasis, transport, mystic transport; meditation, contemplation; **rapture;** yoga trance, dharana, dhyana, samadhi; hypnosis 22.7

4 **incantation, conjuration,** magic words *or* formula, invocation, evocation, chant; hocus-pocus, abracadabra, mumbo jumbo; open sesame, abraxas, paternoster

5 **charm, amulet, talisman, fetish,** periapt, phylactery; **voodoo, hoodoo,** juju, obeah, mumbo jumbo; **good-luck charm,** good-luck piece, **lucky piece** *or* **charm,** rabbit's-foot, lucky bean, four-leaf clover, whammy <nf>; mascot; madstone; love charm, philter; scarab, scarabaeus, scarabee; veronica, sudarium; swastika, fylfot, gammadion; potion; bell, book, and candle

6 **wish-bringer,** wish-giver; **wand, magic wand,** Aaron's rod; Aladdin's lamp, magic ring, magic belt, magic spectacles, magic carpet, seven-league boots; wishing well, wishing stone, wishing cap, Fortunatus's cap; cap of darkness, Tarnkappe, Tarnhelm; fern seed; **wishbone,** wishing bone, merrythought <Brit>

VERBS 7 **cast a spell,** spell, **spellbind; entrance,** trance, put in a trance; **hypnotize, mesmerize**

8 **charm,** becharm, **enchant, fascinate,** captivate, glamour

9 **bewitch,** witch, **hex, jinx;** voodoo, hoodoo; **possess, obsess;** bedevil, diabolize, demonize; hagride; overlook, look on with the evil eye, cast the evil eye

10 **put a curse on,** put a hex on, put a juju on, put obeah on, give the evil eye, give the *malocchio,* give a whammy <nf>

ADJS 11 **bewitching, witching;** illusory, illusive, illusionary; **charming, enchanting, entrancing, spellbinding, fascinating,** glamorous, Circean

12 **enchanted, charmed,** becharmed, charmstruck, charm-bound; **spellbound,** spell-struck, spell-caught; **fascinated,** captivated; **hypnotized, mesmerized;** under a spell, in a trance

13 **bewitched,** witched, witch-charmed, witch-held, witch-struck; hag-ridden; **possessed,** taken over, obsessed

692 PIETY

NOUNS 1 **piety, piousness,** pietism; **religion, faith; religiousness, religiosity,** religionism, religious-mindedness; theism; love of God, adoration; **devoutness,** devotion, devotedness, worship 696, worshipfulness, prayerfulness, cultism; faithfulness, dutifulness, observance, churchgoing, conformity 867; sanctimony; **reverence,** veneration; discipleship, followership; daily communion; deism, mysticism, spirituality

2 **godliness,** godlikeness; fear of God; **sanctity,** sanctitude; odor of sanctity, beauty of holiness; **righteousness, holiness,** goodness; **spirituality,** spiritual-mindedness, holy-mindedness, heavenly-mindedness, godly-mindedness; **purity,** pureness, pure-heartedness, pureness of heart; **saintliness,** saintlikeness; saintship, sainthood; angelicalness, seraphicalness; heavenliness; **unworldliness,** unearthliness, other-worldliness

3 **zeal,** zealousness, zealotry, zealotism; unction; **evangelism, revival,** evangelicalism, revivalism; pentecostalism, charismatic movement; charismatic renewal, baptism in the spirit; charismatic gift, gift of tongues, glossolalia; **overreligiousness, religiosity,** overpiousness, overrighteousness, **overzealousness,**

overdevoutness; bibliolatry; fundamentalism, militance, **fanaticism** 925.11; **sanctimony** 693

4 believer, truster, accepter, receiver; God-fearing man, pietist, religionist, saint, theist; **devotee,** devotionalist, votary; **zealot,** zealotist, fundamentalist, militant; **churchgoer,** churchman, churchite; pillar of the church; communicant, daily communicant; **convert,** proselyte, neophyte, catechumen; **disciple,** follower, servant, faithful servant; **fanatic**

5 the believing, the faithful, the righteous, the good; the elect, the chosen, the saved; the children of God, the children of light; Christendom, the Church 687.3

VERBS **6 be pious, be religious; have faith,** trust in God, love God, fear God; witness, bear witness, affirm, **believe** 952.10; keep the faith, fight the good fight, let one's light shine, praise and glorify God, walk humbly with one's God; be observant, follow righteousness

7 be converted, get religion <nf>, receive *or* accept Christ, stand up for Jesus, be washed in the blood of the Lamb; be born again, see the light, meet God, enter the church

ADJS **8 pious,** pietistic; **religious,** religious-minded; theistic; **devout,** devoted, devotional, dedicated, worshipful, prayerful, cultish, cultist, cultistic; **reverent,** reverential, venerative, venerational, adoring, solemn; faithful, dutiful, worshipful; orthodox; affirming, witnessing, believing 953.21; keeping the faith; **observant, practicing**

9 godly, godlike; God-fearing; righteous, holy, good; **spiritual,** spiritual-minded, holy-minded, godly-minded, heavenly-minded; **pure,** purehearted, pure in heart; **saintly,** saintlike; **angelic, angelical,** seraphic, seraphical; heavenly; **unworldly,** unearthly, otherwordly, not of the earth, not of this world

10 regenerate, regenerated, **converted, redeemed, saved,** God-fearing, theopathic, humble, prostrate; reborn, **born-again;** sanctified 685.8

11 zealous, zealotical; ardent, unctuous; **overreligious,** ultrareligious, overpious, overrighteous, **overzealous,** overdevout; holier-than-thou; crusading, missionary, Bible-thumping; **fanatical** 926.32; sanctimonious 693.5

693 SANCTIMONY

NOUNS **1 sanctimony, sanctimoniousness; pietism,** piety, **piousness,** pietisticalness, false piety; religionism, religiosity; **self-righteousness;** goodiness *and* goody-goodiness <nf>; pharisaism, pharisaicalness; Tartuffery, Tartuffism; **falseness, insincerity, hypocrisy** 354.6; affectation 500; **cant,** mummery, snivel, snuffle; unction, unctuousness,

oiliness, smarm *and* smarminesss <nf>, mealymouthedness

2 lip service, mouth honor, mouthing, lip homage *or* worship *or* devotion *or* praise *or* reverence; formalism, solemn mockery; BOMFOG *or* brotherhood of man and fatherhood of God

3 pietist, religionist, **hypocrite,** religious hypocrite, canting hypocrite, pious fraud, religious *or* spiritual humbug, whited sepulcher, **pharisee,** Holy Willie <Robert Burns>, "a saint abroad and a devil at home"—Bunyan; bleeding heart <nf>; **canter,** ranter, snuffler, sniveler; dissembler, dissimulator; affecter, poser 500.8; **lip server,** lip worshiper, formalist; Pharisee, scribes and Pharisees; Tartuffe, Pecksniff, Mawworm, Joseph Surface

VERBS **4 be sanctimonious,** be hypocritical; cant, snuffle, snivel; give mouth honor, render *or* pay lip service

ADJS **5 sanctimonious,** sanctified, **pious, pietistic, pietistical,** self-righteous, pharisaic, pharisaical, **holier-than-thou,** holier-than-the-pope <nf>; goody *and* goody-goody *and* goo-goo <nf>; **false, insincere, hypocritical** 354.32; affected 500.15; Tartuffish, Tartuffian; canting, sniveling, unctuous, mealymouthed, smarmy <nf>

694 IMPIETY

NOUNS **1 impiety, impiousness;** ungodliness, godlessness; **irreverence,** undutifulness; desertion, renegadism, apostasy, recreancy; backsliding, recidivism, lapse, fall *or* lapse from grace; **atheism, irreligion; unsanctity** 686

2 sacrilege, blasphemy, blaspheming, impiety; **profanity,** profaneness; sacrilegiousness, blasphemousness; **desecration, profanation;** tainting, pollution, contamination

3 sacrilegist, blasphemer, Sabbath-breaker; deserter, renegade, apostate, recreant; backslider, recidivist; **atheist,** unbeliever 695.11

VERBS **4 desecrate, profane,** dishonor, unhallow, commit sacrilege

5 blaspheme; vilify, abuse 513.7; curse, swear 513.6; take in vain; taint, pollute, contaminate

ADJS **6 impious, irreverent,** undutiful; **profane,** profanatory; **sacrilegious, blasphemous;** renegade, apostate, recreant, backsliding, recidivist *or* recidivistic, lapsed, fallen, lapsed *or* fallen from grace; atheistic, **irreligious** 695.17; **unsacred** 686.3

695 NONRELIGIOUSNESS

NOUNS **1 nonreligiousness, unreligiousness; undevoutness;** indevoutness, indevotion,

undutifulness, nonobservance; adiaphorism,
indifferentism, Laodiceanism, lukewarm piety;
indifference 102; **laicism,** unconsecration;
deconsecration, secularization, laicization,
desacralization

2 **secularism, worldliness,** earthliness, earthiness,
mundaneness; **unspirituality,** carnality; worldly-
mindedness, earthly-mindedness, carnal-
mindedness; materialism, Philistinism

3 **ungodliness,** godlessness, **unrighteousness,
irreligion, unholiness,** unsaintliness,
unangelicalness; unchristianliness, un-Christliness;
impiety 694; **wickedness, sinfulness** 654.4

4 **unregeneracy,** unredeemedness, **reprobacy,**
gracelessness, shriftlessness

5 **unbelief, disbelief** 955.1; infidelity, infidelism,
faithlessness; **atheism;** nullifidianism,
minimifidianism

6 **agnosticism; skepticism, doubt, incredulity,**
Pyrrhonism, Humism; scoffing 508.1

7 **freethinking,** free thought, **latitudinarianism;
humanism,** secular humanism

8 antireligion; antichristianism, antichristianity;
antiscripturism

9 **iconoclasm,** iconoclasticism, image breaking

10 **irreligionist; worldling,** earthling; **materialist;**
iconoclast, idoloclast; anti-Christian, antichrist

11 **unbeliever, disbeliever,** nonbeliever; **atheist,
infidel, pagan, heathen,** heretic; nullifidian,
minimifidian; secularist; **gentile** 688.6

12 **agnostic; skeptic, doubter,** dubitante, **doubting
Thomas,** scoffer, Pyrrhonist, Humist

13 **freethinker, latitudinarian,** *esprit fort* <Fr>;
humanist, secular humanist

VERBS 14 **disbelieve,** doubt 955.6; scoff 508.9;
laicize, deconsecrate, **secularize,** desacralize

ADJS 15 **nonreligious, unreligious,** having no
religious preference; **undevout,** indevout,
indevotional, undutiful, nonobservant,
nonpracticing; adiamorphic, indifferentist *or*
indifferentistic, Laodicean, lukewarm, indifferent
102.6; unconsecrated, **deconsecrated, secularized,**
laicized, desacralized

16 **secularist, secularistic, worldly, earthly,** earthy,
terrestrial, **mundane,** temporal; **unspiritual,
profane,** carnal, **secular;** humanistic, secular-
humanistic; worldly minded, earthly minded,
carnal-minded; **materialistic,** material, Philistine

17 **ungodly,** godless, **irreligious, unrighteous, unholy,**
unsaintly, unangelic, unangelical; impious 694.6;
wicked, sinful 654.16

18 **unregenerate,** unredeemed, **unconverted,** godless,
reprobate, graceless, shriftless, **lost, damned;**
lapsed, fallen, recidivist, recidivistic

19 **unbelieving, disbelieving, faithless; infidel,**
infidelic; **pagan, heathen; atheistic,** atheist;
nullifidian, minimifidian

20 **agnostic; skeptic, skeptical, doubtful, dubious,
incredulous,** Humean, Pyrrhonic; Cartesian

21 **freethinking, latitudinarian**

22 **antireligious;** antichristian; antiscriptural;
iconoclastic

696 WORSHIP

NOUNS 1 **worship,** worshiping, **adoration, devotion,
homage, veneration, reverence,** honor; adulation,
esteem; cult, cultus, cultism; latria, dulia,
hyperdulia; falling down and worshiping,
prostration; co-worship; idolatry 697

2 **glorification,** glory, **praise,** extolment, laudation,
laud, exaltation, magnification, dignification

3 **paean,** laud; hosanna, hallelujah, alleluia; **hymn,**
hymn of praise, **doxology, psalm, anthem,** motet,
canticle, chorale; **chant,** versicle; mantra, Vedic
hymn *or* chant; plainsong, carol, gospel song;
Introit, Miserere; Gloria, Gloria in Excelsis, Gloria
Patri; Te Deum, Agnus Dei, Benedicite, Magnificat,
Nunc Dimittis; response, responsory, report,
answer; Trisagion; antiphon, antiphony; offertory,
offertory sentence *or* hymn; hymnody, hymnology,
hymnography, psalmody; hymnal

4 **prayer,** praying, **supplication, invocation,**
imploration, impetration, entreaty, beseechment,
appeal, petition, suit, aid prayer, bid *or* bidding
prayer, request, petitionary prayer, orison,
obsecration, obtestation, confession, rogation,
devotions; genuflection, prostration; silent prayer,
meditation, contemplation, communion;
intercession *or* intercessory prayer, suffrage; **grace,
thanks, thanksgiving;** litany; breviary, canonical
prayers; collect, collect of the Mass, collect of the
Communion; Angelus; Paternoster, the Lord's
Prayer; Hail Mary, Ave, Ave Maria; Kyrie Eleison;
Pax; chaplet; rosary, beads, beadroll; Kaddish,
Mourner's Kaddish; prayer wheel *or* machine

5 **benediction, blessing,** benison, invocation,
benedicite; sign of the cross; laying on of hands

6 **propitiation,** appeasement 465.1; atonement 658

7 **oblation, offering, sacrifice, immolation,** incense;
libation, drink offering; burnt offering, holocaust;
thank offering, votive *or* ex voto offering; heave
offering, peace offering, sacramental offering, sin
or piacular offering, whole offering; human
sacrifice, mactation, infanticide, hecatomb; self-
sacrifice, self-immolation; sutteeism; scapegoat,
suttee; offertory, collection; penitence

8 divine service, **service,** public worship, **liturgy**
701.3, office, duty, exercises, **devotions;** meeting;
church service, church, celebration; **revival,** revival

meeting, camp meeting, tent meeting, praise
meeting; watch meeting, watch-night service,
watch night; **prayer meeting,** prayers, prayer, call
to prayer; morning devotions *or* services *or*
prayers, matins, lauds; prime, prime song; tierce,
undersong; sext; none, nones; novena; evening
devotions *or* services *or* prayers, vesper, vespers,
vigils, evensong; compline, night song *or* prayer;
bedtime prayer; Mass; pilgrimage, hajj

9 **worshiper,** adorer, venerator, votary, adulator,
communicant, daily communicant, celebrant,
churchgoer, chapelgoer, parishioner, follower;
prayer, suppliant, supplicant, supplicator,
petitioner; orans, orant; beadsman; revivalist,
evangelist; congregation; **idolater** 697.4; flock,
sheep, congregation, concourse, minyan <Heb>

10 <sacred object> cross, crucifix, chalice, relic,
incense, holy water, thurible, censer, chrism, rosary
beads, votive candle, vigil light; phylactery, tefillin,
mezuzah, menorah; totem, talisman, charm, amulet

VERBS 11 **worship, adore, reverence, venerate,
revere, honor,** respect, adulate, do *or* pay homage
to, pay divine honors to, do service, lift up the
heart, bow down and worship, humble oneself
before, prostrate, genuflect; **idolize** 697.5

12 **glorify, praise, laud, exalt, extol,** magnify, bless,
celebrate; praise God, praise *or* glorify the Lord,
bless the Lord, praise God from whom all
blessings flow; praise Father, Son, and Holy Ghost;
give thanks; sing praises, sing the praises of, sound
or resound the praises of; doxologize, hymn

13 **pray, supplicate,** invoke, petition, make
supplication, *daven* <Yiddish>; **implore, beseech**
440.11, obtest; offer a prayer, send up a prayer,
commune with God; **say one's prayers;** tell one's
beads, recite the rosary; **say grace, give** *or* **return
thanks;** pray over

14 **bless, give one's blessing,** give benediction, confer
a blessing upon, invoke benefits upon; cross, make
the sign of the cross over *or* upon; lay hands on

15 **propitiate,** make propitiation; appease 465.7; **offer
sacrifice,** sacrifice, make sacrifice to, immolate
before, offer up an oblation

ADJS 16 **worshipful,** worshiping; **adoring,** adorant;
devout, devotional; pious; **reverent,** reverential,
dedicated; **venerative,** venerational; solemn; at the
feet of; **prayerful,** praying, penitent, **supplicatory,**
supplicant, suppliant; precatory, precative,
imploring, honoring, on one's knees, on bended
knee; prone *or* prostrate before, in the dust;
blessing, benedictory, benedictional; propitiatory

INTERJS 17 **hallelujah!,** alleluia!, **hosanna!, praise
God!,** praise the Lord!, praise ye the Lord!, amen!,
"praise Him all His hosts!"—Bible, Heaven be
praised!, glory to God!, glory be to God!, glory be

to God in the highest!, bless the Lord!, "bless the
Lord, O my soul, and all that is within me, bless
His holy name!," "hallowed be Thy Name!"—both
Bible, praise God from whom all blessings flow;
thanks be to God!, *Deo gratias!* <L>; sursum
corda! <Hindu>; om!, om mani padme hum!

18 O Lord!, our Father which art in heaven!; God
grant!, pray God that!; God bless!, God save!, God
forbid!

697 IDOLATRY

NOUNS 1 **idolatry,** idolatrousness, idolism,
idolodulia, **idol worship;** heathenism, paganism;
image worship, iconolatry, iconoduly; cult, cultism;
totemism; **fetishism** *or* fetichism; **demonism,**
demonolatry, demon *or* devil worship, Satanism;
animal worship, snake worship, fire worship,
pyrolatry, Parsiism, Zoroastrianism; sun worship,
star worship, Sabaism; tree worship, plant
worship, Druidism, nature worship; phallic
worship, phallicism; hero worship; idolomancy

2 **idolization,** fetishization; **deification,** apotheosis

3 **idol; fetish,** totem, joss; **graven image, golden calf,**
effigy; devil-god, "the god of my idolatry"—
Shakespeare; Baal, Jaganatha *or* Juggernaut;
sacred cow

4 **idolater,** idolatress, idolizer, idolatrizer, iconolater,
cultist, idolist, idol worshiper, image-worshiper;
fetishist, totemist; demon *or* devil worshiper,
demonolater, chthonian; animal worshiper,
zoolater, theriolater, therolater, snake worshiper,
ophiolater; fire worshiper, pyrolater, Parsi,
Zoroastrian; sun worshiper, heliolater; star
worshiper, Sabaist; tree worshiper, arborolater,
dendrolater, plant worshiper, Druid, nature
worshiper; phallic worshiper; anthropolater,
archaeolater, etc; groupie, hero-worshiper

VERBS 5 **idolatrize,** idolize, idolify, idol; fetishize,
fetish, totemize; **make an idol of, deify,** apotheosize;
idealize, lionize, hero-worship, look up to

6 **worship idols,** worship the golden calf, *adorer le
veau d'or* <Fr>

ADJS 7 **idolatrous,** idolatric *or* idolatrical, **idol
worshiping;** idolistic, idolizing, iconolatrous,
cultish, fetishistic, totemistic; heathen, pagan;
demonolatrous, chthonian; heliolatrous;
bibliolatrous; zoolatrous; hero-worshiping,
lionizing

698 THE MINISTRY

NOUNS 1 **the ministry, pastorate,** pastorage, pastoral
care, cure *or* care of souls, **the Church,** the cloth,
the pulpit, the desk; **priesthood,** priestship;

apostleship; call, vocation, sacred calling; holy orders; rabbinate

2 ecclesiasticalism, ecclesiology, priestcraft

3 **clericalism**, sacerdotalism; priesthood; priestism; episcopalianism; ultramontanism

4 **monasticism**, monachism, monkery, **monkhood**, friarhood; celibacy 565

5 ecclesiastical office <see list>, church office, dignity

6 **papacy**, papality, **pontificate**, popedom, the Vatican, Apostolic See, See of Rome, the Church

7 hierarchy, hierocracy; theocracy

8 **diocese, see**, archdiocese, bishopric, archbishopric; province; synod, conference; **parish**

9 **benefice**, living, **incumbency**, glebe, advowson; curacy, cure, charge, cure or care of souls; prelacy, rectory, vicarage

10 **holy orders, orders** 699.4, major orders, apostolic orders, minor orders; calling, election, nomination, appointment, preferment, induction, institution, installation, investiture; conferment, presentation; **ordination**, ordainment, consecration, canonization, reading in <Brit>

VERBS 11 **be ordained, take holy orders,** take orders, take vows, read oneself in <Brit>; **take the veil,** wear the cloth

12 **ordain,** frock, **canonize, consecrate;** saint

ADJS 13 **ecclesiastic, ecclesiastical, churchly;** ministerial, clerical, sacerdotal, **pastoral; priestly,** priestish; prelatic, prelatical, prelatial; episcopal, episcopalian; archiepiscopal; primatal, primatial, primatical; canonical; capitular, capitulary; abbatical, abbatial; ultramontane; **evangelistic;** rabbinic, rabbinical; priest-ridden; parochial

14 **monastic,** monachal, **monasterial, monkish;** conventual

15 **papal, pontific, pontifical,** apostolic, apostolical; **popish** or papist or papistic or papistical or papish <nf>

16 **hierarchical,** hierarchal, hieratic; hierocratic; theocratic, theocratist

17 **ordained;** in orders, in holy orders, of the cloth

18 **ecclesiastical offices**

abbacy
archbishopric or
  archiepiscopate or
  archiepiscopacy
archdeaconry
bishopric or bishopdom
canonry or canonicate
cardinalate or cardinalship
chaplaincy or chaplainship
curacy
deaconry or deaconship
deanery or deanship
episcopate or episcopacy
ministry

pastorate or pastorship or
  pastorage
pontificate or papacy or
  popedom
prebend or prebendaryship
  or prebendal stall
prelacy or prelature or
  prelateship or
  prelatehood
presbytery or presbyterate
primacy or primateship
rabbinate
rectorate or rectorship
vicariate or vicarship

699 THE CLERGY

NOUNS 1 **clergy, ministry,** the cloth; clerical order, clericals; **priesthood;** priestery; presbytery; prelacy; Sacred College; rabbinate; hierocracy, pastorage; clerical venue

2 **clergyman,** clergywoman, man or woman of the cloth, **divine, ecclesiastic, churchman, cleric,** clerical; clerk, clerk or person in holy orders, tonsured cleric; **minister, minister of the Gospel, parson, pastor,** abbé and curé <Fr>, **rector,** curate, vicar, man or woman of God, servant of God, shepherd, sky pilot and Holy Joe <nf>, reverend <nf>; supply minister or preacher, supply clergy; **chaplain;** military chaplain, padre <nf>; the Reverend, the Very or Right Reverend; Doctor of Divinity or DD; elder

3 **preacher,** sermoner, sermonizer, sermonist, homilist; pulpiter, pulpiteer; predicant, predikant; preaching friar; circuit rider; televison or TV preacher, telepreacher <nf>

4 holy orders, major orders, priest or presbyter, deacon or diaconus, subdeacon or subdiaconus; minor orders, acolyte or acolytus, exorcist or exorcista, reader or lector, doorkeeper or ostiarius; ordinand, candidate for holy orders

5 **priest,** gallach <Heb>, **father,** father in Christ, **padre,** cassock, presbyter; curé, parish priest; confessor, father confessor, spiritual father or director or leader, holy father; penitentiary

6 **evangelist,** revivalist, evangel, evangelicalist; **missionary,** missioner; missionary apostolic, missionary rector, colporteur; television or TV evangelist, televangelist <nf>

7 benefice-holder, beneficiary, **incumbent;** resident, residentiary

8 church dignitary, ecclesiarch, ecclesiast, hierarch; minor or lay officer

9 <Catholic> pope, pontiff; cardinal, dean, archbishop, bishop, provost, high priest, ecclesiarch, canon, monsignor

10 <Mormon> deacon, teacher, priest, elder, **Seventy,** high priest, bishop, patriarch, apostle; Aaronic priesthood, Melchizedek priesthood

11 <Jewish> **rabbi,** rebbe, rabbin; chief rabbi; baal kore <Yiddish>; cantor; priest, kohen <Heb>, high priest; maggid; Levite; scribe

12 <Muslim> imam, qadi, sheikh, mullah, murshid, mufti, hajji, muezzin, dervish, abdal, fakir, santon, ayatollah

13 <Hindu> Brahman, pujari, purohit, pundit, guru, bashara, vairagi or bairagi, Ramwat, Ramanandi; sannyasi; yogi, yogin; bhikshu, bhikhari

14 <Buddhist> bonze, bhikku, poonghie, talapoin; lama; Grand Lama, Dalai Lama, Panchen Lama

15 <pagan> Druid, Druidess; flamen; hierophant, hierodule, hieros, daduchus, mystes, epopt
16 **religious,** *religieux* <Fr>; **monk,** monastic; brother, lay brother; cenobite, conventual; caloyer, hieromonach; **mendicant, friar;** pilgrim, palmer; stylite, pillarist, pillar saint; beadsman; prior, claustral *or* conventual prior, grand prior, general prior; abbot; lay abbot, abbacomes; hermit 584.5; ascetic 667.2; celibate 565.2
17 **nun,** sister, *religieuse* <Fr>, clergywoman, conventual; abbess, prioress; **mother superior,** lady superior, superioress, the reverend mother, holy mother; canoness, regular *or* secular canoness; novice, postulant
18 **religious orders**

Augustinian *or* Austin Friars	Friars Minor
Augustinian Hermit	Friars Preacher
Barnabite	Gilbertine
Benedictine *or* Black Monks	Holy Cross
	Hospitaler
Bernardine	Jesuit *or* Loyolite
Bonhomme	Lorettine
Brigittine	Marist
Capuchin	Maryknoll
Carmelite *or*	Maturine
White Friars	Minorite
Carthusian	Observant
Cistercian	Oratorian
Cluniac	Pallottine Fathers and
Conventual	Brothers
Crosier	preaching Friars *or*
Crutched Friars *or*	brothers
Crossed Friars	Premonstratensian
Discalced Carmelite	Recollect *or* Recollet
Dominican *or*	Redemptorist
Black Friars	Salesian
Franciscan *or* Gray Friars	Templar
	Trappist

700 THE LAITY

NOUNS 1 **the laity, lay persons,** laymen, laywomen, nonclerics, nonordained persons, seculars; brothers, sisters, brethren, sistren <nf>, people; flock, fold, sheep; **congregation,** parishioners, churchgoers, assembly; *minyan* <Heb>; **parish,** society; class
2 **layman,** laic, secular, churchman, **parishioner,** church member; brother, sister, lay brother, lay sister; laywoman, churchwoman; catchumen; communicant
ADJS 3 **lay,** laic *or* laical; **nonecclesiastical,** nonclerical, nonministerial, nonpastoral, nonordained; nonreligious; **secular,** secularist; secularistic; temporal, popular, civil; congregational

701 RELIGIOUS RITES

NOUNS 1 **ritualism,** rituality, ritualization, **ceremonialism, formalism,** liturgism; symbolism, symbolics; **cult,** cultus, cultism; sacramentalism, sacramentarianism; sabbatism, Sabbatarianism; ritualization, **solemnization,** solemn observance, **celebration;** liturgics, liturgiology
2 **ritualist, ceremonialist,** celebrant, liturgist, **formalist,** formulist, formularist; sacramentalist, sacramentarian; sabbatist, Sabbatarian; High-Churchman, High-Churchist; crucifer, thurifer, acolyte
3 **rite** <see list>, **ritual,** rituality, **liturgy,** holy rite; service, order of worship; **ceremony, ceremonial; observance,** ritual observance; **formality,** solemnity; **form,** formula, formulary, form of worship *or* service, mode of worship; prescribed form; service, function, duty, office, practice; **sacrament,** sacramental, mystery; ordinance; institution
4 **seven sacraments,** mysteries: baptism, confirmation, the Eucharist, penance, extreme unction, holy orders, matrimony
5 **unction,** sacred unction, sacramental anointment, chrism *or* chrisom, chrismation, chrismatory; **extreme unction, last rites,** viaticum; ointment; chrismal
6 **baptism,** baptizement; **christening; immersion,** total immersion; **sprinkling,** aspersion, aspergation; affusion, infusion; baptism for the dead; baptismal regeneration; baptismal gown *or* dress *or* robe, chrismal; baptistery, baptistry, **font; confirmation,** bar *or* bas mitzvah <Jewish>
7 **Eucharist, Lord's Supper, Last Supper, Communion,** Holy Communion, **the Sacrament,** the Holy Sacrament; intinction; consubstantiation, impanation, subpanation, transubstantiation; real presence; elements, consecrated elements, bread and wine, body and blood of Christ; Host, wafer, loaf, bread, altar bread, consecrated bread; Sacrament Sunday
8 **Mass,** *Missa* <L>, Eucharistic rites; **the Liturgy,** the Divine Liturgy; **parts of the Mass,** High Mass, Low Mass
9 <non-Christian rites> initiation, rite of passage; circumcision; bar mitzvah *and* bas mitzvah <Jewish>; Kaddish, shivah; female circumcision; ritual cleaning, ritual bathing; fertility rite; sun dance, rain dance, war dance, ghost dance, potlatch; witches' Sabbath, black mass; hara-kiri
10 **sacred object** *or* **article; ritualistic manual,** Book of Common Prayer, breviary, canon, haggadah <Jewish>, missal *or* Mass book, book of hours, lectionary, prayer book; siddur *and* mahzor <Jewish>

11 psalter, psalmbook; Psalm Book, Book of Common Order; the Psalms, Book of Psalms, the Psalter, the Psaltery

12 holy day, hallowday <nf>, holytide, holiday; feast, fast, fast day; Sabbath; Sunday, Lord's day; saint's day; church calendar, ecclesiastical calendar

13 Christian holy days <see list>; Jewish holy days <see list>

14 <Muslim holy days> Ramadan <month>, Bairam, Muharram

VERBS **15 celebrate, observe, keep, solemnize;** ritualize; celebrate Mass; communicate, administer Communion; attend Communion, receive the Sacrament, partake of the Lord's Supper; attend Mass

16 minister, officiate, do duty, **perform a rite,** perform service or divine service; administer a sacrament, administer the Eucharist, etc; anoint, chrism, bless; confirm, impose, lay hands on; make the sign of the cross

17 baptize, christen; dip, immerse; sprinkle, asperge; circumcise

18 confess, make confession, receive absolution; **shrive,** hear confession; **absolve,** administer absolution; administer extreme unction

ADJS **19 ritualistic, ritual; ceremonial, ceremonious;** formal, formular, formulaic, formulary; liturgic, liturgical, **liturgistic, liturgistical;** solemn, consecrated; High-Church; **sacramental,** sacramentarian; eucharistic, eucharistical, baptismal; paschal; Passover; matrimonial, nuptial; funereal

20 religious rites

ablution	litany
absolution	love feast or agape
anointing of the sick	lustration
aspersion or asperges	offertory
celebration	pax or kiss of peace
cleansing or purification	penitence
confession or auricular	processional
confession or the	reciting the rosary or
confessional or the	telling one's beads
confessionary	sign of the cross or
confirmation	signum crucis <L>
greater or lesser litany	or signing or
high celebration	crossing oneself
imposition or laying on	sprinkling
of hands	Stations of the Cross
invocation	thurification or
invocation of saints	censing
last rites	viaticum

21 Western Christian holy days

Advent <pre-Christmas>
All Saints' Day or Allhallows <Nov 1>
All Souls' Day <Nov 2>
Annunciation or Lady Day <Mar 25>
Ascension Day or Holy Thursday <40 days after Easter>
Ash Wednesday <start of Lent>
Assumption <Aug 15>
Candlemas or Candlemas Day or Presentation <Feb 2>
Christmas <Dec 25>
Circumcision or Holy Name Day <Jan 1>
Corpus Christi <Thurs after Trinity Sun>
Easter or Eastertide <1st Sunday after 1st full moon after vernal equinox>
Easter Even or Holy Saturday
Ember days <beginning of seasons>
Epiphany or Three Kings' Day <Jan 6>
Good Friday <Fri before Easter>
Hallowmas or Allhallowmas or Allhallowtide or Halloween or Allhallows or All Saints' Day or All Souls' Day <Oct 31>
Holy Thursday or Maundy Thursday <before Easter>
Holy Week or Passion Week <before Easter>
Lammas or Lammas Day or Lammastide or Feast of St Peter's Chains <Aug 1>
Lent or Lententide <40 days before Easter>
Martinmas <Nov 11>
Michaelmas or Michaelmas Day or Michaelmastide <Sept 29>
Palm Sunday <Sun before Easter>
Pentecost or Whitsuntide or Whitsun or Whitsunday <7th Sun after Easter>
Quadragesima or Quadragesima Sunday
Septuagesima
Shrove Tuesday or Mardi Gras or Carnival or Pancake Day <Tues before Ash Wednesday>
Solemnity of Mary <Jan 1>
Trinity Sunday <Sun after Pentecost>
Twelfth-tide or Twelfth-night or Twelfth-day <night before Epiphany>
Whitweek and Whitmonday and Whit-Tuesday, etc <after Pentecost>

22 Jewish holy days

Fast of Av or Ninth of Av or Tishah b'Av
Hanukkah or Feast of the Dedication or Feast of Lights
High Holy Days <between Rosh Hashanah and Yom Kippur>
Lag b'Omer
Passover or Pesach
Purim
Rosh Hashanah or New Year
Rosh Hodesh or Rosh Chodesh
Shabuoth or Shavuoth or Pentecost or Feast of Weeks
Shemini Atzeres
Simhath Torah or Rejoicing over the Law
Sukkoth or Feast of Tabernacles
Yom Kippur or Day of Atonement

702 ECCLESIASTICAL ATTIRE

NOUNS **1 canonicals,** clericals <nf>, robes, cloth; **vestments,** vesture; regalia; liturgical garments, ceremonial attire; pontificals, pontificalia, episcopal vestments; habit, veil

2 robe, frock, mantle, gown, cloak, surplice, scapular, cassock, cope, hood, clerical collar, etc
3 staff, pastoral staff, **crosier, cross,** cross-staff, crook, paterissa
ADJS **4 vestmental,** vestmentary

703 RELIGIOUS BUILDINGS

NOUNS **1 church,** kirk <Scot>, bethel, **meetinghouse,** church house, **house of God,** place of worship, house of worship *or* prayer; conventicle; **mission;** basilica, major *or* patriarchal basilica, minor basilica; **cathedral,** cathedral church, *duomo* <Ital>; collegiate church
2 temple, fane; **tabernacle; synagogue,** *shul* <Yiddish>; **mosque,** masjid; dewal, girja; pagoda; kiack; pantheon; wat, ziggurat
3 chapel, chapel of ease, chapel royal, side chapel, school chapel, sacrament chapel, Lady chapel, oratory, oratorium; chantry; sacellum, sacrarium
4 shrine, holy place, dagoba, cella, naos; sacrarium, sanctum sanctorum, holy of holies, delubrum; tope, stupa; reliquary, *reliquaire* <Fr>
5 sanctuary, holy of holies, sanctum, sanctum sanctorum, adytum, sacrarium
6 cloister, monastery, house, abbey, friary; priory, priorate; lamasery; **convent, nunnery;** ashram, hermitage, retreat
7 parsonage, pastorage, pastorate, manse, **church house,** clergy house; presbytery, **rectory,** vicarage, deanery; glebe; chapter house
8 bishop's palace; **Vatican;** Lambeth, Lambeth Palace
9 <church interior> vestry, sacristy, sacrarium, sanctuary, diaconicon *or* diaconicum; baptistery; aisle, ambry, apse, blindstory, chancel, choir, choir screen, cloisters, confessional, confessionary <old>, crypt, Easter sepulcher, narthex, nave, porch, presbytery, rood loft, rood stair, rood tower *or* spire *or* steeple, transept, triforium; organ loft
10 <church furnishings> piscina; stoup, holy-water stoup *or* basin; baptismal font; patent; reredos; jube, rood screen, rood arch, chancel screen; altar cloth, cerecloth, chrismal; communion *or* sacrament cloth, corporal, fanon, oblation cloth; rood cloth; baldachin, *baldacchino* <Ital>; kneeling stool, *prie-dieu* <Fr>; prayer rug *or* carpet *or* mat
11 <vessels> cruet; chalice; ciborium, pyx; chrismal, chrismatory; monstrance, ostensorium; reliquary; font, holy-water font
12 altar, scrobis; bomos, eschara, hestia; **Lord's table,** holy table, **Communion table,** chancel table, table of the Lord, God's board; rood altar; altar desk, missal stand; credence, prothesis, table *or* altar of prothesis, predella; superaltar, retable, retablo,

ancona, gradin; altarpiece, altar side, altar rail, altar carpet, altar stair; altar facing *or* front, frontal; altar slab, altar stone, mensal
13 pulpit, rostrum, ambo; **lectern,** desk, reading desk
14 <seats> **pew; stall;** mourners' bench, anxious bench *or* seat, penitent form; amen corner; sedilia
ADJS **15 churchly,** churchish, **ecclesiastical;** churchlike, templelike; cathedral-like, cathedralesque; tabernacular; synagogical, synagogal; pantheonic
16 claustral, cloistered; monastic, monachal, **monasterial; coventual,** conventical

704 SHOW BUSINESS, THEATER

NOUNS **1 show business,** show biz <nf>, the entertainment industry; **the theater, the footlights, the stage, the boards,** the bright lights, Broadway, the Great White Way, the scenes <old>, traffic of the stage; avant-garde theater, contemporary theater, experimental theater, total theater, epic theater, theater of the absurd, theater of cruelty, guerrilla theater, street theater; stagedom, theater world, stage world, stageland, playland; **drama,** legitimate stage *or* theater, legit <nf>, off Broadway, off-off-Broadway; music *or* musical theater, fringe theater; café theater, dinner theater; regional theater; repertory drama *or* theater, stock; summer theater, summer stock, straw hat *or* straw hat circuit <nf>; **vaudeville,** variety; **burlesque; circus,** carnival; magic show; theatromania, theatrophobia
2 dramatics; dramatization, dramaticism, dramatism; **theatrics,** theatricism, **theatricalism,** theatricality, staginess; theatricals, amateur theatricals; **histrionics,** histrionism; dramatic *or* histrionic *or* Thespian art; dramatic stroke, *coup de théâtre* <Fr>; **melodramatics,** sensationalism; **dramaturgy,** dramatic structure, play construction, dramatic form; dramatic irony, tragic irony
3 theatercraft, stagecraft, stagery, scenecraft; **showmanship**
4 stage show, show; play, stage play, piece, vehicle, work; **hit** *or* hit show <nf>, gasser <nf>, success, critical success, audience success, word-of-mouth success, box-office hit, long run; short run, failure, **flop** *and* bomb *and* turkey <nf>
5 tragedy, tragic drama, melodrama; tragic flaw; buskin, cothurnus; tragic muse, Melpomene
6 comedy; comic relief; comic muse, Thalia; black comedy, satire, farce; sock, coxcomb, cap and bells, motley, bladder, slapstick, burlesque; historic comedy
7 act, scene, number, turn, bit *and* shtick <nf>,

routine <nf>; curtain raiser *or* lifter; introduction; expository scene; monologue, soliloquy; **prologue,** epilogue; **entr'acte,** intermezzo, intermission, interlude, *divertissement* <Fr>, *divertimento* <Ital>, climax; **finale,** afterpiece; exodus, exode; chaser <nf>; curtain call, curtain; encore, ovation; hokum *or* hoke act <nf>; song and dance; burlesque act; stand-up comedy act; sketch, skit

8 **acting, playing,** playacting, performing, **performance,** taking a role *or* part, role-playing; **representation, portrayal, characterization,** interpretation, projection, enactment; **impersonation,** personation, miming, mimicking, mimicry, mimesis; pantomiming, mummery; Method acting; improvisation; ham *and* hammy acting *and* hamming *or* hamming up <nf>, camping it up <nf>, overacting, histrionics; stage presence; stage directions, **business,** stage business, *jeu de théâtre* <Fr>, acting device; stunt *and* gag <nf>; hokum *or* hoke <nf>; buffoonery, slapstick; patter; stand-up comedy; crossover

9 **repertoire, repertory;** stock

10 **role, part,** piece <nf>; cue, **lines,** side; cast; **character,** person, personage; lead, starring *or* lead *or* leading role, fat part, leading man, leading woman *or* lady, hero, heroine; antihero; title role, top billing, protagonist, principal character; supporting role, supporting character; ingenue, *jeune première* or *jeune premier* <Fr>, romantic lead; <Fr>; *soubrette* <Fr>; villain, heavy <nf>, bad guy <nf>, antagonist, deuteragonist; bit, bit part, minor role, speaking part; feed *or* feeder, straight part; walking part, walk-on, extra; double, stand-in, stunt person, stunt man *or* woman, understudy; top banana, second banana; chorus, Greek chorus; stock part *or* character; **actor 707.2**

11 **engagement,** playing engagement, booking; **run; stand,** one-night stand *or* one-nighter; **circuit,** barnstorming, vaudeville circuit, borscht circuit; **tour, bus-and-truck, production tour;** date, gig <nf>

12 theatrical performance, **performance, show, presentation,** presentment, **production,** entertainment, stage presentation *or* performance; bill; **exhibit, exhibition;** benefit performance, benefit; personal appearance; showcase, tryout, preview; premiere, premier performance, debut, opening night; farewell performance, swan song <nf>; command performance; matinee; sellout, full house

13 **production,** mounting, staging, putting on; stage management; **direction,** *mise-en-scène* <Fr>; blocking; **rehearsal,** dress rehearsal, walk-through, run-through, technical *or* tech rehearsal *or* run, final dress, gypsy rehearsal *or* run-through *or* run

14 **theater, playhouse, house,** theatron, odeum; auditorium; **opera house,** opera; **hall,** music hall, concert hall; **amphitheater;** circle theater, arena, stadium, theater-in-the-round; vaudeville theater; burlesque theater; **little theater,** community theater; open-air theater, outdoor theater; Greek theater; children's theater; Elizabethan theater, Globe Theatre; showboat; dinner theater; cabaret, nightclub, club, night spot, *boîte de nuit* <Fr>

15 **auditorium,** seating; parquet, orchestra, **pit** <Brit>; **orchestra circle,** parquet circle, parterre; **dress circle;** fauteuil *or* theatre stall *or* **stall** <Brit>; **box,** box seat, **loge,** *baignoire* <Fr>; stage box; proscenium boxes, parterre boxes; balcony, gallery, mezzanine; **peanut gallery** and paradise <nf>; standing room; box office

16 **stage,** the boards; acting area, playing *or* performing area; thrust stage, three-quarter-round stage, theater-in-the-round; apron, passerelle, apron stage, forestage; proscenium stage, proscenium arch, proscenium; bridge; revolving stage; orchestra, pit, orchestra pit; **bandstand,** shell, band shell; stage right, R; stage left, L; upstage, downstage, backstage, center stage; **wings,** coulisse; dressing room, greenroom; flies, fly gallery, fly floor; gridiron, grid <nf>; board, lightboard, switchboard; dock; prompter's box; curtain, grand drape, safety curtain, asbestos curtain, fire curtain; stage door

17 <stage requisites> **property, prop;** practical piece *or* prop <nf>, handprop; costume 5.9; theatrical makeup, makeup, greasepaint, blackface, clown white; spirit gum

18 stage lighting, lights, instruments; **footlights,** foots <nf>, floats; floodlight, flood; bunch light; battens, houselights; **limelight,** follow spot, spotlight *or* spot <nf>, following spot <nf>, arc light, arc, klieg *or* kleig light; color filter, color wheel, medium, gelatin *or* gel; projector, stroboscope *or* strobe *or* strobe light; lightboard; dimmer; marquee; light plot

19 **setting, stage setting,** stage set, **set,** *mise-en-scène* <Fr>; location, locale

20 **scenery,** decor; **scene;** screen, **flat;** cyclorama *or* cyc; batten; side scene, **wing,** coulisse; border; tormentor, **teaser;** wingcut, woodcut; transformation, transformation scene; flipper; counterweight; **curtain,** rag <nf>, hanging; **drop,** drop scene, drop curtain, scrim, cloth; **backdrop,** back cloth <Brit>; act drop *or* curtain; tab, tableau curtain

21 **playbook, script,** text, **libretto;** promptbook; book, book of words; **score; scenario,** continuity, shooting script; scene plot; lines, actor's lines, cue, sides; stage direction; prompt book

22 **dramatist; playwright,** playwriter, dramaturge;

doctor *and* play doctor *and* play fixer <nf>; dramatizer; **scriptwriter, scenario writer,** scenarist, **scenarioist, screenwriter; gagman,** gag writer, joke writer, jokesmith; **librettist;** tragedian, comedian; farcist, *farceur* and *farceuse* <Fr>, farcer; melodramatist; monodramatist; mimographer; **choreographer**

23 **theater man,** theatrician; **showman,** exhibitor, **producer, impresario; director,** auteur; stage director, **stage manager;** set designer, scenewright; costume designer, costumer, *costumier* and *costumière* <Fr>, wardrobe master *or* mistress; dresser; hair *or* wigmaker *or* designer; makeup artist, visagiste; propsmaster *or* propsmistress; prompter; callboy; playreader; master of ceremonies, MC *or* emcee <nf>; box-office staff; ticket collector; usher, usherer, usherette, doorkeeper; ringmaster, equestrian director; barker, ballyhoo man *and* spieler <nf>

24 **stage technician, stagehand,** stage crew, machinist <old>, sceneman, scene master, **sceneshifter;** flyman; carpenter; **electrician;** sound man; scene painter, scenic artist, scenewright

25 **agent, actor's agent,** playbroker, ten-percenter <nf>; **booking agent;** advance agent, advance man; press agent; publicity man *or* agent; business manager, publicity manager

26 **patron,** patroness; **backer, angel** <nf>, promoter; Dionysus

27 **playgoer, theatergoer;** attender 221.5, spectator 918, audience 48.6, house; moviegoer, **motion-picture fan** <nf>; first-nighter; standee, groundling <old>; *claqueur* <Fr>, hired applauder; pass holder, deadhead <nf>, stage-door Johnny; critic, reviewer, talent scout

VERBS 28 **dramatize,** theatricalize; melodramatize; scenarize; **present, stage, produce, mount, put on,** put on the stage, adapt for the stage; **put on a show;** try out, preview; give a performance; premiere; **open,** open a show, open a show cold <nf>; set the stage; ring up the curtain, ring down the curtain; **star, feature** <nf>, bill, **headline,** give top billing to; succeed, make *or* be a hit *and* have legs <nf>, be a gas *or* gasser *and* run out of gas <nf>; fail, flop *and* bomb *and* bomb out <nf>; script

29 **act, perform, play,** playact, tread the boards, strut one's stuff <nf>; appear, **appear on the stage;** act like a trouper; register; emotionalize, emote <nf>; pantomime, mime; patter; sketch; troupe, barnstorm <nf>; improvise, ad-lib, wing it <nf>; steal the show, upstage, steal the spotlight; **debut,** make one's debut *or* bow, come out, take the stage, make an entrance; act as foil *or* feeder, stooge <nf>, be straight man for; **star,** play the lead, get

top billing, have one's name in lights, costar, understudy

30 **enact, act out; represent, depict, portray;** act *or* play *or* perform a part *or* role, role-play, take a part, sustain a part, act *or* play the part of; create a role *or* character; **impersonate,** personate; play opposite, support

31 **overact,** overdramatize, chew up the scenery <nf>, act all over the stage; **ham** *and* ham it up <nf>, camp it up; play to the gallery; **mug** <nf>, grimace; spout, rant, roar, declaim, "out-herod Herod"—Shakespeare; milk a scene, milk it; **underact,** underplay, fluff, go blank, throw away <nf>

32 **rehearse, practice,** go through, walk *or* run through, go over; block; go through one's part, read one's lines; learn one's lines, memorize, con *or* study one's part; be a fast *or* slow study; interpret the part, get into character

ADJS 33 **dramatic,** dramatical <old>, **dramaturgic, dramaturgical; theatric, theatrical, histrionic, thespian;** scenic; **stagy;** theaterlike, stagelike; rehearsed, staged, interpreted, improvised; **spectacular; melodramatic;** ham *or* hammy *or* campy <nf>; overacted, overplayed, milked <nf>; underacted, underplayed, thrown away; musical, choral; **operatic;** choreographic, terpsichorean; ballet, balletic; legitimate; stellar, all-star; stagestruck, starstruck; stageworthy, actor-proof

34 **tragic,** heavy; buskined, cothurned; tragicomic *or* tragicomical

35 **comic, light;** tragicomical, **farcical, slapstick;** camp *or* campy <nf>; burlesque

ADVS 36 **on the stage** *or* boards, before an audience, before the footlights; **in the limelight** *or* spotlight; onstage; downstage, upstage; backstage, off stage, behind the scenes; down left *or* DL; down right *or* DR; up left *or* UL; up right *or* UR

705 DANCE

NOUNS 1 **dancing** <see list>, terpsichore, dance; the light fantastic; **choreography;** dance drama, choreodrama; **hoofing** <nf>

2 **dance, hop** <nf>, dancing party, **shindig** *and* shindy <nf>; **ball, bal** <Fr>; masked ball, masque, mask, masquerade ball, masquerade, *bal masqué* <Fr>, *bal costumé* <Fr>, fancy-dress ball, cotillion *or* cotillon; promenade, **prom** <nf>, formal <nf>; country dance, square dance, barn dance, hoedown; mixer, stag dance; record hop; dinner-dance, tea dance, *thé dansant* <Fr>, dinner dance

3 **dancer,** danseur, terpsichorean, **hoofer** <nf>, step dancer, tap dancer, clog dancer, go-go dancer, foxtrotter, etc; **ballet dancer; ballerina,** danseur,

danseuse, coryphée; *première danseuse* and *danseur noble* <Fr>, corps de ballet; classical dancer; **modern dancer;** *corps de ballet* <Fr>; figurant, figurante; **chorus girl, chorine,** chorus boy *or* man; chorus line; geisha *or* geisha girl; nautch girl, bayadere; hula girl; taxi dancer; topless dancer; burlesque dancer, strip-teaser, stripper *and* bump-and-grinder <nf>; choreographer

4 **ballroom, dance hall,** dancery; dance palace; discotheque, disco; dance floor; nightclub, casino

VERBS 5 **dance, trip the light fantastic,** go dancing, "trip it as we go, on the light fantastic toe"— Milton, trip, skip, hop, foot, prance <nf>, **hoof** *and* hoof it <nf>, clog, tap-dance, fold-dance, etc; shake, shimmy, shuffle; waltz, one-step, two-step, foxtrot, etc; choreograph

ADJS 6 **dancing, dance, terpsichorean;** balletic; choreographic

7 **kinds of dancing**

aerobic dancing	jazz tap
ballet	jitterbugging
ballroom dancing	lap dancing
belly dancing	line dancing
break dancing	marathon dancing
character dancing	modern ballet
choral dancing	modern dance
classical ballet	morris dancing
clog dancing	ritual dancing
comedy ballet	round dancing
country dancing	slam dancing
dirty dancing	social dancing
disco dancing	soft-shoe dancing
fan dancing	solo dancing
flamenco	square dancing
folklorico	step dancing
folk dancing	sword dancing
go-go dancing	tap dancing
interpretive dancing	taxi dancing
jazz dancing	

706 MOTION PICTURES

NOUNS 1 **motion pictures, movies, the movies, the pictures,** moving pictures, films, the films, the cinema, the screen, the big screen, the silver screen, the flicks *and* the flickers <nf>, motion-picture industry, moviedom, filmdom, Hollywood; **motion picture, movie, picture, film,** flick *and* flicker <nf>, picture show, motion-picture show, moving-picture show, photoplay, photodrama; **sound film,** silent film *or* silent; cinéma vérité *or* direct cinema; vérité; magic realism; **documentary film** *or* **movie,** docudrama, docutainment; **feature,** feature film, feature-length film, main attraction; theatrical film, big-screen film; **motion-picture genre** *or* **type;** TV film *or* movie, made-for-television movie *or* film, cable movie, miniseries;

short, short movie, short subject; preview, sneak preview; independent film, indie; **B-movie,** B-picture, Grade B movie, low-budget picture; **educational film** *or* **movie,** training film, promotional film, trigger film; **underground film** *or* **movie,** experimental film *or* movie, avant-garde film *or* movie, representational film, art film *or* movie, surrealistic film *or* movie; **cartoon,** animated cartoon, animation, cel animation, claymation, computer graphics; animatron, audioanimatron; video <nf>, rental movie, pay-per-view movie; **rated movie** *or* **film,** rating system, rating, G *or* general audience, PG *or* parental guidance suggested, PG-13 *or* parents strongly cautioned, R *or* restricted *or* children under 17 require accompanying parent or guardian, NC-17 *or* X *or* no children under 17 admitted; filmmaking

2 <movie type> drama, comedy, musical, love story, mystery, thriller, adventure, romance, Western, shoot-em-up <nf>, historical film, epic film, futuristic film, science-fiction *or* sci-fi film, foreign *or* foreign-language film, film noir, cult movie, girl flick

3 **script, screenplay,** motion-picture play *or* script, shooting script, storyboard, scenario, treatment, original screenplay, screen adaptation; plot, subplot, story; **dialogue,** book, lines; **role,** lead, romantic lead, stock character, ingenue, soubrette, cameo, bit, silent bit

4 **motion-picture studio, movie studio,** film studio, dream factory <nf>, animation studio, lot, back lot, sound stage, location; **set, motion-picture set, film set,** *mise-en-scène* <Fr>, properties *or* props, set dressing; **motion-picture company, film company,** production company; **producer,** filmmaker, moviemaker, **director,** auteur, screenwriter *or* scriptwriter *or* scenarist, editor *or* film editor, **actor, actress, film actor, film actress,** player, cinemactor, cinemactress, star, starlet, character actor, featured player, supporting actor *or* actress, supporting player, bit player, extra; **crew,** film crew

5 **motion-picture photography, photography,** cinematography, camera work, cinematics, camera work, camera angle, camera position, **shot, take,** footage, retake; screen test; **special effects,** rear-screen projection, mechanical effects, optical effects, process photography, FX; **color photography,** Technicolor *and* CinemaScope <trademark>; black-and-white, color, colorization; **cameraman** *or* **camerawoman, motion-picture cameraman** *or* **camerawoman,** cinematographer, director of photography *or* DP, first cameraman, lighting cameraman

6 motion-picture editing, film editing, editing, cutting, arranging, synchronizing; **transition,** fade, fade-out/fade-in, dissolve, lap *or* overlap dissolve, out-focus-dissolve, match dissolve, cross-dissolve, mix; colorizing, colorization; freeze-frame

7 motion-picture theater, movie theater, picture theater *or* house, film theater, cinema <Brit>, movie house *or* palace, dream palace <nf>, circuit theater, drive-in theater *or* movie, grind house <nf>, fleapit <Brit>; **screen,** movie screen, motion-picture screen, silver screen, aspect ratio *or* format, screen proportion, wide-screen, Cinerama *and* Cinemascope *and* VistaVision *and* Ultra-Panavision <trademarks>

VERBS **8 film, shoot,** cinematize, filmmake; colorize

ADJS **9 motion-picture, movie, film,** cinema, cinematic, filmistic, filmic; colorized; black-and-white; animated; animatronic, audioanimatronic

707 ENTERTAINER

NOUNS **1 entertainer,** public entertainer, performer; artist, artiste; impersonator, female impersonator; **vaudevillian,** vaudevillist; dancer 705.3, hoofer <nf>; song and dance man; chorus girl, show girl, chorine <nf>; coryphée; chorus boy *or* man; burlesque queen <nf>, **stripteaser,** exotic dancer, ecdysiast; stripper *and* peeler *and* stripteuse *and* bump-and-grinder <nf>; dancing girl, nautch girl, belly dancer; go-go dancer; geisha, geisha girl; mountebank; **magician,** conjurer, prestidigitator, sleight-of-hand artist; circus performer, clown; mummer, guiser <Scot>, guisard; singer, musician 710; performance artist

2 actor, actress, player, stage player *or* performer, playactor, histrion, histrio, thespian, Roscius, theatrical <nf>, trouper; child actor; mummer, pantomime, pantomimist; monologist, diseur, diseuse, reciter; dramatizer; mime, mimer, mimic; strolling player, stroller; barnstormer <nf>; character actor *or* actress, character man *or* woman, character; **villain,** antagonist, **bad guy** *or* **heavy** *or* black hat <nf>, villainess; juvenile, ingenue; *jeune premier* and *jeune première* <Fr>; soubrette; foil, feeder *and* stooge <nf>, straight man *or* person; utility man *or* person; protean actor; featured actor, leading man *or* lady, lead actor *or* actress; Method actor; matinee idol <nf>, star of stage and screen; romantic lead

3 circus artist *or* performer; trapeze artist, aerialist, flier <nf>; high-wire artist, tightrope walker, slack-roper artist, equilibrist; acrobat, tumbler; bareback rider; juggler; lion tamer, sword swallower; snake charmer; clown; ringmaster, equestrian director

4 motion-picture actor, movie actor; **movie star,** film star; starlet; day player, under-five player, contract player

5 ham *or* ham actor <nf>; grimacer

6 lead, leading man *or* lady, leading actor *or* actress, principal, **star,** superstar, megastar, headliner, headline *or* feature attraction; costar; **hero, heroine,** protagonist; juvenile lead, *jeune premier or jeune première* <Fr>; first tragedian, heavy lead <nf>; **prima donna,** diva, singer 710.13; première danseuse, prima ballerina, *danseur noble* <Fr>

7 supporting actor *or* **actress; support,** supporting cast; **supernumerary,** super *or* supe <nf>, spear-carrier <nf>, **extra;** bit player; walking gentleman *or* lady <nf>, walk-on, mute; figurant, figurante; **understudy, stand-in,** standby, substitute, swing

8 tragedian, tragedienne

9 comedian, comedienne, **comic, funnyman;** farcist, farcer, *farceur* and *farceuse* <Fr>; stand-up comic *or* comedian <nf>, light comedian, genteel comedian, low comedian, slapstick comedian, hokum *or* hoke comic <nf>

10 buffoon, *buffo* <Ital>, **clown, fool, jester, zany, merry-andrew,** jack-pudding, pickle-herring, **motley fool,** motley, wearer of the cap and bells; harlequin; Pierrot; Pantaloon, Pantalone; Punch, Punchinello, Pulcinella, Polichinelle; Punch and Judy; Hanswurst; Columbine; Harlequin; Scaramouch

11 cast, cast of characters, characters, persons of the drama, *dramatis personae* <L>; supporting cast; **company,** acting company, outfit, **troupe;** repertory company, stock company, touring company; ensemble, chorus, *corps de ballet* <Fr>; circus troupe

708 MUSIC

NOUNS **1 music** <see list>, harmonious sound, "the only universal tongue"—Samuel Rogers, "the universal language of mankind"—Longfellow

2 melody, melodiousness, **tunefulness,** musicalness, musicality; **tune, tone,** musical sound, musical quality, tonality; sweetness, dulcetness, mellifluence, mellifluousness

3 harmony, concord, concordance, concert, consonance *or* consonancy, consort, accordance, **accord,** monochord, concentus, symphony, diapason; synchronism, synchronization; **attunement,** tune, attune; chime, chiming; unison, unisonance, homophony, monody; **euphony;** chime; light *or* heavy harmony; two-part *or* three-part harmony, etc; harmony *or* music of the spheres; harmonics 709

4 air, aria, **tune, melody,** line, melodic line, refrain, note, **song,** solo, solo part, soprano part, treble, lay, descant, lilt, **strain,** measure; canto, cantus

5 piece, opus, **composition,** production, work; **score; arrangement,** adaptation, orchestration, harmonization, setting; **form;** transcription, accompaniment

6 classical music, classic; concert music, serious music, longhair music <nf>, symphonic music, chamber music, operatic music; semiclassic, semiclassical music

7 popular music, pop music, pop, light music, popular song *or* air *or* tune, **ballad;** hit, song hit, hit tune; Tin Pan Alley; karaoke

8 dance music, ballroom music, **dances;** syncopated music, **syncopation; ragtime** *or* rag, doo-wop; modern dance music

9 jazz; hot jazz, Dixieland, Basin Street, New Orleans, Chicago, traditional jazz *or* trad <Brit nf>; **swing,** jive <nf>; bebop, bop <nf>; mainstream jazz; avant-garde jazz, the new music <nf>, modern jazz, progressive jazz, third-stream jazz, cool jazz, acid jazz; boogie *or* boogie-woogie; rhythm-and-blues *or* R and B, blues; walking bass, stride *or* stride piano

10 rock-and-roll, rock music, rock-'n'-roll, rock, hard rock, soft rock, acid rock, folk rock, country rock, rockabilly, hard core, full-tilt boogie, heavy metal, punk rock, New Wave, fusion, grunge

11 folk music, folk songs, ethnic music, ethnomusicology; folk ballads, balladry; border ballads; country music, hillbilly music; country-and-western music, western swing; old-time country music *or* old-timey music; bluegrass; field holler; ethnic music, soul, reggae, ska

12 march, martial *or* military music; military march, quick *or* quickstep march; processional march, recessional march; funeral *or* dead march; wedding march

13 vocal music, song; singing, caroling, warbling, lyricism, vocalism, **vocalization;** operatic singing, bel canto, coloratura, bravura; choral singing; folk singing; croon, crooning; yodel, yodeling; scat, scat singing; intonation; hum, humming; solmization, tonic sol-fa, solfeggio, solfège, sol-fa, sol-fa exercise

14 song, lay, *Lied* <Ger>, *chanson* <Fr>, carol, **ditty,** canticle, lilt; **ballad,** ballade, *ballata* <Ital>; *canzone* <Ital>; canzonet, *canzonetta* <Ital>; aubade, serenade, lullaby, barcarole, glee, lay, chantey *or* chanty *or* shantey, chant, plainsong, canticle, chorale, carol, hymn, psalm, anthem

15 solo; karaoke; **aria;** operatic aria

16 <Italian terms for arias> arietta, arioso; aria buffa, aria da capo, aria d'agilità, aria da chiesa, aria d'imitazione, aria fugata, aria parlante; bravura, aria di bravura; coloratura, aria di coloratura; cantabile, aria cantabile; recitativo

17 sacred music, church music, liturgical music; **hymn,** hymn-tune, hymnody, hymnology; **psalm,** psalmody; **chorale,** choral fantasy, anthem; motet; **oratorio;** passion; **mass;** requiem mass, requiem, missa brevis, missa solemnis; offertory, offertory sentence *or* hymn; **cantata;** doxology, introit, canticle, paean, prosodion; recessional

18 part music, polyphonic music, part song, part singing, ensemble music, ensemble singing; **duet,** duo, *duettino* <Ital>; **trio,** terzet, *terzetto* <Ital>; **quartet; quintet; sextet,** sestet; **septet,** septuor; **octet;** cantata, lyric cantata; madrigal, *madrigaletto* <Ital>; **chorus** 710.16, chorale, glee club, choir; choral singing; four-part, soprano-alto-tenor-base *or* SATB; barbershop quartet

19 round, rondo, rondeau, **roundelay,** catch, troll; rondino, rondoletto; **fugue,** canon, fugato

20 polyphony, polyphonism; **counterpoint,** contrapunto; **plainsong,** Gregorian chant, Ambrosian chant; *faux-bourdon* <Fr>; musica ficta, false music

21 monody, monophony, homophony

22 part, melody *or* voice part, **voice** 709.5, **line;** descant, canto, cantus, cantus planus *or* firmus, plain song, plain chant; prick song, cantus figuratus; soprano, tenor, treble, alto, contralto, baritone, bass, bassus; undersong; drone; **accompaniment;** continuo, basso continuo, figured bass, thorough bass; ground bass, basso ostinato; drone, drone bass, bourdon, burden

23 response, responsory report, answer; echo; antiphon, antiphony, antiphonal chanting *or* singing

24 passage, phrase, musical phrase, strain, part, motive, motif, theme, subject, figure; leitmotiv; **movement;** introductory phrase, anacrusis; statement, exposition, development, variation; division; period, musical sentence; section; **measure;** figure; **verse, stanza;** burden, bourdon; **chorus, refrain,** response; folderol, **ornament** 709.18, cadence 709.23, harmonic close, resolution; **coda,** tailpiece; ritornello; intermezzo, interlude; bass passage; tutti, tutti passage; bridge, bridge passage

25 <fast, slow, etc passages> presto, prestissimo; allegro, allegretto; scherzo, scherzando; adagio, adagietto; andante, andantino; largo, larghetto, larghissimo; crescendo; diminuendo, decrescendo; rallentando, ritardando; ritenuto; piano, pianissimo; forte, fortissimo; staccato, marcato, marcando; pizzicato; spiccato; legato; stretto

26 overture, prelude, *Vorspiel* <Ger>, **introduction,** operatic overture, dramatic overture, concert overture, voluntary, descant, vamp; curtain raiser

27 impromptu, extempore, improvisation, interpolation; cadenza; **ornament** 709.18, flourish, ruffles and flourishes, grace note, appoggiatura, mordent, upper mordent, inverted mordent; **run,** melisma; vamp; lick, hot lick, riff

28 score, musical score *or* copy, **music,** notation, musical notation, written music, copy, draft, transcript, transcription, version, edition, text, arrangement; part; full *or* orchestral score, compressed *or* short score, piano score, vocal score, instrumental score; tablature, lute tablature; opera score, opera; **libretto;** sheet music; **songbook,** songster; hymnbook, hymnal; music paper; music roll

29 staff, stave <Brit>; line, ledger line; bar, bar line; space, degree; brace

30 execution, performance; rendering, rendition, music-making, **touch, expression;** fingering; pianism; intonation; repercussion; pizzicato, staccato, spiccato, parlando, legato, cantando, rubato, demilegato, mezzo staccato, slur; glissando

31 musicianship; musical talent *or* flair, musicality; virtuosity; pianism; musical ear, ear for music; musical sense, sense of rhythm; absolute *or* perfect pitch; relative pitch

32 musical occasion; choral service, service of lessons and carols, service of song, sing <nf>, singing, community singing *or* sing, singfest, songfest, sing-in; karaoke; folk-sing *and* hootenanny <nf>; **festival,** music festival; opera festival; folk-music festival, jazz festival, rock festival; *Sängerfest* <Ger>, *eisteddfod* <Welsh>; jam session <nf>

33 performance, musical performance, **program,** musical program, program of music; **concert,** symphony concert, chamber concert; philharmonic concert, philharmonic; popular concert, pops *and* pop concert <nf>; promenade concert, prom <nf>; band concert; **recital;** service of music; concert performance <of an opera>; **medley,** potpourri; swan song, farewell performance

34 musical theater, music theater, lyric theater, musical stage, lyric stage; **music drama,** lyric drama; song-play, *Singspiel* <Ger>; **opera,** grand opera, light opera, ballad opera; comic opera, *opéra bouffe* <Fr>, *opera buffa* <Ital>; **operetta; musical comedy; musical;** Broadway musical; musical drama; **ballet,** *opéra ballet* <Fr>, comedy ballet, *ballet d'action* <Fr>, *ballet divertissement* <Fr>; dance drama; chorus show; **song-and-dance act;** minstrel, minstrel show

VERBS **35 harmonize,** be harmonious, be in tune *or* concert, chord, **accord,** symphonize, synchronize, **chime, blend,** blend in, symphonize, segue; tune, attune, atone, sound together, sound in tune; assonate; melodize, musicalize

36 tune, tune up, attune, atone, chord, **put in tune;** voice, string; tone up, tone down

37 strike up, strike up a tune, **strike up the band,** break into music, pipe up, pipe up a song, yerk out <nf>, **burst into song**

38 sing, vocalize, carol, descant, lilt, troll, line out *and* belt out *and* tear off <nf>; **warble,** trill, tremolo, quaver, shake; **chirp,** chirrup, twit <Brit nf>, **twitter;** pipe, whistle, tweedle, tweedledee; **chant; intone,** intonate; **croon; hum; yodel;** roulade; chorus, choir, sing in chorus; **hymn,** anthem, psalm, "make a joyful noise unto the Lord"—Bible; sing the praises of; minstrel; ballad; **serenade;** sol-fa, do-re-mi, solmizate

39 play, perform, execute, render, do; interpret; make music; concertize; symphonize; chord; accompany; play by ear; play at, pound out *and* saw away at <nf>

40 strum, thrum, pluck, plunk, **pick,** twang, sweep the strings

41 fiddle <nf>, play violin *or* the violin; scrape *and* saw <nf>

42 blow a horn, sound *or* wind the horn, sound, blow, wind, **toot,** tootle, pipe, tweedle; bugle, carillon, clarion, fife, flute, trumpet, whistle; bagpipe, doodle <Brit nf>; lip, tongue, double-tongue, triple-tongue

43 syncopate, play jazz, swing, jive <nf>, rag <nf>, jam <nf>, riff <nf>

44 beat time, keep time, tap, tap out the rhythm, keep tempo; count, count the beats; beat the drum, **drum** 55.4, play drum *or* the drums, thrum, beat, thump, pound; tomtom; ruffle; beat *or* sound a tattoo

45 conduct, direct, lead, wield the baton

46 compose, write, arrange, score, set, set to music, put to music; musicalize, melodize, **harmonize; orchestrate;** instrument, instrumentate; **adapt,** make an adaptation; transcribe, transpose

ADJS **47 musical, musically inclined,** musicianly, with an ear for music; virtuoso, virtuose, virtuosic; **music-loving,** music-mad, musicophile, philharmonic; absolute, aleatory

48 melodious, melodic; **musical,** music-like; **tuneful,** tunable; fine-toned, tonal, **pleasant-sounding,** agreeable-sounding, pleasant, appealing, agreeable, catchy, singable; **euphonious** *or* euphonic, **lyric, lyrical,** melic; **lilting,** songful, songlike; **sweet, dulcet,** sweet-sounding, achingly sweet, sweet-flowing; honeyed, mellifluent, mellifluous, mellisonant, music-flowing; rich, mellow; sonorous, canorous; golden, golden-toned; silvery, silver-toned; sweet-voiced, golden-voiced, silver-voiced, silver-tongued, golden-tongued, music-tongued; ariose, arioso, cantabile

49 harmonious, harmonic, symphonious; harmonizing, **chiming,** blending, well-blended, blended; **concordant,** consonant, accordant, according, **in accord,** in concord, in concert; synchronous, synchronized, in sync <nf>, symphonic, **in tune,** tuned, attuned; in unison, in chorus; unisonous, unisonant; homophonic, monophonic, monodic; assonant, assonantal; rhythmic

50 vocal, singing; **choral,** choric; four-part; operatic; hymnal; psalmic, psalmodic, psalmodial; sacred, liturgical; treble, soprano, tenor, alto, falsetto; coloratura, lyric, bravura, dramatic, heroic; baritone; bass

51 instrumental, orchestral, symphonic, concert; dramatico-musical; jazz, syncopated, jazzy, rock, swing

52 polyphonic, contrapuntal

ADJS, ADVS **53** <directions, style> legato; staccato; spiccato; pizzicato; forte, fortissimo; piano, pianissimo; sordo; crescendo, accrescendo; decrescendo, diminuendo, morendo; dolce; amabile; affettuoso, con affetto; amoroso, con amore lamentabile; agitato, con agitazione; leggiero; agilmente, con agilità; capriccioso, a capriccio; scherzando, scherzoso; appassionato, appassionatamente; abbandono; brillante; parlando; a cappella; trillando, tremolando, tremoloso; sotto voce; stretto

54 <slowly> largo, larghetto, allargando; adagio, adagietto; andante, andantino, andante moderato; calando; a poco; lento; ritardando, rallentando

55 <fast> presto, prestissimo; veloce; accelerando; vivace, vivacissimo; desto, con anima, con brio; allegro, allegretto; affrettando, moderato

56 varieties of music

absolute music	classical music
acid rock	country-and-western music
Afro-beat	country music
aleatory music	country rock
art music	dance hall
art rock	dance music
atonal music *or* atonalism	deca-rock *or* glitter rock
ballet music	Delta blues
baroque music	disco
beach music	ear candy <nf>
big band	easy listening music
bluegrass	electronic *or* synthesized
bubblegum	music
calypso	elevator music *or* Muzak
cathedral music	<trademark>
chamber music	ensemble music
church music	field music
circus music	folk music

folk rock	program music
funk	progressive rock
fusion	progressive soul
gospel music	psychobilly
Gregorian chant	punkabilly
grunge	punk rock
hard rock	raga-rock
heavy metal	ragtime music *or* ragtime
heavy rock	rap music
hillbilly music	reggae
hiphop	rhythm and blues *or* R and
house music *or* House	B *or* the blues
inspirational music	rock music *or* rock'n'roll
instrumental music	rockabilly
jazz music *or* jazz	rococo music
jazz rock	romantic music
Latin rock	sacred music
light music	salon music
loft jazz	semiclassical music
martial *or* military music	ska
new age *or* new wave	soul music
operatic music	swing music *or* swing
organ music	technopop
part music	thirdstream music
piped music	through-composed music
plainsong	twelve-tone music *or*
political rock	serialism
pomp rock	vocal music
polyphonic music	wind music
pop-rock	Zopf music
popular *or* pop music	zydeco

709 HARMONICS, MUSICAL ELEMENTS

NOUNS **1 harmonics,** harmony; melodics; rhythmics; musicality; music, **music theory,** theory; musicology; musicography

2 harmonization; orchestration, instrumentation; arrangement, setting, adaptation, transcription; accompaniment; harmonic progression, chordal progression; phrasing, modulation, intonation, preparation, suspension, solution, resolution; tone painting

3 tone, tonality 50.3

4 pitch, tuning, tune, **tone, key, note,** register, tonality; height, depth; pitch range, tessitura; classical pitch, high pitch, diapason *or* normal *or* French pitch, international *or* concert *or* new philharmonic pitch, standard pitch, low pitch, Stuttgart *or* Scheibler's pitch, philharmonic pitch, philosophical pitch; temperament, equal temperament; absolute pitch, perfect pitch

5 voice, voce <Ital>; voce di petto <Ital>, chest voice; voce di testa <Ital>, head voice; **soprano,** mezzo-soprano, dramatic soprano, soprano spinto, lyric soprano, coloratura soprano; boy soprano; male soprano, castrato; alto, contralto; tenor, lyric tenor, operatic tenor, heldentenor *or* heroic tenor *or* Wagnerian tenor; countertenor *or* male alto; baritone, light *or* lyric baritone; **bass,** basso, basso profundo, basso cantante *or* lyric bass, basso buffo *or* comic bass; treble, falsetto, castrato

6 **scale, gamut,** register, compass, range, diapason; diatonic scale, chromatic scale, modal scale, enharmonic scale, major scale, minor scale, natural *or* harmonic *or* melodic minor, whole-tone scale; great scale; octave scale, dodecuple scale, pentatonic scale; tetrachordal scale; twelve-tone *or* dodecuple scale, tone block, tone row, tone cluster

7 **sol-fa,** tonic sol-fa, do-re-mi; Guidonian syllables, ut, re, mi, fa, sol, la; sol-fa syllables, do, re, mi, fa, sol, la, ti *or* si, do; solmization, solfeggio; fixed-do system, movable-do system; solmization; bobization

8 <diatonic series> tetrachord, chromatic tetrachord, enharmonic tetrachord, Dorian tetrachord; hexachord, hard hexachord, natural hexachord, soft hexachord; pentachord

9 **octave,** *ottava* <Ital>, eighth; *ottava alta* <Ital>, *ottava bassa* <Ital>; small octave, great octave; contraoctave, subcontraoctave, double contraoctave; one-line octave, two-line octave, four-line octave, two-foot octave, four-foot octave; tenor octave

10 **mode,** octave species; major mode, minor mode; Greek mode, Ionian mode, Dorian mode, Phrygian mode, Lydian mode, mixolydian mode, Aeolian mode, Locrian mode; hypoionian mode, hypodorian mode, hypophrygian mode, hypolydian mode, hypoaeolian mode, hypomixolydian mode, hypolocrian mode; Gregorian *or* ecclesiastical *or* church *or* medieval mode; plagal mode, authentic mode; Indian *or* Hindu mode, raga

11 **form,** arrangement, pattern, model, design; song *or* lied form, primary form; **sonata form,** sonata allegro, ternary form, symphonic form, canon form, toccata form, fugue form, rondo form

12 **notation,** character, mark, symbol, signature, sign, *segno* <Ital>; proportional notation; chart *or* paper <nf>, dot; custos, direct; cancel; bar, measure; measure *or* time signature, key signature; tempo mark, metronome *or* metronomic mark; fermata, hold, pause; *presa* <Ital>, lead; slur, tie, ligature, vinculum, enharmonic tie; swell; accent, accent mark, expression mark; ledger, staff, stave, line, space, brace, rest, interval

13 **clef;** C clef, soprano clef, alto *or* viola clef, tenor clef; F *or* bass clef, G *or* treble clef

14 **note,** musical note, notes of a scale; **tone** 50.2; **sharp, flat, natural; accidental;** double whole note, breve; whole note, semibreve; half note, minim;

quarter note, crotchet; eighth note, quaver; sixteenth note, semiquaver; thirty-second note, demisemiquaver; sixty-fourth note, hemidemisemiquaver; tercet, triplet; sustained note, dominant, dominant note; enharmonic, enharmonic note; separation, hammering, staccato, spiccato; connected, smooth, legato; responding note, report; shaped note, patent note

15 **key,** key signature, tonality, sharps and flats; **keynote,** tonic; tonic key; major, minor, major *or* minor key, tonic major *or* minor; supertonic, mediant, submediant, dominant, subdominant, subtonic; pedal point, organ point

16 **harmonic,** harmonic tone, overtone, upper partial tone; flageolet tone

17 **chord,** *concento* <Ital>, combination of tones *or* notes; major *or* minor chord, primary *or* secondary chord, tonic chord, dominant chord; tertiary chord, third, fourth, etc; interval, major *or* minor interval

18 **ornament,** grace, arabesque, embellishment, *fioritura* <Ital>; **flourish,** roulade, flight, run; passage, division 708.24; florid phrase *or* passage; coloratura; incidental, incidental note; grace note, appoggiatura, arpeggio, acciaccatura; rubato; mordent, single mordent, double *or* long mordent; inverted mordent, pralltriller; turn, back *or* inverted turn; cadence, cadenza

19 **trill,** trillo; trillet, *trilleto* <Ital>; **tremolo,** tremolant, tremolando; quaver, quiver, tremble, tremor, flutter, falter, shake; **vibrato,** *Bebung* <Ger>

20 **interval,** degree, **step,** note, tone; second, third, fourth, fifth, sixth, seventh, octave; prime *or* unison interval, major *or* minor interval, harmonic *or* melodic interval, enharmonic interval, diatonic interval; parallel *or* consecutive intervals, parallel fifths, parallel octaves; whole step, major second; half step, halftone, semitone, minor second; augmented interval; diminished interval; diatonic semitone, chromatic semitone, less semitone, quarter semitone, tempered *or* mean semitone; quarter step, enharmonic diesis; diatessaron, diapason; *tierce de Picardie* <Fr> *or* Picardy third; augmented fourth *or* tritone

21 **rest,** pause; whole rest, breve rest, semibreve rest, half rest, minim, quarter rest, eighth rest, sixteenth rest, thirty-second rest, sixty-fourth rest

22 **rhythm, beat, meter, measure,** number *or* numbers, movement, **lilt, swing;** prosody, metrics; rhythmic pattern *or* phrase

23 **cadence** *or* cadency, authentic cadence, plagal cadence, mixed cadence, perfect *or* imperfect cadence, half cadence, deceptive *or* false cadence, interrupted *or* suspended cadence

24 tempo, time, beat, time pattern, timing; time signature; simple time *or* measure, compound time *or* measure; two-part *or* duple time, three-part *or* triple time, triplet, four-part *or* quadruple time, five-part *or* quintuple time, six-part *or* sextuple time, seven-part *or* septuple time, nine-part *or* nonuple time; two-four time, six-eight time, etc; tempo rubato, rubato; mixed times; **syncopation,** syncope; **ragtime,** rag <nf>; waltz time, three-four *or* three-quarter time, andante tempo, march tempo, etc; largo, etc; presto, etc

25 accent, accentuation, rhythmical accent *or* accentuation, ictus, emphasis, stress arsis, thesis

26 beat, throb, pulse, pulsation; downbeat, upbeat, offbeat; bar beat

ADJS **27 tonal,** tonic; chromatic, enharmonic; semitonic

28 rhythmic, rhythmical, cadent, cadenced, **measured, metric, metrical;** in rhythm, in numbers; beating, throbbing, pulsing, pulsating, pulsative, pulsatory

29 syncopated; ragtime, ragtimey <nf>; **jazz;** jazzy *and* jazzed *and* jazzed up <nf>, hot, swingy <nf>

ADVS **30 in time,** in tempo 709.24, *a tempo* <Ital>

710 MUSICIAN

NOUNS **1 musician,** musico, **music maker,** professional musician; performer, executant, interpreter, tunester, artiste, artist, concert artist, player, **virtuoso,** virtuosa; maestro; recitalist; **soloist,** duettist; singer; street musician, busker <chiefly Brit>

2 popular *or* **pop musician;** ragtime musician; **jazz musician, jazzman;** swing musician; big-band musician; **rock** *or* **rock'n'roll musician**

3 player, instrumentalist, instrumental musician; bandman, bandsman; orchestral musician; symphonist; concertist; accompanist, accompanyist

4 wind player, wind-instrumentalist, horn player, French-horn player *or* hornist, horner, piper, tooter; bassoonist, bugler, clarinetist, cornettist, fifer, oboist, piccoloist, saxophonist, trombonist; trumpeter, trumpet major; fluegelhornist; flutist *or* flautist

5 string musician, strummer, picker <nf>, thrummer, twanger; banjoist, banjo-picker <nf>, citharist, guitarist, guitar-picker <nf>, classical guitarist, folk guitarist, lute player, lutenist, lutist, lyrist, mandolinist, theorbist; violinist, fiddler <nf>; bass violinist, bassist, bass player, contrabassist; violoncellist, cellist, celloist; violist; harpist, harper; zitherist, psalterer

6 xylophonist, marimbaist, vibist *or* vibraphonist

7 pianist, pianiste, pianofortist, piano player, ivory tickler *or* thumper <nf>; keyboard player *or* keyboardist; harpsichordist, clavichordist, monochordist; accordionist, concertinist

8 organist, organ player

9 organ-grinder, hurdy-gurdist, hurdy-gurdyist, hurdy-gurdy man

10 drummer, percussionist, tympanist *or* timpanist, kettle-drummer; taborer

11 cymbalist, cymbaler; bell-ringer, **carilloneur,** campanologist, campanist; triangle player

12 orchestra, band, ensemble, combo <nf>, group; strings, woodwind *or* woodwinds, brass *or* brasses, string *or* woodwind *or* brass section, string *or* woodwind *or* brass choir; desks

13 singer, vocalist, vocalizer, voice, songster, songbird, warbler, lead singer, backup vocalist, caroler, melodist, minstrel, cantor; songstress, singstress, cantatrice, chanteuse, song stylist, canary <nf>; chanter, chantress; aria singer, lieder singer, opera singer, diva, prima donna; improvisator; rap singer; blues singer, torch singer <nf>; crooner, rock *or* rock-and-roll singer; yodeler; country singer, folk singer *or* folkie <nf>; psalm singer, hymner; Meistersinger; **singing voice, voice** 709.5

14 minstrel, ballad singer, balladeer, **bard,** rhapsode, rhapsodist; wandering *or* strolling minstrel, **troubadour,** trovatore, trouvère, minnesinger, scop, gleeman, fili, jongleur; street singer, wait; serenader; **folk singer,** folk-rock singer; country-and-western singer

15 choral singer, choir member, chorister, chorus singer, choralist; choirman, **choirboy; chorus girl,** chorine <nf>

16 chorus, chorale, choir, choral group, choral society, oratorio society, chamber chorus *or* Kammerchor <Ger>, men's *or* women's chorus, male chorus *or* Männerchor <Ger>, mixed chorus, ensemble, voices; **glee club,** Liedertafel and Liederkranz <Ger>, singing club *or* society; *a cappella* choir; choral symphony

17 conductor, leader, maestro, symphonic conductor, **music director,** director, Kapellmeister <Ger>; **orchestra leader, band leader, bandmaster,** band major, drum major

18 choirmaster, choral director *or* conductor, chorus master, song leader, Kapellmeister <Ger> *or* maestro di cappella <Ital>; choir chaplain, minister of music, precentor, cantor, chorister

19 concertmaster, concertmeister, Konzertmeister <Ger>, first violinist; first chair

20 composer, scorer, arranger, musicographer; melodist, melodizer; harmonist, harmonizer; **orchestrator;** adapter; symphonist; tone poet; ballad maker *or* writer, balladeer, balladist, balladmonger; madrigalist; lyrist; hymnist, hymnographer, hymnologist; contrapuntist; song writer *or* songwriter, songsmith, tunesmith; lyricist, librettist; musicologist, ethnomusicologist; music teacher

21 **music lover,** philharmonic person, **music fan** *and* music buff <nf>, musicophile; musicmonger; concertgoer, operagoer, opera lover; tonalist

22 <patrons> the Muses, the Nine, sacred Nine, tuneful Nine, Pierides; Apollo, Apollo Musagetes; Orpheus; Erato, Euterpe, Polymnia *or* Polyhymnia, Terpsichore, St Cecilia

23 **songbird,** singing bird, **songster,** feathered songster, warbler; nightingale, Philomel; bulbul, canary, cuckoo, lark, mavis, mockingbird, oriole, ringdove, song sparrow, thrush

711 MUSICAL INSTRUMENTS

1 **musical instrument,** instrument of music; electronic instrument, synthesizer, Mellotron <trademark>, Moog synthesizer <trademark>

2 **string** *or* **stringed instrument,** chordophone; strings, string choir

3 **harp, lyre**

4 **plucked stringed instrument** <see list>

5 **viol** *or* **violin family** <see list>, chest of viols; Stradivarius, Stradivari, Strad <nf>; Amati, Cremona, Guarnerius; bow, fiddlestick, fiddlebow; bridge, sound hole, soundboard, fingerboard, tuning peg, scroll; string, G string, D string, A string, E string

6 **wind instrument, wind;** aerophone; **horn,** pipe, tooter; mouthpiece, embouchure, lip, chops <nf>; valve, bell, reed, double reed, key, slide

7 **brass wind** <see list> brass *or* brass-wind instrument; brasses, brass choir

8 **woodwind** <see list>, wood *or* woodwind instrument; woods, woodwind choir; reed instrument, **reed;** double-reed instrument, **double reed; single-reed instrument,** single reed

9 **bagpipe** *or* bagpipes, pipes, union pipes, war pipes, Irish pipes, doodlesack, *Dudelsack* <Ger>; cornemuse, musette; sordellina; chanter, drone; pipe bag

10 **mouth organ,** mouth harp, harp, French harp <nf>, **harmonica,** harmonicon; jaws *or* Jew's harp, mouth bow; kazoo

11 **accordion,** piano accordion; **concertina;** squeeze box <nf>; mellophone; bandonion

12 keyboard instrument <see list>, **piano, harpsichord, clavichord, player piano;** music roll, piano player roll

13 **organ,** keyboard wind instrument

14 **hurdy-gurdy,** vielle, **barrel organ,** hand organ, grind organ, street organ

15 **music box,** musical box; orchestrion, orchestrina

16 **percussion instrument** <see list>, percussion, **drum;** drumstick, jazz stick, tymp stick

17 **keyboard,** fingerboard; console, **keys,** manual, claviature; piano keys, ivories <nf>, eighty-eight <nf>, organ manual, great, swell, choir, solo, echo; pedals

18 **carillon,** chimes 711.18, chime of bells; electronic carillon

19 **organ stop,** stop rank, register

20 string, chord, steel string, wound string, nylon string; fiddlestring, catgut; horsehair; music wire, piano wire

21 plectrum, plectron, pick

22 <aids> metronome, rhythmometer; tone measurer, monochord, sonometer; tuning fork, tuning bar, diapason; pitch pipe, tuning pipe; mute; music stand, music lyre; baton, conductor's baton, stick <nf>; MIDI

23 **plucked stringed instruments**

acoustic guitar	F-hole guitar
angelica *or* angel lute	gittern
Appalachian dulcimer	harp
Autoharp <trademark>	Hawaiian guitar
archlute	lute
balalaika	lyre
bandore	mando-bass
bandurria <Sp>	mando-cello
banjo	mandolin *or* mandola
banjolin	mandolute
banjorine	mandore
banjo-ukulele *or* banjuke *or*	oud
banjulele *or* banjo-uke	pandora
banjo-zither	psaltery
bass guitar	samisen
bouzouki	sitar
centerhole guitar	Spanish guitar
chitarra	steel guitar
cittern	tamboura *or* tambura
classical guitar	theorbo
colascione	troubadour fiddle
concert guitar	ukulele *or* uke <nf>
Dobro guitar <trademark>	vina
electric guitar	zither

24 **viol or violin family**

alto *or* tenor viol	bass viol *or* bass *or*
baritone viol *or* viola	doghouse *or* bass fiddle
d'amore	*or* bull fiddle <nf>
baryton	gusla *or* gusle
basso da camera <Ital>	kit
bass viol *or* viola da gamba	kit violin
contrabass	lira da braccio
crowd <old>	lira da gamba
crwth	lyra viol
descant viol	nyckelharpa
double bass *or* violone *or*	pocket *or* kit fiddle

rebab
rebec
treble viol
trumpet marine *or* tromba
  marina
vielle
viol *or* viola da braccio
viol *or* viola da spalla
viol *or* viola di bordone
viol *or* viola di fagotto
viola *or* tenor

viola alta
viola bastarda
viola d'amore
viola pomposa
violette
violin *or* fiddle <nf>
violinette
violino piccolo
violoncello *or* cello
violoncello piccolo
violotta

25 brass wind instruments and brasses

alpenhorn *or* alphorn
althorn *or* alto horn
ballad horn
baritone horn
bass horn
bombardon
buccina
bugle *or* bugle horn
clarion
cornet *or* cornet-à-pistons
cornopean
double-bell euphonium
E-flat horn
euphonium
F horn
flugelhorn
French horn
helicon
horn
hunting horn *or corno di
  caccia* <Ital>
key trumpet
lituus
lur

mellophone
nyas taranga
oliphant
ophicleide
orchestral horn
pocket trumpet
post horn
sackbut
saxcornet
saxhorn
saxophone
saxtuba
serpent
slide trombone *or* sliphorn
  <nf>
sousaphone
tenor tuba
tromba
trombone
trumpet
tuba
valve trombone
valve trumpet

26 woodwinds

aulos
bagpipe
bass *or* basset oboe
bass clarinet
basset horn
bassoon
bombarde
bombardon
clarinet *or* licorice stick
  <nf>
contrabassoon *or*
  contrafagotto
double bassoon
English horn *or* cor anglais
  <Fr>
fife
fipple flute *or* pipe
flageolet
flute
heckclarina
heckelphone *or* bass oboe

hornpipe
krummhorn *or* cromorne
  or cromorna *or*
  crumhorn
musette
nose-flute
oaten reed
oboe *or* hautboy *or*
  hautbois
oboe d'amore <Ital>
oboe da caccia <Ital>
ocarina *or* sweet potato
  <nf>
Pandean pipe
panpipe
pibgorn *or* pibcorn
piccolo
pipe
pommer
recorder
saxophone *or* sax <nf>

shakuhachi
shawm
sonorophone
syrinx *or* shepherd's pipe
tabor pipe

tenoroon
tin-whistle *or* penny-
  whistle
transverse flute
whistle

27 keyboard stringed instruments

baby grand
cembalo
clarichord
clavichord
clavicittern
clavicymbal *or*
  clavicembalo
clavicytherium
clavier
concert grand
console piano
cottage piano
couched harp
digital piano
dulcimer harpsichord
electronic keyboard
fortepiano
grand piano
hammer dulcimer
harmonichord
harpsichord

lyrichord
manichord
melodion
melopiano
monochord
pair of virginals
parlor grand
pianette
pianino
piano *or* pianoforte
piano-violin
Pianola <trademark>
player *or* mechanical
  piano
sostinente pianoforte
spinet
square piano
street piano
upright *or* upright piano
violin piano
virginal

28 percussion instruments and drums

anvil
bass drum
bells
bones
bongo drum
carillon
castanets
celesta
chimes
clappers
conga
cowbell
crash cymbal
cymbals *or* potlids <nf>
drumhead
drumskin
finger cymbals
gamelan
glockenspiel
gong
handbells
highhat cymbal <nf>
kazoo
kettledrum *or* timbal *or*
  timpani
lithophone
lyra
maraca
marimba
mbira *or* kalimba

membranophone
metallophone
mirliton
musical glasses *or* glass
  harmonica
musical saw
nagara <India>
naker
orchestral bells
rattle
rattlebones
ride cymbal
side drum
sizzler
snappers
snare drum
spoons
tabor
tambourine
tam-tam
tenor drum
thumb piano
timbale
timbrel
timpani *or* kettledrums
tintinnabula
tom-tom
tonitruone
triangle
troll-drum

tubular bells	war drum
vibraphone *or* vibraharp *or*	xylophone
vibes <nf>	xylorimba

29 reed organs

accordion	melodeon
concertina	mouth organ
harmonica	organ
harmonium	reed organ

712 VISUAL ARTS

NOUNS **1** **visual arts; art, artwork,** the arts; **fine arts,** *beaux arts* <Fr>; arts of design, **design,** designing; art form; abstract art, representative art; **graphic arts** 713; plastic art; **arts and crafts;** primitive art, cave art; folk art; calligraphy; commercial art, applied art, industrial art; sculpture 715; ceramics 742; photography 714; etching, engraving 713.2; decoration 498.1; artist 716

2 "the conveyance of spirit by means of matter"—Salvador de Madariaga, "an instant arrested in eternity"—James Huneker, "life upon the larger scale"—E B Browning, "the conscious utterance of thought, by speech or action, to any end"—Emerson, "the wine of life"—Jean Paul Richter, "a shadow of the divine perfection"—Michelangelo, "life seen through a temperament"—Zola, "a form of catharsis"—Dorothy Parker

3 **craft, manual art,** industrial art, **handicraft,** arts and crafts, artisan work, craftwork, artisanship; industrial design; woodcraft, woodwork, carpentry, woodworking, metalcraft, stonecraft; ceramics, glassmaking

4 <act or art of painting> **painting,** coloring, "a noble and expressive language"—Ruskin; the brush

5 <art of drawing> **drawing, draftsmanship, sketching, delineation; black and white,** charcoal; mechanical drawing, drafting; freehand drawing

6 scenography, ichnography, orthographic *or* orthogonal projection

7 **artistry, art, talent,** artistic skill, flair, artistic flair, artistic invention; artiness *and* arty-craftiness *and* artsy-craftiness <nf>; artistic temperament, artistic taste; virtu, artistic quality

8 **style;** lines; genre; **school,** movement <see list>; the grand style

9 **treatment; technique,** draftsmanship, brushwork, painterliness; **composition, design,** arrangement; grouping, balance; **color,** values; atmosphere, tone; shadow, shading; **line;** perspective

10 **work of art, object of art,** objet d'art, art object, art work, artistic production *or* creation, piece, **work, study, design, composition;** creation, brainchild; virtu, article *or* object *or* piece of virtu; **masterpiece,** *chef d'œuvre* <Fr>, masterwork,

master <old>, old master, classic; museum piece; grotesque; statue; mobile, stabile; nude, still life; pastiche, *pasticcio* <Ital>; artware, artwork; bric-a-brac; kitsch

11 **picture; image, likeness, representation,** tableau; "a poem without words"—Horace; photograph 714.3; **illustration,** illumination; miniature; copy, reproduction; print, color print; engraving 713.2, stencil, block print; daub; abstraction, abstract; mural, fresco, wall painting; cyclorama, panorama; montage, collage, assemblage; still life, study in still life; tapestry, mosaic, stained glass, stained glass window, **icon,** altarpiece, diptych, triptych

12 **scene, view, scape; landscape;** waterscape, riverscape, seascape, seapiece; airscape, skyscape, cloudscape; snowscape; cityscape, townscape; farmscape; pastoral; treescape; diorama; exterior, interior

13 **drawing; delineation;** line drawing; **sketch, draft; black and white,** chiaroscuro; **charcoal, crayon, pen-and-ink,** pencil drawing, charcoal drawing, pastel, pastel painting, crayon drawing; silhouette; vignette; doodle; rough draft *or* copy, rough outline, study, design; caricature; cartoon, sinopia, **study,** design; *brouillon* and *ébauche* and *esquisse* <Fr>; diagram, graph; mechanical drawing; silver-print drawing, tracing; doodle, graffito, scribble

14 **painting, canvas,** easel-picture, "silent poetry"—Simonides, "the intermediate somewhat between a thought and a thing"—Coleridge; **oil painting,** oil; **watercolor,** water, aquarelle, wash, wash drawing; acrylic; finger painting; tempera, egg tempera; *gouache* <Fr>

15 **portrait, portraiture, portrayal;** head; profile; silhouette, shadow figure; nude; miniature

16 **cartoon, caricature; comic strip;** comic section, comics, funny paper *and* funnies <nf>; comic book; animated cartoon

17 **studio,** atelier <Fr>; **gallery** 386.9

18 <art equipment> palette; easel; paintbox; art paper, drawing paper; sketchbook, sketchpad; canvas, artists' canvas; canvas board; scratchboard; lay figure; camera obscura, camera lucida; maulstick; palette knife, spatula; brush, paintbrush; air brush, spray gun; pencil, drawing pencil; pen, ink, marker, highlighter; crayon, charcoal, chalk, pastel; stump; painter's cream; ground; pigments, medium; siccative, drier; fixative, varnish; **paint** 35.8

VERBS **19** **portray, picture,** picturize, **depict, limn,** draw *or* paint a picture; **paint** 35.14; brush, brush in; color, tint, colorize; spread *or* lay on a color; **daub** <nf>; scumble; **draw, sketch, delineate;**

draft; pencil, chalk, crayon, charcoal; draw in, pencil in; dash off, scratch <nf>; doodle; design; diagram; cartoon; copy, trace; stencil; touch up; hatch, crosshatch, shade; doodle

ADJS **20 artistic,** painterly; **arty** or arty-crafty or artsy-craftsy or artsy-fartsy <nf>; **art-minded,** art-conscious; imaginative, creative, stylized, **aesthetic; tasteful; beautiful; decorative, ornamental** 498.10; **well-composed,** well-grouped, well-arranged, well-varied; of consummate art; in the grand style

21 pictorial, pictural, **graphic, picturesque;** picturable; photographic 714.17; scenographic; painty, pastose; scumbled; monochrome, polychrome; freehand

22 art schools, groups, movements

abstract expressionism	Madrid
action painting	Mannerist
American scene painting	Milanese
art deco	Modenese
Art Nouveau	modernism
Arts and Crafts movement	Momentum
Ashcan school or the Eight	'N'
avant-garde	Neapolitan
Barbizon school	neoclassicism
baroque	Neonism
Bauhaus	New Objectivity
Biedermeier	New York
Bolognese	op art
British	Origine
classical abstraction	Paduan
Cobra	Parisian
cubism	Phases
Dada	plein-air or pleinairism
De Stijl	pointillism
Der Blaue Reiter	pre-Columbian
Die Brücke	Pre-Raphaelite
Dutch	Raphaelite
eclectic	realism
expressionism	Reflex
fauvism or Les Fauves	Restany
Flemish	Rocky Mountain
Florentine	rococo
Fontainebleau	Roman or Romanesque
French	romanticism
Glasgow	Scottish Colorists
Gothic	Sienese
Honfleur	Spur
Hudson River	Suprematism
impressionism	tachisme
International Gothic or International	tenebrists
	The Ten
Italian	Tuscan
Jugendstil	Umbrian
L'Age d'or	Unit One
letrist	Venetian
Lombard	Wanderers
Madinensor	Washington

713 GRAPHIC ARTS

NOUNS **1 graphic arts, graphics; printmaking; painting; drawing; relief-carving; photography** 714; **printing** 548; graphic artist 716.8

2 engraving <see list>, engravement, graving, enchasing, **tooling,** chiseling, incising, incision, lining, scratching, slashing, scoring; **inscription,** inscript; type-cutting; **marking,** line, scratch, slash, score; hatching, cross-hatching; etch, etching; stipple, stippling; tint, demitint, half tint; burr; photoengraving 548.1

3 lithography, planography, autolithography, artist lithography; chromolithography; photolithography, offset lithography 548.1

4 stencil printing, stencil; silk-screen printing, serigraphy; monotype; glass printing, decal, decalcomania; cameography

5 print, numbered print, imprint, impression, first impression, impress; negative; color print; **etching; lithograph;** autolithograph; chromolithograph; lithotype; crayon engraving, graphotype; **block, block print,** linoleum-block print, rubber-block print, wood engraving, **woodprint,** xylograph, **cut, woodcut,** woodblock; vignette

6 plate, steel plate, copperplate, chalcograph; zincograph; stone, lithographic stone; printing plate 548.8

7 proof, artist's proof, proof before letter, open-letter proof, remarque proof

8 engraving tool, graver, burin, tint tool, style, point, etching point, needle, etching needle; etching ball; etching ground or varnish; scorper; rocker; **die,** punch, stamp, intaglio, seal

VERBS **9 engrave, grave, tool, enchase, incise, sculpture, inscribe,** character, **mark,** line, crease, score, scratch, scrape, cut, carve, chisel; groove, furrow 290.3; stipple, cribble; hatch, crosshatch; lithograph, autolithograph; **be a printmaker** or graphic artist; make prints or graphics; print 548.14

10 etch, eat, eat out, corrode, bite, bite in

ADJS **11 engraved, graven,** graved, glypt- or glypto-; tooled, enchased, chased, inscribed, incised, marked, lined, creased, cut, carved, glyphic, **sculptured,** insculptured, "insculp'd upon"—Shakespeare; grooved, furrowed 290.4; **printed, imprinted, impressed, stamped,** numbered

12 glyptic, glyptical, glyptographic, lapidary, lapidarian; xylographic, wood-block; lithographic, autolithographic, chromolithographic; aquatint, aquatinta, mezzotint

13 kinds of engraving

acid-blast	cerography
aquatint	chalcography
black-line engraving	chalk engraving

chasing
copperplate engraving
crayon engraving
cribbling *or manière*
  criblée <Fr>
drypoint *or* draw-point
  engraving
eccentric engraving
electric engraving
etching
gem engraving
glass-cutting
glyptics *or* glyptography
intaglio
lignography
line cut
line engraving
linocut
lithograph
metal cut
metal engraving

mezzotint
photochemical engraving
  or photoetching
photoengraving
plate engraving
pyrography *or* pyrogravure
  or pokerwork
relief etching
relief method
soft-ground etching
steel engraving
stipple engraving
woodburning *or*
  xylopyrography
woodcut *or* wood
  engraving
xylography
zinc etching
zincography *or* zinc
  engraving

714 PHOTOGRAPHY

NOUNS **1 photography** <see list>, picture-taking;
cinematography, motion-picture photography;
color photography, black-and-white photography;
photochromy, heliochromy; **3-D,** three-dimensional
photography; photofinishing; photogravure;
radiography, X-ray photography; photogrammetry,
phototopography

2 photographer 716.5, shutter-bug <nf>,
photojournalist, press photographer, paparazzo,
lensman, shooter *and* photog <nf>

3 photograph, photo <nf>, heliograph, **picture,** shot
<nf>; **snapshot,** snap <nf>, image; black-and-
white photograph; color photograph, color print,
heliochrome; Polaroid <trademark>; slide,
diapositive, transparency; candid photograph;
take; still, still photograph; photomural; montage,
photomontage; aerial photograph, photomap;
facsimile *or* fax transmission; telephotograph,
Telephoto <trademark>, Wirephoto <trademark>;
photomicrograph, microphotograph; metallograph;
microradiograph; electron micrograph;
photochronograph, chronophotograph;
radiograph, X ray; **portrait,** closeup; action shot,
action sequence; pinup <nf>, cheesecake *and*
beefcake <nf>; police photograph, **mug** *or* mug
shot <nf>; rogues' gallery; photobiography

4 tintype *or* ferrotype, ambrotype, **daguerreotype,**
calotype *or* talbotype, collotype *or* albertype *or*
artotype *or* heliotype, photocollotype, autotype,
vitrotype

5 print, photoprint, positive; glossy, matte, semi-
matte; **enlargement, blowup;** photocopy, Photostat
<trademark>, photostatic copy, stat <nf>, Xerox

<trademark>, Xerox copy; microfilm, microfiche,
microphotocopy, microprint, microcopy; blueprint,
cyanotype; **slide,** transparency, lantern slide;
contact printing, projection printing;
photogravure; hologram

6 shadowgraph, shadowgram, skiagraph, skiagram;
radiograph, radiogram, scotograph; **X ray,** X-ray
photograph, roentgenograph, roentgenogram;
photofluorogram; photogram

7 spectrograph, spectrogram; spectroheliogram

8 <motion pictures> **shot; take, retake;** close-up,
long shot, medium shot, full shot, group shot,
deuce shot, matte shot, process shot, boom shot,
travel shot, trucking shot, follow-focus shot, pan
shot *or* panoramic shot, rap shot, reverse *or*
reverse-angle shot, wild shot, zoom shot; motion
picture; kinescope

9 exposure, time exposure; shutter speed; f-stop, lens
opening; film rating, **film speed,** film gauge, ASA
number, **DIN** *or Deutsche Industrie Normen*
number, DX code; exposure meter, light meter

10 film; negative; printing paper, photographic paper;
plate; dry plate; vehicle; motion-picture film,
panchromatic film, monochromatic film,
orthochromatic film, black-and-white film, color
film, color negative film, color reversal film,
Polaroid film <trademark>; microfilm, bibliofilm;
sound-on-film, sound film; sound track,
soundstripe; Super-8, videotape, 35mm; roll,
cartridge; pack, bipack, tripack; frame; emulsion,
dope, backing

11 camera, Kodak *and* Polaroid <trademark>;
disposable camera; photo booth; video camera,
camcorder; TV camera, motion-picture camera,
cinematograph *or* kinematograph <Brit>; security
camera

12 projector; motion-picture projector, cineprojector,
cinematograph *or* kinematograph <Brit>,
vitascope; **slide projector,** magic lantern,
stereopticon; slide viewer

13 processing solution; developer, soup <nf>; fixer,
fixing bath, sodium thiosulfate *or* sodium
hyposulfite *or* hypo; acid stop, stop bath, short-
stop, short-stop bath; emulsion

VERBS **14 photograph, shoot** <nf>, **take a
photograph,** take a picture, take one's picture;
snap, snapshot, snapshoot; **film,** get *or* capture on
film; **mug** <nf>; daguerreotype, talbotype,
calotype; Photostat <trademark>; xerox;
microfilm; photomap; pan; **X-ray,** radiograph,
roentgenograph

15 process; develop; print; blueprint; **blow up,
enlarge**

16 project, show, screen

ADJS **17 photographic,** photo; **photogenic,**

picturesome; photosensitive, photoactive; panchromatic; telephotographic, telephoto; tintype; three-dimensional, 3-D

18 types of photography

acoustical holography
aerophotography *or* aerial photography *or* air photography
animation photography
architectural photography
astrophotography
available-light photography
candid photography
chronophotography
cinematography *or* motion-picture photography
cinephotomicrography
color photography
documentary photography
electrophotography
fashion photography
flash photography
heliophotography
holography
infrared photography
integral photography
landscape photography
laser photography
macrophotography
microfilming
microphotography
miniature photography
motion-picture photography

phonophotography
photoheliography
photojournalism
photomacrography
photomicrography
photoreproduction
phototopography
portraiture
pyrophotography
radiation-field *or* Kirlian photography
radiography
reprography
schlieren photography
skiagraphy
spectroheliography
spectrophotography
sports photography
stereophotography
still-life photography
stroboscopic photography
studio photography
telephotography
thermography
time-lapse photography
underwater photography
uranophotography
wildlife photography
xerography
X-ray photography

715 SCULPTURE

NOUNS **1 sculpture, sculpturing;** plastic art, **modeling; statuary; stonecutting;** gem-cutting, masonry; **carving,** stone carving, bone-carving, cameo carving, scrimshaw, *taille directe* <Fr>, whittling, woodcarving *or* xyloglyphy; embossing, **engraving** 713.2, **chasing,** toreutics, founding, casting, molding, plaster casting, lost-wax process, *cire perdue* <Fr>; sculptor 716.6

2 <sculptured piece> **sculpture; glyph; statue;** marble, bronze, terra cotta, scrimshaw, woodcarving; mobile, stabile; cast 785.6; found object, *objet trouvé* <Fr>; collage, assemblage

3 relief, relievo; **embossment,** boss; half relief, *mezzo-rilievo* <Ital>; high relief, *alto-rilievo* <Ital>; low relief, bas-relief, *basso-rilievo* <Ital>, *rilievo stiacciato* <Ital>; sunk relief, *cavo-rilievo* <Ital>, coelanaglyphic sculpture, **intaglio,** *intaglio rilievo or intaglio rilevato* <Ital>; *repoussé* <Fr>; glyph, anaglyph; glyptograph; **mask;** plaquette; **medallion; medal; cameo,** cameo glass, sculptured glass; cut glass

4 <tools, materials> chisel, point, mallet, burin, modeling tool, spatula; cutting torch, welding torch, soldering iron; solder; modeling clay, Plasticine <trademark>, sculptor's wax; plaster

VERBS **5 sculpture, sculp** *or* **sculpt** <nf>, insculpture <old>; **carve,** chisel, cut, grave, engrave, chase; weld, solder; assemble; **model, mold;** cast, found

ADJS **6 sculptural,** sculpturesque, sculptitory; statuary; **statuesque,** statuelike; **monumental,** marmoreal; plastic

7 sculptured, sculpted; sculptile; **molded, modeled,** ceroplastic; **carved,** chiseled; **graven,** engraven, engraved, incised; in relief, in high *or* low relief; glyphic, glyptic, anaglyphic, anaglyptic; anastatic; embossed, chased, hammered, toreutic; *repoussé* <Fr>; tactile

716 ARTIST

NOUNS **1 artist,** *artiste* <Fr>, "a dreamer consenting to dream of the actual world"—Santayana, creator, maker; master, **old master;** dauber, daubster; copyist; **craftsman, artisan** 726.6

2 limner, delineator, depicter, picturer, portrayer, imager; **illustrator;** illuminator; calligrapher; commercial artist; drawer, renderer, doodler, scribbler; pastelist

3 draftsman, draftswoman, sketcher, delineator; graphic artist; drawer, architectural draftsman; crayonist, charcoalist, pastelist; **cartoonist, caricaturist,** animator

4 painter, *artiste-peintre* <Fr>; **colorist;** luminist, luminarist; **oil painter,** oil-colorist; **watercolorist;** aquarellist; finger painter; monochromist, polychromist; genre painter, historical painter, landscape painter, landscapist, miniaturist, portrait painter, portraitist, marine painter, still-life painter, animal painter, religious painter; pavement artist; sign painter; scene painter, scenewright, scenographer

5 photographer, photographist, lensman, **cameraperson,** camerawoman, cameraman; **cinematographer;** snapshotter, snap shooter, shutterbug <nf>; daguerreotypist, calotypist, talbotypist; skiagrapher, shadowgraphist, radiographer, X-ray technician

6 sculptor, sculptress, sculpturer; earth artist, environmental artist; statuary; figurer, figurist, *figuriste* <Fr>, **modeler,** molder, wax modeler, clay modeler; graver, chaser, carver; molder, caster; stonecutter, mason, monumental mason, wood carver, xyloglyphic artist, whittler; ivory carver, bone carver, shell carver; gem carver, glyptic *or* glyptographic artist; engraver, etcher; lapidary

7 ceramist, ceramicist, potter; china decorator *or*

painter, tile painter, majolica painter; glassblower, glazer, glass decorator, pyroglazer, glass cutter; enamelist, enameler

8 **printmaker,** graphic artist; **engraver,** graver, burinist; inscriber, carver; **etcher;** line engraver; **lithographer,** autolithographer, chromolithographer; serigrapher, silk-screen artist; cerographer, cerographist; chalcographer; gem engraver, glyptographer, lapidary; wood engraver, xylographer; pyrographer, xylopyrographer; zincographer

9 **designer, stylist,** styler; costume designer, dress designer, *couturier* <Fr>, *couturière* <Fr fem>; furniture designer, rug designer, textile designer

10 **architect,** civil architect; landscape architect, landscape gardener; city *or* urban planner, urbanist; functionalist

11 **decorator,** expert in decor, ornamentist, ornamentalist; **interior decorator** *or* designer, house decorator, room decorator, floral decorator, table decorator; window decorator *or* dresser; confectionery decorator

717 ARCHITECTURE, DESIGN

NOUNS 1 **architecture,** architectural design, building design, the art and technique of building, "inhabited sculpture"—Brancusi, "music in space"—Schelling, "the art of significant forms in space"—Claude Bragdon; **architectural science,** architectural engineering, structural engineering, architectural technology, building science, building technology; architectonics, tectonics; **architectural style** <see list>; **architectural specialty**; landscape architecture, landscape gardening 1069.2

2 **architectural element; ornamentation, architectural ornamentation;** column order, Doric, Ionic, Corinthian, Composite; **type of construction,** building type

3 **architect,** building designer; landscape architect, landscape gardener 1069.6; architectural engineer; city *or* urban planner, urbanist, urbanologist

4 **design, styling,** patterning, planning, shaping, "the conscious effort to impose meaningful order"— Victor Papanek; **design specialty**

5 <design specialties> accessory design, appearance design, architectural design, automotive design, book design, clothing design, costume design, ergonomics *or* ergonomy *or* human engineering *or* human factors engineering, fashion design, furniture design, graphics design, industrial *or* product design, interior design, jewelry design, landscape architecture, lighting design, package design, pottery design, reverse engineering, stage design, textile design, typographic design

6 **designer, stylist,** styler

ADJS 7 **architectural,** architectonic, tectonic; **design, designer**

8 **architectural styles and types**

absolute	Gothic
academic	Great West Road
action	Greco-Roman
additive	Greek
American colonial	Greek Revival
American Georgian	hard
Anglo-Saxon	high Gothic
Art Deco *or* Art Moderne	high Renaissance
Art Nouveau	hi-tech
arts and crafts	indeterminate
baroque	international *or*
Bauhaus	international Gothic
Beaux Arts	Islamic
brutalist	Italianate
Byzantine	Italian Gothic
Carolingian	Italian Mannerism
Chicago School	Italian Renaissance
Chinese	Jacobean
churrigueresque *or*	Japanese
churrigueresco	Jesuit
cinquecento	kinetic
Cistercian	Louis XIV
classical	Louis XV
colonial	mannerism
conceptual *or* invisible *or*	medieval
imaginary *or* nowhere	Mesopotamian
Decorated	Mestizo
de Stijl	mission
directed *or*	moderne *or* modernism
programmed	neo-Gothic
duck	neoclassical
early American	new brutalist
early English	New England colonial
early Gothic	Norman
early Renaissance	organicist
earthwork	Palladian
eclectic	perpendicular *or*
ecological	rectilinear
Edwardian	Persian
Egyptian	pneumatic
Elizabethan	postmodern
Empire	Prairie
endless	Queen Anne
English decorated Gothic	Regency
English Georgian	Renaissance
English Renaissance	rococo
flamboyant Gothic	Roman
formalist	Romanesque
Francois Premier	Romanesque Revival
French colonial	Romantic
French Renaissance	Shingle
functionalist	Southern colonial
Georgian	Spanish
German Renaissance	Stuart
gingerbread	tensile

Tudor
Utopian *or* fantastic *or*
  visionary
vernacular
Victorian
Victorian Gothic

9 architectural specialties

church *or* religious *or*
  ecclesiastical
  architecture
civic architecture
college architecture
commercial architecture
domestic architecture
governmental architecture

industrial architecture
institutional architecture
landscape architecture
library architecture
military architecture
museum architecture
recreational architecture

718 LITERATURE

NOUNS **1 literature, letters, belles lettres,** polite
literature, humane letters, *litterae humaniores*
<L>, republic of letters; **work, literary work, text,
literary text; works, complete works, oeuvre,
canon, literary canon, author's canon;** serious
literature; **classics,** ancient literature; medieval
literature, Renaissance literature, etc; national
literature, English literature, French literature, etc;
ethnic literature, black *or* Afro-American literature,
Latino literature, etc; contemporary literature;
underground literature; pseudonymous literature;
folk literature; travel literature; wisdom literature;
erotic literature, erotica; pornographic literature,
pornography, porn *and* hard porn *and* soft porn
<nf>, obscene literature, scatological literature;
popular literature, pop literature <nf>; kitsch

2 authorship, writing, authorcraft, pencraft,
wordsmanship, **composition,** the art of
composition, inditing, inditement; one's pen;
creative writing, literary art, verbal art, literary
composition, literary production, verse-writing,
short-story writing, novel-writing, playwriting,
drama-writing; essay-writing; **expository writing;**
technical writing; journalism, newspaper writing,
editorial-writing, feature-writing, rewriting;
magazine writing; songwriting, lyric-writing,
libretto-writing; artistry, literary power, literary
artistry, literary talent *or* flair, skill with words *or*
language, facility in writing, ready pen; **writer's
itch,** graphomania, scribblemania, graphorrhea,
cacoëthes scribendi <L>

3 writer, scribbler <nf>, **penman,** pen, penner; pen
or pencil driver *or* pusher <nf>, word-slinger,
inkslinger *and* ink spiller *and* inkstained wretch
<nf>, knight of the plume *or* pen *or* quill <nf>

4 author, writer, scribe <nf>, composer, inditer,
penman, wordsmith; authoress, penwoman;
creative writer, *littérateur* <Fr>, literary artist,
literary craftsman *or* artisan *or* journeyman,
belletrist, man of letters, literary scholar; word
painter; freelance, freelance writer; ghostwriter,

ghost <nf>; collaborator, coauthor; prose writer,
logographer; fiction writer, fictioneer <nf>; story
writer, **short story writer;** storyteller, narrator;
novelist; novelettist; diarist; chronicler, historian,
historiographer; biographer; **newspaperman;
annalist; poet** 720.13; **dramatist,** humorist 489.12;
scriptwriter, scenario writer, scenarist; nonfiction
writer; article writer, magazine writer; **essayist;**
monographer; reviewer, critic, literary critic, music
critic, art critic, drama critic, dance critic; cultural
commentator; columnist; pamphleteer; technical
writer; copywriter, advertising writer; compiler,
encyclopedist, bibliographer

5 hack writer, hack, literary hack, Grub Street writer
<Brit>, **penny-a-liner, scribbler** <nf>, **potboiler**
<nf>

VERBS **6 write,** author, pen, **compose, indite,**
formulate, produce, prepare; dash off, knock off *or*
out <nf>, throw on paper, pound *or* crank *or* grind
or churn out; freelance; collaborate, coauthor;
ghostwrite, ghost <nf>; novelize; scenarize;
pamphleteer; editorialize

ADJS **7 literary,** belletristic, lettered; classical

8 auctorial, authorial

719 HISTORY

NOUNS **1 history,** the historical discipline, the
investigation of the past, the record of the past, the
story of mankind, study of the past; historical
research; **annals, chronicles,** memorabilia,
chronology; chronicle, record 549; historical
method, historical approach, philosophy of history,
historiography; cliometrics; documentation,
recording; narrative history, **oral history,** oral
record, survivors' *or* witnesses' accounts;
biography, memoir, memorial, **life,** story, **life story,**
adventures, fortunes, reminiscences, experiences;
résumé, vita, curriculum vitae *or* CV; life and
letters, track record <nf>; legend, saint's legend,
hagiology, hagiography; **autobiography, memoirs,**
memorials, archive; **journal, diary,** confessions;
profile, biographical sketch; obituary, necrology,
martyrology; photobiography; case history;
historiography, theory of history; epigraphy,
archaeology; Clio, Muse of history; **the past** 837;
record, recording 549; herstory <nf>

2 "a set of lies agreed upon"—Napoleon, "a cyclic
poem written by Time upon the memories of
man"—Shelley, "the essence of innumerable
biographies"—Carlyle, "philosophy learned from
examples"—Dionysius of Halicarnassus, "History
is more or less bunk"—Henry Ford

3 story, tale, yarn, account, narrative, narration,
chronicle, tradition, legend, folk tale, folk history;

anecdote, anecdotage; **epic,** epos, **saga;** minutes, notes; file, dossier

4 **historian,** cliometrician, historiographer; **chronicler,** annalist, recorder, archivist; **biographer,** memorialist, Boswell; autobiographer, autobiographist; diarist, Pepys; epigrapher, archaeologist

VERBS 5 **chronicle,** write history, historify; historicize; biograph, biography, biographize; immortalize; document, report, **record** 549.16

6 **narrate, tell, relate,** recount, report, **recite,** rehearse, give an account of; commentate, voice over

ADJS 7 **historical, historic,** historied, historically accurate; fact-based; historicized; historiographical; cliometric; **chronicled;** chronologic, chronological; **traditional, legendary;** biographical, autobiographic, autobiographical; documentary, documented, archival; hagiographic, hagiographical, martyrologic, martyrological; necrologic, necrological; retro

8 **narrative,** narrational; **fictional**

ADVS 9 **historically,** historically speaking; as chronicled, as history tells us, according to or by all accounts; as the record shows; retrospectively

720 POETRY

NOUNS 1 **poetry,** poesy, **verse, song, rhyme;** "musical thought"—Carlyle, "the supreme fiction"—Wallace Stevens, "the spontaneous overflow of powerful feelings recollected in tranquility"—Wordsworth, "painting with the gift of speech"—Simonides, "the poet's innermost feeling issuing in rhythmic language"—John Keble, "the journal of a sea animal living on land, wanting to fly in the air," "the achievement of the synthesis of hyacinths and biscuits"—both Sandburg, "not the thing said but a way of saying it"—A E Housman, "the art of uniting pleasure with truth, by calling imagination to the help of reason"—Samuel Johnson, "the music of the soul, and above all of great and of feeling souls"—Voltaire

2 **poetics,** poetcraft, versecraft, versification, versemaking, ars poetica <L>; "my craft and sullen art"—Dylan Thomas; **poetic language,** poetic diction, poeticism; **poetic license, poetic justice**

3 **bad poetry,** doggerel, versemongering, poetastering, poetastery; poesy; crambo, crambo clink or jingle <Scot>, Hudibrastic verse; nonsense verse, amphigory; macaronics, macaronic verse; lame verses, limping meters, halting meters

4 **poem, verse, rhyme,** "imaginary gardens with real toads in them"—Marianne Moore; verselet, versicle

5 **book of verse,** garland, **collection, anthology;** poetic works, poesy

6 **metrics, prosody, versification; scansion,** scanning; metrical pattern or form, prosodic pattern or form, meter, numbers, measure; quantitative meter, syllabic meter, accentual meter, accentual-syllabic meter, duple meter, triple meter; free verse, vers libre <Fr>; alliterative meter, Stabreim <Ger>

7 **meter, measure,** numbers; **rhythm, cadence,** movement, lilt, jingle, swing; sprung rhythm; **accent,** accentuation, metrical accent, stress, emphasis, ictus, **beat;** arsis, thesis; quantity, mora; metrical unit; **foot, metrical foot** <see list>; triseme, tetraseme; metrical group, metron, colon, period; dipody, syzygy, tripody, tetrapody, pentapody, hexapody, heptapody; monometer, dimeter, trimeter, tetrameter, pentameter, hexameter, heptameter, octameter; **iambic pentameter, dactylic hexameter;** Alexandrine; Saturnian meter; elegiac, elegiac couplet or distich, elegiac pentameter; heroic couplet; sprung rhythm; counterpoint; caesura, diaeresis, masculine caesura, feminine caesura; catalexis; anacrusis

8 **rhyme;** clink, crambo; **consonance, assonance; alliteration;** eye rhyme; male or masculine or single rhyme, female or feminine or double rhyme; initial rhyme, end rhyme; tail rhyme, rhyme royal; broken rhyme, half rhyme, near rhyme, pararhyme, slant rhyme; internal rhyme; terza rima, ottava rima <Ital>; rime riche, identical rhyme; rhyme scheme; rhyming dictionary; unrhymed poetry, blank verse

9 <poetic divisions> **measure, strain; syllable; line;** verse; stanza, stave; strophe, antistrophe, epode; **canto,** book; **refrain, chorus,** burden; envoi; monostich, distich, tristich, tetrastich, pentastich, hexastich, heptastich, octastich; ·**couplet;** triplet; tercet, terza rima <Ital>; **quatrain;** sextet, sestet; septet; octave, octet, ottava rima <Ital>; rhyme royal; Spenserian stanza

10 **Muse;** the Muses, Pierides, Camenae <L>; Apollo, Apollo Musagetes; Calliope, Polyhymnia, Erato, Euterpe; Helicon, Parnassus; Castilian Spring, Pierian Spring, Hippocrene; Bragi; **poetic genius,** poesy, afflatus, fire of genius, **creative imagination** 986.2, **inspiration** 920.8

11 **poet,** poetess, poetress <old>, maker <old>; "the painter of the soul"—Disraeli, "a nightingale who sits in darkness and sings to cheer its own solitude with sweet sounds"— Shelley, "all who love, who feel great truths, and tell them"—Philip James Bailey, "literalists of the imagination"—Marianne Moore; ballad maker; **bard, minstrel,** scop, fili, baird, skald, **jongleur, troubadour,** trovatore <Ital>, trouveur, trouvère <Fr>, Meistersinger <Ger>,

minnesinger; minor poet, major poet, arch-poet; laureate, **poet laureate;** occasional poet; **lyric poet;** epic poet; pastoral poet, pastoralist, idyllist, bucoliast <old>; rhapsodist, rhapsode; vers-librist, *vers libriste* <Fr>; elegist, librettist; lyricist, lyrist; odist; satirist; sonneteer; modernist, imagist, symbolist; Parnassian; beat poet

12 **bad poet;** rhymester, rhymer; metrist; versemaker, versesmith, versifier, verseman, versemonger; poetling, **poetaster,** poeticule; balladmonger

VERBS 13 **poetize, versify,** verse, write *or* compose poetry, build the stately rime, sing deathless songs, make immortal verse; tune one's lyre, climb Parnassus, mount Pegasus; **sing;** elegize; poeticize

14 **rhyme,** assonate, alliterate; **scan;** jingle; cap verses *or* rhymes

ADJS 15 **poetic, poetical,** poetlike; **lyrical, narrative,** dramatic, lyrico-dramatic; bardic; runic, skaldic; epic, heroic; mock-heroic, Hudibrastic; pastoral, bucolic, eclogic, idyllic, Theocritean; didactic; elegiac, elegiacal; dithyrambic, rhapsodic, rhapsodical, Alcaic, Anacreontic, Homeric, Pindaric, sapphic; Castalian, Pierian; Parnassian, Sapphic; poetico-mythological; poetico-mystical, poetico-philosophic; comic, concrete, epic, erotic, folk, metaphysical, nonsense, pattern, satirical, tragic

16 **metric, metrical, prosodic, prosodical; rhythmic, rhythmical, measured,** cadenced, scanning, scanned; accentual; iambic, dactylic, spondaic, pyrrhic, trochaic, anapestic, antispastic, etc

17 **rhyming; assonant,** assonantal; **alliterative,** onomatopoeic; resonant; jingling; musical, lilting

ADVS 18 **poetically, lyrically; metrically, rhythmically,** in measure; musically

19 **metrical feet**

amphibrach	iamb *or* iambus *or*
amphimacer	iambic
anapest	ionic
antispast	molossus
bacchius	paeon
choriambus *or* choriamb	proceleusmatic
cretic *or* amphimacer	pyrrhic *or* dibrach
dactyl	spondee
dochmiac	tribrach
epitrite	trochee

721 PROSE

NOUNS 1 **prose,** "words in their best order"— Coleridge; prose fiction, nonfiction prose, expository prose; prose rhythm; prose style; poetic prose, polyphonic prose, prose poetry

2 **prosaism, prosaicism, prosaicness,** prosiness, pedestrianism, **unpoeticalness; matter-of-factness,** unromanticism, unidealism; **unimaginativeness**

987; **plainness,** commonness, commonplaceness, unembellishedness; insipidness, flatness, vapidity; **dullness** 117

VERBS 3 **prose,** write prose *or* in prose; pedestrianize

ADJS 4 **prose,** in prose; unversified, nonpoetic, nonmetricalf

5 **prosaic, prosy, prosing;** unpoetical, poetryless; **plain, common, commonplace, ordinary,** unembellished, mundane; **matter-of-fact, unromantic, unidealistic,** unimpassioned; pedestrian, **unimaginative** 987.5; insipid, vapid, flat; humdrum, tiresome, **dull** 117.6

722 FICTION

NOUNS 1 **fiction,** narrative, narrative literature, imaginative narrative, prose fiction; **narration,** relation, relating, recital, rehearsal, telling, retelling, recounting, recountal, review, portrayal, graphic narration, description, delineation, presentation; **storytelling,** tale-telling, yarn-spinning *and* yarning <nf>; narrative poetry; operatic libretto; computer *or* interactive fiction; pulp fiction

2 **narration, narrative, relation, recital,** rehearsal, telling, retelling, recounting, recountal, review; **storytelling,** tale-telling, yarn spinning *or* yarning <nf>

3 **story** <see list>, **short story,** tale, narrative, yarn, account, narration, chronicle, relation, version; **novel** <see list>, *roman* <Fr>

4 <story elements> **plot,** fable, argument, story, line, story line, subplot, secondary plot, mythos; **structure,** plan, architecture, architectonics, scheme, design; **subject, topic, theme,** motif; thematic development, development, continuity; **action,** movement; incident, episode; **complication;** rising action, turning point, climax, falling action, *peripeteia* <Gk>, switch <nf>; *anagnorisis* <Gk>, recognition; denouement, catastrophe; *deus ex machina* <L>; catharsis; device, contrivance, **gimmick** <nf>; angle *and* slant *and* twist <nf>; **character,** characterization; **speech,** dialogue; **tone, atmosphere,** mood; **setting,** locale, world, milieu, background, region, local color

5 **narrator,** relator, reciter, recounter, *raconteur* <Fr>; **anecdotist; storyteller,** storier, taleteller, teller of tales, spinner of yarns *and* yarn spinner <nf>; word painter; **persona,** central consciousness, the I of the story; point-of-view <see list>; **author, writer,** short-story writer, **novelist,** novelettist, fictionist; fabulist, fableist, fabler, mythmaker, mythopoet; romancer, romancist; sagaman

VERBS 6 **narrate, tell, relate, recount,** report, **recite,** rehearse, give an account of; tell a story, unfold a tale, a tale unfold, fable, fabulize; storify, fictionalize; romance; novelize; mythicize, mythify, mythologize, allegorize; retell

ADJS **7 fictional,** fictionalized; **novelistic,** novelized, novelettish; mythical, mythological, **legendary, fabulous;** mythopoeic, mythopoetic or mythopoetical; **allegorical** or allegoric, parabolic or parabolical; **romantic,** romanticized; historical, historicized, fact-based

8 narrative, narrational; storied, storified; **anecdotal,** anecdotic; epic or epical

9 types of stories

adventure story	horror story or chiller and
allegory	chiller-diller <nf>
apologue	lai
beast fable	legend
bedtime story	love story
chivalric romance	Milesian tale
classical detective story	mystery or mystery story
conte <Fr>	myth or mythos
crime story	nursery tale
detective story or	parable
detective yarn or	romance
whodunit <nf>	romantic adventure
dime novel or penny	saga
dreadful <nf>	saint's legend
epic or epos	science fiction story or sci-
exemplum or didactic tale	fi story <nf>
or moral tale	short short story or short-
fable	short
fabliau	short story
fairy tale or	sketch
Märchen <Ger>	spy story
fantasy	supernatural tale
folktale or folk story	suspense story
gest or geste	thriller or thriller-diller
ghost story	<nf>
hard-boiled detective story	vignette
or tough-tec story <nf>	Western or Western story
hero tale	or cowboy story

10 types of novels

adventure novel	epistolary novel
antinovel or anti-roman or	erotic novel
nouveau roman	experimental novel
autobiographical novel	fantasy novel
Bildungsroman <Ger>	fictional or fictionalized
bodice ripper <nf>	biography
cliffhanger	Gothic novel
collage novel	historical novel
comic novel	historical romance or
detective novel	bodice-ripper <nf>
dime novel	Kunstlerroman <Ger>
dystopia or cacotopia or	lyrical novel
dystopian	naturalistic novel
entertainment	nouveau roman
epic novel	novel of character

novel of ideas	roman-fleuve <Fr> or
novel of incident	river novel
novel of manners	romance novel
novel of sensibility or	satirical novel
sentimental novel	science-fiction or sci-fi
novel of the soil	novel
novelette	sentimental novel
novella or nouvelle <Fr>	social melodrama
penny dreadful <Brit>	sociological novel
picaresque novel	stream-of-consciousness
political novel	novel
pornographic novel	surrealistic novel
problem novel	techno-thriller
proletarian novel	thesis novel
propaganda novel	thriller or psychological
psychological novel	thriller
psychological thriller	utopia or utopian novel
realistic novel	Victorian novel
regional novel	Western
roman à clef <Fr>	

11 narrative points of view

documentary or camera-	omniscient observer
eye observer	stream of consciousness or
fallible observer	interior monologue
first-person past narrator	third-person past narrator
first-person present	third-person present
narrator	narrator

723 CRITICISM OF THE ARTS

NOUNS **1 criticism,** criticism of the arts, esthetic or artistic criticism, aesthetic or artistic evaluation, aesthetic or artistic analysis, aesthetic or artistic interpretation, critical commentary, critique, critical analysis, critical interpretation, critical evaluation, metacriticism, exegetics, hermeneutics; **art criticism,** formalist criticism, expressionist criticism, neoformalist criticism; music criticism; dramatic criticism; dance criticism; aesthetics

2 review, critical notice, commentary, compte rendu critique <Fr>, critical treatment or treatise

3 literary criticism, Lit-Crit <nf>, literary analysis or evaluation or interpretation or exegetics or hermeneutics, poetics; **critical approach or school; literary theory,** theory of literature, critical theory, theory of criticism

4 critic, interpreter, exegete, analyst, explicator, theoretician, aesthetician; reviewer

VERBS **5 criticize,** critique, evaluate, interpret, explicate, analyze, judge; theorize

ADJS **6 critical,** evaluative, interpretive, exegetical, analytical, explicative

724 OCCUPATION

NOUNS **1 occupation, work, job, employment,** business, employ, **activity, function,** enterprise, undertaking, **affairs,** labor; thing *and* bag <nf>; **affair, matter, concern,** concernment, **interest,** lookout <nf>; what one is doing *or* about; **commerce** 731

2 **task, work, stint, job,** labor, toil, industry, piece of work, **chore,** chare, odd job; **assignment, charge,** project, errand, **mission,** commission, **duty,** service, exercise; things to do, matters in hand, irons in the fire, fish to fry; homework, take-home work; busywork, makework

3 **function, office, duty, job,** province, place, **role,** *rôle* <Fr>, part; **capacity,** character, **position**

4 <sphere of work or activity> **field, sphere,** profession, trade, province, bailiwick, turf <nf>, department, area, discipline, subdiscipline, orb, orbit, realm, arena, domain, walk; **specialty, niche,** speciality <Brit>, line of country <Brit nf>; beat, round; shop

5 **position, job,** employment, gainful employment, situation, **office, post, place,** station, berth, billet, **appointment,** engagement, gig <nf>; incumbency, tenure; opening, vacancy; second job, moonlighting <nf>

6 **vocation, occupation, business, work, line, line of work,** line of business *or* endeavor, number <nf>, walk, **walk of life, calling,** mission, **profession, practice, pursuit, specialty,** specialization, *métier* <Fr>, mystery <old>, **trade,** racket *and* game <nf>; **career,** lifework, life's work; career track, Mommy track <nf>; **craft,** art, handicraft; careerism, career building

7 **avocation, hobby,** hobbyhorse <old>, sideline, by-line, side interest, pastime, spare-time activity; amateur pursuit, amateurism; unpaid work, volunteer work

8 **professionalism,** professional standing *or* status

9 **nonprofessionalism, amateurism,** amateur standing *or* status

VERBS **10** **occupy, engage, busy,** devote, spend, **employ,** occupy oneself, busy oneself, go about one's business, devote oneself; pass *or* employ *or* spend the time; occupy one's time, take up one's time; attend to business, attend to one's work; mind one's business, mind the store <nf>, stick to one's last *or* knitting <nf>; telecommute

11 **busy oneself with,** do, occupy *or* engage oneself with, employ oneself in *or* upon, pass *or* employ *or* spend one's time in; **engage in, take up,** devote oneself to, apply oneself to, address oneself to, have one's hands in, turn one's hand to; concern oneself with, make it one's business; **be about, be doing,** be occupied with, be engaged *or* employed in, be at work on; practice, follow as an occupation

12 **work,** work at, work for, have a job, be employed,

ply one's trade, labor in one's vocation, do one's number <nf>, follow a trade, practice a profession, carry on a business *or* trade, keep up; **do** *or* **transact business,** carry on *or* conduct business; set up shop, set up in business, hang out one's shingle <nf>; stay employed, hold down a job <nf>; moonlight <nf>, consult; labor, toil 725.13,14

13 **officiate, function, serve; perform as, act as,** act *or* play one's part, **do duty,** discharge *or* perform *or* exercise the office *or* duties *or* functions of, serve in the office *or* capacity of

14 **hold office,** fill an office, occupy a post

ADJS **15** **occupied, busy,** working; practical, realistic 987.6; banausic, moneymaking, breadwinning, utilitarian 387.18; materialistic 695.16; workaday, workday, prosaic 117.8; **commercial** 731.21

16 **occupational, vocational,** functional; **professional,** pro <nf>; official; technical, industrial; all in the day's work

17 **avocational,** hobby, amateur, nonprofessional

ADVS **18** **professionally,** vocationally; as a profession *or* vocation; in the course of business

725 EXERTION

NOUNS **1** **exertion, effort, energy,** elbow grease; **endeavor** 403; **trouble, pains;** great *or* mighty effort, might and main, muscle, one's back, nerve and sinew, hard *or* strong *or* long pull, "a long pull, a strong pull, and a pull all together"—Dickens

2 **strain,** straining, **stress,** stressfulness, **stress and strain,** taxing, **tension,** stretch, rack; tug, pull, haul, heave; overexertion, overstrain, overtaxing, overextension, overstress

3 **struggle, fight, battle, tussle, scuffle, wrestle,** hassle <nf>

4 **work, labor, employment, industry, toil,** moil, travail, toil and trouble, sweat of one's brow; **drudgery, sweat,** slavery, spadework, rat race <nf>; treadmill; unskilled labor, hewing of wood *and* drawing of water; dirty work, grunt work *and* donkey work *and* shit-work *and* scut work <nf>, thankless task; **makework,** tedious *or* stupid *or* idiot *or* tiresome work, humdrum toil, grind <nf>, fag <chiefly Brit>; rubber room work *or* job *or* assignment, no-work job; **manual labor,** handwork, handiwork; forced labor; hand's turn, stroke of work, stroke; lick *and* lick of work *and* stitch of work <nf>; man-hour; **workload,** work schedule; task 724.2; fatigue 21

5 **hard work** *or* **labor, backbreaking work,** moil, warm work, uphill work, long haul, hard *or* tough grind <nf>, the hard way; **hard job** 1013.2; labor of Hercules; **laboriousness, toilsomeness,**

effortfulness, **strenuousness, arduousness,** operosity, operoseness; onerousness, oppressiveness, burdensomeness; troublesomeness

6 exercise 84, exercising; **practice, drill, workout,** preparation; yoga; constitutional <nf>, stretch; violent exercise; physical education

7 exerciser; horizontal bar, parallel bars, horse, side horse, long horse, rings; trapeze; trampoline; Indian club; medicine ball; punching bag; rowing machine; weight, dumbbell, barbell

VERBS **8 exert, exercise, ply, employ, use, put forth,** put out *and* make with <nf>; practice

9 exert oneself, use some elbow grease <nf>, spread oneself, put forth one's strength, bend every effort, bend might and main, spare no effort, put on a full-court press <nf>, tax one's energies, break a sweat <nf>; put *or* lay oneself out <nf>, go all out <nf>; endeavor 403.4; **do one's best; apply oneself,** come to grips with; hump *and* hump it *and* hump oneself <nf>, **buckle** *or* **knuckle** *or* bear <nf>, lay to; lay to the oars, ply the oar

10 strain, tense, stress, stretch, tax, press, rack; **pull, tug,** haul, **heave;** strain the muscles, strain every nerve *or* every nerve and sinew; put one's back into it <nf>; sweat blood; overwork, work night and day, take on too much, spread oneself too thin, overexert, overstrain, overtax, overextend; drive *or* whip *or* flog oneself

11 struggle, strive, contend, fight, battle, buffet, scuffle, tussle, wrestle, hassle <nf>, work *or* fight one's way, agonize, huff and puff, grunt and sweat, sweat it <nf>, make heavy weather of it

12 work, labor; busy oneself 724.10,11; turn a hand, do a hand's turn, do a lick of work, earn one's keep; chore, do the chores, char *or* do chars, chare <Brit>

13 work hard; scratch *and* **hustle** *and* **sweat** <nf>, **slave, sweat and slave** <nf>, slave away, toil away, hammer at; **hit the ball** *and* bear down *and* pour it on <nf>; burn the candle at both ends; work one's head off <nf>, work one's fingers to the bone, break one's back, bust one's hump *or* ass <nf>; put one's heart and soul into it; beaver *or* beaver away <Brit nf>, work like a beaver, work like a horse *or* cart horse *or* dog, work like a slave *or* galley slave, work like a coal heaver, work like a Trojan; work overtime, be a workaholic <nf>, overwork, do double duty, work double hours *or* tides, **work day and night,** work late, **burn the midnight oil;** lucubrate, elucubrate; overwork 993.10

14 drudge, grind *and* **dig** <nf>, fag <Brit>, **grub, toil,** moil, toil and moil, travail, **plod, slog, peg, plug** <nf>, hammer, peg away *or* along, plug away *or* along <nf>, hammer away, pound away, struggle along, struggle on, work away; **get** *or* **keep one's nose to the grindstone;** wade through

15 set to work, get rolling, get busy, get down to business *or* **work,** roll up one's sleeves, spit on one's hands, gird up one's loins; **fall to work, fall to, buckle** *or* **knuckle down to** <nf>, **turn to, set to** *or* **about,** put *or* set one's hand to, start in, set up shop, enter on *or* upon, launch into *or* upon; **get on the job** *and* get going <nf>; **go to it** *and* **get with it** *and* get cracking *and* have at it *and* get one's teeth into it <nf>; hop *or* jump to it <nf>; **attack,** set at, **tackle** <nf>; **plunge into,** dive into; **pitch in** *or* **into** <nf>; light into *and* wade into *and* tear into *and* sail into <nf>, put *or* lay one's shoulder to the wheel, put one's hand to the plow; take on, undertake 404.3

16 task, work, busy, keep busy, fag <Brit>, sweat <nf>, **drive, tax;** overtask, overtax, **overwork,** overdrive; burden, oppress 297.13

ADJS **17 laboring, working; struggling, striving,** straining; **drudging, toiling,** slaving, sweating *and* grinding <nf>, grubbing, **plodding,** slogging, pegging, plugging <nf>, persevering; hardworking; busy, industrious, hard at it

18 laborious, toilsome, arduous, strenuous, painful, effortful, operose, troublesome, onerous, oppressive, burdensome; wearisome, tiring, exhausting; **heavy,** hefty <nf>, tough <nf>, uphill, **backbreaking,** grueling, punishing, crushing, killing, Herculean; uphill; **labored,** forced, strained; straining, tensive, painstaking, **intensive;** hard-fought, hard-won, hard-earned

ADVS **19 laboriously, arduously, toilsomely, strenuously,** operosely; effortfully, with effort, **hard,** by the sweat of one's brow; the hard way; with all one's might, for all one is worth, with a will, **with might and main,** with a strong hand, manfully; **hammer and tongs, tooth and nail,** *bec et ongles* <Fr>, heart and soul; **industriously** 330.27

726 WORKER, DOER

NOUNS **1 doer, agent,** actor, **performer, worker, practitioner,** perpetrator; **producer, maker,** creator, fabricator, **author,** mover, prime mover; architect; **agent,** medium; **executor,** executant, executrix; **operator,** operative, operant, hand; subject *and* agent <gram>; coworker, colleague

2 worker, laborer, toiler, moiler; member of the working class, proletarian, prole <Brit nf>, blue-collar *or* lunch-bucket worker, laboring man, stiff *and* working stiff <nf>; **workman, working man; workwoman, working woman,** workfolk, workpeople; working girl, workgirl; **factory worker,**

industrial worker; autoworker, steelworker; construction worker; **commuter;** home worker, telecommuter; **office worker, white-collar worker;** career woman, career girl; **jobholder,** wageworker, **wage earner,** salaried worker; **breadwinner;** wage slave; employee, servant 577; **hand, workhand,** hourly worker; **laborer,** common laborer, **unskilled laborer,** navvy <Brit>, day laborer, roust-about; casual, casual laborer; **agricultural worker** 1069.5; migrant worker, migrant; menial, flunky; piece-worker, jobber; factotum, jack-of-all-trades; full-time worker, part-time worker; temporary employee, temporary, office temporary, temp <nf>; freelance worker, freelance, freelancer, self-employed person, independent contractor, consultant; volunteer; domestic worker, clerical worker, sales worker, service worker, repair worker, artistic worker, technical worker; **labor force, work force,** crew, shop floor <Brit>, factory floor; personnel; labor market

3 **drudge, grub, hack, fag, plodder, slave,** galley slave, **workhorse,** beast of burden, slogger; "hewers of wood and drawers of water"—Bible; grind *and* greasy grind <nf>, swot <Brit nf>; slave labor, sweatshop labor; busy bee *and* beaver *and* ant <nf>

4 **professional,** member of a learned profession, professional practitioner; businessman, businesswoman, career woman; executive; pro *and* old pro <nf>, seasoned professional; gownsman; doctor, lawyer, member of the clergy, teacher, accountant; social worker; health-care professional, military professional; law-enforcement professional, etc

5 **amateur, nonprofessional, layman,** member of the laity, laic

6 **skilled worker,** skilled laborer, **journeyman,** mechanic; **craftsman, handicraftsman;** craftswoman; craftsperson; craftspeople; **artisan,** artificer, artist; **maker,** *fabbro* <Ital>; **wright; technician;** apprentice, prentice <nf>; **master,** master craftsman, master workman, master carpenter, etc

7 **engineer,** professional engineer; **technician,** technical worker, techie <nf>; engineering, technology

8 **smith;** farrier <Brit>, forger, forgeman, metalworker; Vulcan, Hephaestus, Wayland *or* Völund

727 UNIONISM, LABOR UNION

NOUNS 1 **unionism,** trade unionism, trades unionism <Brit>, labor unionism; **unionization; collective bargaining; arbitration,** nonbinding arbitration; industrial relations, labor relations, work relations; employee rights, employer rights; salary negotiations, labor negotiations, negotiated *or* negotiation points, employee demands, management demands

2 **labor union,** trade union, trades union <Brit>; organized labor; collective bargaining; **craft union,** guild, horizontal union; **industrial union,** vertical union; **local,** union local, local union; company union

3 **union shop,** preferential shop, **closed shop;** open shop; nonunion shop; **labor contract, union contract,** sweetheart contract, yellow-dog contract; maintenance of membership

4 **unionist, labor unionist, trade unionist, union member,** trades unionist <Brit>, organized *or* unionized worker, cardholder; shop steward, bargainer, negotiator; business agent; union officer; union *or* labor organizer, organizer, labor union official; union contractor

5 **strike, walkout** *or* tie-up <nf>, industrial action <Brit>, **job action;** slowdown, rulebook slowdown, sick-in *and* sickout *and* blue flu <nf>; work stoppage, sit-down strike, sit-down, wildcat strike, out-law strike, called strike, organized strike; sympathy strike; **slowdown,** work-to-rule, rule-book slowdown; general strike; **boycott,** boy-cottage, picketing, picket; buyer's *or* consumer's strike; **lock-out;** revolt 327.4

6 **striker,** picket; sitdown striker; holdout <nf>

7 <strike enforcer> **picket; goon** <nf>, strong-arm man; flying squadron *or* squad, goon squad <nf>

8 **strikebreaker, scab** *and* **rat** *and* **fink** *and* scissorbill <nf>, goon, **blackleg** <Brit>

VERBS 9 **organize, unionize;** bargain, bargain collectively; arbitrate; submit to arbitration

10 **strike, go on strike, go out, walk, walk out;** hit the bricks <nf>, shut it down; slow down; sit down; **boycott;** picket; hold out <nf>; **lock out;** revolt 327.7

11 **break a strike; scab** *and* **rat** *and* **fink** <nf>, **blackleg** <Brit>

728 MONEY

NOUNS 1 **money, currency, legal tender, medium of exchange,** circulating medium, sterling <Brit>, **cash,** hard cash, cold cash; specie, coinage, mintage, coin of the realm, gold; **silver;** dollars; pounds, shillings, and pence; **the wherewithal,** the wherewith; lucre, **filthy lucre** <nf>, the almighty dollar, pelf, root of all evil, mammon; "the ruling spirit of all things"—Publilius Syrus, "coined liberty"—Dostoyevsky; **hard currency,** soft currency; fractional currency; managed currency; necessity money, scrip, emergency money; monetary unit, monetary denomination

2 <nf terms> **dough, bread, jack, kale,** bucks, scratch, change, mazuma, mopus, gelt, gilt, coin, spondulicks, oof, ooftish, wampum, possibles, moolah, boodle, blunt, dinero, do-re-mi, **sugar,** brass, tin, rocks, simoleons, shekels, berries, chips, **bucks,** green, green stuff, the needful, grease, ointment, palm oil, gravy, cabbage, lettuce, whip-out, the necessary, loot

3 **wampum,** wampumpeag, peag, sewan, roanoke, shell money; cowrie

4 **specie,** hard money; coinage; coin, piece, piece of money, piece of silver *or* gold; roll of coins, rouleau; **gold piece;** ten-dollar gold piece, eagle; five-dollar gold piece, half eagle; twenty-dollar gold piece, double eagle; guinea, sovereign, pound sovereign, crown, half crown; doubloon; ducat; napoleon, louis d'or; moidore

5 **paper money;** cash; **bill,** dollar bill, etc; **note,** negotiable note *or* instrument, legal-tender note; **bank note,** bill of exchange, Federal Reserve note; national bank note; government note, treasury note; silver certificate; gold certificate; scrip; fractional note, shinplaster <nf>; fiat money, assignat

6 <nf terms> **folding money, green stuff,** the long green, folding green, lean green, mint leaves, lettuce, greenbacks, frogskins, skins

7 <US denominations> mill; cent, penny, copper, red cent <nf>; five cents, nickel; ten cents, dime; twenty-five cents, quarter, two bits <nf>; fifty cents, half-dollar, four bits <nf>; dollar, dollar bill; buck *and* smacker *and* frogskin *and* fish *and* skin <nf>; silver dollar, beau dollar <old>, cartwheel *and* iron man <nf>; two-dollar bill, two-spot <nf>; five-dollar bill; fiver *and* five-spot *and* fin <nf>; ten-dollar bill; tenner *and* ten-spot *and* sawbuck <nf>; twenty-dollar bill, double sawbuck <nf>; fifty-dollar bill, half a C <nf>; hundred-dollar bill; C *and* C-note *and* century *and* bill <nf>; five hundred dollars, half grand <nf>, five-hundred-dollar bill, half G <nf>; thousand dollars, G *and* grand <nf>, thousand-dollar bill, G-note *and* yard *and* big one <nf>

8 <British denominations> mite; farthing; halfpenny *or* ha'penny, bawbee <nf>, mag *or* meg <nf>; penny; pence, p; new pence, np; two-pence *or* tuppence; threepence *or* thrippence, threepenny bit *or* piece; fourpence, fourpenny, groat; sixpence, tanner <nf>, teston; shilling, bob <nf>; florin; half crown, half-dollar <nf>; crown, dollar <nf>; pound, quid <nf>; guinea; fiver <£5>, tenner <£10>, pony <£25>, monkey <£500>, plum <£100,000>, marigold <£1,000,000> <nf>

9 **foreign money,** foreign denominations; **convertibility, foreign exchange;** rate of exchange *or* exchange rate; parity of exchange; agio

10 counterfeit, counterfeit money, funny *or* phony *or* bogus money <nf>, false *or* bad money, queer <nf>, base coin, green goods <nf>; **forgery,** bad check, rubber check *and* bounced check *and* kite <nf>

11 **negotiable instrument** *or* **paper,** commercial paper, paper, bill; **bill of exchange,** bill of draft; certificate, certificate of deposit *or* CD; **check,** cheque <Brit>; blank check; bank check, teller's check; treasury check; cashier's check, certified check; traveler's check *or* banker's check; letter of credit, commercial letter of credit; **money order** *or* MO; postal order *or* postoffice order <Brit>; draft, warrant, voucher, debenture; **promissory note, note, IOU;** note of hand; credit note; acceptance, acceptance bill, bank acceptance, trade acceptance; due bill; demand bill, sight bill, demand draft, sight draft; time bill, time draft; exchequer bill *or* treasury bill <Brit>; checkbook

12 **token, counter,** slug; **scrip, coupon; check, ticket,** tag; hat check, baggage check

13 **sum,** amount of money; round sum, lump sum

14 **funds, finances, moneys,** exchequer, purse, budget, pocket; treasury, treasure, substance, **assets,** resources, total assets, worth, net worth, **pecuniary resources, means,** available means *or* resources *or* funds, cash flow, wherewithal, command of money; balance; pool, **fund, kitty** <nf>, petty cash; war chest; checking account, bank account; Swiss bank account, unnumbered *or* unregistered bank account; reserves, cash reserves; savings, savings account, nest egg <nf>; life savings; bottom dollar <nf>; automated teller machine *or* ATM

15 **capital, fund;** moneyed capital; principal, corpus; circulating capital, floating capital; fixed capital, working capital, equity capital, **risk** *or* **venture capital;** capital structure; capital gains distribution; capitalization

16 **money market,** supply of short-term funds; tight money, cheap money; **borrowing** 621; **lending** 620; discounting, note discounting, note shaving, dealing in commercial paper

17 **bankroll;** roll *or* wad <nf>

18 **cash, ready money** *or* **cash,** the ready <nf>, available funds, money in hand, cash in hand, balance in hand, immediate resources, **liquid assets,** cash supply, **cash flow;** treasury

19 **petty cash, pocket money, pin money,** spending money, mad money, **change,** small change; nickels and dimes *and* chicken feed *and* peanuts <nf>, pittance

20 precious metals; **gold,** yellow stuff <nf>; nugget, gold nugget; **silver, copper, nickel,** coin gold *or* silver; bullion, ingot, bar

21 standard of value, gold standard, silver standard; monometallism, bimetallism; money of account

22 <science of coins> **numismatics,** numismatology; numismatist, numismatologist

23 monetization; issuance, circulation; remonetization; demonetization; revaluation, devaluation

24 **coining,** coinage, mintage, striking, stamping; **counterfeiting, forgery;** coin-clipping

25 **coiner,** minter, mintmaster, moneyer; **counterfeiter, forger;** coin-clipper

VERBS **26** monetize; **issue,** utter, **circulate;** remonetize, reissue; demonetize; revalue, devalue, devaluate

27 discount, discount notes, deal in commercial paper, shave; borrow, lend 620.5

28 **coin, mint; print,** stamp; **counterfeit, forge;** utter, pass *or* shove the queer <nf>; pass a bad check, kite a check

29 **cash,** cash in <nf>, liquidate, convert into cash, realize

ADJS **30** **monetary, pecuniary,** nummary, nummular, **financial,** fiduciary; capital; fiscal; sumptuary; numismatic; sterling

31 convertible, liquid, negotiable

729 FINANCE, INVESTMENT

NOUNS **1** **finance, finances, money matters;** world of finance, financial world, financial industry, **high finance,** investment banking, international banking, Wall Street banking, Lombard Street; the gnomes of Zurich; economics 731; purse strings

2 **financing, funding, backing,** financial backing, **sponsorship, patronization,** support, financial support; **stake** *and* **grubstake** <nf>; subsidy 478.8; **capitalizing,** capitalization, provision of capital; deficit financing

3 personal finance; bank account, savings account, checking account; budget; pension, 401K, Individual Retirement Account *or* IRA, Keogh plan

4 **investment, venture, risk,** plunge <nf>, speculation; prime investment; ethical *or* conscience investment; money market, mutual fund, stock market, bond market; **divestment,** disinvestment

5 **banking,** money dealing, money changing; investment banking; banking industry

6 **financial condition,** state of the exchequer; **credit rating,** Dun & Bradstreet rating

7 **solvency,** soundness, solidity; credit standing, creditworthiness; unindebtedness

8 **crisis,** financial crisis; dollar crisis, dollar gap

9 **financier,** moneyman, **capitalist,** finance capitalist; Wall Streeter; investor; financial expert, economist, authority on money and banking; international banker

10 **financier, backer,** funder, **sponsor, patron, supporter,** angel <nf>, Maecenas; cash cow *and* staker *and* grubstaker <nf>, meal ticket <nf>; **fundraiser**

11 **banker, money dealer,** moneymonger; money broker; discounter, note broker, bill broker <Brit>; moneylender 620.3; money changer, cambist; investment banker; bank president, bank manager, bank officer, loan officer, trust officer, banking executive; bank clerk, cashier, teller

12 **treasurer,** financial officer, bursar, purser, purse bearer, **cashier,** cashkeeper; accountant, auditor, controller *or* comptroller, bookkeeper; chamberlain, curator, steward, trustee; depositary, depository; receiver, liquidator; **paymaster;** Secretary of the Treasury, Chancellor of the Exchequer

13 **treasury, treasure-house;** subtreasury; **depository,** repository; storehouse 386.6; gold depository, Fort Knox; **strongbox, safe,** money chest, **coffer, locker, chest;** piggy bank, penny bank, bank; **vault,** strong room; safe-deposit *or* safety-deposit box *or* vault; cashbox, coin box, cash register, **till;** bursary; exchequer, fisc; **public treasury,** public funds, taxpayer funds *or* money, pork barrel, public crib *or* trough *or* till <nf>

14 **bank,** banking house, lending institution, savings institution; automated teller machine *or* ATM, cash machine; **central bank,** Bank of England *or* the Old Lady of Threadneedle Street, Bank of France; Federal Reserve Bank *or* System; World Bank, International Monetary Fund; clearing house

15 **purse, wallet, pocketbook, bag, handbag,** clutch, shoulder bag, porte-monnaie, **billfold,** money belt, money clip, poke <nf>, **pocket;** fanny pack; moneybag; purse strings

VERBS **16** **finance, back, fund, sponsor, patronize, support,** provide for, capitalize, provide capital *or* money for, pay for, bankroll <nf>, angel <nf>, put up the money, hold the purse strings; **stake** *or* **grubstake** <nf>; subsidize 478.19; set up, set up in business; refinance

17 **invest,** place, put, sink; **risk, venture;** make an investment, lay out money, place out *or* put out at interest; reinvest, roll over, plow back into <nf>; **invest in, put money in,** sink money in, pour money into, tie up one's money in; buy in *or* into, buy a piece *or* share of; financier; plunge <nf>, speculate 737.23; play the big board, play the stock exchange

ADJS **18 solvent,** sound, substantial, solid, good, sound as a dollar, creditworthy; **able to pay,** good for, unindebted 624.23, out of the hole *or* the red

19 insolvent, unsound, indebted 623.8

20 financial, monetary, fiscal, pecuniary, economic; bull, bear

730 BUSINESSMAN, MERCHANT

NOUNS **1 businessman,** businesswoman, businessperson, businesspeople; enterpriser, entrepreneur, man of commerce; small *or* little businessman; big businessman, magnate, tycoon <nf>, baron, king, top executive, business leader; director, manager 574.1; big boss; **industrialist,** captain of industry; banker, financier; robber baron; intrapreneur

2 merchant, merchandiser, marketer, **trader,** trafficker, **dealer,** monger, chandler; **tradesman,** tradeswoman; **storekeeper, shopkeeper;** regrater; **wholesaler,** jobber, middleman; importer, exporter; **distributor; retailer,** retail merchant, retail dealer *or* seller; **dealership, distributorship;** franchise; concession

3 salesman, seller, salesperson, salesclerk; **saleswoman,** saleslady, salesgirl; **clerk,** shop clerk, store clerk, shop assistant; floorwalker; **agent, sales agent,** selling agent; sales engineer; sales manager; salespeople, sales force, sales personnel; scalper *and* ticket scalper <nf>

4 traveling salesman, traveler, commercial traveler, traveling agent, traveling man *or* woman, road warrior, knight of the road, bagman <Brit>, drummer <old>; detail man; door-to-door salesman, canvasser

5 vendor, peddler, huckster, hawker, butcher <old>, higgler, cadger <Scot>, colporteur, chapman <Brit>; cheap-jack *and* cheap-john <nf>; coster *or* costermonger <Brit>; sidewalk salesman

6 solicitor, canvasser

7 <nf terms> tout, touter, **pitch-man** *or* **-woman** *or* person, barker, spieler, ballyhooer, **ballyhoo man**

8 auctioneer, auction agent

9 broker, note broker, bill broker <Brit>, discount broker, cotton broker, hotel broker, insurance broker, mortgage broker, diamond broker, furniture broker, ship broker, grain broker; stockbroker 737.10; pawnbroker 620.3; money broker, money changer, cambist; land broker, real estate broker, realtor, real estate agent, estate agent <Brit>

10 ragman, old-clothesman, rag-and-bone man <Brit>; **junkman,** junk dealer

11 tradesmen, tradespeople, tradesfolk, **merchantry**

ADJS **12 business, commercial,** mercantile; entrepreneurial

731 COMMERCE, ECONOMICS

NOUNS **1 commerce, trade, traffic,** truck, intercourse, **dealing, dealings; business,** business dealings *or* affairs *or* relations, commercial affairs *or* relations; the business world, the world of trade *or* commerce, the marketplace; merchantry, mercantile business; **market,** marketing, state of the market, buyers' market, sellers' market; **industry** 725.4; big business, small business; fair trade, free trade, reciprocal trade, unilateral trade, multilateral trade; most favored nation; balance of trade; restraint of trade

2 trade, trading, doing business, trafficking; barter, bartering, **exchange,** interchange, swapping <nf>; give-and-take, horse trading <nf>, **dealing, deal-making,** wheeling and dealing <nf>; **buying and selling; wholesaling,** jobbing; brokerage, agency; **retailing,** merchandising 734.2; commercial trade, export and import

3 negotiation, bargaining, haggling, higgling, **dickering, chaffering,** chaffer, haggle; hacking out *or* working out *or* hammering out a deal, coming to terms; horse trading; collective bargaining, package bargaining, pattern bargaining

4 transaction, business *or* commercial transaction, **deal,** business deal, negotiation <old>, operation, turn; package deal

5 bargain, deal <nf>, dicker; agreement, contract; **trade, swap** <nf>; horse trade <nf>; trade-in; blind bargain, pig in a poke; hard bargain

6 custom, customers, clientele, patronage, patrons, trade; **goodwill,** repute, good name

7 economy, economic system, market, capitalist *or* capitalistic economy, free-enterprise *or* free-trade *or* private-enterprise economy, market economy, free-market economy, socialist *or* socialistic economy, collectivized economy; hot *or* overheated economy; healthy *or* sound economy, weak economy; **gross national product** *or* **GNP;** economic sector, public sector, private sector; economic self-sufficiency, autarky; economic policy, fiscal policy, monetary policy; microeconomics, macroeconomics; privatization, nationalization, denationalization, supply-side economics; economic theory; open market

8 standard of living, standard of life, standard of comfort; real wages, take-home pay *or* take-home; **cost of living;** cost-of-living index, consumer price index

9 economic indicator, econometrics; gross national

product *or* GNP, price index, consumer price index, retail price index, cost-of-living index; unemployment rate, national debt, budget deficit

10 business cycle, economic cycle, business fluctuations; peak, peaking; low, bottoming out <nf>; prosperity, boom <nf>; boomlet *or* miniboom; crisis, **recession, depression,** slowdown, cooling off, slump *and* bust <nf>, downturn, downtick <nf>; upturn, uptick <nf>; expanding economy, recovery; **growth,** economic growth, business growth, high growth rate, expansion, market expansion, **economic expansion; trade cycle;** trade deficit, trade gap, balance of payments; **monetary cycle; inflation,** deflation, stagflation

11 economics, eco *or* econ <nf>, economic science, the dismal science; political economy; dynamic economics; theoretical economics, plutology; classical economics; Keynesian economics, Keynesianism; supply side economics; econometrics; economism, economic determinism

12 economist, economic expert *or* authority; political economist

13 commercialism, mercantilism; industrialism; mass marketing

14 commercialization; industrialization

VERBS 15 trade, deal, traffic, truck, buy and sell, do business; barter; exchange, change, interchange, give in exchange, take in exchange, **swap** <nf>, switch; swap horses *and* horse-trade <nf>; trade off; trade in; trade sight unseen, make a blind bargain, sell a pig in a poke; **ply one's trade** 724.12

16 deal in, trade in, traffic in, handle, carry, be in; market, merchandise, **sell,** retail, wholesale, job

17 trade with, deal with, traffic with, traffic in, do business with, have dealings with, have truck with, transact business with; frequent as a customer, shop at, trade at, **patronize,** take one's business *or* trade to; open an account with, have an account with; export, import; market, merchandise

18 bargain, drive a bargain, negotiate, haggle, higgle, chaffer, huckster, **deal, dicker,** barter, make a deal, do a deal <Brit>, hack out *or* work out *or* hammer out a deal, do a deal; **bid,** bid for, cheapen, beat down; underbid, outbid; drive a hard bargain; hold out for

19 strike a bargain, make a bargain, make a dicker, **make a deal,** get oneself a deal, put through a deal, shake hands, shake on it <nf>; bargain for, agree to; **come to terms** 332.10; be a bargain, be a go *and* be a deal <nf>, be on <nf>; network

20 put on a business basis *or* footing, make businesslike; commercialize; industrialize

21 <adjust the economy> cool *or* cool off the economy; heat *or* heat up the economy

ADJS 22 commercial, business, trade, trading, **mercantile,** merchant; commercialistic, mercantilistic; industrial; wholesale, retail

23 economic, fiscal, monetary, pecuniary, financial, budgetary; inflationary, deflationary; socio-economic, politico-economic *or* -economical

732 ILLICIT BUSINESS

NOUNS 1 illicit business, illegitimate business, illegal operations, illegal commerce *or* traffic, shady dealings, **racket** <nf>; **the rackets** <nf>, the syndicate, **organized crime, Mafia,** Cosa Nostra; **black market,** gray market; **drug** *or* **narcotics traffic;** narcoterrorism; **prostitution,** streetwalking; **pimping,** traffic in women, white slavery; usury 623.3, loan-sharking *and* shylocking <nf>; protection racket; bootlegging, moon-shining <nf>; gambling 759.7

2 smuggling, contrabandage, contraband; narcotics smuggling, dope smuggling <nf>, jewel smuggling, cigarette smuggling; gunrunning, rumrunning

3 contraband, smuggled goods; narcotics, drugs, dope <nf>, jewels, cigarettes; bootleg liquor; stolen goods *or* property, hot goods *or* items <nf>

4 racketeer; Mafioso; **black marketeer,** gray marketeer; bootlegger, moonshiner <nf>; pusher *and* dealer <nf>, narcotics *or* dope *or* drug pusher <nf>; **drug lord;** Medellin cartel

5 smuggler, contrabandist, runner; drug smuggler, mule <nf>; gunrunner, rumrunner

6 fence, receiver, **receiver of stolen goods,** swagman *and* swagsman <nf>, bagman, bagwoman

VERBS 7 <deal in illicit goods> push *and* shove <nf>; **sell under the counter; black-market,** black-marketeer; bootleg, moonshine <nf>; fence <nf>

8 smuggle, run, sneak

733 PURCHASE

NOUNS 1 purchase, buying, purchasing, acquisition; shopping, marketing; shopping around, comparison shopping; window-shopping; impulse buying; shopping spree; repurchase, rebuying; mail-order buying, catalog shopping; teleshopping, home shopping, online shopping; installment buying, hire purchase <Brit>; layaway purchase; **buying up,** cornering, coemption <old>; **buying** *or* **purchasing power; consumerism;** consumer society, consumer sovereignty, consumer power, acquisitive society; retail *or* consumer price index; wholesale price index; shopping list

2 option, first option, **first refusal,** refusal,

preemption, right of preemption, prior right of purchase

3 **market,** public, purchasing public; urban market, rural market, youth market, suburban market, etc; **clientele, customers,** clientage, **patronage, custom,** trade; carriage trade; demand, consumer demand

4 **customer, client; patron,** patronizer <nf>, regular customer *or* buyer, regular; clientele; **prospect;** mark *or* sucker <nf>

5 **buyer,** purchaser, emptor, **consumer,** vendee; **shopper,** shopaholic, impulse buyer, marketer; bargain-hunter; bidder; window-shopper, browser; purchasing agent, customer agent

6 by-bidder, decoy, come-on man *and* shill <nf>

VERBS 7 **purchase, buy,** procure, make *or* complete a purchase, make a buy, make a deal for, blow oneself to <nf>; **buy up,** regrate, **corner,** monopolize, engross, hoard; buy out; buy in, buy into, buy a piece of; repurchase, rebuy, buy back; buy on credit, buy on the installment plan, charge; buy sight unseen *or* blind; trade up

8 **shop, market, go shopping,** go marketing; **shop around;** window-shop, comparison-shop, **browse,** graze; impulse-buy; shop till one drops *and* hit the shops <nf>

9 **bid,** make a bid, offer, offer to buy, make an offer; give the asking price; by-bid, shill <nf>; bid up; bid in

ADJS 10 **purchasing, buying,** in the market; cliental

11 **bought,** store-bought, boughten *or* store-boughten <nf>, purchased

734 SALE

NOUNS 1 **sale; wholesale, retail; market, demand,** outlet; buyers' market, sellers' market; mass market; conditional sale; tie-in sale, tie-in; turnover; bill of sale; cash sale, cash-and-carry

2 **selling, merchandising, marketing; wholesaling,** jobbing; **retailing;** direct selling; sell-through; telemarketing; mail-order selling, direct-mail selling, catalog selling; television *or* video selling; online selling, e-commerce; **vending, peddling, hawking, huckstering;** hucksterism; market *or* marketing research, consumer research, consumer preference study, consumer survey, data warehousing; sales campaign, promotion, sales promotion; **salesmanship,** high-pressure salesmanship, hard sell <nf>, low-pressure salesmanship, soft sell <nf>; cold call; sellout

3 **sale,** sellout, closing-out sale, going-out-of-business sale, inventory-clearance sale, distress sale, fire sale; bazaar; rummage sale, white elephant sale, garage sale, tag sale, yard sale, flea market; tax sale

4 **auction,** auction sale, vendue, outcry, sale at *or* by

auction, sale to the highest bidder; Dutch auction; **auction block, block**

5 **sales talk, sales pitch,** patter; **pitch** *or* spiel *or* ballyhoo <nf>

6 **sales resistance,** consumer *or* buyer resistance

7 **salability,** salableness, commerciality, merchandisability, **marketability,** vendibility

VERBS 8 **sell, merchandise, market,** move, turn over, sell off, make *or* effect a sale; convert into cash, turn into money; **sell out,** close out; sell up <Brit>; **retail,** sell retail, sell over the counter; **wholesale,** sell wholesale, job, be jobber *or* wholesaler for; dump, unload, flood the market with, get rid of; sacrifice, sell at a sacrifice *or* loss; sell off, remainder; resell, sell over; undersell, undercut, cut under; sell short; sell on consignment

9 **vend,** dispense, **peddle, hawk, huckster;** tout

10 **put up for sale,** put up, ask bids *or* offers for, offer for sale, offer at a bargain

11 **auction, auction off, auctioneer,** sell at auction, sell by auction, put up for auction, **put on the block,** bring under the hammer; knock down, sell to the highest bidder

12 **be sold, sell,** bring, realize, sell for; change hands; sell like hotcakes, be in demand

ADJS 13 **sales,** selling, market, **marketing, merchandising, retail,** retailing, wholesale, wholesaling; vending

14 **salable, marketable,** retailable, merchandisable, merchantable, commercial, vendible; in demand

15 **unsalable,** nonsalable, **unmarketable;** on one's hands, on the shelves, not moving, not turning over, unbought, unsold

ADVS 16 **for sale,** to sell, up for sale, in *or* on the market, in the marts of trade; at a bargain, marked down

17 **at auction,** at outcry, at public auction *or* outcry, by auction, **on the block,** under the hammer

735 MERCHANDISE

NOUNS 1 **merchandise, commodities, wares, goods,** effects, vendibles; **items,** oddments; **consumer goods,** consumer items, retail goods, goods for sale; **stock, stock-in-trade;** staples; **inventory; line,** line of goods; sideline; job lot; mail-order goods, catalog goods; **luxury goods,** high-ticket *or* big-ticket *or* upscale items

2 **commodity, ware,** vendible, **product, article, item,** article of commerce *or* merchandise; staple, staple item, standard article; special, feature, leader, lead item, loss leader; seconds; drug, drug on the market

3 **dry goods, soft goods;** textiles; yard goods, white

goods, linens, napery; men's wear, ladies' wear, children's wear, infants' wear; sportswear, sporting goods; leatherware, leather goods

4 **hard goods, durables, durable goods;** fixtures, white goods, **appliances** 385.4; tools and machinery 1040; **hardware,** ironmongery <Brit>; sporting goods, **housewares,** home furnishings, kitchenware; tableware, dinnerware; flatware, hollow ware; metalware, brassware, copperware, silverware, ironware, tinware; woodenware; glassware; chinaware, earthenware, clayware, stoneware, graniteware; enamelware; ovenware

5 **furniture** 229, furnishings, home furnishings

6 **notions, sundries,** novelties, knickknacks, odds and ends; toilet goods, toiletries; cosmetics; giftware

7 **groceries,** grocery <Brit>, food items, edibles, victuals, baked goods, packaged goods, canned goods, tinned goods <Brit>; green goods, **produce,** truck

736 MARKET
<place of trade>

NOUNS 1 **market, mart, store, shop,** salon, boutique, wareroom, emporium, house, establishment, *magasin* <Fr>; **retail store; wholesale house, discount store, discount house, outlet store;** warehouse, megastore; mail-order house; **general store,** country store; **department store;** warehouse store, superstore; **co-op** <nf>, cooperative; **variety store,** variety shop, **dime store; ten-cent store** or five-and-ten or five-and-dime <nf>; convenience store, corner store, mom-and-pop store; chain store; concession; **trading post,** post; **supermarket**

2 **marketplace, mart, market, open market,** market overt, agora; **shopping center, shopping plaza** or **mall,** plaza, mall, arcade, shopping or shop or commercial complex; warehouse; emporium, rialto; staple; **bazaar, fair,** trade fair, show, auto show, boat show, etc, exposition; flea market, flea fair, street market, farmers' market, fish market, meat market, *marché aux puces* <Fr>; trading post; home shopping, e-commerce or electronic commerce

3 **booth, stall, stand;** newsstand, kiosk, news kiosk; pushcart; roadside stand

4 **vending machine,** vendor, coin machine, coin-operated machine, slot machine, automat; redeemer or reverse vending machine

5 **salesroom,** wareroom; showroom; auction room

6 **counter,** shopboard <old>; notions counter; showcase; peddler's cart, pushcart

737 STOCK MARKET

NOUNS 1 **stock market, the market, Wall Street;** securities market, commodity market; ticker market; open market, competitive market; steady market, strong market, hard or stiff market; unsteady market, spotty market; weak market; long market; top-heavy market; market index, stock price index, Dow-Jones Industrial Average

2 **active market,** brisk market, lively market

3 **inactive market,** slow market, stagnant market, flat market, tired market, sick market; investors on the sidelines

4 **rising market,** booming market, buoyant market; **bull market,** bullish market, bullishness

5 **declining market,** sagging market, retreating market, off market, soft market; **bear market,** bearish market, bearishness; **slump,** sag; break, break in the market; profit-taking, selloff; **crash,** smash

6 **rigged market,** manipulated market, pegged market, put-up market; **insider trading**

7 **stock exchange, exchange,** Wall Street, change <Brit>, **stock market,** bourse, **board;** the Exchange, New York Stock Exchange, the Big Board; American Stock Exchange, Amex, curb, curb market, curb exchange; over-the-counter market, telephone market, outside market; third market; exchange floor; commodity exchange, pit, corn pit, wheat pit, etc; quotation board; **ticker,** stock ticker; ticker tape

8 **financial district,** Wall Street, the Street; Lombard Street

9 **stockbrokerage,** brokerage, brokerage house, brokerage office; wire house; bucket shop *and* boiler room <nf>

10 **stockbroker,** sharebroker <Brit>, **broker,** jobber, stockjobber, dealer, stock dealer; Wall Streeter; stock-exchange broker, *agent de bourse* <Fr>; floor broker, floor trader, floorman, specialist, market maker; pit man; curb broker; odd-lot dealer; two-dollar broker; day trader, night trader; broker's agent, customer's broker or customer's man, registered representative; bond crowd

11 **speculator,** adventurer, operator; big operator, smart operator; **plunger,** gunslinger; scalper; stag <Brit>; lame duck; margin purchaser; **arbitrager** or arbitrageur or arb <nf>; inside trader

12 **bear,** short, short seller; shorts, short interest, short side; short account, bear account

13 **bull,** long, longs, long interest, long side; long account, bull account

14 **stockholder,** stockowner, **shareholder, shareowner;** bondholder, coupon-clipper <nf>; stockholder of record

15 **stock company,** joint-stock company; issuing company; stock insurance company

16 trust, investment company; investment trust, holding company; closed-end investment company, closed-end fund; open-end fund, mutual fund, money-market fund; unit trust <Brit>; load fund, no-load fund, low-load fund, back-end fund; growth fund, income fund, dual purpose fund; trust fund; blind trust

17 pool, bear pool, bull pool, blind pool

18 stockbroking, brokerage, stockbrokerage, jobbing, stockjobbing, stockjobbery, stock dealing; bucketing, legal bucketing

19 trading, stock-market trading, market-trading; computer *or* programmed selling; playing the market <nf>; **speculation,** stockjobbing, stockjobbery; **venture,** flutter; flier, plunge; scalping; liquidation, profit taking; **arbitrage,** arbitraging; buying in, covering shorts; short sale; spot sale; round trade *or* transaction, turn; risk *or* venture capital, equity capital; money-market trading, foreign-exchange trading, agiotage; **buyout, takeover,** hostile takeover, takeover bid; leveraged buyout; greenmail; **leverage**

20 manipulation, rigging; raid, bear raid, bull raid; **corner,** corner in, corner on the market, monopoly; washing, washed *or* wash sale

21 option, stock option, right, **put, call,** put and call, right of put and call; straddle, spread; strip; strap

22 panic, bear panic, rich man's panic

VERBS **23 trade, speculate,** venture, operate, **play the market,** buy *or* sell *or* deal in futures; **arbitrage; plunge,** take a flier <nf>; scalp; bucket, bucketshop; stag *or* stag the market <Brit>; trade on margin; pyramid; be long, go long, be long of the market, be on the long side of the market; be short, be short of the market, be on the short side of the market; margin up, apply *or* deposit margin; wait out the market, hold on; be caught short, miss the market, overstay the market; scoop the market, make a scoop *or* killing *or* bundle *or* pile <nf>

24 sell, convert, liquidate; throw on the market, dump, unload; **sell short,** go short, make a short sale; cover one's short, fulfill a short sale; make delivery, clear the trade; close out, sell out, terminate the account

25 manipulate the market, **rig the market;** bear, **bear the market;** bull, **bull the market;** raid the market; hold *or* peg the market; whipsaw; wash sales

26 corner, get a corner on, **corner the market;** monopolize, engross; buy up, absorb

738 SECURITIES

NOUNS **1 securities** <see list>, **stocks and bonds,** investment securities; arbitrage, program trading

2 stock <see list>, shares <Brit>, equity, equity security, corporate stock; stock split, split; reverse split; stock list; stock ledger, share ledger <Brit>; **holdings, portfolio,** investment portfolio

3 share, lot; preference share; dummy share; holding, holdings, stockholding, stockholdings; block; round lot, full lot, even lot, board lot; odd lot, fractional lot

4 stock certificate, certificate of stock; street certificate; interim certificate; **coupon**

5 bond <see list>; nominal rate, coupon rate, current yield, yield to maturity

6 issue, issuance; **flotation;** stock issue, secondary issue; bond issue; poison pill <nf>

7 dividend; regular dividend; extra dividend, special dividend, plum *and* melon <nf>; payout ratio; cumulative dividend, accumulated dividends, accrued dividends; interim dividend; cash dividend; stock dividend; optional dividend; scrip dividend; liquidating dividend; phony dividend; **interest** 623.3; **return, yield,** return on investment, payout, payback

8 assessment, Irish dividend

9 price, quotation; bid-and-asked prices, bid price, asked *or* asking *or* offering price; actual *or* delivery *or* settling price, put price, call price; opening price, closing price; high, low; market price, quoted price, flash price; issue price; fixed price; parity; **par,** issue par; par value, nominal value, face value; stated value; book value; market value; bearish prices, bullish prices; swings, fluctuations; flurry, flutter; rally, decline

10 margin; thin margin, shoestring margin; exhaust price

11 <commodities> spots, spot grain, etc; futures, future grain, etc

VERBS **12 issue, float,** put on the market; issue stock, go public <nf>; float a bond issue

13 declare a dividend, cut a melon <nf>

ADVS **14** dividend off, ex dividend; dividend on, cum dividend; coupon off, ex coupon; coupon on, cum coupon; warrants off, ex warrants; warrants on, cum warrants; when issued

15 kinds of securities

active securities	corporation securities
American Depository Receipts *or* ADRs	debenture *or* certificate of indebtedness
banker's acceptance	digested securities
callable securities	fixed-income securities
certificate of accrual on treasury securities *or* CATS	foreign securities
	futures contract
	gilt-edged securities
certificate of deposit *or* CD	government securities
	international securities
convertible securities *or* convertibles *or* CVs	junior securities
	legal securities

liquid yield option notes *or*
  LYONs
listed securities
margined securities
marketable securities
money-market certificate
mortgage-based securities
municipal securities
negotiable securities *or*
  negotiables
noncallable securities
note
obsolete securities
outside securities
outstanding securities
over-the-counter securities
pass-throughs *or*
  participation certificate
program trading
registered securities

senior securities
separate trading of
  registered interest *and*
  principal securities *or*
  STRIPS
short-term note
speculative securities *or*
  cats and dogs <nf>
stamped securities
treasury bill
treasury bond
treasury certificate
treasury investment growth
  receipts *or* TIGRs
treasury note
undigested securities
unlisted securities
unregistered securities
warrant

16 kinds of stock

active stock
assessable stock
authorized capital stock
blue chip stock *or* blue chip
borrowed stock
capital stock
common stock *or* ordinary
  shares <Brit>
convertible preferred stock
cumulative convertible
  preferred stock
cumulative preferred stock
cyclical stock
debenture stock
defensive stock
deferred stock
eighth stock
floating stock
growth stock
guaranteed stock
high-grade stock
hypothecated stock
inactive stock
income stock
industrials *or* rails *or*
  utilities, etc
initial public offering
issued capital stock
letter stock

loaned stock
long stock
new issue
no-par stock
nonassessable stock
nonvoting stock
over-the-counter stock
pale blue chip
participating preferred
  stock
penny stock
preferred stock *or*
  preference stock <Brit>
protective stock
quality stock
quarter stock
seasoned stock
short stock
small cap stock
special situation stock
specialty stock
speculative stock
standard stock
ten-share unit stock
treasury stock
unissued capital stock
voting stock
voting-right certificate
watered stock

17 kinds of bond

adjustment bond
annuity bond
appreciation bond
assented bond
asset-backed bond
assumed bond
baby bond
bearer bond

bearer certificate
bond anticipation note
callable bond
collateral trust bond
consolidated annuities *or*
  consols *or* bank
  annuities <Brit>
consolidated stock

convertible bond
convertible debenture
corporate bond
corporation stock <Brit>
coupon bond
current income bond
deep-discount bond
defense bond
deferred bond
definitive bond
discount bond
equipment bond
equipment note
equipment trust
equipment trust bond
equipment trust certificate
extended bond
Fannie Mae bond
Federal Agency bond
FICO bond
first mortgage bond *or* first
foreign bond
Freddie Mac bond
general mortgage bond
general obligation bond
gilt-edged bond
Ginnie Mae bond
government bond
guaranteed bond
high-grade bond
high-yield bond *or* junk
  bond <nf>
income bond
indenture
installment bond
interchangeable bond
interim bond
joint bond
junk bond
Liberty bond
long-term bond
mortgage-backed bond

municipal bond
negotiable bond
noncallable bond
nonnegotiable bond
optional bond
par bond
participating bond
perpetual bond
premium bond
purchase money bond
redeemable bond
refunding bond
registered bond
registered certificate
revenue bond
savings bond
second mortgage bond *or*
  second
secured bond
serial bond
Series EE bond
Series HH bond
short-term bond
sinking-fund bond
small bond
state bond
subordinated bond
tax anticipation note
tax-exempt bond
tax-free bond
treasury bill
treasury bond
treasury note
trust indenture
trustee mortgage bond
turnpike bond
unsecured bond
voting bond
war bond
Z-bond *or* accrual bond *or*
  accretion bond
zero coupon bond

18 kinds of mutual fund

aggressive growth mutual
  fund
asset management mutual
  fund
balanced mutual fund
bond mutual fund
capital appreciation
  mutual fund
closed-end mutual fund
corporate bond mutual
  fund
double tax-exempt bond
  mutual fund
equity mutual fund
equity-income mutual
  fund

federal municipal bond
  mutual fund
federal municipal money
  market mutual fund
fixed-income mutual fund
global bond mutual fund
global mutual fund
government bond mutual
  fund
growth and income mutual
  fund
growth mutual fund
index mutual fund
international mutual fund
large-cap mutual fund
load mutual fund

mid-cap mutual fund
money market mutual fund
mutual funds of mutual fund
no-load mutual fund
small-cap mutual fund
speciality or sector mutual fund
state municipal bond mutual fund
state municipal money market mutual fund
state tax-exempt income mutual fund
stock mutual fund
tax-exempt income mutual fund
tax-exempt money market fund
triple tax-exempt bond mutual fund
U.S. Government money market fund

739 WORKPLACE

NOUNS **1 workplace,** worksite, **workshop, shop;** shop floor, workspace, working space, work area, loft; **bench,** workbench, worktable; counter, worktop; **work station; desk,** desktop; **workroom; studio,** *atelier* <Fr>, library; parlor, beauty parlor, funeral parlor, etc; **establishment, facility,** installation; **company,** institution, house, firm, concern, agency, organization, **corporation; financial institution, stock exchange** 737, **bank** 729; **market, store** 736, mall, shopping mall; **restaurant, eating place** 8.17; hotel, motel; gas station; construction site, building site; dockyard, shipyard; farm, ranch, nursery; power station; government office

2 hive, hive of industry, beehive; factory *or* mill *or* manufacturing town; hub of industry, center of manufacture, industrial town

3 plant, factory, works, manufactory <old>, manufacturing plant, installation, shop floor, *usine* <Fr>; main plant, assembly plant, subassembly plant, feeder plant; foreign-owned plant, transplant; push-button plant, automated *or* cybernated *or* automatic *or* robot factory; assembly *or* production line; defense plant, munitions plant, armory, arsenal; **power plant** 1032.19; atomic energy plant; **machine shop; mill,** sawmill, flour mill, etc; **yard,** yards, railroad yard, brickyard, shipyard, dockyard, boatyard; rope-walk; mint; refinery, oil refinery, sugar refinery, etc; distillery, brewery, winery; boilery; bindery, bookbindery; packinghouse; cannery; dairy, creamery; pottery; tannery; sweatshop; **factory district,** industrial zone *or* area, industrial park, industrial estate <Brit>; factory belt, manufacturing quarter; enterprise zone

4 foundry, works, metalworks; steelworks, steelyard, steel mill; refinery, forge, furnace, bloomery; smelter; smithy, smithery, stithy, blacksmith shop *or* blacksmith's shop; brickworks; quarry, mine, colliery, coal mine; mint

5 repair shop, fix-it shop <nf>; **garage;** roundhouse; hangar

6 laboratory, lab <nf>; research laboratory, research installation *or* facility *or* center *or* park

7 office, shop <nf>; home *or* head *or* main office, headquarters, executive office, corporate *or* company headquarters; office suite, executive suite; chambers <chiefly Brit>; closet, cabinet <old>, **study,** den, carrell; **embassy,** consulate, legation, chancery, chancellery; box office, booking office, ticket office; branch, branch office, local office, subsidiary office, bureau, business house; office *or* executive park

8 <home workplace> home office, office, den, study; kitchen, laundry room, sewing room, workbench

740 WEAVING

NOUNS **1 weaving,** weave, warpage, weftage, warp and woof *or* weft, texture, tissue; **fabric, web,** webbing; **interweaving,** interweavement, intertexture; **interlacing,** interlacement, interlacery; crisscross; **intertwining,** intertwinement; intertieing, interknitting, interthreading, intertwisting; **lacing,** enlacement; **twining,** entwining, entwinement; wreathing, knitting, twisting; **braiding,** plaiting, plashing

2 braid, plait, pigtail, **wreath,** wreathwork

3 warp; woof, weft, filling; shoot, pick

4 weaver, interlacer, webster <old>, knitter, spinner; weaverbird, weaver finch, whirligig beetle

5 loom, weaver; hand loom; Navajo loom; knitting machine; spinning wheel; shuttle, distaff

VERBS **6 weave,** loom, tissue; **interweave, interlace, intertwine,** interknit, interthread, intertissue, intertie, intertwist; inweave, intort; web, net; **lace,** enlace; **twine,** entwine; **braid,** plait, pleach, **wreathe,** raddle, **knit,** twist, mat, wattle; crisscross; twill, loop, noose; splice; felt, mat, brush, nap; interconnect

ADJS **7 woven,** loomed, textile; **interwoven, interlaced,** interthreaded, **intertwined,** interknit, intertissued, intertied, intertwisted; handwoven; **laced,** enlaced; **wreathed,** fretted, raddled, knit, knitted; **twined,** entwined; **braided,** plaited, platted, pleached; hooked; webbed; loomed

8 weaving, twining, entwining; **intertwining, interlacing,** interweaving, crosswise, crossways

741 SEWING

NOUNS **1 sewing, needlework,** stitchery, stitching; mending, basting, darning, hemming, quilting, embroidery, cross-stitching; **fancywork;** tailoring, garment making 5.31; suture

2 sewer, needleworker, seamstress, sempstress, needlewoman; seamster, sempster, **tailor,** needleman <old>, needler <Brit>; embroiderer, embroideress; knitter; garmentmaker 5.33

3 sewing machine, sewer, embroidery hoop
VERBS **4 sew, stitch,** needle; mend, baste; stitch up,
　sew up; **tailor**

742 CERAMICS

NOUNS **1 ceramics** <see list>, **pottery;** potting
　2 ceramic ware, ceramics; pottery, crockery; china,
　porcelain; enamelware; refractory, cement; bisque,
　biscuit; pot, crock, vase, urn, jug, bowl; tile,
　tiling; brick, firebrick, refractory brick, adobe;
　glass 1029.2; industrial ceramics; ceramist,
　ceramicist, potter
　3 <materials> clay; potter's clay *or* earth, fireclay,
　refractory clay; argil, adobe, terra cotta; porcelain
　clay, kaolin, china clay, china stone, marl, feldspar,
　petuntze *or* petuntse; flux; slip; glaze, overglaze,
　underglaze; crackle
　4 potter's wheel, wheel; kick wheel, pedal wheel,
　hand-turned wheel, power wheel
　5 kiln, oven, stove, furnace; acid kiln, brick kiln,
　cement kiln, enamel kiln, muffle kiln, limekiln,
　bottle kiln, beehive kiln, reverberatory,
　reverberatory kiln; pyrometer, pyrometric cone,
　Seger cone
VERBS **6** pot, shape, **throw,** throw *or* turn a pot; cast,
　mold; **fire,** bake; glaze
ADJS **7 ceramic,** earthen, clay, enamel, china,
　porcelain; fired, baked, glazed; refractory; hand-
　turned, hand-painted, thrown; industrial
　8 ceramics

agateware	cottage china
Albion ware	crackle *or* crackleware
Allervale pottery	creamware
Aretine ware	crockery
Arita ware	crouch ware
Arretine ware *or* terra	Crown Derby ware
sigillata	Dedham pottery
basalt *or* basaltes *or*	delft *or* delftware
basaltware	Derby porcelain
Belleek ware	Doulton ware
Berlin ware	Dresden china
biscuit *or* bisque ware	earthenware
blackware	eggshell porcelain
blue and white ware	enamel *or*
bone china	enamelware
Castleford ware	faience
Castor ware	glassware
champlevé *or* champlevé	glazed ware
enamel	gombroon
Chelsea porcelain	hard-paste porcelain
china *or* chinaware	Hirado ware
Ch'ing porcelain	Hizen porcelain
clayware	Imari ware
cloisonné *or* cloisonné	industrial ceramics
enamel	ironstone *or* ironstone
Coalport	china

istoriato ware	Royal Worcester porcelain
Jackfield ware	salt-glazed ware
jasper *or* jasperware	Samian ware
Kakiemon ware	sanda ware
Kinkozan ware	Satsuma ware
lambrequin	semiporcelain
Leeds pottery	Sèvres *or* Sèvres ware
Limoges *or* Limoges ware	Seto ware
Lowestoft ware	slipware
lusterware *or* luster pottery	soft-paste porcelain
majolica	Spode
Meissen ware	spongeware
mezza-majolica	Staffordshire *or*
Nabeshima ware	Staffordshire ware
Nanking ware	stoneware
Old Worcester ware	Sung ware
ovenware	T'ang ware
Palissy ware	terra cotta
Parian ware	terra sigillata *or* Arretine
Pennsylvania Dutch *or*	ware
German ware	Tiffany glass
porcelain	ting ware *or* ting yao
porcelain enamel	Toft ware
queensware	tulip ware
redware	Wedgwood *or* Wedgwood
refractory ware	ware
Rockingham ware	whiteware *or* white pottery
Royal Copenhagen	willowware
porcelain	Worcester ware
Royal Doulton	yi-hsing ware *or* yi-hsing
porcelain	yao

743 AMUSEMENT

NOUNS **1 amusement, entertainment, diversion,**
　solace, divertisement, *divertissement* <Fr>,
　recreation, relaxation, regalement; **pastime,** *passe-*
　temps <Fr>; **mirth** 109.5; **pleasure, enjoyment** 95
　2 fun, action <nf>; funmaking, fun and games, **play,**
　sport, game; **good time,** lovely time, pleasant time;
　big time *and* **high time** *and* high old time <nf>,
　picnic *and* laughs *and* lots of laughs *and* ball <nf>,
　great fun, time of one's life; a short life and a
　merry one; wild oats
　3 festivity, merrymaking, merriment, gaiety, jollity,
　jollification <nf>, **joviality, conviviality,** whoopee
　and hoopla <nf>; larking <nf>, cavorting,
　skylarking, racketing, mafficking <Brit nf>, holiday-
　making; **revelry,** revelment, reveling, revels; nightlife
　4 festival, festivity, festive occasion, *fiesta* <Sp>,
　fete, gala, **gala affair, blowout** <nf>, **jamboree**
　<nf>; **high jinks,** do, great doings <nf>; *fête*
　champêtre <Fr>; **feast, banquet** 8.9; picnic 8.6;
　party 582.11; waygoose <Brit nf>, wayzgoose; fair,
　carnival; kermis; *Oktoberfest* <Ger>; Mardi Gras;
　Saturnalia; harvest festival, harvest home <Brit>;
　field day; gala day, feria

5 frolic, play, romp, rollick, frisk, gambol, caper, dido <nf>

6 revel, lark, escapade, ploy; **celebration** 487; **party** 582.11; **spree, bout, fling,** wingding *and* randan <nf>, randy <Scot>; **carouse, drinking bout** 88.5

7 round of pleasure, mad round, **whirl,** merry-go-round, the rounds, the dizzy rounds

8 sports 744; **athletics,** agonistics; athleticism

9 game; card game; board game; parlor game, role-playing game; children's game; computer game, video game; gambling game; table game; word game; indoor game, outdoor game; **play; contest** 457.3; race 457.12; **event, meet; bout, match,** go <nf>; gambling 759

10 tournament, tourney, gymkhana, **field day;** rally; **regatta**

11 playground; field, athletic field, playing field; football field, gridiron; baseball field, diamond; infield, outfield; soccer field; archery ground, cricket ground, polo ground, croquet ground *or* lawn, bowling green; bowling alley; links, golf links, golf course; fairway, putting green; **gymnasium,** gym <nf>; **court,** badminton court, basketball court, tennis court, racket court, squash court; billiard parlor, poolroom, pool hall; racecourse, track, course turf, oval; stretch; rink, glaciarium, ice rink, skating rink; **playroom** 197.12

12 swimming pool, pool, swimming bath <Brit>, plunge, plunge bath, natatorium; swimming hole; wading pool

13 entertainment; entertainment industry, show business, show biz <nf>; **theater;** dinner theatre; **cabaret, tavern, roadhouse;** café dansant, chantant; nightclub, night spot *or* nitery *and* hot spot <nf>, *boîte* and *boîte de nuit* <Fr>; juke joint <nf>, discothèque *or* disco <nf>; dance hall, dancing pavilion, ballroom, dance floor; casino; **resort** 228.27

14 park, public park, pleasure garden *or* ground, pleasance, paradise, common, commons, playground; **amusement park,** Tivoli, fun fair, carnival; fairground; **theme park,** safari park

15 ride, merry-go-round, carousel, roundabout, ride, whirligig, whip, flying horses; Ferris wheel; seesaw, teeter-totter; slide; swing; roller coaster; chutes, chute-the-chute; funhouse, arcade; -drome

16 toy, plaything, sport; bauble, knickknack, gimcrack, gewgaw, kickshaw, whim-wham, trinket; **doll,** paper doll, golliwog, rag doll, stuffed animal, teddy bear, puppet, glove puppet, marionette, toy soldier, tin soldier; **dollhouse,** doll carriage; **hobbyhorse,** cockhorse, rocking horse; **hoop,** hula hoop; **top,** spinning top, teetotum; pinwheel; **jack-in-the-box;** jacks, jackstones; **jackstraws,** pick-up sticks; **blocks; checkerboard,** chessboard; **marble,**

mig, agate, steelie, taw; pop-gun, BB gun, air gun; slingshot, catapult <Brit>; ball; blocks, building blocks

17 chessman, man, piece; **bishop, knight, king, queen, pawn, rook** *or* castle

18 player, frolicker, frisker, **funmaker,** funster, gamboler; **pleasure-seeker,** pleasurer, pleasurist, **playboy** <nf>; **reveler, celebrant, merrymaker,** rollicker, skylarker, **carouser,** cutup <nf>; contestant 452.2

19 athlete, jock <nf>, **player,** sportsman, sportswoman, contender, amateur athlete, professional athlete, competitor, sportsman; letter man

20 master of ceremonies, MC *or* **emcee** <nf>, compère <Brit>, marshal; **toastmaster;** host, master of the revels, revel master; Lord of Misrule, Abbot of Unreason <Scot>; social director

VERBS **21 amuse, entertain, divert,** regale, beguile, solace, recreate, refresh, enliven, exhilarate, put in good humor; **relax,** loosen up; **delight, tickle, titillate,** tickle pink *or* to death <nf>, tickle the fancy; **make one laugh, strike one as funny,** raise a smile *or* laugh, convulse, set the table on a roar, be the death of; wow *and* slay *and* knock dead *and* kill *and* break one up *and* crack one up *and* fracture one <nf>; have them rolling in the aisles; keep them in stitches

22 amuse oneself, pleasure oneself, take one's pleasure, give oneself over to pleasure; get one's kicks *or* jollies <nf>; **relax,** let oneself go, loosen up; **have fun, have a good time,** have a ball *and* have lots of laughs <nf>, live it up *and* laugh it up <nf>; drown care, drive dull care away; beguile the time, kill time, while away the time; get away from it all

23 play, sport, disport; frolic, rollick, gambol, frisk, **romp, caper,** cut capers <nf>, lark about <Brit nf>, antic, curvet, cavort, caracole, flounce, trip, skip, dance; **cut up** <nf>, cut a dido <nf>, horse around <nf>, fool around, carry on <nf>

24 make merry, revel, roister, jolly, lark <nf>, skylark, **make whoopee** <nf>, let oneself go, **blow** *or* **let off steam;** cut loose, let loose, let go, let one's hair down <nf>, whoop it up, **kick up one's heels;** hell around *and* raise hell *and* blow off the lid <nf>; step out <nf>, go places and do things, go on the town, see life, **paint the town red** <nf>; go the dizzy rounds, go on the merry-go-round <nf>; **celebrate** 487.2; spree, **go on a spree,** go on a bust *or* toot *or* bender *or* binge *or* rip *or* tear <nf>; carouse, jollify <nf>, wanton, debauch, pub-crawl <chiefly Brit>; **sow one's wild oats, have one's fling**

25 "eat, drink, and be merry"—Bible, feast, banquet

ADJS **26 amused,** entertained; diverted, **delighted,** tickled, tickled pink *or* to death <nf>, titillated

27 amusing, entertaining, diverting, beguiling; **fun,** funsome *and* more fun than a barrel of monkeys <nf>; recreative, recreational; **delightful,** titillative, titillating; humorous 488.4

28 festive, festal; merry, gay, jolly, jovial, joyous, joyful, gladsome, convivial, gala, hilarious; merrymaking, on the loose <nf>; on the town, out on the town

29 playful, sportive, sportful; **frolicsome,** gamesome, rompish, larkish, capersome; waggish 322.6

30 sporting, sports; **athletic,** agonistic; **gymnastic,** palaestral; **acrobatic**

ADVS **31 in fun,** for amusement, for fun, for the fun of it; for kicks *and* for laughs <nf>, for the devil *or* heck *or* hell of it <nf>; just to be doing

744 SPORTS

NOUNS **1 sport, sports, athletics,** athletic competition, game, sports activity, play, contest, match; round, set, tournament; aeronautical *or* air sport <see list>; animal sport <see list>; water *or* aquatic sport <see list>; **ball game; track and field** 755; **gymnastics** <see list>; indoor sport; **outdoor sport** <see list>; **winter sport** <see list>; contact sport; **combat sport,** martial art <see list>; **decathlon; triathlon,** biathlon; **bicycling,** bicycle touring, cross-country cycling, cyclo-cross, bicycle moto-cross, road racing, off-road racing, track racing; **motor sport,** automobile racing 756, go-carting, jet-skiing, water skiing, motorcycling, moto-cross, dirt-biking, snowmobiling, soapbox racing; **in-line skating** *or* blading *or* Roller-blading <trademark>, roller skating, roller hockey, skateboarding; **target sport,** archery, field archery, darts, marksmanship, target shooting, skeet shooting, trap shooting; **throwing sport** <see list>; **weightlifting, bodybuilding,** iron-pumping <nf>, Olympic lifting, powerlifting, weight training; blood sport; extreme sport

VERBS **2 play, compete;** practice, train, work out; try out, go out for; follow

3 aeronautical or air sports

aerial skiing	helicopter flying
aerobatics	hydroplane racing
aeromodeling	kiting
aerotow	microlighting
ballooning	parachuting
bungee jumping	paragliding
flying	parasailing
freefalling	sky-diving
gliding	soaring
hang gliding	sports parachuting

4 animal sports

barrel racing	horseback riding
bronc riding *and* bronco busting	horsemanship
	horse racing
bullfighting	pack riding
bull riding	pigeon racing
calf roping	point-to-point
camel racing	polo
carriage driving	rodeo
cockfighting	show jumping
cross-country riding	steeplechase
dog racing	steer roping
dogsled racing	steer wrestling
dressage	team penning
driving	team roping
endurance riding	three-day event
equestrian sport	trail riding
falconry	trotting
greyhound racing	vaulting
harness racing 463	Western riding

5 aquatic or water sports

birling	sailing
boating	sailplaning
body surfing	scuba diving
canoeing	sculling
canoe polo	skin diving
canoe slalom	snorkeling
distance swimming	surfing *or* surfboarding
diving	swimming
dragon boat racing	synchronized swimming
fin swimming	underwater diving
fishing	underwater hockey
inner tube water polo	underwaterball
jet skiing	water polo
kayaking	water skiing
lifesaving	whitewater canoeing
motorboat racing	whitewater rafting
offshore yacht racing	windsurfing *or*
powerboat racing	boardsailing *or*
rafting	sailboarding
rowing	yachting

6 gymnastics

balance beam	rhythmic gymnastics
floor exercises	rings
horizontal bar	trampolining
mini-trampolining	tumbling
parallel bars	uneven parallel bars
pommel horse	vaulting

7 outdoor sports

backpacking	orienteering
camping	rock climbing
Frisbee <trademark>	speleology *or* spelunking
hiking	<nf>
ice climbing	superalpinism *or* Alpine
mountaineering *or*	climbing
alpinism	wilderness survival

8 winter sports

Alpine combined event	mogul skiing
Alpine skiing	Nordic combined
bandy	event
biathlon	off-piste skiing
bobsledding	short-track speed
broomball	skating
cross-country skiing *or*	skating
Nordic skiing *or*	skibob racing
langlauf	skiing
curling	skijoring
downhill skiing	ski jumping
figure skating	ski mountaineering
freestyle skiing *or*	slalom
hotdogging <nf>	sledding
giant slalom	snowboarding
heli-skiing	snowmobiling
hockey	snowshoeing
ice boating *or* sailing	snow tubing
ice dancing	speed skating
ice sailing	super giant slalom
luge	tobogganing

9 combat sports, martial arts

aikido *or* aiki-jutsu	karate
arm *and* wrist wrestling	kendo
arnis	kenipo
bando	kenjutsu
bersilat	kiaijutsu
bojutsu	kick boxing
boxing	kobu-jutsu
capoeira	kung-fu
Cornish wrestling	kyujutsu
dumog	laido
escrima	lua
fencing	main tindju
freestyle wrestling	mud wrestling
glimae	naginata-jutsu
go-ti	ninjutsu
Greco-Roman wrestling	pankation
Greek boxing	pentjak-silat
hapkido	pukulan
hwarang-do	sambo wrestling
Iaido	savate
Iaijutsu	self-defence
Icelandic wrestling	stick fighting
jeet kune do	sumo wrestling
jobajutsu	tae kwon do
jojutsu	t'ai chi
jousting	tang soo do
judo	tegumi
jujitsu *or* jujutsu	Thai kick boxing
jukendo	wrestling
kalari payat	wu shu *or* wushu

10 throwing sports

boomeranging	hammer throw
discus throw	horseshoe pitching
Frisbee <trademark>	javelin throw

shot put	ultimate skate Frisbee
ultimate Frisbee	<trademark>
<trademark> *or* ultimate	
or airborne soccer	

11 target sports

archery	golf
boccie *or* bocci	green bowling
bowling	horseshoe pitching
Canadian 5-pin	pistol shooting
bowling	pool
candlepins	rifle shooting
carom billiards	skittles <Brit>
clay pigeon shooting	sharpshooting
croquet	skeet *or* skeet shooting
curling	snooker
darts	tenpins
duckpins	trapshooting

12 team games

Australian rules	ice hockey
football	lacrosse
bandy	netball
baseball	roller hockey
basketball	rounders <Brit>
Canadian football	rugby
cricket	soccer *or* association
curling	football <Brit>
field hockey	softball
football	speedball
Gaelic football	team handball
hurling	volleyball

13 court sports

badminton	squash
court tennis	table tennis *or* Ping-Pong
handball	<trademark>
jai alai *or* pelota	tennis
racquetball	

745 BASEBALL

NOUNS **1 baseball, ball,** the national pastime, hardball; **organized baseball, league,** loop, circuit, **major league,** big league, the majors *and* the big time *and* the bigs <nf>, professional baseball, the National League *or* Senior Circuit, the American League *or* Junior Circuit; **minor league,** triple-A, the minors *and* bush leagues *and* the bushes <nf>, college baseball; Little League baseball; division championship, playoff, League Championship Series, league championship *or* pennant, World Series, All-Star Game; **farm team,** farm club, farm, farm system; rotisserie league; **ball park, ball field,** field, park; **stands, grandstand,** boxes, lower deck, upper deck, outfield stands, bleachers; **diamond;** dugout; **home plate, the plate,** platter *and* dish <nf>; **base line, line,** base path; **base, bag,** sack, **first,** first base, **second,** second base, keystone *and* keystone sack <nf>, **third,** third base, hot corner

<nf>; **infield,** infield grass *or* turf; **outfield,** warning track, fences; foul line, foul pole; **mound,** pitcher's mound, hill; **equipment** <see list>, gear

2 **baseball team, team, nine,** roster, squad, the boys of summer, **club,** ball club, personnel, crew; **starting lineup, lineup batting order; starter, regular;** substitute, sub, utility player, benchwarmer *and* bench jockey <nf>, the bench; **pitcher,** hurler <nf>, motion, pitching motion, herky-jerky motion <nf>, **right-hander,** right-hand pitcher, righty <nf>, **left-hander, left-hand pitcher, lefty** *and* **southpaw** *and* portsider <nf>; **starting pitcher, starter,** fifth starter, spot starter; starting rotation, rotation, pitching rotation; **relief pitcher, reliever,** fireman *and* closer *and* stopper <nf>, long reliever, middle *or* inner reliever, short reliever, the bull pen; **battery; catcher,** backstop *and* receiver <nf>; **fielder,** glove man, outfielder, infielder, cover man, cut-off man, relay man; **first baseman,** first bagger *and* first sacker <nf>; **second baseman,** second bagger *and* second sacker *and* keystone bagger *and* keystone sacker <nf>; **third baseman,** third bagger *and* third sacker *and* hot-corner man <nf>; shortstop; **outfielder,** left fielder, center fielder, right fielder; pinch hitter; designated hitter *or* DH *or* desi; **batter, hitter,** man at the plate, man in the box *or* batter's box, **stance,** batting stance, pull hitter, power hitter, long-ball hitter, slugger <nf>, spray hitter, contact hitter, banjo hitter <nf>, switch hitter, leadoff hitter, cleanup hitter, closer; base runner, runner, designated runner; **manager, pilot, coach,** batting coach, pitching coach, bench coach, bullpen coach, first-base coach, third-base coach; official scorer; scout, talent scout

3 **game, ball game,** play, strategy; **umpire,** home-plate umpire, plate umpire, umpire in chief, umpire crew, first-base umpire, second-base umpire, third-base umpire; **pitch** <see list>, set, windup, kick, delivery, stuff, offering; **strike zone,** wheelhouse *and* kitchen <nf>; **throwing arm,** arm, cannon *and* soupbone <nf>; **balk; count,** balls and strikes, full count; **hit, base hit,** tater *and* bingle *and* dinger <nf>, opposite-field hit; hard-hit ball, shot *and* bullet *and* scorcher <nf>; **single,** seeing-eye hit *and* excuse-me hit *and* banjo hit <nf>; **double,** two-base hit, two-base shot, two-bagger; **triple,** three-base hit *or* three-base shot, three-bagger; **home run, homer,** four-bagger, tater *and* round trip *and* round tripper *and* circuit clout *and* big salami *and* dinger <nf>, one you can hang the wash on <nf>, grand-slam home run, grand-slammer, cheap homer *and* Chinese homer <nf>; **fly,** pop fly, pop-up, can of corn *and* looper *and* blooper *and* bloop *and* Texas Leaguer <nf>,

sacrifice fly *or* sac fly <nf>; **line drive, liner,** line shot, rope *and* clothesline <nf>; **ground ball,** grounder, wormburner <nf>, slow roller, roller, bunt, drag bunt, bleeder *and* squibbler *and* nubber *and* dying quail <nf>, come-backer, chopper; **foul ball, foul; base on balls, walk,** intentional pass, free ticket *and* free ride <nf>; error, passed ball, unearned run, earned run; **out,** strikeout *or* K *or* punchout, put-out, foul-out, force-out, double play, DP, double killing *and* twin killing <nf>, triple play, triple killing <nf>, assist; **catch,** shoestring catch, basket catch, circus catch; squeeze play, hit-and-run play, pickoff play, pickoff, pitch-out; **base runner,** baseburner <nf>, pinch-runner; **run; inning,** frame, top of the inning, bottom of the inning, extra innings

4 **statistics,** averages, stats and numbers <nf>, percentages; batting average, earned-run average *or* ERA, slugging average *or* slugging percentage, fielding average, run batted in *or* RBI, ribby <nf>; **the record book,** the book

VERBS 5 **play,** play ball, take the field; **umpire,** call balls and strikes, officiate; **pitch, throw,** deliver, fire, offer, offer up, bring it *and* burn it *and* throw smoke *and* blow it by *and* throw seeds <nf>; throw a bean ball, dust the batter off, back the batter off; **relieve,** put out the fire <nf>; **bat, be up,** step up to the plate, be in the batter's box; **hit,** belt *and* clout *and* connect <nf>, golf, chop, tomahawk; **fly,** hit a fly, sky it *and* pop *and* pop up <nf>; **ground,** bounce, lay it down, lay down a bunt; **sacrifice,** hit a sacrifice fly; **hit,** get a base hit, put on one's hitting shoes <nf>; **connect,** blast it *and* cream it *and* tear the cover off *and* hit it right on the screws *and* hit it right on the button *and* hit with the good wood *and* get good wood on it <nf>; **hit a home run, homer,** hit it out; **single, double, triple;** get aboard, be a base runner; **walk, get a free ride** *or* free pass <nf>; **strike out,** go down *or* out on strikes, go down swinging, fan *and* whiff <nf>, be called out on strikes, be caught looking <nf>; ground out, fly out, pop out; catch, haul in, grab *and* glove *and* flag down <nf>; misplay, make an error, bobble *and* boot <nf>; take a trip to the showers <nf>

6 **baseball equipment**

bar mask	birdcage mask
base	catcher's mask
baseball *or* ball; pill *or*	chest protector
apple <nf>	cleats
bat; lumber *or* Louisville	glove
slugger <nf>	pine-tar rag
batting cage	rosin bag
batting glove	shin pads *or*
batting helmet	shin guards

7 baseball pitches

back door	forkball
beanball *or* beaner	gopher ball
bender	intentional walk *or* pass
breaking ball *or* breaker	knuckleball *or* knuckler
brush-off *or* brushing *or* dust-off	knucklecurve
	off-speed pitch
Captain Hook	palmball
change-up *or* change-of-pace ball	reverse curve
	roundhouse curve
curve ball *or* curve *or* breaking ball *or* bender *or* Captain Hook *or* slurve	sailing fastball
	screwball
	screwgy <nf>
	sinker
cut fastball	slider
dime	slow ball
duster	spitball *or* spitter
eefus ball	split-finger fastball
fadeaway	splitter
fast ball *or* smoke *or* bullet *or* heater *or* hummer	Uncle Charlie
	wild pitch
floater	

746 FOOTBALL

NOUNS **1 football, ball,** American football; **organized football, college football,** NCAA football, conference, league; conference championship, post-season game, bowl invitation, Cotton Bowl, Gator Bowl, Orange Bowl, Rose Bowl, Sugar Bowl, Fiesta Bowl, national championship *or* mythical national championship; **professional football,** pro football <nf>, National Football League *or* NFL; division championship, playoff, Super Bowl, Super Bowl championship, Pro Bowl; high school football; Pop Warner football, Pee Wee football; **stadium,** bowl, domed stadium, dome; **field, gridiron; line,** sideline, end line, end zone, goal line, goalpost, crossbar, yard line, midfield stripe, inbounds marker *or* hash mark; **equipment** <see list>, gear, armament; official, sideline crew, chain gang <nf>, zebra <nf>; fantasy football

2 football team, eleven, team, squad, roster, personnel; first team, regulars, starting lineup, offensive team *or* platoon, defensive team *or* platoon, special team, kicking team; substitute *or* sub, benchwarmer; **ball,** football, pigskin *and* oblate spheroid <nf>; **line, linemen, forward wall,** offensive linemen, front four, **end, tackle, nose tackle, guard, noseguard, center,** flanker, **tight end; backfield,** back, **quarterback,** signal-caller *or* field general <nf>, passer; **halfback, fullback,** kicker, punter, tailback, plunging back, slotback, flanker back, running back, wingback, blocking back, linebacker, defensive back, cornerback, safety, free safety, strong safety, weak safety; **pass receiver, receiver,** wide receiver *or* wide out, primary receiver

3 game, strategy, game plan, ball control; **official** <see list>, zebra <nf>; **kickoff,** kick, coin-toss *or* -flip, place kick, squib kick, free kick, onside kick, runback, kickoff return; **play** <see list>, down, first down, second down, third down, fourth down; **line,** line of scrimmage *or* scrimmage line, flat; **lineup, formation** <see list>; **pass from center, snap,** hand-to-hand snap; live ball, ball in play, ball out of play, dead ball, play stopped, ball whistled dead; **running play, passing play, kick; ball-carrier,** ball-handling, tuck, feint, hand-off, pocket, straightarm; **block,** blocking, body block, brush block, chop block, cross block, lead block, screen block, shoulder block; **tackle,** neck tackle, shirt tackle, face-mask tackle, sack; **yardage,** gain, loss, long yardage, short yardage; **forward pass, pass,** pass pattern <see list>, pitchout, screen pass, quick release, bomb <nf>, incomplete pass, completed pass, pass completion; **pass rush,** blitz; **possession,** loss of possession, turnover, fumble, pass interception, interception, turnover; in bounds, out of bounds; **penalty** <see list>, infraction, foul, flag on the play; **punt, kick,** quick kick, squib kick *or* knuckler; punt return, fair catch; **touchdown,** conversion, field goal, safety; **period, quarter, half,** halftime, intermission, two-minute warning, thirty-second clock, sudden-death overtime; **gun,** final gun

4 statistics, averages, stats *and* numbers <nf>, average running yardage, average passing yardage, average punting yardage, average punt-return yardage

VERBS **5 play,** kick, kick off, run, scramble, pass, punt; complete a pass, catch a pass; **block, tackle,** double-team, blindside, sack, blitz, red-dog; **lose possession,** fumble, bobble <nf>, give up the ball; **score,** get on the scoreboard; **officiate,** blow the whistle, whistle the ball dead, drop a flag, call a penalty

6 football equipment

cleats	mouth guard
face mask	numbers
football	pads
helmet	pants
hip pads	shirt *or* jersey
jersey	shoes
kicking tee	shoulder pads
kneepads	thigh pads

7 football officials

back judge	referee
chain gang <nf>	side judge
field judge	umpire
head linesman	zebra <nf>
line judge	

8 football plays and calls

automatic *or* audible	naked bootleg
blitz *or* red dog	naked reverse
bomb	off-tackle slant
bootleg	option
buck lateral	pass
conversion	pitchout
counter	play-action pass
cutback	plunge
draw	power sweep
end around	quarterback sneak
end run	quick kick
fair catch	reverse
flare pass	rollout
flea-flicker	scramble
hail-Mary	screen pass
hand-off	slant
inside run	Statue of Liberty
keeper	sweep
lateral pass *or* lateral	trap
man in motion	two-point
mousetrap	conversion

9 football formations

3-4 defense	shotgun offense
4 3 2 2	short punt formation
4-3 defense	single coverage
6 2 2 1	single wing *or*
7 diamond	wingback
dime defense	slot
double coverage	split end
double wing *or*	split T
wingback	straight T
flexbone *or* flex defense	strong side
huddle	T formation
I	tight end
man-to-man defense	undershift
nickel defense	veer
Notre Dame box	weak side
option	wedge *or*
overshift	flying wedge
power I	wing T
prevent defense	wishbone T
pro set	zone blocking
run-and-shoot offense	zone defense

10 football pass patterns

buttonhook	screen pass
circle	sideline pass
crossing pattern	slant-in pattern
curl	spot pass
down and out	square-in
flag pattern	square-out
flare *or* swing pass	streak pattern
flood	up the middle *or*
fly	the gut
hook pattern	zig in
look-in pass	zig out
option pass	Z pattern
post pattern	

11 football penalties

5-yard penalty	illegal use of hands
10-yard penalty	ineligible receiver
15-yard penalty	intentional grounding
clipping	kick-catching interference
crackback block	late hit <nf>
dead-ball foul	more than 11 players on
delay of game	the field
encroachment	offside
excessive timeouts	out-of-bounds kickoff
false start	pass interference
grabbing the face mask *or*	personal foul
facemask	piling on
holding	roughing the kicker
illegal blocking below the	roughing the passer
waist	running into the kicker
illegal formation	tackling by the facemask
illegal motion	tripping
illegal position	unnecessary roughness
illegal procedure	unsportsmanlike conduct
illegal shift	

747 BASKETBALL

NOUNS **1 basketball,** hoop, hoop sport, ball; **organized basketball, college basketball,** NCAA *or* National Collegiate Athletic Association; **professional basketball,** pro basketball <nf>, National Basketball Association *or* NBA; **tournament,** competition, championship, Olympic Games, NCAA *or* National Collegiate Athletic Association Tournament, March Madness, NIT *or* National Invitational Tournament, Sweet 16, Final Four, NAIA *or* National Association of Intercollegiate Athletics Tournament; **basketball court, court,** hardwood *and* pine <nf>, forecourt, midcourt, backcourt, end line *or* base line, sideline, basket *or* hoop, iron <nf>, backboard, glass <nf>, defensive board, offensive board, free throw line, charity line <nf>, free throw lane *or* foul lane, key *and* keyhole <nf>, foul line *or* the line

2 basketball team, five, team, roster, squad, personnel; **basketball player,** hoopster, cager, center, right forward, left forward, corner man, right guard, left guard, point guard, shooting guard, point player *or* playmaker, swingman, trailer, backcourt man, disher-upper, gunner, sixth man

3 basketball game, game, play, strategy, defense <see list>, offense <see list>; **official, referee,** umpire, official scorekeeper, timer; **foul,** violation <see list>, infraction; **play, strategy,** running game, fast break, passing game, draw and kick game; **jump,** center jump, jump ball, live ball; **pass,** passing, pass ball, assist, bounce pass, dish *and* feed <nf>; rebound; **tactics, action,** dribble, fake, hand-off, ball control, ball-handling, boxing out, sky shot *or* air ball, clear-out or outlet pass, basket hanging, freelancing, pivot or post, high post, low post, one-on-one, screening, pick, pick and roll, trap, turnover, steal or burn, out-of-bounds, dead ball, throw-in, corner throw, buzzer play; **restrictions,** three-second rule, five-second rule, ten-second rule, twenty-four-second rule, thirty-second rule; **shot** <see list>, **score, basket** or **field goal,** bucket <nf>, three-point play or three-pointer, free throw or foul shot; **quarter,** half, overtime period or overtime

VERBS **4 play,** play basketball, play ball, ride the pine <nf>, **dribble,** fake, pass, dish <nf>, work the ball around, take it coast to coast, give and go, sky it, clear the ball, hand off, **guard,** play tight, play loose, double-team, hand-check, block, screen, pick, press, set a pick, steal, burn, freelance, shoot, score, sink one and can and swish <nf>, finger-roll, tip it in, use the backboard, dunk, slam dunk, make a free throw, shoot a brick <nf>, rebound, clear the board, freeze the ball, kill the clock; **foul,** commit a foul or violation, foul out

5 basketball defensive strategies

box-and-one defense	sagging or collapsing
combination defense	defense
man-to-man defense	set pattern
matchup defense	slough
multiple defense	stack defense
pressure or pressing	zone defense or zone
defense	

6 basketball offensive strategies

ball-control offense	low post
clear out one side	motion offense
delay offense	press
fast-break offense	pressure offense
flip-flop offense	rotation offense
full-court press	run and gun offense
full-court zone press	running offense
gap offense	shuffle offense
give and go offense	stack offense
half-court press	stall offense
high post	

7 basketball fouls

blocking	palming
charging	personal foul or personal
disqualifying foul	pushing off
double dribble	stepping over the line
double foul	<free throw, throw-in>
force-out	technical foul or technical
goaltending	ten-second backcourt
hacking	violation
held ball	three-second lane violation
intentional foul	traveling or walking or
kicking the ball	running with the ball
multiple foul	tripping
offensive foul	

8 basketball shots

bank shot	jump shot or jumper
brick <nf>	lay-up
bunny <nf>	one-and-one
charity toss and charity	one-hand shot
throw and charity shot	pivot shot
<nf>	penalty free throw
cripple <nf>	scoop shot
dunk <nf>	set shot
finger-roll	slam dunk <nf>
free throw or foul shot or	swish <nf>
penalty shot	tip-in
hook shot or hook	two-hand shot

748 TENNIS

NOUNS **1 tennis,** lawn tennis, indoor tennis, outdoor tennis, singles, doubles, mixed doubles, Canadian doubles, team tennis; court or real or royal tennis; table tennis, Ping-Pong <trademark>; **organized tennis,** International Tennis Federation or ITF, United States Tennis Association or USTA; **tournament,** tennis competition, championship, crown, match, trophy; **tennis ball, ball, tennis racket, racket,** aluminum racket, Fiberglas racket, graphite racket, wooden racket, bat <nf>, sweet spot; **tennis court, court,** sideline, alley, doubles sideline, baseline, center mark, service line, half court line, backcourt, forecourt, midcourt, net, band; **surface,** slow surface, fast surface, grass surface or grass or grass court, hard court, clay court, competition court, all-weather court; squash, squash racquets, squash tennis, badminton

2 game, strategy, serve-and-volley, power game; **official, umpire,** baseline umpires or linesmen, line umpires or linesmen, service-line umpire or linesman, net-court judge; **play,** coin-toss, racket-flip, grip, Eastern grip, Continental grip, Western grip, two-handed grip, **stroke** <see list>, **shot,** service or serve, return, spin, top-spin, let ball or let, net-cord ball, rally, fault, double fault, foot fault; error, unforced error; **score, point,** service ace or ace, love, deuce, advantage or ad, game point, service break, break point, set point, match point, tiebreaker, lingering death <nf>, game, set, match; Van Alen Streamlined Scoring System or VASSS

VERBS **3 play tennis, play,** serve, return, drive, volley, smash, lob, place the ball, serve and volley, play serve-and-volley tennis, fault, foot-fault, double-fault, make an unforced error; **score** or **make a point,** score, ace one's opponent, break service, break back

4 tennis strokes

approach shot	backhand drive
backhand	chop

drive
drop shot
forehand
forehand drive
ground drive
ground stroke
half-volley
lob
lob volley
overhead

passing shot
reverse twist service
service *or* serve
slice
smash *or* overhead
   smash
topspin
twist service
two-handed backhand
volley

749 HOCKEY

NOUNS **1 hockey,** ice hockey, Canadian national sport; **professional hockey,** National Hockey League *or* NHL, Clarence Campbell Conference, Smythe Division, Norris Division, Prince of Wales Conference, Patrick Division, Adams Division; **amateur hockey,** bantam hockey, midget hockey, pee-wee hockey, junior hockey, Canadian Amateur Hockey Association, Amateur Hockey Association of the United States, International Ice Hockey Federation; **competition,** series, championship, cup, Olympic Games, Stanley Cup, All-Star Game; **rink,** ice rink, hockey rink, boards, end zone, defending *or* defensive zone, attacking *or* offensive zone, neutral zone *or* center ice, blue line, red line, goal line, crease, goal *and* net *and* cage, face-off spot, face-off circle, penalty box, penalty bench, players' bench; **equipment,** gear <see list>

2 hockey team, team, skaters, squad, bench; line, forward line, center, forward, winger, right wingman, left wingman, linesman; **defense,** defender, right defenseman, left defenseman, goaltender *or* goalie, goalkeeper, goalminder; specialized player, playmaker, penalty killer, point *or* point man, enforcer <nf>

3 game, match; **referee,** linesman, goal judge, timekeepers, scorer; **foul,** penalty <see list>, infraction, offside, icing *or* icing the puck; **play,** skating, stick *or* puck handling, ragging, deking, checking, backchecking, forechecking, passing, shooting; **pass,** blind pass, drop pass, through-pass; **check; offense,** breakout, Montreal offense, headmanning, Toronto offense, play-off hockey, give-and-go, breakaway, peel-off, screening; **shot,** slap shot, wrist shot, backhand shot, flip, sweep shot; power play; **score,** point, finish off a play, feed, assist, hat trick; **period,** overtime *or* overtime period, sudden death overtime, shoot-out

4 field hockey, banty *or* bandy, hurley *or* hurling, shinty *or* shinny; International Hockey Board, *Fédération Internationale de Hockey* <Can Fr>, International Federation of Women's Hockey Associations, United States Field Hockey Association, Field Hockey Association of America;

hockey field, field, pitch, goal line, center line, center mark, bully circle, sideline, 7-yard line, alley, 25-yard line, striking *or* shooting circle, goalpost, goal, goal mouth; **equipment,** gear, stick, ball, shin pads

5 team, attack, outside left, inside left, center forward, inside right, outside right, defense, left halfback, center halfback, right halfback, left fullback, wing half, right fullback, goalkeeper

6 game, match; **umpire,** timekeeper; **foul,** infraction, advancing, obstructing, sticks, undercutting, **penalty,** free hit, corner hit, defense hit, penalty bully, penalty shot; **play, bully, bully-off,** pass-back, stroke, marking, pass, tackle, circular tackle, out-of-bounds, roll-in *or* push-in, hit-in; **goal,** point, score; **period,** half

VERBS **7 play, skate,** pass, check, block, stick-handle *or* puck-handle, face off, rag, deke, give-and-go, headman, break out, shoot, score, clear, dig, freeze the puck, center, ice *or* ice the puck; tackle, mark; make a hat trick

8 hockey equipment

abdominal protector
catching glove
chest protector
elbow pads
face mask
gloves
goaltender's stick
helmet
hip pads
knee pads

left-handed stick
leg pads
neutral stick
puck
right-handed stick
shin guards
shoulder pads
skates
stick
stick glove

9 hockey fouls and penalties

bench minor penalty
board-checking *or*
  boarding
body-checking
butt-ending
charging
clipping
crosschecking
ejection
elbowing
falling on the puck
fighting
handling the puck
high-sticking
holding
hooking

icing
interference
kneeing
match penalty
major *or* five-minute
  penalty
minor *or* two-minute
  penalty
misconduct penalty
offsides
penalty shot
poke checking
roughing
slashing
spearing
tripping

750 BOWLING

NOUNS **1 bowling,** kegling *or* kegeling <nf>, tenpin bowling *or* tenpins, candlepin bowling *or* candlepins, duckpin bowling *or* duckpins, fivepin bowling, rubberband duckpin bowling, ninepins, skittles <Brit>; **bowling organization,** league,

American Bowling Congress or ABC, Women's International Bowling Congress or WIBC, American Junior Bowling Congress; amateur bowling, league bowling; **professional bowling,** pro bowling <nf>, tour, Professional Bowlers Association or PBA, Professional Women's Bowling Association; **tournament,** competition, match-play tournament, round-robin tournament; **alley, lane,** gutter, foul line, rear cushion, bed, spot, pin spot, 1-3-strike pocket; **equipment, pin,** candlepin, duckpin, fivepin, rubberband duckpin, tenpin; automatic pinsetter; **ball,** two-hole ball, three-hole ball, bowling shoes; bowling bag

2 **game** or string, frame; **delivery,** grip, two-finger grip, three-finger grip, conventional grip, semi-fingertip grip, full-fingertip grip, **approach,** three-step approach or delivery, four-step approach, five-step approach, push-away, downswing, backswing, timing step, release, follow-through, straight ball, curve ball, backup, hook ball, gutter ball; **pocket,** Brooklyn side, Brooklyn hit or Jersey hit or crossover, **strike** or ten-strike, mark, double, turkey, foundation; **spare,** mark, leave, spare leave, split <see list>, railroad, open frame; **score,** pinfall, miss, perfect game or 300 game, Dutch

3 **lawn bowling,** green bowling, lawn bowls, bowling on the green, bowls; American Lawn Bowling Association; **bowling green,** green, crown green, level green, rink, ditch; **ball,** bowl, jack or kitty, mat or footer; **team,** side, rink, lead or leader, second player, third player, skip

4 **spare leaves and splits**

baby split	fence
bed posts or fenceposts or goal posts	fit-in split
	Golden Gate
bucket	left fence
Christmas tree	mother-in-law
Cincinnati	right fence
converted split	washout
double pinochle	Woolworth
double wood or tandem	

751 GOLF

NOUNS 1 **golf,** the royal and ancient; **professional golf,** pro golf <nf>, tour, Professional Golfers Association of America or PGA, Ladies' Professional Golfers' Association or LPGA; **amateur golf,** club, United States Golf Association or USGA; **tournament,** championship, title, cup; **golf course,** course, links, 9-hole course, 18-hole course, penal course, strategic course, green, tee, teeing ground, back or championship marker, middle or men's marker, front or womens' marker, hole, par-3 hole, par-4 hole, par-5 hole, front nine or side, back nine or side, water hole, fairway,

dogleg, obstruction, rub of the green, casual water, rough, hazard, water hazard, bunker, sand hazard, sand trap, beach <nf>, collar, apron, fringe, putting green, grass green, sand green, out of bounds, pin, flagstick, flag, lip, cup; **equipment** <see list>

2 **golfer,** player, scratch golfer or player, handicapped golfer, dub and duffer and hacker <nf>, linksman, putter; **team,** twosome, threesome, foursome; caddie

3 **round,** 9 holes, 18 holes, 72 holes, match, stroke play, match play, medal play, four-ball match, three-ball match, best ball, mixed foursome, Scotch foursome; **official,** referee, official observer, marker; **play,** golfing grip, overlapping or Vardon grip, reverse overlap, interlocking grip, full-finger grip, address, stance, closed stance, square stance, open stance, waggle, swing, backswing, downswing, follow-through, pivot, body pivot, tee-off; **stroke, shot** <see list>, backspin, bite, distance, carry, run, lie, plugged lie, blind, stymie; **score,** scoring, strokes, eagle, double eagle, birdie, par, bogey, double bogey, penalty, hole-in-one and ace, halved hole, gross, handicap, net

VERBS 4 **play, shoot,** tee up, tee off, drive, hit, sclaff, draw, fade, pull, push, hook, slice, top, sky, loft, dunk, putt, can <nf>, borrow, hole out, sink, shoot par, eagle, double eagle, birdie, par, bogey, double bogey, make a hole in one, ace; play through; concede, default

INTERJ 5 **fore!**

6 **golf equipment**

1 iron or driving iron	number 1 wood or driver
2 iron or midiron	
3 iron or mid mashie	number 2 wood or brassie
4 iron or mashie iron	
5 iron or mashie	number 3 wood or spoon
6 iron or spade mashie	
7 iron or mashie niblick	number 4 wood or cleek or short spoon
8 iron or pitching niblick	
9 iron or niblick	number 5 wood or baffy
ball or pill <nf>	pitching wedge
chipping iron club	putter
club cover	sand iron
driver	sand wedge
golf bag	short iron
golf cart	tee
golf glove	Texas wedge
iron	track iron
lofter or lofting iron	utility iron
long iron	wedge
middle iron	wood

7 **golf shots**

approach shot or approach	chip shot or chip
blast	chip-and-run
bunker shot	cut shot

draw	Mulligan *or* Shapiro
drive	pitch
dubbed shot	pitch-and-run
duck hook	pull
fade	punch
fairway wood shot	putt
full shot	recovery shot
gimme <nf>	run-up
hole in one	sand shot
hole out	sclaff
hook	slice
lag	snake
lob	tee shot
lofted shot	water shot
long iron shot	

752 SOCCER

NOUNS **1 soccer,** football, association football <Brit>, soccer football; **league,** college soccer, Intercollegiate Soccer Football Association of America, National Collegiate Athletic Association *or* NCAA, Federation of International Football Associations *or* FIFA; **tournament,** competition, championship, cup; **professional soccer,** pro soccer, North American Soccer League *or* NASL; **soccer field,** field, soccer pitch, pitch, goal line, touch line, halfway line, penalty area, penalty spot *or* penalty-kick mark, goal area, goal, goalpost, crossbar, 6-yard box, 18-yard box, corner area, corner flag, center mark, center circle; **equipment,** gear, ball, suit, uniform, shirt, shorts, knee socks, shin guards, soccer shoes

2 team, squad, side, footballer <Brit>, forward, striker, outside right, inside right, center forward, lineman, midfielder, inside left, outside left, right half, center half, left half, defender, back, center back, right back, left back, winger, back four, sweeper, stopper, goalkeeper *or* goaltender *or* goalie

3 game, match; official, referee, linesman; **play,** coin-toss *or* -flip, 3-3-4 offense, 5-2 offense, man-to-man offense, kickoff, kick <see list>, throw-in, goal kick, corner kick *or* corner, offside, ball-control, pass, back-heel pass, outside-of-the-foot pass, push pass, back pass, tackle, sliding tackle, sliding block tackle, trap, chest trap, thigh trap, breakaway, header *or* head, shot, save; **rule,** law; **foul** <see list>; **penalty,** caution, red card, free kick, direct free kick, indirect free kick, caution, penalty kick, yellow card; **goal,** score, point, tie-breaker, series of penalty kicks, shootout, bonus point; **period,** quarter, overtime period

VERBS **4 play,** kick, kick off, trap, pass, dribble, screen, head, center, clear, mark, tackle, save

5 soccer kicks

bicycle kick	lofted kick
chip	long pass
corner kick	low drive
direct free kick	overhead volley
flick kick	penalty kick
free kick	punt
goal kick	scissors kick
half-volley	volley *or* volley kick
instep *or* inside-of-the-foot kick	

6 soccer fouls

charging dangerously	jumping at an opponent
charging from behind	kicking an opponent
charging the goalkeeper	obstruction
continual breaking of rules	offside
dangerous play	onside
dissenting from referee's decision	pushing an opponent
	spitting at an opponent
foul *or* abusive language	striking an opponent
handling the ball	tripping an opponent
holding an opponent	ungentlemanly conduct

753 SKIING

NOUNS **1 skiing,** snow-skiing, Alpine skiing, downhill skiing, **Nordic skiing,** cross-country skiing *or* langlauf, snowboarding, ski-jumping, jumping, freestyle skiing *or* hotdog skiing *or* hotdogging, ballet skiing, mogul skiing, skijoring, helicopter skiing *or* heli-skiing, off-trail skiing, mountain skiing, grass-skiing, ski mountaineering; **organized skiing,** competitive skiing, *Fédération Internationale de Ski* <Fr> *or* FIS, International Freestyle Skiers Association, World Hot Dog Ski Association; **competition, championship,** cup, race; **slope,** ski slope, ski run, nursery *or* beginner's slope, expert's slope, intermediate slope, expert's trail, marked trail, moguled trail, course, trail, mogul; **ski lift, lift,** ski tow, rope tow, J-bar, chairlift, T-bar, poma; **race course,** downhill course, slalom course, giant slalom course, super giant slalom course, parallel *or* dual slalom course; starting gate, fall line, drop *or* vertical drop, control gate, obligatory gate, flagstick, open gate, closed *or* blind gate, hairpin, flush, H, men's course, women's course, **ski-jump,** ramp, inrun, outrun, hill rating, 60-point hill, normal hill, big hill, cross-country course; equipment, gear <see list>

2 skier, snow-skier, cross-country skier, ski-jumper, racer, downhill racer, slalom racer, giant slalom racer, mogul racer, snowboarder, freestyle skier, touring skier, forerunner, forejumper, skimeister

3 race, downhill race, slalom, giant slalom, super giant slalom *or* super G, slalom pole, rapid slalom pole, parallel *or* dual slalom, Alpine race, cross-country race, biathlon; **technique,** style, Arlberg technique, Lilienfeld technique, wedeln, **position,** tuck *and* egg, Vorlage, sitting position, inrun position, fish position, flight position; **maneuver, turn** <see list>

VERBS **4 ski,** run, schuss, traverse, turn, check; hot dog, ski freestyle; snowboard

5 skiing equipment

aluminum alloy pole	laminated wood ski
Alpine boots	metal ski
Arlberg *or* safety strap	molded boot
basket *or* snow basket	plastic ski
bent pole	pole *or* stick
cross-country binding	racing ski
cross-country pole	release binding
cross-country ski	short ski
double boot	ski boots
downhill pole	ski wax
downhill ski	slalom ski
fiberglass pole	snowboard
giant slalom ski	step-in binding
jumping ski	toe clamp

6 skiing maneuvers and turns

carved turn	schuss
check	short swing
Christiania *or* christie	sideslip
climb	sidestep
diagonal stride	snap
double-pole stride	snowplow *or* double stem
double-poling	*or* wedge
edging	snowplow turn
Gelondesprung	stem turn
herringbone	stem christie
hockey stop	step acceleration
jet turn	step turn
jump turn	Telemark
kick turn	tempo
parallel christie	traverse
parallel swing	tuck
parallel turn	unweighting
pole plant	uphill christie
rotation turn	wedeln

754 BOXING

NOUNS **1 boxing, prizefighting,** fighting, pugilism, noble *or* manly art of self-defense, the noble *or* sweet science, fisticuffs, the fistic sport, the fights *and* the fight game <nf>, the ring; **amateur boxing,** Olympic Games, International Amateur Boxing Association *or* IABA, Amateur Athletic Union *or* AAU, Gold *or* Golden Gloves; **professional boxing,** International Boxing Federation, World Boxing Council *or* WBC, World Boxing Association *or* WBA, European Boxing Union, club boxing *or* fighting; Queensbury rules, Marquess of Queensbury rules; shadowboxing; **boxing ring, ring,** prize ring, square circle *or* ring,

canvas, corner, ropes, bell; **equipment, gloves,** mitts *and* mittens <nf>, boxing shorts, tape, bandages, sparring helmet, mouthpiece; boxing purse

2 boxer, fighter, pugilist, prizefighter, pug *and* palooka <nf>, slugger, mauler; **weight** <see list>; division; **manager; trainer; handler,** second, sparring partner

3 fight, match, bout, prizefight, battle, duel, slugfest *or* haymaker <nf>; **official, referee,** ref <nf>, judge, timekeeper; **strategy, fight-plan, style,** stance, footwork, **offense, punch** <see list>, blow, belt *and* biff *and* sock <nf>, sparring, jabbing, socking, pummeling; **defense,** blocking, ducking, parrying, slipping, feint, clinching; **foul; win, knockout** *or* **KO,** technical knockout *or* TKO, decision, unanimous decision, split decision, win on points; **round,** canto *and* stanza <nf>

VERBS **4 fight, box,** punch, spar, mix it up <nf>, prizefight, jab, sock, clinch, break, block, catch, slip a punch, duck, feint, parry, heel, thumb, knock down, knock out, slug, maul, land a rabbit punch, hit below the belt; go down, go down for the count, hit the canvas <nf>, shadow-box

5 boxing weight divisions

light flyweight	welterweight
flyweight	light middleweight
bantamweight	middleweight
super bantamweight	light heavyweight
featherweight	cruiserweight
junior lightweight	heavyweight
lightweight	super-heavyweight
light welterweight	

6 boxing punches

backhand *or* backhander	Long Melford
backstroke	mishit *or* mislick
body blow *or* body slam	rabbit punch
bolo punch	right *or* right-hander
chop	round-arm blow
combination	roundhouse
corkscrew punch	short-arm blow
counter-punch	sideswipe
cross	sidewinder
flanker	sneak punch *or* sucker
follow-up	punch
haymaker	solar-plexus punch
hook	straight punch
jab	swing
knockdown punch	swipe
knockout punch	the one-two *or* the old one-
left *or* left-hander *or*	two
portsider	uppercut

755 TRACK AND FIELD

NOUNS **1 track, track and field,** athletics <Brit>, light athletics <Ger>; governing organization, International Amateur Athletic Federation *or* IAAF,

Amateur Athletic Union of the US *or* AAU, Amateur Athletic Federation of Canada, Amateur Athletic Union of Canada, National Federation of State High School Athletic Associations; **games,** competition, cup; **stadium, arena,** oval, armory, field house; **track,** oval, lane, start line, starting block, finish line, **infield;** lap, lap of honor, victory lap

2 track meet, meet, games, program; **running event,** race, run *or* running, heat, sprint racing, middle-distance running, long-distance running, relay racing, hurdles, cross-country racing; **field event** <see list>; **all-around event,** decathlon <see list>, heptathlon <see list>, pentathlon <see list>; triathlon <see list>, biathlon <see list>; **walking, race walking,** the walk, heel-and-toe racing

3 field events

discus throw	multi-event contest
hammer throw	pole vault
high jump	shot put
javelin throw	triple jump
long jump *or* broad jump	

4 heptathlon

100-meter hurdles	javelin
200-meter run	long jump
800-meter run	shot put
high jump	

5 decathlon

100-meter run	high jump
110-meter hurdles	javelin
400-meter run	long jump
1500-meter run	pole vault
discus	shot put

6 pentathlon

100-meter hurdles	javelin
200-meter run	long jump
high jump	

7 triathlon

100-meter dash	shot put
high jump	

8 biathlon

cross-country skiing	rifle shooting

756 AUTOMOBILE RACING

NOUNS **1 automobile racing, auto racing, car racing,** motor sport; Indy car racing, stock-car racing, drag racing, Formula car racing, midget-car racing, hot-rod racing, autocross, go-karting; **racing association; race,** competition, championship; **track,** speedway, Indianapolis Motor Speedway *or* the Brickyard <nf>, closed course, road course *or* circuit, dirt track, grasstrack, super speedway; **car, racing car** <see list>, racer; **racing engine; supercharger,** turbocharger, blower *and* windmill <nf>; **tires, racing tires,** shoes <nf>, slicks; **body,** body work, spoiler, sidepod, roll bar, roll cage; **wheel,** wire wheel *or* wire, magnesium wheel *or* mag; **fuel, racing fuel,** methanol, nitromethane *or* nitro, blend, pop *and* juice <nf>

2 race driving, racing driver, driver, fast driver *or* leadfoot <nf>, slow driver *or* balloon foot, novice driver *or* yellowtail

3 race, driving, start, Le Mans start, flying start, paced start, grid start; **position,** qualifying, qualifying heat, starting grid, inside position, pole *or* pole position, bubble; **track,** turn, curve, hairpin, switchback, banked turn, corner, chicane, groove, shut-off, drift, straightaway *or* chute, pit, pit area; **signal,** black flag, white flag, checkered flag; **lap,** pace lap, victory lap *or* lane

VERBS **4 drive, race,** start, jump, rev, accelerate, put the hammer down <nf>, slow down, back off, stroke it, draft, fishtail, nerf, shut the gate

ADVS **5 at top speed,** flat-out, full-bore, ten-tenths ride the rail, spin, spin out, crash, t-bone

6 racing cars

championship car	hobby car
compact sprint car	Indy car
dirt car	late-model sportsman
dragster	midget car
experimental car *or* X-car	modified stock car
Formula A	production car
formula car	prototype
Formula F	quarter-midget car
Formula One	Formula SCCA
Formula Super Vee	sportsman
Formula Vee	sports car
fuel dragster *or* slingshot *or* rail job	sprint car *or* big car
	stock car
fueler	supercharger
funny car	touring car
gas dragster	turbine car
grand touring car *or* GT	turbocharger

757 HORSE RACING

NOUNS **1 horse racing, the turf,** the sport of kings, the turf sport, the racing world *or* establishment; **flat racing; harness racing,** trotting, pacing; steeplechase, hurdle race, point-to-point race; **Jockey Club,** Trotting Horse Club, Thoroughbred Racing Association *or* TRA, Thoroughbred Racing Protective Bureau *or* TRPB, state racing commission; **General Stud Book, American Stud Book,** Wallace's Trotting Register; **Triple Crown,** Kentucky Derby, Preakness Stakes, Belmont Stakes; Grand National, Derby, 2000 Guineas, Sty Leger, Gold Cup Race, Oaks; **racetrack, track,** racecourse, turf, oval, course, strip; rail, inside rail, infield, paddock, post; turf track, steeplejack course; gate *and* barrier; **track locations** <see list> *and* **calls; track conditions**, footing, racing equipment, tack

2 **jockey,** jock, rider, race rider, pilot, bug boy <nf>, money rider; apprentice jockey, bug <nf>; breeder, owner; trainer; steward, racing secretary; **railbird** *and* race bird <nf>, turf-man; **racehorse, pony,** thoroughbred, standardbred, mount, flyer, running horse, trotter, pacer, quarter horse, bangtail *and* daisy-cutter *and* filly *and* gee-gee <nf>; **sire, dam,** stallion, stud, stud horse, racing stud, mare, brood mare, gelding, ridgeling *or* rigling; **horse,** aged horse, three-year-old, sophomore, two-year-old, juvenile, colt, racing colt, filly, baby, foal, tenderfoot, bug, maiden *or* maiden horse, yearling, weanling; **favorite,** chalk, choice, odds-on favorite, public choice, top horse; runner, front-runner, pacesetter; strong horse, router, stayer; winner *or* win horse, place horse, show horse, also-ran; **nag** *and* race-nag *and* beagle *and* beetle *and* hayburner *and* nine of hearts *and* palooka *and* pelter *and* pig *and* plater *and* selling plater <nf>; **rogue,** bad actor, cooler

3 **horse race, race;** race meeting, race card, scratch sheet; **starters,** field, weigh-in *or* weighing-in, post parade, post time, post position *or* PP; **start, break,** off; easy race, romp, shoo-in, armchair ride, hand ride; **finish,** dead heat, blanket finish, photo finish, Garison finish; **dishonest race,** boat race *and* fixed race <nf>

4 **statistics, records,** condition book, chart, **form, racing form,** daily racing form, past performance, **track record,** dope *or* tip *or* tout sheet <nf>, par time, parallel-time chart; **betting;** pari-mutuel 759.4; horse-racing bets

VERBS 5 **race, run; start, break, be off;** air *and* breeze; make a move, drive, extend, straighten out; fade, come back; screw in *or* through; ride out, run wide; **win,** romp *or* breeze in; **place, show,** be in the money; be out of the money

ADJS 6 **winning, in the money;** losing, out of the money; on the chinstrap; out in front, on the Bill Daley

7 **horse track locations or calls**

backstretch	post
clubhouse turn	quarter pole *or* post
eighth pole *or* post	sixteenth pole *or* post
far turn	straightaway *or* home
five-eighths pole *or* post	stretch *or* home straight
half-mile pole *or* post	winner's circle
mile pole *or* post	

758 CARDPLAYING

NOUNS 1 **cardplaying** *or* card playing, shuffling, cutting, cut, dealing, deal; **card game,** game; gambling 759, gambling games

2 **card, playing card,** board, pasteboard; **deck, pack; suit,** hearts, diamonds, spades, clubs, puppy-feet <nf>; hand; **face card,** blaze, coat card, coat, count card, court card, paint, paint-skin, picture card, redskin; **king,** figure, cowboy *and* sergeant from K Company <nf>, one-eyed king, king of hearts *or* suicide king; queen, bitch *and* hen *and* lady *and* mop-squeezer *and* whore <nf>, queen of spades, Black Maria *and* Maria *and* slippery Anne <nf>; **jack,** knave, boy *and* fishhook *and* j-bird *and* j-boy *and* john <nf>, one-eyed jack, jack of trumps *or* right bower, left bower; **joker,** bower, best bower; spot card, rank card, plain card; **ace,** bull *and* bullet *and* seed *and* spike <nf>, ace of diamonds *or* pig's eye <nf>, ace of clubs *or* puppyfoot <nf>; **two, deuce,** two-spot, duck <nf>, two of spades *or* curse of Mexico <nf>; **three, trey,** three-spot; **four,** four-spot, four of clubs *or* devil's bedposts <nf>; **five,** five-spot, fever <nf>; **six,** six-spot; **seven,** seven-spot, fishhook <nf>; **eight,** eight-spot; **nine,** nine-spot, nine of diamonds *or* curse of Scotland <nf>; **ten,** ten-spot; wild card

3 **bridge,** auction bridge, contract bridge, rubber bridge, duplicate *or* tournament bridge; **bridge player,** partner, dummy, North and South, East and West, left hand opponent *or* LHO, bidder, responder, declarer, senior, dummy; **suit,** major suit, minor suit, trump suit *or* trumps, lay suit *or* plain suit *or* side suit; **call, bid** <see list>; pass; **hand** <see list>; **play,** lead, opening lead, **trick,** quick trick *or* honor trick, high-card trick, overtrick, odd trick, finesse, ruff, crossruff; **score,** adjusted score, grand slam, little slam *or* small slam, game, rubber, premium, honors *or* honors cards, yarborough, set *or* setback

4 **poker,** draw poker, stud poker, five-card stud, six-card stud, seven-card stud, eight-card stud, strip poker; poker hand, five of a kind, straight flush, royal flush, four of a kind, full house, flush, straight, three of a kind, two pairs, one pair; pot, jackpot, pool, ante, chip, stake, call, checking, raise

VERBS 5 **shuffle,** make up, make up the pack, fan *and* wash <nf>; cut; **deal,** serve, pitch <nf>

6 **bridge bids**

asking bid	insufficient bid
bidding convention	jump bid
borderline bid	no-trump bid
business double	opening bid
demand bid	original bid
double	overbid *or* overcall
forcing bid	pass
forcing pass	rebid
free bid	redouble

renege
response
sacrifice bid
score bid
shut-out bid

sign-off
skip bid
suit bid
takeout double
underbid

7 bridge hands

balanced hand
doubleton
exposed hand
long trump
long suit
major tenace
minor tenace
offensive strength
perfect tenace

piano hand
pianola hand
side strength
singleton
short suit
tenace
unbalanced hand
void
yarborough

759 GAMBLING

NOUNS **1 gambling, playing, betting, action,** wagering, punting, hazarding, risking, staking, gaming, laying, taking *or* giving *or* laying odds, sporting <old>; **speculation, play;** drawing *or* casting lots, tossing *or* flipping a coin, sortition

2 gamble, chance, risk, risky thing, hazard; gambling *or* **gambler's chance,** betting proposition, bet, matter of chance, sporting chance, **luck of the draw,** hazard of the die, roll *or* cast *or* throw of the dice, turn *or* roll of the wheel, turn of the table, turn of the cards, fall of the cards, flip *or* toss of a coin, toss-up, toss; heads or tails, touch and go; blind bargain, pig in a poke; leap in the dark, shot in the dark; potshot, random shot, potluck; **speculation, venture,** flier *and* plunge <nf>; calculated risk; uncertainty 970; fortune, luck 972.1

3 bet, wager, stake, hazard, lay, play *and* chunk *and* shot <nf>; cinch bet *or* sure thing, mortal cinch *and* mortal lock *and* nuts <nf>; long shot; **ante;** parlay, double or nothing; **dice bet, craps bet,** golf bet, **horse-racing bet, poker bet,** roulette bet, telebet

4 betting system; pari-mutuel, off-track betting *or* OTB; perfecta, exacta, win, place, show, all-way bet, daily double

5 pot, jackpot, pool, stakes, kitty; bank; office pool

6 gambling odds, odds, price; **even** *or* **square odds,** even break; **short odds, long odds,** long shot; even chance, good chance, small chance, no chance 971.10; **handicapper,** odds maker, pricemaker

7 gambling game <see list>, game of chance, game, friendly game; card games

8 dice, bones *and* rolling bones *and* ivories *and* babies *and* cubes *and* devil's bones *or* teeth *and* galloping dominoes *and* golf balls *and* marbles *and* Memphis dominoes *and* Mississippi marbles *and* Missouri marbles <nf>, **craps,** crap shooting, crap

game, bank craps *or* casino craps, muscle craps, African dominoes *and* African golf *and* alley craps *and* army craps *and* blanket craps *and* army marbles *and* Harlem tennis *and* poor man's roulette <nf> floating crap game, floating game, sawdust game; poker dice; **false** *or* crooked *or* loaded dice

9 <throw of dice> **throw, cast, rattle, roll, shot,** hazard of the die; dice points and rolls <see list>

10 poker, draw poker *or* draw *or* five-card draw *or* open poker, stud poker *or* stud *or* closed poker, five-card stud *or* seven-card stud, up card *or* open card, down card *or* closed card; common *or* community *or* communal card; highball, high-low, lowball; **straight** *or* **natural poker,** wild-card poker; **poker hand,** duke *and* mitt <nf>, good hand *or* cards, lock *or* cinch *or* cinch hand *or* ironclad hand *or* iron duke *or* mortal cinch *or* nut hand *or* nuts *or* immortals; bad hand *or* cards, trash *and* rags <nf>; **openers,** progressive openers, bet, raise *or* kick *or* bump *or* pump *or* push, showdown

11 blackjack *or* **twenty-one** *or* vingt-et-un; deal, card count, stiff, hard seventeen, hard eighteen, soft count, soft hand, soft eighteen, hit, blackjack *or* natural *or* snap *or* snapper, California blackjack; cut card *or* indicator card *or* sweat card; card-counting *or* ace-count *or* number count

12 roulette, American roulette, European roulette; **wheel,** American wheel, European wheel, wheel well, canoe, fret; **layout,** column, damnation alley, outside; zero, double zero, knotholes *or* house numbers

13 cheating, cheating scheme, cheating method, angle, con *and* grift *and* move *and* racket *and* scam *and* sting <nf>; deception 356

14 lottery, drawing, sweepstakes *or* sweepstake *or* sweep; draft lottery; **raffle; state lottery,** Lotto, Pick Six, Pick Four; tombola <Brit>; number lottery, numbers pool, **numbers game** *or* policy, Chinese lottery <nf>; interest lottery, Dutch *or* class lottery; tontine; grab bag *or* barrel *or* box

15 bingo, slow death <nf>, beano, keno, lotto; bingo card, banker, counter

16 <gambling device> gambling wheel, wheel of fortune, big six wheel, Fortune's wheel, raffle wheel *or* paddle wheel; roulette wheel, American wheel, European wheel; raffle wheel; cage, birdcage; goose *or* shaker, gooseneck; pinball machine; slot machine, slot, the slots, one-armed bandit <nf>; **layout** *or* green cloth, gambling table, craps table, Philadelphia layout, roulette table; **cheating device,** gaff *and* gimmick *and* tool <nf>

17 pari-mutuel, pari-mutuel machine; totalizator, totalizer, tote *and* tote board <nf>, odds board

18 **chip, check, counter** bean *and* fish <nf>

19 **casino, gambling house, house,** store *and* shop <nf>, gaming house, betting house, betting parlor, gambling den, gambling hall, sporting house <old>, gambling hell <nf>; luxurious casino, carpet joint *and* rug joint <nf>; honest gambling house, right joint <nf>; disreputable gambling house, crib *and* dive *and* joint *and* sawdust joint *and* store *and* toilet <nf>; illegal gambling house, cheating gambling house, brace house *and* bust-out joint *and* clip joint *and* deadfall *and* flat joint *and* flat store *and* hell *and* juice joint *and* low den *and* nick joint *and* peek store *and* skinning house *and* snap house *and* sneak joint *and* steer joint *and* wire joint *and* wolf trap <nf>; **handbook, book,** sports book, bookie joint <nf>, racebook, horse parlor, horse room, off-track betting parlor, OTB

20 **bookmaker, bookie** <nf>, turf accountant; **tout,** turf consultant; numbers runner; bagman

21 **gambler, player,** gamester, sportsman *or* sporting man <old>, sport, hazarder <old>; **speculator,** venturer, adventurer; **bettor,** wagerer, punter; high-stakes gambler, money player, high roller, plunger; petty gambler, low roller, piker *and* tinhorn *and* tinhorn gambler <nf>; professional gambler, pro *and* nutman <nf>; skillful gambler, sharp, shark, sharper, dean *and* professor *and* river gambler *and* dice gospeller *and* sharpie <nf>; cardsharp *or* cardshark, cardsharper; card counter, counter, caser, matrix player; crap shooter *and* boneshaker <nf>; compulsive gambler; spectator, kibitzer, lumber *and* sweater *and* wood <nf>

22 **cheater,** cheat, air bandit *and* bilk *and* bunco artist *and* dildock *and* grec *and* greek *and* grifter *and* hustler *and* mechanic *and* mover *and* rook *and* worker <nf>; deceiver 357; **dupe, victim,** coll *and* flat *and* john *and* lamb *and* lobster *and* mark *and* monkey *and* patsy *and* **sucker** <nf>

VERBS **23** **gamble,** game, sport <old>, play, **try one's luck** *or* **fortune; speculate; run** *or* **bank a game;** draw lots, draw straws, lot, cut lots, **cast lots;** cut the cards *or* deck; match coins, toss, flip a coin, call, call heads or tails; shoot craps, play at dice, roll the bones <nf>; play the ponies <nf>; raffle off

24 **chance, risk, hazard,** set at hazard, **venture,** wager, take a flier <nf>; **gamble on,** take a gamble on; **take a chance,** take one's chance, take the chances of, try the chance, **chance it,** "stand the hazard of the die"—Shakespeare; **take** *or* **run the risk,** run a chance; **take chances,** tempt fortune; **leave** *or* **trust to chance** *or* **luck,** rely on fortune, take a leap in the dark; buy a pig in a poke; take potluck

25 **bet, wager, gamble, hazard, stake,** punt, lay, lay down, put up, **make a bet, lay a wager,** give *or* take *or* lay odds, make book, get a piece of the action <nf>; plunge <nf>; **bet on** *or* **upon, back;** bet *or* play against; play *or* follow the ponies <nf>; parlay; **ante, ante up; cover, call,** match *or* meet a bet, see, fade; **check, sandbag** <nf>, **pass,** stand pat *or* stand stiff

26 **cheat, pluck** *and* skin *and* rook <nf>; load the dice, mark the cards

ADJS **27** speculative, **uncertain** 971.15; **hazardous, risky** 1006.10, dicey <nf>; **lucky,** winning, hot *and* red hot *and* on a roll <nf>; **unlucky,** losing, cold <nf>

28 **gambling games**

all fours	lotto
auction bridge	lowball poker
baccarat	monte
bezique	numbers *or* policy
bingo	old maid
blind poker	ombre
bridge	paddle wheel *or* raffle
canasta	wheel
casino	penny ante
crazy eights	picquet
chemin de fer	pinball
chuck-a-luck *or* birdcage	pinochle
contract bridge *or* contract	pitch and toss
craps	poker
cribbage	poker dice
draw poker	quinze
écarté	rouge et noir
euchre	roulette
fan tan	rum
faro	rummy
fish *or* go fish	seven-up
gin	stud poker
gin rummy	three-card monte
hazard	trente-et-quarante
hearts	twenty-one *or* blackjack *or*
high, low, jack and the	vingt-et-un
game	war
keno	wheel of fortune *or* big
loo	six wheel
lottery	whist

29 **dice points and rolls**

blanket roll *or* soft-pad roll	even roll
boxes *or* hard eight	fimps *or* hard ten
craps	five *or* fee-bee *or* fever *or*
doublet	phoebe *or* little
drop shot	Phoebe
dump over shot	four *or* little Dick Fisher *or*
eight *or* eighter from	little Dick *or* little joe *or*
Decatur *or* Ada from	little joe from Baltimore
Decatur *or* Ada Ross *or*	*or* little joe from Chicago
Ada Ross the stable	*or* little joe from
hoss	Kokomo
English *or* ass English *or*	greek shot
body English *or* Jonah	little natural *or* slow crap

nine *or* carolina *or* carolina nina *or* nina from caroliner *or* nina from carolina
number *or* point
puppy feet
seven *or* natural *or* little natural *or* pass *or* craps *or* skinny Dugan
six *or* captain hicks *or* sister hicks *or* Jimmy

Hicks *or* sixie from dixie *or* sixty days *or* sice
ten *or* big dick *or* big Joe from Boston *or* slow crap
three *or* cock-eyes
twelve *or* boxcars *or* high noon *or* Gary Cooper
two *or* snake eyes *or* Dolly Parton

760 OTHER SPORTS

NOUNS 1 **billiards,** pool, pocket billiards, snooker; billiard table, pool table, pocket, cue ball, cue stick, chalk; pool hall, billiards club

2 **boating,** sailing, canoeing, rowing, sculling, windsurfing, sailboarding, surfing, rafting, whitewater rafting; yachting, competitive sailing, day sailing; sailboat, canoe, catamaran, rowboat, kayak; regatta, America's Cup; sailor, yachtsman, yachtswoman, canoeist, rower, oarsman *or* oar, sculler, windsurfer, surfer, sailboarder; mariner, boater

3 **martial arts;** judo, the way of gentleness; karate, the way of the empty hand, sport karate, recreational karate; tae kwon do, the way of the foot and fist; aikido, the way of harmony of the spirit, competition aikido; belt, grade, dan grade; dojo

4 **fencing;** foil fencing, épée fencing, saber fencing, *escrime* <Fr>; en garde, parry, riposte, thrust, feint, lunge

5 **gymnastics;** floor exercise, tumbling, vaulting, trampolining, balance beam, horizontal bar, uneven parallel bars, pommel *or* side horse, stationary rings

6 **mountain climbing,** mountaineering, rock climbing, bouldering, free climbing, clean climbing, aid climbing, big wall climbing, snow climbing, ice climbing, Alpine-style climbining, alpinism; climbing expedition, base camp, advance camp; rock face

7 **ice skating,** figure skating, free skating, pairs skating, ice dancing, speed skating; Olympic skating, professional skating; compulsory figure, loop, salchow, jump, axel jump, double axel, triple axel, toe jump, spin, camel spin, lay-back spin, sit spin

8 **swimming,** natation; synchronized swimming, diving, scuba, snorkeling, skinny-dipping <nf>, dog-paddling, Olympic swimming; crawl *or* American crawl *or* Australian crawl, back crawl, backstroke, breaststroke, butterfly stroke; flutter kick, scissors kick, back kick, wedge kick, frog kick, whip kick; lifeguarding, lifesaving; swimming pool, natatorium

761 EXISTENCE

NOUNS 1 **existence, being;** subsistence, entity, essence, isness, absolute *or* transcendental essence, *l'être* <Fr>, pure being, *Ding-an-sich* <Ger, thing-in-itself>, noumenon; **occurrence,** presence, monadism; **materiality** 1052, **substantiality** 763; **life** 306

2 **reality, actuality,** factuality, empirical *or* demonstrable *or* objective existence, the here and now; historicity; necessity; the real thing; facticity; **truth** 972; **authenticity;** sober *or* grim reality, hardball *and* the nitty-gritty <nf>, not a dream, more truth than poetry; thing, something, ens, entity, being, object, substance, phenomenon

3 **fact,** the case, fact *or* truth of the matter, not opinion, not guesswork, what's what *and* where it's at <nf>; **matter of fact; bare fact,** naked fact, bald fact, **simple fact,** sober fact, simple *or* sober truth; **cold fact,** hard fact, **stubborn fact, brutal fact,** painful fact, the nitty-gritty *and* the bottom line <nf>; **actual fact,** positive fact, absolute fact; **self-evident fact,** axiom, postulate, premise, accomplished fact, *fait accompli* <Fr>; **accepted fact,** conceded fact, admitted fact, fact of experience, well-known fact, established fact, inescapable fact, irreducible fact, indisputable fact, undeniable fact; **demonstrable fact,** provable fact; empirical fact; protocol, protocol statement *or* sentence *or* proposition; given fact, given, donné datum, **circumstance** 766; **salient fact,** significant fact; factoid

4 **the facts,** the information 551, the particulars, the details, the specifics, **the data;** the dope *and* the scoop *and* the score *and* the skinny *and* the inside skinny <nf>; the picture <nf>, the gen <Brit nf>, what's what <nf>; the fact *or* facts *or* truth of the matter, the facts of the case, the whole story <nf>; "irreducible and stubborn facts"—W James; essentials, basic *or* essential facts, brass tacks *or* nitty-gritty <nf>

5 **self-existence,** uncreated being, noncontingent existence, aseity, innascibility

6 **mere existence,** simple existence, **vegetable existence, vegetation,** mere tropism

7 <philosophy of being> ontology, metaphysics, existentialism

VERBS 8 **exist, be,** be in existence, be extant, have being; breathe, **live** 306.9; subsist, stand, obtain, hold, prevail, be the case; **occur,** be present, be there, be found, be true, be met with, happen to be

9 **live on,** continue to exist, persist, last, stand the test of time, abide, endure 827.6

10 **vegetate,** merely exist, just be, pass the time

11 **exist in, consist in,** subsist in, lie in, rest in, repose in, reside in, abide in, inhabit, dwell in, **inhere in,** be present in, be a quality of, be comprised in, be contained in, be constituted by, be coextensive with

12 **become,** come to be, go, get, get to be, turn out to be, materialize; be converted into, turn into 858.17; grow 861.5; be changed

ADJS 13 **existent, existing,** in existence, de facto; **subsistent,** subsisting; **being,** in being; **living** 306.13; **present, extant, prevalent, current,** in force or effect, afoot, on foot, under the sun, on the face of the earth

14 **self-existent,** self-existing, innascible; uncreated, increate

15 **real, actual,** factual, veritable, for real <nf>, de facto, simple, sober, **hard; absolute, positive; self-evident,** axiomatic; accepted, conceded, stipulated, given; admitted, well-known, **established, inescapable, indisputable, undeniable; demonstrable,** provable; empirical, **objective,** historical; **true** 973.12; honest-to-God <nf>, genuine, card-carrying <nf>, **authentic; substantial** 763.6

ADVS 16 **really, actually; factually; genuinely,** veritably, basically, **truly; in reality,** in actuality, in effect, in fact, de facto, in point of fact, as a matter of fact; positively, absolutely; no buts about it <nf>; no ifs, ands, or buts <nf>; obviously, manifestly 348.14

WORD ELEMENTS 17 onto-

762 NONEXISTENCE

NOUNS 1 **nonexistence,** nonsubsistence; **nonbeing,** unbeing, not-being, nonentity; **nothingness,** nothing, nullity, nihility, invalidity; vacancy, deprivation, emptiness, inanity, vacuity 222.2; vacuum, void 222.3; nix <nf>; negativeness, negation, negativity; nonoccurrence, nonhappening; **unreality,** nonreality, unactuality; nonpresence, absence 222

2 **nothing, nil,** nihil <L>, nichts <Ger>, nada <Sp>, **naught, aught;** zero, 0, cipher; nothing whatever, nothing at all, nothing on earth or under the sun, no such thing; thing of naught 764.2

3 <nf terms> **zilch, zip,** zippo, nix, goose egg, Billy be damn, diddly, shit, diddly shit, squat, diddly squat, Sweet Fanny Adams <Brit>, bubkes, beans, a hill of beans, a hoot, **a fart,** a fuck, fuck all and bugger all <Brit>, jack-shit, a rat's ass

4 **none,** not any, none at all, not a one, not a blessed one <nf>, never a one, ne'er a one, nary one <nf>; **not a bit,** not a whit, not a hint, not a smitch or smidgen <nf>, not a speck, not a mite, not a particle, not an iota, not a jot, not a one, not a sausage <Brit>, not a scrap, not a trace, not a lick or a whiff <nf>, not a shadow, not a suspicion, not a shadow of a suspicion, neither hide nor hair

VERBS 5 **not exist,** not be in existence, not be met with, not occur, not be found, found nowhere, be absent or lacking or wanting, be null and void

6 **cease to exist** or **be, be annihilated,** be destroyed, **be wiped out,** be extirpated, be eradicated; **go, vanish,** be no more, leave no trace; **vanish, disappear** 34.2, evaporate, fade, fade away or out, fly, flee, dissolve, melt away, die out or away, pass, pass away, pass out of the picture <nf>, turn to nothing or naught, peter out <nf>, come to an end, wind down, tail off and trail off <nf>, reach an all-time low; **perish, expire,** pass away, **die** 307.19

7 **annihilate** 395.13, **exterminate** 395.14, eradicate, extirpate, **eliminate,** liquidate, **wipe out, stamp out,** waste and take out and nuke and zap <nf>, put an end to 395.12

ADJS 8 **nonexistent,** unexistent, inexistent, nonsubsistent, unexisting, without being, nowhere to be found; **minus, missing,** lacking, wanting; **null, void,** devoid, empty, inane, vacuous; **negative,** less than nothing; absent

9 **unreal,** unrealistic, unactual, not real; merely nominal; **immaterial** 1053.7; **unsubstantial** 764.5; **imaginary, imagined,** make believe, **fantastic, fanciful, fancied** 985.19–22; illusory

10 **uncreated, unmade,** unborn, unbegotten, unconceived, unproduced

11 **no more, extinct, defunct, dead** 307.30, expired, passed away; vanished, gone glimmering; perished, obsolete, annihilated; gone, all gone; all over with, had it <nf>, finished and phut and pffft and kaput <nf>, down the tube and down the drain and up the spout <nf>, done for and dead and done for <nf>

ADVS 12 **none, no,** not at all, in no way, to no extent

WORD ELEMENTS 13 nulli-

763 SUBSTANTIALITY

NOUNS 1 **substantiality,** substantialness; materiality 1052; **substance, body,** mass; **solidity,** density, concreteness, **tangibility,** palpability, ponderability; **sturdiness, stability,** soundness, firmness, steadiness, stoutness, toughness, **strength,** durability

2 **substance, stuff, fabric, material, matter** 1052.2, medium, the tangible; **elements,** constituent

elements, constituents, ingredients, components, atoms, building blocks, parts

3 **something, thing,** an existence; **being, entity,** unit, individual, entelechy, monad; **person,** persona, personality, body, soul; **creature,** created being, contingent being; **organism,** life form, living thing, life; **object** 1052.4

4 **embodiment, incarnation,** materialization, substantiation, concretization, hypostasis, reification

VERBS 5 **embody,** incarnate, **materialize,** concretize, body forth, lend substance to, reify, entify, hypostatize

ADJS 6 **substantial,** substantive; **solid, concrete; tangible,** sensible, appreciable, palpable, ponderable; **material** 1052.9; **real** 761.15; **created,** creatural, organismic or organismal, contingent

7 **sturdy,** stable, **solid,** sound, firm, steady, tough, stout, **strong,** rugged; **durable,** lasting, enduring; **hard, dense,** unyielding, steely, adamantine; **well-made,** well-constructed, well-built, well-knit; **well-founded,** well-established, well-grounded; **massive,** bulky, heavy, chunky

ADVS 8 **substantially,** essentially, materially

WORD ELEMENTS 9 stere-, ont-

764 UNSUBSTANTIALITY

NOUNS 1 **unsubstantiality,** insubstantiality, unsubstantialness; **immateriality** 1053; bodilessness, incorporeality, unsolidity, unconcreteness; **intangibility,** impalpability, imponderability; **thinness, tenuousness,** attenuation, tenuity, evanescence, subtlety, subtility, fineness, airiness, mistiness, vagueness, ethereality; **fragility, frailness; flimsiness** 16.2; **transience** 828, **ephemerality,** ephemeralness, fleetingness, fugitiveness

2 thing of naught, nullity, zero; **nonentity, nobody** and nonstarter and nebbish <nf>, nonperson, unperson, cipher, man of straw, jackstraw <old>, lay figure, puppet, dummy, hollow man; flash in the pan, dud <nf>; **trifle** 998.5; nugae <L>; nothing 761.2

3 **spirit,** air, **thin air,** breath, mere breath, smoke, vapor, mist, ether, **bubble,** "such stuff as dreams are made on"—Shakespeare, **shadow,** mere shadow; illusion 976; phantom 988.1

VERBS 4 **spiritualize, disembody,** dematerialize; etherealize, **attenuate,** subtilize, rarefy, fine, refine; **weaken,** enervate, sap

ADJS 5 **unsubstantial,** insubstantial, nonsubstantial, unsubstanced; intangible, impalpable, imponderable; **immaterial** 1053.7; **bodiless,** incorporeal, unsolid, unconcrete; weightless 298.10; **transient** 828.7, ephemeral, fleeting, fugitive

6 **thin, tenuous,** subtile, subtle, evanescent, fine, overfine, refined, rarefied; **ethereal,** airy, windy, spirituous, vaporous, gaseous; air-built, cloud-built; **chimerical,** gossamer, gossamery, gauzy, shadowy, phantomlike 988.7; dreamlike, **illusory, unreal;** fatuous, fatuitous, inane; **imaginary,** fanciful 986.20

7 **fragile, frail** 1050.4; **flimsy,** shaky, weak, papery, paper-thin, **unsound,** infirm 16.15

8 **baseless, groundless,** ungrounded, **without foundation,** unfounded, not well-founded, built on sand, "writ on water"—Keats

WORD ELEMENTS 9 pseudo-

765 STATE

NOUNS 1 **state,** mode, modality; **status, situation,** status quo or status in quo, position, standing, footing, location, bearings, spot, walk of life; **rank,** estate, station, place, place on the ladder, **standing; condition,** circumstance 766; **case, lot; predicament, plight,** pass, pickle and picklement and fix and jam and spot and bind <nf>

2 **the state of affairs,** the nature or shape of things, the way it shapes up <nf>, the way of the world, how things stack up <nf>, **how things stand,** how things are, the way of things, the way it is, like it is, where it's at <nf>, **the way things are,** the way of it, the way things go, how it goes, the way the cookie crumbles, **how it is,** the status quo or status in quo, the size of it <nf>; how the land lies, the lay of the land; shape, phase, state of the art

3 **good condition, bad condition;** adjustment, fettle, form, order, repair, **shape** <nf>, trim

4 **mode, manner, way,** tenor, vein, fashion, style, lifestyle, way of life, preference, thing and bag <nf>; **form,** shape, guise, complexion, make-up; **role,** capacity, character, part; modus vivendi, modus operandi

VERBS 5 **be in** or **have a certain state,** be such or so or thus, **fare,** go on or along; **enjoy** or **occupy** a certain position; **get on** or **along,** come on or along <nf>; **manage** <nf>, **contrive, make out** <nf>, come through, get by; **turn out,** come out, stack up <nf>, shape up <nf>

ADJS 6 conditional, modal, formal, situational, statal

7 **in condition** or **order** or repair or shape; **out of order,** out of commission and **out of kilter** or kelter and out of whack <nf>

766 CIRCUMSTANCE

NOUNS 1 **circumstance, occurrence, occasion, event** 831, **incident;** juncture, conjuncture, contingency, eventuality; **condition** 765.1

2 circumstances, total situation, existing conditions *or* situation, set of conditions, terms of reference, **environment** 209, environing circumstances, context, frame, setting, surround, surrounding conditions, parameters, status quo *or* status in quo, setup; state of affairs; **the picture,** the whole picture, full particulars, ins and outs, ball game <nf>, the score <nf>, how things stand, lay of the land, layout, play-by-play description, blow-by-blow account

3 particular, instance, item, detail, point, count, case, fact, matter, article, datum, element, part, ingredient, factor, facet, aspect, thing; **respect, regard,** angle; minutia, minutiae <pl>, trifle, petty *or* trivial matter; incidental, minor detail

4 circumstantiality, particularity, specificity, thoroughness, minuteness of detail; accuracy

5 circumstantiation, itemization, particularization, specification, spelling-out, detailing, anatomization, atomization, analysis 801

VERBS **6 itemize, specify,** circumstantiate, particularize, **spell out, detail,** go *or* enter into detail, descend to particulars, give full particulars, put in context, atomize, anatomize; **analyze** 801.6; **cite,** instance, adduce, document, give *or* quote chapter and verse; **substantiate**

ADJS **7 circumstantial,** conditional, provisional; **incidental,** occasional, contingent, adventitious, **accidental, chance,** fortuitous, casual, aleatory, unessential *or* inessential *or* nonessential; background

8 environmental, environing, surrounding, conjunctive, conjoined, contextual, attending, attendant, limiting, determining, parametric; grounded, based

9 detailed, minute, full, particular, meticulous, fussy, finicky *or* finicking *or* finical, persnickety, picayune, picky <nf>, nice <old>, precise, exact, specific, special

ADVS **10 thus, thusly,** <nf>, in such wise, thuswise, this way, this-a-way <nf>, thus and thus, thus and so, **so,** just so, like so *and* yea <nf>, like this, like that, just like that; similarly 784.18, precisely

11 accordingly, in that case, in that event, at that rate, that being the case, such being the case, that being so, **under the circumstances,** the condition being such, as it is, as matters stand, as the matter stands, **therefore** 888.7, **consequently; as the case may be,** as it may be, according to circumstances; as it may happen *or* turn out, as things may fall; **by the same token,** equally

12 circumstantially, conditionally, provisionally; provided 959.12

13 fully, in full, in detail, minutely, specifically, particularly, in particular, wholly 792.13, *in toto* <L>, completely 793.14, **at length,** *in extenso* <L>, *ad nauseam* <L>

767 INTRINSICALITY

NOUNS **1 intrinsicality,** internality, innerness, **inwardness; inbeing,** indwelling, immanence; **innateness, inherence,** indigenousness; essentiality, fundamentality; **subjectivity,** internal reality, nonobjectivity

2 essence, substance, stuff, very stuff, inner essence, essential nature, quiddity; **quintessence, epitome,** embodiment, incarnation, model, pattern, purest type, typification, perfect example *or* exemplar, elixir, flower; **essential,** principle, essential principle, fundamental, hypostasis, postulate, axiom; **gist,** gravamen, **nub** <nf>, nucleus, center, focus, kernel, **core, pith,** meat; **heart,** soul, heart and soul, spirit, sap, lifeblood, marrow, entelechy

3 <nf terms> **meat and potatoes,** nuts and bolts, the nitty-gritty, the guts, the name of the game, the bottom line, where it's at, what it's all about, the ball game, the payoff, the score, where the rubber meets the road; back to basics

4 nature, character, quality, suchness; **constitution,** crasis <old>, composition, **characteristics,** makeup, constituents, building blocks; physique 262.4, physio; **build,** body-build, somatotype, frame, constitution, genetic make-up, system; complexion <old>, humor *and* humors <old>; **temperament,** temper, fiber, **disposition,** spirit, ethos, genius, dharma; **way, habit,** tenor, cast, hue, tone, grain, vein, streak, stripe, mold, brand, stamp; **kind** 809.3, **sort, type,** ilk; **property, characteristic** 865.4; **tendency** 896; the way of it, the nature of the beast <nf>

5 inner nature, inside, insides <nf>, internal *or* inner *or* esoteric *or* intrinsic reality, iniety, true being, essential nature, what makes one tick <nf>, center of life, vital principle, nerve center; **spirit, indwelling spirit, soul, heart, heart and soul, breast, bosom, inner person,** heart of hearts, secret heart, inmost heart *or* soul, secret *or* innermost recesses of the heart, heart's core, bottom *or* cockles of the heart; vitals, the quick, depths of one's being, guts *and* kishkes <nf>, where one lives <nf>; **vital principle,** archeus, life force, *élan vital* <Fr>

VERBS **6 inhere,** indwell, belong to *or* permeate by nature, makes one tick <nf>; run in the blood, run in the family, inherit, be born so, have it in the genes, be made that way, be built that way <nf>, be part and parcel of

ADJS **7 intrinsic,** internal, **inner,** inward; **inherent,** resident, implicit, immanent, indwelling; inalienable, unalienable, uninfringeable, unquestionable, unchallengeable, irreducible, qualitative; **ingrained,** in the very grain; infixed, implanted, inwrought, deep-seated; **subjective,** esoteric, private, secret

8 **innate, inborn,** born, congenital; **native, natural,** natural to, connatural, native to, indigenous; **constitutional,** bodily, physical, temperamental, organic; **inbred, genetic, hereditary,** inherited, bred in the bone, in the blood, running in the blood *or* race *or* strain, radical, rooted; connate, connatal, coeval; **instinctive,** instinctual, atavistic, primal

9 **essential,** of the essence, **fundamental; primary,** primitive, primal, elementary, elemental, simple, bare-bones *and* no-frills *and* bread-and-butter <nf>, original, *ab ovo* <L>, **basic, gut** <nf>, basal, underlying; **substantive,** substantial, material; constitutive, constituent; mandatory, compulsory

ADVS 10 **intrinsically, inherently,** innately; internally, inwardly, immanently; originally, primally, primitively; **naturally, congenitally,** genetically, **by birth, by nature**

11 **essentially, fundamentally, primarily, basically; at bottom,** *au fond* <Fr>, at heart; in essence, at the core, in substance, in the main; substantially, materially, most of all; per se, of *or* in itself, as such, qua

WORD ELEMENTS 12 physi-, physic-

768 EXTRINSICALITY

NOUNS 1 **extrinsicality,** externality, outwardness, extraneousness, otherness, discreteness; foreignness; **objectivity,** nonsubjectivity, impersonality

2 **nonessential,** inessential *or* unessential, nonvitalness, carrying coals to Newcastle, gilding the lily; **accessory, extra,** collateral; the other, not-self; **appendage,** appurtenance, auxiliary, supernumerary, **supplement,** addition, addendum, superaddition, adjunct 254; **subsidiary,** subordinate, secondary; **contingency,** contingent, incidental, accidental, accident, happenstance, mere chance; **superfluity,** superfluousness; fifth wheel *and* tits on a boar <nf>; triviality

ADJS 3 **extrinsic, external,** outward, outside, outlying; **extraneous,** foreign; **objective,** nonsubjective, impersonal, extraorganismic *or* extraorganismal; not of this world

4 **unessential,** inessential *or* nonessential, unnecessary, nonvital, superfluous; **accessory, extra,** collateral, auxiliary, supernumerary;

adventitious, appurtenant, adscititious; **additional, supplementary,** supplemental, superadded, supervenient, make-weight; **secondary,** subsidiary, subordinate; **incidental,** circumstantial, contingent; trivial, throwaway; **accidental, chance,** fortuitous, casual, aleatory; **indeterminate, unpredictable,** capricious

769 ACCOMPANIMENT

NOUNS 1 **accompaniment,** concomitance *or* concomitancy, withness and togetherness <nf>; synchronism, **simultaneity** 836, simultaneousness; coincidence, co-occurrence, concurrence, concurrency, coexistence, symbiosis; parallelism; coagency

2 **company, association,** consociation, **society,** community; **companionship, fellowship,** consortship, partnership; cohabitation

3 **attendant,** concomitant, corollary, **accessory,** appendage; **adjunct** 254

4 **accompanier, accompanist; attendant, companion, fellow, mate,** comate, consort, **partner;** companion piece

5 **escort, conductor, usher,** shepherd; **guide,** tourist guide, cicerone; **squire,** esquire, swain, cavalier; **chaperon,** duenna; **bodyguard,** guard, **convoy,** muscle <nf>; companion, sidekick <nf>, fellow traveler, travel companion, satellite, outrider

6 **attendance, following, cortege, retinue, entourage,** suite, followers, followership, rout, train, body of retainers; **court,** cohort; parasite 138.5

VERBS 7 **accompany,** bear *or* keep one company, **keep company with,** companion, go *or* travel *or* run with, go together, go along for the ride <nf>, **go along with, attend,** wait on *or* upon; **associate with,** assort with, sort with, **consort with,** couple with, hang around with *and* hang out with *and* hang with <nf>, go hand in hand with; **combine** 804.3, **associate,** consociate, confederate, flock *or* band *or* herd together

8 **escort, conduct,** have in tow <nf>, marshal, **usher,** shepherd, **guide, lead; convoy,** guard; **squire,** esquire, **attend,** wait on *or* upon, **take out** <nf>; **chaperon;** attend, dance attendance on

ADJS 9 **accompanying, attending, attendant, concomitant,** accessory, collateral; **combined** 805.5, **associated,** coupled, paired; **fellow, twin, joint, joined** 800.13, conjoint, hand-in-hand, hand-in-glove, mutual; **simultaneous, concurrent,** coincident, synchronic, synchronized; correlative; parallel; complementary, accessory

ADVS 10 **hand in hand** *or* glove, arm in arm, side by side, cheek by jowl, shoulder to shoulder; therewith, therewithal, herewith

11 together, collectively, mutually, jointly, unitedly, in conjunction, conjointly, *en masse* <Fr>, communally, corporately, **in a body,** all at once, *ensemble* <Fr>, in association, in company; simultaneously, coincidentally, concurrently, at once

PREPS **12 with, in company with, along with, together with,** in association with, coupled *or* paired *or* partnered with, in conjunction with

WORD ELEMENTS **13** co-, con-, col-, com-, cor-, meta-, syn-, sym-

770 ASSEMBLAGE

NOUNS **1 assemblage, assembly, collection, gathering,** ingathering, forgathering, **congregation,** assembling; concourse, concurrence, conflux, confluence, convergence; collocation, juxtaposition, junction 800.1; combination 805; mobilization, call-up, muster, *attroupement* <Fr>; roundup, rodeo, corralling, shepherding, marshaling; **comparison** 943; canvass, census, data-gathering, survey, inventory

2 assembly <of persons>, *assemblée* <Fr>, **gathering, forgathering, congregation,** congress, conference, convocation, concourse, **meeting,** meet, **get-together** *and* turnout <nf>; convention, conventicle, synod, council, diet, **conclave,** levee; caucus; mass meeting, **rally,** sit-in, demonstration, demo <nf>; **session,** séance, sitting, sit-down <nf>; **panel,** forum, symposium, colloquium; committee, commission; *eisteddfod* <Welsh>; plenum, quorum; **party, festivity** 743.4, fete, at home, housewarming, soiree, reception, **dance,** ball, prom, do <chiefly Brit>, shindig *and* brawl <nf>; rendezvous, date, assignation

3 company, group, grouping, groupment, network, **party, band, knot, gang, crew,** complement, cast, outfit, pack, cohort, troop, troupe, tribe, **body,** corps, stable, bunch *and* mob *and* crowd <nf>; squad, platoon, battalion, regiment, brigade, division, fleet; **team,** squad, string; covey, bevy; posse, detachment, contingent, detail, *posse comitatus* <L>; phalanx; **party, faction,** movement, wing, persuasion; in-group, old-boy network, out-group, peer group, age group; coterie, salon, clique, **set;** junta, cabal

4 throng, multitude, horde, host, heap <nf>, army, panoply, legion; flock, cluster, galaxy; **crowd,** press, crush, flood, spate, deluge, mass, surge, storm, squeeze; **mob,** mass, rabble, rout, ruck, jam, *cohue* <Fr>, everybody and his uncle *or* his brother <nf>, all and them some

5 <animals> **flock, bunch, pack,** colony, host, troop, army, **herd, drove,** drive, drift, trip; pride <of lions>, sloth <of bears>, skulk <of foxes>, gang <of elk>, kennel <of dogs>, clowder <of cats>, pod <of seals>, gam <of whales>, **school** *or* shoal <of fish>; <animal young> **litter**

6 <birds, insects> **flock,** flight, **swarm,** cloud; covey <of partridges>, bevy <of quail>, skein <of geese in flight>, gaggle <of geese on water>, watch <of nightingales>, charm <of finches>, murmuration <of starlings>, spring <of teal>; hive <of bees>, plague <of locusts>

7 bunch, group, grouping, groupment, crop, **cluster, clump,** knot, wad; grove, copse, thicket; **batch, lot,** slew <nf>, **mess** <nf>; tuft, wisp; tussock, hassock; shock, stook; arrangement, nosegay, posy, spray

8 bundle, bindle <nf>, **pack, package,** packet, deck, budget, **parcel,** fardel <nf>, sack, bag, poke <nf>, rag-bag <nf>, bale, truss, **roll,** rouleau, bolt; fagot, fascine, fasces; quiver, sheaf; bouquet, nosegay, posy

9 accumulation, cumulation, gathering, **amassment,** congeries, acervation, collection, collecting, grouping; agglomeration, conglomeration, glomeration, conglomerate, agglomerate; **aggregation,** aggregate; conglobation; **mass, lump,** gob <nf>, chunk *and* hunk <nf>, wad; snowball; stockpile, stockpiling

10 pile, heap, stack, mass; mound, hill; molehill, anthill; bank, embankment, dune; haystack, hayrick, haymow, haycock, cock, mow, rick; drift, snowdrift; pyramid

11 collection, collector's items, collectibles *or* collectables; **holdings,** fund, treasure, hoard; corpus, corpora, **body,** data, raw data; compilation, collectanea; ana; anthology, florilegium, treasury, store, stockpile; *Festschrift* <Ger>; chrestomathy; **museum, library,** zoo, menagerie, aquarium

12 set, suit, suite, series, outfit *and* kit <nf>

13 miscellany, miscellanea, collectanea; **assortment, medley, variety, mixture** 797; mixed bag, hodgepodge, conglomerate, **conglomeration,** omnium-gatherum <nf>, potpourri, smorgasbord; **sundries,** oddments, **odds and ends,** bits and pieces

14 <a putting together> **assembly,** assemblage; assembly line, production line; assembly-line production

15 collector, gatherer, accumulator, connoisseur, fancier, enthusiast, pack rat *and* magpie <nf>, hoarder; beachcomber; collection agent, bill collector, dunner; tax collector, tax man, exciseman <Brit>, customs agent, *douanier* <Fr>; **miser** 484.4

VERBS **16 come together, assemble, congregate,**

collect, come from far and wide, come *or* arrive in a body; league 805.4, ally; **unite** 800.5; muster, **meet, gather, forgather,** gang up <nf>, mass, amass; **merge,** converge, flow together, fuse; group, flock, flock together; herd together; **throng, crowd,** swarm, teem, hive, surge, seethe, mill, stream, horde; **be crowded,** be mobbed, burst at the seams, be full to overflowing; **cluster,** bunch, bunch up, clot; gather around, gang around <nf>; rally, rally around; **huddle,** go into a huddle, close ranks; rendezvous, date; **couple,** copulate, link, link up

17 **convene, meet,** hold a meeting *or* session, sit; **convoke,** summon, call together

18 <bring or gather together> **assemble, gather;** drum up, muster, rally, **mobilize; collect,** collect up, fund-raise, take up a collection, raise, take up; **accumulate,** cumulate, **amass,** mass, bulk, batch; agglomerate, conglomerate, aggregate; **combine** 805.3, **network, join** 800.5, **bring together,** get together, **gather together,** draw *or* lump *or* batch *or* bunch together, pack, pack in, cram, cram in; **bunch,** bunch up; **cluster,** clump; **group,** aggroup; **gather in,** get *or* whip in; scrape *or* scratch together, scrape up, together, rake *or* dredge *or* dig up; round up, corral, drive together; **put together,** make up, compile, colligate; collocate, **juxtapose,** pair, match, partner; hold up together, **compare** 942.4

19 **pile, pile on, heap, stack,** heap *or* pile *or* stack up; mound, hill, bank, bank up; rick; pyramid; drift; stockpile, build up

20 **bundle,** bundle up, **package,** parcel, parcel up, **pack,** bag, sack, truss, truss up; bale; wrap, **wrap up,** do *or* tie *or* bind up; roll up

ADJS 21 **assembled, collected, gathered;** congregate, congregated; meeting, in session; **combined** 805.5; **joined** 799.13; joint, leagued 805.6; **accumulated,** cumulate, massed, **amassed;** heaped, stacked, piled; glomerate, agglomerate, conglomerate, aggregate; **clustered,** bunched, lumped, clumped, knotted; bundled, packaged, wrapped up; fascicled, fasciculated; herded, shepherded, rounded up

22 **crowded, packed, crammed;** bumper-to-bumper <nf>, jam-packed, packed *or* crammed like sardines <nf>, chockablock; **compact,** firm, solid, dense, close, serried; **teeming, swarming, crawling,** seething, bristling, populous, milling, **full** 794.11

23 **cumulative,** accumulative, total, overall

771 DISPERSION

NOUNS 1 **dispersion** *or* **dispersal, scattering,** scatter, scatteration, diffraction; ripple effect; **distribution, spreading,** strewing, sowing, broadcasting, **broadcast, spread,** narrowcast, publication 352, **dissemination,** propagation, dispensation; **radiation,** divergence 171; expansion, splay; **diffusion,** circumfusion; **dilution,** attenuation, thinning, thinning-out, watering, watering-down, weakening; **evaporation,** volatilization, dissipation; fragmentation, shattering, pulverization; sprinkling, spattering; peppering, buckshot *or* shotgun pattern; deployment

2 **decentralization,** deconcentration

3 **disbandment,** dispersion *or* dispersal, diaspora, separation, parting; breakup, split-up <nf>; **demobilization,** deactivation, **release,** detachment; dismissal 908.5; dissolution, disorganization, disintegration 806; population drift, urban sprawl, sprawl

VERBS 4 **disperse, scatter,** diffract; **distribute, broadcast, sow,** narrowcast, disseminate, propagate, pass around *or* out, publish 352.10; **diffuse, spread,** dispread, circumfuse, strew, bestrew, dot; **radiate,** diverge 171.5; expand, splay, branch *or* fan *or* spread out; **issue, deal out,** dole out, retail, utter, dispense; sow broadcast, scatter to the winds; overscatter, overspread, oversow; sunder, hive off <nf>

5 **dissipate, dispel,** dissolve, attenuate, dilute, thin, thin out, water, water down, weaken; **evaporate,** volatilize; drive away, clear away, cast forth, blow off

6 **sprinkle,** besprinkle, asperge, **spatter,** splatter, splash; **dot,** spot, speck, speckle, freckle, stud; **pepper,** powder, dust; flour, crumb, bread, dredge

7 **decentralize,** deconcentrate

8 **disband, disperse, scatter, separate, part,** break up, split up; part company, go separate ways, bug out <nf>; **demobilize,** demob <nf>, deactivate, muster out, debrief, **release,** detach, discharge, let go; dismiss 909.18; **dissolve,** disorganize, disintegrate 806.3

ADJS 9 **dispersed, scattered, distributed,** dissipated, disseminated, strown, strewn, broadcast, **spread,** dispread; **widespread,** diffuse, discrete, sparse; **diluted,** thinned, thinned-out, watered, watered-down, weakened; **sporadic;** straggling, straggly; all over the lot *or* place <nf>, few and far between, from hell to breakfast <nf>

10 **sprinkled,** spattered, splattered, asperged, splashed, **peppered,** spotted, dotted, powdered, dusted, specked, speckled, **studded,** freckled

11 dispersive, **scattering, spreading,** diffractive *or* diffractional, **distributive,** disseminative, diffusive, dissipative, attenuative

ADVS 12 **scatteringly, dispersedly,** diffusely, sparsely, **sporadically,** *passim* <L>, **here and there;** in places, **in spots** <nf>; at large, everywhere, throughout, wherever you look *or* turn <nf>, in all quarters

772 INCLUSION

NOUNS **1 inclusion, comprisal, comprehension,** coverage, envisagement, embracement, encompassment, incorporation, embodiment, assimilation, reception; **membership,** participation, admission, admissibility, eligibility, legitimation, legitimization; **power-sharing,** enablement, enfranchisement; **completeness** 794, **inclusiveness, comprehensiveness,** exhaustiveness; **whole** 792; openness, toleration *or* tolerance; universality, generality

2 entailment, involvement, implication; assumption, presumption, presupposition, subsumption

VERBS **3 include, comprise, contain, comprehend,** hold, **take in; cover,** cover a lot of ground <nf>, occupy, take up, fill; fill in *or* out, build into, **complete** 794.6; **embrace,** encompass, enclose, encircle, incorporate, assimilate, embody, constitute, admit, receive, envisage; **legitimize,** legitimatize; **share power,** enable, enfranchise, cut in *and* deal in *and* give a piece of the action <nf>; among, count in, work in; **number among,** take into account *or* consideration

4 <include as a necessary circumstance or consequence> **entail, involve, implicate,** imply, assume, presume, presuppose, subsume, affect, take in, contain, comprise, **call for, require,** take, bring, lead to

ADJS **5 included, comprised,** comprehended, envisaged, embraced, encompassed, added-in, covered, subsumed; bound up with, forming *or* making a part of, built-in, tucked-in, integrated; **involved** 898.3

6 inclusive, including, containing, comprising, covering, embracing, encompassing, enclosing, encircling, assimilating, incorporating, envisaging; counting, numbering; broad-brush *and* ballpark <nf>, all-in

7 comprehensive, sweeping, complete 794.9; whole 792.9; **all-comprehensive,** all-inclusive 863.14; without omission *or* exception, **overall,** universal, global, wall-to-wall <nf>, around-the-world, **total,** blanket, omnibus, umbrella, across-the-board; encyclopedic, compendious; synoptic; bird's-eye, panoramic

773 EXCLUSION

NOUNS **1 exclusion, barring,** debarring, debarment, preclusion, exception, omission, nonadmission, cutting-out, leaving-out, omission; **restriction,** circumscription, narrowing, demarcation; **rejection,** repudiation; **ban,** bar, taboo, injunction; relegation; prohibition, embargo, blockade; boycott, lockout; inadmissibility, excludability, exclusivity

2 elimination, riddance, culling, culling out, winnowing-out, shakeout, eviction, chasing, bum's rush <nf>; **severance** 802.2; withdrawal, **removal,** detachment, disjunction 802.1; discard, eradication, clearance, **ejection,** expulsion, suspension; **deportation, exile,** expatriation, ostracism, outlawing *or* outlawry; disposal, disposition; **liquidation, purge;** obliteration

3 exclusiveness, narrowness, tightness; **insularity,** snobbishness, parochialism, ethnocentrism, ethnicity, xenophobia, know-nothingism; special case, exemption; **segregation, separation, separationism,** division; **isolation,** insulation, seclusion; quarantine; racial segregation, apartheid, color bar, Jim Crow, race hatred; **out-group; outsider,** non-member, stranger, the other, they; **foreigner, alien** 774.3, outcast 586.4, outlaw; *persona non grata* <L>; blacklist, blackball; monopoly; sexual discrimination

VERBS **4 exclude, bar,** debar, bar out, lock out, **shut out, keep out,** count out <nf>, close the door on, close out, cut out, cut off, preclude; **reject, repudiate,** blackball *and* turn thumbs down on <nf>, read *or* drum out, ease *or* freeze out *and* leave *or* keep out in the cold <nf>, cold-shoulder, send to Coventry <Brit>, ostracize, wave off *or* aside; **ignore,** turn a blind eye, turn a deaf ear, filter out, tune out; **ban,** prohibit, proscribe, taboo, **leave out,** omit, pass over, ignore; relegate; **blockade,** embargo; **tariff,** trade barrier

5 eliminate, get rid of, rid oneself of, **get quit of,** get shut of <nf>, **dispose of, remove,** abstract, eject, expel, give the bum's rush <nf>, kick downstairs, cast off *or* out, chuck <nf>, throw over *or* overboard <nf>; **deport, exile,** outlaw, expatriate; clear, clear out, clear away, clear the decks; **weed out,** pick out; **cut out,** strike off *or* out, elide, censor; eradicate, root up *or* out; **purge, liquidate**

6 segregate, separate, separate out *or* off, divide, cordon, cordon off; **isolate,** insulate, seclude; **set apart,** keep apart; **quarantine,** put in isolation; put beyond the pale, ghettoize; **set aside,** lay aside, put aside, keep aside, box off, wall off, fence off; **sort** *or* **pick out,** cull out, sift, screen, sieve, bolt, riddle, winnow, winnow out; thresh, thrash, gin

ADJS **7 excluded, barred,** debarred, precluded, kept-out, **shut-out, left-out,** left out in the cold <nf>, passed-over; not included, not in it, not in the picture <nf>; excepted, excused; **ignored;** cold-shouldered; relegated; **banned,** prohibited,

proscribed, tabooed; **expelled,** ejected, **purged,**
liquidated; deported, exiled; **blockaded,** embargoed

8 **segregated, separated, cordoned-off, divided;**
isolated, insulated, secluded; **set apart,**
sequestered; **quarantined; ghettoized,** beyond the
pale; peripheral

9 **exclusive, excluding,** exclusory; seclusive,
preclusive, exceptional, inadmissible, prohibitive,
preventive, prescriptive, restrictive; separative,
segregative, closed-door; select, selective; narrow,
insular, parochial, ethnocentric, xenophobic,
snobbish; racist, sexist

PREPS 10 **excluding, barring,** bar, exclusive of,
precluding, omitting, without, absent, **leaving out;
excepting, except, except for,** with the exception
of, outside of <nf>, **save,** saving, save and except,
let alone; **besides,** beside, **aside from**

774 EXTRANEOUSNESS

NOUNS 1 **extraneousness, foreignness;** otherness,
alienism, alienage, alienation; **extrinsicality** 768;
exteriority 206; nonassimilation, nonconformity;
intrusion

2 **intruder,** foreign body *or* element, foreign intruder
or intrusion, interloper, encroacher; **impurity,**
blemish 1004; speck 258.7, spot, macula, blot;
mote, splinter *or* sliver, **weed,** misfit 789.4; oddball
870.4; black sheep

3 **alien, stranger, foreigner, outsider,** non-member,
not one of us, not our sort, not the right sort, the
other, outlander, *Uitlander* <Afrikaans>,
tramontane, ultramontane, barbarian, foreign
devil <Chin>, *gringo* <Sp Amer>; **exile,** outcast,
outlaw, wanderer, refugee, émigré, displaced
person *or* DP, *déraciné* <Fr>; the Wandering Jew

4 **newcomer, new arrival,** *novus homo* <L>; *arriviste*
<Fr>, Johnny-come-lately <nf>, new boy <Brit>;
tenderfoot, greenhorn; settler, emigrant,
immigrant; recruit, rookie <nf>; **intruder,
squatter,** gate-crasher, stowaway

ADJS 5 **extraneous, foreign, alien,** strange, exotic,
foreign-looking; unearthly, extraterrestrial 1072.26;
exterior, **external;** extrinsic 768.3; ulterior, outside,
outland, outlandish; barbarian, barbarous,
barbaric; foreign-born; intrusive

ADVS 6 **abroad,** in foreign parts; oversea, **overseas,**
beyond seas; on one's travels

WORD ELEMENTS 7 ep-, epi-, eph-, ex-, exo-, ef-,
xen-, xeno-

775 RELATION

NOUNS 1 **relation, relationship, connection;**
relatedness, connectedness, **association** 617,
affiliation, filiation, bond, union, alliance, **tie,** tie-
in <nf>, link, linkage, linking, linkup, liaison,
addition 253, adjunct 254, junction 799.1,
combination 805, assemblage 770; deduction
255.1, disjunction 802.1, **contrariety** 779,
disagreement 789, negative *or* bad relation;
positive *or* **good relation, affinity, rapport,** mutual
attraction, sympathy, accord 455; **closeness,**
propinquity, **proximity,** approximation, contiguity,
nearness 223, intimacy; **relations, dealings,** affairs,
business, transactions, doings *and* truck <nf>,
intercourse; **similarity** 784, homology

2 **relativity,** dependence, contingency; **relativism,**
indeterminacy, uncertainty, variability, variance;
interrelation, correlation 777

3 **kinship,** common source *or* stock *or* descent *or*
ancestry, consanguinity, agnation, cognation,
enation, relationship by blood 559; family
relationship, affinity 564.1

4 **relevance, pertinence,** pertinency, cogency,
relatedness, materiality, **appositeness,**
germaneness; application, applicability, effect,
appropriateness; **connection,** reference, **bearing,**
concern, concernment, interest, respect, regard

VERBS 5 **relate to,** refer to, **apply to, bear on** *or*
upon, respect, regard, **concern, involve,** touch,
affect, interest; **pertain, pertain to,** appertain,
appertain to, belong to, fit; **agree, agree with,**
answer to, correspond to, chime with; **have to do
with,** have connection with, link with *or* link up
with, connect, put in context, tie in with <nf>,
liaise with <nf>, deal with, treat of, touch upon

6 **relate, associate, connect,** interconnect, ally, link,
link up, wed, marry, marry up, weld, bind, tie,
couple, bracket, equate, identify; bring into
relation with, bring to bear upon, apply; **parallel,**
parallelize, draw a parallel; symmetrize;
interrelate, relativize, **correlate** 777.4

ADJS 7 **relative, comparative,** relational; **relativistic,**
indeterminate, uncertain, variable; **connective,
linking,** associative; **relating,** pertaining,
appertaining, pertinent, referring, referable

8 **approximate,** approximating, approximative,
proximate; **near, close** 223.14; **comparable,**
relatable, commensurable; **proportional,**
proportionate, proportionable; correlative; **like,**
homologous, **similar** 784.10

9 **related, connected; linked,** tied, coupled, knotted,
twinned, wedded, wed, married *or* married up,
welded, conjugate, bracketed, bound, yoked,
spliced, conjoined, conjoint, conjunct, joined
799.13; **associated, affiliated,** filiated, **allied,**
associate, affiliate; interlocked, **interrelated,**
interlinked, involved, implicated, overlapping,
interpenetrating, relevant, **correlated;** in the same

category, of that kind or sort or ilk, corresponding; parallel, collateral; **congenial,** *en rapport* <Fr>, sympathetic, compatible, affinitive

10 kindred, akin, related, of common source or stock or descent or ancestry, agnate, cognate, enate, connate, connatural, congeneric or congenerous, consanguine or consanguineous, genetically related, related by blood 559.6, affinal 564.4

11 relevant, pertinent, appertaining, **germane, apposite,** cogent, material, admissible, applicable, applying, pertaining, belonging, involving, appropriate, **apropos,** *à propos* <Fr>, to the purpose, **to the point,** in point, *ad rem* <L>

ADVS **12 relatively,** comparatively, proportionately, not absolutely, to a degree, to an extent, to some extent; **relevantly,** pertinently, appositely, germanely

PREPS **13 with** or **in relation to,** with or in reference to, **with** or **in regard to,** with respect to, in respect to or of, in what concerns, relative to, **relating** or **pertaining to,** pertinent to, appertaining to, referring to, in relation with, **in connection with,** apropos of, speaking of; **as to,** as for, as respects, as regards; in the matter of, on the subject of, in point of, on the score of; re, *in re* <L>; **about,** anent, of, on, upon, **concerning,** touching, respecting, **regarding**

776 UNRELATEDNESS

NOUNS **1 unrelatedness,** irrelativeness, irrelation; **irrelevance,** irrelevancy, impertinence, inappositeness, uncogency, ungermaneness, immateriality, inapplicability; inconnection or disconnection, inconsequence, independence; **unconnectedness,** separateness, delinkage, discreteness, dissociation, disassociation, disjuncture, disjunction 802.1

2 misconnection, misrelation, wrong or invalid linking, **mismatch,** mismatching, misalliance, *mésalliance* <Fr>; misapplication, misapplicability, misreference

3 an irrelevance, or irrelevancy, quite another thing, something else again *and* a whole nother thing *and* a whole different story *and* a whole different ball game <nf>

VERBS **4 not concern,** not involve, not imply, not implicate, not entail, not relate to, not connect with, have nothing to do with, have no business with, cut no ice *and* make no never mind <nf>, have no bearing

5 foist, drag in 213.6; impose on 643.7

ADJS **6 unrelated,** irrelative, unrelatable, unrelational, **unconnected,** unallied, unlinked, **unassociated,** unaffiliated or disaffiliated;

disrelated, disconnected, dissociated, detached, discrete, disjunct, removed, **separated,** segregated, apart, other, independent, marked off, bracketed; **isolated,** insular; **foreign, alien,** strange, exotic, outlandish; incommensurable, incomparable; inconsistent, inconsonant; extraneous 768.3

7 irrelevant, irrelative; **impertinent, inapposite,** ungermane, uncogent, inconsequent, inapplicable, immaterial, inappropriate, inadmissible; wide of or away from the point, *nihil ad rem* <L>, **beside the point,** beside the mark, wide of the mark, **beside the question,** off the subject, not to the purpose, **nothing to do with the case,** not at issue, out-of-the-way; **unessential,** nonessential, extraneous, extrinsic 768.3; incidental, parenthetical

8 farfetched, remote, distant, out-of-the-way, strained, forced, dragged in, neither here nor there, brought in from nowhere; **imaginary** 986.19; improbable 969.3

ADVS **9 irrelevantly,** irrelatively, impertinently, inappositely, ungermanely, uncogently, amiss; without connection, without reference or regard

777 CORRELATION
<reciprocal or mutual relation>

NOUNS **1 correlation,** corelation; correlativity, correlativism; **reciprocation,** reciprocity, reciprocality, two-edged sword, relativity 774.2; **mutuality,** communion, community, commutuality, common ground; **common denominator,** common factor; proportionality, direct or inverse relationship, direct or inverse ratio, direct or inverse proportion, covariation; **equilibrium, balance,** symmetry 264; **correspondence, equivalence,** equipollence, coequality

2 interrelation, interrelationship; **interconnection,** interlocking, interdigitation, intercoupling, interlinking, interlinkage, interalliance, interassociation, interaffiliation, interdependence, interdependency, codependency; dovetail

3 interaction, interworking, intercourse, intercommunication, **interplay;** alternation, seesaw; **meshing,** intermeshing, mesh, engagement; **complementation,** complementary relation, complementary distribution; **interweaving,** interlacing, intertwining 740.1; **interchange** 863, tit for tat, trade-off, *quid pro quo* <L>; **concurrence** 899, coaction, **cooperation** 450, compromise; codependency

4 correlate, correlative; **correspondent,** analogue, counterpart; reciprocator, reciprocatist; each other, one another

VERBS **5 correlate,** corelate; **interrelate, interconnect,** interassociate, interlink, intercouple, interlock, interdigitate, interally, intertie, interjoin, interdepend; interface; find common ground; dovetail

6 **interact,** interwork, **interplay;** mesh, intermesh, engage, fit, fit like a glove, dovetail, mortise; **interweave,** interlace, intertwine; **interchange;** coact, **cooperate;** codepend

7 **reciprocate, correspond,** correspond to, respond to, answer, answer to, go tit-for-tat; **complement,** coequal; **cut both ways,** cut two ways; counteract

ADJS 8 **correlative,** corelative, correlational, corelational; **correlated,** corelated; **interrelated, interconnected,** interassociated, interallied, interaffiliated, interlinked, interlocked, intercoupled, intertied, interdependent; interchanged, converse

9 **interacting,** interactive, interworking, interplaying; in gear, in mesh; dovetailed, mortised; cooperative, **cooperating** 450.5

10 **reciprocal,** reciprocative, tit-for-tat, seesaw, seesawing; **corresponding,** correspondent, answering, analogous, homologous, equipollent, tantamount, equivalent, coequal; **complementary,** complemental

11 **mutual,** commutual, **common, joint, communal,** shared, sharing, conjoint; respective, two-way, cooperative

ADVS 12 **reciprocally,** back and forth, backward and forward, backwards and forwards, alternately, seesaw, to and fro; vice versa

13 **mutually, commonly,** communally, **jointly;** respectively, each to each; *entre nous* <Fr>, *inter se* <L>

WORD ELEMENTS 14 equi-

778 SAMENESS

NOUNS 1 **sameness, identity,** identicalness, selfsameness, indistinguishability, undifferentiation, nondifferentiation, two peas in a pod; **coincidence,** correspondence, agreement, congruence; **equivalence, equality** 790, coequality; **synonymousness,** synonymity, synonymy; **oneness, unity,** homogeneity, consubstantiality

2 **identification,** likening, unification, coalescence, combination, union, fusion, merger, blending, melding, synthesis

3 **the same, selfsame,** very same, one and the same, identical same, no other, none other, very *or* actual thing, a distinction without a difference, the same difference <nf>; **equivalent** 783.3; **synonym;** homonym, homograph, homophone; ditto <nf>, *idem* <L>, *ipsissima verba* <L, the very words>; **duplicate,** double, clone *and* cookie-cutter copy <nf>, *Doppelgänger* <Ger>, twin, very image,

look-alike, dead ringer <nf>, the image of, the picture of, spitting image *and* spit and image <nf>, **exact counterpart, copy** 785.1,3–5, replica, facsimile, carbon copy

VERBS 4 **coincide, correspond,** agree, chime with, match, tally, go hand in glove with, twin; complement

5 **identify,** make one, **unify,** unite, join, combine, coalesce, synthesize, merge, blend, meld, fuse 805.3

6 **reproduce,** copy, reduplicate, **duplicate,** ditto <nf>, clone

ADJS 7 **identical,** identic; **same, selfsame,** one, **one and the same,** all the same, all one, of the same kidney; **indistinguishable,** without distinction, without difference, undifferent, undifferentiated; **alike, all alike, like** 784.10, just alike, exactly alike, like two peas in a pod; **duplicate,** reduplicated, copied, twin; **homogeneous,** consubstantial; redundant, tautological

8 **coinciding,** coincident, coincidental; **corresponding,** correspondent, congruent; complementary; **synonymous, equivalent,** six of one and half a dozen of the other <nf>; **equal** 789.7, coequal, coextensive, coterminous; in *or* at parity

ADVS 9 **identically,** synonymously, **alike;** coincidentally, correspondently, correspondingly, congruently; **equally** 790.11, coequally, coextensively, coterminously; on the same footing, on all fours with; **likewise,** the same way, just the same, as is, ditto, same here <nf>; *ibid and ibidem* <L>

779 CONTRARIETY

NOUNS 1 **contrariety, oppositeness, opposition** 451; **antithesis, contrast,** contraposition 215, counterposition, contradiction, contraindication, contradistinction; **antagonism,** repugnance, oppugnance, oppugnancy, **hostility,** perversity, nay-saying, negativeness, orneriness <nf>, inimicalness, **antipathy,** scunner <nf>; **confrontation,** showdown, standoff, Mexican standoff <nf>, clashing, collision, cross-purposes 456.2, conflict; polarity; discrepancy, inconsistency, **disagreement** 788; antonymy

2 **the opposite, the contrary, the antithesis, the reverse,** the other way round *or* around, the inverse, the converse, the obverse, the counter; **the other side,** the mirror *or* reverse image, the other side of the coin, the flip *or* B side <nf>; the direct *or* polar opposite, the other *or* opposite extreme, other end of the spectrum; antipode, antipodes; countercheck *or* counterbalance *or* counterpoise,

offset, setoff; **opposite pole,** antipole, counterpole, counterpoint; opposite number <nf>, vis-à-vis; **antonym,** opposite, opposite term, counterterm

3 <contrarieties when joined or coexisting> self-contradiction, **paradox** 789.2, antinomy, oxymoron, ambivalence, **irony,** enantiosis, equivocation, **ambiguity**

VERBS **4 go contrary to, run counter to,** counter, contradict, contravene, controvert, fly in the face of, be *or* play at cross-purposes, go against; **oppose,** be opposed to, go *or* run in opposition to, run counter to, side against; **conflict with,** come in conflict with, oppugn, conflict, clash; contrast with, **offset,** set off, countercheck *or* counterbalance, countervail; **counteract,** counterwork; counterpose *or* contrapose, counterpoise, juxtapose in opposition

5 reverse, invert, obvert, **transpose** 205.5, flip <nf>

ADJS **6 contrary;** contrarious, perverse, **opposite,** antithetic, antithetical, **contradictory,** counter, contrapositive, contrasted; **converse, reverse,** obverse, inverse; **adverse,** adversative *or* adversary, adversarial, **opposing, opposed,** oppositive, oppositional; anti <nf>, dead against; **antagonistic,** repugnant, oppugnant, perverse, contrarious, ornery <nf>, nay-saying, negative, hostile, combative, bellicose, belligerent, inimical, antipathetic, antipathetical, discordant; inconsistent, discrepant, conflicting, clashing, at cross-purposes, confronting, **confrontational,** confrontive, squared off <nf>, face to face, vis-à-vis, eyeball to eyeball *and* toe-to-toe <nf>, at loggerheads; contradistinct; antonymous; countervailing, counterpoised, balancing, counterbalancing, compensating

7 diametric, diametrical, diametrically opposite, diametrically opposed, at opposite poles, in polar opposition, antipodal *or* antipodean; opposite as black and white *or* light and darkness *or* day and night *or* fire and water *or* the poles, etc, "Hyperion to a satyr"—Shakespeare

8 self-contradictory, **paradoxical,** antinomic, oxymoronic, ambivalent, **ironic;** equivocal, **ambiguous**

ADVS **9** contrarily, contrariwise, counter, conversely, inversely, **vice versa,** topsy-turvy, upside down, arsy-varsy <nf>, **on the other hand,** *per contra* <L>, **on** *or* **to the contrary,** *tout au contraire* <Fr>, at loggerheads, in flat opposition; rather, nay rather, quite the contrary, otherwise 780.11, just the other way, just the other way around, **oppositely,** just the opposite *or* reverse; by contraries, by way of opposition; against the grain, *à rebours* <Fr>; contrariously, perversely, ornerily <nf>

PREPS **10 opposite,** over against, contra, in contrast with, contrary to, vis-à-vis

WORD ELEMENTS **11** con-, contra-, counter-

780 DIFFERENCE

NOUNS **1 difference,** otherness, separateness, discreteness, distinctness, **distinction;** unlikeness, **dissimilarity** 787; **variation,** variance, variegation, variety, **mixture** 797, **heterogeneity, diversity; deviation,** divergence *or* divergency, departure; **disparity,** gap, inequality 790, odds; **discrepancy,** inconsistency, inconsonance, incongruity, discongruity, unconformity *or* nonconformity, disconformity, **strangeness** 870, unorthodoxy 688, incompatibility, irreconcilability; culture gap; **disagreement, dissent** 333, disaccord *or* disaccordance, inaccordance, discordance, dissonance, inharmoniousness, inharmony; **contrast,** opposition, **contrariety** 779; a far cry, a whale of a difference <nf>; biodiversity

2 margin, wide *or* narrow margin, **differential;** differentia, distinction, point of difference; **nicety, subtlety,** refinement, delicacy, nice *or* fine *or* delicate *or* subtle distinction, fine point; shade *or* particle of difference, **nuance,** hairline; **seeming difference,** distinction without a difference

3 a different thing, a different story <nf>, **something else,** something else again <nf>, *tertium quid* <L, a third something>, *autre chose* <Fr>, another kettle of fish <nf>, another tune, different breed of cat <nf>, another can of worms, horse of a different color, bird of another feather; **nothing of the kind,** no such thing, **quite another thing; other, another,** tother *and* whole nother thing *and* different ball game *and* whole different ball game <nf>, special case, exception to the rule

4 differentiation, differencing, **discrimination,** distinguishing, **distinction;** demarcation, limiting, drawing the line; **separation, separateness,** discreteness 801.1, division, atomization, anatomization, analysis, disjunction, segregation, severance, severalization; **modification, alteration, change** 852, tweak, variation, diversification, disequalization; **particularization,** specification, individualization, individuation, personalization, specialization

VERBS **5 differ, vary,** diverge, stand apart, be distinguished *or* distinct; **deviate from,** diverge from, divaricate from, depart from; **disagree with,** disaccord with, conflict with, contrast with, stand over against, clash with, jar with; not be like, bear no resemblance to 787.2, not square with, not accord with, not go on all fours with; ring the changes

6 **differentiate,** difference; **distinguish, make a distinction, discriminate, secern; separate,** sever, severalize, segregate, divide; **demarcate,** mark, mark out *or* off, set off, set apart, draw a line, set limits; **modify,** vary, diversify, disequalize, **change** 852.5,6; **particularize,** individualize, individuate, personalize, specify, specialize; atomize, analyze, anatomize, disjoin; split hairs, sharpen *or* refine a distinction, chop logic

ADJS 7 **different,** differing; unlike, not like, **dissimilar** 787.4; **distinct,** distinguished, differentiated, discriminated, discrete, separated, separate, disjoined 802.21, widely apart; **various,** variant, varying, varied, heterogeneous, multifarious, motley, assorted, variegated, diverse, divers, **diversified** 783.4; **several,** many; **divergent,** deviative, diverging, deviating, departing; **disparate,** unequal 790.4; **discrepant,** inconsistent, inconsonant, incongruous, incongruent, unconformable, incompatible, irreconcilable; **disagreeing,** in disagreement; **at odds,** at variance, clashing, inaccordant, disaccordant, discordant, dissonant, inharmonious, out of tune; **contrasting,** contrasted, poles apart, poles asunder, worlds apart; **contrary** 779.6; **discriminable,** separable, severable

8 **other, another,** whole nother <nf>, else, otherwise, other than *or* from; not the same, not the type <nf>, not that sort, of another sort, of a sort *and* of sorts <nf>; **unique,** one of a kind, rare, **special,** peculiar, *sui generis* <L, of its own kind>, in a class by itself

9 **differentiative,** differentiating, diacritic, diacritical, differential; **distinguishing,** discriminating, discriminative, discriminatory, characterizing, individualizing, individuating, personalizing, differencing, separative; diagnostic; **distinctive,** contrastive, characteristic, peculiar, idiosyncratic

ADVS 10 **differently,** diversely, variously; in a different manner, in another way, with a difference; differentiatingly, distinguishingly

11 **otherwise,** in other ways, **in other respects;** elsewise, else, or else; than; other than; **on the other hand;** contrarily 779.9; alias

WORD ELEMENTS 12 all-, de-, dis-, heter-, xen-

equilibrium, unruffledness, serenity, tranquility, calm, calmness, cool <nf>

2 **regularity, constancy,** invariability, unvariation, undeviation, even tenor *or* pace, smoothness, clockwork regularity; **sameness** 778, **monotony,** monotonousness, undifferentiation, the same old thing <nf>, the daily round *or* routine, the treadmill; monotone, drone, dingdong, singsong, monologue

VERBS 3 **persist, prevail,** persevere, run true to form *or* type, continue the same; drag on *or* along; hum, drone

4 **make uniform,** uniformize; **regulate,** regularize, normalize, stabilize, damp; **even, equalize,** symmetrize, harmonize, balance, balance up, equilibrize; **level,** level out *or* off, smooth, smooth out, even, even out, flatten; **homogenize, assimilate,** standardize, stereotype; clone <nf>

ADJS 5 **uniform, equable,** equal, **even; level,** flat, smooth; **regular, constant,** steadfast, persistent, continuous; **unvaried,** unruffled, unbroken, seamless, undiversified, undifferentiated, unchanged; invariable, unchangeable, immutable; **unvarying,** undeviating, unchanging, steady, stable; cloned *or* clonish *and* cookie-cutter <nf>; **ordered,** balanced, measured; **orderly,** methodical, systematic, mechanical, faceless, robotlike, automatic; **consistent,** consonant, correspondent, accordant, homogeneous, **alike,** all alike, all of a piece, of a piece, consubstantial, monolithic; nonsexist, inclusive, nondiscriminatory

6 **same,** wall-to-wall, back-to-back; **monotonous, humdrum,** unrelieved, repetitive, drab, gray, ho-hum <nf>, samey <Brit nf>, usual, as usual; tedious, boring

ADVS 7 **uniformly,** equably, **evenly;** monotonously, in a rut *or* groove, dully, tediously, routinely, unrelievedly

8 **regularly; constantly, steadily,** continually; **invariably,** without exception, at every turn, every time one turns around, all the time, all year round, week in week out, year in year out, day in day out, never otherwise; methodically, orderly, systematically; **always** 829.11; like clockwork

WORD ELEMENTS 9 equi-, hol-, hom-, is-, mon-

781 UNIFORMITY

NOUNS 1 **uniformity, evenness,** equability; **steadiness,** stability 855, steadfastness, firmness, unbrokenness, seamlessness, constancy, unwaveringness, undeviatingness, persistence, perseverance, continuity, **consistency;** consonance, correspondence, accordance; unity, **homogeneity,** consubstantiality, monolithism; **equanimity,**

782 NONUNIFORMITY

NOUNS 1 **nonuniformity, unevenness, irregularity,** raggedness, crazy-quilt, choppiness, jerkiness, **disorder** 810; **difference** 780; inequality; **inconstancy, inconsistency,** variability, changeability, changeableness, mutability, capriciousness, mercuriality, wavering, **instability, unsteadiness; variation, deviation,** deviance, divergence, differentiation, divarication, ramification; versatility, **diversity,** diversification, nonformalization; **nonconformity,** nonconformism, unconformity, unconformism, **unorthodoxy; pluralism,** variegation, variety, variousness, motleyness, dappleness; multiculturalism, multiculturism

VERBS **2 diversify, vary,** variegate 47.7, chop and change, waver, mutate; **differentiate,** divaricate, diverge, ramify; **differ** 780.5; dissent 333.4; **disunify,** break up, break down, fragment, partition, **analyze** 801.6

ADJS **3 nonuniform,** ununiform, **uneven, irregular,** ragged, erose, choppy, jerky, jagged, rough, disorderly, unsystematic; **different** 779.7, unequal, unequable; **inconstant, inconsistent, variable,** varying, **changeable,** changing, mutable, capricious, impulsive, mercurial, erratic, spasmodic, sporadic, wavery, wavering, **unstable, unsteady;** deviating, deviative, deviatory, divergent, divaricate, ramified; **diversified,** variform, diversiform, nonformal; **nonconformist,** unorthodox; **pluralistic,** variegated, various, motley 47.9,12; multicultural, multiracial

ADVS **4 nonuniformly,** ununiformly, unequally, **unevenly, irregularly,** inconstantly, **inconsistently,** unsteadily, erratically, spasmodically, by fits and starts, capriciously, impulsively, sporadically; unsystematically, chaotically, helter-skelter, higgledy-piggledy; in all manner of ways, every which way <nf>, all over the shop *and* all over the ball park <nf>; here there and everywhere

WORD ELEMENTS **5** diversi-, vari-, heter-

783 MULTIFORMITY

NOUNS **1 multiformity,** multifariousness, **variety,** nonuniformity 782, **diversity,** diversification, variation, variegation 47, variability, versatility, proteanism, manifoldness, multiplicity, heterogeneity; omniformity, omnifariousness; pluralism, multiculturalism; everything but the kitchen sink <nf>, all colors of the rainbow, polymorphism, heteromorphism; allotropy *or* allotropism <chemistry>; Proteus, shapeshifting, shapeshifter; "her infinite variety"—Shakespeare

VERBS **2 diversify, vary,** change form, change shape, shift shape, ring changes, cover the spectrum, **variegate** 47.7; branch out, spread one's wings; have many irons in the fire

ADJS **3 multiform,** diversiform, variable, versatile; **protean,** proteiform; **manifold,** multifold, multiplex, multiple, multifarious, multiphase; polymorphous, polymorphic, heteromorphous, heteromorphic, metamorphic; omniform,

omniformal, omnifarious, omnigenous; allotropic *or* allotropical <chemistry>

4 diversified, varied, assorted, heterogeneous, nonuniform; **various,** many and various, divers <old>, diverse, sundry, **several, many;** of all sorts *or* conditions *or* kinds *or* shapes *or* descriptions *or* types; multiethnic, multicultural

ADVS **5 variously, severally,** sundrily, multifariously, diversely, manifoldly

WORD ELEMENTS **6** allo-, diversi-, heter-, multi-, omni-, parti-, party-, poecil- *or* poikil-, poly-, vari-

784 SIMILARITY

NOUNS **1 similarity, likeness,** alikeness, **sameness,** similitude; **resemblance,** semblance; **analogy, correspondence,** conformity, accordance, agreement, comparability, commensurability, comparison, **parallelism, parity,** community, alliance, consimilarity; **approximation,** approach, closeness, nearness; assimilation, likening, **simile, metaphor,** parable, allegory; **simulation, imitation,** copying, aping, mimicking, taking-off, takeoff, burlesque, pastiche, *pasticcio* <Ital>; identity 778.1; equivalence

2 kinship, affinity, connection, family resemblance *or* likeness, family favor, generic *or* genetic resemblance; connaturality *or* connaturalness, connature, connateness, congeneracy; compatibility

3 likeness, like, the like of *or* the likes of <nf>, point of likeness, point in common; suchlike, such; **analogue, parallel;** cognate, congener; **counterpart, complement, correspondent,** pendant, similitude, tally; **approximation,** rough idea, sketch; coordinate, reciprocal, obverse, equivalent; correlate, correlative; **close imitation** *or* reproduction *or* copy *or* facsimile *or* replica, near duplicate, simulacrum; **close match, match-up, fellow, mate;** soul mate, kindred spirit *or* soul, **companion, twin,** brother, sister, brother *or* sister under the skin; *mon semblable* <Fr>, second self, alter ego; a chip off the old block; **look-alike,** the image of, the picture of, shadow, another edition

4 close *or* **striking resemblance,** startling *or* marked *or* decided resemblance; close *or* near likeness; **faint** *or* **remote resemblance,** mere hint *or* shadow

5 set, group, matching pair *or* set, his and hers <nf>, couple, pair, twins, look-alikes, two of a kind, birds of a feather, peas in a pod

6 <of words or sounds> assonance, alliteration, rhyme, slant rhyme, near rhyme, jingle, clink; pun, paronamasia

VERBS **7** resemble, be like, bear resemblance; put one in mind of <nf>, remind one of, bring to mind, be reminiscent of, suggest, evoke, call up, call to mind; **look like,** favor <nf>, mirror; **take after,** partake of, follow, appear *or* seem like, sound like; savor *or* smack of, be redolent of; **have all the earmarks of,** have every appearance of, have all the features of, have all the signs of, have every sign *or* indication of; **approximate,** approach, near, come near, come close; **compare with,** stack up with <nf>; **correspond, match, parallel,** connect, relate; not tell apart, not tell one from the other; **imitate** 336.5, **simulate,** copy, ape, mimic, take off, counterfeit; nearly reproduce *or* duplicate *or* reduplicate

8 **similarize,** approximate, assimilate, bring near; connaturalize

9 **assonate,** alliterate, rhyme, chime; pun

ADJS 10 **similar, like, alike,** something like, not unlike; **resembling,** resemblant, following, favoring <nf>, savoring *or* smacking of, suggestive of, **on the order of;** consimilar; **simulated, imitated,** imitation, copied, aped, mimicked, taken off, fake *or* phony <nf>, counterfeit, **mock,** synthetic, ersatz; nearly reproduced *or* duplicated *or* reduplicated; uniform with, homogeneous, identical 778.7

11 **analogous,** comparable; **corresponding,** correspondent, equivalent; **parallel,** paralleling; **matching,** cast in the same mold, of a kind, of a size, of a piece; duplicate, twin, of the same hue *or* stripe

12 **such as,** suchlike, so

13 **akin,** affinitive, related; connatural, connate, cognate, agnate, enate, conspecific, correlative; congenerous, congeneric, congenerical; brothers *or* sisters under the skin

14 **approximating,** approximative, approximate, approximable; **near, close;** much of a muchness <Brit nf>, much the same, much at one, nearly the same, same but different, "like—but oh! how different"—Wordsworth; quasi, pseudo

15 **very like, mighty like,** powerful like <nf>, uncommonly like, remarkably like, extraordinarily like, strikingly like, **ridiculously like, for all the world like,** as like as can be; a lot alike, pretty much the same, the same difference *and* damned little difference <nf>; as like as two peas in a pod, *comme deux gouttes d'eau* <Fr, like two drops of water>; faintly *or* remotely like

16 **lifelike,** speaking, faithful, living, breathing, to the life, **true to life** *or* nature; **realistic, natural**

17 <of words or sounds> assonant, assonantal, alliterative, alliteral; **rhyming,** jingling, chiming, punning

ADVS 18 **similarly,** correspondingly, **like, likewise,** either; in the same manner, **in like manner,** in

kind; in that way, like that, like this; **thus** 765.10; so; by the same token, by the same sign; identically 778.9

19 **so to speak,** in a manner of speaking, **as it were,** in a manner, in a way; kind of *and* sort of <nf>

785 COPY

NOUNS 1 **copy, representation, facsimile, image, likeness** 784.3, **resemblance,** semblance, similitude, picture, portrait, life mask, death mask, icon, simulacrum; ectype; pastiche, *pasticcio* <Ital>; fair copy, faithful copy; certified copy; **imitation** 336.3, **counterfeit** 354.13, forgery, fake *and* phony <nf>

2 **reproduction, duplication, reduplication;** reprography; transcription; tracing, rubbing; mimeography, xerography, hectography

3 **duplicate, duplication,** dupe *and* ditto <nf>; **double,** cookie-cutter copy, clone; representation, **reproduction, replica,** repro <nf>, reduplication, facsimile, model, **counterpart;** a chip off the old block; triplicate, quadruplicate, etc; repetition 849

4 **transcript, transcription,** apograph, tenor <law>; **transfer,** tracing, rubbing, **carbon copy,** carbon; manifold <old>; microcopy, microform; microfiche, fiche; recording

5 **print,** offprint; **impression,** impress; **reprint,** proof, reproduction proof, repro proof *and* repro <nf>, second edition; photostatic copy, Photostat <trademark>, stat <nf>; mimeograph copy, Ditto copy <trademark>, hectograph copy, xerographic copy, Xerox copy <trademark> *or* Xerox <trademark>; **facsimile,** fax <nf>; **photograph,** positive, negative, print, enlargement, contact print, photocopy

6 **cast,** casting; mold, **molding,** die, stamp, seal

7 **reflection,** reflex; **shadow,** silhouette, outline 211.2; **echo**

VERBS 8 **copy, reproduce,** replicate, **duplicate,** dupe <nf>; clone; reduplicate; **transcribe;** trace; double; triplicate, quadruplicate, etc; manifold <old>, multigraph, mimeograph, mimeo, Photostat <trademark>, stat <nf>, facsimile, fax <nf>, hectograph, ditto, Xerox <trademark>; microcopy, microfilm

ADVS 9 in duplicate, in triplicate, etc

786 MODEL
   <thing copied>

NOUNS 1 **model, pattern, standard, criterion,** classic example, rule, mirror, paradigm; showpiece, showplace; **original,** urtext, *locus classicus* <L>;

type, **prototype**, antetype, **archetype**, genotype, biotype, type specimen, type species; **precedent**

2 **example**, exemplar; **representative**, type, symbol, emblem, exponent; **exemplification**, illustration, demonstration, explanation; **instance**, relevant instance, **case**, typical example *or* case, case in point, object lesson

3 **sample, specimen**; piece, taste, swatch; instance, for-instance <nf>

4 **ideal**, beau ideal, ego ideal, ideal type, acme, highest *or* perfect *or* best type; cynosure, apotheosis, idol; **shining example**, role-model, **hero, superhero; model**, the very model, mirror, paragon, epitome; cult figure

5 artist's model, dressmaker's model, photographer's model, mannequin; dummy, lay figure; clay model, wood model, pilot model, mock-up

6 **mold, form** 262, cast, template, matrix, negative; **die**, punch, stamp, intaglio, seal, mint; last, shoe last

VERBS 7 **set an example**, set the pace, lead the way; **exemplify**, epitomize, fit the pattern; **emulate**, follow, hold up as a model, model oneself on

ADJS 8 **model, exemplary**, precedential, typical, paradigmatic, representative, standard, normative, classic; ideal

9 **prototypal**, prototypic, prototypical, archetypal, archetypic, archetypical, antitypic, antitypical

787 DISSIMILARITY

NOUNS 1 **dissimilarity**, unsimilarity; **dissimilitude**, dissemblance, **unresemblance; unlikeness**, unsameness; **disparity**, diversity, divergence, gap, **contrast, difference** 780; nonuniformity 782; uncomparability, uncomparableness, incomparability, incomparableness, uncommensurableness, uncommensurability, incommensurableness, incommensurability, no resemblance, no common ground; culture gap; **disguise**, dissimilation, camouflage, masking; cosmetics; poor imitation, bad likeness *or* copy, botched copy, mere caricature *or* counterfeit

VERBS 2 **not resemble, bear no resemblance**, not look like, **not compare with; differ** 780.5; have little *or* nothing in common; diverge, deviate

3 disguise, dissimilate, camouflage; do a cosmetic job on; vary 852.6

ADJS 4 **dissimilar**, unsimilar, unresembling, unresemblant; **unlike, unalike**, unidentical; **disparate**, diverse, divergent, **contrasting, different** 779.7; nonuniform 782.3; scarcely like, hardly like, a bit *or* mite different; **off**, a bit on the off side, offbeat <nf>; unmatched, odd, counter, out

5 **nothing like**, not a bit alike, not a bit of it, **nothing**

of the sort, nothing of the kind, something else, something else again <nf>, different as night from day, quite another thing, cast in a different mold, not the same thing at all; not so you could tell it *and* not that you would know it and **far from it** *and* far other <nf>; way off, away off, a mile off, way out, no such thing, no such a thing <nf>; "no more like than an apple to an oyster"—Sir Thomas More

6 **uncomparable**, not comparable, not to be compared, incomparable; incommensurable, uncommensurable, uncommensurate, incommensurate; unrelated, extraneous

ADVS 7 **dissimilarly, differently** 780.10, with a difference, disparately, contrastingly

788 AGREEMENT

NOUNS 1 **agreement, accord** 455, accordance; **concord**, concordance; **harmony, cooperation** 450, peace 464, *rapport* <Fr>, concert, consort, **consonance**, unisonance, **unison**, union, chorus, oneness; **correspondence**, coincidence, intersection, overlap, parallelism, symmetry, tally, equivalence 778.1; congeniality, compatibility, affinity; **conformity**, conformance, conformation, uniformity 780; congruity, congruence, congruency; **consistency**, self-consistency, coherence; synchronism, sync <nf>, timing; **assent** 332

2 **understanding**, entente; mutual *or* cordial understanding, consortium, *entente cordiale* <Fr>; **compact** 437

3 <general agreement> consensus, consentaneity, consentaneousness, *consensus omnium* <L, consent of all> and *consensus gentium* <L, consent of the people>, sense, **unanimity** 332.5; **likemindedness**, meeting *or* intersection *or* confluence of minds, sense of the meeting; family feeling; good vibrations <nf>

4 **adjustment, adaptation**, mutual adjustment, **compromise**, coaptation, arbitration, arbitrament; **regulation**, attunement, harmonization, **coordination**, accommodation, squaring, integration, assimilation; reconciliation, reconcilement, synchronization; consensus-building *or* -seeking

5 **fitness** *or* fittedness, **suitability, appropriateness**, propriety, admissibility; **aptness**, aptitude, qualification; **relevance** 775.4, felicity, appositeness, applicability

VERBS 6 **agree, accord** 455.2, **harmonize, concur** 332.9, have no problem with, go along with <nf>, **cooperate** 450.3, **correspond, conform**, coincide, parallel, intersect, overlap, **match**, tally, hit, register, lock, interlock, check <nf>, square, dovetail, jibe <nf>; **be consistent,** cohere, stand *or* hold *or* hang together, fall in together, fit together, chime, chime with, chime in with; **assent** 332.8, come to an agreement 332.10, be of one *or* the same *or* like mind, subscribe to, see eye to eye, sing in chorus, have a meeting of the minds, climb on the bandwagon; **go together,** go with, conform with, be uniform with, square with, sort *or* assort with, go on all fours with, consist with, register with, answer *or* respond to

7 <make agree> **harmonize,** coordinate, bring into line, accord, make uniform 781.4, equalize 790.6, similarize, assimilate, homologize; pull together; **adjust, set,** regulate, **accommodate, reconcile,** synchronize, sync <nf>; adapt, fit, tailor, measure, proportion, adjust to, trim to, cut to, gear to, key to; fix, **rectify,** true, true up, right, set right, make plumb; **tune,** attune, put in tune

8 suit, fit, suit *or* fit to a tee, fit like a glove, **qualify, do,** serve, answer, be OK <nf>, do thejob *and* do the trick *and* fill the bill *and* cut the mustard <nf>

ADJS **9 agreeing, in agreement; in accord, concurring,** positive, affirmative, in rapport, *en rapport* <Fr>, **in harmony,** in accordance, in sync <nf>, **at one,** on all fours, of one *or* the same *or* like mind, **like-minded,** consentient, consentaneous, **unanimous** 332.15, unisonous *or* unisonant; **harmonious,** accordant, **concordant,** consonant; **consistent,** self-consistent; uniform, coherent, conformable, of a piece, equivalent, **coinciding** 778.8, coincident, corresponding *or* correspondent; answerable, reconcilable; commensurate, proportionate; **congruous,** congruent; **agreeable,** congenial, compatible, cooperating *or* cooperative 450.5, coexisting *or* coexistent, symbiotic; **synchronized,** synchronous, synchronic; empathetic

10 apt, apposite, appropriate, suitable; applicable, relevant, pertinent, likely, sortable, seasonable, opportune; **fitting,** befitting, **suiting,** becoming; **fit,** fitted, qualified, **suited,** adapted, geared, tailored, dovetailing, meshing; **right,** just right, well-chosen, **pat,** happy, felicitous, just what the doctor ordered <nf>; to the point, to the purpose, *ad rem* <L>, *à propos* <Fr>, **apropos,** on the button *and* on the money <nf>, spot-on <Brit nf>

ADVS **11 in step,** in concert, **in unison,** in chorus, **in line, in conformity, in keeping,** hand in glove, just right; with it <nf>; **unanimously, as one, with one voice, harmoniously,** concordantly, consonantly, in synchronization, in sync <nf>, **by consensus;** agreeably, congenially, compatibly; fittingly

PREPS **12** in agreement with, together with, with, right with, in there with, right along there with; in line with, in keeping with; together on

PHRS **13** that's it, that's the thing, that's just the thing, that's the very thing, that's the idea *and* that's the ticket <nf>; right on <nf>; touché

789 DISAGREEMENT

NOUNS **1 disagreement, discord,** discordance *or* discordancy; **disaccord** 456, disaccordance, inaccordance; disunity, disunion; **disharmony,** unharmoniousness; dissonance, dissidence; **jarring,** clashing; **difference** 780, **variance,** divergence, diversity; **disparity,** discrepancy, inequality; antagonism, **opposition** 451, **conflict,** controversy, faction, oppugnancy, repugnance, dissension 456.3, argumentation 935.4; **dissent** 333, negation 335, contradiction; parting of the ways

2 inconsistency, incongruity, asymmetry, inconsonance, incoherence; **incompatibility,** irreconcilability, incommensurability; disproportion, disproportionateness, nonconformity *or* unconformity, nonconformability *or* unconformability, heterogeneity, heterodoxy, unorthodoxy, heresy; self-contradiction, paradox, antinomy, oxymoron, **ambiguity** 539.2, ambivalence, equivocality, equivocalness, mixed message *or* signal

3 unfitness, inappropriateness, unsuitability, impropriety; **inaptness,** inaptitude, **inappositeness, irrelevance** *or* irrelevancy, infelicity, uncongeniality, inapplicability, inadmissibility; abnormality, anomaly; **maladjustment,** misjoining, misjoinder; mismatch, mismatchment; misalliance, *mésalliance* <Fr>

4 misfit, nonconformist, individualist, inner-directed person, oddball <nf>; **freak,** sport, anomaly; naysayer, crosspatch, dissenter; a fish out of water, a square peg in a round hole <nf>

VERBS **5 disagree, differ** 780.5, vary, not see eye-to-eye, be at cross-purposes, tangle assholes <nf>, **disaccord** 456.8, **conflict,** clash, **jar,** jangle, jostle, collide, square off, cross swords, break, break off; **mismatch,** mismate, mismarry, misally; part company, split up; **dissent** 333.4, agree to disagree, object, **negate** 335.3, **contradict,** counter; be *or* march out of step, "hear a different drummer" —Thoreau

ADJS **6 disagreeing, differing** 780.7, **discordant** 456.15, disaccordant; dissonant, dissident; **inharmonious,** unharmonious, disharmonious; discrepant, disproportionate; divergent, variant; at variance, **at odds,** at war, at daggers drawn, at opposite poles, at loggerheads, at cross-purposes; **hostile,** antipathetic, antagonistic, repugnant;

inaccordant, out of accord, out of whack <nf>; **jarring,** clashing, grating, jangling; **contradictory, contrary; disagreeable,** cross, cranky, disputatious, ornery <nf>, negative, uncongenial, incompatible; immiscible <chem>

7 **inappropriate, inapt,** unapt, inapposite, misplaced, **irrelevant,** malapropos, *mal à propos* <Fr>; **unsuited,** ill-suited; **unfitted,** ill-fitted; **maladjusted,** unadapted, ill-adapted; ill-sorted, ill-assorted, ill-chosen; ill-matched, ill-mated, mismatched, mismated, mismarried, misallied; **unfit,** inept, unqualified; unfitting, unbefitting; **unsuitable,** improper, **unbecoming,** unseemly; infelicitous, inapplicable, inadmissible; **unseasonable, untimely,** ill-timed; **out of place,** out of line, out of keeping, out of character, out of proportion, out of joint, out of tune, out of time, out of season, out of its element

8 **inconsistent, incongruous, inconsonant,** inconsequent, incoherent, **incompatible,** irreconcilable; incommensurable, incommensurate; disproportionate, out of proportion, self-contradictory, paradoxical, oxymoronic, **absurd; abnormal,** anomalous; misfitting; ambivalent, ambiguous

9 **nonconformist,** individualistic, inner-directed, perverse; **unorthodox,** heterodox, heretical

PREPS 10 **in disagreement with, against,** agin <nf>, counter to, clean counter to, **contrary to,** in defiance of, in contempt of, in opposition to; out of line with, not in keeping with

WORD ELEMENTS 11 contra-, counter-, dis-, ill-, mal-, mis-

790 EQUALITY

NOUNS 1 **equality, parity,** par, equation, **identity** 778.1; equivalence *or* equivalency, convertibility, **correspondence,** parallelism, equipollence, coequality; **likeness,** levelness, evenness, coextension; **balance,** poise, equipoise, **equilibrium,** equiponderance; symmetry, proportion; level playing field; **justice** 649, equity, equal rights

2 **equating, equation; equalizing,** equilibration, evening, evening up; coordination, integration, accommodation, adjustment; **even break** *and* fair shake <nf>, affirmative action, equal opportunity

3 **the same** 778.3; **tie, draw, standoff** *and* Mexican standoff *and* wash *and* dead heat <nf>, stalemate, deadlock, impasse, neck-and-neck race, photo finish, even money; tied *or* knotted score, deuce; a distinction without a difference, six of one and half a dozen of the other, Tweedledum and Tweedledee

4 **equal, match,** mate, twin, fellow, **like, equivalent,** opposite number, counterpart, answer <nf>, vis à vis, equipollent, coequal, parallel, ditto <nf>; **peer,** compeer, colleague, peer group

VERBS 5 **equal, match, rival, correspond, be even-steven,** be tantmount to, be equal to; **keep pace with, keep step with, run abreast; amount to,** come to, come down to, run to, reach, touch; **measure up to,** come up to, stack up with <nf>, match up with; lie on a level with, **balance, parallel,** ditto <nf>; break even <nf>; **tie, draw,** knot; go shares, go halves, go Dutch

6 **equalize; equate; even,** equal out, equal, even up, even off, square, level, level out, level off, make both ends meet, synchronize; **balance,** strike a balance, poise, balance out, balance the accounts, balance the books; **compensate,** make up for, counterpoise; countervail, counterbalance, cancel; coordinate, integrate, proportion; fit, accommodate, adjust

ADJS 7 **equal, equalized,** like, **alike, even,** level, par, **on a par,** at par, at parity, au pair, commensurate, proportionate, flush; on the same level, on the same plane, on the same *or* equal footing; on terms of equality, **on even** *or* **equal terms,** on even ground; on a level, on a level playing field, on a footing, in the same boat; **square,** quits, zero-sum, even-steven <nf>; half-and-half, **fifty-fifty;** nip and tuck, **drawn, tied,** neck-and-neck <nf>, abreast, too close to call, deadlocked, stalemated, knotted

8 **equivalent, tantamount,** equiparant, equipollent, coequal, coordinate; **identical** 778.7; corresponding *or* correspondent; convertible, much the same, as broad as long, neither more nor less, **all one,** all the same, neither here nor there

9 **balanced, poised,** apoise, **on an even keel;** equibalanced, equiponderant *or* equiponderous

10 **equisized,** equidimensional, equiproportional, equispaced; equiangular, isogonic, isometric; equilateral, equisided; coextensive

ADVS 11 **equally, correspondingly, proportionately,** equivalently, **evenly; identically** 778.9; without distinction, indifferently; to the same degree, *ad eundem* <L>; as, **so;** as well; to all intents and purposes, other things being equal, *ceteris paribus* <L>; as much as to say

12 **to a standoff** <nf>, to a tie *or* draw

WORD ELEMENTS 13 co-, equi-, aequi-, homal-, is-, pari-

791 INEQUALITY

NOUNS 1 **inequality, disparity, unevenness, contrariety** 779, **difference** 780; **irregularity,** nonuniformity 782, heterogeneity; **disproportion,** asymmetry; **unbalance,** imbalance, disequilibrium, overbalance, inclination of the balance, overcompensation, tippiness; **inadequacy,** insufficiency, shortcoming; **odds,** handicap; **injustice,** inequity, tilting of the scales, unfair discrimination, second-class citizenship, untouchability; unfair advantage, loaded dice

VERBS **2 unequalize,** disproportion

3 unbalance, disbalance, disequilibrate, overbalance, overcompensate, **throw off balance,** upset, skew, destabilize

ADJS **4 unequal,** disparate, **uneven; irregular** 782.3; disproportionate, **out of proportion,** skew, skewed, asymmetric *or* asymmetrical; mismatched *or* ill-matched, ill-sorted; **inadequate,** insufficient; at a disadvantage

5 unbalanced, ill-balanced, overbalanced, off-balance, tippy, listing, heeling, leaning, canting, top-heavy, off-center; **lopsided,** slaunchways *and* cockeyed *and* skewgee *and* skygodlin <nf>, skew-whiff <Brit nf>; **unstable,** unsteady, tender <nautical>

ADVS **6 unequally,** disparately, disproportionately, variously, **unevenly;** nonuniformly 782.4

792 WHOLE

NOUNS **1 whole, totality, entirety,** collectivity; complex; integration, embodiment; **unity, integrity, wholeness;** organic unity, oneness; integer

2 total, sum, sum total, sum and substance, **the amount,** whole *or* gross amount, grand total; entity

3 all, the whole, the entirety, everything, all the above *or* all of the above <nf>, the aggregate, the assemblage, one and all, all and sundry, each and every <nf>, complete works; **package,** set, complement, package deal; **the lot,** the corpus, all she wrote <nf>, **the ensemble; be-all,** be-all and end-all, beginning and end, "alpha and omega"—Bible, A to Z, A to izzard, the whole range *or* spectrum, length and breadth, sum and substance; everything from soup to nuts *and* everything but the kitchen sink <nf>; grand design, world view, big picture

4 <nf terms> **whole bunch, whole mess, whole caboodle, the kit and caboodle, whole kit and caboodle,** whole kit and boodle, whole bit *or* shtick, whole megillah, **whole shooting match,** whole hog, whole animal <old>, **whole deal,** whole schmear, **whole shebang,** whole works, the works, the full monty <Brit nf>, whole ball of wax, whole show, whole nine yards

5 wholeness, totality, **completeness** 794, **unity, fullness,** inclusiveness, exhaustiveness, comprehensiveness; holism, holistic *or* total approach; universality

6 major part, best part, better part, **most; majority,** generality, plurality; **bulk, mass,** body, main body;

lion's share; **substance,** gist, meat, essence, thrust, gravamen

VERBS **7 form** *or* **make a whole,** constitute a whole; **integrate,** unite, form a unity

8 total, amount to, come to, run to *or* **into,** mount up to, add up to, tot *or* tot up to <nf>, tote *or* tote up to <nf>, reckon up to <nf>, aggregate to; aggregate, unitize; **number, comprise,** contain, encompass

ADJS **9** <not partial> **whole, total, entire,** aggregate, gross, all; integral, integrated; **one,** one and indivisible; **inclusive,** all-inclusive, **exhaustive,** comprehensive, omnibus, all-embracing, across-the-board, global; holistic; universal

10 intact, untouched, undamaged 1002.8, all in one piece <nf>, unimpaired, virgin, pristine, unspoiled, pure

11 undivided, uncut, unsevered, unclipped, uncropped, unshorn; **undiminished,** unreduced, complete

12 unabridged, uncondensed, unexpurgated

ADVS **13** <not partially> **wholly, entirely,** all; **totally,** *in toto* <L>, from start to finish, from soup to nuts <nf>, from A to Z, from A to izzard, across the board; **altogether, all put together,** in its entirety, *tout ensemble* <Fr>; **in all,** on all counts, in all respects, at large; **as a whole, in the aggregate,** in the lump, in the gross, in bulk, in the mass, *en masse* <Fr>, *en bloc* <Fr>; **collectively, corporately,** bodily, in a body, as a body; lock, stock, and barrel; hook, line, and sinker

14 on the whole, in the long run, over the long haul, all in all, to all intents and purposes, on balance, **by and large, in the main, mainly, mostly, chiefly,** substantially, essentially, effectually, **for the most part,** almost entirely, for all practical purposes, **virtually;** approximately, nearly, all but

WORD ELEMENTS **15** pan-, pant-, panta-, coen-

793 PART

NOUNS **1 part, portion, fraction;** percentage; **division** 802.1; **share,** parcel, dole, quota, piece *or* piece of the action <nf>; cut *and* slice *and* vigorish <nf>; **section,** sector, **segment;** quarter, quadrant; **item,** detail, particular; installment; **subdivision,** subset, subgroup, subspecies; detachment, contingent; **cross section,** sample, random sample, sampling; **component** 796.2, module, constituent, ingredient; **adjunct** 254; **remainder** 256; minority

2 <part of writing> section, front *or* back matter, prologue, epilogue, foreword, preface, introduction, afterword, text, chapter, verse, article; sentence, clause, phrase, segment, string, constituent, paragraph, passage; number, book, fascicle; sheet, folio, page, signature, gathering

3 piece, particle, bit, scrap 248.3, bite, **fragment, morsel, crumb,** shard, potsherd, snatch, snack, appetizer; **cut,** cutting, clip, clipping, paring, shaving, rasher, snip, snippet, chip, slice, collop, dollop, scoop; **tatter, shred,** stitch; **splinter,** sliver; **shiver, smithereen** <nf>; **lump,** gob <nf>, gobbet, **hunk, chunk; stump,** butt, end, butt-end, fag-end, tail-end; modicum 248.2, moiety; bits and pieces, odds and ends; sound bite, outtake

4 member, organ; appendage; **limb; branch,** imp, bough, twig, sprig, spray, switch; runner, tendril; **off-shoot,** ramification, scion, spur; **arm** 906.5, **leg,** tail; hand 474.4; **wing,** pinion, lobe, lobule, hemisphere; facet, feature, integrant, integral part

5 dose, portion; slug *and* shot *and* nip *and* snort *and* dram <nf>; helping

VERBS **6 separate,** apportion, share, share out, distribute, cut, cut up, slice, slice up, divide 802.18; **analyze** 800.6

ADJS **7 partial,** part; **fractional,** sectional, componential, partitive; segmentary, segmental, modular; **fragmentary;** incomplete 794.4, open-ended

ADVS **8 partly, partially,** part, **in part**

9 piece by piece, bit by bit, part by part, **little by little,** inch by inch, foot by foot, drop by drop; **piecemeal,** piecewise, bitwise, inchmeal, by inchmeal; **by degrees,** by inches; **by** *or* **in snatches,** by *or* in installments, in lots, in small doses, in driblets, in dribs and drabs; in detail

WORD ELEMENTS **10** organo-; chir-; ali-, pter-, pterus-, pteryg-

794 COMPLETENESS

NOUNS **1 completeness, totality; wholeness** 792.5, **entireness, entirety; unity,** integrity, integrality, undividedness, intactness, untouchedness, unbrokenness; solidity, solidarity; **thoroughness,** exhaustiveness, unstintedness, inclusiveness, comprehensiveness, universality; pervasiveness, ubiquity, omnipresence; **universe,** cosmos, plenum

2 fullness, full; **amplitude, plenitude;** impletion, **repletion,** plethora; saturation, saturation point, satiety, congestion

3 full measure, fill, full house; max <nf>; **load, capacity, complement,** lading, **charge;** the whole bit <nf>; bumper, brimmer; bellyful *and* snootful <nf>, skinful *or* mouthful <nf>; **crush,** cram <nf>, jam-up <nf>

4 completion, fulfillment, consummation, culmination, perfection, realization, actualization, fruition, **accomplishment** 407, topping-off, closure

5 limit, end 820, **extremity,** extreme, **acme,** apogee, climax, **maximum,** max <nf>, ceiling, **peak,** summit, **pinnacle,** crown, top; **utmost,** uttermost, utmost extent, highest degree, nth degree *or* power, *ne plus ultra* <L>; **all, the whole** 792.3,4, the whole hog <nf>

VERBS **6** <make whole> **complete,** bring to completion *or* fruition, mature; **fill in, fill out,** piece out, top off, eke *or* eke out, round out; **make up,** make good, replenish, refill; **accomplish** 407.4, fulfill

7 fill, charge, load, lade, freight, weight; **stuff, wad,** pad, **pack,** crowd, **cram,** jam, jam-pack, ram in, chock; **fill up,** fill to the brim, brim, top up *or* top off, fill to overflowing, fill the measure of; supercharge, saturate, satiate, congest; overfill 993.15, make burst at the seams, surfeit

8 <be thorough> **go to all lengths, go all out, go the limit** <nf>, go the whole way, **go the whole hog** <nf>, cover a lot of ground, make a federal case of *and* make a big deal of *and* do up brown *and* do with a vengeance <nf>, **see it through** <nf>, follow out *or* up, follow *or* prosecute to a conclusion; leave nothing undone, not overlook a bet *and* use every trick in the book <nf>; **move heaven and earth, leave no stone unturned;** put the finishing touches to

ADJS **9 complete, whole, total,** global, **entire,** intact, solid; **full, full-fledged,** full-dress, **full-scale;** full-grown, mature, matured, ripe, developed; **uncut,** unabbreviated, undiminished, unexpurgated

10 thorough, thoroughgoing, thorough-paced, exhaustive, intensive, broad-based, wall-to-wall <nf>, house-to-house *and* door-to-door <nf>, A-to-Z, comprehensive, all-embracing, all-encompassing, omnibus, radical, sweeping; **pervasive,** all-pervading, ubiquitous, omnipresent, **universal; unmitigated, unqualified, unconditional,** unrestricted, unreserved, **all-out,** wholesale, whole-hog <nf>; **out-and-out, through-and-through,** outright, downright, straight; congenital, born, **consummate,** unmitigated, unalloyed, perfect, veritable, egregious, deep-dyed, dyed-in-the-wool; **utter, absolute, total; sheer,** clear, clean, **pure,** plumb <nf>, **plain,** regular <nf>

11 full, filled, **replete,** plenary, capacity, flush, round; **brimful,** brimming; **chock-full,** chock-a-block, chuck-full, **cram-full,** topful, no room to spare; **jam-full, jam-packed, overcrowded;** stuffed, overstuffed, **packed, crammed,** *farci* <Fr>; **swollen** 259.13, bulging, bursting, bursting at the seams, ready to burst, full to bursting, fit to bust <nf>; as full as a tick, packed like sardines *or* herrings; standing room only *or* SRO; **saturated,** satiated, soaked; fully laden, coming out of one's ears; congested; overfull 993.20, surfeited

12 fraught, freighted, **laden, loaded, charged,** burdened; heavy-laden; full-laden, full-fraught, full-charged, super-charged

13 completing, fulfilling, filling; completive *or* completory, consummative *or* consummatory, culminative, perfective; **complementary,** complemental

ADVS **14 completely, totally,** globally, **entirely, wholly, fully,** integrally, roundly, **altogether,** hundred percent, **exhaustively,** inclusively, comprehensively, bag and baggage *and* lock, stock, and barrel <nf>; **unconditionally,** unrestrictedly, unreservedly, with no strings attached, no ifs, ands, or buts; **one and all;** outright, *tout à fait* <Fr>; **thoroughly,** inside out <nf>; in full, in full measure; to the hilt

15 absolutely, perfectly, quite, right, stark, clean, sheer, plumb <nf>, plain; irretrievably, unrelievedly, irrevocably

16 utterly, to the utmost, all the way, **all out,** flat out <Brit>, *à outrance* <Fr>, *à toute outrance* <Fr>, hammer and tongs *and* tooth and nail <nf>, **to the full, to the limit,** to the max <nf>, mondo <nf>, to the backbone, to the marrow, to the nth degree *or* power, to the sky *or* skies, to the top of one's bent, **to a fare-thee-well,** to a fare-you-well *or* fare-ye-well, to beat the band *or* the Dutch *and* nine ways to Sunday <nf>, with a vengeance, all hollow <nf>

17 throughout, all over, overall, **inside and out, through and through;** through thick and thin, down to the ground <nf>, **from the ground up,** from the word 'go' *and* from the git-go <nf>; **to the end** *or* **bitter end,** to the death; **at full length,** *in extenso* <L>, *ad infinitum* <L>; every inch, every whit, every bit; root and branch, head and shoulders, heart and soul; to the brim, to the hilt, neck deep, up to the ears, up to the eyes; **in every respect,** in all respects, you name it <nf>; **on all counts,** at all points, for good and all

18 from beginning to end, from start to finish, from end to end, **from first to last, from A to Z,** from A to izzard, from soup to nuts *and* from hell to breakfast <nf>, from cover to cover; **from top to bottom,** *de fond en comble* <Fr>; from top to toe, **from head to foot,** *a capite ad calcem* <L>, cap-a-pie; **from stem to stern,** from clew to earing, fore and aft; *ab ovo usque ad mala* <L, from eggs to apples>—Horace

WORD ELEMENTS **19** hol-, integri-, pan-, per-, tel-, teleut-

795 INCOMPLETENESS

NOUNS **1 incompleteness,** incompletion; **deficiency,** defectiveness, imperfection, **inadequacy;** underdevelopment, hypoplasia, **immaturity,** callowness, arrestment; **sketchiness,** scrappiness, patchiness; short measure *or* weight; lick and a promise

2 <part lacking> **deficiency,** want, **lack, need, deficit,** defect, **shortage,** shortfall, underage; wantage, outage, ullage, slippage; defalcation, arrearage, default; **omission,** gap, hiatus, hole, vacuum, break, lacuna, discontinuity, interval

VERBS **3 lack** 991.7, want, want for; fall short 910.2; be arrested, underdevelop, undergrow

ADJS **4 incomplete, uncompleted, deficient,** defective, unfinished, imperfect, unperfected, **inadequate; undeveloped,** underdeveloped, undergrown, stunted, hypoplastic, **immature,** callow, infant, arrested, embryonic, **wanting, lacking,** needing, missing, **partial,** part, failing; in default, in arrear *or* arrears; **in short supply,** scanty; **short,** scant, shy <nf>; **sketchy,** patchy, scrappy; left hanging

5 mutilated, garbled, hashed, **mangled, butchered,** docked, hacked, lopped, truncated, castrated, cut short; abridged

ADVS **6 incompletely, partially,** by halves, by *or* in half measures, in installments, in *or* by bits and pieces; **deficiently,** imperfectly, inadequately

WORD ELEMENTS **7** semi-, parti-

796 COMPOSITION
<manner of being composed>

NOUNS **1 composition,** constitution, construction, formation, fabrication, fashioning, shaping, organization; **embodiment,** incorporation, incarnation; **make, makeup,** getup *or* setup <nf>; **building,** buildup, structure, structuring, shaping-up; **assembly,** assemblage, putting *or* piecing together; synthesis, syneresis; **combination** 804; **compound** 796.5; **junction** 799.1; **mixture** 796

2 component, constituent, ingredient, integrant, makings *and* fixings <nf>, **element, factor, part** 792, player, module, part and parcel; appurtenance, adjunct 254; **feature,** aspect, specialty, circumstance, detail, item

VERBS **3 compose, constitute,** construct, fabricate; **incorporate,** embody, incarnate; **form, organize,** structure, shape, shape up; **enter into,** go into, go to make up; **make, make up, build,** build up, assemble, put *or* piece together; **consist of,** be a feature of, form a part of, combine *or* unite in, merge in; **consist,** be made up of, be constituted of, contain; **synthesize; combine** 804.3; **join** 799.5; **mix**

ADJS **4 composed of,** formed of, **made of,** made up of, made out of, compact of, consisting of; composing, comprising, constituting, including, inclusive of, containing, incarnating, embodying, subsuming; contained in, embodied in

5 component, constituent, modular, integrant, integral; **formative,** elementary

797 MIXTURE

NOUNS **1 mixture,** mixing, blending; **admixture,** composition, commixture, immixture, intermixture, **mingling,** minglement, commingling *or* comminglement, intermingling *or* interminglement, interlarding *or* interlardment; **eclecticism,** syncretism; **pluralism,** melting pot, multiculturism *or* multiculturalism, ethnic *or* racial *or* cultural diversity; **fusion,** interfusion, conflation; amalgamation, **integration,** alloyage, coalescence; **merger, combination** 804

2 imbuement, impregnation, infusion, suffusion, decoction, infiltration, instillment, instillation, permeation, pervasion, interpenetration, penetration; saturation, steeping, soaking, marination

3 adulteration, corruption, contamination, denaturalization, **pollution, doctoring** <nf>; fortifying, lacing, spiking <nf>; **dilution,** cutting <nf>, watering, watering down; debasement, bastardizing

4 crossbreeding, crossing, **interbreeding,** miscegenation; **hybridism,** hybridization, mongrelism, mongrelization; intermarriage

5 compound, mixture, admixture, intermixture, immixture, commixture, **composite, blend,** meld, composition, confection, concoction, **combination,** combo <nf>, ensemble, marriage; amalgam, alloy; paste, magma; cocktail

6 hodgepodge, hotchpotch, hotchpot; **medley, miscellany,** mélange, pastiche, *pasticcio* <Ital>, **conglomeration, assortment,** assemblage, mixed bag, ragbag, grab bag, olio, *olla podrida* <Sp>, **scramble, jumble,** mingle-mangle, **mix,** mishmash, **mess,** can of worms <nf>, dog's breakfast <Can nf>, mare's nest, rat's nest, hurrah's nest <nautical nf>, hash, patchwork, salad, gallimaufry, salmagundi, sundries, **potpourri,** stew, gumbo, sauce, slurry, omnium-gatherum, Noah's ark, **odds and ends,** oddments, all sorts, everything but the kitchen sink <nf>, all colors of the rainbow, broad spectrum, what you will

7 <slight admixture> **tinge, tincture, touch, dash, smack,** taint, tinct, tint, **trace,** vestige, hint, inkling, intimation, soupçon, suspicion, suggestion, whiff, modicum, thought, shade, tempering; sprinkling, seasoning, sauce, spice, infusion

8 hybrid, crossbreed, cross, mixed-blood, mixblood, **half-breed,** half-bred, half blood, half-caste; **mongrel,** cur; *ladino* <Sp>; mustee *or* mestee, *mestizo* <Sp>, *mestiza* <Sp fem>, *métis* <Fr>, *métisse* <Fr fem>; Eurasian; **mulatto,** high yellow <nf>, quadroon, quintroon, octoroon; sambo, zambo, *cafuso* <Brazil Pg>, Cape Colored <S Africa>, griqua <S Africa>; griffe; zebrule, zebrass, cattalo, mule, hinny, liger, tigon; tangelo, citrange, plumcot; alley cat

9 mixer, blender, beater, agitator, food processor, shaker; cement mixer, eggbeater, churn; homogenizer, colloid mill, emulsifier; crucible, melting pot

VERBS **10 mix,** admix, commix, immix, **intermix, mingle,** bemingle, commingle, immingle, **intermingle,** interlace, interweave, intertwine, interlard, intersperse, interleave; syncretize; **blend,** interblend, stir in; **amalgamate, integrate,** alloy, coalesce, **fuse, merge,** meld, compound, compose, conflate, concoct; **combine** 805.3; mix up, hash, stir up, **scramble,** conglomerate, shuffle, **jumble,** jumble up, mingle-mangle, throw *or* toss together, entangle; knead, work; homogenize, emulsify

11 imbue, imbrue, **infuse,** suffuse, transfuse, breathe, **instill,** infiltrate, **impregnate, permeate,** pervade, penetrate, leaven; **tinge, tincture,** entincture, temper, color, dye, flavor, season, dredge, besprinkle; **saturate,** steep, decoct, brew

12 adulterate, corrupt, contaminate, **debase,** infect, denaturalize, pollute, denature, bastardize, **tamper with, doctor** *and* doctor up <nf>; **fortify,** spike <nf>, pep up <nf>, lace; **dilute,** cut <nf>, water, water down <nf>

13 hybridize, crossbreed, cross, interbreed, miscegenate, mongrelize

ADJS **14 mixed, mingled,** blended, compounded, amalgamated; **combined** 805.5; **composite,** compound, **complex,** many-sided, multifaceted, intricate; **conglomerate,** pluralistic, multiracial, multicultural, multiethnic, multinational, heterogeneous, varied, **miscellaneous,** medley, motley, dappled, patchy, sundry, divers; promiscuous, indiscriminate, **scrambled, jumbled,** thrown together; half-and-half, fifty-fifty <nf>; amphibious; equivocal, **ambiguous,** ambivalent, ironic; syncretic, eclectic

15 hybrid, mongrel, interbred, **crossbred,** crossed, cross; **half-breed,** half-bred, half-blooded, half-caste

16 miscible, mixable, assimilable, integrable

PREPS **17 among,** amongst, 'mongst; **amid,** mid, amidst, midst, **in the midst of, in the thick of; with,** together with

798 SIMPLICITY
<freedom from mixture or complexity>

NOUNS **1 simplicity, purity,** simpleness, **plainness,** no frills, starkness, severity; unmixedness, monism; **unadulteration,** unsophistication, unspoiledness, intactness, fundamentality, elementarity, primitiveness *or* primitivity, primariness, naturalness; **singleness,** oneness, unity, integrity, homogeneity, uniformity 781; homeyness, unpretentiousness; unadornment

2 simplification, streamlining, refinement, purification, distillation; **disentanglement,** disinvolvement; uncluttering, unscrambling, unsnarling, unknotting; stripping, stripping away *or* down, paring down, narrowing, confining, bracketing; **analysis** 801; deconstruction

3 oversimplification, oversimplicity, oversimplifying; **simplism,** reductivism; intellectual childishness *or* immaturity, conceptual crudity

VERBS **4 simplify,** streamline, **reduce,** reduce to elements *or* essentials, factorize; purify, refine, distill; strip, strip down; narrow, confine, bracket, zero in <nf>; streamline; oversimplify; **analyze** 801.6

5 disinvolve, disintricate, unmix, disembroil, **disentangle,** untangle, **unscramble, unsnarl,** unknot, untwist, unbraid, unweave, untwine, unwind, uncoil, unthread, **unravel,** ravel; **unclutter,** clarify, clear up, disambiguate, sort out, get to the core *or* nub *or* essence

ADJS **6 simple, plain,** bare, bare-bones *and* no-frills <nf>, mere; **single,** uniform, homogeneous, of a piece; **pure,** simon-pure, pure and simple; **essential,** elementary, indivisible, **primary,** primal, primitive, prime, pristine, **irreducible, fundamental,** basic; undifferentiable *or* undifferentiated, undifferenced, monolithic; **austere,** chaste, unadorned, uncluttered, spare, stark, severe; homely, homespun, grass-roots, bread-and-butter, down-home *and* vanilla *or* plain-vanilla *and* white-bread <nf>; beginning, entry-level; common *or* garden, everyday; unpretentious; unadorned, natural

7 unmixed, unmingled, unblended, **uncombined,** uncompounded; unleavened; **unadulterated,** unspoiled, untouched, intact, virgin, uncorrupted, unsophisticated, unalloyed, untinged, undiluted, unfortified; **clear,** clarified, purified, refined, **distilled,** rectified; **neat, straight,** absolute, sheer, naked, bare

8 uncomplicated, uninvolved, incomplex, straightforward

9 simplified, streamlined, stripped down

10 oversimplified, oversimple; **simplistic,** reductive; intellectually childish *or* immature, conceptually crude

ADVS **11 simply, plainly, purely;** merely, barely; **singly, solely,** only, **alone,** exclusively, just, simply and solely

WORD ELEMENTS **12** hapl-

799 COMPLEXITY

NOUNS **1 complexity, complication, involvement,** complexness, involution, convolution, tortuousness, Byzantinism, *chinoiserie* <Fr>, tanglement, **entanglement,** perplexity, **intricacy,** intricateness, ramification, crabbedness, technicality, subtlety

2 complex, perplex <nf>, tangle, tangled skein, **mess** *and* snafu *and* fuck-up <nf>, ravel, snarl, snarl-up; knot, Gordian knot; **maze,** meander, Chinese puzzle, **labyrinth;** webwork, mesh; **wilderness, jungle,** morass, quagmire; Rube Goldberg contraption, Heath Robinson device <Brit>, wheels within wheels; mare's nest, rat's nest, hurrah's nest <nautical nf>, can of worms <nf>, snake pit; hard nut to crack, riddle of the Sphinx, squaring the circle

VERBS **3 complicate, involve, perplex,** ramify; **confound, confuse,** muddle, **mix up,** mess up *and* ball up *and* bollix up *and* screw up *and* foul up *and* fuck up *and* snafu *and* muck up *and* louse up <nf>, implicate; **tangle,** entangle, embrangle, **snarl, snarl up,** ravel, knot, tie in knots

ADJS **4 complex, complicated,** many-faceted, multifarious, ramified, perplexed, **confused,** confounded, **involved,** implicated, crabbed, **intricate,** elaborate, involuted, convoluted, multilayered, multilevel; **mixed up,** balled up *and* bollixed up *and* screwed up *and* loused up *and* fouled up *and* fucked up *and* snafued *and* mucked up *and* messed up <nf>; **tangled,** entangled, tangly, embrangled, **snarled,** knotted, matted, twisted, raveled; mazy, daedal, **labyrinthine,** labyrinthian, meandering; **devious,** roundabout, deep-laid, Byzantine, subtle

5 inextricable, irreducible, unknottable, unsolvable

800 JOINING

NOUNS **1 joining, junction,** joinder, jointure, **connection, union,** unification, bond, bonding, connectedness *or* connectivity, conjunction, conjoining, conjugation, liaison, marriage, hookup <nf>, splice, tie, tie-up *and* tie-in <nf>, knotting, entanglement, commerce; merger, merging; symbiosis; **combination** 805; conglomeration, **aggregation,** agglomeration, congeries; **coupling,** copulation, accouplement, coupledness, **bracketing,** yoking, pairing, splicing, wedding; **linking,** linkup, linkage, bridging, **concatenation,** chaining, articulation, agglutination; **meeting,** meeting place *or* point, confluence, convergence, concurrence, concourse, gathering, massing, clustering; communication, intercommunication, intercourse

2 **interconnection,** interjoinder, **interlinking,** interlocking, interdigitation; **interassociation,** interaffiliation

3 **fastening, attachment, affixation,** annexation; ligature, ligation, ligating; **binding,** bonding, gluing, sticking, tying, lashing, splicing, knotting, linking, trussing, girding, hooking, clasping, zipping, buckling, buttoning; knot <see list>; adhesive 803.4; splice, bond, fastener, Velcro

4 **joint,** join, joining, **juncture, union, connection,** link, connecting link, **coupling, accouplement;** clinch, embrace; articulation <anatomy and botany>, symphysis <anatomy>; **pivot, hinge; knee; elbow; wrist; ankle; knuckle; hip; shoulder; neck,** cervix; ball-and-socket joint, pivot joint, hinged joint, gliding joint; toggle joint; connecting rod, tie rod; seam, suture, stitch, closure, mortise and tenon, miter, butt, scarf, dovetail, rabbet, weld; boundary, interface

VERBS 5 **put together, join,** conjoin, **unite,** unify, bond, **connect,** associate, league, band, merge, **assemble,** accumulate; **join up,** become a part of, associate oneself, enter into, come aboard <nf>; **gather,** mobilize, marshal, mass, amass, **collect,** conglobulate; **combine** 805.3; **couple,** pair, accouple, copulate, conjugate, marry, wed, tie the knot <nf>, **link,** link up, build bridges, yoke, knot, splice, tie, chain, bracket, ligate; **concatenate,** articulate, agglutinate; glue, tape, cement, solder, weld; **put together,** fix together, lay together, piece together, clap together, tack together, stick together, lump together, roll into one; bridge over *or* between, span; **include,** encompass, take in, cover, embrace, comprise

6 **interconnect, interjoin,** intertie, interassociate, interaffiliate, **interlink,** interlock, interdigitate

7 **fasten, fix, attach, affix,** annex, put to, set to; graft, engraft; **secure,** anchor, moor; cement, knit, set, grapple, belay, **make fast;** clinch, clamp, cramp; tighten, trim, trice up, screw up; cinch *or* cinch up

8 **hook,** hitch; **clasp,** hasp, clip, snap; **button,** buckle, zipper; lock, latch; **pin,** skewer, peg, nail, nail up, tack, staple, toggle, screw, bolt, rivet; **sew,** stitch; **wedge,** jam, stick; rabbet, butt, scarf, mortise, miter, dovetail; batten, batten down; cleat; **hinge,** joint, articulate

9 **bind, tie,** brace, truss, **lash,** leash, rope, strap, lace, wire, chain; handcuff; **splice,** bend; **gird,** girt, belt, girth, girdle, band, cinch; **tie up,** bind up, do up, batten; **wrap,** wrap up, bundle; shrink-wrap; **bandage,** bandage up, swathe, swaddle

10 **yoke, hitch up,** hook up; harness, harness up; halter, bridle; saddle; tether, fetter

11 <be joined> **join, connect, unite, meet,** meet up, link up, merge, converge, **come together;** communicate, intercommunicate, network, interface; knit, grow together; cohere, adhere, hang *or* hold together, clinch, embrace

ADJS 12 **joint, combined,** joined, **conjoint,** conjunct, conjugate, corporate, compact, cooperative, cooperating; concurrent, coincident; inclusive, comprehensive; coherent

13 **joined, united, connected,** copulate, **coupled,** linked, knit, bridged, tight-knit, knitted, bracketed, associated, conjoined, incorporated, integrated, **merged,** gathered, assembled, accumulated, **collected; associated,** joined up, on board; **allied,** leagued, banded together; hand-in-hand, hand-in-glove, intimate, liaising; unseparated, undivided; **wedded,** matched, married, paired, yoked, mated; **tied, bound,** knotted, spliced, lashed

14 **fast, fastened, fixed,** secure, firm, close, tight, set, zipped up; **bonded,** glued, cemented, taped; **jammed,** wedged, stuck, frozen, seized, seized up

15 **inseparable,** impartible, **indivisible,** undividable, indissoluble, inalienable, inseverable, bound up in *or* with

16 **joining, connecting,** meeting; **communicating,** intercommunicating; **connective,** connectional; conjunctive, combinative, combinatorial, copulative, linking, bridging, binding

17 jointed, articulate

ADVS 18 jointly, conjointly, corporately, **together; in common,** in partnership, mutually, in concord; **all together,** as one, in unison, in agreement, in harmony; concurrently, at once, at *or* in one fell swoop

19 **securely, firmly, fast,** tight; **inseparably,** indissolubly

20 **knots**

anchor knot	constrictor knot
barrel knot *or* blood knot	crossing knot
becket knot	crown knot
Blackwall hitch	cuckold's neck
bow	diamond knot
bowknot	double hitch
bowline	Englishman's tie
bowline knot	eye splice
builder's knot	figure-eight knot
butcher's knot	figure-of-eight bend
carrick bend	fisherman's bend
cat's-paw	fisherman's knot
clinch	flat knot
clove hitch	Flemish knot

French shroud knot
German knot
granny knot
half crown
half hitch
half-Windsor knot
hangman's knot
harness hitch
hawser bend
hawser fastening
heaving-line bend
inside clinch
lanyard knot
long splice
loop knot
magnus hitch
manrope knot
marlinespike hitch
marling hitch
masthead knot
Matthew Walker knot
mesh knot
midshipman's hitch
monkey's fist
netting knot
open hand knot
outside clinch
overhand knot
prolonge knot
reef knot
reeving-line bend
ring hitch *or* lark's head

ring knot
rolling hitch
rope-yarn knot
round seizing
round turn and half hitch
running bowline
running knot
sennit knot
sheepshank
Shelby knot
short splice
shroud knot
single knot
slide knot
slipknot *or* nooseknot
square knot
star knot
stevedore's knot
stopper's knot
studding-sail halyard
 bend
stunner hitch
surgeon's knot
sword knot
tack bend
timber knot *or* hitch
truckman's knot
truelove knot
Turk's-head
wall knot
weaver's knot *or* hitch
Windsor knot

801 ANALYSIS

NOUNS **1 analysis,** analyzation, **breakdown,** breaking down, breakup, breaking up; anatomy, anatomizing, dissection; separation, **division, subdivision,** segmentation, reduction to elements *or* parts; chemical analysis, **assay** *or* assaying, resolution, titration, docimasy <old>, qualitative analysis, quantitative analysis, volumetric analysis, gravimetric analysis; ultimate analysis, proximate analysis; microanalysis, semimicroanalysis; profiling

2 itemization, enumeration, detailing, breakout, isolation; outlining, schematization, blocking, blocking out; resolution; scansion, parsing

3 classification, categorization, sorting, taxonomy, sorting out, sifting, sifting out, grouping, factoring, winnowing, shakeout, pigeonholing, categorizing; **weighing, evaluation,** gauging, assessment, appraisal, position statement *or* paper, **judgment** 946; impact statement

4 outline, structural outline, **plan,** scheme, schema, chart, flow chart, graph; table, table of contents, index; **diagram,** block diagram, exploded view, **blueprint; catalog,** *catalogue raisonné* <Fr>

5 analyst, analyzer, examiner 938.16; taxonomist
VERBS **6 analyze, break down,** break up, anatomize, dissect, atomize, unitize; **divide, subdivide,** segment; assay, titrate; separate, make discrete, isolate, reduce, reduce to elements, resolve

7 itemize, enumerate, factorize, number, detail, break out; **outline,** schematize, block out, diagram, graph, chart; resolve; scan, parse

8 classify, class, **categorize,** catalog, sort, sort out, sift, group, factor, winnow, thrash out; weigh, weigh up, **evaluate, judge,** gauge 946.9, assess, appraise 946.9

ADJS **9 analytical,** analytic; segmental; classificatory, enumerative; schematic
ADVS **10 analytically,** by parts *or* divisions *or* sections; by categories *or* types

802 SEPARATION

NOUNS **1 separation, disjunction,** severalty, disjointure, disjointing, split-up, splitting-up, demerger, delinkage, disarticulation, **disconnection,** disconnectedness, discontinuity, incoherence, disengagement, disunion, nonunion, disassociation, segregation; **parting,** alienation, estrangement, **removal,** withdrawal, isolation, detachment, sequestration, abstraction; **subtraction** 255; divorce, divorcement; **division,** subdivision, partition, compartmentalization, segmentation, marking off; districting, zoning; **dislocation,** luxation; separability, partibility, dividableness, divisibility; separatism; **separateness,** discreteness, singleness, monism, unitariness

2 severance, disseverment *or* disseverance, **sunderance,** scission, fission, cleavage, dichotomy, parting; **cutting, slitting,** slashing, **splitting,** slicing; **rending, tearing,** ripping, laceration, hacking, chopping, butchering, mutilation; section, resection; **surgery**

3 disruption, dissolution, abruption, cataclasm; revolution 860; **disintegration** 806, breakup, crack-up, shattering, splintering, fragmentizing, fragmentation; **bursting,** dissilience *or* dissiliency; **scattering,** dispersal, diffusion; **stripping,** scaling, exfoliation

4 break, breakage, **breach,** burst **rupture, fracture; crack,** cleft, **fissure, cut, split,** slit; slash, slice; **gap, rift,** rent, rip, tear; chip, splinter, scale; dividing line, caesura, solidus

5 dissection, analysis 801, vivisection, resolution, breakdown, diaeresis; anatomy

6 disassembly, dismantlement, taking down *or* apart, dismemberment, dismounting; undoing, unbuilding; **stripping,** stripping away *or* down, divestiture, divestment, defoliation, deprivation; disrobing, unclothing, doffing

7 **separator,** sieve, centrifuge, ultracentrifuge; creamer, cream separator; breaker, stripper, mincer; slicer, cutter, microtome; analyzer

VERBS 8 **separate, divide, disjoin, disunite,** draw apart, dissociate, disassociate, grow apart, **disjoint,** disengage, disarticulate, **disconnect;** uncouple, unyoke; **part,** cut the knot, **divorce,** estrange; **alienate, segregate,** separate off, factor out, sequester, isolate, curtain off, shut off, set apart *or* aside, split off, cut off *or* out *or* loose *or* adrift; **withdraw, leave, depart,** take one's leave, cut out *and* split <nf>; pull out *or* away *or* back, stand apart *or* aside *or* aloof, step aside; subtract 255.9; delete 255.12; **expel,** eject, throw off *or* out, cast off *or* out

9 **come apart,** spring apart, fly apart, come unstuck, come unglued, come undone, come apart at the seams, **come *or* drop** *or* fall to pieces, **disintegrate, come to pieces,** go to pieces, fall apart, fall apart at the seams, fall to pieces, atomize, unitize, fragmentize, pulverize, break up, bust up <nf>, unravel; come *or* fall off, peel off, carry away; get loose, give way, start

10 **detach, remove,** disengage, take *or* lift off, doff; **unfasten, undo,** unattach, unfix; **free, release,** liberate, loose, unloose, unleash, unfetter; **unloosen,** loosen; cast off, weigh anchor; **unhook,** unhitch, unclasp, unclinch, unbuckle, unbutton, unsnap, unscrew, unpin, unbolt; **untie,** unbind, unknit, unbandage, unlace, unzip, unstrap, unchain; unstick, unglue

11 **sever, dissever,** cut off *or* away *or* loose, shear off, hack through, hack off, ax, amputate; **cleave, split,** fissure; sunder, cut in two, dichotomize, halve, bisect; **cut,** incise, carve, **slice,** pare, prune, trim, trim away, resect, excise 255.10; slit, snip, lance, scissor; **chop, hew,** hack, **slash;** gash, whittle, butcher; saw, jigsaw; **tear, rend,** rive, rend asunder

12 **break, burst,** bust <nf>, breach; **fracture, rupture; crack,** split, check, craze, fissure; snap; chip, scale, exfoliate

13 **shatter, splinter,** shiver, break to *or* into pieces, fragmentize, break to *or* into smithereens <nf>; **smash,** crush, crunch, squash, squish <nf>; **disrupt,** demolish, break up, smash up; **scatter,** disperse, diffuse; **fragment,** fission, atomize; **pulverize** 1051.9, grind, cut to pieces, mince, make mincemeat of, make hamburger of <nf>

14 **tear *or* rip apart,** take *or* pull apart, **pick *or* rip** *or* **tear to pieces,** tear to rags *or* tatters, **shred,** rip to shreds; **dismember,** tear limb from limb, draw and quarter; **mangle,** lacerate, mutilate, maim; skin, flay, strip, peel, denude; defoliate

15 **disassemble,** take apart *or* down, tear down; **dismantle, demolish,** dismount, unrig <nautical>

16 **disjoint,** unjoint, **unhinge,** disarticulate, **dislocate,** luxate, throw out of joint, unseat

17 **dissect, analyze** 801.6, vivisect, anatomize, break down

18 **apportion, portion,** section, partition, compartmentalize, segment; **divide,** divide up, divvy *and* divvy up <nf>, **parcel,** parcel up *or* out, **split,** split up, cut up, subdivide; district, zone

19 **part company, part, separate,** split up, dispel, disband, scatter, **disperse,** break up, break it up <nf>, **go separate ways,** diverge

ADJS 20 **separate, distinct, discrete; unjoined, unconnected, unattached,** unaccompanied, unattended, unassociated; **apart,** asunder, **in two;** discontinuous, noncontiguous, divergent; **isolated,** insular, detached, detachable, free-standing, free-floating, autonomous; **independent,** self-contained, stand-alone <nf>; noncohesive, noncohering, incoherent 804.4; bipartite, dichotomous, multipartite, multisegmental; **subdivided,** partitioned, curtained-off, marked-off, compartmentalized

21 **separated,** disjoined, disjoint, disjointed, disjunct, **disconnected,** disengaged, detached, **disunited, divided,** removed, divorced, **alienated,** estranged, distanced, **segregated,** sequestered, isolated, cloistered, shut off; **scattered,** dispersed, helter-skelter; disarticulated, dislocated, luxated, out of joint

22 **unfastened, unbound,** uncaught, unfixed, **undone, loose, free,** loosened, unloosened, clear; **untied, unbound,** unknit, unleashed, unfettered, unchained, unlaced, unbandaged, unhitched; unstuck, unglued; unclasped, unclinched, unbuckled, unbuttoned, unzipped, unsnapped; unscrewed, unpinned, unbolted; **unanchored,** adrift, afloat, floating, free, free-floating

23 **severed, cut,** cleaved, cleft, cloven, riven, hewn, sheared; **splintered,** shivered, cracked, **split,** slit, reft; **rent, torn;** tattered, shredded, in shreds; quartered, **dismembered,** in pieces

24 **broken,** busted <nf>, **burst, ruptured,** dissilient; sprung; **shattered,** broken up, broken to pieces *or* bits, fragmentized, fragmentary, fragmented, in shards, in smithereens <nf>

25 **separating, dividing,** parting, distancing; separative, disjunctive

26 **separable,** severable, **divisible,** alienable, cleavable, partible; **fissionable,** fissile, scissile; dissoluble, dissolvable

ADVS 27 **separately,** severally, piecemeal, one by one; **apart,** adrift, asunder, **in two,** in twain; apart from, away from, aside from; abstractly, in the abstract, objectively, impersonally

28 disjointedly, unconnectedly, sporadically, spasmodically, discontinuously, by bits and pieces, by fits and starts

29 to pieces, all to pieces, **to bits, to smithereens** <nf>, to splinters, to shards, to tatters, to shreds

803 COHESION

NOUNS **1 cohesion,** cohesiveness, **coherence, adherence, adhesion, sticking,** sticking together, cling, clinging, binding, colligation, inseparability; cementation, conglutination, agglutination; concretion, condensation, accretion, solidification, set, congelation, congealment, clotting, coagulation, curdling; **conglomeration,** conglobation, compaction, agglomeration, consolidation; inspissation, incrassation; **clustering,** massing, bunching, nodality; colloidality, emulsification

2 consistency 788.1, connection, connectedness; junction 800.1; continuity, seriality, sequence 815, sequentialness, consecutiveness 812.1, orderliness

3 tenacity, tenaciousness, **adhesiveness,** cohesiveness, retention, adherence; **tightness,** snugness; stickiness, **tackiness,** gluiness, gumminess, **viscidity,** consistency, viscosity, glutinosity, mucilaginousness; gelatinousness, jellylikeness, gelatinity; pulpiness; persistence *or* persistency, **stick-to-itiveness** <nf>, toughness, **stubbornness, obstinacy 361,** bulldoggedness *or* bulldoggishness, bullheadedness

4 <something adhesive or tenacious> **adhesive,** adherent, adherer; **bulldog,** barnacle, leech, limpet, remora; burr, cocklebur, clotbur, bramble, brier, prickle, thorn; sticker, bumper sticker, decalcomania, decal <nf>; **glue, cement,** gluten, mucilage, epoxy resin, paste, stickum *and* gunk <nf>; gum; resin, tar; **plaster,** adhesive plaster, court plaster; putty, size; syrup, molasses, honey; mucus; thickener; pulper; fixative; tape, Scotch tape <trademark>, masking tape; Band-Aid <trademark>

5 conglomeration, consolidation, conglomerate, breccia <geology>, agglomerate, agglomeration, cluster, bunch, mass, clot; concrete, concretion; compaction

VERBS **6 cohere, adhere, stick, cling,** cleave, hold; **persist,** stay, stay put <nf>; cling to, freeze to <nf>; hang on, hold on; take hold of, clasp, grasp, hug, embrace, clinch; **stick together, hang** *or* **hold together;** grow to, grow together; **solidify, set,** conglomerate, agglomerate, conglobate; **congeal,** coagulate, clabber <nf>, **clot; cluster,** mass, bunch

7 be consistent 788.6, **connect,** connect with, follow; **join** 800.11, link up

8 hold fast, stick close, stick like glue, stick like a wet shirt *or* wet T-shirt *or* second skin, hug *or* mold to the figure; stick closer than a brother, stick like a barnacle *or* limpet *or* leech, cling like ivy *or* a burr, hold on like a bulldog

9 stick together, cement, bind, colligate, paste, glue, agglutinate, conglutinate, gum; **weld,** fuse, **solder,** braze; gum up <nf>

ADJS **10 cohesive,** cohering, coherent; adhering, **sticking, clinging,** inseparable, cleaving, holding together; **cemented,** stuck, agglutinative, agglutinated, agglutinate, conglutinate, conglutinated; **concrete, condensed, solidified, set, congealed,** clotted, coagulated; conglomerated, conglobate, **compacted, consolidated,** agglomerated; **clustered,** massed, bunched, nodal

11 consistent 788.9, **connected;** continuous 812.8, **serial,** uninterrupted, contiguous, sequential, sequent, **consecutive** 812.9; orderly, tight; **joined** 800.13

12 adhesive, adherent, stickable, self-adhesive, retentive; **tenacious,** clingy; **sticky, tacky,** gluey, gummy, gummous, glutenous, **viscid,** viscous, viscose, glutinous; inspissate, incrassate; colloidal; gooey *and* gunky <nf>; **persistent,** tough, **stubborn, obstinate** 361.8, bulldoggish *or* bulldogged *or* bulldoggy, bullheaded; stick-to-it-ive <nf>

804 NONCOHESION

NOUNS **1 noncohesion,** uncohesiveness, incoherence, inconsistency, discontinuity 813, nonadhesion, unadhesiveness, unadherence, untenacity, immiscibility; **separateness,** discreteness, aloofness, standoffishness <nf>; **disjunction** 802.1, unknitting, unraveling, dismemberment; **dislocation; dissolution, chaos** 810.2, anarchy, **disorder** 810, confusion, entropy; **scattering,** dispersion *or* dispersal; diffusion

2 looseness, slackness, bagginess, **laxness,** laxity, relaxation, floppiness; sloppiness, shakiness, ricketiness

VERBS **3 loosen, slacken, relax;** slack, slack off; ease, ease off, let up; **loose, free,** let go, unleash; **disjoin,** unknit, unravel, dismember, undo, unfasten, unpin; **sow confusion,** open Pandora's box; unstick, unglue; **scatter,** disperse, diffuse

ADJS **4 incoherent,** uncoherent, noncoherent, **inconsistent, uncohesive, unadhesive,** nonadhesive, noncohesive, nonadherent, like grains of sand, **untenacious, unconsolidated,** tenuous; unjoined 802.20, disconnected, unconnected, unraveled, dismembered, gapped, open; **disordered** 810.12, chaotic, anarchic, anomic, confused; **discontinuous** 813.4, broken, detached, discrete, aloof, standoffish <nf>

5 **loose, slack, lax, relaxed,** easy, sloppy; shaky, rickety; flapping, streaming; loose-fitting, hanging, drooping, dangling; bagging, baggy

805 COMBINATION

NOUNS 1 **combination,** combine, combo <nf>, composition; **union, unification,** marriage, wedding, coupling, accouplement, linking, linkage, yoking; **incorporation,** aggregation, agglomeration, conglomeration, congeries; **amalgamation, consolidation,** assimilation, **integration,** solidification, **encompassment,** inclusion, ecumenism; **junction** 800.1; conjunction, conjugation; **alliance,** affiliation, reaffiliation, **association** 617, **merger,** league, hookup <nf>, tie-up <nf>; **taking** 480, buyout, takeover, leveraged buyout; **federation, confederation,** confederacy; collaboration; federalization, centralization, cartel; **fusion,** blend, blending, meld, melding; coalescence, coalition; **synthesis,** syncretism, syneresis; syndication; **conspiracy,** cabal, junta; *enosis* <Gk>, *Anschluss* <Ger>; package, package deal; collection; **agreement** 788; **addition** 253

2 **mixture** 797, **compound** 797.5

VERBS 3 **combine, unite, unify,** marry, wed, couple, link, yoke, yoke together; **incorporate, amalgamate, consolidate,** assimilate, **integrate,** solidify, coalesce, compound, put *or* lump together, roll into one, come together, make one, unitize; **connect, join** 800.5; **mix; add** 253.4; **merge,** meld, **blend,** stir in, merge *or* blend *or* meld *or* shade into, **fuse,** flux, melt into one, conflate; interfuse, interblend; **encompass,** include, comprise; **take,** take over, buy out; **synthesize,** syncretize; syndicate; reembody

4 **league, ally, affiliate, associate,** consociate; unionize, organize, cement a union; **federate, confederate,** federalize, centralize; **join forces,** join *or* unite with, join *or* come together, join up with <nf>, hook up with <nf>, tie up *or* in with <nf>, **throw in with** <nf>, stand up with, go *or* be in cahoots <nf>, **pool one's interests, join fortunes with,** stand together, close ranks, make common cause with; **marry, wed, couple, yoke,** yoke together, link; **band together,** club together, bunch, bunch up <nf>, gang up <nf>, gang, club; team with, **team up with** <nf>, couple, pair, double up, buddy up <nf>, pair off, partner; go in partnership, go in partners <nf>; **conspire,** cabal, put heads together

ADJS 5 **combined, united, amalgamated, incorporated, consolidated, integrated,** assimilated, one, unitary, unitive, unitized, **joined** 799.13, joint 800.12, conjoint; conjunctive, combinative *or* combinatory, connective, conjugate; **merged,** blended, fused; **mixed; synthesized,** syncretized, syncretistic, eclectic

6 **leagued,** enleagued, **allied, affiliated,** affiliate, **associated,** associate, corporate; federated, confederated, federate, confederate; **in league,** in cahoots <nf>, in with; **conspiratorial,** cabalistic; partners with, in partnership; teamed, coupled, paired, married, wed, wedded, yoked, yoked together, linked, linked up

7 **combining, uniting,** unitive, unitizing, incorporating; merging, blending, fusing; combinative, combinatory; associative; federative, federal; corporative, incorporative, corporational; coalescent, symphystic

806 DISINTEGRATION

NOUNS 1 **disintegration, decomposition, dissolution, decay,** coming-apart, resolution, disorganization, degradation, breakup, breakdown, fragmentation, atomization; corruption; ruin, **ruination,** destruction 395; **erosion,** corrosion, crumbling, dilapidation, wear, wear and tear, waste, wasting, wasting away, ablation, ravagement, ravages of time; **disjunction** 802.1; **incoherence** 803.1; **impairment** 393

2 dissociation; electrolysis, catalysis, dialysis, hydrolysis, proteolysis, thermolysis, photolysis <all chemistry>, catabolism; catalyst, hydrolyst <chemistry>; hydrolyte <chemistry>; **decay,** fission <physics>, splitting, atom smashing

VERBS 3 **disintegrate, decompose, decay,** biodegrade, dissolve, come apart, disorganize, **break up** 395.22, go to rack and ruin 395.24, crack up, disjoin, unknit, split, fission, atomize, **come** *or* **fall to pieces; erode,** corrode, ablate, consume, wear *or* waste away, molder, molder away, crumble, crumble into dust

4 <chemical terms> dissociate; catalyze, dialyze, hydrolyze, electrolyze, photolyze; split, fission, atomize

ADJS 5 **disintegrative,** decomposing, disintegrating, disruptive, disjunctive; **destructive,** ruinous 395.26; chaotic; **erosive,** corrosive, ablative; resolvent, solvent, separative; **dilapidated,** disintegrated, ruinous, shacky, worn-out, worn, clapped-out <Brit nf>, moldering, ravaged, wrecked, totaled <nf>; disintegrable, decomposable, degradable, biodegradable

6 <chemical terms> dissociative; catalytic, dialytic,

hydrolytic, proteolytic, thermolytic, electrolytic, photolytic; catabolic

WORD ELEMENTS 7 -lysis, lyso-, lysi-, -lyte

807 ORDER

NOUNS 1 **order, arrangement** 808; **organization** 808.2; **disposition,** disposal, deployment, marshaling; prioritization, putting in order; **formation, structure, configuration,** array, makeup, lineup, setup, layout; system, scheme, schedule; routine, even tenor, standard operating procedure; **peace,** quiet, quietude, **tranquillity; regularity,** uniformity 781; symmetry, proportion, concord, **harmony,** order, the music of the spheres, Tao or Dào

2 **continuity,** logical order, serial order, reverse order, ascending or descending order, alphabetical order, numerical order; **degree** 245; **hierarchy,** pecking order, ontology, **gradation,** subordination, superordination, rank, place, position, status; progression; **sequence** 815; category, class

3 **orderliness, trimness, tidiness, neatness;** good shape <nf>, good condition, fine fettle, good trim, apple-pie order <nf>, a place for everything and everything in its place; **discipline,** method, methodology, methodicalness, system, systematicness; anality, compulsiveness, compulsive neatness

VERBS 4 **order, arrange** 808.8, get it together <nf>, **organize, regulate;** dispose, deploy, marshal; form, form up, configure, structure, array, pull it together, get or put one's ducks in a row <nf>, straighten it out, get or put one's house in order, run a tight ship, line up, set up, lay out; **pacify,** quiet, cool off or down <nf>, **tranquilize; regularize,** harmonize; **systematize,** methodize, normalize, standardize, routinize; hierarchize, categorize, classify, grade, rank, prioritize

5 **form, take form,** take order, **take shape,** crystallize, **shape up;** arrange or range itself, place itself, take its place, fall in, **fall or drop into place,** fall into line or order or series, fall into rank, take rank; come together, draw up, gather around, rally round; put to rights, whip into shape

ADJS 6 **orderly,** ordered, **regular, well-regulated, well-ordered, methodical, formal,** regular as clockwork, punctilious, uniform 780.5, **systematic,** symmetrical, **harmonious;** businesslike, routine, steady, normal, habitual, usual, en règle, in hand; **arranged** 808.14; scientific, businesslike; hierarchical, taxonomic, ontological

7 in order, in trim, to rights and in apple-pie order <nf>; **in condition,** in good condition, in kilter or kelter <nf>, in shape, in good shape <nf>, in

perfect order, in good form, in fine fettle, in good trim, in the pink <nf>, in the pink of condition; **in repair,** in commission, in adjustment, in working order, fixed; up to scratch or snuff <nf>

8 **tidy, trim, natty, neat,** spruce, sleek, slick and slick as a whistle <nf>, smart, trig, dinky <Brit nf>, snug, tight, **shipshape,** shipshape and Bristol fashion; **well-kept,** well-kempt, well-cared-for, well-groomed; neat as a button or pin <nf>, not a hair out of place

ADVS 9 **methodically, systematically, regularly,** through channels, uniformly, harmoniously, like clockwork

10 **in order, in turn, in sequence, in succession,** hierarchically, in series, seriatim <L>; step by step, by stages

808 ARRANGEMENT
<putting in order>

NOUNS 1 **arrangement, ordering,** structuring, shaping, forming, configurating, configuration, constitution; **disposition, disposal, deployment,** placement, marshaling, **arraying; distribution,** collation, collocation, allocation, allotment, apportionment; **formation,** formulation, **configuration,** form, array; regimentation; syntax; **order** 807

2 **organization, methodization,** ordering, planning, charting, codification, regulation, regularization, routinization, normalization, rationalization; **adjustment,** harmonization, tuning, fine-tuning, tune-up, tinkering; **systematization,** ordination, coordination

3 **grouping, classification** 809, categorization, taxonomy; **gradation,** subordination, superordination, **ranking,** placement; **sorting,** sorting out, assortment, sifting, screening, triage, culling, selection, shakeout

4 **table,** code, digest, **index, inventory,** census; table of organization

5 **arranger, organizer,** coordinator, spreadsheet; **sorter,** sifter, **sieve,** riddle, **screen,** bolter, colander, grate, grating

6 <act of making neat> **cleanup,** red-up <nf>; tidy-up, trim-up, police-up <nf>

7 **rearrangement, reorganization,** reconstitution, **reordering, restructuring,** perestroika <Russ>, shake-up <nf>; **redeployment,** redisposition, realignment

VERBS 8 **arrange,** order 807.4, reduce to order, **put or get or set in order,** right, prioritize, put first things first, get one's ducks in a row <nf>; **put or set to rights, get it together** <nf>, **pull it together,** put in or into shape, whip into shape <nf>, sort out <chiefly Brit>, unsnarl, make sense out of <nf>

9 **dispose, distribute, fix, place,** set out, collocate, allocate, **compose,** space, **marshal,** rally, array; align, line, **line up,** form up, range; regiment; **allot, apportion,** parcel out, deal, **deal out**

10 **organize,** methodize, **systematize,** rationalize, regularize, get *or* put one's house in order; **harmonize,** synchronize, **tune,** tune up; **regularize,** routinize, normalize, standardize; **regulate,** adjust, coordinate, fix, settle; **plan,** chart, codify

11 **classify** 809.6, **group,** categorize; grade, gradate, rank, subordinate; **sort,** sort out <chiefly Brit>, assort; **separate,** divide; collate; **sift,** size, sieve, **screen,** bolt, riddle

12 tidy, **tidy up,** neaten, trim, **put in trim,** trim up, trig up <chiefly Brit>, **straighten up,** fix up <nf>, **clean up,** police *and* police up <nf>, groom, spruce *and* spruce up <nf>, **clear up,** clear the decks

13 **rearrange, reorganize,** reconstitute, **reorder, restructure,** reshuffle, rejigger <nf>, tinker *or* tinker with, tune, tune up, fine-tune; **shake up,** shake out; redispose, redistribute, reallocate, realign

ADJS 14 **arranged, ordered, disposed,** configured, composed, constituted, fixed, placed, aligned, ranged, arrayed, marshaled, grouped, ranked, **graded;** organized, methodized, **regularized,** routinized, normalized, standardized, **systematized;** regulated, harmonized, synchronized; **classified** 809.8, categorized, **sorted,** assorted; **orderly** 807.6

15 **organizational,** formational, structural

WORD ELEMENTS 16 tax-, taxi-, -taxia, -taxis

809 CLASSIFICATION

NOUNS 1 **classification, categorization,** classing, placement, ranging, **pigeonholing,** compartmentalizing, **sorting, grouping; grading,** stratification, ranking, rating, classing; division, subdivision; **cataloging,** codification, tabulation, rationalization, indexing, filing; **taxonomy,** typology; ontology; analysis 801, **arrangement** 807

2 **class, category, head, order, division,** branch, set, **group,** grouping, bracket, pigeonhole; **section,** heading, rubric, **label,** title; **grade,** rank, rating, status, estate, stratum, level, station, position; **caste,** clan, race, strain, blood, kin, sept; **subdivision,** subgroup, suborder, subclass, subcategory, subset; hyponym, hypernym, superordinate, subordinate

3 **kind, sort, ilk, type,** breed of cat <nf>, lot <nf>, **variety, species, genus,** *genre* <Fr>, phylum,

denomination, designation, description, style, strain, manner, **nature, character,** persuasion, the like *or* likes of <nf>; **stamp, brand,** feather, color, stripe, line, grain, kidney; **make,** mark, label, shape, cast, form, mold, model; tribe, clan, race, strain, blood, kin, breed; league, realm, domain, sphere

4 **hierarchy,** class structure, power structure, pyramid, establishment, pecking order; natural hierarchy, order *or* chain of being, domain, realm, **kingdom,** animal kingdom, vegetable kingdom, mineral kingdom

5 <botanical and zoological classifications, in descending order> **kingdom;** subkingdom, **phylum** <zoology>, branch <botany>; superclass, **class,** subclass, superorder, **order,** suborder, superfamily, **family,** subfamily, tribe, subtribe, **genus,** subgenus, series, section, superspecies, **species;** subspecies, **variety,** subvariety, scion; biotype, genotype

VERBS 6 **classify,** class, assign, designate; **categorize,** type, put down as, **pigeonhole,** place, **group, arrange** 807.8, range; **order** 807.4, put in order, rank, rate, **grade; sort,** assort; distribute; **divide,** analyze 801.6, subdivide, break down; **catalog,** list, file, tabulate, rationalize, **index,** alphabetize, digest, codify

ADJS 7 **classificational,** classificatory; **categorical, taxonomic** *or* taxonomical, typologic *or* typological; ordinal; divisional, divisionary, subdivisional; ontological; **typical,** typal; **special,** specific, characteristic, particular, peculiar, denominative, differential, distinctive, defining, varietal

8 **classified, classed, cataloged, pigeonholed,** indexed, ordered, sorted, assorted, **graded, grouped,** ranked, rated, stratified, hierarchic, hierarchical, pyramidal; placed; filed, on file; tabular, indexical

ADVS 9 **any kind** *or* sort, **of any description, at all,** whatever, soever, whatsoever

WORD ELEMENTS 10 speci-, specie-, gen-

810 DISORDER

NOUNS 1 **disorder, disorderliness, disarrangement,** derangement, disarticulation, disjunction 802.1, **disorganization;** discomposure, **dishevelment, disarray,** upset, disturbance, discomfiture, disconcertedness; **irregularity,** randomness, turbulence, perturbation, ununiformity *or* nonuniformity, unsymmetry *or* nonsymmetry, no rhyme or reason, **disproportion, disharmony;** indiscriminateness, promiscuity, promiscuousness, haphazardness; **randomness,** randomicity, vagueness, trendlessness; entropy; **disruption** 802.3, destabilization; **incoherence** 804.1, unintelligibility; untogetherness <nf>;

disintegration 806; "most admired disorder"—
Shakespeare, "inharmonious harmony"—Horace

2 **confusion, chaos,** anarchy, misrule, license,
madhouse; **Babel,** cognitive dissonance; **muddle,**
morass, **mix-up** and foul-up and fuck-up and snafu
and screw-up <nf>, ball-up <nf>, balls-up <Brit
nf>, hoo-ha and fine how-de-do <nf>, pretty kettle
of fish, pretty piece of business, nice piece of work

3 **jumble, scramble, tumble, snarl-up, mess,** bloody
or holy or unholy or god-awful mess <nf>, pickle
<nf>, shemozzle <Brit>, **turmoil,** welter,
mishmash, hash, helter-skelter, farrago, crazy-quilt,
higgledy-piggledy; shambles, tohubohu; **clutter,**
litter, hodgepodge 797.6, rat's nest, mare's nest,
hurrah's nest <nautical>; topsy-turviness or topsy-
turvydom, arsy-varsiness, hysteron proteron

4 **commotion, hubbub, Babel, tumult,** turmoil,
uproar, racket, riot, **disturbance, rumpus** <nf>,
ruckus and ruction <nf>, disruption, **fracas,**
hassle, shemozzle <Brit nf>, shindy <nf>,
hullabaloo, rampage; **ado,** to-do <nf>, trouble,
bother, pother, dustup <Brit nf>, stir <nf>, **fuss,**
brouhaha, foofaraw <nf>, aggro <Brit, Austral>;
row and hassle <nf>, **brawl,** free-for-all <nf>,
donnybrook or donnybrook fair, broil,
embroilment, melee, scramble; helter-skelter, pell-
mell, **roughhouse, rough-and-tumble**

5 **pandemonium, hell, bedlam,** witches' Sabbath,
Babel, confusion of tongues; **cacophony,** din,
noise, static, racket

6 slovenliness, **slipshodness,** carelessness,
negligence; **untidiness,** uneatness, looseness,
messiness <nf>, **sloppiness,** dowdiness, seediness,
shabbiness, tawdriness, chintziness <nf>,
shoddiness, tackiness <nf>, grubbiness <nf>,
frowziness, blowziness; **slatternliness,**
frumpishness <nf>, sluttishness; **squalor,**
squalidness, sordidness; derangement

7 **slob** <nf>, **slattern, sloven,** frump <nf>, sloppy
Joe, schlep, schlump; drab, **slut, trollop; pig,**
swine; **litterbug**

VERBS **8** lapse into disorder, fall into confusion,
come apart, come apart at the seams, dissolve into
chaos, slacken 804.3, come unstuck or unglued
<nf>, disintegrate 806.3, degenerate, detune,
untune

9 **disorder, disarrange** 811.2, **disorganize,** dishevel;
confuse 811.3, sow confusion, open Pandora's box,
muddle, jumble, jumble up, mix up; **discompose**
811.4, **upset,** destabilize, unsettle, **disturb,** perturb

10 **riot, roister,** roil, carouse; **create a disturbance,**
make a commotion, make trouble, cause a stir or
commotion, **make an ado** or to-do, create a riot,
cut loose, run wild, run riot, run amok, go on a
rampage, go berserk

11 <nf terms> **kick up a row,** kick up a shindy or a
fuss or a storm, piss up a storm, **raise the devil,**
raise the deuce or dickens, raise a rumpus or a
storm, raise a ruckus, raise Cain, **raise hell,** raise
sand, raise the roof, whoop it up, hell around,
horse around or about; **carry on,** go on, maffick
<Brit>; **cut up,** cut up rough, roughhouse

ADJS **12** **unordered, orderless, disordered,**
unorganized, random, entropic, unarranged,
ungraded, unsorted, unclassified; untogether <nf>;
unmethodical, immethodical; **unsystematic,**
systemless, nonsystematic; disjunct, unjoined
802.20; disarticulated, **incoherent** 804.4;
discontinuous; **formless,** amorphous, inchoate,
shapeless; ununiform or nonuniform,
unsymmetrical or nonsymmetrical,
disproportionate, misshapen; **irregular, haphazard,**
desultory, **erratic,** sporadic, spasmodic, fitful,
promiscuous, indiscriminate, casual, frivolous,
capricious, random, hit-or-miss, vague, dispersed,
wandering, planless, undirected, **aimless,**
straggling, straggly; senseless, meaningless,
gratuitous

13 **disorderly, in disorder,** disordered, **disorganized,**
disarranged, discomposed, dislocated, deranged,
convulsed; **upset, disturbed,** perturbed, unsettled,
discomfited, disconcerted; **turbulent,** turbid, roily;
out of order, **out of place,** misplaced, shuffled; **out**
of kilter or kelter <nf>, **out of whack** <nf>, out
of gear, out of joint, out of tune, on the fritz <nf>,
haywire; **cockeyed** and skewgee and slaunchways
and skygodlin <nf>, skew-whiff <Brit nf>, awry,
amiss, askew, on the blink and haywire <nf>

14 **disheveled, mussed up** <nf>, messed up <nf>,
slobby <nf>, **rumpled,** tumbled, ruffled, snarled,
snaggy; **tousled,** tously; uncombed, shaggy,
matted; windblown

15 **slovenly, slipshod, careless, loose, slack,**
nonformal, negligent; **untidy, unsightly,** unneat,
slobby and scuzzy <nf>, **unkempt; messy** <nf>,
mussy <nf>, **sloppy** <nf>, scraggly, poky, seedy
<nf>, **shabby,** shoddy, schlocky <nf>, lumpen,
chintzy, grubby <nf>, **frowzy, blowzy,** tacky <nf>;
slatternly, sluttish, frumpish, frumpy,
draggletailed, drabbletailed, draggled, bedraggled;
down at the heel, out at the heels, out at the
elbows, in rags, ragged, raggedy-ass or ragged-ass
<nf>, raggedy, tattered; **squalid,** sordid;
dilapidated, ruinous, **beat-up** and shacky <nf>

16 **confused, chaotic,** anarchic, **muddled, jumbled,**
scattered, scatterbrained, helter-skelter <nf>,
higgledy-piggledy, hugger-mugger, skimble-
skamble, in a mess; **topsy-turvy,** arsy-varsy, upside-
down, ass-backwards <nf>; **mixed up, balled** or
bollixed up <nf>, **screwed up** <nf>, mucked up

<nf>, **fouled up** *and* fucked up *and* snafu *and* snafued <nf>; discomposed, discombobulated

ADVS **17 in disorder, in disarray, in confusion,** Katy bar the door <nf>, in a jumble, in a tumble, in a muddle, in a mess; higgledy-piggledy, helter-skelter <nf>, hugger-mugger, skimble-skamble, harum-scarum <nf>, willy-nilly <nf>, all over, all over hell <nf>, **all over the place, all over the shop** <nf>

18 haphazardly, unsystematically, unmethodically, irregularly, desultorily, **erratically,** capriciously, promiscuously, indiscriminately, **sloppily** <nf>, **carelessly,** randomly, **fitfully;** by *or* at intervals, sporadically, spasmodically, by fits, **by fits and starts,** by *or* in snatches, in spots <nf>; every now and then *and* every once in a while <nf>; **at random,** at haphazard, **by chance, hit** *or* **miss**

19 chaotically, anarchically, turbulently, **riotously; confusedly,** dispersedly, vaguely, wanderingly, **aimlessly,** planlessly, senselessly

811 DISARRANGEMENT
<bringing into disorder>

NOUNS **1 disarrangement, derangement,** misarrangement, convulsion, dislocation; **disorganization,** shuffling; **discomposure,** disturbance, perturbation, disconcertedness; **disorder** 810; insanity 926

VERBS **2 disarrange, derange,** misarrange; **disorder,** disorganize, disorient, throw out of order, put out of gear, dislocate, upset the apple-cart, **disarray; dishevel,** rumple, ruffle; tousle <nf>, muss *and* **muss up** <nf>, mess *and* **mess up** <nf>; **litter, clutter,** scatter

3 confuse, muddle, jumble, confound, garble, tumble, scramble, snarl, tie in knots, fumble, pi; **shuffle,** riffle; **mix up,** snarl up, **ball** *or* **bollix up** <nf>, **foul up** *and* fuck up *and* **screw up** *and* muck up *and* snafu <nf>; make a hash *or* mess of <nf>, play hob with <nf>; disrupt

4 discompose, throw into confusion, **upset, unsettle, disturb,** trip up, perturb, trouble, distract, throw <nf>, throw into a tizzy *or* snit *or* stew <nf>, agitate, convulse, embroil; **psych** *and* spook *and* bug <nf>; put out, inconvenience

ADJS **5 disarranged** 810.13, **confused** 810.16, **disordered** 810.12

812 CONTINUITY
<uninterrupted sequence>

NOUNS **1 continuity, uninterruption, uninterruptedness,** uninterrupted course, featurelessness, unrelievedness, monotony, unintermittedness, unbrokenness, **uniformity** 781, undifferentiation; fullness, plenitude; seamlessness, jointlessness, gaplessness, smoothness; **consecutiveness,** successiveness; continuousness, **endlessness, ceaselessness, incessancy;** constancy 847.2, continualness, constant flow; steadiness, steady state, equilibrium, stability 855

2 series, succession, run, **sequence,** consecution, progression, course, gradation; one thing after another; **continuum,** plenum; lineage, descent, filiation; **connection, concatenation,** catenation, catena, **chain,** chaining, linkup, articulation, reticulation, nexus; chain reaction, powder train; **train,** range, rank, **file, line, string,** thread, queue, **row,** bank, tier; windrow, swath; single file, Indian file; array; **round, cycle,** rotation, routine, the daily grind <nf>, recurrence, periodicity, flywheel effect, pendulum; endless belt *or* chain, Möbius band *or* strip, *la ronde* <Fr>, endless round; gamut, spectrum, scale; drone, monotone, hum, buzz

3 procession, train, column, line, string, cortège; stream, steady stream; cavalcade, caravan, motorcade; **parade,** pomp; dress parade; promenade, review, march-past, flyover, flypast <Brit>, funeral; skimmington <Brit>; chain gang, coffel; mule train, pack train; queue, crocodile <Brit>

VERBS **4 continue,** be continuous, not stop, **connect, connect up, concatenate,** continuate, catenate, join 800.5, link *or* link up, **string together,** string, thread, chain *or* chain up, follow in *or* form a series, run on, maintain continuity

5 align, line, line up, string out, rank, array, range, arrange, get *or* put in a row

6 line up, get in *or* **get on line,** queue *or* queue up <Brit>, make *or* form a line, get in formation, get in line, **fall in,** fall in *or* into line, fall into rank, take rank, take one's place

7 file, defile, file off; **parade,** go on parade, promenade, march past, fly over, fly past <Brit>

ADJS **8 continuous,** continued, **continual,** continuing; **uninterrupted, unintermittent,** unintermitted, featureless, unrelieved, monotonous; **connected, joined** 800.13, linked, chained, concatenated, catenated, articulated; **unbroken,** serried, **uniform** 781.5, homogeneous, homogenized, cloned *or* clonish *and* cookie-cutter <nf>, undifferentiated, wall-to-wall *and* back-to-back <nf>, seamless, jointless, gapless, smooth, unstopped; unintermitting, unremitting; **incessant, constant,** steady, stable, **ceaseless,** unceasing, **endless,** unending, never-ending, **interminable,** perpetual, perennial; **cyclical,** repetitive, **recurrent,** periodic; straight, running, **nonstop; round-the-clock,** twenty-four-hour, all-hours; immediate, direct

9 consecutive, successive, successional, back-to-back <nf>, in order, running; progressive; **serial,** ordinal, seriate, catenary; sequent, **sequential;** linear, lineal, in-line; chronological

ADVS **10 continuously, continually; uninterruptedly, unintermittently; without cease,** without stopping, with every other breath, without a break, back-to-back *and* wall-to-wall <nf>, unbrokenly, gaplessly, seamlessly, jointlessly, **connectedly,** together, cumulatively, on end; unceasingly, **endlessly,** *ad infinitum* <L>, perennially, **interminably,** again and again, repeatedly, time after time, time and again, time and time again, repetitively, cyclically, monotonously, unrelievedly, week in week out, year in year out, year-round, on and on, at *or* on a stretch; round the clock, all day long, all the livelong day

11 consecutively, progressively, sequentially, successively, **in succession,** one after the other, back-to-back <nf>, **in turn,** turn about, turn and turn about; step by step; running, hand running <nf>; **serially,** in a series, *seriatim* <L>; **in a line,** in a row, in column, in file, in a chain, in single file, in Indian file

813 DISCONTINUITY
<interrupted sequence>

NOUNS **1 discontinuity,** discontinuousness, discontinuation, discontinuance, noncontinuance; **incoherence** 804.1, **disconnectedness,** disconnection, delinkage, decoupling, discreteness, **disjunction** 802.1; **nonuniformity** 782; irregularity, **intermittence,** fitfulness 851.1; brokenness; nonseriality, nonlinearity, non sequitur; incompleteness 795; episode, parenthesis; time lag, time warp; broken thread, missing link; digression, non sequitur, parenthesis

2 interruption, suspension, break, fissure, breach, gap, hiatus, lacuna, caesura, crevasse; **interval, pause,** interim 826, lull, cessation, letup <nf>, **intermission**

VERBS **3 discontinue, interrupt** 857.10, **break,** break off, **disjoin,** disconnect; disarrange 811.2; intermit 851.2; pause; digress

ADJS **4 discontinuous,** noncontinuous, unsuccessive, **incoherent** 804.4, nonserial, nonlinear, nonsequential, discontinued, **disconnected,** unconnected, unjoined 802.20, delinked, decoupled, *décousu* <Fr>, **broken;** nonuniform 782.3, irregular; broken, broken off, fragmentary, **interrupted,** suspended; disjunctive, discrete, discretive; **intermittent,** fitful 851.3, stop-and-go, on-again off-again; scrappy, snatchy, spotty, patchy, jagged; choppy, chopped-off, herky-jerky <nf>, jerky, spasmodic; episodic, parenthetic

ADVS **5 discontinuously, disconnectedly,** brokenly, fragmentarily; at intervals; **haphazardly** 810.18, randomly, occasionally, infrequently, now and then, now and again, intermittently, fitfully, **by fits and starts,** by fits, by snatches, by catches, by jerks, spasmodically, episodically, by skips, skippingly, *per saltum* <L>; willy-nilly, **here and there,** in spots, sporadically, patchily

814 PRECEDENCE
<in order>

NOUNS **1 precedence** *or* precedency, antecedence *or* antecedency, anteposition, anteriority, precession; the lead, front position, front seat, pole position, first chair; **priority,** preference, urgency; top priority, taking precedence, preemption; prefixation, prothesis; **superiority** 249; **dominion** 417.6; **precursor** 816; prelude 816.2; preliminaries, run-up *and* walk-up <nf>; preceding 165.1

VERBS **2 precede,** antecede, **come first,** come *or* go before, **go ahead of, go in advance,** stand first, stand at the head, **head,** head up <nf>, front, **lead** 165.2, take precedence, have priority, preempt; lead off, kick off, usher in; pilot, lead the way, blaze a trail, spearhead; head the table *or* board, sit on the dais; rank, outrank, rate; anticipate, foreshadow

3 <place before> prefix, preface, premise, prelude, prologize, preamble, introduce

ADJS **4 preceding,** precedent, **prior,** antecedent, anterior, precessional, **leading** 165.3; preemptive; **preliminary,** precursory, prevenient, prefatory, exordial, prelusive, preludial, proemial, preparatory, initiatory, propaedeutic, inaugural; **first, foremost,** headmost, **chief** 249.14

5 former, foregoing, erstwhile, one-time, late, previous; aforesaid, aforementioned, beforementioned, above-mentioned, aforenamed, forenamed, forementioned, said, named, same

ADVS **6 before** 216.12; above, hereinbefore, hereinabove, *supra* <L>, *ante* <L>

815 SEQUENCE

NOUNS **1 sequence,** logical sequence, **succession,** successiveness, consecution, **consecutiveness,** following, coming after, accession; descent, lineage, line, family tree; **series** 812.2, serialization; **order,** order of succession; **priority; progression,** procession, rotation; **continuity** 812; **continuation,** prolongation, extension, posteriority; suffixation, subjunction, postposition; subsequence, sequel

VERBS **2 succeed, follow, ensue,** come *or* go after, **come next; inherit,** take the mantle of, step into the shoes *or* place of, take over; segue; tailgate, follow on the heels of, tail <nf>

3 <place after> suffix, append, subjoin

ADJS **4 succeeding, successive, following, ensuing,** sequent, sequential, sequacious, posterior, **subsequent,** consequent; proximate, **next;** appendant, suffixed, postpositive, postpositional; serial; progressive; tailgating

816 PRECURSOR

NOUNS **1 precursor, forerunner,** foregoer, *voorlooper* <Dutch>, vaunt-courier, avant-courier, front- *or* lead-runner; pioneer, *voortrekker* <Dutch>, frontiersman, bushwhacker; scout, pathfinder, explorer, point, point man, trailblazer *or* trailbreaker, guide; **leader** 574.6, leadoff man *or* woman, bellwether, fugleman; **herald,** announcer, *buccinator* <L>, messenger, harbinger, stormy petrel; **predecessor,** forebear, precedent, antecedent, **ancestor; vanguard, avant-garde,** avant-gardist, innovator, groundbreaker

2 curtain raiser, countdown, run-up *and* walk-up <nf>, lead-in, warm-up, kickoff, opening gun *or* shot; **opening episode,** first episode, prequel; **prelude, preamble, preface,** prologue, foreword, introduction, *avant-propos* <Fr>, protasis, proem, proemium, prolegomenon *or* prolegomena, exordium; **prefix,** prefixture; frontispiece; **preliminary,** front matter; overture, voluntary, verse; premise, presupposition, postulate, prolepsis; **innovation, breakthrough** <nf>, leap

VERBS **3 go before, pioneer,** blaze *or* break the trail, break new ground, be in the van *or* vanguard; guide; **lead** 165.2, lead *or* show the way; **precede** 814.2; herald, count down, run up, lead in, forerun, usher in, introduce

ADJS **4 preceding** 814.4; preliminary, exploratory, pioneering, trailblazing, door-opening, kickoff, inaugural; **advanced,** avant-garde, original 337.5

817 SEQUEL

NOUNS **1 sequel,** sequela *or* sequelae, sequelant, sequent, sequitur, **consequence** 887.1; **continuation,** continuance, **follow-up** *or* **follow-through** <nf>, perseverance; caboose; **supplement,** addendum, appendix, back matter; postfix, suffix; postscript *or* PS, subscript, postface; postlude, **epilogue,** conclusion, peroration, codicil; refrain, chorus, coda; envoi, colophon, tag; afterthought, second thought, double take <nf>, *arrière-pensée* <Fr>, *esprit d'escalier* <Fr>; parting *or* Parthian

shot; last words, swan song, dying words, famous last words

2 afterpart, afterpiece; **wake,** trail, train, queue; **tail,** tailpiece, rear, rear end; tab, tag, trailer

3 aftermath, afterclap, afterglow, afterimage, aftereffect, side effect, by-product, spin-off, aftertaste; **aftergrowth,** aftercrop; **afterbirth,** placenta, secundines; afterpain

4 successor, replacement, backup, backup man *or* woman, substitute, stand-in; **descendant,** posterity, **heir,** inheritor

VERBS **5 succeed,** follow, come next, come after, come on the heels of; **follow through,** carry through, take the next step, drop the other shoe

818 BEGINNING

NOUNS **1 beginning, commencement, start,** running *or* flying start, starting point, square one <nf>, **outset,** outbreak, **onset,** oncoming; dawn; **creation, foundation, establishment, establishing, institution, origin,** origination, setting-up, setting in motion; **launching,** launch, launch *or* launching pad; alpha, A; **opening,** rising of the curtain; day one; first crack out of the box <nf>, leadoff, kickoff *and* jump-off *and* send-off *and* start-off *and* take-off *and* blast-off *and* git-go <nf>, the word 'go' <nf>; fresh start, new departure; **opening wedge,** leading edge, cutting edge, thin end of the wedge; entry level, bottom rung, bottom of the ladder, low place on the totem pole; daybreak

2 beginner, neophyte, tyro; newcomer 774.4, new arrival, Johnny-come-lately <nf>; entry-level employee, low man on the totem pole; entrant, **novice,** novitiate, probationer, catechumen; **recruit,** raw recruit, rookie <nf>; **apprentice,** trainee, learner, student; baby, infant, newborn; nestling, fledging; freshman 572.6; tenderfoot, greenhorn, greeny <nf>, initiate; debutant, deb <nf>; starter

3 first, first ever, prime, primal, primary, **initial,** alpha; **initiation,** initialization, first move, opening move, gambit, **first step,** baby step, *le premier pas* <Fr>, openers, starters, first lap, first round, first inning, first stage, first leg; breaking-in, warming-up; first blush, first glance, first sight, first impression; early days

4 origin, origination, **genesis, inception,** incipience *or* incipiency, inchoation; **divine creation,** creationism, creation science; **birth,** birthing, bearing, parturition, pregnancy, nascency *or* nascence, nativity; **infancy,** babyhood, childhood, youth; freshman year; incunabula, beginnings, cradle; fountainhead, wellspring, source

5 inauguration, installation *or* installment,

induction, **introduction,** initiation; inception; setting in motion; embarkation *or* embarkment, **launching,** floating, flotation, unveiling; debut, first appearance, coming out <nf>; opener <nf>, preliminary, curtain raiser *or* lifter; maiden speech, inaugural address

6 **basics, essentials, rudiments, elements, nuts and bolts** <nf>; **principles,** principia, first principles, first steps, **outlines, primer,** hornbook, first reader, grammar, alphabet, **ABC's,** abecedarium; introduction, induction; groundwork, spacework

VERBS 7 **begin, commence, start; start up, kick** *or* **click in** <nf>; **start in, start off, start out, set out,** set sail, set in, set to *or* about, go *or* swing into action, get to *or* down to, **turn to,** fall to, pitch in <nf>, dive in <nf>, plunge into, head into <nf>, **go ahead,** let her rip <nf>, fire *or* blast away <nf>, take *or* jump *or* kick *or* tee *or* blast *or* send off <nf>, get the show on the road <nf>, get *or* set *or* start the ball rolling <nf>, roll it *and* let it roll <nf>

8 **make a beginning,** make a move <nf>, **start up,** get going <nf>, get off, set forth, set out, launch forth, get off the ground <nf>, **get under way,** set up shop, get in there <nf>; set a course, **get squared away** <nf>; make an auspicious beginning, **get off to a good start,** make a dent; get in on the ground floor <nf>; **break in, warm up,** get one's feet wet <nf>, cut one's teeth

9 enter, **enter on** *or* **upon** *or* **into, embark in** *or* **on** *or* **upon,** take up, go into, have a go at <chiefly Brit>, take a crack *or* whack *or* shot at <nf>; **debut,** make one's debut

10 **initiate, originate, create,** invent; **precede** 814.2, **take the initiative, take the first step,** take the lead, pioneer 815.3; **lead,** lead off, lead the way; **ahead,** head up <nf>, stand at the head, stand first; **break the ice,** take the plunge, break ground, cut the first turf, lay the first stone, get one's feet wet

11 **inaugurate,** institute, **found, establish,** set up <nf>; **install,** initiate, induct; **introduce,** broach, bring up, lift up, raise; **launch,** float; christen <nf>; **usher in,** ring in <nf>; **set on foot,** set abroach, set agoing, turn on, kick-start *and* jump-start <nf>, start up, start going, start the ball rolling <nf>, get cracking <nf>

12 **open,** open up, breach, open the door to, cut the ribbon; open fire

13 **originate, take** *or* **have origin,** be born, take birth, get started, come into the world, **become,** come to be, get to be <nf>, see the light of day, rise, **arise,** take rise, take its rise, **come forth, issue,** issue forth, come out, spring *or* crop up; burst forth, break out, erupt, irrupt; debut

14 **engender, beget, procreate** 78.8; **give birth to, bear,** birth, bring to birth, bring into the world; father, mother, sire

ADJS 15 **beginning, initial,** initiatory *or* initiative; incipient, inceptive, **introductory,** inchoative, inchoate; inaugural *or* inauguratory; **prime,** primal, **primary,** primitive, primeval; **original, first,** first ever, first of all; aboriginal, autochthonous; **elementary,** elemental, **fundamental,** foundational; **rudimentary,** rudimental, abecedarian; **ancestral,** primogenital *or* primogenitary; **formative, creative,** procreative, inventive; embryonic, in embryo, in the bud, budding, fetal, gestatory, parturient, pregnant, in its infancy, formative; infant, infantile, incunabular; **natal,** nascent, prenatal, antenatal, neonatal; early

16 **preliminary, prefatory,** preludial, proemial, precursory, preparatory; entry-level, door-opening; prepositive, prefixed

17 **first, foremost,** front, frontal, up-front <nf>, **head, chief, principal,** premier, **leading, main,** flagship, foremost; maiden

ADVS 18 **first,** firstly, **at first,** first off, first thing, for openers *or* starters <nf>, as a gambit, up front <nf>, **in the first place,** first and foremost, before everything, *primo* <L>; **principally,** mainly, chiefly, most of all; **primarily,** initially; **originally, in the beginning,** *in limine* <L>, **at the start,** at first glance *or* first blush, at the outset, at the first go-off <nf>; from the ground up, from the foundations, from the beginning, **from scratch** <nf>, from the first, **from the word 'go'** *and* from the git-go <nf>, *ab origine* <L>, *ab initio* <L>; *ab ovo* <L>

WORD ELEMENTS 19 acro-, arche-, eo-, ne-, neo-, proto-; *Ur-* <Ger>

819 MIDDLE

NOUNS 1 **middle,** median, midmost, **midst;** thick, thick of things; **center** 208.2, inside; **heart, core,** nucleus, kernel, heart of the matter; **mean** 246, midpoint; interior 207.2; midriff, diaphragm; **waist,** waistline, zone, girth, tummy *and* belly girt <nf>; equator; diameter; midday, midnight

2 **mid-distance,** middle distance; **equidistance; half,** moiety; **middle ground,** middle of the road, centrism; halfway point *or* place, midway, midcourse, midstream, halfway house; bisection; neutral ground, gray area, happy medium

VERBS 3 seek the middle, bisect, split down the middle; center, focus; average 246.2; double, fold, middle <nautical>; straddle, compromise

ADJS 4 **middle, medial,** median, mesial, middling, mediocre, average, **medium** 246.3, mezzo

<music>, **mean,** mid; **midmost,** middlemost;
central 208.11, core, nuclear; focal, pivotal;
interior, inside, internal; **intermediate,**
intermediary; equidistant, halfway, midway,
equatorial, diametral, midfield, midcourse,
midstream; midland, mediterranean; midships,
amidships; centrist, moderate, middle-of-the-road;
center-seeking, centripetal

ADVS **5 midway, halfway, in the middle,** betwixt and
between <nf>, halfway in the middle <nf>; plump
or smack *or* slap- *or* smack-dab in the middle
<nf>; half-and-half, neither here nor there, *mezzo-
mezzo* <Ital>; medially, mediumly; in the mean; *in
medias res* <L>; **in the midst of,** in the thick of;
midships, amidships

WORD ELEMENTS **6** mid-, medi-, medio-, mes-,
meso-, mesio-; intermedi-, intermedio-

820 END

NOUNS **1 end,** end point, ending, perfection, be-all
and end-all, **termination, terminus, terminal,**
terminating, term, period, **expiration,** expiry,
phaseout, phasedown, discontinuation, closeout,
cessation 857, ceasing, consummation,
culmination, close, **conclusion, finish, finis, finale,**
the end, finishing, finalizing *or* finalization, a wrap
<nf>, quietus, stoppage, windup *and* payoff <nf>,
curtain, curtains <nf>, all she wrote <nf>, fall of
the curtain, end of the road *or* line <nf>; decease,
taps, **death** 307; **last,** demise, "latter end"—Bible,
last gasp *or* breath, final twitch, last throe, last
legs, last hurrah <nf>; omega, à, izzard, Z; **goal,**
destination, stopping place, resting place, finish
line, tape *and* wire <nf>, journey's end, last stop;
denouement, catastrophe, apocalypse, final
solution, resolution; last *or* final words, peroration,
swan song, dying words, envoi, coda, epilogue;
fate, destiny, last things, eschatology, last trumpet,
Gabriel's trumpet, crack of doom, doom; **effect**
887; **happy ending,** Hollywood ending, walking
into the sunset

2 extremity, extreme; limit 794.5, ultimacy,
definitiveness, **boundary,** farthest bound, jumping-
off place, Thule, *Ultima Thule* <L>, **pole; tip,**
point, nib; tail, **tail end,** butt end, tag, tag end, fag
end; bitter end; stub, stump, butt; bottom dollar
<nf>, bottom of the barrel <nf>

3 close, closing, cessation; decline, lapse;
homestretch, last lap *or* **round** *or* **inning** <nf>,
ninth inning, last stage; beginning of the end;
deadline, closing time

4 finishing stroke, ender, **end-all,** quietus, stopper,
deathblow, death stroke, *coup de grâce* <Fr>, kiss
of death, mortal blow; **finisher,** clincher, equalizer,
crusher, **settler;** knockout *and* knockout blow
<nf>; sockdolager, KO *or* kayo *and* kayo punch
<nf>; final stroke, finishing *or* perfecting *or*
crowning touch, last dab *or* lick <nf>, last straw
<nf>

VERBS **5 end, terminate,** determine, close, close out,
close the books on, phase out *or* down, **finish,**
conclude, finish with, resolve, finish *or* wind up
<nf>; **put an end to,** put a period to, put paid to
<Brit>, put *or* lay to rest, **make an end of,** bring to
an end, bring to a close *or* halt, end up; **get it over,**
get over with *or* through with <nf>, be done with;
bring down *or* drop the curtain; put the lid on
<nf>, fold up <nf>, wrap *and* wrap up <nf>, sew
up <nf>; call off <nf>, call all bets off <nf>;
dispose of, polish off <nf>; kibosh *and* put the
kibosh on <nf>, put the skids under <nf>; **stop,**
cease 857.6; perorate; abort; scrap *and* scratch
<nf>; **kill** 308.14, extinguish, scrag *and* waste *and*
take out *and* zap <nf>, **give the quietus,** put the
finisher *or* settler on <nf>, knock on *or* in the
head, knock out <nf>, kayo *or* KO <nf>, shoot
down *and* shoot down in flames <nf>, stop dead
in one's tracks, wipe out <nf>; **cancel, delete,**
expunge, censor, censor out, blank out, erase

6 come to an end, draw to a close, expire, die
307.19, come to rest, end up, land up; lapse,
become void *or* extinct *or* defunct, run out, run its
course, have its time *and* have it <nf>, pass, **pass
away,** die away, wear off *or* away, go out, blow
over, be all over, be no more; peter out, fizzle out

7 complete 794.6, perfect, finish, finish off, finish up,
polish off, put the last *or* final *or* finishing touches
on, finalize <nf>

ADJS **8 ended, at an end, terminated, concluded,**
finished, complete 794.9, perfected, settled,
decided, set at rest; **over, all over,** all up <nf>; all
off <nf>, all bets off <nf>; **done,** done with, over
with, over and done with, through *and* through
with <nf>; wound up <nf>, washed up <nf>; all
over but the shouting <nf>; **dead** 307.30, defunct,
extinct; **finished,** defeated, out of action, disabled,
hors de combat <Fr>; **canceled, deleted,**
expunged, censored *or* censored out, blanked *or*
blanked out, bleeped *or* bleeped out; scrapped

9 <nf terms> **belly-up, dead meat,** kaput, shot, done
for, SOL *or* shit out of luck, scragged, shot down,
shot down in flames, down in flames, wasted,
zapped, pffft *or* phut, wiped out, washed up, down
and out, down the tubes, totaled

10 ending, closing, concluding, finishing,
culminating *or* culminative, consummative *or*
consummatory, **ultimate,** definitive, perfecting *or*
perfective, terminating, crowning, capping,
conclusive

11 final, terminal, terminating *or* terminative, determinative, definitive, **conclusive; last,** last-ditch <nf>, last but not least, eventual, farthest, extreme, boundary, border, limbic, limiting, polar, endmost, ultimate; caudal, tail, tail-end

ADVS **12 finally,** in fine; **ultimately, eventually, as a matter of course; lastly,** last, **at last,** at the last *or* end *or* conclusion, at length, at long last; **in conclusion, in sum;** conclusively, once and for all

13 to the end, to the bitter end, all the way, to the last gasp, the last extremity, **to a finish,** *à outrance* <Fr>, till hell freezes over <nf>, "to the edge of doom," "to the last syllable of recorded time"—both Shakespeare

PHRS **14 that's all for, that's final, that's that,** that's all she wrote *and* that buttons it up <nf>, that's the end of the matter, so much for that, nuf said *and* enough said <nf>; the subject is closed, the matter is ended, the deal is off <nf>; "the rest is silence"—Shakespeare

WORD ELEMENTS **15** acr-, acro-, tel-, telo-, tele-

821 TIME

NOUNS **1 time, duration,** *durée* <Fr>, lastingness, continuity 812, term, while, tide, space; real time; psychological time; biological time; tense 530.12; **period** 824, time frame; time warp; cosmic time; kairotic time; quality time; space-time 158.6; the past 837, the present 838, the future 838; timebinding; **chronology** 832.1, chronometry, chronography, horology; tempo

2 Time, **Father Time,** Cronus, Kronos; "the illimitable, silent, never-resting thing called Time"—Carlyle, "a sandpile we run our fingers in"—Sandburg

3 tract of time, corridors of time, whirligig of time, glass *or* hourglass of time, sands of time, ravages of time, noiseless foot of Time, scythe of Time, time's winged chariot

4 passage of time, course of time, lapse of time, progress of time, process of time, succession of time, time-flow, flow *or* flowing *or* flux of time, sweep of time, stream *or* current *or* tide of time, time and tide, march *or* step of time, flight of time, time's caravan, "Time's revolving wheels"—Petrarch, "Time's wingèd chariot"—Andrew Marvell; timeframe

VERBS **5 elapse,** lapse, **pass, expire,** run its course, run out, go *or* pass by; **flow,** tick away *or* by *or* on, run, proceed, advance, roll *or* press on, roll by, flit, fly, slip, slide, glide; drag by *or* on; **continue** 812.4, last, **endure,** go *or* run *or* flow on

6 spend time, pass time, put in time, employ *or* use time, fill *or* occupy time, kill time <nf>, consume time, take time, take up time, while away the time; find *or* look for time; race with *or* against time, buy time, work against time, run out of time, make time stand still; weekend, winter, summer; keep time, mark time, measure time

ADJS **7 temporal, chronological;** chronometric, chronographic; durational, durative; lasting, continuous 812.8; temporary, pending

ADVS **8 when, at which time,** what time *and* whenas <old>, at which moment *or* instant, on which occasion, **upon which, whereupon,** at which, in which time, at what time, in what period, on what occasion, whenever

9 at that time, on that occasion, at the same time as, at the same time *or* moment that, then, concurrently, simultaneously, contemporaneously

10 in the meantime, meanwhile 826.5; during the time; for the duration; at a stretch

11 then, thereat, thereupon, **at that time,** at that moment *or* instant, in that case *or* instance, on that occasion; **again,** at another time, at some other time, anon

12 whenever, whene'er, whensoever, whensoe'er, **at whatever time,** at any time, anytime, no matter when; if ever, once

13 in the year of our Lord, *anno Domini* <L>, AD, in the Common *or* Christian Era, CE; *ante Christum* <L>, AC, before Christ, BC, before the Common *or* Christian era, BCE; *anno urbis conditae* <L>, AUC; *anno regni* <L>, AR

PREPS **14 during,** pending, *durante* <law>; **in the course of,** in the process of, in the middle of; **in the time of,** at the time of, in the age *or* era of; over, through, **throughout,** throughout the course of, **for the period of;** until the conclusion of

15 until, till, to, unto, **up to,** up to the time of

16 CONJS **when, while,** whilst <chiefly Brit>, the while; **during the time that,** at the time that, at the same time that, at *or* during which time; **whereas, as long as,** as far as

17 PHRS **time flies,** *tempus fugit* <L>, time runs out, time marches on, "Time and tide stayeth for no man"—Richard Braithwaite

WORD ELEMENTS **18** chron-, chrono-, -chronous

822 TIMELESSNESS

NOUNS **1 timelessness,** neverness, datelessness, eternity 829.1,2; no time, no time at all, running out of time; time out of time, stopping time; everlasting moment; immortality

2 <a time that will never come> Greek calends *or* kalends, when hell freezes over, the thirtieth of February

ADJS **3 timeless, dateless**

ADVS **4 never,** ne'er, **not ever,** at no time, on no occasion, not at all; **nevermore;** never in the world, never on earth; not in donkey's years <Brit>, never in all one's born days <nf>, never in my life, *jamais de la vie* <Fr>

5 without date, *sine die* <L>, open, open-ended

823 INFINITY

NOUNS **1 infinity,** infiniteness, infinitude, the all, the be-all and end-all; **boundlessness, limitlessness, endlessness;** illimitability, interminability, termlessness; **immeasurability,** unmeasurability, immensity, incalculability, innumerability, incomprehensibility; measurelessness, countlessness, unreckonability, numberlessness; exhaustlessness, inexhaustibility; universality, "world without end"—Bible; **all-inclusiveness,** all-comprehensiveness; **eternity** 829.1,2, **perpetuity** 829, forever; vastness; bottomless pit

VERBS **2 have no limit** *or* **bounds** *or* **end,** know no limit *or* bounds *or* end, be without end, **go on and on,** go on forever, never cease *or* end; last forever, perpetuate

ADJS **3 infinite, boundless, endless, limitless,** termless, shoreless; unbounded, uncircumscribed, **unlimited,** illimited, infinitely continuous *or* extended, stretching *or* extending everywhere, without bound, without limit *or* end, no end of *or* to, bottomless; illimitable, **interminable,** interminate; **immeasurable,** incalculable, unreckonable, innumerable, incomprehensible, beyond comprehension, unfathomable; measureless, countless, sumless; **unmeasured,** unmeasurable, immense, unplumbed, untold, unnumbered, without measure *or* number *or* term; exhaustless, inexhaustible; **all-inclusive,** all-comprehensive 864.14, **universal** 864.14; **perpetual,** eternal 828.7; "as boundless as the sea"—Shakespeare; mind-boggling <nf>

ADVS **4 infinitely, illimitably,** boundlessly, limitlessly, **interminably; immeasurably,** measurelessly, immensely, incalculably, innumerably, incomprehensibly; **endlessly,** without end *or* limit; *ad infinitum* <L>, to infinity; **forever, eternally** 829.10, in perpetuity, "to the last syllable of recorded time"—Shakespeare

824 PERIOD
<portion or point of time>

NOUNS **1 period, point, juncture,** stage; **interval,** lapse of time, time frame, space, span, timespan, stretch, time-lag, time-gap; **time,** while, **moment,** minute, instant, hour, day, **season;** psychological moment; pregnant *or* fateful moment, fated moment, kairos, moment of truth; **spell** 825; "this bank and shoal of time"—Shakespeare

2 <periods> **moment, second,** millisecond, microsecond, nanosecond; **minute,** New York minute <nf>; hour, man-hour; **day,** sun; weekday; **week;** fortnight; **month,** moon, lunation; calendar month, lunar month; **quarter; semester,** trimester, term, session, academic year; **year,** annum, sun, twelvemonth; common year, regular year, intercalary year, leap year, bissextile year, defective year, perfect *or* abundant year; solar year, lunar year, sidereal year; fiscal year; calendar year; quinquennium, lustrum, luster; **decade,** decennium, decennary; **century; millennium**

3 term, time, duration, **tenure;** spell 825

4 age, generation, time, day, date, cycle; eon *or* aeon; Platonic year, great year, *annus magnus* <L>

5 era, epoch, age; Golden Age, Silver Age; Ice Age, glacial epoch; Stone Age, Bronze Age, Iron Age, Steel Age; Middle Ages, Dark Ages; Era of Good Feeling; Jacksonian Age; Reconstruction Era *and* Gilded Age <1870s and 1880s>; Gay Nineties *and* Naughty Nineties *and* Mauve Decade *and* Golden Age *and* Gilded Age <1890s>; Roaring Twenties *and* Golden Twenties *and* Mad Decade *and* Age of the Red-Hot Mamas *and* Jazz Age *and* Flapper Era <1920s>; Depression Era; New Deal Era; Prohibition Era

6 <modern age> Technological Age, Automobile Age, Air Age, Jet Age, Supersonic Age, Atomic Age, Electronic Age, Computer Age, Space Age, Age of Anxiety, Age of Aquarius

7 geological time periods

Algonkian	Mississippian
Archean	Oligocene
Archeozoic	Ordovician
Cambrian	Paleocene
Carboniferous	Paleozoic
Cenozoic	Pennsylvanian
Comanchean	Permian
Cretaceous	Pleistocene
Devonian	Pliocene
Eocene	Precambrian
Glacial	Proterozoic
Holocene *or* Recent Epoch	Quaternary
Jurassic	Silurian
Lower Cretaceous	Tertiary
Lower Tertiary	Triassic
Mesozoic	Upper Cretaceous
Miocene	Upper Tertiary

825 SPELL
<period of duty, etc>

NOUNS **1 spell,** fit, stretch, go <nf>

2 turn, bout, round, inning, innings <Brit>, time,

time at bat, place, say, whack *and* go <nf>; opportunity, chance; **relief, spell;** one's turn, one's move <nf>, one's say

3 **shift,** work shift, **tour,** tour of duty, stint, bit, **watch, trick,** time, **turn,** relay, spell *or* turn of work; day shift, night shift, swing shift, graveyard shift <nf>, dogwatch, anchor watch; lobster trick *or* tour, sunrise watch; split shift, split schedule; flextime *or* flexitime; half-time, part-time, full-time; **overtime**

4 **term,** time; **tenure,** continuous tenure, tenure in *or* of office; **enlistment, hitch** <nf>, tour; prison term, stretch <nf>; fiscal year; biorhythm, circadian rhythm, biological clock

VERBS 5 **take one's turn,** have a go <nf>; **take turns,** alternate, turn and turn about; **time off, spell** *and* **spell off** <nf>, **relieve,** cover, **fill in for,** take over for; put in one's time, work one's shift; **stand one's watch** *or* **trick,** keep a watch; have one's innings <Brit>; do a stint; hold office, have tenure *or* tenure of appointment; **enlist,** sign up; reenlist, re-up <nf>; do a hitch <nf>, do a tour *or* tour of duty; serve *or* do time

826 INTERIM

<intermediate period>

NOUNS 1 **interim, interval, interlude, intermission,** pause, break, **time-out,** recess, coffee break, halftime *or* halftime intermission, interruption; **lull,** quiet spell, resting point, point of repose, plateau, letup, relief, vacation, holiday, time off, off-time; downtime; **respite** 20.2; **intermission,** interval <Brit>, entr'acte; *intermezzo* <Ital>; interregnum

2 **meantime, meanwhile,** while, the while

VERBS 3 **intervene,** interlude, interval; **pause,** break, **recess,** declare a recess; call a halt *or* break *or* intermission; **call time** *or* time-out; take five *and* ten, etc *and* take a break <nf>

ADJS 4 **interim, temporary,** tentative, provisional, provisory

ADVS 5 **meanwhile, meantime, in the meanwhile** *or* **meantime,** in the interim, *ad interim* <L>; between acts *or* halves *or* periods, betweenwhiles, betweentimes, between now and then; till *or* until then; *en attendant* <Fr>, in the intervening time, during the interval, at the same time, for the nonce, for a time *or* season; *pendente lite* <L>

827 DURATION

NOUNS 1 **durability, endurance,** duration, durableness, **lastingness,** *longueur* <Fr>, perenniality, abidingness, long-lastingness,

perdurability; **continuance,** perseverance, maintenance, **steadfastness,** constancy, **stability** 855, **persistence, permanence** 853, standing, long standing; **longevity,** long-livedness; **antiquity, age; survival,** survivability, viability, defiance *or* defeat of time; **service life,** serviceable life, useful life, shelf life, mean life; **perpetuity** 828

2 **protraction, prolongation,** continuation, extension, lengthening, drawing- *or* stretching- *or* dragging- *or* spinning-out, lingering; perpetuation; procrastination 845.5

3 **length of time,** distance of time, vista *or* stretch *or* desert of time; corridor *or* tunnel of time

4 **long time,** long while, long; **age** *and* **ages** <nf>, **aeon, century, eternity,** years, **years on end,** time immemorial, coon's age <nf>, donkey's years <Brit nf>, month of Sundays <nf>, right smart spell <nf>

5 **lifetime, life,** life's duration, life expectancy, lifespan, expectation of life, "threescore years and ten"—Bible, period of existence, all the days of one's life; **generation, age;** all one's born days *or* natural life <nf>

VERBS 6 **endure, last** *or* **last out,** bide, **abide,** dwell, perdure, **continue,** run, extend, **go on,** carry on, hold on, keep on, stay on, run on, stay the course, go the distance, go through with, grind *or* slog on, grind *or* plug away; live, **live on,** continue to be, subsist, exist, tarry; get *or* keep one's head above water; **persist,** persevere; hang in *and* hang in there *and* hang tough <nf>; maintain, sustain, **remain, stay,** keep, hold, stand, prevail, last long, hold out; **survive,** defy *or* defeat time; live to fight another day; perennate; live on, live through; wear, wear well; stand the test of time

7 **linger on,** linger, tarry, go on, **go on and on, wear on,** crawl, creep, drag, **drag on,** drag along, drag its slow length along, drag a lengthening chain

8 **outlast, outstay,** last out, outwear, **outlive, survive**

9 **protract, prolong,** continue, **extend, lengthen,** lengthen out, **draw out, spin out,** drag *or* stretch out; linger on, dwell on; dawdle, procrastinate, temporize, drag one's feet

ADJS 10 **durable,** perdurable, **lasting, enduring,** perduring, **abiding, continuing,** remaining, staying, **stable** 854.12, persisting, **persistent,** perennial; inveterate, agelong; **steadfast, constant,** intransient, immutable, unfading, evergreen, sempervirent, **permanent** 853.7, perennial, **long-lasting,** long-standing, of long duration *or* standing, diuturnal; long-term; **long-lived,** tough, hardy, vital, longevous *or* longeval; **ancient,** aged, antique; macrobiotic; chronic; **perpetual** 828.7

11 **protracted, prolonged,** extended, lengthened; **long,** overlong, time-consuming, interminable,

marathon, lasting, **lingering,** languishing; long-continued, long-continuing, long-pending; drawn- *or* stretched- *or* dragged- *or* spun-out, long-drawn, **long-drawn-out;** long-winded, prolix, verbose 538.12

12 daylong, nightlong, weeklong, monthlong, yearlong

13 lifelong, livelong, lifetime, for life

ADVS **14 for a long time, long, for long, interminably,** unendingly, undyingly, persistently, protractedly, enduringly; for ever so long <nf>, for many a long day, for life *or* a lifetime, for an age *or* ages, for a coon's *or* dog's age <nf>, for a month of Sundays <nf>, for donkey's years <Brit nf>, **forever and a day, forever and ever, for years on end, for days on end,** etc; all the year round, all the day long, the livelong day, as the day is long; morning, noon, and night; hour after hour, day after day, month after month, year after year; day in day out, month in month out, year in year out; till hell freezes over <nf>, till you're blue in the face <nf>, till the cows come home <nf>, till shrimps learn to whistle <nf>, till doomsday, from now till doomsday, from here to eternity, till the end of time; since time began, from way back, long ago, long since, time out of mind, time immemorial

828 TRANSIENCE
<short duration>

NOUNS **1 transience** *or* transiency, transientness, **impermanence** *or* impermanency, transitoriness, changeableness 854, rootlessness, **mutability, instability, temporariness,** fleetingness, **momentariness;** finitude; **ephemerality,** ephemeralness, short duration; evanescence, volatility, fugacity, **short-livedness; mortality,** death, perishability, corruptibility, caducity; **expedience** 995, ad hoc, ad hockery *or* ad hocism, adhocracy

2 brevity, briefness, shortness; swiftness 174, fleetness

3 short time, little while, little, **instant,** moment 830.3, mo <nf>, small space, span, spurt, **short spell;** no time, less than no time; bit *or* **little bit,** a breath, the wink of an eye, pair of winks <nf>; **two shakes** *and* two shakes of a lamb's tail <nf>, half a mo <nf>; just a second

4 transient, transient guest *or* boarder, temporary lodger; **sojourner;** passer, passerby, **wanderer; vagabond,** drifter, derelict, homeless person, bag person, tramp, hobo, bum <nf>; caller, guest, visitor

5 ephemeron, ephemera, ephemeral; ephemerid, ephemeris, ephemerides <pl>; mayfly; bubble,

smoke; nine days' wonder, flash in the pan, passing fancy; snows of yesteryear, *neiges d'antan* <Fr>; shooting star, meteor; ship that passes in the night

VERBS **6** <be transient> **flit, fly,** fleet; **pass, pass away, vanish, evaporate,** dissolve, evanesce, disappear, fade, melt, sink; fade like a shadow *or* dream, vanish like a dream, vanish into thin air, burst like a bubble, **go up in smoke,** melt like snow

ADJS **7 transient, transitory,** transitive; **temporary,** temporal; **impermanent,** unenduring, undurable, nondurable, nonpermanent; frail, brittle, fragile, insubstantial; changeable 854.6, **mutable, unstable,** inconstant 854.7; capricious, fickle, impulsive, impetuous; **short-lived, ephemeral,** fly-by-night, evanescent, volatile, **momentary;** deciduous; **passing,** fleeting, flitting, flying, fading, dying; fugitive, fugacious; perishable, mortal, corruptible; "as transient as the clouds"—Robert Green Ingersoll, here today and gone tomorrow; **expedient** 995.5, ad-hoc

8 brief, short, short-time, quick, brisk, swift, fleet, speedy, "short and sweet"—Thomas Lodge; meteoric, cometary, flashing, flickering; short-term, short-termed

ADVS **9 temporarily,** for the moment, for the time, *pro tempore* <L>, pro tem, for the nonce, **for the time being,** for a time, awhile

10 transiently, impermanently, evanescently, transitorily, changeably, mutably, ephemerally, fleetingly, flittingly, flickeringly, **briefly, shortly,** swiftly, quickly, **for a little while,** for a short time; **momentarily,** for a moment; **in an instant** 830.7

829 PERPETUITY
<endless duration>

NOUNS **1 perpetuity,** perpetualness; **eternity,** eternalness, sempiternity, infinite duration; everness, foreverness, **everlastingness, permanence** 852, ever-duringness, duration 827, perdurability, indestructibility; **constancy,** stability, immutability, continuance, perseverance, continualness, perennialness *or* perenniality, **ceaselessness,** unceasingness, incessancy; timelessness 822; **endlessness,** never-endingness, **interminability; infinity** 823; coeternity

2 forever, an eternity, endless time, **time without end;** "a moment standing still for ever"—James Montgomery, "a short parenthesis in a long period"—Donne

3 immortality, eternal life, **deathlessness,** imperishability, undyingness, incorruptibility *or* incorruption, athanasy *or* athanasia, life everlasting; eternal youth, fountain of youth

4 perpetuation, preservation, eternalization, immortalization; eternal re-creation, eternal return *or* recurrence; steady-state universe

VERBS **5 perpetuate, preserve,** preserve from oblivion, keep fresh *or* alive, perennialize, **eternalize,** eternize, **immortalize;** monumentalize; freeze, embalm

6 last *or* endure forever, **go on forever,** go on and on, live forever, **have no end,** have no limits *or* bounds *or* term, never cease *or* end *or* die *or* pass

ADJS **7 perpetual, everlasting,** everliving, ever-being, ever-abiding, ever-during, ever-durable, permanent 853.7, perdurable, indestructible; **eternal,** sempiternal, eterne <old>, **infinite** 823.3, aeonian *or* eonian; dateless, ageless, timeless, immemorial; **endless,** unending, never-ending, without end, **interminable,** nonterminous, nonterminating; **continual,** continuous, steady, **constant, ceaseless,** nonstop, unceasing, never-ceasing, **incessant,** unremitting, unintermitting, uninterrupted, "continuous as the stars that shine"—Wordsworth; coeternal

8 perennial, indeciduous, **evergreen,** sempervirent, ever-new, ever-young; ever-blooming, ever-bearing

9 immortal, everlasting, **deathless,** undying, never-dying, **imperishable,** incorruptible, amaranthine; fadeless, **unfading,** never-fading, ever-fresh; frozen, embalmed

ADVS **10 perpetually,** in perpetuity, **everlastingly, eternally,** permanently 853.9, perennially, perdurably, indestructibly, **constantly,** continually, steadily, **ceaselessly,** unceasingly, never-ceasingly, **incessantly,** never-endingly, **endlessly,** unendingly, **interminably,** without end, world without end, time without end, "from everlasting to everlasting"—Bible; **infinitely,** *ad infinitum* <L> 823.4

11 always, all along, all the time, all the while, at all times, *semper et ubique* <L, always and everywhere>; ever and always, **invariably,** without exception, never otherwise, *semper eadem* <L, ever the same; Elizabeth I>

12 forever, forevermore, for ever and ever, forever and aye; forever and a day <nf>, now and forever, *ora e sempre* <Ital>, "yesterday and today and forever"—Bible; **ever, evermore,** ever and anon, ever and again; aye, for aye; **for good,** for keeps <nf>, for good and all, for all time; throughout the ages, from age to age, in all ages, "for ages of ages"—Douay Bible; **to the end of time,** till time stops *or* runs out, "to the last syllable of recorded time"—Shakespeare, to the crack of doom, to the last trumpet, till doomsday; till you're blue in the face <nf>, till hell freezes over <nf>, till the cows come home <nf>

13 for life, for all one's natural life, for the term of one's days, while life endures, while one draws breath, in all one's born days <nf>; from the cradle to the grave, from the womb to the tomb; **till death,** till death do us part

830 INSTANTANEOUSNESS
<imperceptible duration>

NOUNS **1 instantaneousness** *or* **instantaneity,** momentariness, **momentaneousness** <old>, **immediateness** *or* immediacy, near-simultaneity *or* -simultaneousness; simultaneity 836

2 suddenness, abruptness, precipitateness, precipitance *or* precipitancy; **unexpectedness,** unanticipation, inexpectation 131

3 instant, moment, second, sec <nf>, split second, millisecond, microsecond, nanosecond, half a second, half a mo <Brit nf>, minute, **trice,** twinkle, **twinkling, twinkling** *or* **twinkle of an eye,** twink, **wink,** bat of an eye <nf>, **flash,** crack, tick, stroke, coup, breath, twitch; two shakes of a lamb's tail *and* two shakes *and* shake *and* half a shake *and* jiffy *and* jiff *and* half a jiffy <nf>

ADJS **4 instantaneous,** instant, momentary, momentaneous <old>, **immediate,** presto, quick as thought *or* lightning; lightning-like, lightning-swift; nearly simultaneous; simultaneous; split-second; urgent, on-the-spot; fast-food, convenience-food; ready-to-wear, off-the-rack

5 sudden, abrupt, precipitant, **precipitate, precipitous; hasty,** headlong, impulsive, impetuous; speedy, swift, quick; **unexpected** 131.10, unanticipated, unpredicted, unforeseen, unlooked-for; **surprising** 131.11, startling, electrifying, shocking, nerve-shattering

ADVS **6 instantly,** instanter, momentaneously <old>, momentarily, momently, **instantaneously, immediately, right off the bat** <nf>; on the instant, on the dot <nf>, on the nail

7 quickly, in an instant, in a trice, in a second, in a moment, in a mo *or* half a mo <Brit nf>, in a bit *or* little bit, in a jiff *or* jiffy *or* half a jiffy <nf>, in a flash, in a wink <nf>, in a twink, **in a twinkling, in the twinkling of an eye, as quick as a wink,** as quick as greased lightning <nf>, in two shakes *or* a shake *or* half a shake <nf>, in two shakes of a lamb's tail <nf>, before you can say 'Jack Robinson' <nf>; **in no time,** in less than no time, in nothing flat <nf>, in short order; at the drop of a hat *or* handkerchief, like a shot, like a shot out of hell <nf>; with the speed of light

8 at once, at once and on the spot, **then and there, now, right now, right away, right off,** straightway, straightaway, forthwith, this minute, this very

minute, **without delay,** without the least delay, in a
hurry <nf>, *pronto* <Sp>, *subito* <Ital>;
simultaneously, at the same instant, in the same
breath; **all at once,** all together, at one time, at a
stroke, at one stroke, at a blow, at one blow, at one
swoop, "at one fell swoop"—Shakespeare; at one
jump, *per saltum* <L>, *uno saltu* <L>

9 **suddenly,** sudden, of a sudden, on a sudden, **all of
a sudden, all at once: abruptly,** sharp;
precipitously or precipitately, precipitantly,
impulsively, impetuously, hastily; dash; smack,
bang, slap, plop, plunk, plump, pop; **unexpectedly**
131.14, out of a clear blue sky, when least
expected, before you know it; on short notice,
without notice or warning, without further ado,
unawares, **surprisingly** 131.15, startlingly, like a
thunderbolt or thunderclap, like a flash, like a bolt
from the blue

10 PHRS no sooner said than done

831 EVENT

NOUNS 1 **event, eventuality,** eventuation, effect 887,
issue, outcome, result, aftermath, consequence;
realization, materialization, coming to be or pass,
incidence; contingency, contingent; accident 972.6

2 **event, occurrence, incident, episode, experience,**
adventure, hap, **happening,** happenstance,
phenomenon, fact, matter of fact, reality,
particular, circumstance, **occasion,** turn of events;
nonevent, pseudo-event, media event or
happening, photo opportunity; what's happening

3 **affair, concern, matter,** thing, concernment,
interest, **business,** job <nf>, **transaction,**
proceeding, doing; current affairs or events; cause
célèbre, matter of moment

4 **affairs, concerns, matters,** circumstances,
relations, **dealings, proceedings,** doings, goings-on
<nf>; course or run of events, run of things, the
way of things, the way things go, what happens,
current of events, march of events; the world, life,
the times; order of the day; **conditions, state of
affairs,** environing or ambient phenomena, state or
condition of things

VERBS 5 **occur, happen** 972.11, hap, eventuate, **take
place,** come or go down <nf>, go on, **transpire,** be
realized, come, **come off** <nf>, **come about,** come
true, **come to pass,** pass, pass off, go off, fall,
befall, betide; **be found,** be met with

6 **turn up, show up** <nf>, **come along,** come one's
way, cross one's path, come into being or existence,
chance, **crop up,** spring up, pop up <nf>, arise,
come forth, come or draw on, appear, approach,
materialize, present itself, be destined for one

7 **turn out, result** 887.5

8 **experience, have, know, feel,** taste; **encounter,
meet,** meet with, meet up with <nf>, run up
against <nf>; **undergo, go through,** pass through,
be subjected to, be exposed to, stand under, labor
under, **endure, suffer,** sustain, pay, spend

ADJS 9 **happening, occurring, current, actual,**
passing, taking place, on, **going on,** ongoing <nf>,
prevalent, prevailing, that is, that applies, in the
wind, afloat, afoot, under way, in hand, **on foot,**
ado, doing; incidental, circumstantial,
accompanying; accidental; occasional; resultant;
eventuating

10 **eventful, momentous, stirring,** bustling, full of
incident; phenomenal

11 **eventual, coming, final,** last, **ultimate; contingent,**
collateral, secondary, indirect

ADVS 12 **eventually, ultimately, finally, in the end,
after all is said and done, in the long run, over the
long haul;** in the course of things, in the natural
way of things, as things go, as times go, as the
world goes, as the tree falls, the way the cookie
crumbles <nf>, as things turn out, as it may be or
happen or turn out, as luck or fate or destiny wills

CONJS 13 **in the event that, if, in case,** if it should
happen that, just in case, in any case, in either
case, in the contingency that, in case that;
provided 959.12

832 MEASUREMENT OF TIME

NOUNS 1 **chronology,** timekeeping, timing, clocking,
horology, **chronometry,** horometry, chronoscopy,
chronography; watch- or clock-making;
scheduling, calendar-making; **dating,** carbon-14
dating, radiocarbon dating, dendrochronology

2 **time of day, time** 821, **the time,** the exact time;
time of night; **hour,** minute; stroke of the hour,
time signal, bell

3 standard time, civil time, zone time, slow time
<nf>; mean time, solar time, mean solar time,
sidereal time, apparent time, local time; universal
time or Greenwich time or Greenwich mean time
or GMT, Eastern time, Central time, Mountain
time, Pacific time; Atlantic time; Alaska time,
Yukon time; daylight-saving time; fast time <nf>,
summer time <Brit>; **time zone**

4 **date,** point of time, time, day; postdate, antedate;
datemark; date line, International Date Line;
calends, nones, ides; name day, saint's day; red-
letter day, anniversary

5 epact, annual epact, monthly or menstrual epact

6 **timepiece,** timekeeper, **timer, chronometer,** ship's
watch; horologe, horologium; **clock,** Big Ben, ticker
<nf>, **watch,** turnip <nf>; hourglass, sundial;
watch or clock movement, clockwork, watchworks

7 almanac, The Old Farmer's Almanac, Nautical Almanac, Poor Richard's Almanac, World Almanac

8 calendar, calends; calendar stone, chronogram; almanac *or* astronomical calendar, ephemeris; perpetual calendar; Chinese calendar, church *or* ecclesiastical calendar, Cotsworth calendar, Gregorian calendar, Hebrew *or* Jewish calendar, Hindu calendar, international fixed calendar, Julian calendar, Muslim calendar, Republican *or* Revolutionary calendar, Roman calendar, ordo calendar

9 chronicle, chronology, register, registry, record; **annals,** journal, diary; time sheet, time book, **log,** daybook; timecard, time ticket, clock card, check sheet; datebook; date slip; **timetable,** schedule, timeline, time schedule, time chart, schedule; time scale; time study, motion study, time and motion study

10 chronologist, chronologer, chronographer, horologist, horologer; watchmaker *or* clockmaker; timekeeper, timer; chronicler, annalist, diarist, historian, historiographer; calendar maker, calendarist

VERBS 11 time, fix *or* **set the time,** mark the time; **keep time,** mark time, measure time, beat time; **clock** <nf>; watch the clock; set the alarm; synchronize

12 punch the clock *and* punch in *and* punch out *and* **time in** *and* **time out** <nf>; ring in, ring out; clock in, clock out; check in, check out; check off

13 date, be dated, date at *or* from, date back, bear a date of, bear the date of, carry a date; fix *or* set the date, make a date; **predate,** backdate, antedate; **postdate; update,** bring up to date; datemark; date-stamp; dateline

14 chronologize, chronicle, calendar, intercalate

ADJS 15 chronologic *or* **chronological,** temporal, timekeeping; **chronometric** *or* chronometrical, chronoscopic, chronographic *or* chronographical, chronogrammatic *or* chronogrammatical, horologic *or* horological, horometric *or* horometrical, metronomic *or* metronomical, calendric *or* calendrical, intercalary *or* intercalated; dated; annalistic, diaristic; calendarial

ADVS 16 o'clock, of the clock, by the clock; half past, half *or* half after <Brit>; a quarter of *or* to, a quarter past *or* after

833 ANACHRONISM

<false estimation or knowledge of time>

NOUNS 1 anachronism, chronological *or* historical error, **mistiming, misdating,** misdate, postdating, antedating; parachronism, metachronism,

prochronism; prolepsis, anticipation; earliness, lateness, tardiness, unpunctuality

VERBS 2 mistime, misdate; antedate, foredate, postdate; lag

ADJS 3 anachronous *or* anachronistical *or* **anachronistic,** parachronistic, metachronistic, prochronistic, unhistorical, unchronological; **mistimed, misdated;** antedated, foredated, postdated; ahead of time, **beforehand, early;** behind time, **behindhand, late,** unpunctual, tardy; **overdue,** past due; unseasonable, out of season; **dated,** out-of-date

834 PREVIOUSNESS

NOUNS 1 previousness, earliness 845, **antecedence** *or* antecedency, priority, **anteriority, precedence** *or* precedency 814, precession; *status quo ante* <L>, previous *or* prior state, earlier state; preexistence; **anticipation,** predating, antedating; antedate; **past time** 836

2 antecedent, precedent, premise; forerunner, **precursor** 816, ancestor

VERBS 3 be prior, be before *or* early *or* earlier, come on the scene *or* appear earlier, **precede, antecede, forerun,** come *or* go before, set a precedent; **herald,** usher in, proclaim, announce; **anticipate,** antedate, predate; **preexist**

ADJS 4 previous, prior, early 845.7, **earlier,** *ci-devant* *or* *ci-dessus* <Fr>, **former,** fore, prime, first, **preceding** 165.3, foregoing, above, anterior, **anticipatory,** antecedent; **preexistent;** older, elder, senior

5 prewar, ante-bellum, before the war; prerevolutionary; premundane *or* antemundane; prelapsarian, before the Fall; antediluvian, before the Flood; protohistoric, prehistoric 836.10; precultural; pre-Aryan; pre-Christian; premillenarian, premillennial; anteclassical, preclassical, pre-Roman, pre-Renaissance, pre-Romantic, pre-Victorian, etc

ADVS 6 previously, priorly, **hitherto, heretofore,** thitherto, theretofore; **before, early** 845.11, **earlier,** ere, erenow, ere then, or ever; already, yet; before all; **formerly** 837.13

PREPS 7 prior to, previous to, before, in advance of, in anticipation of, in preparation for

WORD ELEMENTS 8 ante-, anti-, fore-, pre-, pro-, prot-, proto-, proter-, protero-, supra-

835 SUBSEQUENCE

<later time>

NOUNS 1 subsequence, posteriority, **succession, ensuing, following** 166, sequence, coming after, supervenience, supervention; lateness 846; afterlife, next life; remainder 256, hangover <nf>; postdating; postdate; future time 838

2 **sequel** 817, **follow-up,** sequelae, **aftermath; consequence, effect** 887; **posterity,** offspring, descendant, heir, inheritor; **successor;** replacement, line, **lineage,** dynasty, family

VERBS 3 **come** or **follow** or **go after, follow, follow on** or **upon,** succeed, replace, take the place of, displace, overtake, supervene; **ensue,** issue, emanate, attend, **result;** follow up, trail, track, come close on or tread on the heels of, "follow hard upon"—Shakespeare, dog the footsteps of; **step into** or fill the shoes of, don the mantle of, assume the robe of

ADJS 4 **subsequent, after, later,** after-the-fact, *post factum* and *ex post facto* <L>, posterior, **following, succeeding,** successive, sequent, lineal, consecutive, ensuing, attendant; **junior,** cadet, puisne <law>, younger

5 **posthumous,** afterdeath; **postprandial,** postcibal, postcenal, after-dinner; **post-war,** *postbellum* <L>, after the war; **postdiluvian,** postdiluvial, after the flood, postlapsarian, after the Fall, post-industrial, post-modern, post-millenial, etc

ADVS 6 **subsequently, after, afterwards,** after that, after all, **later, next,** since; **thereafter,** thereon, thereupon, therewith, **then;** in the process or course of time, as things worked out, in the sequel; at a subsequent or later time, in the aftermath; *ex post facto* <L>; hard on the heels or on the heels

7 **after which, on** or **upon which, whereupon,** whereon, whereat, whereto, whereunto, wherewith, wherefore, on, upon; hereinafter

PREPS 8 **after, following, subsequent to,** later than, past, beyond, behind; below, farther down or along

WORD ELEMENTS 9 ante-, anti-, fore-, pre-, pro-, prot-, proto-, proter-, protero-, supra-; epi-, eph-, infra-, meta-, post-

836 SIMULTANEITY

NOUNS 1 **simultaneity** or **simultaneousness,** coincidence, co-occurrence, concurrence or concurrency, concomitance or concomitancy; **coexistence; contemporaneousness** or contemporaneity, coetaneousness or coetaneity, coevalness or coevalneity; unison; **synchronism,** synchronization, sync <nf>; isochronism; accompaniment 769, agreement 788

2 **contemporary,** coeval, concomitant, compeer; age group, peer group

3 **tie,** dead heat, draw, wash <nf>

VERBS 4 **coincide,** co-occur, concur; **coexist;** coextend; **synchronize,** isochronize, put or be in

phase, be in time, keep time, time; contemporize; **accompany** 769.7, **agree** 788.6, match, go along with, go hand in hand, keep pace with, keep in step; sync <nf>

ADJS 5 **simultaneous, concurrent,** co-occurring, coinstantaneous, concomitant; **tied,** neck-and-neck; coexistent, coexisting; **contemporaneous,** contemporary, coetaneous, coeval; coterminous, conterminous; unison, unisonous; photo-finish; isochronous, isochronal; coeternal; accompanying 769.9, collateral; agreeing 788.9

6 **synchronous,** synchronized, synchronic or synchronal, in sync <nf>, isochronal, isochronous; **in time,** in step, in tempo, in phase, with or on the beat, in sync <nf>

ADVS 7 **simultaneously, concurrently,** coinstantaneously; **together,** all together, **at the same time,** at one and the same time, as one, as one man, in concert with, in chorus, with one voice, in unison, in a chorus, in the same breath; at one time, at a clip <nf>; synchronously, **synchronically,** isochronously, in phase, **in sync** <nf>, with or on the beat, on the downbeat

837 THE PAST

NOUNS 1 **the past,** past, foretime, former times, past times, times past, water under the bridge, **days** or **times gone by, bygone times** or **days,** bygones, **yesterday, yesteryear;** recent past, just or only yesterday; history, past **history;** dead past, dead hand of the past; the years that are past, "the days that are no more"—Tennyson, "the irrevocable Past"—Longfellow

2 **old** or **olden times,** early times, **old** or **olden days,** the olden time, times of old, **days of old, days** or **times of yore,** yore, yoretime, foretime, eld <old>, good old times or days, the way it was, lang syne or auld lang syne <Scot>, **the long ago,** time out of mind, days beyond recall; the old story, the same old story

3 **antiquity, ancient times,** time immemorial, ancient history, prehistory, protohistory, remote age or time, remote or far or dim or **distant past,** distance of time, past age, way back when; geological past, ice age; "the dark backward and abysm of time"—Shakespeare; ancientness 842

4 **memory** 989, **remembrance, recollection, reminiscence, fond remembrance, retrospection,** retrospective, musing on the past, looking back, reprise; "the remembrance of things past"—Shakespeare, *"la recherche du temps perdu"*—Proust; **reliving,** reexperiencing; revival 396.3; youth 301

5 <grammatical terms> past tense, preterit, perfect

tense, past perfect tense, pluperfect, historical present tense, past progressive tense, past participle; aorist; perfective aspect; preterition

VERBS 6 pass, be past, **be a thing of the past,** be history, elapse, lapse, slip by *or* away, be gone, fade, fade away, be dead and gone, be all over, have run its course, have run out, have had its day; pass into history; **disappear** 34.2; **die** 307.19

ADJS 7 past, gone, by, **gone-by, bygone,** gone glimmering, bypast, ago, **over,** departed, passed, passed away, elapsed, lapsed, vanished, faded, no more, lost forever, long gone, irrecoverable, never to return, not coming back; **dead** 307.30, dead as a dodo, expired, extinct, dead and buried, defunct, deceased; run out, blown over, finished, forgotten, wound up; **passé, obsolete,** has-been, dated, antique, **antiquated**

8 reminiscent 989.22, **retrospective, remembered** 989.23, **recollected; relived, reexperienced; restored, revived;** retro; diachronic

9 <grammatical terms> past, preterit *or* preteritive, pluperfect, past perfect; aorist, aoristic; perfective

10 former, past, fore, **previous,** late, recent, **once, onetime,** sometime, **erstwhile,** then, quondam; obsolescent; retired, emeritus, superannuated; **prior** 833.4; **ancient, immemorial,** early, primitive, primeval, prehistoric; **old,** olden

11 foregoing, aforegoing, **preceding** 814.4; last, latter

12 back, backward, into the past; early; retrospective, retro, retroactive, *ex post facto* <L>, *a priori* <L>

ADVS 13 formerly, previously, priorly 834.6; **earlier, before,** before now, erenow, erst, whilom, erewhile, **hitherto, heretofore,** thitherto, aforetime, beforetime, **in the past,** in times past; then; **yesterday,** only yesterday, recently; **historically,** prehistorically, in historic *or* prehistoric times

14 once, once upon a time, one day, one fine morning, time was

15 ago, since, gone by; back, back when; backward, to *or* into the past; **retrospectively,** reminiscently, retroactively

16 long ago, long since, **a long while** *or* **time ago,** some time ago *or* since, some time back, a way *or* away back <nf>, ages ago, **years ago,** donkey's years ago <Brit nf>; **in times past,** in times gone by, in the old days, in the good old days; **anciently, of old, of yore,** in ancient times, in olden times, in the olden times, **in days of yore,** early, in the memory of man, time out of mind

17 since, ever since, until now; **since long ago, long since,** from away back <nf>, since days of yore, ages ago, **from time immemorial,** from time out of mind, aeons ago, since the world was made, since the world was young, since time began, since the

year one, since Hector was a pup and since God knows when <nf>

WORD ELEMENTS 18 archae-, archaeo-, archeo-; pale-, paleo-, praeter-, preter-, retro-; -ed, y- <old>

838 THE PRESENT

NOUNS 1 the present, presentness, present time, the here and now; **now,** the present juncture *or* occasion, the present hour *or* moment *or* minute, this instant *or* second *or* moment, **the present day** *or* **time** etc; **the present age; today,** this day, **this day and age; this point,** this stage, this hour, **now,** nowadays, the now, the way things are, the nonce, **the time being; the times,** our times, these days, modern times; **contemporaneousness** *or* contemporaneity, nowness, actuality, topicality; **newness** 841, modernity; the Now Generation, the me generation; historical present *and* present tense <gram>, present participle

ADJS 2 present, immediate, latest, current, running, extant, **existent,** existing, actual, topical, being, that is, as is, that be; **present-day,** present-time, present-age, **modern** 841.13, modern-day; **contemporary,** contemporaneous; up-to-date, up-to-the-minute, fresh, with it <nf>, **new** 841.7

ADVS 3 now, at present, at this point, at this juncture, at this stage *or* at this stage of the game, on the present occasion, **at this time,** at this moment *or* instant, at the present time; **today,** this day, in these days, **in this day and age,** in our time, **nowadays;** this night, **tonight;** here, hereat, **here and now,** *hic et nunc* <L>, even now, but now, **just now,** as of now, as things are; on the spot; for the nonce, for the time being; for this occasion

4 until now, hitherto, till now, thitherto, **hereunto,** heretofore, until this time, by this time, **up to now,** up to the present, up to this time, to this day, to the present moment, to this very instant, **so far,** thus far, **as yet, to date,** yet, already, still, now *or* then as previously

WORD ELEMENTS 5 ne-, neo-, nov-, novo-; cen-, ceno-, caen-, caeno-, -cene

839 THE FUTURE

NOUNS 1 the future, future, futurity, what is to come, imminence 840, subsequence 834, eventuality 831.1, **hereafter,** aftertime, afteryears, **time to come,** years to come, etc; **futurism,** futuristics; **tomorrow,** the morrow, the morning after, *mañana* <Sp>; **immediate** *or* **near future,** time just ahead, immediate prospect, offing, next period; **distant future,** remote *or* deep *or* far future, long run, long term; **by-and-by,** the sweet by-and-by <nf>; time ahead, course ahead, **prospect,** outlook, anticipation, expectation, project, probability, prediction, extrapolation, forward look, foresight, prevision, prevenience, envisionment, envisagement, prophecy, divination, clairvoyance, crystal ball; what is to be *or* come; determinism; future tense, future perfect; futurism; the womb of time

2 **destiny** 964.2, **fate,** doom, karma, kismet, what bodes *or* looms, what is fated *or* destined *or* doomed, what is written, what is in the books, "whatever limits us"—Emerson; the Fates, the Parcae *or* Parcae Fates, Lachesis, Clotho, Atropos, Moira, Moirai, **the hereafter,** the great hereafter, a better place, Paradise, Heaven, Elysian Fields, Happy Isles, the Land of Youth *or* Tir na n'Og, Valhalla; Hades, the Underworld, Hell, Gehenna; **the afterworld,** the otherworld, **the next world,** the world to come, life *or* world beyond the grave, **the beyond,** the great beyond, the unknown, the great unknown, **the grave,** home *or* abode *or* world of the dead, eternal home; "the great world of light, that lies behind all human destinies"—Longfellow; a**fterlife, postexistence,** future state, **life to come,** life after death

3 **doomsday,** doom, day of doom, day of reckoning, crack of doom, trumpet *or* trump of doom; **Judgment Day,** Day of Judgment, the Judgment; eschatology, last things, **last days**

4 **futurity;** ultimateness, eventuality, finality

5 **advent, coming, approach of time,** time drawing on

VERBS 6 **come,** come on, **approach,** near, **draw on** *or* **near;** be to be *or* come; be fated *or* destined *or* doomed, be in the books, be in the cards; **loom,** threaten, await, stare one in the face, be imminent 840.2; lie ahead *or* in one's course, lie just around the corner; **predict,** foresee, envision, envisage, see ahead, previse, foretell, prophesy; **anticipate, expect,** hope, hope for, look for, look forward to, **project,** plot, plan, scheme, think ahead, extrapolate, take the long view

7 **live on,** postexist, survive, get by *or* through, make it <nf>

ADJS 8 **future, later,** hereafter; **coming, forthcoming, imminent** 840.3, approaching, nearing, close at hand, waiting in the wings, nigh, **prospective;** eventual 831.11, ultimate, to-be, **to come; projected,** plotted, planned, looked- *or* hoped-for, desired, emergent, **predicted,** prophesied, foreseen, anticipated, anticipatory, previsional, prevenient, envisioned, envisaged, probable, extrapolated; determined, fatal, fatidic, fated, destinal, destined, doomed; eschatological; futuristic

ADVS 9 **in the future,** in aftertime, **afterward** *or* afterwards, **later,** at a later time, after a time *or*

while, anon; **by and by,** in the sweet by-and-by <nf>; **tomorrow,** *mañana* <Sp>, the day after tomorrow; *proximo* <L>, prox, **in the near** *or* **immediate future,** just around the corner, **imminently** 839.4, **soon, before long;** probably, predictably, hopefully; fatally, by destiny *or* necessity

10 in future, **hereafter,** hereinafter, thereafter, **henceforth, henceforward** *or* henceforwards, thence, **thenceforth,** thenceforward *or* thenceforwards, over the long haul *or* short haul <nf>, from this time forward, from this day on *or* forward, from this point, from this *or* that time, from then on, **from here** *or* **now on,** from now on in <nf>, from here in *or* out <nf>, from this moment on

11 **in time, in due time,** in due season *or* course, all in good time, **in the fullness of time,** in God's good time, in the course *or* process of time, **eventually** 830.12, **ultimately,** in the long run

12 **sometime, someday, some of these days,** one of these days, some fine day *or* morning, one fine day *or* morning, some sweet day, sometime or other, somewhen, sooner or later, when all is said and done

PREPS 13 **about to, at** *or* **on the point of,** on the eve of, on the brink *or* edge *or* verge of, near to, close upon, in the act of

840 IMMINENCE
   <future event>

NOUNS 1 **imminence** *or* **imminency,** impendence *or* impendency, forthcomingness; **forthcoming,** coming, **approach, loom;** immediate *or* near future; futurity 839.1

VERBS 2 **be imminent, impend, overhang,** hang *or* lie over, **loom,** hang over one's head, hover, **threaten, menace,** lower; brew, gather; **come** *or* **draw on,** draw near *or* nigh, rush up on one, forthcome, **approach, loom up, near,** be on the horizon, be in the offing, be just around the corner, await, face, **confront, loom,** stare one in the face, be in store, breathe down one's neck, be about to be borning

ADJS 3 **imminent, impending,** impendent, **overhanging,** hanging over one's head, waiting, lurking, **threatening, looming,** lowering, **menacing,** lying in ambush; **brewing,** gathering, preparing; **coming, forthcoming, upcoming, to come,** about to be, about *or* going to happen, **approaching, nearing,** looming, looming up, looming in the distance *or* future; **near, close,** immediate, instant, soon to be, **at hand,** near at hand, close at hand; **in the offing,** on the horizon, **in prospect,** already in sight, just around the corner, in view, in one's eye, in store, in reserve, **in the wind,** in the womb of time; on the knees *or* lap of the gods, in the cards <nf>; that will be, that is to be; future 839.8

ADVS **4 imminently,** impendingly; **any time,** any time now, any moment, any second, any minute, any hour, any day; **to be expected,** as may be expected, as may be

CONJS **5 on the point of, on the verge of,** on the eve of

841 NEWNESS

NOUNS **1 newness,** freshness, maidenhood, dewiness, pristineness, mint condition, new-mintedness, newbornness, virginity, intactness, greenness, immaturity, rawness, callowness, brand-newness; presentness, nowness; **recentness,** recency, lateness; **novelty,** gloss of novelty, newfangledness *or* newfangleness; originality 337.1; **uncommonness,** unusualness, strangeness, unfamiliarity

2 novelty, innovation, neology, neologism, newfangled device *or* contraption <nf>, neoism, neonism, **new** *or* **latest wrinkle** <nf>, **the last word** *or* **the latest thing** <nf>, *dernier cri* <Fr>; what's happening *and* what's in *and* the in thing *and* where it's at <nf>; new ball game; new look, latest fashion *or* fad; advance guard, vanguard, **avant-garde;** neophilia, neophiliac; start-up

3 modernity, modernness; modernism; modernization, updating, *aggiornamento* <Ital>; state of the art; postmodernism, space age

4 modern, modern man; modernist; modernizer; neologist, neoterist, neology, neologism, neoterism, neoteric; modern *or* rising *or* new generation; neonate, fledgling, stripling, neophyte, *novus homo* <L>, new man, upstart, *arriviste* <Fr>, *nouveau riche* <Fr>, parvenu; Young Turk, bright young man, comer <nf>; trendsetter; new kid on the block <nf>

VERBS **5 innovate, invent,** make from scratch *or* from the ground up, coin, new-mint, mint, inaugurate, neologize, neoterize; **renew,** renovate 396.17; give a new lease on life

6 modernize, streamline; update, **bring up to date,** keep *or* stay current, move with the times

ADJS **7 new,** young, **fresh,** fresh as a daisy, fresh as the morning dew; **unused, firsthand, original;** untried, untouched, unhandled, unhandseled, untrodden, unbeaten; virgin, virginal, intact, maiden, maidenly; green, vernal; dewy, pristine, ever-new, sempervirent, evergreen; **immature,** undeveloped, raw, callow, fledgling, unfledged, nestling; neological, neologistic, neophytic

8 fresh, additional, further, other, another; **renewed**

9 new-made, new-built, new-wrought, new-shaped, new-mown, new-minted, new-coined, uncirculated, in mint condition, mint, new-begotten, new-grown, new-laid; **newfound;** newborn, neonatal, new-fledged; **new-model,** late-model, like new, factory-new, factory-fresh, oven-fresh, in its original carton

10 <nf terms> **brand-new,** fire-new, **brand-spanking new,** spanking, **spanking new; just out; hot,** hottest, hot off the fire *or* griddle *or* spit, hot off the press; newfangled *or* newfangle

11 novel, original, unique, different; strange, unusual, uncommon; unfamiliar, unheard-of; **first, first ever** 818.15

12 recent, late, newly come, of yesterday; latter, later

13 modern, contemporary, present-day, present-time, twentieth-century, latter-day, space-age, neoteric, now <nf>, topical, **newfashioned,** fashionable, modish, mod, *à la mode* <Fr>, **up-to-date,** up-to-datish, **up-to-the-minute, in,** abreast of the times; **advanced,** progressive, forward-looking, modernizing, **avant-garde;** ultramodern, ultra-ultra, ahead of its time, far out, way out, modernistic, modernized, streamlined; postmodern, trendy, faddish

14 state-of-the-art, newest, latest, the very latest, up-to-the-minute, last, most recent, newest of the new, farthest out

ADVS **15 newly,** freshly, new, **anew,** once more, from the ground up, from scratch <nf>, *ab ovo* <L>, *de novo* <L>, **afresh, again;** as new

16 now, recently, lately, latterly, **of late,** not long ago, a short time ago, the other day, only yesterday; just now, right now <nf>; neoterically

842 OLDNESS

NOUNS **1 oldness, age,** eld <old>, hoary eld; elderliness, seniority, senior citizenship, senility, **old age** 303.5; **ancientness, antiquity,** dust of ages, rust *or* cobwebs of antiquity; venerableness, eldership, primogeniture, great *or* hoary age, "the ancient and honourable"—Bible; old order, old style, *ancien régime* <Fr>; **primitiveness,** primordialism *or* primordiality, aboriginality; atavism

2 tradition, custom, immemorial usage, immemorial wisdom; Sunna <Muslim>; Talmud *and* Mishnah <Jewish>, ancient wisdom, ways of the fathers; traditionalism *or* traditionality; oral tradition; myth, mythology, legend, lore, folklore, folktale, folk motif, folk history; racial memory, archetypal myth *or* image *or* pattern, archetype; collective unconscious; "Spiritus Mundi"—Yeats

3 antiquation, superannuation, staleness, disuse; **old-fashionedness,** unfashionableness, out-of-dateness; **old-fogyishness,** fogyishness, stuffiness, stodginess, fuddy-duddiness

4 antiquarianism; classicism, medievalism, Pre-Raphaelitism, longing *or* yearning *or* nostalgia for the past; **archaeology;** Greek archaeology, Roman archaeology, etc, Assyriology, Egyptology, Sumerology; crisis archeology, industrial archeology, underwater *or* marine archeology, paleology, epigraphy, paleontology, human paleontology, paleethnology, paleonanthropology, paleoethnography; paleozoology, paleornithology, prehistoric anthropology

5 antiquarian, antiquary, *laudator temporis acti* <L>; dryasdust, the Rev Dr Dryasdust, Jonathan Oldbuck, Herr Teufelsdrö-ckh; **archaeologist;** classicist, medievalist, Miniver Cheevy, Pre-Raphaelite; antique dealer, antique collector, antique-car collector; archaist

6 antiquity, antique, archaism; **relic,** relic of the past; **remains,** survival, vestige, ruin *or* ruins; old thing, oldie *and* golden oldie <nf>; monument; **fossil,** index fossil, zone fossil, trace fossil, fossil record; petrification, petrified wood, petrified forest; **artifact,** artefact, eolith, mezzolith, microlith, neolith, paleolith, plateaulith; cave painting, petroglyph; ancient manuscript 547.11; museum piece

7 ancient, man *or* woman *or* person of old, old Homo, **prehistoric mankind** <see list>; preadamite, antediluvian; anthropoid, humanoid, primate, fossil man, protohuman, prehuman, missing link, apeman, hominid; **primitive, aboriginal,** aborigine, bushman, autochthon; **caveman,** cave dweller, troglodyte; bog man, bog body, Lindow man; Stone Age man, Bronze Age man, Iron Age man

8 <antiquated person> back number <nf>; pop *and* pops *and* dad <nf>, dodo *and* old dodo <nf>; fossil *and* antique *and* relic <nf>; **mossback** <nf>, longhair *and* square <nf>, **mid-Victorian,** antediluvian; old liner, old believer, conservative, hard-shell, traditionalist, reactionary; has-been; **fogy, old fogy,** regular old fogy, old poop *or* crock <nf>, **fud** *and* **fuddy-duddy** <nf>; granny <nf>, **old woman,** matriarch; **old man,** patriarch, elder, *starets* <Russ>, old-timer <nf>, Methuselah

VERBS **9 age,** grow old 303.10, grow *or* have whiskers; **antiquate,** fossilize, date, **superannuate,** outdate; obsolesce, go out of use *or* style, molder, fust, rust, fade, perish; lose currency *or* novelty; become obsolete *or* extinct; belong to the past, be a thing of the past; deteriorate, crumble

ADJS **10 old, age-old,** auld <Scot>, olden <old>, old-time, old-timey <nf>; **ancient,** antique, archaic, venerable, hoary; of old, of yore; dateless, timeless, ageless; **immemorial,** old as Methuselah *or* Adam, old as God, old as history, old as time, old as the hills, out of the Ark; **elderly** 303.16

11 primitive, prime, **primeval,** primogenial, primordial, pristine; atavistic; **aboriginal,** autochthonous; ancestral, patriarchal; **prehistoric,** protohistoric, preglacial, preadamite, antepatriarchal; prehuman, protohuman, humanoid; archetypal

12 traditional; mythological, heroic; **legendary,** unwritten, oral, handed down; true-blue, tried and true; **prescriptive, customary,** conventional, understood, admitted, recognized, acknowledged, received; **hallowed, time-honored,** immemorial; **venerable,** hoary, worshipful; **long-standing, of long standing,** long-established, established, fixed, inveterate, rooted; folk, of the folk, folkloric, legendary

13 antiquated, grown old, **superannuated, antique, old,** age-encrusted, of other times, old-world; Victorian, mid-Victorian; historic, classical, medieval, Gothic; antediluvian; **fossil,** fossilized, petrified

14 stale, fusty, musty, rusty, dusty, moldy, mildewed; **worn, timeworn,** time-scarred; **moth-eaten,** moss-grown, crumbling, moldering, gone to seed, dilapidated, ruined, ruinous

15 obsolete, passé, extinct, gone out, gone-by, dead, past, run out, **outworn**

16 old-fashioned, old-fangled, old-timey <nf>, **dated, out, out-of-date, outdated, outmoded,** out of style *or* fashion, out of use, disused, out of season, **unfashionable,** styleless, **behind the times,** of the old school, old hat *and* back-number *and* has-been <nf>

17 old-fogyish, fogyish, old-fogy; fuddy-duddy, square *and* corny *and* cornball <nf>; **stuffy, stodgy;** aged 303.16, senile, bent *or* wracked *or* ravaged with age

18 secondhand, used, worn, previously owned, **unnew,** not new, pawed-over; hand-me-down *and* reach-me-down <nf>

19 older, senior, Sr, major, elder, dean; **oldest,** eldest; first-born, firstling, primogenitary; former 837.10

20 archaeological, paleological; antiquarian; archaic; paleolithic, eolithic, neolithic, mezzolithic

ADVS **21** anciently 837.16

22 Stone Age cultures

Acheulean	Combe-Capelle
Aurignacian	Cro-Magnon
Azilian	Dabban
Capsian	Eolithic
Chellean	Goodwin

Magdalenian
Middle Awash
Mousterian
Neolithic
Oldowan

Olduvai
Paleolithic
Pre-Chellean
Solutrean

23 prehistoric men and manlike primates

Aurignacian man
Australanthropus
Australopithecus
Australopithecus afarensis
Australopithecus africanus
Australopithecus boisei
Australopithecus robustus
Bronze Age man
Brünn race
caveman *or* cave dweller
Cro-Magnon man
Dawn man <the Piltdown hoax>
eolithic man
Florisbad man
Furfooz *or* Grenelle man
Galley Hill man
Gigantopithecus
Grimaldi man
Heidelberg man
hominid

Homo erectus
Homo habilis
Iron Age man
Java man
Lucy
Meganthropus
Neanderthal man
neolithic man
Oreopithecus
paleolithic man
Paranthropus
Peking man
Piltdown man <hoax>
Pithecanthropus
Plesianthropus
protohuman
Rhodesian man
Sinanthropus
Stone Age man
Swanscombe man
Zinjanthropus

24 prehistoric animals

allosaurus
ammonite
anatosaurus
ankylosaurus
apatosaurus
archaeohippus
archaeopteryx
archaeornis
archaeotherium
archelon
archosaur
arthrodiran
atlantosaurus
aurochs
baryonyx Walker
bothriolepis
brachiosaurus
brontops
brontosaurus
brontothere
camarasaurus
cantius trigonodus
ceratopsid
ceratosaurus
cetiosaurus
coccostean
coelacanth
coelodont
compsognathus
coryphodon

cotylosaur
creodont
crossopterygian
cynodictis
cynodont
deinonychus
denversaurus
diacodexis
diatryma
dimetrodon
dinichthyid
dinosaur
dinothere
diplodocus
dipnoan
diprotodon
dodo
duck-billed dinosaur
edaphosaurid
elasmosaurus
eohippus
eryopsid
eurypterid
eurypterus remipes
giant sloth
glyptodont
gorgosaurus
hadrosaurus
hesperornis
hoplophoneus

hyaenodon
hyracodont
hyracothere
ichthyornis
ichthyosaurus
iguanodon
imperial mammoth *or* elephant
labyrinthodont
machairodont
mamenchisaurus
mammoth
mastodon
megalosaurus
megathere
merodus
merychippus
merycoidodon
merycopotamus
mesohippus
mesosaur
miacis
mosasaurus
nummulite
ornithomimid
ornithopod
ostracoderm
palaeodictyopteron
palaeomastodon
palaeoniscid
palaeophis
palaeosaur
palaeospondylus
pelycosaur
phytosaur
pinchosaurus
plesiosaurus

pliosaur
protoceratops
protohippus
protylopus
pteranodon
pteraspid
pterichthys
pterodactyl
pterosaur
quetzalcoatlus northropii
raptor
rhamphorhynchus
saber-toothed cat *or* tiger
sauropod
scelidosaurus
smilodon
stegocephalian
stegodon
stegosaurus
struthiomimus
teleoceras
therapsid
theriodont
theropod
thrinaxodon liorhinus
titanosaurus
titanothere
trachodon
triceratops
trilobite
tyrannosaurus *or* tyrannosaurus rex
uintathere
urus
woolly *or* northern mammoth

843 TIMELINESS

NOUNS **1 timeliness, seasonableness, opportuneness,** convenience; **expedience** *or* **expediency,** meetness, fittingness, fitness, appropriateness, rightness, propriety, suitability; **favorableness, propitiousness,** auspiciousness, felicitousness; **ripeness,** pregnancy, cruciality, criticality, criticalness, expectancy, loadedness, chargedness

2 opportunity, chance, time, occasion; opening, room, scope, space, place, liberty; clear stage, fair field, level playing field, fair game, fair shake *and* even break <nf>; **opportunism;** equal opportunity, nondiscrimination, affirmative action, positive discrimination <Brit>; trump card; a leg up, stepping-stone, rung of the ladder; time's forelock; window of opportunity

3 good opportunity, good chance, favorable opportunity, golden opportunity, well-timed opportunity, the chance of a lifetime, a once-in-alifetime chance, happy coincidence, lucky break, "a tide in the affairs of men"—Shakespeare; suitable occasion, proper occasion, suitable *or* proper time, **good time,** high time, due season; propitious *or* well-chosen moment; window of opportunity

4 crisis, critical point, crunch, crucial period, climax, climacteric; **turning point,** hinge, turn, turn of the tide, cusp, nexus; **emergency, exigency,** juncture *or* conjuncture *or* convergence of events, critical juncture, crossroads; **pinch,** clutch <nf>, rub, push, pass, strait, extremity, spot <nf>; **emergency,** state of emergency, red alert, race against time

5 crucial moment, critical moment, loaded *or* charged moment, decisive moment, kairotic moment, kairos, pregnant moment, defining moment, turning point, climax, **moment of truth,** crunch *and* when push comes to shove <nf>, when the balloon goes up <Brit nf>, point of no return; **psychological moment,** right moment; nick of time, eleventh hour; **zero hour,** H-hour, D-day, A-day, target date, deadline

VERBS **6 be timely,** suit *or* befit the time *or* season *or* occasion, come *or* fall just right

7 take *or* **seize the opportunity,** use the occasion, take the chance; take the bit in the teeth, leap into the breach, take the bull by the horns, bite the bullet, **make one's move,** cross the Rubicon, *prendre la balle au bond* <Fr, take the ball on the rebound>; **commit oneself,** make an opening, drive an entering wedge

8 improve the occasion, "improve each shining hour"—Isaac Watts, turn to account *or* good account, avail oneself of, **take advantage of,** put to advantage, profit by, **cash in** *or* **capitalize on;** take time by the forelock, seize the opportunity, seize the present hour, *carpe diem* <L, seize the day>, make hay while the sun shines; strike while the iron is hot; not be caught flatfooted, not be behindhand, not be caught looking <nf>, don't let the chance slip by, get going *and* get off the dime <nf>

ADJS **9 timely, well-timed, seasonable, opportune,** *in loco* <L>, convenient; **expedient,** meet, fit, fitting, befitting, suitable, sortable, appropriate; **favorable, propitious,** ripe, auspicious, lucky, providential, heaven-sent, fortunate, happy, felicitous; heaven-sent

10 critical, crucial, pivotal, climactic, climacteric *or* climacterical, decisive; pregnant, kairotic, loaded, charged; exigent, emergent; eleventh-hour

11 incidental, occasional, casual, accidental; parenthetical, by-the-way

ADVS **12 opportunely, seasonably, propitiously,**

auspiciously, in proper time *or* season, in due time *or* course *or* season, in the fullness of time, **in good time,** all in good time; in the nick of time, just in time, at the eleventh hour; now *or* never

13 incidentally, by the way, by the by; while on the subject, speaking of, *à propos* <Fr>, apropos *or* apropos of; **in passing,** *en passant* <Fr>; parenthetically, by way of parenthesis, *par parenthèse* <Fr>; for example, *par exemple* <Fr>

14 a bird in the hand is worth two in the bush, better late than never, every minute *or* moment counts; live for the moment, you can't take it with you

844 UNTIMELINESS

NOUNS **1 untimeliness, unseasonableness,** inopportuneness, inopportunity, unripeness, inconvenience; **inexpedience,** irrelevance *or* irrelevancy; **awkwardness,** inappropriateness, impropriety, unfitness, unfittingness, wrongness, unsuitability; **unfavorableness,** unfortunateness, inauspiciousness, unpropitiousness, infelicity; **intrusion,** interruption; **prematurity** 844.2; **lateness** 846, afterthought, thinking too late, *l'esprit de l'escalier* <Fr>

2 wrong time, bad time, wrong *or* bad *or* poor timing, unsuitable time, unfortunate time; evil hour, unlucky day *or* hour, off-year, *contretemps* <Fr>; inopportune moment

VERBS **3 ill-time, mistime,** miss the time; **lack the time,** not have time, have other *or* better things to do, be otherwise occupied, be engaged, be preoccupied, have other fish to fry <nf>

4 talk out of turn, speak inopportunely, interrupt, **put one's foot in one's mouth** <nf>, intrude, butt in *and* stick one's nose in <nf>, **go off half-cocked** <nf>, open one's big mouth *or* big fat mouth <nf>; blow it <nf>, speak too late *or* too soon

5 miss an opportunity, miss the chance, miss out, miss the boat, miss one's turn, lose the opportunity, ignore opportunity's knock, lose the chance, blow the chance <nf>, throw away *or* waste *or* neglect the opportunity, allow the occasion to go by, let slip through one's fingers, be left at the starting gate *or* post, be caught looking <nf>, oversleep, lock the barn door after the horse is stolen

ADJS **6 untimely, unseasonable, inopportune, ill-timed,** ill-seasoned, mistimed, unripe, unready, ill-considered, too late *or* soon, out of phase *or* time *or* sync; ill-starred; **inconvenient,** unhandy, discommodious; **inappropriate,** irrelevant, improper, unfit, wrong, out of line, off-base, unsuitable, **inexpedient,** unfitting, unbefitting, untoward, malapropos, *mal à propos* <Fr>, intrusive; **unfavorable,** unfortunate, infelicitous, inauspicious, **unpropitious,** unhappy, unlucky, misfortuned; **premature** 845.8; not in time, **late** 845.16

ADVS **7 inopportunely, unseasonably,** inconveniently, inexpediently; **unpropitiously,** inauspiciously, unfortunately, in an evil hour, at just the wrong time

845 EARLINESS

NOUNS **1 earliness,** early hour, time to spare; **head start,** running start, ground floor, first crack, early start, beginnings, first *or* early stage, very beginning, preliminaries; **anticipation, foresight,** prevision, prevenience; advance notice, lead time, a stitch in time, readiness, preparedness, preparation

2 prematurity, prematureness; **untimeliness** 844; precocity, **precociousness,** forwardness; precipitation, precipitancy, haste, hastiness, **overhastiness,** rush, impulse, impulsivity, impulsiveness

3 promptness, promptitude, punctuality, punctualness, readiness; instantaneousness 830, immediateness *or* immediacy, summariness, decisiveness, **alacrity,** quickness 174.1, speediness, swiftness, rapidity, expeditiousness, expedition, dispatch

4 early bird <nf>, early riser, early *or* first comer, first arrival, first on the scene; Johnny-on-the-spot <nf>; **precursor** 816

VERBS **5 be early,** be ahead of time, take time by the forelock, be up and stirring, be beforehand *or* betimes, be ready and waiting, be off and running; gain time, draw on futurity *or* on the future; get there first; get a wiggle on *or* hop to it <nf>

6 anticipate, foresee, foreglimpse, previse, see the handwriting on the wall, foretaste, pave the way for, prevent <old>; **forestall,** forerun, go before, **get ahead of,** win the start, break out ahead, get a head start, steal a march on, beat someone to the punch *or* the draw <nf>; **jump the gun,** beat the gun, go off half-cocked <nf>; preempt; take the words out of one's mouth

ADJS **7 early,** bright and early *and* with the birds <nf>, **beforetime,** in good time *or* season; **forehand,** forehanded; foresighted, **anticipative** *or* **anticipatory,** prevenient, previsional

8 premature, too early, too soon, oversoon; previous *and* a bit previous <nf>, prevenient; **untimely; precipitate,** hasty 830.5, **overhasty,** too soon off the mark, too quick on the draw *or* trigger *or* uptake <nf>; **unprepared,** unripe, impulsive, rushed, unmatured; unpremeditated, unmeditated, ill-

considered, **half-cocked** *and* **half-baked** <nf>, unjelled, uncrystallized, not firm; **precocious, forward, advanced,** far ahead, born before one's time

9 prompt, punctual, immediate, instant, instantaneous 830.4, **quick** 174.19, speedy, swift, expeditious, summary, decisive, apt, alert, **ready,** alacritous, Johnny-on-the-spot <nf>; as soon as possible *or* ASAP

10 earlier, previous 834.4

ADVS **11 early, bright and early, beforehand, beforetime,** early on, betimes, precociously, **ahead of time,** foresightedly, in advance, in anticipation, ahead, before, **with time to spare**

12 in time, in good time, soon enough, time enough, early enough; just in time, **in the nick of time,** with no time to spare, just under the wire, without a minute to spare

13 prematurely, too soon, oversoon, untimely, too early, before its *or* one's time; **precipitately,** impulsively, in a rush, hastily, **overhastily;** at half cock <nf>

14 punctually, precisely, exactly, sharp; **on time,** on the minute *or* instant, to the minute *or* second, **on the dot** <nf>, spot on *and* bang on <Brit nf>, at the gun

15 promptly, without delay, without further delay *or* ado, directly, **immediately,** immediately if not sooner <nf>, **instantly** 830.6, instanter, on the instant, on the spot, **at once,** right off, **right away, straightway,** straightaway, **forthwith,** *pronto* <Sp>, *subito* <Ital>, PDQ *or* pretty damned quick <nf>, **quickly,** swiftly, speedily, with all speed, **summarily,** decisively, smartly, expeditiously, apace, in no time, in less than no time; no sooner said than done

16 soon, presently, directly, shortly, in a short time *or* while, **before long,** ere long, in no long time, in a while, **in a little while, after a while, by and by,** anon, betimes, *bientôt* <Fr>, in due time, in due course, at the first opportunity; in a moment *or* minute, *tout à l'heure* <Fr>

PHRS **17** the early bird gets the worm

846 LATENESS

NOUNS **1 lateness, tardiness, belatedness, unpunctuality;** late hour, small hours; eleventh hour, last minute, high time; unreadiness, unpreparedness; untimeliness 844

2 delay, stoppage, jam *and* logjam <nf>, obstruction, tie-up *and* bind <nf>, **block,** blockage, **hang-up** <nf>; delayed reaction, double take, afterthought; **retardation** *or* retardance, slow development, slowdown *and* slow-up <nf>, slowness, lag, time lag, lagging, dragging, dragging one's feet *and* foot-dragging <nf>, pigeonholing; **detention,** suspension, holdup <nf>, **obstruction, hindrance;** delaying action, delaying tactics; **wait, halt, stay, stop,** down-time, break, pause, interim 826, respite; reprieve, stay of execution; moratorium; **red tape,** red-tapery, red-tapeism, bureaucratic delay, *paperasserie* <Fr>

3 **waiting,** cooling one's heels <nf>, **tarrying,** tarriance <old>; **lingering, dawdling,** dalliance, dallying, dillydallying; back burner

4 **postponement, deferment** *or* **deferral,** prorogation, putting-off, tabling, holding up, holding in suspension, carrying over; **prolongation,** protraction, continuation, extension of time; **adjournment** *or* adjournal, adjournment sine die

5 **procrastination,** "the thief of time"—Edward Young, hesitation 362.3; **temporization, a play for time, stall** *and* tap-dancing <nf>; Micawberism, Fabian policy; **dilatoriness,** slowness, backwardness, remissness, slackness, laxness

6 **latecomer,** late arrival, Johnny-come-lately; slow starter, dawdler, dallier, dillydallier; late bloomer *or* developer; retardee; late riser, slug-abed; ten o'clock scholar

VERBS 7 **be late, not be on time,** be overdue, be behindhand, show up late, miss the boat; keep everyone waiting; **stay late,** stay up late *or* into the small hours, burn the midnight oil, keep late hours; get up late, keep banker's hours; oversleep

8 **delay, retard, detain,** make late, slacken, lag, drag, drag one's feet *and* stonewall <nf>, dilly-dally, slow down, **hold up** <nf>, hold *or* keep back, check, **stay, stop,** arrest, impede, **block,** hinder, obstruct, throw a monkey wrench in the works <nf>, confine; tie up with red tape

9 **postpone, delay, defer, put off,** give one a rain check <nf>, shift off, hold off *or* up <nf>, prorogue, put on hold *or* ice *or* the back burner <nf>, reserve, waive, **suspend,** hang up, stay, hang fire; protract, drag *or* stretch out <nf>, **prolong, extend,** spin *or* string out, continue, adjourn, recess, take a recess, prorogue; **hold over,** lay over, stand over, let the matter stand, **put aside,** lay *or* set *or* push aside, lay *or* set by, **table,** lay on the table, pigeonhole, **shelve,** put on the shelf, put on ice <nf>; consult one's pillow about, sleep on

10 **be left behind,** be outrun *or* outdistanced, make a slow start, be slow *or* late *or* last off the mark, be left at the post *or* starting gate; bloom *or* develop late

11 **procrastinate,** be dilatory, hesitate, let something slide, hang, hang back, hang fire; **temporize,** gain *or* make time, **play for time,** drag one's feet <nf>, hold off <nf>; **stall,** stall off, **stall for time,** stall *or*

stooge around *and* tap-dance <nf>; talk against time, filibuster

12 **wait, delay, stay,** bide, abide, **bide** *or* **abide one's time; take one's time,** take time, mark time; **tarry, linger, loiter,** dawdle, dally, dillydally; hang around *or* about *or* out <nf>, stick around <nf>; **hold on** <nf>, sit tight <nf>, hold one's breath; wait a minute *or* second, wait up; hold everything *and* hold your horses *and* hold your water *and* keep your shirt on <nf>; wait *or* stay up, sit up; **wait and see,** bide the issue, see which way the cat jumps, see how the cookie crumbles *or* the ball bounces <nf>, let sleeping dogs lie; wait for something to turn up; **await** 130.8

13 wait impatiently, tear one's hair *and* sweat it out *and* champ *or* chomp at the bit <nf>

14 be kept waiting, be stood up <nf>, be left; **cool one's heels** <nf>

15 **overstay,** overtarry

ADJS 16 **late, belated, tardy,** slow, slow on the draw *or* uptake *or* trigger <nf>, **behindhand,** never on time, backward, back, **overdue, long-awaited, untimely; unpunctual,** unready; latish; **delayed,** detained, **held up** <nf>, **retarded, arrested,** blocked, **hung up** *and* in a bind <nf>, obstructed, stopped, jammed, congested; weather-bound; **postponed, in abeyance,** held up, put off, **on hold** *or* put on hold <nf>, on the back burner *or* put on the back burner <nf>; delayed-action; moratory

17 **dilatory, delaying,** Micawberish; slow *or* late *or* last off the mark; **procrastinating,** procrastinative *or* procrastinatory, go-slow; **obstructive,** obstructionist *or* obstructionistic, bloody-minded <Brit nf>; **lingering,** loitering, lagging, dallying, dillydallying, **slow,** sluggish, laggard, foot-dragging, shuffling, backward; easygoing, **lazy, lackadaisical; remiss,** slack, work-shy, lax

18 later 835.4; last-minute, eleventh-hour, deathbed

ADVS 19 **late, behind, behindhand, belatedly,** backward, slow, **behind time,** after time; far on, deep into; late in the day, at the last minute, at the eleventh hour, none too soon, in the nick of time, under the wire

20 **tardily, slow, slowly,** deliberately, dilatorily, sluggishly, lackadaisically, leisurely, at one's leisure, lingeringly; until all hours, into the night

847 FREQUENCY

NOUNS 1 **frequency,** frequence, **oftenness; commonness,** usualness, prevalence, **common occurrence,** routineness, habitualness; **incidence,** relative incidence; radio frequency

2 **constancy, continualness,** steadiness, sustainment, **regularity,** noninterruption *or* uninterruption,

nonintermission *or* unintermission, incessancy, ceaselessness, constant flow, continuity 812; perpetuity 829; repetition 849; **rapidity** 174.1; rapid recurrence *or* succession, rapid *or* quick fire, tattoo, **staccato,** chattering, stuttering; **vibration,** shuddering, juddering <Brit>, pulsation, **oscillation** 916

VERBS 3 be frequent, occur often, have a high incidence, continue 812.4, recur 850.5; shudder, judder <Brit>, vibrate, oscillate 916.10; frequent, hang out at <nf>

ADJS 4 frequent, oftentime, many, many times, **recurrent,** recurring, **oft-repeated,** thick-coming; **common,** of common occurrence, not rare, thick on the ground <Brit>, **prevalent,** usual, routine, habitual, ordinary, everyday; frequentative

5 constant, continual 812.8, **perennial; steady,** sustained, **regular;** periodic; **incessant, ceaseless, unceasing,** unintermitting, unintermittent *or* unintermitted, unremitting, relentless, unrelenting, unchanging, unvarying, uninterrupted, unstopped, unbroken; **perpetual** 829.7; repeated 848.12; **rapid, staccato,** stuttering, chattering, machine gun; pulsating, juddering <Brit>, vibrating, **oscillating** 916.15

ADVS 6 frequently, commonly, usually, ordinarily, routinely, habitually; **often,** oft, **oftentimes,** oft times; **repeatedly** 848.16, **again and again, time after time; most often** *or* frequently, in many instances, **many times,** many a time, full many a time, many a time and oft, as often as can be, as often as not, more often than not; **in quick** *or* **rapid succession;** often enough, not infrequently, not seldom, unseldom; as often as you wish *or* like, whenever you wish *or* like

7 constantly, continually 812.10, **steadily,** sustainedly, **regularly,** as regular as clockwork, with every other breath, every time one turns around, right along <nf>, unvaryingly, uninterruptedly, unintermittently, **incessantly,** unceasingly, **ceaselessly,** without cease *or* ceasing, perennially, all the time, at all times, ever, ever and anon, on and on, without letup *or* break *or* intermission, without stopping; **perpetually, always** 829.11; **rapidly;** all year round, every day, every hour, every moment; daily, hourly, daily and hourly; **night and day,** day and night; **morning, noon, and night;** hour after hour, day after day, month after month, year after year; **day in day out,** month in month out, year in year out

848 INFREQUENCY

NOUNS 1 infrequency, infrequence, unfrequentness, seldomness; occasionalness; **rarity, scarcity,**

scarceness, rareness, **uncommonness,** uniqueness, unusualness; **sparsity** 885.1; **slowness** 175; one-time offer

ADJS 2 infrequent, unfrequent, **rare,** scarce, scarce as hens' teeth, scarcer than hens' teeth, **uncommon,** unique, unusual, almost unheard-of, seldom met with, seldom seen, few and far between, **sparse** 885.5; one-time, one-shot, once in a lifetime; **slow** 175.10; like snow in August; unprecedented

3 occasional, casual, incidental; odd, sometime, extra, side, off, off-and-on, out-of-the-way, spare, sparetime, **part-time**

ADVS 4 infrequently, unfrequently, **seldom, rarely, uncommonly,** scarcely, hardly, **scarcely** *or* hardly ever, very seldom, not often, only now and then, at infrequent intervals, unoften, off-and-on; **sparsely** 885.8

5 occasionally, on occasion, **sometimes, at times,** at odd times, every so often <nf>, at various times, on divers occasions, **now and then,** every now and then <nf>, now and again, **once in a while,** every once in a while <nf>, every now and again, once and again, once or twice, betweentimes, betweenwhiles, at intervals, **from time to time;** only occasionally, only when the spirit moves, only when necessary, only now and then, at infrequent intervals, once in a blue moon *and* once in a coon's age <nf>; irregularly, sporadically

6 once, one-time, on one occasion, just *or* only once, just this once, once and no more, once for all, once and for all *or* always

849 REPETITION

NOUNS 1 repetition, reproduction, duplication 874, reduplication, doubling, redoubling; **recurrence,** reoccurrence, cyclicality, return, reincarnation, rebirth, reappearance, renewal, resumption; resurfacing, reentry; echo, reecho, parroting; regurgitation, rehearsal, rote recitation; **quotation; imitation** 336; plagiarism 621.2; reexamination, second *or* another look

2 iteration, reiteration, recapitulation, recap *and* wrapup <nf>, retelling, recounting, recountal, **recital, rehearsal, restatement,** rehash <nf>; reissue, reprint; review, summary, précis, résumé, summing up, peroration; going over *or* through, practicing; reassertion, reaffirmation; elaboration, dwelling upon; **copy** 785

3 redundancy, tautology, tautologism, pleonasm, macrology, battology; stammering, stuttering; padding, filling, filler, expletive

4 repetitiousness, repetitiveness, stale *or* unnecessary repetition; harping; **monotony,** monotone, drone; **tedium** 118, daily round *or*

grind, same old story; **humdrum,** dingdong, singsong, chime, jingle, jingle-jangle, trot, pitter-patter; **rhyme, alliteration,** assonance, slant *or* near rhyme; echolalia, **repeated sounds** 55

5 **repeat,** repetend, bis, ditto <nf>, echo; **refrain,** burden, chant, undersong, chorus, bob; bob wheel, bob and wheel; ritornel, *ritornello* <Ital>; rerun; rehash; reprint, reissue; remake; second helping

6 **encore,** repeat performance, repeat, **reprise;** replay, replaying, return match; repeat order

VERBS 7 **repeat, redo,** do again, do over, do a repeat, **reproduce, duplicate** 874.3, reduplicate, double, redouble, ditto <nf>, **echo, parrot,** reecho; **rattle off,** reel off, regurgitate; renew, reincarnate, revive; come again *and* run it by again <nf>, say again, repeat oneself, **quote,** repeat word for word *or* verbatim, repeat like a broken record; **copy, imitate** 336.5; plagiarize 621.4, 336.5; **reexamine,** take *or* have a second look, take *or* have another look

8 **iterate, reiterate, rehearse, recapitulate, recount,** rehash <nf>, **recite, retell,** retail, **restate,** reword, review, run over, sum up, summarize, précis, resume, encapsulate; reissue, reprint; do *or* say over again, **go over** *or* **through,** practice, say over, go over the same ground, give an encore, quote oneself, go the same round, fight one's battles over again; **tautologize,** battologize, pad, fill; **reaffirm,** reassert

9 **dwell on** *or* **upon,** insist upon, **harp on,** beat a dead horse, have on the brain, constantly recur *or* revert to, labor, belabor, hammer away at, always trot out, sing the same old song *or* tune, play the same old record, plug the same theme, never hear the last of; **thrash** *or* **thresh over,** cover the same ground, go over again and again, go over and over

10 **din, ding;** drum 55.4, beat, hammer, pound; **din in the ear,** din into, drum into, say over and over

11 <be repeated> **repeat, recur,** reoccur, **come again,** come round again, go round again, come up again, resurface, reenter, **return, reappear, resume;** resound, reverberate, echo; revert, turn *or* go back; keep coming, come again and again, happen over and over, run through like King Charles's head

ADJS 12 **repeated,** reproduced, doubled, redoubled; **duplicated,** reduplicated; regurgitated, recited by rote; **echoed,** reechoed, parroted; **quoted,** plagiarized; **iterated, reiterated,** reiterate; retold, **twice-told;** warmed up *or* over, *réchauffé* <Fr>

13 **recurrent,** recurring, **returning,** reappearing, revenant, ubiquitous, ever-recurring, cyclical, periodic, yearly, monthly, weekly, daily, circadian, thick-coming, frequent, incessant, continuous

812.8, year-to-year, month-to-month, week-to-week, etc; haunting, thematic

14 **repetitious,** repetitive, repetitional *or* repetitionary, repeating; **duplicative,** reduplicative; **imitative** 336.9, parrotlike; echoing, reechoing, echoic; **iterative, reiterative,** reiterant; recapitulative, recapitulatory; battological, **tautological** *or* **tautologous, redundant**

15 **monotonous,** monotone, **tedious;** harping, labored, belabored, cliché-ridden; **humdrum,** singsong, chiming, chanting, dingdong <nf>, jog-trot, jingle-jangle; **rhymed, rhyming, alliterative,** alliterating, assonant

ADVS 16 **repeatedly, often, frequently, recurrently, every time one turns around,** with every other breath, like a tolling bell, **again and again, over and over,** over and over again, many times over, time and again, **time after time,** times without number, **ad nauseam;** year in year out, week in week out, etc, year after year, day after day, day by day, "tomorrow and tomorrow and tomorrow"—Shakespeare; **many times,** several times, a number of times, many a time, many a time and oft, full many a time and oft; every now and then, every once in a while

17 **again,** over, over again, **once more,** *encore* and *bis* <Fr>, two times, twice over, ditto; **anew,** *de novo* <L>, afresh; from the beginning, *da capo* <Ital>

INTERJS 18 **encore!,** *bis!* <Fr>, once more!, again!

850 REGULARITY OF RECURRENCE

NOUNS 1 **regularity,** regularness, clockwork regularity, predictability, punctuality, smoothness, **steadiness, evenness, unvariableness, methodicalness,** systematicalness; **repetition** 849; **uniformity** 781; **constancy** 847.2

2 **periodicity,** periodicalness; cyclical motion, piston motion, pendulum motion, regular wave motion, undulation, **pulsation; intermittence** *or* intermittency, alternation; rhythm 709.22, meter, beat; **oscillation** 916; **recurrence,** go-round, reoccurrence, reappearance, return, the eternal return, **cyclicalness,** cyclicality, seasonality; resurfacing, reentry

3 **round, revolution, rotation, cycle,** circle, wheel, **circuit; beat,** upbeat, downbeat, thesis, arsis, **pulse;** systole, diastole; course, series, **bout, turn,** rota <Brit>, spell 825

4 **anniversary, commemoration;** immovable feast, annual holiday; biennial, triennial, quadrennial, quinquennial, sextennial, septennial, octennial, nonennial, decennial, tricennial, jubilee, silver jubilee, golden jubilee, diamond jubilee; centennial, centenary; quasquicentennial;

sesquicentennial; bicentennial, bicentenary; tercentennial, tercentenary, tricentenary; quincentennial, quincentenary; **wedding anniversary,** silver wedding anniversary, golden wedding anniversary; **birthday,** birthdate, natal day; saint's day, name day; leap year, bissextile day; annual holiday, government holiday, bank holiday; **religious holiday,** holy day

VERBS **5** <occur periodically> **recur, reoccur, return, repeat** 849.7, reappear, **come again,** come up again, be here again, resurface, reenter, **come round** or around, come round again, come in its turn; **rotate, revolve,** turn, circle, wheel, cycle, **roll around,** roll about, wheel around, go around, go round; **intermit,** alternate, **come and go,** ebb and flow; undulate 916.11; **oscillate** 916.10, **pulse, pulsate** 916.12; commute, shuttle

ADJS **6 regular, systematic** or systematical, methodical, ordered, orderly, regular as clockwork; everyday; **uniform** 780.5; **constant** 847.5

7 periodic or periodical, seasonal, epochal, **cyclic** or cyclical, serial, isochronal, metronomic; measured, steady, even, **rhythmic** or rhythmical 709.28; **recurrent,** recurring, reoccurring; **intermittent,** reciprocal, alternate, every other; circling, wheeling, rotary, rotational, wavelike, undulant, undulatory, oscillatory 915.15, pulsing, beating 916.18

8 momentary, momently, **hourly; daily,** diurnal, quotidian, circadian, nightly, tertian; biorhythmic; **weekly,** tertian, hebdomadal, hebdomadary; biweekly, semiweekly; fortnightly; **monthly,** menstrual, catamenial, estrous; bimonthly, semimonthly; quarterly; biannual, semiannual, semiyearly, half-yearly, semestral; **yearly, annual;** perennial; biennial, triennial, decennial, etc; centennial, centenary; bissextile; secular

ADVS **9 regularly, systematically, methodically,** like clockwork, at regular intervals, punctually, steadily; at stated times, at fixed or established periods; intermittently, every so often, every now and then; **uniformly** 781.7; **constantly** 847.7

10 periodically, recurrently, seasonally, cyclically, epochally; rhythmically, on the beat, in time, synchronously, **hourly, daily,** etc; every hour, every day, etc; hour by hour, day by day, etc; from hour to hour, from day to day, *de die in diem* <L>

11 alternately, by turns, in turns, in rotation, turn about, **turn and turn about,** reciprocally, every other, one after the other; to and fro, up and down, from side to side; off and on, make and break, round and round

PHRS **12 what goes around comes around,** *plus ça change plus c'est la même chose* <Fr>

851 IRREGULARITY OF RECURRENCE

NOUNS **1 irregularity,** unmethodicalness, unsystematicness; **inconstancy, unevenness, unsteadiness,** uncertainty, desultoriness; **variability,** capriciousness, unpredictability, whimsicality, eccentricity; stagger, wobble, weaving, erraticness; roughness; **fitfulness, sporadicity** or sporadicalness, spasticity, jerkiness, fits and starts, patchiness, spottiness, choppiness, brokenness, disconnectedness, discontinuity 813; **intermittence, fluctuation;** nonuniformity 781; arrhythmia *and* fibrillation <medical>; assymetry; unusualness

VERBS **2 intermit, fluctuate,** vary, lack regularity, go by fits and starts; break, disconnect

ADJS **3 irregular,** unregular, unsystematic, unmethodical or immethodical; **inconstant, unsteady, uneven, unrhythmical,** unmetrical, rough, unequal, uncertain, unsettled; **variable,** deviative, heteroclite; **capricious, erratic,** off-again-on-again, eccentric; wobbly, wobbling, weaving, staggering, lurching, careening; **fitful, spasmodic** or spasmodical, spastic, spasmic, **jerky,** herky-jerky <nf>, halting; **sporadic,** patchy, spotty, scrappy, snatchy, catchy, choppy, halting, **broken, disconnected, discontinuous** 813.4; **nonuniform** 782.3; **intermittent,** intermitting, **desultory, fluctuating, wavering,** wandering, rambling, veering; flickering, guttering; haphazard, disorderly

ADVS **4 irregularly,** unsystematically, unmethodically; **inconstantly, unsteadily, unevenly,** unrhythmically, roughly, uncertainly; **variably,** capriciously, unpredictably, whimsically, eccentrically, wobblingly, lurchingly, erratically; **intermittently, disconnectedly, discontinuously** 813.5; **nonuniformly** 781.4; **brokenly, desultorily,** patchily, spottily, in spots, in snatches; **by fits and starts,** by fits, by jerks, by snatches, by catches; **fitfully, sporadically, jerkily, spasmodically,** haltingly; **off and on,** at irregular intervals, sometimes and sometimes not; when the mood strikes, when the spirit moves, at random

852 CHANGE

NOUNS **1 change, alteration, modification; variation,** variety, difference, diversity, diversification; **deviation,** diversion, aberrance or aberrancy, **divergence; switch, switchover, changeover, turn,** change of course, turnabout, about-face, U-turn, **reversal,** flip-flop <nf>; apostasy, defection, change of heart, change of mind; **shift,** transition, **modulation,** qualification; **conversion, renewal,** revival, revivification, retro; remaking, reshaping,

re-creation, redesign, restructuring, *perestroika*
<Russ>; realignment, **adaptation, adjustment,**
accommodation, fitting, tweaking, tweak; **reform,**
reformation, **improvement,** amelioration,
melioration, mitigation, constructive change,
betterment, change for the better; **take** *and* **new
take** <nf>; **social mobility,** vertical mobility,
horizontal mobility, upward *or* downward
mobility; gradual change, progressive change,
continuity 812; **degeneration, deterioration,**
worsening, degenerative change, change for the
worse, disorder 810, entropy; changeableness 854;
"the ever whirling wheels of Change"—Spenser,
"Nature's mighty law"—Robert Burns, "the
changes and chances of this mortal life"—Book of
Common Prayer

2 **revolution,** revolt, **break,** break with the past,
sudden change, radical *or* revolutionary *or* violent
or total change, catastrophic change, **upheaval,**
overthrow, **quantum jump** *or* **leap,** sea change;
discontinuity 813

3 **transformation,** transmogrification; **translation;**
metamorphosis, metamorphism; makeover;
mutation, transmutation, permutation, vicissitude;
mutant, mutated form, sport; **transfiguration** *or*
transfigurement; metathesis, transposition,
translocation, **displacement,** metastasis,
heterotopia; **transubstantiation,** consubstantiation;
transanimation, transmigration, reincarnation,
metempsychosis avatar; metasomatism,
metasomatosis; catalysis; metabolism, anabolism,
catabolism; metagenesis; transformism;
redecoration

4 **innovation, introduction,** discovery, invention,
launching; neologism, neoterism, coinage;
breakthrough, leap, quantum jump *or* leap, new
phase; **novelty** 840.2

5 **transformer,** transmogrifier, **innovator,**
innovationist, introducer; precursor 816; **alterant,**
alterer, alterative, **agent,** catalytic agent, catalyst;
the wind *or* winds of change; **leaven,** yeast,
ferment; **modifier,** modificator; magician

VERBS 6 **be changed, change, undergo a change,** go
through a change, sing *or* dance to a different tune
<nf>, be converted into, turn into 857.17; **alter,**
mutate, modulate; **vary,** checker, diversify; **deviate,
diverge,** turn, take a turn, take a new turn, turn
aside, turn the corner, **shift,** veer, jibe, tack, come
about, come round *or* around, haul around, chop,
chop and change, swerve, warp; change sides,
change horses in midstream; **revive,** be renewed,
feel like a new person; **improve,** ameliorate,
meliorate, mitigate, turn the corner; **degenerate,
deteriorate, worsen;** hit bottom, bottom out <nf>,
reach the nadir, flop <nf>

7 **change, work** *or* **make a change, alter,** change
someone's tune; **mutate; modify;** adapt; modulate,
accommodate, adjust, fine-tune, fit, **qualify; vary,
diversify; convert, renew, recast, revamp** <nf>,
change over, exchange, **revive;** remake, reshape, re-
create, redesign, **rebuild,** reconstruct, restructure;
realign; refit; **reform, improve,** better, ameliorate,
meliorate, mitigate; **revolutionize,** turn upside
down, subvert, overthrow, break up; worsen,
deform, denature; ring the changes; give a turn to,
give a twist to, turn the tide, turn the tables, turn
the scale *or* balance; shift the scene; shuffle the
cards; turn over a new leaf; **about-face,** do an
about-face, do a 180 <nf>, change direction,
reverse oneself, turn one's coat, sing *or* dance to a
different tune, flip-flop <nf>, make a U-turn,
change one's mind

8 **transform, transfigure, transmute,** transmogrify;
translate; transubstantiate, metamorphose;
metabolize; perform magic, conjure

9 **innovate,** make innovations, invent, discover, make
a breakthrough, make a quantum jump *or* leap,
pioneer 816.3, **revolutionize, introduce,** introduce
new blood; neologize, neoterize, coin

ADJS 10 **changed, altered, modified,** qualified,
transformed, transmuted, **metamorphosed;**
translated, metastasized; deviant, aberrant,
mutant; divergent; **converted, renewed,** revived,
rebuilt, remodeled; **reformed,** improved, **better,**
ameliorative, ameliatory; before-and-after;
degenerate, worse, unmitigated; subversive,
revolutionary; changeable 854.6,7

11 **innovational,** innovative, ameliorative

12 **metamorphic, metabolic,** anabolic, catabolic;
metastatic, **catalytic**

13 presto, presto chango, hey presto <Brit>

PHRS 14 the shoe is on the other foot

853 PERMANENCE

NOUNS 1 **permanence** *or* permanency, **immutability,
changelessness,** unchangingness, invariableness *or*
invariability; **unchangeableness,** unchangeability,
unchangingness, inalterability *or* inalterableness,
inconvertibility *or* inconvertibleness; **fixedness,
constancy,** steadfastness, firmness, solidity,
immovableness *or* immovability, persistence *or*
persistency, establishment, faithfulness,
lastingness, abidingness, endurance, duration,
continuance, perseverance, continuity, standing,
long standing, inveteracy; durableness, durability
827; **perpetualness** 829.1; **stability** 855;
unchangeability 855.4; **immobility,** stasis,
frozenness, hardening, **rigidity; quiescence,** torpor,
coma

2 maintenance, preservation 397, **conservation**

3 conservatism, conservativeness, opposition *or* resistance to change, unprogressiveness, fogyism, fuddy-duddyism, backwardness, old-fashionedness, standpattism <nf>; ultraconservatism, arch-conservatism; misocainea, misoneism; political conservatism, rightism 611.1; laissez-faireism 329.1; old school tie <Brit>; "adherence to the old and tried, against the new and untried"—Lincoln

4 conservative, conservatist; conservationist; ultraconservative, arch-conservative, knee-jerk conservative <nf>, **diehard,** standpat *and* standpatter <nf>, **old fogy,** fogy, stick-in-the-mud <nf>, mossback <nf>, *laudator temporis acti* <L>, rightist, right-winger 611.9, "the leftover progressive of an earlier generation"—Edmund Fuller; old school

VERBS **5 remain, endure** 827.6, last, stay, persist, bide, abide, stand, hold, subsist; be ever the same; take root, be here to stay; cast in stone

6 be conservative, save, preserve, oppose change, stand on ancient ways; stand pat *and* stand still <nf>; **let things take their course,** leave things as they are, let be, let *or* leave alone, stick with it *and* let it ride <nf>, follow a hands-off policy, let well enough alone, do nothing; stop *or* turn back the clock

ADJS **7 permanent, changeless, unchanging, immutable,** unvarying, unshifting; unchanged, unchangeable, unvaried, **unaltered,** inalterable, inviolate, undestroyed, intact; **constant, persistent,** sustained, fixed, firm, solid, steadfast, like the Rock of Gibraltar, faithful; unchecked, unfailing, unfading; **lasting, enduring,** abiding, remaining, staying, continuing; **durable** 827.10, entrenched; **perpetual** 829.7; stable 855.12; **unchangeable** 854.17; **immobile, static,** stationary, frozen, **rigid,** rocklike; **quiescent,** torpid, comatose, vegetable

8 conservative, preservative, old-line, **diehard,** standpat <nf>, opposed to change; backward, backward-looking, old-fashioned, **unprogressive,** nonprogressive, unreconstructed, status-quo, stuck-in-the-mud; ultraconservative, misoneistic, fogyish, **old-fogyish; right-wing** 611.17; *laissez-faire* <Fr>, hands-off; noninvasive, noninterventionist

ADVS **9 permanently,** abidingly, lastingly, steadfastly, unwaveringly, changelessly, unchangingly; enduringly, **perpetually,** invariably, **forever, always** 829.11; statically, rigidly, inflexibly

10 *in status quo* <L>, as things are, **as is, as usual,** as per usual <nf>; at a stand *or* standstill, without a shadow of turning

PHRS **11** *plus ça change, plus c'est la même chose* <Fr, the more it changes, the more it's the same thing>; if it isn't broken don't fix it, let sleeping dogs lie

854 CHANGEABLENESS

NOUNS **1 changeableness,** changefulness, **changeability, alterability,** convertibility, modifiability; **mutability,** permutability, impermanence, **transience,** transitoriness; mobility, motility, movability; plasticity, malleability, workability, rubberiness, fluidity; **resilience, adaptability,** adjustability, **flexibility,** suppleness; **nonuniformity** 781

2 inconstancy, instability, changefulness, unstableness, **unsteadiness,** unsteadfastness, unfixedness, unsettledness, rootlessness; **uncertainty,** undependability, inconsistency, shiftiness, unreliability; **variability,** variation, variety, restlessness, deviability; unpredictability, irregularity 851.1; **desultoriness,** waywardness, wantonness; **erraticism, eccentricity;** freakishness, freakery; flightiness, impulsiveness *or* impulsivity, mercuriality, moodiness, whimsicality, **capriciousness,** caprice, **fickleness** 364.3

3 changing, fluctuation, vicissitude, **variation, shiftingness;** alternation, oscillation, **vacillation,** pendulation; **mood swings; wavering,** shifting, shuffling, teetering, tottering, seesawing, teeter-tottering; **exchange,** trading, musical chairs; bobbing and weaving

4 <comparisons> Proteus, kaleidoscope, chameleon, shifting sands, rolling stone, April showers, cloud shapes, feather in the wind; water; wheel of fortune; whirligig; mercury, quicksilver; the weather, weathercock, weather vane; moon, phases of the moon; iridescence

VERBS **5 change, fluctuate, vary; shift; alternate, vacillate,** tergiversate, oscillate, pendulate, waffle <Brit nf>, blow hot and cold <nf>; ebb and flow, wax and wane; go through phases, waver, shuffle, swing, sway, wobble, wobble about, flounder, stagger, teeter, totter, **seesaw, teeter-totter;** back and fill, turn, blow hot and cold, ring the changes, have as many phases as the moon; **exchange,** trade, play musical chairs; metamorphose

ADJS **6 changeable, alterable,** alterative, modifiable; mutable, permutable, impermanent, transient, **transitory; variable,** checkered, ever-changing, many-sided, kaleidoscopic, variegated; **movable,** mobile, motile; plastic, malleable, rubbery, fluid; **resilient, adaptable,** adjustable, **flexible,** supple, able to adapt, able to roll with the punches *or* bend without breaking; protean, proteiform; metamorphic; **nonuniform** 782.3

7 inconstant, changeable, changeful, changing,

shifting, uncertain, inconsistent, in a state of flux; **shifty,** unreliable, undependable; **unstable, unfixed,** infirm, restless, **unsettled,** unstaid, **unsteady,** wishy-washy, spineless, shapeless, amorphous, indecisive, irresolute, waffling <Brit nf>, blowing hot and cold <nf>, like a feather in the wind, unsteadfast, unstable as water; **variable,** deviable, dodgy <nf>; unaccountable, unpredictable; vicissitudinous *or* vicissitudinary; whimsical, **capricious, fickle** 364.6, off-again-on-again; **erratic, eccentric,** freakish; volatile, giddy, dizzy, ditzy <nf>, scatterbrained, mercurial, moody, flighty, impulsive, impetuous; **fluctuating,** alternating, **vacillating, wavering,** wavery, wavy, mazy, flitting, flickering, guttering, fitful, shifting, shuffling; irregular, spasmodic 851.3; **desultory,** rambling, roving, vagrant, homeless, wanton, wayward, wandering, afloat, adrift; **unrestrained, undisciplined,** irresponsible, uncontrolled, fast and loose

ADVS **8 changeably, variably, inconstantly,** shiftingly, shiftily, uncertainly, **unsteadily,** unsteadfastly, whimsically, capriciously, desultorily, erratically, waveringly; **impulsively, impetuously,** precipitately; back and forth, to and fro, in and out, off and on, on and off, round and round

855 STABILITY

NOUNS **1 stability, firmness, soundness, substantiality, solidity; security,** secureness, securement; **rootedness,** fastness; reliability 969.4; **steadiness,** steadfastness; constancy 847.2, invariability, undeflectability; **imperturbability,** unflappability <nf>, nerve, steady *or* unshakable nerves, nerves of steel, unshakableness, unsusceptibility, unimpressionability, stolidness *or* stolidity, stoicism, **cool** <nf>, *sang-froid* <Fr>; iron will; **equilibrium, balance,** stable state, stable equilibrium, homeostasis; steady state; emotional stability, balanced personality; aplomb; **uniformity** 781

2 fixity, fixedness, fixture, fixation; infixion, implantation, embedment; **establishment, stabilization,** confirmation, entrenchment; inveteracy, deep-rootedness, **deep-seatedness**

3 immobility, immovability, unmovability, immovableness, irremovability, immotility; inextricability; **firmness,** solidity, unyieldingness, rigidity, **inflexibility** 1044.3; inertia, *vis inertiae* <L>, inertness; immobilization

4 unchangeableness, unchangeability, unalterability, inalterability, unmodifiability, **immutability,** incommutability, inconvertibility; nontransferability; lastingness, **permanence** 852; irrevocability, indefeasibility, **irreversibility;**

irretrievability, unreturnableness, unrestorableness; intransmutability

5 indestructibility, imperishability, incorruptibility, inextinguishability, immortality, **deathlessness;** invulnerability, invincibility, inexpugnability, impregnability; ineradicability, indelibility, ineffaceability, inerasableness

6 <comparisons> rock, Rock of Gibraltar, bedrock, pillar *or* tower of strength, foundation; leopard's spots

VERBS **7 stabilize,** stabilitate *or* stabilify <old>; **firm, firm up** <nf>; **steady, balance,** counterbalance, ballast; **immobilize,** freeze, keep, retain; **transfix,** stick, hold, pin *or* nail down <nf>; set *or* cast *or* write in stone

8 secure, make sure *or* secure, firm up, tie, tie off *or* up, chain, tether; cleat, belay; **wedge, jam, seize; make fast, fasten,** fasten down; **anchor,** moor; batten *and* batten down; "build one's house upon a rock"—Bible; **confirm,** ratify

9 fix, define, set, **settle; establish,** found, ground, lodge, seat, **entrench; root;** infix, ingrain, set in, plant, implant, engraft, bed, embed; **print,** imprint, **stamp,** inscribe, **etch,** engrave, impress; deep-dye, **dye in the wool;** stereotype

10 <become firmly fixed> **root, take root,** strike root, settle down; **stick,** stick fast; seize, seize up, freeze; **catch, jam,** lodge, foul

11 stand fast, stand *or* remain firm, **stand pat** <nf>, stay put <nf>, hold fast, not budge, not budge an inch, **stand *or* hold one's ground,** persist, persevere, hold one's own, dig in one's heels, take one's stand, **stick to one's guns,** put one's foot down <nf>; **hold out,** stick *or* gut *or* tough it out *and* hang tough <nf>, stay the course; **hold up; weather,** weather the storm, ride it out, get home free <nf>; be imperturbable, be unflappable *and* not bat an eye *or* eyelash *and* keep one's cool <nf>

ADJS **12 stable, substantial, firm, solid, sound,** stabile; firm as Gibraltar, solid as a rock, rock-like, built on bedrock; **fast, secure; steady,** unwavering, steadfast; **balanced,** in equilibrium, in a stable state; **well-balanced; imperturbable,** unflappable <nf>, unshakable, **cool** <nf>, unimpressionable, unsusceptible, impassive, stolid, stoic; without nerves, without a nerve in one's body, unflinching, iron-willed; **reliable** 970.17, predictable; fiducial

13 established, stabilized, **entrenched,** vested, firmly established; **well-established,** well-founded, **well-grounded,** on a rock, in *or* on bedrock, aground; old-line, long-established; **confirmed, inveterate; settled, set;** well-settled, well-set, in place, entrenched; **rooted,** well-rooted; **deep-rooted, deep-seated,** deep-set, deep-settled, deep-fixed, deep-dyed, deep-engraven, deep-grounded, deep-laid; **infixed, ingrained,** implanted, engrafted, embedded, ingrown, inwrought; impressed, indelibly impressed, imprinted; engraved, etched, graven, embossed; **dyed-in-the-wool**

14 **fixed,** fastened, anchored, riveted; **set, settled, stated;** staple

15 **immovable,** unmovable, **immobile,** immotile, unmoving, **irremovable, stationary,** frozen, not to be moved, at a standstill, on dead center; **firm, unyielding,** adamant, adamantine, rigid, **inflexible** 1046.12; pat, standpat <nf>; at anchor

16 **stuck, fast,** stuck fast, **fixed, transfixed, caught,** fastened, tied, chained, tethered, anchored, moored, held, inextricable; **jammed,** impacted, congested, packed, wedged; seized, seized up, frozen; aground, grounded, stranded, high and dry

17 **unchangeable,** not to be changed, changeless, unchanged, unchanging, unvarying, unvariable, **unalterable,** unaltered, unalterative, **immutable,** incommutable, inconvertible, unmodifiable; insusceptible of change; **constant, invariable,** undeviating, undeflectable; lasting, unremitting, **permanent** 853.7; irrevocable, indefeasible, **irreversible,** nonreversible, reverseless; irretrievable, unrestorable, unreturnable, nonreturnable; intransmutable, inert, noble <chemistry>

18 **indestructible,** undestroyable, **imperishable,** nonperishable, incorruptible; **deathless,** immortal, undying; **invulnerable, invincible,** inexpugnable, impregnable, indivisible; **ineradicable,** indelible, ineffaceable, inerasable; **inextinguishable,** unquenchable, quenchless, undampable

PHRS 19 **stet, let it stand; what's done is done**

856 CONTINUANCE
<continuance in action>

NOUNS 1 **continuance, continuation, ceaselessness,** unceasingness, uninterruptedness, unremittingness, **continualness** 812.1; **prolongation, extension, protraction, perpetuation,** lengthening, spinning *or* stringing out; **survival** 827.1, holding out, hanging on *or* in; **maintenance,** sustenance, sustained action *or* activity; pursuance; run, way, straight *or* uninterrupted course; **progress,** progression; **persistence, perseverance** 360; **endurance** 826.1, **stamina,** staying power; **continuity** 812; **repetition** 849

2 **resumption, recommencement,** rebeginning, reestablishment, revival, recrudescence, resuscitation, **renewal,** reopening, reentrance, reappearance; **fresh start,** new beginning; another try, another shot *or* crack *or* go <nf>

VERBS 3 **continue** 812.4, keep *or* stay with it, keep *or*

stay at it, carry on; **remain,** bide, **abide, stay,** tarry, linger; **go on,** go along, **keep on,** keep on keeping on, keep going, carry on, see it through, stay on, hold on, hold one's way *or* course *or* path, hold steady, run on, jog on, drag on, bash ahead *or* on <nf>, slog on, soldier on, plug away <nf>, grind away *or* on, stagger on, put one foot in front of the other; never cease, cease not; **endure** 827.6

4 **sustain, protract, prolong, extend,** perpetuate, lengthen, spin *or* string out; **maintain,** keep, hold, retain, preserve; **keep up,** keep going, keep alive, **survive** 826.6

5 **persist, persevere,** keep at it 360.2, stick it out, stick to it, stick with it, never say die, see it through, hang in *and* hang tough *and* not know when one is licked <nf>; survive, make out, manage, get along, get on, eke out an existence, keep the even tenor of one's way; go on, go on with, go on with the show <nf>, press on; perseverate, iterate, reiterate, **harp,** go on about, chew one's ear off *and* run off at the mouth <nf>, beat a dead horse

6 **resume, recommence,** rebegin, **renew,** reestablish; **revive,** resuscitate, recrudesce; reenter, reopen, **return to,** go back to, begin again, take up again, make a new beginning, make a fresh start, start all over, have another try, have another shot *or* crack *or* go <nf>

ADJS 7 **continuing, abiding** 827.10; staying, remaining, sticking; **continuous** 811.8, **ceaseless, unceasing,** unending, endless, incessant, unremitting, steady, sustained, protracted, undying, indefatigable, **persistent; repetitious,** repetitive 848.14; **resumed,** recommenced, rebegun, renewed, reopened

857 CESSATION

NOUNS 1 **cessation, discontinuance,** discontinuation, phaseout, phasedown, scratching *and* scrubbing *and* breakoff <nf>; **desistance,** desinence, cease, surcease, **ceasing,** ending, halting, stopping, termination; **close,** closing, shutdown; sign-off; log-off; **relinquishment,** renunciation, abandonment, breakup

2 **stop,** stoppage, **halt, stay, arrest,** check, cutoff <nf>; stand, **standstill;** full stop, dead stop, screaming *or* grinding *or* shuddering *or* squealing halt; **strike** 727.7, walkout, work stoppage, sit-down strike, lockout; sick-out *and* blue flu <nf>; **end,** ending, endgame, final whistle, gun, bell, checkmate; **tie,** stalemate, deadlock, wash *and* toss-up <nf>, standoff *and* Mexican standoff <nf>; **terminal,** end of the line, rest stop, stopping place, terminus; closure

3 pause, rest, break, caesura, fermata, **recess, intermission,** interim 826, intermittence, interval, interlude, *intermezzo* <Ital>; **respite,** letup <nf>; **interruption, suspension,** time-out, break in the action, breathing spell, cooling-off period; **postponement** 846.4, rain-out; **remission;** abeyance, stay, drop, lull, lapse; truce, cease-fire, stand-down; **vacation, holiday,** time off, day off, recess, playtime, leisure

4 <grammatical terms> pause, juncture, boundary, caesura; <punctuation> stop *or* point *or* period, comma, colon, semicolon

5 <legislatures> **cloture,** *clôture* <Fr>; cloture by compartment, kangaroo cloture; guillotine <Brit>; closure of debate

VERBS **6 cease, discontinue, end, stop, halt,** end-stop, terminate, close the books on, close the books, put paid to <Brit>, abort, cancel, scratch *and* scrub <nf>, hold, **quit,** stay, belay <nf>; **desist, refrain,** leave off, lay off <nf>, give over, **have done with;** cut it out *and* drop it *and* knock it off <nf>, relinquish, renounce, abandon; **come to an end** 819.6, draw to a close; hang up, ring off <nf>

7 stop, come to a stop *or* halt, halt, stop in one's tracks, skid to a stop, stop dead, **stall; bring up, pull up,** pull in, head in, draw up, **fetch up; stop short,** come up short, bring up short, come to a screaming *or* squealing *or* grinding *or* shuddering halt, stop on a dime <nf>, come to a full stop, put on the brake, come to a standstill, grind to a halt, fetch up all standing; **stick,** jam, hang fire, seize, seize up, freeze; **cease fire,** stand down; run into a brick wall

8 <stop work> lay off, knock off <nf>, call it a day <nf>, call it quits <nf>; lay down one's tools, **shut up shop,** close shop, shut down, lock up, close down, secure <nautical nf>; **strike,** walk out, call a strike, go *or* go out on strike, stand down; work to rule

9 pause, rest, let up *and* take it easy <nf>, **relax,** rest on one's oars; **recess,** take *or* call a recess; call time-out; **take a break,** break, take five *or* ten; hang fire

10 interrupt, suspend, intermit, **break, break off,** take a break <nf>, cut off, break *or* snap the thread

11 put a stop to, call a halt to, get it over with, blow the whistle on <nf>, **put an end to** 820.5, put paid to <Brit nf>, call off the dogs <nf>; **stop, stay, halt, arrest, check,** flag down, wave down; block, brake, dam, stem, stem the tide *or* current; pull up, draw rein, put on the brakes, hit the brake pedal; **bring to a stand** *or* **standstill,** bring to a close *or* halt, freeze, bring to, bring up short, **stop dead** *or* dead in one's tracks, set one back on his heels, stop cold, stop short, cut short, check in full career; checkmate, stalemate, deadlock; thwart; do in <nf>

12 turn off, shut off, shut, shut down, close; **phase out,** phase down, taper off, wind up *or* down; **kill, cut,** cut off short, switch off

INTERJS **13 cease!, stop!, halt!,** *halte!* <Fr>, hold!, freeze!, stay!, desist!, quit it!; **let up!,** easy!, take it easy!, relax!, get off it!, **leave off!,** *arrêtez!* <Fr>, stop it!, forget it!, no more!, have done!, *tenez!* <Fr>, **hold everything!, hold it!,** hold to!, hold on!, whoa!, that's it!, that's enough!, that will do!, enough!, enough is enough!, genug!, all right already!, *basta!* <Ital>

14 <nf terms> cut it out!, cool it!, bag it!, chill out!, call it quits!, can it!, turn it off!, chuck it!, stow it!, drop it!, lay off!, all right already!, come off it!, **knock it off!,** break it off!, break it up!

858 CONVERSION
<change to something different>

NOUNS **1 conversion,** reconversion, **change-over,** turning into, becoming; convertibility; **change** 852, sea change, **transformation,** transubstantiation, transmutation, metamorphosis; **transition,** transit, **switch** *and* **switchover** <nf>, passage, **shift; reversal,** about-face *and* flip-flop <nf>, *volte-face* <Fr>; makeover; **relapse,** lapse, descent; **breakthrough; growth,** progress, development; transcendence; **resolution** 940.1; reduction, simplification; **assimilation,** naturalization, adoption, assumption; processing; alchemy

2 new start, new beginning, fresh start, clean slate, square one <nf>; **reformation, reform, regeneration, revival, reclamation,** redemption, amendment, improvement 392, renewal, recrudescence, **rebirth,** renascence, new birth, **change of heart;** change of mind *or* commitment *or* allegiance *or* loyalty *or* conviction

3 apostasy, renunciation, **defection, desertion,** treason, crossing-over, abandonment; degeneration 393.3

4 rehabilitation, reconditioning, recovery, readjustment, reclamation, restoration; **reeducation,** reinstruction; **repatriation**

5 indoctrination, reindoctrination, counterindoctrination; **brainwashing,** menticide; subversion, alienation, corruption

6 conversion, proselytization, proselytism, evangelization, persuasion 375.3; indoctrination; spiritual rebirth

7 convert, proselyte, neophyte, catechumen, disciple, new man *or* woman, born-again person

8 apostate, defector, turncoat, traitor, deserter, **renegade**

9 converter, proselyter, proselytizer, **missionary, apostle, evangelist,** televangelist; reformer, rehabilitator

10 <instruments> philosopher's stone, melting pot, crucible, alembic, test tube, caldron, retort, mortar; potter's wheel, anvil, lathe; converter, transformer, transducer, engine, motor, machine 1040.4

VERBS 11 convert, reconvert; **change over,** switch *and* switch over <nf>, **shift,** slide into; **do over,** re-do, make over, rejigger <nf>; **change, transform** 852.5,8, transmute, metamorphose; **change into, turn into, become,** resolve into, assimilate to, bring to, reduce to, naturalize; **make,** render; **reverse,** do an about-face; change one's tune, sing a different tune, dance to another tune; turn back 859.5

12 re-form, remodel, reshape, refashion, recast; regroup, redeploy, rearrange 808.13; **renew,** new-model; be reborn, be born again, be a new person, feel like a new person; get it together *and* get one's act *or* shit together *and* get one's ducks in a row <nf>; **regenerate, reclaim,** redeem, amend, set straight; **reform, rehabilitate,** set on the straight and narrow, make a new man of, restore self-respect; mend *or* change one's ways, **turn over a new leaf,** put on the new man, undergo a personality change

13 defect, renege, wimp *or* chicken *or* cop out <nf>, turn one's coat, desert, apostatize, change one's colors, turn against, turn traitor; leave *or* desert a sinking ship; lapse, relapse; degenerate

14 rehabilitate, recondition, reclaim, recover, restore, readjust; **reeducate,** reinstruct; **repatriate**

15 indoctrinate, brainwash, reindoctrinate, counterindoctrinate; subvert, alienate, win away, corrupt

16 convince, persuade, wean, bring over, sweep off one's feet <nf>, **win over;** proselyte, **proselytize,** evangelize

17 be converted into, **turn into** *or* **to, become** 761.12, **change into,** alter into, run *or* fall *or* pass into, slide *or* glide into, **grow into,** ripen into, **develop** *or* **evolve into,** merge *or* blend *or* melt into, shift into, lapse into, open into, resolve itself *or* settle into, come round to

ADJS 18 convertible, changeable, resolvable, transmutable, **transformable, transitional, modifiable;** reformable, reclaimable, renewable

19 converted, changed, transformed; naturalized, assimilated; **reformed,** regenerated, renewed, redeemed, reborn, born-again; liquidated; brainwashed

20 apostate, treasonable, traitorous, degenerate, renegade

859 REVERSION
<change to a former state>

NOUNS 1 reversion, reverting, retroversion, retrogradation, **retrogression,** retrocession, regress, **relapse** 394, **regression, backsliding,** lapse, slipping back, backing, recidivism, recidivation; reconversion; **reverse, reversal,** turnabout, about-face, right about-face, 180-degree shift, flip-flop <nf>, **turn; return,** returning, retreat; disenchantment; **reclamation, rehabilitation,** redemption, return to the fold; **reinstatement,** restitution, restoration; retroaction; turn of the tide

2 throwback, atavism

3 returnee, repeater; prodigal son, lost lamb; reversioner, reversionist; recidivist, habitual criminal *or* offender, two-time loser <nf>; backslider

VERBS 4 revert, retrovert, **regress, retrogress,** retrograde, retrocede, **reverse, return,** return to the fold; backslide, slip back, recidivate, lapse, lapse back, relapse 394.4

5 turn back, change back, go back, hark back, cry back, break back, **turn,** turn around *or* about; make a round trip; do an about-face *and* flip-flop *and* do a flip-flop *and* hang a 180 <nf>, ricochet; undo, turn back the clock, put the genie back into the bottle, put the toothpaste back into the tube; go back to go *or* to square one *or* to the drawing board <nf>

6 revert to, return to, recur to, go back to; hark *or* cry back to

ADJS 7 reversionary, reversional, **regressive,** recessive, **retrogressive, retrograde;** reactionary; recidivist *or* recidivistic, recidivous, lapsarian; retroverse, retrorse; retroactive; atavistic; revertible, returnable, reversible, recoverable

WORD ELEMENTS 8 retro-

860 REVOLUTION
<sudden or radical change>

NOUNS 1 revolution, radical *or* **total change, violent change,** striking alteration, sweeping change, clean sweep, clean slate, square one <nf>, tabula rasa; transilience, quantum leap *or* jump; **overthrow,** overturn, upset, *bouleversement* <Fr>, convulsion, spasm, subversion, coup d'état; breakup, breakdown; **cataclysm, catastrophe,** debacle, *débâcle* <Fr>; **revolution,** revolutionary war, war of national liberation; bloodless revolution, palace revolution; technological revolution, electronic *or* communications *or* computer *or* information revolution; green revolution; counterrevolution; **revolt** 327.4

2 **revolutionism,** revolutionariness, anarchism, syndicalism, terrorism; Bolshevism *or* Bolshevikism <Russ>, Carbonarism <Ital>, Sinn Feinism <Ir>, Jacobinism <Fr>; sans-culottism <Fr>, *sans-culotterie* <Fr>, Castroism <Cuba>, Maoism <Chin>, Shining Path <Peru>, Sandinistism <Nicaragua>

3 **revolutionist, revolutionary,** revolutionizer; **rebel** 327.5; anarchist, anarch, syndicalist, criminal syndicalist, terrorist 671.9; subversive; red; Red Republican <Fr>, *bonnet rouge* <Fr>; Jacobin <Fr>, sans-culotte, sans-culottist; Yankee *or* Yankee Doodle *or* Continental <US>; Puritan *or* Roundhead <Brit>; Bolshevik *or* Bolshevist *or* Bolshie <Russ>, Marxist, Leninist, Communist, Commie <nf>, Red, Trotskyite *or* Trotskyist, Castroist *or* Castroite <Cuba>, Guevarist, Maoist; Vietcong *or* VC *and* Cong *and* Charley <Vietnam>; *Carbonaro* <Ital>, Carbonarist <Ital>; Sinn Feiner, Fenian <Ir>; revolutionary junta

VERBS **4** **revolutionize, make a radical change,** make a clean sweep, break with the past; **overthrow, overturn,** throw the rascals out *and* let heads roll <nf> *boulverse* <Fr>, upset; revolt 327.7

ADJS **5** **revolutionary;** revulsive, revulsionary; transilient; cataclysmic, catastrophic; **radical,** sweeping 794.10; **insurrectionary** 327.11

6 **revolutionist, revolutionary,** anarchic *or* anarchical, syndicalist, terrorist *or* terroristic, agin the government <nf>; Bolshevistic, Bolshevik; sans-culottic, sans-culottish; Jacobinic *or* Jacobinical, Carbonarist, Fenian, Marxist, Leninist, Communist, Trotskyist *or* Trotskyite, Guevarist, Castroist *or* Castroite, Maoist, Vietcong, Mau-Mau

861 EVOLUTION

NOUNS **1** **evolution, evolving,** evolvement; evolutionary change, gradual change, step-by-step change, peaceful *or* nonviolent change; **development, growth,** rise, incremental change, developmental change, natural growth *or* development; flowering, blossoming; ripening, coming of age, maturation 303.6; accomplishment 407; **advance,** advancement, furtherance; **progress,** progression; **elaboration,** enlargement, amplification, **expansion;** devolution, degeneration 393.3

2 **unfolding,** unfoldment, unrolling, unfurling, unwinding; revelation, gradual revelation

3 <biological terms> **genesis;** phylogeny, phylogenesis; ontogeny, ontogenesis; physiogeny, physiogenesis; **biological evolution,** speciation, convergent evolution, parallel evolution; natural selection, adaptation; horotely, bradytely, tachytely

4 **evolutionism,** theory of evolution; **Darwinism,** Darwinianism, punctuated equilibrium, Neo-Darwinism, organic evolution, survival of the fittest; Haeckelism, Lamarckism *or* Lamarckianism, Neo-Lamarckism, Lysenkoism, Weismannism, Spencerianism; social Darwinism, social evolution

VERBS **5** **evolve; develop, grow,** wax, change gradually *or* step-by-step; **progress, advance,** come a long way; accomplish 407.4; ripen, mellow, mature 303.9, maturate; flower, bloom, blossom, bear fruit; degenerate

6 **elaborate, develop, work out,** enlarge, enlarge on *or* upon, amplify, **expand,** expand on *or* upon, detail, go *or* enter into detail, go into, flesh out, **pursue,** spell out <nf>; complete 407.6

7 unfold, unroll, unfurl, unwind, unreel, uncoil, reveal, reveal *or* expose gradually

ADJS **8** **evolutionary,** evolutional, evolutionist *or* evolutionistic; **evolving, developing, unfolding; maturing,** maturational, maturative; **progressing, advancing;** devolutionary, degenerative; genetic, phylogenetic, ontogenetic, physiogenetic; horotelic, bradytelic, tachytelic

862 SUBSTITUTION

<change of one thing for another>

NOUNS **1** **substitution, exchange, change,** switch, switcheroo <nf>, swap, commutation, subrogation; **surrogacy;** vicariousness, **representation,** deputation, **delegation;** deputyship, **agency, power of attorney; supplanting,** supplantation, succession; **replacement,** displacement, shuffle; provision, provisionalness *or* provisionality, adhocracy, ad hockery *or* ad hocery, ad hocism; superseding, supersession *or* supersedure; tit for tat, *quid pro quo* <L>; job sharing

2 **substitute,** sub <nf>, **substitution, replacement,** backup, second *or* third string <nf>, secondary, utility player, succedaneum; **change, exchange; ersatz,** phony *and* fake <nf>, counterfeit, imitation 336, copy 785; surrogate; reserves, bench <nf>, backup, backup personnel, spares; **alternate,** alternative, next best thing, lesser of two evils; **successor,** supplanter, superseder, capper <nf>; **proxy,** dummy, ghost; vicar, agent, representative; **deputy** 576; locum tenens, vice, vice-president, vice-regent, etc; **relief, fill-in, stand-in, understudy, pinch hitter** *or* runner <nf>; double; **equivalent,** equal; ringer <nf>; ghostwriter; **analogy,** comparison; **metaphor,** metonymy, synecdoche <all grammar>; **symbol, sign,** token, icon; makeshift 995.2

3 scapegoat, goat <nf>, fall guy *and* can-carrier *and* patsy *and* catch dog <nf>, whipping boy, lamb to the slaughter

VERBS **4 substitute, exchange, change,** take *or* ask *or* offer in exchange, switch, swap, ring in <nf>, **put in the place of,** change for, make way for, give place to; commute, redeem, compound for; **pass off,** pawn *or* foist *or* palm *or* fob off; rob Peter to pay Paul; dub in; make do with, shift with, put up with; shuffle

5 substitute for, sub for <nf>, subrogate; **act for,** double for *or* as, stand *or* sit in for, understudy for, fill in for, serve as proxy, don the mantle of, change places with, swap places with <nf>, stand in the stead of, step into *or* fill the shoes of, pinch-hit *and* pinch-run <nf>; deputize; relieve, spell *and* spell off <nf>, cover for; ghost, ghostwrite; **represent** 576.14; **supplant, supersede,** succeed, **replace,** displace, **take the place of,** crowd out, cut out <nf>

6 <nf terms> **cover up for,** front for; **take the rap for** *and* take the fall for <nf>, carry the can *and* be the goat *or* patsy *or* fall guy <nf>

7 delegate, deputize, commission, give the nod to <nf>, designate an agent *or* a proxy

ADJS **8 substitute, alternate, alternative,** other, tother <nf>, equivalent, token, dummy, pinch, utility, backup, secondary; ad hoc, provisional; **vicarious,** ersatz, mock, phony *and* fake *and* bogus <nf>, counterfeit, imitation 336.8; **proxy,** deputy; makeshift, reserve, **spare,** stopgap, temporary, provisional, tentative

9 substitutional, substitutionary, substitutive, provisional, supersessive; **substituted,** substituent

10 replaceable, substitutable, supersedable, expendable

ADVS **11 instead, rather,** *faute de mieux* <Fr>; in its stead *or* place; in one's stead, in one's behalf, in one's place, in one's shoes; by proxy; as an alternative; *in loco parentis* <L>

PREPS **12 instead of,** in the stead of, rather than, sooner than, **in place of,** in the place of, **in** *or* **on behalf of, in lieu of; for,** as proxy for, as a substitute for, as representing, in preference to, as an alternative to; **replacing,** as a replacement for, vice

WORD ELEMENTS **13** pro-, vice-, quasi-, pseudo-

863 INTERCHANGE
<double or mutual change>

NOUNS **1 interchange, exchange,** counterchange; **transposition,** transposal; mutual transfer *or* replacement; mutual admiration, mutual support; **cooperation** 450; commutation, permutation, intermutation; alternation; **interplay, tradeoff, compromise, reciprocation** 777.1, reciprocality, reciprocity, mutuality, two-way traffic; give-and-take, something for something, *quid pro quo* <L>, measure for measure, tit for tat, an eye for an eye, "an eye for an eye and a tooth for a tooth"—Bible; retaliation, *lex talionis* <L>; cross fire; battledore and shuttlecock; repartee

2 trading, swapping <nf>; trade, swap <nf>, even trade, even-steven trade, **switch;** barter 731.2; logrolling, back scratching, pork barrel; pawning, castling <chess>

3 interchangeability, exchangeability, changeability, standardization; convertibility, commutability, permutability

VERBS **4 interchange, exchange,** change, counterchange; alternate; **transpose;** convert, commute, permute; **trade, swap** <nf>, **switch;** bandy, bandy about, play at battledore and shuttlecock; **reciprocate, trade off,** compromise, settle, settle for, respond, keep a balance; **give and take,** give tit for tat, give a Roland for an Oliver, give as much as one takes, give as good as one gets, return the compliment *or* favor, pay back, compensate, **requite,** return; **retaliate,** get back at, get even with, be quits with; logroll, scratch each other's back, **cooperate** 450.3

ADJS **5 interchangeable, exchangeable,** changeable, standard; equivalent; **even,** equal; returnable, **convertible,** commutable, permutable; commutative; retaliatory, equalizing; **reciprocative** *or* reciprocating, reciprocatory, reciprocal, traded-off, two-way; **mutual,** give-and-take; **exchanged, transposed,** switched, **swapped** <nf>, traded, **interchanged;** requited, reciprocated

ADVS **6 interchangeably, exchangeably; in exchange, in return; even, evenly,** *au pair* <Fr>; **reciprocally,** mutually; **in turn,** each in its turn, every one in his turn, by turns, turn about, turn and turn about

PHRS **7** one good turn deserves another; you scratch my back I scratch yours

864 GENERALITY

NOUNS **1 generality, universality,** cosmicality, inclusiveness 772.1; worldwideness, globality *or* globalism, globaloney <nf>, ecumenicity *or* ecumenicalism; catholicity; **internationalism,** cosmopolitanism; **generalization,** universalization, globalization, ecumenization, internationalization; **labeling,** stereotyping

2 **prevalence, commonness,** commonality, usualness, **currency,** occurrence; **extensiveness,** widespreadness, pervasiveness, sweepingness, rifeness, rampantness; **normality,** normalness, averageness, ordinariness, routineness, habitualness, standardness

3 **average,** ruck, **run,** general *or* common *or* average *or* ordinary run, **run of the mill;** any Tom, Dick, *or* Harry; Everyman; common *or* average man, the man in the street, John Q Public, John *or* Jane Doe, ordinary Joe, Joe Six-pack, Joe Blow, lowest common denominator; girl next door; everyman, everywoman; *homme moyen sensuel* <Fr>

4 **all, everyone, everybody, each and every one, one and all,** all comers *and* all hands *and* every man Jack *and* every mother's son <nf>, every living soul, **all the world,** everyone and his brother, *tout le monde* <Fr>, the devil and all <nf>, **whole, totality** 792.1; **everything,** all kinds *or* all manner of things; you name it *and* what have you *and* all the above <nf>

5 **any, anything,** any one, aught, either; **anybody, anyone**

6 **whatever,** whate'er, **whatsoever,** whatsoe'er, **what, whichever,** anything soever which, no matter what *or* which, what have you, what you will

7 **whoever,** whoso, **whosoever, whomever,** whomso, **whomsoever,** anyone, no matter who, anybody

8 <idea or expression> **generalization,** general idea, **abstraction,** generalized proposition; glittering generality, sweeping statement, vague generalization; **truism, platitude, conventional wisdom,** commonplace, *lieu commun* <Fr>, *locus communis* <L>; **cliché,** tired cliché, bromide, trite *or* hackneyed expression; labeling, stereotyping

VERBS 9 **generalize, universalize,** catholicize, ecumenicize, globalize, internationalize; **broaden, widen, expand,** extend, spread; make a generalization, deal in generalities *or* abstractions; **label,** stereotype

10 **prevail, predominate, obtain,** dominate, reign, rule; be in force *or* effect; be the rule *or* fashion, be the rage *or* thing <nf>, have currency, be in <nf>

ADJS 11 **general, generalized, nonspecific,** generic, **indefinite,** indeterminate, vague, abstract, nebulous, unspecified, undifferentiated, featureless, uncharacterized, bland, neutral

12 **prevalent, prevailing, common,** popular, **current,** running; regnant, reigning, **ruling, predominant,** predominating, **dominant; rife, rampant,** pandemic, epidemic, besetting; **ordinary, normal, average, usual,** routine, standard, par for the course <nf>, stereotyped, stereotypical; public, communal

13 **extensive, broad, wide,** liberal, diffuse, large-scale, broad-scale, broad-scope, broadly-based, wide-scale, **sweeping; cross-disciplinary,** interdisciplinary; widespread, far-spread, far-stretched, **far-reaching,** far-going, far-embracing, far-extending, far-spreading, far-flying, far-ranging, **far-flung,** wide-flung, wide-reaching, wide-extending, wide-extended, wide-ranging, wide-stretching; **wholesale, indiscriminate;** rife; panoramic, bird's-eye

14 **universal,** cosmic *or* cosmical, heaven-wide, galactic, planetary, world-wide, transnational, planet-wide, **global; total,** allover, holistic; catholic, **all-inclusive,** all-including, **all-embracing,** all-encompassing, all-comprehensive, all-comprehending, all-filling, all-pervading, all-covering, encyclopedic; nonsectarian, nondenominational, ecumenic *or* ecumenical; omnipresent, ubiquitous; **cosmopolitan,** international; **national,** nation-wide, country-wide, state-wide

15 **every, all,** any, whichever, whichsoever; **each,** each one; every one, each and every, each and all, **one and all, all and sundry,** all and some

16 **trite, commonplace,** hackneyed, platitudinous, truistic, overworked, quotidian; common *or* garden

ADVS 17 **generally, in general; generally speaking,** speaking generally, **broadly,** broadly speaking, **roughly,** roughly speaking, as an approximation; **usually, as a rule, ordinarily, commonly, normally,** routinely, as a matter of course, in the usual course; **by and large,** at large, altogether, overall, over the long haul <nf>, **all things considered,** taking one thing with another, taking all things together, on balance, **all in all,** taking all in all, taking it for all in all, **on the whole,** as a whole, **in the long run,** for the most part, for better *or* for worse; **prevailingly, predominantly, mostly,** chiefly, mainly

18 **universally,** galactically, cosmically; **everywhere, all over,** the world over, all over the world, internationally; in every instance, without exception, **invariably, always,** never otherwise

WORD ELEMENTS 19 glob-, globo-, omn-, omni-, pan-, pano-, pant-, panto-, panta-

865 PARTICULARITY

NOUNS 1 **particularity, individuality, singularity, differentiation,** differentness, distinctiveness, uniqueness; identity, individual *or* separate *or* concrete identity; **personality,** personship, personal identity; soul; **selfness,** selfhood, **egohood,** self-

identity, "a single separate person"—Whitman;
oneness 871.1, wholeness, integrity; personal
equation, human factor; **nonconformity** 868;
individualism, particularism; nominalism

2 **speciality, specialness,** specialty, specificality,
specificness, definiteness; special case; specialty of
the house, soup du jour, flavor of the month,
today's specials

3 the **specific,** the special, **the particular,** the
concrete, the individual, the unique; "all things
counter, original, spare, strange"—G M Hopkins

4 **characteristic, peculiarity, singularity,**
particularity, specialty, individualism, **character,**
property, nature, **trait,** quirk, point of character,
bad point, good point, saving grace, redeeming
feature, mannerism, keynote, trick, **feature,**
distinctive feature, lineament; claim to fame,
expertise, métier, forte; **mark,** marking, **earmark,**
hallmark, index, signature; badge, token; **brand,**
cast, stamp, cachet, seal, mold, cut, figure, shape,
configuration; impress, impression; differential,
differentia; **idiosyncrasy,** idiocrasy, eccentricity,
peculiarity; **quality, property, attribute;** savor,
flavor, taste, gust, aroma, odor, smack, tang, taint

5 **self, ego; oneself, I,** myself, me, my humble self,
number one <nf>, yours truly <nf>; yourself,
himself, herself, itself; ourselves, yourselves;
themselves; you; he, she; him, her; they, them; it;
inner self, inner man; subliminal *or* subconscious
self; superego, better self, ethical self; other self,
alter ego, alter, *alterum* <L>

6 **specification, designation, stipulation,** specifying,
designating, stipulating, singling-out, featuring,
highlighting, focusing on, denomination;
allocation, attribution, fixing, selection,
assignment, pinning down; specifications,
particulars, minutiae, fine print

7 **particularization, specialization;** individualization,
peculiarization, personalization; localization;
itemization 766.5; special interest, pursuit,
vocation, field

8 **characterization,** distinction, **differentiation;**
definition, description

VERBS 9 **particularize, specialize; individualize,**
peculiarize, personalize; **descend to particulars,** go
into detail, get precise, get down to brass tacks *or*
to cases <nf>, get down to the nitty-gritty <nf>,
come to the point, lay it on the line <nf>, spell
out; **itemize** 766.6, detail, spell out

10 **characterize, distinguish, differentiate, define,
describe; mark, earmark,** mark off, mark out,
demarcate, **set apart,** make special *or* unique;
keynote <nf>, sound the keynote, set the tone *or*
mood, set the pace; be characteristic, **be a feature
or trait of**

11 **specify,** specialize, **designate, stipulate,** determine,
single out, feature, highlight, focus on, mention,
select, pick out, **fix,** set, assign, pin down; **name,**
denominate, name names, state, mark, check,
check off, **indicate, signify,** point out, put *or* lay
one's finger on; mention, cite, quote, attribute

ADJS 12 **particular, special, especial, specific,
express,** precise, **concrete; singular, individual,**
individualist *or* individualistic, unique; **personal,**
private, intimate, inner, solipsistic, esoteric;
respective, several; **fixed, definite, defined,** distinct,
different, different as night and day, determinate,
certain, absolute; **distinguished,** noteworthy,
exceptional, extraordinary; minute, detailed

13 **characteristic, peculiar, singular,** single,
quintessential, intrinsic, unique, qualitative,
distinctive, marked, distinguished, notable,
nameable; appropriate, proper; idiosyncratic,
idiocratic, **in character, true to form,** typical

14 **this,** this and no other, this one, this single; **these;
that,** that one; those

ADVS 15 **particularly, specially, especially,
specifically, expressly,** concretely, exactly, precisely,
in particular, to be specific; **definitely, distinctly;
minutely,** in detail, item by item, singly, separately

16 **personally,** privately, idiosyncratically, **individually;
in person,** in the flesh, *in propria persona* <L>; as
for me, for all of me, **for my part,** as far as I am
concerned

17 **characteristically, peculiarly,** singularly,
intrinsically, **uniquely,** markedly, **distinctively,** in
its own way, like no other

18 **namely,** nominally, **that is to say,** *videlicet* <L>,
viz, *scilicet* <L>, scil, sc, **to wit**

19 **each, apiece;** severally, respectively, one by one,
each to each; *per annum* or *per diem* or *per capita*
<L>

PREPS 20 **per, for each**

WORD ELEMENTS 21 -ness, -hood, -dom; aut-, auto-,
idio-, self-; -acean, -aceous, -ey, -y, -ious, -ous, -ish,
-ist, -istic, -istical, -itious, -itic, -ose, -some

866 SPECIALTY
<object of special attention or preference>

NOUNS 1 **specialty,** speciality, **line, pursuit, pet
subject,** business, **line of business, line of country**
<Brit>, **field,** area, main interest; **vocation** 724.6;
forte, métier, strong point, long suit; specialism,
specialization; technicality; **way,** manner, **style,**
type; **lifestyle,** way of life, preferences; cup of tea
and bag *and* thing *and* thang *and* weakness <nf>

2 **special, feature,** main feature; **leader,** lead item,
leading card

3 **specialist,** specializer, **expert, authority,** savant,

scholar, connoisseur, maven <nf>; technical expert, technician, techie <nf>, nerd <nf>; pundit, critic; amateur, dilettante; fan, buff, freak *and* nut <nf>, aficionado

VERBS **4 specialize, feature; narrow, restrict,** limit, confine; specialize in, **go in for,** be into <nf>, have a weakness *or* taste for, be strong in, follow, pursue, **make one's business;** major in, minor in; do one's thing <nf>

ADJS **5 specialized,** specialist, specialistic; down one's alley <nf>, cut out for one, fits one like a glove; technical; **restricted, limited,** confined; **featured,** feature; **expert, authoritative,** knowledgeable

867 CONFORMITY

NOUNS **1 conformity; conformance,** conformation, other-directedness; **compliance,** acquiescence, goose step, lockstep, obedience, observance, subordination, traditionalism, **orthodoxy;** strictness; **accordance,** accord, **correspondence,** harmony, agreement, **uniformity** 781; **consistency,** congruity; **accommodation,** adaptation, adaption, pliancy, malleability, flexibility, adjustment; reconciliation, reconcilement; **conventionality** 579.1

2 conformist, conformer, sheep, trimmer, parrot, yes-man, organization man, company man, lackey; **conventionalist,** Mrs Grundy, Babbitt, Philistine, middle-class type, button-down *or* white-bread type <nf>, **bourgeois,** burgher, Middle American, plastic person *and* clone *and* square <nf>, three-piecer *and* yuppie <nf>, Barbie Doll <trademark nf>; model child; teenybopper <nf>; **formalist,** methodologist, perfectionist, precisianist *or* precisian, stick-in-the-mud; anal character, compulsive character; pedant

VERBS **3 conform, comply, correspond,** accord, harmonize; **adapt,** adjust, **accommodate,** bend, meet, suit, fit, shape; **comply with,** agree with, tally with, chime *or* fall in with, go by, be guided *or* regulated by, observe, follow, bend, yield, take the shape of; **adapt to,** adjust to, gear to, assimilate to, **accommodate to *or* with; reconcile,** settle, compose; rub off corners; **make conform,** shape, lick into shape, mold, force into a mold; straighten, rectify, correct, **discipline**

4 follow the rule, toe the mark, do it according to Hoyle *or* by the book <nf>, play the game <nf>; go through channels; **fit in, follow the crowd,** go with the crowd, follow the fashion, swim *or* go with the stream *or* tide *or* current, get on the bandwagon, trim one's sails to the breeze, follow the beaten path, **do as others do, get *or* stay in line,** fall in *or* into line, fall in with; run true to

form; **keep in step,** goose-step, walk in lockstep; keep up to standard, pass muster, come up to scratch <nf>

ADJS **5 conformable, adaptable,** adaptive, adjustable; **compliant,** pliant, complaisant, malleable, flexible, plastic, acquiescent, unmurmuring, other-directed, submissive, tractable, obedient

6 conformist, conventional 579.5, bourgeois, plastic *and* square *and* straight *and* white-bread *and* white-bready *and* button-down *and* buttoned-down <nf>, cloned *and* clonish *and* cookie-cutter <nf>; **orthodox,** traditionalist *or* traditionalistic; kosher; **formalistic,** legalistic, precisianistic, anal, compulsive; pedantic, stuffy *and* hidebound <nf>, strait-laced, uptight <nf>; in accord, in keeping, in line, in step, in lockstep; **corresponding,** accordant, concordant, harmonious

ADVS **7** conformably, conformingly, in conformity, **obediently, pliantly,** flexibly, malleably, complaisantly, yieldingly, **compliantly,** submissively; **conventionally,** traditionally; anally, **compulsively;** pedantically

8 according to rule, *en règle* <Fr>, according to regulations; **according to Hoyle *and* by the book *and* by the numbers <nf>

PREPS **9 conformable to, in conformity with,** in compliance with; **according to, in accordance with, consistent with, in harmony with,** in agreement with, in correspondence to; adapted to, adjusted to, accommodated to; proper to, suitable for, agreeable to, agreeably to; answerable to, in obedience to; congruent with, uniform with, in uniformity with; **in line with,** in step with, in lock-step with, **in keeping with; after, by, per, as per**

PHRS **10 don't rock the boat, don't make waves,** get in line, shape up, shape up or ship out <nf>; when in Rome do as the Romans do

868 NONCONFORMITY

NOUNS **1 nonconformity,** unconformity, nonconformism, **inconsistency,** incongruity; **inaccordance,** disaccord, disaccordance; originality 337.1; **nonconformance,** disconformity; **nonobservance, noncompliance,** nonconcurrence, **dissent** 333, **protest** 333.2, rebellion, disagreement, contrariety, recalcitrance, refractoriness, recusance *or* recusancy; **deviation** 870.1, deviationism

2 unconventionality, unorthodoxy 688, revisionism, heterodoxy, heresy, originality, Bohemianism, beatnikism, hippiedom, counterculture, iconoclasm; eccentricity; alternative lifestyle *or* society *or* medicine

3 nonconformist, unconformist, **original,** eccentric, gonzo <nf>, deviant, deviationist, maverick <nf>, dropout, Bohemian, beatnik, free spirit, freethinker, hippie, hipster, freak <nf>, flower child, New-Age Traveler; **misfit,** square peg in a round hole, ugly duckling, fish out of water; *enfant terrible* <Fr>; **dissenter** 333.3; **heretic** 688.5; sectary, sectarian; nonjuror

VERBS **4 not conform,** nonconform, not comply; **get out of line** *and* **rock the boat** *and* make waves <nf>, **leave the beaten path, go out of bounds,** upset the apple cart, break step, break bounds; drop out, opt out; **dissent** 333.4, swim against the current *or* against the tide *or* upstream, **protest** 333.5; "hear a different drummer"—Thoreau

ADJS **5 nonconforming,** unconforming, nonconformable, unadaptable, unadjustable; **uncompliant,** unsubmissive; **nonobservant;** contrary, recalcitrant, refractory, recusant; **deviant,** deviationist, atypic *or* atypical, unusual; **dissenting** 333.6, **dissident;** antisocial

6 unconventional, unorthodox, eccentric, gonzo <nf>, heterodox, heretical; unfashionable, not done, not kosher, not cricket <Brit nf>; offbeat <nf>, way out *and* far out *and* kinky *and* out in left field <nf>, fringy, breakaway, **out-of-the-way; original,** maverick, Bohemian, beat, hippie, counterculture; **nonformal,** free and easy <nf>, "at ease and lighthearted"—Whitman

7 out of line, out of keeping, out of order *or* place, misplaced, **out of step,** out of turn <nf>, out of tune

869 NORMALITY

NOUNS **1 normality,** normalness, typicality, normalcy, **naturalness;** health, wholesomeness, propriety, **regularity;** naturalism, naturism, realism; **order** 806

2 usualness, ordinariness, commonness, commonplaceness, averageness, mediocrity; **generality** 864, **prevalence,** currency

3 the normal, the usual, the ordinary, the common, the commonplace, the day-to-day, the way things are, the normal order of things; common *or* garden variety, the run of the mine *or* the mill

4 rule, law, principle, standard, criterion, canon, code, code of practice, maxim, prescription, guideline, rulebook, the book <nf>, regulation, reg *or* regs <nf>; **norm, model,** rule of behavior, ideal, ideal type, specimen type, exemplar; **rule** *or* **law** *or* **order of nature,** natural *or* universal law; **form, formula,** formulary, formality, prescribed *or* set form; standing order, standard operating procedure; **hard-and-fast rule,** Procrustean law

5 normalization, standardization, regularization; codification, formalization

VERBS **6 normalize, standardize, regularize; codify,** formalize

7 do the usual thing, make a practice of, carry on, carry on as usual, do business as usual

ADJS **8 normal, natural; general** 864.11; typical, unexceptional; **normative,** prescribed, model, ideal, desired, white-bread *or* white-bready <nf>; naturalistic, naturistic, realistic; orderly 807.6

9 usual, regular; customary, habitual, accustomed, wonted, normative, prescriptive, standard, regulation, conventional; **common, commonplace, ordinary, average, everyday,** mediocre, familiar, household, vernacular, stock; **prevailing, predominating,** current, popular; **universal** 864.14

ADVS **10 normally, naturally; normatively,** prescriptively, **regularly; typically,** usually, commonly, ordinarily, customarily, habitually, generally; mostly, chiefly, mainly, for the most part, most often *or* frequently; **as a rule,** as a matter of course; **as usual,** as per usual <nf>; **as may be expected,** to be expected, as things go

WORD ELEMENTS **11** norm-, normo-

870 ABNORMALITY

NOUNS **1 abnormality,** abnormity; **unnaturalness,** unnaturalism, strangeness; **anomaly,** anomalousness, anomalism; **aberration,** aberrance *or* aberrancy; **atypicality,** atypicalness; **irregularity, deviation,** divergence, **difference** 780; **eccentricity,** erraticism, unpredictability, unpredictableness, randomness, chaos; **monstrosity,** teratism, amorphism, heteromorphism; **subnormality; inferiority** 250; **superiority** 249; **derangement** 811.1

2 unusualness, uncommonness, unordinariness, unwontedness, exceptionalness, exceptionality, extraordinariness; **rarity,** rareness, **uniqueness; prodigiousness,** marvelousness, wondrousness, fabulousness, mythicalness, remarkableness, stupendousness; **incredibility** 955.3, increditability, inconceivability, **impossibility** 966

3 oddity, queerness, curiousness, quaintness, **peculiarity, absurdity** 967.1, singularity; **strangeness,** outlandishness; bizarreness, *bizarrerie* <Fr>; fantasticality, anticness; **freakishness, grotesqueness,** grotesquerie, strangeness, weirdness, gonzo <nf>, monstrousness, monstrosity, malformation, deformity, teratism

4 <odd person> oddity, **character** <nf>, type, **case** <nf>, natural, original, odd fellow, queer specimen; **oddball** *and* **weirdo** <nf>, odd *or* queer fish, queer duck, rum one <Brit nf>; **rare bird,** *rara avis* <L>; flake, eccentric 927.3; *meshuggenah* <Yiddish>; **freak** *and* **screwball** *and* **crackpot** *and* kook *and* **nut** *and* bird *and* gonzo <nf>; **fanatic, crank,** zealot; **outsider, alien,** foreigner; **alien,** extraterrestrial, Martian, little green man, visitor from another planet; pariah, loner, lone wolf, solitary, hermit; hobo, tramp; maverick; **outcast,** outlaw, scapegoat; **nonconformist** 868.3

5 <odd thing> **oddity, curiosity, wonder,** funny *or* peculiar *or* strange thing; **abnormality, anomaly; rarity,** improbability, exception, one in a thousand *or* million; **prodigy,** prodigiosity; curio, conversation piece; museum piece

6 **monstrosity, monster** <see list>, miscreation, abortion, teratism, abnormal *or* defective birth, abnormal *or* defective fetus; **freak,** freak of nature, *lusus naturae* <L>

7 **supernaturalism,** supernaturalness, supernaturality, supranaturalism, supernormalness, **preternaturalism,** supersensibleness, superphysicalness, superhumanity; **the paranormal;** numinousness; **unearthliness,** unworldliness, **otherworldliness,** eeriness; transcendentalism; New Age; the supernatural, **the occult,** the supersensible; **paranormality;** supernature, supranature; **mystery,** mysteriousness, miraculousness, strangeness; faerie, witchery, elfdom

8 **miracle, sign, signs and portents, prodigy, wonder,** wonderwork, ferlie <Scot>; thaumatology, thaumaturgy; fantasy, enchantment

ADJS 9 **abnormal, unnatural; anomalous,** anomalistic; **irregular,** eccentric, erratic, deviative, divergent, **different** 779.7; **aberrant,** stray, straying, wandering; heteroclite, heteromorphic; formless, shapeless, amorphous; **subnormal**

10 **unusual,** unordinary, **uncustomary,** unwonted, **uncommon, unfamiliar,** atypic *or* atypical, unheard-of, *recherché* <Fr>; **rare, unique,** *sui generis* <L, of its own kind>; **out of the ordinary,** out of this world, out-of-the-way, out of the common, out of the pale, **off the beaten track,** offbeat, breakaway; unexpected, not to be expected, unthought-of, undreamed-of

11 **odd, queer, peculiar, absurd** 967.7, **singular, curious, oddball** <nf>, weird *and* kooky *and* freaky *and* freaked-out <nf>, quaint, **eccentric,** gonzo <nf>, funny, rum <Brit nf>; **strange, outlandish, off-the-wall** <nf>, surreal, not for real <nf>, passing strange, "wondrous strange"— Shakespeare; **weird,** unearthly; off, out

12 **fantastic,** fantastical, fanciful, antic, **unbelievable** 955.10, **impossible, incredible,** logic-defying, incomprehensible, unimaginable, unexpected, unaccountable, inconceivable

13 **freakish,** freak *or* freaky <nf>; **monstrous, deformed,** malformed, misshapen, **misbegotten,** teratogenic, teratoid; **grotesque, bizarre,** baroque, rococo

14 **extraordinary, exceptional, remarkable,** noteworthy, **wonderful, marvelous,** fabulous, mythical, legendary; **stupendous,** stupefying, prodigious, portentous, phenomenal; unprecedented, unexampled, unparalleled, not within the memory of man; indescribable, unspeakable, ineffable

15 **supernatural,** supranatural, **preternatural; supernormal,** hypernormal, preternormal, **paranormal; superphysical,** hyperphysical; numinous; supersensible, **supersensual,** pretersensual; **superhuman,** preterhuman, unhuman, nonhuman; **supramundane,** extramundane, transmundane, extraterrestrial; **unearthly, unworldly, otherworldly, eerie;** fey; psychical, **spiritual, occult; transcendental; mysterious,** arcane, esoteric

16 **miraculous, wondrous,** wonder-working, thaumaturgic *or* thaumaturgical, necromantic, **prodigious; magical,** enchanted, bewitched

ADVS 17 **unusually, uncommonly, incredibly, unnaturally,** abnormally, unordinarily, **uncustomarily,** unexpectedly; **rarely, seldom,** seldom if ever, once in a thousand years, hardly, hardly ever

18 **extraordinarily, exceptionally, remarkably, wonderfully, marvelously,** prodigiously, fabulously, unspeakably, ineffably, phenomenally, stupendously

19 **oddly, queerly, peculiarly, singularly, curiously,** quaintly, **strangely,** outlandishly, **fantastically,** fancifully; **grotesquely, monstrously; eerily, mysteriously,** supernaturally

WORD ELEMENTS 20 terat-, terato-; medus-, medusi-, -pagus, anom-, anomo-, anomal-, anomalo-, anomali-, dys-, dis-, mal-, ne-, neo-, par-, para-, poly-, pseud-, pseudo-

21 **mythical and imaginary monsters**

abominable snowman *or* yeti	dipsas
	dragon
Argus	drake <old>
basilisk	Echidna
Bigfoot *or* Sasquatch	Erebus
Briareus	Frankenstein
bucentur	Geryon
Cacus	Gigantes
Caliban	Gorgon
centaur	green-eyed monster
Cerberus	Grendel
Ceto	griffin
Charybdis	Harpy
chimera	hippocampus
cockatrice	hippocentaur
Cyclops	hippocerf

hippogriff
hircocervus
Hydra
Jabberwock
Kraken
Ladon
Lamia
Leviathan
Loch Ness monster
manticore
Medusa
mermaid
merman
Midgard serpent
Minotaur
Mylodont
nixie
ogre
ogress
opinicus
Orthos *or* Orthros
Pegasus
Pongo
Python

roc
Sagittary
salamander
Sasquatch
satyr
Scylla
sea horse
sea serpent
simurgh *or* simug
siren
Sphinx
Talos
troll
Typhoeus
Typhon
unicorn
vampire
werewolf
windigo
wivern *or* wyvern
xiphopagus
yowie
zombie

871 LIST

NOUNS **1 list, enumeration, itemization,** listing, shopping list *and* laundry list *and* want list *and* wish list *and* hit list *and* shit list *and* drop-dead list <nf>, items, **schedule, register,** registry; **inventory,** repertory, tally; database *and* data base; **spreadsheet,** electronic spreadsheet; **checklist;** tally sheet; active list, civil list <Brit>, retired list, sick list; waiting list; blacklist; short list; reading list; syllabus

2 table, contents, table of contents; computer listing, menu; chart

3 catalog; classified catalog, *catalogue raisonné* <Fr>; **card catalog, bibliography,** finding list, handlist, reference list; filmography, discography; publisher's catalog *or* list; **file,** filing system, letter file, pigeonholes

4 dictionary, word list, **lexicon, glossary, thesaurus, Roget's, vocabulary,** terminology, nomenclator; promptorium, gradus; **gazetteer; almanac;** telephone directory, address book; book of lists

5 bill, statement, account, itemized account, invoice; ledger, books; **bill of fare, menu,** carte, wine list, dessert menu; **bill of lading,** manifest, waybill, docket

6 roll, roster, scroll, rota; **roll call,** muster, **census,** nose *or* head count <nf>, **poll,** questionnaire, returns, census report *or* returns; property roll, tax roll, cadastre; muster roll; checkroll, checklist; jury list *or* panel; calendar, docket, **agenda,** order of business; daybook, journal, agenda book, diary;

program, dramatis personae, credits, lineup; honor roll, dean's list; timetable, schedule, itinerary, prospectus

7 index, listing, tabulation; **cataloging, itemization,** filing, card file, card index, Rolodex <trademark>, thumb index, indexing; **registration,** registry, enrollment

VERBS **8 list, enumerate, itemize, tabulate, catalog,** tally; **register,** post, enter, **enroll, book;** impanel; **file,** pigeonhole, classify; **index;** inventory; calendar; score, keep score; **schedule,** program, put on the agenda; diarize; short-list

ADJS **9 listed, enumerated, entered, itemized, cataloged,** tallied, inventoried; filed, **indexed, tabulated; scheduled,** programmed; put on the agenda; inventorial, glossarial, cadastral, classificatory, taxonomic; registered, recorded, noted

872 ONENESS
<state of being one>

NOUNS **1 oneness, unity, singleness,** singularity, **individuality,** identity, selfsameness; **particularity** 865; **uniqueness;** intactness, inviolability, purity, simplicity 798, irreducibility, **integrity,** integrality; **unification,** uniting, integration, fusion, combination 804; **solidification,** solidity, solidarity, **indivisibility,** undividedness, **wholeness** 792.5; univocity, organic unity; uniformity 780; "the sacredness of private integrity"—Emerson

2 aloneness, loneness, **loneliness, lonesomeness,** soleness, singleness; **privacy,** solitariness, **solitude;** separateness, aloofness, detachment, seclusion, sequestration, **withdrawal, alienation,** standing *or* moving *or* keeping apart, **isolation,** "splendid isolation"—Sir William Goschen; celibacy, single blessedness

3 one, I, 1, **unit,** ace, atom; monad; one and only, none else, no other, nothing else, nought beside

4 individual, single, unit, **integer, entity,** singleton, **item,** article, point, module; person, wight <old>, persona, soul, body, warm body <nf>; **individuality,** personhood; isolated case, single instance

VERBS **5 unify,** reduce to unity, unitize, make one; **integrate,** unite 805.3

6 stand alone, stand *or* move *or* keep apart, keep oneself to oneself, withdraw, alienate *or* seclude *or* sequester *or* isolate oneself, feel out of place; individuate, become an individual; go solo, paddle one's own canoe, do one's own thing <nf>

ADJS **7 one, single, singular, individual, sole, unique,** a certain, **solitary, lone;** exclusive; **integral,** indivisible, irreducible, monadic, monistic, unanalyzable, noncompound, atomic, unitary, unitive, unary, undivided, solid, whole-cloth, seamless, uniform 781.5, simple 798.6, whole 792.9; an, any, any one, either

8 **alone, solitary,** solo, *solus* <L>; isolated, insular, apart, separate, separated, alienated, withdrawn, aloof, standoffish, detached, removed; **lone, lonely, lonesome,** lonely-hearts; **private,** reserved, reticent, reclusive, shy, nonpublic, ungregarious; **friendless,** kithless, homeless, rootless, companionless, **unaccompanied,** unescorted, unattended; **unaided,** unassisted, unabetted, unsupported, unseconded; **single-handed,** solo, one-man, one-woman, one-person

9 **sole, unique,** singular, absolute, unrepeated, **alone,** lone, **only,** only-begotten, **one and only,** first and last; odd, impair, unpaired, azygous; celibate

10 **unitary, integrated,** integral, integrant; **unified,** united, rolled into one, composite

11 **unipartite,** unipart, **one-piece;** monadic *or* monadal; **unilateral, one-sided;** unilateralist, uniangulate, unibivalent, unibranchiate, unicameral, unicellular, unicuspid, unidentate, unidigitate; **unidimensional, unidirectional;** uniflorous, unifoliate, unifoliolate, unigenital, uniglobular, unilinear, uniliteral, unilobed, unilobular, unilocular, unimodular, unimolecular, uninuclear, uniocular, unisexual, unisex; unipolar, **univalent, univocal;** one-size; monolingual, monochromatic

12 **unifying, uniting,** unific; **combining,** combinative 805.5,7, combinatory; connective, connecting, connectional; conjunctive 799.16, conjunctival; coalescing, coalescent

ADVS 13 **singly, individually,** particularly, severally, one by one, one at a time; **singularly,** in the singular; **alone,** by itself, *per se* <L>; **by oneself,** by one's lonesome <nf>, on one's own, under one's own steam, **single-handedly, solo,** unaided, separately, apart; **once** 848.6

14 **solely, exclusively, only,** merely, **purely,** simply; **entirely,** wholly, totally; **integrally, indivisibly,** irreducibly, unanalyzably, undividedly

873 DOUBLENESS

NOUNS 1 **doubleness, duality,** dualism, duplexity, **twoness;** twofoldness, biformity; polarity; conjugation, pairing, coupling, yoking; **doubling,** duplication 874, twinning, bifurcation; **dichotomy,** bisection 875, halving, splitting down the middle *or* fifty-fifty; **duplicity,** two-facedness, double-think, hypocrisy, Dr. Jekyll and Mr. Hyde; **irony,** enantiosis, ambiguity, equivocation, equivocality, **ambivalence;** Janus

2 **two,** 2, II, twain <old>; **couple, pair, matching**

pair, twosome, set of two, duo, duet, brace, team, span, yoke, double harness; match, matchup, mates; **couplet,** distich, double, doublet; duad, dyad; the two, **both;** Darby and Joan; tandem

3 **deuce;** pair, doubleton; **craps** *and* **snake eyes** <gambling>

4 **twins,** pair of twins <nf>, identical twins, fraternal twins, exact mates, look-alikes, dead ringers <nf>, mirror image, carbon copy, Doppelganger, spit and image *or* spitting image; Tweedledum and Tweedledee, Siamese twins; Twin stars, Castor and Pollux, Gemini

VERBS 5 **double,** duplicate, replicate, dualize, twin; **halve,** split down the middle *or* fifty-fifty <nf>, bifurcate, dichotomize, bisect, transect; team, **yoke,** yoke together, span, double-team, double-harness; **mate, match,** couple, conjugate; **pair,** pair off, pair up, couple up, team up, match up, buddy up <nf>; talk out of both sides of one's mouth at once; square; copy, mirror, echo

ADJS 6 **two,** twain <old>; **dual, double,** duple, duplex, doubled, twinned, duplicated, replicated, dualized; **dualistic;** dyadic; duadic; biform; bipartite, bipartisan, bilateral, either-or, two-sided, double-sided, binary; dichotomous; bifurcated, bisected, dichotomized, split down the middle *or* fifty fifty <nf>; twin, identical, matched, twinned, duplicated; **two-faced,** duplicitous, hypocritical, double-faced, Janus-like; second, secondary; two-way, two-ply, dual-purpose, two-dimensional

7 **both,** the two, the pair; for two, tête-à-tête, *à deux* <Fr>

8 coupled, paired, yoked, yoked together, matched, matched up, mated, paired off, paired up, teamed up, buddied up <nf>; **bracketed;** conjugate, conjugated; biconjugate, bigeminate; bijugate

PHRS 9 it takes two to tango *and* it's not a one-way street <nf>

WORD ELEMENTS 10 ambi-, amph-, amphi-, bi-, bin-, bis-, deut-, deuto-, deuter-, deutero-, di-, dis-, didym-, didymo-, duo-, dyo-, gem-, twi-, zyg-, zygo-

874 DUPLICATION

NOUNS 1 **duplication, reduplication,** replication, conduplication; **reproduction, repro** <nf>, **doubling;** twinning, gemination, ingemination; **repetition** 849, iteration, reiteration, echoing; **imitation** 336, parroting; **copying** 336.1; **duplicate** 785.3

2 repeat, encore, repeat performance; echo

VERBS 3 **duplicate,** dupe <nf>, ditto <nf>; **double,** double up; multiply by two; twin, geminate, ingeminate; **reduplicate, reproduce,** replicate, redouble; **repeat** 849.7; **copy**

ADJS **4 double, doubled, duplicate,** duplicated, reproduced, replicated, cloned, twinned, geminate, geminated, dualized

ADVS **5 doubly; twofold,** as much again, twice as much; twice, two times

6 secondly, second, secondarily, **in the second place** *or* instance

7 again, another time, **once more,** once again, over again, yet again, *encore* and *bis* <Fr>; **anew,** afresh, new, freshly, newly

WORD ELEMENTS **8** bi-, bis-, deuter-, deutero-, di-, dis-, diphy-, diphyo-, dipl-, diplo-, diss-, disso-, twi-

875 BISECTION

NOUNS **1 bisection,** halving, bipartition, bifidity; **dichotomy, halving, division, in half** *or* **by two,** splitting *or* dividing *or* cutting in two, splitting *or* dividing fifty-fifty <nf>; subdivision; bifurcation, forking, ramification, branching

2 half, moiety; hemisphere, semisphere, semicircle, **fifty percent;** half-and-half *and* fifty-fifty <nf>

3 bisector, diameter, equator, halfway mark, divider, partition 213.5, line of demarcation, boundary 211.3

VERBS **4 bisect, halve, divide, in half** *or* **by two,** transect, subdivide; cleave, fission, **divide** *or* split *or* **cut in two,** share and share alike, go halfers *or* go Dutch <nf>, **dichotomize;** bifurcate, fork, ramify, branch

ADJS **5 half, part, partly, partial,** halfway

6 halved, bisected, divided; dichotomous; bifurcated, forked *or* forking, ramified, branched, branching; riven, **split,** cloven, cleft

7 bipartite, bifid, biform, bicuspid, biaxial, bicameral, binocular, binomial, binominal, biped, bipetalous, bipinnate, bisexual, bivalent, unibivalent

ADVS **8 in half,** in halves, **in two,** in twain, by two, down the middle; half-and-half *and* fifty-fifty <nf>; apart, asunder

WORD ELEMENTS **9** bi-, demi-, dich-, dicho-, hemi-, semi-, sesqui-

876 THREE

NOUNS **1 three,** 3, III, **trio,** trey, **threesome,** trialogue, set of three, tierce <cards>, leash, troika; **triad,** trilogy, trine, **trinity,** triunity, ternary, ternion; **triplet,** tercet, terzetto; trefoil, shamrock, clover; tripod, trivet; **triangle,** tricorn, trihedron, trident, trisul, triennium, trimester, trinomial, trionym, triphthong, triptych, triplopy, trireme, triseme, triskelion, triumvirate; triple crown, triple threat; trey *and* threespot <cards>,

deuce-ace <dice>; triple-decker; ménage à trois; hat trick

2 threeness, triplicity, triality, tripleness, trebleness, threefoldness; triunity, trinity

ADJS **3 three, triple,** triplex, trinal, trine, trial; triadic *or* triadical; triune, three-in-one, *tria juncta in uno* <L>; triform; treble; **triangular,** deltoid, fan-shaped

WORD ELEMENTS **4** tri-, ter-, ternati-

877 TRIPLICATION

NOUNS **1 triplication,** triplicity, trebleness, **threefoldness;** triplicate

VERBS **2 triplicate, triple, treble, multiply by three,** threefold; cube

ADJS **3 triple,** triplicate, **treble, threefold,** trifold, triplex, trinal, trine, tern, ternary, ternal, ternate; three-ply; trilogic *or* trilocial

4 third, tertiary

ADVS **5 triply, trebly,** trinely; **threefold; thrice,** three times, again and yet again

6 thirdly, in the third place

WORD ELEMENTS **7** cub-, cubo-, cubi-; ter-; tert-, trit-, trito-

878 TRISECTION

NOUNS **1 trisection,** tripartition, trichotomy, trifurcation

2 third, tierce, third part, one-third; *tertium quid* <L, a third something>

VERBS **3 trisect, divide in thirds** *or* **three,** third, trichotomize; trifurcate

ADJS **4 tripartite,** trisected, triparted, **three-parted,** trichotomous; three-sided, trihedral, trilateral; **three-dimensional;** three-forked, three-pronged, trifurcate; trident, tridental, tridentate, trifid; tricuspid; three-footed, tripodic, tripedal; trifoliate, trifloral, triflorate, triflorous, tripetalous, triadelphous, triarch; trimerous, 3-merous; three-cornered, tricornered, tricorn; trigonal, trigonoid; triquetrous, triquetral; trigrammatic, triliteral; **triangular,** triangulate, deltoid

879 FOUR

NOUNS **1 four,** 4, IV, tetrad, quatern, quaternion, quaternary, quaternity, **quartet, quadruplet, foursome;** quatre; Little Joe *and* Little Joe from Kokomo *and* Little Dick Fisher <gambling>; quadrennium; tetralogy; tetrapody; tetraphony, four-part diaphony; quadrille, square dance; quatrefoil *or* quadrifoil, four-leaf clover; tetragram, tetragrammaton; quadrangle, quad <nf>, rectangle; tetrahedron; tetragon, square; biquadrate; quadrinomial; quadrature, squaring; quadrilateral

2 fourness, quaternity, quadruplicity, fourfoldness

VERBS **3 square, quadrate,** form *or* make four; form fours *or* squares; **cube, dice**

ADJS **4 four;** foursquare; quaternary, quartile, quartic, quadric, quadratic; tetrad, tetradic; quadrinomial, biquadratic; tetractinal, four-rayed, **quadruped,** four-legged; quadrivalent, tetravalent; quadrilateral 278.9

WORD ELEMENTS **5** quadr-, quadri-, quadru-, tetr-, tetra-, tessar-, tessara-, tri-, trip-, tripl-, triplo-, tris-

880 QUADRUPLICATION

NOUNS **1 quadruplication,** quadruplicature, quadruplicity, fourfoldness

VERBS **2 quadruple, quadruplicate,** fourfold, form *or* make four, multiply by four; quadrate, biquadrate, quadruplex

ADJS **3 quadruplicate, quadruple,** quadraple, **quadruplex, fourfold,** four-ply, four-part, tetraploid, quadrigeminal, biquadratic

WORD ELEMENTS **4** quadr-, quadri-, quadru-, quater-, tetr-, tetra-, tetrakis-

881 QUADRISECTION

NOUNS **1 quadrisection,** quadripartition, **quartering**

2 fourth, one-fourth, **quarter,** one-quarter, fourth part, twenty-five percent, twenty-five cents, two bits <old nf>; quartern; quart; farthing; quarto *or* 4to *or* 4°

VERBS **3 divide by four** *or* **into four; quadrisect, quarter**

ADJS **4 quadrisected, quartered,** quarter-cut; quadripartite, quadrifid, quadriform; quadrifoliate, quadrigeminal, quadripinnate, quadriplanar, quadriserial, quadrivial, quadrifurcate, quadrumanal *or* quadrumanous

5 fourth, quarter

ADVS **6 fourthly,** in the fourth place; quarterly, by quarters

882 FIVE AND OVER

NOUNS **1 five,** V, cinque <cards and dice>, Phoebe *and* Little Phoebe *and* fever <gambling>; **quintet, fivesome,** quintuplets, quints <nf>, cinquain, quincunx, pentad; fifth; **five dollars,** fiver *and* fin *and* finniff *and* five bucks <nf>; pentagon, pentahedron, pentagram; pentapody, pentameter, pentastich; pentarchy; Pentateuch; pentachord; pentathlon; five-pointed star, pentacle, pentalpha, mullet <heraldry>; five-spot <nf>; quinquennium

2 six, VI, sixie from Dixie *and* sister Hicks *and* Jimmy Hicks *and* Captain Hicks <gambling>, **half a dozen, sextet,** sestet, sextuplets, hexad; hexagon, hexahedron, hexagram, six-pointed star, estoile <heraldry>, Jewish star, star of David, *Magen David* <Heb>; hexameter, hexapody, hexastich; hexapod; hexarchy; Hexateuch; hexastyle; hexachord; six-shooter; sixth sense; six-pack

3 seven, VII, heptad, little natural <crapshooting>; septet, heptad; heptagon, heptahedron; heptameter, heptastich; septemvir, heptarchy; Septuagint, Heptateuch; heptachord; **week;** seven deadly sins; seven seas; Seven Wonders of the World

4 eight, VIII, ogdoad, eighter *or* Ada from Decatur <crapshooting>, Ada Ross *and* Ada Ross the stable hoss <gambling>; octad, octonary; octagon, octahedron; octastylos *or* oktostylos; octave, octavo *or* 8vo; octachord; octet *or* octal, octameter; Octateuch; piece of eight; Eightfold Path

5 nine, IX, niner <radio communication>, Nina from Carolina *and* Nina Ross the stable hoss *and* Nina Nina ocean liner <gambling>; ennead; nonagon *or* enneagon, enneahedron; novena; enneastylos; nine days' wonder

6 ten, X, Big Dick *and* Big Dick from Battle Creek <gambling>; **decade;** decagon, decahedron; decagram, decigram, decaliter, deciliter, decare, decameter, decimeter, decastere; decapod; decastylos; decasyllable; decemvir, decemvirate, decurion; decennium, decennary; Ten Commandments *or* Decalogue; tithe; decathlon

7 <eleven to ninety> **eleven; twelve, dozen,** boxcar *and* boxcars <gambling>, duodecimo *or* twelvemo *or* 12mo; **teens; thirteen,** long dozen, baker's dozen; **fourteen,** two weeks, fortnight; **fifteen,** quindecima, quindene, quindecim, quindecennial; **sixteen,** sixteenmo *or* 16mo; **twenty, score; twenty-four,** four and twenty, two dozen, twenty-fourmo *or* 24mo; **twenty-five,** five and twenty, quarter of a hundred *or* century; thirty-two, thirty-twomo *or* 32mo; **forty,** twoscore; **fifty,** L, half a hundred; **sixty,** sexagenary; Sexagesima; sexagenarian, threescore; **sixty-four,** sixty-fourmo *or* 64mo *or* sexagesimo-quarto; **seventy,** septuagenarian, threescore and ten; **eighty,** octogenarian, fourscore; **ninety,** nonagenarian, four-score and ten

8 hundred, century, C, one C <nf>; centennium, centennial, centenary; centenarian; cental, centigram, centiliter, centimeter, centare, centistere; hundredweight *or* cwt; hecatomb; centipede; centumvir, centumvirate, centurion; <120> great *or* long hundred; <144> gross; <150> sesquicentennial, sesquicentenary;

<200> bicentenary, bicentennial; <300> tercentenary, tercentennial, etc

9 five hundred, D, five centuries; five C's <nf>

10 thousand, M, chiliad; **millennium;** G *and* grand *and* thou *and* yard <nf>; chiliagon, chiliahedron *or* chiliaüdron; chiliarchia *or* chiliarch; millepede; milligram, milliliter, millimeter, kilogram *or* kilo, kiloliter, kilometer; kilocycle, kilohertz; kilobyte; gigabyte; **ten thousand,** myriad; **one hundred thousand,** *lakh* <India>

11 million; ten million, *crore* <India>

12 billion, thousand million, milliard

13 trillion, quadrillion, quintillion, sextillion, septillion, octillion, nonillion, decillion, undecillion, duodecillion, tredecillion, quattuordecillion, quindecillion, sexdecillion, septendecillion, octodecillion, novemdecillion, vigintillion; googol, googolplex; zillion *and* jillion <nf>

14 <division into five or more parts> quinquesection, quinquepartition, sextipartition, etc; decimation, decimalization; fifth, sixth, etc; **tenth, tithe,** decima

VERBS **15** <divide by five, etc> quinquesect; decimalize

16 <multiply by five, etc> fivefold, sixfold, etc; quintuple, quintuplicate; sextuple, sextuplicate; centuple, centuplicate

ADJS **17 fifth,** quinary; **fivefold, quintuple,** quintuplicate; quinquennial; quinquepartite, pentadic, quinquefid; quincuncial; pentastyle; pentad, pentavalent, quinquevalent; pentagonal

18 sixth, senary; **sixfold, sextuple;** sexpartite, hexadic, sextipartite, hexapartite; hexagonal, hexahedral, hexangular; hexad, hexavalent; sextuplex, hexastyle; sexennial; hexatonic

19 seventh, septimal; **sevenfold, septuple,** septenary; septempartite, heptadic, septemfid; heptagonal, heptahedral, heptangular; heptamerous; hebdomal

20 eighth, octonary; **eightfold, octuple;** octadic; octal, octofid, octaploid; octagonal, octahedral, octan, octangular; octosyllabic; octastyle

21 ninth, novenary, nonary; **ninefold, nonuple,** enneadic; enneahedral, enneastyle, nonagonal

22 tenth, denary, **decimal,** tithe; **tenfold, decuple;** decagonal, decahedral; decasyllabic; decennial

23 eleventh, undecennial, undecennary

24 twelfth, duodenary, duodenal; duodecimal

25 thirteenth, fourteenth, etc; eleventeenth, umpteenth <nf>; in one's teens

26 twentieth, vicenary, vicennial, vigesimal, vicesimal

27 sixtieth, sexagesimal, sexagenary

28 seventieth, septuagesimal, septuagenary

29 hundredth, centesimal, **centennial,** centenary, centurial; **hundredfold, centuple,** centuplicate; secular; centigrado

30 thousandth, millenary, **millennial; thousandfold**

31 millionth; billionth, quadrillionth, quintillionth, etc

WORD ELEMENTS **32** pent-, penta-, pen-, quinqu-, quinque-, quintquinti-; hex-, hexa-, sex-, sexi-, sexti-; hept-, hepta-, sept-, septi-; oct-, octa-, octo-; non-, nona-, ennea-; deca-, deka-, deci-; undec-, hendec-, hendeca-; dodec-, dodeca-; icos-, icosa-, icosi-, eicos-, eicosa-; cent-, centi-, hect-, hecto-, hecato-, hecaton; kilo-, milli-; meg-, mega-, micro-; giga-, nano-; pico-

883 PLURALITY
<more than one>

NOUNS **1 plurality,** pluralness; a greater number, a certain number; **several,** some, a few 885.2, more; plural number, the plural; compositeness, nonsingleness, nonuniqueness; **pluralism** 782.1, variety; numerousness 884

2 majority, plurality, more than half, the greater number, the greatest number, **most,** preponderance *or* preponderancy, greater *or* better part, **bulk, mass;** lion's share

3 pluralization, plurification <old>

4 multiplication, multiplying, proliferation, **increase** 251; duplication 874; multiple, multiplier, multiplicand, product, factor; factorization, exponentiation; multiplication table; lowest *or* least common multiple, greatest common divisor, highest *or* greatest common factor; prime factor, submultiple, power, square, cube, fourth power, exponent, index, square root, cube root, surd, root mean square, factorial

VERBS **5 pluralize,** plurify <old>; raise to *or* make more than one

6 multiply, proliferate, **increase** 251.4,6, duplicate 874.3

ADJS **7 plural,** pluralized, more than one, more, several, severalfold; **some,** certain; not singular, composite, nonsingle, nonunique; plurative <logic>; **pluralistic** 782.3, various; many, beaucoup <nf>, numerous 884.6

8 multiple, multiplied, multifold, **manifold** 884.6; **increased** 251.7; multinomial *and* polynomial <mathematics>

9 majority, most, the greatest number

ADVS **10 in the majority;** and others, et al, et cetera 253.14; plurally

WORD ELEMENTS **11** multi-; -fold

884 NUMEROUSNESS

NOUNS **1 numerousness, multiplicity, manyness,** manifoldness, multifoldness, multitudinousness, multifariousness, teemingness, swarmingness, rifeness, profuseness, profusion; **plenty,** abundance 991.2; **countlessness,** innumerability, infinitude, infinity

2 <indefinite number> **a number,** a certain number, one or two, two or three, **a few, several,** parcel, passel <nf>; eighteen *and* umpteen <nf>

3 <large number> **multitude, throng** 770.4; a many, numbers, quantities, lots 247.4, flocks, **scores, scads;** an abundance of, all kinds *or* sorts of, no end of, quite a few, tidy sum; muchness, any number of, **large amount; host, army,** more than one can shake a stick at, fistful *and* slew *and* shitload *and* shithouse full <nf>, legion, rout, ruck, mob, jam, clutter; **swarm, flock** 770.5, flight, cloud, hail, bevy, covey, shoal, hive, nest, pack, litter, bunch 769.7; a world of, a mass of, worlds of, masses of

4 <immense number> **a myriad,** a thousand, **a thousand and one,** *a lakh* <India>, *a crore* <India>, a million, a billion, a quadrillion, a nonillion, etc 881.13; umpteen, a zillion *or* jillion <nf>; googol, googolplex

VERBS 5 **teem with,** overflow with, **abound with,** burst with, bristle with, pullulate with, **swarm with,** throng with, creep with, **crawl with, be alive with, have coming out of one's ears** *and* **have up the gazoo** *and* **kazoo** <nf>; clutter, crowd, jam, pack, overwhelm, overflow; multiply 883.6; outnumber; overcrowd

ADJS 6 **numerous, many, manifold,** not a few, no few; **very many,** full many, **ever so many,** considerable *and* quite some <nf>, quite a few; **multitudinous,** multitudinal, multifarious, multifold, multiple, **myriad,** thousand, million, billion; zillion *and* jillion <nf>; heaped-up; numerous as the stars, numerous as the sands, numerous as the hairs on the head

7 **several,** divers, **sundry,** various; fivish, sixish, etc; some five or six, etc; upwards of

8 **abundant,** copious, ample, plenteous, **plentiful** 991.7, thick on the ground <Brit>

9 **teeming, swarming, crowding,** thronging, overflowing, overcrowded, overwhelming, bursting, **crawling, alive with,** lousy with <nf>, populous, prolific, proliferating, crowded, packed, jammed, bumper-to-bumper <nf>, jam-packed, like sardines in a can <nf>, thronged, studded, bristling, rife, lavish, prodigal, superabundant, **profuse,** in profusion, thick, **thick with,** thick-coming, thick as hail *or* flies

10 **innumerable, numberless,** unnumbered, countless, uncounted, **uncountable,** unreckonable, untold, incalculable, immeasurable, unmeasured, measureless, inexhaustible, endless, infinite,

without end *or* limit, more than one can tell, more than you can shake a stick at <nf>, no end of *or* to; countless as the stars *or* sands; **astronomical,** galactic; millionfold, trillionfold, etc

11 **and many more,** *cum multis aliis* <L>, and what not, and heaven knows what

ADVS 12 **numerously,** multitudinously, **profusely,** swarmingly, teemingly, thickly, copiously, **abundantly, prodigally; innumerably,** countlessly, infinitely, incalculably, inexhaustibly, immeasurably; in throngs, in crowds, in swarms, in heaps, *acervatim* <L>; **no end** <nf>

WORD ELEMENTS 13 multi-, myri-, myrio-, pluri-, poly-

885 FEWNESS

NOUNS 1 **fewness,** infrequency, **sparsity,** sparseness, **scarcity, paucity, scantiness, meagerness,** miserliness, niggardliness, tightness, thinness, stringency, restrictedness; chintziness *and* chinchiness *and* stinginess <nf>, scrimpiness *and* skimpiness <nf>; **rarity,** exiguity; smallness 258.1; unsubstantiality *or* insubstantiality; skeleton staff

2 **a few,** too few, mere *or* piddling *or* piddly few, only a few, **small number,** limited *or* piddling *or* piddly number, not enough to count *or* matter, not enough to shake a stick at, **handful, scattering,** corporal's guard, sprinkling, trickle; low *or* poor turnout, too few to mention

3 **minority,** least; the minority, the few; minority group; "we happy few"—Shakespeare; minimum; less, least

ADJS 4 **few, not many;** hardly *or* scarcely any, precious little *or* few, of small number, to be counted on one's fingers, too few

5 **sparse,** scant, **scanty,** exiguous, **infrequent,** sporadic, scarce, scarce as hen's teeth <nf>, poor, piddling, piddly, thin, slim, **meager,** not much; miserly, niggardly, cheeseparing, tight; chintzy *and* chinchy *and* stingy <nf>, scrimpy *and* skimpy <nf>, skimping *and* scrimping <nf>; **scattered,** sprinkled, spotty, **few and far between; rare,** seldom met with, seldom seen, not thick on the ground <Brit>

6 **fewer, less,** smaller, not so much *or* many, reduced, minimal

7 **minority,** least

ADVS 8 **sparsely,** *sparsim* <L>, **scantily, meagerly,** exiguously, piddlingly; stingily *and* scrimpily *and* skimpily <nf>, thinly; **scarcely,** rarely, infrequently; **scatteringly,** scatteredly, spottily, in dribs and drabs *and* in bits and pieces <nf>, **here and there,** in places, in spots

886 CAUSE

NOUNS **1 cause, occasion,** antecedents, **grounds,** ground, background, stimulus, base, **basis,** element, principle, factor; **determinant,** determinative; causation, causality, cause and effect; etiology

2 reason, reason why, rationale, reason for *or* behind, underlying reason, rational ground, **explanation,** answer, **the why,** the wherefore, the whatfor *or* whyfor <nf>, **the why and wherefore,** the idea <nf>, the big idea <nf>; stated cause, pretext, pretense, excuse

3 immediate cause, proximate cause, trigger, spark; **domino effect,** causal sequence, chain *or* nexus of cause and effect, ripple effect, slippery slope, contagion effect, knock-on *or* knock-on effect <chiefly Brit>; transient cause, occasional cause; formal cause; efficient cause; ultimate cause, immanent cause, remote cause, causing cause, *causa causans* <L>, first cause; **final cause,** *causa finalis* <L>, **end,** end in view, teleology; provocation, **last straw,** straw that broke the camel's back, match in the powder barrel; butterfly effect *or* strange attraction *or* sensitive dependence on initial conditions; planetary influence, astrological influence

4 author, agent, **originator,** generator, begetter, engenderer, producer, maker, beginner, **creator,** mover, inventor; **parent, mother, father,** sire; **prime mover,** *primum mobile* <L>; causer, effector; inspirer, instigator, catalyst; motivator, inspiration

5 source, origin, genesis, original, origination, **derivation, rise, beginning,** conception, inception, commencement, **head;** provenance, provenience, background; **root,** radix, radical, taproot, grass roots; stem, stock

6 fountainhead, headwater, headstream, riverhead, springhead, headspring, **mainspring,** wellspring, wellhead, well, **spring, fountain,** fount, font, *fons et origo* <L>; mine, quarry

7 vital force *or* **principle,** *élan vital* <Fr>, reproductive urge, a gleam in one's father's eye <nf>; **egg,** ovum 305.12, **germ,** germen <old>, spermatozoon 305.11, nucleus 305.7, **seed; embryo** 305.14; bud 310.23; loins; **womb,** matrix, uterus

8 birthplace, breeding place, breeding ground, birthsite, rookery, hatchery; **hotbed,** forcing bed; incubator, brooder; **nest,** nidus; **cradle,** nursery

9 <a principle or movement> **cause, principle,** interest, issue, burning issue, commitment, faith, great cause, lifework; reason for being, *raison d'être* <Fr>; **movement,** mass movement, activity; **drive, campaign, crusade;** zeal, passion, fanaticism

VERBS **10 cause,** be the cause of, lie at the root of; bring about, bring to pass, effectuate, **effect,** bring to effect, realize; **impact,** impact on, influence; **occasion, make, create, engender,** generate, **produce,** breed, work, do; **originate,** give origin to, give occasion to, **give rise to,** spark, spark off, set off, trigger, trigger off; **give birth to, beget,** bear, bring forth, labor *or* travail and bring forth, author, **father,** sire, sow the seeds of; gestate, **conceive,** have the idea, have a bright idea <nf>; set up, set afloat, **set on foot;** found, establish, inaugurate, institute; engineer

11 induce, lead, procure, get, obtain, contrive, **effect,** bring, **bring on,** draw on, **call forth, elicit, evoke, provoke,** inspire, influence, instigate, egg on, **motivate;** draw down, open the door to; suborn; superinduce; incite, kindle

12 determine, decide, turn the scale, have the last word, tip the scale; **necessitate,** entail, require; contribute to, have a hand in, lead to, conduce to; **advance, forward,** influence, subserve; **spin off,** hive off <Brit>

ADJS **13 causal,** causative; chicken-and-egg <nf>; occasional; originative, institutive, constitutive; **at the bottom of,** behind the scenes; **formative,** determinative, effectual, decisive, pivotal; etiological

14 original, primary, primal, primitive, pristine, primo <nf>, primeval, aboriginal, **elementary,** elemental, **basic,** basal, **rudimentary,** crucial, central, radical, **fundamental;** embryonic, in embryo, *in ovo* <L>, germinal, seminal, pregnant; **generative,** genetic, protogenic; effectual

WORD ELEMENTS **15** uter-, utero-, metr-, metro-, -metrium, venter; etio-, aetio-, prot-, proto-; -facient, -factive, -fic, -ic, -ical, -etic

887 EFFECT

NOUNS **1 effect, result,** resultant, **consequence,** consequent, sequent, sequence, sequel, sequela, sequelae; event, eventuality, eventuation, **upshot, outcome,** logical outcome, possible outcome, scenario; **outgrowth,** spin-off, offshoot, offspring, issue, aftermath, legacy; side effect; **product** 893, precipitate, distillate, **fruit,** first fruits, crop, harvest, payoff; development, corollary; derivative, derivation, by-product; net result, end result

2 impact, force, **repercussion,** reaction; backwash, backlash, reflex, recoil, response; mark, print, imprint, impress, impression; significance, import, meaning

3 aftereffect, aftermath, aftergrowth, aftercrop, **afterclap,** aftershock, afterimage, afterglow, aftertaste; wake, trail, track; domino effect

VERBS **4 result, ensue, issue, follow,** attend, accompany; **turn out, come out,** fall out, redound,

work out, pan out <nf>, fare; have a happy result, turn out well, come up roses <nf>; turn out to be, prove, prove to be; **become of,** come of, come about; **develop,** unfold; **eventuate,** terminate, end; **end up,** land up <Brit>, come out, wind up

5 **result from,** be the effect of, be due to, originate in *or* from, **come from,** come out of, grow from, **grow out of,** follow from *or* on, proceed from, descend from, emerge from, issue from, ensue from, emanate from, flow from, **derive from,** accrue from, rise *or* arise from, take its rise from, **spring from, stem from,** sprout from, bud from, germinate from; **spin off; depend on,** hinge *or* pivot *or* turn on, hang on, be contingent on; pay off, bear fruit

ADJS 6 **resultant, resulting, following, ensuing; consequent,** consequential, following, sequent, sequential, sequacious; necessitated, entailed, required; **final;** derivative, derivational

ADVS 7 **consequently, as a result,** as a consequence, in consequence, in the event, naturally, *naturellement* <Fr>, necessarily, of necessity, inevitably, of course, as a matter of course, and so, it follows that; **therefore; accordingly** 766.11; **finally**

CONJS 8 **resulting from,** coming from, arising from, deriving *or* derivable from, consequent to, in consequence of; **owing to, due to;** attributed *or* attributable to, dependent *or* contingent on; **caused by,** occasioned by, **at the bottom of;** required by, entailed by, following from, following strictly from

PHRS 9 one thing leads to another, *post hoc, ergo propter hoc* <L>, what goes up must come down <nf>, what goes around comes around <nf>

888 ATTRIBUTION
<assignment of cause>

NOUNS 1 **attribution, assignment,** assignation, **ascription, imputation,** arrogation, placement, application, attachment, saddling, **charge, blame; indictment; responsibility,** answerability; **credit,** honor; accounting for, reference to, derivation from, connection with; etiology

2 **acknowledgment,** citation, tribute; confession; **reference;** trademark, signature; **by-line,** credit line

VERBS 3 **attribute, assign, ascribe, impute,** give, place, put, apply, attach, refer

4 **attribute to, ascribe to, impute to,** assign to, **lay to,** put *or* set down to, apply to, refer to, point to; **pin on,** pinpoint <nf>, fix on *or* upon, attach to, acrete to, connect with, fasten upon, hang on <nf>, **saddle on *or* upon,** place upon, **father upon,** settle upon, saddle with; blame, **blame for,** blame on *or*

upon, charge on *or* upon, place *or* put the blame on, place the blame *or* responsibility for, indict, **fix the responsibility for,** point to one, put the finger on *and* finger <nf>, fix the burden of, **charge to,** lay to one's charge, place to one's account, set to the account of, account for, lay at the door of, bring home to; acknowledge, confess; **credit *or* accredit with;** put words in one's mouth

5 **trace to,** follow the trail to; **derive from,** trace the origin *or* derivation of; affiliate to, filiate to, father, fix the paternity of

ADJS 6 **attributable, assignable, ascribable, imputable,** traceable, referable, accountable, explicable; owing, **due,** assigned *or* referred to, derivable from, derivative, derivational; **charged,** alleged, imputed, putative; **credited, attributed**

ADVS 7 **hence, therefore,** therefor, **wherefore,** wherefrom, whence, then, thence, *ergo* <L>, for which reason; **consequently** 886.7; **accordingly** 766.11; **because of that,** for that, by reason of that, for that reason, for the reason that, in consideration of something, from *or* for that cause, **on that account,** on that ground, threat; **because of this, on this account,** for this cause, on account of this, *propter hoc* <L>, for this reason, hereat; thus, thusly <nf>, thuswise; on someone's head, on *or* at someone's doorstep

8 **why,** whyever, whyfor *and* for why <nf>, how come <nf>, how is it that, **wherefore, what for,** for which, **on what account,** on account of what *or* which, for what *or* whatever reason, from what cause, *pourquoi* <Fr>

PREPS 9 **because of,** by reason of, **as a result of,** by *or* in virtue of, **on account of,** on the score of, for the sake of, **owing to, due to,** thanks to; **considering,** in consideration of, **in view of;** after

CONJS 10 **because,** *parce que* <Fr>, **since,** as, for, **whereas, inasmuch as, forasmuch as, insofar as, insomuch as,** as things go; in that, for the cause that, for the reason that, in view of the fact that, taking into account that, **seeing that,** seeing as how <nf>, being as how <nf>; **resulting from** 887.8

889 OPERATION

NOUNS 1 **operation, functioning, action, performance,** performing, **working, work,** workings, exercise, practice; agency; implementation; operations; **management** 573, **direction, conduct, running, carrying-on *or* -out,** execution, seeing to, overseeing, oversight; **handling,** manipulation; responsibility 641.2; **occupation** 724; joint operation

2 **process, procedure,** proceeding, course; what

makes it tick; **act,** step, measure, initiative, *démarche* <Fr>, move, maneuver, motion

3 **workability, operability,** operativeness, performability, negotiability <nf>, manageability, compassability, manipulatability, maneuverability; **practicability, feasibility,** viability

4 **operator,** operative, operant; **handler,** manipulator; **manager** 574.1, **executive** 574.3; functionary, agent; driver

VERBS 5 **operate, function, run, work; manage, direct** 573.8, **conduct; carry on** *or* **out** *or* **through,** make go *or* work, carry the ball <nf>, perform; **handle,** manipulate, maneuver; deal with, see to, take care of; occupy oneself with 724.10; be responsible for 641.6

6 operate on, **act on** *or* **upon, work on, affect, influence,** bear on, impact, impact on; have to do with, treat, focus *or* concentrate on; bring to bear on

7 <be operative> **operate, function, work, act, perform, go, run,** be in action *or* operation *or* commission; percolate *and* perk *and* tick <nf>; be effective, go into effect, have effect, take effect, militate; be in force; have play, have free play

8 **function as,** work as, **act as,** act *or* play the part of, have the function *or* role *or* job *or* mission of; do one's thing <nf>

ADJS 9 **operative, operational,** go <nf>, **functional, practical,** in working order; **effective,** effectual, efficient, efficacious; relevant, significant

10 **workable, operable,** operatable, **performable,** actable, **doable,** manageable, compassable, negotiable, manipulatable, maneuverable; **practicable, feasible,** practical, viable, useful

11 **operating, operational, working, functioning,** operant, functional, acting, active, running, **going,** going on, ongoing; **in operation,** in action, **in practice, in force,** in play, in exercise, at work, on foot; **in process,** in the works, on the fire, in the pipe *or* pipeline <nf>, in hand, up and going

12 operational, functional; **managerial** 573.12; agential, agentive *or* agentival; manipulational

WORD ELEMENTS 13 -age, -al, -ance, -ence, -ation, -ing, -ion, -ism, -ization, -isation, -ment, -osis, -sis, -th, -ure

890 PRODUCTIVENESS

NOUNS 1 **productiveness, productivity,** productive capacity; **fruitfulness,** fructification, procreativeness, progenitiveness, **fertility,** fecundity, fecundation, prolificness, prolificity, prolificacy; **pregnancy; luxuriance, exuberance,** generousness, bountifulness, plentifulness, plenteousness, richness, lushness, **abundance**

991.2, superabundance, copiousness, teemingness, swarmingness; teeming womb *or* loins

2 proliferation, multiplication, fructification, pullulation, teeming; **reproduction** 78, **production** 891

3 **fertilization, enrichment,** fecundation; propagation, pollination; insemination; impregnation 78.4

4 **fertilizer,** dressing, top dressing, enricher, richener, procreator, propagator; organic fertilizer, manure, muck, mulch, night soil, dung, guano, compost, leaf litter, leaf mold, humus, peat moss, castor-bean meal, bone meal, fish meal; commercial fertilizer, inorganic fertilizer, chemical fertilizer, phosphate, superphosphate, ammonia, nitrogen, nitrate, potash, ammonium salts, sulfate, lime, marl

5 <goddesses of fertility> Demeter, Ceres, Isis, Astarte *or* Ashtoreth, Venus of Willenburg; <gods> Frey, Priapus, Dionysus, Pan, Baal; fertility cult

6 <comparisons> rabbit, Hydra, warren, seed plot, hotbed, rich soil, land flowing with milk and honey

VERBS 7 **produce, be productive, proliferate,** pullulate, fructify, be fruitful, **multiply,** procreate, propagate, generate, multiply, mushroom, spin off, hive off <Brit>, engender, beget, teem; **reproduce** 78.7,8

8 **fertilize, enrich,** make fertile, richen, fatten, feed; fructify, fecundate, fecundify, prolificate; inseminate, impregnate 78.10; pollinate, germinate, seed; cross-fertilize, cross-pollinate; dress, top-dress; manure, compost, feed, mulch, marl

ADJS 9 **productive, fruitful,** fructiferous, fecund; **fertile, pregnant,** seminal, **rich,** flourishing, thriving, blooming; **prolific,** proliferous, uberous, **teeming,** swarming, bursting, bursting out, plenteous, **plentiful,** copious, generous, bountiful, **abundant** 991.7, **luxuriant, exuberant, lush,** superabundant; creative

10 **bearing, yielding, producing;** fruitbearing, fructiferous

11 **fertilizing, enriching,** richening, fattening, fecundatory, fructificative, **seminal,** germinal

891 UNPRODUCTIVENESS

NOUNS 1 **unproductiveness,** unproductivity, ineffectualness 19.3; **unfruitfulness,** fruitlessness, **barrenness,** nonfruition, dryness, aridity, dearth, famine; sterileness, **sterility,** unfertileness, **infertility,** infecundity; wasted *or* withered loins, dry womb; **birth control, contraception,** family planning, planned parenthood; abortion; impotence 19, incapacity

2 wasteland, waste, desolation, barren *or* **barrens,** barren land, "An old man in a dry season"— T S Eliot; heath; **desert,** Sahara, "a barren waste, a wild of sand"—Addison, sands, desert sands, karroo <Africa>, badlands, dust bowl, salt flat, Death Valley, Arabia Deserta, lunar waste *or* landscape; desert island; wilderness, howling **wilderness,** wild, wilds; treeless plain; bush, brush, outback <Austral>; fallowness, aridness; desertification, desertization

VERBS **3** be unproductive, **come to nothing,** come to naught, prove infertile, hang fire <nf>, flash in the pan, fizzle *or* peter out <nf>; **lie fallow;** stagnate, run to seed

ADJS **4 unproductive,** nonproductive *or* nonproducing; **infertile, sterile,** unfertile *or* nonfertile, **unfruitful,** unfructuous, acarpous <botany>, infecund, unprolific *or* nonprolific; **impotent,** gelded 19.19; **ineffectual** 19.15; **barren, desert, arid,** dry, dried-up, sere, exhausted, drained, leached, sucked dry, wasted, gaunt, **waste, desolate,** jejune; **childless,** issueless, without issue, *sine prole* <L>; fallow, unplowed, unsown, untilled, uncultivated, unfecundated; celibate; virgin; menopausal

5 uncreative, noncreative, nonseminal, nongerminal, unfructified, unpregnant; uninventive, unoriginal, derivative

892 PRODUCTION

NOUNS **1 production, creation, making, origination, invention, conception,** innovation, originating, engenderment, engendering, genesis, beginning; **devising,** hatching, fabrication, **concoction,** coinage, mintage, **contriving,** contrivance; **authorship;** creative effort, **generation** 78.6; improvisation, making do; **gross national product** *or* GNP, net national product *or* NNP, national production of goods and services

2 production, manufacture *or* **manufacturing, making, producing,** devising, design, fashioning, framing, forming, formation, formulation; engineering, tooling-up; processing, conversion; casting, **shaping,** molding; machining, milling, finishing; **assembly,** composition, elaboration; **workmanship, craftsmanship,** skill 413; **construction, building,** erection, architecture; **fabrication,** prefabrication; handiwork, handwork, handicraft, crafting; **mining,** extraction, smelting, **refining; growing,** cultivation, **raising,** harvesting

3 industrial production, industry, mass production, volume production, **assembly-line production;** production line, assembly line; modular production *or* assembly, standardization; division of labor, industrialization; **cottage industry;** piecework, farmed-out work

4 establishment, foundation, constitution, institution, installation, formation, **organization,** inauguration, **inception, setting-up,** realization, materialization, effectuation; spinning-off, hiving-off <Brit>

5 performance, execution, doing, accomplishment, achievement, productive effort *or* effect, realization, bringing to fruition, fructification, effectuation, operation 888; overproduction, glut; underproduction, scarcity; **productiveness** 890, fructuousness

6 bearing, yielding, birthing; fruition, fruiting, fructification

7 producer, maker, craftsman, wright, smith; **manufacturer,** industrialist; **creator,** begetter, engenderer, **author,** mother, **father,** sire; **ancestors** 560.7; **precursor** 816; **originator,** initiator, establisher, inaugurator, introducer, institutor, beginner, mover, prime mover, motive force, instigator; **founder,** organizer, founding father, founding *or* founder member, founding partner, cofounder; **inventor,** discoverer, deviser; developer; engineer; **builder,** constructor, artificer, **architect,** planner, **conceiver,** designer, **shaper,** master *or* leading spirit; executor, executrix; facilitator, animator; **grower,** raiser, cultivator; effector, realizer; **apprentice, journeyman, master,** master craftsman *or* workman, artist, past master

VERBS **8 produce, create, make, manufacture, form,** formulate, evolve, mature, elaborate, fashion, **fabricate,** prefabricate, cast, shape, configure, carve out, mold, extrude, frame; **construct, build,** erect, put up, set up, run up, raise, rear; make up, get up, prepare, compose, write, indite, devise, design, concoct, compound, churn out *and* crank out *and* pound out *and* hammer out *and* grind out *and* rustle up *and* gin up <nf>; **put together, assemble,** piece together, patch together, whomp up *and* fudge together *and* slap up *or* together <nf>, improvise 365.8; **make to order,** custom-make, custom-build, purpose-build <Brit>

9 process, convert 858.11; mill, machine; carve, chisel; **mine,** extract, pump, smelt, **refine; raise,** rear, **grow,** cultivate, harvest

10 establish, found, constitute, institute, install, form, **set up, organize,** equip, endow, inaugurate, realize, materialize, effect, effectuate

11 perform, do, work, act, execute, **accomplish, achieve** 407.4, **deliver,** come through with, realize, engineer, effectuate, **bring about,** bring to fruition *or* into being, cause; mass-produce, volume-produce, industrialize; overproduce; underproduce; **be productive** 890.7

12 originate, invent, conceive, discover, **make up, devise, contrive,** concoct, fabricate, coin, mint, frame, hatch, hatch *or* cook up, strike out; improvise, make do with; think up, think out, dream up, **design,** plan, formulate, set one's wits to work; **generate, develop,** mature, **evolve;** breed, engender, beget, spawn, hatch; bring forth, give rise to, give being to, bring *or* call into being; procreate 78.8

13 bear, yield, produce, furnish; **bring forth,** usher into the world; fruit, **bear fruit,** fructify; spawn

ADJS **14 productional, creational,** formational; executional; **manufacturing,** manufactural, fabricational, **industrial,** smokestack

15 constructional, structural, building, housing, edificial; **architectural,** architectonic

16 creative, originative, causative, **productive** 890.9, **constructive,** formative, fabricative, demiurgic; inventive; generative 78.16

17 produced, made, caused, brought about; effectuated, executed, performed, done; grown, raised

18 made, man-made; **manufactured,** created, crafted, formed, shaped, molded, cast, forged, machined, milled, fashioned, **built, constructed,** fabricated; **mass-produced,** volume-produced, assembly-line; **well-made,** well-built, well-constructed; **homemade,** homespun, **handmade,** handcrafted, handicrafted, self-made, DIY *or* do it yourself; machine-made; **processed; assembled,** put together; **custom-made,** custom-built, purpose-built <Brit>, custom, made to order, bespoke; **ready-made,** ready-formed, ready-prepared, ready-to-wear, ready-for-wear, off-the-shelf, off-the-rack; prefabricated, prefab <nf>; **mined,** extracted, smelted, **refined; grown, raised,** harvested, gathered

19 invented, originated, **conceived,** discovered, newfound; fabricated, coined, minted, new-minted; **made-up,** made out of whole cloth

20 manufacturable, producible, productible

ADVS **21 in production;** in the works, in hand, on foot; under construction; in the pipeline; on-line

893 PRODUCT

NOUNS **1 product,** end product, production, manufacture; **work,** *œuvre* <Fr>, **handiwork, artifact; creation;** creature; **offspring,** child, fruit, fruit of one's loins; **result,** effect 887, issue, outgrowth, outcome; **invention,** origination, coinage, mintage *or* new mintage, brainchild; **concoction,** composition; opus, opuscule; apprentice work; journeyman work; **masterwork, masterpiece,** *chef d'œuvre* <Fr>, *Meisterstück*

<Ger>, work of an artist *or* a master *or* a past master, crowning achievement; gross national product 892.1

2 production, produce, proceeds, net, **yield, output,** throughput; **crop,** harvest, take <nf>, return, bang <nf>

3 extract, distillation, essence; **by-product,** secondary *or* incidental product, spin-off, outgrowth, offshoot; **residue,** leavings, waste, waste product, industrial waste, solid waste, lees, dregs, ash, slag

4 <amount made> make, making; batch, lot, run, boiling

894 INFLUENCE

NOUNS **1 influence,** influentiality; **power** 18, force, clout <nf>, potency, pressure, effect, indirect *or* incidental power, **say,** the final say, the last word, say-so *and* a lot to do with *or* to say about <nf>, veto power; **prestige,** favor, good feeling, credit, esteem, repute, personality, leadership, charisma, magnetism, charm, enchantment; **weight,** moment, consequence, importance, eminence; **authority** 417, control, domination, hold; **sway** 612.1, reign, rule; **mastery,** ascendancy, supremacy, dominance, predominance, preponderance; upper hand, whip hand, trump card; leverage, purchase; **persuasion** 375.3, suasion, suggestion, subtle influence, insinuation

2 favor, special favor, **interest; pull** *and* drag *and* suction <nf>; **connections,** the right people, inside track <nf>; amicus curiae

3 backstairs influence, intrigues, deals, schemes, **games,** Machiavellian *or* Byzantine intrigues, ploys; **wires** *and* **strings** *and* ropes <nf>; **wire-pulling** <nf>; **influence peddling;** lobbying, lobbyism; Big Brother

4 sphere of influence, orbit, ambit; bailiwick, vantage, stamping ground, footing, **territory,** turf, home turf, constituency, **power base,** niche

5 influenceability, swayableness, movability; **persuadability,** persuadableness, persuasibility, suasibility, openness, open-mindedness, get-at-ableness <Brit nf>, perviousness, accessibility, receptiveness, responsiveness, amenableness; **suggestibility, susceptibility,** impressionability, malleability; weakness 16; putty in one's hands

6 <influential person or thing> **influence,** good influence; bad influence, sinister influence; **person** *or* **woman** *or* **man of influence,** an influential, an affluential, a presence, a palpable presence, a mover and shaker <nf>, a person to be reckoned with, a player *or* player on the scene; heavyweight, big wheel *and* biggie *and* heavy *or* long-ball hitter *and* piledriver <nf>, very important person *or* VIP <nf>, big shot *or* bigwig *or* big cheese <nf>; wheeler-dealer <nf>, influencer, **wire-puller** <nf>; **powerbroker; power behind the throne,** gray eminence, *éminence grise* <Fr>, hidden hand, manipulator, friend at *or* in court, kingmaker; **influence peddler,** five-percenter, lobbyist; Svengali, Rasputin; **pressure group,** special-interest group, special interests, single-issue group, PAC *or* political action committee; lobby; the Establishment, ingroup, court, powers that be 575.15, superpower, lords of creation; **key,** key to the city, access, open sesame

VERBS **7 influence,** make oneself felt, **affect,** weigh with, **sway,** bias, bend, incline, dispose, predispose, **move,** prompt, lead; color, tinge, tone, slant, impart spin; **induce,** persuade 375.23, jawbone *and* twist one's arm *and* hold one's feet to the fire <nf>, work, work *or* bend to one's will; lead by the nose <nf>, wear down, soften up; win friends and influence people, ingratiate oneself

8 <exercise influence over> **govern** 612.12, **rule, control** 612.13, order, **regulate,** direct, guide; **determine,** decide, dispose; have the say *or* say-so, have veto power over, have the last word, call the shots *and* be in the driver's seat *and* wear the pants <nf>; charismatize

9 exercise *or* **exert influence, use one's influence, bring pressure to bear upon,** lean on <nf>, act on, **work on,** bear upon, throw one's weight around *or* into the scale, say a few words to the right person *or* in the right quarter; charismatize; draw, draw on, lead on, magnetize; **approach,** go up to with hat in hand, make advances *or* overtures, make up to *or* get cozy with <nf>; get at *or* get the ear of <nf>; **pull strings** *or* **wires** *or* **ropes,** wire-pull <nf>; lobby, lobby through; wheel and deal <nf>

10 have influence, be influential, carry weight, weigh, tell, count, cut ice, throw a lot of weight <nf>, have a lot to do with *or* say about <nf>; be the decisive factor *or* the one that counts, have pull *or* suction *or* drag *or* leverage <nf>; have a way with one, have personality *or* magnetism *or* charisma, charm the birds out of the trees, charm the pants off one <nf>, be persuasive; have an in <nf>, have the inside track <nf>; have full play; have friends in high places

11 have influence *or* power *or* a hold over, have pull *or* clout with <nf>; **lead by the nose, twist** *or* **turn** *or* **wind around one's little finger,** have in one's pocket, keep under one's thumb, make sit up and beg *or* lie down and roll over; hypnotize, mesmerize, **dominate** 612.15

12 gain influence, **get in with** <nf>, ingratiate oneself with, get cozy with <nf>; make peace, **mend**

fences; gain a footing, take hold, move in, take root, strike root in, make a dent in; gain a hearing, make one's voice heard, make one sit up and take notice, be listened to, be recognized; get the mastery *or* control of, get the inside track <nf>, gain a hold upon; change the preponderance, turn the scale *or* balance, turn the tables

ADJS **13 influential, powerful** 18.12, affluential, potent, strong, to be reckoned with; **effective,** effectual, efficacious, telling; **weighty,** momentous, important, consequential, substantial, earth-shattering, **prestigious,** estimable, authoritative, reputable; **persuasive,** suasive, personable, **winning,** magnetic, charming, enchanting, charismatic

14 <in a position of influence> **well-connected,** favorably situated, near the seat of power; **dominant** 612.18, **predominant,** preponderant, prepotent, prepollent, regnant, ruling, swaying, prevailing, prevalent, on the throne, in the driver's seat <nf>; **ascendant,** in the ascendant, in ascendancy

15 influenceable, swayable, movable; persuadable, persuasible, suasible, open, open-minded, pervious, accessible, receptive, responsive, amenable; **under one's thumb,** in one's pocket, on one's payroll; coercible, bribable, compellable, vulnerable; **plastic, pliant,** pliable, malleable; **suggestible, susceptible, impressionable,** weak 16.12

895 ABSENCE OF INFLUENCE

NOUNS **1 lack of influence** *or* **power** *or* **force,** uninfluentiality, **unauthoritativeness,** powerlessness, forcelessness, impotence 19, impotency; **ineffectiveness,** inefficaciousness, inefficacy, ineffectuality; **no say,** no say-so, nothing to do with *or* say about <nf>; unpersuasiveness, lack of personality *or* charm, lack of magnetism *or* charisma; **weakness** 16, wimpiness *or* wimpishness <nf>

2 uninfluenceability, unswayableness, unmovability; **unpersuadability,** impersuadability, impersuasibility, unreceptiveness, imperviousness, unresponsiveness; unsuggestibility, **unsusceptibility,** unimpressionability; invulnerability; **obstinacy** 361

ADJS **3 uninfluential, powerless,** forceless, impotent 19.13; **weak** 16.12, wimpy *or* wimpish <nf>; unauthoritative; **ineffective,** ineffectual, inefficacious; **of no account,** no-account, without any weight, featherweight, lightweight

4 uninfluenceable, unswayable, unmovable; unpliable, unyielding, inflexible; **unpersuadable**

361.13, impersuadable, impersuasible, unreceptive, unresponsive, unamenable; impervious, closed to; **unsuggestible, unsusceptible,** unimpressionable; invulnerable; **obstinate** 361.8

5 **uninfluenced, unmoved, unaffected, unswayed**

896 TENDENCY

NOUNS 1 **tendency, inclination, leaning,** penchant, proneness, conatus, weakness, susceptibility; liability 897, readiness, willingness, eagerness, aptness, aptitude, **disposition, proclivity, propensity,** predisposition, **predilection,** a thing for <nf>, affinity, prejudice, **liking,** delight, soft spot, penchant; **yen,** lech <nf>, hunger, thirst; instinct or feeling for, sensitivity to; **bent, turn, bias,** slant, tilt, spin <nf>, cast, warp, twist; probability 968; diathesis <medicine>, tropism <biology>

2 **trend, drift, course, current,** *Tendenz* <Ger>, flow, stream, mainstream, main current, movement, glacial movement, motion, run, **tenor,** tone, **set,** set of the current, swing, bearing, line, direction, the general tendency or drift, the main course, the course of events, the way the wind blows, **the way things go,** sign of the times, spirit of the age or time, time spirit, *Zeitgeist* <Ger>; climate; the way it looks

VERBS 3 **tend,** have a tendency, **incline,** be disposed, **lean, trend,** have a penchant, set, **go,** head, lead, point, verge, turn, warp, tilt, bias, bend to, work or gravitate or set toward; show a tendency or trend or set or direction, swing toward, point to, look to; **conduce,** contribute, serve, redound to; bode well

ADJS 4 **tending;** tendentious or tendential; **leaning, inclining,** inclinatory, inclinational; **mainstream,** main-current, mainline

PREPS 5 **tending to, conducive to,** leading to, inclined toward, inclining toward, heading or moving or swinging or working toward, pointing to

6 **inclined to, leaning to, prone to, disposed to,** drawn to, predisposed to, given to; **apt to, likely to, liable to** 897.6, calculated to, minded to, ready to, in a fair way to

897 LIABILITY

NOUNS 1 **liability, likelihood** or **likeliness;** probability 968, contingency, chance 972, eventuality 831.1; weakness, **proneness** 896.1; **possibility** 965; **responsibility** 641.2, legal responsibility; **indebtedness** 623.1, financial commitment, pecuniary obligation

2 **susceptibility, liability,** susceptivity, liableness, **openness, exposure; vulnerability** 1006.4

VERBS 3 **be liable; be subjected** or **subjected to,** be a pawn or plaything of, be the prey of, lie under; **expose oneself to, lay** or **leave oneself open to,** open the door to; **gamble,** stand to lose or gain, stand a chance, **run the chance** or **risk,** let down one's guard or defenses; **admit of,** open the possibility of, be in the way of, bid or stand fair to; **owe,** be in debt or indebted for

4 **incur, contract, invite,** welcome, run, **bring on, bring down,** bring upon or down upon, bring upon or down upon oneself; **be responsible for** 641.6; fall into, fall in with; get, gain, acquire

ADJS 5 **liable, likely, prone; probable; responsible,** legally responsible, answerable; **in debt, indebted,** financially burdened, heavily committed, overextended; **exposed, susceptible, at risk,** overexposed, open, like a sitting duck, **vulnerable**

6 **liable to, subject to,** standing to, in a position to, incident to, dependent on; **susceptible** or **prone to,** susceptive to, **open** or vulnerable or **exposed to,** naked to, in danger of, within range of, at the mercy of; **capable of,** ready for; **likely to,** apt to 896.6; obliged to, responsible or answerable for

CONJS 7 **lest,** that, **for fear that**

898 INVOLVEMENT

NOUNS 1 **involvement,** involution, **implication, entanglement,** enmeshment, engagement, involuntary presence or cooperation, embarrassment; relation 775; **inclusion** 772; **absorption** 983.3

VERBS 2 **involve, implicate,** tangle, **entangle,** embarrass, enmesh, engage, **draw in,** drag or hook or suck into, catch up in, **make a party to;** interest, concern; **absorb** 983.13

3 **be involved, be into** <nf>, partake, participate, take an interest, interest oneself, have a role or part

ADJS 4 **involved, implicated;** interested, concerned, a party to; **included** 772.5

5 **involved in, implicated in,** tangled or entangled in, enmeshed in, **caught up in,** tied up in, wrapped up in, all wound up in, dragged or hooked or sucked into; in deep, deeply involved, **up to one's neck** or **ears in,** up to one's elbows or ass in, head over heels in, **absorbed in** 983.17, immersed or submerged in, far-gone

899 CONCURRENCE

NOUNS 1 **concurrence, collaboration,** coaction, **coworking,** collectivity, combined effort or operation, united or concerted action, concert, synergy; **cooperation** 450; **agreement** 788; me-tooism; **coincidence,** simultaneity 835, synchronism;

concomitance, accompaniment 769; **union,**
junction 800.1, **conjunction,** combination 805,
association, alliance, consociation; conspiracy,
collusion, cahoots <nf>; concourse, confluence;
accordance 455.1, concordance, correspondence,
consilience; symbiosis, parasitism; saprophytism
VERBS **2 concur, collaborate,** coact, **co-work,**
synergize; **cooperate** 450.3; conspire, collude,
connive, be in cahoots <nf>; **combine** 805.3,
unite, associate 805.4, coadunate, join, conjoin;
harmonize; **coincide,** synchronize, happen
together; **accord** 455.2, correspond, **agree** 788.6
3 go with, **go along with, go hand in hand with,** be
hand in glove with, team *or* join up with, buddy up
with <nf>; keep pace with, run parallel to
ADJS **4 concurrent,** concurring; **coacting,** coactive,
collaborative, collective, **co-working,** cooperant,
synergetic *or* synergic *or* synergistic; **cooperative**
450.5; conspiratorial, collusive; **united, joint,**
conjoint, **combined, concerted,** associated,
associate, coadunate; **coincident,** synchronous,
synchronic, in sync, coordinate; concomitant,
accompanying 769.9; meeting, uniting, combining;
accordant, agreeing 788.9, concordant,
harmonious, consilient, at one with; symbiotic,
parasitic, saprophytic
ADVS **5 concurrently,** coactively, **jointly, conjointly,**
concertedly, in concert, in harmony *or* unison
with, synchronously, **together; with one accord,**
with one voice, as one, as one man; hand in hand,
hand in glove, shoulder to shoulder, cheek by jowl

900 COUNTERACTION

NOUNS **1 counteraction, counterworking;** opposition
451, opposure, counterposition *or* contraposition,
confutation, **contradiction; antagonism,**
repugnance, oppugnance *or* oppugnancy,
antipathy, conflict, friction, interference, clashing,
collision; reaction, repercussion, **backlash, recoil,**
kick, backfire, boomerang effect; resistance,
recalcitrance, dissent 333, revolt 327.4,
perverseness, nonconformity 868, crankiness,
crotchetiness, orneriness <nf>, renitency; going
against the current *or* against the tide, swimming
upstream; **contrariety** 779
2 neutralization, nullification, annulment,
cancellation, voiding, invalidation, vitiation,
frustration, thwarting, undoing; **offsetting,**
counterbalancing, countervailing, balancing;
negation
3 counteractant, counteractive, **counteragent;**
counterirritant; **antidote,** remedy, preventive *or*
preventative, prophylactic, contraceptive;
neutralizer, nullifier, offset; antacid, buffer

4 counterforce, countervailing force,
counterinfluence, counterpressure; counterpoise,
counterbalance, counterweight; countercurrent,
crosscurrent, undercurrent; counterblast;
headwind, foul wind, crosswind; friction, drag
5 countermeasure, counterattack, counterstep;
counterblow *or* counterstroke *or* countercoup *or*
counterblast, counterfire; counterrevolution,
counterinsurgency; counterterrorism;
counterculture; **retort,** comeback <nf>; defense
460
VERBS **6 counteract,** counter, counterwork,
counterattack, countervail; counterpose *or*
contrapose, **oppose,** antagonize, **go in opposition**
to, go *or* **run counter to, go** *or* **work against,** go
clean counter to, go *or* fly in the face of, run
against, beat against, militate against; **resist,** fight
back, bite back, lift a hand against, defend oneself;
dissent, dissent from; **cross,** confute, **contradict,**
contravene, oppugn, **conflict,** be antipathetic *or*
hostile *or* inimical, interfere *or* conflict with, come
in conflict with, **clash,** collide, meet head-on, lock
horns; rub *or* go against the grain; swim upstream
or against the tide *or* against the current;
boomerang
7 neutralize, nullify, annul, cancel, cancel out,
negate, negative, negativate, invalidate, vitiate,
void, frustrate, stultify, thwart, come *or* bring to
nothing, undo; **offset,** counterbalance 338.5; buffer
ADJS **8** counteractive *or* counteractant,
counteracting, counterworking,
counterproductive, countervailing; **opposing,**
oppositional; contradicting, contradictory;
antagonistic, hostile, antipathetic, inimical,
oppugnant, repugnant, **conflicting, clashing;**
reactionary; resistant, recalcitrant, dissentient,
dissident, revolutionary, breakaway,
nonconformist, perverse, cranky, crotchety, ornery
<nf>, renitent
9 neutralizing, nullifying, stultifying, annulling,
canceling, negating, invalidating, vitiating, voiding;
balanced, counterbalanced, poised, in poise, offset,
zero-sum; offsetting, counterbalancing,
countervailing; antacid, buffering; antidotal
ADVS **10** counteractively, antagonistically, opposingly,
in opposition to, counter to
WORD ELEMENTS **11** ant-, anti-, anth-, contra-,
counter-

901 SUPPORT

NOUNS **1 support, backing, aid** 449; upholding,
upkeep, carrying, carriage, maintenance,
sustaining, sustainment, sustenance, sustentation;
reinforcement, backup; subsidy, subvention;

support services, infrastructure; moral support; emotional *or* psychological support, security blanket <nf>; reassurance; **power base, constituency, party;** supportive relationship, supportive therapy; strokes <nf>; **approval** 509; **assent,** concurrence 332; **reliance** 953.1; life-support, life-sustainment

2 **supporter, support; upholder,** bearer, carrier, sustainer, maintainer; staff 273.2, stave, cane, stick, walking stick, alpenstock, crook, crutch; **advocate** 616.9; **stay, prop,** fulcrum, **bracket, brace,** bracer, guy, guywire *or* guyline, shroud, rigging, standing rigging; bulwark, anchor; buttress, shoulder, arm, good right arm; mast, sprit, yard, yardarm; **mainstay,** backbone, spine, neck, cervix; athletic supporter, jock *and* jockstrap <nf>, G-string <nf>; brassiere, bra <nf>, bandeau, corset, girdle, foundation garment; **reinforcement,** reinforce, reinforcing, reinforcer, strengthener, stiffener; back, backing; rest, resting place

3 <mythology> Atlas, Hercules, Telamon, the tortoise that supports the earth

4 **buttress,** buttressing; abutment, shoulder; **bulwark,** rampart; **embankment,** bank, retaining wall, bulkhead, bulkheading, plank buttress, piling; **breakwater,** seawall, mole, **jetty,** jutty, groin; **pier,** pier buttress, buttress pier; flying buttress, *arc-boutant* <Fr>, arch buttress; hanging buttress; **beam**

5 **footing, foothold, toehold,** hold, perch, **purchase** 906; **standing,** stand, stance, standing place, pou sto, *point d'appui* <Fr>, *locus standi* <L>; footrest, footplate, footrail

6 **foundation,** *fond* <Fr>, firm foundation, **base, basis, footing,** basement, pavement, **ground,** grounds, **groundwork, seat,** sill, floor *or* flooring, fundament; bed, bedding; **substructure,** substruction, substratum; infrastructure; **understructure,** understruction, underbuilding, undergirding, undercarriage, underpinning, bearing wall; stereobate, stylobate; firm *or* solid ground, *terra firma* <L>; solid rock *or* bottom, rock bottom, bedrock; hardpan; riprap; **fundamental** 997.6, **principle, premise** 957.1; grounds, precedent; root, radical; rudiment

7 **foundation stone,** footstone; **cornerstone, keystone,** headstone, first stone, quoin

8 **base, pedestal; stand,** standard; **shaft** 273, **upright, column, pillar, post,** jack, pole, staff, stanchion, pier, pile *or* piling, king-post, queen-post, pilaster, newel-post, banister, baluster, balustrade, colonnade, caryatid; dado, die; plinth, subbase; surbase; socle; **trunk,** stem, **stalk,** pedicel, peduncle, footstalk

9 **sill,** groundsel; mudsill; window sill; doorsill, threshold; doorstone

10 **frame,** underframe, infrastructure, chassis, **skeleton;** armature; **mounting,** mount, **backing, setting;** surround

11 **handle, hold,** grip, grasp, haft, helve

12 **scaffold,** scaffolding, *échafaudage* <Fr>; stage, staging

13 **platform; stage,** estrade, dais, floor; **rostrum, podium, pulpit,** speaker's platform *or* stand, **soapbox** <nf>; hustings, **stump;** tribune, tribunal; emplacement; catafalque; landing stage, landing; heliport, landing pad; launching pad; **terrace,** step terrace, deck; **balcony, gallery**

14 **shelf, ledge,** shoulder, corbel, beam-end; mantel, mantelshelf, mantelpiece; retable, superaltar, gradin, *gradino* <Ital>, predella; hob

15 **table,** board, **stand; bench,** workbench; **counter,** bar, buffet; **desk,** writing table, **secretary,** *secrétaire* <Fr>, escritoire; **lectern,** reading stand, ambo, reading desk

16 **trestle, horse; sawhorse,** buck *or* sawbuck; clotheshorse; trestle board *or* table, trestle and table; trestlework, trestling; A-frame

17 **seat, chair;** saddle

18 <saddle parts> **pommel,** horn; jockey; girth, girt, surcingle, bellyband; cinch, stirrup

19 sofa, **bed; couch;** the sack *and* the hay *and* kip *and* doss <nf>; futon; bedstead; **litter, stretcher,** gurney

20 **bedding,** underbed, underbedding; **mattress,** paillasse, pallet; air mattress, foam-rubber mattress, innerspring mattress; sleeping bag; pad, mat, rug; litter, bedstraw; **pillow,** cushion, bolster; **springs,** bedsprings, box springs; futon

VERBS 21 **support, bear,** carry, **hold, sustain, maintain, bolster, reinforce,** back, back up, shoulder, give *or* furnish *or* afford *or* supply *or* lend support; go to bat for <nf>; **hold up, bear up,** bolster up, keep up, buoy up, keep afloat, back up; **uphold,** upbear, upkeep; **brace, prop,** crutch, buttress; shore, **shore up;** stay, mainstay; underbrace, undergird, underprop, underpin, underset; **underlie,** be at the bottom of, form the foundation of; cradle; cushion, pillow; **subsidize;** subvene; assent 332.8; concur 332.9; **approve** 509.9

22 **rest on, stand on, lie on,** recline on, repose on, bear on, **lean on,** abut on; **sit on,** perch, ride, piggyback on; **straddle,** bestraddle, stride, bestride; be based on, rely on

ADJS 23 **supporting, supportive, bearing,** carrying, burdened; **holding,** upholding, maintaining, sustaining, sustentative, suspensory; bracing, propping, shoring, bolstering, buttressing; life-sustaining; collaborative, corroborative, cooperative

24 supported, borne, upborne, held, buoyed-up, **upheld, sustained,** maintained; **braced,** guyed, stayed, propped, shored *or* shored up, bolstered, buttressed; based *or* founded *or* grounded on

ADVS **25 on, across, astride, astraddle,** straddle, straddle-legged, straddleback, on the back of; horseback, on horseback; pickaback *or* piggyback

902 IMPULSE, IMPACT
<driving and striking force>

NOUNS **1 impulse,** impulsion, impelling force, impellent; **drive,** driving force *or* power; **motive power,** power 18; **force,** irresistible force; clout <nf>; **impetus; momentum;** moment, moment of force; propulsion 904.1; incitement 375.4, incentive 375.7, compulsion 424

2 thrust, push, shove, boost <nf>; **pressure; stress;** press; **prod, poke, punch, jab,** dig, nudge; **bump,** jog, joggle, jolt; **jostle,** hustle; **butt,** bunt; head <of water, steam, etc>

3 impact, collision, clash, appulse, **encounter,** meeting, impingement, **bump, crash,** crump, whomp; **carom,** carambole, cannon; sideswipe <nf>; smash *and* crunch <nf>; **shock, brunt; concussion,** percussion; **thrusting, ramming,** bulling, **bulldozing,** shouldering, muscling, steamrollering, railroading; hammering, smashing, mauling, sledgehammering; onslaught 459.1

4 hit, blow, stroke, knock, rap, pound, slam, bang, crack, **whack, smack, thwack,** smash, dash, swipe, swing, **punch, poke, jab,** dig, drub, thump, pelt, cut, chop, dint, slog; drubbing, drumming, tattoo, fusillade; beating 604.4

5 <nf terms> sock, bang, bash, bat, belt, bonk, bust, clip, clout, duke, swat, yerk, plunk, larrup, paste, lick, biff, clump, clunk, clonk, wallop, whop, slam, slug, whomp, swack

6 punch, boxing punch, blow, belt, sock

7 tap, rap, pat, dab, chuck, touch, tip; love-tap; **snap, flick, flip,** fillip, flirt, whisk, brush; **peck,** pick

8 slap, smack, flap; **box, cuff,** buffet; **spank;** whip, **lash,** cut, stripe

9 kick, boot; punt, drop kick, place kick, kicking, calcitration <old>

10 stamp, stomp <nf>, drub, clump, clop

VERBS **11 impel,** give an impetus, **set going** *or* agoing, put *or* set in motion, give momentum; **drive, move,** animate, actuate, forward; **thrust,** power; drive *or* whip on; goad; **propel;** motivate, incite 375.17; compel 424.4

12 thrust, push, shove, boost <nf>; press, stress, **bear,** bear upon, bring pressure to bear upon; **ram,** ram down, tamp, pile drive, jam, crowd, cram;

bull, bulldoze, muscle, steamroller, railroad; **drive, force,** run; **prod, goad, poke, punch, jab,** dig, nudge; **bump,** jog, joggle, jolt, shake, rattle; **jostle,** hustle, hurtle; elbow, shoulder; **butt,** bunt, buck <nf>, run *or* bump *or* butt against, bump up against, knock *or* run one's head against; assault

13 collide, come into collision, be on a collision course, **clash,** meet, encounter, confront each other, impinge; percuss, concuss; **bump, hit, strike, knock, bang; run into, bump into,** bang into, slam into, smack into, **crash into, impact,** smash into, dash into, carom into, cannon into <Brit>; rear-end; **hit against,** strike against, knock against; foul, fall *or* run foul *or* afoul of; hurtle, hurt; **carom,** cannon <chiefly Brit>; **sideswipe** <nf>; **crash,** smash, crump, whomp; smash up *or* crack up *or* crunch <nf>

14 hit, strike, knock, knock down *or* out, smite; land a blow, draw blood; **poke, punch, jab,** thwack, **smack,** clap, crack, swipe, **whack;** deal, fetch, swipe at, take a punch at, throw one at <nf>, deal *or* fetch a blow, hit a clip <nf>, let have it; **thump,** snap; strike at 459.16

15 <nf terms> belt, bat, clout, bang, slam, bash, biff, paste, wham, whop, clump, bonk, wallop, clip, cut, plunk, swat, soak, sock, slog, slug, yerk <old>, clunk, clonk

16 pound, beat, hammer, maul, sledgehammer, **knock, rap, bang,** thump, **drub,** buffet, **batter,** pulverize, paste <nf>, patter, pommel, pummel, pelt, baste, lambaste; thresh, thrash; flail; spank, flap; whip

17 <nf terms> clobber, knock for a loop, marmelize <Brit>, knock cold, dust off, bash up, punch out, rough up, slap down, smack down, sandbag, work over, deck, coldcock, wallop, larrup

18 tap, rap, pat, dab, chuck, touch, tip; **snap, flick, flip,** fillip, tickle, flirt, whisk, **graze,** brush; bunt; **peck,** pick, beak

19 slap, smack, flap; **box, cuff,** buffet; **spank;** whip

20 club, cudgel, blackjack, sandbag, cosh <Brit>

21 kick, boot, kick about *or* around, calcitrate <old>; kick downstairs <old>; kick out; knee

22 stamp, stomp <nf>, trample, tread, drub, clump, clop

ADJS **23 impelling,** impellent; impulsive, pulsive, **moving,** motive, animating, actuating, **driving;** thrusting

24 concussive, percussive, crashing, smashing

903 REACTION

NOUNS **1 reaction, response,** respondence, feedback; reply, answer 940.1, **rise** <nf>; **reflex,** reflection, **reflex action;** echo, bounce back, reverberation, resonance, sympathetic vibration; return; reflux, refluence; action and reaction; opposite response, negative response, retroaction, revulsion; predictable response, automatic *or* autonomic reaction, knee-jerk *and* knee-jerk response <nf>, spontaneous *or* unthinking response, spur-of-the-moment response; conditioned reflex

2 recoil, rebound, resilience, repercussion, *contrecoup* <Fr>; **bounce, bound, spring,** bounce-back; **repulse, rebuff; backlash,** backlashing, kickback, **kick,** a kick like a mule <nf>, recalcitration <old>; **backfire, boomerang;** ricochet, carom, cannon <Brit>

3 <a drawing back or aside> **retreat,** recoil, fallback, pullout, pullback, contingency plan, backup plan; evasion, avoidance, sidestepping; **flinch,** wince, cringe; **side step,** shy; **dodge, duck** <nf>

4 reactionary, reactionist, recalcitrant

VERBS **5 react, respond,** reply, answer, riposte, snap back, come back at <nf>; rise to the fly, take the bait; go off half-cocked *or* at half cock

6 recoil, rebound, resile; **bounce, bound, spring; spring** *or* **fly back,** bounce *or* bound back, snap back; repercuss, have repercussions; **kick,** kick back, kick like a mule <nf>, recalcitrate <old>; **backfire, boomerang;** backlash, lash back; ricochet, carom, cannon *and* cannon off <Brit>

7 pull *or* **draw back,** retreat, recoil, fade, **fall back,** reel back, hang back, start back, shrink back, give ground; **shrink, flinch, wince, cringe,** blink, blench, quail; **shy,** shy away, start *or* turn aside, evade, avoid, sidestep, weasel, weasel out, cop out <nf>; **dodge, duck** <nf>; jib, swerve, sheer off, give a wide berth

8 get a reaction, get a response, evoke a response, ring a bell, strike a responsive chord, strike fire, strike *or* hit home, hit a nerve, get a rise out of <nf>

ADJS **9 reactive,** reacting, merely reactive; **responsive,** respondent, responding, antiphonal; **quick on the draw** *or* trigger *or* uptake; **reactionary;** retroactionary, retroactive; revulsive; **reflex,** reflexive, knee-jerk <nf>; refluent

10 recoiling, rebounding, **resilient; bouncing,** bouncy, bounding, springing, springy; repercussive; recalcitrant

ADVS **11 on the rebound,** on the return, on the bounce; on the spur of the moment, off the top of the head

904 PUSHING, THROWING

NOUNS **1 pushing, propulsion, propelling; shoving,** butting; **drive, thrust,** motive power, driving force, means of propulsion; **push, shove;** butt, bunt; shunt, impulsion 902.1

2 throwing, projection, jaculation, ejaculation, trajection, flinging, slinging, **pitching, tossing,** casting, hurling, lobbing, chucking, chunking <nf>, heaving, firing *and* burning *and* pegging <nf>; bowling, rolling, **shooting,** firing, gunnery, gunning, musketry; trap-shooting, skeet *or* skeet shooting; archery

3 throw, toss, fling, sling, cast, hurl, chuck, chunk <nf>, lob, **heave,** shy, **pitch,** peg <nf>; **flip;** put, shot-put; <football> pass, forward pass, lateral pass, lateral; <tennis> serve, service; bowl; <baseball> pitch

4 shot, discharge; ejection 909; detonation 56.3; gunfire; gun, cannon; bullet; **salvo, volley,** fusillade, tattoo, spray; bowshot, gunshot, stoneshot, potshot

5 projectile; ejecta, ejectamenta; **missile;** ball; discus, quoit

6 propeller, prop <nf>, airscrew, prop-fan; propellant, propulsor, driver; screw, wheel, screw propeller, twin screws; bow thruster; paddle wheel; turbine; fan, impeller, rotor; piston

7 thrower, pitcher, hurler, bowler <cricket>, chucker, chunker <nf>, **heaver, tosser,** flinger, slinger, caster, jaculator, ejaculator; bowler; shot-putter; javelin thrower; discus thrower, discobolus

8 shooter, shot; gunner, gun, **gunman, rifleman,** musketeer, carabineer, pistoleer; cannoneer, artilleryman; Nimrod, hunter 382.5; trapshooter; archer, bowman, toxophilite; **marksman, markswoman,** targetshooter, **sharpshooter,** sniper; good shot, dead shot, deadeye, **crack shot**

VERBS **9 push, propel,** impel, **shove,** thrust 902.11; **drive, move,** forward, advance, traject; sweep, sweep along; butt, bunt; shunt; pole, row; pedal, treadle; **roll,** troll, bowl, trundle

10 throw, fling, sling, pitch, toss, cast, hurl, heave, chuck, chunk *and* peg <nf>, lob, shy, fire, burn, pepper <nf>, launch, dash, let fly, let go, let rip, let loose; catapult; **flip,** snap, jerk; bowl; pass; serve; put, put the shot; bung <Brit nf>; dart, lance, tilt; fork, pitchfork; pelt 459.27

11 project, jaculate, ejaculate

12 shoot, fire, fire off, let off, let fly, **discharge,** eject 909.13; detonate 56.8; gun <nf>, pistol; sharpshoot; shoot at 459.22, gun for <nf>; strike, hit, plug <nf>; shoot down, fell, drop, stop in one's tracks; **riddle, pepper,** pelt, pump full of lead <nf>; snipe, pick off; torpedo; pot; potshoot, potshot, take a potshot; load, prime, charge; cock

13 start, start off, start up, give a start, crank up, give a push *or* shove <nf>, jump-start, kick-start, **put** *or* **set in motion, set on foot,** set going *or* agoing, start going; **kick off** *and* **start the ball rolling** <nf>; get off the ground *or* off the mark, **launch,**

launch forth *or* out, float, set afloat; send, send off
or forth; bundle off

ADJS **14 propulsive,** propulsory, **propellant,**
propelling; **motive; driving, pushing, shoving**

15 projectile, trajectile, jaculatory, ejaculatory;
ballistic, missile; ejective

16 jet-propelled, rocket-propelled, steam-propelled,
gasoline-propelled, gas-propelled, diesel-propelled,
wind-propelled, self-propelled, etc

17 <means of propulsion> battery, diesel, diesel-
electric, electric, gas *or* gasoline, gravity, jet,
plasma-jet, prop-fan, pulse-jet, ram-jet, reaction,
resojet, rocket, spring, steam, turbofan, turbojet,
turbopropeller *or* turboprop, wind

905 PULLING

NOUNS **1 pulling, traction, drawing,** draft, dragging,
heaving, tugging, towing; pulling *or* tractive power,
pull; tug-of-war; towing, towage; towrope, towbar,
towing cable *or* hawser; tow car, wrecker; **hauling,**
haulage, drayage; man-hauling, man-haulage;
attraction 907; extraction 192

 2 pull, draw, heave, haul, tug, tow, lug, a long pull
and a strong pull, strain, drag

 3 jerk, yank <nf>, quick *or* sudden pull; **twitch,**
tweak, pluck, hitch, wrench, snatch, start, bob;
flip, flick, flirt, flounce; jig, **jiggle;** jog, joggle

VERBS **4 pull, draw, heave, haul,** hale, lug, **tug, tow,**
take in tow; trail, train; **drag,** man-haul, draggle,
snake <nf>; troll, trawl

 5 jerk, yerk <nf>, **yank** <nf>; **twitch,** tweak, pluck,
snatch, hitch, wrench, snake <nf>; **flip,** flick, flirt,
flounce; **jiggle,** jig, jigget, jigger; jog, joggle

ADJS **6 pulling, drawing,** tractional, tractive, hauling,
tugging, towing, towage; man-hauled

906 LEVERAGE, PURCHASE
 *<mechanical advantage applied to moving or
 raising>*

NOUNS **1 leverage,** fulcrumage; **pry,** prize <nf>

 2 purchase, hold, advantage; **foothold,** toehold,
footing; differential purchase; collier's purchase;
traction

 3 fulcrum, axis, pivot, bearing, rest, resting point,
point d'appui <Fr>; thole, tholepin, rowlock,
oarlock

 4 lever; pry, prize <nf>; **bar,** pinch bar, crowbar,
crow, pinchbar, iron crow, wrecking bar, ripping
bar, claw bar; cant hook, peavey; **jimmy;**
handspike, marlinespike; boom, spar, beam,
outrigger; pedal, treadle, crank; limb

 5 arm; forearm; wrist; elbow; upper arm, biceps

 6 tackle, purchase

 7 windlass; capstan <nautical>; **winch,** crab; reel;
Chinese windlass, Spanish windlass

VERBS **8** get a purchase, get leverage, get a foothold;
pry, prize, lever, wedge; pry *or* prize out; **jimmy,**
crowbar, pinchbar

 9 reel in, wind in, bring in, draw in, pull in, crank
in, trim, tighten, tauten, draw taut, take the strain;
windlass, winch, crank, reel; tackle

907 ATTRACTION
 <a drawing toward>

NOUNS **1 attraction,** traction 905.1, attractiveness,
attractivity; mutual attraction *or* magnetism;
pulling power, **pull,** drag, draw, tug; magnetism
1032.7; gravity, gravitation; centripetal force;
capillarity, capillary attraction; adduction; **affinity,
sympathy; allurement** 377

 2 attractor, attractant, attrahent; adductor; cynosure,
focus, center, center of attraction *or* attention;
crowd-pleaser *or* drawer, charismatic figure; **lure**
377.2

 3 magnet, artificial magnet, field magnet, bar
magnet, horseshoe magnet, electromagnet,
solenoid, paramagnet, permanent magnet, keeper,
superconducting magnet, electromagnetic lifting
magnet, magnetic needle; lodestone, magnetite;
magnetic pole, magnetic north; lodestar, polestar;
siderite

VERBS **4 attract, pull, draw,** drag, tug, pull *or* draw
towards, have an attraction; **magnetize,** magnet, be
magnetic; **lure;** adduct

ADJS **5** attracting, drawing, pulling, dragging,
tugging; eye-catching; **attractive, magnetic;**
charismatic; magnetized, attrahent; sympathetic;
alluring; adductive, adducent; associative

ADVS **6** attractionally, attractively; magnetically;
charismatically

908 REPULSION
 <a thrusting away>

NOUNS **1 repulsion,** repellence *or* repellency,
repelling; mutual repulsion, polarization;
disaffinity; centrifugal force; magnetic repulsion,
diamagnetism; antigravity; ejection 909

 2 repulse, rebuff; dismissal, cold shoulder, snub,
spurning, brush-off, cut; kiss-off <nf>; turn-off
<nf>; rejection; refusal; discharge 909.5

VERBS **3 repulse, repel, rebuff, turn back,** put back,
beat back, drive *or* push *or* thrust back; drive away,
chase, chase off *or* away; send off *or* away, send
about one's business, **send packing,** pack off,
dismiss; snub, cut, brush off, drop; kiss off <nf>;
show someone the door; spurn, refuse; **ward off,**

hold off, keep off, fend off, fight off, push off, keep at arm's length; slap *or* smack down <nf>; eject 909.13, discharge 909.19

ADJS **4 repulsive,** repellent, **repelling;** diamagnetic, of opposite polarity, centrifugal, abducent, abductive; off-putting

ADVS **5** repulsively, repellently

909 EJECTION

NOUNS **1 ejection,** ejectment, throwing out, **expulsion, discharge,** extrusion, obtrusion, detrusion, **ousting, ouster,** removal, kicking *or* booting *or* chucking out <nf>; throwing *or* kicking downstairs; the boot *and* the bounce *and* the bum's rush *and* the old heave-ho <nf>, the chuck *or* the push <Brit nf>; defenestration; **rejection** 372; jettison

2 eviction, ousting, dislodgment, dispossession, expropriation; **ouster,** throwing overboard

3 depopulation, dispeoplement, unpeopling; devastation, desolation

4 banishment, relegation, exclusion 773; **excommunication,** disfellowship; **disbarment,** unfrocking, defrocking; proscription; **expatriation, exile,** exilement; outlawing *or* outlawry, fugitation <Scot>; **ostracism,** ostracization, thumbs-down, thumbing-down, *pollice verso* <L>, blackballing, silent treatment, sending to Coventry, cold shoulder; **deportation,** transportation, **extradition;** rustication; degradation, **demotion** 447, stripping, depluming, displuming; deprivation

5 dismissal, discharge, forced separation, *congé* <Fr>; outplacement; **firing** *and* canning <nf>, **cashiering,** drumming out, dishonorable discharge, rogue's march; disemployment, **layoff,** removal, surplusing, displacing, furloughing; suspension; **retirement;** marching orders, the elbow, the bounce, **the sack** *and* the chuck <Brit nf>, heave-ho <nf>; the boot *and* the gate *and* the ax *and* the sack <nf>; walking papers *or* ticket <nf>, pink slip <nf>; deposal 447

6 evacuation, voidance, voiding; **elimination,** removal; **clearance, clearing,** clearage; unfouling, freeing; scouring *or* cleaning out, unclogging; exhaustion, exhausting, venting, emptying, depletion; **unloading,** off-loading, discharging cargo *or* freight; draining, drainage; egress 190.2; **excretion,** defecation 12.2,4

7 disgorgement, disemboguement, expulsion, ejaculation, **discharge,** emission; **eruption,** eructation, extravasation, **blowout, outburst;** outpour, jet, spout, squirt, spurt

8 vomiting, vomition, **disgorgement, regurgitation,** egestion, emesis, the pukes *and* the heaves <nf>;

retching, heaving, gagging; nausea; vomit, vomitus, puke *and* puking *and* barf *and* barfing <nf>, spew, egesta; the dry heaves <nf>; vomiturition

9 belch, burp <nf>, belching, wind, gas, eructation; **hiccup**

10 fart <nf>, **flatulence** *or* flatulency, flatuosity, flatus, breaking wind, passing gas, gas, wind

11 ejector, expeller, -fuge; **ouster,** evictor; **bouncer** *and* chucker <nf>, chucker-out <Brit nf>

12 dischargee, expellee; ejectee; evictee

VERBS **13 eject, expel, discharge,** extrude, obtrude, detrude, exclude, **reject,** cast, remove; **oust, bounce** *and* give the hook <nf>, **put out, turn out,** thrust out; **throw out,** run out <nf>, cast out, chuck out, give the chuck to <Brit nf>, toss out, heave out, throw *or* kick downstairs; kick *or* boot out <nf>; give the bum's rush *or* give the old heave-ho *or* throw out on one's ear <nf>; defenestrate; jettison, throw overboard, discard, junk, throw away; **be rid of,** be shut of, see the last of

14 drive out, run out, chase out, chase away, run off, **rout out;** drum out, read out; freeze out <nf>, push out, force out, send packing, send about one's business; **hunt out,** harry out; **smoke out,** drive into the open; run out of town, ride on a rail

15 evict, oust, dislodge, dispossess, put out, turn out, **turn out of doors,** turn out of house and home, turn *or* put out bag and baggage, throw into the street; unhouse, unkennel

16 depopulate, dispeople, unpeople; devastate, desolate

17 banish, expel, cast out, thrust out, relegate, **ostracize,** disfellowship, exclude, send down, **blackball,** spurn, thumb down, turn thumbs down on, snub, cut, give the cold shoulder, send to Coventry, give the silent treatment; **excommunicate; exile, expatriate, deport,** transport, send away, **extradite; deport;** outlaw, fugitate <Scot>, ban, proscribe; rusticate

18 dismiss, send off *or* **away, turn off** *or* **away,** bundle, bundle off *or* out, hustle out, pack off, **send packing,** send about one's business, send to the showers <nf>; bow out, **show the door,** show the gate; **give the gate** *or* the air <nf>

19 dismiss, discharge, expel, cashier, drum out, disemploy, outplace, separate forcibly *or* involuntarily, **lay off,** suspend, surplus, furlough, turn off, make redundant, riff <nf>, turn out, release, let go, let out, remove, displace, replace, strike off the rolls, give the pink slip ; unfrock, defrock; degrade, demote, strip, deplume, displume, deprive; depose, disbar 447.4; break, bust <nf>; **retire,** put on the retired list; pension off, superannuate, put out to pasture; read out of; kick upstairs

20 <nf terms> **fire, can, sack, bump,** bounce, kick, boot, give the ax, give the gate, give one the sack *or* the ax *or* the boot *or* the gate *or* the air *or* one's walking papers, send one to the showers, show one the door *or* gate

21 **do away with, exterminate, annihilate;** purge, liquidate; **shake off,** shoo, dispel; **throw off,** fling off, cast off; **eliminate,** get rid of 772.5; throw away 390.7

22 **evacuate, void; eliminate,** remove; **empty,** empty out, deplete, **exhaust,** vent, drain; **clear, purge,** clean *or* scour out, clear off *or* away, clear, unfoul, unclog, flush out, blow, blow out, sweep out, make a clean sweep, clear the decks; defecate 12.13

23 **unload,** off-load, unlade, unpack, disburden, unburden, **discharge, dump;** unship, break bulk; pump out

24 **let out, give vent to,** give out *or* off, throw off, blow off, **emit, exhaust,** evacuate, let go; **exhale,** expire, breathe out, let one's breath out, blow, puff; fume, steam, vapor, smoke, reek; open the sluices *or* floodgates, turn on the tap

25 **disgorge,** debouch, disembogue, **discharge, exhaust, expel,** ejaculate, throw out, **cast forth,** send out *or* forth; **erupt,** eruct, **blow out,** extravasate; **pour out** *or* **forth,** pour, outpour, decant; spew, jet, spout, squirt, **spurt**

26 **vomit,** spew, **disgorge, regurgitate,** egest, **throw up,** bring up, be sick <Brit>, sick up <Brit nf>, cast *or* heave the gorge; **retch,** keck, **heave, gag;** reject; be seasick, feed the fish

27 <nf terms> **puke,** upchuck, chuck up, urp, oops, oops up, shoot *or* blow *or* toss one's cookies *or* lunch, barf, ralph, ralph up, blow grits

28 **belch, burp** <nf>, eruct, eructate; **hiccup**

29 **fart** <nf>, let *or* lay *or* cut a fart <nf>, let *or* break wind

ADJS **30** **ejective, expulsive,** ejaculative, emissive, extrusive; eliminant; vomitive, vomitory; eructative; flatulent, flatuous; **rejected** 372.3, rejective

INTERJS **31** **go away!,** begone!, get you gone!, go along!, get along!, **run along!, get along with you!,** away!, away with you!, **off with you!,** off you go!, on your way!, go about your business!, be off!, **get out of here!,** get out!, clear out!, leave!, *allez!* <Fr>, *allez-vous-en!* <Fr>, *va-t'-en!* <Fr>, *raus mit dir!* <Ger>, *heraus!* <Ger>, *¡váyase!* <Sp>, *via!* or *va' via!* <Ital>, shoo!, scat!, git! <nf>, "stand not on the order of your going, but go at once"— Shakespeare, "go and hang yourself"—Plautus

32 <nf terms> **beat it!, scram!,** buzz off!, bug off!, shoo!, skiddoo!, skedaddle!, vamoose!, cheese it!, make yourself scarce!, **get lost!,** take a walk!, take a hike!, go chase yourself!, go play in the traffic!, get the hell out!, push off!, shove off!, take a powder!, blow!

910 OVERRUNNING

NOUNS **1** **overrunning, overgoing, overpassing;** overrun, overpass; **overspreading,** overgrowth; inundation, whelming, overwhelming; burying, burial; seizure, taking 480; overflowing 238.6; exaggeration 355; surplus, excess 992; superiority 249

2 **infestation,** infestment; **invasion,** swarming, swarm, teeming, ravage, plague; **overrunning, overswarming,** overspreading; lousiness, pediculosis

3 **overstepping, transgression, trespass,** inroad, usurpation, incursion, intrusion, **encroachment,** infraction, **infringement**

VERBS **4** **overrun, overgo, overpass,** overreach, go beyond; overstep, overstride, overstep the mark *or* bounds; overleap, overjump; **overshoot,** overshoot the mark, overshoot the field; exaggerate 355.3; superabound, exceed, **overdo** 993.10

5 **overspread,** bespread, spread over, spill over; **overgrow,** grow over, run riot, cover, swarm over, teem over

6 **infest, beset,** invade, swarm, ravage, plague; **overrun, overswarm,** overspread; **creep with, crawl with,** swarm with; seize 480.14

7 **run over,** overrun; **ride over,** override, **run down,** ride down; **trample, trample on** *or* **upon,** trample down, tread upon, step on, walk on *or* over, trample underfoot, **ride roughshod over;** hit-and-run; **inundate, whelm, overwhelm;** overflow 238.17; shout down

8 **pass, go** *or* **pass by,** get *or* shoot ahead of; bypass; **pass over, cross,** go across, ford; step over, overstride, bestride, straddle

9 **overstep, transgress, trespass,** intrude, break bounds, overstep the bounds, go too far, know no bounds, **encroach, infringe,** invade, breach, irrupt, make an inroad *or* incursion *or* intrusion, advance upon; usurp

ADJS **10** **overrun, overspread,** overpassed, bespread; overgrown; inundated, whelmed, overwhelmed; buried

11 **infested,** beset, ravaged, teeming, lagued; lousy, pediculous, pedicular; wormy, grubby; ratty

911 SHORTCOMING
<motion or action short of>

NOUNS **1** **shortcoming,** falling short, not measuring up, coming up short, **shortfall; shortage,** short

measure, underage, deficit; **inadequacy** 794.1;
insufficiency 992; delinquency; **default,**
defalcation; arrear, **arrears,** arrearage; decline,
slump; defectiveness, imperfection 1002;
inferiority 250; **undercommitment;** failure 410

VERBS **2 fall short, come short, run short,** stop
short, not make the course, not reach; not measure
up, not hack it *and* not make the grade *and* not
make the cut <nf>, not make it, not make out;
want, want for, lack, not have it <nf>, **be found
wanting,** not answer, not fill the bill, not suffice;
not reach to, not stretch; decline, lag, lose ground,
slump, collapse, fall away, run out of gas *or* steam;
lose out, fail 410.9

3 fall through, fall down, **fall to the ground,** fall flat,
collapse, break down; get bogged down, get mired,
get mired down, get hung up, come to nothing,
come to naught, end up *or* go up in smoke; **fizzle** *or*
peter *or* poop out <nf>; fall *or* drop by the wayside,
end "not with a bang but a whimper"—T S Eliot

4 miss, miscarry, go amiss, go astray, **miss the mark,**
miss by a mile <nf>; misfire; **miss out,** miss the
boat *or* bus; miss stays, miss one's mooring

ADJS **5 short of,** short, fresh *or* clean out of <nf>,
not all *or* what it is cracked up to be; **deficient,**
inadequate 794.4; **insufficient** 992.9;
undercommitted; **inferior** 250.6; **lacking,** wanting,
minus; unreached

ADVS **6 behind, behindhand, in arrears** *or* arrear

7 amiss, astray, beside the mark, below the mark,
beside the point, far from it, to no purpose, in
vain, vainly, fruitlessly, bootlessly

912 ELEVATION
<act of raising>

NOUNS **1 elevation, raising, lifting,** upping, boosting
and hiking <nf>; **rearing,** escalation, **erection;**
uprearing, uplifting; upbuoying; **uplift,** upheaval,
upthrow, upcast, upthrust; **exaltation;** apotheosis,
deification; beatification, canonization;
enshrinement, assumption; *sursum corda* <L>;
height 272; ascent 193; increase 251; antigravity

2 lift, boost *and* **hike** <nf>, hoist, heave; a leg up;
promotion

3 lifter, erector; crane, derrick, gantry crane, crab;
jack, jackscrew; **hoist,** lift, hydraulic lift; forklift;
hydraulic tailgate; lever 906.4; windlass 906.7;
tackle; yeast, leaven

4 elevator, *ascenseur* <Fr>, **lift** <Brit>; escalator,
moving staircase *or* stairway, ski lift, chair lift;
dumbwaiter

VERBS **5 elevate, raise, rear,** escalate, up, boost *and*
hike <nf>; **erect, heighten, lift,** levitate, boost <nf>,

hoist, heist <nf>, heft, heave; raise up, rear up, lift
up, hold up, set up; stick up, cock up, perk up; buoy
up, upbuoy; **upraise, uplift,** uphold, uprear, uphoist;
upheave, upthrow, upcast; throw up, cast up; jerk
up, hike <nf>; knock up, lob, loft; sky <nf>

6 exalt, elevate, ensky; deify, apotheosize; beatify,
canonize; enshrine; put on a pedestal

7 give a lift, give a boost, give a leg up <nf>, **help
up,** put on; mount, horse; enhance, upgrade

8 pick up, take up, pluck up, **gather up;** draw up,
fish up, haul up, drag up; dredge, dredge up

ADJS **9 raised, lifted, elevated;** upraised, **uplifted,**
upcast; **reared,** upreared; rearing, rampant;
upthrown, upflung; **exalted, lofty;** deified,
apotheosized; canonized, sainted, beatified;
enshrined, sublime; antigravitational; stilted, on
stilts; erect, upright 200.11; high 272.19

10 elevating, elevatory, escalatory; lifting; **uplifting;**
erective, erectile; levitative

913 DEPRESSION
<act of lowering>

NOUNS **1 depression, lowering; sinking;** ducking,
submergence, pushing *or* thrusting under, down-
thrust, down-thrusting, detrusion, pushing *or*
pulling *or* hauling down; reduction, de-escalation,
diminution; demotion 447, debasement,
degradation; concavity, hollowness 284.1; descent
194; decrease 252; deflation

2 downthrow, downcast; **overthrow,** overturn 205.2;
precipitation, fall, downfall; downpour,
downpouring

3 crouch, stoop, bend, squat; **bow,** genuflection,
kneeling, kowtow, kowtowing, salaam, reverence,
obeisance, **curtsy;** bob, duck, nod; prostration,
supination; crawling, groveling; abasement, self-
abasement

VERBS **4 depress, lower,** let *or* take down, debase,
de-escalate, **sink,** bring low, deflate, reduce, couch;
pull *or* haul down, take down a peg <nf>; bear
down, downbear, squash; thrust *or* press *or* push
down, detrude; indent 284.14

5 fell, drop, bring down, fetch down, down <nf>,
take down, take down a peg, lay low, reduce to the
ranks, cashier; **raze,** rase, raze to the ground; **level,**
lay level; pull down, pull about one's ears; **cut
down,** chop down, hew down, whack down <nf>,
mow down; **knock down,** dash down, send
headlong, **floor,** deck *and* lay out <nf>, lay by the
heels, ground, **bowl down** *or* **over** <nf>; trip, trip
up, topple, tumble; **prostrate,** supinate; throw, **throw**
or fling *or* cast down, **precipitate;** bulldog; spread-
eagle <nf>, pin, pin down; blow over *or* down

6 overthrow, overturn 205.6; depose 447.4; demote 447.3

7 drop, let go of, let drop *or* fall

8 crouch, duck, cringe, **cower; stoop, bend, stoop down, squat,** squat down, get down, hunker *and* hunker down *and* get down on one's hunkers <nf>; hunch, hunch down, hunch over, scrooch *or* scrouch down <nf>

9 bow, bend, kneel, genuflect, bend the knee, **curtsy,** make a low bow, make a leg, make a reverence *or* an obeisance, salaam, bob, duck; **kowtow,** prostrate oneself; crawl, grovel; wallow, welter

10 sit down, seat oneself, park oneself <nf>, **be seated** 173.10

11 lie down, couch, drape oneself, recline 201.5; **prostrate,** supinate, prone <nf>; flatten oneself, prostrate oneself; hit the ground *or* the dirt <nf>

ADJS **12 depressed, lowered,** debased, reduced, **fallen,** deflated; sunk, **sunken,** submerged; downcast, downthrown; prostrated, prostrate 201.8; low, at a low ebb; falling, precipitous

914 CIRCUITOUSNESS

NOUNS **1 circuitousness,** circuity, circuition <old>; **roundaboutness,** indirection, ambagiousness <old>, meandering, deviance *or* deviancy, **deviation** 164; deviousness, **digression,** circumlocution 538.5; **excursion,** excursus; **circling, wheeling,** circulation, rounding, orbit, **orbiting; spiraling,** spiral, gyring, gyre; circumambulation, circumambience *or* circumambiency, circumflexion, circumnavigation, circummigration; turning, **turn** 164.1; circularity 280; convolution 281

2 circuit, round, revolution, **circle,** full circle, go-round, **cycle,** orbit, ambit; pass; round trip, *aller retour* <Fr>; **beat,** rounds, **walk,** tour, turn, lap, loop; round robin

3 detour, bypass, roundabout way, roundabout, ambages <old>, circuit, circumbendibus <nf>, the long way around, digression, deviation, excursion

VERBS **4 go roundabout,** meander, deviate, go around Robin Hood's barn, take *or* go the long way around, twist and turn; **detour,** make a detour, **go around,** go round about, go out of one's way, **bypass;** deviate 164.3; digress 538.9; **talk in circles,** say in a roundabout way; equivocate 936.9, shilly-shally; dodge 368.8

5 circle, circuit, describe a circle, make a circuit, move in a circle, **circulate; go round** *or* **around,** go about; **wheel,** orbit, go into orbit, round; make a

pass; come full circle, close the circle, make a round trip, return to the starting point; cycle; spiral, gyre; go around in circles, chase one's tail, go round and round; revolve 915.9; **compass,** encompass, encircle, surround; skirt, flank; go the round, make the round of, make one's rounds, circuiteer <old>; lap; circumambulate, circummigrate; circumnavigate, girdle, girdle the globe, "put a girdle round about the earth" —Shakespeare

6 turn, go around, round, turn *or* round a corner, corner, round a bend, double *or* round a point

ADJS **7 circuitous, roundabout, out-of-the-way, devious, oblique, indirect,** ambagious <old>, meandering, backhanded; **deviative** 164.7, **deviating,** digressive, discursive, excursive; equivocatory 936.14; evasive 368.15; vacillating 362.10; **circular** 280.11, **round,** wheel-shaped, O-shaped; spiral, helical; orbital; rotary 915.15

8 circumambient, circumambulatory, circumforaneous, circumfluent, circumvolant, circumnavigatory, circumnavigable

ADVS **9 circuitously, deviously, obliquely,** ambagiously <old> **indirectly, round about,** about it *and* about, round Robin Hood's barn, in a roundabout way, by a side door, by a side wind; circlewise, wheelwise

915 ROTATION

NOUNS **1 rotation, revolution,** roll, **gyration, spin,** circulation; axial motion, rotational motion, angular motion, angular momentum, angular velocity; circumrotation, circumgyration, circumvolution, full circle; **turning, whirling,** swirling, **spinning,** wheeling, reeling, whir; **spiraling,** twisting upward *or* downward, gyring, volution, turbination; centrifugation; swiveling, pivoting, swinging; **rolling,** trolling, trundling, bowling, volutation <old>

2 whirl, wheel, reel, **spin, turn,** round; spiral, helix, helicoid, gyre; pirouette; **swirl,** twirl, **eddy,** gurge, surge; vortex, **whirlpool,** maelstrom, Charybdis; dizzy round, rat race; tourbillion, **whirlwind** 318.14, twister; rotary, traffic circle

3 revolutions, revs <nf>; revolutions per minute *or* rpm

4 rotator, rotor; roller, rundle; **whirler,** whirligig, **top,** whirlabout; **merry-go-round,** carousel, roundabout; **wheel,** disk; Ixion's wheel; rolling stone; revolving door; spit

5 axle, axis; pivot, gudgeon, trunnion, **swivel, spindle,** arbor, pole, radiant; fulcrum 901.2; pin, pintle; **hub,** nave; axle shaft, axle spindle, axle bar, axle-tree;

distaff; mandrel; gimbal; **hinge,** hingle <nf>; rowlock, oarlock

6 **axle box,** journal, journal box; hotbox; universal joint

7 **bearing,** ball bearing, journal bearing, saw bearing, tumbler bearing, main bearing, needle bearing, roller bearing, thrust bearing, bevel bearing, bushing; jewel; headstock

8 <science of rotation> trochilics, gyrostatics

VERBS 9 **rotate, revolve, spin, turn,** round, **go round** *or* **around,** turn round *or* around; **spiral, gyrate,** gyre, whirl like a dervish; circumrotate, circumvolute; circle, circulate; **swivel, pivot, wheel,** swing; pirouette, turn a pirouette; wind, twist, screw, crank; wamble

10 **roll,** trundle, troll, **bowl;** roll up, **furl**

11 **whirl,** whirligig, twirl, **wheel, reel, spin,** spin like a top *or* teetotum, whirl like a dervish; centrifuge, centrifugate; **swirl,** gurge, surge, **eddy,** whirlpool

12 <move around in confusion> **seethe, mill,** mill around *or* about, stir, roil, moil, be turbulent

13 <roll about in> **wallow, welter,** grovel, roll, flounder, tumble

ADJS 14 **rotating, revolving, turning,** gyrating; **whirling, swirling,** twirling, **spinning,** wheeling, **reeling; rolling,** trolling, bowling

15 **rotary, rotational,** rotatory, rotative; trochilic, vertiginous; circumrotatory, circumvolutory, circumgyratory; spiral, spiralling, helical, gyral, gyratory, gyrational, gyroscopic, gyrostatic; whirly, swirly, gulfy; whirlabout, whirligig; vortical, cyclonic, tornadic, whirlwindy, whirlwindish

ADVS 16 **round, around,** round about, **in a circle; round and round,** in circles, like a horse in a mill; in a whirl, in a spin; head over heels, heels over head; clockwise, counterclockwise, anticlockwise, widdershins

916 OSCILLATION
<motion to and fro>

NOUNS 1 **oscillation, vibration,** vibrancy; to-and-fro motion; harmonic motion, simple harmonic motion; libration, nutation; pendulation; **fluctuation,** vacillation, wavering 362.2; electrical oscillation, mechanical oscillation, oscillating current; libration of the moon, libration in latitude *or* longitude; vibratility; **frequency,** frequency band *or* spectrum; resonance, resonant *or* resonance frequency; **periodicity** 850.2

2 **waving,** wave motion, **undulation,** undulancy; **brandishing, flourishing,** flaunting, shaking; brandish, flaunt, flourish; wave 238.14

3 **pulsation, pulse, beat, throb;** beating, throbbing; systole, diastole; rat-a-tat, staccato, rataplan,

drumming 55.1; **rhythm,** tempo 709.24; **palpitation,** flutter, arrhythmia, pitter-patter, pit-a-pat; fibrillation, ventricular fibrillation, tachycardia, ventricular tachycardia <all medicine>; **heartbeat,** heartthrob

4 **wave,** wave motion, ray; transverse wave, longitudinal wave; electromagnetic wave, electromagnetic radiation; **light** 1025; **radio wave** 1034.11; mechanical wave; acoustic wave, **sound wave** 50.1; seismic wave, **shock wave;** de Broglie wave; diffracted wave, guided wave; one- *or* two- *or* three-dimensional wave; periodic wave; standing wave, node, antinode; sea wave, surface wave, **tidal wave,** tsunami, seismic sea wave; traveling wave; surge, storm surge; amplitude, crest, trough; scend; **surf,** roller, curler, comber, whitecap, white horse; tube; wavelength; frequency, frequency band *or* spectrum; resonance, resonant *or* resonance frequency; period; wave number; diffraction; reinforcement, interference; in phase, out of phase; wave equation, Schrödinger equation; Huygens' principle

5 **alternation, reciprocation;** regular *or* rhythmic play, **coming and going,** to-and-fro, back-and-forth, ebb and flow, *va-et-vien* <Fr>, flux and reflux, systole and diastole, ups and downs, wax and wane, systole and diastole; sine wave, Lissajous figure *or* curve; **seesawing,** teetering, tottering, **teeter-tottering;** seesaw, teeter, teeter-totter, wigwag; zig-zag, zig-zagging, zig, zag

6 **swing,** swinging, **sway,** swag; **rock, lurch, roll, reel,** careen; wag, waggle; wave, waver; swing of the pendulum

7 seismicity, seismism; seismology, seismography, seismometry

8 <instruments> oscilloscope, oscillograph, oscillometer; wavemeter; harmonograph; vibroscope, vibrograph; kymograph; seismoscope, seismograph, seismometer; wave gauge

9 **oscillator, vibrator;** pendulum, pendulum wheel; metronome; swing; seesaw, teeter, teeter-totter, teeterboard, teetery-bender; rocker, rocking chair, cradle; rocking stone, logan stone, shuttle; shuttlecock

VERBS 10 **oscillate, vibrate,** librate, nutate; pendulate; **fluctuate,** vacillate, waver, wave; resonate; **swing, sway,** swag, dangle, **reel, rock, lurch, roll,** careen, toss, pitch; **wag,** waggle; **wobble,** coggle <Scot>, wamble; **bob,** bobble; shake, flutter 917.10,12

11 **wave, undulate; brandish, flourish,** flaunt, shake, swing, wield; float, fly; **flap, flutter;** wag, wigwag

12 **pulsate, pulse, beat, throb,** not miss a beat; **palpitate,** go pit-a-pat; miss a beat; beat time, beat out, tick, ticktock; drum 55.4

13 **alternate,** reciprocate, swing, **go to and fro,** to-

and-fro, **come and go,** pass and re-pass, ebb and flow, wax and wane, ride and tie, hitch and hike, back and fill; **seesaw, teeter, teeter-totter;** shuttle, shuttlecock, battledore and shuttlecock; **wigwag,** wibble-wabble; zigzag

14 <move up and down> **pump, shake,** bounce

ADJS **15 oscillating,** oscillatory; **vibrating,** vibratory, harmonic; vibratile; librational, libratory; nutational; **periodic,** pendular, pendulous; **fluctuating,** fluctuational, fluctuant; wavering; vacillating, vacillatory; resonant

16 waving, undulating, undulatory, undulant; seismic

17 swinging, swaying, dangling, **reeling, rocking, lurching,** careening, **rolling,** tossing, pitching

18 pulsative, pulsatory, pulsatile; **pulsating, pulsing, beating, throbbing, palpitating,** palpitant, pit-a-pat, staccato; rhythmic 709.28

19 alternate, reciprocal, reciprocative; sine-wave; **back-and-forth, to-and-fro,** up-and-down, seesaw

20 seismatical, seismological, seismographic, seismometric; successive, successatory, sussultatory

ADVS **21 to and fro, back and forth,** backward and forward, backwards and forwards, **in and out, up and down,** seesaw, shuttlewise, from side to side, from pillar to post, off and on, ride and tie, hitch and hike, round and round, like buckets in a well

917 AGITATION
<irregular motion>

NOUNS **1 agitation, perturbation,** hecticness, conturbation <old>; **frenzy,** excitement 105; **trepidation** 127.5, trepidity, fidgets *and* jitters *and* ants in the pants <nf>, antsiness *and* jitteriness <nf>, heebie-jeebies <nf>, jumpiness, nervousness, yips <nf>, nerviness <Brit>, nervosity, twitter, upset; **unrest, malaise, unease,** restlessness; fever, feverishness, febrility; **disquiet,** disquietude, inquietude, discomposure, hand-wringing; **stir, churn, ferment,** fermentation, foment; seethe, seething, ebullition, boil, boiling; embroilment, roil, turbidity, fume, **disturbance, commotion,** moil, **turmoil,** turbulence 671.2, **swirl, tumult,** tumultuation, hubbub, shemozzle <Brit nf>, rout, fuss, row, to-do, bluster, fluster, flurry, flutteration, hoo-ha *and* flap <nf>, bustle, brouhaha, bobbery, hurly-burly; maelstrom; **disorder** 810

2 shaking, quaking, palsy, **quivering, quavering, shivering, trembling,** tremulousness, **shuddering, vibration;** juddering <Brit>, succussion; jerkiness, fits and starts, spasms; jactation, jactitation; joltiness, bumpiness, the shakes *and* the shivers *and* the cold shivers <nf>, ague, chattering;

chorea, rigor, St Vitus's dance; delirium tremens *or* the DT's

3 shake, quake, quiver, quaver, falter, **tremor, tremble, shiver, shudder,** twitter, didder, dither; **wobble; bob,** bobble; **jog,** joggle; **shock, jolt,** jar, jostle; **bounce,** bump; **jerk, twitch,** tic, grimace, rictus, vellication; jig, jiggle; the shakes <nf>

4 flutter, flitter, flit, **flicker, waver,** dance; shake, quiver 917.3; **sputter, splutter; flap,** flop <nf>; **beat,** beating; **palpitation,** throb, pit-a-pat, pitter-patter

5 twitching, jerking, vellication; **fidgets,** fidgetiness; itchiness, formication, pruritus

6 spasm, convulsion, cramp, **paroxysm,** throes; **orgasm,** sexual climax; epitasis, eclampsia; **seizure,** grip, attack, **fit,** access, ictus; epilepsy, falling sickness; stroke, apoplexy

7 wiggle, wriggle; wag, waggle; writhe, **squirm**

8 flounder, flounce, stagger, totter, stumble, falter; wallow, welter; **roll, rock, reel, lurch,** careen, **swing, sway; toss, tumble,** pitch, plunge

9 <instruments> **agitator,** shaker, jiggler, vibrator; beater, stirrer, paddle, whisk, eggbeater; churn; blender

VERBS **10 agitate, shake, disturb, perturb,** shake up, perturbate, **disquiet, discompose, upset, trouble, unsettle, stir,** swirl, flurry, flutter, flutter the dovecot, fret, roughen, ruffle, rumple, ripple, ferment, convulse; **churn,** whip, whisk, beat, paddle; **excite** 105.11; **stir up,** cause a stir *or* commotion, muddy the waters, shake up a hornet's nest <nf>; work up, shake up, churn up, whip up, beat up; roil, rile <nf>; disarrange 811.2

11 shake, quake, vibrate, jactitate; **tremble, quiver, quaver,** falter, **shudder, shiver,** twitter, didder, chatter; shake in one's boots *or* shoes, quake *or* shake *or* tremble like an aspen leaf, have the jitters *or* the shakes <nf>, have ants in one's pants <nf>; have an ague; **wobble; bob,** bobble; jiggle, **jog,** joggle; **shock, jolt,** jar, jostle, hustle, jounce, **bounce,** jump, bump

12 flutter, flitter, flit, flick, **flicker,** gutter, bicker, wave, **waver,** dance; **sputter, splutter; flap,** flop <nf>, flip, beat, slat; **palpitate,** pulse, throb, pitter-patter, go pit-a-pat

13 twitch, jerk, vellicate; itch; **jig, jiggle,** jigger *or* jigget <nf>; **fidget,** have the fidgets

14 wiggle, wriggle; wag, waggle; **writhe, squirm,** twist and turn; have ants in one's pants <nf>

15 flounder, flounce, **stagger,** totter, stumble, falter, blunder, wallop; **struggle,** labor; **wallow, welter; roll, rock, reel, lurch,** career, **swing, sway; toss, tumble,** thrash about, **pitch, plunge,** pitch and plunge, toss and tumble, toss and turn, be the sport of winds and waves; **seethe**

ADJS **16 agitated, disturbed, perturbed, disquieted,**

discomposed, **troubled, upset, ruffled,** flurried, flustered, unsettled; stirred up, shaken, shaken up, all worked up, all shook up <nf>; troublous, feverish, fidgety *and* jittery *and* antsy <nf>, jumpy, nervous, nervy <Brit>, restless, uneasy, unquiet, unpeaceful; all of a twitter <nf>, all of a flutter, giddy, in a spin; turbulent; excited 105.18,20,22

17 **shaking, vibrating,** chattering; **quivering, quavering, quaking, shivering, shuddering, trembling, tremulous,** palsied, aspen; successive, successatory; **shaky,** quivery, quavery, shivery, trembly; wobbly; juddering

18 **fluttering, flickering, wavering,** guttering, dancing; sputtering, spluttering, sputtery; fluttery, flickery, bickering, flicky, wavery, unsteady, desultory

19 **jerky,** herky-jerky <nf>, twitchy *or* twitchety, jerking, **twitching, fidgety, jumpy,** jiggety <nf>, vellicative; **spastic, spasmodic,** eclamptic, orgasmic, convulsive; fitful, saltatory

20 **jolting,** jolty, **joggling,** joggly, jogglety, jouncy, **bouncy, bumpy,** choppy, rough; **jarring,** bone-bruising

21 **wriggly,** wriggling, crawly, creepy-crawly <nf>; **wiggly,** wiggling; squirmy, squirming; writhy, writhing, antsy <nf>

ADVS 22 **agitatedly, troublously, restlessly,** uneasily, unquietly, unpeacefully, nervously, feverishly; **excitedly**

23 **shakily,** quiveringly, quaveringly, quakingly, **tremblingly,** shudderingly, tremulously; flutteringly, waveringly, unsteadily, desultorily; **jerkily,** spasmodically, fitfully, by jerks, by snatches, saltatorily, by fits and starts, "with many a flirt and flutter"—Pope

918 SPECTATOR

NOUNS 1 **spectator, observer; looker, onlooker,** looker-on, **watcher,** gazer, gazer-on, gaper, goggler, **viewer,** seer, beholder, perceiver, percipient; spectatress, spectatrix; **witness, eyewitness; bystander,** passerby; innocent bystander; sidewalk superintendent; kibitzer; girl-watcher, ogler, drugstore cowboy <nf>; bird-watcher; **viewer,** television-viewer, televiewer, video-gazer, TV-viewer, couch potato <nf>

2 **attender** 221.5, attendee; theatergoer; **audience** 48.6, house, crowd, gate, fans

3 **sightseer,** excursionist, **tourist,** rubberneck *or* **rubbernecker** <nf>; slummer; tour group

4 **sight-seeing,** rubbernecking <nf>, lionism <Brit nf>; **tour,** walking tour, bus tour, sightseeing tour *or* excursion, **rubberneck tour** <nf>

VERBS 5 spectate <nf>, witness, see 27.12, look on, eye, **ogle, gape;** take in, **look at, watch;** attend 221.8

6 **sight-see,** see the sights, take in the sights, lionize *or* see the lions <Brit nf>; **rubberneck** <nf>; go slumming; go on a tour, join a tour

ADJS 7 spectating, spectatorial; onlooking; sight-seeing, rubberneck <nf>; passing by, caught in the cross-fire *or* in the middle

919 INTELLECT
   <mental faculty>

NOUNS 1 **intellect, mind,** *mens* <L>; mental *or* intellectual faculty, nous, **reason, rationality,** rational *or* reasoning faculty, power of reason, *Vernunft* <Ger>, *esprit* <Fr>, *raison* <Fr>, ratio, discursive reason, "discourse of reason"— Shakespeare, **intelligence,** mentality, mental capacity, **understanding,** reasoning, intellection, conception; cognition, perception; **brain, brains,** brainpower, smarts *and* gray matter <nf>; **thought** 931; head, headpiece

2 **wits, senses, faculties,** parts, capacities, intellectual gifts *or* talents, mother wit; intellectuals <old>; consciousness 928.2

3 **inmost mind,** inner recesses of the mind, mind's core, deepest mind, center of the mind; inner man; subconscious, subconscious mind; inmost heart

4 **psyche, spirit,** spiritus, **soul,** geist, *âme* <Fr>, **heart, mind,** inner mind, inner being, anima, *anima humana* <L>, animus; shade, shadow, manes; breath, pneuma, breath of life, divine breath; *atman* and *purusha* and *buddhi* and *jiva* and *jivatma* <all Skt>; *ba* and *khu* <Egyptian myth>; *ruach* and *nephesh* <Heb>; spiritual being, inner man, "the Divinity that stirs within us"— Addison; **ego,** the self, the I

5 **life principle,** vital principle, vital spirit *or* soul, *élan vital* <Fr>, **vital force,** *prana* <Hindu>; essence *or* substance of life, individual essence, *ousia* <Gk>; divine spark, vital spark *or* flame

6 **brain** 2.15, seat *or* organ of thought; sensory, sensorium; encephalon; gray matter, head, cerebrum, pate *and* sconce *and* noddle <nf>; noodle *or* noggin *or* bean *or* upper story <nf>; sensation 24

ADJS 7 **mental, intellectual, rational, reasoning, thinking,** noetic, conceptive, conceptual, phrenic; intelligent 920.12; noological; endopsychic, psychic, psychical, psychologic, psychological, spiritual; cerebral; subjective, internal

920 INTELLIGENCE, WISDOM
   <mental capacity>

NOUNS 1 **intelligence, understanding,** *Verstand* <Ger>, **comprehension,** apprehension, mental *or* intellectual grasp, prehensility of mind, intellectual power, brainpower, thinking power, power of mind *or* thought; ideation, conception; integrative power, esemplastic power; rationality, reasoning *or* deductive power, ratiocination; **sense, wit,** mother wit, natural *or* native wit; **intellect** 919; **intellectuality,** intellectualism; capacity, mental capacity, **mentality,** caliber, reach *or* compass *or* scope of mind; **IQ** *or* intelligence quotient, mental ratio, mental age; sanity 925; knowledge 928

2 **smartness, braininess,** smarts *and* savvy <nf>, **brightness, brilliance, cleverness,** aptness, aptitude, native cleverness, mental alertness, nous, **sharpness, keenness,** acuity, acuteness; high IQ, **mental ability** *or* **capability,** gift, gifts, giftedness, **talent, flair, genius;** quickness, nimbleness, quickness *or* nimbleness of wit, adroitness, dexterity; sharp-wittedness, keen-wittedness, quick-wittedness, nimble-wittedness; nimble mind, mercurial mind, quick parts, clear *or* quick thinking; ready wit, quick wit, sprightly wit, *esprit* <Fr>

3 **shrewdness, artfulness, cunning,** cunningness, canniness, **craft, craftiness,** wiliness, guilefulness, slickness <nf>, **slyness,** pawkiness <Brit>, foxiness <nf>, peasant *or* animal cunning, low cunning; subtility, subtilty, **subtlety;** insinuation, insidiousness, deviousness

4 **sagacity,** sagaciousness, **astuteness, acumen,** longheadedness; **foresight,** foresightedness, providence; **farsightedness,** farseeingness, longsightedness; **discernment, insight,** intuition, penetration, acuteness, acuity; perspicacity, perspicaciousness, perspicuity, perspicuousness; incisiveness, trenchancy, cogency; **percipience** *or* percipiency, **perception,** apperception; **sensibility** 24.2

5 **wisdom,** ripe wisdom, seasoned understanding, mellow wisdom, wiseness, sageness, sapience, good *or* sound understanding; Sophia <female personification of wisdom>; erudition 927.5; **profundity,** profoundness, depth; broad-mindedness 979; **conventional wisdom,** received wisdom, prudential judgment

6 **sensibleness, reasonableness,** reason, rationality, sanity, saneness, **soundness; practicality,** practical wisdom, practical mind; **sense,** good *or* common *or* plain sense, **horse sense** <nf>; due sense of; level head, cool head, **levelheadedness,** balance, coolheadedness, coolness; soberness, sobriety, **sober-mindedness;** savvy, smarts

7 **judiciousness, judgment,** good *or* sound judgment, cool judgment, soundness of judgment; **prudence,** prudentialism, providence, policy, polity; weighing,

consideration, circumspection, circumspectness, reflection, reflectiveness, **thoughtfulness; discretion,** discreetness; **discrimination**

8 **genius,** *Geist* <Ger>, spirit, soul; daimonion, demon, daemon; **inspiration,** afflatus, divine afflatus; Muse; fire of genius; **creativity;** talent 413.4; creative thought 986.2

9 <intelligent being> **intelligence, intellect,** head, brain, mentality, consciousness; **wise man** 921; intellectual, thinker, academic, savant, scholar, walking encyclopedia

VERBS 10 have all one's wits about one, have all one's marbles *and* have smarts *or* savvy <nf>, have a head on one's shoulders *and* have one's head screwed on right <nf>; have method in one's madness; use one's head *or* wits, get *or* keep one's wits about one; know what's what, know the score <nf>, be wise as a serpent *or* an owl; be reasonable, listen to reason

11 be brilliant, **scintillate,** sparkle, coruscate

ADJS 12 intelligent, intellectual <old>; ideational, conceptual, conceptive, discursive; sophic, noetic, phrenic; **knowing, understanding, reasonable, rational, sensible, bright;** sane 925.4; not so dumb <nf>, strong-minded

13 **clear-witted,** clearheaded, clear-eyed, clear-sighted; no-nonsense; awake, **wide-awake,** alive, **alert,** on the ball <nf>

14 **smart, brainy** <nf>, **bright, brilliant,** scintillating; **clever,** apt, **gifted,** talented; **sharp,** keen; **quick,** nimble, adroit, astute, dexterous; **sharp-witted,** keen-witted, needle-witted, **quick-witted,** quick-thinking, steel-trap, nimble-witted, quick on the trigger *or* uptake <nf>; smart as a whip, sharp as a tack <nf>; nobody's fool *and* no dumbbell *and* not born yesterday <nf>, all there <nf>

15 **shrewd, artful, cunning, knowing, crafty, wily,** guileful, canny, slick, sly, pawky <Brit>, smart as a fox, foxy *and* crazy like a fox <nf>; **subtle,** subtile; insinuating, insidious, devious, Byzantine, calculating

16 **sagacious, astute,** longheaded, argute; **understanding, discerning,** penetrating, incisive, acute, trenchant, cogent, piercing; **foresighted,** foreseeing; forethoughted, forethoughtful, provident; **farsighted,** farseeing, longsighted; **perspicacious,** perspicuous; **perceptive, percipient,** apperceptive, appercipient

17 **wise, sage,** sapient, seasoned, **knowing,** knowledgeable; **learned** 928.21; **profound,** deep; wise as an owl *or* a serpent, wise as Solomon; wise beyond one's years, in advance of one's age, wise in one's generation; broad-minded 979.8

18 **sensible, reasonable, reasoning, rational, logical; practical,** pragmatic; philosophical; commonsense,

commonsensical <nf>; **levelheaded,** balanced, coolheaded, cool, clearheaded, **sound, sane,** sober, **sober-minded,** well-balanced, lucid; realistic, ratiocinative; well thought-out; profound

19 **judicious,** judicial, judgmatic, judgmatical, **prudent,** prudential, politic, careful, provident, **considerate,** circumspect, sapient, **thoughtful,** reflective, reflecting; **discreet;** discriminative, discriminating; **well-advised,** well-judged, enlightened

ADVS 20 **intelligently, understandingly,** knowingly, discerningly; **reasonably,** rationally, sensibly; **smartly, cleverly; shrewdly,** artfully, cunningly; **wisely,** sagaciously, astutely; **judiciously, prudently,** discreetly, providently, considerately, circumspectly, thoughtfully

921 WISE PERSON

NOUNS 1 **wise man, wise woman, sage,** sapient, man *or* woman of wisdom; **master, mistress,** authority, mastermind, master spirit of the age, oracle; **philosopher,** thinker, lover of wisdom; "he who, seeing the furthest, has the deepest love for mankind"—Maurice Maeterlinck; rabbi; doctor; great soul, mahatma, guru, rishi; *starets* <Russ>, elder, wise old man, elder statesman; illuminate; seer; mentor; intellect, man of intellect; mandarin, **intellectual** 929; savant, **scholar** 929.3; logician, dialectician, sophist, syllogist, metaphysician

2 Solomon, Socrates, Plato, Mentor, Nestor, Confucius, Buddha, Gandhi, Albert Schweitzer, Martin Luther King Jr

3 **the wise,** the intelligent, the sensible, the prudent, the knowing, the understanding

4 Seven Wise Men of Greece, Seven Sages, Seven Wise Masters; Solon, Chilon, Pittacus, Bias, Periander, Epimenides, Cleobulus, Thales

5 Magi, Three Wise Men, Wise Men of the East, Three Kings; Three Kings of Cologne; Gaspar *or* Caspar, Melchior, Balthasar

6 **wiseacre,** wisehead, wiseling, **witling,** wisenheimer <nf>, wise guy, smart ass <nf>; wise fool; Gothamite, wise man of Gotham, wise man of Chelm

922 UNINTELLIGENCE

NOUNS 1 **unintelligence,** unintellectuality <old>, unwisdom, unwiseness, intellectual *or* mental weakness; **senselessness, witlessness, mindlessness,** brainlessness, primal stupidity, *Urdummheit* <Ger>, reasonlessness, lackwittedness, lackbrainedness, slackwittedness, slackmindedness; **irrationality;** ignorance 930;

foolishness 922; incapacity, ineptitude; low IQ, low mental age

2 **unperceptiveness,** imperceptiveness, insensibility, impercipience *or* impercipiency, undiscerningness, unapprehendingness, **incomprehension,** nonunderstanding; **blindness,** mindblindness, purblindness; **unawareness,** lack of awareness, unconsciousness, lack of consciousness; **shortsightedness,** nearsightedness, dim-sightedness

3 **stupidity,** stupidness, *bêtise* <Fr>, **dumbness** <nf>, **doltishness,** boobishness, duncery <old>, dullardism, blockishness, cloddishness, lumpishness, sottishness, **asininity,** ninnyism, simplemindedness, simpletonianism; oafishness, oafdom, yokelism, loutishness; **density,** denseness, opacity; grossness, crassness, crudeness, boorishness; **dullness,** dopiness <nf>, **obtuseness,** sluggishness, bovinity, cowishness, slowness, lethargy, stolidity, hebetude; **dim-wittedness,** dimness, **dull-wittedness,** slow-wittedness, beef-wittedness, dull-headedness, **thick-wittedness,** thick-headedness, unteachability, ineducability; wrongheadedness

4 <nf terms> **blockheadedness,** woodenheadedness, klutziness, dunderheadedness, goofiness, jolterheadedness *or* joltheadedness <Brit>, chowderheadedness, chuckleheadedness, beetleheadedness, chumpiness, numskulledness *or* numskullery, cabbageheadedness, sapheadedness, muttonheadedness, meatheadedness, fatheadedness, boneheadedness, knuckleheadedness, blunderheadedness

5 **muddleheadedness,** addleheadedness, addlepatedness, puzzleheadedness

6 **empty-headedness,** empty-mindedness, absence of mind, airheadedness *and* bubbleheadedness <nf>; **vacuity,** vacuousness, vacancy, vacuum, emptiness, mental void, blankness, hollowness, inanity, vapidity, jejunity

7 **superficiality, shallowness, unprofundity,** lack of depth, unprofoundness, thinness; shallow-wittedness, shallow-mindedness; **frivolousness,** flightiness, lightness, fluffiness, frothiness, volatility, dizziness *and* ditziness <nf>

8 **feeblemindedness,** weak-mindedness; infirmity, weakness, feebleness, softness, mushiness <nf>

9 **mental deficiency,** mental retardation, amentia, mental handicap, subnormality, mental defectiveness; brain damage; **arrested development,** infantilism, retardation, retardment, backwardness; **simplemindedness,** simple-wittedness, simpleness, simplicity; **idiocy,** idiotism <old>, profound idiocy, **imbecility, half-wittedness,** blithering idiocy; moronity, moronism,

cretinism; mongolism, mongolianism, mongoloid idiocy, Down's syndrome; insanity 926

10 **senility,** senilism, senile weakness, senile debility, caducity, decrepitude, senectitude, decline; **childishness, second childhood, dotage, dotardism;** anility; senile dementia, senile psychosis, Alzheimer's disease

11 **puerility,** puerilism, immaturity, **childishness; infantilism,** babyishness

VERBS 12 **be stupid,** show ignorance, not have all one's marbles; drool, slobber, drivel, dither, blither, blather, maunder, dote, burble; not see an inch beyond one's nose, not have enough sense to come in out of the rain, not find one's way to first base; lose one's mind *or* marbles; not be all there; have a low IQ

ADJS 13 **unintelligent,** unintellectual <old>, **unthinking, unreasoning, irrational,** unwise, inept, **not bright;** ungifted, untalented; **senseless,** insensate; **mindless, witless, reasonless, brainless,** pin-brained, pea-brained, of little brain, headless, empty-headed; **lackwitted,** lackbrained, slackwitted, slackminded, lean-minded, lean-witted, short-witted; **foolish** 922.8; **ignorant** 930.12

14 **undiscerning, unperceptive,** imperceptive, impercipient, insensible, unapprehending, uncomprehending, nonunderstanding; **shortsighted,** myopic, nearsighted, dim-sighted; **blind,** purblind, mind-blind, blind as a bat; blinded, blindfold, blindfolded

15 **stupid, dumb,** dullard, **doltish,** blockish, klutzy *and* klutzish <nf>, duncish, duncical, cloddish, clottish <Brit>, chumpish <nf>, lumpish, **oafish,** boobish, sottish, **asinine,** lamebrained, Boeotian; **dense,** thick <nf>, opaque, gross, crass, fat; bovine, cowish, beef-witted, beef-brained, beefheaded; unteachable, ineducable; wrongheaded

16 **dull,** dull of mind, **dopey** <nf>, **obtuse,** blunt, dim, wooden, heavy, sluggish, slow, **slow-witted,** hebetudinous, **dim-witted, dull-witted,** blunt-witted, dull-brained, dull-headed, dull-pated, **thick-witted,** thick-headed, thick-pated, thick-skulled, thick-brained, fat-witted, gross-witted, gross-headed

17 <nf terms> **blockheaded,** woodenheaded, stupidheaded, dumbheaded, dunderheaded, blunderheaded, clueless *or* jolterheaded *or* joltheaded *or* jingle-brained <Brit>, chowderheaded, chuckleheaded, beetleheaded, nitwitted, numskulled, cabbageheaded, pumpkin-headed, sapheaded, lunkheaded, muttonheaded, meatheaded, fatheaded, boneheaded, knuckleheaded, clodpated; dead from the neck up, dead above *or* between the ears, muscle-bound

between the ears; featherheaded, airheaded, bubbleheaded, out to lunch, lunchy, dufus, dufus-assed, spastic, spazzy, three bricks shy of a load, without brain one, not playing with a full deck, not sixteen ounces to the pound, not all there, soft in the head

18 **muddleheaded, fuddlebrained** *and* scramblebrained <nf>, mixed-up, muddled, addled, addleheaded, **addlepated,** addlebrained, muddybrained, puzzleheaded, blear-witted; dizzy <nf>, muzzy, foggy

19 **empty-headed,** empty-minded, empty-noddled, empty-pated, empty-skulled; **vacuous,** vacant, empty, hollow, inane, vapid, jejune, blank, airheaded *and* bubbleheaded <nf>; **rattlebrained,** rattleheaded; scatterbrained 985.16

20 **superficial, shallow, unprofound;** shallow-witted, shallow-minded, shallow-brained, shallow-headed, shallow-pated; **frivolous,** dizzy *and* ditzy <nf>, flighty, light, volatile, frothy, fluffy, **featherbrained, birdwitted, birdbrained**

21 **feebleminded, weak-minded,** weak, feeble, infirm, soft, soft in the head, weak in the upper story <nf>

22 **mentally deficient,** mentally defective, mentally handicapped, retarded, **mentally retarded,** backward, arrested, subnormal, not right in the head, **not all there** <nf>; **simpleminded,** simplewitted, simple, simpletonian; **half-witted,** half-baked <nf>; **idiotic, moronic, imbecile,** imbecilic, cretinous, cretinistic, mongoloid, spastic <nf>; crackbrained, cracked, crazy; babbling, driveling, slobbering, drooling, blithering, dithering, maundering, burbling; brain-damaged

23 **senile,** decrepit, doddering, doddery; **childish,** childlike, in one's second childhood, **doting**

24 **puerile,** immature, **childish;** childlike; **infantile,** infantine; **babyish,** babish

ADVS 25 **unintelligently, stupidly;** insensately, foolishly

923 FOOLISHNESS

NOUNS 1 **foolishness, folly,** foolery, foolheadedness, **stupidity, asininity,** *niaiserie* <Fr>; *bêtise* <Fr>; **inanity, fatuity,** fatuousness; ineptitude; **silliness; frivolousness,** frivolity, giddiness; triviality, triflingness, nugacity, desipience; **nonsense,** tomfoolery, poppycock; **senselessness, insensateness, witlessness, thoughtlessness,** brainlessness, mindlessness; **idiocy, imbecility; craziness, madness,** lunacy, **insanity,** daftness; **eccentricity, queerness,** crankiness, crackpottedness; weirdness; screwiness *and* nuttiness *and* wackiness *and* goofiness *and* daffiness *and* battiness *and* sappiness <nf>;

zaniness, zanyism, **clownishness, buffoonery,** clowning, fooling *or* horsing *or* dicking around <nf>

2 **unwiseness,** unwisdom, **injudiciousness, imprudence;** indiscreetness, **indiscretion,** inconsideration, thoughtlessness, witlessness, inattention, unthoughtfulness, lack of sensitivity; **unreasonableness, unsoundness, unsensibleness,** senselessness, reasonlessness, **irrationality, unreason,** inadvisability; recklessness; childishness, immaturity, puerility, callowness; gullibility, bamboozlability <nf>; inexpedience 996; unintelligence 922; pompousness, stuffiness

3 **absurdity,** absurdness, **ridiculousness;** ludicrousness 488.1; **nonsense,** nonsensicality, stuff and nonsense, codswallop <Brit nf>, horseshit *and* bullshit <nf>; **preposterousness,** fantasticalness, monstrousness, wildness, **outrageousness**

4 <foolish act> **folly, stupidity,** act of folly, absurdity, *sottise* <Fr>, foolish *or* stupid thing, dumb thing to do <nf>; fool *or* fool's trick, dumb trick <nf>; **imprudence, indiscretion,** imprudent *or* unwise step; blunder 975.5, blooper <nf>, gaffe

5 stultification; infatuation; trivialization

VERBS 6 **be foolish**; be stupid 922.12; **act *or* play the fool**; get funny, do the crazy act *or* bit *or* shtick <nf>; **fool,** tomfool <nf>, **trifle,** frivol; **fool *or* horse around** <nf>, dick around <nf>, clown, clown around; **make a fool of oneself,** make a monkey of oneself <nf>, stultify oneself, invite ridicule, put oneself out of court, play the buffoon; **lose one's head, take leave of one's senses,** go haywire; pass from the sublime to the ridiculous; strain at a gnat and swallow a camel; tilt at windmills; tempt fate, never learn

7 stultify, infatuate, turn one's head, befool; gull, dupe; **make a fool of,** make a monkey of *and* play for a sucker *and* put on <nf>

ADJS 8 **foolish,** fool <nf>, foolheaded <nf>, **stupid, dumb** <nf>, clueless <Brit nf>, **asinine,** wet <Brit>; buffoonish; **silly,** apish, dizzy <nf>; **fatuous,** fatuitous, inept, **inane;** futile; **senseless, witless, thoughtless,** insensate, brainless; **idiotic,** moronic, imbecile, imbecilic, spastic <nf>; **crazy, mad,** daft, **insane;** infatuated, besotted, credulous, gulled, befooled, beguiled, fond, doting, gaga; sentimental, maudlin; dazed, fuddled

9 <nf terms> **screwy, nutty,** cockeyed, wacky, goofy, daffy, loony, batty, sappy, kooky, flaky, damn-fool, out of it, out to lunch, lunchy, dorky, dippy, bird-brained, spaced-out, doodle-brained, lame, ditzy, dizzy, loony-tune, dopey, fluffheaded, loopy, scatty, zerking

10 **unwise,** injudicious, **imprudent,** unpolitic, impolitic, contraindicated, **counterproductive;** indiscreet; inconsiderate, thoughtless, mindless, witless, unthoughtful, unthinking, unreflecting, unreflective; **unreasonable, unsound, unsensible,** senseless, insensate, reasonless, **irrational,** reckless, inadvisable; inexpedient 995.5; **ill-advised, ill-considered,** ill-gauged, ill-judged, ill-imagined, ill-contrived, ill-devised, on the wrong track, unconsidered; unadvised, misadvised, misguided; undiscerning; unforeseeing, unseeing, shortsighted, myopic; suicidal, self-defeating

11 **absurd, nonsensical,** insensate, ridiculous, laughable, ludicrous 488.4; **foolish, crazy;** preposterous, cockamamie <nf>, fantastic, fantastical, grotesque, monstrous, wild, weird, **outrageous,** incredible, beyond belief, *outré* <Fr>, extravagant, **bizarre;** high-flown

12 foolable, befoolable, gullible, bamboozlable <nf>; naive, artless, guileless, inexperienced, impressionable; malleable, like putty; persuasible, biddable

ADVS 13 foolishly, stupidly, sillily, idiotically; **unwisely,** injudiciously, imprudently, indiscreetly, inconsiderately; myopically, blindly, senselessly, unreasonably, thoughtlessly, witlessly, imsensately, unthinkingly; absurdly, ridiculously

924 FOOL

NOUNS 1 **fool, damn fool,** tomfool, perfect fool, born fool; *schmuck* <Yiddish>; **ass,** jackass, stupid ass, egregious ass; zany, **clown, buffoon,** doodle; sop, milksop; mome <old>, mooncalf, softhead; figure of fun; **lunatic** 926.15; **ignoramus** 930.8

2 **stupid person, dolt, dunce,** clod, Boeotian, **dullard,** *niais* <Fr>, donkey, yahoo, thickwit, **dope, nitwit,** dimwit, lackwit, half-wit, lamebrain, putz, lightweight, witling

3 <nf terms> **chump, boob,** booby, sap, prize sap, klutz, basket case, dingbat, dingdong, ding-a-ling, **ninny,** ninnyhammer, **nincompoop,** looby, noddy, saphead, mutt, jerk, jerk-off, asshole, goof, schlemiel, sawney <Brit>, galoot, gonzo, dumbo, dweeb, dropshop, dipshit, nerd, twerp, yo-yo

4 <nf terms> **blockhead, airhead,** bubblehead, fluffhead, featherhead, woodenhead, dolthead, dumbhead, dummy, dum-dum, dumbo, dumb cluck, dodo head, doodoohead, dumbbell, dumb bunny, stupidhead, dullhead, bufflehead, bonehead, jughead, thickhead, thickskull, numskull, putz, lunkhead, chucklehead, knucklehead, chowderhead, headbanger *and* jolterhead <Brit>, muttonhead, beefhead, meathead, noodle, noodlehead, thimblewit, pinhead, pinbrain, peabrain, cabbagehead,

pumpkin head, fathead, blubberhead, muddlehead, puzzlehead, addlebrain, addlehead, addlepate, tottyhead <old>, puddinghead, stupe, mushhead, blunderhead, dunderhead, dunderpate, clodpate, clodhead, clodpoll, jobbernowl *and* gaby *and* gowk <Brit>, vegetable, dim-bulb, twit, sucker

5 oaf, lout, boor, lubber, oik <Brit>, **gawk,** gawky, **lummox,** yokel, rube, hick, hayseed, bumpkin, clod, clodhopper

6 silly, silly Billy <nf>, **silly ass, goose**

7 scatterbrain, scatterbrains *and* shatterbrain *or* shatterplate <old>, ditz <nf>, **rattlebrain,** rattlehead, rattlepate, **harebrain,** featherbrain, shallowbrain, shallowpate <old>, featherhead, giddybrain, giddyhead, giddypate, **flibbertigibbet**

8 idiot, driveling *or* blithering *or* adenoidal *or* congenital idiot; **imbecile, moron, half-wit,** natural, natural idiot, born fool, natural-born fool, mental defective, defective; cretin, basket case *and* spastic *and* spaz <nf>; simpleton, simp <nf>, juggins *and* jiggins <nf>, clot *and* berk <Brit nf>, golem

9 dotard, senile; fogy, **old fogy,** fuddy-duddy, old fart *or* fud

925 SANITY

NOUNS **1 sanity, saneness,** sanemindedness, soundness, **soundness of mind,** soundmindedness, sound mind, healthy mind, right mind <nf>, senses, reason, **rationality,** reasonableness, intelligibility, lucidity, coherence, stability, balance, wholesomeness; normalness, normality, normalcy; **mental health;** mental hygiene; mental balance *or* poise *or* equilibrium; sobriety, sober senses; a sound mind in a sound body, a healthy mind in a healthy body; contact with reality; lucid interval; knowing right from wrong; good sense, common sense, wits

VERBS **2 come to one's senses,** sober down *or* up, recover one's sanity *or* balance *or* equilibrium, get things into proportion; see in perspective; have all one's marbles <nf>; have a good head on one's shoulder; have one's wits about one

3 bring to one's senses, bring to reason

ADJS **4 sane,** sane-minded, not mad, **rational,** reasonable, sensible, **lucid,** normal, wholesome, clearheaded, clearminded, sober, balanced, **sound,** mentally sound, of sound mind, *compos mentis* <L>, sound-minded, healthy-minded, right, right in the head, **in one's right mind,** in possession of one's faculties *or* senses, together *and* all there <nf>; in touch with reality; with both oars in the water *and* playing with a full deck <nf>

926 INSANITY, MANIA

NOUNS **1 insanity,** insaneness, unsaneness, **lunacy, madness,** *folie* <Fr>, **craziness, daftness,** oddness, strangeness, queerness, abnormality; loss of touch *or* contact with reality, loss of mind *or* reason; dementedness, dementia, athymia, brainsickness, mindsickness, mental sickness, sickness; **criminal insanity,** homicidal mania, hemothymia; **mental illness, mental disease;** brain damage; rabidness, **mania,** furor; alienation, aberration, mental disturbance, **derangement,** distraction, disorientation, mental derangement *or* disorder, unbalance, mental instability, unsoundness, **unsoundness of mind;** unbalanced mind, diseased *or* unsound mind, **sick mind,** disturbed *or* troubled *or* clouded mind, shattered mind, mind overthrown *or* unhinged, darkened mind, disordered mind *or* reason; senselessness, witlessness, reasonlessness, irrationality; possession, pixilation; mental deficiency 922.9

2 <nf terms> **nuttiness,** craziness, daffiness, battiness, screwiness, goofiness, kookiness, wackiness, dottiness, pottiness, *mishegas* <Yiddish>, looniness, lunchiness, balminess; bats in the belfry, a screw loose, one wheel in the sand, one sandwich short of a picnic; lame brains

3 psychosis, psychopathy, psychopathology, psychopathic condition; certifiability; **neurosis;** psychopathia sexualis, sexual pathology 75.18; pathological drunkenness *or* intoxication, dipsomania; pharmacopsychosis, drug addiction 87.1; moral insanity, psychopathic personality, *folie du doute* and *folie à deux* <Fr>, abulia 362.4

4 schizophrenia, dementia praecox, mental dissociation, dissociation of personality; catatonic schizophrenia, catatonia, residual schizophrenia, hebephrenia, hebephrenic schizophrenia; schizothymia; schizophasia; thought disorder; schizoid personality, split personality, schizotypal personality; **paranoia,** paraphrenia, paranoiac *or* paranoid psychosis; paranoid schizophrenia; schizoaffective disorder

5 depression, melancholia, depressive psychosis, dysthymia, barythymia, lypothymia, "moping, melancholy and moonstruck madness"—Milton; melancholia hypochrondriaca; involutional melancholia *or* psychosis; stuporous melancholia, melancholia attonita; flatuous melancholia; melancholia religiosa; postpartum depression; **manic-depressive disorder, manic-depression, bipolar disorder;** cyclothymia, poikilothymia, mood swings

6 rabies, hydrophobia, lyssa, canine madness; dumb *or* sullen rabies, paralytic rabies; furious rabies

7 frenzy, furor, fury, maniacal excitement, fever, **rage; seizure,** attack, acute episode, episode, **fit,** paroxysm, spasm, **convulsion; snit,** *crise* <Fr>; amok, murderous insanity *or* frenzy, homicidal mania, hemothymia; psychokinesia; furor epilepticus

8 delirium, deliriousness, brainstorm; calenture of the brain, afebrile delirium, lingual delirium, delirium mussitans; incoherence, wandering, raving, ranting; exhaustion delirium *or* infection, exhaustion psychosis

9 delirium tremens, mania *or* dementia a potu, delirium alcoholicum *or* ebriositatis

10 <nf terms> **the DT's,** the horrors, the shakes, the heebie-jeebies, the jimjams, the screaming meemies; blue Johnnies, blue devils, pink elephants, pink spiders, snakes, snakes in the boots

11 fanaticism, fanaticalness, **rabidness, overzealousness,** overenthusiasm, ultrazealousness, zealotry, zealotism, bigotry, perfervidness; extremism, extremeness, extravagance, excessiveness, overreaction; overreligiousness 692.3

12 mania <see lists>, **craze, infatuation, enthusiasm,** passion, fascination, crazy fancy, bug <nf>, rage, furor; manic psychosis; megalomania

13 obsession, prepossession, preoccupation, **hang-up** <nf>, **fixation,** tic, complex, fascination; hypercathexis; **compulsion,** morbid drive, obsessive compulsion, irresistible impulse; **monomania,** ruling passion, fixed idea, *idée fixe* <Fr>, one-track mind; **possession**

14 insane asylum, asylum, lunatic asylum, **madhouse,** mental institution, mental home, bedlam; **bughouse** *and* nuthouse *and* laughing academy *and* **loony bin** *and* **booby hatch** *and* funny farm <nf>; mental hospital, psychopathic hospital *or* ward, psychiatric hospital *or* ward; padded cell, rubber room

15 lunatic, madman, madwoman, dement, phrenetic *and* fanatic <old>, *fou* and *aliéné* <Fr>, non compos, *bacayaro* <Japanese>; bedlamite, Tom o' Bedlam; demoniac, energumen; mental case, **maniac,** raving lunatic; homicidal maniac, psychopathic killer, berserk *or* berserker; borderline case; mental defective, idiot 924.8; hypochondriac; melancholic, depressive; neurotic; headcase

16 <nf terms> **nut,** nutso, nutter, nutball, nutbar, nutcase, loon, loony, loony tune, headcase <Brit>, crazy, psycho, crackpot, screwball, weirdie, weirdo, kook, flake, crackbrain, *meshugana* <Yiddish>, fruitcake, schizo, wack, wacko, sickie, sicko, space cadet

17 psychotic, psycho <nf>, mental, mental case, certifiable case, **psychopath,** psychopathic case; psychopathic personality; paranoiac, paranoid; schizophrenic, schizophrene, schizoid; schiz *and* schizy *and* schizo <nf>; catatoniac; hebephreniac; manic-depressive; megalomaniac

18 fanatic, infatuate, **bug** <nf>, **nut** <nf>, **buff** *and* **fan** <nf>, freak <nf>, *fanatico* and *aficionado* <Sp>, devotee, **zealot, enthusiast,** energumen; monomaniac, crank <nf>; lunatic fringe

19 psychiatry, alienism, psychiatric care, psychotherapy; psychiatrist, alienist, psychotherapist

VERBS 20 be insane, be out of one's mind, not be in one's right mind, not be right in the head, **not be all there** <nf>, have a demon *or* devil; have bats in the belfry *and* have a screw loose, not have all one's buttons *or* marbles <nf>, not play with a full deck *and* not have both oars in the water <nf>; **wander, ramble; rave,** rage, **rant,** have a fit; dote, babble; drivel, drool, slobber, slaver; froth *or* foam at the mouth, run mad, run amok, go berserk

21 go mad, take leave of one's senses, lose one's mind *or* senses *or* reason *or* wits, **crack up,** go off one's head <nf>

22 <nf terms> **go crazy, go bats,** go cuckoo, go bughouse, go nuts, go nutso, go out of one's gourd *or* skull *or* tree, go off one's nut *or* rocker, go off the track *or* trolley, go off the deep end, blow one's top *or* stack, pop one's cork, flip one's lid *or* wig, wig out, go ape *or* apeshit, schiz out, go bananas, go crackers *and* go bonkers <Brit>, go bonzo, blow one's mind, freak out, flip out, go hog wild, go round the bend <Brit>, have a screw loose, have bats in one's belfry, have rocks in one's head, lose one's marbles

23 addle the wits, **affect one's mind, go to one's head**

24 madden, dement, **craze,** mad <old>, make mad, send mad, **unbalance,** unhinge, undermine one's reason, **derange,** distract, frenzy, shatter, **drive insane** *or* mad *or* **crazy,** put *or* send out of one's mind, overthrow one's mind *or* reason, drive up the wall <nf>

25 obsess, possess, beset, infatuate, **preoccupy,** be uppermost in one's thoughts, have a thing about <nf>; grip, hold, get a hold on, not let go; **fixate; drive,** compel, impel

ADJS 26 insane, unsane, **mad,** stark-mad, mad as a hatter, mad as a march hare, **stark-staring mad,** maddened, **sick,** crazed, **lunatic,** moonstruck, **daft, non compos mentis,** non compos, *baca* <Japanese>, **unsound,** of unsound mind, **demented, deranged,** deluded, disoriented, unhinged, **unbalanced,** unsettled, distraught, wandering, mazed, crackbrained, brainsick, sick *or* soft in the head, not right, not in one's right mind, **touched,** touched in the head, **out of one's mind,**

out of one's senses *or* wits, bereft of reason, reasonless, irrational, deprived of reason, senseless, witless; hallucinated; manic; queer, queer in the head, odd, strange, off, flighty <old>; abnormal 870.9, mentally deficient 921.22

27 <nf terms> **crazy, nutty,** daffy, dotty, dippy, crazy as a bedbug *or* coot *or* loon, loony, loony-tune, goofy, wacky, balmy *or* barmy, flaky, kooky, potty, batty, ape, apeshit, wiggy, lunchy, out to lunch, bonzo, bats, nuts, nutso, nutty as a fruitcake, fruity, fruitcakey, screwy, screwball, screwballs, crackers <Brit>, bananas, bonkers <Brit>, loopy, beany, buggy, bughouse, bugs, cuckoo, slaphappy, flipped, freaked-out, off-the-wall, gaga, haywire, off in the upper story, off one's nut *or* rocker, off the track *or* trolley, off the hinges, round the bend <Brit>, minus some buttons, nobody home, with bats in the belfry, just plain nuts, loco, mental <Brit>, psycho, cracked, not right in the head, tetched, off one's head, out of one's head, out of one's gourd *or* skull, out of one's tree, not all there, *meshuga* or *meshugga* <Yiddish>, not tightly wrapped, three bricks shy of a load, rowing with one oar in the water, up the wall, off the wall, schizzy, schizoid, schizo

28 **psychotic, psychopathic, psychoneurotic, mentally ill,** mentally sick, certifiable; sociopathic; traumatized, deluded, disturbed, neurotic; schizophrenic, schizoid, schiz *or* schizy <nf>; hypochondriacal; dissociated, disconnected; depressed, depressive; manic; manic-depressive; maniacal; paranoiac, **paranoid;** catatonic; brain-damaged, brain-injured

29 **possessed,** possessed with a demon *or* devil, **pixilated, bedeviled,** demonized, devil-ridden, demonic, demonical, demoniacal

30 **rabid, maniac** *or* **maniacal,** manic, raving mad, stark-raving mad, **frenzied, frantic,** frenetic; **mad,** madding, **wild, furious, violent;** desperate; hysterical, **beside oneself,** like one possessed, uncontrollable; **raving, raging,** ranting; frothing *or* foaming at the mouth; **amok, berserk,** running wild; maenadic, corybantic, bacchic, Dionysiac

31 **delirious,** out of one's head <nf>, off one's head <nf>, off, deluded; **giddy,** dizzy, lightheaded; hallucinating, **wandering, rambling, raving, ranting,** babbling, incoherent

32 **fanatic, fanatical, rabid; overzealous,** ultrazealous, **overenthusiastic,** zealotic, bigoted, perfervid; **extreme,** extremist, extravagant, inordinate; **unreasonable, irrational; wild-eyed,** wild-looking, haggard; overreligious

33 **obsessed, possessed,** prepossessed, infatuated, preoccupied, fixated, **hung up** <nf>, besotted, gripped, held; monomaniac *or* monomaniacal

34 **obsessive,** obsessional; **obsessing, possessing, preoccupying,** gripping, holding; driving, impelling, **compulsive, compelling**

ADVS 35 madly, insanely, crazily; deliriously; fanatically, rabidly, etc

36 **manias by subject**

<activity> ergasiomania
<acute mania> hypermania
<alcohol> alcoholomania
<alcoholic beverages> dipsomania
<animals> zoomania
<ablutomania> bathing
<Beatles> Beatlemania
<becoming larger> macromania
<becoming smaller> micromania
<bed rest> clinomania
<bees> apimania
<being in vehicles> amaxomania
<birds> ornithomania
<blushing> erythromania
<book theft> bibliokleptomania
<books> bibliomania
<bullets> ballistomania
<buying> oniomania
<cats> ailuromania
<China> Chinamania
<cliffs> cremnomania
<complaints> paramania
<counting> arithmomania
<crossing bridges> gephyromania
<crowds> demomania *or* ochlomania
<dancing> choreomania
<Dante> Dantomania
<death; the dead> necromania
<death> thanatomania
<deep melancholy> lypemania
<delirium tremens> tromomania
<demonic possession> cacodemonomania
<dogs> cynomania
<drinking water> hydrodipsomania
<drinking> potomania
<England> Anglomania
<erotica> eroticomania

<erotic literature> erotographomania
<falsities> pseudomania
<female lust> nymphomania
<fires> pyromania
<fish> ichthyomania
<flowers> anthomania
<food; eating> phagomania
<food> sitomania
<foreigners> xenomania
<foul speech> coprolalomania
<France> Francomania *or* Gallomania
<freedom> eleuthromania
<fur> doramania
<gaiety> cheromania
<genitals> edeomania
<Germany> Germanomania *or* Teutonomania
<God> theomania
<great wealth> cresomania *or* plutomania
<Greece> Grecomania
<grinding one's teeth> bruxomania
<hair> trichomania
<home> oikomania
<homesickness> philopatridomania
<horses> hippomania
<hypnosis> mesmeromania
<icons> iconomania
<idols> idolomania
<imagined disease> nosomania
<incurable insanity> acromania
<insects> entomomania
<Italy> Italomania
<lies; exaggerations> mythomania
<light> photomania
<lycanthropy> lycomania
<male lust> satyromania
<marriage> gamomania

<medicines>
  pharmacomania
<melancholia> tristimania
<men> andromania
<mice> musomania
<mild mania> hypomania
  or submania
<money> chrematomania
<moral insanity>
  pathomania
<movement> kinesomania
<murder> homicidomania
<music> melomania or
  musicomania
<nakedness>
  gymnomania
<narcotics> letheomania
<night> noctimania
<noise> phonomania
<novelty> kainomania
<nudity> nudomania
<nymphomania>
  hysteromania or
  oestromania or
  uteromania
<one's own wisdom>
  sophomania
<one's self> egomania
<one subject> monomania
<open spaces>
  agoramania
<opium> opiomania
<own importance>
  megalomania
<penis> mentulomania
<picking at growths>
  phaneromania
<pinching off one's hair>
  trichorrhexomania
<plants> florimania
<pleasing delusions>
  amenomania
<pleasure> hedonomania
<politics> politicomania
<pornography>
  pornographomania
<postage stamps>
  timbromania
<priests> hieromania
<public employment>
  empleomania
<railroad travel>
  siderodromomania
<religion> entheomania
<reptiles> ophidiomania
<return home>
  nostomania

<running away>
  drapetomania
<Russia> Russomania
<satyriasis> gynecomania
<sea> thalassomania
<second coming of
  Christ> parousiamania
<several subjects>
  oligomania
<sexual pleasure>
  aphrodisiomania or
  erotomania
<sin> hamartomania
<sitting> kathisomania
<sleep> hypnomania
<snow> chionomania
<solitude> automania
<speech> lalomania
<spending>
  squandermania
<stealing> kleptomania
<stillness> eremiomania
<suicide>
  autophonomania
<sun> heliomania
<surgery> tomomania
<symmetry>
  symmetromania
<talking> logomania
<testicles> orchidomania
<theater> theatromania
  phronemomania
<travel> hodomania
<traveling> dromomania
<tuberculosis>
  phthisiomania
<United States>
  Americamania
<wandering>
  ecdemiomania
<wanderlust> poriomania
<washing, bathing>
  ablutomania
<water> hydromania
<wine> enomania or
  oinomania
<woods> hylomania
<words> verbomania
<work> ergomania
<writing for publication>
  typomania
<writing verse>
  metromania
<writing> graphomania or
  scribblemania or
  scribomania

37 manias by name

ablutomania <washing,
  bathing>
acromania <incurable
  insanity>
agoramania <open
  spaces>
agromania <living alone>
agyiomania <streets>
ailuromania <cats>
alcoholomania <alcohol>
amaxomania <being in
  vehicles>
amenomania <pleasing
  delusions>
Americamania
  <United States>
andromania <men>
Anglomania <Eng>
anthomania <flowers>
aphrodisiomania or
  erotomania <sexual
  pleasure>
apimania <bees>
arithmomania <counting>
automania <solitude>
autophonomania
  <suicide>
ballistomania <bullets>
Beatlemania <the Beatles>
bibliomania <books>
bibliokleptomania <book
  theft>
bruxomania <grinding
  one's teeth>
cacodemonomania
  <demonic possession>
cheromania <gaiety>
Chinamania <Chin>
chionomania <snow>
choreomania <dancing>
chrematomania <money>
cleptomania <stealing>
clinomania <bed rest>
coprolalomania <foul
  speech>
cremnomania <cliffs>
cresomania <great
  wealth>
cynomania <dogs>
Dantomania <Dante>
demomania <crowds>
dipsomania <alcoholic
  beverages>
doramania <fur>
drapetomania <running
  away>

dromomania <traveling>
ecdemiomania
  <wandering>
edeomania <genitals>
egomania <one's self>
eleuthromania <freedom>
empleomania <public
  employment>
enomania <wine>
entheomania <religion>
entomomania <insects>
eremiomania <stillness>
ergasiomania <activity>
ergomania <work>
eroticomania <erotica>
erotographomania <erotic
  literature>
erotomania <sexual
  desire>
erythromania <blushing>
etheromania <ether>
ethnomania <ethnic or
  racial autonomy>
florimania <plants>
Francomania <Fr>
Gallomania <Fr>
gamomania <marriage>
gephyromania <crossing
  bridges>
glazomania
  <list making>
Germanomania <Ger>
Gorbymania <Mikhail S
  Gorbachev>
graphomania <writing>
Grecomania <Greece>
gymnomania <nakedness>
gynecomania <male lust>
hamartomania <sin>
hedonomania <pleasure>
heliomania <sun>
hieromania <priests>
hippomania <horses>
hodomania <travel>
homicidomania <murder>
hydrodipsomania
  <drinking water>
hydromania <water>
hylomania <woods>
hypermania <acute
  mania>
hypnomania <sleep>
hypomania <mild mania>
hysteromania <female
  lust>
ichthyomania <fish>

iconomania <icons>
idolomania <idols>
Italomania <Italy>
kainomania <novelty>
kathisomania <sitting>
kinesomania <movement>
kleptomania <stealing>
lalomania <speech>
letheomania <narcotics>
litigiomania <legal
 disputes>
logomania <talking>
lycomania
 <lycanthropy>
lypemania <deep
 melancholy>
macromania <becoming
 larger>
megalomania <self-
 importance>
melomania <music>
mentulomania <penis>
mesmeromania
 <hypnosis>
metromania <writing>
micromania <becoming
 smaller>
monomania <one idea or
 subject>
musicomania <music>
musomania <mice>
mythomania <lying,
 exaggerations>
necromania <death; the
 dead>
nesomania <islands>
noctimania <night>
nosomania <imagined
 disease>
nostomania
 <homesickness>
nudomania <nudity>
nymphomania <female
 lust>
ochlomania <crowds>
oestromania
 <female lust>
oikomania <home>
oinomania <wine>
oligomania <several
 subjects>
oniomania <buying>
onomatomania <words,
 names>
ophidiomania <reptiles>
orchidomania <testicles>
ornithomania <birds>

paramania <complaints>
parousiamania <second
 coming of Christ>
pathomania <moral
 insanity>
phagomania <food;
 eating>
phaneromania <growths
 on one's body>
pharmacomania
 <medicines>
philopatridomania
 <homesickness>
phonomania <noise>
photomania <light>
phronemomania
phthisiomania
 <tuberculosis>
plutomania <great
 wealth>
politicomania <politics>
poriomania <wanderlust>
pornographomania
 <pornography>
potomania <drinking;
 delirium tremens>
pseudomania <falsities>
pyromania <fire>
Russomania <Russ>
satyromania <male lust>
scribblemania <writing>
scribomania <writing>
siderodromomania
 <railroad travel>
sitomania <food>
sophomania <wisdom>
squandermania
 <spending>
submania <mild mania>
symmetromania
 <symmetry>
Teutonomania <Ger>
thalassomania <sea>
thanatomania <death>
theatromania <theater>
theomania <God>
timbromania <postage
 stamps>
tomomania <surgery>
trichomania <hair>
trichotillomania <pulling
 out one's hair>
tristimania <melancholia>
tromomania <delirium
 tremens>
Turkomania <Turk>

typomania <writing for
 publication>
uteromania <female lust>

verbomania <words>
xenomania <foreigners>
zoomania <animals>

927 ECCENTRICITY

NOUNS **1 eccentricity, idiosyncrasy,** idiocrasy,
erraticism, erraticness, queerness, oddity,
peculiarity, strangeness, singularity, freakishness,
freakiness, quirkiness, crotchetiness, dottiness,
crankiness, crankism, crackpotism; whimsy,
whimsicality; abnormality, anomaly,
unnaturalness, irregularity, deviation, deviancy,
differentness, divergence, aberration;
nonconformity, unconventionality 868.2

2 quirk, twist, kink, crank, quip, trick, mannerism,
crotchet, conceit, whim, maggot, maggot in the
brain, bee in one's bonnet or head <nf>

3 eccentric, erratic, character; odd person 870.4;
nonconformist 868.3, recluse 584.5

4 freak, character, crackpot, nut, screwball, weirdie,
weirdo, kook, queer potato, oddball, flake,
strange duck, odd fellow, crank, bird, goofus,
wack, wacko

ADJS **5 eccentric, erratic,** idiocratic, idiocratical,
idiosyncratic, idiosyncratical, **queer,** queer in the
head, **odd, peculiar,** strange, fey, singular,
anomalous, freakish, funny; unnatural, abnormal,
irregular, divergent, deviative, deviant, different,
exceptional; unconventional 868.6; **crotchety,**
quirky, dotty, maggoty <Brit>, cranky, crank,
crankish, whimsical, twisted; solitary, reclusive,
antisocial

6 <nf terms> **kooky, goofy,** birdy, funny, kinky,
loopy, goofus, haywire, squirrely, screwy, screwball,
nutty, wacky, flaky, oddball, wacko, lunch, out to
lunch, nobody home, weird

928 KNOWLEDGE

NOUNS **1 knowledge,** knowing, knowingness, ken;
command, reach; **acquaintance, familiarity,**
intimacy; private knowledge, privity; **information,**
data, database, datum, items, facts, factual base,
corpus; **certainty,** sure or certain knowledge 970;
protocol, protocol statement or sentence or
proposition; intelligence; practical knowledge,
experience, know-how, expertise, métier; technic,
technics, technique; self-knowledge; *ratio
cognoscendi* <L>

2 cognizance; cognition, noesis; **recognition,
realization; perception,** insight, apperception,
sudden insight, illumination, dawning, aha
reaction, flashing <nf>; **consciousness, awareness,**

mindfulness, note, notice; altered state of consciousness *or* ASC; **sense,** sensibility; appreciation, appreciativeness

3 **understanding, comprehension, apprehension,** intellection, prehension; conception, conceptualization, ideation; hipness *and* savvy <nf>; **grasp,** mental grasp, grip, **command,** mastery; precognition, familiarity, foreknowledge 961.3, clairvoyance 689.8; intelligence, wisdom 920; savoir-faire, *Aufklarung* <Ger>

4 **learning, enlightenment, education, schooling, instruction,** edification, illumination; acquirements, acquisitions, attainments, accomplishments, skills; sophistication; store of knowledge; liberal education; acquisition of knowledge 570

5 **scholarship, erudition,** eruditeness, **learnedness,** reading, letters; **intellectuality,** intellectualism; **literacy;** computer literacy, computeracy, numeracy; **culture, literary culture, high culture,** book learning, booklore; **bookishness,** bookiness, **pedantry,** pedantism, donnishness <Brit>; bluestockingism; bibliomania, book madness, bibliolatry, bibliophilism; classicism, classical scholarship, humanism, humanistic scholarship

6 **profound knowledge,** deep knowledge, total command *or* mastery; specialism, specialized *or* special knowledge; expertise, proficiency 413.1; wide *or* vast *or* extensive knowledge, generalism, general knowledge, interdisciplinary *or* cross-disciplinary knowledge; **encyclopedic knowledge,** polymathy, polyhistory, pansophy; **omniscience,** all-knowingness

7 slight knowledge 930.6

8 tree of knowledge, tree of knowledge of good and evil; forbidden fruit; bo *or* bodhi tree

9 **lore, body of knowledge,** corpus, body of learning, store of knowledge, system of knowledge, treasury of information; common knowledge; **canon;** literature, literature of the field, publications, materials; bibliography; encyclopedia, cyclopedia

10 **science,** -ology <see list>, **art, study, discipline; field,** field of inquiry, concern, province, domain, area, arena, sphere, branch *or* field of study, branch *or* department of knowledge, specialty, academic specialty, academic discipline; **technology, technics,** technicology, high technology, high-tech *or* hi-tech <nf>; social science, natural science; applied science, pure science, experimental science; Big Science

11 **scientist,** man of science; **technologist;** practical scientist, experimental scientist; boffin <Brit>; savant, **scholar** 929.3; authority, expert, maven <nf>; technocrat; intellectual; egghead <nf>

VERBS 12 **know, perceive, apprehend,** prehend, cognize, recognize, discern, see, make out; conceive, conceptualize; **realize, appreciate, understand, comprehend,** fathom; dig *and* savvy <nf>; wot *or* wot of <Brit nf>, ken <Scot>; have, possess, **grasp,** seize, have hold of; have knowledge of, be informed, be apprised of, command, master, have a good command of, have information about, be acquainted with, be conversant with, be cognizant of, be conscious *or* aware of; know something by heart *or* by rote *or* from memory

13 **know well, know full well,** know damn well *or* darn well <nf>, have a good *or* thorough knowledge of, be well-informed, be learned in, be proficient in, **be up on** <nf>, be master of, command, be thoroughly grounded in, retain, **have down pat** *or* **cold** <nf>, have it taped <Brit nf>, have at one's fingers' ends *or* fingertips, have in one's head, **know by heart** *or* rote, **know like a book,** know like the back of one's hand, **know backwards,** know backwards and forwards, **know inside out,** know down to the ground <nf>, **know one's stuff** *and* know one's onions <nf>, know a thing or two, know one's way around; be expert in; **know the ropes,** know all the ins and outs, know the score <nf>, know all the answers <nf>; know what's what

14 learn <acquire knowledge> 570.6,9–11; come to one's knowledge 551.15

ADJS 15 **knowing,** knowledgeable, informed; **cognizant, conscious, aware, mindful, sensible;** intelligent 920.12; **understanding, comprehending,** apprehensive, apprehending; **perceptive,** insightful, apperceptive, percipient, perspicacious, appercipient, prehensile; shrewd, sagacious, wise 920.17; omniscient, all-knowing

16 **cognizant of, aware of, conscious of, mindful of, sensible to** *or* **of, appreciative of,** appreciatory of, no stranger to, seized of <Brit>; privy to, in the secret, let into, in the know <nf>, behind the scenes *or* curtain; alive to, awake to; **wise to** <nf>, hep to *and* on to <nf>; streetwise, street-smart; apprised of, informed of; undeceived, undeluded

17 <nf terms> **hep, hip,** on the beam, go-go, **with it,** into, really into, groovy; chic, clued-up, clued in, in the know, trendy

18 **informed, enlightened, instructed,** versed, well-versed, educated, schooled, **taught;** posted, briefed, primed, trained; **up on,** up-to-date, abreast of, *au courant* <Fr>, *au fait* <Fr>, in the picture, wise to <nf>

19 **versed in, informed in,** read *or* well-read in, up on, strong in, at home in, master of, expert *or* authoritative in, proficient in, **familiar with,** at

home with, **conversant with, acquainted with,** intimate with

20 well-informed, well-posted, well-educated, **well-grounded, well-versed, well-read,** widely read

21 learned, erudite, educated, cultured, cultivated, lettered, literate, civilized, **scholarly,** scholastic, studious; wise 920.17; **profound,** deep, abstruse; **encyclopedic,** pansophic, polymath *or* polymathic, polyhistoric

22 book-learned, book-read, **literary,** book-taught, book-fed, book-wise, book-smart, **bookish,** booky, book-minded; book-loving, bibliophilic, bibliophagic; **pedantic,** donnish <Brit>, scholastic, inkhorn; **bluestocking**

23 intellectual, intellectualistic; **highbrow** *and* highbrowed *and* highbrowish <nf>; elitist

24 self-educated, self-taught, autodidactic

25 knowable, cognizable, recognizable, **understandable, comprehensible,** apprehendable, apprehensible, prehensible, graspable, seizable, discernible, conceivable, appreciable, perceptible, distinguishable, ascertainable, discoverable

26 known, recognized, ascertained, conceived, grasped, apprehended, prehended, seized, perceived, discerned, appreciated, **understood, comprehended,** realized; pat *and* **down pat** <nf>

27 well-known, well-understood, well-recognized, **widely known,** commonly known, universally recognized, generally *or* universally admitted; **familiar,** familiar as household words, household, **common, current; proverbial;** public, notorious; known by every schoolboy; talked-of, talked-about, in everyone's mouth, **on everyone's tongue** *or* **lips;** commonplace, trite 117.9, hackneyed, platitudinous, truistic

28 scientific; technical, technological, technicological; high-tech *or* hi-tech <nf>; **scholarly;** disciplinary

ADVS **29 knowingly, consciously, wittingly,** with forethought, understandingly, intelligently, studiously, learnedly, eruditely, as every schoolboy knows

30 to one's knowledge, **to the best of one's knowledge,** as far as one can see *or* tell, as far as one knows, as well as can be said

31 -ologies by name

abiology <inanimate things>
acarology <lice and ticks>
acrology <initial sounds or signs>
adenology <glands>
aesthology <sensory organs>
agrology <soil>
alethology <truth>
algology *or* phycology <algae, seaweeds>
ambrology <amber>
anatripsology <friction>
andrology <male diseases>
angiology <blood vessels>
anorganology <inorganic things>

anthropology <mankind>
apiology *or* melittology <bees>
arachnology *or* araneology <spiders>
archeology *or* archaeology <ancient or historical artifacts>
archology <government>
areology <Mars>
argyrology <money boxes>
aristology <dining>
arthrology <joints>
asthenology <diseases of debility>
astrolithology <meteorites>
astrology <stellar and planetary influence>
atmology <water vapor>
audiology <hearing disorders>
auxology <growth>
axiology <values, ethics>
azoology <inanimate things>
bacteriology <bacteria>
balneology <therapeutic baths>
barology <weight>
batology <brambles>
bibliology <books>
bioecology <biological interrelationships>
biology <life, living things>
biometeorology <organic-atmospheric interrelationships>
bromatology <food>
brontology <thunder>
bryology *or* muscology <mosses>
Buddhology <Buddha, Buddhahood>
caliology <bird nests>
campanology <bells; bell-ringing>
carcinology <crustaceans>
cardiology <heart>
carpology *or* pomology <fruits>
cartology <maps>
cephalology <the head>
cetology <whales, dolphins>
cholology *or* choledology <bile>

choreology <dance notation>
chorology <geographical boundaries>
chrondrology <cartilage>
chronology <dates, time>
climatology <climate>
coleopterology <beetles>
conchology <shells>
cosmology <universe>
craniology <skull>
criminology <criminal behavior>
crustaceology <crustaceans>
cryology <snow and ice>
cryptology <codes and ciphers>
curiology <picture writing>
cyesiology <pregnancy>
cytology <cells>
cytopathology <cell pathology>
dactylology <fingers>
deltiology <picture postcards>
demology <human activities>
dendrochronology <tree-ring dating>
dendrology <trees, shrubs>
deontology <ethics>
dermatology <skin>
desmology <ligaments>
diabiology <the devil, devils>
dipteriology <flies>
dittology <double interpretation>
docimology <metal assaying>
dolorology <pain>
dosiology <dosage>
dysteleology <purposelessness>
ecclesiology <churches; church history>
ecology <environment>
edaphology <soils>
Egyptology <ancient Egypt>
eidology <mental imagery>
electrology <electricity>
embryology <embryos>
endocrinology <endocrine glands>

enterology <internal organs>

entomology <insects>

epiphuytology <plant diseases>

epistemology <human knowledge>

eremology <deserts>

ergology <work and its effects>

eschatology <last things, esp final judgment>

ethnology <races and ethnic groups>

ethology <animal behavior>

etiology <causes, esp of disease>

etymology <derivation and history of words>

exobiology <life on other planets>

faunology <animal distribution>

fetology <fetus>

fluviology <watercourses, rivers>

garbology or garbageology <garbage, refuse>

gastrology <stomach>

gemology <gemstones>

geology <Earth's crust>

geomorphology <origin of geological features>

geratology <approaching extinction>

gerontology <old age>

glaciology <glaciers>

glossology <linguistics>

gnotobiology <germ-free biology>

grammatology <systems of writing>

graphology <handwriting>

gynecology <women's health>

hagiology <saints>

hamartiology <sin>

hedonology <pleasure>

helcology <ulcers>

heliology <Sun>

helminthology <worms, esp parasitic worms>

hematology <blood>

heortology <religious festivals>

hepatology <liver>

heresiology <heresies>

herpetology <reptiles>

hierology <sacred things>

hippology <horses>

hippopathology <diseases of the horse>

histology or histiology <tissues and organs>

historology <history>

horology <time, clocks>

hydrology <water>

hyetology <rainfall>

hygiology <health and hygiene>

hygrology <humidity>

hymenology <membranes>

hymenopterology <wasps, bees, ants>

hypnology <sleep; hypnotism>

hysterology <uterus>

iatrology <healing, medicine>

ichnolithology or ichnology <fossil footprints>

ichthyology or piscology <fish>

immunology <immunity to diseases>

irenology <peace>

journology <newspapers>

kalology <beauty>

kinesiology <bodily movement>

lalopathology <speech therapy>

laryngology <larynx>

lexicology <word forms and meanings>

lepidopterology <butterflies, moths>

limnology <lakes and ponds>

lithology or lithoidology <rock, stone>

loimology <infectious diseases>

malacology <mollusks>

malacostracology <crustaceology>

mantology <divination>

mastology <mammals>

meteorology <atmosphere and weather>

metrology <weights and measures>

microbiology <microorganisms>

micrology <tiny things>

microseismology <earthquake tremors>

morphology <form, shape>

muscology <mosses>

musicology <music>

mycology <fungi>

myology <muscles>

myrmecology <ants>

naology <church buildings>

nasology or rhinology <nose>

neonatology <newborns>

nephology <clouds>

nephrology <kidneys>

neurology <nervous system>

neuropathology <nervous system pathology>

neurypnology <hypnotism>

nomology <law>

noology <intuition>

nosology <classification of diseases>

nostology <old age, geriatrics>

numerology <numbers>

numismatology <coins>

odontology <the teeth>

oenology or enology <wine>

olfactology <smells>

ombrology <rain>

oncology <tumors>

oneirology <dreams>

onomasiology or onomatology <names, naming>

ontology <being, metaphysics>

oology <eggs, esp birds'>

ophiology <snakes>

ophthalmology <eyes>

organology <body organs>

orismology <terminology>

ornithology <birds>

orology or oreology <mountains>

oryctology <fossils>

osmology <odors>

osteology <bones>

otolaryngology <ear, nose, throat>

otology <ear>

paleobiology <fossil life>

paleoethnology <prehistoric mankind>

paleoichtyology <fossil fishes>

paleontology <early history of life>

paleoornithology <fossil birds>

paleopedology <early soils>

paleoetiology <explanation of past phenomena>

paleozoology or zoogeeology <fossil animals>

palynology <pollen, spores>

parapsychology <beyond psychology>

parasitology <parasites>

paroemiology <proverbs>

pathology <diseases>

pedology <soil science>

penology <punishment>

petrology or stromatology <rocks>

pharmacology <drugs>

phenology <natural cycles>

philology <languages>

phitology <political economy>

phlebology <blood vessels>

phonology <vocal sounds>

photology <light and optics>

phrenology <skull shape>

phycology <algae>

physicotheology <natural theology>

physiology <living body>

phytology <plants>

phytopathology <plant diseases>

phytophysiology <plant physiology>

phytoserology <plant viruses>

piscatology <fishing>

pistology <religious faith>

planetology <planets>

pleology <running water>

pneumatology <spirit>

pomology <fruits>

ponerology <evil>

posology <drug administration>

potamology <rivers>

proctology <anus, rectum>

promorphology <fundamental shapes and forms>

psephology <election statistics>

psychology <the mind>

psychonosology <mental diseases>

psychopathology <insanity>

psychophysiology <body and mind>

pteridology <ferns>

pterology <insect wings>

pterylology <feathers>

ptochology <pauperism, unemployment>

pyretology <fever>

pyrgology <towers>

pyrology <fire and heat>

radiology or Röntgenology <X-rays>

reflexology <reflexes and behavior>

rheology <flow and deformation of matter>

rhinology <nose>

roentgenology <medical X-rays>

runology <runes>

satanology <devil worship>

scatology <feces>

seismology <earthquakes>

selenology <the Moon>

semasiology <word meanings>

sematology or semeiology <symptoms>

semiology <signs, symbols>

serology <serums>

silphology <larval forms>

sinology <China>

siphonapterology <fleas>

sitology <diet, dietetics>

sociobiology <biology and behavior>

sociology <society>

somatology <organic bodies>

sophiology <ideas>

soteriology <salvation>

speciology <species>

spectrology <ghosts, phantoms>

speleology <caves>

spermatology <sperm>

sphygmoology <the pulse>

splanchnology <the viscera>

splenology <the spleen>

stereology <2-, 3- dimensional figures>

stoichiology <fundamental laws>

stomatology <mouth>

storiology <folklore>

suicidology <suicide>

symbology <symbols>

synchronology <comparative chronology>

synecology <plant, animal communities>

systematology <ordered arrangements>

taxology <scientific classification>

technology <mechanical and manufacturing arts>

tectology <structural morphology>

teleology <aims, determined ends>

teratology <tall tales; monsters>

terminology <system of names or terms>

thanatology <death>

thaumatology <miracles>

theology <divinity>

thermology or thermatology <heat>

therology <mammals>

thremmatology <plant or animal breeding>

threpsology <nutrition>

tidology <tides>

timbrology <stamps, stamp-collecting>

timology <values>

tocology <obstetrics>

tonology <tones, speech>

toxicology <poisons>

traumatology <wounds; shock>

tribology <friction; interacting surfaces>

trichology <hair>

typhology <blindness>

ufology <UFOs>

uranology <astronomy>

urbanology <cities>

urology <urogenital organs and diseases>

venereology <veneral disease>

vermiology <worms>

vexillology <flags>

victimology <victims>

virology <viruses>

vvulcanology <volcanoes>

xyloology <the structure of wood>

zoology <animal life>

zoonosology <animal diseases>

zoophysiology <animal physiology>

zymology or zymotechnology <fermentation>

32 -ologies by subject

<aims, determined ends> teleology

<ancient or historical artifacts> archeology

<animal behavior> ethology

<animal diseases> zoonosology

<animal distribution> faunology

<animal life> zoology

<animal physiology> zoophysiology

<ants> myrmecology

<anus, rectum> proctology

<astronomy> uranology

<atmosphere and weather> meteorology

<beauty> kalology

<bees> apiology or melittology

<beetles> coleopterology

<being, metaphysics> ontology

<bells; bell-ringing> campanology

<bile> chology or choledology

<biological interrelationships> bioecology

<bird nests> caliology

<birds> ornithology

<blindness> typhology

<blood vessels> angiology or phlebology

<blood> hematology

<body and mind> psychophysiology

<body organs> organology

<bones> osteology

<books> bibliology

<cartilage> chrondrology

<causes of disease> etiology

<caves> speleology

<cell pathology> cytopathology

<cells> cytology

<China> sinology

<church buildings> naology

<churches; church history> ecclesiology

<cities> urbanology

<classification of diseases> nosology

<clouds> nephology

<codes and ciphers> cryptology

<coins> numismatology

<comparative chronology> synchronology

<crustaceans> carcinology or crustaceology

<crustaceology> malacostracology

<dance notation> choreology

<dates, dating> chronology

<death> thanatology

<derivation and history of words> etymology

<deserts> eremology

<devil worship> satanology

<didactic literature> gnomology

<diet> sitology

<dining> aristology

<diseases of debility> asthenology

<diseases> pathology

<divination> mantology

<divinity> theology

<dosage> dosiology or dosology or posology

<double interpretation> dittology

<dreams> oneirology

<drugs> pharmacology

<ear> otology

<early history of life> paleontology

<early soils> paleopedology

<Earth's crust> geology

<earthquake tremors> microseismology

<earthquakes> seismology
<eggs> oology
<election statistics> psephology
<electricity> electrology
<embryos> embryology
<endocrine glands> endocrinology
<environment> ecology or environmentology
<evil> ponerology
<explanation of past phenomena> paleoetiology
<extinction> geratology
<eyes> ophthalmology
<feathers> pterylology
<female health and disease> gynecology
<fermentation> zymology or zymotechnology
<ferns> pteridology
<fetus> fetology
<fever> pyretology
<fingers> dactylology
<fire and heat> pyrology
<fish> ichthyology or piscology
<fishing> piscatology
<flags> vexillology
<fleas> siphonapterology
<flies> dipteriology
<flow and deformation of matter> rheology
<folklore> storiology
<food> bromatology
<form, shape> morphology
<fossil animals> paleozoology or zoogeolology
<fossil birds> paleoornithology
<fossil excrement> scatology
<fossil fishes> paleoichtyology
<fossil footprints> ichnolithology or ichnology
<fossil life> paleobiology
<fossils> oryctology
<friction> anatripsology
<fruits> carpology or pomology
<fundamental laws> stoichiology
<fundamental shapes and forms> promorphology

<fungi> mycology
<garbage, refuse> garbology or garbageology
<geographical boundaries> chorology
<germ-free biology> gnotobiology
<glands> adenology
<government> archology
<growth> auxology
<hair> trichology
graphology
<head> cephalology
<healing, medicine> iatrology
<health and hygiene> hygiology
<hearing disorders> audiology
<heart> cardiology
<heat> thermology or thermatology
<heresies> heresiology
<history> historology
<horses> hippology
<human activities> demology
<human knowledge> epistemology
<humidity> hygrology
<hypnotism> neurypnology
<ideas> sophiology
<immunity to diseases> immunology
<inanimate things> abiology or azoology
<infectious diseases> loimology
<initial sounds or signs> acrology
<inorganic things> anorganology
<insanity> psychopathology
<insect wings> pterology
<insects> entomology
<interacting surfaces> tribology
<internal organs> enterology
<intuition> noology
<joints> arthrology
<lakes and ponds> limnology
<language meaning> semasiology
<languages> philology

<larval forms> silphology
<larynx> laryngology
<last things, esp final judgment> eschatology
<law> nomology
<lice and ticks> acarology
<life on other planets> exobiology
<life, living things> biology
<ligaments> desmology
<light and optics> photology
<linguistics> glossology
<liver> hepatology
<living body> physiology
<male diseases> andrology
<mammals> mastology or therology
<mankind> anthropology
<maps> cartology
<Mars> areology
<mechanical and manufacturing arts> technology
<membranes> hymenology
<mental diseases> psychonosology
<mental imagery> eidology
<metal assaying> docimology
<meteorites> astrolithology
<microorganisms> microbiology
<miracles> thaumatology
<mollusks> mallacology
<monsters> teratology
<moral obligation> deontology
<mosses> bryology or muscology
<mountains> orology or oreology
<mouth diseases> stomatology
<muscles> myology
<names, naming> onomasiology or onomatology
<natural cycles> phenology
<natural theology> physicotheology
<nervous system> neurology

<newspapers> journology
<nose> nasology or rhinology
<nutrition> threpsology
<obstetrics> tocology
<odors> osmology
<old age, geriatrics> nostology
<old age> gerontology
<ordered arrangements> systematology
<organic bodies> somatology
<organic-atmospheric interrelationships> biometeorology
<pain> dolorology
<pathology of the nervous system> neuropathology
<peace> irenology
<physiology of the nervous system> neurophysology
<picture postcards> deltiology
<picture writing> curiology
<plant diseases> epiphuytology or phytopathology
<plant or animal breeding> thremmatology
<plant physiology> phytophysiology
<plant viruses> phytoserology
<plants> phytology
<poisons> toxicology
<political economy> phitology
<pollen> palynology
<pregnancy> cyesiology
<prehistoric mankind> paleoethnology
<proverbs> paroemiology
<punishment of crime> penology
<purposelessness> dysteleology
<races and peoples> ethnology
<rain> ombrology
<rainfall> hyetology
<religious faith> pistology
<religious festivals> heortology
<reptiles> herpetology
<rivers> potamology
<rock, stone> lithology or lithoidology

<rocks> petrology or stromatology
<runes> runology
<running water> pleology
<sacred things> hierology
<saints> hagiology
<salvation> soteriology
<scientific classification> taxology
<seaweeds> algology or phycology
<sensory organs> aesthology
<serums> serology
<shells> conchology
<sin> hamartiology
<skin> dermatology
<skull shape> phrenology
<skull> craniology
<sleep> hypnology
<smells> olfactology
<snakes> ophiology
<society> sociology
<soils> edaphology or pedology
<species> speciology
<spectroscopic analysis> spectrology
<sperm> spermatology
<spiders> arachnology or araneology
<spirit> pneumatology
<spleen> splenology
<stamps, stamp-collecting> timbrology
<stellar and planetary influence> astrology
<stomach> gastrology
<structural morphology> tectology
<structure of wood> xyloology
<suicide> suicidology
<Sun> heliology
<symptoms> sematology or semeiology
<system of names or terms> terminology
<teeth> odontology
<terminology> orismology
<the devil, devils> diabiology

<the mind> psychology
<the Moon> selenology
<the pulse> sphygmoology
<therapeutic agents> acology
<therapeutic baths> balneology
<thunder> brontology
<tides> tidology
<time, clocks> horology
<tiny things> micrology
<tissues and organs> histology or histiology
<towers> pyrgology
<tree-ring dating> dendrochronology
<trees> dendrology
<truth> alethology
<tumors> oncology
<ulcers> helcology
<universe> cosmology
<urogenital organs and diseases> urology
<uterus> hysterology
<values> timology
<victims> victimology
<viscera> splanchnology
<vocal sounds> phonology
<volcanoes> vulcanology
<wasps, bees, ants> hymenopterology
<water vapor> atmology
<water> hydrology
<weight> barology
<weights and measures> metrology
<whales and dolphins> cetology
<wine> oenology or enology
<words and meanings> lexicology
<work and its effects> ergology
<worms, esp parasitic worms> helminthology
<worms> vermiology
<wounds, shock> traumatology
<X-rays> radiology or Röentgenology

929 INTELLECTUAL

NOUNS **1 intellectual, intellect,** intellectualist, literate, member of the intelligentsia, white-collar intellectual; "someone whose mind watches itself"—Camus; brainworker, thinker; brain *and* rocket scientist *and* brain surgeon <nf>; **pundit,**

Brahmin, **mandarin,** egghead *and* pointy-head <nf>; **highbrow** <nf>; wise man 921

2 intelligentsia, literati, illuminati; intellectual elite; clerisy

3 scholar, scholastic <old>, clerk *or* learned clerk <old>; a gentleman and a scholar; student 572; **learned person,** man of learning, giant of learning, colossus of knowledge, mastermind, **savant,** pundit; genius 413.12; polymath, polyhistor *or* polyhistorian, **mine of information,** walking encyclopedia; literary man, *littérateur* <Fr> *or* litterateur, **man of letters;** philologist, philologue; philomath, lover of learning; philosopher, philosophe; bookman, **academician,** academic, schoolman; classicist, classicalist, Latinist, humanist; Renaissance man *or* woman

4 bookworm, bibliophage; **grind** *and* greasy grind <nf>; **booklover, bibliophile,** bibliophilist, philobiblist, bibliolater, bibliolatrist; bibliomaniac, bibliomane

5 pedant; formalist, precisionist, precisian, purist, *précieux* <Fr>, **bluestocking,** *bas bleu* <Fr>, *précieuse* <Fr fem>; Dr Pangloss <Voltaire>, Dryasdust <Rev Dr Carlyle>

6 dilettante, half scholar, sciolist, **dabbler,** dabster, amateur, trifler, smatterer; grammaticaster, philologaster, criticaster, philosophaster, Latinitaster

930 IGNORANCE

NOUNS **1 ignorance,** ignorantness, **unknowingness,** unknowing, nescience; lack of information, knowledge-gap, hiatus of learning; empty-headedness, blankmindedness, vacuousness, vacuity, inanity; tabula rasa; **unintelligence** 922; **unacquaintance, unfamiliarity; greenness,** greenhornism, rawness, callowness, unripeness, green in the eye, **inexperience** 414.2; innocence, ingenuousness, simpleness, simplicity; crass *or* gross *or* primal *or* pristine ignorance; ignorantism, know-nothingism, obscurantism; agnosticism

2 "the mother of prejudice"—John Bright, "the dominion of absurdity"—J A Froude

3 incognizance, unawareness, unconsciousness, insensibility, unwittingness, nonrecognition; deniability; nonrealization, incomprehension; **unmindfulness;** mindlessness; blindness 30, deafness 49

4 unenlightenment, benightedness, benightment, dark, darkness; savagery, barbarism, paganism, heathenism, Gothicism; age of ignorance, dark age; rural idiocy

5 unlearnedness, inerudition, ineducation, unschooledness, unletteredness; **unscholarliness,**

unstudiousness; **illiteracy,** illiterateness, functional illiteracy, semiliteracy; **unintellectuality,** unintellectualism, Philistinism, bold ignorance

6 **slight knowledge,** vague notion, imperfect knowledge, a little learning, glimmering, glimpse <old>, smattering, **smattering of knowledge,** smattering of ignorance, **half-learning,** semi-learning, semi-ignorance, sciolism; **superficiality,** shallowness, surface-scratching; **dilettantism,** dilettantship, amateurism

7 **the unknown,** the unknowable, the strange, the unfamiliar, the incalculable; **matter of ignorance,** sealed book, riddle, enigma, mystery, puzzle 971.3; *terra incognita* <L>, unexplored ground *or* territory; frontier, frontiers of knowledge, **unknown quantity,** x, y, z, n; dark horse; guesswork, anybody's guess; complete blank; closed *or* sealed book; all Greek <nf>

8 **ignoramus, know-nothing;** no scholar, puddinghead, dunce, fool 924; simpleton; **illiterate;** aliterate; **lowbrow** <nf>; unintelligentsia, illiterati; **greenhorn,** greeny <nf>, beginner, tenderfoot, neophyte, novice, duffer <nf>; **dilettante,** dabbler 929.6; layperson; **middlebrow** <nf>

VERBS 9 **be ignorant,** be green, have everything to learn, **know nothing,** know from nothing <nf>; wallow in ignorance; not know any better; **not know what's what,** not know what it is all about, not know the score <nf>, not be with it <nf>, not know any of the answers; not know the time of day *or* what o'clock it is, not know beans, not know the first thing about, not know one's ass from one's elbow <nf>, not know the way home, not know enough to come in out of the rain, not know chalk from cheese, **not know up from down,** not know which way is up

10 **be in the dark,** be blind, labor in darkness, walk in darkness, be benighted, grope in the dark, have nothing to go on, have a lot to learn

11 **not know,** not rightly know <nf>, know not, know not what, know nothing of, wot not of <Brit nf>, be innocent of, have no idea *or* notion *or* conception, **not have the first idea, not have the least** *or* **remotest idea,** be clueless *and* not have a clue <nf> not have idea one, not have the foggiest <nf>, **not pretend to say,** not take upon oneself to say; be stumped; not know the half of it; not know from Adam, not know from the man in the moon; wonder, wonder whether; half-know, have a little learning, scratch the surface, know a little, smatter, dabble, toy with, coquet with; pass, give up

ADJS 12 **ignorant,** nescient, **unknowing,** uncomprehending, **know-nothing;** simple, **dumb** <nf>, empty, empty-headed, blank, blankminded, vacuous, inane, **unintelligent** 922.13; **ill-informed, uninformed, unenlightened,** unilluminated, unapprized, unposted <nf>, clueless <nf>, pig-ignorant <Brit nf>; **unacquainted, unconversant,** unversed, uninitiated, **unfamiliar,** strange to; **inexperienced** 414.17; **green,** callow, innocent, ingenuous, gauche, awkward, naive, unripe, raw; groping, tentative, unsure

13 **unaware, unconscious, insensible, unknowing, incognizant;** mindless, witless; unprehensive, unrealizing, nonconceiving, **unmindful,** unwitting, unsuspecting; unperceiving, impercipient, unhearing, unseeing, uninsightful; unaware of, in ignorance of, unconscious of, unmindful of, insensible to, out of it <nf>, not with it <nf>; **blind to, deaf to,** dead to, a stranger to; asleep, napping, **off one's guard,** caught napping, caught tripping

14 **unlearned, inerudite,** unerudite, **uneducated,** unschooled, uninstructed, untutored, unbriefed, untaught, unedified, unguided; ill-educated, misinstructed, misinformed, mistaught, led astray; hoodwinked, deceived; **illiterate,** functionally illiterate, unlettered, grammarless; **unscholarly,** unscholastic, unstudious; **unliterary, unread,** unbookish, unbook-learned, bookless <old>, unbooked; **uncultured,** uncultivated, unrefined, rude, Philistine; barbarous, pagan, heathen; Gothic; nonintellectual, **unintellectual; lowbrow** *and* lowbrowed *and* lowbrowish <nf>

15 **half-learned,** half-baked <nf>, half-cocked *and* half-assed <nf>, sciolistic; semiskilled; **shallow, superficial;** immature, sophomoric, sophomorical; **dilettante,** dilettantish, smattering, dabbling, amateur, amateurish, inexperienced; **wise in one's own conceit**

16 **benighted, dark,** in darkness, in the dark

17 **unknown,** unbeknown <nf>, unheard <old>, **unheard-of,** unapprehended, unapparent, unperceived, unsuspected; unexplained, unascertained; uninvestigated, unexplored; unidentified, unclassified, uncharted, unfathomed, unplumbed, virgin, untouched; undisclosed, unrevealed, undivulged, undiscovered, unexposed, sealed; **unfamiliar,** strange; incalculable, **unknowable,** incognizable, undiscoverable; enigmatic 522.17, mysterious, puzzling

ADVS 18 **ignorantly, unknowingly,** unmindfully, unwittingly, witlessly, unsuspectingly, **unawares;** unconsciously, insensibly; for anything *or* aught one knows, not that one knows

INTERJS 19 **God knows!,** God only knows!, Lord knows!, Heaven knows!, nobody knows!, damned if I know!, search me!, **beats me!,** beats the hell *or* heck *or* shit out of me!, your guess is as good as mine!, it has me guessing!, it's Greek to me!; **search me!,** you've got me!, I give up!, I pass!, **who knows?,** how should I know?, I don't know what!

931 THOUGHT
<exercise of the intellect>

NOUNS **1 thought, thinking, cogitation,** cerebration, ideation, noesis, mentation, intellection, intellectualization, ratiocination; using one's head *or* noodle <nf>; workings of the mind; **reasoning** 935; **brainwork, headwork,** mental labor *or* effort, mental act *or* process, act of thought, mental *or* intellectual exercise; deep-think <nf>; **way of thinking,** logic, habit of thought *or* mind, thought-pattern; heavy thinking, straight thinking; conception, conceit <old>, conceptualization; abstract thought, imageless thought; excogitation, thinking out *or* through; thinking aloud; **idea** 932; creative thought 985.2

2 consideration, contemplation, reflection, speculation, meditation, musing, rumination, deliberation, lucubration, brooding, study, **pondering,** weighing, revolving, turning over in the mind, looking at from all angles, noodling *or* noodling around <nf>; lateral thought *or* thinking; advisement, counsel

3 thoughtfulness, contemplativeness, speculativeness, reflectiveness; **pensiveness,** wistfulness, reverie, musing, melancholy; **preoccupation, absorption, engrossment,** abstraction, brown study, intense *or* deep *or* profound thought; **concentration,** study, close study; deep thinking

4 thoughts, burden of one's mind, mind's content; inmost *or* innermost thoughts *or* mind, secret thoughts, mind's core, one's heart of hearts; **train of thought,** current *or* flow of thought *or* ideas, succession *or* sequence *or* chain of thought *or* ideas; **stream of consciousness; association,** association of ideas

5 mature thought, developed thought, ripe idea; **afterthought,** *arrière-pensée* <Fr>, *esprit d'escalier* <Fr>, second thought *or* thoughts; **reconsideration,** reappraisal, revaluation, rethinking, re-examination, review, thinking over

6 introspection, self-communion, self-counsel, self-consultation, subjective inspection *or* speculation, head trip <nf>

7 subject for thought, food for thought, something to chew on, something to get one's teeth into

VERBS **8 think, cogitate,** cerebrate, put on one's thinking *or* considering cap <nf>, intellectualize, ideate, conceive, conceptualize, form ideas,

entertain ideas; **reason** 935.15; **use one's head** *or* brain, use one's noodle *or* noggin <nf>, use *or* exercise the mind, set the brain *or* wits to work, bethink oneself, have something on one's mind, have a lot on one's mind

9 think hard, think one's head off, **rack** *or* **ransack one's brains,** crack one's brains <nf>, **beat** *or* **cudgel one's brains,** work one's head to the bone, do some heavy thinking, bend *or* apply the mind, knit one's brow; sweat *or* stew over <nf>, hammer *or* hammer away at; puzzle, **puzzle over**

10 concentrate, concentrate the mind *or* thoughts, concentrate on *or* upon, attend closely to, brood on, **focus on** *or* **upon,** give *or* devote the mind to, glue the mind to, cleave to the thought of, fix the mind *or* thoughts upon, bend the mind upon, bring the mind to bear upon; get to the point; gather *or* collect one's thoughts, pull one's wits together, focus *or* fix one's thoughts, marshal *or* arrange one's thoughts *or* ideas

11 think about, cogitate, **give** *or* **apply the mind to,** put one's mind to, apply oneself to, bend *or* turn the mind *or* thoughts to, direct the mind upon, **give thought to, trouble one's head about,** occupy the mind *or* thoughts with; think through *or* out, puzzle out, sort out, reason out, excogitate, ratiocinate, work out, take stock of

12 consider, contemplate, speculate, reflect, wonder, study, ponder, perpend, **weigh, deliberate, debate, meditate, muse, brood, ruminate,** chew the cud <nf>, digest; introspect, be abstracted; wrinkle one's brow; fall into a brown study, retreat into one's mind *or* thoughts; **toy with, play with,** play around with, flirt *or* coquet with the idea

13 think over, ponder over, brood over, muse over, mull over, reflect over, con over, **deliberate over,** run over, **meditate over,** ruminate over, chew over, digest, turn over, **revolve,** revolve *or* turn over in the mind, deliberate upon, meditate upon, muse on *or* upon, bestow thought *or* consideration upon, noodle *or* noodle around <nf>

14 take under consideration, entertain, take under advisement, take under active consideration, inquire into, **think it over,** have a look at *and* see about <nf>; **sleep upon,** consult with *or* advise with *or* take counsel of one's pillow

15 reconsider, re-examine, review; revise one's thoughts, reappraise, revaluate, rethink; view in a new light, have second thoughts, think better of

16 think of, bethink oneself of, seize on, flash on <nf>; tumble to <nf>; **entertain the idea of,** entertain thoughts of; conceive of; have an idea of, have thoughts about; **have in mind, contemplate, consider, have under consideration;** take it into one's head; **bear in mind, keep in mind,** hold the thought; harbor an idea, keep *or* hold an idea, cherish *or* foster *or* nurse *or* nurture an idea; ideate, premise, theorize, invent

17 <look upon mentally> **contemplate, look upon, view, regard,** see, view with the mind's eye, **envisage,** envision, **visualize** 986.15, imagine, image

18 **occur to,** occur to one's mind, occur, **come to mind,** rise to mind, rise in the mind, come into one's head, impinge on one's consciousness, claim one's mind *or* thoughts, pass through one's head *or* mind, dawn upon one, **enter one's mind,** pass in the mind *or* thoughts, cross one's mind, race *or* tumble through the mind, flash on *or* across the mind; **strike,** strike one, strike the mind, grab one <nf>, **suggest itself,** present itself, offer itself, present itself to the mind *or* thoughts, give one pause

19 **impress, make an impression, strike, grab** <nf>, hit; catch the thoughts, arrest the thoughts, seize one's mind, sink *or* penetrate into the mind, embed itself in the mind, lodge in the mind, **sink in** <nf>

20 **occupy the mind** *or* **thoughts,** engage the thoughts, monopolize the thoughts, fasten itself on the mind, seize the mind, fill the mind, take up one's thoughts; **preoccupy,** occupy, **absorb, engross,** absorb *or* enwrap *or* engross the thoughts, obsess the mind, run in the head; foster in the mind; come uppermost, be uppermost in the mind; have in *or* on one's mind, **have on the brain** <nf>, have constantly in one's thoughts

ADJS 21 **cognitive,** prehensive, **thought,** conceptive, conceptual, conceptualized, ideative, ideational, noetic, **mental,** cerebral; **rational** 935.18, logical, ratiocinative; **thoughtful,** cogitative, **contemplative, reflective, speculative, deliberative, meditative, ruminative,** ruminant, in a brown study, museful <old>; **pensive,** wistful, musing; introspective; thinking, reflecting, contemplating, pondering, deliberating, excogitating, excogitative, meditating, ruminating, musing; reasoned, cogitative; studious, studying; sober, serious, deepthinking; concentrating, concentrative, concentrated, attentive

22 absorbed *or* engrossed in thought, **absorbed, engrossed,** introspective, rapt, **wrapped in thought, lost in thought,** pensive, abstracted, immersed in thought, buried in thought, engaged in thought, occupied, **preoccupied**

ADVS 23 **thoughtfully,** contemplatively, reflectively, meditatively, ruminatively, musefully <old>, cogitatively, introspectively; **pensively,** wistfully; on reconsideration, on second thought

24 **on one's mind, on the brain** *and* on one's chest

<nf>, in the thoughts; in the heart, *in petto* <Ital>, in one's inmost *or* innermost thoughts

932 IDEA

NOUNS 1 **idea; thought,** mental *or* intellectual object, **notion, concept,** conception, conceit, fancy; **perception, sense, impression,** mental impression, image, **mental image,** picture in the mind, mental picture, representation, recept, visualization; imago, ideatum, noumenon, essence; memory trace; **sentiment,** apprehension; reflection, observation; **opinion** 952.6; viewpoint, point of view; supposition, **theory** 951; plan, scheme

2 <philosophy> ideatum, ideate; noumenon; universal, universal concept *or* conception; idée-force; Platonic idea *or* form, archetype, prototype, subsistent form, eternal object, transcendent universal, eternal universal, pattern, model, exemplar, ideal, transcendent idea *or* essence, universal essence, innate idea; Aristotelian form, form-giving cause, formal cause; complex idea, simple idea; percept; construct of memory and association; Kantian idea, supreme principle of pure reason, regulative first principle, highest unitary principle of thought, transcendent nonempirical concept; Hegelian idea, highest category, the Absolute, the Absolute Idea, the Self-determined, the realized ideal; logical form *or* category; noosphere <Teilhard de Chardin>; history of ideas, *Geistesgeschichte* <Ger>; **idealism** 1053.3

3 **abstract idea, abstraction,** general idea, generality, abstract

4 **main idea,** intellectual *or* philosophical basis, leading *or* principal idea, fundamental *or* basic idea, *idée-maitresse* <Fr>, guiding principle, crowning principle, **big idea** <nf>, precept, premise

5 **novel idea,** intellectual *or* conceptual breakthrough, new *or* **latest wrinkle** <nf>, new slant *or* twist *or* take <nf>

6 **good idea, great idea,** not a bad idea; **bright thought,** bright *or* brilliant idea, **insight; brainchild** *and* **brainstorm** <nf>, brain wave <nf>, **inspiration;** quantum leap

7 **absurd idea,** crazy idea, fool notion *and* brainstorm <nf>

8 **ideology,** system of ideas, body of ideas, system of theories; world view, *Weltanschauung* <Ger>; philosophy; **ethos**

ADJS 9 ideational, ideal, **conceptual, conceptive,** notional, fanciful, imaginative; **intellectual;** theoretical 950.13; **ideological**

10 ideaed, notioned, thoughted

933 ABSENCE OF THOUGHT

NOUNS **1 thoughtlessness,** thoughtfreeness; **vacuity, vacancy, emptiness of mind, empty-headedness,** blankness, mental blankness, blankmindedness; fatuity, inanity, foolishness 923; tranquillity, calm of mind; **nirvana,** ataraxia, calm *or* tranquillity of mind; **oblivion,** forgetfulness, lack *or* loss of memory, amnesia; mental block; quietism, passivity, apathy; blank mind, fallow mind, tabula rasa; unintelligence 922; ignorance; head in the clouds

VERBS **2 not think, make the mind a blank,** let the mind lie fallow; **not think of,** not consider, be unmindful of; **not enter one's mind** *or* **head,** be far from one's mind *or* head *or* thoughts; pay no attention *or* mind

3 get it off one's mind, get it off one's chest <nf>, clear the mind, relieve one's mind; **put it out of one's thoughts,** dismiss from the mind *or* thoughts, push from one's thoughts, put away thought

ADJS **4 thoughtless, thoughtfree,** incogitant, **unthinking,** unreasoning; unideaed; unintellectual; **vacuous,** vacant, blank, blankminded, relaxed, empty, **empty-headed,** fallow, fatuous, inane 922.19; unoccupied; calm, tranquil; nirvanic; oblivious, ignorant; quietistic, passive

5 unthought-of, undreamed-of, unconsidered, unconceived, unconceptualized; unimagined, unimaged; imageless

934 INTUITION, INSTINCT

NOUNS **1 intuition, intuitiveness, sixth sense;** intuitive reason *or* knowledge, direct perception *or* apprehension, immediate apprehension *or* perception, unmediated perception *or* apprehension, subconscious perception, unconscious *or* subconscious knowledge, immediate cognition, knowledge without thought *or* reason, flash of insight; intuitive understanding, tact, spontaneous sense; **revelation,** epiphany, moment of illumination; **insight,** inspiration, aperçu; precognition, anticipation, a priori knowledge; *satori* <Japanese>, *buddhi* <Skt>; woman's intuition; second sight, second-sightedness, precognition 961.3, clairvoyance 689.8, extrasensory perception, presentiment; intuitionism, intuitivism

2 instinct, natural instinct, unlearned capacity, innate *or* inborn proclivity, native *or* natural tendency, **impulse,** blind *or* unreasoning impulse, vital impulse; **libido, id,** primitive self; archetype, archetypal pattern *or* idea; unconscious *or* subconscious urge *or* drive; collective unconscious, race memory; "the *not ourselves,* which is in us

and all around us"—Matthew Arnold, "an unfathomable Somewhat, which is *Not we*"—Carlyle, "that which is imprinted upon the spirit of man by an inward instinct"—Francis Bacon; **reflex,** spontaneous reaction, unthinking response, knee-jerk, Pavlovian response, gut reaction <nf>

3 hunch <nf>, sense, **presentiment, premonition,** preapprehension, intimation, foreboding; suspicion, **impression,** intuition, intuitive impression, **feeling,** forefeeling, vague feeling *or* idea, funny feeling <nf>, feeling in one's bones, gut feeling <nf>, flash

VERBS **4 intuit, sense, feel,** feel intuitively, **feel** *or* **know in one's bones** <nf>, **have a feeling,** have a funny feeling <nf>, **get** *or* **have the impression,** have a hunch <nf>, just know, know instinctively; grok <nf>; perceive, divine

ADJS **5 intuitive,** intuitional, sensing, sensitive, perceptive, feeling; second-sighted, precognitive 961.7, telepathic, clairvoyant

6 instinctive, natural, **inherent, innate,** unlearned; unconscious, subliminal; **involuntary, automatic,** spontaneous, impulsive, reflex, knee-jerk <nf>; **instinctual,** libidinal

ADVS **7 intuitively,** by intuition; **instinctively,** automatically, spontaneously, on *or* by instinct, **instinctually**

935 REASONING

NOUNS **1 reasoning, reason,** logical thought, discursive reason, rationalizing, rationalization, ratiocination; the divine faculty, "a harmony among irrational impulses"—Santayana; **rationalism, rationality,** discourse *or* discourse of reason <old>; sweet reason, reasonableness; demonstration, proof 957; specious reasoning, sophistry 936; philosophy 952

2 logic, logics; **dialectics,** dialectic, dialecticism; art of reason, science of discursive thought, "the art of making truth prevail"—La Bruyère; formal logic, material logic; doctrine of terms, doctrine of the judgment, doctrine of inference, traditional *or* Aristotelian logic, Ramist *or* Ramistic logic, modern *or* epistemological logic, pragmatic *or* instrumental *or* experimental logic; psychological logic, psychologism; symbolic *or* mathematical logic, logistic; propositional calculus, calculus of individuals, functional calculus, combinatory logic, algebra of relations, algebra of classes, set theory, Boolean algebra

3 <methods> a priori reasoning, a fortiori reasoning, a posteriori reasoning; discursive reasoning; **deduction, deductive reasoning,** syllogism, syllogistic reasoning; hypothetico-deductive method; **induction, inductive reasoning,** epagoge; philosophical induction, inductive *or* Baconian method; **inference; generalization,** particularization; synthesis, analysis; hypothesis and verification

4 **argumentation, argument, controversy, dispute, disagreement, disputation, polemic, debate,** disceptation <old>, eristic, art of dispute; **contention, wrangling, bickering,** hubbub 53.3, quibble, bicker, setto <nf>, rhubarb *and* hassle <nf>, passage of arms; war of words, verbal engagement *or* contest, logomachy, flyting; paper war, *guerre de plume* <Fr>; adversarial procedure, confrontational occasion; academic disputation, defense of a thesis; defense, apology, apologia, apologetics; dialectics, dialecticism; pilpul, casuistry; polemics; litigation; examination, cross-examination

5 **argument,** *argumentum* <L>; **case, plea,** pleading, *plaidoyer* <Fr>, brief; special pleading; **reason, consideration; refutation,** elenchus, ignoratio elenchi; stance, position; grounds, evidence; pros, cons, **pros and cons;** talking point; **dialogue,** reasoning together, dialectic; formal argument; rationale, pretext, premise

6 **syllogism;** prosyllogism; mode; figure; mood; pseudosyllogism, paralogism; sorites, progressive *or* Aristotelian sorites, regressive *or* Goclenian sorites; categorical syllogism; enthymeme; dilemma; **rule,** rule of deduction, transformation rule; modus ponens, modus tollens

7 **premise, proposition, position,** assumed position, sumption, **assumption,** supposal, presupposition, **hypothesis, thesis, theorem,** lemma, **statement,** affirmation, categorical proposition, premise, assertion, basis, ground, foundation; **postulate, axiom, postulation,** postulatum; data; major premise, minor premise; first principles; a priori principle, apriorism; philosophical proposition, philosopheme; hypothesis ad hoc; sentential *or* propositional function, truth-function, truth table, truth-value

8 **conclusion** 946.4

9 **reasonableness,** reasonability, **logicalness,** logicality, **rationality, sensibleness, soundness,** justness, justifiability, admissibility, cogency; sense, common sense, sound sense, sweet reason, **logic, reason;** plausibility 968.3

10 **good reasoning, right thinking,** sound reasoning, ironclad reasoning, irrefutable logic; cogent argument, **cogency;** strong argument, knockdown argument; good case, good reason, sound evidence, strong point

11 **reasoner,** ratiocinator, **thinker; rationalist;** rationalizer; synthesizer; **logician,** logistician;

logicaster; dialectician; syllogist, syllogizer; **sophist** 935.6; philosopher 952.8

12 **arguer, controversialist, disputant,** plaintiff, defendant, **debater,** eristic, argufier <nf>, advocate, wrangler, proponent, litigator, mooter, lawyer, jurist, Philadelphia lawyer <nf>, guardhouse *or* latrine *or* forecastle lawyer <nf>, disceptator <old>, pilpulist, casuist; polemic, polemist, polemicist; logomacher, logomachist; apologist

13 **contentiousness,** litigiousness, **quarrelsomeness,** argumentativeness, disputatiousness, testiness, feistiness <nf>, combativeness; ill humor 110

14 **side,** interest; **the affirmative,** pro, yes, aye, yea; **the negative,** con, no, nay

VERBS 15 **reason;** logicalize, logicize; rationalize, provide a rationale; intellectualize; bring reason to bear, apply *or* use reason, put two and two together; construe, **deduce, infer, generalize; synthesize, analyze, work out; theorize,** hypothesize; premise; philosophize; syllogize; ratiocinate

16 **argue,** argufy <nf>, **dispute,** discept <old>, dissent, disagree, logomachize, polemize, polemicize, moot, **bandy words, chop logic, plead,** pettifog <nf>, join issue, give and take, cut and thrust, try conclusions, cross swords, lock horns, **contend, contest,** spar, **bicker, wrangle,** hassle <nf>, have it out, have words; thrash out; take one's stand upon, **put up an argument** <nf>; take sides, take up a side; argue to no purpose; **quibble, squabble,** cavil 936.9; litigate

17 **be reasonable, be logical, make sense,** figure <nf>, **stand to reason,** be demonstrable, be irrefutable; hold good, hold water <nf>; have a leg to stand on; show wisdom

ADJS 18 **reasoning, rational,** ratiocinative *or* ratiocinatory; analytic, analytical; conceptive, conceptual; cerebral, noetic, phrenic

19 **argumentative, argumental, dialectic, dialectical, controversial, disputatious, contentious,** quarrelsome, dissenting, disputing, litigious, combative, factious, testy, feisty <nf>, petulant, ill-humored 110.18, eristic, eristical, polemic, polemical, logomachic, logomachical, pilpulistic, pro and con; diectic, apodeictic, aporetic; at cross-purposes, at odds

20 **logical, reasonable, rational, cogent, sensible, sane, wise, sound,** well-thought-out, legitimate, just, justifiable, admissible; credible 953.24; plausible 968.7; as it should be, as it ought to be; well-argued, **well-founded, well-grounded**

21 **reasoned, advised, considered,** calculated, meditated, contemplated, deliberated, studied, weighed, thought-out, well-reasoned

22 dialectic, dialectical, maieutic; syllogistic, syllogistical, enthymematic, enthymematical, soritical, epagogic, inductive, deductive, inferential, synthetic, synthetical, analytic, analytical, discursive, heuristic; a priori, a fortiori, a posteriori; categorical, hypothetical, propositional, postulated, conditional

23 deducible, derivable, inferable; sequential, following

ADVS **24 reasonably, logically, rationally,** by the rules of logic, **sensibly,** sanely, soundly; syllogistically, analytically; realistically, pragmatically, plausibly; **in reason,** in all reason, within reason, within the bounds *or* limits of reason, within reasonable limitations, **within bounds,** within the bounds of possibility, as far as possible, in all conscience

936 SOPHISTRY

<specious reasoning>

NOUNS **1 sophistry,** sophistication, sophism, philosophism, **casuistry,** Jesuitry, Jesuitism, subtlety, oversubtlety; **false *or* specious reasoning, rationalization,** evasive reasoning, vicious reasoning, sophistical reasoning, special pleading; **fallacy,** fallaciousness; **speciousness,** speciosity, superficial *or* apparent soundness, plausibleness, plausibility; **insincerity, disingenuousness; equivocation,** equivocalness; fudging *and* waffling <nf>, fudge and mudge <Brit nf>; perversion, distortion, misapplication; vicious circle, circularity; mystification, obfuscation, obscurantism; reduction, trivialization

2 illogicalness, illogic, illogicality, **unreasonableness, irrationality, reasonlessness, senselessness, unsoundness,** unscientificness, invalidity, untenableness, inconclusiveness; **inconsistency,** incongruity, antilogy; invalidity

3 <specious argument> sophism, sophistry, insincere argument, mere rhetoric, philosophism, solecism; paralogism, pseudosyllogism; claptrap, moonshine, empty words, doubletalk, doublespeak, "sound and fury, signifying nothing"—Shakespeare; bad case, weak point, flawed argument, circular argument, "lame and impotent conclusion"—Shakespeare; **fallacy,** logical fallacy, formal fallacy, material fallacy, verbal fallacy; *argumentum ad hominem, argumentum ad baculum, argumentum ad captandum, argumentum ad captandum vulgus* <all L>, crowd-pleasing argument, argument by analogy, *tu quoque* <L>, argument, *petitio principii* <L>, begging the question, **circular argument,** undistributed middle, *non sequitur* <L>, *hysteron*

proteron <Gk>, *post hoc* and *ergo propter hoc* <L>, paradox; contradiction in terms

4 quibble, quiddity, quodlibet, quillet <old>, Jesuitism, **cavil;** quip, quirk, shuffle, dodge

5 quibbling, caviling, boggling, captiousness, nit-picking, **bickering; logic-chopping,** choplogic, **hairsplitting,** trichoschistism; subterfuge, chicane, chicanery, pettifoggery; **equivocation,** tergiversation, prevarication, **evasion, hedging, pussyfooting** <nf>, **sidestepping,** dodging, shifting, shuffling, fencing, parrying, boggling, paltering, beating around the bush

6 sophist, sophister, philosophist <old>, **casuist,** Jesuit; choplogic <old>, logic-chopper; paralogist

7 quibbler, caviler, pettifogger, hairsplitter, captious *or* picayune critic, nitpicker; **equivocator,** Jesuit, mystifier, mystificator, obscurantist, prevaricator, palterer, tergiversator, shuffler, mudger <Brit nf>; **hedger;** pussyfoot *or* **pussyfooter** <nf>, waffler <nf>

VERBS **8** reason speciously, reason ill, paralogize, reason in a circle, argue insincerely, pervert, distort, misapply; explain away, rationalize; prove that black is white and white black; not have a leg to stand on

9 quibble, cavil, bicker, boggle, chop logic, **split hairs,** nitpick, pick nits; Jesuitize; **equivocate,** mystify, obscure, prevaricate, tergiversate, doubletalk, doublespeak, tap-dance <nf>, misrepresent, misinform, fudge, palter, fence, parry, shift, shuffle, **dodge,** shy, **evade,** sidestep, hedge, skate around <Brit nf>, pussyfoot <nf>, evade the issue; twist, slant; **beat about *or* around the bush,** avoid the issue, not come to the point, **beg the question;** pick holes in, pick to pieces; blow hot and cold; strain at a gnat and swallow a camel

ADJS **10 sophistical,** sophistic, philosophistic, philosophistical <old>, casuistic, casuistical, Jesuitic, Jesuitical, **fallacious, specious,** colorable, plausible, hollow, superficially *or* apparently sound; deceptive, illusive, empty; overrefined, oversubtle, **insincere, disingenuous**

11 illogical, unreasonable, irrational, reasonless, contrary to reason, **senseless,** without reason, **without rhyme *or* reason;** unscientific, nonscientific, unphilosophical; **invalid,** inauthentic, unauthentic, faulty, flawed, paralogical, fallacious; inconclusive, inconsequent, inconsequential, not following; **inconsistent,** incongruous, absonant <old>, loose, unconnected; contradictory, **self-contradictory,** self-annulling, self-refuting, oxymoronic

12 unsound, unsubstantial, insubstantial, weak, feeble, poor, flimsy, unrigorous, inconclusive, unproved, unsustained, poorly argued

13 baseless, groundless, ungrounded, **unfounded,** ill-founded, unbased, **unsupported,** unsustained, invalid, **without foundation,** without basis *or* sound basis; **untenable, unsupportable,** unsustainable; **unwarranted,** idle, empty, vain

14 quibbling, caviling, equivocatory, equivocal, captious, nitpicky *and* nit-picking <nf>, bickering; picayune, petty, trivial, trifling; paltering, shuffling, hedging, pussyfooting <nf>, **evasive; hairsplitting,** trichoschistic, logic-chopping, choplogic *or* choplogical <old>

ADVS **15 illogically, unreasonably, irrationally, reasonlessly, senselessly;** baselessly, groundlessly; untenably, unsupportably, unsustainably; out of all reason, out of all bounds

937 TOPIC

NOUNS **1 topic, subject,** subject of thought, **matter, subject matter,** what it is about, **concern,** focus of interest *or* attention, discrete matter, category; field, branch, discipline; **theme,** burden, **text,** motif, motive, angle, business at hand, **case,** matter in hand, **question, problem, issue,** bone of contention; **point,** point at issue, point in question, topic for discussion, main point, gist 997.6; plot; item on the agenda; head, heading, chapter, rubric, category; contents, substance, meat, essence, material part, basis; living issue, topic of the day; thesis

2 caption, title, heading, head, superscription, rubric; **headline;** overline; banner, banner head *or* line, streamer; **scarehead,** screamer; spread, spreadhead; drop head, dropline, hanger; running head *or* title, jump head; **subhead, subheading,** subtitle; legend, motto, epigraph; title page

VERBS **3** focus on, have regard to, distinguish, lift up, set forth, specify, zero in on <nf>, center on, be concerned with; include; caption, title, head, head up <nf>; **headline;** subtitle, subhead

ADJS **4 topical, thematic**

938 INQUIRY

NOUNS **1 inquiry,** inquiring, probing, **inquest** 307.18, inquirendo; inquisition; interpellation; inquiring mind; analysis 801

2 examination, school examination, examen, **exam** <nf>, **test, quiz;** oral examination, oral, doctor's oral, master's oral, viva voce examination, viva <nf>; catechesis, catchization; **audition, hearing;** multiple-choice test, multiple-guess test <nf>; written examination, written <nf>, blue book <nf>, test paper; course examination, midterm, midyear, midsemester; qualifying examination, preliminary examination, prelim <nf>; take-home examination; unannounced examination, pop *or* shotgun *or* surprise quiz <nf>; final examination, **final** <nf>, comprehensive examination, comps <nf>, great go <old> *or* greats <Oxford>; honors <Brit>, tripos <Cambridge>

3 examination, inspection, scrutiny; survey, review, perusal, look-over, once over *and* look-see <nf>, perlustration, **study,** look-through, scan, run-through; visitation; overhaul, overhauling; quality control; confirmation, cross-check

4 investigation, indagation <old>, **research,** legwork <nf>, inquiry into; data-gathering, gathering *or* amassing evidence; perscrutation, **probe,** searching investigation, close inquiry, exhaustive study; police inquiry *or* investigation, criminal investigation, detective work, detection, sleuthing; investigative bureau *or* agency, bureau *or* department of investigation; legislative investigation, Congressional investigation, hearing; witch-hunt, fishing expedition, Inquisition

5 preliminary *or* tentative examination; quick *or* cursory inspection, glance, quick look, first look, once-over-lightly <nf>

6 checkup, check; spot check; physical examination, **physical,** physical checkup, health examination; self-examination; exploratory examination; testing, drug testing, alcohol testing, random testing

7 re-examination, reinquiry, recheck, **review,** reappraisal, revaluation, rethinking, revision, rebeholding, second *or* further look

8 reconnaissance; recce *and* recco *and* recon <nf>; **reconnoitering,** reconnoiter, exploration, **scouting**

9 surveillance, shadowing, following, trailing, tailing <nf>, 24-hour surveillance, observation, stakeout <nf>; **spying, espionage,** espial, **intelligence,** military intelligence, intelligence work, cloak-and-dagger work <nf>; intelligence agency, secret service, secret police; counterespionage, counterintelligence; wiretap, wiretapping, bugging <nf>, electronic surveillance; tagging

10 question, query, inquiry, demand <old>, **interrogation,** interrogatory; interrogative; frequently asked question *or* FAQ; **problem, issue,** topic 936, case *or* point in question, bone of contention, controversial point, question before the house, debating point, controversy, question *or* point at issue, **moot point** *or* case, question mark, *quodlibet* <L>; difficult question, vexed *or* knotty question, burning question; sixty-four-thousand-dollar question; leader, leading question; feeler, trial balloon, fishing question; trick question, poser, stumper, tough nut to crack, conundrum, enigma, mind-boggler <nf>; trivia question; cross-question, rhetorical question; cross-interrogatory; catechism, catechizing; easy question

11 **interview,** press conference, press opportunity, photo opportunity, photo op <nf>

12 **questioning, interrogation, querying,** asking, seeking, pumping, probing, inquiring; **quiz,** quizzing, **examination;** challenge, dispute; interpellation, bringing into question; catechizing, catechization; catechetical method, Socratic method *or* induction

13 **grilling,** the grill <nf>, inquisition, pumping; police interrogation; **the third-degree** <nf>; direct examination, redirect examination, **cross-examination,** cross-interrogation, **cross-questioning**

14 **canvass, survey, inquiry, questionnaire,** questionary; exit poll; **poll, public-opinion poll,** opinion poll *or* survey, statistical survey, opinion sampling, voter-preference survey; consumer-preference survey, market-research survey; consumer research, market research

15 **search,** searching, **quest, hunt,** hunting, stalk, stalking, still hunt, dragnet, posse, search party; search warrant; search-and-destroy operation *or* mission; **rummage, ransacking,** turning over *or* upside down; **forage;** house-search, perquisition, domiciliary visit; exploration, probe; **body search,** frisk *and* toss *and* shake *and* shakedown *and* skin-search *and* body-shake *and* pat-down search <nf>

16 **inquirer, asker, prober,** querier, querist, **questioner,** questionist, interrogator; interviewer; interrogatrix; interpellator; **quizzer,** examiner, catechist; inquisitor, inquisitionist; cross-questioner, cross-interrogator, **cross-examiner;** interlocutor; **pollster,** poller, sampler, canvasser, opinion sampler; **interviewer; detective** 576.10; secret agent 576.9; quiz-master

17 **examiner,** examinant, **tester; inspector,** scrutinizer, scrutator, scrutineer, quality-control inspector; **monitor,** reviewer; fact-checker; check-out pilot; observer; visitor, visitator; **investigator,** indagator <old>; editor, copy editor, proofreader

18 seeker, hunter, searcher, perquisitor; rummager, ransacker; digger, delver; zetetic; **researcher, fact finder,** researchist, research worker, market researcher, consumer researcher; surveyor

19 **examinee,** examinant, examinate, questionee, quizzee; interviewee; informant, subject, interviewee; witness; candidate; defendant, plaintiff, suspect

VERBS 20 **inquire, ask, question, query; make inquiry,** take up *or* institute *or* pursue *or* follow up *or* conduct *or* carry on an inquiry, ask after, inquire after, ask about, ask questions, put queries; inquire of, require an answer, ask a question, put a question to, pose *or* set *or* propose *or* propound a question; bring into question, interpellate; **demand** <old>, **want to know;** introspect

21 **interrogate, question, query, quiz, test, examine;** catechize; **pump,** pump for information, shoot questions at, pick the brains of, worm out of; interview; draw one out

22 **grill,** put on the grill <nf>, inquisition, pump, make inquisition; roast <nf>, put the pressure on *and* put the screws to *and* go over <nf>; **cross-examine, cross-question,** cross-interrogate; third-degree <nf>, give *or* put through the third degree <nf>; put to the question; extract information, pry *or* prize out; run *or* put through the mill <nf>

23 **investigate,** indagate <old>, sift, **explore, look into,** peer into, **search into, go into, delve into,** dig into, poke into, pry into; fact-find; **probe, sound, plumb, fathom; check into, check on, check out,** nose into, see into; poke about, root around *or* about, scratch around *or* about, cast about *or* around

24 **examine, inspect, scrutinize, survey,** canvass, **look at,** peer at, eyeball <nf>, **observe, scan, peruse, study; look over,** give the once-over <nf>, run the eye over, cast *or* pass the eyes over, scope out <nf>; go over, run over, pass over, pore over; overlook, overhaul; **monitor, review,** pass under review; set an examination, give an examination; **take stock of,** size *or* size up, take the measure <nf>; **check, check out, check over *or* through; check up on;** autopsy, postmortem 307.18; soul-search

25 **make a close study of, research, scrutinize,** examine thoroughly, vet <Brit>, **go deep into,** look closely at, probe; examine point by point, go over with a fine-tooth comb, go over step by step, subject to close scrutiny, view *or* try in all its phases, get down to nuts and bolts <nf>; perscrutate, perlustrate

26 **examine cursorily,** take a cursory view of, give a quick *or* cursory look, give a once-over-lightly <nf>, give a dekko <Brit nf>, **scan, skim, skim over *or* through,** slur, slur over, slip *or* skip over *or* through, **glance at,** give the once-over <nf>, pass over lightly, zip through, **dip into, touch upon,** touch upon lightly *or* in passing, **hit the high spots; thumb through,** flip through the pages, turn over the leaves, leaf *or* page *or* flick through

27 **re-examine,** recheck, reinquire, **reconsider,** reappraise, revaluate, rethink, **review,** revise, rebehold, take another *or* a second *or* a further look; retrace, retrace one's steps, go back over; rejig *or* rejigger <nf>; take back to the old drawing board

28 **reconnoiter,** make a reconnaissance, case <nf>, scout, **scout out,** spy, **spy out,** play the spy, peep;

watch, put under surveillance, stake out <nf>; bug
<nf>; check up on, check up

29 **canvass, survey,** make a survey; **poll,** conduct a
poll, sample, **questionnaire** <nf>

30 **seek, hunt,** look <old>, **quest, pursue,** go in
pursuit of, follow, go in search of, prowl after, see
to, try to find; **look up, hunt up; look for,** look
around or about for, look for high and low, look
high and low, search out, **search for,** seek for, **hunt
for,** cast or beat about for; shop around for; **fish
for, angle for,** bob for, dig for, delve for, go on a
fishing expedition; **ask for,** inquire for; **gun for,** go
gunning for; still-hunt <nf>

31 **search, hunt, explore;** research; read up on; **hunt
through, search through, look through, go
through;** dig, delve, burrow, root, pick over, poke,
pry; look round or around, poke around, nose
around, smell around; beat the bushes; forage;
frisk <nf>

32 **grope,** grope for, **feel for,** fumble, grabble, scrabble,
feel around, poke around, pry around, beat about,
grope in the dark; **feel** or **pick one's way**

33 **ransack, rummage, rake, scour, comb;** rifle; **look
everywhere,** look into every hole and corner, **look
high and low,** look upstairs and downstairs, **look
all over,** look all over hell <nf>, search high
heaven, turn upside down, turn inside out, **leave
no stone unturned;** shake down and shake and
toss <nf>

34 **search out, hunt out, spy out,** scout out, **ferret
out,** fish out, pry out, winkle out <Brit nf>, dig
out, root out, grub up

35 **trace, stalk, track, trail; follow,** follow up, shadow,
tail <nf>, dog the footsteps of, have or keep an
eye on; nose, nose out, **smell** or **sniff out,** follow
the trail or scent or spoor of; follow a clue; **trace
down, hunt down, track down, run down, run to
earth**

ADJS 36 **inquiring, questioning, querying,** quizzing;
quizzical, curious; interrogatory, interrogative,
interrogational; inquisitorial, inquisitional;
visitatorial, visitorial; catechistic, catechistical,
catechetic, catechetical

37 **examining,** examinational; scrutatorial,
examinatorial; **testing,** trying, **tentative;** groping,
feeling; inspectional; **inspectorial;** interpellant;
investigative, indagative <old>; zetetic; heuristic,
investigatory, investigational; **exploratory,**
explorative, explorational; fact-finding; analytic,
analytical; curious

38 **searching, probing, prying, nosy** <nf>; poking,
digging, fishing, delving; in search or quest of,
looking for, **out for,** on the lookout for, **in the
market for,** loaded or out for bear <nf>; all-
searching; fact-finding, knowledge-seeking

ADVS 39 **in question, at issue,** in debate or dispute,
under consideration, under active consideration,
under advisement, subjudice <L>, under
examination, under investigation, under
surveillance, up or open for discussion; **before the
house, on the docket, on the agenda, on the table,
on the floor**

939 ANSWER

NOUNS 1 **answer, reply, response,** responsion,
replication; answering, respondence; riposte,
uptake <nf>, **retort, rejoinder,** reaction 902,
return, **comeback** and **take** <nf>, back answer,
short answer, back talk, backchat <nf>; **repartee,**
backchat, clever or ready or witty reply or retort,
snappy comeback <nf>, witty repartee; yes-and-no
answer, evasive reply; **acknowledgment,** receipt,
confirmation; rescript, rescription; antiphon; **echo,**
reverberation 54.2

2 **rebuttal, counterstatement,** counterreply,
counterclaim, counterblast, counteraccusation,
countercharge, tu quoque <L, you too>, defense,
contraremonstrance; **rejoinder,** replication,
defense, rebutter, surrebutter or surrebuttal,
surrejoinder; confutation, refutation; last word,
parting shot

3 **answerer, replier,** responder, **respondent,**
responser; defendant

VERBS 4 **answer,** make or give answer, return answer,
return for answer, offer, proffer, **reply, respond,**
say, say in reply; **retort,** riposte, **rejoin,** return,
throw back, flash back; come back and come back
at and come right back at <nf>, answer back and
talk back and shoot back <nf>, **react;
acknowledge,** make or give acknowledgement;
echo, reecho, reverberate 54.7

5 **rebut,** make a rebuttal; **rejoin,** surrebut, surrejoin;
counterclaim, countercharge; confute, refute; have
the last word, have the final say; fire the parting
shot; lip off <nf>

ADJS 6 **answering, replying, responsive,** respondent,
responding; rejoining, returning; antiphonal;
echoing, echoic, reechoing 54.12; confutative,
refutative; acknowledging, confirming

ADVS 7 in answer, in reply, in response, in return, in
rebuttal

940 SOLUTION
<answer to a problem>

NOUNS 1 **solution,** resolution, **answer, reason,**
explanation 341.4; **finding,** conclusion,
determination, ascertainment, verdict, judgment;
outcome, upshot, denouement, **result,** issue, end

820, end result; accomplishment 407; **solving,** working, **working-out,** finding-out, resolving, **clearing up,** cracking; **unriddling,** riddling, unscrambling, unraveling, sorting out, untwisting, unspinning, unweaving, untangling, disentanglement; **decipherment, deciphering, decoding,** decryption; interpretation 341; **happy ending** or outcome, the answer to one's prayers, the light at the end of the tunnel; possible solution, **scenario**

VERBS **2 solve, resolve,** find the solution or answer, **clear up,** get, get right, do, work, **work out, find out, figure out,** dope and dope out <nf>; **straighten out, iron out,** sort out, puzzle out; debug; psych and psych out <nf>; **unriddle,** riddle, unscramble, undo, untangle, disentangle, untwist, unspin, unweave, **unravel,** ravel, ravel out; **decipher, decode,** decrypt, crack; **make out,** interpret 341.9; **answer,** explain 341.10; unlock, pick or open the lock; find the key of, find a clue to; **get to the bottom** or **heart of,** fathom, plumb, bottom; have it, hit it, hit upon a solution, hit the nail on the head, hit it on the nose <nf>; guess, divine, guess right; end happily, work out right and come up roses <nf>

ADJS **3 solvable,** soluble, **resolvable,** open to solution, capable of solution, workable, doable, answerable; explainable, explicable, determinable, ascertainable; **decipherable,** decodable

941 DISCOVERY

NOUNS **1 discovery, finding, detection,** spotting, catching, catching sight of, sighting, espial; recognition, determination, distinguishment; locating, **location; disclosure, exposure, revelation, uncovering, unearthing,** digging up, exhumation, excavation, bringing to light or view; **find,** trove, treasure trove, *trouvaille* <Fr>, strike, lucky strike; accidental or chance discovery, happening or stumbling upon, tripping over, casual discovery; serendipity; **learning, finding out,** determining, becoming conscious or cognizant of, becoming aware of; self-discovery; realization, enlightenment; rediscovery; invention; archaeology

VERBS **2 discover, find,** get; strike, hit; put or lay one's hands on, lay one's fingers on, **locate** 159.10; **hunt down,** search out, trace down, track down, **run down, run** or **bring to earth;** trace; **learn, find out,** determine, become cognizant or conscious of, become aware of, get it <nf>; discover or find out the hard way, discover to one's cost; discover or find oneself; rediscover; invent

3 come across, run across, meet with, meet up with

<nf>, fall in with, **encounter, run into,** bump into <nf>, come or run up against <nf>, **come on** or **upon, hit on** or **upon,** strike on, light on or upon, alight on or upon, fall on, tumble on or upon; **chance on** or **upon,** happen on or upon or across, **stumble on** or **upon,** or **across** or **into,** stub one's toe on or upon, trip over, bump up against, blunder upon, discover serendipitously

4 uncover, unearth, dig up, disinter, exhume, excavate; **disclose, expose, reveal,** blow the lid off, crack wide open, **bring to light,** lay bare; **turn up,** root up, rootle up <Brit>, fish up; worm out, ferret out, winkle out <Brit>, pry out

5 detect, spot <nf>, **see, lay eyes on,** catch sight of, catch a glimpse of, perceive, **spy,** espy, descry, sense, pick up, notice, discern, **perceive, make out, recognize,** distinguish, identify

6 scent, catch the scent of, sniff, smell, get a whiff of <nf>, **get wind of;** sniff or scent or smell out, nose out; be on the right scent, be near the truth, be warm <nf>, burn <nf>, have a fix on, place

7 catch, catch out; catch off side, catch off base; catch tripping, **catch napping, catch off-guard,** catch asleep at the switch; **catch at,** catch in the act, **catch red-handed,** catch in *flagrante delicto,* **catch with one's pants down** <nf>, catch flat-footed, have the goods on <nf>, ensnare

8 <detect the hidden nature of> **see through, penetrate,** see as it really is, see in its true colors, see the inside of, read between the lines, see the cloven hoof; open the eyes to, tumble to, catch on to, wise up to <nf>; **be on to, be wise to, be hep to** <nf>, have one's measure, **have one's number,** have dead to rights <nf>, read someone like a book

9 turn up, show up, be found; discover itself, expose or betray itself; hang out <nf>; materialize, **come to light,** come out; come along, come to hand; show one's true colors

ADJS **10** on the right scent, **on the right track,** on the trail of; **hot** and **warm** <nf>; **discoverable,** determinable, findable, **detectable,** spottable, disclosable, exposable, locatable, **discernible;** exploratory

INTERJS **11 eureka!,** I have it!, at last!, at long last!, finally!, *thalassa!* or *thalatta!* <Gk>; ah hah!

942 EXPERIMENT

NOUNS **1 experiment, experimentation;** experimental method; testing, trying, trying-out, **trial;** research and development or R and D; running it up the flagpole <nf>, trying it on or out <nf>, exploration; **trial and error,** hit and miss, cut and try <nf>; empiricism, experimentalism, pragmatism, instrumentalism; **rule of thumb;** tentativeness, tentative method; control experiment, controlled experiment, **control;** experimental design; experimental proof *or* verification; noble experiment; single-blind experiment, double-blind experiment; guesswork

2 **test, trial, try;** essay; check; docimasy <old>, assay; determination, blank determination; **proof, verification;** touchstone, standard, criterion 300.2; crucial test; acid test, litmus *or* litmus-paper test; ordeal, crucible; probation; **feeling out, sounding out;** test case; first *or* rough draft, rough sketch, mock-up; stab *and* crack *and* whack <nf>; *brouillon* <Fr>

3 **tryout,** workout, **rehearsal,** practice; pilot plan *or* program; **dry run,** dummy run, practice run; *Gedankenexperiment* <Ger>; road test; **trial run,** practical test; shakedown, shakedown cruise, bench test; flight test, test flight *or* run; audition, hearing

4 **feeler, probe,** sound, sounder; **trial balloon,** *ballon d'essai* <Fr>, pilot balloon, barometer; weather vane, weathercock; straw to show the wind, straw vote; sample, random sample, experimental sample

5 **laboratory, lab** <nf>, research laboratory, research center *or* establishment *or* facility *or* institute, experiment station, field station, research and development *or* R and D establishment; **proving ground;** think tank <nf>, workshop

6 **experimenter,** experimentist, experimentalist, empiricist, bench scientist, **researcher,** research worker, R and D worker; experimental engineer; **tester,** tryer-out, test driver, test pilot; essayer; assayer; analyst, analyzer, investigator

7 **subject, experimental subject,** experimentee, testee, patient, sample; laboratory animal, experimental *or* test animal, **guinea pig,** lab rat

VERBS 8 **experiment,** experimentalize, **research,** make an experiment, **run an experiment,** run a sample *or* specimen; **test, try,** essay, cut and try <nf>, **test *or* try out,** have a dry run *or* dummy run *or* rehearsal *or* test run, rehearse; run it up the flagpole and see who salutes <nf>; put to the test, **put to the proof, prove, verify,** validate, substantiate, confirm, put to trial, bring to test, make a trial of, give a trial to; **give a try,** have a go, give it a go <nf>, have *or* take a stab *or* crack *or* whack at <nf>; sample, taste; assay; play around *or* fool around with <nf>; try out under controlled conditions; give a tryout *or* workout <nf>, **road-test,** shake down; try one out, put one through his paces; experiment *or* practice upon; try it on; try on, try it for size <nf>; try one's strength, see what one can do

9 **sound out, check out, feel out, sound,** get a sounding *or* reading *or* sense, probe, **feel the pulse,** read; **put *or* throw out a feeler,** put out feelers, send up a trial balloon, fly a kite; **see which way the wind blows,** see how the land lies, test out, test the waters; take a straw vote, take a random sample, use an experimental sample

10 **stand the test, stand up, hold up, hold up in the wash,** pass, **pass muster,** get by <nf>, make it *and* hack it *and* cut the mustard <nf>, meet *or* satisfy requirements

ADJS 11 **experimental, test, trial;** pilot; testing, proving, trying; probative, probatory, verificatory; probationary; **tentative,** provisional; empirical; trial-and-error, hit-or-miss, cut-and-try; heuristic

12 **tried, well-tried, tested, proved,** verified, confirmed, tried and true

ADVS 13 **experimentally,** by rule of thumb, by trial and error, by hit and miss, hit or miss, by guess and by God

14 **on trial,** under examination, **on *or* under probation,** under suspicion, **on approval**

943 COMPARISON

NOUNS 1 **comparison,** compare, examining side by side, matching, matchup, holding up together, proportion <old>, comparative judgment *or* estimate; **likening,** comparing, **analogy;** parallelism; comparative relation; weighing, balancing; opposing, opposition, **contrast;** contrastiveness, distinctiveness, distinction 944.3; confrontment, confrontation; **relation** 775, relating, relativism; correlation 777; simile, similitude, metaphor, allegory, figure *or* trope of comparison; comparative degree; comparative method; comparative linguistics, comparative grammar, comparative literature, comparative anatomy, etc

2 **collation,** comparative scrutiny, point-by-point comparison; **verification, confirmation, checking;** check, cross-check

3 **comparability,** comparableness, comparativeness; analogousness, equivalence, **commensurability;** proportionateness *or* proportionability <old>; ratio, proportion, balance; **similarity** 784

VERBS 4 **compare, liken,** assimilate, similize, liken to, compare with; **make *or* draw a comparison,** run a comparison, do a comparative study, bring into comparison; **analogize,** bring into analogy; relate 775.6; metaphorize; **draw a parallel,** parallel; **match,** match up; examine side by side, view together, hold up together; weigh *or* measure against; confront, bring into confrontation, **contrast, oppose,** set in opposition, set off against, set in contrast, **put** *or* **set over against,** set *or* place against, counterpose; compare and contrast, note similarities and differences; **weigh,** balance

5 **collate,** scrutinize comparatively, compare point by point, painstakingly match; **verify, confirm, check, cross-check**

6 **compare notes,** exchange views *or* observations, match data *or* findings, put heads together <nf>

7 **be comparable, compare, compare to** *or* **with,** not compare with 787.2, admit of comparison, be commensurable, be of the same order *or* class, be worthy of comparison, be fit to be compared; **measure up to, come up to,** match up with, stack up with <nf>, hold a candle to <nf>; **match, parallel;** vie, vie with, rival; **resemble** 784.7

ADJS 8 **comparative, relative** 775.7, **comparable,** commensurate, commensurable, parallel, matchable, **analogous;** analogical; collatable; **correlative;** much at one, much of a muchness <nf>; **similar** 784.10; something of the sort *or* to that effect

9 **incomparable,** incommensurable, not to be compared, of different orders; apples and oranges; **unlike, dissimilar** 787.4

ADVS 10 **comparatively, relatively;** comparably; dollar for dollar, pound for pound, ounce for ounce, etc; on the one hand, on the other hand

PREPS 11 **compared to, compared with,** as compared with, by comparison with, **in comparison with, beside,** over against, taken with; than

944 DISCRIMINATION

NOUNS 1 **discrimination,** discriminateness, discriminatingness, discriminativeness; seeing *or* making distinctions, appreciation of differences; analytic power *or* faculty; **criticalness; finesse,** refinement, delicacy; niceness of distinction, nicety, subtlety, refined discrimination, critical niceness; **tact, tactfulness,** feel, feeling, sense, sensitivity 24.3, **sensibility** 24.2; intuition, instinct 934; appreciation, appreciativeness; judiciousness 920.7; taste, discriminating taste, aesthetic *or* artistic judgment; palate, fine *or* refined palate; ear, good ear, educated ear; eye, good eye; connoisseurship, savvy <nf>, selectiveness, fastidiousness 495

2 **discernment,** critical discernment, penetration, **perception,** perceptiveness, **insight,** perspicacity; **flair; judgment,** acumen 920.4; analysis 801

3 **distinction,** contradistinction, distinctiveness <old>; **distinguishment,** differentiation 780.4, winnowing, shakeout, separation, separationism, division, segregation, segregationism, demarcation; nice *or* subtle *or* fine distinction,

nuance, shade of difference, microscopic distinction; hairsplitting, trichoschistism

VERBS 4 **discriminate, distinguish,** draw *or* make distinctions, contradistinguish, compare and contrast, pick and choose, secern, distinguish in thought, **separate,** separate out, divide, analyze 801.6, subdivide, **segregate,** sever, severalize, **differentiate,** demark, demarcate, mark the interface, set off, **set apart,** grade, graduate, sift, sift out, sieve, sieve out, winnow, screen, screen out, sort, classify, sort out; **pick out,** select 371.14; separate the sheep from the goats, separate the men from the boys, separate the wheat from the tares *or* chaff, winnow the chaff from the wheat; **draw the line,** fix *or* set a limit; **split hairs,** draw *or* make a fine *or* overfine *or* nice *or* subtle distinction, subtilize

5 **be discriminating,** discriminate, exercise discrimination, tell which is which; **be tactful,** show *or* exercise tact; be tasteful, use one's palate; shop around, pick and choose; use advisedly

6 **distinguish between, make** *or* **draw a distinction,** appreciate differences, see nuances *or* shades of difference, see the difference, tell apart, tell one thing from another, know which is which, know what's what <nf>, not confound *or* mix up; "know a hawk from a handsaw"—Shakespeare, know one's ass from one's elbow <nf>

ADJS 7 **discriminating, discriminate,** discriminative, selective; discriminatory; **tactful, sensitive;** appreciative, appreciatory; **critical;** distinctive <old>, **distinguishing;** differential; precise, accurate, exact; nice, fine, delicate, subtle, subtile, refined; fastidious 495.9; distinctive, contrastive

8 **discerning, perceptive,** perspicacious, insightful; **astute,** judicious 920.19; perfectionist, choosy

9 **discriminable, distinguishable,** separable, differentiable, contrastable, opposable

ADVS 10 **discriminatingly,** discriminatively, discriminately; with finesse; **tactfully; tastefully**

945 INDISCRIMINATION

NOUNS 1 **indiscrimination,** indiscriminateness, undiscriminatingness, undiscriminativeness, unselectiveness, **uncriticalness, unparticularness;** syncretism; unfastidiousness; lack of refinement, coarseness *or* crudeness *or* crudity of intellect; **casualness,** promiscuousness, **promiscuity; indiscretion,** indiscreetness, **imprudence** 922.2; **untactfulness,** tactlessness, lack of feeling, insensitivity, **insensibility** 25, unmeticulousness, unpreciseness 340.4, inexactitude; **generality** 864, catholicity, catholic tastes; indifference; color blindness, tone-deafness; impartiality

2 indistinction, indistinctness, vagueness 32.2; **indefiniteness** 971.4; uniformity 780; facelessness, impersonality; indistinguishableness, **undistinguishableness,** indiscernibility; a distinction without a difference; randomness, generality, universality

VERBS **3 confound, confuse,** mix, mix up, muddle, tumble, jumble, jumble together, **blur,** blur distinctions, overlook distinctions; lump together, take as one, roll into one

4 use loosely, use unadvisedly

ADJS **5 undiscriminating, indiscriminate,** indiscriminative, undiscriminative, undifferentiating, unselective; wholesale, **general** 863.11, **blanket; uncritical,** uncriticizing, undemanding, nonjudgmental; **unparticular,** unfastidious; unsubtle; **casual, promiscuous;** undiscerning; unexacting, unmeticulous 340.13; **indiscreet,** undiscreet, **imprudent; untactful,** tactless, insensitive; catholic; indifferent; color-blind

6 indistinguishable, undistinguishable, undistinguished, indiscernible, **indistinct,** indistinctive, **without distinction,** not to be distinguished, undiscriminated, nondiscriminatory, inclusive, unindividual, unindividualized, undifferentiated, **alike,** six of one and half a dozen of the other <nf>; desultory; undefined, **indefinite;** faceless, impersonal; standard, interchangeable, stereotyped, uniform 781.5; random; miscellaneous, motley

946 JUDGMENT

NOUNS **1 judgment,** judging, adjudgment, adjudication, judicature, deeming <old>; judgment call <nf>; arbitrament, arbitration 466.2; **resolution** 359; good judgment 920.7; **choice** 371; **discrimination** 943

2 criticism; censure 510.3; **approval** 509; **critique,** review, notice, critical notice, report, comment; book review, critical review, thumbnail review; literary criticism, art criticism, music criticism, etc, critical journal, critical bibliography

3 estimate, estimation; view, opinion 953.6; **assessment,** assessing, **appraisal,** appraisement, appraising, appreciation, reckoning, **stocktaking,** valuation, valuing, **evaluation,** evaluating, value judgment, evaluative criticism, analyzing, weighing, weighing up, gauging, ranking, rank-ordering, **rating;** measurement 300; comparison 943; second opinion; public opinion

4 conclusion, deduction, inference, consequence, consequent, corollary; derivation, illation; induction; judgment day

5 verdict, decision, resolution <old>, **determination, finding,** holding; diagnosis, prognosis; **decree, ruling,** consideration, order, **pronouncement,** deliverance; **award,** action, **sentence; condemnation,** doom; dictum; precedent; edict, decree; execution of judgment

6 judge, judger, adjudicator, justice; arbiter 596.1; referee, umpire

7 critic, criticizer; connoisseur, *cognoscente* <Ital>; literary critic, man of letters; textual critic; editor; social critic, muckraker; captious critic, smellfungus, caviler, carper, faultfinder; criticaster, criticule, critickin; **censor,** censurer; **reviewer, commentator,** commenter; scholiast, annotator

VERBS **8 judge,** exercise judgment *or* the judgment; make a judgment call <nf>; adjudge, adjudicate; be judicious *or* judgmental; **consider, regard,** hold, **deem, esteem, count, account,** think of; allow <nf>, **suppose,** presume 951.10, opine, form an opinion, give *or* pass *or* express an opinion, weigh in *and* put in one's two cents' worth <nf>

9 estimate, form an estimate, make an estimation; **reckon,** call, guess, figure <nf>; **assess, appraise,** give an appreciation, **gauge, rate, rank,** rank-order, put in rank order, class, mark, **value,** deem, **evaluate,** valuate, place *or* set a value on, weigh, weigh up, prize, appreciate; size up *or* take one's measure <nf>, **measure** 300.11

10 conclude, draw a conclusion, be forced to conclude, **come to *or* arrive at a conclusion, come up with a conclusion** *and* end up <nf>; find, hold; deduce, derive, take as proved *or* demonstrated, extract, **gather,** collect, glean, fetch; **infer,** draw an inference; induce; **reason,** reason that; put two and two together

11 decide, determine; **find,** hold, ascertain; **resolve** 359.7, **settle,** fix; make a decision, come to a decision, **make up one's mind,** settle one's mind, come down <nf>, settle the matter

12 sit in judgment, hold the scales, hold court; **hear,** give a hearing to; **try** 598.18; **referee, umpire,** officiate; arbitrate 466.6

13 pass judgment, pronounce judgment, utter a judgment, deliver judgment; agree on a verdict, return a verdict, hand down a verdict, **bring in a verdict, find,** find for *or* against; pronounce on, act on, **pronounce,** report, **rule,** decree, order; **sentence,** pass sentence, hand down a sentence, doom, condemn; charge the jury

14 criticize, critique; **censure** 510.13, pick holes in, pick to pieces; **approve** 509.9; **review;** comment upon, annotate; moralize upon; pontificate; vet <nf>

15 rank, rate, count, be regarded, be thought of, be in one's estimation

ADJS **16 judicial, judiciary,** judicative, judgmental;

juridic, juridical, juristic, juristical; **judicious**
920.19; **evaluative; critical;** approbatory 509.16
ADVS **17 all things considered, on the whole, taking
one thing with another,** on balance, taking
everything into consideration *or* account;
everything being equal, other things being equal,
ceteris paribus <L>, taking into account,
considering, after all, this being so; therefore,
wherefore; on the one hand, on the other hand,
having said that; *sub judice* <L>, in court, before
the bench *or* bar *or* court

947 PREJUDGMENT

NOUNS **1 prejudgment,** prejudication, forejudgment;
**preconception, presumption, supposition,
presupposition,** presupposal, presurmise,
preapprehension, prenotion, **prepossession;
predilection,** predisposition; preconsideration,
predetermination, predecision, preconclusion,
premature judgment; ulterior motive, hidden
agenda, *parti pris* <Fr>, an ax to grind, **prejudice**
980.3
VERBS **2 prejudge,** forejudge; **preconceive,
presuppose, presume,** presurmise; **be predisposed;**
predecide, predetermine, preconclude, judge
beforehand *or* prematurely, judge before the
evidence is in, have one's mind made up; **jump to a
conclusion,** go off half-cocked *or* at half cock *and*
beat the gun *and* jump the gun *and* shoot from the
hip <nf>
ADJS **3 prejudged,** forejudged, **preconceived,**
preconceptual, **presumed, presupposed,**
presurmised; predetermined, predecided,
preconcluded, judged beforehand *or* prematurely;
predisposed, predispositional; prejudicial,
prejudging, prejudicative

948 MISJUDGMENT

NOUNS **1 misjudgment,** poor judgment, error in
judgment, warped *or* flawed *or* skewed judgment;
miscalculation, miscomputation, **misreckoning,
misestimation,** misappreciation, misperception,
misevaluation, misvaluation, misconjecture, wrong
impression; **misreading,** wrong construction,
misconstruction, **misinterpretation** 342;
inaccuracy, error 975; unmeticulousness 340.4;
injudiciousness 923.2; wrong end of the stick
VERBS **2 misjudge,** judge amiss, **miscalculate,
misestimate, misreckon,** misappreciate,
misperceive, get a wrong impression, misevaluate,
misvalue, miscompute, misdeem, misesteem,
misthink, misconjecture; **misread,** misconstrue,
put the wrong construction on things, get wrong,

misread the situation *or* case; **misinterpret** 342.2;
err 975.9; fly in the face of facts; get hold of the
wrong end of the stick <nf>

949 OVERESTIMATION

NOUNS **1 overestimation,** overestimate,
overreckoning, overcalculation, **overrating,**
overassessment, overvaluation, overappraisal;
overreaction; **overstatement, exaggeration** 355,
hype <nf>
VERBS **2 overestimate, overreckon,** overcalculate,
overcount, overmeasure, see more than is there;
overrate, overassess, overappraise, overesteem,
overvalue, overprize, overprice, think *or* make too
much of, put on a pedestal, idealize, see only the
good points of; overreact to; **overstate,** exaggerate
355.3; pump up *and* jump up *and* make a big deal
or federal case <nf>; hype <nf>
ADJS **3 overestimated, overrated,** puffed up, pumped
up <nf>, overvalued, on the high side;
exaggerated 355.4

950 UNDERESTIMATION

NOUNS **1 underestimation,** misestimation,
underestimate, **underrating,** underreckoning,
undervaluation, misprizing, misprizal, misprision;
belittlement, depreciation, deprecation,
minimization, disparagement 512; conservative
estimate; negative outlook, pessimism
VERBS **2 underestimate,** misestimate, **underrate,**
underreckon, **undervalue,** underprize, **misprize,**
underprice; **make little of,** set at little, set at
naught, set little by, attach little importance to, not
do justice to, sell short, think little of, make *or*
think nothing of, see less than is there, miss on the
low side, set no store by, make light of, shrug off,
soft-pedal <nf>; **depreciate, deprecate,** minimize,
belittle, bad-mouth *and* poor-mouth *and* put down
and run down <nf>, take someone for an idiot *or*
a fool; disparage 512.8; play down, understate
ADJS **3 underestimated, underrated,** undervalued, on
the low side; unvalued, unprized, misprized;
underpriced, cheap

951 THEORY, SUPPOSITION

NOUNS **1 theory,** theorization, *theoria* <Gk>;
theoretics, theoretic, theoric <old>; **hypothesis,**
hypothecation, hypothesizing; **speculation,** mere
theory; doctrinairism, doctrinality, doctrinarity;
analysis, **explanation,** abstraction; theoretical basis
or justification; body of theory, theoretical
structure *or* construct; unified theory

2 theory, explanation, proposed *or* tentative explanation, rationalization, proposal, proposition, statement covering the facts *or* evidence; **hypothesis,** working hypothesis

3 supposition, supposal, supposing; **presupposition,** presupposal; **assumption, presumption, conjecture, inference, surmise, guesswork; postulate,** postulation, *postulatum* <L>, set of postulates; **proposition, thesis, concept, premise** 935.7; **axiom** 974.2

4 guess, conjecture, unverified supposition, perhaps, speculation, guesswork, surmise, educated guess; guesstimate *and* hunch *and* shot *and* stab <nf>; rough guess, wild guess, blind guess, bold conjecture, shot in the dark <nf>, crude estimate

5 <vague supposition> **suggestion,** bare suggestion, **suspicion, inkling, hint, clue, sense, feeling, feeling in one's bones, intuition** 934, **intimation, impression, notion,** mere notion, hunch *and* sneaking suspicion <nf>, instinct, trace of an idea, half an idea, vague idea, hazy idea, **idea** 932

6 supposititiousness, presumptiveness, presumableness, theoreticalness, hypotheticalness, conjecturableness, speculativeness

7 theorist, theorizer, theoretic, **theoretician,** notionalist <old>; **speculator;** hypothesist, hypothesizer; doctrinaire, doctrinarian; inquirer; synthesizer; armchair authority *or* philosopher; thinker; researcher, experimenter

8 supposer, assumer, surmiser, **conjecturer, guesser,** guessworker, speculator, gambler

VERBS **9 theorize, hypothesize, hypothecate,** form a hypothesis, **speculate,** postulate, have *or* entertain a theory, espouse a theory, generalize

10 suppose, assume, presume, surmise, expect, **suspect, infer, understand, gather, conclude, deduce, consider,** reckon, reason, derive, divine, imagine, **fancy,** dream, conceive, **believe, deem,** repute, feel, **think,** be inclined to think, opine, say, daresay, be afraid <nf>; take, take it, take it into one's head, take for, take to be, take for granted, take as a precondition, **presuppose, presurmise,** prefigure; provisionally accept *or* admit *or* agree to, take one up on <nf>, grant, stipulate, take it as given, let, let be, say *or* assume for argument's sake, say for the hell of it <nf>; draw a mental picture

11 conjecture, guess, guesstimate <nf>, give a guess, talk off the top of one's head <nf>, hazard a conjecture, venture a guess, risk assuming *or* stating, tentatively suggest, go out on a limb <nf>

12 postulate, predicate, posit, set forth, lay down, put forth, assert; pose, advance, **propose,** propound 439.5

ADJS **13 theoretical, hypothetical,** hypothetic; postulatory, notional; **speculative, conjectural,** blue-sky; impressionistic, intuitive 933.5; general, generalized, abstract, ideal; unverified, merely theoretical, academic, moot; impractical, armchair, thought-provoking

14 supposed, suppositive, **assumed, presumed, conjectured, inferred,** understood, deemed, **reputed,** putative, alleged, accounted as; suppositional, supposititious; assumptive, **presumptive;** guessed; given, granted, taken as *or* for granted, agreed, stipulated; **postulated,** postulational, premised; granted for the sake of argument

15 supposable, presumable, assumable, conjecturable, surmisable, imaginable, premissable

ADVS **16 theoretically, hypothetically,** *ex hypothesi* <L>, notionally, conceptually, ideally; **in theory,** in idea, in the ideal, in the abstract, on paper, in Never-Neverland <nf>

17 supposedly, supposably, **presumably,** presumedly, assumably, assumedly, presumptively, assumptively, reputedly, presumingly; suppositionally, supposititiously; **seemingly,** in seeming, quasi; as it were; on the assumption that

18 conjecturably, **conjecturally;** to guess, to make a guess, **as a guess,** as a rough guess *or* an approximation, speculatively

CONJS **19 supposing,** supposing that, **assuming that,** allowing that, if we assume that, let's say that, granting *or* granted that, given that, on the assumption *or* supposition that; if, as if, as though, by way of hypothesis

952 PHILOSOPHY

NOUNS **1 philosophy,** "life's guide"—Cicero, "a handmaid to religion"—Francis Bacon; philosophical inquiry *or* investigation, philosophical speculation; inquiry *or* investigation into first causes; branch of philosophy <see list>, department *or* division of philosophy; school of philosophy <see list>, philosophic system, school of thought; philosophic doctrine, philosophic theory; theory of knowledge; philosophastry, philosophastering; sophistry 936

2 viewpoint, point of view, outlook, attitude, opinion; feeling, sentiment, idea, thought, notion; tenet, dogma, doctrine, canon, principle; assertion, proposition, premise, assumption, precept, thesis, postulate, hypothesis, concept; supposition, presupposition, conjecture, speculation; maxim, axiom; rationalization, justification; conclusion, judgment; philosophical system, belief system, value system, set of beliefs *or* values, ethics, morals, school of thought, moral code, code of conduct, value judgment, standards, principles, ideology

3 Platonic philosophy, Platonism, philosophy of the Academy; Aristotelian philosophy, Aristotelianism, philosophy of the Lyceum, Peripateticism, Peripatetic school; Stoic philosophy, Stoicism, philosophy of the Porch *or* Stoa; Epicureanism, philosophy of the Garden

4 materialism; idealism 1053.3

5 monism, philosophical unitarianism, mind-stuff theory; pantheism, cosmotheism; hylozoism

6 pluralism; dualism, mind-matter theory

7 <political and economic philosophy> anarchism, capitalism, collectivism, communism, internationalism, isolationism, Marxism, monetarism, nationalism, socialism, utilitarianism, utopianism

8 philosopher, philosophizer, philosophe; philosophaster; **thinker,** speculator; casuist; metaphysician, cosmologist, logician, dialectician, syllogist; sophist 935.6; idealist, idealogue, visionary, dreamer

VERBS **9 philosophize,** reason 935.15, probe

ADJS **10 philosophical,** philosophic, sophistical 936.10; philosophicohistorical, philosophicolegal, philosophicojuristic, philosophicopsychological, philosophicoreligious, philosophicotheological; notional, abstract, esoteric, ideological, ideational, hypothetical, theoretical

11 absurdist, acosmistic, aesthetic, African, agnostic, Alexandrian, analytic, animalistic, animist *or* animistic, atomistic, etc <see list of schools and doctrines>

12 Aristotelian, Peripatetic; Augustinian, Averroist *or* Averroistic, Bergsonian, Berkeleian, Cartesian, Comtian, Hegelian, Neo-Hegelian, Heideggerian, Heraclitean, Humean, Husserlian, Kantian, Leibnizian, Parmenidean, Platonic, Neoplatonic, pre-Socratic, Pyrrhonic, Pyrrhonian, Pythagorean, Neo-Pythagorean, Sartrian, Schellingian, Schopenhauerian, Scotist, Socratic, Spencerian, Thomist *or* Thomistic, Viconian, Wittgensteinian

13 branches or departments of philosophy

aesthetics *or* theory of beauty *or* philosophy of art
analytic philosophy
axiology *or* value theory
casuistry
commonsense *or* naïve realism
cosmology
deontology
ethics *or* moral philosophy
logic *or* theory of argument
metaphysics *or* first philosophy *or* theory of existence
ontology *or* science of being
phenomenology
philosophy of biology
philosophy of education
philosophy of history
philosophy of language *or* semantics
philosophy of law
philosophy of logic
philosophy of nature
philosophy of physics
philosophy of religion
philosophy of science
philosophy of signs *or* semiotics
political philosophy
sentential *or* propositional calculus
teleology
theology
theory of knowledge *or* epistemology *or* gnosiology

14 schools and doctrines of philosophy

Augustinianism
Aristotelianism
Atomism
Augustinianism
Averroism
Baconism
Bergsonism
Berkeleianism
Bonaventurism
Bradleianism
Brahmanism
Buddhism
Cartesianism
Comtism
Confucianism
cosmotheism
criticism *or* critical philosophy
Cynicism
Cyrenaic hedonism *or* Cyrenaicism
deconstructionism
deism
dialectical materialism
dualism
eclecticism
egoism
egoistic hedonism
Eleaticism *or* the Elean school
empiricism
Epicureanism
Eretrian school
eristic school
essentialism
ethicism
ethics
eudaemonism
existentialism *or* existential philosophy
Fabianism
Fichteanism
Gnosticism
hedonism
Hegelianism
Heideggerianism
Heracliteanism
Herbartianism
Hinduism
Hobbism
humanism
Humism
hylomorphism
hylotheism
hylozoism
idealism
immaterialism
individualism
instrumentalism
intuitionism
Ionian school
Jainism
Juddaism
Kantianism
Leibnizianism
linguistic *and* analytic philosophy
logical empiricism *or* logical positivism
Manichaeism
Marxism
materialism
mechanism
Megarianism
mentalism
Mimamsa
Mithraism
monism
mysticism
naturalism
Neo-Hegelianism
Neo-Platonism
Neo-Pythagoreanism
Neo-Scholasticism
neocriticism
Neoplatonism
new ethical movement
nominalism
noumenalism
Nyaya
ontologism
ontology
optimism
ordinary language philosophy
organic mechanism

organicism
panlogism
panpneumatism
panpsychism
pantheism
panthelism
Parmenidean school
patristic philosophy
patristicism
Peripateticism
pessimism
phenomenalism
phenomenology
philosophy of organism
philosophy of signs
philosophy of the ante-
  Nicene Fathers
philosophy of the post-
  Nicene Fathers
physicalism
physicism
Platonism
pluralism
positivism
pragmatism *or*
  pragmaticism
probabilism
Protestantism
psychism
psychological hedonism
Puritanism
Purva Mimamsa
Pyrrhonism
Pythagoreanism
rationalism
realism

Sankhya
Sartrianism
Satyagraha
Schellingism
Scholasticism
Schopenhauerism
Scotism
secular humanism
semiotic *or* semiotics *or*
  semi-idiotics <nf>
sensationalism
sensism
Shintoism
Sikhism
skepticism
Socratism *or* Socratic
  philosophy
solipsism
Sophism *or* Sophistry
Spencerianism
Spinozism
Stoicism
substantialism
syncretism
Taoism
theism
Thomism
transcendentalism
universalistic hedonism
utilitarianism
Uttara Mimamsa
Valsheshika
vitalism
voluntarism
zetetic philosophy

953 BELIEF

NOUNS **1 belief,** credence, credit, believing, faith, trust; hope; **confidence,** assuredness, convincedness, persuadedness, **assurance;** sureness, surety, **certainty** 970; **reliance, dependence,** reliance on *or* in, dependence on, stock *and* store <nf>; acceptation, acception, acceptance; reception, acquiescence; blind faith, full faith and credit; suspension of disbelief; fideism; **credulity** 954

2 a belief, tenet, dogma, precept, **principle, principle** *or* **article of faith,** premise, canon, maxim, axiom; **doctrine,** teaching

3 system of belief; religion, faith 675.1, belief-system; **school, cult, ism,** philosophy, **ideology,** *Weltanschauung* <Ger>, world view; political faith *or* belief *or* philosophy; **creed, credo,** credenda, dogma, canon; articles of religion, articles of faith, creedal *or* doctrinal statement, formulated *or* stated belief; gospel; catechism

4 statement of belief *or* **principles,** manifesto, position paper; solemn declaration; deposition, affidavit, sworn statement

5 conviction, persuasion, certainty; firm belief, moral certainty, implicit *or* staunch belief, settled judgment, mature judgment *or* belief, fixed opinion, unshaken confidence, steadfast faith, rooted *or* deep-rooted belief

6 opinion, sentiment, feeling, sense, impression, reaction, **notion, idea, thought,** mind, thinking, **way of thinking, attitude,** stance, posture, position, mindset, **view,** viewpoint, eye, sight, lights, observation, **conception,** concept, conceit, **estimation,** estimate, consideration, angle, **theory** 951, conjecture, supposition, assumption, presumption, **conclusion,** judgment 946, personal judgment; **point of view** 978.2; public opinion, public belief, general belief, prevailing belief *or* sentiment, *consensus gentium* <L>, common belief, community sentiment, popular belief, conventional wisdom, vox pop, *vox populi* <L>, climate of opinion; ethos; mystique

7 profession, confession, declaration, **profession** *or* **confession** *or* **declaration of faith**

8 believability, persuasiveness, believableness, convincingness, **credibility, credit, trustworthiness, plausibility,** tenability, acceptability, conceivability; **reliability** 969.4

9 believer, truster; religious believer; true believer; the assured, the faithful, the believing; fideist; ideologist, ideologue; conformist; innocent, naïf

VERBS **10 believe, credit, trust, accept,** receive, buy <nf>; give credit *or* credence to, give faith to, put faith in, take stock in *or* set store by <nf>, take to heart, attach weight to; be led to believe; accept implicitly, believe without reservation, rest assured, take for granted, take *or* accept for gospel, take as gospel truth <nf>, take *or* accept on faith, take on trust *or* credit, pin one's faith on; take at face value; **take one's word for,** trust one's word, take at one's word; fall for; **buy** *and* **buy into** <nf>, **swallow** 953.6; **be certain** 970.9

11 think, opine, be of the opinion, be persuaded, be convinced; be afraid <nf>, **have the idea,** have an idea, **suppose, assume, presume, judge** 945.8, **guess, surmise, suspect,** have a hunch <nf>, have an inkling, expect <nf>, have an impression, be under the impression, have a sense *or* the sense, conceive, ween *and* trow <old>, **imagine, fancy,** daresay; **deem, esteem, hold, regard, consider, maintain,** reckon, estimate; hold as, account as, set down as *or* for, view as, look upon as, take for, take, take it, get it into one's head

12 state, assert, swear, swear to God <nf>, declare, **affirm,** vow, avow, avouch, warrant, asseverate, confess, be under the impression, profess, express the belief, swear to a belief; depose, make an affidavit *or* a sworn statement

13 **hold the belief, have the opinion,** entertain a belief *or* an opinion, adopt *or* embrace a belief, take as an article of faith; foster *or* nurture *or* cherish a belief, be wedded to *or* espouse a belief; get hold of an idea, get it into one's head, form a conviction

14 **be confident,** have confidence, **be satisfied, be convinced, be certain,** be easy in one's mind about, be secure in the belief, **feel sure, rest assured,** rest in confidence; doubt not, **have no doubt,** have no misgivings *or* diffidence *or* qualms, have no reservations, have no second thoughts

15 **believe in, have faith in,** pin one's faith to, confide in, **have confidence in,** place *or* repose confidence in, place reliance in, put onself in the hands of, **trust in,** put trust in, have simple *or* childlike faith in, rest in, repose in *or* hope in <old>; give *or* get the benefit of the doubt

16 **rely on** *or* **upon, depend on** *or* **upon,** place reliance on, rest on *or* upon, repose on, lean on, **count on,** calculate on, reckon on, **bank on** *or* **upon** <nf>; **trust to** *or* **unto,** swear by, take one's oath upon; **bet on** *and* gamble on *and* lay money on *and* bet one's bottom dollar on *and* make book on <nf>; take one's word for

17 **trust, confide in, rely on, depend on,** repose, place trust *or* confidence in, have confidence in, **trust in** 953.15, trust utterly *or* implicitly, deem trustworthy, think reliable *or* dependable, take one's word, take at one's word

18 **convince; convert, win over,** lead one to believe, bring over, bring round, take in, talk over, talk around, bring to reason, bring to one's senses, **persuade, lead to believe, give to understand; satisfy, assure;** put one's mind at rest on; sell *and* sell one on <nf>; make *or* carry one's point, bring *or* drive home to; cram down one's throat *and* beat into one's head <nf>; be convincing, carry conviction; inspire belief *or* confidence; evangelize, proselytize, propagandize

19 **convince oneself, persuade oneself,** sell oneself <nf>, make oneself easy about, make oneself easy on that score, satisfy oneself on that point, make sure of, make up one's mind

20 **find credence, be believed,** be accepted, be received; be swallowed *and* go down *and* pass current <nf>; produce *or* carry conviction; have the ear of, gain the confidence of

ADJS 21 **believing,** of belief, preceptive, principled; attitudinal; **believing, undoubting, undoubtful,** doubtless <old>; faithful <old>, God-fearing, pious, pietistic, observant, **devout;** under the impression, impressed with; **convinced, confident,**

positive, dogmatic, secure, **persuaded,** sold on, **satisfied, assured;** born-again; **sure, certain** 970.13,20; fideistic

22 **trusting, trustful,** trusty <old>, **confiding, unsuspecting, unsuspicious,** without suspicion; childlike, innocent, guileless, naive 416.5; **knee-jerk, credulous** 954.8; relying, depending, reliant, dependent; gullible, naive

23 **believed, credited, held, trusted, accepted;** received, of belief, authoritative, maintained; **undoubted,** unsuspected, **unquestioned,** undisputed, uncontested

24 **believable, credible, creditable; tenable,** conceivable, **plausible,** colorable, realistic; worthy of faith, trustworthy, trusty; fiduciary; reliable 969.17; unimpeachable, unexceptionable, **unquestionable** 970.15

25 fiducial, fiduciary; convictional

26 **convincing,** convictional, well-founded, **persuasive,** assuring, impressive, satisfying, satisfactory, confidence-building; decisive, absolute, conclusive, determinative; authoritative

27 **doctrinal, creedal,** preceptive, canonical, dogmatic, confessional, mandatory, of faith

ADVS 28 **believingly, undoubtingly,** undoubtfully, without doubt *or* question *or* quibble, unquestioningly; **trustingly,** trustfully, unsuspectingly, unsuspiciously; piously, devoutly; with faith; **with confidence,** on *or* upon trust, on faith, on one's say-so

29 **in one's opinion, to one's mind,** in one's thinking, **to one's way of thinking,** the way one thinks, **in one's estimation,** according to one's lights, **as one sees it, to the best of one's belief;** in the opinion of, in the eyes of

954 CREDULITY

NOUNS 1 **credulity, credulousness,** inclination *or* disposition to believe, ease of belief, will *or* willingness to believe, wishful belief *or* thinking; **blind faith,** unquestioning belief, knee-jerk response *or* agreement <nf>; uncritical acceptance, premature *or* unripe acceptation, hasty *or* rash conviction; **trustfulness, trustingness, unsuspiciousness,** unsuspectingness; uncriticalness, unskepticalness; overcredulity, overcredulousness, overtrustfulness, overopenness to conviction *or* persuasion, gross credulity; infatuation, fondness, dotage; one's blind side

2 **gullibility, dupability,** bamboozlability <nf>, cullibility <old>, **deceivability,** seduceability, persuadability, hoaxability; biddability; easiness <nf>, softness, weakness; **simpleness,** simplicity,

ingenuousness, unsophistication; greenness, naïveness, **naïveté,** naivety

3 **superstition,** superstitiousness; popular belief, **old wives' tale;** tradition, lore, folklore; charm, spell 691

4 trusting soul; **dupe** 358; sucker *and* patsy *and* easy mark *and* pushover <nf>

VERBS **5** **be credulous,** accept unquestioningly; not boggle at anything, **believe anything,** be easy of belief *or* persuasion, be uncritical, believe at the drop of a hat, be a dupe, think the moon is made of green cheese, buy a pig in a poke

6 <nf terms> kid oneself, fall for, swallow, swallow anything, swallow whole, not choke *or* gag on; swallow hook, line, and sinker; eat up, lap up, devour, gulp down, gobble up *or* down, buy, buy into, bite, nibble, rise to the fly, take the bait, swing at, go for, tumble for, be taken in, be suckered, be a sucker *or* a patsy *or* an easy mark

7 **be superstitious;** knock on wood, keep one's fingers crossed

ADJS **8** **credulous, knee-jerk** <nf>, easy of belief, ready *or* inclined to believe, easily taken in; **undoubting** 953.21; **trustful, trusting; unsuspicious, unsuspecting;** unthinking, uncritical, unskeptical; overcredulous, overtrustful, overtrusting, overconfiding; fond, infatuated, doting; **superstitious**

9 **gullible, dupable,** bamboozlable <nf>, cullible <old>, **deceivable, foolable, deludable, exploitable,** victimizable, seduceable, persuadable, hoaxable, humbugable, hoodwinkable; biddable; soft, easy <nf>, **simple; ingenuous, unsophisticated, green, naive** 416.5

955 UNBELIEF

NOUNS **1** **unbelief, disbelief,** nonbelief, unbelievingness, discredit; refusal *or* inability to believe; **incredulity** 955; **unpersuadedness,** unconvincedness, lack of conviction; **denial** 335.2, **rejection** 372; misbelief, heresy 688.2; infidelity, atheism, **agnosticism** 695.6; minimifidianism, nullifidianism

2 **doubt, doubtfulness, dubiousness,** dubiety; half-belief; **reservation, question,** question in one's mind; **skepticism,** skepticalness; total skepticism, Pyrrhonism; **suspicion,** suspiciousness, wariness, leeriness, **distrust, mistrust, misdoubt,** distrustfulness, mistrustfulness; **misgiving,** self-doubt, diffidence; qualm; scruple *and* scrupulousness <old>; hesitation; apprehension 127.4; **uncertainty** 971; shadow of doubt

3 **unbelievability,** unbelievableness, **incredibility, implausibility,** impossibility, improbability, inconceivability, untenableness, untenability;

unpersuasiveness, unconvincingness; **doubtfulness, questionableness;** credibility gap; unreliability 971.6

4 doubter, doubting Thomas; scoffer, skeptic, cynic, pooh-pooher, nay-sayer, disbeliever, nonbeliever, unbeliever 695.11

VERBS **5** **disbelieve,** unbelieve, misbelieve, **not believe,** find hard to believe, not admit, refuse to admit, not buy <nf>, take no stock in *and* set no store by <nf>; **discredit,** refuse to credit, refuse to give credence to, give no credit *or* credence to; gag on, **not swallow** 956.3; negate, **deny** 335.4, nay-say, say nay; scoff at, pooh-pooh; **reject** 372.2

6 **doubt, be doubtful, be dubious, be skeptical,** doubt the truth of, beg leave to doubt, **have one's doubts,** have *or* harbor *or* entertain doubts *or* suspicions, half believe, have reservations, **take with a grain of salt,** be from Missouri <nf>, scruple <old>, **distrust, mistrust,** misgive, cross one's fingers; **be uncertain** 971.9; **suspect,** smell a rat *and* see something funny <nf>; **question,** query, **challenge, contest, dispute,** cast doubt on, greet with skepticism, keep one's eye on, treat with reserve, bring *or* call into question, raise a question, throw doubt upon, awake a doubt *or* suspicion; **doubt one's word,** give one the lie; doubt oneself, be diffident

7 **be unbelievable,** be incredible, be hard to swallow, defy belief, pass belief, be hard to believe, strain one's credulity, **stagger belief;** shake one's faith, undermine one's faith; perplex, boggle the mind, stagger, fill with doubt

ADJS **8** **unbelieving, disbelieving,** nonbelieving; faithless, without faith; unconfident, unconvinced, unconverted; nullifidian, minimifidian, creedless; **incredulous** 956.4; repudiative; **heretical** 688.9; **irreligious** 695.17

9 **doubting, doubtful, in doubt, dubious; questioning; skeptical,** Pyrrhonic, from Missouri <nf>; **distrustful, mistrustful, untrustful,** mistrusting, untrusting; **suspicious,** suspecting, scrupulous <old>, shy, wary, leery; **agnostic; uncertain**

10 **unbelievable, incredible,** unthinkable, **implausible,** unimaginable, inconceivable, not to be believed, **hard to believe,** hard of belief, beyond belief, unworthy of belief, not meriting *or* not deserving belief, tall <nf>; **defying belief,** staggering belief, passing belief; **mind-boggling,** preposterous, absurd, ridiculous, unearthly, ungodly; **doubtful, dubious,** doubtable, dubitable, **questionable,** problematic, problematical, **unconvincing,** open to doubt *or* suspicion; **suspicious,** suspect, funny; so-called, self-styled; thin *and* a bit thin <nf>; thick *and* a bit thick *and* a little too thick <nf>

11 under a cloud, unreliable
12 **doubted, questioned,** disputed, contested, moot; **distrusted,** mistrusted; **suspect,** suspected, **under suspicion,** under a cloud; **discredited,** exploded, rejected, **disbelieved**
ADVS 13 **unbelievingly,** doubtingly, **doubtfully, dubiously,** questioningly, **skeptically,** suspiciously; **with a grain of salt,** with reservations, with some allowance, with caution
14 **unbelievably, incredibly,** unthinkably, implausibly, inconceivably, unimaginably, staggeringly

956 INCREDULITY

NOUNS 1 **incredulity, incredulousness,** uncredulousness, refusal *or* disinclination to believe, resistance *or* resistiveness to belief, tough-mindedness, hardheadedness, **inconvincibility,** unconvincibility, unpersuadability, unpersuasibility; **suspiciousness,** suspicion, wariness, leeriness, guardedness, cautiousness, caution; **skepticism** 955.2
2 **ungullibility,** uncullibility <old>, **undupability, undeceivability,** unhoaxability, unseduceability; **sophistication**
VERBS 3 **refuse to believe,** resist believing, **not allow oneself to believe,** be slow to believe *or* accept; not kid oneself <nf>; **disbelieve** 954.5; **be skeptical** 955.6; **not swallow,** not be able to swallow *or* down <nf>, not go for *and* **not fall for** <nf>, not be taken in by; **not accept, not buy** *or* **buy into** <nf>, **reject** 372.2
ADJS 4 **incredulous,** uncredulous, **hard of belief,** shy of belief, disposed to doubt, indisposed *or* disinclined to believe, unwilling to accept; impervious to persuasion, **inconvincible,** unconvincible, unpersuadable, unpersuasible; **suspicious, suspecting,** wary, leery, cautious, guarded; **skeptical** 955.9
5 **ungullible,** uncullible <old>, **undupable, undeceivable, unfoolable, undeludable,** unhoaxable, unseduceable, hoaxproof; **sophisticated, wise, hardheaded,** practical, realistic, tough-minded; nobody's fool, not born yesterday, nobody's sucker *or* patsy <nf>

957 EVIDENCE, PROOF

NOUNS 1 **evidence, proof; reason to believe,** reason, grounds for belief; **ground, grounds,** material grounds, **facts, data,** information, record, premises, basis for belief; piece *or* item of evidence, **fact,** datum, relevant fact; **indication, manifestation, sign, symptom,** mark, token, mute witness; body of evidence, documentation;

muniments, title deeds and papers; chain of evidence; **clue;** exhibit; intelligence; lowdown <nf>
2 **testimony, attestation,** attest <old>, **witness;** testimonial, testimonium <old>; **statement, declaration, assertion,** asseveration, affirmation 334, avouchment, avowal, averment, allegation, admission, **disclosure** 351, profession, word; confession; **deposition,** legal evidence, sworn evidence *or* testimony; *procès-verbal* <Fr>; compurgation; affidavit, sworn statement; instrument in proof, *pièce justificative* <Fr>
3 **proof, demonstration,** ironclad proof, incontrovertible proof; **determination, establishment, settlement; conclusive evidence,** indisputable evidence, incontrovertible evidence, damning evidence, unmistakable sign, sure sign, absolute indication, smoking gun <nf>; open-and-shut case; burden of proof, onus, *onus probandi* <L>; the proof of the pudding
4 **confirmation, substantiation,** proof, proving, proving out, bearing out, affirmation, attestation, **authentication, validation, certification,** ratification, **verification; corroboration, support,** supporting evidence, corroboratory evidence, fortification, buttressing, bolstering, backing, backing up, reinforcement, undergirding, strengthening, circumstantiation, fact sheet; **documentation**
5 **citation, reference,** quotation; **exemplification,** instance, example, case, case in point, particular, item, illustration, demonstration; cross reference
6 **witness, eyewitness,** spectator, earwitness; **bystander,** passerby; **deponent, testifier,** attestant, attester, attestator, voucher, swearer; **informant,** informer; character witness; cojuror, compurgator
7 **provability, demonstrability,** determinability; confirmability, supportability, verifiability
VERBS 8 **evidence, evince,** furnish evidence, **show, go to show, mean,** tend to show, witness to, testify to; **demonstrate, illustrate,** exhibit, manifest, display, express, set forth; approve; **attest; indicate, signify,** signalize, symptomatize, mark, **denote, betoken, point to,** give indication of, show signs of, bear on, touch on; **connote, imply, suggest,** involve; argue, breathe, tell, bespeak; **speak for itself,** speak volumes
9 **testify, attest, give evidence,** witness, witness to, **give** *or* **bear witness;** disclose 351.4; vouch, state one's case, **depose,** depone, **warrant, swear,** take one's oath, acknowledge, avow, **affirm,** avouch, aver, allege, asseverate, **certify, give one's word;** turn state's evidence, rat *and* squeal *and* sing <nf>; grass <Brit nf>
10 **prove, demonstrate, show,** afford proof of, prove

to be, prove true; **establish**, fix, **determine, ascertain,** make out, remove all doubt; **settle,** settle the matter; **set at rest;** clinch *and* cinch *and* nail down <nf>; **prove one's point,** make one's case, bring home to, make good, have *or* make out a case; hold good, hold water; follow, follow from, follow as a matter of course

11 **confirm,** affirm, **attest,** warrant, uphold <Brit nf>, **substantiate, authenticate, validate, certify,** ratify, **verify;** circumstantiate, **corroborate, bear out,** support, buttress, **sustain,** fortify, bolster, back, back up, reinforce, undergird, strengthen; **document;** probate, prove; double-check

12 **adduce,** produce, **advance, present,** bring to bear, **offer,** proffer, invoke, obtest, allege <old>, plead, **bring forward,** bring on; rally, marshal, deploy, array; call to witness, call to *or* put in the witness box

13 **cite, name,** call to mind; **instance,** cite a particular *or* particulars, cite cases *or* a case in point, itemize, particularize, produce an instance, give a for-instance <nf>; **exemplify,** example <old>, **illustrate,** demonstrate; **document; quote,** quote chapter and verse

14 **refer to,** direct attention to, **appeal to,** invoke; make reference to; cross-refer, make a cross-reference; reference, cross-reference

15 **have evidence** *or* **proof,** have a case, possess incriminating evidence, **have something on** <nf>; **have the goods on** *and* have dead to rights *or* bang to rights <nf>

ADJS 16 **evidential,** evidentiary, **factual,** symptomatic, **significant, relevant, indicative,** attestative, attestive, probative; founded on, grounded on, based on; implicit, suggestive; material, telling, convincing, weighty; overwhelming, damning; **conclusive,** determinative, **decisive,** final, incontrovertible, irresistible, indisputable, irrefutable, sure, certain, absolute; documented, documentary; **valid, admissible;** adducible; firsthand, authentic, reliable 970.17, empirical, eyewitness; hearsay, circumstantial, presumptive, nuncupative, cumulative, ex parte

17 **demonstrative,** demonstrating, demonstrational, telltale; evincive, apodictic

18 **confirming,** confirmatory, confirmative, certificatory; substantiating, **verifying,** verificative; **corroborating,** corroboratory, **corroborative,** supportive, **supporting**

19 **provable, demonstrable,** demonstratable, apodictic, evincible, attestable, **confirmable,** checkable, **substantiatable, establishable,** supportable, sustainable, **verifiable,** validatable, authenticatable

20 **proved, proven, demonstrated,** shown;

established, fixed, **settled, determined,** nailed down <nf>, ascertained; evident, self-evident; **confirmed, substantiated,** attested, **authenticated, certified, validated, verified;** circumstantiated, **corroborated,** borne out; cross-checked, double-checked; collated; ostensible

21 **unrefuted,** unconfuted, unanswered, uncontroverted, uncontradicted, **undenied;** unrefutable 970.15

ADVS 22 **evidentially,** according to the evidence, on the evidence, as attested by, judging by; **in confirmation, in corroboration of, in support of;** at first hand, at second hand; dead to rights *or* bang to rights *and* with a smoking gun *and* with one's pants down <nf>

23 **to illustrate,** to prove the point, as an example, as a case in point, to name an instance, by way of example, **for example, for instance,** to cite an instance, as an instance, e.g., *exempli gratia* <L>; as, **thus**

24 **which see, q.v.,** *quod vide* <L>; *loco citato* <L>, loc cit; *opere citato* <L>, op cit

PHRS 25 **it is proven,** *probatum est* <L>, there is nothing more to be said, it must follow; QED, *quod erat demonstrandum* <L>

958 DISPROOF

NOUNS 1 **disproof,** disproving, disproval, **invalidation,** disconfirmation, explosion, negation, redargution <old>; exposure, exposé; *reductio ad absurdum* <L>; circumstantial evidence, hearsay evidence, inadmissible evidence, incriminating evidence

2 **refutation, confutation,** confounding, refutal, **rebuttal, answer,** complete answer, crushing *or* effective rejoinder, squelch, comeback; discrediting; **overthrow,** overthrowal, upset, upsetting, subversion, undermining, demolition; renunciation; contention; **contradiction,** controversion, **denial** 335.2

3 **conclusive argument, elenchus, knockdown argument, floorer,** sockdolager <nf>; **clincher** *or* crusher *or* **settler** *and* finisher *and* squelcher <nf>

VERBS 4 **disprove, invalidate,** disconfirm, discredit, prove the contrary, belie, give the lie to, redargue <old>; **negate,** negative; **expose, show up;** explode, blow up, blow sky-high, **puncture,** deflate **shoot** *or* **poke full of holes, cut to pieces, cut the ground from under; knock the bottom out of** <nf>, knock the props *or* chocks out from under, knock down, take the ground from under, undercut, cut the ground from under one's feet, not leave a leg to stand on, have the last word, leave nothing to say, put *or* lay to rest

5 **refute, confute, confound, rebut,** parry, answer, **answer conclusively,** dismiss, dispose of; **overthrow,** overturn, overwhelm, upset, subvert, defeat, demolish, undermine; argue down, argue into a corner; show what's what; floor *and* finish *and* settle *and* squash *and* squelch <nf>, crush, smash all opposition; silence, put *or* reduce to silence, shut up, stop the mouth of; nonplus, take the wind out of one's sails; **contradict,** controvert, counter, run counter, **deny** 335.4

ADJS 6 **refuting, confuting,** confounding, confutative, refutative, refutatory, discomfirmatory; contradictory, contrary 335.5

7 **disproved,** disconfirmed, **invalidated,** negated, negatived, discredited, belied; **exposed,** shown up; **punctured,** deflated, **exploded; refuted,** confuted, confounded; **upset, overthrown,** overturned; **contradicted,** disputed, denied, impugned; dismissed, discarded, rejected 372.3

8 **unproved,** not proved, unproven, **undemonstrated,** unshown, not shown; **untried,** untested; **unestablished,** unfixed, **unsettled, undetermined,** unascertained; **unconfirmed, unsubstantiated,** unattested, **unauthenticated,** unvalidated, uncertified, **unverified; uncorroborated,** unsustained, **unsupported,** unsupported by evidence, **groundless,** without grounds *or* basis, **unfounded** 935.13; **inconclusive,** indecisive; **moot,** sub judice; not following

9 **unprovable,** controvertible, **undemonstrable,** undemonstratable, unattestable, unsubstantiatable, **unsupportable,** unconfirmable, unsustainable, unverifiable

10 **refutable,** confutable, **disprovable,** defeasible

959 QUALIFICATION

NOUNS 1 **qualification, limitation, limiting, restriction,** circumscription, **modification,** hedge, hedging; setting conditions, conditionality, provisionality, circumstantiality; specification; **allowance, concession,** cession, grant; grain of salt; **reservation, exception,** waiver, exemption; **exclusion,** ruling out, including out <nf>; specialness, special circumstance, special case, special treatment; **mental reservation,** salvo <old>, *arrière-pensée* <Fr>, crossing one's fingers; extenuating circumstances

2 **condition, provision, proviso, stipulation,** whereas; definition; frame of reference; **specification,** parameter, given, *donnée* <Fr>, **limitation,** limiting condition, boundary condition; **contingency,** circumstance 766; **catch** *and* joker *and* kicker *and* string *and* a string to it <nf>; **requisite, prerequisite,** obligation; *sine qua non*

<L>, *conditio sine qua non* <L>; clause, escape clause, escapeway, escape hatch, saving clause; escalator clause; **terms,** provisions; grounds; small *or* fine print *and* fine print at the bottom <nf>; ultimatum

VERBS 3 **qualify, limit,** condition <old>, hedge, hedge about, **modify, restrict,** restrain, circumscribe, delimit, set limits *or* conditions, box in <nf>, narrow, set criteria; adjust to, regulate by; alter 852.6; **temper, season,** leaven, soften, modulate, moderate, assuage, **mitigate,** palliate, abate, reduce, diminish

4 **make conditional,** make contingent, **condition;** make it a condition, attach a condition *or* proviso, **stipulate;** insist upon, make a point of; **have a catch** *and* have a joker *or* kicker *and* have a joker in the deck *and* have a string attached <nf>; cross one's fingers behind one's back

5 **allow for, make allowance for,** make room for, provide for, open the door to, take account of, **take into account** *or* **consideration, consider,** consider the circumstances; allow, **grant, concede,** admit, admit exceptions, see the special circumstances; **relax,** relax the condition, **waive, set aside,** ease, lift temporarily, pull one's punches <nf>; disregard, **discount,** leave out of account; consider the source, take with a grain of salt

6 **depend,** hang, rest, hinge; **depend on** *or* **upon,** hang on *or* upon, **rest on** *or* **upon,** rest with, repose upon, lie on, lie with, stand on *or* upon, be based on, be bounded *or* limited by, be dependent on, be predicated on, **be contingent** *or* **conditional on; hinge on** *or* **upon, turn on** *or* **upon, revolve on** *or* **upon,** have as a fulcrum

ADJS 7 **qualifying,** qualificative, qualificatory, **modifying,** modificatory, altering; **limiting, limitational, restricting,** limitative, restrictive, bounding; circumstantial, contingent; **extenuating,** extenuatory, **mitigating,** mitigative, mitigatory, modulatory, palliative, assuasive, lenitive, softening

8 **conditional, provisional,** provisory, stipulatory; parametric; specificative; **specified, stipulated,** defined, fixed, stated, given; **temporary,** expedient

9 **contingent, dependent, depending;** contingent on, **dependent on, depending on,** predicated on, based on, hanging *or* hinging on, turning on, revolving on; depending on circumstances; circumscribed by, hedged *or* hedged about by; boxed in <nf>; **subject to,** incidental to, incident to

10 **qualified, modified, conditioned, limited, restricted,** delimited, hedged, hedged about; **tempered, seasoned,** leavened, palliative, softened, moderated, **mitigated,** modulated

ADVS 11 **conditionally, provisionally,** with

qualifications, with a string *or* catch *or* joker *or* kicker to it <nf>; with a reservation *or* an exception, with a grain of salt; **temporarily,** for the time being

CONJS **12 provided,** provided that, provided always, **providing,** with this proviso, it being provided; **on condition,** on condition that, **with the stipulation,** with the understanding, according as, subject to

13 granting, admitting, allowing, admitting that, allowing that, seeing that; exempting, waiving

14 if, an *or* an' <old>, if and when, only if, if only, if and only if, if it be so, if it be true that, if it so happens *or* turns out

15 so, just so, so that <old>, **so as, so long as, as long as**

16 unless, unless that, **if not, were it not,** were it not that; **except, excepting,** except that, with the exception that, save, **but; without,** absent

960 NO QUALIFICATIONS

NOUNS **1 unqualifiedness,** unlimitedness, **unconditionality,** unrestrictedness, **unreservedness,** uncircumscribedness; categoricalness; **absoluteness,** definiteness, **explicitness;** decisiveness

ADJS **2 unqualified, unconditional,** unconditioned, **unrestricted,** unhampered, **unlimited,** uncircumscribed, unmitigated, **categorical,** straight, **unreserved,** without reserve; unaltered, unadulterated, intact; **implicit,** unquestioning, undoubting, unhesitating; **explicit, express, unequivocal,** clear, unmistakable; **peremptory,** indisputable, inappealable; **without exception,** admitting no exception, unwaivable; **positive, absolute, flat,** definite, definitive, determinate, decided, decisive, fixed, final, conclusive; **complete, entire, whole, total,** global; **utter,** perfect, downright, outright, out-and-out, straight-out <nf>, all-out, flat-out <nf>

ADVS **3** <nf terms> **no ifs, ands, or buts;** no strings attached, no holds barred, no catch *or* joker *or* kicker, no joker in the deck, no small print *or* fine print, no fine print at the bottom; downright, that's that, what you see is what you get

961 FORESIGHT

NOUNS **1 foresight,** foreseeing, looking ahead, **prevision,** divination 962.2, forecast; **prediction** 961; **foreglimpse,** foreglance, foregleam; preview, prepublication; **prospect,** prospection; **anticipation,** contemplation, envisionment, envisagement; **foresightedness; farsightedness,** longsightedness, farseeingness; sagacity,

providence, discretion, preparation, provision, forehandedness, readiness, consideration, prudence 920.7

2 forethought, premeditation, predeliberation, preconsideration 380.3; caution 494; lead time, advance notice; run-up; plan, long-range plan, contingency plan; prospectus

3 foreknowledge, foreknowing, forewisdom, **precognition,** prescience, presage, presentiment, foreboding; clairvoyance 689.8; foreseeability 961.8; insight; premonition, expectation

4 foretaste, antepast <old>, prelibation

VERBS **5 foresee,** see beforehand *or* ahead, foreglimpse, foretaste, **anticipate,** contemplate, envision, envisage, **look forward to,** look ahead, look beyond, look *or* pry *or* peep into the future; **predict** 962.9; think ahead *or* beforehand; have an eye to the future

6 foreknow, know beforehand, precognize, know in advance, have prior knowledge; smell in the wind, scent from afar; **have a presentiment,** have a premonition 133.11; see the handwriting on the wall, have a hunch *or* feel in one's bones <nf>, just know, intuit 934.4

ADJS **7 foreseeing, foresighted; foreknowing, precognizant,** precognitive, prescient; divinatory 962.11; **forethoughted,** forethoughtful; anticipant, anticipatory, expectant; **farseeing, farsighted,** longsighted; sagacious, provident, providential, forehanded, prepared, ready, prudent 920.19; intuitive 933.5; clairvoyant, telepathic

8 foreseeable 962.13; foreseen 962.14; predictable; intuitable

ADVS **9 foreseeingly, foreknowingly,** with foresight; against the time when, for a rainy day

962 PREDICTION

NOUNS **1 prediction, foretelling,** foreshowing, forecasting, **prognosis,** prognostication, presage <old>, presaging; **prophecy,** prophesying, vaticination; **soothsaying,** soothsay; prefiguration, prefigurement, prefiguring; preshowing, presignifying, presigning <old>; **forecast, promise;** apocalypse; prospectus; foresight 961; presentiment, foreboding; omen 133.3,6; **guesswork,** speculation, guestimation <nf>, hunch, feeling; **probability** 968, statistical prediction, actuarial prediction; improbability 969

2 divination, divining, **augury,** haruspication, haruspicy, pythonism, mantic, mantology <old>; **fortunetelling,** crystal gazing, palm-reading, palmistry, tea-leaf reading, tarot reading, I Ching; crystal ball; astrology, horoscopy, astrology 1072.20; sorcery 690; clairvoyance 689.8, telepathy

3 dowsing, witching, water witching; **divining rod** or stick, wand, witch or witching stick, dowsing rod, doodlebug; water diviner, dowser, water witch or witcher; hydromancy

4 **predictor, foreteller, prognosticator,** seer, foreseer, forecaster, foreknower, presager <old>, prefigurer; **forecaster;** prophet, prophesier, soothsayer, vates <L>; **diviner,** divinator; augur; psychic 689.13; clairvoyant; prophetess, seeress, divineress, pythoness; Druid; **fortuneteller;** crystal gazer; palmist; geomancer; haruspex or aruspex, astrologer 1070.23; weather prophet 317.6; prophet of doom, calamity howler, Cassandra; religious prophets 684; speculator

5 <nf terms> **dopester, tipster, tout** or touter

6 **sibyl;** Pythia, Pythian, Delphic sibyl; Babylonian or Persian sibyl, Cimmerian sibyl, Cumaean sibyl, Erythraean sibyl, Hellespontine or Trojan sibyl, Libyan sibyl, Phrygian sibyl, Samian sibyl, Tiburtine sibyl

7 **oracle;** Delphic or Delphian oracle, Python, Pythian oracle; Delphic tripod, tripod of the Pythia; Dodona, oracle or oak of Dodona; sage

8 **predictability,** divinability, foretellableness, **calculability, foreseeability,** foreknowableness

VERBS **9** **predict,** make a prediction, **foretell, soothsay,** prefigure, **forecast, prophesy, prognosticate,** call <nf>, make a prophecy or prognosis, vaticinate, forebode, presage, see ahead, see or tell the future, read the future, see in the crystal ball; **foresee** 961.5; dope and dope out <nf>; call the turn and call one's shot <nf>; **divine;** witch or dowse for water; **tell fortunes,** fortune-tell, cast one's fortune; read one's hand, read palms, read tea leaves, cast a horoscope or nativity; **guess,** speculate, guesstimate <nf>, make an educated guess; **bet, bet on, gamble**

10 **portend,** foretoken 133.12, foreshow, foreshadow

ADJS **11** **predictive,** predictory, predictional; **foretelling,** forewarning, forecasting; prefiguring, prefigurative, presignifying, presignificative; **prophetic,** prophetical, fatidic, fatidical, apocalyptic, apocalyptical; vatic, vaticinatory, vaticinal, mantic, sibyllic, sibylline, fatidic, fatidical; **divinatory, oracular,** auguring, augural; haruspical; **foreseeing** 960.7; presageful, presaging; **prognostic,** prognosticative, prognosticatory; fortunetelling; weather-wise

12 **ominous,** premonitory, foreboding 133.17, unfavorable, adverse

13 **predictable, divinable, foretellable, calculable,** anticipatable; **foreseeable, foreknowable,** precognizable; **probable** 968.6; improbable 969.3

14 **predicted,** prophesied, presaged, **foretold, forecast,** foreshown; foreseen, foreglimpsed, **foreknown**

963 NECESSITY

NOUNS **1** **necessity,** necessariness, necessitude <old>, necessitation, entailment; mandatoriness, mandatedness, obligatoriness, **obligation,** obligement; compulsoriness, **compulsion,** duress 424.3

2 **requirement, requisite,** requisition; **necessity, need, want,** occasion; need for, **call for, demand,** demand for; desideratum, desideration; **prerequisite,** prerequirement; **must,** must item; sine qua non; **essential,** indispensable; the necessary, the needful; necessities, necessaries, essentials, bare necessities, fundamentals

3 **needfulness,** requisiteness; **essentiality,** essentialness, vitalness; **indispensability,** indispensableness; irreplaceability; irreducibleness, irreducibility

4 **urgent need, dire necessity; exigency** or exigence, **urgency,** imperative, imperativeness, immediacy, pressingness, pressure; "necessity's sharp pinch"— Shakespeare; matter of necessity, case of need or emergency, **matter of life and death;** predicament 1013.4

5 **involuntariness,** unwilledness, **instinctiveness;** compulsiveness; reflex action, Pavlovian reaction, conditioning, automatism; echolalia, echopraxia; automatic writing; **instinct,** impulse 365; blind impulse or instinct, knee-jerk reaction, sheer chemistry

6 **choicelessness,** no choice, no alternative, lack of choice, **Hobson's choice,** only choice, zero option, coercion; that or nothing; not a pin to choose, six of one and half a dozen of the other, distinction without a difference; indiscrimination 945

7 **inevitability,** inevitableness, **unavoidableness,** necessity, inescapableness, inevasibleness, unpreventability, undeflectability, ineluctability; irrevocability, indefeasibility; uncontrollability; relentlessness, inexorability, unyieldingness, inflexibility; fatedness, fatefulness, **certainty,** sureness; force majeure <Fr>, vis major, act of God, inevitable accident, unavoidable casualty; **predetermination;** God's will, will of Allah; doom, karma, one's lot, **fate** 964.2

VERBS **8** **necessitate, oblige,** dictate, **constrain;** coerce, impel, force, mandate; insist upon, **compel** 424.4

9 **require, need, want,** lack, must have, feel the want of, have occasion for, be in need of, be hurting for <nf>, stand in need of, not be able to dispense with, not be able to do without; **call for,** cry for, cry out for, clamor for; **demand,** ask, claim, exact; prerequire <old>; need or want doing, take doing <nf>, be indicated

10 **be necessary,** lie under a necessity, be one's fate; be a must <nf>; can't be avoided, can't be helped; be under the necessity of, be in for; be obliged, **must,** need *or* needs must <old>, **have to,** have got to <nf>, should, need, **need to,** have need to; not able to keep from, not able to help, **cannot help but,** cannot do otherwise; be forced *or* driven

11 have no choice *or* **alternative,** have one's options reduced *or* closed *or* eliminated, have no option but, cannot choose but, be robbed *or* relieved of choice; be pushed to the wall, be driven into a corner; take it or leave it *and* like it or lump it <nf>, have that or nothing

ADJS **12 necessary, obligatory, compulsory,** entailed, mandatory, fundamental; **exigent, urgent,** necessitous, importunate, **imperative;** choiceless, without choice, out of one's hands *or* control

13 requisite, needful, required, needed, necessary, **wanted, called for,** indicated, imperative; **essential, vital, indispensable,** unforgoable, irreplaceable; irreducible, irreductible; prerequisite

14 involuntary, instinctive, automatic, mechanical, reflex, reflexive, knee-jerk <nf>, autonomic, conditioned; **unconscious,** unthinking, blind; **unwitting,** unintentional, independent of one's will, unwilling, unwilled, against one's will; compulsory, **compulsive;** forced; **impulsive** 365.9

15 inevitable, unavoidable, necessary, **inescapable,** inevasible, unpreventable, undeflectable, ineluctable, irrevocable, indefeasible; uncontrollable, unstoppable; relentless, inexorable, unyielding, inflexible; irresistible, resistless; **certain,** fateful, **sure,** sure as fate, sure as death, sure as death and taxes; preordained, predestined, **destined, fated** 964.9; necessitarian, deterministic

ADVS **16 necessarily, needfully,** requisitely; **of necessity,** from necessity, need *or* needs <old>, perforce; without choice; **willy-nilly,** *nolens volens* <L>, willing or unwilling, *bon gré mal gré* <Fr>, whether one will or not; come what may; compulsorily

17 if necessary, if need be, if worst comes to worst; for lack of something better, *faute de mieux* <Fr>

18 involuntarily, instinctively, automatically, mechanically, by reflex, reflexively; blindly, **unconsciously,** unthinkingly, without premeditation; **unwittingly,** unintentionally; **compulsively; unwillingly** 325.8

19 inevitably, unavoidably, necessarily, **inescapably,** come hell *or* high water <nf>, inevasibly, unpreventably, ineluctably; irrevocably, indefeasibly; uncontrollably; relentlessly, inexorably, unyieldingly, inflexibly; fatefully, **certainly, surely**

PHRS **20 it is necessary, it must be,** if need be, it needs must be *or* it must needs be <old>, it will

be, there's no two ways about it, it must have its way; it cannot be helped, there is no helping it *or* help for it, that's the way the cookie crumbles *or* the ball bounces <nf>, what will be will be, it's God's will; the die is cast; it is fated 963.11

964 PREDETERMINATION

NOUNS **1 predetermination, predestination,** foredestiny, **preordination,** foreordination, foreordainment; decree; foregone conclusion, par for the course <nf>, preconceived notion *or* opinion; **necessity** 963; foreknowledge, prescience 960.3

2 fate, fatality, **fortune, lot,** cup, **portion,** appointed lot, karma, kismet, weird, *moira* <Gk>, future 839; **destiny,** destination, **end,** final lot; **doom,** foredoom <old>, God's will, will of Heaven; **inevitability** 963.7; "a tyrant's authority for crime and a fool's excuse for failure"—Ambrose Bierce; the handwriting on the wall; book of fate; Fortune's wheel, wheel of fortune *or* chance; astral influences, stars, planets, constellation, astrology 1070.20; unlucky day, ides of March, Friday, Friday the thirteenth, *dies funestis* <L>

3 Fates, *Fata* <L>, Parcae, *Moirai* <Gk>, Clotho, Lachesis, Atropos; Nona, Decuma, Morta; Weird Sisters, Weirds; Norns; Urdur, Verthandi, Skuld; Fortuna, Lady *or* Dame Fortune, *Tyche* <Gk>; Providence, Heaven, "a divinity that shapes our ends, rough-hew them how we will"—Shakespeare

4 determinism, fatalism, necessitarianism, necessarianism, predeterminism; predestinarianism, Calvinism, election

5 determinist, fatalist, necessitarian, necessarian; predestinationist, predestinarian, Calvinist

VERBS **6 predetermine, predecide,** preestablish, preset; **predestine,** predestinate, **preordain,** foreordain; agree beforehand, preconcert

7 destine, predestine, necessitate 963.8, destinate <old>, **ordain,** fate, mark, appoint, decree, intend; come with the territory <nf>; have in store for; **doom,** foredoom

ADJS **8 determined, predetermined, predecided,** preestablished, **predestined,** predestinate, **preordained,** foreordained; foregone; open-and-shut; arranged

9 destined, fated, fateful, fatal <old>, ordained, written, in the cards, marked, appointed <old>, in store, cut-and-dried; **doomed,** foredoomed; devoted; inevitable 962.15

10 deterministic, fatalistic, necessitarian, necessarian

PHRS **11 it is fated, it is written,** it's in the cards; what will be will be, *che sarà sarà* <Ital>, *que será será* <Sp>; *c'est la vie* and *c'est la guerre* <Fr>

965 PREARRANGEMENT

NOUNS **1 prearrangement,** preordering, preconcertedness; premeditation, plotting, planning, scheming; directed verdict; **reservation,** booking; overbooking

2 <nf terms> **put-up job,** packed *or* rigged game *or* jury, packed deal, stacked deck, cold deck, boat race, tank job; **frame-up,** frame, setup

3 schedule, program, programma, **bill,** card, **calendar,** docket, slate; playbill; batting order, **lineup, roster,** rota <chiefly Brit>; blueprint, budget; **prospectus;** schedule *or* program of operation, **order of the day,** things to be done, **agenda,** list of agenda; protocol; laundry list *and* wish list <nf>; **bill of fare, menu,** *carte du jour* <Fr>

VERBS **4 prearrange,** precontrive, predesign <old>, preorder, preconcert; premeditate, plot, plan, scheme; **reserve,** book, overbook

5 <nf terms> **fix, rig,** pack, cook, cook up; **stack the cards,** cold-deck, pack the deal; put in the bag, sew up; frame, frame-up, set up; **throw,** tank, go in the tank, hold a boat race

6 schedule, line up <nf>, **slate, book,** book in, bill, program, calendar, docket, budget, put on the agenda

ADJS **7 prearranged,** precontrived, predesigned <old>, preordered, preconcerted, cut out; premeditated, plotted, planned, schemed; cut-and-dried, cut-and-dry

8 <nf terms> **fixed, rigged, put-up,** packed, stacked, cooked, cooked-up; **in the bag,** on ice, iced, cinched, sewed up; **framed, framed-up,** set-up

9 scheduled, slated, booked, billed, booked-in, to come

966 POSSIBILITY

NOUNS **1 possibility,** possibleness, **the realm of possibility,** the domain of the possible, conceivableness, **conceivability,** thinkability, thinkableness, imaginability; **probability,** likelihood 968; what may be, what might be, what is possible, what one can do, what can be done, the possible, the attainable, the feasible; **potential, potentiality,** virtuality; contingency, eventuality; **chance, prospect, odds; outside chance** <nf>, off chance, remote possibility, ghost of a chance; hope, outside hope, small hope, slim odds; **good possibility, good chance,** even chance 972.7; bare possibility 972.9

2 practicability, practicality, feasibility; workability, operability, actability, performability, realizability, negotiability; **viability,** viableness; **achievability,** doability, compassability, **attainability;** surmountability, superability; realm of possibility

3 accessibility, access, **approachability, openness,** reachableness, come-at-ableness *and* get-at-ableness <nf>; **penetrability,** perviousness; **obtainability,** obtainableness, **availability, donability, procurability,** procurableness, securableness, getableness, acquirability

VERBS **4 be possible,** could be, might be, **have *or* stand a chance *or* good chance,** bid fair to

5 make possible, **enable,** permit, permit of, clear the road *or* path for, smooth the way for, open the way for, open the door to, open up the possibility of, give a chance to

ADJS **6 possible,** within the bounds *or* realm *or* range *or* domain of possibility, in one's power, in one's hands, humanly possible; **probable,** likely 968.6; **conceivable,** conceivably possible, **imaginable, thinkable,** cogitable; plausible 968.7; **potential,** virtual; contingent; able, apt

7 practicable, practical, feasible; workable, actable, performable, effectible <old>, realizable, compassable, operable, negotiable, doable, swingable, bridgeable; **viable; achievable, attainable;** surmountable, superable, overcomable

8 accessible, approachable, come-at-able *and* get-at-able <nf>, **reachable,** within reach; **open,** open to; **penetrable,** get-in-able <nf>, pervious; **obtainable, attainable, available,** procurable, securable, findable, easy to come by, getable, to be had, donable

ADVS **9 possibly, conceivably,** imaginably, feasibly; within the realm of possibility; **perhaps,** perchance, haply; maybe, it may be, for all *or* aught one knows

10 by any possibility, by any chance, by any means, **by any manner of means;** in any way, in any possible way, **at any cost, at all,** if at all, ever; on the bare possibility, on the off chance, by merest chance

11 if possible, if humanly possible, **God willing,** *Deo volente* <L>, wind and weather permitting, Lord willing and the creek don't rise

967 IMPOSSIBILITY

NOUNS **1 impossibility,** impossibleness, the realm *or* domain of the impossible, **inconceivability,** unthinkability, unimaginability, what cannot be, what can never be, what cannot happen, hopelessness, Chinaman's chance *and* a snowball's chance in hell <nf>, **no chance** 972.10; **self-contradiction,** unreality, absurdity, paradox, oxymoron, logical impossibility; impossible, the impossible, impossibilism; no-no <nf>

2 impracticability, unpracticability, **impracticality, unfeasibility; unworkability,** inoperability, unperformability; **unachievability, unattainability;** unrealizability, uncompassability; insurmountability, **insuperability**

3 inaccessibility, unaccessibility; **unapproachability,** un-come-at-ableness <nf>, unreachableness; **impenetrability,** imperviousness; **unobtainability,** unobtainableness, **unattainability, unavailability,** unprocurableness, unsecurableness, ungettableness <nf>, unacquirability; undiscoverability, unascertainableness

VERBS **4 be impossible,** be an impossibility, **not have a chance,** be a waste of time; **contradict itself,** be a logical impossibility, be a paradox; fly in the face of reason

5 attempt the impossible, try for a miracle, look for a needle in a haystack *or* in a bottle of hay, try to be in two places at once, try to fetch water in a sieve *or* catch the wind in a net *or* weave a rope of sand *or* get figs from thistles *or* gather grapes from thorns *or* make bricks from straw *or* make cheese of chalk *or* make a silk purse out of a sow's ear *or* change the leopard's spots *or* get blood from a turnip; ask the impossible, cry for the moon; turn back time; walk on water

6 make impossible, rule out, disenable, disqualify, close out, **bar,** prohibit, put out of reach, leave no chance, make things difficult

ADJS **7 impossible, not possible,** beyond the bounds of possibility *or* reason, contrary to reason, at variance with the facts; **inconceivable, unimaginable, unthinkable, not to be thought of, out of the question;** hopeless; **absurd,** ridiculous, preposterous; **self-contradictory,** paradoxical, oxymoronic, logically impossible; **ruled-out,** excluded, closed-out, **barred,** prohibited, forbidden; self-contradictory, self-defeating

8 impracticable, impractical, unpragmatic, unfeasible; unworkable, unviable, unperformable, inoperable, undoable, unnegotiable, unbridgeable; **unachievable, unattainable,** uneffectible <old>; unrealizable, uncompassable; insurmountable, unsurmountable, **insuperable,** unovercomable; **beyond one,** beyond one's power, beyond one's control, out of one's depth, too much for

9 inaccessible, unaccessible; **unapproachable,** un-come-at-able <nf>; **unreachable,** beyond reach, out of reach; **impenetrable,** impervious; closed to, denied to, lost to, closed forever to; **unobtainable, unattainable, unavailable,** unprocurable, unsecurable, ungettable <nf>, unacquirable; not to be had, **not to be had for love or money;** undiscoverable, unascertainable

ADVS **10 impossibly, inconceivably,** unimaginably, unthinkably; not at any price

PHRS **11** no can do, no way, no way José <nf>

968 PROBABILITY

NOUNS **1 probability, likelihood,** likeliness, liability, aptitude, verisimilitude; **chance, odds; expectation, outlook,** prospect; favorable prospect, well-grounded hope, some *or* reasonable hope, fair expectation; **good chance** 972.8; presumption, presumptive evidence; tendency; probable cause, reasonable ground *or* presumption; probabilism; possibility 966

2 mathematical probability, statistical probability, statistics, **predictability;** probability theory, game theory, theory of games; operations research; probable error, standard deviation; stochastic *or* statistical independence, stochastic variable; probability curve, frequency curve, frequency polygon, frequency distribution, probability function, probability density function, probability distribution, cumulative distribution function; **statistical mechanics,** quantum mechanics, uncertainty *or* indeterminancy principle, Maxwell-Boltzmann distribution law, Bose-Einstein statistics, Fermi-Dirac statistics; **mortality table,** actuarial table, life table, combined experience table, Commissioners Standard Ordinary table; blip, hiccup

3 plausibility; reasonability 935.9; **credibility** 953.8; verisimilitude

VERBS **4 be probable, seem likely,** could be, offer a good prospect, offer the expectation, have *or* run a good chance, be in the running, come as no surprise; **promise,** be promising, make fair promise, **bid fair to,** stand fair to, show a tendency, be in the cards, have the makings of, have favorable odds, lead one to expect; **make probable,** probabilize, make more likely, smooth the way for; increase the chances

5 think likely, daresay, venture to say; anticipate; **presume,** suppose 951.10

ADJS **6 probable, likely, liable, apt,** verisimilar, in the cards, odds-on; **promising, hopeful,** fair, in a fair way; foreseeable, **predictable; presumable,** presumptive; **statistical,** actuarial; mathematically *or* statistically probable, predictable within limits; prone, apt

7 plausible, colorable, apparent <old>; **reasonable** 935.20; credible 953.24; **conceivable** 966.6

ADVS **8 probably, in all probability or likelihood,** likely, **most likely, very likely;** as likely as not, very like *and* like enough *and* like as not <nf>; **doubtlessly,** doubtless, **no doubt,** indubitably; **presumably,** presumptively; by all odds, ten to one, a hundred to one, dollars to doughnuts

PHRS **9 there is reason to believe,** I am led to believe, it can be supposed, it would appear, it stands to reason, it might be thought, one can assume, appearances are in favor of, the chances *or* odds are, you can bank on it, you can make book on it, you can bet on it, you can bet your bottom dollar, you can just bet, you can't go wrong; I daresay, I venture to say

969 IMPROBABILITY

NOUNS 1 **improbability, unlikelihood,** unlikeliness; **doubtfulness,** dubiousness, **questionableness; implausibility,** incredibility 954.3; little expectation, low order of probability, poor possibility, bare possibility, faint likelihood, poor prospect, poor outlook, a ghost of a chance, fat chance <nf>, chance in a million; **small chance** 971.9

VERBS 2 **be improbable, not be likely,** be a stretch of the imagination, strain one's credulity, go beyond reason, go beyond belief, go far afield, go beyond the bounds of reason *or* probability, be far-fetched *or* fetched from afar

ADJS 3 **improbable, unlikely,** unpromising, hardly possible, logic-defying, scarcely to be expected *or* anticipated; statistically improbable; **doubtful,** dubious, **questionable,** doubtable, dubitable, more than doubtful; far-fetched, **implausible,** incredible 955.10; unlooked-for, unexpected, unpredictable

PHRS 4 **not likely!**, no fear!, never fear!, I ask you!, you should live so long! <nf>, don't hold your breath!, don't bet *or* make book on it <nf>

970 CERTAINTY

NOUNS 1 **certainty, certitude,** certainness, **sureness,** surety, **assurance, assuredness,** certain knowledge; **positiveness, absoluteness, definiteness,** dead *or* moral *or* absolute certainty; unequivocalness, unmistakableness, unambiguity, nonambiguity, univocity, univocality; **infallibility,** infallibilism, inerrability, inerrancy; **necessity,** determinacy, determinateness, noncontingency, Hobson's choice, ineluctability, predetermination, predestination, **inevitability** 963.7; **truth** 972; **proved fact,** probatum

2 <nf terms> **sure thing,** dead certainty, dead cert <Brit nf>, dead-sure thing, sure bet, sure card, aces wired, cinch, lead-pipe cinch, dead cinch, lock, mortal lock, shoo-in, open-and-shut case

3 **unquestionability, undeniability,** indubitability, indubitableness, **indisputability,** incontestability, incontrovertibility, **irrefutability,** unrefutability, unconfutability, irrefragability, unimpeachability; **doubtlessness, questionlessness; demonstrability,**

provability, verifiability, confirmability; factuality, **reality,** actuality 761.2

4 **reliability, dependability, dependableness, validity, trustworthiness,** faithworthiness; unerringness; predictability, calculability; stability, substantiality, firmness, **soundness,** solidity, staunchness, steadiness, **steadfastness;** secureness, **security;** invincibility 15.4; **authoritativeness, authenticity**

5 **confidence,** confidentness, conviction, belief 953, fixed *or* settled belief, **sureness, assurance, assuredness,** surety, security, certitude; **faith,** subjective certainty; trust 953.1; **positiveness, cocksureness; self-confidence, self-assurance, self-reliance;** poise 106.3; courage 492; **overconfidence, oversureness,** overweening <old>, overweeningness, hubris; pride 136, arrogance 141, pomposity 501.7, self-importance 140.1

6 **dogmatism,** dogmaticalness, pontification, **positiveness,** positivism, peremptoriness, **opinionatedness,** self-opinionatedness; bigotry; infallibilism

7 **dogmatist,** dogmatizer, opinionist, doctrinaire, bigot; positivist; infallibilist

8 **ensuring, assurance;** reassurance, reassurement; **certification;** ascertainment, **determination,** establishment; **verification, corroboration,** substantiation, validation, collation, check, cross-check, double-check, checking; independent *or* objective witness; **confirmation**

VERBS 9 **be certain, be confident,** feel sure, rest assured, have sewed up <nf>, **have no doubt,** doubt not; know, just know, know for certain; **bet on** *and* gamble on *and* bet one's bottom dollar on *and* bet the ranch on <nf>; admit of no doubt; **go without saying,** *aller sans dire* <Fr>, be axiomatic *or* apodictic, bet one's life <nf>

10 **dogmatize,** lay down the law, pontificate, oracle, oraculate, proclaim, assert oneself

11 **make sure, make certain,** make sure of, make no doubt, make no mistake; remove *or* dismiss *or* expunge *or* erase all doubt; **assure, ensure,** insure, **certify; ascertain, get a fix** *or* **lock on** <nf>; **find out,** get at, see to it, see that; **determine,** decide, **establish,** settle, fix, lock in *and* nail down *and* clinch *and* cinch <nf>, pin down, clear up, sort out, set at rest; assure *or* satisfy oneself, make oneself easy about *or* on that score; **reassure**

12 **verify, confirm,** test, prove, audit, **collate,** validate, check, check up *or* on *or* out <nf>, check over *or* through, **double-check,** triple-check, cross-check, recheck, check and doublecheck, check up and down, check over and through, check in and out, "make assurance double sure"—Shakespeare, measure twice cut once

ADJS **13 certain, sure,** sure-enough <nf>; well-founded; bound; **positive, absolute, definite,** perfectly sure, apodictic; decisive, conclusive; clear, clear as day, clear and distinct, unequivocal, unmistakable, unambiguous, nonambiguous, univocal; **necessary,** determinate, ineluctable, predetermined, predestined, **inevitable** 962.15; true 973.12

14 <nf terms> dead sure, sure as death, sure as death and taxes, sure as fate, sure as can be, sure as shooting, sure as God made little green apples, sure as hell *or* the devil, shit-sure, as sure as I live and breathe

15 obvious, patent, unquestionable, unexceptionable, undeniable, self-evident, axiomatic; indubitable, unarguable, indisputable, incontestable, **irrefutable,** unrefutable, unconfutable, incontrovertible, irrefragable, unanswerable, inappealable, unimpeachable, absolute; admitting no question *or* dispute *or* doubt *or* denial; **demonstrable,** demonstratable, provable, verifiable, testable, confirmable; well-founded, well-established, well-grounded; factual, **real,** historical, actual 761.15

16 undoubted, not to be doubted, indubious, **unquestioned, undisputed, uncontested,** uncontradicted, unchallenged, uncontroverted, uncontroversial; **doubtless, questionless,** beyond a shade *or* shadow of doubt, past dispute, beyond question

17 reliable, dependable, sure, surefire <nf>, **trustworthy, trusty,** faithworthy, **to be depended** *or* **relied upon,** to be counted *or* reckoned on; predictable, calculable; **secure, solid, sound, firm,** fast, **stable, substantial,** staunch, steady, **steadfast, faithful, unfailing;** true to one's word; invincible

18 authoritative, authentic, magisterial, **official;** cathedral, ex cathedra; standard, approved, accepted, received, pontific; from *or* straight from the horse's mouth

19 infallible, inerrable, inerrant, unerring

20 assured, made sure; **determined, decided, ascertained; settled, established,** fixed, cinched *and* iced *and* sewed up *and* taped <nf>, set, stated, determinate, secure; **certified,** attested, guaranteed, warranted, tested, tried, proved; wired *and* cinched *and* open-and-shut *and* nailed down *and* in the bag *and* on ice <nf>

21 confident, sure, secure, **assured,** reassured, decided, determined; **convinced,** persuaded, positive, **cocksure; unhesitating,** unfaltering, unwavering; **undoubting** 952.21; **self-confident, self-assured, self-reliant,** sure of oneself; poised 106.13; unafraid; **overconfident, oversure,** overweening, hubristic; proud 136.8, arrogant 141.9, pompous 501.22, self-important 140.8

22 dogmatic, dogmatical, dogmatizing, pronunciative, didactic, **positive,** positivistic, peremptory, pontifical, oracular; **opinionated,** opinioned, opinionative, conceited 140.11; **self-opinionated,** self-opinioned; doctrinarian, doctrinaire; bigoted

ADVS **23 certainly, surely, assuredly, positively, absolutely, definitely,** decidedly; without batting an eye <nf>; decisively, distinctly, clearly, unequivocally, unmistakably; **for certain,** for sure *and* for a fact <nf>, in truth, certes *or* forsooth <old>, and no mistake <nf>; **for a certainty,** to a certainty, *à coup sûr* <Fr>; **most certainly,** most assuredly; **indeed,** indeedy <nf>; truly; **of course,** as a matter of course; **by all means,** by all manner of means; at any rate, at all events; nothing else but <nf>, no two ways about it, no buts about it <nf>; no ifs, ands, or buts

24 surely, sure, to be sure, sure enough, for sure <nf>; sure thing *and* surest thing you know <nf>

25 unquestionably, without question, undoubtedly, beyond the shadow of a doubt, beyond a reasonable doubt, indubitably, admittedly, undeniably, unarguably, indisputably, incontestably, incontrovertibly, irrefutably, irrefragably; **doubtlessly,** doubtless, **no doubt, without doubt,** beyond doubt *or* question, out of question

26 without fail, unfailingly, whatever may happen, **come what may,** come hell or high water <nf>; cost what it may, *coûte que coûte* <Fr>; rain or shine, live or die, sink or swim

PHRS **27 it is certain,** there is no question, there is not a shadow of doubt, that's for sure <nf>; that goes without saying, *cela va sans dire* <Fr>; that is evident, that leaps to the eye, *cela saute aux yeux* <Fr>

971 UNCERTAINTY

NOUNS **1 uncertainty, incertitude, unsureness,** uncertainness; indemonstrability, unverifiability, unprovability, unconfirmability; **unpredictability,** unforeseeableness, incalculability, unaccountability; **indetermination,** indeterminacy, indeterminism; **relativity,** relativism, contingency, conditionality; **randomness, chance,** chanciness, hit-or-missness, **luck;** entropy; **indecision,** indecisiveness, undecidedness, undeterminedness; **hesitation, hesitancy; suspense,** suspensefulness, agony *or* state of suspense; **fickleness, capriciousness,** whimsicality, **erraticness,** erraticism, **changeableness** 853; **vacillation, irresolution** 362; trendlessness; Heisenberg *or* indeterminacy *or* uncertainty principle; question mark

2 doubtfulness, dubiousness, doubt, dubiety,

dubitancy, dubitation <old>; **questionableness, disputability,** contestability, controvertibility, refutability, confutability, deniability; disbelief 955.1

3 **bewilderment,** disconcertion, disconcertedness, disconcert, disconcertment, **embarrassment, confoundment,** discomposure, unassuredness, **confusion,** cognitive dissonance; **perplexity, puzzlement,** baffle, **bafflement,** predicament, plight, **quandary, dilemma,** horns of a dilemma, nonplus; **puzzle,** problem, riddle, conundrum, mystery, enigma; fix *and* jam *and* pickle *and* scrape *and* stew <nf>; perturbation, **disturbance, upset, bother,** pother

4 **vagueness, indefiniteness, indecisiveness,** indeterminateness, indeterminableness, indefinableness, **unclearness, indistinctness,** haziness, fogginess, mistiness, murkiness, blurriness, fuzziness; **obscurity,** obscuration; **looseness, laxity, inexactness,** inaccuracy, imprecision; **broadness, generality,** sweepingness; ill-definedness, amorphousness, shapelessness, blobbiness; inchoateness, disorder, incoherence

5 **equivocalness,** equivocality, polysemousness, ambiguity 539

6 **unreliability, undependability, untrustworthiness,** unfaithworthiness, treacherousness, treachery; **unsureness, insecurity, unsoundness, infirmity,** insolidity, unsolidity, **instability,** insubstantiality, unsubstantiality, **unsteadfastness,** unsteadiness, desultoriness, shakiness; **precariousness,** hazard, danger, risk, riskiness, diceyness *and* dodginess <Brit nf>, knife-edge, moment of truth, tightrope walking, peril, perilousness, ticklishness, slipperiness, shiftiness, shiftingness; speculativeness; **unauthoritativeness,** unauthenticity

7 **fallibility,** errability, errancy, liability to error

8 <an uncertainty> **gamble, guess,** piece of guesswork, question mark, estimate, guesstimate *and* ball-park figure <nf>; **chance, wager; toss-up** *and* **coin-toss** <nf>, **touch and go;** contingency, double contingency, possibility upon a possibility; **question, open question;** undecided issue, loose end; wild guess, **gray area,** twilight zone, borderline case; blind bargain, pig in a poke, sight-unseen transaction; leap in the dark; enigma

VERBS 9 **be uncertain, feel unsure; doubt,** have one's doubts, **question,** puzzle over, agonize over; **wonder,** wonder whether, wrinkle one's brow; not know what to make of, not be able to make head *or* tail of; be at sea, float in a sea of doubt; be at one's wit's end, **not know which way to turn,** be of two minds, be at sixes and sevens, not know where one stands, have mixed feelings, not know whether one stands on one's head or one's heels, be in a dilemma *or* quandary, flounder, grope, beat about, thrash about, not know whether one is coming or going, go around in circles; go off in all directions at once

10 **hang in doubt,** stop to consider, think twice; **falter,** dither, **hesitate,** vacillate 362.8

11 **depend,** all depend, be contingent *or* conditional on, hang on *or* upon; **hang, hang in the balance,** be touch and go, tremble in the balance, **hang in suspense; hang by a thread,** cliffhang, hang by a hair, hang by the eyelids

12 **bewilder, disconcert,** discompose, **upset,** perturb, **disturb, dismay,** tie one in knots; abash, **embarrass, put out,** pother, **bother,** moider <Brit nf>, flummox <nf>, keep one on tenterhooks

13 **perplex, baffle, confound,** daze, amaze <old>, maze, addle, fuddle, muddle, **mystify, puzzle,** nonplus, put to one's wit's end; keep one guessing, keep in suspense

14 <nf terms> **stump,** boggle <Brit>, buffalo, bamboozle, stick, floor, throw, get, beat, beat the shit out of, lick

15 **make uncertain, obscure, muddle, muddy,** fuzz, fog, **confuse** 985.7

ADJS 16 **uncertain, unsure; doubting,** agnostic, skeptical, unconvinced, unpersuaded; chancy, dicey <Brit>, touch-and-go; **unpredictable,** unforeseeable, incalculable, uncountable, unreckonable, unaccountable, undivinable; indemonstrable, unverifiable, unprovable, unconfirmable; **equivocal,** polysemous, inexplicit, imprecise, ambiguous; **fickle, capricious,** whimsical, **erratic,** variable, wavering, irresponsible, changeable 854.6; **hesitant,** hesitating; **indecisive,** irresolute 362.9

17 **doubtful,** iffy <nf>; **in doubt,** *in dubio* <L>; dubitable, doubtable, **dubious, questionable, problematic, problematical, speculative,** conjectural, suppositional; debatable, moot, arguable, **disputable,** contestable, controvertible, **controversial,** refutable, confutable, deniable; mistakable; **suspicious,** suspect; open to question *or* doubt; in question, in dispute, at issue

18 **undecided, undetermined, unsettled,** unfixed, unestablished; untold, uncounted; pendent, dependent, **pending,** depending, contingent, conditional, conditioned; **open,** in question, at issue, **in the balance, up in the air,** up for grabs <nf>, **in suspense,** in a state of suspense, suspenseful

19 **vague, indefinite, indecisive, indeterminate,** indeterminable, **undetermined,** unpredetermined, undestined; **random,** stochastic, entropic, **chance,** chancy <nf>, dicey *and* dodgy <Brit nf>, aleatory

or aleatoric, hit-or-miss; indefinable, undefined, ill-defined, unclear, unplain, **indistinct,** fuzzy, **obscure, confused, hazy,** shadowy, shadowed forth, misty, foggy, fog-bound, murky, blurred, blurry, veiled; **loose, lax, inexact, inaccurate,** imprecise; nonspecific, unspecified; **broad, general,** sweeping; amorphous, shapeless, blobby; inchoate, disordered, orderless, chaotic, incoherent

20 **unreliable, undependable, untrustworthy,** unfaithworthy, treacherous, unsure, not to be depended *or* relied on; **insecure, unsound, infirm,** unsolid, **unstable,** unsubstantial, insubstantial, **unsteadfast,** unsteady, desultory, shaky; **precarious,** hazardous, dangerous, perilous, risky, ticklish; shifty, shifting, slippery, slippery as an eel; provisional, tentative, temporary

21 **unauthoritative, unauthentic, unofficial,** nonofficial, apocryphal; **uncertified, unverified,** unchecked, unconfirmed, uncorroborated, unauthenticated, unvalidated, unattested, unwarranted; **undemonstrated, unproved**

22 **fallible, errable,** errant, liable *or* open to error, error-prone

23 **unconfident, unsure, unassured, insecure,** unsure of oneself; unselfconfident, unselfassured, unselfreliant

24 **bewildered, dismayed,** distracted, distraught, abashed, **disconcerted, embarrassed,** discomposed, **put-out, disturbed, upset,** perturbed, **bothered,** all hot and bothered <nf>; **confused** 985.12; clueless, without a clue, guessing, mazed, in a maze; turned around, going around in circles, like a chicken with its head cut off <nf>; in a fix *or* stew *or* pickle *or* jam *or* scrape <nf>; **lost,** astray, abroad, adrift, **at sea,** off the track, out of one's reckoning, out of one's bearings, disoriented

25 **in a dilemma,** on the horns of a dilemma; **perplexed, confounded, mystified, puzzled, nonplussed, baffled,** bamboozled <nf>, buffaloed <nf>; **at a loss, at one's wit's end,** fuddled, addled, muddled, dazed; **on tenterhooks,** in suspense

26 <nf terms> **beat,** licked, stuck, floored, stumped, thrown, buffaloed, boggled <Brit>

27 **bewildering, confusing, distracting, disconcerting,** discomposing, **dismaying, embarrassing,** disturbing, **upsetting,** perturbing, bothering; **perplexing, baffling, mystifying, mysterious, puzzling,** funny, funny peculiar, confounding; **problematic** *or* problematical; intricate 799.4; **enigmatic** 522.17

ADVS 28 **uncertainly,** in an uncertain state, **unsurely; doubtfully, dubiously;** in suspense, at sea, on the horns of a dilemma, at sixes and sevens;

perplexedly, disconcertedly, confusedly, dazedly, mazedly, in a daze, in a maze, around in circles

29 **vaguely, indefinitely,** indeterminably, indefinably, **indistinctly,** indecisively, **obscurely; broadly, generally,** in broad *or* general terms

972 CHANCE
<absence of assignable cause>

NOUNS 1 **chance,** happenstance, hap, "heedless hap"—Spenser; **luck;** good luck *or* fortune, serendipity, happy chance, dumb luck <nf>, rotten *and* tough luck <nf>; **fortune,** fate, **destiny,** whatever comes, *moira* <Gk>, lot 964.2; **fortuity, randomness,** randomicity, fortuitousness, adventitiousness, indeterminateness *or* indeterminacy, problematicness, uncertainty 971, flukiness <nf>, casualness, flip of a coin, crazy quilt, patternlessness, trendlessness, accidentality; **break** <nf>, the breaks <nf>, run of luck, the luck of the draw, the rub of the green, run *or* turn of the cards, fall *or* throw of the dice, the way things fall, the way the cards fall, how they fall, the way the cookie crumbles *or* the ball bounces <nf>; uncertainty principle, principle of indeterminacy, Heisenberg's principle; **probability** 967, stochastics, theory of probability, law of averages, statistical probability, actuarial calculation; random sample, **risk, risk-taking, chancing,** gamble 759; **opportunity** 843.2

2 Chance, Fortune, Lady *or* Dame Fortune, wheel of fortune, Fortuna, the fickle finger of fate <nf>; Luck, Lady Luck; "a nickname of Providence"—de Chamfort, "blind Chance"—Lucan, "the pseudonym of God when He did not want to sign"—Anatole France

3 **purposelessness, causelessness,** randomness, dysteleology, **unpredictability** 971.1, designlessness, **aimlessness;** lack of motive, no attributable cause, nonintention

4 **haphazard,** chance-medley <law>, **random;** random shot; potluck; spin of the wheel

5 **vicissitudes,** vicissitudes of fortune, ins and outs, **ups and downs,** ups and downs of life, chapter of accidents, feast and famine, "the various turns of chance"—Dryden; **chain of circumstances,** concatenation of events, chain reaction, vicious circle, causal nexus, **domino effect**

6 <chance event> **happening,** hap, happenstance; **fortuity, accident,** casualty, adventure, hazard; contingent, contingency; **fluke** <nf>, freak, freak occurrence *or* accident, coincidence; chance hit, lucky shot, long shot, one in a million, long odds

7 **even chance,** even break *and* fair shake <nf>, even *or* square odds, level playing field, touch and go,

odds; **half a chance,** fifty-fifty; toss, **toss-up,** standoff <nf>

8 **good chance, sporting chance,** good opportunity, good possibility; odds-on, odds-on chance, **likelihood,** possibility 966, probability 968, favorable prospect, well-grounded hope; **sure bet,** sure thing *and* dollars to doughnuts <nf>; **best bet,** main chance, winning chance

9 **small chance,** little chance, dark horse, **poor prospect** *or* prognosis, poor lookout <nf>, little opportunity, poor possibility, **unlikelihood,** improbability 968, hardly a chance, not half a chance; **off chance, outside chance** <nf>, **remote possibility,** bare possibility, a ghost of a chance, slim chance, gambling chance, **fighting chance** <nf>; poor bet, long odds, long shot <nf>, hundred-to-one shot <nf>, one chance in a million

10 **no chance,** not a Chinaman's chance *and* not a snowball's chance in hell <nf>, Buckley's chance <Austral nf>, not a prayer; **impossibility** 966, hopelessness

VERBS 11 **chance,** bechance <old>, betide, come *or* happen by chance, hap, hazard, **happen** 831.5, happen *or* fall on, come, come *or* happen along, bump into <nf>, **turn up,** pop up <nf>, **befall;** fall to one's lot, be one's fate

12 **risk,** take a chance, run a risk, push *or* press one's luck, lay one's ass on the line *and* put one's money where one's mouth is <nf>, **gamble,** bet 759.19; risk one's neck *and* shoot the works *and* go for broke <nf>; **predict** 962.9, prognosticate, make book <nf>; call someone's bluff

13 have a chance *or* an opportunity, **stand a chance, run a good chance, bid** *or* **stand fair to,** admit of; be in it *or* in the running <nf>; have *or* take a chance at, have a fling *or* shot at <nf>; have a small *or* slight chance, be a dark horse, barely have a chance

14 **not have** *or* **stand a chance,** have no chance *or* opportunity, not have a prayer, not have a Chinaman's chance <nf>, not stand a snowball's chance in hell <nf>; not be in it <nf>, be out of it <nf>, **be out of the running**

ADJS 15 **chance;** chancy <nf>, dicey <Brit nf>, **risky** <nf>; **fortuitous, accidental,** aleatory; **lucky,** fortunate, blessed by fortune, serendipitous; **casual,** adventitious, incidental, contingent, iffy <nf>; **causeless,** uncaused; indeterminate, undetermined; **unexpected** 131.10, **unpredictable,** unforeseeable, unlooked-for, **unforeseen; fluky** <nf>; fatal, fatidic, destinal

16 **purposeless, causeless,** designless, **aimless,** driftless, undirected, objectless, unmotivated, mindless; **haphazard, random,** dysteleological, stochastic, stray, inexplicable, unaccountable,

promiscuous, indiscriminate, casual, leaving much to chance

17 **unintentional,** unintended, **unmeant, unplanned,** undesigned, unpurposed, unthought-of; **unpremeditated,** unmeditated, unprompted, unguided, unguarded; **unwitting, unthinking,** unconscious, involuntary

18 impossible 967.7; **improbable** 969.3; certain 970.13; **probable** 968.6

ADVS 19 **by chance,** perchance, **by accident, accidentally, casually,** incidentally, by coincidence, **unpredictably, fortuitously, out of a clear blue sky;** by a piece of luck, by a fluke <nf>, by good fortune; **as it chanced, as luck would have it,** by hazard, as it may happen, as it may be, as the case may be, as it may chance, as it may turn up *or* out; somehow, in some way, in some way or other, somehow or other, for some reason

20 **purposelessly, aimlessly; haphazardly, randomly,** dysteleologically, stochastically, inexplicably, unaccountably, promiscuously, indiscriminately, casually, **at haphazard, at random,** at hazard

21 **unintentionally, without design, unwittingly,** unthinkingly, unexpectedly, unconsciously, involuntarily

INTERJS 22 break a leg!, best of luck!, good luck!

PHR 23 it's a crapshoot

973 TRUTH
<conformity to fact or reality>

NOUNS 1 **truth, trueness, verity,** veridicality, conformity to fact *or* reality *or* the evidence *or* the data, simple *or* unadorned truth, very truth, sooth *or* good sooth <old>; more truth than poetry; **unerroneousness, unfalseness,** unfallaciousness; historical truth, **objective truth, actuality,** historicity, impersonality; **fact, actuality,** reality 761.2, the real world, things as they are; the true, ultimate truth; eternal verities; truthfulness, veracity 644.3

2 **a truth, a self-evident truth, an axiomatic truth, an axiom;** a premise, a given, a donnée *or* donné, an accomplished fact *or fait accompli* <Fr>

3 **the truth,** the truth of the matter, the case; the home truth, the unvarnished truth, the simple truth, the basic truth, indisputable truth, the unadorned truth, the naked truth, the plain truth, the unqualified truth, the honest truth, the sober truth, the exact truth, the straight truth; the absolute truth, the intrinsic truth, the unalloyed truth, the cast-iron truth, the hard truth, the stern truth, gospel, gospel truth, Bible truth, revealed truth; the truth the whole truth and nothing but the truth

4 <nf terms> **what's what,** how it is, how things are, like it is, where it's at, dinkum oil <Austral>, the straight of it, the straight goods *or* skinny *or* scoop, the honest-to-God truth, God's truth, the real thing, the very model, the genuine article, the very thing, it, the article, the goods, the McCoy, the real McCoy, no imitation, chapter and verse, the gospel, the gospel truth, the lowdown, the skinny

5 **accuracy, correctness,** care for truth, attention to fact, right, subservience to the facts *or* the data, **rightness, trueness, rigor, rigorousness, exactness, exactitude; preciseness, precision;** mathematical precision, pinpoint accuracy *or* precision, scientific exactness *or* exactitude; factualness, factualism; **faultlessness,** perfection, absoluteness, flawlessness, impeccability, unimpeachability; **faithfulness, fidelity;** literalness, literality, literalism, textualism, the letter, literal truth; strictness, severity, rigidity; niceness, nicety, delicacy, subtlety, fineness, refinement; **meticulousness** 339.3; attention to detail; pinpoint accuracy, mathematical precision, clockwork precision

6 **validity, soundness,** solidity, substantiality, **justness;** authority, **authoritativeness; cogency,** weight, force, persuasiveness

7 **genuineness, authenticity,** bona fides, bona fideness, **legitimacy; realness, realism,** photographic realism, absolute realism, realistic representation, **naturalism,** naturalness, truth to nature, **lifelikeness,** truth to life, slice of life, *tranche de vie* <Fr>, kitchen sink, true-to-lifeness, verisimilitude, *vraisemblance* <Fr>, faithful rendering, verism, verismo, faithfulness; absolute likeness, **literalness,** literality, literalism, truth to the letter; socialist realism; inartificiality, unsyntheticness; **unspuriousness,** unspeciousness, unfictitiousness, artlessness, unaffectedness; **honesty, sincerity;** unadulteration 797.1

VERBS **8** **be true,** be the case; conform to fact, square *or* chime with the facts *or* evidence; **prove true,** prove to be, **prove out,** be so in fact; **hold true, hold good, hold water** <nf>, hold *or* stick together <nf>, **hold up, hold up in the wash** <nf>, wash <nf>, **stand up,** stand the test, be consistent *or* self-consistent, **hold,** remain valid; **be truthful**

9 seem true, ring true, sound true, **carry conviction,** convince, persuade, win over, hold *or* have the ring of truth

10 **be right, be correct,** be just right, get it straight; be OK <nf>, add up; **hit the nail on the head,** hit it on the nose *or* on the money *and* say a mouthful <nf>, hit the bull's-eye, score a bull's-eye

11 **be accurate, dot one's i's and cross one's t's,** draw *or* cut it fine <nf>, be precise; make precise, precise, particularize; stick to the letter, go by the book

12 **come true, come about,** attain fulfillment, **turn out, come to pass** *or* **to be,** happen as expected, become a reality

ADJS **13** **true, truthful; unerroneous,** not in error, in conformity with the facts *or* the evidence *or* reality, on the up-and-up *or* strictly on the up-and-up <nf>; gospel, **hard,** cast-iron; unfalse, unfallacious, unmistaken; **real, veritable,** veracious, sure-enough <nf>, objective, true to the facts, in conformity with the facts *or* the evidence *or* the data *or* reality, **factual,** actual 761.15, effectual, **historical,** documentary; objectively true; **certain,** undoubted, unquestionable 970.15; unrefuted, unconfuted, undenied; **ascertained, proved, proven, verified,** validated, **certified,** demonstrated, confirmed, determined, established, attested, substantiated, **authenticated,** corroborated; true as gospel; substantially true, categorically true; **veracious** 644.16

14 **valid, sound, well-grounded, well-founded,** conforming to the facts *or* the data *or* the evidence *or* reality, hard, solid, substantial; consistent, self-consistent, logical; **good, just,** sufficient; **cogent, weighty, authoritative; legal, lawful,** legitimate, **binding**

15 **genuine, authentic,** veridic, veridical, **real, natural, realistic, naturalistic,** true to reality, **true to nature, lifelike,** true to life, verisimilar, veristic; **literal,** following the letter, letter-perfect, *au pied de la lettre* <Fr>, true to the letter; verbatim, verbal, word-perfect, **word-for-word;** true to the spirit; **legitimate,** rightful, lawful; **bona fide,** card-carrying <nf>, **good,** sure-enough <nf>, **sincere, honest;** candid, honest-to-God <nf>, dinkum <Austral nf>; **inartificial, unsynthetic;** unspurious, unspecious, unsimulated, unfaked, unfeigned, **undisguised, uncounterfeited, unpretended, unaffected, unassumed; unassuming, simple,** unpretending, unfeigning, undisguising; **unfictitious,** unfanciful, unfabricated, unconcocted, uninvented, unimagined; unromantic; **original,** unimitated, uncopied; unexaggerated, undistorted; unflattering, unvarnished, uncolored, unqualified; **unadulterated** 798.7, honest-to-goodness; **pure,** simon-pure; **sterling,** twenty-four carat, all wool and a yard wide <nf>

16 **accurate, correct, right,** proper, just; all right *or* OK *or* okay <nf>, just right as rain, right, dead right, on target *and* on the money *and* on the nose *and* on the button <nf>, bang on <Brit nf>, straight, straight-up-and-down; **faultless,** flawless, impeccable, unimpeachable, unexceptionable; **absolute, perfect,** letter-perfect; meticulous 339.12; factual, literal

17 **exact, precise,** express; even, square; absolutely *or* definitely *or* positively right; **faithful;** direct; **unerring, undeviating, constant; infallible, inerrant, inerrable; strict,** close, severe, **rigorous,** rigid; mathematically exact, mathematical; mechanically *or* micrometrically precise; scientifically exact, scientific; religiously exact, religious; **nice,** delicate, subtle, **fine,** refined; pinpoint, microscopic

ADVS 18 **truly, really,** really-truly <nf>, **verily,** veritably, forsooth *or* in very sooth <old>, **in truth,** in good *or* very truth, **actually,** historically, objectively, impersonally, rigorously, strictly, strictly speaking, unquestionably, without question, **in reality, in fact,** factually, technically, in point of fact, as a matter of fact, for that matter, for the matter of that, to tell the truth, if you want to know the truth, to state the fact *or* truth, of a truth, with truth; **indeed,** indeedy <nf>; **certainly; indubitably,** undoubtedly 970.25; no buts about it <nf>, nothing else but

19 **genuinely, authentically, really,** naturally, **legitimately, honestly,** veridically; warts and all; unaffectedly, unassumedly, from the heart, in one's heart of hearts, with all one's heart and soul

20 **accurately, correctly,** rightly, properly, straight; **perfectly, faultlessly,** flawlessly, impeccably, unimpeachably, unexceptionably; **just right,** just so; **so,** sic

21 **exactly, precisely,** to a T, expressly; **just, dead,** right, straight, even, square, **plumb,** directly, squarely, point-blank; unerringly, undeviatingly; verbatim, **literally,** *literatim* <L>, verbally, word-perfectly, word for word, word by word, word for word and letter for letter, *verbatim et litteratim* <L>, in the same words, *ipsissimis verbis* <L>, to the letter, according to the letter, *au pied de la lettre* <Fr>; **faithfully, strictly, rigorously,** rigidly; **definitely, positively, absolutely; in every respect,** in all respects, for all the world, neither more nor less

22 **to be exact, to be precise, strictly, technically, strictly speaking,** not to mince the matter, by the book

23 **to a nicety,** to a T *or* tittle, to a turn, to a hair, to *or* within an inch

PHRS 24 **right!, that's right, that is so,** amen!, that's it, that's just it, just so, it is that, *c'est ça* <Fr>; **you are right,** right you are, right as rain, it is for a fact, you speak truly, as you say, **right;** believe it or not; touché!

25 <nf terms> **right on!,** you better believe it!, you've got something there, I'll say, I'll tell the world, I'll drink to that, righto, quite, rather!, you got it!, you said it, you said a mouthful, now you're talking, you can say that again, you're not kidding, that's for sure, ain't it the truth?, you're damn tootin', don't I know it?, you're telling me?, you're not just whistling Dixie, bet your ass *or* sweet ass *or* bippy *or* boots *or* life *or* you bet the rent, fucking ay, fucking ay right

974 WISE SAYING

NOUNS 1 **maxim, aphorism,** apothegm *or* apophthegm, **epigram, dictum, adage, proverb,** gnome, words of wisdom, **saw, saying,** witticism, sentence, expression, phrase, catchword, catchphrase, word, byword, mot, motto, moral; **precept,** prescript, teaching, text, verse, sutra, distich, sloka; golden saying, proverbial saying; common *or* current saying, stock saying, pithy saying, wise saying *or* expression, oracle, sententious expression *or* saying; **conventional wisdom, common knowledge; ana, analects, proverbs, wisdom, wisdom literature, collected sayings**

2 **axiom, truth,** a priori truth, postulate, truism, self-evident truth, general *or* universal truth, home truth, obvious truth, intrinsic truth; theorem; **proposition;** brocard, **principle,** *principium* <L>, settled principle; **formula; rule, law,** dictate <old>, **dictum;** golden rule

3 **platitude, cliché, saw, old saw, commonplace, banality,** bromide, **chestnut** <nf>, corn <nf>, triticism <old>, tired phrase, trite saying, hackneyed *or* stereotyped saying, stock phrase, commonplace expression, *lieu commun* <Fr>, *locus communis* <L>, **familiar tune** *or* **story,** old song *or* story, old song and dance <nf>, twice-told tale, retold story; reiteration 849.2; prosaicism, prosaism; prose; old joke 489.9

4 **motto, slogan,** watchword, catchword, catchphrase, tag line *or* tag, byword; **device;** epithet; inscription, epigraph

VERBS 5 aphorize, apothegmatize, epigrammatize, coin a phrase; proverb

ADJS 6 **aphoristic, proverbial,** epigrammatic, epigrammatical, **axiomatical; sententious, pithy,** gnomic, pungent, succinct, enigmatic, pointed; formulistic, formulaic; **cliché** *or* clichéd, banal, tired, stock, trite, tritical <old>, **platitudinous** 117.9

ADVS 7 **proverbially,** to coin a phrase, in a nutshell, **as the saying is** *or* **goes,** as they say, as the fellow says <nf>, as it has been said, as it was said of old

975 ERROR

NOUNS 1 error, erroneousness; untrueness,
untruthfulness, **untruth; wrongness, wrong;**
falseness, falsity; fallacy, fallaciousness, self-
contradiction; fault, **faultiness,** defectiveness; **sin**
655, sinfulness, peccancy, flaw, flawedness,
hamartia <Gk>; misdoing, misfeasance; errancy,
aberrancy, aberration, **deviancy,** wrongdoing;
heresy, unorthodoxy, heterodoxy; perversion,
distortion; mistaking, misconstruction,
misapplication, misprision <old>; **delusion,**
illusion 976; misjudgment 948; **misinterpretation**
342; faulty reasoning, flawed logic; fallibility,
human error

2 inaccuracy, inaccurateness, **incorrectness,**
uncorrectness, inexactness, unfactualness,
inexactitude, **unpreciseness,** imprecision,
unspecificity, looseness, laxity, unrigorousness;
tolerance, allowance; negligence; approximation;
deviation, standard deviation, probable error,
predictable error, range of error; uncertainty 971

3 mistake, error, *erratum* <L>, *corrigendum* <L>;
fault, *faute* <Fr>; gross error, bevue; human error;
misconception, misapprehension,
misunderstanding; misstatement, misquotation;
misreport; **misprint, typographical error,** typo
<nf>, printer's error, typist's error; clerical error;
misidentification; **misjudgment,** miscalculation
948.1; misplay; misdeal; miscount; misuse; failure,
miss, miscarriage

4 slip, slipup *and* miscue <nf>; **lapse,** *lapsus* <L>,
oversight, omission, balk <old>, inadvertence *or*
inadvertency, loose thread; **misstep,** trip, stumble,
false *or* wrong step, wrong *or* bad *or* false move;
false note; **slip of the tongue,** *sus linguae* and
lapsus linguae <L>; **slip of the pen,** *lapsus calami*
<L>; Freudian slip

5 blunder, faux pas, gaffe, solecism; stupidity,
indiscretion 923.4; **botch,** bungle 414.5

6 <nf terms> **goof, boo-boo,** muff, flub, foozle,
bloomer, bloop, blooper, boot, bobble, boner,
bonehead play *or* trick, dumb trick, boob stunt,
fool mistake; howler, clanger <Brit>, screamer;
fuck-up, screw-up, foul-up, snafu, muck-up, balls-
up <Brit>, louse-up; pratfall, whoops

7 grammatical error, solecism, anacoluthon,
anacoluthia, misusage, faulty syntax, missaying,
mispronunciation; **bull, Irish bull,** fluff,
malapropism, malaprop, Mrs Malaprop <R B
Sheridan>; Pickwickian sense; spoonerism,
marrow-sky; hypercorrection, hyperform; folk
etymology; catachresis; misspelling

VERBS 8 not hold water *and* not hold together <nf>,
not stand up, not square, not figure <nf>, not add
up, **not hold up, not hold up in the wash** *and*
not wash <nf>

9 err, fall into error, **go wrong, go amiss,** go astray,
go *or* get out of line, go awry, stray, get off-base
<nf>, **deviate,** wander, transgress, sin; **lapse, slip,**
slip up, trip, stumble; **miscalculate** 948.2

10 be wrong, mistake oneself, be mistaken, be in
error, be at fault, be out of line, be off the track,
be in the wrong, miss the truth, miss the point,
miss by a mile <nf>, have another think coming
<nf>; take wrong, receive a false impression, take
the shadow for the substance, misconstrue,
misinterpret, be misled, be misguided; deceive
oneself, be deceived, delude oneself; labor under a
false impression, get it wrong

11 bark up the wrong tree, back the wrong horse,
count one's chickens before they are hatched

12 misdo, do amiss; misuse, misemploy, misapply;
misconduct, mismanage; miscall, miscount,
miscalculate, misdeal, misplay, misfield; misprint,
miscite, misquote, misread, misreport, misspell

13 mistake, make a mistake; miscue *and* make a
miscue <nf>; **misidentify; misunderstand,**
misapprehend, misconceive, **misinterpret** 342.2;
confuse 811.3, mix up, not distinguish

14 blunder, make a blunder, make a faux pas, blot
one's copy book, make a colossal blunder, make a
false *or* wrong step, make a misstep; **misspeak,**
misspeak oneself, trip over one's tongue;
embarrass oneself, have egg on one's face <nf>;
blunder into; **botch,** bungle 414.11

15 <nf terms> **make** *or* **pull a boner** *or* boo-boo *or*
blooper; drop a brick <Brit>, goof, fluff, duff
<Brit>, foozle, boot, bobble, blow, blow it, drop
the ball; fuck up, screw up, foul up, muck up,
louse up; put *or* stick one's foot in it *or* in one's
mouth; muff one's cue, muff *or* blow *or* fluff one's
lines, fall flat on one's face *or* ass, step on one's
dick, trip up

ADJS 16 erroneous, untrue, not true, **not right;**
unfactual, **wrong,** all wrong; peccant, perverse,
corrupt; **false, fallacious,** self-contradictory;
illogical 936.11; **unproved** 958.8; **faulty,** faultful,
flawed, defective, **at fault;** out, off, all off, off the
track *or* rails; **wide** <old>, wide of the mark,
beside the mark; amiss, awry, askew, deviant,
deviative, deviational; erring, errant, **aberrant;**
straying, astray, adrift; **heretical,** unorthodox,
heterodox; abroad, all abroad; perverted, **distorted;**
delusive, deceptive, **illusory**

17 inaccurate, incorrect, inexact, unfactual,
unprecise, imprecise, unspecific, loose, lax,
unrigorous; negligent; **vague;** approximate,
approximative; out of line, out of plumb, out of
true, out of square; off-base <nf>

18 mistaken, in error, erring, under an error, **wrong, all wet** <nf>, full of bull *or* shit *or* hot air *or* it *or* prunes *or* crap *or* beans <nf>; off *or* out in one's reckoning; in the wrong box, in the right church but the wrong pew

19 unauthentic *or* **inauthentic, unauthoritative, unreliable** 971.20; **misstated,** misreported, miscited, misquoted, **garbled;** unfounded 936.13; spurious

ADVS **20 erroneously, falsely,** by mistake, fallaciously; faultily, faultfully; **untrue** <old>, untruly; **wrong,** wrongly; **mistakenly;** amiss, astray, on the wrong track

21 inaccurately, incorrectly, inexactly, unprecisely, by guess and by God *or* by golly <nf>

INTERJS **22** whoops! *and* sorry about that! <nf>

PHRS **23 you are wrong, you are mistaken,** you're all wet *or* you're way off *or* you have another guess coming *or* don't kid yourself <nf>

976 ILLUSION

NOUNS **1 illusion, delusion,** deluded belief; **deception** 356, **trick;** self-deception, self-deceit, self-delusion; dereism, autism; **misconception, misbelief,** false belief, wrong impression, warped *or* distorted conception; **bubble, chimera,** vapor, "airy nothing"—Shakespeare; wishful thinking, *ignis fatuus* <L>, will-o'-the-wisp; **dream,** dream vision; dreamworld, dreamland, dreamscape; **daydream;** pipe dream *and* trip <nf>; fool's paradise, castle in the air, fond illusion, dreamscape; maya, confabulation

2 illusoriness, illusiveness, delusiveness; **falseness,** fallaciousness; **unreality,** unactuality; unsubstantiality, airiness, immateriality; **idealization** 985.7; **seeming,** semblance, simulacrum, **appearance,** false *or* specious appearance, show, false show, false light; **magic,** sorcery 690, illusionism, sleight of hand, prestidigitation, magic show, magic act; magician, **sorcerer** 690.5, illusionist, Prospero <Shakespeare>; Mahamaya <Hindu>

3 fancy, phantasy, imagination 986

4 phantom, phantasm, phantasma, wraith, specter; shadow, shade; phantasmagoria; **fantasy,** wildest dream; **figment of the imagination** 986.5, phantom of the mind; **apparition, appearance; vision,** waking dream, image <old>; shape, form, figure, presence; eidolon, idolum; "such stuff as dreams are made on"—Shakespeare

5 optical illusion, trick of eyesight; afterimage, spectrum, ocular spectrum

6 mirage, fata morgana, will-o'-the-wisp, looming

7 hallucination; hallucinosis; tripping <nf>, mind-expansion; consciousness-expansion; delirium tremens 926.9,10; dream 985.9

VERBS **8 go on a trip** *and* **blow one's mind** <nf>, freak out <nf>; **hallucinate;** expand one's consciousness; make magic, prestidigitate

ADJS **9 illusory,** illusive; illusional, illusionary; Barmecide *or* Barmecidal; **delusory,** delusive; delusional, delusionary, deluding; dereistic, autistic; **dreamy, dreamlike; visionary;** imaginary 986.19; **erroneous** 975.16; **deceptive;** self-deceptive, self-deluding; **chimeric, chimerical, fantastic; unreal,** unactual, unsubstantial 764.5, airy; unfounded 936.13; **false,** fallacious, misleading; **specious, seeming,** apparent, ostensible, supposititious, all in the mind; spectral, apparitional, phantom, phantasmal; phantasmagoric, surreal

10 hallucinatory, hallucinative, hallucinational; hallucinogenic, psychedelic, consciousness-expanding, mind-expanding, mind-blowing <nf>

977 DISILLUSIONMENT

NOUNS **1 disillusionment,** disillusion, **disenchantment,** undeception, unspelling, return to reality, loss of one's illusions, loss of innocence, cold light of reality, enlightenment, bursting of the bubble; awakening, rude awakening, bringing back to earth; disappointment 132; debunking <nf>

VERBS **2 disillusion,** disillude, disillusionize; **disenchant,** unspell, uncharm, break the spell *or* charm; **disabuse, undeceive;** correct, **set right** *or* **straight,** put straight, tell the truth, enlighten, let in on, put one wise <nf>; clear the mind of; open one's eyes, awaken, wake up, unblindfold; disappoint 132.2; dispel *or* dissipate one's illusions, rob *or* strip one of one's illusions; bring one back to earth, let down easy <nf>; **burst** *or* **prick the bubble,** puncture one's balloon <nf>; let the air out of, take the wind out of; knock the props out from under, take the ground from under; debunk <nf>; expose, show up 351.4

3 be disillusioned, be disenchanted, get back to earth, get one's feet on the ground, have one's eyes opened, return to *or* embrace reality; charge to experience; have another thing *or* guess coming <nf>

ADJS **4 disillusioning,** disillusive, disillusionary, **disenchanting,** disabusing, undeceiving, enlightening

5 disillusioned, disenchanted, unspelled, uncharmed, **disabused,** undeceived, stripped *or* robbed of illusion, enlightened, set right, put straight; with one's eyes open, sophisticated, **blasé;** disappointed 132.5

978 MENTAL ATTITUDE

NOUNS 1 **attitude,** mental attitude; psychology; **position, posture,** stance; **way of thinking; feeling, sentiment,** the way one feels; feeling tone, affect, affectivity, emotion, emotivity; opinion 953.6

2 **outlook,** mental outlook; *Anschauung* <Ger>, **point of view, viewpoint, standpoint, perspective,** *optique* <Fr>; position, stand, place, situation; side; footing, basis; where one is *or* sits *or* stands; **view,** sight, light, eye; respect, regard; angle, angle of vision, slant, way of looking at things, slant on things, where one is coming from <nf>; **frame of reference,** intellectual *or* ideational frame of reference, framework, arena, world, universe, world *or* universe of discourse, system, reference system; phenomenology

3 **disposition, character, nature, temper, temperament,** mettle, constitution, complexion *and* humor <old>, makeup, stamp, type, stripe, kidney, make, mold; **turn of mind, inclination,** mind, **tendency,** grain, vein, set, mental set, mindset, **leaning,** animus, propensity, proclivity, predilection, preference, predisposition; **bent, turn, bias,** slant, cast, warp, twist; idiosyncrasy, eccentricity, individualism; diathesis, aptitude; strain, streak

4 **mood, humor, feeling, feelings, temper, frame of mind, state of mind,** mindset, **morale,** cue *or* frame <old>, tone, note, **vein; mind,** heart, spirit *or* **spirits**

5 <pervading attitudes> **climate,** mental *or* intellectual climate, spiritual climate, moral climate, mores, norms, climate of opinion, **ethos,** ideology, *Weltanschauung* <Ger>, world view; *Zeitgeist* <Ger>, spirit of the time *or* the age

VERBS 6 **take the attitude,** feel about it, look at it, **view,** look at in the light of; **be disposed to,** tend *or* incline toward, prefer, lean toward, be bent on

ADJS 7 **attitudinal; temperamental, dispositional,** inclinational, constitutional; emotional, affective; mental, intellectual, ideational, ideological; spiritual; characteristic 865.13; innate

8 **disposed,** dispositioned, **predisposed, prone, inclined, given,** bent, bent on, apt, likely, **minded, in the mood** *or* **humor**

ADVS 9 **attitudinally; temperamentally, dispositionally,** constitutionally; emotionally; mentally, intellectually, ideationally, ideologically; morally, spiritually; **by temperament** *or* **disposition,** by virtue of mind-set, by the logic of character *or* temperament; from one's standpoint *or* viewpoint *or* angle, from where one stands *or* sits, from where one is; within the frame of reference *or* framework *or* reference system *or* universe of discourse

979 BROAD-MINDEDNESS

NOUNS 1 **broad-mindedness,** wide-mindedness, large-mindedness; **breadth,** broadness, broad gauge, latitude; **unbigotedness,** unhideboundness, unprovincialism, noninsularity, unparochialism, cosmopolitanism; ecumenicity, ecumenicism, ecumenicalism, ecumenism; broad mind, spacious mind

2 **liberalness, liberality,** catholicity, **liberalmindedness;** liberalism, libertarianism, latitudinarianism; freethinking, free thought

3 **open-mindedness, openness,** receptiveness, receptivity; **persuadableness, persuadability,** persuasibility; open mind

4 **tolerance,** toleration; **indulgence,** lenience *or* **leniency** 427, condonation, lenity; **forbearance, patience,** long-suffering; easiness, **permissiveness; charitableness,** charity, **generousness, magnanimity** 652.2; **compassion** 427.1, sympathy; sensitivity

5 **unprejudicedness, unbiasedness; impartiality** 649.4, evenhandedness, equitability, **justice** 649, **fairness** 649.3, justness, **objectivity, detachment, dispassionateness, disinterestedness,** impersonality; indifference, neutrality; unopinionatedness

6 **liberal,** liberalist; libertarian; freethinker, latitudinarian, ecumenist, ecumenicist; big person, broad-gauge person; bleeding heart, bleeding-heart liberal

VERBS 7 **keep an open mind,** be big <nf>, judge not, not write off, suspend judgment, listen to reason, open one's mind to, see both sides, judge on the merits; **live and let live;** lean over backwards, **tolerate** 134.5; **accept,** be easy with, **view with indulgence, condone,** brook, abide with, be content with; **live with** <nf>; shut one's eyes to, look the other way, wink at, blink at, **overlook, disregard, ignore;** "swear allegiance to the words of no master"—Horace

ADJS 8 **broad-minded,** wide-minded, large-minded, **broad, wide,** wide-ranging, broad-gauged, catholic, spacious of mind; **unbigoted,** unfanatical, **unhidebound,** unprovincial, cosmopolitan, noninsular, unparochial; ecumenistic, ecumenical

9 **liberal, liberal-minded,** liberalistic; libertarian; freethinking, latitudinarian; bleeding-heart

10 **open-minded, open, receptive,** rational, admissive; **persuadable,** persuasible; unopinionated, **unopinioned,** unwedded to an opinion; **unpositive, undogmatic;** uninfatuated, unbesotted, unfanatical

11 **tolerant** 134.9, tolerating; **indulgent,** lenient 427.7, **condoning;** forbearing, forbearant <old>, **patient, long-suffering; charitable, generous, magnanimous** 652.6; compassionate 427.7, sympathetic, sensitive

12 unprejudiced, unbiased, unprepossessed, unjaundiced; impartial, evenhanded, **fair,** just 649.8, equitable, **objective, dispassionate, impersonal, detached, disinterested;** indifferent, neutral; **unswayed, uninfluenced,** undazzled; nonsexist, inclusive

13 liberalizing, liberating, broadening, enlightening

980 NARROW-MINDEDNESS

NOUNS **1 narrow-mindedness,** narrowness, illiberality, uncatholicity; little-mindedness, **small-mindedness, smallness, littleness, meanness, pettiness; bigotry,** bigotedness, fanaticism, *odium theologicum* <L>; insularity, insularism, provincialism, parochialism; **hideboundness,** straitlacedness, stuffiness <nf>; authoritarianism; **shortsightedness,** nearsightedness, purblindness; blind side, blind spot, tunnel vision, blinders; closed mind, mean mind, petty mind, shut mind; narrow views *or* sympathies, cramped ideas; *parti pris* <Fr>, an ax to grind

2 intolerance, intoleration; **uncharitableness,** ungenerousness; unforbearance; noncompassion, insensitivity

3 prejudice, prejudgment, forejudgment, **predilection, prepossession,** preconception; **bias,** bent, leaning, inclination, twist; **jaundice,** jaundiced eye; **partiality,** partialism, partisanship, favoritism, onesidedness, undispassionateness, undetachment

4 discrimination, social discrimination, minority prejudice; xenophobia, know-nothingism; **chauvinism,** ultranationalism, superpatriotism; fascism; **class consciousness,** class prejudice, class distinction, class hatred, class war; anti-Semitism; redbaiting <nf>; **racism,** racialism, race hatred, **race prejudice,** race snobbery, racial discrimination; white *or* black supremacy, white *or* black power; **color line,** color bar; **social barrier,** Jim Crow, Jim Crow law; **segregation,** apartheid; sex discrimination, sexism, manism, masculism, male chauvinism, feminism, womanism; ageism, age discrimination; class prejudice, class hatred, social prejudice; glass ceiling

5 bigot, intolerant, illiberal, little person; **racist,** racialist, racial supremacist, white *or* black supremacist, pig <nf>; **chauvinist,** ultranationalist, jingo, superpatriot; **sexist,** male chauvinist, male chauvinist pig *or* MCP <nf>, manist, masculist, feminist, female chauvinist, womanist, **dogmatist,** doctrinaire 970.7; fanatic

VERBS **6 close one's mind,** shut the eyes of one's mind, take narrow views, put on blinders, blind oneself, have a blind side *or* spot, have tunnel

vision, constrict one's views; not see beyond one's nose *or* an inch beyond one's nose; **view with a jaundiced eye,** see but one side of the question, look only at one side of the shield

7 prejudge, forejudge, judge beforehand, precondemn, prejudicate <old>, take one's opinions ready-made, accede to prejudice

8 discriminate against, draw the line, draw the color line; bait, **bash;** red-bait

9 prejudice, prejudice against, prejudice the issue, prepossess, **jaundice, influence, sway, bias,** bias one's judgment; warp, twist, bend, distort

ADJS **10 narrow-minded,** narrow, narrow-gauged, closed, closed-minded, cramped, constricted, pofaced <Brit>, *borné* <Fr>, little-minded, small-minded, mean-minded, petty-minded, narrow-hearted, narrow-souled, narrow-spirited, mean-spirited, small-souled; **small, little, mean, petty;** uncharitable, ungenerous; bigot, **bigoted,** fanatical; **illiberal,** unliberal, uncatholic; provincial, insular, parochial; **hidebound,** creedbound, **straitlaced,** stuffy <nf>; authoritarian; **shortsighted,** nearsighted, purblind; deaf, deaf-minded, deaf to reason

11 intolerant, untolerating; **unindulgent,** uncondoning, unforbearing

12 discriminatory; prejudiced, prepossessed, **biased, jaundiced,** colored; **partial,** one-sided, partisan; influenced, swayed, warped, twisted; interested, nonobjective, **undetached,** undispassionate; xenophobic, know-nothing; **chauvinistic,** ultranationalist, superpatriotic; **racist,** racialist, anti-Negro, antiblack, antiwhite; anti-Semitic; sexist; dogmatic, doctrinaire, **opinionated** 969.22

981 CURIOSITY

NOUNS **1 curiosity,** curiousness, **inquisitiveness; interest,** interestedness, lively interest; thirst *or* desire *or* lust *or* itch for knowledge, mental acquisitiveness, inquiring *or* curious mind; **attention** 983; **alertness, watchfulness,** vigilance; **nosiness** *and* snoopiness <nf>, prying, snooping <nf>; eavesdropping; officiousness, meddlesomeness 214.2; **morbid curiosity, ghoulishness;** voyeurism, scopophilia, prurience, prurient interest; rubbernecking <nf>

2 inquisitive person, quidnunc; **inquirer,** questioner, querier, querist, inquisitor, inquisitress; detective; **busybody,** gossip, *yenta* <Yiddish>, **pry,** Paul Pry, **snoop,** snooper, nosy Parker <nf>; eavesdropper; sightseer; rubbernecker *or* rubberneck <nf>; watcher, Peeping Tom, voyeur, scopophiliac; Lot's wife; explorer

VERBS **3 be curious, want to know, take an interest in,** take a lively interest, burn with curiosity; be alert, alert oneself, watch, be watchful, be vigilant; prick up one's ears, keep one's ear to the ground; eavesdrop; interrogate, quiz, question, inquire, query; keep one's eyes open, keep one's eye on, stare, gape, peer, gawk, rubber *and* rubberneck <nf>; seek, dig up, dig around for, nose out, nose around for; investigate

4 pry, snoop, peep, peek, spy, nose, nose into, have a long *or* big nose, poke *or* stick one's nose in; meddle 214.7

ADJS **5 curious, inquisitive,** inquisitorial, inquiring, interested, quizzical; **alert,** keen, tuned in <nf>, **attentive** 982.15; burning with curiosity, eaten up *or* consumed with curiosity, curious as a cat; agape, agog, all agog, openmouthed, open-eyed; gossipy; overcurious, supercurious; morbidly curious, **morbid, ghoulish; prurient,** itchy, voyeuristic, scopophiliac; rubbernecking <nf>

6 prying, snooping, **nosy** *and* **snoopy** <nf>; meddlesome 214.9

982 INCURIOSITY

NOUNS **1 incuriosity,** incuriousness, **uninquisitiveness;** boredom; **inattention** 984; **uninterestedness,** disinterest, disinterestedness, **unconcern,** uninvolvement, detachment, **indifference** 102, indifferentness, indifferentism, uncaring, **apathy,** passivity, passiveness, impassivity, impassiveness, listlessness, stolidity, **lack of interest;** carelessness, heedlessness, regardlessness, insouciance, unmindfulness; unperturbability; aloofness, detachment, withdrawal, reclusiveness; intellectual inertia; catatonia, autism; gullibility, credulity, blind faith; objectivity

VERBS **2 take no interest in, not care;** mind one's own business, pursue the even tenor of one's way, glance neither to the right nor to the left, keep one's nose out, keep an open mind; be indifferent, not care less <nf>, lack emotion; disregard; take it *or* leave it; take on trust; live and let live

ADJS **3 incurious, uninquisitive,** uninquiring; bored; **inattentive** 984.6; **uninterested,** unconcerned, disinterested, uninvolved, nonaligned, detached, **indifferent,** impersonal, **apathetic,** passive, impassive, stolid, phlegmatic, imperturbable, listless; careless, heedless, regardless, insouciant, mindless, unmindful; aloof, detached, distant, withdrawn, reclusive, sequestered, eremitic; catatonic, autistic; apathetic, not bothered; lackadaisical; unbiased, objective

983 ATTENTION

NOUNS **1 attention, attentiveness,** mindfulness, regardfulness, heedfulness; **attention span; heed,** ear; consideration, thought, mind; **awareness, consciousness,** alertness 339.5; **observation,** observance, advertence, advertency, **note, notice,** remark, put one's finger on, **regard,** respect; **intentness,** intentiveness, concentration; diligence, assiduity, assiduousness, earnestness; **care** 339.1; **curiosity** 981

2 interest, concern, concernment; **curiosity** 981; **enthusiasm,** passion, ardor, zeal; cathexis; matter of interest, special interest; solicitude

3 engrossment, absorption, intentness, single-mindedness, **concentration, application,** study, studiousness, **preoccupation,** engagement, **involvement, immersion,** submersion; obsession, monomania; rapt attention, absorbed attention *or* interest; deep study, deep *or* profound thought, contemplation, meditation

4 close attention, close study, scrutiny, fixed regard, rapt *or* fascinated attention, whole *or* total *or* undivided attention; minute *or* meticulous attention, attention to detail, microscopic *or* microscopical scrutiny, finicalness, finickiness; constant *or* unrelenting attention, close observance, harping, strict attention; special consideration

VERBS **5 attend to,** look to, **see to,** advert to, be aware of; **pay attention to,** pay regard to, give mind to, pay mind to <nf>, not forget, spare a thought for, **give heed to;** bethink, bethink oneself; have a look at; **turn to,** give thought to, trouble one's head about; give one's mind to, direct one's attention to, turn *or* bend *or* set the mind *or* attention to; **devote oneself to,** devote the mind *or* thoughts to, fix *or* rivet *or* focus the mind *or* thoughts on, set one's thoughts on, apply the mind *or* attention to, apply oneself to, **occupy oneself with, concern oneself with,** give oneself up to, be absorbed *or* engrossed in, be into <nf>; sink one's teeth, take an interest in, take hold of; **have a lot on one's mind** *or* **plate;** be preoccupied with; **lose oneself in; hang on one's words,** hang on the lips; **drink in,** drink in with rapt attention; be solicitous, suck up to <nf>, brown-nose <nf>

6 heed, attend, be heedful, tend, **mind, watch, observe, regard,** look, see, view, mark, remark, animadvert <old>, **note, notice,** take note *or* notice, get a load of <nf>

7 hearken to, hark, **listen, hear,** give ear to, lend an ear to, incline *or* bend an ear to, prick up the ears, strain one's ears, **keep one's ears open,** unstopper one's ears, have *or* keep an ear to the ground, listen with both ears, **be all ears**

8 **pay attention** *or* **heed,** take heed, give heed, **look out, watch out** <nf>, **take care** 339.7; look lively *or* alive, **look sharp,** stay *or* be alert, sit up and take notice; be on the ball *or* keep one's eye on the ball *or* not miss a trick *or* not overlook a bet <nf>, keep a weather eye out *or* on; miss nothing; get after, seize on, keep one's eyes open 339.8; attend to business, mind one's business; pay close *or* strict attention, strain one's attention, not relax one's concern, give one's undivided attention, give special attention to, dance attendance on; keep in the center of one's attention, keep uppermost in one's thought; **concentrate on,** focus *or* fix on; **study,** scrutinize, survey; be obsessed with; cathect

9 **take cognizance of, take note** *or* **notice of,** take heed of, **take account of, take into consideration** *or* **account,** bear in mind, keep *or* hold in mind, reckon with, keep in sight *or* view, not lose sight of, have in one's eye, have an eye to, have regard for

10 **call attention to,** direct attention to, **bring under** *or* **to one's notice,** hold up to notice, bring to attention, **mention,** mention in passing, touch on; **single out,** pick out, lift up, focus on, call *or* bring to notice, direct to the attention, **feature,** highlight, brightline; **direct to,** address to; **mention,** specify, mention in passing, touch on, cite, **refer to,** allude to; **alert one,** call to one's attention, put one wise *and* put one on <nf>; **point out, point to,** point at, put *or* lay one's finger on; **excite** *or* **stimulate attention,** drum up attention

11 **meet with attention,** fall under one's notice; **catch the attention,** strike one, impress one, draw *or* hold *or* focus the attention, take *or* catch *or* meet *or* strike the eye, get *or* catch one's ear, attract notice *or* attention, arrest *or* engage attention, fix *or* rivet one's attention, arrest the thoughts, awaken the mind *or* thoughts, **excite notice,** arouse notice, arrest one's notice, invite *or* solicit attention, claim *or* demand attention, act as a magnet

12 **interest, concern,** involve in *or* with, affect the interest, give pause; **pique, titillate,** tantalize, tickle, tickle one's fancy, **attract,** invite, **fascinate, provoke, stimulate, arouse, excite,** pique one's interest, excite interest, excite *or* whet one's interest, arouse one's passion *or* enthusiasm, turn one on <nf>

13 **engross, absorb,** immerse, **occupy, preoccupy, engage,** involve, monopolize, exercise, take up; **obsess; grip, hold, arrest, hold the interest, fascinate, enthrall,** spellbind, **hold spellbound,** grab <nf>, charm, enchant, mesmerize, hypnotize, catch; absorb the attention, claim one's

thoughts, engross the mind *or* thoughts, engage the attention, involve the interest, occupy the attention, monopolize one's attention, engage the mind *or* thoughts

14 **come to attention,** stand at attention

ADJS **15** **attentive, heedful, mindful, regardful,** advertent; intent, intentive, on top of <nf>, diligent, assiduous, intense, earnest, concentrated; **careful** 339.10, on guard, vigilant; **observing,** observant; watchful, aware, conscious, alert 339.14; **curious** 981.5; agog, openmouthed; open-eared, open-eyed, **all eyes, all ears,** all eyes and ears; on the job <nf>, on the ball *and* Johnny-on-the-spot <nf>; **meticulous** 339.12, sedulous, nice, finical, finicky, finicking, niggling

16 **interested,** concerned; **alert to, sensitive to, on the watch;** curious 981.5; tantalized, piqued, titillated, tickled, **attracted,** fascinated, excited, turned-on <nf>; keen on *or* about, enthusiastic, passionate; fixating, cathectic

17 **engrossed, absorbed,** totally absorbed, single-minded, **occupied, preoccupied, engaged,** devoted, devoted to, intent, intent on, monopolized, obsessed, monomaniacal, swept up, taken up with, **involved, caught up in,** wrapped in, **wrapped up in,** engrossed in, **absorbed in** *or* with *or* by, **lost in, immersed in,** submerged in, buried in; over head and ears in, head over heels in <nf>, up to one's elbows in, up to one's ears in; contemplating, contemplative, studying, studious, meditative, meditating; solicitous, indulgent

18 **gripped, held, fascinated, enthralled, rapt, spellbound,** charmed, enchanted, mesmerized, **hypnotized,** fixed, caught, riveted, **arrested,** switched on <nf>

19 **interesting, stimulating, provocative,** provoking, thought-provoking, thought-challenging, thought-inspiring; **titillating,** tickling, **tantalizing, inviting, exciting; piquant,** lively, racy, juicy, succulent, spicy, rich; readable

20 **engrossing, absorbing,** consuming, **gripping,** riveting, holding, **arresting,** engaging, attractive, **fascinating, enthralling, spellbinding,** enchanting, magnetic, hypnotic, mesmerizing, mesmeric; obsessive, obsessing

ADVS **21** **attentively,** with attention; **heedfully,** mindfully, regardfully, advertently; observingly, observantly; **interestedly,** with interest; **raptly,** with rapt attention; engrossedly, absorbedly, preoccupiedly; devotedly, **intently,** without distraction, **with undivided attention**

INTERJS **22** **attention!, look!,** see!, look you!, look here!, looky! <nf>, witness!; tah-dah! <nf>, presto!, hey presto! <Brit>, voilà!; lo!, behold!, lo and behold!; **hark!,** listen!, listen up! <nf>, hark ye!, hear ye!, oyez!; *nota bene* <L, note well>, NB; mark my words!

23 **hey!, hail!, ahoy!, hello!,** hollo!, hallo!, halloo!, halloa!, ho!, heigh!, hi!, hist!; hello there!, ahoy there!, yo!

984 INATTENTION

NOUNS 1 **inattention,** inattentiveness, **heedlessness, unheedfulness, unmindfulness, thoughtlessness,** inconsideration; **incuriosity** 981, **indifference** 102; inadvertence *or* inadvertency; unintentness, unintentiveness; disregard, disregardfulness, regardlessness, apathy; **flightiness** 984.5, giddiness 985.4, lightmindedness, dizziness *and* ditziness <nf>, scattiness <Brit nf>; levity, frivolousness, flippancy; shallowness, superficiality; **inobservance,** unobservance, nonobservance; **unalertness,** unwariness, unwatchfulness; **obliviousness,** unconsciousness, unawareness; **carelessness,** negligence 340.1, oversight; distraction, **absentmindedness, woolgathering,** daydreaming 985.2, head in the clouds; attention deficit disorder *or* ADD, attention deficit hyperactivity disorder *or* ADHD

VERBS 2 **be inattentive, pay no attention,** pay no mind <nf>, not attend, not notice, **take no note** *or* **notice of,** take no thought *or* account of, miss, not heed, give no heed, pay no regard to, not listen, hear nothing, not hear a word; **disregard, overlook, ignore,** pass over *or* by, have no time for, let pass *or* get by *or* get past; think little of, think nothing of, **slight,** make light of; **close** *or* **shut one's eyes to,** see nothing, be blind to, turn a blind eye, **look the other way, blink at, wink at,** connive at; stick *or* bury *or* hide one's head in the sand; **turn a deaf ear to,** stop one's ears, let come in one ear and go out the other, tune out <nf>; let well enough alone; not trouble oneself with, not trouble one's head with *or* about; **be unwary,** be off one's guard, be caught out

3 **wander, stray,** divagate, wander from the subject, ramble; have no attention span, have a short attention span, let one's attention wander, allow one's mind to wander, get off the track <nf>; **fall asleep at the switch** <nf>, woolgather, **daydream** 985.9

4 **dismiss,** dismiss *or* drive from one's thoughts; **put out of mind,** put out of one's head *or* thoughts, wean *or* force one's thoughts from, **think no more of, forget, forget it,** forget about it, **let it go** <nf>, let slip, not give it another *or* a second thought, **drop the subject,** give it no more thought; turn one's back upon, turn away from, turn one's attention from, walk away, abandon, leave out in

the cold <nf>; put *or* set *or* lay aside, push *or* thrust aside *or* to one side, wave aside; put on the back burner *or* on hold <nf>; **turn up one's nose at,** sneeze at; **shrug off, brush off** *or* **aside** *or* **away,** blow off *and* laugh off *or* away <nf>, dismiss with a laugh; slight 157.6, kiss off *and* slap *or* smack down <nf>

5 **escape notice** *or* **attention,** escape one, get by, be missed, pass one by, not enter one's head, never occur to one, fall on deaf ears, not register, go over one's head

ADJS 6 **inattentive, unmindful,** inadvertent, thoughtless, **incurious** 982.3, **indifferent** 102.6; **heedless,** unheeding, unheedful, regardless, *distrait* <Fr>, **disregardful,** disregardant; **unobserving,** inobservant, unobservant, unnoticing, unnoting, unremarking, unmarking; **distracted** 985.10; **careless,** negligent 340.10; **scatterbrained,** giddy 985.16, ditzy <nf>, scatty <Brit nf>, flighty; absent-minded, out to lunch <nf>

7 **oblivious, unconscious,** insensible, dead to the world, out of it *and* not with it <nf>; blind, deaf; **preoccupied** 985.11; in a world of one's own

8 **unalert, unwary, unwatchful, unvigilant,** uncautious, incautious; **unprepared,** unready; unguarded, **off one's guard,** off-guard; **asleep,** sleeping, nodding, napping, **asleep at the switch** *and* asleep on the job *and* **not on the job** *and* goofing off *and* looking out the window <nf>; daydreaming, woolgathering

985 DISTRACTION, CONFUSION

NOUNS 1 **distraction,** distractedness, **diversion,** separation *or* withdrawal of attention, divided attention, competing stimuli; too much on one's mind *or* on one's plate, cognitive dissonance, sensory overload; inattention 984

2 **abstractedness, abstraction, preoccupation, absorption,** engrossment, depth of thought, fit of abstraction; **absentmindedness, absence of mind; bemusement,** musing, musefulness <old>; **woolgathering,** mooning <nf>, moonraking <old>, stargazing, **dreaming, daydreaming,** fantasying, pipe-dreaming <nf>, castle-building; **brown study,** study, reverie, muse, dreamy abstraction, quiet *or* muted ecstasy, trance; dream, **daydream,** fantasy, pipe dream <nf>; daydreamer, Walter Mitty

3 **confusion, fluster,** flummox <nf>, **flutter,** flurry, ruffle; disorientation, **muddle, muddlement,** fuddle *and* fuddlement <nf>, befuddlement, muddleheadedness, daze, maze <nf>; unsettlement, disorganization, **disorder,** chaos, **mess** *and* mix-up *and* snafu <nf>, balls-up *and*

shemozzle <Brit nf>, shuffle, jumble,
discomfiture, discomposure, disconcertion,
discombobulation <nf>, **bewilderment,**
embarrassment, disturbance, perturbation, **upset,**
frenzy, pother, bother, botheration *and* stew <nf>,
pucker <old>; tizzy *and* swivet *and* sweat <nf>;
haze, fog, mist, cloud; maze; **perplexity** 971.3

4 **dizziness, vertigo,** vertiginousness, spinning head,
swimming, swimming of the head, **giddiness,**
wooziness <nf>, **lightheadedness;** tiddliness <Brit
nf>, **drunkenness** 88.1,3

5 **flightiness, giddiness,** volatility, mercuriality;
thoughtlessness, witlessness, brainlessness, empty-
headedness, frivolity, frivolousness, dizziness *and*
ditziness <nf>, scattiness <Brit nf>, foolishness
923; **scatterbrain,** flibbertigibbet 924.7

VERBS 6 **distract, divert,** detract, distract the
attention, divert *or* detract attention, divert the
mind *or* thoughts, draw off the attention, call
away, take the mind off of, relieve the mind of,
cause the mind to stray *or* wander, put off the
track, derail, throw off the scent, lead the mind
astray, beguile; throw off one's guard, catch off
balance, put off one's stride, trip up

7 **confuse,** throw into confusion *or* chaos, entangle,
mix up, fluster; flummox <nf>, **flutter,** put into a
flutter, **flurry, rattle, ruffle,** moider <Brit nf>;
muddle, fuddle <nf>, **befuddle, addle,** addle the
wits, **daze,** maze, **dazzle,** bedazzle; **upset, unsettle,**
raise hell, disorganize; throw into a tizzy *or* swivet;
disconcert, discomfit, discompose,
discombobulate <nf>, disorient, disorientate,
bewilder, embarrass, put out, disturb, perturb,
bother, pother, bug <nf>; fog, mist, cloud,
becloud; **perplex** 971.13

8 **dizzy, make one's head swim,** cause vertigo, send
one spinning, whirl the mind, swirl the senses,
make one's head reel *or* whirl *or* spin *or* revolve, go
to one's head; **intoxicate** 88.22

9 **muse, moon** <nf>, **dream, daydream,** pipe-dream
<nf>, fantasy; abstract oneself, be lost in thought,
let one's attention wander, let one's mind run on
other things, dream of *or* muse on other things;
wander, stray, ramble, divagate, let one's thoughts
or mind wander, give oneself up to reverie,
woolgather, go woolgathering, let one's wits go
bird's nesting, **be in a brown study,** be absent, be
somewhere else, stargaze, be out of it *and* be not
with it <nf>

ADJS 10 **distracted, distraught,** *distrait* <Fr>;
wandering, rambling; wild, frantic, beside oneself

11 **abstracted, bemused,** museful <old>, **musing,**
preoccupied, absorbed, engrossed, taken up;
absentminded, absent, faraway, elsewhere,
somewhere else, not there; pensive, meditative;

lost, **lost in thought,** wrapped in thought; rapt,
transported, ecstatic; dead to the world,
unconscious, oblivious; dreaming, dreamy,
drowsing, dozing, nodding, half-awake, betwixt
sleep and waking, napping; **daydreaming,**
daydreamy, pipe-dreaming <nf>; **woolgathering,**
mooning *and* moony <nf>, moonraking <old>,
castle-building, in the clouds, off in the clouds,
stargazing, in a reverie

12 **confused, mixed-up,** crazy mixed-up <nf>;
flustered, fluttered **ruffled, rattled,** fussed <nf>;
upset, unsettled, off-balance, off one's stride;
disorganized, disordered, disoriented,
disorientated, chaotic, jumbled, in a jumble,
shuffled; shaken, shook <nf>, **disconcerted,**
discomposed, discombobulated <nf>,
embarrassed, put-out, disturbed, perturbed,
bothered, all hot and bothered <nf>; in a stew *or*
botheration <nf>, in a pucker <old>; in a tizzy *or*
swivet *or* sweat <nf>, in a pother; **perplexed**

13 **muddled,** in a muddle; fuddled <nf>, **befuddled;**
muddleheaded, fuddlebrained <nf>;
puzzleheaded, puzzlepated; **addled,** addleheaded,
addlepated, addlebrained; adrift, at sea, foggy,
fogged, in a fog, hazy, muzzy <nf>, misted, misty,
cloudy, beclouded

14 **dazed,** mazed **dazzled,** bedazzled, in a daze; **silly,**
knocked silly, cockeyed <nf>; **groggy** <nf>, **dopey**
<nf>, woozy <nf>; **punch-drunk** *and* punchy *and*
slap-happy <nf>

15 **dizzy, giddy,** vertiginous, spinning, swimming,
turned around, going around in circles;
lightheaded, tiddly <Brit nf>, **drunk, drunken**
88.31

16 **scatterbrained,** shatterbrained *or* shatterpated
<old>, rattlebrained, rattleheaded, rattlepated,
scramblebrained, harebrain, harebrained, **giddy,**
dizzy *and* ditzy *and* gaga <nf>, scatty <Brit nf>,
giddy-brained, giddy-headed, giddy-pated, giddy-
witted, giddy as a goose, fluttery, frivolous,
featherbrained, featherheaded; **thoughtless,**
witless, brainless, empty-headed 922.19

17 **flighty,** volatile, mercurial

986 IMAGINATION

NOUNS 1 **imagination,** imagining, imaginativeness,
fancy, fantasy, conceit <old>; mind's eye, "that
inward eye which is the bliss of solitude"—
Wordsworth, "the mad boarder"—Malebranche;
flight of fancy, fumes of fancy; fantasticism

2 **creative thought,** conception; lateral thinking,
association of ideas; productive *or* constructive *or*
creative imagination, creative power *or* ability,
esemplastic imagination *or* power, shaping

imagination, poetic imagination, artistic imagination; mythopoeia, *mythopoesis* <Gk>; mythification, mythicization; inspiration, stimulus, muse; Muses: Calliope <poetry>, Clio <history>, Erato <lyric and love poetry>, Euterpe <music>, Melpomene <tragedy>, Polyhymnia <sacred song>, Terpsichore <dancing and choral song>, Thalia <comedy>, Urania <astronomy>; genius 920.8; afflatus, divine afflatus; frenzy, ecstasy

3 **invention, inventiveness, originality, creativity, fabrication,** creativeness, **ingenuity;** productivity, prolificacy, **fertility,** fecundity; rich *or* teeming imagination, fertile *or* pregnant imagination, seminal *or* germinal imagination, fertile mind; imagineering; **fiction,** fictionalization

4 **lively imagination,** active fancy, **vivid imagination,** colorful *or* highly colored *or* lurid imagination, warm *or* ardent imagination, fiery *or* heated imagination, excited imagination, bold *or* daring *or* wild *or* fervent imagination; verve, vivacity of imagination

5 **figment of the imagination,** creature of the imagination, creation *or* coinage of the brain, fiction of the mind, maggot <old>, whim, whimsy, figment, imagination, invention; caprice, vagary; brainchild; **imagining,** fancy, idle fancy, vapor, "thick-coming fancies"—Shakespeare, imagery; **fantasy, make-believe;** fabrication; phantom, vision, apparition, insubstantial image, eidolon, **phantasm** 976.4; **fiction,** myth, romance; wildest dreams, **stretch** of the imagination; **chimera, bubble, illusion** 976; hallucination, delirium, sick fancy; trip *or* drug trip <nf>

6 **visualization, envisioning,** envisaging, picturing, objectification, imaging, calling to *or* before the mind's eye, figuring *or* portraying *or* representing in the mind; depicting *or* delineating in the imagination; conceptualization; **picture, vision, image,** mental image, mental picture, visual image, visualization, vivid *or* lifelike image, eidetic image, concept, **conception,** mental representation *or* presentation, *Vorstellung* <Ger>; image-building, **imagery,** word-painting; poetic image, poetic imagery; imagery study; imagism, imagistic poetry

7 **idealism, idealization; ideal,** ideality; rose-colored glasses; visionariness, **utopianism;** flight of fancy, play of fancy, imaginative exercise; **romanticism,** romanticizing, romance; **quixotism,** quixotry; dreamery; **impracticality,** unpracticalness, **unrealism,** unreality; **wishful thinking,** wish fulfillment, wish-fulfillment fantasy, dream come true; autistic thinking, dereistic thinking, autism, dereism, autistic distortion

8 **dreaminess,** dreamfulness, musefulness, pensiveness; dreamlikeness; **dreaming, musing;**

daydreaming, pipe-dreaming <nf>, dreamery, fantasying, castlebuilding

9 **dream; reverie, daydream, pipe dream** <nf>, wishful thinking; **brown study** 985.2; **vision; nightmare,** incubus, bad dream

10 **air castle, castle in the air,** castle in the sky *or* skies, castle in Spain; Xanadu *and* pleasure dome of Kubla Khan, pie in the sky, end of the rainbow

11 **utopia** *or* Utopia <Sir Thomas More>, **paradise,** heaven 681, **heaven on earth;** millennium, kingdom come; dreamland, dream world, lotus land, land of dreams, land of enchantment, land of heart's desire, wonderland, cloudland, fairyland, land of faerie, faerie; Eden, Garden of Eden; the Promised Land, land of promise, land of plenty, land of milk and honey, Canaan, Goshen; Shangri-la, New Atlantis <Francis Bacon>, Arcadia, Agapemone, Happy Valley, land of Prester John, Eldorado, Seven Cities of Cibola, Quivira; Laputa; Cockaigne, Big Rock-Candy Mountain, Fiddler's Green, never-never land, Never-land, Cloudcuckooland *or* Nephelococcygia, Erewhon, Land of Youth, Tir-na-n'Og <Ir>; dystopia *or* kakotopia; Pandemonium

12 **imaginer, fancier,** fantast; fantasist; mythmaker, mythopoet; mythifier, mythicizer; **inventor; creative artist,** composer, poet, creative writer; imagineer

13 **visionary, idealist;** prophet, **seer; dreamer, daydreamer,** dreamer of dreams, castle-builder, lotus-eater, **wishful thinker; romantic,** romanticist, romancer; Quixote, Don Quixote; utopian, utopianist, utopianizer; escapist, ostrich; enthusiast, rhapsodist

VERBS 14 **imagine, fancy, conceive,** conceit <old>, conceptualize, ideate, figure to oneself; **invent, create, originate, make,** think up, dream up, shape, mold, coin, hatch, concoct, fabricate, produce; **suppose** 951.10; **fantasize;** fictionalize; use one's imagination; give free rein to the imagination, let one's imagination riot *or* run riot *or* run wild, allow one's imagination to run away with one; experience imaginatively *or* vicariously

15 **visualize,** vision, **envision, envisage, picture, image,** objectify; picture in one's mind, picture to oneself, **view with the mind's eye,** contemplate in the imagination, form a mental picture of, represent, **see,** just see, have a picture of; call up, summon up, conjure up, **call to mind,** realize; have an inspiration

16 **idealize,** utopianize, quixotize, rhapsodize; **romanticize,** romance; paint pretty pictures of, paint in bright colors; see through rose-colored glasses; **build castles in the air** *or* **Spain;** live in a dream world

17 dream; dream of, dream on; **daydream,** pipe-dream <nf>, get *or* have stars in one's eyes, have one's head in the clouds, indulge in wish fulfillment; fantasy, conjure up a vision, "see visions and dream dreams"—Bible; blow one's mind *and* go on a trip *and* trip *and* freak out <nf>

ADJS **18 imaginative,** conceptual, conceptive, ideational, ideative, notional; perceptive; **inventive, original,** innovative, originative, esemplastic, shaping, **creative, ingenious, resourceful; productive, fertile,** fecund, prolific, seminal, germinal, teeming, pregnant; **inspired,** visioned

19 imaginary, imaginational, notional; **imagined, fancied; unreal,** unrealistic, airy-fairy <Brit>, unactual, nonexistent, never-never; visional, supposititious, **all in the mind; illusory;** not of this world

20 fanciful, notional, notiony <nf>, whimsical, maggoty <Brit>; airy-fairy <nf>; brain-born; fancy-bred, fancy-born, fancy-built, fancy-framed, fancy-woven, fancy-wrought; dream-born, dream-built, dream-created; **fantastic, fantastical,** fantasque, extravagant, preposterous, outlandish, wild, baroque, rococo, florid; Alice-in-Wonderland, bizarre, grotesque, Gothic

21 fictitious, make-believe, figmental, fictional, fictive, fabricated, fictionalized; nonhistorical, nonfactual, nonactual, nonrealistic; **fabulous, mythic, mythical,** mythological, legendary; mythified, mythicized

22 chimeric, chimerical, aerial, ethereal, phantasmal; vaporous, vapory; gossamer; air-built, cloud-built, cloud-born, cloud-woven

23 ideal, idealized; utopian, Arcadian, Edenic, paradisal; pie in the sky <nf>; heavenly, celestial; millennial

24 visionary, idealistic, quixotic; romantic, romanticized, romancing, romanticizing; poetic *or* poetical; storybook; **impractical, unpractical, unrealistic;** wish-fulfilling, autistic, dereistic; starry-eyed, dewy-eyed; in the clouds, with one's head in the clouds; airy, **otherworldly,** transmundane, transcendental

25 dreamy, dreamful; dreamy-eyed, dreamy-minded, dreamy-souled; dreamlike; day-dreamy, **dreaming, daydreaming,** pipe-dreaming <nf>, castle-building; **entranced,** tranced, in a trance, dream-stricken, enchanted, spellbound, spelled, charmed

26 imaginable, fanciable, conceivable, thinkable, cogitable; **supposable** 951.15

987 UNIMAGINATIVENESS

NOUNS **1 unimaginativeness,** unfancifulness; **prosaicness,** prosiness, prosaism, prosaicism, unpoeticalness; **staidness, stuffiness** <nf>; stolidity; **dullness, dryness;** aridness, aridity, barrenness, infertility, infecundity; **unoriginality,** uncreativeness, uninventiveness, dearth of ideas

2 <practical attitude> **realism,** realisticness, **practicalness, practicality, practical-mindedness,** sober-mindedness, sobersidedness, **hardheadedness, matter-of-factness;** down-to-earthness, earthiness, worldliness, secularism; real world, the here and now; nuts and bolts, no nonsense, no frills; **pragmatism,** pragmaticism, positivism, scientism; unidealism, unromanticalness, unsentimentality; sensibleness, saneness, reasonableness, rationality; freedom from illusion, lack of sentimentality; lack of feelings 94

3 realist, pragmatist, positivist, practical person, hardhead

VERBS **4 keep both feet on the ground,** stick to the facts, call a spade a spade; **come down to earth,** come down out of the clouds, know when the honeymoon is over.

ADJS **5 unimaginative, unfanciful;** unidealized, unromanticized; **prosaic,** prosy, prosing, unpoetic, unpoetical; **literal,** literal-minded; earthbound, mundane; **staid, stuffy** <nf>; stolid; **dull, dry;** arid, barren, infertile, infecund; **unoriginal,** uninspired; hedged, undaring, unaspiring, **uninventive** 891.5

6 realistic, realist, **practical;** pragmatic, pragmatical, scientific, scientistic, positivistic; **unidealistic,** unideal, **unromantic, unsentimental, practical-minded,** sober-minded, sobersided, **hardheaded,** straight-thinking, **matter-of-fact, down-to-earth, with both feet on the ground;** worldly, earthy, secular; sensible, sane, reasonable, rational, sound, sound-thinking; **reductive, simplistic**

988 SPECTER

NOUNS **1 specter, ghost,** spectral ghost, **spook** <nf>, **phantom,** phantasm, phantasma, **wraith, shade,** shadow, fetch, **apparition,** appearance, presence, shape, form, eidolon, idolum, revenant, larva; **spirit;** sprite, shrouded spirit, disembodied spirit, departed spirit, restless *or* wandering spirit *or* soul, soul of the dead, dybbuk; oni; Masan; astral spirit, astral; unsubstantiality, immateriality, incorporeal, incorporeity, incorporeal being *or* entity; walking dead man, zombie; jinn *or* dijn, genie; duppy; vision, theophany; materialization; haunt *or* hant <nf>; banshee; poltergeist; control, guide; manes, lemures; grateful dead

2 White Lady, White Lady of Avenel, White Ladies of Normandy; Brocken specter; Wild Hunt; Flying Dutchman

3 double, etheric double *or* self, co-walker, *Doppelgänger* <Ger>, doubleganger, fetch, wraith

4 eeriness, ghostliness, weirdness, uncanniness, spookiness <nf>

5 possession, spirit control; obsession

VERBS **6 haunt,** hant <nf>, spook <nf>; **possess,** control; obsess

ADJS **7 spectral,** specterlike; **ghostly,** ghostish, ghosty, ghostlike; **spiritual, psychic,** psychical; **phantomlike,** phantom, phantomic *or* phantomical, phantasmal, phantasmic, **wraithlike,** wraithy, shadowy; etheric, ectoplasmic, astral, ethereal 764.6; incorporeal 1053.7; **occult, supernatural** 870.15

8 disembodied, bodiless, immaterial 1053.7, discarnate, decarnate, decarnated

9 weird, eerie, eldritch, **uncanny,** unearthly, macabre; **spooky** *and* spookish *and* hairy <nf>

10 haunted, spooked *and* spooky <nf>, spirit-haunted, ghost-haunted, specter-haunted; **possessed,** ghost-ridden; obsessed

989 MEMORY

NOUNS **1 memory, remembrance, recollection,** mind, *souvenir* <Fr>; memory trace, engram; mind's eye, eye of the mind, mirror of the mind, tablets of the memory; corner *or* recess of the memory, inmost recesses of the memory; Mnemosyne, mother of the Muses; short-term memory, long-term memory, anterograde memory; computer memory, information storage; group memory, collective memory, mneme, racial memory; atavism; cover *or* screen memory, affect memory; eye *or* visual memory, kinesthetic memory; skill, verbal response, emotional response

2 "that inward eye"—Wordsworth, "the warder of the brain"—Shakespeare, "the treasury and guardian of all things"—Cicero, "storehouse of the mind, garner of facts and fancies"—M F Tupper, "the diary that we all carry around with us"—Oscar Wilde

3 retention, retentiveness, retentivity, memory span; good memory, retentive memory *or* mind; total memory, eidetic memory *or* imagery, photographic memory, total recall; camera-eye

4 remembering, remembrance, recollection, recollecting, exercise of memory, **recall,** recalling; reflection, reconsideration; **retrospect,** retrospection, hindsight, looking back, harking back; flashback, **reminiscence,** review, contemplation of the past, review of things past, nostalgia; **memoir; memorization,** memorizing, **rote,** rote memory, rote learning, learning by heart, commitment to memory; déjà vu

5 recognition, identification, reidentification, distinguishment; realization 928.2

6 reminder, remembrance, remembrancer; **prompt,** prompter, tickler; prompting, cue, hint; jogger <nf>, flapper; *aide-mémoire* <Fr>, **memorandum** 549.4

7 memento, remembrance, token, trophy, souvenir, keepsake, relic, favor, token of remembrance; commemoration, memorial 549.12; *memento mori* <L>; **memories, memorabilia,** memorials; history, memoirs

8 memorability, rememberability

9 mnemonics, memory training, mnemotechny, mnemotechnics, mnemonization; mnemonic, mnemonic device, *aide-mémoire* <Fr>

VERBS **10 remember, recall, recollect,** flash on *and* mind <nf>; have a good *or* ready memory, remember clearly, remember as if it were yesterday; have total recall, remember everything; reflect; **think of,** bethink oneself <old>; **call** *or* **bring to mind,** recall to mind, call up, summon up, conjure up, evoke, reevoke, revive, recapture, call back, bring back, "call back yesterday, bid time return"—Shakespeare; **think back,** go back, **look back,** cast the eyes back, carry one's thoughts back, look back upon things past, use hindsight, retrospect, **see in retrospect,** go back over, hark back, retrace, reconstruct, review, hark back, turn back time; review, review in retrospect; write one's memoirs

11 reminisce, rake *or* dig up the past

12 recognize, know, tell, distinguish, make out; identify, place, have; spot *and* nail *and* peg *and* cotton on <nf>, **reidentify,** know again, recover *or* recall knowledge of, know by sight; realize 928.12

13 keep in memory, bear in mind, keep *or* hold in mind, hold *or* retain the memory of, **keep in view,** have in mind, hold *or* carry *or* retain in one's thoughts, store in the mind, **retain, keep;** tax *or* burden the memory, **treasure, cherish,** treasure up in the memory, enshrine *or* embalm in the memory, cherish the memory of; keep up the memory of, keep the memory alive, keep alive in one's thoughts; brood over, dwell on *or* upon, fan the embers, let fester in the mind, let rankle in the breast

14 be remembered, sink in, penetrate, make an impression; live *or* dwell in one's memory, be easy to recall, remain in one's memory, be green *or* fresh in one's memory, stick in the mind, remain indelibly impressed on the memory, be stamped on one's memory, **never be forgotten; haunt one's thoughts,** obsess, run in the head, be in one's thoughts, be on one's mind; be burnt into one's memory, plague one; be like King Charles's head; **rankle,** rankle in the breast, fester in the mind

15 recur, recur to the mind, return to mind, come back, resurface, reenter

16 come to mind, pop into one's head, come to me, come into one's head, flash on the mind, pass in review

17 memorize, commit to memory, con; study; **learn by heart,** get by heart, learn *or* get by rote, get word-perfect *or* letter-perfect, learn word for word, learn verbatim; know by heart *or* from memory, have by heart *or* rote, have at one's fingers' ends *or* tips; repeat by heart *or* rote, give word for word, recite, repeat, parrot, repeat like a parrot, say one's lesson, rattle *or* reel off; be a quick study; retain

18 fix in the mind *or* memory, instill, infix, inculcate, impress, imprint, stamp, inscribe, etch, grave, engrave; **impress on the mind, get into one's head,** drive *or* hammer into one's head, get across, get into one's thick head *or* skull <nf>; **burden the mind with,** task the mind with, load *or* stuff *or* cram the mind with; inscribe *or* stamp *or* rivet in the memory, set in the tablets of memory, etch indelibly in the mind

19 refresh the memory, review, restudy, **brush up, rub up,** polish up *and* bone up <nf>, get up on; **cram** <nf>, swot up <Brit nf>

20 remind, put in mind, remember, put in remembrance, bring back, bring to recollection, refresh the memory of; **remind one of, recall,** suggest, **put one in mind of; take one back,** carry back, carry back in recollection; **jog the memory,** awaken *or* arouse the memory, flap the memory, give a hint *or* suggestion, refresh one's memory; **prompt,** prompt the mind, give the cue, hold the promptbook; nudge, pull by the sleeve, nag; brush up; make a note

21 try to recall, think hard, rack *or* ransack one's brains, **cudgel one's brains,** crack one's brains <nf>; have on the tip of one's tongue, have on the edge of one's memory *or* consciousness

ADJS **22 recollective, memoried;** mnemonic; retentive; **retrospective,** in retrospect; **reminiscent,** nostalgic, **mindful, remindful, suggestive,** redolent, evocative

23 remembered, recollected, recalled; retained, pent-up in the memory, kept in remembrance, enduring, lasting, **unforgotten;** present to the mind, lodged in one's mind, stamped on the memory; vivid, eidetic, fresh, green, alive

24 remembering, mindful, keeping *or* bearing in mind, holding in remembrance; unable to forget, haunted, plagued, obsessed, nagged, rankled

25 memorable, rememberable, recollectable; notable

26 unforgettable, never to be forgotten, never to be erased from the mind, **indelible,** indelibly impressed on the mind, fixed in the mind;

haunting, persistent, recurrent, nagging, plaguing, rankling, festering; obsessing, obsessive

27 memorial, commemorative

ADVS **28 by heart,** *par cœur* <Fr>, **by rote, by** *or* **from memory,** without book; **memorably; rememberingly**

29 in memory of, to the memory of, in remembrance *or* commemoration, *in memoriam* <L>; *memoria in aeterna* <L>, in perpetual remembrance

990 FORGETFULNESS

NOUNS **1 forgetfulness,** unmindfulness, absentmindedness, **memorylessness;** short memory, short memory span, little retentivity *or* recall, mind *or* memory like a sieve; loose memory, vague *or* fuzzy memory, dim *or* hazy recollection; **lapse of memory,** decay of memory; **obliviousness, oblivion,** nirvana; obliteration; Lethe, Lethe water, waters of Lethe *or* oblivion, river of oblivion; insensibility; trance; nepenthe; **forgetting;** heedlessness 340.2; forgiveness 148

2 loss of memory, memory loss, amnesia, failure; **memory gap,** blackout <nf>; fugue; agnosia, unrecognition, body-image agnosia, ideational agnosia, astereognosis *or* astereocognosy; paramnesia, retrospective falsification, false memory, misremembrance; amnesiac

3 block, blocking, **mental block,** memory obstruction; repression, suppression, defense mechanism, conversion, sublimation, symbolization

VERBS **4 be forgetful,** suffer memory loss, be absentminded, have a short memory, have a mind *or* memory like a sieve, have a short memory span, be unable to retain, have little recall, forget one's own name, be oblivious; misremember

5 forget, clean forget <nf>; **not remember,** disremember *and* disrecollect <nf>, fail to remember, forget to remember, **have no remembrance** *or* **recollection of,** be unable to recollect *or* recall, draw a blank <nf>; lose, lose sight of, lose one's train of thought, lose track of what one was saying; have on the tip of the tongue; blow *or* go up in *or* fluff one's lines, forget one's lines, dry up; misremember, misrecollect

6 efface *or* erase from the memory, consign to oblivion, unlearn, obliterate, **dismiss from one's thoughts** 984.4; forgive 148.3,5

7 be forgotten, escape one, miss, **slip one's mind,** fade *or* die away from the memory, slip *or* escape the memory, drop from one's thoughts; fall *or* sink into oblivion, go in one ear and out the other

ADJS **8 forgotten,** clean forgotten <nf>, **unremembered,** disremembered *and* disrecollected

<nf>, **unrecollected, unretained, unrecalled,** past recollection *or* recall, out of the mind, lost, erased, effaced, obliterated, gone out of one's head *or* recollection, beyond recall, consigned to oblivion, buried *or* sunk in oblivion; out of sight out of mind; misremembered, misrecollected; half-remembered; on the tip of one's tongue

9 **forgetful, forgetting,** inclined to forget, **memoryless, unremembering, unmindful,** absentminded, **oblivious,** insensible to the past, with a mind *or* memory like a sieve; blank, vacant, vacuous, empty-headed, absent-minded; suffering from *or* stricken with amnesia, amnesic, amnestic; blocked, repressed, suppressed, sublimated, converted; heedless 340.11; Lethean; in a trance, preoccupied, spaced-out <nf>, out to lunch <nf>

10 **forgettable,** unrememberable, unrecollectable; effaceable, eradicable, erasable

ADVS 11 **forgetfully,** forgettingly, unmindfully, absentmindedly, **obliviously**

991 SUFFICIENCY

NOUNS 1 **sufficiency,** sufficientness, **adequacy,** adequateness, **enough,** a competence *or* competency; satisfactoriness, satisfaction, satisfactory amount, enough to go around; good *or* adequate supply; exact measure, right amount, no more and no less; bare sufficiency, minimum, bare minimum, just enough, enough to get by on, enough to live on; self-sufficiency

2 **plenty,** plenitude, plentifulness, plenteousness, muchness <old>; myriad, myriads, numerousness 884; **amplitude,** ampleness; substantiality, substantialness; **abundance, copiousness;** exuberance, riotousness; **bountifulness,** bounteousness, liberalness, **liberality,** generousness, **generosity; lavishness, extravagance, prodigality;** luxuriance, fertility, teemingness, productiveness 890; **wealth, opulence** *or* opulency, richness, affluence; more than enough; maximum; **fullness,** full measure, repletion, repleteness; **overflow, outpouring,** flood, inundation, flow, shower, spate, stream, gush, avalanche; landslide; **prevalence,** profuseness, **profusion,** riot; **superabundance** 993.2; **overkill;** no end of, great abundance, great plenty, quantities, much, as much as one could wish, one's fill, more than one can shake a stick at, lots, a fistful <nf>, **scads** 247.4; bumper crop, rich harvest, foison <old>; rich vein, bonanza, oodles *and* luau <nf>; an ample sufficiency, enough and to spare, enough and then some; fat of the land

3 cornucopia, horn of plenty, horn of Amalthea, endless supply, bottomless well

VERBS 4 **suffice, do,** just do, serve, **answer,** quench; work, be equal to, **avail;** answer *or* serve the purpose, do the trick <nf>, **suit;** qualify, meet, fulfill, **satisfy,** meet requirements; **pass muster,** make the grade *or* the cut *and* hack it *and* cut the mustard *and* **fill the bill** <nf>, measure up to, prove acceptable; get by *and* scrape by <nf>, do it, do'er <nf>, do in a pinch, **pass,** pass in the dark <nf>; hold, stand, stand up, take it, bear; stretch <nf>, reach, go around; rise to the occasion

5 **abound,** be plentiful, exuberate <old>, teem, **teem with,** creep with, crawl with, swarm with, be lousy with <nf>, bristle with; proliferate 890.7; **overflow,** run over, flood; flow, stream, rain, **pour,** shower, gush; flow with milk and honey, rain cats and dogs *and* stink of *and* roll in <nf>

ADJS 6 **sufficient,** sufficing; **enough, ample,** substantial, **plenty, satisfactory, adequate,** decent, due; competent, up to the mark, up to snuff; commensurate, proportionate, corresponding 788.9; suitable, fit 788.10; good, **good enough,** plenty good enough <nf>; sufficient for *or* to *or* unto, up to, equal to; barely sufficient, minimal, minimum; hand-to-mouth

7 **plentiful,** plenty, **plenteous,** plenitudinous; **galore** *and* a gogo *and* up the gazoo *or* kazoo *and* up to the ass in <nf>, in plenty, in quantity *or* quantities, aplenty <nf>; numerous 884.6; beaucoup <nf>, much, many 247.8; **ample,** all-sufficing; wholesale; well-stocked, well-provided, well-furnished, well-found; abundant, abounding, **copious,** exuberant, riotous; flush; **bountiful,** bounteous, **lavish, generous, liberal, extravagant, prodigal; luxuriant,** fertile, productive 890.9, **rich,** fat, **wealthy, opulent, affluent;** maximal; **full,** replete, well-filled, running over, overflowing; inexhaustible, exhaustless, bottomless; **profuse,** profusive, effuse, diffuse; **prevalent,** prevailing, rife, rampant, epidemic; lousy with <nf>, teeming 884.9; **superabundant** 993.19; a dime a dozen

ADVS 8 **sufficiently, amply,** substantially, **satisfactorily, enough;** competently, **adequately;** minimally

9 **plentifully,** plenteously, **aplenty** <nf>, **in plenty,** in quantity *or* quantities, in good supply; **abundantly,** in abundance, copiously, no end <nf>; **superabundantly** 992.24; **bountifully,** bounteously, **lavishly, generously, liberally, extravagantly, prodigally;** maximally; **fully,** in full measure, to the full, overflowingly; inexhaustibly, exhaustlessly, bottomlessly; exuberantly, luxuriantly, riotously; richly, opulently, affluently; **profusely,** diffusely, effusely; beyond one's wildest dreams, beyond the dreams of avarice

992 INSUFFICIENCY

NOUNS **1 insufficiency, inadequacy,** insufficientness, inadequateness; short supply, seller's market; none to spare; unsatisfactoriness, nonsatisfaction, nonfulfillment, coming *or* falling short *or* shy, slippage, shortfall; **undercommitment;** disappointment, too little too late; a band-aid <nf>, a drop in the bucket *or* the ocean, a lick and a promise, a cosmetic measure; **incompetence,** incompetency, unqualification, unsuitability 789.3

2 meagerness, exiguousness, exiguity, scrimpiness, skimpiness, scantiness, spareness; meanness, miserliness, niggardliness, narrowness <nf>, stinginess, parsimony; smallness, slightness, puniness, paltriness; thinness, leanness, slimness, slim pickings <nf>, slenderness, scrawniness; jejuneness, jejunity; austerity; skeleton crew, corporal's guard

3 scarcity, scarceness, **sparsity,** sparseness; **scantiness,** scant sufficiency; **dearth, paucity,** poverty; **rarity,** rareness, uncommonness

4 want, lack, need, deficiency, deficit, shortage, shortfall, wantage, **incompleteness,** defectiveness, shortcoming 911, imperfection; **absence 222,** omission; **destitution,** impoverishment, beggary, deprivation; starvation, famine, drought, drying-up

5 pittance, dole, scrimption <nf>; drop in the bucket *or* the ocean; **mite,** bit 248.2; short allowance, short commons, half rations, cheeseparings and candle ends; mere subsistence, starvation wages; widow's mite

6 dietary deficiency, vitamin deficiency; undernourishment, undernutrition, **malnutrition,** starvation diet, half rations, bread and water; Lenten fare, Spartan fare

VERBS **7 want, lack, need, require;** miss, feel the want of, be sent away empty-handed; run short of

8 be insufficient, not qualify, be found wanting, leave a lot to be desired, kick the beam, not make it *and* not hack it *and* not make the cut *and* not cut it *and* not cut the mustard <nf>, be beyond one's depth *or* ken, be in over one's head, **fall short,** fall shy, come short, not come up to; run short; want, want for, lack, fail, fail of *or* in; cramp one's style <nf>

ADJS **9 insufficient,** unsufficing, **inadequate;** found wanting, defective, incomplete, imperfect, deficient, lacking, failing, wanting; **too few,** undersupplied, low on, light on; **too little,** not enough, precious little, a trickle *or* mere trickle; **unsatisfactory,** unsatisfying; cosmetic, merely cosmetic, surface, superficial, symptomatic, merely symptomatic; **incompetent,** unequal to, unqualified, not up to it, not up to snuff, beyond one's depth *or* over one's head, outmatched; short-staffed, understaffed, short-handed

10 meager, slight, scrimpy, skimp, skimpy, exiguous; scant, **scanty,** spare; miserly, niggardly, stingy, narrow <nf>, parsimonious, mean; hard to find, out of stock; austere, Lenten, Spartan, abstemious, ascetic; stinted, frugal, sparing; poor, impoverished; small, puny, paltry; thin, lean, slim, slender, scrawny; dwarfish, dwarfed, stunted, undergrown; straitened, limited; jejune, watered, watery, unnourishing, unnutritious; subsistence, starvation

11 scarce, sparse, scanty; in short supply, at a premium; **rare,** uncommon, infrequent; scarcer than hen's teeth <nf>; not to be had, not to be had for love *or* money, not to be had at any price; out of print, out of stock *or* season, nonexistent; few and far between

12 ill-provided, ill-furnished, ill-equipped, ill-found, ill off; **unprovided,** unsupplied, unreplenished; bare-handed; unfed, underfed, undernourished; shorthanded, undermanned; **empty-handed, poor,** pauperized, impoverished, beggarly; hungry, starved, half-starved, on short commons, starving, starveling, famished, anorectic

13 wanting, lacking, needing, missing, in want of; for want of, in default of, in the absence of; short, **short of,** scant of; shy, **shy of** *or* **on;** out of, clean *or* fresh out of <nf>, destitute of, bare of, void of, empty of, devoid of, forlorn of, bereft of, deprived of, denuded of, unpossessed of, unblessed with, bankrupt in; out of pocket; at the end of one's rope *or* tether

ADVS **14 insufficiently; inadequately,** unsubstantially, incompletely

15 meagerly, slightly, sparely, punily, scantily, poorly, frugally, sparingly

16 scarcely, sparsely, scantily, skimpily, scrimpily; **rarely,** uncommonly

PREPS **17 without,** minus, less, sans, absent

WORD ELEMENTS **18** hyp-, hypo-, under-, mal-, ill-, sub-

993 EXCESS

NOUNS **1 excess, excessiveness, inordinance,** inordinateness, nimiety, **immoderateness,** immoderacy, immoderation, **extravagance** *or* extravagancy, intemperateness, incontinence, overindulgence, **intemperance** 669; unrestrainedness, abandon; gluttony 672; **extreme,** extremity, **extremes; boundlessness** 823.1; overlargeness, overgreatness, monstrousness, enormousness 247.1; overgrowth, overdevelopment, hypertrophy, gigantism, giantism, elephantiasis; **overmuch,** overmuchness, too much, too-muchness; **exorbitance** *or* exorbitancy, undueness, **outrageousness,** unconscionableness, **unreasonableness;** radicalism, extremism 611.4; egregiousness; fabulousness, hyperbole, **exaggeration** 355

2 **superabundance,** overabundance, superflux, **plethora,** redundancy, overprofusion, too many, too much, too much of a good thing, **overplentifulness,** overplenteousness, overplenty, **oversupply,** overstock, overaccumulation, **oversufficiency,** overmuchness, overcopiousness, overlavishness, overluxuriance, overbounteousness, overnumerousness; lavishness, **extravagance** or extravagancy, **prodigality; plenty** 991.2; **more than enough, enough and to spare,** enough in all conscience; **overdose,** overmeasure, "enough, with over-measure"—Shakespeare, one too many; too much of a good thing, egg in one's beer <nf>; more than one knows what to do with, drug on the market; spate, avalanche, landslide, deluge, flood, inundation; *embarras de richesses* <Fr>, money to burn <nf>; overpopulation; spare tire, fifth wheel; lagniappe

3 **overfullness,** plethora, **surfeit, glut;** satiety 994; engorgement, repletion, congestion; hyperemia; **saturation,** supersaturation; **overload,** overburden, overcharge, surcharge, overfreight, overweight; **overflow,** overbrimming, overspill; **insatiability,** insatiableness; all the market can bear

4 **superfluity,** superfluousness, fat; **redundancy,** redundance; unnecessariness, needlessness; fifth wheel *and* tits on a boar <nf>; featherbedding, payroll padding; duplication, duplication of effort, overlap; **luxury,** extravagance, frill *and* **frills** *and* bells and whistles *and* gimcrackery <nf>; frippery, froufrou, overadornment, bedizenment, gingerbread; **ornamentation,** embellishment 498.1; expletive, **padding, filling;** pleonasm, tautology; verbosity, prolixity 538.2; more than one really wants to know

5 **surplus,** surplusage, leftovers, plus, **overplus,** overstock, **overage,** overset, overrun, **overmeasure, oversupply;** margin; **remainder, balance, leftover, extra, spare,** something extra *or* to spare; bonus, dividend; lagniappe <nf>; gratuity, tip, *pourboire* <Fr>

6 **overdoing,** overcarrying, **overreaching,** supererogation; **overkill;** piling on <nf>, overimportance, overemphasis; overuse; overreaction; **overwork, overexertion,** overexercise, overexpenditure, overtaxing, overstrain, tax, strain; too much on one's plate, too many irons in the fire, too much at once; **overachievement,** overachieving

7 **overextension, overdrawing,** drawing *or* spreading too thin, **overstretching,** overstrain, overstraining, stretching, straining, stretch, strain, tension, extreme tension, snapping *or* breaking point; **overexpansion;** inflation, distension, overdistension, edema, turgidity, swelling, bloat, bloating 259.2

VERBS 8 **superabound,** overabound, **know no bounds, swarm,** pullulate, run riot, luxuriate, **teem;** overflow, flood, overbrim, overspill, spill over, overrun, overspread, overswarm, overgrow, fill, saturate; meet one at every turn; hang heavy on one's hands, remain on one's hands; burst at the seams

9 **exceed, surpass, pass, top, transcend, go beyond;** overpass, overstep, overrun, **overreach,** overshoot, overshoot the mark

10 **overdo, go too far,** do twice over, do it to death <nf>, pass all bounds, know no bounds, overact, **carry too far,** overcarry, go to an extreme, **go to extremes,** go overboard, go *or* jump off the deep end; **run** *or* **drive into the ground; make a big deal of** *and* make a federal case of <nf>; overemphasize, overstress; max out; overplay, overplay one's hand <nf>; **overreact,** protest too much; overreach oneself; **overtax,** overtask, overexert, overexercise, overstrain, overdrive, overspend, exhaust, overexpend, overuse; overtrain; **overwork,** overlabor; overelaborate, overdevelop, tell more than one wants to know; overstudy; burn the candle at both ends; **spread oneself too thin, take on too much,** have too much on one's plate, have too many irons in the fire, do too many things at once; **exaggerate** 355.3; **overindulge** 669.5

11 **pile it on,** lay it on, **lay it on thick,** lay it on with a trowel <nf>, talk too much, exaggerate

12 **carry coals to Newcastle,** teach fishes to swim, teach one's grandmother to suck eggs, kill the slain, beat *or* flog a dead horse, labor the obvious, butter one's bread on both sides, preach to the converted, paint *or* gild the lily, "to gild refined gold, to paint the lily, to throw a perfume on the violet"—Shakespeare

13 **overextend, overdraw, overstretch, overstrain,** stretch, strain; reach the breaking *or* snapping point; **overexpand,** overdistend, overdevelop, inflate, swell 259.4

14 **oversupply, overprovide,** overlavish, overfurnish, overequip; **overstock;** overprovision, overprovender; overdose; flood the market, oversell; **flood, deluge,** inundate, engulf, swamp, whelm, overwhelm; lavish with, be prodigal with

15 **overload,** overlade, **overburden,** overweight, **overcharge,** surcharge; **overfill,** stuff, crowd, cram, jam, pack, jam-pack, **congest,** choke; **overstuff,**

overfeed; gluttonize 672.4; **surfeit, glut, gorge,** satiate 994.4; **saturate,** soak, drench, supersaturate, supercharge

ADJS **16 excessive, inordinate, immoderate,** overweening, hubristic, **intemperate, extravagant,** incontinent; unrestrained, unbridled, abandoned; gluttonous 672.6; **extreme; overlarge, overgreat,** overbig, larger than life, monstrous, enormous, jumbo, elephantine, gigantic 247.7; overgrown, overdeveloped, hypertrophied; **overmuch,** too much, a bit much, de trop; **exorbitant, undue, outrageous,** unconscionable, **unreasonable;** fancy *and* high *and* stiff *and* steep <nf>; **out of bounds** *or* **all bounds,** out of sight *and* out of this world <nf>, **boundless** 823.3; egregious; fabulous, hyperbolic, hyperbolical, **exaggerated** 355.4

17 superfluous, redundant; excess, in excess, duplicative; unnecessary, unessential, nonessential, **needless,** otiose, expendable, dispensable, needless, unneeded, gratuitous, uncalled-for; expletive; pleonastic, tautologous, tautological; verbose, prolix 538.12; *de trop* <Fr>, supererogatory, supererogative; spare, to spare; on one's hands

18 surplus, overplus; **remaining,** unused, **leftover;** over, **over and above; extra, spare,** supernumerary, for lagniappe <nf>, as a bonus

19 superabundant, overabundant, plethoric, **overplentiful,** overplenteous, overplenty, **oversufficient, overmuch; lavish, prodigal,** overlavish, overbounteous, overgenerous, overliberal; overcopious, overluxuriant, riotous, overexuberant; overprolific, overnumerous; **swarming,** pullulating, **teeming,** overpopulated, overpopulous; plentiful 991.7

20 overfull, overloaded, overladen, overburdened, overfreighted, overfraught, overweighted, **overcharged,** surcharged, **saturated,** drenched, soaked, supersaturated, supercharged; **surfeited, glutted,** gorged, overfed, bloated, replete, swollen, satiated 994.6, **stuffed,** overstuffed, **crowded, overcrowded, crammed,** jammed, packed, jam-packed, like sardines in a can *or* tin, bumper-to-bumper <nf>; choked, **congested,** stuffed up; **overstocked, oversupplied; overflowing,** in spate, running over, filled to overflowing; plethoric, hyperemic; **bursting,** ready to burst, bursting at the seams, at the bursting point, overblown, distended, **swollen,** bloated 259.13

21 overdone, overwrought; overdrawn, overstretched, overstrained; overwritten, overplayed, overacted

ADVS **22 excessively, inordinately, immoderately, intemperately,** overweeningly, hubristically, **overly,** over, **overmuch,** too much; **too,** too-too <nf>;

exorbitantly, unduly, unreasonably, unconscionably, **outrageously**

23 in *or* **to excess,** to extremes, to the extreme, all out *and* to the max <nf>, flat out <Brit nf>, to a fault, too far, out of all proportion

24 superabundantly, overabundantly, **lavishly, prodigally, extravagantly;** more than enough, plentifully 991.9; without measure, out of measure, beyond measure

25 superfluously, redundantly, supererogatorily; tautologously; unnecessarily, needlessly, beyond need, beyond reason, to a fare-thee-well <nf>

PREPS **26 in excess of,** over, beyond, past, above, **over and above,** above and beyond

WORD ELEMENTS **27** arch-, hyper-, over-, super-, sur-, ultra-, extra-

994 SATIETY

NOUNS **1 satiety, satiation, satisfaction, fullness, surfeit, glut,** repletion, engorgement; contentment; **fill, bellyful** *and* skinful <nf>; **saturation,** oversaturation, saturatedness, supersaturation; saturation point; more than enough, enough in all conscience, all one can stand *or* take; too much of a good thing, much of a muchness <nf>

2 satedness, surfeitedness, cloyedness, jadedness; overfullness, fed-upness <nf>

3 cloyer, surfeiter, sickener; **overdose;** a diet of cake; warmed-over cabbage

VERBS **4 satiate, sate, satisfy,** slake, allay; **surfeit, glut, gorge,** engorge; **cloy,** jade, pall; **fill,** fill up; saturate, oversaturate, supersaturate; **stuff,** overstuff, cram; **overfill,** overgorge, overdose, overfeed

5 have enough, have about enough of, have quite enough, **have one's fill;** have too much, have too much of a good thing, **have a bellyful** *or* skinful <nf>, have an overdose, **be fed up** <nf>, have all one can take *or* stand, have it up to here *and* up the gazoo *or* kazoo <nf>, have had it

ADJS **6 satiated, sated, satisfied,** slaked, allayed; **surfeited, gorged,** replete, engorged, **glutted; cloyed,** jaded; **full,** full of, with one's fill of, **overfull,** saturated, oversaturated, supersaturated; **stuffed,** overstuffed, crammed, overgorged, overfed; **fed up** *and* fed to the gills *or* fed to the teeth *and* stuffed to the gills <nf>; **with a bellyful** *or* skinful <nf>, with enough of; disgusted, **sick of,** tired of, sick and tired of

7 satiating, sating, satisfying, filling; surfeiting, overfilling; jading, **cloying,** cloysome

INTERJS **8** enough!, *basta* <Ital>, *genug!* and *genug shayn!* <Yiddish>, all right already!, enough already!

995 EXPEDIENCE

NOUNS **1 expedience** *or* **expediency, advisability,** politicness, **desirability,** recommendability; **fitness, fittingness, appropriateness,** propriety, decency <old>, seemliness, **suitability,** rightness, feasibility, **convenience;** seasonableness, timeliness, **opportuneness;** usefulness 387.3; **advantage, advantageousness,** beneficialness, **profit,** profitability, percentage *and* mileage <nf>, worthwhileness, fruitfulness; wisdom, prudence 920.7; **temporariness, provisionality**

 2 expedient, means, means to an end, **provision, measure, step, action,** effort, **stroke,** stroke of policy, coup, **move,** countermove, **maneuver,** demarche, course of action; tactic, **device,** contrivance, artifice, stratagem, **shift; gimmick** *and* dodge *and* trick <nf>; **resort,** resource; answer, solution; quick-and-dirty solution <nf>; working proposition, working hypothesis; **temporary expedient, improvisation,** ad hoc measure, ad hoc *or* ad hockery *or* ad hocism; **fix** *and* **quick fix** <nf>, jury-rigged expedient, **makeshift,** stopgap, shake-up, jury-rig; last expedient, **last resort** *or* resource, *pis aller* <Fr>, last shift, trump

VERBS **3 expedite one's affair,** work to one's advantage, not come amiss, come in handy, be just the thing, be just what the doctor ordered <nf>, fit to a T *or* like a glove *or* like a second skin; forward, advance, promote, profit, advantage, benefit; **work, serve,** answer, answer *or* serve one's purpose, fill the bill *and* do the trick <nf>; suit the occasion, **be fitting,** fit, befit, be right

 4 make shift, make do, make out <nf>, rub along <Brit>, cope, manage, manage with, get along on, get by on, do with; do as well as *or* the best one can; use a last resort, scrape the bottom of the barrel

ADJS **5 expedient, desirable,** to be desired, much to be desired, **advisable, politic,** recommendable; **appropriate, meet, fit, fitting,** befitting, **right, proper,** good, decent <old>, **becoming,** seemly, likely, congruous, **suitable,** sortable, feasible, doable, swingable <nf>, **convenient,** happy, heaven-sent, felicitous; timely, seasonable, opportune, well-timed, in the nick of time; **useful** 387.18; **advantageous,** favorable; **profitable,** fructuous, worthwhile, worth one's while; **wise** 920.17

 6 practical, practicable, pragmatic *or* pragmatical, banausic; feasible, workable, operable, realizable; **efficient,** effective, **effectual**

 7 makeshift, makeshifty, **stopgap,** band-aid <nf>, improvised, improvisational, **jury-rigged; last-ditch; ad hoc;** quick *and* dirty <nf>; temporary, provisional, tentative

ADVS **8 expediently, fittingly,** fitly, **appropriately, suitably,** sortably, congruously, rightly, properly, decently <old>, feasibly, conveniently; practically; seasonably, opportunely; desirably, advisably; advantageously, to advantage, all to the good; as a last resort

PHRS **9** there's more than one way to skin a cat, where there's a will there's a way

996 INEXPEDIENCE

NOUNS **1 inexpedience** *or* inexpediency, **undesirability, inadvisability,** impoliticness *or* impoliticalness; **unwiseness** 922.2; **unfitness, unfittingness, inappropriateness, unaptness, unsuitability,** incongruity, **unmeetness,** wrongness, unseemliness; **inconvenience** *or* inconveniency, awkwardness; ineptitude, inaptitude; unseasonableness, untimeliness, inopportuneness; unfortunateness, infelicity; disadvantageousness, unprofitableness, unprofitability, worthlessness, futility, uselessness 391

 2 disadvantage, drawback, liability; detriment, impairment, prejudice, loss, damage, hurt, harm, mischief, injury; **a step back** *or* **backward,** a loss of ground; **handicap** 1012.6, disability; drag, millstone around one's neck

 3 inconvenience, discommodity, incommodity, disaccommodation <old>, **trouble, bother;** inconvenientness, inconveniency, **unhandiness,** awkwardness, clumsiness, unwieldiness, troublesomeness, clunkiness <nf>; gaucheness, gaucherie

VERBS **4 inconvenience,** put to inconvenience, **put out, discommode,** incommode, disaccommodate <old>, disoblige, **burden, embarrass; trouble, bother,** put to trouble, put to the trouble of, **impose upon;** harm, disadvantage 1000.6

ADJS **5 inexpedient, undesirable, inadvisable, counterproductive,** impolitic, impolitical, unpolitic, not to be recommended, contraindicated; **impractical, impracticable,** dysfunctional, unworkable; **ill-advised, ill-considered, unwise; unfit, unfitting,** unbefitting, **inappropriate, unsuitable,** unmeet, inapt, inept, unseemly, **improper, wrong,** bad, out of place, out of order, incongruous, ill-suited; malapropos, *mal à propos* <Fr>, inopportune, untimely, ill-timed, badly timed, unseasonable; infelicitous, unfortunate, unhappy; unprofitable 391.12; futile 391.13

 6 disadvantageous, unadvantageous, **unfavorable;** unprofitable, profitless, unrewarding, worthless, useless 391.9; **detrimental,** deleterious, injurious, harmful, prejudicial, disserviceable

7 inconvenient, incommodious, discommodious; **unhandy, awkward,** clumsy, unwieldy, troublesome, onerous; gauche

ADVS **8 inexpediently, inadvisably,** impoliticly *or* impolitically, **undesirably; unfittingly, inappropriately, unsuitably,** ineptly, inaptly, incongruously; inopportunely, unseasonably; infelicitously, unfortunately, unhappily

9 disadvantageously, unadvantageously, unprofitably, unrewardingly; uselessly 391.15; **inconveniently,** unhandily, with difficulty, ill

997 IMPORTANCE

NOUNS **1 importance, significance, consequence,** consideration, **import,** note, mark, **moment, weight, gravity;** materiality; concern, concernment, interest; **first order,** high order, high rank; **priority,** primacy, precedence, preeminence, paramountcy, superiority, **supremacy;** value, worth, merit, excellence 999.1; self-importance 140.1; emphasis, oomph <nf>

2 notability, noteworthiness, remarkableness, salience, memorability; **prominence, eminence, greatness,** distinction, magnitude; prestige, esteem, repute, reputation, honor, glory, renown, dignity, **fame** 662.1; **stardom,** celebrity, celebrity-hood, superstardom; semicelebrity

3 gravity, graveness, seriousness, solemnity, weightiness; *gravitas* <L>, grave affair; no joke, no laughing matter, nothing to sneeze at <nf>, hardball <nf>, matter of life and death, heavy scene <nf>

4 urgency, imperativeness, exigence *or* exigency; **momentousness, crucialness, cruciality;** consequentiality, consequentialness; **press,** pressure, high pressure, **stress,** tension, **pinch;** clutch *and* crunch <nf>; **crisis, emergency;** moment of truth, turning point, climax, defining moment; crunch

5 matter of importance *or* **consequence,** thing of interest, point of interest, matter of concern, object of note, one for the book *and* something to write home about <nf>, something special, no tea party, no picnic; not chicken feed <nf>; vital concern *or* interest; notabilia, memorabilia, great doings

6 salient point, cardinal point, high point, great point, key point; important thing, chief thing, **the point, main point,** main thing, essential matter, **essence,** the name of the game *and* the bottom line *and* what it's all about *and* where it's at <nf>, substance, gravamen, *sine qua non* <L>, issue, real issue, front-burner issue <nf>, prime issue; **essential,** fundamental, substantive point, material point; **gist, nub** <nf>, **heart,** meat, pith, kernel,

core; **crux,** crucial *or* pivotal *or* critical point, pivot; turning point, **climax, cusp, crisis;** keystone, cornerstone; landmark, milestone, bench mark; linchpin; secret weapon, trump card

7 feature, highlight, high spot, main attraction, centerpiece, pièce de résistance; outstanding feature; best part, cream

8 personage, important person, person of importance *or* consequence, **great man** *or* **woman,** man *or* woman of mark *or* note, **somebody, notable,** notability, figure; **celebrity,** famous person, person of renown, personality; name, big name, megastar, nabob, **mogul,** captain of industry, panjandrum, person to be reckoned with, very important person, heavyweight; sachem; mover and shaker, lord of creation; **worthy,** pillar of society, salt of the earth, elder, father; **dignitary,** dignity; **magnate;** tycoon <nf>, baron; power; power elite, Establishment; interests; brass, top brass; top people, the great; ruling circle, lords of creation, "the choice and master spirits of the age"—Shakespeare; the top, the summit

9 <nf terms> **big shot,** wheel, **big wheel,** big boy, big cat, big fish, biggie, big cheese, big noise, big-timer, big-time operator, **bigwig,** big man, big gun, **high-muck-a-muck** *or* high-muckety-muck, kingpin, lion, something, **VIP,** brass hat, high man on the totem pole, suit; sacred cow, little tin god, tin god; big man on campus *or* BMOC; 800-pound gorilla; queen bee, heavy momma; first fiddle; mega-

10 chief, principal, chief executive, chief executive officer *or* CEO, paramount, lord of the manor, overlord, **king,** queen, monarch, electronics king, etc; leading light, luminary, master spirit, **star,** superstar, superman, superwoman, prima donna, lead 707.6

11 <nf terms> **boss, honcho,** big enchilada, biggest frog in the pond, big man, top *or* high man on the totem pole, top dog, Mr Big, head cheese, his nibs, himself, man upstairs

VERBS **12 matter,** import <old>, signify, **count, tell, weigh, carry weight,** cut ice *and* cut some ice <nf>, be prominent, stand out, mean much; be something, be somebody, amount to something; have a key to the executive washroom; be featured, star, get top billing, take the limelight

13 value, esteem, treasure, prize, appreciate, respect, **rate highly,** think highly of, think well of, **think much of,** set store by; give *or* attach *or* ascribe importance to; make much of, make a fuss *or* stir about, make an ado *or* much ado about; hold up as an example

14 emphasize, stress, lay emphasis *or* stress upon, feature, highlight, brightline, place emphasis on, give emphasis to, **accent, accentuate, punctuate,**

point up, bring to the fore, put in the foreground, put in bright lights; prioritize; **highlight,** spotlight; **star, underline, underscore,** italicize; overemphasize, overstress, overaccentuate, hammer home, rub in; harp on; dwell on, belabor; attach too much importance to, make a big deal *or* federal case of <nf>, make a mountain out of a molehill; pull no punches <nf>

15 **feature,** headline <nf>; **star,** give top billing to

16 **dramatize, play up** <nf>, splash, make a production of; put on the map

ADJS 17 **important, major, consequential, momentous, significant, considerable,** substantial, material, **great,** grand, big; superior, world-shaking, earthshaking; big-time *and* big-league *and* major-league *and* heavyweight <nf>; high-powered <nf>, double-barreled <nf>; bigwig *and* bigwigged <nf>; name *and* big-name <nf>, self-important 140.8; mega; A-1 <nf>

18 **of importance, of significance, of consequence,** of note, of moment, of weight; of concern, of concernment, of interest, not to be overlooked *or* despised, not hay *and* not chopped liver *and* not to be sneezed at <nf>; viable

19 **notable, noteworthy, celebrated, remarkable, marked, standout** <nf>, of mark, signal; **memorable,** rememberable, unforgettable, classic, historic, never to be forgotten; striking, telling, salient; **eminent, prominent,** conspicuous, noble, **outstanding, distinguished;** prestigious, esteemed, estimable, elevated, sublime, reputable 662.15; **extraordinary,** *extraordinaire* <Fr>, out of the ordinary, **exceptional, special,** rare; top-ten

20 **weighty,** heavy, **grave,** sober, sobering, **solemn, serious,** earnest; portentous, fateful, fatal; formidable, awe-inspiring, imposing, larger than life; world-shaking, earth-shattering

21 **emphatic, decided, positive, forceful,** forcible; **emphasized, stressed,** accented, accentuated, punctuated, pointed; underlined, underscored, starred, italicized, highlighted; red-letter, in red letters, in letters of fire

22 **urgent, imperative,** imperious, **compelling, pressing,** high-priority, high-pressure, crying, clamorous, insistent, instant, exigent; crucial, critical, pivotal, acute; fateful

23 **vital, all-important,** crucial, of vital importance, life-and-death *or* life-or-death; earth-shattering, epoch-making; **essential,** fundamental, indispensable, basic, substantive, bedrock, material; **central,** focal; bottom-line *and* meat-and-potatoes *and* gut <nf>; grass-roots

24 **paramount, principal, leading, foremost, main, chief,** number one <nf>, premier, **prime, primary,** preeminent, **supreme,** capital <old>, cardinal;

highest, uppermost, topmost, toprank, ranking, of the first rank, world-class, **dominant,** predominant, master, controlling, **overruling,** overriding, all-absorbing

ADVS 25 **importantly, significantly,** consequentially, materially, momentously, greatly, grandly; eminently, prominently, conspicuously, outstandingly, saliently, signally, notably, markedly, remarkably

26 **at the decisive moment,** in the clutch *and* when the chips are down *and* when push comes to shove <nf>

998 UNIMPORTANCE

NOUNS 1 **unimportance, insignificance,** inconsequence, inconsequentiality, indifference, **immateriality;** inessentiality; ineffectuality; unnoteworthiness, unimpressiveness; inferiority, secondariness, low order of importance, low priority, dispensability, expendability, marginality; lack of substance; **smallness,** littleness, slightness, inconsiderableness, negligibility; irrelevancy, meaninglessness; **pettiness,** puniness, pokiness, picayune, picayunishness; marginalization; irrelevance 776.1

2 **paltriness,** poorness, **meanness,** sorriness, sadness, pitifulness, contemptibleness, pitiableness, despicableness, miserableness, wretchedness, vileness, crumminess <nf>, shabbiness, shoddiness, cheapness, cheesiness, beggarliness, worthlessness, uselessness, unworthiness, meritlessness; tawdriness, meretriciousness, gaudiness 501.3

3 **triviality,** trivialness, triflingness, nugacity, nugaciousness; **superficiality,** shallowness; slightness, slenderness, slimness, flimsiness; **frivolity,** frivolousness, lightness, levity; **foolishness,** silliness; inanity, emptiness, vacuity; triteness, vapidity; vanity, idleness, futility; **much ado about nothing,** tempest *or* storm in a teacup *or* teapot, much cry and little wool, piss *and* wind *and* big deal <nf>; pettiness; snap of the fingers

4 **trivia, trifles; trumpery,** *nugae* <L>, gimcrackery, knickknackery, bric-a-brac; **rubbish,** trash, chaff; peanuts *and* chicken feed *and* chickenshit *and* Mickey Mouse <nf>, small change; small beer; froth, "trifles light as air"—Shakespeare; minutiae, details, minor details; inessential, nonessential

5 **trifle, triviality, oddment, bagatelle,** fribble, **gimcrack, gewgaw,** frippery, froth, **trinket,** bibelot, curio, **bauble,** gaud, toy, **knickknack,** knickknackery, kickshaw, minikin <old>, whim-wham, folderol; pin, button, hair, straw, rush, feather, fig, bean, hill of beans <nf>, molehill, row

of pins *or* buttons <nf>, sneeshing <Brit nf>, pinch of snuff; bit, snap; a curse, a continental, a hoot *and* a damn *and* a darn *and* a shit <nf>, a tinker's damn; picayune, rap, sou, halfpenny, farthing, brass farthing, cent, red cent, two cents, twopence *or* tuppence <Brit>, penny, dime, plugged nickel; peppercorn; drop in the ocean *or* the bucket; fleabite, pinprick; joke, jest, farce, mockery, child's play; small potatoes

6 **an insignificancy,** an inessential, a marginal matter *or* affair, a trivial *or* paltry affair, a small *or* trifling *or* minor matter, **no great matter;** a little thing, *peu de chose* <Fr>, hardly *or* scarcely anything, matter of no importance *or* consequence, matter of indifference; **a nothing, a big nothing, a naught,** a mere nothing, nothing in particular, nothing to signify, nothing to speak *or* worth speaking of, nothing to think twice about, nothing to boast of, nothing to write home about, thing of naught, *rien du tout* <Fr>, nullity, nihility; **technicality,** mere technicality; red herring

7 **a nobody, insignificancy,** hollow man, jackstraw <old>, **nonentity,** nonperson, empty suit *and* nebbish <nf>, an obscurity, a nothing, cipher, little man, nobody one knows; lightweight, mediocrity; whippersnapper *and* whiffet *and* pip-squeak *and* squirt *and* shrimp *and* scrub *and* runt <nf>; squit <Brit nf>, punk <nf>; small potato, small potatoes; **the little fellow,** the little guy <nf>, **the man in the street;** common man 864.3; man of straw, dummy, figurehead; **small fry,** Mr and Mrs Nobody, John Doe and Richard Roe *or* Mary Roe; Tom, Dick, and Harry; Brown, Jones, and Robinson

8 **trifling,** dallying, **dalliance,** flirtation, flirtiness, coquetry; toying, fiddling, playing, fooling, **puttering,** tinkering, pottering, piddling; dabbling, smattering; loitering, idling 331.4

9 <nf terms> **monkeying, monkeying around,** buggering around, diddling around, fiddling around, frigging around, horsing around, fooling around, kidding around, messing around, pissing around, playing around, screwing around, mucking around, farting around; jerking off

10 **trifler, dallier,** fribble; **putterer,** potterer, piddler, tinkerer, smatterer, dabbler; amateur, dilettante, Sunday painter; **flirt, coquet**

VERBS 11 **be unimportant,** be of no importance, not signify, **not matter,** not count, signify nothing, matter little, **not make any difference; cut no ice, not amount to anything,** make no never mind *and* not amount to a hill of beans *or* a damn <nf>; have no clout *or* pull

12 **attach little importance to,** give little weight to; make little of, underplay, de-emphasize, downplay, play down, **minimize,** marginalize, disregard, **make light of,** think little of, throw away, **make** *or* **think nothing of,** take no account of, set little by, set no store by, set at naught; snap one's fingers at; not care a straw about; not give a shit *or* a hoot *or* two hoots for <nf>, not give a damn about, not give a dime a dozen for; bad-mouth <nf>, deprecate, depreciate 512.8; **trivialize**

13 **make much ado about nothing,** make mountains out of molehills, have a storm *or* tempest in a teacup *or* teapot

14 **trifle, dally;** flirt, coquet; **toy,** fribble, **play, fool,** play at, **putter, potter,** tinker, **piddle; dabble,** smatter; toy with, fiddle with, fool with, play with; idle, loiter 331.12,13; nibble, niggle, nickel-and-dime <nf>

15 <nf terms> **monkey, monkey around,** fiddle, fiddle around, fiddle-faddle, frivol, horse around, fool around, play around, mess around, kid around, **screw around,** muck around, muck about <Brit>, fart around, piss around, bugger around, diddle around, frig around; jerk off

ADJS 16 **unimportant, of no importance,** of little *or* small importance, of no great importance, **of no account,** of no significance, of no concern, of no matter, of little *or* no consequence, no great shakes <nf>; no skin off one's nose *or* elbow *or* ass <nf>; inferior, secondary, of a low order of importance, low-priority, expendable; marginal; one-dimensional, two-dimensional; not apropos, not related, irrelevant

17 **insignificant** 248.6, **inconsequential, immaterial,** of no consequence, insubstantial; nonessential, unessential, inessential, **not vital,** back-burner <nf>, dispensable; unnoteworthy, unimpressive; **inconsiderable,** inappreciable, negligible; **small, little,** minute, footling, petit <old>, minor, inferior; technical

18 <nf terms> **measly, small-time, two-bit,** Mickey Mouse, chickenshit, nickel-and-dime, low-rent, piddly, pissy-ass, dinky, poky <Brit>, tinhorn, punk; not worth a dime *or* a red cent *or* beans *or* a hill of beans *or* bubkes *or* shit, not worth a second thought; **one-horse, two-by-four,** jerkwater

19 **trivial, trifling;** fribble, fribbling, nugacious, nugatory; catchpenny; **slight,** slender, flimsy; **superficial, shallow; frivolous, light,** windy, airy, frothy; idle, futile, vain, otiose; **foolish,** fatuous, asinine, **silly; inane,** empty, vacuous; trite, vapid; unworthy of serious consideration

20 **petty, puny, piddling,** piffling, niggling, pettifogging, technical, picayune, picayunish; small-beer

21 **paltry, poor,** common, **mean, sorry, sad,** pitiful, pitiable, pathetic, **despicable, contemptible,**

beneath contempt, **miserable, wretched,** beggarly, vile, **shabby,** scrubby, scruffy, shoddy, scurvy, scuzzy <nf>, scummy, **crummy** *and* cheesy <nf>, **trashy,** rubbishy, garbagey <nf>, trumpery, gimcracky <nf>; tinpot <nf>; **cheap,** worthless, valueless, twopenny *or* twopenny-halfpenny <Brit>, two-for-a-cent *or* -penny, dime-a-dozen; tawdry, meretricious, gaudy 501.20; mickey mouse *or* rinky-dink <nf>

22 **unworthy, worthless,** meritless, unworthy of regard *or* consideration, beneath notice; no great shakes <nf>

ADVS 23 **unimportantly, insignificantly, inconsequentially,** immaterially, unessentially; **pettily,** paltrily; **trivially,** triflingly; superficially, shallowly; frivolously, lightly, idly

PHRS 24 **it does not matter,** it matters not, it does not signify, mox nix <nf>, **it is of no consequence** *or* **importance,** it makes no difference, it makes no never mind <nf>, it cannot be helped, it is all the same; *n'importe* and *de rien* and *ça ne fait rien* <Fr>; it will all come out in the wash <nf>, it will be all the same a hundred years from now

25 **no matter, never mind,** think no more of it, do not give it another *or* a second thought, don't lose any sleep over it, let it pass, let it go <nf>, ignore it, forget it <nf>, skip it *and* drop it <nf>; fiddle-dee-dee

26 **what does it matter?, what matter?, what's the difference?,** what's the diff? <nf>, what do I care?, what of it?, what boots it?, what's the odds?, so what?, what else is new?; for aught one cares, big deal <nf>

999 GOODNESS
<good quality or effect>

NOUNS 1 **goodness, excellence, quality,** class <nf>; **virtue,** grace; **merit,** desert; **value, worth; fineness,** goodliness, fairness, niceness; **superiority,** first-rateness, **skillfulness** 413.1, proficiency; wholeness, **soundness,** healthiness 81.1; **virtuousness** 653.1; **kindness, benevolence,** benignity 143.1; beneficialness, helpfulness 449.10; favorableness, auspiciousness 133.9; expedience, advantageousness 995.1; **usefulness** 387.3; pleasantness, agreeableness 97.1; cogency, validity; profitableness, rewardingness 472.4

2 **superexcellence,** supereminence, preeminence, supremacy, primacy, paramountcy, peerlessness, unsurpassedness, matchlessness, superfineness; **superbness,** exquisiteness, **magnificence,** splendidness, splendiferousness, marvelousness, distinction

3 **tolerableness,** tolerability, goodishness,

passableness, fairishness, **adequateness, satisfactoriness,** acceptability, admissibility; sufficiency 991

4 **good, welfare,** well-being, **benefit;** public weal, common good; **interest, advantage; behalf,** behoof, edification; blessing, benison, boon; **profit,** avail <old>, gain, betterment; world of good; favor, advantage; use, usefulness

5 **good thing,** a thing to be desired, "a consummation devoutly to be wish'd"— Shakespeare; **treasure,** gem, jewel, diamond, pearl; boast, pride, **pride and joy;** prize, trophy, plum; winner *and* no slouch *and* nothing to sneeze at <nf>; catch, find <nf>, *trouvaille* <Fr>; godsend, windfall; tour de force, chef-d'oeuvre, masterpiece; bestseller; collector's item; hit

6 **first-rater, topnotcher, world-beater; wonder, prodigy,** genius, virtuoso, **star, superstar;** luminary, leading light, one in a thousand *or* a million; hard *or* tough act to follow <nf>

7 <nf terms> **dandy, jim dandy, dilly, humdinger, pip,** pippin, **peach,** ace, beaut, **lulu, daisy,** darb, doozy, honey, sweetheart, dream, lollapalooza, bitch, hot shit *or* poo, pisser, pistol, corker, whiz, blinger, **crackerjack,** knockout, something else, something else again, barn-burner, killer, killer-diller, smash, smash hit, the nuts, the cat's pajamas *or* balls *or* meow, bitch-kitty, whiz, whizbang, wow, wowser

8 **the best,** the very best, the best ever, the top of the heap *or* the line <nf>, head of the class, tops; **quintessence,** essence, prime, optimum, superlative; **choice, pick, select, elect, elite,** *corps d'élite* <Fr>, chosen; **cream, flower,** fat; cream *or* pick of the crop, *crème de la crème* <Fr>, grade A, salt of the earth; *pièce de résistance* <Fr>; prize, champion, queen; nonesuch, paragon, nonpareil; gem of the first water

9 **harmlessness,** hurtlessness, uninjuriousness, **innocuousness,** benignity, benignancy; unobnoxiousness, inoffensiveness; innocence; heart of gold, kindness of heart, milk of human kindness

VERBS 10 **do good, profit,** avail; do a world of good; **benefit, help, serve,** be of service, advance, advantage, favor 449.11,14,17,19; be the making of, make a man *or* woman of; do no harm, break no bones

11 **excel, surpass,** outdo, pass, do *or* go one better, transcend; do up brown *or* in spades <nf>, do with a vengeance; be as good as, equal, emulate, rival, vie, vie with, challenge comparison, go one-on-one with <nf>; **make the most of, optimize,** exploit; cream off <Brit>, skim off the cream

ADJS 12 **good, excellent,** *bueno* <Sp>, *bon* <Fr>,

bonny <Brit>, **fine, nice,** goodly, fair; **splendid, capital, grand,** elegant <nf>, braw <Scot>, famous <nf>, noble; royal, regal, fit for a king; very good, *très bon* <Fr>; commendable, laudable, **estimable** 509.20; skillful 413.22; **sound,** healthy 81.5; virtuous; kind, benevolent 143.15; beneficial, helpful 449.21; profitable; favorable, auspicious 133.18; expedient, advantageous 995.5; useful 387.18; pleasant 97.6; cogent, valid 973.13

13 <nf terms> **great,** swell, dandy, bitchin', jim dandy, neat, neato, cool, super, super-duper, bully <old>, tough, mean, gnarly, heavy, bad, groovy, out of sight, fab, fantabulous, marvy, gear, something else, ducky, dynamite, keen, killer, hot, nifty, sexy, spiffy, spiffing, ripping, nobby, peachy, peachy-keen, delicious, scrumptious, not too shabby, tits, out of this world, hunky-dory, crackerjack, boss, stunning, corking, smashing, solid, all wool and a yard wide; rum *or* wizard <Brit>, bonzer <Austral>; bang-up, jam-up, slap-up, ace-high, fine and dandy, just dandy, but good, OK, okay, A-OK; copacetic; phat

14 **superior,** above par, head and shoulders above, **crack** <nf>; **high-grade, high-class,** high-quality, high-caliber, high-test, **world-class,** grade A; impressive

15 **superb,** super <nf>, **superexcellent, supereminent,** superfine, **exquisite; magnificent,** splendid, splendiferous, tremendous, immense, **marvelous, wonderful,** glorious, divine, heavenly, terrific, sensational; sterling, golden; gilt-edged *and* gilt-edge, blue-chip; of the highest type, of the best sort, of the first water, as good as good can be, as good as they come, as good as they make 'em *and* out of this world <nf>

16 **best,** very best, greatest *and* top-of-the-line <nf>, **prime,** optimum, optimal; **choice, select, elect,** elite, **picked,** handpicked; **prize, champion; supreme,** paramount, **unsurpassed,** surpassing, unparalleled, unmatched, unmatchable, matchless, makeless <old>, **peerless;** quintessential; for the best, all for the best

17 **first-rate, first-class,** in a class by itself; of the first *or* highest degree; unmatched, matchless; champion, record-breaking

18 <nf terms> **A-1, A number one,** primo, first-chop, tip-top, top-notch, topflight, top-drawer, tops; topping *or* top-hole <Brit>

19 **up to par,** up to standard, **up to snuff** <nf>; **up to the mark,** up to the notch *and* **up to scratch** <nf>

20 **tolerable, goodish, fair, fairish,** moderate, tidy <nf>, **decent,** respectable, presentable, good enough, **pretty good, not bad,** not amiss, not half bad, not so bad, **adequate, satisfactory, all right,** OK *or* okay <nf>; better than nothing; **acceptable,** admissible, **passable,** unobjectionable, unexceptionable; workmanlike; sufficient 991.6

21 **harmless,** hurtless, unhurtful; well-meaning, well-meant; **uninjurious,** undamaging, **innocuous,** innoxious, innocent; unobnoxious, inoffensive; nonmalignant, **benign;** nonpoisonous, nontoxic, nonvirulent, nonvenomous

ADVS 22 **excellently, nicely,** finely, **capitally, splendidly, famously,** royally; **well,** very well, **fine** <nf>, right, aright; one's best, at one's best, at the top of one's bent

23 **superbly,** exquisitely, **magnificently,** tremendously, immensely, terrifically, **marvelously, wonderfully,** gloriously, divinely

24 **tolerably, fairly,** fairishly, moderately, respectably, **adequately, satisfactorily,** passably, **acceptably,** unexceptionably, presentably, decently; fairly well, well enough, pretty well; **rather, pretty**

1000 BADNESS
<bad quality or effect>

NOUNS 1 **badness, evil,** evilness, viciousness, damnability, reprehensibility; moral badness, dereliction, peccancy, iniquity, sinfulness, wickedness 654.4; unwholesomeness, unhealthiness 82.1; inferiority 1005.3; unskillfulness 414.1; unkindness, malevolence 144; inauspiciousness, unfavorableness 133.8; inexpedience 996; unpleasantness 98; invalidity 19.3; inaccuracy 975.2; improperness 638.1; deviltry

2 **terribleness, dreadfulness,** direness, **awfulness** <nf>, horribleness; **atrociousness, outrageousness,** heinousness, nefariousness; **notoriousness, egregiousness,** scandalousness, shamefulness, **infamousness; abominableness,** odiousness, **loathsomeness, detestableness,** despicableness, contemptibleness, hatefulness; **offensiveness,** grossness, obnoxiousness; squalor, squalidness, sordidness, **wretchedness,** filth, **vileness,** fulsomeness, **nastiness,** rankness, **foulness,** noisomeness; disgustingness, repulsiveness; uncleanness 80; beastliness, bestiality, brutality; **rottenness** *and* lousiness <nf>; the pits <nf>; shoddiness, shabbiness; scurviness, **baseness** 661.3; **worthlessness** 998.2

3 **evil, bad, wrong,** ill; **harm, hurt, injury, damage, detriment; destruction** 395; despoliation; mischief, havoc; outrage, atrocity; crime, foul play; abomination, grievance, vexation, woe, crying evil; poison 1001.3; blight, venom, toxin, **bane** 1001; **corruption,** pollution, infection, befoulment, defilement; environmental pollution, fly in the ointment, worm in the apple *or* rose; skeleton in

the closet; snake in the grass, Pandora's Box; "something rotten in the state of Denmark"— Shakespeare; ills the flesh is heir to, "all ills that men endure"—Abraham Cowley; the worst

4 bad influence, malevolent influence, evil star, **ill wind;** evil genius, **hoodoo** *and* **jinx** <nf>, **Jonah; curse,** enchantment, whammy *and* double *or* triple whammy <nf>, spell, hex, voodoo; **evil eye,** *malocchio* <Ital>; malediction

5 harmfulness, hurtfulness, injuriousness, banefulness, balefulness, detrimentalness, deleteriousness, perniciousness, mischievousness, noxiousness, venomousness, poisonousness, toxicity, virulence, noisomeness, **malignance** *or* **malignancy, malignity, viciousness;** unhealthiness 82.1; disease 85; deadliness, lethality 308.9; ominousness 133.7

VERBS **6** work evil, do ill; **harm, hurt; injure,** scathe, wound, **damage; destroy** 395.10; despoil, prejudice, disadvantage, impair, disserve, distress; **wrong,** do wrong, do wrong by, aggrieve, do evil, do a mischief, do an ill office to; **molest,** afflict; lay a hand on; get into trouble; **abuse,** bash <nf>, batter, outrage, violate, maltreat, mistreat 389.5; torment, **harass,** hassle <nf>, persecute, savage, crucify, torture 96.18; play mischief *or* havoc with, wreak havoc on, play hob with <nf>; **corrupt,** deprave, taint, pollute, infect, befoul, defile; poison, envenom, blight; **curse,** put a whammy on <nf>, give the evil eye, hex, jinx, bewitch; spell *or* mean trouble, threaten, menace 514.2; doom; condemn 602.3

ADJS **7 bad, evil, ill,** untoward, black, sinister; **wicked, wrong,** peccant, iniquitous, **vicious;** sinful 654.16; criminal; unhealthy 82.5; **inferior** 1005.9; unskillful 414.15; unkind, malevolent 144.19; inauspicious, unfavorable 133.17; inexpedient 996.5; unpleasant 98.17; invalid 19.15; inaccurate 975.17; improper 638.3

8 <nf terms> **lousy,** punk, bum, badass, shitty, crappy, cruddy, cheesy, dog-ass, gnarly, gross, raunchy, piss-poor, rat-ass, **crummy,** grim, low-rent, low-ride, putrid, icky, skanky, yecchy, vomity, barfy, stinking, stinky, creepy, hairy, god-awful, gosh-awful

9 terrible, dreadful, awful <nf>, dire, horrible, horrid; atrocious, outrageous, heinous, villainous, nefarious; enormous, monstrous; **deplorable,** lamentable, regrettable, pitiful, pitiable, woeful, woesome <old>, grievous, sad 98.20; flagrant, **scandalous,** shameful, **shocking,** infamous, **notorious,** arrant, **egregious;** unclean 80.20; shoddy, schlocky <nf>, shabby, scurvy, **base** 661.12; **odious, obnoxious,** offensive, gross, **disgusting,** repulsive, loathsome, **abominable, detestable, despicable, contemptible,** beneath

contempt, hateful; blameworthy, **reprehensible;** rank, fetid, foul, filthy, vile, fulsome, noisome, **nasty,** squalid, sordid, **wretched;** beastly, brutal; as bad as they come, as bad as they make 'em <nf>, as bad as bad can be; worst; too bad; below par, subpar, not up to scratch *or* snuff *or* the mark, poor-quality, **worthless**

10 execrable, damnable; damned, accursed, cursed 513.9; infernal, hellish, devilish, fiendish, satanic, ghoulish, demoniac, demonic, demonical, diabolic, diabolical, unholy, ungodly

11 evil-fashioned, ill-fashioned, evil-shaped, ill-shaped, evil-qualitied, evil-looking, ill-looking, evil-favored, ill-favored, evil-hued, evil-faced, evil-minded, evil-eyed, ill-affected <old>, evil-gotten, ill-gotten, ill-conceived

12 harmful, hurtful, scatheful, **baneful,** baleful, distressing, **injurious, damaging, detrimental,** deleterious, counterproductive, **pernicious,** mischievous; noxious, mephitic, venomous, venenate, poisonous, venenous, veneniferous, toxic, virulent, noisome; malignant, malign, malevolent, malefic, vicious; prejudicial, disadvantageous, disserviceable; corruptive, corrupting, corrosive, corroding; deadly, lethal; ominous 133.17

ADVS **13 badly,** bad <nf>, **ill,** evil, evilly, wrong, wrongly, amiss; to one's cost

14 terribly, dreadfully, dreadful <nf>, **horribly,** horridly, **awfully** <nf>, **atrociously, outrageously;** flagrantly, scandalously, shamefully, shockingly, infamously, notoriously, egregiously, grossly, offensively, nauseatingly, fulsomely, odiously, **vilely,** obnoxiously, **disgustingly,** loathsomely; wretchedly, sordidly, shabbily, basely, abominably, detestably, despicably, contemptibly, foully, nastily; brutally, bestially, savagely, viciously; something fierce *or* terrible <nf>

15 harmfully, hurtfully, banefully, balefully, **injuriously, damagingly, detrimentally,** deleteriously, counterproductively, **perniciously,** mischievously; noxiously, venomously, poisonously, toxically, virulently, noisomely; **malignantly,** malignly, malevolently, malefically, **viciously;** prejudicially, disadvantageously, disserviceably; corrosively, corrodingly

1001 BANE

NOUNS **1 bane, curse, affliction,** infliction, visitation, **plague, pestilence,** pest, calamity, scourge, **torment,** open wound, running sore, grievance, woe, burden, crushing burden; disease 85; death 307; evil, harm 1000.3; destruction 395; vexation 96.2; thorn, thorn in the flesh *or* side, pea in the shoe; bugbear, **bête noire,** bogy, bogeymen, nemesis, arch-nemesis

2 blight, blast; canker, cancer; mold, fungus, mildew, smut, must, rust; rot, dry rot; **pest;** worm, worm in the apple *or* rose; moth <old>

3 poison, venom, venin, virus <old>, toxic, toxin, toxicant; eradicant, **pesticide; insecticide,** insect powder, bug bomb <nf>; roach powder, roach paste; stomach poison, contact poison, systemic insecticide *or* systemic, fumigant, chemosterilant; chlorinated hydrocarbon insecticide, organic chlorine; organic phosphate insecticide; carbamate insecticide, sheepdip; termiticide, miticide, acaricide, vermicide, anthelminthic; rodenticide, ratsbane, rat poison; **herbicide,** defoliant, Agent Orange, paraquat, **weed killer;** fungicide; microbicide, germicide, antiseptic, disinfectant, antibiotic; **toxicology;** toxic waste, **environmental pollutant;** hemlock, arsenic, cyanide; carcinogen

4 miasma, mephitis, malaria <old>; effluvium, exhaust, exhaust gas; coal gas, chokedamp, blackdamp, firedamp; air *or* atmospheric pollution, smoke, smog, exhaust fumes, carbon monoxide; secondhand smoke; acid rain

5 sting, stinger, dart; **fang,** tang <nf>; beesting, snakebite

6 poisonous plants

aconite	laburnum
amanita	larkspur
angel's trumpet	locoweed
banewort	marijuana
bearded darnel	mayapple
belladonna	mescal bean
black henbane	monkshood
black nightshade	nightshade
bleeding heart	nux vomica
castor-oil plant	opium poppy
chinaberry	poinsettia
corn cackle	poison bean
cowbane	poisonberry
datura	poison bush
deadly nightshade	poison hemlock *or* parsley
death camas	poison ivy
death cup *or* angel	poison oak
devil's trumpet	poison rye grass
elderberry	poison sumac
ergot	poison tobacco
fiddleneck	poisonweed
foxglove	pokeweed
gastrolobium	sheep laurel
hairy vetch	thornapple
hellebore	tobacco
hemlock	upas
henbane	water hemlock
horsetail	white snakeroot
jack-in-the-pulpit	wisteria
jimsonweed	wolfsbane

1002 PERFECTION

NOUNS 1 perfection, faultlessness, flawlessness, defectlessness, indefectibility, impeccability, absoluteness; infallibility; spotlessness, stainlessness, taintlessness, purity, immaculateness; sinlessness; chastity 664

2 soundness, integrity, intactness, wholeness, entireness, completeness; **fullness,** plenitude; finish; mint condition

3 acme of perfection, pink, pink of perfection, culmination, perfection, height, top, acme, ultimate, summit, pinnacle, peak, highest pitch, climax, consummation, *ne plus ultra* <L>, **the last word,** a dream come true

4 pattern *or* standard *or* mold *or* norm of perfection, very model, quintessence; archetype, prototype, exemplar, mirror, **epitome;** *ne plus ultra* <L>, perfect specimen, highest type; **classic,** masterwork, masterpiece, *chef d'œuvre* <Fr>, crowning achievement, showpiece; **ideal** 786.4; role model; **paragon** 659.4; a 10 <nf>

VERBS 5 perfect, develop, flesh out, ripen, mature; improve 392.7; crown, culminate, put on the finishing touch; lick *or* whip into shape, fine-tune; complete 407.6; do to perfection 407.7

ADJS 6 perfect, ideal, faultless, flawless, unflawed, defectless, not to be improved, **impeccable,** absolute; **just right,** just so; spotless, stainless, taintless, unblemished, untainted, unspotted, immaculate, **pure,** uncontaminated, unadulterated, unmixed; sinless; chaste 664.4; indefective <old>, indefectible, trouble-free; infallible; beyond all praise, irreproachable, unfaultable, *sans peur et sans reproche* <Fr>, **matchless,** peerless 249.15; A-1, world-class, number-one

7 sound, intact, whole, entire, complete, integral; **full;** total, utter, unqualified 960.2

8 undamaged, unharmed, unhurt, uninjured, unscathed, **unspoiled,** virgin, inviolate, **unimpaired;** harmless, scatheless; **unmarred,** unmarked, unscarred, unscratched, undefaced, unbruised; **unbroken,** unshattered, untorn; undemolished, undestroyed; undeformed, unmutilated, unmangled, unmaimed; unfaded, unworn, unwithered, bright, fresh, untouched, pristine, mint; none the worse for wear, right as rain

9 perfected, finished, polished, refined; done to a T *or* to a turn; **classic, classical,** masterly, masterful, expert, proficient; ripened, ripe, matured, mature, developed, fully developed; thorough-going, thorough-paced; **consummate,** quintessential, archetypical, exemplary, model

ADVS 10 perfectly, ideally; **faultlessly, flawlessly,**

impeccably; just right; spotlessly; immaculately, purely; infallibly; wholly, entirely, completely, fully, thoroughly, totally, absolutely 794.15

11 to perfection, to a turn, to a T, to a finish, to a nicety; to a fare-thee-well or fare-you-well or fare-ye-well <nf>; to beat the band <nf>

1003 IMPERFECTION

NOUNS 1 imperfection, imperfectness, room for improvement; unperfectedness; faultiness, defectiveness, defectibility; shortcoming, deficiency, lack, want, shortage, inadequacy, inadequateness; erroneousness, fallibility; inaccuracy, inexactness, inexactitude 975.2; unsoundness, incompleteness, patchiness, sketchiness, unevenness; impairment 393; mediocrity 1005; immaturity, undevelopment 406.4; impurity, adulteration 797.3

2 fault, faute <Fr>, defect, deficiency, inadequacy, imperfection, kink, defection <old>, hangup; flaw, hole, bug <nf>; something missing; catch <nf>, fly in the ointment, problem, little problem, curate's egg <Brit>, snag, drawback; crack, rift; weakness, frailty, infirmity, failure, failing, foible, shortcoming; weak point, Achilles' heel, vulnerable place, chink in one's armor, weak link, soft spot, underbelly; blemish, taint 1004; malfunction, glitch <nf>

VERBS 3 fall short, come short, miss, miss out, miss the mark, miss by a mile <nf>, not qualify, fall down <nf>, not measure up, not come up to par, not come up to the mark, not come up to scratch or to snuff <nf>, not pass muster, not bear inspection, not hack it and not make it and not cut it and not make the cut <nf>; not make the grade; fail

ADJS 4 imperfect, not perfect, less than perfect; good in parts; unperfected; defective, faulty, inadequate, deficient, short, not all it's cracked up to be <nf>, lacking, wanting, found wanting, "weighed in the balance and found wanting"—Bible; off; erroneous, fallible; inaccurate, inexact, imprecise 974.17; unsound, incomplete, unfinished, partial, patchy, sketchy, uneven, unthorough; makeshift 995.7; damaged, impaired 393.27; mediocre 1005.7; blemished 1004.8; half-baked <nf>, immature, undeveloped 406.12; impure, adulterated, mixed

ADVS 5 imperfectly, inadequately, deficiently; incompletely, partially; faultily, defectively

1004 BLEMISH

NOUNS 1 blemish, disfigurement, disfiguration, defacement; scar, keloid, cicatrix; needle scar, track or crater <nf>; scratch; scab; blister, vesicle,

bulla, bleb; weal, wale, welt, wen, sebaceous cyst; port-wine stain or mark, hemangioma, strawberry mark, macula; pock, pustule; pockmark, pit; nevus, birthmark, mole; freckle, lentigo; milium, whitehead, blackhead, comedo, pimple, zit <nf>, hickey <nf>, sty; crud; wart, verruca; crack, craze, check, rift, split; deformity, deformation, warp, twist, kink, distortion; flaw, defect, fault 1003.2

2 discoloration, discolorment, discolor <old>; bruise; foxing

3 stain, taint, tarnish; mark, brand, stigma; maculation, macule, macula; spot, blot, blur, blotch, patch, speck, speckle, fleck, flick, flyspeck; daub, dab; smirch, smudge, smutch or smouch, smut, smear; splotch, splash, splatter, spatter; bloodstain; eyesore; caste mark, tattoo, brand

VERBS 4 blemish, disfigure, deface, flaw, mar; scab; scar, cicatrize, scarify; crack, craze, check, split; deform, warp, twist, kink, distort

5 spot, bespot, blot, blotch, speck, speckle, bespeckle, maculate <old>; freckle; flyspeck; spatter, splatter, splash, splotch

6 stain, bestain, discolor, smirch, besmirch, taint, attaint, tarnish; mark, stigmatize, brand; smear, besmear, daub, bedaub, slubber <Brit nf>; blur, slur <nf>; darken, blacken; smoke, besmoke; scorch, singe, sear; dirty, soil 80.16

7 bloodstain, bloody, ensanguine

ADJS 8 blemished, disfigured, defaced, marred, scarred, keloidal, cicatrized, scarified, stigmatized, scabbed, scabby; pimpled, pimply; cracked, crazed, checked, split; deformed, warped, twisted, kinked, distorted; faulty, flawed, defective 1003.4

9 spotted, spotty, maculate, maculated, macular, blotched, blotchy, splotched, splotchy; speckled, speckly, bespeckled; freckled, freckly, freckle-faced; spattered, splattered, splashed

10 stained, discolored, foxed, foxy, tainted, tarnished, smirched, besmirched; stigmatized, stigmatic, stigmatiferous; darkened, blackened, murky, smoky, inky; polluted, soiled 80.21

11 bloodstained, blood-spattered, bloody, sanguinary, gory, ensanguined

1005 MEDIOCRITY

NOUNS 1 mediocrity, mediocreness, fairishness, modestness, modesty, moderateness, middlingness, indifference; respectability, passableness, tolerableness 999.3; dullness, lackluster, tediousness 117.1

2 ordinariness, averageness, normalness, normality, commonness, commonplaceness; unexceptionality, unremarkableness, unnoteworthiness; conventionality

3 inferiority, inferiorness, **poorness,** lowliness, humbleness, **baseness, meanness, commonness,** coarseness, tackiness, tack; **second-rateness,** third-rateness, fourth-rateness

4 low grade, low class, low quality, poor quality; second best, next best

5 mediocrity, second-rater, third-rater, fourth-rater, nothing *or* nobody special, no great shakes <nf>, no prize, no prize package, no brain surgeon, no rocket scientist, not much of a bargain, small potatoes *and* small beer <nf>; tinhorn <nf>; **nobody, nonentity** 998.7; middle class, bourgeoisie, burgherdom; suburbia, the burbs <nf>; Middle America, silent majority

6 irregular, second, third; schlock <nf>

ADJS **7 mediocre, middling, indifferent, fair, fairish, fair to middling** <nf>, moderate, modest, medium, betwixt and between; respectable, passable, tolerable; so-so, *comme ci comme ça* <Fr>; of a kind, of a sort, of sorts <nf>; nothing to brag about, not much to boast of, nothing to write home about; bush-league; dull, lackluster, tedious 117.6; insipid, vapid, wishy-washy, namby-pamby

8 ordinary, average, normal, **common, commonplace,** garden *and* garden-variety <nf>, run-of-mine *or* -mill, run-of-the-mine *or* -mill, vanilla <nf>; **unexceptional, unremarkable, unnoteworthy,** unspectacular, nothing *or* nobody special *and* no great shakes <nf>, no prize, no prize package, no brain surgeon, no rocket scientist; conventional; middle-class, bourgeois, plastic <nf>; suburban; usual, regular

9 inferior, poor, punk <nf>, **base, mean, common,** coarse, cheesy *and* tacky <nf>, tinny; shabby, seedy; cheap, Mickey Mouse <nf>, paltry; irregular; second-best; **second-rate,** third-rate, fourth-rate; **second-class,** third-class, fourth-class, etc; **low-grade, low-class,** low-quality, low-test, low-rent *and* low-ride <nf>

10 below par, below standard, **below the mark** <nf>, substandard, **not up to scratch** *or* snuff *or* the mark <nf>, not up to sample *or* standard *or* specification, off

ADVS **11 mediocrely, middlingly,** fairly, fairishly, middling well, fair to middling <nf>, moderately, modestly, **indifferently, so-so;** passably, **tolerably**

12 inferiorly, poorly, basely, meanly, commonly

1006 DANGER

NOUNS **1 danger, peril, endangerment, imperilment, jeopardy, hazard, risk,** cause for alarm, **menace, threat** 514; **crisis, emergency,** hot spot, nasty *or* tricky spot, pass, pinch, strait, plight, predicament 1013.4; powder keg, time bomb; dangerous *or* unpredictable *or* uncontrollable person, loose cannon <nf>; rocks *or* breakers *or* white water ahead, gathering clouds, storm clouds; dangerous ground, yawning *or* gaping chasm, quicksand, thin ice; hornet's nest; house of cards, cardhouse; hardball <nf>, no tea party, no picnic; desperate situation

2 dangerousness, hazardousness, riskiness, treachery, precariousness 971.6, chanciness, dodginess <chiefly Brit nf>, diceyness <nf>, **perilousness; unsafeness,** unhealthiness <nf>; criticalness; **ticklishness,** slipperiness, touchiness, delicacy, ticklish business *and* shaky ground <nf>; **insecurity,** unsoundness, instability, unsteadiness, shakiness, totteriness, wonkiness <Brit nf>; sword of Damocles; **unreliability,** undependability, untrustworthiness 971.6; **unsureness,** unpredictability, **uncertainty,** doubtfulness, dubiousness 971.2

3 exposure, openness, liability, nonimmunity, susceptibility; **unprotectedness, defenselessness,** nakedness, helplessness; lamb, sitting duck; roadkill <nf>; naiveté

4 vulnerability, pregnability, penetrability, assailability, vincibility; weakness 16; vulnerable point, **weak link, weak point, soft spot,** heel of Achilles, chink, chink in one's armor, "the soft underbelly"—Sir Winston Churchill; tragic flaw, fatal flaw

5 <hidden danger> snags, rocks, reefs, ledges; coral heads; shallows, shoals; sandbank, sandbar, sands; quicksands; crevasses; rockbound *or* ironbound coast, lee shore; undertow, undercurrent; **pitfall;** snake in the grass; trap, booby trap, springe, snare, tripwire, pitfall; snarling dog, ticking package; cloud on the horizon

VERBS **6 endanger, imperil,** peril; **risk, hazard, gamble, gamble with; jeopardize,** jeopard, jeopardy, compromise, put in danger, **put in jeopardy,** put on the spot *and* lay on the line <nf>; **expose,** lay open; incur danger, run into *or* encounter danger

7 take chances, take a chance, chance, risk, stake, gamble, hazard, press *or* push one's luck, **run the chance** *or* **risk** *or* **hazard;** risk one's neck, run a risk, go out on a limb, stick one's neck out<nf>, **expose oneself,** bare one's breast, lower one's guard, **lay oneself open to,** leave oneself wide open, open the door to, let oneself in for; drive recklessly; **tempt Providence** *or* **fate,** forget the odds, **defy danger,** skate on thin ice, court destruction, dance on the razor's edge, go in harm's way, hang by a hair *or* a thread, stand *or* sleep on a volcano, sit on a barrel of gunpowder, build a house of cards, put one's head in the lion's mouth, "beard the lion in his den"—Sir Walter Scott, march up to the cannon's mouth, play with fire, go through fire and water, go out of one's depth, go to sea in a sieve, carry too much sail, sail too near the wind; risk one's life, throw caution to the wind, **take one's life in one's hand, dare, face up to,** brave 492.11

8 **be in danger,** be in peril, be *in extremis*, be in a desperate case, have one's name on the danger list, have the chances *or* odds against one, have one's back to the wall, have something hanging over one's head; be despaired of; hang by a thread; tremble on the verge, totter on the brink, teeter on the edge; feel the ground sliding from under one; have to run for it; race against time *or* the clock; be threatened, be on the spot *or* in a bind <nf>

ADJS 9 **dangerous,** dangersome <nf>, **perilous,** periculous, parlous, jeopardous, bad, ugly, serious, critical, explosive, attended *or* beset *or* fraught with danger; alarming, too close for comfort *or* words, **menacing,** threatening 514.3

10 **hazardous, risky, chancy,** dodgy <chiefly Brit nf>, dicey <nf>, hairy <nf>, aleatory, riskful, full of risk; **adventurous,** venturous, venturesome; **speculative,** wildcat

11 **unsafe,** unhealthy <nf>; **unreliable, undependable, untrustworthy,** treacherous, **insecure, unsound,** unstable, unsteady, shaky, tottery, wonky <Brit nf>, rocky; **unsure, uncertain,** unpredictable, doubtful, dubious; on the brink *or* verge

12 **precarious, ticklish, touchy,** touch-and-go, **critical, delicate;** slippery, slippy; on thin ice, on slippery ground; hanging by a thread, trembling in the balance; nerve-racking

13 **in danger, in jeopardy, in peril, at risk,** in a bad way; **endangered, imperiled, jeopardized,** *in periculo* <L>, at the last extremity, *in extremis* <L>, in deadly peril, *in periculo mortis* <L>, in desperate case; threatened, up against it, in a bad way, on the spot *and* on *or* in the hot seat <nf>; sitting on a powder keg; between the hammer and the anvil, between Scylla and Charybdis, between two fires, between the devil and the deep blue sea, between a rock and a hard place <nf>; in a predicament 1013.21; cornered

14 **unprotected, unshielded, unsheltered,** uncovered, unscreened, **unguarded, undefended,** unattended, unwatched, unfortified; armorless, unarmored, **unarmed,** bare-handed, weaponless; guardless, ungarrisoned, insecure, **defenseless, helpless;** unwarned, unsuspecting

15 **exposed, open,** out in the open, naked, bare; out on a limb <nf>; liable, susceptible, nonimmune

16 **vulnerable,** naïve, **pregnable,** penetrable, expugnable; assailable, attackable, surmountable; conquerable, beatable <nf>, vincible; weak 16.12–14

ADVS 17 **dangerously, perilously, hazardously, riskily,** critically, unsafely; **precariously,** ticklishly; at gun point

1007 SAFETY

NOUNS 1 **safety,** safeness, **security,** surety <old>, assurance; risklessness, immunity, clear sailing; **protection,** safeguard 1007.3; harmlessness 999.9; airworthiness, crashworthiness, roadworthiness, seaworthiness; invulnerability 15.4; safety in numbers; wide berth, safe distance; safekeeping

VERBS 2 **be safe, be on the safe side; keep safe, come through;** weather, ride out, weather the storm; keep one's head above water, tide over; keep a safe distance; land on one's feet; save one's bacon <nf>, save one's neck; lead a charmed life, have nine lives

3 **play safe** <nf>, **keep on the safe side,** give danger a wide berth, watch oneself, watch out, take precautions 494.6, demand assurances; assure oneself, make sure, keep an eye *or* a weather eye out, look before one leaps; **save, protect** 1008.18

ADJS 4 **safe, secure, safe and sound,** not at risk; immune, immunized; insured; **protected** 1008.21; on the safe side; unthreatened, unmolested; unhurt, unharmed, unscathed, intact, untouched, with a whole skin, undamaged, whole

5 **unhazardous, undangerous, unperilous, unrisky,** riskless, **unprecarious;** fail-safe, trouble-free; recession-proof; guaranteed, warranteed; dependable, reliable, trustworthy, sound, stable, steady, firm 970.17; "founded upon a rock"—Bible; as safe as houses; harmless; invulnerable; -proof

6 **in safety, out of danger,** past danger, out of the meshes *or* toils, in, home, out of the woods *and* over the hump *or* home free <nf>, free and dry <Brit nf>, **in the clear, out of harm's reach** *or* **way;** under cover, under lock and key; in shelter, in harbor *or* port, at anchor *or* haven, in the shadow of a rock; on sure *or* solid ground, on *terra firma*, high and dry, above water; in safe keeping

7 **snug, cozy,** home free; crashworthy, roadworthy, airworthy, seaworthy, seakindly

ADVS 8 **safely, securely,** reliably, dependably; with safety, **with impunity**

INTERJS 9 **all's well!,** all clear!, all serene!, A-OK!; ally-ally out'n free!

PHRS 10 the danger is past, the storm has blown over, the coast is clear

1008 PROTECTION

NOUNS **1 protection, guard, shielding, safekeeping; policing, law enforcement; patrol, patroling,** community policing, professional *or* bureaucratic policing; eye, protectiveness, watchfulness, vigilance, watchful eye, shepherding; house-sitting <nf>; protective custody; **safeguarding, security,** security industry, public safety, safety 1007; **shelter, cover,** shade, shadow <old>, windbreak, lee; **refuge** 1009; preservation 397; **defense** 460; protective coating, Teflon coating <trademark>

2 protectorship, guardianship, stewardship, custodianship; **care, charge, keeping, nurture, nurturing, nurturance, custody, fostering, fosterage,** cocooning, fatherly *or* motherly eye; **hands,** safe hands, wing; **auspices, patronage, tutelage, guidance; ward,** wardship, wardenship, watch and ward; cure, pastorship, pastorage, pastorate; **oversight,** jurisdiction, management, ministry, administration, government, governance; **child care,** infant care, day-care, family service; baby-sitting, baby-minding <Brit>

3 safeguard, palladium, **guard,** preventive measure, precautionary steps; **shield, screen,** aegis; umbrella, protective umbrella; patent, copyright; **bulwark** 460.4; backstop; fender, mudguard, **bumper, buffer, cushion,** pad, padding; seat *or* safety belt; protective clothing; shin guard, knuckle guard, knee guard, nose guard, hand guard, arm guard, ear guard, finger guard, foot guard; goggles, mask, face mask, welder's mask, fencer's mask; safety shoes; helmet, hard hat <nf>, crash helmet, sun helmet; cowcatcher, pilot; dashboard; windshield, windscreen <Brit>; dodger *and* cockpit dodger <Brit>; life preserver 397.6; lifeline, safety rail, guardrail, handrail; governor; safety, safety switch, interlock; safety valve, safety plug; fuse, circuit breaker; insulation; safety glass, laminated glass; lightning rod, lightning conductor; **anchor,** bower, sea anchor, sheet anchor, drogue; **parachute; safety net;** prophylactic, preventive 86.20; contraceptive 86.23

4 insurance, assurance <Brit>; **annuity,** variable annuity; **social security** 611.7; nest egg, savings account, provision; **insurance company,** stock company, mutual company; **insurance policy,** policy, certificate of insurance; deductible; insurance man, underwriter, insurance broker, insurance agent, insurance adjuster, actuary; lemon law

5 protector, keeper, protectress, safekeeper, minder; patron, patroness; tower, pillar, strong arm, tower of strength, rock; champion, **defender** 460.7

6 guardian, warden, governor; **custodian,** steward, **keeper, caretaker,** warder <Brit>, attendant; caregiver; next friend, prochein ami, guardian *ad litem;* **curator,** conservator; janitor; castellan; **shepherd,** herd, cowherd; **game warden,** gamekeeper; **ranger,** forest ranger, forester; lifeguard, lifesaver <Brit>; air warden; guardian angel

7 chaperon, duenna; **governess;** escort

8 nurse, nursemaid, nurserymaid, nanny <chiefly Brit>, amah, ayah, mammy <nf>; dry nurse, wet nurse; **baby-sitter,** baby-minder <Brit>, sitter <nf>

9 guard, guarder, guardsman <old>, warder; **outguard, outpost; picket,** outlying picket, inlying picket, outrider; advance guard, **vanguard,** van; **rear guard;** coast guard; armed guard, security guard; jailer 429.10; bank guard; railway *or* train guard; goalkeeper, goaltender, goalie <nf>; garrison; cordon, *cordon sanitaire* <Fr>

10 watchman, watch, watcher; watchkeeper; **lookout,** lookout man; **sentinel,** picket, **sentry; scout,** vedette; **point,** forward observer, spotter; **patrol, patrolman,** patroller, roundsman; night watchman, Charley <nf>; fireguard, fire patrolman, fire warden; airplane spotter; Argus

11 watchdog, bandog, guard dog, attack dog; sheep dog; Cerberus

12 doorkeeper, doorman, gatekeeper, Cerberus, warden, **porter, janitor,** commissionaire <Brit>, *concierge* <Fr>, ostiary, usher; receptionist

13 picket, picketer, demonstrator, picket line; counterdemonstrator

14 bodyguard, safeguard; **convoy, escort;** guards, praetorian guard; guardsman; yeoman *or* yeoman of the guard *or* beefeater, gentleman-at-arms, Life Guardsman <all England>

15 policeman, policewoman, constable, officer, police officer, *flic* <Fr nf>, *gendarme* <Fr>, *carabiniere* <Ital>; peace officer, law enforcer, law enforcement agent, arm of the law; military policeman *or* MP; detective 576.10; police matron; patrolman, police constable <Brit>; trooper, mounted policeman, state police, state trooper; reeve, portreeve; **sheriff, marshal;** deputy sheriff, deputy, bound bailiff, catchpole, beagle <nf>, bombailiff <Brit nf>; sergeant, police sergeant; roundsman; lieutenant, police lieutenant; captain, police captain; inspector, police inspector; superintendent, chief of police; commissioner, police commissioner; government man, federal, fed *and* G-man <nf>; narc <nf>; **bailiff,** tipstaff, tipstaves <pl>; mace-bearer, lictor, sergeant at arms; beadle; traffic officer, meter maid; detective

16 <nf terms> cop, copper, John Law, bluecoat, bull, flatfoot, gumshoe, gendarme, shamus, dick, pig, flattie, bizzy *and* bobby *and* peeler <Brit>,

Dogberry; the cops, the law, the fuzz, feds, heat; New York's finest; tec, op

17 police, police force, law enforcement agency; the force, forces of law and order, long arm of the law; **constabulary;** state police, troopers *or* state troopers, highway patrol, county police, provincial police; security force; special police; tactical police, riot police; SWAT *or* special weapons and tactics, SWAT team, **posse,** *posse comitatus* <L>; **vigilantes,** vigilance committee; secret police, political police; Federal Bureau of Investigation *or* FBI; military police *or* MP; shore patrol *or* SP; Scotland Yard <Brit>; *Sûreté* <Fr>; Cheka, NKVD, MVD, OGPU <Russ>; Gestapo <Ger>; Royal Canadian Mounted Police *or* RCMP *and* Mounties <Can>; Interpol, International Criminal Police Commission; neighborhood watch

VERBS 18 protect, guard, safeguard, secure, keep, bless, make safe, **police, enforce the law;** keep from harm; **insure,** underwrite; ensure, guarantee 438.9; patent, copyright, register; **cushion;** champion, go to bat for <nf>; ride shotgun <nf>, fend, defend 460.8; **shelter, shield, screen, cover,** cloak, shroud <old>, temper the wind to the shorn lamb; **harbor, haven;** nestle; compass about, fence; arm, armor; put in a safe place, keep under cover

19 care for, take care of; preserve, conserve; provide for, support; take charge of, **take under one's wing,** make one a protégé; **look after,** see after, **attend to, minister to,** look *or* see to, look *or* watch out for <nf>, have *or* keep an eye on *or* upon, keep a sharp eye on *or* upon, **watch over,** keep watch over, **watch, mind, tend;** keep tab *or* tabs on <nf>; **shepherd,** ride herd on <nf>; **chaperon,** matronize; baby-sit <nf>; **foster, nurture, cherish, nurse; mother,** be a mother *or* father to

20 watch, keep watch, keep guard, keep watch over, keep vigil, keep watch and ward; stand guard, stand sentinel; be on the lookout 339.8; mount guard; **police,** patrol, pound a beat <nf>, go on one's beat

ADJS 21 protected, guarded, safeguarded, defended; safe 1006.4–6; patented, copyrighted; **sheltered, shielded,** screened, covered, cloaked; policed; armed 460.14; invulnerable

22 under the protection of, under the shield of, under the auspices of, under the aegis of, **under one's wing,** under the wing of, under the shadow of one's wing

23 protective, custodial, guardian, tutelary; curatorial; vigilant, watchful, on the watch, on top of; prophylactic, preventive; immunizing; protecting, guarding, safeguarding, sheltering, **shielding,** screening, covering; fostering, parental; defensive 460.11; Teflon-coated <trademark>

1009 REFUGE

NOUNS 1 refuge, sanctuary, safehold, **asylum, haven, port,** harborage, **harbor;** harbor of refuge, port in a storm, snug harbor, safe haven; game sanctuary, bird sanctuary, preserve, forest preserve, game preserve; stronghold 460.6; **political asylum;** Rock of Gibraltar

2 recourse, resource, resort; last resort *or* resource, *dernier ressort* and *pis aller* <Fr>; **hope; expedient** 995.2

3 shelter, cover, covert, coverture; concealment 346; *abri* <Fr>, dugout, cave, earth, funk hole <Brit nf>, foxhole; **bunker;** trench; storm cellar, storm cave, cyclone cellar; air-raid shelter, bomb shelter, bombproof, fallout shelter, safety zone *or* isle *or* island; stockade, fort

4 asylum, home, retreat; **poorhouse,** almshouse, workhouse <Brit>, poor farm; **orphanage; hospice,** hospitium; old folks' home, rest home, nursing home, old soldiers' home, sailors' snug harbor; foster home; safe house; halfway house; retirement home *or* village *or* community, life-care home, continuing-care retirement community *or* CCRC

5 retreat, recess, hiding place, **hideaway,** hideout, hidey-hole <nf>, priest hole; **sanctum, inner sanctum, sanctum sanctorum,** holy ground, holy of holies, adytum; private place, privacy <old>, secret place; **den,** lair, mew; safe house; **cloister,** hermitage, ashram, cell; **ivory tower;** study, library

6 harbor, haven, port, seaport, port of call, free port, treaty port, home port; hoverport; harborage, **anchorage,** anchorage ground, protected anchorage, moorage, moorings; **roadstead,** road, roads; berth, slip; **dock,** dockage, marina, basin; dry dock; shipyard, dockyard; **wharf, pier,** quay; harborside, dockside, pierside, quayside, landing, landing place *or* stage, jetty, jutty <old>; breakwater, mole, groin; seawall, embankment, bulkhead

VERBS 7 take refuge, take shelter, seek refuge, **claim sanctuary,** claim refugee status, ask for political asylum; run into port; fly to, throw oneself into the arms of; bar the gate, lock *or* bolt the door, raise the drawbridge, let the portcullis down; take cover 346.8

8 find refuge *or* sanctuary, make port, reach safety; seclude *or* sequester oneself, dwell *or* live in an ivory tower; make port

1010 PROSPERITY

NOUNS 1 prosperity, prosperousness, thriving *or* flourishing condition; **success** 409; **welfare, well-being,** weal, happiness, felicity; quality of life;

comfortable *or* easy circumstances, **comfort, ease, security; life of ease,** life of Riley <nf>, **the good life; clover** *and* **velvet** <nf>, **bed of roses, luxury,** lap of luxury, Easy Street *and* Fat City *and* hog heaven <nf>; the affluent life, gracious life, gracious living; fat of the land; fleshpots, fleshpots of Egypt; milk and honey, loaves and fishes; a chicken in every pot, a car in every garage; purple and fine linen; high standard of living; upward mobility; **affluence,** wealth 618

2 **good fortune** *or* **luck,** happy fortune, **fortune, luck,** the breaks <nf>; **fortunateness, luckiness,** felicity <old>; blessing, smiles of fortune, fortune's favor

3 **stroke of luck,** piece of good luck; blessing; **fluke** *and* lucky strike *and* scratch hit *and* **break** <nf>, **good** *or* **lucky break** <nf>; **run** *or* **streak of luck** <nf>; bonanza; Midas touch

4 **good times,** piping times, bright *or* palmy *or* halcyon days, days of wine and roses, rosy era; heyday; prosperity, era of prosperity; fair weather, sunshine; golden era, **golden age,** golden time, golden days, Saturnian age, reign of Saturn, *Saturnia regna* <L>; honeymoon; holiday; prime, youth; age of Aquarius, millennium; **utopia** 986.11; **heaven** 681

5 **roaring trade, land-office business** <nf>, bullishness, bull *or* bullish market, seller's market; **boom,** booming economy, expanding economy

6 **lucky dog** <nf>, lucky devil, fortune's favorite, favorite of the gods, fortune's child, destiny's darling

VERBS 7 **prosper,** enjoy prosperity, **fare well,** get on well, do well, have it made *or* hacked <nf>, have a good thing going, have everything going one's way, get on swimmingly, go great guns <nf>; **turn out well, go well,** take a favorable turn; **succeed;** come on *or* along <nf>, come a long way, get on <nf>; **advance,** progress, make progress, make headway, get ahead <nf>, move up in the world, pull oneself up by one's own boot-straps

8 **thrive, flourish,** boom; blossom, bloom, flower; batten, fatten, grow fat; be fat, dumb, and happy <nf>

9 **be prosperous, make good, make one's mark,** rise *or* get on in the world, make a noise in the world <nf>, do all right by oneself <nf>, **make one's fortune;** grow rich; drive a roaring trade, do a land-office business <nf>, rejoice in a seller's market

10 **live well, live in clover** *or* on velvet <nf>, **live a life of ease,** live *or* lead the life of Riley, **live high, live high on the hog** <nf>, live on *or* off the fat of the land, ride the gravy train *and* piss on ice <nf>, roll in the lap of luxury; bask in the sunshine, have one's place in the sun; have a good *or* fine time of it

11 **be fortunate, be lucky,** be in luck, luck out <nf>, have all the luck, have one's moments <nf>, **lead** *or* **have a charmed life;** fall into the shithouse *and* come up with a five-dollar gold piece <nf>; **get a break** *and* get the breaks <nf>; hold aces *and* turn up trumps *or* roses <nf>; have a run of luck *and* hit a streak of luck <nf>; have it break good for one <nf>, have a stroke of luck; strike it lucky *and* make a lucky strike *and* strike oil <nf>, **strike it rich** <nf>, hit it big <nf>, strike a rich vein, come into money, drop into a good thing

ADJS 12 **prosperous,** in good case; **successful,** rags-to-riches; **well-paid, high-income,** higher-income, well-heeled *and* upscale <nf>; **affluent, wealthy; comfortable,** comfortably situated, **easy;** on Easy Street *and* in Fat City *and* in hog heaven <nf>, **in clover** *and* **on velvet** <nf>, on a bed of roses, in luxury, high on the hog <nf>; up in the world, on top of the heap <nf>

13 **thriving, flourishing, prospering, booming** <nf>; vigorous, exuberant; in full swing, going strong <nf>; halcyon, palmy, balmy, rosy, piping, clear, fair; blooming, blossoming, flowering, fruiting; fat, sleek, in good case; fat, dumb, and happy <nf>

14 **fortunate, lucky, providential;** in luck; **blessed,** blessed with luck, favored; born under a lucky star, born with a silver spoon in one's mouth, born on the sunny side of the hedge; out of the woods, over the hump; **auspicious**

ADVS 15 **prosperously, thrivingly, flourishingly,** boomingly, swimmingly <nf>

16 **fortunately, luckily, providentially**

1011 ADVERSITY

NOUNS 1 **adversity,** adverse circumstances, difficulties, hard knocks *and* rough going <nf>, **hardship, trouble,** troubles, "sea of troubles"— Shakespeare, **rigor,** vicissitude, care, stress, pressure, stress of life; hard case *or* plight, **hard life,** dog's life, vale of tears; wretched *or* miserable *or* hard *or* unhappy lot, tough *or* hard row to hoe <nf>, ups and downs of life, things going against one; bitter cup, bitter pill; bummer *and* downer <nf>; the bad part, the downside <nf>; annoyance, irritation, aggravation; **difficulty** 1012; **trial,** tribulation, cross, bane, curse, blight, **affliction** 96.8; plight, predicament 1013.4; the pits <nf>, raw deal <nf>

2 **misfortune, mishap,** ill hap, **misadventure, mischance,** *contretemps* <Fr>, grief; **disaster, calamity, catastrophe,** meltdown, cataclysm, **tragedy;** missed chance; **shock, blow,** hard *or* nasty *or* staggering blow; **accident,** casualty, collision, crash, plane *or* car crash; **wreck,** shipwreck; smash

and smashup *and* crack-up *and* pileup <nf>; bad news <nf>

3 reverse, reversal, reversal of fortune, **setback,** check, severe check, backset *and* throwback <nf>; **comedown,** descent, down

4 unfortunateness, unluckiness, lucklessness, ill success; unprosperousness; starcrossed *or* ill-fated life; "the slings and arrows of outrageous fortune"—Shakespeare; inauspiciousness 133.8

5 bad luck, ill luck, **hard luck,** hard lines <Brit>, **tough** *or* **rotten luck** <nf>, raw deal <nf>, bad *or* tough *or* rotten break <nf>, devil's own luck; **ill fortune,** bad fortune, evil fortune, evil star, ill wind, evil dispensation; frowns of fortune

6 hard times, bad times, sad times; evil day, ill day; rainy day; hard *or* stormy *or* heavy weather, storm clouds; **depression,** recession, **slump,** economic stagnation, **bust** <nf>; rough patch, bad spell; winter of discontent

7 unfortunate, poor unfortunate, the plaything *or* toy *or* sport of fortune, fortune's fool; **loser** *and* sure loser *and* non-starter <nf>, born loser; hard case *and* sad sack *and* hard-luck guy <nf>; *schlemiel* or *schlimazel* <Yiddish>; odd man out; the underclass, the dispossessed, the homeless, the wretched of the earth; victim 96.11, victim of fate; martyr

VERBS **8 go hard with,** go ill with; run one hard; **oppress, weigh on** *or* **upon,** weigh heavy on, weigh down, **burden,** overburden, load, overload, bear hard upon, lie on, lie hard *or* heavy upon; try one, put one out

9 have trouble; be born to trouble, be born under an evil star, be "born unto trouble, as the sparks fly upward"—Bible; **have a hard time of it,** be up against it <nf>, make heavy weather of it, meet adversity, have a bad time, lead *or* live a dog's life, have a tough *or* hard row to hoe; bear the brunt, bear more than one's share; be put to one's wit's end, not know which way to turn; **be unlucky, have bad** *or* **rotten luck,** be misfortuned, get the short *or* shitty end of the stick <nf>, hit the skids <nf>

10 come to grief, have a mishap, suffer a misfortune, fall, be stricken, be staggered, be shattered, be poleaxed, be felled, come a cropper <Brit nf>, be clobbered <nf>; run aground, go on the rocks *or* shoals, split upon a rock; sink, drown; **founder**

11 fall on evil days, go *or* **come down in the world,** go downhill, slip, be on the skids <nf>, come down, have a comedown, fall from one's high estate; deteriorate, **degenerate,** run *or* go to seed, sink, decline; **go to pot** <nf>, go to the dogs, go belly up <nf>; reach the depths, touch bottom, hit rock bottom; have seen better days

12 bring bad luck; hoodoo *and* hex *and* jinx *and*

Jonah *and* put the jinx on <nf>; put the evil eye on, whammy <nf>, put the *or* a double whammy on <nf>

ADJS **13 adverse, untoward, detrimental, unfavorable;** sinister; hostile, antagonistic, inimical; contrary, counter, counteractive, conflicting, opposing, opposed, opposite, in opposition; **difficult, troublesome, troublous, hard,** trying, rigorous, stressful; wretched, miserable 96.26; **not easy;** harmful 1000.12

14 unfortunate, unlucky, unprovidential, unblessed, **unprosperous,** sad, unhappy, hapless, fortuneless, misfortuned, luckless, donsie <Brit nf>; **out of luck,** short of luck; **down on one's luck** <nf>, badly *or* ill off, down in the world, in adverse circumstances; underprivileged, depressed; ill-starred, evil-starred, born under a bad sign, born under an evil star, planet-stricken, planet-struck, star-crossed; fatal, dire, doomful, funest <old>, **ominous, inauspicious** 133.17; **in a jam** *and* in a pickle *or* pretty pickle *and* in a tight spot *and* between a rock and a hard place <nf>, between the devil and the deep blue sea, caught in the crossfire *or* middle; up a tree *and* up the creek *or* up shit creek without a paddle *and* up to one's ass in alligators <nf>

15 disastrous, calamitous, catastrophic, cataclysmic, cataclysmal, **tragic,** ruinous, wreckful <old>, fatal, dire, black, woeful, sore, baneful, grievous; destructive 395.26; **life-threatening, terminal**

ADVS **16 adversely, untowardly,** detrimentally, **unfavorably;** contrarily, conflictingly, opposingly, oppositely

17 unfortunately, unluckily, unprovidentially, sadly, unhappily, **as ill luck would have it;** by ill luck, by ill hap; in adverse circumstances, if worse comes to worse

18 disastrously, calamitously, catastrophically, cataclysmically, grievously, woefully, sorely, banefully, tragically, crushingly, shatteringly

INTERJS **19 tough luck!,** tough tiddy! *and* tough shit! *and* tough darts! <nf>

1012 HINDRANCE

NOUNS **1 hindrance,** hindering, **hampering,** let, let *or* hindrance; **check, arrest,** arrestment, arrestation; fixation; **impediment,** holdback; **resistance,** opposition 451; suppression, **repression, restriction,** restraint 428; **obstruction,** blocking, blockage, clogging, occlusion; **bottleneck,** traffic jam, gridlock; speed bump, sleeping policeman <Brit>; **interruption,** interference; **retardation,** retardment, **detention,** detainment, **delay,** holdup, setback; **inhibition;** constriction, squeeze, stricture, cramp, stranglehold; **closure,** closing up *or* off; obstructionism, bloody-mindedness <Brit>, negativism, foot-dragging <nf>; nuisance value

2 **prevention, stop, stoppage, stopping,** arrestation, estoppel; stay, staying, halt, halting; **prohibition,** forbiddance; debarment; **determent,** deterrence, **discouragement; forestalling, preclusion, obviation,** foreclosure

3 **frustration, thwarting, balking, foiling; discomfiture, disconcertion,** bafflement, confounding; **defeat,** upset; check, checkmate, balk, foil <old>; derailing, derailment; vicious circle

4 **obstacle, obstruction,** obstructer; **hang-up** <nf>; **block,** blockade, cordon, curtain; **difficulty,** hurdle, hazard; **deterrent,** determent; **drawback,** objection; **stumbling block,** stumbling stone, stone in one's path; fly in the ointment, one small difficulty, **hitch,** hang-up <nf>, **catch,** joker <nf>, a "but," a "however"; bureaucracy, red tape, regulations

5 **barrier, bar;** gate, portcullis; **fence, wall,** stone wall, brick wall, impenetrable wall; seawall, jetty, groin, mole, breakwater; **bulwark, rampart,** defense, buffer, bulkhead, parapet, breastwork, work, earthwork, mound; bank, embankment, levee, dike; ditch, moat; dam, weir, leaping weir, barrage, milldam, beaver dam, cofferdam, wicket dam, shutter dam, bear-trap dam, hydraulic-fill dam, rock-fill dam, arch dam, arch-gravity dam, gravity dam; boom, jam, logjam; roadblock; speed bump; backstop; iron curtain, bamboo curtain; glass ceiling

6 **impediment,** embarrassment, hamper; encumbrance, cumbrance; **trouble,** difficulty 1013; **handicap,** disadvantage, inconvenience, penalty; white elephant; **burden,** burthen <old>, imposition, onus, cross, weight, deadweight, ball and chain, millstone around one's neck; **load,** pack, cargo, freight, charge; impedimenta, lumber; technical difficulty, flat tire, gremlin, glitch, bug <nf>, hiccup <nf>

7 **curb, check,** countercheck, arrest, **stay, stop,** damper, holdback; **brake,** clog, drag, drogue, remora; chock, scotch, spoke, spoke in one's wheel; doorstop; check-rein, bearing rein, martingale; bit, snaffle, pelham, curb bit; shackle, chain, fetter, trammel 428.4; sea anchor, drift anchor, drift sail, drag sail *or* sheet; boot *or* Denver boot

8 **hinderer,** impeder, **marplot,** obstructer; frustrater, thwarter; obstructionist, negativist; filibuster, filibusterer

9 **spoilsport,** wet blanket, **killjoy,** grouch, grinch *and* sourpuss <nf>, malcontent, **dog in the manger** <nf>, party pooper <nf>

VERBS 10 **hinder, impede, inhibit, arrest, check,** countercheck, scotch, **curb,** snub; **resist,** oppose 451.3; stonewall <nf>, stall, stall off; **suppress,** repress 428.8; **interrupt,** intercept <old>; intervene, interfere, intermeddle, meddle 214.7; damp, dampen, pour *or* dash *or* throw cold water; **retard,** slacken, **delay,** detain, **hold back, keep back,** set back, hold up <nf>; **restrain** 428.7; keep *or* hold in check, bottle up, dam up

11 **hamper, impede, cramp,** embarrass; trammel, entrammel, enmesh, entangle, ensnarl, entrap, entwine, involve, entoil, toil, net, lime, tangle, snarl; fetter, shackle; **handcuff,** tie one's hands; **encumber,** cumber, **burden,** lumber, **saddle with,** weigh *or* weight down, press down; hang like a millstone round one's neck; **handicap,** put at a disadvantage; lame, cripple, hobble, hamstring; cramp one's style, crab one's deal; gum up *or* gum up the works <nf>

12 **obstruct, get *or* stand in the way; dog, block,** block the way, put up a roadblock, blockade, block up, occlude; **jam,** crowd, pack; **bar,** barricade, bolt, lock; **debar,** shut out; shut off, **close,** close off *or* up, close tight, shut tight; constrict, squeeze, squeeze shut, **strangle,** strangulate, **stifle,** suffocate, **choke,** choke off, chock; stop up 293.7

13 **stop, stay, halt,** bring to a stop, put a stop *or* end to, bring to a shuddering *or* screeching halt <nf>; **brake,** slow down, put on the brakes, hit the brakes <nf>; **block, stall, stymie,** deadlock; nip in the bud

14 **prevent, prohibit, forbid; bar,** estop; save, help, **keep from; deter, discourage,** dishearten; **avert, parry, keep off, ward off, stave off, fend off,** fend, repel, deflect, turn aside; **forestall,** foreclose; **preclude,** exclude, debar, **obviate,** anticipate; rule out

15 **thwart, frustrate, foil, cross, balk;** spike, scotch, checkmate; **counter,** contravene, counteract, countermand, counterwork; stand in the way of, confront, brave, defy, challenge; **defeat** 412.6,8,9; **discomfit,** upset, **disrupt, confound,** flummox <nf>, discountenance, put out of countenance, **disconcert, baffle,** nonplus, perplex, stump <nf>; throw on one's beam ends, trip one up, throw one for a loss <nf>; **circumvent,** elude; sabotage, **spoil, ruin,** dish <nf>, dash, blast; **destroy** 395.10; throw a wrench in the machinery, **throw a monkey wrench *or* spanner** <Brit> **into the works** <nf>; put a spoke in one's wheel, scotch one's wheel, spike one's guns, put one's nose out of joint <nf>, upset one's applecart; **derail;** take the wind out of one's sails, steal one's thunder, cut the ground from under one, knock the chocks *or* props from under one, knock the bottom out of <nf>; tie one's hands, clip one's wings

16 <nf terms> **queer, crab, foul up, louse up,** snafu,
bollix or bollix up, gum, **gum up,** gum up the
works; crimp, cramp, **put a crimp in,** cramp one's
style; cook one's goose, cut one down to size; give
one a hard time

ADJS 17 **hindering,** troublesome; **inhibitive,**
inhibiting, suppressive, repressive; constrictive,
strangling, stifling, choking; restrictive 428.12;
obstructive, obstructing, occlusive, obstruent
<old>; cantankerous <nf>, bloody-minded
<Brit>, contrary, crosswise; interruptive,
interrupting; in the way

18 **hampering, impeding, counterproductive,**
impedimental, impeditive; onerous, oppressive,
burdensome, cumbersome, cumbrous,
encumbering

19 **preventive,** preventative, avertive, prophylactic;
prohibitive, forbidding; deterrent, deterring,
discouraging; preclusive, forestalling; foot-dragging

20 **frustrating,** confounding, disconcerting, baffling,
defeating

ADVS 21 under handicap, at a disadvantage, on the
hip <old>, with everything against one

1013 DIFFICULTY

NOUNS 1 **difficulty,** difficultness; "the nurse of
greatness"—William Cullen Bryant; **hardness,**
toughness <nf>, strain, the hard way <nf>, **rigor,**
rigorousness, ruggedness; **arduousness,**
laboriousness, strenuousness, toilsomeness,
severity; **troublesomeness,** bothersomeness;
onerousness, oppressiveness, burdensomeness;
formidability, hairiness <nf>; complication,
intricacy, **complexity** 799; abstruseness 522.2

2 **tough proposition** and **tough one** and **toughie**
<nf>, large or tall order <nf>; **hard job, tough job**
and heavy lift <nf>, big undertaking, backbreaker,
ballbuster <nf>, **chore,** man-sized job; brutal task,
Herculean task, Augean task; uphill work or going,
rough go <nf>, **heavy sledding,** hard pull <nf>,
dead lift <old>; tough lineup to buck <nf>, hard
road to travel; hard or tough nut to crack and hard
or tough row to hoe and hard row of stumps <nf>;
bitch <nf>; **handful** <nf>, all one can manage, no
easy task

3 **trouble, the matter;** headache <nf>, problem,
besetment, **inconvenience,** disadvantage; the bad
part, the downside <nf>; **ado,** great ado; peck of
troubles, "sea of troubles"—Shakespeare; hornet's
nest, Pandora's box, can of worms <nf>; **evil** 1000.3;
bother, annoyance 98.7; **anxiety,** worry 126.2

4 **predicament, plight,** spot of trouble, **strait,** straits,
parlous straits, tightrope, knife-edge, thin edge;
pinch, bind, pass, clutch, situation, emergency;

pretty pass, nice or pretty predicament, pretty or
fine state of affairs, **sorry plight;** slough, quagmire,
morass, swamp, quicksand; **embarrassment,**
embarrassing position or situation; **complication,**
imbroglio; the devil to pay

5 <nf terms> **pickle,** crunch, hobble, pretty pickle,
fine kettle of fish, how-do-you-do, fine how-do-you-
do; **spot, tight spot; squeeze, tight squeeze,**
ticklish or tricky spot, hot spot, hot seat, sticky
wicket <Brit>; **scrape, jam, hot water,** tail in a
gate, tit in the wringer; **mess,** holy or unholy mess,
mix, stew; hell to pay; no-win situation

6 **impasse, corner** and **box** and **hole** <nf>, cleft
stick; **cul-de-sac, blind alley, dead end,** dead-end
street, blank wall; **extremity, end of one's rope**
or **tether,** wit's end, nowhere to turn; **stalemate,**
deadlock; stand, standoff, standstill, logjam,
halt, stop

7 **dilemma,** horns of a dilemma, double bind,
damned-if-you-do-and-damned-if-you-don't, no-
win situation, **quandary,** nonplus, conundrum;
vexed question, thorny problem, knotty point,
knot, crux, node, nodus, Gordian knot, hard nut to
crack, can of worms, headache, poser, teaser,
perplexity, puzzle, enigma 522.8; paradox,
oxymoron; asses' bridge, *pons asinorum* <L>; bad
hair day

8 **crux, hitch, pinch, rub,** snag, hurdle, catch, joker
<nf>, where the shoe pinches, complication

9 **unwieldiness, unmanageability; unhandiness,**
inconvenience, impracticality; **awkwardness,**
clumsiness; cumbersomeness, ponderousness,
bulkiness, hulkiness; ham-handedness

VERBS 10 **be difficult, present difficulties, pose**
problems, take some doing <nf>

11 **have difficulty, have trouble,** have a rough time
<nf>, hit a snag, have a hard time of it, have one's
hands full, have one's work cut out, get off to a
bad start or on the wrong foot; be hard put, have
much ado with; labor under difficulties, labor
under a disadvantage, have the cards stacked
against one and have two strikes against one
<nf>; struggle, **flounder,** beat about, make heavy
weather of it; have one's back to the wall, not
know where to turn, come to a dead end or
standstill, not know whether one is coming or
going, go around in circles, swim against the
current; walk a tightrope, walk on eggshells or hot
coals, dance on a hot griddle

12 **get into trouble,** plunge into difficulties; **let**
oneself in for, put one's foot in it <nf>; **get in a**
jam or **hot water** or **the soup** <nf>, **get into a**
scrape <nf>, **get in a mess** or **hole** or **box** or
bind <nf>; paint oneself into a corner <nf>, get
one's ass in a bind and put oneself in a spot <nf>,

put one's foot in one's mouth, strike a bad patch, be up a tree; have a tiger by the tail; burn one's fingers; get all tangled *or* snarled *or* wound up, get all balled *or* bollixed up <nf>

13 trouble, beset; **bother,** pother, get one down, <nf>, **disturb, perturb,** irk, plague, **torment,** drive one up the wall <nf>, give one gray hair, make one lose sleep; **harass, vex, distress** 96.16; inconvenience, **put out,** put out of the way, discommode 996.4; **concern, worry** 126.3; **puzzle, perplex** 971.13; put to it, give one trouble, complicate matters; give one a hard time *and* give one a bad time *and* make it tough for <nf>; be too much for; ail, be the matter; tree <nf>

14 cause trouble, bring trouble, "sow the wind and reap the whirlwind"—Bible; ask for trouble, ask for it <nf>, bring down upon one, bring down upon one's head, bring down around one's ears; **stir up a hornet's nest,** kick up *or* piss up a fuss *or* storm *or* row <nf>; stir up a hornet's nest, open Pandora's box, open a can of worms <nf>, put fire to tow; **raise hob** *or* **hell** <nf>; raise merry hell *and* play hob *and* play hell <nf>, play the deuce *or* devil <nf>

15 put in a hole <nf>, put in a spot <nf>; **embarrass; involve,** enmesh, entangle

16 corner, run *and* drive into a corner <nf>, **tree** <nf>, chase up a tree *or* stump <nf>, drive *or* force to the wall, push one to the wall, put one's back to the wall, have one on the ropes <nf>

ADJS **17 difficult,** difficile; **not easy,** no picnic, hairy; **hard, tough** *and* **rough** *and* **rugged** <nf>, rigorous, brutal, severe; wicked *and* mean *and* hairy <nf>, **formidable; arduous, strenuous, toilsome, laborious,** operose, Herculean; steep, uphill; hard-fought; hard-earned; jawbreaking; knotty, knotted; thorny, spiny, set with thorns; delicate, ticklish, tricky, sticky <nf>, critical, easier said than done, like pulling teeth; exacting, demanding; intricate, complex 799.4; abstruse 522.16; hard-ass <nf>

18 troublesome, besetting; **bothersome,** irksome, vexatious, painful, plaguey <nf>, problematic, annoying 98.22; **burdensome,** oppressive, onerous, heavy *and* hefty <nf>, crushing, backbreaking; **trying,** grueling

19 unwieldy, unmanageable, unhandy; inconvenient, impractical; **awkward, clumsy, cumbersome,** unmaneuverable; contrary, perverse, crosswise; ponderous, bulky, hulky, hulking, ungainly

20 troubled, trouble-plagued, beset, sore beset; **bothered, vexed,** irked, annoyed 96.21; plagued, **harassed** 96.24; distressed, perturbed 96.22; inconvenienced, embarrassed; put to it *and* hard put to it <nf>; **worried, anxious** 126.6,7; puzzled

21 in trouble, in deep trouble, in a predicament, in a sorry plight, in a pretty pass; in deep water, out of one's depth

22 <nf terms> in deep shit *or* doo-doo, in a jam, in a pickle, in a pretty pickle, in a spot, in a tight spot, in a fix, in a hole, in a bind, in a box; in a mess, in a scrape, in hot water, in the soup; up a tree, up to one's ass in alligators, up the creek, up shit creek without a paddle, in Dutch, on the spot, behind the eight ball, on Queer Street, out on a limb, on the hot seat

23 in a dilemma, on the horns of a dilemma, **in a quandary;** between two stools; between Scylla and Charybdis, between the devil and the deep blue sea, between a rock and a hard place <nf>

24 at an impasse, at one's wit's end, at a loss, at a stand *or* standstill, deadlocked; **nonplussed,** at a nonplus; **baffled, perplexed, bewildered,** mystified, stuck *and* stumped <nf>, stymied

25 cornered, in a corner, with one's back to the wall; **treed** *and* **up a tree** *and* up a stump <nf>; **at bay,** *aux abois* <Fr>

26 straitened, reduced to dire straits, in desperate straits, **pinched,** sore *or* sorely pressed, **hard-pressed, hard up** <nf>, **up against it** <nf>; driven from pillar to post; **desperate, in extremities,** *in extremis* <L>, **at the end of one's rope** *or* **tether**

27 stranded, grounded, aground, **on the rocks,** high and dry; **stuck,** stuck *or* set fast; foundered, swamped; castaway, marooned, wrecked, shipwrecked

ADVS **28 with difficulty,** difficultly, with much ado; hardly, painfully; the hard way, **arduously, strenuously, laboriously,** toilsomely

29 unwieldily, unmanageably, unhandily, inconveniently; **awkwardly, clumsily, cumbersomely;** ponderously

1014 FACILITY

NOUNS **1 facility, ease, easiness,** facileness, effortlessness; lack of hindrance, **smoothness,** freedom; clear coast, clear road *or* course; smooth road, royal road, highroad; easy going, plain sailing, smooth *or* straight sailing; clarity, intelligibility 521; uncomplexity, uncomplicatedness, **simplicity** 797

2 handiness, wieldiness, wieldableness, handleability, manageability, **manageableness,** maneuverability; **convenience,** practicality, practicableness, untroublesomeness; **flexibility,** pliancy, **pliability,** ductility, malleability; adaptability, feasibility

3 easy thing, mere child's play, simple matter, mere twist of the wrist; easy target, sitting duck <nf>; sinecure

4 <nf terms> **cinch, snap,** pushover, breeze, waltz, duck soup, velvet, picnic, pie, cherry pie, apple pie, cakewalk, piece of cake <Brit>, kid stuff, turkey shoot, no-brainer, setup, high road, walkover, no sweat

5 facilitation, facilitating, easing, smoothing, smoothing out, smoothing the way; **speeding,** expediting, expedition, quickening, hastening; streamlining; lubricating, greasing, oiling

6 disembarrassment, disentanglement, disencumbrance, disinvolvement, uncluttering, uncomplicating, unscrambling, unsnarling, disburdening, unburdening, unhampering; **extrication,** disengagement, **freeing,** clearing; deregulation; **simplification** 798.2

VERBS **7 facilitate, ease; grease the wheels** <nf>; **smooth, smooth** or **pave the way,** ease the way, grease or soap the ways <nf>, prepare the way, **clear the way,** make all clear for, make way for; run interference for <nf>, open the way, open the door to; not stand in the way of; **open up, unclog,** unblock, unjam, unbar, loose 431.6; **lubricate,** make frictionless or dissipationless, remove friction, grease, oil; **speed, expedite,** quicken, hasten; **help along,** help on its way; **aid** 449.11; **explain,** make clear 521.6; **simplify** 798.4

8 do easily, make short work of, do with one's hands tied behind one's back, do with both eyes shut, do standing on one's head, do hands down, sail or dance or waltz through, wing it <nf>, take to like a duck to water

9 disembarrass, disencumber, unload, relieve, disburden, unhamper, get out from under; **disentangle,** disembroil, disinvolve, unclutter, unscramble, unsnarl; **extricate,** disengage, **free,** free up, clear; liberate 431.4

10 go easily, run smoothly, work well, work like a machine, go like clockwork or a sewing machine; present no difficulties, give no trouble, be painless, be effortless; flow, roll, glide, slide, coast, sweep, sail

11 have it easy, have it soft <nf>, have it all one's own way, have the game in one's hands, have it in the bag; win easily; breeze in <nf>, walk over the course <nf>, win in a walk or in a canter or hands down <nf>

12 take it easy and **go easy** <nf>, swim with the stream, drift with the current, go with the tide; cool it and not sweat it <nf>; take the line of least resistance; take it in one's stride, make little or light of, think nothing of

ADJS **13 easy, facile, effortless,** smooth, painless; soft <nf>, cushy <nf>; plain, uncomplicated, straightforward, **simple** 797.6, Mickey Mouse <nf>, simple as ABC <nf>, easy as pie and easy as

falling off a log <nf>, downhill all the way, like shooting fish in a barrel, like taking candy from a baby, no sooner said than done; **clear;** glib; **light,** unburdensome; nothing to it; casual, throwaway <nf>

14 smooth-running, frictionless, dissipationless, easy-running, easy-flowing; well-lubricated, well-oiled, well-greased

15 handy, wieldy, wieldable, handleable; tractable; flexible, pliant, yielding, malleable, ductile, pliable, **manageable,** maneuverable; **convenient,** foolproof, goofproof <nf>, practical, untroublesome, user-friendly; adaptable, feasible

ADVS **16 easily,** facilely, **effortlessly, readily, simply,** lightly, swimmingly <nf>, without difficulty; no sweat and like nothing and slick as a whistle <nf>; hands down <nf>, with one hand tied behind one's back, with both eyes closed, standing on one's head; like a duck takes to water; **smoothly,** frictionlessly, like clockwork; on easy terms

1015 UGLINESS

NOUNS **1 ugliness, unsightliness, unattractiveness,** uncomeliness, unhandsomeness, unbeautifulness, unprettiness, unloveliness, unaestheticness, unpleasingness 98.1; unprepossessingness, ill-favoredness, inelegance; **homeliness,** plainness; unshapeliness, shapelessness; ungracefulness, gracelessness, clumsiness, ungainliness 414.3; **uglification, uglifying, disfigurement,** defacement; dysphemism; cacophony

2 hideousness, horridness, horribleness, frightfulness, dreadfulness, terribleness, awfulness <nf>; **repulsiveness** 98.2, repugnance, repugnancy, repellence, repellency, offensiveness, forbiddingness, loathsomeness; ghastliness, gruesomeness, grisliness; **deformity,** misshapenness

3 forbidding countenance, vinegar aspect, wry face, face that would stop a clock

4 eyesore, blot, blot on the landscape, blemish, **sight** <nf>, **fright, horror, mess,** no beauty, no beauty queen, ugly duckling; baboon; **scarecrow,** gargoyle, monster, **monstrosity,** teratism; witch, bag and dog <nf>, **hag,** harridan; something the cat dragged in, back end of a bus

VERBS **5 offend,** offend the eye, offend one's aesthetic sensibilities, **look bad;** look something terrible and look like hell and look like the devil and look a sight or a fright or a mess or like something the cat dragged in <nf>; **uglify, disfigure,** deface, blot, blemish, mar, scar, spoil; dysphemize

ADJS **6 ugly, unsightly, unattractive, unhandsome, unpretty, unlovely,** uncomely, **inelegant;**

unbeautiful, unbeauteous, beautiless, unaesthetic, unpleasing 98.17; **homely, plain;** not much to look at, not much for looks, short on looks <nf>, hard on the eyes <nf>; ugly as sin, ugly as the wrath of God, ugly as hell, homely as a mud fence, homely enough to sour milk, homely enough to stop a clock, not fit to be seen, grotty <nf>; **uglified, disfigured,** defaced, blotted, blemished, marred, spoiled; dysphemized, dysphemistic; cacophonous, cacophonic

7 **unprepossessing, ill-favored,** hard-favored, evil-favored, ill-featured; ill-looking, evil-looking; hard-featured, hard-visaged; grim, grim-faced, grim-visaged; hatchet-faced, horse-faced

8 **unshapely,** shapeless, **ill-shaped,** ill-made, ill-proportioned; **deformed,** misshapen, misproportioned, malformed, misbegotten; grotesque, scarecrowish, gargoylish; monstrous, teratic, cacogenic

9 **ungraceful,** ungraced, graceless; clumsy, clunky <nf>, **ungainly** 414.20

10 **inartistic,** unartistic, **unaesthetic; unornamental, undecorative**

11 **hideous, horrid, horrible, frightful, dreadful, terrible, awful** <nf>; **repulsive** 98.18, repellent, repelling, rebarbative, **repugnant,** offensive, foul, forbidding, loathsome, loathly <old>, revolting; **ghastly,** gruesome, grisly

ADVS 12 **uglily,** homelily, uncomelily, **unattractively, unhandsomely, unbeautifully, unprettily**

13 **hideously, horridly, horribly, frightfully, dreadfully, terribly, awfully** <nf>; **repulsively, repugnantly,** offensively, forbiddingly, loathsomely, revoltingly; gruesomely, ghastly

1016 BEAUTY

NOUNS 1 **beauty, beautifulness,** beauteousness, **prettiness, handsomeness,** attractiveness 97.2, **loveliness, pulchritude, charm,** grace, elegance, exquisiteness; bloom, glow; the beautiful; source of aesthetic pleasure *or* delight; beauty unadorned

2 "God's handwriting"—Emerson, "a form of genius"—Oscar Wilde, "the power by which a woman charms a lover and terrifies a husband"—Ambrose Bierce

3 **comeliness, fairness,** sightliness, personableness, becomingness, pleasingness 97.1, goodliness, bonniness, agreeability, agreeableness; charisma

4 **good looks,** good appearance, good effect; good proportions, aesthetic proportions; **shapeliness,** good figure, good shape, *belle tournure* <Fr>, nice body, lovely build, physical *or* bodily charm, curvaceousness, curves <nf>, pneumaticness, sexy body, sexiness; good bone structure; bodily grace, **gracefulness,** gracility; good points, **beauties, charms, delights,** perfections, good features, delicate features

5 **daintiness, delicacy,** delicateness; **cuteness** *or* cunningness <nf>

6 **gorgeousness,** ravishingness; **gloriousness,** heavenliness, sublimity; **splendor,** splendidness, splendiferousness, splendorousness *or* splendrousness, sublimeness, resplendence; **brilliance,** brightness, radiance, luster; **glamour** 377.1

7 **thing of beauty,** vision, picture <nf>, poem, eyeful <nf>, **sight for sore eyes** <nf>, cynosure; masterpiece

8 **beauty, charmer,** *charmeuse* <Fr>; beauty queen, beauty contest winner, Miss America, bathing beauty; **glamour girl,** cover girl, model; sex goddess; **belle,** reigning beauty, great beauty, lady fair; beau ideal, paragon; enchantress; "the face that launch'd a thousand ships"—Marlowe

9 <nf terms> **doll, dish, cutie,** angel, angelface, babyface, beaut, honey, dream, looker, good-looker, stunner, dazzler, dreamboat, fetcher, bird *and* crumpet <Brit>, peach, knockout, raving beauty, centerfold, pinup girl, pinup, bunny, cutie *or* cutesy pie, cute *or* slick chick, pussycat, sex kitten, ten; treasure; babe, hunk

10 <famous beauties> Venus, Venus de Milo; Aphrodite, Hebe; Adonis, Appollo, Apollo Belvedere, Hyperion, Antinoüs, Narcissus; Astarte; Balder, Freya; Helen of Troy, Cleopatra; the Graces, houri, peri

11 **beautification,** prettification, cutification <nf>, **adornment;** decoration 498.1; **beauty care,** beauty treatment, cosmetology; facial <nf>; manicure; hairdressing; cosmetic surgery, plastic surgery

12 **makeup, cosmetics, beauty products, beauty-care products;** war paint *and* drugstore complexion <nf>; pancake makeup; powder, talcum, talcum powder; foundation, base; rouge, blush *or* blusher, paint; lip rouge, **lipstick,** lip color; **nail polish;** greasepaint, clown white; eye makeup, eyeliner, mascara, eye shadow, kohl; cold cream, hand cream *or* lotion, vanishing cream, foundation cream; mudpack; eyebrow pencil; puff, powder puff; makeup brush; compact, vanity case; toiletries, shampoo, soap, deodorant, perfume

13 **beautician,** beautifier, cosmetologist, makeup artist, cosmetician; hairdresser, *coiffeur* and *coiffeuse* <Fr>, hairstylist; barber; manicurist, pedicurist

14 **beauty parlor** *or* salon *or* shop, *salon de beauté* <Fr>, hairdressing salon, hair salon; barbershop, barber

15 hairdressing, hair styling, hair coloring, barbering; shave, depilation, tweezing, electrolysis, waxing; hair replacement; hairstyle, hairdo; haircut, trim, permanent, perm; crop, bob, cut, ponytail, plait, cornrows, braids, pigtails, bangs, chignon, bun, beehive, pompadour, pageboy, dreadlocks, sideburns, crewcut, flattop, ducktail, **DA,** Mohawk, Afro

VERBS **16 beautify, prettify,** cutify <nf>, pretty up *or* gussy up *or* doll up <nf>, grace, **adorn; decorate** 498.8; set off, set off to advantage *or* good advantage, become one; **glamorize; make up,** paint *and* put on one's face <nf>, titivate, cosmetize, cosmeticize; primp

17 look good; look like a million *and* look fit to kill *and* knock dead *and* knock one's eyes out <nf>; take the breath away, beggar description; shine, beam, **bloom, glow**

ADJS **18 beautiful, beauteous,** endowed with beauty; **pretty, handsome, attractive** 97.7, pulchritudinous, **lovely, graceful,** gracile; elegant; esthetic, aesthetically appealing; **cute;** pretty as a picture, "lovely as the day"—Longfellow, "fair as is the rose in May"—Chaucer; tall dark and handsome; picturesque, scenic

19 comely, fair, good-looking, nice-looking, well-favored, **personable,** presentable, agreeable, becoming, pleasing 97.6, goodly, bonny, likely <nf>, **sightly;** pleasing to the eye, lovely to behold; **shapely,** well-built, built, well-shaped, well-proportioned, well-made, well-formed, stacked *or* well-stacked <nf>, shapely, curvaceous, curvy <nf>, pneumatic, amply endowed, built for comfort *or* built like a brick shithouse <nf>, buxom, callipygian, callipygous; Junoesque, statuesque, goddess-like; slender 270.16; Adonis-like, hunky <nf>

20 fine, exquisite, flowerlike, **dainty, delicate;** *mignon* <Fr>

21 gorgeous, ravishing; glorious, heavenly, divine, sublime; **resplendent,** splendorous *or* splendrous, splendiferous, **splendid; brilliant,** bright, radiant, shining, beaming, glowing, blooming, abloom, sparkling, **dazzling; glamorous**

22 <nf terms> **eye-filling, easy on the eyes,** not hard to look at, long on looks, looking fit to kill, dishy <chiefly Brit>; cutesy, cutesy-poo; raving, devastating, **stunning,** killing

23 beautifying, cosmetic; decorative 498.10; cosmetized, cosmeticized, beautified, made-up, mascaraed, titivated

ADVS **24 beautifully,** beauteously, **prettily, handsomely, attractively, becomingly,** comelily; elegantly, exquisitely; charmingly, enchantingly

25 daintily, delicately; cutely

26 gorgeously, ravishingly; ravingly *and* devastatingly *and* stunningly <nf>; **gloriously,** divinely, sublimely; **resplendently,** splendidly, splendorously, splendrously; **brilliantly,** brightly, radiantly, glowingly, **dazzlingly**

WORD ELEMENTS **27** cal-, calo-, callo-, cali-, calli-

1017 MATHEMATICS

NOUNS **1 mathematics** <see list>, math <US nf>, maths <Brit nf>, mathematic, **numbers, figures;** pure mathematics, abstract mathematics, applied mathematics, higher mathematics, elementary mathematics, classical mathematics, metamathematics, new mathematics; algorithm, logarithm; mathematical element <see list>

2 <mathematical operations> notation, **addition** 253, **subtraction** 255, **multiplication, division,** numeracy, calculation, computation, reckoning, proportion, practice, equation, extraction of roots, inversion, reduction, involution, evolution, approximation, interpolation, extrapolation, transformation, differentiation, integration; arithmetic operation, algebraic operation, logical operation, associative operation, distributive operation

3 number <see list>, **numeral,** *numero* <Sp and Ital>, no *or* n, digit, binary digit *or* bit, **cipher,** character, symbol, sign, notation, figure, base; decimal

4 <number systems> **Arabic numerals,** algorism *or* algorithm, Roman numerals; **decimal system,** binary system, octal system, duodecimal system, hexadecimal system; place-value notation, positional notation, fixed-point notation, floating-point notation

5 large number, astronomical number, boxcar number <nf>, zillion *and* jillion <nf>; googol, googolplex; infinity, infinite number, transfinite number, infinitude 822.1; billion, trillion, etc 882.13

6 sum, summation, difference, product, **number, count,** x number, n number; account, cast, **score, reckoning, tally,** tale, the story *and* whole story *and* all she wrote <nf>, the bottom line <nf>, **aggregate, amount,** quantity 244; **whole** 792, **total** 792.2, running total; box score <nf>

7 ratio, rate, proportion; quota, quotum; **percentage,** percent; **fraction,** proper fraction, improper fraction, compound fraction, continued fraction, decimal fraction; common *or* vulgar fraction; geometric ratio *or* proportion, arithmetical proportion, harmonic proportion; rule of three; numerator, denominator

8 series, progression; arithmetical progression,

geometrical progression, harmonic progression; Fibonacci numbers

9 numeration, enumeration, numbering, counting, count, accounting, census, inventorying, telling, tally, tallying, scoring; page numbering, pagination, foliation; counting on the fingers, dactylonomy; **measurement** 300; quantification, quantifying, quantization

10 calculation, computation, estimation, reckoning, figuring, number work, mental arithmetic, calculus; adding, footing, casting, ciphering, totaling, toting *or* totting <nf>; rounding up, rounding down, rounding off

11 summation, summary, summing, summing up, recount, recounting, rehearsal, capitulation, **recapitulation,** recap *and* rehash <nf>, statement, **reckoning, count,** bean-counting <nf>, repertory, census, inventory, head count, nose count, body count; account, accounts; **table,** reckoner, ready reckoner

12 division; long division, short division, divisibility; quotient, ratio, proportion, percentage, fraction; reciprocal, inverse, dividend, divisor, aliquot part, remainder, residue; numerator, denominator, common denominator

13 account of, count of, a reckoning of, **tab** *or* **tabs of** <nf>, tally of, check of, track of

14 figures, statistics, indexes *or* indices; vital statistics

15 calculator <see list>, **computer** 1042.2; estimator, figurer, reckoner, abacist, pollster; statistician, actuary; number-cruncher <nf>; accountant, bookkeeper 628.7

16 mathematician, arithmetician; geometer, geometrician; algebraist, trigonometrician, statistician, geodesist, mathematical physicist, topologist; analyst

VERBS **17 number,** numerate, number off, **enumerate, count, tell, tally,** give a figure to, put a figure on, call off, name, call over, run over; **count noses** *or* **heads** <nf>, call the roll; census, poll; page, paginate, foliate; **measure** 300.11; **round,** round out *or* off *or* down; quantify, quantitate, quantize

18 calculate, compute, estimate, reckon, figure, solve, reckon at, put at, cipher, cast, tally, score; **figure out,** work out, dope out <nf>, determine; take account of, figure in *and* figure on <nf>; **add,** add up, sum, **subtract,** take away, **multiply, divide,** multiply out, cross-multiply, times, algebraize, extract roots, raise to the power of, cube, square, decimalize; factor, factor out, factorize; **measure** 300.11

19 sum up, sum, summate, say it all <nf>; aggregate, **figure up,** cipher up, reckon up, **count up, add up,** foot up, cast up, score up, **tally up; total,** total up,

tote *or* tot up <nf>; **summarize, recapitulate,** recap *and* rehash <nf>, **recount,** rehearse, recite, relate; detail, itemize, inventory; round up, round down, round off

20 keep account of, keep count of, **keep track of, keep tab** *or* **tabs** <nf>, keep tally, keep a check on *or* of

21 check, verify 970.12, double-check, check on *or* out; **prove,** demonstrate; balance, balance the books; **audit,** overhaul; take stock, inventory

ADJS **22 mathematical,** numeric *or* numerical, numerary, arithmetic *or* arithmetical, algebraic *or* algebraical, geometric *or* geometrical, trigonometric *or* trigonometrical, analytic *or* analytical, combinatorial, topological, statistical

23 numeric *or* **numerical,** numeral, numerary, numerative; **odd,** impair, **even,** pair; arithmetical, algorismic *or* algorithmic; **cardinal, ordinal;** figural, **figurate,** figurative, **digital;** aliquot, submultiple, **reciprocal,** prime, fractional, decimal, exponential, **logarithmic,** logometric, differential, integral; positive, negative; rational, irrational, transcendental; surd, radical; real, imaginary; possible, impossible, finite, infinite, transfinite; integral, whole; decenary, binary, ternary; signed, unsigned, nonnegative

24 numerative, enumerative; calculative, computative, estimative; **calculating,** computing, computational, estimating; statistical; quantifying, quantizing

25 calculable, computable, **reckonable,** estimable, countable, numberable, enumerable, numerable; **measurable,** mensurable, quantifiable; addable, subtractive, multipliable, dividable

26 branches and kinds of mathematics

addition algebra	complex *or* double algebra
affine geometry	control theory
algebra	denumerative geometry
algebraic geometry	descriptive geometry
algebraic topology	differential calculus
analysis	differential geometry
analytic geometry	division algebra
applied mathematics	elementary arithmetic
arithmetic	elementary *or* ordinary
associative algebra	algebra
binary arithmetic	equivalent algebras
Boolean algebra	Euclidean geometry
calculus	Fourier analysis
calculus of differences	functional analysis
category theory	game theory
circle geometry	geodesic geometry
combinatorial	geodesy
mathematics *or*	geometry
combinatorics	Gödel's proof
combinatorial topology	graphic algebra
commutative algebra	group theory

harmonic analysis
higher algebra
higher arithmetic
homological algebra
hyperalgebra
hyperbolic geometry
infinitesimal calculus
integral calculus
intuitional geometry
invariant subalgebra
inverse geometry
Lagrangian function
Laplace's equation
linear algebra
line geometry
mathematical biology
mathematical biophysics
mathematical computing
mathematical ecology
mathematical geography
mathematical logic
mathematical physics
matrix algebra
measure theory
metageometry
modular arithmetic
multiple algebra
natural geometry
nilpotent algebra
noncommutative algebra
non-Euclidean geometry
n-tuple linear algebra

number theory
numerical analysis
operational calculus
operations research
plane geometry
plane trigonometry
point-set topology
political arithmetic
potential theory
probability theory
projective geometry
proper subalgebra
quadratics
quaternian algebra
reducible algebra
Riemannian geometry
semisimple algebra
set theory
simple algebra
solid geometry
speculative geometry
sphere geometry
spherical trigonometry
statistics
subalgebra
systems analysis *or* theory
topology
trigonometry *or* trig <nf>
universal algebra
universal geometry
vector algebra
zero algebra

fraction
function
greatest common divisor
    or GCD
haversine
hyperbolic
i
increment
index
integral
Laplace transform
least common
    denominator *or* LCD
least common multiple
    or LCM
logarithm *or* log
mantissa
matrix
minuend
minus sign
mixed decimal
modulus
monomial
multinomial
multiple
multiplicand
multiplicator
multiplier
norm
numerator
parameter
part
permutation
pi <π>

plus sign
polynomial
power
quadratic equation
quaternion
quotient
radical
radix
reciprocal
repeating *or* circulating
    decimal
root
secant
sequence
series
set
simultaneous equations
sine
solution
square root
submultiple
subtrahend
summand
tangent
tensor
topological group
topological space
variable
vector
vector product
vector sum
versed sine *or* versine
vulgar fraction

27 mathematical elements

addend
algorithm
aliquot
antilogarithm
argument
auxiliary equation
base
Bessel function
binomial
characteristic
characteristic equation
characteristic function
characteristic polynomial
characteristic root *or*
    characteristic value *or*
    eigenvalue *or* latent root
    or proper value
characteristic vector
coefficient
combination
common divisor *or*
    measure
complement
congruence
coordinate
constant

cosecant
cosine
cotangent
cube
cube root
decimal
denominator
derivative
determinant
difference *or* remainder
differential
discriminate
dividend
division sign
divisor
e
elliptical function
empty set *or* null set
equal sign
equation
exponent
exponential
expression
factor
factorial
formula

28 kinds of numbers

abundant number
algebraic number
Avogadro's
cardinal number *or*
    cardinal
complex *or* Gaussian
    integer
complex number
composite *or* rectangular
    number
deficient *or* defective
    number
directed number
even number *or* pair
Fermat number
figurate number
finite number
fraction
imaginary number *or* pure
    imaginary
infinity
integer *or* whole number
irrational number *or*
    irrational

Mersenne number
mixed number
natural number
negative number
nonnegative number
odd number *or* impair
ordinal number *or* ordinal
perfect number
polygonal number
positive number
prime *or* rectilinear
    number *or* prime
pyramidal number
random number
rational number
    or rational
real number *or* real
round *or* rounded number
serial number
signed number
surd *or* surd quantity
transcendental number
transfinite number
whole number

29 calculators

abacus
adding machine
analog computer
arithmograph
arithmometer
calculating machine
cash register
compass
computer
counter
difference engine
digital computer
Napier's bones *or* rods
number-cruncher <nf>

online calculator
pari-mutuel machine
pocket calculator
programmable calculator
quipu
rule
scientific calculator
score card
slide rule *or* sliding scale
suan pan <Chin>
tabulator
tally *or* tally stick
totalizator
Turing machine

1018 PHYSICS

NOUNS 1 physics; natural *or* physical science; philosophy *or* second philosophy *or* natural philosophy *or* physic <old>; **branch of physics** <see list>; physical theory, quantum theory, relativity theory, special relativity theory, general relativity theory, unified field theory, grand unified theory *or* GUT, superunified theory *or* theory of everything *or* TOE, eightfold way, superstring theory, kinetic theory, wave theory, electromagnetic theory

2 physicist, aerophysicist, astrophysicist, biophysicist, etc

ADJS 3 physical; aerophysical, astrophysical, biophysical, etc

4 branches of physics

acoustics
aerodynamics
aerophysics
applied physics
astrophysics
basic conductor physics
biophysics
chaos theory *or* chaos
   dynamics *or* chaology
chemical physics *or*
   chemicophysics
classical physics *or*
   Newtonian physics
condensed-matter physics
cryogenics
crystallography
cytophysics
dynamics
electricity
electrodynamics
electromagnetism
electron optics
electronics *or* electron
   physics
electrophysics
fluid dynamics

fluid mechanics
geometric optics
geophysics
high-energy physics
hyperphysics
hypophysics
iatrophysics
kinematics
macrophysics
magnetism
mathematical physics
mechanics
medicophysics
microphysics
molecular physics
morphophysics
myophysics
Newtonian mechanics
nuclear physics
optics
organismic physics
physical chemistry *or*
   physicochemistry
physical optics
physicomathematics
plasma physics

psychophysics
quantum physics
radiation physics
radionics
solar physics
solid-state physics

statics
stereophysics
theoretical physics
thermodynamics
X-ray crystallography
zoophysics

1019 HEAT

NOUNS 1 heat, hotness, heatedness; superheat, superheatedness; calidity *or* caloric <old>; **warmth,** warmness; incalescence; radiant heat, thermal radiation, induction heat, convector *or* convected heat, coal heat, gas heat, oil heat, hot-air heat, steam heat, electric heat, solar heat, dielectric heat, ultraviolet heat, atomic heat, molecular heat; latent heat, specific heat; animal heat, body heat, blood heat, hypothermia; fever heat, fever, pyrexia, feverishness, flush, calescence; heating, burning 1020.5; smoke detector

2 <metaphors> **ardor,** ardency, **fervor,** fervency, fervidness, fervidity; eagerness 101; excitement 105; **anger** 152.5,8,9; **sexual desire** 75.5; love 104

3 temperature, temp <nf>; room temperature, comfortable temperature; comfort index, temperature-humidity index *or* THI; flash point; boiling point; melting point, freezing point; dew point; recalescence point; zero, absolute zero; thermometry, pyrometry

4 lukewarmness, tepidness, tepidity; tepidarium

5 torridness, torridity; extreme heat, intense heat, torrid heat, red heat, white heat, tropical heat, sweltering heat, African heat, Indian heat, Bengal heat, summer heat, oppressive heat; "where the sun beats, and the dead tree gives no shelter, the cricket no relief"—T S Eliot; **hot wind** 318.7; incandescence, flash point

6 sultriness, stuffiness, closeness, oppressiveness; **humidity, humidness, mugginess,** stickiness <nf>, swelter, fug; tropical heat; overheating

7 hot weather, sunny *or* sunshiny weather; sultry weather, stuffy weather, humid weather, muggy weather, sticky weather <nf>; summer, midsummer, high summer; Indian Summer, **dog days,** canicular days, canicule; **heat wave,** hot wave, hot spell, warm front; broiling sun, midday sun; vertical rays; warm weather, fair weather; global warming, greenhouse effect

8 hot day, summer day; **scorcher** *and* **roaster** *and* broiler *and* sizzler *and* swelterer <nf>

9 hot air, superheated air; thermal; firestorm

10 hot water, boiling water; **steam,** vapor; volcanic water; hot *or* warm *or* thermal spring, thermae; geyser, Old Faithful; steaminess; boiling point

11 <hot place> **oven, furnace,** fiery furnace, inferno, hell; heater, warmer, burner; steam bath, sauna, solarium; **tropics,** subtropics, Torrid Zone, Sahara, Dearth Valley; equator; melting point

12 glow, incandescence, fieriness; **flush, blush, bloom,** redness 41, rubicundity, rosiness; whiteness 37; thermochromism; hectic, hectic flush; sunburn

13 fire; blaze, flame, ingle, devouring element; **combustion, ignition,** ignition temperature *or* point, flash *or* flashing point; **conflagration;** flicker 1024.8, wavering *or* flickering flame, "lambent flame"—Dryden; smoldering fire, sleeping fire; marshfire, fen fire, ignis fatuus, will-o'-the-wisp; fox fire; witch fire, St Elmo's fire, corposant; **cheerful fire,** cozy fire, crackling fire; **roaring fire,** blazing fire; **raging fire,** sheet of fire, sea of flames; bonfire, balefire; beacon fire, beacon, signal beacon, watch fire; towering inferno; alarm fire, two-alarm fire, three-alarm fire, etc; wildfire, prairie fire, forest fire; backfire; brushfire; open fire; campfire; smudge fire; death fire, pyre, funeral pyre, crematory; burning ghat; fireball; first-degree burn, second-degree burn, third-degree burn

14 flare, flare-up, **flash,** flash fire, **blaze,** burst, outburst; deflagration

15 spark, sparkle; **scintillation,** scintilla; ignescence

16 coal, live coal, brand, firebrand, **ember,** burning ember; **cinder**

17 fireworks <see list>, **pyrotechnics** *or* pyrotechny

18 <perviousness to heat> transcalency; adiathermancy, athermancy

19 thermal unit; British thermal unit *or* BTU; Board of Trade unit *or* BOT; centigrade thermal unit; centigrade *or* Celsius scale, Fahrenheit scale; **calorie,** mean calorie, centuple *or* rational calorie, small calorie, large *or* great calorie, kilocalorie, kilogram-calorie; therm; joule

20 thermometer, thermal detector; mercury, glass; thermostat; calorimeter; thermograph, thermostat

21 <science of heat> thermochemistry, thermology, thermotics, thermodynamics; volcanology; pyrology, pyrognostics; pyrotechnics *or* pyrotechny, ebulliometry; calorimetry

VERBS **22** <be hot> **burn** 1020.24, **scorch,** parch, scald, **swelter, roast,** toast, cook, bake, fry, broil, sizzle, boil, seethe, simmer, stew; **be in heat;** shimmer with heat, give off waves of heat, radiate heat; **blaze,** combust, spark, **catch fire,** flame 1020.23, flame up, **flare,** flare up; **flicker** 1025.25; **glow,** incandesce, flush, blush, bloom; smolder; steam; sweat 12.16; gasp, pant; **suffocate, stifle,** smother, choke; keep warm; run a temperature; sunbathe

23 smoke, fume, reek, smolder; smudge; carbonize

ADJS **24 warm,** calid <old>, **thermal,** thermic; **toasty** <nf>, warm as toast; **sunny,** sunshiny, sunbaked; fair, mild, genial; summery, aestival; **temperate,**

warmish; balmy, **tropical,** equatorial, subtropical; semitropical; **tepid, lukewarm,** luke; room-temperature; blood-warm, blood-hot; unfrozen

25 hot, heated, torrid, thermal, thermic; **sweltering,** sweltry, canicular; **burning,** parching, scorching, searing, scalding, blistering, baking, roasting, toasting, broiling, grilling, simmering, sizzling; **boiling,** seething, ebullient; **piping hot,** scalding hot, burning hot, roasting hot, scorching hot, sizzling hot, smoking hot; **red-hot,** white-hot; ardent; flushed, sweating, sweaty, sudorific; overwarm, overhot, overheated; hot as fire, hot as a three-dollar pistol <nf>, hot as hell *or* blazes, hot as the hinges of hell, hot enough to roast an ox, hot enough to fry an egg on, so hot you can fry eggs on the sidewalk <nf>, like a furnace *or* an oven; feverish

26 fiery, igneous, firelike, pyric; combustive, conflagrative

27 burning, ignited, kindled, enkindled, **blazing,** ablaze, ardent, flaring, flaming, aflame, inflamed, alight, **afire, on fire,** in flames, in a blaze, flagrant <old>; conflagrant, comburent; live, living; molten; **glowing,** aglow, in a glow, incandescent, candescent, candent; sparking, scintillating, scintillant, ignescent; **flickering,** aflicker, guttering; unquenched, unextinguished; slow-burning; **smoldering; smoking,** fuming, reeking

28 sultry, stifling, suffocating, stuffy, close, oppressive, steamy; **humid, sticky** <nf>, **muggy**

29 warm-blooded, hot-blooded

30 isothermal, isothermic; centigrade, Fahrenheit

31 diathermic, diathermal, transcalent; adiathermic, adiathermal, athermanous

32 pyrological, pyrognostic, pyrotechnic *or* pyrotechnical; pyrogenic *or* pyrogenous *or* pyrogenetic; thermochemical; thermodynamic, thermodynamical

WORD ELEMENTS **33** igni-, pyr-, pyro-; therm-, thermo-, -thermous

34 fireworks

Bengali-light	flowerpot
bomb	fountain
candlebomb	girandole
cannon cracker	ladyfinger
cap	mandarin cracker
Catherine wheel	maroon
chaser	pastille
cherry bomb	peeoy
colored fire	petard
cracker	pinwheel
cracker bonbon	rocket
firecracker	Roman candle
fizgig *or* fisgig	serpent
fizzer	six-inch salute
flare	skyrocket

snake	tourbillion
sparkler	Vesuvius fountain
squib	volcano
tantrum	wheel
throwdown	whiz-bang
torpedo	

1020 HEATING

NOUNS **1 heating, warming,** calefaction, torrefaction, increase *or* raising of temperature; superheating; pyrogenesis; decalescence, recalescence; preheating; **heating system** <see list>, heating method; solar radiation, insolation; dielectric heating; induction heating; heat exchange; cooking 11

2 boiling, seething, **stewing,** ebullition, ebullience *or* ebulliency, coction; decoction; **simmering;** boil; simmer

3 melting, fusion, liquefaction, liquefying, liquescence, running; **thawing,** thaw; liquation; fusibility; thermoplasticity

4 ignition, lighting, lighting up *or* off, **kindling,** firing; reaching flash point *or* flashing point

5 burning, combustion, blazing, flaming, **scorching,** parching, singeing; **searing,** branding; **blistering,** vesication; **cauterization,** cautery; **incineration; cremation;** suttee, self-cremation, self-immolation; the stake, burning at the stake, *auto da fé* <Pg>; scorification; carbonization; oxidation, oxidization; calcination; cupellation; deflagration; distilling, distillation; refining, smelting; pyrolysis; cracking, thermal cracking, destructive distillation; **spontaneous combustion,** thermogenesis

6 burn, scald, scorch, singe; sear; brand; sunburn, sunscald; windburn; mat burn; first- *or* second- *or* third-degree burn

7 incendiarism, arson, torch job <nf>, fire-raising <Brit>; **pyromania;** pyrophilia; pyrolatry, fire worship

8 incendiary, arsonist, torcher <nf>; pyromaniac, firebug <nf>; pyrophile, fire buff <nf>; pyrolater, fire worshiper

9 flammability, inflammability, combustibility; spontaneous combustion

10 heater, warmer; stove, oven, furnace; cooker, cookery; firebox; tuyere, tewel <old>; burner, jet, gas jet, pilot light *or* burner, element, heating element, Bunsen burner; heat lamp; heating pipe, steam pipe, hot-water pipe; heating duct, caliduct

11 fireplace, hearth, ingle; **fireside,** hearthside, ingleside, inglenook, ingle cheek <Scot>, chimney corner; hearthstone; hob, hub; fireguard, fireboard, fire screen, fender; chimney, chimney piece, chimney-breast, chimney-pot, chimney-stack, flue, grate; smokehole; brazier, kiln, smelter, forge; pyre

12 fire iron; andiron, firedog; tongs, pair of tongs, fire tongs, coal tongs; poker, stove poker, salamander, fire hook; lifter, stove lifter; pothook, crook, crane, chain; trivet, tripod; spit, turnspit; grate, grating; gridiron, grid, griddle, grill, griller; damper

13 incinerator, cinerator, burner; solid-waste incinerator, garbage incinerator; **crematory,** cremator, crematorium, burning ghat; calcinatory

14 blowtorch, blowlamp <Brit>, blast lamp, torch, alcohol torch, butane torch; soldering torch; blowpipe; **burner; welder;** acetylene torch *or* welder, cutting torch *or* blowpipe, oxyacetylene blowpipe *or* torch, welding blowpipe *or* torch

15 cauterant, cauterizer, cauter, cautery, thermocautery, actual cautery; hot iron, **branding iron,** brand iron, brand; moxa; electrocautery; **caustic, corrosive,** mordant, escharotic, potential cautery; acid; lunar caustic; radium

16 <products of combustion> scoria, sullage, slag, dross; **ashes,** ash; **cinder,** clinker, coal; coke, charcoal, brand, lava, carbon, calx; **soot,** smut, coom <Brit nf>; **smoke,** smudge, fume, reek

VERBS **17 heat,** raise *or* increase the temperature, heat up, hot *or* hot up <Brit>, **warm,** fire, fire up, stoke up; chafe; take the chill off; tepefy; gas-heat, oil-heat, hot-air-heat, hot-water-heat, steam-heat, electric-heat, solar-heat; superheat; overheat; preheat; **reheat,** recook, warm over *or* up; mull; steam; foment; cook 11.5; glow; cook, roast, toast, bake, braise, broil, fry

18 <metaphors> **excite, inflame;** incite, **kindle, arouse** 375.17,19; anger, **enrage**

19 insolate, sun-dry; **sun,** bask, bask in the sun, sun oneself, sunbathe, suntan, get a tan, tan

20 boil, stew, simmer, seethe; distill; scald, parboil, steam

21 melt, melt down, liquefy; **run,** colliquate, **fuse,** flux; refine, smelt; render; **thaw,** thaw out, unfreeze; defrost, de-ice

22 ignite, set fire to, fire, set on fire, set alight, kindle, enkindle, inflame, **light,** light up, strike a light, put a match *or* torch to, torch <nf>, touch off, **burn,** conflagrate; **build a fire;** rekindle, relight, relume; feed, feed the fire, **stoke,** stoke the fire, add fuel to the flame; bank; poke *or* stir the fire, blow up the fire, fan the flame; open the draft; reduce to ashes

23 catch fire, catch on fire, catch, take fire, **burn, flame,** combust, blaze, **blaze up, burst into flames,** go up in flames

24 burn, torrefy, **scorch, parch, sear; singe,** swinge; **blister,** vesicate; **cauterize,** brand, burn in; char, coal, carbonize; scorify; calcine; pyrolyze, crack; solder, weld, fuse, lag; vulcanize; cast, found; oxidize, oxidate; deflagrate; cupel; burn off; blaze, flame 1019.22

25 burn up, incendiarize, **incinerate, cremate,** consume, burn *or* reduce to ashes, **burn to a crisp,** burn to a cinder; **burn down,** burn to the ground, **go up in smoke;** burn at the stake

ADJS **26 heating, warming,** chafing, calorific; calefactory, calefactive, calefacient, calorifacient, calorigenic; fiery, burning 1018.25,27; cauterant, cauterizing; calcinatory

27 inflammatory, inflammative, **inflaming, kindling,** enkindling, lighting; **incendiary,** incendive; arsonous

28 flammable, inflammable, combustible, burnable

29 heated, het *or* het up <nf>, hotted up <Brit>, **warmed,** warmed up, centrally heated, gas-heated, oil-heated, kerosene-heated, hot-water-heated, hot-air-heated, steam-heated, solar-heated, electric-heated, baseboard-heated; superheated; overheated; preheated; **reheated,** recooked, **warmed-over,** *réchauffé* <Fr>; hot 1019.25

30 burned, burnt, burned to the ground, incendiarized, torched <nf>, burned-out *or* -down, gutted; **scorched, blistered, parched, singed, seared, charred,** pyrographic, adust; sunburned; **burnt-up,** incinerated, cremated, consumed, consumed by fire; ashen, ashy, carbonized, pyrolyzed, pyrolytic

31 molten, melted, fused, liquefied; liquated; meltable, fusible; thermoplastic

32 heating systems

baseboard heating	hypocaust
central heating	kerosene heating
convection heating	oil heating
electric heating	panel heating
furnace heating	radiant heating
gas heating	solar heating
heat pump	space heating
hot-air heating	steam heating
hot-water heating	stove heating

1021 FUEL

NOUNS **1 fuel** <see list>, energy source; heat source, firing, combustible *or* inflammable *or* flammable material, burnable, combustible, inflammable, flammable; fossil fuel, nonrenewable energy *or* fuel source; alternate *or* alternative energy source, renewable energy *or* fuel source; solar energy, solar radiation, insolation; wind energy; geothermal energy, geothermal heat, geothermal gradient; synthetic fuels *or* synfuels; solid fuel; fuel starter; fuel additive, dope, fuel dope; propellant; **oil** 1054; gas 1067

2 slack, coal dust, coom *or* comb <Brit nf>, culm

3 firewood, stovewood, wood; woodpile; **kindling,** kindlings, kindling wood; brush, brushwood; fagot, bavin <Brit>; log, backlog, yule log *or* yule clog <old>

4 lighter, light, igniter, sparker; pocket lighter, cigar *or* cigarette lighter, butane lighter; **torch,** flambeau, taper, spill; brand, **firebrand;** portfire; **flint,** flint *and* steel; **detonator,** fuse, spark plug, ignition system

5 match, matchstick, lucifer; friction match, locofoco *and* vesuvian *and* vesta *and* fusee *and* Congreve *or* Congreve match <old>; safety match; matchbook

6 tinder, touchwood; **punk,** spunk, German tinder, amadou; tinder fungus; pyrotechnic sponge; tinderbox

7 renewable energy, soft energy; solar power, solar energy; photovoltaic cell, solar cell; wind power; geothermal energy; water power, hydroelectric power; wave power, tidal power; biomass

VERBS **8 fuel,** fuel up; fill up, top off; refuel; coal, oil, **stoke, feed,** add fuel to the flame; detonate, explode

ADJS **9 fuel,** energy, heat; fossil-fuel; alternate- *or* alternative-energy; oil-fired, coal-fired, etc; gas-powered, oil-powered, wind-powered, etc; water-driven, hydroelectric, etc; wood-burning; coaly, carbonaceous, carboniferous; anthracite; clean-burning; bituminous; high-sulfur; lignitic; peaty; gas-guzzling

10 fuels

alcohol	glance coal
anthracite *or* hard coal	grate coal
aviation fuel *or* gas	heptane
benzine	hexane
bituminous *or* soft coal	high-octane
blind coal	gasoline
briquette *or* briquet	isooctane
broken coal	jet fuel
buckwheat coal	kerosene *or* paraffin
butane	<Brit>
cannel *or* cannel coal	leaded gasoline
carbon	lignite *or* brown coal
charcoal	liquid oxygen
chestnut coal	lump coal
coal	methane
coal gas	methanol
coke	motor fuel
crude oil	mustard-seed coal
diesel fuel *or* diesel *or*	naphtha
diesel oil *or* derv <Brit>	natural gas
egg coal	nuclear power *and* nuclear
electricity	energy
ethane	nut coal
ethanol	octane
ethyl gasoline	oil *or* petroleum
flaxseed coal	pea coal
gas carbon	peat *or* turf
gasohol	pentane
gasoline *or* gas	petrol <Brit>

premium *or* high-test
  gasoline
producer *or* air gas
propane
propellant
regular gasoline
renewable energy
rocket fuel
sea coal

solar power
steamboat coal
stove coal
unleaded *or* lead-free
  gasoline
water power
white gasoline
wind power
wood

1022 INCOMBUSTIBILITY

NOUNS **1 incombustibility, uninflammability,**
noninflammability, **nonflammability;**
unburnableness; fire resistance

2 extinguishing, extinguishment, extinction,
quenching, dousing <nf>, **snuffing,** putting out;
choking, damping, stifling, smothering,
smotheration; controlling; fire fighting; going out,
dying, burning out, flame-out, burnout

3 extinguisher, fire extinguisher; fire apparatus, fire
engine, hook-and-ladder, ladder truck; ladder pipe,
snorkel, deluge set, deck gun; pumper, super-
pumper; **foam,** carbon-dioxide foam, Foamite
<trademark>, foam extinguisher; drypowder
extinguisher; carbon tetrachloride, carbon tet;
water, soda, acid, wet blanket; sprinkler, automatic
sprinkler, sprinkler system, sprinkler head;
hydrant, fire hydrant, fireplug; fire hose

4 fire fighter, fireman, fire-eater <nf>; pumpman;
forest fire fighter, fire warden, fire-chaser,
smokechaser, smokejumper; volunteer fireman,
vamp <nf>; fire department, fire brigade <chiefly
Brit>

5 fireproofing; fire resistance; fireproof *or* fire-
resistant *or* fire-resisting *or* fire-resistive *or* fire-
retardant material, fire retardant; asbestos;
amianthus, earth flax, mountain flax; asbestos
curtain, fire wall; fire break, fire line

VERBS **6 fireproof,** flameproof

7 fight fire; extinguish, put out, quench, out, douse
<nf>, **snuff,** snuff out, blow out, stamp out; stub
out, dinch <nf>; **choke, damp, smother, stifle,**
slack; bring under control, contain

8 burn out, go out, die, die out *or* down *or* away;
fizzle *and* **fizzle out** <nf>; flame out

ADJS **9 incombustible, noncombustible,**
uninflammable, noninflammable, noncombustive,
nonflammable, unburnable; asbestine, asbestous,
asbestoid, asbestoidal; amianthine

10 fireproof, flameproof, fireproofed, fire-retarded,
fire-resisting *or* -resistant *or* -resistive, fire-
retardant

11 extinguished, quenched, snuffed, **out;** contained,
under control

1023 COLD

NOUNS **1 cold, coldness; coolness,** coolth, freshness;
low temperature, arctic temperature, drop *or*
decrease in temperature, lack of heat; **chilliness,**
nippiness, freshness, crispness, briskness,
sharpness, bite; **chill, nip,** sharp air; **frigidity,**
iciness, frostiness, extreme *or* intense cold, gelidity,
algidity, algidness; **rawness,** bleakness, keenness,
sharpness, bitterness, severity, inclemency, rigor;
freezing point; cryology; cryonics; cryogenics;
absolute zero

2 <sensation of cold> **chill,** chilliness, chilling,
shivering, chills, **shivers,** cold shivers, shakes,
didders <Brit nf>, dithers, chattering of the teeth;
creeps, **cold creeps** <nf>; **gooseflesh, goose**
pimples, goose *or* duck bumps <nf>, horripilation;
frostbite, chilblains, kibe, cryopathy; ache, aching;
ice-cream headache

3 cold weather, bleak weather, raw weather, bitter
weather, wintry weather, arctic weather, **freezing**
weather, zero weather, subzero weather; **cold**
wave, snap, **cold snap,** cold spell, cold front;
freeze, frost, hard frost, deep freeze, arctic frost,
big freeze, hard freeze; winter, wintriness, depths
of winter, hard winter, arctic conditions; wintry
wind 318.8; coolness, chill, nip in the air, chilliness,
nippiness; chill factor, wind-chill factor; ice age

4 <cold place> Siberia, Hell, Novaya Zemlya,
Alaska, Iceland, the Hebrides, Greenland,
"Greenland's icy mountains"—Reginald Heber, the
Yukon, Tierra del Fuego, Lower Slobbovia <Al
Capp>; North Pole, South Pole; Frigid Zones; the
Arctic, Arctic Circle *or* Zone; Antarctica, the
Antarctic; Antarctic Circle *or* Zone; tundra; the
freezer, the deep-freeze, igloo

5 ice, frozen water; ice needle *or* crystal; **icicle,**
iceshockle <Brit nf>; cryosphere; ice sheet, ice
field, ice barrier, ice front; **floe, ice floe,** sea ice, ice
island, ice raft, ice pack; ice foot, ice belt; shelf ice,
sheet ice, pack ice, bay ice, berg ice, field ice;
iceberg, berg, growler; calf; snowberg; **icecap,**
jokul <Iceland>; ice pinnacle, serac, nieve
penitente; **glacier,** glacieret, glaciation, ice dike,
"motionless torrents, silent cataracts"—Samuel
Taylor Coleridge; piedmont glacier; icefall; ice
banner; ice cave; **sleet,** glaze, glazed frost, verglas;
snow ice; névé, black ice, granular snow, firn;
ground ice, anchor ice, frazil; lolly; sludge, slob *or*
slob ice <chiefly Can>; ice cubes; crushed ice; Dry
Ice <trademark>, solid carbon dioxide; icequake;
ice storm, freezing rain

6 hail, hailstone; soft hail, graupel, snow pellets,
tapioca snow; **hailstorm**

7 frost, Jack Frost; **hoarfrost,** hoar, rime, rime frost,

white frost; black frost; hard frost, sharp frost;
killing frost; frost smoke; frost line; permafrost;
silver frost; glaze frost; ground frost

8 snow; granular snow, corn snow, spring corn,
spring snow, powder snow, wet snow, tapioca
snow; **snowfall; snowstorm,** snow blast, snow
squall, snow flurry, flurry, snow shower, blizzard,
whiteout; **snowflake,** snow-crystal, flake, crystal;
snow dust; **snowdrift,** snowbank, snow cover, snow
blanket, snow mantle, snow wreath <Brit nf>,
driven snow, drifting snow; snowcap; snow
banner; snow blanket; snow bed, snowpack,
snowfield, mantle of snow; snowscape; snowland;
snowshed; snow line; snowball, snowman;
snowslide, snowslip, avalanche; snow slush, **slush,**
slosh, snowmelt, melt, meltwater; snowbridge;
snow fence; snowhouse, igloo; mogul

VERBS 9 freeze, be cold, grow cold, lose heat; **shiver,
quiver,** shiver to death, quake, shake, tremble,
shudder, didder <Brit nf>, dither; **chatter; chill,**
have a chill, have the cold shivers; **freeze,** freeze to
death, freeze one's balls off <nf>, die *or* perish
with the cold, horripilate, have goose pimples,
have goose *or* duck bumps <nf>; have chilblains;
get frostbite

10 <make cold> **freeze, chill,** chill to the bone *or*
marrow, make one shiver, make one's teeth chatter;
nip, bite, cut, **pierce,** penetrate, penetrate to the
bone, go through *or* right through; freshen; air-
condition; glaciate; freeze-dry; **freeze** 1024.11; frost,
frostbite; numb, benumb; **refrigerate** 1023.10

11 hail, sleet, snow; snow in; snow under; **frost,** ice,
ice up, ice over, glaze, glaze over, freeze over

ADJS 12 cool, coolish, temperate; chill, **chilly,** parky
<Brit nf>; **fresh,** brisk, crisp, bracing, sharpish,
invigorating, stimulating

13 unheated, unwarmed; unmelted, unthawed

14 cold, freezing, freezing cold, **crisp, brisk,** nipping,
nippy, snappy <nf>, **raw, bleak, keen, sharp,**
bitter, biting, pinching, cutting, **piercing,**
penetrating, perishing; inclement, severe, rigorous;
snowcold; sleety; slushy; **icy,** icelike, **ice-cold,**
glacial, ice-encrusted; cryospheric; supercooled;
frigid, bitter *or* bitterly cold, gelid, algid; below
zero, subzero; numbing; **wintry,** wintery,
winterlike, winterbound, hiemal, brumal, hibernal;
arctic, Siberian, boreal, hyperborean; stone-cold,
cold as death, cold as ice, cold as marble, cold as
charity, "cold as the north side of a gravestone in
winter"—Anon

15 <nf terms> **cold as hell,** cold as a welldigger's ass,
cold as a witch's tit *or* kiss, cold enough to freeze
the tail *or* balls off a brass monkey, cold as a
bastard *or* a bitch, colder than hell *or* the deuce *or*
the devil

16 <feeling cold> **cold, freezing; cool, chilly,** nippy;
shivering, shivery, shaky, dithery; algid, aguish,
aguey; chattering, with chattering teeth; **frozen**
1023.14, half-frozen, frozen to death, chilled to the
bone, blue with cold, *figé de froid* <Fr>, so cold
one could spit ice cubes

17 frosty, frostlike; **frosted,** frosted-over, frost-beaded,
frost-covered, frost-chequered, rimed, **hoary,**
hoar-frosted, rime-frosted; frost-riven, frost-rent;
frosty-faced, frosty-whiskered; frostbound,
frost-fettered

18 snowy, snowlike, niveous, nival; snow-blown,
snow-drifted, snow-driven; **snow-covered,** snow-
clad, snow-mantled, snow-robed, snow-blanketed,
snow-sprinkled, snow-lined, snow-encircled, snow-
laden, snow-loaded, snow-hung; **snow-capped,**
snow-peaked, snow-crested, snow-crowned, snow-
tipped, snow-topped; snow-bearded; snow-
feathered; snow-still

19 frozen out *or* in, **snowbound,** snowed-in, **icebound**

20 cold-blooded, hypothermic, heterothermic,
poikilothermic; cryogenic; cryological

WORD ELEMENTS 21 cryo- *or* kryo-, frigo-, psychro-;
glacio-; chio-, chion-

1024 REFRIGERATION
<reduction of temperature>

NOUNS 1 refrigeration, infrigidation, reduction of
temperature; **cooling, chilling; freezing,**
glacification, glaciation, congelation, congealment;
refreezing, regelation; mechanical refrigeration,
electric refrigeration, electronic refrigeration, gas
refrigeration; food freezing, quick freezing, deep
freezing, sharp freezing, blast freezing,
dehydrofreezing; adiabatic expansion, adiabatic
absorption, adiabatic demagnetization; cryogenics;
super-cooling; air conditioning, **air cooling,**
climatisation <Fr>; climate control

2 refrigeration anesthesia, crymoanesthesia,
hypothermia *or* hypothermy; crymotherapy, cryo-
aerotherapy; cold cautery, cryocautery; cryopathy

3 cooler, chiller; water cooler, air cooler, air
conditioner; ventilator; fan; surface cooler; ice
cube, ice pail *or* bucket, wine cooler; ice bag, ice
pack, cold pack

4 refrigerator, refrigeratory, **icebox,** ice chest;
Frigidaire <trademark>, fridge <nf>, electric
refrigerator, electronic refrigerator, gas
refrigerator, refrigerator-freezer; refrigerator car,
refrigerator truck, reefer <nf>; freezer ship; ice
house

5 freezer, deep freeze, deep-freezer, quick-freezer,
sharp-freezer; ice-cream freezer; ice machine, ice-
cube machine, freezing machine, refrigerating

machine *or* engine; **ice plant,** icehouse, refrigerating plant

6 **cold storage; frozen-food locker,** locker, freezer locker, locker plant; coolhouse; coolerman; frigidarium; cooling tower

7 <cooling agent> **coolant; refrigerant;** cryogen; ice, Dry Ice <trademark>, ice cubes; freezing mixture, liquid air, ammonia, carbon dioxide, Freon <trademark>, ether; ethyl chloride; liquid air, liquid oxygen *or* lox, liquid nitrogen, liquid helium, etc

8 **antifreeze,** coolant, radiator coolant, alcohol, ethylene glycol

9 refrigerating engineering, refrigerating engineer

VERBS 10 **refrigerate; cool, chill;** refresh, freshen; ice, ice-cool; water-cool, air-cool; **air-condition;** ventilate

11 **freeze** 1023.9,10, ice, glaciate, congeal; **deep-freeze,** quick-freeze, sharp-freeze, blast-freeze; freeze solid; freeze-dry; **nip,** blight, blast; refreeze, regelate

ADJS 12 **refrigerative,** refrigeratory, refrigerant, frigorific, algific; **cooling, chilling; freezing,** congealing; quick-freezing, deep-freezing, sharp-freezing, blast-freezing; freezable, glaciable

13 **cooled, chilled; air-conditioned;** iced, ice-cooled; air-cooled, water-cooled; super-cooled

14 **frozen,** frozen solid, glacial, gelid, congealed; icy, ice-cold, icy-cold, ice, icelike; deep-frozen, quick-frozen, sharp-frozen, blast-frozen; frostbitten, frostnipped

15 antifreeze, antifreezing

1025 LIGHT

NOUNS 1 **light,** radiant *or* luminous energy, visible radiation, radiation in the visible spectrum, **illumination,** illuminance, **radiation, radiance** *or* radiancy, irradiance *or* irradiancy, irradiation, emanation; "God's first creature"—Francis Bacon, "the first of painters"—Emerson, "the white radiance of eternity"—Shelley; light wave; highlight; sidelight; photosensitivity; light source 1026; **invisible light,** black light, infrared light, ultraviolet light

2 **shine,** shininess, **luster, sheen, gloss,** glint, glister; **glow, gleam,** flush, sunset glow; light emission; lambency; **incandescence,** candescence; shining light; afterglow; skylight, air glow, night glow, day glow, twilight glow

3 **lightness, luminousness,** lightedness, luminosity, luminance; **lucidity,** lucence *or* lucency, translucence *or* translucency; backlight

4 **brightness, brilliance** *or* brilliancy, **splendor,** radiant splendor, **glory, radiance** *or* radiancy,

resplendence *or* resplendency, **vividness,** luminance, contrast, flamboyance *or* flamboyancy; effulgence, refulgence *or* refulgency, fulgentness, fulgidity, fulgor; **glare,** blare, blaze; bright light, brilliant light, blazing light, glaring light, dazzling light, blinding light; TV lights, Klieg light, footlights, house lights; streaming light, flood of light, burst of light

5 **ray,** radiation 1037, **beam, gleam,** leam <Scot>, **stream, streak, pencil, patch,** ray of light, beam of light; "slant of light"—Emily Dickinson; ribbon, ribbon of light, streamer, stream of light; electromagnetic radiation; violet ray, ultraviolet ray, infrared ray, X ray, gamma ray, invisible radiation; actinic ray *or* light, actinism; atomic beam, atomic ray; laser beam; solar rays; photon; visible spectrum

6 **flash, blaze, flare, flame, gleam, glint, glance;** blaze *or* flash *or* gleam of light; green flash; solar flare, solar prominence, facula; Bailey's beads

7 **glitter, glimmer, shimmer, twinkle, blink; sparkle,** spark; **scintillation,** scintilla; coruscation; **glisten,** glister, spangle, tinsel, glittering, glimmering, shimmering, twinkling; stroboscopic *or* strobe light <nf>, blinking; firefly, glowworm

8 **flicker, flutter, dance, quiver;** flickering, fluttering, bickering, guttering, dancing, quivering, lambency; wavering *or* flickering light, play, play of light, dancing *or* glancing light; light show; "the lambent easy light"—Dryden

9 **reflection;** reflected *or* incident light; reflectance, albedo; blink, iceblink, ice sky, snowblink, waterblink, water sky

10 **daylight,** dayshine, day glow, light of day; day, daytime, daytide; **natural light; sunlight, sunshine,** shine; noonlight, white light, midday sun, noonday *or* noontide light, "the blaze of noon"—Milton; broad day *or* daylight, full sun; bright time; dusk, twilight 315.3; the break *or* crack of dawn, cockcrow, dawn 314.4; sunburst, sunbreak; **sunbeam,** sun spark, ray of sunshine; green flash; solar energy

11 **moonlight, moonshine,** moonglow; **moonbeam,** moonrise

12 **starlight,** starshine; earthshine

13 **luminescence;** luciferin, luciferase; phosphor, luminophor; **ignis fatuus, will-o'-the-wisp,** will-with-the-wisp, wisp, jack-o'-lantern, marshfire; friar's lantern; fata morgana; fox fire; St Elmo's light *or* fire, corona discharge, wild fire, witch fire, corposant; double corposant; bioluminescence, thermoluminescence, fluorescence, phosphorescence, radioluminescence

14 **halo, nimbus,** aura, **aureole,** circle, ring, glory; **rainbow,** solar halo, lunar halo, ring around the

sun *or* moon; white rainbow *or* fogbow; **corona,** solar corona, lunar corona; parhelion, parhelic circle *or* ring, mock sun, sun dog; anthelion, antisun, countersun; paraselene, mock moon, moon dog

15 <nebulous light> nebula 1072.7; zodiacal light, gegenschein, counterglow, streamers

16 polar lights, **aurora; northern lights, aurora borealis,** merry dancers; southern lights, **aurora australis;** aurora polaris; aurora glory; streamer *or* curtain *or* arch aurora; polar ray

17 **lightning, flash** *or* **stroke of lightning,** fulguration, fulmination, bolt, lightning strike, **bolt of lightning,** streak, bolt from the blue, **thunderbolt,** thunderstroke, thunderball, fireball, firebolt, levin bolt *or* brand; "the lightning's gleaming rod"— Joaquin Miller, fork *or* forked lightning, chain lightning, globular *or* ball lightning, summer *or* heat lightning, sheet lightning, dark lightning; Jupiter Fulgur *or* Fulminator; Thor

18 **iridescence,** opalescence, nacreousness, pearliness; **rainbow;** nacre, mother-of-pearl; nacreous *or* mother-of-pearl cloud

19 **lighting, illumination,** artificial light *or* lighting; lamp light, arc light, calcium light, candlelight, electric light, fluorescent light, gaslight, incandescent light, mercury-vapor light, neon light, sodium light, strobe light, torchlight, streetlight, floodlight, spotlight; Christmas tree lights, safety light; tonality; light and shade, black and white, chiaroscuro, clairobscure, contrast, highlights; photoemission, light-emitting diode *or* LED, liquid-crystal display *or* LCD, light pen

20 **illuminant,** luminant; electricity; gas, illuminating gas; oil, petroleum, benzine; gasoline, petrol <Brit>; kerosene, paraffin <Brit>, coal oil; light source 1025; fire, lantern

21 <measurement of light> **candle power,** luminous intensity, luminous power, luminous flux, flux, intensity, light; quantum, **light quantum, photon;** unit of light, unit of flux; lux, candle-meter, lumen meter, lumeter, lumen, candle lumen; **exposure meter,** light meter, ASA scale, Scheiner scale

22 <light units> *bougie décimale* <Fr>, British candle, candle, candle-foot, candle-hour, decimal candle, foot-candle, Hefner candle, international candle, lamp-hour, lumen-hour

23 <science of light> photics, photology, photometry; **optics,** geometrical optics, physical optics; dioptrics, catoptrics, fiber optics; actinology, actinometry; heliology, heliometry, heliography

VERBS 24 **shine,** shine forth, **burn, give light,** incandesce; glow, beam, gleam, glint, luster, glance; **flash, flare, blaze, flame,** fulgurate; **radiate,** shoot, shoot out rays, send out rays; spread *or*

diffuse light; be bright, shine brightly, beacon; **glare;** daze, blind, dazzle, bedazzle

25 **glitter, glimmer, shimmer, twinkle, blink,** spangle, tinsel, coruscate; **sparkle,** spark, **scintillate; glisten,** glister, glisk <Scot>

26 **flicker,** bicker, gutter, **flutter, waver, dance,** play, quiver

27 **luminesce,** phosphoresce, fluoresce; iridesce, opalesce

28 **grow light,** grow bright, light, **lighten,** brighten; dawn, break

29 **illuminate,** illumine, illume, luminate, **light, light up, lighten,** enlighten, brighten, brighten up, irradiate; bathe *or* flood with light; relumine, relume; **shed light upon,** cast *or* throw light upon, shed luster on, shine upon, overshine; spotlight, highlight; floodlight; beacon

30 **strike a light,** light, **turn** *or* **switch on the light,** open the light <nf>, make a light, shine a light

ADJS 31 **luminous,** luminant, luminative, luminificent, luminiferous, luciferous *or* lucific <old>, luciform, illuminant; **incandescent,** candescent; **lustrous,** orient; **radiant,** irradiative; **shining,** shiny, burning, lamping, streaming; **beaming,** beamy; **gleaming,** gleamy, glinting; **glowing,** aglow, suffused, blushing, flushing; rutilant, rutilous; **sunny, sunshiny,** bright and sunny, light as day; starry, starlike, starbright

32 **light,** lightish, lightsome; **lucid,** lucent, luculent, relucent; translucent, translucid, pellucid, diaphanous, transparent; **clear,** serene; **cloudless,** unclouded, unobscured

33 **bright, brilliant, vivid, splendid,** splendorous, splendent, **resplendent,** bright and shining; fulgid <old>, fulgent, effulgent, refulgent; **flamboyant,** flaming; **glaring,** glary, garish; **dazzling,** bedazzling, blinding, pitiless; shadowless, shadeless

34 **shiny,** shining, **lustrous, glossy,** glassy, *glacé* <Fr>, bright as a new penny, **sheeny, polished,** burnished, shined

35 **flashing,** flashy, **blazing, flaming, flaring, burning,** fulgurant, fulgurating; aflame, ablaze; meteoric

36 **glittering, glimmering, shimmering, twinkling, blinking, glistening,** glistering; glittery, glimmery, glimmerous, shimmery, twinkly, blinky, spangly, tinselly; **sparkling, scintillating,** scintillant, scintillescent, coruscating, coruscant

37 **flickering,** bickering, **fluttering, wavering, dancing,** playing, quivering, lambent; flickery, flicky <nf>, aflicker, fluttery, wavery, quivery; blinking, flashing, stroboscopic

38 **iridescent,** opalescent, nacreous, pearly, pearl-like; rainbowlike

39 **luminescent,** photogenic; autoluminescent, bioluminescent

40 illuminated, luminous, **lightened,** enlightened, brightened, **lighted,** lit, **lit up,** well-lit, flooded *or* bathed with light, floodlit; irradiated, irradiate; **alight, glowing,** aglow, lambent, suffused with light; ablaze, blazing, in a blaze, fiery; lamplit, lanternlit, candlelit, torchlit, gaslit, firelit; sunlit, moonlit, starlit; spangled, bespangled, tinseled, studded; starry, starbright, star-spangled, star-studded

41 illuminating, illumining, **lighting, lightening,** brightening

42 luminary, photic; photologic *or* photological; photometric *or* photometrical; heliological, heliographic; actinic, photoactinic; catoptric *or* catoptrical; luminal

43 photosensitive; photophobic; phototropic

WORD ELEMENTS **44** phot-, photo-, lumin-, lumino-, lumini-; fluoro- *or* fluori-; irido-; actino-, actini-

1026 LIGHT SOURCE

NOUNS **1 light source,** source of light, **luminary,** illuminator, luminant, illuminant, incandescent body *or* point, **light,** glim; **lamp,** light bulb, electric light bulb, lantern, candle, taper, torch, flame; match; **fluorescent light, fluorescent tube,** fluorescent lamp; starter, ballast; "a lamp unto my feet, and a light unto my path"—Bible; fire 1019.13; sun, moon, stars 1072.4

2 candle, taper; dip, farthing dip, tallow dip; tallow candle; wax candle, bougie; bayberry candle; rush candle, rushlight; corpse candle; votary candle

3 torch, flaming torch, flambeau, cresset, link <old>; **flare,** signal flare, fusee; beacon

4 traffic light *or* light, stop-and-go light; stop *or* red light, go *or* green light, caution *or* amber light, pedestrian light

5 firefly, lightning bug, lampyrid, **glowworm,** fireworm; fire beetle; lantern fly, candle fly; luciferin, luciferase; phosphor, luminophor

6 chandelier, gasolier, electrolier, hanging *or* ceiling fixture, luster; corona, corona lucis, crown, circlet; light holder, light fixture, candlestick

7 wick, taper; candlewick, lampwick

1027 DARKNESS, DIMNESS

NOUNS **1 darkness, dark, lightlessness; obscurity,** obscure, tenebrosity, tenebrousness, leadenness; **night** 315.4, dead of night, deep night; sunlessness, moonlessness, starlessness; **pitch-darkness,** pitch-blackness, utter *or* thick *or* total darkness, intense darkness, velvet darkness, Cimmerian *or* Stygian *or* Egyptian darkness, Stygian gloom, Erebus; "the

suit of night"—Shakespeare, "darkness which may be felt"—Bible; **blackness,** swarthiness 38.2; darkest hour

2 darkishness, darksomeness, **duskiness,** duskness; **murkiness, murk; dimness,** dim, dimming; **semidarkness,** semidark, partial darkness, bad light, dim light, half-light, *demi-jour* <Fr>; gloaming, crepuscular light, **dusk,** twilight 314.4,315.3; romantic lighting, dimmed lights

3 shadow, shade, shadiness; umbra, umbrage, umbrageousness; thick *or* dark shade, gloom; mere shadow; penumbra; silhouette; skiagram, skiagraph

4 gloom, gloominess, somberness, sombrousness, somber; lowering, lower

5 dullness, flatness, lifelessness, **drabness, deadness,** somberness, **lackluster, lusterlessness,** lack of sparkle *or* sheen; matte, matte finish

6 darkening, dimming, bedimming; obscuration, obscurement, obumbration, obfuscation; eclipsing, occulting, blocking the light; **shadowing, shading,** overshadowing, overshading, overshadowment, **clouding,** overclouding, obnubilation, gathering of the clouds, overcast; blackening 38.5; extinguishment 1022.2; hatching, cross-hatching

7 blackout, dimout, brownout; fadeout

8 eclipse, occultation; total eclipse, partial eclipse, central eclipse, annular eclipse; solar eclipse, lunar eclipse

VERBS **9 darken,** bedarken; **obscure,** obfuscate, obumbrate; **eclipse,** occult, occultate, block the light; **black out,** brown out; black, brown; blot out; **overcast,** darken over; **shadow, shade,** cast a shadow, spread a shadow *or* shade over, encompass with shadow, overshadow; **cloud,** becloud, encloud, cloud over, overcloud, obnubilate; gloom, begloom, somber, cast a gloom over, murk; **dim, bedim,** dim out; blacken 38.7

10 dull, mat, deaden; **tone down**

11 turn *or* switch off the light, close the light <nf>; extinguish 1022.7

12 grow dark, darken, darkle, lower *or* lour; gloom <old>, gloam <Scot>; dusk; **dim, grow dim;** go out

ADJS **13 dark, black,** darksome, darkling; **lightless,** beamless, rayless, unlighted, **unilluminated,** unlit; obscure, caliginous, **obscured,** obfuscated, eclipsed, occulted, clothed *or* shrouded *or* veiled *or* cloaked *or* mantled in darkness; tenebrous, tenebrific, tenebrious, tenebrose; Cimmerian, Stygian; **pitch-dark,** pitch-black, pitchy, dark as pitch, "dark as a wolf's mouth"—Sir Walter Scott, dark as the inside of a black cat; ebon, ebony; night-dark, night-black, dark *or* black as night; night-clad, night-cloaked, night-enshrouded, nightmantled, night-veiled, night-hid, night-filled; sunless, moonless, starless

14 gloomy, gloomful <old>, glooming, dark and gloomy, Acheronian, Acherontic, **somber,** sombrous; lowering; **funereal;** stormy, cloudy, clouded, overcast; ill-lighted, ill-lit

15 darkish, darksome, **semidark; dusky,** dusk; fuscous, subfuscous, subfusc; **murky,** murksome, murk <old>; **dim,** dimmed, bedimmed, dimmish, dimpsy <Brit nf>, half-lit, semidark; dark-colored 38.9

16 shadowy, shady, shadowed, shaded, casting a shadow, tenebrous, darkling, umbral, umbrageous; overshadowed, overshaded, obumbrate, obumbrated; penumbral

17 lackluster, lusterless; dull, dead, deadened, **lifeless,** somber, **drab,** wan, **flat,** mat, murky

18 obscuring, obscurant

ADVS **19 in the dark,** darkling, in darkness; in the night, in the dark of night, in the dead of night, at *or* by night; dimly, wanly

1028 SHADE
<a thing that shades>

NOUNS **1 shade,** shader, **screen, light shield, curtain,** drape, drapery, blind, veil; **awning,** sunblind <Brit>; **sunshade,** parasol, **umbrella,** beach umbrella; cover 295.2; shadow 1027.3; partial eclipse

2 eyeshade, eyeshield, visor, bill; goggles, colored spectacles, smoked glasses, dark glasses, **sunglasses,** shades <nf>

3 lamp shade; moonshade; globe, light globe

4 light filter, filter, diffusing screen; smoked glass, frosted glass, ground glass; stained glass; butterfly; gelatin filter, celluloid filter; frosted lens; lens hood; sunscreen

VERBS **5 shade, screen,** veil, curtain, shutter, draw the curtains, put up *or* close the shutters; cover 295.19; **shadow** 1027.9; cast a shadow

ADJS **6 shading, screening,** veiling, curtaining; shadowing; covering

7 shaded, screened, veiled, curtained; sunproof; visored; shadowed, shady 1027.16

1029 TRANSPARENCY

NOUNS **1 transparency,** transparence, transpicuousness, show-through, transmission *or* admission of light; **lucidity,** pellucidity, **clearness, clarity,** limpidity; nonopacity, uncloudedness; **crystallinity,** crystal-clearness; **glassiness,** glasslikeness, vitreousness, vitrescence; vitreosity, hyalescence; **diaphanousness,** diaphaneity,

sheerness, thinness, **gossameriness,** filminess, gauziness; colorlessness

2 transparent substance, diaphane; **glass** <see list>, glassware, glasswork; vitrics; stemware; window, pane, windowpane, light, windowlight, shopwindow; vitrine; showcase, display case; watch crystal *or* glass; water, air

VERBS **3** be transparent, show through; pass *or* transmit light; vitrify; reveal; crystallize

ADJS **4 transparent,** transpicuous, light-pervious; show-through, see-through, peekaboo, revealing; **lucid,** lucent, pellucid, **clear,** limpid; nonopaque, colorless, unclouded, **crystalline,** crystal, **crystal-clear,** clear as crystal; **diaphanous,** diaphane <old>, sheer, thin; **gossamer,** gossamery, filmy, flimsy, gauzy, open-textured; insubstantial

5 glass, glassy, glasslike, clear as glass, vitric, vitreous, vitriform, hyaline, hyalescent; hyalinocrystalline

WORD ELEMENTS **6** vitri-

7 glass

agate glass	lace glass
antimony glass	Lalique glass
arsenic glass	laminated glass *or*
Baccarat glass	laminated safety glass
basalt glass	lead crystal
Bilbao glass	lead glass
borax glass	milk glass
blown glass	mirror
bone glass	obsidian
bottle glass	opal glass
bulletproof glass	opaline
camphor glass	optical glass
carnival glass	ornamental glass
Chevalier glass	Orrefors glass
coralene	photosensitive glass
cranberry glass	plastic glass
crown glass	plate glass
cryolite glass	porcelain glass
crystal *or* crystal glass	pressed glass
custard glass	prism glass
cut glass	Pyrex <trademark>
etched glass	quartz glass
Fiberglas <trademark>	reinforced glass
flashed glass	rhinestone
flat glass	rock crystal
flint glass	ruby glass
float glass	safety glass
Fostoria <trademark>	Sandwich glass
frosted glass	satin glass
fused quartz	sheet glass
glass bead	show glass
glass brick	Silex glass <trademark>
glass wool	stained glass
ground glass	Steuben glass
hobnail glass	Swedish glass
ice glass	Syracuse watch glass

tempered glass *or*
   tempered safety glass
uranium glass
uviol glass
Venetian glass

Vitaglass <trademark>
vitreous silica
Waterford glass
window glass
wire *or* wired glass

1030 SEMITRANSPARENCY

NOUNS **1 semitransparency,** semipellucidity,
semidiaphaneity; semiopacity
  2 translucence, translucency, lucence, lucency,
translucidity, pellucidity, lucidity; transmission *or*
admission of light; milkiness, pearliness,
opalescence
VERBS **3 frost,** frost over
ADJS **4 semitransparent,** semipellucid,
semidiaphanous, semiopaque; frosty, frosted;
milky, pearly, opalescent, opaline
  5 translucent, lucent, translucid, lucid, pellucid;
semitranslucent, semipellucid

1031 OPAQUENESS

NOUNS **1 opaqueness,** opacity, intransparency,
nontranslucency, imperviousness to light,
adiaphanousness; roil, roiledness, turbidity,
turbidness; cloudiness; blackness; **darkness,
obscurity,** inscrutability, **dimness** 1027
VERBS **2** opaque, **darken, obscure** 1027.9; **cloud,**
becloud; devitrify
ADJS **3 opaque,** intransparent, nontransparent,
nontranslucent, adiaphanous, impervious to light,
impenetrable; **dark,** black, **obscure** 1026.13,
lightproof; **cloudy,** roiled, roily, grumly <Scot>,
turbid; covered; semiopaque

1032 ELECTRICITY, MAGNETISM

NOUNS **1 electricity; electrical science** <see list>;
electrical *or* **electric unit,** unit of measurement
  2 current, electric current <see list>, current flow,
amperage, electric stream *or* flow, juice <nf>
  3 electric *or* **electrical field,** static field, electrostatic
field, field of electrical force; tube of electric force,
electrostatic tube of force; **magnetic field,**
magnetic field of currents; **electromagnetic field;**
variable field
  4 circuit, electrical circuit, path
  5 charge, electric *or* **electrical charge,** positive
charge, negative charge; live wire
  6 discharge, arc, electric discharge; **shock,**
electroshock, galvanic shock
  7 magnetism, magnetic attraction;
electromagnetism; magnetization; diamagnetism,
paramagnetism, ferromagnetism; residual

magnetism, magnetic remanence; magnetic
memory, magnetic retentiveness; magnetic
elements; magnetic dip *or* inclination, magnetic
variation *or* declination; hysteresis, magnetic
hysteresis, hysteresis curve, magnetic friction,
magnetic lag *or* retardation, magnetic creeping;
permeability, magnetic permeability, magnetic
conductivity; magnetic circuit, magnetic curves,
magnetic figures; magnetic flux, gilbert, weber,
maxwell; magnetic moment; magnetic potential;
magnetic viscosity; magnetics
  8 polarity, polarization; **pole, positive pole, anode,
negative pole, cathode,** magnetic pole, magnetic
axis; north pole, N pole; south pole, S pole
  9 magnetic force *or* **intensity,** magnetic flux density,
gauss, oersted; magnetomotive force;
magnetomotivity; magnetic tube of force; line of
force; **magnetic field, electromagnetic field**
 10 electromagnetic radiation, light, radio wave,
microwave, infrared radiation, visible radiation,
ultraviolent radiation *or* UV, UVA, UVB, X-rays,
gamma rays; radar; electromagnetic spectrum,
visible spectrum, radio spectrum
 11 electroaffinity, electric attraction; electric repulsion
 12 voltage, volt, **electromotive force** *or* EMF,
electromotivity, potential difference; **potential,
electric potential;** tension, high tension, low
tension
 13 resistance, ohm, ohms, ohmage, ohmic resistance,
electric resistance; surface resistance, skin effect,
volume resistance; insulation resistance;
reluctance, magnetic **reluctance** *or* resistance;
specific reluctance, reluctivity; **reactance,**
inductive reactance, capacitive reactance;
impedance
 14 conduction, electric conduction; **conductance,**
conductivity, mho; superconductivity; gas
conduction, ionic conduction, metallic
conduction, liquid conduction, photoconduction;
conductor, semiconductor, superconductor;
nonconductor, dielectric, insulator
 15 induction; electrostatic induction, magnetic
induction, electromagnetic induction,
electromagnetic induction of currents; self-
induction, mutual induction; **inductance,**
inductivity, henry
 16 capacitance, capacity, farad; collector junction
capacitance, emitter junction capacitance,
resistance capacitance
 17 gain, available gain, current gain, operational gain
 18 electric power, wattage, watts; electric
horsepower; hydroelectric power, hydroelectricity;
power load
 19 powerhouse, power station, power plant, central
station; oil-fired power plant, coal-fired power

plant; hydroelectric plant; nuclear *or* atomic power plant; power grid, distribution system

20 blackout, power failure, power cut, power loss; **brownout,** voltage drop, voltage loss

21 electrical device, electrical appliance; **battery** <see list>, accumulator, storage battery, storage device; **electric meter,** meter; **wire, cable,** electric wire, electric cord, cord, power cord, power cable

22 electrician, electrotechnician; radio technician 1034.24; wireman; **lineman,** linesman; rigger; groundman; power worker

23 electrotechnologist, electrobiologist, electrochemist, electrometallurgist, electrophysicist, electrophysiologist, **electrical engineer**

24 electrification, electrifying, supplying electricity

25 electrolysis; ionization; galvanization, electrogalvanization; electrocoating, electroplating, electrogilding, electrograving, electroetching; ion, cation, anion; electrolyte, ionogen; nonelectrolyte

VERBS **26 electrify, galvanize,** energize, **charge;** wire, wire up; shock; **generate,** step up, amplify, stiffen; step down; plug in, loop in; switch on *or* off, turn on *or* off, turn on *or* off the juice <nf>; short-circuit, short

27 magnetize; electromagnetize; demagnetize, degauss

28 electrolyze; ionize; galvanize, electrogalvanize; electroplate, electrogild

29 insulate, isolate; **ground**

ADJS **30 electric, electrical, electrifying;** galvanic, voltaic; dynamoelectric, hydroelectric, photoelectric, piezoelectric, etc; electrothermal, electrochemical, electromechanical, electropneumatic, electrodynamic, static, electrostatic; electromotive; electrokinetic; electroscopic, galvanoscopic; electrometric, galvanometric, voltametric; **electrified,** electric-powered, battery-powered, cordless; solar-powered

31 magnetic, electromagnetic; diamagnetic, paramagnetic, ferromagnetic; **polar**

32 electrolytic; hydrolytic; ionic, anionic, cationic; ionogenic

33 electrotechnical; electroballistic, electrobiological, electrochemical, electrometallurgical, electrophysiological

34 charged, electrified, live, hot; high-tension, low-tension

35 positive, plus, electropositive; **negative,** minus, electronegative

36 nonconducting, nonconductive, insulating, dielectric

WORD ELEMENTS **37** electr-, electro-; rheo-; magnet-, magneto-

38 electrical sciences

electrical engineering	electrophysiology
electroacoustics	electrostatics
electroballistics	electrotechnology *or*
electrobiology	electrotechnics
electrochemistry	electrotherapeutics *or*
electrodynamics	electrotherapy
electrokinematics	electrothermics
electrokinetics	galvanism
electromagnetics	hydroelectricity
electromechanics	magnetics
electrometallurgy	magnetometry
electrometry	photoelectricity
electronics	pyroelectricity
electro-optics	thermionics
electrophotomicrography	thermoelectricity
electrophysics	voltaism

39 electric currents

absorption current	low-frequency current
active current	magnetizing current
alternating current *or* AC	multiphase current
conduction current	oscillating current
convection current	pulsating direct current
delta current	reactive current
dielectric displacement current	rotary current
direct current *or* DC	single-phase alternating current
displacement current	stray current
eddy current	supercurrent
emission current	thermionic current
exciting current	thermoelectric current
free alternating current	three-phase alternating current
galvanic current	current
high-frequency current	transient current
induced current	voltaic current
induction current	watt current
ionization current	wattless *or* idle current
juice <nf>	

40 batteries

A battery	Leyden battery
AA battery	Leyden jar
AAA battery	mercury cell
acid cell	nickel-cadmium battery
accumulator	nine-volt battery
air cell	primary battery
alkaline cell	primary cell
atomic battery	secondary battery
B battery	secondary cell
C battery	solar battery
cell	solar cell
D battery	storage battery
dry battery	storage cell
dry cell	voltaic battery
electronic battery	voltaic cell
fuel cell	voltaic pile
lead-acid battery	wet cell

1033 ELECTRONICS

NOUNS **1 electronics,** radionics, radioelectronics; electron physics, electrophysics, electron dynamics; electron optics; semiconductor physics, transistor physics; photoelectronics, photoelectricity; microelectronics; electronic engineering; avionics; electron microscopy; nuclear physics 1038; radio 1033; television 1035; radar 1036; automation 1041

2 <electron theory> electron theory of atoms, electron theory of electricity, electron theory of solids, free electron theory of metals, band theory of solids

3 electron <see list>, negatron, cathode particle, beta particle; thermion; electron capture, electron transfer; electron spin; electron state, energy level; ground state, excited state; electron pair, lone pair, shared pair, electron-positron pair, duplet, octet; electron cloud; shells, electron layers, electron shells, valence shell, valence electrons, subvalent electrons; electron affinity, relative electron affinity

4 electronic effect; Edison effect, thermionic effect, photoelectric effect

5 electron emission; thermionic emission; photoelectric emission, photoemission; collision emission, bombardment emission, secondary emission; field emission; grid emission, thermionic grid emission; electron ray, electron beam, cathode ray, anode ray, positive ray, canal ray; glow discharge, cathode glow, cathodoluminescence, cathodofluorescence; electron diffraction

6 electron flow, electron stream, electron *or* **electronic current;** electric current 1032.2; electron gas, electron cloud, space charge

7 electron volt; ionization potential; input voltage, output voltage; base signal voltage, collector signal voltage, emitter signal voltage; battery supply voltage; screen-grid voltage; inverse peak voltage; voltage saturation

8 electronic circuit, transistor circuit, semiconductor circuit; vacuum-tube circuit, thermionic tube circuit; **printed circuit, microcircuit; chip, silicon chip,** microchip; **circuitry**

9 conductance, electronic conductance; **resistance,** electronic resistance

10 electron tube, vacuum tube, tube, valve <Brit>, thermionic tube; radio tube, television tube; **special-purpose tube; vacuum tube component**

11 photoelectric tube *or* **cell, phototube,** photocell; electron-ray tube, **electric eye;** photosensitivity, **photosensitive devices**

12 transistor, semiconductor *or* solid-state device

13 electronic device, electronic meter, electronic measuring device; **electronic tester,** electronic testing device

14 electronics engineer, electronics physicist

ADJS **15 electronic;** photoelectronic, **photoelectric;** autoelectronic; microelectronic; thermoelectronic; thermionic; anodic, cathodic; transistorized

16 electrons

beta particle	p-electron
bonding electron	peripheral electron
bound electron	photoelectron
conduction electron	planetary electron
d-electron	positive electron
delta ray	primary electron
excess electron	recoil electron
extranuclear electron	secondary electron
f-electron	s-electron
free electron	spinning electron
negaton <old>	surface-bound electron
nuclear electron	valence electron
orbital electron	wandering electron

1034 RADIO

NOUNS **1 radio, wireless** <Brit>; radiotelephony, radiotelegraphy; radio communications, telecommunication 347.1

2 radiotechnology, radio engineering, communication engineering; radio electronics, radioacoustics; radiogoniometry; conelrad *or* Control of Electromagnetic Radiation for Civil Defense <old>, emergency warning network

3 radio, radio receiver <see list>; radio telescope; **radio set, receiver,** receiving set, **wireless** *and* wireless set <Brit>, set; cabinet, console, housing; chassis; receiver part

4 radio transmitter <see list>, **transmitter;** transmitter part; microphone 50.9, radiomicrophone; **antenna,** aerial

5 radiomobile, mobile transmitter, remote-pickup unit

6 radio station, transmitting station, **studio,** studio plant; AM station, FM station, shortwave station, ultrahigh-frequency station, clear-channel station; direction-finder station, RDF station; relay station, radio relay station, microwave relay station; amateur station, ham station <nf>, ham shack <nf>; pirate radio station, offshore station

7 control room, mixing room, monitor room, monitoring booth; **control desk,** console, master control desk, instrument panel, control panel *or* board, jack field, mixer <nf>

8 network, net, radio links, **hookup,** communications net, circuit, network stations, network affiliations, affiliated stations; coaxial network, circuit network, coast-to-coast hookup

9 radio circuit, radio-frequency circuit, audio-frequency circuit, superheterodyne circuit, amplifying circuit; electronic circuit 1033.8

10 radio signal, radio-frequency *or* RF signal, direct signal, shortwave signal, AM signal, FM signal; reflected signal, bounce; unidirectional signal, beam; signal-noise ratio; **radio-frequency** *or* **RF amplifier,** radio-frequency *or* RF stage

11 radio wave, electric wave, electromagnetic wave, hertzian wave; shortwave, long wave, microwave, high-frequency wave, low-frequency wave, medium wave; ground wave, sky wave; carrier, carrier wave; **wavelength**

12 frequency; radio frequency *or* RF, intermediate frequency *or* IF, audio frequency *or* AF; high frequency *or* HF; very high frequency *or* VHF; ultrahigh frequency *or* UHF; superhigh frequency *or* SHF; extremely high frequency *or* EHF; medium frequency *or* MF; low frequency *or* LF; very low frequency *or* VLF; upper frequencies, lower frequencies; **carrier frequency;** spark frequency; spectrum, frequency spectrum; cycles, CPS, hertz, Hz, **kilohertz, kilocycles; megahertz, megacycles**

13 band, frequency band, standard band, broadcast band, amateur band, citizens band, police band, shortwave band, FM band; **channel,** radio channel, broadcast channel

14 modulation; amplitude modulation *or* AM; frequency modulation *or* FM; phase modulation *or* PM; sideband, side frequency, single sideband, double sideband

15 amplification, radio-frequency *or* RF amplification, audio-frequency *or* AF amplification, intermediate-frequency *or* IF amplification, high-frequency amplification

16 radio broadcasting, broadcasting, the air waves, radiocasting; **airplay, airtime;** commercial radio, public radio, college radio, satellite radio, Citizens Band *or* CB, amateur radio, ham radio; AM broadcasting, FM broadcasting, shortwave broadcasting; **transmission, radio transmission;** direction *or* beam transmission, asymmetric *or* vestigial transmission; multipath transmission, multiplex transmission; mixing, volume control, sound *or* tone control, fade-in, fade-out; broadcasting regulation, Federal Communications Commission *or* FCC

17 pickup, outside pickup, **remote pickup,** spot pickup

18 radiobroadcast, broadcast, radiocast, **radio program;** rebroadcast, rerun; simulcast; electronic *or* broadcast journalism, broadcast news, newscast, newsbreak, newsflash; all-news radio *or* format; sportscast; **talk radio;** talk show, audience-participation show, call-in *or* phone-in show, interview show; network show; commercial program, commercial; sustaining program, sustainer; serial, soap opera <nf>; taped program, canned show <nf>, electrical transcription; sound effects

19 signature, station identification, call letters, call sign; theme song; **station break,** pause for station identification

20 commercial, commercial announcement, commercial message, message, **spot announcement,** spot *and* plug <nf>

21 reception; fading, fade-out; **drift,** creeping, crawling; **interference,** noise interference, station interference; **static,** atmospherics, noise; blasting, blaring; blind spot; **jamming,** deliberate interference

22 radio listener, listener-in *and* tuner-inner <nf>; radio audience, listeners, **listenership**

23 broadcaster, radiobroadcaster, radiocaster; newscaster, sportscaster; commentator, news commentator; anchor, news anchor, anchorman *or* anchorwoman; host, talk-show host, talk jockey <nf>; veejay *or* VJ; announcer, voiceover; disk jockey *or* DJ *or* deejay <nf>; shock jock <nf>; master of ceremonies, MC *or* emcee <nf>; program director, programmer; sound-effects man, sound man; American Federation of Radio *and* Television Artists *or* AFTRA

24 radioman, radio technician, radio engineer; radiotrician, radio electrician, radio repairman; **radio operator;** control engineer, volume engineer; mixer; **amateur radio operator, ham** *and* ham operator <nf>, radio amateur; Amateur Radio Relay League *or* ARRL; monitor; radiotelegrapher 347.16

VERBS **25 broadcast,** radiobroadcast, radiocast, simulcast, **radio, wireless** <Brit>, radiate, **transmit,** send; narrowcast; shortwave; beam; newscast, sportscast, put *or* go on the air, sign on; go off the air, sign off

26 monitor, check

27 listen in, tune in; tune up, tune down, tune out, tune off

ADJS **28 radio, wireless** <Brit>; radiosonic; neutrodyne; heterodyne; superheterodyne; shortwave; radio-frequency, audio-frequency; high-frequency, low-frequency, etc; radiogenic

29 radio receivers

all-wave receiver	citizens band *or* CB radio
AM receiver	*or* CB
AM tuner	clock radio
AM-FM receiver	communications
AM-FM tuner	receiver
antenna	crystal set
aviation radio	direction finder
battery radio	facsimile receiver *or* fax
boom box <nf>	FM receiver
car radio	FM tuner

ghetto blaster *or* box *or*
  beat box
headband receiver
loudspeaker
mobile radio
multiplex receiver
pager *or* beeper
pocket radio
portable radio
radar receiver
radio direction finder
  or RDF
radio-phonograph
radio-record player
radiophone
railroad radio
receiver
rechargeable-battery radio
regenerative receiver
relay receiver
scanner

ship-to-shore radio
shortwave receiver
single-signal receiver
six-band receiver
stereo receiver
superheterodyne
telephone receiver
three-way *or* three-power
  receiver
transceiver
transistor radio
transmit-receiver
transponder
tuner
two-way radio
universal receiver
VHF-FM receiver
walkie-talkie
Walkman <trademark>
weather radio
wireless

30 radio transmitters

AM transmitter
amateur *or* ham
  transmitter *or* rig <nf>
arc *or* spark transmitter
continuous-wave *or* CW
  transmitter
Dictograph <trademark>
facsimile transmitter *or* fax
fan marker
FM transmitter
link transmitter
microphone
picture transmitter
portable transmitter
pulse transmitter
radio beacon
radio marker
radio range beacon

radiometeorograph
radiosonde
radiotelephone transmitter
relay transmitter
RT transmitter
shortwave transmitter
spark transmitter
standby transmitter
tape transmitter
teleprinter
television transmitter
Telex
transceiver
transmitter receiver *or*
  transceiver
vacuum-tube transmitter
VHF-FM transmitter
walkie-talkie

1035 TELEVISION

NOUNS **1 television, TV, video,** telly <Brit nf>; the
small screen *or* the tube <nf>, the boob tube
<nf>; **network television,** free television, local
television; the dream factory; subscription
television, pay TV; cable television, cable TV, cable-
television system *or* cable system, cable; closed-
circuit television *or* closed circuit TV; public-access
television *or* public-access TV; satellite
broadcasting, satellite television

2 television broadcast, telecast, TV show; direct
broadcast, live show <nf>; taped show, canned
show <nf>; prime time, prime-time show *or*
attraction; syndicated program; television drama
or play, teleplay, made-for-television *or* -TV movie;

telefilm; series, dramatic series, miniseries;
situation comedy *or* sitcom <nf>; variety show;
game show; **serial,** daytime serial, soap opera *or*
soap <nf>; quiz show; giveaway show; panel
show; talk show; electronic *or* broadcast
journalism, broadcast news, newscast, news show;
documentary, docudrama; telethon; public service
announcement; edutainment, infotainment; film
pickup; colorcast; simulcast; childrens' television,
kidvid <nf>; television *or* TV performer, television
or TV personality; news anchor, anchor, anchor
man, anchor woman, anchor person; ratings,
Nielsen rating, sweeps; people meter

3 televising, telecasting; facsimile broadcasting;
monitoring, mixing, shading, blanking, switching;
scanning, parallel-line scanning, interlaced
scanning

4 <transmission> photoemission, audioemission;
television channel, TV band; video *or* picture
channel, audio *or* sound channel, video frequency;
picture carrier, sound carrier; beam, scanning
beam, return beam; triggering pulse, voltage pulse,
output pulse, timing pulse, equalizing pulse;
synchronizing pulse, vertical synchronizing pulse,
horizontal synchronizing pulse; video signal, audio
signal; IF video signal, IF audio signal;
synchronizing signal, blanking signal

5 <reception> **picture, image; color television,** dot-
sequential *or* field-sequential *or* line-sequential
color television; **black-and-white television;** HDTV
or high-definition television; definition, blacker
than black synchronizing; shading, black spot,
hard shadow; test pattern, scanning pattern, grid;
vertical interference, rain; granulation,
scintillation, snow, snowstorm; flare, bloom,
woomp; picture shifts, blooping, rolling; double
image, multiple image, ghost; video static, noise,
picture noise; signal-to-noise ratio; fringe area

6 television studio, TV station

7 mobile unit, TV mobile; video truck, audio truck,
transmitter truck

8 transmitter, televisor; audio transmitter, video
transmitter; transmitter part, adder, encoder;
television mast, television tower; satellite
transmitter

9 relay links, boosters, booster amplifiers, relay
transmitters, **booster** *or* **relay stations;** microwave
link; aeronautical relay, stratovision;
communication satellite, satellite relay; Telstar,
Intelsat, Syncom; Comsat

10 television camera, telecamera, pickup camera,
pickup; **camera tube,** iconoscope, orthicon,
vidicon; video camera, camcorder; mobile camera

11 television receiver, television *or* **TV set,** TV, telly
<Brit nf>, televisor, boob tube *and* idiot box <nf>;

picture tube, cathode-ray tube, kinescope, monoscope, projection tube; receiver part, amplifier, detector, convertor, electron tube, deflector, synchronizer, limiter, mixer; portable television *or* TV set; **screen**, telescreen, videoscreen; raster; **video-cassette recorder** *or* **VCR**, videorecorder, video-tape recorder; video tape, video-cassette; videophone, Picturephone <trademark>; satellite dish, dish <nf>; television recording, videocassette, videocassette recorder *or* VCR, videotape

12 televiewer, viewer; television *or* viewing audience; viewership

13 **television technician**, TV man *or* woman, television *or* TV repairman *or* repairwoman, television engineer; monitor, sound *or* audio monitor, picture *or* video monitor; pickup unit man, cameraman, camerawoman, sound man, sound woman; media personality, host, newscaster, newsreader, commentator, announcer

VERBS 14 **televise, telecast;** colorcast; simulcast

15 **teleview**, watch television *or* TV; telerecord, record, tape; channel-surf, graze <nf>; zap <nf>

ADJS 16 **televisional**, televisual, televisionary, **video;** telegenic, videogenic; in synchronization, in sync <nf>, locked in

WORD ELEMENTS 17 tele-, video-, TV-

1036 RADAR, RADIOLOCATORS

NOUNS 1 **radar**, radio detection *and* ranging; **radar set**, radiolocator <Brit>; radar part; oscilloscope, radarscope; radar antenna; radar reflector

2 airborne radar, aviation radar; **navar**, navigation *and* ranging; **teleran**, television radar air navigation; radar bombsight, K-1 bombsight; radar dome, radome

3 **loran**, long range aid to navigation; **shoran**, short range aid to navigation; GEE navigation, consolan

4 **radiolocator;** direction finder, radio direction finder *or* RDF; radiogoniometer, high-frequency direction finder *or* HFDF, huff-duff <nf>; radio compass, wireless compass <Brit>

5 **radar speed meter**, electronic cop <nf>; radar highway patrol; **radar detector**, Fuzzbuster <trademark>

6 **radar station**, control station; Combat Information Center *or* CIC; Air Route Traffic Control Center *or* ARTCC; beacon station, display station; fixed station, home station; portable field unit, mobile trailer unit; tracking station; direction-finder station, radio compass station; triangulation stations

7 **radar beacon, racon;** transponder; radar beacon buoy, marker buoy, radar marked beacon, ramark

8 <radar operations> data transmission, scanning, scan conversion, flector tuning, signal modulation, triggering signals; phase adjustment, locking signals; triangulation, three-pointing; mapping; range finding; tracking, automatic tracking, locking on; precision focusing, pinpointing; radar-telephone relay; radar navigation

9 <applications> detection, interception, ranging, ground control of aircraft, air-traffic control, blind flying, blind landing, storm tracking, hurricane tracking; radar fence *or* screen; radar astronomy

10 **pulse**, radio-frequency *or* RF pulse, high-frequency *or* HF pulse, intermediate-frequency *or* IF pulse, trigger pulse, echo pulse

11 **signal**, radar signal; transmitter signal, output signal; return signal, echo signal, video signal, reflection, picture, target image, display, signal display, trace, reading, return, **echo, bounces, blips, pips;** spot, CRT spot; three-dimensional *or* 3-D display, double-dot display; deflection-modulated *or* DM display, intensity-modulated *or* IM display; radio-frequency *or* RF echoes, intermediate-frequency *or* IF signal; beat signal, Doppler signal, local oscillator signal; beam, beavertail beam

12 **radar interference**, deflection, refraction, superrefraction; atmospheric attenuation, signal fades, blind spots, false echoes; clutter, ground clutter, sea clutter

13 <radar countermeasure> **jamming, radar jamming;** tinfoil, aluminum foil, chaff, window <Brit>

14 **radar technician**, radar engineer, radarman; air-traffic controller; jammer

VERBS 15 **transmit, send**, radiate, beam; **jam**

16 **reflect**, return, echo, bounce back

17 **receive, tune in**, pick up, spot, home on; pinpoint; identify, trigger; lock on; sweep, scan; map

1037 RADIATION, RADIOACTIVITY

NOUNS 1 **radiation**, radiant energy; ionizing radiation; **radioactivity**, activity, radioactive radiation *or* emanation, atomic *or* nuclear radiation; natural radioactivity, artificial radioactivity; curiage; specific activity, high-specific activity; actinic radiation, ultra-violet *or* violet radiation; radiotransparency, radiolucence *or* radiolucency; radiopacity; radiosensitivity, radiosensibility; half-life; radiocarbon dating; contamination, decontamination; saturation point; radiac *or* radioactivity detection identification *and* computation; fallout 1038.16; China syndrome, nuclear winter

2 **radioluminescence, autoluminescence;** cathode luminescence; Cerenkov radiation, synchrotron radiation

3 ray, radiation <see list>, cosmic ray bombardment, electron shower; electron emission 1033.5

4 radioactive particle; alpha particle, beta particle; heavy particle; high-energy particle; meson, mesotron; cosmic particle, solar particle, aurora particle, V-particle

5 <radioactive substance> **radiator;** alpha radiator, beta radiator, gamma radiator; fluorescent paint, radium paint; radium; fission products; radiocarbon, radiocopper, radioiodine, radiothorium, etc; mesothorium; **radioactive element** <see list>, radioelement; radioisotope; tracer, tracer element, tracer atom; radioactive waste

6 <units of radioactivity> curie, dose equivalent, gray, half-life, megacurie, microcurie, millicurie, multicurie, rad, roentgen

7 counter, radioscope, radiodetector, **atom-tagger;** ionization chamber; ionizing event; X-ray spectrograph, X-ray spectrometer

8 radiation physics, radiological physics; radiobiology, radiochemistry, radiometallography, radiography, roentgenography, roentgenology, radiometry, spectroradiometry, radiotechnology, radiopathology; radiology; radiotherapy; radioscopy, curiescopy, roentgenoscopy, radiostereoscopy, fluoroscopy, photofluorography, orthodiagraphy; X-ray photometry, X-ray spectrometry; tracer investigation, atom-tagging; **unit of radioactivity;** exposure, dose, absorbed dose

9 radiation physicist; radiobiologist, radiometallographer, radiochemist, etc; radiologist

VERBS **10 radioactivate,** activate, **irradiate,** charge; radiumize; **contaminate,** poison, infect

ADJS **11 radioactive,** activated, radioactivated, irradiated, charged, **hot; contaminated,** infected, poisoned; exposed; radiferous; radioluminescent, autoluminescent

12 radiable; radiotransparent, radioparent, radiolucent; radiopaque, radium-proof; radiosensitive

13 rays, radiation

actinic ray	extraordinary ray
alpha ray *or* radiation	gamma ray *or* radiation
anode ray	Grenz ray
Becquerel ray	infraroentgen ray
beta ray *or* radiation	Leonard ray
canal ray	nuclear radiation
cathode ray	ordinary ray
cosmic ray *or* radiation	positive ray
crepuscular ray	Roentgen ray
delta ray	X ray *or* radiation

14 radioactive elements

actinium	neptunium
americium	nobelium
astatine	plutonium
berkelium	polonium
californium	promethium
curium	protactinium
einsteinium	radium
fermium	radon *or* radium
francium	emanation
hahnium	technetium
lawrencium	thorium
mendelevium	uranium

1038 NUCLEAR PHYSICS

NOUNS **1 nuclear physics,** particle physics, nucleonics, atomics, atomistics, atomology, atomic science; quantum mechanics, wave mechanics; molecular physics; thermionics; mass spectrometry, mass spectrography; radiology 1037.8

2 <atomic theory> quantum theory, Bohr theory, Dirac theory, Rutherford theory, Schrödinger theory, Lewis-Langmuir *or* octet theory, Thomson's hypothesis; law of conservation of mass, law of definite proportions, law of multiple proportions, law of Dulong and Petit, law of parity, correspondence principle; Standard Model; supersymmetry theory, unified field theory; atomism; quark model

3 atomic scientist, nuclear physicist, particle physicist; radiologist 1037.9

4 atom <see list>; tracer, tracer atom, tagger atom; atomic model, nuclear atom; nuclide; **ion; shell,** subshell, planetary shell, valence shell; **atomic unit;** atomic constant; atomic mass, atomic weight, atomic number, proton number, mass number, nucleon number, neutron number

5 isotope; protium, deuterium *or* heavy hydrogen *and* tritium <of hydrogen>; radioactive isotope, **radioisotope;** carbon 14, strontium 90, uranium 235; artificial isotope; isotone; isobar, isomer, nuclear isomer

6 elementary particle, fundamental particle, atomic particle, **subatomic particle** <see list>, subnuclear particle, ultraelementary particle; **atomic nucleus, nucleus,** *Kern* <Ger>; **nuclear particle,** nucleon; proton, neutron <see list>; deuteron *or* deuterium nucleus, triton *or* tritium nucleus, alpha particle *or* helium nucleus; **nuclear force,** weak force *or* weak nuclear force, strong force *or* strong nuclear force; weak interaction, strong interaction; fifth force; nucleosynthesis; nuclear resonance, Mössbauer effect, nuclear magnetic resonance *or* NMR; strangeness; charm

7 atomic cluster, molecule; radical, simple radical, compound radical, chain, straight chain, branched chain, side chain; ring, closed chain, cycle; homocycle, heterocycle; benzene ring *or* nucleus, Kekulé formula; lattice, space-lattice

8 **fission, nuclear fission,** fission reaction; **atom-smashing,** atom-chipping, **splitting the atom;** atomic reaction; atomic disintegration *or* decay, alpha decay, beta decay, gamma decay; stimulation, dissociation, photodisintegration, ionization, nucleization, cleavage; neutron reaction, proton reaction, etc; reversible reaction, nonreversible reaction; thermonuclear reaction; **chain reaction;** exchange reaction; breeding; disintegration series; bombardment, atomization; bullet, target; proton gun

9 **fusion, nuclear fusion,** fusion reaction, thermonuclear reaction, thermonuclear fusion, laser-induced fusion, cold fusion

10 **fissionable material,** nuclear fuel; fertile material; **critical mass,** noncritical mass; parent element, daughter element; end product

11 **accelerator** <see list>, **particle accelerator,** atomic accelerator, atom smasher, atomic cannon

12 mass spectrometer, mass spectrograph

13 **reactor** <see list>, **nuclear reactor, pile,** atomic pile, reactor pile, chain-reacting pile, chain reactor, **furnace,** atomic *or* nuclear furnace, neutron factory; fast pile, intermediate pile, slow pile; lattice; bricks; rods; radioactive waste

14 atomic engine, **atomic** *or* **nuclear power plant,** reactor engine

15 **atomic energy, nuclear energy** *or* **power,** thermonuclear power; activation energy, binding energy, mass energy; energy level; atomic research, atomic project; Atomic Energy Commission *or* AEC

16 **atomic explosion, atom blast, A-blast; thermonuclear explosion,** hydrogen blast, **H-blast;** ground zero; blast wave, Mach stem; Mach front; mushroom cloud; **fallout,** airborne radioactivity, fission particles, dust cloud, radioactive dust; flash burn; **atom bomb** *or* **atomic bomb** *or* **A-bomb, hydrogen bomb,** thermonuclear bomb, nuke <nf>; A-bomb shelter, fallout shelter

VERBS 17 **atomize,** nucleize; activate, accelerate; bombard, cross-bombard; cleave, fission, **split** *or* **smash the atom**

ADJS 18 **atomic;** atomistic; atomiferous; monatomic, diatomic, triatomic, tetratomic, pentatomic, hexatomic, heptatomic; heteratomic, heteroatomic; subatomic, subnuclear, ultraelementary; dibasic, tribasic; cyclic, isocyclic, homocyclic, heterocyclic; isotopic, isobaric, isoteric

19 **nuclear, thermonuclear,** isonuclear, homonuclear, heteronuclear, extranuclear

20 **fissionable,** fissile, scissile

21 **atoms**

acceptor atom	impurity atom
anion	isobar
antiatom	isotere
asymmetric carbon atom	isotopic isobar
	labeled atom
Bohr atom	neutral atom
cation	normal atom
diradical *or* biradical	nuclear isomer
discrete atom	nuclide
excited atom	radiation atom
free radical	recoil atom
hot atom	stripped atom

22 **subatomic** *or* **elementary particles**

alpha particle	omega *or* omega-zero *or* omega nought particle
antibaryon	
antielectron	phi-meson
antilepton	photino
antimeson	photon
antineutrino	pion *or* pi-meson
antineutron	positron *or* positive electron
antiparticle	
antiproton	proton
antiquark	quark
b *or* bottom quark	quark color
baryon	quark flavor
beta particle	quarkonium
B meson *or* B particle	rho particle
boson	s *or* strange quark
cascade particle	sigma particle
D meson *or* D particle	slepton
deuteron	squark
electron	strange particle
energy particle	subnuclear particle
fermion	superstring
flavor	tachyon
gauge boson	tardyon
gluino	tau *or* tauon *or* tau lepton
gravitino	
graviton	tau meson
hadron	tau neutrino *or* tauonic neutrino
Higgs boson	
hyperon	technifermion
intermediate-vector boson	t *or* top quark
	triton
J/psi *or* J *or* psi particle	u *or* up quark
kaon *or* K meson *or* K particle	upsilon
	virtual particle
lambda particle	weakon
lepton	WIMP *or* weakly interactive massive particle
magnetic monopole	
matter particle	
meson *or* mesotron	W particle
muon *or* mu-meson	xi-particle
neucleon	zino
neutrino	Z particle
neutron	Z-zero particle

23 neutrons

delayed neutron	resonance neutron
fast neutron	slow neutron
monoenergetic neutron	thermal neutron
photoneutron	

24 accelerators

atom smasher	induction accelerator
betatron	linear accelerator
bevatron	microwave linear
cascade transformer	accelerator
charge-exchange	particle accelerator
accelerator	positive-ion accelerator
Cockcroft-Walton voltage	superconducting
multiplier	supercollider *or* SSC
colliding-beam machine *or*	synchrocyclotron
collider	synchrotron
cosmotron	tevatron
cyclotron	tokamak
electron accelerator	Van de Graaff generator
electrostatic generator	wake-field accelerator

25 reactors

boiling water reactor	homogeneous reactor
breeder reactor	nuclear reactor
CANDU *or* Canada	plutonium reactor
deuterium oxide-	power-breeder reactor
uranium reactor	power reactor
gas-cooled reactor	pressurized-water
fast-breeder reactor	reactor
fusion reactor	stellarator
heterogeneous reactor	uranium reactor

1039 MECHANICS

NOUNS **1 mechanics** <see list>; leverage 906; tools and machinery 1040

2 statics <see list>

3 dynamics <see list>, **kinetics,** energetics

4 hydraulics, fluid dynamics, hydromechanics, hydrokinetics, fluidics, hydrodynamics, hydrostatics; hydrology, hydrography, hydrometry, fluviology

5 pneumatics, pneumatostatics; aeromechanics, aerophysics, aerology, aerometry, aerography, aerotechnics, aerodynamics, aerostatics

6 engineering, mechanical engineering, jet engineering, etc; engineers

ADJS **7 mechanical,** mechanistic, mechanized; locomotive, locomotor; motorized, power-driven; hydraulic, electronic; labor-saving; zoomechanical, biomechanical, aeromechanical, hydromechanical, etc

8 static; biostatic, electrostatic, geostatic, etc

9 dynamic, dynamical, kinetic, kinetical, kinematic, kinematical; geodynamic, radiodynamic, electrodynamic, etc

10 pneumatic, pneumatological; aeromechanical, aerophysical, aerologic, aerological, aerotechnical, aerodynamic, aerostatic, aerographic, aerographical

11 hydrologic, hydrometric, hydrometrical, hydromechanic, hydromechanical, hydrodynamic, hydrostatic, hydraulic

12 kinds and branches of mechanics

aerodynamics	matrix mechanics
aeromechanics	mechanical arts
animal mechanics	Newtonian mechanics
applied mechanics	micromechanics
atomechanics	practical mechanics
auto mechanics	pure *or* abstract
biomechanics	mechanics
celestial mechanics	quantum mechanics
classical mechanics	rational mechanics
dynamics	servomechanics
electromechanics	statistical mechanics
fluid mechanics	telemechanics
hydromechanics *or*	theoretical *or* analytical
hydrodynamics	mechanics
kinematics	wave mechanics
kinetics	zoomechanics *or*
magnetohydrodynamics *or*	biomechanics
MHD	

13 kinds and branches of statics

aerostatics	hydrostatics
biostatics	hygrostatics
electrostatics	magnetostatics
geostatics	rheostatics
gnathostatics	social statics
graphostatics	stereostatics
gyrostatics	thermostatics
hemastatics *or*	
hematostatics	

14 kinds and branches of dynamics

aerodynamics	megadynamics
astrodynamics	myodynamics
barodynamics	pharmacodynamics
biodynamics	photodynamics
cardiodynamics	phytodynamics
chromodynamics	pneodynamics *or*
electrodynamics	pneumatics
fluid dynamics	pneumodynamics
geodynamics	quantum chromodynamics
gnathodynamics	radiodynamics
hemadynamics *or*	thermodynamics
hematodynamics	trophodynamics
hydrodynamics	zoodynamics
kinesiology	
magnetohydrodynamics *or*	
magnetofluid dynamics	

1040 TOOLS, MACHINERY

NOUNS **1 tool, instrument, implement, utensil; apparatus, device,** mechanical device, contrivance, contraption <nf>, gadget, gizmo, gimcrack, gimmick <nf>, means, mechanical means; gadgetry; **hand tool; power tool;** machine tool; speed tool; precision tool *or* instrument; garden tool, agricultural tool <see list>; **mechanization,** mechanizing; motorizing

2 **cutlery,** edge tool <see list>; **knife, ax,** dagger, sword, blade, cutter, whittle; steel, cold steel, naked steel; shiv *and* pigsticker *and* toad stabber *and* toad sticker <nf>; perforator, piercer, puncturer, point; sharpener; **saw;** trowel; shovel; plane; drill; valve 239.10

3 **machinery,** enginery; **machine, mechanism,** mechanical device; heavy machinery, earthmoving machinery, earthmover; farm machinery; mill; welder; pump; **engine,** motor; engine part; power plant, **power source,** drive, motive power, prime mover; **appliance,** convenience, facility, utility, home appliance, mechanical aid; fixture; labor-saving device

4 **mechanism,** machinery, **movement,** movements, **action, motion, works,** workings, inner workings, what makes it work, innards, nuts and bolts, what makes it tick; drive train, power train; wheelwork, **wheelworks,** wheels, gear, wheels within wheels, epicyclic train; clockworks, watchworks, servomechanism 1040.13; robot, automaton

5 **simple machine;** lever, wheel and axle, pulley, inclined plane; machine part, gear, gearwheel, shaft, crank, rod, hub, cam, coupling, bearing, ball bearing, roller bearing, journal, bush, differential

6 **machine tool;** drill, press drill, borer, lathe, mill, broaching machine, facing machine, threading machine, tapping machine, grinder, planer, shaper <see list>, saw

7 **hand tool;** hammer <see list>, screwdriver <see list>, drill <see list>, punch, awl, wrench <see list>, pliers, clamp, vise, chisel, wedge, ax, knife, saw <see list>, lever, crowbar, jack, pulley, wheel

8 **garden tool;** spade, shovel <see list>, trowel, fork, rake, hoe, tiller, plow, hedge trimmer, shears, lawn mower

9 **gear,** gearing, gear train; gearwheel, cogwheel, rack; **gearshift;** low, intermediate, high, neutral, reverse; differential, differential gear *or* gearing; **transmission,** gearbox; automatic transmission; selective transmission; standard transmission, stick shift, manual transmission, five-speed, five on the floor; synchronized shifting, synchromesh; spur gear, rack and pinion, helical gear, bevel gear, skew gear, worm gear, internal gear, external gear; gear tooth

10 **clutch,** cone clutch, plate clutch, dog clutch, disk clutch, multiple-disk clutch, rim clutch, friction clutch, cone friction clutch, slip friction clutch, spline clutch, rolling-key clutch

11 **tooling,** tooling up; **retooling;** instrumentation, industrial instrumentation; servo instrumentation

12 **mechanic,** mechanician; grease monkey <nf>;

artisan, artificer; machinist, machiner; auto mechanic, aeromechanic, etc

VERBS 13 **tool,** tool up, instrument; retool; **machine,** mill; **mechanize,** motorize; sharpen

ADJS 14 **mechanical;** machinelike; power, powered, power-driven, motor-driven, motorized; **mechanized,** mechanistic; electronic; labor-saving

15 **agricultural, gardening tools**

baler	pick
billhook	pickax
binder	pitchfork
blower	plow
brush cutter	pruner
cant hook	pruning saw
chisel plow	rake
colter	reaper
combine	roller
crop duster	rototiller
cultivator	scuffle hoe
dibble *or* dibber	scythe
draw hoe	shears
edger	shovel
flail	shredder
grub hoe	sickle
harvester	spade
hayfork	spading fork
hay rake	sprinkler
hedge clipper	tiller
hoe	tractor
lawn mower	trowel
loy	weed trimmer
mattock	wheelbarrow
maul	

16 **blacksmithing tools**

anvil	hoof tester
ball peen hammer	hot chisel
blower	mandrel
chisel	nipper
clinch cutter	post drill
clincher	post vise
clipping hammer	power hammer
cold chisel	pritchel
creaser	puncher
cross peen hammer	rasp
dipper	set hammer
drift	sledge hammer
drill	straight peen hammer
fileflatter	swage
floor mandrel	swage block
forge	swedge
fuller	swedge block
hammer	tongs
hardie	treadle hammer
hoof gauger	vise

17 **cutting, pointed, edged tools**

adz	bill
awl	blade
ax	bodkin

bolster chisel
burin
butcher knife
carving knife
chisel
cleaver
clipper
cold chisel
drove or boaster
firmer chisel
gouge
graver
hardy
hatchet
hook
jackknife
knife

machete
masonry chisel
paring chisel
pick
pinking shears
pipe cutter
punch
razor
router
scissors
scorper
scraper
scythe
shears
sickle
square-end chisel
wire cutter

18 drills

auger
bench drill
bit
bore
bow drill
breast drill
broach
cordless drill
corkscrew
countersink
diamond drill
drill press
eggbeater drill

electric drill
gimlet
hand drill
portable drill
power drill
push drill
reamer
rose reamer
seed drill
twist drill
wimble
woodborer

19 fastening, gripping tools

adjustable bar clamp
band clamp
bar clamp
bench dog
bench vise
bent-nose pliers
brace
C-clamp
channel-type pliers
chuck
clamp
claw
clip
corner clamp
cutting pliers
diagonal-cutting pliers
electric riveter
forceps
glue gun
grip
hand vise
holddown clamp
joint fastener
lineman's pliers
locking pliers

long-nose pliers
nail puller
needlenose pliers
pincers
pinchcock
pipe clamp
plate joiner
pliers
power nailer
pucellas
puller
riveter
screw clamp
slip-joint pliers
snap ring pliers
spring clamp
staple gun
stapler
toggle clamp
tongs
tweezers
vise
vise grip
web clamp

20 hammers, mallets

ball peen hammer
beetle
blacksmith's hammer
brick hammer
bushhammer
chipping hammer
claw hammer
cross peen hammer
demolition hammer
double-claw hammer
drywall hammer
electric hammer
engineer's hammer
framing hammer
fuller
joiner's mallet
long-handled hammer
machinist's hammer

maul
peen hammer
pile hammer
rip hammer
rubber mallet
scutch
shingler's hammer
shoemaker's hammer
sledgehammer
small anvil
soft-faced hammer
soft-faced mallet
stonemason's hammer
tack hammer
tilt hammer
triphammer
Warington hammer
wooden mallet

21 measuring, marking tools

bevel
butt gauge
caliper
carpenter's level
carpenter's pencil
carpenter's square
center punch
chalk liner
combination square
compass
depth gauge
dividers
electronic level
feeler gauge
folding rule
framing square
gauge
level
line level
marking gauge
mason's level
micrometer

miter box
miter square
mortise gage
plumb bob
plumb rule
protractor
rafter square
rule
ruler
scale
scratch awl
scriber
slide caliper
square
steel rule
straight edge
studfinder
tape measure
torpedo level
T square
turning caliper
wing divider

22 saws

backsaw
band saw
bench saw
bucksaw
butcher's saw
buzz saw
chain saw
circular saw
compass saw
coping saw
crosscut saw
crown saw
cutoff saw
diamond saw
dovetail saw

dry-wall saw
electric saw
flooring saw
flush cut saw
folding saw
frame saw
fretsaw
hacksaw
hand saw
jeweler's saw
jigsaw
keyhole saw
log saw
lumberman's saw
meat saw

one-man crosscut saw
pad saw
panel saw
pit saw
plumber's saw
portable circular saw
power saw
radial arm saw
reciprocating saw
ripsaw

saber saw
scroll saw
stationary circular saw
table saw
tree saw
two-handed saw
two-man crosscut saw
utility saw
vertical saw

23 screwdrivers

auger screwdriver
cabinet-pattern screwdriver
clutch-head tip screwdriver
cordless screwdriver
electric screwdriver
flat-head screwdriver
impact driver
magnetic screwdriver

offset screwdriver
Phillips screwdriver
ratcheting screwdriver
screw gun
spiral ratchet screwdriver
stubby screwdriver
Yankee screwdriver

24 shaping, smoothing tools

adz
anvil
beading plane
belt sander
bench plane
block plane
brick trowel
buffer
bullnose plane
chamfering plane
circular file
corner trowel
die
disk sander
double cut file
drum sander
electric sander
emery wheel
file
finishing sander
flat file
flatter
float
fore plane
grinder
grinding wheel
grindstone
grooving plane
half-round file
hand sander
hone
jack plane

lathe
machine tool
multiplane
oilstone
plane
planer
power sander
putty knife
rasp
round file
router
router plane
sander
sandpaper
scraper
shaper
sharpener
shavehook
single cut file
slipstone
smoothing plane
spokeshave
stone
swage
swage block
tamper
thickness planer
trimming plane
trowel
trying plane
waterstone
whetstone

25 shovels, diggers

bail
bar spade
bull tongue

coal shovel
cultivator
ditch spade

draw hoe
fire shovel
fork
garden spade
garden trowel
grub hoe
hoe
irrigating shovel
loy
mattock
peat spade
pitchfork
plow

posthole digger
power shovel
rake
scoop
scooper
power shovel
rake
scoop
scooper
spade
spatula
spud
trowel

26 wrenches

adjustable wrench
Allen wrench
alligator wrench
bicycle wrench
box wrench
box-end wrench
box *or* open-end wrench
crescent Wrench
crowfoot wrench
flare-nut wrench
gooseneck wrench
hexagonal wrench
lug wrench

monkey wrench
obstruction wrench
open-end wrench
pin wrench
pipe-gripping wrench
pipe wrench
ratcheting box-end wrench
socket wrench
spanner
spark plug wrench
Stillson wrench
torque wrench
valve wrench

1041 AUTOMATION

NOUNS **1 automation,** automatic control; robotization, cybernation; **self-action,** self-activity; self-movement, self-motion, **self-propulsion;** self-direction, self-determination, self-government, automatism, self-regulation; automaticity, automatization; servo instrumentation; computerization

2 autonetics, automatic *or* automation technology, automatic electronics, automatic engineering, automatic control engineering, servo engineering, **servomechanics,** system engineering, systems analysis, feedback system engineering; robotics, **cybernetics;** telemechanics; radiodynamics, radio control; systems planning, systems design; circuit analysis; bionics; communication *or* communications theory, information theory

3 automatic control, cybernation, servo control, robot control, robotization; cybernetic control; electronic control, electronic-mechanical control; feedback control, digital feedback control, analog feedback control; cascade control, piggyback control <nf>; supervisory control; action, control action; derivative *or* rate action, reset action; control agent; control means

4 semiautomatic control; **remote control,** push-button control, remote handling, tele-action; radio control; telemechanics; telemechanism; telemetry, telemeter, telemetering; transponder; bioinstrument, bioinstrumentation

5 control system, **automatic control system,** servo system, robot system; closed-loop system; open-sequence system; linear system, nonlinear system; carrier-current system; integrated system, complex control system; data system, data-handling system, data-reduction system, data-input system, data-interpreting system, digital data reducing system; process-control system, annunciator system, flow-control system, motor-speed control system; automanual system; automatic telephone system; electrostatic spraying system; automated factory, automatic *or* robot factory, push-button plant; servo laboratory, servolab; electronic banking; electronic cottage

6 **feedback,** closed sequence, feedback loop, closed loop; multiple-feed closed loop; process loop, quality loop; feedback circuit, current-control circuit, direct-current circuit, alternating-current circuit, calibrating circuit, switching circuit, flip-flop circuit, peaking circuit; multiplier channels; open sequence, linear operation; positive feedback, negative feedback; reversed feedback, degeneration

7 <functions> accounting, analysis, automatic electronic navigation, automatic guidance, braking, comparison of variables, computation, coordination, corrective action, fact distribution, forecasts, impedance matching, inspection, linear *or* nonlinear calibrations, manipulation, measurement of variables, missile guidance, output measurement, processing, rate determination, record keeping, statistical communication, steering, system stabilization, ultrasonic *or* supersonic flow detection

8 **process control,** bit-weight control, color control, density control, dimension control, diverse control, end-point control, flavor control, flow control, fragrance control, hold control, humidity control, light-intensity control, limit control, liquid-level control, load control, pressure control, precision-production control, proportional control, quality control, quantity control, revolution control, temperature control, time control, weight control

9 variable, process variable; simple variable, complex variable; manipulated variable; steady state, transient state

10 values, target values; set point; differential gap; proportional band; dead band, dead zone; neutral zone

11 time constants; time lead, gain; time delay, dead time; lag, process lag, hysteresis, holdup, output lag; throughput

12 automatic device, automatic; semi-automatic; self-actor, self-mover; **robot, automation,** mechanical man; cyborg; bionic man, bionic woman

13 **servomechanism,** servo; cybernion, automatic machine; **servomotor;** synchro, selsyn, autosyn; synchronous motor, synchronous machine

14 **system component; control mechanism; regulator, control,** controller, **governor;** servo control, servo regulator; control element

15 **automatic detector;** automatic analyzer; automatic indicator

16 **control panel,** console; coordinated panel, graphic panel; panelboard, set-up board

17 **computer, computer science** 1042, electronic computer, electronic brain; electronic organizer; information machine, thinking machine; computer unit, hardware, computer hardware

18 <automatic devices> automatic pilot *or* autopilot, automaton, guided missile, robot, self-starter, speedometer

19 **control engineer,** servo engineer, system engineer, systems analyst, automatic control system engineer, feedback system engineer, automatic technician, robot specialist; computer engineer, computer technologist, computer technician, **computer programmer;** cybernetic technologist, cyberneticist

VERBS 20 **automate,** automatize, robotize; robot-control, servo-control; program; computerize

21 **self-govern,** self-control, **self-regulate,** selfdirect

ADJS 22 **automated,** cybernated, robotized; **automatic,** automatous, **spontaneous; self-acting,** self-active; **self-operating,** self-operative, self-working; **self-regulating,** self-regulative, self-governing, self-directing; **self-regulated, self-controlled,** self-governed, self-directed, self-steered; self-adjusting, self-closing, self-cocking, self-cooking, self-dumping, self-emptying, self-lighting, self-loading, self-opening, self-priming, self-rising, self-sealing, self-starting, self-winding, automanual; semiautomatic; computerized, computer-controlled

23 **self-propelled,** self-moved, horseless; **self-propelling,** self-moving, self-propellent; self-driven, self-drive; **automotive,** automobile, automechanical; **locomotive,** locomobile

24 **servomechanical,** servo-controlled; **cybernetic;** isotronic

25 **remote-control,** remote-controlled, telemechanic; telemetered, telemetric; by remote control

WORD ELEMENTS 26 aut-, auto-, automat-, automato-, self-

1042 COMPUTER SCIENCE

NOUNS 1 **computer science** <see list>, computer systems *and* applications, computer hardware *and* software, computers, digital computers, computing, machine computation, number-crunching <nf>; **computerization,** digitization;

data processing, electronic data processing *or* EDP, data storage and retrieval; data bank; **information science,** information processing, informatics; computer security; computer crime *or* fraud, computer virus *or* worm; hacking

2 **computer,** electronic data processor, information processor, electronic brain, digital computer, general purpose computer, analog computer, hybrid computer, machine, **hardware,** computer hardware, microelectronics device; **processor,** central processing unit *or* CPU, multiprocessor, microprocessor, coprocessor, mainframe computer *or* mainframe, dataflow computer, hybrid computer, work station, minicomputer, microcomputer, personal computer *or* PC, home computer, desktop computer, laptop computer, notebook computer, briefcase computer, pocket computer, handheld computer, personal organizer, personal digital assistant *or* PDA, minisupercomputer, superminicomputer, supermicrocomputer, supercomputer, graphoscope, array processor, neurocomputer; multimedia computer; neural net *or* network, semantic net *or* network; management information system *or* MIS; clone; abacus, calculator

3 **circuitry,** circuit, integrated circuit, logic circuit, **chip,** silicon chip, gallium arsenide chip, semiconductor chip, hybrid chip, wafer chip, superchip, microchip, neural network chip, transputer, **board,** printed circuit board *or* PCB, card, motherboard; **peripheral,** peripheral device *or* unit, input device, output device; expansion slot; **port,** channel interface, serial interface, serial port, parallel port; **read-write head;** vacuum tube, transistor, bus, LED, network adapter, small computer systems interface *or* SCSI, register

4 **input device,** keyboard, keypad; reader, tape reader, card punch, scanner, optical scanner, optical character reader, optical character recognition *or* OCR device, data tablet *or* tablet, touchscreen, light pen, mouse, joystick, trackball, wand

5 **drive, disk drive,** floppy disk drive, hard disk drive *or* Winchester drive, tape drive, removable drive

6 **disk, magnetic disk, floppy disk** *or* floppy <nf> *or* diskette, minifloppy, microfloppy, hard *or* fixed *or* Winchester disk, removable disk, optical disk, disk pack; magnetic tape *or* mag tape <nf>, magnetic tape unit, magnetic drum; CD-ROM, compact-disk read-only memory, magneto-optical disk

7 **memory, storage,** memory bank, memory chip, firmware; **main memory,** main storage *or* store, cache memory *or* cache, random-access memory *or* RAM, read-only memory *or* ROM, programmable read-only memory *or* PROM, semiconductor memory, magnetic core memory, core, core storage

or store, solid-state memory, auxiliary *or* secondary memory, disk pack, magnetic disk, primary storage, backing store, read/write memory, optical disk memory, bubble memory; read-only memory *or* ROM, programmable read-only memory *or* PROM

8 **retrieval, access,** random access, sequential access, direct access, data capture, capture

9 **output device,** peripheral, terminal, workstation, video terminal, video display terminal *or* VDT, video display unit *or* VDU, visual display unit *or* VDU, graphics terminal, **monitor,** screen, display, cathode ray tube *or* CRT, monochrome monitor, color monitor, RGB monitor, active matrix display, window; **printer,** color printer, **serial printer,** character printer, impact printer, dot-matrix printer, daisy-wheel *or* printwheel printer, drum printer, **line printer,** line dot-matrix printer, chain printer, **page printer,** nonimpact printer, laser printer, electronic printer, graphics printer, color graphics printer, ink-jet printer, thermal printer, bubble-jet printer, electrostatic printer; plotter; **modem** *or* modulator-demodulator

10 **forms, computer forms, computer paper,** continuous stationery

11 **software, program,** computer program, source program, object program, binary file, binary program; program suite, suite of applications; bundle; software package, courseware, groupware, routine, subroutine, intelligent agent *or* agent; applet; shareware, freeware

12 **systems program, operating system** *or* **OS,** disk operating system *or* DOS, system software; Microsoft <trademark> disk operating system *or* MS-DOS <trademark>; UNIX; control program monitor *or* CPM; **word processor,** text editor, editor, print formatter, WYSIWYG *or* what-you-see-is-what-you-get word processor, post-formatted word processor; spreadsheet, electronic spreadsheet, desktop publishing program, database management system *or* DBMS, authoring tool, utility program, screen saver, computer game; **computer application** <see list>, applications program, application software, bootloader *or* bootstrap loader

13 **language** <see list>, assembler *or* assemblage language, programming language, machine language, machine-readable language, conventional programming language, computer language, high-level language, fourth generation language, macro language, preprocessor language, compiler, interpreter, low-level language, application development language, assembly language, assembly code, object code, job-control language *or* JCL, procedural language, problem-oriented language, query language; **computer** *or* **electronic virus,** computer worm, phantom bug,

Trojan horse, logic bomb; source code, machine code; loader, parser, debugger; Java, HTML, SGML

14 bit, binary digit, infobit, kilobit, megabit, gigabit, terbit; **byte,** kilobyte, megabyte

15 data, information, database, data capture, database management, file, record, data bank, input, input-output or I/O; **file,** data set, record, data record, data file, text file

16 network, computer network, communications network, local area network or LAN, workgroup computing, mesh; neural network, neural net; **on-line system,** interactive system, on-line service; intranet; Internet

17 programmer, liveware, wetware; software engineer, computer engineer, computer scientist; systems programmer, system software specialist, application programmer, systems analyst, systems engineer, system operator or sysop; computer designer, computer architect, operator, technician, key puncher, keyboarder; techie; hacker <nf>

18 <computer terms> access, archive, authoring, backup, bandwidth, batch processing, baud rate, benchmark, beta test, binary tree, bit, bitmap, block, boot, bootstrap, bug, byte, click, clock rate, command, compatibility, computerate, computer-literate, controller, crash, cursor, data, desktop, diagnostic, digital, direct access, directory, display, download, downtime, emulator, escape key, field, file, file folder, footprint, FTP, function key, gigabyte, gopher, graphics, hacking, helpdesk, home page, icon, input, interactive, interface, job, key, kilobyte, login, logon, logoff, megabyte, menu, millennium bug, morphing, mouse potato, multimedia, multitasking, mouse potato <nf>, output, parity, password, plug-and-play, power user, pulldown, queue, random access, real time, record, save, scrollable, sector, sequential access, signature, sleep mode, smiley, spell-check, turnkey operation, upload, virus, WYSIWYG or what you see is what you get

19 <computer communications> Internet, the Net <nf>, World Wide Web or Web or WWW, cyberspace, information superhighway; Internet service provider or ISP, electronic mail or e-mail or email, mailbox, website, communications protocol; compression, encryption; intranet; Usenet; local area network or LAN, wide area network or WAN, file server, client-server; browser; gateway; search engine; bulletin board service or BBS, chat room, newsgroup, workgroup; netizen, surfer; spam

20 artificial intelligence, knowledge engineering, knowledge representation, intelligent retrieval, natural language processing, expert systems, speech synthesis, robotics, hypertext, hypermedia, intelligent agent

VERBS 21 computerize, digitize; **program,** boot, boot up, initialize, log in, log out, run, load, download, upload, **compute,** crunch numbers <nf>; capture; **keyboard,** key in, input; browse, surf; search; cut and paste; export, import

ADJS 22 computerized; wired; machine-usable, computer-usable; computer-aided, computer-assisted; computer-driven, computer-guided, computer-controlled, computer-governed; computer-literate, computerate

23 branches of computer science

artificial intelligence or AI	information retrieval or IR
automata theory	information storage and
combinatorial processes	retrieval
compiler design	information technology or
computer-aided design or	IT
CAD	language processing
computer-aided or	logical design
computer-assisted	machine organization
learning or CAL	management information
computer-aided	system or MIS
manufacturing or CAM	natural language
computer-aided molecular	processing
design or CAMD	neural networks
computer-aided testing or	nonnumerical applications
CAT	numerical analysis
computer applications	numerical applications
computer architecture	office automation
computer-based learning	operating systems
computer graphics	optimization
computer-integrated	programming
manufacture or CIM	programming languages
computer-managed	robotics
instruction or CMI	simulation
computer systems	switching theory
cybernetics	symbol manipulation
data entry	systems analysis
data processing	theory of computation
desktop publishing	theory of formal languages
electronic data processing	utility programs

24 computer applications

authoring tool	desktop publishing
batch processing	or DTP
communications software	electronic publishing
computer art	Internet access or Internet
computer bulletin boards	service provider software
computer conferencing	musical instrument digital
computer games	interface program or
computer graphics	MIDI
computer typesetting	office automation program
computer-aided design	presentation software
computer-aided engineering	screen saver
computer-aided	simulation software
manufacturing	spell checking
computer-assisted	spreadsheet program
instruction	time-sharing
database management	Web design software
system	word processing

25 computer languages

ADA
ALGOL *or* algorithmic-oriented language
APL *or* a programming language
APT *or* automatic programmed tools
awk *or* Aho Weinberger and Kernighan
BAL *or* basic assembly language
BASIC *or* beginners all-purpose symbolic instruction code
BCPL
C
C++
COBOL *or* common business-oriented language
COMIT
COMPACT II
CPL
efl
eqn
FLOWMATIC
FORMAC
FORTH
FORTRAN *or* formula translator
GPSS
HTML
IPL-V
Java
JOSS
JOVIAL
Lex
LISP *or* list-processing
Logo
MUMPS
OCCAM
PASCAL
Perl
pic
PILOT *or* programmed inquiry learning *or* teaching
PL/1 *or* programming language 1
Ratfor
RPG II
SNOBOL *or* sno *or* string-oriented symbolic language
SOL
yacc *or* yet another computer compiler

1043 ENGINEERING

NOUNS **1 engineering**, mechanical engineering, civil engineering, chemical engineering, electrical engineering, mining and metallurgy, industrial engineering; automotive engineering, aerospace engineering, aeronautical engineering, astronautical engineering, marine engineering, agricultural engineering; structural engineering, transportation engineering, hydraulic engineering, geotechnical engineering, construction engineering; material engineering, biochemical engineering, environmental engineering

2 engineer, registered engineer; mechanical engineer, civil engineer, chemical engineer, electrical engineer, mining engineer, metallurgical engineer, industrial engineer; automotive engineer, aerospace engineer, aeronautical engineer, astronautical engineer, marine engineer, agricultural engineer; structural engineer, transportation engineer, hydraulic engineer, construction engineer; material engineer, biochemical engineer, biomedical engineer, environmental engineer; electronics engineer; mechanic, technician

3 <engine types> internal-combustion, external-combustion; Wankel, reciprocating, steam, gasoline, diesel, jet, turboprop, turbojet, rocket, Stirling, locomotive; automotive, aircraft, marine, railroad

VERBS **4 engineer,** construct, build, erect, survey, map, excavate, dig, grade, dredge, drill, tunnel, blast, pave; process, manufacture, measure; reverse-engineer

1044 FRICTION

NOUNS **1 friction, rubbing,** rub, frottage; frication *and* confrication *and* perfrication <old>; **drag,** skin friction; **resistance,** frictional resistance; static friction, rolling friction, internal friction, sliding friction, slip friction

2 abrasion, attrition, erosion, wearing away, wear, detrition, ablation; rubbing against *or* together; ruboff; **corrosion;** erasure, erasing, rubbing away *or* off *or* out, obliteration; **grinding, filing,** rasping, limation; fretting; galling; **chafing, chafe;** levigation; **scraping,** grazing, scratching, scuffing; scrape, scratch, **scuff;** scrubbing, scrub; scouring, scour; **polishing,** burnishing, sanding, smoothing, dressing, buffing, shining; sandblasting; abrasive; brass-rubbing, heelball rubbing, graphite rubbing

3 massage, massaging, stroking, kneading; **rubdown;** massotherapy; whirlpool bath, Jacuzzi <trademark>; vibrator; facial massage, facial

4 massager, masseur, masseuse; massotherapist

5 <mechanics> force of friction; force of viscosity; coefficient of friction; friction head; friction clutch, friction drive, friction gearing, friction pile, friction saw, friction welding

VERBS **6 rub,** frictionize; **massage,** knead, rub down; caress, pet, stroke 73.8; pulverize; smooth, iron

7 abrade, abrase, gnaw, gnaw away; **erode,** erode away, ablate, wear, wear away, corrode; erase, rub away *or* off *or* out, rub against; **grind, rasp, file, grate; chafe,** fret, gall; **scrape,** scratch, **graze,** raze <old>, **scuff,** bark, skin; **fray,** frazzle; **scrub, scour**

8 buff, burnish, polish, rub up, sandpaper, **sand,** smooth, dress, shine, furbish, sandblast; brush, curry

ADJS **9 frictional,** friction; fricative; **rubbing**

10 abrasive, abradant, attritive, gnawing, erosive, ablative; scraping; **grinding, rasping;** chafing, fretting, galling

1045 DENSITY

NOUNS **1 density,** denseness, **solidity, solidness,** firmness, **compactness, closeness,** spissitude <old>; **congestion,** congestedness, crowdedness, jammedness; **impenetrability,** impermeability, imporosity; hardness 1046; incompressibility; specific gravity, relative density; **consistency,** consistence, thick consistency, thickness; viscidity, viscosity, **viscousness, thickness,** gluiness, ropiness

2 **indivisibility, inseparability,** impartibility, infrangibility, indiscerptibility; indissolubility; cohesion, coherence 803; unity 791; insolubility, infusibility

3 **densification, condensation, compression, concentration,** inspissation, concretion, consolidation, conglobulation; hardening, **solidification** 1046.5; agglutination, clumping, clustering

4 **thickening,** inspissation; congelation, **congealment, coagulation,** clotting, **setting,** concretion; gelatinization, gelatination, jellification, jellying, **jelling,** gelling; **curdling,** clabbering; **distillation**

5 **precipitation,** deposit, sedimentation; precipitate

6 **solid,** solid body, body, mass, bulk; lump, clump, cluster; block, cake; node, knot; concrete, concretion; conglomerate, conglomeration

7 **clot,** coagulum, coagulate; blood clot, grume, embolus, crassamentum; **coagulant,** coagulator, clotting factor, coagulase, coagulose, thromboplastin *or* coagulin; casein, caseinogen, paracasein, legumin; **curd,** clabber, loppered milk *and* bonnyclabber <nf>, clotted cream, Devonshire cream

8 <instruments> densimeter, densitometer; aerometer, hydrometer, lactometer, urinometer, pycnometer

VERBS 9 **densify,** inspissate, densen; **condense, compress,** compact, **consolidate, concentrate,** come to a head; **congest; squeeze, press, crowd,** cram, jam, pack, ram down; steeve; pack *or* jam in; **solidify** 1046.8

10 **thicken,** thick <old>; inspissate, incrassate; **congeal, coagulate, clot,** set, concrete; gelatinize, gelatinate, jelly, jellify, **jell,** gel; **curdle,** curd, clabber, lopper <nf>; cake, lump, clump, cluster, knot

11 **precipitate,** deposit, sediment, sedimentate

ADJS 12 **dense, compact, close;** close-textured, close-knit, close-woven, tight-knit; serried, **thick, heavy,** massy, thickset, thick-packed, thick-growing, thick-spread, thick-spreading; **condensed, compressed,** compacted, concrete, consolidated, concentrated; **crowded, jammed,** packed, jam-packed, packed *or* jammed in, packed *or* jammed in like sardines; **congested,** crammed, crammed full; **solid,** firm, substantial, massive; impenetrable, impermeable, imporous, nonporous; hard 1046.10; incompressible; viscid, viscous, ropy, gluey; thick enough to be cut with a knife <nf>

13 **indivisible,** nondivisible, undividable, **inseparable,** impartible, infrangible, indiscerptible, indissoluble; cohesive, coherent 803.10; unified; insoluble, indissolvable, infusible

14 **thickened,** inspissate *or* inspissated, incrassate; **congealed, coagulated, clotted,** grumous; **curdled,** curded, clabbered; **jellied,** jelled *or* gelled, gelatinized; lumpy, lumpish; caked, cakey; coagulant, coagulating

ADVS 15 **densely,** compactly, **close,** closely, **thick,** thickly, heavily; solidly, firmly

1046 HARDNESS, RIGIDITY

NOUNS 1 **hardness,** durity <old>, induration; **callousness,** callosity; stoniness, rock-hardness, flintiness, steeliness; **strength,** toughness 1047; solidity, impenetrability, density 1045; restiveness, resistance 453; obduracy 361.1; hardness of heart 94.3

2 **rigidity, rigidness,** rigor <old>; **firmness,** renitence *or* renitency, incompressibility; nonresilience *or* nonresiliency, inelasticity; **tension,** tensity, **tenseness,** tautness, tightness

3 **stiffness, inflexibility,** unpliability, unmalleability, intractability, unbendingness, unlimberness, starchiness; **stubbornness,** unyieldingness 361.2; **unalterability,** immutability; immovability 855.3; inelasticity, irresilience *or* irresiliency; inextensibility *or* unextensibility, unextendibility, inductility

4 **temper,** tempering; chisel temper, die temper, razor temper, saw file temper, set temper, spindle temper, tool temper; precipitation hardening, heat treating; hardness test, Brinell test; hardness scale, Brinell number *or* Brinell hardness number *or* Bhn; indenter; hardener, hardening, hardening agent

5 **hardening, toughening,** induration, firming; **strengthening; tempering,** case hardening, steeling; seasoning; **stiffening,** rigidification, starching; **solidification, setting,** curing, caking, concretion; crystallization, granulation; callusing; sclerosis, arteriosclerosis, atherosclerosis, hardening of the arteries; lithification; lapidification <old>; **petrification,** fossilization, ossification; glaciation; cornification, hornification; calcification; vitrification, vitrifaction

6 <comparisons> stone, rock 1059, adamant, granite, flint, marble, diamond; steel, iron, nails; concrete, cement; brick; oak, heart of oak; bone

VERBS 7 **harden,** indurate, firm, **toughen** 1049.3; **callous; temper,** anneal, oil-temper, heat-temper, **case-harden,** steel; season; **petrify,** lapidify <old>, fossilize; lithify; vitrify; calcify; ossify; cornify, hornify

8 solidify, concrete, **set,** take a set, cure, cake; condense, thicken 1045.10; **crystallize,** granulate, candy; hard-boil; anneal; freeze

9 stiffen, rigidify, starch; **strengthen,** toughen 1049.3; back, brace, reinforce, shore up; **tense, tighten,** tense up, tension; trice up, screw up

ADJS **10 hard, solid,** dure <old>, lacking give, **tough** 1049.4; resistive, resistant, steely, steellike, iron-hard, ironlike; **stony,** rocky, stonelike, rock-hard, rocklike, lapideous, lapidific, lapidifical, lithoid *or* lithoidal; diamondlike, adamant, adamantine; flinty, flintlike; marble, marblelike; granitic, granitelike; gritty; concrete, cement, cemental; horny; bony, osseous, ossific; petrifactive; vitreous; hard-boiled; hard as nails *or* a rock, etc 1044.6; dense 1045.12; obdurate 361.10; hard-hearted 94.12

11 rigid, stiff, firm, renitent, incompressible; **tense, taut, tight,** unrelaxed; nonresilient, inelastic; **rodlike,** virgate; ramrod-stiff, ramrodlike, pokerlike; stiff as a poker *or* rod *or* board, stiff as buckram; starched, starchy

12 inflexible, unflexible, **unpliable, unpliant, unmalleable, intractable,** untractable, intractile, **unbending,** unlimber, **unyielding** 361.9, ungiving, **stubborn, unalterable,** immutable; **immovable** 855.15; **adamant,** adamantine; **inelastic,** nonelastic, irresilient; inextensile, inextensible, unextensible, inextensional, unextendible, nonstretchable, inductile; intransigent

13 hardened, toughened, steeled, indurate, indurated, fortified; **callous,** calloused; **solidified,** set; crystallized, granulated; petrified, lapidified <old>, fossilized; vitrified; sclerotic; ossified; cornified, hornified; calcified; crusted, crusty, incrusted; **stiffened, strengthened,** rigidified, backed, reinforced; frozen solid

14 hardening, toughening, indurative; petrifying, petrifactive

15 tempered, case-hardened, heat-treated, **annealed,** oil-tempered, heat-tempered, tempered in fire; seasoned; indurate, indurated

1047 SOFTNESS, PLIANCY

NOUNS **1 softness,** give, nonresistiveness, insolidity, unsolidity, nonrigidity; **gentleness,** easiness, delicacy, tenderness; *morbidezza* <Ital>; lenity, leniency 427; mellowness; fluffiness, flossiness, downiness, featheriness; velvetiness, plushiness, satininess, silkiness; sponginess, pulpiness

2 pliancy, pliability, plasticity, flexibility, flexility, flexuousness, bendability, ductility, ductibility <old>, tensileness, tensility, tractility, **tractability,** amenability, adaptability, facility, give, **suppleness,**

willowiness, **litheness, limberness;** elasticity 1048, **resilience,** springiness, resiliency, rubberiness; sponginess, pulpiness, doughiness, compressibility; malleability, moldability, fictility, sequacity <old>; **impressionability,** susceptibility, responsiveness, receptiveness, sensibility, sensitiveness; formability, formativeness; extensibility, extendibility; agreeability 324.1; submissiveness 433.3

3 flaccidity, flaccidness, **flabbiness, limpness,** rubberiness, floppiness; **looseness,** laxness, laxity, laxation, relaxedness, relaxation

4 <comparisons> putty, clay, dough, blubber, rubber, wax, butter, soap, pudding; velvet, plush, satin, silk; wool, fleece; pillow, cushion; kapok; baby's bottom; puff; fluff, floss, flue; down, feathers, feather bed, eiderdown, swansdown, thistledown; breeze, zephyr; foam; snow

5 softening, softening-up; **easing,** padding, cushioning; mollifying, mollification; **relaxation,** laxation; mellowing; tenderizing

VERBS **6 soften,** soften up; unsteel; **ease,** cushion; gentle, mollify, milden; **subdue,** tone *or* tune down; mellow; tenderize; **relax,** laxate, loosen; limber, limber up, supple; massage, knead, plump, plump up, fluff, fluff up, shake up; **mash,** whip, **smash,** squash, pulp, pulverize; masticate, macerate; thaw, liquefy

7 yield, give, relent, relax, bend, unbend, give way; comply; mellow, loosen up, chill out <nf>; submit 433.6,9

ADJS **8 soft,** nonresistive, nonrigid; mild, **gentle, easy, delicate, tender;** complaisant 427.8; mellow, mellowy <old>; **softened,** mollified; whisper-soft, soft as putty *or* clay *or* dough, etc 1047.4, soft as a kiss *or* a sigh *or* a whisper *or* a baby's bottom

9 pliant, pliable, flexible, flexile, flexuous, **plastic,** elastic 1048.7, **ductile,** sequacious *or* facile <old>, tractile, **tractable, yielding,** giving, bending; adaptable, **malleable,** moldable, shapable, fabricable, fictile; compliant 324.5, submissive 433.12; **impressionable,** impressible, susceptible, responsive, receptive, sensitive; **formable,** formative; **bendable; supple,** willowy, **limber; lithe,** lithesome, lissome, double-jointed, loose-limbed, whippy; **elastic,** resilient, springy; extensile, extensible, extendible; putty, waxy, doughy, pasty, puttylike

10 flaccid, flabby, limp, rubbery, flimsy, floppy; **loose,** lax, relaxed, slack, unstrung

11 spongy, pulpy, pithy, medullary; edematous; foamy; juicy

12 pasty, doughy; loamy, clayey, argillaceous

13 squashy, squishy, squushy, squelchy

14 fluffy, flossy, **downy,** pubescent, feathery; fleecy, flocculent, woolly, lanate; furry

15 velvety, velvetlike, velutinous; plushy, plush; **satiny,** satinlike; cottony; **silky,** silken, silklike, sericeous, soft as silk

16 softening, easing; subduing, mollifying, emollient; demulcent; **relaxing,** loosening

ADVS **17 softly, gently,** easily, delicately, tenderly; compliantly 324.9, submissively 433.17

1048 ELASTICITY

NOUNS **1 elasticity, resilience** *or* resiliency, **give;** snap, **bounce,** bounciness; **stretch, stretchiness,** stretchability; extensibility; tone, tonus, tonicity; **spring, springiness;** rebound 903.2; **flexibility** 1047.2; **adaptability,** responsiveness; **buoyancy** *or* buoyance; **liveliness** 330.2

2 stretching; extension; distension 259.2; **stretch, tension, strain**

3 elastic; elastomer; **rubber,** gum elastic; stretch fabric, latex, spandex; gum, chewing gum 1062.6; whalebone, baleen; rubber band, rubber ball, handball, tennis ball; sponge rubber, crepe rubber; spring; springboard; trampoline; racket, battledore; gutta-percha; neoprene; spring, shock absorber

VERBS **4 stretch;** extend; distend 259.4; flex

5 give, yield 1047.7; bounce, spring, snap back, recoil, rebound, spring back 903.6

6 elasticize; rubberize, rubber; vulcanize, plasticize

ADJS **7 elastic, resilient, springy,** bouncy; **stretchable, stretchy,** stretch; extensile; **flexible** 1047.9; flexile; **adaptable,** adaptive, responsive; buoyant; lively 330.17; tensile

8 rubber, **rubbery,** rubberlike; rubberized

1049 TOUGHNESS

NOUNS **1 toughness, resistance, ruggedness; strength, hardiness, vitality,** stamina 15.1, sturdiness; stubbornness, stiffness; **unbreakableness** *or* **unbreakability,** infrangibility; cohesiveness, tenacity, viscidity 803.3; durability, lastingness 826.1; **hardness** 1046; **leatheriness,** leatherlikeness; stringiness; staying power

2 <comparisons> leather; gristle, cartilage

VERBS **3 toughen,** harden, stiffen, work-harden, **temper,** strengthen; season; be tough; **endure, hang tough** <nf>

ADJS **4 tough, resistant;** shockproof, shock-resistant, impactproof, impact-resistant; stubborn, stiff; **heavy-duty;** hard *or* tough as nails; **strong, hardy,** vigorous; cohesive, **tenacious,** viscid; **durable,** lasting 827.10; untiring; **hard** 1046.10; chewy <nf>; leathery, leatherlike, coriaceous, tough as leather; sinewy, wiry; gristly, cartilaginous; stringy, fibrous; long-lasting

5 unbreakable, nonbreakable, infrangible, unshatterable, shatterproof, chip-proof, fractureproof; bulletproof, bombproof, fireproof; indestructible

6 toughened, hardened, tempered, annealed; seasoned; casehardened; vulcanized

1050 BRITTLENESS, FRAGILITY

NOUNS **1 brittleness, crispness,** crispiness; **fragility, frailty,** damageability, delicacy 16.2, flimsiness, **breakability,** breakableness, frangibility, fracturableness, crackability, crackableness, crunchability, crushability, crushableness; lacerability; fissility; friability, friableness, crumbliness 1051, flakiness; vulnerableness, **vulnerability** 1006.4; inelasticity

2 <comparisons> eggshell, old bone, piecrust, peanut brittle; matchwood, balsa, old paper, parchment, rice paper, dead leaf; glass, glass jaw, china, ice, icicle, glass house; house of cards; lamina, shale, slate, pottery

VERBS **3 break, shatter,** fragment, fragmentize, fragmentate, fall to pieces, shard, fracture, chip off, flake, shiver, **disintegrate** 805

ADJS **4 brittle, crisp,** crispy; **fragile, frail,** delicate 16.14, flimsy, **breakable,** frangible, crushable, crackable, crunchable, fracturable; lacerable; **shatterable,** shattery, shivery, splintery; friable, crumbly 1051.13, flaky; fissile, scissile; brittle as glass; **vulnerable** 1005.16; wafer-thin, papery; inelastic

1051 POWDERINESS, CRUMBLINESS

NOUNS **1 powderiness,** pulverulence, dustiness; chalkiness; **mealiness,** flouriness, branniness; efflorescence, bloom

2 granularity, graininess, granulation; **sandiness, grittiness,** gravelliness, sabulosity, sandiness

3 friability, pulverableness, crispness, crumbliness, flakiness; brittleness 1050

4 pulverization, comminution, trituration, attrition, detrition; levigation; reduction to powder *or* dust, pestling; fragmentation, sharding; brecciation; atomization, micronization; **powdering, crumbling,** flaking; abrasion 1044.2; **grinding,** milling, grating, shredding; granulation, granulization; **beating, pounding, shattering,** flailing, mashing, smashing, crushing; disintegration 806, decomposition

5 powder, dust, chalk; dust ball *or* kitten *or* bunny, slut's wool <Brit nf>, lint; efflorescence; **crumb,** crumble; **meal,** bran, flour, farina, grist; grits, groats; filings, raspings, sawdust; soot, smut;

particle, particulate, particulates, airborne particles, air pollution; fallout; cosmic dust; dust cloud, dust devil; spore, pollen

6 **grain,** granule, granulet; **grit, sand; gravel,** shingle; detritus, debris; breccia, collapse breccia; speck, mote, particle

7 **pulverizer,** comminutor, triturator, levigator; **crusher; mill; grinder;** granulator, pepper grinder, pepper mill; **grater,** cheese grater, nutmeg grater; **shredder;** pestle, **mortar and pestle; masher;** pounder; grindstone, millstone, quern, quernstone, muller; roller, steamroller; hammer; abrasive

8 koniology; konimeter

VERBS 9 **pulverize, powder,** comminute, triturate, contriturate, levigate, bray, pestle, disintegrate, reduce to powder *or* dust, grind to powder *or* dust, grind up; **fragment,** shard, shatter; brecciate; atomize, micronize; **crumble,** crumb, chip, flake; **granulate,** granulize, grain; **grind, grate, shred,** abrade 1044.7; **mill,** flour; **beat, pound, mash, smash, crush,** crunch, flail, squash, scrunch <nf>; grate, shred, mince, kibble

10 <be reduced to powder> **powder,** come *or* fall to dust, **crumble,** crumble to *or* into dust, **disintegrate** 806, fall to pieces, break up; effloresce; granulate, grain

ADJS 11 **powdery, dusty,** powder, pulverulent, pulverous, lutose; **pulverized,** pulverant, powdered, disintegrated, comminute, gone to dust, reduced to powder, dust-covered; **particulate; ground, grated,** pestled, milled, stone-ground, comminuted, triturated, levigated; sharded, **crushed; fragmented; shredded;** sifted; **fine,** impalpable; **chalky,** chalklike; **mealy,** floury, farinaceous; branny; furfuraceous, scaly, scurfy; flaky 296.7; detrited, detrital; scobiform, scobicular; efflorescent

12 **granular, grainy,** granulate, **granulated; sandy, gritty,** sabulous, arenarious, arenaceous, arenose; shingly, shingled, pebbled, pebbly; **gravelly;** breccial, brecciated

13 **pulverable, pulverizable,** pulverulent, triturable; **friable,** crimp <old>, crisp, **crumbly**

1052 MATERIALITY

NOUNS 1 **materiality,** materialness; **corporeity,** corporality, corporeality, corporealness, bodiliness, embodiment, existence; **substantiality** 762, concreteness 763.1; **physicalness,** physicality; tangibility; palpability

2 **matter, material,** materiality, **substance** 763, **stuff,** hyle; raw material, organic matter; **primal matter,** initial substance, xylem; brute matter; **element;** chemical element 1060.1; the four elements; earth,

air, fire, water; elementary particle, fundamental particle; elementary unit, building block, unit of being, monad; constituent, component; **atom** 1038.4; atomic particles 1037.6; **molecule;** material world, physical world, real world, nature, natural world; hypostasis, substratum; plenum; antimatter

3 **body,** physical body, material body, corpus <nf>, anatomy <nf>, person, **figure, form,** frame, **physique,** carcass <nf>, bones, flesh, clay, clod, hulk; soma; **torso, trunk;** warm body <nf>

4 **object, article, thing,** material thing, affair, something, entity; whatsit <nf>, what's-its-name 528.2; something *or* other, *etwas* <Ger>, *eppes* <Yiddish>, *quelque chose* <Fr>; artifact; inanimate object; animate being

5 <nf terms> gadget 1040.1; thingum, **thingamabob,** thingumadad, thingy, thingumadoodle, **thingamajig** *or* thingumajig, thingumajigger, thingumaree, thingummy, **doodad,** dofunny, **dojigger,** dojiggy, domajig, domajigger, **dohickey** *or* doohickey, dowhacky, flumadiddle, gigamaree, **gimmick, gizmo,** dingus, hickey, jigger, hootmalalie, hootenanny, whatchy, widget, whatsis *or* whatsit, gismo *or* gizmo

6 **materialism,** physicism, epiphenomenalism, identity theory of mind, atomism, mechanism; physicalism, behaviorism, instrumentalism, pragmatism, pragmaticism; historical materialism, dialectical materialism, Marxism; **positivism,** logical positivism, positive philosophy, empiricism, **naturalism;** realism, natural realism, commonsense realism, commonsense philosophy, naïve realism, new realism, critical realism, representative realism, epistemological realism; substantialism; hylomorphism; hylotheism; hylozoism; worldliness, earthliness, animalism, secularism, temporality

7 **materialist,** physicist, atomist; historical *or* dialectical materialist, Marxist; **naturalist;** realist, natural realist, commonsense realist, commonsense philosopher, epistemological realist; humanist, positivist; physical scientist

8 **materialization,** corporealization; substantialization, substantiation; **embodiment, incorporation,** personification, **incarnation,** manifestation; **reincarnation,** reembodiment, transmigration, metempsychosis

VERBS 9 **materialize** 763.5, corporalize; substantialize, substantify, substantiate; **embody** 763.5, body, **incorporate,** corporify, personify, **incarnate; reincarnate,** reembody, transmigrate; externalize

ADJS 10 **material,** materiate, hylic, **substantial** 763.6, tangible; **corporeal,** corporeous, corporal, **bodily;**

physical, somatic, somatical, somatous; **fleshly;**
worldly, earthly, here-and-now, **secular,** temporal,
unspiritual, nonspiritual; empirical,
spatiotemporal; objective, clinical
11 **embodied,** bodied, **incorporated, incarnate**
12 **materialist** or **materialistic,** atomistic, mechanist,
mechanistic; Marxian, Marxist; **naturalist,
naturalistic, positivist, positivistic;** commonsense,
realist, realistic; hylotheistic; hylomorphous;
hylozoic, hylozoistic

1053 IMMATERIALITY

NOUNS 1 **immateriality,** immaterialness;
incorporeity, incorporeality, incorporealness,
bodilessness; unsubstantiality 763,
unsubstantialness; **intangibility,** impalpability,
imponderability; inextension, nonextension;
nonexteriority, nonexternality; **unearthliness,
unworldliness,** ethereality, unreality;
supernaturalism 689.2; **spirituality,** spiritualness,
spirituousness <old>, otherworldliness,
ghostliness, shadowiness; occultism 689, the
occult, occult phenomena; ghost-raising, ghost-
hunting, ghostbusting <nf>; psychism, psychics,
psychic or psychical research, psychicism; spirit
world, astral plane
2 incorporeal, incorporeity, immateriality,
unsubstantiality 764
3 **immaterialism, idealism,** philosophical idealism,
metaphysical idealism; objective idealism; absolute
idealism; epistemological idealism; monistic
idealism, pluralistic idealism; critical idealism;
transcendental idealism; subjectivism; solipsism;
subjective idealism; **spiritualism;** personalism;
panpsychism, psychism, animism, hylozoism,
animatism; Platonism, Platonic realism,
Berkeleianism, Cambridge Platonism, Kantianism,
Hegelianism, New England Transcendentalism;
Neoplatonism; Platonic idea or ideal or form, pure
form, form, universal; transcendental object;
transcendental
4 immaterialist, **idealist;** Berkeleian, Platonist,
Hegelian, Kantian; Neoplatonist; **spiritualist;**
psychist, panpsychist, animist; **occultist** 689.11;
medium; ghost-raiser, ghost-hunter, ghostbuster
<nf>
5 dematerialization; **disembodiment,** disincarnation;
spiritualization
VERBS 6 dematerialize, immaterialize,
unsubstantialize, insubstantialize,
desubstantialize, **disembody,** disincarnate;
spiritualize, spiritize; meditate
ADJS 7 **immaterial,** nonmaterial; **unsubstantial** 764.5,
insubstantial, **intangible,** impalpable,

imponderable; unextended, extensionless;
incorporeal, incorporate, incorporeous; **bodiless,**
unembodied, without body, asomatous;
disembodied, disbodied, discarnate, decarnate,
decarnated; metaphysical; **unphysical,**
nonphysical; **unfleshly;** airy, ghostly, spectral,
phantom, shadowy, ethereal; **spiritual,** astral,
psychic or psychical; **unearthly, unworldly,
otherworldly,** extramundane, transmundane;
supernatural; **occult;** parapsychological
8 **idealist, idealistic,** immaterialist, immaterialistic;
solipsistic; spiritualist, spiritualistic; panpsychist,
panpsychistic; animist, animistic; Platonic,
Platonistic, Berkeleian, Hegelian, Kantian;
Neoplatonic, Neoplatonistic

1054 MATERIALS

NOUNS 1 **materials,** substances, stuff, matter; **raw
material, staple, stock,** grist, basic material;
material resources or means; store, supply 386;
strategic materials; matériel; natural resource
2 <building materials> sticks and stones, lath and
plaster, bricks and mortar, wattle and daub;
roofing, roofage, tiles, shingles; walling, siding;
flooring, pavement, paving material, paving,
paving stone; masonry, stonework, flag, flagstone,
ashlar, stone 1059.1; covering materials; mortar,
plasters; **cement, concrete,** cyclopean concrete,
ferroconcrete, prestressed concrete, reinforced
concrete, slag concrete, cinder concrete; brick,
firebrick; cinder block, concrete block; clinker,
adobe, clay; **tile,** tiling; glass, steel, slate, cobble,
tar, asphalt, gravel
3 **wood** <see list>, **lumber, timber,** forest-product;
hardwood, softwood; stick, stick of wood, stave;
billet; log, pole, post, beam 273.3, **board,** plank;
deal; two-by-four, three-by-four, etc; slab,
puncheon; slat, splat, lath; boarding, timbering,
timberwork, planking; lathing, lathwork; sheeting;
paneling, panelboard, panelwork; plywood,
plyboard; sheathing, sheathing board; siding,
sideboard; weatherboard, clapboard; shingle,
shake; log; driftwood; firewood, kindling,
stovewood; cordwood; cord, cordage; brushwood;
dead wood; pulpwood, sapwood, alburnum,
heartwood, duramen; early wood, late wood,
springwood, summerwood
4 cane, bamboo, rattan
5 **paper** <see list>, paper stock, stock; sheet, leaf,
page; quire, ream, stationery; cardboard
6 **plastic** <see list>; thermoplastic; thermosetting
plastic; resin plastic; cellulose plastic; protein
plastic; cast plastic, molded plastic, extruded
plastic; molding compounds; laminate; adhesive;

plasticizer; polymer <see list>; **synthetic;** synthetic fabric *or* textile *or* cloth; synthetic rubber

VERBS 7 gather *or* procure materials; **store, stock,** stock up 386.11, lay in, restock; **process,** utilize

8 woods

acacia	lancewood
alder	larch
applewood	laurel
ash	lignum vitae
aspen	linden
balsa	loblolly pine
balsam	locust
banyan	logwood
bass *or* basswood	magnolia
beech *or* beechwood	mahogany
betel palm	maple
birch	mesquite
boxwood	monkeypod
brierwood	myrtle
burl	oak
buttonwood	olive
cacao	palm
cedar *or* cedarwood	pear
cherry	pecan
chestnut	pine
citrus	poplar
coconut	redwood
cork	rosewood
cottonwood	rubber
cypress	sandalwood
dogwood	satinwood
ebony	sequoia
elder	sisal
elm *or* elmwood	sour gum
eucalyptus	spruce
fig	sugar maple
fir	sumac
fruit wood	sycamore
gum *or* gumwood	teak *or* teakwood
hawthorn	tulipwood
hazel *or* hazelwood	tupelo
hemlock	walnut
hickory	willow
ironwood	yew
juniper	zebrawood
knotty pine	

9 plastics

acetate	cellulose nitrate
acetate nitrate	cellulosic
acrylic	coumarone-indene
alkyd	epoxy
aminoplast	fluorocarbon plastic
Bakelite <trademark>	Formica <trademark>
casein plastic	furane
cellophane	laminate
celluloid	lignin
cellulose acetate	Lucite <trademark>
cellulose ether	melamine

multiresin	polyurethane
Mylar <trademark>	polyvinyl chloride *or* PVC
neoprene	polyvinyl-formaldehyde
nitrate	resinoid
nylon	silicone resin
phenolic	Styrofoam <trademark>
phenolic urea	Teflon <trademark>
Plexiglas <trademark>	terpene
polyester	tetrafluoroethylene
polyethylene	urea
polymeric amide	urea formaldehyde
polypropylene	vinyl
polystyrene	Vinylite <trademark>

10 polymers

addition polymer	polyester
atactic polymer	polyethylene *or* polyethene *or* polythene
chloroprene rubber	
condensation polymer	polypropylene *or* polypropene
copolymer	
epoxide resin	polystyrene
homopolymer	polyurethane
isoprene rubber	polyvinyl chloride *or* PVC
isotactic polymer	resin
macromolecule	stereoregular polymer
monomer	syndiotactic polymer
nylon	Teflon <trademark>
plasticizer	thermosetting plastic
Plexiglas <trademark>	vulcanite
polycarbonate	

11 paper

bond paper	posterboard
carbon paper	rag paper
cardboard	rice paper
computer paper	stationery
crepe paper	tissue paper
fiberboard	toilet paper
foolscap	tracing paper
glossy paper	typing paper
laminated paper	watermarked paper
newsprint	wax paper
onionskin	wrapping paper
paper towel	writing paper

1055 INORGANIC MATTER

NOUNS 1 inorganic matter, nonorganic matter; inanimate *or* lifeless *or* nonliving matter, inorganized *or* unorganized matter, inert matter, dead matter, **brute matter;** mineral kingdom *or* world; matter, mere matter

2 inanimateness, inanimation, **lifelessness,** inertness; **insensibility,** insentience, insensateness, senselessness, unconsciousness, unfeelingness

3 inorganic chemistry; chemicals 1060

ADJS 4 inorganic, unorganic, nonorganic; **mineral,** nonbiological; unorganized, inorganized; material 1052.9

5 inanimate, inanimated, unanimated, exanimate,

azoic, nonliving, dead, **lifeless,** soulless; inert; insentient, unconscious, nonconscious, **insensible,** insensate, senseless, unfeeling; dumb, mute

1056 OILS, LUBRICANTS

NOUNS **1 oil,** *oleum* <L>; **fat,** lipid, **grease;** sebum, tallow, vegetable oil, animal oil; **ester,** glyceryl ester; fixed oil, fatty oil, nonvolatile oil, volatile oil, essential oil; saturated fat, hydrogenated fat, unsaturated fat, polyunsaturated fat; drying oil, semidrying oil, nondrying oil; glycerol, wax

2 lubricant, lubricator, lubricating oil, lubricating agent, antifriction; graphite, plumbago, black lead; silicone; glycerin *or* glycerine; silicone; wax, cerate; mucilage, mucus, synovia; spit, spittle, saliva; Vaseline <trademark>, petroleum jelly, K-Y <trademark>; soap, lather

3 ointment, balm, salve, lotion, cream, unguent, unguentum, inunction, inunctum, unction, chrism *or* chrisom; soothing syrup, lenitive, embrocation, demulcent, emollient, liniment; spikenard, nard; balsam; **pomade,** pomatum, brilliantine; styling mousse, styling gel; cold cream, hand lotion, face cream, lanolin; eyewash, collyrium; sun-block, sun-tan lotion, tanning cream

4 petroleum, rock oil, fossil oil, shale oil, coal oil; **fuel;** fuel oil; mineral oil; crude oil, crude; motor oil; gasoline *or* gas; kerosene, paraffin

5 oiliness, greasiness, unctuousness, unctiousness, unctuosity; **fattiness,** fatness, pinguidity; richness; sebaceousness; adiposis, adiposity; **soapiness,** saponacity *or* saponaceousness; smoothness, slickness, sleekness, **slipperiness,** lubricity; waxiness; creaminess; soapiness, saponaceousness

6 lubrication, lubricating, **oiling, greasing,** lubrification <old>; nonfriction; lubricity, lube <nf>, grease *or* lube job <nf>; **anointment,** unction, inunction; chrismatory, chrismation

7 lubritorium, lubritory; grease rack, grease pit; lubricator, oilcan, grease gun

VERBS **8 oil,** grease; **lubricate,** lubrify <old>; **anoint,** salve, unguent, embrocate, dress, pour oil *or* balm upon; smear, daub; slick, slick on <nf>; pomade; lard; glycerolate, glycerinate, glycerinize; wax, beeswax; smooth the way *and* soap the way *and* grease the wheels <nf>; soap, lather

ADJS **9 oily, greasy; unctuous,** unctional; unguinous; **oleaginous,** oleic; unguentary, **unguent,** unguentous; chrismal, chrismatory; **fat, fatty,** adipose; pinguid, pinguedinous, pinguescent; rich; sebaceous; blubbery, tallowy, suety; lardy, lardaceous; buttery, butyraceous; soapy, saponaceous; paraffinic; mucoid; smooth, slick, sleek, **slippery;** creamy; waxy, waxen, cereous, cerated

10 lubricant, lubricating, **lubricative,** lubricatory, lubricational; lenitive, unguentary, emollient, soothing, moisturizing

WORD ELEMENTS **11** ole-, oleo-, oli-; lip-, lipo-, lipar-, liparo-; cer-, cero-; sebo-, sebi-; steat-, steato-; petr-, petro-, petri-

1057 RESINS, GUMS

NOUNS **1 resin; gum,** gum resin; oleoresin; hard *or* varnish resin, vegetable resin; synthetic resin, plastic, resinoid; resene; **rosin,** colophony, colophonium, colophonone, resinate

VERBS **2** resin, resinize, resinate; rosin

ADJS **3 resinous,** resinic, resiny; resinoid; rosiny; **gummy,** gummous, gumlike; pitchy

1058 MINERALS, METALS

NOUNS **1 mineral** <see list>; inorganic substance, lifeless matter found in nature; extracted matter *or* material; **mineral world** *or* **kingdom;** mineral resources; mineraloid, gel mineral, mineral aggregate; mineralization; crystalline element *or* compound; inorganic mineral, natural mineral, silicate, carbonate, oxide, sulfide, sulfate etc

2 ore <see list>, mineral; mineral-bearing material; unrefined *or* untreated mineral; natural *or* native mineral

3 metal, elementary metal, metallic element <see list>; metallics; native metals, alkali metals, earth metals, alkaline-earth metals, noble metals, precious metals, base metals, rare metals, rare-earth metals *or* elements; metalloid, semimetal, nonmetal; gold *or* silver bullion; gold dust; leaf metal, metal leaf, metal foil; metalwork, metalware; metallicity, metalleity

4 alloy, alloyage, fusion, compound; **amalgam**

5 cast, casting; ingot, bullion; pig, sow; sheet metal; button, gate, regulus

6 mine, pit; **quarry; diggings, workings;** open cut, opencast; bank; shaft; coal mine, colliery; strip mine; gold mine, silver mine, etc

7 deposit, mineral deposit, pay dirt; **vein, lode,** seam, dike, ore bed; shoot *or* chute, ore shoot *or* chute; chimney; stock; placer, placer deposit, placer gravel; country rock; lodestuff, gangue, matrix, veinstone

8 mining; coal mining, gold mining, etc; long-wall mining; room-and-pillar mining; strip mining; placer mining; hydraulic mining; prospecting; mining claim, lode claim, placer claim; gold fever; gold rush

9 miner, mineworker, pitman; coal miner, collier <Brit>; gold miner, gold digger; gold panner;

placer miner; quarry miner; **prospector,** desert rat
<nf>, sourdough; wildcatter; **forty-niner;** hand
miner, rockman, powderman, driller, draw man;
butty

10 **mineralogy;** mineralogical chemistry;
crystallography; **petrology,** petrography,
micropetrography; **geology;** mining geology,
mining engineering

11 **metallurgy;** metallography, metallurgical
chemistry, metallurgical engineering, physical
metallurgy, powder metallurgy, electrometallurgy,
hydrometallurgy, pyrometallurgy, production
metallurgy, extractive metallurgy

12 **mineralogist; metallurgist,** electrometallurgist,
metallurgical engineer; **petrologist,** petrographer;
geologist; mining engineer

VERBS **13** mineralize; petrify 1046.7

14 **mine;** quarry; pan, pan for gold; prospect; hit pay
dirt; mine out

ADJS **15** **mineral;** inorganic 1055.4; mineralized,
petrified; asbestine, carbonous, graphitic,
micaceous, alabastrine, quartzose, silicic;
sulfurous, sulfuric; ore-bearing, ore-forming

16 **metal, metallic,** metallike, metalline, metalloid *or*
metalloidal, metalliform; semimetallic;
nonmetallic; metallo-organic *or* metallorganic,
organometallic; bimetallic, trimetallic;
metalliferous, metalbearing

17 brass, brassy, brazen; bronze, bronzy; copper,
coppery, cuprous, cupreous; gold, golden, gilt,
aureate; nickel, nickelic, nickelous, nickeline;
silver, silvery; iron, ironlike, ferric, ferrous,
ferruginous; steel, steely; tin, tinny; lead, leaden;
pewter, pewtery; mercurial, mercurous,
quicksilver; gold-filled, gold-plated, silver-plated,
etc

18 **mineralogical, metallurgical,** petrological,
crystallographic

19 minerals

alabaster	brookite
amphibole	brucite
anhydrite	calcite
antimony	carbon
apatite	carnelian
argillite	chalcedony
arsenic	chert
asbestos	chlorite
asphalt	chromite
augite	clay
azurite	coal
barite	coke
bauxite	corundum
bitumen	cryolite
boron	diamond
brimstone	diatomite
bromine	dolomite

elaterite	monazite
emery	moonstone
epidote	obsidian
epsomite	olivine
feldspar	orthoclase
flint	ozokerite
fluorite	peat
fluorspar	peridot
fool's gold	perlite
garnet	phosphate rock
glauconite	phosphorus
graphite	pitchblende
gypsum	pumice
holosiderite	pumicite
hornblende	pyrite
ilmenite	pyroxene
iolite	quartz
iron pyrites	realgar
jet	red clay
kaolinite	rhodonite
kyanite	rock salt
lazurite	serpentine
lignite	siderite
lime	silica
magnesite	silicate
malachite	silicon
maltha	sodalite
marcasite	spar
marl	spinel
meerschaum	sulfur
mica	talc
microlite	tellurium
microlith	topaz
mineral charcoal	tourmaline
mineral coal	tripoli
mineral oil	umber
mineral salt	vermiculite
mineral tallow	wollastonite
mineral tar	wulfenite
mineral wax	zeolite
molybdenite	zircon

20 ores

amblygonite	cuprite
argentite	galena
arsenopyrite *or* mispickel	garnierite
azurite	goethite
barite	hematite
bauxite	hemimorphite
beryl	hydrozincite
bornite	ilmenite
calaverite	iron ore
carnotite	ironstone
cassiterite	limonite
celestite	lodestone
cerussite	magnetite
chalcocite	malachite
chalcopyrite	molybdenite
chromite	monazite
cinnabar	niobite

pitchblende	sylvanite
pyrargyrite	tetrahedrite
pyrite	tinstone
scheelite	turgite
siderite	uranitite
smithsonite	wolframite
sphalerite	zincite
stibnite	

21 metallic elements

actinium	niobium
aluminum	osmium
americium	palladium
antimony	phosphorus
barium	platinum
beryllium	polonium
bismuth	potassium
cadmium	praseodymium
cerium	promethium
cesium	protactinium
chromium	quicksilver
cobalt	radium
copper	rhenium
dysprosium	rhodium
erbium	rubidium
europium	ruthenium
gadolinium	samarium
gallium	scandium
germanium	silver
gold	sodium
hafnium	strontium
holmium	tantalum
indium	technetium
iridium	terbium
iron	thallium
lanthanum	thorium
lawrencium	thulium
lead	tin
lithium	titanium
lutetium	tungsten
magnesium	uranium
manganese	vanadium
mercury	ytterbium
molybdenum	yttrium
neodymium	zinc
nickel	zirconium

1059 ROCK

NOUNS **1 rock, stone** <see list>; living rock, rock formation; **igneous rock,** plutonic *or* abyssal rock, hypabyssal rock, magmatic rock, acid rock, mafic rock, felsic rock, ultrabasic rock, ultramafic rock; volcanic rock, extrusive *or* effusive rock, scoria; magma, intrusive rock; granite, basalt, porphyry, **lava,** aa *and* pahoehoe <Hawaiian>; **sedimentary rock,** lithified sediment, stratified rock, clastic rock, nonclastic rock; limestone, sandstone; **metamorphic rock,** schist, gneiss; conglomerate,

pudding stone, breccia, rubble, rubblestone, scree, talus, tuff, tufa, brash; sarsen, sarsen stone, druid stone; monolith; crag, craig <Scot>; bedrock; mantlerock, regolith; saprolite, geest, laterite; building stone

2 sand; grain of sand; sands of the sea; sand pile, sand dune, sand hill; sand reef, sandbar

3 gravel, shingle, chesil <Brit>

4 pebble, pebblestone, gravelstone; jackstone *and* checkstone <nf>; fingerstone; slingstone; drakestone; spall

5 boulder, river boulder, shore boulder, glacial boulder

6 geological sediment, organic sediment, inorganic sediment, oceanic sediment, alluvial deposit, lake sediment, glacial deposit, eolian deposit; mud, sand, silt, clay, loess; rock, boulder, stone, gravel, granule, pebble

7 precious stone, gem, gemstone <see list>; stone: crystal, crystal lattice, crystal system; semiprecious stone; gem of the first water; birthstone

8 petrification, petrifaction, lithification, crystallization; rock cycle, sedimentation, deposition, consolidation, cementation, compaction, magmatism, metamorphosis, recrystallization, foliation

9 geology, petrology, crystallography; petrochemistry; petrogenesis

VERBS **10** petrify, lithify, crystallize, turn to stone; harden 1046.7

ADJS **11 stone, rock,** lithic; petrified; petrogenic, petrescent; adamant, adamantine; flinty, flintlike; marbly, marblelike; granitic, granitelike; slaty, slatelike

12 stony, rocky, lapideous; stonelike, rocklike, lithoid *or* lithoidal; sandy, gritty 1051.12; gravelly, shingly, shingled; pebbly, pebbled; porphyritic, trachytic; crystal, crystalline; bouldery, rock- *or* boulder-strewn, rock-studded, rock-ribbed; craggy; monolithic

WORD ELEMENTS **13** petr-, petro-, petri-, saxi-, lith-, litho-, -lith; grano-; blast-, blasto-, -blast, orth-, ortho-, par-; para-; -clast; -lithic, litic; -clastic; crystall-, crystallo-

14 stones

anthraconite	diabase
aplite	diorite
basalt	dolerite
beetlestone	dolmen
boulder	dolomite
brimstone	dripstone
brownstone	eaglestone
buhr *or* buhrstone	emery
cairngorm	fieldstone
chalk	flag *or* flagstone
clinkstone	flint
dendrite	floatstone

freestone
geode
gneiss
goldstone
granite
granulite
graywacke
greenstone
grit
gritrock *or* gritstone
hairstone
hoarstone
ironstone
lava
limestone
lodestone
Lydian stone
marble
megalith
menhir
milkstone
monolith
mudstone
obsidian
omphalos
pitchstone
porphyry

pumice
quarrystone
quartz
quartzite
rance
rottenstone
sandstone
serpentine
shale
slab
slate
smokestone
snakestone
soapstone
stalactite
stalagmite
starstone
steatite
stinkstone
stone
tinstone
touchstone
trap *or* traprock
tufa
wacke
whitestone

15 gemstones

achroite
agate
alexandrite
amethyst
aquamarine
beryl
black opal
bloodstone
brilliant
carbuncle
carnelian
cat's-eye
chalcedony
chrysoberyl
chrysolite
chrysoprase
citrine
coral
demantoid *or* Uralian
    emerald
diamond
emerald
fire opal
garnet
girasol
harlequin opal
heliotrope
hyacinth
jacinth

jade *or* jadestone
jargoon
jasper
kunzite
lapis lazuli
moonstone
morganite
onyx
opal
pearl
peridot
plasma
rhodolite
rose quartz
ruby
sapphire
sard
sardonyx
siberite
spinel *or* spinel ruby
sunstone
tanzanite
tiger's eye
topaz
tourmaline
turquoise
water sapphire
white sapphire
zircon

1060 CHEMISTRY, CHEMICALS

NOUNS **1 chemistry,** chemical science, science of substances, science of matter; branch of chemistry <see list>

2 element <see list>, chemical element; table of elements, periodic table, periodic table of elements; **radical group;** free radical, diradical; **ion,** anion, cation; atom 1037.4; **molecule,** macromolecule; trace element, microelement, micronutrient, minor element; **chemical, chemical compound;** organic chemical, biochemical, inorganic chemical; fine chemicals, heavy chemicals; agent, **reagent;** metal, nonmetal, semimetal, metalloid, heavy metal, alkali metal, noble metal; alkaline-earth element, transition element, noble gas, rare-earth element, lanthanide, actinide, transuranic element, supertransuranic element, superheavy element; inert gas, rare gas; period, short period, long period; family, group; s-block, p-block, d-block, f-block

3 acid; hydracid, oxyacid, sulfacid; acidity; **base, alkali,** nonacid; pH; neutralizer, antacid; alkalinity

4 valence, valency <Brit>, positive valence, negative valence; monovalence, univalence, bivalence, trivalence, tervalence, quadrivalence, tetravalence, etc, multivalence, polyvalence; covalence, electrovalence

5 atomic weight, atomic mass, atomic volume, mass number; **molecular weight,** molecular mass, molecular volume; atomic number, valence number

6 chemicalization, chemical process <see list>, chemical action, chemism; **chemical apparatus,** beaker, Bunsen burner, burette, centrifuge, condenser, crucible, graduated cylinder *or* graduate, pipette, test tube

7 chemist, chemical scientist; agricultural chemist, analytical chemist, astrochemist, biochemist, inorganic chemist, organic chemist, physical chemist, physiochemist, theoretical chemist, etc

VERBS **8 chemicalize,** chemical; alkalize, alkalinize, alkalify; acidify, acidulate, acetify; borate, carbonate, chlorinate, hydrate, hydrogenate, hydroxylate, nitrate, oxidize, reduce, pepsinate, peroxidize, phosphatize, sulfate, sulfatize, sulfonate; calcify, carburize, deuterate, esterify, fluorinate, fluoridate, halogenate, tritrate; isomerize, metamerize, polymerize, copolymerize, homopolymerize; ferment, work; catalyze 806.4; electrolyze; bond, intercalate, invert, neutralize, ionize

ADJS **9 chemical;** astrochemical, biochemical, chemicobiologic; physicochemical, physiochemical, chemicophysical,

chemicobiological, chemicophysiologic *or*
chemicophysiological, chemicodynamic,
chemicoengineering, chemicomechanical,
chemicomineralogical, chemicopharmaceutical,
chemurgic, electrochemical, iatrochemical,
chemotherapeutic *or* chemotherapeutical,
chemophysiologic *or* chemophysiological,
macrochemical, microchemical, physicochemical,
phytochemical, photochemical, radiochemical,
thermochemical, zoochemical; organic, inorganic;
elemental, elementary; acid; alkaline, alkali,
nonacid, basic; isomeric, isomerous, metameric,
metamerous, heteromerous, polymeric,
polymerous, copolymeric, copolymerous,
monomeric, monomerous, dimeric, dimerous, etc

10 valent; univalent, monovalent, monatomic, bivalent,
trivalent, tervalent, quadrivalent, tetravalent, etc,
multivalent, polyvalent; covalent, electrovalent

WORD ELEMENTS 11 chem-, chemo-, chemi-,
chemic-, chemico-; -mer, -merous, -meric; -valent

12 branches of chemistry

actinochemistry	macrochemistry
agricultural chemistry	magnetochemistry
alchemy *or* alchemistry	metachemistry
analytical chemistry	metallurgy
applied chemistry	microchemistry
astrochemistry	mineralogical chemistry
atomic chemistry	natural product chemistry
biochemistry	neurochemistry
biogeochemistry	nuclear chemistry
business chemistry	organic chemistry
capillary chemistry	pathological chemistry *or*
catalysis	pathochemistry
chemiatry	petrochemistry
chemical dynamics	pharmaceutical chemistry
chemical engineering	phonochemistry
chemical physics	photochemistry
chemicobiology	physical chemistry *or*
chemicoengineering	physiochemistry
chemophysiology	physiological chemistry *or*
chemurgy <old>	physiochemistry
colloid chemistry	phytochemistry
colorimetry *or* colorimetric	piezochemistry
analysis	pneumatochemistry
crystallography	polymer chemistry
cytochemistry	psychobiochemistry *or*
electrochemistry	psychochemistry
engineering chemistry	pure chemistry
galactochemistry	quantum chemistry
galvanochemistry	radiochemistry
geochemistry	soil chemistry
histochemistry	spectrochemistry
hydrochemistry	stereochemistry
iatrochemistry	structural chemistry
immunochemistry	surface chemistry
industrial chemistry	synthetic chemistry
inorganic chemistry	technochemistry
lithochemistry	theoretical chemistry

thermochemistry
topochemistry
ultramicrochemistry

zoochemistry *or* zoochemy
zyochemistry *or* zymurgy

13 chemical elements

actinium *or* Ac	neodymium *or* Nd
aluminum *or* Al	neon *or* Ne
americium *or* Am	neptunium *or* Np
antimony *or* Sb	nickel *or* Ni
argon *or* Ar *or* A	niobium *or* Nb
arsenic *or* As	nitrogen *or* N
astatine *or* At	nobelium *or* No
barium *or* Ba	osmium *or* Os
berkelium *or* Bk	oxygen *or* O
beryllium *or* Be	palladium *or* Pd
bismuth *or* Bi	phosphorus *or* P
boron *or* B	platinum *or* Pt
bromine *or* Br	plutonium *or* Pu
cadmium *or* Cd	polonium *or* Po
calcium *or* Ca	potassium *or* K
californium *or* Cf	praseodymium *or* Pr
carbon *or* C	promethium *or* Pm
cerium *or* Ce	protactinium *or* Pa
cesium *or* Cs	radium *or* Ra
chlorine *or* Cl	radon *or* Rn
chromium *or* Cr	rhenium *or* Re
cobalt *or* Co	rhodium *or* Rh
copper *or* Cu	rubidium *or* Rb
curium *or* Cm	ruthenium *or* Ru
dysprosium *or* Dy	samarium *or* Sm
einsteinium *or* Es *or* E	scandium *or* Sc
erbium *or* Er	selenium *or* Se
europium *or* Eu	silicon *or* Si
fermium *or* Fm	silver *or* Ag
fluorine *or* F	sodium *or* Na
francium *or* Fr	strontium *or* Sr
gadolinium *or* Gd	sulfur *or* S
gallium *or* Ga	tantalum *or* Ta
germanium *or* Ge	technetium *or* Tc
gold *or* Au	tellurium *or* Te
hafnium *or* Hf	terbium *or* Tb
helium *or* He	thallium *or* Tl
holmium *or* Ho	thorium *or* Th
hydrogen *or* H	thulium *or* Tm
indium *or* In	tin *or* Sn
iodine *or* I	titanium *or* Ti
iridium *or* Ir	tungsten *or* wolfram *or* W
iron *or* Fe	unnihexium *or* Unh
krypton *or* Kr	unnilpentium *or* Unp *or*
lanthanum *or* La	hahnium
lawrencium *or* Lw	unnilquadrium *or* Unq *or*
lead *or* Pb	rutherfordium
lithium *or* Li	uranium *or* U
lutetium *or* Lu	vanadium *or* V
magnesium *or* Mg	xenon *or* Xe
manganese *or* Mn	ytterbium *or* Yb
mendelevium *or* Md *or* Mv	yttrium *or* Y
mercury *or* Hg	zinc *or* Zn
molybdenum *or* Mo	zirconium *or* Zr

14 chemical processes

acetification
acidification *or*
  acidulation
alkalization *or*
  alkalinization
aromatization
carbonation
catalysis
chain reaction
chlorination
condensation
copolymerization
cyclization
electrolysis
electrophilic reaction
fermentation *or* ferment
geometric isomerization
heterolysis
heterolytic fission
homolysis
homolytic fission
homopolymerization
hydration
hydrogenation
hydroxylation

ionization
isomerization
isotope effect
metamerization
neutralization
nitration
nucleophilic reaction
optical isomerization
oxidation
oxidization
phosphatization
photochemical reaction
polymerization
position isomerization
pyrolysis
radiochemical reaction
reduction
ring opening
saturization
sulfation
sulfatization
sulfonation
synthesis
tautoisomerization

1061 LIQUIDITY

NOUNS **1 liquidity, fluidity,** fluidness, liquidness, liquefaction 1064; wateriness; rheuminess, runniness; **juiciness,** sappiness, succulence; milkiness, lactescence; lactation; chylifaction, chylification; serosity; suppuration; **moisture,** wetness 1065.1; **fluency,** flow, flowage, flux, fluxion, fluxility <old>; **circulation;** turbulence, turbidity, turbulent flow; streamline flow; hemorrhage; suppuration, secretion; liquid state; solubleness; fluid mechanics, hydrology

2 fluid, liquid; liquor 10.49, drink, beverage; liquid extract, fluid extract, condensation; **juice, sap,** latex, extract; milk, whey, buttermilk, ghee; water 1065.3; **body fluid, blood;** stock, meat juice, gravy, sauce, soup; semiliquid 1062.5; fluid mechanics, hydraulics, etc 1039.4; solvent, liquefier, liquefacient; solution, infusion, decoction

3 flowmeter, fluidmeter, hydrometer, sphygmomanometer

ADJS **4 fluid,** fluidal, fluidic, **fluent, flowing,** fluxible *or* fluxile <old>, fluxional, fluxionary, runny; circulatory, **circulation,** turbid; **liquid,** liquidy; watery 1065.16; **juicy,** sappy, succulent, moist; **wet** 1065.15; uncongealed, unclotted; rheumy; bloody; liquefied, liquefying, liquefiable

5 milky, lacteal, lacteous, **lactic;** lactescent, lactiferous; milk, milch

1062 SEMILIQUIDITY

NOUNS **1 semiliquidity,** semifluidity; butteriness, creaminess; pulpiness 1063

2 viscosity, viscidity, viscousness, slabbiness, lentor <old>; thickness, spissitude <old>, heaviness, stodginess; **stickiness, tackiness,** glutinousness, glutinosity, toughness, tenaciousness, tenacity, **adhesiveness,** clinginess, clingingness, **gumminess,** gauminess <nf>, gumlikeness; **ropiness, stringiness;** clamminess, sliminess, mucilaginousness; gooeyness *and* gunkiness <nf>; **gluiness,** gluelikeness; syrupiness, treacliness <Brit>; gelatinousness, jellylikeness, gelatinity, gelation; colloidality; doughiness, pastiness; **thickening,** curdling, clotting, coagulation, incrassation, inspissation, clabbering *and* loppering *or* lobbering <nf>, jellification

3 mucosity, mucidness, mucousness, pituitousness <old>, snottiness <nf>; **sliminess**

4 muddiness, muckiness, miriness, **slushiness,** sloshiness, sludginess, **sloppiness,** slobbiness, slabbiness <old>, squashiness, squelchiness, **ooziness; turbidity,** turbidness, dirtiness

5 semiliquid, semifluid; **goo** *and* goop *and* gook *and* gunk *and* glop <nf>, sticky mess, gaum <nf>; **paste,** pap, pudding, putty, **butter,** cream; **pulp** 1063.2; **jelly,** gelatin *or* gelatine, jell, gel, jam, agar, isinglass; **glue;** size; **gluten;** mucilage; mucus; **dough,** batter; mousse, pudding; **syrup,** molasses, treacle <Brit>, honey; egg white, albumen, glair; starch, cornstarch; **curd,** clabber, bonnyclabber; gruel, porridge, loblolly <nf>; soup, gumbo, gravy, purée, pulp; yogurt

6 gum 1057, chewing gum, bubble gum; chicle, chicle gum

7 emulsion, emulsoid; emulsification; emulsifier; **colloid,** colloider

8 mud, muck, mire, slush, slosh, sludge, slob <Ir>, squash, swill, **slime; slop, ooze, mire;** clay, slip; gumbo; gook *or* gunk *or* gook *or* glop *or* guck <nf>

9 mud puddle, puddle, loblolly <nf>, slop; **mudhole,** slough, muckhole, chuckhole, chughole <nf>; hog wallow

VERBS **10 emulsify,** emulsionize; colloid, colloidize; cream; churn, whip, beat up; **thicken,** inspissate, incrassate, curdle, clot, coagulate, congeal, clabber *and* lopper <nf>; jell, jelly, jellify, gel

ADJS **11 semiliquid,** semifluid, semifluidic; buttery; creamy; emulsive, colloidal; **pulpy** 1063.6; half-frozen, half-melted

12 viscous, viscid, viscose, slabby; **thick,** heavy, stodgy, soupy, thickened, inspissated, incrassated; curdled, clotted, grumous, coagulated, clabbered *and*

loppered <nf>; **sticky, tacky,** tenacious, adhesive,
clingy, clinging, tough; gluey, gluelike, glutinous,
glutenous, glutinose; gumbo, gumbolike; **gummy,**
gaumy <nf>, gummous, gumlike, **syrupy;** treacly
<Brit>; ropy, stringy; mucilaginous, clammy, slimy,
slithery; gooey *and* gunky *and* gloppy *and* goopy
and gooky <nf>; **gelatinous,** jellylike, jellied,
jelled; tremelloid *or* tremellose; glairy, **doughy,
pasty;** starchy, amylaceous; pulpy, soft, mushy

13 **mucous,** muculent, mucoid, mucinous, pituitous
<old>, phlegmy, snotty <nf>; mucific, muciferous

14 **slimy; muddy,** miry, mucky, **slushy, sloshy,** sludgy,
sloppy, slobby, slabby <old>, splashy, **squashy,**
squishy, **squelchy, oozy,** sloughy, plashy, sposhy
<nf>; **turbid, dirty**

1063 PULPINESS

NOUNS 1 **pulpiness,** pulpousness; softness 1047;
flabbiness; **mushiness,** mashiness, squashiness,
creaminess; **pastiness,** doughiness; **sponginess,**
pithiness; fleshiness, overripeness, succulence

2 **pulp, paste, mash, mush,** smash, squash, crush;
tomato paste *or* pulp; pudding, porridge, sponge;
sauce, butter; poultice, cataplasm, plaster; pith;
paper pulp, wood pulp, sulfate pulp, sulfite pulp,
rag pulp; pulpwood; pulp lead, white lead; dental
or tooth pulp

3 **pulping,** pulpification, pulpefaction; blending,
steeping; digestion; **maceration,** mastication

4 **pulper,** pulpifier, macerator, pulp machine *or*
engine, digester; **masher,** smasher, potato masher,
ricer, beetle; blender, food processor, food mill

VERBS 5 **pulp,** pulpify; **macerate,** masticate, chew;
regurgitate; **mash,** smash, squash, crush

ADJS 6 **pulpy,** pulpous, pulpal, pulpar, pulplike,
pulped; **pasty,** doughy; pultaceous; **mushy;**
macerated, masticated, chewed; regurgitated;
squashy, squelchy, squishy; soft, flabby; fleshy,
succulent; **spongy,** pithy

1064 LIQUEFACTION

NOUNS 1 **liquefaction,** liquefying, liquidizing,
liquidization, fluidification, fluidization;
liquescence *or* liquescency, deliquescence,
deliquiation *and* deliquium <old>; **solution,**
dissolution, dissolving; **infusion,** soaking, steeping,
brewing; **melting,** thawing, running, fusing, fusion;
decoagulation, unclotting; solubilization;
colliquation; lixiviation, percolation, leaching

2 **solubility,** solubleness, dissolvability,
dissolvableness, dissolubility, dissolubleness;
meltability, fusibility

3 **solution;** decoction, infusion, mixture; chemical
solution; lixivium, leach, leachate; **suspension,**
colloidal suspension; **emulsion,** gel, aerosol

4 **solvent** <see list>, dissolvent, dissolver, dissolving
agent, resolvent, resolutive, **thinner,** diluent;
anticoagulant; liquefier, liquefacient; menstruum;
universal solvent, alkahest; flux

VERBS 5 **liquefy,** liquidize, liquesce, fluidify, fluidize;
melt, run, thaw, colliquate; melt down; fuse, flux;
deliquesce; **dissolve,** solve; thin, cut; solubilize;
hold in solution; unclot, decoagulate; leach,
lixiviate, percolate; **infuse,** decoct, steep, soak, brew

ADJS 6 **liquefied, melted, molten,** thawed; unclotted,
decoagulated; in solution, in suspension,
liquescent, deliquescent; colloidal

7 **liquefying,** liquefactive; colliquative, melting,
fusing, thawing; **dissolving,** dissolutive,
dissolutional

8 **solvent,** dissolvent, resolvent, resolutive, thinning,
cutting, diluent; alkahestic

9 liquefiable; **meltable,** fusible, thawable; **soluble,
dissolvable,** dissoluble; water-soluble

10 **solvents**

acetone	furfural
alcohol	gasoline
alkahest	glycerol
amyl alcohol	glycol
benzene	kerosene
benzine *or* benzol	methyl alcohol
carbolic acid	naphtha
carbon disulfide	pentane
carbon tetrachloride *or*	phenol
carbon tet <nf>	propylene glycol
chloroform	pyridine
denatured alcohol	toluene
ether	turpentine
ethyl acetate	urethane
ethyl chloride	xylene *or* xylol

1065 MOISTURE

NOUNS 1 **moisture,** damp, wet; **dampness,
moistness,** moistiness, **wetness,** wettedness,
wettishness, **wateriness,** humor *or* humectation
<old>; soddenness, soppiness, soppingness,
sogginess; swampiness, bogginess, marshiness;
dewiness; mistiness, fogginess 319.4; raininess,
pluviosity, showeriness; rainfall; exudation 190.6;
secretion 13

2 **humidity,** humidness, **dankness,** dankishness,
mugginess, closeness, stickiness, sweatiness;
absolute humidity, relative humidity; dew point,
saturation, saturation point; humidification

3 **water,** *aqua* <L>, *agua* <Sp>, *eau* <Fr>; Adam's
ale *or* wine, **H$_2$O;** hydrol; hard water, soft water;

heavy water; water supply, water system, waterworks; drinking water, tap water; rain water, rain 316; snowmelt, melt water; **groundwater,** underground water, subsurface water, subterranean water; water table, aquifer, artesian basin, artesian spring, sinkhole; spring water, well water; seawater, salt water; limewater; fresh water; standing water; mineral water *or* waters; soda water, carbonated water; steam, water vapor; hydrosphere; hydrometeor; head, hydrostatic head; hydrothermal water; distilled water; wetting agent, wetting-out agent, liquidizer, moisturizer; humidifier; bottled water, commercially bottled water, designer water <nf>; water cycle, hydrological cycle, evaporation, transpiration, precipitation, runoff, percolation

4 **dew, dewdrops,** dawn *or* morning dew, night dew, evening damp; fog drip, false dew; guttation; haze, mist, fog, cloud

5 **sprinkle, spray,** sparge, shower; spindrift, spume, froth, foam; **splash,** plash, swash, slosh; **splatter,** spatter

6 **wetting, moistening, dampening,** damping; humidification; dewing, bedewing; **watering, irrigation;** hosing, wetting *or* hosing down; **sprinkling, spraying,** spritzing <nf>, sparging, aspersion, aspergation; **splashing,** swashing, splattering, spattering; affusion, baptism; bath, bathing, rinsing, laving; **flooding,** drowning, inundation, deluge; **immersion,** submersion 367.2

7 **soaking,** soakage, soaking through, sopping; **drenching,** imbruement, sousing; ducking, dunking <nf>; soak, drench, souse; **saturation,** permeation; waterlogging; **steeping,** maceration, seething, infusion, brewing, imbuement; injection, impregnation; infiltration, percolation, leaching, lixiviation; pulping 1063.3

8 **sprinkler,** sparger, sparge, sprayer, speed sprayer, concentrate sprayer, mist concentrate sprayer, spray, spray can, atomizer, aerosol; nozzle; aspergil, aspergillum; **shower,** shower bath, shower head, needle bath; syringe, fountain syringe, douche, enema, clyster; sprinkling *or* watering can; water pistol *or* gun, squirt gun; lawn sprinkler; sprinkling system, sprinkler head; hydrant, irrigator

9 <sciences> hygrology, hygrometry, psychrometry, hydrography, hydrology; hydraulics; hydrotherapy, hydrotherapeutics, taking the waters

10 <instruments> hygrometer, hair hygrometer, hygrograph, hygrodeik, hygroscope, hygrothermograph; psychrometer, sling psychrometer; hydrostat; rain gauge *or* pluviometer; hydrograph; humidor; hygrostat

VERBS 11 be damp, not have a dry thread; **drip,** weep; **seep, ooze,** percolate; exude 190.15; sweat; secrete 13.5

12 **moisten, dampen,** moisturize, damp, **wet,** wet down; humidify, humect *or* humectate <old>; **water, irrigate;** dew, bedew; **sprinkle,** besprinkle, **spray,** spritz <nf>, sparge, asperge; bepiss; **splash,** dash, **swash, slosh, splatter, spatter,** bespatter; dabble, paddle; slop, slobber; hose, hose down; syringe, douche; sponge; dilute, adulterate

13 **soak, drench,** imbrue, **souse, sop,** sodden; **saturate,** permeate; **bathe,** lave, wash, rinse, douche, flush; water-soak, waterlog **steep,** seethe, macerate, infuse, imbue, brew, impregnate, inject, injest; infiltrate, percolate, leach, lixiviate

14 **flood,** float, **inundate, deluge,** turn to a lake *or* sea, swamp, whelm, overwhelm, drown; duck, dip, dunk <nf>; **submerge** 367.7; sluice, pour on, flow on; rain 316.10

ADJS 15 **moist,** moisty; **damp,** dampish; **wet,** wettish; undried, tacky; **humid, dank, muggy, sticky;** dewy, bedewed, roric *and* roriferous <old>; rainy 316.11; marshy, swampy, fenny, boggy

16 **watery,** waterish, **aqueous, aquatic;** liquid; **splashy,** plashy, sloppy, swashy <Brit>; hydrous, hydrated; hydraulic; moist; hydrodynamic, hydraulic

17 **soaked, drenched,** soused, bathed, steeped, macerated; **saturated,** permeated; **watersoaked, waterlogged; soaking, sopping; wringing wet,** soaking wet, sopping wet, wet to the skin, like a drowned rat; **sodden,** soppy, **soggy,** soaky; dripping, **dripping wet;** dribbling, seeping, weeping, oozing; flooded, overflowed, whelmed, swamped, engulfed, inundated, deluged, drowned, submerged, submersed, immersed, dipped, dunked <nf>; awash, weltering

18 wetting, dampening, moistening, watering, humectant; **drenching, soaking,** sopping; **irrigational,** irriguous <old>

19 hygric, hygrometric, hygroscopic, hygrophilous, hygrothermal

WORD ELEMENTS 20 hydr-, hydro-, hydrat-, hydrato-, aqui-, aqua-; hygr-, hygro-

1066 DRYNESS

NOUNS 1 **dryness, aridness,** aridity, waterlessness, siccity; **drought;** juicelessness, saplessness; **thirst,** thirstiness, dehydration, xerostomia; corkiness; watertightness, watertight integrity; parchedness

2 <comparisons> desert, dust, bone, parchment, stick, mummy, biscuit, cracker

3 **drying, desiccation,** drying up, exsiccation; **dehydration,** anhydration; evaporation; air-drying; blow-drying; freeze-drying; insolation, sunning; drainage; withering, mummification; dehumidification; blotting

4 **drier,** desiccator, desiccative, siccative, exsiccative,

exsiccator, **dehydrator,** dehydrant; dehumidifier; evaporator; hair-drier, blow-dryer; clothes dryer; tumbler-dryer; absorbent; clothesline

VERBS **5** thirst; drink up, soak up, sponge up; parch

6 dry, desiccate, exsiccate, dry up, **dehydrate,** anhydrate; evaporate; dehumidify; air-dry; drip-dry; dry off; insolate, sun, sun-dry; hang out to dry, air; spin-dry, tumbler-dry; blow-dry; freeze-dry; smoke, smoke-dry; cure; torrefy, burn, fire, kiln, **bake, parch,** scorch, sear; **wither, shrivel;** wizen, weazen; mummify; sponge, blot, soak up; **wipe,** rub, swab, brush; towel; drain 192.12; evaporate

ADJS **7 dry, arid; waterless,** unwatered, undamped, anhydrous; **bone-dry,** dry as dust, dry as a bone; like parchment, parched; droughty; juiceless, sapless; moistureless; **thirsty,** thirsting, athirst; high and dry; sandy, dusty; desert, Saharan

8 rainless, fine, fair, bright and fair, pleasant

9 dried, dehydrated, desiccated, dried-up, exsiccated; evaporated; squeezed dry; **parched, baked,** sunbaked, burnt, scorched, **seared,** sere, sun-dried, adust; wind-dried, air-dried; drip-dried; blow-dried; freeze-dried; **withered, shriveled,** wizened, weazened; corky; mummified

10 drying, dehydrating, desiccative, desiccant, exsiccative, exsiccant, siccative, siccant; evaporative

11 watertight, waterproof, moistureproof, dampproof, leakproof, seepproof, dripproof, stormproof, stormtight, rainproof, raintight, showerproof, floodproof; dry-shod

1067 VAPOR, GAS

NOUNS **1 vapor,** volatile; **fume, reek,** exhalation, breath, effluvium, expiration; fluid; **miasma,** mephitis, malaria <old>, fetid air, fumes; **smoke,** smudge; smog; wisp *or* plume *or* puff of smoke; **damp,** chokedamp, blackdamp, firedamp, afterdamp; **steam,** water vapor; **cloud** 319

2 gas <see list>; rare *or* noble *or* inert gas, halogen gas; fluid, compressible fluid; **atmosphere, air** 317; pneumatics, aerodynamics 1039.5

3 vaporousness, vaporiness; vapor pressure *or* tension; **aeriness; ethereality,** etherialism; **gaseousness,** gaseous state, gassiness, gaseity; **gas,** stomach gas, gassiness, flatulence, flatus, wind, windiness, farting <nf>, flatuosity <old>; burping; fluidity

4 volatility, vaporability, vaporizability, evaporability

5 vaporization, evaporation, volatilization, gasification; sublimation; distillation, fractionation; etherification; aeration, aerification; fluidization; atomization; exhalation; fumigation; smoking; steaming; etherealization; exhalation

6 vaporizer, evaporator; atomizer, aerosol, spray; propellant; condenser; still, retort

7 vaporimeter, manometer, pressure gauge; gas meter, gasometer; pneumatometer, spirometer; aerometer, airometer; eudiometer

VERBS **8 vaporize, evaporate,** volatilize, **gasify;** sublimate, sublime; distill, fractionate; etherify; **aerate,** aerify; carbonate, oxygenate, hydrogenate, chlorinate, halogenate, etc; atomize, spray; fluidize; **reek, fume;** exhale, give off, emit, send out, exhale; **smoke; steam;** fumigate, perfume; **etherize**

ADJS **9 vaporous,** vaporish, vapory, vaporlike; **airy, aerial, ethereal,** atmospheric; **gaseous,** in the gaseous state, gasified, gassy, gaslike, gasiform, fizzy, carbonated; vaporing; **reeking,** reeky; miasmic *or* miasmal *or* miasmatic, mephitic, fetid, effluvial; **fuming,** fumy; smoky, smoking, smoggy; steamy, steaming; ozonic; oxygenous; oxyacetylene; pneumatic, aerostatic, aerodynamic

10 volatile, volatilizable; **vaporable,** vaporizable, vaporescent, vaporific; **evaporative,** evaporable

WORD ELEMENTS **11** vapo-, vapori-, atm-, atmo-; aer-, aero-, mano-, pneum-, pneumo-, pneumat-, pneumato-

12 gases

acetylene *or* ethyne	hydrogen cyanide
air *or* producer gas	hydrogen fluoride
ammonia	hydrogen iodide
argon	hydrogen sulfide
avgas	ideal *or* perfect gas
biogas	illuminating gas
blister gas	inert gas
bottled gas	ketene
butane	krypton
carbon dioxide	lewisite
carbon monoxide	liquid oxygen
carbonic-acid gas	marsh *or* swamp gas
carbureted-hydrogen gas	mephitis
chlorine	methane
chlorofluorocarbon	mustard gas
coal gas	natural gas
damp	neon
ethane	nerve gas
ether *or* ethyl ether	nitric oxide
ethyl chloride	nitrogen
ethylene *or* ethene *or*	nitrogen dioxide
olefiant gas	nitrous oxide *or* laughing
ethylene oxide	gas
fluorocarbon	noble gas
fluorine	oil gas
formaldehyde	oxygen
Freon <trademark>	ozone
helium	phosgene *or* carbon
hydrogen	oxychloride
hydrogen bromide	phosphine
hydrogen chloride	Pintsch gas

poison gas
propane
propylene
radon
refrigerator gas
sewer gas
sneeze gas

synthesis gas
tear gas *or* lachrymatory
  gas
vesicatory gas
vinyl chloride
water *or* blue gas
xenon

1068 BIOLOGY

NOUNS 1 biology <see list>, biological science, life
science, the science of life, the study of living
things; **botany** <see list>, plant biology,
phytobiology, phytology, plant science; **plant
kingdom,** vegetable kingdom; **plants** 310, flora,
plantlife; **zoology** <see list>, animal biology,
animal science; **animal kingdom,** kingdom
Animalia, phylum, class, order, family, genus,
species; **animals** 311, fauna, animal life

2 biologist, naturalist, life scientist; **botanist,** plant
scientist, plant biologist, phytobiologist,
phytologist; **zoologist,** animal biologist, animal
scientist <for other NOUNS add -ist *or* -er to
names of branches listed>

3 life science; natural history, biological science;
anatomy, biochemistry, biology, biophysics, botany,
cell biology, embryology, ethnobiology,
microbiology, paleontology, pathology, physiology,
zoology; taxonomy, systematics

ADJS 4 biological, biologic, microbiological;
botanical, botanic, plant, phytological, phytologic,
phytobiological; **zoological,** zoologic, faunal <for
other ADJS add -ic *or* -ical to the names of
branches listed>

5 branches of biology

aerobiology
agrobiology
anatomy
aquatic biology
aquatic microbiology
autoecology
bacteriology
biobehavioral science
biochemical genetics
biochemistry
biodynamics
bioecology
biogeography
biometry *or* biometrics *or*
  biostatistics
bionics
biophysics
biostatistics
biotechnology *or* biotech
  <nf>
biothermodynamics
biophysics
botany

cell biology
cell physiology
chronobiology
cryobiochemistry
cryobiology
cytogenetics
cytology
cytotaxonomy
ecology *or* bioecology *or*
  bionomics
electrobiology
electrophysiology
embryology
enzymology
ethnobiology
eugenics
evolution
exobiology *or* astrobiology
  or bioastronautics *or*
  space biology *or* space
  bioscience *or*
  xenobiology
genetics

gnotobiosis
histology
human ecology
hydrobiology
hydrology *or* hydrogeology
  or geohydrology
limnology
marine biology
mathematical biology
medicine
microbiology
molecular biology
morphology
natural classification
natural history
neurobiology
neurochemistry
neuroendocrinology
neurogenetics
neuroscience

organology
paleontology
palynology
parasitology
phylogenetic classification
  or phyletic classification
  or phyletics
physiology
population biology
population genetics
radiobiology
sociobiology
somatology
synecology
taxonomy *or* systematics
virology
zoogeography *or* animal
  geography
zoology

6 branches of botany

agriculture
agrobiology
agronomy
algology
applied botany
aquiculture
bacteriology
botanical histochemistry
bryology
dendrology
economic botany
ethnobotany
evolution
floriculture
forestry
fungology
genetics
geobotany
gnotobiology
histology
horticulture
hydroponics
mycology
olericulture
paleobotany
palynology
phycology
physiology
phytobiology

phytochemistry
phytoecology
phytography
phytology
phytosociology
plant anatomy *or*
  phytotomy
plant biochemistry *or*
  phytochemistry
plant breeding
plant cytology
plant ecology *or*
  phytoecology
plant geography *or*
  phytogeography
plant morphology
plant pathology *or*
  phytopathology *or*
  vegetable pathology
plant physiology *or*
  vegetable physiology
plant taxonomy
pomology
pteridology
research botany
seed biology
silviculture
systematic botany *or*
  taxonomy

7 branches of zoology

anatomy
animal behavior
animal chemistry *or*
  zoochemistry
animal pathology *or*
  zoopathology
animal physiology *or*
  zoonomy

animal psychology
apiculture
applied zoology
arachnology
behavioral ecology
biochemistry
biometrics
biophysics

comparative anatomy *or* zootomy
comparative embryology
comparative psychology
conchology
cytogenetics
cytology
ecology
embryology
endocrinology
entomology
ethology
evolution
genetics
helminthology
herpetology
histology
ichthyology
invertebrate zoology
malacology

mammalogy
marine biology
morphology
ophiology
ornithology
paleontology
parasitology
physiological chemistry
physiology
protozoology
research zoology
sociobiology
systematic zoology *or* systematics *or* taxonomy
vertebrate zoology
veterinary medicine
wildlife management
zoogeography
zoography

1069 AGRICULTURE

NOUNS **1 agriculture, farming** <see list>, husbandry; cultivation, culture, geoponics, tillage, tilth; green revolution; agrology, agronomy, agronomics, agrotechnology, agricultural science, agroscience, agriscience; thremmatology; agroecosystem; agrogeology, agricultural geology; agrochemistry; agricultural engineering; agricultural economics; rural economy *or* economics, farm economy *or* economics, agrarian economy *or* economics, agrarianism; agribusiness *or* agrobusiness, agribiz <nf>, agroindustry; sharecropping; intensive farming, factory farming, mixed farming, crop farming, organic farming, subsistence farming

2 horticulture, gardening; landscape gardening, landscape architecture, groundskeeping; truck gardening, market gardening, olericulture; flower gardening, flower-growing, floriculture; viniculture, viticulture; orcharding, fruit-growing, pomiculture, citriculture; arboriculture, silviculture; indoor gardening

3 forestry, arboriculture, tree farming, silviculture, forest management; Christmas tree farming; forestation, afforestation, reforestation; lumbering, logging; deforestation; woodcraft

4 <agricultural deities> vegetation spirit *or* daemon, fertility god *or* spirit, year-daemon, forest god *or* spirit, green man, corn god, Ceres, Demeter, Gaea, Triptolemus, Dionysus, Persephone, Kore, Flora, Aristaeus, Pomona, Frey

5 agriculturist, agriculturalist; agrologist, agronomist; **farmer,** granger, husbandman, **yeoman,** cultivator, tiller, sodbuster, **tiller of the soil;** rural economist, agrotechnician; boutique farmer, contour farmer, crop-farmer, dirt farmer

<nf>, truck farmer, etc; gentleman-farmer; **peasant,** *campesino* <Sp>, *Bauer* <Ger>, countryman, rustic, **grower,** raiser; **planter,** tea-planter, coffee-planter, etc; peasant holder *or* proprietor, *kulak* and *muzhik* <Russ>; tenant farmer, crofter <Brit>, peasant farmer; sharecropper, cropper, collective farm worker, *kolkhoznik* <Russ>, *kibbutznik* <Yiddish>; **agricultural worker, farm worker,** farmhand, farm laborer, migrant *or* migratory worker *or* laborer, bracero, picker; plowman, plowboy; farmboy, farmgirl; planter, sower; reaper, harvester, harvestman; haymaker

6 horticulturist, nurseryman, gardener, grower, green thumb, propagator; landscape gardener, landscapist, landscape architect; truck gardener, market gardener, olericulturist; **florist,** floriculturist; vinegrower, viniculturist, viticulturist, vintager; *vigneron* <Fr>; vinedresser; orchardist, orchardman, fruitgrower

7 forester, arboriculturist, arborist, silviculturist, dendrologist, verderer, tree farmer, topiarist; conservationist; **ranger,** forest ranger, forest manager; woodsman, woodman <Brit>, woodcraftsman, woodlander; **logger, lumberman,** timberman, lumberjack, lumberer; woodcutter, wood chopper; tapper; tree surgeon

8 farm, farmplace, farmstead, farmhold <old>, farmery <Brit>, **grange,** location <Austral>, pen <Jamaica>; boutique farm, crop farm, dirt farm, tree farm, etc; **plantation,** cotton plantation, etc, *hacienda* <Sp>; croft, homecroft <Brit>; **homestead,** steading; toft <Brit>; mains <Brit nf>; demesne, homefarm, demesne farm, manor farm; **barnyard,** farmyard, barton <Brit nf>; collective farm, *kolkhoz* <Russ>, *kibbutz* <Heb>; farmland, cropland, arable land, plowland, fallow; grassland, pasture 310.8

9 field, tract, plat, **plot, patch,** piece *or* parcel of land; cultivated land; clearing; hayfield, corn field, wheat field, etc; paddy, paddy field, rice paddy

10 garden, *jardin* <Fr>; bed, **flower bed,** border, ornamental border; paradise; garden spot; **vineyard,** vinery, grapery, grape ranch; herbarium; botanical garden; compost pile *or* heap, seed tray

11 nursery; conservatory, greenhouse, glasshouse <Brit>, forcing house, summerhouse, lathhouse, **hothouse,** coolhouse; potting shed; force *or* forcing bed, forcing pit, **hotbed,** cold frame; seedbed; cloche; pinery, orangery

12 growing, raising, rearing, cultivation; **green thumb**

13 cultivation, cultivating, culture, **tilling,** dressing, working; harrowing, plowing, contour plowing, furrowing, listing, fallowing, weeding, hoeing, pruning, thinning; overcropping, overcultivation; irrigation, overirrigation

14 planting, setting; **sowing, seeding,** semination, insemination; breeding, hydridizing; **dissemination,** broadcast, broadcasting; transplantation, resetting; retimbering, reforestation

15 harvest, harvesting, **reaping, gleaning,** gathering, cutting; nutting; cash crop, root crop, **crop** 472.5

VERBS **16 farm, ranch, work the land; grow, raise,** rear; crop; dryfarm; sharecrop; **garden; have a green thumb**

17 cultivate, culture, **dress, work, till,** till the soil, dig, delve, spade; mulch; **plow,** plow in, plow under, plow up, list, fallow, backset <W US>, double-dig, rototill, fork; take cuttings, graft; irrigate; **harrow,** rake; **weed,** weed out, hoe, cut, prune, thin, thin out; force; overcrop, overcultivate; slash and burn; top-dress, compost, fertilize 889.8

18 plant, implant <old>, **set,** put in; **sow, seed,** seed down, seminate, inseminate; **disseminate,** broadcast, sow broadcast, scatter seed; drill; bed; dibble; transplant, reset, pot, **transplant;** vernalize; **forest,** afforest; deforest; retimber, reforest

19 harvest, reap, crop, **glean, gather,** gather in, bring in, get in the harvest, reap and carry; **pick,** pluck; dig, grabble <S US>; mow, cut; hay; nut; crop herbs

ADJS **20 agricultural, agrarian,** agro-, geoponic, geoponical, agronomic, agronomical; farm, **farming;** arable; rustic, bucolic, **rural** 233.6

21 horticultural; olericultural; vinicultural, viticultural; arboricultural, silvicultural

22 types of farming

boutique farming	livestock farming
contour farming	mixed farming
crop farming	organic farming
dirt farming <nf>	sharecropping
dry farming	share farming
dryland farming	slash-and-burn
factory farming	strip farming
fruit farming	stubble-mulch farming or
grain farming	trash farming
hydroponics or tank	subsistence farming
farming	tree farming
intensive farming	truck farming

1070 ANIMAL HUSBANDRY

NOUNS **1 animal husbandry,** animal rearing *or* raising *or* culture, stock raising, **ranching;** zooculture, zootechnics, zootechny; thremmatology; gnotobiotics; herding, grazing, keeping flocks and herds, running livestock, livestock farming; transhumance; breeding, stockbreeding, stirpiculture; horse training, dressage, manège; horsemanship; pisciculture, fish culture; apiculture, bee culture, beekeeping; cattle raising; sheepherding; stock farming, fur farming; factory farming; pig-keeping; dairy-farming, chicken-farming, pig-farming, etc; cattle-ranching, mink-ranching, etc

2 stockman, stock raiser, stockkeeper <Austral>; breeder, stockbreeder; sheepman; cattleman, cow keeper, cowman, grazier <Brit>; **rancher,** ranchman, ranchero; ranchhand; dairyman, dairy farmer; milkmaid; **stableman,** stableboy, **groom,** hostler, equerry; trainer, breaker, tamer; broncobuster *and* buckaroo <nf>; **blacksmith,** horseshoer, farrier

3 herder, drover, herdsman, herdboy; **shepherd,** shepherdess, **sheepherder,** sheepman; goatherd; swineherd, pigman, pigherd, hogherd; gooseherd, gooseboy, goosegirl; swanherd; **cowherd,** neatherd <Brit>; cowboy, cowgirl, cowhand, puncher *and* **cowpuncher** *and* cowpoke <nf>, waddy <W US>, cowman, cattleman, *vaquero* <Sp>, gaucho; horseherd, **wrangler,** horse wrangler

4 apiarist, apiculturist, **beekeeper,** beeherd

5 farm, stock farm, animal farm; **ranch,** rancho, rancheria; station <Austral>; horse farm, stable, stud farm; **cattle ranch;** dude ranch; pig farm, piggery; chicken farm *or* ranch, turkey farm, duck farm, poultry farm; sheep farm *or* ranch; fur farm *or* ranch, mink farm *or* ranch; **dairy farm;** factory farm; animal enclosure

VERBS **6 raise, breed,** rear, grow, hatch, feed, nurture, fatten; keep, run; ranch, farm; culture; back-breed

7 tend; groom, rub down, brush, curry, currycomb; water, drench, feed, fodder; bed, bed down, litter; milk; harness, saddle, hitch, bridle, yoke; gentle, handle, manage; tame, train, break

8 drive, herd, drove <Brit>, herd up, punch cattle, **shepherd,** ride herd on; spur, goad, prick, lash, whip; wrangle, round up; corral, cage

1071 EARTH SCIENCE

NOUNS **1 earth science, earth sciences** <see list>; geoscience; geography, geology, rock hunting *and* rock hounding <nf>, geological science, oceanography, oceanographic science, meteorology, atmospheric science, planetary science, space science

2 earth scientist, geoscientist; **geologist,** rock hound *and* rock hunter <nf>, **geographer, oceanographer, astronomer,** star-gazer <nf>, **meteorologist,** weather man <for other NOUNS, add -ist *or* -er to names of branches listed below>

3 earth sciences

aerology
aeronomy
astrogeology
bathymetry
biogeography
biostratigraphy
chronostratigraphy
climatology
crystallography
economic geology
engineering geology
environmental geology
geobotanical prospecting
geobotany
geochemistry
geochronology
geochronometry
geocosmogony
geodesy
geodynamics
geography
geological cartography
geology
geomagnetism
geomorphology
geophysics
geopolitics
glacial geology
glaciology
gravimetry
historical geology
hydrography
igneous petrology
invertebrate paleontology
hydrology *or* geohydrology
   or hydrogeology
lithostratigraphy
magnetostratigraphy
marine geology
metamorphic petrology
meteorology
micropaleontology
mineralogy

mining geology
oceanography
oceanology
paleobiogeography
paleobotany
paleoclimatology
paleogeography
paleogeophysics
paleolimnology
paleomagnetism
paleontology
paleopedology
palynology
pedology *or* soil science
petrochemistry
petrogenesis
petrography
petroleum geology
petrology *or* lithology
physical climatology
physical geography *or*
   physiography
physical geology
physical oceanography
planetology
plate *or* global tectonics
radiometric dating
sedimentary petrology
sedimentology
seismography
seismology
stratigraphy
structural geology
submarine geology
tectonic *or* geotectonic *or*
   structural geology
tectonics
tectonophysics
thalassography
topography
urban geology
vertebrate paleontology
volcanology *or* vulcanology

1072 THE UNIVERSE, ASTRONOMY

NOUNS 1 **universe, world, cosmos,** cosmological model; creation, created universe, created nature, all, **all creation,** all tarnation <nf>, all *or* everything that is, all being, totality, totality of being, sum of things; omneity, allness; nature, system; wide world, whole wide world, "world without end"—Bible; plenum; **macrocosm,** macrocosmos, megacosm; metagalaxy; open universe, closed universe, inflationary universe, flat universe, oscillating universe, steady-state universe, expanding universe, pulsating universe;

Einsteinian universe, Newtonian universe, Friedmann universe; Ptolemaic universe, Copernican universe; sidereal universe

2 **the heavens,** heaven, **sky, firmament;** empyrean, welkin, *caelum* <L>, lift *or* lifts <nf>; **the blue,** blue sky, azure, cerulean, the blue serene; **ether, air,** hyaline; vault, cope, canopy, vault *or* canopy of heaven, "the arch of heaven"—Vergil, "that inverted bowl they call the sky"—Omar Khayyám, starry sphere, celestial sphere, starry heaven *or* heavens, "this majestical roof fretted with golden fire"—Shakespeare; Caelus

3 **space, outer space,** cosmic space, deep space, empty space, ether space, pressureless space, celestial spaces, interplanetary *or* interstellar *or* intergalactic *or* intercosmic space, metagalactic space, **the void,** the void above, ocean of emptiness; chaos; outermost reaches of space; astronomical unit, light-year, parsec; interstellar medium

4 **stars,** fixed stars, starry host, "living sapphires"—Milton, "the burning tapers of the sky"—Shakespeare, "the mystical jewels of God"—Robert Buchanan, "golden fruit upon a tree all out of reach"—George Eliot; music *or* harmony of the spheres; orb, sphere; **heavenly body,** celestial body *or* sphere; **comet; comet cloud; morning star,** daystar, Lucifer, Phosphor, Phosphorus; **evening star,** Vesper, Hesper, Hesperus, Venus; **North Star,** polestar, polar star, lodestar, Polaris; Dog Star, Sirius, Canicula; Bull's Eye, Aldebaran

5 **constellation** <see list>, **configuration,** asterism, stellar group, stellar population; zodiacal constellation; cluster, **star cluster,** galactic cluster, open cluster, globular cluster, stellar association, supercluster; Magellanic clouds

6 **galaxy, island universe,** galactic nebula; spiral galaxy *or* nebula, spiral; barred spiral galaxy *or* nebula, barred spiral; elliptical *or* spheroidal galaxy; disk galaxy; irregular galaxy; radio galaxy; lenticular galaxy; active galaxy; Seyfert galaxy, starburst galaxy; **the Local Group; the Galaxy, the Milky Way,** the galactic circle, *Via Lactea* <L>; galactic cluster, supergalaxy; great attractor; chaotic attractor; continent of galaxies, great wall *or* sheet of galaxies; galactic coordinates, galactic pole, galactic latitude, galactic longitude; galactic noise, cosmic noise; galactic nucleus, active galactic nucleus; cosmic string; Hubble classification

7 **nebula,** nebulosity; gaseous nebula; hydrogen cloud; dark nebula; dust cloud; dark matter; interstellar cloud; planetary nebula; whirlpool nebula; cirro-nebula; ring nebula; diffuse nebula; emission nebula; reflection nebula; absorption nebula; galactic nebula; anagalactic nebula; bright

diffuse nebula; dark nebula, dark cloud, coalsack; Nebula of Lyra *or* Orion, Crab Nebula, the Coalsack, Black Magellanic Cloud; nebulous stars; nebular hypothesis

8 **star** <see list>; **quasar,** quasi-stellar radio source; **pulsar,** pulsating star, eclipsing binary X-ray pulsar; luminary; Nemesis, the Death Star; Hawking radiation; magnitude, stellar magnitude, visual magnitude; relative magnitude, absolute magnitude, apparent nebula; star *or* stellar populations; mass-luminosity law; spectrum-luminosity diagram, Hertzsprung-Russell diagram; star catalog, star atlas, star chart, sky atlas, sky survey, Messier catalog, Dreyer's New General Catalog *or* NGC; star cloud, star cluster, globular cluster, open cluster; Pleiades *or* Seven Sisters, Hyades, Beehive; stellar evolution, stellar birth, protostar, molecular cloud, main sequence, gravitational collapse, dying star, red giant, white dwarf; nova, supernova, supernova remnant, neutron star, pulsar, **black hole,** giant black hole, mini-black hole, starving black hole, supermassive black hole, frozen black hole, event horizon, singularity, white hole, active galactic nucleus

9 **planet,** wanderer, wandering star, terrestrial planet, inferior planet, superior planet, secondary planet, major planet; minor planet, planetoid, asteroid; asteroid belt; Earth; Jupiter; Mars, the Red Planet; Mercury; Neptune; Pluto; Saturn; Uranus; Venus; solar system; syzygy

10 **Earth,** planet Earth, third planet, **the world,** *terra* <L>; **globe,** terrestrial globe, Spaceship Earth, the blue planet; geosphere, biosphere, magnetosphere; vale, vale of tears; "this goodly frame, the earth," "a stage where every man must play a part"—both Shakespeare; Mother Earth, Ge *or* Gaea *or* Gaia, Tellus *or* Terra; whole wide world, four corners of the earth, "the round earth's imagined corners"—Donne, the length and breadth of the land; geography; Gaia hypothesis

11 **moon, satellite,** natural satellite; orb of night, queen of heaven, queen of night; silvery moon; **new moon,** wet moon; **crescent moon,** crescent, increscent moon, increscent, waxing moon, waxing crescent moon, first quarter, last quarter; decrescent moon, decrescent, waning moon, waning crescent moon; gibbous moon; **half-moon,** demilune; **full moon, harvest moon,** hunter's moon; horned moon; **eclipse,** lunar eclipse, eclipse of the moon; artificial satellite 1075.6,14

12 <moon goddess, the moon personified> Diana, Phoebe, Cynthia, Artemis, Hecate, Selene, Luna, Astarte, Ashtoreth; man in the moon

13 **sun;** orb of day, daystar; sunshine, solar radiation, sunlight; solar disk; "the glorious lamp of Heav'n, the radiant sun"—Dryden, "that orbed continent, the fire that severs day from night"—Shakespeare; photosphere, chromosphere, corona; sunspot; sunspot cycle; solar flare, solar prominence; solar wind; **eclipse,** eclipse of the sun, solar eclipse, total eclipse, partial eclipse, central eclipse, annular eclipse; corona, solar corona, Baily's beads

14 <sun god or goddess, the sun personified> Sol, Helios, Hyperion, Titan, Phaëthon, Phoebus, Phoebus Apollo, Apollo, Ra *or* Amen-Ra, Shamash, Surya, Savitar, Amaterasu

15 **meteor;** falling *or* shooting star, meteoroid, fireball, bolide; **meteorite,** meteorolite; micrometeoroid, micrometeorite; aerolite; chondrite; siderite; siderolite; tektite; meteor dust, cosmic dust; meteor trail, meteor train; meteor swarm; meteor *or* meteoric shower; radiant, radiant point; meteor crater

16 **orbit, circle, trajectory;** circle of the sphere, great circle, small circle; **ecliptic; zodiac;** zone; meridian, celestial meridian; colures, equinoctial colure, solstitial colure; equator, celestial equator, equinoctial, equinoctial circle *or* line; equinox, vernal equinox, autumnal equinox; longitude, celestial longitude, geocentric longitude, heliocentric longitude, galactic longitude, astronomical longitude, geographic *or* geodetic longitude; apogee, perigee; aphelion, perihelion; period; revolution, eccentric inclination, rotation, rotational axis, rotational period; parabolic orbit, hyperbolic orbit

17 **observatory,** astronomical observatory; radio observatory, orbiting astronomical observatory *or* OAO, orbiting solar observatory *or* OSO; ground-based observatory, optical observatory, infrared observatory; **planetarium;** orrery; **telescope,** astronomical telescope; planisphere, astrolabe, flux collector; reflector, refractor, Newtonian telescope, Cassegrainian telescope; **radio telescope,** radar telescope; **spectroscope,** spectrograph; spectrohelioscope, spectroheliograph; coronagraph; heliostat, coelostat; **observation;** seeing, bright time, dark time

18 **cosmology,** cosmography, **cosmogony;** stellar cosmogeny, astrogony; cosmism, cosmic philosophy, cosmic evolution; nebular hypothesis; **big bang** *or* expanding universe theory, oscillating *or* pulsating universe theory, steady state *or* continuous creation theory, plasma theory; creationism, creation science

19 **astronomy, stargazing,** uranology, starwatching, astrognosy, astrography, uranography, uranometry; astrophotography, stellar photometry; spectrography, spectroscopy, radio astronomy,

radar astronomy, X-ray astronomy; **astrophysics,**
solar physics; celestial mechanics, gravitational
astronomy; astrolithology; meteoritics;
astrogeology; stellar statistics; astrochemistry,
cosmochemistry; optical astronomy, observational
astronomy; infrared astronomy, ultraviolet
astronomy; exobiology, astrobotany

20 **astrology,** astromancy, **horoscopy;** astrodiagnosis;
natural astrology; judicial *or* mundane astrology;
genethliacism, genethlialogy, genethliacs,
genethliac astrology; **horoscope,** nativity; zodiac,
signs of the zodiac; house, mansion; house of life,
mundane house, planetary house *or* mansion;
aspect

21 **cosmologist;** cosmogenist, cosmogener;
cosmographer, cosmographist; cosmic philosopher,
cosmist

22 **astronomer,** stargazer, observer, uranologist,
uranometrist, uranographer, uranographist,
astrographer, astrophotographer; radio
astronomer, radar astronomer; **astrophysicist,**
solar physicist; astrogeologist; cosmochemist

23 **astrologer,** astrologian, astromancer, stargazer,
Chaldean, astroalchemist, horoscoper, horoscopist,
genethliac <old>

ADJS **24** **cosmic,** cosmical, **universal;** cosmologic *or*
cosmological, cosmogonal, cosmogonic *or*
cosmogonical; cosmographic, cosmographical

25 **celestial, heavenly, empyrean,** empyreal; uranic;
astral, starry, stellar, stellary, sphery; star-spangled,
star-studded; cometary; galactic, intergalactic,
extragalactic; side-real; zodiacal; equinoctial;
astronomic *or* **astronomical,** astrophysical,
astrologic *or* astrological, astrologistic,
astrologous; **planetary,** planetarian, planetal,
circumplanetary; planetoidal, planetesimal,
asteroidal; **solar,** heliacal; terrestrial; **lunar,**
lunular, lunate, lunulate, lunary, cislunar,
translunar, Cynthian; semilunar; meteoric,
meteoritic; extragalactic, anagalactic; galactic;
nebular, nebulous, nebulose; interstellar,
intersidereal; interplanetary; intercosmic

26 **extraterrestrial,** exterrestrial, extraterrene,
extramundane, alien, space; **transmundane,**
otherworldly, transcendental; extra-solar

ADVS **27** **universally,** everywhere

28 star types

A star	blue-white giant
alpha	brown dwarf
astral body	C star *or* carbon star
B star	Cepheid *or* Cepheid
beta	variable
binary star	circumpolar star
black dwarf	close binary star
blaze star	comparison star

dark star	nebulous star
delta	neutron star
double star	nova
dwarf star	O-type star
early-type star	quasar
eclipsing binary	quasi-stellar radio source
eclipsing variable	R star
eruptive variable	radio star
evening star	red dwarf
F star	red giant
fixed star	red supergiant
flare star	RR Lyrae star
gamma	runaway star
giant star	semiregular variable
gravity star	silicon star
Greenwich star	solar *or* sun star
G star	spectroscopic binary
hydrogen star	standard star
intrinsic variable	supermassive star
irregular star	supernova
K star	variable star
late-type star	visible *or* visual binary
long-period variable	white dwarf
M star	x-ray binary star
main sequence star	x-ray star
morning star	yellow dwarf
multiple star	yellow giant
N star	zenith star
nautical star	

29 constellations

Air Pump *or* Pump	Canis Minor *or* the Lesser
Andromeda *or* the Chained	Dog
Lady	Capricorn *or* the Goat
Antlia *or* Antlia Pneumatica	Carina *or* the Keel
or the Air Pump	Cassiopeia *or* the Lady in
Apus *or* the Bird of	the Chair
Paradise	Centaurus *or* the Centaur
Aquarius *or* the Water	Cepheus *or* the Monarch
Bearer	Cetus *or* the Whale
Aquila *or* the Eagle	Chamaeleon *or* the
Ara *or* the Altar	Chameleon
Argo *or* Argo Navis *or* the	Circinus *or* the Compasses
Ship Argo	Columba *or* Columba Noae
Aries *or* the Ram	*or* Noah's Dove
Auriga *or* the Charioteer	Coma Berenices *or*
Big Dipper *or* Ursa Major	Berenice's Hair
or Charles' Wain	Corona Australis *or* the
Bootes *or* the Herdsman	Wreath *or* the Southern
Caelum *or* Caela Sculptoris	Crown
or the Sculptor's Tool *or*	Corona Borealis *or* the
Chisel	Northern Crown
Camelopardalis *or*	Corvus *or* the Crow
Camelopardus *or* the	Crater *or* the Cup
Giraffe	Crux *or* the Southern Cross
Cancer *or* the Crab	Cygnus *or* the Swan
Canes Venatici *or* the	Delphinus *or* the Dolphin
Hunting Dogs	Dorado *or* Swordfish
Canis Major the Larger	Draco *or* the Dragon
Dog *or* Orion's Hound	Equuleus *or* the Foal

Eridanus *or the River*
Fornax *or the Furnace*
Gemini *or the Twins*
Grus *or the Crane*
Hercules
Horologium *or the Clock*
Hydra *or the Sea Serpent*
Hydrus *or the Water Snake*
Indus *or the Indian*
Lacerta *or the Lizard*
Leo *or the Lion*
Leo Minor *or the Lesser Lion*
Lepus *or the Hare*
Libra *or the Balance*
Little Dipper *or Ursa Minor*
Lupus *or the Wolf*
Lynx *or the Lynx*
Lyra *or the Lyre*
Malus *or the Mast*
Mensa *or the Table*
Microscopium *or the Microscope*
Monoceros *or the Unicorn*
Musca *or the Fly*
Norma *or the Rule*
Northern Cross
Octans *or the Octant*
Ophiuchus *or the Serpent Bearer*
Orion *or the Giant Hunter*
Orion's Belt
Orion's Sword
Pavo *or the Peacock*
Pegasus *or the Winged Horse*

Perseus
Phoenix
Pictor *or the Painter*
Pisces *or the Fishes*
Piscis Australis *or the Southern Fish*
Puppis *or the Stern*
Pyxis *or Mariner's Compass*
Reticulum *or the Net*
Sagitta *or the Arrow*
Sagittarius *or the Archer*
Scorpio *or Scorpius or the Scorpion*
Sculptor
Scutum *or the Shield*
Serpens *or the Serpent*
Sextans *or the Sextant*
Southern Cross
Taurus *or the Bull*
Telescopium *or the Telescope*
Triangulum *or the Triangle*
Triangulum Australe *or the Southern Triangle*
Tucana *or the Toucan*
Ursa Major *or the Great Bear or the Big Dipper*
Ursa Minor *or the Lesser Bear or the Little Dipper*
Vela *or the Sails*
Virgo *or the Virgin or Maiden*
Volans *or Piscis Volans or the Flying Fish*
Vulpecula *or the Little Fox*

30 signs of the zodiac

Capricorn the Goat
  <Dec 23–Jan 19>
Aquarius the Water
  Carrier <Jan 20–
  Feb 19>
Pisces the Fishes
  <Feb 20–Mar 21>
Aries the Ram
  <Mar 22–Apr 20>
Taurus the Bull
  <Apr 21–May 21>
Gemini the Twins
  <May 22–June 22>

Cancer the Crab
  <June 23–July 23>
Leo the Lion
  <July 24–Aug 23>
Virgo the Virgin
  <Aug 24–Sept 23>
Libra the Scales *or the Balance*
  <Sept 24–Oct 23>
Scorpio the Scorpion
  <Oct 24–Nov 22>
Sagittarius the Archer
  <Nov 23–Dec 22>

1073 THE ENVIRONMENT

NOUNS **1 the environment,** the natural world, the ecology, global ecology, ecosystem, global ecosystem, the biosphere, the ecosphere, the balance of nature, macroecology, microecology;

ecology, bioregion; **environmental protection,** environmental policy; **environmental control,** environmental management; environmental assessment, environmental auditing, environmental monitoring, environmental impact analysis; emission control; **environmental science** <see list>, environmentology

2 environmental destruction, ecocide, ecocatastrophe; environmental pollution, pollution, contamination; **air pollution,** atmospheric pollution, air quality; **water pollution,** stream pollution, lake pollution, ocean pollution, groundwater pollution, pollution of the aquifer; **environmental pollutant** <see list>; eutrophication; **biodegradation,** biodeterioration, microbial degradation

3 environmentalist, conservationist, preservationist, nature-lover, environmental activist, doomwatcher <Brit>, duck-squeezer *and* ecofreak *and* tree-hugger *and* eagle freak <nf>; Green Panther

4 environmental sciences

autecology
bioecology *or* bionomics
ecology
environmental archaeology
environmental biology
environmental chemistry
environmental design
environmental engineering
environmental geology
environmental health
environmental horticulture
environmental management
environmental toxicology
human ecology
land management
synecology
wildlife management
zoo-ecology

5 environmental pollutants

acid rain
aerosol sprays
aircraft noise
asbestos
automobile exhaust
azo compounds
benzene
beryllium
calcium carbonates
carbon dioxide
carbon monoxide
carbon tetrachloride
carcinogens
chemical waste
chlordane
chlorine
chlorobenzenes
chloroethanes
chlorofluorocarbons *or* CFCs
chlorohydrocarbons
chloromethane
chlorophenol
chloropropanones
chlorpropham
chromium
coal smoke
dibromochloropropane *or* DBCP
dichlorides
dichloroacetate
dichlorobenzenes
dichlorodiphenyltrichloroethane *or* DDT
dichloroethanes
dichlorophenol
dichloropropane
dioxins
endosulfan
endrin
ethanes
ethylene
ethylene dibromide *or* EDB
ethylene glycol
ethylene oxide
exhaust fumes
fenoxaprop ethyl
fluorenes
fluorocarbons
fluorohydrocarbons

formaldehyde
fungicides
gasoline
halon
heptachlor
herbicides
hexachlorethane
hexone
hydrocarbons
hydrochlorofluorocarbon
  or HCFC
industrial particulate
  matter
isocyanuric acid
kepone
lead
lead paint
leaded gasoline
leptophos
malathion
mercury
metalaxyl
methyl ethyl ketone
methyl parathion
mining waste
mirex
nabam
naphthalene
nitro compounds
nitrogen oxides
nitroso compounds

noise
nuclear waste
paraquat dichloride
parathion
pentachloraphenol *or* PCP
pesticides
phosphate
polybrominated biphenyls
  or PBBs
polychlorinated biphenyls
  or PCBs
radon
radionuclides
secondhand smoke
sewage
smog
smoke
solid waste
sulfur oxides
sulfuric acid
tobacco smoke
toxaphene
toxic waste
trichloroacetic acid
trichlorobenzene
trichloroethylene *or* TCE
trimethylbenzenes
triphenyltin hydroxide *or*
  DuTer <trademark>
ultraviolet radiation
vinyl chloride

1074 ROCKETRY, MISSILERY

NOUNS **1 rocketry,** rocket science *or* engineering *or*
research *or* technology; **missilery,** missile science
or engineering *or* research *or* technology; rocket *or*
missile testing; ground test, firing test, static firing;
rocket *or* missile project *or* program;
instrumentation; telemetry

2 rocket, rocket engine *or* **motor,** reaction engine *or*
motor; rocket thruster, thruster; retrorocket; rocket
exhaust; plasma jet, plasma engine; ion engine;
jetavator

3 rocket, missile <see list>, **ballistic missile, guided
missile; torpedo;** projectile rocket, ordnance
rocket, combat *or* military *or* war rocket; bird
<nf>; **payload; warhead,** nuclear *or*
thermonuclear warhead, atomic warhead; multiple
or multiple-missile warhead

4 rocket bomb, flying bomb *or* torpedo, cruising
missile; **robot bomb,** robomb, *Vergeltungswaffe*
<Ger>, V-weapon, P-plane; **buzzbomb,**
bumblebomb, doodle-bug

5 multistage rocket, step rocket; two- *or* three-stage
rocket, two- *or* three-step rocket; single-stage
rocket, single-step rocket, one-step rocket; **booster,**
booster unit, booster rocket, takeoff booster *or*

rocket; piggyback rocket

6 test rocket, research rocket, high-altitude research
rocket, registering rocket, instrument rocket,
instrument carrier, test instrument vehicle, rocket
laboratory; probe

7 proving ground, testing ground; firing area; impact
area; control center, mission control, bunker; radar
tracking station, tracking station, visual tracking
station; meteorological tower

8 rocket propulsion, reaction propulsion, jet
propulsion, blast propulsion; **fuel, propellant,** solid
fuel, liquid fuel, hydrazine, liquid oxygen *or* lox;
charge, propelling *or* propulsion charge, powder
charge *or* grain, high-explosive charge; **thrust,**
constant thrust; **exhaust,** jet blast, backflash

9 rocket launching *or* **firing,** ignition, launch, shot,
shoot; countdown; **lift-off,** blast-off; guided *or*
automatic control, programming; flight, trajectory;
burn; burnout, end of burning; velocity peak,
Brennschluss <Ger>; altitude peak, ceiling;
descent; airburst; impact

10 rocket launcher, projector; **launching** *or* **launch
pad,** launching platform *or* rack, firing table; **silo;**
takeoff ramp; tower projector, launching tower;
launching mortar, launching tube, projector tube,
firing tube; rocket gun, bazooka, antitank rocket,
Panzerfaust <Ger>; superbazooka; multiple
projector, calliope, Stalin organ, Katusha;
antisubmarine projector, Mark 10, hedgehog <nf>;
Minnie Mouse launcher, mousetrap <nf>;
Meilewagon

11 rocket scientist *or* technician, rocketeer *or*
rocketer, rocket *or* missile man, rocket *or* missile
engineer

VERBS **12 rocket, skyrocket**

13 launch, project, **shoot, fire,** blast off; abort

14 rockets, missiles

AAM *or* air-to-air
  missile
AA target rocket
ABM *or* antiballistic
  missile
airborne rocket
anchor rocket
antiaircraft rocket
antimine rocket
antimissile
antiradar rocket
antisubmarine *or* antisub
  rocket
antitank rocket
ASM *or* air-to-surface
  missile
ATA missile *or* air-to-air
ATG rocket *or* air-to-
  ground

atom-rocket
ATS *or* air-to-ship
AUM *or* air-to-underwater
  missile
barrage rocket
bat bomb
bazooka rocket
bombardment rocket
booster
chemical rocket
combat high-explosive
  rocket
Congreve rocket
countermissile
demolition rocket
fin-stabilized rocket
fireworks rocket
flare rocket
flying tank

GAPA *or* ground-to-air
  pilotless aircraft
glide bomb
GTA rocket *or* ground-to-air
GTG rocket *or* ground-to-
  ground
guided missile
harpoon rocket
high-altitude rocket
homing rocket
HVAR *or* high velocity
  aircraft rocket
ICBM *or* intercontinental
  ballistic missile
incendiary antiaircraft
  rocket
incendiary rocket
ion rocket
IRBM *or* intermediate
  range ballistic missile
launch vehicle *or* launcher
line-throwing rocket
liquid-fuel rocket
long-range rocket
MIRV *or* multiple
  independently targetable
  re-entry vehicle
MRV *or* multiple re-entry
  vehicle
multistage rocket
ram rocket
retro-float light
retrorocket
rockoon
SAM *or* surface-to-air
  missile
scud

signal rocket
skyrocket
smart rocket
smokeless powder rocket
smoke rocket
snake *or* antimine
solid-fuel rocket
solid rocket booster *or*
  SRB
space rocket
spinner
spin-stabilized rocket
SSM *or* surface-to-surface
  missile
STS rocket *or* ship-to-shore
submarine killer
supersonic rocket
target missile
torpedo rocket
training rocket *or* missile
trajectory missile
transoceanic rocket
ullage rocket
vernier *or* vernier rocket
window rocket *or* antiradar
winged rocket
XAAM *or* experimental air-
  to-air missile
XASM *or* experimental air-
  to-surface missile
XAUM *or* experimental air-
  to-underwater missile
XSAM *or* experimental
  surface-to-air missile
XSSM *or* experimental
  surface-to-surface
  missile

1075 SPACE TRAVEL

NOUNS **1 space travel, astronautics,** cosmonautics,
space flight, navigation of empty space;
interplanetary travel, space exploration; manned
flight; space walk; space navigation, astrogation;
space science, space technology *or* engineering;
aerospace science, aerospace technology *or*
engineering; space *or* aerospace research; space *or*
aerospace medicine, bioastronautics; astrionics;
escape velocity; rocketry 1074; multistage flight,
step flight, shuttle flights; trip to the moon, trip to
Mars, grand tour; space terminal, target planet;
space age; science fiction, cyberpunk

2 spacecraft <see list>, **spaceship, space rocket,**
rocket ship, manned rocket, interplanetary rocket;
rocket 1074.2; orbiter; **shuttle,** space shuttle;
capsule, space capsule, ballistic capsule; **nose
cone, heat shield,** heat barrier, thermal barrier;
module, command module, lunar excursion

module *or* LEM, lunar module *or* LM; moon ship,
Mars ship, etc; deep-space ship; exploratory ship,
reconnaissance rocket; ferry rocket, tender rocket,
tanker ship, fuel ship; **multistage rocket** 1074.5,
shuttle rocket, retrorocket, rocket thruster *or*
thruster, attitude-control rocket, main rocket;
burn; space docking, docking, docking maneuver;
orbit, parking orbit, geostationary orbit; earth
orbit, apogee, perigee; lunar *or* moon orbit,
apolune, perilune, apocynthion, pericynthion;
guidance system, terrestrial guidance; soft landing,
hard landing; injection, insertion, lunar insertion,
Earth insertion; **reentry, splashdown**

3 flying saucer, unidentified flying object *or* UFO

4 rocket engine 1074.2; atomic power plant; solar
battery; power cell

5 space station, astro station, **space island,** island
base, cosmic stepping-stone, halfway station,
advance base; manned station; inner station, outer
station, transit station, space airport, **spaceport,**
spaceport station, space platform, space dock,
launching base, research station, space laboratory,
space observatory; tracking station, radar tracking
station; radar station, radio station; radio relay
station, radio mirror; space mirror, solar mirror;
moon station, moon base, lunar base, lunar city,
observatory on the moon

6 artificial satellite <see list>, **satellite,** space
satellite, robot satellite, unmanned satellite,
sputnik; communications satellite, active
communications satellite, communications relay
satellite, weather satellite, earth satellite,
astronomical satellite, meteorological satellite,
geostationary satellite, geosynchronous satellite,
spy satellite, orbiting observatory, space
observatory, geophysical satellite, navigational
satellite, geodetic satellite, research satellite,
interplanetary monitoring satellite, automated
satellite; **probe, space probe** <see list>, geo probe,
interplanetary explorer, planetary probe; orbiter,
lander

7 <satellite telemetered recorders> micro-
instrumentation; aurora particle counter, cosmic
ray counter, gamma ray counter, heavy particle
counter, impulse recorder, magnetometer, solar
ultraviolet detector, solar X-ray detector,
telecamera

8 astronaut, astronavigator, cosmonaut, **spaceman,
spacewoman,** space crew member, shuttle crew
member, space traveler, rocketeer, rocket pilot;
space doctor; space crew; planetary colony, lunar
colony; extraterrestrial visitor, alien, saucerman,
man from Mars, Martian, little green man

9 rocketry, rocket propulsion; burn, thrust, escape
velocity, orbit, parking orbit, transfer orbit,

insertion, injection, trajectory, flyby, rendezvous, docking, reentry, splashdown, soft landing, hard landing; launch vehicle, multistage rocket, payload, retrorocket, solid rocket booster, engine, booster, propellant, liquid fuel, solid fuel; **rocket society,** American Rocket Society, American Interplanetary Society, British Interplanetary Society

10 <space hazards> cosmic particles, intergalactic matter, aurora particles, radiation, cosmic ray bombardment; rocket *or* satellite debris, space junk <nf>; meteors, meteorites; asteroids; meteor dust impacts, meteoric particles, space bullets; extreme temperatures; the bends, blackout, weightlessness

11 space suit, pressure suit, G suit, anti-G suit; space helmet

VERBS 12 travel in space, go into outer space; launch, lift off, blast off, enter orbit, orbit the earth, go into orbit, orbit the moon, etc; navigate in space, astrogate; escape earth, break free, leave the atmosphere, shoot into space; rocket to the moon, park in space, hang *or* float in space, space-walk

ADJS 13 astronautical, cosmonautical, spacetraveling, spacefaring; astrogational; rocketborne, spaceborne

14 spacecraft, artificial satellites, space probes

A-1	communications satellites
Alouette	*or* comsats
Anik	Comsat
Anna	Copernicus
Apollo	cosmic background
Ariane	explorer *or* COBE
Ariel	Cosmos
Astro	Courier
ATDA	D1-C
Atlas-Score	D2-D
ATS	Deep Space
Aurora 7 <Mercury>	Diapason
Biosatellite	Discoverer
Cassini	Early Bird

Echo	OGO *or* orbiting
Einstein	geophysical observatory
Elektron	orbiter
ERS	OSO *or* orbiting solar
ESSA *or* environmental	observatory
survey satellite	OV1
Explorer	OV3
Explorer 760	Pageos
Faith 7 <Mercury>	Pegasus
FR-1	Pioneer
Freedom 7 <Mercury>	Polyot
Friendship 7 <Mercury>	probe
Galileo	Proton
GATV	Ranger
Gemini	Relay
Geostationary Operational	ROSAT
Environmental Satellite	Samos
or GOES	San Marco
Greb	Secor
Hubble Space Telescope	Sigma 7 <Mercury>
Injun	Skylab
Intelsat	Solar Max
killersat	Soyuz
Lageos *or* laser	Spacelab
geodynamic satellite	space shuttle *or* shuttle
Lani Bird	space station
Liberty Bell 7	Spartan
<Mercury>	Sputnik
Lofti	Stardust
Luna	Surveyor
Lunar Orbiter	Syncom
Lunar Prospector	Tardis
Lunik	Telstar
Mariner	TIROS *or* television and
Mars Global Surveyor	infrared observation
Mars Pathfinder	satellite
Mars Sojourner	Transit
Mars Surveyor	Ulysses
Mercury	Vanguard
Midas	Venera
MIR	Viking
Molniya	Voskhod
Nimbus	Vostok
OAO *or* orbiting	WRESAT
astronomical observatory	Zondd

Index

How to Use This Index

Numbers after index entries refer to categories and paragraphs in the front section of this book, not to page numbers. The part of the number before the decimal point refers to the category in which you will find synonyms and related words for the word you are looking up. The part of the number after the decimal point refers to the paragraph or paragraphs within the category. Look at the index entry for **abdomen** on the next page:

abdomen 2.18

This entry listing tells you that you can find words related to **abdomen** in paragraph 18 of category 2.

Words, of course, frequently have more than one meaning. Each of those meanings may have synonyms or associated related words. Look at the entry for **abhor**:

abhor dislike 99.3
hate 103.5

This tells you that you will find synonyms for **abhor** in the sense meaning "dislike" in category 99, paragraph 3. It also tells you that you will find synonyms for **abhor**, meaning "hate," in category 103, paragraph 5.

In many cases, words are spelled the same as nouns, verbs, adjectives, etc. Look at the entry for **abandon** and notice that here you are directed to **abandon** when it is used as a noun and when it is used as a verb in a variety of meanings. Here, as in the examples above, you are referred to the category and paragraph number.

Not all words in the main part of the book are included in the index. Many adverbs ending with **-ly** have been left out of the index, but you will find the common adverbs ending in **-ly** here, such as **lightly** or **easily**. If you can't find the adverb ending in **-ly** that you are looking for, look up the word in its adjective form and go to that category. Frequently, you can use the words in the adjective paragraphs you find and convert them into the adverb you are looking for by simply adding **-ly** to the adjective.

To make it easier to find phrases, we have indexed them according to their first word, unless that first word is an article such as **a**, **the**, or **an**. You do not have to guess what the main word of the phrase is to find it in the index. Simply look up the first word in the phrase. For example, **hot air** will be found in the Hs, **fat cat** in the Fs, and **let go** in the Ls.

A-1 important 997.17
 perfect 1002.6
abaft aft 182.69
 after 217.14
abandon
 n zeal 101.2
 fury 105.8
 carelessness 340.2
 unrestraint 430.3
 turpitude 654.5
 excess 993.1
 v quit 188.9
 leave undone 340.7
 desert 370.5
 break the habit 374.3
 discard 390.7
 surrender 433.8
 disregard 435.3
 relinquish 475.3
 swear off 668.8
 cease 857.6
 dismiss 984.4
abandoned
 zealous 101.9
 frenzied 105.25
 available 222.15
 neglected 340.14
 forsaken 370.8
 disused 390.10
 unrestrained 430.24
 relinquished 475.5
 forlorn 584.12
 outcast 586.10
 corrupt 654.14
 profligate 665.25
 excessive 993.16
abase debase 137.5
 demote 447.3
abashed
 distressed 96.22
 humiliated 137.14
 bewildered 971.24
abate weaken 16.10
 relieve 120.5
 decrease 252.6
 bate 252.8
 subtract 255.9
 discount 631.2
 moderate 670.6
 relax 670.9
 qualify 959.3
abatement
 weakening 16.5
 relief 120.1
 decrease 252.1
 discount 631.1
 modulation 670.2
abattoir 308.12
abbé 699.2
abbess
 mistress 575.2
 nun 699.18
abbey 703.6
abbot 699.16
abbreviate
 delete 255.12
 contract 260.7
 shorten 268.6
 be brief 537.5
abbreviated
 short 268.8

shortened 268.9
 concise 537.6
abbreviation
 deletion 255.5
 contraction 260.1
 shortening 268.3
 shortening 537.4
 abridgment 557.1
ABC's
 writing system 546.3
 elementary education 568.5
 basics 818.6
abdicate give up 370.7
 cease to use 390.4
 resign 448.2
abdication 475.1
abdomen 2.18
abdominal 2.31
abduct seize 480.14
 abduce 482.20
abduction
 seizure 480.2
 kidnapping 482.9
abductor 483.10
abeam 218.11
abed 20.11
Abélard and Héloïse 104.18
aberrant
 deviative 164.7
 wrong 638.3
 changed 852.10
 abnormal 870.9
 erroneous 975.16
aberration
 deviation 164.1
 divergence 171.1
 obliquity 204.1
 abnormality 870.1
 insanity 926.1
 eccentricity 927.1
 error 975.1
abet advance 162.5
 encourage 375.21
 aid 449.11
 encourage 449.14
abettor
 prompter 375.10
 accomplice 616.3
 supporter 616.9
abeyance
 inertness 173.4
 discontinuance 390.2
 pause 857.3
abhor dislike 99.3
 hate 103.5
abhorrent
 offensive 98.18
 unlikable 99.7
 hating 103.7
abide await 130.8
 endure 134.5
 inhabit 225.7
 live on 761.9
 endure 827.6
 wait 846.12
 remain 853.5
 continue 856.3
abide by
 assent 332.8
 observe 434.2
 execute 437.9

abide in 761.11
abiding
 n habitation 225.1
 adj resident 225.13
 durable 827.10
 permanent 853.7
 continuing 856.7
ability
 capability 18.2
 means 384.2
 preparedness 405.4
 skill 413.1
 talent 413.4
abject penitent 113.9
 humblehearted 137.11
 obsequious 138.14
 submissive 433.12
 base 661.12
abjure
 n recant 363.8
 v deny 335.4
 give up 370.7
 reject 372.2
 cease to use 390.4
 relinquish 475.3
ablate decrease 252.6
 consume 388.3
 wear 393.20
 waste 473.5
 disintegrate 806.3
 abrade 1044.7
ablaze fervent 93.18
 burning 1019.27
 flashing 1025.34
 illuminated 1025.39
able
 capable 18.14
 fitted 405.17
 competent 413.24
 possible 966.6
able-bodied 15.16
abloom floral 310.38
 ripe 407.13
 gorgeous 1016.21
ablution 79.5
ably capably 18.16
 skillfully 413.31
abnormal wrong 638.3
 inconsistent 789.8
 unnatural 870.9
 insane 926.26
 eccentric 927.5
abnormality
 disease 85.1
 wrong 638.1
 unfitness 789.3
 unnaturalness 870.1
 fluke 870.1
 oddity 870.5
 insanity 926.1
 eccentricity 927.1
aboard here 159.23
 on board 182.62
abode location 159.1
 habitation 225.1
 dwelling 228
 living place 228.1
abolish nullify 395.13
 repeal 445.2
abolition
 extinction 395.6

repeal 445.1
A-bomb 1038.16
abominable
 offensive 98.18
 wrong 638.3
 wicked 654.16
 base 661.12
 terrible 1000.9
abominate 103.5
abomination
 defilement 80.4
 hostility 99.2
 hate 103.1
 hated thing 103.3
 horror 638.2
 iniquity 654.3
 evil 1000.3
aborigine native 227.3
 ancient 842.7
abort miscarry 410.15
 end 820.5
 cease 857.6
 launch 1074.13
abortion
 miscarriage 410.5
 monstrosity 870.6
 unproductiveness 891.1
abortive
 fruitless 391.12
 unsuccessful 410.18
abound
 teem with 884.5
 exuberate 991.5
about
 adv around 209.12
 near 223.20
 approximately 244.6
 prep around 223.26
 in relation to 775.13
about-face
 n reverse 163.3
 denial 335.2
 switch 363.1
 change 852.1
 conversion 858.1
 reversion 859.1
 v regress 163.10
 change 852.7
about to
 adj prepared 405.16
 prep at the point of 839.13
above
 adj superior 249.12
 higher 272.19
 previous 834.4
 adv additionally 253.11
 on high 272.21
 before 814.6
 prep on 295.37
 beyond 522.26
 in excess of 993.26
above all 249.17
above all that 141.12
above and beyond 993.26
aboveboard
 adj straight 644.14
 adv openly 348.15
above it all 94.13
above suspicion 657.8
above water
 unindebted 624.23

in safety 1007.6
ab ovo
 adj essential 767.9
 adv first 818.18
 newly 841.15
abracadabra 691.4
abrade subtract 255.9
 grind 287.8
 injure 393.13
 wear 393.20
 abrase 1044.7
 pulverize 1051.9
abrasion trauma 85.38
 subtraction 255.1
 roughness 288.1
 attrition 1044.2
 pulverization 1051.4
abrasive
 n cleanser 79.17
 smoother 287.4
 abrasion 1044.2
 pulverizer 1051.7
 adj unpleasant 98.17
 out of humor 110.17
 rugged 288.7
 abradant 1044.10
abreast
 in parallel 203.7
 beside 218.11
 informed 928.18
abridge reduce 252.7
 delete 255.12
 abbreviate 268.6
 take from 480.21
 shorten 557.5
abridged
 shortened 268.9
 concise 537.6
 condensed 557.6
 mutilated 795.5
abridgment
 decrease 252.1
 deletion 255.5
 shortening 268.3
 deprivation 480.6
 aphorism 537.3
 compendium 557.1
abroad
 adj nonresident 222.12
 bewildered 971.24
 erroneous 975.16
 adv extensively 158.12
 outdoors 206.11
 far and wide 261.16
 wide 261.19
 in foreign parts 774.6
abrogate
 abolish 395.13
 repeal 445.2
abrupt steep 204.18
 blunt 286.3
 precipitate 401.10
 commanding 420.13
 gruff 505.7
 sudden 830.5
abruptly short 268.13
 precipitately 401.15
 gruffly 505.9
abscess
 symptom 85.9
 sore 85.37

abscissa 300.5
abscond quit 188.9
 flee 368.10
absconded 222.11
absconder 368.5
absence
 nonpresence 222.1
 nonattendance 222.4
 nonexistence 762.1
 want 992.4
absent
 adj not present 222.11
 abstracted 985.11
 prep lacking 222.19
 excluding 773.10
 without 992.17
 conj unless 959.16
absentee 222.5
absentee ballot vote 371.6
 ballot 609.19
absentminded
 abstracted 985.11
 forgetful 990.9
absolute
 omnipotent 18.13
 downright 247.12
 affirmative 334.8
 authoritative 417.15
 imperious 417.16
 mandatory 420.12
 unrestricted 430.27
 governmental 612.17
 musical 708.47
 real 761.15
 thorough 794.10
 unmixed 798.7
 particular 865.12
 sole 872.9
 convincing 953.26
 evidential 957.16
 unqualified 960.2
 certain 970.13
 obvious 970.15
 accurate 973.16
 perfect 1002.6
absolutely
 adv extremely 247.22
 affirmatively 334.10
 really 761.16
 fully 794.15
 certainly 970.23
 exactly 973.21
 perfectly 1002.10
 interj yes 332.18
absoluteness 1002.1
absolve
 forgive 148.3
 exempt 430.14
 acquit 601.4
 declare a moratorium
  625.9
 confess 701.18
absorb digest 7.18
 adsorb 187.13
 consume 388.3
 understand 521.7
 acquire 570.7
 corner 737.26
 involve 898.2
 occupy the thoughts 931.20
 engross 983.13

absorbed
 engrossed in thought 931.22
 occupied 983.17
 abstracted 985.11
absorbent
 n sorption 187.6
 drier 1066.4
 adj sorbent 187.17
absorbing
 deep-felt 93.24
 engrossing 983.20
absorption
 body function 2.17
 digestion 7.8
 sorption 187.6
 permeation 221.3
 consumption 388.1
 ingestion 570.2
 involvement 898.1
 thoughtfulness 931.3
 engrossment 983.3
 abstractedness 985.2
abstain refrain 329.3
 not use 390.5
 remain neutral 467.5
 deny oneself 667.3
 abstain from 668.7
abstainer ascetic 667.2
 abstinent 668.4
abstemious
 continent 664.6
 abstinent 668.10
 meager 992.10
abstention disuse 390.1
 neutrality 467.1
 abstinence 668.2
abstinence disuse 390.1
 fasting 515.1
 continence 664.3
 asceticism 667.1
 refraining 668.2
 moderation 670.1
abstract
 n shortening 268.3
 abridgment 557.1
 picture 712.11
 abstract idea 932.3
 v subtract 255.9
 shorten 268.6
 steal 482.13
 eliminate 773.5
 adj recondite 522.16
 general 864.11
 theoretical 951.13
abstracted shortened 268.9
 absorbed in thought 931.22
 bemused 985.11
abstraction subtraction 255.1
 theft 482.1
 picture 712.11
 separation 802.1
 generalization 864.8
 thoughtfulness 931.3
 abstract idea 932.3
 theory 951.1
 abstractedness 985.2
abstruse
 concealed 346.11
 recondite 522.16
 learned 928.21
 difficult 1013.17

absurd vain 391.13
 humorous 488.4
 nonsensical 520.7
 inconsistent 789.8
 odd 870.11
 foolish 923.11
 unbelievable 955.10
 impossible 967.7
abulia weak will 362.4
 psychosis 926.3
abundance
 quantity 247.3
 store 386.1
 wordiness 538.2
 numerousness 884.1
 productiveness 890.1
 plenty 991.2
abundant much 247.8
 diffuse 538.11
 copious 884.8
 productive 890.9
 plentiful 991.7
abuse
 n misuse 389.1
 mistreatment 389.2
 berating 510.7
 vilification 513.2
 seduction 665.6
 v exploit 387.16
 misuse 389.4
 mistreat 389.5
 berate 510.19
 vilify 513.7
 seduce 665.20
 blaspheme 694.5
 work evil 1000.6
abusive caustic 144.23
 insulting 156.8
 condemnatory 510.22
 disparaging 512.13
 cursing 513.8
 threatening 514.3
abut adjoin 223.9
 juxtapose 223.13
 rest on 901.22
abysmal huge 257.20
 abyssal 275.11
abyss crack 224.2
 something deep 275.2
 ocean depths 275.4
 pit 284.4
 hell 682.1
academia 567.5
academic
 n teacher 571.1
 adj learning 567.13
 scholastic 568.19
 studious 570.17
 pedagogic 571.11
 theoretical 951.13
academician 929.3
academic journal 555.1
academy school 567.1
 secondary school 567.4
accede assent 332.8
 submit 433.6
 consent 441.2
 be instated 615.13
accelerate
 speed up 174.10
 intensify 251.5
 hasten 401.4

drive 756.4
atomize 1038.17
acceleration
quickening 174.4
intensification 251.2
hastening 401.3
accelerator 1038.11
accent
n regional accent 524.8
enunciation 524.10
notation 709.12
accentuation 709.25
meter 720.7
v emphasize 997.14
accept
take for granted 123.2
condone 134.7
forgive 148.4
assent 332.8
acknowledge 332.11
ratify 332.12
adopt 371.15
undertake 404.3
submit 433.6
consent 441.2
take 479.6
approve 509.9
receive 585.7
believe 953.10
keep an open mind 979.7
acceptable
desirable 100.30
admissible 107.12
eligible 371.24
welcome 585.12
tolerable 999.20
acceptance
composure 106.2
contentment 107.1
patience 134.1
admission 187.2
assent 332.1
acknowledgment 332.3
ratification 332.4
adoption 371.4
lenience 427.1
submission 433.1
consent 441.1
receiving 479.1
approval 509.1
usage 518.4
negotiable instrument
    728.11
accepted
allowed 332.14
chosen 371.26
customary 373.13
undertaken 404.7
received 479.10
approved 509.19
conventional 579.5
orthodox 687.7
real 761.15
believed 953.23
authoritative 970.18
accepter
assenter 332.6
recipient 479.3
believer 692.4
accepting
content 107.7

patient 134.9
lenient 427.7
submissive 433.12
access
n seizure 85.6
outburst 152.9
approach 167.1
entree 187.3
ingress 189.1
entrance 189.5
increase 251.1
passageway 383.3
influence 894.6
spasm 917.6
accessibility 966.3
retrieval 1042.8
v arrive 186.6
enter 189.7
accessibility 223.1
accessible
approachable 167.5
present 221.12
permeable 292.21
communicative 343.10
published 352.17
handy 387.20
obtainable 472.14
influenceable 894.15
possible 966.8
accession
approach 167.1
increase 251.1
addition 253.1
adjunct 254.1
assent 332.1
authority 417.12
acquisition 472.1
installation 615.3
accessory
n adjunct 254.1
belongings 471.2
participator 476.4
litigant 598.11
accomplice 616.3
nonessential 768.2
attendant 769.3
adj additional 253.10
helping 449.20
participating 476.8
unessential 768.4
accompanying 769.9
accident
nonessential 768.2
event 831.1
chance event 972.6
misfortune 1011.2
accidental
n note 709.14
nonessential 768.2
adj circumstantial 766.7
unessential 768.4
happening 831.9
incidental 843.11
chance 972.15
accident-prone
bungling 414.20
reckless 493.8
acclaim
n applause 509.2
repute 662.1
v assent 332.8

applaud 509.10
acclaimed
approved 509.19
distinguished 662.16
acclamation
unanimity 332.5
applause 509.2
acclimated 373.15
acclivity 204.6
accolade
praise 509.5
citation 646.4
accommodate
be kind 143.9
orient 161.11
accustom 373.9
provide 385.7
furnish accommodations
    385.10
arrange 437.8
oblige 449.19
reconcile 465.8
compromise 468.2
make agree 788.7
equalize 790.6
change 852.7
conform 867.3
accommodating
resigned 134.10
considerate 143.16
indulgent 427.8
courteous 504.14
accommodation
orientation 161.4
quarters 228.4
capacity 257.2
habituation 373.7
lodgings 385.3
compact 437.1
facility 449.9
appeasement 465.4
compromise 468.1
giving 478.1
loan 620.2
adjustment 788.4
equating 790.2
change 852.1
conformity 867.1
accommodation address
hiding place 346.4
address 553.9
accommodation ladder 193.4
accompaniment
adjunct 254.1
part 708.22
togetherness 769.1
concomitance 769.1
simultaneity 836.1
concurrence 899.1
accompanist
player 710.3
accompanier 769.4
accompany play 708.39
keep one company 769.7
coincide 836.4
result 887.4
accompanying
attending 769.9
happening 831.9
simultaneous 836.5
concurrent 899.4

accomplice
participator 476.4
cohort 616.3
accomplice in crime 616.3
accomplish
arrive 186.6
do 328.6
perform 328.9
achieve 407.4
succeed with 409.11
complete 794.6
evolve 861.5
finish 892.11
accomplished
achieved 407.10
skilled 413.26
accomplishment
arrival 186.1
superiority 249.1
development 328.2
act 328.3
fulfillment 407.1
achievement 407.1
success 409.1
acquirement 413.8
completion 794.4
evolution 861.1
performance 892.5
learning 928.4
solution 940.1
accord
n unanimity 332.5
compact 437.1
consent 441.1
relationship 455
accordance 455.1
peace 464.1
harmony 708.3
relation 775.1
agreement 788.1
conformity 867.1
v consent 332.9
permit 443.9
get along 455.2
give 478.12
harmonize 708.35
agree 788.6
make agree 788.7
conform 867.3
concur 899.2
accordingly
in that case 766.11
consequently 887.7
hence 888.7
according to 867.9
according to Hoyle
adj right 637.3
adv according to rule 867.8
accordion 711.11
accost
n greeting 585.4
v approach 167.3
address 524.26
greet 585.10
account
n recounting 349.3
record 549.1
report 549.7
information 551.1
credit account 622.2
fee 624.5

reckoning 628.2
statement 628.3
worth 630.2
esteem 662.3
story 719.3
tale 722.3
bill 871.5
sum 1017.6
summary 1017.11
v judge 946.8
accountability 130.4
accountable
interpretable 341.17
responsible 641.17
attributable 888.6
accountant
recorder 550.1
bookkeeper 628.7
professional 726.4
treasurer 729.12
calculator 1017.15
accountant general 628.7
account for
explain 341.10
justify 600.9
attribute to 888.4
accounting
n report 549.7
accountancy 628.6
numeration 1017.9
automation 1041.7
adj bookkeeping 628.12
accredit ratify 332.12
authorize 443.11
commission 615.10
attribute to 888.4
accredited
authorized 443.17
commissioned 615.19
accretion 472.2
accrue grow 251.6
be received 479.8
mature 623.7
result from 887.5
acculturate
naturalize 226.4
accustom 373.9
make better 392.9
accumulate grow 251.6
store up 386.11
collect 472.11
assemble 770.18
put together 800.5
accumulation
increase 251.1
store 386.1
collection 472.2
cumulation 770.9
accuracy
meticulousness 339.3
circumstantiality 766.4
correctness 973.5
accurate
meticulous 339.12
discriminating 944.7
correct 973.16
accurately
meticulously 339.16
correctly 973.20
accursed cursed 513.9
execrable 1000.10

accusation charge 599.1
accusal 599.1
accusatory 599.13
accuse
bring accusation 599.7
censure 510.13
accused
n defendant 599.6
adj charged 599.15
accuser 599.5
accustomed
wont 373.15
usual 869.9
ace military pilot 185.3
short distance 223.2
modicum 248.2
superior 249.4
skillful person 413.14
friend 588.4
game 748.2
round 751.4
card 758.2
one 872.3
first-rate 999.7
acedia apathy 94.4
wretchedness 96.6
unconcern 102.2
dejection 112.3
despair 125.2
languor 331.6
ace in the hole
advantage 249.2
reserve 386.3
aceldama
place of killing 308.12
battlefield 463.2
acerbic bitter 64.6
sour 67.5
pungent 68.6
caustic 144.23
resentful 152.26
acetify sour 67.4
chemicalize 1060.8
ache
n aching 26.5
pain 96.5
cold 1023.2
v suffer 26.8
discomfort 96.19
grieve 112.17
ache for 100.16
achievable 966.7
achieve arrive 186.6
do 328.6
accomplish 407.4
succeed with 409.11
perform 892.11
achievement
arrival 186.1
production 328.2
act 328.3
accomplishment 407.1
exploit 492.7
heraldry 647.2
performance 892.5
Achilles' heel
weak point 16.4
fault 1003.2
aching
n ache 26.5
pain 96.5

yearning 100.5
cold 1023.2
adj achy 26.12
pained 96.23
desirous of 100.22
achromatic 36.7
acid
n sour 67.2
LSD 87.10
bitterness 152.3
cauterant 1020.15
extinguisher 1022.3
hydracid 1060.3
adj acrimonious 17.14
acidulous 67.6
pungent 68.6
out of humor 110.17
caustic 144.23
resentful 152.26
vigorous 544.11
chemical 1060.9
acidhead 87.21
acidic
caustic 144.23
resentful 152.26
acidify sour 67.4
chemicalize 1060.8
acidity acrimony 17.5
sourness 67.1
pungency 68.1
causticity 144.8
bitterness 152.3
acid 1060.3
acid rain 1001.4
acid rock 708.10
acid test 942.2
acidulous
acrimonious 17.14
acid 67.6
caustic 144.23
resentful 152.26
acknowledge
thank 150.4
admit 332.11
confess 351.7
reply 553.11
pay for 624.18
attribute to 888.4
answer 939.4
testify 957.9
acknowledged
accepted 332.14
conventional 579.5
traditional 842.12
acknowledgment
thanks 150.2
recognition 332.3
confession 351.3
commendation 509.3
letter 553.2
receipt 627.2
due 639.2
apology 658.2
citation 888.2
answer 939.1
acme
summit 198.2
supremacy 249.3
height 272.2
ideal 786.4
limit 794.5

culmination 1002.3
acne 85.35
acolyte assistant 616.6
holy orders 699.4
acoustic
n sound 50.1
adj auditory 48.13
sonic 50.17
phonetic 524.30
acoustics 50.5
acquaint inform 551.8
introduce 587.14
acquaintance
information 551.1
acquaintedness 587.4
friend 588.1
knowledge 928.1
acquiesce
be willing 324.3
assent 332.8
submit 433.6
comply 441.3
acquiescent
resigned 134.10
willing 324.5
obedient 326.3
assenting 332.13
submissive 433.12
consenting 441.4
conformable 867.5
acquire get 472.8
receive 479.6
take 480.13
absorb 570.7
receive 627.3
incur 897.4
acquired immune deficiency
syndrome or AIDS
deficiency diseases 85.11
venereal disease or VD 85.18
acquisition
acquirement 472.1
gaining 472.1
receiving 479.1
taking 480.1
purchase 733.1
acquisitive
greedy 100.27
acquiring 472.15
selfish 651.5
acquit
bring in a verdict 598.20
clear 601.4
acquit oneself
behave 321.4
meet an obligation 641.11
keep faith 644.9
acquittal
observance 434.1
judgment 598.9
exculpation 601.1
acquittance 601.1
payment 624.1
acreage 158.1
acres land 234.1
real estate 471.6
acrid
acrimonious 17.14
bitter 64.6
pungent 68.6
caustic 144.23

sharp 285.8
hostile 589.10
acrimonious
  acrid 17.14
  caustic 144.23
  resentful 152.26
  violent 671.16
acrimony acridity 17.5
  causticity 144.8
  bitterness 152.3
  berating 510.7
  animosity 589.4
  violence 671.1
acrobat 707.3
acrobatic
  n maneuvers 184.13
  adj sporting 743.30
acromegaly 257.5
acronym 526.4
across
  adj crosswise 170.9
  transverse 204.19
  adv crosswise 170.13
  transversely 204.24
  on 901.25
  prep opposite to 215.7
  beyond 261.21
across the board
  comprehensive 772.7
  wholly 792.13
acrostic
  wordplay 489.8
  word form 526.4
acrylic 712.14
act
  n doing 328.1
  action 328.3
  legislation 613.5
  law 673.3
  scene 704.7
  process 889.2
  v behave 321.4
  serve 328.4
  impersonate 349.12
  sham 354.21
  stage 704.29
  be operative 889.7
  perform 892.11
act as
  impersonate 349.12
  officiate 724.13
  function as 889.8
act for
  be instrumental 384.7
  represent 576.14
  substitute for 862.5
acting
  n action 328.1
  impersonation 349.4
  sham 354.3
  playing 704.8
  adj performing 328.10
  deputy 576.16
  operating 889.11
acting-out 92.25
actinic 1025.41
action behavior 321.1
  activity 328.1
  doing 328.1
  act 328.3
  activeness 330.1

undertaking 404.1
fight 457.4
military operation 458.5
lawsuit 598.1
plot 722.4
fun 743.2
basketball game 747.3
gambling 759.1
operation 889.1
verdict 946.5
expedient 995.2
mechanism 1040.4
automatic control 1041.3
actionable
  litigious 598.21
  legal 673.11
  illegal 674.6
activate
  reactivate 17.12
  militarize 458.20
  radioactivate 1037.10
  atomize 1038.17
active
  n voice 530.14
  adj energetic 17.13
  moving 172.7
  lively 330.17
  effectual 387.21
  observant 434.4
  operating 889.11
activewear 5.2
activist
  n man of action 330.8
  instigator 375.11
  adj energetic 17.13
  active 330.17
  enterprising 330.23
activity animation 17.4
  motion 172.1
  behavior 321.1
  active 328.1
  movement 330.1
  action 330.1
  occupation 724.1
  cause 886.9
  radiation 1037.1
act of God 963.7
act of grace 143.7
act on
  take action 328.5
  operate on 889.6
  exercise influence 894.9
  pass judgment 946.13
act on behalf of 576.14
actor deceiver 357.1
  phony 500.7
  role 704.10
  motion-picture studio
    706.4
  actress 707.2
  doer 726.1
actual real 761.15
  happening 831.9
  present 838.2
  obvious 970.15
  true 973.13
actuality reality 761.2
  the present 838.1
  unquestionability 970.3
  truth 973.1
actualize 206.5

actually
  positively 247.19
  really 761.16
  truly 973.18
actuarial 968.6
actuary
  accountant 628.7
  insurance 1008.4
  calculator 1017.15
actuate
  set in motion 172.6
  motivate 375.12
  impel 902.11
act up 322.4
acuity sharpness 285.1
  alertness 339.5
  smartness 920.2
  sagacity 920.4
acumen sagacity 920.4
  discernment 944.2
acupuncture anesthetic 25.3
  practice of medicine
    90.13
acute energetic 17.13
  sensitive 24.13
  painful 26.10
  shrill 58.14
  deep-felt 93.24
  sharp 285.8
  pointed 285.9
  cunning 415.12
  violent 671.16
  sagacious 920.16
  urgent 997.22
acutely 247.20
ad advertisement 352.6
AD 821.13
adage 529.1
adagio
  n music 708.25
  adj music 708.54
adamant
  n hardness 1046.6
  adj unyielding 361.9
  immovable 855.15
  hard 1046.10
  inflexible 1046.12
  stone 1059.11
Adam's apple 524.18
adapt orient 161.11
  accustom 373.9
  fit 405.8
  compose 708.46
  make agree 788.7
  change 852.7
  conform 867.3
adaptable
  handy 387.20
  versatile 413.25
  changeable 854.6
  conformable 867.5
  facile 1014.15
  pliant 1047.9
  elastic 1048.7
adaptation
  orientation 161.4
  fitting 405.2
  piece 708.5
  harmonization 709.2
  adjustment 788.4
  change 852.1

evolution 861.3
conformity 867.1
adapter 710.2
add plus 253.4
  combine 805.3
  calculate 1017.18
added-in 772.5
addendum
  adjunct 254.1
  nonessential 768.2
  sequel 817.1
add fuel to the fire
  excite 105.12
  aggravate 119.2
  intensify 251.5
  sow dissension 456.14
addict
  drug addict 87.21
  desirer 100.12
  enthusiast 101.4
  addiction 373.8
addiction
  substance abuse 87.1
  addict 373.8
addictive 375.27
adding machine 253.3
add insult to injury
  aggravate 119.2
  offend 156.5
  impair 393.9
  pick a quarrel 456.13
addition increase 251.1
  attachment 253.1
  accession 253.1
  component 254.1
  adjunct 254.3
  expansion 259.1
  acquisition 472.1
  nonessential 768.2
  relation 775.1
  combination 805.1
  notation 1017.2
additional
  additive 253.8
  supplementary 253.10
  unessential 768.4
  fresh 841.8
additive
  n adjunct 254.1
  adj additional 253.8
addle intoxicate 88.22
  perplex 971.13
  confuse 985.7
addled
  intoxicated 88.31
  muddleheaded 922.18
  in a dilemma 971.25
  befuddled 985.13
address
  n abode 228.1
  behavior 321.1
  skill 413.1
  request 440.1
  remark 524.3
  speech 543.2
  name and address 553.9
  greeting 585.4
  round 751.3
  v solicit 440.14
  speak to 524.26
  make a speech 543.9

direct 553.13
court 562.21
greet 585.10
address book 871.4
addressee
inhabitant 227.2
recipient 479.3
correspondent 553.8
address oneself to
practice 328.8
undertake 404.3
busy oneself with 724.11
add to increase 251.4
augment 253.5
enlarge 259.4
adduction 907.1
add up compute 253.6
be right 973.10
sum up 1017.19
adenoidal 525.12
adept
n expert 413.11
occultist 689.11
adj skillful 413.22
adequacy ability 18.2
satisfactoriness 107.3
mean 246.1
sufficiency 991.1
adequate able 18.14
satisfactory 107.11
sufficient 991.6
tolerable 999.20
adhere join 800.11
cohere 803.6
adherent
n hanger-on 138.6
associate 166.2
commender 509.8
follower 616.8
adhesive 803.4
adj adhesive 803.12
adhere to
observe 434.2
execute 437.9
hold 474.6
adhesion retention 474.1
fidelity 644.7
cohesion 803.1
adhesive
n fastening 800.3
adherent 803.4
plastic 1054.6
adj adherent 803.12
viscous 1062.12
ad hoc
n transience 828.1
expedient 995.2
adj extemporaneous 365.12
unprepared 406.8
transient 828.7
substitute 862.8
makeshift 995.7
ad hominem attack 512.2
adieu
n leave-taking 188.4
interj farewell! 188.22
ad infinitum
lengthily 267.10
throughout 794.17
continuously 812.10
infinitely 823.4

perpetually 829.10
adios! 188.22
adipose
corpulent 257.18
oily 1056.9
adiposity
corpulence 257.8
oiliness 1056.5
adit
entrance 189.5
channel 239.1
adjacent 223.16
adjective 530.3
adjoin
border 211.10
join 223.9
juxtapose 223.13
add 253.4
adjoining 223.16
adjourn 846.9
adjournment 846.4
adjudicate 946.8
adjunct
n thing added 253.1
addition 254.1
expansion 259.1
associate 616.1
nonessential 768.2
attendant 769.3
relation 775.1
part 793.1
component 796.2
adj added 253.9
adjure
administer an oath 334.7
entreat 440.11
adjust
orient 161.11
size 257.15
accustom 373.9
fit 405.8
arrange 437.8
reconcile 465.8
settle 466.7
compromise 468.2
make agree 788.7
equalize 790.6
organize 808.10
change 852.7
conform 867.3
adjustable
versatile 413.25
changeable 854.6
conformable 867.5
adjusted
accustomed 373.15
fitted 405.17
adjustment
rehabilitation 92.27
orientation 161.4
habituation 373.7
fitting 405.2
compact 437.1
accommodation 465.4
compromise 468.1
good condition 765.3
adaptation 788.4
equating 790.2
organization 808.2
change 852.1
conformity 867.1

adjutant 616.6
adjuvant
n adjunct 254.1
adj remedial 86.39
helping 449.20
ad lib
n improvisation 365.5
unpreparedness 406.1
adv at will 323.5
extemporaneously 365.15
ad-lib
v improvise 365.8
be unprepared 406.6
adj extemporaneous 365.12
unprepared 406.8
administer
execute 437.9
parcel out 477.8
give 478.12
administrate 573.11
administer justice 594.5
govern 612.12
give 643.6
administer to 577.13
administration
performance 328.2
governance 417.5
distribution 477.2
principal 571.8
executive function 573.3
government 612.1
giving 643.2
protectorship 1008.2
administrative authoritative 417.15
governmental 612.17
administrative assistant 577.3
administrator
principal 571.8
director 574.1
admirable
endearing 104.25
praiseworthy 509.20
admiral 575.20
admire
cherish 104.21
respect 155.4
approve 509.9
admirer
enthusiast 101.4
lover 104.12
supporter 616.9
admissible
acceptable 107.12
receptive 187.16
eligible 371.24
permissible 443.15
justifiable 600.14
relevant 775.11
logical 935.20
evidential 957.16
tolerable 999.20
admission
admittance 187.2
entrance 189.1
naturalization 226.3
acknowledgment 332.3
confession 351.3
permission 443.1
receiving 479.1
fee 630.6

inclusion 772.1
testimony 957.2
admit receive 187.10
enter 189.7
naturalize 226.4
acknowledge 332.11
confess 351.7
permit 443.9
take in 479.6
welcome 585.7
include 772.3
allow for 959.5
admit of
be liable 897.3
have a chance 972.13
admitted
accepted 332.14
disclosive 351.10
permitted 443.16
received 479.10
approved 509.19
conventional 579.5
real 761.15
traditional 842.12
admixture
addition 253.1
mixture 797.1
compound 797.5
admonish
dissuade 379.3
warn 399.5
exhort 422.6
reprove 510.17
admonition
dissuasion 379.1
warning 399.1
advice 422.1
reproof 510.5
ad nauseam
lengthily 267.10
at length 538.16
fully 766.13
repeatedly 849.16
ado
n agitation 105.4
bustle 330.4
commotion 810.4
trouble 1013.3
adj happening 831.9
adobe
n ceramic ware 742.2
building material 1054.2
adj earthy 234.5
adolescence 303.1
adolescent
n youngster 302.1
adj grown 14.3
pubescent 301.13
immature 406.11
Adonis 1016.10
adopt naturalize 226.4
approve 371.15
use 384.5
appropriate 480.19
borrow 621.4
usurp 640.8
adoptive parent 560.8
adorable
desirable 100.30
endearing 104.25
adore enjoy 95.13

cherish 104.21
respect 155.4
worship 696.11
adorn ornament 498.8
make grandiloquent 545.7
honor 662.12
beautify 1016.16
adrift
adj afloat 182.61
unfastened 802.22
inconstant 854.7
bewildered 971.24
erroneous 975.16
muddled 985.13
adv separately 802.27
adroit skillful 413.22
smart 920.14
adsorb 187.13
adsorption 187.6
adulation praise 509.5
flattery 511.1
adult
n grownup 304.1
adj grown 14.3
mature 303.12
lascivious 665.29
obscene 666.9
adult education 567.5
adulterate dilute 16.11
rarefy 299.3
tamper with 354.17
weaken 393.12
corrupt 797.12
adulterated
diluted 16.19
rare 299.4
imperfect 1003.4
adulterer 665.13
adulterous 665.27
adultery
copulation 75.7
love affair 104.6
illicit sex 665.7
adulthood 303.1
adumbrate
foreshow 133.10
image 349.11
hint 551.10
advance
n progression 162.1
approach 167.1
course 172.2
increase 251.1
improvement 392.1
offer 439.1
promotion 446.1
furtherance 449.5
lending 620.1
loan 620.2
evolution 861.1
v progress 162.2
further 162.5
approach 167.3
move 172.5
grow 251.6
be instrumental 384.7
improve 392.7
make better 392.9
make good 409.10
propose 439.5
promote 446.2

be useful 449.17
lend 620.5
elapse 821.5
evolve 861.5
determine 886.12
push 904.9
postulate 951.12
adduce 957.12
expedite one's affair 995.3
do good 999.10
prosper 1010.7
advance! 459.32
advanced front 216.10
aged 303.16
improved 392.13
preceding 816.4
modern 841.13
premature 845.8
advancement
progression 162.1
improvement 392.1
promotion 446.1
furtherance 449.5
lending 620.1
evolution 861.1
advantage
n vantage 249.2
benefit 387.4
facility 449.9
game 748.2
purchase 906.2
expedience 995.1
good 999.4
v avail 387.17
be useful 449.17
expedite one's affair 995.3
do good 999.10
advantageous
useful 387.18
gainful 472.16
expedient 995.5
good 999.12
advent approach 167.1
arrival 186.1
coming 839.5
adventitious
circumstantial 766.7
unessential 768.4
chance 972.15
adventure act 328.3
emprise 404.2
exploit 492.7
event 831.2
happening 972.6
adventurer
traveler 178.1
mercenary 461.17
daredevil 493.4
upstart 606.7
speculator 737.11
gambler 759.21
adventurous
dynamic 330.23
enterprising 404.8
daring 492.22
foolhardy 493.9
hazardous 1006.10
adverb 530.3
adverbial 530.3
adversarial
contrapositive 215.5

oppositional 451.8
contrary 779.6
adversarial procedure 935.4
adversary
n opponent 452.1
enemy 589.6
adj oppositional 451.8
adverse
oppositional 451.8
contrary 779.6
untoward 1011.13
adversity 1011
advertent 983.15
advertise
publish 352.10
publicize 352.15
flaunt 501.17
inform 551.8
advertisement 352.6
advertising 352.5
advice counsel 422
tip 551.3
news 552.1
message 552.4
advisable 995.5
advise warn 399.5
counsel 422.5
inform 551.8
advised
intentional 380.8
reasoned 935.21
advisement advice 422.1
adviser counsel 422.3
informant 551.5
advisory
recommendatory 422.8
conciliar 423.5
informative 551.18
advocacy
promotion 352.5
advice 422.1
patronage 449.4
recommendation 509.4
advocate
n defender 460.7
deputy 576.1
friend 588.1
lawyer 597.1
justifier 600.8
associate 616.9
supporter 901.2
arguer 935.12
v urge 375.14
advise 422.5
abet 449.14
defend 460.8
commend 509.11
defend 600.10
aegis patronage 449.4
safeguard 1008.3
aeon age 824.4
long time 827.4
aerate air 317.11
foam 320.5
vaporize 1067.8
aerial
n radio transmitter 1034.4
adj aviation 184.49
high 272.14
airy 317.12
chimeric 986.22

vaporous 1067.9
aerialist 707.3
aerification 1067.5
aerify 317.11
aerobe 85.42
aerobics 84.2
aerodynamic
aviation 184.49
pneumatic 1039.10
vaporous 1067.9
aerodynamics
pneumatics 1039.5
gas 1067.2
aerography
meteorology 317.5
pneumatics 1039.5
aerology
meteorology 317.5
pneumatics 1039.5
aerometer
density 1045.8
vaporimeter 1067.7
aerometry 1039.5
aeronaut aviator 185.1
balloonist 185.7
aeronautical 184.49
aeronautical engineering
1043.1
aeronautics 184.1
aeroplane
n aircraft 181.1
v fly 184.36
aerosol
solution 1064.3
sprinkler 1065.8
vaporizer 1067.6
aerospace
n atmosphere 184.32
adj aviation 184.49
aerospace engineering 1043.1
aerospace technology 1075.1
aerostatic
aviation 184.49
pneumatic 1039.10
vaporous 1067.9
aerostatics 1039.5
aerotechnics 1039.5
aery 317.12
aesthete 496.6
aesthetic
tasteful 496.8
artistic 712.20
absurdist 952.11
aesthetician 723.4
aesthetics
artistic taste 496.5
criticism 723.1
aestival green 44.4
seasonal 313.9
warm 1019.24
aestivate
hibernate 22.15
lie idle 331.16
AF tone 50.2
frequency 1034.12
afar 261.15
afeared 127.22
affable pleasant 97.6
good-natured 143.14
indulgent 427.8
courteous 504.14

informal 581.3
sociable 582.22
cordial 587.16
affair
love affair 104.6
undertaking 404.1
social gathering 582.10
occupation 724.1
concern 831.3
object 1052.4
affaire d'honneur 457.7
affairs action 328.1
occupation 724.1
relation 775.1
concerns 831.4
affect
n feeling 93.1
attitude 978.1
v wear 5.44
touch 93.14
impress 93.15
move 145.5
imitate 336.5
manifest 348.5
sham 354.21
assume 500.12
entail 772.4
relate to 775.5
operate on 889.6
influence 894.7
affectation
behavior 321.1
sham 354.3
pretension 500.1
airs 500.1
style 532.2
elegance 533.3
grandiloquence 545.1
sanctimony 693.1
affecting
touching 93.22
distressing 98.20
pitiful 145.8
affection
disease 85.1
feeling 93.1
liking 100.2
love 104.1
amorousness 104.3
friendship 587.1
affectionate
loving 104.27
kind 143.13
affective
emotional 93.17
attitudinal 978.7
affectless
insensible 25.6
unfeeling 94.9
affiance
n betrothal 436.3
v be engaged 436.6
affianced
n fiancé 104.17
adj promised 436.8
affidavit
deposition 334.3
certificate 549.6
declaration 598.7
statement of principles 953.4
testimony 957.2

affiliate
n branch 617.10
member 617.11
v naturalize 226.4
adopt 371.15
cooperate 450.3
join 617.14
league 805.4
adj related 775.9
leagued 805.6
affiliates 617.12
affiliation
naturalization 226.3
adoption 371.4
alliance 450.2
blood relationship 559.1
lineage 560.4
association 582.6
sect 675.3
relation 775.1
combination 805.1
affinity
inclination 100.3
preference 371.5
accord 455.1
marriage relationship 564.1
familiarity 587.5
relation 775.1
kinship 775.3
similarity 784.2
agreement 788.1
tendency 896.1
attraction 907.1
affirm
ratify 332.12
assert 334.5
announce 352.12
say 524.23
be pious 692.6
state 953.12
testify 957.9
confirm 957.11
affirmation
ratification 332.4
assertion 334.1
declaration 334.1
deposition 334.3
consent 441.1
remark 524.3
premise 935.7
testimony 957.2
confirmation 957.4
affirmative
n yes 332.2
consent 441.1
adj affirming 334.8
consenting 441.4
agreeing 788.9
affix
n added to writing 254.2
morphology 526.3
v add 253.4
fasten 800.7
afflatus
inspiration 375.9
revelation 683.10
Muse 720.10
genius 920.8
afflict pain 26.7
disorder 85.50
distress 96.16

aggrieve 112.19
work evil 1000.6
affliction
disease 85.1
infliction 96.8
bane 1001.1
adversity 1011.1
affluent
n tributary 238.3
adj flowing 238.24
wealthy 618.14
plentiful 991.7
prosperous 1010.12
afflux approach 167.1
influx 189.2
flow 238.4
afford provide 385.7
give 478.12
furnish 478.15
have money 618.11
well afford 626.7
yield 627.4
affordable 633.7
afforestation
woodland 310.13
forestry 1069.3
affray 457.4
affright
n fear 127.1
v frighten 127.15
affront
n provocation 152.11
indignity 156.2
v offend 152.21
disrespect 156.5
confront 216.8
oppose 451.5
defy 454.3
brave 492.11
affusion baptism 701.6
wetting 1065.6
afghan 295.10
aficionado
enthusiast 101.4
attender 221.5
supporter 616.9
specialist 866.3
fanatic 926.18
afield 261.19
afire fervent 93.18
zealous 101.9
inspired 375.31
burning 1019.27
afloat
adj floating 182.60
adrift 182.61
flooded 238.25
afoot 405.23
reported 552.15
unfastened 802.22
happening 831.9
inconstant 854.7
adv on board 182.62
at sea 240.10
afoot
adj astir 330.19
on foot 405.23
existent 761.13
happening 831.9
adv walking 177.43
aforementioned 814.5

aforethought
n intentionality 380.3
adj premeditated 380.9
afoul of sail into 182.41
collide 902.13
afraid scared 127.22
weak-willed 362.12
cowardly 491.10
afresh newly 841.15
repeated 849.17
again 874.7
African-American 312.3
aft
adj rear 217.9
adv abaft 182.69
after 217.14
after
adj rear 217.9
subsequent 835.4
adv behind 166.6
aft 217.14
like 336.12
in pursuit of 382.12
subsequently 835.6
following 835.8
conformable to 867.9
because of 888.9
after a fashion
limited 248.10
somehow 384.11
after all
notwithstanding 338.8
subsequently 835.6
all things considered 946.17
afterglow
remainder 256.1
aftermath 817.3
aftereffect 887.3
shine 1025.2
afterimage
remainder 256.1
aftermath 817.3
aftereffect 887.3
optical illusion 976.5
afterlife 681.2
aftermath yield 472.5
afterclap 817.3
event 831.1
sequel 835.2
result 887.1
aftereffect 887.3
afternoon
n post meridiem 315.1
adj post meridian 315.7
aftertaste taste 62.1
aftermath 817.3
aftereffect 887.3
afterthought
change of mind 363.1
sequel 817.1
untimeliness 844.1
delay 846.2
mature thought 931.5
afterwards
subsequently 835.6
in the future 839.9
afterword 254.2
afterworld
the hereafter 681.2
destiny 839.2
aftmost 217.9

again
    adv additionally 253.11
    notwithstanding 338.8
    then 821.11
    newly 841.15
    over 849.17
    another time 874.7
    interj encore! 849.18
again and again
    continuously 812.10
    frequently 847.6
    repeatedly 849.16
against
    adj disapproving 510.21
    prep toward 161.26
    contraposed 215.7
    up against 223.25
    in preparation for 405.24
    opposed to 451.10
    in disagreement with 789.10
against the grain
    adj unlikable 99.7
    adv backwards 163.13
    crosswise 170.13
    cross-grained 288.12
    in opposition 451.9
    contrarily 779.9
agape love 104.1
    benevolence 143.4
    accord 455.1
agape
    wondering 122.9
    expectant 130.11
    gaping 292.18
    curious 981.5
age
    n time of life 303.1
    years 303.1
    generation 824.4
    era 824.5
    durability 827.1
    long time 827.5
    duration 827.5
    oldness 842.1
    v ripen 303.10
    grow old 842.9
aged ripe 303.13
    elderly 303.16
    mature 304.7
    durable 827.10
    old-fogyish 842.17
agee 204.14
ageism class 607.1
    discrimination 980.4
ageless perpetual 829.7
    old 842.10
agency
    instrumentality 384.3
    commission 615.1
    trade 731.2
    workplace 739.1
    substitution 862.1
    operation 889.1
agenda
    record book 549.11
    roll 871.6
    schedule 965.3
agent
    intermediary 213.4
    instrument 384.4
    mediator 466.3

director 574.1
    representative 576.1
    deputy 576.3
    lawyer 597.1
    assignee 615.9
    assistant 616.6
    advance man 704.25
    doer 726.1
    salesman 730.3
    transformer 852.5
    substitute 862.2
    author 886.4
    operator 889.4
    element 1060.2
agent provocateur
    shill 357.5
    instigator 375.11
age-old 842.10
ages 827.4
agglomeration
    accumulation 770.9
    joining 800.1
    cohesion 803.1
    conglomeration 803.5
    combination 805.1
agglutination
    addition 253.1
    joining 800.1
    cohesion 803.1
    densification 1045.3
agglutinative 803.10
aggrandize
    increase 251.4
    enlarge 259.4
    exaggerate 355.3
    promote 446.2
    glorify 662.13
aggravate annoy 96.13
    irritate 96.14
    vex 98.15
    worsen 119.2
    provoke 152.24
    intensify 251.5
    impair 393.9
    sow dissension 456.14
    antagonize 589.7
aggravating
    annoying 98.22
    exasperating 119.5
aggravation annoyance 96.2
    irritation 96.3
    vexatiousness 98.7
    excitation 105.11
    worsening 119.1
    increase 119.1
    resentment 152.1
    intensification 251.2
    adversity 1011.1
aggregate
    n accumulation 770.9
    sum 1017.6
    v math term 253.2
    assemble 770.18
    total 792.8
    adj assembled 770.21
    whole 792.9
aggregation
    accumulation 770.9
    joining 800.1
    combination 805.1
aggression
    enterprise 330.7

warlikeness 458.11
    attack 459.1
aggressive energetic 17.13
    enterprising 330.23
    partisan 456.17
    warlike 458.21
    offensive 459.30
    gruff 505.7
aggressor 459.12
aggrieve pain 96.17
    oppress 112.19
    offend 152.21
    work evil 1000.6
aghast
    wondering 122.9
    terrified 127.26
agile fast 174.15
    quick 330.18
    alert 339.14
    nimble 413.23
agility quickness 330.3
    alertness 339.5
    nimbleness 413.2
aging
    n maturation 303.6
    adj growing old 303.17
agitated
    distressed 96.22
    perturbed 105.23
    anxious 126.7
    jittery 128.12
    bustling 330.20
    disturbed 917.16
agitation
    perturbation 105.4
    excitation 105.11
    anxiety 126.1
    trepidation 127.5
    nervousness 128.1
    bustle 330.4
    incitement 375.4
    turbulence 671.2
    violence 917
    stimulation 917.1
agitator rebel 327.5
    instigator 375.11
    troublemaker 593.2
    mixer 797.9
    shaker 917.9
agitprop
    instigator 375.11
    propaganda 569.2
aglow burning 1019.27
    luminous 1025.30
    illuminated 1025.39
agnate
    n kinfolk 559.2
    lineage 560.4
    adj related 559.6
    lineal 560.18
    kindred 775.10
    akin 784.13
agnostic
    n skeptic 695.12
    adj skeptic 695.20
    absurdist 952.11
    doubting 955.9
    uncertain 971.16
ago
    adj past 837.7
    adv since 837.15

agog eager 101.8
    excited 105.20
    wondering 122.9
    expectant 130.11
    curious 981.5
    attentive 983.15
agonize pain 26.7
    suffer 26.8
    torture 96.18
    cause upleasantness 96.19
    excruciate 98.12
    grieve 112.17
    struggle 725.11
    be uncertain 971.9
agony anguish 26.6
    wretchedness 96.6
    harshness 98.4
    sorrow 112.10
    moribundity 307.9
agrarian rustic 233.6
    agricultural 1069.20
agree be willing 324.3
    assent 332.8
    concur 332.9
    come to an agreement
        332.10
    contract 437.5
    get along 455.2
    relate to 775.5
    be the same 778.4
    accord 788.6
    coincide 836.4
    collaborate 899.2
agreeable tasty 63.8
    pleasant 97.6
    desirable 100.30
    acceptable 107.12
    good-natured 143.14
    considerate 143.16
    willing 324.5
    indulgent 427.8
    submissive 433.12
    consenting 441.4
    in accord 455.3
    courteous 504.14
    welcome 585.12
    friendly 587.15
    melodious 708.48
    agreeing 788.9
    comely 1016.19
agreed
    adj assenting 332.13
    contracted 437.11
    supposed 951.14
    interj so be it 332.20
agreement assent 332.1
    unanimity 332.5
    obligation 436.2
    compact 437.1
    consent 441.1
    harmony 455.1
    sameness 778.1
    similarity 784.1
    accord 788.1
    understanding 788.2
    combination 805.1
    simultaneity 836.1
    conformity 867.1
    concurrence 899.1
agree to assent 332.8
    commit 436.5

contract 437.5
consent 441.2
strike a bargain 731.19
agree with
make for health 81.4
assent 332.8
concur 332.9
come to an agreement 332.10
get along 455.2
relate to 775.5
conform 867.3
agricultural
rustic 233.6
agrarian 1069.20
agricultural engineering
1043.1
agriculturalist 1069.5
agriculture
farming 1069.1
working the land 1069.1
agronomic 1069.20
agronomist 1069.5
agronomy 1069.1
aground
adj stuck 855.16
stranded 1013.27
adv on the rocks 182.73
ague symptom 85.9
shaking 917.2
aguey 1023.16
ah! 122.20
aha! 509.22
ahead
v initiate 818.10
adj front 216.10
superior 249.12
adv forward 162.8
before 216.12
early 845.11
ahead of time
adj anachronous 833.3
adv early 845.11
ahimsa peaceableness 464.4
moderation 670.1
ahoy! greeting 585.16
hey! 983.23
aid
n remedy 86.1
support 449.1
help 449.1
subsidy 478.8
benefactor 592.1
assistant 616.6
backing 901.1
v advance 162.5
help 449.11
subsidize 478.19
benefit 592.3
facilitate 1014.7
aid and abet
encourage 375.21
abet 449.14
aid and comfort 121.4
aide
commissioned officer 575.18
assistant 616.6
aidless 19.18
ail pain 26.8
suffer 85.46
trouble 1013.13
ailing 85.56

ailment 85.1
aim
n direction 161.1
motive 375.1
intention 380.1
objective 380.2
meaning 518.2
v direct 161.5
head for 161.7
intend 380.4
endeavor 403.5
aim at desire 100.14
direct 161.5
intend 380.4
pull the trigger 459.22
aimless useless 391.9
meaningless 520.6
discursive 538.13
unordered 810.12
purposeless 972.16
aim to 403.8
air
n looks 33.4
milieu 209.3
lightness 298.2
ether 317.1
atmosphere 317.2
breeze 318.5
behavior 321.1
aria 708.4
spirit 764.3
gas 1067.2
the heavens 1072.2
v air out 317.11
divulge 351.5
publish 352.10
make public 352.11
flaunt 501.17
discuss 541.12
race 757.5
air a grievance 115.15
airborne 184.50
air-built thin 764.6
chimeric 986.22
airburst 1074.9
air conditioner 1024.3
air conditioner 317.10
air conditioning
ventilation 317.9
refrigeration 1024.1
air corps 461.29
aircraft vehicle 179.1
air travel mode 181
airplane 181.1
internal-combustion 1043.3
aircraft carrier 180.8
aircrew 185.4
air-cushion vehicle
hovercraft 179.22
flying platform 181.7
airdrop 184.9
air duct 239.13
airfield 184.22
Air Force
service branch 461.21
air corps 461.29
air force
military aircraft 181.9
aeronautical organization
184.7
combat pilot 185.3

airfreight
n transportation 176.3
air travel 184.10
v send 176.15
airhead
vanguard 216.2
fool 924.4
air hole
atmosphere 184.32
air passage 239.13
airing ride 177.7
walk 177.10
ventilation 317.9
publication 352.1
discussion 541.7
air lane airway 184.33
route 383.1
airless 173.16
airlift
n transportation 176.3
flight 184.9
v fly 184.36
airline 184.10
air line airway 184.33
shortcut 268.5
straight line 277.2
air lock entrance 189.5
floodgate 239.11
airmail send 176.15
mail 553.12
airman 185.1
air mass
atmosphere 317.2
weather map 317.4
air out air 317.11
flee 368.11
airplane
n aircraft 181.1
v fly 184.36
airplay repute 662.1
radio broadcasting 1034.16
air pocket 184.32
air pollution
unhealthfulness 82.1
miasma 1001.4
powder 1051.5
environmental destruction
1073.2
airport airfield 184.22
destination 186.5
air pressure 317.4
air raid
Air Force mission 184.11
raid 459.4
air route 184.33
airs contempt 157.1
affectation 500.1
pretensions 501.2
air shaft 239.13
airship 181.11
air shuttle 184.10
airsick nauseated 85.57
aviation 184.49
air space room 158.1
open space 158.4
region 231.1
plot 231.4
air strike 459.4
airstrip 184.23
airtight resistant 15.20
close 293.12

air-traffic control 184.1
air-traffic controller
aviation 184.1
radar technician 1036.14
airward 272.21
airway air lane 184.33
air passage 239.13
airworthy
aviation 184.49
snug 1007.7
airy
lighthearted 109.12
thin 270.16
high 272.14
light 298.10
rare 299.4
atmospheric 317.12
windy 318.22
careless 340.11
unsubstantial 764.6
illusory 976.9
visionary 986.24
trivial 998.19
immaterial 1053.7
vaporous 1067.9
aisle passageway 383.3
church interior 703.9
ait 235.2
ajar clashing 61.5
gaping 292.18
akimbo 278.6
akin in accord 455.3
related 559.6
kindred 775.10
affinitive 784.13
alabaster
n whiteness 37.2
smoothness 287.3
adj whitish 37.8
à la carte 8.11
alack 98.31
alacrity
eagerness 101.1
willingness 324.1
quickness 330.3
hastiness 401.2
promptness 845.3
Aladdin's lamp 691.6
à la mode
stylish 578.12
fashionably 578.17
modern 841.13
alarm
n fear 127.1
warning 399.1
danger signal 400.1
red light 400.1
signal 517.15
call 517.16
v frighten 127.15
alert 400.3
alarm clock 400.1
alarming
frightening 127.28
dangerous 1006.9
alarmist 127.8
alas 98.31
albeit 338.8
albinism
faulty eyesight 28.1
whiteness 37.1

albino
  n whiteness 37.1
  adj albinic 37.10
album
  record book 549.11
  compilation 554.7
albumen egg 305.15
  semiliquid 1062.5
albuminous 305.23
alchemist 690.5
alchemy sorcery 690.1
  conversion 858.1
alcohol sedative 86.12
  spirits 88.13
  antifreeze 1024.8
alcoholic
  n addict 87.21
  drinker 88.11
  adj spirituous 88.37
alcoholism
  substance abuse 87.1
  dipsomania 88.3
alcove nook 197.3
  summerhouse 228.12
  recess 284.7
alderman
  public official 575.17
  legislator 610.3
aleatory
  musical 708.47
  circumstantial 766.7
  unessential 768.4
  vague 971.19
  chance 972.15
  hazardous 1006.10
alee leeward 182.68
  downwind 218.9
alehouse 88.20
alert
  n warning sign 399.3
  alarm 400.1
  v warn 399.5
  alarm 400.3
  tip off 551.11
  adj awake 23.8
  wary 339.14
  prepared 405.16
  prompt 845.9
  clear-witted 920.13
  curious 981.5
  attentive 983.15
alfresco
  outdoor 206.8
  exterior 206.11
  airy 317.12
algae 310.4
algebraic 1017.22
algebraic operation 1017.2
algesia 26.4
algid
  cold 1023.14
  frigid 1023.16
algorithm
  mathematics 1017.1
  Arabic numerals 1017.4
alias
  n pseudonym 527.8
  adj nominal 527.15
  adv otherwise 780.11
alibi
  n pretext 376.1

justification 600.4
  v excuse 600.11
alien
  n exclusiveness 773.3
  stranger 774.3
  oddity 870.4
  astronaut 1075.8
  v transfer 629.3
  adj extraterritorial 206.9
  oppositional 451.8
  extraneous 774.5
  unrelated 776.6
  extraterrestrial 1072.26
alienate
  sow dissension 456.14
  antagonize 589.7
  transfer 629.3
  separate 802.8
  indoctrinate 858.15
alienation
  defense mechanism 92.23
  dissent 333.1
  falling-out 456.4
  disaccord 589.2
  transfer 629.1
  extraneousness 774.1
  separation 802.1
  indoctrination 858.5
  aloneness 872.2
  insanity 926.1
alight
  v land 184.43
  arrive 186.8
  light upon 194.7
  adj burning 1019.27
  illuminated 1025.39
alight upon
  light upon 194.10
  meet 223.11
  come across 941.3
align level 201.6
  parallelize 203.5
  dispose 808.9
  line 812.5
alignment
  orientation 161.4
  parallelism 203.1
  affiliation 450.2
align oneself with
  back 449.13
  side with 450.4
alike identical 778.7
  congruent 778.9
  uniform 781.5
  similar 784.10
  equal 790.7
  indistinguishable 945.6
alimentary 7.21
alimentation
  nutrition 7.1
  food 10.3
alimony 478.8
aliquot 1017.23
alive living 306.13
  active 330.17
  alert 339.14
  clear-witted 920.13
  remembered 989.23
alive and kicking
  healthy 83.9
  living 306.13

alive to sensible 24.11
  cognizant of 928.16
alkali
  n acid 1060.3
  adj chemical 1060.9
alkali metal 1060.1
alkaline-earth element 1060.1
alkalinity 1060.3
alkalizer 86.25
all
  n the whole 792.3
  limit 794.5
  everyone 864.4
  universe 1072.1
  adj whole 792.9
  every 864.15
  adv wholly 792.13
the all 823.1
all aboard 182.62
all-absorbing 997.24
Allah 677.2
all along 829.11
all and sundry
  n all 792.3
  adj every 864.15
all around
  handy 387.20
  versatile 413.25
all-around event 755.2
all at once
  together 769.11
  abruptly 830.8
  suddenly 830.9
allay gratify 95.8
  relieve 120.5
  pacify 465.7
  moderate 670.6
  satiate 994.4
all but nearly 223.22
  on the whole 792.14
all clear
  n alarm 400.1
  adj unindebted 624.23
  interj all's well! 1007.9
all-consuming 395.27
all creation 1072.1
all ears listening 48.14
  vigilant 339.13
  attentive 983.15
allegation
  affirmation 334.1
  claim 376.2
  remark 524.3
  declaration 598.7
  accusation 599.1
  testimony 957.2
allege affirm 334.5
  pretext 376.3
  state 524.23
  accuse 599.7
  testify 957.9
  adduce 957.12
alleged affirmed 334.9
  pretexted 376.5
  attributable 888.6
  supposed 951.14
allegiance
  obedience or obediency
  326.1
  duty 641.1
  fidelity 644.7

allegorical
  meaningful 518.10
  symbolic 519.10
  fictional 722.7
allegorist 341.7
allegory symbol 517.2
  implication 519.2
  similarity 784.1
  comparison 943.1
allegro
  n music 708.25
  adv actively 330.25
  music 708.55
alleluia
  n cheer 116.2
  paean 696.3
  interj hallelujah! 696.17
all-embracing
  whole 792.9
  thorough 794.10
  universal 864.14
allergen allergy 85.34
  antitoxin 86.27
allergic sensitive 24.12
  anemic 85.61
  averse 99.8
allergy sensitivity 24.3
  allergic disorder 85.34
  hostility 99.2
alleviate relieve 120.5
  abate 252.8
  lighten 298.6
  moderate 670.6
alleviation relief 120.1
  decrease 252.1
  lightening 298.3
  modulation 670.2
alleviative
  n palliative 86.10
  moderator 670.3
  adj palliative 86.40
  relieving 120.9
  lightening 298.16
  sedative 670.16
alley
  passageway 383.3
  tennis 748.1
  field hockey 749.4
  bowling 750.1
all eyes and ears
  vigilant 339.13
  attentive 983.15
all for
  adj favorable 449.22
  prep in favor of 509.21
all fours 177.17
alliance treaty 437.2
  affiliation 450.2
  blood relationship 559.1
  marriage 563.1
  association 617.1
  relation 775.1
  similarity 784.1
  combination 805.1
  concurrence 899.1
allied akin 559.6
  related 775.9
  joined 800.13
  leagued 805.6
alligator 311.25
all in 21.8

all in all
on the average 246.5
on the whole 792.14
generally 864.17

all-inclusive
comprehensive 772.7
whole 792.9
infinite 823.3
universal 864.14

all in the mind
illusory 976.9
imaginary 986.19

alliteration
rhyme 720.8
assonance 784.6
repetitiousness 849.4

alliterative
rhyming 720.17
assonant 784.17
monotonous 849.15

all-knowing
almighty 677.17
knowing 928.15

allocate locate 159.11
allot 477.9
dispose 808.9

allocation
placement 159.6
allotment 477.3
arrangement 808.1
specification 865.6

allocution 543.2

all of a sudden
short 268.13
suddenly 830.9

all off ended 820.8
erroneous 975.16

all one's got 403.4

allopathic 90.15

allot quantify 244.4
lot 477.9
give 478.12
dispose 808.9

allotment rations 10.6
amount 244.2
assignment 477.3
portion 477.5
subsidy 478.8
arrangement 808.1

allottee 479.4

all out
at full speed 174.20
extremely 247.22
actively 330.25
utterly 794.16
thorough 794.10
unqualified 960.2
to excess 993.23

allover 864.14

all over
adj ended 820.8
adv everywhere 158.13
throughout 794.17
in disorder 810.17
universally 864.18
prep over 159.28

all over the place
adj dispersed 771.9
adv everywhere 158.13
in every direction 161.25
in disorder 810.17

all over with
completed 407.11
no more 762.11

allow
acknowledge 332.11
permit 443.9
give 478.12
discount 631.2
judge 946.8
qualify 959.5

allowable
permissible 443.15
giveable 478.23
justifiable 600.14

allowance
n rations 10.6
acknowledgment 332.3
permission 443.1
portion 477.5
subsidy 478.8
extenuation 600.5
fee 624.5
discount 631.1
qualification 959.1
inaccuracy 975.2
v budget 477.10

allowed
accepted 332.14
permitted 443.16
given 478.24

allow for
condone 148.4
extenuate 600.12
make allowance for 959.5

alloy
n compound 797.5
amalgam 1058.4
v corrupt 393.12
mix 797.10

all-pervading
thorough 794.10
universal 864.14

all points bulletin 382.1

all-powerful
omnipotent 18.13
almighty 677.17

all-presence 221.2

all right
adj well 83.10
acceptable 107.12
accurate 973.16
tolerable 999.20
interj congratulations! 149.5
yes 332.18

all round
everywhere 158.13
in every direction 161.25
all about 209.13

all said and done 407.11

all-seeing 677.18

all set 405.16

all sorts 797.6

all sorts of 884.3

all the better for 392.14

all the more 249.17

all there 925.4

all the same
adj identical 778.7
equivalent 790.8
adv notwithstanding 338.8

all the time
regularly 781.8

always 829.11
constantly 847.7

all the way
through thick and thin
360.10
utterly 794.16
to the end 820.13

all the worse for 393.27

all things considered
on the average 246.5
generally 864.17
on the whole 946.17

all through over 159.28
through 161.27

all thumbs 414.20

all together
unanimously 332.17
jointly 800.18
at once 830.8
simultaneously 836.7

allude to
designate 517.18
imply 519.4
remark 524.24
hint 551.10
call attention to
983.10

allurement
loveableness 104.7
inducement 375.3
enticement 377.1
allure 377.1
attraction 907.1

alluring
provocative 375.27
fascinating 377.8
attracting 907.5

allusion 519.2

allusive
suggestive 519.6
figurative 536.3

allusory 519.6

alluvium deposit 176.9
land 234.1
overflow 238.6
dregs 256.2

all wet 975.18

ally
n country 232.1
associate 616.1
v cooperate 450.3
come together 770.16
relate 775.6
league 805.4

alma mater 567.5

almanac reference book 554.9
The Old Farmer's Almanac
832.7
calendar 832.8
dictionary 871.4

almighty
adj powerful 18.13
omnipotent 677.17
adv very 247.18

almost 223.22

alms act of kindness 143.7
donation 478.6

almsgiver
philanthropist 143.8
giver 478.11

almshouse 1009.4

almsman
beneficiary 479.4
poor man 619.4

aloft on board 182.62
on high 272.21

aloha
n leave-taking 188.4
interj farewell! 188.22
greetings! 585.15

alone
adj secluded 584.11
solitary 872.8
sole 872.9
adv independently 430.33
simply 798.11
singly 872.13

along
v walk 177.27
adv forward 162.8
lengthwise 267.11

alongside
adj side 218.6
adv board and board
182.70
in parallel 203.7
aside 218.10
prep beside 218.11

along with also 253.13
with 769.12

aloof
adj apathetic 94.13
unsociable 141.12
reticent 344.10
standoffish 583.6
incoherent 804.4
alone 872.8
incurious 982.3
adv at a distance 261.14
on high 272.21

aloofness 261.1

aloud audibly 50.18
loudly 53.14

alp 237.6

alpen 272.18

alpha beginning 818.1
first 818.3

alphabet
n representation 349.1
symbols 546.3
writing 547.1
letter 547.9
basics 818.6
v letter 546.6

alphabetic
literal 546.8
ideographic 547.26

alphabetical order 807.2

alphabetize letter 546.6
classify 809.6

alpine highland 237.8
hilly 272.18

alpinist traveler 178.1
climber 193.6

already
previously 834.6
until now 838.4

alright 107.12

also
adv additionally 253.11
conj and 253.13

also known as 527.15

also-ran failure 410.8
  loser 412.5
  candidate 610.9
  jockey 757.2
altar 703.12
altarpiece altar 703.12
  picture 712.11
alter
  n self 865.5
  v castrate 255.11
  be changed 852.6
  change 852.7
  qualify 959.3
alterable 854.6
alteration
  differentiation 780.4
  change 852.1
altercation
  quarrel 456.5
  contention 457.1
alter ego deputy 576.1
  friend 588.1
  right-hand man 616.7
  likeness 784.3
  self 865.5
alterer 852.5
alternate
  n deputy 576.1
  substitute 862.2
  v vacillate 362.8
  take one's turn 825.5
  recur 850.5
  change 854.5
  interchange 863.4
  reciprocate 916.13
  adj periodic 850.7
  substitute 862.8
  reciprocal 916.19
alternating 854.7
alternation
  interaction 777.3
  periodicity 850.2
  changing 854.3
  interchange 863.1
  reciprocation 916.5
alternative
  n loophole 369.4
  option 371.2
  substitute 862.2
  adj elective 371.22
  substitute 862.8
alternative energy 17.1
alternative medicine
  practice of medicine 90.13
  unconventionality 868.2
although 338.8
altimeter 272.9
altitude
  height 272.1
  coordinates 300.5
alto
  n high voice 58.6
  part 708.22
  harmonics 709.5
  adj high 58.13
  vocal 708.50
altogether
  additionally 253.11
  wholly 792.13
  completely 794.14
  generally 864.17

the altogether 6.3
alto-rilievo
  protuberance 283.2
  relief 715.3
altruism
  benevolence 143.4
  public spirit 591.1
  unselfishness 652.1
altruist 143.8
altruistic
  benevolent 143.15
  unselfish 652.5
alum 260.6
alumna 572.8
alumnus 572.8
alveolar
  indented 284.17
  phonetic 524.30
alveolus
  cavity 284.2
  indentation 284.6
  speech organ 524.18
always regularly 781.8
  all along 829.11
  constantly 847.7
  permanently 853.9
  universally 864.14
Alzheimer's disease 85.25
AM morning 314.1
  modulation 1034.14
amalgam
  compound 797.5
  alloy 1058.4
amalgamate
  cooperate 450.3
  mix 797.10
  combine 805.3
amalgamation
  affiliation 450.2
  mixture 797.1
  combination 805.1
amanuensis
  writer 547.13
  recorder 550.1
  agent 576.3
amass store up 386.11
  collect 472.11
  assemble 770.18
  put together 800.5
amassed stored 386.14
  assembled 770.21
amateur
  n enthusiast 101.4
  connoisseur 496.7
  nonprofessional 726.5
  specialist 866.3
  dilettante 929.6
  trifler 998.10
  adj avocational 724.17
  half-learned 930.15
amateurish
  unskilled 414.16
  half-learned 930.15
amateurism
  inexperience 414.2
  avocation 724.7
  nonprofessionalism 724.9
  slight knowledge 930.6
amatory
  amorous 104.26
  lovemaking 562.23

amaze
  n wonder 122.1
  v astonish 122.6
  perplex 971.13
amazement
  wonder 122.1
  marvel 122.2
amazing 122.12
amazon
  mannish female 76.9
  giantess 257.13
Amazon 461.6
ambages
  convolution 281.1
  circumlocution 538.5
  detour 914.3
ambassador 576.6
ambergris 70.2
ambidextrous
  ambidextral 219.6
  falsehearted 354.31
  versatile 413.25
  treacherous 645.21
ambience
  environment 209.1
  milieu 209.3
ambiguity
  unintelligibility 522.1
  complexity of meaning 539.1
  gray area 539.1
  equivoque 539.2
  self-contradiction 779.3
  inconsistency 789.2
  doubleness 873.1
  equivocalness 971.5
ambiguous
  unintelligible 522.13
  equivocal 539.4
  self-contradictory 779.8
  mixed 797.14
  uncertain 971.16
ambition
  ambitiousness 100.10
  desire 100.11
  motive 375.1
  intention 380.1
ambitious
  aspiring 100.28
  agressive 330.23
  enterprising 404.8
  ostentatious 501.18
ambivalence
  psychological stress 92.17
  irresolution 362.1
  self-contradiction 779.3
  inconsistency 789.2
  doubleness 873.1
ambivalent
  irresolute 362.9
  self-contradictory 779.8
  mixed 797.14
amble
  n walk 177.10
  gait 177.12
  v go slowly 175.6
  stride 177.28
  go on horseback 177.34
amblyopia 28.2
ambrosia
  delicacy 10.8
  sweetening 66.2

  perfumery 70.2
ambulance chaser 597.3
ambulate 177.27
ambulatory
  n passageway 383.3
  adj traveling 177.36
ambush
  n trap 346.3
  v surprise 131.7
  ambuscade 346.10
  attack 459.14
ameliorate
  improve 392.7
  make better 392.9
  be changed 852.6
  change 852.7
amelioration
  improvement 392.1
  change 852.1
amen
  n affirmative 332.2
  v ratify 332.12
  adv right! 973.24
  interj yes 332.18
  so be it 332.20
amenable
  resigned 134.10
  willing 324.5
  consenting 441.4
  responsible 641.17
  influenceable 894.15
amend improve 392.7
  make better 392.9
  revise 392.12
  remedy 396.13
  re-form 858.12
amendment
  improvement 392.1
  revision 392.4
  new start 858.2
amends
  compensation 338.1
  reparation 396.6
  restitution 481.2
  recompense 624.3
  atonement 658.1
amenities
  creature comforts 121.3
  courtesies 504.7
  etiquette 580.3
amenity
  pleasantness 97.1
  facility 449.9
  polite act 504.1
  courtesy 504.6
amentia 922.9
America
  world region 231.6
  United States 232.3
American Indian 312.3
Americanism
  language 523.8
  patriotism 591.2
Americanize 226.4
American Sign Language
  523.12
amiable pleasant 97.6
  good-natured 143.14
  indulgent 427.8
  sociable 582.22
  hospitable 585.11

friendly 587.15
amicable pleasant 97.6
  favorable 449.22
  in accord 455.3
  friendly 587.15
amicus curiae
  deputy 576.1
  lawyer 597.1
  favor 894.2
amid between 213.12
  among 797.17
amidships
  adj middle 819.4
  adv midway 819.5
amidst between 213.12
  among 797.17
amigo 588.3
amino acid 7.6
amiss
  adj disorderly 810.13
  erroneous 975.16
  adv irrelevantly 776.9
  astray 911.7
  erroneously 975.20
  badly 1000.13
amity accord 455.1
  friendship 587.1
ammonia
  fertilizer 890.4
  coolant 1024.7
ammunition 462.13
amnesia trance 92.19
  thoughtlessness
    933.1
  loss of memory 990.2
amnesty
  n pardon 148.2
  peace treaty 464.7
  peace offer 465.2
  exemption 601.2
  v forgive 148.3
  acquit 601.4
amoeba 85.42
amoebic 258.15
amok
  n frenzy 926.7
  adj frenzied 105.25
  rabid 926.30
among
  v include 772.3
  prep at 159.27
  between 213.12
  amongst 797.17
amor 104.9
Amor love god 104.1
  deity 104.8
amoral
  dishonest 645.16
  vice-prone 654.11
amorality
  unmorality 636.4
  vice 654.1
amorous sexual 75.25
  amatory 104.26
amorphous
  formless 263.4
  obscure 522.15
  unordered 810.12
  inconstant 854.7
  abnormal 870.9
  vague 971.19

amortization
  payment 624.1
  transfer 629.1
amount count 244.1
  quantity 244.2
  degree 245.1
  price 630.1
  sum 1017.6
amount to cost 630.13
  equal 790.5
  total 792.8
amour 104.6
amperage power 18.1
  current 1032.2
amphibian
  n seaplane 181.8
  plant 310.3
  creature 311.3
  batrachian 311.27
  adj reptile 311.48
amphibious
  versatile 413.25
  mixed 797.14
amphitheater
  hall 197.4
  arena 463.1
  schoolroom 567.11
  theater 704.14
ample
  satisfactory 107.11
  spacious 158.11
  much 247.8
  voluminous 257.17
  broad 269.6
  abundant 884.8
  sufficient 991.6
  plentiful 991.7
amplification
  aggravation 119.1
  increase 251.1
  expansion 259.1
  translation 341.3
  exaggeration 355.1
  expatiation 538.6
  evolution 861.1
  radio-frequency
    amplification 1034.15
amplifier
  listening device 48.8
  audio 50.10
amplify
  aggravate 119.2
  increase 251.4
  enlarge 259.4
  exaggerate 355.3
  expatiate 538.7
  elaborate 861.6
  electrify 1032.26
amplitude sound 50.1
  loudness 53.1
  spaciousness 158.5
  quantity 244.1
  greatness 247.1
  size 257.1
  breadth 269.1
  wordiness 538.2
  fullness 794.2
  wave 916.4
  plenty 991.2
amputate
  excise 255.10

sever 802.11
amputation 255.3
amputee 85.45
amulet 691.5
amusement
  pleasure 95.1
  merriment 109.5
  diversion 743.1
  entertainment 743.1
amusing
  humorous 488.4
  witty 489.15
  entertaining 743.27
ana archives 549.2
  compilation 554.7
  excerpts 557.4
  collection 770.11
  maxim 974.1
anabolism
  body function 2.20
  metabolism 7.12
  transformation 852.3
anachronism
  false estimation of time 833
  chronological error 833.1
anachronistic 833.3
anaerobe 85.42
anagram
  wordplay 489.8
  riddle 522.9
anal retentive 474.8
  overfastidious 495.12
  conformist 867.6
analects
  compilation 554.7
  excerpts 557.4
  maxim 974.1
analeptic
  n remedy 86.1
  tonic 86.8
  adj refreshing 9.3
  remedial 86.39
  tonic 86.44
  restorative 396.22
analgesic
  n anesthetic 25.3
  sedative 86.12
  adj deadening 25.9
  sedative 86.45
  relieving 120.9
analogy
  parallelism 203.1
  similarity 784.1
  substitute 862.2
  comparison 943.1
analysis
  psychoanalysis 92.6
  discussion 541.7
  commentary 556.2
  circumstantiation 766.5
  differentiation 780.4
  simplification 798.2
  breaking down 801.1
  analyzation 801.1
  dissection 802.5
  classification 809.1
  reasoning 935.3
  inquiry 938.1
  discernment 944.2
  theory 951.1
  automation 1041.7

analyst
  psychologist 92.10
  critic 723.4
  analyzer 801.5
  experimenter 942.6
analytic
  schematic 801.9
  reasoning 935.18
  dialectic 935.22
  examining 938.37
  absurdist 952.11
  mathematical 1017.22
analyze
  grammaticize 530.16
  discuss 541.12
  criticize 723.5
  itemize 766.6
  differentiate 780.6
  diversify 782.2
  separate 793.6
  simplify 798.4
  break down 801.6
  dissect 802.17
  classify 809.6
  reason 935.15
  discriminate 944.4
anaphylactic 24.12
anaphylaxis 24.3
anarchic
  formless 263.4
  lawless 418.6
  turbulent 671.18
  unruly 671.19
  illegal 674.6
  incoherent 804.4
  confused 810.16
  revolutionist 860.6
anarchist
  law-breaker 418.3
  radical 611.12
  revolutionist 860.3
anarchy
  formlessness 263.1
  lawlessness 418.2
  illegality 674.1
  noncohesion 804.1
  confusion 810.2
anathema
  hated thing 103.3
  censure 510.3
  curse 513.1
anathematize
  censure 510.13
  curse 513.5
  condemn 602.3
anatomical 266.6
anatomize
  itemize 766.6
  differentiate 780.6
  analyze 801.6
  dissect 802.17
anatomy body 2.1
  human form 262.4
  structure 266.1
  anthropology 312.10
  analysis 801.1
  dissection 802.5
  physical being 1052.3
ancestor parent 560.8
  precursor 816.1
  antecedent 834.2

anticipate expect 130.5
be prior 834.3
come 839.6
foresee 845.6
predict 961.5
prevent 1012.14
anticipating
pregnant 78.18
expectant 130.11
anticipation
expectation 130.1
carefulness 339.1
anachronism 833.1
previousness 834.1
the future 839.1
earliness 845.1
intuition 934.1
foresight 961.1
anticipatory
expectant 130.11
previous 834.4
future 839.8
early 845.7
foreseeing 961.7
anticlimax 488.3
anticoagulant 1064.4
antidepressant
n drug 87.3
adj psychochemical 86.46
antidotal 900.9
antidote
counterpoison 86.26
counteractant 900.3
antiestablishment 333.6
antifreeze
n coolant 1024.8
adj antifreezing 1024.15
antigen blood 2.25
immunity 83.4
antitoxin 86.27
antihero 704.10
antinomian
n anarchist 418.3
heretic 688.5
adj anarchic 418.6
unorthodox 688.9
antinomy
self-contradiction 779.3
inconsistency 789.2
antipasto 10.9
antipathetic
oppositional 451.8
hostile 589.10
contrary 779.6
disagreeing 789.6
counteractive 900.8
antipathy
dislike 99.2
loathing 103.1
hated thing 103.3
refusal 325.1
hostility 451.2
enmity 589.3
contrariety 779.1
counteraction 900.1
antiphon paean 696.3
response 708.23
answer 939.1
antipodes
opposites 215.2
remote region 261.4

poles 779.2
Antipodes 231.6
antipyretic
n febrifuge 86.14
adj antidotal 86.41
antiquarian
n antiquary 842.5
adj archaeological 842.20
antiquated
disused 390.10
past 837.7
grown old 842.13
antique
n relic 842.6
back number 842.8
adj disused 390.10
durable 827.10
past 837.7
old 842.10
antiquated 842.13
antiquity
durability 827.1
ancient times 837.3
oldness 842.1
antique 842.6
antireligious 695.22
anti-Semitism
hate 103.1
discrimination 980.4
antiseptic
n disinfectant 86.21
poison 1001.3
adj sanitary 79.27
disinfectant 86.43
antisocial
misanthropic 590.3
eccentric 927.5
antithesis
contraposition 215.1
contrariety 779.1
antithetical
contrapositive 215.5
oppositional 451.8
contrary 779.6
antitoxin
antitoxic serum 86.27
inoculation 91.16
antler 285.4
antonym word 526.1
the opposite 779.2
antrum 284.2
antsy
excited 105.23
restless 105.27
apprehensive 127.24
impatient 135.6
agitated 917.16
wriggly 917.21
anus
digestive system 2.18
asshole 292.5
anvil ear 2.10
instrument of conversion 858.10
anxiety
unpleasure 96.1
eagerness 101.1
apprehensiveness 126.1
anxiousness 126.1
fear 127.4
suspense 130.3

impatience 135.1
trouble 1013.3
anxious
pleasureless 96.20
eager 101.8
concerned 126.7
apprehensive 127.24
in suspense 130.12
impatient 135.6
troubled 1013.20
any
n some 244.3
anything 864.5
adj quantitative 244.5
every 864.15
one 872.7
anybody 864.5
anyhow
carelessly 340.18
anyway 384.10
any kind 809.9
anyone any 864.5
whoever 864.7
any one
n any 864.5
adj one 872.7
anyplace 159.22
anything some 244.3
any 864.5
anytime
whenever 821.12
imminently 840.4
anyway 384.10
anywhere
adj addicted 87.25
adv wherever 159.22
aorta 2.23
apace swiftly 174.17
hastily 401.12
promptly 845.15
apart
adj distant 261.8
secluded 584.8
unrelated 776.6
separate 802.20
alone 872.8
adv away 261.17
privately 345.19
separately 802.27
singly 872.13
in half 875.8
apartheid
seclusion 584.1
exclusiveness 773.3
discrimination 980.4
apartment 228.13
apathetic insensible 25.6
incurious 982.3
apathy
insensibility 25.1
lack of feeling 94.4
unconcern 102.2
despair 125.2
inertness 173.4
languor 331.6
indifference 467.2
thoughtlessness 933.1
incuriosity 982.1
ape
n strong man 15.7
wild animal 311.23

imitator 336.4
ruffian 593.4
violent person 671.10
v mimic 336.6
impersonate 349.12
gesture 517.21
resemble 784.7
adj crazy 926.27
aperçu
treatise 556.1
abridgment 557.1
intuition 934.1
apéritif appetizer 10.9
drink 88.9
aperture
opening 292.1
passageway 383.3
apex summit 198.2
height 272.2
angle 278.2
speech organ 524.18
aphasia muteness 51.2
loss of speech 525.6
aphorism
witticism 489.7
epigram 537.3
maxim 974.1
aphrodisiac
love potion 75.6
aphroditous 75.26
Aphrodite Love 104.8
beauty 1016.10
apical 198.10
apiece 865.19
apish imitative 336.9
representational 349.13
foolish 923.8
aplenty
adj sufficient 991.7
adv plentifully 991.9
aplomb
equanimity 106.3
verticalness 200.1
self-control 359.5
stability 855.1
apnea 85.9
apocalypse
disclosure 351.1
revelation 683.10
prediction 962.1
Apocalypse 683.4
apocalyptic
ominous 133.17
scriptural 683.11
predictive 962.11
apocryphal
spurious 354.26
unorthodox 688.9
unauthoritative 971.21
apogee summit 198.2
boundary 211.3
long way 261.2
limit 794.5
orbit 1072.16
spacecraft 1075.2
Apollo music 710.22
Muse 720.10
sun 1072.14
apologetic
n apology 600.3
justifier 600.8

adj penitent 113.9
justifying 600.13
atoning 658.7
apologia apology 600.3
argumentation 935.4
apologist
defender 460.7
justifier 600.8
supporter 616.9
arguer 935.12
apologize
repent 113.7
beg pardon 658.5
apology
penitence 113.4
pretext 376.1
apologia 600.3
excuse 658.2
argumentation 935.4
apophthegm 974.1
apoplectic
n sick person 85.43
adj anemic 85.61
apoplexy seizure 85.6
paralysis 85.27
upheaval 671.5
spasm 917.6
apostasy dissent 333.1
denial 335.2
recreancy 363.2
desertion 370.2
backsliding 394.2
nonobservance 435.1
Protestantism 675.10
impiety 694.1
change 852.1
renunciation 858.3
apostate
n dissenter 333.3
turncoat 363.5
backslider 394.3
Protestant 675.20
sacrilegist 694.3
defector 858.8
adj recreant 363.11
relapsing 394.5
Protestant 675.28
impious 694.6
treasonable 858.20
apostle disciple 572.2
religion 684.2
clergy 699.10
converter 858.9
apostolic
abstinent 668.10
scriptural 683.11
papal 698.15
apostrophe
remark 524.3
soliloquy 542.1
apothecary 86.35
apothegm
witticism 489.7
maxim 974.1
apotheosis
respect 155.1
praise 509.5
glorification 662.8
removal to heaven 681.11
idolization 697.2
ideal 786.4

elevation 912.1
appall offend 98.11
terrify 127.17
dismay 127.19
appalling horrid 98.19
terrible 127.30
remarkable 247.10
appanage 471.5
apparatus
equipment 385.4
impedimenta 471.3
tool 1040.1
apparel
n clothing 5.1
v outfit 5.39
apparent visible 31.6
appearing 33.11
exterior 206.7
manifest 348.8
specious 354.27
plausible 968.7
illusory 976.9
apparently visibly 31.8
seemingly 33.12
externally 206.10
manifestly 348.14
falsely 354.35
apparition ghost 33.1
appearance 33.5
phantom 976.4
figment of the imagination
986.5
specter 988.1
appeal
n delightfulness 97.2
desirability 100.13
loveableness 104.7
allurement 377.1
entreaty 440.2
appeal motion 598.10
prayer 696.4
v attract 377.6
entreat 440.11
appealing
delightful 97.7
alluring 377.8
imploring 440.17
melodious 708.48
appeal to
entreat 440.11
address 524.26
refer to 957.14
appear show 31.4
become visible 33.8
seem 33.10
attend 221.8
come out 348.6
be revealed 351.8
be published 352.16
act 704.29
turn up 831.6
appearance
showing-up 33.1
appearing 33.1
exterior 33.2
apparition 33.5
arrival 186.1
front 206.1
lineaments 262.3
manifestation 348.1
sham 354.3

illusoriness 976.2
phantom 976.4
specter 988.1
appear for 576.14
appease gratify 95.8
relieve 120.5
pacify 465.7
calm 670.7
propitiate 696.15
appeasement
relief 120.1
pacification 465.1
foreign policy 609.5
propitiation 696.6
appellate 595.7
appellation
naming 527.2
nomenclature 527.3
append add 253.4
place after 815.3
appendage member 2.7
hanger-on 138.6
follower 166.2
adjunct 254.1
belongings 471.2
nonessential 768.2
attendant 769.3
part 793.4
appendix
digestive system 2.18
added to writing 254.2
sequel 817.1
appertaining
relative 775.7
relevant 775.11
appertain to
belong to 469.7
relate to 775.5
appetite eating 8.1
craving 100.6
stomach 100.7
eagerness 101.1
will 323.1
sensuality 663.1
appetizer bite 8.2
food 10.9
sample 62.4
piece 793.3
appetizing
mouth-watering 63.10
desirable 100.30
alluring 377.8
applaud cheer 116.6
congratulate 149.2
assent 332.8
acclaim 509.10
applause
cheer 116.2
congratulation 149.1
plaudit 509.2
apple pie 1014.4
apple-polisher 138.4
applet 1042.11
appliance
instrument 384.4
use 387.1
facility 449.9
machinery 1040.3
applicable
usable 387.23
legal 673.11

relevant 775.11
apt 788.10
applicant 440.7
application
dressing 86.33
industry 330.6
perseverance 360.1
use 387.1
request 440.1
study 570.3
administration 643.2
relevance 775.4
attribution 888.1
engrossment 983.3
application software 1042.12
applied 387.24
appliqué 295.4
apply
cover 295.19
put to use 387.11
petition 440.10
administer 643.6
relate 775.6
attribute 888.3
apply for 440.9
apply oneself
practice 328.8
endeavor 403.5
undertake 404.3
study 570.12
busy oneself with 724.11
exert oneself 725.9
think about 931.11
attend to 983.5
appoint
elect 371.20
equip 385.8
prescribe 420.9
allot 477.9
assign 615.11
destine 964.7
appointee 615.9
appointment
election 371.9
authority 417.12
decree 420.4
allotment 477.3
engagement 582.8
assignment 615.2
commission 615.4
holy orders 698.10
position 724.5
appointments
equipment 385.4
belongings 471.2
Apollo 1016.10
apportion
quantify 244.4
share 476.6
mete out 477.6
separate 793.6
portion 802.18
dispose 808.9
apposite
relevant 775.11
apt 788.10
apposition 223.3
appraisal
measurement 300.1
valuation 630.3
classification 801.3

estimate 946.3
appreciable
 weighable 297.19
 measurable 300.14
 substantial 763.6
 knowable 928.25
appreciate
 savor 63.5
 enjoy 95.13
 be grateful 150.3
 respect 155.4
 grow 251.6
 measure 300.10
 understand 521.7
 know 928.12
 estimate 946.9
 value 997.13
appreciation
 gratitude 150.1
 respect 155.1
 increase 251.1
 acknowledgment 332.3
 commendation 509.3
 cognizance 928.2
 discrimination 944.1
 estimate 946.3
appreciative
 grateful 150.5
 approbatory 509.16
 aware of 928.16
 discriminating 944.7
apprehend sense 24.6
 fear 127.10
 forebode 133.11
 arrest 429.15
 capture 480.18
 understand 521.7
 know 928.12
apprehension
 anxiety 126.1
 apprehensiveness 127.4
 suspense 130.3
 foreboding 133.2
 arrest 429.6
 seizure 480.2
 intelligence 920.1
 understanding 928.3
 idea 932.1
 doubt 955.2
apprehensive
 anxious 126.7
 misgiving 127.24
 nervous 128.11
 in suspense 130.12
 knowing 928.15
apprentice
 n novice 572.9
 skilled worker 726.6
 beginner 818.2
 producer 892.7
 v train 568.13
 indenture 615.18
 adj indentured 615.21
apprenticeship 432.3
apprise 551.8
apprised of 928.16
approach
 n motion towards 167
 access 167.1
 convergence 169.1
 landing 184.18

arrival 186.1
 entrance 189.5
 nearness 223.1
 plan 381.1
 manner 384.1
 attempt 403.2
 offer 439.1
 game 750.2
 similarity 784.1
 imminence 840.1
 v come close 167.3
 converge 169.2
 arrive 186.6
 near 223.7
 be around 223.8
 communicate with 343.8
 bribe 378.3
 use 384.5
 attempt 403.6
 make advances 439.7
 address 524.26
 cultivate 587.12
 resemble 784.7
 turn up 831.6
 be in the future 839.6
 be imminent 840.2
 exercise influence 894.9
approachable
 accessible 167.5
 communicative 343.10
 bribable 378.4
 possibility 966.8
approbation
 respect 155.1
 ratification 332.4
 consent 441.1
 approval 509.1
 esteem 662.3
appropriate
 v take possession 472.10
 adopt 480.19
 steal 482.13
 plagiarize 482.19
 borrow 621.4
 usurp 640.8
 adj useful 387.18
 decorous 496.10
 fit 533.7
 right 637.3
 due 639.8
 relevant 775.11
 apt 788.10
 timely 843.9
 characteristic 865.13
 expedient 995.5
appropriation
 allotment 477.3
 taking over 480.4
 theft 482.1
 plagiarism 482.8
 adoption 621.2
 usurpation 640.3
approval
 respect 155.1
 ratification 332.4
 consent 441.1
 high marks 509.5
 approbation 509.1
 esteem 662.3
 support 901.1
 criticism 946.2

approve
 ratify 332.12
 adopt 371.15
 consent 441.2
 accept 509.9
 support 901.21
 criticize 946.14
 evidence 957.8
approved
 accepted 332.14
 chosen 371.26
 received 479.10
 favored 509.19
 conventional 579.5
 orthodox 687.7
 authoritative 970.18
approximate
 v be around 223.8
 imitate 336.5
 resemble 784.7
 similarize 784.8
 adj approaching 167.4
 near 223.14
 approximating 775.8
 similar 784.14
 inaccurate 975.17
 v approach 167.3
approximately
 also 223.23
 nearly 244.6
 on the whole 792.14
approximation
 approach 167.1
 nearness 223.1
 measurement 300.1
 reproduction 336.3
 relation 775.1
 similarity 784.1
 likeness 784.3
 inaccuracy 975.2
 notation 1017.2
appurtenance
 adjunct 254.1
 equipment 385.4
 facility 449.9
 belongings 471.2
 prerogative 642.1
 nonessential 768.2
 component 796.2
apron clothing 5.17
 runway 184.23
 stage 704.16
 golf 751.1
apropos
 relevant 775.11
 apt 788.10
 incidentally 843.13
apse arch 279.4
 church 703.9
apt skillful 413.22
 appropriate 533.7
 teachable 570.18
 apposite 788.10
 prompt 845.9
 smart 920.14
 probable 968.6
 disposed 978.8
aptitude
 innate skill 413.5
 teachableness 570.5
 fitness 788.5

tendency 896.1
 smartness 920.2
 probability 968.1
 disposition 978.3
apt to
 adj liable to 897.6
 prep inclined to 896.6
aquarium
 vivarium 228.24
 collection 770.11
aquatic
 n creatures 311.3
 adj water-dwelling 182.58
 watery 1065.16
aquatics 182.11
aqueduct
 watercourse 239.2
 trench 290.2
aqueous 1065.16
aquiline hooked 279.8
 birdlike 311.49
aquiver 105.20
Arab 178.4
arabesque
 n network 170.3
 detailed design 498.2
 ornament 709.18
 adj ornate 498.12
Arabesque 554.15
Arabic numerals 1017.4
arable 1069.20
arachnid 311.33
arbiter
 arbitrator 466.4
 connoisseur 496.7
 referee 596.1
 judge 946.6
arbitrage
 n stocks 737.19
 v trade 737.23
arbitrary
 voluntary 324.7
 capricious 364.5
 unthinking 365.10
 imperious 417.16
arbitration
 arbitrament 466.2
 unionism 727.1
 adjustment 788.4
 judgment 946.1
arbitrator arbiter 466.4
 go-between 576.4
 judge 596.1
arbor
 summerhouse 228.12
 axle 915.5
arboreal forked 171.10
 arborical 310.39
arboretum 397.7
arc
 n curve 279.2
 lights 704.18
 discharge 1032.6
 v curve 279.6
arcade corridor 197.18
 fence 212.4
 pillar 273.5
 arch 279.4
 passageway 383.3
Arcadian rustic 233.6
 natural 416.6

ideal 986.23
arcane secret 345.11
  implied 519.7
  recondite 522.16
  supernatural 870.15
arch
  n foot 199.5
  span 279.4
  monument 549.12
  v curve 279.6
  adj chief 249.14
  mischievous 322.6
  cunning 415.12
archaeological 842.20
archaeologist 842.5
archaeology oldness 842.4
  discovery 941.1
archaic language 523.2
archaism
  archaicism 526.12
  antiquity 842.6
archangel 679.1
archbishop 699.9
archdiocese
  region 231.5
  diocese 698.8
arched bowed 279.10
  convex 283.13
archenemy
  opponent 452.1
  enemy 589.6
archer 904.8
archery ballistics 462.3
  sport 744.1
  throwing 904.2
archetypal 842.11
archetype
  engram 92.29
  form 262.1
  original 337.2
  model 786.1
  philosophy 932.2
  instinct 934.2
  standard of perfection 1002.4
archetypical
  unimitated 337.6
  prototypal 786.9
  perfected 1002.9
archipelago 235.2
architect planner 381.6
  draftsman 716.10
  landscape planner 717.3
  doer 726.1
  producer 892.7
architectonics 717.1
architectural
  structural 266.6
  design 717.7
  constructional 892.15
architecture
  structure 266.1
  design 717.4
  construction 717.1
  plot 722.4
  production 892.2
archives
  storehouse 386.6
  preserve 397.7
  public records 549.2
  registry 549.3
archivist 550.1

archway 279.4
arctic unfeeling 94.9
  northern 161.14
  seasonal 313.9
  cold 1023.14
ardent alcoholic 88.37
  fervent 93.18
  zealous 101.9
  amorous 104.26
  willing 324.5
  industrious 330.22
  vehement 544.13
  cordial 587.16
  fiery 671.22
  hot 1019.25
  burning 1019.27
ardor animation 17.4
  passion 93.2
  desire 100.1
  zeal 101.2
  love 104.1
  willingness 324.1
  industry 330.6
  vehemence 544.5
  interest 983.2
  heat 1019.2
arduous
  laborious 725.18
  difficult 1013.17
area space 158.1
  location 159.1
  region 231.1
  size 257.1
  study 568.8
  occupation 724.4
  specialty 866.1
  science 928.10
arear 163.13
arena space 158.1
  hall 197.4
  setting 209.2
  enclosed place 212.3
  sphere 231.2
  sports venue 463.1
  scene of action 463.1
  occupation 724.4
  track 755.1
  science 928.10
  outlook 978.2
argosy ship 180.1
  fleet 180.10
  navy 461.27
argot
  Greek 522.7
  jargon 523.9
arguable 971.17
argue
  affirm 334.5
  signify 517.17
  mean 518.8
  support 600.10
  reason 935.16
  evidence 957.8
argument
  quarrel 456.5
  contention 457.1
  pleadings 598.6
  testimony 598.8
  defense 600.2
  plot 722.4
  reason 935.4

  case 935.5
  specious argument 936.3
aria
  air 708.4
  solo 708.15
arid
  dull 117.6
  unproductive 891.4
  unimaginative 987.5
  dry 1066.7
aright 999.22
arise
  get up 23.6
  appear 33.8
  emerge 190.11
  ascend 193.8
  rise 200.8
  revolt 327.7
  originate 818.13
  turn up 831.6
arise from 887.5
aristocracy
  the best 249.5
  mastership 417.7
  upper class 607.2
  social status 607.3
  noble rank 608
  nobility 608.1
  aristocracy 608.1
  blue blood 608.2
  government 612.4
aristocrat
  patrician 607.4
  nobleman 608.4
aristocratic
  dignified 136.12
  lordly 141.11
  imperious 417.16
  upper-class 607.10
  noble 608.10
  governmental 612.17
arithmetic 1017.22
arithmetical 1017.22
arithmetic operation 1017.2
arm
  n appendage 2.7
  inlet 242.1
  branch 617.10
  game 745.3
  member 793.4
  supporter 901.2
  forearm 906.5
  v empower 18.10
  equip 385.8
  fortify 460.9
  protect 1008.18
armada 461.27
armament
  provision 385.1
  equipment 385.4
  arms 462.1
  football 746.1
armchair 951.13
armed provided 385.13
  prepared 405.16
  embattled 458.23
  heeled 460.14
  protected 1008.21
armed forces 461.20
arm in arm
  adj near 223.14

  adv sociably 582.25
  amicably 587.22
  hand in hand 769.10
armistice 465.5
armor
  n callousness 94.3
  shell 295.15
  armature 460.3
  v fortify 460.9
  protect 1008.18
armory
  storehouse 386.6
  arsenal 462.2
  insignia 647.1
  heraldry 647.2
  plant 739.3
  track 755.1
arms
  military science 458.6
  matériel 462.1
  weapons 462.1
  heraldry 647.2
arms control peace treaty 464.7
  disarmament 465.6
arms race 458.10
arm-twisting
  inducement 375.3
  coercion 424.3
  threat 514.1
army branch 461.21
  military units 461.22
  forces 461.23
  throng 770.4
  group of animals 770.5
  multitude 884.3
aroma odor 69.1
  fragrance 70.1
  characteristic 865.4
aromatherapy odorousness
  69.2
  fragrance 70.1
aromatic
  n perfumery 70.2
  adj odorous 69.9
  fragrant 70.9
around
  adv in every direction 161.25
  round 209.12
  near 223.20
  rotating 915.16
  prep through 161.27
  about 223.26
arousal
  awakening 23.2
  stimulation 105.1
  excitation 105.11
  elicitation 192.5
  incitement 375.4
arouse energize 17.10
  wake someone up 23.5
  excite 105.12
  provoke 152.24
  elicit 192.14
  incite 375.17
  rouse 375.19
  alarm 400.3
  interest 983.12
  heat 1020.18
arousing
  n excitation 105.11
  adj aphrodisiac 75.26

extractive 192.17
arraignment
  censure 510.3
  indictment 598.3
  accusation 599.1
arrange plan 381.8
  prepare 405.6
  settle 437.8
  mediate 466.7
  compose 708.46
  order 807.4
  align 808.8
  classify 809.6
arranged
  planned 381.12
  contracted 437.11
  orderly 807.6
  composed 808.14
arrangement
  form 262.1
  structure 266.1
  plan 381.1
  preparation 405.1
  compact 437.1
  adjustment 465.4
  compromise 468.1
  ornamentation 498.1
  appointment 582.8
  piece 708.5
  score 708.28
  harmonization 709.2
  music 709.11
  treatment 712.9
  order 807.1
  configuration 808.1
  organization 808.1
  classification 809.1
arrant
  downright 247.12
  conspicuous 348.12
  wicked 654.16
  base 661.12
  terrible 1000.9
array
  n clothing 5.1
  army 461.23
  order 807.1
  arrangement 808.1
  series 812.2
  v clothe 5.39
  ornament 498.8
  order 807.4
  dispose 808.9
  align 812.5
  adduce 957.12
arrayed clothing 5.45
  embattled 458.23
  arranged 808.14
arrears debt 623.2
  shortcoming 911.1
arrest
  n seizure 85.6
  slowing 175.4
  restraint 428.1
  arrestment 429.6
  confinement 480.2
  stop 857.2
  hindrance 1012.1
  curb 1012.7
  v slow 175.9
  restrain 428.7

confine 429.15
capture 480.18
delay 846.8
put a stop to 857.11
engross 983.13
hinder 1012.10
arrested
  retarded 175.12
  undeveloped 406.12
  restrained 428.13
  incomplete 795.4
  late 846.16
  mentally deficient 922.22
  gripped 983.18
arrested development
  fixation 92.21
  mental deficiency 922.9
arrival
  landing 184.18
  entrant 186.1
  incomer 189.4
arrive
  appear 33.8
  arrive at 186.6
  make good 409.10
arrivederci! 188.22
arriving
  adj approaching 186.9
  adv on arrival 186.10
arriviste
  vulgarian 497.6
  upstart 606.7
  newcomer 774.4
  modern 841.4
arrogant
  vain 136.9
  proud 140.9
  overbearing 141.9
  insolent 142.9
  contemptuous 157.8
  imperious 417.16
  defiant 454.7
  confident 970.21
arrogate
  take command 417.14
  appropriate 480.19
  usurp 640.8
arrow
  n swiftness 174.6
  shaft 462.6
  pointer 517.4
  v be straight 277.4
arsenal
  storehouse 386.6
  armory 462.2
  plant 739.3
arson 1020.7
arsonist
  destroyer 395.8
  incendiary 1020.8
art
  representation 349.1
  knack 413.6
  science 413.7
  cunning 415.1
  stratagem 415.3
  visual arts 712.1
  artistry 712.7
  vocation 724.6
  science 928.10
artefact 842.6

arterial 2.33
arteriosclerosis 1046.5
artery duct 2.23
  passageway 383.3
artful
  falsehearted 354.31
  deceitful 356.22
  cunning 415.12
  insincere 645.18
  shrewd 920.15
arthritic
  n sick person 85.43
  adj anemic 85.61
arthropod animal 311.3
  insect 311.32
article
  n definite article 530.6
  writing 547.10
  news item 552.3
  part 554.13
  treatise 556.1
  commodity 735.2
  particular 766.3
  part of grammar 793.2
  individual 872.4
  object 1052.4
  v accuse 599.7
  indenture 615.18
articulate
  v say 524.22
  put together 800.5
  hook 800.8
  adj audible 50.16
  intelligible 521.10
  speaking 524.31
  eloquent 544.8
  jointed 800.17
articulation
  uttering 524.5
  speech sound 524.12
  word 526.1
  joining 800.1
  joint 800.4
  series 812.2
artifact antiquity 842.6
  product 893.1
  object 1052.4
artifice
  falseheartedness 354.4
  chicanery 356.4
  trick 356.6
  intrigue 381.5
  cunning 415.1
  stratagem 415.3
  affectation 533.3
  expedient 995.2
artificial
  spurious 354.26
  put on 500.15
  affected 533.9
artificial coloring 35.8
artificial insemination 78.3
artificial intelligence 1042.2
artillery ballistics 462.3
  cannon 462.11
artilleryman
  artillerist 461.11
  shooter 904.8
artisan expert 413.11
  worker 607.9
  artist 716.1

skilled laborer 726.6
  mechanic 1040.12
artist expert 413.11
  entertainer 707.1
  musician 710.1
  visual arts 712.1
  creator 716.1
  artiste 716.1
  skilled worker 726.6
  producer 892.7
artistic
  skillful 413.22
  tasteful 496.8
  painterly 712.20
artistry skill 413.1
  authorship 547.2
  art 712.7
  talent 718.2
artless natural 406.13
  unskillful 414.15
  simple 416.5
  candid 644.17
  foolable 923.12
artlessness
  naturalness 406.3
  simplicity 416.1
  ingenuousness 416.1
  candor 644.4
  genuineness 973.7
arts and crafts 712.1
artsy-craftsy 712.20
artwork
  visual arts 712.1
  work of art 712.10
arty 712.20
as
  adv how 384.9
  equally 790.11
  to illustrate 957.23
  conj because
    888.10
as a matter of course
  finally 820.12
  generally 864.17
  normally 869.10
  consequently 887.7
  certainly 970.23
as a matter of fact
  really 761.16
  truly 973.18
as a rule
  generally 864.17
  normally 869.10
asbestos 1022.5
ascend move 172.5
  climb 184.39
  fly 193.8
  rise 200.8
  incline 204.10
  tower 272.10
  levitate 298.9
ascendancy
  superiority 249.1
  victory 411.1
  dominance 417.6
  influence 894.1
ascendant
  rising 193.14
  superior 249.12
  victorious 411.7
  authoritative 417.15

governing 612.18
influential 894.14
ascending
n course 172.2
rising 200.5
adj flowing 172.8
in the ascendant 193.14
sloping upward 204.17
high 272.14
ascension ascent 193.1
rising 200.5
removal to heaven 681.11
ascent course 172.2
motion upward 193
ascension 193.1
rising 200.5
acclivity 204.6
increase 251.1
lightness 298.1
improvement 392.1
elevation 912.1
ascertain learn 570.6
decide 946.11
prove 957.10
make sure 970.11
ascertained
known 928.26
proved 957.20
assured 970.20
true 973.13
ascetic
n recluse 584.5
puritan 667.2
abstainer 668.4
religious 699.16
adj plain-speaking 535.3
atoning 658.7
austere 667.4
abstinent 668.10
meager 992.10
asceticism
penance 658.3
self-denial 667.1
austerity 667.1
abstinence 668.2
ascribable
due 639.10
attributable 888.6
ascribe accuse 599.7
attribute 888.3
aseptic 79.27
asexual 75.29
as far as to 261.20
when 821.16
as for 775.13
as good as 223.22
ash dregs 256.2
extract 893.3
combustion product 1020.16
ashamed
regretful 113.8
humiliated 137.14
ashen colorless 36.7
gray 39.4
terrified 127.26
burned 1020.30
ashes corpse 307.16
combustion product 1020.16
ashore 234.8
ashram
community 617.2

retreat 1009.5
aside
n interjection 213.2
byplay 490.1
soliloquy 542.1
adv in an undertone 52.22
laterally 218.8
on one side 218.10
apart 261.17
privately 345.19
in reserve 386.17
aside from
adv separately 802.27
prep excluding 773.10
as if 951.19
asinine
ungulate 311.46
stupid 922.15
foolish 923.8
trivial 998.19
as is
adj present 838.2
adv identically 778.9
as it were
by interpretation 341.18
figuratively 536.4
so to speak 784.19
supposedly 951.17
ask demand 421.5
request 440.9
invite 440.13
charge 630.12
inquire 938.20
require 963.9
ask about 938.19
askance
obliquely 204.14
askew 204.22
laterally 218.8
warily 494.13
disapprovingly 510.26
askew skew 204.14
awry 204.22
distorted 265.10
disorderly 810.13
erroneous 975.16
ask for
encourage 375.21
demand 421.5
request 440.9
seek 938.30
ask for it defy 454.3
be rash 493.5
cause trouble 1013.14
asking price offer 439.1
price 738.9
ask no quarter 430.20
aslant
adj inclining 204.15
adv slantingly 204.23
asleep sleeping 22.22
insensible 25.6
unconscious 25.8
dead 307.30
unaware 930.13
unalert 984.8
as long as
prep when 821.16
conj so 959.15
aslope
adj inclining 204.15

adv slantingly 204.23
as much as 244.7
as new 841.15
as of now 838.3
as one
unanimously 332.17
cooperatively 450.6
in step 788.11
jointly 800.18
simultaneously 836.7
concurrently 899.5
aspect look 33.3
navigation 159.3
perfective 530.13
particular 766.3
component 796.2
astrology 1072.20
as per 867.9
asperity
pungency 68.1
ill humor 110.1
causticity 144.8
bitterness 152.3
roughness 288.1
aspersion
indignity 156.2
criticism 510.4
slur 512.4
stigma 661.6
baptism 701.6
wetting 1065.6
asphalt
n ground covering 199.3
pavement 383.6
v floor 295.22
asphyxiate
suffocate 307.24
strangle 308.19
suppress 428.8
asphyxiation
symptom 85.9
violent death 307.6
suffocation 308.6
aspic 10.13
aspirant desirer 100.12
optimist 124.6
petitioner 440.7
candidate 610.9
aspiration
breathing 2.21
murmur 52.4
reaching high 100.9
hope 124.1
inhaling 187.5
drawing 192.3
motive 375.1
intention 380.1
speech sound 524.12
aspire
be ambitious 100.20
take off 193.10
aspiring
ambitious 100.28
hopeful 124.11
high 272.14
as regards 775.13
ass sex object 75.4
copulation 75.7
beast of burden 176.8
buttocks 217.5
donkey 311.16

adv slantingly 204.23
as much as 244.7
obstinate person 361.6
fool 924.1
assail attack 459.14
criticize 510.20
incriminate 599.10
assailant
opponent 452.1
assailer 459.12
assailing
n attack 459.1
berating 510.7
adj attacking 459.29
assassin
alarmist 127.8
killer 308.11
assassination 308.2
assault
n attack 459.1
berating 510.7
incrimination 599.2
unruliness 671.3
v attack 459.14
rage 671.11
thrust 902.12
assay
n measurement 300.1
attempt 403.2
analysis 801.1
test 942.2
v measure 300.10
attempt 403.6
analyze 801.6
experiment 942.8
ass-backwards
adj backward 163.12
misinterpreted 342.3
botched 414.22
confused 810.16
adv backwards 163.13
clumsily 414.24
assemblage
association 617.1
picture 712.11
gathering 770.1
assembly 770.1
all 770.14
relation 775.1
composition 796.1
hodgepodge 797.6
assemble
collect 472.11
sculpture 715.5
come together 770.16
gather 770.18
compose 796.3
join 800.5
produce 892.8
assembly
council 423.1
legislature 613.1
the laity 700.1
assemblage 770.1
bunch 770.2
meeting 770.14
composition 796.1
production 892.2
assembly code 1042.13
assembly hall 567.11
assembly line
plant 739.3
assembly 770.14
industrial production 892.3

assembly-line 892.18
assemblyman 610.3
assent
  n agreement 332
  acquiescence 332.1
  submission 433.1
  consent 441.1
  vote yes 788.1
  support 901.1
  v acquiesce 332.8
  submit 433.6
  consent 441.2
  agree 788.6
  support 901.21
assenting
  agreeing 332.13
  submissive 433.12
  consenting 441.4
assert
  affirm 334.5
  insist 421.8
  state 524.23
  defend 600.10
  postulate 951.12
  maintain 953.12
assertative 334.8
assertion
  affirmation 334.1
  remark 524.3
  premise 935.7
  testimony 957.2
assertive 334.8
assert oneself 348.6
assess
  measure 300.10
  price 630.11
  charge 630.12
  classify 801.8
  estimate 946.9
assessment
  measurement 300.1
  fee 624.5
  valuation 630.3
  tax 630.9
  Irish dividend 738.8
  classification 801.3
  estimate 946.3
assessor
  measurer 300.9
  tax collector 630.10
assets
  supply 386.2
  means 471.7
  wealth 618.1
  accounts 628.1
  funds 728.14
asseverate
  affirm 334.5
  speech 524.23
  state 953.12
  testify 957.9
asshole anus 292.5
  bad person 660.5
  fool 924.3
assiduous
  industrious 330.22
  painstaking 339.11
  persevering 360.8
  attentive 983.15
assign
  n beneficiary 479.4

v locate 159.11
  transfer 176.10
  allot 477.9
  commit 478.16
  give homework 568.17
  commission 615.10
  appoint 615.11
  transfer property 629.3
  classify 809.6
  specify 865.11
  attribute 888.3
assignation
  rendezvous 582.9
  transfer 629.1
  assembly 770.2
  attribution 888.1
assignee
  beneficiary 479.4
  appointee 615.9
assignment
  placement 159.6
  authority 417.12
  allotment 477.3
  commitment 478.2
  lesson 568.7
  commission 615.1
  appointment 615.2
  transfer 629.1
  duty 641.1
  task 724.2
  specification 865.6
  attribution 888.1
assimilate digest 7.18
  absorb 187.13
  internalize 207.5
  naturalize 226.4
  consume 388.3
  understand 521.7
  conform 570.7
  include 772.3
  make uniform 781.4
  similarize 784.8
  make agree 788.7
  combine 805.3
  compare 943.4
assimilation
  digestion 2.17
  metabolism 2.20
  nutrition 7.8
  body function 7.12
  sorption 187.6
  naturalization 226.3
  consumption 388.1
  speech sound 524.12
  absorption 570.2
  inclusion 772.1
  similarity 784.1
  adjustment 788.4
  combination 805.1
  conversion 858.1
assist
  n helping hand 449.2
  baseball 745.3
  basketball game 747.3
  hockey 749.3
  v be instrumental 384.7
  aid 449.11
  subsidize 478.19
  benefit 592.3
assistance remedy 86.1
  aid 449.1

subsidy 478.8
assistant
  n subordinate 432.5
  helper 449.7
  academic rank 571.3
  employee 577.3
  aid 616.6
  adj helping 449.20
assisted suicide 307.6
ass-kisser
  yes-man 138.4
  assenter 332.6
  flatterer 511.4
associate
  n academic rank 571.3
  companion 588.3
  partner 616.2
  confederate 616.1
  member 617.11
  v cooperate 450.3
  join 617.14
  accompany 769.7
  relate 775.6
  put together 800.5
  league 805.4
  concur 899.2
  adj related 775.9
  leagued 805.6
  concurrent 899.4
associate oneself with
  undertake 404.3
  back 449.13
  participate 476.5
  espouse 509.13
  defend 600.10
  join 617.14
association
  association of ideas 92.33
  council 423.1
  affiliation 450.2
  participation 476.1
  social set 582.5
  consociation 582.6
  society 617.1
  social grouping 617.1
  company 769.2
  relation 775.1
  combination 805.1
  concurrence 899.1
  thoughts 931.4
assonance rhyme 720.8
  repetitiousness 849.4
assonant
  harmonious 708.49
  rhyming 720.17
  monotonous 849.15
assorted different 780.7
  diversified 783.4
  arranged 808.14
  classified 809.8
assortment
  miscellany 770.13
  hodgepodge 797.6
  grouping 808.3
assuage gratify 95.8
  relieve 120.5
  moderate 670.6
  qualify 959.3
assuasive
  n palliative 86.10
  adj palliative 86.40

relieving 120.9
  moderating 670.16
  qualifying 959.7
as such 767.11
assume don 5.43
  imitate 336.5
  sham 354.21
  undertake 404.3
  take command 417.14
  receive 479.6
  appropriate 480.19
  affect 500.12
  imply 519.4
  adopt 621.4
  presume 640.6
  usurp 640.8
  entail 772.4
  suppose 951.10
  think 953.11
assumed
  spurious 354.26
  undertaken 404.7
  put-on 500.16
  implied 519.7
  supposed 951.14
assumed name 527.8
assuming 141.10
assumption
  hope 124.1
  presumptuousness 141.2
  authority 417.12
  receiving 479.1
  appropriation 480.4
  implication 519.2
  adoption 621.2
  presumption 640.2
  usurpation 640.3
  removal to heaven
     681.11
  entailment 772.2
  conversion 858.1
  elevation 912.1
  premise 935.7
  supposition 951.3
  opinion 953.6
assumptive 951.14
assurance
  equanimity 106.3
  consolation 121.4
  hope 124.1
  insolence 142.1
  oath 334.4
  promise 436.1
  security 438.1
  encouragement 492.9
  belief 953.1
  certainty 970.1
  confidence 970.5
  ensuring 970.8
  safety 1007.1
  insurance 1008.4
assure comfort 121.6
  give hope 124.10
  depose 334.6
  promise 436.4
  secure 438.9
  encourage 492.16
  convince 953.18
  make sure 970.11
assured
  composed 106.13

hopeful 124.11
insolent 142.9
promised 436.8
secured 438.11
belief 953.21
made sure 970.20
confident 970.21
assuredly 332.18
assuring
comforting 121.13
convincing 953.26
assymetry 851.1
astern
backwards 163.13
aft 182.69
in reverse 217.14
asteroid 1072.9
as the crow flies 161.23
asthma
symptom 85.9
allergy 85.34
asthmatic
n breathing 2.21
adj respiratory 2.32
as though 951.19
astigmatic 28.11
astigmatism
faulty eyesight 28.1
bad likeness 350.2
astir
adj stirring 330.19
afoot 405.23
adv under way 172.9
as to 775.13
astonish
amaze 122.6
surprise 131.7
astonishing
amazing 122.12
surprising 131.11
remarkable 247.10
astonishment
marvel 122.2
surprise 131.2
astound astonish 122.6
dismay 127.19
astounded
wondering 122.9
terrified 127.26
astounding
astonishing 122.12
terrible 127.30
astral
n astral body 689.17
specter 988.1
adj spectral 988.7
immaterial 1053.7
celestial 1072.25
astray
adj bewildered 971.24
erroneous 975.16
adv wide 261.19
amiss 911.7
erroneously 975.20
astride 901.25
astringency
acrimony 17.5
acridness 64.2
pungency 68.1
harshness 144.9
contraction 260.1

strictness 425.1
astringent
n contractor 260.6
adj acrimonious 17.14
bitter 64.6
pungent 68.6
penetrating 105.31
harsh 144.24
contractive 260.11
strict 425.6
astrologer
predictor 962.4
astrologian 1072.23
astrological 1072.25
astrology
divination 962.2
fate 964.2
astromancy 1072.20
astronaut
traveler 178.1
aviator 185.1
astronavigator 1075.8
astronautical engineering
1043.1
astronomer
earth scientist 1071.2
stargazer 1072.22
astronomical
large 247.7
huge 257.20
innumerable 884.10
the universe 1072.25
astronomy
cosmos 1072.1
stargazing 1072.19
astrophysical
physical 1018.3
celestial 1072.25
astrophysics 1072.19
astute cunning 415.12
sagacious 920.16
discerning 944.8
asunder
adj distant 261.8
separate 802.20
adv separately 802.27
in half 875.8
as usual
adj same 781.6
adv in status quo 853.10
normally 869.10
as well
additionally 253.11
equally 790.11
as yet 838.4
asylum
hiding place 346.4
infirmary 926.14
refuge 1009.1
home 1009.4
asymmetric
distorted 265.10
unequal 791.4
asymmetry
distortion 265.1
inconsistency 789.2
inequality 791.1
asymptotic 169.3
at by 159.27
in 207.13
at all anyhow 384.10

any kind 809.9
by any possibility 966.10
at all costs 338.9
at a loss
adj in a dilemma 971.25
at an impasse 1013.24
adv unprofitably 473.9
at any rate
limited 248.10
notwithstanding 338.8
anyhow 384.10
certainly 970.23
ataraxy apathy 94.4
unconcern 102.2
inexcitability 106.1
quiescence 173.1
at arm's length 261.14
at a standstill
adj motionless 173.13
inactive 331.17
immovable 855.15
at an impasse 1013.24
adv at a halt 329.7
in status quo 853.10
at a stretch
continuously 812.10
in the meantime 821.10
atavism
inversion 205.1
relapse 394.1
oldness 842.1
throwback 859.2
memory 989.1
atavistic
inverted 205.7
innate 767.8
primitive 842.11
reversionary 859.7
at bay
adj cornered 1013.25
adv defensively 460.16
at best 248.10
at bottom deep 275.16
essentially 767.11
at cost 633.10
at cross-purposes
adj at odds 456.16
at outs 589.12
contrary 779.6
disagreeing 789.6
adv in opposition 451.9
at ease
adj content 107.7
comfortable 121.12
adv at rest 20.11
atelier library 197.6
studio 712.17
workplace 739.1
at fault
blameworthy 510.25
guilty 656.3
erroneous 975.16
at first sight
vision 27.22
apparently 33.12
at hand
adj present 221.12
handy 387.20
imminent 840.3
adv near 223.20
at heart 767.11

atheism
infidelity 688.3
impiety 694.1
unorthodoxy 695.5
unbelief 955.1
atheist
n sacrilegist 694.3
impious person 695.11
adj unbelieving 695.19
atherosclerosis 1046.5
athlete 743.19
athletic able-bodied 15.16
sporting 743.30
athletics sports 743.8
gymnastics 744.1
track 755.1
athletic shoes 5.27
at home
n social gathering 582.10
assembly 770.2
adj at ease 121.12
adv in the bosom of one's
family 225.16
at home with
used to 373.16
friends with 587.17
versed in 928.19
athwart
adj transverse 170.9
oblique 204.19
adv crosswise 170.13
transversely 204.24
in opposition 451.9
prep opposed to 451.10
atilt
adj inclining 204.15
adv slantingly 204.23
at issue
adj doubtful 971.17
undecided 971.18
adv in opposition 451.9
in question 938.39
at it 330.21
at large
adj escaped 369.11
free 430.21
adv at length 538.16
scatteringly 771.12
wholly 792.13
generally 864.17
atlas pillar 273.5
reference book 554.9
Atlas strong man 15.6
support 901.3
at last
adv finally 820.12
interj eureka! 941.11
at least 248.10
at length
lengthily 267.10
lengthwise 267.11
ad nauseam 538.16
fully 766.13
finally 820.12
at liberty idle 331.18
free 430.21
at loose ends
idle 331.18
irresolute 362.9
atmosphere
milieu 209.3

aerosphere 317.2
treatment 712.9
plot 722.4
gas 1067.2
atmospheric 317.12
at most 248.10
at odds
  adj unwilling 325.5
  oppositional 451.8
  at variance 456.16
  at outs 589.12
  different 780.7
  disagreeing 789.6
  adv in opposition 451.9
atoll 235.2
atom modicum 248.2
  particle 258.8
  one 872.3
  tracer 1038.4
  matter 1052.2
  element 1060.2
atom bomb
  n atomic explosion 1038.16
  v bomb 459.23
atomic
  infinitesimal 258.14
  one 872.7
  atomistic 1038.18
atomic energy 1038.15
atomic nucleus 1038.6
atomic number 1060.5
atomic scientist 1038.3
atomic war 458.1
atomic weight
  unit of measure 297.5
  weight 297.8
  chemistry 1060.5
atomize
  demolish 395.17
  itemize 766.6
  differentiate 780.6
  analyze 801.6
  come apart 802.9
  shatter 802.13
  disintegrate 806.3
  nucleize 1038.17
  pulverize 1051.9
  vaporize 1067.8
atomizer perfume 70.6
  sprinkler 1065.8
  vaporizer 1067.6
atom smasher 1038.11
atonal 61.4
atonality 61.1
at once hastily 401.12
  together 769.11
  jointly 800.18
  at once 830.8
  promptly 845.15
atone
  compensate 338.4
  make restitution 481.5
  repay 624.11
  make amends 658.4
  harmonize 708.35
  tune 708.36
at one
  unanimous 332.15
  in accord 455.3
  agreeing 788.9
atonement
  compensation 338.1

peace offer 465.2
restitution 481.2
recompense 624.3
reparation 658.1
function of Christ
  677.14
propitiation 696.6
at one's disposal
  at one's command 326.4
  handy 387.20
  possessed 469.8
at one's fingertips
  adj handy 387.20
  adv near 223.20
at one's mercy 432.14
at one's wit's end
  in a dilemma 971.25
  at an impasse 1013.24
at one with
  unanimous 332.15
  concurrent 899.4
atop on top 198.15
  on high 198.16
at par 790.7
at present 838.3
at random
  haphazardly 810.18
  irregularly 851.4
  purposelessly 972.20
at rest
  adj at ease 121.12
  quiescent 173.12
  dead 307.30
  adv at ease 20.11
  beneath the sod 309.23
at risk
  liable 897.5
  in danger 1006.13
atrocious
  painful 26.10
  horrid 98.19
  cruel 144.26
  insulting 156.8
  wrong 638.3
  wicked 654.16
  base 661.12
  savage 671.21
  terrible 1000.9
atrocity
  dreadfulness 98.3
  act of cruelty 144.12
  indignity 156.2
  mistreatment 389.2
  abomination 638.2
  injustice 650.4
  iniquity 654.3
  misdeed 655.2
  violence 671.1
  evil 1000.3
atrophy
  n symptom 85.9
  shrinking 260.3
  emaciation 270.6
  waste 393.4
  v waste 393.19
at sea
  adj bewildered 971.24
  muddled 985.13
  adv under way 182.63
  on the water 240.10
at stake 438.12

attach add 253.4
  annex 480.20
  fasten 800.7
  attribute 888.3
attaché expert 413.11
  diplomat 576.6
attached to 104.30
attachment love 104.1
  addition 253.1
  adjunct 254.1
  annexation 480.5
  fidelity 644.7
  fastening 800.3
  attribution 888.1
attack
  n seizure 85.6
  plan 381.1
  manner 384.1
  war 458.1
  assault 459.1
  accusation 459.1
  berating 510.7
  articulation 524.5
  incrimination 599.2
  unruliness 671.3
  team 749.5
  spasm 917.6
  frenzy 926.7
  v use 384.5
  undertake 404.3
  raise one's hand against
    457.14
  make war on 458.15
  assault 459.14
  criticize 510.20
  incriminate 599.10
  rage 671.11
  set to work 725.15
  interj advance! 459.32
attacker 459.12
attain arrive 186.6
  accomplish 407.4
attainable
  approachable 167.5
  obtainable 472.14
  practicable 966.7
  accessible 966.8
attainder 602.2
attainment
  arrival 186.1
  accomplishment 407.1
  skill 413.8
  acquisition 472.1
  learning 928.4
attempt
  n trial 403.2
  undertaking 404.1
  v try 403.6
  undertake 404.3
  presume 640.6
attend
  v listen 48.10
  be at 221.8
  aid 449.18
  serve 577.13
  accompany 769.7
  escort 769.8
  come after 835.3
  result 887.4
  spectate 918.5
  heed 983.6

  interj hark! 48.16
attendant
  n hospital staff 90.11
  follower 166.2
  tender 577.5
  assistant 616.6
  concomitant 769.3
  accompanier 769.4
  guardian 1008.6
  adj present 221.12
  serving 577.14
  environmental 766.8
  accompanying 769.9
  subsequent 835.4
attending
  serving 577.14
  environmental 766.8
  accompanying 769.9
attend to
  listen 48.10
  observe 434.2
  punish 604.11
  look to 983.5
  care for 1008.19
attention
  n hearing 48.1
  audition 48.2
  carefulness 339.1
  alertness 339.5
  courtesy 504.6
  curiosity 981.1
  attentiveness 983.1
  respects 983.1
  interj hark! 48.16
  look! 983.22
attention deficit disorder or
    ADD 984.1
attention deficit hyperactivity
    disorder or ADHD 984.1
attentive
  listening 48.14
  considerate 143.16
  respectful 155.8
  careful 339.10
  meticulous 339.12
  alert 339.14
  courteous 504.14
  curious 981.5
  heedful 983.15
attenuate
  v weaken 16.10
  dilute 16.11
  abate 252.8
  shrink 260.9
  thin 270.12
  rarefy 299.3
  spiritualize 764.4
  dissipate 771.5
  adj thin 270.16
  smooth 294.8
  rare 299.4
attenuated
  diluted 16.19
  reduced 252.10
  shrunk 260.13
  thin 270.16
  haggard 270.20
  smooth 294.8
  rare 299.4
attest
  n testimony 957.2

v depose 334.6
secure 438.9
evidence 957.8
testify 957.9
confirm 957.11
attestation
deposition 334.3
certificate 549.6
testimony 957.2
confirmation 957.4
attested affirmed 334.9
proved 957.20
assured 970.20
true 973.13
at the bottom of
adj responsible 641.17
causal 886.13
conj resulting from 887.8
at the drop of a hat
willingly 324.8
quickly 830.7
at the end of one's rope
dying 307.33
poor 619.7
wanting 992.13
straitened 1013.26
at the mercy of 897.6
at the pleasure of 432.17
at the point of
near 223.24
about to 839.13
at the same time
additionally 253.11
notwithstanding 338.8
meanwhile 826.5
simultaneously 836.7
at the wheel 417.21
attic room 197.16
storehouse 386.6
Attic witty 489.15
tasteful 496.8
simple 499.6
elegant 533.6
Attila 144.14
at times 848.5
attire
n clothing 5.1
v clothe 5.39
attitude
navigation 159.3
opinion 953.6
mental disposition 978.1
attitudinal
belief 953.21
temperamental 978.7
attitudinize 500.13
attorney steward 574.4
deputy 576.1
lawyer 597.1
attorney general 597.1
attract enamor 104.23
allure 377.6
pull 907.4
interest 983.12
attraction
desirability 100.13
allurement 377.1
lure 377.3
pulling 905.1
a drawing toward 907
traction 907.1

attractive
delightful 97.7
desirable 100.30
alluring 377.8
attracting 907.5
engrossing 983.20
beautiful 1016.18
attributable
adj due 639.10
assignable 888.6
conj resulting from 887.8
attribute
n syntax 530.2
insignia 647.1
characteristic 865.4
v assign 888.3
attribution
specification 865.6
assignment of cause 888
designation 888.1
attrition
weakening 16.5
regret 113.1
decrement 252.3
reduction 255.2
consumption 388.1
abrasion 1044.2
pulverization 1051.4
attune
n harmony 708.3
v fit 405.8
harmonize 708.35
tune 708.36
make agree 788.7
attuned in accord 455.3
harmonious 708.49
at variance
adj at odds 456.16
at outs 589.12
different 780.7
disagreeing 789.6
adv in opposition 451.9
at war
adj at odds 456.16
disagreeing 789.6
adv up in arms 458.24
at which 821.8
atwitter 105.20
at worst 248.10
atypical
nonconforming 868.5
unusual 870.10
auburn
reddish-brown 40.4
redheaded 41.10
au courant 928.18
auction
n sale 734.4
v sell 734.11
auctioneer
n auction agent 730.8
v sell 734.11
audacious
insolent 142.9
defiant 454.7
daring 492.22
foolhardy 493.9
audacity
insolence 142.1
defiance 454.1
daring 492.5

foolhardiness 493.3
audible auditory 48.13
hearable 50.16
audience audition 48.2
auditory 48.6
attender 221.5
recipient 479.3
conference 541.6
playgoer 704.27
spectator 918.2
audio 48.13
audio frequency
n tone 50.2
frequency 1034.12
adj radio 1034.28
audiologist 90.11
audio-visual 48.13
audit
n accounting 628.6
v be taught 570.11
take account of 628.9
verify 970.12
check 1017.21
audition recital 48.1
hearing 48.2
examination 938.2
tryout 942.3
auditor listener 48.5
recipient 479.3
student 572.1
superintendent 574.2
accountant 628.7
treasurer 729.12
auditorium hall 197.4
arena 463.1
schoolroom 567.11
theater 704.14
parquet 704.15
auditory
n audience 48.6
adj audio 48.13
auf Wiedersehen! 188.22
auger
n point 285.3
v perforate 292.15
aught some 244.3
nothing 762.2
any 864.5
augment
aggravate 119.2
increase 251.4
add to 253.5
enlarge 259.4
augur
n predictor 962.4
v hint 133.12
augur well 124.10
augury omen 133.3
divination 962.2
august dignified 136.12
venerable 155.12
eminent 247.9
au naturel 11.6
aunt 559.3
au pair girl 577.8
aura milieu 209.3
illustriousness 662.6
ectoplasm 689.7
halo 1025.14
aural eye 2.28
auditory 48.13

aureole radiation 171.2
circle 280.2
halo 1025.14
au revoir! 188.22
auricle
the hearing sense 2.10
ear 310.29
auricular
auditory 48.13
confidential 345.14
aurora dawn 314.3
foredawn 314.4
polar lights 1025.16
Aurora 314.2
auscultate 48.10
auspices
patronage 449.4
supervision 573.2
protectorship 1008.2
auspicious
promising 124.13
of good omen 133.18
timely 843.9
good 999.12
fortunate 1010.14
austere harsh 144.24
strict 425.6
inornate 499.9
plain-speaking 535.3
ascetic 667.4
simple 798.6
meager 992.10
austerity
harshness 144.9
strictness 425.1
inornateness 499.4
plain speech 535.1
thrift 635.1
asceticism 667.1
meagerness 992.2
autarchy
independence 430.5
government 612.4
absolutism 612.9
auteur
theater man 704.23
motion-picture studio 706.4
authentic
original 337.5
straight 644.14
orthodox 687.7
real 761.15
evidential 957.16
authoritative 970.18
genuine 973.15
authenticate
ratify 332.12
confirm 957.11
authenticated
accepted 332.14
proved 957.20
true 973.13
authenticity
nonimitation 337.1
candor 644.4
orthodoxy 687.1
reality 761.2
reliability 970.4
genuineness 973.7
author
n writer 547.15

discourser 556.3
literary person 718.4
narrator 722.5
doer 726.1
agent 886.4
producer 892.7
v write 547.21
pen 718.6
cause 886.10
authoritarian
authoritative 417.15
imperious 417.16
strict 425.6
governmental 612.17
narrow-minded 980.10
authoritative
powerful 18.12
skillful 413.22
vested with authority 417.15
imperious 417.16
preceptive 419.4
commanding 420.13
orthodox 687.7
specialized 866.5
influential 894.13
convincing 953.26
authentic 970.18
valid 973.14
the authorities
the powers that be 575.15
the government 612.3
authority
power 18.1
supremacy 249.3
expert 413.11
sanction 417.12
prerogative 417.1
authoritativeness 417.2
prestige 417.4
governance 417.5
command 420.1
authorization 443.3
connoisseur 496.7
certificate 549.6
informant 551.5
direction 573.1
commission 615.1
prerogative 642.1
specialist 866.3
influence 894.1
wise man 921.1
scientist 928.11
validity 973.6
authorize
empower 18.10
ratify 332.12
prescribe 420.9
sanction 443.11
commission 615.10
legalize 673.9
authorized
authoritative 417.15
empowered 443.17
commissioned 615.19
legal 673.11
authorship
creation 547.2
writing 718.2
production 892.1
autism
defense mechanism 92.23

unfeeling 94.1
unsociability 583.1
selfishness 651.1
illusion 976.1
incuriosity 982.1
idealism 986.7
autistic unfeeling 94.9
unsociable 583.5
selfish 651.5
illusory 976.8
incurious 982.3
visionary 986.24
auto 179.9
autobiographical 719.7
autobiography 719.1
autocracy
government 612.4
absolutism 612.9
autocrat 575.14
autocratic
authoritative 417.15
imperious 417.16
governmental 612.17
auto-da-fé killing 308.1
burning 1020.5
autoerotic
homosexual 75.30
vain 140.8
autoeroticism
masturbation 75.8
sexual preference 75.10
vanity 140.1
autograph
n holograph 337.3
signature 527.10
handwriting 547.3
writing 547.10
v ratify 332.12
adj written 547.22
automat
restaurant 8.17
vending machine 736.4
automate 1041.20
automated 1041.22
**automated teller machine or
    ATM** credit 622.3
funds 728.14
automatic
n automatic device 1041.12
adj unpremeditated 365.11
habitual 373.14
uniform 781.5
instinctive 934.6
involuntary 963.14
automated 1041.22
automatic pilot 574.7
automatic transmission 1040.9
automatic writing
authorship 547.2
psychic phenomena 689.6
involuntariness 963.5
automation
electronics 1033.1
robotics 1041.2
automatic control 1041.1
automatic device 1041.12
automatism
habit 373.3
psychic phenomena 689.6
involuntariness 963.5
self-action 1041.1

automaton figure 349.6
mechanism 1040.4
automatic device 1041.18
automaton automatous
    1041.22
automobile
n car 179.9
adj self-propelled 1041.23
automotive
vehicular 179.23
self-propelled 1041.23
automotive engineering 1043.1
autonomous
voluntary 324.7
independent 430.22
governmental 612.17
separate 802.20
autonomy
voluntariness 324.2
independence 430.5
government 612.4
autopsy
n postmortem 307.18
v examine 938.24
autosuggestion 22.8
autumn
n fall 313.4
adj seasonal 313.9
autumnal 313.9
auxiliaries
reinforcements 449.8
reserves 461.25
auxiliary
n verb 530.4
assistant 616.6
nonessential 768.2
adj additional 253.10
helping 449.20
unessential 768.4
avail
n utility 387.3
benefit 387.4
good 999.4
v be of use 387.17
aid 449.11
suffice 991.4
do good 999.10
availability
presence 221.1
utility 387.3
accessibility 966.3
available
present 221.12
open 222.15
idle 331.18
handy 387.20
prepared 405.16
obtainable 472.14
accessible 966.8
avail oneself of
make use of 387.14
take advantage of 387.15
improve the occasion 843.8
avalanche
n slide 194.4
plenty 991.2
superabundance 993.2
snow 1023.8
v slide 194.9
avant-garde
n vanguard 216.2

precursor 816.1
novelty 841.2
adj original 337.5
preceding 816.4
modern 841.13
avarice greed 100.8
stinginess 484.3
selfishness 651.1
avaricious greedy 100.27
stingy 484.9
selfish 651.5
avatar appearance 33.1
manifestation 348.1
avenge 507.4
avenger 507.3
avenue outlet 190.9
passageway 383.3
aver affirm 334.5
state 524.23
testify 957.9
average
n mean 246.1
ruck 864.3
v strike a balance 246.2
seek the middle 819.3
adj medium 246.3
middle 819.4
prevalent 864.12
usual 869.9
ordinary 1005.8
average man
common man 606.5
average 864.3
averages
statistics 745.4
numbers 746.4
averred 334.9
averse allergic 99.8
unwilling 325.5
aversion hostility 99.2
loathing 103.1
hated thing 103.3
refusal 325.1
avert avoid 164.6
prevent 1012.14
avian 311.49
aviary 228.23
aviation
n aeronautics 184.1
adj aeronautic 184.49
aviator flier 185.1
airman 185.1
avid greedy 100.27
eager 101.8
avidly
greedily 100.32
eagerly 101.13
avocation 724.7
avoid detour 157.7
evade 164.6
shun 368.6
abstain 668.7
pull back 903.7
avoidable 368.14
avoidance
working around 368.1
shunning 368.1
abstinence 668.2
retreat 903.3
avoidance mechanism 92.23
avoirdupois 297.1

avouch
  n promise 436.1
  v affirm 334.5
  promise 436.4
  state 953.12
  testify 957.9
avow
  n oath 334.4
  v acknowledge 332.11
  affirm 334.5
  confess 351.7
  pretext 376.3
  state 953.12
  testify 957.9
avowal
  acknowledgment 332.3
  affirmation 334.1
  confession 351.3
  testimony 957.2
avulsion 192.1
avuncular 559.6
await wait 130.8
  come 839.6
  be imminent 840.2
  be in the future 846.12
awake
  v get up 23.4
  revive 23.5
  excite 105.12
  come to life 306.10
  adj conscious 23.8
  alert 339.14
  clear-witted 920.13
awaken
  get up 23.4
  revive 23.5
  excite 105.12
  come to life 306.10
  rouse 375.19
  disillusion 977.2
awakening
  wakening 23.2
  disillusionment 977.1
awake to 928.16
award
  n giving 478.1
  gift 478.4
  reward 646.2
  verdict 946.5
  v give 478.12
aware sensible 24.11
  knowing 928.15
  attentive 983.15
awash
  floating 182.60
  flooded 238.25
  soaked 1065.17
away
  adj gone 34.4
  absent 222.11
  distant 261.8
  adv backwards 163.13
  hence 188.20
  aside 218.10
  elsewhere 222.18
  at a distance 261.14
  apart 261.17
  interj go away! 909.31
away from
  adv separately 802.27
  prep departed 188.21

awe
  n wonder 122.1
  fear 127.1
  respect 155.1
  v astonish 122.6
  terrify 127.17
  daunt 127.18
  command respect 155.7
awe-inspiring
  awesome 122.11
  terrible 127.30
  venerable 155.12
  grandiose 501.21
  weighty 997.20
awesome awful 122.11
  terrible 127.30
  venerable 155.12
  large 247.7
  grandiose 501.21
  eminent 662.18
  sacred 685.7
awestruck
  wondering 122.9
  terrified 127.26
  reverent 155.9
awful horrid 98.19
  awesome 122.11
  terrible 127.30
  venerable 155.12
  remarkable 247.11
  grandiose 501.21
  sacred 685.7
  ugly 1000.9
  hideous 1015.11
awfully
  awesomely 122.15
  frightfully 127.34
  very 247.18
  distressingly 247.21
  terribly 1000.14
  hideously 1015.13
awhile 828.9
awkward
  mortifying 98.21
  bulky 257.19
  bungling 414.20
  stiff 534.3
  ignorant 930.12
  inconvenient 996.7
  unwieldy 1013.19
awning 1028.1
AWOL
  n absence 222.4
  flight 368.4
  adj truant 222.13
awry
  adj askew 204.14
  disorderly 810.13
  erroneous 975.16
  adv askew 204.22
ax
  n blade 462.5
  execution 605.5
  cutlery 1040.2
  v sever 802.11
axial
  flowing 172.8
  central 208.11
axiom fact 761.3
  essence 767.2
  premise 935.7

  supposition 951.3
  a belief 953.2
  truth 974.2
axiomatic
  manifest 348.8
  real 761.15
  obvious 970.15
  aphoristic 974.6
axis center 208.2
  straight line 277.2
  stem 310.21
  association 617.1
  fulcrum 906.3
  axle 915.5
axle 915.5
an ax to grind
  prejudgment 947.1
  narrow-mindedness 980.1
aye
  n affirmative 332.2
  vote 371.6
  consent 441.1
  side 935.14
  adv forever 829.12
  interj yes 332.18
azimuth
  navigation 159.3
  position 161.1
  direction 161.2
  horizon 201.4
  coordinates 300.5
azure
  n blueness 45.1
  heraldry 647.2
  the heavens 1072.2
  v blue 45.2
  adj blue 45.3
Babbitt
  vulgarian 497.6
  conformist 867.2
babble
  n nonsense 520.2
  Greek 522.7
  chatter 540.3
  v ripple 52.11
  betray 351.6
  talk nonsense 520.5
  be incomprehensible 522.10
  chatter 540.5
  be insane 926.20
babbling
  n divulgence 351.2
  v chattering 540.10
  adj rippling 52.19
  mentally deficient 922.22
  delirious 926.31
babe woman 77.6
  gal 302.7
  infant 302.9
  dupe 358.1
  simple soul 416.3
  endearment term 562.6
  innocent 657.4
Babel clash 61.2
  Greek 522.7
  confusion 810.2
  commotion 810.4
  pandemonium 810.5
baboon 1015.4
baby
  n weakling 16.6

  loved one 104.11
  ladylove 104.15
  miniature 258.6
  youngster 302.1
  gal 302.7
  infant 302.9
  simple soul 416.3
  coward 491.5
  endearment term 562.6
  innocent 657.4
  jockey 757.2
  beginner 818.2
  adj miniature 258.12
  infant 301.12
baby boom
  reproduction 78.1
  intensification 251.2
babyish infant 301.12
  puerile 922.24
Babylon 654.7
baby-sit 1008.19
baby-sitter 1008.8
baccalaureate 648.6
bacchanal spree 88.5
  drinker 88.11
bacchic 926.30
Bacchus 88.2
bachelor
  single man 565.3
  knight 608.5
  degree 648.6
bachelor girl
  woman 77.5
  single woman 565.4
bachelorhood independence
    430.5
  unmarried 565.1
bacillus 85.42
back
  n exterior 206.2
  setting 209.2
  rear 217.1
  dorsum 217.3
  speech organ 524.18
  type 548.6
  makeup 554.12
  football team 746.2
  soccer team 752.2
  supporter 901.2
  v reverse 163.7
  move 172.5
  backwater 182.34
  mount 193.12
  be behind 217.8
  secure 438.9
  back up 449.13
  commend 509.11
  benefit 592.3
  support 609.41
  finance 729.16
  bet 759.25
  subsidize 901.21
  confirm 957.11
  stiffen 1046.9
  adj backward 163.12
  flowing 172.8
  rear 217.9
  hinterland 233.9
  phonetic 524.30
  due 623.10
  past 837.12

late 846.16
adv backwards 163.13
in compensation 338.7
in reserve 386.17
ago 837.15
backache
ache 26.5
symptom 85.9
back and forth
n alternation 916.5
adj alternate 916.19
adv reciprocally 777.12
changeably 854.8
to and fro 916.21
back away 163.7
backbiting
n slander 512.3
adj disparaging 512.13
backbone pluck 359.3
fearlessness 492.4
supporter 901.2
backbreaking
laborious 725.18
troublesome 1013.18
back burner
n discontinuance 390.2
adj insignificant
998.17
back country
n open space 158.4
hinterland 233.2
adj country 233.9
backdoor 345.12
back door rear 217.1
secret passage 346.5
byway 383.4
back down
n recant 363.8
v retreat 163.6
hesitate 362.7
yield 433.7
backdrop setting 209.2
scenery 704.20
backer giver 478.11
friend 588.1
benefactor 592.1
supporter 616.9
patron 704.26
financer 729.10
backfill 266.3
backfire
n explosion 671.7
counteraction 900.1
recoil 903.2
fire 1019.13
v explode 671.14
recoil 903.6
backflow 238.12
background
setting 209.2
the distance 261.3
experience 413.9
arena 463.1
motif 498.7
plot 722.4
cause 886.1
source 886.5
backhanded
insulting 156.8
oblique 204.13
circuitous 914.7

backing
n regress 163.3
course 172.2
means 384.2
consent 441.1
patronage 449.4
bookbinding 554.14
film 714.10
financing 729.2
reversion 859.1
support 901.1
supporter 901.2
frame 901.10
confirmation 957.4
adj approving 509.17
benefitting 592.4
backlash
n retaliation 506.1
impact 887.2
counteraction 900.1
recoil 903.2
v recoil 903.6
backlist 558.4
backlog
n store 386.1
reserve 386.3
firewood 1021.3
v store up 386.11
back matter
added to writing 254.2
makeup 554.12
part of a book 793.2
sequel 817.1
back number
n edition 554.5
old man 842.8
adj trite 117.9
old-fashioned 842.16
back off retreat 163.6
reverse 163.7
hesitate 362.7
not interfere 430.17
drive 756.4
back out
n recant 363.8
v retreat 163.6
abandon 370.5
lose one's nerve 491.8
backpack 177.30
backpedal
reverse 163.7
slow 175.9
back room 381.1
back scratching
n obsequiousness 138.2
political influence 609.29
trading 863.2
adj obsequious 138.14
back seat
rear 217.1
inferiority 250.1
subservience 432.2
backseat driver
traveler 178.10
meddler 214.4
adviser 422.3
back side
rear 217.1
buttocks 217.5
golf 751.1
back side forward 205.7

backslapper 511.4
backslide
regress 163.5
invert 205.5
relapse 394.4
go wrong 654.9
revert 859.4
backstage
n stage 704.16
adv on the boards 704.36
back stairs
n stairs 193.3
secret passage 346.5
byway 383.4
adj covert 345.12
backstop
baseball team 745.2
safeguard 1008.3
barrier 1012.5
backstroke 182.11
back talk sass 142.4
answer 939.1
back to back
following 166.5
opposite 215.6
behind 217.13
cooperatively 450.6
same 781.6
continuously 812.8
consecutively 812.9
ongoing 812.10
sequentially 812.11
backtrack
n reverse 163.3
v reverse 163.7
backup
n reverse 163.3
reserve 386.3
deputy 576.1
game 750.2
successor 817.4
substitute 862.2
support 901.1
adj substitute 862.8
back up
reverse 163.7
move 172.5
be behind 217.8
back 449.13
represent 576.14
second 609.41
support 901.21
confirm 957.11
backward
adj reserved 139.11
reversed 163.12
flowing 172.8
retarded 175.12
inverted 205.7
rear 217.9
reluctant 325.6
distorted 342.3
reticent 344.10
undeveloped 406.12
back 837.12
late 846.16
dilatory 846.17
conservative 853.8
mentally deficient 922.22
adv inversely 205.8
rearward 217.15

ago 837.15
late 846.19
backwater
n eddy 238.12
recant 363.8
v reverse 163.7
slow 175.9
back 182.34
back when 837.15
backwoods
n hinterland 233.2
adj country 233.9
backyard rear guard
217.2
area 231.1
bacteria 85.42
bacterial 258.15
bactericide 86.21
bad
n vice 593.1
iniquity 654.3
evil 1000.3
adj nasty 64.7
malodorous 71.5
unhealthful 82.5
ill 85.56
diseased 85.60
ominous 133.17
dying 307.33
misbehaving 322.5
crippled 393.30
decayed 393.40
wicked 654.16
inexpedient 996.5
excellent 999.13
evil 1000.7
dangerous 1006.9
adv badly 1000.13
bad blood
bad feeling 93.7
malevolence 144.4
hostility 451.2
disaccord 456.1
animosity 589.4
bad chemistry 93.7
bad egg 660.4
bad faith
falseheartedness 354.4
violation 435.2
infidelity 645.5
bad for 82.5
badge sign 517.1
identification 517.11
insignia 647.1
military symbol 647.5
characteristic 865.4
badger annoy 96.13
wrest 480.22
bad guy
evildoer 593.1
actor 707.2
bad hand
handwriting 547.6
poker 759.10
badinage 490.1
badlands 891.2
bad lot
reprobate 660.4
bad person 660.5
badly off poor 619.7
unfortunate 1011.14

bad-mouth
be disrespectful 156.6
defame 512.9
underestimate 950.2
attach little importance to 998.12
bad move 975.4
bad name 661.1
bad news
good news 552.2
bad person 660.1
bad press 510.4
bad rap 650.4
bad taste
unsavoriness 64.1
vulgarity 497.1
inelegance 534.1
bad temper
ill humor 110.1
malevolence 144.4
temper 152.6
bad trip 87.1
bad turn 144.13
bad vibes 93.7
bad word oath 513.4
barbarism 526.6
baffle
n silencer 51.4
bewilderment 971.3
v muffle 51.9
disappoint 132.2
be incomprehensible 522.10
perplex 971.13
thwart 1012.15
baffled
disappointed 132.5
in a dilemma 971.25
at an impasse 1013.24
bafflement
disappointment 132.1
discomfiture 412.2
bewilderment 971.3
frustration 1012.3
baffling
bewildering 971.27
frustrating 1012.20
bag
n genitals 2.13
contraceptive 86.23
dose 87.20
sack 195.2
hang 202.2
quantity 247.3
breast 283.6
old woman 304.3
preference 371.5
take 480.10
occupation 724.1
purse 729.15
baseball 745.1
mode 765.4
bundle 770.8
specialty 866.1
eyesore 1015.4
v load 159.15
hang 202.6
package 212.9
bulge 283.11
acquire 472.9
catch 480.17
rob 482.16

bundle 770.20
bag and baggage
n impedimenta 471.3
adv free and clear 469.12
completely 794.14
bagatelle
hardly anything 248.5
trifle 998.5
baggage
freight 176.6
container 195.1
impedimenta 471.3
strumpet 665.14
baggy
drooping 202.10
formless 263.4
bulging 283.15
loose 804.5
bag of tricks 384.2
bag lady 619.4
bagman
traveling salesman 730.4
fence 732.6
bookmaker 759.20
bag person displaced person 160.4
vagabond 178.3
transient 828.4
baignoire 704.15
bail
n pledge 438.2
arraignment 598.3
v ladle 176.17
bailiff steward 574.4
policeman 1008.15
bailiwick area 231.2
region 231.5
arena 463.1
bureau 594.4
occupation 724.4
sphere of influence 894.4
bail out
n rescue 398.1
aid 449.1
v parachute 184.47
emerge 190.11
escape 369.6
pledge 438.10
aid 449.11
bait
n snare 356.13
incentive 375.7
lure 377.3
v annoy 96.13
lure 377.5
discriminate against 980.8
baited 96.24
bake cook 11.5
pot 742.6
be hot 1019.22
dry 1066.6
baker 11.3
baker's dozen
extra 254.4
gratuity 478.5
thirteen 882.7
bakery food preparation 11.4
sweetness 66.1
baking
n cooking 11.2
adj hot 1019.25

balance
n equanimity 106.3
mean 246.1
difference 255.8
remainder 256.1
symmetry 264.1
offset 338.2
supply 386.2
harmony 533.2
account 628.2
justice 649.1
moderation 670.1
treatment 712.9
funds 728.14
correlation 777.1
equality 790.1
stability 855.1
sensibleness 920.6
sanity 925.1
comparability 943.3
surplus 993.5
v symmetrize 264.3
weigh 297.10
offset 338.5
hesitate 362.7
keep accounts 628.8
make uniform 781.4
equal 790.5
make the same 790.6
stabilize 855.7
compare 943.4
check 1017.21
balanced
composed 106.13
symmetric 264.4
harmonious 533.8
just 649.8
uniform 781.5
poised 790.9
stable 855.12
neutralizing 900.9
sensible 920.18
sane 925.4
balance sheet 628.4
balance the books
keep accounts 628.8
equalize 790.6
check 1017.21
balcony
gallery 197.22
auditorium 704.15
platform 901.13
bald hairless 6.17
uncovered 292.17
open 348.10
unadorned 499.8
plain-speaking 535.3
balderdash
nonsense 520.2
bombast 545.2
bale
n wretchedness 96.6
burden 297.7
bundle 770.8
v bundle 770.20
balk
n disappointment 132.1
discomfiture 412.2
game 745.3
slip 975.4

frustration 1012.3
v disappoint 132.2
refuse 325.3
stickle 361.7
thwart 1012.15
balky
reluctant 325.6
obstinate 361.8
ball
n sphere 282.2
shot 462.19
dance 705.2
fun 743.2
baseball 745.1
prolate spheroid 746.1
football team 746.2
basketball 747.1
tennis 748.1
field hockey 749.4
bowling 750.1
bocci 750.3
soccer 752.1
assembly 770.2
projectile 904.5
v copulate 75.21
snowball 282.7
have a party 582.21
ballad
n popular music 708.7
song 708.14
v sing 708.38
balladeer
minstrel 710.14
composer 710.20
balladry 708.11
ball and chain
wife 563.8
impediment 1012.6
ballast
n counterbalance 297.4
offset 338.2
light source 1026.1
v trim ship 182.49
weight 297.12
stabilize 855.7
ball bearing 915.7
ballerina 705.3
ballet
n musical theater 708.34
adj dramatic 704.33
balletic
dramatic 704.33
dancing 705.6
ball game 766.2
ballistic 904.15
ballistics 462.3
ball of fire
energizer 17.6
man of action 330.8
balloon
n aerostat 181.11
bag 195.2
sphere 282.2
bubble 320.1
v grow 14.2
fly 184.36
increase 251.6
enlarge 259.5
ball 282.7
bulge 283.11

ballooning
n aviation 184.1
increase 251.1
adj drooping 202.10
bulging 283.15
balloonist 185.7
ballot
n vote 371.6
slate 609.19
v vote 371.18
ballpark figure
measurement 300.1
gamble 971.8
ballroom hall 197.4
dance emporium 705.4
entertainment 743.13
balls genitals 2.13
fearlessness 492.4
bull 520.3
ballsy 492.19
ball up
n confusion 810.2
v spoil 393.11
complicate 799.3
confuse 811.3
ballyhoo
n publicity 352.4
exaggeration 355.1
sales talk 734.5
v publicize 352.15
exaggerate 355.3
balm anesthetic 25.3
perfumery 70.2
remedy 86.1
medicine 86.4
lotion 86.11
condolence 147.1
moderator 670.3
ointment 1056.3
balmy fragrant 70.9
palliative 86.40
bright 97.11
relieving 120.9
crazy 926.27
thriving 1010.13
balneal 79.28
baloney
humbug 354.14
bullshit 520.3
balsa 180.11
balsam perfumery 70.2
remedy 86.1
medicine 86.4
balm 86.11
ointment 1056.3
balsamic
palliative 86.40
relieving 120.9
balustrade fence 212.4
post 273.4
base 901.8
bambino 302.9
bamboo grass 310.5
cane 1054.4
bamboo curtain
frontier 211.5
veil of secrecy 345.3
barrier 1012.5
bamboozle
deceive 356.14
stump 971.14

ban
n prohibition 444.1
disapproval 510.1
curse 513.1
ostracism 586.3
exclusion 773.1
v excise 255.10
prohibit 444.3
disapprove 510.10
ostracize 586.6
exclude 773.4
banish 909.17
banal trite 117.9
medium 246.3
aphoristic 974.6
banality triteness 117.3
platitude 974.3
bananas 926.27
band
n stripe 47.5
dressing 86.33
strip 271.4
circle 280.3
layer 296.1
jewel 498.6
line 517.6
association 617.1
orchestra 710.12
tennis 748.1
company 770.3
frequency 1034.13
v variegate 47.7
encircle 209.7
cooperate 450.3
put together 800.5
bind 800.9
bandage
n dressing 86.33
strip 271.4
wrapper 295.18
v blind 30.7
treat 91.24
bind 800.9
Band-Aid 86.33
band-aid
n pretext 376.1
adj makeshift 995.7
B and B 228.15
bandeau brassiere 5.24
heraldry 647.2
supporter 901.2
banded 47.15
bandied about 552.15
bandit
military aircraft 181.9
brigand 483.4
banditry theft 482.3
plundering 482.6
bandmaster 710.17
bandstand 704.16
band together
cooperate 450.3
accompany 769.7
league 805.4
the bandwagon 578.5
bandwidth 1042.18
bandy
n field hockey 749.4
v interchange 863.4
adj deformed 265.12
bowed 279.10

bandy about
publish 352.10
interchange 863.4
bandy-legged 265.12
bane death 307.1
killing 308.1
end 395.2
destroyer 395.8
enemy 589.6
evil 1000.3
affliction 1001.1
curse 1001.1
baneful
unhealthful 82.5
horrid 98.19
ominous 133.17
deadly 308.23
harmful 1000.12
disastrous 1011.15
bang
n tuft 3.6
energy 17.3
power 18.1
noise 53.3
report 56.1
detonation 56.3
dose 87.20
excitement 105.3
gunfire 459.8
explosion 671.7
production 893.2
hit 902.4
blow 902.5
v din 53.7
crack 56.6
blast 56.8
close 293.6
collide 902.13
strike 902.15
pound 902.16
adv suddenly 830.9
interj boom! 56.13
banging crashing 56.11
large 257.21
bangle 498.6
**bang one's head against a
     brick wall**
be impotent 19.7
be useless 391.8
bangs 3.6
banish
ostracize 586.6
expel 909.17
banishment
ostracism 586.3
relegation 909.4
banister
post 273.4
base 901.8
bank
n incline 204.4
border 211.4
side 218.1
shore 234.2
slope 237.2
shoal 276.2
storehouse 386.6
preserve 397.7
lending institution 620.4
treasury 729.13
banking house 729.14

workplace 739.1
pot 759.5
pile 770.10
series 812.2
buttress 901.4
barrier 1012.5
mine 1058.6
v maneuver 184.40
incline 204.10
store 386.10
fortify 460.9
pile 770.19
ignite 1020.22
bankable useful 387.18
valuable 387.22
gainful 472.16
paying 624.21
bank account
account 622.2
funds 728.14
bankbook 628.4
banker
lender 620.3
money dealer 729.11
businessman 730.1
bingo 759.15
bank holiday 20.4
banking
maneuvers 184.13
money dealing 729.5
bank note 728.5
bank on
hope 124.7
plan 380.6
rely upon 953.16
bankroll
n means 384.2
roll 728.17
v subsidize 478.19
finance 729.16
bankrupt
n failure 410.7
poor man 619.4
insolvent 625.4
v impoverish 619.6
ruin 625.8
adj ruined 395.28
destitute 619.9
insolvent 625.11
bankruptcy
impairment 393.1
failure 410.1
insolvency 625.3
bank statement 627.2
bank upon
rely on 953.16
plan 380.6
banned
prohibited 444.7
excluded 773.7
banner
n poster 352.7
rallying device 458.12
sign 517.1
trophy 646.3
flag 647.7
caption 937.2
adj chief 249.14
banns
betrothal 436.3
wedding 563.3

banquet
n feast 8.9
festival 743.4
v feast 8.24
banshee
fairy 678.8
specter 988.1
Bantam 311.29
bantam
n runt 258.4
adj miniature 258.12
bantamweight
n weight 297.3
adj lightweight 298.13
banter
n buffoonery 489.5
kidding 490.1
badinage 490.1
ridicule 508.1
v twit 490.5
banty
n runt 258.4
poultry 311.29
field hockey 749.4
adj miniature 258.12
banzai
n call to arms 458.8
interj attack! 459.32
baptism
admission 187.2
submergence 367.2
naming 527.2
christening 701.6
wetting 1065.6
baptismal
introductory 187.18
ritualistic 701.19
baptistery
baptism 701.6
church 703.9
baptize
dilute 16.11
wash 79.19
submerge 367.7
name 527.11
christen 701.17
bar
n stripe 47.5
barroom 88.20
island 235.2
line 267.3
shaft 273.1
shoal 276.2
obstruction 293.3
wild animal 311.23
lock 428.5
line 517.6
legal profession 597.4
heraldry 647.2
military insignia 647.5
staff 708.29
notation 709.12
precious metals 728.20
exclusion 773.17
table 901.15
lever 906.4
barrier 1012.5
v variegate 47.7
cross 170.6
fence 212.7
excise 255.10

close 293.6
stop 293.7
prohibit 444.3
exclude 773.4
make impossible 967.6
obstruct 1012.12
prevent 1012.14
prep excluding 773.10
barb
n whiskers 3.10
feather part 3.17
bristle 288.3
arrow 462.6
v sharpen 285.7
barbarian
n savage 497.7
evildoer 593.5
alien 774.3
adj unrefined 497.12
extraneous 774.5
barbaric
cruel 144.26
unrefined 497.12
inelegant 534.2
savage 671.21
extraneous 774.5
barbarism
unrefinement 497.3
corruption 526.6
solecism 531.2
inelegance 534.1
unenlightenment
930.4
barbecue
n meal 8.6
meat 10.13
v cook 11.5
barbed 285.9
barbel
whiskers 3.10
feeler 73.4
bristle 288.3
barbell fitness 84.1
exerciser 725.7
barber
n beautician 1016.13
v cut the hair 3.22
barbershop 1016.14
barbershop quartet 708.18
barbiturates 87.5
bar code
n mark 517.5
v label 517.20
bard
minstrel 710.14
poet 720.11
bare
v divest 6.5
unclose 292.12
disclose 351.4
adj naked 6.14
vacant 222.14
mere 248.8
open 292.17
uncovered 348.10
worn 393.31
unadorned 499.8
plain-speaking 535.3
simple 798.6
unmixed 798.7
bare-boned 270.17

bare bones
n base 199.2
adj mere 248.8
essential 767.9
simple 798.6
bared 6.12
barefaced
bare 6.16
brazen 142.11
barefoot unshod 6.15
ascetic 667.4
bare-handed
bare 6.16
ill-provided 992.12
unprotected 1006.14
bare-headed 6.16
barely nakedly 6.19
scarcely 248.9
narrowly 270.22
simply 798.11
bare minimum 991.1
bare necessities 963.2
barf
n vomiting 909.8
v feel disgust 99.4
vomit 909.27
barfly 88.11
barfy nasty 64.7
filthy 80.23
nauseated 85.57
bad 1000.8
bargain
n compact 437.1
compromise 468.1
advantageous purchase 633.3
deal 731.5
v plan 380.6
contract 437.5
treat with 437.6
mediate 466.6
confer 541.11
organize 727.9
haggle 731.18
make a deal 731.19
bargain-basement 633.8
bargain-hunter 733.5
barge haul 176.13
way of walking 177.28
barge in enter 189.7
intrude 214.5
baritone
n part 708.22
voice 709.5
adj deep 54.11
vocal 708.50
bark
n detonation 56.3
cry 59.1
animal noise 60.1
ship 180.1
skin 295.3
hull 295.16
v peel 6.8
blast 56.8
cry 59.6
yelp 60.2
publicize 352.15
injure 393.13
berate 510.19
speak 524.25
abrade 1044.7

barker publicist 352.9
theater man 704.23
solicitor 730.7
barley 10.4
barmaid
liquor dealer 88.19
waiter 577.7
bar mitzvah 701.6
barmy leavening 298.17
foamy 320.7
crazy 926.27
barn 228.20
barnacle parasite 138.5
adhesive 803.4
barnstorm
pilot 184.37
act 704.29
Barnumesque 105.32
barnyard 1069.8
barometer
measure 300.2
weather instrument 317.8
feeler 942.4
barometric 317.13
baron nobleman 608.4
businessman 730.1
personage 997.8
baronet
nobleman 608.4
knight 608.5
baroque
n ornateness 498.2
adj ornate 498.12
freakish 870.13
fanciful 986.20
barracks
n camp 228.29
v restrict 428.9
barrage
n staccato 55.1
volley 459.9
barrier 1012.5
v pull the trigger 459.22
barred striped 47.15
netlike 170.11
enclosed 212.10
closed 293.9
prohibited 444.7
excluded 773.7
impossible 967.7
barrel
n feather part 3.17
quantity 247.3
cylinder 282.4
wealth 618.3
v speed 174.9
package 212.9
barrel-chested 15.16
barrel organ 711.14
barren
n wasteland 891.2
adj ineffective 19.15
dull 117.6
vacant 222.14
fruitless 391.12
unproductive 891.4
unimaginative 987.5
barrens 891.2
barricade fortify 460.9
obstruct 1012.12
barrier boundary 211.3

fence 212.4
partition 213.5
obstruction 293.3
lock 428.5
fortification 460.4
horse racing 757.1
bar 1012.5
barring
  n exclusion 773.1
  prep off 255.14
  excluding 773.10
barrio 230.6
barrister 597.1
barroom 88.20
barrow hill 237.4
  tomb 309.16
  swine 311.9
  monument 549.12
bartender
  liquor dealer 88.19
  waiter 577.7
barter
  n transfer 629.1
  commerce 731.2
  trading 863.2
  v transfer 629.3
  trade 731.15
basal basic 199.8
  essential 767.9
  original 886.14
basalt 1059.1
base
  n station 159.2
  point of departure 188.5
  basement 199.2
  headquarters 208.6
  bottom 274.4
  baseball 745.1
  cause 886.1
  foundation 901.6
  pedestal 901.8
  makeup 1016.12
  acid 1060.3
  v establish 159.16
  adj offensive 98.18
  servile 138.13
  inadequate 250.7
  dastardly 491.12
  vulgar 497.15
  populational 606.8
  knavish 645.17
  wicked 654.16
  low 661.12
  terrible 1000.9
  inferior 1005.9
baseboard 199.2
baseborn
  populational 606.8
  illegitimate 674.7
base camp 760.6
based on
  supported 901.24
  evidential 957.16
  contingent 959.9
baseless
  unsubstantiated 764.8
  groundless 936.13
baseline
  point of departure 188.5
  baseball 745.1
  basketball 747.1

tennis 748.1
basement latrine 12.10
  cellar 197.17
  base 199.2
  storehouse 386.6
  foundation 901.6
base metals 1058.3
baseness 497.1
base pay 624.4
bash
  n attempt 403.3
  party 582.12
  blow 902.5
  v injure 393.13
  censure 510.13
  strike 902.15
  discriminate against 980.8
  work evil 1000.6
bashful fearful 127.23
  shy 139.12
  demurring 325.7
  unsociable 583.5
  reticent 344.10
bashing
  persecution 389.3
  censure 510.3
basic basal 199.8
  essential 767.9
  simple 798.6
  original 886.14
  vital 997.23
  chemical 1060.9
basics
  elementary education 568.5
  essentials 818.6
basic training
  preparation 405.1
  training 568.3
basilar 199.8
basilica 703.1
basin washbasin 79.12
  container 195.1
  bed 199.4
  plain 236.1
  valley 237.7
  cavity 284.2
  harbor 1009.6
basis
  point of departure 188.5
  motive 375.1
  warrant 600.6
  cause 886.1
  foundation 901.6
  premise 935.7
  topic 937.1
  outlook 978.2
bask 1020.19
basket
  n genitals 2.13
  container 195.1
  basketball 747.1
  score 747.3
  v package 212.9
basket case
  fool 924.3
  idiot 924.8
basketwork 170.3
bask in 95.13
bas-relief
  protuberance 283.2
  relief 715.3

bass
  n part 708.22
  voice 709.5
  adj deep 54.11
  vocal 708.50
bassist 710.5
basso 709.5
basso continuo 708.22
bastard
  n man 76.5
  illegitimate 561.5
  bad person 660.5
  adj spurious 354.26
  illegitimate 674.7
bastardize 797.12
baste cook 11.5
  whip 604.13
  pound 902.16
bastille 429.8
bastion 460.6
bat
  n the blind 30.4
  drinking spree 88.6
  tennis 748.1
  blow 902.5
  v play 745.5
  strike 902.15
batch
  n amount 244.2
  lot 247.4
  lump 257.10
  bunch 770.7
  product 893.4
  v assemble 770.18
bate decrease 252.6
  abate 252.8
  subtract 255.9
  blunt 286.2
  discount 631.2
  relax 670.9
bated muffled 52.17
  reduced 252.10
bath
  n bathe 79.8
  dip 79.9
  shower 79.10
  washbasin 79.12
  wetting 1065.6
  v wash 79.19
bathe
  n bath 79.8
  aquatics 182.11
  v wash 79.19
  treat 91.24
  swim 182.56
  soak 1065.13
bather 182.12
bathetic 93.21
bathhouse 79.10
bathing
  balneation 79.7
  aquatics 182.11
  wetting 1065.6
bathing suit 5.29
bathos
  sentimentality 93.8
  sadness 112.1
  anticlimax 488.3
bathrobe 5.21
bathroom
  latrine 12.10

bathing place 79.10
  lavatory 197.26
baths
  bathing place 79.10
  health resort 91.23
  spa 228.27
bathtub 79.12
bathysphere 367.5
bat of an eye 830.3
baton staff 273.2
  scepter 417.9
  insignia 647.1
  heraldry 647.2
  stigma 661.6
  illegitimacy 674.2
  music 711.22
batrachian
  n amphibian 311.27
  adj reptile 311.48
bats 926.27
battalion
  military unit 461.22
  company 770.3
batten
  n strip 271.4
  scenery 704.20
  v close 293.6
  gluttonize 672.4
  hook 800.8
  secure 855.8
  thrive 1010.8
batter
  n baseball team 745.2
  semiliquid 1062.5
  v mistreat 389.5
  injure 393.13
  thrash soundly 604.14
  rage 671.11
  pound 902.16
  work evil 1000.6
battered 393.33
battering trauma 85.38
  unruliness 671.3
battery
  military unit 461.22
  artillery 462.11
  corporal punishment 604.4
  baseball team 745.2
  electrical device 1032.21
battle
  n contention 457.4
  war 458.1
  operation 458.5
  struggle 725.3
  fight 754.3
  v oppose 451.4
  quarrel 456.11
  contend 457.13
  war 458.14
  fortify 460.9
  struggle 725.11
battle-ax 110.12
battle cry cry 59.1
  challenge 454.2
  call to arms 458.8
  call 517.16
battledore
  textbook 554.10
  elastic 1048.3
battle fatigue 92.14
battlefield 463.2

battlefront
vanguard 216.2
battlefield 463.2
battlement 289.3
battleship 180.7
batty foolish 923.9
crazy 926.27
bauble trinket 498.4
toy 743.16
trifle 998.5
bawd 665.18
bawdy
lascivious 665.29
obscene 666.9
bawdyhouse 665.9
bawl
n cry 59.1
lament 115.3
v sob 59.6
cry 60.2
weep 115.12
wail 115.13
speak 524.25
bawl out 510.18
bay
n blare 53.5
nook 197.3
shore 234.2
ocean 240.3
inlet 242.1
recess 284.7
horse 311.11
storehouse 386.6
v blare 53.10
cry 60.2
adj reddish-brown 40.4
bay at the moon
cry 60.2
wail 115.13
be useless 391.8
bayonet 459.25
bayou tributary 238.3
inlet 242.1
bayside
n shore 234.2
adj coastal 234.7
bay window 2.19
bazaar sale 734.3
marketplace 736.2
bazooka
weapon 462.21
rocket launcher
1074.10
BC 821.13
be exist 761.8
be able 18.11
beach
n shore 234.2
golf 751.1
v shipwreck 182.42
beachcomber
vagabond 178.3
bum 331.9
wretch 660.2
beachfront
n shore 234.2
adj coastal 234.7
beachhead
vanguard 216.2
stronghold 460.6
beachside 234.7

beacon
n observation post 27.8
flying marker 184.19
alarm 400.1
signal 517.15
fire 1019.13
torch 1026.3
v lead 165.2
shine 1025.23
illuminate 1025.28
bead
n drop 282.3
v ball 282.7
figure 498.9
beaded beady 282.10
ornamented 498.11
beaded brow 12.7
beading 211.7
beadle 1008.15
beads jewel 498.6
prayer 696.4
beagle detective 576.11
jockey 757.2
policeman 1008.15
beak
n prow 216.3
spout 239.8
nose 283.8
judge 596.1
v tap 902.18
beaked 279.8
be-all and end-all
end 820.1
supremacy 249.3
all 792.3
beam
n smile 116.3
flying marker 184.19
side 218.1
breadth 269.1
shaft 273.3
buttress 901.4
lever 906.4
ray 1025.5
radio wave 1034.10
television 1035.4
signal 1036.11
wood 1054.3
v be pleased 95.12
exude cheerfulness 109.6
smile 116.7
look good 1016.17
shine 1025.23
broadcast 1034.25
transmit 1036.15
be a man 492.10
beaming happy 95.16
cheerful 109.11
gorgeous 1016.21
luminous 1025.30
beam out 171.6
bean man 76.5
head 198.6
plant 310.4
brain 919.6
trifle 998.5
beanery 8.17
beanpole slim 270.8
longlegs 272.7
beans vegetables 10.35
mescaline 87.13

nothing 762.3
beanstalk 270.8
bear
n sorehead 110.11
wild animal 311.23
short 737.12
v give birth 1.3
endure 134.5
take direction 161.7
transport 176.12
submit 433.6
suffer 443.10
aid 449.12
hold 474.7
afford 626.7
exert oneself 725.9
manipulate the market 737.25
engender 818.14
cause 886.10
yield 892.13
support 901.21
thrust 902.12
suffice 991.4
bearable 107.13
bear arms 458.18
beard
n genitals 2.13
whiskers 3.8
type 548.6
v defy 454.3
brave 492.11
beardless hairless 6.17
childish 301.11
bear down
aggrieve 112.19
work hard 725.13
depress 913.4
bear down on
approach 167.3
sail for 182.35
press 424.6
bearer carrier 176.7
mourner 309.7
supporter 901.2
bear false witness
swear falsely 354.20
trump up a charge 599.12
bear fruit ripen 407.8
evolve 861.5
bear 892.13
bear hug hold 474.2
wrestling 474.3
embrace 562.3
bearing
n looks 33.4
navigation 159.3
direction 161.1
transportation 176.3
behavior 321.1
yield 472.5
gesture 517.14
meaning 518.1
relevance 775.4
origin 818.4
producing 892.6
trend 896.2
fulcrum 906.3
ball bearing 915.7
adj born 1.4
yielding 890.10
supporting 901.23

bearings location 159.1
navigation 159.3
orientation 161.4
heraldry 647.2
state 765.1
bear in mind think of 931.16
take cognizance of 983.9
keep in memory 989.13
bearish
irascible 110.19
ursine 311.44
gruff 505.7
bear malice
harshen 144.15
bear ill will 589.8
bear market 737.5
bear on
weigh on 297.11
relate to 775.5
operate on 889.6
rest on 901.22
evidence 957.8
bear one's cross 134.5
bear out
support 449.12
confirm 957.11
bear the brunt
endure 134.5
have trouble 1011.9
bear up
not weaken 15.10
be of good cheer 109.10
comfort 121.6
approach 167.3
buoy 298.8
stay with it 360.4
support 449.12
resist 453.2
keep up one's courage 492.15
support 901.21
bear upon
exercise influence 894.9
thrust 902.12
bear with endure 134.5
condone 148.4
be easy on 427.5
suffer 443.10
bear witness
be pious 692.6
testify 957.9
beastly hoggish 80.24
offensive 98.18
horrid 98.19
cruel 144.26
animal 311.40
gruff 505.7
carnal 663.6
terrible 1000.9
beast of burden
pack animal 176.8
drudge 726.3
beat
n staccato 55.1
parasite 138.5
sphere 231.2
routine 373.5
route 383.1
accent 524.10
news item 552.3
rhythm 709.22
tempo 709.24

throb 709.26
meter 720.7
occupation 724.4
periodicity 850.2
round 850.3
circuit 914.2
pulsation 916.3
flutter 917.4
v get tired 21.6
drum 55.4
sail near the wind 182.25
change course 182.30
best 249.7
foam 320.5
deceive 356.19
hunt 382.9
injure 393.13
vanquish 411.5
defeat 412.9
whip 604.13
time 708.44
din 849.10
pound 902.16
pulsate 916.12
agitate 917.10
flutter 917.12
stump 971.14
pulverize 1051.9
adj tired 21.8
defeated 412.15
without money 619.10
unconventional 868.6
licked 971.26
beat about
change course 182.30
grope 938.32
be uncertain 971.9
have difficulty 1013.11
beat a dead horse
be useless 391.8
dwell on 849.9
persist 856.5
carry coals to Newcastle 993.12
beat around the bush
dodge 368.8
circumlocute 538.10
quibble 936.9
beat back 908.3
beat down
sadden 112.18
raze 395.19
subdue 432.9
domineer 612.16
cheapen 633.6
bargain 731.18
beaten burnt-out 21.10
bubbly 320.6
habitual 373.14
defeated 412.14
beaten path
routine 373.5
path 383.2
beater hunter 382.5
mixer 797.9
agitator 917.9
beatific happy 95.16
blissful 97.9
heavenly 681.12
beatified happy 95.16
eminent 662.18

angelic 679.6
heavenly 681.12
sanctified 685.8
raised 912.9
beatify gladden 95.9
glorify 662.13
sanctify 685.5
exalt 912.6
beating
n staccato 55.1
defeat 412.1
corporal punishment 604.4
hit 902.4
pulsation 916.3
flutter 917.4
pulverization 1051.4
adj staccato 55.7
rhythmic 709.28
periodic 850.7
pulsative 916.18
beat into one's head
inculcate 568.12
convince 953.18
beat it
v depart 188.7
leave 222.10
flee 368.11
interj go away! 909.31
beatitude
happiness 95.2
sanctification 685.3
beatnik 868.3
beat one's brains 931.9
beat one's breast 115.11
beat out best 249.7
pulsate 916.12
beat someone to the punch 845.6
beat the drum for
publicize 352.15
espouse 509.13
beat the rap
get off 369.7
go free 431.9
beat the system 409.13
beat time
keep rhythm 708.44
time 832.11
pulsate 916.12
beat up
v punish 604.15
agitate 917.10
emulsify 1062.10
adj tired 21.8
spoiled 393.29
dilapidated 393.33
slovenly 810.15
beau
n inamorato 104.13
dandy 500.9
v court 562.21
Beau Brummel
dandy 500.9
person of fashion 578.7
beaucoup
adj much 247.8
plural 883.7
plentiful 991.7
adv greatly 247.15
beau monde noble 608.1

the rich 618.6
beaut
first-rate 999.7
beauty 1016.9
beautician 1016.13
beautification
development 392.2
prettification 1016.11
beautified
improved 392.13
beautifying 1016.23
beautiful
adj artistic 712.20
beauteous 1016.18
interj bravo! 509.22
beautiful people 578.6
beautify
develop 392.10
ornament 498.8
prettify 1016.16
beauty harmony 533.2
attractiveness 1016.1
beautifulness 1016.1
charmer 1016.8
beauty parlor
workplace 739.1
salon de beauté 1016.14
beauty queen 1016.8
beauty sleep 22.2
beaux arts 712.1
beaver
n beard 3.8
man of action 330.8
v work hard 725.13
bebop 708.9
becalm 173.11
becalmed 173.17
because 888.10
bechance 972.11
becharm
delight 95.10
enamor 104.23
fascinate 377.7
charm 691.8
beck and call 420.5
beckon
n gesture 517.14
v attract 377.6
gesture 517.21
becloud fog 319.7
conceal 346.6
confuse 985.7
darken 1027.9
opaque 1031.2
become behoove 641.4
come to be 761.12
originate 818.13
convert 858.11
change into 858.17
become of 887.4
become one
get married 563.15
beautify 1016.16
becoming
n conversion 858.1
adj decorous 496.10
rightful 639.8
decent 664.5
apt 788.10
expedient 995.5
comely 1016.19

bed
n bottom 199.1
floor 199.4
furniture 229.1
watercourse 239.2
layer 296.1
accommodations 385.3
presswork 548.9
marriage 563.1
bowling 750.1
foundation 901.6
sofa 901.19
garden 1069.10
v rest 20.6
retire 22.17
put to bed 22.19
inset 191.5
house 225.10
fix 855.9
plant 1069.18
tend 1070.7
bed and board 385.3
bed and breakfast 228.15
bedarken blacken 38.7
darken 1027.9
bedaub soil 80.16
coat 295.24
stain 1004.6
bedazzle blind 30.7
astonish 122.6
confuse 985.7
shine 1025.23
bedazzled
blinded 30.10
dazed 985.14
bedbug 311.38
bedchamber 197.7
bedding blanket 295.10
layer 296.1
foundation 901.6
underbed 901.20
bedecked clothing 5.45
ornamented 498.11
bedevil annoy 96.13
demonize 680.16
bewitch 691.9
bedeviled
tormented 96.24
possessed 926.29
bedew 1065.12
bedfast 85.59
bedfellow companion 588.3
associate 616.1
bedim 1027.9
bedimming
inconspicuousness 32.2
decoloration 36.3
darkening 1027.6
bedizen dress up 5.42
color 35.14
ornament 498.8
bedizened
ornamented 498.11
grandiloquent 545.8
bedlam
noise 53.3
pandemonium 810.5
insane asylum 926.14
bed of roses
comfort 121.1
prosperity 1010.1

Bedouin 178.4
bedpan 12.11
bedraggled
  soiled 80.21
  slovenly 810.15
bedrape 5.39
bedridden 85.59
bedrock
  n bottom 199.1
  base 274.4
  stability 855.6
  foundation 901.6
  rock 1059.1
  adj bottom 199.7
  deepest 275.15
  vital 997.23
bedroom
  n boudoir 197.7
  v restrict 428.9
bedsheet 295.10
bedsore 85.37
bedspread 295.10
bedsprings 901.20
bedstead 901.19
bedtime sleep 22.2
  night 315.4
bedwarf 252.9
bee honeybee 311.35
  quilting bee 582.14
beef
  n food 10.14
  muscularity 15.2
  power 18.1
  complaint 115.5
  weight 297.1
  cattle 311.6
  objection 333.2
  bone of contention 456.7
  v be discontented 108.6
  complain 115.16
  object 333.5
beefcake sex object 75.4
  photo 714.3
beefeater 1008.14
beefheaded 922.15
beefing
  n complaint 115.5
  adj discontented 108.8
  complaining 115.20
beefsteak 10.18
beef up
  strengthen 15.13
  intensify 251.5
  add to 253.5
beefy strong 15.15
  corpulent 257.18
beehive nest 228.25
  hive 739.2
bee in one's bonnet 927.2
beekeeper 1070.4
beekeeping 1070.1
beeline
  shortcut 268.5
  straight line 277.2
Beelzebub 680.4
beep
  n noise 53.5
  v blare 53.10
beeper
  telephone 347.4
  alarm 400.1

beer 88.16
beerbelly 2.19
beer garden 88.20
beery
  intoxicated 88.31
  sentimental 93.21
beeswax 1056.8
beetle
  n insect 311.33
  jockey 757.2
  pulper 1063.4
  v overhang 202.7
  adj overhanging 202.11
beetle-browed
  sullen 110.24
  overhanging 202.11
befall occur 831.5
  chance 972.11
befit behoove 641.4
  expedite one's affair 995.3
befitting apt 788.10
  timely 843.9
  expedient 995.5
befog cover 295.19
  cloud 319.7
  conceal 346.6
befool fool 356.15
  stultify 923.7
before
  adv in front 165.4
  ahead 216.12
  preferably 371.29
  above 814.6
  previously 834.6
  formerly 837.13
  early 845.11
  prep in the presence of 221.18
  prior to 834.7
beforehand
  adj anachronistic 833.3
  adv early 845.11
before long in the future 839.9
  soon 845.16
beforementioned 814.5
before one's eyes
  adj visible 31.6
  adv before 216.12
  openly 348.15
before the bar
  adv all things considered 946.17
  phrs in litigation 598.22
before the house 938.38
beforetime
  adj early 845.7
  adv formerly 837.13
  early 845.11
befoul defile 80.17
  misuse 389.4
  work evil 1000.6
befouling 393.2
befriend aid 449.11
  make friends with 587.10
  benefit 592.3
befrilled
  ornamented 498.11
  ornate 545.11
befringed 211.12
befuddle
  intoxicate 88.22
  confuse 985.7

befuddled 985.13
beg
  n governor 575.13
  v evade 368.7
  find means 384.6
  entreat 440.11
  scrounge 440.15
beget procreate 78.8
  engender 818.14
  cause 886.10
  produce 890.7
  originate 892.12
begetter parent 560.8
  author 886.4
  producer 892.7
beggar
  n vagabond 178.3
  bum 331.9
  nonworker 331.11
  mendicant 440.8
  poor man 619.4
  wretch 660.2
  v strip 480.24
  impoverish 619.6
beggar description
  stagger belief 122.8
  look good 1016.17
beggarly
  obsequious 138.14
  low 497.15
  indigent 619.8
  base 661.12
  ill-provided 992.12
  paltry 998.21
begild color 35.14
  yellow 43.3
begin 818.7
begin again 856.6
beginner novice 572.9
  neophyte 818.2
  author 886.4
  producer 892.7
beginning
  n start 818
  commencement 818.1
  source 886.5
  production 892.1
  adj simple 798.6
  initial 818.15
beginnings
  origin 818.4
  earliness 845.1
beg off abandon 370.5
  refuse 442.3
begone
  v depart 188.6
  interj go away! 909.31
beg pardon
  repent 113.7
  apologize 658.5
begrime 80.15
begrudge envy 154.3
  refuse 325.3
  deny 442.4
  stint 484.5
beg the question
  dodge 368.8
  quibble 936.9
beg to differ 333.4
beguile
  deceive 356.14

  fascinate 377.7
  amuse 743.21
  distract 985.6
beguiled
  wondering 122.9
  foolish 923.8
beguiling
  n allurement 377.1
  adj wonderful 122.10
  deceptive 356.21
  alluring 377.8
  amusing 743.27
be had 632.8
behalf benefit 387.4
  good 999.4
behave act 321.4
  conduct oneself 321.5
  be good 328.4
behavior
  conditioning 92.26
  tendency 321
  conduct 321.1
  action 328.1
behavioral
  behaviorist 321.7
  acting 328.10
behaviorism
  behavioral science 321.3
  materialism 1052.6
behaviorist 321.7
behavior modification
  92.6
behead 604.17
behemoth 257.14
behest 420.1
behind
  n rear 217.1
  buttocks 217.5
  adj retarded 175.12
  adv after 166.6
  in the rear 217.13
  late 846.19
  short 911.6
  prep back of 449.27
  after 835.8
behindhand
  adj defaulting 625.10
  anachronous 833.3
  late 846.16
  adv late 846.19
  in arrears 911.6
behind the eight ball
  1013.22
behind the scenes
  adj invisible 32.5
  manipulation 415.4
  causal 886.13
  cognizant of 928.16
  adv behind 217.13
  secretly 345.17
  on the stage 704.36
behind the times 842.16
behold
  v see 27.12
  interj attention! 983.22
beholden
  grateful 150.5
  obliged 641.16
beholder
  recipient 479.3
  spectator 918.1

behoof
 benefit 387.4
 good 999.4
behoove 641.4
beige brown 40.3
 yellow 43.4
being
 n heart 93.3
 organism 305.2
 person 312.5
 existence 761.1
 something 763.3
 adj existent 761.13
 present 838.2
being as how 888.10
be it so 332.20
bejeweled 498.11
belabor whip 604.13
 dwell on 849.9
 emphasize 997.14
belabored 849.15
belaboring 604.4
belated 846.16
belay fasten 800.7
 secure 855.8
 cease 857.6
bel canto 708.13
belch
 n rasp 58.3
 outburst 671.6
 burp 909.9
 v sound harshly 58.9
 erupt 671.13
 burp 909.28
beldam bitch 110.12
 old woman 304.3
 witch 593.7
 violent person 671.9
beleaguer annoy 96.13
 enclose 212.5
 besiege 459.19
belfry 272.6
belie deny 335.4
 misrepresent 350.3
 falsify 354.16
 contradict 451.6
 disprove 958.4
belied 958.7
belief
 n religion 675.1
 trust 953.1
 credence 953.1
 confidence 970.5
 adj of belief 953.21
belief system 952.2
believable 953.24
believe be pious 692.6
 suppose 951.10
 credit 953.10
 have faith in 953.15
believer
 religionist 675.15
 truster 692.4
 zealot 953.9
belittle minimize 252.9
 disparage 512.8
 underestimate 950.2
belittled 252.10
belittle oneself 137.7
bell
 n gong 54.4

 marker 517.10
 signal 517.15
 wind instrument 711.6
 time of day 832.2
 stop 857.2
 v blare 53.10
 cry 60.2
belle
 fine lady 500.10
 beauty 1016.8
belles lettres
 writing 547.12
 literature 718.1
bellhop
 errand boy 353.4
 attendant 577.5
bellicose
 contentious 110.26
 partisan 456.17
 warlike 458.21
 contrary 779.6
bellied
 rotund 282.8
 bulged 283.16
belligerent
 n combatant 461.1
 adj contentious 110.26
 partisan 456.17
 warlike 458.21
 hostile 589.10
 contrary 779.6
bellow
 n cry 59.1
 v roar 59.6
 cry 60.2
 be excitable 105.16
 speak 524.25
bellowing 105.25
bellows lungs 2.22
 blower 318.18
bell-shaped 279.13
bell the cat
 brave 492.11
 court danger 493.6
bellwether
 n sheep 311.7
 leader 574.6
 precursor 816.1
 adj original 337.5
belly
 n digestive system 2.18
 bottom 199.1
 sphericity 282.1
 type 548.6
 v bulge 283.11
bellyache
 n ache 26.5
 complaint 115.5
 v be discontented 108.6
 complain 115.16
belly dancer 707.1
bellyful
 full measure 794.3
 satiety 994.1
bellying
 n convexity 283.1
 protuberance 283.2
 adj bulging 283.15
bellyland 184.43
belly laugh
 n laughter 116.4

 joke 489.6
 v laugh 116.8
belly up
 v die 307.20
 go bankrupt 625.7
 adj ruined 395.29
 insolvent 625.11
 ended 820.9
belong
 have place 159.9
 hold membership 617.15
belonging 775.11
belongings 471.2
belong to
 pertain to 469.7
 relate to 775.5
beloved
 n sweetheart 104.10
 adj loved 104.24
below
 adv down 194.13
 on earth 234.9
 underneath 274.10
 hellishly 682.9
 prep under 274.11
 subordinate to 432.17
 after 835.8
below par
 adj ill 85.56
 terrible 1000.9
 sub-standard 1005.10
 adv beneath norm 274.10
 at a discount 631.3
below the belt 650.10
below the mark
 below 274.10
 amiss 911.7
belt
 n waistband 5.19
 stripe 47.5
 excitement 105.3
 region 231.1
 inlet 242.1
 strip 271.4
 circle 280.3
 layer 296.1
 attempt 403.3
 victory 411.1
 slap 604.3
 whip 605.1
 trophy 646.3
 fight 754.3
 blow 902.5
 punch 902.6
 v encircle 209.7
 whip 604.13
 play 745.5
 bind 800.9
 strike 902.15
belt out 708.38
belt-tightening
 strictness 425.1
 thrift 635.1
 asceticism 667.1
belvedere
 observation post 27.8
 cigar 89.4
bemingle 797.10
bemire dirty 80.15
 mire 243.2
bemist 319.7

bemoan regret 113.6
 lament 115.10
bemuse 88.22
bemused
 intoxicated 88.31
 abstracted 985.11
be my guest 440.20
bench
 fitness 84.1
 plateau 272.4
 authority 417.10
 council 423.1
 seat of justice 595.5
 team 617.7
 workplace 739.1
 hockey players 749.2
 substitute 862.2
 table 901.15
bench mark
 location 159.1
 marker 517.10
 salient point 997.6
bench warrant 598.12
bend
 n obeisance 155.2
 deviation 164.1
 bias 204.3
 diagonal 204.7
 angle 278.2
 bending 279.3
 heraldry 647.2
 crouch 913.3
 v bow 155.6
 direct 161.5
 deviate 164.3
 deflect 164.5
 oblique 204.9
 distort 265.5
 angle 278.5
 curve 279.6
 conquer 412.10
 subdue 432.9
 submit 433.10
 bind 800.9
 conform 867.3
 influence 894.7
 crouch 913.8
 depress 913.9
 prejudice 980.9
 yield 1047.7
bend an ear
 listen 48.10
 hearken to 983.7
bender 88.6
bending
 n deflection 164.2
 bend 279.3
 deliberate falsehood 354.9
 adj pliant 1047.9
bend one's ear 524.20
bend over backwards
 be willing 324.3
 make a special effort 403.11
 jump at 101.6
 be careful 339.7
 be just 649.6
the bends 1075.10
bene! 509.22
beneath
 below 274.11
 under 432.17

beneath one's dignity
inferior 250.6
disgraceful 661.11
Benedict Arnold 357.10
benediction
thanks 150.2
blessing 696.5
benedictory 696.16
benefaction
act of kindness 143.7
benefit 478.7
benefactor helper 449.7
philanthropist 592.1
benefactress 592.1
benefice 698.9
beneficence 143.4
beneficent
benevolent 143.15
favorable 449.22
beneficial
healthful 81.5
useful 387.18
helpful 449.21
good 999.12
beneficiary
proprietor 470.2
allottee 479.4
benefice-holder 699.7
beneficience 133.9
benefit
n act of kindness 143.7
use 387.4
aid 449.1
estate 471.4
benefaction 478.7
theatrical performance
704.12
good 999.4
v do a favor 143.12
avail 387.17
aid 449.11
help 592.3
expedite one's affair 995.3
do good 999.10
benevolence
auspiciousness 133.9
good nature 143.2
charity 143.4
act of kindness 143.7
pity 145.1
forgiveness 148.1
compliance 427.2
benefit 478.7
magnanimity 652.2
goodness 999.1
benevolent
charitable 143.15
forgiving 148.6
favorable 449.22
magnanimous 652.6
indulgent 427.8
good 999.12
benighted blind 30.9
night-overtaken 315.10
dark 930.16
benign
healthful 81.5
auspicious 133.18
kind 143.13
indulgent 427.8
favorable 449.22

harmless 999.21
benignity
auspiciousness 133.9
kindness 143.1
act of charity 143.7
compliance 427.2
goodness 999.1
harmlessness 999.9
benison
benediction 696.5
good 999.4
bent
n inclination 100.3
direction 161.1
bias 204.3
preference 371.5
aptitude 413.5
tendency 896.1
disposition 978.3
prejudice 980.3
adj high 87.24
drunk 88.33
distorted 265.10
angular 278.6
curved 279.7
disposed 978.8
benthic 275.14
bent on
desirous of 100.22
determined upon 359.16
disposed 978.8
bent out of shape 152.30
benumb deaden 25.4
numb 94.8
relieve 120.5
freeze 1023.10
benumbed
insensible 25.6
apathetic 94.13
languid 331.20
be off
v depart 188.6
set out 188.8
race 757.5
interj go away! 909.31
be on to 941.8
bequeath will 478.18
transfer 629.3
bequeathal
bequest 478.10
inheritance 479.2
transfer 629.1
bequest
bequeathal 478.10
inheritance 479.2
be quiet! 51.14
bereave leave 307.28
take from 480.21
widow 566.6
bereaved bereft 307.35
sorrowful 473.8
indigent 619.8
bereavement
deathliness 307.11
loss 473.1
deprivation 480.6
bereft bereaved 307.35
at a loss 473.8
indigent 619.8
wanting 992.13
berg 1023.5

beribboned 498.11
berm shore 234.2
path 383.2
Bermuda shorts pants 5.18
berry fruit 10.38
plant 310.31
berserk
n violent person 671.9
lunatic 926.15
adj frenzied 105.25
rabid 926.30
berth
n anchor 180.16
quarters 228.4
position 724.5
harbor 1009.6
v inhabit 225.7
house 225.10
beseech entreat 440.11
pray 696.13
beset
v annoy 96.13
make anxious 126.5
enclose 212.5
persecute 389.7
importune 440.12
besiege 459.19
infest 910.6
obsess 926.25
trouble 1013.13
adj distressed 96.22
tormented 96.24
worried 126.8
enclosed 212.10
infested 910.11
troubled 1013.20
besetting
prevalent 864.12
troublesome 1013.18
beside
adj side 218.6
adv in juxtaposition
223.21
additionally 253.11
prep alongside 218.11
excluding 773.10
compared to 943.11
beside oneself
overjoyed 95.17
frenzied 105.25
angry 152.28
rabid 926.30
distracted 985.10
beside the point
adj irrelevant 776.7
adv amiss 911.7
besiege enclose 212.5
importune 440.12
lay siege to 459.19
besmear color 35.14
soil 80.16
coat 295.24
stain 1004.6
besmirch blacken 38.7
soil 80.16
vilify 512.10
stigmatize 661.9
stain 1004.6
besmirched
dingy 38.11
soiled 80.21

unchaste 665.23
stained 1004.10
besot deaden 25.4
intoxicate 88.22
besotted
intoxicated 88.31
foolish 923.8
obsessed 926.33
bespangled
spotted 47.13
ornamented 498.11
illuminated 1025.39
bespatter
spatter 80.18
vilify 512.10
stigmatize 661.9
moisten 1065.12
bespeak outfit 5.41
request 440.9
signify 517.17
mean 518.8
address 524.26
employ 615.14
evidence 957.8
bespeckle
variegate 47.7
spot 1004.5
bespoke tailored 5.48
made 892.18
best
v excel 249.6
beat 249.7
vanquish 411.5
defeat 412.6
adj superlative 249.13
reduced 633.9
the tops 999.16
n creature comforts 121.3
the top of the line 249.5
choice 999.8
best bet 972.8
best case
n hope 124.1
adj promising 124.13
bestial cruel 144.26
animal 311.40
unrefined 497.12
carnal 663.6
savage 671.21
bestiality
perversion 75.11
cruelty 144.11
sadism 144.12
unrefinement 497.3
carnality 663.2
terribleness 1000.2
be still 51.14
bestir oneself
stir 330.11
make haste 401.5
best man
wedding party 563.4
assistant 616.6
bestow spend 387.13
give 478.12
administer 643.6
bestraddle
mount 193.12
rise above 272.11
overlie 295.30
rest on 901.22

bestride mount 193.12
  rise above 272.11
  overlie 295.30
  dominate 612.15
  rest on 901.22
  pass 910.8
best seller
  great success 409.3
  book 554.1
best wishes
  congratulation 149.1
  regards 504.8
  greetings 585.3
bet
  n gamble 759.2
  wager 759.3
  poker 759.10
  v ante 759.25
  predict 962.9
  risk 972.12
betake oneself 177.18
beta particle
  electron 1033.3
  radioactive particle 1037.4
beta test 1042.18
bête noire
  frightener 127.9
  enemy 589.6
  bugbear 680.9
  bane 1001.1
be that as it may 338.8
bethink oneself
  think 931.8
  attend to 983.5
  remember 989.10
betide occur 831.5
  chance 972.11
betimes early 845.11
  soon 845.16
bétise stupidity 922.3
  foolishness 923.1
betoken augur 133.12
  manifest 348.5
  signify 517.17
  mean 518.8
  evidence 957.8
bet on bet 759.25
  rely on 953.16
  predict 962.9
  be certain 970.9
betray inform 351.6
  deceive 356.14
  defect 370.6
  rat on 551.12
  double-cross 645.14
  seduce 665.20
betrayal
  divulgence 351.2
  apostasy 363.2
  desertion 370.2
  betrayment 645.8
  seduction 665.6
betrayed 132.5
betrothal love affair 104.6
  promise 436.3
betrothed
  n fiancé 104.17
  adj promised 436.8
better
  v excel 249.6
  improve 392.9

change 852.7
  adj superior 249.12
  preferable 371.25
  augmented 392.14
  changed 852.10
better half
  spouse 563.6
  wife 563.8
betterment
  improvement 392.1
  change 852.1
better self
  compunction 113.2
  self 865.5
betting parlor 759.19
bettor 759.21
between 213.12
between the devil and the
  deep blue sea
  in danger 1006.13
  unfortunate 1011.14
  in a dilemma 1013.23
between the lines 519.5
betweentimes
  meanwhile 826.5
  occasionally 848.5
betwixt 213.12
betwixt and between
  adj ambiguous 539.4
  mediocre 1005.7
  adv midway 819.5
  prep between 213.12
bet your life 973.25
bevel
  n incline 204.4
  instrument 278.4
  type 548.6
  adj inclining 204.15
beveled 204.15
beverage liquid 8.4
  drink 10.49
  spirits 88.13
  fluid 1061.2
bevy company 770.3
  assemblage 770.6
  multitude 884.3
bewail regret 113.6
  lament 115.10
beware 494.7
bewhiskered
  bearded 3.25
  trite 117.9
bewilder
  astonish 122.6
  disconcert 971.12
  confuse 985.7
bewildered
  wondering 122.9
  dismayed 971.24
  at an impasse 1013.24
bewildering
  wonderful 122.10
  confusing 971.27
bewitch
  delight 95.10
  enamor 104.23
  fascinate 377.7
  demonize 680.16
  cast a spell 690.13
  witch 691.9
  work evil 1000.6

bewitched
  enamored 104.28
  wondering 122.9
  witched 691.13
  miraculous 870.16
bewitching
  delightful 97.7
  alluring 377.8
  witching 691.11
bey
  ruler 575.9
  governor 575.13
beyond
  adv additionally 253.11
  prep distant 261.21
  past 522.26
  after 835.8
  in excess of 993.26
the beyond 839.2
beyond a shadow of doubt
  970.16
beyond belief
  absurd 923.11
  unbelievable 955.10
beyond compare
  adj peerless 249.15
  adv extremely 247.22
beyond measure
  extremely 247.22
  superabundantly 993.24
beyond one
  adj hard to understand
    522.14
  impracticable 967.8
  adv unrealistic 19.20
beyond question
  adj undoubted 970.16
  adv unquestionably 970.25
beyond recall 125.15
beyond the call of duty 492.1
beyond the pale
  prohibited 444.7
  unpraiseworthy 510.24
  segregated 773.8
beyond words 98.19
biannual 850.8
bias
  n inclination 100.3
  deviation 164.1
  bend 204.3
  diagonal 204.7
  preference 371.5
  partiality 650.3
  tendency 896.1
  disposition 978.3
  prejudice 980.3
  v deflect 164.5
  oblique 204.9
  pervert 265.6
  influence 894.7
  tend 896.3
  prejudice 980.9
  adj inclining 204.15
  transverse 204.19
  adv diagonally 204.25
biaxial 875.7
bib
  n apron 5.17
  v drink 8.29
  tipple 88.24
bibacious 88.35

bibelot trinket 498.4
  trifle 998.5
Bible scripture 683.1
  Holy Bible 683.2
Biblical 683.11
bibliographer
  writer 547.15
  author 718.4
bibliography
  makeup 554.12
  bibliology 554.19
  Modern Language Association
    Bibliography 558.4
  directory 574.10
  catalog 871.3
  lore 928.9
bibliolatry
  strictness 687.5
  zeal 692.3
  scholarship 928.5
bibliophile
  booklover 554.18
  bookworm 929.4
bibliophilic 928.22
bibulous
  bibacious 88.35
  sorbent 187.17
  intemperate 669.7
bicameral
  legislative 613.11
  bipartite 875.7
bicentenary 850.4
bicentennial
  anniversary 850.4
  hundred 882.8
biceps member 2.7
  arm 906.5
bicker
  n quarrel 456.5
  argumentation 935.4
  v quarrel 456.11
  flutter 917.12
  argue 935.16
  quibble 936.9
  flicker 1025.25
bickerer 461.1
bicolored 47.9
bicorn 279.11
bicuspid
  n teeth 2.8
  adj bipartite 875.7
bicycle
  n cycle 179.8
  v exercise 84.4
  ride 177.33
bicycling
  riding 177.6
  sport 744.1
bicyclist 178.11
bid
  n attempt 403.2
  offer 439.1
  entreaty 440.2
  invitation 440.4
  bridge 758.3
  v command 420.8
  offer 439.6
  bargain 731.18
  bet 733.9
bid come
  summon 420.11

invite 440.13
bidding
command 420.1
summons 420.5
invitation 440.4
biddy woman 77.6
female animal 77.10
poultry 311.29
maid 577.8
bide expect 130.8
endure 134.5
be still 173.7
sit through 827.6
wait 846.12
remain 853.5
continue 856.3
bide one's time
expect 130.8
be still 173.7
do nothing 329.2
wait 846.12
bidet washbasin 79.12
hunter 311.13
bid fair to
be liable 897.3
be possible 966.4
be probable 968.4
have a chance 972.13
biennial
n plant 310.3
anniversary 850.4
adj momentary 850.8
bier 309.13
biff
n energy 17.3
fight 754.3
blow 902.5
v strike 902.15
bifid 875.7
bifocals 29.3
bifurcated
forked 171.10
two 873.6
halved 875.6
bifurcation
forking 171.3
angle 278.2
doubleness 873.1
bisection 875.1
big enthusiastic 101.10
arrogant 141.9
large 257.16
adult 303.12
inflated 502.12
magnanimous 652.6
eminent 662.18
important 997.17
bigamist 563.11
bigamous 563.19
the Big Board 737.7
Big Brother 894.3
big bucks 618.3
big business 731.1
big cheese chief 575.4
important person 997.9
big deal
n triviality 998.3
phrs what does it matter?
998.26
big game
animal life 311.1

quarry 382.7
biggety conceited 140.11
impudent 142.10
biggie influence 894.6
important person 997.9
big gun 997.9
big hand 509.2
bighearted
benevolent 143.15
liberal 485.4
magnanimous 652.6
bight inlet 242.1
angle 278.2
big league
n baseball 745.1
adj important 997.17
big mouth
braggart 502.5
talkativeness 540.1
big-mouthed
talkative 540.9
boastful 502.10
big name
n celebrity 662.9
personage 997.8
adj important 997.17
bigot
n hater 103.4
obstinate person 361.6
prejudiced person 687.6
dogmatist 970.7
intolerant 980.5
adj narrow-minded 980.10
bigotry hate 103.1
obstinacy 361.1
strictness 687.5
fanaticism 926.11
dogmatism 970.6
narrow-mindedness 980.1
the big picture 381.1
big shot superior 249.4
politics 610.7
important person 997.9
big talk
exaggeration 355.1
boasting 502.2
grandiloquence 545.1
big talker 540.4
big ticket
n high price 632.3
adj expensive 632.11
big time
n fun 743.2
adj important 997.17
big wheel
influence 894.6
important person 997.9
bigwig
n important person 997.9
adj important 997.17
bijou 498.6
bike
n cycle 179.8
v ride 177.33
biker 178.11
bikini 5.29
bilateral sided 218.7
two 873.6
bile digestion 2.17
body function 7.8
secretion 13.2

ill humor 110.1
bitterness 152.3
bilge
n offal 80.9
receptacle of filth 80.12
bulge 283.3
bullshit 520.3
v bulge 283.11
bilgewater offal 80.9
refuse 391.4
bilingual 523.16
bilious anemic 85.61
sour 110.23
bilk
n cheater 759.22
v disappoint 132.2
cheat 356.18
bill
n nose 283.8
point of land 283.9
poster 352.7
advertising matter 352.8
declaration 598.7
omnibus bill 613.9
debt 623.1
fee 624.5
account 628.3
law 673.3
theatrical performance
704.12
paper money 728.5
legal tender 728.7
negotiable instrument
728.11
statement 871.5
schedule 965.3
eyeshade 1028.2
v publicize 352.15
send a statement 628.11
dramatize 704.28
schedule 965.6
bill and coo 562.14
billboard 352.7
bill collector
creditor 622.4
collector 770.15
billed hooked 279.8
scheduled 965.9
billet
n letter 553.2
heraldry 647.2
position 724.5
wood 1054.3
v house 225.10
billfold 729.15
billiards 760.1
billion
n thousand million 882.12
large number 1017.5
adj numerous 884.6
billionaire 618.7
billionth 882.31
bill of attainder 602.2
bill of fare menu 8.14
bill 871.5
schedule 965.3
bill of goods 356.9
bill of health
pass 443.7
certificate 549.6
bill of particulars 599.1

Bill of Rights
right 430.2
constitution 673.6
bill of sale 734.1
billow
n wave 238.14
v surge 238.22
bulge 283.11
billowy curved 279.7
wavy 281.10
bulging 283.15
billy goat
male animal 76.8
goat 311.8
bimbo
roughneck 593.4
strumpet 665.14
violent person 671.10
bimonthly
n periodical 555.1
adj momentary 850.8
bin 386.6
binary digit
number 1017.3
bit 1042.14
bind
n state 765.1
delay 846.2
predicament 1013.4
v border 211.10
stop 293.7
compel 424.4
restrain 428.10
commit 436.5
indenture 615.18
obligate 641.12
relate 775.6
tie 800.9
stick together 803.9
binder
dressing 86.33
wrapper 295.18
payment 624.1
binding
n edging 211.7
wrapper 295.18
bookbinding 554.14
fastening 800.3
cohesion 803.1
adj preceptive 419.4
mandatory 420.12
compulsory 424.11
obligatory 641.15
joining 800.16
valid 973.14
bind up
bundle 770.20
bind 800.9
binge
n celebration 487.1
v stuff 8.25
drink 88.6
celebrate 487.2
overindulge 669.5
bingo 759.15
binocular optic 29.9
bipartite 875.7
binoculars 29.4
binomial
terminological 527.17
bipartite 875.7

biochemical
n element 1060.2
adj chemical 1060.9
biochemistry 1068.3
biodegradable
degradable 393.47
disintegrative 806.5
bioethics 636.1
biographer 719.4
biographical 719.7
biography
n history 719.1
v chronicle 719.5
biohazard 85.32
biological
organic 305.17
related 559.6
botanical 1068.4
biological clock 306.3
biological urge 75.5
biologist 1068.2
biology
organic matter 305.1
animal life 311.1
the study of living things 1068.1
biological science 1068.1
bioluminescence 1025.13
biomechanical 1039.7
bionics 1041.2
biophysicist 1018.2
biopsy 91.12
biorhythm life force 306.3
term 825.4
biosphere
organic matter 305.1
ecosphere 306.8
atmosphere 317.2
Earth 1072.10
biotic 305.17
bipartisan
partisan 609.44
two 873.6
bipartisanship 450.1
bipartite
separate 802.20
two 873.6
bifid 875.7
biped
n creature 311.3
adj bipartite 875.7
birch
n rod 605.2
v whip 604.13
bird poultry 10.22
man 76.5
woman 77.6
fowl 311.28
oddity 870.4
freak 927.4
beauty 1016.9
rocket 1074.3
birdbrained 922.20
birdcage gambling wheel 759.16
birdhouse 228.23
birdcall
animal noise 60.1
call 517.16
birdhouse 228.23
bird in hand 469.1

bird of passage
wanderer 178.2
bird 311.28
bird of prey
hunter 311.28
extortionist 480.12
bird sanctuary
preserve 397.7
refuge 1009.1
bird's-eye 864.13
bird's-eye view
viewpoint 27.7
appearance 33.6
abridgment 557.1
birds of a feather 784.5
bird song 60.1
bird-watcher 918.1
birth
n genesis 1.1
beginning 1.1
generation 78.6
life 306.1
lineage 560.4
heredity 560.6
aristocracy 607.3
nobility 608.2
origin 818.4
v engender 818.14
adj related 559.6
birth control 891.1
birth control device 86.23
birthday 850.4
birthday suit 6.3
birth defect 85.1
birthmark mark 517.5
blemish 1004.1
birth parent 560.8
birthplace
fatherland 232.2
breeding place 886.8
birthright
inheritance 479.2
prerogative 642.1
birthstone 1059.7
biscuit sinker 10.30
cookie 10.43
ceramic ware 742.2
dryness 1066.2
bisect sever 802.11
seek the middle 819.3
double 873.5
halve 875.4
bisector 875.3
bisexual
n homosexual 75.14
adj homosexual 75.30
bipartite 875.7
bisexuality
sexuality 75.2
sexual preference 75.10
bishop clergy 699.10
chessman 743.17
bishopric region 231.5
mastership 417.7
diocese 698.8
bison 311.6
bisque 742.2
bistro restaurant 8.17
bar 88.20
bit short distance 223.2
modicum 248.2

point 285.3
portion 477.5
information theory 551.7
act 704.7
role 704.10
script 706.3
piece 793.3
shift 825.3
short time 828.3
pittance 992.5
trifle 998.5
curb 1012.7
binary digit 1042.14
a bit to a degree 245.7
scarcely 248.9
bit by bit
by degrees 245.6
piece by piece 793.9
bitch
n woman 77.6
female animal 77.10
shrew 110.12
complaint 115.5
dog 311.17
objection 333.2
strumpet 665.14
card 758.2
first-rate 999.7
tough proposition 1013.2
v be discontented 108.6
sulk 110.14
complain 115.16
object 333.5
bungle 414.12
bitchy irascible 110.20
malicious 144.20
spiteful 144.21
disparaging 512.13
bite
n morsel 8.2
light meal 8.7
acrimony 17.5
pang 26.2
sip 62.2
zest 68.2
modicum 248.2
minute 258.7
hold 474.2
portion 477.5
vigor 544.3
round 751.3
piece 793.3
cold 1023.1
v chew 8.27
pain 26.7
nip 68.5
come to a point 285.6
hold 474.6
etch 713.10
kid oneself 954.6
freeze 1023.10
bite off more than one can chew
overextend oneself 404.6
overindulge 669.5
bite one's tongue
n change one's tune 363.6
v be silent 51.5
regret 113.6
be humiliated 137.9
keep to oneself 344.6

bite the bullet
endure 134.6
submit 433.6
brave 492.11
seize the opportunity 843.7
bite the dust die 307.20
be destroyed 395.22
lose 412.12
bite the hand that feeds one
be ungrateful 151.3
play one false 645.13
biting
acrimonious 17.14
painful 26.10
pungent 68.6
penetrating 105.31
caustic 144.23
witty 489.15
vigorous 544.11
cold 1023.14
a bit much
insufferable 98.25
excessive 993.16
bits and pieces miscellany 770.13
parts 793.3
bitter
v sour 110.16
adj acrimonious 17.14
flavored 62.9
galling 64.6
pungent 68.6
unpleasant 98.17
distressing 98.20
sour 110.23
caustic 144.23
resentful 152.26
hostile 589.10
cold 1023.14
bitter end 820.2
bitterly
caustically 144.32
distressingly 247.21
bitter pill
acridness 64.2
affliction 96.8
bittersweet
flavored 62.9
sweet 66.4
ambiguous 539.4
bituminous 1021.9
bivalent bipartite 875.7
valent 1060.10
bivouac
n settlement 228.29
campground 463.3
v settle 159.17
camp 225.11
biweekly
n periodical 555.1
adj momentary 850.8
bizarre
awesome 122.11
humorous 488.4
freakish 870.13
absurd 923.11
fanciful 986.20
blabber
n nonsense 520.2
chatter 540.3
gabber 540.4

informer 551.6
v betray 351.6
talk nonsense 520.5
chatter 540.5
blabbermouth 551.6
black
n pitch 38.1
mourning 115.7
Caucasian 312.3
v blacken 38.7
soil 80.16
darken 1027.9
adj black as ink 38.8
dark-skinned 38.10
sullen 110.24
gloomy 112.24
ominous 133.17
wicked 654.16
bad 1000.7
disastrous 1011.15
dark 1027.13
black-and-blue mark 85.38
black and white
opposites 215.2
motion-pictures 706.5
drawing 712.5
photographs 712.13
lighting 1025.19
blackball
n disapproval 510.1
ostracism 586.3
v reject 372.2
disapprove 510.10
ostracize 586.6
exclude 773.4
banish 909.17
black belt
the country 233.1
trophy 646.3
black box 549.1
black comedy 704.6
blackdamp
miasma 1001.4
vapor 1067.1
blacken cook 11.5
black 38.7
soil 80.16
berate 510.19
vilify 512.10
stigmatize 661.9
stain 1004.6
darken 1027.9
black eye
trauma 85.38
stigma 661.6
blackface
n theater 704.17
adj typographic 548.20
blackguard
n rascal 660.3
v vilify 513.7
blackhead 1004.1
blackhearted 654.15
black hole prison 429.8
star 1072.8
black humor 489.1
blackjack
n deal 759.11
twenty-one 759.11
v coerce 424.7
club 902.20

blackleg
n disease 85.41
cheater 357.4
strikebreaker 727.8
v break a strike 727.11
black light 1025.1
blacklist
n ostracism 586.3
list 871.1
v reject 372.2
ostracize 586.6
condemn 602.3
black look 510.8
black magic Satanism
680.14
the black art 690.2
blackmail
n demand 421.1
extortion 480.8
booty 482.11
fee 624.5
v demand 421.5
wrest 480.22
black man 312.3
black mark 661.6
black market
n illicit business 732.1
v illicit goods 732.7
adj illegal 674.6
Black Mass 680.14
blackout
unconsciousness 25.2
disappearance 34.1
grayout 184.21
veil of secrecy 345.3
loss of memory 990.2
dimout 1027.7
power failure 1032.20
space hazard 1075.10
black out
faint 25.5
gray out 184.46
cover up 345.8
darken 1027.9
black sheep
reprobate 660.4
intruder 774.2
blacktop
n ground covering 199.3
pavement 383.6
v floor 295.22
bladder bag 195.2
sphere 282.2
bubble 320.1
comedy 704.6
blade sled 179.20
leaf 310.19
combatant 461.1
sword 462.5
dandy 500.9
vocal organ 524.18
cutlery 1040.2
blah
n apathy 94.4
bullshit 520.3
adj apathetic 94.13
dull 117.6
tedious 118.9
blahs apathy 94.4
blues and blue devils and
mulligrubs 112.6

blame
n censure 510.3
accusation 599.1
attribution 888.1
v censure 510.13
accuse 599.8
attribute to 888.4
blamed curse 513.10
accused 599.15
blameless
honest 644.13
innocent 657.6
blameworthy
blamable 510.25
wicked 654.16
terrible 1000.9
blanch cook 11.5
suffer 26.8
pale 36.5
lose color 36.6
whiten 37.5
change color 105.19
blanched
bleached 36.8
terrified 127.26
weatherworn 393.34
bland
wishy-washy 16.17
insipid 65.2
vacant 222.14
suave 504.18
flattering 511.8
moderate 670.10
general 864.11
blandishment
inducement 375.3
allurement 377.1
importunity 440.3
flattery 511.1
endearment 562.5
blank
n absence 222.1
void 222.3
document 549.5
adj dull 117.6
vacant 222.14
closed 293.9
reticent 344.10
unadorned 499.8
inexpressive 522.20
empty-headed 922.19
thoughtless 933.4
blank check
latitude 430.4
carte blanche 443.4
privilege 642.2
negotiable paper 728.11
blanket
n coverlet 295.10
coating 295.12
v cover 295.19
conceal 346.6
adj comprehensive 772.7
undiscriminating 945.5
blankminded
ignorant 930.12
thoughtless 933.4
blank out 820.5
blank slate 222.3
blank verse 720.8
blank wall 293.3

blare
n blast 53.5
rasp 58.3
brightness 1025.4
v blast 53.10
sound harshly 58.9
cry 60.2
proclaim 352.13
speak 524.25
blaring
n reception 1034.21
adj noisy 53.13
blarney
n flattery 511.1
bullshit 520.3
style 532.2
v flatter 511.6
blasé apathetic 94.13
nonchalant 106.15
weary 118.11
languid 331.20
sophistication 413.9
experienced 413.28
disillusioned 977.5
blaspheme
curse 513.5
vilify 694.5
blasphemous
cursing 513.8
impious 694.6
blasphemy
curse 513.1
sacrilege 694.2
blast
n noise 53.3
blare 53.5
detonation 56.3
excitement 105.3
gust 318.6
success 409.4
charge 462.16
party 582.12
explosion 671.7
blight 1001.2
v din 53.7
blare 53.10
detonate 56.8
use 87.22
kill 308.14
blow 318.20
blow up 395.18
pull the trigger 459.22
curse 513.5
explode 671.14
thwart 1012.15
freeze 1024.11
interj damn! 513.12
blasted high 87.24
disappointed 132.5
blighted 393.42
ruined 395.28
curse 513.10
blast off
v begin 818.7
launch 1074.13
n beginning 818.1
rocket launching 1074.9
blat
n blare 53.5
rasp 58.3
v blare 53.10

sound harshly 58.9
cry 60.2
speak 524.25
blatant
noisy 53.13
vociferous 59.10
howling 60.6
conspicuous 348.12
gaudy 501.20
blatantly
distressingly 247.21
conspicuously 348.16
gaudily 501.27
blather
n nonsense 520.2
chatter 540.3
v talk nonsense 520.5
chatter 540.5
be stupid 922.12
blaze
n outburst 105.9
notch 289.1
pointer 517.4
mark 517.5
card 758.2
fire 1019.13
flare 1019.14
brightness 1025.4
flash 1025.6
v notch 289.4
proclaim 352.13
mark 517.19
be hot 1019.22
catch fire 1020.23
burn 1020.24
shine 1025.23
blaze up
flare up 152.19
catch fire 1020.23
blazon
n display 501.4
heraldry 647.2
v proclaim 352.13
ornament 498.8
bleach
n decoloration 36.3
bleacher 36.4
v decolor 36.5
pale 36.6
whiten 37.5
clean 79.18
bleached
decolored 36.8
clean 79.25
vacant 222.14
weatherworn 393.34
bleachers
observation post 27.8
baseball 745.1
bleak distressing 98.20
gloomy 112.24
hopeless 125.12
windblown 318.24
cold 1023.14
bleakness
distressfulness 98.5
gloom 112.7
vacancy 222.2
cold 1023.1
bleary-eyed 28.13
bleat 60.2

bleb sore 85.37
bulge 283.3
bubble 320.1
blemish 1004.1
bleed
hemorrhage 12.17
let blood 91.27
suffer 96.19
grieve 112.17
pity 145.3
exude 190.15
draw off 192.12
exploit 387.16
take from 480.21
strip 480.24
overprice 632.7
bleeding
n hemorrhage 12.8
decoloration 36.3
symptom 85.9
bloodletting 91.20
drawing 192.3
adj bloody 12.23
pained 96.23
pitying 145.7
bleeding heart
n sentimentality 93.8
wretchedness 96.6
heartache 112.9
philanthropist 143.8
compassionateness 145.2
pietist 693.3
liberal 979.6
adj liberal 611.19
pious 979.9
bleed white
exploit 387.16
consume 388.3
strip 480.24
overprice 632.7
bleep out excise 255.10
suppress 428.8
blemish
n mark 517.5
intruder 774.2
fault 1003.2
disfigurement 1004.1
blot 1004.1
eyesore 1015.4
v deform 265.7
mark 517.19
disfigure 1004.4
offend 1015.5
injure 393.13
blemished
deformed 265.12
unvirtuous 654.12
imperfect 1003.4
disfigured 1004.8
ugly 1015.6
blench flinch 127.13
demur 325.4
pull back 903.7
blend
n hybrid word 526.11
automobile racing 756.1
compound 797.5
combination 805.1
v harmonize 708.35
identify 778.5
mix 797.10

combine 805.3
blender mixer 797.9
agitator 917.9
blend in with 455.2
bless gladden 95.9
congratulate 149.2
thank 150.4
approve 509.9
praise 509.12
sanctify 685.5
glorify 696.12
give one's blessing 696.14
protect 1008.18
blessed happy 95.16
curse 513.10
heavenly 681.12
sanctified 685.8
fortunate 1010.14
blessed event 1.1
blessed with 469.9
blessing
n act of kindness 143.7
congratulation 149.1
consent 441.1
godsend 472.7
benefit 478.7
approval 509.1
sanctification 685.3
benediction 696.5
good 999.4
good fortune 1010.2
stroke of luck 1010.3
adj worshipful 696.16
blight
n disease 85.1
evil 1000.3
blast 1001.2
adversity 1011.1
v spoil 393.10
work evil 1000.6
freeze 1024.11
blighted
disappointed 132.5
spoiled 393.28
blasted 393.42
ruined 395.28
blighter 660.2
blimp aerostat 181.11
heavyweight 257.12
stuffed shirt 501.9
blind
n aviation 184.1
ambush 346.3
trick 356.6
pretext 376.1
stratagem 415.3
round 751.3
shade 1028.1
v cover the eyes 30.7
conceal 346.6
hoodwink 356.17
shine 1025.23
adj insensible 25.6
poor-sighted 28.11
sightless 30.9
high 87.24
closed 293.9
concealed 346.11
unpersuadable 361.13
obscure 522.15
undiscerning 922.14

involuntary 963.14
oblivious 984.7
blind alley
n obstruction 293.3
impasse 1013.6
adj closed 293.9
blind date 582.8
blinders blindfold 30.5
narrow-mindedness 980.1
blind faith 954.1
blindfold
n eye patch 30.5
v blind 30.7
hoodwink 356.17
adj blinded 30.10
undiscerning 922.14
blinding
n blindness 30.1
adj obscuring 30.11
garish 35.20
rainy 316.11
bright 1025.32
blindness
insensibility 25.1
faulty eyesight 28.1
sightlessness 30.1
total darkness 30.1
carelessness 340.2
unpersuadableness 361.5
unperceptiveness 922.2
incognizance 930.3
blindsided 131.12
blind spot
blindness 30.1
narrow-mindedness 980.1
reception 1034.21
blind to
insensible 94.10
unaware 930.13
blink
n glance 27.4
glitter 1025.7
reflection 1025.9
v wink 28.10
flinch 127.13
slight 340.8
pull back 903.7
glitter 1025.24
blink at
be blind 30.8
condone 148.4
suffer 443.10
keep an open mind 979.7
be inattentive 984.2
blinkers
spectacles 29.3
blindfold 30.5
signals 517.15
blinking
n winking 28.7
glitter 1025.7
adj poor-sighted 28.11
glittering 1025.35
flickering 1025.36
blintz 10.45
blips 1036.11
bliss happiness 95.2
pleasantness 97.1
heaven 681.5
blissful happy 95.16
pleasant 97.6

dine 8.21
ship activity 182.48
embark 188.15
mount 193.12
face 295.23
provision 385.9
accommodate 385.10
raid 459.20
boarder eater 8.16
lodger 227.8
board game 743.9
boardinghouse 228.15
board meeting 423.3
the boards
show business 704.1
stage 704.16
boardwalk 383.2
boast
n boasting 502.1
good thing 999.5
v be stuck on oneself 140.6
possess 469.4
brag 502.6
praise 509.12
boastful vain 136.9
proud 140.9
boasting 502.10
boat
n car 179.10
watercraft 180.1
ship 180.1
v navigate 182.13
boathouse 197.27
boating 182.1
boatload 196.2
boat person 368.5
boatswain
ship's officer 183.7
superintendent 574.2
boatyard 739.3
bob
n obeisance 155.2
float 180.11
instrument 200.6
weight 297.6
greeting 585.4
money 728.8
repeat 849.5
jerk 905.3
crouch 913.3
shake 917.3
v cut the hair 3.22
bow 155.6
excise 255.10
shorten 268.6
caper 366.6
fish 382.10
depress 913.9
oscillate 916.10
shake 917.11
bobble
n bungle 414.5
shake 917.3
goof 975.6
v bungle 414.12
mishandle 745.5
play 746.5
oscillate 916.10
shake 917.11
make a boner 975.15
bobby 1008.16

bobbysoxer 302.8
bobcat 311.22
bob up burst forth 33.9
be unexpected 131.6
arrive 186.6
shoot up 193.9
bode 133.11
bodice 5.15
bodiless
unsubstantial 764.5
disembodied 988.8
immaterial 1053.7
bodily
adj carnal 663.6
innate 767.8
material 1052.10
adv in person 221.17
wholly 792.13
body
n the one 2.1
man 76.5
population 227.1
size 257.1
human form 262.4
thickness 269.2
corpse 307.16
person 312.5
type 548.6
association 617.1
community 617.2
sect 675.3
automobile racing 756.1
substantiality 763.1
something 763.3
company 770.3
collection 770.11
major part 792.6
individual 872.4
solid 1045.6
physical being 1052.3
v materialize 1052.9
bodybuilding
exercise 84.2
sport 744.1
body count
obituary 307.14
summation 1017.11
body double 576.1
bodyguard escort 769.5
safeguard 1008.14
body language 517.14
body politic
population 227.1
country 232.1
the people 606.1
body snatcher
thief 483.1
executive search agency 615.5
boffo 409.4
bog
n receptacle of filth 80.12
marsh 243.1
v mire 243.2
bog down 243.2
bogey
n frightener 127.9
military aircraft 181.9
bugbear 680.9
round 751.3
v play 751.4

bogeyman
frightener 127.9
bugbear 680.9
bogeymen 1001.1
boggle
n demur 325.2
bungle 414.5
v astonish 122.6
start 127.12
demur 325.4
object 333.5
not know one's own mind 362.6
bungle 414.11
lose one's nerve 491.8
quibble 936.9
stump 971.14
boggle the mind
astonish 122.6
be unbelievable 955.7
boggy marshy 243.3
moist 1065.15
bogus
spurious 354.26
substitute 862.8
Bohemian
n nomad 178.4
nonconformist 868.3
adj informal 581.3
unconventional 868.6
boil
n dish 10.7
sore 85.37
swelling 283.4
turbulence 671.2
agitation 917.1
heating 1020.2
v cook 11.5
sanitize 79.24
be angry 152.15
bubble 320.4
seethe 671.12
be hot 1019.22
stew 1020.20
boil down 268.6
boiler room
noisemaker 53.6
confidence game 356.10
stockbrokerage 737.9
boiling over
fervent 93.18
heated 105.22
boiling point 1019.1
boisterous noisy 53.13
turbulent 105.24
blustering 503.4
rampageous 671.20
bold insolent 142.9
brazen 142.11
seaworthy 180.18
steep 204.18
protruding 283.14
in relief 283.18
conspicuous 348.12
defiant 454.7
courageous 492.17
foolhardy 493.9
immodest 666.6
boldfaced
brazen 142.11
typographic 548.20

bole cylinder 282.4
stem 310.21
boll sphere 282.2
seed vessel 310.30
bollix up spoil 393.11
bungle 414.12
complicate 799.3
confuse 811.3
hinder 1012.16
Bolshevik
n radical 611.12
Communist 611.13
revolutionist 860.3
adj Communist 611.21
revolutionist 860.6
bolster
n bedding 901.20
v comfort 121.6
aid 449.12
encourage 492.16
support 901.21
confirm 957.11
bolt
n a length 267.2
apostasy 363.2
change one's mind 363.7
flight 368.4
desertion 370.2
lock 428.5
arrow 462.6
missile 462.18
bundle 770.8
lightning 1025.17
v gobble 8.23
refine 79.22
speed 174.8
close 293.6
flee 368.10
defect 370.6
gluttonize 672.4
segregate 773.6
hook 800.8
classify 808.11
obstruct 1012.12
bolt-hole
hiding place 346.4
secret passage 346.5
means of escape 369.3
bolt out of the blue 131.2
bolt upright
vertical 200.11
straight 200.13
bolus bite 8.2
pill 86.7
sphere 282.2
bomb
n marijuana 87.11
surprise 131.2
failure 410.2
bombshell 462.20
stage show 704.4
game 746.3
v fall flat 117.4
blow up 395.18
fail 410.10
attack 459.23
dramatize 704.28
bombardier crew 185.4
artilleryman 461.11
bombardment
bombing 459.7

fission 1038.8
bombast
  n boasting 502.1
  nonsense 520.2
  bombastry 545.2
  v talk big 545.6
bombastic
  pompous 501.22
  inflated 502.12
  stiff 534.3
  fustian 545.9
bombed out 87.24
bomber alarmist 127.8
  destroyer 395.8
  artilleryman 461.11
  violent person 671.9
bombshell
  surprise 131.2
  bomb 462.20
bomb shelter 346.4
bona fide
  adj straight 644.14
  genuine 973.15
  adv faithfully 644.25
bonanza
  source of supply 386.4
  rich source 618.4
  plenty 991.2
bon appetit! 8.35
bond
  n shackle 428.4
  compact 437.1
  security 438.1
  pledge 438.2
  fidelity 644.7
  nominal rate 738.5
  relation 775.1
  joining 800.1
  fastening 800.3
  v secure 438.9
  pledge 438.10
  put together 800.5
  adj subjugated 432.14
bondage 432.1
bondholder 737.14
bondsman
  subject 432.7
  guarantor 438.6
bone
  n the skeleton 2.2
  whiteness 37.2
  hardness 1046.6
  dryness 1066.2
  v study 570.12
  adj skeleton 2.26
bonehead
  bungler 414.9
  fool 924.4
bone of contention
  apple of discord 456.7
  question 938.10
boner bungle 414.5
  goof 975.6
bones heart 93.3
  corpse 307.16
  refuse 391.4
  dice 759.8
  body 1052.3
bone to pick
  bone of contention 456.7
  grudge 589.5

bone up
  study up 570.14
  refresh the memory 989.19
bonfire 1019.13
bonhomie
  good nature 143.2
  hospitality 585.1
  cordiality 587.6
bon jour! 585.15
bonkers 926.27
bon mot 489.7
bonnet cloak 5.40
  top 295.21
bonny good 999.12
  comely 1016.19
bon ton custom 373.1
  fashion 578.1
  chic 578.2
  upper class 607.2
bonus extra 254.4
  find 472.6
  gratuity 478.5
  premium 624.6
  surplus 993.5
bon vivant
  eater 8.16
  connoisseur 496.7
  sociable person 582.16
  boon companion 588.5
  sensualist 663.3
bon voyage! 188.22
bony
  skeleton 2.26
  lean 270.17
  hard 1046.10
boo
  n marijuana 87.11
  booing 508.3
  v hiss 508.10
  interj bah! 157.10
boob dupe 358.2
  fool 924.3
boo-boo
  bungle 414.5
  goof 975.6
boobs 283.7
boob tube 1035.11
booby loser 412.5
  fool 924.3
booby hatch 926.14
booby prize 646.2
booby trap
  ambush 346.3
  deception 356.12
  hidden danger 1006.5
boodle bribe 378.2
  booty 482.11
  spoils of office 609.35
  money 728.2
boogie-woogie 708.9
boo-hoo 115.12
book
  n publication 352.1
  volume 554.1
  edition 554.1
  printed product 554.3
  part 554.13
  periodical 555.1
  playbook 704.21
  script 706.3
  poetry 720.9

casino 759.19
  part of writing 793.2
  v depose 334.6
  flee 368.11
  curse 513.5
  record 549.15
  accuse 599.7
  employ 615.14
  keep accounts 628.8
  list 871.8
  prearrange 965.4
  schedule 965.6
bookbinding 554.14
bookcase
  storehouse 386.6
  bookbinding 554.14
  bookholder 554.17
bookdealer 554.2
book end 554.17
bookie 759.20
booking
  registration 549.14
  engagement 615.4
  show 704.11
  prearrangement 965.1
bookish learned 570.17
  studentlike 572.12
  book-smart 928.22
bookkeeper
  recorder 550.1
  accountant 628.7
  treasurer 729.12
  calculator 1017.15
bookkeeping
  n accounting 628.6
  adj recording 628.12
book learning 928.5
booklet 554.11
booklover
  philobiblist 554.18
  bookworm 929.4
bookmaker 759.20
bookmark 517.10
book review 946.2
book reviewer 556.4
books
  account book 628.4
  bill 871.5
bookseller 554.2
bookshelf 554.17
bookstore 554.16
book value 738.9
bookworm
  booklover 554.18
  nerd 572.10
  bibliophage 929.4
boom
  n noise 53.3
  reverberation 54.2
  volume 56.4
  float 180.11
  intensification 251.2
  explosion 671.7
  business cycle 731.10
  lever 906.4
  roaring trade 1010.5
  barrier 1012.5
  v hum 52.13
  din 53.7
  reverberate 54.7
  thunder 56.9

speed 174.9
  ship activity 182.48
  grow 251.6
  speak 524.25
  thrive 1010.8
  interj bang! 56.13
boom box 50.11
boomerang
  n missile 462.18
  retaliation 506.1
  recoil 903.2
  v return 903.6
booming
  n hum 52.7
  reverberation 54.2
  explosion 56.4
  adj humming 52.20
  loud 53.11
  reverberating 54.12
  thundering 56.12
  thriving 1010.13
boon
  n godsend 472.7
  benefit 478.7
  good 999.4
  adj convivial 582.23
boondocks
  open space 158.4
  hinterland 233.2
  remote region 261.4
  woodland 310.13
boor bungler 414.8
  vulgarian 497.6
  peasant 606.6
  oaf 924.5
boorish insensible 25.6
  countrified 233.7
  bungling 414.20
  churlish 497.13
  ill-bred 505.6
boost
  n increase 251.1
  improvement 392.1
  promotion 446.1
  assist 449.2
  theft 482.4
  commendation 509.3
  thrust 902.2
  lift 912.2
  v cheer 109.7
  increase 251.4
  publicize 352.15
  make better 392.9
  promote 446.2
  be useful 449.17
  rob 482.16
  commend 509.11
  thrust 902.12
  elevate 912.5
booster dose 86.6
  inoculation 91.16
  enthusiast 101.5
  publicist 352.9
  thief 483.1
  commender 509.8
  multistage rocket
    1074.5
boot
  n excitement 105.3
  navy man 183.4
  recruit 461.18

novice 572.9
torture 605.4
kick 902.9
goof 975.6
v cloak 5.40
play 745.5
kick 902.21
dismiss 909.20
make a boner 975.15
computerize 1042.21
bootblack 577.5
boot camp 461.6
booth
  compartment 197.2
  hut 228.9
  stall 736.3
bootleg
  v distill 88.30
  illicit goods 732.7
  adj illegal 674.6
bootlegger
  liquor dealer 88.19
  racketeer 732.4
bootless
  ineffective 19.15
  fruitless 391.12
  unsuccessful 410.18
bootlicker
  flatterer 138.4
  assenter 332.6
bootmaker 5.38
boot out 909.13
booty gain 472.3
  take 480.10
  spoil 482.11
booze
  n spirits 88.13
  v imbibe 8.29
  use 87.22
  drink 88.25
bop 708.9
bordello
  disapproved place 228.28
  brothel 665.9
border
  n exterior 206.2
  limbus 211.4
  frontier 211.5
  partition 213.5
  side 218.1
  sphere 231.2
  size 257.1
  scenery 704.20
  garden 1069.10
  v edge 211.10
  side 218.4
  adjoin 223.9
  adj final 820.11
bordering
  n edging 211.7
  adj environing 209.8
  fringing 211.11
  adjacent 223.16
borderland
  frontier 211.5
  sphere 231.2
  hinterland 233.2
borderline 211.11
borderline case
  lunatic 926.15
  gamble 971.8

bore
  n annoyance 96.2
  crashing bore 118.4
  wave 238.14
  diameter 269.3
  hole 292.3
  v give no pleasure 96.12
  leave one cold 118.7
  excavate 284.15
  perforate 292.15
boreal
  northern 161.14
  seasonal 313.9
  windy 318.22
  cold 1023.14
boredom
  unpleasure 96.1
  weariness 118.3
  languor 331.6
  incuriosity 982.1
borehole 292.3
borer 285.3
boring
  n hole 292.3
  adj irritating 26.13
  wearying 118.10
  same 781.6
born
  given birth 1.4
  innate 767.8
  thorough 794.10
born-again
  redeemed 685.9
  regenerate 692.10
  converted 858.19
borne 901.24
borne out 957.20
born for 413.29
born yesterday 416.5
borough town 230.1
  region 231.5
  election district 609.16
borrow
  imitate 336.5
  rob 482.16
  plagiarize 482.19
  take a loan of 621.3
  go in debt 623.6
  discount 728.27
  play 751.4
borrowing
  plagiarism 482.8
  loan word 526.7
  appropriation 621.2
  money-raising 621.1
  debt 623.1
  money market 728.16
borscht circuit 704.11
borstal
  prison 429.8
  reform school 567.9
bosh humbug 354.14
  bullshit 520.3
bos'n 183.7
bosom
  n heart 93.3
  interior 207.2
  breast 283.6
  inner nature 767.5
  v keep secret 345.7
  conceal 346.7

  hold 474.7
  embrace 562.18
bosom buddy 588.4
bosomy
  corpulent 257.18
  bulging 283.15
  pectoral 283.19
boss
  n superior 249.4
  bulge 283.3
  print 517.7
  superintendent 574.2
  master 575.1
  politics 610.7
  important person
    997.11
  v emboss 283.12
  roughen 288.4
  direct 573.8
  supervise 573.10
  adj supervising 573.13
  governing 612.18
  excellent 999.13
bossism
  authoritativeness 417.3
  politics 609.1
bossy
  n female animal 77.10
  cattle 311.6
  adj in relief 283.18
  imperious 417.16
botanical
  vegetable 310.36
  biological 1068.4
botanical garden 1069.1
botany biology 1068.1
  plants 310.1
botch
  n slipshodness 340.3
  bad likeness 350.2
  fiasco 410.6
  bungle 414.5
  blunder 975.5
  v do carelessly 340.9
  misdraw 350.4
  spoil 393.10
  miss 410.14
  bungle 414.11
  blunder 975.14
both
  n two 873.2
  adj the two 873.7
bother
  n annoyance 96.2
  dither 105.6
  bustle 330.4
  imposition 643.1
  commotion 810.4
  bewilderment 971.3
  confusion 985.3
  inconvenience 996.3
  trouble 1013.3
  v annoy 96.13
  distress 96.16
  vex 98.15
  concern 126.4
  presume upon 640.7
  bewilder 971.12
  confuse 985.7
  inconvenience 996.4
  trouble 1013.13

bothered
  annoyed 96.21
  distressed 96.22
  anxious 126.7
  bewildered 971.24
  confused 985.12
  troubled 1013.20
bothersome
  annoying 98.22
  troublesome 126.10
  difficult 1013.18
bottle
  n container 195.1
  v package 212.9
  put up 397.11
bottleneck
  convergence 169.1
  contraction 260.1
  narrow place 270.3
  obstruction 293.3
  hindrance 1012.1
bottle up enclose 212.6
  secrete 346.7
  suppress 428.8
  confine 429.12
  retain 474.5
  hinder 1012.10
bottom
  n ship 180.1
  under side 199.1
  bed 199.4
  buttocks 217.4
  marsh 243.1
  base 274.4
  valley 284.9
  pluck 359.3
  fortitude 492.6
  v base on 199.6
  solve 940.2
  adj bottommost 199.7
  reduced 633.9
bottom dollar
  funds 728.14
  extremity 820.2
bottoming out 731.10
bottomless
  greedy 100.27
  abysmal 275.11
  plentiful 991.7
bottomless pit
  depths 275.3
  infinity 823.1
the bottom line
  essential content 196.5
  fact 761.3
  essence 767.3
  salient point 997.6
  sum 1017.6
bottom of the barrel 820.2
bottom out
  base on 199.6
  be changed 852.6
boudoir 197.7
bouffant 259.13
bough branch 310.20
  member 793.4
bought 733.11
bougie 1026.2
bouillabaisse 10.11
bouillon 10.14
boulder 1059.5

bounce
  n lightheartedness 109.3
  leap 366.1
  swagger 501.8
  recoil 903.2
  shake 917.3
  radio signal 1034.10
  elasticity 1048.1
  v leap 366.5
  caper 366.6
  bluster 503.3
  play 745.5
  recoil 903.6
  eject 909.13
  dismiss 909.20
  alternate 916.14
  shake 917.11
  give 1048.5
bounce a check 625.6
bounce back
  n reaction 903.1
  v reverberate 54.7
  recover 396.19
  recoil 903.6
  reflect 1036.16
bouncer 909.11
bouncing
  n leaping 366.3
  adj strong 15.15
  hale 83.12
  active 330.17
  leaping 366.7
  recoiling 903.10
bound
  n boundary 211.3
  leap 366.1
  recoil 903.2
  v speed 174.8
  circumscribe 210.4
  limit 210.5
  separate 211.8
  border 211.10
  enclose 212.5
  leap 366.5
  recoil 903.6
  adj limited 210.7
  enclosed 212.10
  stopped 293.11
  resolute 359.11
  tied 428.16
  promised 436.8
  obliged 641.16
  related 775.9
  joined 800.13
  certain 970.13
boundary
  n limitation 210.2
  bound 211.3
  border 211.3
  fence 212.4
  size 257.1
  joint 800.4
  extremity 820.2
  grammar 857.4
  bisector 875.3
  adj bordering 211.11
  final 820.11
bounder
  vulgarian 497.6
  cad 660.7
bound for 161.26

boundless large 247.7
  almighty 677.17
  infinite 823.3
  excessive 993.16
bound over 615.21
bountiful liberal 485.4
  productive 890.9
  plentiful 991.7
bounty gratuity 478.5
  subsidy 478.8
  liberality 485.1
  bonus 624.6
bouquet fragrance 70.1
  nosegay 310.25
  compliment 509.6
  bundle 770.8
bourgeois
  n townsman 227.6
  vulgarian 497.6
  member of the middle class
    607.6
  conformist 867.2
  adj common 497.14
  upper-class 607.10
  capitalist 611.23
  conformist 867.6
  ordinary 1005.8
bourgeoisie
  middle class 607.5
  mediocrity 1005.5
bout spree 88.5
  contest 457.3
  boxing 457.9
  revel 743.6
  game 743.9
  fight 754.3
  turn 825.2
  round 850.3
boutique 736.1
boutonniere 310.25
bovine
  n cattle 311.6
  adj unconcerned 102.7
  inexcitable 106.10
  complacent 107.10
  ungulate 311.46
  stupid 922.15
bow curve 279.2
  bend 279.3
  bulge 283.3
  longbow 462.7
  violin family 711.5
bow
  n obeisance 155.2
  prow 216.3
  greeting 585.4
  crouch 913.3
  v fawn 138.7
  make obeisance
    155.6
  curve 279.6
  lose 412.12
  submit 433.10
  bend 913.9
bowdlerize
  clean 79.18
  delete 255.12
  shorten 268.6
bowel movement
  defecation 12.2
  feces 12.4

bowels
  digestive system 2.18
  insides 207.4
  depths 275.3
bower
  summerhouse 228.12
  card 758.2
  safeguard 1008.3
Bowery 230.6
bowl
  n tableware 8.12
  cavity 284.2
  arena 463.1
  ceramic ware 742.2
  football 746.1
  lawn bowling 750.3
  throw 904.3
  v be concave 284.12
  hollow 284.13
  push 904.9
  throw 904.10
  roll 915.10
bowl down
  astonish 122.6
  startle 131.8
  fell 913.5
bowlegged 265.12
bowlegs 265.3
bowl over
  astonish 122.6
  startle 131.8
  fell 913.5
bow out quit 188.9
  exit 190.12
  absent oneself 222.8
  die 307.20
  dismiss 909.18
box
  n container 195.1
  compartment 197.2
  cottage 228.8
  coffin 309.11
  storehouse 386.6
  gift 478.4
  slap 604.3
  auditorium 704.15
  slap 902.8
  impasse 1013.6
  v package 212.9
  wrap 295.20
  restrict 428.9
  contend 457.13
  hit 604.12
  fight 754.4
  slap 902.19
boxed packed 212.12
  covered 295.31
boxer pugilist 461.2
  fighter 754.2
box in enclose 212.5
  confine 212.6
  restrict 428.9
  qualify 959.3
boxing packaging
    212.2
  fighting 457.9
  sports 754
  prizefighting 754.1
box office
  attendance 221.4
  receipts 627.1

  office 739.7
box score 1017.6
boy
  n heroin 87.9
  lad 302.5
  man 577.4
  card 758.2
  interj goody! 95.21
boycott
  n objection 333.2
  ostracism 586.3
  strike 727.5
  exclusion 773.1
  v object 333.5
  ostracize 586.6
  strike 727.10
boyfriend admirer 104.13
  friend 588.1
boyhood
  childhood 301.2
  young people 302.2
boyish thin 270.16
  childish 301.11
  immature 406.11
boy wonder 413.12
bra brassiere 5.24
  supporter 901.2
brace
  n dressing 86.33
  verticalness 200.1
  staff 708.29
  two 873.2
  supporter 901.2
  v refresh 9.2
  strengthen 15.13
  stand 200.7
  bind 800.9
  support 901.21
  stiffen 1046.9
bracelet circle 280.3
  jewel 498.6
brace oneself
  be determined 359.8
  prepare oneself 405.13
bracer refreshment 9.1
  tonic 86.8
  drink 88.8
  supporter 901.2
brace up refresh 9.2
  strengthen 15.13
  cheer up 109.9
  recuperate 396.19
  take courage 492.14
  encourage 492.16
bracing
  n refreshment 9.1
  adj refreshing 9.3
  energizing 17.15
  healthful 81.5
  tonic 86.44
  supporting 901.23
  cool 1023.12
bracket
  n boundary 211.3
  class 809.2
  supporter 901.2
  v parenthesize 212.8
  grammaticize 530.16
  relate 775.6
  simplify 798.4
  put together 800.5

brackish nasty 64.7
  salty 68.9
bract 310.28
brag
  n boasting 502.1
  braggart 502.5
  v boast 502.6
  bluster 503.3
  praise 509.12
braggart
  n egotist 140.5
  boaster 502.5
  blusterer 503.2
  adj boastful 502.10
Brahman cattle 311.6
  nobleman 608.4
  clergy 699.13
Brahmin snob 141.7
  aristocrat 607.4
  intellectual 929.1
braid
  n hair 3.7
  cord 271.2
  plait 740.2
  v spin 271.6
  weave 740.6
Braille 30.6
brain
  n encephalon 2.15
  sensory area 919.1
  seat of thought 919.6
  intelligence 920.9
  intellectual 929.1
  v strike dead 308.18
  adj nerve 2.30
brainchild
  writing 547.10
  work of art 712.10
  product 893.1
  good idea 932.6
  figment of the imagination
    986.5
brain-damaged 926.28
brain death
  fatal disease 85.2
  death 307.1
brainless
  unintelligent 922.13
  foolish 923.8
  scatterbrained 985.16
brainstorm
  caprice 364.1
  impulse 365.1
  delirium 926.8
  good idea 932.6
  absurd idea 932.7
brainteaser 522.9
brain trust 423.1
brain twister 522.8
brainwash
  inculcate 568.12
  propagandize 569.4
  indoctrinate 858.15
brainy 920.14
braise cook 11.5
  brown 40.2
brake
  n thicket 310.15
  curb 1012.7
  v slow 175.9
  put a stop to 857.11

  halt 1012.13
bramble
  thorn 285.5
  shrubbery 310.9
  adhesive 803.4
brambly 285.10
bran feed 10.4
  hull 295.16
  powder 1051.5
branch
  n divergence 171.4
  stream 238.1
  tributary 238.3
  fork 310.20
  part of the service 461.21
  lineage 560.4
  offshoot 561.4
  organ 617.10
  sect 675.3
  office 739.7
  member 793.4
  class 809.2
  arm 809.5
  v fork 171.7
  spread 259.6
  angle 278.5
  bisect 875.4
branching
  n forking 171.3
  bisection 875.1
  adj forked 171.10
  leafy 310.41
  halved 875.6
branch off deviate 164.3
  fork 171.7
branch out fork 171.7
  spread 259.6
  disperse 771.4
brand
  n mark 517.5
  label 517.13
  stigma 661.6
  nature 767.4
  kind 809.3
  characteristic 865.4
  stain 1004.3
  coal 1019.16
  burn 1020.6
  cauterant 1020.15
  combustion product
    1020.16
  lighter 1021.4
  v mark 517.19
  label 517.20
  stigmatize 661.9
  stain 1004.6
  burn 1020.24
brandish
  n waving 916.2
  v manifest 348.5
  flaunt 501.17
  wave 916.11
brand-new 841.10
brandy 88.15
brash
  n rainstorm 316.2
  rock 1059.1
  adj impudent 142.10
  defiant 454.7
  rash 493.7
  gruff 505.7

brass
  n impudence 142.3
  rashness 493.1
  monument 549.12
  orchestra 710.12
  money 728.2
  personage 997.8
  adj brazen 1058.17
the brass the best 249.5
  directorate 574.11
  commissioned officer 575.18
brassiere bra 5.24
  supporter 901.2
brass knuckles 462.4
brass tacks 761.4
brass wind instrument 711.7
brassy noisy 53.13
  raucous 58.15
  brazen 142.11
  defiant 454.7
  immodest 666.6
  brass 1058.17
brat urchin 302.4
bravado defiance 454.1
  daring 492.5
  boasting 502.1
  bluster 503.1
brave
  n military man 461.6
  brave person 492.8
  v endure 134.5
  confront 216.8
  defy 454.3
  face 492.11
  take chances 1006.7
  thwart 1012.15
  adj courageous 492.17
  showy 501.19
bravery courage 492.1
  finery 498.3
bravo
  n killer 308.11
  combatant 461.1
  blusterer 503.2
  ruffian 593.3
  interj congratulations!
    149.4
  bravissimo! 509.22
bravura
  n skill 413.1
  daring 492.5
  display 501.4
  vocal music 708.13
  aria 708.16
  adj skillful 413.22
  showy 501.19
  vocal 708.50
brawl
  n noise 53.3
  quarrel 456.5
  free-for-all 457.5
  party 582.12
  turbulence 671.2
  assembly 770.2
  commotion 810.4
  v be noisy 53.9
  quarrel 456.11
  contend 457.13
brawler rebel 327.5
  oppositionist 452.3
  combatant 461.1

brawling noisy 53.13
  vociferous 59.10
brawn
  muscularity 15.2
  organic matter 305.1
brawny
  able-bodied 15.16
  corpulent 257.18
bray
  n blare 53.5
  rasp 58.3
  v blare 53.10
  sound harshly 58.9
  cry 60.2
  speak 524.25
  pulverize 1051.9
brazen
  v brave 492.11
  adj reddish-brown 40.4
  noisy 53.13
  raucous 58.15
  insolent 142.11
  defiant 454.7
  gaudy 501.20
  hardened 654.17
  immodest 666.6
  brass 1058.17
  rash 493.7
brazen it out 360.4
breach
  n crack 224.2
  violation 435.2
  falling-out 456.4
  misdeed 655.2
  break 802.4
  interruption 813.2
  v cleave 224.4
  rupture 292.14
  violate 435.4
  break 802.12
  open 818.12
breach of confidence 645.5
breach of faith 645.6
bread
  n food 10.1
  pain 10.28
  support 449.3
  Eucharist 701.7
  money 728.2
  v feed 8.18
  sprinkle 771.6
breadth space 158.1
  size 257.1
  width 269.1
  expanse 269.1
  extent 300.3
  broad-mindedness 979.1
breadwinner 726.2
break
  n respite 20.2
  trauma 85.38
  act of kindness 143.7
  start 188.2
  boundary 211.3
  crack 224.2
  escape 369.1
  falling-out 456.4
  cheapening 633.4
  declining market 737.5
  horse race 757.3
  deficiency 795.2

breezy
lighthearted 109.12
airy 317.12
windy 318.22
active 330.17
brethren brother 559.3
the laity 700.1
brevet decree 420.4
grant 443.5
commission 615.1
brevity shortness 268.1
taciturnity 344.2
conciseness 537.1
briefness 828.2
brew
n spirits 88.13
beer 88.16
concoction 405.3
v cook 11.5
grow 14.2
distill 88.30
expand 259.7
blow 318.20
plot 381.9
make up 405.7
imbue 797.11
be imminent 840.2
liquefy 1064.5
soak 1065.13
brewer 88.19
brewery
distillery 88.21
plant 739.3
bribable
corruptible 378.4
improbity 645.23
influenceable 894.15
bribe
n incentive 375.7
bribe money 378.2
gratuity 478.5
v throw a sop to 378.3
bribery
graft 378.1
bribing 378.1
bric-a-brac
trinket 498.4
work of art 712.10
trivia 998.4
brick
n pavement 383.6
good person 659.2
ceramic ware 742.2
hardness 1046.6
building material 1054.2
v face 295.23
brickbat
n indignity 156.2
disrespect 156.3
missile 462.18
v pelt 459.27
brick wall 1012.5
brickyard 739.3
bridal
n wedding 563.3
adj matrimonial 563.18
bride 563.5
bridegroom 563.5
bridesmaid 563.4
bridge
n observation post 27.8

railway 383.7
span 383.9
stage 704.16
passage 708.24
violin family 711.5
auction bridge 758.3
v overlie 295.30
bridged 800.13
bridgehead
vanguard 216.2
stronghold 460.6
bridging
n joining 800.1
adj overlying 295.36
joining 800.16
bridle
n shackle 428.4
v give oneself airs 141.8
anger 152.17
restrain 428.7
bind 428.10
mince 500.14
yoke 800.10
tend 1070.7
brief
n airmanship 184.3
report 549.7
abridgment 557.1
argument 935.5
v give a briefing 184.48
outline 381.11
advise 422.5
inform 551.8
give instructions 568.15
employ 615.14
adj short 268.8
taciturn 344.9
concise 537.6
abridged 557.6
transient 828.8
briefing
airmanship 184.3
preparation 405.1
advice 422.1
information 551.1
instructions 568.6
engagement 615.4
briefly
shortly 268.12
concisely 537.7
transiently 828.10
brier thorn 285.5
shrubbery 310.9
adhesive 803.4
brig prison 429.8
jail 429.9
brigade
military unit 461.22
company 770.3
brigadier 575.18
brigand 483.4
bright
n tobacco 89.2
adj colorful 35.19
clean 79.25
sunny 97.11
cheerful 109.11
optimistic 124.12
auspicious 133.18
alert 339.14
teachable 570.18

illustrious 662.19
intelligent 920.12
smart 920.14
undamaged 1002.8
gorgeous 1016.21
brilliant 1025.32
bright and early 845.7
brighten
make pleasant 97.5
cheer 109.7
grow light 1025.27
illuminate 1025.28
bright side
cheerfulness 97.4
optimism 124.3
brilliant
colorful 35.19
skillful 413.22
witty 489.15
illustrious 662.19
smart 920.14
gorgeous 1016.21
bright 1025.32
brim
n border 211.4
v fill 794.7
brimming 794.11
brim over 238.17
brimstone
n bitch 110.12
witch 593.7
adj hellish 682.8
brindle 47.15
brine
n saltiness 68.4
preservative 397.4
v preserve 397.9
bring fetch 176.16
induce 375.22
cost 630.13
inflict 643.5
be sold 734.12
entail 772.4
cause 886.11
bring about
change course 182.30
do 328.6
prompt 375.13
bring to pass 407.5
cause 886.10
perform 892.11
bring back fetch 176.16
revive 396.16
restore 481.4
remember 989.10
remind 989.20
bring down
n disrespect 156.3
v abase 137.5
strike dead 308.18
raze 395.19
disparage 512.8
incur 897.4
fell 913.5
bring down the curtain 820.5
bring forth
elicit 192.14
manifest 348.5
cause 886.10
originate 892.12
bear 892.13

bring forward
confront 216.8
manifest 348.5
make better 392.9
propose 439.5
call to witness 598.17
adduce 957.12
bring home to
impress upon 93.16
accuse of 599.9
condemn 602.3
attribute to 888.4
convince 953.18
prove 957.10
bring in
introduce 187.14
yield 627.4
cost 630.13
reel in 906.9
harvest 1069.19
bring into play 387.14
bring into question
inquire 938.20
doubt 955.6
bring off do 328.6
carry out 328.7
bring about 407.5
succeed with 409.11
bring on induce 886.11
incur 897.4
adduce 957.12
bring oneself 324.3
bring out
elicit 192.14
externalize 206.5
manifest 348.5
issue 352.14
print 548.14
bring pressure to bear upon
urge 375.14
press 424.6
exercise influence 894.9
thrust 902.12
bring round
change course 182.30
persuade 375.23
cure 396.15
revive 396.16
convince 953.18
bring to
sail against the wind
182.24
revive 396.16
put a stop to 857.11
convert 858.11
bring to a head
aggravate 119.2
focus 208.10
ripen 407.8
bring to bear upon
apply 387.11
relate 775.6
bring together
add 253.4
reconcile 465.8
collect 472.11
assemble 770.18
bring to light
elicit 192.14
disclose 351.4
uncover 941.4

bring to mind
imply 519.4
resemble 784.7
remember 989.10
bring to one's senses
persuade 375.23
bring to reason 925.3
convince 953.18
bring to pass do 328.6
bring about 407.5
cause 886.10
bring to terms
subdue 432.9
reconcile 465.8
settle 466.7
bring up confront 216.8
propose 439.5
train 568.13
inaugurate 818.11
stop 857.7
vomit 909.26
bring upon inflict 643.5
incur 897.4
bring up the rear
follow 166.3
be behind 217.8
brink 211.4
brinkmanship
foolhardiness 493.3
foreign policy 609.5
brio 17.4
brisk
v refresh 9.2
adj refreshing 9.3
energetic 17.13
zestful 68.7
penetrating 105.31
windy 318.22
active 330.17
brief 828.8
cool 1023.12
cold 1023.14
bristle
n hair 3.2
thorn 285.5
barb 288.3
v anger 152.17
provoke 152.24
rise 200.8
ruffle 288.5
bristle with
come to a point 285.6
teem with 884.5
abound 991.5
bristling bristly 288.9
crowded 770.22
teeming 884.9
Britain 232.4
britches 5.18
brittle frail 16.14
wasted 393.35
transient 828.7
crisp 1050.4
broach
n hole 292.3
v draw off 192.12
open 292.11
perforate 292.15
make public 352.11
propose 439.5
inaugurate 818.11

broad
n woman 77.6
gal 302.7
strumpet 665.14
adj spacious 158.11
voluminous 257.17
wide 269.6
comic 488.6
burlesque 508.14
phonetic 524.30
candid 644.17
vulgar 666.8
extensive 864.13
vague 971.19
open-minded 979.8
broadcast
n publication 352.1
dispersion 771.1
radiobroadcast 1034.18
planting 1069.14
v communicate 343.7
publish 352.10
disperse 771.4
radiobroadcast 1034.25
plant 1069.18
adj published 352.17
dispersed 771.9
broadcasting 343.5
broaden
increase 251.4
grow 251.6
enlarge 259.4
expand 259.5
widen 269.4
generalize 864.9
broadening
n increase 251.1
expansion 259.1
adj liberalizing 979.13
broad humor 489.1
broadly
extensively 158.12
far and wide 261.16
humorously 488.7
candidly 644.23
generally 864.17
vaguely 971.29
broad-minded
nonrestrictive 430.25
wise 920.17
wide-minded 979.8
broadsheet 352.8
broad-shouldered
able-bodied 15.16
virile 76.13
broadside
n side 218.1
announcement 352.2
advertising matter
352.8
volley 459.9
information 551.1
adv laterally 218.8
breadthwise 269.9
Broadway 704.1
brochure advertising matter
352.8
booklet 554.11
brogue 524.8
broil
n dish 10.7

cooking 11.2
quarrel 456.5
free-for-all 457.5
turbulence 671.2
commotion 810.4
v cook 11.5
quarrel 456.11
contend 457.13
be hot 1019.22
broke bereft 473.8
without money 619.10
insolvent 625.11
broken
domesticated 228.34
rough 288.6
impaired 393.27
in disrepair 393.37
ruined 395.28
conquered 412.17
subdued 432.15
meek 433.15
insolvent 625.11
busted 802.24
incoherent 804.4
discontinuous 813.4
irregular 851.3
broken-down
overcome 112.29
dilapidated 393.33
brokenhearted 112.29
broken-in 373.15
broken record 118.5
broker
intermediary 213.4
go-between 576.4
businessman 730.9
stockbroker 737.10
brokerage fee 630.6
trade 731.2
commerce 737.9
stockbroking 737.18
bromide
generalization 864.8
platitude 974.3
bronchial 2.32
bronco 311.10
broncobuster
rider 178.8
stockman 1070.2
Bronx cheer 508.3
bronze
n sculpture 715.2
v brown 40.2
adj reddish-brown 40.4
brass 1058.17
brooch 498.6
brood
n race 559.4
family 559.5
offspring 561.1
v be pregnant 78.12
consider 931.12
brooder
sourpuss 112.13
coop 228.22
poultry 311.29
birthplace 886.8
brood over
grieve 112.17
harbor revenge 507.5
think over 931.13

keep in memory 989.13
brook
n stream 238.1
v endure 134.5
submit 433.6
suffer 443.10
keep an open mind 979.7
broom 79.23
broomstick 270.8
brothel
disapproved place 228.28
sewer 654.7
house of prostitution 665.9
brother buddy 559.3
friend 588.1
associate 616.1
member 617.11
religious 699.16
layman 700.2
likeness 784.3
brotherhood
kindness 143.1
blood relationship 559.1
fellowship 587.2
association 617.3
brotherly love
love 104.1
benevolence 143.4
accord 455.1
brouhaha noise 53.3
outcry 59.4
excitement 105.4
turbulence 671.2
commotion 810.4
agitation 917.1
brow eyelashes 3.12
looks 33.4
summit 198.2
head 198.6
border 211.4
forehead 216.5
browbeat
intimidate 127.20
domineer 612.16
browbeaten 432.16
brown
n brownness 40.1
heroin 87.9
v cook 11.5
embrown 40.2
darken 1027.9
adj brownish 40.3
brownie flatterer 138.4
dwarf 258.5
fairy 678.8
Brownie points 662.3
brown-nose
n flatterer 138.4
assenter 332.6
v fawn 138.7
brownout
n darkness 1027.7
blackout 1032.20
v darken 1027.9
brown study
thoughtfulness 931.3
abstractedness 985.2
dream 986.9
browse feed on 8.28
scan 570.13
shop 733.8

browser 1042.19
bruise
  n trauma 85.38
  discoloration 1004.2
  v pain 96.17
  mistreat 389.5
  injure 393.13
  thrash soundly 604.14
bruiser ruffian 593.4
  violent person 671.10
bruit
  n report 552.6
  v publish 352.10
bruit about 352.10
brumal seasonal 313.9
  cold 1023.14
brunch 8.6
brunet
  n hair color 35.9
  adj black-haired 38.13
  brown 40.3
  brown-haired 40.5
brunt 902.3
brush
  n plant beard 3.9
  touch 73.1
  tail 217.6
  contact 223.5
  hinterland 233.2
  scrub 310.16
  fight 457.4
  art equipment 712.18
  wasteland 891.2
  tap 902.7
  firewood 1021.3
  v touch lightly 73.7
  sweep 79.23
  speed 174.9
  contact 223.10
  portray 712.19
  tap 902.18
  dry 1066.6
  tend 1070.7
brush aside
  dismiss 984.4
  reject 372.2
brush off
  n rejection 372.1
  repulse 908.2
  v sweep 79.23
  repulse 908.3
  dismiss 984.4
brush up groom 79.20
  perfect 392.11
  study up 570.14
  refresh the memory 989.19
brusque taciturn 344.9
  gruff 505.7
  concise 537.6
  candid 644.17
brutal cruel 144.26
  deadly 308.23
  animal 311.40
  unrefined 497.12
  carnal 663.6
  savage 671.21
  terrible 1000.9
  difficult 1013.17
brutality
  cruelty 144.11
  unkindness 144.12

  unrefinement 497.3
  carnality 663.2
  violence 671.1
  terribleness 1000.2
brutalize callous 94.6
  bear malice 144.15
  rage 671.11
brute
  n beast 144.14
  animal 311.2
  barbarian 497.7
  savage 593.5
  violent person 671.9
  adj cruel 144.26
  animal 311.40
  carnal 663.6
brute force
  power 18.1
  force 424.2
bub boy 302.5
  brother 559.3
bubble
  n airy hope 124.5
  structure 266.2
  sphere 282.2
  bulge 283.3
  lightness 298.2
  globule 320
  bleb 320.1
  race 756.3
  spirit 764.3
  ephemeron 828.5
  illusion 976.1
  figment of the imagination 986.5
  fragility 1050.2
  v ripple 52.11
  foam up 320.4
bubble over
  be enthusiastic 101.7
  carbonate 320.4
bubbly light 298.10
  burbly 320.6
  active 330.17
buccaneer
  n mariner 183.1
  hijacker 483.7
  v pirate 482.18
buck
  n male animal 76.8
  boy 302.5
  hoofed animal 311.5
  goat 311.8
  hare 311.24
  leap 366.1
  money 728.7
  trestle 901.16
  v leap 366.5
  contend against 451.4
  thrust 902.12
buckaroo
  rider 178.8
  stockman 1070.2
bucket
  n ship 180.1
  basketball game 747.3
  v ladle 176.17
  trade 737.23
buck for 375.14
buckle
  n distortion 265.1

  v distort 265.5
  exert oneself 725.9
  hook 800.8
buckled 265.10
buckle down to
  undertake 404.3
  set to work 725.15
buck-passing 415.5
bucks 728.2
buckskin 311.11
bucktooth 2.8
buck up
  refresh 9.2
  cheer up 109.9
  take courage 492.14
  encourage 492.16
bucolic rustic 233.6
  natural 416.6
  poetic 720.15
bud
  n boy 302.5
  burgeon 310.23
  brother 559.3
  friend 588.4
  vital force 886.7
  v graft 191.6
  vegetate 310.34
Buddha Deity 677.4
  religious founder 684.4
  Solomon 921.2
Buddhism 675.14
budding
  n bodily 14.1
  growth 259.3
  vegetation 310.32
  adj grown 14.3
  expanding 259.12
  immature 301.10
  beginning 818.15
buddy boy 302.5
  brother 559.3
  friend 588.4
  henchman 610.8
  partner 616.2
  co-worker 616.5
buddy-buddy 587.20
budge 172.5
budget
  n amount 244.2
  store 386.1
  portion 477.5
  expenses 626.3
  accounts 628.1
  funds 728.14
  bundle 770.8
  schedule 965.3
  v ration 477.10
  spend 626.5
  schedule 965.6
  adj accounting 628.12
  cheap 633.7
buenos días! 585.15
buff
  n enthusiast 101.5
  follower 166.2
  attender 221.5
  commender 509.8
  supporter 616.9
  specialist 866.3
  fanatic 926.18
  v polish 287.7

  burnish 1044.8
  adj yellow 43.4
the buff nudity 6.3
  skin 295.3
buffalo
  n cattle 311.6
  v stump 971.14
buffer
  n partition 213.5
  counteractant 900.3
  safeguard 1008.3
  barrier 1012.5
  v neutralize 900.7
buffer state 223.6
buffer zone 465.5
buffet feast 8.9
  restaurant 8.17
  table 901.15
buffet
  n disappointment 132.1
  knock 604.3
  slap 902.8
  v mistreat 389.5
  injure 393.13
  contend against 451.4
  slap 604.12
  whip 604.13
  struggle 725.11
  pound 902.16
  knock 902.19
buffoon
  mischief-maker 322.3
  buffo 707.10
  fool 924.1
buffoonery
  clownishness 489.5
  acting 704.8
  foolishness 923.1
bug
  n microphone 50.9
  germ 85.42
  enthusiast 101.5
  insect 311.33
  bugbear 680.9
  jockey 757.2
  mania 926.12
  fanatic 926.18
  fault 1003.2
  v listen 48.10
  annoy 96.13
  bulge 283.11
  importune 440.12
  nag 510.16
  discompose 811.4
  reconnoiter 938.28
  confuse 985.7
bugbear
  frightener 127.9
  false alarm 400.2
  bugaboo 680.9
  bane 1001.1
bug-eyed
  cross-eyed 28.12
  bulged 283.16
bugger
  n sexual pervert 75.16
  man 76.5
  mischief-maker 322.3
  bad person 660.5
  bugbear 680.9
  v disable 19.9

cuddle 562.17
swaddle 770.20
bind 800.9
dismiss 909.18
bundle off start 904.13
dismiss 909.18
bundle up clothe 5.39
bundle 770.20
bung
  n anus 292.5
  stopper 293.4
  v stop 293.7
  injure 393.13
bungalow 228.8
bungle
  n fiasco 410.6
  blunder 414.5
  error 975.5
  v do carelessly 340.9
  miss 410.14
  blunder 414.11
  fail 975.14
bunion sore 85.37
  swelling 283.4
bunk
  n humbug 354.14
  boasting 502.2
  bullshit 520.3
  v inhabit 225.7
  house 225.10
bunker
  n cellar 197.17
  cave 284.5
  storehouse 386.6
  entrenchment 460.5
  stronghold 460.6
  golf 751.1
  shelter 1009.3
  proving ground 1074.7
  v provision 385.9
bunkum
  humbug 354.14
  boasting 502.2
  flattery 511.1
  bullshit 520.3
  political jargon
    609.37
bunny hare 311.24
  beauty 1016.9
bunt
  n game 745.3
  thrust 902.2
  pushing 904.1
  v thrust 902.12
  tap 902.18
  push 904.9
bunting 647.7
buoy
  n float 180.11
  life preserver 397.6
  marker 517.10
  v lighten up 298.8
buoyant
  lighthearted 109.12
  floaty 298.14
  recuperative 396.23
  elastic 1048.7
buoy up cheer 109.7
  buoy 298.8
  support 901.21
  elevate 912.5

burble
  n flow 184.29
  v ripple 52.11
  bubble 320.4
  be stupid 922.12
burden
  n affliction 96.8
  load 196.2
  capacity 257.2
  burthen 297.7
  duty 641.1
  charge 643.3
  guilt 656.1
  part 708.22
  passage 708.24
  poetry 720.9
  repeat 849.5
  topic 937.1
  bane 1001.1
  impediment 1012.6
  v distress 96.16
  oppress 98.16
  load 159.15
  add 253.4
  burthen 297.13
  task 725.16
  inconvenience 996.4
  go hard with 1011.8
  hamper 1012.11
burdened
  weighted 297.18
  fraught 794.12
  supporting 901.23
burden of proof 957.3
burdensome
  oppressive 98.24
  onerous 297.17
  laborious 725.18
  hampering 1012.18
  troublesome 1013.18
bureau 594.4
bureaucracy
  routine 373.5
  the authorities 575.15
  officialism 612.11
bureaucratic
  governmental 612.17
  executive 612.19
burg 230.1
burgeon
  n branch 310.20
  bud 310.23
  v grow 14.2
  expand 259.7
  vegetate 310.34
burgher
  townsman 227.6
  respectable citizen 659.3
  conformist 867.2
burglar 483.3
burglary 482.5
burial interment 309.1
  funeral 309.5
  tomb 309.16
  concealment 346.1
  submergence 367.2
  overrunning 910.1
buried
  underground 275.12
  underwater 275.13
  concealed 346.11

overrun 910.10
engrossed 983.17
burl 283.3
burlesque
  n imitation 336.1
  reproduction 336.3
  bad likeness 350.2
  exaggeration 355.1
  wit 489.1
  lampoon 508.6
  disparagement 512.5
  show business 704.1
  similarity 784.1
  v misrepresent 350.3
  exaggerate 355.3
  ridicule 508.11
  lampoon 512.12
  adj comical 488.6
  farcical 508.14
burly
  able-bodied 15.16
  corpulent 257.18
burn
  n smart 26.3
  trauma 85.38
  stream 238.1
  deception 356.9
  theft 482.4
  basketball game 747.3
  scald 1020.6
  rocket launching 1074.9
  spacecraft 1075.2
  v pain 26.7
  brown 40.2
  be angry 152.15
  cremate 309.20
  deceive 356.19
  injure 393.13
  rob 482.16
  execute 604.17
  rage 671.11
  play 747.4
  throw 904.10
  scent 941.6
  be hot 1019.22
  ignite 1020.22
  catch fire 1020.23
  torrefy 1020.24
  shine 1025.23
  dry 1066.6
burner destroyer 395.8
  heater 1020.10
  incinerator 1020.13
  blowtorch 1020.14
burn in effigy 661.9
burning
  n smart 26.3
  cremation 309.2
  discard 390.3
  capital punishment 604.7
  throwing 904.2
  heat 1019.1
  combustion 1020.5
  adj sore 26.11
  colorful 35.19
  zestful 68.7
  in heat 75.28
  feverish 85.58
  fervent 93.18
  zealous 101.9
  excited 105.22

resentful 152.26
seething 152.29
near 223.14
vehement 544.13
hot 1019.25
ignited 1019.27
heating 1020.26
luminous 1025.30
flashing 1025.34
burnish
  n polish 287.2
  smoother 287.4
  v polish 287.7
  buff 1044.8
burn one's bridges
  leave home 188.17
  be determined 359.8
burnout fatigue 21.1
  apathy 94.4
  extinguishing 1022.2
  rocket launching 1074.9
burn out fatigue 21.4
  get tired 21.5
  go out 1022.8
burnt
  red-complexioned 41.9
  burned 1020.30
  dried 1066.9
burn the candle at both ends
  squander 486.3
  dissipate 669.6
  overdo 993.10
burn the midnight oil
  study 570.12
  work hard 725.13
  be late 846.7
burn up annoy 96.13
  consume 388.3
  incendiarize 1020.25
burp
  n belch 909.9
  v expel 909.28
burr
  n rasp 58.3
  thorn 285.5
  seed vessel 310.30
  accent 524.8
  engraving 713.2
  adhesive 803.4
  v hum 52.13
  sound harshly 58.9
burro 311.16
burrow
  n lair 228.26
  cave 284.5
  v settle 159.17
  excavate 284.15
  hide 346.8
  search 938.31
bursar payer 624.9
  treasurer 729.12
burst
  n report 56.1
  detonation 56.3
  outburst 105.9
  resentment 152.9
  run 174.3
  bustle 330.4
  volley 459.9
  violence 671.6
  explosion 671.7

separate 802.4
flare 1019.14
v blast 56.8
break 393.23
explode 671.14
break 802.12
adj impaired 393.27
broken 802.24
burst forth
break forth 33.9
emerge 190.11
vegetate 310.34
erupt 671.13
originate 818.13
burst in enter 189.7
intrude 214.5
breach 292.14
bursting
n disruption 802.3
adj banging 56.11
excited 105.20
explosive 671.24
full 794.11
teeming 884.9
productive 890.9
brimming 993.20
burst one's bubble
sadden 112.18
shatter one's hopes 125.11
burst out erupt 671.13
exclaim 59.7
laugh 116.8
bury inter 309.19
secrete 346.7
submerge 367.7
bury oneself in 570.12
bury the hatchet
forget 148.5
make peace 465.9
bus
n car 179.10
public vehicle 179.13
v haul 176.13
ride 177.33
busboy 577.7
bush
marijuana 87.11
lining 196.3
hinterland 233.2
shrubbery 310.9
woodland 310.13
brush 310.16
wasteland 891.2
bushed 21.8
bush-league 1005.7
bushwhack
surprise 131.7
kill 308.14
attack 459.15
bushwhacker
irregular 461.16
precursor 816.1
bushy hairy 3.24
arboreal 310.39
sylvan 310.40
business
n action 328.1
activity 330.1
undertaking 404.1
company 617.9
duty 641.1

acting 704.8
occupation 724.1
vocation 724.6
commerce 731.1
relation 775.1
affair 831.3
specialty 866.1
adj occupational 730.12
commercial 731.22
the business 356.9
businesslike 807.6
businessman
businessperson 730.1
businesswoman 730.1
business manager 704.25
busman's holiday 20.3
buss
n kiss 562.4
v kiss 562.19
bust
n drinking spree 88.6
breast 283.6
figure 349.6
failure 410.2
washout 410.8
arrest 429.6
demotion 447.1
monument 549.12
insolvency 625.3
business cycle 731.10
blow 902.5
hard times 1011.6
v flunk 410.17
arrest 429.16
domesticate 432.11
demote 447.3
depose 447.4
go under 625.7
bankrupt 625.8
explode 671.14
break 802.12
dismiss 909.19
busted
impaired 393.27
without money 619.10
insolvent 625.11
broken 802.24
bust in enter 189.7
breach 292.14
bustle
n excitement 105.4
fuss 330.4
haste 401.1
bluster 503.1
agitation 917.1
v fuss 330.12
hasten 401.4
move quickly 401.5
bustling
fussing 330.20
eventful 831.10
bust out 431.8
busty
corpulent 257.18
pectoral 283.19
busy
v occupy 724.10
task 725.16
adj meddlesome 214.9
full of business 330.21
ornate 498.12

occupied 724.15
busybody
n meddler 214.4
newsmonger 552.9
inquisitive person 981.2
v meddle 214.7
adj meddlesome 214.9
busywork 724.2
but
notwithstanding 338.8
unless 959.16
butch
n mannish female 76.9
adj homosexual 75.30
butcher
n killer 308.11
vendor 730.5
v slaughter 308.17
misdraw 350.4
bungle 414.11
rage 671.11
sever 802.11
butchered
botched 414.21
mutilated 795.5
butler steward 574.4
man 577.4
major-domo 577.10
butt
n cigarette 89.5
buttocks 217.5
remainder 256.1
objective 380.2
laughingstock 508.7
piece 793.3
joint 800.4
extremity 820.2
thrust 902.2
pushing 904.1
v adjoin 223.9
hook 800.8
thrust 902.12
push 904.9
butte plateau 237.3
hill 237.4
butter
n suavity 504.5
softness 1047.4
semiliquid 1062.5
pulp 1063.2
v coat 295.24
flatter 511.6
butterfingers 414.9
butterflies 128.2
buttery
n storehouse 386.6
larder 386.8
adj slippery 287.12
suave 504.18
flattering 511.8
oily 1056.9
semiliquid 1062.11
butt in intrude 214.5
mediate 466.6
talk out of turn 844.4
buttinsky 422.3
buttocks bottom 199.1
rump 217.4
button
n chin 216.6
runt 258.4

bulge 283.3
insignia 647.1
trifle 998.5
cast 1058.5
v close 293.6
hook 800.8
buttoned-down 867.6
buttonhole
n bouquet 310.25
v bore 118.7
importune 440.12
address 524.26
button up
be silent 51.6
close 293.6
complete 407.6
butt out
v not interfere 430.17
phrs none of your business 214.10
buttress
n supporter 901.2
buttressing 901.4
v strengthen 15.13
help 449.12
support 901.21
confirm 957.11
buxom
merry 109.15
corpulent 257.18
comely 1016.19
buy
n bargain 633.3
v assent 332.8
bribe 378.3
take advice 422.7
purchase 733.7
believe 953.10
kid oneself 954.6
buyer 733.5
buyers' market
low price 633.2
cheapening 633.4
commerce 731.1
sale 734.1
buy into
take advice 422.7
invest 729.17
purchase 733.7
believe 953.10
kid oneself 954.6
buyout
n trading 737.19
combination 805.1
v purchase 733.7
combine 805.3
buzz
n sibilation 57.1
rasp 58.3
tingle 74.1
substance abuse 87.1
telephone call 347.13
report 552.6
series 812.2
v hum 52.13
sibilate 57.2
sound harshly 58.9
flathat 184.42
telephone 347.19
publish 352.10
speak 524.25

tip off 551.11
buzzer 400.1
buzzing
  n hum 52.7
  flathatting 184.17
  adj humming 52.20
buzz off
  v depart 188.7
  interj go away! 909.31
by
  adj past 837.7
  adv in reserve 386.17
  prep at 159.27
  through 161.27
  beside 218.11
  by means of 384.13
  conformable to 867.9
by all means
  adv certainly 970.23
  interj yes 332.18
by all odds
  by far 247.17
  probably 968.8
by and by
  in the future 839.9
  soon 845.16
by and large
  approximately 244.6
  on the whole 792.14
  generally 864.17
by any means
  anyhow 384.10
  by any possibility 966.10
by bits and pieces
  incompletely 795.6
  disjointedly 802.28
by chance
  haphazardly 810.18
  perchance 972.19
by degrees
  degreewise 245.6
  piece by piece 793.9
by design 380.10
by dint of
  adv usefully 387.26
  prep by virtue of 18.18
  by means of 384.13
by ear 365.15
bye-bye 22.2
by far 247.17
by fits and starts
  nonuniformly 782.4
  disjointedly 802.28
  haphazardly 810.18
  discontinuously 813.5
  irregularly 851.4
  shakily 917.23
bygone 837.7
by hand 176.19
by heart 989.28
by hook or by crook 384.11
by inches
  by degrees 245.6
  piece by piece 793.9
bylaw 673.3
by law 673.13
by leaps and bounds
  in progress 162.7
  swiftly 174.17
by-line
  avocation 724.7

acknowledgment 888.2
by means of
  through the agency of
    384.13
  helped by 449.25
by nature 767.10
by no means
  adv noway 248.11
  interj by no manner of means
    335.9
  God forbid! 510.27
  phrs I refuse 442.7
by oneself
  adj solitary 584.11
  adv independently 430.33
  singly 872.13
bypass
  n byway 383.4
  detour 914.3
  v pass 910.8
  go roundabout 914.4
by-product
  aftermath 817.3
  effect 887.1
  extract 893.3
by proxy
  indirectly 576.18
  instead 862.11
by rights 637.4
bystander
  neighbor 223.6
  spectator 918.1
  witness 957.6
by storm 18.17
byte 1042.14
by the board
  adj lost 473.7
  adv overboard 182.74
by the same token
  additionally 253.11
  accordingly 766.11
  similarly 784.18
by the way
  discursive 538.13
  incidental 843.11
  timely 843.13
by virtue of
  by dint of 18.18
  by means of 384.13
  by authority of 417.20
  because of 888.9
by virtue of office 417.18
byway
  bypath 383.4
  digression 538.4
by way of
  through 161.27
  by means of 384.13
byword
  laughingstock 508.7
  catchword 526.9
  name 527.3
  disgrace 661.5
  maxim 974.1
Byzantine
  n Aldine 554.15
  adj convolutional 281.6
  scheming 381.13
  complex 799.4
  shrewd 920.15
c'est la vie 964.11

cab 179.13
cabal
  n intrigue 381.5
  fellowship 617.3
  clique 617.6
  company 770.3
  combination 805.1
  v plot 381.9
  league 805.4
cabalistic secret 345.11
  occult 689.23
  leagued 805.6
caballero beau 104.13
  rider 178.8
  knight 608.5
cabaret bar 88.20
  theater 704.14
  entertainment 743.13
cabbagehead 924.4
cabdriver driver 178.9
  chauffeur 178.10
cabin
  n stateroom 197.9
  cottage 228.8
  v confine 212.6
cabin boy hand 183.6
  attendant 577.5
cabinet container 195.1
  sanctum 197.8
  furniture 229.1
  council 423.1
  directorate 574.11
  ministry 613.3
  office 739.7
  radio 1034.3
cable
  n cord 271.2
  telegram 347.14
  line 347.17
  electrical device 1032.21
  v telegraph 347.20
caboose kitchen 11.4
  sequel 817.1
cache
  n hiding place 346.4
  reserve 386.3
  v secrete 346.7
  store 386.10
cache memory 1042.7
cachet
  label 517.13
  characteristic 865.4
cachinnation noise 53.3
  cry 59.1
cackle
  n rasp 58.3
  laughter 116.4
  chatter 540.3
  v sound harshly 58.9
  bird sound 60.5
  laugh 116.8
  speak 524.25
cacophony
  raucousness 58.2
  discord 61.1
  inelegance 534.1
  turbulence 671.2
  pandemonium 810.5
  ugliness 1015.1
cactus mescaline 87.13
  peyote 87.17

thorn 285.5
cad vulgarian 497.6
  bounder 660.7
cadastral 871.9
cadaver 307.16
cadaverous
  tired-looking 21.9
  colorless 36.7
  haggard 270.20
  deathly 307.29
caddie carrier 176.7
  attendant 577.5
cadence sinkage 194.2
  accent 524.10
  passage 708.24
  ornament 709.18
  harmony 709.23
  meter 720.7
cadenza
  impromptu 708.27
  ornament 709.18
cadet
  n navy man 183.4
  undergraduate 572.6
  adj subsequent 835.4
cadger
  nonworker 331.11
  beggar 440.8
  vendor 730.5
cadre frame 266.4
  military unit 461.22
  directorate 574.11
  clique 617.6
caduceus 417.9
caesar ruler 575.9
  tyrant 575.14
caesura
  interval 224.1
  meter 720.7
  interruption 813.2
  pause 857.3
  grammar 857.4
café
  restaurant 8.17
  bar 88.20
cafeteria
  restaurant 8.17
  dining room 197.11
caftan 5.21
cage
  n place of confinement
    429.7
  hockey 749.1
  gambling wheel 759.16
  v enclose 212.5
  confine 429.12
  drive 1070.8
cagey evasive 368.15
  cunning 415.12
  wary 494.9
cahoots
  affiliation 450.2
  concurrence 899.1
Cain 308.11
cairn marker 517.10
  monument 549.12
cajole deceive 356.14
  urge 375.14
  lure 377.5
  importune 440.12
  flatter 511.5

cake
n food 10.42
solid 1045.6
v thicken 1045.10
solidify 1046.8
caked 1045.14
calamitous
destructive 395.26
disastrous 1011.15
calamity fatality 308.8
bane 1001.1
misfortune 1011.2
calcify 1046.7
calcimine
n whitening agent 37.4
v color 35.14
whitewash 37.6
calculable
measurable 300.14
predictable 962.13
reliable 970.17
computable 1017.25
calculate
measure 300.10
intend 380.6
premeditate 380.7
plan 381.8
compute 1017.18
calculated
intentional 380.8
planned 381.12
reasoned 935.21
calculating
deceitful 356.22
scheming 381.13
sly 645.18
shrewd 920.15
numerative 1017.24
calculation
measurement 300.1
intentionality 380.3
plan 381.1
caution 494.1
computation 1017.10
calculator adding 253.3
strategist 415.7
accountant 628.7
computer 1017.15
calculus 1017.10
caldron 858.10
calefacient 1020.26
calendar
n record book 549.11
reference book 554.9
bill 613.9
calends 832.8
roll 871.6
schedule 965.3
v record 549.15
chronologize 832.14
list 871.8
schedule 965.6
calender 287.6
calf member 2.7
leg 177.14
fledgling 302.10
cattle 311.6
ice 1023.5
caliber ability 18.2
degree 245.1
size 257.1

diameter 269.3
talent 413.4
intelligence 920.1
calibrate
graduate 245.4
measure 300.10
calico 47.12
caliper 300.10
caliph 575.10
calisthenics
exercise 84.2
physical education 568.9
call
n audition 48.2
yell 59.1
cry 59.1
animal noise 60.1
telephone message
347.13
command 420.5
demand 421.1
entreaty 440.2
invitation 440.4
summons 517.16
visit 582.7
warrant 600.6
enlistment 615.7
the ministry 698.1
option 737.21
bridge 758.3
v cry 59.6
wail 60.2
bird sound 60.5
telephone 347.19
summon 420.11
invite 440.13
name 527.11
bill 628.11
gamble 759.23
estimate 946.9
predict 962.9
call a halt to 857.11
call a spade a spade
be frank 644.12
keep both feet on the ground
987.4
call attention to
remark 524.24
direct attention to 983.10
call down 510.18
caller
telephoner 347.11
errand boy 353.4
guest 585.6
call for
n requirement 963.2
v fetch 176.16
summon 420.11
demand 421.5
oblige 424.5
request 440.9
entail 772.4
require 963.9
call forth excite 105.12
elicit 192.14
prompt 375.13
summon 420.11
induce 886.11
call girl 665.16
calligrapher
writer 547.13

limner 716.2
calligraphy
handwriting 547.3
fine writing 547.5
visual arts 712.1
calling motive 375.1
summons 420.5
invitation 440.4
naming 527.2
holy orders 698.10
vocation 724.6
calling card 517.11
call into question
contradict 451.6
doubt 955.6
call it a day
take a rest 20.8
complete 407.6
stop work 857.8
call names offend 156.5
vilify 512.10
curse 513.7
call off end 820.5
number 1017.17
call on urge 375.14
command 420.8
petition 440.10
entreat 440.11
visit 582.19
call one's bluff 454.6
callous
v harden 94.6
numb 1046.7
adj insensible 25.6
calloused 94.12
impenitent 114.5
heartless 144.25
hardened 654.17
unfeeling 1046.13
call out vociferate 59.8
elicit 192.14
summon 420.11
demand 421.5
defy 454.3
callow
immature 301.10
unprepared 406.11
inexperienced 414.17
incomplete 795.4
new 841.7
ignorant 930.12
call sign 1034.19
call someone's bluff
confront 216.8
risk 972.12
call the shots
command 420.8
direct 573.8
control 612.13
exercise influence 894.8
call time 826.3
call to account
censure 510.13
reprove 510.17
punish 604.10
obligate 641.12
call to arms 457.13
call up excite 105.12
elicit 192.14
telephone 347.19
prompt 375.13

summon 420.11
call to arms 458.19
enlist 615.17
conjure 690.11
resemble 784.7
visualize 986.15
remember 989.10
call-up
call to arms 458.8
enlistment 615.7
assemblage 770.1
call upon
petition 440.10
entreat 440.11
visit 582.19
urge 375.14
avail oneself of 387.14
command 420.8
callus 85.39
calm
n composure 106.2
unastonishment 123.1
lull 173.5
moderation 670.1
uniformity 781.1
v be cool 106.6
quiet 173.8
pacify 465.7
moderate 670.7
adj placid 106.12
unastonished 123.3
unnervous 129.2
quiescent 173.12
pacific 464.9
equable 670.13
thoughtless 933.4
calmative
n sedative 86.12
moderator 670.3
adj sedative 86.45
palliative 670.16
calming
n pacification 465.1
modulation 670.2
adj tranquilizing 670.15
calorie energy unit 17.7
thermal unit 1019.19
calorific 1020.26
calumnious
insulting 156.8
disparaging 512.13
cursing 513.8
calumny slander 512.3
vilification 513.2
Calvinist
n determinist 964.5
adj Protestant 675.28
camaraderie
affiliation 450.2
fellowship 582.2
companionship 587.2
camber arch 279.4
convexity 283.1
camel
beast of burden 176.8
hoofed animal 311.5
camelback
n deformity 265.3
adj humpbacked 265.13
cameo
description 349.2

script 706.3
relief 715.3
camera lens 29.2
Kodak 714.11
cameraman
motion-picture photography 706.5
photographer 716.5
television technician 1035.13
camisole 428.4
camouflage
n cover 356.11
dissimilarity 787.1
v conceal 346.6
misrepresent 350.3
falsify 354.16
disguise 787.3
camouflaged
invisible 32.5
disguised 346.13
camp
n camping 225.4
encampment 228.29
settlement 463.3
vulgarity 497.1
political party 609.24
association 617.4
v settle 159.17
encamp 225.11
adj comic 704.35
campaign
n journey 177.5
war 458.4
politics 609.13
cause 886.9
v journey 177.21
undertake operations 458.17
electioneer 609.40
go into politics 610.13
campaigner
veteran 461.19
electioneer 610.10
campaign for 509.13
campanile 272.6
camper traveler 178.1
vehicle 179.19
trailer 228.17
campfire 1019.13
camp follower
follower 166.2
associate 616.8
campground 463.3
campo plain 236.1
grassland 310.8
campus arena 463.1
schoolhouse 567.10
can
n latrine 12.10
toilet 12.11
battleship 180.7
buttocks 217.5
jail 429.9
marker 517.10
v be able 18.11
package 212.9
put up 397.11
may 443.13
sink 747.4
play 751.4
dismiss 909.20

canal
n duct 2.23
channel 239.1
watercourse 239.2
inlet 242.1
narrow place 270.3
trench 290.2
v furrow 290.3
canape 62.4
canard
fabrication 354.10
report 552.6
canary
n singer 710.13
songbird 710.23
adj yellow 43.4
cancel
n obliteration 395.7
repeal 445.1
notation 709.12
v excise 255.10
delete 255.12
abolish 395.13
obliterate 395.16
repeal 445.2
declare a moratorium 625.9
equalize 790.6
end 820.5
cease 857.6
neutralize 900.7
canceled forgiven 148.7
ended 820.8
cancellate 170.11
cancer growth 85.39
blight 1001.2
cancerous 85.61
candescent
burning 1019.27
luminous 1025.30
candid
v talkative 540.9
adj communicative 343.10
artless 416.5
free-acting 430.23
natural 499.7
plain-speaking 535.3
frank 644.17
genuine 973.15
candidacy 609.10
candidate
desirer 100.12
petitioner 440.7
aspirant 610.9
assignee 615.9
candle
light source 1026.1
taper 1026.2
candlelit 1025.39
can do
v be able 18.11
adj energetic 17.13
active 330.17
candor
communicativeness 343.3
artlessness 416.1
plain speech 535.1
talkativeness 540.1
candidness 644.4
fairness 649.3
candy
n sweets 10.40

amyl nitrate 87.5
v sweeten 66.3
solidify 1046.8
candy store 66.1
candy-stripe
n stripe 47.5
adj striped 47.15
cane
n blind 30.6
staff 273.2
grass 310.5
stem 310.21
rod 605.2
supporter 901.2
bamboo 1054.4
v whip 604.13
canicular
seasonal 313.9
hot 1019.25
canine
n teeth 2.8
creature 311.3
dog 311.17
adj doggish 311.42
canker
n sore 85.37
blight 1001.2
v corrupt 393.12
corrode 393.21
decay 393.22
cankered
diseased 85.60
irascible 110.19
decayed 393.40
cannibal
n eater 8.16
killer 308.11
creature 311.3
savage 593.5
adj eating 8.31
cannibalize 365.8
cannon
n artillery 462.11
game 745.3
impact 902.3
recoil 903.2
shot 904.4
v pull the trigger 459.22
collide 902.13
recoil 903.6
cannonade
n boom 56.4
volley 459.9
v pull the trigger 459.22
cannonball
swiftness 174.6
plunge 367.1
shot 462.19
cannot 19.8
canny cunning 415.12
cautious 494.8
economical 635.6
shrewd 920.15
canoe
n roulette 759.12
v navigate 182.13
can of worms
hodgepodge 797.6
complex 799.2
trouble 1013.3
canon music 280.9

measure 300.2
precept 419.2
literature 547.12
compilation 554.7
law 673.3
Bible 683.2
round 708.19
scripture 718.1
rule 869.4
lore 928.9
a belief 953.2
canonical
preceptive 419.4
theological 676.4
scriptural 683.11
orthodox 687.7
ecclesiastic 698.13
doctrinal 953.27
canonize
glorify 662.13
sanctify 685.5
ordain 698.12
exalt 912.6
canopy
n the heavens 1072.2
v cover 295.19
cant
n inclination 204.2
angle 278.2
hypocrisy 354.6
Greek 522.7
jargon 523.9
sanctimony 693.1
v change course 182.30
careen 182.43
incline 204.10
be hypocritical 354.23
speak 523.18
be sanctimonious 693.4
cantankerous
irascible 110.20
perverse 361.11
hindering 1012.17
cantata
sacred music 708.17
part music 708.18
canteen 8.17
canter
n run 174.3
hypocrite 357.8
pietist 693.3
v speed 174.8
go on horseback 177.34
canticle paean 696.3
song 708.14
sacred music 708.17
cantilever 202.3
cantina 8.17
canto air 708.4
part 708.22
poetry 720.9
fight 754.3
canton region 231.5
heraldry 647.2
cantor clergy 699.11
singer 710.13
choirmaster 710.18
canvas sail 180.14
tent 295.8
arena 463.1
painting 712.14

art equipment 712.18
boxing 754.1
canvass
  n vote 371.6
  solicitation 440.5
  campaign 609.13
  assemblage 770.1
  survey 938.14
  v vote 371.18
  solicit 440.14
  discuss 541.12
  electioneer 609.40
  examine 938.24
  survey 938.29
canvasser
  traveling salesman 730.4
  solicitor 730.6
canyon 237.7
cap
  n headdress 5.25
  LSD 87.10
  summit 198.2
  top part 198.4
  architectural topping 198.5
  cover 295.5
  fuse 462.15
  type 548.6
  v cloak 5.40
  top 198.9
  excel 249.6
  cover 295.21
  complete 407.6
  give in kind 506.6
capability ability 18.2
  preparedness 405.4
  skill 413.1
  talent 413.4
capable able 18.14
  fitted 405.17
  competent 413.24
  liable to 897.6
capacious
  spacious 158.11
  voluminous 257.17
capacitate 405.8
capacities 919.2
capacity
  n ability 18.2
  spaciousness 158.5
  volume 257.2
  means 384.2
  skill 413.1
  talent 413.4
  function 724.3
  mode 765.4
  full measure 794.3
  intelligence 920.1
  capacitance 1032.16
  adj full 794.11
caparison
  n wardrobe 5.2
  horsecloth 295.11
  harness 385.5
  v outfit 5.41
cape 283.9
caper
  n dido 366.2
  prank 489.10
  frolic 743.5
  v exude cheerfulness 109.6
  rejoice 116.5

leap 366.6
play 743.23
capillary
  n duct 2.23
  adj circulatory 2.33
  hairlike 3.23
  threadlike 271.7
capital
  n architectural topping 198.5
  metropolis 208.7
  city 230.4
  means 384.2
  supply 386.2
  type 548.6
  fund 728.15
  adj top 198.10
  chief 249.14
  literal 546.8
  monetary 728.30
  paramount 997.24
  good 999.12
capitalism
  noninterference 430.9
  political system 611.8
capitalist
  n coupon-clipper 611.15
  rich man 618.7
  financier 729.9
  adj bourgeois 611.23
capitalize letter 546.6
  keep accounts 628.8
  finance 729.16
capitalize on
  take advantage of 387.15
  profit 472.12
  improve the occasion 843.8
capital punishment
  condemnation 602.1
  execution 604.7
capital sin 655.2
capitol 613.4
capitulate 433.8
capitulation
  surrender 433.2
  treaty 437.2
  summation 1017.11
a cappella 708.53
capping
  topping 198.11
  superior 249.12
  ending 820.10
caprice whim 364.1
  impulse 364.1
  capriciousness 364.2
  thoughtlessness 365.3
capricious
  irresolute 362.9
  whimsical 364.5
  unthinking 365.10
  unessential 768.4
  nonuniform 782.3
  unordered 810.12
  transient 828.7
  irregular 851.3
  inconstant 854.7
  uncertain 971.16
capriole
  n leap 366.1
  caper 366.2
  v leap 366.5
  caper 366.6

capsize
  n overturn 205.2
  v upset 182.44
  tumble 194.8
  overturn 205.6
capstone 407.3
capsule
  n pill 86.7
  hull 295.16
  seed vessel 310.30
  abridgment 557.1
  spacecraft 1075.2
  v package 212.9
  abridge 557.5
  adj shortened 268.9
captain
  n ship's officer 183.7
  aviator 185.1
  governor 575.6
  commissioned officer 575.18
  naval officer 575.20
  policeman 1008.15
  v direct 573.8
  govern 612.12
caption
  n title 937.2
  v focus on 937.3
captious
  critical 510.23
  quibbling 936.14
captivate delight 95.10
  enamor 104.23
  persuade 375.23
  fascinate 377.7
  charm 691.8
captivated
  enamored 104.28
  wondering 122.9
  enchanted 691.12
captivating
  delightful 97.7
  alluring 377.8
captive
  n prisoner 429.11
  subject 432.7
  adj subjugated 432.14
capture
  n arrest 429.6
  seizure 480.2
  take 480.10
  v triumph 411.3
  arrest 429.15
  acquire 472.8
  apprehend 480.18
car
  vehicle 179.9
  railway car 179.15
  automobile racing 756.1
carabineer
  infantryman 461.9
  shooter 904.8
caracole
  n caper 366.2
  v exude cheerfulness 109.6
  rejoice 116.5
  go on horseback 177.34
  caper 366.6
  play 743.23
carapace
  shell 295.15

armor 460.3
caravan wagon 179.2
  trailer 179.19
  train 228.17
  procession 812.3
carbohydrate 7.5
carbon
  radiotherapy 91.8
  transcript 785.4
  combustion product 1020.16
  isotope 1038.5
carbonated bubbly 320.6
  vaporous 1067.9
carbon copy
  the same 778.3
  transcript 785.4
carboniferous 1021.9
carbonize 1020.24
carbonous 1058.15
carbuncle sore 85.37
  swelling 283.4
carcass body 2.1
  corpse 307.16
  wreck 393.8
  dead thing 1052.3
carcinogen 85.42
carcinogenic 85.61
carcinoma 85.39
card
  n identification 517.11
  recording media 549.10
  postcard 553.3
  playing card 758.2
  schedule 965.3
  v comb 79.21
cardboard 1054.5
card-carrying
  real 761.15
  genuine 973.15
card game game 743.9
  cardplaying 758.1
cardholder
  member 617.11
  unionist 727.4
cardinal red 41.6
  chief 249.14
  paramount 997.24
  numeric 1017.23
cardiovascular disease 85.19
cardsharp cheat 357.3
  gambler 759.21
care
  n medicine 90.1
  affliction 96.8
  sorrow 112.10
  anxiety 126.1
  carefulness 339.1
  usage 387.2
  custody 429.5
  observance 434.1
  support 449.3
  patronage 449.4
  caution 494.1
  supervision 573.2
  commission 615.1
  thrift 635.1
  attention 983.1
  protectorship 1008.2
  adversity 1011.1
  v respond 93.11
  mind 339.6

adj helping 449.20

careen
  n swing 916.6
  flounder 917.8
  v list 182.43
  tumble 194.8
  incline 204.10
  overturn 205.6
  oscillate 916.10
  flounder 917.15

career
  n progression 162.1
  course 172.2
  vocation 724.6
  v speed 174.8
  flounder 917.15
  adj skilled 413.26

careerism
  ambition 100.10
  selfishness 651.1
  vocation 724.6

care for treat 91.24
  love 104.19
  minister to 387.12
  foster 449.16
  serve 577.13
  protect 1008.19

carefree content 107.7
  lighthearted 109.12

careful
  adj heedful 339.10
  cautious 494.8
  economical 635.6
  conscientious 644.15
  judicious 920.19
  attentive 983.15
  interj be careful! 494.14

caregiver nurse 90.10
  guardian 1008.6

care-giving
  n support 449.3
  adj helping 449.20

careless
  unconcerned 102.7
  heedless 340.11
  unthinking 365.10
  bungling 414.20
  lax 426.4
  reckless 493.8
  ungrammatic 531.4
  slovenly 810.15
  incurious 982.3
  inattentive 984.6

caress
  n touch 73.1
  contact 223.5
  endearment 562.5
  v stroke 73.8
  contact 223.10
  pet 562.16
  rub 1044.6

caretaker keeper 429.1
  guardian 1008.6

careworn
  sorrowful 112.26
  heavy-laden 126.9

carfare 630.6

cargo freight 176.6
  load 196.2
  burden 297.7
  charge 643.3

impediment 1012.6

caricature
  n bad likeness 350.2
  exaggeration 355.1
  wit 489.1
  burlesque 508.6
  cartoon 712.16
  v misrepresent 350.3
  exaggerate 355.3
  burlesque 508.11

caries 85.40

carillon
  n bell 54.4
  chimes 711.18
  v blow a horn 708.42

caring
  n sympathy 93.5
  love 104.1
  carefulness 339.1
  support 449.3
  adj careful 339.10
  helping 449.20

carjacking theft 482.3
  piracy 482.7

carmine
  v make red 41.4
  adj red 41.6

carnage
  massacre 308.4
  destruction 395.1

carnal sexual 75.25
  unvirtuous 654.12
  sensual 663.6
  lascivious 665.29
  secularist 695.16

carnality sexuality 75.2
  amorousness 104.3
  vice 654.1
  sensuality 663.2
  lasciviousness 665.5
  secularism 695.2

carnival treat 95.3
  show business 704.1
  festival 743.4
  park 743.14

carnivore eater 8.16
  creature 311.3

carnivorous 8.31

carol
  n song 708.14
  v bird sound 60.5
  rejoice 116.5
  sing 708.38

carom
  n impact 902.3
  recoil 903.2
  v collide 902.13
  recoil 903.6

carouse
  n spree 88.5
  dissipation 669.2
  revel 743.6
  v go on a spree 88.28
  dissipate 669.6
  make merry 743.24
  riot 810.10

carousel
  merry-go-round 743.15
  rotator 915.4

carp 510.15

carpentry 712.3

carpet
  n ground covering 199.3
  rug 295.9
  v floor 295.22

carpetbagger 357.3

carping
  n criticism 510.4
  adj critical 510.23

carriage looks 33.4
  transportation 176.3
  vehicle 179.1
  four-wheeler 179.4
  behavior 321.1
  gesture 517.14
  freightage 630.7
  support 901.1

carriage trade
  society 578.6
  market 733.3

carried away
  overjoyed 95.17
  excited 105.20
  frenzied 105.25

carrier infection 85.4
  vector 85.44
  conveyer 176.7
  vehicle 179.1
  aircraft ship 180.8
  messenger 353.1
  mail deliverer 353.6
  supporter 901.2
  radio wave 1034.11

carrion
  n filth 80.7
  offal 80.9
  corpse 307.16
  rot 393.7
  adj dead 307.30

carry
  n range 158.2
  transportation 176.3
  round 751.3
  v be pregnant 78.12
  use 87.22
  extend 158.9
  transport 176.12
  adopt 371.15
  induce 375.22
  triumph 411.3
  give credit 622.6
  keep accounts 628.8
  deal in 731.16
  support 901.21

carry a torch for 104.20

carry away delight 95.10
  enamor 104.23
  remove 176.11
  kill 308.13
  fascinate 377.7
  triumph 411.3
  abduct 482.20
  come apart 802.9

carry off
  remove 176.11
  kill 308.13
  carry out 328.7
  bring about 407.5
  succeed with 409.11
  triumph 411.3
  seize 480.14
  abduct 482.20

carry on
  be patient 134.4
  be angry 152.15
  misbehave 322.4
  practice 328.8
  keep going 330.15
  persevere 360.2
  direct 573.8
  rage 671.11
  play 743.23
  create disorder 810.11
  endure 827.6
  continue 856.3
  do the usual thing 869.7
  operate 889.5

carry out
  reach out 261.5
  carry through 328.7
  apply 387.11
  bring about 407.5
  perform 434.3
  execute 437.9
  operate 889.5

carry over
  n thing added 254.1
  v transfer 176.10
  keep accounts 628.8

carry the day 411.3

carry through
  be patient 134.4
  carry out 328.7
  not hesitate 359.10
  prosecute to a conclusion
    360.5
  bring about 407.5
  perform 434.3
  execute 437.9
  succeed 817.5
  operate 889.5

carry weight
  weigh 297.10
  have influence 894.10
  matter 997.12

carsick 85.57

cart
  n two-wheeler 179.3
  v haul 176.13

carte blanche
  latitude 430.4
  blank check 443.4
  privilege 642.2

cartel compact 437.1
  treaty 437.2
  company 617.9
  combination 805.1

carter carrier 176.7
  driver 178.9

cartilage
  n the skeleton 2.2
  the muscles 2.3
  toughness 1049.2
  adj skeleton 2.26

cart off 176.11

cartographer
  map 159.5
  measurer 300.9

carton 212.9

cartoon
  n diagram 381.3
  motion pictures 706.1
  drawing 712.13

caricature 712.16
v portray 712.19
cartoonist 716.3
cartridge
  sound reproduction system
    50.11
  record 50.12
  cartouche 462.17
  film 714.10
carve form 262.7
  furrow 290.3
  apportion 477.6
  record 549.15
  engrave 713.9
  sculpture 715.5
  sever 802.11
  process 892.9
carving figure 349.6
  sculpture 715.1
Casanova
  deceiver 357.1
  philanderer 562.12
  libertine 665.10
cascade
  n descent 194.1
  waterfall 238.11
  outburst 671.6
  v descend 194.5
  hang 202.6
  overflow 238.17
case
  n sick person 85.43
  infatuation 104.4
  container 195.1
  frame 266.4
  blanket 295.10
  hull 295.16
  casing 295.17
  grammar 530.9
  type 548.6
  bookbinding 554.14
  lawsuit 598.1
  state 765.1
  particular 766.3
  example 786.2
  oddity 870.4
  argument 935.5
  topic 937.1
  citation 957.5
  v package 212.9
  wrap 295.20
  reconnoiter 938.28
the case fact 761.3
  the truth 973.3
casebook
  reference book 554.9
  text 554.10
case-hardened
  callous 94.12
  obstinate 361.8
  accustomed 373.15
  hardened 654.17
  tempered 1046.15
case history
  medical history 91.10
  record 719.1
casement frame 266.4
  window 292.7
caseworker 143.8
cash
  n payment 624.1

dollars 728.1
  ready money 728.18
  v pay 624.17
  transact 728.29
  adv cash on the barrelhead
    624.25
cashbook
  record book 549.11
  account book 628.4
cashbox 729.13
cashier
  n payer 624.9
  banker 729.11
  treasurer 729.12
  v depose 447.4
  dismiss 909.19
cash in die 307.20
  cash 728.29
cash in on
  take advantage of 387.15
  profit 472.12
  improve the occasion
    843.8
casing frame 266.4
  case 295.17
casino
  resort 228.27
  ballroom 705.4
  entertainment 743.13
  gambling house 759.19
cask
  n container 195.1
  cylinder 282.4
  v package 212.9
casket
  n coffin 309.11
  v confine 212.6
Cassandra
  pessimist 125.7
  warner 399.4
  predictor 962.4
casserole 10.7
cassette 50.12
cassette tape 549.1
cassock 699.5
cast
  n slough 2.5
  glance 27.4
  strabismus 28.5
  looks 33.4
  color 35.1
  dressing 86.33
  hint 248.4
  form 262.1
  team 617.7
  role 704.10
  cast of characters 707.11
  sculpture 715.2
  throw 759.9
  nature 767.4
  company 770.3
  copy 785.6
  mold 786.6
  kind 809.3
  characteristic 865.4
  tendency 896.1
  throw 904.3
  disposition 978.3
  sum 1017.6
  casting 1058.5
  v give birth 1.3

shed 6.10
  place violently 159.13
  change course 182.30
  form 262.7
  plan 381.8
  discard 390.7
  sculpture 715.5
  produce 892.8
  throw 904.10
  eject 909.13
  calculate 1017.18
  burn 1020.24
  adj born 1.4
  formative 262.9
  made 892.18
cast about
  change course 182.30
  investigate 938.23
cast aside
  put away 390.6
  discard 390.7
castaway
  n derelict 370.4
  discard 390.3
  outcast 586.4
  adj abandoned 370.8
  discarded 390.11
  outcast 586.10
  stranded 1013.27
cast down
  v chagrin 96.15
  sadden 112.18
  disappoint 132.2
  raze 395.19
  fell 913.5
  adj distressed 96.22
  dejected 112.22
caste rank 245.2
  social status 607.1
  community 617.2
  class 809.2
cast forth
  dissipate 771.5
  disgorge 909.25
castigate
  criticize 510.20
  punish 604.10
casting sculpture 715.1
  copy 785.6
  production 892.2
  throwing 904.2
  calculation 1017.10
  cast 1058.5
cast-iron strong 15.15
  unyielding 361.9
  true 973.13
castle estate 228.7
  stronghold 460.6
  chessman 743.17
castle-building
  n abstractedness 985.2
  dreaminess 986.8
  adj abstracted 985.11
  dreamy 986.25
cast lots 759.23
castoff derelict 370.4
  discard 390.3
cast off take off 6.6
  weigh anchor 182.18
  discard 390.7
  waste 473.5

eliminate 773.5
  separate 802.8
  detach 802.10
  do away with 909.21
cast-off adrift 182.61
  discarded 390.11
  outcast 586.10
cast out
  eliminate 773.5
  separate 802.8
  eject 909.13
  banish 909.17
castrate unman 19.12
  feminize 77.13
  geld 255.11
  cripple 393.14
  domineer 612.16
castrated
  unmanned 19.19
  unsexual 75.29
  crippled 393.30
  mutilated 795.5
cast the first stone
  censure 510.13
  incriminate 599.10
cast up erect 200.9
  elevate 912.5
  sum up 1017.19
casual
  n irregular 461.16
  poor man 619.4
  worker 726.2
  adj in dishabille 5.47
  unconcerned 102.7
  nonchalant 106.15
  careless 340.11
  unpremeditated 365.11
  informal 581.3
  circumstantial 766.7
  unessential 768.4
  unordered 810.12
  incidental 843.11
  occasional 848.3
  undiscriminating 945.5
  chance 972.15
  purposeless 972.16
  easy 1014.13
casualty fatality 308.8
  chance event 972.6
  misfortune 1011.2
casuistry
  insincerity 354.5
  ethical philosophy 636.2
  argumentation 935.4
  sophistry 936.1
cat sharp vision 27.11
  man 76.5
  bitch 110.12
  feline 311.21
  whip 605.1
catabolism
  the body 2.20
  metabolism 7.12
  transformation 852.3
cataclasm 802.3
cataclysm
  overflow 238.6
  debacle 395.4
  upheaval 671.5
  revolution 860.1
  misfortune 1011.2

catacombs 309.16
catalepsy
  stupor 22.6
  unconsciousness 25.2
  paralysis 85.27
  trance 92.19
  inertness 173.4
catalog
  n description 349.2
  record 549.1
  book 549.11
  reference 554.9
  directory 574.10
  account book 628.4
  outline 801.4
  classified list 871.3
  v record 549.15
  classify 801.8
  represent 809.6
  list 871.8
catalysis
  dissociation 806.2
  transformation
    852.3
catalyst
  instigator 375.11
  dissociation 806.2
  transformer 852.5
  author 886.4
catamaran 760.2
cataplexy
  paralysis 85.27
  trance 92.19
catapult
  n takeoff 184.8
  sling 462.9
  toy 743.16
  v throw 904.10
cataract
  n blindness 30.1
  descent 194.1
  waterfall 238.11
  v descend 194.5
  overflow 238.17
catastrophe
  debacle 395.4
  upheaval 671.5
  plot 722.4
  end 820.1
  revolution 860.1
  misfortune 1011.2
catatonic
  unconscious 25.8
  unfeeling 94.9
  inert 173.14
  unsociable 583.5
  psychotic 926.28
  incurious 982.3
catcall
  n noisemaker 53.6
  boo 508.3
  v boo 508.10
catch
  n desire 100.11
  lover 104.12
  surprise 131.2
  trick 356.6
  proviso 421.3
  lock 428.5
  seizure 480.2
  take 480.10

round 708.19
  game 745.3
  condition 959.2
  good thing 999.5
  fault 1003.2
  obstacle 1012.4
  crux 1013.8
  v hear 48.11
  take sick 85.47
  jump at 101.6
  row 182.53
  attend 221.8
  trap 356.20
  acquire 472.8
  hook 472.9
  take 480.17
  understand 521.7
  play 745.5
  fight 754.4
  fix 855.10
  discover 941.7
  engross 983.13
  flame up 1020.23
catch at straws
  be hopeful 124.8
  be rash 493.5
  find fault 510.15
catcher taker 480.11
  baseball team 745.2
catch fire
  be excitable 105.16
  succeed 409.7
  catch on 578.8
  be hot 1019.22
  heat up 1020.23
catching
  n seizure 480.2
  discovery 941.1
  adj poisonous 82.7
  contagious 85.62
  alluring 377.8
  taking 480.25
catch it 604.20
catch on succeed 409.7
  understand 521.7
  become popular 578.8
catch one's breath
  take a rest 20.8
  recuperate 396.19
catch short 131.7
catch the eye show 31.4
  appear 33.8
  meet with attention 983.11
catch up
  overtake 174.13
  seize 480.14
catchword
  call to arms 458.8
  clue 517.9
  phrase 526.9
  makeup 554.12
  maxim 974.1
  motto 974.4
catchy
  deceptive 356.21
  melodious 708.48
  irregular 851.3
catechism
  doctrine 676.2
  question 938.10
  system of belief 953.3

catechize teach 568.10
  inculcate 568.12
  interrogate 938.21
catechumen
  novice 572.9
  believer 692.4
  beginner 818.2
  convert 858.7
categorical
  classificational 809.7
  dialectic 935.22
  unqualified 960.2
categorize
  analyze 801.8
  arrange 808.11
  classify 809.6
category class 809.2
  topic 937.1
catenary
  n sinkage 194.2
  curve 279.2
  adj consecutive 812.9
cater 385.9
catercorner
  v cut 204.11
  adj transverse 204.19
  adv diagonally 204.25
caterer 11.3
catering cooking 11.1
  provision 385.1
caterpillar larva 302.12
  insect 311.33
cater to toady to 138.8
  indulge 427.6
  serve 449.18
caterwaul
  n screech 58.4
  cry 59.1
  animal noise 60.1
  v screech 58.8
  cry 59.6
  wail 60.2
catharsis
  defecation 12.2
  cleansing 79.2
  purgation 92.25
  release 120.2
cathartic
  n cleanser 79.17
  laxative 86.17
  adj cleansing 79.28
  laxative 86.48
  relieving 120.9
cathedral
  n church 703.1
  adj authoritative
    970.18
catheter 239.6
cathexis
  cathection 92.34
  feeling 93.1
  interest 983.2
cathode 1032.8
cathode ray 1033.5
catholic
  universal 864.14
  broad-minded 979.8
Catholic
  n Roman Catholic 675.19
  adj religious denomination
    675.29

cathouse
  disapproved place 228.28
  brothel 665.9
cation
  electrolysis 1032.25
  element 1060.2
cat man 483.3
catnap
  n nap 22.3
  v sleep 22.13
cat-o'-nine-tails 605.1
cat's-paw
  sycophant 138.3
  breeze 318.5
  dupe 358.1
  instrument 384.4
  deputy 576.1
  agent 576.3
  follower 616.8
cattle
  animal life 311.1
  kine 311.6
  rabble 606.3
cattleman
  stockman 1070.2
  herder 1070.3
cattle rustler 483.8
catty peevish 110.22
  spiteful 144.21
  feline 311.43
  disparaging 512.13
cattycorner
  adj transverse 204.19
  adv diagonally 204.25
catwalk 383.2
Caucasian race 312.2
  white man 312.3
caucus
  n legislative gathering 609.9
  election 609.15
  party 617.4
  assembly 770.2
  v politick 609.38
caudal tail 217.11
  final 820.11
caught stuck 855.16
  gripped 983.18
caught short
  surprised 131.12
  unprepared 406.8
caught up in
  involved in 898.5
  engrossed 983.17
caulk 293.7
cause
  n motive 375.1
  lawsuit 598.1
  warrant 600.6
  reason 886.2
  occasion 886.1
  principle 886.9
  v prompt 375.13
  compel 424.4
  reason 886.10
  perform 892.11
cause célèbre
  report 552.6
  affair 831.3
caused by 887.8
causeless
  chance 972.15

purposeless 972.16
causerie chat 541.4
  treatise 556.1
causeway 295.22
caustic
  n curve 279.2
  cauterant 1020.15
  adj acrimonious 17.14
  bitter 64.6
  pungent 68.6
  penetrating 105.31
  out of humor 110.17
  mordant 144.23
  resentful 152.26
  satiric 508.13
  hostile 589.10
cauterant
  n cauterizer 1020.15
  adj heating 1020.26
cauterize 1020.24
caution
  n wariness 339.1
  hesitation 362.3
  dissuasion 379.1
  warning 399.1
  advice 422.1
  collateral 438.3
  carefulness 494.1
  cautiousness 494.1
  tip-off 551.3
  game 752.3
  incredulity 956.1
  forethought 961.2
  v dissuade 379.3
  warn 399.5
  admonish 422.6
cautious slow 175.10
  careful 339.10
  hesitant 362.11
  wary 494.8
  incredulous 956.4
cavalcade 812.3
cavalier
  n beau 104.13
  rider 178.8
  gallant 504.9
  knight 608.5
  escort 769.5
  adj disdainful 141.13
  gruff 505.7
cave
  n lair 228.26
  cavern 284.5
  debacle 395.4
  shelter 1009.3
  v sink 194.6
  collapse 260.10
  hollow 284.13
caveat dissuasion 379.1
  warning 399.1
  advice 422.1
cave in weaken 16.9
  sink 194.6
  collapse 260.10
  hollow 284.13
  breach 292.14
  break down 393.24
  yield 433.7
cave-in collapse 260.4
  debacle 395.4
caveman real man 76.6

ancient 842.7
cavern 284.5
cavernous
  abysmal 275.11
  concave 284.16
cavil
  n criticism 510.4
  quibble 936.4
  v find fault 510.15
  argue 935.16
  quibble 936.9
cavity
  compartment 197.2
  crack 224.2
  pit 275.2
  concavity 284.2
  opening 292.1
cavort
  n caper 366.2
  v caper 366.6
  play 743.23
caw
  n rasp 58.3
  v sound harshly 58.9
  bird sound 60.5
cay 235.2
cease
  n cessation 857.1
  v disappear 34.2
  quiet 173.8
  close shop 293.8
  give up 370.7
  perish 395.23
  end 820.5
  discontinue 857.6
  interj stop! 857.13
cease-fire truce 465.5
  pause 857.3
ceaseless nonstop 812.8
  perpetual 829.7
  constant 847.5
  continuing 856.7
cede give up 370.7
  yield 433.7
  surrender 433.8
  relinquish 475.3
  transfer 629.3
ceiling
  distinctness 31.2
  atmosphere 184.32
  boundary 211.3
  height 272.1
  roof 295.6
  price index 630.4
  limit 794.5
  rocket launching 1074.9
celebrate party 487.2
  praise 509.12
  formalize 580.5
  glorify 696.12
  observe 701.15
  make merry 743.24
celebrated
  distinguished 662.16
  notable 997.19
celebration
  spree 88.5
  treat 95.3
  rejoicing 116.1
  observance 487.1
  ceremony 580.4

ritualism 701.1
revel 743.6
celebrity glory 247.2
  publicity 352.4
  repute 662.1
  man of mark 662.9
  notability 997.2
  personage 997.8
celerity velocity 174.1
  quickness 330.3
celestial
  n angel 679.1
  adj divine 677.16
  angelic 679.6
  heavenly 681.12
  ideal 986.23
  the universe 1072.25
celibate
  n abstainer 565.2
  religious 699.16
  adj monastic 565.6
  continent 664.6
  abstinent 668.10
  sole 872.9
  unproductive 891.4
cell
  compartment 197.2
  bioplast 305.4
  prison 429.8
  refuge 584.6
  clique 617.6
  retreat 1009.5
cellar cellarage 197.17
  storehouse 386.6
cell biology 1068.3
cellist 710.5
cellular 305.19
cellulose 305.6
Celsius scale 1019.19
cement
  n pavement 383.6
  ceramic ware 742.2
  adhesive 803.4
  hardness 1046.6
  building material 1054.2
  v floor 295.22
  plaster 295.25
  put together 800.5
  fasten 800.7
  stick together 803.9
  adj hard 1046.10
cemetery 309.15
cenotaph tomb 309.16
  monument 549.12
censer 70.6
censor
  n restrictionist 428.6
  faultfinder 510.9
  conscience 636.5
  critic 946.7
  v delete 255.12
  cover up 345.8
  suppress 428.8
  end 820.5
censorious averse 99.8
  fastidious 495.9
  prudish 500.19
  disapproving 510.22
  condemnatory 602.5
censorship
  suppression 92.24

deletion 255.5
veil of secrecy 345.3
restraint 428.2
censure
  n reprehension 510.3
  incrimination 599.2
  condemnation 602.1
  stigma 661.6
  criticism 946.2
  v reprehend 510.13
  incriminate 599.10
  condemn 602.3
  stigmatize 661.9
  criticize 946.14
census
  n contents 196.1
  population 227.1
  assemblage 770.1
  table 808.4
  roll 871.6
  numeration 1017.9
  summation 1017.11
  v number 1017.17
cent money 728.7
  trifle 998.5
centenarian
  old man 304.2
  hundred 882.8
centennial
  n anniversary 850.4
  hundred 882.8
  adj momentary 850.8
  hundredth 882.29
center
  n interior 207.2
  centrum 208.2
  mean 246.1
  middle course 467.3
  moderatism 611.2
  core 611.10
  football team 746.2
  basketball team 747.2
  hockey team 749.2
  essence 767.2
  median 819.1
  attractor 907.2
  v converge 169.2
  centralize 208.9
  play 749.7
  position 752.4
centerpiece
  focus 208.4
  feature 997.7
center stage 704.16
centigrade scale 1019.19
centipede
  insect 311.33
  hundred 882.8
central
  n exchange 347.7
  telephone operator 347.9
  adj interior 207.6
  centric 208.11
  medium 246.3
  chief 249.14
  phonetic 524.30
  middle 819.4
  original 886.14
  vital 997.23
centralize
  converge 169.2

center 208.9
league 805.4
centrifugal 171.8
centrifugal force
centripetal force 18.6
repulsion 908.1
centrifuge
n separator 802.7
v whirl 915.11
centripetal
converging 169.3
focal 208.13
middle 819.4
centripetal force
centrifugal force 18.6
attraction 907.1
centrist
n nonpartisan 609.28
political follower 611.10
moderate 670.4
adj neutral 467.7
moderate 611.18
middle 819.4
centurion
Army noncommissioned
officer 575.19
hundred 882.8
century money 728.7
moment 824.2
long time 827.4
eleven 882.7
hundred 882.8
cephalic 198.14
ceramic 742.7
ceramics
visual arts 712.1
pottery 742.1
earthenware 742.1
ceramic ware 742.2
cereal
n breakfast food 10.34
grass 310.5
adj vegetable 310.36
cerebellum 2.15
cerebral nerve 2.30
mental 919.7
cerebrate 931.8
cerebrum brain part 2.15
mental capacity 919.6
ceremonial
n formality 580.1
ceremony 580.4
rite 701.3
adj solemn 580.8
ritualistic 701.19
ceremonious
respectful 155.8
gallant 504.15
solemn 580.8
ritualistic 701.19
ceremony
celebration 487.1
formality 580.1
function 580.4
rite 701.3
cerise 41.6
certain
expectant 130.11
quantitative 244.5
secured 438.11
particular 865.12

plural 883.7
evidential 957.16
inevitable 963.15
sure 970.13
impossible 972.18
true 973.13
belief 953.21
certainly 332.18
certainty
expectation 130.1
knowledge 928.1
belief 953.1
conviction 953.5
inevitability 963.7
sureness 970.1
certitude 970.1
certifiable 926.28
certificate
n certification 549.6
negotiable instrument 728.11
v authorize 443.11
certification
ratification 332.4
deposition 334.3
authorization 443.3
credential 549.6
confirmation 957.4
ensuring 970.8
certified
accepted 332.14
affirmed 334.9
secured 438.11
proved 957.20
assured 970.20
true 973.13
certify ratify 332.12
depose 334.6
secure 438.9
authorize 443.11
testify 957.9
confirm 957.11
make sure 970.11
cerulean
n the heavens 1072.2
adj blue 45.3
cervix genitals 2.13
contraction 260.1
joint 800.4
supporter 901.2
cessation
standstill 173.3
abandonment 370.1
disuse 390.2
interruption 813.2
end 820.1
close 820.3
stop 857.2
discontinuance 857.1
cession
abandonment 370.3
surrender 433.2
relinquishment 475.1
transfer 629.1
qualification 959.1
cesspool 80.12
chafe
n trauma 85.38
irritation 96.3
abrasion 1044.2
v pain 26.7
irritate 96.14

feel anxious 126.6
be impatient 135.4
be angry 152.15
provoke 152.24
injure 393.13
heat 1020.17
abrade 1044.7
chaff
n remainder 256.1
hull 295.16
lightness 298.2
refuse 391.4
rabble 606.3
trivia 998.4
radar 1036.13
v banter 490.5
scoff 508.9
chagrin
n distress 96.4
humiliation 137.2
v embarrass 96.15
chain
n mountain 237.6
jewel 498.6
insignia 647.1
series 812.2
curb 1012.7
fire iron 1020.12
atomic cluster 1038.7
v bind 428.10
put together 800.5
join 800.9
continue 812.4
secure 855.8
chain gang
prisoner 429.11
procession 812.3
chain reaction
series 812.2
vicissitudes 972.5
fission 1038.8
chains 428.4
chain-smoke
n smoking 89.10
v use 87.22
smoke 89.14
chair
n furniture 229.1
mastership 417.7
authority 417.10
instructorship 571.10
chairman 574.5
seat 901.17
v administer 573.11
govern 612.12
install 615.12
the chair
capital punishment 604.7
execution 605.5
chairmanship
mastership 417.7
directorship 573.4
chairperson 574.5
chaise 179.4
chalet 228.8
chalice 703.11
chalk
n whiteness 37.2
art equipment 712.18
jockey 757.2
v whiten 37.5

mark 517.19
record 549.15
portray 712.19
chalky white 37.7
powdery 1051.11
challenge
n objection 333.2
opposition 451.1
resistance 453.1
dare 454.2
declaration of war 458.7
questioning 938.12
v confront 216.8
object 333.5
demand 421.5
claim 421.6
contradict 451.6
offer resistance 453.3
defy 454.3
compete 457.18
make war on 458.15
doubt 955.6
thwart 1012.15
challenging
provocative 375.27
defiant 454.7
chamber
n toilet 12.11
room 197.1
compartment 197.2
bedroom 197.7
council 423.1
v enclose 212.5
chamberlain
major-domo 577.10
treasurer 729.12
chambermaid 577.8
chamber music 708.6
chamber of commerce 617.9
chamber pot 12.11
chambers
apartment 228.13
office 739.7
chameleon
variegation 47.6
timeserver 363.4
changeableness 854.4
champ
n bite 8.2
victor 411.2
champion 413.15
v chew 8.27
champ at the bit
have energy 17.11
be impatient 135.4
wait impatiently 846.13
champion
n superior 249.4
victor 411.2
champ 413.15
defender 460.7
deputy 576.1
justifier 600.8
supporter 616.9
the best 999.8
protector 1008.5
v back 449.13
defend 460.8
justify 600.10
protect 1008.18
adj peerless 249.15

best 999.16
first-rate 999.17
chance
    n gamble 759.2
    turn 825.2
    opportunity 843.2
    liability 897.1
    possibility 966.1
    probability 968.1
    uncertainty 971.1
    lottery 971.8
    absence of assignable cause
        972
    happenstance 972.1
    v attempt 403.6
    risk 759.24
    turn up 831.6
    bechance 972.11
    take a gamble 1006.7
    adj circumstantial 766.7
    unessential 768.4
    vague 971.19
    iffy 972.15
chancellery
    mastership 417.7
    office 739.7
chancellor
    principal 571.8
    executive 574.3
    head of state 575.7
    public official 575.17
    diplomat 576.6
chancery registry 549.3
    office 739.7
chance upon 941.3
chancre 85.37
chandelier 1026.6
chandler
    provider 385.6
    merchant 730.2
change
    n custody 429.5
    money 728.2
    petty cash 728.19
    stock exchange 737.7
    differentiation 780.4
    alteration 852.1
    modification 852.1
    conversion 858.1
    substitution 862.1
    surrogate 862.2
    v don 5.43
    move 172.5
    vacillate 362.8
    trade 731.15
    differentiate 780.6
    alter 852.6
    make a change 852.7
    fluctuate 854.5
    convert 858.11
    substitute 862.4
    interchange 863.4
changeable
    wishy-washy 16.17
    irresolute 362.9
    fickle 364.6
    nonuniform 782.3
    transient 828.7
    changed 852.10
    alterable 854.6
    inconstant 854.7

convertible 858.18
interchangeable 863.5
uncertain 971.16
change hands 629.4
changeless
    almighty 677.17
    permanent 853.7
    unchangeable 855.17
changeling 680.11
change of heart
    penitence 113.4
    conversion 852.1
    new start 858.2
change of life 303.7
change one's mind
    n sing a different tune 363.6
    v repent 113.7
    vacillate 362.8
changing
    n fluctuation 854.3
    adj nonuniform 782.3
    inconstant 854.7
channel
    n seaway 182.10
    outlet 190.9
    bed 199.4
    stream 238.1
    conduit 239.1
    pipe 239.1
    narrow place 270.3
    trench 290.2
    passageway 383.3
    informant 551.5
    communication theory 551.7
    band 1034.13
    v transport 176.14
    focus 208.10
    direct 239.15
    furrow 290.3
    guide 573.9
chant
    n paean 696.3
    repeat 849.5
    v speak 524.25
    sing 708.38
chanting 849.15
chaos
    formlessness 263.1
    anarchy 418.2
    turbulence 671.2
    noncohesion 804.1
    disorder 810.2
    confusion 985.3
    space 1072.3
chaotic formless 263.4
    anarchic 418.6
    turbulent 671.18
    incoherent 804.4
    disordered 810.16
    vague 971.19
    confused 985.12
chap man 76.5
    crack 224.2
chapel hall 197.4
    branch 617.10
    religious building 703.3
chaperon
    n maid 577.8
    escort 769.5
    duenna 1008.7
    v escort 769.8

care for 1008.19
chapfallen
    distressed 96.22
    glum 112.25
    disappointed 132.5
    humiliated 137.14
chaplain 699.2
chapter
    ecclesiastical council 423.4
    part 554.13
    branch 617.10
    part of writing 793.2
    topic 937.1
char
    n cleaner 79.14
    v work 725.12
    burn 1020.24
character
    n man 76.5
    description 349.2
    recommendation 509.4
    sign 517.1
    letter 546.1
    phonetic symbol 546.2
    heredity 560.6
    probity 644.1
    repute 662.1
    role 704.10
    actor 707.2
    notation 709.12
    plot 722.4
    function 724.3
    mode 765.4
    nature 767.4
    kind 809.3
    characteristic 865.4
    oddity 870.4
    eccentric 927.3
    freak 927.4
    disposition 978.3
    number 1017.3
    v represent 349.8
    describe 349.9
    letter 546.6
    engrave 713.9
character assassination
    defamation 512.2
    scandal 552.8
    smear campaign 609.14
characteristic
    n habit 373.3
    sign 517.1
    nature 767.4
    peculiarity 865.4
    adj typical 349.15
    differentiative 780.9
    classificational 809.7
    peculiar 865.13
    attitudinal 978.7
characterization
    representation 349.1
    description 349.2
    impersonation 349.4
    indication 517.3
    acting 704.8
    plot 722.4
    distinction 865.8
characterless
    dull 117.6
    vacant 222.14
    formless 263.4

charade gesture 517.14
    riddle 522.9
charcoal
    n blackness 38.4
    blacking 38.6
    drawing 712.5
    sketching 712.13
    art equipment 712.18
    combustion product 1020.16
    v blacken 38.7
    portray 712.19
charge
    n power 18.1
    cathexis 92.34
    excitement 105.3
    load 196.2
    burden 297.7
    precept 419.1
    injunction 420.2
    dependent 432.6
    attack 459.1
    load 462.16
    supervision 573.2
    arraignment 598.3
    accusation 599.1
    commission 615.1
    price 630.1
    fee 630.6
    duty 641.1
    imposition 643.3
    heraldry 647.2
    benefice 698.9
    task 724.2
    full measure 794.3
    attribution 888.1
    protectorship 1008.2
    impediment 1012.6
    electrical charge 1032.5
    rocket propulsion 1074.8
    v energize 17.10
    burden 297.13
    prime 405.9
    command 420.8
    admonish 422.6
    rush 459.18
    accuse 599.7
    commission 615.10
    receive credit 622.7
    demand 630.12
    impose 643.4
    fill 794.7
    shoot 904.12
    electrify 1032.26
    radioactivate 1037.10
    interj attack! 459.32
charge card 622.3
chargé d'affaires 576.6
charge in 214.5
charge off
    n discount 631.1
    v forget 148.5
    keep accounts 628.8
    discount 631.2
charger animal 311.10
    war-horse 461.30
charisma power 18.1
    allurement 377.1
    illustriousness 662.6
    influence 894.1
charismatic
    alluring 377.8

illustrious 662.19
influential 894.13
attracting 907.5
charitable
loving 104.27
kind 143.13
benevolent 143.15
pitying 145.7
philanthropic 478.22
gratuitous 634.5
tolerant 979.11
charity love 104.1
benevolence 143.4
patronage 449.4
accord 455.1
almsgiving 478.3
donation 478.6
cardinal virtues 653.4
tolerance 979.4
charity case 619.4
charity event 478.9
charlatan
n impostor 357.6
adj quack 354.28
charlatanism 354.7
charley horse 26.2
charm
n delightfulness 97.2
loveableness 104.7
allurement 377.1
lure 377.3
jewel 498.6
sorcery 690.1
magic spell 691.1
spell 691.1
amulet 691.5
assemblage 770.6
influence 894.1
superstition 954.3
beauty 1016.1
elementary particle 1038.6
v delight 95.10
enamor 104.23
persuade 375.23
fascinate 377.7
becharm 691.8
engross 983.13
charmer deceiver 357.1
tempter 377.4
slyboots 415.6
bewitcher 690.9
beauty 1016.8
charming
delightful 97.7
endearing 104.25
alluring 377.8
bewitching 691.11
influential 894.13
charnel house
mortuary 309.9
tomb 309.16
chart
n map 159.5
representation 349.1
diagram 381.3
statistics 757.4
outline 801.4
v locate 159.11
represent 349.8
plot 381.10
itemize 801.7

organize 808.10
charter
n exemption 430.8
permission 443.1
grant 443.5
rental 615.6
v authorize 443.11
commission 615.10
hire 615.15
rent out 615.16
chartreuse 44.4
chary wary 494.9
economical 635.6
chase
n furrow 290.1
woodland 310.13
pursuit 382.1
hunting 382.2
v follow 166.3
emboss 283.12
pursue 382.8
hunt 382.9
make haste 401.5
court 562.21
sculpture 715.5
repulse 908.3
chase away
repulse 908.3
drive out 909.14
chaser drink 88.9
pursuer 382.4
act 704.7
sculptor 716.6
chasm crack 224.2
pit 275.2
concavity 284.4
opening 292.1
chassis base 199.2
structure 266.4
frame 901.10
radio 1034.3
chaste tasteful 496.8
celibate 499.6
elegant 533.6
immaculate 653.7
virtuous 664.4
abstinent 668.10
simple 798.6
perfect 1002.6
chasten
simplify 499.5
punish 604.10
moderate 670.6
chastened meek 433.15
restrained 670.11
chastise reprove 510.17
punish 604.10
chastity elegance 533.1
purity 653.3
celibacy 664.3
virtue 664.1
abstinence 668.2
perfection 1002.1
chat
n talk 540.3
cozy chat 541.4
v chatter 540.5
visit 541.10
château 228.7
chatelaine jewel 498.6
mistress 575.2

governor 575.6
chattel subject 432.7
property 471.1
chatter
n rattle 55.3
speech 524.1
jabber 540.3
v rattle 55.6
bird sound 60.5
speak 524.19
protract 538.8
talk 540.5
shake 917.11
freeze 1023.9
chatty
v talkative 540.9
adj conversational 541.13
intimate 582.24
chauffeur
n driver 178.10
man 577.4
v ride 177.33
chauvinist
n militarist 461.5
misanthrope 590.2
patriot 591.3
bigot 980.5
adj militaristic 458.22
public-spirited 591.4
cheap
adj worthless 391.11
stingy 484.9
inexpensive 633.7
disgraceful 661.11
paltry 998.21
inferior 1005.9
adv cheaply 633.10
cheapen corrupt 393.12
depreciate 633.6
bargain 731.18
cheat
n fake 354.13
fraud 356.8
cheater 357.3
deceiver 759.22
v victimize 356.18
be dishonest 645.11
be promiscuous 665.19
rook 759.26
check
n plaid 47.4
trauma 85.38
slowing 175.4
crack 224.2
opening 292.1
measure 300.2
discomfiture 412.2
restraint 428.1
confinement 429.1
mark 517.5
label 517.13
speech sound 524.12
statement 628.3
negotiable instrument
  728.11
token 728.12
game 749.3
chip 759.18
stop 857.2
checkup 938.6
collation 943.2

ensuring 970.8
blemish 1004.1
reverse 1011.3
hindrance 1012.1
frustration 1012.3
curb 1012.7
v look 27.13
variegate 47.7
slow 175.9
cleave 224.4
injure 393.13
thwart 412.11
restrain 428.7
confine 429.12
fend off 460.10
mark 517.19
play 749.7
ski 753.4
bet 759.25
agree 788.6
break 802.12
delay 846.8
put a stop to 857.11
specify 865.11
examine 938.24
collate 943.5
verify 970.12
blemish 1004.4
hinder 1012.10
recalculate 1017.21
monitor 1034.26
adj checked 47.14
checkered
checked 47.14
changeable 854.6
check in arrive 186.6
die 307.20
record 549.15
punch the clock 832.12
checking account
finances 622.2
funds 728.14
checklist
directory 574.10
list 871.1
roll 871.6
checkmate
n discomfiture 412.2
stop 857.2
frustration 1012.3
v defeat 412.11
put a stop to 857.11
thwart 1012.15
check out look 27.13
depart 188.7
clock out 188.13
die 307.20
qualify 405.15
punch out 832.12
investigate 938.23
examine 938.24
verify 970.12
check 1017.21
cheek impudence 142.3
side 218.1
rashness 493.1
cheek by jowl
adj near 223.14
adv hand in glove 769.10
concurrently 899.5
phrs side by side 218.12

cheeky
impudent 142.10
defiant 454.7
cheer
n food 10.1
cry 59.1
happiness 95.2
cheerfulness 109.1
hurrah 116.2
applause 509.2
conviviality 582.3
v refresh 9.2
cry 59.6
please 95.9
gladden 109.7
rejoice 116.6
comfort 121.6
give hope 124.10
assent 332.8
encourage 492.16
applaud 509.10
cheerful happy 95.16
pleasant 97.6
glad 109.11
cheering 109.16
optimistic 124.12
homelike 228.33
cheerless
pleasureless 96.20
distressing 98.20
unhappy 112.21
hopeless 125.12
cheese 10.48
cheesecake 714.3
cheeseparing
n parsimony 484.1
economizing 635.2
adj parsimonious 484.7
economical 635.6
sparse 885.5
cheesy base 661.12
paltry 998.21
bad 1000.8
inferior 1005.9
chef 11.3
chef d'œuvre
masterpiece 413.10
work of art 712.10
product 893.1
standard of perfection 1002.4
chemical
n element 1060.2
v chemicalize 1060.8
adj biochemical 1060.9
chemical engineering 1043.1
chemist
pharmacist 86.35
drugstore 86.36
chemistry science of matter
1060.1
chemical science 1060.1
cheque 728.11
cherish
hold dear 104.21
foster 449.16
retain 474.7
keep in memory 989.13
care for 1008.19
cherry bomb 53.6
cherub child 302.3
endearment term 562.6

angel 679.1
chessboard check 47.4
toy 743.16
chest
n breast 283.6
storehouse 386.6
treasury 729.13
adj pectoral 283.19
chestnut
n horse 311.11
old joke 489.9
platitude 974.3
adj reddish-brown 40.4
redheaded 41.10
chesty conceited 140.11
corpulent 257.18
pectoral 283.19
chevalier rider 178.8
gallant 504.9
knight 608.5
chevron zigzag 204.8
angle 278.2
heraldry 647.2
military insignia 647.5
chew
n bite 8.2
chewing tobacco 89.7
v masticate 8.27
smoke 89.14
disapprove 510.18
pulp 1063.5
chewed-up 393.27
chewing gum
elastic 1048.3
gum 1062.6
chew out 510.18
chew the fat 541.9
chewy delightful 97.8
tough 1049.4
chiaroscuro
drawing 712.13
lighting 1025.19
chic
n smartness 578.3
adj dressed up 5.46
smart 578.13
knowledgeable 928.17
chicanery
quackery 354.7
chicane 356.4
trick 356.6
stratagem 415.3
knavery 645.2
quibbling 936.5
chichi ornate 498.12
showy 501.19
ultrafashionable 578.14
chick woman 77.6
gal 302.7
fledgling 302.10
bird 311.28
poultry 311.29
endearment term 562.6
chicken
n weakling 16.6
homosexual 75.14
effeminate male 77.11
poultry 311.29
dupe 358.2
coward 491.5
military insignia 647.5

v lose one's nerve 491.8
adj weak 16.12
effeminate 77.15
irresolute 362.12
cowardly 491.10
chicken feed
feed 10.4
petty cash 728.19
trivia 998.4
chicken out
hesitate 362.7
compromise 468.2
lose one's nerve 491.8
defect 858.13
chide 510.17
chief
n superior 249.4
superintendent 574.2
master 575.1
head 575.3
potentate 575.8
heraldry 647.2
principal 997.10
adj leading 165.3
top 198.10
front 216.10
main 249.14
directing 573.12
governing 612.18
preceding 814.4
first 818.17
paramount 997.24
chiefly
mainly 249.17
on the whole 792.14
first 818.18
generally 864.17
normally 869.10
chieftain 575.8
chiffon
n finery 498.3
adj bubbly 320.6
chigger 311.37
chignon braid 3.7
false hair 3.13
chilblain sore 85.37
cold 1023.2
child one 302.3
person 312.5
simple soul 416.3
descendant 561.3
innocent 657.4
product 893.1
child's play 998.5
childbearing 1.1
childhood
preteens 301.2
origin 818.4
childishness
childlikeness 301.4
senility 922.10
puerility 922.11
unwiseness 923.2
childless 891.4
childlike
childish 301.11
artless 416.5
innocent 657.6
senile 922.23
puerile 922.24
trusting 953.22

children
young people 302.2
family 559.5
offspring 561.1
chill
n symptom 85.9
unfeeling 94.1
indifference 102.1
dejection 112.3
deterrent 379.2
aloofness 583.2
enmity 589.1
cold 1023.1
frost 1023.2
v disincline 379.4
freeze 1023.9
frost 1023.10
refrigerate 1024.10
adj unfeeling 94.9
unfriendly 589.9
cool 1023.12
chilling
n cold 1023.2
refrigeration 1024.1
adj frightening 127.28
refrigerative 1024.12
chill out 1047.7
chilly unfeeling 94.9
aloof 141.12
reticent 344.10
unsociable 583.6
unfriendly 589.9
cool 1023.12
feeling cold 1023.16
chime
n ringing 54.3
harmony 708.3
repetitiousness 849.4
v ring 54.8
interrupt 214.6
say 524.22
harmonize 708.35
assonate 784.9
agree 788.6
chimera
airy hope 124.5
illusion 976.1
figment of the imagination
986.5
chimerical
thin 764.6
illusory 976.9
imaginary 986.22
chimney valley 237.7
flue 239.14
fireplace 1020.11
deposit 1058.7
chimpanzee 311.23
chin
n point of the chin 216.6
v speak 524.20
converse 541.9
china
n tableware 8.12
ceramic ware 742.2
fragility 1050.2
adj ceramic 742.7
chink
n thud 52.3
ringing 54.3
crack 224.2

furrow 290.1
vulnerability 1006.4
v thud 52.15
ring 54.8
open 292.11
stop 293.7
chink in one's armor
weak point 16.4
fault 1003.2
vulnerability 1006.4
chinoiserie 498.2
chinook 318.7
chintzy stingy 484.9
vulgar 497.10
base 661.12
slovenly 810.15
sparse 885.5
chip
n trauma 85.38
scrap 248.3
flake 296.3
lightness 298.2
check 759.18
piece 793.3
break 802.4
electronic circuit 1033.8
component 1042.3
v use 87.22
injure 393.13
break 802.12
chip away at 252.7
chip in
interrupt 214.6
participate 476.5
contribute 478.14
pay for 624.18
a chip off the old block
descendant 561.3
likeness 784.3
duplicate 785.3
chip on one's shoulder
challenge 454.2
warlikeness 458.11
chipper healthy 83.9
pert 109.13
active 330.17
chippy
n strumpet 665.14
v use 87.22
chiropractor 90.4
chirp
n insect sound 58.5
v stridulate 58.7
bird sound 60.5
exude cheerfulness 109.6
rejoice 116.5
speak 524.25
sing 708.38
chisel
n sculpture tool 715.4
v form 262.7
furrow 290.3
deceive 356.19
engrave 713.9
sculpture 715.5
process 892.9
chiseler 357.4
chiseling
n fraud 356.8
engraving 713.2
adj deceitful 356.22

chit
runt 258.4
child 302.3
gal 302.7
letter 553.2
chitchat
conversation 541.5
gossip 552.7
chits 623.1
chivalry
military science 458.6
courage 492.1
gallantry 504.2
aristocracy 608.1
magnanimity 652.2
chivy
n hunting 382.2
v annoy 96.13
pursue 382.8
chlorinate
sanitize 79.24
chemicalize 1060.8
vaporize 1067.8
chloroform deaden 25.4
kill 308.13
chlorophyll 44.1
chock
n curb 1012.7
v fill 794.7
obstruct 1012.12
chock-full 794.11
chocolate 40.3
choice
n will 323.1
loophole 369.4
selection 371.1
option 371.1
free will 430.6
elegance 533.1
jockey 757.2
judgment 946.1
the best 999.8
adj tasteful 496.8
best 999.16
choicy 495.9
choir
n church 703.9
part music 708.18
chorus 710.16
keyboard 711.17
v sing 708.38
choirboy 710.15
choirmaster
leader 574.6
choral conductor
710.18
choke
n asphyxiation 307.6
suffocation 308.6
v silence 51.8
gag 99.4
contract 260.7
close 293.6
stop 293.7
asphyxiate 307.24
strangle 308.19
extinguish 395.15
overload 993.15
obstruct 1012.12
be hot 1019.22
fight fire 1022.7

choke back 106.8
choked raucous 58.15
contracted 260.12
closed 293.9
stopped 293.11
inarticulate 525.12
overfull 993.20
chokedamp
miasma 1001.4
vapor 1067.1
choked up mute 51.12
closed 293.9
stopped 293.11
choleric
n personality type 92.12
adj sour 110.23
resentful 152.26
cholesterol 7.7
chomp
n bite 8.2
v chew 8.27
chomp at the bit 846.13
choose desire 100.14
will 323.2
elect 371.13
choosing
n choice 371.1
adj selective 371.23
choosy selective 371.23
fastidious 495.9
chop
n feed 10.4
cutlet 10.19
side 218.1
wave 238.14
roughness 288.2
hit 902.4
v notch 289.4
play 745.5
sever 802.11
be changed 852.6
chop down raze 395.19
fell 913.5
chop logic
differentiate 780.6
argue 935.16
quibble 936.9
chopped-off 813.4
chopper cycle 179.8
rotor plane 181.5
game 745.3
choppy rough 288.6
nonuniform 782.3
discontinuous 813.4
irregular 851.3
jolting 917.20
chops mouth 292.4
wind instrument 711.6
choral 708.50
chorale paean 696.3
sacred music 708.17
part music 708.18
chorus 710.16
chord
n sympathy 93.5
straight line 277.2
concento 709.17
string 711.20
v harmonize 708.35
tune 708.36
play 708.39

chore
n task 724.2
tough proposition 1013.2
v serve 577.13
work 725.12
chorea 917.2
choreographer
dramatist 704.22
dancer 705.3
choreography
representation 349.1
dancing 705.1
chorister
choral singer 710.15
choirmaster 710.18
chorographic
locational 159.19
measuring 300.12
chortle
n laughter 116.4
v laugh 116.8
chorus
n unanimity 332.5
cast 707.11
part music 708.18
passage 708.24
chorale 710.16
poetry 720.9
agreement 788.1
sequel 817.1
repeat 849.5
v imitate 336.5
say 524.22
sing 708.38
chorus line 705.3
chosen
n legislator 610.3
the best 999.8
adj superior 249.12
selected 371.26
chow 10.2
chowder 10.11
chrismal
n unction 701.5
baptism 701.6
church 703.10
holy vessels 703.11
adj oily 1056.9
Christ 677.10
christen name 527.11
baptize 701.17
inaugurate 818.11
Christendom
Christianity 675.7
the believing 692.5
Christian
n respectable citizen 659.3
Nazarene 675.17
adj kind 143.13
honest 644.13
orthodox 687.7
Christianity 675.7
Christian name 527.4
Christian Scientist 675.24
Christlike
humblehearted 137.11
kind 143.13
divine 677.16
Christmas
n Yuletide 313.6
v vacation 20.9

chromatic
  colorational 35.16
  tonal 709.27
chromatics 35.10
chromatography 35.10
chromosome
  allosome 305.8
  heredity 560.6
chronic
  confirmed 373.18
  durable 827.10
chronicle
  n record 549.1
  history 719.1
  annals 719.3
  story 722.3
  chronology 832.9
  v record 549.15
  write history 719.5
  chronologize 832.14
chronicler annalist 550.2
  historian 719.4
  chronologist 832.10
chronography time 821.1
  chronology 832.1
chronological
  historical 719.7
  temporal 821.7
chronology
  history 719.1
  time 821.1
  timekeeping 832.1
  chronicle 832.9
chronometer
  navigation 182.2
  timepiece 832.6
chrysalis 302.12
chthonian
  n Satanist 680.15
  idolater 697.4
  adj hellish 682.8
  idolatrous 697.7
chubby
  corpulent 257.18
  stubby 268.10
chuck
  n food 10.2
  tap 902.7
  throw 904.3
  v bird sound 60.5
  place violently 159.13
  reject 372.2
  discard 390.7
  eliminate 773.5
  tap 902.18
  throw 904.10
chuckhole
  pothole 284.3
  mud puddle 1062.9
chuckle
  n ripple 52.5
  laughter 116.4
  v laugh 116.8
chuck up 909.27
chug-a-lug 88.25
chum
  n friend 588.4
  v associate with 582.18
chummy 587.20
chump dupe 358.2
  fool 924.3

chunk
  n amount 244.2
  lump 257.10
  portion 477.5
  bet 759.3
  accumulation 770.9
  piece 793.3
  throw 904.3
  v throw 904.10
chunky
  corpulent 257.18
  stubby 268.10
  sturdy 763.7
church school 617.5
  sect 675.3
  divine service 696.8
  kirk 703.1
the Church
  the true church 687.3
  the believing 692.5
  the ministry 698.1
  papacy 698.6
churchgoer
  attender 221.5
  believer 692.4
  worshiper 696.9
  the laity 700.1
churchly
  ecclesiastic 698.13
  churchish 703.15
churchman
  believer 692.4
  clergyman 699.2
  layman 700.2
Church of England 675.11
churchyard 309.15
churlish
  irascible 110.19
  countrified 233.7
  boorish 497.13
  gruff 505.7
churn
  n mixer 797.9
  blend 917.1
  agitator 917.9
  v seethe 671.12
  agitate 917.10
  emulsify 1062.10
churn out write 547.21
  pen 718.6
  produce 892.8
chute parachute 181.13
  outlet 190.9
  incline 204.4
  rapids 238.10
  gutter 239.3
  race 756.3
  deposit 1058.7
chutzpah
  impudence 142.3
  rashness 493.1
  fearlessness 492.4
CIA man 576.9
ciao! 188.22
cicatrix mark 517.5
  blemish 1004.1
cicerone
  traveler 178.1
  interpreter 341.7
  guide 574.7
  escort 769.5

cigar 89.4
cigarette 89.5
cilia
  eyelashes 3.12
  organelle 305.5
cinch
  n dupe 358.2
  sure success 409.2
  poker 759.10
  saddle parts 901.18
  certainty 970.2
  easy 1014.4
  v fasten 800.7
  bind 800.9
  prove 957.10
  make sure 970.11
cincture
  n surrounding 209.5
  enclosed place 212.3
  circle 280.3
  v encircle 209.7
cinder dregs 256.2
  coal 1019.16
  combustion product
    1020.16
cinder block 1054.2
cinema
  n motion-picture theater
    706.7
  adj motion-picture 706.9
cinematic 706.9
cinematographer
  motion-picture photography
    706.5
  photographer 716.5
cinerary 309.22
cinereous colorless 36.7
  gray 39.4
cipher
  n discord 61.1
  cryptography 345.6
  symbol 517.2
  Greek 522.7
  signature 527.10
  letter 546.1
  nothing 762.2
  thing of naught 764.2
  a nobody 998.7
  number 1017.3
  v code 345.10
  calculate 1017.18
circa
  adv approximately 244.6
  prep about 223.26
circadian
  recurrent 849.13
  momentary 850.8
circle
  n environment 209.1
  region 230.9
  sphere 231.2
  curve 279.2
  circus 280.2
  jewel 498.6
  clique 617.6
  round 850.3
  circuit 914.2
  halo 1025.14
  orbit 1072.16
  v move 172.5
  encircle 209.7

  round 280.10
  recur 850.5
  circuit 914.5
  rotate 915.9
circuit
  n journey 177.5
  environment 209.1
  sphere 231.2
  circle 280.2
  route 383.1
  engagement 704.11
  baseball 745.1
  routine 850.3
  round 914.2
  detour 914.3
  electrical circuit 1032.4
  network 1034.8
  circuitry 1042.3
  v circle 914.5
circuitous
  deviative 164.7
  oblique 204.13
  convolutional 281.6
  circumlocutory 538.14
  roundabout 914.7
circuitry
  electronic circuit 1033.8
  computer parts 1042.3
circular
  n announcement 352.2
  advertising matter 352.8
  booklet 554.11
  adj round 280.11
  circuitous 914.7
circularity
  curvature 279.1
  roundness 280.1
  orbit 280.1
  circuitousness 914.1
  sophistry 936.1
circulate
  distribute 352.10
  be published 352.16
  deliver 478.13
  monetize 728.26
  circle 914.5
  rotate 915.9
circulation
  n blood 2.25
  publication 352.1
  monetization 728.23
  circuitousness 914.1
  rotation 915.1
  liquidity 1061.1
  adj fluid 1061.4
circumcise 701.17
circumcision 685.4
circumference
  exterior 206.2
  bounds 211.1
  circle 280.2
circumferential
  environing 209.8
  outlining 211.14
circumlocution
  convolution 281.1
  roundaboutness 538.5
  circuitousness 914.1
circumnavigate
  navigate 182.13
  circle 914.5

circumscribe
  bound 210.4
  limit 211.8
  contract 260.7
  restrict 428.9
  qualify 959.3
circumscription
  restriction 210.2
  limiting 210.1
  confines 211.1
  boundary 211.3
  enclosure 212.1
  contraction 260.1
  restraint 428.3
  exclusion 773.1
  qualification 959.1
circumspect
  slow 175.10
  careful 339.10
  cautious 494.8
  judicious 920.19
circumstance
  pomp 501.6
  fact 761.3
  state 765.1
  existing conditions 766.2
  occurrence 766.1
  component 796.2
  event 831.2
  qualification 959.2
circumstances
  environment 209.1
  assets 471.7
  total situation 766.2
  affairs 831.4
circumstantial
  conditional 766.7
  unessential 768.4
  happening 831.9
  evidential 957.16
  qualifying 959.7
circumstantiate
  itemize 766.6
  confirm 957.11
circumvent
  deceive 356.14
  avoid 368.6
  evade 368.7
  outwit 415.11
  thwart 1012.15
circus town 230.9
  circle 280.2
  arena 463.1
  show business 704.1
cirrous
  threadlike 271.7
  cloudy 319.8
cirrus filament 271.1
  coil 281.2
cist 309.16
cistern 241.1
citadel 460.6
citation
  incrimination 599.2
  eulogy 646.4
  acknowledgment 888.2
  reference 957.5
Citation 311.15
cite summon 420.11
  accuse 599.7
  honor 646.8

itemize 766.6
  name 957.13
  call attention to 983.10
citified 230.11
citizen national 227.4
  freeman 430.11
  noncombatant 464.5
citizenry
  population 227.1
  the people 606.1
citizens band 1034.13
citizenship
  native-born citizenship 226.2
  public spirit 591.1
citrus fruit 10.38
city
  n metropolis 230
  town 230.1
  region 231.5
  adj urban 230.11
city dweller 227.6
city father
  public official 575.17
  legislator 610.3
city hall
  town hall 230.5
  political party 609.24
  capitol 613.4
city planner
  artist 716.10
  architect 717.3
city planning 230.10
city slicker
  townsman 227.6
  sophisticate 413.17
city-state 232.1
civic urban 230.11
  public 312.16
  public-spirited 591.4
  political 609.43
  governmental 612.17
civics 609.2
civil public 312.16
  decorous 496.10
  courteous 504.14
  sociable 582.22
  governmental 612.17
  lay 700.3
civil ceremony 563.3
civil code 673.5
civil disobedience 327.1
civil disorder 327.4
civil engineering 1043.1
civilian dress 5.8
civilian life 465.6
civility
  cultivation 392.3
  decorousness 496.3
  courtesy 504.1
  manners 504.6
  amenities 504.7
  social convention 579.1
  etiquette 580.3
  sociability 582.1
civilization
  culture 373.2
  cultivation 392.3
  courtesy 504.1
civilize
  humanize 312.12
  make better 392.9

teach 568.10
civilized
  improved 392.13
  elegant 496.9
  learned 928.21
civil law 673.5
civil liberties
  freedom 430.2
  human rights 642.3
civil rights
  freedom 430.2
  human rights 642.3
civil servant 575.16
civil war 458.1
civvies 5.8
clabber
  n clot 1045.7
  semiliquid 1062.5
  v cohere 803.6
  thicken 1045.10
  emulsify 1062.10
clack
  n noisemaker 53.6
  rattle 55.3
  snap 56.2
  chatter 540.3
  v rattle 55.6
  snap 56.7
  bird sound 60.5
  chatter 540.5
clad 5.45
cladding exterior 206.2
  plating 295.13
  lamina 296.2
claim
  n extortion 192.6
  profession 376.2
  demand 421.1
  possession 469.1
  estate 471.4
  declaration 598.7
  prerogative 642.1
  v extort 192.15
  pretext 376.3
  demand 421.5
  pretend to 421.6
  possess 469.4
  take 480.13
  require 963.9
claimant
  petitioner 440.7
  accuser 599.5
clairvoyance ESP 689.8
  the future 839.1
  understanding 928.3
  intuition 934.1
  foreknowledge 961.3
  divination 962.2
clairvoyant 962.4
clam
  n discord 61.1
  marine animal 311.30
  man of few words 344.5
  v fish 382.10
clambake meal 8.6
  party 582.12
  electioneering 609.12
clamber
  n ascent 193.1
  v climb 193.11
clammy sweaty 12.22

viscous 1062.12
clamor
  n noise 53.3
  outcry 59.4
  clash 61.2
  entreaty 440.2
  v be noisy 53.9
  vociferate 59.8
  complain 115.15
clamor for
  wish for 100.16
  demand 421.5
  entreat 440.11
  require 963.9
clamorous noisy 53.13
  vociferous 59.10
  turbulent 105.24
  demanding 421.9
  urgent 997.22
clamp
  n contractor 260.6
  hold 474.2
  v squeeze 260.8
  fasten 800.7
clampdown 428.1
clamp down on
  restrain 428.7
  suppress 428.8
  domineer 612.16
clam up
  v be silent 51.6
  keep to oneself 344.6
  keep secret 345.7
  interj silence! 51.14
clan race 559.4
  community 617.2
  clique 617.6
  class 809.2
  kind 809.3
clandestine 345.12
clangor
  n noise 53.3
  ringing 54.3
  rasp 58.3
  v be noisy 53.9
  ring 54.8
  sound harshly 58.9
clank
  n ringing 54.3
  rasp 58.3
  v ring 54.8
  sound harshly 58.9
  speak poorly 525.7
clannish
  contemptuous 157.8
  exclusive 495.13
  racial 559.7
  cliquish 617.18
clansman 559.2
clap
  n noise 53.3
  report 56.1
  applause 509.2
  v crack 56.6
  place violently 159.13
  close 293.6
  applaud 509.10
  hit 902.14
clapboard
  n wood 1054.3
  v face 295.23

clapper
noisemaker 53.6
bell 54.4
claptrap
humbug 354.14
nonsense 520.2
bull 520.3
specious argument 936.3
claque 509.8
clarification
refinement 79.4
explanation 341.4
clarify refine 79.22
explain 341.10
make clear 521.6
disinvolve 798.5
clarinetist 710.4
clarion call 458.8
clarity
distinctness 31.2
clearness 521.2
elegance 533.1
facility 1014.1
transparency 1029.1
clash
n report 56.1
rasp 58.3
jangle 61.2
disaccord 456.1
fight 457.4
hostility 589.3
impact 902.3
v conflict 35.15
crack 56.6
sound harshly 58.9
strike a sour note 61.3
disagree 456.8
contend 457.13
go contrary to 779.4
fight 789.5
counteract 900.6
collide 902.13
clasp
n hold 474.2
embrace 562.3
v stay near 223.12
hold 474.6
seize 480.14
embrace 562.18
hook 800.8
cohere 803.6
class
n rank 245.2
nomenclature 527.1
race 559.4
form 572.11
social class 607.1
community 617.2
school 617.5
the laity 700.1
category 809.2
classifications 809.5
goodness 999.1
biology 1068.1
v analyze 801.8
classify 809.6
estimate 946.9
classic
n book 554.1
classical music 708.6
work of art 712.10

standard of perfection 1002.4
adj simple 499.6
elegant 533.6
model 786.8
perfected 1002.9
classical
downright 247.12
tasteful 496.8
simple 499.6
elegant 533.6
literary 547.24
artistic 718.7
antiquated 842.13
perfected 1002.9
classicist purist 533.4
antiquarian 842.5
scholar 929.3
classification
veil of secrecy 345.3
nomenclature 527.1
analysis 801.3
grouping 808.3
categorization 809.1
listing 809.1
classify
keep secret 345.7
analyze 801.8
group 808.11
class 809.6
discriminate 944.4
classmate
schoolchild 572.3
companion 588.3
classroom
n schoolroom 567.11
adj scholastic 567.13
classy
ostentatious 501.18
chic 578.13
clatter
n noise 53.3
rattle 55.3
chatter 540.3
v rattle 55.6
chatter 540.5
gossip 552.12
clause phrase 529.1
part 554.13
bill 613.9
part of writing 793.2
condition 959.2
clavichord 711.12
claw torture 96.18
injure 393.13
seize 480.14
clawed tortured 96.25
pedal 199.9
prehensile 474.9
claws governance 417.5
clutches 474.4
control 612.2
clay
n pipe 89.6
land 234.1
corpse 307.16
humankind 312.1
person 312.5
ceramics 742.3
softness 1047.4
body 1052.3
mud 1062.8

adj ceramic 742.7
clayey earthy 234.5
pasty 1047.12
clean
v cleanse 79.18
adj pure 79.25
shapely 264.5
skillful 413.22
honest 644.13
virtuous 653.7
spotless 657.7
chaste 664.4
thorough 794.10
adv cleanly 79.29
absolutely 794.15
clean bill of health
healthiness 83.2
pass 443.7
certificate 549.6
clean-cut distinct 31.7
shapely 264.5
clear 521.11
clean-limbed 264.5
cleanliness
purity 79.1
innocence 657.1
chastity 664.1
clean out clean 79.18
strip 480.24
evacuate 909.22
cleanse clean 79.18
release 120.6
sanctify 685.5
cleanser
sweeper 79.16
cleaner 79.17
clean-shaven 6.17
cleansing
n cleaning 79.2
release 120.2
adj cleaning 79.28
relieving 120.9
atoning 658.7
clean slate void 222.3
innocence 657.1
new start 858.2
revolution 860.1
cleanup gain 472.3
red-up 808.6
clean up clean 79.18
complete 407.6
triumph 411.3
profit 472.12
tidy 808.12
clear
n clarity 521.2
v refine 79.22
take off 184.38
rise above 272.11
unclose 292.12
leap 366.5
manage 409.12
extricate 431.7
profit 472.12
justify 600.9
acquit 601.4
pay in full 624.13
pass 749.7
play 752.4
eliminate 773.5
evacuate 909.22

disembarrass 1014.9
adj distinct 31.7
audible 50.16
vacant 222.14
open 292.17
manifest 348.8
free 430.21
unhampered 430.26
quit 430.31
crystal-clear 521.11
legible 521.12
elegant 533.6
unindebted 624.23
innocent 657.6
thorough 794.10
unmixed 798.7
unfastened 802.22
unqualified 960.2
certain 970.13
thriving 1010.13
easy 1014.13
light 1025.31
transparent 1029.4
adv wide 261.19
clearance room 158.3
open space 158.4
altitude 184.35
interval 224.1
distance 261.1
latitude 430.4
authorization 443.3
pass 443.7
justification 600.1
acquittal 601.1
payment 624.1
elimination 773.2
evacuation 909.6
clear-cut
distinct 31.7
lost 473.7
clear 521.11
clearheaded
sober 516.3
clear-witted 920.13
sane 925.4
clearing opening 292.1
extrication 431.3
justification 600.1
acquittal 601.1
evacuation 909.6
disembarrassment 1014.6
field 1069.9
clearing house 729.14
clearly visibly 31.8
audibly 50.18
positively 247.19
manifestly 348.14
intelligibly 521.13
certainly 970.23
clear out
v disappear 34.2
clean 79.18
depart 188.7
flee 368.11
eliminate 773.5
evacuate 909.22
interj go away! 909.31
clear sailing 1007.1
clear-sighted
clear-eyed 27.21
clear-witted 920.13

clear the air
  explain 341.10
  pacify 465.7
  moderate 670.6
clear the decks
  trim ship 182.49
  prepare 405.6
  take precautions 494.6
  eliminate 773.5
  tidy 808.12
  evacuate 909.22
clear the way
  prepare the way 405.12
  facilitate 1014.7
clear up explain 341.10
  disinvolve 798.5
  tidy 808.12
  solve 940.2
  make sure 970.11
cleavage
  falling-out 456.4
  severance 802.2
  fission 1038.8
cleave crack 224.4
  open 292.11
  demolish 395.17
  sever 802.11
  cohere 803.6
  bisect 875.4
  atomize 1038.17
cleft
  n crack 224.2
  notch 289.1
  opening 292.1
  falling-out 456.4
  break 802.4
  adj cut 224.7
  severed 802.23
  halved 875.6
cleft palate 265.3
clemency pity 145.1
  leniency 427.1
clench
  n hold 474.2
  v hold 474.6
  seize 480.14
clerestory floor 197.23
  top 198.1
clergy priesthood 699.1
  ministry 699.1
clerical
  n clergyman 699.2
  adj secretarial 547.28
  ecclesiastic 698.13
clerical worker 726.2
clerk writer 547.13
  recorder 550.1
  agent 576.3
  accountant 628.7
  clergyman 699.2
  salesman 730.3
  scholar 929.3
clever skillful 413.22
  well-laid 413.30
  cunning 415.12
  witty 489.15
  teachable 570.18
  smart 920.14
cliché
  n triteness 117.3
  catchword 526.9

  generalization 864.8
  platitude 974.3
  adj aphoristic 974.6
click
  n thud 52.3
  snap 56.2
  v thud 52.15
  snap 56.7
  succeed 409.7
  befriend 587.11
clicking
  n ticking 55.2
  adj staccato 55.7
client
  n advisee 422.4
  dependent 432.6
  customer 733.4
  adj subject 432.13
clientele 733.3
cliff precipice 200.3
  slope 237.2
climacteric
  n change of life 303.7
  crisis 843.4
  adj critical 843.10
climactic top 198.10
  critical 843.10
climate
  milieu 209.3
  zone 231.3
  weather 317.3
  mental climate 978.5
climatic 317.13
climatology 317.5
climax
  n copulation 75.7
  summit 198.2
  finishing touch 407.3
  upheaval 671.5
  plot 722.4
  limit 794.5
  crisis 843.4
  crucial moment 843.5
  urgency 997.4
  salient point 997.6
  acme of perfection 1002.3
  v come 75.24
  top 198.9
  complete 407.6
climb
  n ascent 193.1
  acclivity 204.6
  v move 172.5
  ascend 184.39
  clamber 193.11
  incline 204.10
climb down
  n recant 363.8
  v humble oneself 137.7
  get down 194.7
climber
  traveler 178.1
  ascender 193.6
  plant 310.4
  upstart 606.7
clime zone 231.3
  weather 317.3
clinch
  n hold 474.2
  joint 800.4
  v hold 474.6

  seize 480.14
  fight 754.4
  fasten 800.7
  join 800.11
  cohere 803.6
  prove 957.10
  make sure 970.11
clincher
  finishing stroke 820.4
  conclusive argument 958.3
cling
  n hold 474.2
  cohesion 803.1
  v stay near 223.12
  hold 474.6
  retain 474.7
  cohere 803.6
clinic facility 91.21
  hospital room 197.25
clinical 90.15
clink
  n thud 52.3
  ringing 54.3
  jail 429.9
  rhyme 720.8
  assonance 784.6
  v thud 52.15
  ring 54.8
clinker
  discord 61.1
  dregs 256.2
  combustion product
    1020.16
  building material 1054.2
clip
  n velocity 172.4
  excerpt 557.3
  piece 793.3
  blow 902.5
  v speed 174.9
  excise 255.10
  shorten 268.6
  deceive 356.19
  hold 474.6
  retain 474.7
  rob 482.16
  abridge 557.5
  overprice 632.7
  hook 800.8
  strike 902.15
clipper 181.8
clippings 557.4
clique
  n social set 582.5
  coterie 617.6
  company 770.3
  v associate with 582.18
cliquish
  contemptuous 157.8
  exclusive 495.13
  clannish 617.18
clitoris 2.13
cloak
  n overgarment 5.12
  cover 295.2
  pretext 376.1
  robe 702.2
  v mantle 5.40
  cover 295.19
  conceal 346.6
  protect 1008.18

cloak-and-dagger
  sensational 105.32
  covert 345.12
cloakroom 197.15
clobber
  best 249.7
  defeat 412.9
  punish 604.15
  beat 902.17
clock
  n furniture 229.1
  timepiece 832.6
  v check out 188.13
  time 832.11
clock in
  arrive 186.6
  punch the clock 832.12
clock watcher
  idler 331.8
  shirker 368.3
clockwise
  adj right 219.4
  adv rightward 161.24
  round 915.16
clod land 234.1
  lump 257.10
  bungler 414.8
  peasant 606.6
  stupid person 924.2
  oaf 924.5
  body 1052.3
cloddish
  countrified 233.7
  boorish 497.13
  stupid 922.15
clog
  n obstruction 293.3
  curb 1012.7
  v stop 293.7
  dance 705.5
clogs 5.27
cloister
  n corridor 197.18
  enclosed place 212.3
  passageway 383.3
  monastery 703.6
  retreat 1009.5
  v enclose 212.6
  confine 429.12
cloistered
  quiescent 173.12
  walled off 212.10
  enclosing 212.11
  confined 429.19
  recluse 584.10
  claustral 703.16
  separated 802.21
clone
  n the same 778.3
  duplicate 785.3
  conformist 867.2
  v reproduce 778.6
  make uniform 781.4
  copy 785.8
close
  n completion 407.2
  closing 820.3
  cessation 857.1
  v approach 167.3
  converge 169.2
  surround 209.6

shut 293.6
arrange 437.8
contend 457.13
end 820.5
turn off 857.12
obstruct 1012.12
close
  n enclosed place 212.3
  plot 231.4
  adj stuffy 173.16
  near 223.14
  narrow 270.14
  tight 293.12
  meticulous 339.12
  taciturn 344.9
  secret 345.11
  secretive 345.15
  concealed 346.11
  stingy 484.9
  phonetic 524.30
  concise 537.6
  unsociable 583.5
  familiar 587.19
  crowded 770.22
  approximate 775.8
  approximating 784.14
  fast 800.14
  imminent 840.3
  exact 928.17
  sultry 1019.28
  dense 1045.12
  adv around 209.12
  nigh 223.20
  nearly 223.22
  densely 1045.15
close call 369.2
closed shut 293.9
  secret 345.11
  inhospitable 586.7
  narrow-minded 980.10
closed-minded
  unpersuadable 361.13
  narrow-minded 980.10
close down
  close shop 293.8
  suppress 428.8
  stop work 857.8
closefisted 484.9
close in approach 167.3
  converge 169.2
  enclose 212.5
closemouthed
  taciturn 344.9
  secretive 345.15
close one's eyes to
  be blind 30.4
  condone 148.4
  be inattentive 984.2
close out
  n end 820.1
  v reject 372.2
  complete 407.6
  keep accounts 628.8
  deal 734.8
  sell 737.24
  exclude 773.4
  end 820.5
  make impossible 967.6
close shave 369.2
closet
  n latrine 12.10

sanctum 197.8
clothes room 197.15
bathroom 197.26
storehouse 386.6
office 739.7
  v confine 212.6
  adj secret 345.11
close up
  n motion picture 714.8
  v converge 169.2
  shut 293.6
  close shop 293.8
  heal 396.21
  complete 407.6
  obstruct 1012.12
closing arguments 598.8
closure shutting 293.1
  closing 293.1
  completion 794.4
  joint 800.4
  hindrance 1012.1
clot
  n bungler 414.8
  conglomeration 803.5
  idiot 924.8
  coagulum 1045.7
  v come together 770.16
  cohere 803.6
  thicken 1045.10
  emulsify 1062.10
cloth material 4.1
  sail 180.14
  canonicals 702.1
  scenery 704.20
clothe enclothe 5.39
  empower 18.10
  cover 295.19
  equip 385.8
clothes apparel 5.1
  blanket 295.10
clothes-conscious 578.13
clotheshorse
  dandy 500.9
  person of fashion 578.7
  trestle 901.16
clothier 5.33
clothing
  n apparel 5.1
  wear 5.1
  adj dress 5.45
cloture
  legislative procedure 613.6
  cessation 857.5
cloud
  high fog 319.1
  assemblage 770.6
  multitude 884.3
  confusion 985.3
  vapor 1067.1
  v cover 295.19
  becloud 319.7
  conceal 346.6
  confuse 985.7
  darken 1027.9
  opaque 1031.2
cloudburst 316.2
cloudless 1025.31
cloud nine
  happiness 95.2
  summit 198.2
cloudy stormy 318.23

nebulous 319.8
obscure 522.15
muddled 985.13
gloomy 1027.14
opaque 1031.3
clout
  n power 18.1
  authoritativeness 417.2
  vigor 544.3
  influence 894.1
  impulse 902.1
  blow 902.5
  v play 745.5
  strike 902.15
cloven cleft 224.7
  severed 802.23
  halved 875.6
clover feed 10.4
  comfort 121.1
  three 876.1
  prosperity 1010.1
cloverleaf 170.2
clown
  n bungler 414.8
  humorist 489.12
  vulgarian 497.6
  peasant 606.6
  circus performer 707.3
  buffoon 707.10
  fool 924.1
  v be foolish 923.6
cloying nasty 64.7
  oversweet 66.5
  sentimental 93.21
  satiating 994.7
club
  n resort 228.27
  fist 462.4
  rod 605.2
  fellowship 617.3
  theater 704.14
  baseball team 745.2
  golf 751.1
  v whip 604.13
  league 805.4
  cudgel 902.20
clubby 582.22
clubfoot
  foot 199.5
  deformity 265.3
clubhouse 228.27
clubwoman
  person of fashion 578.7
  sociable person 582.16
  member 617.11
cluck 60.5
clue cue 517.9
  tip-off 551.3
  hint 551.4
  evidence 957.1
clue one in 351.4
clump
  n thud 52.3
  lump 257.10
  bulge 283.3
  growth 310.2
  bunch 770.7
  blow 902.5
  stamp 902.10
  solid 1045.6
  v thud 52.15

way of walking 177.28
assemble 770.18
strike 902.15
stamp 902.22
thicken 1045.10
clumsy
  n bungler 414.9
  adj bulky 257.19
  slipshod 340.12
  bungling 414.20
  inelegant 534.2
  inconvenient 996.7
  unwieldy 1013.19
  ungraceful 1015.9
clunk
  n thud 52.3
  blow 902.5
  v thud 52.15
  strike 902.15
cluster
  n throng 770.4
  bunch 770.7
  conglomeration 803.5
  solid 1045.6
  v come together 770.16
  assemble 770.18
  cohere 803.6
  thicken 1045.10
clutch
  n amount 244.2
  hold 474.2
  offspring 561.2
  crisis 843.4
  urgency 997.4
  predicament 1013.4
  cone clutch 1040.10
  v hold 474.6
  seize 480.14
clutch at straws 124.8
clutches
  governance 417.5
  claws 474.4
  control 612.2
clutter
  n jumble 810.3
  multitude 884.3
  radar interference
    1036.12
  v disarrange 811.2
  teem with 884.5
coach
  n preparer 405.5
  tutor 571.5
  trainer 571.6
  baseball team 745.2
  v advise 422.5
  tutor 568.11
coach-and-four 179.5
coachman driver 178.9
  man 577.4
coact cooperate 450.3
  interact 777.6
  concur 899.2
coactive
  compulsory 424.10
  cooperative 450.5
  concurrent 899.4
coadjutant
  n assistant 616.6
  adj cooperative
    450.5

coagulate
  n clot 1045.7
  v cohere 803.6
  thicken 1045.10
  emulsify 1062.10
coagulation
  thickening 1045.4
  viscosity 1062.2
coal
  n blackness 38.4
  live coal 1019.16
  combustion product
    1020.16
  v provision 385.9
  burn 1020.24
  fuel 1021.8
coalesce
  cooperate 450.3
  identify 778.5
  mix 797.10
  combine 805.3
coalescent 872.12
coalition
  affiliation 450.2
  front 609.33
  association 617.1
  combination 805.1
coarse raucous 58.15
  bitter 64.6
  offensive 98.18
  thick 269.8
  rough 288.6
  textured 294.6
  undeveloped 406.12
  gross 497.11
  ill-bred 505.6
  inelegant 534.2
  populational 606.8
  carnal 663.6
  vulgar 666.8
  inferior 1005.9
coarsened 94.12
coast
  n slide 194.4
  border 211.4
  side 218.1
  shore 234.2
  v be still 173.7
  glide 177.35
  navigate 182.13
  sail coast-wise 182.39
  slide 194.9
  do nothing 329.2
  take it easy 331.15
  go easily 1014.10
coastal
  bordering 211.11
  littoral 234.7
coast guard
  rescuer 398.2
  branch 461.21
  navy 461.27
  guard 1008.9
coastguardsman 183.4
coat
  n hair 3.2
  outerwear 5.13
  color 35.8
  cover 295.2
  blanket 295.12
  lamina 296.2

  card 758.2
  v cloak 5.40
  color 35.14
  spread on 295.24
coating
  n color 35.8
  painting 35.12
  covering 295.1
  blanket 295.12
  lamina 296.2
  adj covering 295.35
coat of arms 647.2
coattails 449.4
coauthor
  n writer 547.15
  collaborator 616.4
  author 718.4
  v write 547.21
  publish 718.6
coax
  n prompter 375.10
  v urge 375.14
  lure 377.5
  importune 440.12
coaxial 208.14
coaxial cable 347.17
cob ear 310.29
  race horse 311.14
cobalt 91.8
cobbler
  shoemaker 5.38
  mender 396.10
cobblestone
  n pavement 383.6
  v floor 295.22
cobelligerent 232.1
cobweb filament 271.1
  lightness 298.2
  snare 356.13
coccus 85.42
co-chairman 574.5
cochlear 281.8
cock
  n male animal 76.8
  valve 239.10
  stopper 293.4
  poultry 311.29
  weather vane 318.17
  pile 770.10
  v regress 163.5
  prime 405.9
  shoot 904.12
cock-a-doodle-doo 60.5
cockamamie 923.11
cock-and-bull story 354.11
cockatrice
  traitor 357.10
  heraldry 647.2
cockeyed
  cross-eyed 28.12
  drunk 88.33
  askew 204.14
  distorted 265.10
  unbalanced 791.5
  disorderly 810.13
  foolish 923.9
  dazed 985.14
cockle
  n wrinkle 291.3
  marine animal 311.30
  v wrinkle 291.6

cockles of the heart
  heart 93.3
  inner nature 767.5
Cockney 523.7
cockpit 463.1
cockroach 311.37
cocksure 970.21
cocktail 88.9
cocktail hour 315.2
cocktail lounge 88.20
cocky conceited 140.11
  impudent 142.10
  defiant 454.7
cocoa 40.3
coconspirator
  schemer 381.7
  accomplice 616.3
cocoon 302.12
coction 1020.2
coda adjunct 254.1
  added to writing 254.2
  passage 708.24
  sequel 817.1
  end 820.1
coddle cook 11.5
  indulge 427.6
  foster 449.16
  caress 562.16
code
  n cryptography
    345.6
  telegraph 347.2
  precept 419.2
  Greek 522.7
  ethics 636.1
  digest 673.5
  table 808.4
  rule 869.4
  v encode 345.10
code of honor 641.2
codependency 777.3
code word
  cryptography 345.6
  implication 519.2
  catchword 526.9
codex
  manuscript 547.11
  rare book 554.6
codicil
  added to writing 254.2
  bequest 478.10
  sequel 817.1
codification 673.6
codify digest 673.10
  organize 808.10
  classify 809.6
  normalize 869.6
co-ed 572.5
coeducational 568.18
coequal
  n equal 790.4
  v reciprocate 777.7
  adj symmetric 264.4
  reciprocal 777.10
  coinciding 778.8
  equivalent 790.8
coerce
  use violence 424.7
  domineer 612.16
coercion 424.3
coercive 424.12

coeternal
  perpetual 829.7
  simultaneous 836.5
coeval
  n contemporary 836.2
  adj innate 767.8
  simultaneous 836.5
coexistence
  foreign policy 609.5
  simultaneity 836.1
coexisting
  agreeing 788.9
  simultaneous 836.5
coextend parallel 203.4
  coincide 836.4
coextensive
  parallel 203.6
  coinciding 778.8
coffee 40.3
coffee break meal 8.7
  respite 20.2
  interim 826.1
coffee shop 8.17
coffer
  n treasury 729.13
  v store 386.10
coffin
  n casket 309.11
  v confine 212.6
  inter 309.19
cofounder 892.7
cog
  n inferior 250.2
  projection 285.4
  v cheat 356.18
cogent powerful 18.12
  relevant 775.11
  sagacious 920.16
  logical 935.20
  valid 973.14
  good 999.12
cogitate
  ruminate 931.8
  think about 931.11
cognate
  n root 526.2
  kinfolk 559.2
  lineage 560.4
  likeness 784.3
  adj related 559.6
  lineal 560.18
  kindred 775.10
  akin 784.13
cognition 928.2
cognitive 931.21
cognizance
  thanks 150.2
  due 639.2
  cognition 928.2
cognizant
  sensible 24.11
  knowing 928.15
cognomen name 527.3
  surname 527.5
  nomenclature 527.6
  nickname 527.7
cognoscente
  connoisseur 496.7
  critic 946.7
cogwheel 1040.9
cohabit copulate 75.21

inhabit 225.7
live together 563.17
cohabitation 769.2
cohere agree 788.6
join 800.11
adhere 803.6
coherent clear 521.11
agreeing 788.9
clinging 803.10
indivisible 1045.13
cohesion adhesion 803.1
sticking 803.1
indivisibility 1045.2
cohesive
cohering 803.10
indivisible 1045.13
tough 1049.4
cohort hanger-on 138.6
military unit 461.22
henchman 610.8
associate 616.1
accomplice 616.3
attendance 769.6
company 770.3
coif
n hairdo 3.15
v cut the hair 3.22
cloak 5.40
top 295.21
coiffure
n hairdo 3.15
v cut the hair 3.22
coil
n braid 3.7
a length 267.2
whorl 281.2
v curl 281.5
coin
n angle 278.2
money 728.2
specie 728.4
v mint 728.28
innovate 841.5
change 852.9
originate 892.12
imagine 986.14
coinage
neologism 526.8
money 728.1
coining 728.24
innovation 852.4
production 892.1
result 893.1
coin a phrase 974.5
coincide assent 332.9
correspond 778.4
agree 788.6
co-occur 836.4
concur 899.2
coincidence
accompaniment 769.1
sameness 778.1
agreement 788.1
simultaneity 836.1
concurrence 899.1
coincidental 778.8
coital 75.25
coitus 75.7
coke cocaine 87.7
combustion product
1020.16

col ridge 237.5
valley 237.7
colander refinery 79.13
porousness 292.8
arranger 808.5
cold
n low temperature 1023.1
chilliness 1023.1
adj unconscious 25.8
chromatic 35.16
unsexual 75.29
unfeeling 94.9
indifferent 102.6
dull 117.6
insolent 142.9
heartless 144.25
stone-dead 307.31
reticent 344.10
aloof 583.6
unfriendly 589.9
speculative 759.27
freezing 1023.14
chilly 1023.16
cold blood 94.1
cold-blooded
unfeeling 94.9
heartless 144.25
hypothermic 1023.20
cold comfort 108.1
cold cream
cleanser 79.17
makeup 1016.12
ointment 1056.3
cold feet 491.4
coldhearted
unfeeling 94.9
heartless 144.25
cold shoulder
n aloofness 583.2
repulse 908.2
banishment 909.4
v snub 157.5
slight 340.8
cold sore allergy 85.34
sore 85.37
cold spell 1023.3
cold storage
storage 386.5
discontinuance 390.2
frozen-food locker 1024.6
cold sweat sweat 12.7
hostility 99.2
trepidation 127.5
nervousness 128.2
cold turkey 87.1
cold water 379.2
colic ache 26.5
symptom 85.9
colicky aching 26.12
anemic 85.61
coliseum 463.1
collaborate
be willing 324.3
cooperate 450.3
write 547.21
act the traitor 645.15
co-author 718.6
concur 899.2
collaboration 805.1
collaborator
subversive 357.11

apostate 363.5
author 547.15
cooperator 616.4
author 718.4
collage 712.11
collapse
n weakness 16.1
exhaustion 21.2
breakdown 85.8
descent 194.1
decline 252.2
prostration 260.4
impairment 393.1
debacle 395.4
crash 410.3
defeat 412.1
insolvency 625.3
v weaken 16.9
burn out 21.5
take sick 85.47
descend 194.5
cave 260.10
break down 393.24
fail 410.12
go bankrupt 625.7
fall short 911.2
fall through 911.3
collapsible 260.11
collar
n circle 280.3
foam 320.2
shackle 428.4
arrest 429.6
insignia 647.1
golf 751.1
v arrest 429.16
acquire 472.9
capture 480.18
collate classify 808.11
scrutinize comparatively
943.5
verify 970.12
collateral
n security 438.3
kinfolk 559.2
nonessential 768.2
adj parallel 203.6
additional 253.10
related 559.6
unessential 768.4
accompanying 769.9
related 775.9
eventual 831.11
simultaneous 836.5
collation
light meal 8.7
arrangement 808.1
comparative scrutiny 943.2
ensuring 970.8
colleague
companion 588.3
associate 616.1
equal 790.4
collect
n prayer 696.4
v store up 386.11
gather 472.11
come together 770.16
assemble 770.18
put together 800.5
conclude 946.10

collected
composed 106.13
stored 386.14
assembled 770.21
joined 800.13
collection
store 386.1
gathering 472.2
donation 478.6
edition 554.5
compilation 554.7
excerpts 557.4
oblation 696.7
book of verse 720.5
assemblage 770.1
collector's items 770.11
collective
cooperative 450.5
communal 476.9
concurrent 899.4
collective bargaining
unionism 727.1
labor union 727.2
negotiation 731.3
collective unconscious
842.2
collectivism
cooperation 450.1
communion 476.2
socialism 611.6
government 612.8
collectivize
communize 476.7
attach 480.20
collect oneself 106.7
collector desirer 100.12
enthusiast 101.4
connoisseur 496.7
governor 575.13
gatherer 770.15
collector's items 770.11
colleen 302.6
college university 567.5
association 617.1
collegiality
affiliation 450.2
communion 476.2
social life 582.4
collegiate
n college student 572.5
adj scholastic 567.13
studentlike 572.12
collide clash 35.15
sail into 182.41
disagree 456.8
contend 457.13
argue 789.5
counteract 900.6
come into collision 902.13
collier 1058.9
collimation
orientation 161.4
parallelism 203.1
collision
crash 184.20
opposition 451.2
hostility 589.3
contrariety 779.1
counteraction 900.1
impact 902.3
misfortune 1011.2

understanding 928.3
v rule 249.11
rise above 272.11
will 323.2
order 420.8
possess 469.4
direct 573.8
govern 612.12
know well 928.13
command performance 704.12
commandant
jailer 429.10
governor 575.6
commissioned officer 575.18
commandeer
attach 480.20
enlist 615.17
commander ship's officer
183.7
superior 249.4
governor 575.6
commissioned officer 575.18
naval officer 575.20
commanding
authoritative 417.15
imperious 420.13
directing 573.12
governing 612.18
commandment
rule 419.2
command 420.1
commandos 461.15
command post 208.6
commemoration
celebration 487.1
anniversary 850.4
memento 989.7
commemorative
celebrative 487.3
memorial 989.27
commence 818.7
commencement
ceremony 580.4
beginning 818.1
source 886.5
commend
commit 478.16
speak highly of 509.11
commendable
praiseworthy 509.20
good 999.12
commensal eating 8.31
cooperative 450.5
commensurable
approximate 775.8
comparative 943.8
commensurate
satisfactory 107.11
agreeing 788.9
equal 790.7
comparative 943.8
sufficient 991.6
comment
n word of explanation 341.5
commentary 556.2
criticism 946.2
v remark 524.24
commentary
added to writing 254.2
comment 341.5
treatise 556.2

review 723.2
commentator
interpreter 341.7
reviewer 556.4
critic 946.7
broadcaster 1034.23
commerce
copulation 75.7
communication 343.1
social life 582.4
occupation 724.1
trade 731.1
business 731.1
commercial
n advertisement 352.6
radiobroadcast 1034.18
announcement 1034.20
adj occupied 724.15
business 730.12
trade 731.22
salable 734.14
commercialism 731.13
commercialize
profit 472.12
put on a business footing
731.20
commingle 797.10
comminute
v pulverize 1051.9
adj powdery 1051.11
commiserate pity 145.3
condole with 147.2
commissar
tyrant 575.14
public official 575.17
delegate 576.2
commissary
provisions 10.5
provider 385.6
store 386.1
delegate 576.2
commission
n performance 328.2
precept 419.1
injunction 420.2
portion 477.5
deputy 576.13
legislature 613.1
delegation 615.1
assignment 615.1
dividend 624.7
task 724.2
assembly 770.2
v repair 396.14
command 420.8
represent 576.14
authorize 615.10
delegate 862.7
commissioner
public official 575.17
delegate 576.2
policeman 1008.15
commit do 328.6
confine 429.17
engage 436.5
agree 436.5
contract 437.5
dedicate 477.11
consign 478.16
commission 615.10
obligate 641.12

commitment
zeal 101.2
resolution 359.1
undertaking 404.1
committal 429.4
obligation 436.2
dedication 477.4
consignment 478.2
devotion 587.7
commission 615.1
duty 641.1
unselfishness 652.1
cause 886.9
commit oneself
be determined 359.8
undertake 404.3
take the responsibility 641.9
seize the opportunity 843.7
commit suicide 308.22
committed
zealous 101.9
resolute 359.11
promised 436.8
devoted 587.21
obliged 641.16
unselfish 652.5
committee
subcommittee 423.2
delegation 576.13
assembly 770.2
commixture
mixture 797.1
compound 797.5
commodious
comfortable 121.11
spacious 158.11
useful 387.18
commodity 735.2
commodity market 737.1
commodore 575.20
common
n green 310.7
estate 471.4
park 743.14
the normal 869.3
adj trite 117.9
medium 246.3
inferior 250.6
public 312.16
cooperative 450.5
communal 476.9
commonplace 497.14
simple 499.6
vernacular 523.20
plain-speaking 535.3
populational 606.8
prosaic 721.5
mutual 777.11
frequent 847.4
prevalent 864.12
usual 869.9
well-known 928.27
paltry 998.21
ordinary 1005.8
inferior 1005.9
common denominator 777.1
commoner
student 572.7
common man 606.5
common good 999.4
common ground 777.1

common knowledge
n publicity 352.4
information 551.1
maxim 974.1
adj published 352.17
common-law wife 563.8
common man
commoner 606.5
average 864.3
a nobody 998.7
commonplace
n generalization 864.8
platitude 974.3
adj dull 117.9
common 497.14
simple 499.6
plain-speaking 535.3
populational 606.8
prosaic 721.5
trite 864.16
usual 869.9
well-known 928.27
ordinary 1005.8
common practice 373.4
commons
nutriment 10.3
rations 10.6
dining room 197.11
the people 606.1
park 743.14
common sense
sensibleness 920.6
reasonableness 935.9
common touch 581.1
commonweal
welfare 143.5
country 232.1
commonwealth
population 227.1
country 232.1
government 612.4
community 617.2
commotion
noise 53.3
excitement 105.4
bustle 330.4
turbulence 671.2
hubbub 810.4
agitation 917.1
communal
public 312.16
cooperative 450.5
common 476.9
associational 617.17
mutual 777.11
commune region 231.5
participation 476.1
community 617.2
commune with
communicate 343.6
converse 541.9
communicable
poisonous 82.7
contagious 85.62
transferable 176.18
impartable 343.11
giveable 478.23
communicant
informant 551.5
believer 692.4
worshiper 696.9

layman 700.2
communicate
transfer 176.10
be in touch 343.6
impart 343.7
give 478.12
say 524.22
converse 541.9
inform 551.8
celebrate 701.15
join 800.11
communication
n transferal 176.1
intercourse 343.1
communion 343.1
passageway 383.3
giving 478.1
speech 524.1
conversation 541.1
information 551.1
message 552.4
letter 553.2
social life 582.4
joining 800.1
adj telephonic 347.21
communications
n electronic communications
343.5
signaling 347.1
the press 555.3
radio 1034.1
adj telephonic 347.21
communicative
v talkative 540.9
adj talkative 343.10
conversational 541.13
informative 551.18
sociable 582.22
communion
communication 343.1
accord 455.1
community 476.2
conversation 541.1
social life 582.4
school 617.5
sect 675.3
prayer 696.4
correlation 777.1
communiqué
announcement 352.2
information 551.1
message 552.4
communism
cooperation 450.1
communion 476.2
Bolshevism 611.5
participation 612.4
government 612.8
Communist
n Bolshevist 611.13
revolutionist 860.3
adj cooperative 450.5
communistic 611.21
Marxist 860.6
community
population 227.1
humankind 312.1
cooperation 450.1
accord 455.1
communion 476.2
social life 582.4

the people 606.1
society 617.2
sect 675.3
company 769.2
correlation 777.1
similarity 784.1
community center 230.5
community chest 478.9
communize
communalize 476.7
attach 480.20
politicize 611.16
commutation
travel 177.1
compensation 338.1
substitution 862.1
interchange 863.1
commute travel 177.18
substitute 862.4
interchange 863.4
commuter
traveler 178.1
worker 726.2
compact
n contract 437
pact 437.1
understanding 788.2
makeup 1016.12
v contract 260.7
squeeze 437.5
densify 1045.9
adj miniature 258.12
contracted 260.12
short 268.8
close 293.12
concise 537.6
crowded 770.22
joint 800.12
dense 1045.12
compacted
contracted 260.12
crowded 437.11
cohesive 803.10
dense 1045.12
compaction petrification
1059.8
conglomeration 803.5
companion
n lover 104.12
stairs 193.3
image 349.5
maid 577.8
fellow 588.3
knight 608.5
associate 616.1
accompanier 769.4
escort 769.5
likeness 784.3
v accompany 769.7
companionable 582.22
companionship
association 582.6
fellowship 587.2
company 769.2
company
military unit 461.22
association 582.6
guest 585.6
companion 588.3
team 617.7
firm 617.9

cast 707.11
workplace 739.1
association 769.2
actors 770.3
company headquarters 739.7
comparable
approximate 775.8
analogous 784.11
comparative 943.8
comparative 943.8
compare
n comparison 943.1
v assemble 770.18
liken 943.4
be comparable 943.7
comparison
assemblage 770.1
similarity 784.1
substitute 862.2
examining side by side
943.1
compare 943.1
estimate 946.3
compartment 197.2
compartmentalize 802.18
compass
n range 158.2
environment 209.1
bounds 211.1
boundary 211.3
degree 245.1
distance 261.1
magnetic compass 574.9
scale 709.6
v surround 209.6
enclose 212.5
accomplish 407.4
succeed with 409.11
circle 914.5
compassion
sensitivity 24.3
kindness 143.1
pity 145.1
leniency 427.1
tolerance 979.4
compatible
pleasant 97.6
in accord 455.3
sociable 582.22
related 775.9
agreeing 788.9
compatriot
fellow citizen 227.5
associate 616.1
compeer
companion 588.3
associate 616.1
equal 790.4
compel
motivate 375.12
force 424.4
domineer 612.16
impel 902.11
obsess 926.25
necessitate 963.8
compelling
motivating 375.25
commanding 420.13
compulsory 424.10
obsessive 926.34
urgent 997.22

compendious
short 268.8
concise 537.6
abridged 557.6
comprehensive 772.7
compendium 557.1
compensate
symmetrize 264.3
make compensation 338.4
remedy 396.13
make restitution 481.5
requite 506.5
pay 624.10
atone 658.4
equalize 790.6
interchange 863.4
compensation
defense mechanism 92.23
symmetrization 264.2
repayment 338.1
recompense 338.1
reparation 396.6
reimbursement 481.2
reprisal 506.2
penalty 603.1
damages 624.3
pay 624.4
atonement 658.1
compete
contend 457.18
play 744.2
competence
power 18.1
ability 18.2
preparedness 405.4
skill 413.1
authority 417.1
competent able 18.14
fitted 405.17
capable 413.24
authoritative 417.15
legal 673.11
sufficient 991.6
competitive
oppositional 451.8
competitory 457.23
competitor
contestant 452.2
combatant 461.1
athlete 743.19
compilation
omnibus 554.7
code 673.5
collection 770.11
compile codify 673.10
assemble 770.18
compiler 1042.13
complacent
bovine 107.10
vain 140.8
complain
dissatisfy 108.5
groan 115.15
object 333.5
offer resistance 453.3
accuse 599.7
complainer
malcontent 108.3
lamenter 115.8
faultfinder 510.9
complaint disease 85.1

grievance 115.4
objection 333.2
resistance 453.1
disapproval 510.1
arraignment 598.3
declaration 598.7
accusation 599.1
complaisant
pleasant 97.6
considerate 143.16
indulgent 427.8
submissive 433.12
courteous 504.14
conformable 867.5
soft 1047.8
complement
n hand 183.6
adjunct 254.1
syntax 530.2
team 617.7
company 770.3
likeness 784.3
all 792.3
full measure 794.3
v reciprocate 777.7
complementary
reciprocal 777.10
completing 794.13
complete
v perform 328.9
perfect 407.6
execute 437.9
include 772.3
bring to fruition 794.6
end 820.7
elaborate 861.6
develop 1002.5
adj downright 247.12
perfect 407.12
comprehensive 772.7
undivided 792.11
whole 794.9
ended 820.8
unqualified 960.2
sound 1002.7
completely 766.13
completion
performance 328.2
completing 407.2
execution 437.4
fulfillment 794.4
complex
n inferiority complex
  92.22
culture 373.2
whole 792.1
perplex 799.2
obsession 926.13
adj hard to understand
  522.14
mixed 797.14
complicated 799.4
difficult 1013.17
complexion
n looks 33.4
color 35.1
personality 92.11
mode 765.4
nature 767.4
disposition 978.3
v color 35.14

complexity
convolution 281.1
abstruseness 522.2
complication 799.1
difficulty 1013.1
compliance
resignation 134.2
willingness 324.1
obedience 326.1
assent 332.1
complaisance 427.2
submission 433.1
observance 434.1
consent 441.1
conformity 867.1
complicate
intensify 251.5
add 253.4
make unintelligible 522.12
involve 799.3
complication
disease 85.1
abstruseness 522.2
plot 722.4
complexity 799.1
difficulty 1013.1
predicament 1013.4
complicity
intrigue 381.5
cooperation 450.1
participation 476.1
guilt 656.1
compliment
n congratulation 149.1
regards 504.8
polite commendation
  509.6
flattery 511.1
v congratulate 149.2
pay a compliment 509.14
flatter 511.5
complimentary
congratulatory 149.3
approbatory 509.16
flattering 511.8
gratuitous 634.5
comply obey 326.2
assent 332.8
submit 433.6
acquiesce 441.3
conform 867.3
component
n part 793.1
constituent 796.2
matter 1052.2
adj constituent 796.5
components
contents 196.1
substance 763.2
comportment 321.1
compose
make up 405.7
arrange 437.8
reconcile 465.8
settle 466.7
compromise 468.2
pen 547.21
set 548.16
calm 670.7
write 708.46
author 718.6

constitute 796.3
mix 797.10
dispose 808.9
conform 867.3
produce 892.8
composed
collected 106.13
content 107.7
unastonished 123.3
arranged 808.14
composer
songwriter 547.15
scorer 710.20
author 718.4
composite
n compound 797.5
adj mixed 797.14
unitary 872.10
plural 883.7
composition
contents 196.1
form 262.1
structure 266.1
concoction 405.3
compromise 468.1
diction 532.1
written piece 547.2
writing 547.10
typesetting 548.2
atonement 658.1
piece 708.5
treatment 712.9
work of art 712.10
authorship 718.2
nature 767.4
construction 796.1
constitution 796.1
mixture 797.1
compound 797.5
combination 805.1
production 892.2
product 893.1
compositor 554.2
compost 890.4
compost heap 391.7
composure
countenance 106.2
contentment 107.1
unastonishment 123.1
quiescence 173.1
self-control 359.5
compound
n word form 526.4
composition 796.1
mixture 797.5
combination 805.2
alloy 1058.4
v make up 405.7
compromise 468.2
mix 797.10
combine 805.3
produce 892.8
adj mixed 797.14
comprehend
understand 521.7
include 772.3
know 928.12
comprehension
inclusion 772.1
intelligence 920.1
understanding 928.3

comprehensive
great 247.6
voluminous 257.17
broad 269.6
sweeping 772.7
whole 792.9
thorough 794.10
joint 800.12
compress
n dressing 86.33
v reduce 252.7
contract 260.7
squeeze 260.8
shorten 268.6
densify 1045.9
compressed
contracted 260.12
shortened 268.9
concise 537.6
dense 1045.12
comprise
internalize 207.5
include 772.3
entail 772.4
total 792.8
put together 800.5
combine 805.3
compromise
n adjustment 465.4
middle course 467.3
mutual concession 468
composition 468.1
foreign policy 609.5
atonement 658.1
agreement 788.4
interchange 863.1
v reconcile 465.8
reach an agreement
  468.1
interchange 863.4
endanger 1006.6
compromise oneself 661.7
comptroller
superintendent 574.2
accountant 628.7
treasurer 729.12
compulsion power 18.1
urge 375.6
obligation 424.1
duty 424.1
impulse 902.1
obsession 926.13
necessity 963.1
compulsive
driving 424.10
overfastidious 495.12
conformist 867.6
obsessive 926.34
involuntary 963.14
compulsory
mandatory 420.12
driving 424.10
obligatory 424.11
necessary 963.12
compunction
qualm 113.2
demur 325.2
objection 333.2
computation
adding 253.3
measurement 300.1

calculation 1017.10
  automation 1041.7
compute
  add up 253.6
  measure 300.10
  calculate 1017.18
  computerize 1042.21
computer
  calculator 1017.15
  computer science 1041.17
  electronic data processor
    1042.2
computer engineer 1042.17
computer game program
    1042.12
  game 743.9
computerized
  automated 1041.22
  machine-usable 1042.22
computer language 523.12
computer-literate 1042.18
computer program 1042.11
computer scientist 1042.17
comrade
  companion 588.3
  associate 616.1
  member 617.11
comradeship
  affiliation 450.2
  camaraderie 582.2
  fellowship 587.2
con
  n prisoner 429.11
  cheating 759.13
  side 935.14
  v cheat 356.18
  persuade 375.23
  study 570.12
  memorize 989.17
  adj oppositional 451.8
  disapproving 510.21
  prep opposed to 451.10
con artist 357.4
concatenation
  association 92.33
  joining 800.1
  series 812.2
concave
  n cavity 284.2
  v hollow 284.13
  adj bowed 279.10
  concaved 284.16
concavity
  compartment 197.2
  crack 224.2
  curvature 279.1
  hollowness 284.1
  imprint 284.1
  cavity 284.2
  print 517.7
  depression 913.1
conceal
  keep secret 345.7
  hide 346.6
concealment
  invisibility 32.1
  secrecy 345.1
  hiding 346.1
  veil 346.1
  hiding place 346.4
  shelter 1009.3

concede
  acknowledge 332.11
  confess 351.7
  play 751.4
  allow for 959.5
conceit
  n pride 136.1
  conceitedness 140.4
  caprice 364.1
  witticism 489.7
  foppery 500.4
  boasting 502.1
  quirk 927.2
  thought 931.1
  idea 932.1
  opinion 953.6
  imagination 986.1
  v flatter 511.5
  imagine 986.14
conceited
  vain 136.9
  self-proud 140.11
  contemptuous 157.8
  foppish 500.17
  boastful 502.10
  dogmatic 970.22
conceivable
  knowable 928.25
  believable 953.24
  possible 966.6
  plausible 968.7
  imaginable 986.26
conceive
  get in the family way 78.11
  vivify 306.11
  understand 521.7
  phrase 532.4
  cause 886.10
  originate 892.12
  know 928.12
  think 931.8
  suppose 951.10
  believe 953.11
  imagine 986.14
concentrate
  n extract 192.8
  v converge 169.2
  extraction 192.16
  focus 208.10
  intensify 251.5
  contract 260.7
  narrow thoughts 931.10
  densify 1045.9
concentration
  convergence 169.1
  extract 192.7
  formula 192.8
  centralization 208.8
  intensification 251.2
  contraction 260.1
  industry 330.6
  firmness 359.2
  perseverance 360.1
  thoughtfulness 931.3
  attention 983.1
  engrossment 983.3
  densification 1045.3
concentration camp
  camp 228.29
  place of killing 308.12
  prison 429.8

concentric 208.14
concept
  idea 932.1
  opinion 953.6
  visualization 986.6
conception
  conceiving 78.4
  plan 381.1
  source 886.5
  production 892.1
  intellect 919.1
  intelligence 920.1
  understanding 928.3
  thought 931.1
  idea 932.1
  opinion 953.6
  creative thought 986.2
  visualization 986.6
conceptual
  mental 919.7
  intelligent 920.12
  cognitive 931.21
  ideational 932.9
  imaginative 986.18
conceptualize
  know 928.12
  think 931.8
  imagine 986.14
concern
  n sensitivity 24.3
  sympathy 93.5
  anxiety 126.1
  considerateness 143.3
  carefulness 339.1
  undertaking 404.1
  company 617.9
  occupation 724.1
  workplace 739.1
  relevance 775.4
  affair 831.3
  science 928.10
  topic 937.1
  interest 983.2
  importance 997.1
  v give anxiety 126.4
  relate to 775.5
  involve 898.2
  interest 983.12
  trouble 1013.13
concerning 775.13
concert
  n unanimity 332.5
  cooperation 450.1
  harmony 708.3
  performance 708.33
  agreement 788.1
  concurrence 899.1
  v plan 381.8
  cooperate 450.3
  adj instrumental 708.51
concerted
  cooperative 450.5
  concurrent 899.4
concert hall hall 197.4
  theater 704.14
concession
  acknowledgment 332.3
  confession 351.3
  grant 443.5
  compromise 468.1
  giving 478.1

discount 631.1
  merchant 730.2
  market 736.1
  qualification 959.1
concierge 1008.12
conciliate 465.7
conciliatory
  forgiving 148.6
  unbelligerent 464.10
  pacificatory 465.12
concise short 268.8
  taciturn 344.9
  brief 537.6
conclave council 423.1
  ecclesiastical council
    423.4
  conference 541.6
  political convention 609.8
  assembly 770.2
conclude resolve 359.7
  complete 407.6
  arrange 437.8
  end 820.5
  draw a conclusion 946.10
  suppose 951.10
conclusion
  affirmation 334.1
  completion 407.2
  signing 437.3
  sequel 817.1
  end 820.1
  reasonableness 935.8
  solution 940.1
  deduction 946.4
  opinion 953.6
conclusive
  completing 407.9
  mandatory 420.12
  final 820.11
  convincing 953.26
  evidential 957.16
  unqualified 960.2
  certain 970.13
concoct
  fabricate 354.18
  plot 381.9
  make up 405.7
  mix 797.10
  produce 892.8
  originate 892.12
  imagine 986.14
concoction
  fabrication 354.10
  decoction 405.3
  compound 797.5
  production 892.1
  product 893.1
concomitant
  n adjunct 254.1
  attendant 769.3
  contemporary 836.2
  adj accompanying 769.9
  simultaneous 836.5
  concurrent 899.4
concord
  n unanimity 332.5
  treaty 437.2
  cooperation 450.1
  accord 455.1
  harmony 708.3
  agreement 788.1

order 807.1
v cooperate 450.3
concordance
  unanimity 332.5
  cooperation 450.1
  accord 455.1
  reference book 554.9
  harmony 708.3
  agreement 788.1
  concurrence 899.1
concordant
  unanimous 332.15
  cooperative 450.5
  in accord 455.3
  pacific 464.9
  harmonious 708.49
  agreeing 788.9
  conformist 867.6
  concurrent 899.4
concourse
  convergence 169.1
  flow 238.4
  assemblage 770.1
  assembly 770.2
  joining 800.1
  concurrence 899.1
concrete
  n ground covering 199.3
  pavement 383.6
  conglomeration 803.5
  solid 1045.6
  hardness 1046.6
  building material
    1054.2
  v floor 295.22
  plaster 295.25
  thicken 1045.10
  solidify 1046.8
  adj substantial 763.6
  cohesive 803.10
  particular 865.12
  dense 1045.12
  hard 1046.10
concubine
  subject 432.7
  wife 563.8
  mistress 665.17
concupiscence
  sexual desire 75.5
  desire 100.1
  lasciviousness 665.5
concur accord 332.9
  cooperate 450.3
  agree 788.6
  coincide 836.4
  collaborate 899.2
  support 901.21
concurrence
  convergence 169.1
  parallelism 203.1
  assent 332.1
  unanimity 332.5
  cooperation 450.1
  accompaniment 769.1
  assemblage 770.1
  interaction 777.3
  joining 800.1
  simultaneity 836.1
  collaboration 899.1
  agreement 899.1
  support 901.1

concussion
  trauma 85.38
  shock 671.8
  impact 902.3
condemn
  destroy 395.10
  censure 510.13
  damn 602.3
  pass judgment 946.13
  work evil 1000.6
condemnation
  censure 510.3
  judgment 598.9
  conviction 602.1
  damnation 602.1
  verdict 946.5
condemnatory
  censorious 510.22
  accusing 599.13
  damnatory 602.5
condensation 1061.2
condense trickle 238.18
  intensify 251.5
  contract 260.7
  shorten 268.6
  be brief 537.5
  abridge 557.5
  densify 1045.9
  solidify 1046.8
condescend deign 137.8
  give oneself airs 141.8
  consent 441.2
condescending 141.9
condescension
  humility 137.3
  arrogance 141.1
condign right 637.3
  due 639.8
condiment
  cooking 11.1
  flavoring 63.3
condition
  n fitness 84.1
  disease 85.1
  rank 245.2
  preparedness 405.4
  stipulation 421.2
  state 765.1
  circumstance 766.1
  provision 959.2
  v limit 210.5
  accustom 373.9
  repair 396.14
  fit 405.8
  inculcate 568.12
  train 568.13
  qualify 959.3
  make conditional 959.4
conditional
  n mood 530.11
  adj modal 765.6
  circumstantial 766.7
  dialectic 935.22
  provisional 959.8
  undecided 971.18
conditioning
  n classical conditioning
    92.26
  habituation 373.7
  fitting 405.2
  inculcation 568.2

training 568.3
  involuntariness 963.5
  adj healthful 81.5
condolence
  comfort 121.4
  pity 145.1
  consolation 147
  reassurance 147.1
condom 86.23
condominium
  apartment house 228.14
  participation 476.1
condone accept 134.7
  overlook 148.4
  suffer 443.10
  keep an open mind 979.7
conducive
  adj modal 384.8
  helpful 449.21
  prep tending to 896.5
conduct
  n behavior 321.1
  performance 328.2
  direction 573.1
  operation 889.1
  v transport 176.12
  channel 239.15
  practice 328.8
  perform 328.9
  direct 573.8
  lead an orchestra 708.45
  escort 769.8
  operate 889.5
conduction
  transferal 176.1
  electric conduction 1032.14
conductor
  trainman 178.13
  director 574.1
  leader 574.6
  musician 710.17
  escort 769.5
  conduction 1032.14
conduit
  channel 239.1
  passageway 383.3
cone
  n loudspeaker 50.8
  conoid 282.5
  plant 310.27
  v round 282.6
confabulation
  deliberate falsehood 354.9
  talk 541.3
  conference 541.6
confection sweets 10.40
  concoction 405.3
  compound 797.5
confectionery 66.1
confederacy
  intrigue 381.5
  affiliation 450.2
  association 617.1
  combination 805.1
confederate
  n associate 616.1
  accomplice 616.3
  v cooperate 450.3
  accompany 769.7
  league 805.4
  adj leagued 805.6

confer advise 422.5
  give 478.12
  hold a conference 541.11
  transfer 629.3
conference
  audition 48.2
  council 423.1
  forum 423.3
  ecclesiastical council 423.4
  congress 541.6
  discussion 541.7
  diocese 698.8
  football 746.1
  assembly 770.2
confess
  acknowledge 332.11
  break down 351.7
  make confession 701.18
  attribute to 888.4
  state 953.12
confession assent 332.3
  disclosure 351.3
  school 617.5
  apology 658.2
  acknowledgment 888.2
  profession 953.7
confessor
  penitent 113.5
  priest 699.5
confetti 47.6
confidant
  adviser 422.3
  friend 588.1
  right-hand man 616.7
confide hope 124.7
  divulge 351.5
  commit 478.16
  tip off 551.11
confide in
  believe in 953.15
  trust 953.17
confidence
  equanimity 106.3
  hope 124.1
  expectation 130.1
  secret 345.5
  fearlessness 492.3
  belief 953.1
  confidentness 970.5
confident
  composed 106.13
  hopeful 124.11
  expectant 130.11
  unafraid 492.20
  belief 953.21
  sure 970.21
confidential 345.14
configuration
  aspect 33.3
  gestalt 92.32
  environment 209.1
  outline 211.2
  form 262.1
  forming 262.5
  structure 266.1
  order 807.1
  arrangement 808.1
  characteristic 865.4
  constellation 1072.5
confine
  n boundary 211.3

enclosed place 212.3
v limit 210.5
immure 212.6
narrow 270.11
restrict 428.9
shut in 429.12
simplify 798.4
delay 846.8
specialize 866.4
confinement
birth 1.1
limitation 210.2
enclosure 212.1
narrowness 270.1
restriction 428.3
imprisonment 429.3
locking up 429.1
punishment 604.2
confirm
strengthen 15.13
ratify 332.12
accustom 373.9
secure 438.9
minister 701.16
stabilize 855.8
experiment 942.8
collate 943.5
affirm 957.11
verify 970.12
confirmation
ratification 332.4
seven sacraments 701.4
baptism 701.6
fixity 855.2
examination 938.3
collation 943.2
substantiation 957.4
ensuring 970.8
confirmed
accepted 332.14
inveterate 373.18
established 855.13
tried 942.12
proved 957.20
true 973.13
confiscate
demand 421.5
attach 480.20
conflagration 1019.13
conflict
n psychological stress 92.17
hostility 451.2
disaccord 456.1
contention 457.1
fight 457.4
enmity 589.3
contrariety 779.1
disagreement 789.1
counteraction 900.1
v clash 35.15
hit a sour note 61.3
disaccord 456.8
go contrary to 779.4
disagree 789.5
counteract 900.6
confluence
convergence 169.1
flow 238.4
assemblage 770.1
joining 800.1
concurrence 899.1

conform obey 326.2
observe the proprieties 579.4
agree 788.6
comply 867.3
conformation
form 262.1
forming 262.5
structure 266.1
agreement 788.1
conformity 867.1
conformist
n imitator 336.4
conventionalist 579.3
conformer 867.2
adj customary 373.13
conventional 867.6
conformity
symmetry 264.1
obedience 326.1
custom 373.1
observance 434.1
social convention 579.1
piety 692.1
similarity 784.1
agreement 788.1
compliance 867.1
conformance 867.1
confound chagrin 96.15
astonish 122.6
dismay 127.19
corrupt 393.12
destroy 395.10
overwhelm 412.8
curse 513.5
complicate 799.3
disarrange 811.3
confuse 945.3
refute 958.5
perplex 971.13
thwart 1012.15
confrere
companion 588.3
associate 616.1
confront
approach 167.3
contrapose 215.4
front 216.8
meet 223.11
affront 451.5
offer resistance 453.3
defy 454.3
brave 492.11
be imminent 840.2
compare 943.4
thwart 1012.15
confrontation
contraposition 215.1
meeting 223.4
conference 541.6
contrariety 779.1
comparison 943.1
Confucius
Buddha 684.4
Solomon 921.2
confuse chagrin 96.15
deform 263.3
complicate 799.3
disorder 810.9
muddle 811.3
confound 945.3
make uncertain 971.15

mistake 975.13
throw into chaos 985.7
confused
inconspicuous 32.6
clashing 61.5
distressed 96.22
shy 139.12
formless 263.4
complex 799.4
incoherent 804.4
chaotic 810.16
disarranged 811.5
vague 971.19
bewildered 971.24
mixed-up 985.12
confusion chagrin 96.4
shyness 139.4
formlessness 263.1
discomfiture 412.2
anarchy 418.2
noncohesion 804.1
chaos 810.2
bewilderment 971.3
distractedness 985.1
fluster 985.3
confute
counteract 900.6
rebut 939.5
refute 958.5
con game 356.10
congeal cohere 803.6
freeze 1024.11
thicken 1045.10
congenial pleasant 97.6
in accord 455.3
sociable 582.22
friendly 587.15
related 775.9
agreeing 788.9
congenital innate 767.8
thorough 794.10
congested
diseased 85.60
stopped 293.11
full 794.11
late 846.16
stuck 855.16
overfull 993.20
dense 1045.12
congestion
obstruction 293.3
fullness 794.2
overfullness 993.3
density 1045.1
conglomerate
n accumulation 770.9
miscellany 770.13
cohesive object 803.5
solid 1045.6
rock 1059.1
v assemble 770.18
mix 797.10
cohere 803.6
adj assembled 770.21
mixed 797.14
conglomeration
accumulation 770.9
miscellany 770.13
hodgepodge 797.6
joining 800.1
cohesion 803.1

conglomerate 803.5
combination 805.1
solid 1045.6
congratulate
gratulate 149.2
compliment 509.14
congratulations
n appplause 149.1
interj take a bow! 149.4
bravo! 509.22
congregate
v come together 770.16
adj assembled 770.21
congregation
audience 48.6
ecclesiastical council 423.4
worshiper 696.9
the laity 700.1
assemblage 770.1
assembly 770.2
congress
copulation 75.7
convergence 169.1
communication 343.1
council 423.1
conference 541.6
social life 582.4
legislature 613.1
assembly 770.2
congressional 613.11
congressman 610.3
congruent
in accord 455.3
coinciding 778.8
agreeing 788.9
congruity
symmetry 264.1
agreement 788.1
conformity 867.1
congruous
in accord 455.3
agreeing 788.9
expedient 995.5
conic 282.12
conjectural
theoretical 951.13
doubtful 971.17
conjecture
n supposition 951.3
guess 951.4
v guess 951.11
conjoined added 253.9
environmental 766.8
related 775.9
joined 800.13
conjoint
communal 476.9
accompanying 769.9
related 775.9
mutual 777.11
joint 800.12
combined 805.5
concurrent 899.4
conjugal loving 104.27
matrimonial 563.18
conjugate
n word form 526.4
v grammaticize 530.16
put together 800.5
double 873.5
adj lexical 526.19

related 775.9
joint 800.12
combined 805.5
coupled 873.8
conjugation
fertilization 78.3
juxtaposition 223.3
morphology 526.3
joining 800.1
combination 805.1
doubleness 873.1
conjunction
juxtaposition 223.3
part of speech 530.3
joining 800.1
combination 805.1
concurrence 899.1
conjure deceive 356.14
summon 420.11
entreat 440.11
make up 690.11
conjurer
trickster 357.2
sorcerer 690.5
entertainer 707.1
conjure up
summon 420.11
make appear 690.11
visualize 986.15
remember 989.10
conk out weaken 16.9
stall 184.45
die 307.20
be impaired 393.26
perish 395.23
fail 410.16
con man cheater 357.4
thief 483.1
connate innate 767.8
kindred 775.10
akin 784.13
connect use 87.22
converge 169.2
adjoin 223.9
succeed 409.7
play 745.5
apply to 775.5
relate 775.6
put together 800.5
join 800.11
be consistent 803.7
combine 805.3
continue 812.4
connection
copulation 75.7
addict 87.21
intermediary 213.4
juxtaposition 223.3
communication 343.1
passageway 383.3
mediator 466.3
blood relationship
559.1
marriage 564.1
go-between 576.4
relation 775.1
relevance 775.4
joining 800.1
joint 800.4
consistency 803.2
series 812.2

connections
kinfolk 559.2
favor 894.2
conniption 152.8
connivance
chicanery 356.4
intrigue 381.5
consent 441.1
sufferance 443.2
connive plot 381.9
concur 899.2
connive at
condone 148.4
consent 441.2
suffer 443.10
be inattentive 984.2
conniving
scheming 381.13
cooperative 450.5
connoisseur
expert 413.11
judge 496.7
collector 770.15
specialist 866.3
critic 946.7
connoisseurship
aesthetic taste 496.5
discrimination 944.1
connotation
meaning 518.1
implication 519.2
connote signify 517.17
mean 518.8
imply 519.4
evidence 957.8
connubial 563.18
conquer
vanquish 412.10
subdue 432.9
appropriate 480.19
conqueror 411.2
conquistador 461.5
consanguinity
blood relationship 559.1
lineage 560.4
kinship 775.3
conscience
n psyche 92.28
grace 636.5
v confess 351.7
conscience-stricken 113.8
conscientious
meticulous 339.12
observant 434.4
fastidious 495.9
dutiful 641.13
proper 644.15
conscientious objector pacifist
464.6
dissenter 333.3
conscious awake 23.8
sensible 24.11
shy 139.12
living 306.13
intentional 380.8
knowing 928.15
attentive 983.15
consciousness
wakefulness 23.1
sensation 24.1
wits 919.2

intelligence 920.9
cognizance 928.2
attention 983.1
consciousness-expanding
976.10
conscript
n recruit 461.18
v call to arms 458.19
enlist 615.17
conscription 458.9
consecrate
dedicate 477.11
sanctify 685.5
ordain 698.12
consecration
authority 417.12
dedication 477.4
unselfishness 652.1
sanctification 685.3
holy orders 698.10
consecutive
following 166.5
consistent 803.11
successive 812.9
subsequent 835.4
consensus
n unanimity 332.5
cooperation 450.1
agreement 788.3
adj cooperative 450.5
consent
n willingness 324.1
obedience 326.1
assent 332.1
unanimity 332.5
submission 433.1
approval 441.1
authorization 441.1
permission 443.1
v be willing 324.3
assent 332.8
submit 433.6
approve 441.2
permit 443.9
consequence
glory 247.2
prestige 417.4
meaning 518.1
distinction 662.5
sequel 817.1
event 831.1
subsequence 835.2
effect 887.1
influence 894.1
conclusion 946.4
importance 997.1
consequential
vain 140.8
great 247.6
authoritative 417.15
prominent 662.17
resultant 887.6
influential 894.13
important 997.17
consequently
accordingly 766.11
as a result 887.7
hence 888.7
conservation
storage 386.5
preservation 397.1

maintenance 853.2
conservationist
n preserver 397.5
conservative 853.4
forester 1069.7
environmentalist
1073.3
adj preservative 397.12
conservative
n right side 219.1
political party 611.9
moderate 670.4
back number 842.8
conservatist 853.4
adj right 219.4
preservative 397.12
right-wing 611.17
unexcessive 670.12
permanence 853.8
conservatory
n summerhouse 228.12
storehouse 386.6
nursery 1069.11
adj preservative 397.12
conserve
n sweets 10.40
v reserve 386.12
preserve 397.8
care for 1008.19
consider
be considerate 143.10
care 339.6
discuss 541.12
contemplate 931.12
think of 931.16
judge 946.8
suppose 951.10
believe 953.11
allow for 959.5
considerable
n lot 247.4
adj great 247.6
large 257.16
authoritative 417.15
numerous 884.6
important 997.17
adv greatly 247.15
considerate
sensitive 24.12
thoughtful 143.16
careful 339.10
courteous 504.14
judicious 920.19
consideration
thoughtfulness 143.3
respect 155.1
offset 338.2
carefulness 339.1
motive 375.1
gratuity 478.5
courtesy 504.1
discussion 541.7
recompense 624.3
esteem 662.3
judiciousness 920.7
contemplation 931.2
argument 935.5
verdict 946.5
opinion 953.6
attention 983.1
importance 997.1

considered
intentional 380.8
reasoned 935.21
considering
adv all things considered 946.17
prep because of 888.9
consign transfer 176.10
send 176.15
commit 429.17
give 478.16
commission 615.10
transfer 629.3
consignment
freight 176.6
confinement 429.4
commitment 478.2
commission 615.1
transfer 629.1
consistency
symmetry 264.1
clearness 521.2
uniformity 781.1
agreement 788.1
connection 803.2
tenacity 803.3
conformity 867.1
density 1045.1
consistent
clear 521.11
faithful 644.20
uniform 781.5
agreeing 788.9
connected 803.11
valid 973.14
consist of 796.3
consolation
solace 121.4
condolence 147.1
function of Holy Ghost 677.15
console
n keyboard 711.17
radio 1034.3
control room 1034.7
panel 1041.16
v comfort 121.6
condole with 147.2
consolidate
intensify 251.5
contract 260.7
cooperate 450.3
combine 805.3
densify 1045.9
consolidation
intensification 251.2
contraction 260.1
affiliation 450.2
cohesion 803.1
combination 805.1
densification 1045.3
consonance
harmony 708.3
rhyme 720.8
uniformity 781.1
agreement 788.1
consonant
n speech sound 524.12
adj phonetic 524.30
harmonious 708.49
uniform 781.5

agreeing 788.9
consort spouse 563.6
companion 588.3
associate 616.1
harmony 708.3
accompanier 769.4
agreement 788.1
consortium
compact 437.1
company 617.9
understanding 788.2
consort with
associate with 582.17
accompany 769.7
conspicuous
distinct 31.7
remarkable 247.10
noticeable 348.12
prominent 662.17
notable 997.19
conspiracy
chicanery 356.4
intrigue 381.5
stratagem 415.3
combination 805.1
concurrence 899.1
conspirator
traitor 357.10
schemer 381.7
conspire plot 381.9
cooperate 450.3
league 805.4
concur 899.2
constable 1008.15
constabulary
bureau 594.4
police 1008.17
constant
deep-dyed 35.18
firm 359.12
persevering 360.8
habitual 373.14
observant 434.4
devoted 587.21
faithful 644.20
uniform 781.5
continuous 812.8
durable 827.10
perpetual 829.7
continual 847.5
regular 850.6
permanent 853.7
unchangeable 855.17
exact 973.17
constantly
faithfully 644.25
uniformly 781.8
perpetually 829.10
continually 847.7
regularly 850.9
constellation
celebrity 662.9
fate 964.2
configuration 1072.5
consternation 127.1
constipated 293.11
constipation
symptom 85.9
obstruction 293.3
constituency
population 227.1

means 384.2
electorate 609.22
membership 617.12
sphere of influence 894.4
support 901.1
constituent
n piece 793.1
part of writing 793.2
component 796.2
matter 1052.2
adj selective 371.23
essential 767.9
component 796.5
constitute
legislate 613.10
legalize 673.9
compose 796.3
establish 892.10
constitution
structure 266.1
legislation 613.5
written document 673.6
nature 767.4
composition 796.1
arrangement 808.1
establishment 892.4
disposition 978.3
constitutional
n exercise 84.2
walk 177.10
fitness 725.6
adj healthful 81.5
governmental 612.17
legal 673.11
innate 767.8
attitudinal 978.7
constitutional law 673.5
constrain compel 424.4
restrain 428.7
confine 429.12
moderate 670.6
necessitate 963.8
constraint
reserve 139.3
reticence 344.3
self-control 359.5
urge 375.6
compulsion 424.1
restraint 428.1
confinement 429.1
temperance 668.1
moderation 670.1
constrict
contract 260.7
narrow 270.11
close 293.6
obstruct 1012.12
constricted
contracted 260.12
narrow 270.14
closed 293.9
narrow-minded 980.10
construct
n structure 266.2
v build 266.5
compose 796.3
produce 892.8
construction
structure 266.1
frame 266.2
interpretation 341.1

explanation 518.3
word form 526.4
phrase 529.1
composition 796.1
production 892.2
constructive
interpretative 341.14
helpful 449.21
creative 892.16
construe
interpret 341.9
translate 341.12
consular 576.17
consulate house 228.5
mastership 417.7
office 739.7
consult 541.11
consultant
expert 413.11
adviser 422.3
consultation
advice 422.1
conference 541.6
consume devour 8.22
decrease 252.6
shrink 260.9
use 387.13
spend 388.3
impair 393.19
destroy 395.10
lose 473.5
waste 486.4
expend 626.5
disintegrate 806.3
burn up 1020.25
consumer
eater 8.16
user 387.9
buyer 733.5
consuming
n consumption 388.1
adj agonizing 98.23
destructive 395.26
engrossing 983.20
consummate
v top 198.9
accomplish 407.4
adj top 198.10
downright 247.12
complete 407.12
thorough 794.10
perfected 1002.9
consumption
eating 8.1
tuberculosis 85.17
decrement 252.3
shrinking 260.3
use 387.1
using up 388.1
consuming 388.1
impairment 393.4
destruction 395.1
waste 473.2
expenditure 626.1
contact
n touch 73.1
addict 87.21
nearness 223.5
communication 343.1
go-between 576.4
v be heard 48.12

come near 223.10
communicate with 343.8
contact sport 744.1
contagious
poisonous 82.7
infectious 85.62
transferable 176.18
communicable 343.11
contain
internalize 207.5
limit 210.5
enclose 212.5
close 293.6
restrain 428.7
include 772.3
entail 772.4
total 792.8
compose 796.3
fight fire 1022.7
container
receptacle 195.1
can 195.1
enclosed place 212.3
cavity 284.2
containment
surrounding 209.5
enclosure 212.1
foreign policy 609.5
contaminate
defile 80.17
infect 85.51
corrupt 393.12
blaspheme 694.5
adulterate 797.12
radioactivate 1037.10
contamination
defilement 80.4
unhealthfulness 82.1
infection 85.4
corruption 393.2
hybrid word 526.11
sacrilege 694.2
adulteration 797.3
radiation 1037.1
environmental destruction
1073.2
contemn disdain 157.3
reject 372.2
contemplate
scrutinize 27.14
expect 130.5
meditate 380.5
study 570.12
consider 931.12
think of 931.16
mull over 931.17
foresee 961.5
contemplation
scrutiny 27.6
expectation 130.1
quiescence 173.1
inaction 329.1
study 570.3
revelation 683.10
trance 691.3
prayer 696.4
consideration 931.2
foresight 961.1
engrossment 983.3
contemporary
n coeval 836.2

adj simultaneous 836.5
present 838.2
modern 841.13
contempt hate 103.1
insolence 142.1
indignity 156.2
disdain 157.1
disrespect 157.1
rejection 372.1
defiance 454.1
deprecation 510.2
disparagement 512.1
contemptible
offensive 98.18
base 661.12
paltry 998.21
terrible 1000.9
hateful 103.8
contemptuous
hating 103.7
arrogant 141.13
insolent 142.9
insulting 156.8
disdainful 157.8
rejective 372.4
defiant 454.7
condemnatory 510.22
disparaging 512.13
contend
contrapose 215.4
affirm 334.5
insist 421.8
contest 457.13
compete 457.18
struggle 725.11
argue 935.16
contender
competitor 452.2
combatant 461.1
contend for
try for 403.9
strive for 457.20
defend 600.10
contend with
treat 387.12
offer resistance 453.3
engage with 457.17
content
components 196.1
n material within 196.1
stuffing 196.1
capacity 257.2
makeup 554.12
table 871.2
content
n pleasure 95.1
contentment 107.1
v satisfy 107.4
adj pleased 95.15
contented 107.7
willing 324.5
assenting 332.13
consenting 441.4
contention
contraposition 215.1
opposition 451.1
disaccord 456.1
quarrel 456.5
contest 457.1
fight 457.1
hostility 589.3

argumentation 935.4
contentious
quarrelsome 110.26
aggravating 119.5
warlike 458.21
argumentative 935.19
contest
n contention 457.1
engagement 457.3
game 743.9
sport 744.1
v deny 335.4
contend against 451.4
contradict 451.6
oppose 457.13
dispute 457.21
argue 935.16
doubt 955.6
contestant
n competitor 452.2
combatant 461.1
player 743.18
adj contending 457.22
context
environment 209.1
circumstances 766.2
contiguity
juxtaposition 223.3
relation 775.1
contiguous
adjacent 223.16
consistent 803.11
continence
limitation 210.2
celibacy 565.1
abstemiousness 664.3
abstinence 668.2
moderation 670.1
continent
n world region 231.6
mainland 235.1
adj abstemious 664.6
abstinent 668.10
contingency
circumstance 766.1
nonessential 768.2
relativity 775.2
event 831.1
liability 897.1
condition 959.2
possibility 966.1
uncertainty 971.1
gamble 971.8
chance event 972.6
contingency plan 961.2
contingent
n portion 477.5
nonessential 768.2
company 770.3
part 793.1
event 831.1
chance event 972.6
adj in contact 223.17
substantial 763.6
circumstantial 766.7
unessential 768.4
eventual 831.11
qualifying 959.7
dependent 959.9
possible 966.6
undecided 971.18

chance 972.15
contingent on 887.8
continual
continuous 812.8
perpetual 829.7
constant 847.5
continuation
adjunct 254.1
payment 624.1
sequence 815.1
sequel 817.1
protraction 827.2
postponement 846.4
continuance 856.1
continue lengthen 267.6
persevere 360.2
be continuous 812.4
elapse 821.5
endure 827.6
protract 827.9
postpone 846.9
be frequent 847.3
stay with it 856.3
continuing
persevering 360.8
continuous 812.8
durable 827.10
permanent 853.7
abiding 856.7
continuity
playbook 704.21
plot 722.4
uniformity 781.1
consistency 803.2
logical order 807.2
uninterruption 812.1
cohesion 812.1
sequence 815.1
time 821.1
constancy 847.2
change 852.1
continuance 856.1
continuous
omnipresent 221.13
uniform 781.5
consistent 803.11
continued 812.8
temporal 821.7
perpetual 829.7
recurrent 849.13
continuing 856.7
continuum space 158.1
omnipresence 221.2
series 812.2
contort deflect 164.5
distort 265.5
convolve 281.4
misinterpret 342.2
contortion
n deflection 164.2
distortion 265.1
adj torsional 265.9
contour
n outline 211.2
tournure 262.2
v outline 211.9
contra
n oppositionist 452.3
adj negative 335.5
oppositional 451.8
adv in opposition 451.9

prep opposed to
451.10
opposite 779.10
contraband
n prohibition 444.1
smuggling 732.2
illicit goods 732.3
adj prohibited 444.7
illegal 674.6
contraceptive
birth control device
86.23
safeguard 1008.3
contract
n make small 258.9
undertaking 404.1
obligation 436.2
compact 437.1
v take sick 85.47
compress 260.7
shorten 268.6
narrow 270.11
close 293.6
commit 436.5
be engaged 436.6
compact 437.5
acquire 472.8
incur 897.4
contraction
decrease 252.1
compression 260.1
narrowing 270.2
abbreviation 537.4
stenography 547.8
contractive
decreasing 252.11
compressible 260.11
contractual 437.10
contradict deny 335.4
reject 372.2
cross 451.6
go contrary to 779.4
disagree 789.5
counteract 900.6
refute 958.5
contradiction
denial 335.2
rejection 372.1
refusal 442.1
opposition 451.1
ambiguity 539.1
contrariety 779.1
disagreement 789.1
counteraction 900.1
refutation 958.2
contradictory
negative 335.5
oppositional 451.8
contrary 779.6
disagreeing 789.6
counteractive 900.8
illogical 936.11
refuting 958.6
contradistinction
contrariety 779.1
distinction 944.3
contraindicated
prohibited 444.7
unwise 923.10
inexpedient 996.5
contraindication 379.1

contralto
n part 708.22
voice 709.5
adj deep 54.11
contraposition
opposition 215.1
anteposition 215.1
contrast 451.1
contrariety 779.1
counteraction 900.1
contraption
novelty 841.2
tool 1040.1
contrariety
offensiveness 98.2
contraposition 215.1
hostility 451.2
relation 775.1
oppositeness 779.1
difference 780.1
inequality 791.1
nonconformity 868.1
counteraction 900.1
contrary
adj negative 335.5
perverse 361.11
oppositional 451.8
contrarious 779.6
different 780.7
disagreeing 789.6
nonconforming 868.5
refuting 958.6
adverse 1011.13
hindering 1012.17
unwieldy 1013.19
adv opposite 215.6
contrast
n contraposition 215.1
contrariety 779.1
difference 780.1
dissimilarity 787.1
comparison 943.1
lighting 1025.19
v contrapose 215.4
compare 943.4
contravene deny 335.4
violate 435.4
contradict 451.6
break the law 674.5
go contrary to 779.4
counteract 900.6
thwart 1012.15
contretemps
wrong time 844.2
misfortune 1011.2
contribute
provide 385.7
participate 476.5
subscribe 478.14
tend 896.3
contribute to
advance 162.5
be useful 449.17
subscribe 478.14
determine 886.12
contribution
demand 421.1
participation 476.1
giving 478.1
donation 478.6
treatise 556.1

tax 630.9
contributor 478.11
contributory
additional 253.10
helpful 449.21
donative 478.25
contrite 113.9
contrition regret 113.1
apology 658.2
contrivance
plan 381.1
intrigue 381.5
instrument 384.4
stratagem 415.3
plot 722.4
production 892.1
expedient 995.2
tool 1040.1
contrive plan 381.8
manage 409.12
maneuver 415.10
fare 765.5
induce 886.11
originate 892.12
control
n supremacy 249.3
self-control 359.5
skill 413.1
governance 417.5
restraint 428.1
subjection 432.1
direction 573.1
mastery 612.2
moderation 670.1
familiar spirit 678.12
influence 894.1
experiment 942.1
specter 988.1
system component 1041.14
v pilot 184.37
possess authority 417.13
restrain 428.7
direct 573.8
hold in hand 612.13
moderate 670.6
exercise influence 894.8
haunt 988.6
controller
superintendent 574.2
accountant 628.7
treasurer 729.12
system component 1041.14
controlling
n extinguishing 1022.2
adj authoritative 417.15
restraining 428.11
directing 573.12
governing 612.18
paramount 997.24
control oneself
compose oneself 106.7
restrain oneself 668.6
controversial
contentious 110.26
argumentative 935.19
doubtful 971.17
controversy
quarrel 456.5
contention 457.1
disagreement 789.1
argumentation 935.4

controvert deny 335.4
contradict 451.6
discuss 541.12
go contrary to 779.4
refute 958.5
controvertible
unprovable 958.9
doubtful 971.17
contumacious
defiant 327.10
ungovernable 361.12
contumely
insolence 142.1
indignity 156.2
contempt 157.1
berating 510.7
vilification 513.2
contusion 85.38
conundrum
riddle 522.9
bewilderment 971.3
convalescence 396.8
convalescent 396.23
convalescent home 91.21
convection 176.1
convene
summon 420.11
meet 770.17
convenience
latrine 12.10
comfortableness 121.2
benefit 387.4
leisure 402.1
facility 449.9
timeliness 843.1
expedience 995.1
handiness 1014.2
machinery 1040.3
convenience store 736.1
convenient
comfortable 121.11
nearby 223.15
handy 387.20
timely 843.9
expedient 995.5
convent 703.6
convention
custom 373.1
rule 419.2
ecclesiastical council 423.4
compact 437.1
treaty 437.2
conference 541.6
fashion 578.1
social rule 579.1
etiquette 580.3
political convention 609.8
assembly 770.2
conventional
customary 373.13
preceptive 419.4
contractual 437.10
decorous 579.5
ceremonious 580.8
orthodox 687.7
traditional 842.12
conformist 867.6
usual 869.9
ordinary 1005.8
conventional medicine
90.13

converge
come together 169.2
focus 208.10
near 223.7
assemble 770.16
join 800.11

convergence
coming together 169
meeting 169.1
centralization 208.8
nearness 223.1
assemblage 770.1
joining 800.1

conversant with
used to 373.16
versed in 928.19

conversation
communication 343.1
speech 524.1
interchange of speech 541.1
converse 541.1
social life 582.4

conversational
v talkative 540.9
adj communicational 343.9
vernacular 523.20
colloquial 541.13

conversation piece 870.5

converse
v communicate 343.6
speak 524.19
talk together 541.9

converse
n inverse 205.4
opposite side 215.3
communication 343.1
conversation 541.1
social life 582.4
adj contrapositive 215.5
contrary 779.6

convert
n apostate 363.5
disciple 572.2
believer 692.4
proselyte 858.7
v invert 205.5
misuse 389.4
redeem 685.6
sell 737.24
change 852.7
reconvert 858.11
interchange 863.4
process 892.9
convince 953.18

converted
improved 392.13
redeemed 685.9
regenerate 692.10
altered 852.10
changed 858.19
forgetful 990.9

convertible
liquid 728.31
equivalent 790.8
changeable 858.18
interchangeable 863.5

convertor 1035.11

convex
n bulge 283.3
adj bowed 279.10
rotund 282.8

convexed 283.13

convey
transport 176.12
channel 239.15
communicate 343.7
say 524.22
transfer 629.3

conveyability
transferability 176.2
communicability 343.4

conveyable
transferable 176.18
communicable 343.11
moveable 629.5

conveyance
transportation 176.3
vehicle 179.1
informing 343.2
theft 482.1
transfer 629.1

conveyor 176.7

convict
n prisoner 429.11
criminal 660.9
v bring in a verdict 598.20
condemn 602.3

conviction hope 124.1
condemnation 602.1
persuasion 953.5
confidence 970.5

convince
persuade 375.23
cause to believe 858.16
convert 953.18
seem true 973.9

convinced belief 953.21
confident 970.21

convincing
convictional 953.26
evidential 957.16

conviviality
joviality 582.3
festivity 743.3

convocation
summons 420.5
ecclesiastical council 423.4
ceremony 580.4
assembly 770.2

convolution
curvature 279.1
involution 281.1
grandiloquence 545.1
complexity 799.1
circuitousness 914.1

convoy
n escort 769.5
bodyguard 1008.14
v maneuver 182.46
escort 769.8

convulse pain 26.7
torture 96.18
amuse 743.21
discompose 811.4
agitate 917.10

convulsion seizure 85.6
symptom 85.9
outburst 105.9
laughter 116.4
fit 152.8
fall 395.3
upheaval 671.5

disarrangement 811.1
revolution 860.1
spasm 917.6
frenzy 926.7

coo murmur 52.10
bird sound 60.5
speak 524.25

co-occurrence 836.1

cook
n chef 11.3
maid 577.8
v prepare food 11.5
tamper with 354.17
spoil 393.11
do for 395.11
prearrange 965.5
be hot 1019.22
heat 1020.17

cookbook 11.4

cookery
cooking 11.1
kitchen 11.4
heater 1020.10

cookie biscuit 10.43
man 76.5

cookout 8.6

cook up cook 11.5
fabricate 354.17
improvise 365.8
plot 381.9
originate 892.12
prearrange 965.5

cool
n composure 106.2
unastonishment 123.1
moderation 670.1
uniformity 781.1
stability 855.1
v disincline 379.4
restrain 428.7
pacify 465.7
calm 670.7
refrigerate 1024.10
adj chromatic 35.16
unfeeling 94.9
indifferent 102.6
calm 106.12
unastonished 123.3
aloof 141.12
insolent 142.9
quiescent 173.12
reticent 344.10
cautious 494.8
unsociable 583.6
unfriendly 589.9
equable 670.13
stable 855.12
sensible 920.18
excellent 999.13
chilly 1023.12
feeling cold 1023.16

coolant
refrigerant 1024.7
antifreeze 1024.8

cooler jail 429.9
jockey 757.2
chiller 1024.3

coolheaded
calm 106.12
unnervous 129.2
sensible 920.18

coolie 176.7

cool off
compose oneself 106.7
restrain 428.7
order 807.4

cool one's heels
await 130.8
do nothing 329.2
be kept waiting 846.14

coop
n enclosed place 212.3
chicken house 228.22
place of confinement 429.7
jail 429.9
participation 476.1
v enclose 212.5
confine 429.12

co-op
apartment house 228.14
market 736.1

cooperation
working together 450.1
collaboration 450.1
communion 476.2
association 582.6
interaction 777.3
agreement 788.1
interchange 863.1
concurrence 899.1

cooperative
n participation 476.1
association 617.1
market 736.1
adj willing 324.5
favorable 449.22
collaborative 450.5
communal 476.9
interacting 777.9
agreeing 788.9
joint 800.12
concurrent 899.4

co-opt 371.13

co-option 371.1

coordinate
n likeness 784.3
v symmetrize 264.3
make agree 788.7
equalize 790.6
organize 808.10
adj symmetric 264.4
equivalent 790.8
concurrent 899.4

coordinated 413.22

coordinates
bounds 211.1
Cartesian coordinates 300.5

cop
n cone 282.5
police 1008.16
v acquire 472.9
rob 482.16

copacetic 999.13

cop a plea
confess 351.7
get off 369.7

cope
n the heavens 1072.2
v cover 295.19
support oneself 385.12
compete 457.18

make shift 995.4
cope with treat 321.6
  perform 328.9
  deal 387.12
  contend with 457.17
copious much 247.8
  voluminous 257.17
  diffuse 538.11
  abundant 884.8
  productive 890.9
  plentiful 991.7
cop out hesitate 362.7
  get off 369.7
  remain neutral 467.5
  compromise 468.2
  seclude oneself 584.7
  defect 858.13
  pull back 903.7
cop-out
  neutrality 467.1
  compromise 468.1
  excuse 600.4
copper
  n money 728.7
  precious metals 728.20
  police 1008.16
  adj reddish-brown 40.4
  brass 1058.17
copse
  grove 310.14
  thicket 310.15
  bunch 770.7
copula 530.3
copulate
  v couple 75.21
  procreate 78.8
  make love 562.14
  come together 770.16
  join 800.5
  adj joined 800.13
copy
  n duplicate 78.1
  imitation 336.3
  image 349.5
  diagram 381.3
  writing 547.10
  printer's copy 548.4
  news item 552.3
  edition 554.5
  score 708.28
  picture 712.11
  the same 778.3
  reproduction 785.2
  representation 785.1
  iteration 849.2
  substitute 862.2
  v reproduce 78.7
  imitate 336.5
  impersonate 349.12
  write 547.19
  adopt 621.4
  portray 712.19
  mimic 778.6
  resemble 784.7
  substitute 785.8
  repeat 849.7
  duplicate 874.3
copycat
  n imitator 336.4
  v mimic 336.6
copy-edit 548.17

copyreader
  proofreader 548.13
  journalist 555.4
copyright
  n patent 210.3
  privilege 642.2
  safeguard 1008.3
  v limit 210.5
  preserve 397.8
  protect 1008.18
copywriter
  publicist 352.9
  writer 547.15
  author 718.4
coquette lover 104.12
  tempter 377.4
  flirt 562.11
coquettish fickle 364.6
  alluring 377.8
  amatory 562.23
coral 41.8
coral reef island 235.2
  shoal 276.2
  point of land 283.9
cord line 271.2
  electrical device 1032.21
  wood 1054.3
cordage capacity 257.2
  cording 271.3
cordial
  n refreshment 9.1
  tonic 86.8
  liqueur 88.15
  adj refreshing 9.3
  fervent 93.18
  pleasant 97.6
  good-natured 143.14
  receptive 187.16
  informal 581.3
  hospitable 585.11
  genial 587.16
cordless 1032.30
cordon
  n quarantine 429.2
  decoration 646.5
  guard 1008.9
  obstacle 1012.4
  v enclose 212.5
  quarantine 429.13
  segregate 773.6
cordon bleu
  expert 413.11
  decoration 646.5
corduroy
  n roughness 288.2
  adj furrowed 290.4
core
  n essential content 196.5
  interior 207.2
  center 208.2
  city district 230.6
  summary 557.2
  essence 767.2
  middle 819.1
  salient point 997.6
  memory 1042.7
  adj urban 230.11
  middle 819.4
cork
  n float 180.11
  stopper 293.4

skin 295.3
  lightness 298.2
  v blacken 38.7
  stop 293.7
  top 295.21
  suppress 428.8
corkscrew
  n extractor 192.9
  coil 281.2
  opener 292.10
  v convolve 281.4
  adj spiral 281.8
corn
  n feed 10.4
  growth 85.39
  swelling 283.4
  grass 310.5
  old joke 489.9
  platitude 974.3
  v preserve 397.9
corncob pipe 89.6
  ear 310.29
cornea 2.9
corner
  n deviation 164.1
  nook 197.3
  small space 258.3
  angle 278.2
  recess 284.7
  hiding place 346.4
  monopoly 469.3
  manipulation 737.20
  boxing 754.1
  race 756.3
  impasse 1013.6
  v monopolize 469.6
  purchase 733.7
  get a corner on 737.26
  turn 914.6
  run into a corner 1013.16
cornerstone
  foundation 901.7
  salient point 997.6
corn-fed 257.18
cornice 198.5
cornified pointed 285.9
  hardened 1046.13
cornucopia store 386.1
  source of supply 386.4
  horn of plenty 991.3
corny trite 117.9
  old-fogyish 842.17
corollary adjunct 254.1
  attendant 769.3
  effect 887.1
  conclusion 946.4
corona
  n cigar 89.4
  radiation 171.2
  circle 280.2
  flower 310.28
  halo 1025.14
  chandelier 1026.6
  sun 1072.13
  adj circular 280.11
coronation
  authority 417.12
  installation 615.3
coroner doctor 90.4
  autopsy 307.18
coronet circle 280.2

jewel 498.6
  heraldry 647.2
  royal insignia 647.3
corporal
  n Army noncommissioned
    officer 575.19
  naval officer 575.20
  church 703.10
  adj material 1052.10
corporate
  associated 617.16
  joint 800.12
  leagued 805.6
corporation goozle 2.19
  workplace 739.1
corporeal 1052.10
corps branch 461.21
  military unit 461.22
  association 617.1
  company 770.3
corpse slim 270.8
  dead body 307.16
corpulent stout 257.18
  thick 269.8
corpus capital 728.15
  collection 770.11
  knowledge 928.1
  lore 928.9
  body 1052.3
corpuscle blood 2.25
  cell 305.4
corpus delicti 307.16
corral enclose 212.5
  acquire 472.9
  assemble 770.18
  drive 1070.8
correct
  v revise 392.12
  remedy 396.13
  reprove 510.17
  punish 604.10
  conform 867.3
  disillusion 977.2
  adj meticulous 339.12
  mannerly 504.16
  grammatical 530.17
  appropriate 533.7
  conventional 579.5
  right 637.3
  orthodox 687.7
  accurate 973.16
correction
  measurement 300.1
  revision 392.4
  reparation 396.6
  reproof 510.5
  punishment 604.1
corrective
  n remedy 86.1
  adj remedial 86.39
  emendatory 392.16
  punishing 604.23
correlation
  relativity 775.2
  reciprocal relation 777
  mutuality 777.1
  comparison 943.1
correlative
  n correspondent 777.4
  likeness 784.3
  adj accompanying 769.9

approximate 775.8
correlative 777.8
akin 784.13
comparative 943.8
correspondence
symmetry 264.1
communication 343.1
accord 455.1
record 549.1
written communication 553.1
letter writing 553.1
correlation 777.1
sameness 778.1
uniformity 781.1
similarity 784.1
agreement 788.1
equality 790.1
conformity 867.1
concurrence 899.1
correspondent
n letter writer 553.8
journalist 555.4
correlate 777.4
likeness 784.3
adj reciprocal 777.10
coinciding 778.8
uniform 781.5
analogous 784.11
agreeing 788.9
equivalent 790.8
corridor airway 184.33
entrance 189.5
hall 197.18
region 231.1
passageway 383.3
corrigible
improvable 392.17
remediable 396.25
manageable 433.14
corroborate 957.11
corrode
decrease 252.6
erode 393.21
etch 713.10
disintegrate 806.3
corrosion
decrement 252.3
decay 393.6
disintegration 806.1
corrosive
n cauterant 1020.15
adj acid 110.17
caustic 144.23
corrupting 393.44
vigorous 544.11
disintegrative 806.5
harmful 1000.12
corrugated rough 288.6
rugged 288.7
furrowed 290.4
wrinkled 291.8
corrupt
v defile 80.17
bribe 378.3
debase 393.12
decay 393.22
misteach 569.3
sully 654.10
adulterate 797.12
indoctrinate 858.15
work evil 1000.6

adj bribable 378.4
decayed 393.40
dishonest 645.16
corrupted 654.14
erroneous 975.16
corruptible
bribable 378.4
venal 645.23
transient 828.7
corruption filth 80.7
perversion 265.2
bribery 378.1
pollution 393.2
decay 393.6
wordplay 489.8
mispronunciation 525.5
barbarism 526.6
solecism 531.2
misteaching 569.1
improbity 645.1
turpitude 654.2
adulteration 797.3
indoctrination 858.5
evil 1000.3
corsage shirt 5.15
bouquet 310.25
corsair 483.7
corset stays 5.23
supporter 901.2
cortege funeral 309.5
attendance 769.6
procession 812.3
cortex exterior 206.2
skin 295.3
shell 295.15
armor 460.3
cosmetic
exterior 206.7
shallow 276.5
hasty 401.9
insufficient 992.9
beautifying 1016.23
cosmetics
appearance 33.2
exteriority 206.1
pretext 376.1
notions 735.6
dissimilarity 787.1
makeup 1016.12
cosmetic surgery 90.2
cosmic large 247.7
universal 864.14
cosmologic 1072.24
cosmology 1072.18
cosmonaut 1075.8
cosmopolitan
n citizen 227.4
sophisticate 413.17
adj traveled 177.40
public 312.16
experienced 413.28
chic 578.13
universal 864.14
broad-minded 979.8
cosmos
completeness 794.1
universe 1072.1
cossack 461.12
cosset
n favorite 104.16
v indulge 427.6

foster 449.16
caress 562.16
cost
n loss 473.1
expenses 626.3
value 630.1
high price 632.3
v spend 626.5
sell for 630.13
cost-effective 635.6
costive 293.11
costly 632.11
cost of living
expenses 626.3
standard of living 731.8
costume
n clothing 5.1
suit 5.6
costumery 5.9
theater 704.17
v outfit 5.41
costume design 717.5
cot 228.8
coterie
social set 582.5
clique 617.6
company 770.3
coterminous
adjacent 223.16
coinciding 778.8
simultaneous 836.5
cottage
cot 228.8
Aldine 554.15
cottager 227.1
cotton 86.33
cotton-picking 661.12
cotton to
fall in love 104.22
get along 455.2
be friends 587.9
couch
n lair 228.26
sofa 901.19
v rest 20.6
lie low 274.5
lurk 346.9
say 524.22
phrase 532.4
depress 913.4
lie down 913.11
the couch 92.6
couchant
recumbent 201.8
low 274.7
couch potato
idler 331.8
spectator 918.1
cougar 311.22
cough 2.21
cough drops 86.16
coughing 85.9
cough up 624.16
council
n advice 422.1
committee 423.2
conclave 423.1
conference 541.6
directorate 574.11
tribunal 595.1
cabinet 613.3

association 617.1
assembly 770.2
adj conciliar 423.5
councilman
public official 575.17
legislator 610.3
counsel
n advice 422.1
adviser 422.3
lawyer 597.1
legal representation 597.4
consideration 931.2
v advise 422.5
confer 541.11
counseling 92.6
counselor
psychologist 92.10
adviser 422.3
lawyer 597.1
count
n amount 244.2
accusation 599.1
nobleman 608.4
returns 609.21
game 745.3
particular 766.3
total 1017.6
summation 1017.11
v quantify 244.4
beat time 708.44
have influence 894.10
judge 946.8
rank 946.15
matter 997.12
number 1017.17
countdown
rocket launching 1074.9
curtain-raiser 816.2
countenance
n looks 33.4
composure 106.2
face 216.4
authorization 443.3
patronage 449.4
approval 509.1
v accept 134.7
encourage 375.21
suffer 443.10
abet 449.14
approve 509.9
counter
n stern 217.7
retaliation 506.1
type 548.6
token 728.12
shopboard 736.6
workplace 739.1
bingo 759.15
gambler 759.21
table 901.15
radioscope 1037.7
v deny 335.4
oppose 451.3
contend against 451.4
fend off 460.10
retaliate 506.4
defend 600.10
go contrary to 779.4
disagree 789.5
counteract 900.6
refute 958.5

thwart 1012.15
adj backward 163.12
oppositional 451.8
contrary 779.6
dissimilar 787.4
adverse 1011.13
adv opposite 215.6
in opposition 451.9
contrarily 779.9
counteract
contrapose 215.4
offset 338.5
oppose 451.3
go contrary to 779.4
counter 900.6
thwart 1012.15
counterattack
n attack 459.1
countermeasure 900.5
v launch an attack
459.17
counteract 900.6
counterbalance
n makeweight 297.4
offset 338.2
the opposite 779.2
counterforce 900.4
v weigh 297.10
offset 338.5
go contrary to 779.4
equalize 790.6
stabilize 855.7
neutralize 900.7
countercharge
n recrimination 599.3
rebuttal 939.2
v recriminate 599.11
rebut 939.5
counterclockwise
adj left 220.4
adv clockwise 161.24
backwards 163.13
round 915.16
counterculture
n dissent 333.1
unconventionality 868.2
countermeasure 900.5
adj dissenting 333.6
unconventional 868.6
counterespionage 938.9
counterfeit
n fake 354.13
phony money 728.10
copy 785.1
substitute 862.2
v imitate 336.5
fabricate 354.18
sham 354.21
affect 500.12
coin 728.28
resemble 784.7
adj imitation 336.8
spurious 354.26
similar 784.10
substitute 862.8
counterforce 900.4
counterinsurgency 900.5
counterintelligence
secret service 576.12
surveillance 938.9
counterirritant 900.3

countermand
n take back 445.1
v repeal 445.2
thwart 1012.15
countermeasure 900.5
countermine
n entrenchment 460.5
v plot 381.9
countermove 995.2
counteroffensive 459.1
counterorder
n countermand 445.1
v repeal 445.2
counterpane 295.10
counterpart
correlate 777.4
likeness 784.3
duplicate 785.3
equal 790.4
counterpoint
polyphony 708.20
meter 720.7
the opposite 779.2
counterpose
go contrary to 779.4
counteract 900.6
compare 943.4
counterproductive
ineffective 19.15
counteractive 900.8
unwise 923.10
inexpedient 996.5
harmful 1000.12
hampering 1012.18
counterrevolution
revolution 860.1
countermeasure 900.5
countersign
n identification 517.11
password 517.12
signature 527.10
v ratify 332.12
promise 436.4
counterspy 576.9
counterstatement
defense 600.2
rebuttal 939.2
counter to
counteractively 900.10
opposed to 451.10
in disagreement with 789.10
countervailing
n neutralization 900.2
adj compensating 338.6
contrary 779.6
counteractive 900.8
neutralizing 900.9
counterweight
offset 338.2
scenery 704.20
counterforce 900.4
countess 608.6
counting
n numeration 1017.9
adj inclusive 772.6
countless much 247.8
infinite 823.3
innumerable 884.10
count on hope 124.7
look forward to 130.6
plan 380.6

rely on 953.16
count out 773.4
countrified 233.7
country
n region 231.1
nation 232.1
land 232.1
jury 596.6
adj rustic 233.6
country bumpkin 606.6
country house 228.5
countryman
fellow citizen 227.5
peasant 606.6
agriculturist 1069.5
country music 708.11
countryside 233.1
count sheep 23.3
count up 1017.19
county region 231.5
country 232.1
county seat 230.4
coup act 328.3
attempt 403.2
stratagem 415.3
seizure 480.2
instant 830.3
expedient 995.2
coup d'état revolt 327.4
seizure 480.2
revolution 860.1
couple
n set 784.5
two 873.2
v copulate 75.21
wed 563.14
get married 563.15
come together 770.16
relate 775.6
put together 800.5
combine 805.3
league 805.4
double 873.5
couplet poetry 720.9
two 873.2
coupon token 728.12
stock certificate 738.4
courage pluck 359.3
fortitude 492.6
bravery 492.1
confidence 970.5
courageous
resolute 359.14
plucky 492.17
courier
messenger 353.1
guide 574.7
course
n serving 8.10
dish 10.7
direction 161.1
progression 162.1
career 172.2
travel 177.1
journey 177.5
voyage 182.6
heading 184.34
flow 238.4
channel 239.1
layer 296.1
policy 381.4

route 383.1
manner 384.1
arena 463.1
track 517.8
study 568.8
golf 751.1
skiing 753.1
horse racing 757.1
series 812.2
round 850.3
process 889.2
trend 896.2
v travel 177.18
traverse 177.20
flow 238.16
hunt 382.9
adv under way 182.63
course of action 995.2
courser swiftness 174.6
horse 311.10
hunter 382.5
war-horse 461.30
court
n enclosed place 212.3
estate 228.7
council 423.1
courtship 562.7
judiciary 594.2
law court 595.2
courthouse 595.6
legislature 613.1
playground 743.11
basketball 747.1
tennis 748.1
attendance 769.6
influence 894.6
v curry favor 138.9
solicit 440.14
woo 562.21
cultivate 587.12
adj tribunal 595.7
courteous
sensitive 24.12
respectful 155.8
polite 504.14
sociable 582.22
courtesan 665.15
courtesy
sensitivity 24.3
act of kindness 143.7
respect 155.1
good behavior 321.2
politeness 504.1
courteousness 504.1
civility 504.6
sociability 582.1
courthouse
town hall 230.5
court 595.6
capitol 613.4
courtier
sycophant 138.3
follower 166.2
flatterer 511.4
courtliness
proud bearing 136.2
gallantry 504.2
courtesy 504.6
etiquette 580.3
courtly
dignified 136.12

gallant 504.15
flattering 511.8
court-martial
  military court 595.4
  trial 598.5
courtroom 595.6
courtship 562.7
courtyard 212.3
cousin 559.3
couturier
  dressmaker 5.36
  designer 716.9
cove man 76.5
  nook 197.3
  inlet 242.1
  arch 279.4
  cave 284.5
  recess 284.7
coven 690.8
covenant
  n compact 437.1
  v come to an agreement 332.10
  contract 437.5
cover
  n serving 8.10
  food service 8.11
  dish 10.7
  Air Force mission 184.11
  ground covering 199.3
  covering 295.2
  lid 295.5
  blanket 295.10
  concealment 346.1
  veil 346.2
  hiding place 346.4
  disguise 356.11
  pretext 376.1
  anonymity 528.1
  bookbinding 554.14
  protection 1008.1
  shelter 1009.3
  shade 1028.1
  v color 35.14
  copulate 75.21
  be pregnant 78.12
  extend 158.9
  traverse 177.20
  close 293.6
  stop 293.7
  cover up 295.19
  compensate 338.4
  explain 341.10
  conceal 346.6
  hide under 376.4
  bet 759.25
  include 772.3
  put together 800.5
  take one's turn 825.5
  overspread 910.5
  protect 1008.18
  shade 1028.5
coverage size 257.1
  scope 295.1
  protection 295.2
  news 552.1
  inclusion 772.1
cover charge
  food service 8.11
  fee 630.6
cover for 862.5

cover girl 1016.8
covert
  n plumage 3.18
  lair 228.26
  cover 295.2
  thicket 310.15
  hiding place 346.4
  shelter 1009.3
  adj covered 295.31
  clandestine 345.12
  concealed 346.11
  latent 519.5
cover-up
  veil of secrecy 345.3
  pretext 376.1
covet crave 100.18
  envy 154.3
covey company 770.3
  assemblage 770.6
  multitude 884.3
cow
  n female animal 77.10
  cattle 311.6
  v intimidate 127.20
  domineer 612.16
coward
  n jellyfish 491.5
  adj cowardly 491.10
cowardice frailty 16.2
  fear 127.1
  weak will 362.4
  submission 433.1
  spinelessness 491.2
  cowardliness 491.1
cowardly weak 16.12
  fearful 127.23
  weak-willed 362.12
  coward 491.10
cowboy rider 178.8
  violent person 671.10
  card 758.2
  herder 1070.3
cower be weak 16.8
  fawn 138.7
  quail 491.9
  crouch 913.8
cowl
  n cover 295.2
  v hood 295.19
cowlick 3.6
co-worker 616.5
coxcomb dandy 500.9
  comedy 704.6
coxswain
  n steersman 183.8
  guide 574.7
  v pilot 182.14
coy shy 139.12
  amatory 562.23
coyote 311.20
cozen 356.18
cozy pleased 95.15
  comfortable 121.11
  homelike 228.33
  conversational 541.13
  intimate 582.24
  snug 1007.7
crab
  n malcontent 108.4
  complainer 115.9
  marine animal 311.30

vermin 311.37
windlass 906.7
lifter 912.3
  v be discontented 108.6
  complain 115.16
  maneuver 184.40
  hinder 1012.16
  adj sour 67.5
crabbed sour 67.5
  irascible 110.19
  stricken in years 303.18
  hard to understand 522.14
  stiff 534.3
  complex 799.4
crack
  n stripe 47.5
  report 56.1
  snap 56.2
  detonation 56.3
  trauma 85.38
  cocaine 87.7
  cleft 224.2
  furrow 290.1
  opening 292.1
  attempt 403.3
  witticism 489.7
  remark 524.3
  break 802.4
  instant 830.3
  hit 902.4
  fault 1003.2
  blemish 1004.1
  v clap 56.6
  snap 56.7
  blast 56.8
  lose self-control 128.8
  cleave 224.4
  furrow 290.3
  open 292.11
  unclose 292.12
  explain 341.10
  injure 393.13
  break 393.23
  separate 802.12
  hit 902.14
  solve 940.2
  blemish 1004.4
  burn 1020.24
  adj skillful 413.22
  superior 999.14
crack down on
  restrain 428.7
  suppress 428.8
  attack 459.15
cracked raucous 58.15
  dissonant 61.4
  cleft 224.7
  gaping 292.18
  impaired 393.27
  severed 802.23
  mentally deficient 922.22
  crazy 926.27
  blemished 1004.8
cracker
  biscuit 10.30
  noisemaker 53.6
  wilderness settler 227.10
  dryness 1066.2
crackerjack
  n skillful person 413.14
  good person 659.2

first-rate 999.7
  adj skillful 413.22
  excellent 999.13
crackle
  n snap 56.2
  trauma 85.38
  v pop 56.7
crackpot oddity 870.4
  lunatic 926.16
  freak 927.4
crack the whip 573.1
crack up
  n exhaustion 21.2
  collapse 85.8
  mental disorder 92.14
  frayed nerves 128.4
  crash 184.20
  impairment 393.1
  debacle 395.4
  disruption 802.3
  misfortune 1011.2
  v burn out 21.5
  laugh 116.8
  lose self-control 128.8
  crash 184.44
  disintegrate 806.3
  collide 902.13
  go mad 926.21
cradle
  n refinery 79.13
  fatherland 232.2
  infancy 301.5
  origin 818.4
  birthplace 886.8
  v put to bed 22.19
  foster 449.16
  calm 670.7
  support 901.21
craft ship 180.1
  deceit 356.3
  skill 413.1
  art 413.7
  cunning 415.1
  stratagem 415.3
  manual work 712.3
  vocation 724.6
  shrewdness 920.3
crafted 892.18
craftsman
  expert 413.11
  artist 716.1
  skilled worker 726.6
  producer 892.7
crafty
  falsehearted 354.31
  deceitful 356.22
  cunning 415.12
  cautious 494.8
  sly 645.18
  shrewd 920.15
crag
  precipice 200.3
  mountain 237.6
  projection 285.4
  rock 1059.1
craggy rugged 288.7
  stony 1059.12
cram
  n study 570.3
  full measure 794.3
  v stuff 8.25

tutor 568.11
study up 570.14
gluttonize 672.4
assemble 770.18
fill 794.7
thrust 902.12
refresh the memory 989.19
overload 993.15
satiate 994.4
densify 1045.9
cramp
    n pang 26.2
    seizure 85.6
    pain 96.5
    restriction 428.3
    spasm 917.6
    hindrance 1012.1
    v weaken 16.10
    confine 212.6
    contract 260.7
    squeeze 260.8
    restrict 428.9
    fasten 800.7
    hamper 1012.11
    hinder 1012.16
    adj narrow 270.14
    hard to understand 522.14
cramped limited 210.7
    enclosed 212.10
    little 258.10
    contracted 260.12
    constricted 270.14
    restricted 428.15
    stiff 534.3
    narrow-minded 980.10
cramp one's style 1012.16
cramps 85.29
crane
    n lifter 912.3
    fire iron 1020.12
    v gaze 27.15
    be long 267.5
    demur 325.4
cranium 198.7
crank
    n amphetamines 87.4
    malcontent 108.4
    sorehead 110.11
    complainer 115.9
    angle 278.2
    caprice 364.1
    punishment 605.3
    oddity 870.4
    lever 906.4
    fanatic 926.18
    quirk 927.2
    freak 927.4
    v zigzag 204.12
    angle 278.5
    reel in 906.9
    rotate 915.9
    adj eccentric 927.5
cranky
    discontented 108.8
    irascible 110.19
    complaining 115.20
    capricious 364.5
    disagreeing 789.6
    counteractive 900.8
    eccentric 927.5
cranny nook 197.3

crack 224.2
furrow 290.1
hiding place 346.4
crap
    n defecation 12.2
    feces 12.4
    heroin 87.9
    humbug 354.14
    bull 520.3
    v defecate 12.13
crape 115.7
craps dice 759.8
    deuce 873.3
crapulent
    intoxicated 88.31
    intemperate 669.7
    gluttonous 672.6
crash
    n noise 53.3
    report 56.1
    substance abuse 87.1
    crack-up 184.20
    descent 194.1
    decline 252.2
    impairment 393.1
    debacle 395.4
    collapse 410.3
    defeat 412.1
    insolvency 625.3
    declining market 737.5
    impact 902.3
    misfortune 1011.2
    v sleep 22.14
    go to bed 22.18
    din 53.7
    boom 56.6
    use 87.22
    crack up 184.44
    penetrate 189.8
    descend 194.5
    intrude 214.5
    inhabit 225.7
    billow 238.22
    break down 393.24
    fall 410.12
    go bankrupt 625.7
    cheapen 633.6
    collide 902.13
    adv at top speed 756.5
crash diet fast 515.2
    diet 7.13
crass downright 247.12
    thick 269.8
    coarse 497.11
    ill-bred 505.6
    stupid 922.15
crate
    n car 179.10
    storehouse 386.6
    v package 212.9
    wrap 295.20
crater valley 237.7
    pit 275.2
    cavity 284.2
    blemish 1004.1
crave covet 100.18
    request 440.9
    entreat 440.11
craven
    n dastard 491.6
    adj cowardly 491.12

craving
    n coveting 100.6
    adj desiring 100.24
craw
    digestive system 2.18
    narrow place 270.3
crawl
    n slow motion 175.2
    creeping 177.17
    aquatics 182.11
    v feel creepy 74.7
    fawn 138.7
    go slow 175.6
    creep 177.26
    lie 201.5
    get low 274.5
    linger on 827.7
    bow 913.9
crawl with
    pervade 221.7
    teem with 884.5
    infest 910.6
    abound 991.5
crayon
    n drawing 712.13
    art equipment 712.18
    v portray 712.19
craze
    n stripe 47.5
    trauma 85.38
    greed 100.8
    eagerness 101.1
    fury 105.8
    crack 224.2
    caprice 364.1
    fad 578.5
    mania 926.12
    blemish 1004.1
    v cleave 224.4
    injure 393.13
    break 802.12
    madden 926.24
    blemish 1004.4
crazy
    n lunatic 926.16
    adj variegated 47.9
    distorted 265.10
    mentally deficient 922.22
    foolish 923.8
    absurd 923.11
    nutty 926.27
    adv swiftly 174.18
crazy about
    enthusiastic 101.11
    nuts about 104.31
creak
    n screech 58.4
    insect sound 58.5
    v stridulate 58.7
    screech 58.8
cream
    n whiteness 37.2
    cleanser 79.17
    superior 249.5
    upper class 607.2
    the best 999.8
    ointment 1056.3
    semiliquid 1062.5
    v foam 320.5
    defeat 412.9
    emulsify 1062.10

    adj whitish 37.8
    yellow 43.4
cream of the crop 578.6
crease
    n fold 291.1
    wrinkle 291.3
    hockey 749.1
    v fold 291.5
    wrinkle 291.6
    engrave 713.9
create form 262.7
    originate 337.4
    initiate 818.10
    cause 886.10
    produce 892.8
    imagine 986.14
creation
    forming 262.5
    structure 266.1
    divine function 677.13
    work of art 712.10
    beginning 818.1
    production 892.1
    work 893.1
    universe 1072.1
creative
    nonimitative 337.5
    falsehearted 354.31
    wrong 638.3
    dishonest 645.16
    illegal 674.6
    almighty 677.17
    beginning 818.15
    productive 890.9
    originative 892.16
    imaginative 986.18
creative writer 986.12
creativity
    nonimitation 337.1
    genius 920.8
    invention 986.3
creator artist 716.1
    doer 726.1
    author 886.4
    producer 892.7
creature
    sycophant 138.3
    inferior 250.2
    organism 305.2
    animal 311.2
    person 312.5
    assenter 332.6
    instrument 384.4
    dependent 432.6
    figurehead 575.5
    deputy 576.1
    retainer 577.1
    follower 616.8
    something 763.3
    product 893.1
credence altar 703.12
    belief 953.1
credential
    preparedness 405.4
    recommendation 509.4
    identification 517.11
    certificate 549.6
credibility
    honesty 644.3
    believability 953.8
    plausibility 968.3

credibility gap
untruthfulness 354.8
deceitfulness 645.3
unbelievability 955.3
credible logical 935.20
believable 953.24
plausible 968.7
credit
n thanks 150.2
difference 255.8
trust 622.1
receipts 627.1
entry 628.5
due 639.2
honor 646.1
esteem 662.3
attribution 888.1
influence 894.1
belief 953.1
credible 953.8
v thank 150.4
pay 622.5
keep accounts 628.8
believe 953.10
creditable
praiseworthy 509.20
honest 644.13
reputable 662.15
creditor 622.4
credit union
association 617.1
lending institution 620.4
credit 622.1
credo religion 675.1
doctrine 676.2
system of belief 953.3
credulous foolish 923.8
trusting 953.22
knee-jerk 954.8
creed affirmation 334.1
policy 381.4
religion 675.1
doctrine 676.2
system of belief 953.3
creedbound strict 687.8
narrow-minded 980.10
creek stream 238.1
inlet 242.1
creep
n slow motion 175.2
crawling 177.17
bad person 660.5
v feel creepy 74.7
fawn 138.7
go slow 175.6
crawl 177.26
lurk 346.9
linger on 827.7
creep in enter 189.7
intrude 214.5
join 617.14
creeps
creeping of the flesh 74.4
trepidation 127.5
nervousness 128.2
cold 1023.2
creep with
pervade 221.7
teem with 884.5
infest 910.6
abound 991.5

creepy crawly 74.11
spooky 127.31
bad 1000.8
cremation
incineration 309.2
burning 1020.5
crematorium
mortuary 309.9
incinerator 1020.13
crenellated
notched 289.5
fortified 460.12
creole 523.11
crêpe 10.45
crepitant 56.10
crepuscular 315.8
crepuscule
foredawn 314.4
dusk 315.3
crescendo
n loudness 53.1
increase 251.1
expansion 259.1
music 708.25
v din 53.7
grow 251.6
enlarge 259.4
increase 259.5
adj music 708.53
crescent
n circle 230.9
curve 279.5
semicircle 280.8
heraldry 647.2
moon 1072.11
adj grown 14.3
increasing 251.8
expanding 259.12
curving 279.11
crest
n feather 3.16
summit 198.2
top part 198.4
mountain 237.6
notching 289.2
heraldry 647.2
wave 916.4
v top 198.9
crestfallen glum 112.25
disappointed 132.5
humiliated 137.14
cretin 924.8
cretinism 922.9
crevasse
n valley 237.7
pit 275.2
v open 292.11
crevice 224.2
crew aircrew 185.4
staff 577.11
clique 617.6
team 617.7
motion-picture studio 706.4
baseball team 745.2
company 770.3
crewcut 1016.15
crib
n compartment 197.2
quarters 228.4
hut 228.9
translation 341.3

storehouse 386.6
garner 386.7
brothel 665.9
casino 759.19
v enclose 212.6
imitate 336.5
cheat 356.18
confine 429.12
rob 482.16
plagiarize 482.19
crick
n pang 26.2
insect sound 58.5
stream 238.1
v stridulate 58.7
cricket
noisemaker 53.6
locust 311.36
propriety 637.2
fairness 649.3
crier 353.3
crime
wrongdoing 655.1
misdeed 655.2
offense 674.4
criminal
n evildoer 593.1
perpetrator 645.10
felon 660.9
adj wrong 638.3
dishonest 645.16
wicked 654.16
evil 655.5
guilty 656.3
illegal 674.6
bad 1000.7
criminalize prohibit 444.3
ostracize 586.6
criminal law 673.5
criminology 673.7
crimp
n lock 3.5
trench 290.2
fold 291.1
wrinkle 291.3
cheat 357.3
abductor 483.10
v curl 281.5
notch 289.4
furrow 290.3
fold 291.5
wrinkle 291.6
abduct 482.20
hinder 1012.16
adj pulverable 1051.13
crimson
v color 41.4
redden 41.5
change color 105.19
blush 139.8
adj red 41.6
cringe
n retreat 903.3
v be weak 16.8
flinch 127.13
fawn 138.7
retract 168.3
cower 491.9
pull back 903.7
crouch 913.8

crinkle
n convolution 281.1
wrinkle 291.3
v rustle 52.12
convolve 281.4
ruffle 288.5
wrinkle 291.6
cripple
n defective 85.45
v weaken 16.10
disable 19.9
lame 393.14
hamper 1012.11
crisis
financial trouble 729.8
business cycle 731.10
critical point 843.4
urgency 997.4
salient point 997.6
danger 1006.1
crisp
v curl 281.5
fold 291.5
adj refreshing 9.3
curly 281.9
clear 521.11
concise 537.6
aphoristic 974.6
cool 1023.12
cold 1023.14
brittle 1050.4
pulverable 1051.13
crisscross
v cross 170.6
adj cross 170.8
adv crosswise 170.13
criterion
measure 300.2
model 786.1
rule 869.4
test 942.2
critic
opinion maker 341.7
connoisseur 496.7
faultfinder 510.9
columnist 547.15
commentator 556.4
judge 596.1
author 718.4
interpreter 723.4
specialist 866.3
criticizer 946.7
critical
meticulous 339.12
explanatory 341.15
fastidious 495.9
faultfinding 510.23
dissertational 556.6
evaluative 723.6
crucial 843.10
discriminating 944.7
judicial 946.16
urgent 997.22
dangerous 1006.9
precarious 1006.12
difficult 1013.17
criticism
exegetics 341.8
adverse reaction 510.4
commentary 556.2
review of the arts 723.1

censure 946.2
criticize pan 510.14
  write upon 556.5
  critique 723.5
  judge 946.14
critter animal 311.2
  cattle 311.6
  horse 311.10
croak
  n rasp 58.3
  speech defect 525.1
  v sound harshly 58.9
  bird sound 60.5
  complain 115.15
  forebode 133.11
  die 307.20
  kill 308.14
  speak poorly 525.7
crock
  n horse 311.12
  ceramic ware 742.2
  v intoxicate 88.23
crocodile 311.25
Croesus 618.8
croft 231.4
Cronus 821.2
crony
  companion 588.3
  associate 616.1
cronyism 609.35
crook
  n deviation 164.1
  bias 204.3
  shaft 273.2
  angle 278.2
  curve 279.2
  cheater 357.4
  scepter 417.9
  thief 483.1
  evildoer 593.1
  ecclesiastical insignia 647.4
  criminal 660.9
  staff 702.3
  supporter 901.2
  fire iron 1020.12
  v deflect 164.5
  oblique 204.9
  distort 265.5
  angle 278.5
  curve 279.6
crooked askew 204.14
  zigzag 204.20
  distorted 265.10
  fake 265.11
  angular 278.6
  hooked 279.8
  falsehearted 354.31
  dishonest 645.16
crooner 710.13
crop
  n digestive system 2.18
  head of hair 3.4
  breast 283.6
  growth 310.2
  yield 472.5
  whip 605.1
  bunch 770.7
  effect 887.1
  production 893.2
  harvest 1069.15
  v feed on 8.28

excise 255.10
  shorten 268.6
  farm 1069.16
  harvest 1069.19
crop out
  be exposed 31.5
  appear 33.8
crop up
  originate 818.13
  turn up 831.6
crosier shaft 273.2
  scepter 417.9
  ecclesiastical insignia 647.4
  staff 702.3
cross
  n affliction 96.8
  crux 170.4
  staff 273.2
  signature 527.10
  monument 549.12
  execution 605.5
  insignia 647.1
  heraldry 647.2
  rood 702.3
  hybrid 797.8
  adversity 1011.1
  impediment 1012.6
  v disappoint 132.2
  converge 169.2
  crisscross 170.6
  traverse 177.20
  navigate 182.13
  deny 335.4
  oppose 451.3
  contradict 451.6
  bless 696.14
  hybridize 797.13
  counteract 900.6
  pass 910.8
  thwart 1012.15
  adj irascible 110.19
  angry 152.28
  crossing 170.8
  transverse 170.9
  cruciform 170.10
  oppositional 451.8
  disagreeing 789.6
  hybrid 797.15
  adv crosswise 170.13
  in opposition 451.9
crossbow 462.7
crossbreed
  n hybrid 797.8
  v procreate 78.8
  hybridize 797.13
cross-check
  n examination 938.3
  collation 943.2
  ensuring 970.8
  v collate 943.5
  verify 970.12
cross-country racing 755.2
crosscurrent flow 238.4
  wind 318.1
  opposition 451.1
  counterforce 900.4
crossed
  disappointed 132.5
  cross 170.8
  cruciform 170.10
  hybrid 797.15

cross-examination
  trial 598.5
  argumentation 935.4
  grilling 938.13
cross-eyed 28.12
cross-fertilization 78.3
cross-fertilize
  reproduce 78.10
  fertilize 890.8
cross fire 863.1
crossgrained
  adj irascible 110.19
  rough 288.6
  coarse 294.6
  negative 335.5
  perverse 361.11
  adv crosswise 170.13
  against the grain 288.12
cross-hatching
  network 170.3
  line 517.6
  engraving 713.2
crossing-over 858.3
cross-interrogation 938.13
cross one's fingers
  be hopeful 124.8
  await 130.8
  doubt 955.6
cross one's heart
  depose 334.6
  promise 436.4
cross one's mind 931.18
cross out delete 255.12
  obliterate 395.16
crosspatch
  sorehead 110.11
  misfit 789.4
crosspiece 170.5
cross purposes
  hostility 451.2
  disagreement 456.2
  contrariety 779.1
crossroads
  convergence 169.1
  village 230.2
  crisis 843.4
cross section
  crossing 170.1
  representative 349.7
  part 793.1
crosswind airflow 318.1
  counterforce 900.4
crosswise
  adj transverse 170.9
  oblique 204.19
  hindering 1012.17
  unwieldy 1013.19
  adv decussatively 170.13
  transversely 204.24
crotch genitals 2.13
  fork 171.4
crotchet angle 278.2
  caprice 364.1
  note 709.14
  quirk 927.2
crotchety
  capricious 364.5
  counteractive 900.8
  eccentric 927.5
crouch
  n stoop 913.3

v fawn 138.7
  lie low 274.5
  bow down 433.10
  cower 491.9
  duck 913.8
crow
  n blackness 38.4
  laughter 116.4
  speech defect 525.1
  lever 906.4
  v bird sound 60.5
  laugh 116.8
  put up a bold front 454.5
  exult 502.9
  speak 524.25
crow's-feet 291.3
crowbar
  n extractor 192.9
  lever 906.4
  v get a purchase 906.8
crowd
  n audience 48.6
  social circle 582.5
  the masses 606.2
  clique 617.6
  company 770.3
  throng 770.4
  attender 918.2
  v make one's way 162.4
  hurry 401.4
  make haste 401.5
  come together 770.16
  fill 794.7
  teem with 884.5
  thrust 902.12
  overload 993.15
  obstruct 1012.12
  densify 1045.9
crowd in enter 189.7
  thrust in 191.7
  intrude 214.5
crown
  n summit 198.2
  top part 198.4
  architectural topping 198.5
  head 198.6
  supremacy 249.3
  circle 280.2
  finishing touch 407.3
  victory 411.1
  jewel 498.6
  volume 554.4
  trophy 646.3
  heraldry 647.2
  royal insignia 647.3
  specie 728.4
  money 728.8
  tennis 748.1
  limit 794.5
  chandelier 1026.6
  v top 198.9
  cover 295.21
  complete 407.6
  take command 417.14
  install 615.12
  honor 646.8
  glorify 662.13
  perfect 1002.5
the Crown
  sovereignty 417.8
  the government 612.3

crowning
topping 198.11
chief 249.14
completing 407.9
ending 820.10
crowning achievement 1002.4
crown of thorns 96.8
crucial critical 843.10
original 886.14
urgent 997.22
vital 997.23
crucible mixer 797.9
instrument of conversion 858.10
test 942.2
crucifix 170.4
crucifixion
agony 26.6
torment 96.7
capital punishment 604.7
crucify pain 26.7
torture 96.18
execute 604.17
stigmatize 661.9
work evil 1000.6
crude
n raw material 406.5
petroleum 1056.4
adj garish 35.20
offensive 98.18
raw 406.10
undeveloped 406.12
coarse 497.11
gaudy 501.20
ill-bred 505.6
inelegant 534.2
base 661.12
crudity
undevelopment 406.4
coarseness 497.2
baseness 661.3
cruel painful 26.10
cruel-hearted 144.26
pitiless 146.3
murderous 308.24
savage 671.21
cruelty
cruelness 144.11
unkindness 144.10
pitilessness 146.1
cruise
n journey 177.5
voyage 182.6
v journey 177.21
navigate 182.13
fly 184.36
make good 409.10
cruiser traveler 178.1
police car 179.11
motorboat 180.4
battleship 180.7
cruller 10.44
crumb
n scrap 248.3
minute 258.7
piece 793.3
powder 1051.5
v sprinkle 771.6
pulverize 1051.9
crumble
n powder 1051.5

v weaken 16.9
decrease 252.6
decay 393.22
be destroyed 395.22
disintegrate 806.3
pulverize 1051.9
powder 1051.10
crumbly frail 16.14
brittle 1050.4
pulverable 1051.13
crummy base 661.12
paltry 998.21
bad 1000.8
crumple
n wrinkle 291.3
v distort 265.5
ruffle 288.5
wrinkle 291.6
crunch
n rasp 58.3
poverty 619.1
concussion 671.8
crisis 843.4
crucial moment 843.5
impact 902.3
urgency 997.4
predicament 1013.5
v grate 58.10
shatter 802.13
collide 902.13
pulverize 1051.9
crunched 265.10
crusade
n campaign 458.4
cause 886.9
v espouse 509.13
crush
n liking 100.2
infatuation 104.4
squeezing 260.2
throng 770.4
full measure 794.3
pulp 1063.2
v sadden 112.18
aggrieve 112.19
unnerve 128.10
abase 137.5
squeeze 260.8
conquer 412.10
suppress 428.8
subdue 432.9
shatter 802.13
refute 958.5
pulverize 1051.9
pulp 1063.5
crushing
n wretchedness 96.6
suppression 428.2
subdual 432.4
pulverization 1051.4
adj mortifying 98.21
oppressive 98.24
humiliating 137.15
laborious 725.18
troublesome 1013.18
crust
n bread 10.28
impudence 142.3
exterior 206.2
land 234.1
incrustation 295.14

upper class 607.2
v incrust 295.27
crustacean
n marine animal 311.30
invertebrate 311.32
adj invertebrate 311.51
crusty
irascible 110.20
impudent 142.10
gruff 505.7
hardened 1046.13
crutch
n genitals 2.13
fork 171.4
staff 273.2
aid 901.2
v support 449.12
help 901.21
crux cross 170.4
enigma 522.8
salient point 997.6
dilemma 1013.7
hitch 1013.8
cry
n yell 59.1
call 59.1
animal noise 60.1
weeping 115.2
lament 115.3
cheer 116.2
publicity 352.4
entreaty 440.2
catchword 526.9
report 552.6
v call 59.6
yelp 60.2
weep 115.12
wail 115.13
cheer 116.6
proclaim 352.13
crybaby 16.6
cry for wish for 100.16
demand 421.5
entreat 440.11
require 963.9
cry havoc warn 399.5
alarm 400.3
crying
n weeping 115.2
adj vociferous 59.10
howling 60.6
tearful 115.21
demanding 421.9
urgent 997.22
cryogenics cold 1023.1
refrigeration 1024.1
crypt compartment 197.2
understructure 266.3
cavity 284.2
tomb 309.16
church 703.9
cryptic secret 345.11
latent 519.5
implied 519.7
enigmatic 522.17
cryptography
exegetics 341.8
cryptanalysis 345.6
writing 547.1
crystal
n amphetamines 87.4

snow 1023.8
adj transparent 1029.4
stony 1059.12
crystal ball
the future 839.1
divination 962.2
crystallize form 807.5
solidify 1046.8
petrify 1059.10
crystallography
mineralogy 1058.10
geology 1059.9
cry uncle weaken 16.9
flinch 127.13
cry wolf 400.3
cub
n boy 302.5
fledgling 302.10
adj unaccustomed 374.4
immature 406.11
cubbyhole nook 197.3
small space 258.3
hiding place 346.4
cube triplicate 877.2
square 879.3
cubes 759.8
cubic spatial 158.10
quadrangular 278.9
cubicle nook 197.3
bedroom 197.7
cuckold 665.22
cuckoldry
love affair 104.6
illicit sex 665.7
cuckoo
n imitator 336.4
songbird 710.23
v bird sound 60.5
adj crazy 926.27
cud bite 8.2
chewing tobacco 89.7
cuddle comfort 121.10
snuggle 562.17
cuddly 104.25
cudgel whip 604.13
club 902.20
cue braid 3.7
tail 217.6
clue 517.9
tip 551.3
hint 551.4
role 704.10
playbook 704.21
mood 978.4
reminder 989.6
cuff
n slap 604.3
punishment 902.8
v slap 604.12
hit 902.19
cuffs 428.4
cuisine food 10.1
cooking 11.1
kitchen 11.4
cul-de-sac
obstruction 293.3
impasse 1013.6
culinary 11.6
cull excise 255.10
select 371.14
collect 472.11

culling
elimination 773.2
grouping 808.3
culmination
summit 198.2
completion 407.2
accomplishment 794.4
end 820.1
acme of perfection 1002.3
culpable
blameworthy 510.25
guilty 656.3
culprit 660.8
cult ism 675.2
worship 696.1
ritualism 701.1
system of belief 953.3
cultist
n religionist 675.15
adj pious 692.8
cultivate
sensitize 24.7
develop 392.10
foster 449.16
train 568.13
nurture 587.12
process 892.9
culture 1069.17
cultivated
improved 392.13
elegant 496.9
well-bred 504.17
learned 928.21
cultural 568.18
culture
n humankind 312.1
society 373.2
cultivation 392.3
taste 496.1
good breeding 504.4
scholarship 928.5
agriculture 1069.1
cultivation 1069.13
v growth 1069.17
raise 1070.6
cultured
improved 392.13
elegant 496.9
well-bred 504.17
learned 928.21
culvert 239.2
cumbersome
bulky 257.19
onerous 297.17
bungling 414.20
hampering 1012.18
unwieldy 1013.19
cumbrous
bulky 257.19
onerous 297.17
stiff 534.3
hampering 1012.18
cum laude 646.11
cumulate
v store up 386.11
assemble 770.18
adj assembled 770.21
cumulative
additive 253.8
accumulative 770.23
evidential 957.16

cuneiform
n phonetic symbol
546.2
adj triangular 278.8
cunning
n falseheartedness 354.4
deceit 356.3
skill 413.1
craftiness 415.1
artfulness 415.1
shrewdness 920.3
adj falsehearted 354.31
deceitful 356.22
skillful 413.22
well-laid 413.30
crafty 415.12
shrewd 920.15
cup
n container 195.1
cupful 196.4
cavity 284.2
victory 411.1
monument 549.12
trophy 646.3
hockey 749.1
golf 751.1
soccer 752.1
skiing 753.1
track 755.1
fate 964.2
v bleed 91.27
ladle 176.17
be concave 284.12
hollow 284.13
cupboard
container 195.1
storehouse 386.6
Cupid symbol 104.9
Love 104.8
cupidity 100.8
cupola tower 272.6
arch 279.4
roof 295.6
cupping
bloodletting 91.20
drawing 192.3
cur mongrel 311.19
beast 660.6
curable 396.25
curate 699.2
curative
remedial 86.39
tonic 396.22
curator steward 574.4
treasurer 729.12
guardian 1008.6
curb
n kerb 211.6
pavement 383.6
restraint 428.1
stock exchange 737.7
check 1012.7
v slow 175.9
restrain 428.7
hinder 1012.10
curd
n clot 1045.7
semiliquid 1062.5
v thicken 1045.10
curdle thicken 1045.10
emulsify 1062.10

cure
n remedy 86.1
treatment 91.14
curing 396.7
commission 615.1
benefice 698.9
protectorship 1008.2
v remedy 86.38
treat 91.24
disaccustom 374.2
restore 396.15
preserve 397.9
prepare 405.6
solidify 1046.8
dry 1066.6
curé 699.5
cure-all 86.3
curfew 315.5
curio oddity 870.5
trifle 998.5
curiosity desire 100.1
marvel 122.2
oddity 870.5
inquisitiveness 981
alertness 981.1
attention 983.1
interest 983.2
curious careful 339.10
odd 870.11
inquiring 938.36
inquisitive 981.5
attentive 983.15
interested 983.16
curl
n lock 3.5
exercise 84.2
curve 279.2
coil 281.2
v curve 279.6
coil 281.5
curler
curling iron 281.3
wave 916.4
curlicue 281.2
curl up rest 20.6
snuggle 121.10
curly 281.9
curmudgeon
sorehead 110.11
niggard 484.4
currency
publicity 352.4
fashionableness 578.2
money 728.1
prevalence 864.2
usualness 869.2
current
n direction 161.1
course 172.2
flow 238.4
wind 318.1
trend 896.2
thoughts 931.4
electricity 1032.2
v follow the rule 867.4
adj published 352.17
customary 373.13
reported 552.15
fashionable 578.11
existent 761.13
happening 831.9

present 838.2
prevalent 864.12
usual 869.9
well-known 928.27
current affairs 552.1
curriculum 568.8
curried cooked 11.7
zestful 68.7
curry
n stew 10.11
v cook 11.5
comb 79.21
tend 1070.7
curry favor 138.9
curse
n affliction 96.8
malediction 513
hex 513.1
oath 513.4
spell 691.1
bad influence 1000.4
bane 1001.1
adversity 1011.1
v accurse 513.5
swear 513.6
blaspheme 694.5
work evil 1000.6
cursed
accursed 513.9
execrable 1000.10
cursive 547.22
cursory
insignificant 248.6
shallow 276.5
unwilling 325.5
careless 340.11
hasty 401.9
curt short 268.8
taciturn 344.9
gruff 505.7
concise 537.6
curtail reduce 252.7
subtract 255.9
contract 260.7
shorten 268.6
restrain 428.7
take from 480.21
curtain
n cover 295.2
partition 345.3
veil 346.2
act 704.7
stage 704.16
scenery 704.20
end 820.1
obstacle 1012.4
shade 1028.1
v cover 295.19
conceal 346.6
shade 1028.5
curtain call 704.7
curtain raiser act 704.7
overture 708.26
countdown 816.2
inauguration 818.5
curtains death 307.1
end 820.1
curtsy
n obeisance 155.2
greeting 585.4
crouch 913.3

v bow 155.6
show respect 433.10
greet 585.10
be polite 913.9
curvaceous
curved 279.7
comely 1016.19
curvature curving 279.1
turn 279.1
curve
n deviation 164.1
angle 278.2
sinus 279.2
trick 356.6
race 756.3
v deviate 164.3
deflect 164.5
angle 278.5
turn 279.6
adj curved 279.7
curvy crooked 204.20
wavy 279.7
comely 1016.19
cushion
n silencer 51.4
partition 213.5
moderator 670.3
bedding 901.20
safeguard 1008.3
softness 1047.4
v muffle 51.9
relieve 120.5
absorb the shock 670.8
support 901.21
protect 1008.18
soften 1047.6
cushioned 121.11
cushy
comfortable 121.11
easy 1014.13
cusp point 285.3
crisis 843.4
salience 997.6
cuss
n oath 513.4
v curse 513.6
cussedness
ill humor 110.3
malice 144.5
perversity 361.3
custodian cleaner 79.14
hospital staff 90.11
jailer 429.10
steward 574.4
guardian 1008.6
custodianship
vigilance 339.4
usage 387.2
preservation 397.1
custody 429.5
thrift 635.1
protectorship 1008.2
custody vigilance 339.4
storage 386.5
preservation 397.1
custodianship 429.5
directorship 573.4
protectorship 1008.2
custom
n behavior 321.1
convention 373.1

rite 373.1
habit 373.3
fashion 578.1
social more 579.1
patronage 731.6
market 733.3
tradition 842.2
adj made 892.18
customary
wonted 373.13
conventional 579.5
orthodox 687.7
traditional 842.12
usual 869.9
customer man 76.5
client 733.4
custom-made
tailored 5.48
made 892.18
customs 630.10
cut
n trauma 85.38
pain 96.5
indignity 156.2
snub 157.2
absence 222.4
crack 224.2
degree 245.1
gains 251.3
curtailment 252.4
reduction 255.2
form 262.1
shortcut 268.5
notch 289.1
furrow 290.1
trench 290.2
lamina 296.2
attempt 403.3
thrust 459.3
portion 477.5
gibe 508.2
mark 517.5
dividend 624.7
discount 631.1
cheapening 633.4
print 713.5
part 793.1
piece 793.3
break 802.4
characteristic 865.4
hit 902.4
slap 902.8
repulse 908.2
v dilute 16.11
pain 26.7
bite 68.5
hurt 96.17
offend 152.21
snub 157.5
slant across 204.11
leave 222.10
cleave 224.4
reduce 252.7
excise 255.10
delete 255.12
form 262.7
shorten 268.6
come to a point 285.6
notch 289.4
furrow 290.3
open 292.11

rarefy 299.3
leave undone 340.7
injure 393.13
discard 442.5
apportion 477.6
record 549.15
abridge 557.5
whip 604.13
discount 631.2
cheapen 633.6
engrave 713.9
sculpture 715.5
shuffle 758.5
separate 793.6
adulterate 797.12
sever 802.11
turn off 857.12
strike 902.15
repulse 908.3
banish 909.17
freeze 1023.10
liquefy 1064.5
cultivate 1069.17
harvest 1069.19
adj diluted 16.19
pained 96.23
cleft 224.7
formative 262.9
furrowed 290.4
rare 299.4
impaired 393.27
concise 537.6
reduced 633.9
engraved 713.11
severed 802.23
cut across
v cross 170.6
slice 204.11
take a short cut 268.7
adj cross 170.8
cut-and-dried
trite 117.9
ready-made 405.19
prearranged 965.7
cutaneous
n injection 91.17
adj cuticular 2.27
covering 295.32
cutback
n curtailment 252.4
economizing 635.2
adj reduced 252.10
cut back reduce 252.7
shorten 268.6
retrench 635.5
cut corners
take a short cut 268.7
slight 340.8
retrench 635.5
cut down reduce 252.7
shorten 268.6
kill 308.13
strike dead 308.18
raze 395.19
retrench 635.5
fell 913.5
cute deceitful 356.22
skillful 413.22
cunning 415.12
tricky 645.18
beautiful 1016.18

cuticle 295.3
cutie gal 302.7
beauty 1016.9
cut in intrude 214.5
interrupt 214.6
include 772.3
cut it be able 18.11
do 328.6
cut it out
v cease 857.6
interj stop! 857.13
cutlery tableware 8.12
edge tool 1040.2
cutlet 10.19
cut loose release 120.6
ship activity 182.48
escape 369.6
let oneself go 430.19
loose 431.6
extricate 431.7
run amok 671.15
make merry 743.24
separate 802.8
sever 802.11
riot 810.10
cutoff boundary 211.3
shortcut 268.5
end 395.2
stop 857.2
cut off
v excise 255.10
kill 308.13
put an end to 395.12
take from 480.21
dispossess 480.23
exclude 773.4
separate 802.8
sever 802.11
interrupt 857.10
adj bereft 473.8
cut out
v depart 188.7
extract 192.10
leave 222.10
excise 255.10
reject 372.2
plan 381.8
cease to use 390.4
exterminate 395.14
exclude 773.4
eliminate 773.5
separate 802.8
substitute for 862.5
adj talented 413.29
prearranged 965.7
cut-rate 633.9
cut short
v shorten 268.6
destroy 395.12
put a stop to 857.11
adj shortened 268.9
mutilated 795.5
cutter teeth 2.8
garmentmaker 5.34
shortener 268.4
separator 802.7
cutlery 1040.2
cut the mustard
be able 18.11
do 328.6
manage 409.12

suit 788.8
stand the test 942.10
suffice 991.4
cutthroat
  n killer 308.11
  ruffian 593.3
  adj murderous 308.24
  competitive 457.23
  overpriced 632.12
cutting
  n reduction 255.2
  plant 310.3
  apportionment 477.1
  morphology 526.3
  syntax 530.2
  abbreviation 537.4
  motion-picture editing 706.6
  piece 793.3
  adulteration 797.3
  severance 802.2
  harvest 1069.15
  adj acrimonious 17.14
  pungent 68.6
  penetrating 105.31
  caustic 144.23
  sharp 285.8
  vigorous 544.11
  violent 671.16
  cold 1023.14
  solvent 1064.8
cutting edge
  leading 165.1
  border 211.4
  vanguard 216.2
  sharp 285.2
  beginning 818.1
cutting remark 508.2
cutup
  mischief-maker 322.3
  humorist 489.12
  player 743.18
cut up
  v pain 96.17
  aggrieve 112.19
  misbehave 322.4
  apportion 477.6
  find fault 510.15
  play 743.23
  separate 793.6
  divide 802.18
  create disorder 810.11
  adj wretched 96.26
  sorrowful 112.26
  overcome 112.29
cyanosis blueness 45.1
  symptom 85.9
cybernetic
  n autonetic 1041.2
  adj servomechanical 1041.24
cyberspace 1042.19
cycle
  n wheel 179.8
  circle 280.2
  series 812.2
  age 824.4
  round 850.3
  circuit 914.2
  atomic cluster 1038.7
  v ride 177.33
  recur 850.5
  circle 914.5

cycles 1034.12
cyclical circular 280.11
  continuous 812.8
  recurrent 849.13
  periodic 850.7
cyclist 178.11
cyclone outburst 105.9
  weather map 317.4
  whirlwind 318.14
  storm 671.4
cyclonic
  climatal 317.13
  stormy 318.23
  rotary 915.15
cyclopedia reference book
  554.9
  lore 928.9
Cyclops 15.6
cygnet 311.28
cylinder 282.4
cylindrical
  tubular 239.16
  columnar 282.11
cynic pessimist 125.7
  disparager 512.6
  misanthrope 590.2
  doubter 955.4
cynical
  pessimistic 125.16
  satiric 508.13
  critical 510.23
  misanthropic 590.3
cynosure focus 208.4
  guiding star 574.8
  celebrity 662.9
  ideal 786.4
  attractor 907.2
cyst growth 85.39
  swelling 283.4
cytoplasm 305.4
czar ruler 575.9
  tyrant 575.14
dab
  n fish 10.24
  modicum 248.2
  tap 902.7
  stain 1004.3
  v color 35.14
  smooth 287.5
  coat 295.24
  tap 902.18
dabble spatter 80.18
  waste time 331.13
  not know 930.11
  trifle 998.14
  moisten 1065.12
dabbler
  dilettante 929.6
  ignoramus 930.8
  trifler 998.10
da capo 849.17
dactylic 720.16
dad father 560.10
  patriarch 842.8
dado
  n base 199.2
  furrow 290.1
  support 901.8
  v furrow 290.3
daedal variegated 47.9
  skillful 413.22

complex 799.4
daemon spirit 678.5
  familiar 678.12
  genius 920.8
  agricultural deity 1069.4
daft foolish 923.8
  insane 926.26
dagger
  n cross 170.4
  sword 462.5
  cutlery 1040.2
  v stab 459.25
daguerreotype
  n tintype 714.4
  v photograph 714.14
daily
  n cleaner 79.14
  periodical 555.1
  newspaper 555.2
  adj recurrent 849.13
  momentary 850.8
dainty
  n delicacy 10.8
  adj edible 8.33
  frail 16.14
  tasty 63.8
  clean 79.25
  delicate 248.7
  smooth 294.8
  light 298.12
  nice 495.11
  elegant 496.9
  fine 1016.20
dairy larder 386.8
  plant 739.3
dairyman 1070.2
dais authority 417.10
  platform 901.13
daisy 999.7
dale valley 237.7
  concavity 284.9
dalliance
  love affair 104.6
  dawdling 175.3
  lovemaking 562.1
  flirtation 562.9
  waiting 846.3
  trifling 998.8
dally dawdle 175.8
  dillydally 331.14
  make love 562.14
  wait 846.12
  trifle 998.14
dam
  n lake 241.1
  mother 560.11
  jockey 757.2
  barrier 1012.5
  v close 293.7
  put a stop to 857.11
damage
  n impairment 393.1
  loss 473.1
  price 630.1
  disadvantage 996.2
  evil 1000.3
  v impair 393.9
  work evil 1000.6
damages fine 603.3
  recompense 624.3
dame female 77.5

damsel 77.6
  woman 77.9
  gal 302.7
  old woman 304.3
  teacher 571.2
  mistress 575.2
  noblewoman 608.6
damn
  n trifle 998.5
  v destroy 395.10
  censure 510.13
  curse 513.5
  vilify 513.7
  condemn 602.3
  doom 682.6
  adj cursed 513.9
  interj damn it! 513.11
damnable cursed 513.9
  wicked 654.16
  execrable 1000.10
damnation
  destruction 395.1
  censure 510.3
  curse 513.1
  condemnation 602.1
damndest 403.16
damned
  n evil spirits 680.1
  adj cursed 513.9
  demoniac 680.17
  unregenerate 695.18
  execrable 1000.10
damning 957.16
damp
  n silencer 51.4
  killjoy 112.14
  deterrent 379.2
  moisture 1065.1
  vapor 1067.1
  v weaken 16.10
  muffle 51.9
  sadden 112.18
  reduce 252.7
  disincline 379.4
  moderate 670.6
  cushion 670.8
  make uniform 781.4
  hinder 1012.10
  fight fire 1022.7
  moisten 1065.12
  adj moist 1065.15
damp down 428.8
damper silencer 51.4
  killjoy 112.14
  deterrent 379.2
  curb 1012.7
  fire iron 1020.12
damsel 302.6
dance
  n dancing 705.1
  ball 705.1
  hop 705.2
  assembly 770.2
  flutter 917.4
  flicker 1025.8
  v exude cheerfulness 109.6
  rejoice 116.5
  trip the light fantastic 705.5
  play 743.23
  flutter 917.12
  flicker 1025.25

day of rest 20.5
daytime 1025.10
daze
  n trance 92.19
  confusion 985.3
  v blind 30.7
  astonish 122.6
  perplex 971.13
  confuse 985.7
  shine 1025.23
dazed stupefied 25.7
  blinded 30.10
  foolish 923.8
  in a dilemma 971.25
  mazed 985.14
dazzle
  n showiness 501.3
  v blind 30.7
  astonish 122.6
  cut a dash 501.13
  confuse 985.7
  shine 1025.23
dazzling
  blinding 30.11
  gorgeous 1016.21
  bright 1025.32
D-day zero hour 459.13
  crucial moment 843.5
deacon
  holy orders 699.4
  clergy 699.10
deactivate
  disarm 465.11
  disband 771.8
dead
  n silence 51.1
  corpse 307.16
  the majority 307.17
  adj tired 21.8
  asleep 22.22
  insensible 25.6
  unconscious 25.8
  colorless 36.7
  muffled 52.17
  insipid 65.2
  dull 117.6
  inert 173.14
  closed 293.9
  lifeless 307.30
  languid 331.20
  no more 762.11
  ended 820.8
  past 837.7
  obsolete 842.15
  lackluster 1027.17
  inanimate 1055.5
  adv directly 161.23
  extremely 247.22
  exactly 973.21
deadbeat 138.5
dead duck 125.8
deaden weaken 16.10
  desensitize 25.4
  muffle 51.9
  numb 94.8
  relieve 120.5
  moderate 670.6
  cushion 670.8
  dull 1027.10
dead end
  n obstruction 293.3

  impasse 1013.6
  adj closed 293.9
deadening
  n weakening 16.5
  relief 120.1
  modulation 670.2
  adj numbing 25.9
  anesthetic 86.47
  relieving 120.9
  mitigating 670.14
deadeye 904.8
dead giveaway 351.2
deadhead
  freeloader 634.3
  playgoer 704.27
dead letter 520.1
deadline
  boundary 211.3
  plan 381.1
  crucial moment 843.5
deadlock
  n standstill 173.3
  the same 790.3
  stop 857.2
  impasse 1013.6
  v put a stop to 857.11
  halt 1012.13
deadly
  poisonous 82.7
  remarkable 247.11
  deathly 307.29
  lethal 308.23
  destructive 395.26
  harmful 1000.12
dead march dirge 115.6
  slow motion 175.2
  funeral 309.5
  march 708.12
dead of night
  silence 51.1
  midnight 315.6
  darkness 1027.1
deadpan
  adj inexpressive
    522.20
  adv unfeelingly 94.14
dead reckoning
  location 159.3
  navigation 182.2
dead ringer
  image 349.5
  the same 778.3
dead set against
  unwilling 325.5
  oppositional 451.8
  disapproving 510.21
dead set on 359.16
dead to the world
  asleep 22.22
  unconscious 25.8
  oblivious 984.7
  abstracted 985.11
deadweight
  n impediment 1012.6
  weight 297.1
  onerousness 297.2
  burden 297.7
  adj heavy 297.16
deadwood
  branch 310.20
  refuse 391.4

deaf
  hard of hearing 49.6
  unpersuadable 361.13
  narrow-minded 980.10
  oblivious 984.7
deafen stun 49.5
  muffle 51.9
  din 53.7
deafening intense 15.22
  loud 53.11
deaf-mute
  n the deaf 49.2
  mute 51.3
  adj deaf 49.6
deafness
  hardness of hearing 49
  handicap 49.1
  ear disease 85.15
  unpersuadableness 361.5
  incognizance 930.3
deaf to insensible 94.10
  unconsenting 442.6
  unaware 930.13
deal
  n amount 244.2
  lot 247.4
  lamina 296.2
  act 328.3
  undertaking 404.1
  compact 437.1
  compromise 468.1
  portion 477.5
  transaction 731.4
  bargain 731.5
  blackjack 759.11
  wood 1054.3
  v use 87.22
  parcel out 477.8
  give 478.12
  trade 731.15
  bargain 731.18
  shuffle 758.5
  dispose 808.9
  hit 902.14
dealer merchant 730.2
  racketeer 732.4
  stockbroker 737.10
dealings act 328.3
  communication 343.1
  commerce 731.1
  relation 775.1
  affairs 831.4
deal one in 477.6
deal with treat 321.6
  perform 328.9
  communicate 343.6
  use 387.12
  accomplish 407.4
  discuss 541.12
  write upon 556.5
  punish 604.10
  trade with 731.17
  relate to 775.5
  operate 889.5
dean
  n superior 249.4
  senior 304.5
  principal 571.8
  executive 574.3
  chief 575.3
  gambler 759.21

  adj older 842.19
dear
  n sweetheart 104.10
  endearment term 562.6
  adj beloved 104.24
  precious 632.10
  expensive 632.11
  adv dearly 632.13
  interj my! 122.21
dearth
  unproductiveness 891.1
  scarcity 992.3
death fatal disease 85.2
  dying 307.1
  finality 307.1
  destruction 395.2
  end 820.1
  transience 828.1
  bane 1001.1
deathbed
  n moribundity 307.9
  adj later 846.18
deathblow
  early death 307.5
  death stroke 308.10
  end 395.2
  defeat 412.1
  finishing stroke 820.4
death-defying 493.9
death grip 474.2
death knell dirge 115.6
  death 307.1
  end 395.2
deathless
  immortal 829.9
  indestructible 855.18
deathly
  deathlike 307.29
  deadly 308.23
death penalty 602.1
death song dirge 115.6
  swan song 307.10
death struggle
  moribundity 307.9
  life-and-death struggle 457.6
deathwatch
  moribundity 307.9
  last offices 309.4
debacle descent 194.1
  disaster 395.4
  defeat 412.1
  revolution 860.1
debar prohibit 444.3
  exclude 773.4
  obstruct 1012.12
  prevent 1012.14
debarkation 186.2
debase abase 137.5
  lower 274.6
  misuse 389.4
  corrupt 393.12
  demote 447.3
  disparage 512.8
  disgrace 661.8
  adulterate 797.12
  depress 913.4
debased low 274.7
  corrupt 654.14
  base 661.12
  depressed 913.12
debatable 971.17

debate
n contention 457.1
discussion 541.7
speech 543.2
legislative procedure 613.6
argumentation 935.4
v hesitate 362.7
discuss 541.12
declaim 543.10
consider 931.12
debauch
n spree 88.5
dissipation 669.2
v go on a spree 88.28
corrupt 393.12
be promiscuous 665.19
seduce 665.20
dissipate 669.6
make merry 743.24
debauchery
profligacy 665.3
dissipation 669.2
debenture 728.11
debilitate 252.8
debilitated weak 16.12
ineffective 19.15
unmanned 19.19
tired 21.7
unhealthy 85.54
stricken in years 303.18
languid 331.20
debility weakness 16.1
fatigue 21.1
unhealthiness 85.3
old age 303.5
debit
n loss 473.1
expenditure 626.1
entry 628.5
v keep accounts 628.8
debonair 109.12
debouch
n outlet 190.9
v burst forth 33.9
emerge 190.11
find vent 369.10
disgorge 909.25
debrief brief 184.48
disband 771.8
debris deposit 176.9
remainder 256.1
rubbish 391.5
grain 1051.6
debt borrowing 621.1
liability 623
indebtedness 623.1
debtor borrowing 621.1
borrower 623.4
debug 940.2
debunk 977.2
debunker 512.6
debut
n coming out 582.15
theatrical performance
704.12
inauguration 818.5
v act 704.29
enter 818.9
debutante 578.7
decade moment 824.2
ten 882.6

decadent
deteriorating 393.45
corrupt 654.14
decal
stencil printing 713.4
adhesive 803.4
decalogue 636.1
decamp depart 188.6
break camp 188.14
flee 368.10
decant ladle 176.17
draw off 192.12
disgorge 909.25
decapitate 604.17
decathlon sport 744.1
track meet 755.2
decay
n filth 80.7
decomposition 393.6
rot 393.7
disintegration 806.1
dissociation 806.2
v decompose 393.22
disintegrate 806.3
decease
n death 307.1
end 820.1
v die 307.19
deceased
n corpse 307.16
adj dead 307.30
past 837.7
deceit
falseness 356.3
stratagem 415.3
deceitful
falsehearted 354.31
false 356.22
cunning 415.12
improper 645.18
deceive lie 354.19
beguile 356.14
live by one's wits 415.9
outwit 415.11
impose on 643.7
be dishonest 645.11
seduce 665.20
deceiver imitator 336.4
misleader 357.1
deluder 357.1
evildoer 593.1
con man 645.10
criminal 660.9
seducer 665.12
cheater 759.22
deceleration
slowing 175.4
decline 252.2
restraint 428.1
decent kind 143.13
indulgent 427.8
decorous 496.10
conventional 579.5
right 637.3
honest 644.13
modest 664.5
sufficient 991.6
expedient 995.5
tolerable 999.20
decentralization
divergence 171.1

deconcentration 771.2
deception
concealment 346.1
sham 354.3
falseness 356.3
calculated lie 356.1
hoax 356.7
cheating 759.13
illusion 976.1
deceptive
deceiving 356.21
sophistical 936.10
erroneous 975.16
illusory 976.9
decibel 50.7
decide
resolve 359.7
induce 375.22
determine 886.12
exercise influence 894.8
judge 946.11
make sure 970.11
will 323.2
decide against 444.5
decided
downright 247.12
affirmative 334.8
resolute 359.11
ended 820.8
unqualified 960.2
assured 970.20
confident 970.21
emphatic 997.21
decide upon 371.16
deciduous
descending 194.11
arboreal 310.39
perennial 310.44
transient 828.7
decimal tenth 882.22
numeric 1017.23
decimate
slaughter 308.17
destroy 395.10
decipher
explain 341.10
make clear 521.6
solve 940.2
decipherable
intelligible 521.10
legible 521.12
solvable 940.3
decision will 323.1
resolution 359.1
choice 371.1
judgment 598.9
fight 754.3
verdict 946.5
decisive
resolute 359.11
mandatory 420.12
critical 843.10
prompt 845.9
causal 886.13
convincing 953.26
evidential 957.16
unqualified 960.2
certain 970.13
deck
n dose 87.20
ground covering 199.3

layer 296.1
card 758.2
bundle 770.8
platform 901.13
v clothe 5.39
overcome 412.7
ornament 498.8
beat 902.17
fell 913.5
deckhand 183.6
declaim
proclaim 352.13
speak 524.19
hold forth 543.10
overact 704.31
declamatory
elocutionary 543.12
grandiloquent 545.8
declaration
acknowledgment 332.3
affirmation 334.1
announcement 352.2
decree 420.4
remark 524.3
statement 598.7
profession 953.7
testimony 957.2
declare affirm 334.5
announce 352.12
command 420.8
speak 524.23
state 953.12
declare war
contend 457.13
make war on 458.15
déclassé
n outcast 586.4
adj upper-class 607.10
decline
n sinkage 194.2
declivity 204.5
declension 252.2
deterioration 393.3
cheapening 633.4
price 738.9
close 820.3
shortcoming 911.1
senility 922.10
v weaken 16.9
fail 85.48
recede 168.2
sink 194.6
slope 204.10
decrease 252.6
age 303.10
reject 372.2
sink 393.17
refuse 442.3
grammaticize 530.16
cheapen 633.6
fall short 911.2
fall on evil days
1011.11
declivity descent 204.5
slope 237.2
decoction extract 192.7
product 192.8
concoction 405.3
imbuement 797.2
boiling 1020.2
solution 1064.3

emigration 190.7
denial 335.2
apostasy 363.2
desertion 370.2
nonpayment 625.1
change 852.1
conversion 858.3
fault 1003.2
defective
  n cripple 85.45
  idiot 924.8
  adj incomplete 795.4
  erroneous 975.16
  insufficient 992.9
  imperfect 1003.4
  blemished 1004.8
defend guard 460.8
  offer in defense 600.10
  protect 1008.18
defendant
  oppositionist 452.3
  litigant 598.11
  accused 599.6
defender
  champion 460.7
  justifier 600.8
  supporter 616.9
  team 752.2
  protector 1008.5
defense protection 460
  front 460.1
  pleadings 598.6
  plea 600.2
  basketball game 747.3
  hockey strategy 749.2
  team 749.5
  fight 754.3
  countermeasure 900.5
  argumentation 935.4
  rebuttal 939.2
  wall 1008.1
  barrier 1012.5
defenseless
  helpless 19.18
  forlorn 584.12
  unprotected 1006.14
defense mechanism
  reaction 92.23
  avoidance 368.1
  instinct 460.1
  block 990.3
defensive
  defending 460.11
  protective 1008.23
defer retreat 163.6
  retract 168.3
  postpone 846.9
deference respect 155.1
  obedience 326.1
  submission 433.1
  observance 434.1
  courtesy 504.1
  duty 641.1
deferential
  respectful 155.8
  obedient 326.3
  obeisant 433.16
  courteous 504.14
  dutiful 641.13
defer to respect 155.4
  obey 326.2

submit to 433.9
observe 434.2
defiance
  impenitence 114.2
  refractoriness 327.2
  ungovernability 361.4
  resistance 453.1
  defying 454
  disobedience 454.1
  declaration of war 458.7
defiant
  impenitent 114.5
  disobedient 327.8
  refractory 327.10
  ungovernable 361.12
  defying 454.7
deficiency
  inadequacy 250.3
  incompleteness 795.1
  want 795.2
  lack 992.4
  imperfection 1003.1
  fault 1003.2
deficient
  inadequate 250.7
  slipshod 340.12
  incomplete 795.4
  short of 911.5
  insufficient 992.9
  imperfect 1003.4
deficit difference 255.8
  debt 623.1
  arrears 623.2
  deficiency 795.2
  shortcoming 911.1
  want 992.4
defile
  n valley 237.7
  narrow place 270.3
  passageway 383.3
  v foul 80.17
  march 177.30
  misuse 389.4
  corrupt 393.12
  vilify 512.10
  impair 654.10
  stigmatize 661.9
  seduce 665.20
  file 812.7
  work evil 1000.6
define
  circumscribe 210.4
  interpret 341.9
  mark 517.19
  name 527.11
  fix 855.9
  characterize 865.10
defined distinct 31.7
  circumscribed 210.6
  clear 521.11
  particular 865.12
defining
  limiting 210.9
  classificational 809.7
definite distinct 31.7
  audible 50.16
  circumscribed 210.6
  resolute 359.11
  clear 521.11
  particular 865.12
  unqualified 960.2

certain 970.13
definite article 530.6
definition
  distinctness 31.2
  circumscription 210.1
  interpretation 341.1
  explanation 518.3
  clearness 521.2
  naming 527.2
  characterization 865.8
  television reception 1035.5
definitive
  limiting 210.9
  downright 247.12
  ending 820.10
  final 820.11
  unqualified 960.2
deflate disable 19.10
  humiliate 137.4
  reduce 252.7
  collapse 260.10
  cheapen 633.6
  disprove 958.4
deflation
  humiliation 137.2
  decrease 252.1
  contraction 260.4
  collapse 410.3
  cheapening 633.4
  business cycle 731.10
deflect deviate 164.5
  oblique 204.9
  curve 279.6
  disincline 379.4
  prevent 1012.14
deflection
  bending 164.2
  obliquity 204.1
  angle 278.2
  curve 279.3
  radar interference 1036.12
deflector 1035.11
deflower
  corrupt 393.12
  possess sexually 480.15
  seduce 665.20
defluxion outflow 190.4
  descent 194.1
  stream 238.4
defoliant 1001.3
defoliate 802.14
deforestation 1069.3
deform distort 263.3
  misshape 265.7
  change 852.7
  blemish 1004.4
deformation
  disfigurement 265.3
  misrepresentation 350.1
  deterioration 393.3
  blemish 1004.1
deformed
  malformed 265.12
  freakish 870.13
  blemished 1004.8
  unshapely 1015.8
deformity disease 85.1
  cripple 85.45
  deformation 265.3
  oddity 870.3
  blemish 1004.1

hideousness 1015.2
defraud cheat 356.18
  steal 482.13
defray 624.18
defrock depose 447.4
  disgrace 661.8
  dismiss 909.19
defrost 1020.21
deft 413.22
defunct dead 307.30
  no more 762.11
  ended 820.8
  past 837.7
defuse relieve 120.5
  keep the peace 464.8
  pacify 465.7
  moderate 670.6
defy
  n challenge 454.2
  v confront 216.8
  disobey 327.6
  violate 435.4
  bid defiance 454.3
  dare 492.10
  resist 453.2
  make war on 458.15
  thwart 1012.15
dégagé
  nonchalant 106.15
  careless 340.11
  informal 581.3
degenerate
  n reprobate 660.4
  v corrupt 393.12
  deteriorate 393.16
  go wrong 654.9
  lapse into disorder 810.8
  be changed 852.6
  defect 858.13
  evolve 861.5
  fall on evil days 1011.11
  adj deteriorating 393.45
  corrupt 654.14
  changed 852.10
  apostate 858.20
degradable
  biodegradable 393.47
  disintegrative 806.5
degradation
  deterioration 393.3
  decay 393.6
  demotion 447.1
  knavery 645.2
  turpitude 654.5
  baseness 661.3
  infamy 661.4
  disintegration 806.1
  banishment 909.4
  depression 913.1
degrade abase 137.5
  corrupt 393.12
  demote 447.3
  disparage 512.8
  disgrace 661.8
  dismiss 909.19
degree grade 245.1
  rank 245.1
  measure 300.2
  extent 300.3
  class 607.1
  academic honor 648.6

staff 708.29
interval 709.20
continuity 807.2
degrees
points of the compass 161.3
graduate 572.8
dehumanize 144.15
dehumidify 1066.6
dehydrate
preserve 397.9
dry 1066.6
dehydration 1066.1
deice 1020.21
deification
respect 155.1
praise 509.5
glorification 662.8
idolization 697.2
elevation 912.1
deify respect 155.4
praise 509.12
glorify 662.13
idolatrize 697.5
exalt 912.6
deign condescend 137.8
give oneself airs 141.8
consent 441.2
deism 675.5
deist 675.16
deity divinity 677.1
spirit 677.1
god 678.2
déjà vu 689.6
remembering 989.4
deject 112.18
dejected sullen 110.24
depressed 112.22
dejection
defecation 12.2
excrement 12.3
sullenness 110.8
depression 112.3
de jure 673.13
delay
n slowing 175.4
stoppage 846.2
hindrance 1012.1
v dawdle 175.8
slow 175.9
do nothing 329.2
put away 390.6
retard 846.8
postpone 846.9
wait 846.12
hinder 1012.10
delectable tasty 63.8
delicious 97.10
delectation 95.2
delegate
n legate 576.2
v commit 478.16
commission 615.10
deputize 862.7
delegation
authority 417.12
commitment 478.2
deputation 576.13
commission 615.1
substitution 862.1
delete erase 255.12
obliterate 395.16

separate 802.8
end 820.5
deleted absent 222.11
ended 820.8
deleterious
disadvantageous 996.6
harmful 1000.12
deliberate
v hesitate 362.7
confer 541.11
discuss 541.12
consider 931.12
adj slow 175.10
intentional 380.8
leisurely 402.6
cautious 494.8
deliberated
intentional 380.8
reasoned 935.21
deliberation
slowness 175.1
intentionality 380.3
leisureliness 402.2
caution 494.1
discussion 541.7
legislative procedure 613.6
consideration 931.2
deliberative
conciliar 423.5
legislative 613.11
cognitive 931.21
delicacy tidbit 10.8
frailty 16.2
sensitivity 24.3
unhealthiness 85.3
sensibility 93.4
tenderness 93.6
considerateness 143.3
insignificance 248.1
thinness 270.4
smoothness 294.3
lightness 298.1
meticulousness 339.3
nicety 495.3
taste 496.1
decency 664.2
margin 780.2
discrimination 944.1
accuracy 973.5
dangerousness 1006.2
daintiness 1016.5
softness 1047.1
brittleness 1050.1
delicate frail 16.14
sensitive 24.12
soft-colored 35.22
tasty 63.8
feeling 93.20
considerate 143.16
dainty 248.7
thin 270.16
smooth 294.8
light 298.12
meticulous 339.12
nice 495.11
elegant 496.9
decent 664.5
discriminating 944.7
exact 973.17
precarious 1006.12
difficult 1013.17

fine 1016.20
soft 1047.8
brittle 1050.4
delicatessen 8.17
delicious edible 8.33
tasty 63.8
delightful 97.7
delectable 97.10
excellent 999.13
delight
n happiness 95.2
tendency 896.1
v delectate 95.10
be pleased 95.12
rejoice 116.5
exult 502.9
amuse 743.21
delighted pleased 95.15
amused 743.26
delightful tasty 63.8
exquisite 97.7
amusing 743.27
Delilah 665.15
delimit
circumscribe 210.4
mark 517.19
delimitation
circumscription 210.1
boundary 211.3
delineate outline 211.9
represent 349.8
describe 349.9
plan 381.11
portray 712.19
delineation
outline 211.2
representation 349.1
description 349.2
diagram 381.3
line 517.6
drawing 712.5
sketch 712.13
fiction 722.1
delineator limner 716.2
draftsman 716.3
delinquency
misbehavior 322.1
disobedience 327.1
nonobservance 435.1
nonpayment 625.1
wrong 638.1
vice 654.1
misdeed 655.2
lawbreaking 674.3
shortcoming 911.1
delinquent
n evildoer 593.1
defaulter 625.5
wrongdoer 660.8
adj defaulting 625.10
wrong 638.3
deliquescent
decreasing 252.11
liquefied 1064.6
delirious feverish 85.58
fervent 93.18
overzealous 101.12
frenzied 105.25
out of one's head 926.31
delirium fever 85.7
fury 105.8

deliriousness 926.8
figment of the imagination
986.5
delirium tremens
alcoholism 88.3
shaking 917.2
mania 926.9
hallucination 976.7
deliver release 120.6
transfer 176.10
do 328.6
rescue 398.3
accomplish 407.4
succeed 409.7
liberate 431.4
hand 478.13
say 524.22
send 629.3
play 745.5
perform 892.11
deliverance
release 120.2
escape 369.1
rescue 398.1
liberation 431.1
giving 478.1
transfer 629.1
verdict 946.5
deliverer
preserver 397.5
savior 592.2
delivery birth 1.1
transportation 176.3
escape 369.1
rescue 398.1
liberation 431.1
giving 478.1
articulation 524.5
transfer 629.1
pitch 745.3
game 750.2
dell highland 237.7
valley 284.9
delocalize 176.11
delouse 79.24
Delphic oracle 962.7
delta fork 171.4
plain 236.1
point of land 283.9
deltoid
diverging 171.8
spread 259.11
triangular 278.8
three 876.3
tripartite 878.4
delude deceive 356.10
be mistaken 975.10
deluded 926.26
deluge
n torrent 238.5
overflow 238.6
rainstorm 316.2
throng 770.4
superabundance 993.2
wetting 1065.6
v overflow 238.17
submerge 367.7
oversupply 993.14
flood 1065.14
delusion sham 354.3
deception 356.1

error 975.1
illusion 976.1
delusional 356.21
deluxe 501.21
delve
excavate 284.15
search 938.31
cultivate 1069.17
demagnetize 1032.27
demagogue
n instigator 375.11
speaker 543.4
v declaim 543.10
demand
n extortion 192.6
stipulation 421.2
claim 421.1
request 440.1
fee 630.6
prerogative 642.1
imposition 643.1
sale 734.1
question 938.10
requirement 963.2
v extort 192.15
prescribe 420.9
summon 420.11
ask 421.5
oblige 424.5
request 440.9
charge 630.12
impose 643.4
inquire 938.20
require 963.9
demanding
meticulous 339.12
exacting 421.9
strict 425.6
importunate 440.18
difficult 1013.17
demarcate
circumscribe 210.4
mark 517.19
differentiate 780.6
characterize 865.10
discriminate 944.4
demarcation
circumscription 210.1
exclusion 773.1
differentiation 780.4
distinction 944.3
demasculinize
unman 19.12
feminize 77.13
demean 137.5
demeaning
inferior 250.6
disgraceful 661.11
demeanor looks 33.4
behavior 321.1
demented
turbulent 671.18
insane 926.26
dementia 926.1
demesne
sphere 231.2
real estate 471.6
farm 1069.8
Demeter
fertility 890.5
agricultural deity 1069.4

demigod
brave person 492.8
hero 659.5
godling 678.3
demilitarize 465.11
demimonde 665.15
demise
n death 307.1
transfer 629.1
v transfer 629.3
demobilize
release 431.5
disarm 465.11
disband 771.8
democracy
communion 476.2
government 612.4
democratic centralism
611.5
demographic
human 312.13
populational 606.8
demography
population 227.1
anthropology 312.10
the people 606.1
demolish
wreck 395.17
shatter 802.13
disassemble 802.15
refute 958.5
demolition
demolishment 395.5
refutation 958.2
demon
enthusiast 101.5
monster 593.6
violent person 671.9
spirit 678.5
familiar spirit 678.12
fiend 680.6
genius 920.8
demonic
frenzied 105.25
diabolic 654.13
demoniac 680.17
possessed 926.29
execrable 1000.10
demonism
Satanism 680.14
black magic 690.2
idolatry 697.1
demonology 690.2
demonstrable
manifested 348.13
real 761.15
provable 957.19
obvious 970.15
demonstrate
object 333.5
explain 341.10
manifest 348.5
image 349.11
flaunt 501.17
teach 568.10
evidence 957.8
prove 957.10
cite 957.13
check 1017.21
demonstrated
manifested 348.13

proved 957.20
true 973.13
demonstration
objection 333.2
explanation 341.4
manifestation 348.2
representation 349.1
display 501.4
assembly 770.2
example 786.2
reasoning 935.1
proof 957.3
citation 957.5
demonstrative
emotional 93.17
loving 104.27
explanatory 341.15
communicative 343.10
manifesting 348.9
indicative 517.23
evincive 957.17
demonstrator
interpreter 341.7
picket 1008.13
demoralize
intimidate 127.20
unnerve 128.10
corrupt 654.10
demos 606.1
Demosthenes 543.6
demote degrade 447.3
dismiss 909.19
overthrow 913.6
demotion
deterioration 393.3
downgrading 447.1
degrading 447.1
infamy 661.4
banishment 909.4
depression 913.1
demulcent
n balm 86.11
ointment 1056.3
adj palliative 86.40
relieving 120.9
moderate 670.16
softening 1047.16
demur
n scruple 325.2
objection 333.2
resistance 453.1
v scruple 325.4
object 333.5
hesitate 362.7
demure solemn 111.3
shy 139.12
prudish 500.19
demurrer
objection 333.2
dissenter 333.3
pleadings 598.6
defense 600.2
demystify 521.6
demythologize 341.10
den sanctum 197.8
lair 228.26
disapproved place 228.28
hiding place 346.4
sewer 654.7
office 739.7
retreat 1009.5

denature
corrupt 393.12
adulterate 797.12
change 852.7
deniability
incognizance 930.3
doubtfulness 971.2
denial
disaffirmation 335.2
disavowal 335.2
recantation 363.3
rejection 372.1
refusal 442.1
prohibition 444.1
opposition 451.1
loss 473.1
defense 600.2
temperance 668.1
unbelief 955.1
refutation 958.2
denied rejected 372.3
disproved 958.7
denied to 967.9
denigrate blacken 38.7
deprecate 510.12
vilify 512.10
denizen
n inhabitant 227.2
v people 225.9
den of iniquity
sewer 654.7
brothel 665.9
denomination
indication 517.3
naming 527.2
name 527.3
school 617.5
sect 675.3
kind 809.3
specification 865.6
denominator division
1017.12
ratio 1017.7
denotation
indication 517.3
meaning 518.1
denote signify 517.17
designate 517.18
mean 518.8
evidence 957.8
denouement plot 722.4
end 820.1
solution 940.1
denounce
censure 510.13
threaten 514.2
accuse 599.7
condemn 602.3
dense thick 269.8
luxuriant 310.43
sturdy 763.7
crowded 770.22
stupid 922.15
compact 1045.12
hard 1046.10
density
substantiality 763.1
stupidity 922.3
solidness 1045.1
compactness 1045.1
hardness 1046.1

dent
  n indentation 284.6
  print 517.7
  v indent 284.14
dental hygienist 81.3
dentate notched 289.5
  prehensile 474.9
denticulate 285.14
dentist 90.6
dentistry 90.3
denude divest 6.5
  strip 480.24
  tear apart 802.14
denuded divested 6.12
  bereft 473.8
denuded of 992.13
denunciation
  censure 510.3
  curse 513.1
  threat 514.1
  accusation 599.1
  condemnation 602.1
deny
  n recant 363.8
  v not admit 335.4
  reject 372.2
  withhold 442.4
  prohibit 444.3
  contradict 451.6
  disbelieve 955.5
  refute 958.5
deny oneself
  abstain 667.3
  restrain oneself 668.6
  detemperate 668.7
deodorant 72.3
deodorize
  fumigate 72.4
  falsify 354.16
Deo volente 966.11
depart disappear 34.2
  deviate 164.3
  make off 188.6
  exit 190.12
  absent oneself 222.8
  die 307.19
  flee 368.10
  abandon 370.5
  digress 538.9
  differ 780.5
  separate 802.8
departed
  left 188.19
  absent 222.11
  dead 307.30
  past 837.7
department
  region 231.1
  sphere 231.2
  bureau 594.4
  occupation 724.4
department store 736.1
departure
  disappearance 34.1
  deviation 164.1
  leaving 188.1
  leave-taking 188.4
  egress 190.2
  absence 222.4
  death 307.1
  digression 538.4

difference 780.1
depend pend 202.6
  hang 959.6
  all depend 971.11
dependability
  trustworthiness 644.6
  reliability 970.4
dependable
  trustworthy 644.19
  reliable 970.17
  unhazardous 1007.5
dependence hope 124.1
  pendency 202.1
  tutelage 432.3
  supporter 616.9
  relativity 775.2
  belief 953.1
dependency
  pendency 202.1
  tutelage 432.3
  dependent 432.6
  possession 469.1
dependent
  n hanger-on 138.6
  follower 166.2
  charge 432.6
  retainer 577.1
  adj pendent 202.9
  subject 432.13
  trusting 953.22
  contingent 959.9
  undecided 971.18
depend on
  be at the mercy of 432.12
  result from 887.5
  rely on 953.16
  trust 953.17
  depend 959.6
depersonalization 92.20
depict
  represent 349.8
  describe 349.9
  enact 704.30
  portray 712.19
depiction
  representation 349.1
  description 349.2
depilation 1016.15
depilatory 6.4
deplane 186.8
deplete consume 388.3
  waste 473.5
  evacuate 909.22
depletion
  decrement 252.3
  reduction 255.2
  consumption 388.1
  waste 473.2
  evacuation 909.6
deplorable
  distressing 98.20
  regrettable 113.10
  disgraceful 661.11
  terrible 1000.9
deplore
  regret 113.6
  lament 115.10
deploy locate 159.11
  diverge 171.5
  spread 259.6
  prepare 405.6

order 807.4
  adduce 957.12
deployment
  placement 159.6
  divergence 171.1
  expansion 259.1
  battle array 458.3
  order 807.1
  arrangement 808.1
deplume
  demote 447.3
  strip 480.24
  disgrace 661.8
  dismiss 909.19
depopulate
  slaughter 308.17
  dispeople 909.16
deport transfer 176.10
  emigrate 190.16
  eliminate 773.5
  banish 909.17
deportment 321.1
depose dislodge 160.6
  depone 334.6
  remove from office 447.4
  dismiss 909.19
  overthrow 913.6
  state 953.12
  testify 957.9
deposit
  n placement 159.6
  sediment 176.9
  collateral 438.3
  payment 624.1
  precipitation 1045.5
  mineral deposit 1058.7
  v lay 78.9
  repose 159.14
  secrete 346.7
  store 386.10
  pledge 438.10
  precipitate 1045.11
deposition
  placement 159.6
  dregs 256.2
  sworn statement 334.3
  deposal 447.2
  certificate 549.6
  declaration 598.7
  statement of belief 953.4
  testimony 957.2
depository
  storehouse 386.6
  trustee 470.5
  treasurer 729.12
  treasury 729.13
depot 386.6
deprave
  corrupt 393.12
  work evil 1000.6
depravity
  turpitude 654.5
  baseness 661.3
deprecate
  discommend 510.12
  underestimate 950.2
  attach little importance to
    998.12
deprecatory
  self-effacing 139.10
  condemnatory 510.22

disparaging 512.13
depreciate
  reduce 252.7
  subtract 255.9
  waste 473.5
  depreciate 510.12
  disparage 512.8
  discount 631.2
  cheapen 633.6
  underestimate 950.2
  attach little importance to
    998.12
depreciation
  decrease 252.1
  reduction 255.2
  deterioration 393.3
  waste 473.2
  deprecation 510.2
  disparagement 512.1
  discount 631.1
  cheapening 633.4
  underestimation 950.1
depredate
  destroy 395.10
  plunder 482.17
depress
  sadden 112.18
  reduce 252.7
  lower 274.6
  deepen 275.8
  indent 284.14
  press down 913.4
depressant
  n sedative 86.12
  drug 87.3
  adj sedative 86.45
  depressing 112.30
depressed
  pleasureless 96.20
  dejected 112.22
  low 274.7
  indented 284.17
  lowered 913.12
  unfortunate 1011.14
depression
  mental disorder 92.14
  wretchedness 96.6
  distressfulness 98.5
  dejection 112.3
  decrease 252.1
  lowness 274.1
  deepening 275.7
  concavity 284.1
  cavity 284.2
  notch 289.1
  business cycle 731.10
  lowering 913.1
  melancholia 926.5
  hard times 1011.6
Depression Era 824.5
deprivation
  absence 222.1
  refusal 442.1
  deposal 447.2
  loss 473.1
  divestment 480.6
  indigence 619.2
  nonexistence 762.1
  disassembly 802.6
  banishment 909.4
  want 992.4

deprive
take from 480.21
dismiss 909.19
deprived limited 210.7
bereaved 307.35
indigent 619.8
deprived of
bereft 473.8
wanting 992.13
depth space 158.1
interiority 207.1
size 257.1
thickness 269.2
deepness 275.1
pit 275.2
pitch 709.4
wisdom 920.5
deputation
authority 417.12
delegation 576.13
commission 615.1
substitution 862.1
deputize
empower 18.10
represent 576.14
commission 615.10
delegate 862.7
deputy
n mediator 466.3
director 574.1
representative 576.1
proxy 576.1
lawyer 597.1
assignee 615.9
assistant 616.6
substitute 862.2
policeman 1008.15
adj deputative 576.16
deracinate
dislodge 160.6
extract 192.10
exterminate 395.14
derail miscarry 410.15
distract 985.6
thwart 1012.15
derange afflict 85.50
disarrange 811.2
madden 926.24
derangement
disorder 810.1
disarrangement 811.1
abnormality 870.1
insanity 926.1
derby contest 457.3
race 457.12
Derby 757.1
deregulate
not interfere 430.16
politicize 611.16
deregulation
noninterference 430.9
disembarrassment
1014.6
derelict
n bum 331.9
castoff 370.4
outcast 586.4
wretch 660.2
transient 828.4
adj negligent 340.10
abandoned 370.8

dilapidated 393.33
outcast 586.10
unfaithful 645.20
dereliction
disobedience 327.1
neglect 340.1
desertion 370.2
nonobservance 435.1
infidelity 645.5
misdeed 655.2
badness 1000.1
deride disdain 157.3
flout 454.4
ridicule 508.8
have the audacity 142.7
de rigueur
conventional 579.5
obligatory 641.15
derisive
impudent 142.10
disrespectful 156.7
defiant 454.7
ridiculing 508.12
condemnatory 510.22
disparaging 512.13
derivation
receiving 479.1
root 526.2
morphology 526.3
etymology 526.15
lineage 560.4
adoption 621.2
source 886.5
effect 887.1
conclusion 946.4
derivative
n root 526.2
effect 887.1
adj resultant 887.6
attributable 888.6
uncreative 891.5
derive elicit 192.14
acquire 472.8
receive 479.6
conclude 946.10
derive from
receive 479.6
adopt 621.4
result from 887.5
trace to 888.5
dermal
cutaneous 2.27
covering 295.32
dermis the skin 2.4
skin 295.3
dernier cri 841.2
derogation
reduction 255.2
deterioration 393.3
disparagement 512.1
derogatory
disparaging 512.13
disreputable 661.10
derrick tower 272.6
lifter 912.3
derriére 217.4
derring-do 492.5
dervish ascetic 667.2
Muslim 675.23
clergy 699.12
désœuvré 331.18

descant
n treatise 556.1
air 708.4
part 708.22
overture 708.26
v amplify 538.7
write upon 556.5
sing 708.38
descend
condescend 137.8
give oneself airs 141.8
move 172.5
land 184.43
go down 194.5
incline 204.10
gravitate 297.15
change hands 629.4
incur disgrace 661.7
descendant
offspring 561.3
successor 817.4
sequel 835.2
descending
n course 172.2
descent 194.1
adj flowing 172.8
descendant 194.11
sloping downward 204.16
descend upon
light upon 194.10
attack 459.14
descent
humiliation 137.2
course 172.2
motion downward 194
descending 194.1
declivity 204.5
deterioration 393.3
lineage 560.4
offspring 561.1
series 812.2
sequence 815.1
conversion 858.1
depression 913.1
reverse 1011.3
rocket launching 1074.9
describe
interpret 341.9
portray 349.9
characterize 865.10
description
interpretation 341.1
portrayal 349.2
portrait 349.5
fiction 722.1
kind 809.3
characterization 865.8
descriptive
interpretative 341.14
depictive 349.14
linguistic 523.19
descry see 27.12
perceive 521.9
detect 941.5
desecrate misuse 389.4
corrupt 393.12
profane 694.4
desecration
misuse 389.1
abomination 638.2
sacrilege 694.2

desensitize deaden 25.4
dull 94.7
desensitization 25.3
desert
n open space 158.4
plain 236.1
wasteland 891.2
dryness 1066.2
adj unproductive 891.4
dry 1066.7
desert
n reprisal 506.2
goodness 999.1
v quit 188.9
apostatize 363.7
flee 368.10
abandon 370.5
be unfaithful 645.12
defect 858.13
deserted available 222.15
neglected 340.14
abandoned 370.8
disused 390.10
forlorn 584.12
deserter apostate 363.5
desertion 370.2
sacrilegist 694.3
apostate 858.8
desertion
departure 188.1
apostasy 363.2
flight 368.4
defection 370.2
forlornness 584.4
impiety 694.1
apostasy 858.3
deserts reprisal 506.2
just deserts 639.3
deserve 639.5
deserved
warranted 639.9
just 649.8
deserving
praiseworthy 509.20
due 639.10
desex 19.12
déshabillé 5.20
desiccate
languish 393.18
preserve 397.9
dry 1066.6
desideratum
desire 100.11
intention 380.1
requirement 963.2
design
n trick 356.6
intention 380.1
plan 381.1
diagram 381.3
stratagem 415.3
motif 498.7
intent 518.2
makeup 554.12
form 709.11
visual arts 712.1
treatment 712.9
work of art 712.10
drawing 712.13
architectural design 717.1
styling 717.4

plot 722.4
production 892.2
v intend 380.4
plan 381.8
portray 712.19
produce 892.8
originate 892.12
designate
nominate 371.19
commit 436.5
specify 517.18
name 527.11
appoint 615.11
classify 809.6
specify 865.11
designation
nomination 371.8
obligation 436.2
indication 517.3
naming 527.2
name 527.3
appointment 615.2
kind 809.3
specification 865.6
designer planner 381.6
theater man 704.23
stylist 716.9
architect 717.6
producer 892.7
designing
n visual arts 712.1
adj scheming 381.13
cunning 415.12
desirable sexual 75.25
pleasant 97.6
sought-after 100.30
eligible 371.24
welcome 585.12
expedient 995.5
desire
n sexual desire 75.5
want 100.1
wish 100.1
heart's desire 100.11
love 104.1
hope 124.1
will 323.1
intention 380.1
request 440.1
v lust 75.20
desiderate 100.14
jump at 101.6
hope 124.7
will 323.2
intend 380.4
request 440.9
desired wanted 100.29
welcome 585.12
future 839.8
normal 869.8
desirous
keen on 100.21
eager 101.8
amorous 104.26
desirous of
keen on 100.22
envious 154.4
desist
v cease to use 390.4
cease 857.6
interj cease! 857.13

desk furniture 229.1
pulpit 703.13
workplace 739.1
table 901.15
desktop computer 1042.2
desktop publishing program
1042.12
desolate
v agonize 98.12
aggrieve 112.19
destroy 395.10
depopulate 909.16
adj wretched 96.26
distressing 98.20
disconsolate 112.28
forlorn 584.12
unproductive 891.4
desolation
wretchedness 96.6
harshness 98.4
disconsolateness
112.12
destruction 395.1
forlornness 584.4
wasteland 891.2
depopulation 909.3
despair
n wretchedness 96.6
dejection 112.3
desperation 125.2
v lose heart 112.16
despair of 125.10
desperado
killer 308.11
ruffian 593.3
criminal 660.9
desperate
hopeless 125.12
reckless 493.8
rabid 926.30
straitened 1013.26
desperation 125.2
despicable
offensive 98.18
base 661.12
paltry 998.21
terrible 1000.9
despise hate 103.5
disdain 157.3
reject 372.2
flout 454.4
deprecate 510.12
despite
n hate 103.1
spite 144.6
indignity 156.2
contempt 157.1
defiance 454.1
adv in spite of 338.9
despoil
corrupt 393.12
destroy 395.10
strip 480.24
plunder 482.17
seduce 665.20
work evil 1000.6
despoliation
destruction 395.1
loss 473.1
plundering 482.6
evil 1000.3

despondency
n wretchedness 96.6
dejection 112.3
despair 125.2
v lose heart 112.16
despondent
dejected 112.22
hopeless 125.12
despot 575.14
despotic
imperious 417.16
governmental 612.17
despotism
absolutism 612.9
tyranny 612.10
dessert serving 8.10
delicacy 10.8
desserts 604.1
destabilize 810.9
destigmatize
justify 600.9
acquit 601.4
destination goal 186.5
objective 380.2
address 553.9
end 820.1
fate 964.2
destined future 839.8
inevitable 963.15
fated 964.9
destiny portion 477.5
end 820.1
predestiny 839.2
fate 964.2
chance 972.1
destitute bereft 473.8
down-and-out 619.9
insolvent 625.11
destitution
indigence 619.2
want 992.4
destroy excise 255.10
kill 308.13
spoil 393.10
deal destruction 395.10
defeat 412.6
rage 671.11
work evil 1000.6
thwart 1012.15
destroyer
battleship 180.7
ruiner 395.8
savage 593.5
destructible 16.14
destruction
excision 255.3
killing 308.1
impairment 393.1
ruin 395.1
defeat 412.1
loss 473.1
violence 671.1
disintegration 806.1
evil 1000.3
bane 1001.1
destructive
poisonous 82.7
deadly 308.23
destroying 395.26
violent 671.16
disintegrative 806.5

disastrous 1011.15
desuetude
abandonment 370.1
disuse 390.1
desultory
deviative 164.7
discursive 538.13
unordered 810.12
irregular 851.3
inconstant 854.7
fluttering 917.18
unreliable 971.20
detach
commission 615.10
enlist 615.17
disband 771.8
remove 802.10
detached
apathetic 94.13
reticent 344.10
free 430.21
aloof 583.6
secluded 584.8
impartial 649.10
unrelated 776.6
distinct 802.20
separated 802.21
incoherent 804.4
alone 872.8
unprejudiced 979.12
incurious 982.3
detachment
apathy 94.4
unconcern 102.2
reticence 344.3
military unit 461.22
aloofness 583.2
seclusion 584.1
impartiality 649.4
company 770.3
disbandment 771.3
elimination 773.2
part 793.1
separation 802.1
aloneness 872.2
unprejudicedness 979.5
incuriosity 982.1
detail
n meticulousness 339.3
military unit 461.22
motif 498.7
particular 766.3
company 770.3
part 793.1
component 796.2
v allot 477.9
amplify 538.7
commission 615.10
itemize 766.6
analyze 801.7
elaborate 861.6
particularize 865.9
sum up 1017.19
details
description 349.2
trivia 998.4
detain
slow 175.9
confine 429.12
delay 846.8
hinder 1012.10

detect 941.5
detectable
  visible 31.6
  discoverable 941.10
detection
  investigation 938.4
  discovery 941.1
  radar 1036.9
detective
  operative 576.10
  inquirer 938.16
  policeman 1008.15
détente
  pacification 465.1
  foreign policy 609.5
detention
  slowing 175.4
  imprisonment 429.3
  delay 846.2
  hindrance 1012.1
deter daunt 127.18
  disincline 379.4
  prevent 1012.14
detergent 79.17
deteriorate
  aggravate 119.2
  impair 393.9
  sicken 393.16
  be changed 852.6
  degenerate 1011.11
determinant
  n boundary 211.3
  heredity 560.6
  cause 886.1
  adj bordering 211.11
determinate
  circumscribed 210.6
  particular 865.12
  unqualified 960.2
  certain 970.13
  assured 970.20
determination
  circumscription 210.1
  measurement 300.1
  will 323.1
  resolution 359.1
  obstinacy 361.1
  intention 380.1
  endeavor 403.1
  solution 940.1
  discovery 941.1
  test 942.2
  verdict 946.5
  proof 957.3
  ensuring 970.8
determine
  direct 161.5
  circumscribe 210.4
  will 323.2
  resolve 359.7
  induce 375.22
  intend 380.4
  learn 570.6
  end 820.5
  specify 865.11
  decide 886.12
  exercise influence 894.8
  discover 941.2
  decide 946.11
  prove 957.10
  make sure 970.11

determined
  circumscribed 210.6
  resolute 359.11
  trial 403.16
  future 839.8
  proved 957.20
  predetermined 964.8
  assured 970.20
  confident 970.21
  true 973.13
determinism
  the future 839.1
  fatalism 964.4
deterrent
  n determent 379.2
  obstacle 1012.4
  adj frightening 127.28
  dissuasive 379.5
  warning 399.7
  preventive 1012.19
detest dislike 99.3
  hate 103.5
detestable
  offensive 98.18
  hateful 103.8
  terrible 1000.9
dethrone 447.4
detonate blast 56.8
  explode 671.14
  shoot 904.12
  fuel 1021.8
detour
  n deviation 164.1
  byway 383.4
  bypass 914.3
  v deviate 164.3
  go roundabout 914.4
detoxification 87.1
detoxify 516.2
detract subtract 255.9
  distract 985.6
detraction
  minimization 252.5
  reduction 255.2
  disparagement 512.1
detrain 186.8
detriment
  impairment 393.1
  loss 473.1
  disadvantage 996.2
  evil 1000.3
detrimental
  disadvantageous 996.6
  harmful 1000.12
  adverse 1011.13
detritus deposit 176.9
  remainder 256.1
  grain 1051.6
de trop
  excessive 993.16
  superfluous 993.17
deuce game 748.2
  card 758.2
  pair 873.3
deuced 513.10
deus ex machina 722.4
devaluate
  cheapen 633.6
  monetize 728.26
devalue corrupt 393.12
  monetize 728.26

devastate
  destroy 395.10
  depopulate 909.16
devastation
  destruction 395.1
  depopulation 909.3
develop
  age 14.2
  grow 251.6
  enlarge 259.4
  become larger 259.5
  expand 259.7
  mature 303.9
  manifest 348.5
  disclose 351.4
  improve 392.7
  elaborate 392.10
  amplify 538.7
  train 568.13
  process 714.15
  turn into 858.17
  evolve 861.5
  get better 861.6
  result 887.4
  originate 892.12
  perfect 1002.5
developer
  planner 381.6
  processing solution
    714.13
  producer 892.7
development
  bodily development 14.1
  birth 78.6
  increase 251.1
  growth 259.3
  maturation 303.6
  refinement 392.2
  amplification 538.6
  training 568.3
  passage 708.24
  plot 722.4
  conversion 858.1
  evolution 861.1
  effect 887.1
deviance
  deviation 164.1
  obliquity 204.1
  wrong 638.1
  nonuniformity 782.1
  circuitousness 914.1
deviant
  n sexual pervert 75.16
  nonconformist 868.3
  adj homosexual 75.30
  deviative 164.7
  oblique 204.13
  wrong 638.3
  changed 852.10
  nonconforming 868.5
  eccentric 927.5
  erroneous 975.16
deviate
  n sexual pervert 75.16
  v depart from 164.3
  deflect 164.5
  oblique 204.9
  digress 538.9
  go wrong 654.9
  misbelieve 688.8
  be changed 852.6

  go roundabout 914.4
  err 975.9
deviation
  orientation 161.4
  divergence 164.1
  deviance 164.1
  divergency 171.1
  obliquity 204.1
  distortion 265.1
  digression 538.4
  difference 780.1
  nonuniformity 782.1
  change 852.1
  nonconformity 868.1
  abnormality 870.1
  circuitousness 914.1
  detour 914.3
  eccentricity 927.1
  inaccuracy 975.2
device
  surgery 91.19
  trick 356.6
  pretext 376.1
  plan 381.1
  instrumentality 384.3
  instrument 384.4
  stratagem 415.3
  sign 517.1
  signature 527.10
  figure of speech 536.1
  letter 546.1
  heraldry 647.2
  plot 722.4
  motto 974.4
  expedient 995.2
  tool 1040.1
devil
  n beast 144.14
  dust storm 318.13
  mischief-maker 322.3
  daredevil 493.4
  printer 548.12
  enemy 589.6
  ruffian 593.3
  monster 593.6
  wretch 660.2
  rascal 660.3
  violent person 671.9
  diable 680.2
  demon 680.6
  v cook 11.5
  annoy 96.13
devilish cruel 144.26
  mischievous 322.6
  diabolic 654.13
  demoniac 680.17
  hellish 682.8
  execrable 1000.10
devil-may-care
  unconcerned 102.7
  nonchalant 106.15
  reckless 493.8
deviltry 1000.1
devil worship
  Satanism 680.14
  idolatry 697.1
devious
  deviative 164.7
  oblique 204.13
  dishonest 645.16
  complex 799.4

circuitous 914.7
shrewd 920.15
devise
  n bequest 478.10
  v plan 381.8
  bequeath 478.18
  produce 892.8
  originate 892.12
devitalize
  weaken 16.10
  unman 19.12
  afflict 85.50
devoid
  vacant 222.14
  nonexistent 762.8
devoid of 992.13
devoir 641.1
devolve
  relapse 394.4
  commission 615.10
  change hands 629.4
devote
  spend 387.13
  dedicate 477.11
  sanctify 685.5
  occupy 724.10
devoted
  zealous 101.9
  loving 104.27
  obedient 326.3
  resolute 359.11
  observant 434.4
  dedicated 587.21
  faithful 644.20
  unselfish 652.5
  sanctified 685.8
  pious 692.8
  destined 964.9
  engrossed 983.17
devotee
  desirer 100.12
  enthusiast 101.4
  lover 104.12
  believer 692.4
  fanatic 926.18
devote oneself to
  practice 328.8
  be determined 359.8
  undertake 404.3
  espouse 509.13
  busy oneself with 724.11
  attend to 983.5
devotion
  zeal 101.2
  love 104.1
  resolution 359.1
  dedication 477.4
  commitment 587.7
  duty 641.1
  fidelity 644.7
  unselfishness 652.1
  sanctification 685.3
  piety 692.1
  worship 696.1
devour
  swallow 8.22
  enjoy 95.13
  ingest 187.11
  destroy 395.10
  gluttonize 672.4
  kid oneself 954.6

devouring
  n eating 8.1
  adj greedy 100.27
devout
  zealous 101.9
  observant 434.4
  pious 692.8
  worshipful 696.16
  belief 953.21
dew
  n dewdrops 1065.4
  v moisten 1065.12
dew point
  temperature 1019.3
  humidity 1065.2
dewy
  young 301.9
  immature 301.10
  new 841.7
  moist 1065.15
dewy-eyed 986.24
dexterity
  rightness 219.2
  skill 413.1
  smartness 920.2
dexterous
  right-handed 219.5
  skillful 413.22
  smart 920.14
diabetic 85.61
diabolic cruel 144.26
  diabolical 654.13
  demoniac 680.17
  execrable 1000.10
diabolism
  Satanism 680.14
  black magic 690.2
diacritical mark
  punctuation 530.15
  letter 546.1
diadem circle 280.2
  jewel 498.6
  royal insignia 647.3
diaeresis meter 720.7
  dissection 802.5
diagnosis
  examination 91.12
  interpretation 341.1
  verdict 946.5
diagnostic
  interpretative 341.14
  indicative 517.23
  differentiative 780.9
diagonal
  crosspiece 170.5
  oblique 204.7
  straight line 277.2
  line 517.6
diagram
  n representation 349.1
  plot 381.3
  drawing 712.13
  outline 801.4
  v represent 349.8
  plot 381.10
  grammaticize 530.16
  portray 712.19
  itemize 801.7
diagrammatic 517.23
dial 216.4
dialect language 523.1

idiom 523.7
  diction 532.1
dialectic
  n discussion 541.7
  logic 935.2
  argument 935.5
  adj argumentative 935.19
  dialectical 935.22
dialogue talk 541.3
  script 706.3
  plot 722.4
  argument 935.5
diameter size 257.1
  bore 269.3
  straight line 277.2
  middle 819.1
  bisector 875.3
diametric 779.7
diamond
  n good person 659.1
  playground 743.11
  baseball 745.1
  good thing 999.5
  hardness 1046.6
  v figure 498.9
Diana 1072.12
diapason range 158.2
  harmony 708.3
  scale 709.6
  interval 709.20
  music 711.22
diaper 5.19
diaphanous
  dainty 248.7
  thin 270.16
  light 1025.31
  transparent 1029.4
diaphragm
  digestive system 2.18
  loudspeaker 50.8
  contraceptive 86.23
  partition 213.5
  middle 819.1
diarist writer 547.15
  author 718.4
  historian 719.4
  chronologist 832.10
diarrhea
  defecation 12.2
  symptom 85.9
diary
  record book 549.11
  periodical 555.1
  history 719.1
  chronicle 832.9
diaspora 771.3
diastole
  distension 259.2
  round 850.3
  pulsation 916.3
diatonic scale 709.6
diatribe berating 510.7
  speech 543.2
dice
  n gambling device 759.8
  v square 879.3
dicey
  speculative 759.27
  uncertain 971.16
  vague 971.19
  chance 972.15

hazardous 1006.10
dichotomy
  severance 802.2
  doubleness 873.1
  bisection 875.1
dichromatic
  chromatic 35.16
  variegated 47.9
dick detective 576.10
  gumshoe 576.11
  police 1008.16
dick around 923.6
dicker
  n compact 437.1
  bargain 731.5
  v bargain 731.18
Dick Turpin 483.11
dictate
  n precept 419.1
  command 420.1
  law 673.3
  axiom 974.2
  v command 420.8
  prescribe 420.9
  oblige 424.5
  dominate 612.15
  necessitate 963.8
dictator 575.14
dictatorial
  lordly 141.11
  imperious 417.16
  governmental 612.17
dictatorship
  mastership 417.7
  directorship 573.4
  government 612.4
  absolutism 612.9
diction phrasing 529.2
  word-usage 532
  words 532.1
dictionary
  reference book 554.9
  word list 871.4
dictum
  affirmation 334.1
  rule 419.2
  decree 420.4
  remark 524.3
  verdict 946.5
  maxim 974.1
  axiom 974.2
didactic
  preceptive 419.4
  advisory 422.8
  educational 568.18
  poetic 720.15
  dogmatic 970.22
diddle
  n deception 356.9
  v copulate 75.21
  waste time 331.13
  dally 331.14
  deceive 356.14
  fake 356.19
die
  n engraving tool 713.8
  cast 785.6
  mold 786.6
  base 901.8
  v disappear 34.2
  decease 307.19

wait 846.12
dilute
 v cut 16.11
 abate 252.8
 thin 270.12
 rarefy 299.3
 dissipate 771.5
 adulterate 797.12
 adj insipid 65.2
 rare 299.4
diluvium deposit 176.9
 dregs 256.2
dim
 n darkishness 1027.2
 v blind 30.7
 blur 32.4
 decolor 36.5
 darken 1027.9
 grow dark 1027.12
 adj dim-sighted 28.13
 inconspicuous 32.6
 colorless 36.7
 faint 52.16
 obscure 522.15
 dull 922.16
 darkish 1027.15
dime
 n money 728.7
 v inform on 551.13
dime-a-dozen
 dirt cheap 633.8
 plentiful 991.7
 common 998.21
dimension space 158.1
 size 257.1
dime store 736.1
diminish relieve 120.5
 abase 137.5
 recede 168.2
 decrease 252.6
 reduce 252.7
 subtract 255.9
 narrow 270.11
 languish 393.18
 extenuate 600.12
 moderate 670.6
 qualify 959.3
diminution relief 120.1
 decrease 252.1
 reduction 255.2
 modulation 670.2
 depression 913.1
diminutive
 n runt 258.4
 nickname 527.7
 adj miniature 258.12
 nominal 527.15
dimple
 n indentation 284.6
 v indent 284.14
dim view 510.1
dimwit 924.2
din
 n noise 53.3
 pandemonium 810.5
 v boom 53.7
 ding 849.10
dine feed 8.18
 dinner 8.21
diner meal 8.6
 eater 8.16

restaurant 8.17
 dining room 197.11
ding
 n ringing 54.3
 disrespect 156.3
 v ring 54.8
 din 849.10
ding-a-ling
 ringing 54.3
 fool 924.3
dingdong
 n ringing 54.3
 regularity 781.2
 repetitiousness 849.4
 fool 924.3
 v ring 54.8
 adj monotonous 849.15
dingy colorless 36.7
 grimy 38.11
 gray 39.4
 dirty 80.22
dining room
 restaurant 8.17
 cafeteria 197.11
dinky inferior 250.6
 little 258.10
 tidy 807.8
 insignificant 998.18
dinner
 n meal 8.6
 v dine 8.21
dinner party 8.9
dinnerware 735.4
dinosaur
 behemoth 257.14
 reptile 311.25
dint
 n power 18.1
 indentation 284.6
 print 517.7
 hit 902.4
 v indent 284.14
diocese region 231.5
 see 698.8
Dionysus
 bibulousness 88.2
 patron 704.26
 fertility 890.5
 agricultural deity 1069.4
diorama spectacle 33.7
 scene 712.12
dip
 n bath 79.9
 declivity 204.5
 cavity 284.2
 submergence 367.2
 pickpocket 483.2
 candle 1026.2
 v color 35.14
 ladle 176.17
 maneuver 184.40
 incline 204.10
 submerge 367.7
 signal 517.22
 baptize 701.17
 flood 1065.14
diphthong 524.12
diploma grant 443.5
 certificate 549.6
diplomacy skill 413.1
 Machiavellianism 415.2

foreign policy 609.5
diplomat expert 413.11
 Machiavellian 415.8
 diplomatist 576.6
diplomatic
 n diplomat 576.6
 foreign policy 609.5
 adj skillful 413.22
 cunning 415.12
 ambassadorial 576.17
 political 609.43
diplomatic agent 576.6
dipsomania
 substance abuse 87.1
 alcoholism 88.3
 psychosis 926.3
diptych
 record book 549.11
 picture 712.11
dire horrid 98.19
 terrible 127.30
 ominous 133.17
 bad 1000.9
 unfortunate 1011.14
 disastrous 1011.15
dire straits 619.1
direct
 v exercise influence 894.8
 adj directional 161.12
 straight 277.6
 artless 416.5
 free-acting 430.23
 natural 499.7
 clear 521.11
 elegant 533.6
 plain-speaking 535.3
 lineal 560.18
 candid 644.17
 continuous 812.8
 exact 973.17
 adv directly 161.23
direction bearing 161.1
 directionality 161.1
 motivation 375.2
 precept 419.1
 directive 420.3
 advice 422.1
 pointer 517.4
 address 553.9
 teaching 568.1
 supervision 573.2
 management 573.1
 government 612.1
 production 704.13
 operation 889.1
 trend 896.2
directive
 n direction 420.3
 adj directable 161.13
 motivating 375.25
 commanding 420.13
 advisory 422.8
 directing 573.12
director librarian 558.3
 person in charge 574.1
 directeur 574.1
 governor 575.6
 theater man 704.23
 motion-picture studio 706.4
 conductor 710.17
 businessman 730.1

directorship 417.1
directory
 n council 423.1
 register 549.9
 information 551.1
 reference book 554.9
 guidebook 574.10
 directorate 574.11
 adj directing 573.12
dirge
 n funeral song 115.6
 last offices 309.4
 funeral 309.5
 v lament 115.10
dirigible
 n aerostat 181.11
 adj directable 161.13
dirt
 n grime 80.6
 land 234.1
 scandal 552.8
 obscenity 666.4
 v dirty 80.15
dirt cheap 633.8
dirty
 v dirty up 80.15
 stain 1004.6
 adj dingy 38.11
 grimy 80.22
 stormy 318.23
 cloudy 319.8
 cursing 513.8
 unfair 650.10
 evil-minded 654.15
 base 661.12
 lascivious 665.29
 obscene 666.9
 slimy 1062.14
dirty look 27.5
dirty pool
 juggling 356.5
 smear campaign 609.14
 treachery 645.6
 unfairness 650.2
dirty trick trick 356.6
 treachery 645.6
dirty word oath 513.4
 barbarism 526.6
disability
 inability 19.2
 disease 85.1
 handicap 603.2
 disadvantage 996.2
disable
 disenable 19.9
 afflict 85.50
 cripple 393.14
disabled
 weakened 16.18
 incapacitated 19.16
 crippled 393.30
 ended 820.8
disabled person 85.45
disabuse 977.2
disaccord
 n dissent 333.1
 hostility 451.2
 unharmonious relationship 456
 discord 456.1
 ruffled feelings 589.2

difference 780.1
disagreement 789.1
nonconformity 868.1
v discord 456.8
disagree 789.5
disaccustomed 374.4
disadvantage
  n handicap 603.2
  drawback 996.2
  impediment 1012.6
  trouble 1013.3
  v inconvenience 996.4
  work evil 1000.6
disadvantaged
  inferior 250.6
  indigent 619.8
the disadvantaged
  the underprivileged 606.4
  the poor 619.3
disaffected
  averse 99.8
  alienated 589.11
  unfaithful 645.20
disaffirm 335.4
disagree dissent 333.4
  refuse 442.3
  differ 456.8
  dispute 789.5
disagreeable
  unsavory 64.5
  unpleasant 98.17
  irascible 110.19
  unkind 144.16
  disagreeing 789.6
disagreement
  dissent 325.1
  dissidence 333.1
  refusal 442.1
  difficulty 456.2
  disapproval 510.1
  relation 775.1
  contrariety 779.1
  difference 780.1
  disaccord 789
  discord 789.1
  nonconformity 868.1
disagree with
  not be good for 82.4
  dissent 333.4
  differ 780.5
disallow deny 335.4
  refuse 442.3
  prohibit 444.3
  disapprove 510.10
  not pay 625.6
disappear
  be invisible 32.3
  vanish 34.2
  quit 188.9
  absent oneself 222.8
  hide 346.8
  perish 395.23
  cease to exist 762.6
  flit 828.6
  pass 837.6
disappearance
  invisibility 32.1
  vanishing 34.1
  disappearing 34.1
  absence 222.4
  flight 368.4

disappoint
  dissatisfy 108.5
  shatter one's hopes 125.11
  defeat expectation 132.2
  disillusion 977.2
disappointed
  discontented 108.7
  bitterly disappointed 132.5
  unaccomplished 408.3
  disapproving 510.21
  disillusioned 977.5
disappointment 992.1
disapprobation
  dislike 99.1
  resentment 152.1
  dissent 333.1
  disapproval 510.1
  disrepute 661.1
disapproval
  dislike 99.1
  resentment 152.1
  dissent 333.1
  rejection 372.1
  disapprobation 510.1
  disparagement 512.1
disapprove reject 372.2
  disfavor 510.10
  stigmatize 661.9
disarm disable 19.9
  lay down one's arms 465.11
disarmament 465.6
disarming 504.18
disarrange
  dislocate 160.5
  disorder 810.9
  derange 811.2
  discontinue 813.3
  agitate 917.10
disarray
  n disorder 810.1
  v undress 6.7
  disarrange 811.2
disassemble
  demolish 395.17
  take apart 802.15
disassociation
  unrelatedness 776.1
  separation 802.1
disaster
  fatality 308.8
  debacle 395.4
  upheaval 671.5
  misfortune 1011.2
disastrous
  destructive 395.26
  convulsive 671.23
  calamitous 1011.15
disavow
  n recant 363.8
  v deny 335.4
disavowal denial 335.2
  recantation 363.3
  rejection 372.1
disband disarm 465.11
  disperse 771.8
  part company 802.19
disbar depose 447.4
  dismiss 909.19
disbelief
  nonreligious 695.5
  unbelief 955.1

doubtfulness 971.2
disbelieve doubt 695.14
  unbelieve 955.5
  refuse to believe 956.3
disburden ease 120.7
  lighten 298.6
  confess 351.7
  unload 909.23
  disembarrass 1014.9
disburse
  parcel out 477.8
  spend 626.5
disc record 50.12
  recording media 549.10
discard
  n derelict 370.4
  rejection 372.1
  discarding 390.3
  elimination 773.2
  v abandon 370.5
  reject 372.2
  eliminate 390.7
  eject 909.13
discern see 27.12
  perceive 521.9
  know 928.12
  detect 941.5
discernible visible 31.6
  manifest 348.8
  knowable 928.25
  on the right scent 941.10
discerning
  sagacious 920.16
  perceptive 944.8
discharge
  n humor 2.24
  excretion 12.1
  excrement 12.3
  detonation 56.3
  release 120.2
  emergence 190.1
  outflow 190.4
  performance 328.2
  accomplishment 407.1
  exemption 430.8
  freedom 431.2
  observance 434.1
  execution 437.4
  acquittal 601.1
  payment 624.1
  acknowledgment 627.2
  explosion 671.7
  shot 904.4
  repulse 908.2
  ejection 909.1
  dismissal 909.5
  disgorgement 909.7
  arc 1032.6
  v excrete 12.12
  blast 56.8
  exude 190.15
  perform 328.9
  accomplish 407.4
  exempt 430.14
  release 431.5
  perform 434.3
  execute 437.9
  acquit 601.4
  pay in full 624.13
  erupt 671.13
  explode 671.14

disband 771.8
shoot 904.12
repulse 908.3
eject 909.13
dismiss 909.19
unload 909.23
disgorge 909.25
disciple
  enthusiast 101.4
  follower 166.2
  protégé 572.2
  associate 616.8
  religion 684.2
  believer 692.4
  convert 858.7
disciplinarian 575.14
discipline
  n limitation 210.2
  self-control 359.5
  strictness 425.1
  training 568.3
  study 568.8
  punishment 604.1
  government 612.1
  temperance 668.1
  occupation 724.4
  orderliness 807.3
  science 928.10
  v limit 210.5
  hold a tight hand upon 425.4
  train 568.13
  punish 604.10
  govern 612.12
  conform 867.3
disclaim
  n recant 363.8
  v deny 335.4
  reject 372.2
  refuse 442.3
disclose unclose 292.12
  manifest 348.5
  reveal 351.4
  signify 517.17
  say 524.22
  inform 551.8
  uncover 941.4
  testify 957.9
disclosure
  appearance 33.1
  opening 292.1
  informing 343.2
  manifestation 348.1
  revelation 351.1
  publicizing 351.1
  indication 517.3
  discovery 941.1
  testimony 957.2
disco 743.13
discolor
  n discoloration 1004.2
  v decolor 36.5
  mark 517.19
  stain 1004.6
discombobulate
  agitate 105.14
  confuse 985.7
discomfit chagrin 96.15
  dismay 127.19
  overwhelm 412.8
  confuse 985.7
  thwart 1012.15

discomfiture
chagrin 96.4
disappointment 132.1
rout 412.2
disorder 810.1
confusion 985.3
frustration 1012.3
discomfort
n pain 26.1
unpleasure 96.1
distressfulness 98.5
v chagrin 96.16
distress 98.14
disconcert
n bewilderment 971.3
v chagrin 96.15
mortify 98.13
agitate 105.14
dismay 127.19
bewilder 971.12
confuse 985.7
thwart 1012.15
disconnect 802.8
disconnected
unrelated 776.6
separated 802.21
incoherent 804.4
discontinuous 813.4
irregular 851.3
disconsolate
wretched 96.26
inconsolable 112.28
hopeless 125.12
discontent
n unpleasure 96.1
dissatisfaction 108.1
discontentment 108.1
ill humor 110.1
unhappiness 112.2
resentment 152.1
disapproval 510.1
v give no pleasure 96.12
dissatisfy 108.5
discontinue
break the habit 374.3
cease to use 390.4
swear off 668.8
interrupt 813.3
cease 857.6
discontinuity
dislocation 160.1
interval 224.1
deficiency 795.2
separation 802.1
noncohesion 804.1
interrupted sequence 813
discontinuousness 813.1
irregularity 851.1
revolution 852.2
discontinuous
separate 802.20
incoherent 804.4
unordered 810.12
noncontinuous 813.4
irregular 851.3
discord
noise 53.3
raucousness 58.2
dissonant sounds 61
discordance 61.1
disaccord 456.1

disagreement 789.1
discordance
dissonance 61.1
disaccord 456.1
difference 780.1
disagreement 789.1
discordant
off-color 35.21
dissonant 61.4
disaccordant 456.15
contrary 779.6
different 780.7
disagreeing 789.6
discotheque 743.13
discount
n deduction 631.1
cut 631.1
v reject 372.2
price 630.11
cut 631.2
discount notes 728.27
allow for 959.5
discourage
sadden 112.18
daunt 127.18
disincline 379.4
prevent 1012.14
discouragement
dejection 112.3
deterrent 379.2
prevention 1012.2
discourse
n speech 524.1
conversation 541.1
lecture 543.3
treatise 556.1
lesson 568.7
reasoning 935.1
v make a speech 543.9
write upon 556.5
expound 568.16
discourteous
disrespectful 156.7
uncourteous 505.4
discourtesy
insensibility 25.1
disrespect 156.1
bad behavior 321.2
misbehavior 322.1
impoliteness 505.1
discourteousness 505.1
discover see 27.12
disclose 351.4
learn 570.6
innovate 852.9
originate 892.12
find 941.2
discovery
disclosure 351.1
find 472.6
innovation 852.4
finding 941.1
discredit
n disrepute 661.1
unbelief 955.1
v disparage 512.8
disgrace 661.8
disbelieve 955.5
disprove 958.4
discreet reticent 344.10
secretive 345.15

cautious 494.8
judicious 920.19
discrepancy
difference 255.8
contrariety 779.1
differentness 780.1
disagreement 789.1
discrete
dispersed 771.9
unrelated 776.6
different 780.7
separate 802.20
incoherent 804.4
discontinuous 813.4
discretion
will 323.1
reticence 344.3
secrecy 345.1
option 371.2
free will 430.6
caution 494.1
judiciousness 920.7
foresight 961.1
discriminate
favor 650.8
differentiate 780.6
distinguish 944.4
be discriminating 944.5
discriminate against 980.8
discriminating
selective 371.23
fastidious 495.9
elegant 496.9
differentiative 780.9
judicious 920.19
discriminate 944.7
discrimination
selectivity 371.10
fastidiousness 495.1
taste 496.1
elegance 533.1
partiality 650.3
differentiation 780.4
judiciousness 920.7
critical discernment 944.2
discriminateness 944.1
judgment 946.1
social discrimination
980.4
discursive
deviative 164.7
wandering 177.37
aimless 538.13
circuitous 914.7
intelligent 920.12
dialectic 935.22
discuss confer 541.11
debate 541.12
write upon 556.5
discussion
conference 541.6
debate 541.7
treatise 556.1
disdain
n disdainfulness 141.5
insolence 142.1
contempt 157.1
rejection 372.1
defiance 454.1
v scorn 157.3
reject 372.2

flout 454.4
be hard to please 495.8
deprecate 510.12
disease
n illness 85.1
harmfulness 1000.5
bane 1001.1
v infect 85.51
disembark
anchor 182.15
land 186.8
disembarrass
lighten 120.7
extricate 431.7
disencumber 1014.9
disembody
spiritualize 689.20
unsubstantiate 764.4
dematerialize 1053.6
disembowel 192.13
disembroil
extricate 431.7
disinvolve 798.5
disembarrass 1014.9
disenchanted
averse 99.8
disapproving 510.21
disillusioned 977.5
disencumber
relieve 120.7
lighten 298.6
disembarrass 1014.9
disenfranchise 432.8
disengage
retreat 163.6
extricate 431.7
separate 802.8
detach 802.10
disembarrass 1014.9
disentangle
extract 192.10
straighten 277.5
extricate 431.7
disinvolve 798.5
solve 940.2
disembarrass 1014.9
disfavor
n dislike 99.1
falling-out 456.4
disapproval 510.1
disrepute 661.1
v dislike 99.3
disapprove 510.10
disfigure deform 265.7
blemish 1004.4
offend 1015.5
disfranchise 432.8
disgorge
relinquish 475.3
erupt 671.13
debouch 909.25
vomit 909.26
disgrace
n humiliation 137.2
disparagement 512.1
abomination 638.2
iniquity 654.3
scandal 661.5
v humiliate 137.4
disparage 512.8
dishonor 661.8

disgraceful
wrong 638.3
wicked 654.16
shameful 661.11
disgruntled
discontented 108.7
disapproving 510.21
disguise
n costume 5.9
veil 346.2
sham 354.3
cover 356.11
dissimilarity 787.1
v conceal 346.6
misrepresent 350.3
falsify 354.16
dissimilate 787.3
disgust
n hostility 99.2
v repel 64.4
offend 98.11
displease 99.6
disgusted
pleasureless 96.20
hating 103.7
satiated 994.6
disgusting filthy 80.23
offensive 98.18
horrid 98.19
base 661.12
terrible 1000.9
dish
n serving 8.10
tableware 8.12
culinary preparation 10.7
cooking 11.1
baseball 745.1
basketball game 747.3
beauty 1016.9
v ladle 176.17
be concave 284.12
hollow 284.13
do for 395.11
play 747.4
thwart 1012.15
dishabille 5.20
disharmony
discord 61.1
disaccord 456.1
disagreement 789.1
disorder 810.1
dishearten
dissatisfy 108.5
sadden 112.18
daunt 127.18
prevent 1012.14
dishevel
disorder 810.9
disarrange 811.2
dishonest
falsehearted 354.31
insincere 354.32
untruthful 354.34
dishonorable 645.16
dishonesty
falseheartedness 354.4
untruthfulness 354.8
fraud 356.8
improbity 645.1
dishonor
n disrespect 156.1

nonpayment 625.1
improbity 645.1
disrepute 661.1
v offend 156.5
not pay 625.6
disgrace 661.8
desecrate 694.4
dish out
ladle 176.17
parcel out 477.8
give 478.12
administer 643.6
dishpan 79.12
dish up
ladle 176.17
provide 385.7
propose 439.5
dishwasher
washbasin 79.12
washer 79.15
dishwater
symbol of weakness 16.7
offal 80.9
refuse 391.4
dishy delightful 97.8
desirable 100.30
alluring 377.8
beautiful 1016.22
disillusion
n disapproval 510.1
disillusionment 977.1
v disappoint 132.2
disillude 977.2
disincentive 379.2
disinclination
dislike 99.1
refusal 325.1
disinfect 79.24
disinfectant
n cure 86.21
poison 1001.3
adj antiseptic 86.43
disingenuous
insincere 354.32
deceitful 645.18
sophistical 936.10
disinherit 480.23
disintegrate
weaken 16.9
strike dead 308.18
decay 393.22
break 393.23
demolish 395.17
be destroyed 395.22
disband 771.8
come apart 802.9
decompose 806.3
lapse into disorder 810.8
be brittle 1050.3
pulverize 1051.9
powder 1051.10
disintegration
frailty 16.2
decay 393.6
destruction 395.1
disbandment 771.3
disruption 802.3
coming-apart 806.1
decomposition 806.1
disorder 810.1
pulverization 1051.4

disinterest
n apathy 94.4
unconcern 102.2
impartiality 649.4
unselfishness 652.1
incuriosity 982.1
v disincline 379.4
disinterested
apathetic 94.13
unconcerned 102.7
impartial 649.10
unselfish 652.5
unprejudiced 979.12
incurious 982.3
disinvolve
extricate 431.7
disintricate 798.5
disembarrass 1014.9
disjoin
differentiate 780.6
separate 802.8
loosen 804.3
disintegrate 806.3
discontinue 813.3
disjointed
dislocated 160.9
separated 802.21
disjunction
elimination 773.2
relation 775.1
unrelatedness 776.1
differentiation 780.4
separation 802.1
noncohesion 804.1
disintegration 806.1
disorder 810.1
discontinuity 813.1
disk circle 280.2
lamina 296.2
recording media
549.10
rotator 915.4
magnetic disk 1042.6
diskette
recording media 549.10
disk 1042.6
disk jockey 1034.23
dislike
n unpleasure 96.1
distaste 99.1
hate 103.1
v mislike 99.3
have it in for 103.6
dislocate
displace 160.5
disjoint 802.16
disarrange 811.2
dislocation
displacement 160.1
separation 802.1
noncohesion 804.1
disarrangement 811.1
dislodge
unplace 160.6
remove 176.11
extricate 431.7
evict 909.15
disloyal
apostate 363.11
unfaithful 645.20
dismal gray 39.4

distressing 98.20
gloomy 112.24
dull 117.6
hopeless 125.12
pessimistic 125.16
funereal 309.22
dismantle
demolish 395.17
disassemble 802.15
dismay
n fear 127.1
v distress 98.14
disconcert 127.19
bewilder 971.12
dismayed
frightened 127.25
cowardly 491.10
bewildered 971.24
dismember
torture 604.16
tear apart 802.14
loosen 804.3
dismiss slight 157.6
reject 372.2
release 431.5
depose 447.4
acquit 601.4
disband 771.8
repulse 908.3
send off 909.18
discharge 909.19
refute 958.5
dismiss from one's thoughts
984.4
dismissal snub 157.2
rejection 372.1
release 431.2
deposal 447.2
acquittal 601.1
disbandment 771.3
repulse 908.2
discharge 909.5
dismount
dislodge 160.6
get down 194.7
disassemble 802.15
disobedience
refusal 325.1
noncompliance 327.1
nonobedience 327.1
lawlessness 418.1
refusal 442.1
disoblige offend 156.5
inconvenience 996.4
disorder
n disease 85.1
formlessness 263.1
misbehavior 322.1
anarchy 418.2
nonuniformity 782.1
noncohesion 804.1
disarrangement 810.1
disorderliness 810.1
change 852.1
agitation 917.1
vagueness 971.4
confusion 985.3
v afflict 85.50
deform 263.3
disorganize 810.9
disarrange 811.2

snub 157.2
neglect 340.1
rejection 372.1
nonobservance 435.1
defiance 454.1
inattention 984.1
v take 134.8
condone 148.4
slight 157.6
disobey 327.6
neglect 340.6
reject 372.2
lose sight of 435.3
flout 454.4
allow for 959.5
keep an open mind 979.7
be inattentive 984.2

disrepair
uselessness 391.1
impairment 393.1

disreputable
n bad person 660.1
adj discreditable 661.10

disrepute 661.1

disrespect
n impudence 142.2
irreverence 156.1
low esteem 156.1
disobedience 327.1
discourteousness 505.2
disapproval 510.1
v not respect 156.4

disrobe 6.7

disrupt shatter 802.13
thwart 1012.15

disruption
misbehavior 322.1
destruction 395.1
anarchy 418.2
falling-out 456.4
dissolution 802.3
disorder 810.1

dissatisfaction
unpleasure 96.1
discontent 108.1
disappointment 132.1
resentment 152.1
dissent 333.1
disapproval 510.1

dissatisfied
discontented 108.7
disappointed 132.5
disapproving 510.21

dissect analyze 801.6
separate 802.17

dissemblance sham 354.3
dissimilarity 787.1

dissemble conceal 346.6
sham 354.21

dissembler
imitator 336.4
deceiver 357.1
pietist 693.3

disseminate
transfer 176.10
communicate 343.7
publish 352.10
disperse 771.4
plant 1069.18

dissension
dissent 333.1

hostility 451.2
dissent 456.3
disagreement 789.1

dissent
n complaint 115.4
dissension 325.1
dissidence 333.1
refusal 442.1
resistance 453.1
dissension 456.3
disapproval 510.1
Protestantism 675.10
difference 780.1
disagreement 789.1
nonconformity 868.1
counteraction 900.1
v dissent from 333.4
refuse 442.3
offer resistance 453.3
diversify 782.2
disagree 789.5
not conform 868.4
counteract 900.6

dissertation 556.1

disservice
bad deed 144.13
injustice 650.4

dissident
n dissenter 333.3
oppositionist 452.3
adj dissenting 333.6
disaccordant 456.15
disagreeing 789.6
nonconforming 868.5
counteractive 900.8

dissimilar
different 780.7
unsimilar 787.4
incomparable 943.9

dissimilitude 787.1

dissimulate 354.20

dissimulator
imitator 336.4
deceiver 357.1
pietist 693.3

dissipate
disappear 34.2
spend 387.13
waste 473.5
go to waste 473.6
squander 486.3
be promiscuous 665.19
plunge into dissipation 669.6
dispel 771.5

dissociate
separate 802.8
chemical terms 806.4

dissociated 776.6

dissociate oneself from 510.10

dissoluble
separable 802.26
liquefiable 1064.9

dissolute
corrupt 654.14
profligate 665.25
licentious 669.8

dissolution
disappearance 34.1
decrement 252.3
death 307.1
decay 393.6

destruction 395.1
disbandment 771.3
disruption 802.3
noncohesion 804.1
disintegration 806.1
liquefaction 1064.1

dissolvable
separable 802.26
liquefiable 1064.9

dissolve
n motion-picture editing
706.6
v disappear 34.2
destroy 395.10
cease to exist 762.6
dissipate 771.5
disband 771.8
disintegrate 806.3
flit 828.6
liquefy 1064.5

dissonant
discordant 61.4
different 780.7
disagreeing 789.6

dissuade 379.3

distaff
n woman 77.5
axle 915.5
adj feminine 77.14

distance
n station 159.2
setting 209.2
farness 261.1
remoteness 261.1
length 267.1
extent 300.3
reticence 344.3
aloofness 583.2
round 751.3
v outdistance 249.10

distance learning 567.5

distant faint 52.16
aloof 141.12
distal 261.8
reticent 344.10
aloof 583.6
farfetched 776.8
incurious 982.3

distaste dislike 99.1
refusal 325.1
disapproval 510.1

distasteful
unsavory 64.5
unpleasant 98.17
unlikable 99.7

distemper
n color 35.8
illness 85.1
disease 85.41
v color 35.14
annoy 96.13

distended
corpulent 257.18
dilated 259.13
bulging 283.15
overfull 993.20

distension
expanding 259.2
swelling 283.4
overextension 993.7
stretching 1048.2

distich poetry 720.9
two 873.2
maxim 974.1

distill refine 79.22
brew 88.30
leak 190.14
extraction 192.16
trickle 238.18
simplify 798.4
boil 1020.20
vaporize 1067.8

distillation
refinement 79.4
leakage 190.5
take out 192.7
extract 192.8
essential content 196.5
trickle 238.7
simplification 798.2
product 893.3
burning 1020.5
thickening 1045.4
vaporization 1067.5

distinct plain 31.7
audible 50.16
manifest 348.8
clear 521.11
different 780.7
separate 802.20
particular 865.12

distinction glory 247.2
elegance 533.1
nobility 608.2
honor 646.1
mark 662.5
difference 780.1
margin 780.2
differentiation 780.4
characterization 865.8
comparison 943.1
contradistinction
944.3
notability 997.2

distinctive
audible 50.16
typical 349.15
differentiative 780.9
classificational 809.7
characteristic 865.13
discriminating 944.7

distinguish see 27.12
honor 662.12
differentiate 780.6
characterize 865.10
focus on 937.3
detect 941.5
discriminate 944.4
recognize 989.12

distinguished
eminent 247.9
superior 249.12
honored 646.9
distingué 662.16
different 780.7
particular 865.12
characteristic 865.13
notable 997.19

distort deflect 164.5
deform 263.3
contort 265.5
misinterpret 342.2

misrepresent 350.3
falsify 354.16
corrupt 393.12
reason speciously 936.8
prejudice 980.9
blemish 1004.4
distortion
audio distortion 50.13
deflection 164.2
twistedness 265
torsion 265.1
misinterpretation 342.1
misrepresentation 350.1
bad likeness 350.2
deliberate falsehood
354.9
sophistry 936.1
error 975.1
blemish 1004.1
distract
disincline 379.4
discompose 811.4
madden 926.24
divert 985.6
distracted
frenzied 105.25
bewildered 971.24
inattentive 984.6
distraught 985.10
distraught
insane 926.26
bewildered 971.24
distracted 985.10
distress
n pain 26.1
chagrin 96.4
unpleasantness 96.5
affliction 96.8
distressfulness 98.5
anxiety 126.1
attachment 480.5
fine 603.3
v pain 26.7
afflict 96.16
dismay 98.14
concern 126.4
work evil 1000.6
trouble 1013.13
distribute
publish 352.10
parcel out 477.8
give 478.12
deliver 478.13
disperse 771.4
separate 793.6
dispose 808.9
distributor
intermediary 213.4
merchant 730.2
district
n location 159.1
area 231.1
region 231.5
v apportion 802.18
distrust
n suspiciousness 153.2
wariness 494.2
doubt 955.2
v suffer pangs of jealousy
153.3
doubt 955.6

disturb
annoy 96.13
distress 96.16
mortify 98.13
excite 105.14
concern 126.4
disorder 810.9
discompose 811.4
agitate 917.10
bewilder 971.12
confuse 985.7
trouble 1013.13
disturbed
neurotic 92.39
annoyed 96.21
distressed 96.22
excited 105.23
anxious 126.7
disorderly 810.13
agitated 917.16
psychotic 926.28
bewildered 971.24
confused 985.12
disunity
falling-out 456.4
disagreement 789.1
ditch
n crack 224.2
channel 239.1
trench 290.2
entrenchment 460.5
lawn bowling 750.3
barrier 1012.5
v land 184.43
cleave 224.4
furrow 290.3
evade 368.7
discard 390.7
dither
n tizzy 105.6
shake 917.3
v vacillate 362.8
chatter 540.5
be stupid 922.12
hang in doubt 971.10
freeze 1023.9
ditto
n the same 778.3
duplicate 785.3
equal 790.4
repeat 849.5
v concur 332.9
imitate 336.5
reproduce 778.6
copy 785.8
equal 790.5
repeat 849.7
duplicate 874.3
adv identically 778.9
again 849.17
ditty 708.14
ditzy inconstant 854.7
superficial 922.20
foolish 923.9
inattentive 984.6
scatterbrained 985.16
diuretic
n cleanser 79.17
laxative 86.17
adj cleansing 79.28
cathartic 86.48

diurnal 850.8
diva lead 707.6
singer 710.13
divaricate
v deviate 164.3
diverge 171.5
fork 171.7
open 292.11
diversify 782.2
adj diverging 171.8
nonuniform 782.3
dive
n bar 88.20
submarines 182.8
maneuvers 184.13
tumble 194.3
disapproved place 228.28
decline 252.2
plunge 367.1
cheapening 633.4
brothel 665.9
casino 759.19
v submarines 182.47
swim 182.56
nose-dive 184.41
decrease 252.6
deepen 275.8
plunge 367.6
cheapen 633.6
dive into
rush into 401.7
set to work 725.15
diverge deviate 164.3
deflect 164.5
divaricate 171.5
oblique 204.9
fall out 456.10
disperse 771.4
differ 780.5
diversify 782.2
part company 802.19
be changed 852.6
divergence
deviation 164.1
divarication 171.1
obliquity 204.1
distance 261.1
falling-out 456.4
dispersion 771.1
difference 780.1
nonuniformity 782.1
dissimilarity 787.1
disagreement 789.1
change 852.1
abnormality 870.1
eccentricity 927.1
diverse different 780.7
diversified 783.4
dissimilar 787.4
diversify
differentiate 780.6
diverge 782.2
vary 783.2
be changed 852.6
change 852.7
diversion
deviation 164.1
misuse 389.1
attack 459.1
amusement 743.1
change 852.1

distraction 985.1
diversity dissent 333.1
difference 780.1
nonuniformity 782.1
multiformity 783.1
dissimilarity 787.1
disagreement 789.1
change 852.1
divert deflect 164.5
disincline 379.4
misuse 389.4
amuse 743.21
distract 985.6
divest strip 6.5
take from 480.21
take 480.24
divested stripped 6.12
bereft 473.8
divestment
unclothing 6.1
loss 473.1
deprivation 480.6
investment 729.4
disassembly 802.6
divide
n watershed 272.5
v diverge 171.5
bound 211.8
partition 213.8
quantify 244.4
open 292.11
measure 300.10
vote 371.18
fall out 456.10
sow dissension 456.14
apportion 477.6
segregate 773.6
differentiate 780.6
part 793.6
analyze 801.6
separate 802.8
apportion 802.18
arrange 808.11
classify 809.6
bisect 875.4
discriminate 944.4
calculate 1017.18
dividend portion 477.5
royalty 624.7
receipts 627.1
regular dividend 738.7
surplus 993.5
divination
sorcery 689.10
augury 690.1
the future 839.1
foresight 961.1
divining 962.2
divine
n theologian 676.3
clergyman 699.2
v augur 133.12
solve 940.2
suppose 951.10
predict 962.9
adj blissful 97.9
theological 676.4
heavenly 677.16
godlike 678.16
sacred 685.7
superb 999.15

gorgeous 1016.21
divine right 417.1
diving 760.8
divinity theology 676.1
deity 677.1
god 678.2
sanctity 685.1
division
divergence 171.1
partition 213.5
region 231.1
vote 371.6
disagreement 456.2
falling-out 456.4
military unit 461.22
navy 461.27
apportionment 477.1
class 607.1
legislative procedure 613.6
party 617.4
branch 617.10
sect 675.3
passage 708.24
ornament 709.18
boxer 754.2
company 770.3
exclusiveness 773.3
differentiation 780.4
part 793.1
analysis 801.1
separation 802.1
classification 809.1
class 809.2
bisection 875.1
distinction 944.3
notation 1017.2
divorce
n dissolution of marriage 566
divorcement 566.1
separation 802.1
v separate 566.5
sever 802.8
divot wig 3.14
turf 310.6
divulge
manifest 348.5
divulgate 351.5
make public 352.11
divvy
n apportionment 477.1
v apportion 477.6
separate 802.18
Dixie 231.7
dizzy
v make one's head swim 985.8
adj weak 16.12
intoxicated 88.31
inconstant 854.7
muddleheaded 922.18
superficial 922.20
giddy 923.8
foolish 923.9
delirious 926.31
giddy 985.15
scatterbrained 985.16
DJ 1034.23
DNA
genetic material 305.9
heredity 560.6
DNA double helix 305.9

DNA print 517.11
do
n party 582.12
festival 743.4
assembly 770.2
v cook 11.5
be satisfactory 107.6
travel 177.19
traverse 177.20
attend 221.8
average 246.2
behave 321.4
effect 328.6
practice 328.8
imitate 336.5
impersonate 349.12
deceive 356.19
avail 387.17
accomplish 407.4
perform 434.3
play 708.39
busy oneself with 724.11
suit 788.8
cause 886.10
perform 892.11
solve 940.2
suffice 991.4
interj please 440.20
do all right by oneself
make good 409.10
grow rich 618.10
be prosperous 1010.9
do a number on
deceive 356.19
defame 512.9
do away with
kill 308.13
commit suicide 308.22
put an end to 395.12
repeal 445.2
exterminate 909.21
do business
cooperate 450.3
work 724.12
trade 731.15
docile willing 324.5
tractable 433.13
teachable 570.18
dock
n hangar 184.24
tail 217.6
storehouse 386.6
courthouse 595.6
stage 704.16
harbor 1009.6
v anchor 182.15
land 186.8
excise 255.10
shorten 268.6
docket
n label 517.13
memorandum 549.4
document 549.5
record book 549.11
roll 871.6
schedule 965.3
v record 549.15
keep accounts 628.8
schedule 965.6
doctor
n physician 90.4

mender 396.10
degree 648.6
dramatist 704.22
professional 726.4
wise man 921.1
v practice medicine 90.14
treat 91.24
undergo treatment 91.29
tamper with 354.17
repair 396.14
aid 449.11
adulterate 797.12
doctoral 568.19
doctorate 648.6
doctrinaire
n theorist 951.7
dogmatist 970.7
bigot 980.5
adj dogmatic 970.22
discriminatory 980.12
doctrine religion 675.1
dogma 676.2
a belief 953.2
document
n writing 547.10
official document 549.5
v itemize 766.6
confirm 957.11
cite 957.13
documentary
n television broadcast 1035.2
adj documentational 549.18
evidential 957.16
true 973.13
documentation
record 549.1
evidence 957.1
confirmation 957.4
doddering
unsteady 16.16
stricken in years 303.18
senile 922.23
dodge
n trick 356.6
fraud 356.8
avoidance 368.1
stratagem 415.3
retreat 903.3
quibble 936.4
expedient 995.2
v avoid 157.7
deviate 164.6
slight 340.8
prevaricate 344.7
duck 368.8
shirk 368.9
live by one's wits 415.9
pull back 903.7
go roundabout 914.4
quibble 936.9
doe
female animal 77.10
hoofed animal 311.5
goat 311.8
hare 311.24
dog
n member 2.7
male animal 76.8
foot 199.5
horse 311.12
canine 311.17

telephone 347.4
beast 660.6
eyesore 1015.4
v annoy 96.13
make anxious 126.5
follow 166.3
pursue 382.8
hunt 382.9
obstruct 1012.12
dog days summer 313.3
hot weather 1019.7
dog-eared eared 48.15
folded 291.7
worn 393.31
dog-eat-dog 146.3
dogged
tormented 96.24
worried 126.8
persevering 360.8
obstinate 361.8
doggerel
n bad poetry 720.3
adj burlesque 508.14
inelegant 534.2
doghouse
kennel 228.21
small space 258.3
dog in the manger
self-seeker 651.3
spoilsport 1012.9
dog-in-the-manger 108.7
dog it shirk 368.9
flee 368.11
dogleg 204.9
dogma
doctrine 676.2
a belief 953.2
dogmatic
obstinate 361.8
unpersuadable 361.13
strict 687.8
belief 953.21
doctrinal 953.27
positive 970.22
discriminatory 980.12
do good
do a favor 143.12
aid 449.11
profit 999.10
dog tag 517.11
dog-tired 21.10
doohickey 1052.5
do in fatigue 21.4
get tired 21.6
kill 308.14
do for 395.11
put an end to 395.12
defeat 412.9
do it yourself 892.18
do justice to
feast 8.24
savor 63.5
enjoy 95.13
observe 434.2
justify 600.9
do one's duty 641.10
be just 649.6
doldrums
blues 112.6
calm 173.5
prevailing wind 318.10

dole
  n modicum 248.2
  distribution 477.2
  portion 477.5
  donation 478.6
  subsidy 478.8
  part 793.1
  pittance 992.5
  v parcel out 477.8
  give 478.12
the dole 143.5
doleful
  sorrowful 112.26
  pitiful 145.8
doll woman 77.6
  ladylove 104.15
  miniature 258.6
  gal 302.7
  figure 349.6
  endearment term 562.6
  good person 659.2
  toy 743.16
  beauty 1016.9
dollar currency 728.7
  money 728.8
dollars to doughnuts
  n good chance 972.8
  adv probably 968.8
dollhouse
  small space 258.3
  toy 743.16
dollop 793.3
doll up dress up 5.42
  ornament 498.8
  beautify 1016.16
dolorous
  distressing 98.20
  sorrowful 112.26
dolphin 311.30
dolt bungler 414.8
  stupid person 924.2
domain sphere 231.2
  country 232.1
  real estate 471.6
  occupation 724.4
  hierarchy 809.4
  science 928.10
dome
  n hall 197.4
  head 198.6
  highlands 237.1
  mountain 237.6
  tower 272.6
  arch 279.4
  football 746.1
  v curve 279.6
  top 295.21
domestic
  n servant 577.2
  adj residential 228.32
  recluse 584.10
domesticate
  settle 159.17
  accustom 373.9
  tame 432.11
domicile
  n abode 228.1
  v inhabit 225.7
  house 225.10
dominance
  dominion 417.6

influence 894.1
dominant
  n note 709.14
  key 709.15
  adj chief 249.14
  victorious 411.7
  authoritative 417.15
  governing 612.18
  prevalent 864.12
  influential 894.14
  paramount 997.24
dominate show 31.4
  rise above 272.11
  subjugate 432.8
  predominate 612.15
  prevail 864.10
  have influence over 894.11
domineering
  n arrogance 141.1
  authoritativeness 417.3
  despotism 612.10
  adj arrogant 141.9
  imperious 417.16
dominion
  sphere 231.2
  country 232.1
  supremacy 249.3
  governance 417.5
  dominance 417.6
  ownership 469.2
  control 612.2
  precedence 814.1
domino effect
  immediate cause 886.3
  aftereffect 887.3
  vicissitudes 972.5
don
  n man 76.7
  teacher 571.1
  v put on 5.43
donate provide 385.7
  give 478.12
done
  adj well-done 11.8
  tired 21.8
  worn-out 393.36
  completed 407.11
  ended 820.8
  produced 892.17
  interj so be it 332.20
done deal act 328.3
  accomplishment 407.1
done for dead 307.30
  dying 307.33
  spoiled 393.29
  ruined 395.29
  defeated 412.14
  no more 762.11
  ended 820.9
done with
  disused 390.10
  completed 407.11
  ended 820.8
Don Juan
  beau 104.13
  deceiver 357.1
  tempter 377.4
  philanderer 562.12
  libertine 665.10
donkey ass 311.16
  obstinate person 361.6

stupid person 924.2
donnybrook noise 53.4
  quarrel 456.5
  commotion 810.4
donor provider 385.6
  giver 478.11
do-nothing
  passive 329.6
  indolent 331.19
Don Quixote
  knight 608.5
  visionary 986.13
doodad 498.4
doodle
  n drawing 712.13
  fool 924.1
  v waste time 331.13
  dally 331.14
  scribble 547.20
  blow a horn 708.42
  portray 712.19
doohickey 1052.5
doom
  n death 307.1
  destruction 395.2
  condemnation 602.1
  end 820.1
  destiny 839.2
  doomsday 839.3
  verdict 946.5
  fate 964.2
  v condemn 602.3
  damn 682.6
  pass judgment 946.13
  destine 964.7
  work evil 1000.6
do one's bit
  lay down one's life for one's
    country 307.25
  be willing 324.3
  do one's duty 641.10
do one's duty feast 8.24
  perform 434.3
  perform one's duty 641.10
do one's heart good
  please 95.6
  gratify 95.8
  make proud 136.6
do one's own thing disregard
    435.3
  stand alone 872.6
  function as 889.8
do one's part
  be willing 324.3
  do 328.6
  share 476.6
  do one's duty 641.10
door entrance 189.5
  porch 189.6
  outlet 190.9
  doorway 292.6
doormat wig 3.14
  weakling 16.6
  dupe 358.2
doorstep 193.5
doorway porch 189.6
  door 292.6
do out of cheat 356.18
  take from 480.21
do over
  reproduce 78.7

repeat 849.7
  convert 858.11
dope
  n anesthetic 25.3
  drug 87.3
  film 714.10
  contraband 732.3
  stupid person 924.2
  fuel 1021.1
  v put to sleep 22.20
  deaden 25.4
  medicate 91.25
  relieve 120.5
  solve 940.2
  predict 962.9
the dope
  information 551.1
  the facts 761.4
dopey inert 173.14
  languid 331.20
  dull 922.16
  foolish 923.9
  dazed 985.14
Doppelgänger
  the same 778.3
  double 988.3
do right by 143.9
dormant
  asleep 22.22
  inert 173.14
  passive 329.6
  languid 331.20
  latent 519.5
dormitory
  bedroom 197.7
  inn 228.15
dorsal 217.10
DOS 1042.12
dose
  n venereal disease 85.18
  draft 86.6
  hit 87.20
  amount 244.2
  portion 793.5
  radiation physics 1037.8
  v medicate 91.25
  administer 643.6
a dose of one's own medicine
    506.2
dossier 549.5
dot
  n spottiness 47.3
  modicum 248.2
  minute 258.7
  endowment 478.9
  mark 517.5
  notation 709.12
  v variegate 47.7
  interspace 224.3
  mark 517.19
  disperse 771.4
  sprinkle 771.6
dotage old age 303.5
  senility 922.10
  credulity 954.1
dote on 104.19
do the honors
  extend courtesy
    504.12
  entertain 585.8
  introduce 587.14

do the right thing
  behave oneself 321.5
  do one's duty 641.10
  be good 653.5
do the right thing by
  observe 434.2
  be just 649.6
do the trick do 328.6
  avail 387.17
  accomplish 407.4
  succeed with 409.11
  suit 788.8
  suffice 991.4
  expedite one's affair 995.3
do time
  be imprisoned 429.18
  take one's turn 825.5
dotty
  spotted 47.13
  crazy 926.27
  eccentric 927.5
double
  n deviation 164.1
  fold 291.1
  image 349.5
  game 745.3
  string 750.2
  the same 778.3
  duplicate 785.3
  substitute 862.2
  etheric double 988.3
  v turn back 163.8
  intensify 251.5
  fold 291.5
  play 745.5
  copy 785.8
  seek the middle 819.3
  repeat 849.7
  double 873.5
  duplicate 874.3
  adj falsehearted 354.31
  treacherous 645.21
  two 873.6
  doubled 874.4
double agent
  traitor 357.10
  secret agent 576.9
double-check
  n ensuring 970.8
  v verify 970.12
  check 1017.21
double-cross
  deceive 356.14
  betray 645.14
double-dealing
  n falseheartedness 354.4
  treachery 645.6
  adj falsehearted 354.31
  treacherous 645.21
double-edged
  acrimonious 17.14
  sharp 285.8
double entendre
  joke 489.6
  ambiguity 539.1
  equivocation 539.2
double meaning 539.1
double or nothing 759.3
doubles 748.1
double standard 354.4
doublet root 526.2

two 873.2
double take
  sequel 817.1
  delay 846.2
double-talk
  n nonsense 520.2
  speech sound 524.12
  specious argument 936.3
  v quibble 936.9
double vision 28.1
doubt
  n apprehension 127.4
  suspiciousness 153.2
  agnosticism 695.6
  doubtfulness 955.2
  uncertainty 971.2
  v suffer pangs of jealousy
    153.3
  disbelieve 695.14
  be doubtful 955.6
  be uncertain 971.9
doubtful
  dishonest 645.16
  agnostic 695.20
  doubting 955.9
  unbelievable 955.10
  improbable 969.3
  iffy 971.17
  unsafe 1006.11
doubting Thomas
  agnostic 695.12
  doubter 955.4
doubtless
  adj belief 953.21
  undoubted 970.16
  adv probably 968.8
  unquestionably 970.25
douche
  n washing 79.5
  bath 79.8
  sprinkler 1065.8
  v wash 79.19
  moisten 1065.12
  soak 1065.13
dough soldier 461.7
  money 728.2
  softness 1047.4
  semiliquid 1062.5
doughboy 461.7
doughnut 10.44
doughty strong 15.15
  courageous 492.17
doughy pasty 1047.12
  viscous 1062.12
  pulpy 1063.6
dour sullen 110.24
  harsh 144.24
  unyielding 361.9
  strict 425.6
  firm 425.7
douse take off 6.6
  submerge 367.7
  fight fire 1022.7
dove bird 311.28
  simple soul 416.3
  pacifist 464.6
  innocent 657.4
dovecote 228.23
dovetail
  n joint 800.4
  v interact 777.6

agree 788.6
  hook 800.8
dowager woman 77.5
  old woman 304.3
  widow 566.4
  mistress 575.2
  aristocrat 607.4
dowdiness 810.6
dowdy
  n pastry 10.41
  adj shabby 393.32
dowel 283.3
do well 1010.7
dower
  n talent 413.4
  endowment 478.9
  v endow 478.17
  adj endowed 478.26
do without
  not use 390.5
  relinquish 475.3
  abstain 668.7
Dow-Jones Industrial Average
  737.1
down
  n beard 3.8
  fluff 3.19
  descent 194.1
  plain 236.1
  hill 237.4
  smoothness 294.3
  lightness 298.2
  game 746.3
  reverse 1011.3
  softness 1047.4
  v devour 8.22
  tipple 88.24
  take 134.8
  descend 194.5
  thin 270.12
  change 852.7
  fell 913.5
  adj ill 85.56
  laid up 85.59
  dejected 112.22
  motionless 173.13
  descending 194.11
  lower 274.8
  defeated 412.14
  recorded 549.17
  adv downward 194.13
  cash 624.25
Down's syndrome 922.9
down-and-out
  n poor man 619.4
  adj ruined 395.28
  destitute 619.9
  ended 820.9
down-at-the-heel
  shabby 393.32
  indigent 619.8
  slovenly 810.15
downbeat
  n beat 709.26
  round 850.3
  adj depressing 112.30
  pessimistic 125.16
downcast
  n downthrow 913.2
  adj dejected 112.22
  downturned 194.12

depressed 913.12
downer annoyance 96.2
  dejection 112.3
  adversity 1011.1
downers 87.5
downfall descent 194.1
  rainstorm 316.2
  fall 395.3
  collapse 410.3
  defeat 412.1
  downthrow 913.2
downgrade
  n descent 194.1
  declivity 204.5
  v reduce 252.7
  demote 447.3
  adj sloping downward 204.16
  adv down 194.13
  slantingly 204.23
downhearted 112.22
downhill
  n declivity 204.5
  adj descending 194.11
  sloping downward 204.16
  adv down 194.13
  slantingly 204.23
down-home
  comfortable 121.11
  informal 581.3
  simple 798.6
down in the dumps 112.22
download 1042.18
down on averse 99.8
  disapproving 510.21
down on one's luck 1011.14
down pat 928.26
down payment 624.1
downplay
  minimize 252.9
  moderate 670.6
  attach little importance to
    998.12
downpour
  descent 194.1
  flow 238.4
  rainstorm 316.2
  downthrow 913.2
downright
  adj vertical 200.11
  outright 247.12
  candid 644.17
  thorough 794.10
  unqualified 960.2
  adv down 194.13
  extremely 247.22
  no ifs, ands, or buts 960.3
the downside
  adversity 1011.1
  trouble 1013.3
downsize 252.7
downstage
  n stage 704.16
  adv on the stage 704.36
downstairs
  down 194.13
  below 274.10
down the drain
  lost 473.7
  wasted 486.9
  no more 762.11
down the hatch! 88.38

down the tube
  ruined 395.29
  lost 473.7
  no more 762.11
downtime respite 20.2
  leisure 402.1
  interim 826.1
  delay 846.2
down-to-earth 987.6
downtown
  n city district 230.6
  adj urban 230.11
  adv down 194.13
downtrodden 432.16
downturn
  descent 194.1
  decline 252.2
  deterioration 393.3
  business cycle 731.10
down under 231.6
downward
  adj flowing 172.8
  descending 194.11
  adv down 194.13
downward mobility
  deterioration 393.3
  class 607.1
  change 852.1
downy feathery 3.27
  smooth 287.10
  smooth-textured 294.8
  light 298.10
  fluffy 1047.14
do wonders 409.7
dowry
  n talent 413.4
  endowment 478.9
  adj endowed 478.26
doxology paean 696.3
  sacred music 708.17
doyen senior 304.5
  chief 575.3
doze
  n sleep 22.2
  v sleep 22.13
dozen 882.7
drab
  n strumpet 665.14
  slob 810.7
  adj brown 40.3
  same 781.6
  lackluster 1027.17
Draconian 144.26
Dracula 127.9
draft
  n beverage 8.4
  dose 86.6
  drink 88.7
  submergence 275.6
  wind 318.1
  diagram 381.3
  demand 421.1
  recruit 461.18
  writing 547.10
  abridgment 557.1
  enlistment 615.7
  score 708.28
  drawing 712.13
  negotiable instrument
   728.11
  pulling 905.1

  v draw off 192.12
  outline 381.11
  write 547.19
  enlist 615.17
  portray 712.19
  drive 756.4
drag
  n substance abuse 87.1
  smoking 89.10
  annoyance 96.2
  killjoy 112.14
  tedious person 118.5
  slowing 175.4
  gait 177.12
  resistance 184.27
  burden 297.7
  favor 894.2
  pull 905.2
  attraction 907.1
  disadvantage 996.2
  curb 1012.7
  friction 1044.1
  v use 87.22
  smoke 89.14
  lag 166.4
  go slow 175.6
  dawdle 175.8
  way of walking 177.28
  hang 202.6
  smooth 287.5
  linger on 827.7
  delay 846.8
  pull 905.4
  attract 907.4
drag in
  interpose 213.6
  foist 776.5
drag into 898.2
dragnet
  snare 356.13
  seizure 480.2
  search 938.15
dragon
  sorehead 110.11
  violent person 671.9
drag on
  be tedious 118.6
  persist 781.3
  linger on 827.7
  continue 856.3
drag one's feet
  go slow 175.6
  hesitate 362.7
  protract 827.9
  delay 846.8
  procrastinate 846.11
dragoon
  n cavalryman 461.12
  v intimidate 127.20
  compel 424.4
  coerce 424.7
drag out go slow 175.6
  elicit 192.14
  lengthen 267.6
  diffuse 538.8
  protract 827.9
  postpone 846.9
drag queen 75.15
drag racing 756.1
drain
  n receptacle of filth 80.12

  outflow 190.4
  sough 239.5
  consumption 388.1
  demand 421.1
  waste 473.2
  v disable 19.9
  decolor 36.5
  run out 190.13
  draw off 192.12
  subtract 255.9
  exploit 387.16
  consume 388.3
  waste 473.5
  take from 480.21
  strip 480.24
  evacuate 909.22
  dry 1066.6
drake
  male animal 76.8
  poultry 311.29
dram
  n beverage 8.4
  drink 88.7
  modicum 248.2
  dose 793.5
  v tipple 88.24
drama
  show business 704.1
  representation 349.1
dramatic
  emotionalistic 93.19
  theatrical 501.24
  thespian 704.33
  vocal 708.50
  poetic 720.15
dramatist
  author 547.15
  playwright 704.22
  writer 718.4
dramatize
  manifest 348.5
  affect 500.12
  theatricalize 704.28
  play up 997.16
drape
  n pendant 202.4
  cover 295.2
  shade 1028.1
  v clothe 5.39
  hang 202.6
drastic 671.16
drat! 513.12
draw
  n attendance 221.4
  valley 237.7
  lure 377.3
  poker 759.10
  the same 790.3
  tie 836.3
  pull 905.2
  attraction 907.1
  v smoke 89.14
  extract 192.10
  draw off 192.12
  contract 260.7
  lengthen 267.6
  represent 349.8
  describe 349.9
  lure 377.5
  acquire 472.8
  receive 479.6

  portray 712.19
  play 751.4
  equal 790.5
  exercise influence 894.9
  pull 905.4
  attract 907.4
draw a blank
  fail 410.10
  forget 990.5
draw and quarter
  torture 604.16
  tear apart 802.14
draw apart
  antagonize 589.7
  separate 802.8
drawback
  discount 631.1
  disadvantage 996.2
  fault 1003.2
  obstacle 1012.4
drawer lure 377.3
  storehouse 386.6
draftsman 716.3
draw in retract 168.3
  suck 187.12
  contract 260.7
  narrow 270.11
  lure 377.5
  portray 712.19
  involve 898.2
  reel in 906.9
drawing
  n extraction 192.1
  drafting 192.3
  representation 349.1
  diagram 381.3
  draftsmanship 712.5
  delineation 712.13
  graphic arts 713.1
  lottery 759.14
  pulling 905.1
  adj pulling 905.6
  attracting 907.5
drawing card 377.3
drawing room
  parlor 197.5
  room on train 197.10
  society 578.6
drawl
  n slowness 175.1
  accent 524.8
  v speak 524.25
  speak poorly 525.7
draw lots 759.23
drawn
  tired-looking 21.9
  lengthened 267.8
  equal 790.7
draw out
  extract 192.10
  elicit 192.14
  lengthen 267.6
  diffuse 538.8
  protract 827.9
draw the line at 325.3
draw up
  write 547.19
  form 807.5
  stop 857.7
  pick up 912.8
dray 179.2

dread
n unpleasure 96.1
anxiety 126.1
fear 127.1
suspense 130.3
v fear 127.10
expect 130.5
adj terrible 127.30
dreadful
adj horrid 98.19
terrible 127.30
venerable 155.12
remarkable 247.11
bad 1000.9
hideous 1015.11
adv terribly 1000.14
dream
n aspiration 100.9
airy hope 124.5
illusion 976.1
hallucination 976.7
abstractedness 985.2
reverie 986.9
first-rate 999.7
beauty 1016.9
v suppose 951.10
muse 985.9
dream of 986.17
dreamland sleep 22.2
illusion 976.1
utopia 986.11
dream up
originate 892.12
imagine 986.14
dreamy sleepy 22.21
tranquilizing 670.15
illusory 976.9
abstracted 985.11
dreamful 986.25
dreary gray 39.4
distressing 98.20
gloomy 112.24
dull 117.6
tedious 118.9
ominous 133.17
dredge
n excavator 284.10
v extract 192.10
excavate 284.15
sprinkle 771.6
imbue 797.11
pick up 912.8
dredge up
extract 192.10
assemble 770.18
pick up 912.8
dregs grounds 256.2
refuse 391.4
rabble 606.3
extract 893.3
drench
n inhibition 8.4
drink 88.7
soaking 1065.7
v overload 993.15
soak 1065.13
tend 1070.7
dress
n clothing 5.1
suit 5.6
gown 5.16

insignia 647.1
v clothe 5.39
groom 79.20
smooth 287.5
equip 385.8
prepare 405.6
ornament 498.8
fertilize 890.8
buff 1044.8
oil 1056.8
cultivate 1069.17
adj clothing 5.45
dressage 1070.1
dress down
dress up 5.42
disapprove 510.18
punish 604.15
dressed to kill
dressed up 5.46
chic 578.13
dressing clothing 5.1
stuffing 10.27
application 86.33
disapproval 510.6
fertilizer 890.4
abrasion 1044.2
cultivation 1069.13
dressing room
closet 197.15
stage 704.16
dress rehearsal 704.13
dried-up shrunk 260.13
wasted 393.35
unproductive 891.4
dried 1066.9
drift
n direction 161.1
deviation 164.1
course 172.2
deposit 176.9
drift angle 184.28
flow 238.4
meaning 518.1
race 756.3
group of animals 770.5
pile 770.10
trend 896.2
reception 1034.21
v stray 164.4
wander 177.23
drift off course 182.29
float 182.54
fly 184.36
do nothing 329.2
take it easy 331.15
pile 770.19
drifter
displaced person 160.4
wanderer 178.2
bum 331.9
fisher 382.6
wretch 660.2
transient 828.4
drift off 22.16
driftwood 1054.3
drill
n exercise 84.2
point 285.3
action 328.1
rule 373.4
training 568.3

study 570.3
exercise 725.6
cutlery 1040.2
v deepen 275.8
excavate 284.15
perforate 292.15
train 568.13
study 570.12
plant 1069.18
drink
n potation 8.4
beverage 10.49
dram 88.7
cocktail 88.9
spirits 88.13
ocean 240.1
fluid 1061.2
v drink in 8.29
use 87.22
tipple 88.24
ingest 187.11
absorb 187.13
drink in drink 8.29
absorb 187.13
learn 570.7
attend to 983.5
drinking habit 87.1
drink to drink 8.29
toast 88.29
drink up drink 8.29
tipple 88.24
absorb 187.13
thirst 1066.5
drip
n tedious person 118.5
leakage 190.5
trickle 238.7
v leak 190.14
trickle 238.18
be damp 1065.11
drive
n vim 17.2
power 18.1
desire 100.1
acceleration 174.4
ride 177.7
enterprise 330.7
motive 365.1
urge 375.6
haste 401.1
campaign 458.4
attack 459.1
vigor 544.3
group of animals 770.5
cause 886.9
impulse 902.1
pushing 904.1
machinery enginery 1040.3
disk drive 1042.5
v set in motion 172.6
ride 177.33
drift off course 182.29
pilot 184.37
excavate 284.15
hustle 330.13
hunt 382.9
compel 424.4
launch an attack 459.17
guide 573.9
task 725.16
play tennis 748.3

play 751.4
race 756.4
ride 757.5
impel 902.11
thrust 902.12
push 904.9
obsess 926.25
herd 1070.8
drive a bargain 731.18
drive at 380.4
drive away
dissipate 771.5
repulse 908.3
drive crazy 926.24
drive home to 953.18
drive-in movie 706.7
drive insane 926.24
drive-in theater 706.7
drivel
n saliva 13.3
nonsense 520.2
v salivate 13.6
talk nonsense 520.5
be incomprehensible 522.10
be stupid 922.12
be insane 926.20
drive on
make one's way 162.4
hustle 330.13
urge on 375.16
hasten 401.4
impel 902.11
driver reinsman 178.9
motorist 178.10
tyrant 575.14
man 577.4
race driving 756.2
operator 889.4
propeller 904.6
driver's license 443.6
driver's seat 417.10
drive up the wall
annoy 96.13
madden 926.24
driving
n riding 177.6
race 756.3
adj moving 172.7
rainy 316.11
enterprising 330.23
motivating 375.25
compulsory 424.10
attacking 459.29
vigorous 544.11
impelling 902.23
propulsive 904.14
obsessive 926.34
drizzle
n rain 316.1
v rain 316.10
droit 642.1
droll
humorous 488.4
witty 489.15
dromedary
beast of burden 176.8
hoofed animal 311.5
drone
n slowpoke 175.5
bee 311.35
nonworker 331.11

mumbling 525.4
part 708.22
bagpipes 711.9
regularity 781.2
series 812.2
repetitiousness 849.4
v hum 52.13
mumble 525.9
persist 781.3
drool
n saliva 13.3
nonsense 520.2
v salivate 13.6
talk nonsense 520.5
be stupid 922.12
be insane 926.20
droop
n gait 177.12
sinkage 194.2
hang 202.2
v weaken 16.9
burn out 21.5
fail 85.48
lose heart 112.16
sink 194.6
hang 202.6
languish 393.18
drooping weak 16.12
languishing 16.21
tired 21.7
dejected 112.22
descending 194.11
limp 202.10
deteriorating 393.45
loose 804.5
drop
n drink 88.7
leakage 190.5
descent 194.1
declivity 204.5
trickle 238.7
modicum 248.2
advantage 249.2
decline 252.2
minute 258.7
droplet 282.3
hiding place 346.4
plunge 367.1
deterioration 393.3
address 553.9
execution 605.5
scenery 704.20
skiing 753.1
pause 857.3
v give birth 1.3
take off 6.6
weaken 16.9
burn out 21.5
faint 25.5
lay 78.9
snub 157.5
leak 190.14
descend 194.5
incline 204.10
trickle 238.18
decrease 252.6
gravitate 297.15
strike dead 308.18
plunge 367.6
give up 370.7
break the habit 374.3

cease to use 390.4
lose 473.4
relinquish 475.3
cheapen 633.6
shoot 904.12
repulse 908.3
fell 913.5
let go of 913.7
drop a hint 551.10
drop a line
communicate with 343.8
correspond 553.10
drop anchor
settle 159.17
land 186.8
drop by go to 177.25
enter 189.7
visit 582.19
drop cloth 295.9
drop dead 307.22
drop in go to 177.25
enter 189.7
visit 582.19
drop in on 131.7
drop in the bucket
pittance 992.5
trifle 998.5
drop off
go to sleep 22.16
descend 194.5
decrease 252.6
die 307.20
drop out
dissent 333.4
abandon 370.5
not conform 868.4
drops 86.4
dropsy symptom 85.9
distension 259.2
drop the ball
fail 410.10
bungle 414.12
make a boner 975.15
drop the other shoe 817.5
drop the subject 984.4
dross dregs 256.2
combustion product
1020.16
drought
appetite 100.7
want 992.4
dryness 1066.1
drove
n group of animals 770.5
v drive 1070.8
drown choke 307.24
strangle 308.19
submerge 367.7
suppress 428.8
come to grief 1011.10
flood 1065.14
drown out 53.8
drowsy sleepy 22.21
tranquilizing 670.15
drub
n hit 902.4
stamp 902.10
v defeat 412.9
whip 604.13
pound 902.16
stamp 902.22

drudge
n servant 577.2
grub 726.3
v be busy 330.10
keep doggedly at 360.3
serve 577.13
grind and dig 725.14
drug
n anesthetic 25.3
medicine 86.4
narcotic drug 86.5
narcotic 87.3
moderator 670.3
commodity 735.2
v put to sleep 22.20
deaden 25.4
medicate 91.25
numb 94.8
moderate 670.6
drug abuse 87.1
drug addict 87.21
drugged 25.8
drug habit 87.1
drug pusher 732.4
drugstore 86.36
drug trafficking 87.2
Druid
idolater 697.4
pagan clergy 699.15
predictor 962.4
drum
n staccato 55.1
cylinder 282.4
percussion instrument 711.16
v thrum 55.4
bird sound 60.5
rain 316.10
beat time 708.44
din 849.10
pulsate 916.12
drum out
depose 447.4
exclude 773.4
drive out 909.14
dismiss 909.19
drumstick
fowl part 10.23
leg 177.14
percussion instrument 711.16
drum up acquire 472.9
assemble 770.18
drunk
n drinking spree 88.6
drinker 88.11
lush 88.12
adj intoxicated 88.31
fervent 93.18
dizzy 985.15
druthers
preference 371.5
free will 430.6
dry
n conservative 611.9
prohibitionist 668.5
v preserve 397.9
strip 480.24
desiccate 1066.6
adj raucous 58.15
sour 67.5
thirsty 100.26
dull 117.6

tedious 118.9
right 219.4
satiric 508.13
sober 516.3
plain-speaking 535.3
conservative 611.17
prohibitionist 668.11
unproductive 891.4
unimaginative 987.5
arid 1066.7
dry-clean 79.18
dry goods 735.3
dry goods dealer 5.33
drying
n shrinking 260.3
food preservation 397.2
desiccation 1066.3
adj dehydrating 1066.10
dry land 234.1
dry out use 87.22
sober up 516.2
swear off 668.8
dry run
Air Force mission 184.11
preparation 405.1
operation 458.5
tryout 942.3
dry up
v shrink 260.9
be consumed 388.4
languish 393.18
dry 1066.6
interj silence! 51.14
dual
n number 530.8
adj two 873.6
dualism theism 675.5
doubleness 873.1
pluralism 952.6
dualist 675.16
dub
n bungler 414.9
golfer 751.2
v smooth 287.5
name 527.11
dub in 862.4
dubious
deceptive 356.21
irresolute 362.9
dishonest 645.16
agnostic 695.20
doubting 955.9
unbelievable 955.10
improbable 969.3
doubtful 971.17
unsafe 1006.11
ducal 608.10
ducat 728.4
duchess 608.6
duchy region 231.5
country 232.1
duck
n man 76.5
poultry 311.29
submergence 367.2
avoidance 368.1
loser 412.5
endearment term 562.6
card 758.2
retreat 903.3
crouch 913.3

v avoid 164.6
retract 168.3
prevaricate 344.7
submerge 367.7
dodge 368.8
shirk 368.9
fight 754.4
pull back 903.7
crouch 913.8
bow 913.9
flood 1065.14
duck out
absent oneself 222.8
flee 368.11
slip away 368.12
duck soup 1014.4
ducky
n ladylove 104.15
adj excellent 999.13
duct vessel 2.23
channel 239.1
ductile docile 433.13
handy 1014.15
pliant 1047.9
dud
n impotent 19.6
false alarm 400.2
failure 410.2
abortion 410.5
flop 410.8
candidate 610.9
thing of naught 764.2
v clothe 5.39
dude man 76.5
dandy 500.9
dudgeon 152.7
duds clothing 5.1
garment 5.3
due
n debt 623.1
one's due 639.2
prerogative 642.1
adj expected 130.13
owed 623.10
right 637.3
payable 639.7
entitled to 639.10
just 649.8
attributable 888.6
sufficient 991.6
adv directly 161.23
duel
n single combat 457.7
fight 754.3
v contend 457.13
duelist 461.1
dues debt 623.1
fee 630.6
deserts 639.3
duet cooperation 450.1
part music 708.18
two 873.2
due to
conj resulting from 887.8
prep because of 888.9
duffel equipment 385.4
impedimenta 471.3
duffer
incompetent 414.7
bungler 414.9
golfer 751.2

dugout cave 284.5
hiding place 346.4
entrenchment 460.5
baseball 745.1
shelter 1009.3
dugs 283.6
duke nobleman 608.4
poker 759.10
blow 902.5
duke it out 457.17
dulcet pleasant 97.6
melodious 708.48
dulcify sweeten 66.3
pacify 465.7
calm 670.7
dull
v weaken 16.10
deaden 25.4
decolor 36.5
muffle 51.9
blunt 94.7
relieve 120.5
blunt 286.2
moderate 670.6
mat 1027.10
adj weak 16.12
insensible 25.6
colorless 36.7
gray 39.4
muffled 52.17
unfeeling 94.9
apathetic 94.13
inexcitable 106.10
dry 117.6
tedious 118.9
inert 173.14
blunt 286.3
languid 331.20
plain-speaking 535.3
prosaic 721.5
dull of mind 922.16
unimaginative 987.5
mediocre 1005.7
lackluster 1027.17
dullard 924.2
dumb
adj mute 51.12
animal 311.40
taciturn 344.9
stammering 525.13
stupid 922.15
foolish 923.8
ignorant 930.12
inanimate 1055.5
dumbbell
exerciser 725.7
fool 924.4
dumbfound
silence 51.8
astonish 122.6
dumbstruck
mute 51.12
wondering 122.9
dumbwaiter 912.4
dummy
n mute 51.3
reproduction 336.3
figure 349.6
fake 354.13
instrument 384.4
composition 548.2

figurehead 575.5
deputy 576.1
follower 616.8
bridge 758.3
thing of naught 764.2
artist's model 786.5
substitute 862.2
fool 924.4
a nobody 998.7
adj spurious 354.26
substitute 862.8
dump
n sty 80.11
receptacle of filth 80.12
humiliation 137.2
disrespect 156.3
hovel 228.11
disapproved place 228.28
derelict 370.4
store 386.1
storehouse 386.6
trash pile 391.6
armory 462.2
v abase 137.5
place 159.12
load 159.15
discard 390.7
relinquish 475.3
sell 734.8
divest 737.24
unload 909.23
dumpling 10.33
dump on
abase 137.5
be disrespectful 156.6
disdain 157.3
dumps
sulks 110.10
blues 112.6
dumpy
corpulent 257.18
dwarf 258.13
stubby 268.10
dun
n horse 311.11
creditor 622.4
statement 628.3
v importune 440.12
bill 628.11
adj brown 40.3
dunce
stupid person 924.2
ignoramus 930.8
dunderhead 924.4
dune hill 237.4
pile 770.10
dung
n feces 12.4
fertilizer 890.4
v defecate 12.13
dungeon 429.8
dunghill
n manure pile 80.10
adj dastardly 491.12
dunk
submerge 367.7
play 751.4
flood 1065.14
duo
part music 708.18
two 873.2

duodecimal system 1017.4
duodenal 882.24
dupe
n sycophant 138.3
dupable person 358
gull 358.1
instrument 384.4
simple soul 416.3
laughingstock 508.7
agent 576.3
cheater 759.22
duplicate 785.3
trusting soul 954.4
v deceive 356.14
copy 785.8
duplicate 874.3
stultify 923.7
duplex
n apartment house
228.14
adj two 873.6
duplicate
n image 349.5
the same 778.3
replica 785.3
duplication 874.1
v reproduce 78.7
re-create 778.6
copy 785.8
repeat 849.7
double 873.5
dupe 874.3
multiply 883.6
adj identical 778.7
analogous 784.11
double 874.4
duplication
remake 78.1
replica 336.3
reproduction 785.2
clone 785.3
repetition 849.1
doubleness 873.1
replication 874.1
reduplication 874.1
multiplication 883.4
superfluity 993.4
duplicity
falseheartedness 354.4
deceit 356.3
treachery 645.6
doubleness 873.1
durable sturdy 763.7
perdurable 827.10
permanent 853.7
tough 1049.4
duration time 821.1
term 824.3
lastingness 827
durability 827.1
perpetuity 829.1
permanence 853.1
duress power 18.1
coercion 424.3
imprisonment 429.3
necessity 963.1
during 821.14
dusk
n dusking time 315.3
daylight 1025.10
darkishness 1027.2

v grow dark 1027.12
adj dark 38.9
evening 315.8
darkish 1027.15

dust
n dirt 80.6
cocaine 87.7
drugs 87.18
land 234.1
lightness 298.2
corpse 307.16
refuse 391.4
rubbish 391.5
powder 1051.5
dryness 1066.2
v clean 79.18
dirty 80.15
sprinkle 771.6

dust bowl
the country 233.1
wasteland 891.2

dust jacket
wrapper 295.18
bookbinding 554.14

dusty gray 39.4
dirty 80.22
dull 117.6
tedious 118.9
wayworn 177.41
stale 842.14
powdery 1051.11
dry 1066.7

Dutch courage 87.1
Dutch uncle 422.3
dutiful respectful 155.8
obedient 326.3
observant 434.4
duteous 641.13
pious 692.8

duty respect 155.1
function 387.5
demand 421.1
tax 630.9
obligation 641.1
charge 643.3
divine service 696.8
rite 701.3
task 724.2
job 724.3

duty-free 630.16
duvet 295.10
dwarf
n modicum 248.2
dwarfling 258.5
fairy 678.8
v minimize 252.9
adj dwarfed 258.13

dwell inhabit 225.7
endure 827.6

dwell in
be present 221.6
exist in 761.11

dwelling
n habitation 225.1
abode 228.1
house 228.5
adj resident 225.13

dwell on
harp on 118.8
harbor revenge 507.5
protract 827.9

insist upon 849.9
keep in memory 989.13
emphasize 997.14

dwindle disappear 34.2
fail 85.48
recede 168.2
quiet 173.8
decrease 252.6

dyad 873.2
dybbuk demon 680.6
specter 988.1

dye
n color 35.8
v infuse 35.14
imbue 797.11

dyed-in-the-wool
deep-dyed 35.18
confirmed 373.18
thorough 794.10
established 855.13

dying
n decrease 252.1
death 307.1
terminal case 307.15
deterioration 393.3
extinguishing 1022.2
adj unhealthy 85.54
impatient 135.6
receding 168.5
terminal 307.33
transient 828.7

dying breath 307.9
dying to
wanting 100.21
desirous of 100.22
eager 101.8

dying words
sequel 817.1
end 820.1

dyke 76.9
dynamic
energetic 17.13
powerful 18.12
enterprising 330.23
dynamical 1039.9

dynamite 999.13
dynastic 417.17
dynasty 835.2
dyne 17.7
dysentery
defecation 12.2
symptom 85.9

dysfunction 638.1
dyspeptic
n sick person 85.43
adj anemic 85.61
sour 110.23

each
adj every 864.15
adv apiece 865.19

each other 777.4
eager
desirous 100.21
anxious 101.8
expectant 130.11
impatient 135.6
willing 324.5
active 330.17
enterprising 404.8
prepared 405.16
consenting 441.4

eagle
n sharp vision 27.11
swiftness 174.6
ascent 193.7
bird 311.28
insignia 647.1
heraldry 647.2
military insignia 647.5
specie 728.4
round 751.3
v play 751.4

eagle eye
sharp eye 27.10
vigilance 339.4

ear
n auditory apparatus 2.10
hearing 48.1
audition 48.2
lug 48.7
bulge 283.3
spike 310.29
discrimination 944.1
attention 983.1
adj eye 2.28

earache ache 26.5
ear disease 85.15

an ear for
good hearing 48.3
aptitude 413.5

earful 524.3
earl 608.4
earlier
adj lower 274.8
previous 834.4
prior 845.10
adv previously 834.6
formerly 837.13

earliest 216.10
ear lobe ear 2.10
pendant 202.4

early
adj anachronous 833.3
previous 834.4
former 837.10
back 837.12
bright 845.7
adv previously 834.6
long ago 837.16
bright and early 845.11

early bird 845.4
earmark
n sign 517.1
mark 517.5
characteristic 865.4
v commit 436.5
allot 477.9
label 517.20
characterize 865.10

earn acquire 472.8
be paid 624.20
deserve 639.5

earnest
n pledge 438.2
payment 624.1
adj zealous 101.9
solemn 111.3
resolute 359.11
attentive 983.15
weighty 997.20

earnings
acquisition 472.1

gain 472.3
pay 624.4
receipts 627.1

earn one's keep
make a living 385.11
work 725.12

earphone 50.8
ear-piercing
loud 53.11
shrill 58.14

earring circle 280.3
jewel 498.6

earshot earreach 48.4
short distance 223.2

ear-splitting 58.14
earth
n ground covering 199.3
horizontal 201.3
lair 228.26
land 234.1
corpse 307.16
shelter 1009.3
adj terrestrial 234.4

Earth planet 1072.9
the world 1072.10

earthborn human 312.13
populational 606.8

earthbound
terrestrial 234.4
unimaginative 987.5

earthen earthy 234.5
ceramic 742.7

earthling person 312.5
irreligionist 695.10

earthly
terrestrial 234.4
secularist 695.16
material 1052.10

earthquake 671.5
earthshaking
loud 53.11
important 997.17

earthworm 311.39
earthy earthen 234.5
human 312.13
coarse 497.11
populational 606.8
carnal 663.6
vulgar 666.8
secularist 695.16
realistic 987.6

ease
n rest 20.1
pleasure 95.1
contentment 107.1
relief 120.1
comfort 121.1
leisure 402.1
aid 449.1
elegance 533.1
fluency 544.2
informality 581.1
prosperity 1010.1
facility 1014.1
v relax 20.7
relieve 120.5
release 120.6
comfort 121.6
abate 252.8
lighten 298.6
liberalize 430.13

aid 449.11
extenuate 600.12
calm 670.7
relax 670.9
loosen 804.3
allow for 959.5
facilitate 1014.7
soften 1047.6
ease in 191.3
easel 712.18
ease off
  let up 20.7
  avoid 164.6
  slow 175.9
  relax 670.9
  loosen 804.3
ease out 773.4
ease up relax 20.7
  slow 175.9
  relax 670.9
ease up on
  have pity 145.4
  be easy on 427.5
east
  n points of the compass 161.3
  adj northern 161.14
  adv E 161.17
East 231.6
East Coast 231.7
easter
  n north wind 318.9
  v go west 161.8
eastward
  n points of the compass 161.3
  adv east 161.17
easy
  adj pleased 95.15
  nonchalant 106.15
  content 107.7
  comfortable 121.11
  at ease 121.12
  good-natured 143.14
  slow 175.10
  light 298.12
  indolent 331.19
  leisurely 402.6
  unstrict 426.5
  lenient 427.7
  elegant 533.6
  fluent 544.9
  informal 581.3
  cheap 633.7
  wanton 665.26
  loose 804.5
  gullible 954.9
  prosperous 1010.12
  facile 1014.13
  soft 1047.8
  adv cautiously 494.12
  interj careful! 494.14
  cease! 857.13
easy come 486.8
easy does it
  interj take it easy! 402.8
  careful! 494.14
  phrs take it easy 175.15
easygoing
  unconcerned 102.7
  nonchalant 106.15
  content 107.7

careless 340.11
unstrict 426.5
lenient 427.7
free 430.21
informal 581.3
dilatory 846.17
easy mark dupe 358.2
  trusting soul 954.4
easy money 472.6
easy on the eyes 1016.22
easy pickings 358.2
Easy Street 1010.1
easy target 1014.3
eat feed 8.20
  take 134.8
  ingest 187.11
  consume 388.3
  corrode 393.21
  etch 713.10
eat away
  subtract 255.9
  corrode 393.21
eat crow
  n recant 363.8
  v humble oneself 137.7
  eat dirt 433.11
eat humble pie
  n recant 363.8
  v humble oneself 137.7
  eat dirt 433.11
eating disorder mental
    disorder 92.14
  gluttony 672.1
eat one's words
  n recant 363.8
  v humble oneself 137.7
eat up
  v devour 8.22
  feast 8.24
  enjoy 95.13
  consume 388.3
  kid oneself 954.6
  interj chow down! 8.35
eau de Cologne 70.3
eaves 295.6
eavesdrop
  listen 48.10
  be curious 981.3
eaves trough 239.3
ebb
  n standstill 173.3
  tide 238.13
  decline 252.2
  deterioration 393.3
  v recede 168.2
  move 172.5
  quiet 173.8
  flow 238.16
  decrease 252.6
  decline 393.17
ebb and flow
  n tide 238.13
  alternation 916.5
  v billow 238.22
  change 854.5
  alternate 916.13
ebony
  n blackness 38.1
  darkness 38.4
  adj black 38.8
  dark 1027.13

ebullient
  excited 105.20
  bubbly 320.6
  active 330.17
  hot 1019.25
eccentric
  n nonconformist 868.3
  oddity 870.4
  erratic 927.3
  adj off-center 160.12
  humorous 488.4
  irregular 851.3
  inconstant 854.7
  unconventional 868.6
  abnormal 870.9
  odd 870.11
  erratic 927.5
eccentricity
  humorousness 488.1
  irregularity 851.1
  inconstancy 854.2
  abnormality 870.1
  foolishness 923.1
  idiosyncrasy 927.1
  disposition 978.3
ecclesiastic
  n clergyman 699.2
  adj ministerial 698.13
ecdysiast
  nudity 6.3
  entertainer 707.1
ECG 91.9
echelon
  flight formation 184.12
  rank 245.2
  battle array 458.3
echo
  n reverberation 54.2
  sympathy 93.5
  imitator 336.4
  response 708.23
  keyboard 711.17
  reflection 785.7
  repetition 849.1
  repeat 849.5
  duplicate 874.2
  reaction 903.1
  answer 939.1
  signal 1036.11
  v reverberate 54.7
  respond 93.11
  concur 332.9
  imitate 336.5
  repeat 849.7
  recurrence 849.11
  answer 939.4
  reflect 1036.16
éclat publicity 352.4
  display 501.4
  applause 509.2
  repute 662.1
eclectic
  selective 371.23
  mixed 797.14
  combined 805.5
eclecticism
  selectivity 371.10
  sectarianism 675.4
  mixture 797.1
eclipse
  n disappearance 34.1

covering 295.1
occultation 1027.8
moon 1072.11
sun 1072.13
v blind 30.7
overshadow 249.8
cover 295.19
conceal 346.6
darken 1027.9
ecological 209.9
ecology 1073.1
e-commerce 736.2
economic cheap 633.7
  thrifty 635.6
  socio-economic 731.23
economic indicator 731.9
economics
  finance 729.1
  trade 731.1
  eco 731.11
economist
  economizer 635.3
  financier 729.9
  economic expert 731.12
economy
  n parsimony 484.1
  thrift 635.1
  economic system 731.7
  adj cheap 633.7
ecosphere
  organic matter 305.1
  biosphere 306.8
  atmosphere 317.2
  the environment 1073.1
ecosystem 1073.1
ecru brown 40.3
  yellow 43.4
ecstasy
  amphetamines 87.4
  passion 93.2
  happiness 95.2
  amorousness 104.3
  fury 105.8
  revelation 683.10
  trance 691.3
ecstatic
  n psychic 689.13
  adj overjoyed 95.17
  frenzied 105.25
  abstracted 985.11
ectomorph 92.12
ectoplasm cell 305.4
  exteriorized protoplasm
    689.7
ecumenical
  cooperative 450.5
  universal 864.14
  broad-minded 979.8
ecumenism
  cooperation 450.1
  moderation 670.1
  combination 805.1
  broad-mindedness 979.1
eczema 85.34
eddy
  n agitation 105.4
  back stream 238.12
  whirl 915.2
  v gurge 238.21
  whirl 915.11
edema symptom 85.9

increase 251.1
distension 259.2
swelling 283.4
overextension 993.7
Eden 986.11
edge
    n acrimony 17.5
    pungency 68.1
    summit 198.2
    border 211.4
    advantage 249.2
    straight line 277.2
    sharpness 285.1
    sharp edge 285.2
    v border 211.10
    side 218.4
    go sideways 218.5
    sharpen 285.7
edge in enter 189.7
    interpose 213.6
    intrude 214.5
edge out outdo 249.9
    triumph 411.3
    defeat 412.6
edgy
    excitable 105.28
    nervous 128.11
    impatient 135.6
edible 8.33
edict
    announcement 352.2
    decree 420.4
    law 673.3
edification
    teaching 568.1
    learning 928.14
edifice house 228.5
    structure 266.2
edify
    make better 392.9
    teach 568.10
edit delete 255.12
    comment upon 341.11
    revise 392.12
    write 547.19
edition rendering 341.2
    issue 554.5
    score 708.28
editor interpreter 341.7
    publisher 554.2
    journalist 555.4
    commentator 556.4
    motion-picture studio 706.4
    examiner 938.17
    critic 946.7
    systems program 1042.12
editorial
    n commentary 556.2
    adj explanatory 341.15
    journalistic 555.5
educate
    make better 392.9
    teach 568.10
educated
    improved 392.13
    learned 570.16
    informed 928.18
    scholarly 928.21
educated guess 951.4
education
    cultivation 392.3

teaching 568.1
learning 570.1
erudition 928.4
educational 551.18
educe 192.14
EEG 91.9
eel 10.24
eerie awesome 122.11
    creepy 127.31
    deathly 307.29
    supernatural 870.15
    weird 988.9
efface 395.16
effect
    n power 18.1
    aspect 33.3
    intention 380.1
    meaning 518.1
    relevance 775.4
    end 820.1
    event 831.1
    sequel 835.2
    consequence 887.1
    result 887.1
    product 893.1
    influence 894.1
    v do 328.6
    use 384.5
    accomplish 407.4
    execute 437.9
    cause 886.10
    induce 886.11
    establish 892.10
effective
    powerful 18.12
    able 18.14
    effectual 387.21
    vigorous 544.11
    operative 889.9
    influential 894.13
    practical 995.6
effects
    equipment 385.4
    property 471.1
    merchandise 735.1
effectual able 18.14
    effective 387.21
    causal 886.13
    operative 889.9
    influential 894.13
    true 973.13
    practical 995.6
effeminate
    n mama's boy 77.11
    v feminize 77.13
    adj frail 16.14
    homosexual 75.30
    womanish 77.15
effervescence
    sibilation 57.1
    agitation 105.4
    bubbling 320.3
    liveliness 330.2
effervescent
    sibilant 57.3
    excited 105.20
    bubbly 320.6
    active 330.17
effete weak 16.12
    weakened 16.18
    ineffective 19.15

dull 117.6
used up 388.5
worn-out 393.36
deteriorating 393.45
efficacious able 18.14
    effectual 387.21
    operative 889.9
    influential 894.13
efficiency
    ability 18.2
    utility 387.3
    skill 413.1
efficient able 18.14
    effectual 387.21
    competent 413.24
    economical 635.6
    operative 889.9
    practical 995.6
effigy 349.5
efflorescence
    skin eruption 85.36
    flowering 310.26
    powderiness 1051.1
    powder 1051.5
effluent
    n excrement 12.3
    tributary 238.3
    refuse 391.4
    adj outgoing 190.19
effluvium odor 69.1
    ectoplasm 689.7
    miasma 1001.4
    vapor 1067.1
effluxion 190.4
effort act 328.3
    endeavor 403.1
    attempt 403.2
    undertaking 404.1
    exertion 725.1
    expedient 995.2
effortless 1014.13
effrontery 142.1
effulgence 1025.4
effuse
    v excrete 12.12
    emerge 190.11
    exude 190.15
    adj plentiful 991.7
effusive
    v talkative 540.9
    adj outgoing 190.19
    communicative 343.10
    diffuse 538.11
egalitarianism 612.4
egest excrete 12.12
    vomit 909.26
egestion excretion 12.1
    vomiting 909.8
egg
    n ovum 305.12
    ovule 305.15
    race 753.3
    vital force 886.7
    v pelt 459.27
egghead snob 141.7
    intellectual 929.1
egg on urge on 375.16
    induce 886.11
egg on one's face
    chagrin 96.4
    mortification 98.6

humiliation 137.2
eggshell
    n egg 305.15
    fragility 1050.2
    adj soft-colored 35.22
    whitish 37.8
ego psyche 92.28
    egotism 140.3
    self 865.5
    psyche 919.4
egocentric
    n egotist 140.5
    adj unfeeling 94.9
    egotistic 140.10
egoist
    proudling 136.3
    egotist 140.5
egomaniac 140.1
egotism egoism 140.3
    selfishness 651.1
egotist egoist 140.5
    self-seeker 651.3
egotistical
    self-centered 140.10
    selfish 651.5
ego trip vanity 140.1
    selfishness 651.1
egregious
    remarkable 247.10
    downright 247.12
    thorough 794.10
    excessive 993.16
    terrible 1000.9
egress
    n departure 188.1
    exit 190.2
    outlet 190.9
    channel 239.1
    evacuation 909.6
    v exit 190.12
eiderdown
    down 3.19
    blanket 295.10
    softness 1047.4
eidetic 989.23
eidolon aspect 33.3
    phantom 976.4
    figment of the imagination
        986.5
    specter 988.1
eight team 617.7
    card 758.2
    number 882.4
eighth
    n octave 709.9
    adj octonary 882.20
eighty-six 390.7
Einstein theory 158.6
either
    n any 864.5
    adj one 872.7
    adv similarly 784.18
either-or
    ambiguous 539.4
    two 873.6
ejaculate exclaim 59.7
    climax 75.24
    project 904.11
    disgorge 909.25
eject erupt 671.13
    eliminate 773.5

separate 802.8
shoot 904.12
repulse 908.3
expel 909.13
ejection
excretion 12.1
excrement 12.3
outburst 190.3
elimination 773.2
shot 904.4
repulsion 908.1
discharge 909.1
ejectment 909.1
eke out
support oneself 385.12
be poor 619.5
complete 794.6
EKG 91.9
el 179.14
elaborate
v develop 392.10
amplify 538.7
ornament 545.7
develop 861.6
produce 892.8
adj painstaking 339.11
ornate 498.12
grandiose 501.21
complex 799.4
elaborated 533.9
elaboration
development 392.2
ornamentation 498.1
amplification 538.6
iteration 849.2
evolution 861.1
production 892.2
élan animation 17.4
eagerness 101.1
gaiety 109.4
elapse lapse 821.5
pass 837.6
elastic
n elastomer 1048.3
adj expansive 259.9
recuperative 396.23
pliant 1047.9
resilient 1048.7
elate
v exalt 109.8
make proud 136.6
adj overjoyed 95.17
rejoicing 116.10
crowing 502.13
elbow
n member 2.7
angle 278.2
joint 800.4
arm 906.5
v angle 278.5
thrust 902.12
elbow bender 88.12
elbow grease 725.1
elbowroom room 158.3
latitude 430.4
elder
n old man 304.2
senior 304.5
master 575.1
public official 575.17
clergy 699.10

back number 842.8
wise man 921.1
personage 997.8
adj previous 834.4
older 842.19
elder statesman
expert 413.11
statesman 610.2
wise man 921.1
elect
n elite 371.12
upper class 607.2
aristocracy 608.1
the best 999.8
v choose 371.13
vote in 371.20
support 609.41
adj chosen 371.26
exclusive 495.13
best 999.16
the elect 692.5
election
choice 371.1
appointment 371.9
authority 417.12
general election 609.15
holy orders 698.10
determinism 964.4
electioneer
n campaigner 610.10
v campaign 609.40
elective
voluntary 324.7
volitional 371.22
selective 371.23
electorate
population 227.1
region 231.5
selector 371.7
electors 609.22
Electra complex 92.22
electric
n streetcar 179.17
adj exciting 105.30
provocative 375.27
galvanic 1032.30
electrical engineering 1043.1
electric chair 605.5
electric current
current 1032.2
electron flow 1033.6
electric field 1032.3
electrician
stage technician 704.24
electrotechnician 1032.22
electricity
swiftness 174.6
telegraph 347.2
illuminant 1025.20
electrical science 1032.1
electric power
manpower 18.4
wattage 1032.18
electrify energize 17.10
agitate 105.14
startle 131.8
galvanize 1032.26
electrolysis 1032.25
electromagnetic field
electric field 1032.3
magnetic force 1032.9

electron atom 258.8
negatron 1033.3
electronic device 1033.13
electronic mail computer
networking 347.18
delivery 353.5
correspondence 553.1
mail 553.4
postal service 553.7
computer communications
1042.19
electronic media 551.5
electronics radio 347.3
electron physics 1033.1
radionics 1033.1
electron theory of atoms
1033.2
electrostatic
electric 1032.30
static 1039.8
eleemosynary
benevolent 143.15
philanthropic 478.22
gratuitous 634.5
elegance
parsimony 484.1
taste 496.1
ornateness 498.2
overniceness 500.5
grandeur 501.5
good breeding 504.4
refinement 533.1
grace 533.1
fluency 544.2
smartness 578.3
etiquette 580.3
decency 664.2
beauty 1016.1
elegant graceful 496.9
ornate 498.12
overnice 500.18
grandiose 501.21
tasteful 533.6
fluent 544.9
chic 578.13
decent 664.5
good 999.12
beautiful 1016.18
elegiac
n meter 720.7
adj dirgelike 115.22
poetic 720.15
elegy 115.6
element
natural environment 209.4
particular 766.3
component 796.2
cause 886.1
heater 1020.10
matter 1052.2
chemical element 1060.2
elemental
n elemental spirit 678.6
adj basic 199.8
climatal 317.13
essential 767.9
beginning 818.15
original 886.14
chemical 1060.9
elementary basic 199.8
essential 767.9

component 796.5
simple 798.6
beginning 818.15
original 886.14
chemical 1060.9
elementary school 567.3
elements
contents 196.1
elementary education 568.5
Eucharist 701.7
substance 763.2
basics 818.6
the elements 317.3
elephant drugs 87.18
beast of burden 176.8
behemoth 257.14
pachyderm 311.4
elephantine dull 117.6
bulky 257.19
huge 257.20
elephantlike 311.47
stiff 534.3
excessive 993.16
elevate elate 109.8
erect 200.9
heighten 272.13
make better 392.9
promote 446.2
glorify 662.13
raise 912.5
exalt 912.6
elevated
n train 179.14
adj drunk 88.33
lofty 136.11
eminent 247.9
increased 251.7
high 272.14
lofty 544.14
grandiloquent 545.8
magnanimous 652.6
eminent 662.18
raised 912.9
elevation ascent 193.1
erection 200.4
increase 251.1
height 272.1
steep 272.2
diagram 381.3
promotion 446.1
loftiness 544.6
magnanimity 652.2
distinction 662.5
glorification 662.8
raising 912.1
elevator
people mover 176.5
garner 386.7
ascenseur 912.4
eleven team 617.7
football team 746.2
twelve 882.7
eleventh hour
curfew 315.5
crucial moment 843.5
lateness 846.1
elf dwarf 258.5
brat 302.4
mischief-maker 322.3
fairy 678.8
imp 680.7

elfish
mischievous 322.6
fairy 678.17
impish 680.18
elicit educe 192.14
prompt 375.13
induce 886.11
elide shorten 268.6
eliminate 773.5
eligibility
qualification 371.11
inclusion 772.1
eligible
n eligibility 371.11
adj qualified 371.24
eliminate excrete 12.12
excise 255.10
murder 308.16
discard 390.7
exterminate 395.14
annihilate 762.7
get rid of 773.5
do away with 909.21
evacuate 909.22
elimination
excretion 12.1
disappearance 34.1
excision 255.3
homicide 308.2
discard 390.3
extinction 395.6
riddance 773.2
evacuation 909.6
elision
shortening 268.3
abbreviation 537.4
elite
n superior 249.5
elect 371.12
society 578.6
upper class 607.2
aristocracy 608.1
clique 617.6
the best 999.8
adj exclusive 495.13
socially prominent
578.16
best 999.16
elixir panacea 86.3
medicine 86.4
extract 192.8
essential content 196.5
essence 767.2
elk 311.5
ell adjunct 254.3
angle 278.2
ellipse curve 279.2
oval 280.6
ellipsis
shortening 268.3
abbreviation 537.4
ellipsoid
n sphere 282.2
adj parabolic 279.13
spherical 282.9
elliptical
oblong 267.9
shortened 268.9
parabolic 279.13
elocution speech 524.1
public speaking 543.1

elongated
lengthened 267.8
oblong 267.9
elope 368.10
elopement
flight 368.4
wedding 563.3
eloquence
articulateness 524.4
public speaking 543.1
rhetoric 544.1
else
adj other 780.8
adv additionally
253.11
otherwise 780.11
elsewhere
adj abstracted 985.11
adv away 222.18
elucidate
explain 341.10
make clear 521.6
elude evade 368.7
outwit 415.11
thwart 1012.15
elvish
mischievous 322.6
impish 680.18
Elysian blissful 97.9
heavenly 681.12
Elysian Fields
mythological 681.9
destiny 839.2
emaciate
v shrink 260.9
thin 270.12
waste 393.19
adj haggard 270.20
emaciation
symptom 85.9
shrinking 260.3
emaceration 270.6
waste 393.4
emanate radiate 171.6
emerge 190.11
come after 835.3
emanation odor 69.1
radiation 171.2
emergence 190.1
ectoplasm 689.7
light 1025.1
emancipated
free 430.21
liberated 431.10
emasculate
v unman 19.12
feminize 77.13
castrate 255.11
cripple 393.14
adj unmanned 19.19
embalm perfume 70.8
lay out 309.21
mummify 397.10
perpetuate 829.5
embankment
shore 234.2
railway 383.7
pile 770.10
buttress 901.4
harbor 1009.6
barrier 1012.5

embargo
n closure 293.1
prohibition 444.1
exclusion 773.1
v stop 293.7
prohibit 444.3
exclude 773.4
embark send 176.15
get under way 182.19
go aboard 188.15
embark on 818.9
embarrass
chagrin 96.15
mortify 98.13
humiliate 137.4
involve 898.2
bewilder 971.12
confuse 985.7
inconvenience 996.4
hamper 1012.11
put in a hole 1013.15
embarrassed
distressed 96.22
humiliated 137.14
blushing 139.13
indebted 623.8
bewildered 971.24
confused 985.12
troubled 1013.20
embarrassment
chagrin 96.4
mortification 98.6
humiliation 137.2
shyness 139.4
involvement 898.1
bewilderment 971.3
confusion 985.3
impediment 1012.6
predicament 1013.4
embassy house 228.5
message 552.4
foreign office 576.7
commission 615.1
office 739.7
embattled
battled 458.23
fortified 460.12
embed inset 191.5
internalize 207.5
fix 855.9
embellish falsify 354.16
develop 392.10
ornament 498.8
bombast 545.7
embellishment
development 392.2
ornamentation 498.1
ornateness 545.4
ornament 709.18
superfluity 993.4
ember dregs 256.2
coal 1019.16
embezzle misuse 389.4
steal 482.13
embitter sour 110.16
aggrieve 112.19
aggravate 119.2
provoke 152.24
impair 393.9
antagonize 589.7
embittered sour 110.23

embargo
aggravated 119.4
resentful 152.26
impaired 393.27
emblazon color 35.14
ornament 498.8
flaunt 501.17
praise 509.12
emblem symbol 517.2
insignia 647.1
example 786.2
embodiment
manifestation 348.1
impersonation 349.4
representative 349.7
incarnation 763.4
essence 767.2
inclusion 772.1
whole 792.1
composition 796.1
materiality 1052.1
materialization 1052.8
embody manifest 348.5
image 349.11
incarnate 763.5
include 772.3
compose 796.3
materialize 1052.9
embolden
encourage 375.21
abet 449.14
motivate 492.16
embolism 293.3
embossed
in relief 283.18
sculptured 715.7
established 855.13
embouchure
mouth 292.4
wind instrument 711.6
embrace
n hold 474.2
hug 562.3
welcome 585.2
greeting 585.4
joint 800.4
v surround 209.6
wrap 295.20
adopt 371.15
hold 474.6
retain 474.7
seize 480.14
hug 562.18
welcome 585.9
include 772.3
put together 800.5
join 800.11
cohere 803.6
embroider
falsify 354.16
ornament 498.8
grandiloquent 545.7
embroidery exaggeration
355.1
sewing 741.1
embroilment
agitation 105.4
quarrel 456.5
fight 457.4
turbulence 671.2
commotion 810.4
agitation 917.1

embryo
zygote 305.14
vital force 886.7
embryology 1068.3
embryonic
infinitesimal 258.14
germinal 305.22
undeveloped 406.12
incomplete 795.4
beginning 818.15
original 886.14
emcee steward 574.4
theater man 704.23
master of ceremonies 743.20
broadcaster 1034.23
emend
make better 392.9
revise 392.12
remedy 396.13
emendation
explanation 341.4
revision 392.4
emerald 44.4
emerge
show 31.4
appear 33.8
come out 190.11
find vent 369.10
emergency
hospital room 197.25
crisis 843.4
urgency 997.4
danger 1006.1
predicament 1013.4
emergent
emerging 190.18
future 839.8
critical 843.10
emeritus
n academic rank 571.3
adj retired 448.3
emery 287.8
emetic
n nastiness 64.3
cleanser 79.17
vomitive 86.18
adj cleansing 79.28
vomitive 86.49
emigrant
migrant 178.5
goer 190.10
newcomer 774.4
emigrate
migrate 177.22
leave home 188.17
out-migrate 190.16
eminence hill 237.4
glory 247.2
height 272.1
steep 272.2
protuberance 283.2
prestige 417.4
distinction 662.5
influence 894.1
notability 997.2
éminence grise
Machiavellian 415.8
politics 610.6
influence 894.6
eminent
prominent 247.9

superior 249.12
high up 272.14
protruding 283.14
authoritative 417.15
high 662.18
notable 997.19
eminent domain 417.1
emir
Muslim ruler 575.10
prince 608.7
Sir 648.3
emissary
messenger 353.1
delegate 576.2
diplomat 576.6
emit excrete 12.12
exude 190.15
issue 352.14
say 524.22
let out 909.24
vaporize 1067.8
emollient
n balm 86.11
ointment 1056.3
adj palliative 86.40
relieving 120.9
softening 1047.16
lubricant 1056.10
emote
emotionalize 93.13
affect 500.12
act 704.29
emotion feeling 93.1
excitement 105.1
attitude 978.1
emotional
affective 93.17
excitable 105.28
attitudinal 978.7
emotive
feeling 93.17
emotionalistic 93.19
affecting 93.22
empathic
sensitive 24.12
condoling 147.3
in accord 455.3
empathize with
respond 93.11
condole with 147.2
empathy
sensitivity 24.3
sympathy 93.5
accord 455.1
emperor 575.8
emphasis
impressiveness 524.10
accent 709.25
meter 720.7
emphasize 997.14
emphatic
affirmative 334.8
vehement 544.13
decided 997.21
empire country 232.1
dominion 417.5
sovereignty 417.8
government 612.1
empirical
real 761.15
experimental 942.11

empiricism
ethical philosophy 636.2
experiment 942.1
materialism 1052.6
emplacement
location 159.1
placement 159.6
platform 901.13
emplane 188.15
employ
n use 387.1
service 577.12
occupation 724.1
v practice 328.8
use 387.10
spend 387.13
hire 615.14
occupy 724.10
exert 725.8
employee
subordinate 432.5
hireling 577.3
pensioner 577.3
assistant 616.6
worker 726.2
emporium
market 736.1
marketplace 736.2
empower
enable 18.10
authorize 443.11
commission 615.10
empty
v run out 190.13
draw off 192.12
evacuate 909.22
adj ineffective 19.15
hungry 100.25
dull 117.6
vacant 222.14
concave 284.16
insincere 354.32
vain 391.13
meaningless 520.6
inexpressive 522.20
nonexistent 762.8
empty-headed 922.19
ignorant 930.12
thoughtless 933.4
sophistical 936.10
baseless 936.13
trivial 998.19
empty-headed
empty-minded 922.19
ignorant 930.12
thoughtless 933.4
scatterbrained 985.16
emulate follow 336.7
compete 457.18
set an example 786.7
excel 999.11
emulsify mix 797.10
emulsionize 1062.10
emulsion film 714.10
emulsoid 1062.7
solution 1064.3
enable
empower 18.10
fit 405.8
authorize 443.11
include 772.3

make possible 966.5
enact perform 328.9
manifest 348.5
impersonate 349.12
accomplish 407.4
legislate 613.10
legalize 673.9
act out 704.30
enamel
n blanket 295.12
v color 35.14
coat 295.24
adj ceramic 742.7
enamored 104.28
enate
n kinfolk 559.2
lineage 560.4
adj related 559.6
lineal 560.18
kindred 775.10
akin 784.13
encampment
camping 225.4
camp 228.29
campground 463.3
encapsulate
shorten 268.6
wrap 295.20
abridge 557.5
iterate 849.8
encase confine 212.6
package 212.9
wrap 295.20
enchant
delight 95.10
fascinate 377.7
charm 691.8
engross 983.13
enchanted
overjoyed 95.17
enamored 104.28
wondering 122.9
charmed 691.12
miraculous 870.16
gripped 983.18
dreamy 986.25
encipher 345.10
encircle
surround 209.7
enclose 212.5
circle 280.10
besiege 459.19
include 772.3
enclose 914.5
enclave
enclosed place 212.3
plot 231.4
enclitic
added to writing 254.2
morphology 526.3
enclose
internalize 207.5
surround 209.6
circumscribe 210.4
bound 211.8
close in 212.5
confine 429.12
include 772.3
enclosure
the enclosed 196.6
surrounding 209.5

confinement 212.1
enclosed place 212.3
place of confinement 429.7
fortification 460.4
encode 345.10
encomiastic 509.16
encompass
extend 158.9
surround 209.6
enclose 212.5
circle 280.10
wrap 295.20
besiege 459.19
include 772.3
total 792.8
put together 800.5
combine 805.3
encircle 914.5
encore
n repeat performance 849.6
repeat 874.2
v applaud 509.10
adv recurrently 849.17
again 874.7
interj bravo! 509.22
bis! 849.18
encounter
n meeting 223.4
contest 457.3
impact 902.3
v approach 167.3
confront 216.8
meet 223.11
oppose 451.5
come up against 457.15
experience 831.8
collide 902.13
come across 941.3
encourage cheer 109.7
comfort 121.6
hearten 375.21
admonish 422.6
abet 449.14
be useful 449.17
hearten 492.16
encouraging
cheering 109.16
comforting 121.13
promising 124.13
provocative 375.27
encroach intrude 214.5
usurp 640.8
overstep 910.9
encroachment
intrusion 214.1
impairment 393.1
usurpation 640.3
overstepping 910.3
encrust 295.27
encumber add 253.4
burden 297.13
hamper 1012.11
encumbered
weighted 297.18
indebted 623.8
encyclical 352.2
encyclopedia
reference book 554.9
lore 928.9
encyclopedic
comprehensive 772.7

learned 928.21
end
n boundary 211.3
remainder 256.1
death 307.1
motive 375.1
objective 380.2
fatality 395.2
completion 407.2
gain 472.3
portion 477.5
football team 746.2
piece 793.3
limit 794.5
end point 820.1
stop 857.2
immediate cause 886.3
solution 940.1
fate 964.2
v kill 308.13
put an end to 395.12
perish 395.23
complete 407.6
terminate 820.5
cease 857.6
result 887.4
endanger 1006.6
endearing
delightful 97.7
lovable 104.25
endeavor
n act 328.3
effort 403.1
attempt 403.2
exertion 725.1
v strive 403.5
undertake 404.3
exert oneself 725.9
endemic
contagious 85.62
native 226.5
endless wordy 538.12
continuous 812.8
infinite 823.3
perpetual 829.7
continuing 856.7
innumerable 884.10
endocrine
n digestive secretion
13.2
adj glandular 13.8
endomorph 92.12
endorse ratify 332.12
adopt 371.15
secure 438.9
consent 441.2
abet 449.14
approve 509.9
support 609.41
endow empower 18.10
provide 385.7
invest 478.17
establish 892.10
endowed
provided 385.13
talented 413.29
dowered 478.26
end up arrive 186.6
end 820.5
come to an end 820.6
result 887.4

conclude 946.10
endurance
strength 15.1
patience 134.1
perseverance 360.1
durability 827.1
permanence 853.1
continuance 856.1
endure bear 134.5
condone 148.4
keep alive 306.12
persevere 360.2
suffer 443.10
resist 453.2
afford 626.7
live on 761.9
elapse 821.5
last 827.6
experience 831.8
remain 853.5
continue 856.3
toughen 1049.3
enema washing 79.5
cleanser 79.17
clyster 86.19
sprinkler 1065.8
enemy
n opponent 452.1
foe 589.6
adj oppositional 451.8
warlike 458.21
energetic
vigorous 17.13
powerful 18.12
active 330.17
industrious 330.22
energize
dynamize 17.10
vivify 306.11
motivate 375.12
electrify 1032.26
energy
n strength 15.1
vigor 17.1
power 18.1
liveliness 330.2
industry 330.6
exertion 725.1
adj fuel 1021.9
enervate weaken 16.10
unman 19.12
fatigue 21.4
afflict 85.50
spiritualize 764.4
enervation
weakening 16.5
helplessness 19.4
fatigue 21.1
unhealthiness 85.3
languor 331.6
enfant terrible
brat 302.4
mischief-maker 322.3
spoiled child 427.4
enfeeble weaken 16.10
disable 19.9
afflict 85.50
enfeebled
weakened 16.18
tired 21.7
enflame 375.18

enfold
internalize 207.5
surround 209.6
fold 291.5
wrap 295.20
embrace 562.18
enforce apply 387.11
compel 424.4
execute 437.9
legalize 673.9
enfranchise
liberate 431.4
authorize 443.11
include 772.3
enfranchisement
empowerment 18.8
vote 371.6
liberation 431.1
authorization 443.3
inclusion 772.1
engage induce 375.22
attract 377.6
attempt 403.6
commit 436.5
contract 437.5
take on 457.16
employ 615.14
occupy 724.10
interact 777.6
involve 898.2
engross 983.13
engage in
practice 328.8
undertake 404.3
busy oneself with 724.11
engagement
inducement 375.3
undertaking 404.1
obligation 436.2
betrothal 436.3
contest 457.3
participation 476.1
proposal 562.8
appointment 582.8
employment 615.4
playing engagement 704.11
position 724.5
interaction 777.3
involvement 898.1
engrossment 983.3
engaging
delightful 97.7
alluring 377.8
engrossing 983.20
en garde 760.4
engender
procreate 78.8
beget 818.14
cause 886.10
produce 890.7
originate 892.12
engine
instrument of conversion
858.10
machinery enginery 1040.3
engineer
n engineman 178.12
planner 381.6
combat engineer 461.14
professional engineer 726.7
producer 892.7

v plot 381.9
manage 409.12
maneuver 415.10
direct 573.8
perform 892.11
engineering 1043.1
English 341.12
English-speaking 524.31
engorge stuff 8.25
ingest 187.11
destroy 395.10
gluttonize 672.4
satiate 994.4
engrave
impress upon 93.16
indent 284.14
furrow 290.3
figure 498.9
mark 517.19
print 548.14
record 549.15
grave 713.9
sculpture 715.5
fix 855.9
fix in the mind 989.18
engross
absorb 187.13
fatten 259.8
monopolize 469.6
write 547.19
purchase 733.7
corner 737.26
occupy the mind 931.20
take in 983.13
engrossed in 983.17
engulf ingest 187.11
overflow 238.17
submerge 367.7
overwhelm 395.21
oversupply 993.14
enhance
aggravate 119.2
intensify 251.5
make better 392.9
enhancement
aggravation 119.1
intensification 251.2
exaggeration 355.1
improvement 392.1
enigma secret 345.5
mystery 522.8
the unknown 930.7
bewilderment 971.3
dilemma 1013.7
enigmatic
wonderful 122.10
secret 345.11
cryptic 522.17
unknown 930.17
bewildering 971.27
ambiguous 539.4
enjoin command 420.8
admonish 422.6
restrain 428.7
prohibit 444.3
impose 643.4
enjoy savor 63.5
pleasure in 95.13
possess 469.4
enjoyment
pleasure 95.1

amusement 743.1
enkindle
excite 105.12
kindle 375.18
ignite 1020.22
enlace 740.6
enlarge
aggravate 119.2
increase 251.4
size 257.15
expand 259.4
grow 259.5
amplify 538.7
process 714.15
elaborate 861.6
enlargement
aggravation 119.1
increase 251.1
expansion 259.1
exaggeration 355.1
amplification 538.6
print 714.5
photoprint 785.5
evolution 861.1
enlighten
explain 341.10
make better 392.9
inform 551.8
teach 568.10
disillusion 977.2
illuminate 1025.28
enlightening
explanatory 341.15
informative 551.18
educational 568.18
disillusioning 977.4
liberalizing 979.13
enlightenment
explanation 341.4
cultivation 392.3
information 551.1
teaching 568.1
learning 928.4
disillusionment 977.1
enlist install 191.4
induce 375.22
participate 476.5
list 615.17
join 617.14
take one's turn 825.5
enlistee recruit 461.18
member 617.11
enliven refresh 9.2
energize 17.10
stimulate 105.13
cheer 109.7
inspire 375.20
amuse 743.21
en masse
cooperatively 450.6
together 769.11
wholly 792.13
enmesh trap 356.20
catch 480.17
involve 898.2
hamper 1012.11
put in a hole 1013.15
enmity hostility 99.2
bitterness 103.2
hatefulness 451.2
disaccord 456.1

contention 457.1
unfriendliness 589.1
ennoble promote 446.2
glorify 662.13
ennui unpleasure 96.1
weariness 118.3
languor 331.6
enormity
indignity 156.2
greatness 247.1
hugeness 257.7
misdeed 655.2
baseness 661.3
enormous large 247.7
huge 257.20
excessive 993.16
terrible 1000.9
enough
n sufficiency 991.1
adj satisfactory 107.11
sufficient 991.6
sated 994.6
adv satisfactorily 107.15
sufficiently 991.8
interj cease! 857.13
en passant
on the way 176.20
incidentally 843.13
enplane 188.15
en plein air 206.11
enrage excite 105.12
infuriate 152.25
heat 1020.18
enraptured
overjoyed 95.17
enamored 104.28
frenzied 105.25
wondering 122.9
en règle 867.8
enrich
vitaminize 7.20
make better 392.9
ornament 498.8
ornament 545.7
richen 618.9
fertilize 890.8
enrobe 5.39
enroll install 191.4
record 549.15
be taught 570.11
enlist 615.17
join 617.14
list 871.8
en route
on the way 176.20
on the move 177.42
ensconce settle 159.17
conceal 346.6
ensemble
n furniture 229.1
cast 707.11
orchestra 710.12
chorus 710.16
compound 797.5
adv together 769.11
enshrine
enclose 212.5
inter 309.19
glorify 662.13
sanctify 685.5
exalt 912.6

enshroud clothe 5.39
wrap 295.20
conceal 346.6
ensign
Navy officer 575.20
insignia 647.1
flag 647.7
enslave
subjugate 432.8
appropriate 480.19
domineer 612.16
ensnare trap 356.20
lure 377.5
catch 480.17
ensue succeed 815.2
come after 835.3
result 887.4
ensure secure 438.9
make sure 970.11
protect 1008.18
entail
n inheritance 479.2
v bequeath 478.18
signify 517.17
imply 519.4
transfer 629.3
involve 772.4
determine 886.12
entangle trap 356.20
catch 480.17
complicate 799.3
involve 898.2
confuse 985.7
hamper 1012.11
put in a hole 1013.15
entente treaty 437.2
understanding 788.2
enter appear 33.8
go in 189.7
insert 191.3
record 549.15
join 617.14
keep accounts 628.8
enter on 818.9
list 871.8
enter into
participate 476.5
compose 796.3
put together 800.5
enter 818.9
enterprise vim 17.2
act 328.3
enterprisingness 330.7
plan 381.1
endeavor 403.1
undertaking 404.1
daring 492.5
exploit 492.7
company 617.9
occupation 724.1
entertain hold 474.7
have a party 582.20
entertain guests 585.8
amuse 743.21
take under consideration
   931.14
entertainment meal 8.5
pleasure 95.1
party 582.11
theatrical performance 704.12
amusement 743.1

entertainment industry 743.13
enter upon
  undertake 404.3
  set to work 725.15
  enter 818.9
enthrall delight 95.10
  fascinate 377.7
  subjugate 432.8
  engross 983.13
enthrone
  install 615.12
  glorify 662.13
enthusiasm
  animation 17.4
  eagerness 101.1
  willingness 324.1
  vehemence 544.5
  mania 926.12
  interest 983.2
enthusiastic
  energetic 17.13
  fervent 93.18
  enthused and big 101.10
  willing 324.5
  vehement 544.13
  interested 983.16
entice 377.5
entire
  n male animal 76.8
  horse 311.10
  adj whole 792.9
  complete 794.9
  unqualified 960.2
  sound 1002.7
entitle
  authorize 443.11
  name 527.11
entitled
  authorized 443.17
  warranted 639.9
entity existence 761.1
  something 763.3
  individual 872.4
entomb confine 212.6
  inter 309.19
entourage
  follower 166.2
  environment 209.1
  attendance 769.6
entrails
  digestive system 2.18
  insides 207.4
entrance
  put to sleep 22.20
  delight 95.10
  fascinate 377.7
  cast a spell 691.7
entrance entrée 187.3
  access 189.1
  entry 189.1
  opening 189.5
  insertion 191.1
  vestibule 197.19
  intrusion 214.1
  channel 239.1
  door 292.6
entranced
  overjoyed 95.17
  wondering 122.9
  dreamy 986.25
entrant incomer 189.4

competitor 452.2
novice 572.9
beginner 818.2
entrap trap 356.20
  catch 480.17
  hamper 1012.11
entreaty appeal 440.2
  prayer 696.4
entrée serving 8.10
  dish 10.7
  entrée 187.3
  entrance 189.1
entrench
  intrude 214.5
  fortify 460.9
  fix 855.9
entre nous
  confidentially 345.20
  mutually 777.13
entrep(tm)t 386.6
entrepreneuer 381.6
entrepreneur 730.1
entropy
  inertness 173.4
  formlessness 263.1
  information theory 551.7
  noncohesion 804.1
  disorder 810.1
  change 852.1
  uncertainty 971.1
entrust commit 478.16
  commission 615.10
  give credit 622.6
entry entrée 187.3
  entrance 189.1
  opening 189.5
  vestibule 197.19
  door 292.6
  memorandum 549.4
  registration 549.14
  item 628.5
entry fee 630.6
entwine weave 740.6
  hamper 1012.11
enumerate
  quantify 244.4
  itemize 801.7
  list 871.8
  number 1017.17
enunciate affirm 334.5
  announce 352.12
  say 524.22
envelop clothe 5.39
  surround 209.6
  wrap 295.20
  conceal 346.6
envelope
  n exterior 206.2
  wrapper 295.18
  illustriousness 662.6
  v besiege 459.19
enviable 100.30
envious
  discontented 108.7
  jealous 153.5
  envying 154.4
environment
  neighborhood 209.1
  natural environment
    209.4
  surrounding 209.5

circumstances 766.2
the natural world 1073.1
environmental engineering
  1043.1
environs
  environment 209.1
  nearness 223.1
  region 231.1
envision expect 130.5
  contemplate 380.5
  come 839.6
  think of 931.17
  foresee 961.5
  visualize 986.15
envoy delegate 576.2
  diplomat 576.6
envoy extraordinary 576.6
envy
  n discontent 108.1
  jealousy 153.1
  resentfulness 154
  enviousness 154.1
  v be envious of 154.3
enwrap clothe 5.39
  surround 209.6
  package 212.9
  wrap 295.20
enzyme 7.9
eon 824.4
epaulet 647.5
ephemeral
  n plant 310.3
  ephemeron 828.5
  adj mortal 307.34
  perennial 310.44
  unsubstantial 764.5
  transient 828.7
epic
  n story 719.3
  adj huge 257.20
  poetic 720.15
  narrative 722.8
epicedium 115.6
epicenter control center 208.5
  upheaval 671.5
epicureanism
  gastronomy 8.15
  pleasure-loving 95.4
  aesthetic taste 496.5
  sensuality 663.1
  epicurism 672.2
epidemic
  n plague 85.5
  adj contagious 85.62
  prevalent 864.12
  plentiful 991.7
epidermic
  epidermal 2.27
  exterior 206.7
  cutaneous 295.32
epigram
  witticism 489.7
  aphorism 537.3
  maxim 974.1
epigrammatic
  concise 537.6
  aphoristic 974.6
epigraph
  lettering 546.5
  caption 937.2
  motto 974.4

epigraphy 341.8
epilepsy seizure 85.6
  spasm 917.6
epilogue
  added to writing 254.2
  act 704.7
  part of writing 793.2
  sequel 817.1
  end 820.1
epiphany visibility 31.1
  appearance 33.1
  manifestation 348.1
  revelation 683.10
  intuition 934.1
episcopal 698.13
episode
  interjection 213.2
  digression 538.4
  plot 722.4
  discontinuity 813.1
  event 831.2
  frenzy 926.7
epistle 553.2
epitaph 309.18
epithalamium 563.3
epithet
  n oath 513.4
  name 527.3
  nickname 527.7
  motto 974.4
  v vilify 513.7
epitome
  shortening 268.3
  abridgment 557.1
  paragon 659.4
  essence 767.2
  ideal 786.4
  pattern of perfection 1002.4
epitomize
  shorten 268.6
  set an example 786.7
epoch 824.5
epode 720.9
eponym root 526.2
  name 527.3
equal
  n match 790.4
  substitute 862.2
  v parallel 203.4
  match 790.5
  excel 999.11
  adj parallel 203.6
  symmetric 264.4
  proportionate 477.13
  coinciding 778.8
  uniform 781.5
  equalized 790.7
  interchangeable 863.5
equality
  symmetry 264.1
  justice 649.1
  sameness 778.1
  parity 790.1
equalize level 201.6
  symmetrize 264.3
  smooth 287.5
  make uniform 781.4
  make agree 788.7
  equate 790.6
equal opportunity
  equating 790.2

opportunity 843.2
equal rights 790.1
equanimity
equilibrium 106.3
uniformity 781.1
equate
parallelize 203.5
relate 775.6
equalize 790.6
equator zone 231.3
circle 280.3
middle 819.1
bisector 875.3
hot place 1019.11
orbit 1072.16
equestrian
n rider 178.8
adj ungulate 311.46
equidistant
parallel 203.6
central 208.11
middle 819.4
equilibrium
equanimity 106.3
symmetry 264.1
inaction 329.1
harmony 533.2
moderation 670.1
correlation 777.1
uniformity 781.1
equality 790.1
continuity 812.1
stability 855.1
equine
n horse 311.10
adj ungulate 311.46
equinox
vernal equinox 313.7
orbit 1072.16
equip outfit 5.41
furnish 385.8
fit 405.8
establish 892.10
equipment
supplies 385.2
provision 385.1
matériel 385.4
preparation 405.1
fitting 405.2
talent 413.4
baseball 745.1
football 746.1
hockey 749.1
field hockey 749.4
bowling 750.1
golf 751.1
soccer 752.1
skiing 753.1
boxing 754.1
equitable just 649.8
impartial 649.10
unprejudiced 979.12
equity estate 471.4
justice 649.1
stock 738.2
equality 790.1
equivalence
correlation 777.1
sameness 778.1
agreement 788.1
equality 790.1

comparability 943.3
equivalent
n offset 338.2
the same 778.3
likeness 784.3
equal 790.4
substitute 862.2
adj reciprocal 777.10
coinciding 778.8
analogous 784.11
agreeing 788.9
tantamount 790.8
substitute 862.8
interchangeable 863.5
equivocal
n ambiguity 539.2
adj prevaricating 344.11
untruthful 354.34
ambiguous 539.4
self-contradictory 779.8
mixed 797.14
uncertain 971.16
equivocate
prevaricate 344.7
lie 354.19
vacillate 362.8
dodge 368.8
weasel 539.3
go roundabout 914.4
quibble 936.9
era 824.5
eradicate
extract 192.10
excise 255.10
exterminate 395.14
annihilate 762.7
eliminate 773.5
erase delete 255.12
kill 308.14
obliterate 395.16
end 820.5
abrade 1044.7
Erato music 710.22
Muse 720.10
creative thought 986.2
Erebus
nether world deity 682.5
darkness 1027.1
erect
v elevate 200.9
produce 892.8
elevate 912.5
adj proud 136.8
vertical 200.11
honest 644.13
raised 912.9
erection
sexual desire 75.5
erecting 200.4
house 228.5
structure 266.2
production 892.2
elevation 912.1
eremite 584.5
erg 17.7
ergo 888.7
ergonomics 717.5
eristic
n argumentation 935.4
arguer 935.12
adj partisan 456.17

argumentative 935.19
ermine heraldry 647.2
royal insignia 647.3
erode disappear 34.2
recede 168.2
decrease 252.6
subtract 255.9
consume 388.3
wear 393.20
corrode 393.21
waste 473.5
disintegrate 806.3
abrade 1044.7
erogenous 75.25
Eros god 104.1
Love 104.8
erose notched 289.5
nonuniform 782.3
erosion
decrement 252.3
subtraction 255.1
consumption 388.1
wear 393.5
waste 473.2
disintegration 806.1
abrasion 1044.2
erotic sexual 75.25
amorous 104.26
lascivious 665.29
erotica
literature 547.12
pornographic literature 718.1
err stray 164.4
miss 410.14
go wrong 654.9
do wrong 655.4
misbelieve 688.8
misjudge 948.2
fall into error 975.9
errand
commission 615.1
task 724.2
errant
deviative 164.7
wandering 177.37
fallible 971.22
erroneous 975.16
errata 554.12
erratic
n eccentric 927.3
adj deviative 164.7
nonuniform 782.3
unordered 810.12
irregular 851.3
inconstant 854.7
abnormal 870.9
eccentric 927.5
uncertain 971.16
erratum 975.3
erroneous false 354.25
ungrammatic 531.4
unorthodox 688.9
untrue 975.16
illusory 976.9
imperfect 1003.4
error
misinterpretation 342.1
miss 410.4
bungle 414.5
iniquity 654.3
misdeed 655.2

heresy 688.2
muff 745.3
game 748.2
misjudgment 948.1
erroneousness 975.1
mistake 975.3
ersatz
n substitute 862.2
adj imitation 336.8
spurious 354.26
similar 784.10
substitute 862.8
erstwhile 837.10
eruct erupt 671.13
disgorge 909.25
belch 909.28
erudite 570.16
erudition
learning 570.1
wisdom 920.5
scholarship 928.5
erupt
burst forth 33.9
take sick 85.47
emerge 190.11
find vent 369.10
burst out 671.13
originate 818.13
disgorge 909.25
escalator
people mover 176.5
elevator 912.4
escapade 743.6
escape
n defense mechanism 92.23
departure 188.1
outlet 190.9
absence 222.4
avoidance 368.1
getaway 369.1
v absent oneself 222.8
evade 368.7
make one's escape 369.6
free oneself from 431.8
escape clause
loophole 369.4
condition 959.2
escape one
be incomprehensible 522.10
not understand 522.11
escape notice 984.5
be forgotten 990.7
escapism
defense mechanism 92.23
escape 369.1
escargot 10.25
escarpment
precipice 200.3
slope 237.2
eschatology end 820.1
doomsday 839.3
eschew 668.7
escort
n lover 104.12
conductor 769.5
chaperon 1008.7
bodyguard 1008.14
v conduct 769.8
escrow
storage 386.5
pledge 438.2

esker 237.5
esophagus 2.18
esoteric
  n occultist 689.11
  adj secret 345.11
  confidential 345.14
  latent 519.5
  implied 519.7
  recondite 522.16
  occult 689.23
  intrinsic 767.7
  particular 865.12
  supernatural 870.15
ESP
  communication 343.1
  clairvoyance 689.8
espionage
  observation 27.2
  surveillance 938.9
esplanade 383.2
espousal
  adoption 371.4
  betrothal 436.3
espouse
  adopt 371.15
  join with 509.13
  get married 563.15
  defend 600.10
esprit heart 93.3
  gaiety 109.4
  cooperation 450.1
  accord 455.1
  wit 489.1
  intellect 919.1
  smartness 920.2
esprit de corps 587.3
espy see 27.12
  detect 941.5
esquire
  n beau 104.13
  nobleman 608.4
  escort 769.5
  v court 562.21
  escort 769.8
essay
  n attempt 403.2
  writing 547.10
  treatise 556.1
  test 942.2
  v attempt 403.6
  experiment 942.8
essence odor 69.1
  perfumery 70.2
  extract 192.8
  essential content 196.5
  meaning 518.1
  summary 557.2
  existence 761.1
  substance 767.2
  major part 792.6
  intrinsicalness 893.3
  topic 937.1
  salient point 997.6
essential
  n essence 767.2
  requirement 963.2
  adj quintessential 192.18
  basic 199.8
  of the essence 767.9
  simple 798.6
  requisite 963.13

vital 997.23
establish fix 159.16
  publicize 352.15
  accustom 373.9
  legalize 673.9
  inaugurate 818.11
  stable 855.9
  cause 886.10
  found 892.10
  prove 957.10
  make sure 970.11
establishment
  foundation 159.7
  the best 249.5
  structure 266.2
  organization 617.8
  market 736.1
  workplace 739.1
  hierarchy 809.4
  beginning 818.1
  fixity 855.2
  foundation 892.4
  proof 957.3
  ensuring 970.8
the Establishment
  the authorities 575.15
  the government 612.3
  influence 894.6
estate
  mansion 228.7
  rank 245.2
  interest 471.4
  class 607.1
  state 765.1
  category 809.2
esteem
  n respect 155.1
  approval 509.1
  estimation 662.3
  influence 894.1
  notability 997.2
  v cherish 104.21
  respect 155.4
  approve 509.9
  judge 946.8
  think 953.11
  value 997.13
esthetic 1016.18
estimable
  venerable 155.12
  measurable 300.14
  praiseworthy 509.20
  honest 644.13
  reputable 662.15
  influential 894.13
  notable 997.19
  good 999.12
  calculable 1017.25
estimate
  n measurement 300.1
  estimation 946.3
  opinion 953.6
  gamble 971.8
  v measure 300.10
  form an estimate 946.9
  think 953.11
  calculate 1017.18
estivation 313.3
estrange
  sow dissension 456.14
  antagonize 589.7

separate 802.8
estrangement 566.1
estuary outlet 190.9
  inlet 242.1
et al
  adv in the majority 883.10
  phrs et cetera 253.14
et cetera
  adv in the majority 883.10
  phrs and so forth 253.14
etch eat 713.10
  fix 855.9
etching 713.2
eternal
  mandatory 420.12
  almighty 677.17
  infinite 823.3
  perpetual 829.7
eternity
  timelessness 822.1
  infinity 823.1
  long time 827.4
  perpetuity 829.1
an eternity 829.2
ether height 272.2
  lightness 298.2
  air 317.1
  spirit 764.3
  coolant 1024.7
  the heavens 1072.2
ethereal thin 270.16
  high 272.14
  light 298.10
  rare 299.4
  airy 317.12
  heavenly 681.12
  unsubstantial 764.6
  chimeric 986.22
  spectral 988.7
  immaterial 1053.7
  vaporous 1067.9
ethical moral 636.6
  dutiful 641.13
  honest 644.13
ethics principles 636.1
  duty 641.1
ethnic
  n person 312.5
  adj racial 559.7
ethnic cleansing 308.4
ethnicity
  humankind 312.1
  race 559.4
  exclusiveness 773.3
ethology 321.3
ethos culture 373.2
  ethics 636.1
  nature 767.4
  ideology 932.8
  opinion 953.6
  climate 978.5
etiology cause 886.1
  attribution 888.1
etiquette
  good behavior 321.2
  custom 373.1
  mannerliness 504.3
  social convention 579.1
  social code 580.3
etymologist 523.15
etymology 526.15

eugenics
  improvement 392.1
  heredity 560.6
euhemeristic 341.15
eulogy dirge 115.6
  last offices 309.4
  praise 509.5
  speech 543.2
  citation 646.4
eunuch impotent 19.6
  sexlessness 75.9
euphemism
  overniceness 500.5
  catchword 526.9
  affectation 533.3
euphonious
  harmonious 533.8
  melodious 708.48
euphoric pleased 95.15
  content 107.7
  cheerful 109.11
euphuistic
  overnice 500.18
  affected 533.9
  grandiloquent 545.8
eureka! 941.11
Europe
  world region 231.6
  continent 235.1
eurythmic 264.4
Euterpe music 710.22
  Muse 720.10
  creative thought 986.2
euthanasia
  natural death 307.7
  killing 308.1
evacuate defecate 12.13
  quit 188.9
  abandon 370.5
  void 909.22
  let out 909.24
evade avoid 164.6
  prevaricate 344.7
  elude 368.7
  escape 369.6
  outwit 415.11
  remain neutral 467.5
  be dishonest 645.11
  pull back 903.7
  quibble 936.9
evaluate
  measure 300.10
  price 630.11
  criticize 723.5
  classify 801.8
  estimate 946.9
evanescence
  disappearance 34.1
  recession 168.1
  infinitesimalness 258.2
  unsubstantiality 764.1
  transience 828.1
evanescent
  infinitesimal 258.14
  thin 764.6
  transient 828.7
evangelical
  scriptural 683.11
  orthodox 687.7
  strict 687.8
evangelist herald 353.2

sanctified 685.8
raised 912.9
exam 938.2
examination
scrutiny 27.6
diagnosis 91.12
discussion 541.7
treatise 556.1
trial 598.5
argumentation 935.4
school examination 938.2
inspection 938.3
questioning 938.12
examine
scrutinize 27.14
discuss 541.12
study 570.12
interrogate 938.21
inspect 938.24
example
n sample 62.4
representative 349.7
warning 399.1
exemplar 786.2
citation 957.5
v cite 957.13
exasperate annoy 96.13
vex 98.15
aggravate 119.2
provoke 152.24
exasperation
annoyance 96.2
vexatiousness 98.7
excitation 105.11
aggravation 119.1
resentment 152.1
incitement 375.4
ex cathedra
adj authoritative 970.18
adv authoritatively 417.18
excavation
extraction 192.1
crack 224.2
deepening 275.7
pit 284.4
digging 284.11
discovery 941.1
exceed loom 247.5
excel 249.6
overrun 910.4
surpass 993.9
excel superior 249.6
be master of 413.18
surpass 999.11
excellence
superiority 249.1
taste 496.1
distinction 662.5
importance 997.1
goodness 999.1
excellent
adj superior 249.12
skillful 413.22
tasteful 496.8
eminent 662.18
good 999.12
interj bravo! 509.22
excelsior 193.17
except
v excise 255.10
reject 372.2

exempt 430.14
prep off 255.14
excluding 773.10
conj unless 959.16
exception marvel 122.2
objection 333.2
rejection 372.1
stipulation 421.2
exemption 430.8
criticism 510.4
defense 600.2
exclusion 773.1
oddity 870.5
qualification 959.1
excerpt
n extract 557.3
v select 371.14
excess
n surplus 256.4
exaggeration 355.1
exorbitance 632.4
undueness 640.1
intemperance 669.1
overrunning 910.1
overabundance 993.2
excessiveness 993.1
adj superfluous 993.17
exchange
n communication 343.1
telephone number 347.12
banter 490.1
retaliation 506.1
conversation 541.1
transfer 629.1
trade 731.2
stock exchange 737.7
changing 854.3
substitution 862.1
substitute 862.2
transpose 863.1
v transfer 629.3
trade 731.15
change 852.7
interchange 854.5
substitute 862.4
transpose 863.4
exchange rate 728.9
exchequer
storehouse 386.6
funds 728.14
treasury 729.13
excise
extract 192.10
cut out 255.10
sever 802.11
excitable
emotional 105.28
irascible 110.19
nervous 128.11
excitation
arousal 105.11
incitement 375.4
excite sensitize 24.7
impassion 105.12
incite 375.17
agitate 917.10
interest 983.12
heat 1020.18
excitement
passion 93.2
stimulation 105

emotion 105.1
excitation 105.11
impatience 135.1
incitement 375.4
agitation 917.1
heat metaphor 1019.2
exciting
desirable 100.30
thrilling 105.30
provocative 375.27
alluring 377.8
vehement 544.13
interesting 983.19
exclaim
give an exclamation 59.7
remark 524.24
speak 524.25
exclaim at
object 333.5
offer resistance 453.3
exclamation
ejaculation 59.2
remark 524.3
exclude excise 255.10
close 293.6
reject 372.2
prohibit 444.3
disapprove 510.10
bar 773.4
eject 909.13
banish 909.17
prevent 1012.14
exclusion
excision 255.3
closure 293.1
rejection 372.1
prohibition 444.1
disapproval 510.1
barring 773.1
banishment 909.4
qualification 959.1
exclusive
n news item 552.3
adj contemptuous 157.8
limiting 210.9
closed 293.9
selective 371.23
prohibitive 444.6
selective 495.13
aloof 583.6
cliquish 617.18
excluding 773.9
one 872.7
exclusivity
contempt 157.1
selectness 495.5
seclusiveness 583.3
partisanism 617.13
exclusion 773.1
excogitate 931.11
excommunication
deposal 447.2
curse 513.1
condemnation 602.1
banishment 909.4
excoriation
unclothing 6.1
torment 96.7
censure 510.3
excrement
dejection 12.3

filth 80.7
excretion discharge 12
egestion 12.1
secretion 13.1
exuding 190.6
evacuation 909.6
excruciating
sensitive 24.13
painful 26.10
agonizing 98.23
exculpate
forgive 148.3
justify 600.9
acquit 601.4
excursion
deviation 164.1
journey 177.5
obliquity 204.1
digression 538.4
circuitousness 914.1
detour 914.3
excursus
deviation 164.1
digression 538.4
treatise 556.1
circuitousness 914.1
excuse
n pardon 148.2
pretext 376.1
cop-out 600.4
acquittal 601.1
apology 658.2
reason 886.2
v forgive 148.3
exempt 430.14
alibi 600.11
acquit 601.4
execrable
offensive 98.18
cursed 513.9
wicked 654.16
base 661.12
damnable 1000.10
execration hate 103.1
hated thing 103.3
berating 510.7
curse 513.1
execute kill 308.13
perform 328.9
accomplish 407.4
perform 434.3
complete 437.9
put to death 604.17
play 708.39
produce 892.11
execution
killing 308.1
action 328.2
accomplishment 407.1
observance 434.1
completion 437.4
attachment 480.5
capital punishment 604.7
performance 708.30
operation 889.1
performance 892.5
executive
n officer 574.3
governor 575.6
operator 889.4
adj grandiose 501.21

expecting
pregnant 78.18
unastonished 123.3
expectant 130.11
expectorate 13.6
expedience
transience 828.1
timeliness 843.1
advisability 995.1
goodness 999.1
expedient
n instrumentality
384.3
stratagem 415.3
means 995.2
recourse 1009.2
adj useful 387.18
transient 828.7
timely 843.9
conditional 959.8
desirable 995.5
good 999.12
expedite
advance 162.5
send 176.15
hasten 401.4
be useful 449.17
facilitate 1014.7
expedition
velocity 174.1
journey 177.5
quickness 330.3
adventure 404.2
furtherance 449.5
campaign 458.4
promptness 845.3
facilitation 1014.5
expeditious fast 174.15
quick 330.18
hasty 401.9
prompt 845.9
expel
transfer 176.10
depose 447.4
eliminate 773.5
separate 802.8
eject 909.13
banish 909.17
dismiss 909.19
disgorge 909.25
expend
spend 387.13
consume 388.3
waste 486.4
pay out 624.14
spend 626.5
expendable
consumable 388.6
replaceable 862.10
superfluous 993.17
unimportant 998.16
expenditure use 387.1
consumption 388.1
waste 473.2
spending 626.1
price 630.1
expense loss 473.1
expenditure 626.1
charges 626.3
price 630.1
expensive 632.11

experience
n sensation 24.1
practice 413.9
event 831.2
knowledge 928.1
v sense 24.6
feel 93.10
have 831.8
experienced
accustomed 373.15
practiced 413.28
experiment
n attempt 403.2
testing 942.1
trial 942.1
v see what one can do 403.10
experimentalize 942.8
expert
n adept 413.11
adviser 422.3
connoisseur 496.7
specialist 866.3
scientist 928.1
adj skillful 413.22
specialized 866.5
perfected 1002.9
expertise skill 413.1
aesthetic taste 496.5
knowledge 928.1
profound knowledge 928.6
expert systems 1042.2
expiate
compensate 338.4
atone 658.4
expiration
breathing 2.21
death 307.1
end 820.1
expire die 307.19
perish 395.23
cease to exist 762.6
come to an end 820.6
elapse 821.5
let out 909.24
explain
explicate 341.10
make clear 521.6
expound 568.16
justify 600.9
excuse 600.11
solve 940.2
facilitate 1014.7
explain away
explain 341.10
extenuate 600.12
reason speciously 936.8
explainer 341.7
explain oneself 341.10
explanation
explication 341.4
definition 518.3
justification 600.1
example 786.2
reason 886.2
solution 940.1
theory 951.1
theorization 951.2
expletive
n exclamation 59.2
oath 513.4
redundancy 849.3

superfluity 993.4
adj superfluous 993.17
explicable
interpretable 341.17
attributable 888.6
solvable 940.3
explicate
explain 341.10
make clear 521.6
amplify 538.7
criticize 723.5
explicit manifest 348.8
clear 521.11
candid 644.17
unqualified 960.2
explode blast 56.8
be excitable 105.16
fly into a rage 152.20
grow 251.6
destruct 395.18
come to nothing 410.13
blow up 671.14
disprove 958.4
fuel 1021.8
exploit
n act 328.3
feat 492.7
v take advantage of 387.15
use 387.16
overprice 632.7
exploration
adventure 404.2
reconnaissance 938.8
search 938.15
exploratory
preceding 816.4
examining 938.37
explore
investigate 938.23
search 938.31
explosion
detonation 56.3
outbreak 105.9
outburst 152.9
intensification 251.2
discharge 671.7
disproof 958.1
explosive
n high explosive 462.14
speech sound 524.12
adj banging 56.11
excitable 105.28
hot-tempered 110.25
bursting 671.24
dangerous 1006.9
exponent
interpreter 341.7
representative 349.7
deputy 576.1
supporter 616.9
example 786.2
export
n transferal 176.1
exporting 190.8
v transfer 176.10
send 176.15
send abroad 190.17
expose
divest 6.5
unclose 292.12
disclose 351.4

stigmatize 661.9
uncover 941.4
disprove 958.4
disillusion 977.2
endanger 1006.6
exposé
disclosure 351.1
disproof 958.1
expose oneself to 897.3
exposition
spectacle 33.7
explanation 341.4
display 348.2
disclosure 351.1
treatise 556.1
lesson 568.7
passage 708.24
marketplace 736.2
expository
explanatory 341.15
manifesting 348.9
dissertational 556.6
expostulate
object 333.5
dissuade 379.3
admonish 422.6
exposure
unclothing 6.1
visibility 31.1
distinctness 31.2
appearance 33.1
navigation 159.3
display 348.2
disclosure 351.1
publicity 352.4
repute 662.1
time exposure 714.9
susceptibility 897.2
discovery 941.1
disproof 958.1
openness 1006.3
radiation physics 1037.8
expound
explain 341.10
exposit 568.16
express
n carrier 176.7
train 179.14
messenger 353.1
message 552.4
v send 176.15
extraction 192.16
affirm 334.5
manifest 348.5
describe 349.9
signify 517.17
say 524.22
phrase 532.4
evidence 957.8
adj fast 174.15
manifest 348.8
clear 521.11
particular 865.12
unqualified 960.2
exact 973.17
adv posthaste 401.13
expression
extraction 192.1
extract 192.7
manifestation 348.1
indication 517.3

remark 524.3
word 526.1
phrase 529.1
diction 532.1
eloquence 544.1
execution 708.30
maxim 974.1
expressive
  manifesting 348.9
  descriptive 349.14
  indicative 517.23
  meaningful 518.10
  graphic 544.10
express mail 553.4
expropriate
  attach 480.20
  dispossess 480.23
expulsion
  transferal 176.1
  deposal 447.2
  elimination 773.2
  ejection 909.1
  disgorgement 909.7
expunge
  delete 255.12
  obliterate 395.16
  end 820.5
expurgate clean 79.18
  delete 255.12
exquisite
  n dandy 500.9
  adj sensitive 24.13
  painful 26.10
  tasty 63.8
  delightful 97.7
  meticulous 339.12
  nice 495.11
  overnice 500.18
  chic 578.13
  superb 999.15
  fine 1016.20
exsanguineous 36.7
exsiccated 1066.9
extant remaining 256.7
  existent 761.13
  present 838.2
extemporaneous
  extemporary 365.12
  unprepared 406.8
extemporize
  improvise 365.8
  be unprepared 406.6
extend reach 158.9
  increase 251.4
  enlarge 259.4
  grow 259.5
  spread 259.6
  reach out 261.5
  be long 267.5
  lengthen 267.6
  broaden 269.4
  straighten 277.5
  offer 439.4
  give 478.12
  diffuse 538.8
  race 757.5
  endure 827.6
  protract 827.9
  postpone 846.9
  sustain 856.4
  generalize 864.9

stretch 1048.4
extension
  space 158.1
  increase 251.1
  adjunct 254.1
  addition 254.3
  size 257.1
  expansion 259.1
  length 267.1
  lengthening 267.4
  telephone 347.4
  meaning 518.1
  sequence 815.1
  protraction 827.2
  continuance 856.1
  stretching 1048.2
extensive
  spacious 158.11
  large 247.7
  voluminous 257.17
  expansive 259.9
  long 267.7
  broad 269.6
  general 864.13
extensive knowledge 928.6
extent space 158.1
  spaciousness 158.5
  quantity 244.1
  degree 245.1
  size 257.1
  distance 261.1
  length 267.1
  breadth 269.1
  measure 300.3
extenuate
  weaken 16.10
  abate 252.8
  mitigate 600.12
  moderate 670.6
extenuating
  justifying 600.13
  qualifying 959.7
exterior
  n appearance 33.2
  external 206.2
  scene 712.12
  adj external 206.7
  extraneous 774.5
exterminate kill 308.13
  eliminate 395.14
  annihilate 762.7
  do away with 909.21
extermination
  killing 308.1
  extinction 395.6
external
  n exterior 206.2
  adj exterior 206.7
  extrinsic 768.3
  extraneous 774.5
exterrestrial
  extraterritorial 206.9
  space 1072.26
exterritorial 206.9
extinct gone 34.4
  no more 762.11
  ended 820.8
  past 837.7
  obsolete 842.15
extinction
  disappearance 34.1

excision 255.3
  death 307.1
  extermination 395.6
  extinguishing 1022.2
extinguish
  overshadow 249.8
  excise 255.10
  quench 395.15
  suppress 428.8
  end 820.5
  fight fire 1022.7
  turn off the light 1027.11
extirpate
  excise 255.10
  exterminate 395.14
  annihilate 762.7
extol praise 509.12
  glorify 696.12
extort exact 192.15
  demand 421.5
  wrest 480.22
  steal 482.13
extortionate
  extractive 192.17
  demanding 421.9
  rapacious 480.26
  overpriced 632.12
extra
  n bonus 254.4
  newspaper 555.2
  motion-picture studio 706.4
  supporting actor 707.7
  nonessential 768.2
  surplus 993.5
  adj additional 253.10
  unused 390.12
  unessential 768.4
  occasional 848.3
  surplus 993.18
  adv additionally 253.11
extract
  n perfumery 70.2
  extraction 192.8
  excerpt 557.3
  distillation 893.3
  v refine 79.22
  take out 192.10
  subtract 255.9
  select 371.14
  rescue 398.3
  process 892.9
  conclude 946.10
extraction
  refinement 79.4
  egress 190.2
  taking out 192
  withdrawal 192.1
  extract 192.8
  reduction 255.2
  excerpt 557.3
  lineage 560.4
  production 892.2
  pulling 905.1
extracurricular 568.20
extradite
  transfer 176.10
  restore 481.4
  banish 909.17
extramarital 665.27
extramural
  extraterritorial 206.9

scholastic 567.13
extraneous
  extrinsic 768.3
  foreign 774.5
  unrelated 776.6
  irrelevant 776.7
extraordinary
  wonderful 122.10
  unexpected 131.10
  remarkable 247.10
  particular 865.12
  exceptional 870.14
  notable 997.19
extrapolate 839.6
extrapolation
  adjunct 254.1
  the future 839.1
  notation 1017.2
extrasensory 689.24
extrasensory perception
  intuition 934.1
  mental state 22.5
extraterrestrial
  n oddity 870.4
  adj extraterritorial 206.9
  heavenly 681.12
  extraneous 774.5
  supernatural 870.15
  otherworldly 1072.26
extravagant
  exaggerated 355.4
  prodigal 486.8
  gaudy 501.20
  grandiose 501.21
  inflated 502.12
  diffuse 538.11
  overpriced 632.12
  intemperate 669.7
  violent 671.16
  absurd 923.11
  fanatic 926.32
  fanciful 986.20
  plentiful 991.7
  excessive 993.16
extravaganza 354.10
extravagation 501.3
extreme
  n exaggeration 355.1
  limit 794.5
  extremity 820.2
  excess 993.1
  adj sensitive 24.13
  bordering 211.11
  great 247.13
  farthest 261.12
  rebellious 327.11
  exaggerated 355.4
  radical 611.20
  intemperate 669.7
  violent 671.16
  final 820.11
  fanatic 926.32
  excessive 993.16
extremes 993.1
extremism
  rebelliousness 327.3
  reform 392.5
  radicalism 611.4
  fanaticism 926.11
  excess 993.1

sect 675.3
company 770.3
disagreement 789.1
factitious 354.25
factoid 761.3
factor
 n heredity 560.6
 steward 574.4
 agent 576.3
 particular 766.3
 component 796.2
 cause 886.1
 v classify 801.8
 calculate 1017.18
factory 739.3
factotum 577.9
facts
 information 551.1
 knowledge 928.1
 evidence 957.1
the facts 761.4
factual real 761.15
 evidential 957.16
 obvious 970.15
 true 973.13
faculty
 ability 18.2
 talent 413.4
 authority 417.1
 staff 571.9
 prerogative 642.1
 intellect 919.2
fad
 caprice 364.1
 great success 409.3
 craze 578.
fade
 n motion-picture editing 706.6
 v weaken 16.9
 disappear 34.2
 decolor 36.5
 lose color 36.6
 fail 85.48
 recede 168.2
 age 303.10
 decline 393.17
 languish 393.18
 play 751.4
 race 757.5
 bet 759.25
 cease to exist 762.6
 flit 828.6
 pass 837.6
 age 842.9
 pull back 903.7
 adj insipid 65.2
 trite 117.9
fag
 n homosexual 75.15
 cigarette 89.5
 work 725.4
 drudge 726.3
 v get tired 21.6
 drudge 725.14
 task 725.16
fail weaken 16.9
 lose strength 85.48
 be inferior 250.4
 age 303.10
 neglect 340.6
 decline 393.17

neglect 408.2
be unsuccessful 410.9
flunk 410.17
go bankrupt 625.7
be unfaithful 645.12
dramatize 704.28
fall short 911.2
be insufficient 992.8
failing
 n deterioration 393.3
 vice 654.2
 fault 1003.2
 adj languishing 16.21
 unhealthy 85.54
 deteriorating 393.45
 unsuccessful 410.18
 incomplete 795.4
 insufficient 992.9
fail-safe 1007.5
failure
 ineffectiveness 19.3
 disappointment 132.1
 inadequacy 250.3
 neglect 340.1
 deterioration 393.3
 nonaccomplishment 408.1
 unsuccessfulness 410.1
 flash in the pan 410.7
 defeat 412.1
 nonobservance 435.1
 bankruptcy 625.3
 insolvent 625.4
 vice 654.2
 misdeed 655.2
 stage show 704.4
 shortcoming 911.1
 mistake 975.3
 loss of memory 990.2
 fault 1003.2
faint
 n unconsciousness 25.2
 v weaken 16.9
 burn out 21.5
 swoon 25.5
 adj weak 16.12
 tired 21.7
 inconspicuous 32.6
 colorless 36.7
 low 52.16
 ill 85.56
 weak-willed 362.12
fainthearted
 weak-willed 362.12
 cowardly 491.10
fair
 n marketplace 736.2
 festival 743.4
 adj whitish 37.8
 clean 79.25
 pleasant 97.6
 bright 97.11
 auspicious 133.18
 courteous 504.14
 legible 521.12
 rightful 639.8
 honest 644.13
 just 649.8
 probable 968.6
 unprejudiced 979.12
 good 999.12
 tolerable 999.20

mediocre 1005.7
thriving 1010.13
comely 1016.19
warm 1019.24
rainless 1066.8
adv pleasantly 97.12
justly 649.11
fair game
 laughingstock 508.7
 opportunity 843.2
fair-haired boy 104.16
fairly to a degree 245.7
 limited 248.10
 legibly 521.14
 justly 649.11
 tolerably 999.24
 mediocrely 1005.11
fair-minded 649.9
fair name 662.2
fairway seaway 182.10
 runway 184.23
 green 310.7
 playground 743.11
 golf 751.1
fair-weather friend 357.8
fairy
 n homosexual 75.15
 lightness 298.2
 sprite 678.8
 adj elfin 678.17
fairy tale 354.11
fait accompli
 act 328.3
 accomplishment 407.1
 fact 761.3
 a truth 973.2
faith zeal 101.2
 hope 124.1
 obedience 326.1
 observance 434.1
 promise 436.1
 school 617.5
 fidelity 644.7
 cardinal virtues 653.4
 religion 675.1
 piety 692.1
 cause 886.9
 belief 953.1
 system of belief 953.3
 confidence 970.5
the faith 687.2
faithful
 n person of honor 644.8
 adj zealous 101.9
 loving 104.27
 obedient 326.3
 descriptive 349.14
 persevering 360.8
 observant 434.4
 devoted 587.21
 loyal 644.20
 orthodox 687.7
 pious 692.8
 lifelike 784.16
 permanent 853.7
 belief 953.21
 reliable 970.17
 exact 973.17
the faithful
 the believing 692.5
 believer 953.9

faith healer 90.9
faithless
 falsehearted 354.31
 apostate 363.11
 unfaithful 645.20
 atheistic 695.19
 unbelieving 955.8
fake
 n fakement 354.13
 hoax 356.7
 impostor 357.6
 affecter 500.7
 basketball game 747.3
 copy 785.1
 substitute 862.2
 v imitate 336.5
 tamper with 354.17
 fabricate 354.17
 sham 354.21
 improvise 365.8
 affect 500.12
 play 747.4
 adj imitation 336.8
 spurious 354.26
 assumed 500.16
 similar 784.10
 substitute 862.8
faker imitator 336.4
 deceiver 357.1
 impostor 357.6
fakir ascetic 667.2
 clergy 699.12
falafel 10.9
falcate 279.11
falcon
 n bird 311.28
 heraldry 647.2
 v hunt 382.9
fall
 n false hair 3.13
 descent 194.1
 tumble 194.3
 hang 202.2
 declivity 204.5
 waterfall 238.11
 decline 252.2
 autumn 313.4
 rain 316.1
 plunge 367.1
 deterioration 393.3
 backsliding 394.2
 downfall 395.3
 collapse 410.3
 defeat 412.1
 original sin 655.3
 downthrow 913.2
 v descend 194.5
 tumble 194.8
 hang 202.6
 incline 204.10
 decrease 252.6
 die 307.19
 rain 316.10
 plunge 367.6
 decline 393.17
 relapse 394.4
 be destroyed 395.22
 fall down 410.12
 lose 412.12
 cheapen 633.6
 go wrong 654.9

fantastic 870.12
ideational 932.9
notional 986.20
fan club 509.8
fancy
　n desire 100.1
　inclination 100.3
　love 104.1
　will 323.1
　caprice 364.1
　impulse 365.1
　preference 371.5
　idea 932.1
　phantasy 976.3
　imagination 986.1
　figment of the imagination
　　986.5
　v desire 100.14
　love 104.19
　suppose 951.10
　think 953.11
　imagine 986.14
　adj edible 8.33
　skillful 413.22
　ornate 498.12
　ostentatious 501.18
　grandiose 501.21
　grand 545.11
　expensive 632.11
　overpriced 632.12
　excessive 993.16
　interj imagine! 122.22
fancy-free 565.7
fancy that! 122.22
fanfare blare 53.5
　celebration 487.1
　Aldine 554.15
fang teeth 2.8
　sting 1001.5
fanged toothlike 285.14
　prehensile 474.9
fangs 474.4
fan mail 553.4
fanny 217.5
fan out diverge 171.5
　spread 259.6
　disperse 771.4
fantasize
　fabricate 354.18
　imagine 986.14
fantastic
　wonderful 122.10
　remarkable 247.10
　fabricated 354.29
　capricious 364.5
　unreal 762.9
　unbelievable 870.12
　absurd 923.11
　illusory 976.9
　fanciful 986.20
fantasy
　n defense mechanism 92.23
　desire 100.1
　caprice 364.1
　miracle 870.8
　phantom 976.4
　abstractedness 985.2
　imagination 986.1
　figment of the imagination
　　986.5
　v muse 985.9

dream 986.17
fan the flame
　excite 105.12
　incite 375.17
　sow dissension 456.14
　ignite 1020.22
far
　adj distant 261.8
　adv by far 247.17
　far off 261.15
far and away
　by far 247.17
　superlatively 249.16
farce stuffing 10.27
　wit 489.1
　burlesque 508.6
　trifle 998.5
farcical comic 488.6
　witty 489.15
　burlesque 508.14
　comic 704.35
fare
　n food 10.1
　traveler 178.1
　fee 630.6
　v eat 8.20
　travel 177.18
　journey 177.21
　be in a certain state 765.5
　result 887.4
farewell
　n leave-taking 188.4
　v take leave 188.16
　adj departing 188.18
　interj good-bye! 188.22
fare well succeed 409.7
　prosper 1010.7
farfetched 776.8
far-flung long 267.7
　extensive 864.13
far from it
　adj nothing like 787.5
　adv amiss 911.7
　interj no 335.8
　by no means 335.9
far-gone
　intoxicated 88.31
　worn-out 393.36
　involved in 898.5
farm
　n house 228.5
　baseball 745.1
　farmplace 1069.8
　stock farm 1070.5
　v ruralize 233.5
　die 307.20
　rent out 615.16
　ranch 1069.16
　raise 1070.6
　adj rustic 233.6
　agricultural 1069.20
farmer
　peasant 606.6
　tax collector 630.10
　agriculturist 1069.5
farm out 615.16
farmers' market 736.2
far out
　extreme 247.13
　modern 841.13
　unconventional 868.6

farrow
　n offspring 561.2
　v give birth 1.3
farsighted
　clear-sighted 27.21
　poor-sighted 28.11
　sagacious 920.16
　foreseeing 961.7
fart
　n stinker 71.3
　bad person 660.5
　zilch 762.3
　flatulence 909.10
　v let a fart 909.29
farther
　adj additional 253.10
　thither 261.10
　adv additionally 253.11
farthing
　modicum 248.2
　money 728.8
　fourth 881.2
　trifle 998.5
fasces scepter 417.9
　insignia 647.1
　bundle 770.8
fascinate
　delight 95.10
　enamor 104.23
　thrill 105.15
　captivate 377.7
　charm 691.8
　interest 983.12
　engross 983.13
fascinating
　delightful 97.7
　wonderful 122.10
　alluring 377.8
　bewitching 691.11
　engrossing 983.20
fascination
　delightfulness 97.2
　inclination 100.3
　eagerness 101.1
　amazement 122.1
　wonderfulness 122.3
　allurement 377.1
　bewitchment 691.2
　mania 926.12
　obsession 926.13
fascism
　government 612.4
　despotism 612.8
　discrimination 980.4
fashion
　n aspect 33.3
　form 262.1
　structure 266.1
　custom 373.1
　manner 384.1
　mode 532.2
　style 578.1
　mode 765.4
　v form 262.7
　produce 892.8
fashion design garment
　　making 5.32
　design specialty 717.5
fast
　n lack of food 515.2
　abstinence 668.2

holy day 701.12
　v not eat 515.4
　adj deep-dyed 35.18
　swift 174.15
　close 293.12
　confirmed 373.18
　devoted 587.21
　profligate 665.25
　fastened 800.14
　stable 855.12
　stuck 855.16
　reliable 970.17
　adv swiftly 174.17
　securely 800.19
fasten close 293.6
　bind 428.10
　fix 800.7
　secure 855.8
fasten upon
　seize on 480.16
　blame 599.8
　impose 643.4
　attribute to 888.4
fast food 10.1
fast-food restaurant 8.17
fast-forward
　run 174.3
　hastening 401.3
fastidious
　clean 79.25
　particular 495.9
　elegant 496.9
　conscientious 644.15
　discriminating 944.7
fasting
　n abstinence from food
　　515.1
　penance 658.3
　asceticism 667.1
　adj hungry 100.25
　uneating 515.5
fast lane dissipation 669.2
　aspiring 100.28
fast track 174.3
fat
　n glyceride 7.7
　superfluity 993.4
　the best 999.8
　oil 1056.1
　v fatten 259.8
　adj corpulent 257.18
　distended 259.13
　stubby 268.10
　thick 269.8
　heavy 297.16
　gainful 472.16
　wealthy 618.14
　stupid 922.15
　plentiful 991.7
　thriving 1010.13
　oily 1056.9
fatal
　deadly 308.23
　destructive 395.26
　future 839.8
　destined 964.9
　chance 972.15
　weighty 997.20
　unfortunate 1011.14
　disastrous 1011.15
fatal flaw 1006.4

fatalism
  composure 106.2
  resignation 134.2
  determinism 964.4
fatality
  ominousness 133.7
  inauspiciousness 133.8
  fatal accident 308.8
  deadliness 308.9
  fate 964.2
fat cat 618.7
fat chance
  n improbability 969.1
  interj nope 335.10
fate
  n doom 395.2
  portion 477.5
  end 820.1
  destiny 839.2
  inevitability 963.7
  fatality 964.2
  chance 972.1
  v allot 477.9
  destine 964.7
fateful
  ominous 133.17
  destructive 395.26
  inevitable 963.15
  destined 964.9
  weighty 997.20
fathead 924.4
father
  n senior 304.5
  brother 559.3
  sire 560.9
  priest 699.5
  author 886.4
  producer 892.7
  personage 997.8
  v procreate 78.8
  engender 818.14
  cause 886.10
  trace to 888.5
fatherland 232.2
fathom
  sound 275.9
  measure 300.10
  understand 521.7
  know 928.12
  investigate 938.23
  solve 940.2
fatigue
  n weakness 16.1
  weakening 16.5
  tiredness 21.1
  symptoms 85.9
  languor 331.6
  work 725.4
  v tire 21.4
  burn out 21.5
  be tedious 118.6
fatten nourish 8.19
  increase 251.4
  size 257.15
  fat 259.8
  thicken 269.5
  make better
    392.9
  fertilize 890.8
  thrive 1010.8
  raise 1070.6

fatuous
  ineffective 19.15
  vain 391.13
  thin 764.6
  foolish 923.8
  thoughtless 933.4
  trivial 998.19
faucet valve 239.10
  stopper 293.4
fault
  n crack 224.2
  vice 654.2
  misdeed 655.2
  game 748.2
  error 975.1
  mistake 975.3
  defect 1003.2
  blemish 1004.1
  v complain 115.15
  deprecate 510.12
  play tennis 748.3
faultfinding
  n complaint 115.4
  critisism 510.4
  disparagement 512.1
  adj discontented 108.7
  plaintive 115.19
  critical 510.23
faultless
  innocent 657.6
  accurate 973.16
  perfect 1002.6
faulty
  ungrammatic 531.4
  guilty 656.3
  illogical 936.11
  erroneous 975.16
  imperfect 1003.4
  blemished 1004.8
fauna
  animal life 311.1
  biology 1068.1
Faust 690.5
faux pas 975.5
favor
  n looks 33.4
  inclination 100.3
  act of kindness 143.7
  pity 145.1
  respect 155.1
  face 216.4
  superiority 249.1
  preference 371.5
  patronage 449.4
  benefit 478.7
  approval 509.1
  letter 553.2
  good terms 587.3
  privilege 642.2
  esteem 662.3
  influence 894.1
  special favor 894.2
  memento 989.7
  v desire 100.14
  be kind 143.9
  respect 155.4
  choose 371.17
  make better 392.9
  indulge 427.6
  aid 449.11
  abet 449.14

  be useful 449.17
  oblige 449.19
  approval 509.9
  prefer 650.8
  resemble 784.7
  do good 999.10
favorable
  promising 124.13
  auspicious 133.18
  willing 324.5
  consenting 441.4
  propitious 449.22
  approving 509.17
  friendly 587.15
  timely 843.9
  expedient 995.5
  good 999.12
favorite
  n preference 104.16
  jockey 757.2
  adj beloved 104.24
  approved 509.19
favoritism
  partiality 650.3
  prejudice 980.3
fawn
  n fledgling 302.10
  hoofed animals 311.5
  v give birth 1.3
  truckle 138.7
  adj brown 40.3
fawning
  n obsequiousness
    138.2
  flattery 511.1
  adj obsequious 138.14
  flattering 511.8
fax
  n Telephoto 347.15
  print 785.5
  v copy 785.8
fay
  n fairy 678.8
  adj fairy 678.17
faze 127.18
FBI detective 576.10
  police 1008.17
FBI agent 576.10
fealty
  obedience 326.1
  duty 641.1
  fidelity 644.7
fear
  n anxiety 126.1
  terror 127.1
  fright 127.1
  nervousness 128.1
  weak will 362.4
  cowardice 491.1
  v be afraid 127.10
  hesitate 362.7
fearful
  anxious 126.7
  fearing 127.23
  frightening 127.28
  nervous 128.11
  remarkable 247.11
  cowardly 491.10
fearsome
  fearful 127.23
  frightening 127.28

feasible
  workable 889.10
  practicable 966.7
  expedient 995.5
  practical 995.6
  handy 1014.15
feast
  n banquet 8.9
  food 10.1
  holiday 20.4
  treat 95.3
  holy day 701.12
  festival 743.4
  v banquet 8.24
  gratify 95.8
feat act 328.3
  masterpiece 413.10
  exploit 492.7
feather
  n quill 3.16
  plumage 3.18
  lightness 298.2
  kind 809.3
  trifle 998.5
  v fledge 3.21
  row 182.53
  maneuver 184.40
  fill 196.7
  figure 498.9
featherbrained
  superficial 922.20
  scatterbrained 985.16
feather in one's cap
  victory 411.1
  trophy 646.3
featherweight
  n runt 258.4
  weight 297.3
  adj lightweight 298.13
  uninfluential 895.3
feature
  n aspect 33.3
  looks 33.4
  treatise 556.1
  motion pictures 706.1
  commodity 735.2
  component 796.2
  characteristic 865.4
  special 866.2
  highlight 997.7
  v manifest 348.5
  dramatize 704.28
  specify 865.11
  specialize 866.4
  call attention to 983.10
  emphasize 997.14
  headline 997.15
  adj specialized 866.5
febrile feverish 85.58
  fervent 93.18
  overzealous 101.12
  heated 105.22
fecal
  excremental 12.20
  malodorous 71.5
  filthy 80.23
feces feculence 12.4
  dregs 256.2
feckless
  ineffective 19.15
  useless 391.9

improvident 406.15

fecund
diffuse 538.11
productive 890.9
invention 986.18

fecundity
wordiness 538.2
productiveness 890.1
invention 986.3

federal
n policeman 1008.15
adj governmental 612.17
combining 805.7

federation
affiliation 450.2
government 612.4
association 617.1
combination 805.1

fed up weary 118.11
satiated 994.6

fee
n gratuity 478.5
stipend 624.5
charge 630.1
dues 630.6
v pay 624.10

feeble weak 16.12
impotent 19.13
inconspicuous 32.6
faint 52.16
unhealthy 85.54
stricken in years 303.18
weak-willed 362.12
feebleminded 922.21
unsound 936.12

feebleminded
weak-willed 362.12
weak-minded 922.21

feed
n meal 8.5
fodder 10.4
basketball game 747.3
game 749.3
v nourish 7.17
dine 8.18
eat 8.20
gratify 95.8
encourage 375.21
provision 385.9
foster 449.16
fertilize 890.8
ignite 1020.22
fuel 1021.8
raise 1070.6
tend 1070.7

feedback
audio distortion 50.13
reaction 903.1
closed sequence 1041.6

feeder eater 8.16
tributary 238.3
role 704.10
actor 707.2

feed the fire
excite 105.12
incite 375.17
vomit 909.26
ignite 1020.22

feel
n touch 73.1
milieu 209.3

texture 294.1
knack 413.6
discrimination 944.1
v sense 24.6
appear to be 33.10
touch 73.6
entertain a feeling 93.10
contact 223.10
caress 562.16
experience 831.8
intuit 934.4
suppose 951.10

feeler
tactile organ 73.4
offer 439.1
question 938.10
probe 942.4

feel for
pity 145.3
grope 938.32

feel good
enjoy good health 83.6
please 95.6
be pleased 95.12

feeling
n sensation 24.1
touch 73.1
handling 73.2
emotion 93.1
pity 145.1
milieu 209.3
hunch 934.3
discrimination 944.1
suggestion 951.5
opinion 953.6
attitude 978.1
mood 978.4
adj emotional 93.17
intuitive 934.5
examining 938.37

feelings emotion 93.1
mood 978.4

feel in one's bones
feel 93.10
foreshow 133.10
intuit 934.4
foreknow 961.6

feel one's way
be blind 30.8
make one's way 162.4
be careful 339.7
see what one can do 403.10
be cautious 494.5
grope 938.31

feign sham 354.21
affect 500.12

feint
n sham 354.3
trick 356.6
pretext 376.1
stratagem 415.3
thrust 459.3
game 746.3
fight 754.3
v lash out at 459.16
fight 754.4

feisty
hot-tempered 110.25
defiant 327.10
plucky 359.14
perverse 361.11

partisan 456.17
argumentative 935.19

felicitation 149.1

felicitous pleasant 97.6
decorous 496.10
appropriate 533.7
eloquent 544.8
apt 788.10
timely 843.9
expedient 995.5

felicity happiness 95.2
aptitude 413.5
decorousness 496.3
elegance 533.1
eloquence 544.1
fitness 788.5
prosperity 1010.1
good fortune 1010.2

feline
n creature 311.3
cat 311.21
adj felid 311.43
covert 345.12
cunning 415.12

fell
n fur 4.2
plain 236.1
plateau 237.3
hill 237.4
skin 295.3
v level 201.6
strike dead 308.18
raze 395.19
conquer 412.10
shoot 904.12
drop 913.5
adj terrible 127.30
cruel 144.26

fellatio 75.7

fellow
n man 76.5
doctor 90.4
beau 104.13
boy 302.5
person 312.5
image 349.5
teacher 571.1
friend 588.1
companion 588.3
associate 616.1
member 617.11
accompanier 769.4
likeness 784.3
equal 790.4
adj cooperative 450.5
accompanying 769.9

fellow feeling 104.1

fellowship
n cooperation 450.1
affiliation 450.2
accord 455.1
subsidy 478.8
instructorship 571.10
camaraderie 582.2
social life 582.4
association 582.6
companionship 587.2
sodality 617.3
scholarship 646.7
sect 675.3
company 769.2

v associate with 582.17

felon sore 85.37
evildoer 593.1
criminal 660.9

felony
misdeed 655.2
offense 674.4

felt 4.1

female
n female being 77.4
adj feminine 77.14

feminine
n gender 530.10
adj female 77.14

feminine caesura 720.7

femininity
femaleness 77.1
feminality 77.1
womankind 77.3
maturity 303.2

feminism
effeminacy 77.2
women's rights 642.4
discrimination 980.4

femme fatale
tempter 377.4
demimonde 665.15

fen 243.1

fence
n wall 212.4
fortification 460.4
receiver 732.6
barrier 1012.5
v wall 212.7
dodge 368.8
contend 457.13
fortify 460.9
illicit goods 732.7
quibble 936.9
protect 1008.18

fence in enclose 212.5
fence 212.7
confine 429.12

fencer 461.1

fence-sitting
n irresolution 362.1
neutrality 467.1
adj irresolute 362.9
repudiative 363.12

fend fend off 460.10
protect 1008.18
prevent 1012.14

fender partition 213.5
safeguard 1008.3
fireplace 1020.11

fend off
ward off 460.10
repulse 908.3
prevent 1012.14

feng shui 498.1

feral frenzied 105.25
cruel 144.26
deadly 308.23
funereal 309.22
animal 311.40
savage 671.21

ferment
n bread 10.28
agitation 105.4
dudgeon 152.7
leavening 298.4

bubbling 320.3
bustle 330.4
turbulence 671.2
transformer 852.5
agitation 917.1
v sour 67.4
leaven 298.7
bubble 320.4
incite 375.17
seethe 671.12
agitate 917.10
chemicalize 1060.8
fermentation
souring 67.3
commotion 105.4
leavening 298.4
bubbling 320.3
agitation 917.1
fern 310.4
ferocious
frenzied 105.25
cruel 144.26
warlike 458.21
savage 671.21
ferret
sharp vision 27.11
wild animal 311.23
ferret out
search out 938.34
uncover 941.4
Ferris wheel 743.15
ferrous 1058.17
ferry
n passageway 383.3
v haul 176.13
fly 184.36
fertile productive 890.9
imaginative 986.18
plentiful 991.7
fertility
wordiness 538.2
productiveness 890.1
invention 986.3
plenty 991.2
fertility rite 701.9
fertilize fructify 78.10
enrich 890.8
cultivate 1069.17
fervent fervid 93.18
zealous 101.9
heated 105.22
industrious 330.22
vehement 544.13
fervid craving 100.24
zealous 101.9
heated 105.22
fervor zeal 101.2
love 104.1
industry 330.6
vehemence 544.5
heat metaphor 1019.2
festal vacational 20.10
festive 743.28
festering
n pus 12.6
soreness 26.4
sore 85.37
corruption 393.2
adj suppurative 12.21
sore 26.11
decayed 393.40

unforgettable 989.26
festination 401.3
festival
musical occasion 708.32
festivity 743.4
festive
convivial 582.23
festal 743.28
festivity treat 95.3
rejoicing 116.1
celebration 487.1
conviviality 582.3
merrymaking 743.3
festival 743.4
assembly 770.2
festoon
n curve 279.2
bouquet 310.25
v ornament 545.7
Festschrift
compilation 554.7
collection 770.11
fetal embryonic 305.22
undeveloped 406.12
beginning 818.15
fetch
n range 158.2
trick 356.6
stratagem 415.3
specter 988.1
double 988.3
v bring 176.16
travel 177.18
sail for 182.35
arrive 186.6
attract 377.6
cost 630.13
hit 902.14
conclude 946.10
fetching delightful 97.7
alluring 377.8
fete festival 743.4
assembly 770.2
fetid
malodorous 71.5
filthy 80.23
offensive 98.18
terrible 1000.9
fetish
n charm 691.5
idol 697.3
v idolatrize 697.5
fetishism
perversion 75.11
animism 675.6
sorcery 690.1
idolatry 697.1
fetlock tuft 3.6
foot 199.5
fetter
n shackle 428.4
curb 1012.7
v bind 428.10
yoke 800.10
hamper 1012.11
fettle
n fitness 84.1
good condition 765.3
v groom 79.20
fettuccine 10.33
fetus 305.14

feud
n quarrel 456.5
possession 469.1
revenge 507.1
animosity 589.4
v quarrel 456.11
contend 457.13
feudal
imperious 417.16
subject 432.13
real 471.9
fever
n feverishness 85.7
symptom 85.9
fever of excitement
105.7
card 758.2
five 882.1
agitation 917.1
frenzy 926.7
heat 1019.1
v take sick 85.47
few insignificant 248.6
least 250.8
not many 885.4
a few plurality 883.1
a number 884.2
too few 885.2
the few 885.3
few and far between
infrequent 848.2
sparse 885.5
fey
supernatural 870.15
eccentric 927.5
fiancé 104.17
fiasco
disappointment 132.1
botch 410.6
fiat decree 420.4
authorization 443.3
fib
n lie 354.11
v lie 354.19
fiber nutrient 7.3
filament 271.1
organic matter 305.1
nature 767.4
fiberglass 295.23
fiber optics optics 29.7
light 1025.22
fibrillation
symptom 85.9
irregularity 851.1
pulsation 916.3
fibrous
threadlike 271.7
tough 1049.4
fickle irresolute 362.9
flighty 364.6
unfaithful 645.20
transient 828.7
inconstant 854.7
uncertain 971.16
fiction
fabrication 354.10
lie 354.11
writing 547.10
story 722
narrative 722.1
invention 986.3

figment of the imagination
986.5
fictional
fabricated 354.29
narrative 719.8
fictionalized 722.7
fictitious 986.21
fictitious
spurious 354.26
fabricated 354.29
make-believe 986.21
fiddle
n deception 356.9
v repair 396.14
play violin 708.41
trifle 998.15
fidelity
perseverance 360.1
observance 434.1
faithfulness 644.7
accuracy 973.5
fidget be excited 105.18
have the fidgets 128.6
twitch 917.13
fidgety jittery 128.12
bustling 330.20
agitated 917.16
jerky 917.19
fiduciary
n trustee 470.5
adj in trust 438.13
believable 953.24
fiducial 953.25
fiefdom 469.1
field space 158.1
airport 184.22
setting 209.2
enclosed place 212.3
sphere 231.2
plot 231.4
latitude 430.4
arena 463.1
battlefield 463.2
study 568.8
heraldry 647.2
occupation 724.4
playground 743.11
baseball 745.1
football 746.1
field hockey 749.4
soccer 752.1
horse race 757.3
specialty 866.1
science 928.10
tract 1069.9
the field 452.2
field goal game 746.3
basketball game 747.3
field hockey 749.4
field of vision
vision 27.1
field of view 31.3
fiend enthusiast 101.5
monster 593.6
violent person 671.9
demon 680.6
fierce frenzied 105.25
passionate 105.29
cruel 144.26
infuriated 152.32
warlike 458.21

violent 671.16
savage 671.21
fiery red 41.6
feverish 85.58
fervent 93.18
zealous 101.9
heated 105.22
passionate 105.29
hot-tempered 110.25
vehement 544.13
hotheaded 671.22
igneous 1019.26
heating 1020.26
illuminated 1025.39
fiesta treat 95.3
festival 743.4
fife 708.42
fifth
n interval 709.20
quinquesection 882.14
adj quinary 882.17
fifth column 357.11
fifth-column 645.22
fifth wheel
nonessential 768.2
superfluity 993.4
fifty-fifty
n half 875.2
even chance 972.7
adj symmetric 264.4
neutral 467.7
proportionate 477.13
equal 790.7
mixed 797.14
in half 875.8
fig clothing 5.1
trifle 998.5
fight
n quarrel 456.5
contest 457.3
battle 457.4
warlikeness 458.11
struggle 725.3
match 754.3
v clash 35.15
contend against 451.4
quarrel 456.11
contend 457.13
war 458.14
struggle 725.11
box 754.4
fighter
combatant 461.1
boxer 754.2
fighting
n contention 457.1
quarreling 457.9
war 458.1
boxing 754.1
adj contending 457.22
warlike 458.21
fight off fend off 460.10
repulse 908.3
fight the good fight
contend 457.13
be good 653.5
be pious 692.6
figment
fabrication 354.10
figment of the imagination
986.5

figurative
representational 349.13
indicative 517.23
meaningful 518.10
symbolic 519.10
tropologic 536.3
ornate 545.11
numeric 1017.23
figurative language 536.1
figure
n aspect 33.3
apparition 33.5
gestalt 92.32
outline 211.2
form 262.1
human form 262.4
figurine 349.6
diagram 381.3
motif 498.7
display 501.4
figure of speech 536.1
ornateness 545.4
price 630.1
repute 662.1
celebrity 662.9
passage 708.24
card 758.2
characteristic 865.4
syllogism 935.6
phantom 976.4
personage 997.8
body 1052.3
v form 262.7
image 349.11
plan 381.8
filigree 498.9
designate 517.18
metaphorize 536.2
be somebody 662.10
be reasonable 935.17
estimate 946.9
calculate 1017.18
figurehead prow 216.3
figure 349.6
nominal head 575.5
deputy 576.1
follower 616.8
insignia 647.1
a nobody 998.7
figure in
participate 476.5
calculate 1017.18
figure of speech
turn of expression 536
figure 536.1
ornateness 545.4
figure on plan 380.6
calculate 1017.18
figure out plan 380.6
solve 940.2
calculate 1017.18
figure skating 760.7
figurine 349.6
filament
feather part 3.17
thread 271
fiber 271.1
filch 482.13
file
n military unit 461.22
document 549.5

recording media 549.10
heraldry 647.2
series 812.2
catalog 871.3
data 1042.15
v march 177.30
sharpen 285.7
grind 287.8
store 386.10
record 549.15
classify 809.6
defile 812.7
list 871.8
abrade 1044.7
filial
loving 104.27
sonly 561.7
filibuster
n legislative procedure 613.6
hinderer 1012.8
v outtalk 540.7
legislate 613.10
procrastinate 846.11
filigree
n extra 254.4
v figure 498.9
filing
legislative procedure 613.6
classification 809.1
index 871.7
abrasion 1044.2
filing card 549.10
filing clerk 550.1
filings remainder 256.1
refuse 391.4
powder 1051.5
fill
n full measure 794.3
satiety 994.1
v load 159.15
pack 196.7
top 198.9
pervade 221.7
stop 293.7
provide 385.7
observe 434.2
possess 469.4
include 772.3
charge 794.7
iterate 849.8
superabound 993.8
satiate 994.4
filler lining 196.3
hunter 311.13
syntax 530.2
fillet strip 271.4
circle 280.3
fill in for
take one's turn 825.5
substitute for 862.5
filling
n lining 196.3
extra 254.4
warp 740.3
redundancy 849.3
superfluity 993.4
adj completing 794.13
satiating 994.7
fill out increase 251.4
enlarge 259.5
round 282.6

execute 437.9
protract 538.8
record 549.15
include 772.3
complete 794.6
fill up shoal 276.3
stop 293.7
provide 385.7
provision 385.9
fill 794.7
satiate 994.4
fuel 1021.8
filly
female animal 77.10
gal 302.7
horse 311.10
jockey 757.2
film
n blanket 295.12
lamina 296.2
fog 319.3
recording media 549.10
motion pictures 706.1
negative 714.10
v blur 32.4
cover 295.19
shoot 706.8
photograph 714.14
adj motion-picture 706.9
filmmaker 706.4
filmmaking 706.2
filmy smooth 294.8
transparent 1029.4
filo 10.41
filter
n refinery 79.13
light filter 1028.4
v refine 79.22
exude 190.15
extraction 192.16
trickle 238.18
filth muck 80.7
cursing 513.3
obscenity 666.4
terribleness 1000.2
filthy obscene 666.9
terrible 1000.9
filtration
refinement 79.4
exuding 190.6
fin money 728.7
five 882.1
finagle cheat 356.18
plot 381.9
maneuver 415.10
final
departing 188.18
completing 407.9
mandatory 420.12
terminal 820.11
eventual 831.11
resultant 887.6
evidential 957.16
unqualified 960.2
finale act 704.7
end 820.1
finalize
accomplish 407.6
complete 820.7
finally
adv in fine 820.12

eventually 831.12
consequently 887.7
interj eureka! 941.11
finance
  n money matters 729
  economics 729.1
  v support 449.12
  subsidize 478.19
  pay for 624.18
  back 729.16
financial district 230.6
financier
  n moneyman 729.9
  businessman 730.1
  v invest 729.17
find
  n finding 472.6
  discovery 941.1
  good thing 999.5
  v arrive 186.6
  provide 385.7
  learn 570.6
  discover 941.2
  conclude 946.10
  decide 946.11
  pass judgment 946.13
finding find 472.6
  solution 940.1
  discovery 941.1
  verdict 946.5
find oneself 941.2
find out learn 570.6
  solve 940.2
  discover 941.2
  make sure 970.11
find time 821.6
find time for 449.13
fine
  v mulct 603.5
  spiritualize 764.4
  adj edible 8.33
  healthy 83.8
  pleasant 97.6
  tiny 258.11
  narrow 270.16
  sharp 285.8
  smooth 294.8
  rare 299.4
  meticulous 339.12
  nice 495.11
  elegant 496.9
  ornate 498.12
  grandiose 501.21
  thin 764.6
  discriminating 944.7
  exact 973.17
  good 999.12
  exquisite 1016.20
  powdery 1051.11
  rainless 1066.8
  adv excellently 999.22
  interj yeah 332.19
  bravo! 509.22
fine arts 712.1
fine fettle
  healthiness 83.2
  orderliness 807.3
fine point 780.2
fine print 959.2
finery clothing 5.1
  frippery 5.10

ornament 498.3
finesse
  n skill 413.1
  cunning 415.1
  taste 496.1
  discrimination 944.1
  v plot 381.9
  live by one's wits 415.9
fine-tune
  improve 392.11
  arrange 437.8
  rearrange 808.13
  change 852.7
  perfect 1002.5
finger
  n digit 73.5
  v touch 73.6
  condemn to death 308.20
  designate 517.18
  inform on 551.13
  accuse 599.7
  attribute to 888.4
finger bowl 79.12
fingerprint print 517.7
  identification 517.11
finicky finical 495.10
  detailed 766.9
  attentive 983.15
finish
  n boundary 211.3
  symmetry 264.1
  polish 287.2
  texture 294.1
  completion 407.2
  accomplishment 413.8
  good breeding 504.4
  elegance 533.1
  horse race 757.3
  end 820.1
  soundness 1002.2
  v polish 287.7
  kill 308.13
  consume 388.3
  perfect 392.11
  put an end to 395.12
  accomplish 407.6
  end 820.5
  complete 820.7
  refute 958.5
finished
  symmetric 264.4
  sleek 287.11
  dead 307.30
  used up 388.5
  spoiled 393.29
  ruined 395.29
  completed 407.11
  skilled 413.26
  elegant 533.6
  no more 762.11
  ended 820.8
  past 837.7
  perfected 1002.9
finish line track 755.1
  end 820.1
finish off kill 308.13
  consume 388.3
  put an end to 395.12
  accomplish 407.6
  complete 820.7
finite limited 210.7

human 312.13
  numeric 1017.23
fink
  n informer 551.6
  strikebreaker 727.8
  v inform on 551.13
  break a strike 727.11
fire
  n vim 17.2
  smart 26.3
  fever 85.7
  passion 93.2
  zeal 101.2
  fever of excitement 105.7
  inspiration 375.9
  gunfire 459.8
  vehemence 544.5
  blaze 1019.13
  light source 1026.1
  v cook 11.5
  energize 17.10
  excite 105.12
  incite 375.17
  kindle 375.18
  inspire 375.20
  explode 671.14
  pot 742.6
  play 745.5
  throw 904.10
  shoot 904.12
  dismiss 909.20
  heat 1020.17
  ignite 1020.22
  dry 1066.6
  launch 1074.13
  interj attack! 459.32
firearm 462.10
fire at
  pull the trigger 459.22
  hurl at 459.28
firebrand
  violent person 671.9
  coal 1019.16
  lighter 1021.4
firecracker 53.6
fired cooked 11.7
  excited 105.20
  inspired 375.31
  ceramic 742.7
fire department 1022.4
fire engine 1022.3
fire escape stairs 193.3
  means of escape 369.3
fire extinguisher 1022.3
firefly glitter 1025.7
  lightning bug 1026.5
fire hydrant
  hydrant 239.12
  extinguisher 1022.3
fireman
  trainman 178.13
  hand 183.6
  baseball team 745.2
  fire fighter 1022.4
fireplace home 228.2
  hearth 1020.11
firepower
  work force 18.9
  gunfire 459.8
fireproof
  v proof 15.14

flameproof 1022.6
  adj resistant 15.20
  flameproof 1022.10
fire-resisting
  resistant 15.20
  fireproof 1022.10
fire sale 734.3
fireside home 228.2
  fireplace 1020.11
fire up
  be excitable 105.16
  flare up 152.19
  heat 1020.17
firewater 88.13
firewood
  stovewood 1021.3
  wood 1054.3
fireworks gunfire
  459.8
  pyrotechnics 1019.17
firing incitement 375.4
  inspiration 375.9
  deposal 447.2
  gunfire 459.8
  throwing 904.2
  dismissal 909.5
  ignition 1020.4
  fuel 1021.1
firing squad 604.7
firm
  n company 617.9
  workplace 739.1
  v stabilize 855.7
  harden 1046.7
  adj sound 15.18
  close 293.12
  staunch 359.12
  unyielding 361.9
  rigid 425.7
  faithful 644.20
  orthodox 687.7
  sturdy 763.7
  crowded 770.22
  fast 800.14
  permanent 853.7
  stable 855.12
  immovable 855.15
  reliable 970.17
  unhazardous 1007.5
  dense 1045.12
  rigid 1046.11
firmament 1072.2
first
  n baseball 745.1
  first ever 818.3
  adj leading 165.3
  front 216.10
  chief 249.14
  preceding 814.4
  beginning 818.15
  foremost 818.17
  previous 834.4
  novel 841.11
  adv before 216.12
  preferably 371.28
  firstly 818.18
first aid 91.14
first base 745.1
first-born
  n senior 304.5
  adj older 842.19

first-class
  superlative 249.13
  first-rate 999.17
first edition
  autograph 337.3
  rare book 554.6
firsthand original 337.5
  new 841.7
  evidential 957.16
first impression
  print 713.5
  first 818.3
first name 527.4
first of all
  chiefly 249.17
  beginning 818.15
first prize
  supremacy 249.3
  victory 411.1
  award 646.2
first-rate
  superlative 249.13
  first-class 999.17
fiscal 728.30
fiscal year 825.4
fish
  n poisson 10.24
  marine animal 311.30
  dupe 358.2
  money 728.7
  chip 759.18
  v go fishing 382.10
fisherman
  mariner 183.1
  fisher 382.6
fishery 382.3
fish for solicit 440.14
  seek 938.30
fishhook snare 356.13
  card 758.2
fish out of water
  misfit 789.4
  nonconformist 868.3
fishpond
  vivarium 228.24
  lake 241.1
fish story lie 354.11
  boasting 502.2
fishtail
  n aquatics 182.11
  v maneuver 184.40
  drive 756.4
fish to fry 724.2
fishy fishlike 311.50
  deceptive 356.21
  inexpressive 522.20
  dishonest 645.16
fission
  n severance 802.2
  dissociation 806.2
  nuclear fission 1038.8
  v shatter 802.13
  disintegrate 806.3
  bisect 875.4
  atomize 1038.17
fissure
  n crack 224.2
  break 802.4
  interruption 813.2
  v open 292.11
  break 393.23

sever 802.11
  separate 802.12
fist clenched fist 462.4
  pointer 517.4
  handwriting 547.3
fistfight 457.4
fit
  n seizure 85.6
  outburst 105.9
  fit of anger 152.8
  bustle 330.4
  fitting 405.2
  upheaval 671.5
  spell 825.1
  spasm 917.6
  frenzy 926.7
  v outfit 5.41
  have place 159.9
  equip 385.8
  condition 405.8
  train 568.13
  relate to 775.5
  interact 777.6
  make agree 788.7
  suit 788.8
  equalize 790.6
  change 852.7
  conform 867.3
  expedite one's affair 995.3
  adj healthy 83.8
  hale 83.12
  eligible 371.24
  fitted 405.17
  competent 413.24
  appropriate 533.7
  right 637.3
  rightful 639.8
  just 649.8
  apt 788.10
  timely 843.9
  sufficient 991.6
  expedient 995.5
fitful unordered 810.12
  discontinuous 813.4
  irregular 851.3
  inconstant 854.7
  jerky 917.19
fit in have place 159.9
  implant 191.8
  follow the rule 867.4
fit like a glove
  interact 777.6
  suit 788.8
  expedite one's affair 995.3
fitness ability 18.2
  health 83.1
  physical conditioning 84.1
  physical fitness 84.1
  eligibility 371.11
  preparedness 405.4
  decorousness 496.3
  propriety 637.2
  suitability 788.5
  timeliness 843.1
  expedience 995.1
fit out outfit 5.41
  equip 385.8
fitted eligible 371.24
  provided 385.13
  adapted 405.17
  competent 413.24

apt 788.10
fitting
  n checking the fit 405.2
  change 852.1
  adj useful 387.18
  decorous 496.10
  appropriate 533.7
  right 637.3
  apt 788.10
  timely 843.9
  expedient 995.5
fit to be tied 152.30
five
  basketball team 747.2
  card 758.2
  V 882.1
five 617.7
five-and-dime 736.1
five-card stud 759.10
fix
  n navigation 159.3
  circumnavigation 182.2
  state 765.1
  bewilderment 971.3
  expedient 995.2
  v locate 159.11
  establish 159.16
  direct 161.5
  circumscribe 210.4
  quantify 244.4
  castrate 255.11
  form 262.7
  perforate 292.15
  kill 308.14
  resolve 359.7
  accustom 373.9
  bribe 378.3
  perfect 392.11
  do for 395.11
  repair 396.14
  prepare 405.6
  defeat 412.9
  prescribe 420.9
  arrange 437.8
  get even with 506.7
  punish 604.11
  make agree 788.7
  fasten 800.7
  dispose 808.9
  organize 808.10
  define 855.9
  specify 865.11
  decide 946.11
  prove 957.10
  prearrange 965.5
  make sure 970.11
fix and toke 87.20
fixate
  psychologize 92.36
  obsess 926.25
fixation
  libido fixation 92.21
  establishment 159.7
  motionlessness 173.2
  fixity 855.2
  obsession 926.13
  hindrance 1012.1
fixative perfumery 70.2
  art equipment 712.18
fixer mender 396.10
  lawyer 597.3

wire-puller 609.30
  processing solution 714.13
fixings 796.2
fixing to
  adj prepared 405.16
  prep in preparation for 405.24
fixity motionlessness 173.2
  fixedness 855.2
fixity of purpose 359.4
fix on direct 161.5
  attribute to 888.4
  pay attention 983.8
fixture adjunct 254.1
  fixity 855.2
  machinery 1040.3
fixtures equipment 385.4
  hard goods 735.4
fix up equip 385.8
  repair 396.14
  cure 396.15
  prepare 405.6
  make up 405.7
  reconcile 465.8
  ornament 498.8
  tidy 808.12
fizz
  n sibilation 57.1
  bubbling 320.3
  v sibilate 57.2
  bubble 320.4
fizzle
  n sibilation 57.1
  disappointment 132.1
  bubbling 320.3
  failure 410.2
  v sibilate 57.2
  be disappointing 132.3
  bubble 320.4
  come to nothing 410.13
  burn out 1022.8
fizzle out weaken 16.9
  be disappointing 132.3
  come to nothing 410.13
  be unproductive 891.3
  fall through 911.3
  burn out 1022.8
fjord 242.1
flabbergast 122.6
flabby weak 16.12
  impotent 19.13
  flaccid 1047.10
  pulpy 1063.6
flaccid weak 16.12
  flabby 1047.10
flack appearance 33.2
  promotion 352.5
  publicist 352.9
flag
  n leaf 310.19
  pavement 383.6
  trophy 646.3
  banner 647.7
  golf 751.1
  building material 1054.2
  v weaken 16.9
  fatigue 21.4
  burn out 21.5
  fail 85.48
  dawdle 175.8
  floor 295.22

flaunting
  n display 501.4
  waving 916.2
  adj garish 35.20
  showy 501.19
  gaudy 501.20
  grandiloquent 545.8
flautist 710.4
flavor
  n taste 62.1
  flavoring 63.3
  odor 69.1
  characteristic 865.4
  v savor 63.7
  imbue 797.11
flavor control 1041.8
flavorless 65.2
flavorsome
  flavorful 63.9
  delectable 97.10
flaw
  n crack 224.2
  gust 318.6
  vice 654.2
  error 975.1
  fault 1003.2
  blemish 1004.1
  v blemish 1004.4
flawed
  unvirtuous 654.12
  illegal 674.6
  illogical 936.11
  erroneous 975.16
  blemished 1004.8
flawless
  accurate 973.16
  perfect 1002.6
flaxen 43.4
flay peel 6.8
  strip 480.24
  criticize 510.20
  tear apart 802.14
flea vermin 311.37
  jumper 366.4
fleabag 228.15
flea-bitten 47.13
flea in one's ear 399.1
a flea in one's ear
  rejection 372.1
  repulse 442.2
  reproof 510.5
flea market sale 734.3
  marketplace 736.2
fleck
  n tuft 3.6
  spottiness 47.3
  modicum 248.2
  minute 258.7
  mark 517.5
  stain 1004.3
  v variegate 47.7
  mark 517.19
fledgling
  n youngster 302.1
  boy 302.5
  birdling 302.10
  bird 311.28
  novice 572.9
  modern 841.4
  adj immature 406.11
  new 841.7

flee disappear 34.2
  run off 188.12
  fly 368.10
  escape 369.6
  cease to exist 762.6
fleece
  n hair 3.2
  head of hair 3.4
  fur 4.2
  whiteness 37.2
  skin 295.3
  softness 1047.4
  v divest 6.5
  cheat 356.18
  strip 480.24
  plunder 482.17
  overprice 632.7
fleet
  n ships 180.10
  navy 461.27
  company 770.3
  v speed 174.8
  flit 828.6
  adj fast 174.15
  agile 413.23
  brief 828.8
fleeting
  vanishing 34.3
  receding 168.5
  unsubstantial 764.5
  transient 828.7
flesh meat 10.13
  sexuality 75.2
  skin 295.3
  organic matter 305.1
  humankind 312.1
  kinfolk 559.2
  carnality 663.2
  · body 1052.3
the flesh 663.2
flesh out amplify 538.7
  elaborate 861.6
  perfect 1002.5
fleshpots
  disapproved place 228.28
  sewer 654.7
  prosperity 1010.1
fleshy corpulent 257.18
  pulpy 1063.6
fleur-de-lis
  insignia 647.1
  heraldry 647.2
flex
  n bend 279.3
  v curve 279.6
flexible folded 291.7
  versatile 413.25
  unstrict 426.5
  docile 433.13
  changeable 854.6
  conformable 867.5
  handy 1014.15
  pliant 1047.9
  elastic 1048.7
flibbertigibbet
  scatterbrain 924.7
  flightiness 985.5
flick
  n thud 52.3
  touch 73.1
  mark 517.5

motion pictures 706.1
  tap 902.7
  jerk 905.3
  stain 1004.3
  v touch 73.6
  tap 902.18
  jerk 905.5
  flutter 917.12
flickering
  n flicker 1025.8
  adj brief 828.8
  irregular 851.3
  inconstant 854.7
  fluttering 917.18
  burning 1019.27
  bickering 1025.36
flier speeder 174.5
  train 179.14
  aviator 185.1
  advertising matter 352.8
  circus artist 707.3
  trading 737.19
  gamble 759.2
flight
  defense mechanism
    92.23
  course 172.2
  velocity 174.1
  migration 177.4
  aviation 184.1
  trip 184.9
  departure 188.1
  fugitation 368.4
  escape 369.1
  air force 461.29
  arrow 462.6
  ornament 709.18
  assemblage 770.6
  multitude 884.3
  rocket launching 1074.9
flight attendant
  crew 185.4
  attendant 577.5
flight of fancy
  imagination 986.1
  idealism 986.7
flight path
  airway 184.33
  route 383.1
flighty fickle 364.6
  inconstant 854.7
  superficial 922.20
  insane 926.26
  inattentive 984.6
  volatile 985.17
flimflam
  n lie 354.11
  humbug 354.14
  deception 356.1
  caprice 364.1
  v deceive 356.19
flimsy
  n writing 547.10
  adj frail 16.14
  thin 270.16
  rare 299.4
  fragile 764.7
  unsound 936.12
  trivial 998.19
  flaccid 1047.10
  brittle 1050.4

flinch
  n retreat 903.3
  v shrink 127.13
  be startled 131.5
  retract 168.3
  demur 325.4
  hesitate 362.7
  pull back 903.7
fling
  n attempt 403.3
  revel 743.6
  throw 904.3
  v place violently 159.13
  speed 174.8
  throw 904.10
fling off
  flounce out 188.11
  say 524.22
  do away with 909.21
fling oneself at
  make advances 439.7
  court 562.21
flint lighter 1021.4
  hardness 1046.6
flinty callous 94.12
  pitiless 146.3
  firm 359.12
  unyielding 361.9
  hard 1046.10
  stone 1059.11
flip
  n reverse 363.1
  game 749.3
  tap 902.7
  throw 904.3
  jerk 905.3
  v get excited 105.17
  lose self-control
    128.8
  talkative 540.9
  reverse 779.5
  tap 902.18
  throw 904.10
  jerk 905.5
  flutter 917.12
  adj impudent 142.10
flip-flop
  n reverse 363.1
  change 852.1
  conversion 858.1
  reversion 859.1
  v change 852.7
  turn back 859.5
flip of a coin
  gamble 759.2
  chance 972.1
flip out
  get excited 105.17
  get angry 152.18
  go mad 926.22
flippant
  impudent 142.10
  careless 340.11
  ridiculing 508.12
flipped 926.27
flipper aquatics 182.11
  scenery 704.20
flip side 215.3
the flip side
  inverse 205.4
  the opposite 779.2

flirt
  n lover 104.12
  tempter 377.4
  coquette 562.11
  tap 902.7
  jerk 905.3
  trifler 998.10
  v lure 377.5
  coquet 562.20
  tap 902.18
  jerk 905.5
  trifle 998.14
flirtation
  love affair 104.6
  allurement 377.1
  flirtiness 562.9
  trifling 998.8
flit
  n homosexual 75.15
  velocity 174.1
  flutter 917.4
  v speed 174.8
  travel 177.18
  migrate 177.22
  wander 177.23
  glide 177.35
  elapse 821.5
  fly 828.6
  flutter 917.12
flitter
  n flutter 917.4
  v flutter 917.12
flitting
  n wandering 177.3
  adj wandering 177.37
  transient 828.7
  inconstant 854.7
float
  n raft 180.11
  v haul 176.13
  ride 182.54
  swim 182.56
  take off 193.10
  buoy 298.8
  levitate 298.9
  issue 738.12
  inaugurate 818.11
  start 904.13
  wave 916.11
  flood 1065.14
float a loan
  lend 620.5
  borrow 621.3
floater wanderer 178.2
  voter 609.23
floating
  n aquatics 182.11
  voting 609.18
  inauguration 818.5
  adj wandering 177.37
  afloat 182.60
  buoyant 298.14
  unfastened 802.22
flocculent hairy 3.24
  flaky 296.7
flock tuft 3.6
  flake 296.3
  the laity 700.1
  throng 770.4
  group of animals 770.5
  assemblage 770.6

multitude 884.3
flock to 450.4
flock together
  associate with 582.17
  accompany 769.7
  come together 770.16
floe 1023.5
flog urge 375.14
  whip 604.13
flood
  n torrent 238.5
  overflow 238.6
  tide 238.13
  quantity 247.3
  increase 251.1
  high tide 272.8
  rainstorm 316.2
  lights 704.18
  throng 770.4
  plenty 991.2
  superabundance 993.2
  v flow 238.16
  overflow 238.17
  abound 991.5
  superabound 993.8
  oversupply 993.14
  float 1065.14
floodgate outlet 190.9
  flood-hatch 239.11
floodlight
  n lights 704.18
  v illuminate 1025.28
flood tide tide 238.13
  high tide 272.8
floor
  n story 197.23
  ground covering 199.3
  bed 199.4
  horizontal 201.3
  boundary 211.3
  layer 296.1
  arena 463.1
  price index 630.4
  foundation 901.6
  platform 901.13
  v carpet 295.22
  overcome 412.7
  fell 913.5
  refute 958.5
  stump 971.14
floor exercise 760.5
floor it speed 174.9
  be active 330.14
floorwalker
  superintendent 574.2
  salesman 730.3
floozy 665.14
flop
  n report 56.1
  tumble 194.3
  failure 410.2
  unsuccessful person 410.8
  stage show 704.4
  flutter 917.4
  v go to bed 22.18
  sink 194.6
  hang 202.6
  fail 410.10
  dramatize 704.28
  be changed 852.6
  flutter 917.12

flophouse 228.15
floppy
  n recording media 549.10
  disk 1042.6
  adj weak 16.12
  drooping 202.10
  flaccid 1047.10
floppy disk
  recording media 549.10
  disk 1042.6
flora 310.1
floral 310.38
florescent grown 14.3
  mature 259.12
  young 301.9
  floral 310.38
florid
  red-complexioned 41.9
  floral 310.38
  ornate 498.12
  grandiloquent 545.11
  fanciful 986.20
florilegium
  compilation 554.7
  excerpts 557.4
  collection 770.11
florist 1069.6
floss down 3.19
  softness 1047.4
flossy feathery 3.27
  threadlike 271.7
  ostentatious 501.18
  fluffy 1047.14
flotation issue 738.6
  inauguration 818.5
flotilla ships 180.10
  navy 461.27
flotsam 370.4
flounce
  n gait 177.12
  edging 211.7
  fold 291.1
  jerk 905.3
  flounder 917.8
  v way of walking 177.28
  fold 291.5
  caper 366.6
  figure 498.9
  play 743.23
  jerk 905.5
  flounder 917.15
flounder
  n fish 10.24
  flounce 917.8
  v pitch 182.55
  tumble 194.8
  bungle 414.11
  change 854.5
  wallow 915.13
  flounce 917.15
  be uncertain 971.9
  have difficulty 1013.11
flour
  n cereal 10.34
  whiteness 37.2
  powder 1051.5
  v sprinkle 771.6
  pulverize 1051.9
flourish
  n extra 254.4
  ornamentation 498.1

display 501.4
  figure of speech 536.1
  ornateness 545.4
  impromptu 708.27
  ornament 709.18
  waving 916.2
  v grow 14.2
  have energy 17.11
  enjoy good health 83.6
  grow 259.7
  mature 303.9
  vegetate 310.34
  manifest 348.5
  ripen 407.8
  flaunt 501.17
  boast 502.6
  ornament 545.7
  be somebody 662.10
  wave 916.11
  thrive 1010.8
flourishing
  n maturation 303.6
  waving 916.2
  adj maturing 14.3
  increasing 251.8
  grown 259.12
  luxuriant 310.43
  productive 890.9
  thriving 1010.13
flout
  n indignity 156.2
  gibe 508.2
  v offend 156.5
  disobey 327.6
  violate 435.4
  disregard 454.4
  scoff 508.9
flow
  n excretion 12.1
  course 172.2
  gliding 177.16
  air flow 184.29
  flowing 238.4
  tide 238.13
  elegance 533.1
  fluency 544.2
  trend 896.2
  plenty 991.2
  liquidity 1061.1
  v move 172.5
  travel 177.18
  glide 177.35
  run out 190.13
  hang 202.6
  stream 238.16
  elapse 821.5
  abound 991.5
  go easily 1014.10
flow chart
  diagram 381.3
  outline 801.4
flower
  n posy 310.24
  figure of speech 536.1
  essence 767.2
  the best 999.8
  v mature 303.9
  be in flower 310.35
  figure 498.9
  evolve 861.5
  thrive 1010.8

flower bed 1069.10
flower child 868.3
flowering
  n florescence 310.26
  evolution 861.1
  adj maturing 14.3
  grown 259.12
  young 301.9
  floral 310.38
  thriving 1010.13
flower power
  power 18.1
  benevolence 143.4
flowery fragrant 70.9
  floral 310.38
  ornate 498.12
  figurative 536.3
  grandiloquent 545.11
flowing
  n gliding 177.16
  flow 238.4
  adj fluent 172.8
  pendent 202.9
  streaming 238.24
  elegant 533.6
  harmonious 533.8
  eloquent 544.9
  written 547.22
  fluid 1061.4
flow on march on 162.3
  coat 295.24
  elapse 821.5
  flood 1065.14
flub
  n bungle 414.5
  goof 975.6
  v bungle 414.12
fluctuate
  vacillate 362.8
  blow hot and cold 364.4
  intermit 851.2
  change 854.5
  oscillate 916.10
fluctuation
  vacillation 362.2
  irregularity 851.1
  changing 854.3
  oscillation 916.1
flue down 3.19
  chimney 239.14
  lightness 298.2
  fireplace 1020.11
  softness 1047.4
fluency flow 238.4
  elegance 533.1
  wordiness 538.2
  talkativeness 540.1
  flow 544.2
  liquidity 1061.1
fluent
  v talkative 540.9
  adj flowing 172.8
  streaming 238.24
  elegant 533.6
  harmonious 533.8
  eloquent 544.9
  fluid 1061.4
fluff
  n down 3.19
  smoothness 294.3
  lightness 298.2

bungle 414.5
  grammatical error 975.7
  softness 1047.4
  v make a boner 975.15
  soften 1047.6
fluffy feathery 3.27
  smooth 294.8
  light 298.10
  superficial 922.20
  flossy 1047.14
fluid
  n liquid 1061.2
  vapor 1067.1
  gas 1067.2
  adj changeable 854.6
  fluidal 1061.4
fluidity
  changeableness 854.1
  liquidity 1061.1
  vaporousness 1067.3
fluid mechanics 1061.1
fluke
  n fish 10.24
  chance event 972.6
  stroke of luck 1010.3
  v triumph 411.3
flume
  n outlet 190.9
  valley 237.7
  watercourse 239.2
  gutter 239.3
  v transport 176.14
flummery 520.2
flummox
  n confusion 985.3
  v fail 410.10
  bewilder 971.12
  confuse 985.7
  thwart 1012.15
flunk
  n abortion 410.5
  v fail 410.9
  disappoint 410.17
flunky sycophant 138.3
  pursuer 166.2
  inferior 250.2
  subordinate 432.5
  retainer 577.1
  lackey 577.6
  follower 616.8
  worker 726.2
fluorescent light 1026.1
flurry
  n agitation 105.4
  velocity 174.1
  rain 316.1
  gust 318.6
  bustle 330.4
  haste 401.1
  bluster 503.1
  price 738.9
  agitation 917.1
  confusion 985.3
  snow 1023.8
  v excite 105.14
  agitate 917.10
  confuse 985.7
flush
  n warmth 35.2
  reddening 41.3
  washing 79.5

health 83.1
  fever 85.7
  thrill 105.2
  blushing 139.5
  jet 238.9
  skiing 753.1
  glow 1019.12
  shine 1025.2
  v redden 41.5
  wash 79.19
  change color 105.19
  elate 109.8
  make proud 136.6
  blush 139.8
  show resentment 152.14
  level 201.6
  flow 238.16
  hunt 382.9
  be hot 1019.22
  soak 1065.13
  adj red-complexioned 41.9
  hale 83.12
  fresh 83.13
  horizontal 201.7
  wealthy 618.14
  full 794.11
  plentiful 991.7
  adv horizontally 201.9
flushed
  red-complexioned 41.9
  fresh 83.13
  feverish 85.58
  fervent 93.18
  overjoyed 95.17
  heated 105.22
  cheerful 109.11
  rejoicing 116.10
  puffed up 136.10
  blushing 139.13
  crowing 502.13
  hot 1019.25
fluster
  n dither 105.6
  bustle 330.4
  bluster 503.1
  agitation 917.1
  confusion 985.3
  v agitate 105.14
  confuse 985.7
flute
  n furrow 290.1
  v furrow 290.3
  fold 291.5
  speak 524.25
  blow a horn 708.42
flutist 710.4
flutter
  n audio distortion 50.13
  staccato 55.1
  trepidation 105.5
  dither 105.6
  bustle 330.4
  haste 401.1
  trill 709.19
  trading 737.19
  price 738.9
  pulsation 916.3
  flitter 917.4
  confusion 985.3
  flicker 1025.8
  v drum 55.4

excite 105.14
  be excited 105.18
  oscillate 916.10
  wave 916.11
  agitate 917.10
  flitter 917.12
  confuse 985.7
  flicker 1025.25
fluvial 238.23
flux
  n excretion 12.1
  defecation 12.2
  symptom 85.9
  course 172.2
  flow 238.4
  tide 238.13
  ceramics 742.3
  measurement of light 1025.21
  liquidity 1061.1
  solvent 1064.4
  v treat 91.24
  combine 805.3
  melt 1020.21
  liquefy 1064.5
fly
  n overlayer 295.4
  insect 311.33
  snare 356.13
  game 745.3
  v disappear 34.2
  speed 174.8
  transport 176.12
  glide 177.35
  be airborne 184.36
  pilot 184.37
  run off 188.12
  take off 193.10
  flee 368.10
  play 745.5
  cease to exist 762.6
  elapse 821.5
  flit 828.6
  wave 916.11
fly at 459.18
flyblown filthy 80.23
  blighted 393.42
fly-by-night
  untrustworthy 645.19
  transient 828.7
flying
  n aviation 184.1
  adj vanishing 34.3
  high 87.24
  flowing 172.8
  fast 174.15
  airborne 184.50
  hasty 401.9
  transient 828.7
flying buttress 901.4
Flying Dutchman
  wanderer 178.2
  mariner 183.1
  White Lady 988.2
fly in the face of
  disobey 327.6
  deny 335.4
  oppose 451.3
  offer resistance 453.3
  flout 454.4
  go contrary to 779.4
  counteract 900.6

fly in the ointment
evil 1000.3
fault 1003.2
obstacle 1012.4
flyleaf 554.12
fly off at a tangent
fly into a rage 152.20
avoid 164.6
diverge 171.5
fly off the handle
get excited 105.17
fly into a rage 152.20
fly on the wall
viewpoint 27.7
listener 48.5
flytrap 356.12
FM signal 1034.10
foal
n fledgling 302.10
horse 311.10
jockey 757.2
v give birth 1.3
foam
n saliva 13.3
whiteness 37.2
lightness 298.2
froth 320.2
extinguisher 1022.3
softness 1047.4
sprinkle 1065.5
v bubble 320.4
froth 320.5
seethe 671.12
foam at the mouth
be angry 152.15
be insane 926.20
foamy light 298.10
foam-flecked 320.7
fob
n bag 195.2
jewel 498.6
v cheat 356.18
fob off on 643.7
focal converging 169.3
confocal 208.13
chief 249.14
vital 997.23
focus
n convergence 169.1
focal point 208.4
centralization 208.8
essence 767.2
attractor 907.2
v focalize 208.10
focus on
specify 865.11
operate on 889.6
concentrate 931.10
have regard to 937.3
pay attention 983.8
call attention to 983.10
fodder
n feed 10.4
v feed 8.18
tend 1070.7
foe
opponent 452.1
enemy 589.6
fog
n atmosphere 184.32
grass 310.5

pea soup 319.3
obscurity 522.3
confusion 985.3
v blur 32.4
cover 295.19
cloud 319.7
make uncertain 971.15
confuse 985.7
foggy
inconspicuous 32.6
soupy 319.10
obscure 522.15
muddleheaded 922.18
vague 971.19
muddled 985.13
foghorn
alarm 400.1
signal 517.15
fogy
old-timer 842.8
conservative 853.4
dotard 924.9
foible
vice 654.2
fault 1003.2
foil
n lamina 296.2
discomfiture 412.2
motif 498.7
actor 707.2
frustration 1012.3
v disappoint 132.2
outwit 415.11
thwart 1012.15
foist 776.5
foist oneself upon 214.5
fold
n enclosed place 212.3
cavity 284.2
crease 291.1
double 291.1
lamina 296.2
the laity 700.1
v collapse 260.10
fold on itself 291.5
close shop 293.8
fail 410.10
embrace 562.18
go bankrupt 625.7
seek the middle 819.3
folder
advertising matter 352.8
booklet 554.11
bookholder 554.17
folderol finery 498.3
nonsense 520.2
passage 708.24
trifle 998.5
fold in 291.5
folding
n mountain 237.6
creasing 291.4
bookbinding 554.14
adj folded 291.7
fold up
collapse 260.10
fold 291.5
close shop 293.8
fail 410.10
go bankrupt 625.7
end 820.5

foliage 310.18
foliation
stratification 296.4
foliage 310.18
numeration 1017.9
folio volume 554.4
makeup 554.12
bookholder 554.17
part of writing 793.2
folk
n population 227.1
race 559.4
family 559.5
the people 606.1
adj traditional 842.12
folk history story 719.3
tradition 842.2
folklore
mythology 678.14
tradition 842.2
superstition 954.3
folk music 708.11
folks
kinfolk 559.2
family 559.5
the people 606.1
folk singer
singer 710.13
minstrel 710.14
folk singing 708.13
folksy 581.3
folktale 842.2
follicle 310.30
follow
n pursuit 382.1
v look 27.13
attach oneself to 138.11
go after 166.3
parallelize 203.5
be behind 217.8
be inferior 250.4
practice 328.8
emulate 336.7
pursue 382.8
take advice 422.7
observe 434.2
understand 521.7
court 562.21
play 744.2
resemble 784.7
set an example 786.7
be consistent 803.7
come next 815.2
succeed 817.5
come after 835.3
specialize 866.4
conform 867.3
result 887.4
seek 938.30
trace 938.35
prove 957.10
follower
enthusiast 101.4
lover 104.12
hanger-on 138.6
successor 166.2
inferior 250.2
pursuer 382.4
apostle 572.2
retainer 577.1
disciple 616.8

believer 692.4
follow from
result from 887.5
prove 957.10
following
n going behind 166
heeling 166.1
follower 166.2
imitation 336.1
pursuit 382.1
attendance 769.6
sequence 815.1
subsequence 835.1
surveillance 938.9
adj trailing 166.5
pursuing 382.11
similar 784.10
succeeding 815.4
subsequent 835.4
resultant 887.6
deducible 935.23
prep after 835.8
follow-through
game 750.2
round 751.3
sequel 817.1
follow up
prosecute to a conclusion
360.5
pursue 382.8
be thorough 794.8
come after 835.3
trace 938.35
follow-up
case history 91.10
pursuit 382.1
news item 552.3
sequel 817.1
subsequence 835.2
folly
foolishness 923.1
foolish act 923.4
foment
n agitation 917.1
v excite 105.12
relieve 120.5
incite 375.17
heat 1020.17
fond
n foundation 901.6
adj loving 104.27
hopeful 124.11
foolish 923.8
credulous 954.8
fondle stroke 73.8
foster 449.16
hold 474.7
caress 562.16
fond of
desirous of 100.22
enamored of 104.30
font jet 238.9
source of supply 386.4
type 548.6
baptism 701.6
church vessels 703.11
fountainhead 886.6
food nutrient 7.3
sustenance 10.1
foodstuff 10.1
food additive preservative 397.4

vitaminization 7.14
food for thought 931.7
food processor 1063.4
foofaraw dither 105.6
  bustle 330.4
  finery 498.3
  turbulence 671.2
  commotion 810.4
foofooraw
  noise 53.4
  quarrel 456.6
fool
  n dupe 358.1
  laughingstock 508.7
  buffoon 707.10
  stupid person 924.2
  damn fool 924.1
  ignoramus 930.8
  v befool 356.15
  be foolish 923.6
  trifle 998.14
  adj foolish 923.8
fool around
  banter 490.6
  play 743.23
  be foolish 923.6
  trifle 998.15
fool around with
  meddle 214.7
  experiment 942.8
foolery
  buffoonery 489.5
  gibe 508.2
  foolishness 923.1
foolhardy
  daring 492.22
  harebrained 493.9
fooling
  n deception 356.1
  buffoonery 489.5
  banter 490.1
  bantering 490.2
  ridicule 508.1
  trifling 998.8
  adj bantering 490.7
  ridiculing 508.12
foolish
  mischievous 322.6
  nonsensical 520.7
  unintelligent 922.13
  fool 923.8
  absurd 923.11
  trivial 998.19
foolproof
  resistant 15.20
  handy 1014.15
fool with meddle 214.7
  trifle 998.14
foot
  n member 2.7
  sail 180.14
  base 199.2
  extremity 199.5
  meter 720.7
  v speed 174.8
  walk 177.27
  way of walking 177.28
  make way 182.21
  float 182.54
  dance 705.5
footage length 267.1

motion-picture photography
  706.5
football sport 746.1
  football team 746.2
  soccer 752.1
foot-dragging
  n slowness 175.1
  refusal 325.1
  delay 846.2
  hindrance 1012.1
  adj slow 175.10
  dilatory 846.17
foothills
  the country 233.1
  highlands 237.1
foothold hold 474.2
  footing 901.5
  purchase 906.2
footing station 159.2
  base 199.2
  hold 474.2
  class 607.1
  fee 624.5
  horse racing 757.1
  state 765.1
  sphere of influence 894.4
  foothold 901.5
  foundation 901.6
  purchase 906.2
  outlook 978.2
  calculation 1017.10
footlights
  show business 701.1
  illumination 701.19
footloose
  wandering 177.37
  free 430.21
footman 577.6
footnote
  comment 341.5
  memorandum 549.4
footprint 517.7
footrest step 193.5
  footing 901.5
foot soldier
  pedestrian 178.6
  infantryman 461.9
footstep stride 177.11
  step 193.5
  print 517.7
foot the bill 624.18
fop dandy 500.9
  person of fashion 578.7
for
  prep to 380.11
  in preparation for 405.24
  on behalf of 449.26
  in favor of 509.21
  instead of 862.12
  conj because 888.10
forage
  n feed 10.4
  search 938.15
  v feed 8.18
  provision 385.9
  plunder 482.17
  search 938.31
forage grass 310.5
forager 483.6
foray
  n raid 459.4

plundering 482.6
  v raid 459.20
  plunder 482.17
forbear
  be patient 134.4
  have pity 145.4
  refrain 329.3
  not use 390.5
  abstain 668.7
forbearance
  patience 134.1
  pity 145.1
  forgiveness 148.1
  avoidance 368.1
  temperance 668.1
  tolerance 979.4
forbid
  v prohibit 444.3
  prevent 1012.14
  adj prohibited 444.7
forbidden fruit
  desire 100.11
  lure 377.3
  prohibition 444.1
  tree of knowledge 928.8
forbidding
  n prohibition 444.1
  adj offensive 98.18
  reticent 344.10
  prohibitive 444.6
  preventive 1012.19
  hideous 1015.11
force
  n strength 15.1
  energy 17.1
  power 18.1
  waterfall 238.11
  quantity 244.1
  enterprise 330.7
  ultima ratio 424.2
  meaning 518.1
  vigor 544.3
  staff 577.11
  violence 671.1
  impact 887.2
  influence 894.1
  impulse 902.1
  validity 973.6
  v motivate 375.12
  compel 424.4
  administer 643.6
  seduce 665.20
  thrust 902.12
  cultivate 1069.17
forced labor 725.4
forced march
  walk 177.10
  hastening 401.3
force-feed 8.19
forceful strong 15.15
  energetic 17.13
  powerful 18.12
  enterprising 330.23
  vigorous 544.11
  emphatic 997.21
force of habit 373.3
forceps 192.9
forces work force 18.9
  army 461.23
force upon
  urge upon 439.9

thrust upon 478.20
  administer 643.6
forcible strong 15.15
  energetic 17.13
  powerful 18.12
  coercive 424.12
  vigorous 544.11
  emphatic 997.21
forcible removal 160.1
forcible seizure
  seizure 480.2
  unruliness 671.3
forcible shift 160.1
for crying out loud! 122.21
ford
  n shoal 276.2
  passageway 383.3
  v pass 910.8
fore
  n front 216.1
  adj front 216.10
  previous 834.4
  former 837.10
  interj golf 751.5
fore and aft
  aft 182.69
  from beginning to end 794.18
forearm
  n member 2.7
  arm 906.5
  v prepare for 405.11
  take precautions 494.6
forebear 816.1
forebearance
  discontinuance 390.2
  leniency 427.1
forebears 560.7
forebode bode 133.11
  forewarn 399.6
  threaten 514.2
  predict 962.9
foreboding
  n feeling 93.1
  anxiety 126.1
  apprehension 127.4
  boding 133.2
  forewarning 399.2
  threat 514.1
  hunch 934.3
  foreknowledge 961.3
  prediction 962.1
  adj anxious 126.7
  ominous 133.17
  forewarning 399.8
  threatening 514.3
  foreshadowing 962.12
forecast
  n foresight 961.1
  prediction 962.1
  v plan 381.8
  predict 962.9
  adj predicted 962.14
forecasting
  n meteorology 317.5
  prediction 962.1
  adj predictive 962.11
foreclose
  dispossess 480.23
  prevent 1012.14
forecourt
  basketball 747.1

tennis 748.1
forefathers 560.7
forefront
  leading 165.1
  border 211.4
  front 216.1
  vanguard 216.2
foregoing
  n leading 165.1
  adj leading 165.3
  former 814.5
  previous 834.4
  aforegoing 837.11
foregone conclusion
  sure success 409.2
  predetermination 964.1
foreground
  front 216.1
  nearness 223.1
forehand
  n front 216.1
  adj front 216.10
  early 845.7
forehead 216.5
foreign
  extraterritorial 206.9
  extrinsic 768.3
  extraneous 774.5
  unrelated 776.6
foreign affairs 609.5
foreign correspondent 555.4
foreigner
  exclusiveness 773.3
  alien 774.3
  oddity 870.4
foreign exchange 728.9
foreign policy 609.5
foreknowledge
  understanding 928.3
  foreknowing 961.3
  predetermination 964.1
foreman
  superintendent 574.2
  juror 596.7
foremost
  adj leading 165.3
  front 216.10
  chief 249.14
  preceding 814.4
  first 818.17
  paramount 997.24
  adv before 165.4
  frontal 216.12
forensic
  n speech 543.2
  adj declamatory 543.12
  jurisprudent 673.12
foreordain 964.6
foreplay 75.7
forerunner
  harbinger 133.5
  herald 353.2
  preparer 405.5
  leader 574.6
  skier 753.2
  precursor 816.1
  antecedent 834.2
foresee
  expect 130.5
  look forward to 130.6
  come 839.6

anticipate 845.6
  see beforehand 961.5
  predict 962.9
foreseeable
  foreseen 961.8
  predictable 962.13
  probable 968.6
foreseeing 961.1
foreshadow
  n omen 133.3
  v foreshow 133.10
  image 349.11
foreshorten 268.6
foreshortening 268.3
foresight plan 381.1
  precaution 494.3
  extrasensory perception 689.8
  the future 839.1
  earliness 845.1
  sagacity 920.4
  looking ahead 961.1
  foreseeing 961.1
  prediction 962.1
forest
  n woodland 310.13
  v plant 1069.18
  adj sylvan 310.40
forestall
  look forward to 130.6
  deceive 356.14
  monopolize 469.6
  anticipate 845.6
  prevent 1012.14
forestation 1069.3
forester
  guardian 1008.6
  arboriculturist 1069.7
forest ranger
  preserver 397.5
  guardian 1008.6
  forester 1069.7
forest reserve 397.7
forestry
  woodland 310.13
  arboriculture 1069.3
foretaste
  n appetizer 10.9
  antepast 961.4
  v anticipate 845.6
  foresee 961.5
foretell come 839.6
  predict 962.9
forethought
  carefulness 339.1
  intentionality 380.3
  plan 381.1
  precaution 494.3
  premeditation 961.2
foretold 962.14
forever
  n infinity 823.1
  an eternity 829.2
  adv for keeps 474.10
  infinitely 823.4
  forevermore 829.12
  permanently 853.9
forewarned 130.11
forewarning
  n warning 133.4
  prewarning 399.2
  adj premonitory 133.16

prewarning 399.8
  predictive 962.11
foreword
  front 216.1
  makeup 554.12
  part of writing 793.2
  curtain-raiser 816.2
for example
  incidentally 843.13
  to illustrate 957.23
for fear that 897.7
forfeit
  n collateral 438.3
  loss 473.1
  fine 603.3
  v lose 473.4
  adj lost 473.7
for fun
  for the hell of it 95.20
  in fun 489.19
  for amusement 743.31
forgathering 770.1
forge
  n foundry 739.4
  v form 262.7
  imitate 336.5
  fabricate 354.18
  coin 728.28
forge ahead
  make one's way 162.4
  be in front 216.7
  hustle 330.13
forgery
  imitation 336.1
  fabrication 354.10
  fake 354.13
  counterfeit 728.10
  coining 728.24
  copy 785.1
forget
  forgive and forget 148.5
  dismiss 984.4
  clean forget 990.5
forget about it 984.4
forgetful
  inconsiderate 144.18
  careless 340.11
  forgetting 990.9
forget it
  v compose oneself 106.7
  dismiss 984.4
  interj nope! 335.10
  cease! 857.13
  phrs no matter 998.25
forgive have pity 145.4
  pardon 148.3
  acquit 601.4
  declare a moratorium 625.9
  efface from the memory
    990.6
forgo refrain 329.3
  give up 370.7
  not use 390.5
  relinquish 475.3
  abstain 668.7
forgone
  relinquished 475.5
  determined 964.8
for good
  for keeps 474.10
  forever 829.12

forgotten
  forgiven 148.7
  unthanked 151.5
  past 837.7
  clean forgotten 990.8
for instance 957.23
fork
  n prong 171.4
  tributary 238.3
  angle 278.2
  branch 310.20
  v furcate 171.7
  ladle 176.17
  angle 278.5
  bisect 875.4
  throw 904.10
for keeps
  to keep 474.10
  forever 829.12
for kicks 743.31
forklift 912.3
fork out give 478.12
  pay out 624.14
  spend 626.5
fork over
  deliver 478.13
  pay out 624.14
forks 8.12
forlorn
  disconsolate 112.28
  hopeless 125.12
  lorn 584.12
form
  n aspect 33.3
  apparition 33.5
  lair 228.26
  shape 262.1
  human form 262.4
  grammar 262.6
  structure 266.1
  standard 373.4
  manner 384.1
  rule 419.2
  formula 419.3
  motif 498.7
  document 549.5
  class 572.11
  social convention 579.1
  formality 580.1
  law 673.3
  rite 701.3
  piece 708.5
  arrangement 709.11
  statistics 757.4
  good condition 765.3
  mode 765.4
  mold 786.6
  ordering 808.1
  kind 809.3
  rule 869.4
  phantom 976.4
  specter 988.1
  body 1052.3
  immaterialism 1053.3
  v formalize 262.7
  be formed 262.8
  construct 266.5
  train 568.13
  compose 796.3
  order 807.4
  take form 807.5

produce 892.8
establish 892.10
formal
n ceremony 580.4
dance 705.2
adj solemn 111.3
formative 262.9
structural 266.6
pompous 501.22
gallant 504.15
nominal 527.15
grammatical 530.17
stiff 534.3
conventional 579.5
formulary 580.7
ritualistic 701.19
conditional 765.6
orderly 807.6
formalist
n pietist 693.3
ritualist 701.2
conformist 867.2
pedant 929.5
adj formal 580.7
formalities
amenities 504.7
etiquette 580.3
formality
solemnity 111.1
overniceness 500.5
pomp 501.6
social convention 579.1
form 580.1
ceremony 580.4
law 673.3
rite 701.3
rule 869.4
formalize form 262.7
sign 437.7
ritualize 580.5
normalize 869.6
format form 262.1
structure 266.1
formation
flight formation 184.12
form 262.1
forming 262.5
structure 266.1
word form 526.4
game 746.3
composition 796.1
order 807.1
arrangement 808.1
production 892.2
establishment 892.4
formative
n morphology 526.3
adj formal 262.9
component 796.5
beginning 818.15
causal 886.13
creative 892.16
pliant 1047.9
former foregoing 814.5
previous 834.4
past 837.10
older 842.19
formidable
terrible 127.30
remarkable 247.10
weighty 997.20

difficult 1013.17
formless
shapeless 263.4
diffuse 538.11
unordered 810.12
abnormal 870.9
formula rule 419.2
form 419.3
law 673.3
rite 701.3
rule 869.4
axiom 974.2
formulary
n formula 419.3
law 673.3
rite 701.3
norm 869.4
adj preceptive 419.4
formal 580.7
ritualistic 701.19
formulate say 524.22
phrase 532.4
write 547.21
legalize 673.9
compose 718.6
produce 892.8
fornicate
copulate 75.21
be promiscuous 665.19
for real
adj real 761.15
adv positively 247.19
forsake abandon 370.5
be unfaithful 645.12
forsaken unloved 99.10
available 222.15
abandoned 370.8
forlorn 584.12
outcast 586.10
forswear
n recant 363.8
v deny 335.4
give up 370.7
reject 372.2
relinquish 475.3
swear off 668.8
forsworn
untruthful 354.34
apostate 363.11
rejected 372.3
relinquished 475.5
deceitful 645.18
fort 460.6
forte
n talent 413.4
music 708.25
specialty 866.1
adj loud 53.11
music 708.53
adv loudly 53.14
forth
adv forward 162.8
hence 188.20
out 190.21
prep out of 190.22
forthcoming
n appearance 33.1
approach 167.1
imminence 840.1
adj approaching 167.4
emerging 190.18

future 839.8
imminent 840.3
in preparation 405.22
for the birds 98.25
for the hell of it
for fun 95.20
in fun 743.31
for the most part
chiefly 249.17
on the whole 792.14
generally 864.17
normally 869.10
for the nonce
meanwhile 826.5
temporarily 828.9
now 838.3
for the period of 821.14
for the sake of
on behalf of 380.11
in order to 449.26
because of 888.9
for the time being
temporarily 828.9
now 838.3
conditionally 959.11
forthright
adj candid 644.17
adv directly 161.23
forthwith at once 830.8
promptly 845.15
fortification
vitaminization 7.14
strengthening 15.5
work 460.4
confirmation 957.4
fortify vitaminize 7.20
refresh 9.2
strengthen 15.13
add to 253.5
embattle 460.9
adulterate 797.12
confirm 957.11
a fortiori
adj dialectic 935.22
adv chiefly 249.17
fortitude strength 15.1
patience 134.1
will power 359.4
hardihood 492.6
cardinal virtues 653.4
Fort Knox 729.13
fortnight
moment 824.2
eleven 882.7
fortress 460.6
fortuitous
circumstantial 766.7
unessential 768.4
chance 972.15
fortuity chance 972.1
chance event 972.6
fortunate
auspicious 133.18
successful 409.14
timely 843.9
chance 972.15
lucky 1010.14
fortune wealth 618.1
gamble 759.2
fate 964.2
chance 972.1

good fortune 1010.2
fortune hunter 651.3
fortuneteller 962.4
forty plot 231.4
eleven 882.7
forty-niner
traveler 178.1
miner 1058.9
forty winks 22.3
forum square 230.8
conference 423.3
arena 463.1
discussion 541.7
tribunal 595.1
assembly 770.2
forward
n team 752.2
v advance 162.5
send 176.15
be instrumental 384.7
make better 392.9
hasten 401.4
be useful 449.17
deliver 478.13
determine 886.12
impel 902.11
push 904.9
expedite one's affair 995.3
adj eager 101.8
insolent 142.9
progressive 162.6
meddlesome 214.9
front 216.10
willing 324.5
strong-willed 359.15
foolhardy 493.9
immodest 666.6
premature 845.8
adv forwards 162.8
frontward 216.13
forward-looking
progressive 162.6
modern 841.13
fosse trench 290.2
entrenchment 460.5
fossil
n remainder 256.1
antiquity 842.6
back number 842.8
adj antiquated 842.13
fossilized
stricken in years 303.18
antiquated 842.13
hardened 1046.13
foster
v nourish 8.19
advance 162.5
look after 339.9
motivate 375.12
encourage 375.21
make better 392.9
nurture 449.16
hold 474.7
train 568.13
care for 1008.19
adj related 559.6
foster-care 449.3
foster child
dependent 432.6
descendant 561.3

fostering
  n accommodations 385.3
  support 449.3
  training 568.3
  protectorship 1008.2
  adj helping 449.20
  protective 1008.23
foul
  n unfairness 650.2
  baseball game 745.3
  football game 746.3
  basketball game 747.3
  hockey game 749.3
  game 749.6
  match 752.3
  fight 754.3
  v defile 80.17
  stop 293.7
  misuse 389.4
  catch 480.17
  play 747.4
  fix 855.10
  collide 902.13
  adj nasty 64.7
  malodorous 71.5
  filthy 80.23
  unhealthful 82.5
  offensive 98.18
  inert 173.14
  stopped 293.11
  stormy 318.23
  decayed 393.40
  cursing 513.8
  unfair 650.10
  wicked 654.16
  base 661.12
  vulgar 666.8
  obscene 666.9
  demoniac 680.17
  terrible 1000.9
  hideous 1015.11
  adv afoul 182.72
foulmouthed
  caustic 144.23
  cursing 513.8
  obscene 666.9
foul play
  homicide 308.2
  chicanery 356.4
  treachery 645.6
  unfairness 650.2
foul-smelling 71.5
foul up spoil 393.11
  bungle 414.12
  complicate 799.3
  confuse 811.3
  make a boner 975.15
  hinder 1012.16
foul-up
  bungler 414.9
  confusion 810.2
  goof 975.6
found
  establish 159.16
  form 262.7
  sculpture 715.5
  inaugurate 818.11
  fix 855.10
  cause 886.10
  set up 892.10
  burn 1020.24

foundation
  settlement 159.7
  base 199.2
  preparation 405.1
  endowment 478.9
  warrant 600.6
  organization 617.8
  game 750.2
  beginning 818.1
  stability 855.6
  establishment 892.4
  fond 901.6
  premise 935.7
  makeup 1016.12
founded on
  supported 901.24
  evidential 957.16
founder
  n producer 892.7
  v go lame 85.49
  capsize 182.44
  descend 194.6
  sink 367.8
  break down 393.24
  fail 410.11
  come to grief 1011.10
founding member 892.7
foundling 370.4
found money 472.6
foundry 739.4
fount jet 238.9
  source of supply 386.4
  fountainhead 886.6
fountain
  n ascent 193.1
  jet 238.9
  source of supply 386.4
  fountainhead 886.6
  v shoot up 193.9
fountain of youth 829.3
four
  n card 758.2
  fourness 879
  tetrad 879.1
  adj foursquare 879.4
four-leaf clover
  charm 691.5
  four 879.1
four-letter word
  oath 513.4
  barbarism 526.6
fourscore 882.7
foursome golfer 751.2
  four 879.1
fourth
  n interval 709.20
  one-fourth 881.2
  adj quarter 881.5
the fourth estate
  news 552.1
  the press 555.3
fourth-rate 1005.9
fowl
  n bird 10.22
  wildfowl 311.28
  poultry 311.29
  v hunt 382.9
fox reynard 311.20
  slyboots 415.6
foxhole cave 284.5
  hiding place 346.4

  entrenchment 460.5
  shelter 1009.3
fox hunt 382.2
foxtrot 705.5
foxy
  reddish-brown 40.4
  canine 311.42
  cunning 415.12
  shrewd 920.15
  stained 1004.10
foyer vestibule 197.19
  home 228.2
fracas noise 53.3
  quarrel 456.5
  free-for-all 457.5
  commotion 810.4
fraction political party 609.24
  part 793.1
  ratio 1017.7
fractious
  irascible 110.19
  unwilling 325.5
  defiant 327.10
  ungovernable 361.12
  oppositional 451.8
  resistant 453.5
fracture
  n trauma 85.38
  crack 224.2
  break 802.4
  v cleave 224.4
  injure 393.13
  impair 393.23
  break 802.12
fragile weak 16.14
  frail 764.7
  transient 828.7
  brittle 1050.4
fragility frailty 16.2
  unhealthiness 85.3
  unsubstantiality 764.1
  damageability 1050.1
  brittleness 1050.1
fragment
  n modicum 248.2
  piece 793.3
  v demolish 395.17
  diversify 782.2
  shatter 802.13
  break 1050.3
  pulverize 1051.9
fragmentary
  unsound 16.15
  partial 793.7
  broken 802.24
  discontinuous 813.4
fragmentate 1050.3
fragmentation
  dispersion 771.1
  disruption 802.3
  disintegration 806.1
  pulverization 1051.4
fragrance odor 69.1
  aroma 70.1
  fragrancy 70.1
fraidy-cat 491.5
frail
  n gal 302.7
  adj slight 16.14
  unhealthy 85.54
  thin 270.16

  human 312.13
  weak-willed 362.12
  unvirtuous 654.12
  fragile 764.7
  transient 828.7
  brittle 1050.4
frailty
  slightness 16.2
  unhealthiness 85.3
  thinness 270.4
  humanness 312.8
  weak will 362.4
  vice 654.2
  fault 1003.2
  brittleness 1050.1
frame
  n body 2.1
  base 199.2
  border 211.4
  form 262.1
  human form 262.4
  structure 266.1
  framing 266.4
  trumped-up charge 599.4
  film 714.10
  game 745.3
  game or string 750.2
  circumstances 766.2
  nature 767.4
  underframe 901.10
  prearrangement 965.2
  mood 978.4
  body 1052.3
  v border 211.10
  form 262.7
  plan 381.8
  plot 381.9
  phrase 532.4
  trump up a charge 599.12
  produce 892.8
  originate 892.12
  prearrange 965.5
frame of mind 978.4
frame up
  plot 381.9
  trump up a charge 599.12
  prearrange 965.5
frame-up fake 354.13
  intrigue 381.5
  trumped-up charge 599.4
  prearrangement 965.2
framework
  the skeleton 2.2
  outline 211.2
  frame 266.4
  outlook 978.2
franchise
  n vote 371.6
  exemption 430.8
  grant 443.5
  suffrage 609.17
  privilege 642.2
  merchant 730.2
  v authorize 443.11
Franciscan
  n ascetic 667.2
  adj ascetic 667.4
frangible frail 16.14
  brittle 1050.4
frank
  n postage 553.5

v talkative 540.9
adj communicative 343.10
artless 416.5
free-acting 430.23
plain-speaking 535.3
candid 644.17
vulgar 666.8
Frankenstein 127.9
frankincense 70.4
frantic
overzealous 101.12
frenzied 105.25
overactive 330.24
turbulent 671.18
rabid 926.30
distracted 985.10
fraternal
kind 143.13
friendly 587.15
fraternity
affiliation 450.2
blood relationship 559.1
association 582.6
companionship 587.2
fellowship 617.3
fraternize
associate with 582.17
act the traitor 645.15
fraternizer 357.11
Frau woman 77.5
female 77.9
fraud sham 354.3
fake 354.13
fraudulence 356.8
impostor 357.6
theft 482.1
affecter 500.7
deceitfulness 645.3
fraudulent
deceitful 356.22
thievish 482.21
wrong 638.3
dishonest 645.16
illegal 674.6
fraught
weighted 297.18
freighted 794.12
fray
n trauma 85.38
fight 457.4
v injure 393.13
wear 393.20
abrade 1044.7
frazzle
n trauma 85.38
v get tired 21.6
concern 126.4
injure 393.13
wear 393.20
abrade 1044.7
freak
n addict 87.21
desirer 100.12
enthusiast 101.5
caprice 364.1
misfit 789.4
specialist 866.3
nonconformist 868.3
oddity 870.4
monstrosity 870.6

fanatic 926.18
character 927.4
chance event 972.6
adj bizarre 870.13
freakish
capricious 364.5
inconstant 854.7
freak 870.13
eccentric 927.5
freak out delight 95.11
lose self-control 128.8
go mad 926.22
go on a trip 976.8
dream 986.17
freckle
n spottiness 47.3
mark 517.5
blemish 1004.1
v variegate 47.7
mark 517.19
spot 1004.5
free
v release 120.6
unclose 292.12
rescue 398.3
liberalize 430.13
exempt 430.14
liberate 431.4
extricate 431.7
acquit 601.4
detach 802.10
loosen 804.3
disembarrass 1014.9
adj available 222.15
open 292.17
voluntary 324.7
idle 331.18
communicative 343.10
escaped 369.11
leisure 402.5
at liberty 430.21
quit 430.31
liberated 431.10
liberal 485.4
gratuitous 634.5
candid 644.17
profligate 665.25
unfastened 802.22
adv freely 430.32
as a gift 478.27
gratuitously 634.6
free and easy
nonchalant 106.15
lighthearted 109.12
careless 340.11
free 430.21
informal 581.3
convivial 582.23
unconventional 868.6
free association 92.33
freebie
n gift 478.4
costlessness 634.1
adj gratuitous 634.5
freedom
leisure 402.1
liberty 430.1
liberality 485.1
privilege 642.2
candor 644.4
facility 1014.1

free enterprise
noninterference 430.9
policy 609.4
capitalism 611.8
free-for-all noise 53.4
knock-down-and-drag-out 457.5
commotion 810.4
freehand
free-acting 430.23
pictorial 712.21
free hand
latitude 430.4
carte blanche 443.4
liberality 485.1
freeholder
householder 227.7
landowner 470.3
legislator 610.3
freeing
n release 120.2
escape 369.1
rescue 398.1
liberation 431.1
freedom 431.2
extrication 431.3
evacuation 909.6
disembarrassment 1014.6
adj benefiting 592.4
free lance
free agent 430.12
mercenary 461.17
writer 547.15
author 718.4
worker 726.2
free-lance
stand on one's own two feet 430.20
author 547.21
write 718.6
freeloader
parasite 138.5
nonworker 331.11
guest 585.6
free rider 634.3
free love
sexology 75.18
love 104.1
illicit sex 665.7
freemasonry
affiliation 450.2
fellowship 587.2
free of
adj quit 430.31
prep absent 222.19
free-range 430.26
free ride
costlessness 634.1
game 745.3
free rider 634.3
free spirit 868.3
free-standing
independent 430.22
separate 802.20
freestyle 182.11
freestyle skiing 753.1
freethinking
n liberalism 430.10
free thought 695.7
liberalness 979.2
adj nonrestrictive 430.25

latitudinarian 695.21
liberal 979.9
free thought
liberalism 430.10
freethinking 695.7
liberalness 979.2
free throw 747.3
free time 402.1
free trade
noninterference 430.9
policy 609.4
commerce 731.1
free up 1014.9
freewheeling 430.22
free will will 323.1
voluntariness 324.2
choice 371.1
free choice 430.6
free with one's money 485.4
freeze
n cold weather 1023.3
v deaden 25.4
numb 94.8
take fright 127.11
terrify 127.17
be still 173.7
preserve 397.9
speak poorly 525.7
perpetuate 829.5
stabilize 855.7
fix 855.10
stop 857.7
put a stop to 857.11
be cold 1023.9
freeze 1023.9
chill 1023.10
ice up 1023.10
ice 1024.11
interj cease! 857.13
the freeze 589.1
freeze-dry
preserve 397.9
freeze 1024.11
dry 1066.6
freeze out
exclude 773.4
drive out 909.14
freezing
n food preservation 397.2
refrigeration 1024.1
adj cold 1023.14
feeling cold 1023.16
refrigerative 1024.12
freight
n transportation 176.3
freightage 176.6
train 179.14
load 196.2
burden 297.7
haulage 630.7
charge 643.3
impediment 1012.6
v load 159.15
transport 176.12
send 176.15
burden 297.13
fill 794.7
freighter carrier 176.7
train 179.14
frenetic
overzealous 101.12

overactive 330.24
rabid 926.30
frenzied
  overzealous 101.12
  frantic 105.25
  overactive 330.24
  turbulent 671.18
  rabid 926.30
frenzy
  n seizure 85.6
  overzealousness 101.3
  fury 105.8
  turbulence 671.2
  agitation 917.1
  furor 926.7
  confusion 985.3
  v excite 105.12
  enrage 152.25
  madden 926.24
frequency
  oftenness 847.1
  routineness 847.1
  oscillation 916.1
  wave 916.4
  radio frequency 1034.12
frequent
  v haunt 221.10
  adj habitual 373.14
  oftentime 847.4
  recurrent 849.13
fresco
  n painting 35.12
  picture 712.11
  v color 35.14
fresh
  n stream 238.1
  torrent 238.5
  adj refreshing 9.3
  clean 79.25
  green 83.13
  impudent 142.10
  additional 253.10
  windy 318.22
  original 337.5
  unused 390.12
  inexperienced 414.17
  present 838.2
  new 841.7
  additional 841.8
  remembered 989.23
  undamaged 1002.8
  cool 1023.12
freshen refresh 9.2
  clean 79.18
  air 317.11
  blow 318.20
  perfect 392.11
  refrigerate 1024.10
freshet stream 238.1
  torrent 238.5
fresh-faced fresh 83.13
  young 301.9
freshman
  undergraduate 572.6
  novice 572.9
  beginner 818.2
fret
  n ache 26.5
  irritation 96.3
  dither 105.6
  dudgeon 152.7

network 170.3
heraldry 647.2
roulette 759.12
v pain 26.7
irritate 96.14
sulk 110.14
grieve 112.17
complain 115.15
make anxious 126.5
feel anxious 126.6
be impatient 135.4
be angry 152.15
provoke 152.24
injure 393.13
wear 393.20
agitate 917.10
abrade 1044.7
fretful
  peevish 110.22
  plaintive 115.19
  impatient 135.6
  bustling 330.20
fretting
  n worry 126.2
  impatience 135.1
  abrasion 1044.2
  adj irritating 26.13
  troublesome 126.10
  impatient 135.6
  abrasive 1044.10
friable
  brittle 1050.4
  pulverable 1051.13
friar 699.16
fricassee
  n stew 10.11
  v cook 11.5
friction
  n touching 73.2
  opposition 451.2
  disaccord 456.1
  hostility 589.3
  counteraction 900.1
  rubbing 1044.1
  adj frictional 1044.9
Friday abstinence 668.2
  fate 964.2
Friday the thirteenth 964.2
fridge 1024.4
fried cooked 11.7
  high 87.24
  drunk 88.33
friend 588.1
friendless
  helpless 19.18
  forlorn 584.12
  alone 872.8
friendly
  comfortable 121.11
  homelike 228.33
  favorable 449.22
  sociable 582.22
  hospitable 585.11
  friendlike 587.15
friendship
  comradeship 587
  friendliness 587.1
fright
  n fear 127.1
  eyesore 1015.4
  v frighten 127.15

frighten fright 127.15
  startle 131.8
  alarm 400.3
frightening
  n intimidation 127.6
  adj frightful 127.28
frighten off
  scare away 127.21
  dissuade 379.3
frightful
  frightening 127.28
  remarkable 247.11
  hideous 1015.11
frigid unsexual 75.29
  unfeeling 94.9
  reticent 344.10
  aloof 583.6
  cold 1023.14
frill
  n edging 211.7
  extra 254.4
  fold 291.1
  finery 498.3
  ornateness 545.4
  superfluity 993.4
  v fold 291.5
frilly ornate 498.12
  showy 501.19
fringe
  n tuft 3.6
  exterior 206.2
  border 211.4
  edging 211.7
  golf 751.1
  adj exterior 206.7
fringe benefits 624.6
frippery finery 5.10
  frills 498.3
  superfluity 993.4
  trifle 998.5
frisk
  n caper 366.2
  frolic 743.5
  search 938.15
  v rejoice 116.5
  go on horseback 177.34
  caper 366.6
  play 743.23
  search 938.31
frisky gay 109.14
  active 330.17
fritter away 486.5
frivolity
  merriment 109.5
  lightness 298.1
  waggishness 489.4
  foolishness 923.1
  flightiness 985.5
  triviality 998.3
frivolous
  merry 109.15
  litigious 598.21
  unordered 810.12
  superficial 922.20
  scatterbrained 985.16
  trivial 998.19
frizz
  n lock 3.5
  v cook 11.5
frizzy 281.9
fro 163.13

frock
  n garment 5.3
  suit 5.6
  dress 5.16
  robe 702.2
  v cloak 5.40
  ordain 698.12
frog
  derogatory names 232.7
  amphibian 311.27
  jumper 366.4
frogman
  swimmer 182.12
  navy man 183.4
  diver 367.4
frolic
  n prank 489.10
  play 743.5
  v exude cheerfulness 109.6
  rejoice 116.5
  play 743.23
from at 159.27
  away from 188.21
  out of 190.22
  off 255.14
from A to Z
  wholly 792.13
  from beginning to end 794.18
from bad to worse 119.6
from scratch
  first 818.18
  newly 841.15
from soup to nuts
  wholly 792.13
  from beginning to end 794.18
from time to time 848.5
frond leaf 310.19
  branch 310.20
front
  n appearance 33.2
  leading 165.1
  atmosphere 184.32
  exteriority 206.1
  facade 206.2
  forepart 216.1
  fore 216.1
  vanguard 216.2
  weather map 317.4
  sham 354.3
  pretext 376.1
  mediator 466.3
  affectation 500.1
  figurehead 575.5
  movement 609.33
  v contrapose 215.4
  be in front 216.7
  confront 216.8
  oppose 451.5
  offer resistance 453.3
  defy 454.3
  brave 492.11
  precede 814.2
  adj frontal 216.10
  phonetic 524.30
  first 818.17
the front 463.2
frontage
  navigation 159.3
  front 216.1

frontal
  n fore 216.1
  altar 703.12
  adj anterior 216.10
front for
  be in front 216.7
  represent 576.14
  take the place of 862.6
frontier
  n boundary 211.3
  border 211.5
  front 216.1
  hinterland 233.2
  remote region 261.4
  the unknown 930.7
  adj bordering 211.11
frontispiece
  front 216.1
  curtain-raiser 816.2
front man front 216.1
  mediator 466.3
  figurehead 575.5
front matter
  front 216.1
  added to writing 254.2
  makeup 554.12
  part of writing 793.2
  curtain-raiser 816.2
front page 216.1
front-page 552.13
front-runner
  vanguard 216.2
  jockey 757.2
  precursor 816.1
front yard 216.1
frost
  n failure 410.2
  enmity 589.1
  cold weather 1023.3
  Jack Frost 1023.7
  v whiten 37.5
  top 198.9
  freeze 1023.10
  hail 1023.11
  frost over 1030.3
frostbite
  n cold 1023.2
  v freeze 1023.10
frosted
  n beverage 10.49
  adj white 37.7
  unfeeling 94.9
  frosty 1023.17
  semitransparent 1030.4
frosting
  sweets 10.40
  whitening 37.3
  topping 198.3
frosty white 37.7
  unfeeling 94.9
  reticent 344.10
  aloof 583.6
  unfriendly 589.9
  frostlike 1023.17
  semitransparent 1030.4
froth
  n saliva 13.3
  dregs 256.2
  lightness 298.2
  foam 320.2
  trivia 998.4

  sprinkle 1065.5
  v bubble 320.4
  foam 320.5
froth at the mouth 926.20
frothy light 298.10
  foamy 320.7
  showy 501.19
  superficial 922.20
  trivial 998.19
froward
  disobedient 327.8
  perverse 361.11
frown
  n scowl 110.9
  offense 152.2
  reproving look 510.8
  v look sullen 110.15
  show resentment 152.14
frozen unfeeling 94.9
  terrified 127.26
  fast 800.14
  immortal 829.9
  permanent 853.7
  immovable 855.15
  stuck 855.16
  feeling cold 1023.16
  frozen solid 1024.14
fructification
  productiveness 890.1
  proliferation 890.2
  performance 892.5
  bearing 892.6
fructuous 995.5
frugal
  parsimonious 484.7
  cheap 633.7
  economical 635.6
  temperate 668.9
  meager 992.10
frugality
  parsimony 484.1
  thrift 635.1
  temperance 668.1
fruit
  n produce 10.38
  homosexual 75.15
  seed 310.31
  yield 472.5
  offspring 561.1
  effect 887.1
  product 893.1
  v bear 892.13
fruitbearing 890.10
fruitcake
  homosexual 75.15
  lunatic 926.16
fruitful 890.9
fruition pleasure 95.1
  accomplishment 407.1
  bearing 892.6
fruitless
  ineffective 19.15
  gainless 391.12
  unsuccessful 410.18
fruits gain 472.3
  receipts 627.1
fruity
  flavorful 63.9
  fragrant 70.9
  vegetable 310.36
  crazy 926.27

frump
  old woman 304.3
  slob 810.7
frustrate
  disappoint 132.2
  thwart 412.11
  outwit 415.11
  neutralize 900.7
  hinder 1012.15
frustrated
  unsexual 75.29
  disappointed 132.5
frustration
  psychological stress 92.17
  disappointment 132.1
  discomfiture 412.2
  circumvention 415.5
  neutralization 900.2
  thwarting 1012.3
fry
  n dish 10.7
  marine animal 311.30
  offspring 561.2
  v cook 11.5
  brown 40.2
  execute 604.17
  be hot 1019.22
fuck copulate 75.21
  deceive 356.19
  mistreat 389.6
a fuck 762.3
fucked-up
  botched 414.22
  complex 799.4
  confused 810.16
fuck off depart 188.7
  leave 222.10
  idle 331.12
fuck-off 331.8
fuck over 389.6
fuck up spoil 393.11
  bungle 414.12
  complicate 799.3
  confuse 811.3
  make a boner 975.15
fuck-up fiasco 410.6
  bungle 414.5
  bungler 414.9
  complex 799.2
  confusion 810.2
  goof 975.6
fuddle
  n intoxication 88.1
  confusion 985.3
  v intoxicate 88.23
  perplex 971.13
  confuse 985.7
fuddy-duddy
  n fussbudget 495.7
  back number 842.8
  dotard 924.9
  adj old-fogyish 842.17
fudge
  n nonsense 520.2
  v slight 340.8
  falsify 354.16
  fabricate 354.18
  cheat 356.18
fuel
  n automobile racing 756.1
  energy source 1021.1

  petroleum 1056.4
  rocket propulsion
    1074.8
  v provision 385.9
  fuel up 1021.8
  adj energy 1021.9
fugitive
  n fleer 368.5
  escapee 369.5
  criminal 660.9
  adj vanishing 34.3
  receding 168.5
  wandering 177.37
  runaway 368.16
  escaped 369.11
  unsubstantial 764.5
  transient 828.7
fugue trance 92.19
  round 708.19
  loss of memory 990.2
führer leader 574.6
  tyrant 575.14
fulcrum
  supporter 901.2
  axis 906.3
  axle 915.5
fulfill
  carry out 328.7
  accomplish 407.4
  observe 434.2
  execute 437.9
  complete 794.6
  suffice 991.4
fulfillment
  adjustment 92.27
  contentment 107.1
  accomplishment 407.1
  observance 434.1
  execution 437.4
  completion 794.4
fuliginous 38.11
full
  n fullness 794.2
  adj colored 35.17
  loud 53.11
  resonant 54.10
  intoxicated 88.31
  great 247.6
  corpulent 257.18
  broad 269.6
  thick 269.8
  stopped 293.11
  unrestricted 430.27
  detailed 766.9
  crowded 770.22
  complete 794.9
  filled 794.11
  plentiful 991.7
  satiated 994.6
  sound 1002.7
full-blooded
  strong 15.15
  red-complexioned 41.9
  upper-class 607.10
  wellborn 608.11
full bloom
  maturity 303.2
  flowering 310.26
full-blown
  full-sized 257.22
  mature 303.13

full-bodied
  flavorful 63.9
  thick 269.8
full circle circuit 914.2
  rotation 915.1
full-fledged
  developed 14.3
  full-sized 257.22
  grown 259.12
  mature 303.13
  complete 794.9
full-grown
  developed 14.3
  full-sized 257.22
  grown 259.12
  mature 303.13
  ripe 407.13
  complete 794.9
full measure fill 794.3
  plenty 991.2
full of beans
  healthy 83.9
  gay 109.14
full of holes 393.32
full of hope 124.11
full of hot air 975.18
full of it 975.18
full of oneself 140.12
full of piss and vinegar
  energetic 17.13
  healthy 83.9
  gay 109.14
  vigorous 544.11
full-scale
  full-sized 257.22
  complete 794.9
full tilt 330.25
full time 825.3
fulminate blast 56.8
  explode 671.14
fulminate against
  censure 510.13
  berate 510.19
  curse 513.5
fulsome nasty 64.7
  malodorous 71.5
  offensive 98.18
  suave 504.18
  uncritical 509.18
  flattering 511.8
  grandiloquent 545.8
  bombastic 545.9
  base 661.12
  obscene 666.9
  terrible 1000.9
fumble
  n bungle 414.5
  game 746.3
  v bungle 414.11
  play 746.5
  confuse 811.3
  grope 938.32
fume
  n odor 69.1
  excitement 105.4
  dudgeon 152.7
  turbulence 671.2
  agitation 917.1
  combustion product 1020.16
  vapor 1067.1
  v decolor 36.5

be angry 152.15
  preserve 397.9
  seethe 671.12
  let out 909.24
  smoke 1019.23
  vaporize 1067.8
fumigate
  perfume 70.8
  deodorize 72.4
  sanitize 79.24
  vaporize 1067.8
fun
  n pleasure 95.1
  pleasantness 97.1
  merriment 109.5
  joke 489.6
  action 743.2
  v joke 489.13
  adj delightful 97.8
  amusing 743.27
function
  n action 328.1
  intention 380.1
  use 387.5
  syntax 530.2
  ceremony 580.4
  duty 641.1
  rite 701.3
  occupation 724.1
  office 724.3
  v act 328.4
  officiate 724.13
  operate 889.5
  be operative 889.7
functional
  psychological 92.37
  acting 328.10
  useful 387.18
  grammatical 530.17
  occupational 724.16
  effective 889.9
  working 889.11
  operational 889.12
functionary
  official 575.16
  agent 576.3
  operator 889.4
functioning
  n action 328.1
  operation 889.1
  adj acting 328.10
  operating 889.11
fund
  n supply 386.2
  finances 728.14
  capital 728.15
  collection 770.11
  v provide 385.7
  support 449.12
  subsidize 478.19
  pay for 624.18
  finance 729.16
fundamental
  n tone 50.2
  essence 767.2
  foundation 901.6
  salient point 997.6
  adj basic 199.8
  essential 767.9
  simple 798.6
  beginning 818.15

original 886.14
  vital 997.23
fundamentalism
  firmness 425.2
  Christianity 675.7
  strictness 687.5
  zeal 692.3
fundamentalist
  n true believer 687.4
  believer 692.4
  adj firm 425.7
  strict 687.8
fund-raise 770.18
fundraiser 729.10
funds means 384.2
  assets 471.7
  finances 728.14
funebrial
  gloomy 112.24
  funereal 309.22
funeral
  n burial 309.5
  procession 812.3
  adj funereal 309.22
funeral march
  dirge 115.6
  slow motion 175.2
  march 708.12
funeral oration
  dirge 115.6
  last offices 309.4
  speech 543.2
funeral pyre 1019.13
funereal dark 38.9
  sad 112.24
  pessimistic 125.16
  funeral 309.22
  gloomy 1027.14
fungus growth 85.39
  germ 85.42
  plant 310.3
  mold 310.4
  blight 1001.2
funicular
  n train 179.14
  cableway 383.8
  adj threadlike 271.7
funk
  n stench 71.1
  fear 127.1
  coward 491.5
  v take fright 127.11
  flinch 127.13
  frighten 127.15
  lose one's nerve 491.8
funky malodorous 71.5
  melancholy 112.23
  cowardly 491.10
funnel
  n convergence 169.1
  tube 239.6
  chimney 239.14
  cone 282.5
  v converge 169.2
  transport 176.14
  channel 239.15
funnies 712.16
funny humorous 488.4
  witty 489.15
  inexplicable 522.18
  ambiguous 539.4

odd 870.11
  eccentric 927.5
  peculiar 927.6
  unbelievable 955.10
  bewildering 971.27
funny farm 926.14
funny feeling
  apprehension 127.4
  nervousness 128.1
  forewarning 399.2
  hunch 934.3
fur
  n hair 3.2
  down 3.19
  pelt 4.2
  skin 295.3
  heraldry 647.2
  v fill 196.7
furbish polish 287.7
  perfect 392.11
  renovate 396.17
  ornament 498.8
  buff 1044.8
furcate
  v fork 171.7
  angle 278.5
  adj forked 171.10
  angular 278.6
the Furies rage 152.10
  avenger 507.3
  Fury 680.10
furious
  overzealous 101.12
  frenzied 105.25
  passionate 105.29
  infuriated 152.32
  hasty 401.9
  reckless 493.8
  violent 671.16
  turbulent 671.18
  rabid 926.30
furlough
  n vacation 20.3
  absence 222.4
  unemployment 331.3
  v dismiss 909.19
furnace foundry 739.4
  kiln 742.5
  hot place 1019.11
  heater 1020.10
  reactor 1038.13
furnish provide 385.7
  equip 385.8
  supply 478.15
  bear 892.13
  fit 405.8
furnishings
  wardrobe 5.2
  furniture 229.1
  equipment 385.4
  merchandise 735.5
furniture
  home furnishings 229
  furnishings 229.1
  equipment 385.4
  composition 548.2
  merchandise 735.5
furor passion 93.2
  greed 100.8
  fury 105.8
  rage 152.10

turbulence 671.2
insanity 926.1
frenzy 926.7
mania 926.12
furrier clothier 5.33
  tailor 5.35
furrow
  n crack 224.2
  indentation 284.6
  groove 290.1
  wrinkle 291.3
  v cleave 224.4
  excavate 284.15
  groove 290.3
  wrinkle 291.6
  engrave 713.9
furry hairy 3.24
  feathery 3.27
  cutaneous 295.32
  fluffy 1047.14
further
  v advance 162.5
  be useful 449.17
  adj additional 253.10
  thither 261.10
  fresh 841.8
  adv additionally 253.11
furtherance
  progression 162.1
  improvement 392.1
  helping along 449.5
  evolution 861.1
furthermore 253.11
further oneself 162.2
furthest
  extreme 247.13
  farthest 261.12
furtive covert 345.12
  in hiding 346.14
  deceitful 356.22
fury
  n passion 93.2
  overzealousness 101.3
  furor 105.8
  sorehead 110.11
  bitch 110.12
  rage 152.10
  witch 593.7
  turbulence 671.2
  violent person 671.9
  frenzy 926.7
  adv swiftly 174.18
fuse
  n detonator 462.15
  safeguard 1008.3
  v cooperate 450.3
  come together 770.16
  identify 778.5
  mix 797.10
  stick together 803.9
  combine 805.3
  melt 1020.21
  liquefy 1064.5
fusillade
  n detonation 56.3
  volley 459.9
  capital punishment 604.7
  hit 902.4
  shot 904.4
  v pull the trigger 459.22
fusion affiliation 450.2

identification 778.2
mixture 797.1
combination 805.1
oneness 872.1
melting 1020.3
nuclear fusion 1038.9
alloy 1058.4
liquefaction 1064.1
fuss
  n dither 105.6
  bustle 330.4
  quarrel 456.5
  fussbudget 495.7
  finery 498.3
  bluster 503.1
  turbulence 671.2
  commotion 810.4
  agitation 917.1
  v agitate 105.14
  complain 115.15
  feel anxious 126.6
  be impatient 135.4
  bustle 330.12
  be hard to please 495.8
fuss at 510.16
fussbudget 495.7
fussy restless 105.27
  bustling 330.20
  meticulous 339.12
  finical 495.10
  ornate 498.12
  detailed 766.9
fustian
  n nonsense 520.2
  bombast 545.2
  adj bombastic 545.9
fusty malodorous 71.5
  trite 117.9
  blighted 393.42
  stale 842.14
futile ineffective 19.15
  vain 125.13
  useless 391.11
  unsuccessful 410.18
  foolish 923.8
  inexpedient 996.5
  trivial 998.19
futility
  ineffectiveness 19.3
  hopelessness 125.1
  vanity 391.2
  failure 410.1
  meaninglessness 520.1
  inexpedience 996.1
  triviality 998.3
future
  n fiancé 104.17
  tense 530.12
  the future 839.1
  fate 964.2
  adj later 839.8
  imminent 840.3
the future 821.1
futures 738.11
fuzz
  n down 3.19
  smoothness 294.3
  lightness 298.2
  v cover 295.19
  make uncertain 971.15
the fuzz 1008.16

Fuzzbuster 1036.5
gab
  n speech 524.1
  chatter 540.3
  v speak 524.19
  babble 524.20
  chatter 540.5
Gabriel herald 353.2
  Azrael 679.4
gad about
  journey 177.21
  wander 177.23
gadfly goad 375.8
  prompter 375.10
gadget tool 1040.1
  thing 1052.5
Gaea
  agricultural deity 1069.4
  Earth 1072.10
gaffe 975.5
gag
  n silencer 51.4
  shackle 428.4
  joke 489.6
  acting 704.8
  v disable 19.10
  silence 51.8
  feel disgust 99.4
  vomit 909.26
gaga 923.8
gage marijuana 87.11
  pledge 438.2
  challenge 454.2
gaggle
  n assemblage 770.6
  v bird sound 60.5
gag order 444.1
gaiety colorfulness 35.4
  happiness 95.2
  gayness 109.4
  finery 498.3
  showiness 501.3
  conviviality 582.3
  festivity 743.3
gain
  n increase 251.1
  profit 472.3
  game 746.3
  good 999.4
  available gain 1032.17
  time constants 1041.11
  v arrive 186.6
  grow 251.6
  persuade 375.23
  improve 392.7
  triumph 411.3
  acquire 472.8
  receive 479.6
  incur 897.4
gainful valuable 387.22
  productive 472.16
gain ground
  progress 162.2
  accelerate 174.10
  improve 392.7
gain on 174.13
gains winnings 251.3
  profit 472.3
  receipts 627.1
gainsay deny 335.4
  contradict 451.6

gait velocity 172.4
  pace 177.12
gal woman 77.6
  dame 302.7
  person 312.5
gala
  n festival 743.4
  adj festive 743.28
galactic spatial 158.10
  large 247.7
  universal 864.14
  innumerable 884.10
  celestial 1072.25
galaxy celebrity 662.9
  throng 770.4
  island universe 1072.6
the Galaxy 1072.6
gale outburst 105.9
  breeze 318.5
  windstorm 318.12
gall
  n digestive secretion
    13.2
  acridness 64.2
  trauma 85.38
  irritation 96.3
  affliction 96.8
  ill humor 110.1
  impudence 142.3
  rancor 144.7
  bitterness 152.3
  bulge 283.3
  rashness 493.1
  v pain 26.7
  irritate 96.14
  injure 393.13
  abrade 1044.7
gallant
  n beau 104.13
  brave person 492.8
  dandy 500.9
  cavalier 504.9
  libertine 665.10
  adj courageous 492.17
  showy 501.19
  chivalrous 504.15
  profligate 665.25
gallantry
  courage 492.1
  gallantness 504.2
  courtship 562.7
  profligacy 665.3
gallbladder 2.16
gallery
  observation post 27.8
  audience 48.6
  hall 197.4
  corridor 197.18
  porch 197.21
  balcony 197.22
  showroom 197.24
  layer 296.1
  passageway 383.3
  museum 386.9
  entrenchment 460.5
  auditorium 704.15
  studio 712.17
  platform 901.13
galley kitchen 11.4
  sailboat 180.3
  proof 548.5

galley slave
boatman 183.5
subject 432.7
drudge 726.3
Gallicism 523.8
gallivant
wander 177.23
flirt 562.20
gallop
n run 174.3
gait 177.12
v speed 174.8
go on horseback 177.34
gallows 605.5
the gallows 604.7
galore
adj plentiful 991.7
adv greatly 247.15
galvanize
energize 17.10
stimulate 105.13
plate 295.26
motivate 375.12
electrify 1032.26
electrolyze 1032.28
gambit trick 356.6
attempt 403.2
stratagem 415.3
first 818.3
gamble
n bet 759.2
guess 971.8
chance 972.1
v game 759.23
bet 759.25
be liable 897.3
predict 962.9
risk 972.12
endanger 1006.6
take chances 1006.7
gamble on
chance 759.24
rely on 953.16
be certain 970.9
gambling
illicit business 732.1
game 743.9
cardplaying 758.1
betting 759
playing 759.1
gambling game 743.9
gambol
n caper 366.2
frolic 743.5
v exude cheerfulness 109.6
rejoice 116.5
caper 366.6
play 743.23
game
n meat 10.13
desire 100.11
sweetheart 104.10
animal life 311.1
objective 380.2
plan 381.1
intrigue 381.5
quarry 382.7
stratagem 415.3
contest 457.3
laughingstock 508.7
vocation 724.6

fun 743.2
card game 743.9
sport 744.1
ball game 745.3
artifice 746.3
basketball game 747.3
strategy 748.2
match 749.3
contest 749.6
frame 750.2
meet 752.3
cardplaying 758.1
bridge 758.3
gambling game 759.7
v gamble 759.23
adj willing 324.5
plucky 359.14
crippled 393.30
resolute 492.18
gamekeeper
guardian 1008.6
hunter 382.5
game plan
plan 381.1
project 381.2
game 746.3
game preserve
preserve 397.7
refuge 1009.1
game reserve 397.7
game room 197.12
game-show 1035.2
gamete 305.10
game warden
preserver 397.5
guardian 1008.6
gamin
vagabond 178.3
brat 302.4
gamut range 158.2
scale 709.6
series 812.2
gamy strong 68.8
malodorous 71.5
tainted 393.41
gander
male animal 76.8
poultry 311.29
a gander 27.3
Gandhi 921.2
gang
n staff 577.11
association 617.1
company 770.3
group of animals 770.5
v league 805.4
gang bang
copulation 75.7
sexual possession 480.3
ganglord 660.10
gangly lean 270.17
giant 272.16
gangplank 189.5
gangrene
n filth 80.7
mortification 85.40
v decay 393.22
gangster bandit 483.4
evildoer 593.1
criminal 660.9
the underworld 660.10

gang up on 459.14
gang up with 582.18
gangway
n entrance 189.5
interj open up! 292.23
the gantlet 604.2
Ganymede
homosexual 75.14
carrier 176.7
attendant 577.5
gap
n interval 224.1
crack 224.2
ridge 237.5
valley 284.9
opening 292.1
difference 780.1
dissimilarity 787.1
deficiency 795.2
break 802.4
interruption 813.2
v cleave 224.4
gape 292.16
gape
n gaze 27.5
crack 224.2
opening 292.1
gaping 292.2
v gaze 27.15
wonder 122.5
gap 292.16
spectate 918.5
be curious 981.3
gaping
n yawning 292.2
adj wondering 122.9
expectant 130.11
cleft 224.7
spread 259.11
abysmal 275.11
yawning 292.18
gapless 812.8
garage carport 197.27
repair shop 739.5
garb
n clothing 5.1
looks 33.4
v clothe 5.39
garbage offal 80.9
heroin 87.9
refuse 391.4
bull 520.3
Greek 522.7
garbage dump
receptacle of filth 80.12
derelict 370.4
trash pile 391.6
garble
n Greek 522.7
v pervert 265.6
misinterpret 342.2
misrepresent 350.3
falsify 354.16
make unintelligible 522.12
confuse 811.3
garçon boy 302.5
man 577.4
garden
n compilation 554.7
horticulture 1069.10
v farm 1069.16

adj floral 310.38
simple 499.6
ordinary 1005.8
gardener man 577.4
horticulturist 1069.6
garden flower 310.24
gardening
flower 310.24
horticulture 1069.2
Garden of Eden 986.11
garden tool garden tool 1040.8
garden variety 869.3
garden-variety
simple 499.6
ordinary 1005.8
Gargantuan large 247.7
huge 257.20
gargle
n dentifrice 86.22
drink 88.7
v wash 79.19
tipple 88.24
gargoyle spout 239.8
eyesore 1015.4
garish lurid 35.20
gaudy 501.20
grandiloquent 545.8
bright 1025.32
garland
n circle 280.2
bouquet 310.25
compilation 554.7
trophy 646.3
heraldry 647.2
book of verse 720.5
v figure 498.9
garment
n vestment 5.3
v clothe 5.39
garner
n granary 386.7
v store up 386.11
garnish
n ornamentation 498.1
v attach 480.20
ornament 498.8
garniture 498.1
garret 197.16
garrison
n stronghold 460.6
military unit 461.22
guard 1008.9
v fortify 460.9
garrote
n suffocation 308.6
capital punishment 604.7
v strangle 308.19
execute 604.17
garrulous 540.9
garter 646.5
gas
n success 409.4
boasting 502.2
poppycock 520.3
chatter 540.3
belch 909.9
fart 909.10
fuel 1021.1
illuminant 1025.20
volatile 1067.1
rare gas 1067.2

vaporousness 1067.3
v provision 385.9
talk nonsense 520.5
chatter 540.5
gas chamber
place of killing 308.12
execution 605.5
the gas chamber 604.7
gasconade
n boasting 502.1
v boast 502.6
bluster 503.3
gaseous rare 299.4
thin 764.6
vaporous 1067.9
gash
n trauma 85.38
crack 224.2
notch 289.1
furrow 290.1
refuse 391.4
mark 517.5
v cleave 224.4
notch 289.4
furrow 290.3
injure 393.13
mark 517.19
sever 802.11
gasket 293.5
gaslit 1025.39
gasoline 1025.20
gasp
n breathing 2.21
v burn out 21.5
speak 524.25
be hot 1019.22
gassiness
distension 259.2
talkativeness 540.1
vaporousness 1067.3
gas station 739.1
gassy
v talkative 540.9
adj distended 259.13
pompous 501.22
inflated 502.12
bombastic 545.9
vaporous 1067.9
gastric 2.31
gastronome 8.16
gastronomy
epicurism 8.15
aesthetic taste 496.5
gourmandise 672.2
gastropod 311.3
gat opening 292.1
gun 462.10
gate entrance 189.5
porch 189.6
channel 239.4
valve 239.10
floodgate 239.11
receipts 627.1
horse racing 757.1
attender 918.2
barrier 1012.5
cast 1058.5
the gate 909.5
gâteau 10.42
gate-crasher
intruder 214.3

guest 585.6
newcomer 774.4
gatehouse 228.9
gatekeeper 1008.12
gather
n fold 291.1
v grow 14.2
expand 259.7
fold 291.5
blow 318.20
collect 472.11
come together 770.16
assemble 770.18
put together 800.5
be imminent 840.2
conclude 946.10
suppose 951.10
harvest 1069.19
gathering
n sore 85.37
collection 472.2
bookbinding 554.14
social gathering 582.10
removal to heaven
681.11
assemblage 770.1
assembly 770.2
accumulation 770.9
part of writing 793.2
joining 800.1
harvest 1069.15
adj imminent 840.3
gauche
bungling 414.20
ignorant 930.12
inconvenient 996.7
gaucho rider 178.8
herder 1070.3
gaudy garish 35.20
coarse 497.11
tawdry 501.20
grandiloquent 545.8
paltry 998.21
gauge
n size 257.1
measure 300.2
v size 257.15
measure 300.10
classify 801.8
estimate 946.9
gaunt lean 270.17
unproductive 891.4
gauntlet 454.2
gauze
dressing 86.33
fog 319.3
gauzy thin 270.16
smooth 294.8
unsubstantial 764.6
transparent 1029.4
gavel 417.9
gawk
n bungler 414.8
oaf 924.5
v gaze 27.15
wonder 122.5
be curious 981.3
gawky
n oaf 924.5
adj lean 270.17
bungling 414.20

gay colorful 35.19
homosexual 75.30
intoxicated 88.31
happy 95.16
gay as a lark 109.14
showy 501.19
convivial 582.23
profligate 665.25
festive 743.28
gaze
n stare 27.5
v gloat 27.15
wonder 122.5
gazebo
observation post 27.8
summerhouse 228.12
gazelle
swiftness 174.6
hoofed animal 311.5
jumper 366.4
gazette
official document 549.8
periodical 555.1
newspaper 555.2
gear
n clothing 5.1
rigging 180.12
cordage 271.3
equipment 385.4
impedimenta 471.3
baseball 745.1
football 746.1
hockey 749.1
field hockey 749.4
golf 751.1
soccer 752.1
skiing 753.1
mechanism 1040.4
gearing 1040.9
v equip 385.8
adj excellent 999.13
geared high 87.24
apt 788.10
gee
v avoid 164.6
interj my! 122.21
geisha dancer 705.3
entertainer 707.1
Geist 920.8
gel
n lights 704.18
semiliquid 1062.5
solution 1064.3
v thicken 1045.10
gelatin
sweets 10.40
lights 704.18
semiliquid 1062.5
geld feminize 77.13
castrate 255.11
gelded
unmanned 19.19
unproductive 891.4
gelding
impotent 19.6
sexlessness 75.9
castration 255.4
horse 311.10
jockey 757.2
gelid cold 1023.14
frozen 1024.14

gem
n jewel 498.6
good person 659.1
good thing 999.5
precious stone 1059.7
v figure 498.9
geminate
v duplicate 874.3
adj double 874.4
Gemini 873.4
Gemütlichkeit
pleasantness 97.1
sociability 582.1
gendarme
officer 1008.15
police 1008.16
gender sex 75.1
masculine 530.10
gene
genetic material 305.9
heredity 560.6
genealogy
register 549.9
pedigree 560.5
general
n commissioned officer
575.18
adj public 312.16
communal 476.9
common 497.14
governing 612.18
generalized 864.11
normal 869.8
undiscriminating 945.5
theoretical 951.13
vague 971.19
general delivery 553.4
general hospital 91.21
generality mean 246.1
major part 792.6
universality 864.1
usualness 869.2
abstract idea 932.3
indiscrimination 945.1
vagueness 971.4
generalization
custom 373.1
generality 864.1
general idea 864.8
reasoning 935.3
generally
approximately 223.23
on the average 246.5
in general 864.17
normally 869.10
vaguely 971.29
general store 736.1
general strike
revolt 327.4
strike 727.5
generate procreate 78.8
cause 886.10
originate 892.12
electrify 1032.26
generation
procreation 78.2
birth 78.6
age 824.4
lifetime 827.5
production 892.1
generation gap 456.1

generator 886.4
generic 864.11
generosity
  benevolence 143.4
  liberality 485.1
  hospitality 585.1
  magnanimity 652.2
  plenty 991.2
generous
  benevolent 143.15
  forgiving 148.6
  much 247.8
  voluminous 257.17
  indulgent 427.8
  philanthropic 478.22
  liberal 485.4
  hospitable 585.11
  magnanimous 652.6
  productive 890.9
  tolerant 979.11
  plentiful 991.7
genesis birth 1.1
  reproduction 78.6
  origin 818.4
  evolution 861.3
  source 886.5
  production 892.1
genetic
  generative 78.16
  protoplasmic 305.18
  related 559.6
  racial 559.7
  hereditary 560.19
  innate 767.8
  evolutionary 861.8
  original 886.14
genetic engineering 560.6
genetics 560.6
genial genetic 78.16
  pleasant 97.6
  cheerful 109.11
  good-natured 143.14
  sociable 582.22
  hospitable 585.11
  cordial 587.16
  warm 1019.24
geniality
  pleasantness 97.1
  cheerfulness 109.1
  good nature 143.2
  sociability 582.1
  hospitality 585.1
  cordiality 587.6
genie 680.6
genitalia
  n reproductive organs 2.13
  sex 75.1
  adj phallic 2.29
  genetic 78.16
genius ability 18.2
  superior 249.4
  inspiration 375.9
  talent 413.4
  talented person 413.12
  master 413.13
  intelligence 678.5
  familiar spirit 678.12
  demon 680.6
  nature 767.4
  smartness 920.2
  Geist 920.8

scholar 929.3
  creative thought 986.2
  first-rater 999.6
genocide killing 308.1
  carnage 308.4
  misdeed 655.2
genre form 262.1
  style 712.8
  kind 809.3
gent male 76.4
  man 76.5
genteel
  decorous 496.10
  well-bred 504.17
  chic 578.13
  upper-class 607.10
  noble 608.10
gentile
  n non-Jew 688.6
  unbeliever 695.11
  adj racial 559.7
  infidel 688.10
gentility
  decorousness 496.3
  good breeding 504.4
  aristocracy 607.3
  nobility 608.2
gentle
  v accustom 373.9
  domesticate 432.11
  calm 670.7
  soften 1047.6
  tend 1070.7
  adj faint 52.16
  good-natured 143.14
  pitying 145.7
  slow 175.10
  light 298.12
  lenient 427.7
  meek 433.15
  well-bred 504.17
  upper-class 607.10
  noble 608.10
  moderate 670.10
  soft 1047.8
gentleman male 76.4
  man 577.4
  aristocrat 607.4
  nobleman 608.4
  person of honor 644.8
  good person 659.1
gentrification 392.1
gentry the people 606.1
  upper class 607.2
  noble rank 608
  gentlefolk 608.3
genuflect bow to 155.6
  bow down 433.10
  bow 913.9
genuine natural 416.6
  straight 644.14
  candid 644.17
  real 761.15
  authentic 973.15
genus
  nomenclature 527.1
  kind 809.3
  classification 809.5
  biology 1068.1
geodesic 300.12
geographer 1071.2

geography
  topography 159.8
  earth science 1071.1
  Earth 1072.10
geology
  mineralogy 1058.10
  petrology 1059.9
  earth science 1071.1
geomancer 962.4
geometric 1017.22
geriatric
  n old man 304.2
  adj aged 303.16
  stricken in years 303.18
germ pathogen 85.42
  embryo 305.14
  vital force 886.7
germane
  related 559.6
  relevant 775.11
germicide
  antiseptic 86.21
  poison 1001.3
germinal
  reproductive 78.15
  infinitesimal 258.14
  embryonic 305.22
  original 886.14
  fertilizing 890.11
  imaginative 986.18
germinate grow 14.2
  expand 259.7
  vegetate 310.34
germination
  bodily development 14.1
  growth 259.3
  vegetation 310.32
germinational 305.22
Geronimo
  n call to arms 458.8
  interj attack! 459.32
gerontology 303.8
gerrymander
  n election district 609.16
  v maneuver 415.10
  politick 609.38
gerrymandering 356.8
gest act 328.3
  exploit 492.7
gestalt aspect 33.3
  pattern 92.32
  environment 209.1
  outline 211.2
Gestapo 1008.17
gestation 78.5
gesticulate 517.21
gesture
  n gesticulation 517.14
  hint 551.4
  v gesticulate 517.21
get
  n gain 472.3
  family 559.5
  offspring 561.2
  receipts 627.1
  v hear 48.11
  procreate 78.8
  take sick 85.47
  annoy 96.13
  speed 174.9
  fetch 176.16

depart 188.7
  kill 308.14
  acquire 472.8
  receive 479.6
  take 480.13
  read one loud and clear 521.8
  learn 570.6
  become 761.12
  induce 886.11
  incur 897.4
  solve 940.2
  discover 941.2
  stump 971.14
get across
  be heard 48.12
  communicate 343.7
  come through 521.5
  make clear 521.6
  teach 568.10
  fix in the mind 989.18
get a fix on
  locate 159.11
  make sure 970.11
get after annoy 96.13
  follow 166.3
  persecute 389.7
  pay attention 983.8
get ahead
  progress 162.2
  lead 165.2
  outdistance 249.10
  grow 251.6
  improve 392.7
  make good 409.10
  prosper 1010.7
get a kick out of 95.13
get a leg up on 411.6
get a life 328.5
get a load of see 27.12
  heed 983.6
get along
  v progress 162.2
  depart 188.6
  age 303.10
  improve 392.7
  manage 409.12
  harmonize 455.2
  be in a certain state 765.5
  persist 856.5
  interj go away! 909.31
get a move on
  v speed 174.9
  make haste 401.6
  interj make haste! 401.17
get around
  journey 177.21
  be published 352.16
  deceive 356.14
  evade 368.7
  know backwards and
    forwards 413.19
  outwit 415.11
  free oneself from 431.8
  flatter 511.6
get at
  arrive at 186.7
  bribe 378.3
  persecute 389.7
  make sure 970.11
getaway
  acceleration 174.4

departure 188.1
start 188.2
escape 369.1
get away depart 188.6
set out 188.8
escape 369.6
get away from it all
vacation 20.9
amuse oneself 743.22
get away with
devour 8.22
get off 369.7
put over 409.11
get back at
retaliate 506.4
interchange 863.4
get behind
regress 163.5
lag 166.4
be behind 217.8
back 449.13
get better 396.19
get by get off 369.7
support oneself 385.12
succeed with 409.11
manage 409.12
be in a certain state 765.5
live on 839.7
stand the test 942.10
escape notice 984.5
suffice 991.4
get cracking
v hurry 401.6
set to work 725.15
interj make haste! 401.17
get down devour 8.22
use 87.22
alight 194.7
crouch 913.8
get even with
even the score 506.7
revenge 507.4
settle with 624.12
interchange 863.4
get going
v depart 188.7
make haste 401.6
undertake 404.3
set to work 725.15
make a beginning 818.8
improve the occasion 843.8
interj make haste! 401.17
get hold of
communicate with 343.8
acquire 472.9
seize 480.14
understand 521.7
learn 570.6
get in
arrive 186.6
enter 189.7
mount 193.12
intrude 214.5
collect 472.11
assemble 770.18
get into don 5.43
penetrate 189.8
join 617.14
get it
read one loud and clear 521.8
be punished 604.20

get it over with
complete 407.6
put a stop to 857.11
get it straight 973.10
get it together
focus 208.10
make better 392.9
order 807.4
arrange 808.8
re-form 858.12
get lost
v depart 188.7
not interfere 430.17
interj go away! 909.31
get next to
ingratiate oneself 138.10
befriend 587.11
get on good terms with 587.13
get nowhere 410.13
get off climax 75.24
use 87.22
depart 188.6
set out 188.8
get down 194.7
escape 369.7
go free 431.9
make a beginning 818.8
get off it 857.13
get on don 5.43
use 87.22
annoy 96.13
depart 188.6
mount 193.12
age 303.10
make good 409.10
manage 409.12
be in a certain state 765.5
persist 856.5
prosper 1010.7
get one's back up
anger 152.17
make angry 152.23
provoke 152.24
get one's dues 639.6
get one's feet wet 818.1
get one's goat
annoy 96.13
make angry 152.23
get one's hands on
acquire 472.9
seize 480.14
get one's way 323.3
get one down
annoy 96.13
sadden 112.18
trouble 1013.13
get on one's nerves
grate on 58.11
irritate 96.14
jangle the nerves 128.9
get on the ball 401.17
get on the bandwagon
attach oneself to 138.11
concur 332.9
follow the fashion 578.10
support 609.41
follow the rule 867.4
get out
v depart 188.7
exit 190.12
extract 192.10

be revealed 351.8
issue 352.14
escape 369.6
extricate 431.7
print 548.14
interj go away! 909.31
get out from under
be relieved 120.8
disembarrass 1014.9
get out of
elicit 192.14
evade 368.7
shirk 368.9
escape 369.6
free oneself from 431.8
go free 431.9
get over move 172.5
communicate 343.7
rally 392.8
recover 396.20
come through 521.5
make clear 521.6
get rid of
murder 308.16
discard 390.7
put an end to 395.12
free oneself from 431.8
relinquish 475.3
eliminate 773.5
do away with 909.21
get rolling
depart 188.7
set to work 725.15
get the better of
win 411.5
defeat 412.6
outwit 415.11
get the drift 521.8
get the hang of
understand 521.7
master 570.9
get the lead out
v speed 174.9
be active 330.14
make haste 401.6
interj make haste! 401.17
get the picture
take action 328.5
read one loud and clear
521.8
get through
penetrate 189.8
carry out 328.7
bring about 407.5
complete 407.6
live on 839.7
get through to
be heard 48.12
communicate with 343.8
get to be heard 48.12
make anxious 126.5
arrive 186.6
extend to 261.6
communicate with 343.8
bribe 378.3
begin 818.7
get together
come to an agreement 332.10
cooperate 450.3
collect 472.11
assemble 770.18

get-together
social gathering 582.10
assembly 770.2
get tough
exert strength 15.12
remain firm 359.9
get under one's skin
affect 93.14
annoy 96.13
get under way
shove off 182.19
depart 188.6
undertake 404.3
make a beginning 818.8
getup wardrobe 5.2
costume 5.9
structure 266.1
enterprise 330.7
composition 796.1
get up dress up 5.42
awake 23.4
get out of bed 23.6
rise 200.8
make up 405.7
study up 570.14
produce 892.8
get-up-and-go
energy 17.3
enterprise 330.7
get up on
master 570.9
study up 570.14
refresh the memory 989.19
get wind of
hear 48.11
know 551.15
scent 941.6
get with it
v take action 328.5
set to work 725.15
interj make haste! 401.17
geyser jet 238.9
hot water 1019.10
ghastly
colorless 36.7
terrible 127.30
deathly 307.29
hideous 1015.11
ghetto
n the inner city 80.11
city district 230.6
adj urban 230.11
ghettoized
indigent 619.8
segregated 773.8
ghost
n frightener 127.9
writer 547.15
author 718.4
substitute 862.2
specter 988.1
television reception 1035.5
v float 182.54
author 547.21
write 718.6
substitute for 862.5
ghostlike
deathly 307.29
spectral 988.7
ghostly
deathly 307.29

spectral 988.7
immaterial 1053.7
ghost story 354.11
ghost town 230.1
ghostwriter
  writer 547.15
  author 718.4
  substitute 862.2
ghoul
  frightener 127.9
  thief 483.1
  monster 593.6
  demon 680.6
ghoulish
  terrible 127.30
  demoniac 680.17
  curious 981.5
  execrable 1000.10
GI 461.7
giant
  n strong man 15.6
  amazon 257.13
  longlegs 272.7
  adj huge 257.20
  gigantic 272.16
gibberish
  nonsense 520.2
  Greek 522.7
  jargon 523.9
gibe
  n indignity 156.2
  witticism 489.7
  scoff 508.2
  v scoff 508.9
giblets viscera 2.16
  food 10.20
  fowl part 10.23
  insides 207.4
Gibraltar 15.8
giddy intoxicated 88.31
  inconstant 854.7
  delirious 926.31
  inattentive 984.6
  dizzy 985.15
  scatterbrained 985.16
gift
  n talent 413.4
  present 478.4
  costlessness 634.1
  smartness 920.2
  v give 478.12
  contribute 478.14
gifted
  talented 413.29
  studentlike 572.12
  smart 920.14
gift of the gab
  style 532.2
  eloquence 544.1
gig
  n position 724.5
  v fish 382.10
gigantic
  herculean 15.17
  large 247.7
  huge 257.20
  giant 272.16
  excessive 993.16
gigantism
  greatness 247.1
  oversize 257.5

hugeness 257.7
excess 993.1
giggle
  n laughter 116.4
  v laugh 116.8
gigolo beau 104.13
  procurer 665.18
gild color 35.14
  yellow 43.3
  make pleasant 97.5
  coat 295.24
  falsify 354.16
  ornament 545.7
Gilded Age 824.5
gild the lily
  make pleasant 97.5
  ornament 545.7
  carry coals to Newcastle
    993.12
gilt
  n swine 311.9
  sham 354.3
  finery 498.3
  money 728.2
  adj yellow 43.4
  brass 1058.17
gimmick trick 356.6
  lure 377.3
  stratagem 415.3
  plot 722.4
  gambling wheel
    759.16
  expedient 995.2
  tool 1040.1
  thing 1052.5
gimmickry
  deception 356.1
  machination 415.4
  finery 498.3
  showiness 501.3
gimmicky
  deceitful 356.22
  cunning 415.12
  showy 501.19
gin
  n trap 356.12
  v trap 356.20
  segregate 773.6
ginger energy 17.3
  zest 68.2
gingerbread
  n finery 498.3
  superfluity 993.4
  adj ornate 498.12
gingerbread man 349.6
gingerly
  adj cautious 494.8
  adv cautiously 494.12
giraffe 311.5
gird strengthen 15.13
  encircle 209.7
  bind 800.9
girdle
  n corset 5.23
  strip 271.4
  circle 280.3
  supporter 901.2
  v encircle 209.7
  surround 280.10
  bind 800.9
  circle 914.5

gird up one's loins
  strengthen 15.13
  prepare oneself 405.13
  militarize 458.20
  set to work 725.15
girl woman 77.5
  cocaine 87.7
  ladylove 104.15
  girlie 302.6
  old woman 304.3
  maid 577.8
girl Friday 577.3
girlfriend
  ladylove 104.15
  companion 588.3
girlhood
  childhood 301.2
  young people 302.2
girlish feminine 77.14
  thin 270.16
  childish 301.11
  immature 406.11
girt
  n circle 280.3
  saddle parts 901.18
  v bind 800.9
  adj encircled 209.11
girth
  n size 257.1
  circle 280.3
  middle 819.1
  saddle parts 901.18
  v bind 800.9
gismo or **gizmo** 1052.5
gist
  essential content 196.5
  meaning 518.1
  summary 557.2
  essence 767.2
  major part 792.6
  topic 937.1
  salient point 997.6
give
  n softness 1047.1
  pliancy 1047.2
  elasticity 1048.1
  v communicate 343.7
  provide 385.7
  donate 478.12
  say 524.22
  present 634.4
  administer 643.6
  attribute 888.3
  soften 1047.7
  yield 1048.5
  transfer 629.3
give and take
  compensate 338.4
  contend 457.13
  compromise 468.2
  retaliate 506.4
  be just 649.6
  interchange 863.4
  argue 935.16
give-and-take
  n offset 338.2
  compromise 468.1
  banter 490.1
  retaliation 506.1
  conversation 541.1
  justice 649.1

trade 731.2
interchange 863.1
adj interchangeable 863.5
giveaway
  n divulgence 351.2
  adj reduced 633.9
give away betray 351.6
  discard 390.7
  break 393.23
  relinquish 475.3
  dispose of 478.21
  join in marriage 563.14
give back
  restore 396.11
  restitute 481.4
give birth bear 1.3
  reproductive 78.13
  vivify 306.11
give in bow to 250.5
  yield 433.7
  deliver 478.13
given
  n fact 761.3
  condition 959.2
  a truth 973.2
  adj allowed 478.24
  gratuitous 634.5
  real 761.15
  supposed 951.14
  conditional 959.8
  disposed 978.8
give notice
  herald 133.14
  announce 352.12
  warn 399.5
  inform 551.8
given that 951.19
given to 896.6
give off excrete 12.12
  exude 190.15
  let out 909.24
  vaporize 1067.8
give oneself airs
  be stuck on oneself 140.6
  hold one's nose in the air
    141.8
  avoid 157.7
  put on airs 501.14
give oneself up to
  lose heart 112.16
  be determined 359.8
  undertake 404.3
  indulge 669.4
  attend to 983.5
give or take 223.26
give out secrete 13.5
  weaken 16.9
  burn out 21.5
  divulge 351.5
  make public 352.11
  be consumed 388.4
  be impaired 393.26
  parcel out 477.8
  give 478.12
  deliver 478.13
  let out 909.24
give over despair 125.10
  give up 370.7
  pass 387.13
  cease to use 390.4
  surrender 433.8

deliver 478.13
cease 857.6
give rise to
cause 886.10
originate 892.12
give room for 443.9
give up despair 125.10
waive 370.7
break the habit 374.3
cease to use 390.4
yield 433.7
surrender 433.8
resign 448.2
relinquish 475.3
not understand 522.11
swear off 668.8
not know 930.11
give way weaken 16.9
lose heart 112.16
despair 125.10
row 182.53
sink 194.6
break 393.23
yield 433.7
compromise 468.2
cheapen 633.6
come apart 802.9
soften 1047.7
give way to
indulge 427.6
let oneself go 430.19
submit to 433.9
glabrous hairless 6.17
smooth 287.10
glacial cold 1023.14
frozen 1024.14
glacier 1023.5
glad pleased 95.15
happy 95.16
cheerful 109.11
cheering 109.16
glade
open space 158.4
marsh 243.1
gladiator 461.1
glamorous
alluring 377.8
illustrious 662.19
bewitching 691.11
gorgeous 1016.21
glamour
n delightfulness 97.2
allurement 377.1
illustriousness 662.6
sorcery 690.1
spell 691.1
gorgeousness 1016.6
v charm 691.8
glance
n glimpse 27.4
touch 73.1
contact 223.5
signal 517.15
preliminary examination
938.5
flash 1025.6
v glimpse 27.17
touch lightly 73.7
avoid 164.6
contact 223.10
polish 287.7

signal 517.22
shine 1025.23
glancing
n touch 73.1
adj side 218.6
in contact 223.17
glandular
glandulous 13.8
emotional 93.17
glare
n gaze 27.5
offense 152.2
publicity 352.4
showiness 501.3
brightness 1025.4
v glower 27.16
blind 30.7
show 31.4
show resentment 152.14
be manifest 348.7
cut a dash 501.13
shine 1025.23
glaring distinct 31.7
garish 35.20
downright 247.12
conspicuous 348.12
gaudy 501.20
bright 1025.32
glass
n lens 29.2
telescope 29.4
mirror 29.6
container 195.1
smoothness 287.3
weather instrument 317.8
jewelry 498.5
ceramic ware 742.2
basketball 747.1
thermometer 1019.20
transparent substance 1029.2
fragility 1050.2
v face 295.23
adj glassy 1029.5
glasses tableware 8.12
spectacles 29.3
glassmaking 712.3
glassy sleek 287.11
inexpressive 522.20
shiny 1025.33
glass 1029.5
glaucoma 30.1
glaze
n sweets 10.40
polish 287.2
ceramics 742.3
ice 1023.5
v color 35.14
sweeten 66.3
polish 287.7
face 295.23
pot 742.6
hail 1023.11
glazed sleek 287.11
inexpressive 522.20
ceramic 742.7
gleam
n hint 248.4
shine 1025.2
ray 1025.5
flash 1025.6
v burst forth 33.9

be somebody 662.10
shine 1025.23
glean select 371.14
collect 472.11
conclude 946.10
harvest 1069.19
glebe land 234.1
benefice 698.9
parsonage 703.7
glee happiness 95.2
merriment 109.5
glee club
part music 708.18
chorus 710.16
glen highland 237.7
valley 284.9
glib
v talkative 540.9
adj suave 504.18
eloquent 544.8
easy 1014.13
glide
n coasting 177.16
maneuvers 184.13
slide 194.4
speech sound 524.12
v coast 177.35
float 182.54
fly 184.36
slide 194.9
elapse 821.5
go easily 1014.10
adj phonetic 524.30
glider 181.12
glimmer
n hint 551.4
glitter 1025.7
v glitter 1025.24
glimmering
n hint 551.4
slight knowledge 930.6
glitter 1025.7
adj glittering 1025.35
glimpse
n glance 27.4
slight knowledge
930.6
v see 27.12
glance 27.17
glint
n shine 1025.2
flash 1025.6
v glance 27.17
shine 1025.23
glissade
n slide 194.4
v glide 177.35
slide 194.9
glisten
n glitter 1025.7
v glitter 1025.24
glitch
impairment 393.1
abortion 410.5
fault 1003.2
glitter
n showiness 501.3
glimmer 1025.7
v cut a dash 501.13
be somebody 662.10
glimmer 1025.24

glitz
appearance 33.2
garishness 35.5
finery 498.3
showiness 501.3
grandiloquence 545.1
gloat gaze 27.15
exult 502.9
glob lump 257.10
sphere 282.2
global
spherical 282.9
comprehensive 772.7
complete 794.9
universal 864.14
unqualified 960.2
global ecosystem 1073.1
globe
n sphere 282.2
lamp shade 1028.3
Earth 1072.10
v ball 282.7
globe-trotter 178.1
globule sphere 282.2
bubble 320.1
gloom
n gloominess 112.7
shadow 1027.3
somberness 1027.4
v look sullen 110.15
eclipse 1027.9
grow dark 1027.12
gloom and doom dejection
112.3
despair 125.2
gloomy dismal 112.24
pessimistic 125.16
ominous 133.17
cloudy 319.8
gloomful 1027.14
gloppy filthy 80.23
viscous 1062.12
glorified
eminent 662.18
angelic 679.6
heavenly 681.12
sanctified 685.8
glorify approve 509.12
glamorize 662.13
sanctify 685.5
praise 696.12
glorious
intoxicated 88.31
eminent 247.9
grandiose 501.21
illustrious 662.19
almighty 677.17
superb 999.15
gorgeous 1016.21
glory
n radiation 171.2
eminence 247.2
circle 280.2
grandeur 501.5
praise 509.5
honor 646.1
repute 662.1
illustriousness 662.6
glorification 696.2
notability 997.2
brightness 1025.4

accumulation 770.9
piece 793.3
go back on
abandon 370.5
repeal 445.2
be unfaithful 645.12
gobble gulp 8.23
bird sound 60.5
ingest 187.11
consume 388.3
destroy 395.10
gluttonize 672.4
gobbledygook
nonsense 520.2
Greek 522.7
jargon 523.9
bombast 545.2
political jargon 609.37
gobbler
male animal 76.8
poultry 311.29
glutton 672.3
gobble up
consume 388.3
destroy 395.10
monopolize 469.6
kid oneself 954.6
go between
interpose 213.6
be instrumental 384.7
mediate 466.6
go-between
intermediary 213.4
interpreter 341.7
messenger 353.1
instrument 384.4
mediator 466.3
middleman 576.4
goblin fairy 678.8
hobgoblin 680.8
gobs lot 247.4
wealth 618.3
go by be called 527.13
elapse 821.5
conform 867.3
pass 910.8
god hero 659.5
deus 678.2
goddesses 678.4
God 677.2
god-awful 1000.8
God bless! 696.18
God bless me! 122.21
God bless you! 188.22
goddam it! 513.11
goddess hero 659.5
deity 678.2
god 678.4
God-fearing
godly 692.9
belief 953.21
God forbid
by no means 335.9
Heaven forbid! 510.27
O Lord! 696.18
godforsaken
available 222.15
out-of-the-way 261.9
forlorn 584.12
God knows! 930.19
godless ungodly 695.17

unregenerate 695.18
godlike great 247.9
eminent 662.18
superhuman 677.16
divine 678.16
godly 692.9
godliness
virtue 653.1
deity 677.1
sanctity 685.1
godlikeness 692.2
godly virtuous 653.6
divine 677.16
godlike 692.9
godown 386.6
go down
capsize 182.44
descend 194.5
sink 194.6
plunge 367.8
decline 393.17
fail 410.11
lose 412.12
play 745.5
fight 754.4
occur 831.5
find credence 953.20
go downhill
weaken 16.9
descend 194.5
incline 204.10
decline 393.17
sink 410.11
fall on evil days 1011.11
go down the tubes regress 163.5
go to waste 473.6
godparent 438.6
godsend boon 472.7
good thing 999.5
Godspeed
n leave-taking 188.4
interj farewell! 188.22
go Dutch
pay for 624.18
bisect 875.4
God willing 966.11
go easy
v swim with the stream
1014.12
interj careful! 494.14
phrs easy does it 175.15
go easy on take pity on 145.4
indulge 427.5
gofer
subordinate 432.5
attendant 577.5
go for love 104.20
head for 161.9
fetch 176.16
pass for 349.10
intend 380.4
abet 449.14
attack 459.15
kid oneself 954.6
go for broke
n call to arms 458.8
v be determined 359.8
persevere 360.7
do one's best 403.14
do to perfection 407.7
court danger 493.6

risk 972.12
go for it
attempt 403.7
do one's best 403.14
go-getter 330.8
go-getting 330.7
goggle
n gaze 27.5
v gaze 27.15
squint 28.9
bulge 283.11
adj bulged 283.16
goggles spectacles 29.3
safeguard 1008.3
eyeshade 1028.2
go in for practice 328.8
adopt 371.15
undertake 404.3
study to be 570.15
specialize 866.4
going-over
apostasy 363.2
iteration 849.2
disapproval 510.6
going rate 630.2
goings-on
behavior 321.1
activity 330.1
affairs 831.4
going steady 104.6
go into enter 189.7
undertake 404.3
participate 476.5
discuss 541.12
write upon 556.5
join 617.14
compose 796.3
embark on 818.9
elaborate 861.6
investigate 938.23
gold
n yellowness 43.1
wealth 618.1
money 728.1
precious metals 728.20
adj yellow 43.4
brass 1058.17
goldbrick
n slowpoke 175.5
idler 331.8
neglecter 340.5
confidence game 356.10
shirker 368.3
v leave undone 340.7
shirk 368.9
golden yellow 43.4
auspicious 133.18
precious 632.10
melodious 708.48
superb 999.15
brass 1058.17
Golden Age 824.5
golden days 1010.4
golden mean
mean 246.1
middle course 467.3
temperance 668.1
moderation 670.1
golden parachute 624.4
golden rule
rule 419.2

ethical philosophy 636.2
axiom 974.2
gold mine
source of supply 386.4
rich source 618.4
mine 1058.6
gold-plated
plated 295.33
expensive 632.11
brass 1058.17
gold rush 1058.8
golf
n sports 751
the royal and ancient 751.1
v play 745.5
golf course
green 310.7
playground 743.11
golf 751.1
golly! 513.12
Gomorrah 654.7
gonads 2.13
gondolier 183.5
gone weak 16.12
tired 21.8
burnt-out 21.10
away 34.4
past hope 125.15
departed 188.19
absent 222.11
dead 307.30
used up 388.5
lost 473.7
no more 762.11
past 837.7
goner 125.8
gong
n bell 54.4
marker 517.10
v ring 54.8
goo sentimentality 93.8
semiliquid 1062.5
good
n utility 387.3
welfare 999.4
adj tasty 63.8
healthful 81.5
pleasant 97.6
auspicious 133.18
kind 143.13
skillful 413.22
praiseworthy 509.20
right 637.3
honest 644.13
just 649.8
virtuous 653.6
almighty 677.17
godly 692.9
solvent 729.18
valid 973.14
genuine 973.15
sufficient 991.6
expedient 995.5
excellent 999.12
adv kindly 143.18
interj yes! 332.18
bravo! 509.22
the good 692.5
good at 413.27
good-bye
n leave-taking 188.4

interj farewell! 188.22
good day 585.15
good enough
  adj acceptable 107.12
  sufficient 991.6
  tolerable 999.20
  interj yes! 332.18
  bravo! 509.22
good faith 644.7
good for
  healthful 81.5
  useful 387.18
  helpful 449.21
  priced 630.14
  solvent 729.18
good-for-nothing
  n bum 331.9
  wretch 660.2
  adj indolent 331.19
  worthless 391.11
good-looking 1016.19
good luck chance 972.1
  happy fortune 1010.2
good-luck charm 691.5
goodly pleasant 97.6
  large 257.16
  good 999.12
  comely 1016.19
good-natured 143.14
goodness
  n savoriness 63.1
  healthfulness 81.1
  pleasantness 97.1
  kindness 143.1
  propriety 637.2
  probity 644.1
  virtue 653.1
  godliness 692.2
  good quality 999
  excellence 999.1
  interj my! 122.21
goods material 4.1
  freight 176.6
  property 471.1
  merchandise 735.1
the goods ability 18.2
  talent 413.4
  information 551.1
  what's what 973.4
good Samaritan 592.1
good shape
  healthiness 83.2
  orderliness 807.3
  good looks 1016.4
good time merriment 109.5
  period of pleasure 95.5
goodwill
  benevolence 143.4
  willingness 324.1
  patronage 449.4
  good terms 587.3
  custom 731.6
goody-goody
  n effeminate male 77.11
  prude 500.11
  adj hypocritical 354.33
  overnice 500.18
  sanctimonious 693.5
gooey
  sentimental 93.21
  viscous 1062.12

goof
  n bungler 414.9
  fool 924.3
  boo-boo 975.6
  v miss 410.14
  bungle 414.12
  make a boner 975.15
go off blast 56.8
  avoid 164.6
  diverge 171.5
  depart 188.6
  decline 393.17
  succeed 409.7
  explode 671.14
  occur 831.5
goof off
  dawdle 175.8
  idle 331.12
  leave undone 340.7
  shirk 368.9
goof-off
  slowpoke 175.5
  idler 331.8
  neglecter 340.5
goofy
  foolish 923.9
  crazy 926.27
  eccentric 927.6
gook
  Caucasian 312.3
  semiliquid 1062.5
goon
  strong man 15.7
  combatant 461.1
  ruffian 593.4
  follower 616.8
  violent person 671.10
  striker 727.7
go on
  be angry 152.15
  progress 162.2
  depart 188.6
  behave 321.4
  persevere 360.2
  manage 409.12
  chatter 540.5
  rage 671.11
  be in a certain state 765.5
  create disorder 810.11
  elapse 821.5
  endure 827.6
  linger on 827.7
  occur 831.5
  continue 856.3
  persist 856.5
go on about
  be enthusiastic 101.7
  protract 538.8
  persist 856.5
go on and on
  have no limit 823.2
  linger on 827.7
  last forever 829.6
go one better
  excel 249.6
  outwit 415.11
  surpass 999.11
go one-on-one with
  confront 451.5
  defy 454.3
  brave 492.11

  surpass 999.11
go on with 856.5
goose
  n poultry 311.29
  gambling wheel 759.16
  silly 924.6
  v goad 375.15
goose bumps
  creeps 74.4
  trepidation 127.5
  roughness 288.2
  cold 1023.2
goose egg 762.3
goose step
  march 177.13
  conformity 867.1
goose-step
  v march 177.30
  follow the rule 867.4
  adj unpremeditated 365.11
  habitual 373.14
go out extend 158.9
  exit 190.12
  reach out 261.5
  die 307.19
  obsolesce 390.9
  strike 727.10
  come to an end 820.6
  burn out 1022.8
go out for
  practice 328.8
  undertake 404.3
  play 744.2
go over
  traverse 177.20
  apostatize 363.7
  succeed 409.7
  study 570.12
  rehearse 704.32
  iterate 849.8
  grill 938.22
  examine 938.23
go overboard
  go by the board 182.45
  overdo 993.10
go over one's head
  be incomprehensible 522.10
  not understand 522.11
  escape notice 984.5
go over the top 193.11
gore
  n blood 2.25
  insert 191.2
  killing 308.1
  v perforate 292.15
  horn 459.26
gorge
  n digestive system 2.18
  valley 237.7
  obstruction 293.3
  v stuff 8.25
  gluttonize 672.4
  overload 993.15
  satiate 994.4
gorgeous
  colorful 35.19
  gaudy 501.20
  ravishing 1016.21
Gorgon 690.9
gorilla strong man 15.7

  killer 308.11
  combatant 461.1
  ruffian 593.4
  violent person 671.10
gormandize 672.4
gormandizer 672.3
go round move 172.5
  surround 209.6
  recur 850.5
  circle 914.5
  rotate 915.9
go-round
  periodicity 850.2
  circuit 914.2
gory
  circulatory 2.33
  sanguine 41.7
  murderous 308.24
  bloodstained 1004.11
gosh! 513.12
gosling
  fledgling 302.10
  poultry 311.29
gospel
  n good news 552.2
  system of belief 953.3
  the truth 973.3
  the real thing 973.4
  adj scriptural 683.11
  true 973.13
the Gospel 683.4
gossamer
  n filament 271.1
  lightness 298.2
  adj dainty 248.7
  thin 270.16
  threadlike 271.7
  smooth 294.8
  unsubstantial 764.6
  chimeric 986.22
  transparent 1029.4
gossip
  n chatter 540.3
  talk 552.7
  newsmonger 552.9
  companion 588.3
  inquisitive person 981.2
  v chatter 540.5
  chat 541.10
  talk over the back fence 552.12
Gothic
  unrefined 497.12
  antiquated 842.13
  unlearned 930.14
  fanciful 986.20
go through
  penetrate 189.8
  carry out 328.7
  squander 486.3
  spend 626.5
  rehearse 704.32
  experience 831.8
  iterate 849.8
  search 938.31
  freeze 1023.10
go through with
  take action 328.5
  carry through 360.5
  endure 827.6
go together 788.6

go to hell
  go to ruin 395.24
  be damned 682.7
go to it 725.15
go to one's head
  intoxicate 88.22
  puff up 140.7
  addle the wits 926.23
  dizzy 985.8
go to pieces
  weaken 16.9
  lose self-control 128.7
  decay 393.22
  be destroyed 395.22
  come apart 802.9
go to pot
  go to ruin 395.24
  go to waste 473.6
  go bankrupt 625.7
  fall on evil days 1011.11
go to press 548.18
go to the dogs
  go to ruin 395.24
  go bankrupt 625.7
  fall on evil days 1011.11
go to the wall
  die 307.20
  go to ruin 395.24
  fail 410.9
  go bankrupt 625.7
gouge
  n indentation 284.6
  furrow 290.1
  v blind 30.7
  excavate 284.15
  furrow 290.3
  deceive 356.19
  overprice 632.7
gouge out
  extract 192.10
  excavate 284.15
  perforate 292.15
goulash 10.11
go under
  go to ruin 395.24
  sink 410.11
  lose 412.12
  go bankrupt 625.7
go up against
  encounter 457.15
  engage 457.16
go up in smoke
  disappear 34.2
  come to nothing 410.13
  go to waste 473.6
  flit 828.6
  fall through 911.3
  burn up 1020.25
gourmand eater 8.16
  connoisseur 496.7
  sensualist 663.3
  glutton 672.3
gourmet
  n eater 8.16
  connoisseur 496.7
  sensualist 663.3
  adj edible 8.33
  tasty 63.8
gout 85.22
goût taste 62.1
  savor 63.2

govern
  restrain 428.7
  direct 573.8
  regulate 612.12
  exercise influence 894.8
governance
  authority 417.5
  direction 573.1
  government 612.1
  protectorship 1008.2
governess
  teacher 571.2
  mistress 575.2
  chaperon 1008.7
government
  region 231.5
  authority 417.5
  direction 573.1
  political science 609.2
  administration 612.1
  governance 612.1
  protectorship 1008.2
governor
  jailer 429.10
  father 560.9
  director 574.1
  ruler 575.6
  administrator 575.13
  safeguard 1008.3
  guardian 1008.6
  system component 1041.14
governor-general 575.13
governorship
  mastership 417.7
  directorship 573.4
go with
  stay near 223.12
  take action 328.5
  concur 332.9
  choose 371.13
  undertake 404.3
  accompany 769.7
  agree 788.6
  go along with 899.3
go without 668.7
go with the flow
  be content 107.5
  take it easy 331.15
  follow the fashion 578.10
gown
  n garment 5.3
  dress 5.16
  robe 702.2
  v cloak 5.40
go wrong
  be disappointing 132.3
  get out of order 393.25
  go to ruin 395.24
  miscarry 410.15
  stray 654.9
  misbelieve 688.8
  err 975.9
goy 688.6
grab
  n seizure 480.2
  v jump at 101.6
  acquire 472.9
  seize 480.14
  capture 480.18
  usurp 640.8
  play 745.5

impress 931.19
  engross 983.13
grab bag lottery 759.14
  hodgepodge 797.6
grace
  n delightfulness 97.2
  benevolence 143.4
  act of kindness 143.7
  pity 145.1
  pardon 148.2
  thanks 150.2
  skill 413.1
  benefit 478.7
  taste 496.1
  elegance 533.1
  fluency 544.2
  reprieve 601.3
  conscience 636.5
  function of Holy Ghost
    677.15
  sanctification 685.3
  prayer 696.4
  ornament 709.18
  goodness 999.1
  beauty 1016.1
  v ornament 498.8
  honor 662.12
  beautify 1016.16
graceful skillful 413.22
  agile 413.23
  tasteful 496.9
  courteous 504.14
  elegant 533.6
  fluent 544.9
  beautiful 1016.18
graceless
  bungling 414.20
  inelegant 534.2
  irreclaimable 654.18
  unregenerate 695.18
  ungraceful 1015.9
the Graces 1016.10
grace with 478.17
gracile thin 270.16
  tasteful 496.9
  elegant 533.6
  beautiful 1016.18
gracious
  adj pleasant 97.6
  kind 143.13
  indulgent 427.8
  liberal 485.4
  elegant 496.9
  courteous 504.14
  informal 581.3
  hospitable 585.11
  interj my! 122.21
gradation
  graduation 245.3
  phonetics 524.13
  class 607.1
  continuity 807.2
  grouping 808.3
  series 812.2
grade
  n incline 204.4
  degree 245.1
  student 572.11
  class 607.1
  category 809.2
  v level 201.6

  incline 204.10
  graduate 245.4
  size 257.15
  smooth 287.5
  order 807.4
  group 808.11
  classify 809.6
grade school 567.3
gradient rising 200.5
  incline 204.4
gradual slow 175.10
  gradational 245.5
graduate
  n expert 413.11
  alumnus 572.8
  v grade 245.4
  size 257.15
  measure 300.10
  improve 392.7
  succeed 409.7
  promote 446.2
  adj scholastic 568.19
  studentlike 572.12
graduation
  gradation 245.3
  promotion 446.1
  ceremony 580.4
graffito inscription 546.5
  drawing 712.13
graft
  n insertion 191.1
  inlay 191.2
  fraud 356.8
  bribery 378.1
  theft 482.1
  booty 482.11
  politics 609.34
  spoils of office 609.35
  v engraft 191.6
  fasten 800.7
grain
  n feed 10.4
  modicum 248.2
  minute 258.7
  texture 294.1
  grass 310.5
  seed 310.31
  nature 767.4
  kind 809.3
  disposition 978.3
  granule 1051.6
  v color 35.14
  coarsen 294.4
  pulverize 1051.9
  powder 1051.10
grain of salt 959.1
grammar
  rules of language 530.1
  diction 532.1
  textbook 554.10
  basics 818.6
grammarian 523.15
grammar school
  elementary school 567.3
  secondary school 567.4
grammatical
  linguistic 523.19
  syntactical 530.17
gramps old man 304.2
  grandfather 560.14
granary 386.7

grand
n money 728.7
thousand 882.10
adj dignified 136.12
great 247.6
large 257.16
grandiose 501.21
lofty 544.14
eminent 662.18
important 997.17
good 999.12
grandeur
proud bearing 136.2
greatness 247.1
sizableness 257.6
grandness 501.5
loftiness 544.6
distinction 662.5
grandfather
n old man 304.2
grandsire 560.13
v exempt 430.14
grandfather clause 430.8
grandiloquence
exaggeration 355.1
pompousness 501.7
long word 526.10
style 532.2
grandiosity 545
magniloquence 545.1
grandiose grand 501.21
grandiloquent 545.8
grandiosity
sizableness 257.6
grandeur 501.5
grandiloquence 545.1
grand-juror 596.7
grandmother
old woman 304.3
grandam 560.15
grand slam score 409.5
victory 411.1
bridge 758.3
grandstand
n observation post 27.8
baseball 745.1
v exercise skill 413.20
show off 501.16
grange farmstead 228.6
farm 1069.8
granite
hardness 1046.6
rock 1059.1
granny
old woman 304.3
fussbudget 495.7
grandmother 560.16
back number 842.8
grant
n concession 443.5
giving 478.1
subsidy 478.8
privilege 642.2
qualification 959.1
v acknowledge 332.11
confess 351.7
consent 441.2
permit 443.9
give 478.12
suppose 951.10
allow for 959.5

granular
infinitesimal 258.14
rough 294.6
grainy 1051.12
granulated
unsmooth 288.6
rough 294.6
hardened 1046.13
granular 1051.12
granulation
unsmoothness 288.1
roughness 294.2
television reception 1035.5
hardening 1046.5
granularity 1051.2
pulverization 1051.4
granule
modicum 248.2
grain 1051.6
grapevine plant 310.4
gossip 551.5
report 552.6
news channel 552.10
graph
n diagram 381.3
letter 546.1
drawing 712.13
outline 801.4
v plot 381.10
itemize 801.7
graphic
representational 349.13
descriptive 349.14
expressive 544.10
written 547.22
pictorial 712.21
graphic arts
printing 548.1
visual arts 712.1
graphics 713.1
graphite 1056.2
grapple
n hold 474.2
v contend 457.13
hold 474.6
seize 480.14
fasten 800.7
grapple with
contest 451.4
contend 457.13
engage with 457.17
brave 492.11
grasp
n hold 474.2
control 612.2
handle 901.11
understanding 928.3
v hold 474.6
seize 480.14
understand 521.7
cohere 803.6
know 928.12
grasping
n greed 100.8
adj greedy 100.27
demanding 421.9
acquisitive 472.15
retentive 474.8
rapacious 480.26
selfish 651.5
graspy greedy 100.27

acquisitive 472.15
rapacious 480.26
selfish 651.5
grass
n marijuana 87.11
gramineous plant 310.5
grassland 310.8
tennis 748.1
v feed 8.18
grasshopper
n locust 311.36
jumper 366.4
adj improvident 406.15
grassland
the country 233.1
land 234.1
plain 236.1
grass 310.8
farm 1069.8
grass roots
bottom 199.1
the country 233.1
source 886.5
grass-roots basic 199.8
populational 606.8
simple 798.6
grassy green 44.4
verdant 310.42
grate
n network 170.3
arranger 808.5
fire iron 1020.12
v pain 26.7
rasp 58.10
sound a sour note 61.3
irritate 96.14
net 170.7
abrade 1044.7
pulverize 1051.9
grateful pleasant 97.6
thankful 150.5
welcome 585.12
grate on jar on 58.11
irritate 96.14
get on one's nerves 128.9
gratify feed 8.18
satisfy 95.8
content 107.4
make proud 136.6
indulge 427.6
gratifying
pleasant 97.6
welcome 585.12
grating
n network 170.3
arranger 808.5
fire iron 1020.12
pulverization 1051.4
adj irritating 26.13
jarring 58.16
dissonant 61.4
unnerving 128.15
disagreeing 789.6
gratis
adj gratuitous 634.5
adv as a gift 478.27
gratuitously 634.6
gratitude
thankfulness 150
gratefulness 150.1

gratuitous
impudent 142.10
voluntary 324.7
given 478.24
gratis 634.5
unordered 810.12
superfluous 993.17
gratuity bribe 378.2
largess 478.5
costlessness 634.1
surplus 993.5
grave
n death 307.1
tomb 309.16
monument 549.12
v record 549.15
engrave 713.9
sculpture 715.5
fix in the mind 989.18
adj painful 26.10
dark 38.9
deep 54.11
sedate 106.14
solemn 111.3
gloomy 112.24
dignified 136.12
great 247.6
heavy 297.16
lofty 544.14
ceremonious 580.8
base 661.12
weighty 997.20
the grave
hell 682.1
destiny 839.2
gravedigger 309.8
gravel
n pavement 383.6
grain 1051.6
shingle 1059.3
v irritate 96.14
graven
engraved 713.11
sculptured 715.7
established 855.13
graveness
darkness 38.2
gravity 997.3
graveyard 309.15
gravidity 78.5
gravitate
descend 194.5
drop 297.15
lean 896.3
gravitation
descent 194.1
weight 297.5
attraction 907.1
gravity
sedateness 106.4
solemnity 111.1
gloom 112.7
proud bearing 136.2
weight 297.5
loftiness 544.6
formality 580.1
attraction 907.1
importance 997.1
graveness 997.3
weight 297.1
gravy find 472.6

gratuity 478.5
bonus 624.6

gray
n grayness 39.1
horse 311.11
v grizzle 39.3
adj colorless 36.7
ashen 39.4
gloomy 112.24
aged 303.16
same 781.6

gray area
middle course 467.3
ambiguity 539.1
gamble 971.8

graybeard
silver-haired person 39.2
old man 304.2

gray-haired
gray-headed 39.5
aged 303.16

gray matter
intellect 919.1
brain 919.6

graze
n touch 73.1
contact 223.5
v feed 8.18
feed on 8.28
touch lightly 73.7
contact 223.10
tap 902.18
abrade 1044.7

grazing
n eating 8.1
touch 73.1
grassland 310.8
abrasion 1044.2
animal husbandry 1070.1
adj in contact 223.17

grease
n gratuity 478.5
flattery 511.1
money 728.2
oil 1056.1
v smooth 287.5
bribe 378.3
facilitate 1014.7
oil 1056.8

grease monkey
aircraftsman 185.6
mechanic 1040.12

greasepaint
theater 704.17
makeup 1016.12

greaser 232.7

grease the palm
bribe 375.23
pay off 378.3
pay 624.16

grease the wheels
facilitate 1014.7
oil 1056.8

greasy
slippery 287.12
oily 1056.9

greasy spoon 8.17

great
n skillful person 413.14
keyboard 711.17

adj pregnant 78.18
grand 247.6
chief 249.14
large 257.16
authoritative 417.15
magnanimous 652.6
eminent 662.18
important 997.17
excellent 999.13
interj bravo! 509.22

the great 997.8

great-coat 5.13

Great Divide
middle of nowhere 261.4
watershed 272.5

greathearted
benevolent 143.15
liberal 485.4
courageous 492.17
magnanimous 652.6

greed
greediness 100.8
selfishness 651.1
gluttony 672.1

greedy
avaricious 100.27
acquisitive 472.15
selfish 651.5
gluttonous 672.6

Greek gibberish 522.7
member 617.11

green
n greenness 44.1
verdigris 44.3
lawn 310.7
money 728.2
lawn bowling 750.3
golf 751.1
adj virid 44.4
sour 67.5
fresh 83.13
jealous 153.5
young 301.10
immature 406.11
inexperienced 414.17
new 841.7
ignorant 930.12
gullible 954.9
remembered 989.23

greenbacks 728.6

Green Berets 461.15

greenery 310.1

greenhorn
n dupe 358.1
incompetent 414.7
novice 572.9
newcomer 774.4
beginner 818.2
ignoramus 930.12
adj unaccustomed 374.4

greenhouse
summerhouse 228.12
nursery 1069.11

Greenland
continent 235.1
remote region 261.4
cold place 1023.4

green light
permission 443.1
signal 517.15
traffic light 1026.4

the green light
start 188.2
ratification 332.4

green plant 310.3

greenroom
anteroom 197.20
stage 704.16

greens
vegetables 10.35
salad 10.37
plants 310.1

green thumb 1069.12

green with jealousy 153.5

greet
n weeping 115.2
v weep 115.12
address 524.26
hail 585.10

greeter 585.5

greeting remark 524.3
salutation 585.4

greetings
n welcome 186.4
regards 504.8
salutations 585.3
interj salutations! 585.15

gregarious
talkative 540.9
sociable 582.22

Gregorian chant 708.20

gremlin
fairy 678.8
imp 680.7

grenadier
longlegs 272.7
infantryman 461.9

greyhound 174.6

grid
n network 170.3
stage 704.16
fire iron 1020.12
television reception 1035.5
v net 170.7

griddle
n fire iron 1020.12
v cook 11.5

griddlecake 10.45

gridiron
network 170.3
stage 704.16
playground 743.11
football 746.1
fire iron 1020.12

gridlock
obstruction 293.3
hindrance 1012.1

grief pain 96.5
wretchedness 96.6
distressfulness 98.5
sorrow 112.10
regret 113.1
misfortune 1011.2

grievance
affliction 96.8
complaint 115.4
objection 333.2
injustice 650.4
evil 1000.3
bane 1001.1

grieve
pain 96.17

distress 98.14
sorrow 112.17
aggrieve 112.19
lament 115.10
move 145.5
offend 152.21

grieving
n lamentation 115.1
adj lamenting 115.18

grievous
distressing 98.20
sorrowful 112.26
pitiful 145.8
terrible 1000.9
disastrous 1011.15

griffin 647.2

grift fraud 356.8
stratagem 415.3
cheating 759.13

grill
n restaurant 8.17
dish 10.7
inquisition 938.13
fire iron 1020.12
v cook 11.5
torture 604.16
put on the grill 938.22

grille 170.3

grilling
n cooking 11.2
the grill 938.13
adj hot 1019.25

grim
pleasureless 96.20
horrid 98.19
sullen 110.24
solemn 111.3
unhappy 112.21
gloomy 112.24
hopeless 125.12
terrible 127.30
harsh 144.24
unyielding 361.9
strict 425.6
bad 1000.8
unprepossessing 1015.7

grimace
n scowl 110.9
wry face 265.4
shake 917.3
v suffer 26.8
shudder at 99.5
look sullen 110.15
make a face 265.8
overact 704.31

grime
n dirt 80.6
v dirty 80.15

Grim Reaper 307.3

grimy dingy 38.11
dirty 80.22

grin
n smile 116.3
v smile 116.7

grin and bear it
be of good cheer 109.10
accept 134.7
submit 433.6

grinch
killjoy 112.14
spoilsport 1012.9

grind
  n rasp 58.3
  routine 373.5
  study 570.3
  swotter 572.10
  work 725.4
  drudge 726.3
  bookworm 929.4
  v chew 8.27
  pain 26.7
  grate 58.10
  sharpen 285.7
  file 287.8
  study 570.12
  domineer 612.16
  drudge 725.14
  shatter 802.13
  abrade 1044.7
  pulverize 1051.9
grind in
  urge 375.14
  inculcate 568.12
grinding
  n study 570.3
  abrasion 1044.2
  pulverization 1051.4
  adj irritating 26.13
  grating 58.16
  oppressive 98.24
  imperious 417.16
  laboring 725.17
  abrasive 1044.10
grind one's teeth 152.14
gringo 774.3
grip
  n acrimony 17.5
  skill 413.1
  governance 417.5
  hold 474.2
  control 612.2
  game 748.2
  game or string 750.2
  handle 901.11
  spasm 917.6
  understanding 928.3
  v hold 474.6
  seize 480.14
  obsess 926.25
  engross 983.13
gripe
  n ache 26.5
  complaint 115.5
  control 612.2
  indigence 619.2
  v pain 26.7
  annoy 96.13
  be discontented 108.6
  complain 115.16
  seize 480.14
gripped
  obsessed 926.33
  held 983.18
gripping
  retentive 474.8
  obsessive 926.34
  engrossing 983.20
grisly
  terrible 127.30
  deathly 307.29
  hideous 1015.11
grist 386.2

gristle 1049.2
grit
  n pluck 359.3
  fortitude 492.6
  grain 1051.6
  v irritate 96.14
grit one's teeth 359.8
grits food 10.2
  powder 1051.5
gritty rough 294.6
  plucky 359.14
  fearless 492.19
  hard 1046.10
  granular 1051.12
  stony 1059.12
grizzled white 37.7
  gray 39.4
grizzly bear 110.11
groan
  n rasp 58.3
  lament 115.3
  complaint 115.4
  v sound harshly 58.9
  wail 115.13
  complain 115.15
  sigh 318.21
groaning board 8.9
groceries
  food 10.2
  provisions 10.5
  grocery 735.7
grog
  n spirits 88.13
  v tipple 88.24
groggy
  unsteady 16.16
  inert 173.14
  dazed 985.14
groin fork 171.4
  buttress 901.4
  harbor 1009.6
  barrier 1012.5
groom
  n newlywed 563.5
  stockman 1070.2
  v dress 79.20
  train 568.13
  tidy 808.12
  tend 1070.7
groomed 405.16
groomsman
  wedding party 563.4
  assistant 616.6
groove
  n crack 224.2
  furrow 290.1
  routine 373.5
  path 383.2
  type 548.6
  race 756.3
  v cleave 224.4
  excavate 284.15
  furrow 290.3
  engrave 713.9
groove on 95.13
groovy
  adj knowledgeable 928.17
  excellent 999.13
  interj goody! 95.21
grope contact 223.10
  feel one's way 938.32

  be uncertain 971.9
gross
  n gain 472.3
  receipts 627.1
  round 751.3
  v profit 472.12
  yield 627.4
  adj nasty 64.7
  filthy 80.23
  offensive 98.18
  downright 247.12
  corpulent 257.18
  thick 269.8
  rough 294.6
  luxuriant 310.43
  coarse 497.11
  ill-bred 505.6
  inelegant 534.2
  base 661.12
  carnal 663.6
  vulgar 666.8
  whole 792.9
  stupid 922.15
  bad 1000.8
  terrible 1000.9
gross out offend 98.11
  repel 99.6
grotesque
  n work of art 712.10
  adj deformed 265.12
  freakish 870.13
  absurd 923.11
  fanciful 986.20
  unshapely 1015.8
grotto 284.5
grouch
  n malcontent 108.4
  sorehead 110.11
  complainer 115.9
  spoilsport 1012.9
  v be discontented 108.6
  sulk 110.14
  complain 115.16
grouchy
  discontented 108.8
  irascible 110.20
  complaining 115.20
ground
  n color 35.8
  station 159.2
  ground covering 199.3
  bed 199.4
  horizontal 201.3
  setting 209.2
  enclosed place (enclosure) 212.3
  region 231.1
  land 234.1
  ocean depths 275.4
  motive 375.1
  arena 463.1
  warrant 600.6
  art equipment 712.18
  cause 886.1
  foundation 901.6
  premise 935.7
  evidence 957.1
  v establish 159.16
  shipwreck 182.42
  limit 210.5
  restrict 428.9

  confine 429.12
  teach 568.10
  play 745.5
  fix 855.9
  fell 913.5
  insulate 1032.29
  adj bottom 199.7
  powdery 1051.11
grounder 745.3
ground floor
  floor 197.23
  earliness 845.1
groundhog
  black clouds 133.6
  excavator 284.10
  wild animal 311.23
grounding
  preparation 405.1
  elementary education 568.5
groundless
  unsubstantial 764.8
  baseless 936.13
  unproved 958.8
grounds nearness 223.1
  dregs 256.2
  green 310.7
  real estate 471.6
  warrant 600.6
  cause 886.1
  foundation 901.6
  evidence 957.1
  condition 959.2
group
  n amount 244.2
  association 617.1
  clique 617.6
  sect 675.3
  orchestra 710.12
  company 770.3
  bunch 770.7
  set 784.5
  class 809.2
  v size 257.15
  assemble 770.18
  analyze 801.8
  arrange 808.11
  classify 809.6
groupie fan 101.5
  idolater 697.4
grouping
  association 617.1
  treatment 712.9
  company 770.3
  bunch 770.7
  analysis 801.3
  arrangement 808.3
  classification 809.1
  class 809.2
grouse
  n complaint 115.5
  v be discontented 108.6
  complain 115.16
grouser
  malcontent 108.4
  complainer 115.9
grout 295.25
grove
  valley 284.9
  woodlet 310.14
  bunch 770.7
grovel fawn 138.7

creep 177.26
lie 201.5
lie low 274.5
bow down 433.10
be promiscuous 665.19
bow 913.9
wallow 915.13
grow develop 14.2
increase 251.6
expand 259.7
grow up 272.12
mature 303.9
vegetate 310.34
become 761.12
evolve 861.5
process 892.9
farm 1069.16
raise 1070.6
growl
n reverberation 54.2
boom 56.4
rasp 58.3
v boom 56.9
sound harshly 58.9
snarl 60.4
complain 115.15
show resentment 152.14
sigh 318.21
speak 524.25
growling
n reverberation 54.2
adj reverberating 54.12
discontented 108.7
irascible 110.19
grown mature 14.3
full-grown 259.12
adult 303.12
produced 892.17
made 892.18
grownup 304.1
grown-up
mature 14.3
grown 259.12
adult 303.12
grow on one
enamor 104.23
become a habit 373.10
grow out of
overdevelop 14.2
expand 259.7
result from 887.5
growth
bodily development
14.1
symptom 85.9
neoplasm 85.39
gain 251.1
increase in size 259
development 259.3
maturation 303.6
stand 310.2
vegetation 310.32
business cycle 731.10
conversion 858.1
evolution 861.1
grow up mature 14.2
ascend 193.8
expand 259.7
grow 272.12
age 303.9
ripen 407.8

grub
n food 10.2
larva 302.12
drudge 726.3
v excavate 284.15
drudge 725.14
grubby dirty 80.22
slovenly 810.15
infested 910.11
grudge
n hostility 99.2
spite 589.5
v envy 154.3
refuse 325.3
deny 442.4
stint 484.5
grudging
n envy 154.1
adj envious 154.4
reluctant 325.6
niggardly 484.8
gruel
n symbol of weakness 16.7
thinness 270.7
semiliquid 1062.5
v weaken 16.10
grueling
weakening 16.20
fatiguing 21.13
punishing 604.23
laborious 725.18
troublesome 1013.18
gruesome
terrible 127.30
deathly 307.29
hideous 1015.11
gruff
raucous 58.15
irascible 110.19
brusque 505.7
grumble
n reverberation 54.2
thunder 56.4
rasp 58.3
v boom 56.9
sound harshly 58.9
growl 60.4
complain 115.15
grumbling
n reverberation 54.2
complaint 115.4
adj discontented 108.7
irascible 110.19
grump
n malcontent 108.4
sorehead 110.11
v be discontented 108.6
sulk 110.14
complain 115.16
Grundyism 579.1
grungy dirty 80.22
filthy 80.23
offensive 98.18
grunt
n animal noise 60.1
dogface 461.10
v snort 60.3
complain 115.15
speak 524.25
G-spot 75.5
G string 711.5

G-string
waistband 5.19
supporter 901.2
guacamole 10.9
guano feces 12.4
fertilizer 890.4
guarantee
n oath 334.4
promise 436.1
security 438.1
guarantor 438.6
v depose 334.6
promise 436.4
secure 438.9
protect 1008.18
guarantor
endorser 332.7
warrantor 438.6
guaranty
n security 438.1
guarantor 438.6
v secure 438.9
guard
n trainman 178.13
vigilance 339.4
jailer 429.10
defense 460.1
defender 460.7
football team 746.2
escort 769.5
protection 1008.1
safeguard 1008.3
guarder 1008.9
v preserve 397.8
restrain 428.7
defend 460.8
play 747.4
escort 769.8
protect 1008.18
guard against
defend 460.8
take precautions 494.6
guarded
vigilant 339.13
reticent 344.10
restrained 428.13
cautious 494.8
incredulous 956.4
protected 1008.21
guardian
n jailer 429.10
steward 574.4
familiar spirit 678.12
warden 1008.6
adj protective 1008.23
guardian angel
penitence 113.4
defender 460.7
conscience 636.5
familiar spirit 678.12
custodian 1008.6
gubernatorial 612.17
guerrilla
irregular 461.16
violent person 671.9
guerrilla warfare 458.1
guess
n conjecture 951.4
gamble 971.8
v solve 940.2
estimate 946.9

conjecture 951.11
think 953.11
predict 962.9
guesstimate 962.9
guesswork
supposition 951.3
guess 951.4
prediction 962.1
guest
n visitor 585.6
v entertain 585.8
guest house 228.15
guest room 197.7
guff bull 520.3
chatter 540.3
guffaw
n laughter 116.4
v laugh 116.8
guidance
navigation 159.3
advice 422.1
patronage 449.4
teaching 568.1
direction 573.1
protectorship 1008.2
guidance counselor 466.5
guide
n gutter 239.3
interpreter 341.7
adviser 422.3
pointer 517.4
teacher 571.1
guider 574.7
familiar spirit 678.12
escort 769.5
precursor 816.1
specter 988.1
v lead 165.2
pilot 182.14
advise 422.5
teach 568.10
steer 573.9
escort 769.8
go before 816.3
exercise influence 894.8
guidebook
information 551.1
handbook 554.8
directory 574.10
guide dog blind 30.6
dog 311.17
guideline plan 381.1
law 419.2
rule 869.4
guidepost pointer 517.4
guide 574.7
guild 617.3
guile deceit 356.3
cunning 415.1
guileful deceitful 356.22
cunning 415.12
shrewd 920.15
guileless
undeceptive 644.18
foolable 923.12
trusting 953.22
guillotine
n capital punishment 604.7
execution 605.5
legislative procedure 613.6
cloture 857.5

v execute 604.17
guilt culpability 656
  guiltiness 656.1
guiltless chaste 653.7
  innocent 657.6
guilty
  adj at fault 656.3
  adv shamefacedly 656.5
guinea pig
  wild animal 311.23
  subject 942.7
guise clothing 5.1
  aspect 33.3
  looks 33.4
  cover 295.2
  behavior 321.1
  pretext 376.1
  manner 384.1
  mode 765.4
guitarist 710.5
gulag 429.8
gulch valley 237.7
  watercourse 239.2
gulf crack 224.2
  eddy 238.12
  ocean 240.3
  cove 242
  inlet 242.1
  hole 275.2
  pit 284.4
  opening 292.1
gull
  n dupe 358.1
  v deceive 356.14
  cheat 356.18
  stultify 923.7
gullible foolable 923.12
  dupable 954.9
gullible person 358.1
Gulliver 178.2
gully
  n valley 237.7
  watercourse 239.2
  v furrow 290.3
gulp
  n breathing 2.21
  drink 8.4
  ingestion 187.4
  v gobble 8.23
  ingest 187.11
  gluttonize 672.4
gum
  n elastic 1048.3
  resin 1057.1
  chewing gum 1062.6
  v chew 8.27
  stick together 803.9
  hinder 1012.16
gumbo
  n semiliquid 1062.5
  mud 1062.8
  adj earthy 234.5
  viscous 1062.12
gummy
  adhesive 803.12
  resinous 1057.3
  viscous 1062.12
gumption 330.7
gumshoe
  n detective 576.11
  police 1008.16

v creep 177.26
  lurk 346.9
gum up disable 19.9
  spoil 393.11
  bungle 414.12
  hinder 1012.16
gun
  n killer 308.11
  artilleryman 461.11
  mercenary 461.17
  firearm 462.10
  ruffian 593.4
  game 746.3
  stop 857.2
  shot 904.4
  shooter 904.8
  v hunt 382.9
  shoot 904.12
gun down
  kill 308.14
  strike dead 308.18
gunfire fire 459.8
  shot 904.4
gung ho
  n call to arms 458.8
  adj energetic 17.13
  enthusiastic 101.10
gunk slime 80.8
  adhesive 803.4
  semiliquid 1062.5
gunky filthy 80.23
  viscous 1062.12
gunman killer 308.11
  mercenary 461.17
  ruffian 593.3
  shooter 904.8
gunner hand 183.6
  crew 185.4
  artilleryman 461.11
  basketball team 747.2
  shooter 904.8
gunrunning 732.2
gunshot
  detonation 56.3
  short distance 223.2
  shot 904.4
gun-shy fearful 127.23
  jittery 128.12
gunslinger 737.11
gurgle ripple 52.11
  trickle 238.18
  bubble 320.4
gurney 901.19
guru teacher 571.1
  master 575.1
  holy man 659.6
  clergy 699.13
  wise man 921.1
gush
  n outflow 190.4
  ascent 193.1
  flow 238.4
  jet 238.9
  increase 251.1
  unction 511.2
  wordiness 538.2
  outburst 671.6
  plenty 991.2
  v emotionalize 93.13
  be enthusiastic 101.7
  run out 190.13

shoot up 193.9
  flow 238.16
  jet 238.20
  chatter 540.5
  abound 991.5
gushiness 540.1
gushing
  n wordiness 538.2
  adj sentimental 93.21
  flowing 238.24
  flattering 511.8
  diffuse 538.11
gushy
  v talkative 540.9
  adj diffuse 538.11
gusset 191.2
gussy up dress up 5.42
  ornament 498.8
  beautify 1016.16
gust taste 62.1
  liking 100.2
  eagerness 101.1
  outburst 105.9
  wind gust 318.6
  characteristic 865.4
gusto vim 17.2
  animation 17.4
  savor 63.2
  passion 93.2
  pleasure 95.1
  liking 100.2
  eagerness 101.1
  gaiety 109.4
gusty tasty 63.8
  windy 318.22
gut
  n goozle 2.19
  heart 93.3
  inlet 242.1
  v eviscerate 192.13
  destroy 395.10
  plunder 482.17
  adj emotional 93.17
  interior 207.6
  unpremeditated 365.11
  essential 767.9
  vital 997.23
gut feeling 934.3
gutless weak 16.12
  uncourageous 491.11
gut reaction
  feeling 93.1
  impulse 365.1
guts viscera 2.16
  goozle 2.19
  strength 15.1
  zest 68.2
  heart 93.3
  contents 196.1
  insides 207.4
  pluck 359.3
  fearlessness 492.4
  nut and bolts 767.3
  inner nature 767.5
gut sensation 93.1
gutsy strong 15.15
  plucky 359.14
  fearless 492.19
gutter
  n trough 239.3
  drain 239.5

trench 290.2
  pavement 383.6
  sewer 654.7
  bowling 750.1
  v flutter 917.12
  flicker 1025.25
  adj disgraceful 661.11
  vulgar 666.8
guttersnipe
  vagabond 178.3
  vulgarian 497.6
guttural raucous 58.15
  inarticulate 525.12
guy man 76.5
  supporter 901.2
guzzle
  n goozle 2.19
  drink 8.4
  drinking spree 88.6
  swig 88.7
  v drink 8.29
  tipple 88.24
  gluttonize 672.4
gym fitness 84.1
  arena 463.1
  playground 743.11
gymnasium
  fitness 84.1
  playroom 197.12
  arena 463.1
  playground 743.11
gymnastics
  exercise 84.2
  physical education 568.9
  sport 744.1
gyp
  n female animal 77.10
  dog 311.17
  deception 356.9
  cheater 357.4
  v deceive 356.19
gypsy 178.4
gypsy cab 179.13
gyrate move 172.5
  rotate 915.9
ha'penny 728.8
haberdasher 5.33
habit
  n clothing 5.1
  suit 5.6
  substance abuse 87.1
  convention 373
  habitude 373.3
  mannerism 500.2
  nature 767.4
  v outfit 5.41
habitat
  environment 209.1
  habitation 225.1
  dwelling 228.1
  home 228.18
habitation
  occupancy 225.1
  inhabiting 225.1
  abode 228.1
habitual regular 373.14
  orderly 807.6
  frequent 847.4
  usual 869.9
habitué
  n attender 221.5

guest 585.6
adj habituated 373.17
hacienda
farmstead 228.6
farm 1069.8
hack
n breathing 2.21
driver 178.9
coachman 178.10
public vehicle 179.13
notch 289.1
horse 311.12
hunter 311.13
attempt 403.3
mark 517.5
hack writer 547.16
politician 610.4
scribbler 718.5
drudge 726.3
v go on horseback 177.34
accomplish 407.4
sever 802.11
hacker
incompetent 414.7
golfer 751.2
liveware 1042.17
hack it
be able 18.11
do 328.6
achieve one's purpose 409.8
manage 409.12
stand the test 942.10
suffice 991.4
hackneyed
trite 117.9
habitual 373.14
hackneyed expression 526.9
hack writer
writing 547.16
hack 718.5
Hades hell 682.1
nether world 682.3
nether world deity 682.5
destiny 839.2
hag old woman 304.3
witch 593.7
sorceress 690.8
eyesore 1015.4
haggard
tired-looking 21.9
colorless 36.7
frenzied 105.25
dejected 112.22
poor 270.20
deathly 307.29
fanatic 926.32
haggle
n negotiation 731.3
v bargain 731.18
hagiography 719.1
ha-ha
n laughter 116.4
trench 290.2
v laugh 116.8
hail
n greeting 585.4
multitude 884.3
hailstone 1023.6
v cry 59.6
assent 332.8
applaud 509.10

signal 517.22
address 524.26
greet 585.10
sleet 1023.11
interj all hail! 509.23
greetings! 585.15
hey! 983.23
hair
pile 3.2
short distance 223.2
modicum 248.2
narrowness 270.1
filament 271.1
skin 295.3
theater man 704.23
trifle 998.5
haircut 3.15
hairdo 3.15
hairdresser 1016.13
hairdressing 1016.11
hair-drier 1066.4
hairless 6.17
hairpiece 3.14
hairpin
n deviation 164.1
zigzag 204.8
skiing 753.1
race 756.3
v deflect 164.5
adj crooked 204.20
hair-raiser 127.9
hair salon beauty parlor or
salon or shop 1016.14
hair shirt
self-reproach 113.3
penance 658.3
hairsplitter 936.7
hairsplitting
n overfastidiousness 495.4
criticism 510.4
quibbling 936.5
distinction 944.3
adj overfastidious 495.12
critical 510.23
quibbling 936.14
hairstyle 3.15
hairy hirsute 3.24
threadlike 271.7
bristly 288.9
nappy 294.7
cutaneous 295.32
weird 988.9
bad 1000.8
difficult 1013.17
hajj 177.5
halcyon bright 97.11
quiescent 173.12
pacific 464.9
thriving 1010.13
hale
v pull 905.4
adj strong 15.15
hearty 83.12
half
n portion 477.5
football game 746.3
basketball game 747.3
game 749.6
mid-distance 819.2
moiety 875.2
adj proportionate 477.13

part 875.5
adv o'clock 832.16
half a mind 323.1
half-assed
slipshod 340.12
unskillful 414.15
botched 414.22
half-learned 930.15
half-baked
immature 406.11
premature 845.8
mentally deficient 922.22
half-learned 930.15
imperfect 1003.4
half-breed
n hybrid 797.8
adj hybrid 797.15
half-cocked
immature 406.11
premature 845.8
half-learned 930.15
half-heard 52.16
halfhearted
wishy-washy 16.17
indifferent 102.6
half-life 1037.6
half-mast 517.22
half-moon
crescent 279.5
heavenly body 1072.11
half nelson 474.3
half note 709.14
halftime game 746.3
shift 825.3
interim 826.1
halftone
color system 35.7
interval 709.20
half-truth 354.11
halfway
adj middle 819.4
half 875.5
adv midway 819.5
halfway house
mid-distance 819.2
asylum 1009.4
half-wit
stupid person 924.2
idiot 924.8
halitosis 71.1
hall entrance 189.5
assembly hall 197.4
corridor 197.18
house 228.5
arena 463.1
schoolhouse 567.10
theater 704.14
hallelujah
n cheer 116.2
paean 696.3
interj alleluia! 696.17
hallmark
n sign 517.1
label 517.13
characteristic 865.4
v label 517.20
hall of famer 413.15
halloo
n cry 59.1
v cry 59.6
address 524.26

interj oh! 122.20
hey! 983.23
hallow celebrate 487.2
sanctify 685.5
hallucinate 976.8
hallucination
deception 356.1
hallucinosis 976.7
figment of the imagination
986.5
hallucinogen
psychoactive drug 86.13
drug 87.3
hallway
entrance 189.5
corridor 197.18
halo radiation 171.2
circle 280.2
illustriousness 662.6
nimbus 1025.14
halt
n respite 20.2
standstill 173.3
delay 846.2
stop 857.2
prevention 1012.2
impasse 1013.6
v be weak 16.8
quiet 173.8
dawdle 175.8
way of walking 177.28
stammer 525.8
cease 857.6
stop 857.7
put a stop to 857.11
hinder 1012.13
adj crippled 393.30
interj cease! 857.13
halter
n shackle 428.4
execution 605.5
v yoke 800.10
halting
n cessation 857.1
prevention 1012.2
adj slow 175.10
crippled 393.30
stammering 525.13
stiff 534.3
irregular 851.3
halve share 476.6
sever 802.11
double 873.5
bisect 875.4
ham
n member 2.7
leg 177.14
village 230.2
acting 704.8
grimacer 707.5
radioman 1034.24
v affect 500.12
overact 704.31
adj dramatic 704.33
hamburger 10.14
hamburger joint 8.17
ham-fisted
bungling 414.20
inelegant 534.2
ham it up
emotionalize 93.13

subsequence 835.1
hang over one's head 840.2
hang together 803.6
hang tough
  be strong 15.11
  use 87.22
  endure 134.6
  confront 216.8
  remain firm 359.9
  persevere 360.7
  offer resistance 453.3
  keep up one's courage 492.15
  last 827.6
  stand fast 855.11
  persist 856.5
  toughen 1049.3
hang up suspend 202.8
  telephone 347.19
  come to nothing 410.13
  postpone 846.9
hang-up delay 846.2
  obsession 926.13
  obstacle 1012.4
hankering
  n yearning 100.5
  adj wistful 100.23
hanky-panky
  love affair 104.6
  juggling 356.5
haphazard
  n chance-medley 972.4
  adj slipshod 340.12
  unprepared 406.8
  unordered 810.12
  purposeless 972.16
hapless 1011.14
happen occur 831.5
  chance 972.11
happening
  n event 831.2
  chance event 972.6
  adj occurring 831.9
happen on
  come across 941.3
  chance 972.11
happy
  intoxicated 88.31
  glad 95.16
  content 107.7
  cheerful 109.11
  auspicious 133.18
  decorous 496.10
  appropriate 533.7
  apt 788.10
  timely 843.9
  expedient 995.5
happy-go-lucky 406.15
happy hour 95.5
happy medium
  mean 246.1
  middle course 467.3
  moderation 670.1
hara-kiri 308.5
harangue
  n speech 543.2
  lesson 568.7
  v declaim 543.10
  expound 568.16
harass
  fatigue 21.4
  annoy 96.13

vex 98.15
  make anxious 126.5
  intimidate 127.20
  persecute 389.7
  besiege 459.19
  work evil 1000.6
  trouble 1013.13
harassment
  annoyance 96.2
  vexatiousness 98.7
  worry 126.2
  persecution 389.3
harbinger
  n forerunner 133.5
  herald 353.2
  precursor 816.1
  v herald 133.14
harbor
  n destination 186.5
  inlet 242.1
  refuge 1009.1
  haven 1009.6
  v house 225.10
  hold 474.7
  doubt 955.6
  protect 1008.18
harbor a grudge 589.8
harbor resentment 152.12
hard
  adj strong 15.15
  painful 26.10
  bitter 64.6
  alcoholic 88.37
  callous 94.12
  impenitent 114.5
  harsh 144.24
  heartless 144.25
  pitiless 146.3
  industrious 330.22
  unyielding 361.9
  obdurate 361.10
  firm 425.7
  hard to understand 522.14
  phonetic 524.30
  hardened 654.17
  lascivious 665.29
  real 761.15
  sturdy 763.7
  true 973.13
  valid 973.14
  adverse 1011.13
  difficult 1013.17
  dense 1045.12
  solid 1046.10
  tough 1049.4
  adv near 223.20
  laboriously 725.19
hard and fast
  aground 182.73
  preceptive 419.4
  mandatory 420.12
hard as nails
  strong 15.15
  pitiless 146.3
  resistant 1046.10
  tough 1049.4
hardball reality 761.2
  gravity 997.3
  danger 1006.1
hard-boiled
  firm 15.18–

obdurate 361.10
  hard 1046.10
hard copy 547.10
hard-core
  unyielding 361.9
  fiery 671.22
hardcover 554.3
hard disk
  recording media 549.10
  disk 1042.6
hard-drinking 88.35
hard drug 87.3
hard-earned
  laborious 725.18
  difficult 1013.17
harden
  strengthen 15.13
  callous 94.6
  accustom 373.9
  indurate 1046.7
  toughen 1049.3
  petrify 1059.10
hardened callous 94.12
  impenitent 114.5
  heartless 144.25
  accustomed 373.15
  hard 654.17
  toughened 1046.13
  tough 1049.6
hard feelings
  bad feeling 93.7
  bitterness 152.3
  animosity 589.4
hard hat patriot 591.3
  conservative 611.9
  safeguard 1008.3
hardheaded
  obstinate 361.8
  ungullible 956.5
  realistic 987.6
hard-hearted
  callous 94.12
  heartless 144.25
  hardened 654.17
  hard 1046.10
hard knocks 1011.1
hard labor
  punishment 604.2
  backbreaking work 725.5
hard line
  unyieldingness 361.2
  strictness 425.1
  warlikeness 458.11
  orthodoxy 687.5
hard-line
  unyielding 361.9
  strict 425.6
  militaristic 458.22
  fiery 671.22
hard liquor 88.13
hard news 552.1
hard-nosed 361.10
hard nut to crack
  enigma 522.8
  tough proposition 1013.2
hard-of-hearing 49.6
hard on 223.24
hard-on 75.5
hard-pressed
  straitened 1013.26
  hurried 401.11

hard rock 708.10
hard sell
  inducement 375.3
  importunity 440.3
  selling 734.2
hard up poor 619.7
  straitened 1013.26
hardware
  hard goods 735.4
  computer hardware 1041.17
  central processing unit
    1042.2
the hard way
  n difficulty 1013.1
  adv laboriously 725.19
  with difficulty 1013.28
hardwood
  n basketball 747.1
  wood 1054.3
  adj arboreal 310.39
hardworking
  industrious 330.22
  laboring 725.17
hardy strong 15.15
  hale 83.12
  insolent 142.9
  perennial 310.44
  courageous 492.17
  durable 827.10
  tough 1049.4
hare
  swiftness 174.6
  leveret 311.24
harebrained
  capricious 364.5
  foolhardy 493.9
  scatterbrained 985.16
harem 563.10
hark
  v listen 48.10
  hearken to 983.7
  interj hark ye! 48.16
  attention! 983.22
hark back
  turn back 859.5
  remember 989.10
harlequin
  n check 47.4
  variegation 47.6
  buffoon 707.10
  v variegate 47.7
  adj variegated 47.9
harlot
  n prostitute 665.16
  adj prostitute 665.28
harm
  n impairment 393.1
  disadvantage 996.2
  evil 1000.3
  bane 1001.1
  v impair 393.9
  inconvenience 996.4
  work evil 1000.6
harmful
  unhealthful 82.5
  malicious 144.20
  disadvantageous 996.6
  hurtful 1000.12
  adverse 1011.13
harmless
  hurtless 999.21

undamaged 1002.8
unhazardous 1007.5
harmonic
n tone 50.2
harmonic tone 709.16
adj harmonious 708.49
oscillating 916.15
harmonica 711.10
harmonious
chromatic 35.16
pleasant 97.6
symmetric 264.4
cooperative 450.5
in accord 455.3
balanced 533.8
friendly 587.15
harmonic 708.49
agreeing 788.9
orderly 807.6
conformist 867.6
concurrent 899.4
harmonize
symmetrize 264.3
cooperate 450.3
get along 455.2
reconcile 465.8
be harmonious 708.35
compose 708.46
make uniform 781.4
agree 788.6
make agree 788.7
order 807.4
organize 808.10
conform 867.3
concur 899.2
harmony
symmetry 264.1
unanimity 332.5
cooperation 450.1
accord 455.1
peace 464.1
proportion 533.2
good terms 587.3
heaven 681.5
concord 708.3
harmonics 709.1
agreement 788.1
order 807.1
conformity 867.1
harness
n wardrobe 5.2
parachute 181.13
caparison 385.5
armor 460.3
v yoke 800.10
tend 1070.7
harp
n lyre 711.3
mouth organ 711.10
v persist 856.5
harp on dwell on 118.8
belabor 849.9
emphasize 997.14
harpoon 480.17
harpsichord 711.12
harpy
extortionist 480.12
monster 593.6
harridan
strumpet 665.14
eyesore 1015.4

harried
tormented 96.24
worried 126.8
harrow
n projection 285.4
v pain 26.7
torture 96.18
smooth 287.5
cultivate 1069.17
harrowing
n cultivation 1069.13
adj painful 26.10
agonizing 98.23
harry annoy 96.13
make anxious 126.5
persecute 389.7
attack 459.14
besiege 459.19
harsh
acrimonious 17.14
painful 26.10
off-color 35.21
raucous 58.15
dissonant 61.4
clashing 61.5
bitter 64.6
pungent 68.6
distressing 98.20
oppressive 98.24
rough 144.24
pitiless 146.3
rugged 288.7
strict 425.6
gruff 505.7
inarticulate 525.12
inelegant 534.2
hart male animal 76.8
hoofed animal 311.5
harum-scarum
adj reckless 493.8
boisterous 671.20
adv in disorder 810.17
harvest
n autumn 313.4
yield 472.5
effect 887.1
production 893.2
harvesting 1069.15
v acquire 472.8
process 892.9
reap 1069.19
has-been
n back number 842.8
adj past 837.7
old-fashioned 842.16
hash
n meat 10.13
hashish 87.8
fiasco 410.6
bungle 414.5
hodgepodge 797.6
jumble 810.3
v mix 797.10
hash house 8.17
hash over 541.12
Hasidic 675.30
hasp 800.8
hassle
n quarrel 456.6
struggle 725.3
commotion 810.4

argumentation 935.4
v vex 98.15
quarrel 456.12
nag 510.16
struggle 725.11
argue 935.16
work evil 1000.6
haste
n impatience 135.1
velocity 174.1
impulsiveness 365.2
hurry 401.1
recklessness 493.2
prematurity 845.2
v speed 174.8
hasten 401.4
hasten
be impatient 135.4
advance 162.5
speed 174.8
accelerate 174.10
haste 401.4
make haste 401.5
be useful 449.17
facilitate 1014.7
hasty
hot-tempered 110.25
impatient 135.6
fast 174.15
impulsive 365.9
hurried 401.9
unprepared 406.8
reckless 493.8
sudden 830.5
premature 845.8
hat
n headdress 5.25
v cloak 5.40
top 295.21
hatch
n porch 189.6
offspring 561.2
v be born 1.2
be pregnant 78.12
fabricate 354.18
plot 381.9
mark 517.19
portray 712.19
engrave 713.9
originate 892.12
imagine 986.14
raise 1070.6
hatchet job demolition
395.5
aspersion 512.4
hatchet man
killer 308.11
combatant 461.1
disparager 512.6
ruffian 593.4
henchman 610.8
hate
n hostility 99.2
aversion 103
malice 103.1
hated thing 103.3
antagonism 589.3
v have deep feelings 93.12
dislike 99.3
detest 103.5
bear ill will 589.8

hateful
offensive 98.18
loathesome 103.8
malicious 144.20
hostile 589.10
terrible 1000.9
hatred hostility 99.2
abhorrence 103.1
antagonism 589.3
haughty vain 136.9
arrogant 141.9
contemptuous 157.8
high 272.14
haul
n distance 261.1
take 480.10
booty 482.11
strain 725.2
pull 905.2
v cart 176.13
sail against the wind 182.24
ship activity 182.48
strain 725.10
pull 905.4
haunch 218.1
haunt
n resort 228.27
specter 988.1
v oppress 98.16
make anxious 126.5
frequent 221.10
hant 988.6
haunted worried 126.8
spooked 988.10
remembering 989.24
haunting
recurrent 849.13
unforgettable 989.26
haute couture 5.32
haute cuisine 11.1
hauteur arrogance 141.1
contempt 157.1
height 272.1
have give birth 1.3
affirm 334.5
deceive 356.19
compel 424.4
suffer 443.10
possess 469.4
hold 474.7
receive 479.6
understand 521.7
experience 831.8
know 928.1
doubt 955.6
recognize 989.12
have it in for
dislike 99.3
loathe 103.6
bear ill will 589.8
have it made
make good 409.10
prosper 1010.7
have it out
contend with 457.17
argue 935.16
haven
n destination 186.5
refuge 1009.1
harbor 1009.6
v protect 1008.18

have to
  be compelled 424.9
  be necessary 963.10
havoc
  n evil 1000.3
  v destroy 395.10
haw avoid 164.6
  stammer 525.8
hawk
  n sharp vision 27.11
  bird 311.28
  militarist 461.5
  patriot 591.3
  v salivate 13.6
  hunt 382.9
  vend 734.9
the hawk 318.8
hawk-eyed
  clear-sighted 27.21
  vigilant 339.13
hay
  n feed 10.4
  marijuana 87.11
  v harvest 1069.19
the hay 901.19
haystack 770.10
haywire
  impaired 393.38
  disorderly 810.13
  crazy 926.27
  eccentric 927.6
hazard
  n golf 751.1
  gamble 759.2
  bet 759.3
  unreliability 971.6
  chance event 972.6
  danger 1006.1
  obstacle 1012.4
  v presume 640.6
  risk 759.24
  bet 759.25
  chance 972.11
  endanger 1006.6
  take chances 1006.7
haze
  n LSD 87.10
  fog 319.3
  confusion 985.3
  v cloud 319.7
  banter 490.5
hazel 40.3
hazy
  inconspicuous 32.6
  formless 263.4
  foggy 319.10
  obscure 522.15
  vague 971.19
  muddled 985.13
he male 76.4
  self 865.5
head
  n member 2.7
  head of hair 3.4
  latrine 12.10
  addict 87.21
  enthusiast 101.5
  sail 180.14
  top part 198.4
  architectural topping 198.5
  headpiece 198.6

front 216.1
headwaters 238.2
superior 249.4
point of land 283.9
plant 310.27
person 312.5
foam 320.2
makeup 554.12
abridgment 557.1
superintendent 574.2
portrait 712.15
class 809.2
source 886.5
thrust 902.2
intellect 919.1
brain 919.6
intelligence 920.9
topic 937.1
caption 937.2
water 1065.3
v take direction 161.7
lead 165.2
top 198.9
be in front 216.7
gravitate 297.15
direct 573.8
govern 612.12
play 752.4
precede 814.2
tend 896.3
focus on 937.3
adj top 198.10
front 216.10
directing 573.12
governing 612.18
first 818.17
headache ache 26.5
  annoyance 96.2
  tedious person 118.5
  trouble 1013.3
head and shoulders above
  superlative 249.13
  superior 999.14
headband 554.14
head count
  population 227.1
  roll 871.6
  summation 1017.11
headdress
  hairdo 3.15
  headgear 5.25
headfirst
  precipitately 401.15
  recklessly 493.11
headhunter
  executive search agency 615.5
  killer 308.11
heading
  n direction 161.1
  leading 165.1
  course 184.34
  top part 198.4
  front 216.1
  supervision 573.2
  class 809.2
  topic 937.1
  caption 937.2
  adj leading 165.3
  topping 198.11
headline
  n caption 937.2

v dramatize 704.28
focus on 937.3
feature 997.15
headlong
  adj fast 174.15
  steep 204.18
  impulsive 365.9
  precipitate 401.10
  reckless 493.8
  sudden 830.5
  adv precipitately
    401.15
  recklessly 493.11
  impulsively 365.13
headmaster 571.8
head off 164.6
head office 739.7
head-on
  adj front 216.10
  adv afoul 182.72
  in opposition 451.9
head over heels
  inversely 205.8
  precipitately 401.15
  recklessly 493.11
  round 915.16
  inverted 205.7
headphone
  loudspeaker 50.8
  radiophone 347.5
headpiece
  headdress 5.25
  top part 198.4
  head 198.6
  intellect 919.1
headquarters
  central station 208.6
  office 739.7
headroom 224.1
heads 215.3
heads or tails 759.2
head start
  advantage 249.2
  earliness 845.1
headstone 901.7
headstrong
  obstinate 361.8
  lawless 418.5
head up
  be in front 216.7
  direct 573.8
  precede 814.2
  initiate 818.10
  focus on 937.3
headway
  progression 162.1
  way 182.9
  improvement 392.1
headwear 5.25
head wind
  atmosphere 184.32
  wind 318.1
  nautical 318.11
  opposition 451.1
  counterforce 900.4
heady
  intoxicating 88.36
  exciting 105.30
  foamy 320.7
  lawless 418.5
heal treat 91.24

cure 396.15
heal over 396.21
health
  n well-being 83.1
  normality 869.1
  adj medical 90.15
health care
  health protection 83.5
  medical care 90.1
  medicine 90.1
health center 91.21
health club
  health care 83.5
  fitness 84.1
health food
  nutrient 7.3
  food 10.1
health insurance
  health care 83.5
  medicine 90.1
  welfarism 611.7
health spa 84.1
healthy
  wellness 81.5
  healthful 83.8
  large 257.16
  good 999.12
heap
  n car 179.10
  amount 244.2
  lot 247.4
  store 386.1
  throng 770.4
  pile 770.10
  v load 159.15
  give 478.12
  pile 770.19
heap up load 159.15
  store up 386.11
  collect 472.11
  pile 770.19
heap upon
  furnish 478.15
  give freely 485.3
hear
  v sense 24.6
  listen 48.10
  catch 48.11
  know 551.15
  try 598.18
  sit in judgment 946.12
  hearken to 983.7
  interj hark! 48.16
  bravo! 509.22
hear a different drummer
  disobey 327.6
  dissent 333.4
hearing
  n senses 24.5
  auditory sense 48.1
  audition 48.1
  aural sense 48.2
  earshot 48.4
  trial 598.5
  examination 938.2
  investigation 938.4
  tryout 942.3
  adj auditory 48.13
hearken 48.10
hearken to obey 326.2
  hark 983.7

hearsay
n report 552.6
adj evidential 957.16
hearse
n funeral car 309.10
v inter 309.19
heart
n viscera 2.16
food 10.20
passion 93.2
soul 93.3
love 104.1
essential content 196.5
interior 207.2
center 208.2
life force 306.3
fortitude 492.6
essence 767.2
inner nature 767.5
middle 819.1
psyche 919.4
mood 978.4
salient point 997.6
v confess 351.7
heartache
wretchedness 96.6
aching heart 112.9
heartbeat
life force 306.3
pulsation 916.3
heartbreak
harshness 98.4
heartache 112.9
heartbreaker 562.12
heartburn ache 26.5
jealousy 153.1
hear tell of hear 48.11
know 551.15
hearten energize 17.10
cheer 109.7
comfort 121.6
motivate 375.21
abet 449.14
encourage 492.16
heartening
n encouragement 492.9
adj cheering 109.16
comforting 121.13
heartfelt 93.24
hearth home 228.2
family 559.5
fireplace 1020.11
heartland inland 207.3
region 231.1
middle America 231.7
heartless unfeeling 94.9
apathetic 94.13
dejected 112.22
unkind 144.25
pitiless 146.3
uncourageous 491.11
hardened 654.17
heartrending
agonizing 98.23
pitiful 145.8
hearts
amphetamines 87.4
card 758.2
heartsick
wretched 96.26
disconsolate 112.28

heartstrings 93.3
heartthrob
loved one 104.11
pulsation 916.3
heart-to-heart
n chat 541.4
adj candid 644.17
heartwarming
delightful 97.7
pleasant 97.6
cheering 109.16
hearty
n mariner 183.1
boon companion 588.5
adj strong 15.15
energetic 17.13
hale 83.12
fervent 93.18
zealous 101.9
gay 109.14
convivial 582.23
hospitable 585.11
cordial 587.16
hear ye
hark! 48.16
attention! 983.22
heat
n sexual desire 75.5
fever 85.7
passion 93.2
zeal 101.2
fever of excitement 105.7
anger 152.5
race 457.12
hotness 1019.1
v cook 11.5
excite 105.12
incite 375.17
raise the temperature
1020.17
adj fuel 1021.9
heated
cooked 11.7
fervent 93.18
zealous 101.9
passionate 105.22
fiery 671.22
hot 1019.25
het 1020.29
heater gun 462.10
warmer 1020.10
heath
plain 236.1
wasteland 891.2
heathen
n pagan 688.7
unbeliever 695.11
adj pagan 688.11
unbelieving 695.19
idolatrous 697.7
unlearned 930.14
heat up
aggravate 119.2
intensify 251.5
incite 375.17
antagonize 589.7
heat wave
weather 317.3
hot weather 1019.7
heave
n wave 238.14

strain 725.2
throw 904.3
pull 905.2
lift 912.2
v feel disgust 99.4
be excited 105.18
ship activity 182.48
pitch 182.55
billow 238.22
strain 725.10
throw 904.10
pull 905.4
vomit 909.26
elevate 912.5
heaven
happiness 95.2
summit 198.2
height 272.2
utopia 986.11
good times 1010.4
the heavens 1072.2
Heaven
abode of the deity and
blessed dead 681
destiny 839.2
Fates 964.3
Heaven forbid! 510.27
Heaven knows! 930.19
heavenly
blissful 97.9
divine 677.16
angelic 679.6
otherworldly 681.12
sacred 685.7
godly 692.9
ideal 986.23
superb 999.15
gorgeous 1016.21
celestial 1072.25
heavenly body 1072.4
heaven-sent
timely 843.9
expedient 995.5
heave to
sail against the wind 182.24
come to a stop 182.33
heaving
n trepidation 105.5
throwing 904.2
pulling 905.1
vomiting 909.8
adj respiratory 2.32
heavy
n heavyweight 257.12
role 704.10
actor 707.2
adj sleepy 22.21
deep 54.11
pregnant 78.18
oppressive 98.24
sad 112.20
dull 117.6
inert 173.14
great 247.6
thick 269.8
ponderous 297.16
luxuriant 310.43
cloudy 319.8
languid 331.20
phonetic 524.30
stiff 534.3

tragic 704.34
laborious 725.18
sturdy 763.7
unintelligent 922.16
weighty 997.20
excellent 999.13
troublesome 1013.18
dense 1045.12
viscous 1062.12
adv heavily 297.21
heavy-duty 1049.4
heavy hand
firm hand 425.3
despotism 612.10
heavy-handed
insensible 25.6
bungling 414.20
inelegant 534.2
heavy heart
wretchedness 96.6
sadness 112.1
heavyset
corpulent 257.18
thick 269.8
heavyweight
n pig 257.12
weight 297.3
influence 894.6
adj heavy 297.16
important 997.17
hebetude apathy 94.4
languor 331.6
stupidity 922.3
Hebrew
n Jew 675.21
adj Jewish 675.30
hecatomb
butchery 308.3
destruction 395.1
oblation 696.7
hundred 882.8
heck! 513.12
heckle comb 79.21
annoy 96.13
hectic
n reddening 41.3
glow 1019.12
adj red-complexioned 41.9
feverish 85.58
overzealous 101.12
heated 105.22
overactive 330.24
hector
n braggart 502.5
blusterer 503.2
v annoy 96.13
intimidate 127.20
bluster 503.3
hedge
n boundary 211.3
caution 494.1
qualification 959.1
v limit 210.5
fence 212.7
dodge 368.8
take precautions 494.6
quibble 936.9
qualify 959.3
hedgehog
wild animal 311.23
launcher 462.21

rocket launcher 1074.10
hedge in
circumscribe 210.4
enclose 212.5
fence 212.7
hedge one's bets 494.6
hedging
n limitation 210.2
caution 494.1
quibbling 936.5
qualification 959.1
adj demurring 325.7
quibbling 936.14
hedonism
pleasure-loving 95.4
ethical philosophy 636.2
selfishness 651.1
sensuality 663.1
hedonistic
pleasure-loving 95.18
selfish 651.5
sensual 663.5
heebie-jeebies 917.1
heed
n carefulness 339.1
observance 434.1
caution 494.1
attention 983.1
v listen 48.10
obey 326.2
care 339.6
observe 434.2
attend 983.6
heedful
considerate 143.16
careful 339.10
cautious 494.8
attentive 983.15
heedless
unconcerned 102.7
inconsiderate 144.18
careless 340.11
unthinking 365.10
improvident 406.15
incurious 982.3
inattentive 984.6
forgetful 990.9
heel
n foot 199.5
rear 217.1
stern 217.7
bad person 660.5
v turn round 163.9
deviate 164.3
follow 166.3
careen 182.43
equip 385.8
fight 754.4
heeled addicted 87.25
provided 385.13
armed 460.14
heel of Achilles 1006.4
heft
n weight 297.1
v weigh 297.10
elevate 912.5
hefty strong 15.15
corpulent 257.18
heavy 297.16
laborious 725.18
troublesome 1013.18

Hegelian
n immaterialist 1053.4
adj Aristotelian 952.12
idealist 1053.8
hegemony
superiority 249.1
supremacy 249.3
dominance 417.6
mastership 417.7
hegira
departure 188.1
flight 368.4
heifer
female animal 77.10
gal 302.7
cattle 311.6
height
degree 245.1
supremacy 249.3
size 257.1
tallness 272
heighth 272.1
rise 272.2
pitch 709.4
elevation 912.1
acme of perfection 1002.3
heighten
increase 272.13
elevate 912.5
heightening
aggravation 119.1
intensification 251.2
exaggeration 355.1
heights
highlands 237.1
altitude 272.2
heinous offensive 98.18
wicked 654.16
base 661.12
terrible 1000.9
heir survivor 256.3
heritor 479.5
successor 817.4
sequel 835.2
heirloom 479.2
heist
n theft 482.4
v rob 482.16
elevate 912.5
held reserved 386.15
possessed 469.8
stuck 855.16
supported 901.24
obsessed 926.33
believed 953.23
gripped 983.18
Helicon 720.10
helicopter 181.5
heliport airport 184.22
platform 901.13
hell blackness 38.4
torment 96.7
depths 275.3
place of confinement 429.7
abode of the damned 682
Hades 682.1
casino 759.19
pandemonium 810.5
hot place 1019.11
Hell
river of death 307.4

destiny 839.2
cold place 1023.4
hell-bent 174.17
hellcat
daredevil 493.4
ruffian 593.3
witch 593.7
violent person 671.9
hellfire 682.2
hellion ruffian 593.4
violent person
671.9
demon 680.6
hellish
frightening 127.28
cruel 144.26
diabolic 654.13
turbulent 671.18
demoniac 680.17
infernal 682.8
execrable 1000.10
hello! oh! 122.20
salutation 585.4
greetings! 585.15
hey! 983.23
helm
n authority 417.10
direction 573.1
reins 573.5
control 612.2
v pilot 182.14
helmet
heraldry 647.2
safeguard 1008.3
helmsman
steersman 183.8
guide 574.7
helot
sycophant 138.3
subject 432.7
help
n serving 8.10
remedy 86.1
aid 449.1
subsidy 478.8
servant 577.2
staff 577.11
benefactor 592.1
assistant 616.6
v do a favor 143.12
aid 449.11
subsidize 478.19
serve 577.13
do good 999.10
prevent 1012.14
helper
subordinate 432.5
assistant 449.7
benefactor 592.1
associate 616.6
helpful
considerate 143.16
modal 384.8
useful 387.18
of use 449.21
good 999.12
helping
n serving 8.10
portion 477.5
adj assisting 449.20
serving 577.14

helpless
defenseless 19.18
dead-drunk 88.32
forlorn 584.12
unprotected 1006.14
helpmeet
wife 563.8
assistant 616.6
helter-skelter
n haste 401.1
jumble 810.3
commotion 810.4
adj carelessly 340.18
hastily 401.12
recklessly 493.11
nonuniformly 782.4
separated 802.21
confused 810.16
in disorder 810.17
hem
n border 211.4
edging 211.7
v border 211.10
fence 212.7
restrict 428.9
stammer 525.8
hem and haw
prevaricate 344.7
hesitate 362.7
dodge 368.8
stammer 525.8
hem in
border 211.10
enclose 212.5
confine 429.12
hemisphere
sphere 231.2
member 793.4
half 875.2
hemlock 604.7
hemmed-in
enclosed 212.10
restricted 428.15
hemorrhage
n bleeding 12.8
symptom 85.9
v bleed 12.17
hemorrhoids 85.37
hemp
marijuana 87.11
execution 605.5
hen woman 77.6
female animal 77.10
old woman 304.3
poultry 311.29
card 758.2
hence thence 188.20
therefore 888.7
henceforth 839.10
henchman
hanger-on 138.6
follower 166.2
cohort 610.8
associate 616.8
henhouse 228.22
henna
v make red 41.4
adj reddish-brown 40.4
henpeck
nag 510.16
domineer 612.16

henpecked
tied to one's apron strings
326.5
downtrodden 432.16
hep 928.17
Hephaestus 726.8
heptagonal
pentagonal 278.10
seventh 882.19
her female 77.4
cocaine 87.7
self 865.5
herald
n foreshadower 133.5
leading 165.1
harbinger 353.2
king of arms 575.21
delegate 576.2
spokesman 576.5
precursor 816.1
v harbinger 133.14
proclaim 352.13
go before 816.3
be prior 834.3
heraldry pomp 501.6
insignia 647.1
herb
remedy 86.4
marijuana 87.11
plant 310.4
herbicide 1001.3
herbivore eater 8.16
creature 311.3
Herculean
Briarean 15.17
huge 257.20
laborious 725.18
difficult 1013.17
Hercules
strong man 15.6
support 901.3
herd
n guide 574.7
the masses 606.2
guardian 1008.6
v guide 573.9
drive 1070.8
herd together
associate with 582.17
accompany 769.7
come together 770.16
here hereat 159.23
there 221.16
now 838.3
hereabouts
here 159.23
near 223.20
hereafter
n the future 839.1
adj future 839.8
adv in future 839.10
the hereafter
the afterworld 681.2
destiny 839.2
here and now
now 838.3
material 1052.10
the here and now
reality 761.2
the present 838.1
realism 987.2

here and there
in places 159.25
discontinuously 813.5
sparsely 885.8
hereby 384.12
hereditary
protoplasmic 305.18
patrimonial 560.19
innate 767.8
heredity
genetic material 305.9
heritage 560.6
herein 207.10
heresy
false doctrine 688.2
inconsistency 789.2
unconventionality 868.2
unbelief 955.1
error 975.1
heretical
unorthodox 688.9
nonconformist 789.9
unconventional 868.6
unbelieving 955.5
erroneous 975.16
hereto 159.23
heretofore
previously 834.6
formerly 837.13
until now 838.4
herewith
therewith 384.12
hand in hand 769.10
heritage
inheritance 479.2
heredity 560.6
hermaphrodite
n intersex 75.17
adj androgynal 75.31
hermeneutics
exegetics 341.8
criticism 723.1
Hermes 353.1
hermetically sealed 293.12
hermetics 345.5
hermit recluse 584.5
ascetic 667.2
religious 699.16
oddity 870.4
hero victor 411.2
brave person 492.8
god 659.5
celebrity 662.9
godling 678.3
role 704.10
lead 707.6
ideal 786.4
heroic eminent 247.9
huge 257.20
courageous 492.17
magnanimous 652.6
vocal 708.50
poetic 720.15
traditional 842.12
heroics
rashness 493.1
boasting 502.1
heroine
brave person 492.8
hero 659.5
celebrity 662.9

godling 678.3
role 704.10
lead 707.6
heroism
glory 247.2
courage 492.1
magnanimity 652.2
hero worship
love 104.1
respect 155.1
praise 509.5
idolatry 697.1
hero-worship
respect 155.4
praise 509.12
Herr 76.7
hesitancy demur 325.2
hesitation 362.3
caution 494.1
uncertainty 971.1
hesitant
demurring 325.7
tentative 362.11
cautious 494.8
uncertain 971.16
hesitate demur 325.4
pause 362.7
stammer 525.8
procrastinate 846.11
hang in doubt 971.10
hesitation demur 325.2
hesitance 362.3
caution 494.1
stammering 525.3
procrastination 846.5
uncertainty 971.1
heterodoxy
unorthodoxy 688.1
inconsistency 789.2
unconventionality 868.2
error 975.1
heterogeneity
difference 780.1
multiformity 783.1
inconsistency 789.2
inequality 791.1
heterogeneous
different 780.7
diversified 783.4
mixed 797.14
heterosexual 75.13
het up
excited 105.22
angry 152.30
heated 1020.29
heuristic
examining 938.37
experimental 942.11
hew form 262.7
sever 802.11
hex
n curse 513.1
sorceress 690.8
spell 691.1
bad influence 1000.4
v curse 513.5
bewitch 691.9
work evil 1000.6
bring bad luck 1011.12
hexagonal
pentagonal 278.10

sixth 882.18
hey oh! 122.20
greetings! 585.15
howdy! 585.16
hail! 983.23
hi greetings! 585.15
hey! 983.23
hiatus interval 224.1
opening 292.1
deficiency 795.2
interruption 813.2
hibernate
aestivate 22.15
do nothing 329.2
lie idle 331.16
be latent 519.3
hibernation sleep 22.2
inactivity 331.1
hiccup
n breathing 2.21
belch 909.9
v belch 909.28
hick
n bungler 414.9
simple soul 416.3
peasant 606.6
oaf 924.5
adj not urbane 233.8
hickey sore 85.37
blemish 1004.1
thing 1052.5
hidden invisible 32.5
secret 345.11
concealed 346.11
latent 519.5
implied 519.7
recondite 522.16
hidden agenda 375.1
hide
n fur 4.2
lamina 296.2
v disappear 34.2
conceal 346.6
conceal oneself 346.8
store up 386.11
defeat 412.9
punish 604.15
hideaway
hiding place 346.4
sanctum 584.6
retreat 1009.5
hideous horrid 98.19
terrible 127.30
ugly 1015.11
hideout
hiding place 346.4
retreat 1009.5
hide out 346.8
hiding
n covering 295.1
concealment 346.1
hiding place 346.4
defeat 412.1
punishment 604.5
adj concealing 346.15
hiding place
hideaway 346.4
retreat 1009.5
hie speed 174.8
travel 177.18
hiemal seasonal 313.9

hippie
 n nonconformist 868.3
 adj unconventional 868.6
hippo
 heavyweight 257.12
 behemoth 257.14
 pachyderm 311.4
hippopotamus
 behemoth 257.14
 pachyderm 311.4
hire
 n rental 615.6
 pay 624.4
 fee 630.6
 v employ 615.14
 rent 615.15
 rent out 615.16
hireling
 n mercenary 461.17
 employee 577.3
 adj employed 615.20
 corruptible 645.23
hirsute hairy 3.24
 feathery 3.27
 bristly 288.9
 nappy 294.7
his nibs 997.11
hiss
 n sibilation 57.1
 boo 508.3
 speech defect 525.1
 v sibilate 57.2
 growl 60.4
 bubble 320.4
 boo 508.10
 speak 524.25
hissing
 n audio distortion 50.13
 sibilation 57.1
 ridicule 508.1
 boo 508.3
 adj sibilant 57.3
 ridiculing 508.12
hist hark! 48.16
 hey! 983.23
historian
 annalist 550.2
 cliometrician 719.4
historical
 historic 719.7
 fictional 722.7
 real 761.15
 obvious 970.15
 true 973.13
historicity
 reality 761.2
 truth 973.1
historiography 719.1
history
 n record 549.1
 the investigation of the past
  719
 the historical discipline
  719.1
 the past 837.1
 adj ruined 395.29
histrionic
 emotionalistic 93.19
 affected 500.15
 theatrical 501.24
 dramatic 704.33

hit
 n dose 87.20
 excitement 105.3
 homicide 308.2
 success 409.4
 score 409.5
 criticism 510.4
 stage show 704.4
 popular music 708.7
 game 745.3
 blackjack 759.11
 blow 902.4
 v impress 93.15
 travel 177.19
 arrive 186.6
 contact 223.10
 kill 308.14
 beg 440.15
 attack 459.14
 criticize 510.14
 swing 745.5
 play 751.4
 agree 788.6
 collide 902.13
 strike 902.14
 shoot 904.12
 impress 931.19
 discover 941.2
hit and miss
 n experiment 942.1
 adj slipshod 340.12
 carelessly 340.18
hit-and-run
 v run over 910.7
 adj dastardly 491.12
hit below the belt
 n unfairness 650.2
 v do wrong 650.6
hit bottom
 base on 199.6
 decline 393.17
 be changed 852.6
hitch
 n pang 26.2
 gait 177.12
 term 825.4
 jerk 905.3
 obstacle 1012.4
 crux 1013.8
 v way of walking 177.28
 beat one's way 177.31
 join in marriage 563.14
 hook 800.8
 jerk 905.5
 tend 1070.7
hitchhike 177.31
hitchhiker 178.6
hitherto
 previously 834.6
 formerly 837.13
hit home 903.8
hit it big 1010.11
hit it off 587.9
hit list 871.1
hit man
 killer 308.11
 violent person 671.9
hit on
 make advances 439.8
 burlesque 508.11
 come across 941.3

hit or miss
 slipshod 340.12
 carelessly 340.18
 unordered 810.12
 haphazardly 810.18
 experimental 942.11
 experimentally 942.13
 vague 971.19
hitter 745.2
hit the books 570.12
hit the jackpot 409.9
hit the nail on the head
 solve 940.2
 be right 973.10
hit the road
 wander 177.23
 depart 188.7
hit the sack 22.18
hit the spot 95.7
hit up beg 440.15
 borrow 621.3
hit upon arrive at 186.7
 light upon 194.10
 come across 941.3
HIV or human immuno-
  deficiency virus 85.42
hive
 n nest 228.25
 hive of industry 739.2
 assemblage 770.6
 multitude 884.3
 v settle 159.17
 come together 770.16
hives allergy 85.34
 skin eruption 85.36
hoar
 n frost 1023.7
 adj white 37.7
 gray 39.4
 gray-haired 39.5
 aged 303.16
hoard
 n store 386.1
 gain 472.3
 v store up 386.11
 not use 390.5
hoarfrost 1023.7
hoarse raucous 58.15
 inarticulate 525.12
hoary white 37.7
 gray 39.4
 gray-haired 39.5
 aged 303.16
 old 842.10
 traditional 842.12
 frosty 1023.17
hoax
 n fake 354.13
 deception 356.7
 v deceive 356.14
hobble
 n slow motion 175.2
 gait 177.12
 shackle 428.4
 predicament 1013.5
 v disable 19.10
 go slow 175.6
 way of walking 177.28
 cripple 393.14
 bind 428.10
 hamper 1012.11

hobby
 n avocation 724.7
 adj avocational 724.17
hobbyhorse
 n avocation 724.7
 toy 743.16
 v pitch 182.55
hobgoblin
 frightener 127.9
 goblin 680.8
Hobgoblin 680.7
hobnob with
 associate with 582.17
 be friends 587.9
hobo
 n vagabond 178.3
 bum 331.9
 beggar 440.8
 wretch 660.2
 transient 828.4
 oddity 870.4
 v wander 177.23
Hobson's choice
 dilemma 371.3
 restriction 428.3
 choicelessness 963.6
 certainty 970.1
hock
 n leg 177.14
 pledge 438.2
 v pledge 438.10
hockey sports 749
 ice hockey 749.1
hocus-pocus
 n juggling 356.5
 trick 356.6
 nonsense 520.2
 occultism 689.1
 incantation 691.4
 v deceive 356.14
 trick 356.19
hodgepodge
 miscellany 770.13
 mix 797.6
 jumble 810.3
hoe 1069.17
hog
 n pig 80.13
 drugs 87.18
 swine 311.9
 self-seeker 651.3
 glutton 672.3
 v monopolize 469.6
 appropriate 480.19
hoggish
 piggish 80.24
 greedy 100.27
 ungulate 311.46
 monopolistic 469.11
 gluttonous 672.6
hogwash
 humbug 354.14
 refuse 391.4
 bull 520.3
hog-wild 105.25
ho-hum dull 117.6
 tedious 118.15
 same 781.6
hoi polloi
 inferior 250.2
 the masses 606.2

hoist
n lift 912.2
lifter 912.3
v elevate 912.5

hoity-toity
n arrogance 141.1
adj arrogant 141.9
upper-class 607.10
interj my! 122.21

hokey 336.8

hokum
humbug 354.14
bull 520.3
acting 704.8

hold
n cellar 197.17
storehouse 386.6
custody 429.5
stronghold 460.6
possession 469.1
purchase 474.2
seizure 480.2
control 612.2
notation 709.12
influence 894.1
footing 901.5
handle 901.11
purchase 906.2
v use 87.22
extend 158.9
refrain 329.3
affirm 334.5
store up 386.11
restrain 428.7
confine 429.12
possess 469.4
grip 474.6
keep 474.7
exist 761.8
include 772.3
cohere 803.6
endure 827.6
remain 853.5
stabilize 855.7
sustain 856.4
cease 857.6
support 901.21
obsess 926.25
judge 946.8
conclude 946.10
decide 946.11
think 953.11
be true 973.8
engross 983.13
suffice 991.4

hold a candle to 943.7

hold a grudge 152.12

hold back
suppress 106.8
slow 175.9
reserve 386.12
not use 390.5
restrain 428.7
deny 442.4
withhold 484.6
restrain oneself 668.6
abstain 668.7
delay 846.8
hinder 1012.10

hold down
suppress 428.8

subjugate 432.8

holder
container 195.1
possessor 470.1
recipient 479.3

hold fast
remain firm 359.9
stay with it 360.4
restrain 428.7
hold 474.6
stick close 803.8
stand fast 855.11

hold forth
offer 439.4
declaim 543.10
expound 568.16

hold in
restrain 428.7
retain 474.5

holding
n possession 469.1
estate 471.4
retention 474.1
share 738.3
verdict 946.5
adj addicted 87.25
possessing 469.9
retentive 474.8
supporting 901.23
obsessive 926.34
engrossing 983.20

holdings
supply 386.2
property 471.1
stock 738.2
share 738.3
collection 770.11

hold it! 857.13

hold off
demur 325.4
not use 390.5
fend off 460.10
postpone 846.9
procrastinate 846.11
repulse 908.3

hold office
hold a post 609.42
fill an office 724.14
take one's turn 825.5

hold on
v direct 161.5
stay with it 360.4
hold 474.6
trade 737.23
cohere 803.6
endure 827.6
wait 846.12
continue 856.3
interj cease! 857.13

hold out
not weaken 15.10
remain firm 359.9
stay with it 360.4
balk 361.7
offer 439.4
resist 453.2
stand fast 453.4
strike 727.10
endure 827.6
stand fast 855.11

holdover
remainder 256.1
officeholder 610.11

hold together
cooperate 450.3

agree 788.6
join 800.11
cohere 803.6
be true 973.8

holdup
slowing 175.4
theft 482.3
overcharge 632.5
delay 846.2
hindrance 1012.1
time constants 1041.11

hold up
not weaken 15.10
slow 175.9
buoy 298.8
stay with it 360.4
restrain 428.7
help 449.12
resist 453.2
rob 482.14
flaunt 501.17
overprice 632.7
delay 846.8
postpone 846.9
stand fast 855.11
support 901.21
elevate 912.5
stand the test 942.10
be true 973.8
hinder 1012.10

hole
n sty 80.11
atmosphere 184.32
compartment 197.2
cellar 197.17
crack 224.2
hovel 228.11
lair 228.26
disapproved place 228.28
small space 258.3
pit 275.2
cavity 284.2
cave 284.5
opening 292.1
perforation 292.3
hiding place 346.4
score 409.5
sewer 654.7
golf 751.1
deficiency 795.2
fault 1003.2
impasse 1013.6
v perforate 292.15

the hole 429.8

hole in one
score 409.5
round 751.3

hole-in-the-wall
nook 197.3
hut 228.9
small space 258.3

holiday
n vacation 20.3
day off 20.4
absence 222.4
celebration 487.1
interim 826.1
pause 857.3
v vacation 20.9
adj vacational 20.10

holier-than-thou
hypocritical 354.33

sanctimonious 693.5

holistic
whole 792.9
universal 864.14

holler
n cry 59.1
complaint 115.5
valley 237.7
v cry 59.6
complain 115.16
object 333.5

hollow
n compartment 197.2
valley 237.7
pit 275.2
cavity 284.2
opening 292.1
v be concave 284.12
hollow out 284.13
adj deep 54.11
dull 117.6
vacant 222.14
concave 284.16
insincere 354.32
vain 391.13
empty-headed 922.19
sophistical 936.10

holly 44.4

holocaust
torment 96.7
slaughter 308.1
butchery 308.3
destruction 395.1
oblation 696.7

the Holocaust 308.4

holograph
n autograph 337.3
handwriting 547.3
writing 547.10
document 549.5
adj written 547.22

holy
almighty 677.17
sacred 685.7
godly 692.9

holy orders
the ministry 698.1
calling 698.10
major orders 699.4
seven sacraments 701.4

holy table 703.12

holy terror
frightener 127.9
brat 302.4
ruffian 593.4
violent person 671.10

homage
respect 155.1
obeisance 155.2
obedience 326.1
submission 433.1
praise 509.5
duty 641.1
fidelity 644.7
worship 696.1

home
n home sweet home 228.2
habitat 228.18
fatherland 232.2
asylum 1009.4
adj residential 228.32
in safety 1007.6

home economics
cooking 11.1

domestic management 573.6
home free 1007.6
the home front 232.2
homeland 232.2
homeless
  n poor man 619.4
  adj unplaced 160.10
  forlorn 584.12
  destitute 619.9
  alone 872.8
the homeless
  the underprivileged 606.4
  the poor 619.3
  unfortunate 1011.7
homely
  comfortable 121.11
  humble 137.10
  homelike 228.33
  common 497.14
  plain 499.6
  plain-speaking 535.3
  informal 581.3
  populational 606.8
  simple 798.6
  ugly 1015.6
homemade 892.18
homemaker 575.2
home office room 197.6
  home workplace 739.8
homeopathic 90.15
homeopathy 90.13
homeowner 227.7
home plate 745.1
homer
  n mail carrier 353.6
  score 409.5
  game 745.3
  v play 745.5
Homeric huge 257.20
  poetic 720.15
home run score 409.5
  game 745.3
home schooling elementary
    school 567.3
  teaching 568.1
  elementary education 568.5
home shopping purchase 733.1
  marketplace 736.2
homesick
  wistful 100.23
  melancholy 112.23
homespun
  n plain speech 535.1
  adj rough 288.6
  natural 416.6
  common 497.14
  plain 499.6
  plain-speaking 535.3
  simple 798.6
  made 892.18
homestead home 228.2
  farm 1069.8
homesteader
  settler 227.9
  tenant 470.4
homestretch 820.3
homeward
  adj arriving 186.9
  adv clockwise 161.24
homework
  lesson 568.7

task 724.2
homey
  comfortable 121.11
  homelike 228.33
  informal 581.3
homicidal 308.24
homicide
  manslaughter 308.2
  killer 308.11
homily lecture 543.3
  treatise 556.1
  lesson 568.7
homing pigeon 353.6
hominid
  n ancient 842.7
  adj manlike 312.14
homoerotic 75.30
homogeneity
  sameness 778.1
  uniformity 781.1
  simplicity 798.1
homogeneous
  identical 778.7
  uniform 781.5
  similar 784.10
  simple 798.6
homogenized 812.8
homonym word 526.1
  the same 778.3
homophone word 526.1
  the same 778.3
Homo sapiens 312.1
homosexual
  n gay person 75.14
  adj homoerotic 75.30
homosexuality
  sexuality 75.2
  sexual preference 75.10
honcho superior 249.4
  chief 575.4
  important person 997.11
hone 285.7
hone for 100.16
honest natural 499.7
  upright 644.13
  veracious 644.16
  genuine 973.15
  virtuous 653.6
honesty
  probity 644.1
  veracity 644.3
  genuineness 973.7
honey
  n sweets 10.40
  sweetening 66.2
  loved one 104.11
  endearment term 562.6
  adhesive 803.4
  first-rate 999.7
  beauty 1016.9
  v sweeten 66.3
  flatter 511.6
honeybee 311.35
honeycomb
  n sweetening 66.2
  indentation 284.6
  porousness 292.8
  v pervade 221.7
  perforate 292.15
  undermine 393.15
  overthrow 395.20

honeydew 66.2
honeyed
  sweet 66.4
  pleasant 97.6
  flattering 511.8
  melodious 708.48
honeymoon
  n wedding 563.3
  v go on a honeymoon 563.16
honk
  n blare 53.5
  v blare 53.10
  quack 60.5
honky-tonk 88.20
honor
  n respect 155.1
  real estate 471.6
  praise 509.5
  probity 644.1
  token of esteem 646
  great honor 646.1
  title 648.1
  esteem 662.3
  prestige 662.4
  chastity 664.1
  attribution 888.1
  notability 997.2
  v respect 155.4
  execute 437.9
  celebrate 487.2
  pay in full 624.13
  recognize 646.8
  confer honor upon 662.12
  worship 696.11
honorable
  venerable 155.12
  honest 644.13
  honorary 646.10
  reputable 662.15
the Honorable 648.8
honorarium
  gratuity 478.5
  subsidy 478.8
  recompense 624.3
honorary
  honorific 646.10
  titular 648.7
honored
  respected 155.11
  distinguished 646.9
  reputable 662.15
  esteemed 662.16
honorific
  n name 527.3
  title 648.1
  adj respectful 155.8
  nominal 527.15
  honorary 646.10
  titular 648.7
hood
  n cover 295.2
  mischief-maker 322.3
  combatant 461.1
  ruffian 593.4
  bad person 660.5
  violent person 671.10
  v cloak 5.40
  cover 295.19
  top 295.21
hooded clothing 5.45
  covered 295.31

hoodlum
  mischief-maker 322.3
  combatant 461.1
  bandit 483.4
  ruffian 593.4
  violent person 671.10
hoodwink blind 30.7
  blindfold 356.17
hooey humbug 354.14
  bull 520.3
hoof
  n foot 199.5
  v dance 705.5
hoofed pedal 199.9
  ungulate 311.46
hoofer pedestrian 178.6
  dancer 705.3
  entertainer 707.1
hoo-ha noise 53.4
  bustle 330.4
  quarrel 456.6
  confusion 810.2
  agitation 917.1
hook
  n anchor 180.16
  angle 278.2
  curve 279.2
  point of land 283.9
  snare 356.13
  lure 377.3
  v angle 278.5
  curve 279.6
  trap 356.20
  persuade 375.23
  acquire 472.9
  catch 480.17
  rob 482.16
  play 751.4
  hitch 800.8
hook, line, and sinker 792.13
hookah 89.6
hooked addicted 87.25
  angular 278.6
  crooked 279.8
hooker ship 180.1
  prostitute 665.16
hookup
  affiliation 450.2
  joining 800.1
  combination 805.1
  network 1034.8
hook up
  cooperate 450.3
  yoke 800.10
hook up with 805.4
hooky 222.4
hooligan
  mischief-maker 322.3
  combatant 461.1
  vulgarian 497.6
  ruffian 593.4
  bad person 660.5
hoop circle 280.3
  toy 743.16
  basketball 747.1
hoopla
  rejoicing 116.1
  publicity 352.4
  festivity 743.3
hooray
  n cheer 116.2

v cheer 116.6

hoot
  n cry 59.1
  boo 508.3
  v cry 59.6
  coo 60.5
  boo 508.10
a hoot nothing 762.3
  trifle 998.5
hootenanny
  musical occasion 708.32
  thing 1052.5
hop
  n opium 87.16
  step 177.11
  flight 184.9
  leap 366.1
  dance 705.2
  v speed 174.9
  way of walking 177.28
  fly 184.36
  leap 366.5
  dance 705.5
hope
  n desire 100.1
  wish 100.11
  aspiration 124
  hopefulness 124.1
  sanguine expectation 130.2
  cardinal virtues 653.4
  belief 953.1
  possibility 966.1
  recourse 1009.2
  v be in hopes 124.7
  expect 130.5
  come 839.6
hoped-for
  desired 100.29
  expected 130.13
  future 839.8
hopeful
  n desirer 100.12
  optimist 124.6
  youngster 302.1
  candidate 610.9
  adj cheerful 109.11
  hoping 124.11
  expectant 130.11
  probable 968.6
hopeless
  apathetic 94.13
  unhopeful 125.12
  dying 307.33
  unskillful 414.15
  impossible 967.7
hopped-up
  high 87.24
  excited 105.20
  impatient 135.6
  increased 251.7
hop to it
  v make haste 401.6
  set to work 725.15
  interj make haste! 401.17
horde
  n the masses 606.2
  throng 770.4
  v come together 770.16
horizon vision 27.1
  field of view 31.3
  skyline 201.4

the distance 261.3
horizontal
  n plane 201.3
  adj level 201.7
  straight 277.6
hormone 13.2
horn
  n loudspeaker 50.8
  noisemaker 53.6
  mountain 237.6
  projection 285.4
  telephone 347.4
  alarm 400.1
  wind instrument 711.6
  saddle parts 901.18
  v gore 459.26
horned
  crescent-shaped 279.11
  pointed 285.9
hornet 311.35
hornet's nest
  nest 228.25
  danger 1006.1
  trouble 1013.3
horn in 214.5
horns of a dilemma
  n bewilderment 971.3
  dilemma 1013.7
  adv uncertainly 971.28
horny lustful 75.27
  pointed 285.9
  lascivious 665.29
  hard 1046.10
horology 832.1
horoscope 1072.20
horrendous
  horrid 98.19
  terrible 127.30
horrible
  horrid 98.19
  terrible 127.30
  remarkable 247.11
  bad 1000.9
  hideous 1015.11
horrid horrible 98.19
  terrible 127.30
  bad 1000.9
  hideous 1015.11
horrific horrid 98.19
  terrible 127.30
horrified 127.26
horrify offend 98.11
  terrify 127.17
horrifying horrid 98.19
  terrible 127.30
horripilation
  trepidation 127.5
  roughness 288.2
  cold 1023.2
horror
  torment 96.7
  hostility 99.2
  fear 127.1
  frighteningness 127.2
  frightener 127.9
  abomination 638.2
  eyesore 1015.4
horror-stricken 127.26
hors d'oeuvre bite 8.2
  appetizer 10.9
  sample 62.4

horse
  n symbol of strength 15.8
  heroin 87.9
  beast of burden 176.8
  horseflesh 311.10
  exerciser 725.7
  jockey 757.2
  trestle 901.16
  v give a lift 912.7
horse around
  misbehave 322.4
  play 743.23
  create disorder 810.11
  be foolish 923.6
  trifle 998.15
horseback
  n ridge 237.5
  adv on horseback 177.44
  astride 901.25
horseback riding 177.6
horsehair
  hair 3.2
  string 711.20
horseman 178.8
horsemanship
  riding 177.6
  skill 413.1
  animal husbandry 1070.1
horse of a different color 780.3
horseplay
  misbehavior 322.1
  buffoonery 489.5
horsepower 18.4
horse race
  contest 457.3
  challenge 457.12
  election 609.15
  race 757.3
horse-race 457.19
horse racing
  the sport of kings 757
  the turf 757.1
horse sense 920.6
horseshoe 279.5
hortatory
  persuasive 375.29
  advisory 422.8
  educational 568.18
horticultural
  floral 310.38
  olericultural 1069.21
horticulture
  flower 310.24
  gardening 1069.2
hosanna
  n cheer 116.2
  paean 696.3
  interj hallelujah! 696.17
hose
  n hosiery 5.28
  tube 239.6
  v deceive 356.19
  moisten 1065.12
hosiery 5.28
hosing deception 356.9
  wetting 1065.6
hospice inn 228.15
  asylum 1009.4
hospitable
  comforting 121.13
  receptive 187.16

liberal 485.4
  sociable 582.22
  welcoming 585.11
  cordial 587.16
hospital 91.21
hospitality
  comfortableness 121.2
  receptivity 187.9
  housing 225.3
  liberality 485.1
  sociability 582.1
  cordiality 585.1
  hospitableness 585.1
  congeniality 587.6
hospitalize 85.50
host
  n army 461.23
  receptionist 585.5
  master of ceremonies 743.20
  throng 770.4
  group of animals 770.5
  multitude 884.3
  broadcaster 1034.23
  v entertain 585.8
Host 701.7
hostage 438.2
hostel 228.15
hostess crew 185.4
  attendant 577.5
  waiter 577.7
  host 585.5
hostile dark 38.9
  unpleasant 98.17
  oppositional 451.8
  warlike 458.21
  antagonistic 589.10
  contrary 779.6
  disagreeing 789.6
  counteractive 900.8
  adverse 1011.13
  dislike 99.8
hostility darkness 38.2
  bad feeling 93.7
  unpleasantness 98.1
  malice 99.2
  contraposition 215.1
  antagonism 451.2
  contention 457.1
  warlikeness 458.11
  hate 589.3
  contrariety 779.1
hot
  v heat 1020.17
  adj red 41.6
  zestful 68.7
  lustful 75.27
  in heat 75.28
  feverish 85.58
  fervent 93.18
  zealous 101.9
  passionate 105.22
  hot-tempered 110.25
  angry 152.30
  near 223.14
  fugitive 368.16
  stolen 482.23
  distinguished 662.16
  lascivious 665.29
  fiery 671.22
  syncopated 709.29
  speculative 759.27

brand-new 841.10
on the right scent 941.10
excellent 999.13
torrid 1019.25
heated 1020.29
charged 1032.34
radioactive 1037.11
hot air boasting 502.2
bull 520.3
chatter 540.3
bombast 545.2
superheated air 1019.9
hotbed birthplace 886.8
productiveness 890.6
nursery 1069.11
hot-blooded
lustful 75.27
zealous 101.9
warm-blooded 1019.29
hot dog
n show-off 501.11
v grandstand 413.20
showboat 501.16
interj oh boy ! 95.21
hotel 228.15
hotheaded
passionate 105.29
hot-tempered 110.25
reckless 493.8
fiery 671.22
hothouse 1069.11
hot line
telephone call 347.13
line 347.17
hot seat
capital punishment 604.7
execution 605.5
predicament 1013.5
hot spot
entertainment 743.13
danger 1006.1
predicament 1013.5
hot spring
health resort 91.23
hot water 1019.10
hot tub bath 79.8
fitness 84.1
hot under the collar
heated 105.22
angry 152.30
hot water
predicament 1013.5
boiling water 1019.10
hound
n enthusiast 101.5
beast 660.6
v annoy 96.13
make anxious 126.5
follow 166.3
pursue 382.8
hunt 382.9
persecute 389.7
hour period 824.1
moment 824.2
time of day 832.2
the present 838.1
hourglass 260.1
hourglass figure 260.1
house
n audience 48.6
cabin 197.9

dwelling 228.5
structure 266.2
council 423.1
race 559.4
family 559.5
lineage 560.4
company 617.9
cloister 703.6
theater 704.14
market 736.1
workplace 739.1
casino 759.19
attender 918.2
astrology 1072.20
v domicile 225.10
accommodate 385.10
house arrest arrest 429.6
form of punishment 604.2
houseboat 228.5
housebound 331.18
housebreak
accustom 373.9
domesticate 432.11
train 568.13
housebreaker 483.3
housebreaking
habituation 373.7
burglary 482.5
training 568.3
housebroken
accustomed 373.15
subdued 432.15
meek 433.15
mannerly 504.16
household
n home 228.2
family 559.5
adj residential 228.32
simple 499.6
usual 869.9
well-known 928.27
household effects
furniture 229.1
property 471.1
householder
homeowner 227.7
proprietor 470.2
housekeeper
steward 574.4
major-domo 577.10
housekeeping
domesticity 228.3
domestic management
573.6
house of cards
weakness 16.1
danger 1006.1
fragility 1050.2
houseplant 310.3
housewares 735.4
housewarming 770.2
housewife 575.2
housing
n hangar 184.24
domiciliation 225.3
abode 228.1
quarters 228.4
cover 295.2
horsecloth 295.11
radio 1034.3
adj constructional 892.15

hovel sty 80.11
dump 228.11
hover fly 184.36
take off 193.10
levitate 298.9
hesitate 362.7
be imminent 840.2
Hovercraft
hovercar 179.22
flying platform 181.7
how 384.9
how come 888.8
how do you do? 585.15
how-do-you-do
greeting 585.4
predicament 1013.5
however
notwithstanding 338.8
anyhow 384.10
howl
n noise 53.3
screech 58.4
cry 59.1
animal noise 60.1
lament 115.3
complaint 115.5
objection 333.2
v screech 58.8
cry 59.6
grunt 60.2
wail 115.13
complain 115.16
sigh 318.21
object 333.5
howler joke 489.6
goof 975.6
howling
n audio distortion 50.13
animal noise 60.1
lamentation 115.1
adj shrill 58.14
yowling 60.6
frenzied 105.25
plaintive 115.19
remarkable 247.11
hoyden
n mannish female 76.9
schoolgirl 302.8
adj mannish 76.14
hub convergence 169.1
center 208.2
axle 915.5
fireplace 1020.11
hubbub noise 53.3
outcry 59.4
bustle 330.4
turbulence 671.2
commotion 810.4
agitation 917.1
argumentation 935.4
hubris
presumptuousness 141.2
insolence 142.1
rashness 493.1
presumption 640.2
confidence 970.5
hubristic lordly 141.11
insolent 142.9
rash 493.7
presumptuous 640.11
confident 970.21

excessive 993.16
huckster
n publicist 352.9
vendor 730.5
v bargain 731.18
vend 734.9
huddle
n conference 541.6
v stay near 223.12
come together 770.16
hue
n color 35.1
color quality 35.6
nature 767.4
v color 35.14
hue and cry noise 53.3
outcry 59.4
publicity 352.4
pursuit 382.1
alarm 400.1
huff
n dudgeon 152.7
v intimidate 127.20
provoke 152.24
enlarge 259.4
blow 318.20
huffing 2.32
huffy irascible 110.20
provoked 152.27
hug
n hold 474.2
embrace 562.3
welcome 585.2
greeting 585.4
v stay near 223.12
hold 474.6
harbor 474.7
seize 480.14
embrace 562.18
welcome 585.9
cohere 803.6
huge
herculean 15.17
large 247.7
immense 257.20
hula hoop 743.16
hulk ship 180.1
largeness 257.11
wreck 393.8
body 1052.3
hulking bulky 257.19
bungling 414.20
unwieldy 1013.19
hull
n ship 180.1
shell 295.16
seed vessel 310.30
v husk 6.9
hullabaloo noise 53.4
outcry 59.4
bustle 330.4
hullo! 585.15
hum
n audio distortion 50.13
humming 52.7
vocal music 708.13
series 812.2
v thrum 52.13
stammer 525.8
sing 708.38
persist 781.3

human
n person 312.5
adj kind 143.13
pitying 145.7
hominal 312.13
human behavior 321.3
human being 312.5
hum and haw
prevaricate 344.7
hesitate 362.7
stammer 525.8
humane kind 143.13
pitying 145.7
lenient 427.7
human error 975.1
humanism
naturalistic humanism 312.11
freethinking 695.7
scholarship 928.5
humanist
freethinker 695.13
scholar 929.3
humanitarian
n philanthropist 143.8
adj benevolent 143.15
humanity
kindness 143.1
pity 145.1
humankind 312.1
human nature 312.6
humanness 312.8
leniency 427.1
humankind
human race 312.1
mankind 312.1
human nature
humanity 312.6
humanness 312.8
human race 312.1
humble
v humiliate 137.4
conquer 412.10
subdue 432.9
demote 447.3
adj penitent 113.9
resigned 134.10
lowly 137.10
modest 139.9
inferior 250.6
meek 433.15
populational 606.8
unselfish 652.5
humbled
penitent 113.9
reduced 137.13
humiliated 137.14
conquered 412.17
subdued 432.15
humbug
n sham 354.3
quackery 354.7
humbuggery 354.14
hoax 356.7
impostor 357.6
nonsense 520.2
v deceive 356.14
humdinger 999.7
humdrum
n tedium 118.1
repetitiousness 849.4
adj tedious 118.9

prosaic 721.5
same 781.6
monotonous 849.15
humectant 1065.18
humid sultry 1019.28
moist 1065.15
humidifier 1065.3
humidify 1065.12
humidity
sultriness 1019.6
humidness 1065.2
humiliate
mortify 98.13
humble 137.4
offend 156.5
subdue 432.9
demote 447.3
disgrace 661.8
humiliating
mortifying 98.21
humiliative 137.15
insulting 156.8
disgraceful 661.11
humiliation
chagrin 96.4
mortification 98.6
embarrassment 137.2
indignity 156.2
snub 157.2
subdual 432.4
demotion 447.1
disgrace 661.5
humility
resignation 134.2
humbleness 137.1
selflessness 137.1
modesty 139.1
inferiority 250.1
meekness 433.5
unselfishness 652.1
hummock 237.4
hummocky 283.15
humongous
remarkable 247.10
huge 257.20
humor
n lymph 2.24
blood 2.25
personality tendency 92.11
caprice 364.1
pleasantry 489.1
wit 489.1
nature 767.4
disposition 978.3
mood 978.4
moisture 1065.1
v indulge 427.6
humorist wit 489.12
writer 547.15
author 718.4
humorless 112.21
humorous funny 488.4
witty 489.15
amusing 743.27
hump
n mountain 237.6
bulge 283.3
v speed 174.9
curve 279.6
be active 330.14
make haste 401.6

exert oneself 725.9
humpbacked
hunchbacked 265.13
bowed 279.10
hun 395.8
hunch
n feeling 93.1
premonition 133.1
bulge 283.3
forewarning 399.2
sense 934.3
guess 951.4
suggestion 951.5
v curve 279.6
crouch 913.8
hunchbacked 265.13
hunch over 913.8
hundred region 231.5
century 882.8
hung 202.9
hunger
n eating 8.1
craving 100.6
appetite 100.7
tendency 896.1
v eat 8.20
hunger for 100.19
hung jury 596.6
hungry
craving 100.24
hungering 100.25
hung up
distressed 96.22
late 846.16
obsessed 926.33
hunk strong man 15.6
hulk 15.7
real man 76.6
amount 244.2
lump 257.10
accumulation 770.9
piece 793.3
hunker down 913.8
hunky strong 15.15
virile 76.13
comely 1016.19
hunky-dory 999.13
hunt
n hunting 382.2
search 938.15
v pursue 382.8
go hunting 382.9
persecute 389.7
seek 938.30
search 938.30
hunter
stalking-horse 311.13
sporting dog 311.18
pursuer 382.4
huntsman 382.5
shooter 904.8
seeker 938.18
hunt for 938.29
hunting
n pursuit 382.1
gunning 382.2
search 938.15
adj pursuing 382.11
hurdle
n leap 366.1
obstacle 1012.4

v leap 366.5
hurdy-gurdy 711.14
hurl
n throw 904.3
v place violently 159.13
throw 904.10
hurler
baseball team 745.2
thrower 904.7
hurling
field hockey 749.4
throwing 904.2
hurly-burly
excitement 105.4
agitation 917.1
hurrah
n cry 59.1
cheer 116.2
v cheer 116.6
interj bravo! 509.22
hurricane
outburst 105.9
windstorm 318.12
storm 671.4
hurried
hasty 401.9
rushed 401.11
reckless 493.8
hurry
n agitation 105.4
velocity 174.1
haste 401.1
v move 172.5
speed 174.8
hasten 401.4
make haste 401.5
hurry up
v accelerate 174.10
hasten 401.4
make haste 401.5
interj make haste! 401.16
hurt
n pain 26.1
discomfort 96.5
impairment 393.1
disadvantage 996.2
evil 1000.3
v pain 26.7
anguish 26.8
afflict 96.17
suffer 96.19
offend 152.21
impair 393.9
injure 393.13
collide 902.13
work evil 1000.6
adj pained 26.9
in pain 96.23
impaired 393.27
hurting
n pain 26.1
impairment 393.1
adj pained 26.9
painful 26.10
hurtle
speed 174.8
thrust 902.12
collide 902.13
hurt one's feelings
pain 96.17
offend 152.21

amphetamines 87.4
smoothness 287.3
jewelry 498.5
frozen water 1023.5
coolant 1024.7
fragility 1050.2
v top 198.9
kill 308.14
play 749.7
hail 1023.11
refrigerate 1024.10
freeze 1024.11
adj frozen 1024.14
iceberg 1023.5
icebox 1024.4
icebreaker 180.6
ice-cold cold 1023.14
frozen 1024.14
ice cream 10.47
ice cubes ice 1023.5
coolant 1024.7
iced prearranged 965.8
assured 970.20
cooled 1024.13
ice hockey 749.1
ice pack ice 1023.5
cooler 1024.3
ice rink 749.1
ice-skate 177.35
ice skates 179.21
ichor humor 2.24
blood 2.25
pus 12.6
icicle 1023.5
icing sweets 10.40
topping 198.3
game 749.3
the icing on the cake 407.3
icky nasty 64.7
filthy 80.23
bad 1000.8
icon aspect 33.3
image 349.5
symbol 517.2
sign 518.6
picture 712.11
copy 785.1
substitute 862.2
computer term 1042.18
iconoclasm 695.9
iconoclast
destroyer 395.8
irreligionist 695.10
iconography 349.1
iconology 517.2
icterus yellow skin 43.2
symptom 85.9
ictus seizure 85.6
accentuation 524.10
accent 709.25
meter 720.7
spasm 917.6
icy unfeeling 94.9
seasonal 313.9
reticent 344.10
aloof 583.6
unfriendly 589.9
cold 1023.14
frozen 1024.14
id psyche 92.28
instinct 934.2

ID 517.11
idea hint 248.4
intention 380.1
plan 381.1
advice 422.1
meaning 518.1
reason 886.2
thinking 931.1
notion 932.1
thought 932.1
suggestion 951.5
opinion 953.6
ideal
n motive 375.1
paragon 659.4
beau ideal 786.4
rule 869.4
philosophy 932.2
idealism 986.7
pattern of perfection 1002.4
adj model 786.8
normal 869.8
ideational 932.9
theoretical 951.13
idealized 986.23
perfect 1002.6
idealism
aspiration 100.9
magnanimity 652.2
philosophy 932.2
materialism 952.4
idealization 986.7
immaterialism 1053.3
idealist
n visionary 986.13
immaterialist 1053.4
adj idealistic 1053.8
idealization
spiritualization 689.19
illusoriness 976.2
idealism 986.7
idealize
spiritualize 689.20
overestimate 949.2
utopianize 986.16
ideate
n philosophy 932.2
v think 931.8
imagine 986.14
idée fixe 926.13
identical
identic 778.7
similar 784.10
equivalent 790.8
two 873.6
identification
sensitivity 24.3
association 92.33
sympathy 93.5
indication 517.3
identification mark 517.11
naming 527.2
likening 778.2
recognition 989.5
identify
signify 517.17
name 527.11
relate 775.6
make one 778.5
detect 941.5
recognize 989.12

receive 1036.17
identify with
respond 93.11
get along 455.2
identity accord 455.1
sameness 778.1
similarity 784.1
equality 790.1
particularity 865.1
oneness 872.1
ideogram
representation 349.1
symbol 517.2
phonetic symbol 546.2
ideographic
n letter 546.1
adj representational 349.13
indicative 517.23
literal 546.8
alphabetic 547.26
ideological
ideational 932.9
attitudinal 978.7
ideology
system of ideas 932.8
system of belief 953.3
climate 978.5
ides of March 964.2
id est 341.18
idiocy
mental deficiency 922.9
foolishness 923.1
idiolect 523.7
idiom language 523.1
dialect 523.7
phrase 529.1
diction 532.1
idiosyncrasy
mannerism 500.2
sign 517.1
characteristic 865.4
eccentricity 927.1
disposition 978.3
idiosyncratic
personal 312.15
indicative 517.23
differentiative 780.9
characteristic 865.13
eccentric 927.5
idiot cripple 85.45
imbecile 924.8
lunatic 926.15
idiot box 1035.11
idiotic
mentally deficient 922.22
foolish 923.8
idle
v stagnate 173.9
go slow 175.6
slow 175.9
do nothing 329.2
while away 486.5
trifle 998.14
adj motionless 173.13
slow 175.10
passive 329.6
inactive 331.17
fallow 331.18
vain 391.13
leisure 402.5
baseless 936.13

trivial 998.19
idle fancy 986.5
idle rich 331.11
idle talk chatter 540.3
gossip 552.7
idol
n favorite 104.16
image 349.5
hero 659.5
celebrity 662.9
god 678.2
fetish 697.3
ideal 786.4
v idolatrize 697.5
idolater
enthusiast 101.4
pagan 688.7
worshiper 696.9
idolatress 697.4
idolatrize 697.5
idolatrous
reverent 155.9
uncritical 509.18
pagan 688.11
idolatric 697.7
idolatry love 104.1
respect 155.1
praise 509.5
overpraise 511.3
paganism 688.4
worship 696.1
idol worship 697.1
idolatrousness 697.1
idolization love 104.1
respect 155.1
fetishization 697.2
idolize
cherish 104.21
respect 155.4
praise 509.12
overpraise 511.7
worship 696.11
idolatrize 697.5
idol worship 697.1
idyllic pacific 464.9
poetic 720.15
if
in the event that 831.13
supposing 951.19
if and when 959.14
iffy doubtful 971.17
chance 972.15
if only 959.14
if possible 966.11
ifs, ands, and buts 421.3
if worse comes to worse
1011.17
igloo house 228.10
arch 279.4
snow 1023.8
igneous 1019.26
ignis fatuus
illusion 976.1
fire 1019.13
luminescence 1025.13
ignite flare up 152.19
set fire to 1020.22
ignition fire 1019.13
lighting 1020.4
rocket launching
1074.9

ignoble
offensive 98.18
low 497.15
disreputable 661.10
ignominious
wrong 638.3
disreputable 661.10
ignominy
abomination 638.2
infamy 661.4
ignoramus
novice 572.9
fool 924.1
know-nothing 930.8
ignorance
unaccustomedness 374.1
inexperience 414.2
unintelligence 922.1
unknowingness 930
ignorantness 930.1
ignorant
unaccustomed 374.4
inexperienced 414.17
unintelligent 922.13
nescient 930.12
ignore take 134.8
condone 148.4
slight 157.6
disobey 327.6
neglect 340.6
reject 372.2
extenuate 600.12
exclude 773.4
keep an open mind 979.7
be inattentive 984.2
ignored
unthanked 151.5
neglected 340.14
rejected 372.3
excluded 773.7
ileum 2.18
ilk nature 767.4
kind 809.3
ill
n evil 1000.3
adj ailing 85.56
ominous 133.17
unkind 144.16
bad 1000.7
adv unkindly 144.27
disadvantageously 996.9
badly 1000.13
ill-advised
unpremeditated 365.11
botched 414.21
unwise 923.10
inexpedient 996.5
ill at ease 96.22
ill-behaved 505.5
ill-bred
ungenteel 505.6
unrefined 497.12
ill-bred fellow 497.6
ill-conceived 1000.11
ill-considered
unpremeditated 365.11
botched 414.21
untimely 844.6
premature 845.8
unwise 923.10
inexpedient 996.5

ill-defined
inconspicuous 32.6
vague 971.19
illegal prohibited 444.7
wrong 638.3
unjust 650.9
unlawful 674.6
illegal drug 87.3
illegality wrong 638.1
injustice 650.1
crime 674.3
unlawfulness 674.1
offense 674.4
illegible 522.19
illegible handwriting 547.6
illegitimate
n bastard 561.5
adj fake 354.26
illegal 674.6
spurious 674.7
ill-equipped
unfitted 406.9
ill-provided 992.12
ill-fated 133.17
ill-favored
evil-fashioned 1000.11
unprepossessing 1015.7
ill-founded 936.13
ill-gotten
dishonest 645.16
evil-fashioned 1000.11
ill health 85.3
ill humor
discontent 108.1
bad temper 110.1
bad humor 110.1
contentiousness 935.13
ill-humored
bad-tempered 110.18
argumentative 935.19
illiberal
n bigot 980.5
adj stingy 484.9
ungenerous 651.6
narrow-minded 980.10
illicit prohibited 444.7
freeloving 665.27
illegal 674.6
illicit business
fraud 356.8
illegality 674.1
illegitimate business 732.1
scam 732.1
ill-informed 930.12
illiteracy 930.5
illiterate
n ignoramus 930.8
adj unlearned 930.14
ill nature
ill humor 110.1
malevolence 144.4
ill-natured
ill-humored 110.18
malevolent 144.19
illness 85.1
ill off poor 619.7
ill-provided 992.12
unfortunate 1011.14
illogic 936.2
illogical
unreasonable 936.11

erroneous 975.16
ill repute 661.1
ill-suited
inappropriate 789.7
inexpedient 996.5
ill-timed
inappropriate 789.7
untimely 844.6
inexpedient 996.5
illuminant
n luminant 1025.20
light source 1026.1
adj luminous 1025.30
illuminate
n wise man 921.1
v color 35.14
explain 341.10
manifest 348.5
figure 498.9
illumine 1025.28
illuminated
drunk 88.33
luminous 1025.39
illuminating
explanatory 341.15
educational 568.18
illumining 1025.40
illumination
coloring 35.11
explanation 341.4
ornamentation 498.1
teaching 568.1
picture 712.11
cognizance 928.2
learning 928.4
light 1025.1
lighting 1025.19
ill-use
n mistreatment 389.2
v exploit 387.16
mistreat 389.5
illusion
deception 356.1
bewitchment 691.2
spirit 764.3
error 975.1
deluded belief 976.1
delusion 976.1
figment of the imagination 986.5
illusionary
bewitching 691.11
illusory 976.9
illusive
deceptive 356.21
bewitching 691.11
sophistical 936.10
illusory 976.9
illusory
deceptive 356.21
bewitching 691.11
unreal 762.9
thin 764.6
erroneous 975.16
illusive 976.9
imaginary 986.19
illustrate
explain 341.10
image 349.11
evidence 957.8
cite 957.13

illustration
explanation 341.4
representation 349.1
picture 712.11
example 786.2
citation 957.5
illustrative
explanatory 341.15
representational 349.13
illustrator 716.2
illustrious 662.19
ill will
malevolence 144.4
animosity 589.4
ill wind
windstorm 318.12
bad influence 1000.4
bad luck 1011.5
image
n appearance 33.2
aspect 33.3
apparition 33.5
engram 92.29
description 349.2
likeness 349.5
affectation 500.1
sign 517.1
figure of speech 536.1
picture 712.11
copy 785.1
idea 932.1
phantom 976.4
visualization 986.6
television reception 1035.5
v mirror 349.11
think of 931.17
visualize 986.15
imagery
representation 349.1
description 349.2
figure of speech 536.1
figment of the imagination 986.5
visualization 986.6
imaginable
supposable 951.15
possible 966.6
fanciable 986.26
imaginary unreal 762.9
thin 764.6
farfetched 776.8
illusory 976.9
imaginational 986.19
numeric 1017.23
imagination
fancy 976.3
creative thought 986.2
imagining 986.1
figment of the imagination 986.5
imaginative
original 337.5
expressive 544.10
conceptual 986.18
imagine
v think of 931.17
suppose 951.10
think 953.11
fancy 986.14
interj fancy! 122.22

imagined
  unreal 762.9
  imaginary 986.19 .
imaging
  catharsis 92.25
  representation 349.1
  visualization 986.6
imagining
  imagination 986.1
  figment of the imagination 986.5
imbalance
  distortion 265.1
  inequality 791.1
imbecile
  n cripple 85.45
  idiot 924.8
  adj weak 16.12
  mentally deficient 922.22
  foolish 923.8
imbecility
  inability 19.2
  mental deficiency 922.9
  foolishness 923.1
imbibe
  drink 8.29
  tipple 88.24
  ingest 187.11
  receive 187.13
  absorb 570.7
imbricate
  v overlie 295.30
  adj overlying 295.36
imbroglio
  quarrel 456.5
  predicament 1013.4
imbrue
  imbue 797.11
  soak 1065.13
imbue color 35.14
  pervade 221.7
  inspire 375.20
  inculcate 568.12
  imbrue 797.11
  soak 1065.13
imbuement
  permeation 221.3
  inculcation 568.2
  impregnation 797.2
  soaking 1065.7
imitate
  copy 336.5
  adopt 621.4
  resemble 784.7
  repeat 849.7
imitation
  n reproduction 78.1
  copying 336
  simulation 336.1
  re-creation 336.3
  impersonation 349.4
  fake 354.13
  burlesque 508.6
  adoption 621.2
  similarity 784.1
  copy 785.1
  repetition 849.1
  substitute 862.2
  duplication 874.1
  adj mock 336.8
  spurious 354.26

similar 784.10
  substitute 862.8
immaculate
  clean 79.25
  honest 644.13
  virtuous 653.7
  spotless 657.7
  chaste 664.4
  perfect 1002.6
immanence
  presence 221.1
  intrinsicality 767.1
immanent
  present 221.12
  intrinsic 767.7
immaterial
  unreal 762.9
  unsubstantial 764.5
  irrelevant 776.7
  disembodied 988.8
  insignificant 998.17
  nonmaterial 1053.7
immateriality
  invisibility 32.1
  rarity 299.1
  unsubstantiality 764.1
  unrelatedness 776.1
  illusoriness 976.2
  specter 988.1
  unimportance 998.1
  incorporealness 1053.1
  immaterialness 1053.1
  incorporeal 1053.2
immaterialize
  spiritualize 689.20
  dematerialize 1053.6
immature
  unadult 301.10
  unripe 406.11
  inexperienced 414.17
  incomplete 795.4
  new 841.7
  puerile 922.24
  half-learned 930.15
  imperfect 1003.4
immaturity
  youthfulness 301.3
  undevelopment 406.4
  inexperience 414.2
  incompleteness 795.1
  newness 841.1
  puerility 922.11
  unwiseness 923.2
  imperfection 1003.1
immeasurable
  large 247.7
  infinite 823.3
  innumerable 884.10
immediacy
  presence 221.1
  nearness 223.1
  instantaneousness 830.1
  promptness 845.3
  urgent need 963.4
immediate
  adj present 221.12
  adjacent 223.16
  nearest 223.19
  hasty 401.9
  continuous 812.8
  instantaneous 830.4

the present 838.2
  imminent 840.3
  prompt 845.9
  interj make haste! 401.16
immemorial
  perpetual 829.7
  former 837.10
  old 842.10
  traditional 842.12
immense large 247.7
  huge 257.20
  infinite 823.3
  superb 999.15
immensity
  greatness 247.1
  hugeness 257.7
  infinity 823.1
immerge 367.7
immerse
  submerge 367.7
  baptize 701.17
  engross 983.13
immersed
  underwater 275.13
  soaked 1065.17
immersion
  submergence 367.2
  baptism 701.6
  engrossment 983.3
  wetting 1065.6
immigrant
  migrant 178.5
  incomer 189.4
  citizen 227.4
  settler 227.9
  newcomer 774.4
immigrate
  migrate 177.22
  in-migrate 189.11
immigration
  migration 177.4
  in-migration 189.3
imminence
  expectation 130.1
  approach 167.1
  threat 514.1
  the future 839.1
  forthcomingness 840.1
  impendence 840.1
imminent
  expected 130.13
  approaching 167.4
  threatening 514.3
  future 839.8
  impending 840.3
immobile
  motionless 173.13
  passive 329.6
  permanent 853.7
  immovable 855.15
immobility
  motionlessness 173.2
  inaction 329.1
  inactivity 331.1
  permanence 853.1
  immovability 855.3
immoderate
  unrestrained 430.24
  overpriced 632.12
  intemperate 669.7
  violent 671.16

excessive 993.16
immodest
  conceited 140.11
  unmodest 666.6
immolate 308.13
immolation
  killing 308.1
  oblation 696.7
immoral
  dishonest 645.16
  vice-prone 654.11
immorality 654.1
immortal
  n celebrity 662.9
  god 678.2
  adj peerless 249.15
  eminent 662.18
  almighty 677.17
  everlasting 829.9
  indestructible 855.18
immortality
  life 306.1
  posthumous fame 662.7
  eternal life 829.3
  indestructibility 855.5
immortalize
  glorify 662.13
  chronicle 719.5
  perpetuate 829.5
immovable
  unfeeling 94.9
  firm 359.12
  unyielding 361.9
  unmovable 855.15
  inflexible 1046.12
immune
  resistant 83.14
  exempt 430.30
  safe 1007.4
immunity
  resistance 83.4
  immunization 91.15
  pardon 148.2
  freedom 430.8
  exemption 601.2
  privilege 642.2
  safety 1007.1
immunization
  immunity 83.4
  immunization therapy 91.15
immunize 91.28
immunology 91.15
immure
  enclose 212.6
  confine 429.12
  imprison 429.14
immured
  enclosed 212.10
  jailed 429.21
immutable
  persevering 360.8
  unyielding 361.9
  almighty 677.17
  uniform 781.5
  durable 827.10
  permanent 853.7
  unchangeable 855.17
  inflexible 1046.12
imp
  n brat 302.4
  mischief-maker 322.3

fairy 678.8
pixie 680.7
member 793.4
v graft 191.6
impact
n power 18.1
meaning 518.1
concussion 671.8
force 887.2
striking force 902
collision 902.3
rocket launching 1074.9
v thrust in 191.7
cause 886.10
operate on 889.6
collide 902.13
impacted 855.16
impair
v subtract 255.9
damage 393.9
work evil 1000.6
adj sole 872.9
numeric 1017.23
impaired
damaged 393.27
imperfect 1003.4
impaired hearing 49.1
impaired vision 28.1
impairment
reduction 255.2
damage 393.1
flaw 393.1
disintegration 806.1
disadvantage 996.2
imperfection 1003.1
impale torture 96.18
perforate 292.15
stab 459.25
punish 604.16
stigmatize 661.9
impalpable
infinitesimal 258.14
unsubstantial 764.5
powdery 1051.11
immaterial 1053.7
impanel
record 549.15
select a jury 598.16
list 871.8
impanelment
registration 549.14
jury selection 598.4
impart transfer 176.10
communicate 343.7
disclose 351.4
give 478.12
say 524.22
impartable
transferable 176.18
communicable 343.11
giveable 478.23
impartial
neutral 467.7
impersonal 649.10
unprejudiced 979.12
impartiality
neutrality 467.1
detachment 649.4
moderation 670.1
unprejudicedness 979.5
imparting 343.2

impasse
obstruction 293.3
the same 790.3
corner 1013.6
impassion
excite 105.12
incite 375.17
impassioned
fervent 93.18
zealous 101.9
amorous 104.26
excited 105.20
vehement 544.13
impassive
unfeeling 94.9
inexcitable 106.10
quiescent 173.12
reticent 344.10
inexpressive 522.20
stable 855.12
incurious 982.3
impatience
eagerness 101.1
restlessness 135.1
anxiety 135.1
impulsiveness 365.2
impatient
eager 101.8
anxious 135.6
impulsive 365.9
impeach
censure 510.13
arraign 598.15
accuse 599.7
impeachable
blameworthy 510.25
guilty 656.3
impeachment
deposal 447.2
censure 510.3
arraignment 598.3
accusation 599.1
impeccable
spotless 657.7
accurate 973.16
perfect 1002.6
impecunious 619.7
impedance 1032.13
impede
slow 175.9
delay 846.8
hinder 1012.10
hamper 1012.11
impediment
obstruction 293.3
hindrance 1012.1
embarrassment 1012.6
impedimenta
freight 176.6
equipment 385.4
luggage 471.3
impediment 1012.6
impel
set in motion 172.6
motivate 375.12
compel 424.4
give an impetus 902.11
push 904.9
obsess 926.25
impelling
moving 172.7

motivating 375.25
impellent 902.23
obsessive 926.34
impend
be as expected 130.10
overhang 202.7
be imminent 840.2
impending
overhanging 202.11
imminent 840.3
impenetrable
impregnable 15.19
impervious 293.13
luxuriant 310.43
unintelligible 522.13
inaccesible 967.9
dense 1045.12
impenitent 114.5
imperative
n rule 419.2
command 420.1
mood 530.11
duty 641.1
urgent need 963.4
adj authoritative 417.15
imperious 417.16
mandatory 420.12
commanding 420.13
compulsory 424.10
binding 424.11
vigorous 544.11
obligatory 641.15
necessary 963.12
urgent 997.22
imperceptible
invisible 32.5
infinitesimal 258.14
imperceptive
insensible 25.6
undiscerning 922.14
imperfect
n tense 530.12
adj inadequate 250.7
impaired 393.27
incomplete 795.4
insufficient 992.9
not perfect 1003.4
imperfection
inadequacy 250.3
vice 654.2
incompleteness 795.1
shortcoming 911.1
want 992.4
defectiveness 1003.1
imperfectness 1003.1
fault 1003.2
imperial
n beard 3.8
volume 554.4
adj imperious 417.16
sovereign 417.17
imperialism
sovereignty 417.8
foreign policy 609.5
government 612.8
imperialist 611.9
imperil 1006.6
imperiled 1006.13
imperious
lordly 141.11
imperial 417.16

sovereign 417.17
commanding 420.13
compulsory 424.10
obligatory 641.15
urgent 997.22
imperishable
immortal 829.9
indestructible 855.18
impermanence
transience 828.1
changeableness 854.1
impermanent
transient 828.7
changeable 854.6
impermeable
impervious 293.13
dense 1045.12
impersonal
reticent 344.10
formal 580.7
impartial 649.10
extrinsic 768.3
indistinguishable 945.6
unprejudiced 979.12
impersonate
mimic 336.6
image 349.11
personate 349.12
pose as 354.22
enact 704.30
impersonation
imitation 336.1
personation 349.4
acting 704.8
impersonator
imitator 336.4
impostor 357.6
masquerader 357.7
entertainer 707.1
impersuadable 895.4
impertinence
impudence 142.2
meddling 214.2
defiance 454.1
unrelatedness 776.1
impertinent
impudent 142.10
meddlesome 214.9
defiant 454.7
irrelevant 776.7
imperturbable
inexcitable 106.10
stable 855.12
impervious
resistant 15.20
callous 94.12
impenetrable 293.13
uninfluenceable 895.4
inaccessible 967.9
impetration
request 440.1
entreaty 440.2
prayer 696.4
impetuous
energetic 17.13
passionate 105.29
impatient 135.6
impulsive 365.9
precipitate 401.10
reckless 493.8
transient 828.7

sudden 830.5
inconstant 854.7
impetus
animation 17.4
acceleration 174.4
impulse 902.1
impiety
irreverence 694.1
impiousness 694.1
sacrilege 694.2
ungodliness 695.3
impinge
intrude 214.5
contact 223.10
collide 902.13
impingement
intrusion 214.1
contact 223.5
impact 902.3
impious
irreverent 694.6
ungodly 695.17
impish
mischievous 322.6
puckish 680.18
implacable
unyielding 361.9
revengeful 507.7
implant graft 191.6
transplant 191.8
inculcate 568.12
fix 855.9
plant 1069.18
implantation
insertion 191.1
inculcation 568.2
fixity 855.2
implanted
confirmed 373.18
intrinsic 767.7
established 855.13
implausible
unbelievable 955.10
improbable 969.3
implement
n instrument 384.4
agent 576.3
tool 1040.1
v carry out 328.7
bring about 407.5
execute 437.9
implementation
performance 328.2
accomplishment 407.1
impliable
unyielding 361.9
firm 425.7
implicate
imply 519.4
incriminate 599.10
entail 772.4
complicate 799.3
involve 898.2
implicated
participating 476.8
implied 519.7
accused 599.15
guilty 656.3
related 775.9
complex 799.4
involved 898.4

implication
meaning 518.1
connotation 519.2
hint 551.4
accusation 599.1
incrimination 599.2
guilt 656.1
entailment 772.2
involvement 898.1
implicative
indicative 517.23
suggestive 519.6
implicit
unspoken 51.11
tacit 519.8
intrinsic 767.7
evidential 957.16
unqualified 960.2
implied meant 518.11
implicated 519.7
tacit 519.8
implode 260.10
implore
admonish 422.6
entreat 440.11
pray 696.13
imploring
n entreaty 440.2
adj entreating 440.17
worshipful 696.16
implosion 260.4
imply
promise 133.13
mean 518.8
implicate 519.4
hint 551.10
accuse 599.7
entail 772.4
evidence 957.8
impolite
unrefined 497.12
discourteous 505.4
impolitic
botched 414.21
unwise 923.10
inexpedient 996.5
imponderable
infinitesimal 258.14
unweighable 298.18
unsubstantial 764.5
immaterial 1053.7
import
n transferal 176.1
bringing in 187.7
entrance 189.1
meaning 518.1
implication 519.2
importance 997.1
v transfer 176.10
bring in 187.14
mean 518.8
imply 519.4
matter 997.12
importance
prestige 417.4
distinction 662.5
influence 894.1
significance 997.1
repute 997.1
important
authoritative 417.15

prominent 662.17
influential 894.13
major 997.17
important person
chief 575.3
celebrity 662.9
personage 997.8
importation
transferal 176.1
bringing in 187.7
entrance 189.1
importunate
annoying 98.22
strong-willed 359.15
demanding 421.9
teasing 440.18
necessary 963.12
importune
v motivate 375.14
make advances 439.7
urge 440.12
adj annoying 98.22
importunity
insistence 421.4
importunateness 440.3
impose
intrude 214.5
prescribe 420.9
demand 421.5
oblige 424.5
compose 548.16
charge 630.12
impose on 643.4
minister 701.16
imposed
mandatory 420.12
inflicted 643.8
impose upon
intrude 214.5
exploit 387.16
presume on 640.7
impose 643.4
take advantage of 643.7
inconvenience 996.4
imposing
dignified 136.12
corpulent 257.18
grandiose 501.21
weighty 997.20
imposition
intrusion 214.1
fraud 356.8
demand 421.1
composition 548.2
tax 630.9
presumption 640.2
inconsiderateness 643.1
infliction 643.1
injustice 650.4
impediment 1012.6
impossibility
hopelessness 125.1
unusualness 870.2
the realm of the impossible
967.1
inconceivability 967.1
no chance 972.10
impossible
n impossibility 967.1
adj unacceptable 108.10
out of the question 125.14

fantastic 870.12
not possible 967.7
improbable 972.18
numeric 1017.23
phrs I refuse 442.7
impost
demand 421.1
tax 630.9
impostor
imitator 336.4
fake 354.13
ringer 357.6
imposture
imitation 336.1
sham 354.3
quackery 354.7
fraud 356.8
impotence
weakness 16.1
powerlessness 19.1
feebleness 19.1
sexuality 75.2
sexlessness 75.9
futility 391.2
laxness 426.1
unproductiveness 891.1
lack of influence 895.1
impotent
n weakling 19.6
adj weak 16.12
powerless 19.13
unsexual 75.29
useless 391.9
lax 426.4
unproductive 891.4
uninfluential 895.3
impound
enclose 212.5
confine 429.12
attach 480.20
impoverish
consume 388.3
strip 480.24
reduce 619.6
bankrupt 625.8
impoverished
used up 388.5
indigent 619.8
meager 992.10
ill-provided 992.12
impractical
theoretical 951.13
impracticable 967.8
visionary 986.24
inexpedient 996.5
unwieldy 1013.19
impracticality
impracticability 967.2
idealism 986.7
unwieldiness 1013.9
imprecation
entreaty 440.2
curse 513.1
imprecise lax 426.4
ungrammatic 531.4
uncertain 971.16
vague 971.19
inaccurate 975.17
imperfect 1003.4
imprecision
unmeticulousness 340.4

laxness 426.1
vagueness 971.4
inaccuracy 975.2
impregnable
impenetrable 15.19
indestructible 855.18
impregnate
reproduce 78.10
inculcate 568.12
imbue 797.11
fertilize 890.8
soak 1065.13
impregnation
reproduction 78.3
inculcation 568.2
imbuement 797.2
fertilization 890.3
soaking 1065.7
impresario
director 574.1
theater man 704.23
impress
n indentation 284.6
character 517.7
etching 548.3
print 713.5
reprint 785.5
characteristic 865.4
impact 887.2
v affect 93.15
indent 284.14
attract 377.6
avail oneself of 387.14
attach 480.20
abduct 482.20
mark 517.19
print 548.14
inculcate 568.12
enlist 615.17
be somebody 662.10
fix 855.9
make an impression 931.19
fix in the mind 989.18
impressed
affected 93.23
engraved 713.11
established 855.13
impression aspect 33.3
feeling 93.1
form 262.1
concavity 284.1
indentation 284.6
imitation 336.1
description 349.2
character 517.7
etching 548.3
edition 554.5
inculcation 568.2
print 713.5
reprint 785.5
characteristic 865.4
impact 887.2
idea 932.1
hunch 934.2
suggestion 951.5
opinion 953.6
impressionable
sensible 24.11
sensitive 93.20
teachable 570.18
influenceable 894.15

foolable 923.12
pliant 1047.9
impressive
sensible 24.11
exciting 105.30
grandiose 501.21
vigorous 544.11
convincing 953.26
impress upon 93.16
imprimatur
ratification 332.4
permit 443.6
imprint
n indentation 284.6
character 517.7
label 517.13
etching 548.3
makeup 554.12
print 713.5
impact 887.2
v indent 284.14
mark 517.19
print 548.14
fix 855.9
fix in the mind 989.18
imprinted
engraved 713.11
established 855.13
imprison enclose 212.5
incarcerate 429.14
imprisoned
enclosed 212.10
jailed 429.21
imprisonment
enclosure 212.1
jailing 429.3
punishment 604.2
improbability
inexpectation 131.1
oddity 870.5
prediction 962.1
unlikelihood 969.1
small chance 972.9
improbable
unexpected 131.10
farfetched 776.8
predictable 962.13
unlikely 969.3
impossible 972.18
improbity
falseheartedness 354.4
dishonesty 645.1
impromptu
n improvisation 365.5
extempore 708.27
adj extemporaneous 365.12
unprepared 406.8
adv extemporaneously 365.15
improper
misbehaving 322.5
vulgar 497.10
ungrammatic 531.4
inelegant 534.2
wrong 638.3
inapt 640.10
wicked 654.16
indecent 666.5
inappropriate 789.7
untimely 844.6
inexpedient 996.5
bad 1000.7

impropriety
misbehavior 322.1
vulgarity 497.1
barbarism 526.6
inelegance 534.1
wrong 638.1
undueness 640.1
injustice 650.1
misdeed 655.2
indecency 666.1
unfitness 789.3
untimeliness 844.1
improve
take advantage of 387.15
grow better 392.7
recuperate 396.19
train 568.13
be changed 852.6
change 852.7
perfect 1002.5
improved
bettered 392.13
changed 852.10
improvement
progression 162.1
betterment 392.1
restoration 396.1
training 568.3
change 852.1
new start 858.2
improvidence
thriftlessness 406.2
rashness 493.1
improvident
prodigal 406.15
rash 493.7
improvisation
extemporization 365.5
unpreparedness 406.1
impromptu 708.27
production 892.1
expedient 995.2
improvise
extemporize 365.8
be unprepared 406.6
produce 892.8
originate 892.12
improvised
extemporaneous 365.12
unprepared 406.8
makeshift 995.7
imprudence
rashness 493.1
unwiseness 923.2
foolish act 923.4
indiscrimination 945.1
imprudent rash 493.7
unwise 923.10
undiscriminating 945.5
impudence
impertinence 142.2
disrespect 156.1
defiance 454.1
rashness 493.1
impudent
impertinent 142.10
disrespectful 156.7
defiant 454.7
rash 493.7
impugn deny 335.4
censure 510.13

incriminate 599.10
impugned
accused 599.15
disproved 958.7
impulse
manpower 18.4
sudden thought 365.1
natural impulse 365.1
urge 375.6
prematurity 845.2
driving force 902
impulsion 902.1
instinct 934.2
involuntariness 963.5
impulsive fickle 364.6
impetuous 365.9
motivating 375.25
precipitate 401.10
nonuniform 782.3
transient 828.7
sudden 830.5
premature 845.8
inconstant 854.7
impelling 902.23
instinctive 934.6
involuntary 963.14
impunity 601.2
impure
unclean 80.20
inelegant 534.2
unvirtuous 654.12
unchaste 665.23
obscene 666.9
imperfect 1003.4
impurity
uncleanness 80.1
inelegance 534.1
vice 654.1
unchastity 665.1
intruder 774.2
imperfection 1003.1
imputable
blameworthy 510.25
attributable 888.6
imputation
criticism 510.4
aspersion 512.4
accusation 599.1
stigma 661.6
attribution 888.1
impute accuse 599.7
attribute 888.3
in
n entrée 187.3
entrance 189.5
adj entering 189.12
participating 476.8
on good terms 587.18
modern 841.13
in safety 1007.6
adv inward 189.13
inside 207.10
by authority of 417.20
prep at 159.27
into 189.14
interior 207.13
in a bad way ill 85.56
worn-out 393.36
in danger 1006.13
inability
incapability 19.2

unskillfulness 414.1
in a bind late 846.16
  in trouble 1013.22
inaccessible
  out-of-the-way 261.9
  reticent 344.10
  aloof 583.6
inaccordance
  difference 780.1
  disagreement 789.1
  nonconformity 868.1
inaccordant
  different 780.7
  disagreeing 789.6
inaccuracy
  unmeticulousness 340.4
  misrepresentation 350.1
  misjudgment 948.1
  vagueness 971.4
  inaccurateness 975.2
  badness 1000.1
  imperfection 1003.1
inaccurate
  unmeticulous 340.13
  vague 971.19
  incorrect 975.17
  bad 1000.7
  imperfect 1003.4
in a class by itself
  peerless 249.15
  other 780.8
  first-rate 999.17
inaction
  motionlessness 173.2
  passivity 329.1
  passiveness 329.1
  inactivity 331.1
in action acting 328.10
  operating 889.11
inactivate 19.9
inactive inert 173.14
  passive 329.6
  unactive 331.17
  leisurely 402.6
inactivity rest 20.1
  motionlessness 173.2
  passivity 329.1
  inaction 331.1
  leisureliness 402.2
in addition 253.11
inadequacy
  inability 19.2
  unsatisfactoriness 108.2
  mediocrity 250.3
  unskillfulness 414.1
  inequality 791.1
  incompleteness 795.1
  shortcoming 911.1
  insufficiency 992.1
  imperfection 1003.1
  fault 1003.2
inadequate
  ineffective 19.15
  unsatisfactory 108.9
  mediocre 250.7
  incompetent 414.19
  unequal 791.4
  incomplete 795.4
  short of 911.5
  insufficient 992.9
  imperfect 1003.4

inadmissible
  unacceptable 108.10
  exclusive 773.9
  irrelevant 776.7
  inappropriate 789.7
in advance ahead 165.4
  before 216.12
  on loan 620.7
  early 845.11
inadvertence
  neglect 340.1
  slip 975.4
  inattention 984.1
inadvertent
  negligent 340.10
  unthinking 365.10
  unpremeditated 365.11
  inattentive 984.6
inadvisable
  unwise 923.10
  inexpedient 996.5
in a fog
  concealed 346.11
  muddled 985.13
in agreement
  adj unanimous 332.15
  cooperative 450.5
  agreeing 788.9
  adv jointly 800.18
  prep together with 788.12
  conformable to 867.9
in a jam
  bewildered 971.24
  unfortunate 1011.14
  in trouble 1013.22
in a jiffy
  in short order 174.19
  hastily 401.12
  quickly 830.7
inalienable
  intrinsic 767.7
  inseparable 800.15
in all conscience
  positively 247.19
  rightly 637.4
  candidly 644.23
  in justice 649.12
  reasonably 935.24
in all fairness 649.12
in all likelihood 968.8
in all respects
  wholly 792.13
  throughout 794.17
  exactly 973.21
in all seriousness
  resolutely 359.17
  candidly 644.23
inalterable
  persevering 360.8
  permanent 853.7
in a manner of speaking
  limited 248.10
  figuratively 536.4
  so to speak 784.19
in a mess
  adj confused 810.16
  in trouble 1013.22
  adv in disorder 810.17
inamorato 104.13
inane
  ineffective 19.15

insipid 65.2
  dull 117.6
  vacant 222.14
  vain 391.13
  meaningless 520.6
  nonexistent 762.8
  thin 764.6
  empty-headed 922.19
  foolish 923.8
  ignorant 930.12
  thoughtless 933.4
  trivial 998.19
inanimate
  n gender 530.10
  adj dead 307.30
  languid 331.20
  inanimated 1055.5
inanity
  ineffectiveness 19.3
  insipidness 65.1
  dullness 117.1
  void 222.3
  futility 391.2
  meaninglessness 520.1
  nonexistence 762.1
  empty-headedness 922.6
  foolishness 923.1
  ignorance 930.1
  thoughtlessness 933.1
  triviality 998.3
in anticipation
  adj expectant 130.11
  in readiness 405.21
  adv early 845.11
in a nutshell
  small 258.16
  shortly 268.12
  concisely 537.8
  in brief 557.7
in any event
  notwithstanding 338.8
  anyhow 384.10
inappetence
  apathy 94.4
  undesirousness 102.3
inapplicable
  unserviceable 391.14
  irrelevant 776.7
  inappropriate 789.7
inapposite
  irrelevant 776.7
  inappropriate 789.7
inappreciable
  infinitesimal 258.14
  insignificant 998.17
inapprehensible 522.13
inappropriate
  vulgar 497.10
  wrong 638.3
  improper 640.10
  indecent 666.5
  irrelevant 776.7
  inapt 789.7
  untimely 844.6
  inexpedient 996.5
inapt
  unskillful 414.15
  inappropriate 789.7
  inexpedient 996.5
inaptitude
  unskillfulness 414.1

unfitness 789.3
  inexpedience 996.1
in arrears
  adj due 623.10
  defaulting 625.10
  incomplete 795.4
  adv behind 911.6
inarticulate
  mute 51.12
  shy 139.12
  unintelligible 522.13
  indistinct 525.12
inartificial
  natural 406.13
  artless 416.6
  plain 499.7
  genuine 973.15
inartistic 1015.10
in a rut
  adj habituated 373.17
  adv uniformly 781.7
inasmuch as 888.10
in a stew
  adj in a dither 105.21
  anxious 126.7
  impatient 135.6
  in a temper 152.31
  bewildered 971.24
  confused 985.12
  adv excitedly 105.33
in a sweat
  adj sweaty 12.22
  in a dither 105.21
  impatient 135.6
  confused 985.12
  adv excitedly 105.33
in a tizzy
  adj in a dither 105.21
  confused 985.12
  adv excitedly 105.33
inattention
  unconcern 102.2
  neglect 340.1
  nonobservance 435.1
  unwiseness 923.2
  incuriosity 982.1
  inattentiveness 984.1
  distraction 985.1
inattentive
  unconcerned 102.7
  negligent 340.10
  unskillful 414.15
  nonobservant 435.5
  incurious 982.3
  unmindful 984.6
inaudible 51.10
inaugural
  n speech 543.2
  ceremony 580.4
  adj preceding 814.4
  prior 816.4
  beginning 818.15
inaugurate insert 191.4
  install 615.12
  institute 818.11
  innovate 841.5
  cause 886.10
  establish 892.10
inauguration
  location 159.7
  admission 187.2

ceremony 580.4
installation 615.3
installment 818.5
establishment 892.4
inauspicious
ominous 133.17
untimely 844.6
bad 1000.7
unfortunate 1011.14
inauthentic
illogical 936.11
unauthoritative 975.19
in a way
to a degree 245.7
limited 248.10
so to speak 784.19
in awe
adj wondering 122.9
reverent 155.9
adv in wonder 122.18
in fear 127.33
in bad taste
vulgar 497.10
inelegant 534.2
in behalf of
adv by proxy 576.18
prep for 449.26
instead of 862.12
in black and white 547.22
inborn 767.8
inbound arriving 186.9
entering 189.12
inbred bred 78.17
innate 767.8
inbreed 78.8
in brief
in short 537.8
in summary 557.7
in cahoots
adj leagued 805.6
adv in cooperation 450.7
incalculable
infinite 823.3
innumerable 884.10
unknown 930.17
uncertain 971.16
incalescence 1019.1
incandesce
be hot 1019.22
shine 1025.23
incandescence
glow 1019.12
shine 1025.2
incandescent
burning 1019.27
luminous 1025.30
incantation
conjuration 690.4
spell 691.4
incapable
n cripple 85.45
incompetent 414.7
adj unable 19.14
unfitted 406.9
incompetent 414.19
incapacitate
disable 19.9
afflict 85.50
cripple 393.14
incapacitated
weakened 16.18

disabled 19.16
crippled 393.30
incapacity
infirmity 16.3
inability 19.2
unskillfulness 414.1
unproductiveness 891.1
unintelligence 922.1
incarcerate
enclose 212.5
imprison 429.14
incarcerated
enclosed 212.10
jailed 429.21
incarceration
enclosure 212.1
imprisonment 429.3
punishment 604.2
incarnate
v manifest 348.5
image 349.11
embody 763.5
compose 796.3
materialize 1052.9
adj divine 677.16
embodied 1052.11
incarnation
appearance 33.1
manifestation 348.1
impersonation 349.4
embodiment 763.4
essence 767.2
composition 796.1
materialization 1052.8
in case 831.13
incautious rash 493.7
unalert 984.8
incendiarism 1020.7
incendiary
n instigator 375.11
violent person 671.9
arsonist 1020.8
adj incitive 375.28
inflammatory 1020.27
incense
n fragrance 70.1
joss stick 70.4
suavity 504.5
flattery 511.1
oblation 696.7
v perfume 70.8
excite 105.12
provoke 152.24
incite 375.17
incensory 70.6
incentive
n inducement 375.7
impulse 902.1
adj incitive 375.28
inception origin 818.4
source 886.5
establishment 892.4
incertitude 971.1
incessancy
continuity 812.1
perpetuity 829.1
constancy 847.2
incessant
continuous 812.8
perpetual 829.7
constant 847.5

recurrent 849.13
continuing 856.7
incest perversion 75.11
illicit sex 665.7
inch go slow 175.6
creep 177.26
in character
to be expected 130.14
characteristic 865.13
in charge
adj under arrest 429.22
supervising 573.13
governing 612.18
adv in authority 417.21
inchmeal
by degrees 245.6
piece by piece 793.9
inchoate formless 263.4
unordered 810.12
vague 971.19
inchoative
n aspect 530.13
adj beginning 818.15
in chorus
adj harmonious 708.49
adv unanimously 332.17
cooperatively 450.6
in step 788.11
simultaneously 836.7
incidence event 831.1
frequency 847.1
incident
plot 722.4
circumstance 766.1
event 831.2
incidental
n ornament 709.18
particular 766.3
nonessential 768.2
adj circumstantial 766.7
unessential 768.4
irrelevant 776.7
happening 831.9
occasional 843.11
infrequent 848.3
chance 972.15
incinerate
strike dead 308.18
cremate 309.20
destroy 395.10
burn up 1020.25
incineration
cremation 309.2
discard 390.3
burning 1020.5
incinerator 1020.13
incipience 818.4
incipient 818.15
incise cleave 224.4
notch 289.4
furrow 290.3
open 292.11
injure 393.13
record 549.15
engrave 713.9
sever 802.11
incised notched 289.5
furrowed 290.4
engraved 713.11
incision trauma 85.38
crack 224.2

notch 289.1
furrow 290.1
engraving 713.2
incisive energetic 17.13
acrimonious 17.14
caustic 144.23
vigorous 544.11
sagacious 920.16
incisor 2.8
incite excite 105.12
instigate 375.17
admonish 422.6
impel 902.11
heat 1020.18
incitement
excitation 105.11
incitation 375.4
incentive 375.7
impulse 902.1
incivility
unrefinement 497.3
discourtesy 505.1
inclemency
harshness 144.9
pitilessness 146.1
violence 671.1
cold 1023.1
inclement harsh 144.24
pitiless 146.3
cold 1023.14
inclination
penchant 100.3
obeisance 155.2
direction 161.1
descent 194.1
leaning 204.2
incline 204.4
will 323.1
preference 371.5
aptitude 413.5
partiality 650.3
tendency 896.1
disposition 978.3
prejudice 980.3
incline
n stairs 193.3
inclination 204.4
slope 237.2
v take direction 161.7
lean 204.10
gravitate 297.15
be willing 324.3
induce 375.22
influence 894.7
tend 896.3
inclined
inclining 204.15
willing 324.5
moved 375.30
disposed 978.8
inclining
inclined 204.15
tending 896.4
in clover
adj pleased 95.15
prosperous 1010.12
adv in comfort 121.15
include
internalize 207.5
enclose 212.5
comprise 772.3

put together 800.5
combine 805.3
included
comprised 772.5
involved 898.4
including
adj inclusive 772.6
composed of 796.4
prep with 253.12
inclusion
surrounding 209.5
enclosure 212.1
affiliation 450.2
incorporation 772.1
comprisal 772.1
combination 805.1
involvement 898.1
inclusive
including 772.6
whole 792.9
joint 800.12
incognito
n privacy 345.2
cover 356.11
masquerader 357.7
anonymity 528.1
adj private 345.13
disguised 346.13
anonymous 528.3
incognizance 930.3
incoherence
dislocation 160.1
unintelligibility 522.1
inconsistency 789.2
separation 802.1
noncohesion 804.1
disintegration 806.1
disorder 810.1
discontinuity 813.1
delirium 926.8
vagueness 971.4
incoherent
unintelligible 522.13
inconsistent 789.8
separate 802.20
uncohesive 804.4
unordered 810.12
discontinuous 813.4
delirious 926.31
vague 971.19
in cold blood
unfeelingly 94.14
heartlessly 144.34
intentionally 380.10
incombustible 1022.9
income entrance 189.1
gain 472.3
pay 624.4
receipts 627.1
incoming
n entrance 189.1
adj arriving 186.9
entering 189.12
incommensurable
unrelated 776.6
uncomparable 787.6
inconsistent 789.8
unlike 943.9
incommensurate
unsatisfactory 108.9
uncomparable 787.6

inconsistent 789.8
incommodious
narrow 270.14
inconvenient 996.7
incommunicable 122.13
incommunicado 346.11
incommutable 855.17
incomparable
peerless 249.15
unrelated 776.6
uncomparable 787.6
incommensurable 943.9
incompatible
unsociable 583.5
unfriendly 589.9
different 780.7
disagreeing 789.6
inconsistent 789.8
incompetence
inability 19.2
inadequacy 250.3
unpreparedness 406.1
unskillfulness 414.1
insufficiency 992.1
incompetent
n impotent 19.6
incapable 414.7
adj unable 19.14
inadequate 250.7
unfitted 406.9
incapable 414.19
insufficient 992.9
incomplete
partial 793.7
uncompleted 795.4
insufficient 992.9
imperfect 1003.4
in compliance with
adv obediently 326.6
prep conformable to 867.9
incomprehensible
wonderful 122.10
unintelligible 522.13
infinite 823.3
fantastic 870.12
incomprehension
unperceptiveness 922.2
incognizance 930.3
incompressible
dense 1045.12
rigid 1046.11
inconceivable
wonderful 122.10
fantastic 870.12
unbelievable 955.10
impossible 967.7
in concert
adj cooperative 450.5
in accord 455.3
harmonious 708.49
adv unanimously 332.17
in step 788.11
concurrently 899.5
inconclusive
illogical 936.11
unsound 936.12
unproved 958.8
in condition
healthy 83.8
hale 83.12
out of order 765.7

in order 807.7
in conformity
adj obedient 326.3
adv in step 788.11
conformably 867.7
incongruity
humorousness 488.1
difference 780.1
inconsistency 789.2
nonconformity 868.1
illogicalness 936.2
inexpedience 996.1
incongruous
off-color 35.21
humorous 488.4
different 780.7
inconsistent 789.8
illogical 936.11
inexpedient 996.5
in conjunction with
additionally 253.12
with 769.12
inconsequence
unrelatedness 776.1
unimportance 998.1
inconsequent
irrelevant 776.7
inconsistent 789.8
illogical 936.11
inconsequential
insignificant 248.6
illogical 936.11
unimportant 998.17
inconsiderable
insignificant 248.6
unimportant 998.17
inconsiderate
unthoughtful 144.18
careless 340.11
unthinking 365.10
ill-bred 505.6
unwise 923.10
inconsistency
contrariety 779.1
difference 780.1
nonuniformity 782.1
incongruity 789.2
noncohesion 804.1
inconstancy 854.2
nonconformity 868.1
illogicalness 936.2
inconsistent
contrary 779.6
different 780.7
nonuniform 782.3
incongruous 789.8
incoherent 804.4
inconstant 854.7
illogical 936.11
inconsolable
sorrowful 112.26
disconsolate 112.28
inconsonant
different 780.7
inconsistent 789.8
inconspicuous 32.6
inconstancy
irresolution 362.1
fickleness 364.3
infidelity 645.5
nonuniformity 782.1

irregularity 851.1
instability 854.2
inconstant
fickle 364.6
nonobservant 435.5
unfaithful 645.20
nonuniform 782.3
transient 828.7
irregular 851.3
changeable 854.7
incontestable
impregnable 15.19
obvious 970.15
incontinence
greed 100.8
unrestraint 430.3
prodigality 486.1
uncontinence 665.2
intemperance 669.1
excess 993.1
incontinent
unrestrained 430.24
prodigal 486.8
uncontinent 665.24
intemperate 669.7
excessive 993.16
incontrovertible
evidential 957.16
obvious 970.15
inconvenience
n imposition 643.1
untimeliness 844.1
inexpedience 996.1
discommodity 996.3
impediment 1012.6
trouble 1013.3
unwieldiness 1013.9
v presume on 640.7
put to inconvenience
996.4
trouble 1013.13
inconvenient
untimely 844.6
incommodious 996.7
unwieldy 1013.19
inconvertible
unpayable 625.13
unchangeable 855.17
inconvincible 956.4
incorporate
include 772.3
compose 796.3
combine 805.3
materialize 1052.9
incorporated
associated 617.16
joined 800.13
combined 805.5
embodied 1052.11
incorporation
affiliation 450.2
inclusion 772.1
composition 796.1
combination 805.1
materialization 1052.8
incorporeal
n specter 988.1
incorporeity 1053.2
adj unsubstantial 764.5
spectral 988.7
immaterial 1053.7

incorrect
ungrammatic 531.4
inelegant 534.2
wrong 638.3
inaccurate 975.17
incorrigible
past hope 125.15
ungovernable 361.12
confirmed 373.18
irreclaimable 654.18
incorrupt
unsinful 653.8
innocent 657.6
incorruptible
trustworthy 644.19
immortal 829.9
indestructible 855.18
incrassate
v thicken 269.5
congeal 1045.10
emulsify 1062.10
adj distended 259.13
thickened 1045.14
increase
n aggravation 119.1
ascent 193.1
gain 251.1
addition 253.1
adjunct 254.1
expansion 259.1
improvement 392.1
multiplication 883.4
elevation 912.1
v develop 14.2
aggravate 119.2
quantify 244.4
graduate 245.4
enlarge 251.4
increase 251.6
add to 253.5
expand 259.4
develop 259.5
grow 259.7
multiply 883.6
increased
aggravated 119.4
heightened 251.7
expanded 259.10
multiple 883.8
incredible
wonderful 122.10
remarkable 247.10
fantastic 870.12
absurd 923.11
unbelievable 955.10
improbable 969.3
incredulity
agnosticism 695.6
unbelief 955.1
ungullibility 956.2
incredulousness
956.1
incredulous
agnostic 695.20
unbelieving 955.8
uncredulous 956.4
increment
increase 251.1
adjunct 254.1
incriminate 599.10
incrimination 599.2

incrustation
covering 295.1
crust 295.14
incubate 78.12
incubation 78.5
incubator 886.8
incubus
frightener 127.9
burden 297.7
demon 680.6
dream 986.9
inculcate
indoctrinate 568.12
fix in the mind 989.18
inculcated 373.18
inculcation 568.2
inculpable 657.8
inculpate 599.10
inculpated
accused 599.15
guilty 656.3
incumbency
burden 297.7
responsibility 641.2
benefice 698.9
position 724.5
incumbent
n inhabitant 227.2
tenant 470.4
officeholder 610.11
benefice-holder 699.7
adj overhanging 202.11
overlying 295.36
onerous 297.17
incur 897.4
incurable
n sick person 85.43
adj past hope 125.15
incuriosity
unconcern 102.2
uninquisitiveness 982.1
incuriousness 982.1
inattention 984.1
incurious
unconcerned 102.7
uninquisitive 982.3
inattentive 984.6
incursion influx 189.2
intrusion 214.1
raid 459.4
overstepping 910.3
incurve curve 279.6
be concave 284.12
incurved
curved 279.7
concave 284.16
indebted grateful 150.5
in debt 623.8
obliged 641.16
insolvent 729.19
liable 897.5
indecency
sexual desire 75.5
vulgarity 497.1
unchastity 665.1
immodesty 666.2
indelicacy 666.1
indecent vulgar 497.10
unchaste 665.23
indelicate 666.5
indecipherable 522.19

indecision
irresolution 362.1
uncertainty 971.1
indecisive
wishy-washy 16.17
formless 263.4
irresolute 362.9
inconstant 854.7
unproved 958.8
uncertain 971.16
vague 971.19
indecorous
vulgar 497.10
inelegant 534.2
wrong 638.3
indecent 666.5
indecorum
vulgarity 497.1
wrong 638.1
indecency 666.1
indeed
adv positively 247.19
chiefly 249.17
certainly 970.23
truly 973.18
interj astonishment 122.19
yes! 332.18
indefatigable
industrious 330.22
persevering 360.8
continuing 856.7
indefeasible
unchangeable 855.17
inevitable 963.15
indefensible
unacceptable 108.10
unjustifiable 650.12
indefinable
indescribable 122.13
inexplicable 522.18
vague 971.19
indefinite
inconspicuous 32.6
formless 263.4
general 864.11
indistinguishable 945.6
vague 971.19
indeliberate 365.11
indelible
deep-dyed 35.18
deep-felt 93.24
indestructible 855.18
unforgettable 989.26
indelicacy
vulgarity 497.1
indecency 666.1
in demand
desired 100.29
salable 734.14
indemnification
compensation 338.1
reparation 481.2
recompense 624.3
atonement 658.1
indemnify
compensate 338.4
make restitution 481.5
requite 506.5
pay 624.10
indemnity
pardon 148.2

compensation 338.1
security 438.1
exemption 601.2
recompense 624.3
atonement 658.1
indemonstrable 971.16
indent
n indentation 284.6
summons 420.5
demand 421.1
request 440.1
appropriation 480.4
print 517.7
v dent 284.14
notch 289.4
summon 420.11
demand 421.5
request 440.9
appropriate 480.19
depress 913.4
indentation
indent 284.6
excavation 284.11
notch 289.1
texture 294.1
print 517.7
indented dented 284.17
notched 289.5
indenture
n indentation 284.6
binding over 615.8
v article 615.18
indentured servant 432.7
independence
pride 136.1
nationhood 232.6
voluntariness 324.2
self-control 359.5
self-determination 430.5
self-help 449.6
rallying device 458.12
neutrality 467.1
nonpartisanism 609.26
wealth 618.1
unrelatedness 776.1
independent
n free agent 430.12
neutral 467.4
nonpartisan 609.28
moderate 611.10
adj proud 136.8
voluntary 324.2
strong-willed 359.15
self-dependent 430.22
self-helpful 449.23
neutral 467.7
nonpartisan 609.45
moderate 611.18
wealthy 618.14
unrelated 776.6
separate 802.20
indescribable
ineffable 122.13
extraordinary 870.14
indestructible
perpetual 829.7
undestroyable 855.18
in detail
meticulously 339.16
at length 538.16
fully 766.13

piece by piece 793.9
particularly 865.15
indeterminate
formless 263.4
obscure 522.15
unessential 768.4
relative 775.7
general 864.11
vague 971.19
chance 972.15
index
n finger 73.5
map 159.5
contents 196.1
prohibition 444.1
sign 517.1
pointer 517.4
hint 551.4
reference book 554.9
makeup 554.12
bibliography 558.4
directory 574.10
outline 801.4
table 808.4
characteristic 865.4
listing 871.7
v record 549.15
classify 809.6
list 871.8
indexed
recorded 549.17
classified 809.8
listed 871.9
Indian 312.3
Indian reservation 397.7
Indian summer
St Martin's summer 313.5
dog days 1019.7
indicate augur 133.12
manifest 348.5
signify 517.17
mean 518.8
hint 551.10
specify 865.11
evidence 957.8
indicated
augured 133.15
implied 519.7
requisite 963.13
indication omen 133.3
manifestation 348.1
signification 517.3
hint 551.4
evidence 957.1
indicative
n mood 530.11
adj premonitory 133.16
manifesting 348.9
indicatory 517.23
meaningful 518.10
suggestive 519.6
evidential 957.16
indicator 517.1
indict
censure 510.13
arraign 598.15
accuse 599.7
attribute to 888.4
indictable
blameworthy 510.25
guilty 656.3

indictment
censure 510.3
arraignment 598.3
accusation 599.1
attribution 888.1
indifference
apathy 94.4
neutrality 102.1
indifferentness 102.1
nonchalance 106.5
inertness 173.4
languor 331.6
carelessness 340.2
laxness 426.1
nonobservance 435.1
neutral 467.2
nonreligiousness 695.1
unprejudicedness 979.5
incuriosity 982.1
inattention 984.1
unimportance 998.1
mediocrity 1005.1
indifferent insipid 65.2
apathetic 94.13
halfhearted 102.6
nonchalant 106.15
reluctant 325.6
careless 340.11
lax 426.4
neutral 467.7
nonreligious 695.15
unprejudiced 979.12
incurious 982.3
inattentive 984.6
mediocre 1005.7
indigence 619.2
indigenous
native 226.5
innate 767.8
indigent
n poor man 619.4
adj poverty-stricken 619.8
indigestible 82.6
indigestion 85.9
indignant angry 152.28
disapproving 510.21
indignation
indignant displeasure 152.4
disapproval 510.1
indignity affront 156.2
disparagement 512.1
indirect deviative 164.7
oblique 204.13
deceitful 356.22
circumlocutory 538.14
dishonest 645.16
eventual 831.11
circuitous 914.7
indirection
deviation 164.1
obliquity 204.1
deceit 356.3
circumlocution 538.5
improbity 645.1
circuitousness 914.1
indiscernible
invisible 32.5
infinitesimal 258.14
indistinguishable 945.6
indiscipline
disobedience 327.1

lawlessness 418.1
unrestraint 430.3
intemperance 669.1
indiscreet rash 493.7
indecent 666.5
unwise 923.10
undiscriminating 945.5
indiscretion
divulgence 351.2
rashness 493.1
misdeed 655.2
indecency 666.1
unwiseness 923.2
foolish act 923.4
indiscrimination 945.1
blunder 975.5
indiscriminate
mixed 797.14
unordered 810.12
extensive 864.13
undiscriminating 945.5
purposeless 972.16
indiscrimination
unconcern 102.2
unparticularness 945.1
indiscriminateness 945.1
choicelessness 963.6
indispensable
n requirement 963.2
adj requisite 963.13
vital 997.23
indispose afflict 85.50
disincline 379.4
indisposed ill 85.56
unwilling 325.5
indisputable
manifest 348.8
real 761.15
evidential 957.16
unqualified 960.2
obvious 970.15
indissoluble
inseparable 800.15
indivisible 1045.13
indistinct
inconspicuous 32.6
faint 52.16
obscure 522.15
inarticulate 525.12
indistinguishable 945.6
vague 971.19
indistinguishable
inconspicuous 32.6
identical 778.7
undistinguishable 945.6
indite pen 547.21
write 718.6
produce 892.8
inditement
writer 547.2
authorship 718.2
individual
n organism 305.2
person 312.5
something 763.3
single 872.4
adj personal 312.15
indicative 517.23
particular 865.12
one 872.7

individualism
egotism 140.3
independence 430.5
capitalism 611.8
selfishness 651.1
particularity 865.1
characteristic 865.4
disposition 978.3
individualist
n egotist 140.5
free agent 430.12
self-seeker 651.3
misfit 789.4
adj particular 865.12
individualistic
independent 430.22
capitalist 611.23
selfish 651.5
nonconformist 789.9
particular 865.12
individuality
person 312.5
particularity 865.1
oneness 872.1
individual 872.4
individualize
differentiate 780.6
particularize 865.9
indivisible
simple 798.6
inseparable 800.15
indestructible 855.18
one 872.7
nondivisible 1045.13
indocile
unwilling 325.5
insubordinate 327.9
ungovernable 361.12
indocility refusal 325.1
disobedience 327.1
ungovernability 361.4
indoctrinate
inculcate 568.12
propagandize 569.4
brainwash 858.15
indoctrinated 226.6
indoctrination
inculcation 568.2
propaganda 569.2
reindoctrination 858.5
indolence
inertness 173.4
slowness 175.1
inaction 329.1
laziness 331.5
indolent
n lazybones 331.7
adj slow 175.10
lazy 331.19
indomitable
impregnable 15.19
persevering 360.8
ungovernable 361.12
indoor
adj interior 207.6
adv indoors 207.12
indraft influx 189.2
wind 318.1
in dribs and drabs
piece by piece 793.9
sparsely 885.8

indubitable
manifest 348.8
obvious 970.15
induce elicit 192.14
prompt 375.22
admonish 422.6
lead 886.11
influence 894.7
conclude 946.10
inducement reason 375.1
enlistment 375.3
incentive 375.7
allurement 377.1
gratuity 478.5
induct insert 191.4
install 615.12
enlist 615.17
inaugurate 818.11
inductee recruit 461.18
novice 572.9
inductile 1046.12
induction
admission 187.2
installation 615.3
enlistment 615.7
holy orders 698.10
inauguration 818.5
basics 818.6
reasoning 935.3
conclusion 946.4
electrostatic induction
1032.15
in due course
in time 839.11
opportunely 843.12
soon 845.16
indulge humor 427.6
suffer 443.10
indulge oneself 669.4
indulged forgiven 148.7
pampered 427.9
indulgence
patience 134.1
considerateness 143.3
forgiveness 148.1
humoring 427.3
sufferance 443.2
privilege 642.2
intemperance 669.1
tolerance 979.4
indulgent patient 134.9
considerate 143.16
compliant 427.8
nonrestrictive 430.25
permissive 443.14
intemperate 669.7
tolerant 979.11
indulge oneself
reject authority 418.4
please oneself 651.4
indulge 669.4
indurate
v callous 94.6
harden 1046.7
adj hard 1046.13
indurated callous 94.12
heartless 144.25
obdurate 654.17
hardened 1046.13
induration
callousness 94.3

impenitence 114.2
heartlessness 144.10
pitilessness 146.1
hardness 1046.1
hardening 1046.5
industrial
occupational 724.16
commercial 731.22
productional 892.14
industrial engineering 1043.1
industrialist
businessman 730.1
producer 892.7
industrialization
commercialization 731.14
industrial production 892.3
industrialize
put on a business basis
731.20
perform 892.11
industrious
assiduous 330.22
painstaking 339.11
persevering 360.8
industry
industriousness 330.6
painstakingness 339.2
perseverance 360.1
company 617.9
work 725.4
commerce 731.1
industrial production 892.3
indwell
be present 221.6
inhere 767.6
indwelling
n intrinsicality 767.1
adj present 221.12
intrinsic 767.7
inebriant
n spirits 88.13
adj intoxicating 88.36
inebriate
n drinker 88.11
v intoxicate 88.22
adj intoxicated 88.31
inebriation 88.1
inedible 64.8
ineducable 922.15
ineffable
indescribable 122.13
sacred 685.7
extraordinary 870.14
in effect
adj in use 387.25
existent 761.13
adv really 761.16
ineffective
unable 19.14
ineffectual 19.15
useless 391.9
unsuccessful 410.18
incompetent 414.19
uninfluential 895.3
ineffectual
ineffective 19.15
useless 391.9
unsuccessful 410.18
incompetent 414.19
unproductive 891.4
uninfluential 895.3

inefficacious
ineffective 19.15
unsuccessful 410.18
uninfluential 895.3
inefficacy
ineffectiveness 19.3
futility 391.2
lack of influence 895.1
inefficiency
inability 19.2
unskillfulness 414.1
inefficient unable 19.14
unskillful 414.15
inelastic
unyielding 361.9
rigid 1046.11
inflexible 1046.12
inelegance
clumsiness 414.3
vulgarity 497.1
unwieldiness 534.1
inelegancy 534.1
indecency 666.1
ugliness 1015.1
inelegant
bungling 414.20
vulgar 497.10
clumsy 534.2
indecent 666.5
ugly 1015.6
ineluctable
inevitable 963.15
certain 970.13
inenarrable
indescribable 122.13
sacred 685.7
inept unable 19.14
unskillful 414.15
inappropriate 789.7
unintelligent 922.13
foolish 923.8
inexpedient 996.5
ineptitude
inability 19.2
unintelligence 922.1
foolishness 923.1
inexpedience 996.1
inequality
roughness 288.1
class 607.1
injustice 650.1
partiality 650.3
difference 780.1
nonuniformity 782.1
disagreement 789.1
disparity 791.1
unevenness 791.1
inequity injustice 650.1
inequality 791.1
ineradicable 855.18
inerasable 855.18
inerrant
infallible 970.19
exact 973.17
inert inactive 173.14
passive 329.6
languid 331.20
unchangeable 855.17
inanimate 1055.5
inertia inertness 173.4
slowness 175.1

inaction 329.1
inactivity 331.1
indolence 331.5
immobility 855.3
inerudite 930.14
inescapable real 761.15
inevitable 963.15
inessential
n nonessential 768.2
adj circumstantial 766.7
accessory 768.4
insignificant 998.17
inestimable 632.10
inevasible 963.15
in every respect
throughout 794.17
exactly 973.21
inevitable
obligatory 424.11
unavoidable 963.15
destined 964.9
certain 970.13
inexact
unmeticulous 340.13
vague 971.19
inaccurate 975.17
imperfect 1003.4
in excess
adj superfluous 993.17
adv intemperately 669.10
to extremes 993.23
inexcitable
unfeeling 94.9
unconcerned 102.7
imperturbable 106.10
dull 117.6
unastonished 123.3
unnervous 129.2
inexcusable 650.12
inexhaustible
infinite 823.3
innumerable 884.10
plentiful 991.7
inexorable
pitiless 146.3
unyielding 361.9
firm 425.7
inevitable 963.15
inexpectation
hopelessness 125.1
unexpectedness 131.1
nonexpectation 131.1
suddenness 830.2
inexpedience
mismanagement 414.6
untimeliness 844.1
unwiseness 923.2
inadvisablity 996.1
undesirability 996.1
badness 1000.1
inexpedient
untimely 844.6
unwise 923.10
undesirable 996.5
bad 1000.7
inexpensive 633.7
inexperience
immaturity 301.3
unaccustomedness 374.1
unfamiliarity 414.2
ignorance 930.1

inexperienced
immature 301.10
unaccustomed 374.4
unpracticed 414.17
foolable 923.12
ignorant 930.12
inexpiable 650.12
inexplicable
unexplainable 522.18
purposeless 972.16
inexplicit
ambiguous 539.4
uncertain 971.16
inexpressible
indescribable 122.13
sacred 685.7
inexpressive 522.20
inexpugnable
impregnable 15.19
indestructible 855.18
inextensible 1046.12
inextinguishable 855.18
in extremis
dying 307.33
in danger 1006.13
straitened 1013.26
inextricable
inexplicable 522.18
irreducible 799.5
stuck 855.16
in fact really 761.16
truly 973.18
infallibility
certainty 970.1
perfection 1002.1
infallible
inerrable 970.19
exact 973.17
perfect 1002.6
infamous wrong 638.3
knavish 645.17
wicked 654.16
disreputable 661.10
terrible 1000.9
infamy
abomination 638.2
iniquity 654.3
infamousness 661.4
infancy inability 19.2
immaturity 301.3
babyhood 301.5
origin 818.4
infant
n youngster 302.1
baby 302.9
simple soul 416.3
schoolchild 572.3
innocent 657.4
beginner 818.2
adj infantile 301.12
incomplete 795.4
beginning 818.15
infantile
infant 301.12
beginning 818.15
puerile 922.24
infantilism
mental deficiency 922.9
puerility 922.11
infantryman
pedestrian 178.6

foot soldier 461.9
infarction 293.3
infatuate
n enthusiast 101.4
lover 104.12
fanatic 926.18
v enamor 104.23
fascinate 377.7
stultify 923.7
obsess 926.25
adj enamored 104.28
infatuated
overzealous 101.12
enamored 104.28
foolish 923.8
obsessed 926.33
credulous 954.8
infatuation liking 100.2
overzealousness 101.3
infatuatedness 104.4
stultification 923.5
mania 926.12
credulity 954.1
in favor of
adj approving 509.17
prep for 449.26
approving of 509.21
infect defile 80.17
disease 85.51
inspire 375.20
corrupt 393.12
work evil 1000.6
radioactivate 1037.10
infected unclean 80.20
diseased 85.60
radioactive 1037.11
infection
defilement 80.4
contagion 85.4
infectious disease 85.13
inspiration 375.9
corruption 393.2
evil 1000.3
infectious
poisonous 82.7
contagious 85.62
infectious disease 85.13
infecund
unproductive 891.4
unimaginative 987.5
infelicitous
ungrammatic 531.4
inelegant 534.2
inappropriate 789.7
untimely 844.6
inexpedient 996.5
infelicity
wretchedness 96.6
unhappiness 112.2
solecism 531.2
inelegance 534.1
unfitness 789.3
untimeliness 844.1
inexpedience 996.1
infer imply 519.4
reason 935.15
conclude 946.10
suppose 951.10
inference
implication 519.2
reasoning 935.3

conclusion 946.4
supposition 951.3
inferential
suggestive 519.6
dialectic 935.22
inferior
n underling 250.2
subordinate 432.5
retainer 577.1
adj unable 19.14
subordinate 250.6
lower 274.8
subject 432.13
short of 911.5
unimportant 998.16
insignificant 998.17
bad 1000.7
poor 1005.9
inferiority
inability 19.2
subordinacy 250.1
subservience 432.2
abnormality 870.1
shortcoming 911.1
unimportance 998.1
badness 1000.1
inferiorness 1005.3
inferiority complex
complex 92.22
self-effacement 139.2
infernal cruel 144.26
diabolic 654.13
hellish 682.8
execrable 1000.10
inferno hell 682.1
hot place 1019.11
inferred implied 519.7
supposed 951.14
infertile
unproductive 891.4
unimaginative 987.5
infertility
unproductiveness 891.1
unimaginativeness 987.1
infest 910.6
infestation 910.2
infidel
n gentile 688.6
unbeliever 695.11
adj infidelic 688.10
unbelieving 695.19
infidelity
love affair 104.6
unfaithfulness 645.5
infidelism 688.3
atheism 695.5
unbelief 955.1
infield playground 743.11
baseball 745.1
track 755.1
horse racing 757.1
infighting
dissension 456.3
contention 457.1
boxing 457.9
infiltrate absorb 187.13
filter in 189.10
intrude 214.5
launch an attack 459.17
imbue 797.11
soak 1065.13

infiltration
sorption 187.6
entrance 189.1
intrusion 214.1
attack 459.1
imbuement 797.2
soaking 1065.7
infiltrator 214.3
infinite
spacious 158.11
omnipresent 221.13
large 247.7
huge 257.20
almighty 677.17
boundless 823.3
perpetual 829.7
innumerable 884.10
numeric 1017.23
infinitesimal 258.14
infinity
omnipresence 221.2
greatness 247.1
distance 261.1
length 267.1
limitlessness 823
infiniteness 823.1
perpetuity 829.1
large number 1017.5
infirm
unsound 16.15
unhealthy 85.54
stricken in years 303.18
weak-willed 362.12
unvirtuous 654.12
fragile 764.7
inconstant 854.7
feebleminded 922.21
unreliable 971.20
infirmity
unsoundness 16.3
disease 85.1
unhealthiness 85.3
old age 303.5
weak will 362.4
vice 654.2
feeblemindedness 922.8
unreliability 971.6
fault 1003.2
infix
n interjection 213.2
added to writing 254.2
morphology 526.3
v implant 191.8
add 253.4
inculcate 568.12
fix 855.9
fix in the mind 989.18
infixed
confirmed 373.18
intrinsic 767.7
established 855.13
inflame energize 17.10
pain 26.7
make red 41.4
excite 105.12
provoke 152.24
incite 375.17
heat 1020.18
ignite 1020.22
inflamed sore 26.11
red 41.6

feverish 85.58
diseased 85.60
excited 105.20
fiery 671.22
burning 1019.27
inflammable
n fuel 1021.1
adj excitable 105.28
flammable 1020.28
inflammation
soreness 26.4
symptom 85.9
inflammatory disease 85.10
excitation 105.11
incitement 375.4
inflammatory
exciting 105.30
incitive 375.28
inflammative 1020.27
inflate puff up 140.7
increase 251.4
enlarge 259.4
exaggerate 355.3
talk big 545.6
heat the economy 632.9
overextend 993.13
inflated
increased 251.7
distended 259.13
exaggerated 355.4
pompous 501.22
swollen 502.12
bombastic 545.9
inflation increase 251.1
distension 259.2
exaggeration 355.1
pompousness 501.7
style 532.2
grandiloquence 545.1
price index 630.4
high price 632.3
business cycle 731.10
overextension 993.7
inflationary
expansive 259.9
overpriced 632.12
inflect curve 279.6
modulate 524.28
grammaticize 530.16
inflection angle 278.2
bend 279.3
intonation 524.6
morphology 526.3
inflexible firm 359.12
unyielding 361.9
strict 425.7
immovable 855.15
uninfluenceable 895.4
inevitable 963.15
intractable 1046.12
inflict do 328.6
wreak 643.5
infliction affliction 96.8
punishment 604.1
imposition 643.1
bane 1001.1
in flight
adj fugitive 368.16
adv on the wing 184.51
inflorescence 310.26
inflorescent 310.38

inflow influx 189.2
flow 238.4
wind 318.1
influence
n power 18.1
supremacy 249.3
motivation 375.2
machination 415.4
prestige 417.4
influentiality 894.1
good influence 894.6
v motivate 375.22
cause 886.10
induce 886.11
determine 886.12
operate on 889.6
make oneself felt 894.7
prejudice 980.9
influence peddler
Machiavellian 415.8
wire-puller 609.30
politician 610.5
influence 894.6
influential
authoritative 417.15
powerful 894.13
influx inflow 189.2
intrusion 214.1
in focus 31.7
infomercial 352.6
in force powerful 18.12
in use 387.25
existent 761.13
operating 889.11
inform
v pervade 221.7
betray 351.6
inspire 375.20
tell 551.8
report 552.11
teach 568.10
adj formless 263.4
informality
unceremoniousness
581.1
informalness 581.1
informant
informer 551.5
examinee 938.19
witness 957.6
information
communication 343.1
facts 551.1
info 551.1
news 552.1
teaching 568.1
arraignment 598.3
accusation 599.1
knowledge 928.1
data 1042.15
information retrieval 551.7
information technology 551.7
information theory
communications 343.5
electronic communications
347.1
data storage 551.7
autonetics 1041.2
informative
informing 551.18
educational 568.18

informed
prepared 405.16
clued-in 551.17
knowing 928.15
cognizant of 928.16
enlightened 928.18
up on 928.19
informer
traitor 357.10
informant 551.5
betrayer 551.6
accuser 599.5
witness 957.6
inform on
disclose 351.6
inform 551.12
accuse 599.7
betray 645.14
infra 274.10
infraction
disobedience 327.1
violation 435.2
wrong 638.1
lawbreaking 674.3
foul 746.3
basketball game 747.3
game 749.3
hockey game 749.6
overstepping 910.3
infrangible
firm 15.18
indivisible 1045.13
unbreakable 1049.5
infrared 41.6
infrastructure
inferior 250.2
understructure 266.3
directorate 574.11
support 901.1
foundation 901.6
frame 901.10
infrequency
seldomness 848
rarity 848.1
fewness 885.1
infrequent
rare 848.2
sparse 885.5
infringe
intrude 214.5
violate 435.4
adopt 621.4
usurp 640.8
break the law 674.5
overstep 910.9
infringement
intrusion 214.1
disobedience 327.1
impairment 393.1
violation 435.2
adoption 621.2
usurpation 640.3
lawbreaking 674.3
overstepping 910.3
in front
adj front 216.10
adv ahead 165.4
before 216.12
prep facing 215.7
in full at length 538.16
fully 766.13

completely 794.14
in full bloom 303.13
in full swing
adj unweakened 15.21
astir 330.19
thriving 1010.13
adv actively 330.25
in fun
mischievously 322.7
in sport 489.19
for amusement 743.31
infundibular
conical 282.12
concave 284.16
infuriate
v excite 105.12
enrage 152.25
antagonize 589.7
adj infuriated 152.32
turbulent 671.18
infuriated 152.32
infuse insert 191.3
extraction 192.16
inspire 375.20
inculcate 568.12
imbue 797.11
liquefy 1064.5
soak 1065.13
infusion
insertion 191.1
extract 192.7
distillation 192.8
inspiration 375.9
inculcation 568.2
baptism 701.6
imbuement 797.2
admixture 797.7
liquefaction 1064.1
solution 1064.3
soaking 1065.7
in general 864.17
ingenious
skillful 413.22
cunning 415.12
imaginative 986.18
ingenue
simple soul 416.3
role 704.10
script 706.3
actor 707.2
ingenuity
skill 413.1
invention 986.3
ingenuous
immature 301.10
artless 416.5
candid 644.17
ignorant 930.12
gullible 954.9
ingest devour 8.22
eat 187.11
consume 388.3
absorb 570.7
ingesta 10.1
ingestion
body function 2.17
digestion 7.8
eating 8.1
reception 187.4
consumption 388.1
absorption 570.2

ingle home 228.2
fire 1019.13
fireplace 1020.11
inglenook home 228.2
recess 284.7
fireplace 1020.11
ingleside home 228.2
fireplace 1020.11
inglorious
humble 137.10
disreputable 661.10
unrenowned 661.14
ingoing
n entrance 189.1
adj introverted 92.40
entering 189.12
in good shape
healthy 83.8
in order 807.7
ingot
precious metals 728.20
cast 1058.5
ingrain color 35.14
fix 855.9
ingrained
deep-dyed 35.18
confirmed 373.18
intrinsic 767.7
established 855.13
ingrate 151.2
ingratiate oneself
insinuate oneself 138.10
influence 894.7
gain influence 894.12
ingratiating
obsequious 138.14
suave 504.18
ingratitude
unthankfulness 151.1
ungratefulness 151.1
ingredient
particular 766.3
part 793.1
component 796.2
ingress
entrance 189.1
inlet 189.5
channel 239.1
ingroup clique 617.6
influence 894.6
ingrown 855.13
inhabit settle 159.17
occupy 225.7
people 225.9
exist in 761.11
inhabitant dweller 227
population 227.1
inhabiter 227.2
inhalant medicine 86.4
drug 87.3
inhalation
breathing 2.21
drawing in 187.5
inhale smell 69.8
smoke 89.14
draw in 187.12
in hand unused 390.12
undertaken 404.7
in preparation 405.22
possessed 469.8
under control 612.20

restrained 670.11
orderly 807.6
happening 831.9
operating 889.11
in production 892.21
inharmonious
off-color 35.21
dissonant 61.4
disaccordant 456.15
different 780.7
disagreeing 789.6
in harmony
in accord 455.3
agreeing 788.9
jointly 800.18
in heat 75.28
inherence
presence 221.1
intrinsicality 767.1
inherent present 221.12
intrinsic 767.7
instinctive 934.6
inherit be heir to 479.7
inhere 767.6
succeed 815.2
inheritable
heritable 560.20
transferable 629.5
inheritance
property 471.1
bequest 478.10
heritance 479.2
heredity 560.6
inherited
hereditary 560.19
innate 767.8
inheritor heir 479.5
successor 817.4
sequel 835.2
inhibit suppress 106.8
restrain 428.7
confine 429.12
prohibit 444.3
retain 474.5
hinder 1012.10
inhibiting
restraining 428.11
hindering 1012.17
inhibition
suppression 92.24
restraint 428.1
prohibition 444.1
retention 474.1
hindrance 1012.1
inhibitive
restraining 428.11
prohibitive 444.6
hindering 1012.17
in honor of 487.4
inhospitable
unkind 144.16
unhospitable 586.7
unfriendly 589.9
inhospitality
unkindness 144.1
uncordialness 586.1
inhospitableness 586.1
enmity 589.1
inhuman
cruel 144.26
savage 671.21

demoniac 680.17
inhumane 144.26
inhumanity
cruelty 144.11
act of cruelty 144.12
violence 671.1
inhume 309.19
inimical
oppositional 451.8
warlike 458.21
unfriendly 589.9
contrary 779.6
counteractive 900.8
adverse 1011.13
inimitable 249.15
in installments
on credit 622.10
piece by piece 793.9
incompletely 795.6
iniquitous
malicious 144.20
unjust 650.9
wicked 654.16
wrongdoing 655.5
bad 1000.7
iniquity
injustice 650.1
evil 654.3
misdeed 655.2
badness 1000.1
initial
n first 818.3
v ratify 332.12
letter 546.6
adj beginning 818.15
initials
identification 517.11
signature 527.10
initiate
n novice 572.9
member 617.11
v install 191.4
preinstruct 568.14
originate 818.10
inaugurate 818.11
adj skilled 413.26
initiation
establishment 159.7
admission 187.2
elementary education 568.5
ceremony 580.4
first 818.3
inauguration 818.5
initiative
n vim 17.2
act 328.3
enterprise 330.7
undertaking 404.1
referendum 613.8
process 889.2
adj introductory 187.18
beginning 818.15
inject use 87.22
insert 191.3
inspire 375.20
soak 1065.13
injection remedy 86.6
narcotic shot 87.20
inoculation 91.16
entrance 189.1
insertion 191.1

interjection 213.2
intrusion 214.1
soaking 1065.7
spacecraft 1075.2
injudicious
rash 493.7
unwise 923.10
injunction
precept 419.1
charge 420.2
court order 420.6
restraint 428.1
prohibition 444.1
exclusion 773.1
injure mistreat 389.5
impair 393.9
hurt 393.13
work evil 1000.6
injured pained 96.23
impaired 393.27
injurious
unhealthful 82.5
impaired 393.27
corrupting 393.44
disadvantageous 996.6
harmful 1000.12
injury pain 96.5
indignity 156.2
mistreatment 389.2
impairment 393.1
loss 473.1
injustice 650.4
misdeed 655.2
disadvantage 996.2
evil 1000.3
injustice
misrepresentation 350.1
presumption 640.2
unjustness 650.1
wrong 650.4
misdeed 655.2
inequality 791.1
ink
n blackness 38.4
v blacken 38.7
in keeping with
in agreement with 788.12
conformable to 867.9
inkling hint 551.4
admixture 797.7
suggestion 951.5
inky black 38.8
stained 1004.10
inland
n inlands 207.3
adj interior 207.7
adv inward 207.11
in-laws 564.2
inlay
n insert 191.2
lining 196.3
v inset 191.5
implant 191.8
fill 196.7
in league in cooperation 450.7
leagued 805.6
inlet entrance 189.5
cove 242.1
opening 292.1
passageway 383.3
in lieu of 862.12

in line in step 788.11
  conformist 867.6
in line with
  adv directly 161.23
  prep in agreement with
    788.12
  conformable to 867.9
in love 104.29
inmate 227.2
in memoriam 989.29
in memory of
  in honor of 487.4
  to the memory of 989.29
in-migrate
  migrate 177.22
  enter 189.11
inmost interior 207.6
  private 345.13
in motion
  moving 172.7
  under way 172.9
inn 228.15
in name only
  pretexted 376.5
  nominal 527.15
innards viscera 2.16
  contents 196.1
  insides 207.4
  mechanism 1040.4
innate
  hereditary 560.19
  inborn 767.8
  instinctive 934.6
  attitudinal 978.7
inner
  n interior 207.2
  adj interior 207.6
  intrinsic 767.7
  particular 865.12
inner circle
  council 423.1
  clique 617.6
inner city 230.6
inner-directed
  introverted 92.40
  moved 375.30
  independent 430.22
  nonconformist 789.9
inner man
  interior 207.2
  self 865.5
  inmost mind 919.3
  psyche 919.4
innermost
  interior 207.6
  private 345.13
inner nature
  interior 207.2
  inside 767.5
inner workings 1040.4
inning game 745.3
  turn 825.2
innocence
  artlessness 416.1
  naturalness 499.2
  purity 653.3
  guiltlessness 657.1
  innocency 657.1
  chastity 664.1
  ignorance 930.1
  harmlessness 999.9

innocent
  n child 302.3
  dupe 358.1
  simple soul 416.3
  baby 657.4
  adj immature 301.10
  artless 416.5
  natural 499.7
  chaste 653.7
  unfallen 657.6
  chaste 664.4
  ignorant 930.12
  trusting 953.22
  harmless 999.21
innocuous
  humble 137.10
  justifiable 600.14
  harmless 999.21
innominable 122.13
innominate 528.3
in no time
  in short order 174.19
  quickly 830.7
  promptly 845.15
innovate
  originate 337.4
  invent 841.5
  make innovations 852.9
innovation
  nonimitation 337.1
  original 337.2
  curtain-raiser 816.2
  novelty 841.2
  introduction 852.4
innovator
  precursor 816.1
  transformer 852.5
innoxious 999.21
innuendo
  sarcasm 508.5
  aspersion 512.4
  implication 519.2
  hint 551.4
  accusation 599.1
innumerable
  infinite 823.3
  numberless 884.10
inobservance
  nonobservance 435.1
  inattention 984.1
inobservant
  nonobservant 435.5
  inattentive 984.6
inoculate
  immunize 91.28
  insert 191.3
  inspire 375.20
  inculcate 568.12
inoculation
  vaccination 86.28
  injection 91.16
  insertion 191.1
  inculcation 568.2
inoffensive
  odorless 72.5
  justifiable 600.14
  harmless 999.21
in on 476.8
in one's power
  under control 612.20
  possible 966.6

inoperable
  past hope 125.15
  unserviceable 391.14
  impracticable 967.8
in operation in use 387.25
  operating 889.11
inoperative
  ineffective 19.15
  unserviceable 391.14
  in disrepair 393.37
inopportune
  untimely 844.6
  inexpedient 996.5
in opposition to
  adv counteractively 900.10
  prep opposite to 215.7
  opposed to 451.10
  in disagreement with 789.10
in order in trim 807.7
  in turn 807.10
in order to 405.24
inordinance 993.1
inordinate
  exaggerated 355.4
  overpriced 632.12
  intemperate 669.7
  fanatic 926.32
  excessive 993.16
inorganic
  unorganic 1055.4
  mineral 1058.15
inornate 499.9
in other words 341.18
in particular
  fully 766.13
  particularly 865.15
in passing
  on the way 176.20
  hastily 401.12
  incidentally 843.13
inpatient
  sick person 85.43
  inhabitant 227.2
in person
  presence 221.17
  personally 865.16
in place located 159.18
  in position 159.20
  present 221.12
  provided 385.13
  established 855.13
in place of 862.12
in plain sight
  visible 31.6
  openly 348.15
inpouring 189.12
in power
  powerful 18.12
  in authority 417.21
in practice
  in use 387.25
  operating 889.11
in process 889.11
in production
  in preparation 405.22
  in the works 892.21
in progress
  in mid-progress 162.7
  undertaken 404.7
  in preparation 405.22
in public openly 348.15

  publicly 352.19
in pursuit of 382.12
input
  n entrance 189.1
  data 1042.15
  v computerize 1042.21
inquest autopsy 307.18
  jury 596.6
  trial 598.5
  inquiry 938.1
in question
  at issue 938.39
  doubtful 971.17
  undecided 971.18
inquietude
  unpleasure 96.1
  excitement 105.5
  anxiety 126.1
  trepidation 127.5
  agitation 917.1
inquire ask 938.20
  be curious 981.3
inquirer student 572.1
  asker 938.16
  inquisitive person 981.2
inquiring
  n inquiry 938.1
  questioning 938.12
  adj questioning 938.36
  curious 981.5
inquiry trial 598.5
  examination 938.2
  inquiring 938.1
  question 938.10
  canvass 938.14
inquisition
  n tribunal 595.1
  trial 598.5
  inquiry 938.1
  grilling 938.13
  v grill 938.22
Inquisition 938.4
inquisitive
  meddlesome 214.9
  curious 981.5
inquisitor
  inquirer 938.16
  inquisitive person 981.2
in rags shabby 393.32
  indigent 619.8
  slovenly 810.15
in reality
  really 761.16
  truly 973.18
in regard to 775.13
in repair
  out of order 765.7
  in order 807.7
in reserve back 386.17
  in readiness 405.21
  imminent 840.3
in return
  in compensation 338.7
  in retaliation 506.9
  interchangeably 863.6
  in answer 939.7
inroad
  n intrusion 214.1
  impairment 393.1
  raid 459.4
  overstepping 910.3

v raid 459.20
inrush influx 189.2
  wind 318.1
ins 610.11
insalubrious 82.5
ins and outs
  circumstances 766.2
  vicissitudes 972.5
insane
  turbulent 671.18
  foolish 923.8
  unsane 926.26
  overzealous 101.12
insanity
  mental disorder 92.14
  disarrangement 811.1
  mental deficiency 922.9
  foolishness 923.1
  mental sickness 926.1
  insaneness 926.1
insatiable
  greedy 100.27
  rapacious 480.26
  gluttonous 672.6
inscribe letter 546.6
  write 547.19
  record 549.15
  engrave 713.9
  fix 855.9
  remember 989.18
inscribed
  written 547.22
  recorded 549.17
  engraved 713.11
inscription
  epitaph 309.18
  lettering 546.5
  writing 547.1
  monument 549.12
  registration 549.14
  makeup 554.12
  engraving 713.2
  motto 974.4
inscrutable 522.13
in season 313.9
insect bug 311.33
  invertebrate 311.33
  bad person 660.6
insecticide 1001.3
insectivore 311.3
insecure
  unreliable 971.20
  unconfident 971.23
  unsafe 1006.11
insecurity
  unreliability 971.6
  dangerousness 1006.2
in self-defense 460.16
inseminate
  reproduce 78.10
  fertilize 890.8
  plant 1069.18
insemination
  reproduction 78.3
  fertilization 890.3
  planting 1069.14
insensate
  insensible 25.6
  cruel 144.26
  turbulent 671.18
  savage 671.21

unintelligent 922.13
  foolish 923.8
  unwise 923.10
  absurd 923.11
  inanimate 1055.5
insensibility
  physical unfeeling 25
  insensibleness 25.1
  callousness 94.2
  unperceptiveness 922.2
  incognizance 930.3
  indiscrimination 945.1
  inanimateness 1055.2
insensible
  unfeeling 25.6
  invisible 32.5
  unconscious 94.10
  undiscerning 922.14
  unaware 930.13
  oblivious 984.7
  inanimate 1055.5
insensitive
  insensible 25.6
  callous 94.12
  inconsiderate 144.18
  heartless 144.25
  ill-bred 505.6
  undiscriminating 945.5
insensitivity
  insensibility 25.1
  callousness 94.3
  unconcern 102.2
  heartlessness 144.10
  discourtesy 505.1
  indiscrimination 945.1
  intolerance 980.2
insentient
  insensible 25.6
  inanimate 1055.5
inseparability
  familiarity 587.5
  cohesion 803.1
  indivisibility 1045.2
inseparable
  familiar 587.19
  impartible 800.15
  cohesive 803.10
  indivisible 1045.13
insert
  n insertion 191.2
  interjection 213.2
  v enter 189.7
  introduce 191.3
  record 549.15
insertion
  entrance 189.1
  putting in 191
  introduction 191.1
  insert 191.2
  interjection 213.2
  registration 549.14
  spacecraft 1075.2
in session
  in council 423.6
  assembled 770.21
inset
  n map 159.5
  insert 191.2
  v inlay 191.5
in shape
  healthy 83.8

hale 83.12
  hearty 765.7
  in order 807.7
in short order
  in no time 174.19
  in a hurry 401.14
  quickly 830.7
inside
  n interior 207.2
  inner nature 767.5
  adj interior 207.6
  confidential 345.14
  adv in 207.10
  prep in 207.13
inside information
  secret 345.5
  private information 551.2
inside job 381.5
inside out
  inverted 205.7
  completely 794.14
insider
  inside information 551.2
  member 617.11
insides
  viscera 2.16
  contents 196.1
  inner parts 207.4
  inner nature 767.5
inside track
  advantage 249.2
  favor 894.2
insidious
  deceitful 356.22
  cunning 415.12
  dishonest 645.16
  shrewd 920.15
insight
  extrasensory perception 689.8
  sagacity 920.4
  cognizance 928.2
  good idea 932.6
  intuition 934.1
  discernment 944.2
insightful
  knowing 928.15
  discerning 944.8
insignia
  sign 517.1
  symbol 647.1
  regalia 647.1
insignificance
  triviality 248.1
  inconsiderableness 248.1
  meaninglessness 520.1
  unimportance 998.1
insignificant
  small 248.6
  meaningless 520.6
  inconsequential 998.17
insincere
  uncandid 354.32
  affected 500.15
  flattering 511.8
  deceitful 645.18
  sanctimonious 693.5
  sophistical 936.10
insincerity
  uncandidness 354.5
  affectation 500.1
  unction 511.2

deceitfulness 645.3
  sanctimony 693.1
  sophistry 936.1
insinuate
  insert 191.3
  intrude 214.5
  advise 422.5
  imply 519.4
  hint 551.10
  accuse 599.7
insinuating
  flattering 511.8
  disparaging 512.13
  suggestive 519.6
  shrewd 920.15
insinuation
  obsequiousness 138.2
  entrance 189.1
  insertion 191.1
  interjection 213.2
  intrusion 214.1
  piece of advice 422.2
  aspersion 512.4
  hint 551.4
  accusation 599.1
  influence 894.1
  shrewdness 920.3
insipid
  wishy-washy 16.17
  tasteless 65.2
  dull 117.6
  vacant 222.14
  prosaic 721.5
  mediocre 1005.7
insist
  affirm 334.5
  urge 375.14
  demand 421.8
  urge upon 439.9
  dwell on 849.9
  make conditional 959.4
  necessitate 963.8
insistence
  perseverance 360.1
  urging 375.5
  exigence 421.4
insistent
  persevering 360.8
  demanding 421.9
  importunate 440.18
  urgent 997.22
insobriety 88.1
insociable 583.5
insofar as 888.10
insolation
  heatstroke 85.28
  heating 1020.1
  fuel 1021.1
  drying 1066.3
insolence
  impenitence 114.2
  arrogance 141.2
  effrontery 142.1
  presumption 142.1
  disrespect 156.1
  defiance 454.1
  rashness 493.1
  impudence 505.2
insolent
  impenitent 114.5
  presumptuous 141.10

impudent 142.9
disrespectful 156.7
insulting 156.8
defiant 454.7
rash 493.7
discourteous 505.4
insoluble
inexplicable 522.18
indivisible 1045.13
insolvable 522.18
insolvency
poverty 619.1
credit 622.1
bankruptcy 625.3
insolvent
n insolvent debtor 625.4
adj destitute 619.9
bankrupt 625.11
unsound 729.19
insomnia
wakefulness 23.1
symptom 85.9
insomniac
n wakefulness 23.1
adj wakeful 23.7
insomuch as 888.10
insouciance
apathy 94.4
unconcern 102.2
carelessness 340.2
incuriosity 982.1
insouciant
apathetic 94.13
unconcerned 102.7
careless 340.11
incurious 982.3
inspect
scrutinize 27.14
examine 938.24
inspection
scrutiny 27.6
study 570.3
examination 938.3
automation 1041.7
inspector
superintendent 574.2
examiner 938.17
policeman 1008.15
inspiration
breathing 2.21
drawing in 187.5
impulse 365.1
motive 375.1
infusion 375.9
encouragement 492.9
function of Holy Ghost
677.15
revelation 683.10
Muse 720.10
genius 920.8
good idea 932.6
intuition 934.1
creative thought 986.2
inspire cheer 109.7
give hope 124.10
draw in 187.12
prompt 375.13
inspirit 375.20
encourage 492.16
induce 886.11
inspired fired 375.31

appropriate 533.7
scriptural 683.11
imaginative 986.18
inspirer
prompter 375.10
author 886.4
inspiring
cheering 109.16
promising 124.13
inspirational 375.26
lofty 544.14
inspirit cheer 109.7
give hope 124.10
vivify 306.11
inspire 375.20
encourage 492.16
inspissate
v broaden 269.5
densify 1045.9
thicken 1045.10
emulsify 1062.10
adj thickened 1045.14
in spite of 338.9
instability
infirmity 16.3
irresolution 362.1
nonuniformity 782.1
transience 828.1
inconstancy 854.2
unreliability 971.6
dangerousness 1006.2
install locate 159.11
establish 159.16
insert 191.4
instate 615.12
inaugurate 818.11
produce 892.10
installation
foundation 159.7
admission 187.2
installment 615.3
holy orders 698.10
workplace 739.1
inauguration 818.5
establishment 892.4
installment
establishment 159.7
admission 187.2
book part 554.13
installation 615.3
payment 624.1
part 793.1
inauguration 818.5
installment plan
borrowing 621.1
credit 622.1
payment 624.1
instance
n urging 375.5
proposal 439.2
particular 766.3
example 786.2
sample 786.3
citation 957.5
v itemize 766.6
cite 957.13
instant
n period 824.1
short time 828.3
moment 830.3
adj hasty 401.9

demanding 421.9
instantaneous 830.4
imminent 840.3
prompt 845.9
urgent 997.22
instantaneous
short 268.8
instant 830.4
prompt 845.9
instate insert 191.4
install 615.12
instead 862.11
instead of 862.12
instep 199.5
in step
in concert 788.11
synchronous 836.6
conformist 867.6
instigate
incite 375.17
induce 886.11
instigation 375.4
instigator
inciter 375.11
author 886.4
producer 892.7
instill inculcate 568.12
imbue 797.11
fix in the mind 989.18
instilled 373.18
instillment
inculcation 568.2
imbuement 797.2
instinct feeling 93.1
impulse 365.1
talent 413.4
intuitiveness 934.1
innateness 934.2
discrimination 944.1
involuntariness 963.5
instinctive
animal 311.40
innate 767.8
natural 934.6
involuntary 963.14
instinctual
animal 311.40
innate 767.8
intuitive 934.6
institute
n school 567.1
organization 617.8
v inaugurate 818.11
cause 886.10
establish 892.10
institution
organization 617.8
law 673.3
holy orders 698.10
rite 701.3
workplace 739.1
beginning 818.1
establishment 892.4
institutionalize 429.17
in store in stock 386.16
in readiness 405.21
possessed 469.8
imminent 840.3
destined 964.9
instruct
command 420.8

advise 422.5
inform 551.8
teach 568.10
instruction
precept 419.1
direction 420.3
advice 422.1
information 551.1
teaching 568.1
orders 568.6
lesson 568.7
learning 928.4
instructive
preceptive 419.4
commanding 420.13
advisory 422.8
informative 551.18
educational 568.18
instructor
aviator 185.1
preparer 405.5
adviser 422.3
teacher 571.1
academic rank 571.3
instrument
n surgery 91.19
sycophant 138.3
measure 300.2
manner 384.4
document 549.5
agent 576.3
tool 1040.1
v compose 708.46
tool 1040.13
instrumental
n case 530.9
adj modal 384.8
helping 449.20
orchestral 708.51
instrumentalist 710.3
instrumentation
measurement 300.1
harmonization 709.2
tooling 1040.11
rocketry 1074.1
insubordinate
n rebel 327.5
adj unsubmissive 327.9
lawless 418.5
insubordination
disobedience 327.1
lawlessness 418.1
insubstantial
thin 270.16
rare 299.4
bodiless 764.5
transient 828.7
unsound 936.12
unreliable 971.20
immaterial 1053.7
insubstantiality
thinness 270.4
rarity 299.1
immateriality 764.1
unreliability 971.6
in succession
in order 807.10
continuously 812.11
insufferable 98.25
insufficiency
inability 19.2

unsatisfactoriness 108.2
insignificance 248.1
inferiority 250.3
shallowness 276.1
inequality 791.1
shortcoming 911.1
inadequacy 992.1
insufficient
unsatisfactory 108.9
inadequate 250.7
unequal 791.4
short of 911.5
unsufficing 992.9
insular
n islander 235.4
adj local 231.9
insulated 235.7
secluded 584.8
exclusive 773.9
unrelated 776.6
separate 802.20
alone 872.8
narrow-minded 980.10
insularity island 235.2
exclusiveness 773.3
narrow-mindedness 980.1
insulate proof 15.14
isolate 235.5
segregate 773.6
nonconduct 1032.29
insulated insular 235.7
segregated 773.8
insulation
exclusiveness 773.3
safeguard 1008.3
insult
n indignity 156.2
contempt 157.1
gibe 508.2
v offend 156.5
disdain 157.3
ridicule 508.8
insulting
insolent 142.9
disrespectful 156.8
insuperable
impregnable 15.19
impracticable 967.8
insupportable 98.25
insuppressible 361.12
insurance
security 438.1
precaution 494.3
assurance 1008.4
insurance company 1008.4
insurance policy 1008.4
insure secure 438.9
make sure 970.11
protect 1008.18
insured
secured 438.11
safe 1007.4
insurer
endorser 332.7
guarantor 438.6
insurgence 327.4
insurgent
n rebel 327.5
adj rebellious 327.11
insurmountable 967.8
insurrection 327.4

insurrectionary
n rebel 327.5
adj rebellious 327.11
revolutionary 860.5
insusceptible 94.9
in suspense
on tenterhooks 130.12
inert 173.14
undecided 971.18
in a dilemma 971.25
uncertainly 971.28
in sync
harmonious 708.49
agreeing 788.9
in step 788.11
synchronous 836.6
simultaneously 836.7
concurrent 899.4
televisional 1035.16
intact
unpierced 293.10
immature 301.10
preserved 397.13
continent 664.6
untouched 792.10
complete 794.9
unmixed 798.7
new 841.7
permanent 853.7
unqualified 960.2
sound 1002.7
safe 1007.4
intaglio
engraving tool 713.8
relief 715.3
mold 786.6
intake entrance 189.1
inlet 189.5
receipts 627.1
intangibility
infinitesimalness 258.2
unsubstantiality 764.1
immateriality 1053.1
intangible
infinitesimal 258.14
unsubstantial 764.5
immaterial 1053.7
intangibles 471.7
integer whole 792.1
individual 872.4
integral whole 792.9
component 796.5
one 872.7
unitary 872.10
sound 1002.7
numeric 1017.23
integrate
symmetrize 264.3
equalize 790.6
form a whole 792.7
mix 797.10
combine 805.3
unify 872.5
integrated
whole 792.9
joined 800.13
combined 805.5
unitary 872.10
integration
symmetrization 264.2
affiliation 450.2

adjustment 788.4
equating 790.2
whole 792.1
mixture 797.1
combination 805.1
oneness 872.1
notation 1017.2
integrity
artlessness 416.1
probity 644.1
wholeness 792.1
completeness 794.1
simplicity 798.1
particularity 865.1
oneness 872.1
soundness 1002.2
integument
exterior 206.2
skin 295.3
intellect
intellectual faculty 919.1
mind 919.1
intelligence 920.1
knowledge 920.9
wise man 921.1
intellectual 929.1
intellectual
n wise man 921.1
scientist 928.11
learned person 929.3
intellect 929.1
adj mental 919.7
intelligent 920.12
knowledgeable 928.23
ideational 932.9
attitudinal 978.7
intellectuality
intelligence 920.1
scholarship 928.5
intellectualize
think 931.8
reason 935.15
intelligence
information 551.1
news 552.1
teachableness 570.5
secret service 576.12
spirit 678.5
intellect 919.1
mental grasp 920.1
understanding 920.1
mental capacity 920.9
knowledge 928.1
brains 928.3
surveillance 938.9
intelligence agent 576.9
intelligence quotient 920.1
intelligence service 576.12
intelligence testing 92.8
intelligence work 938.9
intelligent
teachable 570.18
mental 919.7
intellectual 920.12
knowing 928.15
intelligent agent computer
1042.2
software 1042.11
intelligentsia 929.2
intelligibility
meaningfulness 518.5

comprehensibility 521.1
facility 1014.1
intelligible
meaningful 518.10
comprehensible 521.10
intemperance
bibulousness 88.2
unrestraint 430.3
prodigality 486.1
incontinence 665.2
indulgence 669.1
intemperateness 669.1
gluttony 672.1
excess 993.1
intemperate
unrestrained 430.24
prodigal 486.8
incontinent 665.24
indulgent 669.7
violent 671.16
gluttonous 672.6
excessive 993.16
intend purpose 380.4
plan 381.8
have in mind 518.9
intended
n fiancé 104.17
adj intentional 380.8
promised 436.8
meant 518.11
intense
penetrating 15.22
energetic 17.13
sensitive 24.13
colorful 35.19
fervent 93.18
zealous 101.9
great 247.6
violent 671.16
attentive 983.15
intensified
aggravated 119.4
increased 251.7
intensify pain 26.7
aggravate 119.2
heighten 251.5
grow 251.6
intensity energy 17.1
colorfulness 35.4
loudness 53.1
zeal 101.2
greatness 247.1
violence 671.1
measurement of light 1025.21
intensive
laborious 725.18
thorough 794.10
intent
n intention 380.1
meaning 518.2
adj zealous 101.9
attentive 983.15
engrossed 983.17
intention will 323.1
motive 375.1
aim 380
intent 380.1
plan 381.1
meaning 518.2
inter 309.19
interact 777.6

interacting
  communicational 343.9
  interactive 777.9
interaction
  communication 343.1
  interworking 777.3
inter alia 253.11
interassociation
  interrelation 777.2
  interconnection 800.2
interbreed 797.13
interbreeding 797.4
intercalate
  interpose 213.6
  chronologize 832.14
intercede 466.6
intercept
  listen 48.10
  hinder 1012.10
interception
  game 746.3
  radar 1036.9
intercession
  mediation 466.1
  function of Christ 677.14
  prayer 696.4
intercessional
  mediatory 466.8
  divine 677.16
intercessor
  mediator 466.3
  lawyer 597.1
interchange
  n crossing 170.2
  transferal 176.1
  communication 343.1
  passageway 383.3
  retaliation 506.1
  trade 731.2
  interaction 777.3
  mutual transfer 863
  exchange 863.1
  v communicate 343.6
  get along 455.2
  trade 731.15
  interact 777.6
  exchange 863.4
interchangeable
  transferable 176.18
  exchangeable 863.5
  indistinguishable 945.6
intercollegiate 567.13
intercom
  sound reproduction system
    50.11
  Interphone 347.6
intercommunicate
  communicate 343.6
  join 800.11
intercommunication
  communication 343.1
  social life 582.4
  interaction 777.3
  joining 800.1
intercommunicational 343.9
interconnect
  relate 775.6
  correlate 777.5
  interjoin 800.6
interconnection
  interrelation 777.2

interjoinder 800.2
intercosmic 1072.25
intercourse
  copulation 75.7
  communication 343.1
  conversation 541.1
  social life 582.4
  commerce 731.1
  relation 775.1
  interaction 777.3
  joining 800.1
interdenominational
    675.27
interdependency 777.2
interdependent 777.8
interdict
  n restraint 428.1
  prohibition 444.1
  v prohibit 444.3
interdigitation
  interrelation 777.2
  interconnection 800.2
interdisciplinary
  scholastic 568.19
  extensive 864.13
interest
  n incentive 375.7
  allurement 377.1
  benefit 387.4
  undertaking 404.1
  patronage 449.4
  estate 471.4
  gain 472.3
  portion 477.5
  party 617.4
  lending 620.1
  premium 623.3
  prerogative 642.1
  partiality 650.3
  selfishness 651.1
  occupation 724.1
  dividend 738.7
  relevance 775.4
  affair 831.3
  cause 886.9
  favor 894.2
  side 935.14
  curiosity 981.1
  concern 983.2
  importance 997.1
  good 999.4
  v attract 377.6
  relate to 775.5
  involve 898.2
  concern 983.12
interested
  partisan 617.19
  partial 650.11
  involved 898.4
  discriminatory 980.12
  curious 981.5
  concerned 983.16
interest group
  pressure group 609.31
  party 617.4
interesting
  alluring 377.8
  stimulating 983.19
interest rate
  lending 620.1
  interest 623.3

interface
  boundary 211.3
  middle course 467.3
  joint 800.4
interfere
  intrude 214.5
  hinder 1012.10
interference
  intrusion 214.1
  counteraction 900.1
  wave 916.4
  hindrance 1012.1
  reception 1034.21
interfering 214.8
interfuse
  intersperse 213.7
  combine 805.3
interfusion
  interspersion 213.3
  mixture 797.1
intergalactic 1072.25
interim
  n interval 224.1
  interruption 813.2
  intermediate period 826
  meantime 826.1
  delay 846.2
  pause 857.3
  adj temporary 826.4
interior
  n inside 207.2
  inland 207.3
  scene 712.12
  middle 819.1
  adj internal 207.6
  inland 207.7
  private 345.13
  middle 819.4
interior decorating 498.1
interiority
  inwardness 207.1
  internalness 207.1
  depth 275.1
interjacent 213.10
interject
  insert 191.3
  interpose 213.6
  remark 524.24
interjection
  insertion 191.1
  interpolation 213.2
  intrusion 214.1
  remark 524.3
  part of speech 530.3
interjoin
  correlate 777.5
  interconnect 800.6
interlace weave 740.6
  interact 777.6
  mix 797.10
interlaced
  webbed 170.12
  woven 740.7
interlacing
  n weaving 740.1
  interaction 777.3
  adj weaving 740.8
interlard
  intersperse 213.7
  mix 797.10
interlining 196.3

interlink
  correlate 777.5
  interconnect 800.6
interlinked
  related 775.9
  correlative 777.8
interlock
  n safeguard 1008.3
  v correlate 777.5
  agree 788.6
  interconnect 800.6
interlocked
  related 775.9
  correlative 777.8
interlocking
  interrelation 777.2
  interconnection 800.2
interlocutory
  mediatory 466.8
  conversational 541.13
interlope 214.5
interloper
  intruder 214.3
  outsider 774.2
interloping 214.1
interlude
  n respite 20.2
  act 704.7
  passage 708.24
  interim 826.1
  pause 857.3
  v intervene 826.3
intermarriage 563.1
intermarry 563.15
intermeddle
  meddle 214.7
  hinder 1012.10
intermediary
  n intermedium 213.4
  instrument 384.4
  mediator 466.3
  go-between 576.4
  adj intervening 213.10
  medium 246.3
  modal 384.8
  mediatory 466.8
  middle 819.4
intermediate
  n instrument 384.4
  mediator 466.3
  go-between 576.4
  gear 1040.9
  v mediate 466.6
  adj intervening 213.10
  medium 246.3
  mediatory 466.8
  middle 819.4
intermediator 466.3
interment
  burial 309.1
  concealment 346.1
intermesh 777.6
intermezzo
  act 704.7
  passage 708.24
  interim 826.1
  pause 857.3
interminable 829.7
intermingle 797.10
intermission
  respite 20.2

prep after 382.12
in the midst of
  adv midway 819.5
  prep at 159.27
  between 213.12
  among 797.17
in the mood
  willing 324.5
  disposed 978.8
in the neighborhood of
  adv near 223.20
  at a price 630.17
  prep about 223.26
in the nick of time
  opportunely 843.12
  in time 845.12
  expedient 995.5
in the pink
  healthy 83.9
  in order 807.7
in the red
  at a loss 473.9
  destitute 619.9
  indebted 623.8
in the same boat 790.7
in the same breath
  at once 830.8
  simultaneously 836.7
in the swim 578.11
in the thick of
  adv midway 819.5
  prep between 213.12
  among 797.17
in the wind
  against the wind 182.65
  happening 831.9
  imminent 840.3
in the works
  adj planned 381.12
  undertaken 404.7
  in preparation 405.22
  operating 889.11
  adv in production 892.21
intimacy
  copulation 75.7
  nearness 223.1
  sociability 582.1
  familiarity 587.5
  relation 775.1
  knowledge 928.1
intimate
  n friend 588.1
  v advise 422.5
  imply 519.4
  hint 551.10
  adj interior 207.6
  near 223.14
  homelike 228.33
  private 345.13
  familiar 582.24
  friendly 587.19
  joined 800.13
  particular 865.12
intimate apparel 5.22
intimation
  hint 248.4
  piece of advice 422.2
  sign 517.9
  implication 519.2
  clue 551.4
  admixture 797.7

hunch 934.3
  suggestion 951.5
in time
  in tempo 709.30
  synchronous 836.6
  in due time 839.11
  in good time 845.12
  periodically 850.10
intimidate cow 127.20
  dissuade 379.3
  coerce 424.7
  bluster 503.3
  threaten 514.2
  domineer 612.16
intimidated
  terrified 127.26
  cowardly 491.10
intimidating
  dissuasive 379.5
  threatening 514.3
intimidation
  frightening 127.6
  dissuasion 379.1
  coercion 424.3
  bluster 503.1
  threat 514.1
into
  adj knowledgeable 928.17
  prep in 189.14
  inside 207.13
intolerable
  insufferable 98.25
  unlikable 99.7
  unacceptable 108.10
  downright 247.12
intolerance
  intoleration 135.2
  obstinacy 361.1
  narrow-mindedness 980.2
intolerant
  n bigot 980.5
  adj unforbearing 135.7
  obstinate 361.8
  untolerating 980.11
intonate
  inflect 524.28
  sing 708.38
intonation tone 50.2
  inflection 524.6
  vocal music 708.13
  execution 708.30
  harmonization 709.2
intone 708.38
in toto fully 766.13
  wholly 792.13
intoxicate
  inebriate 88.22
  thrill 105.15
  dizzy 985.8
intoxicated
  under the influence 87.23
  inebriated 88.31
  fervent 93.18
  frenzied 105.25
intoxicating
  intoxicative 88.36
  exciting 105.30
intoxication
  poisoning 85.31
  inebriation 88.1
  happiness 95.2

fury 105.8
intractable
  insubordinate 327.9
  ungovernable 361.12
  inflexible 1046.12
intramural
  intramarginal 207.8
  scholastic 567.13
intransient 827.10
intransigence 361.2
intransigent
  n obstinate person 361.6
  oppositionist 452.3
  adj unyielding 361.9
in transit
  on the way 176.20
  on the move 177.42
intransitive
  n verb 530.4
  adj grammatical 530.17
intransmutable 855.17
intraterritorial 207.8
intravenous 91.17
intrepid 492.17
intricacy
  abstruseness 522.2
  complexity 799.1
  difficulty 1013.1
intricate
  hard to understand 522.14
  mixed 797.14
  complex 799.4
  bewildering 971.27
  difficult 1013.17
intrigue
  n love affair 104.6
  web of intrigue 381.5
  stratagem 415.3
  deceitfulness 645.3
  v fascinate 377.7
  plot 381.9
  maneuver 415.10
intrigued 95.15
intriguing
  delightful 97.7
  alluring 377.8
  scheming 381.13
intrinsic
  interior 207.6
  internal 767.7
  characteristic 865.13
introduce
  bring in 187.14
  insert 191.3
  propose 439.5
  preinstruct 568.14
  present 587.14
  prefix 814.3
  go before 816.3
  inaugurate 818.11
  innovate 852.9
introducer
  transformer 852.5
  producer 892.7
introduction
  bringing in 187.7
  entrance 189.1
  insertion 191.1
  interjection 213.2
  makeup 554.12
  elementary education 568.5

acquaintance 587.4
  legislative procedure 613.6
  act 704.7
  overture 708.26
  part of writing 793.2
  curtain-raiser 816.2
  inauguration 818.5
  basics 818.6
  innovation 852.4
introductory
  introductive 187.18
  educational 568.18
  beginning 818.15
introit 708.17
Introit 696.3
intromission
  admission 187.2
  insertion 191.1
intromit receive 187.10
  insert 191.3
introspect 931.12
introspection 931.6
introspective
  cognitive 931.21
  absorbed in thought 931.22
introversion
  personality tendency 92.11
  inversion 205.1
  interiority 207.1
  reticence 344.3
introvert
  n personality type 92.12
  v invert 205.5
  adj introverted 92.40
introverted
  introvert 92.40
  inverted 205.7
  reticent 344.10
intrude enter 189.7
  interpose 213.6
  obtrude 214.5
  talk out of turn 844.4
  overstep 910.9
intruder incomer 189.4
  interloper 214.3
  foreign body 774.2
  newcomer 774.4
intrusion
  entrance 189.1
  interposition 213.1
  interference 214.1
  obtrusion 214.1
  extraneousness 774.1
  intruder 774.2
  untimeliness 844.1
  overstepping 910.3
intrusive
  entering 189.12
  obtrusive 214.8
  overactive 330.24
  extraneous 774.5
  untimely 844.6
intuit sense 934.4
  foreknow 961.6
intuition
  extrasensory perception
    689.8
  intuitiveness 934.1
  hunch 934.3
  discrimination 944.1
  suggestion 951.5

intuitive
premonitory 133.16
intuitional 934.5
theoretical 951.13
foreseeing 961.7
intumescence
growth 85.39
distension 259.2
swelling 283.4
in tune in accord 455.3
harmonious 708.49
in turn in order 807.10
consecutively 812.11
interchangeably 863.6
inundate
aggrieve 112.19
overflow 238.17
submerge 367.7
overwhelm 395.21
raid 459.20
run over 910.7
oversupply 993.14
flood 1065.14
inundated
overcome 112.29
flooded 238.25
underwater 275.13
overrun 910.10
soaked 1065.17
inundation
overflow 238.6
submergence 367.2
wordiness 538.2
overrunning 910.1
plenty 991.2
superabundance 993.2
wetting 1065.6
in unison
unanimously 332.17
cooperatively 450.6
harmonious 708.49
in step 788.11
jointly 800.18
simultaneously 836.7
inure callous 94.6
accustom 373.9
inured callous 94.12
accustomed 373.15
hardened 654.17
invade intrude 214.5
raid 459.20
usurp 640.8
infest 910.6
overstep 910.9
invader intruder 214.3
assailant 459.12
in vain
unsuccessfully 410.19
amiss 911.7
invalid
n impotent 19.6
sick person 85.43
recluse 584.5
v afflict 85.50
adj ineffective 19.15
unhealthy 85.54
repealed 445.3
illogical 936.11
bad 1000.7
invalidate
disqualify 19.11

abolish 395.13
repeal 445.2
neutralize 900.7
disprove 958.4
invalidated
disabled 19.16
disproved 958.7
invalidation
repeal 445.1
neutralization 900.2
disproof 958.1
invalidity
ineffectiveness 19.3
unhealthiness 85.3
illogicalness 936.2
badness 1000.1
invaluable 632.10
invariable
tedious 118.9
uniform 781.5
unchangeable 855.17
invasion
intrusion 214.1
raid 459.4
usurpation 640.3
infestation 910.2
invasive
entering 189.12
intrusive 214.8
attacking 459.29
invective
n sarcasm 508.5
berating 510.7
vilification 513.2
speech 543.2
adj condemnatory 510.22
inveigh against 510.13
inveigle trap 356.20
lure 377.5
inveiglement 377.1
invent originate 337.4
fabricate 354.18
initiate 818.10
innovate 841.5
change 852.9
produce 892.12
discover 941.2
imagine 986.14
invented
fabricated 354.29
originated 892.19
invention
fabrication 354.10
innovation 852.4
production 892.1
product 893.1
discovery 941.1
inventiveness 986.3
figment of the imagination 986.5
inventive
cunning 415.12
beginning 818.15
creative 892.16
imaginative 986.18
inventor
producer 892.7
imaginer 986.12
inventory
n contents 196.1
store 386.1

record 549.1
account book 628.4
merchandise 735.1
assemblage 770.1
table 808.4
list 871.1
summation 1017.11
v take account of 628.9
list 871.8
sum up 1017.19
check 1017.21
inverse
n reverse 205.4
opposite side 215.3
v invert 205.5
adj contrapositive 215.5
contrary 779.6
inversion
turning over 205
inverting 205.1
notation 1017.2
invert
n homosexual 75.14
v inverse 205.5
invertebrate
n weakling 16.6
creature 311.3
coward 491.5
adj invertebral 311.51
weak-willed 362.12
invest clothe 5.39
empower 18.10
establish 159.16
insert 191.4
surround 209.6
wrap 295.20
provide 385.7
besiege 459.19
endow 478.17
commission 615.10
install 615.12
spend 626.5
place 729.17
invested
clothing 5.45
provided 385.13
endowed 478.26
investigate
discuss 541.12
indagate 938.23
investigation
discussion 541.7
indagation 938.4
investigative journalism 552.1
investigator
detective 576.10
examiner 938.17
investiture clothing 5.1
establishment 159.7
admission 187.2
giving 478.1
commission 615.1
installation 615.3
holy orders 698.10
investment clothing 5.1
empowerment 18.8
provision 385.1
siege 459.5
endowment 478.9
commission 615.1
money matters 729

venture 729.4
investor 729.9
inveteracy
customariness 373.6
permanence 853.1
fixity 855.2
inveterate
confirmed 373.18
durable 827.10
traditional 842.12
established 855.13
invidious
malicious 144.20
jealous 153.5
envious 154.4
in view visible 31.6
expected 130.13
present 221.12
imminent 840.3
in view of 888.9
invigorate refresh 9.2
strengthen 15.13
energize 17.10
stimulate 105.13
cheer 109.7
invigorating
refreshing 9.3
energizing 17.15
healthful 81.5
tonic 86.44
cheering 109.16
cool 1023.12
invincible
impregnable 15.19
peerless 249.15
persevering 360.8
indestructible 855.18
reliable 970.17
inviolable
impregnable 15.19
trustworthy 644.19
sacred 685.7
inviolate honest 644.13
sacred 685.7
permanent 853.7
undamaged 1002.8
invisible
imperceptible 32.5
infinitesimal 258.14
unrevealed 346.12
invitation
incentive 375.7
allurement 377.1
offer 439.1
invite 440.4
invite
n invitation 440.4
v encourage 375.21
attract 377.6
ask 440.13
incur 897.4
interest 983.12
inviting delightful 97.7
receptive 187.16
provocative 375.27
alluring 377.8
invitational 440.19
interesting 983.19
invocation
summons 420.5
entreaty 440.2

conjuration 690.4
prayer 696.4
benediction 696.5
in vogue 578.11
invoice
n statement 628.3
bill 871.5
v bill 628.11
invoke summon 420.11
entreat 440.11
address 524.26
conjure 690.11
pray 696.13
adduce 957.12
refer to 957.14
involuntary
unwilling 325.5
unpremeditated 365.11
obligatory 424.11
intuitive 934.6
instinctive 963.14
unintentional 972.17
involuted
convolutional 281.6
complex 799.4
involution
convolution 281.1
deterioration 393.3
complexity 799.1
involvement 898.1
notation 1017.2
involve surround 209.6
signify 517.17
imply 519.4
ornament 545.7
incriminate 599.10
entail 772.4
relate to 775.5
complicate 799.3
implicate 898.2
evidence 957.8
engross 983.13
hamper 1012.11
put in a hole 1013.15
involved
participating 476.8
implied 519.7
accused 599.15
indebted 623.8
partial 650.11
guilty 656.3
included 772.5
related 775.9
complex 799.4
implicated 898.4
engrossed 983.17
involvement
sympathy 93.5
surrounding 209.5
mediation 466.1
participation 476.1
incrimination 599.2
partiality 650.3
guilt 656.1
entailment 772.2
complexity 799.1
involuntary cooperation 898.1
involution 898.1
engrossment 983.3
invulnerable
impregnable 15.19

indestructible 855.18
uninfluenceable 895.4
unhazardous 1007.5
protected 1008.21
inward
n interior 207.2
adj entering 189.12
in 189.13
interior 207.6
inside 207.11
private 345.13
intrinsic 767.7
inwards
n viscera 2.16
insides 207.4
adv in 189.13
inside 207.11
in with
on good terms 587.18
leagued 805.6
in writing 547.22
ion atom 258.8
electrolysis 1032.25
atom 1038.4
element 1060.2
ionic 1032.32
Ionic 717.2
ionization
electrolysis 1032.25
fission 1038.8
ionize 1032.28
iota modicum 248.2
minute 258.7
IOU 728.11
ipse dixit
affirmation 334.1
decree 420.4
IQ 920.1
irascibility
excitability 105.10
irritability 110.2
perversity 361.3
dissension 456.3
irascible
excitable 105.28
irritable 110.19
perverse 361.11
partisan 456.17
irate 152.28
ire 152.5
irenic
unbelligerent 464.10
pacificatory 465.12
iridesce opalesce 47.8
luminesce 1025.26
iridescence
rainbow 47.2
opalescence 1025.18
iridescent
soft-colored 35.22
rainbowlike 47.10
opalescent 1025.37
iris eye 2.9
sight 27.9
variegation 47.6
Iris 353.1
irk
n tedium 118.1
v annoy 96.13
vex 98.15
be tedious 118.6

trouble 1013.13
irked annoyed 96.21
weary 118.11
troubled 1013.20
irksome
annoying 98.22
wearying 118.10
troublesome 1013.18
iron
n symbol of strength 15.8
cycle 179.8
basketball 747.1
hardness 1046.6
v press 287.6
adj unyielding 361.9
firm 425.7
brass 1058.17
Iron Age 824.5
ironbound
rugged 288.7
firm 425.7
bound 428.16
ironclad firm 425.7
armored 460.13
iron curtain
frontier 211.5
veil of secrecy 345.3
communism 611.5
barrier 1012.5
iron grip 474.2
iron hand
governance 417.5
firm hand 425.3
control 612.2
despotism 612.10
ironic witty 489.15
satiric 508.13
suggestive 519.6
ambiguous 539.4
self-contradictory 779.8
mixed 797.14
iron out reconcile 465.8
solve 940.2
irons 428.4
iron will 359.4
irony wit 489.1
sarcasm 508.5
ambiguity 539.1
self-contradiction 779.3
doubleness 873.1
irradiate
v radiumize 91.26
preserve 397.9
illuminate 1025.28
radioactivate 1037.10
adj illuminated 1025.39
irradiated
illuminated 1025.39
radioactive 1037.11
irradiation
food preservation 397.2
light 1025.1
irrational
unintelligent 922.13
unwise 923.10
insane 926.26
illogical 936.11
numeric 1017.23
irrationality
unintelligence 922.1
unwiseness 923.2

insanity 926.1
illogicalness 936.2
irreclaimable
past hope 125.15
irredeemable 654.18
irreconcilable
n oppositionist 452.3
adj unyielding 361.9
vengeful 507.7
alienated 589.11
different 780.7
inconsistent 789.8
irrecoverable
past hope 125.15
past 837.7
irredeemable
past hope 125.15
unpayable 625.13
irreclaimable 654.18
irreducible
intrinsic 767.7
simple 798.6
inextricable 799.5
one 872.7
requisite 963.13
irreformable
past hope 125.15
irreclaimable 654.18
irrefutable
evidential 957.16
obvious 970.15
irregular
n casual 461.16
second 1005.6
adj distorted 265.10
rough 288.6
informal 581.3
illegal 674.6
nonuniform 782.3
unequal 791.4
unordered 810.12
discontinuous 813.4
unregular 851.3
inconstant 854.7
abnormal 870.9
eccentric 927.5
inferior 1005.9
irregularity
distortion 265.1
roughness 288.1
unsmoothness 294.2
informality 581.1
nonuniformity 782.1
inequality 791.1
disorder 810.1
discontinuity 813.1
unmethodicalness
851.1
inconstancy 854.2
abnormality 870.1
eccentricity 927.1
irrelevance
unrelatedness 776.1
unfitness 789.3
untimeliness 844.1
unimportance 998.1
irrelevant
unrelated 776.7
inappropriate 789.7
untimely 844.6
insignificant 998.17

irreligion
impiety 694.1
ungodliness 695.3
irreligious
impious 694.6
ungodly 695.17
unbelieving 955.8
irremediable
past hope 125.15
ruined 395.28
irremovable 855.15
irreparable 125.15
irreplaceable
used up 388.5
requisite 963.13
irreprehensible 657.8
irrepressible
cheerful 109.11
ungovernable 361.12
unrestrained 430.24
irreproachable
honest 644.13
inculpable 657.8
perfect 1002.6
irresistible
impregnable 15.19
powerful 18.12
delightful 97.7
great 247.6
alluring 377.8
overpowering 412.18
compulsory 424.10
evidential 957.16
inevitable 963.15
irresolute
wishy-washy 16.17
irresolved 362.9
inconstant 854.7
uncertain 971.16
irresolution
frailty 16.2
indecision 362.1
uncertainty 971.1
irrespective of 338.9
irresponsible
lawless 418.5
exempt 430.30
untrustworthy 645.19
inconstant 854.7
irretrievable
past hope 125.15
lost 473.7
unchangeable 855.17
irreverence
disrespect 156.1
impiety 694.1
irreverent
disrespectful 156.7
impious 694.6
irreversible
past hope 125.15
directional 161.12
confirmed 373.18
unchangeable 855.17
irrevocable
past hope 125.15
mandatory 420.12
unchangeable 855.17
inevitable 963.15
irrigate dilute 16.11
wash 79.19

moisten 1065.12
irrigation washing 79.5
wetting 1065.6
cultivation 1069.13
irritability
sensitivity 24.3
excitability 105.10
irascibility 110.2
dissension 456.3
irritable sensitive 24.12
excitable 105.28
irascible 110.19
nervous 128.11
partisan 456.17
irritant
n irritation 96.3
adj irritating 26.13
irritate pain 26.7
displease 96.14
aggravate 119.2
get on one's nerves
128.9
provoke 152.24
impair 393.9
sow dissension 456.14
irritated sore 26.11
annoyed 96.21
aggravated 119.4
provoked 152.27
impaired 393.27
irritating painful 26.13
pungent 68.6
annoying 98.22
aggravating 119.5
irritation
soreness 26.4
annoyance 96.3
excitation 105.11
aggravation 119.1
resentment 152.1
incitement 375.4
adversity 1011.1
irrupt burst forth 33.9
enter 189.7
intrude 214.5
originate 818.13
overstep 910.9
irruption
outburst 105.9
intrusion 214.1
raid 459.4
irruptive
entering 189.12
attacking 459.29
Isis 890.5
Islam 675.13
Islamic 675.31
island
n airport 184.22
isle 235.2
v insulate 235.5
adj insular 235.7
islander 235.4
island-hop 235.5
isle 235.2
ism school 617.5
cult 675.2
system of belief 953.3
isobar
weather map 317.4
isotope 1038.5

isolate
insulate 235.5
excise 255.10
quarantine 429.13
segregate 773.6
analyze 801.6
separate 802.8
nonconduct 1032.29
isolated
quiescent 173.12
insular 235.7
private 345.13
quarantined 429.20
secluded 584.8
segregated 773.8
unrelated 776.6
separate 802.20
separated 802.21
alone 872.8
isolation
defense mechanism 92.23
privacy 345.2
quarantine 429.2
seclusion 584.1
exclusiveness 773.3
itemization 801.2
separation 802.1
aloneness 872.2
isolationism
noninterference 430.9
seclusion 584.1
foreign policy 609.5
isolationist
free agent 430.12
recluse 584.5
isomer 1038.5
isometric
n weather map 317.4
adj climatal 317.13
equisized 790.10
isometrics 84.2
isotherm 317.4
isothermal 1019.30
isothermic 1019.30
isotope 1038.5
Israelite
n Jew 675.21
adj Jewish 675.30
issue
n emergence 190.1
amount 244.2
publication 352.1
escape 369.1
edition 554.5
family 559.5
offspring 561.1
platform 609.7
issuance 738.6
event 831.1
cause 886.9
effect 887.1
product 893.1
topic 937.1
question 938.10
solution 940.1
salient point 997.6
v be born 1.2
appear 33.8
set out 188.8
emerge 190.11
flow 238.16

quantify 244.4
bring out 352.14
be published 352.16
find vent 369.10
parcel out 477.8
give 478.12
print 548.14
monetize 728.26
float 738.12
disperse 771.4
originate 818.13
come after 835.3
result 887.4
issueless 891.4
issue price 738.9
issuing
n appearance 33.1
emergence 190.1
adj emerging 190.18
isthmus
contraction 260.1
narrow place 270.3
it self 865.5
what's what 973.4
italic
n type 548.6
adj written 547.22
italicize 997.14
italicized
written 547.22
emphatic 997.21
it beats me 522.27
itch
n itching 74.3
sexual desire 75.5
craving 100.6
v tingle 74.5
twitch 917.13
itch for lust 75.20
wish for 100.16
itching
n itch 74.3
symptom 85.9
craving 100.6
adj itchy 74.10
lustful 75.27
craving 100.24
lascivious 665.29
itchy sensitive 24.12
itching 74.10
lascivious 665.29
curious 981.5
item
n memorandum 549.4
entry 628.5
commodity 735.2
particular 766.3
part 793.1
component 796.2
individual 872.4
citation 957.5
adv additionally 253.11
itemization
description 349.2
circumstantiation 766.5
enumeration 801.2
particularization 865.7
list 871.1
index 871.7
itemize specify 766.6
enumerate 801.7

particularize 865.9
list 871.8
cite 957.13
sum up 1017.19
items contents 196.1
merchandise 735.1
list 871.1
knowledge 928.1
iterate
reiterate 849.8
persist 856.5
iteration
wordiness 538.2
reiteration 849.2
duplication 874.1
iterative
n aspect 530.13
adj diffuse 538.11
repetitious 849.14
itinerant
n wanderer 178.2
adj traveling 177.36
itinerary
n route 383.1
directory 574.10
adj traveling 177.36
itself 865.5
itsy-bitsy 258.11
IUD 86.23
ivied halls 567.5
ivories teeth 2.8
keyboard 711.17
dice 759.8
ivory
n whiteness 37.2
smoothness 287.3
adj whitish 37.8
ivory tower
seclusion 584.1
retreat 584.6
refuge 1009.5
ivy
n plant 310.4
adj green 44.4
Ivy League 746.1
izzard 820.1
jab
n attack 459.3
thrust 902.2
hit 902.4
v use 87.22
scoff 508.9
thrust 902.12
hit 902.14
jabber
n nonsense 520.2
mumbling 525.4
chatter 540.3
v talk nonsense 520.5
mumble 525.9
chatter 540.5
jabberer 540.4
jack
n mariner 183.1
ass 311.16
flag 647.7
money 728.2
lawn bowling 750.3
card 758.2
base 901.8
lifter 912.3

v hunt 382.9
jackal fox 311.20
follower 616.8
jackass ass 311.16
fool 924.1
jacket
n outerwear 5.13
skin 295.3
hull 295.16
wrapper 295.18
bookbinding 554.14
v cloak 5.40
jackknife 367.1
jack-of-all-trades 413.11
jackpot award 646.2
pot 759.5
jackrabbit hare 311.24
jumper 366.4
jacks 743.16
jack up increase 251.4
disapprove 510.18
jactitation
boasting 502.1
shaking 917.2
Jacuzzi bath 79.8
fitness 84.1
massage 1044.3
jade
n horse 311.12
strumpet 665.14
v fatigue 21.4
burn out 21.5
be tedious 118.6
satiate 994.4
jaded tired 21.7
weary 118.11
languid 331.20
worn-out 393.36
satiated 994.6
jag
n drinking spree 88.6
projection 285.4
notch 289.1
v notch 289.4
jagged angular 278.6
rugged 288.7
notched 289.5
nonuniform 782.3
discontinuous 813.4
jaguar variegation 47.6
wild cat 311.22
jail
n prison 429.8
v enclose 212.5
imprison 429.14
jailbird
prisoner 429.11
criminal 660.9
jailbreak 369.1
jailed
enclosed 212.10
jugged 429.21
jailer gaoler 429.10
penologist 604.9
guard 1008.9
jalopy 179.10
jam
n sweets 10.40
obstruction 293.3
state 765.1
throng 770.4

delay 846.2
multitude 884.3
bewilderment 971.3
barrier 1012.5
predicament 1013.5
semiliquid 1062.5
v drown out 53.8
stop 293.7
have a party 582.21
fill 794.7
hook 800.8
secure 855.8
fix 855.10
stop 857.7
teem with 884.5
thrust 902.12
overload 993.15
obstruct 1012.12
transmit 1036.15
densify 1045.9
jamb leg 177.14
post 273.4
jamboree 743.4
jam in enter 189.7
thrust in 191.7
jammed
stopped 293.11
fast 800.14
late 846.16
stuck 855.16
teeming 884.9
overfull 993.20
dense 1045.12
jamming
reception 1034.21
radar 1036.13
jam-packed
stopped 293.11
crowded 770.22
full 794.11
teeming 884.9
overfull 993.20
dense 1045.12
jam session 708.32
Jane Doe alias 527.8
common woman 606.5
average 864.3
jangle
n noise 53.3
ringing 54.3
rasp 58.3
clash 61.2
disaccord 456.1
v ring 54.8
sound harshly 58.9
grate on 58.11
sound a sour note 61.3
differ 456.8
disagree 789.5
jangling
grating 58.16
clashing 61.5
disagreeing 789.6
janitor
cleaner 79.14
guardian 1008.6
doorkeeper 1008.12
Janus 873.1
japanning 35.12
jape
n joke 489.6

gibe 508.2
v joke 489.13
banter 490.5
scoff 508.9
jar
n rasp 58.3
clash 61.2
start 131.3
disaccord 456.1
shake 917.3
v sound harshly 58.9
sound a sour note 61.3
agitate 105.14
startle 131.8
package 212.9
put up 397.11
differ 456.8
disagree 789.5
shake 917.11
jargon
n nonsense 520.2
Greek 522.7
lingo 523.9
argot 523.11
technical term 526.5
v speak 523.18
jarring
n disaccord 456.1
disagreement 789.1
adj grating 58.16
clashing 61.5
exciting 105.30
unnerving 128.15
surprising 131.11
disagreeing 789.6
jolting 917.20
jaundice
n yellow skin 43.2
symptom 85.9
jealousy 153.1
prejudice 980.3
v yellow 43.3
prejudice 980.9
jaundiced
yellow-faced 43.6
sour 110.23
jealous 153.5
discriminatory 980.12
jaunt
n journey 177.5
walk 177.10
v journey 177.21
wander 177.23
jaunty
lighthearted 109.12
showy 501.19
chic 578.13
javelin 462.8
jaw
n mouth 292.4
v berate 510.19
speak 524.20
chatter 540.5
jawbreaker
long word 526.10
high-sounding words 545.3
jawbreaking
sesquipedalian 545.10
difficult 1013.17
jaws 474.4
jaywalk 177.27

jaywalker 178.6
jazz
 n energy 17.3
 hot jazz 708.9
 adj instrumental 708.51
 syncopated 709.29
Jazz Age 824.5
jazz musician 710.2
jazz up energize 17.10
 stimulate 105.13
 intensify 251.5
jazzy showy 501.19
 instrumental 708.51
 syncopated 709.29
JD 302.4
jealous jaundiced 153.5
 envious 154.4
jealousy
 jealousness 153.1
 resentment 153.1
 envy 154.1
jeans 5.18
jeer
 n indignity 156.2
 gibe 508.2
 v scoff 508.9
jeering
 n indignity 156.2
 ridicule 508.1
 adj ridiculing 508.12
jejune insipid 65.2
 dull 117.6
 haggard 270.20
 shallow 276.5
 unproductive 891.4
 empty-headed 922.19
 meager 992.10
jell
 n semiliquid 1062.5
 v thicken 1045.10
 emulsify 1062.10
jellied
 thickened 1045.14
 viscous 1062.12
jelling 1045.4
jelly
 n sweets 10.40
 semiliquid 1062.5
 v thicken 1045.10
 emulsify 1062.10
jellyfish weakling 16.6
 vacillator 362.5
 coward 491.5
jenny
 female animal 77.10
 spinner 271.5
 ass 311.16
jeopardize 1006.6
jeopardy
 n danger 1006.1
 v endanger 1006.6
Jeremiah 399.4
jerk
 n bad person 660.5
 yank 905.3
 shake 917.3
 fool 924.3
 v be excited 105.18
 preserve 397.9
 throw 904.10
 yerk 905.5

 twitch 917.13
jerking
 n food preservation 397.2
 twitching 917.5
 adj jerky 917.19
jerkwater 998.18
jerky
 n meat 10.13
 beef 10.14
 adj convulsive 671.23
 nonuniform 782.3
 discontinuous 813.4
 irregular 851.3
 herky-jerky 917.19
jerry-built 16.14
jest
 n joke 489.6
 gibe 508.2
 laughingstock 508.7
 trifle 998.5
 v joke 489.13
 banter 490.5
jester humorist 489.12
 buffoon 707.10
jesting
 n bantering 490.2
 adj witty 489.15
Jesuit sophist 936.6
 quibbler 936.7
jesuitic
 insincere 354.32
 sophistical 936.10
jet
 n blackness 38.4
 jet plane 181.3
 ascent 193.1
 spout 238.9
 outburst 671.6
 disgorgement 909.7
 heater 1020.10
 v fly 184.36
 run out 190.13
 shoot up 193.9
 spout 238.20
 disgorge 909.25
Jet Age 824.6
jet-black 38.8
jeté 366.1
jet flight 184.1
jet plane
 swiftness 174.6
 jet 181.3
jet power
 manpower 18.4
 propulsion 184.25
jet-propelled
 flying 184.50
 rocket-propelled 904.16
jet propulsion
 propulsion 184.25
 rocket propulsion 1074.8
jetsam 370.4
jet set traveler 178.1
 society 578.6
jet-setter 178.1
jetstream 184.32
jettison
 n abandonment 370.1
 discard 390.3
 ejection 909.1
 v abandon 370.5

 discard 390.7
 eject 909.13
jetty
 n buttress 901.4
 harbor 1009.6
 barrier 1012.5
 adj black 38.8
jeu d'esprit 489.7
Jew 675.21
jewel
 n favorite 104.16
 bijou 498.6
 good person 659.1
 bearing 915.7
 good thing 999.5
 v figure 498.9
jewelry 498.5
Jewish 675.30
Jezebel
 witch 593.7
 strumpet 665.14
 demimonde 665.15
jib start 127.12
 avoid 164.6
 hesitate 362.7
 pull back 903.7
jibe
 change course 182.30
 agree 788.6
 be changed 852.6
jiffy 830.3
jig
 n snare 356.13
 leap 366.1
 jerk 905.3
 shake 917.3
 v jerk 905.5
 twitch 917.13
jigger
 n drink 88.7
 vermin 311.37
 fisher 382.6
 thing 1052.5
 v jerk 905.5
 twitch 917.13
jiggle
 n jerk 905.3
 shake 917.3
 v jerk 905.5
 twitch 917.13
jillion
 n trillion 882.13
 large number 1017.5
 adj numerous 884.6
jilt
 n deceiver 357.1
 v abandon 370.5
 discard 390.7
jilted 99.10
jilter 357.1
Jim Crow
 seclusion 584.1
 exclusiveness 773.3
 discrimination 980.4
jim-dandy 999.13
jimjams
 trepidation 127.5
 nervousness 128.2
jimmy
 n lever 906.4
 v get a purchase 906.8

jingle
 n ringing 54.3
 meter 720.7
 assonance 784.6
 repetitiousness 849.4
 v ring 54.8
 rhyme 720.14
jingling
 n ringing 54.3
 adj ringing 54.13
 rhyming 720.17
 assonant 784.17
jingo
 n militarist 461.5
 patriot 591.3
 bigot 980.5
 adj militaristic 458.22
jingoism
 warlikeness 458.11
 patriotism 591.2
jingoistic
 militaristic 458.22
 public-spirited 591.4
jinni 680.6
jinx
 n spell 691.1
 bad influence 1000.4
 v bewitch 691.9
 work evil 1000.6
 bring bad luck 1011.12
jitney 179.13
jitters
 nervousness 128.2
 agitation 917.1
jittery
 jumpy 128.12
 agitated 917.16
jive
 n bull 520.3
 jazz 708.9
 v banter 490.6
 syncopate 708.43
job
 n act 328.3
 theft 482.4
 occupation 724.1
 task 724.2
 function 724.3
 position 724.5
 affair 831.3
 v rent 615.15
 hire out 615.16
 deal in 731.16
 sell 734.8
Job 134.3
job action 727.5
jobber
 intermediary 213.4
 worker 726.2
 merchant 730.2
 stockbroker 737.10
jobbing
 Machiavellianism 415.2
 trade 731.2
 selling 734.2
 stockbroking 737.18
jobholder 726.2
jobless 331.18
job lot 735.1
jock real man 76.6
 soldier 461.7

athlete 743.19
jockey 757.2
supporter 901.2
jockey
  n speeder 174.5
  rider 178.8
  jock 757.2
  saddle parts 901.18
  v maneuver 415.10
  compete 457.18
jocose 489.15
jocularity
  merriment 109.5
  wittiness 489.2
jog
  n slow motion 175.2
  gait 177.12
  bulge 283.3
  notch 289.1
  thrust 902.2
  jerk 905.3
  shake 917.3
  v exercise 84.4
  plod 175.7
  walk 177.27
  trot 177.28
  thrust 902.12
  jerk 905.5
  shake 917.11
jogger 989.6
joggle
  n bulge 283.3
  notch 289.1
  thrust 902.2
  jerk 905.3
  shake 917.3
  v thrust 902.12
  jerk 905.5
  shake 917.11
jog on march on 162.3
  continue 856.3
jog the memory 989.20
jog trot run 174.3
  slow motion 175.2
  routine 373.5
jog-trot tedious 118.9
  monotonous 849.15
john latrine 12.10
  toilet 12.11
  card 758.2
  cheater 759.22
John Bull country 232.5
  the government 612.3
John Doe alias 527.8
  the people 606.1
  common man 606.5
  average 864.3
John Hancock
  ratification 332.4
  signature 527.10
johnny latrine 12.10
  toilet 12.11
  man 76.5
Johnny 461.7
johnnycake 10.29
Johnny-come-lately
  newcomer 774.4
  beginner 818.2
  latecomer 846.6
Johnny-on-the-spot
  n benefactor 592.1

adj prompt 845.9
  attentive 983.15
John Q Public
  the people 606.1
  the man in the street 864.3
Johnsonian 545.8
joie de vivre
  animation 17.4
  pleasure 95.1
join
  n joint 800.4
  v adjoin 223.9
  juxtapose 223.13
  flow 238.16
  cooperate 450.3
  side with 450.4
  participate 476.5
  join in marriage 563.14
  associate with 582.17
  enlist 615.17
  join up 617.14
  assemble 770.18
  identify 778.5
  compose 796.3
  put together 800.5
  connect 800.11
  be consistent 803.7
  combine 805.3
  continue 812.4
  concur 899.2
join battle 457.16
joined
  adjacent 223.16
  accompanying 769.9
  assembled 770.21
  related 775.9
  joint 800.12
  united 800.13
  consistent 803.11
  combined 805.5
  continuous 812.8
joiner
  sociable person 582.16
  member 617.11
join forces 805.4
joining
  n meeting 223.4
  addition 253.1
  connection 800.1
  junction 800.1
  joint 800.4
  adj connecting 800.16
joint
  n meat 10.13
  marijuana cigarette 87.12
  crack 224.2
  disapproved place 228.28
  jail 429.9
  sewer 654.7
  brothel 665.9
  casino 759.19
  join 800.4
  v hook 800.8
  adj cooperative 450.5
  communal 476.9
  accompanying 769.9
  assembled 770.21
  mutual 777.11
  connected 800.12
  combined 805.5
  concurrent 899.4

joint effort 450.1
joint operation 450.1
joint ownership 476.1
jointure
  endowment 478.9
  joining 800.1
joke
  n jest 489.6
  laughingstock 508.7
  trifle 998.5
  v jest 489.13
  banter 490.5
joker man 76.5
  surprise 131.2
  mischief-maker 322.3
  trick 356.6
  deceiver 357.1
  proviso 421.3
  humorist 489.12
  bill 613.9
  card 758.2
  condition 959.2
  obstacle 1012.4
  crux 1013.8
jokester
  mischief-maker 322.3
  deceiver 357.1
  humorist 489.12
joking
  n wittiness 489.2
  bantering 490.2
  adj witty 489.15
jollies
  excitement 105.3
  marines 461.28
jollity merriment 109.5
  conviviality 582.3
  festivity 743.3
jolly
  n navy man 183.4
  v banter 490.6
  flatter 511.6
  make merry 743.24
  adj intoxicated 88.31
  merry 109.15
  convivial 582.23
  festive 743.28
jollying
  n bantering 490.3
  adj bantering 490.7
Jolly Roger 647.7
jolt
  n drink 88.7
  excitement 105.3
  start 131.3
  thrust 902.2
  shake 917.3
  v agitate 105.14
  startle 131.8
  way of walking 177.28
  thrust 902.12
  shake 917.11
jolting exciting 105.30
  surprising 131.11
  jolty 917.20
Jonah
  n bad influence 1000.4
  v bring bad luck 1011.12
jongleur
  minstrel 710.14
  poet 720.11

josh joke 489.13
  banter 490.6
joshing
  n wittiness 489.2
  bantering 490.3
  ridicule 508.1
  adj witty 489.15
  ridiculing 508.12
joss 697.3
joss stick 70.4
jostle
  n thrust 902.2
  shake 917.3
  v sound a sour note 61.3
  differ 456.8
  contend 457.13
  rob 482.14
  disagree 789.5
  thrust 902.12
  shake 917.11
jostling
  n theft 482.3
  adj clashing 61.5
jot modicum 248.2
  minute 258.7
  mark 517.5
jounce 917.11
journal
  record book 549.11
  periodical 555.1
  account book 628.4
  history 719.1
  chronicle 832.9
  axle box 915.6
journalese
  n jargon 523.10
  adj journalistic 555.5
journalism
  authorship 547.2
  news 552.1
  the press 555.3
  literature 718.2
journalist 555.4
journey
  n trip 177.5
  v travel 177.21
journeying
  n travel 177.1
  adj traveling 177.36
journeyman
  n expert 413.11
  skilled worker 726.6
  producer 892.7
  adj competent 413.24
joust
  n contest 457.3
  v contend 457.13
jovial merry 109.15
  convivial 582.23
  festive 743.28
joviality
  merriment 109.5
  conviviality 582.3
  festivity 743.3
jowl 218.1
joy
  n happiness 95.2
  merriment 109.5
  v be pleased 95.12
  rejoice 116.5
  exult 502.9

joyful happy 95.16
 merry 109.15
 cheering 109.16
 festive 743.28
joyless
 pleasureless 96.20
 distressing 98.20
 unhappy 112.21
joyous happy 95.16
 merry 109.15
 festive 743.28
joyride
 n ride 177.7
 v ride 177.33
joy stick 87.12
JP 596.1
Jr 301.15
jubilant
 overjoyed 95.17
 rejoicing 116.10
 crowing 502.13
jubilate rejoice 116.5
 celebrate 487.2
 exult 502.9
jubilation treat 95.3
 rejoicing 116.1
 crowing 502.4
jubilee rejoicing 116.1
 celebration 487.1
 anniversary 850.4
Judaic 675.30
Judaism 675.12
Judas
 traitor 357.10
 criminal 660.9
judge
 n arbitrator 466.4
 connoisseur 496.7
 adjudicator 596.1
 magistrate 596.1
 fight 754.3
 judger 946.6
 v mediate 466.6
 administer justice 594.5
 try 598.18
 criticize 723.5
 classify 801.8
 exercise judgment 946.8
 think 953.11
judgeship 594.3
judgment
 judiciary 594.2
 decision 598.9
 condemnation 602.1
 punishment 604.1
 function of Christ 677.14
 classification 801.3
 judiciousness 920.7
 solution 940.1
 discernment 944.2
 assessment 946.3
 judging 946.1
 opinion 953.6
judgmental
 averse 99.8
 fastidious 495.9
 condemnatory 510.22
 judicial 946.16
Judgment Day 839.3
judicature
 judiciary 594.2

tribunal 595.1
 court 595.2
 judgment 946.1
judicial
 jurisdictional 594.6
 tribunal 595.7
 legal 673.11
 judicious 920.19
 judiciary 946.16
judicial process
 judiciary 594.2
 lawsuit 598.1
judicial system 594.2
judiciary
 n judicial system 594.2
 tribunal 595.1
 adj jurisdictional 594.6
 tribunal 595.7
 judicial 946.16
judicious
 cautious 494.8
 moderate 670.10
 intelligent 920.19
 discerning 944.8
 judicial 946.16
jug
 n jail 429.9
 ceramic ware 742.2
 v imprison 429.14
Juggernaut 697.3
juggle
 n trick 356.6
 v tamper with 354.17
 deceive 356.14
juggler trickster 357.2
 cheat 357.3
 circus artist 707.3
juggling 356.5
jughead horse 311.12
 fool 924.4
juice liquor 88.14
 automobile racing 756.1
 current 1032.2
 fluid 1061.2
juiceless 1066.7
juicy tasty 63.8
 delectable 97.10
 immature 301.10
 interesting 983.19
 fluid 1061.4
juju animism 675.6
 sorcery 690.1
 charm 691.5
jukebox 50.11
juke joint 743.13
jumble
 n Greek 522.7
 hodgepodge 797.6
 scramble 810.3
 confusion 985.3
 v deform 263.3
 make unintelligible 522.12
 mix 797.10
 disorder 810.9
 confuse 811.3
 confound 945.3
jumbled
 hard to understand 522.14
 mixed 797.14
 chaotic 810.16
 confused 985.12

jumbo
 n largeness 257.11
 behemoth 257.14
 adj huge 257.20
 excessive 993.16
Jumbo 311.4
jumbo jet 181.3
jump
 n progression 162.1
 step 177.11
 flight 184.9
 ascent 193.1
 interval 224.1
 advantage 249.2
 increase 251.1
 leap 366.1
 promotion 446.1
 basketball game 747.3
 v start 127.12
 be startled 131.5
 way of walking 177.28
 parachute 184.47
 leave undone 340.7
 leap 366.5
 flee 368.10
 escape 369.6
 promote 446.2
 lift one's hand against 457.14
 attack 459.15
 seize on 480.16
 drive 756.4
 shake 917.11
jump down someone's throat
 152.2
jumper leaper 366.4
 diver 367.4
jump in enter 189.7
 mount 193.12
 interrupt 214.6
jumping
 n leaping 366.3
 skiing 753.1
 adj leaping 366.7
jumping-off place
 small town 230.3
 remote region 261.4
 extremity 820.2
jump on
 suppress 428.8
 disapprove 510.18
jump out of one's skin 127.11
jump ship quit 188.9
 play truant 222.9
jump the gun
 be impatient 135.4
 anticipate 845.6
 prejudge 947.2
jump to a conclusion 947.2
jump to it 725.15
jump up
 shoot up 193.9
 rise 200.8
 increase 251.4
 overestimate 949.2
jumpy fearful 127.23
 jittery 128.12
 bustling 330.20
 agitated 917.16
 jerky 917.19
junction
 juxtaposition 223.3

addition 253.1
 passageway 383.3
 railway 383.7
 assemblage 770.1
 relation 775.1
 composition 796.1
 joining 800.1
 consistency 803.2
 combination 805.1
 concurrence 899.1
juncture
 pause 524.9
 circumstance 766.1
 joint 800.4
 period 824.1
 grammar 857.4
jungle 799.2
junior
 n inferior 250.2
 youngster 302.1
 subordinate 432.5
 undergraduate 572.6
 adj inferior 250.6
 Jr 301.15
 subsequent 835.4
junk
 n heroin 87.9
 fake 354.13
 derelict 370.4
 rubbish 391.5
 v abandon 370.5
 scrap 390.8
 eject 909.13
 adj abandoned 370.8
 worthless 391.11
junk dealer 730.10
junket
 n journey 177.5
 v journey 177.21
junk food 10.1
junkie addict 87.21
 enthusiast 101.5
junking 390.3
junk mail 553.4
junkpile car 179.10
 derelict 370.4
 trash pile 391.6
junkyard 391.6
Juno 563.13
Junoesque 1016.19
junta council 423.1
 clique 617.6
 company 770.3
 combination 805.1
Jupiter 1072.9
juridic
 jurisdictional 594.6
 judicial 946.16
jurisdiction
 sphere 231.2
 supremacy 249.3
 governance 417.5
 supervision 573.2
 the confines of the law 594.1
 legal authority 594.1
 control 612.2
 commission 615.1
 legality 673.1
 protectorship 1008.2
jurisprudence 673.7
jurist 597.2

juror 596.7
jury 596.6
jury box 595.6
juryman 596.7
jury-rig
  n improvisation 365.5
  expedient 995.2
  v do carelessly 340.9
  improvise 365.8
jury-rigged
  extemporaneous
    365.12
  makeshift 995.7
jury selection 598.4
jus 673.3
just
  adj appropriate 533.7
  fair 649.8
  virtuous 653.6
  almighty 677.17
  logical 935.20
  valid 973.14
  accurate 973.16
  unprejudiced 979.12
  adv very 247.18
  simply 798.11
  exactly 973.21
  adj rightful 639.8
  honest 644.13
  legal 673.11
just about
  adv nearly 223.22
  prep about 223.26
just around the corner
  near 223.20
  handy 387.20
  in the future 839.9
  imminent 840.3
just deserts
  reprisal 506.2
  deserts 639.3
juste-milieu
  mean 246.1
  temperance 668.1
  moderation 670.1
justice judiciary 594.2
  judge 596.1
  dueness 639.1
  probity 644.1
  justness 649.1
  cardinal virtues 653.4
  legality 673.1
  equality 790.1
  magistrate 946.6
  unprejudicedness 979.5
Justice 649.5
justiceship 594.3
justifiable
  permissible 443.15
  vindicable 600.14
  just 649.8
  logical 935.20
justification
  composition 548.2
  vindication 600.1
  justice 649.1
  sanctification 685.3
justified
  warranted 639.9
  just 649.8
  redeemed 685.9

justify
  compose 548.16
  vindicate 600.9
  acquit 601.4
just in case 831.13
just right apt 788.10
  in step 788.11
  accurately 973.20
  perfect 1002.6
  perfectly 1002.10
just so
  adv how 384.9
  thus 766.10
  accurately 973.20
  phrs right! 973.24
  interj yes 332.18
  conj so 959.15
jut overhang 202.7
  protrude 283.10
  overlie 295.30
jutting
  n overhang 202.3
  adj overhanging 202.11
  protruding 283.14
jutty
  buttress 901.4
  harbor 1009.6
juvenescent 301.9
juvenile
  n youngster 302.1
  book 554.1
  actor 707.2
  jockey 757.2
  adj young 301.9
  immature 406.11
juvenile delinquent 302.4
juvenility 301.1
juxtapose
  appose 223.13
  assemble 770.18
juxtaposition
  apposition 223.3
  addition 253.1
  assemblage 770.1
kaleidoscope 854.4
kama 689.18
Kama 104.8
kamikaze 181.9
kangaroo 366.4
kaolin 742.3
kapok 1047.4
kaput past hope 125.15
  spoiled 393.29
  ruined 395.29
  defeated 412.14
  no more 762.11
  ended 820.9
karaoke popular music 708.7
  solo 708.15
  musical occasion 708.32
karate 760.3
karma destiny 839.2
  fate 964.2
kayo
  n unconsciousness 25.2
  finishing stroke 820.4
  v deaden 25.4
  end 820.5
kazoo
  n mouth organ 711.10
  v teem with 884.5

keel
  n ship 180.1
  base 199.2
  v faint 25.5
  capsize 182.44
  incline 204.10
  overturn 205.6
keelhaul 604.16
keen
  n screech 58.4
  lament 115.3
  dirge 115.6
  v screech 58.8
  lament 115.10
  speak 524.25
  adj energetic 17.13
  acrimonious 17.14
  sensitive 24.13
  shrill 58.14
  pungent 68.6
  fervent 93.18
  deep-felt 93.24
  eager 101.8
  penetrating 105.31
  caustic 144.23
  sharp 285.8
  willing 324.5
  active 330.17
  alert 339.14
  enterprising 404.8
  prepared 405.16
  witty 489.15
  violent 671.16
  smart 920.14
  excellent 999.13
  cold 1023.14
keen on
  desirous of 100.22
  enthusiastic 101.11
  interested 983.16
keep
  n nutriment 10.3
  accommodations 385.3
  custody 429.5
  prison 429.8
  support 449.3
  stronghold 460.6
  v take a course 182.28
  obey 326.2
  provide 385.7
  store up 386.11
  reserve 386.12
  preserve 397.8
  restrain 428.7
  observe 434.2
  support 449.12
  retain 474.5
  hold 474.7
  celebrate 487.2
  practice 701.15
  endure 827.6
  stabilize 855.7
  sustain 856.4
  keep in memory 989.13
  protect 1008.18
  raise 1070.6
keep alive
  keep body and soul together
    306.12
  preserve 397.8
  perpetuate 829.5

  sustain 856.4
keep a low profile
  efface oneself 139.7
  hide 346.8
  beware 494.7
keep an eye on
  look 27.13
  keep informed 551.16
  supervise 573.10
  trace 938.35
  care for 1008.19
keep an eye out
  look 27.13
  be vigilant 339.8
  play safe 1007.3
keep an open mind 982.2
keep a stiff upper lip
  keep cool 106.9
  be of good cheer 109.10
  keep up one's courage 492.15
keep a straight face 111.2
keep at it
  keep going 330.15
  persevere 360.2
  continue 856.3
  persist 856.5
keep away from
  keep one's distance 261.7
  avoid 368.6
keep back slow 175.9
  keep secret 345.7
  reserve 386.12
  not use 390.5
  restrain 428.7
  delay 846.8
  hinder 1012.10
keep books 628.8
keep busy
  keep going 330.15
  task 725.16
keep down
  suppress 428.8
  subjugate 432.8
  domineer 612.16
keeper preserver 397.5
  jailer 429.10
  possessor 470.1
  protector 1008.5
  guardian 1008.6
keep faith 644.9
keep from refrain 329.3
  keep secret 345.7
  avoid 368.6
  restrain 428.7
  abstain 668.7
  prevent 1012.14
keep going
  keep on 330.15
  persevere 360.2
  continue 856.3
  sustain 856.4
keep house
  settle 159.17
  housekeep 228.31
keep in restrain 428.7
  confine 429.12
  retain 474.5
keeping
  n symmetry 264.1
  preservation 397.1
  custody 429.5

observance 434.1
retention 474.1
protectorship 1008.2
adj preservative 397.12
retentive 474.8
keep in mind
think of 931.16
take cognizance of 983.9
keep in memory 989.13
keep in sight look 27.13
be vigilant 339.8
take cognizance of 983.9
keep in touch! 188.22
keep off
fend off 460.10
repulse 908.3
prevent 1012.14
keep on
keep going 330.15
persevere 360.2
endure 827.6
continue 856.3
keep one's cool
be cool 106.6
keep calm 106.9
accept 123.2
be moderate 670.5
stand fast 855.11
keep one's distance
efface oneself 139.7
avoid 157.7
distance oneself 261.7
keep to oneself 344.6
shun 368.6
remain aloof 583.4
keep one's ears open
listen 48.10
hearken to 983.7
keep one's eyes open
keep awake 23.3
look 27.13
be vigilant 339.8
beware 494.7
be curious 981.3
pay attention 983.8
keep one's fingers crossed
be hopeful 124.8
be superstitious 954.7
keep one's head above water
support oneself 385.12
win through 409.13
endure 827.6
be safe 1007.2
keep one's nose to the grindstone
keep going 330.15
keep doggedly at 360.3
drudge 725.14
keep one's shirt on
keep cool 106.9
be patient 134.4
keep one's word 644.9
keep on ice 397.9
keep out 773.4
keep posted 551.16
keep quiet 173.7
keepsake 989.7
keep score 871.8
keep secret 345.7
keep still 51.5

keep tabs on
keep informed 551.16
care for 1008.19
keep the faith
be hopeful 124.8
observe 434.2
be pious 692.6
keep the peace
remain at peace 464.8
be moderate 670.5
calm 670.7
keep time
beat time 708.44
spend time 821.6
time 832.11
coincide 836.4
keep to oneself
be silent 51.5
remain aloof 344.6
keep secret 345.7
retain 474.5
keep oneself to oneself 583.4
keep track of
keep informed 551.16
keep account of 1017.20
keep under wraps 346.6
keep up
not weaken 15.10
persevere 360.2
preserve 397.8
follow the fashion 578.10
work 724.12
sustain 856.4
support 901.21
keister 217.5
kelp 310.4
kelpie 678.10
ken
n vision 27.1
field of view 31.3
knowledge 928.1
v see 27.12
understand 521.7
know 928.12
kennel
n doghouse 228.21
drain 239.5
trench 290.2
dog 311.17
pavement 383.6
group of animals 770.5
v enclose 212.5
keno 759.15
kept reserved 386.15
preserved 397.13
kept woman 665.17
kerchief 5.25
kernel nut 10.39
essential content 196.5
center 208.2
seed 310.31
essence 767.2
middle 819.1
salient point 997.6
kerosene 1025.20
key
n color 35.1
island 235.2
opener 292.10
translation 341.3

telegraph 347.2
clue 517.9
pitch 709.4
key signature 709.15
wind instrument 711.6
basketball 747.1
influence 894.6
v close 293.6
adj central 208.11
keyboard
n fingerboard 711.17
input device 1042.4
v autotype 548.15
computerize 1042.21
keyed up 105.20
keyhole 747.1
keynote
n sign 517.1
key 709.15
characteristic 865.4
v characterize 865.10
keynoter 610.7
keys ecclesiastical insignia 647.4
keyboard 711.17
key signature
notation 709.12
key 709.15
keystone arch 279.4
baseball 745.1
foundation stone 901.7
salient point 997.6
key up excite 105.12
intensify 251.5
khaki 40.3
khakis 5.18
khan ruler 575.9
Muslim ruler 575.10
prince 608.7
Sir 648.3
kibbutz
communion 476.2
farm 1069.8
kibitz meddle 214.7
advise 422.5
kibitzer meddler 214.4
adviser 422.3
gambler 759.21
spectator 918.1
kibosh disable 19.9
end 820.5
kick
n energy 17.3
zest 68.2
excitement 105.3
complaint 115.5
objection 333.2
signal 517.15
hint 551.4
baseball 745.3
football 746.3
soccer 752.3
poker 759.10
counteraction 900.1
boot 902.9
recoil 903.2
v use 87.22
be discontented 108.6
complain 115.16
object 333.5
break the habit 374.3

signal 517.22
swear off 668.8
football 746.5
soccer 752.4
boot 902.21
recoil 903.6
dismiss 909.20
kick around
subdue 432.9
discuss 541.12
domineer 612.16
kick 902.21
kick back relax 20.7
compose oneself 106.7
do nothing 329.2
repay 624.11
discount 631.2
recoil 903.6
kicker
malcontent 108.4
complainer 115.9
surprise 131.2
proviso 421.3
football team 746.2
condition 959.2
kick in die 307.20
provide 385.7
contribute 478.14
pay 624.16
begin 818.7
kick in the teeth 442.2
kickoff
n football 746.3
soccer 752.3
curtain-raiser 816.2
beginning 818.1
adj preceding 816.4
kick off die 307.20
propose 439.5
football 746.5
soccer 752.4
precede 814.2
begin 818.7
start 904.13
kick out kick 902.21
eject 909.13
kickshaw delicacy 10.8
trinket 498.4
toy 743.16
trifle 998.5
kick the bucket 307.20
kick the habit
use 87.22
overcome 412.7
swear off 668.8
kick up a storm
complain 115.16
fly into a rage 152.20
create disorder 810.11
kick upstairs
promote 446.2
depose 447.4
dismiss 909.19
kid
n child 302.3
fledgling 302.10
goat 311.8
v fool 356.15
joke 489.13
banter 490.6
trifle 998.15

kidder
deceiver 357.1
banterer 490.4
kidding
n deception 356.1
banter 490.1
bantering 490.3
adj bantering 490.7
ridiculing 508.12
kid gloves 427.1
kidnap seize 480.14
abduct 482.20
kidnapper 483.10
kidnapping
seizure 480.2
abduction 482.9
kidney viscera 2.16
kind 809.3
disposition 978.3
kill
n stream 238.1
killing 308.1
quarry 382.7
v make laugh 116.9
excise 255.10
delete 255.12
slay 308.13
cover up 345.8
put an end to 395.12
obliterate 395.16
suppress 428.8
veto 444.5
legislate 613.10
amuse 743.21
end 820.5
turn off 857.12
killer
n slayer 308.11
ruffian 593.3
violent person 671.9
first-rate 999.7
adj excellent 999.13
killing
n violent death 307.6
slaying 308.1
gain 472.3
unruliness 671.3
adj fatiguing 21.13
deadly 308.23
laborious 725.18
beautiful 1016.22
killjoy
spoilsport 112.14
pessimist 125.7
hinderer 1012.9
kill oneself 308.22
kill time
waste time 331.13
amuse oneself 743.22
spend time 821.6
kiln
n oven 742.5
v dry 1066.6
kilo 882.10
kilocycle 882.10
kilogram 882.10
kilometer 882.10
kilowatt-hour 17.7
kin kinfolk 559.2
class 809.2
kind 809.3

kind
n race 559.4
nature 767.4
sort 809.3
adj kindly 143.13
forgiving 148.6
indulgent 427.8
favorable 449.22
friendly 587.15
good 999.12
kindergarten 567.2
kindergartner 572.3
kindhearted 143.13
kindle energize 17.10
excite 105.12
flare up 152.19
enkindle 375.18
heat 1020.18
ignite 1020.22
kindling
n ignition 1020.4
firewood 1021.3
adj inflammatory 1020.27
kind of
to a degree 245.7
so to speak 784.19
kindred
n blood relationship 559.1
kinfolk 559.2
adj related 559.6
akin 775.10
kindred soul 784.3
kine 311.6
kinematograph
camera 714.11
projector 714.12
kinescope 714.8
kinesic 517.25
kinesis 172.1
kinetic energetic 17.13
dynamic 1039.9
kinfolk 559.2
king potentate 575.8
prince 608.7
businessman 730.1
chessman 743.17
card 758.2
chief 997.10
kingdom country 232.1
biological classification 305.3
nomenclature 527.1
hierarchy 809.4
classifications 809.5
kingfish 575.4
kingmaker
Machiavellian 415.8
politics 610.6
influence 894.6
kingpin 575.4
kingship
supremacy 249.3
sovereignty 417.8
aristocracy 608.9
king-size great 247.7
large 257.16
huge 257.20
oversize 257.23
kink
n pang 26.2
coil 281.2
caprice 364.1

quirk 927.2
fault 1003.2
blemish 1004.1
v curl 281.5
blemish 1004.4
kinked curly 281.9
blemished 1004.8
kinky curly 281.9
capricious 364.5
unconventional 868.6
eccentric 927.6
kinship
accord 455.1
blood relationship 559.1
common source 775.3
affinity 784.2
kinsmen 559.2
kiosk hut 228.9
summerhouse 228.12
booth 736.3
kipper
n fish 10.24
marine animal 311.30
v preserve 397.9
kirk 703.1
kishkes viscera 2.16
insides 207.4
inner nature 767.5
kismet destiny 839.2
fate 964.2
kiss
n touch 73.1
contact 223.5
buss 562.4
greeting 585.4
v touch lightly 73.7
contact 223.10
osculate 562.19
greet 585.10
kissable 104.25
kiss and make up 465.10
kiss and tell 351.6
kiss ass
bow down 433.10
flatter 511.5
kiss good-bye 473.4
kiss off
relinquish 475.3
repulse 908.3
dismiss 984.4
kit
fledgling 302.10
cat 311.21
equipment 385.4
impedimenta 471.3
set 770.12
kitchen
n restaurant 8.17
cookroom 11.4
storeroom 197.14
baseball 745.3
adj cooking 11.6
kitchen cabinet
council 423.1
cabinet 613.3
kitchen sink
washbasin 79.12
genuineness 973.7
kite
n aircraft 181.1
box kite 181.14

counterfeit 728.10
v take off 193.10
kith and kin 559.2
kitsch vulgarity 497.1
writing 547.12
work of art 712.10
literature 718.1
kitten
n child 302.3
fledgling 302.10
cat 311.21
v give birth 1.3
kittenish
feminine 77.14
gay 109.14
infant 301.12
feline 311.43
kitty cat 311.21
funds 728.14
lawn bowling 750.3
pot 759.5
kittycorner
adj transverse 204.19
adv diagonally 204.25
klutz bungler 414.9
fool 924.3
klutzy
inelegant 534.2
stupid 922.15
knack art 413.6
trinket 498.4
knave
mischief-maker 322.3
rascal 660.3
card 758.2
knavery
stratagem 415.3
roguery 645.2
iniquity 654.3
knavish
mischievous 322.6
roguish 645.17
wicked 654.16
knead stroke 73.8
form 262.7
mix 797.10
rub 1044.6
soften 1047.6
knee
n member 2.7
leg 177.14
angle 278.2
joint 800.4
v kick 902.21
knee-deep deep 275.10
shallow 276.5
knee-high
little 258.10
low 274.7
kneel fawn 138.7
bow 155.6
bend 913.9
kneeling
obeisance 155.2
submission 433.1
crouch 913.3
kneel to
bow down 433.10
entreat 440.11
knell
n ringing 54.3

kneel 155.6
lie 201.5
bow down 433.10
bend 913.9
Kraut vegetables 10.35
derogatory names 232.7
soldier 461.7
kudos praise 509.5
citation 646.4
repute 662.1
kvetch
n malcontent 108.4
complaint 115.5
complainer 115.9
faultfinder 510.9
v be discontented 108.6
complain 115.16
L LSD 87.10
adjunct 254.3
angle 278.2
stage 704.16
eleven 882.7
lab workplace 739.6
laboratory 942.5
label
n tag 517.13
name 527.3
heraldry 647.2
class 809.2
kind 809.3
v tag 517.20
name 527.11
generalize 864.9
labia 2.13
labial 211.13
labor
n birth 1.1
occupation 724.1
task 724.2
work 725.4
v give birth 1.3
be busy 330.10
endeavor 403.5
work 724.12
exert oneself 725.12
dwell on 849.9
flounder 917.15
laboratory
hospital room 197.25
workplace 739.6
lab 942.5
laboratory test 91.12
labor camp 429.8
labored ornate 498.12
stiff 534.3
laborious 725.18
monotonous 849.15
laborer subject 432.7
commoner 607.9
worker 726.2
laboring
n interpretation 341.1
amplification 538.6
adj working 725.17
labor in vain
n labor lost 391.3
v be useless 391.8
fail 410.9
laborious
industrious 330.22
toilsome 725.18

difficult 1013.17
labor of love
act of kindness 143.7
costlessness 634.1
labor organizer 727.4
labor-saving 635.6
labor under ail 85.46
experience 831.8
labor under a disadvantage
1013.11
labor union
association 617.1
trade unionism 727.1
trade union 727.2
labor unionist 727.4
labyrinth 799.2
labyrinthine
deviative 164.7
distorted 265.10
curved 279.7
convolutional 281.6
grandiloquent 545.8
complex 799.4
lace
n material 4.1
network 170.3
strip 271.4
v whip 604.13
weave 740.6
adulterate 797.12
bind 800.9
laced netlike 170.11
woven 740.7
lacerate
v pain 26.7
torture 96.18
injure 393.13
tear apart 802.14
adj notched 289.5
lacerated
pained 26.9
tortured 96.25
notched 289.5
impaired 393.27
laceration
trauma 85.38
torment 96.7
severance 802.2
lachrymal
circulatory 2.33
secretory 13.7
tearful 115.21
lachrymose
secretory 13.7
tearful 115.21
lacing
network 170.3
corporal punishment 604.4
weaving 740.1
adulteration 797.3
lack
n absence 222.1
indigence 619.2
deficiency 795.2
want 992.4
imperfection 1003.1
v be poor 619.5
be incomplete 795.3
fall short 911.2
want 992.7
be insufficient 992.8

lackadaisical
unconcerned 102.7
nonchalant 106.15
languid 331.20
dilatory 846.17
lackey
n retainer 577.1
flunky 577.6
follower 616.8
v serve 577.13
lacking
adj absent 222.11
bereft 473.8
nonexistent 762.8
incomplete 795.4
short of 911.5
insufficient 992.9
wanting 992.13
imperfect 1003.4
prep absent 222.19
lackluster
n colorlessness 36.1
mediocrity 1005.1
dullness 1027.5
adj colorless 36.7
mediocre 1005.7
lusterless 1027.17
lack of feeling
unfeeling 94.1
unconcern 102.2
indiscrimination 945.1
lackwitted 922.13
laconic
n man of few words
344.5
adj taciturn 344.9
concise 537.6
lacquer
n blanket 295.12
v color 35.14
coat 295.24
lacquered 287.11
lactate nourish 8.19
secrete 13.5
lactation humor 2.24
secretion 13.1
liquidity 1061.1
lacteal secretory 13.7
milky 1061.5
lactose intolerance 85.22
lacuna interval 224.1
cavity 284.2
opening 292.1
deficiency 795.2
interruption 813.2
lacustrian
n lake dweller 241.2
adj lakish 241.5
lacy netlike 170.11
thin 270.16
lad man 76.5
boy 302.5
ladder 193.4
lade load 159.15
burden 297.13
fill 794.7
laden weighted 297.18
fraught 794.12
la-di-da 500.15
ladies' man
beau 104.13

dandy 500.9
philanderer 562.12
lading placement 159.6
freight 176.6
load 196.2
burden 297.7
full measure 794.3
ladino 797.8
ladle
n container 195.1
v dip 176.17
lady woman 77.5
female 77.9
cocaine 87.7
ladylove 104.14
wife 563.8
aristocrat 607.4
noblewoman 608.6
person of honor 644.8
good person 659.1
card 758.2
Lady title 648.2
Chance 972.2
lady bountiful
humanitarian 143.8
donor 478.11
cheerful giver 485.2
lady-killer beau 104.13
dandy 500.9
philanderer 562.12
libertine 665.10
ladylike
feminine 77.14
well-bred 504.17
upper-class 607.10
noble 608.10
ladylove 104.14
Lady Luck 972.2
lag
n dawdling 175.3
slowing 175.4
delay 846.2
time constants
1041.11
v lag behind 166.4
dawdle 175.8
be behind 217.8
dally 331.14
mistime 833.2
delay 846.8
fall short 911.2
laggard
n slowpoke 175.5
idler 331.8
adj reluctant 325.6
indolent 331.19
dilatory 846.17
lagging
n dawdling 175.3
delay 846.2
adj dawdling 175.11
dilatory 846.17
lagniappe extra 254.4
gratuity 478.5
bonus 624.6
surplus 993.5
lagoon 241.1
laic
n layman 700.2
amateur 726.5
adj lay 700.3

laid-back
nonchalant 106.15
at ease 121.12
quiescent 173.12
negligent 340.10
leisurely 402.6
unstrict 426.5
laid low ill 85.56
low 274.7
worn-out 393.36
laid up invalided 85.59
stored 386.14
lair den 228.26
disapproved place 228.28
cave 284.5
hiding place 346.4
retreat 584.6
refuge 1009.5
laird proprietor 470.2
nobleman 608.4
laisser aller 329.4
laissez-faire
n inaction 329.1
neglect 340.1
noninterference 430.9
policy 609.4
capitalism 611.8
adj passive 329.6
negligent 340.10
conservative 853.8
lake 241.1
lake dweller 241.2
lakefront
n shore 234.2
adj coastal 234.7
lam depart 188.7
flee 368.11
lama 699.14
lamb
n mutton 10.16
child 302.3
fledgling 302.10
sheep 311.7
simple soul 416.3
endearment term
562.6
innocent 657.4
cheater 759.22
exposure 1006.3
v give birth 1.3
lambaste defeat 412.9
attack 459.15
disapprove 510.18
punish 604.15
pound 902.16
lambent
lightly touching 73.12
flickering 1025.36
illuminated 1025.39
lame
v disable 19.9
cripple 393.14
hamper 1012.11
adj crippled 393.30
unsuccessful 410.18
foolish 923.9
lamebrain 924.2
lame duck
officeholder 610.11
insolvent 625.4
speculator 737.11

lame excuse
pretext 376.1
excuse 600.4
lamellate 296.6
lament
n plaint 115.3
v distress 98.14
mourn 115.10
lamentable
distressing 98.20
sorrowful 112.26
terrible 1000.9
lamentation
distressfulness 98.5
sorrow 112.10
mourning 115.1
lamenting 115.1
lamenter griever 115.8
mourner 309.7
laminate
n plastic 1054.6
v layer 296.5
adj layered 296.6
lamination 296.4
lamp 1026.1
lampoon
n wit 489.1
burlesque 508.6
send-up 512.5
v burlesque 508.11
satirize 512.12
lampooner
humorist 489.12
lampoonist 512.7
lanai 197.21
lance
n cavalryman 461.12
v perforate 292.15
stab 459.25
sever 802.11
throw 904.10
Lancelot 608.5
lancinate 96.18
land
n region 231.1
country 232.1
earth 234.1
ground 234.1
real estate 471.6
v set her down 184.43
come to land 186.8
get down 194.7
meet one's Maker
307.21
acquire 472.9
catch 480.17
land bridge 240.7
landed
possessing 469.9
propertied 471.8
landed gentry
landowner 470.3
gentry 608.3
landfill
receptacle of filth 80.12
derelict 370.4
trash pile 391.6
landholding
n real estate 234.1
ownership 469.2
adj possessing 469.9

landing
coming in 184.18
airport 184.22
landfall 186.2
stairs 193.3
platform 901.13
harbor 1009.6
landlady 470.2
landless 619.9
landlocked 428.15
landloper 178.3
landloping 177.37
landlord
proprietor 470.2
host 585.5
landlubber
mariner 183.2
landsman 234.3
landmark
marker 517.10
salient point 997.6
landmark decision 598.9
landmass
world region 231.6
land 234.1
continent 235.1
land-office business
demand 421.1
roaring trade 1010.5
land on attack 459.15
punish 604.11
landowner 470.3
landscape view 33.6
scene 712.12
landscape architect
artist 716.10
architect 717.3
horticulturist 1069.6
landscape gardener
artist 716.10
architect 717.3
horticulturist 1069.6
land shark cheat 357.3
thief 483.1
landslide slide 194.4
victory 411.1
returns 609.21
plenty 991.2
superabundance 993.2
landsman
fellow citizen 227.5
landman 234.3
friend 588.4
landward
clockwise 161.24
coastward 182.67
lane airway 184.33
passageway 383.3
bowling 750.1
track 755.1
lang syne 837.2
language
n tongue 523.1
communication 523.1
speech 524.1
diction 532.1
assembler language 1042.13
adj speech 524.29
language family 523.12
languid weak 16.12
tired 21.7

landing
sleepy 22.21
apathetic 94.13
inert 173.14
slow 175.10
languorous 331.20
languish weaken 16.9
fail 85.48
lose heart 112.16
decrease 252.6
pine 393.18
languishing
n unhealthiness 85.3
yearning 100.5
adj drooping 16.21
unhealthy 85.54
wistful 100.23
loving 104.27
dejected 112.22
decreasing 252.11
deteriorating 393.45
protracted 827.11
languor weakness 16.1
fatigue 21.1
sleepiness 22.1
apathy 94.4
inertness 173.4
slowness 175.1
languidness 331.6
languorous weak 16.12
inert 173.14
slow 175.10
languid 331.20
lanky
n slim 270.8
adj lean 270.17
tall 272.16
lanolin 1056.3
lantern tower 272.6
roof 295.6
light source 1026.1
lantern jaws 270.5
lap
n drink 8.4
touch 73.1
front 216.1
swash 238.8
overlayer 295.4
lamina 296.2
race 457.12
track 755.1
car race 756.3
circuit 914.2
v clothe 5.39
lap up 8.30
ripple 52.11
lick 73.9
tipple 88.24
lead 165.2
overtake 174.13
surround 209.6
border 211.10
overflow 238.17
plash 238.19
fold 291.5
wrap 295.20
overlie 295.30
cuddle 562.17
circle 914.5
lap dog favorite 104.16
sycophant 138.3
dog 311.17

lapel 291.1
lapidary
  n printmaker 716.8
  adj elegant 533.6
  glyptic 713.12
lapin 311.24
lap of luxury 1010.1
lappet pendant 202.4
  fold 291.1
lapping
  n drinking 8.3
  lap 238.8
  adj rippling 52.19
  overlying 295.36
lapse
  n regression 163.1
  sinkage 194.2
  decline 252.2
  neglect 340.1
  deterioration 393.3
  relapse 394.1
  misdeed 655.2
  impiety 694.1
  close 820.3
  pause 857.3
  conversion 858.1
  reversion 859.1
  slip 975.4
  v regress 163.5
  sink 194.6
  invert 205.5
  neglect 340.6
  decline 393.17
  relapse 394.4
  go wrong 654.9
  come to an end 820.6
  elapse 821.5
  pass 837.6
  defect 858.13
  revert 859.4
  err 975.9
lapsed inverted 205.7
  nonobservant 435.5
  unvirtuous 654.12
  carnal 663.6
  impious 694.6
  unregenerate 695.18
  past 837.7
lapse of memory 990.1
lapse of time
  passage of time 821.4
  period 824.1
laptop computer 1042.2
lap up
  sponge up 8.30
  tipple 88.24
  kid oneself 954.6
larboard
  n left side 220.1
  adj left 220.4
  adv leftward 220.6
larcenous 482.21
larceny 482.2
lard make better 392.9
  oil 1056.8
larder
  provisions 10.5
  store 386.1
  pantry 386.8
lares and penates
  household deity 228.30

property 471.1
  familiar spirit 678.12
large immense 247.7
  sizable 257.16
  liberal 485.4
largehearted
  benevolent 143.15
  liberal 485.4
  magnanimous 652.6
large-minded 979.8
larger than life
  large 257.16
  huge 257.20
  full-sized 257.22
  excessive 993.16
  weighty 997.20
large-scale
  large 257.16
  extensive 864.13
largess gratuity 478.5
  liberality 485.1
largo
  n slow motion 175.2
  music 708.25
  tempo 709.24
  adj music 708.54
lariat 356.13
lark
  n ascent 193.7
  songbird 710.23
  revel 743.6
  v make merry 743.24
larrup punish 604.15
  beat 902.17
larva chrysalis 302.12
  embryo 305.14
  insect 311.33
  specter 988.1
larval 305.22
larynx 524.18
lascivious
  lustful 75.27
  desirous 100.21
  amorous 104.26
  lecherous 665.29
laser surgery 91.19
lash
  n goad 375.8
  whip 605.1
  slap 902.8
  v anchor 182.15
  goad 375.15
  bind 428.10
  criticize 510.20
  whip 604.13
  join 800.9
  drive 1070.8
lashing
  corporal punishment 604.4
  fastening 800.3
lass woman 77.5
  ladylove 104.14
  girl 302.6
lassitude
  weakness 16.1
  fatigue 21.1
  languor 331.6
lasso
  n circle 280.2
  snare 356.13
  v catch 480.17

last
  n mold 786.6
  end 820.1
  v keep alive 306.12
  persevere 360.2
  stay with it 360.4
  live on 761.9
  elapse 821.5
  endure 827.6
  outlast 827.8
  remain 853.5
  adj departing 188.18
  completing 407.9
  final 820.11
  eventual 831.11
  foregoing 837.11
  state-of-the-art 841.14
  adv finally 820.12
last-ditch
  final 820.11
  makeshift 995.7
lasting
  persevering 360.8
  sturdy 763.7
  temporal 821.7
  durable 827.10
  protracted 827.11
  permanent 853.7
  unchangeable 855.17
  remembered 989.23
  tough 1049.4
last minute 846.1
last-minute hasty 401.9
  later 846.18
last name 527.5
last resort
  expedient 995.2
  recourse 1009.2
last rites
  last offices 309.4
  unction 701.5
last straw 886.3
Last Supper 701.7
last word
  supremacy 249.3
  ultimatum 439.3
  meaning 518.1
  administration 573.3
the last word
  the rage 578.4
  novelty 841.2
  influence 894.1
  acme of perfection 1002.3
latch close 293.6
  hook 800.8
late
  adj retarded 175.12
  dead 307.30
  anachronous 833.3
  former 837.10
  recent 841.12
  untimely 844.6
  belated 846.16
  adv behind 846.19
late bloomer 846.6
latecomer 846.6
late lamented
  n corpse 307.16
  adj dead 307.30
latent invisible 32.5
  inert 173.14

secret 345.11
  concealed 346.11
  lurking 519.5
later
  adj subsequent 835.4
  future 839.8
  recent 841.12
  last-minute 846.18
  adv subsequently 835.6
  in the future 839.9
lateral
  n speech sound 524.12
  throw 904.3
  v go sideways 218.5
  adj side 218.6
  sided 218.7
  phonetic 524.30
latest present 838.2
  state-of-the-art 841.14
the latest thing
  the rage 578.4
  novelty 841.2
latex elastic 1048.3
  fluid 1061.2
lath
  n thinness 270.7
  strip 271.4
  wood 1054.3
  v cover 295.23
lathe 858.10
lather
  n sweat 12.7
  dither 105.6
  impatience 135.1
  foam 320.2
  v wash 79.19
  get excited 105.17
  foam 320.5
  defeat 412.9
  punish 604.15
latitude room 158.3
  map 159.5
  zone 231.3
  breadth 269.1
  coordinates 300.5
  scope 430.4
  broad-mindedness 979.1
latitudinarian
  n free agent 430.12
  freethinker 695.13
  liberal 979.6
  adj nonrestrictive 430.25
  freethinking 695.21
  liberal 979.9
latrine
  convenience 12.10
  toilet 12.11
latter foregoing 837.11
  recent 841.12
lattice
  n network 170.3
  frame 266.4
  atomic cluster 1038.7
  reactor 1038.13
  v net 170.7
laud
  n thanks 150.2
  praise 509.5
  glorification 696.2
  paean 696.3
  v praise 509.12

glorify 696.12

laudable
praiseworthy 509.20
good 999.12

laudatory 509.16

lauded 247.9

laugh
n laughter 116.4
joke 489.6
v be pleased 95.12
exude cheerfulness 109.6
burst out laughing 116.8

laughable
humorous 488.4
absurd 923.11

laugh at flout 454.4
ridicule 508.8

laughing
n laughter 116.4
adj happy 95.16
cheerful 109.11

laughingstock 508.7

laugh it up laugh 116.8
amuse oneself 743.22

laughs 743.2

laughter
merriment 109.5
laughing 116.4

launch
n motorboat 180.4
beginning 818.1
rocket launching 1074.9
v propose 439.5
inaugurate 818.11
throw 904.10
start 904.13
project 1074.13

launcher 462.21

launching
beginning 818.1
inauguration 818.5
innovation 852.4

launching pad
beginning 818.1
platform 901.13
rocket launcher 1074.10

launch into
undertake 404.3
set to work 725.15

launder 79.19

laundress 79.15

Laundromat 79.11

laundry
laundering 79.6
washery 79.11

laundry list list 871.1
schedule 965.3

laundry room 739.8

laureate
n superior 249.4
champion 413.15
poet 720.11
adj honored 646.9

laurels
supremacy 249.3
victory 411.1
trophy 646.3

lava
combustion product 1020.16
rock 1059.1

lavatory latrine 12.10

bathing place 79.10
washbasin 79.12
bathroom 197.26

lave wash 79.19
soak 1065.13

lavender 46.3

lavish
v give 478.12
furnish 478.15
spare no expense 485.3
squander 486.3
adj liberal 485.4
prodigal 486.8
ornate 545.11
teeming 884.9
plentiful 991.7
superabundant 993.19

lavish with 993.14

law
n rule 419.2
decree 420.4
prohibition 444.1
lex 673.3
legal system 673.4
jurisprudence 673.7
game 752.3
norm 869.4
axiom 974.2
v sue 598.13

the Law 683.3

the law 1008.16

law-abiding
obedient 326.3
honest 644.13

law and order 464.2

lawbreaker
evildoer 593.1
criminal 660.9

lawbreaking
disobedience 327.1
wrongdoing 655.1
violation 674.3

law enforcement agency
1008.17

law enforcement agent
1008.15

law firm 597.4

lawful
permissible 443.15
just 649.8
legal 673.11
valid 973.14
genuine 973.15

lawgiver 610.3

lawless
disobedient 327.8
licentious 418.5
illegal 674.6

lawmaker 610.3

lawmaking
n legislation 613.5
adj legislative 613.11
legal 673.11

lawn 310.7

law of averages 972.1

law officer 597.1

lawsuit suit 598.1
accusation 599.1

lawyer attorney 597.1
professional 726.4

lax indolent 331.19

negligent 340.10
slack 426.4
lenient 427.7
unrestrained 430.24
nonrestrictive 430.25
permissive 443.14
phonetic 524.30
wanton 665.26
loose 804.5
dilatory 846.17
vague 971.19
inaccurate 975.17
flaccid 1047.10

laxative
n cathartic 86.17
adj cathartic 86.48

laxity neglect 340.1
laxness 426.1
nonobservance 435.1
wantonness 665.4
looseness 804.2
vagueness 971.4
inaccuracy 975.2
flaccidity 1047.3

lay
n navigation 159.3
direction 161.1
air 708.4
song 708.14
bet 759.3
v copulate 75.21
reproduce 78.9
relieve 120.5
place 159.12
deposit 159.14
ship activity 182.48
lie 201.5
level 201.6
smooth 287.5
pacify 465.7
impose 643.4
moderate 670.6
exorcise 690.12
bet 759.25
adj laic 700.3

lay an egg
fall flat 117.4
fail 410.10
bungle 414.12
bomb 459.23

lay aside
remove 176.11
put away 390.6
segregate 773.6
postpone 846.9
dismiss 984.4

lay away store 386.10
put away 390.6

lay back relax 20.7
compose oneself
106.7

lay before
confront 216.8
propose 439.5

lay by lay to 182.17
lie idle 331.16
store 386.10
reserve 386.12
put away 390.6
prepare for 405.11
postpone 846.9

lay down
deposit 159.14
careen 182.43
level 201.6
layer 296.5
affirm 334.5
give up 370.7
store 386.10
prescribe 420.9
pledge 438.10
pay over 624.15
bet 759.25
postulate 951.12

lay down the law
put one's foot down 420.10
direct 573.8
dominate 612.15
dogmatize 970.10

layer
n tier 296.1
thickness 296.1
v lay down 296.5

layette 5.30

lay figure figure 349.6
figurehead 575.5
art equipment 712.18
thing of naught 764.2
artist's model 786.5

lay hands on
attack 459.14
seize 480.14
bless 696.14
minister 701.16

lay in sail for 182.35
store 386.10
gather materials 1054.7

lay into
lift one's hand against 457.14
attack 459.15
punish 604.11

lay it on
exaggerate 355.3
flatter 511.6
talk big 545.6
pile it on 993.11

lay it on thick
coat 295.24
exaggerate 355.3
affect 500.12
boast 502.7
commend 509.11
flatter 511.6
talk big 545.6
pile it on 993.11

lay low weaken 16.10
level 201.6
lie low 274.5
strike dead 308.18
hide 346.8
fell 913.5

layman laic 700.2
amateur 726.5

layoff
unemployment 331.3
dismissal 909.5

lay off
v take a rest 20.8
circumscribe 210.4
measure off 300.11
lie idle 331.16
plot 381.10

cease to use 390.4
cease 857.6
dismiss 909.19
interj cease! 857.14
the lay of the land 765.2
lay on cover 295.19
  coat 295.24
  lift one's hand against 457.14
  blame 599.8
  whip 604.13
  impose 643.4
  administer 643.6
layout form 262.1
  plan 381.1
  composition 548.2
  roulette 759.12
  gambling wheel 759.16
  order 807.1
lay out deaden 25.4
  level 201.6
  form 262.7
  measure off 300.11
  kill 308.14
  embalm 309.21
  plot 381.10
  pledge 438.10
  spend 626.5
  order 807.4
  fell 913.5
layover 225.5
lay over sojourn 225.8
  cover 295.19
  postpone 846.9
lay the foundation
  establish 159.16
  prepare the way 405.12
lay to lay by 182.17
  lie idle 331.16
  exert oneself 725.9
  attribute to 888.4
lay to rest inter 309.19
  abolish 395.13
  end 820.5
  disprove 958.4
lay up afflict 85.50
  lay to 182.17
  layer 296.5
  store up 386.11
lay waste
  destroy 395.10
  raze 671.11
laze go slow 175.6
  idle 331.12
lazy slow 175.10
  indolent 331.19
  careless 340.11
  dilatory 846.17
lazybones 331.7
lea 310.8
leach
  n solution 1064.3
  v refine 79.22
  exude 190.15
  trickle 238.18
  subtract 255.9
  liquefy 1064.5
  soak 1065.13
leached 891.4
lead
  n instrument 200.6
  weight 297.6

v weight 297.12
gravitate 297.15
adj brass 1058.17
lead
  n superiority 249.1
  hunter 311.13
  shackle 428.4
  pointer 517.4
  clue 517.9
  direction 573.1
  role 704.10
  script 706.3
  leading man 707.6
  notation 709.12
  lawn bowling 750.3
  bridge 758.3
  chief 997.10
  v take direction 161.7
  head 165.2
  be in front 216.7
  rule 249.11
  induce 375.22
  direct 573.8
  govern 612.12
  conduct 708.45
  escort 769.8
  precede 814.2
  go before 816.3
  initiate 818.10
  cause 886.11
  influence 894.7
  tend 896.3
lead by the nose
  have subject 432.10
  dominate 612.15
  influence 894.7
  have influence over 894.11
leaden colorless 36.7
  gray 39.4
  dull 117.6
  inert 173.14
  heavy 297.16
  languid 331.20
  stiff 534.3
  brass 1058.17
leader
  vanguard 216.2
  superior 249.4
  hunter 311.13
  commentary 556.2
  director 574.6
  chief 575.3
  conductor 710.17
  commodity 735.2
  lawn bowling 750.3
  precursor 816.1
  special 866.2
  question 938.10
leadership
  supremacy 249.3
  mastership 417.7
  directorship 573.4
  influence 894.1
leading
  n preceding 165.1
  heading 165.1
  direction 573.1
  adj heading 165.3
  front 216.10
  chief 249.14
  authoritative 417.15

directing 573.12
governing 612.18
preceding 814.4
first 818.17
paramount 997.24
leading lady
  role 704.10
  lead 707.6
leading to 896.5
lead item
  commodity 735.2
  special 866.2
lead off
  precede 814.2
  initiate 818.10
lead on lure 377.5
  direct 573.8
  exercise influence 894.9
lead one to expect
  give hope 124.10
  be as expected 130.10
  promise 133.13
  be probable 968.4
lead the way lead 165.2
  set an example 786.7
  go before 816.3
  initiate 818.10
lead time
  preparation 405.1
  earliness 845.1
  forethought 961.2
lead to direct to 161.6
  extend to 261.6
  pave the way 405.12
  entail 772.4
  determine 886.12
lead up the garden path
  356.16
leaf
  n tobacco 89.2
  lamina 296.2
  frond 310.19
  advertising matter 352.8
  makeup 554.12
  paper 1054.5
  v vegetate 310.34
leaflet leaf 310.19
  advertising matter
   352.8
  booklet 554.11
leaf metal 1058.3
leaf through 938.25
leafy green 44.4
  leaved 310.41
league
  n treaty 437.2
  affiliation 450.2
  association 617.1
  baseball 745.1
  football 746.1
  bowling 750.1
  soccer 752.1
  combination 805.1
  v cooperate 450.3
  come together 770.16
  put together 800.5
  ally 805.4
leagued
  assembled 770.21
  joined 800.13
  enleagued 805.6

League of Nations
  supranational government
   12.7
  United Nations 614.1
leak
  n leakage 190.5
  opening 292.1
  divulgence 351.2
  escape 369.1
  v leak out 190.14
  communicate 343.7
  disclose 351.4
  betray 351.6
  go to waste 473.6
  hint 551.10
leakage entrance 189.1
  leaking 190.5
  escape 369.1
  waste 473.2
leak in 189.10
leak out leak 190.14
  be revealed 351.8
  find vent 369.10
leakproof
  resistant 15.20
  watertight 1066.11
leaky exudative 190.20
  apertured 292.19
lean
  n inclination 204.2
  v incline 204.10
  gravitate 297.15
  be willing 324.3
  tend 896.3
  adj thin 270.17
  plain-speaking 535.3
  meager 992.10
leaning
  n desire 100.3
  inclination 204.2
  preference 371.5
  aptitude 413.5
  partiality 650.3
  tendency 896.1
  disposition 978.3
  prejudice 980.3
  adj inclining 204.15
  unbalanced 791.5
  tending 896.4
lean on
  coerce 424.8
  threaten 514.2
  exercise influence 894.9
  rest on 901.22
  rely on 953.16
lean-to 228.9
lean toward
  desire 100.14
  prefer 371.17
  take the attitude 978.6
leap
  n progression 162.1
  ascent 193.1
  interval 224.1
  degree 245.1
  increase 251.1
  jump 366.1
  curtain-raiser 816.2
  innovation 852.4
  v speed 174.8
  jump 366.5

make haste 401.5
leap before one looks 401.7
leapfrog
　n leap 366.1
　v leap 366.5
leaping
　n jumping 366.3
　adj happy 95.16
　ascending 193.14
　jumping 366.7
leap year
　moment 824.2
　anniversary 850.4
learn
　understand 521.7
　come to know 551.14
　get 570.6
　master 570.9
　come to one's knowledge
　　928.14
　discover 941.2
learn by heart 989.17
learned
　educated 570.16
　studentlike 572.12
　wise 920.17
　erudite 928.21
learner
　student 572.1
　beginner 818.2
learning
　intellectual acquirement 570.1
　enlightenment 928.4
　discovery 941.1
lease
　n possession 469.1
　rental 615.6
　v inhabit 225.7
　rent 615.15
　rent out 615.16
leasehold
　n possession 469.1
　adj freehold 471.10
leaseholder 470.4
lease-lend
　rent out 615.16
　lend 620.5
leash
　n shackle 428.4
　three 876.1
　v bind 428.10
　join 800.9
least
　n minority 885.3
　adj humble 137.10
　smallest 250.8
　minority 885.7
leather
　n fur 4.2
　hide 4.3
　toughness 1049.2
　v punish 604.15
leatherneck 183.4
leave
　n vacation 20.3
　leave-taking 188.4
　absence 222.4
　consent 441.1
　permission 443.1
　game 750.2
　v depart 188.6

leave over 256.6
bereave 307.28
vegetate 310.34
leave undone 340.7
abandon 370.5
permit 443.9
resign 448.2
bequeath 478.18
separate 802.8
interj go away! 909.31
leave alone
　let alone 329.4
　not interfere 430.16
　give permission 443.12
　be conservative 853.6
leave behind
　overtake 174.13
　outdistance 249.10
　leave 256.6
　bereave 307.28
　abandon 370.5
leaved
　green 44.4
　leafy 310.41
leaven
　n bread 10.28
　leavening 298.4
　transformer 852.5
　v pervade 221.7
　raise 298.7
　imbue 797.11
　qualify 959.3
leavening
　n bread 10.28
　fermentation 298.4
　adj raising 298.17
leave no stone unturned
　prosecute to a conclusion
　　360.5
　make every effort 403.15
　take precautions 494.6
　be thorough 794.8
　ransack 938.33
leave of absence
　vacation 20.3
　absence 222.4
leave off
　v give up 370.7
　break the habit 374.3
　cease to use 390.4
　cease 857.6
　interj cease! 857.13
leave one cold
　not be affected by 94.5
　fall flat 117.4
　bore 118.7
leave out 773.4
leave-taking 188.4
leave undone
　leave 340.7
　slight 340.8
　neglect 408.2
leave word
　communicate 343.7
　inform 551.8
leaving
　n departure 188.1
　absence 222.4
　abandonment 370.1
　adj departing 188.18
leaving out off 255.14

excluding 773.10
leaving-out 773.1
leavings
　remainder 256.1
　refuse 391.4
　extract 893.3
lecher
　philanderer 562.12
　reprobate 660.4
　satyr 665.11
lechery
　philandering 562.10
　lasciviousness 665.5
lectern pulpit 703.13
　table 901.15
lection 341.2
lector lecturer 571.7
　holy orders 699.4
lecture
　n reproof 510.5
　prelection 543.3
　lesson 568.7
　v reprove 510.17
　prelect 543.11
　expound 568.16
lecturer
　praelector 543.5
　academic rank 571.3
　lector 571.7
lecturing
　n public speaking 543.1
　adj educational 568.18
ledge
　horizontal 201.3
　border 211.4
　layer 296.1
　shelf 901.14
ledger
　record book 549.11
　account book 628.4
　bill 871.5
lee
　n lee side 218.2
　protection 1008.1
　adj side 218.6
leech
　n doctor 90.4
　parasite 138.5
　sail 180.14
　bloodsucker 311.38
　extortionist 480.12
　adhesive 803.4
　v bleed 91.27
leeching 91.20
leer
　n look 27.3
　scornful laugh 508.4
　signal 517.15
　v scrutinize 27.14
　signal 517.22
leering
　n ridicule 508.1
　adj ridiculing 508.12
leery wary 494.9
　doubting 955.9
　incredulous 956.4
lees dregs 256.2
　refuse 391.4
　extract 893.3
leeward
　n lee side 218.2

adj side 218.6
adv clockwise 161.24
to leeward 182.68
downwind 218.9
leeway room 158.3
　way 182.9
　drift 184.28
　interval 224.1
　distance 261.1
　latitude 430.4
left
　n left side 220.1
　liberalism 611.3
　liberal 611.11
　adj departed 188.19
　left-hand 220.4
　remaining 256.7
　abandoned 370.8
　adv leftward 220.6
left-handed
　insulting 156.8
　oblique 204.13
　sinistromanual 220.5
　bungling 414.20
left-hander
　southpaw 220.3
　baseball team 745.2
leftist
　n liberal 611.11
　adj liberal 611.19
left-out 773.7
leftover
　n surplus 993.5
　adj remaining 256.7
　surplus 993.18
leftward
　clockwise 161.24
　to the left 220.6
left wing left side 220.1
　liberalism 611.3
left-wing left 220.4
　liberal 611.19
left-winger
　left side 220.1
　liberal 611.11
lefty
　n left-hander 220.3
　baseball team 745.2
　adj left-handed 220.5
leg
　n body part 2.7
　fowl part 10.23
　limb 177.14
　voyage 182.6
　shank 273.6
　member 793.4
　v walk 177.27
legacy bequest 478.10
　inheritance 479.2
　effect 887.1
legal
　permissible 443.15
　recorded 549.17
　just 649.8
　legitimate 673.11
　valid 973.14
legal age 303.2
legal counselor 597.1
legalistic formal 580.7
　jurisprudent 673.12
　conformist 867.6

legality
permissibility 443.8
justice 649.1
lawfulness 673.1
legitimacy 673.1
legalization
authorization 443.3
legitimation 673.2
legalize
authorize 443.11
legitimize 673.9
legal system
judiciary 594.2
law 673.4
legal tender 728.1
legate delegate 576.2
diplomat 576.6
legatee 479.4
legation
foreign office 576.7
commission 615.1
office 739.7
legato
n music 708.25
execution 708.30
note 709.14
adj music 708.53
legend map 159.5
posthumous fame 662.7
mythology 678.14
history 719.1
tradition 842.2
caption 937.2
legendary
fabricated 354.29
distinguished 662.16
mythic 678.15
historical 719.7
fictional 722.7
traditional 842.12
extraordinary 870.14
fictitious 986.21
legible 521.12
legion
military unit 461.22
throng 770.4
multitude 884.3
legionary 461.6
legislate
make laws 613.10
legalize 673.9
legislation
lawmaking 613.5
legalization 673.2
law 673.3
legislative
legislatorial 613.11
legal 673.11
legislator
public official 575.17
lawmaker 610.3
legislature
council 423.1
legislative body 613.1
legislation 613.5
legit
n show business 704.1
adj legal 673.11
legitimacy
authority 417.1
permissibility 443.8

justifiability 600.7
legality 673.1
genuineness 973.7
legitimate
v authorize 443.11
legalize 673.9
adj permissible 443.15
justifiable 600.14
legal 673.11
dramatic 704.33
logical 935.20
valid 973.14
genuine 973.15
leg man 555.4
legume plant 310.4
seed vessel 310.30
legwork 938.4
lei 310.25
leisure
n idleness 331.2
ease 402.1
pause 857.3
adj idle 331.18
leisured 402.5
leisure class 331.11
leisured
idle 331.18
leisure 402.5
leitmotiv 708.24
lemon
n sour 67.2
failure 410.2
adj yellow 43.4
lend loan 620.5
discount 728.27
lend a hand 449.11
lend an ear 48.10
lender 620.3
lending loaning 620.1
money market 728.16
lend-lease
n rental 615.6
lending 620.1
v rent out 615.16
lend 620.5
length size 257.1
distance 261.1
longness 267.1
extent 300.3
lengthen increase 251.4
prolong 267.6
protract 827.9
sustain 856.4
lengthened
prolonged 267.8
protracted 827.11
lengthening
n prolongation 267.4
protraction 827.2
continuance 856.1
adj increasing 251.8
lengthy long 267.7
giant 272.16
wordy 538.12
leniency patience 134.1
considerateness 143.3
pity 145.1
unstrictness 426.2
mercifulness 427
lenientness 427.1
modulation 670.2

tolerance 979.4
softness 1047.1
lenient patient 134.9
considerate 143.16
pitying 145.7
unstrict 426.5
mild 427.7
permissive 443.14
tolerant 979.11
lenitive
n palliative 86.10
moderator 670.3
ointment 1056.3
adj palliative 86.40
relieving 120.9
moderating 670.16
qualifying 959.7
lubricant 1056.10
lens eye 2.9
glass 29.2
Lent fast day 515.3
penance 658.3
Lenten
fasting 515.5
abstinent 668.10
meager 992.10
lentil 310.4
lento 708.54
leonine 311.43
leopard
variegation 47.6
wild cat 311.22
leper 586.4
leprechaun 678.8
lesbian
n homosexual 75.14
mannish female 76.9
adj homosexual 75.30
lesion sore 85.37
trauma 85.38
pain 96.5
less
adj inferior 250.6
reduced 252.10
fewer 885.6
adv decreasingly 252.12
prep off 255.14
without 992.17
lessee lodger 227.8
tenant 470.4
lessen relieve 120.5
decrease 252.6
reduce 252.7
subtract 255.9
extenuate 600.12
moderate 670.6
lessening
n relief 120.1
decrease 252.1
deterioration 393.3
modulation 670.2
adj decreasing 252.11
mitigating 670.14
lesser inferior 250.6
reduced 252.10
lesson warning 399.1
reproof 510.5
teaching 568.7
lest 897.7
let
n rental 615.6

game 748.2
hindrance 1012.1
v draw off 192.12
permit 443.9
rent 615.15
rent out 615.16
suppose 951.10
adj employed 615.20
let alone
v leave undone 340.7
avoid 368.6
not use 390.5
abstain 668.7
adv additionally 253.11
prep with 253.12
excluding 773.10
let be let alone 329.4
leave undone 340.7
not interfere 430.16
be conservative 853.6
suppose 951.10
letdown
disappointment 132.1
humiliation 137.2
slowing 175.4
collapse 410.3
modulation 670.2
let down
v rest 20.7
disappoint 132.2
slow 175.9
deceive 356.14
deteriorate 393.16
betray 645.14
relax 670.9
depress 913.4
adj discontented 108.7
disappointed 132.5
let drop betray 351.6
remark 524.24
drop 913.7
let fly throw 904.10
shoot 904.12
let go condone 148.4
let pass 329.5
neglect 340.6
leave undone 340.7
cease to use 390.4
exempt 430.14
let oneself go 430.19
release 431.5
relinquish 475.4
acquit 601.4
make merry 743.24
disband 771.8
loosen 804.3
throw 904.10
dismiss 909.19
let out 909.24
lethal deadly 308.23
harmful 1000.12
lethality
deadliness 308.9
harmfulness 1000.5
lethargic sleepy 22.21
apathetic 94.13
languid 331.20
lethargy
sleepiness 22.1
stupor 22.6
apathy 94.4

languor 331.6
stupidity 922.3
let in receive 187.10
welcome 585.7
let in on divulge 351.5
tip 551.11
disillusion 977.2
let it all hang out
lighten 120.7
confess 351.7
let oneself go 430.19
let it go
v forget 148.5
dismiss 984.4
phrs no matter 998.25
let loose
let oneself go 430.19
release 431.5
loose 431.6
make merry 743.24
throw 904.10
let off
v exempt 430.14
release 431.5
acquit 601.4
rent out 615.16
explode 671.14
shoot 904.12
adj exempt 430.30
let on confess 351.7
sham 354.21
let one's hair down
lighten 120.7
divulge 351.5
let oneself go 430.19
chat 541.10
not stand on ceremony
581.2
make merry 743.24
let one have it
attack 459.15
disapprove 510.18
punish 604.11
let out
draw off 192.12
lengthen 267.6
disclose 351.4
divulge 351.5
release 431.5
say 524.22
rent out 615.16
dismiss 909.19
give vent to 909.24
let pass accept 134.7
let go 329.5
be inattentive 984.2
let slip let go 329.5
neglect 340.6
betray 351.6
lose 473.4
dismiss 984.4
letter
n representation 349.1
symbol 546.1
written character 547.9
writing 547.10
type 548.6
message 552.4
epistle 553.2
v initial 546.6
adj epistolary 553.14

letter carrier
carrier 176.7
postman 353.5
lettered literal 546.8
learned 928.21
letterer 547.13
letterhead label 517.13
address 553.9
lettering
initialing 546.5
writing 547.1
handwriting style 547.4
letter of credit
credit instrument 622.3
negotiable instrument 728.11
letter of the law 673.1
letter-perfect 973.15
letterpress
printing 548.1
print 548.3
printed matter 548.10
letters
writing system 546.3
literary work 547.12
record 549.1
literature 718.1
scholarship 928.5
letter writer 553.8
letter writing 553.1
letting go 475.1
letup slowing 175.4
decrease 252.1
modulation 670.2
interruption 813.2
interim 826.1
pause 857.3
let-up 175.9
let up
v relax 20.7
decrease 252.6
ease up 670.9
loosen 804.3
pause 857.9
interj cease! 857.13
let well enough alone
be content 107.5
be inattentive 984.2
leukocyte 2.25
levant
flee 368.10
not pay 625.6
Levant 231.6
levanter
north wind 318.9
defaulter 625.5
levee
social gathering 582.10
assembly 770.2
barrier 1012.5
level
n floor 197.23
horizontal 201.3
plain 236.1
degree 245.1
smoothness 287.3
layer 296.1
class 607.1
classification 809.2
v flatten 201.6
smooth 287.5
raze 395.19

make uniform 781.4
equalize 790.6
fell 913.5
adj horizontal 201.7
straight 277.6
smooth 287.10
just 649.8
uniform 781.5
equal 790.7
adv horizontally 201.9
level at 459.22
level head
equanimity 106.3
sensibleness 920.6
levelheaded
composed 106.13
equable 670.13
sensible 920.18
level off
land 184.43
make uniform 781.4
equalize 790.6
lever
n instrument 384.4
leverage 906.4
lifter 912.3
v get a purchase 906.8
leverage
trading 737.19
influence 894.1
fulcrumage 906.1
mechanics 1039.1
leviathan ship 180.1
behemoth 257.14
Leviathan 311.30
levitate
ascend 193.8
rise 298.9
elevate 912.5
levitation
ascent 193.1
lightness 298.1
psychic phenomena
689.6
levity
lightheartedness 109.3
merriment 109.5
lightness 298.1
fickleness 364.3
waggishness 489.4
ridicule 508.1
inattention 984.1
triviality 998.3
levy
n demand 421.1
call to arms 458.8
recruit 461.18
attachment 480.5
enlistment 615.7
tax 630.9
v demand 421.5
call to arms 458.19
attach 480.20
enlist 615.17
charge 630.12
impose 643.4
lewd lascivious 665.29
obscene 666.9
lex 673.3
lexeme sign 518.6
word 526.1

lexicographer
interpreter 341.7
linguist 523.15
lexicography
exegetics 341.8
lexicology 526.14
lexicologist 523.15
lexicology
semantics 518.7
lexicography 526.14
lexicon
vocabulary 526.13
reference book 554.9
dictionary 871.4
lexigraphic
lexical 526.19
literal 546.8
lexis 526.13
liabilities
expenses 626.3
accounts 628.1
liability debt 623.1
responsibility 641.2
tendency 896.1
indebtedness 897.2
likelihood 897.1
susceptibility 897.2
probability 968.1
disadvantage 996.2
exposure 1006.3
liable chargeable 623.9
responsible 641.17
likely 897.5
probable 968.6
exposed 1006.15
liable to
adj subject to 897.6
prep inclined to 896.6
liaison love affair 104.6
intermediary 213.4
instrument 384.4
relation 775.1
joining 800.1
liar 357.9
libation drink 8.4
alcohol 88.7
oblation 696.7
libel
n monstrous lie 354.12
slander 512.3
declaration 598.7
v slander 512.11
liberal
n left side 220.1
free agent 430.12
left-winger 611.11
liberalist 979.6
adj left 220.4
nonrestrictive 430.25
philanthropic 478.22
free 485.4
hospitable 585.11
liberalistic 611.19
magnanimous 652.6
extensive 864.13
liberal-minded 979.9
plentiful 991.7
liberalism
noninterference 430.9
libertarianism 430.10
progressivism 611.3

liberalness 979.2
Liberalism 609.25
liberality
  giving 478.1
  gratuity 478.5
  generosity 485.1
  liberalness 485.1
  hospitality 585.1
  magnanimity 652.2
  liberalness 979.2
  plenty 991.2
liberalize 430.13
liberate
  rescue 398.3
  liberalize 430.13
  free 431.4
  detach 802.10
  disembarrass 1014.9
liberated free 430.21
  freed 431.10
liberation escape 369.1
  rescue 398.1
  liberalism 430.10
  freeing 431.1
  theft 482.1
liberator 592.2
libertarian
  n free agent 430.12
  liberal 979.6
  adj nonrestrictive 430.25
  liberal 979.9
libertine
  n free agent 430.12
  philanderer 562.12
  swinger 665.10
  adj nonrestrictive 430.25
libertinism
  liberalism 430.10
  profligacy 665.3
liberty vacation 20.3
  freedom 430.1
  exemption 430.8
  permission 443.1
  grant 443.5
  privilege 642.2
  opportunity 843.2
libidinal
  sexual 75.25
  desirous 100.21
  instinctive 934.6
libidinous lustful 75.27
  desirous 100.21
  lascivious 665.29
libido sexuality 75.2
  psyche 92.28
  desire 100.1
  love 104.1
  amorousness 104.3
  instinct 934.2
librarian
  recorder 550.1
  professional librarian 558.3
  steward 574.4
library stacks 197.6
  storehouse 386.6
  preserve 397.7
  edition 554.5
  book depository 558.1
  collection 770.11
  retreat 1009.5
libration 916.1

librettist
  dramatist 704.22
  composer 710.20
  poet 720.11
libretto playbook 704.21
  score 708.28
license
  n lawlessness 418.1
  freedom 430.1
  exemption 430.8
  permission 443.1
  permit 443.6
  commission 615.1
  presumption 640.2
  privilege 642.2
  profligacy 665.3
  confusion 810.2
  v authorize 443.11
  commission 615.10
licensed exempt 430.30
  authorized 443.17
licentious lawless 418.5
  unrestrained 430.24
  presumptuous 640.11
  profligate 665.25
  dissipated 669.8
lichen 310.4
licit permissible 443.15
  legal 673.11
lick
  n sip 62.2
  touch 73.1
  velocity 172.4
  hint 248.4
  attempt 403.3
  impromptu 708.27
  work 725.4
  blow 902.5
  v lap up 8.30
  taste 62.7
  touch 73.9
  best 249.7
  defeat 412.9
  punish 604.15
  stump 971.14
licked defeated 412.15
  beaten 971.26
lickerish lustful 75.27
  desirous 100.21
  lascivious 665.29
lickety-split 174.17
licking eating 8.1
  defeat 412.1
  punishment 604.5
lid body part 2.9
  headdress 5.25
  eye 27.9
  stopper 293.4
  cover 295.5
lido 234.2
lie
  n navigation 159.3
  direction 161.1
  falsehood 354.11
  round 751.3
  v extend 158.9
  be located 159.10
  ride at anchor 182.16
  lie down 201.5
  be present 221.6
  tell a lie 354.19

  be dishonest 645.11
lie detector 92.8
lie down rest 20.6
  lie 201.5
  couch 913.11
lief 324.9
liege
  n subject 432.7
  master 575.1
  retainer 577.1
  adj subject 432.13
lie in give birth 1.3
  be located 159.10
  sail for 182.35
  exist in 761.11
lie in state 309.21
lie in wait 346.9
lie low squat 274.5
  do nothing 329.2
  hide 346.8
  beware 494.7
  be latent 519.3
lien mortgage 438.4
  general lien 438.5
  possession 469.1
lie on weigh on 297.11
  rest on 901.22
  depend 959.6
  go hard with 1011.8
lieu location 159.1
  place 159.4
lieutenant
  subordinate 432.5
  commissioned officer 575.18
  Navy officer 575.20
  deputy 576.1
  assistant 616.6
  policeman 1008.15
life
  n animation 17.4
  energizer 17.6
  eagerness 101.1
  gaiety 109.4
  vitality 306.1
  living 306.1
  person 312.5
  liveliness 330.2
  history 719.1
  existence 761.1
  something 763.3
  lifetime 827.5
  affairs 831.4
  v meet one's Maker 307.21
Life 677.6
life after death
  the hereafter 681.2
  destiny 839.2
life-and-death 997.23
lifeblood blood 2.25
  life force 306.3
lifeboat
  means of escape 369.3
  life preserver 397.6
  rescuer 398.2
life cycle 306.3
life expectancy 306.6
life force
  animation 17.4
  soul 306.3
  inner nature 767.5

life-giving
  reproductive 78.15
  animating 306.14
lifeguard rescuer 398.2
  guardian 1008.6
life insurance 624.6
lifeless dull 117.6
  inert 173.14
  dead 307.30
  languid 331.20
  lackluster 1027.17
  inanimate 1055.5
lifelike
  descriptive 349.14
  similar 784.16
  genuine 973.15
lifeline
  means of escape 369.3
  life preserver 397.6
  safeguard 1008.3
lifelong 827.13
the life of Riley 1010.1
life of the party
  energizer 17.6
  mischief-maker 322.3
  humorist 489.12
  sociable person 582.16
life preserver
  float 180.11
  life jacket 397.6
  safeguard 1008.3
lifer 429.11
lifesaver
  preserver 397.5
  rescuer 398.2
  guardian 1008.6
lifesaving 398.1
life savings 728.14
life science 1068.3
life size 257.3
life-size 257.16
life-style behavior 321.1
  preference 371.5
  custom 373.1
  mode 765.4
  specialty 866.1
life-threatening
  disease-causing 85.53
  deadly 308.23
  disastrous 1011.15
lifetime
  n life 306.1
  existence 827.5
  adj lifelong 827.13
lifework vocation 724.6
  cause 886.9
lift
  n excitement 105.3
  people mover 176.5
  ride 177.7
  lift ratio 184.26
  wave 238.14
  height 272.2
  atmosphere 317.2
  improvement 392.1
  assist 449.2
  skiing 753.1
  boost and hike 912.2
  lifter 912.3
  elevator 912.4
  the heavens 1072.2

v elate 109.8
transport 176.12
billow 238.22
imitate 336.5
make better 392.9
rob 482.16
pay in full 624.13
elevate 912.5
lifter thief 483.1
erector 912.3
fire iron 1020.12
lift-off 1074.9
lift up erect 200.9
inaugurate 818.11
elevate 912.5
focus on 937.3
call attention to 983.10
lift weights 84.4
ligament 271.2
ligature
cord 271.2
type 548.6
notation 709.12
fastening 800.3
light
n aspect 33.3
swiftness 174.6
window 292.7
dawn 314.3
explanation 341.4
information 551.1
wave 916.4
outlook 978.2
lighter 1021.4
illumination 1025.1
radiant energy 1025.1
measurement of light
   1025.21
light source 1026.1
transparent substance 1029.2
v land 184.43
get down 194.7
ignite 1020.22
grow light 1025.27
illuminate 1025.28
strike a light 1025.29
adj frail 16.14
soft-colored 35.22
whitish 37.8
lighthearted 109.12
thin 270.16
shallow 276.5
unheavy 298.10
gentle 298.12
airy 317.12
fickle 364.6
agile 413.23
phonetic 524.30
wanton 665.26
comic 704.35
superficial 922.20
trivial 998.19
easy 1014.13
lightish 1025.31
light bulb 1026.1
lighten
disburden 120.7
make light 298.6
moderate 670.6
grow light 1025.27
illuminate 1025.28

lightened
bleached 36.8
eased 298.11
illuminated 1025.39
lightening
n decoloration 36.3
disburdening 120.3
easing 298.3
modulation 670.2
adj easing 298.16
illuminating 1025.40
lighter
n light 1021.4
v haul 176.13
lightface 548.20
light fingers 482.12
light-footed fast 174.15
agile 413.23
lightheaded weak 16.12
delirious 926.31
dizzy 985.15
light heart 109.3
light holder 1026.6
lighthouse
observation post 27.8
tower 272.6
alarm 400.1
marker 517.10
lighting
n ignition 1020.4
illumination 1025.19
adj inflammatory 1020.27
illuminating 1025.40
light into
lift one's hand against 457.14
attack 459.15
punish 604.11
set to work 725.15
lightless 1027.13
light meter
exposure 714.9
measurement of light 1025.21
lightness frailty 16.2
color quality 35.6
paleness 36.2
whiteness 37.1
lightheartedness 109.3
thinness 270.4
lack of weight 298
levity 298.1
fickleness 364.3
agility 413.2
wantonness 665.4
superficiality 922.7
triviality 998.3
luminousness 1025.3
lightning
swiftness 174.6
flash of lightning 1025.17
lightning rod 1008.3
light opera 708.34
light out 188.10
lights lungs 2.22
instruments 704.18
opinion 953.6
light show
spectacle 33.7
iridescence 47.2
flicker 1025.8
lightsome
lighthearted 109.12

light 1025.31
light source
light 1025.1
illuminant 1025.20
source of light 1026.1
light touch touch 73.1
lightness 298.1
light up excite 105.12
cheer up 109.9
ignite 1020.22
illuminate 1025.28
light upon
arrive at 186.7
alight upon 194.10
meet 223.11
come across 941.3
lightweight
n weakling 16.6
inferior 250.2
runt 258.4
weight 297.3
stupid person 924.2
a nobody 998.7
adj frail 16.14
bantamweight 298.13
uninfluential 895.3
light-year 1072.3
lignitic 1021.9
likable
tasty 63.8
pleasant 97.6
desirable 100.30
endearing 104.25
like
n love 104.1
likeness 784.3
equal 790.4
v savor 63.5
enjoy 95.13
desire 100.14
love 104.19
adj approximate 775.8
identical 778.7
similar 784.10
equal 790.7
adv how 384.9
similarly 784.18
prep in imitation of 336.12
like a bat out of hell 174.18
like a bump on a log
adj passive 329.6
adv inertly 173.20
like a fish out of water 160.11
like a thief in the night
unexpectedly 131.14
surreptitiously 345.18
deceitfully 356.24
dishonestly 645.24
like clockwork
smoothly 287.13
uniformly 781.8
methodically 807.9
regularly 850.9
easily 1014.16
likelihood
liability 897.1
possibility 966.1
probability 968.1
good chance 972.8
likely
adj apt 788.10

liable 897.5
possible 966.6
probable 968.6
disposed 978.8
expedient 995.5
comely 1016.19
adv probably 968.8
likely story 600.4
likely to
adj liable to 897.6
prep inclined to 896.6
like mad swiftly 174.18
excessively 247.23
recklessly 493.11
violently 671.25
like-minded
unanimous 332.15
in accord 455.3
agreeing 788.9
liken 943.4
likeness
aspect 33.3
image 349.5
picture 712.11
similarity 784.1
like 784.3
copy 785.1
equality 790.1
likewise
adv additionally 253.11
identically 778.9
similarly 784.18
interj yeah 332.19
liking desire 100.2
love 104.1
will 323.1
tendency 896.1
Lilliputian
n dwarf 258.5
adj dwarf 258.13
lilt
n air 708.4
song 708.14
rhythm 709.22
meter 720.7
v exude cheerfulness
   109.6
rejoice 116.5
speak 524.25
sing 708.38
lily whiteness 37.2
effeminate male 77.11
lily-livered
weak 16.12
cowardly 491.10
limb member 2.7
leg 177.14
border 211.4
branch 310.20
body part 793.4
lever 906.4
limber
v soften 1047.6
adj weak 16.12
pliant 1047.9
limber up
prepare oneself 405.13
soften 1047.6
limbo
place of confinement 429.7
hell 682.1

eager 101.8
gay 109.14
fast 174.15
active 330.17
spirited 544.12
interesting 983.19
elastic 1048.7
adv actively 330.25
liven energize 17.10
cheer 109.7
live off 138.12
live on feed on 8.28
continue to exist 761.9
endure 827.6
postexist 839.7
live or die
adv without fail 970.26
phrs come what may 359.20
liver viscera 2.16
organ 2.17
digestion 7.8
food 10.20
livery wardrobe 5.2
uniform 5.7
insignia 647.1
livestock 311.1
live through
win through 409.13
endure 827.6
live up to observe 434.2
execute 437.9
live wire
man of action 330.8
charge 1032.5
live with endure 134.5
keep an open mind 979.7
livid colorless 36.7
black and blue 38.12
gray 39.4
blue 45.3
purple 46.3
angry 152.28
deathly 307.29
living
n habitation 225.1
life 306.1
support 449.3
benefice 698.9
adj energetic 17.13
resident 225.13
organic 305.17
alive 306.13
existent 761.13
lifelike 784.16
burning 1019.27
living being
organism 305.2
animal 311.2
living quarters
housing 225.3
quarters 228.4
living room 197.5
lizard 311.25
llama 176.8
llano plain 236.1
grassland 310.8
load
n affliction 96.8
freight 176.6
lading 196.2
quantity 247.3

burden 297.7
charge 462.16
portion 477.5
wealth 618.3
tax 643.3
full measure 794.3
impediment 1012.6
v lade 159.15
fill 196.7
burden 297.13
tamper with 354.17
prime 405.9
fill 794.7
shoot 904.12
go hard with 1011.8
computerize 1042.21
loaded drunk 88.33
weighted 297.18
prepared 405.16
wealthy 618.15
fraught 794.12
critical 843.10
loader 183.9
loading
placement 159.6
burden 297.7
imposition 643.1
loaf
n lump 257.10
Eucharist 701.7
v idle 331.12
loafer vagabond 178.3
idler 331.8
beggar 440.8
loafing 331.4
loamy earthy 234.5
pasty 1047.12
loan
n the lend 620.2
v lend 620.5
loaner 620.3
loaning 620.1
loan shark 620.3
loan-shark 620.5
loan-sharking
lending 620.1
illicit business 732.1
loathe dislike 99.3
hate 103.5
loathing
n hostility 99.2
hate 103.1
adj hating 103.7
loathsome
offensive 98.18
terrible 1000.9
hideous 1015.11
lob
n throw 904.3
v play tennis 748.3
throw 904.10
elevate 912.5
lobar 202.12
lobby
n vestibule 197.19
bungler 414.8
legislative lobby 609.32
influence 894.6
v urge 375.14
exercise influence
894.9

lobbying
inducement 375.3
political influence 609.29
backstairs influence 894.3
lobbyist lobby 609.32
influence 894.6
lobe ear 2.10
pendant 202.4
member 793.4
lobo 311.20
lobster
n marine animal 311.30
cheater 759.22
v row 182.53
local
n bar 88.20
train 179.14
native 227.3
branch 617.10
labor union 727.2
adj localized 231.9
idiomatic 523.22
local color milieu 209.3
plot 722.4
locale location 159.1
area 209.2
arena 463.1
setting 704.19
plot 722.4
localism dialect 523.7
barbarism 526.6
policy 609.4
locality location 159.1
habitat 228.18
localize locate 159.11
restrict 428.9
local yokel 227.3
locate situate 159.11
settle 159.17
discover 941.2
locating
placement 159.6
discovery 941.1
location place 159.1
situation 159.1
placement 159.6
setting 704.19
motion-picture studio
706.4
state 765.1
discovery 941.1
farm 1069.8
loch lake 241.1
inlet 242.1
Loch Ness monster 311.30
lock
n tress 3.5
standstill 173.3
floodgate 239.11
bolt 428.5
wrestling 474.3
poker 759.10
sure thing 970.2
v close 293.6
agree 788.6
hook 800.8
obstruct 1012.12
locker storehouse 386.6
treasury 729.13
cold storage 1024.6
locket 498.6

lock horns
quarrel 456.12
contend with 457.17
counteract 900.6
argue 935.16
lock in imprison 429.14
retain 474.5
make sure 970.11
lockjaw 85.6
lockout exclusion 773.1
stop 857.2
lock out close 293.6
strike 727.10
exclude 773.4
lockup
confinement 429.1
prison 429.8
lock up enclose 212.5
close 293.6
secrete 346.7
imprison 429.14
loco
n disease 85.41
adj crazy 926.27
locomotion
mobility 172.3
travel 177.1
locomotive
traveling 177.36
vehicular 179.23
mechanical 1039.7
self-propelled 1041.23
locus 159.1
locust 311.36
locution
language 523.1
utterance 524.2
word 526.1
phrase 529.1
diction 532.1
lode
source of supply 386.4
rich source 618.4
deposit 1058.7
lodestar focus 208.4
motive 375.1
guiding star 574.8
stars 1072.4
lodestone desire 100.11
magnet 907.3
lodge
n house 228.5
cottage 228.8
lair 228.26
branch 617.10
v deposit 159.14
inhabit 225.7
house 225.10
accommodate 385.10
store 386.10
fix 855.9
repair 855.10
lodger roomer 227.8
tenant 470.4
lodging
n habitation 225.1
housing 225.3
abode 228.1
quarters 228.4
adj resident 225.13
loess deposit 176.9

dregs 256.2
loft
  n library 197.6
  attic 197.16
  workplace 739.1
  v play 751.4
  elevate 912.5
lofty elevated 136.11
  arrogant 141.9
  eminent 247.9
  high 272.14
  ostentatious 501.18
  eloquent 544.14
  grandiloquent 545.8
  impartial 649.10
  magnanimous 652.6
  renowned 662.18
  raised 912.9
log
  n speedometer 174.7
  record book 549.11
  accounts book 628.4
  chronicle 832.9
  firewood 1021.3
  wood 1054.3
  v ship activity 182.48
  record 549.15
  keep accounts 628.8
logarithmic 1017.23
log cabin 228.8
loge 704.15
logger 1069.7
loggia 197.18
logging
  registration 549.14
  forestry 1069.3
logic
  analytic reasoning 935.2
  reasonableness 935.9
logical sensible 920.18
  cognitive 931.21
  reasonable 935.20
  valid 973.14
logic-chopping
  n quibbling 936.5
  adj quibbling 936.14
logician 935.11
login 1042.18
logistics 385.1
logjam delay 846.2
  barrier 1012.5
logo patent 210.3
  symbol 517.2
  label 517.13
  insignia 647.1
logogram
  representation 349.1
  wordplay 489.8
  symbol 517.2
  phonetic symbol 546.2
logomachy
  quarrel 456.5
  contention 457.1
  argumentation 935.4
logomania 540.2
logorrhea
  wordiness 538.2
  logomania 540.2
logotype patent 210.3
  symbol 517.2
  label 517.13

type 548.6
log out 1042.21
logroller
  wire-puller 609.30
  politics 610.6
logrolling
  political influence 609.29
  legislative procedure 613.6
  trading 863.2
logy inert 173.14
  languid 331.20
loin 217.3
loincloth 5.19
loins 886.7
loiter lag 166.4
  dawdle 175.8
  dally 331.14
  wait 846.12
  trifle 998.14
loiterer slowpoke 175.5
  idler 331.8
loitering
  n dawdling 175.3
  idling 331.4
  trifling 998.8
  adj dawdling 175.11
  dilatory 846.17
Loki evil 680.5
  nether world deity 682.5
loll
  n recumbency 201.2
  v rest 20.6
  lie 201.5
lollapalooza 999.7
lolling
  n idling 331.4
  adj recumbent 201.8
lollygag dawdle 175.8
  dally 331.14
  make love 562.15
lollygagging
  n love affair 104.6
  dawdling 175.3
  lovemaking 562.2
  adj dawdling 175.11
lone solitary 584.11
  one 872.7
  alone 872.8
  sole 872.9
loneliness
  solitude 584.3
  aloneness 872.2
lonely solitary 584.11
  alone 872.8
lonely hearts club 563.12
loner recluse 584.5
  self-seeker 651.3
  oddity 870.4
lonesomeness
  solitude 584.3
  aloneness 872.2
lone wolf
  self-seeker 651.3
  oddity 870.4
long
  n bull 737.13
  long time 827.4
  adj lengthy 267.7
  giant 272.16
  wordy 538.12
  protracted 827.11

adv for a long time 827.14
long ago for a long time 827.14
  long since 837.16
longanimity
  patience 134.1
  forgiveness 148.1
  submission 433.1
long distance
  telephone operator 347.9
  telephone call 347.13
long-distance 261.8
long-established
  confirmed 373.18
  traditional 842.12
  established 855.13
longevity haleness 83.3
  old age 303.5
  life 306.1
  durability 827.1
longhair 842.8
longhand 547.22
long haul 261.2
longing
  n yearning 100.5
  adj wistful 100.23
longitude map 159.5
  zone 231.3
  length 267.1
  coordinates 300.5
  orbit 1072.16
long-lasting 827.10
long-lived living 306.13
  durable 827.10
long-lost gone 34.4
  absent 222.11
  lost 473.7
long range 261.2
long-range 261.8
long shot
  motion picture 714.8
  bet 759.3
  gambling odds 759.6
  chance event 972.6
  small chance 972.9
longsighted
  poor-sighted 28.11
  sagacious 920.16
  foreseeing 961.7
long since
  for a long time 827.14
  long ago 837.16
  since 837.17
long-standing
  durable 827.10
  traditional 842.12
long-suffering
  n patience 134.1
  forgiveness 148.1
  submission 433.1
  tolerance 979.4
  adj patient 134.9
  forgiving 148.6
  submissive 433.12
  tolerant 979.11
long suit
  talent 413.4
  specialty 866.1
long-term 827.10
long time length 267.1
  long while 827.4
long way 261.2

long-winded
  tedious 118.9
  lengthened 267.8
  wordy 538.12
  protracted 827.11
long word
  hard word 526.10
  high-sounding words
    545.3
loo 12.10
looby vulgarian 497.6
  peasant 606.6
  fool 924.3
look
  n sight 27.3
  aspect 33.3
  looks 33.4
  hint 248.4
  information 551.4
  v peer 27.13
  gaze 27.15
  appear to be 33.10
  be vigilant 339.8
  seek 938.30
  heed 983.6
  interj attention! 983.22
look after look 27.13
  nurture 339.9
  serve 577.13
  care for 1008.19
look ahead 961.5
look-alikes set 784.5
  twins 873.4
look alive
  v be vigilant 339.8
  pay attention 983.8
  interj make haste! 401.16
look around 938.30
look at look 27.13
  spectate 918.5
  examine 938.24
look back 989.10
look down one's nose
  look askance 27.18
  shudder at 99.5
  give oneself airs 141.8
  be hard to please 495.8
look down upon
  disdain 157.3
  rise above 272.11
looked-for
  expected 130.13
  future 839.8
looker recipient 479.3
  spectator 918.1
  beauty 1016.9
look for hope 124.7
  look forward to 130.6
  solicit 440.14
  come 839.6
  seek 938.30
look for trouble
  defy 454.3
  pick a quarrel 456.13
look forward to
  reckon on 130.6
  come 839.6
  foresee 961.5
look in enter 189.7
  visit 582.19
looking glass 29.6

looking up
promising 124.13
improving 392.15
look like
appear to be 33.10
augur 133.12
resemble 784.7
look on see 27.12
look 27.13
attend 221.8
spectate 918.5
lookout
observation 27.2
observation post 27.8
view 33.6
vigilance 339.4
warner 399.4
occupation 724.1
watchman 1008.10
look out
v be vigilant 339.8
beware 494.7
pay attention 983.8
interj careful! 494.14
look over
scrutinize 27.14
front on 216.9
examine 938.24
looks 33.4
look the other way
be blind 30.8
let alone 329.4
keep an open mind 979.7
be inattentive 984.2
look through 938.30
look-through 938.3
look to
look forward to 130.6
avail oneself of 387.14
prepare for 405.11
tend 896.3
attend to 983.5
care for 1008.19
look up improve 392.7
seek 938.30
look up to 155.4
loom
n weaver 740.5
imminence 840.1
v appear 33.8
ascend 193.8
bulk 247.5
threaten 514.2
weave 740.6
come 839.6
be imminent 840.2
looming
n mirage 976.6
adj ominous 133.17
imminent 840.3
loon 926.16
loony
n lunatic 926.16
adj foolish 923.9
crazy 926.27
loonybin 926.14
loop
n spiral loop 184.16
circle 280.2
bulge 283.3
baseball 745.1

circuit 914.2
v maneuver 184.40
encircle 209.7
curve 279.6
weave 740.6
loophole
observation post 27.8
outlet 190.9
way out 369.4
loose
n freedom 430.1
v set free 431.6
relax 670.9
detach 802.10
loosen 804.3
facilitate 1014.7
adj adrift 182.61
drooping 202.10
negligent 340.10
escaped 369.11
lax 426.4
free 430.21
unrestrained 430.24
ungrammatic 531.4
discursive 538.13
informal 581.3
wanton 665.26
unfastened 802.22
slack 804.5
slovenly 810.15
illogical 936.11
vague 971.19
inaccurate 975.17
flaccid 1047.10
loose ends
slipshodness 340.3
nonaccomplishment 408.1
loosen
loose 431.6
relax 670.9
detach 802.10
slacken 804.3
soften 1047.6
loosening
n laxness 426.1
modulation 670.2
adj softening 1047.16
loosen up
amuse 743.21
amuse oneself 743.22
loose woman 665.14
loot
n booty 482.11
money 728.2
v seize 480.14
plunder 482.17
raze 671.11
looter 483.6
looting
n rapacity 480.9
plundering 482.6
unruliness 671.3
adj plunderous 482.22
lop
n wave 238.14
roughness 288.2
v hang 202.6
excise 255.10
adj drooping 202.10
lope
n run 174.3

v speed 174.8
go on horseback 177.34
lopped 795.5
loppy 202.10
lopsided
distorted 265.10
unbalanced 791.5
loquacity 540.1
loran
ship navigation 182.2
airplane navigation 184.6
long-range navigation 1036.3
lord proprietor 470.2
master 575.1
nobleman 608.4
Lord 648.2
lord it over 612.16
lordly dignified 136.12
arrogant 141.11
imperious 417.16
lordship
supremacy 249.3
mastership 417.7
ownership 469.2
aristocracy 608.9
Lordship 648.2
lore mythology 678.14
tradition 842.2
body of knowledge 928.9
superstition 954.3
Lorelei 377.4
lorgnette 29.3
lorry 179.12
lose fail 410.9
lose out 412.12
incur loss 473.4
waste 486.4
forget 990.5
lose face
bow to 250.5
incur disgrace 661.7
lose ground
regress 163.5
slow 175.9
fall short 911.2
lose heart
despond 112.16
despair 125.10
lose one's head 923.6
lose one's mind
be stupid 922.12
go mad 926.21
loser inferior 250.2
failure 410.2
disappointment 410.8
defeatee 412.5
loss 473.1
insolvent 625.4
unfortunate 1011.7
lose sight of
neglect 340.6
disregard 435.3
forget 990.5
lose track of 340.6
lose weight 270.13
losing streak 473.1
loss
disappearance 34.1
decrement 252.3
impairment 393.1
losing hold of 473

losing 473.1
game 746.3
disadvantage 996.2
loss of memory
thoughtlessness 933.1
amnesia 990.2
loss of speech 525.6
lost vanished 34.4
past hope 125.15
unwon 412.13
gone 473.7
wasted 486.9
irreclaimable 654.18
unregenerate 695.18
bewildered 971.24
abstracted 985.11
forgotten 990.8
the lost 680.1
lost cause 125.8
lost in 983.17
lost in thought
absorbed in thought 931.22
abstracted 985.11
lost soul 660.4
lot
n plot 231.4
amount 244.2
lots 247.4
real estate 471.6
portion 477.5
motion-picture studio 706.4
share 738.3
state 765.1
bunch 770.7
kind 809.3
amount made 893.4
fate 964.2
chance 972.1
v allot 477.9
gamble 759.23
the lot 792.3
Lothario beau 104.13
libertine 665.10
lotion toilet water 70.3
cleanser 79.17
balm 86.11
ointment 1056.3
lots lot 247.4
real estate 471.6
multitude 884.3
plenty 991.2
lottery 759.14
lotus-eater idler 331.8
visionary 986.13
loud
adj intense 15.22
garish 35.20
loud-sounding 53.11
demanding 421.9
coarse 497.11
gaudy 501.20
adv loudly 53.14
loud and clear
adj affirmative 334.8
clear 521.11
adv affirmatively 334.10
loudmouthed
loud-voiced 53.12
vociferous 59.10
loudness
garishness 35.5

sound 50.1
intensity 53.1
coarseness 497.2
showiness 501.3
lounge
　n anteroom 197.20
　v rest 20.6
　lie 201.5
　idle 331.12
lounger 331.8
lounging
　n recumbency 201.2
　idling 331.4
　adj recumbent 201.8
louring 319.8
louse vermin 311.37
　bad person 660.5
louse up spoil 393.11
　bungle 414.12
　complicate 799.3
　goof 975.6
　make a boner 975.15
　hinder 1012.16
lousy infested 910.11
　bad 1000.8
lout bungler 414.8
　simple soul 416.3
　vulgarian 497.6
　peasant 606.6
　oaf 924.5
loutish
　countrified 233.7
　bungling 414.20
　boorish 497.13
　ill-bred 505.6
louver 239.13
lovable
　desirable 100.30
　endearing 104.25
love
　n sexuality 75.2
　liking 100.2
　affection 104.1
　sweetheart 104.10
　benevolence 143.4
　accord 455.1
　regards 504.8
　endearment term 562.6
　friendship 587.1
　cardinal virtues 653.4
　game 748.2
　heat metaphor 1019.2
　v savor 63.5
　have deep feelings
　　93.12
　enjoy 95.13
　desire 100.14
　be fond of 104.19
Love Cupid 104.8
　Deity 677.6
love affair 104.6
love child 561.5
loveless unloved 99.10
　undesirous 102.8
love letter 562.13
love-life 75.2
lovelock 3.5
lovelorn unloved 99.10
　loving 104.27
lovely delightful 97.7
　endearing 104.25

beautiful 1016.18
lovemaking
　sexuality 75.2
　copulation 75.7
　love 104.1
　dalliance 562.1
love nest 582.9
love potion 75.6
lover desirer 100.12
　admirer 104.12
　endearment term 562.6
　friend 588.1
　supporter 616.9
lovesick 104.27
love story 706.2
loving lovesome 104.27
　kind 143.13
　careful 339.10
　almighty 677.17
low
　n weather map 317.4
　business cycle 731.10
　price 738.9
　gear 1040.9
　v cry 60.2
　adj faint 52.16
　deep 54.11
　dejected 112.22
　humble 137.10
　insignificant 248.6
　inferior 250.6
　short 268.8
　unelevated 274.7
　dying 307.33
　base 497.15
　disapproving 510.21
　phonetic 524.30
　inelegant 534.2
　populational 606.8
　cheap 633.7
　wicked 654.16
　base 661.12
　vulgar 666.8
　depressed 913.12
　adv faintly 52.21
　near the ground 274.9
lowball 759.10
lowborn 606.8
lowbrow
　n ignoramus 930.8
　adj unlearned 930.14
Low Church 675.11
low class 1005.4
low-class 1005.9
low-cut 6.13
low-down 661.12
the lowdown
　inside information 551.2
　what's what 973.4
lower
　n scowl 110.9
　gloom 1027.4
　v look sullen 110.15
　sadden 112.18
　forebode 133.11
　show resentment 152.14
　threaten 514.2
　be imminent 840.2
　grow dark 1027.12
lower
　v abase 137.5

sink 194.6
reduce 252.7
debase 274.6
deepen 275.8
excavate 284.15
demote 447.3
cheapen 633.6
depress 913.4
adj inferior 250.6
reduced 252.10
debased 274.8
lower case 548.6
lower-case literal 546.8
　typographic 548.20
lower class
　n inferior 250.2
　commoners 606.1
　social status 607.7
　adj the working class 607.10
lowered humbled 137.13
　reduced 252.10
　low 274.7
　depressed 913.12
lower house 613.1
lower oneself
　condescend 137.8
　give oneself airs 141.8
　incur disgrace 661.7
lowest humble 137.10
　bottom 199.7
　least 250.8
　lower 274.8
　reduced 633.9
lowest common denominator
　clearness 521.2
　average 864.3
lucky charm charm 691.5
low grade 1005.4
low-grade 1005.9
low key reserve 139.3
　reticence 344.3
lowland
　n the country 233.1
　plain 236.1
　lowlands 274.3
　adj rustic 233.6
lowlife 660.2
lowness faintness 52.1
　resonance 54.1
　dejection 112.3
　insignificance 248.1
　inadequacy 250.3
　stubbiness 268.2
　shortness 274.1
　commonness 497.5
　baseness 661.3
low opinion 510.1
low-pitched 54.11
low price 633.2
low priority 998.1
low profile
　distinctness 31.2
　inconspicuousness 32.2
　reserve 139.3
　reticence 344.3
low-profile 32.6
low-spirited
　dejected 112.22
　dull 117.6
low-test 1005.9
low tide tide 238.13

low water 274.2
low voice 52.4
lox fish 10.24
　coolant 1024.7
　rocket propulsion 1074.8
loyal
　zealous 101.9
　obedient 326.3
　firm 359.12
　persevering 360.8
　observant 434.4
　faithful 644.20
loyalist 609.27
loyal opposition 609.24
loyalty
　zeal 101.2
　obedience 326.1
　firmness 359.2
　perseverance 360.1
　duty 641.1
　fidelity 644.7
lozenge pill 86.7
　heraldry 647.2
luau
　source of supply 386.4
　rich source 618.4
　plenty 991.2
lubber
　mariner 183.2
　idler 331.8
　bungler 414.8
　oaf 924.5
lubricant
　n smoother 287.4
　lubricator 1056.2
　adj lubricating 1056.10
lubricate smooth 287.5
　facilitate 1014.7
　oil 1056.8
lubricated drunk 88.33
　slippery 287.12
lubricating
　n facilitation 1014.5
　lubrication 1056.6
　adj lubricant 1056.10
lubrication 1056.6
lubricious
　slippery 287.12
　lascivious 665.29
lubritorium 1056.7
lucid clear 521.11
　elegant 533.6
　sane 925.4
　light 1025.31
　transparent 1029.4
　translucent 1030.5
lucidity
　distinctness 31.2
　clearness 521.2
　elegance 533.1
　extrasensory perception
　　689.8
　sanity 925.1
　lightness 1025.3
　transparency 1029.1
　translucence 1030.2
lucifer 1021.5
Lucifer 1072.4
luck gamble 759.2
　uncertainty 971.1
　chance 972.1

good fortune 1010.2
Luck 972.2
lucky
auspicious 133.18
speculative 759.27
timely 843.9
chance 972.15
fortunate 1010.14
lucky break 1010.3
lucky piece 691.5
lucrative
gainful 472.16
paying 624.21
lucre gain 472.3
wealth 618.1
money 728.1
lucubration
writing 547.10
treatise 556.1
study 570.3
consideration 931.2
ludicrous
humorous 488.4
absurd 923.11
lug
n body part 2.10
ear 48.7
v transport 176.12
pull 905.4
luggage
freight 176.6
container 195.1
impedimenta 471.3
lugubrious
sorrowful 112.26
pessimistic 125.16
lukewarm
unfeeling 94.9
indifferent 102.6
nonreligious 695.15
warm 1019.24
lull
n respite 20.2
silence 51.1
calm 173.5
inactivity 331.1
interruption 813.2
interim 826.1
pause 857.3
v relieve 120.5
quiet 173.8
calm 670.7
lullaby 22.10
lulling
n relief 120.1
modulation 670.2
adj tranquilizing 670.15
lulu 999.7
lumbago 85.9
lumbar region 217.3
lumber
n rubbish 391.5
gambler 759.21
impediment 1012.6
wood 1054.3
v plod 175.7
way of walking 177.28
bungle 414.11
hamper 1012.11
lumbering
n forestry 1069.3

adj slow 175.10
bulky 257.19
bungling 414.20
stiff 534.3
lumberjack 1069.7
lumberyard 386.6
lumen 1025.21
luminary
n celebrity 662.9
chief 997.10
first-rater 999.6
light source 1026.1
adj photic 1025.41
luminesce 1025.26
luminescence 1025.13
luminescent 1025.38
luminous clear 521.11
almighty 677.17
luminant 1025.30
illuminated 1025.39
lummox bungler 414.9
oaf 924.5
lump
n clump 257.10
bulge 283.3
swelling 283.4
bungler 414.9
print 517.7
accumulation 770.9
piece 793.3
solid 1045.6
v thicken 1045.10
lumpen
n the underprivileged 606.4
adj countrified 233.7
idle 331.18
base 661.12
slovenly 810.15
lumpish
countrified 233.7
bulky 257.19
formless 263.4
onerous 297.17
languid 331.20
bungling 414.20
boorish 497.13
stupid 922.15
thickened 1045.14
lump sum 728.13
lump together
assemble 770.18
put together 800.5
combine 805.3
lumpy bulky 257.19
formless 263.4
gnarled 288.8
nappy 294.7
thickened 1045.14
Luna 1072.12
lunacy
foolishness 923.1
insanity 926.1
lunar
crescent-shaped 279.11
celestial 1072.25
lunar eclipse
eclipse 1027.8
moon 1072.11
lunar module 1075.2
lunatic
n fool 924.1

madman 926.15
adj insane 926.26
lunatic fringe
radical 611.12
fanatic 926.18
lunch
n meal 8.6
v dine 8.21
adj eccentric 927.6
lunch counter 8.17
luncheon 8.6
lunchroom 8.17
lung
n viscera 2.16
adj respiratory 2.32
lunge
n thrust 459.3
v way of walking 177.28
lunkhead 924.4
lunkheaded 922.17
lupine
canine 311.42
rapacious 480.26
lurch
n gait 177.12
bias 204.3
swing 916.6
flounder 917.8
v way of walking
177.28
pitch 182.55
tumble 194.8
oscillate 916.10
flounder 917.15
lurching
irregular 851.3
swinging 916.17
lure
n snare 356.13
incentive 375.7
charm 377.3
attractor 907.2
v trap 356.20
induce 375.22
allure 377.5
attract 907.4
lurid garish 35.20
colorless 36.7
brown 40.3
red 41.6
sensational 105.32
deathly 307.29
gaudy 501.20
grandiloquent 545.8
obscene 666.9
lurk couch 346.9
be latent 519.3
lurking
in hiding 346.14
latent 519.5
imminent 840.3
luscious tasty 63.8
oversweet 66.5
delectable 97.10
lush
n drunk 88.12
v drink 88.25
adj tasty 63.8
luxuriant 310.43
ornate 545.11
productive 890.9

lust
n sexual desire 75.5
craving 100.6
greed 100.8
will 323.1
lasciviousness 665.5
v lust after 75.20
desire 100.14
crave 100.18
luster
n polish 287.2
illustriousness 662.6
moment 824.2
gorgeousness 1016.6
shine 1025.2
chandelier 1026.6
v polish 287.7
shine 1025.23
lusterless colorless 36.7
lackluster 1027.17
lustful prurient 75.27
desirous 100.21
lascivious 665.29
lustful leer 27.3
lustral cleansing 79.28
atoning 658.7
lustrous
illustrious 662.19
luminous 1025.30
shiny 1025.33
lusty strong 15.15
energetic 17.13
hale 83.12
corpulent 257.18
Lutheran 675.28
lux 1025.21
luxate dislocate 160.5
disjoint 802.16
luxuriant
flourishing 310.43
ornate 498.12
grandiloquent 545.11
productive 890.9
plentiful 991.7
luxuriate
vegetate 310.34
superabound 993.8
luxuriate in
enjoy 95.13
indulge 669.4
luxurious
delightful 97.7
comfortable 121.11
ornate 498.12
grandiose 501.21
wealthy 618.14
expensive 632.11
sensual 663.5
luxury pleasure 95.1
delightfulness 97.2
grandeur 501.5
sensuality 663.1
superfluity 993.4
prosperity 1010.1
lyceum hall 197.4
secondary school 567.4
lying
n recumbency 201.2
lowness 274.1
untruthfulness 354.8
adj recumbent 201.8

untruthful 354.34
lying-in 1.1
lymph 2.24
lymphatic
  n duct 2.23
  adj circulatory 2.33
  secretory 13.7
  languid 331.20
lynch kill 308.13
  hang 604.18
lynching killing 308.1
  capital punishment 604.7
lynch law 418.2
lynx
  sharp vision 27.11
  wild cat 311.22
lyre 711.3
lyric melodious 708.48
  vocal 708.50
  poetic 720.15
lyricist
  composer 710.20
  poet 720.11
lyric theater 708.34
lysis 395.1
ma 560.12
ma'am 77.9
Mab 678.8
macabre
  terrible 127.30
  deathly 307.29
  weird 988.9
macadam
  ground covering 199.3
  pavement 383.6
macaroni
  noodles 10.33
  dandy 500.9
mace scepter 417.9
  insignia 647.1
macerate
  torture 96.18
  shrink 260.9
  pulp 1063.5
  soak 1065.13
Mach 174.2
Machiavellian
  n deceiver 357.1
  schemer 381.7
  Machiavel 415.8
  politics 610.6
  adj falsehearted 354.31
  scheming 381.13
  cunning 415.12
machinate plot 381.9
  maneuver 415.10
machination
  chicanery 356.4
  intrigue 381.5
  manipulation 415.4
machinator
  traitor 357.10
  schemer 381.7
  strategist 415.7
  politics 610.6
machine
  n automobile 179.9
  political party 609.24
  association 617.1
  instrument of conversion
    858.10

machinery 1040.3
  computer 1042.2
  v process 892.9
  tool 1040.13
machine gun 847.5
machine-made 892.18
machinery
  instrumentality 384.3
  equipment 385.4
  instrument 1040.1
  machine 1040.3
  mechanism 1040.4
machine shop 739.3
machine tool 1040.6
machinist stage technician
    704.24
  mechanic 1040.12
machismo
  male sex 76.2
  courage 492.1
macho
  virile 76.13
  courageous 492.17
macro 257.20
macrobiotic 827.10
macrocosm 1072.1
macroeconomics 731.7
macronutrient 7.11
maculate
  v variegate 47.7
  spot 1004.5
  adj spotted 47.13
  unvirtuous 654.12
  unchaste 665.23
  spotted 1004.9
mad
  n anger 152.5
  v madden 926.24
  adj frenzied 105.25
  angry 152.30
  reckless 493.8
  turbulent 671.18
  foolish 923.8
  insane 926.26
  rabid 926.30
mad about
  enthusiastic 101.11
  crazy about 104.31
madam woman 77.9
  mistress 575.2
  Mrs 648.4
  procurer 665.18
madcap
  n humorist 489.12
  daredevil 493.4
  adj foolhardy 493.9
madden excite 105.12
  enrage 152.25
  antagonize 589.7
  dement 926.24
maddening 105.30
madder 41.4
mad dog ruffian 593.3
  violent person 671.9
made formative 262.9
  successful 409.14
  produced 892.17
  man-made 892.18
mademoiselle
  woman 77.9
  girl 302.6

made of 796.4
made-up
  fabricated 354.29
  invented 892.19
  beautified 1016.23
mad for 100.22
madhouse 926.14
madman 926.15
madness fury 105.8
  foolishness 923.1
  insanity 926.1
Madonna 679.5
madrigal 708.18
maelstrom eddy 238.12
  bustle 330.4
  whirl 915.2
  agitation 917.1
maestro
  teacher 571.1
  musician 710.1
Mae West 397.6
maffick be noisy 53.9
  celebrate 487.2
  create disorder 810.11
Mafia
  the underworld 660.10
  illicit business 732.1
Mafioso
  violent person 671.9
  racketeer 732.4
magazine
  storehouse 386.6
  armory 462.2
  periodical 555.1
magenta 46.3
maggot
  whiteness 37.2
  larva 302.12
  insect 311.33
  caprice 364.1
  quirk 927.2
  figment of the imagination
    986.5
maggoty
  nasty 64.7
  filthy 80.23
  capricious 364.5
  blighted 393.42
  eccentric 927.5
  fanciful 986.20
Magi 921.5
magic
  n illustriousness 662.6
  sorcery 690.1
  illusoriness 976.2
  v summon 420.11
  adj illustrious 662.19
  sorcerous 690.14
magical
  illustrious 662.19
  sorcerous 690.14
  miraculous 870.16
magic carpet 691.6
magician
  trickster 357.2
  master 413.13
  mage 690.6
  entertainer 707.1
  illusoriness 976.2
magic lantern 714.12
magic show 976.2

magic wand 691.6
magisterial
  dignified 136.12
  lordly 141.11
  chief 249.14
  skillful 413.22
  imperious 417.16
  jurisdictional 594.6
  authoritative 970.18
magistracy
  region 231.5
  mastership 417.7
  magistrature 594.3
magistrate
  arbitrator 466.4
  executive 574.3
  public official 575.17
  judge 596.1
Magna Charta 430.2
magna cum laude 646.11
magnanimity
  ambition 100.10
  forgiveness 148.1
  glory 247.2
  liberality 485.1
  magnanimousness 652.2
  tolerance 979.4
magnanimous
  forgiving 148.6
  eminent 247.9
  liberal 485.4
  great-souled 652.6
  tolerant 979.11
magnate
  nobleman 608.4
  businessman 730.1
  personage 997.8
magnet
  n desire 100.11
  focus 208.4
  artificial magnet 907.3
  v attract 907.4
magnetic
  influential 894.13
  attracting 907.5
  engrossing 983.20
  electromagnetic 1032.31
magnetic field
  electric field 1032.3
  magnetic force 1032.9
magnetic force 1032.9
magnetic pole
  magnet 907.3
  polarity 1032.8
magnetic storage 549.1
magnetic tape
  recording media 549.10
  disk 1042.6
magnetism
  desirability 100.13
  allurement 377.1
  influence 894.1
  attraction 907.1
  electrical science 1032
  magnetic attraction
    1032.7
magnetize
  put to sleep 22.20
  exercise influence 894.9
  attract 907.4
  electromagnetize 1032.27

magnification
aggravation 119.1
intensification 251.2
expansion 259.1
exaggeration 355.1
praise 509.5
glorification 662.8
adoration 696.2
magnificence
grandeur 501.5
superexcellence 999.2
magnificent
eminent 247.9
grandiose 501.21
superb 999.15
magnified
aggravated 119.4
increased 251.7
exaggerated 355.4
eminent 662.18
magnify
aggravate 119.2
intensify 251.5
enlarge 259.4
exaggerate 355.3
praise 509.12
glorify 662.13
adore 696.12
magnitude
quantity 244.1
greatness 247.1
size 257.1
star 1072.8
magnum opus 413.1
magpie chatterer 540.4
collector 770.15
magus 690.6
maharani
sovereign queen
575.11
princess 608.8
mahatma
master 413.13
holy man 659.6
occultist 689.11
wise man 921.1
mahogany
n smoothness 287.3
adj reddish-brown 40.4
maid
n girl 302.6
single woman 565.4
maidservant 577.8
v serve 577.13
maiden
n girl 302.6
single woman 565.4
execution 605.5
jockey 757.2
adj childish 301.11
unmarried 565.7
first 818.17
new 841.7
maidenhead
membrane 2.6
childhood 301.2
celibacy 565.1
continence 664.3
maiden lady 565.4
maiden name 527.5
maiden speech 818.5

mail
n plumage 3.18
shell 295.15
armor 460.3
post 553.4
v send 176.15
post 553.12
mailbox 553.6
mail carrier 353.5
mail coach 353.6
maillot 5.29
mailman
postman 353.5
postal service 553.7
mail-order 553.14
mail-order house 736.1
maim disable 19.9
injure 393.13
cripple 393.14
tear apart 802.14
maiming
emasculation 19.5
impairment 393.1
main
n continent 235.1
water main 239.7
ocean 240.1
adj great 247.6
chief 249.14
first 818.17
paramount 997.24
main dish 10.7
main idea 932.4
mainland
n continent 235.1
adj continental
235.6
mainlander 235.3
mainline
v use 87.22
adj tending 896.4
main office
headquarters 208.6
office 739.7
main point
summary 557.2
topic 937.1
salient point 997.6
mainspring
motive 375.1
fountainhead 886.6
mainstay
n supporter 616.9
support 901.2
v support 901.21
mainstream
n trend 896.2
adj tending 896.4
main street 230.6
maintain affirm 334.5
provide 385.7
preserve 397.8
insist 421.8
aid 449.12
retain 474.5
defend 600.10
treat 624.19
endure 827.6
sustain 856.4
support 901.21
think 953.11

maintenance
reparation 396.6
preservation 397.1
aid 449.3
retention 474.1
treatment 624.8
durability 827.1
preservation 853.2
continuance 856.1
support 901.1
maintenance man 396.10
maître d'hôtel
waiter 577.7
major-domo 577.10
majestic
dignified 136.12
eminent 247.9
sovereign 417.17
grandiose 501.21
lofty 544.14
almighty 677.17
majesty
proud bearing 136.2
glory 247.2
sovereignty 417.8
grandeur 501.5
loftiness 544.6
potentate 575.8
Majesty 648.2
major
n adult 304.1
study 568.8
commissioned officer 575.18
key 709.15
adj older 842.19
important 997.17
majordomo
steward 574.4
butler 577.10
major in
study to be 570.15
specialize 866.4
majority
n maturity 303.2
race 312.2
major part 792.6
plurality 883.2
adj most 883.9
the majority
dead 307.17
the masses 606.2
majority leader 610.3
major league 745.1
make
n form 262.1
structure 266.1
yield 472.5
receipts 627.1
composition 796.1
kind 809.3
amount made 893.4
disposition 978.3
v use 87.22
travel 177.19
sail for 182.35
arrive 186.6
flow 238.16
act 328.4
do 328.6
perform 328.9
make up 405.7

accomplish 407.4
compel 424.4
execute 437.9
acquire 472.8
compose 796.3
convert 858.11
cause 886.10
produce 892.8
imagine 986.14
make a beeline
go directly 161.10
take a short cut 268.7
be straight 277.4
make a bid
offer 439.6
bid 733.9
make a clean sweep
revolutionize 860.4
evacuate 909.22
make a deal
contract 437.5
compromise 468.2
bargain 731.18
strike a bargain 731.19
make a dent in
impress 93.15
gain influence 894.12
make advances
communicate with 343.8
approach 439.7
cultivate 587.12
exercise influence 894.9
make a face
shudder at 99.5
grimace 265.8
make a Federal case 949.2
make a fool of
fool 356.15
outwit 415.11
stultify 923.7
make a go of it
succeed 409.7
succeed with 409.11
make a killing
score a success 409.9
triumph 411.3
profit 472.12
trade 737.23
make allowance for
extenuate 600.12
allow for 959.5
make amends
compensate 338.4
make restitution 481.5
requite 506.5
repay 624.11
atone 658.4
make an appearance
appear 33.8
arrive 186.6
attend 221.8
be manifest 348.7
make an example of 604.10
make an impression
be heard 48.12
affect emotionally 93.15
impress 931.19
be remembered 989.14
make a point of
resolve 359.7
contend for 457.20

make conditional 959.4
make a scene 93.13
make a show of
 sham 354.21
 affect 500.12
make believe 354.20
make-believe
 n figment of the imagination
 986.5
 adj spurious 354.26
 fictitious 986.21
make clear
 explain 341.10
 manifest 348.5
 make understandable 521.6
 facilitate 1014.7
make do 995.4
make ends meet
 support oneself 385.12
 economize 635.4
make fun of
 joke 489.13
 ridicule 508.8
make good
 straighten 277.5
 compensate 338.4
 remedy 396.13
 come through 409.10
 observe 434.2
 make restitution 481.5
 grow rich 618.10
 repay 624.11
 meet an obligation 641.11
 keep faith 644.9
 atone 658.4
 complete 794.6
 prove 957.10
 be prosperous 1010.9
make haste
 v speed 174.8
 hasten 401.5
 interj make it quick! 401.16
make hay while the sun shines
 make the most of one's time
 330.16
 improve the occasion 843.8
make headway
 progress 162.2
 make way 182.21
 improve 392.7
 make good 409.10
 prosper 1010.7
make it
 be able 18.11
 arrive 186.6
 make good 409.10
 manage 409.12
 live on 839.7
 stand the test 942.10
make known
 communicate 343.7
 divulge 351.5
 make public 352.11
make light of
 underestimate 950.2
 be inattentive 984.2
 attach little importance to
 998.12
 take it easy 1014.12
make love
 copulate 75.21

procreate 78.8
 bill and coo 562.14
make merry
 celebrate 487.2
 revel 743.24
make money
 profit 472.12
 grow rich 618.10
make no bones about 359.10
make nothing of
 not understand 522.11
 underestimate 950.2
 attach little importance to
 998.12
make one's mark
 make good 409.10
 cut a dash 501.13
 be somebody 662.10
 be prosperous 1010.9
make one's way
 work one's way 162.4
 support oneself 385.12
 make better 392.9
 make good 409.10
make oneself at home 121.8
make out see 27.12
 copulate 75.21
 support oneself 385.12
 manage 409.12
 execute 437.9
 perceive 521.9
 write 547.19
 record 549.15
 make love 562.15
 be in a certain state 765.5
 persist 856.5
 know 928.12
 solve 940.2
 detect 941.5
 prove 957.10
 recognize 989.12
 make shift 995.4
make-out artist 562.12
make over
 reproduce 78.7
 transfer 176.10
 transfer property 629.3
 convert 858.11
make peace
 cease hostilities 465.9
 settle 466.7
 gain influence 894.12
make plain
 explain 341.10
 manifest 348.5
make possible
 permit 443.9
 enable 966.5
make public 352.11
maker artist 716.1
 poet 720.11
 doer 726.1
 skilled worker 726.6
 author 886.4
 producer 892.7
make sense
 be understandable 521.4
 be reasonable 935.17
makeshift
 n improvisation 365.5
 substitute 862.2

expedience 995.2
 adj extemporaneous 365.12
 unprepared 406.8
 substitute 862.8
 expedient 995.7
 imperfect 1003.4
make sure
 take precautions 494.6
 secure 855.8
 make certain 970.11
 play safe 1007.3
make the best of it
 be optimistic 124.9
 accept 134.7
 submit 433.6
make the grade
 be able 18.11
 manage 409.12
 suffice 991.4
make the most of
 take advantage of 387.15
 excel 999.11
make the scene
 appear 33.8
 go to 177.25
 arrive 186.6
 make good 409.10
 participate 476.5
make tracks
 speed 174.9
 run off 188.12
 leave 222.10
 flee 368.11
makeup
 form 262.1
 structure 266.1
 design 554.12
 theater 704.17
 nature 767.4
 composition 796.1
 order 807.1
 disposition 978.3
 cosmetics 1016.12
make up
 fabricate 354.18
 improvise 365.8
 get up 405.7
 arrange 437.8
 shake hands 465.10
 print 548.16
 shuffle 758.5
 assemble 770.18
 complete 794.6
 compose 796.3
 produce 892.8
 originate 892.12
 beautify 1016.16
makeup artist 1016.13
make up one's mind
 resolve 359.7
 choose 371.16
 persuade oneself 375.24
 decide 946.11
 convince oneself 953.19
make up to
 curry favor 138.9
 head for 161.9
 communicate with 343.8
 cultivate 587.12
 repay 624.11
 exercise influence 894.9

make waves
 agitate 105.14
 misbehave 322.4
 oppose 451.3
 offer resistance 453.3
 not conform 868.4
make way
 v gather way 182.21
 make an opening 292.13
 interj open up! 292.23
making
 n reproduction 78.1
 forming 262.5
 structure 266.1
 acquisition 472.1
 production 892.1
 manufacture 892.2
 amount made 893.4
 adj almighty 677.17
makings
 gain 472.3
 component 796.2
maladjusted
 incompetent 414.19
 wrong 638.3
 inappropriate 789.7
maladjustment
 mental disorder 92.14
 unskillfulness 414.1
 wrong 638.1
 unfitness 789.3
maladroit
 inadequate 250.7
 bungling 414.20
malady 85.1
malaise
 pain 26.1
 disease 85.1
 unpleasure 96.1
 discontent 108.1
 dejection 112.3
 anxiety 126.1
 nervousness 128.1
 agitation 917.1
malapropism
 wordplay 489.8
 solecism 531.2
 grammatical error 975.7
malapropos
 inappropriate 789.7
 untimely 844.6
 inexpedient 996.5
malaria miasma 1001.4
 vapor 1067.1
malarial 85.61
malarkey 520.3
malcontent
 n maverick 108.3
 lamenter 115.8
 rebel 327.5
 spoilsport 1012.9
 adj discontented 108.7
mal de mer 85.30
male
 n male being 76.4
 adj masculine 76.12
male chauvinism
 misanthropy 590.1
 discrimination 980.4
male chauvinist
 misanthrope 590.2

bigot 980.5
malediction 513.1
maledictory 513.8
malefactor
 evildoer 593.1
 wrongdoer 660.8
maleness sex 75.1
 masculinity 76.1
 maturity 303.2
male organs 2.13
male sex 76.2
malevolence
 hate 103.1
 inconsiderateness 144.3
 ill will 144.4
 hostility 589.3
 badness 1000.1
malevolent
 n evildoer 593.1
 adj ill-disposed 144.19
 hostile 589.10
 harmful 1000.12
 bad 1000.7
malevolent influence 1000.4
malfeasance
 misbehavior 322.1
 misuse 389.1
 mismanagement 414.6
 wrong 638.1
 wrongdoing 655.1
 misdeed 655.2
malformation
 deformity 265.3
 wrong 638.1
 oddity 870.3
malformed
 deformed 265.12
 freakish 870.13
 unshapely 1015.8
malfunction
 n impairment 393.1
 abortion 410.5
 wrong 638.1
 fault 1003.2
 v get out of order 393.25
malice hate 103.1
 maliciousness 144.5
 hostility 589.3
malicious
 maleficent 144.20
 hostile 589.10
malign
 v defame 512.9
 adj poisonous 82.7
 malicious 144.20
 deadly 308.23
 savage 671.21
 harmful 1000.12
malignancy
 poisonousness 82.3
 malice 144.5
 deadliness 308.9
 harmfulness 1000.5
malignant
 poisonous 82.7
 anemic 85.61
 malicious 144.20
 deadly 308.23
 hostile 589.10
 savage 671.21
 harmful 1000.12

malinger
 leave undone 340.7
 shirk 368.9
malingerer
 neglecter 340.5
 impostor 357.6
 shirker 368.3
malingering
 n shirking 368.2
 adj evasive 368.15
mall path 383.2
 marketplace 736.2
 workplace 739.1
malleable docile 433.13
 teachable 570.18
 changeable 854.6
 conformable 867.5
 influenceable 894.15
 foolable 923.12
 handy 1014.15
 pliant 1047.9
mallet 715.4
malnutrition 992.6
malocchio gaze 27.5
 malevolence 144.4
 curse 513.1
 spell 691.1
 bad influence 1000.4
malodorous nasty 64.7
 bad-smelling 69.9
 fetid 71.5
 filthy 80.23
 offensive 98.18
malpractice
 misuse 389.1
 mismanagement 414.6
 wrong 638.1
 wrongdoing 655.1
maltreat
 mistreat 389.5
 work evil 1000.6
maltreatment 389.2
mama 560.12
mama's boy
 weakling 16.6
 effeminate male 77.11
 spoiled child 427.4
mammal 311.3
mammalian
 pectoral 283.19
 vertebrate 311.41
mammary gland 283.6
mammon wealth 618.1
 money 728.1
mammoth
 n behemoth 257.14
 pachyderm 311.4
 adj large 247.7
 huge 257.20
mammy
 mother 560.12
 nurse 1008.8
man
 n mankind 76.3
 male 76.4
 beau 104.13
 hanger-on 138.6
 adult 304.1
 humankind 312.1
 person 312.5
 husband 563.7

manservant 577.4
 follower 616.8
 chessman 743.17
 v equip 385.8
 fortify 460.9
 interj goody! 95.21
the Man 312.3
mana power 18.1
 the gods 678.1
man-about-town
 sophisticate 413.17
 dandy 500.9
 person of fashion 578.7
 sociable person 582.16
manacle
 n shackle 428.4
 v disable 19.10
 bind 428.10
manacled 428.16
manage pilot 182.14
 perform 328.9
 support oneself 385.12
 use 387.10
 treat 387.12
 accomplish 407.4
 contrive 409.12
 direct 573.8
 govern 612.12
 economize 635.4
 be in a certain state 765.5
 persist 856.5
 operate 889.5
 make shift 995.4
 tend 1070.7
manageability
 governability 433.4
 workability 889.3
 handiness 1014.2
manageable
 governable 433.14
 cheap 633.7
 workable 889.10
 handy 1014.15
management
 supremacy 249.3
 performance 328.2
 usage 387.2
 utilization 387.8
 supervision 573
 direction 573.1
 executive 574.3
 directorate 574.11
 the authorities 575.15
 government 612.1
 thrift 635.1
 operation 889.1
 protectorship 1008.2
manager director 574.1
 governor 575.6
 businessman 730.1
 baseball team 745.2
 boxer 754.2
 operator 889.4
managerial
 directing 573.12
 operational 889.12
mañana
 n the future 839.1
 adv in the future 839.9
man and wife 563.9
manchild 302.5

mandarin
 n snob 141.7
 official 575.16
 wise man 921.1
 intellectual 929.1
 adj studious 570.17
mandate
 n country 232.1
 authority 417.1
 injunction 420.2
 possession 469.1
 referendum 613.8
 commission 615.1
 v command 420.8
mandated 420.12
mandatory
 n country 232.1
 adj preceptive 419.4
 mandated 420.12
 obligatory 424.11
 required 641.15
 doctrinal 953.27
 necessary 963.12
mandibles mouth 292.4
 clutches 474.4
mandrake 22.10
mane 3.2
man-eater eater 8.16
 marine animal 311.30
 savage 593.5
manège riding 177.6
 animal husbandry 1070.1
maneuver
 n exercise 84.2
 act 328.3
 stratagem 415.3
 operation 458.5
 race 753.3
 process 889.2
 expedient 995.2
 v execute a maneuver 182.46
 take action 328.5
 plot 381.9
 manipulate 415.10
 direct 573.8
 operate 889.5
maneuverable
 workable 889.10
 handy 1014.15
maneuvering
 intrigue 381.5
 machination 415.4
man Friday
 employee 577.3
 right-hand man 616.7
mange 85.41
manger 197.2
mangle press 287.6
 tear apart 802.14
mangled
 impaired 393.27
 mutilated 795.5
manhandle
 exert strength 15.12
 remove 176.11
 transport 176.12
 mistreat 389.5
man-hater hater 103.4
 misanthrope 590.2
man-hating
 n misanthropy 590.1

adj misanthropic 590.3
manhood
  bodily development 14.1
  masculinity 76.1
  mankind 76.3
  maturity 303.2
  courage 492.1
man-hour work 725.4
  moment 824.2
mania craving 100.6
  overzealousness 101.3
  mental sickness 926.1
  insanity 926.1
  delirium tremens 926.9
  craze 926.12
maniac
  n lunatic 926.15
  adj frenzied 105.25
  rabid 926.30
maniacal
  frenzied 105.25
  rabid 926.30
manic excited 105.20
  insane 926.26
  psychotic 926.28
manic-depressive
  n psychotic 926.17
  adj psychotic 926.28
manic state 105.1
manicure
  n beautification 1016.11
  v groom 79.20
manicurist 1016.13
manifest
  n statement 628.3
  bill 871.5
  v unclose 292.12
  show 348.5
  disclose 351.4
  flaunt 501.17
  signify 517.17
  evidence 957.8
  adj visible 31.6
  apparent 348.8
manifestation
  visibility 31.1
  appearance 33.1
  expression 348.1
  disclosure 351.1
  display 501.4
  indication 517.3
  evidence 957.1
manifested 348.13
manifesting 348.9
manifesto
  n affirmation 334.1
  announcement 352.2
  statement of belief 953.4
  v affirm 334.5
manifold
  n transcript 785.4
  v copy 785.8
  adj multiform 783.3
  multiple 883.8
manikin dwarf 258.5
  figure 349.6
man in the street 606.5
manipulate touch 73.6
  pilot 184.37
  tamper with 354.17
  use 387.10

exploit 387.16
  maneuver 415.10
  direct 573.8
  operate 889.5
manipulated 354.29
manipulation
  touching 73.2
  masturbation 75.8
  intrigue 381.5
  utilization 387.8
  machination 415.4
  direction 573.1
  rigging 737.20
  operation 889.1
  automation 1041.7
manipulative
  scheming 381.13
  using 387.19
  cunning 415.12
manipulator
  strategist 415.7
  operator 889.4
  influence 894.6
mankind man 76.3
  humankind 312.1
manlike
  masculine 76.12
  anthropoid 312.14
manly masculine 76.12
  courageous 492.17
  honest 644.13
man-made
  spurious 354.26
  made 892.18
manna delicacy 10.8
  support 449.3
  godsend 472.7
  benefit 478.7
manned
  provided 385.13
  armed 460.14
mannequin
  figure 349.6
  artist's model 786.5
manner aspect 33.3
  exteriority 206.1
  behavior 321.1
  custom 373.1
  mode 384
  way 384.1
  style 532.2
  state 765.4
  kind 809.3
  specialty 866.1
mannered
  behavioral 321.7
  affected 500.15
  elegant 533.9
  figurative 536.3
mannerism sham 354.3
  affectation 500.1
  preciosity 500.2
  style 532.2
  elegance 533.3
  characteristic 865.4
  quirk 927.2
manner of speaking
  way of saying 524.7
  phrase 529.1
  style 532.2
  figure of speech 536.1

manners
  behavior 321.1
  custom 373.1
  mannerliness 504.3
  etiquette 580.3
mannish
  homosexual 75.30
  masculine 76.12
  mannified 76.14
man of action 330.8
man of the house 575.1
man of the world
  sophisticate 413.17
  person of fashion 578.7
man-of-war 180.6
manor 471.6
manor house 228.5
manorial
  residential 228.32
  real 471.9
manpower 18.4
manqué 410.18
manse house 228.5
  parsonage 703.7
mansion
  estate 228.7
  astrology 1072.20
manslaughter 308.2
mantel 901.14
mantilla 5.26
mantle
  n cover 295.2
  scepter 417.9
  insignia 647.1
  robe 702.2
  v cloak 5.40
  redden 41.5
  change color 105.19
  blush 139.8
  show resentment
    152.14
  cover 295.19
  foam 320.5
  take command 417.14
mantled clothed 5.45
  covered 295.31
man-to-man
  plain-speaking 535.3
  intimate 582.24
  familiar 587.19
mantra 696.3
manual
  handbook 554.8
  textbook 554.10
  keyboard 711.17
manual art 712.3
manual labor 725.4
manufacture
  n structure 266.1
  preparation 405.1
  production 892.2
  product 893.1
  v fabricate 354.18
  produce 892.8
manufactured
  fabricated 354.29
  made 892.18
manufacturer 892.7
manufacturing
  n production 892.2
  adj productional 892.14

manure
  n feces 12.4
  fertilizer 890.4
  v fertilize 890.8
manure pile 80.10
manuscript
  n handwriting 547.3
  writing 547.10
  copy 548.4
  rare book 554.6
  adj written 547.22
many much 247.8
  different 780.7
  diversified 783.4
  frequent 847.4
  plural 883.7
  numerous 884.6
  plentiful 991.7
many-sided sided 218.7
  versatile 413.25
  mixed 797.14
  changeable 854.6
Maoism
  communism 611.5
  revolutionism 860.2
Maoist
  n Communist 611.13
  revolutionist 860.3
  adj Communist 611.21
  revolutionist 860.6
map
  n chart 159.5
  face 216.4
  representation 349.1
  diagram 381.3
  v locate 159.11
  represent 349.8
  plot 381.10
  receive 1036.17
mapmaker
  charter 159.5
  measurer 300.9
mapped 300.13
mar deform 265.7
  spoil 393.10
  bungle 414.11
  blemish 1004.4
  offend 1015.5
marathon 827.11
maraud 482.17
marauder 483.6
marauding
  n plundering 482.6
  adj plunderous
    482.22
marble
  n variegation 47.6
  smoothness 287.3
  sculpture 715.2
  toy 743.16
  hardness 1046.6
  v variegate 47.7
  adj white 37.7
  hard 1046.10
marbled mottled 47.12
  striped 47.15
marbleize 47.7
marbleized 47.15
marblelike
  hard 1046.10
  stone 1059.11

marcel
  n hairdo 3.15
  v cut the hair 3.22
march
  n progression 162.1
  walk 177.10
  quick gait 177.13
  boundary 211.3
  frontier 211.5
  sphere 231.2
  objection 333.2
  martial music 708.12
  v mush 177.30
  border 211.10
  object 333.5
marcher 178.6
marching orders 909.5
march to a different drummer
  333.4
Mardi Gras treat 95.3
  festival 743.4
mare
  female animal 77.10
  plain 236.1
  horse 311.10
  jockey 757.2
margin
  n room 158.3
  border 211.4
  interval 224.1
  distance 261.1
  latitude 430.4
  collateral 438.3
  thin margin 738.10
  wide margin 780.2
  surplus 993.5
  v border 211.10
marginal
  bordering 211.11
  unimportant 998.16
marginalia
  addition 254.2
  memorandum 549.4
marina 1009.6
marinate 397.9
marination 797.2
marine
  n navy man 183.4
  navy 461.27
  adj nautical 182.57
  oceanic 240.9
marine animal 311.30
marine biology 240.7
marine engineering 1043.1
marine park 228.19
mariner traveler 178.1
  seaman 183.1
marines
  elite troops 461.15
  sea soldiers 461.28
marionette figure 349.6
  toy 743.16
marital 563.18
maritime
  nautical 182.57
  oceanic 240.9
mark
  n boundary 211.3
  degree 245.1
  dupe 358.2
  objective 380.2

sign 517.1
marking 517.5
marker 517.10
signature 527.10
distinction 662.5
notation 709.12
customer 733.4
game 750.2
cheater 759.22
kind 809.3
characteristic 865.4
impact 887.2
evidence 957.1
importance 997.1
stain 1004.3
v celebrate 487.2
signify 517.17
make a mark 517.19
grammaticize 530.16
letter 546.6
engrave 713.9
hockey 749.7
soccer 752.4
differentiate 780.6
characterize 865.10
specify 865.11
estimate 946.9
evidence 957.8
destine 964.7
heed 983.6
stain 1004.6
Mark 684.2
markdown 633.4
mark down
  record 549.15
  price 630.11
  cheapen 633.6
marked
  remarkable 247.10
  superior 249.12
  designated 517.24
  distinguished 662.16
  engraved 713.11
  characteristic 865.13
  destined 964.9
  notable 997.19
marker mark 517.10
  monument 549.12
  recorder 550.1
  round 751.3
market
  n square 230.8
  commerce 731.1
  public 733.3
  sale 734.1
  place of trade 736
  mart 736.1
  marketplace 736.2
  workplace 739.1
  v deal in 731.16
  shop 733.8
  sell 734.8
  adj sales 734.13
the market 737.1
marketable 734.14
market index 737.1
marketing
  n commerce 731.1
  purchase 733.1
  selling 734.2
  adj sales 734.13

marketplace
  square 230.8
  arena 463.1
  mart 736.2
market research
  selling 734.2
  canvass 938.14
market value
  worth 630.2
  price 738.9
marking mark 517.5
  insignia 647.1
  engraving 713.2
  game 749.6
  characteristic 865.4
mark my words 983.22
mark off
  circumscribe 210.4
  measure off 300.11
  plot 381.10
  allot 477.9
  mark 517.19
  differentiate 780.6
  characterize 865.10
marksman
  expert 413.11
  infantryman 461.9
  shooter 904.8
marksmanship
  skill 413.1
  sport 744.1
mark time await 130.8
  be still 173.7
  time 832.11
  wait 846.12
marmalade 10.40
maroon
  v abandon 370.5
  adj red 41.6
marooned
  abandoned 370.8
  stranded 1013.27
marquee poster 352.7
  lights 704.18
marquis 608.4
marred
  deformed 265.12
  spoiled 393.28
  blemished 1004.8
  ugly 1015.6
marriage
  sexuality 75.2
  matrimony 563.1
  wedding 563.3
  joining 800.1
  combination 805.1
marriageable
  grown 14.3
  adolescent 301.13
  adult 303.12
  nubile 563.20
marriage broker
  563.12
marriage license 443.6
marriage vow 436.3
married
  matrimonial 563.18
  wedded 563.21
  related 775.9
  joined 800.13
  leagued 805.6

marrow
  food 10.20
  essential content 196.5
  center 208.2
  essence 767.2
marry
  join in marriage 563.14
  get married 563.15
  relate 775.6
  put together 800.5
  combine 805.3
  league 805.4
Mars war-god 458.13
  planet 1072.9
marsh
  receptacle of filth 80.12
  swamp 243.1
  marshland 243.1
marshal
  n commissioned officer 575.18
  master of ceremonies 743.20
  policeman 1008.15
  v prepare 405.6
  escort 769.8
  put together 800.5
  order 807.4
  dispose 808.9
  adduce 957.12
marshland 243.1
marshy swampy 243.3
  moist 1065.15
mart square 230.8
  market 736.1
  marketplace 736.2
martial 458.21
martial arts 760.3
martial law
  militarization 458.10
  government 612.4
Martian oddity 870.4
  astronaut 1075.8
martinet 575.14
martyr
  n sufferer 96.11
  angel 679.1
  v pain 26.7
  torture 96.18
  kill 308.13
martyrdom agony 26.6
  torment 96.7
  killing 308.1
  punishment 604.2
martyred pained 26.9
  dead 307.30
  angelic 679.6
marvel
  n wonder 122.1
  phenomenon 122.2
  v wonder 122.5
marvelous
  wonderful 122.10
  remarkable 247.10
  extraordinary 870.14
  superb 999.15
Marxism
  communism 611.5
  socialism 611.6
  materialism 1052.6
Marxist
  n Communist 611.13
  socialist 611.14

revolutionist 860.3
materialist 1052.7
adj Communist 611.21
revolutionist 860.6
materialist 1052.12
mascara 1016.12
mascot 691.5
masculine
n male 76.4
gender 530.10
adj male 76.12
masculinity sex 75.1
maleness 76
masculineness 76.1
maturity 303.2
mash
n meal 8.6
feed 10.4
infatuation 104.4
pulp 1063.2
v make advances 439.8
soften 1047.6
pulverize 1051.9
pulp 1063.5
masher dandy 500.9
philanderer 562.12
pulverizer 1051.7
pulper 1063.4
mask
n cover 295.2
reticence 344.3
disguise 356.11
pretext 376.1
dance 705.2
relief 715.3
safeguard 1008.3
v cover 295.19
conceal 346.6
falsify 354.16
masked
covered 295.31
disguised 346.13
masochism 75.11
masochist 75.16
mason 716.6
masonry
sculpture 715.1
building material 1054.2
masque cover 356.11
dance 705.2
masquerade
n costume 5.9
impersonation 349.4
sham 354.3
cover 356.11
dance 705.2
v hide 346.8
masquerader 357.7
mass
n amount 244.1
quantity 247.3
size 257.1
lump 257.10
thickness 269.2
weight 297.5
store 386.1
sacred music 708.17
substantiality 763.1
throng 770.4
accumulation 770.9
major part 792.6

conglomeration 803.5
majority 883.2
solid 1045.6
v load 159.15
come together 770.16
assemble 770.18
put together 800.5
cohere 803.6
adj gravitational 297.20
populational 606.8
adv heavily 297.22
Mass
divine service 696.8
Missa 701.8
massacre
n carnage 308.4
unruliness 671.3
v slaughter 308.17
defeat 412.9
massage
n massaging 1044.3
v stroke 73.8
treat 91.24
rub 1044.6
soften 1047.6
mass communications 343.5
masses lot 247.4
inferior 250.2
the masses 606.2
masseuse 1044.4
massive
large 247.7
bulky 257.19
thick 269.8
heavy 297.16
onerous 297.17
sturdy 763.7
dense 1045.12
mass market 734.1
mass murder
killing 308.1
carnage 308.4
mass-produced 892.18
mass production 892.3
mass spectrography 1038.1
mast spar 180.13
tower 272.6
supporter 901.2
master
n ship's officer 183.7
superior 249.4
boy 302.5
victor 411.2
past master 413.13
proprietor 470.2
teacher 571.1
principal 571.8
lord 575.1
chief 575.3
governor 575.6
degree 648.6
work of art 712.10
artist 716.1
skilled worker 726.6
producer 892.7
wise man 921.1
v conquer 412.10
subdue 432.9
understand 521.7
attain mastery of 570.9
dominate 612.15

adj chief 249.14
governing 612.18
paramount 997.24
Master man 76.7
Sir 648.3
mastered
conquered 412.17
subdued 432.15
masterful lordly 141.11
skillful 413.22
imperious 417.16
perfected 1002.9
mastermind
n master 413.13
wise man 921.1
scholar 929.3
v direct 573.8
master of ceremonies
steward 574.4
theater man 704.23
MC 743.20
broadcaster 1034.23
masterpiece
masterwork 413.10
work of art 712.10
product 893.1
pattern of perfection 1002.4
mastership
supremacy 249.3
skill 413.1
masterhood 417.7
directorship 573.4
control 612.2
mastery
supremacy 249.3
preparedness 405.4
victory 411.1
defeat 412.1
skill 413.1
mastership 417.7
learning 570.1
control 612.2
influence 894.1
understanding 928.3
profound knowledge 928.6
masthead
n label 517.13
v punish 604.10
masticate chew 8.27
pulp 1063.5
mastodon
behemoth 257.14
pachyderm 311.4
masturbate 75.22
masturbation
autoeroticism 75.8
vanity 140.1
mat
n head of hair 3.4
border 211.4
partition 213.5
rug 295.9
arena 463.1
lawn bowling 750.3
bedding 901.20
v weave 740.6
dull 1027.10
adj colorless 36.7
lackluster 1027.17
matador killer 308.11
bullfighter 461.4

match
n image 349.5
contest 457.3
marriage 563.1
amusement 743.9
tennis 748.1
game 749.3
hockey 749.6
round 751.3
soccer 752.3
fight 754.3
equal 790.4
two 873.2
matchstick 1021.5
light source 1026.1
v parallel 203.4
parallelize 203.5
contrapose 215.4
size 257.15
give in kind 506.6
join in marriage 563.14
assemble 770.18
be alike 778.4
resemble 784.7
agree 788.6
equal 790.5
coincide 836.4
double 873.5
compare 943.4
be comparable 943.7
matched
married 563.21
joined 800.13
two 873.6
coupled 873.8
matching
n contest 457.3
marriage 563.1
comparison 943.1
adj chromatic 35.16
analogous 784.11
matchless
peerless 249.15
best 999.16
first-rate 999.17
perfect 1002.6
matchmaker 563.12
mate
n ship's officer 183.7
image 349.5
spouse 563.6
companion 588.3
friend 588.4
partner 616.2
accompanier 769.4
likeness 784.3
equal 790.4
v copulate 75.21
get married 563.15
double 873.5
mated
married 563.21
joined 800.13
coupled 873.8
material
n fabric 4.1
material 4.1
essential content 196.5
store 386.1
substance 763.2
matter 1052.2

adj carnal 663.6
secularist 695.16
substantial 763.6
essential 767.9
relevant 775.11
evidential 957.16
important 997.17
vital 997.23
materiate 1052.10
inorganic 1055.4
materialism
carnality 663.2
secularism 695.2
idealism 952.4
physicism 1052.6
materialist
n irreligionist 695.10
physicist 1052.7
adj atomistic 1052.12
materialistic
carnal 663.6
secularist 695.16
occupied 724.15
atomistic 1052.12
materiality
existence 761.1
substantiality 763.1
relevance 775.4
importance 997.1
substance 1052
materialness 1052.1
matter 1052.2
materialize show 31.4
appear 33.8
be formed 262.8
manifest 348.5
come out 348.6
embody 763.5
happen 831.6
establish 892.10
turn up 941.9
corporalize 1052.9
matériel
equipment 385.4
store 386.1
arms 462.1
materials 1054.1
maternal loving 104.27
native 226.5
ancestral 560.17
maternity
blood relationship 559.1
motherhood 560.3
mathematical
exact 973.17
numeric 1017.22
mathematician 1017.16
mathematics
numbers 1017.1
math 1017.1
matinee 582.10
matinee idol
favorite 104.16
actor 707.2
mating copulation 75.7
fertilization 78.3
mating call
animal noise 60.1
endearment 562.5
matins morning 314.1
divine service 696.8

matriarch
mother 560.11
mistress 575.2
back number 842.8
matriarchal 612.17
matriarchy 612.5
matriculate
record 549.15
be taught 570.11
matriculation 549.14
matrilineage 559.1
matrimonial 563.18
matrimonial bureau 563.12
matrimony 563.1
matrix form 262.1
mold 786.6
vital force 886.7
deposit 1058.7
matron woman 77.5
wife 563.8
mistress 575.2
matronly
feminine 77.14
middle-aged 303.14
matte print 714.5
dullness 1027.5
matted hairy 3.24
complex 799.4
disheveled 810.14
matter
n humor 2.24
excrement 12.3
pus 12.6
essential content 196.5
quantity 244.1
motive 375.1
undertaking 404.1
writing 547.10
copy 548.4
occupation 724.1
substance 763.2
particular 766.3
affair 831.3
topic 937.1
material 1052.2
inorganic matter 1055.1
v fester 12.15
be important 997.12
matter of course 373.4
matter of fact
prosaicness 117.2
fact 761.3
event 831.2
matter-of-fact
prosaic 117.8
simple 499.6
plain-speaking 535.3
prosaic 721.5
realistic 987.6
matter of life and death
urgent need 963.4
point of interest 997.3
mattress 901.20
maturation
bodily development 14.1
growth 259.3
adolescence 301.6
development 303.6
improvement 392.2
completion 407.2
evolution 861.1

mature
v grow 14.2
expand 259.7
grow up 303.9
grow old 304.6
develop 392.10
ripen 407.8
accrue 623.7
complete 794.6
evolve 861.5
produce 892.8
originate 892.12
perfect 1002.5
adj developed 14.3
grown 259.12
adult 303.12
grown old 303.13
middle-aged 304.7
prepared 405.16
ripe 407.13
experienced 413.28
due 623.10
complete 794.9
perfected 1002.9
matured
ripe 407.13
experienced 413.28
complete 794.9
perfected 1002.9
maturing
n bodily development 14.1
growth 259.3
adj evolutionary 861.8
maturity
adulthood 303.2
preparedness 405.4
completion 407.2
debt 623.1
maudlin
intoxicated 88.31
sentimental 93.21
foolish 923.8
maul mistreat 389.5
harm 393.13
injure 393.13
rage 671.11
fight 754.4
pound 902.16
mauled 96.23
mausoleum
tomb 309.16
monument 549.12
mauve 46.3
maven
expert 413.11
adviser 422.3
connoisseur 496.7
specialist 866.3
scientist 928.11
maverick
n cattle 311.6
rebel 327.5
obstinate person 361.6
nonconformist 868.3
oddity 870.4
adj unconventional 868.6
mavis 710.23
maw
digestive system 2.18
mouth 292.4
mawkish nasty 64.7

oversweet 66.5
sentimental 93.21
the max
n supremacy 249.3
adj extreme 247.13
maxim precept 419.2
rule 869.4
a belief 953.2
aphorism 974.1
maximal top 198.10
superlative 249.13
plentiful 991.7
maximize 251.4
maximum
n summit 198.2
supremacy 249.3
limit 794.5
plenty 991.2
adj top 198.10
great 247.6
superlative 249.13
may be able 18.11
can 443.13
maybe 966.9
Mayday 400.1
mayhem 393.1
mayor 575.17
mayoralty
mastership 417.7
magistracy 594.3
Mazda 677.5
maze
n complex 799.2
confusion 985.3
v perplex 971.13
confuse 985.7
mazy deviative 164.7
flowing 238.24
curved 279.7
convolutional 281.6
complex 799.4
inconstant 854.7
MC steward 574.4
theater man 704.23
master of ceremonies 743.20
broadcaster 1034.23
McCarthyism 389.3
MD 90.4
me 865.5
mea culpa
penitence 113.4
apology 658.2
meadow marsh 243.1
grassland 310.8
meager
insignificant 248.6
dwarf 258.13
narrow 270.14
lean 270.17
sparse 885.5
slight 992.10
meal repast 8.5
feed 10.4
cereal 10.34
powder 1051.5
meal ticket
support 449.3
financer 729.10
mealy colorless 36.7
powdery 1051.11
mealymouth 138.3

mediation
instrumentality 384.3
pacification 465.1
intermediation 466.1
mediating 466.1
function of Christ 677.14
mediator
intermediary 213.4
instrument 384.4
intermediator 466.3
go-between 576.4
moderator 670.3
mediatory
mediatorial 466.8
divine 677.16
Medicaid
health care 83.5
welfarism 611.7
medical doctor 90.4
medical examiner
doctor 90.4
autopsy 307.18
medical practice
medicine 90.1
practice of medicine 90.13
Medicare
health care 83.5
welfarism 611.7
medicate 91.25
medication
medicine 86.4
therapy 91.1
treatment 91.14
medicinal
n medicine 86.4
adj remedial 86.39
medicine
n medicament 86.4
liquor 88.14
medical practice 90.1
v medicate 91.25
medicine man 690.7
medico 90.4
medieval 842.13
medievalist 842.5
mediocre
medium 246.3
inadequate 250.7
unskillful 414.15
middle 819.4
usual 869.9
imperfect 1003.4
middling 1005.7
mediocrity mean 246.1
inadequacy 250.3
unskillfulness 414.1
incompetent 414.7
usualness 869.2
a nobody 998.7
imperfection 1003.1
ordinariness 1005.2
mediocreness 1005.1
second-rater 1005.5
meditate
contemplate 380.5
consider 931.12
meditation
inaction 329.1
trance 691.3
prayer 696.4
consideration 931.2

engrossment 983.3
meditative
passive 329.6
cognitive 931.21
engrossed 983.17
abstracted 985.11
medium
n color 35.8
essential content 196.5
natural environment 209.4
intermediary 213.4
mean 246.1
instrument 384.4
mediator 466.3
middle course 467.3
volume 554.4
go-between 576.4
psychic 689.13
lights 704.18
art equipment 712.18
doer 726.1
substance 763.2
immaterialist 1053.4
adj done 11.8
intervening 213.10
mean 246.3
middle 819.4
mediocre 1005.7
medium of exchange 728.1
medley
n performance 708.33
miscellany 770.13
hodgepodge 797.6
adj chromatic 35.16
variegated 47.9
mixed 797.14
Medusa 690.9
meed portion 477.5
recompense 624.3
meek
resigned 134.10
humblehearted 137.11
modest 139.9
gentle 433.15
unbelligerent 464.10
meerschaum 89.6
meet
n contest 457.3
game 743.9
track meet 755.2
assembly 770.2
v converge 169.2
confront 216.8
encounter 223.11
concur 332.9
observe 434.2
oppose 451.5
compete 457.18
brave 492.11
come together 770.16
convene 770.17
join 800.11
experience 831.8
conform 867.3
collide 902.13
suffice 991.4
adj decorous 496.10
conventional 579.5
just 649.8
timely 843.9
expedient 995.5

approachable 167.5
meet halfway
make up 465.10
mediate 466.6
compromise 468.2
meet head-on
contrapose 215.4
meet 223.11
confront 451.5
offer resistance 453.3
brave 492.11
counteract 900.6
meeting
n convergence 169.1
meeting up 223.4
contest 457.3
conference 541.6
rendezvous 582.9
divine service 696.8
assembly 770.2
joining 800.1
impact 902.3
adj converging 169.3
in contact 223.17
assembled 770.21
joining 800.16
concurrent 899.4
meetinghouse
hall 197.4
church 703.1
meeting of minds
unanimity 332.5
consensus 788.3
meet the eye show 31.4
appear 33.8
meet with attention 983.11
mega 257.20
megacycles 1034.12
megaphone 48.8
melancholia
mental disorder 92.14
wretchedness 96.6
melancholy 112.5
depression 926.5
melancholic
n personality type 92.12
sourpuss 112.13
adj melancholy 112.23
weary 118.11
melancholy
n wretchedness 96.6
melancholia 112.5
weariness 118.3
thoughtfulness 931.3
adj sullen 110.24
melancholic 112.23
weary 118.11
n sullenness 110.8
mélange 797.6
melanism 38.1
meld
n compound 797.5
combination 805.1
v identify 778.5
mix 797.10
combine 805.3
melding
identification 778.2
combination 805.1
melee free-for-all 457.5
commotion 810.4

meliorate
improve 392.7
make better 392.9
be changed 852.6
change 852.7
mellifluous sweet 66.4
pleasant 97.6
melodious 708.48
mellow
v mature 303.9
ripen 407.8
evolve 861.5
soften 1047.6
adj soft-colored 35.22
resonant 54.10
intoxicated 88.31
pleasant 97.6
mature 303.13
ripe 407.13
melodious 708.48
soft 1047.8
mellowing
maturation 303.6
softening 1047.5
melodics 709.1
melodist singer 710.13
composer 710.20
melodrama 93.9
melodramatic
emotionalistic 93.19
sensational 105.32
dramatic 704.33
melodramatics
emotionalism 93.9
dramatics 704.2
melody
melodiousness 708.2
air 708.4
melon
political patronage 609.36
dividend 738.7
melt disappear 34.2
affect 93.14
have pity 145.4
move 145.5
flit 828.6
melt down 1020.21
liquefy 1064.5
meltable
molten 1020.31
liquefiable 1064.9
melt away
disappear 34.2
decrease 252.6
cease to exist 762.6
meltdown
outburst 671.6
misfortune 1011.2
melt down
extract 192.16
explode 671.14
melt 1020.21
liquefy 1064.5
melted
penitent 113.9
molten 1020.31
liquefied 1064.6
melting
n disappearance 34.1
fusion 1020.3
liquefaction 1064.1

adj vanishing 34.3
loving 104.27
pitying 145.7
liquefying 1064.7
melting point 1019.11
melting pot
mixture 797.1
mixer 797.9
instrument of conversion 858.10
the melting pot 232.3
member appendage 2.7
affiliate 617.11
organ 793.4
membership
association 582.6
members 617.12
inclusion 772.1
membrane
membrana 2.6
lamina 296.2
memento
monument 549.12
remembrance 989.7
memo 549.4
memoir
memorandum 549.4
treatise 556.1
history 719.1
remembering 989.4
memorabilia
archives 549.2
history 719.1
memento 989.7
matter of importance 997.5
memorable
rememberable 989.25
notable 997.19
memorandum
memo 549.4
reminder 989.6
memorandum book 549.11
memorial
n record 549.1
memorandum 549.4
monument 549.12
history 719.1
memento 989.7
adj celebrative 487.3
commemorative 989.27
memorialize
petition 440.10
celebrate 487.2
memorize
get by rote 570.8
commit to memory 989.17
memory
engram 92.29
celebration 487.1
recording media 549.10
posthumous fame 662.7
retrospection 837.4
recollection 989.1
remembrance 989.1
storage 1042.7
men work force 18.9
mankind 76.3
staff 577.11
menace
n threat 514.1
danger 1006.1

v forebode 133.11
threaten 514.2
be imminent 840.2
work evil 1000.6
menacing
ominous 133.17
threatening 514.3
imminent 840.3
ménage home 228.2
family 559.5
domestic management 573.6
menagerie
zoo 228.19
collection 770.11
mend
n improvement 392.1
v get well 83.7
improve 392.7
make better 392.9
repair 396.14
mendacity
untruthfulness 354.8
lie 354.11
Mendel's law 560.6
mender 396.10
mendicancy
beggary 440.6
indigence 619.2
mendicant
n nonworker 331.11
beggar 440.8
ascetic 667.2
religious 699.16
adj supplicatory 440.16
indigent 619.8
ascetic 667.4
mending
n improvement 392.1
reparation 396.6
adj improving 392.15
menfolk 76.3
menial
n servant 577.2
worker 726.2
adj servile 138.13
serving 577.14
meniscus 279.5
menopause 303.7
menses 12.9
menstrual
bleeding 12.24
regular 850.8
menstrual discharge 12.9
menstruate 12.18
menstruation 12.9
mensuration
measurement 300.1
science of measurement 300.8
menswear 5.1
mental
n psychotic 926.17
adj intellectual 919.7
crazy 926.27
cognitive 931.21
attitudinal 978.7
mental block 990.3
mental capacity 920.1
mental case 926.17
mental deficiency 926.1
mental disorder
emotional disorder 92.14

insanity 926.1
mental health
health 83.1
sanity 925.1
mental hospital 926.14
mental illness
mental disorder 92.14
insanity 926.1
mentality
intellect 919.1
intelligence 920.1
intelligent being 920.9
mentally retarded 922.22
mental picture
idea 932.1
visualization 986.6
mental states 92.1
mental telepathy 689.9
mention
n remark 524.3
information 551.1
citation 646.4
v remark 524.24
specify 865.11
call attention to 983.10
mentor preparer 405.5
adviser 422.3
teacher 571.1
wise man 921.1
Mentor 921.2
menu bill of fare 8.14
statement 871.5
schedule 965.3
meow 60.2
Mephistopheles 680.4
mercantile
business 730.12
commercial 731.22
mercantilism 731.13
mercantilistic 731.22
mercenary
n hireling 461.17
employee 577.3
adj greedy 100.27
employed 615.20
corruptible 645.23
merchandise
n provisions 385.2
goods 735.1
commodities 735.1
v deal in 731.16
sell 734.8
merchandising
n trade 731.2
selling 734.2
adj sales 734.13
merchant
n provider 385.6
businessperson 730
merchandiser 730.2
adj commercial 731.22
merchant marine
ships 180.10
branch 461.21
navy 461.27
merci! 150.6
merciful
kind 143.13
pitying 145.7
lenient 427.7
almighty 677.17

merciless
pitiless 146.3
savage 671.21
mercurial fast 174.15
active 330.17
irresolute 362.9
fickle 364.6
nonuniform 782.3
inconstant 854.7
flighty 985.17
brass 1058.17
mercury
swiftness 174.6
guide 574.7
changeableness 854.4
thermometer 1019.20
Mercury
messenger 353.1
planet 1072.9
mercy kindness 143.1
act of kindness 143.7
pity 145.1
leniency 427.1
mercy killing 308.1
mere
n lake 241.1
marsh 243.1
adj sheer 248.8
simple 798.6
mere caricature 787.1
mere child
simple soul 416.3
innocent 657.4
mere child's play 1014.3
mere existence 761.6
mere facade 500.1
mere farce 489.1
merely adequate 246.3
a mere nothing 998.6
mere show 500.1
mere skin and bones 270.17
mere subsistence 992.5
mere suggestion 551.4
mere technicality 998.6
meretricious
specious 354.27
coarse 497.11
gaudy 501.20
grandiloquent 545.8
prostitute 665.28
paltry 998.21
a mere trickle 992.9
merge
converge 169.2
submerge 367.7
cooperate 450.3
come together 770.16
identify 778.5
mix 797.10
put together 800.5
join 800.11
combine 805.3
merger
convergence 169.1
affiliation 450.2
identification 778.2
mixture 797.1
joining 800.1
combination 805.1
merging
converging 169.3

combining 805.7
meridian
  n map 159.5
  summit 198.2
  zone 231.3
  noon 314.5
  orbit 1072.16
  adj top 198.10
  noon 314.7
meringue sweets 10.40
  foam 320.2
merit
  n importance 997.1
  goodness 999.1
  v deserve 639.5
merited
  warranted 639.9
  just 649.8
meritless 998.22
meritorious
  praiseworthy 509.20
  due 639.10
  reputable 662.15
Merlin 690.6
mermaid
  swimmer 182.12
  spirit of the sea 240.4
  water god 678.10
merriment
  merriness 109.5
  rejoicing 116.1
  waggishness 489.4
  conviviality 582.3
  festivity 743.3
merriness 109.5
merry
  intoxicated 88.31
  mirthful 109.15
  festive 743.28
merry-go-round
  round of pleasure 743.7
  carousel 743.15
  rotator 915.4
merrymaking
  n treat 95.3
  conviviality 582.3
  festivity 743.3
  adj festive 743.28
mesa plain 236.1
  tableland 237.3
  plateau 272.4
mesh
  n network 170.3
  interaction 777.3
  complex 799.2
  network 1042.16
  v net 170.7
  trap 356.20
  catch 480.17
  interact 777.6
meshes
  network 170.3
  snare 356.13
meshing
  n interaction 777.3
  adj apt 788.10
mesmeric
  hypnotic 22.24
  alluring 377.8
  engrossing 983.20
mesmerism 22.8

mesmerize
  hypnotize 22.20
  fascinate 377.7
  cast a spell 691.7
  have influence over 894.11
  engross 983.13
mesmerized
  wondering 122.9
  enchanted 691.12
  gripped 983.18
mesmerizer
  hypnotist 22.9
  deceiver 357.1
mesomorph 92.12
mesomorphism 92.11
meson atom 258.8
  radioactive particle 1037.4
mess
  n meal 8.5
  rations 10.6
  filth 80.7
  dining room 197.11
  amount 244.2
  lot 247.4
  formlessness 263.1
  fiasco 410.6
  bungle 414.5
  portion 477.5
  bunch 770.7
  hodgepodge 797.6
  complex 799.2
  jumble 810.3
  confusion 985.3
  predicament 1013.5
  eyesore 1015.4
  v feed 8.18
  defile 80.17
  disarrange 811.2
message
  communication 343.1
  advertisement 352.6
  information 551.1
  dispatch 552.4
  letter 553.2
  commercial 1034.20
mess around 998.15
messed up
  spoiled 393.29
  botched 414.22
  complex 799.4
  disheveled 810.14
messenger
  n harbinger 133.5
  message-bearer 353.1
  delegate 576.2
  precursor 816.1
  v send 176.15
mess hall
  restaurant 8.17
  dining room 197.11
messiah 574.6
messiness
  uncleanness 80.1
  formlessness 263.1
  slipshodness 340.3
  slovenliness 810.6
messmate 588.3
mess up defile 80.17
  deform 263.3
  spoil 393.11
  bungle 414.12

complicate 799.3
  disarrange 811.2
messy dirty 80.22
  slipshod 340.12
  slovenly 810.15
mestizo 797.8
metabolic
  digestive 2.31
  plasmatic 262.10
  metamorphic 852.12
metabolic rate 2.2
metabolism
  metabolic process 2.20
  basal metabolism 7.12
  transformation 852.3
metabolize digest 7.18
  transform 852.8
metal
  n heraldry 647.2
  elementary metal 1058.3
  v floor 295.22
  adj metallic 1058.16
metallic
  raucous 58.15
  metal 1058.16
metallurgist 1058.12
metallurgy 1058.11
metalworker 726.8
metalworks 739.4
metamorphic
  multiform 783.3
  metabolic 852.12
  changeable 854.6
metamorphosis 852.3
metaphor
  similarity 784.1
  substitute 862.2
  comparison 943.1
metaphorical
  indicative 517.23
  meaningful 518.10
  symbolic 519.10
  figurative 536.3
metaphysician
  parapsychologist 689.12
  philosopher 952.8
metaphysics
  hyperphysics 689.3
  ontology 761.7
metastasis
  transferal 176.1
  grammar 205.3
  transformation 852.3
mete
  n boundary 211.3
  v quantify 244.4
  measure 300.10
  parcel out 477.8
  give 478.12
  administer 643.6
meteor 1072.15
meteoric
  increasing 251.8
  brief 828.8
  flashing 1025.34
  celestial 1072.25
meteorological instrument 317.8
meteorologist
  crew 185.4
  weather scientist 317.6

earth scientist 1071.2
meteorology
  weather science 317.5
  earth science 1071.1
meter
  n measure 300.2
  measurer 300.9
  rhythm 709.22
  metrics 720.6
  prosody 720.7
  periodicity 850.2
  electrical device 1032.21
  v measure 300.10
method
  behavior 321.1
  plan 381.1
  manner 384.1
  means 384.2
  art 413.7
  orderliness 807.3
methodical
  punctilious 580.10
  uniform 781.5
  orderly 807.6
  regular 850.6
methodized
  planned 381.12
  arranged 808.14
methodologist 867.2
methodology
  behavior 321.1
  plan 381.1
  manner 384.1
  orderliness 807.3
Methuselah
  old man 304.2
  back number 842.8
meticulous
  exacting 339.12
  strict 425.6
  observant 434.4
  fastidious 495.9
  punctilious 580.10
  conscientious 644.15
  detailed 766.9
  accurate 973.16
  attentive 983.15
métier talent 413.4
  vocation 724.6
  specialty 866.1
metric
  measuring 300.12
  rhythmic 709.28
  metrical 720.16
metrics
  accent 524.10
  rhythm 709.22
  prosody 720.6
metric system 300.1
métro 179.14
metronome
  notation 709.12
  music 711.22
  oscillator 916.9
metronomic
  chronologic 832.15
  periodic 850.7
metropolis
  capital 208.7
  town 230.1
  region 231.5

mettle
animation 17.4
pluck 359.3
fortitude 492.6
disposition 978.3
mettlesome
energetic 17.13
excitable 105.28
plucky 359.14
resolute 492.18
mew
n lair 228.26
retreat 1009.5
v cry 60.2
enclose 212.5
confine 429.12
mewl 60.2
mews 228.20
mezzanine 197.23
mezzo 819.4
mezzo-soprano
n high voice 58.6
voice 709.5
adj high 58.13
miasma
stench 71.1
mephitis 1001.4
vapor 1067.1
miasmic
malodorous 71.5
poisonous 82.7
offensive 98.18
vaporous 1067.9
Mick 232.7
Mickey Finn
anesthetic 25.3
chloral hydrate 87.6
drink 88.9
Mickey Mouse
n finery 498.3
trivia 998.4
adj vulgar 497.10
insignificant 998.18
inferior 1005.9
easy 1014.13
micro 258.12
microbe germ 85.42
minute 258.7
organism 305.2
microbiology 1068.3
microcosm 258.6
microdot 549.10
microeconomics 731.7
microfiche
recording media 549.10
transcript 785.4
microfilm
n recording media 549.10
film 714.10
v photograph 714.14
copy 785.8
micronutrient 7.11
microorganism
germ 85.42
minute 258.7
organism 305.2
microphone mike 50.9
radio transmitter 1034.4
microscope 29.1
microscopic
telescopic 29.10

infinitesimal 258.14
exact 973.17
microscopy optics 29.7
littleness 258.18
microtome 802.7
microwave
n radio wave 1034.11
v cook 11.5
micturition 12.5
mid
adj phonetic 524.30
middle 819.4
prep between 213.12
among 797.17
Midas 618.8
midday
n noon 314.5
adj noon 314.7
midden dunghill 80.10
derelict 370.4
trash pile 391.6
middle
n center 208.2
mean 246.1
voice 530.14
midpoint 819.1
median 819.1
v centralize 208.9
seek the middle 819.3
adj central 208.11
intervening 213.10
mediatory 466.8
medial 819.4
middle age 303.4
middle-aged
mid-life 303.14
mature 304.7
Middle Ages 824.5
Middle America
inland 207.3
US region 231.7
the people 606.1
middle class 607.5
mediocrity 1005.5
Middle American
n conformist 867.2
adj inland 207.7
middlebrow 930.8
middle class
middle order 607.5
mediocrity 1005.5
middle-class
upper-class 607.10
ordinary 1005.8
the middle class 606.1
Middle East 231.6
middle ground
mean 246.1
middle course 467.3
mid-distance 819.2
middleman
intermediary 213.4
mediator 466.3
go-between 576.4
merchant 730.2
middlemost
central 208.11
middle 819.4
middle of the road
middle course 467.3
moderatism 611.2

mid-distance 819.2
mean 246.1
middle-of-the-road
medium 246.3
moderate 611.18
middle 819.4
middle-of-the-roader
centrist 611.10
moderate 670.4
middle-of-the-roadism 611.2
middle school 567.4
middleweight 297.3
the Middle West 231.7
middling
medium 246.3
middle 819.4
mediocre 1005.7
middy 183.4
Mideast 231.6
midge dwarf 258.5
minute 258.7
midget
n dwarf 258.5
adj dwarf 258.13
midget hockey 749.1
midland
n inland 207.3
adj inland 207.7
middle 819.4
Midland 523.7
midlife crisis 303.4
midmost
n middle 819.1
adj central 208.11
middle 819.4
midnight
n dead of night 315.6
adj black 38.8
nocturnal 315.9
midriff
digestive system 2.18
partition 213.5
middle 819.1
midsection 213.5
midshipman
navy man 183.4
undergraduate 572.6
midst
n middle 819.1
prep between 213.12
among 797.17
midterm 938.2
midtown
n city district 230.6
adj urban 230.11
mid-Victorian
n prude 500.11
back number 842.8
adj prudish 500.19
antiquated 842.13
midway
n mid-distance 819.2
adj neutral 467.7
middle 819.4
adv mediumly 246.4
halfway 819.5
midwife
health care professional 90.8
instrument 384.4
mien looks 33.4
exteriority 206.1

behavior 321.1
miff
n dudgeon 152.7
v annoy 96.13
provoke 152.24
miffed annoyed 96.21
provoked 152.27
might strength 15.1
power 18.1
greatness 247.1
authoritativeness 417.2
might be 966.4
mighty
adj strong 15.15
powerful 18.12
great 247.6
huge 257.20
authoritative 417.15
eminent 662.18
adv very 247.18
migraine 26.5
migrant migrator 178.5
bird 311.28
worker 726.2
migrant worker
migrant 178.5
worker 726.2
agriculturist 1069.5
migrate 177.22
migration
transferal 176.1
transmigration 177.4
departure 188.1
mikado 575.9
mike 50.9
milady woman 77.5
title 648.2
milch 1061.5
milcher 311.6
mild insipid 65.2
bright 97.11
good-natured 143.14
lenient 427.7
meek 433.15
moderate 670.10
warm 1019.24
soft 1047.8
mildew
n fetidness 71.2
decay 393.6
blight 1001.2
v decay 393.22
mildewed
malodorous 71.5
blighted 393.42
stale 842.14
mileage
distance 261.1
length 267.1
benefit 387.4
fee 624.5
expedience 995.1
milepost post 273.4
pointer 517.4
marker 517.10
miles per hour 174.1
milestone
marker 517.10
salient point 997.6
milieu
environment 209.1

ambience 209.3
region 231.1
arena 463.1
plot 722.4
militancy
activity 330.1
warlikeness 458.11
militant
n man of action 330.8
combatant 461.1
believer 692.4
adj active 330.17
warlike 458.21
militarism
warlikeness 458.11
foreign policy 609.5
government 612.4
militarist 461.5
militarization 458.10
militarize 458.20
military 458.21
military court 595.4
military law 673.6
military officer 575.18
military operations
war 458.1
operation 458.5
military police 1008.17
military science 458.6
military tactics 458.6
militate 889.7
militate against
contend against 451.4
counteract 900.6
militia 461.24
milk
n humor 2.24
whiteness 37.2
fluid 1061.2
v draw off 192.12
exploit 387.16
take from 480.21
strip 480.24
tend 1070.7
adj milky 1061.5
milk and honey 1010.1
milk and water 16.7
milker 311.6
milking 192.3
milk run 184.11
milksop weakling 16.6
effeminate male 77.11
coward 491.5
fool 924.1
milky
wishy-washy 16.17
white 37.7
lacteal 1061.5
the Milky Way 1072.6
mill
n money 728.7
plant 739.3
machinery 1040.3
pulverizer 1051.7
v notch 289.4
come together 770.16
process 892.9
seethe 915.12
tool 1040.13
pulverize 1051.9
milled made 892.18

powdery 1051.11
millenarian
n optimist 124.6
adj optimistic 124.12
millennial
thousandth 882.30
ideal 986.23
millennium
moment 824.2
thousand 882.10
utopia 986.11
good times 1010.4
milliner 5.37
millinery
headdress 5.25
garment making 5.32
milling
production 892.2
pulverization 1051.4
million
n ten million 882.11
adj numerous 884.6
millionaire 618.7
millions 618.2
millstone burden 297.7
pulverizer 1051.7
millstone around one's neck
affliction 96.8
disadvantage 996.2
impediment 1012.6
millstream 238.1
mill town 739.2
milord 648.2
milquetoast
n manageability 433.4
coward 491.5
adj henpecked 326.5
manageable 433.14
Milquetoast
weakling 16.6
vacillator 362.5
mime
n imitator 336.4
impersonation 349.4
actor 707.2
v mimic 336.6
impersonate 349.12
gesture 517.21
act 704.29
mimeograph
n printing 548.1
v print 548.14
copy 785.8
mimer imitator 336.4
actor 707.2
mimetic
imitative 336.9
representational 349.13
mimic
n imitator 336.4
actor 707.2
v imitate 336.6
impersonate 349.12
resemble 784.7
adj imitative 336.9
mimicry
mockery 336.2
impersonation 349.4
acting 704.8
miming
impersonation 349.4

acting 704.8
minaret 272.6
minatory 514.3
mince
n meat 10.13
gait 177.12
v walk 177.28
be affected 500.14
speak poorly 525.7
extenuate 600.12
shatter 802.13
mind
n psyche 92.28
desire 100.1
will 323.1
intention 380.1
theosophy 689.18
intellect 919.1
intelligence 919.4
opinion 953.6
disposition 978.3
mood 978.4
attention 983.1
memory 989.1
v take amiss 152.13
refuse 325.3
obey 326.2
care 339.6
beware 494.7
heed 983.6
remember 989.10
care for 1008.19
Mind 677.6
mind-altering drug 87.3
mind-blowing
exciting 105.30
hallucinatory 976.10
mind-boggler 522.8
mind-boggling
deadening 25.9
astonishing 122.12
frightening 127.28
unbelievable 955.10
minded willing 324.5
moved 375.30
disposed 978.8
mind-expanding
psychochemical
86.46
hallucinatory 976.10
mindful
considerate 143.16
careful 339.10
observant 434.4
cautious 494.8
knowing 928.15
attentive 983.15
recollective 989.22
remembering 989.24
mindless
unconcerned 102.7
inconsiderate 144.18
cruel 144.26
animal 311.40
unrefined 497.12
savage 671.21
unintelligent 922.13
unwise 923.10
unaware 930.13
purposeless 972.16
incurious 982.3

mind one's own business
not interfere 430.16
take no interest in 982.2
mind one's P's and Q's
behave oneself 321.5
be careful 339.7
mind one's manners 504.11
mind reader 689.15
mind reading 689.9
mind your own business 214.10
mine
n pit 284.4
trap 356.12
source of supply 386.4
entrenchment 460.5
bomb 462.20
rich source 618.4
fountainhead 886.6
quarry 1058.6
v extract 192.10
deepen 275.8
excavate 284.15
undermine 393.15
blow up 395.18
plant a mine 459.24
fortify 460.9
take from 480.21
process 892.9
quarry 1058.14
miner excavator 284.10
mineworker 1058.9
mineral
n inorganic substance 1058.1
ore 1058.2
adj inorganic 1055.4
inanimate 1058.15
mineral kingdom
mineral 1058.1
hierarchy 809.4
inorganic matter 1055.1
mineralogy 1058.10
mineral oil 1056.4
mineral spring 91.23
mineral water 1065.3
mineworker 1058.9
mingle 797.10
mingling 797.1
mingy niggardly 484.8
ungenerous 651.6
mini
n runt 258.4
miniature 258.6
adj miniature 258.12
miniature
n mini 258.6
image 349.5
picture 712.11
portrait 712.15
adj insignificant 248.6
diminutive 258.12
miniaturization 252.1
miniaturize 258.9
miniaturized
reduced 252.10
miniature 258.12
minim
n modicum 248.2
minute 258.7
note 709.14
rest 709.21
adj least 250.8

minimal least 250.8
  miniature 258.12
  sufficient 991.6
minimization
  reduction 252.5
  underestimation 950.1
minimize
  reduce 252.9
  disparage 512.8
  underestimate 950.2
  attach little importance to
    998.12
minimum
  n modicum 248.2
  sufficiency 991.1
  adj least 250.8
  sufficient 991.6
minimum wage 624.4
mining
  extraction 192.1
  deepening 275.7
  excavation 284.11
  production 892.2
  coal mining 1058.8
mining engineer 1058.12
minion favorite 104.16
  sycophant 138.3
  instrument 384.4
  retainer 577.1
  follower 616.8
minister
  n public official 575.17
  delegate 576.2
  diplomat 576.6
  clergyman 699.2
  v officiate 701.16
ministerial
  modal 384.8
  helping 449.20
  administrative 573.14
  diplomatic 576.17
  executive 612.19
  ecclesiastic 698.13
ministering
  modal 384.8
  helping 449.20
  serving 577.14
minister of state 575.17
minister to treat 91.24
  be instrumental 384.7
  aid 449.18
  serve 577.13
  care for 1008.19
ministration aid 449.1
  service 577.12
ministry aid 449.1
  the authorities 575.15
  service 577.12
  bureau 594.4
  cabinet 613.3
  clergy 699.1
  protectorship 1008.2
minor
  n youngster 302.1
  study 568.8
  key 709.15
  adj inferior 250.6
  immature 301.10
  insignificant 998.17
minority
  n inability 19.2

inferiority 250.1
immaturity 301.3
race 312.2
least 885.3
adj least 885.7
minority group
  party 617.4
  minority 885.3
minority interests 609.31
minority leader 610.3
minority opinion 333.1
minor league 745.1
Minos
  Pontius Pilate 596.5
  justice 649.5
  nether world deity 682.5
minstrel
  n musical theater 708.34
  singer 710.13
  ballad singer 710.14
  poet 720.11
  v sing 708.38
minstrel show 708.34
mint
  n lot 247.4
  gain 472.3
  wealth 618.3
  plant 739.3
  mold 786.6
  v form 262.7
  coin 728.28
  innovate 841.5
  originate 892.12
  adj unused 390.12
  new-made 841.9
  undamaged 1002.8
mintage money 728.1
  coining 728.24
  production 892.1
  product 893.1
mint condition
  healthiness 83.2
  newness 841.1
minted formative 262.9
  invented 892.19
minus
  n math terms 255.6
  deduction 255.7
  adj bereft 473.8
  nonexistent 762.8
  short of 911.5
  positive 1032.35
  prep off 255.14
  without 992.17
minuscule
  n type 548.6
  adj miniature 258.12
  literal 546.8
minute
  n entry 628.5
  period 824.1
  moment 824.2
  instant 830.3
  time of day 832.2
  the present 838.1
  v record 549.15
  keep accounts 628.8
  adj tiny 258.11
  meticulous 339.12
  detailed 766.9
  particular 865.12

insignificant 998.17
minutemen 461.24
minutes
  memorandum 549.4
  report 549.7
minutiae
  modicum 248.2
  detail 258.7
  particular 766.3
  trivia 998.4
minx woman 77.6
  impudent person 142.5
  brat 302.4
  mischief-maker 322.3
miracle marvel 122.2
  sign 870.8
miracle drug 86.29
miracle-worker 690.5
miraculous
  wonderful 122.10
  sorcerous 690.14
  wondrous 870.16
mirage apparition 33.5
  disappointment 132.1
  deception 356.1
  fata morgana 976.6
mire
  n slime 80.8
  receptacle of filth 80.12
  marsh 243.1
  mud 1062.8
  v dirty 80.15
  bemire 243.2
mirror
  n glass 29.6
  furniture 229.1
  paragon 659.4
  model 786.1
  ideal 786.4
  pattern of perfection
    1002.4
  v imitate 336.5
  image 349.11
  resemble 784.7
mirror image 779.2
mirroring
  imitation 336.1
  image 349.5
mirth merriment 109.5
  amusement 743.1
miry dirty 80.22
  marshy 243.3
  slimy 1062.14
misadventure 1011.2
misalliance
  marriage 563.1
  misconnection 776.2
  unfitness 789.3
misanthrope
  hater 103.4
  misanthropist 590.2
misanthropy
  hate 103.1
  people-hating 590
  misanthropism 590.1
misapplication
  misinterpretation 342.1
  misuse 389.1
  misconnection 776.2
  sophistry 936.1
  error 975.1

misapply
  misinterpret 342.2
  misuse 389.4
  reason speciously 936.8
  misdo 975.12
misapprehend
  misinterpret 342.2
  mistake 975.13
misapprehension
  misinterpretation 342.1
  mistake 975.3
misappropriate 389.4
misappropriation 389.1
misbegotten
  deformed 265.12
  illegitimate 674.7
  freakish 870.13
  unshapely 1015.8
misbehave
  behave 321.4
  misdemean 322.4
  transgress 654.8
  do wrong 655.4
misbehavior
  good behavior 321.2
  misconduct 322.1
  wrongdoing 655.1
misbelief
  heresy 688.2
  unbelief 955.1
  illusion 976.1
misbelieve err 688.8
  disbelieve 955.5
misbeliever 688.5
miscalculate
  misjudge 948.2
  err 975.9
miscalculation
  misjudgment 948.1
  mistake 975.3
miscarriage
  abortion 410.5
  mistake 975.3
miscarriage of justice
  650.4
miscarry
  abort 410.15
  miss 911.4
miscegenate
  get married 563.15
  hybridize 797.13
miscegenation
  marriage 563.1
  crossbreeding 797.4
miscellany
  compilation 554.7
  excerpts 557.4
  assortment 770.13
  hodgepodge 797.6
mischance 1011.2
mischief
  mischievousness 322.2
  mischief-maker 322.3
  impairment 393.1
  disaccord 456.1
  disadvantage 996.2
  evil 1000.3
mischief-maker
  mischief 322.3
  instigator 375.11
  troublemaker 593.2

government 612.4
mobster bandit 483.4
evildoer 593.1
criminal 660.9
mock
n indignity 156.2
fake 354.13
gibe 508.2
v offend 156.5
impersonate 349.12
deceive 356.14
joke 489.13
scoff 508.9
adopt 621.4
adj imitation 336.8
spurious 354.26
similar 784.10
substitute 862.8
mocker 336.4
mockery
indignity 156.2
mimicry 336.2
insincerity 354.5
ridicule 508.1
burlesque 508.6
laughingstock 508.7
trifle 998.5
mock-heroic
comic 488.6
poetic 720.15
mocking
n adoption 621.2
adj ridiculing 508.12
mockingbird
imitator 336.4
songbird 710.23
mock-up
reproduction 336.3
artist's model 786.5
mod 841.13
modal
instrumental 384.8
conditional 765.6
modality
form 262.1
manner 384.1
instrumentality 384.3
state 765.1
mode form 262.1
manner 384.1
mood 530.11
style 532.2
fashion 578.1
octave species 709.10
shape 765.1
manner 765.4
syllogism 935.6
model
n form 262.1
measure 300.2
reproduction 336.3
original 337.2
image 349.5
figure 349.6
paragon 659.4
celebrity 662.9
arrangement 709.11
essence 767.2
duplicate 785.3
thing copied 786
pattern 786.1

ideal 786.4
rule 869.4
philosophy 932.2
beauty 1016.8
v form 262.7
sculpture 715.5
adj praiseworthy 509.20
exemplary 786.8
normal 869.8
perfected 1002.9
modeled
formative 262.9
sculptured 715.7
modeler 716.6
modeling
forming 262.5
imitation 336.1
sculpture 715.1
moderate
n centrist 611.10
moderatist 670.4
v slow 175.9
limit 210.5
mediate 466.6
restrain 670.6
qualify 959.3
adj sedate 106.14
slow 175.10
medium 246.3
lenient 427.7
neutral 467.7
centrist 611.18
cheap 633.7
temperate 668.9
moderating 670.10
middle 819.4
tolerable 999.20
mediocre 1005.7
moderation
sedateness 106.4
limitation 210.2
middle course 467.3
temperance 668.1
restraint 670.1
moderateness 670.1
moderato 708.55
moderator
arbitrator 466.4
judge 596.1
mitigator 670.3
modern
n modern man 841.4
adj fashionable 578.11
present 838.2
contemporary
841.13
modernist
poet 720.11
modern 841.4
modernization 841.3
modernize 841.6
modest
humble 137.10
meek 139.9
inferior 250.6
demurring 325.7
reticent 344.10
cheap 633.7
unselfish 652.5
decent 664.5
mediocre 1005.7

modesty
humility 137.1
unpretentiousness 139.1
meekness 139.1
demur 325.2
reticence 344.3
unselfishness 652.1
decency 664.2
mediocrity 1005.1
modicum minim 248.2
portion 477.5
piece 793.3
modifiable
changeable 854.6
convertible 858.18
modification
speech sound 524.12
differentiation 780.4
change 852.1
qualification 959.1
modified
changed 852.10
qualified 959.10
modifier syntax 530.2
transformer 852.5
modify
differentiate 780.6
change 852.7
qualify 959.3
modish dressed up 5.46
stylish 578.12
modern 841.13
modiste 5.36
modular partial 793.7
component 796.5
modulate inflect 524.28
moderate 670.6
be changed 852.6
change 852.7
qualify 959.3
modulation
intonation 524.6
abatement 670.2
harmonization 709.2
change 852.1
amplitude modulation
1034.14
modulator 670.3
module part 793.1
component 796.2
individual 872.4
spacecraft 1075.2
modus operandi 384.1
modus vivendi
behavior 321.1
truce 465.5
mogul skiing 753.1
personage 997.8
snow 1023.8
Mogul 575.10
moiety portion 477.5
community 617.2
piece 793.3
mid-distance
819.2
half 875.2
moil
n work 725.4
agitation 917.1
v drudge 725.14
seethe 915.12

moiré
n variegation 47.6
adj iridescent 47.10
moisten 1065.12
moistening
n wetting 1065.6
adj wetting 1065.18
moisture rain 316.1
liquidity 1061.1
dampness 1065.1
damp 1065.1
moisture-proof 1066.11
moisturizer 1065.3
molar 2.8
molasses
sweetening 66.2
adhesive 803.4
semiliquid 1062.5
mold
n germ 85.42
land 234.1
form 262.1
structure 266.1
plant 310.4
original 337.2
decay 393.6
nature 767.4
cast 785.6
die 786.6
kind 809.3
characteristic 865.4
disposition 978.3
blight 1001.2
v form 262.7
decay 393.22
sculpture 715.5
pot 742.6
conform 867.3
produce 892.8
imagine 986.14
moldable docile 433.13
teachable 570.18
pliant 1047.9
molded
formative 262.9
sculptured 715.7
made 892.18
molder
n sculptor 716.6
v quiet 173.8
decay 393.22
disintegrate 806.3
age 842.9
moldering
quiescent 173.12
blighted 393.42
disintegrative 806.5
stale 842.14
molding
forming 262.5
structure 266.1
sculpture 715.1
cast 785.6
production 892.2
moldy
malodorous 71.5
blighted 393.42
stale 842.14
mole the blind 30.4
growth 85.39
bulge 283.3

mark 517.5
buttress 901.4
blemish 1004.1
harbor 1009.6
barrier 1012.5
molecular 258.14
molecular weight
weight 297.5
chemistry 297.8
atomic weight 1060.5
molecule
modicum 248.2
atom 258.8
atomic cluster 1038.7
matter 1052.2
element 1060.2
molehill hill 237.4
pile 770.10
trifle 998.5
molest annoy 96.13
mistreat 389.5
work evil 1000.6
mollify relieve 120.5
pacify 465.7
calm 670.7
soften 1047.6
mollifying
n softening 1047.5
adj pacificatory 465.12
tranquilizing 670.15
softening 1047.16
mollycoddle
n weakling 16.6
effeminate male 77.11
spoiled child 427.4
v indulge 427.6
molt shed 6.10
waste 473.5
molten melted 1020.31
liquefied 1064.6
mom 560.12
moment prestige 417.4
period 824.1
second 824.2
short time 828.3
instant 830.3
influence 894.1
impulse 902.1
importance 997.1
momentary
transient 828.7
instantaneous 830.4
momently 850.8
moment of truth
period 824.1
crucial moment 843.5
unreliability 971.6
urgency 997.4
momentous
authoritative 417.15
eventful 831.10
influential 894.13
important 997.17
momentum
motion 172.1
course 172.2
impulse 902.1
monad atom 258.8
something 763.3
one 872.3
matter 1052.2

monarch 575.8
monarchic
sovereign 417.17
governmental 612.17
monarchism
radicalism 611.4
government 612.8
monarchist 611.9
monarchy
government 612.4
absolutism 612.9
monasterial
monastic 698.14
claustral 703.16
monastery 703.6
monastic
n celibate 565.2
religious 699.16
adj celibate 565.6
monachal 698.14
claustral 703.16
monasticism
celibacy 565.1
asceticism 667.1
monachism 698.4
monaural system 50.11
monde 578.6
monetary unit 728.1
money wealth 618.1
currency 728.1
moneybags 618.7
money changer
banker 729.11
broker 730.9
money-hungry 100.27
money in hand 728.18
money in the bank 472.6
money-laundering 673.2
moneylender
lender 620.3
banker 729.11
money-mad 100.27
moneymaking
n acquisition 472.1
adj gainful 472.16
paying 624.21
occupied 724.15
moneyman 729.9
money market 728.16
money order 728.11
money-raising 621.1
money-saving 635.6
monger 730.2
mongolism 922.9
mongoloid 922.22
Mongoloid 312.2
mongoloid idiot
924.8
mongrel
n cur 311.19
beast 660.6
hybrid 797.8
adj hybrid 797.15
mongrelization 797.4
mongrelize 797.13
moniker 527.3
monition
dissuasion 379.1
warning 399.1
advice 422.1
tip 551.3

monitor
n warner 399.4
adviser 422.3
shackle 428.4
informant 551.5
teaching fellow 571.4
superintendent 574.2
examiner 938.17
radioman 1034.24
television technician 1035.13
output device 1042.9
v be taught 570.11
examine 938.24
check 1034.26
monitoring
vigilance 339.4
televising 1035.3
monitory
n advice 422.1
adj premonitory
133.16
dissuasive 379.5
warning 399.7
advisory 422.8
informative 551.18
monk
wild animal 311.23
celibate 565.2
religious 699.16
monkey
n temper 152.6
wild animal 311.23
imitator 336.4
dupe 358.1
laughingstock 508.7
cheater 759.22
v trifle 998.15
monkey business 356.5
monkeying 998.9
monkeyshines
buffoonery 489.5
prank 489.10
monkey with 214.7
monkhood 698.4
monkish
inornate 499.9
celibate 565.6
monastic 698.14
mono 50.11
monochrome
n color system 35.7
adj chromatic 35.16
pictorial 712.21
monocle 29.3
monocratic
authoritative 417.15
imperious 417.16
governmental 612.17
monody
dirge 115.6
harmony 708.3
monophony 708.21
monogamist 563.11
monogram
identification 517.11
signature 527.10
letter 546.1
monograph 556.1
monolith
monument 549.12
rock 1059.1

monolithic
uniform 781.5
simple 798.6
stony 1059.12
monologist 542.2
monologue
soliloquy 542.1
regularity 781.2
monomania
obsession 926.13
engrossment 983.3
monomaniac
n fanatic 926.18
adj obsessed 926.33
monopolist
n restrictionist 428.6
self-seeker 651.3
adj monopolistic 469.11
monopolize hog 469.6
appropriate 480.19
purchase 733.7
corner 737.26
engross 983.13
monopoly
restraint 428.1
monopolization 469.3
manipulation 737.20
monorail 179.14
monosyllable 526.1
monotheism 675.5
monotheist 675.16
monotheistic 675.25
monotone
n tone 50.2
regularity 781.2
series 812.2
repetitiousness 849.4
adj sounding 50.15
monotonous 849.15
monotonous
tedious 118.9
same 781.6
continuous 812.8
monotone 849.15
monotony tone 50.2
tedium 118.1
regularity 781.2
continuity 812.1
repetitiousness 849.4
monsieur 76.7
Monsignor 648.5
monsoon season 313.1
wet weather 316.4
monster
n frightener 127.9
beast 144.14
largeness 257.11
behemoth 257.14
fiend 593.6
violent person 671.9
monstrosity 870.6
eyesore 1015.4
adj large 247.7
huge 257.20
monstrosity
hugeness 257.7
deformity 265.3
abnormality 870.1
oddity 870.3
monster 870.6
eyesore 1015.4

monstrous
large 247.7
huge 257.20
deformed 265.12
wicked 654.16
base 661.12
savage 671.21
freakish 870.13
absurd 923.11
excessive 993.16
terrible 1000.9
unshapely 1015.8
montage picture 712.11
photograph 714.3
month 824.2
monthlies 12.9
monthlong 827.12
monthly
n periodical 555.1
adj recurrent 849.13
momentary 850.8
monument
tower 272.6
gravestone 309.17
figure 349.6
marker 517.10
monumental record 549.12
monumental
large 247.7
huge 257.20
high 272.14
sculptural 715.6
monumentalize 829.5
moo 60.2
mooch 440.15
moocher
nonworker 331.11
beggar 440.8
guest 585.6
mooching
n beggary 440.6
adj supplicatory 440.16
mood mode 530.11
plot 722.4
syllogism 935.6
humor 978.4
mood disorder 92.14
moody sullen 110.24
glum 112.25
capricious 364.5
inconstant 854.7
moolah 728.2
moon
n moment 824.2
changeableness 854.4
light source 1026.1
satellite 1072.11
v idle 331.12
muse 985.9
moonbeam 1025.11
moonfaced 257.18
mooning
n abstractedness 985.2
adj abstracted 985.11
moonless 1027.13
moonlight
n moonshine 1025.11
v distill 88.30
work 724.12
moonlighting 724.5
moon-shaped 279.11

moonshine
n liquor 88.14
bootleg liquor 88.18
humbug 354.14
bull 520.3
specious argument 936.3
moonlight 1025.11
v distill 88.30
deal illicitly 732.7
moonshiner
liquor dealer 88.19
racketeer 732.4
moonstruck 926.26
moor
n plain 236.1
highlands 237.1
plateau 237.3
marsh 243.1
v settle 159.17
anchor 182.15
land 186.8
bind 428.10
fasten 800.7
secure 855.8
mooring
establishment 159.7
anchor 180.16
landing 186.2
moose 311.5
moot
v propose 439.5
argue 935.16
adj litigious 598.21
theoretical 951.13
doubted 955.12
unproved 958.8
doubtful 971.17
moot point 938.10
mop
n head of hair 3.4
v wash 79.19
grimace 265.8
mope
n sourpuss 112.13
idler 331.8
v sulk 110.14
grieve 112.17
mopery 331.4
mopey
sullen 110.24
glum 112.25
unsociable 583.5
moping
sullen 110.24
glum 112.25
mop up wash 79.19
complete 407.6
moral
n warning 399.1
rule 419.2
lesson 568.7
maxim 974.1
adj ethical 636.6
dutiful 641.13
honest 644.13
virtuous 653.6
moral climate
ethics 636.1
climate 978.5
moral code 636.1

morale
cooperation 450.1
morality 636.3
virtue 653.1
mood 978.4
moral fiber
will power 359.4
virtue 653.1
moralistic
preceptive 419.4
advisory 422.8
ethical 636.6
morality lesson 568.7
morals 636.3
virtue 653.1
moralize 568.16
morals ethics 636.1
morality 636.3
moral support 901.1
moral turpitude
knavery 645.2
corruption 654.5
morass
marsh 243.1
complex 799.2
confusion 810.2
predicament 1013.4
moratorium
grace period 625.2
delay 846.2
morbid
unwholesome 85.55
diseased 85.60
terrible 127.30
curious 981.5
morbidity disease 85.1
unhealthiness 85.3
morbific 82.5
morceau scrap 248.3
treatise 556.1
mordancy
acrimony 17.5
pungency 68.1
causticity 144.8
vigor 544.3
mordant
n cauterant 1020.15
adj acrimonious 17.14
pungent 68.6
caustic 144.23
witty 489.15
vigorous 544.11
more
n plurality 883.1
adj additional 253.10
plural 883.7
adv increasingly 251.9
additionally 253.11
more or less
approximately 223.23
some 244.6
moreover 253.11
mores custom 373.1
culture 373.2
etiquette 580.3
climate 978.5
more than enough
n plenty 991.2
superabundance 993.2
satiety 994.1
adv superabundantly 993.24

morgue 309.9
moribund
unhealthy 85.54
dying 307.33
languid 331.20
Mormon
Latter-day Saint 675.22
adj Koranic 683.14
morn 314.1
morning
n noonday 314.5
morn 314.1
adj matin 314.6
adv constantly 847.7
Morning 314.2
moron 924.8
moronic
mentally deficient 922.22
foolish 923.8
morose
sullen 110.24
glum 112.25
unsociable 583.5
morpheme
grammar 262.6
sign 518.6
morphology 526.3
Morpheus 22.11
morphine 22.10
morphological
grammar 262.11
structural 266.6
linguistic 523.19
morphemic 526.21
morphology
form 262.6
structure 266.1
morphemics 526.3
grammar 530.1
Morse code 523.12
morsel bite 8.2
delicacy 10.8
scrap 248.3
piece 793.3
mortal
n person 312.5
adj perishable 307.34
deadly 308.23
human 312.13
transient 828.7
mortal blow 308.10
mortality
death rate 307.13
deadliness 308.9
humankind 312.1
humanness 312.8
transience 828.1
mortar
n launcher 462.21
instrument of conversion 858.10
building material 1054.2
v plaster 295.25
pull the trigger 459.22
mortar and pestle 1051.7
mortgage
n mortgage deed 438.4
v pledge 438.10
mortgage company 620.4
mortgaged 623.8

mortgagee
  warrantee 438.7
  lender 620.3
  creditor 622.4
mortgaging 621.1
mortgagor
  guarantor 438.6
  debtor 623.4
mortician 309.8
mortification
  gangrene 85.40
  chagrin 96.4
  embarrassment 98.6
  humiliation 137.2
  penance 658.3
  asceticism 667.1
mortified
  diseased 85.60
  distressed 96.22
  humiliated 137.14
  decayed 393.40
mortify chagrin 96.15
  embarrass 98.13
  humiliate 137.4
  decay 393.22
mortifying
  embarrassing 98.21
  humiliating 137.15
mortise interact 777.6
  hook 800.8
mortuary
  n morgue 309.9
  adj deathly 307.29
  funereal 309.22
mosaic
  n check 47.4
  picture 712.11
  adj checked 47.14
Mosaic 683.11
mosey 175.6
Moslem
  n Muslim 675.23
  adj Muslim 675.31
Moslemism 675.13
mosque 703.2
mosquito 311.38
moss marsh 243.1
  plant 310.4
mossback
  back number 842.8
  conservative 853.4
mossbacked 303.18
mossy 310.42
most
  n supremacy 249.3
  major part 792.6
  majority 883.2
  adj extreme 247.13
  superlative 249.13
  majority 883.9
  adv extremely 247.22
the most 249.16
most likely 968.8
mot witticism 489.7
  maxim 974.1
mote modicum 248.2
  minute 258.7
  lightness 298.2
  stronghold 460.6
  intruder 774.2
motel 228.16

moth-eaten trite 117.9
  stricken in years 303.18
  blighted 393.42
  stale 842.14
mother
  n parent 559.3
  genetrix 560.11
  bad person 660.5
  author 886.4
  producer 892.7
  v procreate 78.8
  foster 449.16
  engender 818.14
  care for 1008.19
  adj native 226.5
Mother 648.5
Mother Earth 1072.10
mother figure 92.31
motherhood
  blood relationship
    559.1
  maternity 560.3
mothering 449.3
mother-in-law 564.2
motherland 232.2
motherless
  helpless 19.18
  bereaved 307.35
  forlorn 584.12
mother lode 618.4
Mother Nature 677.8
mother-of-pearl
  n variegation 47.6
  iridescence 1025.18
  adj soft-colored 35.22
  iridescent 47.10
mother superior
  mistress 575.2
  nun 699.18
mother tongue 523.3
motif edging 211.7
  ornamental motif 498.7
  passage 708.24
  plot 722.4
  topic 937.1
motile moving 172.7
  changeable 854.6
motility
  mobility 172.3
  changeableness 854.1
motion
  n exercise 84.2
  movement 172.1
  travel 177.1
  activity 330.1
  proposal 439.2
  gesture 517.14
  bill 613.9
  baseball team 745.2
  process 889.2
  trend 896.2
  mechanism 1040.4
  v gesture 517.21
motionless
  unmoving 173.13
  passive 329.6
  inactive 331.17
motion picture
  cinematography 706.1
  pictures 714.8
motion sickness 85.30

motivate
  set in motion 172.6
  move 375.12
  induce 886.11
  impel 902.11
motivated
  moved 375.30
  teachable 570.18
motivating force 17.6
motivation
  motion 172.1
  reason 375.1
  moving 375.2
  teachableness
    570.5
motivational
  moving 172.7
  motivating 375.25
motive
  n reason 375.1
  intention 380.1
  passage 708.24
  topic 937.1
  adj moving 172.7
  motivating 375.25
  impelling 902.23
  propulsive 904.14
motive power
  energizer 17.6
  mobility 172.3
  impulse 902.1
  pushing 904.1
  machinery 1040.3
motivity 172.3
mot juste 533.1
motley
  n costume 5.9
  comedy 704.6
  buffoon 707.10
  v variegate 47.7
  adj chromatic 35.16
  variegated 47.9
  mottled 47.12
  different 780.7
  mixed 797.14
  nonuniform 782.3
motor
  n automobile 179.9
  instrument of conversion
    858.10
  machinery 1040.3
  v ride 177.33
  adj moving 172.7
motorboat
  n powerboat 180.4
  v navigate 182.13
motorcade 812.3
motorcar 179.9
motorcycle
  n cycle 179.8
  v ride 177.33
motorcyclist 178.11
motor-driven 1040.14
motoring 177.6
motor inn 228.16
motorist 178.10
motorize 1040.13
motor launch 180.4
motorman 178.12
motor oil 1056.4
motor vehicle 179.9

mottle
  n spottiness 47.3
  mark 517.5
  v variegate 47.7
  mark 517.19
mottled 47.12
motto heraldry 647.2
  caption 937.2
  maxim 974.1
  slogan 974.4
moue scowl 110.9
  grimace 265.4
mound
  n hill 237.4
  monument 549.12
  baseball 745.1
  pile 770.10
  barrier 1012.5
  v pile 770.19
mount
  n ascent 193.1
  mountain 237.6
  horse 311.10
  hunter 311.13
  jockey 757.2
  frame 901.10
  v copulate 75.21
  move 172.5
  go on horseback
    177.34
  soar 184.39
  ascend 193.8
  climb 193.11
  get on 193.12
  rise 200.8
  increase 251.6
  tower 272.10
  grow 272.12
  dramatize 704.28
  give a lift 912.7
mountain mount 237.6
  quantity 247.3
  plateau 272.4
  bulge 283.3
mountain climber 193.6
mountain dew 88.18
mountaineer
  traveler 178.1
  climber 193.6
  wilderness settler 227.10
mountain lion 311.22
mountain man 227.10
mountainous
  hilly 237.8
  large 247.7
  huge 257.20
  high 272.18
mountain range
  mountain 237.6
  plateau 272.4
mountaintop
  summit 198.2
  mountain 237.6
mountebank
  impostor 357.6
  entertainer 707.1
mountebankery 354.7
mounted policeman
  rider 178.8
  policeman 1008.15
Mounties 1008.17

mounting
 n course 172.2
 ascent 193.1
 increase 251.1
 production 704.13
 frame 901.10
 adj flowing 172.8
 ascending 193.14
 high 272.14
Mount Olympus 681.9
mount up to
 cost 630.13
 total 792.8
mourn distress 98.14
 grieve 112.17
 lament 115.10
mourner
 lamenter 115.8
 griever 309.7
mournful
 distressing 98.20
 sorrowful 112.26
 plaintive 115.19
 funereal 309.22
mourning
 n lamentation 115.1
 weeds 115.7
 adj lamenting 115.18
mouse woman 77.6
 trauma 85.38
 shrinking violet 139.6
 runt 258.4
 coward 491.5
 input device 1042.4
mouse-colored 39.4
mouser 311.21
mousetrap trap 356.12
 rocket launcher 1074.10
mousse sweets 10.40
 foam 320.2
mousy gray 39.4
 silent 51.10
 fearful 127.23
 shy 139.12
 rodent 311.45
 cowardly 491.10
mouth
 n digestive system 2.18
 eater 8.16
 inlet 242.1
 maw 292.4
 v chew 8.27
 lick 73.9
 grimace 265.8
 be hypocritical 354.23
 speak 524.19
 mumble 525.9
 declaim 543.10
mouthful bite 8.2
 high-sounding words 545.3
 full measure 794.3
mouthing
 hypocrisy 354.6
 mumbling 525.4
 lip service 693.2
mouth organ 711.10
mouthpiece
 telephone 347.4
 mediator 466.3
 informant 551.5
 spokesman 576.5

 lawyer 597.3
 wind instrument 711.6
 boxing 754.1
mouthwash
 cleanser 79.17
 dentifrice 86.22
mouth-watering
 n saliva 13.3
 adj appetizing 63.10
 desirable 100.30
 alluring 377.8
mouthy 545.9
movable
 transferable 176.18
 changeable 854.6
 influenceable 894.15
movable feast 20.4
movables
 furniture 229.1
 belongings 471.2
move
 n act 328.3
 attempt 403.2
 stratagem 415.3
 cheating 759.13
 process 889.2
 expedient 995.2
 v affect 93.14
 excite 105.12
 touch 145.5
 settle 159.17
 progress 162.2
 budge 172.5
 set in motion 172.6
 remove 176.11
 travel 177.18
 behave 321.4
 act 328.4
 motivate 375.12
 admonish 422.6
 propose 439.5
 sell 734.8
 influence 894.7
 impel 902.11
 push 904.9
move away
 recede 168.2
 depart 188.6
move back 163.6
moved
 affected 93.23
 excited 105.20
 motivated 375.30
move in
 settle 159.17
 inhabit 225.7
 take possession 472.10
 gain influence 894.12
move into
 inhabit 225.7
 undertake 404.3
movement
 defecation 12.2
 feces 12.4
 exercise 84.2
 motion 172.1
 moving 176.4
 travel 177.1
 behavior 321.1
 act 328.3
 activity 330.1

 operation 458.5
 gesture 517.14
 front 609.33
 passage 708.24
 rhythm 709.22
 style 712.8
 meter 720.7
 plot 722.4
 company 770.3
 cause 886.9
 trend 896.2
 mechanism 1040.4
move out 188.6
mover wanderer 178.2
 prompter 375.10
 doer 726.1
 cheater 759.22
 author 886.4
 producer 892.7
mover and shaker 375.1
movie
 n motion pictures 706.1
 adj motion-picture
  706.9
moviegoer
 playgoer 704.27
 attender 221.5
movie star 707.4
moving
 n motion 172.1
 removal 176.4
 travel 177.1
 motivation 375.2
 adj affecting 93.22
 distressing 98.20
 exciting 105.30
 pitiful 145.8
 progressive 162.6
 stirring 172.7
 traveling 177.36
 motivating 375.25
 lofty 544.14
 impelling 902.23
moving spirit
 inspiration 375.9
 prompter 375.10
moving staircase 912.4
mow
 n scowl 110.9
 grimace 265.4
 garner 386.7
 pile 770.10
 v grimace 265.8
 shorten 268.6
 smooth 287.5
 harvest 1069.19
mow down raze 395.19
 fell 913.5
moxie energy 17.3
 power 18.1
 liveliness 330.2
 pluck 359.3
 skill 413.1
 fearlessness 492.4
MP legislator 610.3
 policeman 1008.15
 police 1008.17
Mr common man 606.5
 man 76.7
Mr Universe 15.6
Mrs 77.9

Mrs Grundy
 fussbudget 495.7
 social convention 579.1
 conventionalist 579.3
 conformist 867.2
Ms 77.9
MS 547.10
much
 n quantity 247.3
 plenty 991.2
 adj many 247.8
 plentiful 991.7
 adv greatly 247.15
much ado about nothing
 overreaction 355.2
 triviality 998.3
mucilage
 adhesive 803.4
 lubricant 1056.2
 semiliquid 1062.5
muck
 n filth 80.7
 slime 80.8
 fertilizer 890.4
 mud 1062.8
 v dirty 80.15
muck around 998.15
mucked up
 spoiled 393.29
 complex 799.4
 confused 810.16
muckrake 512.10
muckraker
 disparager 512.6
 critic 946.7
muckraking
 defamation 512.2
 smear campaign 609.14
muck up dirty 80.15
 spoil 393.11
 complicate 799.3
 confuse 811.3
 make a boner 975.15
mucky filthy 80.23
 slimy 1062.14
mucous 1062.13
mucous membrane 2.6
mucus
 digestive secretion 13.2
 filth 80.7
 lubricant 1056.2
 semiliquid 1062.5
mud dirt 80.6
 marsh 243.1
 muck 1062.8
muddle
 n formlessness 263.1
 fiasco 410.6
 disorder 810.2
 confusion 985.3
 v deform 263.3
 bungle 414.11
 complicate 799.3
 disorder 810.9
 disarrange 811.3
 confound 945.3
 perplex 971.13
 make uncertain 971.15
 confuse 985.7
muddled
 intoxicated 88.31

confused 810.16
muddleheaded 922.18
in a dilemma 971.25
in a muddle 985.13
muddlehead 924.4
muddleheaded
fuddlebrained 922.18
muddled 985.13
muddle through
make one's way 162.4
manage 409.12
muddy
v dirty 80.15
make uncertain 971.15
adj colorless 36.7
dingy 38.11
dirty 80.22
marshy 243.3
obscure 522.15
slimy 1062.14
mud flat 243.1
mudhole pothole 284.3
mud puddle 1062.9
mudlark 178.3
mudpack 1016.12
mud puddle 1062.9
mudslinger 512.6
mudslinging
defamation 512.2
smear campaign 609.14
muff
n bungle 414.5
bungler 414.9
goof 975.6
v bungle 414.11
muffin 10.31
muffle
n silencer 51.4
nose 283.8
v proof 15.14
silence 51.8
mute 51.9
cover 295.19
cover up 345.8
muffled muted 52.17
covered 295.31
latent 519.5
muffled tone 52.2
muffler 51.4
muffle up clothe 5.39
cover up 345.8
mufti civilian dress 5.8
disarmament 465.6
judge 596.3
clergy 699.12
mug
n face 216.4
mouth 292.4
dupe 358.2
laughingstock 508.7
ruffian 593.4
photograph 714.3
v grimace 265.8
attack 459.15
rob 482.16
rage 671.11
overact 704.31
photograph 714.14
mugger
assailant 459.12
robber 483.5

nerd 572.10
ruffian 593.4
violent person 671.9
mugging attack 459.1
theft 482.3
muggy sultry 1019.28
moist 1065.15
mug shot 714.3
mugwump
vacillator 362.5
timeserver 363.4
free agent 430.12
neutral 467.4
nonpartisan 609.28
mugwumpery
irresolution 362.1
neutrality 467.1
nonpartisanism 609.26
Muhammad 684.4
Muhammadan
n Muslim 675.23
adj Muslim 675.31
Muhammadanism 675.13
mulatto 797.8
mulch 1069.17
mulct
n fine 603.3
v cheat 356.18
fine 603.5
mule
beast of burden 176.8
spinner 271.5
ass 311.16
obstinate person 361.6
smuggler 732.5
hybrid 797.8
mulish ungulate 311.46
obstinate 361.8
mull
n point of land 283.9
v sweeten 66.3
heat 1020.17
mullion 273.4
mull over 931.13
multicolor
n variegation 47.1
adj variegated 47.9
multifaceted
sided 218.7
mixed 797.14
multifarious
different 780.7
multiform 783.3
complex 799.4
numerous 884.6
multifold
multiform 783.3
multiple 883.8
numerous 884.6
multiform 783.3
multiformity
diversity 783.1
multifariousness 783.1
multilateral
sided 218.7
multiangular 278.11
multilingual 523.16
multimedia 1042.18
multimillionaire 618.7
multinational 797.14
multiparous 78.15

multipartite 802.20
multiphase 783.3
multiple
n multiplication 883.4
adj multiform 783.3
multiplied 883.8
numerous 884.6
multiplication
procreation 78.2
multiplying 883.4
proliferation 890.2
notation 1017.2
multiplication table 883.4
multiplicity
multiformity 783.1
numerousness 884.1
multiplied
increased 251.7
multiple 883.8
multiplier 883.4
multiply procreate 78.8
grow 251.6
proliferate 883.6
teem with 884.5
produce 890.7
calculate 1017.18
multiplying
n multiplication 883.4
adj increasing 251.8
multiracial
nonuniform 782.3
mixed 797.14
multitude
quantity 247.3
assembly 770.4
throng 884.3
multitudinous
much 247.8
numerous 884.6
mum
n silence 51.1
adj mute 51.12
taciturn 344.9
interj silence! 51.14
mumble
n murmur 52.4
mumbling 525.4
v chew 8.27
murmur 52.10
speak 524.25
mutter 525.9
mumbling
n murmur 52.4
muttering 525.4
adj murmuring 52.18
mumbo jumbo
juggling 356.5
obscurity 522.3
jargon 523.9
occultism 689.1
incantation 691.4
charm 691.5
nonsense 520.2
Mumbo Jumbo 680.9
mummer
masquerader 357.7
entertainer 707.1
actor 707.2
mummery
hypocrisy 354.6
cover 356.11

ceremony 580.4
sanctimony 693.1
acting 704.8
mummification
corpse 307.16
embalmment 309.3
preserving 397.3
drying 1066.3
mummify
lay out 309.21
embalm 397.10
dry 1066.6
mummy corpse 307.16
mother 560.12
dryness 1066.2
mumps sulks 110.10
blues 112.6
munch
n bite 8.2
v chew 8.27
munching 8.1
mundane
unsacred 686.3
secularist 695.16
prosaic 721.5
unimaginative 987.5
municipal building 230.5
municipality
town 230.1
bureau 594.4
munificence 485.1
munificent 485.4
munition
n equipment 385.4
v equip 385.8
munitions
equipment 385.4
store 386.1
arms 462.1
mural
n picture 712.11
adj partitioned 213.11
murder
n homicide 308.2
v commit murder 308.16
bungle 414.11
murderer 308.11
murderous
cruel 144.26
slaughterous 308.24
savage 671.21
murderous insanity 926.7
murk
n gloom 112.7
obscurity 522.3
darkishness 1027.2
v blacken 38.7
darken 1027.9
adj darkish 1027.15
murky dingy 38.11
gloomy 112.24
obscure 522.15
vague 971.19
stained 1004.10
darkish 1027.15
murmur
n murmuring 52.4
lament 115.3
v mutter 52.10
complain 115.15
sigh 318.21

speak 524.25
mumble 525.9
murmurer 108.3
murmuring
  n murmur 52.4
  complaint 115.4
  mumbling 525.4
  adj murmurous 52.18
  discontented 108.7
muscle
  n the muscles 2.3
  muscularity 15.2
  exertion 725.1
  v exert strength 15.12
  thrust 902.12
  adj skeleton 2.26
muscle-bound
  firm 425.7
  able-bodied 15.16
muscle in 214.5
muscle man
  strong man 15.6
  hulk 15.7
  ruffian 593.4
  violent person 671.10
muscular skeleton 2.26
  able-bodied 15.16
muscularity 15.2
musculature
  the muscles 2.3
  muscularity 15.2
muse
  n inspiration 375.9
  abstractedness 985.2
  creative thought 986.2
  v remark 524.24
  consider 931.12
  moon 985.9
Muse
  the Muses 720.10
  genius 920.8
museum gallery 386.9
  preserve 397.7
  collection 770.11
museum piece
  work of art 712.10
  oddity 870.5
mush
  n sentimentality 93.8
  face 216.4
  mouth 292.4
  pulp 1063.2
  v march 177.30
mushroom
  n drugs 87.19
  plant 310.4
  v grow 14.2
  expand 259.7
  grow round 282.7
mushy
  wishy-washy 16.17
  sentimental 93.21
  pulpy 1063.6
music
  harmonious sound 708.1
  score 708.28
  harmonics 709.1
musical
  n musical theater 708.34
  adj musically inclined 708.47
  melodious 708.48

rhyming 720.17
musical comedy 708.34
musicality
  melody 708.2
  musicianship 708.31
  harmonics 709.1
music box 711.15
music director 710.17
music festival 708.32
music hall hall 197.4
  theater 704.14
musician
  entertainer 707.1
  music maker 710.1
  musico 710.1
musicianship 708.31
music lover 710.21
music maker 710.1
musicologist 710.20
musicology 709.1
music roll score 708.28
  keyboard instrument 711.12
music school 567.7
musing
  n consideration 931.2
  thoughtfulness 931.3
  abstractedness 985.2
  dreaminess 986.8
  adj cognitive 931.21
  abstracted 985.11
musk 70.2
musketeer
  infantryman 461.9
  shooter 904.8
musketry
  gunfire 459.8
  arms 462.1
  ballistics 462.3
  throwing 904.2
Muslim
  n Muhammadan 675.23
  adj Islamic 675.31
Muslimism 675.13
Muslim rulers 608.7
muss 811.2
mussed up 810.14
mussy 810.15
must
  n fetidness 71.2
  wine 88.17
  duty 641.1
  requirement 963.2
  blight 1001.2
  v be necessary 963.10
  adj in heat 75.28
  mandatory 420.12
  obligatory 641.15
mustache 3.11
mustang 311.10
mustard plaster 86.33
muster
  n call to arms 458.8
  enlistment 615.7
  assemblage 770.1
  roll 871.6
  v avail oneself of 387.14
  summon 420.11
  call to arms 458.19
  enlist 615.17
  come together 770.16
  assemble 770.18

mustering out 465.6
muster roll 871.6
muster up
  prompt 375.13
  summon 420.11
must have 963.9
musty malodorous 71.5
  in heat 75.28
  trite 117.9
  blighted 393.42
  stale 842.14
mutability
  death rate 307.13
  nonuniformity 782.1
  transience 828.1
  changeableness 854.1
mutable mortal 307.34
  irresolute 362.9
  nonuniform 782.3
  transient 828.7
  changeable 854.6
mutant
  n violent person 671.9
  transformation 852.3
  adj savage 671.21
  changed 852.10
mutate diversify 782.2
  be changed 852.6
  change 852.7
mutation
  phonetics 524.13
  transformation 852.3
mute
  n dummy 51.3
  silencer 51.4
  mourner 309.7
  speech sound 524.12
  supporting actor 707.7
  music 711.22
  v muffle 51.9
  adj mum 51.12
  taciturn 344.9
  stammering 525.13
  inanimate 1055.5
muted muffled 52.17
  phonetic 524.30
mutilate excise 255.10
  deform 265.7
  injure 393.13
  tear apart 802.14
mutilated
  deformed 265.12
  impaired 393.27
  garbled 795.5
mutilation
  trauma 85.38
  excision 255.3
  deformity 265.3
  impairment 393.1
  severance 802.2
mutineer
  n rebel 327.5
  anarchist 418.3
  v revolt 327.7
mutinous
  unwilling 325.5
  rebellious 327.11
  lawless 418.5
mutiny
  n revolt 327.4
  lawlessness 418.1

  v revolt 327.7
mutter
  n murmur 52.4
  lament 115.3
  mumbling 525.4
  v murmur 52.10
  complain 115.15
  sigh 318.21
  speak 524.25
  mumble 525.9
mutterer 108.3
muttering
  n murmur 52.4
  mumbling 525.4
  adj murmuring 52.18
  discontented 108.7
mutton mouton 10.16
  sheep 311.7
muttonhead 924.4
muttonheaded 922.17
mutual
  cooperative 450.5
  communal 476.9
  accompanying 769.9
  correlative 777.11
  interchangeable 863.5
mutual attraction
  inclination 100.3
  relation 775.1
  attraction 907.1
mutual company 1008.4
mutual friend 588.1
mutual fund 737.16
mutuality
  cooperation 450.1
  accord 455.1
  correlation 777.1
  interchange 863.1
mutual understanding
  unanimity 332.5
  understanding 788.2
muzzle
  n silencer 51.4
  nose 283.8
  mouth 292.4
  shackle 428.4
  v disable 19.10
  silence 51.8
muzzy drunk 88.33
  inarticulate 525.12
  muddleheaded 922.18
  muddled 985.13
myopia 28.3
myopic
  poor-sighted 28.11
  undiscerning 922.14
  unwise 923.10
myriad
  n thousand 882.10
  plenty 991.2
  adj numerous 884.6
myrmidon
  retainer 577.1
  employee 577.3
  follower 616.8
myrrh 70.2
myself 865.5
mysterious
  awesome 122.11
  secret 345.11
  concealed 346.11

inexplicable 522.18
ambiguous 539.4
occult 689.23
supernatural 870.15
unknown 930.17
bewildering 971.27
mystery
wonderfulness 122.3
secret 345.5
inexplicability 522.6
enigma 522.8
occultism 689.1
rite 701.3
vocation 724.6
supernaturalism 870.7
the unknown 930.7
bewilderment 971.3
mystic
n occultist 689.11
adj latent 519.5
inexplicable 522.18
epiphanic 683.13
occult 689.23
mystical
inexplicable 522.18
epiphanic 683.13
occult 689.23
mysticism
revelation 683.10
occultism 689.1
mystification
concealment 346.1
obscurity 522.3
misteaching 569.1
occultism 689.1
sophistry 936.1
mystified
in a dilemma 971.25
at an impasse 1013.24
mystify
make unintelligible 522.12
misteach 569.3
quibble 936.9
perplex 971.13
mystifying
misteaching 569.6
bewildering 971.27
mystique
illustriousness 662.6
cult 675.2
opinion 953.6
myth
fabrication 354.10
tradition 842.2
figment of the imagination
    986.5
mythical
fabricated 354.29
distinguished 662.16
mythic 678.15
fictional 722.7
extraordinary 870.14
fictitious 986.21
mythical monsters 127.9
mythicize 722.6
mythmaker
narrator 722.5
imaginer 986.12
mythological
mythic 678.15
fictional 722.7

legendary 842.12
fictitious 986.21
mythology
mythicism 678.14
tradition 842.2
mythomania 354.8
nab arrest 429.16
acquire 472.9
capture 480.18
nabbing 480.2
nabob governor 575.13
rich man 618.7
personage 997.8
nacre variegation 47.6
iridescence 1025.18
nacré 47.10
nacreous
soft-colored 35.22
variegated 47.10
iridescent 1025.37
nada 762.2
nadir bottom 199.1
boundary 211.3
base 274.4
nag
n tormentor 96.10
horse 311.10
oatburner 311.12
jockey 757.2
v annoy 96.13
urge 375.14
importune 440.12
niggle 510.16
remind 989.20
nagging
n importunity 440.3
criticism 510.4
adj peevish 110.22
importunate 440.18
critical 510.23
unforgettable 989.26
naiad 678.10
naïf dupe 358.1
simple soul 416.3
nail acquire 472.9
seize 480.14
catch 480.17
punish 604.15
hook 800.8
recognize 989.12
nail down
stabilize 855.7
prove 957.10
make sure 970.11
naive immature 301.10
artless 416.5
natural 499.7
foolable 923.12
ignorant 930.12
trusting 953.22
gullible 954.9
naïveté
artlessness 416.1
naturalness 499.2
gullibility 954.2
naked nude 6.14
visible 31.6
open 292.17
manifest 348.10
unadorned 499.8
unmixed 798.7

exposed 1006.15
naked eye organ 2.9
eye 27.9
field of view 31.3
namby-pamby
n weakling 16.6
sentimentality 93.8
adj frail 16.14
sentimental 93.21
overnice 500.18
mediocre 1005.7
name
n appellation 527.3
repute 662.1
celebrity 662.9
personage 997.8
v nominate 371.19
designate 517.18
denominate 527.11
appoint 615.11
specify 865.11
cite 957.13
number 1017.17
adj important 997.17
name-calling 512.2
named chosen 371.26
called 527.14
former 814.5
name-dropper
snob 141.7
upstart 606.7
self-seeker 651.3
nameless
anonymous 528.3
unrenowned 661.14
name of the game 518.1
namesake 527.3
naming
n nomination 371.8
indication 517.3
calling 527.2
appointment 615.2
adj indicative 517.23
nanny
female animal 77.10
goat 311.8
nurse 1008.8
nap
n snooze 22.3
texture 294.1
v sleep 22.13
napery material 4.1
dry goods 735.3
napkin 8.13
nappies 5.19
napping sleepy 22.21
unaware 930.13
unalert 984.8
abstracted 985.11
nappy feathery 3.27
intoxicated 88.31
pily 294.7
narc detective 576.10
policeman 1008.15
narcissism
perversion 75.11
vanity 140.1
selfishness 651.1
narcissist
sexual pervert 75.16
egotist 140.5

self-seeker 651.3
narcissistic vain 140.8
egotistic 140.10
selfish 651.5
Narcissus egotist 140.5
beauty 1016.10
narcosis stupor 22.6
insensibility 25.1
deadness 94.2
apathy 94.4
narcotic
n anesthetic 25.3
drug 87.3
adj sleep-inducing 22.23
deadening 25.9
sedative 86.45
palliative 670.16
narcotics addict 87.21
narcotics agent 576.10
narcotics pusher 732.4
narcotics traffic 732.1
narcotize
put to sleep 22.20
deaden 25.4
numb 94.8
relieve 120.5
moderate 670.6
narcotized
sleepy 22.21
insensible 25.6
unconscious 25.8
intoxicated 87.23
unfeeling 94.9
nares
olfactory organ 69.5
nose 283.8
narrate tell 719.6
fabricate 722.6
narration
description 349.2
story 719.3
fiction 722.1
narrative 722.2
fabrication 722.3
narrative
n story 719.3
fiction 722.1
narration 722.2
fabrication 722.3
adj narrational 719.8
poetic 720.15
fictional 722.8
narrator 722.5
narrow
n inlet 242.1
narrow place 270.3
v limit 210.5
contract 260.7
constrict 270.11
restrict 428.9
simplify 798.4
specialize 866.4
qualify 959.3
adj limited 210.7
slender 270.14
meticulous 339.12
stingy 484.9
prudish 500.19
phonetic 524.30
poor 619.7
exclusive 773.9

narrow-minded 980.10
  meager 992.10
narrow down 159.11
narrow escape 369.2
narrow-gauge 270.14
narrowing
  n contraction 260.1
  tapering 270.2
  exclusion 773.1
  simplification 798.2
  adj restrictive 428.12
narrow margin 780.2
narrow-mindedness
  small-mindedness 980.1
  narrowness 980.1
narrows inlet 242.1
  narrow place 270.3
narrow the gap
  approach 167.3
  converge 169.2
nasal
  n speech sound 524.12
  adj respiratory 2.32
  phonetic 524.30
  inarticulate 525.12
nasalization 525.1
nasalize 525.10
nascency birth 1.1
  origin 818.4
nascent 818.15
nasty
  v defile 80.17
  adj unpleasant 64.7
  filthy 80.23
  offensive 98.18
  malicious 144.20
  ill-bred 505.6
  obscene 666.9
  terrible 1000.9
nasty crack 489.7
nasty look 510.8
natal native 226.5
  beginning 818.15
nation population 227.1
  country 232.1
  humankind 312.1
  race 559.4
the nation 606.1
national
  n citizen 227.4
  adj public 312.16
  racial 559.7
  populational 606.8
  universal 864.14
national anthem 458.12
national assembly 613.1
national debt 623.1
national defense 460.2
national emergency 458.10
National Guard 461.24
nationalism
  nationhood 232.6
  patriotism 591.2
  foreign policy 609.5
nationalist 591.3
nationality
  nativeness 226.1
  country 232.1
  nationhood 232.6
  humankind 312.1
  patriotism 591.2

nationalization
  naturalization 226.3
  communization 476.3
  attachment 480.5
  socialism 611.6
nationalize
  communize 476.7
  attach 480.20
  politicize 611.16
national park 397.7
native
  n dweller 227.2
  indigene 227.3
  adj indigenous 226.5
  undeveloped 406.13
  natural 416.6
  plain 499.7
  innate 767.8
Native American 312.3
native environment 228.18
native land 232.2
native language 523.3
nativity birth 1.1
  nativeness 226.1
  origin 818.4
  astrology 1072.20
NATO 437.2
natter
  n chatter 540.3
  v speak 524.20
  chatter 540.5
natty chic 578.13
  tidy 807.8
natural
  n sure success 409.2
  talented person 413.12
  note 709.14
  blackjack 759.11
  oddity 870.4
  idiot 924.8
  adj typical 349.15
  native 406.13
  artless 416.6
  plain 499.7
  elegant 533.6
  plain-speaking 535.3
  related 559.6
  informal 581.3
  innate 767.8
  lifelike 784.16
  normal 869.8
  instinctive 934.6
  genuine 973.15
natural history 1068.3
naturalism
  naturalness 416.2
  normality 869.1
  genuineness 973.7
  materialism 1052.6
naturalist
  n materialist 1052.7
  biologist 1068.2
  adj materialist 1052.12
naturalistic
  descriptive 349.14
  typical 349.15
  normal 869.8
  genuine 973.15
  materialist 1052.12
naturalization
  naturalized citizenship 226.3

  habituation 373.7
  conversion 858.1
naturalize
  grant citizenship 226.4
  accustom 373.9
  convert 858.11
naturalized
  adopted 226.6
  accustomed 373.15
  converted 858.19
naturalized citizen 227.4
natural law 869.4
natural resource 1054.1
natural right 642.1
natural science
  science 928.10
  physics 1018.1
natural selection 861.3
natural state 406.3
natural world 1052.2
nature
  naturalness 406.3
  unaffectedness 416.2
  character 767.4
  kind 809.3
  characteristic 865.4
  disposition 978.3
  matter 1052.2
  universe 1072.1
Nature 677.8
naturist 6.3
naturistic naked 6.14
  normal 869.8
naught 762.2
naughty
  misbehaving 322.5
  disobedient 327.8
  wicked 654.16
naughty word 526.6
nausea symptom 85.9
  nauseation 85.30
  unpleasure 96.1
  hostility 99.2
  vomiting 909.8
nauseant
  n nastiness 64.3
  cleanser 79.17
  emetic 86.18
  adj nasty 64.7
nauseate disgust 64.4
  offend 98.11
nauseated
  nauseous 85.57
  pleasureless 96.20
nauseating nasty 64.7
  filthy 80.23
  offensive 98.18
nauseous nasty 64.7
  nauseated 85.57
  pleasureless 96.20
nautical
  marine 182.57
  oceanic 240.9
naval 182.57
naval academy 567.6
naval cadet 183.4
naval officer
  ship's officer 183.7
  fleet admiral 575.20
naval vessel 180.6
navar navigation 184.6

  airborne radar 1036.2
nave center 208.2
  church 703.9
  axle 915.5
navel 208.2
navigate locate 159.11
  journey 177.21
  sail 182.13
  pilot 182.14
  fly 184.36
navigation
  guidance 159.3
  topography 159.8
  direction 161.1
  water travel 182.1
  aviation 184.6
  bearing 573.1
navigational
  locational 159.19
  nautical 182.57
navigator
  mariner 183.1
  hand 183.6
  ship's officer 183.7
  crew 185.4
  guide 574.7
navvy
  excavator 284.10
  worker 726.2
navy
  chewing tobacco 89.7
  ships 180.10
  branch 461.21
  naval forces 461.27
navy man 183.4
nay
  n negation 335.1
  vote 371.6
  refusal 442.1
  side 935.14
  interj no 335.8
nay-sayer
  oppositionist 452.3
  misfit 789.4
  doubter 955.4
nay-saying
  n negation 335.1
  contrariety 779.1
  adj negative 335.5
  contrary 779.6
Nazarene 675.17
Nazism 612.8
NB 983.22
NCO 575.19
Neanderthal
  n barbarian 497.7
  adj unrefined 497.12
neap
  n tide 238.13
  low tide 274.2
  adj low 274.7
near
  v approach 167.3
  come near 223.7
  resemble 784.7
  come 839.6
  be imminent 840.2
  adj approaching 167.4
  left 220.4
  close 223.14
  narrow 270.14

stingy 484.9
familiar 587.19
approximate 775.8
approximating 784.14
imminent 840.3
adv nigh 223.20
nearly 223.22
prep at 159.27
nigh 223.24
nearby
  adj handy 223.15
  adv aside 218.10
  near 223.20
near death 85.56
Near East 231.6
nearer 223.18
nearest 223.19
nearing
  n approach 167.1
  adj approaching 167.4
  near 223.14
  future 839.8
  imminent 840.3
near-miss
  narrow escape 369.2
  crash 184.20
  meeting 223.4
  miss 410.4
nearsighted
  poor-sighted 28.11
  undiscerning 922.14
  narrow-minded 980.10
neat
  n cattle 311.6
  adj shipshape 180.20
  shapely 264.5
  skillful 413.22
  elegant 533.6
  plain-speaking 535.3
  chic 578.13
  unmixed 798.7
  tidy 807.8
  excellent 999.13
neaten 808.12
neat-fingered 413.23
neath 274.11
neb nose 283.8
  point 285.3
nebbish weakling 16.6
  thing of naught 764.2
  a nobody 998.7
nebula light 1025.15
  nebulosity 1072.7
nebulous cloudy 319.8
  obscure 522.15
  general 864.11
  celestial 1072.25
necessaries 963.2
necessary
  n latrine 12.10
  adj obligatory 424.11
  mandatory 641.15
  required 963.12
  requisite 963.13
  inevitable 963.15
  certain 970.13
necessitate
  require 424.5
  determine 886.12
  oblige 963.8
  destine 964.7

necessity
  compulsion 424.1
  indigence 619.2
  prerequisite 963.2
  necessariness 963.1
  requirement 963.2
  inevitability 963.7
  predetermination 964.1
  certainty 970.1
neck
  n fowl part 10.23
  contraction 260.1
  narrow place 270.3
  joint 800.4
  supporter 901.2
  v hang 604.18
neck-and-neck
  equal 790.7
  simultaneous 836.5
necking 562.2
necklace
  circle 280.3
  jewel 498.6
necktie 5.31
necrological
  funereal 309.22
  documentary 549.18
  historical 719.7
necrology
  obituary 307.14
  monument 549.12
  history 719.1
necromancer
  psychic 689.13
  sorcerer 690.5
necromancy
  spiritualism 689.5
  sorcery 690.1
necromantic
  sorcerous 690.14
  miraculous 870.16
necrophilia 75.11
necrophiliac 75.16
necrosis symptom 85.9
  gangrene 85.40
nectar delicacy 10.8
  sweetening 66.2
nectarous tasty 63.8
  sweet 66.4
née 1.4
need
  n desire 100.1
  indigence 619.2
  deficiency 795.2
  requirement 963.2
  want 992.4
  v be poor 619.5
  require 963.9
  be necessary 963.10
  want 992.7
  adv necessarily 963.16
needing
  desirous 100.21
  incomplete 795.4
  wanting 992.13
needle
  n energizer 17.6
  sound reproduction system
    50.11
  mountain 237.6
  point 285.3

thorn 285.5
  leaf 310.19
  pointer 517.4
  compass 574.9
  v annoy 96.13
  perforate 292.15
  goad 375.15
  banter 490.6
  sew 741.4
needless
  unnecessary 391.10
  superfluous 993.17
needlework 741.1
needleworker
  garmentmaker 5.34
  sewer 741.2
needling 375.5
need to 963.10
the needy 619.3
nefarious
  wicked 654.16
  base 661.12
  terrible 1000.9
negate abnegate 335.3
  abolish 395.13
  refuse 442.3
  contradict 451.6
  disagree 789.5
  neutralize 900.7
  disbelieve 955.5
  disprove 958.4
negating
  n negation 335.1
  adj neutralizing 900.9
negation
  disaffirmation 335.2
  negating 335.1
  extinction 395.6
  refusal 442.1
  opposition 451.1
  nonexistence 762.1
  disagreement 789.1
  disproof 958.1
negative
  n math terms 255.6
  negation 335.1
  refusal 442.1
  veto 444.2
  graphic arts 713.5
  film 714.10
  print 785.5
  mold 786.6
  v negate 335.3
  abolish 395.13
  refuse 442.3
  veto 444.5
  neutralize 900.7
  disprove 958.4
  adj pessimistic 125.16
  negatory 335.5
  unconsenting 442.6
  oppositional 451.8
  nonexistent 762.8
  contrary 779.6
  disagreeing 789.6
  numeric 1017.23
  electric 1032.35
  interj no 335.8
negativism
  defense mechanism 92.23
  pessimism 125.6

negation 335.1
  resistance 453.1
  hindrance 1012.1
negativist
  pessimist 125.7
  oppositionist 452.3
  hinderer 1012.8
neglect
  n negligence 340.1
  neglectfulness 340.1
  nonaccomplishment 408.1
  mismanagement 414.6
  nonobservance 435.1
  v slight 157.6
  overlook 340.6
  leave undone 408.2
  disregard 435.3
neglected
  unthanked 151.5
  unattended to 340.14
  needless 391.10
  unaccomplished 408.3
neglecter 340.5
negligee 5.20
negligence
  unconcern 102.2
  neglect 340.1
  thoughtlessness 365.3
  improvidence 406.2
  mismanagement 414.6
  laxness 426.1
  nonobservance 435.1
  slovenliness 810.6
  inaccuracy 975.2
  inattention 984.1
negligent
  n neglecter 340.5
  adj unconcerned 102.7
  neglectful 340.10
  improvident 406.15
  botched 414.21
  lax 426.4
  nonobservant 435.5
  slovenly 810.15
  inaccurate 975.17
  inattentive 984.6
negligible
  insignificant 248.6
  unimportant 998.17
negotiable
  transferable 629.5
  convertible 728.31
  workable 889.10
  practicable 966.7
negotiable instrument 728.5
negotiate leap 366.5
  manage 409.12
  treat with 437.6
  mediate 466.6
  confer 541.11
  transfer 629.3
  bargain 731.18
negotiation
  bargaining 731.3
  transaction 731.4
negotiator
  mediator 466.3
  go-between 576.4
  unionist 727.4
Negro 312.3
neigh 60.2

neighbor
  n neighborer 223.6
  friend 588.1
  v adjoin 223.9
  juxtapose 223.13
  adj adjacent 223.16
neighborhood
  environment 209.1
  nearness 223.1
  region 231.1
neighboring
  environing 209.8
  nearby 223.15
  adjacent 223.16
neighborly
  favorable 449.22
  hospitable 585.11
  friendly 587.15
neither 335.7
nemesis
  punishment 604.1
  justice 649.1
  bane 1001.1
Nemesis rage 152.10
  avenger 507.3
  justice 649.5
  evil 680.5
  star 1072.8
neolith 842.6
neolithic 842.20
neologism
  neology 526.8
  modern 841.4
  innovation 852.4
neonatal
  infant 301.12
  beginning 818.15
  new-made 841.9
neophyte
  novice 572.9
  believer 692.4
  beginner 818.2
  convert 858.7
  ignoramus 930.8
neoplasm 85.39
nepenthe 990.1
nephew 559.3
nephology
  meteorology 317.5
  nephelognosy 319.5
ne plus ultra
  summit 198.2
  supremacy 249.3
  limit 794.5
  acme of perfection
    1002.3
nepotism
  spoils of office 609.35
  partiality 650.3
Neptune
  mariner 183.1
  spirit of the sea 240.4
  water god 678.10
  planet 1072.9
nerd swotter 572.10
  specialist 866.3
  fool 924.3
nerval 24.10
nerve center
  n ganglion 208.5
  inner nature 767.5

nerveless
  weak 16.12
  unmanned 19.19
  unnervous 129.2
nerve-racking 128.15
nerves
  nervous system 2.14
  nervousness 128.1
nerves of steel courage 492.1
  stability 855.1
nervous neural 24.10
  sensitive 24.12
  excitable 105.28
  anxious 126.7
  fearful 127.23
  nervy 128.11
  agitated 917.16
nervous breakdown
  collapse 85.8
  mental disorder 92.14
  frayed nerves 128.4
nervous system 2.14
nervous tension
  anxiety 126.1
  tension 128.3
nervous wreck
  wreck 128.5
  tension 393.8
nervy strong 15.15
  nervous 128.11
  impudent 142.10
  fearless 492.19
  agitated 917.16
nescience 930.1
nest
  n abode 228.1
  nidus 228.25
  fledgling 302.10
  multitude 884.3
  birthplace 886.8
  v snuggle 121.10
  settle 159.17
  inhabit 225.7
nest egg reserve 386.3
  funds 728.14
nester 227.9
nesting
  n habitation 225.1
  adj birdlike 311.49
nestle put to bed 22.19
  snuggle 121.10
  cuddle 562.17
  protect 1008.18
nestling
  n fledgling 302.10
  bird 311.28
  lovemaking 562.1
  beginner 818.2
  adj new 841.7
nestor 422.3
Nestor old man 304.2
  Solomon 921.2
net
  n webbing 170.3
  difference 255.8
  porousness 292.8
  weight 297.1
  snare 356.13
  gain 472.3
  receipts 627.1
  tennis 748.1

  hockey 749.1
  round 751.3
  production 893.2
  network 1034.8
  v web 170.7
  trap 356.20
  arrest 429.15
  acquire 472.8
  profit 472.12
  catch 480.17
  yield 627.4
  weave 740.6
  hamper 1012.11
  adj remaining 256.7
nether 274.8
nethermost 199.7
nether world
  depths 275.3
  hell 682.1
net income pay 624.4
  receipts 627.1
netting webbing 170.3
  arrest 429.6
nettle
  n thorn 285.5
  v annoy 96.13
  provoke 152.24
  incite 375.17
nettled annoyed 96.21
  provoked 152.27
nettle rash 85.36
net wages 624.4
network
  webwork 170.3
  informant 551.5
  company 770.3
networking 450.1
net worth
  assets 471.7
  worth 630.2
  funds 728.14
neural nerve 2.30
  nervous 24.10
neurological
  neural 24.10
  medical 90.15
neurological disease 85.25
neuron 2.14
neurosis
  mental disorder 92.14
  frayed nerves 128.4
  psychosis 926.3
neurotic
  psychoneurotic 92.39
  psychotic 926.28
neuter
  n neutral 467.4
  gender 530.10
  v castrate 255.11
  adj unsexual 75.29
  indifferent 102.6
  passive 329.6
  neutral 467.7
neutral
  n free agent 430.12
  neuter 467.4
  nonpartisan 609.28
  moderate 670.4
  gear 1040.9
  adj wishy-washy 16.17
  colorless 36.7

  unsexual 75.29
  indifferent 102.6
  passive 329.6
  independent 430.22
  neuter 467.7
  nonpartisan 609.45
  impartial 649.10
  general 864.11
  unprejudiced 979.12
neutral ground 467.3
neutrality
  indifference 102.1
  inaction 329.1
  avoidance 368.1
  noninvolvement 467.1
  neutralism 467.1
  impartiality 649.4
  moderation 670.1
  unprejudicedness 979.5
neutralization 900.2
neutralize
  cushion 670.8
  nullify 900.7
neutralizer
  counteractant 900.3
  acid 1060.3
neutron 1038.6
never
  adv noway 248.11
  ne'er 822.4
  interj by no means 335.9
never-dying 829.9
never-ending
  continuous 812.8
  perpetual 829.7
never fear 969.4
never mind
  who cares? 102.11
  no matter 998.25
nevermore 822.4
never-never land 986.11
never say die
  not weaken 15.10
  be hopeful 124.8
  be determined 359.8
  stay with it 360.4
  stand fast 453.4
  persist 856.5
nevertheless
  notwithstanding 338.8
  anyhow 384.10
nevus growth 85.39
  bulge 283.3
  mark 517.5
  blemish 1004.1
new
  adj additional 253.10
  original 337.5
  unaccustomed 374.4
  unused 390.12
  fashionable 578.11
  present 838.2
  young 841.7
  adv newly 841.15
  again 874.7
New Age 870.7
new arrival
  newcomer 774.4
  beginner 818.2
new birth revival 396.3
  redemption 685.4

new start 858.2
newborn born 1.4
 infant 301.12
 new-made 841.9
newcomer
 incomer 189.4
 novice 572.9
 new arrival 774.4
 beginner 818.2
newel 273.4
newfangled 841.10
new-fashioned
 fashionable 578.11
 modern 841.13
New Left 611.4
new life 685.4
new look 841.2
newlywed 563.5
newlyweds 563.9
new money 618.1
new moon 1072.11
news information 552
 tidings 552.1
 newspaper 555.2
newscast
 n radiobroadcast 1034.18
 television broadcast 1035.2
 v broadcast 1034.25
newscaster 1034.23
new slant 932.5
newsletter 552.1
newsman 555.4
news media 552.1
newsmonger
 informant 551.5
 rumormonger 552.9
newspaper news 552.1
 news medium 555.2
newspaperman
 writer 547.15
 newsmonger 552.9
 journalist 555.4
 author 718.4
news report 552.5
newsstand 736.3
newsworthy 552.13
newsy
 v talkative 540.9
 adj communicative 343.10
 newsworthy 552.13
 gossipy 552.14
New Testament 683.4
new to
 unaccustomed 374.4
 inexperienced 414.17
new twist 932.5
New World 231.6
next
 adj adjacent 223.16
 nearest 223.19
 succeeding 815.4
 adv subsequently 835.6
next life 835.1
next of kin 559.2
next to
 v learn 551.14
 prep at 159.27
the next world 839.2
nexus 812.2
Niagara 238.11
nib nose 283.8

point 285.3
 extremity 820.2
nibble
 n bite 8.2
 v feed 8.18
 pick 8.26
 chew 8.26
 kid oneself 954.6
 trifle 998.14
nibbling 8.1
nice tasty 63.8
 pleasant 97.6
 kind 143.13
 meticulous 339.12
 dainty 495.11
 elegant 496.9
 right 637.3
 conscientious 644.15
 detailed 766.9
 discriminating 944.7
 exact 973.17
 attentive 983.15
 good 999.12
nice guy 659.2
nicety
 meticulousness 339.3
 niceness 495.3
 taste 496.1
 margin 780.2
 discrimination 944.1
 accuracy 973.5
niche
 nook 197.3
 recess 284.7
 hiding place 346.4
nick
 n notch 289.1
 jail 429.9
 mark 517.5
 type 548.6
 v notch 289.4
 rob 482.16
 mark 517.19
nickel
 n money 728.7
 precious metals 728.20
 adj brass 1058.17
nickelodeon 50.11
nickname
 n sobriquet 527.7
 v name 527.11
nick of time 843.5
nicotine 89.9
nicotine addict 87.21
nicotine addiction
 substance abuse 87.1
 smoking 89.10
nicotinic 89.15
niece 559.3
nifty chic 578.13
 excellent 999.13
niggard
 n tightwad 484.4
 adj niggardly 484.8
nigger 312.3
niggle
 n criticism 510.4
 v nag 510.16
 trifle 998.14
niggling
 n criticism 510.4

adj insignificant 248.6
 critical 510.23
 attentive 983.15
 petty 998.20
nigh
 v near 223.7
 adj left 220.4
 near 223.14
 adv near 223.20
 nearly 223.22
 prep near 223.24
night
 n blackness 38.4
 close of day 315.2
 nighttime 315.4
 darkness 1027.1
 adj nocturnal 315.9
night and day
 n opposites 215.2
 adv constantly 847.7
night blindness 30.2
nightcap
 sleep-inducer 22.10
 drink 88.9
night clothes 5.21
nightclub bar 88.20
 theater 704.14
 entertainment 743.13
night crawler 311.39
nightdress 5.21
nightfall 315.2
nightgown 5.21
nightie 5.21
nightingale 710.23
night letter 347.14
nightlong
 adj nocturnal 315.9
 continuing 827.12
 adv nightly 315.11
nightmare
 torment 96.7
 frightener 127.9
 dream 986.9
night prayer 696.8
nights 315.11
night spot
 theater 704.14
 entertainment 743.13
nighttime
 n night 315.4
 adj nocturnal 315.9
nightwalk
 creep 177.26
 noctambulate 177.32
 lurk 346.9
nightwalking
 n noctambulation 177.9
 creeping 177.17
 adj noctambulant
 177.38
nihilism
 pessimism 125.6
 anarchy 418.2
 radicalism 611.4
nihilist
 n pessimist 125.7
 destroyer 395.8
 anarchist 418.3
 savage 593.5
 radical 611.12
 adj destructive 395.26

nihilistic
 pessimistic 125.16
 destructive 395.26
 anarchic 418.6
 radical 611.20
 unruly 671.19
nil 762.2
nimble fast 174.15
 quick 330.18
 alert 339.14
 agile 413.23
 smart 920.14
nimble-fingered 413.23
nimble-footed
 agile 413.23
 fast 174.15
nimble-witted
 witty 489.15
 smart 920.14
nimbus
 illustriousness 662.6
 halo 1025.14
Nimrod hunter 382.5
 shooter 904.8
nincompoop 924.3
nine team 617.7
 baseball team 745.2
 card 758.2
 ennead 882.5
nine days' wonder
 marvel 122.2
 great success 409.3
 ephemeron 828.5
ninny 924.3
nip
 n bite 8.2
 drink 8.4
 pang 26.2
 zest 68.2
 liquor 88.7
 scrap 248.3
 squeezing 260.2
 hold 474.2
 dose 793.5
 cold 1023.1
 v pain 26.7
 bite 68.5
 tipple 88.24
 converge 169.2
 speed 174.9
 hasten off 188.10
 excise 255.10
 squeeze 260.8
 shorten 268.6
 put an end to 395.12
 hold 474.6
 seize 480.14
 rob 482.16
 freeze 1023.10
 chill 1024.11
nip and tuck 790.7
nip in the bud
 kill 308.13
 put an end to 395.12
 stop 1012.13
nipped
 contracted 260.12
 shortened 268.9
nipper 302.3
nipple tube 239.6
 breast 283.6

nonbreakable 1049.5
the nonce 838.1
nonce word 526.8
nonchalance
  apathy 94.4
  unconcern 102.2
  casualness 106.5
nonchalant
  apathetic 94.13
  unconcerned 102.7
  blasé 106.15
noncohering 802.20
noncohesion
  nonadhesion 804.1
  uncohesiveness 804.1
noncohesive
  separate 802.20
  incoherent 804.4
noncom 575.19
noncombatant
  n nonbelligerent 464.5
  adj unbelligerent 464.10
noncommissioned officer
  enlisted man 461.8
  superintendent 574.2
noncommittal 494.8
noncommitted 467.7
noncommunicable 122.13
noncompetitive 450.5
noncompletion 408.1
noncompliance
  disobedience 327.1
  nonobservance 435.1
  refusal 442.1
  nonconformity 868.1
non compos mentis 926.26
nonconducting 1032.36
nonconductive 1032.36
nonconductor 1032.14
nonconforming
  disobedient 327.8
  dissenting 333.6
  nonobservant 435.5
  unconforming 868.5
nonconformist
  n rebel 327.5
  dissenter 333.3
  heretic 688.5
  misfit 789.4
  unconformist 868.3
  oddity 870.4
  eccentric 927.3
  adj nonuniform 782.3
  individualistic 789.9
  counteractive 900.8
nonconformity
  obliquity 204.1
  disobedience 327.1
  dissent 333.1
  nonobservance 435.1
  unorthodoxy 688.1
  extraneousness 774.1
  difference 780.1
  nonuniformity 782.1
  inconsistency 789.2
  particularity 865.1
  nonconformance 868.1
  unconformity 868.1
  counteraction 900.1
  eccentricity 927.1
noncontiguous 802.20

nonconvergent 203.6
noncooperation
  disobedience 327.1
  opposition 451.1
  hostility 451.2
  resistance 453.1
  disaccord 456.1
noncooperative
  insubordinate 327.9
  oppositional 451.8
  resistant 453.5
noncreative 891.5
nondenominational
  nonsectarian 675.27
  universal 864.14
nondescript
  formless 263.4
  simple 499.6
nondutiable 630.16
none
  n divine service 696.8
  not any 762.4
  adv no 762.12
nonelastic 1046.12
nonemotional 94.9
nonentity
  weakling 16.6
  nonexistence 762.1
  thing of naught 764.2
  a nobody 998.7
  mediocrity 1005.5
none of your business 214.10
nonessential
  n inessential 768.2
  adj needless 391.10
  circumstantial 766.7
  unessential 768.4
  irrelevant 776.7
  superfluous 993.17
  insignificant 998.17
nonesuch
  marvel 122.2
  the best 999.8
nonetheless
  notwithstanding 338.8
  anyhow 384.10
nonexistence
  absence 222.1
  nonbeing 762.1
  nonsubsistence 762.1
nonexistent gone 34.4
  absent 222.11
  unexistent 762.8
  imaginary 986.19
nonexpectant 131.9
nonfactual 986.21
nonfeasance
  disobedience 327.1
  neglect 340.1
  nonaccomplishment 408.1
  mismanagement 414.6
  nonobservance 435.1
  misdeed 655.2
nonfertile 891.4
nonfiction 547.10
nonflammability 1022.1
nonflammable 1022.9
nonformal
  n substandard language 523.6
  jargon 523.9
  adj in dishabille 5.47

  vernacular 523.20
  nonuniform 782.3
  slovenly 810.15
  unconventional 868.6
nonfulfillment
  nonaccomplishment 408.1
  nonobservance 435.1
  insufficiency 992.1
nonfunctional 391.14
nonhuman 870.15
nonimitation 337.1
nonintellectual 930.14
noninterference
  neglect 340.1
  nonintervention 430.9
  policy 609.4
noninterruption 847.2
nonintervention
  avoidance 368.1
  noninterference 430.9
  policy 609.4
noninvolvement
  inaction 329.1
  avoidance 368.1
  neutrality 467.1
non-Jew 688.6
nonliving 1055.5
nonliving matter 1055.1
nonmalignant 999.21
nonmandatory 324.7
nonmedical therapist 90.9
nonmedical therapy 91.2
nonmetal 1058.3
nonmetallic 1058.16
nonmilitant 464.10
no-no prohibition 444.1
  oath 513.4
nonobjective 980.12
nonobservance
  nonadherence 435.1
  inobservance 435.1
  refusal 442.1
  nonreligiousness 695.1
  nonconformity 868.1
  inattention 984.1
nonobservant
  inobservant 435.5
  nonreligious 695.15
  nonconforming 868.5
nonoccupancy 222.2
nonoccurrence
  absence 222.1
  nonexistence 762.1
nonopposing 433.12
nonopposition 433.1
nonordained 700.3
nonpareil
  marvel 122.2
  superior 249.4
  paragon 659.4
  the best 999.8
nonparticipation 329.1
nonpartisan
  n free agent 430.12
  neutral 467.4
  independent 609.28
  adj autonomous 430.22
  neutral 467.7
  independent 609.45
nonpartisanism
  neutrality 467.1

  independence 609.26
nonpaying 625.10
nonpayment 625.1
nonperformance
  neglect 340.1
  nonaccomplishment 408.1
  nonobservance 435.1
nonperishable 855.18
nonpermanent 828.7
nonphysical 1053.7
nonplus
  n bewilderment 971.3
  dilemma 1013.7
  v refute 958.5
  perplex 971.13
  thwart 1012.15
nonplussed
  in a dilemma 971.25
  at an impasse 1013.24
nonpoetic 721.4
nonpoisonous 999.21
nonpolluted 79.25
nonporous 1045.12
nonproductive 891.4
nonprofessional
  n amateur 726.5
  adj avocational 724.17
nonprofit 617.16
nonrecognition
  ingratitude 151.1
  incognizance 930.3
nonreligious
  unreligious 695.15
  lay 700.3
nonrepresentationalism 350.1
nonresident 222.12
nonresistance
  resignation 134.2
  inaction 329.1
  submission 433.1
  foreign policy 609.5
nonresistive
  submissive 433.12
  soft 1047.8
nonrestrictive
  negligent 340.10
  unrestrictive 430.25
nonreturnable 855.17
nonsectarian
  undenominational 675.27
  universal 864.14
nonsense
  stuff and nonsense 520.2
  foolishness 923.1
  absurdity 923.3
nonsense talk 540.3
nonsense verse 720.3
nonsensical
  silly 520.7
  absurd 923.11
non sequitur
  discontinuity 813.1
  specious argument 936.3
nonsked 184.10
nonsmoker 668.4
non-smoking 89.15
nonspecific
  general 864.11
  vague 971.19
nonspiritual
  carnal 663.6

material 1052.10
nonstop
  continuous 812.8
  perpetual 829.7
nonsubjective 768.3
nontaxable 630.16
nontoxic 999.21
nonuniform
  ununiform 782.3
  dissimilar 787.4
  unordered 810.12
  discontinuous 813.4
  irregular 851.3
  changeable 854.6
nonuniformity
  roughness 288.1
  unevenness 782.1
  multiformity 783.1
  dissimilarity 787.1
  inequality 791.1
  disorder 810.1
  discontinuity 813.1
  irregularity 851.1
  changeableness 854.1
nonunion 802.1
nonunion shop 727.3
nonuple 882.21
nonuse 390.1
nonviable 307.33
nonviolence
  inaction 329.1
  peaceableness 464.4
  moderation 670.1
nonviolent
  unbelligerent 464.10
  moderate 670.10
nonvirulent 999.21
noodle
  n member 2.7
  head 198.6
  brain 919.6
  v think over 931.13
nook corner 197.3
  angle 278.2
  recess 284.7
  hiding place 346.4
noon
  n summit 198.2
  noonday 314.5
  midday 314.5
  adj noonday 314.7
  adv constantly 847.7
no one 222.6
noose
  n circle 280.2
  snare 356.13
  execution 605.5
  v trap 356.20
  catch 480.17
  hang 604.18
  weave 740.6
noosphere
  organic matter 305.1
  biosphere 306.8
  atmosphere 317.2
  philosophy 932.2
nope 335.10
nor 335.7
nor'east 161.19
nor'easter 318.9
norm mean 246.1

measure 300.2
  custom 373.4
  precept 419.2
  ethics 636.1
  paragon 659.4
  rule 869.4
normal
  n vertical 200.2
  mean 246.1
  straight line 277.2
  adj medium 246.3
  right-angled 278.7
  typical 349.15
  customary 373.13
  right 637.3
  orderly 807.6
  prevalent 864.12
  natural 869.8
  sane 925.4
  ordinary 1005.8
normality
  propriety 637.2
  prevalence 864.2
  typicality 869.1
  normalness 869.1
  sanity 925.1
  ordinariness 1005.2
normalize
  make uniform 781.4
  order 807.4
  organize 808.10
  standardize 869.6
normative
  customary 373.13
  preceptive 419.4
  right 637.3
  model 786.8
  normal 869.8
  usual 869.9
north
  n points of the compass
    161.3
  adj northern 161.14
  adv N 161.15
northeast
  n points of the compass
    161.3
  adj northern 161.14
  adv nor'east 161.19
Northener 227.11
norther 318.9
northern 161.14
northern lights 1025.16
North Pole
  opposites 215.2
  remote region 261.4
  cold place 1023.4
north pole 1032.8
North Star
  guiding star 574.8
  stars 1072.4
northward
  n points of the compass
    161.3
  adv north 161.15
northwest
  n points of the compass
    161.3
  adj northern 161.14
  adv nor'west 161.20
north wind 318.9

no say 895.1
nose
  n olfactory organ 69.5
  prow 216.3
  nozzle 239.9
  protuberance 283.8
  person 312.5
  v smell 69.8
  stroke 73.8
  meddle 214.7
  trace 938.35
  pry 981.4
nose around 938.30
nosebleed 12.8
nose count roll 871.6
  summation 1017.11
nose dive
  maneuvers 184.13
  plunge 367.1
  collapse 410.3
  cheapening 633.4
nose-dive dive 184.41
  plunge 367.6
  cheapen 633.6
nosegay fragrance 70.1
  bouquet 310.25
  bundle 770.8
nose ring circle 280.3
  jewel 498.6
nose-tickling 68.6
nosh
  n light meal 8.7
  v pick 8.26
no-show 222.5
nostalgia
  sentimentality 93.8
  wistfulness 100.4
  yearning 100.5
  melancholy 112.5
nostalgic
  sentimental 93.21
  wistful 100.23
  melancholy 112.23
nostril 239.13
no strings attached
  adj unrestricted 430.27
  adv no ifs, ands, or buts
    960.3
nostrum 86.2
no sweat 1014.16
nosy
  meddlesome 214.9
  searching 938.38
  prying 981.6
not 335.8
nota bene 983.22
notability glory 247.2
  distinction 662.5
  celebrity 662.9
  noteworthiness 997.2
  personage 997.8
not a bit
  n none 762.4
  adv noway 248.11
  interj no 335.8
notable
  n celebrity 662.9
  personage 997.8
  adj remarkable 247.10
  conspicuous 348.12
  distinguished 662.16

characteristic 865.13
  memorable 989.25
  noteworthy 997.19
not accept deny 335.4
  not permit 444.4
  refuse to believe 956.3
not admit deny 335.4
  disbelieve 955.5
not allow 444.4
not all there
  mentally deficient 922.22
  crazy 926.27
notarize 332.12
notarized 332.14
notarized statement
  deposition 334.3
  certificate 549.6
notary endorser 332.7
  recorder 550.1
not at all
  adv noway 248.11
  none 762.12
  never 822.4
  interj by no means 335.9
notate
  represent 349.8
  grammaticize 530.16
notation
  comment 341.5
  representation 349.1
  memorandum 549.4
  entry 628.5
  score 708.28
  character 709.12
  addition 1017.2
  number 1017.3
not bad
  adj tolerable 999.20
  interj bravo! 509.22
not believe 955.5
not budge
  do nothing 329.2
  balk 361.7
  stand fast 855.11
not buy refuse 442.3
  disbelieve 955.5
  refuse to believe 956.3
not care
  not mind 102.4
  take no interest in 982.2
not care for
  dislike 99.3
  neglect 340.6
not care to 325.3
notch
  n crack 224.2
  ridge 237.5
  degree 245.1
  indentation 284.6
  cleft 289.1
  nick 289.1
  mark 517.5
  v indent 284.14
  nick 289.4
  mark 517.19
notched
  indented 284.17
  nicked 289.5
notching 289.2
not comparable
  inadequate 250.7

uncomparable 787.6
not compare 250.4
not count 998.11
not counting 255.14
not cricket
  wrong 638.3
  unfair 650.10
  unconventional 868.6
not done
  underdone 11.9
  wrong 638.3
  unfair 650.10
  unconventional 868.6
note
  n observation 27.2
  animal noise 60.1
  milieu 209.3
  added to writing 254.2
  comment 341.5
  sign 517.1
  remark 524.3
  memorandum 549.4
  certificate 549.6
  letter 553.2
  treatise 556.1
  entry 628.5
  distinction 662.5
  air 708.4
  pitch 709.4
  musical note 709.14
  interval 709.20
  paper money 728.5
  negotiable instrument 728.11
  cognizance 928.2
  mood 978.4
  attention 983.1
  importance 997.1
  v signify 517.17
  remark 524.24
  record 549.15
  keep accounts 628.8
  heed 983.6
not easy
  adverse 1011.13
  difficult 1013.17
notebook
  record book 549.11
  book 554.1
notebook computer 1042.2
not enough 992.9
noteworthy
  remarkable 247.10
  particular 865.12
  extraordinary 870.14
  notable 997.19
not have a chance
  be impossible 967.4
  have no chance 972.14
not hesitate 359.10
nothing void 222.3
  nil 762.2
  thing of naught 764.2
nothing doing
  interj nope 335.10
  God forbid! 510.27
  phrs I refuse 442.7
nothing like 787.5
nothingness
  unconsciousness 25.2
  space 158.1
  void 222.3

nonexistence 762.1
nothing of the kind
  n a different thing 780.3
  adj nothing like 787.5
  interj no 335.8
nothing special
  n mediocrity 1005.5
  adj ordinary 1005.8
not hold up 975.8
notice
  n observation 27.2
  announcement 352.2
  press release 352.3
  publicity 352.4
  advertisement 352.6
  warning 399.1
  demand 421.1
  information 551.1
  commentary 556.2
  cognizance 928.2
  criticism 946.2
  attention 983.1
  v see 27.12
  detect 941.5
  heed 983.6
noticeable visible 31.6
  remarkable 247.10
  measurable 300.14
  manifest 348.8
  conspicuous 348.12
notification
  informing 343.2
  announcement 352.2
  warning 399.1
  information 551.1
notify herald 133.14
  warn 399.5
  inform 551.8
not in keeping with 789.10
not in the habit of 374.4
not in the mood 325.5
notion caprice 364.1
  impulse 365.1
  intention 380.1
  plan 381.1
  idea 932.1
  suggestion 951.5
  opinion 953.6
notional
  capricious 364.5
  ideational 932.9
  theoretical 951.13
  imaginative 986.18
  imaginary 986.19
  fanciful 986.20
notions 735.6
not know 930.11
not kosher
  dishonest 645.16
  unfair 650.10
  unconventional 868.6
not likely 442.7
not listen
  disobey 327.6
  be inattentive 984.2
not make sense
  be meaningless 520.4
  be incomprehensible 522.10
not matter 998.11
not mind
  not care 102.4

disobey 327.6
notoriety
  conspicuousness 348.4
  publicity 352.4
  disreputability 661.2
  repute 662.1
notorious
  conspicuous 348.12
  knavish 645.17
  disreputable 661.10
  distinguished 662.16
  immodest 666.6
  well-known 928.27
  terrible 1000.9
not permit 444.4
not remember 990.5
not right
  mentally deficient 922.22
  insane 926.26
  crazy 926.27
  erroneous 975.16
not stand for
  not permit 444.4
  discountenance 510.11
not surprised 130.11
not swallow
  disbelieve 955.5
  refuse to believe 956.3
not there 985.11
not to be believed 955.10
not to be had
  inaccessible 967.9
  scarce 992.11
not tolerate
  not permit 444.4
  discountenance 510.11
not to mention
  adv additionally 253.11
  prep with 253.12
not touch
  avoid 368.6
  not use 390.5
  abstain 668.7
not true false 354.25
  erroneous 975.16
not understand 522.11
not wash 975.8
not with it
  unaware 930.13
  oblivious 984.7
notwithstanding 338.8
not work
  be impotent 19.7
  fail 410.9
noumenon 932.1
noun 530.5
nourish feed 7.17
  nurture 8.19
  encourage 375.21
  foster 449.16
nourishing
  n nutrition 7.1
  adj nutritious 7.21
  eating 8.31
nourishment
  nutrition 7.1
  nutriment 10.3
  support 449.3
nous world spirit 677.7
  intellect 919.1
  smartness 920.2

nouveau riche
  n vulgarian 497.6
  upstart 606.7
  modern 841.4
  adj populational 606.8
nouvelle cuisine food 10.1
  cooking 11.1
nova 10.24
novel
  n book 554.1
  story 722.3
  adj original 337.5
  new 841.11
novelist writer 547.15
  author 718.4
  narrator 722.5
novelty
  nonimitation 337.1
  fad 578.5
  merchandise 735.6
  newness 841.1
  innovation 841.2
  alteration 852.4
novena
  divine service 696.8
  nine 882.5
novice novitiate 572.9
  nun 699.18
  beginner 818.2
  ignoramus 930.8
now
  n the present 838.1
  adj modern 841.13
  adv at once 830.8
  at present 838.3
  recently 841.16
  interj make haste! 401.16
now and then
  discontinuously 813.5
  occasionally 848.5
noway
  adv noways 248.11
  interj by no means 335.9
no way
  n despair 125.2
  interj nope 335.10
  God forbid! 510.27
  phrs I refuse 442.7
  no can do 967.11
nowhere
  n remote region 261.4
  adv in no place 222.17
nowise 248.11
now or never 843.12
noxious nasty 64.7
  malodorous 71.5
  unhealthful 82.5
  poisonous 82.7
  offensive 98.18
  malicious 144.20
  harmful 1000.12
nozzle bib nozzle 239.9
  nose 283.8
  sprinkler 1065.8
nth degree 794.5
nuance degree 245.1
  implication 519.2
  margin 780.2
  distinction 944.3
nub
  essential content 196.5

center 208.2
bulge 283.3
texture 294.1
essence 767.2
salient point 997.6
nubbin runt 258.4
bulge 283.3
nubby studded 283.17
nappy 294.7
nubile grown 14.3
adolescent 301.13
adult 303.12
marriageable 563.20
nuclear
nucleate 208.12
nucleal 305.21
middle 819.4
thermonuclear 1038.19
nuclear bomb 462.2
nuclear energy
energy 17.1
atomic energy 1038.15
nuclear fission 1038.8
nuclear fusion 1038.9
nuclear physicist 1038.3
nuclear physics
electronics 1033.1
atomic science 1038.1
particle physics 1038.1
nuclear power
atomic energy 1038.15
manpower 18.4
nuclear reactor 1038.13
nuclear war 458.1
nuclear weapons 462.1
nucleus center 208.2
cell nucleus 305.7
essence 767.2
middle 819.1
vital force 886.7
elementary particle 1038.6
nude
n work of art 712.10
adj naked 6.14
unadorned 499.8
nudge
n contact 223.5
signal 517.15
hint 551.4
thrust 902.2
v set in motion 172.6
contact 223.10
goad 375.15
importune 440.12
signal 517.22
thrust 902.12
remind 989.20
nudist
n nudity 6.3
adj naked 6.14
nudity nakedness 6.3
unadornment 499.3
nudzh
n tormentor 96.10
v annoy 96.13
nugatory
ineffective 19.15
insignificant 248.6
worthless 391.11
trivial 998.19
nugget lump 257.10

precious metals 728.20
nuisance
annoyance 96.2
tormentor 96.10
bore 118.4
nuisance value 1012.1
null vacant 222.14
meaningless 520.6
nonexistent 762.8
null and void
vacant 222.14
repealed 445.3
nullification
denial 335.2
extinction 395.6
repeal 445.1
policy 609.4
neutralization 900.2
nullify deny 335.4
abolish 395.13
repeal 445.2
declare a moratorium 625.9
neutralize 900.7
nullity
meaninglessness 520.1
nonexistence 762.1
thing of naught 764.2
an insignificancy 998.6
numb
v deaden 25.4
benumb 94.8
relieve 120.5
freeze 1023.10
adj insensible 25.6
apathetic 94.13
unconcerned 102.7
languid 331.20
number
n amount 244.2
deception 356.9
singular 530.8
edition 554.5
act 704.7
rhythm 709.22
vocation 724.6
part of writing 793.2
numeral 1017.3
sum 1017.6
v quantify 244.4
total 792.8
itemize 801.7
numerate 1017.17
number among 772.3
number-cruncher 1017.15
numbering
n numeration 1017.9
adj inclusive 772.6
numberless 884.10
number one
n urine 12.5
victor 411.2
self 865.5
v urinate 12.14
adj governing 612.18
paramount 997.24
numbers
quantity 244.1
rhythm 709.22
metrics 720.6
meter 720.7
statistics 746.4

multitude 884.3
mathematics 1017.1
numbers runner 759.20
numbing
n relief 120.1
adj deadening 25.9
anesthetic 86.47
relieving 120.9
cold 1023.14
numerable
measurable 300.14
calculable 1017.25
numeral
n number 1017.3
adj numeric 1017.23
numerate 1017.17
numeration 1017.9
numerative
measuring 300.12
numeric 1017.23
enumerative 1017.24
numerator ratio 1017.7
division 1017.12
numeric
mathematical 1017.22
numeral 1017.23
numerous
much 247.8
large 257.16
plural 883.7
many 884.6
plentiful 991.7
numinous
awesome 122.11
unintelligible 522.13
illustrious 662.19
almighty 677.17
sacred 685.7
sorcerous 690.14
supernatural 870.15
numismatic 728.30
numismatics 728.22
numskull 924.4
nun marker 517.10
celibate 565.2
sister 699.18
nuncio
messenger 353.1
diplomat 576.6
nunnery 703.6
nuptial
v join in marriage 563.14
adj sexual 75.25
matrimonial 563.18
nuptials 563.3
nurse
n health care professional 90.8
sister 90.10
nursemaid 1008.8
v nourish 8.19
treat 91.24
foster 449.16
hold 474.7
train 568.13
care for 1008.19
nursemaid maid 577.8
nurse 1008.8
nursery bedroom 197.7
hospital room 197.25
preschool 567.2
birthplace 886.8

conservatory 1069.11
nurseryman 1069.6
nursery school 567.2
nursing home 1009.4
nurture
n nutrition 7.1
nutriment 10.3
support 449.3
training 568.3
protectorship 1008.2
v nourish 7.17
feed 8.19
look after 339.9
encourage 375.21
make better 392.9
foster 449.16
hold 474.7
train 568.13
care for 1008.19
raise 1070.6
nut
n food 10.39
enthusiast 101.5
seed 310.31
specialist 866.3
oddity 870.4
lunatic 926.16
fanatic 926.18
freak 927.4
v harvest 1069.19
nuthouse 926.14
Nutrasweet 66.2
nutrient
n nutritive 7.3
adj nutritious 7.21
nutriment
nutrient 7.3
nourishment 10.3
nutrition
nourishment 7.1
eating 8.1
cooking 11.1
nutritionist 7.15
nutritious
nutritive 7.21
eating 8.31
nutritive value 7.1
nutriture 449.3
nuts
n genitals 2.13
bet 759.3
poker 759.10
adj crazy 926.27
nuts about
enthusiastic 101.11
crazy about 104.31
nuts and bolts 1040.4
nutshell
n modicum 248.2
adj shortened 268.9
abridged 557.6
nutty flavorful 63.9
foolish 923.9
crazy 926.27
eccentric 927.6
nuzzle stroke 73.8
cuddle 562.17
nymph larva 302.12
embryo 305.14
insect 311.33
deity 678.9

nymphet
schoolgirl 302.8
strumpet 665.14
nymph 678.9
nymphomania
sexual desire 75.5
lasciviousness 665.5
nymphomaniac
sexual pervert 75.16
strumpet 665.14
oaf bungler 414.8
simple soul 416.3
lout 924.5
oafish bungling 414.20
stupid 922.15
oak
symbol of strength 15.8
hardness 1046.6
oak leaf 647.5
oar paddle 180.15
boatman 183.5
oarsman 183.5
oath vow 334.4
promise 436.1
profane oath 513.4
oats 10.4
obdurate
insensible 25.6
impenitent 114.5
heartless 144.25
tough 361.10
firm 425.7
hardened 654.17
hard 1046.10
obedience
resignation 134.2
compliance 326.1
submission 433.1
conformity 867.1
obedient
resigned 134.10
compliant 326.3
submissive 433.12
dutiful 641.13
conformable 867.5
obeisance
obsequiousness 138.2
reverence 155.2
submission 433.1
crouch 913.3
obeisant
obsequious 138.14
prostrate 155.10
deferential 433.16
obelisk tower 272.6
monument 549.12
Oberon 678.8
obese corpulent 257.18
oversize 257.23
obesity oversize 257.5
corpulence 257.8
obey accept 134.7
mind 326.2
submit 433.6
obfuscate deform 263.3
conceal 346.6
make unintelligible 522.12
misteach 569.3
darken 1027.9
obituary
n obit 307.14

monument 549.12
history 719.1
adj funereal 309.22
documentary 549.18
object
v protest 333.5
offer resistance 453.3
disapprove 510.10
disagree 789.5
object
n objective 380.2
intent 518.2
syntax 530.2
something 763.3
article 1052.4
objectify
externalize 206.5
visualize 986.15
objecting
protesting 333.7
resistant 453.5
objection demur 325.2
protest 333.2
resistance 453.1
disapproval 510.1
defense 600.2
obstacle 1012.4
objectionable
offensive 98.18
unacceptable 108.10
unpraiseworthy 510.24
objective
n will 323.1
object 380.2
adj unfeeling 94.9
impartial 649.10
real 761.15
extrinsic 768.3
true 973.13
unprejudiced 979.12
objectivity
unfeeling 94.1
extrinsicality 768.1
unprejudicedness 979.5
object lesson
warning 399.1
lesson 568.7
example 786.2
objector
dissenter 333.3
oppositionist 452.3
objet d'art 712.10
oblation gift 478.4
offering 696.7
obligate
v commit 436.5
oblige 641.12
adj obliged 641.16
obligated
promised 436.8
chargeable 623.9
obliged 641.16
obligation
act of kindness 143.7
gratitude 150.1
undertaking 404.1
compulsion 424.1
commitment 436.2
security 438.1
debt 623.1
duty 641.1

condition 959.2
necessity 963.1
obligative 530.11
obligatory
mandatory 420.12
compulsory 424.11
binding 641.15
necessary 963.12
oblige be kind 143.9
necessitate 424.5
indulge 427.6
accommodate 449.19
obligate 641.12
require 963.8
obliged grateful 150.5
obligated 641.16
obliging
n indulgence 427.3
adj considerate 143.16
indulgent 427.8
permissive 443.14
courteous 504.14
oblique
n diagonal 204.7
v deviate 204.9
adj transverse 170.9
devious 204.13
circumlocutory 538.14
circuitous 914.7
obliterate
expunge 395.16
declare a moratorium 625.9
efface from the memory 990.6
obliteration
erasure 395.7
moratorium 625.2
forgetfulness 990.1
oblivion
unconsciousness 25.2
insensibility 94.2
carelessness 340.2
thoughtlessness 933.1
forgetfulness 990.1
oblivious asleep 22.22
unconscious 25.8
insensible 94.10
careless 340.11
thoughtless 933.4
inattentive 984.7
abstracted 985.11
forgetful 990.9
oblong
oblongated 267.9
quadrangular 278.9
obloquy criticism 510.4
vilification 513.2
infamy 661.4
obnoxious
offensive 98.18
base 661.12
terrible 1000.9
oboist 710.4
obscene offensive 98.18
cursing 513.8
lascivious 665.29
lewd 666.9
coarse 497.11
obscenity filth 80.7
offensiveness 98.2
coarseness 497.2

cursing 513.3
oath 513.4
lasciviousness 665.5
dirtiness 666.4
obscure
n darkness 1027.1
v blind 30.7
deform 263.3
cover 295.19
cloud 319.7
conceal 346.6
make unintelligible 522.12
misteach 569.3
quibble 936.9
make uncertain 971.15
darken 1027.9
opaque 1031.2
adj inconspicuous 32.6
formless 263.4
concealed 346.11
hard to understand 522.14
vague 522.15
ambiguous 539.4
unrenowned 661.14
uncertain 971.19
dark 1027.13
opaque 1031.3
obscured blinded 30.10
covered 295.31
concealed 346.11
latent 519.5
hard to understand 522.14
dark 1027.13
obscurity
inconspicuousness 32.2
formlessness 263.1
obscuration 522.3
diffuseness 538.1
vagueness 971.4
darkness 1027.1
opaqueness 1031.1
obsequies 309.4
obsequious
servile 138.14
obeisant 155.10
deferential 433.16
flattering 511.8
observable visible 31.6
manifest 348.8
observance regard 27.2
obedience 326.1
vigilance 339.4
custom 373.1
adherence 434.1
observation 434.1
execution 437.4
celebration 487.1
ceremony 580.4
piety 692.1
rite 701.3
conformity 867.1
attention 983.1
observant
vigilant 339.13
respectful 434.4
dutiful 641.13
pious 692.8
belief 953.21
attentive 983.15
observation
regard 27.2

observance 434.1
remark 524.3
idea 932.1
surveillance 938.9
opinion 953.6
attention 983.1
observatory 1072.17
observatory
observation post 27.8
astronomical observatory
1072.17
observe see 27.12
look 27.13
obey 326.2
keep 434.2
execute 437.9
celebrate 487.2
remark 524.24
formalize 580.5
perform a rite 701.15
conform 867.3
examine 938.24
heed 983.6
observer
military pilot 185.3
spectator 918.1
examiner 938.17
obsess oppress 98.16
demonize 680.16
bewitch 691.9
possess 926.25
engross 983.13
haunt 988.6
be remembered 989.14
obsessed affected 93.23
bewitched 691.13
possessed 926.33
engrossed 983.17
haunted 988.10
remembering 989.24
obsession
bewitchment 691.2
prepossession 926.13
engrossment 983.3
possession 988.5
obsessive
obsessional 926.34
engrossing 983.20
unforgettable 989.26
obsolesce
fall into disuse 390.9
age 842.9
obsolescence 390.1
obsolete
n archaism 526.12
adj out of action 19.17
disused 390.10
past 837.7
passé 842.15
obstacle
obstruction 293.3
hindrance 1012.4
obstetric 90.15
obstinacy
strength 15.1
refusal 325.1
defiance 327.2
resolution 359.1
perseverance 360.1
stubbornness 361.1
obstinateness 361.1

firmness 425.2
hostility 451.2
resistance 453.1
tenacity 803.3
uninfluenceability 895.2
obstinate strong 15.15
disobedient 327.8
resolute 359.11
persevering 360.8
stubborn 361.8
firm 425.7
oppositional 451.8
adhesive 803.12
uninfluenceable 895.4
obstreperous
noisy 53.13
vociferous 59.10
defiant 327.10
ungovernable 361.12
unruly 671.19
obstruct slow 175.9
stop 293.7
oppose 451.3
fend off 460.10
delay 846.8
get in the way 1012.12
obstructed
stopped 293.11
late 846.16
obstruction
slowing 175.4
clog 293.3
golf 751.1
delay 846.2
hindrance 1012.1
obstacle 1012.4
obstructionist
oppositionist 452.3
hinderer 1012.8
obstructive
n oppositionist 452.3
adj oppositional 451.8
resistant 453.5
dilatory 846.17
hindering 1012.17
obtain fetch 176.16
elicit 192.14
acquire 472.8
receive 479.6
exist 761.8
prevail 864.10
induce 886.11
obtainable
attainable 472.14
accessible 966.8
obtrude intrude 214.5
eject 909.13
obtrusive
conceited 140.11
insolent 142.9
intrusive 214.8
conspicuous 348.12
gaudy 501.20
obtuse insensible 25.6
unfeeling 94.9
blunt 286.3
negative 335.5
dull 922.16
obverse
n opposite side 215.3
front 216.1

likeness 784.3
adj contrapositive 215.5
contrary 779.6
obviate 1012.14
obvious distinct 31.7
manifest 348.8
patent 970.15
occasion
n pretext 376.1
circumstance 766.1
event 831.2
opportunity 843.2
cause 886.1
requirement 963.2
v be timely 843.6
cause 886.10
occasional
circumstantial 766.7
happening 831.9
incidental 843.11
casual 848.3
causal 886.13
occident 161.3
Occident 231.6
occidental 161.14
occipital 217.10
occlude close 293.6
obstruct 1012.12
occlusion seizure 85.6
closure 293.1
hindrance 1012.1
occlusive
n speech sound 524.12
adj phonetic 524.30
hindering 1012.17
occult
v cover 295.19
conceal 346.6
darken 1027.9
adj secret 345.11
concealed 346.11
latent 519.5
recondite 522.16
esoteric 689.23
supernatural 870.15
spectral 988.7
immaterial 1053.7
the occult secret 345.5
supernaturalism 870.7
immateriality 1053.1
occultation
disappearance 34.1
covering 295.1
concealment 346.1
eclipse 1027.8
occultism
supernaturalism 689.2
esoterics 689.1
immateriality 1053.1
occultist
esoteric 689.11
immaterialist 1053.4
occupancy
habitation 225.1
possession 469.1
occupant
inhabitant 227.2
tenant 470.4
occupation
habitation 225.1
action 328.1

possession 469.1
appropriation 480.4
work 724.1
vocation 724.6
operation 889.1
occupational hazard 85.32
occupational medicine 90.13
occupied
inhabited 225.12
busy 330.21
engaged 724.15
absorbed in thought
931.22
engrossed 983.17
occupy pervade 221.7
inhabit 225.7
possess 469.4
appropriate 480.19
engage 724.10
include 772.3
occupy the mind 931.20
engross 983.13
occur be present 221.6
exist 761.8
happen 831.5
occur to 931.18
occurrence
appearance 33.1
presence 221.1
existence 761.1
circumstance 766.1
event 831.2
prevalence 864.2
ocean
sea 240.1
the deep 240.3
quantity 247.3
ocean depths
ocean 240.1
the deep sea 275.4
oceanic
nautical 182.57
marine 240.9
ocean liner 180.5
oceanographer
thalassographer 240.8
measurer 300.9
earth scientist 1071.2
oceanography
thalassography 240.7
sounding 275.5
earth science 1071.1
Oceanus
spirit of the sea 240.4
water god 678.10
ocelot
variegation 47.6
wild cat 311.22
ocherous orange 42.2
yellow 43.4
Ockham's razor 484.1
octagonal
pentagonal 278.10
eighth 882.20
octave harmonics 709.9
interval 709.20
poetry 720.9
eight 882.4
octet cooperation 450.1
part music 708.18
poetry 720.9

eight 882.4
electron 1033.3
octogenarian
old man 304.2
eighty 882.7
ocular visual 27.20
optic 29.9
oculist
ophthalmologist 29.8
doctor 90.4
OD
n mariner 183.1
ship's officer 183.7
commissioned officer
575.18
v take sick 85.47
commit suicide 308.22
odalisque subject 432.7
demimonde 665.15
odd remaining 256.7
dissimilar 787.4
occasional 848.3
queer 870.11
sole 872.9
insane 926.26
eccentric 927.5
numeric 1017.23
oddball
n intruder 774.2
misfit 789.4
oddity 870.4
freak 927.4
adj odd 870.11
eccentric 927.6
oddity queerness 870.3
character 870.4
curiosity 870.5
eccentricity 927.1
odd job 724.2
odds advantage 249.2
gambling odds 759.6
difference 780.1
inequality 791.1
probability 968.1
even chance 972.7
odds and ends
remainder 256.1
notions 735.6
miscellany 770.13
hodgepodge 797.6
Odin 458.13
odious filthy 80.23
offensive 98.18
unlikable 99.7
base 661.12
terrible 1000.9
odium hate 103.1
infamy 661.4
odor smell 69.1
fragrance 70.1
characteristic 865.4
odorize scent 69.7
perfume 70.8
odorizer 70.6
odorless 72.5
odorous
odoriferous 69.9
fragrant 70.9
malodorous 71.5
odyssey 177.2
Oedipus complex 92.22

oeuvre
literature 547.12
complete works 718.1
of 775.13
of age adult 303.12
marriageable 563.20
of consequence 997.18
of course
adv consequently 887.7
certainly 970.23
interj yes 332.18
off
n horse race 757.3
v kill 308.14
put an end to 395.12
adj dissonant 61.4
right 219.4
idle 331.18
tainted 393.41
dissimilar 787.4
occasional 848.3
odd 870.11
insane 926.26
delirious 926.31
erroneous 975.16
imperfect 1003.4
below par 1005.10
adv hence 188.20
oceanward 240.12
at a distance 261.14
prep from 255.14
offal slough 80.9
refuse 391.4
off and on
adj occasional 848.3
adv infrequently 848.4
alternately 850.11
irregularly 851.4
changeably 854.8
to and fro 916.21
off-balance
eccentric 160.12
unbalanced 791.5
confused 985.12
off-base untimely 844.6
misbehaving 322.5
wrong 638.3
inaccurate 975.17
offbeat
n beat 709.26
adj dissimilar 787.4
unconventional 868.6
unusual 870.10
off-center
eccentric 160.12
distorted 265.10
off chance
possibility 966.1
small chance 972.9
off-color off-tone 35.21
ill 85.56
wrong 638.3
risqué 666.7
off-course 164.8
off duty
on vacation 20.12
idle 331.18
offend
give offense 98.11
provoke 152.21
affront 156.5

do wrong 655.4
offend the eye 1015.5
offender 660.8
offense umbrage 152.2
provocation 152.11
indignity 156.2
violation 435.2
attack 459.1
misdeed 655.2
wrong 674.4
basketball game 747.3
hockey 749.3
fight 754.3
offensive
n attack 459.1
adj nasty 64.7
malodorous 71.5
objectionable 98.18
insulting 156.8
warlike 458.21
combative 459.30
vulgar 497.10
ill-bred 505.6
obscene 666.9
terrible 1000.9
hideous 1015.11
offer
n attempt 403.2
proffer 439.1
offering 439.1
giving 478.1
v put to choice 371.21
attempt 403.6
proffer 439.4
give 478.12
bid 733.9
play 745.5
answer 939.4
adduce 957.12
offered 324.7
offering offer 439.1
gift 478.4
donation 478.6
oblation 696.7
game 745.3
offertory
donation 478.6
paean 696.3
oblation 696.7
sacred music 708.17
off-guard
negligent 340.10
unalert 984.8
offhand
adj nonchalant 106.15
careless 340.11
unpremeditated 365.11
extemporaneous 365.12
informal 581.3
adv carelessly 340.18
extemporaneously 365.15
informally 581.4
office
n act of kindness 143.7
library 197.6
function 387.5
aid 449.1
ceremony 580.4
bureau 594.4
commission 615.1
divine service 696.8

rite 701.3
duty 724.3
position 724.5
shop 739.7
v direct 573.8
office boy
errand boy 353.4
attendant 577.5
officeholder
official 575.16
office-bearer 610.11
officer
n executive 574.3
official 575.16
commissioned officer 575.18
policeman 1008.15
v govern 612.12
official
n executive 574.3
officer 575.16
agent 576.3
football 746.3
basketball 747.3
tennis 748.2
golf 751.3
soccer 752.3
boxing 754.3
adj authoritative 417.15
preceptive 419.4
recorded 549.17
governmental 612.17
executive 612.19
occupational 724.16
correct 970.18
officialdom 575.15
officialese
jargon 523.10
political jargon 609.37
officiate
administer 573.11
minister 701.16
function 724.13
baseball 745.5
football 746.5
sit in judgment 946.12
officious
meddlesome 214.9
overactive 330.24
offing
the distance 261.3
the future 839.1
offish arrogant 141.12
reticent 344.10
aloof 583.6
off-key 61.4
off-limits
restricted 210.8
prohibited 444.7
off-road racing 744.1
offscourings offal 80.9
remainder 256.1
refuse 391.4
rabble 606.3
off-season
n season 313.1
adj seasonal 313.9
offset
n setoff 338.2
printing 548.1
print 548.3
offshoot 561.4

the opposite 779.2
counteractant 900.3
v set off 338.5
cushion 670.8
go contrary to 779.4
neutralize 900.7
adj neutralizing 900.9
offsetting
n compensation 338.1
neutralization 900.2
adj compensating 338.6
neutralizing 900.9
offshoot fork 171.4
adjunct 254.1
sprig 310.20
offset 561.4
party 617.4
branch 617.10
sect 675.3
member 793.4
effect 887.1
extract 893.3
offshore 240.12
offspring child 302.3
family 559.5
posterity 561.1
descendant 561.3
sequel 835.2
effect 887.1
product 893.1
off the beaten track
secluded 584.8
unusual 870.10
off the cuff
adj extemporaneous 365.12
adv extemporaneously 365.15
off the record
adj confidential 345.14
adv confidentially 345.20
off-the-wall
unexpected 131.10
odd 870.11
crazy 926.27
off year 844.2
often frequently 847.6
repeatedly 849.16
ogle
n gaze 27.5
flirtation 562.9
v scrutinize 27.14
gaze 27.15
flirt 562.20
spectate 918.5
ogre frightener 127.9
monster 593.6
oh O! 122.20
my! 122.21
ohm 1032.13
oil
n balm 86.11
flattery 511.1
painting 712.14
fuel 1021.1
illuminant 1025.20
oleum 1056.1
v medicate 91.25
smooth 287.5
provision 385.9
flatter 511.6
facilitate 1014.7
fuel 1021.8

grease 1056.8
oiling
facilitation 1014.5
lubrication 1056.6
oily
slippery 287.12
insincere 354.32
suave 504.18
flattering 511.8
greasy 1056.9
ointment
anesthetic 25.3
balm 86.11
unction 701.5
money 728.2
lubricant 1056.3
okay
n consent 441.1
permission 443.1
v consent 441.2
permit 443.9
adj acceptable 107.12
accurate 973.16
excellent 999.13
tolerable 999.20
interj yeah 332.19
old aged 303.16
disused 390.10
experienced 413.28
former 837.10
age-old 842.10
antiquated 842.13
old age age 303.5
oldness 842.1
the old country
world region 231.6
fatherland 232.2
old days 837.2
older
n senior 304.5
adj mature 304.7
previous 834.4
senior 842.19
oldest
n senior 304.5
adj older 842.19
Old Faithful 1019.10
old-fashioned
disused 390.10
gallant 504.15
old-fangled 842.16
conservative 853.8
old fogy
back number 842.8
conservative 853.4
dotard 924.9
old hand 413.16
old hat trite 117.9
old-fashioned 842.16
old lady
ladylove 104.15
old woman 304.3
wife 563.8
old-line
conservative 611.17
unchanged 853.8
established 855.13
old maid
fussbudget 495.7
prude 500.11
spinster 565.4

old man beau 104.13
elder 304.2
father 560.9
forefather 560.10
grandfather 560.13
husband 563.7
commissioned officer 575.18
back number 842.8
the Old Man
ship's officer 183.7
commissioned officer 575.18
old master
work of art 712.10
artist 716.1
old money 618.1
old pro
veteran 413.16
professional 726.4
old salt mariner 183.3
veteran 413.16
old saw 974.3
old school 853.4
old story 974.3
Old Testament 683.3
old-timer
old man 304.2
veteran 413.16
back number 842.8
old times 837.2
old wives' tale 954.3
old woman
effeminate male 77.11
old lady 304.3
fussbudget 495.7
grandmother 560.16
wife 563.8
back number 842.8
Old World 231.6
old-world
gallant 504.15
antiquated 842.13
olfactories 69.5
olfactory 69.12
olio stew 10.11
hodgepodge 797.6
olive 44.4
olive branch 465.2
ology 928.10
Olympian
apathetic 94.13
arrogant 141.12
high 272.14
reticent 344.10
aloof 583.6
impartial 649.10
heavenly 681.12
Olympics 457.3
Olympus 681.9
ombudsman 466.3
omega 820.1
omelet 10.26
omen
n portent 133.3
warning sign 399.3
prediction 962.1
v foreshow 133.10
ominous
portentous 133.17
threatening 514.3
premonitory 962.12
harmful 1000.12

unfortunate 1011.14
omission
deletion 255.5
neglect 340.1
nonaccomplishment 408.1
mismanagement eating 414.6
nonobservance 435.1
misdeed 655.2
exclusion 773.1
deficiency 795.2
slip 975.4
want 992.4
omit delete 255.12
leave undone 340.7
exclude 773.4
omitting 773.10
omnibus
n public vehicle 179.13
compilation 554.7
adj comprehensive 772.7
whole 792.9
thorough 794.10
omnifarious 783.3
omnipotence 18.3
omnipotent
powerful 18.13
almighty 677.17
omnipresence
all-presence 221.2
completeness 794.1
omnipresent
all-present 221.13
almighty 677.17
thorough 794.10
omniscience 928.6
omniscient
almighty 677.17
knowing 928.15
omnivorous eating 8.31
greedy 100.27
gluttonous 672.6
on
adj addicted 87.25
happening 831.9
adv forward 162.8
on foot 177.43
under way 182.63
after which 835.7
across 901.25
prep at 159.27
toward 161.26
atop 198.16
against 223.25
upon 295.37
with relation to 775.13
on account 622.10
on account of
for 449.26
because of 888.9
on and off 854.8
on and on
increasingly 251.9
continuously 812.10
constantly 847.7
on-again off-again 813.4
on a par 790.7
on approval
at choice 371.27
on trial 942.14
on behalf of for 449.26
instead of 862.12

on board here 159.23
  on shipboard 182.62
  present 221.12
  joined 800.13
on call handy 387.20
  on demand 421.12
  cash 624.25
once
  adj former 837.10
  adv whenever 821.12
  once upon a time
    837.14
  one time 848.6
  singly 872.13
once in a while 848.5
once upon a time 837.14
oncoming
  n approach 167.1
  beginning 818.1
  adj progressive 162.6
  approaching 167.4
on condition 959.12
on demand
  at demand 421.12
  cash 624.25
on duty 330.21
one
  n child 302.3
  person 312.5
  I 872.3
  adj quantitative 244.5
  married 563.21
  almighty 677.17
  identical 778.7
  whole 792.9
  combined 805.5
  single 872.7
one and all
  n entire 792.3
  all 864.4
  adj every 864.15
  adv unanimously 332.17
  completely 794.14
one and only
  n one 872.3
  adj sole 872.9
one-armed bandit 759.16
one at a time 872.13
one by one
  separately 802.27
  each 865.19
  singly 872.13
on edge nervous 128.11
  in suspense 130.12
  impatient 135.6
one-horse
  insignificant 248.6
  inferior 250.6
  little 258.10
  unimportant 998.18
one-horse town 230.3
one mind 332.5
on end
  vertically 200.13
  continuously 812.10
oneness accord 455.1
  sameness 778.1
  agreement 788.1
  whole 792.1
  simplicity 798.1
  particularity 865.1

singleness 872.1
  unity 872.1
one-night stand
  copulation 75.7
  engagement 704.11
one-on-one
  n basketball game 747.3
  adj contrapositive 215.5
  front 216.10
  personal 312.15
  in opposition 451.9
  plain-speaking 535.3
  familiar 587.19
one-piece 872.11
onerous
  oppressive 98.24
  heavy 297.17
  laborious 725.18
  hampering 1012.18
  troublesome 1013.18
oneself 865.5
one-sided sided 218.7
  distorted 265.10
  partial 650.11
  unipartite 872.11
  discriminatory 980.12
onetime 837.10
one time
  adj infrequent 848.2
  adv once 848.6
one-track mind 926.13
one-upmanship
  cunning 415.1
  competition 457.2
one-way 161.12
ongoing
  n progression 162.1
  course 172.2
  adj progressive 162.6
  improving 392.15
  happening 831.9
  operating 889.11
on guard
  adj vigilant 339.13
  cautious 494.8
  adv defensively 460.16
on hand present 221.12
  in store 386.16
  handy 387.20
  possessed 469.8
on high
  high up 272.21
  celestially 681.13
on hold
  neglected 340.14
  late 846.16
on ice
  prearranged 965.8
  assured 970.20
on loan 620.7
onlooker
  neighbor 223.6
  spectator 918.1
onlooking 918.7
only
  adj sole 872.9
  adv limited 248.10
  simply 798.11
  solely 872.14
onomatopoeic
  imitative 336.9

representational 349.13
  lexical 526.19
onomatopoeic word 526.16
on one's knees
  humbled 137.13
  obsequious 138.14
  obeisant 155.10
  deferential 433.16
  supplicatory 440.16
  worshipful 696.16
on one's last legs
  burnt-out 21.10
  stricken in years
    303.18
  dying 307.33
  worn-out 393.36
on one's mind 931.24
on one's own
  at will 323.5
  independently 430.33
  singly 872.13
on one's toes 339.14
on paper
  adj written 547.22
  adv theoretically
    951.16
on purpose 380.10
on record 549.17
onrush course 172.2
  flow 238.4
on schedule 130.14
onset attack 459.1
  printing 548.1
  beginning 818.1
onslaught attack 459.1
  berating 510.7
  unruliness 671.3
  impact 902.3
onstage 704.36
on stream 405.22
on tap 387.20
on tenterhooks
  anxious 126.7
  in suspense 130.12
  in a dilemma 971.25
on the ball alert 339.14
  clear-witted 920.13
  attentive 983.15
on the bare possibility 966.10
on the beam
  laterally 218.8
  straight 277.7
  knowledgeable 928.17
on the blink
  unserviceable 391.14
  impaired 393.38
  disorderly 810.13
on the block 734.17
on the brink 211.15
on the cuff 622.10
on the double
  adj swiftly 174.17
  hurried 401.11
  interj make haste! 401.16
on the fence
  neutral 467.7
  nonpartisan 609.45
on the fritz
  unserviceable 391.14
  impaired 393.38
  disorderly 810.13

on the go
  under way 172.9
  en route 177.42
  busy 330.21
on the house
  adj gratuitous 634.5
  adv as a gift 478.27
  gratuitously 634.6
on the job busy 330.21
  alert 339.14
  attentive 983.15
on the level 644.14
on the lookout 339.13
on the lookout for
  adj expectant 130.11
  searching 938.38
  prep after 382.12
on the loose
  escaped 369.11
  free 430.21
  festive 743.28
on the make
  aspiring 100.28
  out for 403.17
on the mend 392.15
on the move
  under way 172.9
  en route 177.42
  busy 330.21
on the nose
  directable 161.13
  accurate 973.16
on the other hand
  laterally 218.8
  aside 218.10
  notwithstanding 338.8
  contrarily 779.9
  otherwise 780.11
  comparatively 943.10
  all things considered 946.17
on the quiet 345.18
on the rocks
  aground 182.73
  insolvent 625.11
  stranded 1013.27
on the run
  adj busy 330.21
  adv under way 172.9
  on the move 177.42
  hastily 401.12
on the shelf
  neglected 340.14
  disused 390.10
on the side
  aside 218.10
  additionally 253.11
on the spot here 159.23
  hasty 401.9
  now 838.3
  promptly 845.15
  in danger 1006.13
  in trouble 1013.22
on the take 378.4
on the verge 211.15
on the wagon 668.10
on the way
  along the way 176.20
  in preparation 405.22
on the whole
  on the average 246.5
  in the long run 792.14

generally 864.17
all things considered 946.17
on time
 on credit 622.10
 punctually 845.14
on to
 v learn 551.14
 adj cognizant of 928.16
ontogeny 861.3
on top of atop 198.16
 additionally 253.11
 on 295.37
 restraining 428.11
 attentive 983.15
 protective 1008.23
on trial
 adv under examination
 942.14
 phrs in litigation 598.22
on trust
 on credit 622.10
 believingly 953.28
onus duty 641.1
 charge 643.3
 guilt 656.1
 stigma 661.6
 proof 957.3
 impediment 1012.6
onward
 v make one's way 162.4
 adj progressive 162.6
 adv forward 162.8
 frontward 216.13
oodles 247.4
oomph pep 17.3
 importance 997.1
ooze
 n slime 80.8
 exuding 190.6
 mud 1062.8
 v exude 190.15
 be damp 1065.11
opacity obscurity 522.3
 stupidity 922.3
 opaqueness 1031.1
opalescence
 rainbow effect 47.2
 iridescence 1025.18
opalescent
 soft-colored 35.22
 rainbow-like 47.10
 iridescent 1025.37
opaque
 v darken 1031.2
 adj obscure 522.15
 stupid 922.15
 intransparent 1031.3
op cit 957.24
open
 v cleave 224.4
 spread 259.6
 ope 292.11
 disclose 351.4
 dramatize 704.28
 open up 818.12
 adj visible 31.6
 approachable 167.5
 receptive 187.16
 exterior 206.7
 available 222.15
 champaign 236.2

spread 259.11
unclosed 292.17
communicative 343.10
overt 348.10
published 352.17
leisure 402.5
artless 416.5
free-acting 430.23
unrestricted 430.27
liberal 485.4
phonetic 524.30
plain-speaking 535.3
hospitable 585.11
candid 644.17
incoherent 804.4
influenceable 894.15
liable 897.5
accessible 966.8
undecided 971.18
open-minded 979.10
exposed 1006.15
 adv without date 822.5
the open 206.3
open-air outdoor 206.8
 airy 317.12
open and aboveboard 644.14
open-and-shut
 manifest 348.8
 assured 970.20
open-and-shut case
 proof 957.3
 sure thing 970.2
open arms
 reception 187.1
 entree 187.3
 welcome 585.2
 greeting 585.4
open door entree 187.3
 hospitality 585.1
 foreign policy 609.5
opener
 can opener 292.10
 inauguration 818.5
open-eyed
 wondering 122.9
 vigilant 339.13
 curious 981.5
 attentive 983.15
open fire
 n fire 1019.13
 v pull the trigger 459.22
 open 818.12
 interj attack! 459.32
open forum
 forum 423.3
 arena 463.1
 discussion 541.7
openhanded
 liberal 485.4
 magnanimous 652.6
openhearted
 artless 416.5
 liberal 485.4
 hospitable 585.11
 candid 644.17
opening
 appearance 33.1
 entree 187.3
 entrance 189.5
 outlet 190.9
 vacancy 222.2

crack 224.2
aperture 292.1
display 348.2
passageway 383.3
position 724.5
beginning 818.1
opportunity 843.2
opening move 818.3
opening night 704.12
open market
 marketplace 736.2
 stock market 737.1
open mind 979.3
open-minded
 nonrestrictive 430.25
 influenceable 894.15
 open 979.10
openmouthed
 vociferous 59.10
 wondering 122.9
 gaping 292.18
 curious 981.5
 attentive 983.15
 surprised 131.12
openness
 approachability 167.2
 receptivity 187.9
 exteriority 206.1
 communicativeness 343.3
 manifestness 348.3
 artlessness 416.1
 plain speech 535.1
 talkativeness 540.1
 candor 644.4
 inclusion 772.1
 influenceability 894.5
 susceptibility 897.2
 accessibility 966.3
 open-mindedness 979.3
 exposure 1006.3
open question 971.8
the open road 177.3
open season 313.1
open sesame
 n opener 292.10
 password 517.12
 incantation 691.4
 influence 894.6
 interj open up! 292.23
open shop 727.3
open to liable to 897.6
 accessible 966.8
open to question 971.17
open up
 v spread 259.6
 open 292.11
 come out 348.6
 disclose 351.4
 confess 351.7
 make public 352.11
 let oneself go 430.19
 propose 439.5
 begin 818.12
 facilitate 1014.7
 interj open sesame! 292.23
open warfare 458.1
opera theater 704.14
 score 708.28
 musical theater 708.34
operable
 usable 387.23

workable 889.10
practicable 966.7
practical 995.6
opera glasses 29.4
operagoer 710.21
opera house 704.14
operant
 n doer 726.1
 operator 889.4
 adj operating 889.11
opera singer 710.13
operate
 treat 91.24
 pilot 182.14
 act 328.4
 plot 381.9
 use 387.10
 trade 737.23
 function 889.5
 be operative 889.7
operate on treat 91.24
 act on 889.6
operatic
 dramatic 704.33
 vocal 708.50
operating
 n motion 172.1
 adj acting 328.10
 operational 889.11
operating room 197.25
operation
 surgery 90.2
 surgical intervention 91.19
 motion 172.1
 action 328.1
 act 328.3
 function 387.5
 utilization 387.8
 undertaking 404.1
 military operation 458.5
 transaction 731.4
 workings 889.1
 functioning 889.1
 performance 892.5
operational
 acting 328.10
 operative 889.9
 operating 889.11
 functional 889.12
operative
 n secret agent 576.9
 detective 576.10
 doer 726.1
 operator 889.4
 adj powerful 18.12
 acting 328.10
 effectual 387.21
 operational 889.9
operator surgeon 90.5
 man of action 330.8
 telephone operator 347.9
 schemer 381.7
 politics 610.6
 doer 726.1
 speculator 737.11
 operative 889.4
 liveware 1042.17
operetta 708.34
operose
 painstaking 339.11
 laborious 725.18

difficult 1013.17
ophthalmic eye 2.28
  visual 27.20
  optic 29.9
ophthalmologist 29.8
opiate
  sleep-inducer 22.10
  anesthetic 25.3
  drug 87.3
opine remark 524.24
  judge 946.8
  suppose 951.10
  think 953.11
opinion advice 422.1
  idea 932.1
  estimate 946.3
  sentiment 953.6
  attitude 978.1
opinionated
  obstinate 361.8
  dogmatic 970.22
opinion poll 938.14
opium 22.10
opossum 311.23
opponent
  n adversary 452.1
  adj oppositional 451.8
opportune apt 788.10
  timely 843.9
  expedient 995.5
opportunist
  n timeserver 363.4
  schemer 381.7
  adj scheming 381.13
opportunity turn 825.2
  probability 843.2
  chance 972.1
oppose
  contrapose 215.4
  dissent 333.4
  deny 335.4
  counter 451.3
  offer resistance 453.3
  disapprove 510.10
  go contrary to 779.4
  counteract 900.6
  compare 943.4
  hinder 1012.10
oppose change 853.6
opposed
  contrapositive 215.5
  unwilling 325.5
  oppositional 451.8
  disapproving 510.21
  contrary 779.6
  adverse 1011.13
opposed to 451.10
opposed to change 853.8
opposer 452.3
opposing
  n contraposition 215.1
  opposition 451.1
  resistance 453.1
  comparison 943.1
  adj contrapositive 215.5
  dissenting 333.6
  negative 335.5
  oppositional 451.8
  disapproving 510.21
  contrary 779.6
opposing party 452.1

opposing side 452.1
opposite
  n inverse 205.4
  poles 215.2
  contrary 779.2
  adj contrapositive 215.5
  fronting 216.11
  oppositional 451.8
  contrary 779.6
  adverse 1011.13
  adv poles apart 215.6
  prep against 223.25
  over against 779.10
opposite number
  the opposite 779.2
  equal 790.4
opposition
  contraposition 215.1
  refusal 325.1
  dissent 333.1
  opposing 451.1
  resistance 453.1
  disapproval 510.1
  contrariety 779.1
  difference 780.1
  disagreement 789.1
  counteraction 900.1
  comparison 943.1
  hindrance 1012.1
oppositional
  opponent 451.8
  contrary 779.6
  counteractive 900.8
opposition party 609.24
oppress
  burden 98.16
  sadden 112.18
  aggrieve 112.19
  weight down 297.13
  persecute 389.7
  domineer 612.16
  task 725.16
  go hard with 1011.8
oppressed
  sad 112.20
  weighted 297.18
  subjugated 432.14
  downtrodden 432.16
oppression
  affliction 96.8
  dejection 112.3
  stuffiness 173.6
  burden 297.7
  persecution 389.3
  despotism 612.10
oppressive
  burdensome 98.24
  depressing 112.30
  stuffy 173.16
  onerous 297.17
  imperious 417.16
  laborious 725.18
  hampering 1012.18
  troublesome 1013.18
  sultry 1019.28
oppressor 575.14
opprobrium
  vilification 513.2
  infamy 661.4
oppugn
  contradict 451.6

quarrel 456.11
  dispute 457.21
  go contrary to 779.4
  counteract 900.6
opt 371.13
optic
  n eye 2.9
  vision 27.9
  adj eye 2.28
  visual 27.20
  optical 29.9
optical illusion 976.5
optical instrument 29.1
optician 29.8
optics
  optical physics 29.7
  light 1025.22
optimal 999.16
optimism
  cheerfulness 109.1
  optimisticalness 124.3
  sanguine expectation 130.2
optimist 124.6
optimistic
  cheerful 109.11
  upbeat 124.12
  expectant 130.11
optimum
  n the best 999.8
  adj best 999.16
option discretion 371.2
  free will 430.6
  first option 733.2
  stock option 737.21
optional
  voluntary 324.7
  elective 371.22
optometrist
  oculist 29.8
  doctor 90.4
optometry 29.7
opulence wealth 618.1
  plenty 991.2
opulent
  wealthy 618.14
  plentiful 991.7
opus writing 547.10
  book 554.1
  piece 708.5
  product 893.1
or
  n yellowness 43.1
  heraldry 647.2
  adj yellow 43.4
  conj either . . . or 371.29
OR 197.25
oracle
  n wise man 921.1
  Delphic oracle 962.7
  maxim 974.1
  v dogmatize 970.10
oracular
  predictive 962.11
  dogmatic 970.22
oral
  n examination 938.2
  adj mouthlike 292.22
  communicational 343.9
  speech 524.29
  traditional 842.12
oral history 547.12

orange
  n orangeness 42.1
  adj orangeish 42.2
orangery 1069.11
orate 543.10
oration 543.2
orator 543.6
oratorical 543.12
oratorio 708.17
oratory
  public speaking 543.1
  eloquence 544.1
  chapel 703.3
orb
  n eye 2.9
  vision 27.9
  region 231.2
  sphere 282.2
  royal insignia 647.3
  occupation 724.4
  stars 1072.4
  adj spherical 282.9
orbit
  n domain 231.2
  rank 245.2
  circle 280.2
  sphere 282.2
  route 383.1
  occupation 724.4
  sphere of influence 894.4
  circuitousness 914.1
  circuit 914.2
  circle 1072.16
  spacecraft 1075.2
  v encircle 280.10
  circle 914.5
orbiting 914.1
orchard 310.14
orchestra
  audience 48.6
  auditorium 704.15
  stage 704.16
  band 710.12
orchestrate 708.46
orchestration
  piece 708.5
  harmonization 709.2
orchestrator 710.20
ordain install 191.4
  command 420.8
  allot 477.9
  legislate 613.10
  appoint 615.11
  legalize 673.9
  frock 698.12
  destine 964.7
ordained
  in orders 698.17
  destined 964.9
ordeal trial 96.9
  occultism 690.3
  test 942.2
order
  n rank 245.2
  manner 384.1
  precept 419.1
  command 420.1
  demand 421.1
  peacefulness 464.2
  nomenclature 527.1
  harmony 533.2

race 559.4
caste 607.1
community 617.2
fellowship 617.3
school 617.5
decoration 646.5
medal 646.6
sect 675.3
good condition 765.3
arrangement 807.1
taxonomy 807.1
arrangement 808.1
class 809.2
classifications 809.5
sequence 815.1
normality 869.1
verdict 946.5
biology 1068.1
v outfit 5.41
command 420.8
demand 421.5
request 440.9
direct 573.8
organize 807.4
arrange 808.8
classify 809.6
exercise influence 894.8
pass judgment 946.13
ordered
harmonious 533.8
uniform 781.5
orderly 807.6
arranged 808.14
regular 850.6
ordering
direction 573.1
class 607.1
arrangement 808.1
organization 808.2
orderless
formless 263.4
unordered 810.12
vague 971.19
orderly
n hospital staff 90.11
attendant 577.5
adj pacific 464.9
harmonious 533.8
punctilious 580.10
uniform 781.5
consistent 803.11
ordered 807.6
arranged 808.14
regular 850.6
normal 869.8
adv regularly 781.8
order of the day
affairs 831.4
schedule 965.3
ordinal
classificational 809.7
consecutive 812.9
numeric 1017.23
ordinance rule 419.2
decree 420.4
law 673.3
rite 701.3
ordinary
n food service 8.11
heraldry 647.2
the usual 869.3

adj medium 246.3
inferior 250.6
customary 373.13
common 497.14
simple 499.6
populational 606.8
prosaic 721.5
frequent 847.4
prevalent 864.12
usual 869.9
average 1005.8
ordinate
n coordinates 300.5
v appoint 615.11
ordination
admission 187.2
appointment 615.2
holy orders 698.10
organization 808.2
ordnance arms 462.1
artillery 462.11
ordure feces 12.4
filth 80.7
ore raw material 406.5
mineral 1058.2
or else 780.11
organ instrument 384.4
periodical 555.1
branch 617.10
keyboard wind instrument
711.13
member 793.4
organ-grinder 710.9
organic
structural 266.6
organismic 305.17
innate 767.8
organic farming 1069.1
organic matter
living matter 305.1
animate matter 305.1
organism body 2.1
structure 266.1
organization 305.2
something 763.3
organist 710.8
organization
contour 262.2
structure 266.1
organism 305.2
plan 381.1
military unit 461.22
establishment 617.8
sect 675.3
workplace 739.1
composition 796.1
order 807.1
methodization 808.2
production 892.4
organizational
associational 617.17
formational 808.15
organize form 262.7
construct 266.5
plan 381.8
unionize 727.9
compose 796.3
league 805.4
order 807.4
methodize 808.10
establish 892.10

organized drunk 88.33
organic 305.17
planned 381.12
arranged 808.14
organized crime
the underworld 660.10
illicit business 732.1
organized labor 727.2
organizer
planner 381.6
unionist 727.4
arranger 808.5
producer 892.7
organ player 710.8
organ stop 711.19
orgasm
copulation 75.7
fury 105.8
spasm 917.6
orgasmic
lustful 75.27
frenzied 105.25
turbulent 671.18
convulsive 671.23
jerky 917.19
orgiastic
frenzied 105.25
carnal 663.6
incontinent 665.24
saturnalian 669.9
orgy spree 88.5
fury 105.8
dissipation 669.2
oriel 197.3
orient
n points of the compass
161.3
v orientate 161.11
accustom 373.9
adj luminous 1025.30
Orient 231.6
oriental 161.14
Oriental 312.3
orientation
navigation 159.3
direction 161.1
bearings 161.4
habituation 373.7
orienteering 159.3
orienter 422.3
orifice 292.1
origami 291.4
origin
etymology 526.15
beginning 818.1
origination 818.4
source 886.5
original
n real thing 337.2
writing 547.10
model 786.1
nonconformist 868.3
oddity 870.4
source 886.5
adj basic 199.8
native 226.5
actual 337.5
unused 390.12
essential 767.9
preceding 816.4
beginning 818.15

new 841.7
novel 841.11
unconventional 868.6
primary 886.14
genuine 973.15
imaginative 986.18
originality
nonimitation 337.1
newness 841.1
nonconformity 868.1
unconventionality 868.2
invention 986.3
original sin 655.3
originate
invent 337.4
initiate 818.10
take origin 818.13
cause 886.10
result from 887.5
produce 892.12
imagine 986.14
origination
beginning 818.1
origin 818.4
source 886.5
production 892.1
product 893.1
originative
causal 886.13
creative 892.16
imaginative 986.18
originator
author 886.4
producer 892.7
oriole 710.23
orison 696.4
Ormazd 677.5
ornament
n extra 254.4
ornamentation 498.1
figure of speech 536.1
ornateness 545.4
honor 646.1
decoration 646.5
passage 708.24
impromptu 708.27
grace 709.18
v add 253.4
decorate 498.8
make grandiloquent 545.7
ornamental
decorative 498.10
artistic 712.20
ornamentalist 716.11
ornamentation
decoration 498.1
ornament 498.1
ornateness 545.4
architectural element 717.2
superfluity 993.4
ornamented
adorned 498.11
figurative 536.3
ornate elegant 498.12
purple 545.11
ornery irascible 110.20
malicious 144.20
defiant 327.10
negative 335.5
perverse 361.11
oppositional 451.8

contrary 779.6
disagreeing 789.6
counteractive 900.8
orography 237.6
orotund 545.8
orphan
n survivor 256.3
derelict 370.4
v bereave 307.28
adj bereaved 307.35
orphanage 1009.4
orthodontic 90.15
orthodox
n true believer 687.4
adj firm 425.7
conventional 579.5
orthodoxical 687.7
conformist 867.6
Orthodox 675.30
orthodoxy
firmness 425.2
religion 675.1
soundness of doctrine
687
orthodoxness 687.1
conformity 867.1
Orthodoxy 675.9
orthogonal
perpendicular 200.12
right-angled 278.7
quadrangular 278.9
orthography 546.4
orthopedic 90.15
orts remainder 256.1
refuse 391.4
Oscar 646.2
oscillate
vacillate 362.8
be frequent 847.3
recur 850.5
change 854.5
vibrate 916.10
oscillating
vacillating 362.10
constant 847.5
oscillatory 916.15
oscillation
vacillation 362.2
constancy 847.2
periodicity 850.2
changing 854.3
vibration 916.1
oscillator 916.9
oscillatory
vacillating 362.10
periodic 850.7
oscillating 916.15
oscilloscope
instrument 916.8
radar 1036.1
osculate contact 223.10
kiss 562.19
Osiris 682.5
osmose 187.13
osmosis
transferal 176.1
sorption 187.6
ossified skeleton 2.26
hardened 1046.13
ossify callous 94.6
harden 1046.7

ossuary
mortuary 309.9
urn 309.12
tomb 309.16
ostensible
apparent 33.11
conspicuous 348.12
specious 354.27
pretexted 376.5
illusory 976.9
ostentation
display 348.2
conspicuousness 348.4
sham 354.3
ornateness 498.2
pretension 501.1
ostentatiousness 501.1
grandiloquence 545.1
ostentatious
pretentious 501.18
grandiloquent 545.8
ornate 498.12
osteopath 90.4
osteopathy 73.2
ostracism
disapproval 510.1
ostracization 586.3
elimination 773.4
banishment 909.4
ostracize
disapprove 510.4
turn thumbs down 586.6
exclude 773.4
banish 909.17
other
n a different thing 780.3
adj additional 253.10
unrelated 776.6
another 780.8
fresh 841.8
substitute 862.8
other-directed
extroverted 92.41
moved 375.30
conformable 867.5
other self
friend 588.1
self 865.5
other side 215.3
otherwise
adj other 780.8
adv contrarily 779.9
in other ways 780.11
otherworldly
heavenly 681.12
supernatural 870.15
visionary 986.24
immaterial 1053.7
extraterrestrial 1072.26
otic ear 2.28
auditory 48.13
otiose idle 331.18
fruitless 391.12
unserviceable 391.14
trivial 998.19
otology 48.9
ought to 641.3
oui 332.18
Ouija 689.6
ounce
modicum 248.2

weight 297.8
oust depose 447.4
eject 909.13
evict 909.15
ouster
ejection 909.1
eviction 909.2
ejector 909.11
out
n outlet 190.9
excuse 600.4
game 745.3
v be revealed 351.8
fight fire 1022.7
adj asleep 22.22
unconscious 25.8
dead-drunk 88.32
dislocated 160.9
exterior 206.7
disused 390.10
dissimilar 787.4
old-fashioned 842.16
odd 870.11
erroneous 975.16
extinguished 1022.11
adv to the point of
exhaustion 21.14
audibly 50.18
hence 188.20
forth 190.21
externally 206.10
at a loss 473.9
prep from 188.21
out of 190.22
outage 795.2
out-and-out
downright 247.12
thorough 794.10
unqualified 960.2
outback
n open space 158.4
hinterland 233.2
remote region 261.4
wasteland 891.2
adj hinterland 233.9
secluded 584.8
outbalance 297.14
outbrave 492.12
outbreak
emotional outburst 105.9
revolt 327.4
outburst 671.6
beginning 818.1
outbuilding 228.9
outburst
exclamation 59.2
emotional outburst 105.9
outburst of anger 152.9
ejection 190.3
outbreak 671.6
disgorgement 909.7
flare 1019.14
outcast
n recluse 584.5
social outcast 586.4
exclusiveness 773.3
alien 774.3
oddity 870.4
adj unplaced 160.10
forlorn 584.12
cast-off 586.10

outclass outdo 249.9
defeat 412.6
out cold asleep 22.22
unconscious 25.8
dead-drunk 88.32
outcome ending 190.9
event 831.1
effect 887.1
product 893.1
solution 940.1
outcrop
n visibility 31.1
v appear 33.8
outcry
n noise 53.3
vociferation 59.4
lament 115.3
auction 734.4
v vociferate 59.8
outdate 842.9
outdated
disused 390.10
old-fashioned 842.16
outdistance
distance 249.10
reach out 261.5
outdo outrival 249.9
defeat 412.6
excel 999.11
outdoor 206.8
outdoors
n outside 206.3
adv out of doors
206.11
outer 206.7
outermost 206.7
outer space
the universe 158.1
remote region 261.4
depths 275.3
space 1072.3
outface 492.12
outfield
playground 743.11
baseball 745.1
outfielder 745.2
outfit
n wardrobe 5.2
costume 5.9
equipment 385.4
military unit 461.22
impedimenta 471.3
clique 617.6
team 617.7
company 770.3
set 770.12
v costume 5.41
equip 385.8
outflank 415.11
outflow
n outflowing 190.4
flow 238.4
spendings 626.2
v run out 190.13
outflowing
n outflow 190.4
adj outgoing 190.19
out for after 382.12
out to 403.17
searching 938.38
outgoer 190.10

out of work 331.18
out on a limb
  exposed 1006.15
  in trouble 1013.22
outpatient 85.43
outperform 249.9
outpost
  frontier 211.5
  vanguard 216.2
  hinterland 233.2
  remote region 261.4
  guard 1008.9
outpouring
  n outflow 190.4
  plenty 991.2
  adj outgoing 190.19
output yield 472.5
  receipts 627.1
  production 893.2
outrage
  n indignity 156.2
  mistreatment 389.2
  injustice 650.4
  misdeed 655.2
  evil 1000.3
  v offend 152.21
  insult 156.5
  mistreat 389.5
  violate 435.4
  work evil 1000.6
outrageous
  insulting 156.8
  overpriced 632.12
  undue 640.9
  disgraceful 661.11
  violent 671.16
  absurd 923.11
  excessive 993.16
  terrible 1000.9
outré 923.11
outreach
  outdo 249.9
  be long 267.5
  deceive 356.14
  outwit 415.11
outright
  adj downright 247.12
  thorough 794.10
  unqualified 960.2
  adv freely 430.32
  free and clear 469.12
  completely 794.14
outrun
  n skiing 753.1
  v overtake 174.13
  outdo 249.9
  defeat 412.6
outset
  n beginning 818.1
  v set out 188.8
outshine
  outdo 249.9
  defeat 412.6
outside
  n appearance 33.2
  exterior 206.2
  outdoors 206.3
  roulette 759.12
  adj exterior 206.7
  outdoor 206.8
  extrinsic 768.3

extraneous 774.5
  adv externally 206.10
  outdoors 206.11
outside chance
  possibility 966.1
  small chance 972.9
outside of 773.10
outsider
  exclusiveness 773.3
  alien 774.3
  oddity 870.4
outsize
  n oversize 257.5
  adj large 247.7
  oversize 257.23
outskirts
  environment 209.1
  bounds 211.1
  frontier 211.5
  town 230.1
  city district 230.6
  remote region 261.4
outsmart
  deceive 356.14
  outwit 415.11
outspoken
  communicative 343.10
  artless 416.5
  free-acting 430.23
  speaking 524.31
  candid 644.17
outstanding
  exterior 206.7
  eminent 247.9
  remarkable 247.10
  superior 249.12
  superlative 249.13
  remaining 256.7
  protruding 283.14
  conspicuous 348.12
  due 623.10
  prominent 662.17
  notable 997.19
outstare 492.12
outstretched 259.11
outstrip lead 165.2
  overtake 174.13
  loom 247.5
  outdo 249.9
outtalk persuade 375.23
  outspeak 540.7
out to 403.17
outward
  adj apparent 33.11
  exterior 206.7
  formal 580.7
  extrinsic 768.3
  adv forth 190.21
outwear 827.8
outweigh excel 249.6
  overweigh 297.14
outwit outdo 249.9
  deceive 356.14
  outfox 415.11
outworn
  disused 390.10
  obsolete 842.15
oval
  n ovule 280.6
  playground 743.11
  track 755.1

horse racing 757.1
  adj ovate 280.12
ovarian genital 2.29
  glandular 13.8
ovary 2.13
ovation
  celebration 487.1
  applause 509.2
oven kiln 742.5
  hot place 1019.11
over
  adj superior 249.12
  remaining 256.7
  higher 272.19
  ended 820.8
  past 837.7
  surplus 993.18
  adv inversely 205.8
  additionally 253.11
  on high 272.21
  again 849.17
  excessively 993.22
  prep all over 159.28
  through 161.27
  beyond 261.21
  on 295.37
  during 821.14
  in excess of 993.26
overabundance 993.2
overabundant 993.19
overact affect 500.12
  overdramatize 704.31
  overdo 993.10
overacted
  affected 500.15
  dramatic 704.33
  overdone 993.21
overactive 330.24
overactivity 330.9
overage excess 256.4
  surplus 993.5
overall
  adj cumulative 770.23
  comprehensive 772.7
  adv throughout 794.17
  generally 864.17
overall length 267.1
overambitious 101.12
over and above
  adj surplus 993.18
  prep with 253.12
  in excess of 993.26
over and over 849.16
over-anxious
  overzealous 101.12
  anxious 126.7
overassess 949.2
overawe
  daunt 127.18
  domineer 612.16
overbearing
  n authoritativeness 417.3
  adj arrogant 141.9
  imperious 417.16
overblown
  past one's prime 303.15
  overfull 993.20
overboard 182.74
overburden
  n onerousness 297.2
  burden 297.7

overfullness 993.3
  v burden 297.13
  overload 993.15
  go hard with 1011.8
overburdened
  careworn 126.9
  weighted 297.18
  overfull 993.20
overcareful 494.11
overcast
  n atmosphere 184.32
  cloudiness 319.4
  darkening 1027.6
  v cloud 319.7
  darken 1027.9
  adj cloudy 319.8
  gloomy 1027.14
overcautious 494.11
overcharge
  n cathexis 92.34
  surcharge 632.5
  overfullness 993.3
  v exaggerate 355.3
  ornament 545.7
  charge 630.12
  overprice 632.7
  overload 993.15
overclouded 319.8
overcoat 5.13
overcome
  v unnerve 128.10
  excel 249.6
  defeat 411.5
  surmount 412.7
  adj dead-drunk 88.32
  overwrought 105.26
  crushed 112.29
  unnerved 128.14
  defeated 412.14
overcompensation
  defense mechanism 92.23
  inequality 791.1
overconfidence
  rashness 493.1
  confidence 970.5
overconfident
  rash 493.7
  confident 970.21
overconscientious
  overfastidious 495.12
  conscientious 644.15
overcooked 11.8
overcount 949.2
overcritical
  overfastidious 495.12
  critical 510.23
overcrossing 383.9
overcrowded
  full 794.11
  teeming 884.9
  overfull 993.20
overdeveloped
  grown 14.3
  oversize 257.23
  expanded 259.12
  excessive 993.16
overdo
  exaggerate 355.3
  overindulge 669.5
  overrun 910.4
  go too far 993.10

overdone done 11.8
  exaggerated 355.4
  affected 500.15
  grandiloquent 545.8
  overwrought 993.21
overdose
  n superabundance
    993.2
  cloyer 994.3
  v take sick 85.47
  commit suicide 308.22
  oversupply 993.14
  satiate 994.4
overdraft arrears 623.2
  insolvency 625.3
overdraw
  misrepresent 350.3
  exaggerate 355.3
  overspend 486.7
  overextend 993.13
overdrawn
  exaggerated 355.4
  overdone 993.21
overdress 5.42
overdrive task 725.16
  overdo 993.10
overdue
  expected 130.13
  anachronous 833.3
  late 846.16
overeager
  overzealous 101.12
  reckless 493.8
overeat 672.5
overelaborate
  v overdo 993.10
  adj ornate 498.12
  affected 533.9
  grandiloquent 545.8
overemotional
  emotionalistic 93.19
  excitable 105.28
overemphasis
  exaggeration 355.1
  overdoing 993.6
overemphasize
  overdo 993.10
  emphasize 997.14
overenthusiastic
  overzealous 101.12
  reckless 493.8
  fanatic 926.32
overestimate
  n overestimation 949.1
  v exaggerate 355.3
  overpraise 511.7
  overreckon 949.2
overestimated
  exaggerated 355.4
  overrated 949.3
overexcited 105.26
overexercise
  n overdoing 993.6
  v overdo 993.10
overexert strain 725.10
  overdo 993.10
overexpand 993.13
overexpansion 993.7
overextend
  strain 725.10
  overdraw 993.13

overextension
  overactivity 330.9
  strain 725.2
  overdrawing 993.7
overexuberant 993.19
overfed
  oversize 257.23
  overgorged 672.7
  overfull 993.20
  satiated 994.6
overfill fill 794.7
  overload 993.15
  satiate 994.4
overflow
  n spillage 238.6
  wordiness 538.2
  plenty 991.2
  overfullness 993.3
  v flow over 238.17
  teem with 884.5
  run over 910.7
  abound 991.5
  superabound 993.8
overflowing
  n overflow 238.6
  overrunning 910.1
  adj much 247.8
  diffuse 538.11
  teeming 884.9
  plentiful 991.7
  overfull 993.20
overfull full 794.11
  overloaded 993.20
  satiated 994.6
overgarment 5.12
overgrow grow 14.2
  spread 259.6
  expand 259.7
  vegetate 310.34
  overspread 910.5
  superabound 993.8
overgrown grown 14.3
  large 247.7
  oversize 257.23
  overdeveloped 259.12
  luxuriant 310.43
  overrun 910.10
  excessive 993.16
overgrowth
  bodily development 14.1
  oversize 257.5
  growth 259.3
  overrunning 910.1
  excess 993.1
overhang
  n overhanging 202.3
  v hang over 202.7
  overlie 295.30
  be imminent 840.2
overhanging
  n overhang 202.3
  adj overhung 202.11
  imminent 840.3
overhaul
  n reparation 396.6
  examination 938.3
  v overtake 174.13
  repair 396.14
  take account of 628.9
  examine 938.24
  check 1017.21

overhead
  n roof 295.6
  expenses 626.3
  adv on high 272.21
overhear hear 48.11
  know 551.15
overheated hot 1019.25
  heated 1020.29
overindulge
  be intemperate 669.5
  overeat 672.5
  overdo 993.10
overindulgence
  unstrictness 426.2
  indulgence 427.3
  intemperance 669.1
  gluttony 672.1
  excess 993.1
overindulgent
  unstrict 426.5
  indulgent 427.8
  intemperate 669.7
overjoyed 95.17
overkill
  exaggeration 355.1
  attack 459.1
  plenty 991.2
  overdoing 993.6
overland 234.8
overlap
  n overlayer 295.4
  agreement 788.1
  superfluity 993.4
  v overlie 295.30
  agree 788.6
overlapping
  n overlayer 295.4
  adj overlying 295.36
  related 775.9
overlarge
  oversize 257.23
  exaggerated 355.4
  excessive 993.16
overlay
  n overlayer 295.4
  v cover 295.19
  ornament 545.7
overlie 295.30
overload
  n burden 297.7
  overfullness 993.3
  v burden 297.13
  ornament 545.7
  overlade 993.15
  go hard with 1011.8
overloaded
  weighted 297.18
  ornate 545.11
  overfull 993.20
overlong 827.11
overlook
  n observation post 27.8
  v accept 134.7
  condone 148.4
  slight 157.6
  front on 216.9
  rise above 272.11
  neglect 340.6
  suffer 443.10
  supervise 573.10
  bewitch 691.9

  examine 938.24
  keep an open mind 979.7
  be inattentive 984.2
overlooked
  forgiven 148.7
  neglected 340.14
overlord
  master 575.1
  potentate 575.8
  chief 997.10
overlying 295.36
overmaster
  overcome 412.7
  subdue 432.9
  domineer 612.16
overmatched 412.14
overmodest 500.19
overmuch
  n excess 993.1
  adj excessive 993.16
  superabundant 993.19
  adv excessively 993.22
overnice
  overfastidious 495.12
  overprecise 500.18
  affected 533.9
overnight 315.11
over one's head
  adj hard to understand
    522.14
  insufficient 992.9
  adv deep 275.16
overparticular 495.12
overpass
  n crossing 170.2
  passageway 383.3
  bridge 383.9
  overrunning 910.1
  v traverse 177.20
  excel 249.6
  outdistance 249.10
  overrun 910.4
  exceed 993.9
overpay 632.8
overplay
  outdo 249.9
  overdo 993.10
overplayed
  dramatic 704.33
  overdone 993.21
overplus
  n excess 256.4
  surplus 993.5
  adj surplus 993.18
overpopulation 993.2
overpower
  be strong 15.9
  drown out 53.8
  overcome 412.7
overpowered
  overwrought 105.26
  defeated 412.14
overpowering
  impregnable 15.19
  exciting 105.30
  irresistible 412.18
overprice 632.7
overpriced 632.12
overprint 548.14
overrate 949.2
overrated 949.3

overreach
exaggerate 355.3
deceive 356.14
outwit 415.11
overrun 910.4
exceed 993.9
overreact
exaggerate 355.3
overdo 993.10
overrefined
sensitive 24.12
overfastidious 495.12
overnice 500.18
affected 533.9
sophistical 936.10
overreligious
zealous 692.11
fanatic 926.32
override
outdo 249.9
overlie 295.30
conquer 412.10
repeal 445.2
domineer 612.16
run over 910.7
overriding 997.24
overripe nasty 64.7
past one's prime
303.15
overrule repeal 445.2
rule 612.14
overruling chief 249.14
imperious 417.16
paramount 997.24
overrun
n overrunning 910.1
surplus 993.5
v pervade 221.7
overflow 238.17
spread 259.6
vegetate 310.34
appropriate 480.19
compose 548.16
overgo 910.4
infest 910.6
run over 910.7
superabound 993.8
exceed 993.9
adj luxuriant 310.43
overspread 910.10
overrunning
permeation 221.3
overflow 238.6
storm 459.6
inundation 910.1
overgoing 910.1
infestation 910.2
overseas
adj nonresident 222.12
transoceanic 261.11
adv oversea 240.11
abroad 774.6
oversee 573.10
overseer 574.2
oversell
exaggerate 355.3
oversupply 993.14
oversensitive
sensitive 24.12
touchy 110.21
overfastidious 495.12

overset
n overturn 205.2
surplus 993.5
v capsize 182.44
overturn 205.6
overthrow 395.20
overcome 412.7
oversexed 75.25
overshadow
eclipse 249.8
rise above 272.11
cloud 319.7
darken 1027.9
overshoot
land 184.43
overrun 910.4
exceed 993.9
oversight
neglect 340.1
nonobservance 435.1
supervision 573.2
government 612.1
operation 889.1
slip 975.4
protectorship 1008.2
oversimplification
undevelopment 406.4
oversimplicity 798.3
oversize
n outsize 257.5
adj oversized 257.23
oversleep sleep 22.13
miss an opportunity 844.5
be late 846.7
overspend
spend more than one has
486.7
overpay 632.8
overdo 993.10
overspread
v pervade 221.7
cover 295.19
disperse 771.4
bespread 910.5
infest 910.6
superabound 993.8
adj overrun 910.10
overstate
misrepresent 350.3
falsify 354.16
exaggerate 355.3
overestimate 949.2
overstay 846.15
overstep
presume on 640.7
overrun 910.4
transgress 910.9
exceed 993.9
overstrain
n fatigue 21.1
strain 725.2
overdoing 993.6
overextension 993.7
v fatigue 21.4
strain 725.10
overdo 993.10
overextend 993.13
overstuffed
upholstered 295.34
full 794.11
overfull 993.20

satiated 994.6
oversubtle
overfastidious 495.12
sophistical 936.10
oversupply
n superabundance 993.2
surplus 993.5
v overprovide 993.14
oversweet 66.5
overt 348.10
overt act 328.3
overtake
intoxicate 88.23
outstrip 174.13
come after 835.3
overtax
burden 297.13
overprice 632.7
strain 725.10
task 725.16
overdo 993.10
over-the-counter drug 86.4
over the hill
past one's prime 303.15
out of practice 414.18
overthrow
n overturn 205.2
fall 395.3
defeat 412.1
deposal 447.2
change 852.2
revolution 860.1
downthrow 913.2
refutation 958.2
v turn over 205.6
revolt 327.7
destroy 395.20
overcome 412.7
depose 447.4
change 852.7
revolutionize 860.4
overturn 913.6
refute 958.5
overthrown
ruined 395.28
defeated 412.14
disproved 958.7
overtime
basketball game 747.3
hockey 749.3
shift 825.3
overtire 21.4
overtired 21.11
overtone tone 50.2
milieu 209.3
meaning 518.1
implication 519.2
harmonics 709.16
overture
n offer 439.1
prelude 708.26
curtain-raiser 816.2
v make advances 439.7
overturn
n upset 205.2
fall 395.3
defeat 412.1
revolution 860.1
downthrow 913.2
v capsize 182.44
turn over 205.6

destroy 395.20
overcome 412.7
revolutionize 860.4
overthrow 913.6
refute 958.5
overvalue 949.2
overview
scrutiny 27.6
abridgment 557.1
overweening
n presumptuousness
141.2
insolence 142.1
confidence 970.5
adj vain 140.8
presumptuous 141.10
insolent 142.9
rash 493.7
confident 970.21
excessive 993.16
overweight
n oversize 257.5
weight 297.1
overfullness 993.3
v burden 297.13
outweigh 297.14
overload 993.15
adj corpulent 257.18
oversize 257.23
heavy 297.16
overwhelm
be strong 15.9
drown out 53.8
aggrieve 112.19
astonish 122.6
pervade 221.7
overflow 238.17
submerge 367.7
destroy 395.21
whelm 412.8
subdue 432.9
raid 459.20
teem with 884.5
run over 910.7
refute 958.5
oversupply 993.14
overwhelmed
overwrought 105.26
overcome 112.29
wondering 122.9
flooded 238.25
defeated 412.14
overrun 910.10
overwhelming
n permeation 221.3
overflow 238.6
overrunning 910.1
adj impregnable 15.19
exciting 105.30
astonishing 122.12
irresistible 412.18
teeming 884.9
evidential 957.16
overwork
n overdoing 993.6
v work hard 725.13
task 725.16
overdo 993.10
overworked
ornate 498.12
trite 864.16

overwrought
  overexcited 105.26
  exaggerated 355.4
  ornate 498.12
  grandiloquent 545.8
  overdone 993.21
overzealous
  ultrazealous 101.12
  obstinate 361.8
  reckless 493.8
  zealous 692.11
  fanatic 926.32
ovine 311.46
oviparous 305.23
ovoid
  n oval 280.6
  adj oval 280.12
  spherical 282.9
ovule
  oval 280.6
  ovum 305.12
  egg 305.15
ovum egg 305.12
  copulation 75.7
  vital force 886.7
owe be indebted 623.5
  be liable 897.3
owed payable 623.10
  due 639.7
owing payable 623.10
  due 639.7
  attributable 888.6
owing to
  conj resulting from 887.8
  prep because of 888.9
owl bird of ill omen 133.6
  bird 311.28
owlish 570.17
own
  v acknowledge 332.11
  confess 351.7
  have title to 469.5
  adj possessed 469.8
own accord 430.7
owner proprietor 470.2
  jockey 757.2
ownership 469.2
own free will 430.7
owning
  n confession 351.3
  possession 469.1
  adj possessing 469.9
ox
  symbol of strength 15.8
  beast of burden 176.8
  cattle 311.6
  bungler 414.8
oxcart 179.3
oxidation decay 393.6
  burning 1020.5
oxidize corrode 393.21
  burn 1020.24
  chemicalize 1060.8
oxygenate air 317.11
  vaporize 1067.8
oxymoron
  ambiguity 539.1
  self-contradiction 779.3
  inconsistency 789.2
  impossibility 967.1
  dilemma 1013.7

oyez! hark! 48.16
  attention! 983.22
oyster fowl part 10.23
  marine animal 311.30
ozone 317.1
pa 560.10
PA
  sound reproduction system
    50.11
  hospital staff 90.11
  practice of medicine 90.13
pabulum 10.3
pace
  n velocity 172.4
  step 177.11
  gait 177.12
  v lead 165.2
  walk 177.27
  walk back and forth 177.28
  go on horseback 177.34
  row 182.53
  measure 300.10
pacer race horse 311.14
  jockey 757.2
pacesetter leader 574.6
  jockey 757.2
pachyderm 311.4
pacific
  quiescent 173.12
  meek 433.15
  peaceful 464.9
  unbelligerent 464.10
  pacificatory 465.12
pacification
  peacemaking 465.1
  truce 465.5
  modulation 670.2
pacifier
  sedative 86.12
  peacemaker 466.5
  moderator 670.3
pacifism inaction 329.1
  peaceableness 464.4
  moderation 670.1
pacifist
  n pacificist 464.6
  adj unbelligerent 464.10
pacifistic 670.10
pacify quiet 173.8
  conciliate 465.7
  calm 670.7
  order 807.4
pacifying
  pacificatory 465.12
  tranquilizing 670.15
pack
  n freight 176.6
  parachute 181.13
  amount 244.2
  lot 247.4
  stopping 293.5
  film 714.10
  card 758.2
  company 770.3
  group of animals 770.5
  bundle 770.8
  multitude 884.3
  impediment 1012.6
  v load 159.15
  transport 176.12
  fill 196.7

package 212.9
  stop 293.7
  wrap 295.20
  tamper with 354.17
  assemble 770.18
  bundle 770.20
  stuff 794.7
  teem with 884.5
  prearrange 965.5
  overload 993.15
  obstruct 1012.12
package
  n packaging 212.2
  bundle 770.8
  all 792.3
  combination 805.1
  v pack 212.9
  wrap 295.20
  bundle 770.20
packaged
  packed 212.12
  covered 295.31
  assembled 770.21
package deal
  transaction 731.4
  all 792.3
  combination 805.1
package tour
  vacation 20.3
  journey 177.5
packaging 212.2
pack animal 176.8
pack away load 159.15
  store 386.10
packed
  packaged 212.12
  stopped 293.11
  tampered with 354.30
  crowded 770.22
  full 794.11
  stuck 855.16
  teeming 884.9
  prearranged 965.8
  overfull 993.20
  dense 1045.12
packet dose 87.20
  ship 180.1
  wealth 618.3
  bundle 770.8
packet boat 353.6
pack in enter 189.7
  thrust in 191.7
  assemble 770.18
  densify 1045.9
packing
  placement 159.6
  transportation 176.3
  lining 196.3
  packaging 212.2
  stopping 293.5
packinghouse 739.3
pack off repulse 908.3
  dismiss 909.18
pack of troubles 96.8
pack rat 770.15
pact 437.1
pad
  n thud 52.3
  foot 199.5
  partition 213.5
  quarters 228.4

race horse 311.14
  print 517.7
  record book 549.11
  bedding 901.20
  safeguard 1008.3
  v thud 52.15
  relieve 120.5
  creep 177.26
  walk 177.27
  fill 196.7
  protract 538.8
  complete 794.7
  iterate 849.8
padded cell 926.14
padding
  creeping 177.17
  lining 196.3
  extra 254.4
  stopping 293.5
  redundancy 849.3
  superfluity 993.4
  safeguard 1008.3
  softening 1047.5
paddle
  n gait 177.12
  oar 180.15
  rod 605.2
  agitator 917.9
  v way of walking 177.28
  row 182.53
  punish 604.15
  agitate 917.10
  moisten 1065.12
paddle wheel
  gambling wheel 759.16
  propeller 904.6
paddling 604.5
paddy 1069.9
Paddy 232.7
paddy wagon 179.11
padlock
  n lock 428.5
  v close 293.6
padre clergyman 699.2
  priest 699.5
padrone 575.1
paean cheer 116.2
  thanks 150.2
  praise 509.5
  laud 696.3
  sacred music 708.17
paella 10.11
paesano
  fellow citizen 227.5
  friend 588.4
pagan
  n heathen 688.7
  unbeliever 695.11
  adj paganish 688.11
  unbelieving 695.19
  idolatrous 697.7
  unlearned 930.14
paganism
  heathenism 688.4
  idolatry 697.1
  unenlightenment 930.4
page
  n makeup 554.12
  attendant 577.5
  part of writing 793.2
  paper 1054.5

v summon 420.11
number 1017.17
pageant spectacle 33.7
display 501.4
pageantry
spectacle 33.7
display 501.4
paginate 1017.17
pagination 1017.9
pagoda tower 272.6
temple 703.2
paid
employed 615.20
paid-up 624.22
pain
n bread 10.28
physical suffering 26
suffering 26.1
symptom 85.9
annoyance 96.2
distress 96.5
tormentor 96.10
distressfulness 98.5
v give pain 26.7
grieve 96.17
distress 98.14
pained in pain 26.9
grieved 96.23
painful hurtful 26.10
distressing 98.20
laborious 725.18
troublesome 1013.18
pain in the neck
annoyance 96.2
tormentor 96.10
tedious person 118.5
pain killer
anesthetic 25.3
sedative 86.12
painless 1014.13
pains
painstakingness 339.2
punishment 604.1
exertion 725.1
painstaking
n painstakingness 339.2
adj diligent 339.11
paint
n color 35.8
blanket 295.12
horse 311.11
art equipment 712.18
card 758.2
makeup 1016.12
v color 35.14
represent 349.8
describe 349.9
ornament 498.8
figure 498.9
portray 712.19
beautify 1016.16
paintbrush 712.18
painter wild cat 311.22
artist 716.4
painting
paint-work 35.12
coloring 712.4
canvas 712.14
graphic arts 713.1
paint the town red
go on a spree 88.28

make merry 743.24
pair
n rig 179.5
set 784.5
two 873.2
deuce 873.3
v assemble 770.18
put together 800.5
league 805.4
double 873.5
adj numeric 1017.23
paired married 563.21
accompanying 769.9
joined 800.13
leagued 805.6
coupled 873.8
pairing joining 800.1
doubleness 873.1
pair off average 246.2
get married 563.15
league 805.4
double 873.5
paisano 227.5
pajamas 5.21
pal
n friend 588.4
v associate with 582.18
palace 228.7
palace revolution 860.1
paladin defender 460.7
brave person 492.8
palaestra 463.1
palatable edible 8.33
tasty 63.8
desirable 100.30
palate taste 62.1
taste bud 62.5
vocal organ 524.18
discrimination 944.1
palatial
residential 228.32
grandiose 501.21
palaver
n flattery 511.1
nonsense 520.2
speech 524.1
chatter 540.3
talk 541.3
conference 541.6
v flatter 511.5
chatter 540.5
confer 541.11
palazzo 228.7
pale
n bounds 211.1
enclosed place 212.3
sphere 231.2
plot 231.4
leg 273.6
heraldry 647.2
v blur 32.4
decolor 36.5
lose color 36.6
change color 105.19
take fright 127.11
fence 212.7
adj inconspicuous 32.6
soft-colored 35.22
colorless 36.7
whitish 37.8
unhealthy 85.54

dull 117.6
deathly 307.29
paleface 312.3
paleography
exegetics 341.8
linguistics 523.13
writing system 546.3
handwriting 547.3
paleolith 842.6
paleolithic 842.20
paleontology 1068.3
palette 712.18
palindrome
grammar 205.3
wordplay 489.8
palinode 363.3
palisade
n precipice 200.3
fence 212.4
slope 237.2
leg 273.6
v fence 212.7
fortify 460.9
pall
n cover 295.2
graveclothes 309.14
veil of secrecy 345.3
v be tedious 118.6
satiate 994.4
palladium 1008.3
pallbearer 309.7
pallet 901.20
palliate relieve 120.5
extenuate 600.12
moderate 670.6
qualify 959.3
palliative
n alleviative 86.10
extenuation 600.5
moderator 670.3
adj lenitive 86.40
relieving 120.9
justifying 600.13
alleviative 670.16
qualifying 959.7
pallid colorless 36.7
dull 117.6
terrified 127.26
pallor color 35.1
paleness 36.2
dullness 117.1
deathliness 307.12
palm
n clutches 474.4
trophy 646.3
v touch 73.6
take 480.13
steal 482.13
palmate 171.8
palmistry 962.2
palm off on 643.7
palm oil
incentive 375.7
gratuity 478.5
palmy 1010.13
palooka fighter 461.2
boxer 754.2
jockey 757.2
palp 73.4
palpable
touchable 73.11

weighable 297.19
manifest 348.8
substantial 763.6
palpate 73.6
palpitant staccato 55.7
pulsative 916.18
palpitate drum 55.4
be excited 105.18
pulsate 916.12
flutter 917.12
palpitating 916.18
palpitation
staccato 55.1
excitement 105.5
trepidation 127.5
pulsation 916.3
flutter 917.4
palsied
anemic 85.61
stricken in years 303.18
shaking 917.17
palsy
n paralysis 85.27
shaking 917.2
v deaden 25.4
adj chummy 587.20
palsy-walsy
n friend 588.4
v befriend 587.11
adj chummy 587.20
palter
prevaricate 344.7
quibble 936.9
paltry
ungenerous 651.6
base 661.12
meager 992.10
poor 998.21
inferior 1005.9
paludal 243.3
pampas plain 236.1
grassland 310.8
pamper
indulge 427.6
foster 449.16
pampering 427.3
pamphlet 554.11
pan
n container 195.1
face 216.4
v cook 11.5
criticize 510.14
photograph 714.14
mine 1058.14
Pan
forest god 678.11
fertility 890.5
panacea 86.3
panache feather 3.16
showiness 501.3
pancake
n griddlecake 10.45
v land 184.43
panchromatic 714.17
pancreas viscera 2.16
digestive organ 2.17
digestion 7.8
pancreatic 13.8
pandect
treatise 556.1
abridgment 557.1

code 673.5
pandemic
  n epidemic 85.5
  adj contagious 85.62
  prevalent 864.12
pandemonium
  noise 53.3
  turbulence 671.2
Pandemonium
  hell 682.1
  utopia 986.11
pander
  n procurer 665.18
  v vulgarize 497.9
  prostitute oneself 665.21
pandering 665.8
pander to
  toady to 138.8
  aid 449.18
  serve 577.13
pandit 571.1
Pandora's box
  affliction 96.8
  trouble 1013.3
pandowdy 10.41
pane
  bread 10.28
  window 292.7
  lamina 296.2
  transparent substance 1029.2
panegyric
  n praise 509.5
  adj approbatory 509.16
panel
  n partition 213.5
  lamina 296.2
  forum 423.3
  discussion 541.7
  jury 596.6
  litigant 598.11
  assembly 770.2
  v select a jury 598.16
paneling 1054.3
panelist 543.4
panel show 1035.2
pang throe 26.2
  pain 96.5
  compunction 113.2
panhandle 440.15
panhandler
  nonworker 331.11
  beggar 440.8
panhandling 440.6
panic
  n fear 127.1
  nervousness 128.1
  joke 489.6
  bear panic 737.22
  v start 127.12
  put in fear 127.16
  overwhelm 412.8
panicked
  panicky 127.27
  defeated 412.14
panicky
  panic-prone 127.27
  nervous 128.11
  cowardly 491.10
panjandrum 502.5
panning
  n ridicule 508.1

adj ridiculing 508.12
panoply armor 460.3
  throng 770.4
panorama view 33.6
  spectacle 33.7
  picture 712.11
panoramic 772.7
pan out 887.4
pan shot 714.8
pansy weakling 16.6
  homosexual 75.15
pant
  n breathing 2.21
  v burn out 21.5
  be excited 105.18
  speak 524.25
  be hot 1019.22
Pantaloon
  old man 304.2
  buffoon 707.10
pantheism
  religion 675.5
  philosophy 952.5
pantheistic 675.25
pantheon
  the gods 678.1
  temple 703.2
panther 311.22
panting
  n breathlessness 21.3
  trepidation 105.5
  adj respiratory 2.32
  breathless 21.12
  eager 101.8
  precipitate 401.10
pantomime
  n impersonation 349.4
  gesture 517.14
  actor 707.2
  v impersonate 349.12
  gesture 517.21
  act 704.29
pantry closet 197.15
  larder 386.8
pants 5.18
pantywaist
  weakling 16.6
  effeminate male 77.11
pap diet 7.13
  nutriment 10.3
  breast 283.6
  father 560.10
  semiliquid 1062.5
papa 560.10
papacy
  mastership 417.7
  papality 698.6
papal 698.15
Papal Court 595.3
papalism 675.8
paper
  n whiteness 37.2
  thinness 270.7
  writing 547.10
  document 549.5
  newspaper 555.2
  treatise 556.1
  complimentary ticket 634.2
  negotiable instrument 728.11
  paper stock 1054.5
  v face 295.23

paperback 554.3
paper profits 472.3
papers
  naturalization 226.3
  archives 549.2
paper tiger 500.7
paperweight 297.6
papery frail 16.14
  thin 270.16
  wasted 393.35
  fragile 764.7
papilla 283.6
papillary 283.19
papilloma 283.3
papist
  n Catholic 675.19
  adj Catholic 675.29
  papal 698.15
papoose 302.9
pappose 3.25
pappy
  n father 560.10
  adj insipid 65.2
papyrus 547.11
par
  n mean 246.1
  price 738.9
  round 751.3
  equality 790.1
  v golf 751.4
  adj equal 790.7
parabola 279.2
parabolical
  parabolic 279.13
  fictional 722.7
parachute
  n chute 181.13
  life preserver 397.6
  safeguard 1008.3
  v bail out 184.47
  descend 194.5
  plunge 367.6
parachute jump
  parachute 181.13
  plunge 367.1
parachutist 185.8
parade
  n spectacle 33.7
  walk 177.10
  path 383.2
  display 501.4
  procession 812.3
  v go for a walk 177.29
  march 177.30
  manifest 348.5
  flaunt 501.17
  file 812.7
parade ground 463.1
paradiddle 55.1
paradigm
  morphology 526.3
  model 786.1
paradisal
  blissful 97.9
  heavenly 681.12
  ideal 986.23
paradise
  observation 27.8
  happiness 95.2
  preserve 397.7
  auditorium 704.15

park 743.14
  utopia 986.11
  garden 1069.10
Paradise 839.2
paradisiac blissful 97.9
  heavenly 681.12
paradox
  self-contradiction 779.3
  inconsistency 789.2
  impossibility 967.1
  dilemma 1013.7
paradoxical
  self-contradictory 779.8
  inconsistent 789.8
  impossible 967.7
paradoxical sleep 22.5
paraffin 1025.20
paragon superior 249.4
  ideal 659.4
  model 786.4
  the best 999.8
  pattern of perfection
    1002.4
  beauty 1016.8
paragraph
  n phrase 529.1
  part 554.13
  treatise 556.1
  part of writing 793.2
  v diction 532.4
parallel
  n map 159.5
  paralleler 203.2
  zone 231.3
  entrenchment 460.5
  likeness 784.3
  equal 790.4
  v be parallel 203.4
  relate 775.6
  resemble 784.7
  agree 788.6
  equal 790.5
  compare 943.4
  be comparable 943.7
  adj paralleling 203.6
  side 218.6
  accompanying 769.9
  related 775.9
  analogous 784.11
  comparative 943.8
parallel bars 725.7
paralleling
  parallel 203.6
  analogous 784.11
parallelism
  alignment 203
  coextension 203.1
  side 218.1
  symmetry 264.1
  accompaniment 769.1
  similarity 784.1
  agreement 788.1
  equality 790.1
  comparison 943.1
paralogism
  syllogism 935.6
  specious argument 936.3
paralysis
  symptom 85.9
  paralyzation 85.27
  inaction 329.1

paralytic
n cripple 85.45
adj anemic 85.61
passive 329.6
paralyze disable 19.10
deaden 25.4
numb 94.8
astonish 122.6
terrify 127.17
paralyzed
disabled 19.16
drunk 88.33
terrified 127.26
passive 329.6
paramedic
hospital staff 90.11
parachutist 185.8
diver 367.4
parameter
measure 300.2
condition 959.2
paramount
n master 575.1
potentate 575.8
chief 997.10
adj top 198.10
chief 249.14
governing 612.18
principal 997.24
best 999.16
paramountcy
supremacy 249.3
importance 997.1
superexcellence 999.2
paramour lover 104.12
mistress 665.17
paranoia
mental disorder 92.14
dissociation 92.20
schizophrenia 926.4
paranoid
n psychotic 926.17
adj psychotic 926.28
paranymph
wedding party 563.4
deputy 576.1
assistant 616.6
parapet 1012.5
paraphernalia
equipment 385.4
belongings 471.2
paraphilia 75.11
paraphrase
n reproduction 336.3
translation 341.3
v imitate 336.5
rephrase 341.13
paraplegia 85.27
paraplegic 85.45
paraprofessional
teaching fellow 571.4
assistant 616.6
parapsychology 689.4
parasite
barnacle 138.5
follower 166.2
plant 310.4
vermin 311.37
bloodsucker 311.38
nonworker 331.11
attendance 769.6

parasitic
obsequious 138.14
indolent 331.19
rapacious 480.26
concurrent 899.4
parasitism
obsequiousness 138.2
concurrence 899.1
parasol umbrella 295.7
shade 1028.1
paratrooper
parachutist 185.8
diver 367.4
paratroops
elite troops 461.15
army 461.23
parboiled 11.7
Parcae 964.3
parcel
n amount 244.2
real estate 471.6
bundle 770.8
part 793.1
a number 884.2
v package 212.9
quantify 244.4
apportion 477.6
portion out 477.8
bundle 770.20
separate 802.18
dispose 808.9
parceled packed 212.12
apportioned 477.12
parceling 477.1
parcel of land
plot 231.4
field 1069.9
parch shrink 260.9
be hot 1019.22
burn 1020.24
dry 1066.6
parched thirsty 100.26
shrunk 260.13
burned 1020.30
dried 1066.9
parchment
writing 547.10
manuscript 547.11
document 549.5
fragility 1050.2
dryness 1066.2
pardner friend 588.4
partner 616.2
pardon
n pity 145.1
excuse 148.2
acquittal 601.1
v have pity 145.4
forgive 148.3
acquit 601.4
pardonable 600.14
pare peel 6.8
reduce 252.7
excise 255.10
cheapen 633.6
sever 802.11
paregoric
n sedative 86.12
adj sedative 86.45
parent
n progenitor 560.8

author 886.4
v foster 449.16
adj ancestral 560.17
parentage 560.1
parental
loving 104.27
ancestral 560.17
protective 1008.23
parenthesis
grammar 205.3
interjection 213.2
discontinuity 813.1
parenthesize
bracket 212.8
grammaticize 530.16
parenthetical
interjectional 213.9
irrelevant 776.7
incidental 843.11
paresis 85.27
par excellence 249.16
par for the course
n rule 373.4
predetermination 964.1
adj medium 246.3
typical 349.15
prevalent 864.12
parfum 70.2
parget
color 35.14
plaster 295.25
pariah
recluse 584.5
outcast 586.4
oddity 870.4
parietal
enclosing 212.11
partitioned 213.11
parietes 213.5
pari-mutuel
statistics 757.4
betting system 759.4
pari-mutuel machine 759.17
paring flake 296.3
piece 793.3
parish region 231.5
diocese 698.8
the laity 700.1
parishioner 700.2
parity price 738.9
similarity 784.1
equality 790.1
park
n enclosed place 212.3
green 310.7
grassland 310.8
woodland 310.13
preserve 397.7
armory 462.2
public park 743.14
baseball 745.1
v place 159.12
settle 159.17
parlance
language 523.1
diction 532.1
parlay
n bet 759.3
v increase 251.4
bet 759.25

parley
n advice 422.1
peace offer 465.2
conference 541.6
v confer 541.11
parliament 613.1
parliamentarianism 612.8
parliamentary
n train 179.14
adj governmental 612.17
legislative 613.11
parlor
living room 197.5
workplace 739.1
parlor car 197.10
parlous 1006.9
parochial
local 231.9
exclusive 773.9
narrow-minded 980.10
parochialism
exclusiveness 773.3
narrow-mindedness 980.1
parochial school 567.8
parody
n imitation 336.1
reproduction 336.3
bad likeness 350.2
wit 489.1
burlesque 508.6
v imitate 336.5
misrepresent 350.3
burlesque 508.11
lampoon 512.12
parol
n utterance 524.2
adj speech 524.29
parole
n release 431.2
promise 436.1
language 523.1
utterance 524.2
v release 431.5
parolee 429.11
paroxysm pang 26.2
seizure 85.6
outburst 105.9
fit 152.8
upheaval 671.5
spasm 917.6
frenzy 926.7
parquet check 47.4
ground covering 199.3
auditorium 704.15
parrot
n tedium 118.1
imitator 336.4
conformist 867.2
v mimic 336.6
repeat 849.7
memorize 989.17
parrotlike
tedious 118.9
imitative 336.9
diffuse 538.11
repetitious 849.14
parrotry 336.2
parry prevaricate 344.7
dodge 368.8
fend off 460.10
fight 754.4

quibble 936.9
refute 958.5
prevent 1012.14
parrying
prevarication 344.4
fight 754.3
quibbling 936.5
parse
grammaticize 530.16
itemize 801.7
parsimonious
sparing 484.7
economical 635.6
meager 992.10
parsimony
frugality 484
parsimoniousness
484.1
thrift 635.1
meagerness 992.2
parsing grammar 530.1
itemization 801.2
parson 699.2
parsonage house 228.5
pastorage 703.7
part
n contents 196.1
region 231.1
amount 244.2
a length 267.2
function 387.5
estate 471.4
apportioning 477.5
section 554.13
role 704.10
melody part 708.22
passage 708.24
score 708.28
occupation 724.3
mode 765.4
particular 766.3
portion 793.1
component 796.2
v interspace 224.3
open 292.11
die 307.19
apportion 477.6
divorce 566.5
disband 771.8
separate 802.8
part company 802.19
adj partial 793.7
incomplete 795.4
half 875.5
partly 793.8
partake eat 8.20
participate 476.5
take 480.13
be involved 898.3
partaking
n participation 476.1
association 582.6
adj participating 476.8
part and parcel 796.2
parterre 704.15
parthenogenesis 78.6
parthenogenetic 78.16
Parthian shot
leave-taking 188.4
gibe 508.2
remark 524.3

sequel 817.1
partial
n tone 50.2
adj partisan 617.19
interested 650.11
part 793.7
incomplete 795.4
half 875.5
discriminatory 980.12
imperfect 1003.4
partiality
inclination 100.3
love 104.1
preference 371.5
partisanism 617.13
one-sidedness 650.3
prejudice 980.3
partial to
desirous of 100.22
fond of 104.30
partible 802.26
participant
n participator 476.4
adj participating 476.8
participate
take part 476.5
be involved 898.3
participating 476.8
participation
partaking 476.1
association 582.6
inclusion 772.1
participator 476.4
participial 530.17
participle 530.3
particle
modicum 248.2
minute 258.7
part of speech 530.3
piece 793.3
powder 1051.5
parti-color
n variegation 47.1
v variegate 47.7
adj variegated 47.9
particular
n instance 766.3
part 793.1
event 831.2
citation 957.5
adj meticulous 339.12
selective 371.23
proportionate 477.13
fastidious 495.9
detailed 766.9
classificational 809.7
special 865.12
particularity
meticulousness 339.3
fastidiousness 495.1
circumstantiality 766.4
uniqueness 865
individuality 865.1
characteristic 865.4
oneness 872.1
particularization
description 349.2
circumstantiation 766.5
differentiation 780.4
specialization 865.7
reasoning 935.3

particularize
amplify 538.7
itemize 766.6
differentiate 780.6
specialize 865.9
cite 957.13
be accurate 973.11
parting
n departure 188.1
leave-taking 188.4
death 307.1
disbandment 771.3
separation 802.1
adj departing 188.18
separating 802.25
parting shot
leave-taking 188.4
gibe 508.2
sequel 817.1
partisan
n follower 166.2
irregular 461.16
friend 588.1
party member 609.27
supporter 616.9
adj polarizing 456.17
party 609.44
supporting 617.19
partial 650.11
discriminatory 980.12
partisanism
politics 609.1
partisanship 609.25
association 617.13
partiality 650.3
sectarianism 675.4
partisan politics 609.1
partition
n dividing wall 213.5
apportionment 477.1
separation 802.1
bisector 875.3
v set apart 213.8
apportion 477.6
diversify 782.2
separate 802.18
partitioned
walled 213.11
separate 802.20
part music 708.18
partner
n participator 476.4
spouse 563.6
companion 588.3
associate 616.2
bridge 758.3
accompanier 769.4
v cooperate 450.3
assemble 770.18
league 805.4
partner in crime 616.3
partnership
affiliation 450.2
participation 476.1
bar 597.4
association 617.1
company 769.2
part of speech 530.3
parts talent 413.4
substance 763.2
wits 919.2

part time 825.3
part-time 848.3
parturient
pregnant 78.18
beginning 818.15
parturition birth 1.1
origin 818.4
part with discard 390.7
relinquish 475.3
give away 478.21
party
n man 76.5
endorser 332.7
telephoner 347.11
participator 476.4
entertainment 582.11
litigant 598.11
accuser 599.5
political party 609.24
interest 617.4
sect 675.3
festival 743.4
revel 743.6
assembly 770.2
company 770.3
support 901.1
v enjoy oneself 95.14
have a party 582.21
dissipate 669.6
adj partisan 609.44
associating 617.19
party hack
partisan 609.27
politician 610.4
party line
line 347.17
policy 609.4
party pooper 1012.9
par value worth 630.2
price 738.9
parvenu
n vulgarian 497.6
upstart 606.7
rich man 618.7
modern 841.4
adj populational 606.8
pashadom
mastership 417.7
aristocracy 608.9
pass
n ridge 237.5
valley 237.7
narrow place 270.3
ravine 284.9
trick 356.6
passageway 383.3
proposal 439.2
passport 443.7
thrust 459.3
complimentary ticket 634.2
football 746.3
basketball game 747.3
hockey 749.3
hockey game 749.6
soccer 752.3
bridge 758.3
state 765.1
crisis 843.4
circuit 914.2
danger 1006.1
predicament 1013.4

v excrete 12.12
disappear 34.2
progress 162.2
overtake 174.13
transmit 176.10
travel 177.18
average 246.2
outdistance 249.10
die 307.19
ratify 332.12
communicate 343.7
adopt 371.15
spend 387.13
pass away 390.9
perish 395.23
succeed 409.7
promote 446.2
deliver 478.13
bequeath 478.18
not understand 522.11
legislate 613.10
transfer 629.3
change hands 629.4
football 746.5
basketball 747.4
hockey 749.7
soccer 752.4
bet 759.25
cease to exist 762.6
come to an end 820.6
elapse 821.5
flit 828.6
occur 831.5
be past 837.6
throw 904.10
go by 910.8
not know 930.11
stand the test 942.10
suffice 991.4
exceed 993.9
excel 999.11
passable
acceptable 107.12
tolerable 999.20
mediocre 1005.7
passage duct 2.23
progression 162.1
course 172.2
transferal 176.1
travel 177.1
migration 177.4
voyage 182.6
entrance 189.5
corridor 197.18
valley 237.7
channel 239.1
act 328.3
passageway 383.3
part 554.13
excerpt 557.3
legislation 613.5
phrase 708.24
ornament 709.18
part of writing 793.2
conversion 858.1
passageway
n entrance 189.5
corridor 197.18
channel 239.1
opening 292.1
pass 383.3

interj open up! 292.23
pass away 34.2
passbook 628.4
pass by slight 157.6
reject 372.2
be inattentive 984.2
passé past 837.7
obsolete 842.15
passed chosen 371.26
past 837.7
passenger 178.1
passerby traveler 178.1
transient 828.4
spectator 918.1
witness 957.6
pass for go for 349.10
impersonate 349.12
pose as 354.22
passim
here and there 159.25
scatteringly 771.12
passing
n disappearance 34.1
departure 188.1
death 307.1
promotion 446.1
legislation 613.5
basketball game 747.3
hockey 749.3
adj vanishing 34.3
flowing 172.8
traveling 177.36
medium 246.3
hasty 401.9
transient 828.7
happening 831.9
adv awesomely 122.15
passing by
n rejection 372.1
adj spectating 918.7
prep through 161.27
passing fancy
infatuation 104.4
caprice 364.1
passion
sexual desire 75.5
passionateness 93.2
pain 96.5
torment 96.7
desire 100.1
liking 100.2
zeal 101.2
love 104.1
fury 105.8
rage 152.10
will 323.1
vehemence 544.5
turbulence 671.2
sacred music 708.17
cause 886.9
mania 926.12
interest 983.2
passionate lustful 75.27
fervent 93.18
zealous 101.9
amorous 104.26
heated 105.22
fiery 105.29
hot-tempered 110.25
vehement 544.13
turbulent 671.22

interested 983.16
passionless
unfeeling 94.9
undesirous 102.8
passive
n voice 530.14
adj apathetic 94.13
resigned 134.10
inert 173.14
inactive 329.6
submissive 433.12
neutral 467.7
thoughtless 933.4
incurious 982.3
passive resistance
resignation 134.2
disobedience 327.1
inaction 329.1
resistance 453.1
passivity apathy 94.4
resignation 134.2
quiescence 173.1
inertness 173.4
inaction 329.1
languor 331.6
submission 433.1
thoughtlessness 933.1
incuriosity 982.1
passkey 292.10
pass muster
meet with approval 509.15
follow the rule 867.4
stand the test 942.10
suffice 991.4
pass out faint 25.5
disappear 34.2
be drunk 88.27
exit 190.12
die 307.20
issue 352.14
deliver 478.13
disperse 771.4
Passover 701.19
pass over
condone 148.4
consign 176.10
traverse 177.20
die 307.19
neglect 340.6
leave undone 340.7
slight 340.8
deliver 478.13
transfer 629.3
exclude 773.4
pass 910.8
examine 938.24
be inattentive 984.2
passport 443.7
pass the buck
transfer 176.10
outwit 415.11
impose on 643.7
be unfaithful 645.12
pass the hat 440.15
pass the time
waste time 331.13
occupy 724.10
vegetate 761.10
pass through
traverse 177.20
penetrate 189.8

experience 831.8
pass up slight 157.6
leave undone 340.7
reject 372.2
abstain 668.7
password 517.12
past
n tense 530.12
the past 837.1
adj gone 837.7
preterit 837.9
former 837.10
obsolete 842.15
prep beyond 261.21
unintelligible 522.26
after 835.8
in excess of 993.26
pasta 10.33
past due 833.3
paste
n noodles 10.33
fake 354.13
finery 498.3
jewelry 498.5
compound 797.5
adhesive 803.4
blow 902.5
semiliquid 1062.5
pulp 1063.2
v defeat 412.9
stick together 803.9
strike 902.15
pound 902.16
pastel
n softness 35.3
drawing 712.13
art equipment 712.18
adj soft-colored 35.22
pasteurization 79.3
pasteurize 79.24
pasteurized 79.27
pastiche
n imitation 336.1
reproduction 336.3
adoption 621.2
work of art 712.10
similarity 784.1
copy 785.1
hodgepodge 797.6
v imitate 336.5
pastille 70.4
pastime
avocation 724.7
amusement 743.1
past master
master 413.13
producer 892.7
pastor 699.2
pastoral
n scene 712.12
adj rustic 233.6
natural 416.6
pacific 464.9
ecclesiastic 698.13
poetic 720.15
pastoral staff
staff 273.2
ecclesiastical insignia 647.4
attire 702.3
pastorate
the ministry 698.1

parsonage 703.7
protectorship 1008.2
pastrami 10.14
pastry 10.41
pasturage feed 10.4
grassland 310.8
pasture
n eating 8.1
feed 10.4
grassland 310.8
farm 1069.8
v feed 8.18
pasty colorless 36.7
doughy 1047.12
viscous 1062.12
pulpy 1063.6
pat
n thud 52.3
lump 257.10
endearment 562.5
tap 902.7
v thud 52.15
caress 562.16
tap 902.18
adj apt 788.10
immovable 855.15
known 928.26
patch
n spottiness 47.3
plot 231.4
scrap 248.3
mark 517.5
military insignia 647.5
stain 1004.3
ray 1025.5
field 1069.9
v do carelessly 340.9
repair 396.14
patch test 91.15
patch up
do carelessly 340.9
remedy 396.13
repair 396.14
settle 466.7
patchwork check 47.4
hodgepodge 797.6
patchy spotted 47.13
shabby 393.32
incomplete 795.4
mixed 797.14
discontinuous 813.4
irregular 851.3
imperfect 1003.4
pate head 198.6
brain 919.6
pâté 10.21
patent
n copyright 210.3
exemption 430.8
permission 443.1
grant 443.5
privilege 642.2
church 703.10
safeguard 1008.3
v limit 210.5
preserve 397.8
authorize 443.11
protect 1008.18
adj distinct 31.7
manifest 348.8
obvious 970.15

patented limited 210.7
authorized 443.17
protected 1008.21
patent medicine
nostrum 86.2
medicine 86.4
pater father 560.9
ancestor 560.10
paterfamilias
father 560.9
master 575.1
paternal loving 104.27
ancestral 560.17
paternalism 612.9
paternity
blood relationship 559.1
fatherhood 560.2
Paternoster 696.4
path deviation 164.1
airway 184.33
way 383.1
route 383.1
trail 383.2
track 517.8
circuit 1032.4
pathetic affecting 93.22
distressing 98.20
pitiful 145.8
paltry 998.21
pathfinder
traveler 178.1
preparer 405.5
precursor 816.1
pathogen 85.42
pathogenic
unhealthful 82.5
disease-causing 85.53
pathological
unwholesome 85.55
diseased 85.60
pathology 85.1
pathos sympathy 93.5
distressfulness 98.5
sadness 112.1
pity 145.1
pathway 383.2
patience
inexcitability 106.1
forbearance 134.1
patientness 134.1
forgiveness 148.1
perseverance 360.1
leniency 427.1
tolerance 979.4
patient
n sick person 85.43
subject 942.7
adj inexcitable 106.10
armed with patience 134.9
forgiving 148.6
persevering 360.8
lenient 427.7
tolerant 979.11
patina verdigris 44.2
polish 287.2
lamina 296.2
patinate 44.3
patio 197.21
pâtisserie 10.41
pâtissier 11.3
patois dialect 523.7

jargon 523.9
pat on the back
n congratulation 149.1
encouragement 492.9
v comfort 121.6
motivate 375.21
encourage 492.16
compliment 509.14
patria 232.2
patriarch
old man 304.2
father 560.9
master 575.1
clergy 699.10
back number 842.8
patriarchal
aged 303.16
ancestral 560.17
governmental 612.17
primitive 842.11
patrician
n aristocrat 607.4
nobleman 608.4
adj upper-class 607.10
noble 608.10
patrilineage 559.1
patrilineal 559.6
patrimony 479.2
patriot 591.3
patriotic 591.4
patriotism 591.2
patrol
n protection 1008.1
watchman 1008.10
v traverse 177.20
watch 1008.20
patrol car 179.11
patrolman
watchman 1008.10
policeman 1008.15
patron
ship's officer 183.7
attender 221.5
provider 385.6
giver 478.11
master 575.1
benefactor 592.1
associate 616.9
supporter 704.26
financer 729.10
customer 733.4
protector 1008.5
patronage
fosterage 449.4
recommendation 509.4
political patronage 609.36
custom 731.6
market 733.3
protectorship 1008.2
patronize
condescend 137.8
give oneself airs 141.8
sponsor 449.15
finance 729.16
trade with 731.17
patronizing
n arrogance 141.1
adj arrogant 141.9
patroon 575.1
patsy dupe 358.2
cheater 759.22

scapegoat 862.3
trusting soul 954.4
patter
n thud 52.3
staccato 55.1
rain 316.1
jargon 523.9
acting 704.8
sales talk 734.5
v thud 52.15
drum 55.4
rain 316.10
speak 523.18
talk 524.19
chatter 540.5
act 704.29
pound 902.16
pattern gestalt 92.32
form 262.1
structure 266.1
measure 300.2
behavior 321.1
original 337.2
habit 373.3
diagram 381.3
motif 498.7
paragon 659.4
harmonics 709.11
essence 767.2
model 786.1
philosophy 932.2
paucity fewness 885.1
scarcity 992.3
Paul 684.2
paunch 2.18
paunchy 257.18
pauper 619.4
pauperism 619.2
pauperize 619.6
pauperized
indigent 619.8
ill-provided 992.12
pause
n respite 20.2
demur 325.2
juncture 524.9
hiatus 524.9
notation 709.12
rest 709.21
interruption 813.2
interim 826.1
delay 846.2
ceasing 857.3
grammar 857.4
v take a rest 20.8
demur 325.4
hesitate 362.7
intervene 826.3
cease 857.9
pave 295.22
paved 295.31
pavement
ground covering 199.3
rug 295.9
paving 383.6
foundation 901.6
building material 1054.2
pave the way
prepare the way 405.12
facilitate 1014.7
pavilion 228.9

paw
  n member 2.7
  foot 199.5
  v touch 73.6
pawky cunning 415.12
  shrewd 920.15
pawn
  n inferior 250.2
  instrument 384.4
  pledge 438.2
  chessman 743.17
  v pledge 438.10
  borrow 621.3
pawnbroker
  lender 620.3
  lending institution 620.4
  broker 730.9
pawnshop 620.4
paw print 517.7
pax
  n peace 464.1
  interj silence! 51.14
pax vobiscum
  farewell! 188.22
  peace! 464.11
pay
  n punishment 604.1
  payment 624.4
  v do 328.6
  avail 387.17
  be profitable 472.13
  requite 506.5
  punish 604.11
  render 624.10
  spend 626.5
  yield 627.4
  overpay 632.8
  experience 831.8
payable owed 623.10
  due 639.7
pay as you go 624.17
pay a visit 582.19
pay back
  compensate 338.4
  make restitution 481.5
  requite 506.5
  repay 624.11
  interchange 863.4
pay COD 624.17
pay damages 481.5
payday 624.4
pay dearly 632.8
pay dirt 1058.7
payee 479.3
payer 624.9
pay heed 983.8
pay homage to
  show respect for 155.5
  worship 696.11
pay in full 624.13
pay in kind 624.11
pay lip service 693.4
payload freight 176.6
  load 196.2
  charge 462.16
  rocket 1074.3
paymaster payer 624.9
  treasurer 729.12
payment
  incentive 375.7
  punishment 604.1

defrayal 624
paying 624.1
pay 624.4
expenditure 626.1
pay no mind
  not think 933.2
  be inattentive 984.2
pay off
  bring off the wind 182.23
  drift off course 182.29
  bribe 378.3
  avail 387.17
  be profitable 472.13
  requite 506.5
  pay in full 624.13
  yield 627.4
payoff 767.3
payola 378.2
pay one's debt to society
  429.18
pay one's dues
  do one's duty 641.10
  atone 658.4
pay one's respects 504.12
pay out
  parcel out 477.8
  punish 604.11
  settle with 624.12
  fork out 624.14
  spend 626.5
pay phone 347.4
pay respect to 155.5
payroll 624.4
pay the bill
  pay in full 624.13
  pay for 624.18
  treat 624.19
pay the penalty 658.4
pay the piper
  take one's punishment
    604.21
  pay for 624.18
pay through the nose 632.8
pay tribute
  praise 509.12
  honor 646.8
pay TV 1035.1
pay up
  contribute 478.14
  pay in full 624.13
  pay 624.16
PBX 347.8
PBX operator 347.9
PC 1042.2
PCP 87.18
PDQ
  in short order 174.19
  promptly 845.15
pea 310.4
peabrain 924.4
peace silence 51.1
  drugs 87.18
  comfortableness 121.2
  quiescence 173.1
  accord 455.1
  peacefulness 464
  pax 464.1
  truce 465.5
  agreement 788.1
  order 807.1
peace and quiet 464.2

peace be with you!
  farewell! 188.22
  peace! 464.11
peaceful calm 106.12
  comfortable 121.11
  quiescent 173.12
  homelike 228.33
  in accord 455.3
  pacific 464.9
  moderate 670.10
peaceful coexistence
  peaceableness 464.4
  foreign policy 609.5
peacekeeper 466.5
peace-keeping force 465.1
peacemaker
  pacifist 464.6
  make-peace 466.5
  moderator 670.3
peace offering
  peace offer 465.2
  gift 478.4
  atonement 658.1
  oblation 696.7
peace officer 1008.15
peace of mind
  composure 106.2
  contentment 107.1
  peace of heart 464.3
peace pipe pipe 89.6
  peace offer 465.2
peace treaty 464.7
peach
  n first-rate 999.7
  beauty 1016.9
  v betray 351.6
  inform on 551.13
  adj orange 42.2
peaches-and-cream 35.22
peach fuzz beard 3.8
  smoothness 294.3
peachy feathery 3.27
  excellent 999.13
peacock
  n variegation 47.6
  male animal 76.8
  bird 311.28
  strutter 501.10
  v pose 500.13
  strut 501.15
peak
  n summit 198.2
  highland 237.1
  mountain 237.6
  wave 238.14
  plateau 272.4
  projection 285.4
  speech sound 524.12
  business cycle 731.10
  limit 794.5
  acme of perfection 1002.3
  v fail 85.48
  top 198.9
  billow 238.22
peaked unhealthy 85.54
  topped 198.12
  thin 270.20
peal
  n blare 53.5
  ringing 54.3
  boom 56.4

v din 53.7
  blare 53.10
  ring 54.8
  boom 56.9
peanut 258.4
peanut gallery
  observation post 27.8
  auditorium 704.15
peanuts
  petty cash 728.19
  trivia 998.4
pearl
  n whiteness 37.2
  drop 282.3
  good person 659.1
  good thing 999.5
  adj whitish 37.8
  gray 39.4
pearl diver 367.4
Pearl Harbor 459.2
pearly
  soft-colored 35.22
  whitish 37.8
  gray 39.4
  variegated 47.10
  iridescent 1025.37
pearly gates 87.10
pear-shaped 279.14
peasant
  vulgarian 497.6
  countryman 606.6
  agriculturist 1069.5
peas in a pod 784.5
pea soup 319.3
peat bog 243.1
peat moss 890.4
pebble
  n modicum 248.2
  pebblestone 1059.4
  v floor 295.22
pebbled
  granular 1051.12
  stony 1059.12
peccadillo 655.2
peck
  n quantity 247.3
  lot 247.4
  tap 902.7
  v pick 8.26
  tap 902.18
pecking order 809.4
pectoral 283.19
peculiar
  personal 312.15
  indicative 517.23
  other 780.8
  differentiative 780.9
  classificational 809.7
  characteristic 865.13
  odd 870.11
  eccentric 927.5
peculiarity habit 373.3
  mannerism 500.2
  sign 517.1
  characteristic 865.4
  oddity 870.3
  eccentricity 927.1
pecuniary 728.30
pedagogical
  scholastic 568.19
  pedagogic 571.11

pedagogy 568.1
pedal
  n lever 906.4
  v ride 177.33
  push 904.9
  adj plantar 199.9
peddle 734.9
peddler 730.5
peddling 734.2
pedestal 901.8
pedestrian
  n walker 178.6
  adj dull 117.6
  traveling 177.36
  unskillful 414.15
  prosaic 721.5
pediatric 90.15
pedigree register 549.9
  genealogy 560.5
pee
  n urine 12.5
  v urinate 12.14
peek
  n glance 27.4
  v look 27.13
  pry 981.4
peekaboo 1029.4
peel
  n skin 295.3
  lamina 296.2
  stronghold 460.6
  v pare 6.8
  excise 255.10
  tear apart 802.14
peel off pilot 184.37
  come apart 802.9
peel out leave 222.10
  flee 368.11
peep
  n glance 27.4
  v look 27.13
  bird sound 60.5
  reconnoiter 938.28
  pry 981.4
peeper eye 2.9
  sight organ 27.9
peepers 29.3
peephole 27.8
peer
  n nobleman 608.4
  equal 790.4
  v look 27.13
  be curious 981.3
peer group
  company 770.3
  equal 790.4
peerless
  matchless 249.15
  best 999.16
  perfect 1002.6
peeve
  n hated thing 103.3
  complaint 115.4
  grudge 589.5
  v annoy 96.13
  provoke 152.24
peewee
  n runt 258.4
  adj tiny 258.11
peg
  n tooth 2.8

drink 8.4
liquor 88.7
degree 245.1
leg 273.6
bulge 283.3
stopper 293.4
throw 904.3
v plod 175.7
walk 177.27
hustle 177.28
drudge 725.14
hook 800.8
throw 904.10
Pegasus 311.15
pejorative 512.13
pellet
  n sphere 282.2
  shot 462.19
  v pelt 459.27
pell-mell
  agitation 105.4
  commotion 810.4
pelt
  n hair 3.2
  fur 4.2
  skin 295.3
  hit 902.4
  v rain 316.10
  stone 459.27
  pound 902.16
  throw 904.10
  shoot 904.12
pelvis 2.13
pen
  n enclosed place 212.3
  place of confinement 429.7
  prison 429.8
  writing 547.1
  writer 547.13
  author 718.3
  farm 1069.8
  v enclose 212.5
  confine 429.12
  write 547.19
  compose 718.6
penal code 673.5
penal colony 429.8
penal institution 429.8
penalize
  bring in a verdict 598.20
  condemn 602.3
  put a penalty on 603.4
  punish 604.10
penalty
  judgment 598.9
  penance 603.1
  penalization 603.1
  punishment 604.1
  football 746.3
  game 749.3
  sports event 749.6
  golf 751.3
  soccer 752.3
  impediment 1012.6
penalty box 749.1
penalty shot 749.6
penance
  regret 113.4
  penalty 603.1
  penitence 658.3
  seven sacraments 701.4

pen-and-ink
  writing 547.1
  drawing 712.13
penchant
  inclination 100.3
  preference 371.5
  tendency 896.1
pencil
  n art equipment 712.18
  ray 1025.5
  v mark 517.19
  write 547.19
  portray 712.19
pendant hanger 202.4
  adjunct 254.1
  likeness 784.3
pending
  adj pendent 202.9
  overhanging 202.11
  undecided 971.18
  prep during 821.14
pendulous
  pendent 202.9
  oscillating 916.15
pendulum series 812.2
  oscillator 916.9
penetrate bite 68.5
  affect 93.14
  interpenetrate 189.8
  insert 191.3
  pervade 221.7
  perforate 292.15
  get across 521.5
  perceive 521.9
  imbue 797.11
  see through 941.8
  be remembered 989.14
  freeze 1023.10
penetrating
  intense 15.22
  acrimonious 17.14
  shrill 58.14
  pungent 68.6
  strong 69.10
  deep-felt 93.24
  piercing 105.31
  caustic 144.23
  vigorous 544.11
  sagacious 920.16
  cold 1023.14
penile 2.29
peninsula
  continent 235.1
  point of land 283.9
penis 2.13
penitent
  n confessor 113.5
  adj repentant 113.9
penitentiary
  n prison 429.8
  priest 699.5
  adj penitent 113.9
penmanship 547.3
pen name 527.8
pennant flag 647.7
  baseball 745.1
penned enclosed 212.10
  written 547.22
penniless bereft 473.8
  destitute 619.9
Pennsylvania Dutch 523.7

penny money 728.7
  cent 728.8
penny-ante
  insignificant 248.6
  inferior 250.6
  worthless 391.11
penny pincher 484.4
penny-wise and pound-foolish
  parsimonious 484.7
  prodigal 486.8
penologist 604.9
penology 604.1
pen pal 553.8
pension
  n subsidy 478.8
  v depose 447.4
  subsidize 478.19
pensioner
  dependent 432.6
  beneficiary 479.4
  student 572.7
  employee 577.3
pension off scrap 390.8
  depose 447.4
  resign 448.2
  subsidize 478.19
  dismiss 909.19
pensive
  melancholy 112.23
  cognitive 931.21
  abstracted 985.11
pentagon 882.1
pentagram 882.1
pentameter
  meter 720.7
  five 882.1
pentathlon
  contest 755.2
  track meet 755.6
  five 882.1
penthouse house 228.5
  apartment 228.13
  roof 295.6
pent-up
  enclosed 212.10
  confined 429.19
peon sycophant 138.3
  subject 432.7
  retainer 577.1
  peasant 606.6
people
  n population 227.1
  kinfolk 559.2
  race 559.4
  family 559.5
  the laity 700.1
  v settle 159.17
  inhabit 225.9
people's republic 232.1
the people
  human race 312.1
  humankind 312.4
  the population 606.1
  the populace 606.1
pep energy 17.3
  liveliness 330.2
  spirit 544.4
pepper
  n energy 17.3
  v variegate 47.7
  flavor 63.7

pull the trigger 459.22
mark 517.19
sprinkle 771.6
throw 904.10
shoot 904.12
pepper-and-salt 47.12
peppery zestful 68.7
  hot-tempered 110.25
pep pills 87.4
peppy energetic 17.13
  active 330.17
  spirited 544.12
pep rally 375.4
pep talk 543.2
peptic 7.22
peptide 7.6
per by means of 384.13
  for each 865.20
  conformable to 867.9
per annum 865.19
per capita
  proportionate 477.13
  each 865.19
perceive sense 24.6
  see 27.12
  feel 93.10
  understand 521.9
  know 928.12
  detect 941.5
percent 1017.7
percentage
  incentive 375.7
  benefit 387.4
  estate 471.4
  gain 472.3
  portion 477.5
  discount 631.1
  part 793.1
  expedience 995.1
  ratio 1017.7
perceptible visible 31.6
  measurable 300.14
  manifest 348.8
  knowable 928.25
perception
  sensation 24.1
  vision 27.1
  sagacity 920.4
  cognizance 928.2
  idea 932.1
  discernment 944.2
perceptive
  sensible 24.11
  sagacious 920.16
  knowing 928.15
  discerning 944.8
perch
  n birdhouse 228.23
  footing 901.5
  v settle 159.17
  sit 173.10
  get down 194.7
  inhabit 225.7
  rest on 901.22
percolate refine 79.22
  exude 190.15
  trickle 238.18
  be operative 889.7
  liquefy 1064.5
  be damp 1065.11
  soak 1065.13

percolator 79.13
percussion noise 53.3
  concussion 671.8
  percussion instrument 711.16
  impact 902.3
percussionist 710.10
per diem 865.19
peregrine
  n wanderer 178.2
  adj traveling 177.36
perennial
  n plant 310.3
  adj ephemeral 310.44
  continuous 812.8
  durable 827.10
  indeciduous 829.8
  constant 847.5
perestroika
  reproduction 78.1
  reconstruction 396.5
  rearrangement 808.7
  change 852.1
perfect
  n tense 530.12
  v excel 249.6
  touch up 392.11
  accomplish 407.6
  complete 820.7
  develop 1002.5
  adj downright 247.12
  complete 407.12
  unrestricted 430.27
  thorough 794.10
  unqualified 960.2
  accurate 973.16
  ideal 1002.6
perfect binding 554.14
perfected
  improved 392.13
  ended 820.8
  finished 1002.9
perfection
  development 392.2
  accomplishment 407.2
  completion 794.4
  end 820.1
  accuracy 973.5
  flawlessness 1002.1
  faultlessness 1002.1
  acme of perfection 1002.3
perfectionist
  n optimist 124.6
  precision 495.6
  conformist 867.2
  adj optimistic 124.12
perforate
  v pierce 292.15
  adj apertured 292.19
perform
  execute 328.9
  manifest 348.5
  impersonate 349.12
  accomplish 407.4
  practice 434.3
  act 704.29
  play 708.39
  operate 889.5
  be operative 889.7
  do 892.11
performance
  deed 328.2

act 328.3
display 348.2
impersonation 349.4
accomplishment 407.1
observance 434.1
ceremony 580.4
acting 704.8
theatrical performance 704.12
execution 708.30
musical performance 708.33
operation 889.1
production 892.5
performer
  phony 500.7
  entertainer 707.1
  musician 710.1
  doer 726.1
perform one's duty 641.10
perfume
  n fragrance 70.1
  perfumery 70.2
  v odorize 69.7
  scent 70.8
  vaporize 1067.8
perfunctory
  indifferent 102.6
  unwilling 325.5
  reluctant 325.6
  careless 340.11
perfuse
  bleed 91.27
  transfer 176.10
  filter in 189.10
  insert 191.3
  pervade 221.7
perhaps
  n guess 951.4
  adv possibly 966.9
perigee
  juxtaposition 223.3
  orbit 1072.16
  spacecraft 1075.2
peril
  n unreliability 971.6
  danger 1006.1
  v endanger 1006.6
perimeter
  environment 209.1
  bounds 211.1
period
  menstruation 12.9
  degree 245.1
  season 313.1
  phrase 529.1
  passage 708.24
  meter 720.7
  football 746.3
  game 749.3
  hockey 749.6
  soccer 752.3
  end 820.1
  time 821.1
  portion of time 824
  point 824.1
  grammar 857.4
  wave 916.4
  orbit 1072.16
periodic
  continuous 812.8
  recurrent 849.13
  seasonal 850.7

oscillating 916.15
periodical
  n publication 352.1
  magazine 555.1
  serial 555.1
  adj journalistic 555.5
  seasonal 850.7
periodic table 1060.2
peripatetic
  n wanderer 178.2
  pedestrian 178.6
  adj traveling 177.36
  discursive 538.13
peripheral
  n circuitry 1042.3
  adj exterior 206.7
  environing 209.8
  outlining 211.14
peripheral vision 27.1
periscope 367.5
perish
  disappear 34.2
  die 307.19
  expire 395.23
  cease to exist 762.6
  age 842.9
perishable
  mortal 307.34
  transient 828.7
perish the thought! 510.27
perjury
  deliberate falsehood 354.9
  deceitfulness 645.3
perk
  n gain 472.3
  v be operative 889.7
  adj conceited 140.11
perk up refresh 9.2
  energize 17.10
  cheer up 109.9
  improve 392.7
  recuperate 396.19
  elevate 912.5
perky
  lighthearted 109.12
  conceited 140.11
  active 330.17
permanent
  n hairdo 3.15
  adj persevering 360.8
  almighty 677.17
  durable 827.10
  perpetual 829.7
  changeless 853.7
  unchangeable 855.17
permeable
  exudative 190.20
  pervious 292.21
permeate
  pervade 221.7
  imbue 797.11
  soak 1065.13
permission
  ratification 332.4
  exemption 430.8
  consent 441.1
  okay 443.1
  leave 443.1
permissive
  n mood 530.11
  adj negligent 340.10

complaint 115.4
grudge 589.5
petrified
terrified 127.26
antiquated 842.13
hardened 1046.13
mineral 1058.15
stone 1059.11
petroleum
illuminant 1025.20
rock oil 1056.4
petroleum jelly 1056.2
pet subject 866.1
petticoat 77.14
petting touching 73.2
indulgence 427.3
lovemaking 562.2
petty
insignificant 248.6
inadequate 250.7
ungenerous 651.6
base 661.12
quibbling 936.14
narrow-minded 980.10
puny 998.20
petty cash 728.19
petty larceny 482.2
petty officer first class 575.20
petulant
discontented 108.7
peevish 110.22
plaintive 115.19
capricious 364.5
pew
compartment 197.2
church 703.14
pewter 1058.17
pfc 461.8
PG 706.1
PGA 751.1
pH 1060.3
phalanx
military unit 461.22
company 770.3
phallic 2.29
phallic symbol 92.30
phantasm
deception 356.1
phantom 976.4
figment of the imagination
986.5
specter 988.1
phantasmagoric 976.8
phantom
n apparition 33.5
whiteness 37.2
frightener 127.9
spirit 764.3
phantasm 976.4
figment of the imagination
986.5
specter 988.1
adj illusory 976.9
spectral 988.7
immaterial 1053.7
pharaoh ruler 575.9
tyrant 575.14
pharmaceutical 86.50
pharmacist 86.35
pharmacy
pharmacology 86.34

drugstore 86.36
hospital room 197.25
pharynx
digestive system 2.18
vocal organ 524.18
phase 33.3
phase in 245.4
phase out
graduate 245.4
reduce 252.7
cease to use 390.4
end 820.5
turn off 857.12
phases of the moon 854.4
phenom
marvel 122.2
success 409.4
successful person 409.6
talented person 413.12
phenomenal
wonderful 122.10
eventful 831.10
extraordinary 870.14
phenomenology 978.2
phenomenon
apparition 33.5
marvel 122.2
event 831.2
phew! eeyuck! 98.31
oh! 122.20
philanderer
beau 104.13
lover 562.12
libertine 665.10
philanthropic
benevolent 143.15
eleemosynary 478.22
philanthropist
altruist 143.8
giver 478.11
philharmonic
n performance 708.33
adj musical 708.47
Philistine
n vulgarian 497.6
conformist 867.2
adj callous 94.12
common 497.14
secularist 695.16
unlearned 930.14
philosopher
wise man 921.1
scholar 929.3
reasoner 935.11
philosophizer 952.8
philosophical
calm 106.12
patient 134.9
sensible 920.18
philosophic 952.10
philosophize
reason 935.15
be philosophic 952.9
philosophy
composure 106.2
ideology 932.8
reasoning 935.1
school of thought 952.1
physics 1018.1
phlebotomy
bloodletting 91.20

drawing 192.3
phlegm
humor 2.24
apathy 94.4
languor 331.6
phlegmatic
n personality type 92.12
adj apathetic 94.13
inert 173.14
languid 331.20
incurious 982.3
phobia
hated thing 103.3
fear 127.1
phobic neurotic 92.39
afraid 127.22
phoenix 659.5
phone
n sound 50.1
telephone 347.4
speech sound 524.12
v telephone 347.19
phone book
telephone number 347.12
reference book 554.9
directory 574.10
phoneme 524.12
phone number 347.12
phonetic
n phonetic symbol 546.2
adj linguistic 523.19
phonic 524.30
phonetic alphabet 546.3
phonetics hearing 48.9
articulatory phonetics
524.13
spelling 546.4
phonetic spelling 546.4
phonic auditory 48.13
acoustic 50.17
phonetic 524.30
phonograph 50.11
phonograph record
record 50.12
recording media 549.10
phony
n imitator 336.4
fake 354.13
impostor 357.6
hypocrite 357.8
affecter 500.7
copy 785.1
substitute 862.2
adj imitation 336.8
spurious 354.26
assumed 500.16
similar 784.10
substitute 862.8
phosphate 890.4
phosphoresce 1025.26
photic 1025.41
photochemical 1060.9
photochemical process 548.1
photocomposition 548.2
photocopy 714.5
photoelectric
electric 1032.30
electronic 1033.15
photoengraving
printing 548.1
engraving 713.2

photo finish
horse race 757.3
the same 790.3
photogenic
photographic 714.17
luminescent 1025.38
photograph
n description 349.2
picture 712.11
photo 714.3
print 785.5
v shoot 714.14
n image 349.5
photograph album 554.7
photographer
journalist 555.4
shutter-bug 714.2
artist 716.5
photographic
pictorial 712.21
photo 714.17
photographic memory 989.3
photographic reproduction
548.1
photography
optics 29.7
printing 548.1
motion-picture photography
706.5
visual arts 712.1
graphic arts 713.1
picture-taking 714.1
photometry 1025.22
photon
energy unit 17.7
ray 1025.5
measurement of light
1025.21
photo-offset 548.1
photo opportunity
conference 541.6
event 831.2
interview 938.11
photoprint 714.5
photosensitive
photographic 714.17
photophobic 1025.42
photosphere 1072.13
photostatic copy
print 714.5
copy 785.5
phrase
n sign 518.6
remark 524.3
expression 529.1
part 554.13
passage 708.24
part of writing 793.2
maxim 974.1
v say 524.22
express 532.4
adj phrasal 529.4
phraseology
language 523.1
jargon 523.9
vocabulary 526.13
phrasing diction 529.2
harmonics 709.2
phylogenesis 861.3
phylum
nomenclature 527.1

piecemeal
  piece by piece 793.9
  separately 802.27
piece of cake 1014.4
piece of one's mind 510.6
piece of the action
  portion 477.5
  part 793.1
piece out 794.6
piece together
  compose 796.3
  put together 800.5
  produce 892.8
piecework 892.3
pie chart 381.3
piecrust crust 295.14
  fragility 1050.2
pied
  n foot 199.5
  adj mottled 47.12
pied-à-terre 228.8
piedmont 237.1
Pied Piper of Hamelin 377.4
pie-eyed 88.33
pie in the sky 986.23
pier pillar 273.5
  buttress 901.4
  base 901.8
  harbor 1009.6
pierce pain 26.7
  affect 93.14
  hurt 96.17
  penetrate 189.8
  perforate 292.15
  injure 393.13
  stab 459.25
  perceive 521.9
  freeze 1023.10
pierce the ears
  din 53.7
  grate on 58.11
piercing
  n hole 292.3
  stabbing 459.10
  adj intense 15.22
  acrimonious 17.14
  painful 26.10
  loud 53.11
  shrill 58.14
  pungent 68.6
  deep-felt 93.24
  penetrating 105.31
  caustic 144.23
  vigorous 544.11
  violent 671.16
  sagacious 920.16
  cold 1023.10
piety religiousness 692.1
  piousness 692.1
  sanctimony 693.1
piffle
  n bull 520.3
  v talk nonsense 520.5
pig eater 8.16
  pork 10.17
  filthy person 80.13
  cycle 179.8
  heavyweight 257.12
  swine 311.9
  beast 660.6
  glutton 672.3

jockey 757.2
slob 810.7
bigot 980.5
police 1008.16
cast 1058.5
pig's eye 758.2
pigeon
  n bird 311.28
  dupe 358.2
  v deceive 356.14
  cheat 356.18
pigeonhole
  n small space 258.3
  hiding place 346.4
  class 809.2
  v put away 390.6
  legislate 613.10
  classify 809.6
  postpone 846.9
  list 871.8
pigeonholed
  neglected 340.14
  classified 809.8
pigeonholes 871.3
pigeon loft 228.23
pigeon-toed 265.12
pig farm 1070.5
piggish hoggish 80.24
  greedy 100.27
  ungulate 311.46
  gluttonous 672.6
piggy 311.9
piggyback 901.25
piggy bank 729.13
pighead 361.6
pig in a poke
  bargain 731.5
  gamble 759.2
piglet
  fledgling 302.10
  swine 311.9
pigment
  n color 35.8
  paint 712.18
  v color 35.14
pigmentation 35.11
pig out stuff 8.25
  overeat 672.5
pigpen sty 80.11
  hovel 228.11
pigskin 746.2
pigsty sty 80.11
  hovel 228.11
pigtail braid 3.7
  chewing tobacco 89.7
  tail 217.6
  coil 281.2
piker vagabond 178.3
  gambler 759.21
pile
  n hair 3.2
  plant beard 3.9
  down 3.19
  lot 247.4
  structure 266.2
  leg 273.6
  texture 294.1
  leaf 310.19
  store 386.1
  gain 472.3
  wealth 618.3

heap 770.10
base 901.8
reactor 1038.13
v load 159.15
pile on 770.19
piled on 643.8
piledriver
  strong man 15.6
  influence 894.6
pile in 193.12
pile into 459.15
pile it on
  exaggerate 355.3
  talk big 545.6
  lay it on 993.11
piles 85.37
pile up
  shipwreck 182.42
  store up 386.11
  pile 770.19
pilfer misuse 389.4
  steal 482.13
pilgrim
  n traveler 178.1
  religious 699.16
  v journey 177.21
pilgrimage
  n wandering 177.3
  journey 177.5
  adventure 404.2
  v journey 177.21
piling buttress 901.4
  base 901.8
piling on
  cruelty 144.11
  persecution 389.3
  overdoing 993.6
pill bolus 86.7
  tedious person 118.5
  sphere 282.2
  bad person 660.5
the pill 86.23
pillage
  n plundering 482.6
  v seize 480.14
  plunder 482.17
  rage 671.11
pillar tower 272.6
  column 273.5
  cylinder 282.4
  monument 549.12
  base 901.8
  protector 1008.5
pillar of society
  bourgeois 607.6
  good citizen 659.3
  personage 997.8
pillar of strength 855.6
pillbox 460.6
pillory
  n shackle 428.4
  punishment 605.3
  v ridicule 508.8
  punish 604.10
  disgrace 661.8
  stigmatize 661.9
pillow
  n bedding 901.20
  softness 1047.4
  v support 901.21
pillowcase 295.10

pill popper 87.21
pilot
  n steersman 183.8
  aviator 185.1
  guide 574.7
  baseball team 745.2
  jockey 757.2
  safeguard 1008.3
  v steer 182.14
  control 184.37
  guide 573.9
  adj experimental 942.11
piloting 161.1
pilot light 1020.10
pilot program 942.3
pimp
  n reprobate 660.4
  procurer 665.18
  v prostitute oneself 665.21
pimple
  n sore 85.37
  swelling 283.4
  print 517.7
  blemish 1004.1
  v roughen 288.4
pin
  n member 2.7
  stopper 293.4
  jewel 498.6
  insignia 647.1
  bowling 750.1
  golf 751.1
  axle 915.5
  trifle 998.5
  v hook 800.8
  fell 913.5
PIN 517.11
pin a medal on 646.8
pinball machine 759.16
pince-nez 29.3
pincer movement 459.5
pincers
  extractor 192.9
  clutches 474.4
pinch
  n pang 26.2
  modicum 248.2
  small space 258.3
  squeezing 260.2
  urge 375.6
  arrest 429.6
  indigence 619.2
  crisis 843.4
  urgency 997.4
  danger 1006.1
  predicament 1013.4
  crux 1013.8
  v pain 26.7
  converge 169.2
  sail near the wind
    182.25
  squeeze 260.8
  arrest 429.16
  rob 482.16
  stint 484.5
  adj substitute 862.8
pinched limited 210.7
  contracted 260.12
  haggard 270.20
  poor 619.7
  straitened 1013.26

pinch-hit
  represent 576.14
  substitute for 862.5
pinch of snuff
  snuff 89.8
  trifle 998.5
pinch pennies 484.5
pin down locate 159.11
  bind 428.10
  stabilize 855.7
  specify 865.11
  fell 913.5
pine
  n basketball 747.1
  v weaken 16.9
  fail 85.48
  wish for 100.16
  grieve 112.17
  languish 393.18
pine barrens 310.13
pine cone cone 282.5
  plant 310.27
pine needle thorn 285.5
  leaf 310.19
ping 54.3
pinhead top part 198.4
  minute 258.7
  fool 924.4
pinion
  n feather 3.16
  member 793.4
  v bind 428.10
pink
  n pinkness 41.2
  radical 611.12
  acme of perfection 1002.3
  v notch 289.4
  perforate 292.15
  adj pinkish 41.8
  fresh 83.13
  radical 611.20
pink elephants 926.10
pink ladies 87.5
pinko 611.12
pink slip 909.5
pin money 728.19
pinnacle summit 198.2
  mountain 237.6
  tower 272.6
  limit 794.5
  acme of perfection 1002.3
pin on blame 599.8
  attribute to 888.4
pin one's ears back 510.18
pinpoint
  n location 159.1
  minute 258.7
  v locate 159.11
  attribute to 888.4
  receive 1036.17
  adj exact 973.17
pinprick
  shallowness 276.1
  trifle 998.5
pins 177.15
pins and needles
  insensibility 25.1
  tingle 74.1
  anxiety 126.1
pinstripe
  n stripe 47.5

  adj striped 47.15
pinstriper 574.3
pinto
  n horse 311.11
  adj mottled 47.12
pint-size
  insignificant 248.6
  dwarf 258.13
pinup
  photograph 714.3
  beauty 1016.9
pinwheel 743.16
pioneer
  n traveler 178.1
  vanguard 216.2
  settler 227.9
  engineer 461.14
  precursor 816.1
  v be in front 216.7
  go before 816.3
  initiate 818.10
  innovate 852.9
  adj original 337.5
pioneering
  front 216.10
  preceding 816.4
pious
  pietistic 692.8
  sanctimonious 693.5
  believing 953.21
pip disease 85.41
  seed 310.31
  military insignia 647.5
  first-rate 999.7
pipe
  n screech 58.4
  tobacco pipe 89.6
  tube 239.6
  cylinder 282.4
  wind instrument 711.6
  v blare 53.10
  screech 58.8
  bird sound 60.5
  transport 176.14
  channel 239.15
  sigh 318.21
  speak 524.25
  sing 708.38
  blow a horn 708.42
pipe cleaner 89.6
pipe down
  v fall silent 51.7
  interj silence! 51.14
pipe dream
  airy hope 124.5
  illusion 976.1
  abstractedness 985.2
  dream 986.9
pipe-dream muse 985.9
  dream 986.17
pipeline
  n tube 239.6
  inside information 551.2
  news channel 552.10
  v transport 176.14
piper 710.4
pipes
  ship's officer 183.7
  bagpipe 711.9
pipette
  n drawing off 192.9

  tube 239.6
  v draw off 192.12
pipe up
  vociferate 59.8
  blow 318.20
  speak up 524.21
  strike up 708.37
piping hot 1019.25
pippin 999.7
pips 1036.11
pip-squeak runt 258.4
  a nobody 998.7
piquant
  appetizing 63.10
  pungent 68.6
  exciting 105.30
  provocative 375.27
  alluring 377.8
  spirited 544.12
  interesting 983.19
pique
  n offense 152.2
  dudgeon 152.7
  v annoy 96.13
  stimulate 105.13
  provoke 152.24
  incite 375.17
  rouse 375.19
  interest 983.12
piracy
  buccaneering 482.7
  plagiarism 482.8
pirate
  n mariner 183.1
  corsair 483.7
  plagiarist 483.9
  v buccaneer 482.18
  plagiarize 482.19
  adopt 621.4
pirouette
  n whirl 915.2
  v rotate 915.9
piss
  n humor 2.24
  urine 12.5
  v urinate 12.14
  be discontented 108.6
  complain 115.16
  make angry 152.23
piss and vinegar
  energy 17.3
  gaiety 109.4
  liveliness 330.2
piss away 486.5
pissed-off 152.30
piss-poor 1000.8
pistol
  n skillful person 413.14
  first-rate 999.7
  v strike dead 308.18
  shoot 904.12
pistol-whip 604.13
piston 904.6
pit
  n audience 48.6
  deep 275.2
  cavity 284.2
  well 284.4
  indentation 284.6
  texture 294.1
  tomb 309.16

  seed 310.31
  arena 463.1
  sewer 654.7
  auditorium 704.15
  stage 704.16
  stock exchange 737.7
  race 756.3
  blemish 1004.1
  mine 1058.6
  v indent 284.14
the pit 682.1
pit against 456.14
pit bull
  sorehead 110.11
  boxer 461.2
pitch
  n blackness 38.4
  tone 50.2
  summit 198.2
  inclination 204.2
  incline 204.4
  degree 245.1
  plunge 367.1
  intonation 524.6
  speech 543.2
  tuning 709.4
  sales talk 734.5
  baseball 745.3
  field hockey 749.4
  soccer 752.1
  throw 904.3
  flounder 917.8
  v establish 159.16
  toss 182.55
  descend 194.5
  tumble 194.8
  erect 200.9
  incline 204.10
  camp 225.11
  plunge 367.6
  make advances 439.8
  play 745.5
  shuffle 758.5
  throw 904.10
  oscillate 916.10
  flounder 917.15
  adj phonetic 524.30
pitch-black black 38.8
  dark 1027.13
pitched battle 457.4
pitcher
  baseball team 745.2
  thrower 904.7
pitcher's mound 745.1
pitchfork 904.10
pitch in eat 8.20
  set to work 725.15
  begin 818.7
pitchman
  publicist 352.9
  cheat 357.3
pitch pipe 711.22
piteous
  distressing 98.20
  pitiful 145.8
pitfall trap 356.12
  hidden danger 1006.5
pith
  essential content 196.5
  center 208.2
  pluck 359.3

fortitude 492.6
meaning 518.1
summary 557.2
essence 767.2
salient point 997.6
pulp 1063.2

pithy
meaningful 518.10
concise 537.6
aphoristic 974.6
spongy 1047.11
pulpy 1063.6

pitiless unpitying 146.3
savage 671.21
bright 1025.32

pit man 737.10

pit of one's stomach 93.3

the pits bottom 199.1
sewer 654.7
terribleness 1000.2

pittance
modicum 248.2
donation 478.6
dole 992.5

pitted
indented 284.17
rough 288.6
nappy 294.7

pitter-patter
n thud 52.3
staccato 55.1
trepidation 105.5
rain 316.1
repetitiousness 849.4
pulsation 916.3
flutter 917.4
v drum 55.4
rain 316.10
flutter 917.12

pit viper 311.26

pity
n kindness 143.1
sympathy 145.1
leniency 427.1
abomination 638.2
v be sorry for 145.3
condole with 147.2

pivot
n center 208.2
basketball game 747.3
round 751.3
joint 800.4
fulcrum 906.3
axle 915.5
salient point 997.6
v turn round 163.9
rotate 915.9

pivotal
central 208.11
critical 843.10
causal 886.13
urgent 997.22

pivotal point 997.6

pixie
mischief-maker 322.3
fairy 678.8
imp 680.7

pixilated 926.29

pizzazz energy 17.3
power 18.1
liveliness 330.2

vigor 544.3

pizzeria 8.17

PJ's 5.21

placard
n poster 352.7
v publicize 352.15

placate 465.7

place
n serving 8.10
location 159.1
stead 159.4
abode 228.1
square 230.8
region 231.1
rank 245.2
arena 463.1
class 607.1
duty 641.1
function 724.3
position 724.5
state 765.1
continuity 807.2
turn 825.2
opportunity 843.2
outlook 978.2
v locate 159.11
put 159.12
install 615.12
impose 643.4
invest 729.17
race 757.5
dispose 808.9
classify 809.6
attribute 888.3
recognize 989.12

place against 943.4

place an order 421.5

place at one's disposal 439.4

place a value on
price 630.11
estimate 946.9

place before 216.8

placebo 86.4

place confidence in
believe in 953.15
trust 953.17

placed
located 159.18
arranged 808.14
classified 809.8

place emphasis on 997.14

place horse 757.2

place in office
establish 159.16
elect 371.20
install 615.12

a place in the sun 662.1

place itself 807.5

placekick 746.3

place kick 902.9

placement
location 159.1
positioning 159.6
installation 615.3
arrangement 808.1
grouping 808.3
classification 809.1
attribution 888.1

place name 527.3

placenta 817.3

place of residence 228.1

place of worship 703.1

place side by side 223.13

place the blame on
blame 599.8
attribute to 888.4

place trust in 953.17

place under arrest 480.18

place under oath 334.7

place upon 888.4

placid
calm 106.12
quiescent 173.12

placing 159.6

plafond 295.6

plagiarize
imitate 336.5
pirate 482.19
adopt 621.4
repeat 849.7

plague
n epidemic 85.5
assemblage 770.6
infestation 910.2
bane 1001.1
v annoy 96.13
vex 98.15
make anxious 126.5
importune 440.12
infest 910.6
trouble 1013.13

plagued
tormented 96.24
worried 126.8
remembering 989.24
troubled 1013.20

plaid
n check 47.4
adj checked 47.14

plain
n open space 158.4
horizontal 201.3
flat country 236.1
prairie 236.1
adj distinct 31.7
audible 50.16
dull 117.8
humble 137.10
horizontal 201.7
homelike 228.33
champaign 236.2
mere 248.8
manifest 348.8
artless 416.5
uncomplicated 499.6
clear 521.11
elegant 533.6
plain-speaking 535.3
informal 581.3
populational 606.8
candid 644.17
prosaic 721.5
thorough 794.10
simple 798.6
easy 1014.13
ugly 1015.6
adv absolutely 794.15

plain as day
distinct 31.7
manifest 348.8

plain as the nose on one's face
distinct 31.7

manifest 348.8

plainclothesman 576.10

plain English
clearness 521.2
plain speech 535.1

plain folks 606.1

plains
n the country 233.1
plain 236.1
adj rustic 233.6

plain sense 920.6

plaint
lament 115.3
accusation 599.1

plaintiff
oppositionist 452.3
litigant 598.11
accuser 599.5

plaintive
sorrowful 112.26
plangent 115.19

the plain truth 973.3

plait
n braid 3.7
pleat 291.2
lamina 296.2
weave 740.2
v fold 291.5
weave 740.6

plan
n structure 266.1
representation 349.1
intention 380.1
scheme 381.1
undertaking 404.1
intent 518.2
plot 722.4
outline 801.4
v intend 380.4
plan on 380.6
premeditate 380.7
devise 381.8
prepare 405.6
organize 808.10
come 839.6
originate 892.12
prearrange 965.4

plane
n aircraft 181.1
horizontal 201.3
degree 245.1
smoothness 287.3
cutlery 1040.2
v take off 193.10
smooth 287.5
adj horizontal 201.7
smooth 287.10

plane crash 1011.2

planet 1072.9

planetarium 1072.17

planetary
deviative 164.7
circular 280.11
universal 864.14
celestial 1072.25

plangent
loud 53.11
resonant 54.10
sorrowful 112.26
plaintive 115.19

plank
n strip 271.4
lamina 296.2
platform 609.7
wood 1054.3
v place violently 159.13
face 295.23
plankton 311.30
planned
intentional 380.8
devised 381.12
prepared 405.16
future 839.8
prearranged 965.7
planned obsolescence 390.1
planned parenthood 891.1
plant
n vegetable 310.3
shill 357.5
equipment 385.4
factory 739.3
v establish 159.16
people 225.9
secrete 346.7
tamper with 354.17
fix 855.9
implant 1069.18
adj biological 1068.4
plant and animal life 305.1
plantation
establishment 159.7
peopling 225.2
growth 310.2
farm 1069.8
plant biology 1068.1
plant-eating 8.31
plant growth 14.1
plant oneself 159.17
plaque 549.12
plasma 2.25
plaster
n dressing 86.33
sculpture tool 715.4
adhesive 803.4
pulp 1063.2
v intoxicate 88.23
treat 91.24
smooth 287.5
coat 295.24
cover 295.25
adj on 295.43
plastic
n credit instrument 622.3
thermoplastic 1054.6
resin 1057.1
adj formative 262.9
plasmatic 262.10
docile 433.13
teachable 570.18
changeable 854.6
conformable 867.5
conformist 867.6
influenceable 894.15
ordinary 1005.8
pliant 1047.9
plastic surgery surgery 90.2
surgery 91.19
plastic wrap 295.18
plate
n serving 8.10
continent 235.1

plating 295.13
shell 295.15
lamina 296.2
label 517.13
printing surface 548.8
steel plate 713.6
film 714.10
v chromium-plate 295.26
the plate 745.1
plateau
plain 236.1
highlands 237.1
tableland 237.3
degree 245.1
mesa 272.4
interim 826.1
plated
chromium-plated 295.33
layered 296.6
platform
n horizontal 201.3
policy 381.4
arena 463.1
marker 517.10
party platform 609.7
stage 901.13
v make a speech 543.9
platinum 37.7
platinum blond
n hair color 35.9
adj blond 37.9
platitude
generalization 864.8
cliché 974.3
Plato 921.2
Platonic
continent 664.6
Aristotelian 952.12
idealist 1053.8
platoon
military unit 461.22
team 617.7
company 770.3
platter
recording media 549.10
baseball 745.1
plaudit 509.2
plausible
specious 354.27
logical 935.20
sophistical 936.10
believable 953.24
possible 966.6
colorable 968.7
play
n room 158.3
action 328.1
latitude 430.4
joke 489.6
writing 547.10
repute 662.1
stage show 704.4
fun 743.2
frolic 743.5
contest 743.9
sport 744.1
baseball 745.3
football 746.3
basketball game 747.3
tennis 748.2
game 749.3

hockey 749.6
round 751.3
soccer 752.3
bridge 758.3
gambling 759.1
bet 759.3
flicker 1025.8
v jet 238.20
act 328.4
impersonate 349.12
sham 354.21
use 387.10
affect 500.12
stage 704.29
perform 708.39
sport 743.23
compete 744.2
play baseball 745.5
kick 746.5
play basketball 747.4
play tennis 748.3
skate 749.7
play golf 751.4
play soccer 752.4
gamble 759.23
trifle 998.14
flicker 1025.25
playa shore 234.2
plain 236.1
playacting
sham 354.3
acting 704.8
play a joke on 489.14
play along
be willing 324.3
concur 332.9
consent 441.2
play around flirt 562.20
trifle 998.15
play around with
consider 931.12
experiment 942.8
play at cross-purposes
oppose 451.3
go contrary to 779.4
play a waiting game
be patient 134.4
do nothing 329.2
play back 50.14
play ball
cooperate 450.3
play baseball 745.5
play basketball 747.4
playbill 965.3
playbook book 554.1
script 704.21
play both ends against the middle
play a double game 354.24
exploit 387.16
playboy
sociable person 582.16
dissipater 669.3
player 743.18
play by ear
improvise 365.8
be unprepared 406.6
play 708.39
play-by-play description
account 349.3
circumstances 766.2

play by the rules 644.9
play cat and mouse with 389.7
play down
minimize 252.9
moderate 670.6
attach little importance to 998.12
play dumb
be silent 51.6
keep secret 345.7
played out
weakened 16.18
tired 21.8
worn-out 393.36
player
competitor 452.2
participator 476.4
motion-picture studio 706.4
actor 707.2
instrumentalist 710.3
frolicker 743.18
athlete 743.19
golfer 751.2
gambler 759.21
component 796.2
influence 894.6
player piano 711.12
play fair 649.7
play fast and loose with 156.4
play favorites 650.8
play for a sucker
deceive 356.19
exploit 387.16
stultify 923.7
play for time 846.11
playful gay 109.14
mischievous 322.6
waggish 489.17
sportive 743.29
play God 640.8
playground 743.11
play hard to get 562.20
play havoc with
spoil 393.10
bungle 414.11
work evil 1000.6
play hide and seek 346.8
play hooky 222.9
playhouse
small space 258.3
theater 704.14
playing card 758.2
playing field arena 463.1
playground 743.11
playmaker
basketball team 747.2
hockey team 749.2
playmate companion 588.3
mistress 665.17
play musical chairs 854.5
playoff baseball 745.1
football 746.1
play off
symmetrize 264.3
offset 338.5
play one's cards close to one's vest 345.7
play one's cards right 321.5
play one's trump card 415.11
play on words
n wordplay 489.8

v joke 489.13
play opposite 704.30
play out 21.5
play politics 468.2
play possum 354.20
playroom
  recreation room 197.12
  playground 743.11
play Russian roulette 493.6
play safe
  take precautions 494.6
  keep on the safe side 1007.3
playschool 567.2
play second fiddle
  efface oneself 139.7
  retreat 163.6
  retract 168.3
  be inferior 250.4
  depend on 432.12
play the field 562.20
play the fool
  misbehave 322.4
  be foolish 923.6
play the game
  behave oneself 321.5
  conform 579.4
  play fair 649.7
  follow the rule 867.4
play the lead 704.29
play the market 737.23
play the ponies
  gamble 759.23
  bet 759.25
play the same old tune 118.8
plaything dupe 358.1
  instrument 384.4
  toy 743.16
playtime 857.3
play tricks 489.14
play up 997.16
play upon 387.16
play up to
  curry favor 138.9
  flatter 511.6
  cultivate 587.12
play with fire
  not know what one is about 414.14
  court danger 493.6
  take chances 1006.7
playwright 704.22
plaza square 230.8
  marketplace 736.2
plea entreaty 440.2
  pleadings 598.6
  defense 600.2
  argument 935.5
plea-bargain sign 437.7
  compromise 468.2
plea bargaining 598.12
plead entreat 440.11
  enter a plea 598.19
  argue 935.16
  adduce 957.12
plead guilty
  repent 113.7
  confess 351.7
plead ignorance 600.11
plead with 375.14
pleasant pleasing 97.6
  cheerful 109.11

friendly 587.15
  melodious 708.48
  good 999.12
  rainless 1066.8
pleasantry
  pleasantness 97.1
  wit 489.1
  wittiness 489.2
  witticism 489.7
  banter 490.1
please
  v pleasure 95.6
  prefer 371.17
  indulge 427.6
  interj prithee 440.20
pleasing to the eye 1016.19
pleasure
  n enjoyment 95.1
  pleasantness 97.1
  desire 100.1
  will 323.1
  option 371.2
  command 420.1
  amusement 743.1
  v please 95.6
pleasure boat 180.3
pleasure principle
  psyche 92.28
  pleasure-loving 95.4
  desire 100.1
  sensuality 663.1
pleat
  n trench 290.2
  pleating 291.2
  v furrow 290.3
  fold 291.5
pleated furrowed 290.4
  folded 291.7
plebe 572.6
plebeian
  n common man 606.5
  adj common 497.14
  populational 606.8
plebiscite vote 371.6
  referendum 613.8
pledge
  n toast 88.10
  oath 334.4
  promise 436.1
  gage 438.2
  member 617.11
  debt 623.1
  v drink to 88.29
  promise 436.4
  give security 438.10
  contribute 478.14
  obligate 641.12
the pledge 668.2
Pleiades nymph 678.9
  star 1072.8
plenary great 247.6
  unrestricted 430.27
  full 794.11
plenary session 423.1
plenipotentiary
  omnipotent 18.13
  diplomatic 576.17
plenipotentiary power 615.1
plenty
  n quantity 247.3
  store 386.1

numerousness 884.1
  plenitude 991.2
  superabundance 993.2
  adj sufficient 991.6
  plentiful 991.7
  adv greatly 247.15
plenum
  omnipresence 221.2
  council 423.1
  assembly 770.2
  completeness 794.1
  series 812.2
  matter 1052.2
  universe 1072.1
plethora fullness 794.2
  superabundance 993.2
  overfullness 993.3
plexus
  nervous system 2.14
  network 170.3
pliable folded 291.7
  weak-willed 362.12
  usable 387.23
  docile 433.13
  teachable 570.18
  influenceable 894.15
  handy 1014.15
  pliant 1047.9
pliers 192.9
plight
  n promise 436.1
  state 765.1
  bewilderment 971.3
  danger 1006.1
  adversity 1011.1
  predicament 1013.4
  v promise 436.4
plod
  n slow motion 175.2
  v plug 175.7
  way of walking 177.28
  keep doggedly at 360.3
  drudge 725.14
plodder
  slowpoke 175.5
  drudge 726.3
plop
  v place violently 159.13
  sink 194.6
  bubble 320.4
  plunge 367.6
  adv suddenly 830.9
plot
  n plot of ground 231.4
  diagram 381.3
  intrigue 381.5
  stratagem 415.3
  real estate 471.6
  fable 722.4
  field 1069.9
  v premeditate 380.7
  scheme 381.9
  map 381.10
  maneuver 415.10
  come 839.6
  prearrange 965.4
plot a course 182.27
plow maneuver 184.40
  furrow 290.3
  cultivate 1069.17

plow back into 729.17
plow into
  attack 459.15
  criticize 510.14
ploy trick 356.6
  stratagem 415.3
  revel 743.6
pluck
  n spunk 359.3
  courage 492.1
  jerk 905.3
  v divest 6.5
  flunk 410.17
  collect 472.11
  strip 480.24
  strum 708.40
  cheat 759.26
  jerk 905.5
  harvest 1069.19
plucky
  spunky 359.14
  enterprising 404.8
  courageous 492.17
plug
  n hydrant 239.12
  stopper 293.4
  horse 311.12
  publicity 352.4
  snare 356.13
  commendation 509.3
  commercial 1034.20
  v plod 175.7
  stop 293.7
  top 295.21
  publicize 352.15
  keep doggedly at 360.3
  commend 509.11
  drudge 725.14
  shoot 904.12
plug in 1032.26
plum
  desire 100.11
  political patronage 609.36
  money 728.8
  dividend 738.7
  good thing 999.5
plumage 3.18
plumb
  n vertical 200.2
  instrument 200.6
  weight 297.6
  v plumb-line 200.10
  sound 275.9
  measure 300.10
  perceive 521.9
  investigate 938.23
  solve 940.2
  adj perpendicular 200.12
  thorough 794.10
  adv perpendicularly 200.14
  absolutely 794.15
  exactly 973.21
plumbing 385.4
plumb the depths
  lose heart 112.16
  sound 275.9
plume
  n feather 3.16
  v groom 79.20
  adorn 498.9
plume of smoke 1067.1

bundle 770.8
thrust 902.2
hit 902.4
v go slow 175.6
dally 331.14
goad 375.15
signal 517.22
thrust 902.12
hit 902.14
search 938.31
poke at 459.16
poke full of holes 958.4
poke fun at joke 489.13
ridicule 508.8
poke one's nose in
meddle 214.7
pry 981.4
poker
draw poker 759.10
fire iron 1020.12
poker face
unfeeling 94.1
unastonishment 123.1
reticence 344.3
unexpressiveness 522.5
pokey 429.9
poky dull 117.6
slow 175.10
little 258.10
base 661.12
slovenly 810.15
insignificant 998.18
polar
contrapositive 215.5
final 820.11
magnetic 1032.31
polar coordinates 300.5
Polaris
guiding star 574.8
stars 1072.4
Polaroid glasses 29.3
the polar opposite 779.2
pole
n spar 180.13
oar 180.15
summit 198.2
remote region 261.4
tower 272.6
shaft 273.1
beam 273.3
race 756.3
extremity 820.2
base 901.8
axle 915.5
polarity 1032.8
wood 1054.3
v push 904.9
poleax
strike dead 308.18
do for 395.11
polecat
stinker 71.3
wild animal 311.23
beast 660.6
polemic
n quarrel 456.5
contention 457.1
argumentation 935.4
arguer 935.12
adj contentious 110.26
partisan 456.17

argumentative 935.19
pole position
advantage 249.2
race 756.3
precedence 814.1
poles apart
opposite 215.6
different 780.7
pole vault 366.1
police
n policeman
1008.15
police force 1008.17
v tidy 808.12
protect 1008.18
watch 1008.20
police car 179.11
police state 612.4
police station 230.5
policy plan 381.4
polity 609.4
judiciousness 920.7
insurance 1008.4
policyholder 438.7
policy maker 610.7
polio 85.27
polish
n gloss 287.2
smoother 287.4
cultivation 392.3
taste 496.1
good breeding 504.4
elegance 533.1
v shine 287.7
perfect 392.11
buff 1044.8
polish off kill 308.14
accomplish 407.4
end 820.5
polite 504.14
polite society 578.6
political
politic 609.43
governmental 612.17
political action committee
pressure group 609.31
influence 894.6
political activist 330.8
political asylum 1009.41
political convention 609.8
political election 371.9
political influence
machination 415.4
wire-pulling 609.29
political machine
political party 609.24
association 617.1
political party
party 609.24
association 617.4
political philosopher 610.12
political prisoner 429.11
political science 609.2
politician
expert 413.11
Machiavellian 415.8
statesman 610.2
politico 610.1
politicize
politick 609.38
democratize 611.16

politics
Machiavellianism 415.2
statesmanship 609.3
polity 609.1
political science 609.2
polka dot
spottiness 47.3
mark 517.5
poll
n head 198.6
vote 371.6
balloting place 609.20
returns 609.21
roll 871.6
canvass 938.14
v shorten 268.6
vote 371.18
record 549.15
canvass 938.29
number 1017.17
pollen
n sperm 305.11
v fertilize 78.10
pollinate 78.10
polling booth 609.20
pollute defile 80.17
intoxicate 88.23
misuse 389.4
corrupt 393.12
blaspheme 694.5
adulterate 797.12
work evil 1000.6
pollution
defilement 80.4
unhealthfulness 82.1
misuse 389.1
corruption 393.2
sacrilege 694.2
adulteration 797.3
evil 1000.3
environmental destruction
1073.2
Pollyanna 124.6
poltergeist imp 680.7
psychic phenomena 689.6
specter 988.1
polychrome
n variegation 47.1
v variegate 47.7
adj variegated 47.9
pictorial 712.21
polygraph 92.8
polyhedral sided 218.7
multilateral 278.11
polymath 413.12
polymer 1054.6
polymorphous 783.3
Polynesian race 312.2
polynomial 883.8
polyp 85.37
polysaccharide 7.5
polysyllabic 545.10
polyunsaturated fat
fat 7.7
oil 1056.1
pomade
n ointment 1056.3
v oil 1056.8
pommel
n saddle parts 901.18
v whip 604.13

pound 902.16
pomp spectacle 33.7
circumstance 501.6
formality 580.1
procession 812.3
pompadour 3.22
pomp and circumstance 501.6
pom-pom 462.12
pompous stuffy 501.22
stiff 534.3
grandiloquent 545.8
ceremonious 580.8
confident 970.21
pond 241.1
ponder hesitate 362.7
consider 931.12
ponderous dull 117.6
bulky 257.19
heavy 297.16
bungling 414.20
stiff 534.3
unwieldy 1013.19
pone 10.29
pontificate
n mastership 417.7
papacy 698.6
v give oneself airs 501.14
talk big 545.6
criticize 946.14
dogmatize 970.10
Pontius Pilate 596.5
pontoon 180.11
pony
n runt 258.4
horse 311.10
translation 341.3
money 728.8
jockey 757.2
adj miniature 258.12
adv on foot 177.43
ponytail 3.5
pooch
n dog 311.17
v bulge 283.11
pooh-pooh
slight 157.6
scoff 508.9
disbelieve 955.5
pool
landlocked water 241.1
lake 241.1
company 617.9
funds 728.14
bear pool 737.17
swimming pool 743.12
pot 759.5
pool hall 743.11
poop
n energy 17.3
power 18.1
stern 217.7
v get tired 21.6
pooped weak 16.12
tired 21.8
languid 331.20
worn-out 393.36
poor weak 16.15
humble 137.10
haggard 270.20
unskillful 414.15
disapproving 510.21

ill off 619.7
base 661.12
sparse 885.5
unsound 936.12
meager 992.10
ill-provided 992.12
paltry 998.21
inferior 1005.9
poor judgment 948.1
poor man's roulette 759.8
Poor Richard's Almanac 832.7
poor taste 497.1
poor timing 844.2
pop
  n beverage 10.49
  thud 52.3
  detonation 56.3
  vulgarity 497.1
  father 560.10
  grandfather 560.14
  automobile racing
    756.1
  back number 842.8
  v thud 52.15
  blast 56.8
  use 87.22
  bulge 283.11
  play 745.5
  adj common 497.14
  adv suddenly 830.9
pop in enter 189.7
  insert 191.3
pop literature
  writing 547.12
  literature 718.1
pop music 708.7
pop pills 87.22
pop psychology 92.1
poppy 22.10
poppycock
  bull 520.3
  foolishness 923.1
pop quiz 938.2
pop the question
  solicit 440.14
  propose 562.22
populace 227.1
popular
  desired 100.29
  beloved 104.24
  customary 373.13
  communal 476.9
  common 497.14
  approved 509.19
  fashionable 578.11
  populational 606.8
  distinguished 662.16
  lay 700.3
  prevalent 864.12
  usual 869.9
popular belief
  opinion 953.6
  superstition 954.3
populate settle 159.17
  people 225.9
population
  n establishment 159.7
  peopling 225.2
  inhabitants 227.1
  adj populational 606.8
population explosion 251.2

populous
  inhabited 225.12
  crowded 770.22
  teeming 884.9
pop up burst forth 33.9
  be unexpected 131.6
  arrive 186.6
  shoot up 193.9
  play 745.5
  turn up 831.6
  chance 972.11
porcelain
  n ceramic ware 742.2
  adj ceramic 742.7
porch
  propylaeum 189.6
  stoop 197.21
  church 703.9
porcine
  corpulent 257.18
  ungulate 311.46
porcupine 311.23
pore
  n duct 2.23
  outlet 190.9
  opening 292.1
  v scrutinize 27.14
pork food 10.17
  political patronage 609.36
pork barrel
  booty 482.11
  political patronage 609.36
  treasury 729.13
  trading 863.2
pork chop 10.19
porker
  heavyweight 257.12
  swine 311.9
porno film 666.4
pornography
  writing 547.12
  obscenity 666.4
  literature 718.1
porous
  exudative 190.20
  porose 292.20
porpoise
  n marine animal 311.30
  v maneuver 184.40
porridge
  semiliquid 1062.5
  pulp 1063.2
port
  n looks 33.4
  airport 184.22
  destination 186.5
  outlet 190.9
  left side 220.1
  behavior 321.1
  refuge 1009.1
  harbor 1009.6
  circuitry 1042.3
  adj left 220.4
  adv leftward 220.6
portable 176.18
portage
  transportation 176.3
  fee 630.6
portal entrance 189.5
  porch 189.6
  vestibule 197.19

portcullis 1012.5
portent omen 133.3
  ominousness 133.7
  forewarning 399.2
porter carrier 176.7
  trainman 178.13
  doorkeeper 1008.12
portfolio
  scepter 417.9
  bookholder 554.17
  stock 738.2
portico
  vestibule 197.19
  pillar 273.5
  passageway 383.3
port in a storm 1009.1
portion
  n serving 8.10
  remedy 86.6
  fix 87.20
  amount 244.2
  a length 267.2
  share 477.5
  endowment 478.9
  part 793.1
  dose 793.5
  fate 964.2
  v apportion 477.6
  divide 802.18
portly 257.18
port of call 1009.6
portrait
  description 349.2
  image 349.5
  portraiture 712.15
  photograph 714.3
  copy 785.1
portrait painter 716.4
portray represent 349.8
  describe 349.9
  enact 704.30
  picture 712.19
pose
  n behavior 321.1
  sham 354.3
  posing 500.3
  gesture 517.14
  v place 159.12
  propose 439.5
  posture 500.13
  postulate 951.12
pose a question 938.19
Poseidon
  mariner 183.1
  spirit of the sea 240.4
  water god 678.10
posh
  grandiose 501.21
  chic 578.13
  upper-class 607.10
  expensive 632.11
posing against
  contraposition 215.1
  symmetrization 264.2
position
  n location 159.1
  navigation 159.3
  rank 245.2
  affirmation 334.1
  remark 524.3
  class 607.1

  policy 609.4
  prestige 662.4
  function 724.3
  job 724.5
  skiing 753.3
  race 756.3
  state 765.1
  classification 809.2
  premise 935.7
  opinion 953.6
  attitude 978.1
  outlook 978.2
  v locate 159.11
position paper
  affirmation 334.1
  announcement 352.2
  policy 381.4
  platform 609.7
  classification 801.3
  statement of belief 953.4
positive
  n photocopy 714.5
  print 785.5
  adj downright 247.12
  affirmative 334.8
  unpersuadable 361.13
  helpful 449.21
  real 761.15
  agreeing 788.9
  belief 953.21
  unqualified 960.2
  certain 970.13
  confident 970.21
  dogmatic 970.22
  emphatic 997.21
  numeric 1017.23
  plus 1032.35
positive reinforcement 92.26
posse
  military unit 461.22
  company 770.3
  search 938.15
  police 1008.17
possess
  have 469.4
  take 480.13
  demonize 680.16
  bewitch 691.9
  obsess 926.25
  know 928.12
  haunt 988.6
possessed
  overjoyed 95.17
  frenzied 105.25
  owned 469.8
  bewitched 691.13
  possessed with a demon
    926.29
  obsessed 926.33
  haunted 988.10
possessive
  possessory 469.10
  selfish 651.5
possible
  latent 519.5
  within the bounds of
    possibility 966.6
  numeric 1017.23
possum 311.23
post
  n station 159.2

standard 273.4
pillar 273.5
messenger 353.1
stronghold 460.6
mail 553.4
branch 617.10
position 724.5
market 736.1
basketball game 747.3
base 901.8
wood 1054.3
v place 159.12
speed 174.8
send 176.15
publicize 352.15
make haste 401.5
pledge 438.10
record 549.15
wise up 551.9
mail 553.12
commission 615.10
pay 624.16
keep accounts 628.8
list 871.8
adj epistolary 553.14
adv swiftly 174.17
posthaste 401.13
postage 553.5
postage stamp 553.5
postal code 553.9
postal service 553.7
postcard 553.3
postdated 833.3
posted located 159.18
pledged 438.12
recorded 549.17
informed 928.18
poster bill 352.7
mail carrier 353.6
posterior
n rear 217.1
buttocks 217.4
adj rear 217.9
succeeding 815.4
subsequent 835.4
posterity
kinfolk 559.2
progeny 561.1
offspring 561.1
successor 817.4
sequel 835.2
postgraduate
n graduate 572.8
adj scholastic 568.19
studentlike 572.12
posthaste
swiftly 174.17
in posthaste 401.13
posthumous
postmortem 307.36
after death 835.5
post-industrial 835.5
postman
mailman 353.5
postal service 553.7
postmark 553.5
postmaster 353.5
postmortem
n autopsy 307.18
v examine 938.24
adj postmortal 307.36

post office
messenger 353.1
postal service 553.7
postpartum depression 926.5
postpone
put away 390.6
delay 846.9
post position 757.3
postprandial 11.6
postscript
added to writing 254.2
sequel 817.1
post-traumatic stress disorder
92.17
postulate
n fact 761.3
essence 767.2
curtain-raiser 816.2
premise 935.7
supposition 951.3
axiom 974.2
v propose 439.5
predicate 951.12
posture
n looks 33.4
behavior 321.1
sham 354.3
gesture 517.14
opinion 953.6
attitude 978.1
v pose 500.13
posy
n flower 310.24
bouquet 310.25
compliment 509.6
bundle 770.8
adj affected 500.15
ostentatious 501.18
affected 533.9
pot
n abdomen 2.19
marijuana 87.11
container 195.1
lot 247.4
wealth 618.3
trophy 646.3
ceramic ware 742.2
jackpot 759.5
v package 212.9
put up 397.11
shape 742.6
shoot 904.12
plant 1069.18
potable
n beverage 10.49
spirits 88.13
adj drinkable 8.34
potash 890.4
potato 10.35
potato chip 10.30
potbellied
corpulent 257.18
bulging 283.15
potent
strong 15.15
powerful 18.12
sexual 75.25
virile 76.13
authoritative 417.15
influential 894.13
potentate 575.8

potential
n talent 413.4
mood 530.11
possibility 966.1
voltage 1032.12
adj latent 519.5
possible 966.6
potential energy 17.1
pothead 87.21
pothole 284.3
potion drink 8.4
dose 86.6
alcohol 88.7
potluck gamble 759.2
haphazard 972.4
potpourri perfume 70.6
performance 708.33
hodgepodge 797.6
pot roast 10.13
pots and pans 11.4
potshot
n gamble 759.2
shot 904.4
v shoot 904.12
potter
n ceramist 716.7
v waste time 331.13
trifle 998.14
potter's field 309.15
potter's wheel
wheel 742.4
instrument of conversion
858.10
pottery plant 739.3
ceramics 742.1
ceramic ware 742.2
pouch 283.11
poultice
n dressing 86.33
pulp 1063.2
v treat 91.24
relieve 120.5
poultry 311.29
pounce
n descent 194.1
leap 366.1
plunge 367.1
v descend 194.5
leap 366.5
plunge 367.6
pound
n staccato 55.1
kennel 228.21
weight 297.8
place of confinement 429.7
money 728.8
hit 902.4
v suffer 26.8
drum 55.4
pitch 182.55
injure 393.13
confine 429.12
attack 459.14
beat time 708.44
din 849.10
beat 902.16
pulverize 1051.9
pound-foolish 486.8
pound for pound 943.10
pound out
do carelessly 340.9

write 547.21
play 708.39
compose 718.6
produce 892.8
pound the pavement 177.23
pour
n torrent 238.5
rainstorm 316.2
v ladle 176.17
run out 190.13
flow 238.16
rain 316.10
give 478.12
disgorge 909.25
abound 991.5
pour it on speed 174.9
be active 330.14
work hard 725.13
pour oil on the fire
excite 105.12
aggravate 119.2
incite 375.17
pour one's heart out
lighten 120.7
speak up 524.21
pout
n scowl 110.9
grimace 265.4
v look sullen 110.15
grimace 265.8
bulge 283.11
poverty poorness 619.1
scarcity 992.3
POW 429.11
powder
n medicine 86.4
makeup 1016.12
dust 1051.5
v depart 188.7
sprinkle 771.6
pulverize 1051.9
come to dust 1051.10
adj powdery 1051.11
powder keg
threat 514.1
danger 1006.1
powder puff 1016.12
powder room 12.10
power
n strength 15.1
energy 17.1
effective force 18
potency 18.1
country 232.1
greatness 247.1
supremacy 249.3
will power 359.4
means 384.2
talent 413.4
authority 417.1
authoritativeness 417.2
governance 417.5
vigor 544.3
control 612.2
wealth 618.3
prerogative 642.1
influence 894.1
impulse 902.1
personage 997.8
v impel 902.11
adj mechanical 1040.14

power broker 609.30
the power elite 575.15
power failure 1032.20
powerful
  adj strong 15.15
  potent 18.12
  great 247.6
  authoritative 417.15
  vigorous 544.11
  influential 894.13
  adv very 247.18
powerhouse
  strong man 15.7
  man of action 330.8
  power station 1032.19
power-hungry 100.28
powerless weak 16.12
  impotent 19.13
  uninfluential 895.3
power of attorney
  commission 615.1
  substitution 862.1
power plant
  propulsion 184.25
  plant 739.3
  powerhouse 1032.19
  machinery 1040.3
powers talent 413.4
  celestial hierarchy 679.3
the powers that be
  the authorities 575.15
  officeholder 610.11
  the government 612.3
power tool 1040.1
powwow
  n forum 423.3
  conference 541.6
  political convention
    609.8
  v confer 541.11
PR appearance 33.2
  publicity 352.4
  voting 609.18
practical useful 387.18
  usable 387.23
  occupied 724.15
  operative 889.9
  workable 889.10
  sensible 920.18
  ungullible 956.5
  expedient 966.7
  realistic 987.6
  practicable 995.6
  handy 1014.15
practical joke 489.10
practical wisdom 920.6
practice
  n behavior 321.1
  action 328.1
  custom 373.1
  habit 373.3
  manner 384.1
  experience 413.9
  observance 434.1
  training 568.3
  study 570.3
  bar 597.4
  rite 701.3
  vocation 724.6
  exercise 725.6
  operation 889.1

tryout 942.3
  notation 1017.2
  v act 328.4
  put into practice 328.8
  use 384.5
  employ 387.10
  perform 434.3
  train 568.13
  study 570.12
  rehearse 704.32
  busy oneself with
    724.11
  exert 725.8
  play 744.2
  iterate 849.8
practiced
  skilled 413.26
  experienced 413.28
practice law 597.5
practice medicine 90.14
practice what one preaches
  observe 434.2
  keep faith 644.9
practicing
  n iteration 849.2
  adj acting 328.10
  observant 434.4
  pious 692.8
Prado 386.9
pragmatic
  sensible 920.18
  realistic 987.6
  practical 995.6
prairie
  n open space 158.4
  horizontal 201.3
  plain 236.1
  grassland 310.8
  adj rustic 233.6
prairie dog 311.23
praise
  n congratulation 149.1
  thanks 150.2
  approval 509.5
  flattery 511.1
  citation 646.4
  glorification 696.2
  v congratulate 149.2
  give approval 509.12
  flatter 511.5
  honor 646.8
  glorify 696.12
praiseworthy 509.20
pram 179.6
prance
  n gait 177.12
  caper 366.2
  v way of walking 177.28
  go on horseback 177.34
  caper 366.6
  strut 501.15
  dance 705.5
prancer horse 311.10
  race horse 311.14
prank
  n trick 489.10
  v dress up 5.42
  ornament 498.8
pratfall tumble 194.3
  collapse 410.3
  goof 975.6

prattle
  n nonsense 520.2
  speech 524.1
  chatter 540.3
  v talk nonsense 520.5
  chatter 540.5
  chat 541.10
pray
  v petition 440.10
  entreat 440.11
  supplicate 696.13
  interj please 440.20
prayer entreaty 440.2
  supplication 696.4
  divine service 696.8
  worshiper 696.9
prayer book 554.1
preach admonish 422.6
  lecture 543.11
  expound 568.16
preacher lecturer 543.5
  informer 551.6
  teacher 571.7
  sermoner 699.3
preamble
  n curtain-raiser 816.2
  v prefix 814.3
prearrange plan 381.8
  prepare 405.6
  contract 437.5
  precontrive 965.4
precarious
  unreliable 971.20
  ticklish 1006.12
precaution
  n precautiousness 494.3
  v forewarn 399.6
precede lead 165.2
  rule 249.11
  antecede 814.2
  go before 816.3
  initiate 818.10
  be prior 834.3
precedent
  n model 786.1
  precursor 816.1
  antecedent 834.2
  verdict 946.5
  adj leading 165.3
  preceding 814.4
precept
  rule 419
  prescript 419.1
  direction 420.3
  a belief 953.2
  maxim 974.1
precinct
  enclosed place 212.3
  nearness 223.1
  sphere 231.2
  region 231.5
  arena 463.1
  election district 609.16
precious
  n endearment term 562.6
  adj beloved 104.24
  downright 247.12
  overnice 500.18
  affected 533.9
  punctilious 580.10
  dear 632.10

precious few 885.4
precious metals
  gold 728.20
  metal 1058.3
precious stone
  jewel 498.6
  gem 1059.7
precipice cliff 200.3
  slope 237.2
precipitant
  precipitate 401.10
  reckless 493.8
  sudden 830.5
precipitate
  n dregs 256.2
  effect 887.1
  precipitation 1045.5
  v descend 194.5
  gravitate 297.15
  rain 316.10
  hasten 401.4
  fell 913.5
  deposit 1045.11
  adj fast 174.15
  impulsive 365.9
  precipitant 401.10
  unprepared 406.8
  reckless 493.8
  sudden 830.5
  premature 845.8
precipitous
  perpendicular 200.12
  steep 204.18
  precipitate 401.10
  reckless 493.8
  sudden 830.5
précis
  n shortening 268.3
  abridgment 557.1
  iteration 849.2
  v iterate 849.8
precise
  v be accurate 973.11
  adj meticulous 339.12
  fastidious 495.9
  punctilious 580.10
  detailed 766.9
  particular 865.12
  discriminating 944.7
  exact 973.17
precision
  meticulousness 339.3
  fastidiousness 495.1
  elegance 533.1
  accuracy 973.5
preclude
  prohibit 444.3
  exclude 773.4
  prevent 1012.14
precocious 845.8
precognition
  understanding 928.3
  intuition 934.1
  foreknowledge 961.3
preconceive 947.2
preconclusion 947.1
preconscious
  n psyche 92.28
  adj subconscious
    92.42
preconsider 380.7

precursor
harbinger 133.5
leading 165.1
vanguard 216.2
settler 227.9
warning sign 399.3
precedence 814.1
forerunner 816.1
antecedent 834.2
early bird 845.4
transformer 852.5
producer 892.7
predate
date 832.13
be prior 834.3
predator 480.12
predecessor 816.1
predestine
predetermine 964.6
destine 964.7
predetermine
premeditate 380.7
prejudge 947.2
predecide 964.6
predicament
state 765.1
urgent need 963.4
bewilderment 971.3
danger 1006.1
adversity 1011.1
plight 1013.4
predicate
n affirmation 334.1
syntax 530.2
v affirm 334.5
postulate 951.12
predict
look forward to 130.6
foreshow 133.10
come 839.6
foresee 961.5
make a prediction 962.9
risk 972.12
predictable
stable 855.12
divinable 962.13
probable 968.6
reliable 970.17
predilection
inclination 100.3
love 104.1
preference 371.5
tendency 896.1
prejudgment 947.1
disposition 978.3
prejudice 980.3
predispose 894.7
predominant
chief 249.14
governing 612.18
prevalent 864.12
influential 894.14
paramount 997.24
preeminent top 198.10
chief 249.14
authoritative 417.15
paramount 997.24
preempt 480.19
preemptive strike 459.1
preen groom 79.20
ornament 498.8

preexist 834.3
prefabricated
ready-made 405.19
made 892.18
preface
n front 216.1
makeup 554.12
part of writing 793.2
curtain-raiser 816.2
v prefix 814.3
prefect
teaching fellow 571.4
executive 574.3
prefecture 417.7
prefer desire 100.14
have preference 371.17
offer 439.4
propose 439.5
promote 446.2
favor 650.8
take the attitude 978.6
preferable 371.25
prefer charges
arraign 598.15
accuse 599.7
preferential treatment
furtherance 449.5
partiality 650.3
prefix
n front 216.1
added to writing 254.2
morphology 526.3
curtain-raiser 816.2
v add 253.4
preface 814.3
preformed 405.19
pregnable
helpless 19.18
vulnerable 1006.16
pregnant
enceinte 78.18
meaningful 518.10
beginning 818.15
critical 843.10
original 886.14
productive 890.9
imaginative 986.18
preheat 1020.17
prehensile
raptorial 474.9
knowing 928.15
prehistoric
prewar 834.5
former 837.10
primitive 842.11
preindicate 133.12
prejudge
be prejudiced 947.2
forejudge 980.7
prejudice
n preference 371.5
tendency 896.1
prejudgment 947.1
forejudging 980.3
disadvantage 996.2
v prejudice against 980.9
work evil 1000.6
preliminary
n preparation 405.1
curtain-raiser 816.2
inauguration 818.5

adj prior 814.4
preceding 816.4
prefatory 818.16
prelude
n overture 708.26
precedence 814.1
curtain-raiser 816.2
v prefix 814.3
premarital 665.27
premature
untimely 844.6
too early 845.8
premeditate
calculate 380.7
prearrange 965.4
premier
n head of state 575.7
adj first 818.17
paramount 997.24
premiere
n theatrical performance 704.12
v dramatize 704.28
premise
n fact 761.3
curtain-raiser 816.2
antecedent 834.2
foundation 901.6
proposition 935.7
supposition 951.3
v prefix 814.3
premises region 231.1
evidence 957.1
premium
n extra 254.4
gratuity 478.5
interest 623.3
bonus 624.6
discount 631.1
bridge 758.3
adj expensive 632.11
premonition
presentiment 133.1
forewarning 399.2
extrasensory perception 689.8
hunch 934.3
prenatal 818.15
prenuptial agreement 436.3
preoccupy
appropriate 480.19
obsess 926.25
occupy the mind 931.20
engross 983.13
preordained 964.8
prepacked 212.12
prepaid 624.22
preparation
medicine 86.4
provision 385.1
preparing 405.1
training 568.3
harmonization 709.2
earliness 845.1
foresight 961.1
preparatory school 567.4
prepare cook 11.5
provide 385.7
equip 385.8
make ready 405.6
take steps 494.6

write 547.21
train 568.13
formulate 718.6
produce 892.8
preponderance
superiority 249.1
dominance 417.6
majority 883.2
influence 894.1
preposition 530.3
prepossessing
delightful 97.7
alluring 377.8
preposterous
overpriced 632.12
undue 640.9
absurd 923.11
unbelievable 955.10
impossible 967.7
fanciful 986.20
prepped 405.16
preppie 572.3
prerecord 50.14
prerequisite
n preparation 405.1
condition 959.2
requirement 963.2
adj preparatory 405.20
requisite 963.13
prerogative
superiority 249.1
authority 417.1
right 642
presage
n premonition 133.1
foreknowledge 961.3
prediction 962.1
v foreshow 133.10
predict 962.9
preschool
n infant school 567.2
adj scholastic 567.13
prescient 961.7
prescribe
remedy 86.38
require 420.9
advise 422.5
direct 573.8
administer 643.6
legalize 673.9
prescription
remedy 86.1
limitation 210.2
custom 373.1
precept 419.1
formula 419.3
direction 420.3
possession 469.1
prerogative 642.1
law 673.3
rule 869.4
presence looks 33.4
apparition 33.5
being here 221.1
behavior 321.1
existence 761.1
influence 894.6
phantom 976.4
specter 988.1
presence of mind 106.3

present
 n gift 478.4
 tense 530.12
 v manifest 348.5
 put to choice 371.21
 provide 385.7
 offer 439.4
 donate 478.12
 say 524.22
 phrase 532.4
 introduce 587.14
 give 634.4
 dramatize 704.28
 adduce 957.12
 adj attendant 221.12
 existent 761.13
 immediate 838.2
the present time 821.1
 now 838.1
 present tense 838.1
presentable
 giveable 478.23
 tolerable 999.20
 comely 1016.19
presentiment
 feeling 93.1
 premonition 133.1
 forewarning 399.2
 hunch 934.3
 foreknowledge 961.3
 prediction 962.1
present one's case 598.19
preserve
 n sweets 10.40
 reserve 397.7
 refuge 1009.1
 v reserve 386.12
 conserve 397.8
 cure 397.9
 retain 474.5
 perpetuate 829.5
 be conservative 853.6
 sustain 856.4
 care for 1008.19
preserve one's honor 136.7
preset 437.5
preside
 administer 573.11
 entertain 585.8
 administer justice 594.5
president principal 571.8
 executive 574.3
 head of state 575.7
presidential election 609.15
press
 n extractor 192.9
 squeezing 260.2
 urge 375.6
 presswork 548.9
 printing office 548.11
 publisher 554.2
 enlistment 615.7
 throng 770.4
 thrust 902.2
 urgency 997.4
 v squeeze 260.8
 hot-press 287.6
 weigh on 297.11
 urge 375.14
 hasten 401.4
 insist 421.8

bring pressure to bear upon
  424.6
 urge upon 439.9
 importune 440.12
 attach 480.20
 embrace 562.18
 enlist 615.17
 strain 725.10
 thrust 902.12
 densify 1045.9
the press
 informant 551.5
 news 552.1
 journalism 555.3
press charges 599.7
press conference
 conference 541.6
 interview 938.11
press corps 555.4
press into service 387.14
pressman
 printer 548.12
 journalist 555.4
press one's luck
 risk 972.12
 take chances 1006.7
press release
 release 352.3
 message 552.4
pressroom 548.11
press the panic button
  127.11
pressure
 n touching 73.2
 tension 128.3
 squeezing 260.2
 burden 297.7
 urging 375.5
 urge 375.6
 prestige 417.4
 insistence 421.4
 coercion 424.3
 importunity 440.3
 influence 894.1
 thrust 902.2
 urgent need 963.4
 urgency 997.4
 adversity 1011.1
 v urge 375.14
 coerce 424.8
 importune 440.12
pressure group
 interest group 609.31
 party 617.4
 influence 894.6
pressure suit
 blackout 184.21
 space suit 1075.11
pressurize 260.8
presswork 548.9
prestidigitation
 juggling 356.5
 illusoriness 976.2
prestige
 respect 155.1
 superiority 249.1
 authority 417.4
 class 607.1
 honor 662.4
 influence 894.1
 notability 997.2

presto
 n music 708.25
 tempo 709.24
 adj music 708.55
 instantaneous 830.4
 presto chango 852.13
 interj attention! 983.22
presume
 hope 124.7
 expect 130.5
 have the audacity 142.7
 imply 519.4
 assume 640.6
 entail 772.4
 judge 946.8
 prejudge 947.2
 suppose 951.10
 think 953.11
 think likely 968.5
presume upon
 exploit 387.16
 impose on 640.7
 inflict on 643.7
presumption
 hope 124.1
 presumptuousness 141.2
 insolence 142.1
 meddling 214.2
 foolhardiness 493.3
 implication 519.2
 assumption 640.2
 entailment 772.2
 prejudgment 947.1
 supposition 951.3
 opinion 953.6
 probability 968.1
presumptuous
 arrogant 141.10
 insolent 142.9
 meddlesome 214.9
 foolhardy 493.9
 presuming 640.11
presuppose
 imply 519.4
 entail 772.4
 prejudge 947.2
 suppose 951.10
pre-teens 301.2
pretend sham 354.21
 pretext 376.3
 affect 500.12
 presume 640.6
pretender
 impostor 357.6
 phony 500.7
 usurper 640.4
pretentious
 artificial 500.15
 ostentatious 501.18
 inflated 502.12
 affected 533.9
 grandiloquent 545.8
pretext
 n sham 354.3
 loophole 369.4
 pretense 376.1
 reason 886.2
 v make a pretext of 376.3
pretreat 405.6
pretty
 adj beautiful 1016.18

 adv to a degree 245.7
 very 247.18
 tolerably 999.24
a pretty penny 632.3
pretzel 10.30
prevail excel 249.6
 succeed 409.7
 triumph 411.3
 dominate 612.15
 exist 761.8
 persist 781.3
 endure 827.6
 predominate 864.10
prevailing sentiment 953.6
prevailing taste 578.1
prevailing wind 318.10
prevail upon 375.23
prevalent
 customary 373.13
 fashionable 578.11
 governing 612.18
 existent 761.13
 happening 831.9
 frequent 847.4
 prevailing 864.12
 plentiful 991.7
prevaricate
 equivocate 344.7
 lie 354.19
 quibble 936.9
prevent prohibit 444.3
 anticipate 845.6
 hinder 1012.14
preventative
 n prophylactic 86.20
 counteractant 900.3
 adj preventive 1012.19
preventive measure 1008.3
preventive medicine 90.13
prevention
 avoidance 368.1
 prohibition 444.1
 stop 1012.2
preview
 n look 27.3
 motion pictures 706.1
 foresight 961.1
 v dramatize 704.28
previous prior 834.4
 former 837.10
 premature 845.8
 earlier 845.10
prewar 834.5
prewarn 399.6
prey sufferer 96.11
 desire 100.11
 sweetheart 104.10
 objective 380.2
 quarry 382.7
price
 n penalty 603.1
 interest 623.3
 recompense 624.3
 charge 630.1
 cost 630.1
 quotation 738.9
 gambling odds 759.6
 v set a price 630.11
price-fixing 630.5
priceless
 humorous 488.5

precious 632.10
price supports
policy 609.4
price controls 630.5
prick
n pang 26.2
point 285.3
goad 375.8
mark 517.5
bad person 660.5
v hurt 26.7
tingle 74.5
pain 96.17
come to a point 285.6
perforate 292.15
goad 375.15
mark 517.19
drive 1070.8
prickle
n tingle 74.1
point 285.3
thorn 285.5
adhesive 803.4
v tingle 74.5
prickly
sensitive 24.12
tingly 74.8
excitable 105.28
touchy 110.21
pricky 285.10
prick up the ears
listen 48.10
hearken to 983.7
pride self-esteem 136.1
proudness 136.1
vanity 140.2
arrogance 141.1
pomp 501.6
group of animals 770.5
confidence 970.5
good thing 999.5
priest celibate 565.2
holy orders 699.4
parish priest 699.5
teacher 699.10
clergy 699.11
priesthood
the ministry 698.1
clericalism 698.3
clergy 699.1
prig snob 141.7
prude 500.11
prim prudish 500.19
stiff 580.9
prima ballerina 707.6
primacy
supremacy 249.3
dominance 417.6
importance 997.1
superexcellence 999.2
prima donna
lead 707.6
singer 710.13
chief 997.10
prima facie
at sight 27.22
apparently 33.12
primal
n first 818.3
adj basic 199.8
chief 249.14

unimitated 337.6
natural 416.6
innate 767.8
essential 767.9
simple 798.6
beginning 818.15
original 886.14
primary
n color system 35.7
election 609.15
first 818.3
adj basic 199.8
front 216.10
chief 249.14
unimitated 337.6
essential 767.9
simple 798.6
beginning 818.15
original 886.14
paramount 997.24
primary election 609.15
primary school 567.3
primate
wild animal 311.23
ancient 842.7
prime
n maturity 303.2
spring 313.2
dawn 314.3
divine service 696.8
first 818.3
the best 999.8
v color 35.14
coat 295.24
load 405.9
tutor 568.11
shoot 904.12
adj front 216.10
chief 249.14
unimitated 337.6
simple 798.6
beginning 818.15
previous 834.4
primitive 842.11
paramount 997.24
best 999.16
numeric 1017.23
prime interest rate 623.3
prime meridian 231.3
prime minister 575.7
prime of life 303.4
primer color 35.8
fuse 462.15
textbook 554.10
elementary education 568.5
basics 818.6
prime time 1035.2
primeval
beginning 818.15
former 837.10
primitive 842.11
original 886.14
primitive
n native 227.3
simple soul 416.3
root 526.2
ancient 842.7
adj basic 199.8
native 226.5
unimitated 337.6
natural 416.6

unrefined 497.12
essential 767.9
simple 798.6
beginning 818.15
former 837.10
primordial 842.11
original 886.14
primordial 842.11
primp dress up 5.42
ornament 498.8
primrose pink 41.8
yellow 43.4
prince potentate 575.8
nobleman 608.7
good person 659.1
Prince Charming 104.13
princess
sovereign queen 575.11
noblewoman 608.8
principal
n superior 249.4
headmaster 571.8
chief 575.3
lead 707.6
capital 728.15
most important person 997.10
adj chief 249.14
first 818.17
paramount 997.24
principality
region 231.5
country 232.1
dominance 417.6
mastership 417.7
angel 679.1
principle motive 375.1
rule 419.2
essence 767.2
law 869.4
cause 886.1
commitment 886.9
foundation 901.6
a belief 953.2
axiom 974.2
print
n indentation 284.6
mark 517.7
imprint 548.3
type 548.6
picture 712.11
numbered print 713.5
photoprint 714.5
offprint 785.5
copy 785.5
impact 887.2
v represent 349.8
mark 517.19
imprint 548.14
engrave 713.9
process 714.15
fix 855.9
printed written 547.22
in print 548.19
engraved 713.11
printer typist 547.18
printworker 548.12
publisher 554.2
output device 1042.9
printing press 548.9
printmaking
printing 548.1

graphic arts 713.1
the print media 555.3
print run 554.5
print shop 548.11
prior
n religious 699.16
adj leading 165.3
preceding 814.4
previous 834.4
former 837.10
priority leading 165.1
front 216.1
superiority 249.1
prestige 417.4
precedence 814.1
sequence 815.1
previousness 834.1
importance 997.1
prism 29.2
prismatic
chromatic 35.16
variegated 47.9
multilateral 278.11
prison 429.8
prisoner captive 429.11
accused 599.6
prisoner of war 429.11
prissy effeminate 77.15
meticulous 339.12
fastidious 495.9
prudish 500.19
stiff 580.9
pristine
unimitated 337.6
unused 390.12
natural 406.13
unadorned 416.6
innocent 657.6
intact 792.10
simple 798.6
new 841.7
primitive 842.11
original 886.14
undamaged 1002.8
privacy
retirement 345.2
seclusion 584.1
aloneness 872.2
retreat 1009.5
private
n enlisted man 461.8
adj interior 207.6
closed 293.9
personal 312.15
privy 345.13
taking 480.25
privatistic 584.9
intrinsic 767.7
particular 865.12
alone 872.8
private detective 576.10
private enterprise 611.8
private practice 90.13
private sector
capitalism 611.8
economy 731.7
privation loss 473.1
deprivation 480.6
indigence 619.2
privatization 584.1
privatize 611.16

privilege
  n superiority 249.1
  exemption 430.8
  license 642.2
  v authorize 443.11
privileged information
  secret 345.5
  inside information 551.2
privy
  n latrine 12.10
  hut 228.9
  adj covert 345.12
  private 345.13
privy council
  council 423.1
  cabinet 613.3
prix fixe 630.5
prize
  n desire 100.11
  booty 482.11
  monument 549.12
  award 646.2
  leverage 906.1
  lever 906.4
  good thing 999.5
  the best 999.8
  v cherish 104.21
  respect 155.4
  measure 300.10
  price 630.11
  get a purchase 906.8
  estimate 946.9
  value 997.13
  adj best 999.16
prized 104.24
prizefight 457.9
prizewinner 413.15
PR man 352.9
pro
  n expert 413.11
  professional 726.4
  gambler 759.21
  affirmative 935.14
  adj approving 509.17
  occupational 724.16
  prep in favor of 509.21
proactive
  energetic 17.13
  enterprising 330.23
pro and con 935.19
probability
  expectation 130.1
  the future 839.1
  tendency 896.1
  liability 897.1
  prediction 962.1
  possibility 966.1
  likelihood 968.1
  chance 972.1
  good chance 972.8
probable error
  mathematical probability
    968.2
  inaccuracy 975.2
probate
  n bequest 478.10
  v confirm 957.11
probation 942.2
probe
  n nurse 90.10
  investigation 938.4

search 938.15
  feeler 942.4
  test rocket 1074.6
  artificial satellite 1075.6
  v measure 300.10
  investigate 938.23
  sound out 942.9
  philosophize 952.9
probity honesty 644.1
  virtue 653.1
problem
  annoyance 96.2
  enigma 522.8
  topic 937.1
  question 938.10
  bewilderment 971.3
  fault 1003.2
  trouble 1013.3
problematic
  unbelievable 955.10
  doubtful 971.17
  bewildering 971.27
proboscis 283.8
procedure
  behavior 321.1
  rule 373.4
  plan 381.1
  policy 381.4
  manner 384.1
  process 889.2
proceed
  progress 162.2
  behave 321.4
  act 328.4
  take action 328.5
  use 384.5
  elapse 821.5
proceed from 887.5
proceedings
  activity 330.1
  report 549.7
  lawsuit 598.1
  affairs 831.4
proceeds gain 472.3
  yield 472.5
  receipts 627.1
  production 893.2
process
  n manner 384.1
  procedure 889.2
  v cut or dress the hair 3.22
  prepare 405.6
  develop 714.15
  convert 892.9
  gather materials 1054.7
processed
  prepared 405.16
  made 892.18
procession train 812.3
  sequence 815.1
processor 1042.2
proclaim
  herald 133.14
  affirm 334.5
  cry 352.13
  command 420.8
  state 524.23
  be prior 834.3
  dogmatize 970.10
proclamation
  affirmation 334.1

announcement 352.2
  decree 420.4
proclivity
  inclination 100.3
  preference 371.5
  tendency 896.1
  disposition 978.3
proconsul 575.13
procrastinate
  let go 329.5
  leave undone 340.7
  not face up to 368.13
  protract 827.9
  be dilatory 846.11
procrastinator
  slowpoke 175.5
  neglecter 340.5
procreate grow 14.2
  generate 78.8
  develop 259.7
  engender 818.14
  originate 892.12
proctor
  teaching fellow 571.4
  superintendent 574.2
  steward 574.4
  lawyer 597.1
procure fetch 176.16
  elicit 192.14
  induce 375.22
  acquire 472.8
  prostitute oneself 665.21
  purchase 733.7
  cause 886.11
procurement
  provision 385.1
  acquisition 472.1
prod
  n goad 375.8
  thrust 902.2
  v touch 73.6
  goad 375.15
  importune 440.12
  thrust 902.12
prodigal
  n wastrel 486.2
  adj exaggerated 355.4
  improvident 406.15
  extravagant 486.8
  diffuse 538.11
  unvirtuous 654.12
  intemperate 669.7
  teeming 884.9
  plentiful 991.7
  superabundant 993.19
prodigal son
  penitent 113.5
  prodigal 486.2
  returnee 859.3
prodigious
  wonderful 122.10
  large 247.7
  huge 257.20
  extraordinary 870.14
  miraculous 870.16
produce
  n vegetables 10.35
  fruit 10.38
  yield 472.5
  receipts 627.1
  groceries 735.7

production 893.2
  v secrete 13.5
  lengthen 267.6
  do 328.6
  manifest 348.5
  accomplish 407.4
  write 547.21
  dramatize 704.28
  pen 718.6
  cause 886.10
  be productive 890.7
  create 892.8
  bear 892.13
  adduce 957.12
  imagine 986.14
product yield 472.5
  commodity 735.2
  effect 887.1
  end product 893.1
  sum 1017.6
productivity
  power 18.1
  wordiness 538.2
  productiveness 890.1
  invention 986.3
product liability 641.2
profane
  v misuse 389.4
  desecrate 694.4
  adj cursing 513.8
  unsacred 686.3
  impious 694.6
  secularist 695.16
profanity cursing 513.3
  unsanctity 686.1
  sacrilege 694.2
profess affirm 334.5
  sham 354.21
  pretext 376.3
  state 953.12
profession
  acknowledgment 332.3
  affirmation 334.1
  claim 376.2
  occupation 724.4
  vocation 724.6
  confession 953.7
  testimony 957.2
professional
  n expert 413.11
  member of a learned
    profession 726.4
  adj skillful 413.22
  skilled 413.26
  scholastic 568.19
  occupational 724.16
professional ethics 636.1
professor expert 413.11
  teacher 571.1
  academic rank 571.3
  gambler 759.21
proffer
  n offer 439.1
  v offer 439.4
  give 478.12
  answer 939.4
  adduce 957.12
proficient
  n expert 413.11
  adj fitted 405.17
  skillful 413.22

profile
perfected 1002.9
able 18.14

profile
n outline 211.2
side 218.1
contour 262.2
description 349.2
diagram 381.3
portrait 712.15
history 719.1
v outline 211.9

profit
n incentive 375.7
benefit 387.4
gain 472.3
expedience 995.1
good 999.4
v avail 387.17
make profit 472.12
expedite one's affair 995.3
do good 999.10

profitable useful 387.18
valuable 387.22
helpful 449.21
gainful 472.16
paying 624.21
expedient 995.5
good 999.12

profit sharing 476.2

profit-sharing 476.9

profligate
n reprobate 660.4
libertine 665.10
adj prodigal 486.8
corrupt 654.14
licentious 665.25

pro forma 580.11

profound
deep-felt 93.24
downright 247.12
huge 257.20
deep 275.10
recondite 522.16
wise 920.17
learned 928.21

profound thought
thoughtfulness 931.3
engrossment 983.3

profuse
exaggerated 355.4
liberal 485.4
prodigal 486.8
diffuse 538.11
teeming 884.9
plentiful 991.7

progenitor 560.8

progeny family 559.5
offspring 561.1

prognosis
prognostication 91.13
verdict 946.5
prediction 962.1

prognosticate
hope 124.7
predict 962.9
risk 972.12

program
n exercise 84.2
announcement 352.2
plan 381.1
undertaking 404.1

government plan 609.6
platform 609.7
performance 708.33
track meet 755.2
roll 871.6
schedule 965.3
software 1042.11
rocketry 1074.1
v plan 381.8
inculcate 568.12
list 871.8
schedule 965.6
automate 1041.20
computerize 1042.21

programming language
1042.13

progress
n progression 162.1
course 172.2
travel 177.1
journey 177.5
way 182.9
improvement 392.1
continuance 856.1
conversion 858.1
evolution 861.1
v advance 162.2
move 172.5
travel 177.18
improve 392.7
make good 409.10
evolve 861.5
prosper 1010.7

progressive
n left side 220.1
reformer 392.6
liberal 611.11
adj progressing 162.6
flowing 172.8
left 220.4
gradual 245.5
improving 392.15
emendatory 392.16
liberal 611.19
consecutive 812.9
modern 841.13

prohibit
restrain 428.7
forbid 444.3
exclude 773.4
make impossible 967.6
prevent 1012.14

prohibition
restraint 428.1
ban 444.1
forbidding 444.1
prohibitionism 668.3
exclusion 773.1
prevention 1012.2

prohibitive
prohibitory 444.6
overpriced 632.12
exclusive 773.9
preventive 1012.19

project
n intention 380.1
projection 381.2
undertaking 404.1
task 724.2
the future 839.1
v overhang 202.7

externalize 206.5
protrude 283.10
be manifest 348.7
image 349.11
intend 380.4
plan 381.8
show on screen 714.16
lie ahead 839.6
jaculate 904.11
launch 1074.13

projectile
n missile 462.18
ejecta 904.5
adj trajectile 904.15

projector planner 381.6
launcher 462.21
motion-picture projector
714.12
rocket launcher 1074.10

proletarian
n common man 606.5
blue-collar worker 607.9
worker 726.2
adj working-class 607.10

proliferate
procreate 78.8
grow 251.6
multiply 883.6
produce 890.7
abound 991.5

prolific diffuse 538.11
teeming 884.9
productive 890.9
imaginative 986.18

prolix tedious 118.9
lengthened 267.8
wordy 538.12
talkative 540.9
protracted 827.11
superfluous 993.17

prologue act 704.7
part of writing 793.2
curtain-raiser 816.2

prolong lengthen 267.6
protract 827.9
postpone 846.9
sustain 856.4

prom dance 705.2
performance 708.33
assembly 770.2

PROM 1042.7

promenade
n walk 177.10
path 383.2
dance 705.2
procession 812.3
v go for a walk 177.29
file 812.7

prominence
distinctness 31.2
glory 247.2
height 272.1
protuberance 283.2
conspicuousness 348.4
prestige 417.4
distinction 662.5
notability 997.2

prominent
distinct 31.7
eminent 247.9
high 272.14

protruding 283.14
conspicuous 348.12
authoritative 417.15
outstanding 662.17
notable 997.19

promiscuous
slipshod 340.12
wanton 665.26
mixed 797.14
unordered 810.12
undiscriminating 945.5
purposeless 972.16

promise
n hope 124.1
omen 133.3
commitment 436.2
pledge 436.1
compact 437.1
prediction 962.1
v give hope 124.10
suggest 133.13
observe 434.2
make a promise 436.4
contract 437.5
be probable 968.4

the Promised Land 986.11

promising
of promise 124.13
auspicious 133.18
probable 968.6

promissory note 728.11

promo
promotion 352.5
commendation 509.3

promontory 283.9

promote
advance 162.5
publicize 352.15
motivate 375.12
be instrumental 384.7
improve 392.9
upgrade 446.2
be useful 449.17
commend 509.11
expedite one's affair 995.3

promoter
publicist 352.9
planner 381.6
commender 509.8
supporter 616.9

prompt
n hint 551.4
reminder 989.6
v provoke 375.13
induce 375.22
admonish 422.6
hint 551.10
influence 894.7
remind 989.20
adj eager 101.8
fast 174.15
willing 324.5
quick 330.18
alert 339.14
hasty 401.9
consenting 441.4
punctual 845.9

promulgate
publish 352.10
proclaim 352.13
command 420.8

execute 437.9
pronate 205.5
prone
  v lie down 913.11
  adj recumbent 201.8
  low 274.7
  willing 324.5
  deferential 433.16
  liable 897.5
  disposed 978.8
prong fork 171.4
  tributary 238.3
pronoun 530.5
pronounce affirm 334.5
  announce 352.12
  command 420.8
  say 524.22
  pass judgment 946.13
pronounced
  distinct 31.7
  downright 247.12
  affirmed 334.9
  conspicuous 348.12
  speech 524.29
pronounce sentence
  bring in a verdict 598.20
  condemn 602.3
pronto
  in short order 174.19
  at once 830.8
  promptly 845.15
pronunciation 524.5
proof
  n manifestation 348.1
  proof sheet 548.5
  information 551.1
  artist's proof 713.7
  print 785.5
  reasoning 935.1
  test 942.2
  grounds for belief 957.1
  evidence 957.1
  demonstration 957.3
  confirmation 957.4
  v insulate 15.14
  print 548.14
  adj resistant 15.20
proofread 548.17
proofreader
  reader 548.13
  examiner 938.17
prop
  n theater 704.17
  motion-picture studio 706.4
  supporter 901.2
  propeller 904.6
  v strengthen 15.13
  aid 449.12
  support 901.21
propaganda 569.2
propagate
  procreate 78.8
  publish 352.10
  disperse 771.4
propel
  set in motion 172.6
  motivate 375.12
  impel 902.11
  push 904.9
propellant
  n propeller 904.6

fuel 1021.1
  rocket propulsion 1074.8
  adj moving 172.7
  propulsive 904.14
propeller 904.6
propensity
  inclination 100.3
  aptitude 413.5
  tendency 896.1
  disposition 978.3
proper
  downright 247.12
  useful 387.18
  fastidious 495.9
  decorous 496.10
  appropriate 533.7
  conventional 579.5
  right 637.3
  rightful 639.8
  just 649.8
  decent 664.5
  orthodox 687.7
  characteristic 865.13
  accurate 973.16
  expedient 995.5
proper fraction 1017.7
proper noun
  name 527.3
  noun 530.5
property supply 386.2
  legal claim 469.1
  possessions 471.1
  real estate 471.6
  sign 517.1
  wealth 618.1
  theater 704.17
  nature 767.4
  characteristic 865.4
property rights
  possession 469.1
  ownership 469.2
prophecy
  revelation 683.10
  the future 839.1
  prediction 962.1
prophesy come 839.6
  predict 962.9
prophet
  religious founder 684.1
  predictor 962.4
  visionary 986.13
prophet of doom
  pessimist 125.7
  warner 399.4
  predictor 962.4
prophylactic
  n preventive 86.20
  contraceptive 86.23
  counteractant 900.3
  safeguard 1008.3
  adj sanitary 79.27
  preventive 86.42
  precautionary 494.10
  protective 1008.23
  deterrent 1012.19
propitiate pacify 465.7
  atone 658.4
  appease the gods 696.15
propitious
  promising 124.13
  auspicious 133.18

favorable 449.22
  timely 843.9
proponent 600.8
proportion
  n space 158.1
  degree 245.1
  size 257.1
  symmetry 264.1
  portion 477.5
  harmony 533.2
  equality 790.1
  order 807.1
  comparison 943.1
  comparability 943.3
  notation 1017.2
  ratio 1017.7
  v size 257.15
  symmetrize 264.3
  proportionate 477.7
  make agree 788.7
  equalize 790.6
proportional
  spatial 158.10
  proportionate 477.13
  approximate 775.8
proposal
  nomination 371.8
  intention 380.1
  project 381.2
  advice 422.1
  proposition 439.2
  marriage proposal 562.8
  theory 951.2
proposition
  n affirmation 334.1
  project 381.2
  undertaking 404.1
  proposal 439.2
  premise 935.7
  theory 951.2
  supposition 951.3
  axiom 974.2
  v make advances 439.8
proprietary
  n medicine 86.4
  ownership 469.2
  proprietor 470.2
  adj possessive 469.10
  propertied 471.8
proprietor
  householder 227.7
  proprietary 470.2
propriety
  fastidiousness 495.1
  decorousness 496.3
  elegance 533.1
  social convention 579.1
  decorum 637.2
  justice 649.1
  decency 664.2
  fitness 788.5
  timeliness 843.1
  normality 869.1
  expedience 995.1
propter hoc 888.7
propulsion
  manpower 18.4
  impulse 902.1
  pushing 904.1
pro rata
  proportionate 477.13

proportionately 477.14
  priced 630.14
prorate
  proportion 477.7
  charge 630.12
prosaic prose 117.8
  simple 499.6
  plain-speaking 535.3
  prosy 721.5
  occupied 724.15
  unimaginative 987.5
proscenium front 216.1
  stage 704.16
proscribe
  restrain 428.7
  prohibit 444.3
  ostracize 586.6
  condemn 602.3
  exclude 773.4
  banish 909.17
prose
  n prosaicness 117.2
  prose style 721.1
  platitude 974.3
  v platitudinize 117.5
  write prose 721.3
  adj prosaic 117.8
  in prose 721.4
prosecute
  practice 328.8
  pursue 382.8
  execute 437.9
  sue 598.13
prosecutor 599.5
proselytize 858.16
prospect
  n look 27.3
  field of view 31.3
  view 33.6
  hope 124.1
  expectation 130.1
  dueness 639.1
  customer 733.4
  the future 839.1
  foresight 961.1
  possibility 966.1
  probability 968.1
  v mine 1058.14
prospective
  expected 130.13
  future 839.8
prospector 1058.9
prospectus
  intention 380.1
  project 381.2
  prediction 962.1
  schedule 965.3
prosper succeed 409.7
  enjoy prosperity
    1010.7
prosperity
  success 409.1
  wealth 618.1
  business cycle 731.10
  prosperousness 1010.1
  good times 1010.4
Prospero 976.2
prosperous
  auspicious 133.18
  successful 409.14
  wealthy 618.14

in good case 1010.12
prosperous issue 409.1
prostitute
  n harlot 665.16
  v misuse 389.4
  corrupt 393.12
  adj prostituted 665.28
prostrate
  v disable 19.10
  fatigue 21.4
  aggrieve 112.19
  unnerve 128.10
  raze 395.19
  conquer 412.10
  fell 913.5
  lie down 913.11
  adj disabled 19.16
  burnt-out 21.10
  laid up 85.59
  disconsolate 112.28
  overcome 112.29
  unnerved 128.14
  obsequious 138.14
  obeisant 155.10
  recumbent 201.8
  low 274.7
  conquered 412.17
  deferential 433.16
  depressed 913.12
protagonist
  supporter 616.9
  role 704.10
  lead 707.6
protean
  multiform 783.3
  changeable 854.6
protect preserve 397.8
  aid 449.11
  defend 460.8
  play safe 1007.3
  guard 1008.18
protection
  bribe 378.2
  preservation 397.1
  restraint 428.1
  custody 429.5
  pass 443.7
  aid 449.1
  defense 460.1
  precaution 494.3
  policy 609.4
  safety 1007.1
  safeguarding 1008.1
  guard 1008.1
protectionist 428.6
protector
  defender 460.7
  regent 575.12
  keeper 1008.5
protégé 432.6
protein 7.6
pro tem 828.9
proteolytic 806.6
protest
  n complaint 115.4
  demur 325.2
  objection 333.2
  affirmation 334.1
  resistance 453.1
  disapproval 510.1
  nonpayment 625.1

nonconformity 868.1
  v object 333.5
  affirm 334.5
  oppose 451.3
  offer resistance 453.3
  disapprove 510.10
  not pay 625.6
  not conform 868.4
Protestant
  n non-Catholic 675.20
  adj religious 675.28
protocol
  treatment 91.14
  rule 419.2
  compact 437.1
  etiquette 580.3
  fact 761.3
  knowledge 928.1
  schedule 965.3
proton atom 258.8
  elementary particle 1038.6
protoplasm 305.4
prototype form 262.1
  original 337.2
  model 786.1
  philosophy 932.2
  standard of perfection
    1002.4
protozoan
  microbic 258.15
  invertebrate 311.51
protract lengthen 267.6
  extend 538.8
  prolong 827.9
  postpone 846.9
  sustain 856.4
protractor 278.4
protrude
  emerge 190.11
  protuberate 283.10
proud prideful 136.8
  vain 140.9
  arrogant 141.9
  grandiose 501.21
  confident 970.21
provable real 761.15
  demonstrable 957.19
  obvious 970.15
prove print 548.14
  result 887.4
  experiment 942.8
  demonstrate 957.10
  confirm 957.11
  verify 970.12
  check 1017.21
proven
  trustworthy 644.19
  proved 957.20
  true 973.13
provender
  n food 10.1
  feed 10.4
  provisions 10.5
  supplies 385.2
  v provision 385.9
proverb
  n maxim 974.1
  v aphorize 974.5
provide supply 385.7
  prepare 405.6
  furnish 478.15

provide against
  prepare for 405.11
  take precautions 494.6
provided
  adj supplied 385.13
  prepared 405.16
  adv circumstantially 766.12
  conj in the event that
    831.13
  provided that 959.12
provide for
  provide 385.7
  prepare for 405.11
  furnish 478.15
  take precautions 494.6
  finance 729.16
  allow for 959.5
  care for 1008.19
providence
  precaution 494.3
  thrift 635.1
  divine function 677.13
  sagacity 920.4
  judiciousness 920.7
  foresight 961.1
Providence 964.3
provider 385.6
province sphere 231.2
  region 231.5
  country 232.1
  the country 233.1
  duty 641.1
  diocese 698.8
  function 724.3
  occupation 724.4
  science 928.10
provincial
  n governor 575.13
  peasant 606.6
  adj local 231.9
  rustic 233.6
  idiomatic 523.22
  narrow-minded 980.10
proving ground
  laboratory 942.5
  testing ground 1074.7
provision
  n food 10.1
  groceries 10.5
  providing 385.1
  supplies 385.2
  store 386.1
  preparation 405.1
  stipulation 421.2
  support 449.3
  giving 478.1
  precaution 494.3
  substitution 862.1
  condition 959.2
  foresight 961.1
  expedient 995.2
  v feed 8.18
  provender 385.9
provisional government 612.4
proviso
  stipulation 421.2
  bill 613.9
  condition 959.2
provocateur 375.11
provocative
  appetizing 63.10

desirable 100.30
  exciting 105.30
  aggravating 119.5
  provoking 375.27
  alluring 377.8
  hostile 589.10
  interesting 983.19
provoke annoy 96.13
  irritate 96.14
  vex 98.15
  stimulate 105.13
  aggravate 119.2
  be insolent 142.8
  incense 152.24
  prompt 375.13
  incite 375.17
  sow dissension 456.14
  antagonize 589.7
  induce 886.11
  interest 983.12
provost principal 571.8
  executive 574.3
prow 216.3
prowess skill 413.1
  courage 492.1
prowl
  n stealth 345.4
  v wander 177.23
  creep 177.26
  lurk 346.9
prowler 483.1
proximate
  n person 530.7
  v approach 167.3
  adj approaching 167.4
  near 223.14
  approximate 775.8
  succeeding 815.4
proximity
  nearness 223.1
  relation 775.1
proxy
  n vote 371.6
  deputy 576.1
  ballot 609.19
  voter 609.23
  commission 615.1
  substitute 862.2
  adj substitute 862.8
prude 500.11
prudent
  vigilant 339.13
  cautious 494.8
  economical 635.6
  moderate 670.10
  judicious 920.19
  foreseeing 961.7
prune excise 255.10
  shorten 268.6
  sever 802.11
  cultivate 1069.17
prune-faced
  sour 110.23
  aged 303.16
prurient lustful 75.27
  craving 100.24
  lascivious 665.29
  curious 981.5
pruritus itch 74.3
  symptom 85.9
  twitching 917.5

pry
  n meddler 214.4
  leverage 906.1
  lever 906.4
  inquisitive person 981.2
  v look 27.13
  meddle 214.7
  get a purchase 906.8
  search 938.31
  snoop 981.4
pry loose from 480.22
pry open 292.14
pry out extract 192.10
  elicit 192.14
  get a purchase 906.8
  grill 938.22
  search out 938.34
  uncover 941.4
PS 817.1
psalm
  n paean 696.3
  sacred music 708.17
  v sing 708.38
the Psalms 701.11
pseudo
  imitation 336.8
  spurious 354.26
pseudonym 527.8
psyche
  psychic apparatus 92.28
  spirit 919.4
psychedelic
  n psychoactive drug
    86.13
  drug of abuse 87.3
  adj psychochemical 86.46
  hallucinatory 976.10
psyched up 405.16
psychiatric
  psychological 92.37
  psychotherapeutic 92.38
psychiatric hospital 926.14
psychiatrist
  psychologist 92.10
  psychiatry 926.19
psychic
  n spiritualist 689.13
  predictor 962.4
  adj occult 689.24
  supernatural 870.15
  mental 919.7
  spectral 988.7
  immaterial 1053.7
psychic energy 92.28
psychic phenomena 689.6
psychic research 1053.1
psycho
  n lunatic 926.16
  psychotic 926.17
  adj crazy 926.27
psychoactive drug
  hallucinogen 86.13
  drug of abuse 87.3
psychoanalysis 92.6
psychoanalyst 92.10
psychoanalyze 92.36
psychobabble
  psychology 92.1
  jargon 523.10
psychochemical
  n drug 87.3

  adj psychoactive 86.46
psychogenic 92.37
psychokinesis 689.6
psychological
  psychiatric 92.37
  mental 919.7
psychological dependence
  87.1
psychological warfare 127.6
psychologist 92.10
psychology
  science of the mind 92.1
  anthropology 312.10
  attitude 978.1
psychopathic
  psychological 92.37
  psychotic 926.28
psychopathological 92.37
psychophysical 92.37
psychosexual 92.37
psychosis
  mental disorder 92.14
  psychopathy 926.3
psychosocial 92.37
psychosomatic 92.37
psychotherapeutic 92.38
psychotherapy
  therapy 91.1
  science of the mind 92.1
  psychotherapeutics 92.5
psychotic
  n insane 926.17
  adj psychological 92.37
  psychopathic 926.28
psych out
  unnerve 128.10
  solve 940.2
ptomaine poisoning 85.31
pub
  restaurant 8.17
  bar 88.20
puberty
  bodily development 14.1
  adolescence 301.6
pubescence hair 3.2
  bodily development 14.1
  smoothness 294.3
  adolescence 301.6
pubic hair genitals 2.13
  hair 3.2
public
  n bar 88.20
  follower 166.2
  population 227.1
  market 733.3
  adj exterior 206.7
  general 312.16
  published 352.17
  communal 476.9
  common 497.14
  populational 606.8
  well-known 928.27
public acclaim 662.1
public address 543.2
public assistance
  subsidy 478.8
  welfarism 611.7
publication
  informing 343.2
  manifestation 348.1
  dissemination 352.1

  publishing 352.1
  printing 548.1
  information 551.1
  book 554.1
  dispersion 771.1
public baths 79.10
public domain 469.2
public enemy
  enemy 589.6
  evildoer 593.1
  criminal 660.9
public figure 662.9
publicist
  publicizer 352.9
  journalist 555.4
  commentator 556.4
publicity
  publicness 352.4
  information 551.1
  repute 662.1
public library 558.1
public nuisance
  annoyance 96.2
  tormentor 96.10
public official
  official 575.16
  officeholder 610.11
public opinion
  political influence 609.29
  opinion 953.6
public-opinion poll 938.14
public ownership
  communion 476.2
  socialism 611.6
public policy 609.4
public radio 1034.16
public records 549.2
public relations 352.4
public safety 1008.1
public school 567.4
public sector 731.7
public servant
  official 575.16
  officeholder 610.11
public telephone 347.4
public welfare
  welfare 143.5
  subsidy 478.8
publish divulge 351.5
  promulgate 352.10
  print 548.14
  codify 673.10
  disperse 771.4
publisher
  informant 551.5
  book publisher 554.2
publishing house
  press 548.11
  publisher 554.2
puce 41.6
pucker
  n dither 105.6
  anxiety 126.1
  wrinkle 291.3
  confusion 985.3
  v contract 260.7
  wrinkle 291.6
pudding food 10.46
  softness 1047.4
  semiliquid 1062.5
  pulp 1063.2

puddle lake 241.1
  mud puddle 1062.9
pudgy corpulent 257.18
  stubby 268.10
puerile childish 301.11
  immature 406.11
  simple-minded 922.24
puff
  n breathing 2.21
  pastry 10.41
  smoking 89.10
  distension 259.2
  puff of air 318.4
  foam 320.2
  publicity 352.4
  commendation 509.3
  makeup 1016.12
  softness 1047.4
  v burn out 21.5
  use 87.22
  smoke 89.14
  enlarge 259.4
  blow 318.20
  publicize 352.15
  exaggerate 355.3
  boast 502.6
  commend 509.11
  praise 509.12
  let out 909.24
puffy corpulent 257.18
  distended 259.13
  windy 318.22
pug
  n foot 199.5
  fighter 461.2
  print 517.7
  boxer 754.2
  adj stubby 268.10
pugilist fighter 461.2
  boxer 754.2
pugnacious
  partisan 456.17
  warlike 458.21
puissant strong 15.15
  powerful 18.12
  authoritative 417.15
puke
  n vomiting 909.8
  v feel disgust 99.4
  vomit 909.27
pulchritude 1016.1
pule cry 60.2
  whine 115.14
Pulitzer Prize 646.2
pull
  n drink 8.4
  power 18.1
  swig 88.7
  proof 548.5
  strain 725.2
  favor 894.2
  pulling 905.1
  draw 905.2
  attraction 907.1
  v drink 8.29
  smoke 89.14
  deflect 164.5
  row 182.53
  extract 192.10
  lengthen 267.6
  restrain 428.7

print 548.14
strain 725.10
play 751.4
draw 905.4
attract 907.4
pull a boner
  bungle 414.12
  make a boner 975.15
pull a fast one 415.11
pull ahead 249.10
pull a stunt
  deceive 356.19
  trick 489.14
pull away recede 168.2
  dodge 368.8
  separate 802.8
pull back regress 163.5
  withdraw 163.6
  retract 168.3
  demur 325.4
  hesitate 362.7
  dodge 368.8
  separate 802.8
  retreat 903.7
pull down raze 395.19
  acquire 472.9
  receive 479.6
  be paid 624.20
  depress 913.4
  fell 913.5
pullet fledgling 302.10
  poultry 311.29
pull for 403.9
pull in
  retract 168.3
  arrive 186.6
  restrain 428.7
  arrest 429.16
  stop 857.7
  reel in 906.9
pull it together
  order 807.4
  arrange 808.8
Pullman car 197.10
pull off do 328.6
  bring about 407.5
  achieve one's purpose 409.8
  succeed with 409.11
pull one's leg
  fool 356.15
  trick 489.14
  ridicule 508.8
  flatter 511.6
pull one's punches
  limit 210.5
  allow for 959.5
pull one's weight 476.6
pull out retreat 163.6
  retract 168.3
  maneuver 184.40
  depart 188.6
  extract 192.10
  abandon 370.5
  defect 370.6
  separate 802.8
pull out all the stops 430.19
pull rank 424.8
pull strings
  maneuver 415.10
  exercise influence 894.9
pull the plug on 395.11

pull the trigger 459.22
pull the wool over one's eyes
  356.17
pull through
  cure 396.15
  recover 396.20
pull together
  plan 381.8
  cooperate 450.3
pull up
  maneuver 184.40
  extract 192.10
  arraign 598.15
  stop 857.7
  put a stop to 857.11
pull up short 131.7
pull up stakes
  disappear 34.2
  depart 188.7
  decamp 188.14
  leave 222.10
  flee 368.10
pulmonary 2.32
pulp
  n semiliquid 1062.5
  paste 1063.2
  v soften 1047.6
  pulpify 1063.5
pulp fiction 722.1
pulpit rostrum 703.13
  platform 901.13
pulpy insipid 65.2
  spongy 1047.11
  semiliquid 1062.11
  pulpous 1063.6
pulsar 1072.8
pulsate drum 55.4
  recur 850.5
  pulse 916.12
pulse
  n plant 310.4
  beat 709.26
  round 850.3
  pulsation 916.3
  radio-frequency pulse
    1036.10
  v resonate 54.6
  recur 850.5
  pulsate 916.12
  flutter 917.12
pulverize
  demolish 395.17
  come apart 802.9
  shatter 802.13
  pound 902.16
  powder 1051.9
puma 311.22
pumice 287.8
pumice stone 79.17
pummel whip 604.13
  pound 902.16
pump
  n viscera 2.16
  extractor 192.9
  poker 759.10
  machinery 1040.3
  v draw off 192.12
  enlarge 259.4
  process 892.9
  alternate 916.14
  interrogate 938.21

pumped up
  energetic 17.13
  prepared 405.16
  overestimated 949.3
pumping iron 84.2
pumpkin 42.2
pun
  n wordplay 489.8
  ambiguity 539.2
  assonance 784.6
  v joke 489.13
  assonate 784.9
punch
  n energy 17.3
  power 18.1
  zest 68.2
  drink 88.9
  vigor 544.3
  engraving tool 713.8
  fight 754.3
  mold 786.6
  thrust 902.2
  hit 902.4
  boxing punch 902.6
  v indent 284.14
  perforate 292.15
  mark 517.19
  fight 754.4
  thrust 902.12
  hit 902.14
Punch and Judy 707.10
punch bowl
  spirits 88.13
  cavity 284.2
punching bag 725.7
punch line 489.6
punch out
  check out 188.13
  ring in 832.12
  beat 902.17
punch the clock 832.12
punctual
  meticulous 339.12
  observant 434.4
  conscientious 644.15
  prompt 845.9
punctuate mark 517.19
  grammaticize 530.16
  emphasize 997.14
punctuation
  punctuation marks 530.15
  written character 547.9
puncture
  n trauma 85.38
  hole 292.3
  mark 517.5
  v collapse 260.10
  perforate 292.15
  injure 393.13
  mark 517.19
  disprove 958.4
puncture proof
  resistant 15.20
  impervious 293.13
pundit expert 413.11
  teacher 571.1
  clergy 699.13
  specialist 866.3
  intellectual 929.1
  scholar 929.3
pungent intense 15.22

painful 26.10
  bitter 64.6
  sour 67.5
  piquant 68.6
  strong 69.10
  witty 489.15
  spirited 544.12
  aphoristic 974.6
punish
  torture 96.18
  penalize 603.4
  chastise 604.10
  get even with 506.7
punishment
  reprisal 506.2
  penalty 603.1
  disciplinary measure 604.1
punk
  n homosexual 75.14
  brat 302.4
  a nobody 998.7
  tinder 1021.6
  adj insignificant 998.18
  bad 1000.8
  inferior 1005.9
punk rock music 708.1
  type of music 708.11
punt
  n game 746.3
  kick 902.9
  v row 182.53
  compromise 468.2
  play 746.5
  bet 759.25
puny frail 16.14
  little 258.10
  haggard 270.20
  meager 992.10
  petty 998.20
pupa 302.12
pupil eye 2.9
  sight organ 27.9
  student 572.1
puppet
  sycophant 138.3
  miniature 258.6
  figure 349.6
  instrument 384.4
  figurehead 575.5
  deputy 576.1
  agent 576.3
  follower 616.8
  toy 743.16
  thing of naught 764.2
puppet government
  country 232.1
  dependent 432.6
puppy member 2.7
  impudent person 142.5
  boy 302.5
  fledgling 302.10
  dog 311.17
  dandy 500.9
puppy love 104.4
purchase
  n grasp 474.2
  buying 733.1
  influence 894.1
  footing 901.5
  hold 906.2
  tackle 906.6

print 548.14
spend 626.5
exert 725.8
eject 909.13
evict 909.15
bewilder 971.12
confuse 985.7
inconvenience 996.4
trouble 1013.13
fight fire 1022.7
put-out
  n game 745.3
  adj distressed 96.22
  provoked 152.27
  bewildered 971.24
  confused 985.12
put out feelers 942.9
put out of action 19.9
put out of business 625.8
put out of commission 19.9
put out of joint 160.5
put out of one's misery 145.4
put out of reach 967.6
put out of sight
  conceal 346.6
  secrete 346.7
put out the welcome mat 585.7
put out to pasture
  feed 8.18
  scrap 390.8
  depose 447.4
  dismiss 909.19
put over
  bring about 407.5
  succeed with 409.11
  manage 409.12
  make clear 521.6
  impose on 643.7
put pressure on 424.6
putrid
  nasty 64.7
  malodorous 71.5
  filthy 80.23
  decayed 393.40
  bad 1000.8
put right
  direct to 161.6
  remedy 396.13
put sanctions on 603.4
putsch 327.4
put six feet under 309.19
put straight
  v straighten 277.5
  make better 392.9
  remedy 396.13
  arrange 437.8
  disillusion 977.2
  adj disillusioned 977.5
putt 751.4
putter waste time 331.13
  trifle 998.14
put the arm on 621.3
put the best face on 600.12
put the blame on
  blame 599.8
  attribute to 888.4
put the cart before the horse
  invert 205.5
  misinterpret 342.2
  not know what one is about
    414.14

put the fear of God into
  127.16
put the final touches on 820.7
put the finger on
  inform on 551.13
  accuse 599.7
  attribute to 888.4
put the hammer down 756.4
put the heat on
  coerce 424.8
  threaten 514.2
put the icing on the cake
  407.6
put the kibosh on
  disable 19.9
  silence 51.8
  do for 395.11
  end 820.5
put the lid on
  silence 51.8
  close 293.6
  top 295.21
  cover up 345.8
  complete 407.6
  suppress 428.8
  end 820.5
put the pedal to the metal
  174.9
put the pressure on 938.21
put the screws to
  coerce 424.8
  overprice 632.7
  grill 938.22
put the shot 904.10
put the skids under
  do for 395.11
  end 820.5
put through
  channel 239.15
  do 328.6
  carry out 328.7
  bring about 407.5
  succeed with 409.11
  manage 409.12
  execute 437.9
  legislate 613.10
put through the third degree
  938.21
putting 159.6
putting green
  green 310.7
  playground 743.11
  golf 751.1
put to 800.7
put to bed 548.14
put to death
  kill 308.13
  execute 604.17
put together
  v make up 405.7
  assemble 770.18
  compose 796.3
  join 800.5
  combine 805.3
  produce 892.8
  adj made 892.18
put to good use
  apply 387.11
  avail oneself of 387.14
put to music 708.46
put to one side 176.11

put to rest
  abolish 395.13
  end 820.5
  disprove 958.4
put to rights
  remedy 396.13
  arrange 808.8
put to sea
  get under way 182.19
  embark 188.15
put to shame
  humiliate 137.4
  overshadow 249.8
  disgrace 661.8
put to sleep
  lull to sleep 22.20
  deaden 25.4
  kill 308.13
put to the test 942.8
put to use apply 387.11
  avail oneself of 387.14
put two and two together
  reason 935.15
  conclude 946.10
putty softness 1047.4
  semiliquid 1062.5
putty in one's hands 894.5
put under 22.20
put under arrest
  arrest 429.15
  capture 480.18
put under a spell 377.7
put under lock and key
  429.14
put under oath 334.7
put under surveillance 938.27
put up
  v establish 159.16
  suspend 202.8
  house 225.10
  increase 251.4
  sham 354.21
  nominate 371.19
  accommodate 385.10
  store up 386.11
  do up 397.11
  pledge 438.10
  offer 439.4
  pay over 624.15
  put up for sale 734.10
  bet 759.25
  produce 892.8
  adj fabricated 354.29
  pledged 438.12
  prearranged 965.8
put up a fight
  object 333.5
  offer resistance 453.3
  contend 457.13
put up a front
  sham 354.21
  pretext 376.3
  affect 500.12
  give oneself airs 501.14
  defend 600.10
put up an argument 935.16
put up a roadblock 1012.12
put up as collateral
  v pledge 438.10
  adj pledged 438.12
put upon 214.5

put-upon 96.22
put up or shut up 328.5
put up to 375.17
put up with
  endure 134.5
  suffer 443.10
  substitute 862.4
put words in one's mouth
  888.4
putz
  stupid person 924.2
  fool 924.4
puzzle
  n enigma 522.8
  the unknown 930.7
  bewilderment 971.3
  dilemma 1013.7
  v think hard 931.9
  perplex 971.13
  trouble 1013.13
pygmy
  n dwarf 258.5
  human group 312.3
  adj dwarf 258.13
pylon
  flying and landing guides
    marker 184.19
  tower 272.6
pyramid
  n structure 266.2
  tower 272.6
  tomb 309.16
  monument 549.12
  pile 770.10
  hierarchy 809.4
  v increase 251.4
  trade 737.23
  pile 770.19
pyre
  mortuary 309.9
  fire 1019.13
pyromaniac 1020.8
pyrotechnics
  public speaking 543.1
  fireworks 1019.17
  heat 1019.21
pyrrhic 720.16
Pyrrhic victory 411.1
QED 957.25
quack
  n impostor 357.6
  v bird sound 60.5
  adj quackish 354.28
quackery 354.7
quad
  enclosed place 212.3
  plot 231.4
  space 548.7
  four 879.1
quadrant
  instrument 278.4
  semicircle 280.8
  part 793.1
quadratic 879.4
quadrennial 850.4
quadrilateral
  n four 879.1
  adj sided 218.7
  quadrangular 278.9
  four 879.4
quadriplegic 85.45

quadruped
  n creature 311.3
  adj four 879.4
quadruple
  v quadruplicate 880.2
  adj quadruplicate 880.3
quadruplet 879.1
quaff
  n drink 8.4
  v drink 8.29
  tipple 88.24
quagmire
  receptacle of filth 80.12
  marsh 243.1
  complex 799.2
  predicament 1013.4
quail flinch 127.13
  demur 325.4
  cower 491.9
  pull back 903.7
quaint
  humorous 488.4
  odd 870.11
quake
  n upheaval 671.5
  shake 917.3
  v be excited 105.18
  tremble 127.14
  shake 917.11
  freeze 1023.9
qualification
  ability 18.2
  circumscription 210.2
  minimization 252.5
  eligibility 371.11
  fitting 405.2
  preparedness 405.4
  talent 413.4
  stipulation 421.2
  restriction 428.3
  extenuation 600.5
  fitness 788.5
  change 852.1
  provision 959.2
  limitation 959.1
qualifier 530.2
qualify
  circumscribe 210.5
  fit 405.8
  measure up 405.15
  succeed 409.7
  stipulate 421.7
  restrict 428.9
  suit 788.8
  change 852.7
  limit 959.3
  suffice 991.4
qualitative analysis 801.1
quality milieu 209.3
  taste 496.1
  aristocracy 607.3
  nobility 608.2
  nature 767.4
  characteristic 865.4
  goodness 999.1
quality control
  examination 938.3
  process control 1041.8
quality of life
  contentment 107.1
  courtesy 504.1

  prosperity 1010.1
qualm nausea 85.30
  compunction 113.2
  apprehension 127.4
  nervousness 128.1
  demur 325.2
  objection 333.2
  conscientiousness 644.2
quandary
  bewilderment 971.3
  dilemma 1013.7
quantifier 300.9
quantify
  quantize 244.4
  measure 300.10
  number 1017.17
quantity
  quantum 244.1
  amount 244.2
  numerousness 247.3
  capacity 257.2
  lump 257.10
  measure 300.2
  extent 300.3
  vowel quantity 524.11
  meter 720.7
  sum 1017.6
quantum
  energy unit 17.7
  quantity 244.1
  portion 477.5
  measurement of light
    1025.21
quantum leap
  progression 162.1
  improvement 392.1
  innovation 852.4
  revolution 860.1
quantum mechanics
  mathematical probability
    968.2
  nuclear physics 1038.1
quarantine
  n enclosure 212.1
  isolation 429.2
  seclusion 584.1
  exclusiveness 773.3
  v enclose 212.5
  isolate 429.13
  segregate 773.6
quark 258.8
quarrel
  n open quarrel 456.5
  contention 457.1
  fight 457.4
  arrow 462.6
  v dispute 456.11
  contend 457.13
quarry
  n desire 100.11
  sweetheart 104.10
  pit 284.4
  objective 380.2
  game 382.7
  source of supply 386.4
  fountainhead 886.6
  mine 1058.6
  v extract 192.10
  excavate 284.15
  mine 1058.14
quart 881.2

quarter
  n pity 145.1
  direction 161.1
  side 218.1
  region 231.1
  heraldry 647.2
  money 728.7
  game 746.3
  basketball game 747.3
  soccer 752.3
  part 793.1
  moment 824.2
  fourth 881.2
  v house 225.10
  divide by four 881.3
  adj fourth 881.5
quarterback
  n football team 746.2
  v direct 573.8
quarter horse 757.2
quarterly
  n periodical 555.1
  adj momentary 850.8
quartermaster
  ship's officer 183.7
  steersman 183.8
  provider 385.6
quarter note 709.14
quarter rest 709.21
quarters 228.4
quartet
  cooperation 450.1
  part music 708.18
  four 879.1
quasar 1072.8
quash cover up 345.8
  extinguish 395.15
  suppress 428.8
quasi
  adj imitation 336.8
  spurious 354.26
  nominal 527.15
  approximating 784.14
  adv imitatively 336.11
  supposedly 951.17
quaternary
  n four 879.1
  adj four 879.4
quaver
  n trepidation 105.5
  speech defect 525.1
  note 709.14
  trill 709.19
  shake 917.3
  v be weak 16.8
  be excited 105.18
  tremble 127.14
  speak poorly 525.7
  sing 708.38
  shake 917.11
queasy nauseated 85.57
  overfastidious 495.12
queen
  homosexual 75.15
  ant 311.34
  bee 311.35
  sovereign queen 575.11
  princess 608.8
  chessman 743.17
  card 758.2
  the best 999.8

queen bee bee 311.35
  chief 575.4
  important person 997.9
Queensbury rules 754.1
queen size
  n large size 257.4
  adj large 257.16
queer
  n homosexual 75.15
  counterfeit 728.10
  v disable 19.9
  spoil 393.11
  hinder 1012.16
  adj homosexual 75.30
  spurious 354.26
  odd 870.11
  insane 926.26
  eccentric 927.5
quell extinguish 395.15
  conquer 412.10
  suppress 428.8
  subdue 432.9
  calm 670.7
quench gratify 95.8
  disincline 379.4
  extinguish 395.15
  suppress 428.8
  fight fire 1022.7
query
  n question 938.10
  v inquire 938.20
  interrogate 938.21
  doubt 955.6
  be curious 981.3
que serà serà 964.11
quest
  n intention 380.1
  pursuit 382.1
  adventure 404.2
  search 938.15
  v pursue 382.8
  seek 938.30
question
  n enigma 522.8
  remark 524.3
  bill 613.9
  topic 937.1
  query 938.10
  doubt 955.2
  gamble 971.8
  v communicate with
    343.8
  inquire 938.20
  interrogate 938.21
  doubt 955.6
  be uncertain 971.9
  be curious 981.3
questionable
  deceptive 356.21
  dishonest 645.16
  unbelievable 955.10
  improbable 969.3
  doubtful 971.17
questioning
  n interrogation 938.12
  adj communicational 343.9
  inquiring 938.36
  doubting 955.9
question mark
  enigma 522.8
  question 938.10

questionnaire
   n roll 871.6
   canvass 938.14
   v canvass 938.29
queue
   n braid 3.7
   tail 217.6
   series 812.2
   afterpart 817.2
   v line up 812.6
quibble
   n criticism 510.4
   quiddity 936.4
   v find fault 510.15
   argue 935.16
   cavil 936.9
quiche 10.41
quick
   adj eager 101.8
   hot-tempered 110.25
   fast 174.15
   living 306.13
   willing 324.5
   swift 330.18
   alert 339.14
   impulsive 365.9
   hasty 401.9
   skillful 413.22
   teachable 570.18
   brief 828.8
   sudden 830.5
   prompt 845.9
   smart 920.14
   adv swiftly 174.17
the quick
   sore spot 24.4
   provocation 152.11
   the living 306.4
   inner nature 767.5
quick and dirty
   extemporaneous 365.12
   handy 387.20
   makeshift 995.7
quicken refresh 9.2
   energize 17.10
   sensitize 24.7
   stimulate 105.13
   accelerate 174.10
   come to life 306.10
   vivify 306.11
   hasten 401.4
   be useful 449.17
   facilitate 1014.7
quick fix 995.2
quick-freeze
   preserve 397.9
   freeze 1024.11
quick on the draw
   sensitive 24.12
   quick 330.18
   alert 339.14
   impulsive 365.9
   reactive 903.9
quicksand marsh 243.1
   danger 1006.1
   predicament 1013.4
quicksilver
   n swiftness 174.6
   changeableness 854.4
   adj active 330.17
   fickle 364.6

brass 1058.17
quickstep march
   march 177.13
   military march 708.12
quid bite 8.2
   chewing tobacco 89.7
   money 728.8
quid pro quo
   offset 338.2
   tit for tat 506.3
   interaction 777.3
   substitution 862.1
   interchange 863.1
quiescent silent 51.10
   quiet 173.12
   passive 329.6
   inactive 331.17
   permanent 853.7
quiet
   n rest 20.1
   silence 51.1
   composure 106.2
   quiescence 173.1
   peacefulness 464.2
   order 807.1
   v fall silent 51.7
   silence 51.8
   quieten 173.8
   calm 670.7
   order 807.4
   adj vacational 20.10
   soft-colored 35.22
   silent 51.10
   calm 106.12
   reserved 139.11
   quiescent 173.12
   taciturn 344.9
   covert 345.12
   meek 433.15
   pacific 464.9
   tasteful 496.8
   interj silence! 51.14
quill
   n feather 3.16
   feather part 3.17
   thorn 285.5
   v fold 291.5
quilt 295.10
quintessential
   essential 192.18
   typical 349.15
   characteristic 865.13
   best 999.16
   perfected 1002.9
quintet
   cooperation 450.1
   part music 708.18
   five 882.1
quintuplets 882.1
quip
   n witticism 489.7
   gibe 508.2
   quirk 927.2
   quibble 936.4
   v joke 489.13
quirk distortion 265.1
   caprice 364.1
   mannerism 500.2
   characteristic 865.4
   twist 927.2
   quibble 936.4

quirky capricious 364.5
   eccentric 927.5
quit
   v vacate 188.9
   abandon 370.5
   cease to use 390.4
   resign 448.2
   requite 506.5
   repay 624.11
   cease 857.6
   adj clear 430.31
quite
   adv to a degree 245.7
   very 247.18
   positively 247.19
   absolutely 794.15
   interj yes 332.18
   right on! 973.25
quite the contrary
   adv contrarily 779.9
   interj no 335.8
   by no means 335.9
quitter 362.5
quiver
   n thrill 105.2
   trepidation 105.5
   trill 709.19
   bundle 770.8
   shake 917.3
   flutter 917.4
   flicker 1025.8
   v be weak 16.8
   be excited 105.18
   tremble 127.14
   shake 917.11
   freeze 1023.9
   flicker 1025.25
quixotic 986.24
quixotic ideal 124.5
quiz
   n examination 938.2
   questioning 938.12
   v interrogate 938.21
   be curious 981.3
quiz show 1035.2
quizzical
   humorous 488.4
   bantering 490.7
   ridiculing 508.12
   inquiring 938.36
   curious 981.5
Quonset hut 228.9
quorum 770.2
quota portion 477.5
   part 793.1
   ratio 1017.7
quotation price 630.1
   stock price 738.9
   repetition 849.1
   citation 957.5
quote state 524.23
   repeat 849.7
   cite 957.13
quote out of context
   misinterpret 342.2
   distort 350.3
rabbi teacher 571.1
   master 575.1
   supporter 616.9
   clergy 699.11
   wise man 921.1

Rabbi 648.5
rabbinical 698.13
rabbit hare 311.24
   productiveness 890.6
rabbit's-foot 691.5
rabble
   rabblement 606.3
   throng 770.4
rabble-rouser
   instigator 375.11
   speaker 543.4
rabid
   frenzied 105.25
   infuriated 152.32
   maniac 926.30
   fanatic 926.32
rabies disease 85.41
   hydrophobia 926.6
raccoon 311.23
race
   n run 174.3
   stream 238.1
   flow 238.4
   watercourse 239.2
   humankind 312.1
   haste 401.1
   contest of speed 457.12
   people 559.4
   lineage 560.4
   game 743.9
   skiing 753.1
   downhill race 753.3
   automobile racing 756.1
   driving 756.3
   horse race 757.3
   class 809.2
   kind 809.3
   v speed 174.8
   accelerate 174.10
   make haste 401.5
   race with 457.19
   drive 756.4
   run 757.5
race against the clock 1006.8
race against time
   n crisis 843.4
   v spend time 821.6
   be in danger 1006.8
race course 753.1
race hatred hate 103.1
   exclusiveness 773.3
   discrimination 980.4
race horse 311.24
racer speeder 174.5
   skier 753.2
   automobile racing 756.1
racetrack 757.1
race walk 177.27
racial 559.7
racial segregation 773.3
racing
   n track 457.11
   adj flowing 238.24
racing car 756.1
racing form 757.4
racism hate 103.1
   discrimination 980.4
racist
   n hater 103.4
   bigot 980.5
   adj discriminatory 980.12

rack
  n agony 26.6
  torment 96.7
  slow motion 175.2
  gait 177.12
  storehouse 386.6
  destruction 395.1
  punishment 604.2
  torture 605.4
  strain 725.2
  gear 1040.9
  v pain 26.7
  torment 96.18
  way of walking 177.28
  torture 604.16
  strain 725.10
racked pained 26.9
  affected 93.23
  tortured 96.25
racket
  n noise 53.3
  rattle 55.3
  fraud 356.8
  stratagem 415.3
  turbulence 671.2
  vocation 724.6
  illicit business 732.1
  tennis 748.1
  cheating 759.13
  commotion 810.4
  pandemonium 810.5
  elastic 1048.3
  v be noisy 53.9
racketeer
  extortionist 480.12
  bandit 483.4
  evildoer 593.1
  criminal 660.9
  Mafioso 732.4
rack one's brains
  think hard 931.9
  try to recall 989.21
rack up 395.17
racy zestful 68.7
  spirited 544.12
  risqué 666.7
  interesting 983.19
radar
  radio navigation 182.2
  electronic navigation 184.6
  electronics 1033.1
  radio detection 1036.1
radar defenses 460.2
radar tracking station
  proving ground 1074.7
  space station 1075.5
radial
  n divergence 171.1
  adj radiating 171.9
radiant
  n axle 915.5
  meteor 1072.15
  adj happy 95.16
  cheerful 109.11
  illustrious 662.19
  almighty 677.17
  gorgeous 1016.21
  luminous 1025.30
radiant energy
  light 1025.1
  radiation 1037.1

radiant heat 1019.1
radiate
  v exude cheerfulness 109.6
  radiate out 171.6
  disperse 771.4
  shine 1025.23
  broadcast 1034.25
  transmit 1036.15
  adj radiating 171.9
radiation radius 171.2
  dispersion 771.1
  light 1025.1
  beam 1025.5
  radioactive emanation 1037.1
  radiant energy 1037.1
  ray 1037.3
  space hazard 1075.10
radiator 1037.5
radical
  n left side 220.1
  reformer 392.6
  morphology 526.3
  phonetic symbol 546.2
  extremist 611.12
  source 886.5
  foundation 901.6
  atomic cluster 1038.7
  adj basic 199.8
  left 220.4
  utmost 247.13
  emendatory 392.16
  extreme 611.20
  innate 767.8
  thorough 794.10
  revolutionary 860.5
  original 886.14
  numeric 1017.23
radical change
  upheaval 852.2
  revolution 860.1
radical group 1060.2
radical right 611.9
radicle 310.22
radio
  n radiotelephony 347.3
  informant 551.5
  news 552.1
  electronics 1033.1
  radio communications 1034.1
  wireless 1034.1
  radio receiver 1034.3
  v telegraph 347.20
  broadcast 1034.25
  adj communicational 347.21
  wireless 1034.28
radioactive 1037.11
radioactive element 1037.5
radioactive isotope 1038.5
radioactive particle 1037.4
radio broadcasting 1034.16
radiocarbon dating 1037.1
radio frequency 1034.12
radio-frequency 1034.28
radioisotope
  radiotherapy 91.8
  radioactive 1037.5
  isotope 1038.5
radiology
  radiography 91.7
  radiation physics 1037.8
  nuclear physics 1038.1

radioluminescence 1025.13
radioman 1034.24
radio signal 1034.10
radio station
  transmitting station 1034.6
  space station 1075.5
radiotelephone 347.5
radio telescope
  radio 1034.3
  observatory 1072.17
radiotherapy
  radiation therapy 91.6
  radiation physics 1037.8
radio transmitter 1034.4
radium
  radiotherapy 91.8
  cauterant 1020.15
radius
  convergence 169.1
  radiation 171.2
  size 257.1
  diameter 269.3
  straight line 277.2
  circle 280.2
raffle 759.14
raft
  n float 180.11
  lot 247.4
  wealth 618.3
  v haul 176.13
rag
  n material 4.1
  garment 5.3
  sail 180.14
  newspaper 555.2
  rabble 606.3
  scenery 704.20
  dance music 708.8
  tempo 709.24
  v berate 510.19
  syncopate 708.43
  play 749.7
ragamuffin 178.3
rag doll 743.16
rage
  n fury 105.8
  fit 152.8
  passion 152.10
  fad 578.5
  violence 671.1
  turbulence 671.2
  frenzy 926.7
  mania 926.12
  v be excitable 105.16
  be angry 152.15
  blow 318.20
  bluster 503.3
  storm 671.11
  be insane 926.20
ragged
  raucous 58.15
  tormented 96.24
  rugged 288.7
  shabby 393.32
  nonuniform 782.3
  slovenly 810.15
ragging
  n bantering 490.3
  ridicule 508.1
  game 749.3
  adj ridiculing 508.12

raging
  n violence 671.1
  adj frenzied 105.25
  infuriated 152.32
  stormy 318.23
  blustering 503.4
  turbulent 671.18
  rabid 926.30
rags material 4.1
  clothing 5.1
  tatters 5.5
  remainder 256.1
  refuse 391.4
  poker 759.10
rags-to-riches 1010.12
ragtag 606.3
ragtime
  n dance music 708.8
  tempo 709.24
  adj syncopated 709.29
rah 116.2
raid
  n foray 459.4
  plundering 482.6
  manipulation 737.20
  v foray 459.20
  plunder 482.17
raider assailant 459.12
  plunderer 483.6
rail
  n fence 212.4
  thinness 270.7
  railway 383.7
  horse racing 757.1
  v fence 212.7
rail at scoff 508.9
  berate 510.19
railroad
  n railway 383.7
  game 750.2
  v thrust 902.12
railroad through
  hasten 401.4
  legislate 613.10
raiment
  n clothing 5.1
  v clothe 5.39
rain
  n precipitation 316.1
  rainfall 316.1
  television reception 1035.5
  water 1065.3
  v descend 194.5
  precipitate 316.10
  give 478.12
  abound 991.5
  flood 1065.14
rainbow
  n variegation 47.6
  omen 133.6
  halo 1025.14
  iridescence 1025.18
  adj chromatic 35.16
raincoat 5.13
rainfall rain 316.1
  moisture 1065.1
rain on one's parade 393.11
rainy
  showery 316.11
  stormy 318.23
  moist 1065.15

raise
n increase 251.1
height 272.2
promotion 446.1
poker 759.10
v erect 200.9
increase 251.4
enlarge 259.4
emboss 283.12
leaven 298.7
communicate with 343.8
rouse 375.19
make better 392.9
promote 446.2
say 524.22
train 568.13
enlist 615.17
glorify 662.13
conjure 690.11
assemble 770.18
inaugurate 818.11
produce 892.8
process 892.9
elevate 912.5
farm 1069.16
breed 1070.6
raise a hand 453.3
raise an alarm 400.3
raise an objection
dissent 333.4
disapprove 510.10
raise a question 955.6
raise a ruckus 810.11
raise a stink 115.16
raise Cain
be noisy 53.9
be angry 152.15
create disorder 810.11
raised increased 251.7
expanded 259.10
in relief 283.18
produced 892.17
made 892.18
lifted 912.9
raise expectations 124.10
raise eyebrows 661.7
raise money 621.3
raise objections 333.5
raise one's pay 446.2
raise the curtain 351.4
raise the roof
be noisy 53.9
be angry 152.15
create disorder 810.11
raise the spirits 109.7
raison d'etre
objective 380.2
cause 886.9
rake
n inclination 204.2
thinness 270.7
projection 285.4
libertine 665.10
v comb 79.21
incline 204.10
pull the trigger 459.22
be promiscuous 665.19
ransack 938.33
cultivate 1069.17
rake it in profit 472.12
grow rich 618.10

rake over the coals 510.18
rakish showy 501.19
profligate 665.25
rally
n objection 333.2
recovery 396.8
contest 457.3
call to arms 458.8
electioneering 609.12
price 738.9
tournament 743.10
game 748.2
assembly 770.2
v object 333.5
incite 375.17
come about 392.8
recuperate 396.19
recover 396.20
aid 449.11
call to arms 458.19
banter 490.5
scoff 508.9
come together 770.16
assemble 770.18
dispose 808.9
adduce 957.12
rallying cry
cry 59.1
call to arms 458.8
call 517.16
rally round
side with 450.4
form 807.5
ram
n male animal 76.8
sheep 311.7
v sail into 182.41
thrust 902.12
RAM 1042.7
Ramadan
fast day 515.3
holy day 701.14
ramble
n wandering 177.3
walk 177.10
v stray 164.4
wander 177.23
be incomprehensible 522.10
digress 538.9
be insane 926.20
daydream 984.3
muse 985.9
rambunctious 671.20
ramification
forking 171.3
fork 171.4
branch 310.20
nonuniformity 782.1
member 793.4
complexity 799.1
bisection 875.1
ramjet 181.3
ramp
n stairs 193.3
incline 204.4
deception 356.9
skiing 753.1
v be excitable 105.16
climb 193.11
rise 200.8
deceive 356.19

caper 366.6
rage 671.11
rampage
n commotion 810.4
v rage 671.11
rampant
ascending 193.14
vertical 200.11
lawless 418.5
unrestrained 430.24
unruly 671.19
prevalent 864.12
raised 912.9
plentiful 991.7
rampart
fortification 460.4
buttress 901.4
barrier 1012.5
ramrod straight 200.11
ramshackle
unsteady 16.16
dilapidated 393.33
ranch
n farmstead 228.6
farm 1070.5
v farm 1069.16
raise 1070.6
rancher 1070.2
rancid nasty 64.7
malodorous 71.5
tainted 393.41
rancor virulence 144.7
bitterness 152.3
revengefulness 507.2
animosity 589.4
R and D 942.1
random
n haphazard 972.4
adj unordered
810.12
vague 971.19
purposeless 972.16
random testing 938.6
R and R 20.2
range
n vision 27.1
field of view 31.3
earshot 48.4
scope 158.2
direction 161.1
habitat 228.18
highlands 237.1
mountain 237.6
degree 245.1
size 257.1
distance 261.1
grassland 310.8
latitude 430.4
arena 463.1
scale 709.6
series 812.2
v extend 158.9
traverse 177.20
wander 177.23
size 257.15
dispose 808.9
classify 809.6
align 812.5
ranger preserver 397.5
guardian 1008.6
forester 1069.7

rani
amphibian 311.27
sovereign queen 575.11
princess 608.8
rank
n standing 245.2
authority 417.4
military unit 461.22
class 607.1
nobility 608.2
prestige 662.4
state 765.1
continuity 807.2
category 809.2
series 812.2
v rule 249.11
size 257.15
order 807.4
classify 808.11
categorize 809.6
align 812.5
precede 814.2
estimate 946.9
rate 946.15
adj nasty 64.7
strong 68.8
malodorous 71.5
filthy 80.23
downright 247.12
rough 288.6
luxuriant 310.43
tainted 393.41
wicked 654.16
base 661.12
vulgar 666.8
terrible 1000.9
rank and file
army 461.23
the people 606.1
rankle fester 12.15
pain 26.7
provoke 152.24
decay 393.22
be remembered 989.14
rank-order 946.9
ransack plunder 482.17
rummage 938.33
ransom
n rescue 398.1
recovery 481.3
v redeem 396.12
rescue 398.3
recover 481.6
rant
n bluster 503.1
nonsense 520.2
bombast 545.2
v be excitable 105.16
be angry 152.15
bluster 503.3
declaim 543.10
rage 671.11
overact 704.31
be insane 926.20
rap
n thud 52.3
report 56.1
criticism 510.4
discussion 541.7
condemnation 602.1
hit 902.4

tap 902.7
trifle 998.5
v thud 52.15
crack 56.6
criticize 510.14
discuss 541.12
pound 902.16
tap 902.18
rapacious
greedy 100.27
ravenous 480.26
gluttonous 672.6
rape
n sexual possession 480.3
plundering 482.6
seduction 665.6
unruliness 671.3
v possess sexually 480.15
seduce 665.20
rage 671.11
rapid
n rapids 238.10
adj fast 174.15
steep 204.18
constant 847.5
rapid deployment force 461.15
rapid-eye-movement sleep
22.1
rapid fire 847.2
rapids rapid 238.10
outburst 671.6
rapist
sexual pervert 75.16
seducer 665.12
violent person 671.9
rap on the knuckles
n reproof 510.5
slap 604.3
v reprove 510.17
rapping
n speech 524.1
conversation 541.1
adj banging 56.11
rapport
pleasantness 97.1
accord 455.1
good terms 587.3
relation 775.1
rapprochement 587.3
rapt overjoyed 95.17
persevering 360.8
absorbed in thought 931.22
gripped 983.18
abstracted 985.11
rapture happiness 95.2
amorousness 104.3
fury 105.8
trance 691.3
rara avis 870.4
rare underdone 11.9
wonderful 122.10
superior 249.12
thin 270.16
rarefied 299.4
raw 406.10
other 780.8
infrequent 848.2
unusual 870.10
sparse 885.5
scarce 992.11
notable 997.19

rare-earth metals 1058.3
rarefaction 299.2
rarefied diluted 16.19
dainty 248.7
thin 270.16
rare 299.4
tenuous 764.6
rarin' to go 135.6
rascal
mischief-maker 322.3
precious rascal 660.3
rash
n symptom 85.9
skin eruption 85.36
adj impulsive 365.9
precipitate 401.10
brash 493.7
rasp
n scratch 58.3
v pain 26.7
grate 58.10
irritate 96.14
abrade 1044.7
raspberry 508.3
rassle 457.13
rat
n false hair 3.13
traitor 357.10
informer 551.6
bad person 660.5
strikebreaker 727.8
v betray 351.6
inform on 551.13
break a strike 727.11
rat's nest
hodgepodge 797.6
complex 799.2
jumble 810.3
rat-a-tat staccato 55.1
pulsation 916.3
ratchet 285.4
rate
n velocity 172.4
rank 245.2
interest 623.3
price 630.1
worth 630.2
ratio 1017.7
v quantify 244.4
measure 300.10
reprove 510.17
berate 510.19
price 630.11
deserve 639.5
classify 809.6
precede 814.2
estimate 946.9
rank 946.15
rate of exchange 728.9
rate of interest 623.3
rate of pay 624.4
rather
v prefer 371.17
adv to a degree 245.7
notwithstanding 338.8
preferably 371.28
contrarily 779.9
instead 862.11
tolerably 999.24
interj yes 332.18
right on! 973.25

rathole sty 80.11
hovel 228.11
rathskeller 88.20
ratify endorse 332.12
adopt 371.15
consent 441.2
authorize 443.11
secure 855.8
confirm 957.11
rating rank 245.2
measurement 300.1
reproof 510.5
berating 510.7
credit 622.1
valuation 630.3
motion pictures 706.1
classification 809.1
class 809.2
estimate 946.3
ratings 1035.2
ratio degree 245.1
intellect 919.1
comparability 943.3
rate 1017.7
ratiocinate think about 931.11
reason 935.15
ration
n amount 244.2
portion 477.5
v budget 477.10
rational mental 919.7
intelligent 920.12
sensible 920.18
sane 925.4
cognitive 931.21
reasoning 935.18
logical 935.20
open-minded 979.10
realistic 987.6
numeric 1017.23
rationale
explanation 341.4
announcement 352.2
reason 886.2
rationalize
explain 341.10
plan 381.8
justify 600.9
organize 808.10
classify 809.6
reason 935.15
reason speciously 936.8
rations board 10.6
store 386.1
rat race
futility 391.2
work 725.4
whirl 915.2
rattan rod 605.2
cane 1054.4
rattle
n noise 53.3
noisemaker 53.6
rattling 55.3
chatterer 540.4
throw 759.9
v weaken 16.10
ruckle 55.6
agitate 105.14
talk nonsense 520.5
chatter 540.5

thrust 902.12
confuse 985.7
rattle off repeat 849.7
memorize 989.17
ratty rodent 311.45
shabby 393.32
infested 910.11
raucous raucid 58.15
dissonant 61.4
raunchy coarse 497.11
obscene 666.9
bad 1000.8
ravage
n destruction 395.1
plundering 482.6
seduction 665.6
infestation 910.2
v corrupt 393.12
destroy 395.10
plunder 482.17
seduce 665.20
infest 910.6
ravages of time
wear 393.5
disintegration 806.1
tract of time 821.3
rave
n party 582.12
v be enthusiastic 101.7
be excitable 105.16
be angry 152.15
bluster 503.3
rage 671.11
be insane 926.20
raven
n blackness 38.4
bird of ill omen 133.6
v hunger 100.19
plunder 482.17
gluttonize 672.4
adj black 38.8
ravenous
hungry 100.25
greedy 100.27
rapacious 480.26
gluttonous 672.6
ravine valley 237.7
gulch 284.9
ravioli 10.33
ravish delight 95.10
corrupt 393.12
possess sexually 480.15
plunder 482.17
seduce 665.20
raw
n sore spot 24.4
adj naked 6.14
sore 26.11
garish 35.20
callow 301.10
windblown 318.24
crude 406.10
immature 406.11
inexperienced 414.17
coarse 497.11
cursing 513.8
vulgar 666.8
new 841.7
ignorant 930.12
cold 1023.14
the raw 6.3

raw data 770.11
raw deal
  injustice 650.4
  bad luck 1011.5
rawhide
  n fur 4.2
  whip 605.1
  v whip 604.13
raw material
  unlicked cub 263.2
  crude 406.5
  materials 1054.1
raw nerve
  sore spot 24.4
  provocation 152.11
ray
  n divergence 171.2
  wave 916.4
  light 1025.5
  radiation 1037.3
  v radiate 171.6
ray of sunshine
  optimist 124.6
  daylight 1025.10
raze level 201.6
  obliterate 395.16
  rase 395.19
  fell 913.5
  abrade 1044.7
razorback 311.9
razor-edged 285.8
razor-sharp 415.12
razz
  n boo 508.3
  v banter 490.6
razzledazzle 501.3
RBI 745.4
re 775.13
reach
  n earshot 48.4
  range 158.2
  inlet 242.1
  degree 245.1
  size 257.1
  distance 261.1
  length 267.1
  knowledge 928.1
  v be heard 48.12
  move 145.5
  extend 158.9
  travel 177.19
  sail for 182.35
  arrive 186.6
  arrive at 186.7
  extend to 261.6
  communicate with 343.8
  bribe 378.3
  deliver 478.13
  equal 790.5
  suffice 991.4
reachable 966.8
reach a compromise 468.2
reach an agreement 332.10
reach for the sky 100.20
reach maturity 407.8
reach one's goal 409.8
reach orgasm 75.24
reach out
  extend 158.9
  stretch out 261.5
  be long 267.5

reach the breaking point
  993.13
react
  be affected 93.11
  respond 903.5
  answer 939.4
reaction
  mental disorder 92.14
  feeling 93.1
  regression 163.1
  propulsion 184.25
  resistance 453.1
  conservatism 611.1
  impact 887.2
  counteraction 900.1
  response 903.1
  answer 939.1
  opinion 953.6
reactionary
  n malcontent 108.3
  right side 219.1
  conservative 611.9
  back number 842.8
  reactionist 903.4
  adj regressive 163.11
  right 219.4
  conservative 611.17
  reversionary 859.7
  counteractive 900.8
  reactive 903.9
reactivate
  activate 17.12
  restore 396.11
  militarize 458.20
reactive 903.9
reactor 1038.13
read
  interpret 341.9
  understand 521.8
  declaim 543.10
  copyedit 548.17
  study 570.12
  sound out 942.9
read between the lines
  interpret 341.9
  explain 341.10
  see through 941.8
reader
  advertisement 352.6
  lecturer 543.5
  elocutionist 543.7
  proofreader 548.13
  textbook 554.10
  journalist 555.4
  academic rank 571.3
  teacher 571.7
  student 572.1
  holy orders 699.4
  input device 1042.4
reading
  measure 300.2
  interpretation 341.1
  rendering 341.2
  speech 543.2
  elementary education 568.5
  study 570.3
  scholarship 928.5
  signal 1036.11
reading glasses 29.3
read into
  interpret 341.9

  explain 341.10
readjust 858.14
readmit 187.15
read my lips 535.5
read one loud and clear 521.8
read one's mind 689.22
read someone like a book
  perceive 521.9
  see through 941.8
read tea leaves 962.9
read the riot act
  lay down the law 420.10
  reprove 510.17
read up on
  study 570.12
  study up 570.14
  search 938.31
ready
  v repair 396.14
  prepare 405.6
  train 568.13
  adj eager 101.8
  expectant 130.11
  willing 324.5
  quick 330.18
  alert 339.14
  handy 387.20
  prepared 405.16
  skillful 413.22
  cunning 415.12
  consenting 441.4
  teachable 570.18
  prompt 845.9
  foreseeing 961.7
ready-made
  tailored 5.48
  ready-formed 405.19
  made 892.18
ready oneself 570.11
ready-to-wear
  n ready-mades 5.4
  adj tailored 5.48
  ready-made 405.19
  made 892.18
ready wit wit 489.1
  smartness 920.2
reaffirm 849.8
real
  adj land 471.9
  actual 761.15
  substantial 763.6
  obvious 970.15
  true 973.13
  genuine 973.15
  numeric 1017.23
  adv very 247.18
real estate plot 231.4
  land 234.1
  realty 471.6
realign
  parallelize 203.5
  rearrange 808.13
  change 852.7
realism
  normality 869.1
  genuineness 973.7
  realisticness 987.2
  materialism 1052.6
realistic
  descriptive 349.14
  typical 349.15

  occupied 724.15
  lifelike 784.16
  normal 869.8
  ungullible 956.5
  genuine 973.15
  realist 987.6
  materialistic 1052.12
reality actuality 761.2
  event 831.2
  unquestionability 970.3
  truth 973.1
realize
  externalize 206.5
  do 328.6
  image 349.11
  accomplish 407.4
  profit 472.12
  understand 521.7
  be sold 734.12
  cause 886.10
  establish 892.10
  perform 892.11
  know 928.12
  visualize 986.15
  recognize 989.12
reallocate 808.13
really
  astonishment 122.19
  yes 332.18
realm sphere 231.2
  country 232.1
  occupation 724.4
  hierarchy 809.4
the real McCoy 973.4
real time 1042.18
realtor 730.9
realty 471.6
the real world 973.1
ream
  n paper 1054.5
  v masturbate 75.22
  perforate 292.15
  disapprove 510.18
reap shorten 268.6
  acquire 472.8
  harvest 1069.19
Reaper 307.3
reappear
  repeat 849.11
  recur 850.5
reappraise
  reconsider 931.15
  re-examine 938.27
reap the benefit of
  take advantage of 387.15
  get one's deserts 639.6
rear
  n setting 209.2
  hind part 217.1
  rear end 217.1
  rear guard 217.2
  buttocks 217.5
  afterpart 817.2
  v pitch 182.55
  ascend 193.8
  rise 200.8
  erect 200.9
  loom 247.5
  tower 272.10
  foster 449.16
  train 568.13

produce 892.8
process 892.9
elevate 912.5
farm 1069.16
raise 1070.6
adj rearward 217.9
rear admiral 575.20
rear its head 33.8
rearrange
reorganize 808.13
re-form 858.12
rear up ascend 193.8
rise 200.8
elevate 912.5
reason
n explanation 341.4
motive 375.1
warrant 600.6
cause 886.2
intellect 919.1
sensibleness 920.6
sanity 925.1
reasoning 935.1
argument 935.5
reasonableness 935.9
solution 940.1
v discuss 541.12
think 931.8
logicalize 935.15
conclude 946.10
philosophize 952.9
reasonable
justifiable 600.14
cheap 633.7
unexcessive 670.12
intelligent 920.12
sensible 920.18
sane 925.4
logical 935.20
plausible 968.7
realistic 987.6
reasoned 935.21
reasoning
n intellect 919.1
thought 931.1
logical thought 935.1
reason 935.1
adj mental 919.7
rational 935.18
reason to believe 957.1
reassemble 396.18
reassert 849.8
reassess 630.11
reassure comfort 121.6
give hope 124.10
encourage 492.16
make sure 970.11
rebate
n discount 631.1
v discount 631.2
rebel
n malcontent 108.3
revolter 327.5
anarchist 418.3
revolutionist 860.3
v revolt 327.7
object 333.5
adj rebellious 327.11
rebellion
revolt 327.4
objection 333.2

anarchy 418.2
rebel yell
challenge 454.2
call to arms 458.8
call 517.16
rebirth
reproduction 78.1
revival 396.3
redemption 685.4
repetition 849.1
new start 858.2
reborn
renascent 396.24
redeemed 685.9
regenerate 692.10
converted 858.19
rebound
n reverberation 54.2
recoil 903.2
elasticity 1048.1
v reverberate 54.7
play 747.4
recoil 903.6
rebuff
n snub 157.2
rejection 372.1
discomfiture 412.2
refusal 442.2
resistance 453.1
recoil 903.2
repulse 908.2
v snub 157.5
reject 372.2
refuse 442.5
resist 453.2
fend off 460.10
repulse 908.3
rebuild reproduce 78.7
remake 396.18
change 852.7
rebuke
n reproof 510.5
v reprove 510.17
rebuttal
opposition 451.1
pleadings 598.6
defense 600.2
counterstatement 939.2
refutation 958.2
recalcitrant
n reactionary 903.4
adj unwilling 325.5
defiant 327.10
ungovernable 361.12
oppositional 451.8
resistant 453.5
nonconforming 868.5
counteractive 900.8
recoiling 903.10
recall
n repeal 445.1
referendum 613.8
remembering 989.4
v summon 420.11
repeal 445.2
remember 989.10
remind 989.20
recant
n retract 363.8
v deny 335.4
reject 372.2

repeal 445.2
relinquish 475.3
recap
n shortening 268.3
summary 557.2
iteration 849.2
summation 1017.11
v shorten 268.6
re-cover 295.29
repair 396.14
sum up 1017.19
recapture
n recovery 481.3
v recover 481.6
remember 989.10
recast reproduce 78.7
change 852.7
re-form 858.12
recede regress 163.5
retrocede 168.2
receipt
n remedy 86.1
reception 187.1
formula 419.3
receiving 479.1
receipts 627.1
acknowledgment 627.2
answer 939.1
v receive 627.3
receivable
receptive 187.16
due 623.10
receive take in 187.10
assent 332.8
get 479.6
take 480.13
admit 585.7
pocket 627.3
include 772.3
believe 953.10
tune in 1036.17
receive absolution
do penance 658.6
confess 701.18
receiver
container 195.1
telegraph 347.2
telephone 347.4
recipient 479.3
believer 692.4
treasurer 729.12
fence 732.6
baseball team 745.2
football team 746.2
radio 1034.3
receivership 625.3
receive with open arms 585.9
the receiving end 479.3
recent former 837.10
late 841.12
recent past 837.1
receptacle
container 195.1
flower 310.28
reception taking in 187.1
entrance 189.1
receiving 479.1
taking 480.1
social gathering 582.10
welcome 585.2
assembly 770.2

inclusion 772.1
belief 953.1
fading 1034.21
receptionist host 585.5
doorkeeper 1008.12
receptive sensory 24.9
sensible 24.11
sensitive 93.20
recipient 187.16
willing 324.5
receiving 479.9
teachable 570.18
hospitable 585.11
influenceable 894.15
open-minded 979.10
pliant 1047.9
receptor 24.5
recess
n respite 20.2
nook 197.3
interior 207.2
recession 284.7
hiding place 346.4
seclusion 584.1
interim 826.1
pause 857.3
retreat 1009.5
v take a rest 20.8
indent 284.14
intervene 826.3
postpone 846.9
pause 857.9
recessed 284.16
recession
regression 163.1
recedence 168.1
recess 284.7
surrender 433.2
business cycle 731.10
hard times 1011.6
recharge activate 17.12
revive 396.16
recheck
n re-examination
938.7
v re-examine 938.27
verify 970.12
recidivism
regression 163.1
inversion 205.1
ungovernability 361.4
apostasy 363.2
backsliding 394.2
vice 654.1
impiety 694.1
reversion 859.1
recipe remedy 86.1
formula 419.3
recipient
n receiver 479.3
adj receptive 187.16
receiving 479.9
reciprocal
n likeness 784.3
adj cooperative 450.5
communal 476.9
retaliatory 506.8
reciprocative 777.10
periodic 850.7
interchangeable 863.5
alternate 916.19

numeric 1017.23
reciprocate
cooperate 450.3
get along 455.2
retaliate 506.4
correspond 777.7
interchange 863.4
alternate 916.13
recital speech 543.2
lesson 568.7
performance 708.33
fiction 722.1
narration 722.2
iteration 849.2
recite state 524.23
declaim 543.10
narrate 719.6
tell a story 722.6
iterate 849.8
memorize 989.17
sum up 1017.19
reckless
unconcerned 102.7
fast 174.15
careless 340.11
impulsive 365.9
devil-may-care 493.8
unwise 923.10
reckon plan 380.6
estimate 946.9
suppose 951.10
think 953.11
calculate 1017.18
reckoning
amount 244.2
fee 624.5
account 628.2
statement 628.3
estimate 946.3
sum 1017.6
calculation 1017.10
summation 1017.11
reclaim
redeem 396.12
aid 449.11
recover 481.6
re-form 858.12
rehabilitate 858.14
recline rest 20.6
lie 201.5
lie down 913.11
recluse
n loner 584.5
eccentric 927.3
adj reclusive 584.10
recognition
thanks 150.2
acknowledgment 332.3
commendation 509.3
due 639.2
repute 662.1
plot 722.4
cognizance 928.2
discovery 941.1
identification 989.5
recognizance
obligation 436.2
pledge 438.2
recognize see 27.12
thank 150.4
acknowledge 332.11

honor 646.8
perceive 928.12
detect 941.5
know 989.12
recoil
n demur 325.2
retaliation 506.1
impact 887.2
counteraction 900.1
rebound 903.2
retreat 903.3
v shudder at 99.5
flinch 127.13
demur 325.4
dodge 368.8
rebound 903.6
pull back 903.7
recollect 989.10
recommend
n recommendation 509.4
v urge 375.14
advise 422.5
propose 439.5
commend 509.11
recommit
commit 429.17
restore 481.4
recompense
n compensation 338.1
reparation 396.6
restitution 481.2
reprisal 506.2
remuneration 624.3
atonement 658.1
v compensate 338.4
remedy 396.13
make restitution 481.5
requite 506.5
pay 624.10
atone 658.4
recompose
restore 396.11
remake 396.18
reconcile
bring to terms 465.8
make agree 788.7
conform 867.3
reconciliation
contentment 107.1
reconcilement 465.3
adjustment 788.4
conformity 867.1
recondition
repair 396.14
renovate 396.17
rehabilitate 858.14
reconnaissance
Air Force mission 184.11
reconnoitering 938.8
reconnoiter
n reconnaissance 938.8
v look 27.13
traverse 177.20
make a reconnaissance 938.28
reconsider
rethink 931.15
re-examine 938.27
reconstitute
reproduce 78.7
restore 396.11
remake 396.18

rearrange 808.13
reconstruct
reproduce 78.7
remake 396.18
change 852.7
Reconstruction Era 824.5
record
n phonograph record 50.12
supremacy 249.3
preparedness 405.4
documentation 549.1
recording 549.1
report 549.7
history 719.1
chronicle 832.9
data 1042.15
v sound 50.14
write 547.19
put upon record 549.15
chronicle 719.5
teleview 1035.15
record-breaker 249.4
recording
n tape 50.12
record 549.1
registration 549.14
history 719.1
transcript 785.4
adj recordative 549.16
record keeping
registration 549.14
automation 1041.7
record player 50.11
records 757.4
recount
n returns 609.21
summation 1017.11
v narrate 719.6
tell a story 722.6
iterate 849.8
sum up 1017.19
recoup
n recovery 481.3
reimbursement 624.2
v redeem 396.12
recover 481.6
repay 624.11
recourse
instrumentality 384.3
resource 1009.2
recover
get well 83.7
recuperate 392.8
redeem 396.12
rally 396.20
rescue 398.3
regain 481.6
rehabilitate 858.14
re-cover 295.29
recovery
improvement 392.1
reclamation 396.2
rally 396.8
rescue 398.1
regaining 481.3
business cycle 731.10
rehabilitation 858.4
recovery room 197.25
re-create
reproduce 78.7
remake 396.18

change 852.7
recreation
refreshment 9.1
amusement 743.1
recreational drug 87.3
rec room 197.12
recruit
n rookie 461.18
novice 572.9
newcomer 774.4
beginner 818.2
v add to 253.5
provide 385.7
avail oneself of 387.14
restore 396.11
revive 396.16
recuperate 396.19
call to arms 458.19
employ 615.14
enlist 615.17
rectangular
oblong 267.9
right-angled 278.7
quadrangular 278.9
rectify refine 79.22
straighten 277.5
compensate 338.4
revise 392.12
remedy 396.13
make agree 788.7
conform 867.3
recto right side 219.1
makeup 554.12
rector principal 571.8
director 574.1
clergyman 699.2
rectory house 228.5
benefice 698.9
parsonage 703.7
rectum 2.18
recumbency
reclining 201.2
lowness 274.1
recuperate
get well 83.7
rally 392.8
recruit 396.19
recover 481.6
recur be frequent 847.3
repeat 849.11
reoccur 850.5
recur to the mind 989.15
recycle 396.12
red
n redness 41.1
radical 611.12
revolutionist 860.3
adj sore 26.11
reddish 41.6
blushing 139.13
raw 406.10
radical 611.20
Red
n Communist 611.13
revolutionist 860.3
adj Communist 611.21
red, white, and blue 647.7
red alert
warning sign 399.3
crisis 843.4
red-baiting 389.3

red-blooded
strong 15.15
resolute 492.18
redcap carrier 176.7
trainman 178.13
red carpet 580.1
red cent money 728.7
trifle 998.5
red corpuscle 2.25
redden make red 41.4
turn red 41.5
change color 105.19
blush 139.8
show resentment 152.14
reddish 41.6
redecorate 498.8
redeem reclaim 396.12
rescue 398.3
aid 449.11
recover 481.6
pay in full 624.13
pay for 624.18
atone 658.4
regenerate 685.6
re-form 858.12
substitute 862.4
redeeming feature 865.4
redemption
pardon 148.2
reclamation 396.2
rescue 398.1
recovery 481.3
atonement 658.1
function of Christ
677.14
redeemedness 685.4
new start 858.2
reversion 859.1
redesign
n reproduction 78.1
change 852.1
v reproduce 78.7
change 852.7
redevelop
reproduce 78.7
restore 396.11
red flag
warning sign 399.3
signal 517.15
red-handed
adj guilty 656.3
adv in the act 656.4
redhead 35.9
red herring fish 10.24
stratagem 415.3
red-hot fervent 913.18
zealous 101.9
heated 105.22
fiery 671.22
hot 1019.25
red ink 473.3
rediscover 941.2
redistribute 808.13
red-letter day
holiday 20.4
celebration 487.1
red light
warning sign 399.3
alarm 400.1
signal 517.15
traffic light 1026.4

red-light district
city district 230.6
brothel 665.9
redneck
n hater 103.4
wilderness settler 227.10
vulgarian 497.6
adj not urbane 233.8
boorish 497.13
redo reproduce 78.7
ornament 498.8
repeat 849.7
redolent odorous 69.9
fragrant 70.9
recollective 989.22
redouble
intensify 251.5
repeat 849.7
duplicate 874.3
redress
n compensation 338.1
reparation 396.6
restitution 481.2
recompense 624.3
atonement 658.1
v remedy 396.13
make restitution 481.5
requite 506.5
repay 624.11
atone 658.4
red tape routine 373.5
officialism 612.11
delay 846.2
reduce
n make small 258.9
v weaken 16.10
dilute 16.11
afflict 85.50
relieve 120.5
abase 137.5
quantify 244.4
decrease 252.7
subtract 255.9
contract 260.7
shorten 268.6
slenderize 270.13
conquer 412.10
subdue 432.9
demote 447.3
impoverish 619.6
discount 631.2
cheapen 633.6
moderate 670.6
simplify 798.4
analyze 801.6
depress 913.4
qualify 959.3
chemicalize 1060.8
reduce to 858.11
reduction in forces
deposal 447.2
economizing 635.2
redundancy 993.4
redundant
diffuse 538.11
repetitious 849.14
superfluous 993.17
reduplicate
reproduce 778.6
copy 785.8
repeat 849.7

duplicate 874.3
redux 396.24
red wine 88.17
reebok 311.5
reed tube 239.6
grass 310.5
stem 310.21
arrow 462.6
wind instrument 711.6
woodwind 711.8
reeducate teach 568.10
rehabilitate 858.14
reedy 58.14
reef
n island 235.2
shoal 276.2
point of land 283.9
v slow 175.9
reduce sail 182.50
reefer marijuana
cigarette 87.12
refrigerator truck 1024.4
reek
n stench 71.1
combustion product 1020.16
vapor 1067.1
v have an odor 69.6
stink 71.4
exude 190.15
let out 909.24
smoke 1019.23
vaporize 1067.8
reel
n windlass 906.7
whirl 915.2
swing 916.6
flounder 917.8
v be drunk 88.27
pitch 182.55
eddy 238.21
reel in 906.9
whirl 915.11
oscillate 916.10
flounder 917.15
reel in fish 382.10
wind in 906.9
reeling
n rotation 915.1
adj intoxicated 88.31
rotating 915.14
swinging 916.17
reel off chatter 540.5
repeat 849.7
memorize 989.17
reenactment 396.1
reenlist 825.5
reentry
regression 163.1
return 186.3
repetition 849.1
periodicity 850.2
spacecraft 1075.2
reestablish
reproduce 78.7
restore 396.11
resume 856.6
re-examine
reconsider 931.15
recheck 938.27
refashion
reproduce 78.7

remake 396.18
re-form 858.12
refer 888.3
referee
n arbitrator 466.4
judge 596.1
basketball game 747.3
hockey game 749.3
round 751.3
soccer game 752.3
fight 754.3
umpire 946.6
v mediate 466.6
sit in judgment 946.12
reference
n aspect 33.3
recommendation 509.4
meaning 518.1
punctuation 530.15
relevance 775.4
acknowledgment 888.2
citation 957.5
v refer to 957.14
reference book
book 554.1
work of reference 554.9
directory 574.10
referendum vote 371.6
election 609.15
constitutional referendum
613.8
refer to
avail oneself of 387.14
designate 517.18
mean 518.8
remark 524.24
confer 541.11
relate to 775.5
attribute to 888.4
direct attention to 957.14
call attention to 983.10
refill restore 396.11
complete 794.6
refinance 729.16
refine sensitize 24.7
clarify 79.22
extract 192.16
subtract 255.9
spiritualize 764.4
simplify 798.4
process 892.9
melt 1020.21
refinery refiner 79.13
plant 739.3
refit renovate 396.17
change 852.7
reflect curve 279.6
imitate 336.5
image 349.11
remark 524.24
consider 931.12
remember 989.10
return 1036.16
reflectance 1025.9
reflection bend 279.3
image 349.5
criticism 510.4
aspersion 512.4
remark 524.3
stigma 661.6
reflex 785.7

reaction 903.1
judiciousness 920.7
consideration 931.2
idea 932.1
remembering 989.4
reflected light 1025.9
signal 1036.11
reflector mirror 29.6
observatory 1072.17
reflect upon 510.13
reflex
n conditioning 92.26
impulse 365.1
reflection 785.7
impact 887.2
reaction 903.1
instinct 934.2
v curve 279.6
adj backward 163.12
unpremeditated 365.11
reactive 903.9
involuntary 963.14
reflexive
n voice 530.14
adj unpremeditated 365.11
reactive 903.9
involuntary 963.14
refluence
regression 163.1
course 172.2
eddy 238.12
tide 238.13
reaction 903.1
reflux regression 163.1
course 172.2
eddy 238.12
tide 238.13
reaction 903.1
reforestation
woodland 310.13
forestry 1069.3
planting 1069.14
reform
n reformation 392.5
change 852.1
new start 858.2
v repent 113.7
make better 392.9
restore 396.11
redeem 685.6
change 852.7
re-form 858.12
Reform
n Protestantism 675.10
adj Jewish 675.30
Reformationist
n Protestant 675.20
adj Protestant 675.28
reformatory
n prison 429.8
reform school 567.9
adj emendatory 392.16
refracted 164.8
refractory
n ceramic ware 742.2
adj unwilling 325.5
defiant 327.10
ungovernable 361.12
oppositional 451.8
resistant 453.5
ceramic 742.7

nonconforming 868.5
refrain
n air 708.4
passage 708.24
poetry 720.9
sequel 817.1
repeat 849.5
v not do 329.3
not use 390.5
abstain 668.7
cease 857.6
refreeze 1024.11
refresh freshen 9.2
strengthen 15.13
air 317.11
revive 396.16
renovate 396.17
amuse 743.21
refrigerate 1024.10
refresher course 568.8
refreshment
meal 8.5
invigoration 9.1
refection 9.1
nutriment 10.3
strengthening 15.5
ventilation 317.9
revival 396.3
renovation 396.4
refrigerant
n coolant 1024.7
adj refrigerative 1024.12
refrigerate
preserve 397.9
freeze 1023.10
cool 1024.10
refrigerator 1024.4
refuel 1021.8
refuge reception 187.1
hiding place 346.4
pretext 376.1
preserve 397.7
protection 1008.1
sanctuary 1009.1
refugee goer 190.10
fugitive 368.5
alien 774.3
refund
n reparation 481.2
reimbursement 624.2
discount 631.1
v make restitution 481.5
repay 624.11
discount 631.2
refurbish
renovate 396.17
ornament 498.8
refusal
unwillingness 325.1
dissent 333.1
rejection 372.1
denial 442.1
prohibition 444.1
opposition 451.1
option 733.2
repulse 908.2
refuse
n offal 80.9
remainder 256.1
derelict 370.4
discard 390.3

waste 391.4
v be unwilling 325.3
reject 372.2
decline 442.3
prohibit 444.3
repulse 908.3
refuse comment 344.6
refusenik 327.5
refuse to admit
deny 335.4
disbelieve 955.5
refuse to believe 956.3
refuse to pay 625.6
refute deny 335.4
defend 600.10
rebut 939.5
confute 958.5
regain 481.6
regal dignified 136.12
sovereign 417.17
noble 608.10
good 999.12
regale
n refreshment 9.1
treat 95.3
v feed 8.18
feast 8.24
refresh 9.2
gratify 95.8
amuse 743.21
regalia
formal dress 5.11
insignia 647.1
royal insignia 647.3
regard
n observation 27.2
look 27.3
aspect 33.3
love 104.1
considerateness 143.3
respect 155.1
carefulness 339.1
good terms 587.3
esteem 662.3
particular 766.3
relevance 775.4
outlook 978.2
attention 983.1
v look 27.13
cherish 104.21
be considerate 143.10
respect 155.4
care 339.6
observe 434.2
relate to 775.5
think of 931.17
judge 946.8
consider 953.11
heed 983.6
regardless
adj unconcerned 102.7
careless 340.11
incurious 982.3
inattentive 984.6
adv anyhow 384.10
in spite of 338.9
regards
respects 155.3
compliments 504.8
greetings 585.3

regatta
race 457.12
tournament 743.10
regency
mastership 417.7
government 612.4
commission 615.1
regenerate
v reproduce 78.7
revive 396.16
redeem 685.6
re-form 858.12
adj redeemed 685.9
converted 692.10
regent 575.12
regimen diet 7.13
treatment 91.14
government 612.1
regiment
n military unit 461.22
company 770.3
v hold a tight hand upon 425.4
dispose 808.9
regimentation
strictness 425.1
arrangement 808.1
region
location 159.1
area 231.1
territory 231.5
land 234.1
plot 722.4
regional
locational 159.19
territorial 231.8
idiomatic 523.22
register
n range 158.2
record 549.1
memorandum 549.4
record book 549.11
registration 549.14
clerk 550.1
account book 628.4
pitch 709.4
scale 709.6
organ stop 711.19
chronicle 832.9
list 871.1
v be heard 48.12
limit 210.5
represent 349.8
preserve 397.8
get across 521.5
record 549.15
be taught 570.11
act 704.29
agree 788.6
list 871.8
protect 1008.18
register a complaint 115.15
registered trademark
patent 210.3
label 517.13
registered voter 609.23
registrar
recorder 549.13
clerk 550.1
accountant 628.7

permit 443.9
let go 475.4
acquit 601.4
disband 771.8
detach 802.10
dismiss 909.19
relegate commit 478.16
exclude 773.4
banish 909.17
relent have pity 145.4
submit 433.6
be moderate 670.5
yield 1047.7
relentless pitiless 146.3
industrious 330.22
resolute 359.11
persevering 360.8
unyielding 361.9
firm 425.7
constant 847.5
inevitable 963.15
relevant
pertinent 775.11
apt 788.10
reliability
trustworthiness 644.6
stability 855.1
believability 953.8
dependability 970.4
reliable
trustworthy 644.19
stable 855.12
believable 953.24
evidential 957.16
dependable 970.17
unhazardous 1007.5
relic remainder 256.1
corpse 307.16
record 549.1
antiquity 842.6
back number 842.8
memento 989.7
relief remedy 86.1
easement 120.1
consolation 121.4
welfare 143.5
pity 145.1
outline 211.2
protuberance 283.2
lightening 298.3
aid 449.1
reinforcements 449.8
subsidy 478.8
welfarism 611.7
relievo 715.3
turn 825.2
interim 826.1
substitute 862.2
relief pitcher 745.2
relieve give relief 120.5
comfort 121.6
lighten 298.6
aid 449.11
play 745.5
take one's turn 825.5
substitute for 862.5
disembarrass 1014.9
relieve of 480.21
relieve oneself
excrete 12.12
lighten 120.7

speak up 524.21
relight revive 396.16
ignite 1020.22
religion
religious belief 675.1
theology 676.1
piety 692.1
system of belief 953.3
religious
n clergy 699.16
adj meticulous 339.12
conscientious 644.15
theistic 675.25
theological 676.4
sacred 685.7
pious 692.8
exact 973.17
religious ceremony
580.4
religious discourse 543.3
religious faith 675.1
religious holiday 850.4
religious order 675.3
religious rites
celebration 487.1
ritualism 701.1
relinquish
give up 370.7
cease to use 390.4
surrender 433.8
resign 448.2
yield 475.3
discontinue 857.6
reliquary tomb 309.16
monument 549.12
shrine 703.4
church vessels 703.11
relish
n taste 62.1
savor 63.2
flavoring 63.3
zest 68.2
passion 93.2
pleasure 95.1
liking 100.2
appetite 100.7
v eat 8.20
savor 63.5
enjoy 95.13
relocate settle 159.17
remove 176.11
reluctant slow 175.10
renitent 325.6
resistant 453.5
rely on hope 124.7
rest on 901.22
depend on 953.16
trust 953.17
remain be still 173.7
be present 221.6
inhabit 225.7
be left 256.5
endure 827.6
persist 853.5
continue 856.3
remainder
difference 255.8
remains 256.1
part 793.1
subsequence 835.1
surplus 993.5

remains
remainder 256.1
corpse 307.16
record 549.1
antiquity 842.6
remake reproduce 78.7
reconstruct 396.18
change 852.7
remand
n commitment 429.4
restitution 481.1
v imprison 429.17
commit 478.16
restore 481.4
remark
n interjection 213.2
aspersion 512.4
statement 524.3
commentary 556.2
attention 983.1
v comment 524.24
heed 983.6
remarkable
wonderful 122.10
outstanding 247.10
extraordinary 870.14
notable 997.19
remarry 563.15
remedial
curative 86.39
relieving 120.9
tonic 396.22
helpful 449.21
remedy
n cure 86.1
relief 120.1
reparation 396.6
therapy 396.7
aid 449.1
counteractant 900.3
v cure 86.38
treat 91.24
rectify 396.13
heal 396.15
aid 449.11
remember
recall 989.10
remind 989.20
remembrance
celebration 487.1
monument 549.12
posthumous fame 662.7
memory 837.4
recollection 989.1
remembering 989.4
reminder 989.6
memento 989.7
remind 989.20
reminder
memorandum 549.4
remembrance 989.6
reminisce 989.11
reminiscence
memory 837.4
remembering 989.4
remiss indolent 331.19
negligent 340.10
lax 426.4
dilatory 846.17
remission relief 120.1
pardon 148.2

decline 252.2
reduction 255.2
restitution 481.1
acquittal 601.1
modulation 670.2
pause 857.3
remit relieve 120.5
have pity 145.4
forgive 148.3
send 176.15
abate 252.8
imprison 429.17
exempt 430.14
commit 478.16
restore 481.4
acquit 601.4
pay 624.10
be moderate 670.5
relax 670.9
remittance
subsidy 478.8
payment 624.1
remnant
n remainder 256.1
adj remaining 256.7
remodel remake 396.18
re-form 858.12
remonstrate
object 333.5
dissuade 379.3
admonish 422.6
offer resistance 453.3
remora adhesive 803.4
curb 1012.7
remorse regret 113.1
guilt 656.1
remorseless
unregretful 114.4
pitiless 146.3
remote aloof 141.12
distant 261.8
reticent 344.10
standoffish 583.6
secluded 584.8
selfish 651.5
farfetched 776.8
remote control 1041.4
remote past 837.3
remote possibility
possibility 966.1
small chance 972.9
remove
n degree 245.1
v divest 6.5
take off 6.6
release 120.6
move 176.11
quit 188.9
extract 192.10
subtract 255.9
murder 308.16
discard 390.7
exterminate 395.14
depose 447.4
eliminate 773.5
detach 802.10
eject 909.13
dismiss 909.19
evacuate 909.22
removed distant 261.8
reticent 344.10

aloof 583.6
secluded 584.8
unrelated 776.6
separated 802.21
alone 872.8
remove from office 447.4
REM sleep
sleepiness 22.1
deep sleep 22.5
remunerate
remedy 396.13
make restitution 481.5
pay 624.10
renaissance 396.3
Renaissance man 413.3
renascent
reproductive 78.14
redivivus 396.24
rend pain 26.7
injure 393.13
demolish 395.17
wrest 480.22
sever 802.11
render
extraction 192.16
do 328.6
translate 341.12
communicate 343.7
represent 349.8
describe 349.9
execute 437.9
give 478.12
deliver 478.13
pay 624.10
play 708.39
convert 858.11
melt 1020.21
render a service 143.12
render assistance 449.11
rendering extract 192.7
rendition 341.2
representation 349.1
description 349.2
execution 708.30
rendezvous
n tryst 582.9
assembly 770.2
v come together 770.16
rendition extract 192.7
rendering 341.2
representation 349.1
description 349.2
restitution 481.1
execution 708.30
renegade
n apostate 363.5
sacrilegist 694.3
defector 858.8
adj apostate 363.11
impious 694.6
traitorous 858.20
nonobservant 435.5
renege
n recant 363.8
v abandon 370.5
disregard 435.3
repeal 445.2
be unfaithful 645.12
defect 858.13
renew refresh 9.2
stimulate 105.13

revive 396.16
renovate 396.17
innovate 841.5
repeat 849.7
change 852.7
resume 856.6
re-form 858.12
renewable
remediable 396.25
convertible 858.18
renewable energy 1021.7
renitent
reluctant 325.6
resistant 453.5
counteractive 900.8
rigid 1046.11
renounce
n recant 363.8
v deny 335.4
give up 370.7
reject 372.2
cease to use 390.4
surrender 433.8
relinquish 475.3
swear off 668.8
cease 857.6
renovate
reproduce 78.7
renew 396.17
recover 481.6
innovate 841.5
perfect 392.1
renown glory 247.2
repute 662.1
notability 997.2
rent
n trauma 85.38
crack 224.2
rental 615.6
hire 630.8
break 802.4
v cleave 224.4
inhabit 225.7
open 292.11
lease 615.15
rent out 615.16
adj cleft 224.7
impaired 393.27
severed 802.23
rental car 179.13
rent control 630.5
renter lodger 227.8
tenant 470.4
reoccupy 481.6
reoccur repeat 849.11
recur 850.5
reopen 856.6
reorder 808.13
reorganize
reproduce 78.7
rearrange 808.13
repair
n reparation 396.6
good condition
765.3
v perfect 392.11
mend 396.14
atone 658.4
repairman 396.10
repair shop 739.5
repair to 177.25

reparation
compensation 338.1
repair 396.6
restitution 481.2
recompense 624.3
atonement 658.1
repartee
witticism 489.7
conversation 541.1
answer 939.1
repast 8.5
repatriate restore 481.4
rehabilitate 858.14
repave 295.22
repay
compensate 338.4
be profitable 472.13
make restitution 481.5
requite 506.5
pay back 624.11
repeal
n revocation 445.1
v abolish 395.13
revoke 445.2
repeat
n repetend 849.5
encore 849.6
duplication 874.2
v reproduce 78.7
imitate 336.5
publish 352.10
redo 849.7
recur 849.11
become cyclic 850.5
duplicate 874.3
memorize 989.17
repeatedly 847.6
repeat performance
encore 849.6
repeat 874.2
repeat word for word 849.7
repel disgust 64.4
offend 98.11
cause dislike 99.6
reject 372.2
disincline 379.4
rebuff 442.5
resist 453.2
fend off 460.10
repulse 908.3
prevent 1012.14
repellent
offensive 98.18
resistant 453.5
repulsive 908.4
hideous 1015.11
repent
v think better of 113.7
adj creeping 177.39
reptile 311.48
repentant
penitent 113.9
atoning 658.7
repercussion
concussion 671.8
execution 708.30
impact 887.2
counteraction 900.1
recoil 903.2
repertoire store 386.1
repertory 704.9

repertory company 707.11
repetition
reproduction 78.1
triteness 117.3
tediousness 118.2
imitation 336.1
duplicate 785.3
constancy 847.2
redundancy 849.1
regularity 850.1
continuance 856.1
replication 874.1
repetitive
habitual 373.14
diffuse 538.11
same 781.6
continuous 812.8
repetitious 849.14
ceaseless 856.7
rephrase 341.13
replace
restore 396.11
depose 447.4
come after 835.3
substitute for 862.5
dismiss 909.19
replacement
restoration 396.1
deposal 447.2
successor 817.4
sequel 835.2
exchange 862.1
substitute 862.2
replant 91.24
replay 849.6
replenish provide 385.7
restore 396.11
complete 794.6
replete full 794.11
plentiful 991.7
overfull 993.20
satiated 994.6
replica
reproduction 336.3
the same 778.3
duplicate 785.3
replicate copy 785.8
double 873.5
duplicate 874.3
reply
n communication 343.1
retaliation 506.1
letter 553.2
defense 600.2
reaction 903.1
answer 939.1
v acknowledge 553.11
defend 600.10
react 903.5
answer 939.4
répondez s'il vous plaît 553.15
report
n crash 56.1
account 349.3
announcement 352.2
publicity 352.4
bulletin 549.7
information 551.1
rumor 552.6
commentary 556.2
repute 662.1

explosion 671.7
paean 696.3
note 709.14
criticism 946.2
v present oneself 221.11
communicate 343.7
announce 352.12
inform 551.8
give a report 552.11
accuse 599.7
narrate 719.6
tell a tale 722.6
pass judgment 946.13
reportage 552.1
report card 549.7
reporter
informant 551.5
newsmonger 552.9
journalist 555.4
spokesman 576.5
repose
n rest 20.1
respite 20.2
sleep 22.2
quiescence 173.1
recumbency 201.2
leisure 402.1
moderation 670.1
v rest 20.6
be located 159.10
deposit 159.14
be still 173.7
lie 201.5
trust 953.17
repository
storehouse 386.6
friend 588.1
treasury 729.13
repossess 481.6
reprehensible
blameworthy 510.25
wicked 654.16
guilty 656.3
terrible 1000.9
represent
be in front 216.7
manifest 348.5
delineate 349.8
describe 349.9
mediate 466.6
act for 576.14
enact 704.30
substitute for 862.5
visualize 986.15
representation
spectacle 33.7
reproduction 336.3
display 348.2
portrayal 349.1
delineation 349.1
description 349.2
representative 349.7
sham 354.3
vote 371.6
sign 517.1
bar 597.4
acting 704.8
picture 712.11
copy 785.1
duplicate 785.3
substitution 862.1

idea 932.1
representative
n representation 349.7
sign 517.1
deputy 576.1
legislator 610.3
example 786.2
substitute 862.2
adj representational 349.13
descriptive 349.14
indicative 517.23
deputy 576.16
model 786.8
repress inhibit 106.8
blunt 286.2
cover up 345.8
suppress 428.8
prohibit 444.3
retain 474.5
domineer 612.16
hinder 1012.10
reprieve
n release 120.2
pity 145.1
pardon 148.2
respite 601.3
delay 846.2
v release 120.6
have pity 145.4
respite 601.5
reprimand
n reproof 510.5
stigma 661.6
v reprove 510.17
stigmatize 661.9
reprint
n print 548.3
copy 785.5
iteration 849.2
v reproduce 78.7
print 548.14
iterate 849.8
reprisal requital 506.2
revenge 507.1
penalty 603.1
reprise 849.6
repro duplicate 785.3
print 785.5
duplication 874.1
reproach
n reproof 510.5
accusation 599.1
disgrace 661.5
stigma 661.6
v censure 510.13
accuse 599.7
disgrace 661.8
reprobate
n recreant 660.4
v censure 510.13
adj knavish 645.17
corrupt 654.14
wicked 654.16
unsacred 686.3
unregenerate 695.18
reproduce grow 14.2
remake 78.7
grow 259.7
copy 778.6
replicate 785.8
repeat 849.7

duplicate 874.3
produce 890.7
reproduction
bodily development 14.1
remaking 78.1
making 78.1
procreation 78.2
growth 259.3
replication 336.3
picture 712.11
duplication 785.2
double 785.3
repetition 849.1
imitation 874.1
proliferation 890.2
reproductive organs 2.13
reprove 510.17
reptile
n creature 311.3
reptilian 311.25
beast 660.6
adj creeping 177.39
reptilian 311.48
republic country 232.1
government 612.4
republican 612.17
repudiate
n recant 363.8
v deny 335.4
reject 372.2
refuse 442.3
not pay 625.6
exclude 773.4
repugnant
offensive 98.18
negative 335.5
oppositional 451.8
hostile 589.10
contrary 779.6
disagreeing 789.6
counteractive 900.8
hideous 1015.11
repulse
n snub 157.2
rejection 372.1
discomfiture 412.2
refuse 442.2
resistance 453.1
recoil 903.2
rebuff 908.2
v snub 157.5
reject 372.2
rebuff 442.5
resist 453.2
fend off 460.10
repel 908.3
repulsive
malodorous 71.5
filthy 80.23
offensive 98.18
repellent 908.4
terrible 1000.9
hideous 1015.11
reputable
honest 644.13
highly reputed 662.15
influential 894.13
notable 997.19
reputation 997.2
repute
n reputation 662.1

custom 731.6
influence 894.1
notability 997.2
v suppose 951.10
request
n proposal 439.2
expressed desire 440.1
asking 440.1
v ask 440.9
requiem dirge 115.6
last offices 309.4
sacred music 708.17
requiescat in pace 309.24
require
prescribe 420.9
demand 421.5
oblige 424.5
charge 630.12
obligate 641.12
entail 772.4
determine 886.12
need 963.9
want 992.7
requirement
demand 421.1
study 568.8
requisite 963.2
requisite
n condition 959.2
requirement 963.2
adj needful 963.13
requisition
n summons 420.5
demand 421.1
request 440.1
appropriation 480.4
requirement 963.2
v summon 420.11
demand 421.5
request 440.9
appropriate 480.19
requite remedy 396.13
make restitution 481.5
quit 506.5
repay 624.11
interchange 863.4
rerun 1034.18
rescind delete 255.12
repeal 445.2
rescue
n escape 369.1
saving 398.1
deliverance 398.1
liberation 431.1
aid 449.1
v redeem 396.12
come to the rescue 398.3
liberate 431.4
aid 449.11
research
n investigation 938.4
v search 938.31
experiment 942.8
research and development
942.1
researcher
seeker 938.18
experimenter 942.6
research paper 556.1
resection 802.2
resell 734.8

resemble be like 784.7
  be comparable 943.7
resent
  be resentful 152.12
  envy 154.3
reservation
  demur 325.2
  objection 333.2
  preserve 397.7
  stipulation 421.2
  engagement 615.4
  doubt 955.2
  qualification 959.1
  prearrangement 965.1
reserve
  n restraint 139.3
  communicativeness 343.3
  reticence 344.3
  reserves 386.3
  preserve 397.7
  conciseness 537.1
  v save 386.12
  not use 390.5
  allot 477.9
  employ 615.14
  postpone 846.9
  prearrange 965.4
  adj unused 390.12
  substitute 862.8
reserve forces 449.8
reservoir
  n lake 241.1
  reserve 386.3
  storehouse 386.6
  v store 386.10
reset sharpen 285.7
  plant 1069.18
reshape reproduce 78.7
  change 852.7
  re-form 858.12
reshuffle arrange 437.8
  rearrange 808.13
reside settle 159.17
  inhabit 225.7
residence
  habitation 225.1
  abode 228.1
resident
  n doctor 90.4
  inhabitant 227.2
  tenant 470.4
  diplomat 576.6
  benefice-holder 699.7
  adj residentiary 225.13
  intrinsic 767.7
residential 228.32
residual 256.8
residue
  remainder 256.1
  extract 893.3
resign give up 370.7
  cease to use 390.4
  submit 433.6
  demit 448.2
  relinquish 475.3
  deliver 478.13
resign oneself to 134.7
resiliency
  lightheartedness 109.3
  pliancy 1047.2
  elasticity 1048.1

resilient
  lighthearted 109.12
  recuperative 396.23
  changeable 854.6
  recoiling 903.10
  pliant 1047.9
  elastic 1048.7
resin
  n gum 1057.1
  v resinize 1057.2
resist oppose 451.3
  contend against 451.4
  withstand 453.2
  counteract 900.6
  hinder 1012.10
resistance
  immunity 83.4
  defense mechanism 92.23
  suppression 92.24
  drag 184.27
  refusal 325.1
  ungovernability 361.4
  opposition 451.1
  defiance 453.1
  withstanding 453.1
  defense 460.1
  irregular 461.16
  counteraction 900.1
  hindrance 1012.1
  ohm 1032.13
  conductance 1033.9
  friction 1044.1
  hardness 1046.1
  toughness 1049.1
resistance movement revolt
  327.4
  resistance 453.1
resolute
  zealous 101.9
  resolved 359.11
  persevering 360.8
  trial 403.16
  tough 492.18
resolution
  distinctness 31.2
  zeal 101.2
  will 323.1
  determination 359.1
  resolve 359.1
  perseverance 360.1
  intention 380.1
  decay 393.6
  endeavor 403.1
  proposal 439.2
  adjustment 465.4
  fortitude 492.6
  legislation 613.5
  passage 708.24
  harmonization 709.2
  analysis 801.1
  itemization 801.2
  dissection 802.5
  disintegration 806.1
  end 820.1
  conversion 858.1
  solution 940.1
  judgment 946.1
  verdict 946.5
resolve
  n resolution 359.1
  intention 380.1

  v will 323.2
  determine 359.7
  intend 380.4
  endeavor 403.5
  reconcile 465.8
  analyze 801.6
  itemize 801.7
  end 820.5
  solve 940.2
  decide 946.11
resolvent
  n solvent 1064.4
  adj disintegrative 806.5
  solvent 1064.8
resonance
  resoundingness 54.1
  reaction 903.1
  oscillation 916.1
  wave 916.4
resonate vibrate 54.6
  oscillate 916.10
resort haunt 228.27
  instrumentality 384.3
  entertainment 743.13
  expedient 995.2
  recourse 1009.2
resound
  n reverberation 54.2
  v sound 50.14
  din 53.7
  reverberate 54.7
  repeat 849.11
resounding triumph 409.3
resource supply 386.2
  reserve 386.3
  source of supply 386.4
  skill 413.1
  expedient 995.2
  recourse 1009.2
resourceful
  skillful 413.22
  versatile 413.25
  cunning 415.12
respect
  n observation 27.2
  aspect 33.3
  esteem 155.1
  regard 155.1
  observance 434.1
  courtesy 504.1
  approval 509.1
  good terms 587.3
  duty 641.1
  honor 662.3
  particular 766.3
  relevance 775.4
  outlook 978.2
  attention 983.1
  v be considerate 143.10
  entertain respect for 155.4
  observe 434.2
  approve 509.9
  relate to 775.5
respectable
  honest 644.13
  reputable 662.15
  tolerable 999.20
  mediocre 1005.7
respectful
  regardful 155.8
  observant 434.4

  courteous 504.14
  approbatory 509.16
  dutiful 641.13
respective
  proportionate 477.13
  mutual 777.11
  particular 865.12
respects regards 155.3
  compliments 504.8
respiration 2.21
respirator 91.19
respiratory 2.32
respite
  n recess 20.2
  release 120.2
  reprieve 601.3
  interim 826.1
  delay 846.2
  pause 857.3
  v reprieve 601.5
resplendent
  illustrious 662.19
  gorgeous 1016.21
  bright 1025.32
respond sense 24.6
  be affected 93.11
  defend 600.10
  interchange 863.4
  react 903.5
  answer 939.4
respondent
  n accused 599.6
  answerer 939.3
  adj reactive 903.9
  answering 939.6
response sensation 24.1
  feeling 93.1
  sympathy 93.5
  communication 343.1
  meaning 518.1
  defense 600.2
  paean 696.3
  responsory report
  708.23
  passage 708.24
  impact 887.2
  reaction 903.1
  answer 939.1
responsibility
  supervision 573.2
  commission 615.1
  incumbency 641.2
  trustworthiness 644.6
  attribution 888.1
  operation 889.1
  liability 897.1
responsible
  chargeable 623.9
  answerable 641.17
  trustworthy 644.19
  liable 897.5
responsive
  sensitive 24.12
  sympathetic 93.20
  willing 324.5
  communicational 343.9
  influenceable 894.15
  reactive 903.9
  answering 939.6
  pliant 1047.9
  elastic 1048.7

rest
  n respite 20.1
  repose 20.1
  silence 51.1
  quiescence 173.1
  step 193.5
  remainder 256.1
  death 307.1
  leisure 402.1
  musical pause 709.21
  pause 857.3
  supporter 901.2
  fulcrum 906.3
  v repose 20.6
  be situated 159.10
  deposit 159.14
  be still 173.7
  ride at anchor 182.16
  remain 256.5
  do nothing 329.2
  plead 598.19
  calm 670.7
  pause 857.9
  depend 959.6
rest assured
  hope 124.7
  be confident 953.14
  be certain 970.9
restate
  paraphrase 341.13
  iterate 849.8
restaurant
  eating place 8.17
  dining room 197.11
  workplace 739.1
rest easy
  be content 107.5
  persuade oneself 375.24
restful vacational 20.10
  comfortable 121.11
  quiescent 173.12
  pacific 464.9
  tranquilizing 670.15
restimulate 396.16
resting place
  tomb 309.16
  end 820.1
  supporter 901.2
rest in peace 309.24
restitution
  compensation 338.1
  restoration 396.1
  reparation 481.2
  reimbursement 624.2
  recompense 624.3
  atonement 658.1
  reversion 859.1
restive restless 105.27
  discontented 108.7
  impatient 135.6
  reluctant 325.6
  defiant 327.10
  obstinate 361.8
  ungovernable 361.12
restless wakeful 23.7
  restive 105.27
  discontented 108.7
  impatient 135.6
  bustling 330.20
  inconstant 854.7
  agitated 917.16

rest one's case 598.19
rest on one's laurels
  be content 107.5
  take it easy 331.15
restore vitaminize 7.20
  reproduce 78.7
  put back 396.11
  return 481.4
  justify 600.9
  rehabilitate 858.14
  aid 449.11
  recover 481.6
restrain limit 210.5
  compel 424.4
  constrain 428.7
  bind 428.10
  confine 429.12
  simplify 499.5
  moderate 670.6
  qualify 959.3
  hinder 1012.10
restraint
  suppression 92.24
  equanimity 106.3
  reserve 139.3
  limitation 210.2
  reticence 344.3
  self-control 359.5
  compulsion 424.1
  constraint 428.1
  shackle 428.4
  confinement 429.1
  subjection 432.1
  restrainedness 496.4
  elegance 533.1
  temperance 668.1
  moderation 670.1
  hindrance 1012.1
restraint of trade
  restraint 428.1
  commerce 731.1
restrict bound 210.5
  narrow 270.11
  limit 428.9
  confine 429.12
  allot 477.9
  specialize 866.4
  qualify 959.3
restricted
  bounded 210.7
  out of bounds 210.8
  narrow 270.14
  secret 345.11
  limited 428.15
  confined 429.19
  specialized 866.5
  qualified 959.10
Restricted 706.1
rest room latrine 12.10
  bathing place 79.10
  bathroom 197.26
restructure
  reproduce 78.7
  rearrange 808.13
  change 852.7
rest stop 857.2
result
  n event 831.1
  effect 887.1
  product 893.1
  solution 940.1

  v turn out 831.7
  follow after 835.3
  ensue 887.4
resultant
  n effect 887.1
  adj happening 831.9
  resulting 887.6
resume recover 481.6
  iterate 849.8
  repeat 849.11
  recommence 856.6
résumé
  summary 557.2
  history 719.1
  iteration 849.2
resupply 385.1
resurface floor 295.22
  repeat 849.11
  recur 850.5
  recur to the mind 989.15
resurgent
  reproductive 78.14
  renascent 396.24
resurrect
  reproduce 78.7
  revive 396.16
resurrection
  reproduction 78.1
  revival 396.3
  removal to heaven 681.11
resuscitate
  stimulate 105.13
  come to life 306.10
  revive 396.16
  aid 449.11
  resume 856.6
retail
  n sale 734.1
  v publish 352.10
  deal in 731.16
  sell 734.8
  disperse 771.4
  iterate 849.8
  adj commercial 731.22
  sales 734.13
retailer provider 385.6
  merchant 730.2
retail store 736.1
retain reserve 386.12
  keep 474.5
  employ 615.14
  stabilize 855.7
  sustain 856.4
  keep in memory 989.13
retainer
  hanger-on 138.6
  dependent 577.1
  fee 624.5
retaining wall 901.4
retake
  n recovery 481.3
  screen test 706.5
  motion picture 714.8
  v recover 481.6
retaliate
  compensate 338.4
  retort 506.4
  revenge 507.4
  interchange 863.4
retard slow 175.9
  restrain 428.7

  delay 846.8
  hinder 1012.10
retardant 453.5
retardation
  slowing 175.4
  restraint 428.1
  delay 846.2
  mental deficiency 922.9
  hindrance 1012.1
retch feel disgust 99.4
  vomit 909.26
retell narrate 722.6
  iterate 849.8
retention refusal 442.1
  retainment 474.1
  tenacity 803.3
  retentiveness 989.3
rethink
  reconsider 931.15
  re-examine 938.27
reticence 344.3
reticulum
  network 170.3
  cell 305.4
retina 2.9
retinue staff 577.11
  attendance 769.6
retire go to bed 22.17
  efface oneself 139.7
  retreat 163.6
  recede 168.2
  quit 188.9
  be concave 284.12
  be uncommunicative 344.6
  scrap 390.8
  depose 447.4
  resign 448.2
  keep to oneself 583.4
  seclude oneself 584.7
  pay in full 624.13
  dismiss 909.19
retired private 345.13
  disused 390.10
  leisure 402.5
  in retirement 448.3
  secluded 584.8
retirement home 1009.4
retiring
  reserved 139.11
  receding 168.5
  concave 284.16
  reticent 344.10
retold 849.12
retool 1040.13
retort
  n witticism 489.7
  retaliation 506.1
  recrimination 599.3
  instrument of conversion
    858.10
  countermeasure 900.5
  answer 939.1
  vaporizer 1067.6
  v retaliate 506.4
  answer 939.4
retouch
  tamper with 354.17
  perfect 392.11
retrace one's steps
  turn back 163.8
  re-examine 938.26

retract
   n recant 363.8
   v withdraw 168.3
   deny 335.4
   repeal 445.2
   relinquish 475.3
retraction
   recession 168.1
   reduction 255.2
   denial 335.2
   recantation 363.3
   repeal 445.1
   relinquishment 475.1
retread
   n renovation 396.4
   v repair 396.14
   militarize 458.20
retreat
   n reculade 163.2
   recession 168.1
   departure 188.1
   sanctum 197.8
   summerhouse 228.12
   decline 252.2
   evening 315.2
   hiding place 346.4
   surrender 433.2
   seclusion 584.1
   hideaway 584.6
   recoil 903.3
   asylum 1009.4
   recess 1009.5
   v sound a retreat 163.6
   recede 168.2
   quit 188.9
   incline 204.10
   be concave 284.12
   hesitate 362.7
   pull back 903.7
retrenchment
   curtailment 252.4
   reduction 255.2
   shortening 268.3
   restraint 428.1
   economizing 635.2
retrial 598.5
retribution
   reparation 481.2
   reprisal 506.2
   punishment 604.1
   recompense 624.3
retrieval
   reclamation 396.2
   rescue 398.1
   recovery 481.3
   access 1042.8
retrieve
   n recovery 481.3
   v fetch 176.16
   redeem 396.12
   rescue 398.3
   recover 481.6
retroactive
   regressive 163.11
   back 837.12
   reactive 903.9
retrocede regress 163.5
   recede 168.2
   revert 859.4
retroflection motion
      backwards 163.1

inversion 205.1
retrograde
   v regress 163.5
   deteriorate 393.16
   revert 859.4
   adj regressive 163.11
   rear 217.9
   deteriorating 393.45
   reversionary 859.7
retrogress 393.18
retrorocket
   rocket 1074.2
   spacecraft 1075.2
retrospect
   n remembering 989.4
   v remember 989.10
retrospective 837.4
return
   n regression 163.1
   homecoming 186.3
   relapse 394.1
   recovery 396.8
   gain 472.3
   restitution 481.1
   retaliation 506.1
   reimbursement 624.2
   recompense 624.3
   dividend 738.7
   game 748.2
   repetition 849.1
   periodicity 850.2
   reversion 859.1
   production 893.2
   reaction 903.1
   answer 939.1
   signal 1036.11
   v reverberate 54.7
   regress 163.5
   turn back 163.8
   restore 396.11
   give back 481.4
   yield 627.4
   play tennis 748.3
   repeat 849.11
   recur 850.5
   revert 859.4
   interchange 863.4
   answer 939.4
   reflect 1036.16
return a verdict 946.13
returnee 859.3
return match 849.6
returns gain 472.3
   report 549.7
   election returns 609.21
   receipts 627.1
   roll 871.6
return the favor 863.4
return to the fold
   n reversion 859.1
   v revert 859.4
reunion
   reconciliation 465.3
   social gathering 582.10
reunite 465.8
reusable 387.23
Reuters 555.3
rev accelerate 174.10
   drive 756.4
revamp revise 392.12
   renovate 396.17

change 852.7
reveal unclose 292.12
   manifest 348.5
   disclose 351.4
   divulge 351.5
   signify 517.17
   unfold 861.7
   uncover 941.4
revealing
   n disclosure 351.1
   adj disclosive 351.10
   transparent 1029.4
reveille awakening 23.2
   morning 314.1
   call 517.16
revel
   n treat 95.3
   celebration 487.1
   lark 743.6
   v go on a spree 88.28
   rejoice 116.5
   make merry 743.24
revelation
   visibility 31.1
   appearance 33.1
   surprise 131.2
   manifestation 348.1
   disclosure 351.1
   divine revelation 683.10
   unfolding 861.2
   intuition 934.1
   discovery 941.1
Revelation 683.4
reveler drinker 88.11
   player 743.18
revenge
   n compensation 338.1
   reprisal 506.2
   vengeance 507.1
   v avenge 507.4
revenue 627.1
reverberate
   resound 54.7
   repeat 849.11
   answer 939.4
reverence
   n respect 155.1
   obeisance 155.2
   piety 692.1
   worship 696.1
   crouch 913.3
   v respect 155.4
   worship 696.11
Reverend title 648.5
   clergyman 699.2
reverend
   venerable 155.12
   reputable 662.15
reverie trance 92.19
   thoughtfulness 931.3
   abstractedness 985.2
   dream 986.9
reverse
   n reversal 163.3
   inverse 205.4
   opposite side 215.3
   rear 217.1
   about-face 363.1
   relapse 394.1
   discomfiture 412.2
   reversion 859.1

reversal of fortune 1011.3
   gear 1040.9
   v go into reverse 163.7
   backwater 182.34
   invert 205.5
   misinterpret 342.2
   repeal 445.2
   transpose 779.5
   convert 858.11
   revert 859.4
   adj contrapositive 215.5
   contrary 779.6
reversion reverse 163.3
   inversion 205.1
   relapse 394.1
   restoration 396.1
   inheritance 479.2
   devolution 629.2
   change to a former state
      859
   reverting 859.1
revert regress 163.5
   invert 205.5
   be behind 217.8
   relapse 394.4
   repeat 849.11
   retrovert 859.4
revetment 295.12
review
   n discussion 541.7
   periodical 555.1
   commentary 556.2
   abridgment 557.1
   study 570.3
   fiction 722.1
   narration 722.2
   critical notice 723.2
   procession 812.3
   iteration 849.2
   mature thought 931.5
   examination 938.3
   re-examination 938.7
   criticism 946.2
   remembering 989.4
   v discuss 541.12
   write upon 556.5
   study 570.12
   brush up 570.14
   iterate 849.8
   reconsider 931.15
   examine 938.24
   re-examine 938.27
   criticize 946.14
   remember 989.10
   refresh the memory 989.19
reviewer author 547.15
   commentator 556.4
   analyzer 718.4
   critic 723.4
   examiner 938.17
   judge 946.7
revile scoff 508.9
   berate 510.19
   vilify 512.10
revise
   n revision 392.4
   proof 548.5
   v reproduce 78.7
   redact 392.12
   write 547.19
   re-examine 938.27

revisionist
 n reformer 392.6
 Communist 611.13
 adj emendatory
  392.16
 Communist 611.21
revisit 221.9
revitalize 396.16
revival meeting 696.8
revive refresh 9.2
 strengthen 15.13
 reproduce 78.7
 stimulate 105.13
 cheer up 109.9
 come to life 306.10
 perfect 392.11
 revivify 396.16
 recover 396.20
 aid 449.11
 restore 481.6
 repeat 849.7
 be changed 852.6
 change 852.7
 resume 856.6
 remember 989.10
revoke
 n repeal 445.1
 v deny 335.4
 abolish 395.13
 repeal 445.2
revolt
 n rebellion 327.4
 resistance 453.1
 strike 727.5
 revolution 860.1
 counteraction 900.1
 v offend 98.11
 rebel 327.7
 offer resistance 453.3
 strike 727.10
 revolutionize 860.4
revolting
 offensive 98.18
 hideous 1015.11
revolution
 n overturn 205.2
 revolt 327.4
 reform 392.5
 anarchy 418.2
 disruption 802.3
 round 850.3
 break 852.2
 radical change 860.1
 circuit 914.2
 rotation 915.1
 v revolt 327.7
revolutionary
 n rebel 327.5
 reformer 392.6
 radical 611.12
 violent person 671.9
 revolutionist 860.3
 adj rebellious 327.11
 original 337.5
 emendatory 392.16
 radical 611.20
 unruly 671.19
 changed 852.10
 revulsive 860.5
 revolutionist 860.6
 counteractive 900.8

revolve
 invert 205.5
 recur 850.5
 circle 914.5
 rotate 915.9
 think over 931.13
reward
 n death 307.1
 incentive 375.7
 reprisal 506.2
 recompense 624.3
 award 646.2
 v requite 506.5
 pay 624.10
reword
 paraphrase 341.13
 iterate 849.8
rework reproduce 78.7
 revise 392.12
rewrite
 n revision 392.4
 v revise 392.12
 write 547.19
RF 1034.12
rhapsodic
 overjoyed 95.17
 poetic 720.15
rhapsodize
 be enthusiastic 101.7
 idealize 986.16
rhetoric diction 532.1
 style 532.2
 public speaking 543.1
 eloquence 544.1
 grandiloquence 545.1
rhetorical
 declamatory 543.12
 grandiloquent 545.8
rhetorical question 938.10
rheumatic
 n sick person 85.43
 adj arthritic 85.61
rheumy
 circulatory 2.33
 secretory 13.7
Rh factor blood 2.25
 antitoxin 86.27
rhinal 2.32
rhinestone 498.6
rhinoceros 311.4
rhinoceros hide 94.3
rhinovirus 85.42
rhombal 278.9
rhubarb
 vegetables 10.35
 noise 53.4
 quarrel 456.6
 argumentation 935.4
rhyme
 n poetry 720.1
 poem 720.4
 clink 720.8
 assonance 784.6
 repetitiousness 849.4
 v assonate 720.14
 sound similar 784.9
rhymer 720.12
rhythm accent 524.10
 harmony 533.2
 beat 709.22
 meter 720.7

 periodicity 850.2
 pulsation 916.3
rib bulge 283.3
 wife 563.8
ribbed 290.4
ribbing 490.3
ribbon
 n strip 271.4
 monument 549.12
 decoration 646.5
 ray 1025.5
 v figure 498.9
rib cage 2.2
ribonucleic acid 305.9
ribosome 305.5
rib tickler 489.6
rice paddy 1069.9
rich colorful 35.19
 resonant 54.10
 flavorful 63.9
 oversweet 66.5
 humorous 488.5
 ornate 498.12
 wealthy 618.14
 precious 632.10
 melodious 708.48
 productive 890.9
 interesting 983.19
 plentiful 991.7
 oily 1056.9
richly deserve 639.5
rich man
 capitalist 611.15
 wealthy man 618.7
richness of meaning 539.1
rich ore 406.5
rich soil 890.6
rich uncle 618.4
ricketiness
 infirmity 16.3
 old age 303.5
rickety unsteady 16.16
 diseased 85.61
 deformed 265.12
 stricken in years 303.18
 loose 804.5
ricksha 179.3
ricochet 903.2
rid 430.31
riddance
 escape 369.1
 relinquishment 475.1
 elimination 773.2
riddle
 n refinery 79.13
 network 170.3
 porousness 292.8
 conundrum 522.9
 arranger 808.5
 the unknown 930.7
 bewilderment 971.3
 v perforate 292.15
 strike dead 308.18
 mark 517.19
 be incomprehensible 522.10
 segregate 773.6
 classify 808.11
 shoot 904.12
 solve 940.2
ride
 n drive 177.7

 merry-go-round 743.15
 v annoy 96.13
 be disrespectful 156.6
 go for a ride 177.33
 go on horseback 177.34
 ride at anchor 182.16
 weather the storm 182.40
 float 182.54
 banter 490.6
 ridicule 508.8
 rest on 901.22
ride a broomstick 690.10
ride and tie
 n race 457.12
 v alternate 916.13
 adv to and fro 916.21
ride down
 conquer 412.10
 run over 910.7
ride for a fall 493.6
ride full tilt against 459.18
ride herd on
 wield authority 417.13
 hold a tight hand upon 425.4
 supervise 573.10
 dominate 612.15
 care for 1008.19
 drive 1070.8
ride high 298.8
ride it out 855.11
**ride off in all directions at
  once** 105.16
ride on a rail
 torture 604.16
 drive out 909.14
ride out
 race 757.5
 be safe 1007.2
rider
 equestrian 178.8
 added to writing 254.2
 hunter 311.13
 bill 613.9
 jockey 757.2
ride roughshod over
 conquer 412.10
 intimidate 424.7
 domineer 612.16
 run over 910.7
ride shotgun 1008.18
ride the gravy train
 take one's leisure 402.4
 live well 1010.10
ride the high horse 141.8
ride the pine 747.4
ride the sea 182.54
ridge
 n summit 198.2
 head 198.6
 back 217.3
 ridgeline 237.5
 plateau 272.4
 bulge 283.3
 wrinkle 291.3
 v emboss 283.12
 wrinkle 291.6
ridicule
 n impudence 142.2
 disrespect 156.1
 contempt 157.1
 banter 490.1

derision 508.1
deprecation 510.2
v have the audacity 142.7
disrespect 156.4
disdain 157.3
joke 489.13
deride 508.8
deprecate 510.12

ridiculous
humorous 488.4
absurd 923.11
unbelievable 955.10
impossible 967.7

riding 231.5

riding horse 311.13

rid oneself of
break the habit 374.3
discard 390.7
relinquish 475.3
eliminate 773.5

rife reported 552.15
prevalent 864.12
teeming 884.9
plentiful 991.7

riffraff offal 80.9
rubbish 391.5
rabble 606.3

rifle
n military man 461.6
infantryman 461.9
gun 462.10
v furrow 290.3
plunder 482.17
ransack 938.33

rift
n crack 224.2
valley 237.7
falling-out 456.4
break 802.4
fault 1003.2
blemish 1004.1
v open 292.11
adj cleft 224.7

rig
n wardrobe 5.2
suit 5.6
costume 5.9
equipage 179.5
truck 179.12
rigging 180.12
equipment 385.4
ruler 575.9
v outfit 5.41
tamper with 354.17
plot 381.9
equip 385.8
prearrange 965.5

rigamarole 520.2

rigger
aircraftsman 185.6
electrician 1032.22

rigging rig 180.12
cordage 271.3
intrigue 381.5
equipment 385.4
manipulation 737.20
supporter 901.2

right
n right side 219.1
authority 417.1
rights 430.2

estate 471.4
warrant 600.6
conservative 611.9
rightfulness 637.1
due 639.2
prerogative 642.1
justice 649.1
option 737.21
accuracy 973.5
v remedy 396.13
make agree 788.7
arrange 808.8
adj right-hand 219.4
straight 277.6
decorous 496.10
conventional 579.5
rightful 637.3
honest 644.13
just 649.8
orthodox 687.7
apt 788.10
sane 925.4
accurate 973.16
expedient 995.5
adv directly 161.23
rightward 219.7
very 247.18
rightly 637.4
absolutely 794.15
exactly 973.21
right on! 973.24
excellently 999.22
interj yes 332.18

right-about-face
n reverse 163.3
change of mind 363.1
turnabout 859.1
v do an about-face 163.10

right and left
extensively 158.12
all round 209.13
laterally 218.8

right-angle upright 200.2
perpendicular 200.12
right-angled 278.7

right as rain
adj straight 644.14
adv right! 973.24

right away at once 830.8
promptly 845.15

righteous
right 637.3
honest 644.13
virtuous 653.6
godly 692.9

righteous indignation 152.4

rightful right 637.3
condign 639.8
just 649.8
legal 673.11
genuine 973.15

right hand 616.7

right-hand
starboard 219.4
dexterous 219.5

right-handed 219.5

right-hand man
subordinate 432.5
employee 577.3
right hand 616.7

right of eminent domain 480.5

right off the bat 830.6

right-of-way
superiority 249.1
road 383.5

right on
interj congratulations 149.5
yeah 332.19
phrs that's it 788.13
you better believe it!
973.25

the Right Reverend
n clergyman 699.2
adj the Noble 648.8

right side 219.1

the right stuff 413.4

the right thing right 637.1
fairness 649.3
virtue 653.1

right to vote vote 371.6
suffrage 609.17

rightward clockwise 161.24
to the right 219.7

right wing
right side 219.1
conservative 611.9

right with 788.12

rigid firm 15.18
meticulous 339.12
unyielding 361.9
strict 425.7
formal 580.9
permanent 853.7
immovable 855.15
exact 973.17
stiff 1046.11

rigor acrimony 17.5
meticulousness 339.3
firmness 425.2
asceticism 667.1
violence 671.1
accuracy 973.5
adversity 1011.1
difficulty 1013.1
cold 1023.1
rigidity 1046.2

rigor mortis 307.1

rile annoy 96.13
provoke 152.24
agitate 917.10

rill 238.1

rim
n border 211.4
slope 237.2
felly 280.4
v border 211.10

rime 1023.7

rind exterior 206.2
shallowness 276.1
skin 295.3
lamina 296.2

ring
n ringing 54.3
circle 280.2
encircling thing 280.3
bulge 283.3
telephone call 347.13
fighting 457.9
arena 463.1
jewel 498.6
association 617.1
clique 617.6

insignia 647.1
ecclesiastical insignia 647.4
boxing 754.1
halo 1025.14
atomic cluster 1038.7
v din 53.7
tintinnabulate 54.8
check out 188.13
encircle 209.7
telephone 347.19

ring a bell 903.8

ringer impostor 357.6
substitute 862.2

ring in arrive 186.6
inaugurate 818.11
punch the clock 832.12
substitute 862.4

ringing in the ear 54.3

ringleader
instigator 375.11
leader 574.6
politics 610.7

ringlet lock 3.5
circlet 280.5
coil 281.2

ringmaster
theater man 704.23
circus artist 707.3

rings 725.7

ringside seat 27.8

ring true 973.9

rink playground 743.11
hockey 749.1
lawn bowling 750.3

rinse
n washing 79.5
cleanser 79.17
v wash 79.19
soak 1065.13

riot
n revolt 327.4
free-for-all 457.5
joke 489.6
unruliness 671.3
commotion 810.4
plenty 991.2
v vegetate 310.34
revolt 327.7
contend 457.13
rage 671.11
roister 810.10

riot police 1008.17

rip
n trauma 85.38
drinking spree 88.6
disrespect 156.3
tide 238.13
attempt 403.3
libertine 665.10
break 802.4
v torture 96.18
be disrespectful 156.6
speed 174.9
open 292.11
injure 393.13
wrest 480.22

RIP 309.24

rip cord 181.13

ripe
v ripen 407.8
adj mature 303.13

prepared 405.16
seasoned 407.13
experienced 413.28
marriageable 563.20
complete 794.9
timely 843.9
perfected 1002.9
ripen fester 12.15
grow 14.2
enlarge 259.7
mature 303.9
develop 392.10
bloom 407.8
evolve 861.5
perfect 1002.5
ripe old age 303.5
rip into
lift one's hand against 457.14
attack 459.15
criticize 510.14
rip off 482.16
rip-off fake 354.13
hoax 356.7
theft 482.4
ripped high 87.24
drunk 88.33
tortured 96.25
ripping
n extortion 192.6
severance 802.2
adj excellent 999.13
ripple
n splash 52.5
rapids 238.10
wave 238.14
roughness 288.2
wrinkle 291.3
attempt 403.3
v babble 52.11
wrinkle 291.6
agitate 917.10
ripple effect
divergence 171.1
transferal 176.1
permeation 221.3
expansion 259.1
dispersion 771.1
immediate cause 886.3
rip-roaring noisy 53.13
turbulent 671.18
riptide 238.13
rise
n appearance 33.1
ascent 193.1
rising 200.5
acclivity 204.6
slope 237.2
hill 237.4
wave 238.14
increase 251.1
height 272.2
improvement 392.1
promotion 446.1
evolution 861.1
source 886.5
reaction 903.1
v wake up 23.6
appear 33.8
din 53.7
move 172.5
ascend 193.8

arise 200.8
incline 204.10
billow 238.22
grow 251.6
tower 272.10
levitate 298.9
revolt 327.7
make good 409.10
originate 818.13
rise above accept 134.7
loom 247.5
tower above 272.11
defeat 411.5
rise again 306.10
rise and fall 238.22
rise from 887.5
rise in the world
make good 409.10
be prosperous 1010.9
riser 193.5
rise to mind 931.18
rise to the occasion
carry out 328.7
win through 409.13
rise to the surface 190.11
rise up ascend 193.8
rise 200.8
grow 272.12
revolt 327.7
rising
n appearance 33.1
sore 85.37
course 172.2
ascent 193.1
uprising 200.5
acclivity 204.6
swelling 283.4
revolt 327.4
adj flowing 172.8
ascending 193.14
sloping upward 204.17
increasing 251.8
risk
n investment 729.4
gamble 759.2
unreliability 971.6
chance 972.1
v invest 729.17
gamble 759.24
take a chance 972.12
endanger 1006.6
defy danger 1006.7
riskless 1007.5
risk-taking
defiance 454.1
daring 492.5
chance 972.1
risqué cursing 513.8
risky 666.7
rite celebration 487.1
amenity 504.7
ceremony 580.4
ritual 701.3
rite of confession 351.3
rite of passage 580.4
ritual
n custom 373.1
amenity 504.7
formality 580.1
ceremony 580.4
rite 701.3

adj ceremonious 580.8
ritualistic 701.19
ritual murder 308.1
ritual observance
celebration 487.1
rite 701.3
ritzy grandiose 501.21
chic 578.13
rival
n competitor 452.2
combatant 461.1
v contend against 451.4
compete 457.18
equal 790.5
be comparable 943.7
excel 999.11
adj oppositional 451.8
competitive 457.23
rivalry envy 154.1
hostility 451.2
competition 457.2
river stream 238.1
torrent 238.5
river bed 239.2
river gambler 759.21
riverside
n shore 234.2
adj coastal 234.7
rivet 800.8
riveted fixed 855.14
gripped 983.18
riveting alluring 377.8
engrossing 983.20
riviera 234.2
rivulet 238.1
RNA
genetic material 305.9
heredity 560.6
roach
marijuana cigarette 87.12
remainder 256.1
vermin 311.37
road seaway 182.10
inlet 242.1
route 383.1
highway 383.5
harbor 1009.6
ROAD 461.22
roadbed 383.7
roadblock 1012.5
road hog driver 178.10
self-seeker 651.3
roadhouse inn 228.15
entertainment 743.13
road map 574.10
road racing 744.1
road-test 942.8
the road to ruin 395.1
road warrior 730.4
roadwork 84.2
roadworthy 1007.7
roam
n wandering 177.3
v wander 177.23
roan
n horse 311.11
adj reddish-brown 40.4
roar
n noise 53.3
boom 56.4
cry 59.1

v be noisy 53.9
boom 56.9
cry 59.6
animal sound 60.2
laugh 116.8
sigh 318.21
speak 524.25
rage 671.11
overact 704.31
roaring
thundering 56.12
frenzied 105.25
roaring drunk 88.33
roaring fire 1019.13
roaring forties
zone 231.3
prevailing wind 318.10
Roaring Twenties 824.5
roast
n dish 10.7
meat 10.13
celebration 487.1
v cook 11.5
be disrespectful 156.6
banter 490.6
ridicule 508.8
criticize 510.20
grill 938.22
be hot 1019.22
adj cooked 11.7
roast beef 10.14
roaster poultry 311.29
hot day 1019.8
rob
n semiliquid 1062.5
v commit robbery 482.14
robbed of 473.8
robber thief 483.1
holdup man 483.5
robber baron 730.1
robbery loss 473.1
theft 482.3
robe
n garment 5.3
blanket 295.10
frock 702.2
v clothe 5.39
Robin Hood
philanthropist 143.8
thief 483.11
robot 1041.12
robot factory
plant 739.3
control system 1041.5
robotics 1042.2
robotization
automation 1041.1
automatic control 1041.3
robotlike 781.5
rob Peter to pay Paul 862.4
robust strong 15.15
energetic 17.13
hale 83.12
rock
n symbol of strength 15.8
dose 87.20
missile 462.18
rock-and-roll 708.10
stability 855.6
swing 916.6
flounder 917.8

protector 1008.5
hardness 1046.6
stone 1059.1
v impress 93.15
agitate 105.14
pitch 182.55
calm 670.7
oscillate 916.10
flounder 917.15
adj instrumental 708.51
stone 1059.11
rock bottom
bottom 199.1
foundation 901.6
rockbound
rugged 288.7
firm 425.7
rockbound coast
shore 234.2
hidden danger 1006.5
rock climber 193.6
rocker refinery 79.13
marvel 122.2
engraving tool 713.8
oscillator 916.9
rocket
n swiftness 174.6
rocket plane 181.4
ascent 193.7
projectile 462.18
signal 517.15
rocketry 1074.1
rocket engine 1074.2
missile 1074.3
spacecraft 1075.2
v shoot up 193.9
skyrocket 1074.12
rocket engine
rocket 1074.2
atomic power plant 1075.4
rocket fuel 87.18
rocket launcher
launcher 462.21
projector 1074.10
rocket propulsion
propulsion 184.25
reaction propulsion 1074.8
rocketry
ballistics 462.3
missile science 1074.1
space travel 1075.1
rocket scientist
talented person 413.12
intellectual 929.1
rocketeer 1074.11
rock-fill dam 1012.5
rock-hard
unyielding 361.9
hard 1046.10
the Rockies 231.7
rockiness 85.1
rocking
tranquilizing 670.15
swinging 916.17
rocking chair 916.9
rocking horse 743.16
rocklike
unyielding 361.9
stable 855.12
hard 1046.10
stony 1059.12

rock music 708.10
rock'n'roll 708.10
Rock of Gibraltar 855.6
rock pile 604.2
rocks genitals 2.13
money 728.2
hidden danger 1006.5
rock-steady 129.2
rock the boat 868.4
rock to sleep
put to sleep 22.20
calm 670.7
rocky
unsteady 16.16
tired 21.7
ill 85.56
rugged 288.7
unsafe 1006.11
hard 1046.10
stony 1059.12
rococo
n ornateness 498.2
adj ornate 498.12
freakish 870.13
fanciful 986.20
rod shaft 273.1
scepter 417.9
gun 462.10
stick 605.2
royal insignia 647.3
nuclear reactor 1038.13
rodent
n creature 311.3
adj rodential 311.45
rodeo 770.1
rodlike 1046.11
roe fish 10.24
female animal 77.10
egg 305.15
hoofed animal 311.5
Roger 332.19
Roget's
vocabulary 526.13
reference book 554.9
dictionary 871.4
rogue horse 311.12
mischief-maker 322.3
rascal 660.3
jockey 757.2
rogues' gallery 714.3
roil
n agitation 917.1
opaqueness 1031.1
v annoy 96.13
provoke 152.24
riot 810.10
seethe 915.12
agitate 917.10
role function 387.5
part 704.10
script 706.3
occupation 724.3
mode 765.4
role model
paragon 659.4
ideal 786.4
standard of perfection 1002.4
role-player 357.1
role-playing 704.8
roll
n bun 10.31

staccato 55.1
boom 56.4
gait 177.12
barrel roll 184.14
wave 238.14
a length 267.2
coil 281.2
cylinder 282.4
record 549.1
document 549.5
film 714.10
bankroll 728.17
throw 759.9
bundle 770.8
roster 871.6
rotation 915.1
swing 916.6
flounder 917.8
v reverberate 54.7
drum 55.4
boom 56.9
bird sound 60.5
progress 162.2
travel 177.18
way of walking 177.28
pitch 182.55
maneuver 184.40
level 201.6
billow 238.22
ball 282.7
smooth 287.5
press 287.6
rob 482.16
push 904.9
trundle 915.10
wallow 915.13
oscillate 916.10
flounder 917.15
go easily 1014.10
roll around 850.5
rollback
regression 163.1
curtailment 252.4
discount 631.1
economizing 635.2
roll back reduce 252.7
retrench 635.5
roll bar 756.1
roll call
legislative procedure 613.6
roll 871.6
rolled into one 872.10
roller dressing 86.33
billow 238.14
cylinder 282.4
smoother 287.4
game 745.3
rotator 915.4
wave 916.4
pulverizer 1051.7
rollerblade 177.35
roller coaster 743.15
roller-skate 177.35
roller skates 179.21
rollick
n frolic 743.5
v rejoice 116.5
bluster 503.3
play 743.23
roll in arrive 186.6
indulge 669.4

roll-in 749.6
rolling
n progression 162.1
maneuvers 184.13
throwing 904.2
rotation 915.1
television reception 1035.5
adj resonant 54.10
thundering 56.12
hilly 237.8
knobby 272.18
wavy 281.10
rotating 915.14
swinging 916.17
rolling pin 282.4
rolling stone
wanderer 178.2
changeableness 854.4
rotator 915.4
roll in the aisles 116.8
roll into one
put together 800.5
combine 805.3
roll it 818.7
roll of the dice 759.2
roll on march on 162.3
travel 177.18
elapse 821.5
roll out get up 23.6
manifest 348.5
roll out the red carpet
pay homage to 155.5
receive 187.10
welcome 585.9
honor 646.8
roll over 729.17
roll over and play dead 354.20
Rolls-Royce 249.4
roll up one's sleeves
prepare oneself 405.13
set to work 725.15
roll with the punches
keep cool 106.9
accept 134.7
Rolodex 871.7
roly-poly
n heavyweight 257.12
adj corpulent 257.18
roman 548.6
Roman calendar 832.8
Roman candle 517.15
Roman Catholic
n Catholic 675.19
adj Catholic 675.29
romance
n love affair 104.6
fabrication 354.10
figment of the imagination
986.5
idealism 986.7
v narrate 722.6
idealize 986.16
Roman Christianity 675.7
Romanism 675.8
romanization 546.5
Roman numerals 1017.4
romantic
n visionary 986.13
adj sentimental 93.21
loving 104.27
fictional 722.7

visionary 986.24
Romeo 104.13
Romeo and Juliet 104.18
Rome wasn't built in a day
　134.13
romp
　n mannish female 76.9
　schoolgirl 302.8
　victory 411.1
　frolic 743.5
　horse race 757.3
　v exude cheerfulness 109.6
　rejoice 116.5
　caper 366.6
　play 743.23
rompers 5.30
roof
　n top 198.1
　abode 228.1
　home 228.2
　house 228.5
　roofing 295.6
　v top 295.21
rook
　n chessman 743.17
　cheater 759.22
　v deceive 356.19
　cheat 759.26
rookery sty 80.11
　birdhouse 228.23
　birthplace 886.8
rookie recruit 461.18
　novice 572.9
　newcomer 774.4
　beginner 818.2
room
　n latitude 158.3
　compartment 197
　chamber 197.1
　interval 224.1
　quarters 228.4
　capacity 257.2
　latitude 430.4
　opportunity 843.2
　v inhabit 225.7
　house 225.10
room and board 385.3
roomer lodger 227.8
　tenant 470.4
rooming house 228.15
roommate 588.3
room temperature 1019.3
roomy
　comfortable 121.11
　spacious 158.11
　broad 269.6
　airy 317.12
roorback 552.6
roost
　n birdhouse 228.23
　v settle 159.17
　sit 173.10
　inhabit 225.7
rooster
　male animal 76.8
　poultry 311.29
root
　n plant root 310.22
　etymon 526.2
　morphology 526.3
　source 886.5

foundation 901.6
　v vegetate 310.34
　encourage 492.16
　applaud 509.10
　fix 855.9
　lodge 855.10
　search 938.31
root around 938.22
rooted
　confirmed 373.18
　innate 767.8
　traditional 842.12
　established 855.13
rooter enthusiast 101.5
　commender 509.8
rooting out 395.6
root of all evil 728.1
root out dislodge 160.6
　excise 255.10
　exterminate 395.14
　eliminate 773.5
　search out 938.34
rope
　n cigar 89.4
　cord 271.2
　latitude 430.4
　hanging 604.7
　execution 605.5
　game 745.3
　v restrain 428.10
　catch 480.17
　bind 800.9
roped off 429.20
rope enough to hang oneself
　430.4
rope in deceive 356.19
　lure 377.5
rope ladder 193.4
rope off
　circumscribe 210.4
　quarantine 429.13
ropes 894.3
rosary 696.4
rose
　n pinkness 41.2
　nozzle 239.9
　insignia 647.1
　heraldry 647.2
　adj pink 41.8
Rose Bowl 746.1
rose-colored glasses
　optimism 124.3
　idealism 986.7
rosé wine 88.17
rosin
　n gum 1057.1
　v resin 1057.2
roster record 549.1
　baseball team 745.2
　football team 746.2
　basketball team 747.2
　roll 871.6
　schedule 965.3
rostrum prow 216.3
　nose 283.8
　pulpit 703.13
　platform 901.13
rosy pink 41.8
　red-complexioned 41.9
　fresh 83.13
　cheerful 109.11

optimistic 124.12
　thriving 1010.13
rot
　n filth 80.7
　disease 85.41
　rottenness 393.7
　bull 520.3
　blight 1001.2
　v decay 393.22
rota 549.1
rotary flowing 172.8
　periodic 850.7
　circuitous 914.7
　rotational 915.15
rotate move 172.5
　take off 184.38
　invert 205.5
　recur 850.5
　revolve 915.9
rote 989.4
rotgut 88.14
rotor propeller 904.6
　rotator 915.4
rotten unsound 16.15
　nasty 64.7
　malodorous 71.5
　filthy 80.23
　horrid 98.19
　decayed 393.40
　dishonest 645.16
　corrupt 654.14
rotten egg 71.3
rotten luck
　chance 972.1
　ill fortune 1011.5
rotund
　corpulent 257.18
　round 282.8
　convex 283.13
rouge
　n makeup 1016.12
　v make red 41.4
rough
　n roughness 288.2
　diagram 381.3
　combatant 461.1
　vulgarian 497.6
　ruffian 593.3
　golf 751.1
　v roughen 288.4
　mistreat 389.5
　adj acrimonious
　　17.14
　raucous 58.15
　bitter 64.6
　pungent 68.6
　harsh 144.24
　flowing 238.24
　unsmooth 288.6
　coarse 294.6
　undeveloped 406.12
　vulgar 497.11
　gruff 505.7
　violent 671.16
　boisterous 671.20
　nonuniform 782.3
　irregular 851.3
　jolting 917.20
　difficult 1013.17
　adv roughly 288.11
roughage 7.3

rough-and-ready
　unprepared 406.8
　unrefined 497.12
rough-and-tumble
　n commotion 810.4
　adj boisterous 671.20
rough-hew 288.4
roughhouse
　n misbehavior 322.1
　commotion 810.4
　v misbehave 322.4
　create disorder 810.11
rough idea 784.3
rough it 225.11
roughly speaking
　approximately 223.23
　generally 864.17
roughneck
　n vulgarian 497.6
　ruffian 593.3
　adj boorish 497.13
rough sketch 942.2
rough up
　roughen 288.4
　mistreat 389.5
　injure 393.13
　punish 604.15
　beat 902.17
roulette 759.12
round
　n drink 88.7
　step 193.5
　sphere 231.2
　degree 245.1
　circle 280.2
　music 280.9
　routine 373.5
　route 383.1
　rondo 708.19
　occupation 724.4
　18 holes 751.3
　fight 754.3
　series 812.2
　turn 825.2
　revolution 850.3
　circuit 914.2
　whirl 915.2
　v turn round 163.9
　curve 279.6
　encircle 280.10
　round out 282.6
　circle 914.5
　turn 914.6
　rotate 915.9
　number 1017.17
　adj circular 280.11
　rotund 282.8
　elegant 533.6
　candid 644.17
　full 794.11
　circuitous 914.7
　adv about 209.12
　around 915.16
roundhouse
　garage 197.27
　repair shop 739.5
rounding out 407.2
round of applause 509.2
round off
　complete 407.6
　number 1017.17

prohibit 444.3
make impossible 967.6
prevent 1012.14
ruler superior 249.4
straightedge 277.3
governor 575.6
potentate 575.8
rod 605.2
rule the roost 612.15
rule with an iron fist 612.16
ruling
n decree 420.4
law 673.3
verdict 946.5
adj powerful 18.12
chief 249.14
authoritative 417.15
governing 612.18
prevalent 864.12
influential 894.14
ruling class
the best 249.5
mastership 417.7
the authorities 575.15
upper class 607.2
rum
n spirits 88.13
adj odd 870.11
excellent 999.13
rumble
n audio distortion 50.13
noise 53.4
reverberation 54.2
boom 56.4
fight 457.4
report 552.6
v reverberate 54.7
boom 56.9
speak 524.25
rumble seat 217.1
ruminant 931.21
ruminate chew 8.27
consider 931.12
rummage
n search 938.15
v ransack 938.33
rummage sale 734.3
rumor
n report 552.6
v publish 352.10
report 552.11
rump buttocks 217.4
remainder 256.1
rumple
n wrinkle 291.3
v ruffle 288.5
wrinkle 291.3
disarrange 811.2
agitate 917.10
rumpus
n noise 53.4
quarrel 456.6
turbulence 671.2
commotion 810.4
v be noisy 53.9
rumpus room 197.12
rumrunner 732.5
run
n trauma 85.38
direction 161.1
course 172.2

sprint 174.3
migration 177.4
journey 177.5
voyage 182.6
flight 184.9
lair 228.26
stream 238.1
flow 238.4
average 246.1
a length 267.2
routine 373.5
route 383.1
path 383.2
freedom 430.1
race 457.12
engagement 704.11
impromptu 708.27
ornament 709.18
home run 745.3
round 751.3
series 812.2
continuance 856.1
generality 864.3
amount made 893.4
trend 896.2
v fester 12.15
exercise 84.4
extend 158.9
move 172.5
speed 174.8
travel 177.18
migrate 177.22
navigate 182.13
pilot 182.14
sail before the wind 182.22
float 182.54
meet 223.11
flow 238.16
flee 368.10
nominate 371.19
hunt 382.9
injure 393.13
make haste 401.5
print 548.14
direct 573.8
guide 573.9
run for office 609.39
go into politics 610.13
smuggle 732.8
play 746.5
ski 753.4
race 757.5
elapse 821.5
endure 827.6
operate 889.5
be operative 889.7
incur 897.4
thrust 902.12
corner 1013.16
melt 1020.21
computerize 1042.21
liquefy 1064.5
raise 1070.6
runabout 178.2
run across
meet 223.11
come across 941.3
run afoul of 457.15
run aground
shipwreck 182.42
come to grief 1011.10

run amok
go berserk 671.15
riot 810.10
be insane 926.20
the runaround
avoidance 368.1
circumvention 415.5
**run around like a chicken
with its head cut off**
be excitable 105.16
bustle 330.12
run a temperature
take sick 85.47
get excited 105.17
run a tight ship 425.4
runaway
n fugitive 368.5
adj fugitive 368.16
escaped 369.11
run away
run along 188.12
flee 368.10
run circles around
outdo 249.9
defeat 412.9
run counter to
deny 335.4
oppose 451.3
go contrary to 779.4
counteract 900.6
run down
burn out 21.5
fail 85.48
quiet 173.8
sail into 182.41
decline 393.17
arrest 429.15
capture 480.18
disparage 512.8
run over 910.7
trace 938.35
discover 941.2
underestimate 950.2
run-down tired 21.7
unhealthy 85.54
dilapidated 393.33
worn-out 393.36
run dry 388.4
run for it 368.10
run for one's life
run off 188.12
flee 368.10
run for one's money 457.2
run from 182.36
rung step 193.5
degree 245.1
run in sail into 182.41
thrust in 191.7
interpose 213.6
arrest 429.16
capture 480.18
visit 582.19
run-in
n quarrel 456.6
adj accustomed
373.15
run in circles
be impotent 19.7
be useless 391.8
run in opposition to 779.4
run in pursuit of 382.8

run interference for
back 449.13
facilitate 1014.7
run in the family 767.6
run into total 792.8
sail into 182.41
meet 223.11
cost 630.13
be converted into 858.17
collide 902.13
come across 941.3
run into a brick wall 857.7
run into debt
borrow 621.3
go in debt 623.6
run into the ground 993.10
run it by again 849.7
run its course
come to an end 820.6
elapse 821.5
**run it up the flagpole and see
who salutes** 942.8
run neck and neck 174.14
runner speeder 174.5
sled 179.20
channel 239.4
branch 310.20
messenger 353.1
smuggler 732.5
jockey 757.2
member 793.4
runner-up 411.2
running
n pus 12.6
exercise 84.2
motion 172.1
direction 573.1
supervision 573.2
candidacy 609.10
operation 889.1
melting 1020.3
liquefaction 1064.1
adj flowing 172.8
fast 174.15
pouring 238.24
cursive 547.22
continuous 812.8
present 838.2
prevalent 864.12
operating 889.11
adv consecutively
812.11
running away
absence 222.4
flight 368.4
running back 746.2
running commentary 556.2
running head
label 517.13
caption 937.2
running mate 610.9
running sore 1001.1
running start
advantage 249.2
beginning 818.1
earliness 845.1
running wild 926.30
runny exudative 190.20
fluid 1061.4
runoff outflow 190.4
election 609.15

run off
run along 188.12
flee 368.10
print 548.14
drive out 909.14
run off at the mouth
talk nonsense 520.5
chatter 540.5
persist 856.5
run off with
steal 482.13
abduct 482.20
run of luck
chance 972.1
stroke of luck 1010.3
run of the mill
average 864.3
mediocre 1005.8
run on march on 162.3
chatter 540.5
continue 812.4
elapse 821.5
endure 827.6
continue 856.3
run out
v burn out 21.5
exit 190.12
empty 190.13
find vent 369.10
be consumed 388.4
perish 395.23
protract 538.8
come to an end 820.6
elapse 821.5
eject 909.13
drive out 909.14
adj past 837.7
obsolete 842.15
run out of gas
weaken 16.9
stall 410.16
flop 704.28
fall short 911.2
run out on 370.5
run over
overflow 238.17
browse 570.13
iterate 849.8
overrun 910.7
think over 931.13
examine 938.24
abound 991.5
number 1017.17
run parallel to 899.3
run ragged 21.8
run rings around
outdo 249.9
defeat 412.9
run riot revolt 327.7
dissipate 669.6
run amok 671.15
riot 810.10
overspread 910.5
superabound 993.8
run roughshod over 412.10
runs 12.2
run scared 491.8
run short of 992.7
run smoothly 1014.10
runt shrimp 258.4
a nobody 998.7

run the gauntlet 492.11
run the risk
chance 759.24
be liable 897.3
take chances 1006.7
run through
pervade 221.7
perforate 292.15
stab 459.25
squander 486.3
browse 570.13
spend 626.5
rehearse 704.32
run-through
summary 557.2
production 704.13
examination 938.3
run to extend to 261.6
entreat 440.11
cost 630.13
equal 790.5
total 792.8
run together 169.2
run to seed
v waste 393.19
go to ruin 395.24
go to waste 473.6
fall on evil days 1011.11
adj stricken in years 303.18
out of practice 414.18
wasted 486.9
run true to form 781.3
run up grow 251.6
improvise 365.8
go before 816.3
produce 892.8
run-up
preparation 405.1
precedence 814.1
curtain-raiser 816.2
forethought 961.2
run up against
meet 223.11
experience 831.8
come across 941.3
run up a tab 623.6
runway taxiway 184.23
path 383.2
runway lights 184.19
run with the pack 332.9
rupture
n trauma 85.38
crack 224.2
falling-out 456.4
break 802.4
v cleave 224.4
breach 292.14
injure 393.13
be damaged 393.23
break 802.12
rural rustic 233.6
natural 416.6
agricultural 1069.20
ruralist 227.1
ruse trick 356.6
stratagem 415.3
rush
n substance abuse 87.1
thrill 105.2
excitement 105.3
course 172.2

velocity 174.1
run 174.3
flow 238.4
jet 238.9
grass 310.5
haste 401.1
demand 421.1
attack 459.1
outburst 671.6
prematurity 845.2
trifle 998.5
v speed 174.8
flow 238.16
hasten 401.4
make haste 401.5
charge 459.18
rush hour 293.3
rush to the assistance of
449.11
russet 40.4
Russian Orthodox Church
675.9
rust
n fungus 310.4
decay 393.6
blight 1001.2
v brown 40.2
make red 41.4
corrode 393.21
age 842.9
adj reddish-brown 40.4
red 41.6
the Rust Belt 231.7
rustbucket 180.1
rustic
n agriculturist 1069.5
adj rural 233.6
plain-speaking 535.3
rustle
n rustling 52.6
v crinkle 52.12
steal 482.13
rustler 483.8
rustle up cook 11.5
improvise 365.8
provide 385.7
make up 405.7
produce 892.8
rustproof 15.20
rusty
reddish-brown 40.4
red 41.6
stricken in years 303.18
unaccustomed 374.4
corroded 393.43
out of practice 414.18
stale 842.14
rut
n sexual desire 75.5
fever of excitement 105.7
pothole 284.3
furrow 290.1
routine 373.5
path 383.2
v lust 75.20
furrow 290.3
ruthless cruel 144.26
pitiless 146.3
savage 671.21
rutted rough 288.6
furrowed 290.4

RV 179.19
S
adj crescent-shaped 279.11
adv south 161.16
s'il vous plaît 440.20
Sabbath
day of rest 20.5
occultism 690.3
holy day 701.12
sabbatical
n vacation 20.3
adj vacational 20.10
saber 459.25
saber rattling 458.11
sable
n blackness 38.1
heraldry 647.2
adj black 38.8
sabotage
n impairment 393.1
fall 395.3
v disable 19.9
undermine 393.15
oppose 451.3
thwart 1012.15
saboteur 357.11
sac 195.2
saccharin 66.2
sack
n bag 195.2
plundering 482.6
baseball 745.1
tackling 746.3
bundle 770.8
v load 159.15
package 212.9
catch 480.17
plunder 482.17
rage 671.11
tackle 746.5
bundle 770.20
dismiss 909.20
the sack sofa 901.19
dismissal 909.5
sackcloth 115.7
sack out sleep 22.14
go to bed 22.18
sacrament 701.3
the Sacrament 701.7
sacred almighty 677.17
holy 685.7
vocal 708.50
sacred cow idol 697.3
important person 997.9
sacred object 701.10
sacred text 682.7
sacrifice
n killing 308.1
loss 473.1
relinquishment 475.1
unselfishness 652.1
oblation 696.7
v kill 308.13
lose 473.4
relinquish 475.3
give away 478.21
be unselfish 652.3
propitiate 696.15
sell 734.8
play 745.5
sacrificial 633.9

sacrilege
  abomination 638.2
  blasphemy 694.2
sacristy 703.9
sacrosanct 685.7
sad soft-colored 35.22
  dark 38.9
  gray 39.4
  pleasureless 96.20
  distressing 98.20
  saddened 112.20
  disgraceful 661.11
  paltry 998.21
  terrible 1000.9
  unfortunate 1011.14
sadden darken 112.18
  move 145.5
saddle
  n ridge 237.5
  authority 417.10
  seat 901.17
  v burden 297.13
  yoke 800.10
  tend 1070.7
saddler 311.13
saddle stitching 554.14
saddle upon 888.4
saddle with add 253.4
  accuse of 599.9
  obligate 641.12
  impose 643.4
  attribute to 888.4
  hamper 1012.11
sadism
  perversion 75.11
  cruelty 144.11
sadist
  sexual pervert 75.16
  tormentor 96.10
  beast 144.14
  punisher 604.8
sadomasochism 75.11
sadomasochist 75.16
sad sack weakling 16.6
  wretch 660.2
  unfortunate 1011.7
safari 177.5
safari park 743.14
safe
  n treasury 729.13
  adj cautious 494.8
  secure 1007.4
  protected 1008.21
safe-conduct 443.7
safecracker 483.3
safe-deposit box 729.13
safeguard
  n pass 443.7
  precaution 494.3
  safety 1007.1
  palladium 1008.3
  bodyguard 1008.14
  v defend 460.8
  protect 1008.18
safe house
  hiding place 346.4
  retreat 1009.5
safekeeping
  storage 386.5
  preservation 397.1
  custody 429.5

protection 1008.1
safe sex 75.7
safety
  football team 746.2
  game 746.3
  security 1007.1
  safeness 1007.1
  protection 1008.1
  safeguard 1008.3
safety belt
  life preserver 397.6
  safeguard 1008.3
safety catch 428.5
safety net
  precaution 494.3
  safeguard 1008.3
safety valve
  outlet 190.9
  precaution 494.3
  safeguard 1008.3
saffron 43.4
sag
  n sinkage 194.2
  hang 202.2
  cheapening 633.4
  declining market 737.5
  v drift off course
    182.29
  sink 194.6
  hang 202.6
  decrease 252.6
  curve 279.6
  cheapen 633.6
saga 719.3
sage
  n master 413.13
  wise man 921.1
  adj wise 920.17
Sahara 891.2
sahib man 76.7
  master 575.1
  Sir 648.3
said speech 524.29
  former 814.5
sail
  n sailboat 180.3
  canvas 180.14
  voyage 182.6
  v glide 177.35
  navigate 182.13
  get under way 182.19
  float 182.54
  fly 184.36
  go easily 1014.10
sailboat 760.2
sailing ship 180.3
sailor traveler 178.1
  mariner 183.1
sailplane
  n glider 181.12
  v fly 184.36
sail through 1014.8
saint
  n holy man 659.6
  celestial being 679.1
  angel 679.1
  religious prophet 684.2
  believer 692.4
  v glorify 662.13
  sanctify 685.5
  ordain 698.12

sainthood
  sanctification 685.3
  godliness 692.2
Saint Nicholas 678.13
sake motive 375.1
  intention 380.1
salaam
  n obeisance 155.2
  crouch 913.3
  v make obeisance 155.6
  bow 913.9
salad food 10.37
  hodgepodge 797.6
salad bar 8.17
salad days 301.1
salamander
  amphibian 311.27
  spirit 678.6
  fire iron 1020.12
salaried worker
  bourgeois 607.6
  worker 726.2
salary
  n pay 624.4
  v pay 624.10
sale transfer 629.1
  selling 734.2
  wholesale 734.1
  closing-out sale 734.3
sales 734.13
salesmanship
  promotion 352.5
  inducement 375.3
  selling 734.2
salesperson 730.3
sales pitch 734.5
salient
  n region 231.1
  protuberance 283.2
  adj protruding 283.14
  conspicuous 348.12
  notable 997.19
saline 68.9
saliva
  digestive juice 2.17
  humor 2.24
  digestion 7.8
  spittle 13.3
salivary glands
  digestion 2.17
  digestive system 2.18
  ingestion 7.8
salivate 13.6
sallow
  v yellow 43.3
  adj colorless 36.7
  yellow 43.4
  yellow-faced 43.6
sally
  n journey 177.5
  attack 459.1
  witticism 489.7
  v set out 188.8
  emerge 190.11
sally forth set out 188.8
  emerge 190.11
salmon
  n marine animal 311.30
  jumper 366.4
  adj pink 41.8
salon parlor 197.5

museum 386.9
  society 578.6
  social gathering 582.10
  market 736.1
  company 770.3
saloon bar 88.20
  parlor 197.5
  cabin 197.9
salsa 10.9
salt
  n saltiness 68.4
  mariner 183.1
  preservative 397.4
  veteran 413.16
  wit 489.1
  v flavor 63.7
  tamper with 354.17
  preserve 397.9
  falsify accounts 628.10
  adj flavored 62.9
  salty 68.9
  witty 489.15
salt-and-pepper 39.4
salt away 386.10
salt flat plain 236.1
  wasteland 891.2
salt-free diet 7.13
saltine 10.30
salt in the wound 96.3
salt of the earth
  person of honor 644.8
  good citizen 659.3
  the best 999.8
salt water ocean 240.1
  water 1065.3
salud! 88.38
salute
  n obeisance 155.2
  celebration 487.1
  greeting 585.4
  v pay homage to 155.5
  greet another ship 182.52
  praise 509.12
  signal 517.22
  address 524.26
  greet 585.10
  interj toast 88.38
salvage
  n reclamation 396.2
  preservation 397.1
  rescue 398.1
  recovery 481.3
  recompense 624.3
  fee 630.6
  v redeem 396.12
  rescue 398.3
salvageable
  remediable 396.25
  rescuable 398.4
salvager
  mender 396.10
  rescuer 398.2
salvation
  reclamation 396.2
  preservation 397.1
  rescue 398.1
  function of Christ 677.14
  redemption 685.4
salve
  n balm 86.11
  gratuity 478.5

moderator 670.3
ointment 1056.3
v medicate 91.25
relieve 120.5
redeem 396.12
oil 1056.8
salvo detonation 56.3
volley 459.9
celebration 487.1
shot 904.4
qualification 959.1
Samaritan 592.1
same identical 778.7
uniform 781.6
former 814.5
same old story 837.2
same old thing
tedium 118.1
regularity 781.2
sample
n taste 62.4
specimen 786.3
part 793.1
feeler 942.4
subject 942.7
v taste 62.7
canvass 938.29
experiment 942.8
adj typical 349.15
sampler 938.16
Samson 15.6
samurai 608.3
sanctify
glorify 662.13
hallow 685.5
sanctimonious
hypocritical 354.33
prudish 500.19
zealous 692.11
self-righteous 693.5
sanction
n ratification 332.4
consent 441.1
authorization 443.3
approval 509.1
legalization 673.2
v ratify 332.12
consent 441.2
authorize 443.11
approve 509.9
legalize 673.9
sanctioned
authorized 443.17
legal 673.11
sanctity sacredness 685.1
sanctitude 685.1
godliness 692.2
sanctuary
hiding place 346.4
preserve 397.7
holy of holies 703.5
refuge 1009.1
sanctum
sanctum sanctorum 197.8
retreat 584.6
sanctuary 703.5
refuge 1009.5
sand
n grain 1051.6
grain of sand 1059.2
v grind 287.8

buff 1044.8
sandalwood 70.4
sandbag
n weight 297.6
v weight 297.12
defeat 412.9
attack 459.15
bet 759.25
beat 902.17
club 902.20
sandbagger 483.5
sandbar island 235.2
shoal 276.2
hidden danger 1006.5
sand 1059.2
sandblast grind 287.8
buff 1044.8
a sand castle 16.7
sand dune hill 237.4
sand 1059.2
sandhog 284.10
sanding 1044.2
sandman 22.11
sandpaper
n roughness 288.2
v grind 287.8
buff 1044.8
sands shore 234.2
hidden danger 1006.5
sands of time 821.3
sandstone 1059.1
sandstorm 318.13
sand trap 751.1
sandwich
n food 10.32
v interpose 213.6
sandwich board 352.7
sandy yellow 43.4
granular 1051.12
stony 1059.12
dry 1066.7
sane intelligent 920.12
sensible 920.18
sane-minded 925.4
logical 935.20
realistic 987.6
sanguine
n personality type 92.12
adj sanguineous 41.7
red-complexioned 41.9
cheerful 109.11
hopeful 124.11
expectant 130.11
sanitary hygienic 79.27
healthful 81.5
sanitary landfill
receptacle of filth
80.12
derelict 370.4
trash pile 391.6
sanitation
cleansing 79.3
hygiene 81.2
sanity
intelligence 920.1
sensibleness 920.6
saneness 925.1
sans absent 222.19
without 992.17
sans serif 548.6
sans souci 107.7

Santa Claus
giver 478.11
cheerful giver 485.2
Santa 678.13
sap
n essential content 196.5
dupe 358.2
entrenchment 460.5
essence 767.2
fool 924.3
fluid 1061.2
v weaken 16.10
excavate 284.15
undermine 393.15
overthrow 395.20
spiritualize 764.4
sapient 920.19
sapling
youngster 302.1
sprout 302.11
tree 310.10
sapphire 45.3
sappy
sentimental 93.21
immature 301.10
foolish 923.9
fluid 1061.4
sarcasm wit 489.1
irony 508.5
sarcoma 85.39
sarcophagus 309.11
sardonic 508.13
sardonic grin
smile 116.3
scornful laugh 508.4
sartorial
clothing 5.45
tailored 5.48
sash waistband 5.19
frame 266.4
sashay travel 177.18
way of walking 177.28
sass
n back talk 142.4
v talk back 142.8
sassy 142.10
Satan demon 680.6
liar 357.9
the Devil 680.3
nether world deity 682.5
satanic cruel 144.26
diabolic 654.13
demoniac 680.17
execrable 1000.10
Satanist 680.15
sate gratify 95.8
satiate 994.4
sated languid 331.20
satiated 994.6
satellite
hanger-on 138.6
follower 166.2
country 232.1
dependent 432.6
disciple 616.8
escort 769.5
moon 1072.11
artificial satellite 1075.6
satellite communication 347.1
satellite television 1035.1
satiety 107.1

satin
n smooth surface
287.3
fine texture 294.3
softness 1047.4
adj smooth 294.8
satire wit 489.1
sarcasm 508.5
burlesque 508.6
lampoon 512.5
satirist
humorist 489.12
lampooner 512.7
poet 720.11
satirize
burlesque 508.11
lampoon 512.12
satisfaction
pleasure 95.1
contentment 107.1
compensation 338.1
reparation 396.6
observance 434.1
duel 457.7
restitution 481.2
payment 624.1
recompense 624.3
atonement 658.1
sufficiency 991.1
satiety 994.1
satisfactory
satisfying 107.11
convincing 953.26
sufficient 991.6
tolerable 999.20
satisfy feed 8.18
gratify 95.8
content 107.4
indulge 427.6
observe 434.2
pay 624.10
pay in full 624.13
atone 658.4
convince 953.18
suffice 991.4
satiate 994.4
satisfying 97.6
saturate fill 794.7
imbue 797.11
overload 993.15
satiate 994.4
soak 1065.13
saturated fat 1056.1
saturation
colorfulness 35.4
color quality 35.6
fullness 794.2
imbuement 797.2
overfullness 993.3
satiety 994.1
soaking 1065.7
saturation point
fullness 794.2
satiety 994.1
radiation 1037.1
saturation raid 459.4
Saturn 1072.9
satyr
sexual pervert 75.16
lecher 665.11
forest god 678.11

sauce
n cooking 11.1
liquor 88.14
back talk 142.4
hodgepodge 797.6
admixture 797.7
pulp 1063.2
v flavor 63.7
talk back 142.8
saucer tableware 8.12
circle 280.2
saucer eyes
optic part 2.9
eye 27.9
defect 28.6
saucer-shaped
parabolic 279.13
concave 284.16
saucy impudent 142.10
defiant 454.7
sauna bath 79.8
bathing place 79.10
saunter
n slow motion 175.2
walk 177.10
gait 177.12
v go slowly 175.6
wander 177.23
way of walking 177.28
sausage 10.21
sausage meat 10.13
sauté brown 40.2
cook 11.5
savable 398.4
savage
n barbarian 497.7
brute 593.5
violent person 671.9
v torture 96.18
mistreat 389.5
injure 393.13
rage 671.11
work evil 1000.6
adj cruel 144.26
pitiless 146.3
infuriated 152.32
deadly 308.23
warlike 458.21
unrefined 497.12
fierce 671.21
savagery cruelty 144.11
unrefinement 497.3
violence 671.1
unenlightenment 930.4
savanna
horizontal 201.3
the country 233.1
plain 236.1
grassland 310.8
savant expert 413.11
specialist 866.3
wise man 921.1
scientist 928.11
scholar 929.3
save
n soccer action 752.3
v store up 386.11
reserve 386.12
not use 390.5
preserve 397.8
rescue 398.3

aid 449.11
retain 474.5
economize 635.4
redeem 685.6
stop from scoring 752.4
be conservative 853.6
play safe 1007.3
prevent 1012.14
prep off 255.14
excluding 773.10
conj unless 959.16
save-all
n niggard 484.4
adj stingy 484.9
the saved 692.5
saved soul 679.1
save face 136.7
save for a rainy day
reserve 386.12
economize 635.4
save one's neck
rescue 398.3
benefit 592.3
be safe 1007.2
save the day 592.3
save your breath! 51.14
saving grace
extenuation 600.5
characteristic 865.4
savings reserve 386.3
funds 728.14
savings account
account 622.2
funds 728.14
savings institution
lending institution 620.4
bank 729.14
savior preserver 397.5
rescuer 398.2
redeemer 592.2
savoir-faire skill 413.1
mannerliness 504.3
savor
n taste 62.1
relish 63.2
odor 69.1
passion 93.2
characteristic 865.4
v eat 8.20
taste 62.7
relish 63.5
flavor 63.7
enjoy 95.13
savory
n food 10.8
adj edible 8.33
flavored 62.9
tasty 63.8
fragrant 70.9
delectable 97.10
savvy
n skill 413.1
smartness 920.2
understanding 928.3
discrimination 944.1
v understand 521.7
know 928.12
saw
n notching 289.2
maxim 974.1
platitude 974.3

cutlery 1040.2
v fiddle 708.41
sever 802.11
sawbones doctor 90.4
surgeon 90.5
sawbuck money 728.7
trestle 901.16
sawdust
remainder 256.1
powder 1051.5
sawed-off 258.13
sawhorse 901.16
sawmill 739.3
sawtooth
n projection 285.4
adj angular 278.6
rugged 288.7
saw wood 22.13
saxophonist 710.4
say
n supremacy 249.3
affirmation 334.1
vote 371.6
authority 417.1
free will 430.6
remark 524.3
speech 543.2
turn 825.2
influence 894.1
v take leave 188.16
affirm 334.5
announce 352.12
utter 524.22
state 524.23
answer 939.4
suppose 951.10
adv approximately 223.23
say again 849.7
say a good word for 509.11
say amen to 332.12
say a mouthful 973.10
say a word to the wise 399.5
say aye 441.2
say goodbye to 370.5
say hello 585.10
say in a roundabout way
prevaricate 344.7
circumlocute 538.10
go roundabout 914.4
say in defense 600.10
saying
affirmation 334.1
remark 524.3
maxim 974.1
say in reply 939.4
say it all 1017.19
say loud and clear
affirm 334.5
speak up 524.21
say no refuse 442.3
restrain oneself 668.6
say nothing 51.6
sayonara! 188.22
say one's prayers 696.13
say out loud
affirm 334.5
speak up 524.21
say over and over 849.10
say right to one's face 454.3
say-so
affirmation 334.1

command 420.1
free will 430.6
administration 573.3
influence 894.1
say the word
command 420.8
permit 443.9
say to oneself 542.3
say uncle flinch 127.13
lose 412.12
surrender 433.8
say under one's breath 345.9
say what one thinks 644.12
say yes 441.2
scab
n sore 85.37
crust 295.14
strikebreaker 727.8
blemish 1004.1
v crust 295.27
break a strike 727.11
blemish 1004.4
scabies 85.41
scads lot 247.4
plenty 991.2
scaffold
execution 605.5
scaffolding 901.12
scalawag horse 311.12
rascal 660.3
scald
n trauma 85.38
burn 1020.6
v injure 393.13
be hot 1019.22
scalding 1019.25
scale
n range 158.2
map 159.5
ladder 193.4
step 193.5
degree 245.1
size 257.1
blanket 295.12
crust 295.14
flake 296.3
weighing 297.9
measure 300.2
gamut 709.6
break 802.4
series 812.2
v flake 6.11
climb 193.11
layer 296.5
raid 459.20
break 802.12
scale down
n make small 258.9
v reduce 252.7
scales of justice 649.1
scale up 259.4
scaling raid 459.4
disruption 802.3
scallop
n notching 289.2
v cook 11.5
convolve 281.4
notch 289.4
scalloped cooked 11.7
notched 289.5
scalp peel 6.8

trade 737.23
scalper salesman 730.3
  speculator 737.11
scaly flaky 296.7
  powdery 1051.11
scam
  n deception 356.9
  cheating 759.13
  v deceive 356.14
  swindle 356.19
scamp
  n mischief-maker 322.3
  rascal 660.3
  v slight 340.8
  stint 484.5
scamper
  n run 174.3
  haste 401.1
  v speed 174.8
  hasten off 188.10
  make haste 401.5
scan
  n field of view 31.3
  examination 938.3
  v browse 570.13
  rhyme 720.14
  itemize 801.7
  examine 938.24
  examine cursorily 938.26
  receive 1036.17
scandal slander 512.3
  gossip 552.8
  abomination 638.2
  iniquity 654.3
  disgrace 661.5
  immodesty 666.2
scandalize 661.7
scandalmonger 552.9
scandal sheet 555.2
scanner 1042.4
scanning
  n metrics 720.6
  televising 1035.3
  radar 1036.8
  adj metric 720.16
scant
  v limit 210.5
  stint 484.5
  adj narrow 270.14
  incomplete 795.4
  sparse 885.5
  meager 992.10
scantily clad 6.13
scanty narrow 270.14
  incomplete 795.4
  sparse 885.5
  meager 992.10
  scarce 992.11
scapegoat
  sacrifice 696.7
  whipping boy 862.3
  oddity 870.4
scar
  n precipice 200.3
  slope 237.2
  mark 517.5
  blemish 1004.1
  v mark 517.19
  blemish 1004.4
scarab 691.5
scarce infrequent 848.2

in short supply 885.5
  sparse 992.11
scarcely any 885.4
scarcely to be expected 969.3
scarcity
  infrequency 848.1
  fewness 885.1
  underproduction 892.5
  scarceness 992.3
scare
  n fear 127.1
  v frighten 127.15
scarecrow figure 349.6
  eyesore 1015.4
scared to death
  afraid 127.22
  terrified 127.26
scare off 379.3
scare tactics
  terrorization 127.7
  coercion 424.3
  threat 514.1
scare up 472.9
scarf
  n food 10.2
  joint 800.4
  v hook 800.8
scarlet red 41.6
  prostitute 665.28
scarp precipice 200.3
  incline 204.4
  slope 237.2
scary fearful 127.23
  frightening 127.28
scat! 909.31
scathe
  n impairment 393.1
  v criticize 510.20
  work evil 1000.6
scathing
  acrimonious 17.14
  caustic 144.23
scatter
  n deflection 164.2
  rarity 299.1
  dispersion 771.1
  v deflect 164.5
  radiate 171.6
  interspace 224.3
  rarefy 299.3
  overwhelm 412.8
  squander 486.3
  disperse 771.4
  disband 771.8
  shatter 802.13
  part company 802.19
  loosen 804.3
  disarrange 811.2
scatterbrain
  frivolous person 924.7
  flightiness 985.5
scatter to the winds
  squander 486.3
  disperse 771.4
scavenge 79.18
scavenger
  sweeper 79.16
  creature 311.3
scenario project 381.2
  playbook 704.21
  script 706.3

effect 887.1
  solution 940.1
scene look 27.3
  view 33.6
  outburst 152.9
  setting 209.2
  arena 463.1
  act 704.7
  scenery 704.20
  landscape 712.12
scenery view 33.6
  arena 463.1
  decor 704.20
scent
  n odor 69.1
  sense of smell 69.4
  fragrance 70.1
  perfumery 70.2
  track 517.8
  clue 517.9
  hint 551.4
  v odorize 69.7
  smell 69.8
  perfume 70.8
  catch the scent of 941.6
scepter rod 417.9
  royal insignia 647.3
schedule
  n plan 381.1
  chronicle 832.9
  list 871.1
  program 965.3
  v plan 381.8
  allot 477.9
  spend 626.5
  list 871.8
  line up 965.6
scheduled
  planned 381.12
  listed 871.9
  slated 965.9
schematic
  diagrammatic 381.14
  analytical 801.9
scheme
  n trick 356.6
  plan 381.1
  project 381.2
  intrigue 381.5
  stratagem 415.3
  plot 722.4
  outline 801.4
  v premeditate 380.7
  plot 381.9
  maneuver 415.10
  plot 839.6
  prearrange 965.4
schism desertion 370.2
  falling-out 456.4
  sect 675.3
schizoid
  n personality type 92.12
  psychotic 926.17
  adj crazy 926.27
  psychotic 926.28
schizophrenia
  mental disorder 92.14
  dissociation 92.20
  dementia praecox 926.4
schizophrenic
  n psychotic 926.17

adj psychotic 926.28
schlep 175.12
schlock 1005.6
schmaltz 93.8
schnapps 88.13
schnoz 283.8
scholar
  student 572.1
  specialist 866.3
  wise man 921.1
  scientist 928.11
  scholastic 929.3
scholarship
  subsidy 478.8
  studiousness 570.4
  fellowship 646.7
  erudition 928.5
scholastic
  n theologian 676.3
  scholar 929.3
  adj institutional 567.13
  academic 568.19
  studious 570.17
  learned 928.21
  book-learned 928.22
school
  n educational institution 567.1
  teaching 568.1
  order 617.5
  sect 675.3
  style 712.8
  group of animals 770.5
  system of belief 953.3
  v teach 568.10
  adj scholastic 567.13
schoolbook book 554.1
  textbook 554.10
schoolboy boy 302.5
  schoolchild 572.3
schoolbus 179.13
schooled 928.18
schoolgirl
  schoolmaid 302.8
  schoolchild 572.3
schoolhouse 567.10
schooling
  teaching 568.1
  learning 928.4
school library 558.1
school of thought 952.1
schoolroom 567.11
schoolteacher 571.1
sciatic 217.10
science art 413.7
  -ology 928.10
science fiction 1075.1
scientific
  technical 928.28
  exact 973.17
  realistic 987.6
scientist 928.11
scintilla hint 248.4
  spark 1019.15
  glitter 1025.7
scintillate joke 489.13
  be brilliant 920.11
  glitter 1025.24
scintillating
  witty 489.15
  smart 920.14

v grate 58.10
tingle 74.5
excavate 284.15
furrow 290.3
misdraw 350.4
injure 393.13
obliterate 395.16
mark 517.19
scribble 547.20
portray 712.19
engrave 713.9
work hard 725.13
end 820.5
cease 857.6
scratchboard 712.18
scratch each other's back 863.4
scratchiness 58.2
scratch pad 549.11
scratch player 751.2
scratch the surface
  give a lick and a promise
  206.6
  touch upon 276.4
  not know 930.11
scrawl
  n illegibility 522.4
  scribbling 547.7
  v scribble 547.20
scrawny lean 270.17
  meager 992.10
scream
  n screech 58.4
  cry 59.1
  lament 115.3
  joke 489.6
  v screech 58.8
  cry 59.6
  animal cry 60.2
  wail 115.13
  wind sound 318.21
  speak 524.25
scream bloody murder
  cry 59.6
  complain 115.16
screamer caption 937.2
  goof 975.6
screaming garish 35.20
  vociferous 59.10
  gaudy 501.20
screaming halt 857.2
screech
  n shriek 58.4
  cry 59.1
  v shriek 58.8
  cry 59.6
  animal sound 60.2
  wind sound 318.21
  speak 524.25
screen
  n refinery 79.13
  network 170.3
  furniture 229.1
  porousness 292.8
  cover 295.2
  veil 346.2
  pretext 376.1
  scenery 704.20
  motion-picture theater 706.7
  arranger 808.5
  safeguard 1008.3
  shade 1028.1

television picture tube
  1035.11
v refine 79.22
cover 295.19
conceal 346.6
defend 460.8
project 714.16
shield 747.4
play 752.4
segregate 773.6
classify 808.11
discriminate 944.4
protect 1008.18
shade 1028.5
screening
  n refinement 79.4
  network 170.3
  covering 295.1
  concealment 346.1
  basketball game 747.3
  grouping 808.3
  adj covering 295.35
  defensive 460.11
  protective 1008.23
  shading 1028.5
screen pass 746.3
screenplay 706.2
screen test 706.5
screenwriter
  dramatist 704.22
  scriptwriter 706.4
screw
  n distortion 265.1
  coil 281.2
  jailer 429.10
  torture 605.4
  propeller 904.6
  v copulate 75.21
  distort 265.5
  convolve 281.4
  deceive 356.19
  mistreat 389.6
  demand 421.5
  wrest 480.22
  stint 484.5
  overprice 632.7
  hook 800.8
  rotate 915.9
screw around 998.15
screwball
  n oddity 870.4
  lunatic 926.16
  freak 927.4
  adj crazy 926.27
  eccentric 927.6
screwed up spoiled 393.29
  botched 414.22
  complex 799.4
  confused 810.16
a screw loose 926.2
screwy foolish 923.9
  crazy 926.27
  eccentric 927.6
scribble
  n bad likeness 350.2
  illegibility 522.4
  scribbling 547.7
  v misdraw 350.4
  scrabble 547.20
scribbler
  hack writer 547.16

writer 718.3
literary hack 718.5
scribe
  n writer 547.13
  author 547.15
  recorder 550.1
  clergy 699.11
  creative writer 718.4
  v write 547.19
scrimmage fight 457.4
  free-for-all 457.5
scrimmage line 746.3
scrimp stint 484.5
  economize 635.4
scrip writing 547.10
  document 549.5
  money 728.1
  paper money 728.5
  token 728.12
script
  representation 349.1
  writing system 546.3
  handwriting 547.3
  writing 547.10
  type 548.6
  document 549.5
  playbook 704.21
  screenplay 706.3
scripture
  sacred texts 683.1
  scriptures 683.1
Scripture 683.2
scriptwriter
  author 547.15
  dramatist 704.22
  screenwriter 706.4
  creative writer 718.4
scroll
  n coil 281.2
  writing 547.10
  manuscript 547.11
  record 549.1
  document 549.5
  rare book 554.6
  violin part 711.5
  roll 871.6
  v write 547.19
scrooge 484.4
scrotum 2.13
scrounge 440.15
scrounging
  n beggary 440.6
  theft 482.1
  adj indolent 331.19
  supplicatory 440.16
scrub
  n washing 79.5
  shrubbery 310.9
  woodland 310.13
  brush 310.16
  a nobody 998.7
  abrasion 1044.2
  v wash 79.19
  cease 857.6
  abrade 1044.7
scrubby
  dwarf 258.13
  arboreal 310.39
  sylvan 310.40
  vulgar 497.15
  base 661.12

paltry 998.21
scrubland 310.13
scruffy dirty 80.22
  shabby 393.32
  base 661.12
  paltry 998.21
scrumptious
  tasty 63.8
  excellent 999.13
scrunch
  n rasp 58.3
  v grate 58.10
  pulverize 1051.9
scruple
  n compunction 113.2
  modicum 248.2
  demur 325.2
  objection 333.2
  conscientiousness 644.2
  doubt 955.2
  v demur 325.4
  object 333.5
  hesitate 362.7
  doubt 955.6
scrupulous
  demurring 325.7
  meticulous 339.12
  observant 434.4
  fastidious 495.9
  punctilious 580.10
  dutiful 641.13
  conscientious 644.15
  doubting 955.9
scrutinize survey 27.14
  examine 938.24
  make a close study of 938.24
  pay attention 983.8
scrutiny overview 27.6
  examination 938.3
  close attention 983.4
scuba 367.5
scuba diver 367.4
scud
  n run 174.3
  rainstorm 316.2
  gust 318.6
  foam 320.2
  v speed 174.8
  float 182.54
scuff
  n trauma 85.38
  abrasion 1044.2
  v way of walking 177.28
  injure 393.13
  abrade 1044.7
scuffle
  n fight 457.4
  struggle 725.3
  v way of walking 177.28
  contend 457.13
  struggle 725.11
scull
  n oar 180.15
  v navigate 182.13
  row 182.53
sculler 183.5
scullery 11.4
scullery maid
  washer 79.15
  maid 577.8
sculpt form 262.7

sculpture 715.5
sculptor
  sculpture 715.1
  artist 716.6
sculpture
  n forming 262.5
  figure 349.6
  visual arts 712.1
  statuary 715
  sculpturing 715.1
  carving 715.2
  v form 262.7
  engrave 713.9
  sculpt 715.5
scum
  n slime 80.8
  offal 80.9
  dregs 256.2
  blanket 295.12
  lamina 296.2
  sperm 305.11
  foam 320.2
  refuse 391.4
  rabble 606.3
  v cover 295.19
  foam 320.5
scum of the earth
  offal 80.9
  rabble 606.3
  the wicked 660.11
scupper 239.5
scurrilous
  caustic 144.23
  insulting 156.8
  disparaging 512.13
  cursing 513.8
  obscene 666.9
S-curve 279.3
scurvy vulgar 497.15
  base 661.12
  paltry 998.21
  terrible 1000.9
scurvy trick 356.6
scuttle
  n run 174.3
  gait 177.12
  porch 189.6
  haste 401.1
  v speed 174.8
  way of walking
    177.28
  capsize 182.44
  sink 367.8
  do for 395.11
  make haste 401.5
  lose one's nerve 491.8
  bankrupt 625.8
scuttlebutt 552.6
scuzzy filthy 80.23
  offensive 98.18
  slovenly 810.15
  paltry 998.21
scythe 279.5
sea wave 238.14
  ocean 240.1
  open water 240.3
  quantity 247.3
sea anchor
  safeguard 1008.3
  curb 1012.7
seabed bed 199.4

ocean depths 275.4
Seabees 461.27
sea bird 311.28
Seabiscuit 311.15
seaboard 234.2
seaborne 182.57
sea breeze 318.5
sea change 392.1
seacoast 234.2
seafarer 183.1
seafood 10.24
seagoing 182.57
sea ice 1023.5
seal
  n ratification 332.4
  sign 517.1
  print 517.7
  label 517.13
  signature 527.10
  royal insignia 647.3
  engraving tool 713.8
  cast 785.6
  mold 786.6
  characteristic 865.4
  v close 293.6
  ratify 332.12
  resolve 359.7
  sign 437.7
  mark 517.19
  label 517.20
  adj brown 40.3
sea lane seaway 182.10
  route 383.1
sealed close 293.12
  accepted 332.14
  confidential 345.14
  contracted 437.11
  unknown 930.17
sea legs 182.3
sea level 201.3
seal of approval 509.1
seal off close 293.6
  quarantine 429.13
seal one's lips 51.5
seam
  n crack 224.2
  layer 296.1
  joint 800.4
  deposit 1058.7
  v mark 517.19
seamanship
  shipmanship 182.3
  skill 413.1
seamless uniform 781.5
  continuous 812.8
  one 872.7
sea monster 311.30
seamstress
  dressmaker 5.36
  sewer 741.2
seamy 661.10
séance
  conference 541.6
  spiritualism 689.5
  assembly 770.2
sea of grass
  horizontal 201.3
  plain 236.1
seaplane
  n waterplane 181.8
  v fly 184.36

seaport 1009.6
sear
  n burn 1020.6
  v cook 11.5
  shrink 260.9
  languish 393.18
  stain 1004.6
  burn 1020.24
  dry 1066.6
  adj shrunk 260.13
search
  n searching 938.15
  v pursue 382.8
  hunt 938.31
search engine 1042.19
searcher 938.18
search me! 930.19
search warrant 938.15
seascape view 33.6
  scene 712.12
sea serpent 311.30
seashell 295.15
seashore
  n shore 234.2
  adj aquatic 182.58
seasickness 85.30
seaside
  n shore 234.2
  adj coastal 234.7
season
  n time of year 313.1
  period 824.1
  v flavor 63.7
  mature 303.9
  accustom 373.9
  develop 392.10
  preserve 397.9
  imbue 797.11
  be timely 843.6
  qualify 959.3
  harden 1046.7
  toughen 1049.3
seasonable apt 788.10
  timely 843.9
  expedient 995.5
seasonal
  in season 313.9
  periodic 850.7
seasonal affective disorder
  92.14
seasoned zestful 68.7
  mature 303.13
  accustomed 373.15
  ripe 407.13
  experienced 413.28
  wise 920.17
  qualified 959.10
  tempered 1046.15
  toughened 1049.6
seasoning
  flavoring 63.3
  maturation 303.6
  habituation 373.7
  development 392.10
  food preservation 397.2
  preparedness 405.4
  experience 413.9
  admixture 797.7
  hardening 1046.5
seat
  n station 159.2

headquarters 208.6
  abode 228.1
  capital 230.4
  authority 417.10
  foundation 901.6
  chair 901.17
  v place 159.12
  establish 159.16
  fix 855.9
seat belt 1008.3
SEATO 437.2
seat of government 230.4
seat of justice 595.5
Seattle Slew 311.15
seawall
  buttress 901.4
  harbor 1009.6
  barrier 1012.5
seaward
  clockwise 161.24
  oceanward 240.12
seawater 1065.3
seaway 182.10
seaweed 310.4
seaworthy
  sea-kindly 180.18
  snug 1007.7
sebaceous secretory 13.7
  oily 1056.9
secant
  n straight line 277.2
  adj cross 170.8
secede
  n apostatize 363.7
  v revolt 327.7
  dissent 333.4
  defect 370.6
seceder 363.5
secession dissent 333.1
  apostasy 363.2
  desertion 370.2
secluded
  quiescent 173.12
  private 345.13
  concealed 346.11
  seclusive 584.8
  segregated 773.8
seclusion privacy 345.2
  quarantine 429.2
  seclusiveness 583.3
  isolation 584.1
  reclusion 584.1
  exclusiveness 773.3
  aloneness 872.2
second
  n assistant 616.6
  supporter 616.9
  interval 709.20
  second base 745.1
  boxer 754.2
  moment 824.2
  instant 830.3
  irregular 1005.6
  v ratify 332.12
  back 449.13
  adv secondly 874.6
secondary
  n color system 35.7
  inferior 250.2
  subordinate 432.5
  deputy 576.1

nonessential 768.2
substitute 862.2
adj inferior 250.6
unessential 768.4
eventual 831.11
substitute 862.8
unimportant 998.16
secondary disease 85.1
secondary meaning 518.1
secondary product 893.3
secondary school 567.4
secondary smoke 89.1
second banana 704.10
second best 1005.4
second chance 396.3
second childhood
old age 303.5
senility 922.10
second-class 1005.9
second-class citizenship 791.1
second cousin 559.3
second-degree burn
trauma 85.38
burn 1020.6
second down 746.3
second edition 785.5
second estate 607.2
second fiddle
inferiority 250.1
inferior 250.2
subservience 432.2
secondhand
used 387.24
old 842.18
second helping 8.10
second home 228.8
second lieutenant 575.18
second look
repetition 849.1
re-examination 938.7
second mate 183.7
second mortgage 438.4
second nature 373.3
second opinion 946.3
second person 530.7
second prize 646.2
second rank 250.6
second-rate 1005.9
seconds tobacco 89.2
commodity 735.2
second-story thief 483.3
second string
n inferiority 250.1
team 617.7
substitute 862.2
adj inferior 250.6
second thoughts
irresolution 362.1
reverse 363.1
mature thought 931.5
second to none
peerless 249.15
peerlessly 249.18
second wind 396.3
secrecy invisibility 32.1
concealment 345.1
secretness 345.1
hiding 346.1
seclusion 584.1
secret
n confidence 345.5

adj invisible 32.5
close 345.11
secretive 345.15
concealed 346.11
recondite 522.16
intrinsic 767.7
secret agent
operative 576.9
inquirer 938.16
secretariat 594.4
Secretariat
horse 311.15
United Nations 614.2
secretary writer 547.13
recorder 550.1
executive 574.3
public official 575.17
delegate 576.2
agent 576.3
table 901.15
Secretary of the Treasury
729.12
secret ballot 371.6
secrete excrete 12.12
produce 13.5
keep secret 345.7
hide away 346.7
store up 386.11
be damp 1065.11
secretion
excretion 12.1
secreta 13.1
concealment 346.1
moisture 1065.1
secret police
surveillance 938.9
police 1008.17
Secret Service 576.10
secret service
intelligence service 576.12
surveillance 938.9
secret weapon arms 462.1
salient point 997.6
sect party 617.4
school 617.5
system of beliefs 675.1
sectarism 675.3
sectarian
n dissenter 333.3
sectary 675.18
nonconformist 868.3
adj dissenting 333.6
partisan 617.19
sectary 675.26
sectarianism 617.13
section
n region 231.1
plot 231.4
military unit 461.22
part of book 554.13
passage 708.24
part 793.1
part of writing 793.2
severance 802.2
class 809.2
classifications 809.5
v apportion 802.18
sectional
regional 231.8
partisan 617.19
partial 793.7

sector semicircle 280.8
part 793.1
secular
n layman 700.2
adj unsacred 686.3
secularist 695.16
lay 700.3
momentary 850.8
hundredth 882.29
realistic 987.6
material 1052.10
secular humanist 695.13
secure
v fetch 176.16
elicit 192.14
close 293.6
bind 428.10
guarantee 438.9
defend 460.8
acquire 472.8
receive 479.6
fasten 800.7
make sure 855.8
stop work 857.8
protect 1008.18
adj fast 800.14
stable 855.12
belief 953.21
reliable 970.17
assured 970.20
confident 970.21
safe 1007.4
securities 738
security hope 124.1
veil of secrecy 345.3
guaranty 438.1
surety 438.1
stability 855.1
reliability 970.4
confidence 970.5
safety 1007.1
protection 1008.1
prosperity 1010.1
security blanket 901.1
security camera 714.11
Security Council 614.2
security risk 357.11
sedate
v put to sleep 22.20
relieve 120.5
moderate 670.6
adj staid 106.14
solemn 111.3
dignified 136.12
sedative
n sleep-inducer 22.10
anesthetic 25.3
sedative hypnotic 86.12
drug 87.3
moderator 670.3
adj sleep-inducing 22.23
calmative 86.45
palliative 670.16
sedentary inert 173.14
inactive 331.17
sedge 310.5
sediment
n deposit 176.9
dregs 256.2
v precipitate 1045.11
sedimentary rock 1059.1

sedition
rebelliousness 327.3
treason 645.7
seduce enamor 104.23
lure 377.5
betray 665.20
seductive
desirable 100.30
alluring 377.8
see
n diocese 698.8
v sense 24.6
behold 27.12
attend 221.8
perceive 521.9
visit 582.19
bet 759.25
spectate 918.5
know 928.12
think of 931.17
detect 941.5
heed 983.6
visualize 986.15
interj attention! 983.22
see about 931.14
see both sides 979.7
seed
n sperm 305.11
stone 310.31
lineage 560.4
offspring 561.1
card 758.2
vital force 886.7
v plant 1069.18
seedbed 1069.11
seed clouds 316.10
seedling sprout 302.11
plant 310.3
tree 310.10
see double
see badly 28.8
be drunk 88.27
seed pod 310.30
seedy tired 21.7
ill 85.56
shabby 393.32
slovenly 810.15
inferior 1005.9
see eye to eye
concur 332.9
agree 788.6
see fit 371.17
see how the wind blows 494.6
seeing
n vision 27.1
distinctness 31.2
observatory 1072.17
adj visual 27.20
Seeing Eye dog
aid to the blind 30.6
dog 311.17
see in perspective 925.2
see in retrospect 989.10
see into perceive 521.9
investigate 938.23
see it through
prosecute to a conclusion
360.5
be thorough 794.8
continue 856.3
persist 856.5

seek pursue 382.8
  endeavor 403.5
  solicit 440.14
  hunt 938.30
  be curious 981.3
seek refuge 1009.7
seem 33.10
seeming
  n aspect 33.3
  exteriority 206.1
  sham 354.3
  illusoriness 976.2
  adj apparent 33.11
  exterior 206.7
  specious 354.27
  illusory 976.9
seemly decorous 496.10
  appropriate 533.7
  conventional 579.5
  right 637.3
  decent 664.5
  expedient 995.5
see off 188.16
see one's way clear to 441.3
seep
  n exuding 190.6
  v exude 190.15
  trickle 238.18
  be damp 1065.11
seepage
  sorption 187.6
  entrance 189.1
  exuding 190.6
  trickle 238.7
see red 152.18
seesaw
  n playground equipment
    743.15
  interaction 777.3
  alternation 916.5
  oscillator 916.9
  v change 854.5
  alternate 916.13
  adj reciprocal 777.10
  alternate 916.19
  adv reciprocally 777.12
  to and fro 916.21
seethe
  n agitation 917.1
  v be excitable 105.16
  be angry 152.15
  bubble 320.4
  fume 671.12
  come together 770.16
  mill 915.12
  flounder 917.15
  be hot 1019.22
  boil 1020.20
  soak 1065.13
see the cloven hoof 941.8
see the difference 944.6
see the future 962.9
**see the handwriting on the
  wall**
  anticipate 845.6
  foreknow 961.6
see the inside of 941.8
see the last of
  not use 390.5
  relinquish 475.3
  eject 909.13

see the light
  appear 33.8
  come to life 306.10
  be published 352.16
  perceive 521.9
  be converted 692.7
**see the light at the end of the
  tunnel** 124.9
see the light of day
  be born 1.2
  appear 33.8
  be published 352.16
  originate 818.13
see to
  prepare for 405.11
  operate 889.5
  seek 938.30
  attend to 983.5
  care for 1008.19
see what one can do
  see what can be done 403.10
  experiment 942.8
see which way the wind blows
  942.9
see you later! 188.22
segment
  n straight line 277.2
  portion 477.5
  sect 675.3
  part 793.1
  part of writing 793.2
  v analyze 801.6
  apportion 802.18
segregate
  quarantine 429.13
  exclude 773.6
  differentiate 780.6
  separate 802.8
  discriminate 944.4
seismic 671.23
seismic wave 916.4
seismograph 916.8
seismology 916.7
seize
  take command 417.14
  arrest 429.15
  hold 474.6
  take hold of 480.14
  understand 521.7
  usurp 640.8
  secure 855.8
  fix 855.10
  stop 857.7
  infest 910.6
  know 928.12
seize on select 371.14
  fasten upon 480.16
  think of 931.16
  pay attention 983.8
seize the day
  make no provision 406.7
  squander 486.3
seize the opportunity
  use the occasion 843.7
  improve the occasion 843.8
seize up be still 173.7
  fix 855.10
  stop 857.7
seizure pang 26.2
  attack 85.6
  symptom 85.9

  outburst 105.9
  authority 417.12
  arrest 429.6
  hold 474.2
  seizing 480.2
  take 480.10
  usurpation 640.3
  overrunning 910.1
  spasm 917.6
  frenzy 926.7
seldom
  infrequently 848.4
  unusually 870.17
select
  n the best 999.8
  v make a selection
    371.14
  designate 517.18
  appoint 615.11
  specify 865.11
  discriminate 944.4
  adj chosen 371.26
  particular 495.13
  exclusive 773.9
  best 999.16
select a jury 598.16
select committee 423.2
selected works 554.7
selection
  choice 371.1
  indication 517.3
  excerpt 557.3
  appointment 615.2
  grouping 808.3
  specification 865.6
selective service
  service 458.9
  enlistment 615.7
selectman 575.17
self psyche 92.28
  ego 865.5
  soul 919.4
self-abasement
  humiliation 137.2
  unselfishness 652.1
  crouch 913.3
self-absorbed
  unfeeling 94.9
  selfish 651.5
self-abuse 75.8
self-accusing 113.8
self-acting
  voluntary 324.7
  automated 1041.22
self-address 542.1
self-adhesive 803.12
self-adjusting 1041.22
self-admiring vain 140.8
  selfish 651.5
self-admission 351.3
self-adulation 502.3
self-advancement 651.1
self-advertisement
  self-approbation 502.3
  selfishness 651.1
self-analysis 113.3
self-appointed
  presumptuous 141.10
  meddlesome 214.9
self-approbation
  complacency 107.2

  vanity 140.1
  self-praise 502.3
self-assertive 359.15
self-assured
  composed 106.13
  confident 970.21
self-avowal 351.3
self-centered
  unfeeling 94.9
  egotistic 140.10
  selfish 651.5
self-complacent
  complacent 107.10
  vain 140.8
self-conceit 140.4
self-confessed
  accepted 332.14
  disclosive 351.10
self-confidence
  equanimity 106.3
  pride 136.1
  confidence 970.5
self-congratulating 140.8
self-conscious 139.12
self-contained
  independent 430.22
  unsociable 583.5
  selfish 651.5
  separate 802.20
**self-contained underwater
  breathing apparatus**
  367.5
self-content
  n complacency 107.2
  vanity 140.1
  adj complacent 107.10
  vain 140.8
self-contradiction
  inconsistency 789.2
  impossibility 967.1
  error 975.1
self-control
  n equanimity 106.3
  patience 134.1
  self-command 359.5
  restraint 428.1
  temperance 668.1
  moderation 670.1
  v self-govern 1041.21
self-deception
  deception 356.1
  illusion 976.1
self-defeating 923.10
self-defense
  defense 460.1
  justification 600.2
self-deluding 976.8
self-denial
  self-control 359.5
  unselfishness 652.1
  asceticism 667.1
  temperance 668.1
  moderation 670.1
self-dependent 430.22
self-deprecating
  self-abasing 137.12
  self-effacing 139.10
self-destruct
  blow up 395.18
  be destroyed 395.22
self-destruction 308.5

self-destructive
  murderous 308.24
  destructive 395.26
self-determination
  nationhood 232.6
  voluntariness 324.2
  independence 430.5
  rallying device 458.12
  automation 1041.1
self-discipline
  self-control 359.5
  temperance 668.1
self-discovery 941.1
self-doubt
  self-effacement 139.2
  doubt 955.2
self-dramatizing
  n self-approbation 502.3
  adj self-approving 502.11
self-driven 1041.23
self-educated 928.24
self-effacing
  self-modest 139.10
  unselfish 652.5
self-elected 141.10
self-employed person 726.2
self-esteem pride 136.1
  vanity 140.1
  selfishness 651.1
self-evident
  manifest 348.8
  real 761.15
  obvious 970.15
self-examination 938.6
self-explanatory 348.8
self-expression 359.6
self-flagellation 113.3
self-fulfillment 92.27
self-glorification 502.3
self-governing 612.17
self-gratification 95.1
self-hatred 113.3
self-help 449.6
self-help group 449.2
self-humiliating 113.8
self-hypnosis 22.7
self-identity 865.1
self-immolation
  suicide 308.5
  unselfishness 652.1
  oblation 696.7
  burning 1020.5
self-importance
  vanity 140.1
  pompousness 501.7
  confidence 970.5
  importance 997.1
self-improvement 449.6
self-inflicted 643.8
self-interest
  egotism 140.3
  selfishness 651.1
selfish egotistic 140.10
  self-seeking 651.5
self-isolation 651.1
selfless
  impartial 649.10
  unselfish 652.5
self-love vanity 140.1
  selfishness 651.1
self-made 892.18

self-neglect 652.1
self-operating 1041.22
self-opinionated
  conceited 140.11
  dogmatic 970.22
self-pitiful 145.9
self-pity 145.1
self-possessed
  composed 106.13
  strong-willed 359.15
self-praise 502.3
self-preservation 460.1
self-priming 1041.22
self-proclaimed 141.10
self-promoting
  n self-approbation 502.3
  adj self-approving 502.11
  selfish 651.5
self-propelled
  jet-propelled 904.16
  self-moved 1041.23
self-propulsion 1041.1
self-protection 460.1
self-punishment 113.3
self-regulating 1041.22
self-reliance
  pride 136.1
  independence 430.5
  confidence 970.5
self-reproach 113.3
self-respect pride 136.1
  vanity 140.1
self-restraint
  equanimity 106.3
  self-control 359.5
  temperance 668.1
  moderation 670.1
self-righteous 693.5
self-rule
  communion 476.2
  government 612.4
self-sacrifice
  suicide 308.5
  unselfishness 652.1
  oblation 696.7
selfsame
  n the same 778.3
  adj identical 778.7
self-satisfied complacent 107.10
  vain 140.8
self-serving
  n selfishness 651.1
  adj selfish 651.5
self-starter 330.8
self-styled
  spurious 354.26
  nominal 527.15
self-sufficient
  proud 136.8
  vain 140.8
  independent 430.22
  unsociable 583.5
  selfish 651.5
self-support 449.6
self-sustaining 449.23
self-taught
  educated 570.16
  self-educated 928.24
self-winding 1041.22
self-worship 140.1
self-worshiping 140.8

sell publicize 352.15
  urge 375.14
  persuade 375.23
  provision 385.9
  transfer 629.3
  deal in 731.16
  merchandise 734.8
  be sold 734.12
  convert 737.24
  convince 953.18
sell at a loss
  discount 631.2
  sell 734.8
sell at auction 734.11
sell down the river
  defect 370.6
  betray 645.14
seller 730.3
seller's market
  demand 421.1
  insufficiency 992.1
  roaring trade 1010.5
sell for cost 630.13
  be sold 734.12
sell in futures 737.23
selling
  n inducement 375.3
  provision 385.1
  merchandising 734.2
  adj sales 734.13
sell off discard 390.7
  relinquish 475.3
  transfer 629.3
  sell 734.8
sell on credit 622.6
sell one a bill of goods 356.15
sell one on
  persuade 375.23
  convince 953.18
sell oneself
  act the traitor 645.15
  convince oneself 953.19
sell out defect 370.6
  discard 390.7
  inform on 551.13
  betray 645.14
  act the traitor 645.15
  sell 734.8
  sell stocks 737.24
sell short sell 734.8
  sell stocks 737.24
  underestimate 950.2
sell-through 734.2
sell to the highest bidder
  734.11
sell under the counter 732.7
semantic
  indicative 517.23
  meaning 518.12
  linguistic 523.19
semantics
  meaning 518.7
  lexicology 526.14
semaphore 517.15
semblance aspect 33.3
  image 349.5
  sham 354.3
  pretext 376.1
  similarity 784.1
  copy 785.1
  illusoriness 976.2

semen body fluid 13.2
  sperm 305.11
semester 824.2
semi 179.12
semiannual 850.8
semi-automatic 1041.12
semicircle
  crescent 279.5
  half circle 280.8
  half 875.2
semicolon 857.4
semiconductor 1032.14
semiconductor chip 1042.3
semiconductor circuit 1033.8
semiconscious 25.8
semifinalist 452.2
semigloss 35.22
seminal genital 2.29
  secretory 13.7
  reproductive 78.15
  gametic 305.20
  original 886.14
  productive 890.9
  fertilizing 890.11
  imaginative 986.18
seminar
  discussion 541.7
  study 568.8
seminary school 567.1
  secondary school 567.4
semiology symbol 517.2
  semantics 518.7
semiprecious stone 1059.7
semiretired 402.5
semiweekly 850.8
semiyearly 850.8
senary 882.18
senate 423.1
Senate committee 613.2
senator 610.3
send
  n wave 238.14
  v delight 95.11
  remove 176.11
  send off 176.15
  billow 238.22
  communicate 343.7
  mail 553.12
  start 904.13
  broadcast 1034.25
  transmit 1036.15
send abroad 190.17
send after 420.11
send a letter to 553.10
send a message
  communicate 343.7
  announce 352.12
  state 524.23
send a statement 628.11
send away send 176.15
  repulse 908.3
  banish 909.17
send a wire 347.20
send back
  reverberate 54.7
  restore 481.4
send down 909.17
sender 347.2
send flying 412.7
send for 420.11
send forth send 176.15

issue 352.14
start 904.13
disgorge 909.25
send headlong 913.5
sending 343.2
send in one's papers 448.2
send off send 176.15
begin 818.7
start 904.13
repulse 908.3
dismiss 909.18
send-off
leave-taking 188.4
beginning 818.1
send one's condolences 147.2
send one's regards 504.13
send out
commission 615.10
disgorge 909.25
vaporize 1067.8
send packing
reject 372.2
repulse 908.3
drive out 909.14
dismiss 909.18
send the wrong message
pervert 265.6
misrepresent 350.3
send to Davy Jones's locker
367.8
send to hell 682.6
send to jail 429.17
send to kingdom come 308.13
send to the gas chamber 604.17
send up commit 429.17
lampoon 512.12
send-up 512.5
send up a trial balloon 942.9
send up the river
imprison 429.14
commit 429.17
send word
communicate 343.7
inform 551.8
senescence 303.6
senile
n dotard 924.9
adj stricken in years 303.18
old-fogyish 842.17
decrepit 922.23
senior
n superior 249.4
elder 304.5
undergraduate 572.6
chief 575.3
bridge 758.3
adj authoritative 417.15
previous 834.4
older 842.19
senior citizen 304.2
senior high school 567.4
seniority
superiority 249.1
eldership 303.3
prestige 417.4
oldness 842.1
señor 76.7
señora 77.9
señorita 77.9
sensation
physical sensibility 24

sense 24.1
feeling 93.1
thrill 105.2
marvel 122.2
success 409.4
brain 919.6
sensational
emotionalistic 93.19
lurid 105.32
wonderful 122.10
gaudy 501.20
vigorous 544.11
grandiloquent 545.8
superb 999.15
sense
n sensation 24.1
feeling 93.1
milieu 209.3
meaning 518.1
consensus 788.3
intelligence 920.1
sensibleness 920.6
cognizance 928.2
idea 932.1
hunch 934.3
logic 935.9
discrimination 944.1
suggestion 951.5
opinion 953.6
v perceive 24.6
feel 93.10
understand 521.7
intuit 934.4
detect 941.5
senseless
unconscious 25.8
cruel 144.26
meaningless 520.6
unordered 810.12
unintelligent 922.13
foolish 923.8
unwise 923.10
insane 926.26
illogical 936.11
inanimate 1055.5
sense of duty 641.2
sense of hearing 48.1
sense of humor 489.11
sense of relief 120.4
sense of rhythm 708.31
sense of right and wrong
636.5
sense of touch 73.1
sense of wonder 122.1
sense organ 24.5
senses five senses 24.5
wits 919.2
sanity 925.1
sensible sentient 24.11
sensitive 93.20
grateful 150.5
weighable 297.19
cheap 633.7
substantial 763.6
intelligent 920.12
reasonable 920.18
sane 925.4
knowing 928.15
logical 935.20
realistic 987.6
sensitive sensory 24.9

responsive 24.12
sore 26.11
sensible 93.20
excitable 105.28
touchy 110.21
confidential 345.14
fastidious 495.9
discriminating 944.7
tolerant 979.11
pliant 1047.9
sensitize 24.7
sensory
n brain 919.6
adj sensorial 24.9
sensual 663.5
sensual sexual 75.25
sensualist 663.5
lascivious 665.29
sensuous sensory 24.9
delightful 97.7
sensual 663.5
sentence
n remark 524.3
phrase 529.1
judgment 598.9
condemnation 602.1
part of writing 793.2
verdict 946.5
maxim 974.1
v condemn 602.3
pass judgment 946.13
sentence of death 307.1
sentient 24.11
sentiment feeling 93.1
sentimentality 93.8
love 104.1
idea 932.1
opinion 953.6
attitude 978.1
sentimental
maudlin 93.21
loving 104.27
foolish 923.8
sentry warner 399.4
watchman 1008.10
separable
different 780.7
severable 802.26
discriminable 944.9
separate
v refine 79.22
diverge 171.5
bound 211.8
partition 213.8
interspace 224.3
open 292.11
quarantine 429.13
fall out 456.10
sow dissension 456.14
divorce 566.5
disband 771.8
segregate 773.6
differentiate 780.6
apportion 793.6
analyze 801.6
divide 802.8
part company 802.19
classify 808.11
discriminate 944.4
adj secluded 584.8
different 780.7

distinct 802.20
alone 872.8
separate oneself
keep one's distance 261.7
dissent 333.4
separate returns 630.9
**separate the wheat from the
chaff**
select 371.14
discriminate 944.4
separatist
n dissenter 333.3
apostate 363.5
adj repudiative 363.12
separator
extractor 192.9
sieve 802.7
sepia 40.3
seppuku 308.5
septet
cooperation 450.1
part music 708.18
poetry 720.9
seven 882.3
septic unhealthful 82.5
diseased 85.60
putrefactive 393.39
septicemia 85.31
septic tank 80.12
septuagenarian
old man 304.2
seventy 882.7
septum 213.5
sepulcher 309.16
sequel following 166.1
continuation 817.1
consequence 817.1
follow-up 835.2
effect 887.1
sequence
following 166.1
consistency 803.2
continuity 807.2
series 812.2
progression 815.1
subsequence 835.1
effect 887.1
thoughts 931.4
sequester
reserve 386.12
attach 480.20
separate 802.8
sequester oneself
seclude oneself 584.7
stand alone 872.6
find refuge 1009.8
sequitur 817.1
seraglio 563.10
seraph 679.1
sere worn 393.31
wasted 393.35
unproductive 891.4
dried 1066.9
serenade
n courtship 562.7
v court 562.21
sing 708.38
serendipity
discovery 941.1
chance 972.1
serene calm 106.12

pacific 464.9
equable 670.13
light 1025.31
serf sycophant 138.3
  subject 432.7
  retainer 577.1
sergeant
  Army noncommissioned
    officer 575.19
  Navy officer 575.20
  policeman 1008.15
sergeant-at-arms
  ship's officer 183.7
  policeman 1008.15
serial
  n part 554.13
  periodical 555.1
  radiobroadcast 1034.18
  television broadcast 1035.2
  adj journalistic 555.5
  consistent 803.11
  consecutive 812.9
  periodic 850.7
serial killer 308.11
serial number 517.11
series following 166.1
  edition 554.5
  hockey 749.1
  set 770.12
  classifications 809.5
  succession 812.2
  sequence 815.1
  round 850.3
  mathematical progression
    1017.8
serif 548.6
serious zealous 101.9
  sedate 106.14
  solemn 111.3
  great 247.6
  resolute 359.11
  lofty 544.14
  cognitive 931.21
  weighty 997.20
  dangerous 1006.9
sermon
  reproof 510.5
  lecture 543.3
  lesson 568.7
sermonize
  lecture 543.11
  expound 568.16
serpent snake 311.26
  traitor 357.10
  beast 660.6
serpentine
  n variegation 47.6
  v convolve 281.4
  adj deviative 164.7
  flowing 238.24
  curved 279.7
  convolutional 281.6
  coiled 281.7
  reptile 311.48
  cunning 415.12
serrate
  v notch 289.4
  adj angular 278.6
  rugged 288.7
  notched 289.5
serum humor 2.24

blood 2.25
antitoxin 86.27
transfusion 91.18
servant
  hanger-on 138.6
  instrument 384.4
  underling 432.5
  subject 432.7
  employee 577.3
  servitor 577.2
  assistant 616.6
  believer 692.4
  worker 726.2
serve
  n game 748.2
  v copulate 75.21
  be inferior 250.4
  act 328.4
  be instrumental 384.7
  avail 387.17
  summon 420.11
  lend oneself 449.18
  do duty 458.18
  give 478.12
  work for 577.13
  officiate 724.13
  play tennis 748.3
  shuffle 758.5
  suit 788.8
  tend 896.3
  throw 904.10
  suffice 991.4
  expedite one's affair 995.3
  do good 999.10
serve an apprenticeship 570.11
serve-and-volley 748.2
serve as 349.10
serve notice 551.8
serve one right
  requite 506.5
  punish 604.10
  get one's deserts 639.6
  be just 649.6
serve out 477.8
serve time
  be imprisoned 429.18
  take one's turn 825.5
service
  n serving 8.10
  food service 8.11
  act of kindness 143.7
  rigging 180.12
  obedience 326.1
  instrumentality 384.3
  benefit 387.4
  subservience 432.2
  aid 449.1
  military service 458.9
  military branch 461.21
  servanthood 577.12
  ceremony 580.4
  divine service 696.8
  rite 701.3
  task 724.2
  game 748.2
  throw 904.3
  v copulate 75.21
  repair 396.14
serviceable
  modal 384.8
  useful 387.18

helpful 449.21
serviceable life 827.1
service academy 567.6
serviceman
  mender 396.10
  military man 461.6
service medal 646.6
servile slavish 138.13
  inferior 250.6
  subject 432.13
  downtrodden 432.16
  submissive 433.12
  deferential 433.16
  serving 577.14
serving
  n service 8.10
  rigging 180.12
  adj acting 328.10
  helping 449.20
  servitorial 577.14
servitude
  subjection 432.1
  service 577.12
sesquicentennial 850.4
sesquipedality 545.3
session
  ecclesiastical council 423.4
  conference 541.6
  assembly 770.2
  moment 824.2
set
  n navigation 159.3
  direction 161.1
  course 172.2
  flow 238.4
  form 262.1
  sprout 302.11
  edition 554.5
  clique 617.6
  setting 704.19
  motion-picture studio 706.4
  game 745.3
  bridge 758.3
  company 770.3
  collection 770.12
  group 784.5
  all 792.3
  cohesion 803.1
  class 809.2
  trend 896.2
  disposition 978.3
  radio 1034.3
  v be pregnant 78.12
  place 159.12
  establish 159.16
  direct 161.5
  take direction 161.7
  sit 173.10
  sink 194.6
  flow 238.16
  form 262.7
  sharpen 285.7
  heal 396.21
  prime 405.9
  prescribe 420.9
  allot 477.9
  typeset 548.16
  impose 643.4
  put to music 708.46
  make agree 788.7
  fasten 800.7

cohere 803.6
fix 855.9
specify 865.11
tend 896.3
thicken 1045.10
solidify 1046.8
plant 1069.18
adj trite 117.9
located 159.18
circumscribed 210.6
sharp 285.8
firm 359.12
obstinate 361.8
customary 373.13
confirmed 373.18
planned 381.12
prepared 405.16
fast 800.14
cohesive 803.10
established 855.13
fixed 855.14
assured 970.20
hardened 1046.13
set about
  undertake 404.3
  begin 818.7
set above 371.17
set a course 818.8
set afire 375.18
set afloat cause 886.10
  start 904.13
set against
  v offset 338.5
  sow dissension 456.14
  antagonize 589.7
  compare 943.4
  adj oppositional 451.8
  hostile 589.10
set against one another 215.4
set a limit 944.4
set an example 786.7
set apart
  v partition 213.8
  interspace 224.3
  excise 255.10
  reserve 386.12
  allot 477.9
  dedicate 477.11
  sanctify 685.5
  segregate 773.6
  differentiate 780.6
  separate 802.8
  characterize 865.10
  discriminate 944.4
  adj sanctified 685.8
  segregated 773.8
set a precedent 834.3
set a price 630.11
set aside
  remove 176.11
  excise 255.10
  reserve 386.12
  put away 390.6
  repeal 445.2
  segregate 773.6
  separate 802.8
  postpone 846.9
  allow for 959.5
  dismiss 984.4
set astir excite 105.12
  rouse 375.19

conclusive argument 958.3
settle the score
  get even with 506.7
  punish 604.11
settlings 256.2
set to undertake 404.3
  quarrel 456.11
  set to work 725.15
  fasten 800.7
  begin 818.7
set-to 456.6
set to one side 176.11
set to rights
  remedy 396.13
  repair 396.14
  arrange 808.8
set toward 896.3
set to work 725.15
setup structure 266.1
  plan 381.1
  composition 796.1
  order 807.1
  prearrangement 965.2
  easy 1014.4
set up refresh 9.2
  provoke 152.24
  establish 159.16
  erect 200.9
  plan 381.8
  remedy 396.13
  aid 449.11
  trump up a charge
    599.12
  treat 624.19
  glorify 662.13
  finance 729.16
  order 807.4
  inaugurate 818.11
  cause 886.10
  produce 892.8
  found 892.10
  elevate 912.5
  prearrange 965.5
set up barriers 429.13
set up for 354.21
set up in business
  settle 159.17
  work 724.12
  finance 729.16
set upon 459.14
set up shop
  settle 159.17
  practice 328.8
  work 724.12
  set to work 725.15
  make a beginning 818.8
seven
  playing card 758.2
  heptad 882.3
seven-card stud 759.10
sevenfold 882.19
the seven seas 240.1
Seven Sisters 1072.8
seventh
  n interval 709.20
  adj septimal 882.19
seventh heaven
  happiness 95.2
  summit 198.2
  heaven of heavens 681.4
seventy 882.7

sever
  differentiate 780.6
  separate 802.11
  discriminate 944.4
several
  n plurality 883.1
  a number 884.2
  adj proportionate 477.13
  different 780.7
  diversified 783.4
  particular 865.12
  plural 883.7
  divers 884.7
severance
  elimination 773.2
  differentiation 780.4
  disseverment 802.2
severance pay 624.4
severe
  acrimonious 17.14
  painful 26.10
  pungent 68.6
  harsh 144.24
  imperious 417.16
  strict 425.6
  inornate 499.9
  gruff 505.7
  plain-speaking 535.3
  violent 671.16
  simple 798.6
  exact 973.17
  difficult 1013.17
  cold 1023.14
severity acrimony 17.5
  pungency 68.1
  harshness 144.9
  strictness 425.1
  inornateness 499.4
  gruffness 505.3
  plain speech 535.1
  violence 671.1
  simplicity 798.1
  accuracy 973.5
  cold 1023.1
sew stitch 741.4
  hook 800.8
sewage feces 12.4
  offal 80.9
  refuse 391.4
sewed up
  completed 407.11
  prearranged 965.8
  assured 970.20
sewer
  needleworker 741.2
  sewing machine 741.3
sewer
  n receptacle of filth 80.12
  drain 239.5
  cave 284.5
  gutter 654.7
  adj cursing 513.8
sewing
  bookbinding 554.14
  needlework 741.1
sewing machine 741.3
sex
  n gender 75.1
  copulation 75.7
  love 104.1
  v sexualize 75.19

  adj sexual 75.25
sexagenarian
  old man 304.2
  sixty 882.7
sex appeal
  sexual attraction 75.3
  attractiveness 377.2
sex chromosome
  chromosome 305.8
  heredity 560.6
sex discrimination
  misanthropy 590.1
  discrimination 980.4
sex drive 75.2
sex fiend 75.16
sex goddess
  sex object 75.4
  beauty 1016.8
sexism
  sexual preference
    75.10
  misanthropy 590.1
  discrimination 980.4
sexist
  n misanthrope 590.2
  bigot 980.5
  adj misanthropic 590.3
  discriminatory 980.12
sex kitten 1016.9
sexless 75.29
sex life 75.2
sex object
  hot number 75.4
  sweetheart 104.10
sexology 75.18
sex organs 2.13
sex shop 75.7
sex-starved 75.27
sextant
  navigation 182.2
  instrument 278.4
  semicircle 280.8
sextet
  cooperation 450.1
  part music 708.18
  poetry 720.9
  six 882.2
sextuple
  v sixfold 882.16
  adj sixth 882.18
sextuplets 882.2
sexual
  sex 75.25
  gametic 305.20
  lascivious 665.29
  amorous 104.26
  amatory 562.23
sexual abnormality 75.11
sexual abstinence
  celibacy 565.1
  abstinence 668.2
sexual abuse 75.11
sexual advance 439.2
sexual assault
  sexual possession 480.3
  seduction 665.6
sexual climax
  copulation 75.7
  spasm 917.6
sexual counselor 75.18
sexual customs 75.18

sexual desire
  biological urge 75.5
  desire 100.1
  craving 100.6
  will 323.1
  heat metaphor 1019.2
sexual deviation 75.11
sexual excitement 105.7
sexual fantasy
  masturbation 75.8
  defense mechanism 92.23
sexual freedom 75.18
sexual harassment 75.11
sexual intercourse
  copulation 75.7
  lovemaking 562.1
sexuality
  sexual nature 75.2
  lasciviousness 665.5
sexual love 104.1
sexually-transmitted disease
  85.18
sexual magnetism 75.3
sexual maturity 14.1
sexual morality 75.18
sexual mores 75.18
sexual orientation 75.10
sexual pathology
  perversion 75.11
  personality disorder
    92.15
  psychosis 926.3
sexual pleasure 95.1
sexual power 76.2
sexual practices 75.18
sexual preference 75.10
sexual relations 75.7
sexual revolution 75.18
sexual stereotyping 590.1
sexual surrogate 75.18
sexual union 75.7
sexy
  sexual 75.25
  lustful 75.27
  delightful 97.7
  amorous 97.8
  desirable 100.30
  alluring 377.8
  lascivious 665.29
  excellent 999.13
sh! 51.14
shabby
  squalid 80.25
  inadequate 250.7
  worthless 391.11
  shoddy 393.32
  niggardly 484.8
  cheap 633.7
  base 661.12
  slovenly 810.15
  paltry 998.21
  terrible 1000.9
  inferior 1005.9
shack 228.9
shackle
  n restraint 428.4
  curb 1012.7
  v bind 428.10
  confine 429.12
  hamper 1012.11
shack up 75.21

shade
  n color 35.1
  degree 245.1
  hint 248.4
  admixture 797.7
  psyche 919.4
  phantom 976.4
  specter 988.1
  protection 1008.1
  shadow 1027.3
  screen 1028.1
  v color 35.14
  blacken 38.7
  cloud 319.7
  conceal 346.6
  portray 712.19
  darken 1027.9
  screen 1028.5
shade of difference
  margin 780.2
  distinction 944.3
shades spectacles 29.3
  eyeshade 1028.2
shade tree 310.10
shading
  n blackening 38.5
  gradation 245.3
  treatment 712.9
  darkening 1027.6
  televising 1035.3
  television reception 1035.5
  adj screening 1028.6
shadow
  n omen 133.3
  hanger-on 138.6
  follower 166.2
  degree 245.1
  hint 248.4
  remainder 256.1
  thinness 270.7
  slim 270.8
  image 349.5
  treatment 712.9
  spirit 764.3
  reflection 785.7
  psyche 919.4
  phantom 976.4
  specter 988.1
  protection 1008.1
  darkness 1027.3
  shade 1028.1
  v look 27.13
  color 35.14
  blacken 38.7
  foreshow 133.10
  follow 166.3
  cloud 319.7
  lurk 346.9
  image 349.11
  make unintelligible 522.12
  trace 938.35
  darken 1027.9
  shade 1028.5
shadow-box 754.4
shadowing
  n following 166.1
  ambush 346.3
  pursuit 382.1
  surveillance 938.9
  darkening 1027.6
  adj shading 1028.6

shadow of death 307.1
shadow of doubt 955.2
shady dishonest 645.16
  disreputable 661.10
  shadowy 1027.16
  shaded 1028.7
shady character 415.6
shady past 661.6
the shady side 303.5
shaft
  n feather part 3.17
  air passage 239.13
  tower 272.6
  pole 273.1
  hole 275.2
  pit 284.4
  arrow 462.6
  monument 549.12
  base 901.8
  mine 1058.6
  v mistreat 389.6
shag
  n hair 3.2
  head of hair 3.4
  tobacco 89.2
  texture 294.1
  v fetch 176.16
shaggy hairy 3.24
  rough 288.6
  nappy 294.7
  disheveled 810.14
shah 575.9
shake
  n beverage 10.49
  speech defect 525.1
  trill 709.19
  instant 830.3
  quake 917.3
  flutter 917.4
  search 938.15
  wood 1054.3
  v be weak 16.8
  weaken 16.10
  disturb 105.14
  be excited 105.18
  tremble 127.14
  frighten 127.15
  daunt 127.18
  unnerve 128.10
  startle 131.8
  face 295.23
  age 303.10
  evade 368.7
  break the habit
    374.3
  sign 437.7
  speak poorly 525.7
  greet 585.10
  dance 705.5
  sing 708.38
  thrust 902.12
  oscillate 916.10
  wave 916.11
  alternate 916.14
  agitate 917.10
  quake 917.11
  ransack 938.33
  freeze 1023.9
shake a leg
  v be active 330.14
  interj make haste 401.17

shakedown
  extortion 480.8
  search 938.15
  tryout 942.3
shakedown artist 480.12
shakedown cruise
  voyage 182.6
  tryout 942.3
shake hands near 223.7
  sign 437.7
  make up 465.10
  greet 585.10
  strike a bargain 731.19
shaken
  disturbed 105.23
  unnerved 128.14
  startled 131.13
  agitated 917.16
  confused 985.12
shake off evade 368.7
  free oneself from 431.8
  do away with 909.21
shake one's fist at
  defy 454.3
  threaten 514.2
shake on it
  come to an agreement 332.10
  strike a bargain 731.19
shakeout
  elimination 773.2
  classification 801.3
  grouping 808.3
  distinction 944.3
shaker
  gambling wheel 759.16
  agitator 917.9
Shaker
  n abstainer 668.4
  adj abstinent 668.10
the shakes
  shaking 917.2
  delirium tremens 926.10
shake up weaken 16.10
  wake someone up 23.5
  disturb 105.14
  censure 510.13
  rearrange 808.13
  agitate 917.10
  soften 1047.6
shake-up
  rearrangement 808.7
  expedient 995.2
shaky unsteady 16.16
  fearful 127.23
  jittery 128.12
  stricken in years 303.18
  unaccustomed 374.4
  inarticulate 525.12
  fragile 764.7
  loose 804.5
  shaking 917.17
  unreliable 971.20
  unsafe 1006.11
  feeling cold 1023.16
shaky ground 1006.2
shallow
  n shoal 276.2
  v become less deep 276.3
  adj insignificant 248.6
  depthless 276.5
  superficial 922.20

  half-learned 930.15
  trivial 998.19
shallowness
  exteriority 206.1
  depthlessness 276.1
  superficiality 922.7
  slight knowledge 930.6
  inattention 984.1
  triviality 998.3
shallows
  shoal 276.2
  hidden danger 1006.5
shalom!
  farewell! 188.22
  peace! 464.11
sham
  n fakery 354.3
  fake 354.13
  hoax 356.7
  impostor 357.6
  pretext 376.1
  affectation 500.1
  display 501.4
  v fake 354.21
  affect 500.12
  adj imitation 336.8
  spurious 354.26
  assumed 500.16
shaman
  n witch doctor 690.7
  adj sorcerous 690.14
shamble
  n slow motion 175.2
  gait 177.12
  v plod 175.7
  way of walking 177.28
shambles
  butchery 308.3
  place of killing 308.12
  destruction 395.1
  battlefield 463.2
shame
  n chagrin 96.4
  regret 113.1
  humiliation 137.2
  abomination 638.2
  iniquity 654.3
  disgrace 661.5
  decency 664.2
  v humiliate 137.4
  disgrace 661.8
  interj God forbid! 510.27
shamed
  humiliated 137.14
  in disrepute 661.13
shamefaced
  regretful 113.8
  humiliated 137.14
  shy 139.12
shameful
  regretful 113.8
  wrong 638.3
  wicked 654.16
  disgraceful 661.11
  terrible 1000.9
shameless
  unregretful 114.4
  brazen 142.11
  gaudy 501.20
  wrong 638.3
  dishonest 645.16

hardened 654.17
immodest 666.6
shampoo
n washing 79.5
cleanser 79.17
v wash 79.19
shamrock
insignia 647.1
three 876.1
shamus 1008.16
shanghai coerce 424.7
seize 480.14
abduct 482.20
Shangri-la 986.11
shank member 2.7
leg 177.14
shaft 273.6
type 548.6
shanty 228.9
shanty-town 230.6
shape
n aspect 33.3
appearance 33.5
fitness 84.1
form 262.1
human form 262.4
structure 266.1
good condition 765.3
mode 765.4
kind 809.3
characteristic 865.4
illusion 976.4
specter 988.1
v form 262.7
be formed 262.8
plan 381.8
pot 742.6
compose 796.3
conform 867.3
produce 892.8
imagine 986.14
shape a course
pilot 182.14
chart a course
182.27
plan 381.8
shaped
formative 262.9
structural 266.6
planned 381.12
made 892.18
shapeless
formless 263.4
obscure 522.15
unordered 810.12
inconstant 854.7
abnormal 870.9
vague 971.19
unshapely 1015.8
shapely
well-shaped 264.5
comely 1016.19
the shape of things 765.2
shape up
v be formed 262.8
improve 392.7
be in a certain state 765.5
compose 796.3
form 807.5
phrs shape up or ship out
867.10

shard
n refuse 391.4
piece 793.3
v break 1050.3
pulverize 1051.9
share
n amount 244.2
portion 477.5
stockholding 738.3
part 793.1
v respond 93.11
communicate 343.7
share in 476.6
apportion 477.6
separate 793.6
share and share alike
v share 476.6
apportion 477.6
bisect 875.4
adj communal 476.9
proportionately 477.14
sharebroker 737.10
share certificate 622.3
sharecrop 1069.16
sharecropper 1069.5
shared 777.11
shareholder
participator 476.4
stockholder 737.14
share in 476.6
share one's sorrow 147.2
share out
apportion 477.6
separate 793.6
shares 738.2
sharing
n sympathy 93.5
informing 343.2
accord 455.1
participation 476.1
apportionment 477.1
association 582.6
adj participating 476.8
mutual 777.11
shark
marine animal 311.30
cheater 357.4
expert 413.11
extortionist 480.12
savage 593.5
gambler 759.21
sharp
n cheat 357.3
expert 413.11
note 709.14
gambler 759.21
adj acrimonious 17.14
sensitive 24.13
painful 26.10
shrill 58.14
dissonant 61.4
bitter 64.6
pungent 68.6
strong 69.10
deep-felt 93.24
distressing 98.20
penetrating 105.31
caustic 144.23
steep 204.18
angular 278.6
keen 285.8

quick 330.18
alert 339.14
deceitful 356.22
cunning 415.12
witty 489.15
gruff 505.7
chic 578.13
violent 671.16
smart 920.14
cold 1023.14
adv suddenly 830.9
punctually 845.14
sharpen
sensitize 24.7
stimulate 105.13
aggravate 119.2
intensify 251.5
edge 285.7
tool 1040.13
sharpener 1040.2
sharpen the wits 568.10
sharper cheat 357.3
gambler 759.21
sharp eye
keen eye 27.10
vigilance 339.4
sharp pain 26.2
sharps and flats 709.15
sharpshooter
infantryman 461.9
shooter 904.8
sharp-witted 920.14
sharp words 456.5
sharpy
expert 413.11
person of fashion 578.7
shatter
demolish 395.17
splinter 802.13
madden 926.24
break 1050.3
pulverize 1051.9
shattered nerves 128.4
shatterproof
resistant 15.20
unbreakable 1049.5
shave
contact 223.10
excise 255.10
shorten 268.6
smooth 287.5
deceive 356.19
cheapen 633.6
discount 728.27
shaven 6.17
shaver 302.3
shaving
hairlessness 6.4
remainder 256.1
thinness 270.7
flake 296.3
refuse 391.4
piece 793.3
she female 77.4
self 865.5
sheaf 770.8
shear divest 6.5
excise 255.10
shorten 268.6
strip 480.24
sheath 295.17

sheathe clothe 5.39
wrap 295.20
face 295.23
shed
n hangar 184.24
hut 228.9
v cast 6.10
waste 473.5
shed blood bleed 12.17
spill blood 308.15
war 458.14
shed crocodile tears 354.22
she-devil bitch 110.12
witch 593.7
demon 680.6
shed light upon
explain 341.10
illuminate 1025.28
shed tears 115.12
sheen 1025.2
sheep whiteness 37.2
animal 311.7
imitator 336.4
the laity 700.1
conformist 867.2
sheepdip dip 79.9
liquor 88.14
poison 1001.3
sheep dog dog 311.17
watchdog 1008.11
sheep farm 1070.5
sheepherder 1070.3
sheepish penitent 113.9
blushing 139.13
ungulate 311.46
sheepskin 549.6
sheer
n deviation 164.1
bias 204.3
v deviate 164.3
change course 182.30
oblique 204.9
adj perpendicular 200.12
steep 204.18
mere 248.8
thorough 794.10
unmixed 798.7
transparent 1029.4
adv perpendicularly 200.14
absolutely 794.15
sheer drop 200.3
sheer off
avoid 164.6
dodge 368.8
pull back 903.7
sheet whiteness 37.2
blanket 295.10
lamina 296.2
newspaper 555.2
part of writing 793.2
paper 1054.5
sheet ice 1023.5
sheet lightning 1025.17
sheet metal 1058.5
sheet music 708.28
sheet of fire 1019.13
sheet of rain 316.1
sheik 104.13
sheikh ruler 575.9
prince 608.7
clergy 699.12

terrify 127.17
startle 131.8
shake 917.11
electrify 1032.26
shock absorber 670.3
shocking horrid 98.19
frightening 127.30
surprising 131.11
downright 247.12
disgraceful 661.11
sudden 830.5
terrible 1000.9
shock-resistant 1049.4
shock tactics 459.1
shock therapy 92.35
shock troops 461.15
shock wave
air speed 184.31
wave 916.4
shod 5.45
shoddy
n fake 354.13
rubbish 391.5
adj spurious 354.26
worthless 391.11
shabby 393.32
cheap 633.7
base 661.12
slovenly 810.15
paltry 998.21
terrible 1000.9
shoe
n footwear 5.27
bowling 750.1
automobile racing 756.1
v cloak 5.40
the shoe is on the other foot
what goes around comes
around 506.10
permanence 852.14
shoemaker 5.38
shogun 575.9
shoo
v do away with 909.21
interj go away! 909.31
begone 909.32
shoo-in
sure success 409.2
victor 411.2
horse race 757.3
sure thing 970.2
shook startled 131.13
confused 985.12
shook up 128.12
shoot
n pang 26.2
journey 177.5
rapids 238.10
gutter 239.3
sprout 302.11
branch 310.20
offshoot 561.4
warp 740.3
deposit 1058.7
rocket launching 1074.9
v suffer 26.8
inject 87.22
immunize 91.28
speed 174.8
row 182.53
float 182.54

strike dead 308.18
vegetate 310.34
hunt 382.9
pull the trigger 459.22
execute 604.17
explode 671.14
film 706.8
photograph 714.14
play basketball 747.4
play hockey 749.7
play golf 751.4
fire off 904.12
shine 1025.23
launch 1074.13
shoot ahead
spurt 174.12
outdistance 249.10
hustle 330.13
shoot back 939.4
shoot craps 759.23
shoot down
strike dead 308.18
do for 395.11
end 820.5
shoot 904.12
shooter 904.8
shoot from the hip
be impatient 135.4
act on the spur of the
moment 365.7
prejudge 947.2
shoot full of holes 958.4
shooting
n pang 26.2
killing 308.1
hunting 382.2
gunfire 459.8
capital punishment 604.7
hockey game 749.3
throwing 904.2
adj painful 26.10
shooting gallery 87.20
shooting script
playbook 704.21
script 706.3
shooting star
omen 133.6
meteor 1072.15
shoot it out with 457.17
shoot off one's mouth
bluster 503.3
talk nonsense 520.5
speak 524.20
chatter 540.5
shootout 752.3
shoot out 283.10
shoot straight with 649.6
shoot the breeze
speak 524.20
converse 541.9
shoot the works
be determined 359.8
persevere 360.7
do one's best 403.14
do to perfection 407.7
court danger 493.6
risk 972.12
shoot up grow 14.2
inject 87.22
spring up 193.9
increase 251.6

expand 259.7
grow higher 272.12
protrude 283.10
vegetate 310.34
shop
n occupation 724.4
market 736.1
workplace 739.1
office 739.7
casino 759.19
v inform on 551.13
market 733.8
shop around
choose 371.13
shop 733.8
be discriminating 944.5
shop at 731.17
shopkeeper 730.2
shoplift 482.13
shoplifter 483.1
shopper 733.5
shopping-bag lady
homeless person 331.10
poor person 619.4
shopping center
metropolis 208.7
city district 230.6
marketplace 736.2
shopping list 871.1
shopping mall 739.1
shopping spree 733.1
shop steward 727.4
shoptalk 523.10
shopworn 393.31
shore
n border 211.4
side 218.1
coast 234.2
v buttress 449.12
support 901.21
adj aquatic 182.58
coastal 234.7
shore bird 311.28
shore leave 20.3
shoreline
n shore 234.2
adj coastal 234.7
shore patrol 1008.17
shore up
strengthen 15.13
buttress 449.12
support 901.21
stiffen 1046.9
shorn 252.10
shorn of 473.8
short
n car 179.10
motion pictures 706.1
bear account 737.12
v electrify 1032.26
adj insignificant 248.6
little 258.10
brief 268.8
low 274.7
taciturn 344.9
gruff 505.7
concise 537.6
poor 619.7
incomplete 795.4
fleeting 828.8
falling short of 911.5

wanting 992.13
imperfect 1003.4
adv abruptly 268.13
shortage
deficiency 795.2
shortcoming 911.1
want 992.4
imperfection 1003.1
shortchange 356.18
short-circuit 1032.26
shortcoming
inequality 791.1
falling short 911.1
want 992.4
imperfection 1003.1
fault 1003.2
shortcut cut 268.5
straight line 277.2
route 383.1
shorten
n make small 258.9
v reduce 252.7
subtract 255.9
contract 260.7
abbreviate 268.6
be brief 537.5
abridge 557.5
shorten sail
reduce sail 182.50
take precautions 494.6
shorter 252.10
shortfall
deficiency 795.2
shortcoming 911.1
want 992.4
short fuse
irascibility 110.2
hot temper 110.4
shorthand
n phonetic symbol
546.2
stenography 547.8
adj written 547.22
stenographic 547.27
shorthanded 992.12
short list 871.1
short-lived 828.7
short memory 990.1
short odds 759.6
short of breath 21.12
short-order cook 11.3
short range 223.2
short rations 515.2
shorts
bear account 737.12
soccer 752.1
short shrift
pitilessness 146.1
repulse 442.2
shortsighted
poor-sighted 28.11
undiscerning 922.14
unwise 923.10
narrow-minded 980.10
shortstop 745.2
short story 722.3
short story writer
author 547.15
scribe 718.4
short subject 706.1
short supply 992.1

short temper
irascibility 110.2
hot temper 110.4
short-term 828.8
short-term memory 989.1
short time
shortness 268.1
little while 828.3
shortwave
n radio wave 1034.11
v broadcast 1034.25
adj radio 1034.28
shorty 258.4
shot
n detonation 56.3
dose 86.6
fix 87.20
drink 88.7
inoculation 91.16
disrespect 156.3
swiftness 174.6
attempt 403.3
ball 462.19
fee 630.6
cinematography 706.5
photograph 714.3
motion picture segment 714.8
baseball game 745.3
basketball game 747.3
tennis game 748.2
hockey game 749.3
golf stroke 751.3
soccer game 752.3
bet 759.3
throw 759.9
portion 793.5
discharge 904.4
shooter 904.8
guess 951.4
rocket launching 1074.9
adj variegated 47.9
unnerved 128.14
spoiled 393.29
ruined 395.29
ended 820.9
shotgun 308.18
shotgun wedding 563.3
shot in the arm 86.8
shot in the dark
gamble 759.2
guess 951.4
shot-put 904.3
shot through
variegated 47.9
permeated 221.15
apertured 292.19
should
ought to 641.3
be necessary 963.10
shoulder
n bulge 283.3
type 548.6
joint 800.4
supporter 901.2
buttress 901.4
shelf 901.14
v support 901.21
thrust 902.12
shoulder patch 647.5
shoulder to shoulder
adv cooperatively 450.6

hand in hand 769.10
concurrently 899.5
phrs side by side 218.12
shout
n cry 59.1
cheer 116.2
laughter 116.4
v din 53.7
cry 59.6
cheer 116.6
laugh 116.8
be manifest 348.7
proclaim 352.13
shout at the top of one's voice
59.9
shout down
drown out 53.8
run over 910.7
shout hallelujah 116.6
shout out 59.8
shove
n thrust 902.2
pushing 904.1
v set in motion 172.6
illicit goods 732.7
thrust 902.12
push 904.9
shove aside 164.6
shovel
n cutlery 1040.2
v ladle 176.17
excavate 284.15
shove off
v get under way 182.19
sail away from 182.36
depart 188.7
leave 222.10
die 307.20
interj go away 909.32
shoving match 457.4
show
n appearance 33.2
spectacle 33.7
externalization 206.4
exhibition 348.2
sham 354.3
pretext 376.1
affectation 500.1
display 501.4
indication 517.3
stage show 704.4
theatrical performance
704.12
marketplace 736.2
illusoriness 976.2
v show up 31.4
appear 33.8
direct to 161.6
externalize 206.5
explain 341.10
manifest 348.5
disclose 351.4
signify 517.17
teach 568.10
project 714.16
finish third 757.5
evidence 957.8
prove 957.10
show a deficit 623.6
show a lack of respect for
156.4

show a percentage 472.13
show aptitude for 413.18
show a tendency
tend 896.3
be probable 968.4
showboat
n show-off 501.11
theater 704.14
v exercise skill 413.20
show off 501.16
show business
the entertainment industry
704
theater 743.13
showcase
n display 348.2
theatrical performance
704.12
counter 736.6
transparent substance 1029.2
v manifest 348.5
show consideration 670.8
show dog 311.17
showdown poker 759.10
contrariety 779.1
shower
n bath 79.8
showering apparatus 79.12
rain 316.1
plenty 991.2
sprinkle 1065.5
sprinkler 1065.8
v wash 79.19
rain 316.10
give 478.12
abound 991.5
shower head
showering apparatus 79.12
nozzle 239.9
sprinkler 1065.8
show girl 707.1
show good faith 644.9
show horse 757.2
show how
explain 341.10
teach 568.10
showing
n appearance 33.1
externalization 206.4
display 348.2
indication 517.3
adj divested 6.12
visible 31.6
manifesting 348.9
disclosive 351.10
show its colors 351.8
show its face 351.8
show kindness 143.9
showman 704.23
showmanship 704.3
show no mercy 146.2
show off
manifest 348.5
grandstand 501.16
show-off 501.11
show of hands 371.6
show one's hand 351.7
show one's true colors
come out 348.6
confess 351.7
showpiece model 786.1

standard of perfection 1002.4
show pity 670.8
showplace 786.1
show preference 650.8
show promise 133.13
show respect for 155.5
showroom display room
197.24
salesroom 736.5
show signs of
appear to be 33.10
augur 133.12
evidence 957.8
showstopper 409.4
show the door 909.18
show the ropes 568.10
show the way
direct to 161.6
lead 165.2
explain 341.10
go before 816.3
show through
show 31.4
be transparent 1029.3
show up show 31.4
appear 33.8
arrive 186.6
attend 221.8
overshadow 249.8
disclose 351.4
turn up 831.6
be discovered 941.9
disprove 958.4
disillusion 977.2
showy
flaunting 501.19
grandiloquent 545.8
shrapnel 462.19
shred
n scrap 248.3
piece 793.3
v tear apart 802.14
pulverize 1051.9
shredded
severed 802.23
powdery 1051.11
shredder 1051.7
shrew 110.12
shrewd cunning 415.12
artful 920.15
knowing 928.15
shrewish
peevish 110.22
ungovernable 361.12
partisan 456.17
shriek
n blare 53.5
screech 58.4
cry 59.1
laughter 116.4
v blare 53.10
screech 58.8
cry 59.6
wail 115.13
laugh 116.8
sigh 318.21
speak 524.25
shrift pardon 148.2
confession 351.3
shrill
n screech 58.4

v squawk 58.8
adj strident 58.14
dissonant 61.4
shrimp
  n runt 258.4
  a nobody 998.7
  v fish 382.10
shrine
  n tomb 309.16
  monument 549.12
  holy place 703.4
  v enclose 212.5
shrink
  n psychologist 92.10
  v suffer 26.8
  flinch 127.13
  efface oneself 139.7
  recede 168.2
  retract 168.3
  decrease 252.6
  reduce 252.7
  shrivel 260.9
  demur 325.4
  dodge 368.8
  languish 393.18
  waste 473.5
  draw back 903.7
shrink from 99.5
shrinking violet 139.6
shrink-wrap
  package 212.9
  bind 800.9
shrivel shrink 260.9
  age 303.10
  languish 393.18
  dry 1066.6
shroud
  n cover 295.2
  graveclothes 309.14
  supporter 901.2
  v clothe 5.39
  wrap 295.20
  conceal 346.6
  protect 1008.18
shrouded in darkness 1027.13
shrouded in mystery 522.18
shrubbery 310.9
shrug
  n gesture 517.14
  v accept 134.7
  submit 433.6
shrug off
  not care 102.4
  discard 390.7
  submit 433.6
  underestimate 950.2
  dismiss 984.4
shrug the shoulders 517.21
shrunk
  reduced 252.10
  dwarf 258.13
  shrunken 260.13
shtick 704.7
shuck
  n hull 295.16
  v husk 6.9
shudder
  n thrill 105.2
  trepidation 105.5
  shake 917.3
  v be frequent 847.3

shake 917.11
  freeze 1023.9
shuddering halt 857.2
shuffle
  n slow motion 175.2
  gait 177.12
  prevarication 344.4
  quibble 936.4
  confusion 985.3
  v way of walking 177.28
  dance 705.5
  rearrange playing cards 758.5
  mix 797.10
  confuse 811.3
  change 854.5
  quibble 936.9
shuffle off 368.12
shun snub 157.7
  avoid 368.6
  abstain 668.7
shunt
  n pushing 904.1
  v avoid 164.6
  remove 176.11
  push 904.9
shush
  n sibilation 57.1
  v silence 51.8
  sibilate 57.2
  cover up 345.8
  interj silence 51.14
shut
  v close 293.6
  turn off 857.12
  adj closed 293.9
shut away 429.12
shutdown closure 293.1
  cessation 857.1
shut down
  close shop 293.8
  suppress 428.8
  go bankrupt 625.7
  stop work 857.8
  turn off 857.12
shut down on 51.8
shut-eye 22.2
shut in enclose 212.5
  confine 429.12
shut-in
  n sick person 85.43
  recluse 584.5
  adj unhealthy 85.54
  enclosed 212.10
  restricted 428.15
  confined 429.19
  recluse 584.10
shut off
  v separate 802.8
  turn off 857.12
  obstruct 1012.12
  adj secluded 584.8
  separated 802.21
shut one's mouth 51.5
shutout 412.3
shut out
  v close 293.6
  defeat 412.9
  prohibit 444.3
  exclude 773.4
  obstruct 1012.12
  adj defeated 412.16

shutter 1028.5
shutterbug 716.5
shut the door in one's face
  442.5
shut tight 1012.12
shuttle
  n train 179.14
  aircraft 181.1
  air travel 184.10
  loom 740.5
  oscillator 916.9
  spacecraft 1075.2
  v alternate 916.13
shuttlecock
  n oscillator 916.9
  v alternate 916.13
shuttle diplomacy 609.5
shut up
  v be silent 51.6
  enclose 212.5
  close 293.6
  close shop 293.8
  confine 429.12
  refute 958.5
  adj recluse 584.10
  interj silence 51.14
shy
  n avoidance 368.1
  retreat 903.3
  throw 904.3
  v be frightened 127.12
  flinch 127.13
  be startled 131.5
  turn aside 164.6
  retract 168.3
  demur 325.4
  hesitate 362.7
  avoid 368.8
  pull back 903.7
  throw 904.10
  quibble 936.9
  adj fearful 127.23
  timid 139.12
  receding 168.5
  demurring 325.7
  wary 494.9
  incomplete 795.4
  alone 872.8
  doubting 955.9
  wanting 992.13
shy away recede 168.2
  dodge 368.8
  pull back 903.7
shylock 620.3
shyster cheat 357.3
  trickster 415.6
  lawyer 597.3
  rascal 660.3
s' 332.18
siamese connection 239.6
Siamese twins 873.4
Siberia
  remote region 261.4
  cold place 1023.4
Siberian husky 176.8
Siberian tiger 311.22
sibilant 57.3
sibling
  n kinfolk 559.2
  adj related 559.6
sic 973.20

sick ill 85.56
  disconsolate 112.28
  weary 118.11
  insane 926.26
sick and tired of
  weary 118.11
  satiated 994.6
sicken
  disagree with 82.4
  take sick 85.47
  afflict 85.50
  offend 98.11
  deteriorate 393.16
sick joke 489.6
sickle 279.5
sick leave 222.4
sickly colorless 36.7
  unhealthy 85.54
sickness disease 85.1
  insanity 926.1
sic on incite 375.17
  sow dissension 456.14
side
  n aspect 33.3
  conceit 140.4
  incline 204.4
  border 211.4
  flank 218.1
  straight line 277.2
  pretensions 501.2
  boasting 502.1
  bluster 503.1
  lineage 560.4
  faction 617.4
  role 704.10
  playbook 704.21
  lawn bowling 750.3
  team 752.2
  interest 935.14
  outlook 978.2
  v remove 176.11
  border 211.10
  flank 218.4
  adj oblique 204.13
  lateral 218.6
  occasional 848.3
side against
  refuse 442.3
  oppose 451.3
  disapprove 510.10
  go contrary to 779.4
side arms 462.1
sidebar adjunct 254.1
  news item 552.3
sideboard 1054.3
sideburns 3.8
side by side
  adv cooperatively 450.6
  hand in hand 769.10
  phrs cheek to cheek 218.12
side dish 10.7
side door
  secret passage 346.5
  byway 383.4
side effect
  adjunct 254.1
  aftermath 817.3
side-glance glance 27.4
  flirtation 562.9
side horse 725.7
side issue 254.1

sidekick friend 588.4
  henchman 610.8
  partner 616.2
  escort 769.5
sidelight
  information 551.1
  light 1025.1
sideline
  n border 211.4
  avocation 724.7
  merchandise 735.1
  football 746.1
  basketball 747.1
  tennis 748.1
  field hockey 749.4
  v put away 390.6
sidelined 340.14
sidelong
  adj oblique 204.13
  inclining 204.15
  side 218.6
  adv obliquely 204.21
  laterally 218.8
  aside 218.10
side remark 213.2
sidestep avoid 164.6
  go sideways 218.5
  prevaricate 344.7
  dodge 368.8
  compromise 468.2
  pull back 903.7
  quibble 936.9
side street 383.4
sideswipe
  n impact 902.3
  v contact 223.10
  collide 902.13
side-to-side 218.8
sidetrack
  n digression 538.4
  v avoid 164.6
sidewalk 383.2
sideways
  adj flowing 172.8
  lateral 218.6
  adv crosswise 170.13
  obliquely 204.21
  laterally 218.8
sidewheeler 311.14
side with concur 332.9
  back 449.13
  take sides with 450.4
siding side 218.1
  building material 1054.2
  wood 1054.3
sidle
  n gait 177.12
  v avoid 164.6
  creep 177.26
  way of walking 177.28
  incline 204.10
  go sideways 218.5
sidle up to 167.3
siege enclosure 212.1
  besiegement 459.5
sierra 237.6
Sierra Club 397.5
siesta 22.3
sieve
  n refinery 79.13
  network 170.3

porousness 292.8
separator 802.7
arranger 808.5
v refine 79.22
segregate 773.6
classify 808.11
discriminate 944.4
sift refine 79.22
  select 371.14
  discuss 541.12
  segregate 773.6
  analyze 801.8
  classify 808.11
  investigate 938.23
  discriminate 944.4
sigh
  n breathing 2.21
  murmur 52.4
  sighing 52.8
  v murmur 52.10
  moan 52.14
  lament 115.10
  wind sound 318.21
  speak 524.25
sigh of relief 120.4
sight
  n sensation of seeing 24.5
  vision 27.1
  look 27.3
  optical device 29.5
  field of view 31.3
  view 33.6
  spectacle 33.7
  marvel 122.2
  lot 247.4
  opinion 953.6
  outlook 978.2
  eyesore 1015.4
  v see 27.12
sight for sore eyes 1016.7
sighthole
  observation post 27.8
  optical device 29.5
sighting 941.1
sightly 1016.19
sight-see
  journey 177.21
  see the sights 918.6
sight-seeing tour
  journey 177.5
  sight-seeing 918.4
sight-unseen transaction 971.8
sigmoid
  crescent-shaped 279.11
  convolutional 281.6
sign
  n prognosis 91.13
  omen 133.3
  poster 352.7
  telltale sign 517.1
  signal 517.15
  symbol 518.6
  letter 546.1
  hint 551.4
  musical notation 709.12
  substitute 862.2
  miracle 870.8
  evidence 957.1
  number 1017.3
  v ratify 332.12
  shake hands 437.7

secure 438.9
signal 517.22
inscribe 546.6
signal
  n sign 517.1
  beacon 517.15
  hint 551.4
  information theory 551.7
  race 756.3
  radar signal 1036.11
  v make a signal 182.52
  communicate 343.7
  flash 517.22
  adj remarkable 247.10
  communicational 347.21
  notable 997.19
signal flag
  signal 517.15
  flag 647.7
signalman 399.4
signal of distress 400.1
sign a petition 440.10
signatory 332.7
signature
  ratification 332.4
  signing 437.3
  sign 517.1
  identification 517.11
  autograph 527.10
  book part 554.12
  bookbinding 554.14
  musical notation 709.12
  part of writing 793.2
  acknowledgment 888.2
  station identification 1034.19
sign away 629.3
signed, sealed, and delivered 407.11
signed agreement 437.1
signer 332.7
signet
  ratification 332.4
  print 517.7
  label 517.13
  signature 527.10
  royal insignia 647.3
signet ring 498.6
significant
  n sign 518.6
  adj premonitory 133.16
  indicative 517.23
  meaningful 518.10
  prominent 662.17
  evidential 957.16
  important 997.17
significant other
  lover 104.12
  friend 588.1
signify augur 133.12
  betoken 517.17
  mean 518.8
  specify 865.11
  evidence 957.8
  matter 997.12
sign in 186.6
sign language
  deaf-and-dumb alphabet 49.3
  gesture 517.14
  language family 523.12
sign off
  telegraph 347.20

broadcast 1034.25
sign of the cross 696.5
sign of the times 133.3
sign on install 191.4
  telegraph 347.20
  participate 476.5
  employ 615.14
  broadcast 1034.25
sign one's death warrant
  condemn to death 308.20
  condemn 602.3
signor 76.7
signora 77.9
sign out 188.13
sign over 629.3
signpost post 273.4
  pointer 517.4
sign up install 191.4
  employ 615.14
  enlist 615.17
  join 617.14
  take one's turn 825.5
Silas Marner 484.4
silence
  n noiselessness 51
  quiescence 173.1
  taciturnity 344.2
  v disable 19.10
  put to silence 51.8
  strike dead 308.18
  extinguish 395.15
  overcome 412.7
  suppress 428.8
  refute 958.5
  interj hush 51.14
silent
  n motion pictures 706.1
  adj still 51.10
  taciturn 344.9
  unexpressed 519.9
silent majority
  middle class 607.5
  party 617.4
  mediocrity 1005.5
silent partner 616.2
silent treatment 909.4
silhouette
  n outline 211.2
  contour 262.2
  drawing 712.13
  portrait 712.15
  reflection 785.7
  shadow 1027.3
  v outline 211.9
silicon chip
  electronic circuit 1033.8
  circuitry 1042.3
silicone 1056.2
silk material 4.1
  smoothness 287.3
  fine texture 294.3
  softness 1047.4
silk-screen printing
  printing 548.1
  stencil printing 713.4
silk-stocking
  n nobleman 608.4
  adj socially prominent 578.16
silk-stocking district 609.16
silkworm 271.5
silky threadlike 271.7

smooth 287.10
sleek 287.11
fine-textured 294.8
velvety 1047.15
silly
    n fool 924.6
    adj nonsensical 520.7
    foolish 923.8
    dazed 985.14
    trivial 998.19
silo granary 386.7
    rocket launcher 1074.10
silt deposit 176.9
    dregs 256.2
silver
    n tableware 8.12
    whiteness 37.1
    alabaster 37.2
    money 728.1
    precious metals 728.20
    v whiten 37.5
    gray 39.3
    adj white 37.7
    gray 39.4
    eloquent 544.8
    brass 1058.17
Silver 311.15
silver dollar 728.7
silver lining 124.3
silver mine 1058.6
the silver screen 706.1
silver-tongued
    eloquent 544.8
    melodious 708.48
silverware
    tableware 8.12
    hard goods 735.4
silver wedding anniversary
    850.4
simian 311.23
similar
    approximate 775.8
    like 784.10
    comparative 943.8
simile similarity 784.1
    comparible 943.1
simmer
    n boiling 1020.2
    v cook 11.5
    be angry 152.15
    bubble 320.4
    seethe 671.12
    be hot 1019.22
    boil 1020.20
simmer down 106.7
Simon Legree 575.14
simp 924.8
simpatico 587.15
simper
    n smile 116.3
    v smile 116.7
    mince 500.14
simple
    soft-colored 35.22
    humble 137.10
    homelike 228.33
    mere 248.8
    artless 416.5
    tasteful 496.8
    ordinary 499.6
    elegant 533.6

plain-speaking 535.3
informal 581.3
real 761.15
essential 767.9
plain 798.6
one 872.7
mentally deficient 922.22
ignorant 930.12
gullible 954.9
genuine 973.15
easy 1014.13
simple existence 761.6
simple fact 761.3
simple machine 1040.5
simple matter 1014.3
simpleminded
    artless 416.5
    mentally deficient 922.22
simpleton 924.8
simplicity
    prosaicness 117.2
    rusticity 233.3
    decrease 252.1
    artlessness 416.1
    restraint 496.4
    ordinariness 499.1
    clearness 521.2
    elegance 533.1
    plain speech 535.1
    informality 581.1
    simpleness 798.1
    purity 798.1
    oneness 872.1
    mental deficiency 922.9
    ignorance 930.1
    gullibility 954.2
    facility 1014.1
simulate imitate 336.5
    fake 354.21
    affect 500.12
    adopt 621.4
    resemble 784.7
simulation
    imitation 336.1
    sham 354.3
    adoption 621.2
    similarity 784.1
    simultaneous 836.5
sin
    n blackness 38.4
    iniquity 654.3
    wrongdoing 655.1
    misdeed 655.2
    error 975.1
    v do wrong 654.8
    transgress 655.4
since
    adv subsequently 835.6
    ago 837.15
    ever since 837.17
    conj because 888.10
sincere zealous 101.9
    resolute 359.11
    artless 416.5
    candid 644.17
    genuine 973.15
the sincerest form of flattery
    336.1
since time began
    for a long time 827.14
    since 837.17

sine qua non 196.5
sinew muscularity 15.2
    power 18.1
    vigor 544.3
sinewy
    able-bodied 15.16
    vigorous 544.11
    tough 1049.4
sinful wrong 638.3
    immoral 654.16
    wicked 655.5
    ungodly 695.17
    bad 1000.7
sing
    n musical occasion 708.32
    v bird sound 60.5
    be pleased 95.12
    exude cheerfulness 109.6
    rejoice 116.5
    wind sound 318.21
    betray 351.6
    speak 524.25
    inform on 551.13
    vocalize 708.38
    poetize 720.13
sing a different tune
    n change one's mind
        363.6
    v be changed 852.6
    change 852.7
    convert 858.11
singe
    n burn 1020.6
    v stain 1004.6
    burn 1020.24
singer
    entertainer 707.1
    lead 707.6
    vocalist 710.13
Singer 741.3
single
    n celibate 565.2
    baseball hit 745.3
    individual 872.4
    v hit a baseball 745.5
    adj unmarried 565.7
    simple 798.6
    characteristic 865.13
    one 872.7
single file 812.2
single-handed 872.8
single-minded
    resolute 359.11
    persevering 360.8
    artless 416.5
    engrossed 983.17
singleness of purpose 360.1
single out
    select 371.14
    specify 865.11
    call attention to 983.10
single vote 371.6
sing out 59.8
singsong
    n regularity 781.2
    repetitiousness 849.4
    adj tedious 118.9
    monotonous 849.15
sing the blues
    hang one's head 112.15
    lament 115.10

sing the praises of
    praise 509.12
    glorify 696.12
    sing 708.38
sing the same old song
    harp on 118.8
    dwell on 849.9
singular
    n number 530.8
    adj wonderful 122.10
    particular 865.12
    characteristic 865.13
    odd 870.11
    one 872.7
    sole 872.9
    eccentric 927.5
sinister
    adj ominous 133.17
    oblique 204.13
    left 220.4
    dishonest 645.16
    bad 1000.7
    adverse 1011.13
    adv leftward 220.6
sink
    n washbasin 79.12
    receptacle of filth 80.12
    drain 239.5
    cavity 284.2
    den of iniquity 654.7
    v weaken 16.9
    burn out 21.5
    disappear 34.2
    languish 85.48
    lose heart 112.16
    sadden 112.18
    recede 168.2
    move 172.5
    capsize 182.44
    go down 194.6
    decrease 252.6
    deepen 275.8
    be concave 284.12
    excavate 284.15
    gravitate 297.15
    age 303.10
    submerge 367.7
    scuttle 367.8
    spoil 393.11
    decline 393.17
    ruin 395.11
    founder 410.11
    bankrupt 625.8
    invest 729.17
    make a golf shot 751.4
    flit 828.6
    depress 913.4
    come to grief 1011.10
    fall on evil days
        1011.11
sinkhole pothole 284.3
    sewer 654.7
    water 1065.3
sink in
    impress 93.15
    mire 243.2
    get across 521.5
    impress 931.19
    be remembered 989.14
sinking fast 307.33
sinking heart 112.3

sink into despair
  lose heart 112.16
  despair 125.10
sink one's teeth into it 330.11
sink or swim
  adv without fail 970.26
  phrs come what may 359.20
sinner evildoer 593.1
  wrongdoer 660.8
sinuous curved 279.7
  convolutional 281.6
sinus 279.2
sip
  n drink 8.4
  taste 62.2
  nip 88.7
  hint 248.4
  v drink 8.29
  taste 62.7
  tipple 88.24
siphon
  n extractor 192.9
  tube 239.6
  v transport 176.14
  channel 239.15
sir 76.7
Sir 648.3
sire
  n senior 304.5
  father 560.9
  Sir 648.3
  jockey 757.2
  author 886.4
  producer 892.7
  v procreate 78.8
  engender 818.14
  cause 886.10
siren
  n noisemaker 53.6
  spirit of the sea 240.4
  tempter 377.4
  warning sign 399.3
  alarm 400.1
  witch 593.7
  water god 678.10
  bewitcher 690.9
  adj alluring 377.8
Sir Galahad 608.5
sirocco
  hot wind 318.7
  dust storm 318.13
sissy
  n weakling 16.6
  effeminate male 77.11
  spoiled child 427.4
  coward 491.5
  sister 559.3
  adj effeminate 77.15
  cowardly 491.10
sister woman 77.6
  nurse 90.10
  female sibling 559.3
  member 617.11
  nun 699.18
  layman 700.2
  likeness 784.3
Sister 648.5
sister-in-law 564.2
sit be pregnant 78.12
  be seated 173.10
  convene 770.17

sit around 331.12
sit at 221.8
sit at the feet of 570.11
sit back 329.2
sitcom 1035.2
sit-down meal 8.5
  conference 541.6
  strike 727.5
  assembly 770.2
site
  n location 159.1
  arena 463.1
  v locate 159.11
  place 159.12
  establish 159.16
sit idly by 329.3
sit-in
  objection 333.2
  assembly 770.2
sit in 333.5
sit in for 862.5
sit in judgment
  administer justice 594.5
  try 598.18
  hold the scales 946.12
sit in on 48.10
sit it out 329.2
sit on cover up 345.8
  suppress 428.8
  participate 476.5
  appropriate 480.19
  disapprove 510.18
  try 598.18
  rest on 901.22
sit on a barrel of gunpowder
  court danger 493.6
  take chances 1006.7
sit on the fence
  n be a timeserver 363.9
  v hesitate 362.7
  dodge 368.8
  remain neutral 467.5
sit on the sidelines
  do nothing 329.2
  remain neutral 467.5
sitter 1008.8
sit through 134.7
sit tight hide 346.8
  stay with it 360.4
  wait 846.12
sitting duck dupe 358.2
  exposure 1006.3
  easy thing 1014.3
sitting pretty
  cheerful 109.11
  successful 409.14
  victorious 411.7
sitting room 197.5
situate
  v locate 159.11
  adj located 159.18
situation location 159.1
  placement 159.6
  environment 209.1
  occupation 724.5
  state 765.1
  mental outlook 978.2
  predicament 1013.4
sit up rise 200.8
  wait 846.12
sit up and take notice 983.8

sitz bath 79.8
six playing card 758.2
  number 882.2
six feet under
  adj dead 307.30
  adv buried 309.23
sixfold
  v multiply by six 882.16
  adj six times as much 882.18
six of one and half a dozen of
  the other
  n ambiguity 539.1
  the same 790.3
  choicelessness 963.6
  adj coinciding 778.8
  indistinguishable 945.6
sixteen 882.7
sixteenth note 709.14
sixteenth rest 709.21
sixth
  n interval 709.20
  adj ordinal number 882.18
  n fraction 882.14
sixth sense senses 24.5
  extrasensory perception 689.8
  intuition 934.1
sixtieth 882.27
sixty 882.7
sixty-four dollar question
  522.8
sixty-fourth note 709.14
sixty-fourth rest 709.21
sizable large 247.7
  considerable 257.16
size
  n dimension 257.1
  largeness 257.1
  extent 300.3
  semiliquid 1062.5
  v adjust 257.15
  measure 300.10
  classify 808.11
  examine 938.24
size up scrutinize 27.14
  measure 300.10
  examine 938.24
  estimate 946.9
sizzle
  n energy 17.3
  hissing 57.1
  v hiss 57.2
  drug use 87.22
  be angry 152.15
  speed 174.9
sizzler
  speeder 174.5
  hot day 1019.8
skate glide 177.35
  play hockey 749.7
skateboard
  n skates 179.21
  v glide 177.35
skate on thin ice 1006.7
skating rink 743.11
skedaddle
  n flight 368.4
  v be frightened 127.12
  speed 174.9
  depart 188.7
  leave 222.10
  flee 368.11

  lose one's nerve 491.8
  interj go away! 909.32
skeet shooting
  sport 744.1
  trapshooting 904.2
skein cord 271.2
  flock 770.6
skeleton
  n base 199.2
  outline 211.2
  frame 266.4
  thinness 270.7
  thin person 270.8
  corpse 307.16
  diagram 381.3
  wreck 393.8
  abridgment 557.1
  support 901.10
  adj skeletal 2.26
skeleton crew 992.2
skeleton in the closet
  secret 345.5
  evil 1000.3
skeleton key 292.10
skeptic
  n agnostic 695.12
  doubter 955.4
  adj agnostic 695.20
sketch
  n description 349.2
  diagram 381.3
  treatise 556.1
  abridgment 557.1
  act 704.7
  drawing 712.13
  likeness 784.3
  v describe 349.9
  plot 381.10
  outline 381.11
  abridge 557.5
  act 704.29
  portray 712.19
sketchbook
  book 554.1
  art equipment 712.18
sketchy
  incomplete 795.4
  imperfect 1003.4
skew
  n deviation 164.1
  bias 204.3
  v squint 28.9
  deflect 164.5
  diverge 204.9
  go sideways 218.5
  unbalance 791.3
  adj deflective 164.8
  askew 204.14
  unequal 791.4
skewer
  perforate 292.15
  stigmatize 661.9
  hook 800.8
ski
  n skate 179.21
  v glide 177.35
  sport 753.4
skid
  n slide 194.4
  v glide 177.35
  maneuver 184.40

slide 194.9
  go sideways 218.5
skid row 230.6
skier 753.2
skiing gliding 177.16
  sports 753.1
ski jump
  n leap 366.1
  v leap 366.5
ski lift
  cableway 383.8
  transport 753.1
skill superiority 249.1
  expertise 413.1
  skillfulness 413.1
  art 413.7
  production 892.2
  memory 989.1
skilled laborer 726.6
skillful expert 413.22
  good 999.12
skim
  n gliding 177.16
  v touch lightly 73.7
  speed 174.8
  glide 177.35
  float 182.54
  slide 194.9
  contact 223.10
  scratch the surface 276.4
  slight 340.8
  cheat 356.18
  acquire 472.9
  take 480.13
  browse 570.13
  examine cursorily
    938.26
skimp
  v slight 340.8
  stint 484.5
  economize 635.4
  adj meager 992.10
skimpy sparse 885.5
  meager 992.10
skin
  n body covering 2.4
  fur 4.2
  contraceptive 86.23
  exterior 206.2
  shallowness 276.1
  skin 295.3
  blanket 295.12
  lamina 296.2
  money 728.6
  cash 728.7
  v peel 6.8
  best 249.7
  injure 393.13
  strip 480.24
  overprice 632.7
  cheat 759.26
  tear apart 802.14
  abrade 1044.7
skin alive best 249.7
  defeat 412.9
  criticize 510.20
skin and bones
  n shrinking 260.3
  leanness 270.5
  adj wasted 393.35
skin color 35.1

skin-deep
  cutaneous 2.27
  insignificant 248.6
  shallow 276.5
  epidermal 295.32
skin diver 367.4
skin flick 666.4
skinflint 484.4
skin game 356.10
skinny cutaneous 2.27
  lean 270.17
  skinlike 295.32
the skinny
  information 551.1
  the facts 761.4
  the truth 973.4
skinny-dip 182.56
skip
  n step 177.11
  leap 366.1
  wastepaper basket 391.7
  lawn bowling 750.3
  v exude cheerfulness 109.6
  rejoice 116.5
  way of walking 177.28
  depart 188.7
  leave undone 340.7
  leap 366.5
  caper 366.6
  flee 368.11
  escape 369.6
  dance 705.5
  play 743.23
skip it 998.25
skip over slight 340.8
  examine cursorily 938.26
skipper
  n ship's officer 183.7
  v direct 573.8
skirl
  n screech 58.4
  v screech 58.8
skirmish
  n fight 457.4
  v contend 457.13
skirt
  n dress 5.16
  woman 77.6
  border 211.4
  girl 302.7
  v border 211.10
  flank 218.4
  contact 223.10
  evade 368.7
  circle 914.5
skirting
  n edging 211.7
  adj bordering 211.11
  flanking 218.6
ski slope 753.1
skit 704.7
skittish
  sensitive 24.12
  excitable 105.28
  frisky 109.14
  fearful 127.23
  jittery 128.12
  shy 139.12
  fickle 364.6
skoal! 88.38
skulduggery 356.4

skulk
  n shirker 368.3
  group of animals 770.5
  v lurk 346.9
  shirk 368.9
  cower 491.9
skull cranium 198.7
  death 307.3
skull and crossbones
  death 307.3
  warning sign 399.3
  insignia 647.1
skunk
  n stinker 71.3
  wild animal 311.23
  bad person 660.6
  v defeat 412.9
sky
  n summit 198.2
  height 272.2
  the heavens 1072.2
  v hit golf ball 751.4
  elevate 912.5
skycap 176.7
sky dive
  parachute 181.13
  plunge 367.1
sky-high 272.15
skyjack 482.20
skyjacker 483.7
skylark
  n ascent 193.7
  v make merry 743.24
skylight roof 295.6
  shine 1025.2
skyline 201.4
skyrocket
  n ascent 193.7
  v shoot up 193.9
  improve 392.7
  rocket 1074.12
skyscraper
  structure 266.2
  tower 272.6
skyward up 193.16
  on high 272.21
skywriting 184.1
slab lamina 296.2
  wood 1054.3
slack
  n refuse 391.4
  coal dust 1021.2
  v relax 20.7
  leave undone 340.7
  shirk 368.9
  ease up 670.9
  loosen 804.3
  fight fire 1022.7
  adj weak 16.12
  apathetic 94.13
  inert 173.14
  slow 175.10
  indolent 331.19
  negligent 340.10
  lax 426.4
  wanton 665.26
  loose 804.5
  slovenly 810.15
  dilatory 846.17
slacker neglecter 340.5
  shirker 368.3

slack-jawed 292.18
slacks 5.18
slag dregs 256.2
  refuse 391.4
  combustion product 1020.16
slake gratify 95.8
  relieve 120.5
  relax 670.9
  satiate 994.4
slalom 753.3
slam
  n explosive noise 56.1
  disrespect 156.3
  score 409.5
  jail 429.9
  criticism 510.4
  hit 902.4
  blow 902.5
  v make explosive noise 56.6
  be disrespectful 156.6
  close 293.6
  criticize 510.14
  strike 902.15
slammer 429.9
slam the door in one's face
  snub 157.5
  avoid 368.6
  repulse 442.5
slander
  n monstrous lie 354.12
  libel 512.3
  scandal 552.8
  v libel 512.11
slang
  n gibberish 522.7
  nonformal language 523.5
  jargon 523.9
  barbarism 526.6
  v bluster 503.3
  adj jargonish 523.21
slant
  n glance 27.4
  aspect 33.3
  deviation 164.1
  inclination 204.2
  diagonal 204.7
  partiality 650.3
  plot 722.4
  tendency 896.1
  mental outlook 978.2
  disposition 978.3
  v incline 204.10
  go sideways 218.5
  pervert 265.6
  misrepresent 350.3
  falsify 354.16
  favor 650.8
  influence 894.7
  adj inclining 204.15
  transverse 204.19
slap
  n explosive sound 56.1
  punishment 604.3
  smack 902.8
  v make explosive sound 56.6
  place violently 159.13
  punish 604.12
  smack 902.19
  adv suddenly 830.9
slapdash
  n slipshodness 340.3

adj hasty 401.9
reckless 493.8
adv carelessly 340.18
hastily 401.12
recklessly 493.11
slaphappy 926.27
slap in the face
  n provocation 152.11
  indignity 156.2
  repulse 442.2
  slap 604.3
  v offend 156.5
slap on the wrist 604.3
slap shot 749.3
slapstick
  n wit 489.1
  comedy 704.6
  acting 704.8
  adj comical 488.6
  burlesque 508.14
  theatrical 704.35
slash
  n trauma 85.38
  diagonal 204.7
  line 517.6
  discount 631.1
  cheapening 633.4
  engraving 713.2
  break 802.4
  v cut 204.11
  notch 289.4
  injure 393.13
  criticize 510.20
  cheapen 633.6
  sever 802.11
slash and burn 1069.17
slat
  n explosive sound 56.1
  thinness 270.7
  strip 271.4
  lamina 296.2
  wood 1054.3
  v make explosive sound 56.6
  flutter 917.12
slate
  n ballot 609.19
  schedule 965.3
  v cover 295.23
  schedule 965.6
slattern pig 80.13
  slob 810.7
slaughter
  n killing 308.1
  butchery 308.3
  destruction 395.1
  unruliness 671.3
  v butcher 308.17
  put an end to 395.12
  rage 671.11
slaughterhouse 308.12
slave
  n sycophant 138.3
  instrument 384.4
  subject 432.7
  retainer 577.1
  drudge 726.3
  v work hard 725.13
slave driver
  superintendent 574.2
  tyrant 575.14
slavery servility 138.1

subjection 432.1
service 577.12
work 725.4
slay delight 95.11
  make laugh 116.9
  kill 308.13
  amuse 743.21
sleaze 660.5
sled
  n sleigh 179.20
  v glide 177.35
sledgehammer
  v pound 902.16
  adj coercive 424.12
sleek
  v polish 287.7
  adj slick 287.11
  chic 578.13
  tidy 807.8
  thriving 1010.13
  oily 1056.9
sleep
  n rest 20.1
  slumber 22.2
  unconsciousness 25.2
  quiescence 173.1
  death 307.1
  v slumber 22.13
  stagnate 173.9
  neglect 340.6
sleep around 665.19
sleep disorder 92.14
sleep in take a rest 20.8
  sleep 22.13
sleeping bag 901.20
sleeping beauty 22.12
sleeping pill
  anesthetic 25.3
  sedative 86.12
sleeping sickness 22.6
sleepless wakeful 23.7
  industrious 330.22
  vigilant 339.13
  alert 339.14
  persevering 360.8
sleepwalking
  n sleep 22.2
  trance 92.19
  nightwalking 177.9
  adj nightwalking 177.38
sleep with 75.21
sleepy drowsy 22.21
  languid 331.20
sleet
  n ice 1023.5
  v hail 1023.11
sleigh 177.35
sleight chicanery 356.4
  trick 356.6
  stratagem 415.3
sleight of hand
  juggling 356.5
  trick 356.6
  illusoriness 976.2
slender
  narrow 270.14
  thin 270.16
  meager 992.10
  trivial 998.19
  comely 1016.19
sleuth 576.10

slew
  n lot 247.4
  bunch 770.7
  multitude 884.3
  v change course 182.30
slice
  n lamina 296.2
  gain 472.3
  portion 477.5
  part 793.1
  piece 793.3
  break 802.4
  v apportion 477.6
  hit a golf ball 751.4
  separate 793.6
  sever 802.11
slice of life
  description 349.2
  genuineness 973.7
slick
  n blanket 295.12
  lamina 296.2
  v polish 287.7
  oil 1056.8
  adj sleek 287.11
  slippery 287.12
  skillful 413.22
  cunning 415.12
  eloquent 544.8
  tidy 807.8
  shrewd 920.15
  oily 1056.9
  adv cunningly 415.13
slicker
  n outerwear 5.13
  smoother 287.4
  cheater 357.4
  sophisticate 413.17
  v deceive 356.19
slide
  n gliding 177.16
  slip 194.4
  smoothness 287.3
  means of escape 369.3
  wind instrument 711.6
  photograph 714.3
  print 714.5
  playground equipment
    743.15
  v glide 177.35
  slip 194.9
  decline 393.17
  elapse 821.5
  go easily 1014.10
slide back 394.4
slide into 858.17
slide off 368.12
slide projector 714.12
sliding scale 624.4
slight
  n snub 157.2
  nonobservance 435.1
  v ignore 157.6
  turn one's back on 340.8
  flout 454.4
  disparage 512.8
  be inattentive 984.2
  dismiss 984.4
  adj frail 16.14
  little 258.10
  thin 270.16

shallow 276.5
rare 299.4
meager 992.10
trivial 998.19
slightest 250.8
slim
  n thin person 270.8
  v slenderize 270.13
  adj thin 270.16
  sparse 885.5
  meager 992.10
slim chance 972.9
slime
  n filth 80.7
  slop 80.8
  mud 1062.8
  v dirty 80.15
slim pickings 992.2
slimy filthy 80.23
  flattering 511.8
  viscous 1062.12
  muddy 1062.14
sling
  n medical dressing 86.33
  slingshot 462.9
  throw 904.3
  v suspend 202.8
  throw 904.10
slingshot
  sling 462.9
  toy 743.16
slink
  n gait 177.12
  v creep 177.26
  convolve 281.4
  lurk 346.9
  cower 491.9
slink off 368.12
slinky thin 270.16
  covert 345.12
  cowering 491.13
slip
  n anchor 180.16
  slide 194.4
  runt 258.4
  thinness 270.7
  pillowcase 295.10
  youngster 302.1
  girl 302.6
  sprout 302.11
  branch 310.20
  avoidance 368.1
  miss 410.4
  bungle 414.5
  proof 548.5
  recording media 549.10
  misdeed 655.2
  ceramics 742.3
  error 975.4
  harbor 1009.6
  mud 1062.8
  v glide 177.35
  float 182.54
  slide 194.9
  decline 393.17
  sink 410.11
  miss 410.14
  bungle 414.11
  give 478.12
  go wrong 654.9
  elapse 821.5

err 975.9
fall on evil days 1011.11
slip by 837.6
slipcover 554.14
slip in enter 189.7
  insert 191.3
  interpose 213.6
  intrude 214.5
slip off take off 6.6
  absent oneself 222.8
slip of the tongue 975.4
slip on 5.43
slip one's mind 990.7
slip one a Mickey 25.4
slippery slick 287.12
  deceitful 356.22
  evasive 368.15
  cunning 415.12
  dishonest 645.16
  treacherous 645.21
  unreliable 971.20
  precarious 1006.12
  oily 1056.9
slipshod
  careless 340.12
  lax 426.4
  ungrammatic 531.4
  slovenly 810.15
slipstream 184.30
slip through one's fingers
  369.9
slit
  n crack 224.2
  furrow 290.1
  break 802.4
  v cleave 224.4
  furrow 290.3
  open 292.11
  injure 393.13
  sever 802.11
  adj cleft 224.7
  furrowed 290.4
  impaired 393.27
  severed 802.23
slither
  n gait 177.12
  gliding 177.16
  slide 194.4
  v way of walking 177.28
  glide 177.35
  slide 194.9
slit trench 460.5
sliver scrap 248.3
  intruder 774.2
  piece 793.3
slob bungler 414.9
  slattern 810.7
  ice 1023.5
  mud 1062.8
slobber
  n saliva 13.3
  unction 511.2
  v salivate 13.6
  be stupid 922.12
  be insane 926.20
  moisten 1065.12
sloe
  n blackness 38.4
  adj black 38.8
slog
  n walk 177.10

hit 902.4
  v way of walking 177.28
  keep doggedly at 360.3
  drudge 725.14
  strike 902.15
slogan
  call to arms 458.8
  catchword 526.9
  motto 974.4
slop
  n slime 80.8
  offal 80.9
  sentimentality 93.8
  refuse 391.4
  mud 1062.8
  mud puddle 1062.9
  v overflow 238.17
  moisten 1065.12
slope
  n inclination 204.2
  incline 204.4
  declivity 237.2
  skiing 753.1
  v incline 204.10
sloppy filthy 80.23
  sentimental 93.21
  slipshod 340.12
  bungling 414.20
  lax 426.4
  loose 804.5
  slovenly 810.15
  slimy 1062.14
  watery 1065.16
slosh
  n lap 238.8
  snow 1023.8
  mud 1062.8
  sprinkle 1065.5
  v ripple 52.11
  overflow 238.17
  lap 238.19
  moisten 1065.12
sloshed 88.33
slot
  n crack 224.2
  opening 292.1
  syntax 530.2
  gambling wheel 759.16
  v cleave 224.4
sloth
  apathy 94.4
  wretchedness 96.6
  unconcern 102.2
  dejection 112.3
  despair 125.2
  slowness 175.1
  inaction 329.1
  indolence 331.5
  languor 331.21
  group of animals 770.5
slot machine
  vending machine 736.4
  gambling wheel 759.16
slouch
  n slow motion 175.2
  gait 177.12
  idler 331.8
  bungler 414.8
  v way of walking 177.28
  sink 194.6
  idle 331.12

slough
  n shed skin 2.5
  offal 80.9
  gangrene 85.40
  marsh 243.1
  predicament 1013.4
  mud puddle 1062.9
  v shed 6.10
  discard 390.7
slovenly dirty 80.22
  slipshod 340.12
  ungrammatic 531.4
  slipshod 810.15
slow
  v slow down 175.9
  adj dull 117.6
  not fast 175.10
  reluctant 325.6
  indolent 331.19
  languid 331.20
  leisurely 402.6
  late 846.16
  dilatory 846.17
  infrequent 848.2
  dull 922.16
  adv slowly 175.13
  late 846.19
  tardily 846.20
slow burn 152.3
slowdown
  slowing 175.4
  decline 252.2
  economizing 635.2
  strike 727.5
  delay 846.2
slow motion 175.2
slow on the draw 846.16
slowpoke 175.5
slow starter 846.6
slow time
  march 177.13
  time 832.3
slow-up 846.2
slow-witted 922.16
sludge slime 80.8
  refuse 391.4
  ice 1023.5
  mud 1062.8
slug
  n drink 8.4
  slowpoke 175.5
  idler 331.8
  shot 462.19
  line of type 548.2
  type spacing 548.7
  token 728.12
  dose 793.5
  blow 902.5
  v fight 754.4
  strike 902.15
slugger
  baseball player 745.2
  boxer 754.2
sluggish apathetic 94.13
  unconcerned 102.7
  inert 173.14
  slow 175.10
  meandering 238.24
  languid 331.20
  dilatory 846.17
  dull 922.16

sluice
  n outlet 190.9
  watercourse 239.2
  drain 239.5
  floodgate 239.11
  v wash 79.19
  flood 1065.14
slum sty 80.11
  city district 230.6
slumber
  n sleep 22.2
  quiescence 173.1
  v sleep 22.13
  stagnate 173.9
slumlord 470.3
slump
  n sinkage 194.2
  decline 252.2
  deterioration 393.3
  cheapening 633.4
  business cycle 731.10
  declining market 737.5
  shortcoming 911.1
  hard times 1011.6
  v sink 194.6
  decline 393.17
  cheapen 633.6
  fall short 911.2
slur
  n aspersion 512.4
  stigma 661.6
  musical execution 708.30
  musical notation 709.12
  v slight 340.8
  defame 512.9
  stigmatize 661.9
  examine cursorily 938.26
  stain 1004.6
slurp
  n drink 8.4
  ingestion 187.4
  v lap up 8.30
  draw in 187.12
slurry 797.6
slush slime 80.8
  sentimentality 93.8
  talkativeness 540.1
  snow 1023.8
  mud 1062.8
slush fund 609.35
slut female animal 77.10
  unclean person 80.13
  dog 311.17
  neglecter 340.5
  strumpet 665.14
  slob 810.7
sly covert 345.12
  cunning 415.12
  cautious 494.8
  shrewd 920.15
smack
  n explosive sound 56.1
  taste 62.1
  heroin 87.9
  hint 248.4
  attempt 403.3
  kiss 562.4
  punishment 604.3
  admixture 797.7
  characteristic 865.4
  hit 902.4

slap 902.8
v make explosive sound
  56.6
taste 62.7
kiss 562.19
punish 604.12
hit 902.14
slap 902.19
adv suddenly 830.9
smacker 728.7
smack in the middle 819.5
smack of savor of 63.6
  resemble 784.7
smack the lips
  savor 63.5
  enjoy 95.13
small
  adj humble 137.10
  insignificant 248.6
  inadequate 250.7
  little 258.10
  thin 270.16
  ungenerous 651.6
  base 661.12
  narrow-minded 980.10
  meager 992.10
  unimportant 998.17
  adv little 258.16
small business 731.1
small change
  petty cash 728.19
  trivia 998.4
small fry runt 258.4
  young people 302.2
  a nobody 998.7
small-minded 980.10
small potatoes
  a nobody 998.7
  mediocrity 1005.5
small print 959.2
small talk
  chitchat 541.5
  gossip 552.7
small-time 250.7
smarmy
  obsequious 138.14
  insincere 354.32
  suave 504.18
  flattering 511.8
  sanctimonious 693.5
smart
  n smarting 26.3
  v suffer 26.8
  affect emotionally 93.14
  resent 152.12
  adj impudent 142.10
  quick 330.18
  alert 339.14
  witty 489.15
  ridiculing 508.12
  fashionable 578.11
  chic 578.13
  tidy 807.8
  brainy 920.14
smart aleck
  egotist 140.5
  impudent person 142.6
smart money 624.3
smart operator 737.11
smarts intellect 919.1
  smartness 920.2

smash
  n debacle 395.4
  success 409.4
  collapse 410.3
  defeat 412.1
  concussion 671.8
  declining market 737.5
  impact 902.3
  hit 902.4
  misfortune 1011.2
  pulp 1063.2
  v billow 238.22
  demolish 395.17
  raze 395.19
  conquer 412.10
  suppress 428.8
  play tennis 748.3
  shatter 802.13
  collide 902.13
  soften 1047.6
  pulverize 1051.9
  pulp 1063.5
smashed high 87.24
  drunk 88.33
  impaired 393.27
  conquered 412.17
  suppressed 428.14
smash hit 409.4
smashing defeat 412.3
smattering
  n hint 248.4
  slight knowledge 930.6
  trifling 998.8
  adj half-learned 930.15
smear
  n soil 80.5
  defamation 512.2
  stigma 661.6
  stain 1004.3
  v color 35.14
  soil 80.16
  coat 295.24
  defeat 412.9
  vilify 512.10
  stigmatize 661.9
  stain 1004.6
  oil 1056.8
smell
  n senses 24.5
  odor 69.1
  smelling 69.4
  hint 248.4
  v sense 24.6
  have an odor 69.6
  scent 69.8
  stink 71.4
  detect 941.6
smell a rat 955.6
smell out trace 938.35
  detect 941.6
smelly odorous 69.9
  malodorous 71.5
smelt extract 192.10
  process 892.9
  melt 1020.21
smelter extractor 192.9
  foundry 739.4
smidgen 248.2
smile
  n grin 116.3
  greeting 585.4

v be pleased 95.12
  exude cheerfulness 109.6
  grin 116.7
smile at 508.8
smirk
  n smile 116.3
  scornful smile 508.4
  v smile 116.7
  mince 500.14
smithereen scrap 248.3
  piece 793.3
smitten 104.28
smock 5.17
smog
  n fog 319.3
  miasma 1001.4
  v cloud 319.7
smoke
  n blackness 38.4
  marijuana 87.11
  tobacco 89.1
  smoking tobacco 89.3
  puff 89.10
  spirit 764.3
  ephemeron 828.5
  combustion product 1020.16
  vapor 1067.1
  v blacken 38.7
  dirty 80.15
  use marijuana 87.22
  inhale 89.14
  be angry 152.15
  best 249.7
  cloud 319.7
  preserve 397.9
  let out 909.24
  stain 1004.6
  fume 1019.23
  dry 1066.6
  vaporize 1067.8
smoke out 909.14
smoke signal 517.15
smoker addict 87.21
  tobacco user 89.11
  smoking room 89.13
smoke screen
  cover 356.11
  pretext 376.1
smoking gun clue 517.9
  proof 957.3
smoking room
  smoking car 89.13
  kitchen 197.14
Smoky the Bear 397.5
smolder
  be excitable 105.16
  be angry 152.15
  stagnate 173.9
  be latent 519.3
  be hot 1019.22
smooch
  n kiss 562.4
  stigma 661.6
  v make love 562.15
  kiss 562.19
smooth
  n smoothness 287.3
  note 709.14
  v level 201.6
  straighten 277.5
  flatten 287.5

change the texture 294.4
  pacify 465.7
  talkative 540.9
  calm 670.7
  make uniform 781.4
  facilitate 1014.7
  buff 1044.8
  adj hairless 6.17
  quiescent 173.12
  horizontal 201.7
  straight 277.6
  smooth-textured 287.10
  fine 294.8
  cunning 415.12
  suave 504.18
  flattering 511.8
  harmonious 533.8
  eloquent 544.8
  fluent 544.9
  uniform 781.5
  continuous 812.8
  easy 1014.13
  oily 1056.9
smooth customer 415.6
smoothie cheater 357.4
  slyboots 415.6
smooth over
  pacify 465.7
  extenuate 600.12
  calm 670.7
smooth-running 1014.14
smooth sailing 1014.1
smooth talker 415.6
smooth the way
  facilitate 1014.7
  oil 1056.8
smorgasbord
  restaurant 8.17
  appetizer 10.9
smother
  control one's feelings 106.8
  wrap 295.20
  die 307.24
  strangle 308.19
  cover up 345.8
  extinguish 395.15
  suppress 428.8
  moderate 670.6
  be hot 1019.22
  fight fire 1022.7
smothering
  violent death 307.6
  suffocation 308.6
  veil of secrecy 345.3
  suppression 428.2
  extinguishing 1022.2
smudge
  n blackening 38.5
  soil 80.5
  stigma 661.6
  stain 1004.3
  combustion product 1020.16
  vapor 1067.1
  v blacken 38.7
  soil 80.16
  smoke 1019.23
smug
  complacent 107.10
  vain 140.8
  prudish 500.19
  suave 504.18

chic 578.13
smuggle 732.8
smuggler 732.5
smut
  n blackness 38.4
  blackening 38.5
  soil 80.5
  dirt 80.6
  filth 80.7
  dregs 256.2
  fungus 310.4
  obscenity 666.4
  blight 1001.2
  stain 1004.3
  combustion product 1020.16
  powder 1051.5
  v blacken 38.7
  soil 80.16
snack
  n light meal 8.7
  piece 793.3
  v feed 8.18
  pick 8.26
snafu
  n complex 799.2
  mix-up 810.2
  goof 975.6
  confusion 985.3
  v spoil 393.11
  complicate 799.3
  confuse 811.3
  hinder 1012.16
  adj confused 810.16
snag
  n teeth 2.8
  projection 285.4
  proviso 421.3
  fault 1003.2
  hitch 1013.8
  v acquire 472.9
  catch 480.17
snaggle-toothed 285.14
snail shellfish 10.25
  slowpoke 175.5
  marine animal 311.30
snail's pace 175.2
snake
  n serpent 311.26
  traitor 357.10
  bad person 660.6
  v stray 164.4
  creep 177.26
  convolve 281.4
  pull 905.4
  jerk 905.5
snakebite 1001.5
snake charmer 707.3
snake eyes 873.3
snake in the grass
  traitor 357.10
  evil 1000.3
  hidden danger 1006.5
snake oil 86.2
snap
  n bite 8.2
  energy 17.3
  crack 56.2
  zest 68.2
  photograph 714.3
  football play 746.3
  blackjack 759.11

tap 902.7
  trifle 998.5
  easy 1014.4
  cold weather 1023.3
  elasticity 1048.1
  v crack 56.7
  growl 60.4
  show resentment 152.14
  close 293.6
  be damaged 393.23
  speak 524.25
  photograph 714.14
  hook 800.8
  break 802.12
  hit 902.14
  tap 902.18
  throw 904.10
  adj unpremeditated 365.11
  hasty 401.9
  unprepared 406.8
snap back react 903.5
  recoil 903.6
snap decision 365.4
snap one's fingers at
  disdain 157.3
  disobey 327.6
  flout 454.4
  attach little importance to
    998.12
snap out of it
  cheer up 109.9
  recover 396.20
snappy energetic 17.13
  zestful 68.7
  fast 174.15
  active 330.17
  quick 330.18
  cold 1023.14
snapshot
  n photograph 714.3
  v photograph 714.14
snap to it! 401.17
snap up energize 17.10
  seize 480.14
snare
  n springe 356.13
  lure 377.3
  hidden danger 1006.5
  v trap 356.20
  catch 480.17
  rob 482.16
snarl
  n rasp 58.3
  grimace 265.4
  quarrel 456.5
  complex 799.2
  v sound harshly 58.9
  growl 60.4
  show resentment 152.14
  wind sound 318.21
  trap 356.20
  speak 524.25
  complicate 799.3
  confuse 811.3
  hamper 1012.11
snatch
  n seizure 480.2
  piece 793.3
  jerk 905.3
  v jump at 101.6
  seize 480.14

steal 482.13
  abduct 482.20
  jerk 905.5
sneak
  n dastard 491.6
  rascal 660.3
  v creep 177.26
  lurk 346.9
  cower 491.9
  smuggle 732.8
sneak attack
  deceit 356.3
  surprise attack 459.2
sneak in intrude 214.5
  join 617.14
sneaking suspicion 951.5
sneak out of
  shirk 368.9
  slip away 369.9
sneak preview 706.1
sneaky covert 345.12
  deceitful 356.22
  cunning 415.12
  cowering 491.13
sneer
  n snub 157.2
  scornful smile 508.4
  v scoff 508.9
sneeze
  n breathing 2.21
  sibilation 57.1
  v sibilate 57.2
sneeze at disdain 157.3
  dismiss 984.4
snicker
  n laughter 116.4
  scornful laugh 508.4
  v laugh 116.8
snide spiteful 144.21
  disparaging 512.13
  hostile 589.10
sniff
  n breathing 2.21
  sibilation 57.1
  snub 157.2
  drawing in 187.5
  hint 551.4
  v sibilate 57.2
  smell 69.8
  inhale illicit substance 87.22
  draw in 187.12
  scent 941.6
sniff at 157.3
sniff out trace 938.35
  scent 941.6
snifter 88.7
snip
  n deckhand 183.6
  scrap 248.3
  runt 258.4
  minute thing 258.7
  piece 793.3
  v sever 802.11
snipe
  n cigarette 89.5
  v pull the trigger 459.22
  shoot 904.12
sniper
  infantryman 461.9
  shooter 904.8
sniping 115.4

snippet scrap 248.3
  runt 258.4
  minute 258.7
  excerpt 557.3
  piece 793.3
snippy snobbish 141.14
  gruff 505.7
snit dither 105.6
  fit 152.8
  frenzy 926.7
snitch
  n informer 551.6
  v rob 482.16
  inform on 551.13
sniveling
  n weeping 115.2
  adj tearful 115.21
  obsequious 138.14
  sanctimonious 693.5
snob 141.7
snobbish
  snobby 141.14
  contemptuous 157.8
  selective 495.13
  exclusive 773.9
snooker 760.1
snoop
  n listener 48.5
  meddler 214.4
  inquisitive person 981.2
  v meddle 214.7
  pry 981.4
snoot 283.8
snootful 794.3
snooty snobbish 141.14
  contemptuous 157.8
snooze
  n nap 22.3
  v sleep 22.14
snore
  n breathing 2.21
  resonance 54.1
  sibilation 57.1
  rasp 58.3
  v sleep 22.13
  resonate 54.6
  sibilate 57.2
  sound harshly 58.9
snorkel tube 239.6
  diving equipment 367.5
  extinguisher 1022.3
snort
  n drink 8.4
  sibilation 57.1
  drink 88.7
  laughter 116.4
  snub 157.2
  scornful laugh 508.4
  dose 793.5
  v sibilate 57.2
  grunt 60.3
  inhale a drug 87.22
  laugh 116.8
  speak 524.25
snot body fluid 2.24
  filth 80.7
snotty
  snobbish 141.14
  contemptuous 157.8
  mucous 1062.13
snout nozzle 239.9

nose 283.8
snow
  n whiteness 37.2
  cocaine 87.7
  ice 1023.8
  television reception 1035.5
  v deceive 356.14
  give 478.12
  hail 1023.11
snowball
  n accumulation 770.9
  snow 1023.8
  v grow 251.6
  enlarge 259.5
  ball 282.7
a snowball's chance in hell
  967.1
snow-blind
  v blind 30.7
  adj dim-sighted 28.13
  blinded 30.10
snowboarding 753.1
snowdrift pile 770.10
  snow 1023.8
snowfall 1023.8
snowflake 1023.8
snow job
  deception 356.9
  inducement 375.3
snowman figure 349.6
  snow 1023.8
snowmobile 179.20
snowshoes 179.21
snowstorm storm 671.4
  snow 1023.8
  television reception 1035.5
snub
  n rebuff 157.2
  repulse 908.2
  v rebuff 157.5
  shorten 268.6
  restrain 428.7
  refuse 442.5
  repulse 908.3
  banish 909.17
  hinder 1012.10
  adj shortened 268.9
snub-nosed
  deformed 265.12
  stubby 268.10
snuff
  n breathing 2.21
  sibilation 57.1
  tobacco 89.8
  drawing in 187.5
  v sibilate 57.2
  smell 69.8
  draw in 187.12
  kill 308.14
  fight fire 1022.7
snuffbox 89.8
snuff out
  extinguish 395.15
  fight fire 1022.7
snug
  v make comfortable 121.9
  adj comfortable 121.11
  seaworthy 180.18
  homelike 228.33
  close 293.12
  taciturn 344.9

unsociable 583.5
  tidy 807.8
  cozy 1007.7
snuggery nook 197.3
  cottage 228.8
snuggle nestle 121.10
  cuddle 562.17
snug harbor 1009.1
so
  adj suchlike 784.12
  adv greatly 247.15
  very 247.18
  how 384.9
  thus 766.10
  similarly 784.18
  equally 790.11
  accurately 973.20
  conj for 380.11
  just so 959.15
soak
  n drunk 88.12
  soaking 1065.7
  v tipple 88.24
  extraction 192.16
  overprice 632.7
  strike 902.15
  overload 993.15
  liquefy 1064.5
  drench 1065.13
so-and-so 528.2
soap
  n cleanser 79.17
  television broadcast 1035.2
  v wash 79.19
  flatter 511.6
soapbox
  n platform 901.13
  v make a speech 543.9
soapbox racing 744.1
soap opera
  sentimentality 93.8
  radiobroadcast 1034.18
  television broadcast 1035.2
soapy foamy 320.7
  suave 504.18
  flattering 511.8
  oily 1056.9
soar move 172.5
  fly 184.36
  take off 193.10
  loom 247.5
  tower 272.10
soaring costs 632.3
sob
  n sexual pervert 75.16
  lament 115.3
  v sigh 52.14
  weep 115.12
  wind sound 318.21
  speak 524.25
  mumble 525.9
SOB 660.5
sober
  v moderate 670.6
  adj soft-colored 35.22
  dark 38.9
  gray 39.4
  sedate 106.14
  solemn 111.3
  dignified 136.12
  not intoxicated 516.3

plain-speaking 535.3
  temperate 668.9
  moderate 670.10
  real 761.15
  sensible 920.18
  cognitive 931.21
  weighty 997.20
sobering 997.20
sobriety
  darkness 38.2
  sedateness 106.4
  solemnity 111.1
  proud bearing 136.2
  unintoxicatedness 516.1
  temperance 668.1
  moderation 670.1
  sensibleness 920.6
  sanity 925.1
sobriquet 527.7
sob story 93.8
so-called
  spurious 354.26
  pretexted 376.5
  nominal 527.15
soccer 752.1
sociable
  n social gathering 582.10
  v talkative 540.9
  adj communicative 343.10
  informal 581.3
  social 582.22
  friendly 587.15
  associational 617.17
social
  n social gathering 582.10
  adj public 312.16
  communal 476.9
  sociable 582.22
  associational 617.17
social behavior
  good behavior 321.2
  behaviorism 321.3
social class
  social circle 582.5
  class 607.1
  community 617.2
social climbing 100.10
social consciousness 591.1
social convention 580.3
social democracy 612.4
social director 743.20
social disease 85.18
social drinker 88.11
social evolution 861.4
social gathering 582.10
social graces 580.3
social intercourse
  communication 343.1
  social life 582.4
socialism
  communion 476.2
  collective ownership 611.6
  government 612.8
socialite
  n person of fashion 578.7
  aristocrat 607.4
  adj upper-class 607.10
socialize
  make better 392.9
  communize 476.7
  attach 480.20

politicize 611.16
social mobility
  class 607.1
  change 852.1
the social order 606.1
social outcast 586.4
social register 578.6
Social Register
  directory 549.9
  Bluebook 607.2
social security
  welfare 143.5
  subsidy 478.8
  welfarism 611.7
  insurance 1008.4
social services 449.3
social system 617.2
social worker
  philanthropist 143.8
  professional 726.4
society
  n population 227.1
  humankind 312.1
  culture 373.2
  fashionable people 578.6
  association 582.6
  the people 606.1
  alliance 617.1
  community 617.2
  fellowship 617.3
  sect 675.3
  the laity 700.1
  company 769.2
  adj associational 617.17
sociology 312.10
sociopathy 92.15
sock
  n costume 5.9
  comedy 704.6
  fight 754.3
  blow 902.5
  punch 902.6
  v clothe 5.40
  strike 902.15
sock away store 386.10
  not use 390.5
socket 284.2
Socrates 921.2
sod land 234.1
  turf 310.6
soda beverage 10.49
  extinguisher 1022.3
soda fountain 8.17
soda jerk 577.7
sodden
  v soak 1065.13
  adj underdone 11.9
  intoxicated 88.31
  soaked 1065.17
sodomy 75.7
sofa furniture 229.1
  bed 901.19
so far
  thus far 211.16
  limited 248.10
  until now 838.4
soft weak 16.12
  impotent 19.13
  soft-colored 35.22
  faint 52.16
  effeminate 77.15

sensitive 93.20
sentimental 93.21
loving 104.27
comfortable 121.11
pitying 145.7
light 298.12
out of practice 414.18
unstrict 426.5
lenient 427.7
pacific 464.9
cowardly 491.10
unintoxicating 516.4
phonetic 524.30
moderate 670.10
feebleminded 922.21
gullible 954.9
easy 1014.13
nonresistive 1047.8
slimy 1062.14
pulpy 1063.6
soft drink 10.49
soften blur 32.4
muffle 51.9
feminize 77.13
affect 93.14
relieve 120.5
have pity 145.4
move 145.5
extenuate 600.12
moderate 670.6
cushion 670.8
qualify 959.3
soften up 1047.6
softhearted
sensitive 93.20
kind 143.13
pitying 145.7
soft in the head
feebleminded 922.21
insane 926.26
soft landing 1075.2
soft lenses 29.3
soft-pedal
silence 51.8
muffle 51.9
extenuate 600.12
soft pornography 666.4
soft sell
inducement 375.3
selling 734.2
soft-shell crab 311.30
soft-soap
be hypocritical 354.23
urge 375.14
importune 440.12
flatter 511.6
soft-spoken
suave 504.18
speaking 524.31
soft spot
sore spot 24.4
tendency 896.1
vulnerability 1006.4
soft touch 358.2
software 1042.11
softy 16.6
soggy 1065.17
soil
n dirtiness 80.5
region 231.1
land 234.1

v besoil 80.16
vilify 512.10
corrupt 654.10
stigmatize 661.9
seduce 665.20
stain 1004.6
soil one's hands
soil 80.16
condescend 137.8
deign 141.8
incur disgrace 661.7
soiree
social gathering 582.10
assembly 770.2
sojourn
n stay 225.5
v stop 225.8
Sol 1072.14
solace
n consolation 121.4
amusement 743.1
v comfort 121.6
amuse 743.21
solar 1072.25
solar battery 1075.4
solar eclipse
eclipse 1027.8
sun 1072.13
solar energy
energy 17.1
fuel 1021.1
solarium 197.5
solar plexus 2.14
solar power 18.4
solar prominence
flash 1025.6
sun 1072.13
solar system 1072.9
solar wind 1072.13
solder
n sculpture material
715.4
v sculpture 715.5
put together 800.5
stick together 803.9
burn 1020.24
soldier
n ant 311.34
shirker 368.3
military man 461.6
the underworld 660.10
v shirk 368.9
serve 458.18
soldier of fortune 461.17
sold on pleased 95.15
belief 953.21
sole
n fish 10.24
base 199.2
foot 199.5
adj unmarried 565.7
one 872.7
unique 872.9
solecism
ungrammaticism 531.2
specious argument 936.3
blunder 975.5
grammatical error 975.7
solemn
sedate 106.14
dignified 111.3

gloomy 112.24
dull 117.6
reverent 155.9
heavy 297.16
celebrative 487.3
pompous 501.22
lofty 544.14
ceremonious 580.8
pious 692.8
worshipful 696.16
weighty 997.20
solemn oath 334.4
solemn observance
celebration 487.1
ritualism 701.1
solemn promise 436.1
solenoid 907.3
solicit
make advances 439.7
canvass 440.14
solicit advice 422.7
solicitor
petitioner 440.7
lawyer 597.1
canvasser 730.6
solicitous
sensitive 24.12
anxious 126.7
considerate 143.16
careful 339.10
courteous 504.14
solicit votes 609.40
solid
n solid body 1045.6
adj firm 15.18
unanimous 332.15
faithful 644.20
solvent 729.18
substantial 763.6
sturdy 763.7
crowded 770.22
complete 794.9
permanent 853.7
stable 855.12
one 872.7
reliable 970.17
valid 973.14
excellent 999.13
dense 1045.12
hard 1046.10
solidarity
cooperation 450.1
accord 455.1
completeness 794.1
oneness 872.1
solid citizen 607.6
solid fuel 1074.8
solidify contract 260.7
cohere 803.6
combine 805.3
densify 1045.9
set 1046.8
solid-state device 1033.12
solidus 204.7
solid waste
derelict 370.4
refuse 391.4
extract 893.3
soliloquy
self-address 542.1
monology 542.1

solitary
n recluse 584.5
oddity 870.4
adj alone 584.11
unique 872.7
isolated 872.8
eccentric 927.5
solitary confinement 429.8
solo
n flight 184.9
soliloquy 542.1
song 708.4
aria 708.15
keyboard 711.17
v pilot 184.37
adj alone 872.8
adv singly 872.13
soloist 710.1
Solomon judge 596.5
wise person 921.2
so long! 188.22
so long as 959.15
solstice 313.7
soluble solvable 940.3
liquefiable 1064.9
solution
explanation 341.4
harmonization 709.2
answer to a problem 940
resolution 940.1
expedient 995.2
liquefaction 1064.1
decoction 1064.3
solve explain 341.10
resolve 940.2
liquefy 1064.5
solvent
n cleanser 79.17
thinner 270.10
dissolvent 1064.4
adj unindebted 624.23
sound 729.18
disintegrative 806.5
dissolvent 1064.8
soma body 2.1
physical entity 1052.3
somber
n gloom 1027.4
v darken 1027.9
adj soft-colored 35.22
dark 38.9
gray 39.4
solemn 111.3
grim 112.24
ominous 133.17
gloomy 1027.14
lackluster 1027.17
some
n quantity 244.3
plurality 883.1
adj quantitative 244.5
skillful 413.22
plural 883.7
adv approximately 244.6
somebody person 312.5
celebrity 662.9
personage 997.8
someday 839.12
somehow
in some way 384.11
by chance 972.19

someplace 159.26
somersault
  n overturn 205.2
  v capsize 182.44
something
  n some 244.3
  thing 763.3
  important person 997.9
  object 1052.4
  prep about 223.26
something else
  n marvel 122.2
  a different thing 780.3
  first-rate 999.7
  adj nothing like 787.5
  excellent 999.13
something extra
  advantage 249.2
  extra 254.4
  gratuity 478.5
  surplus 993.5
something like 784.10
something out of nothing
  355.3
something special 997.5
something terrible
  distressingly 247.21
  terribly 1000.14
something to fall back on
  386.3
something to spare 993.5
something to write home
  about
  marvel 122.2
  matter of consequence 997.5
sometime
  adj former 837.10
  occasional 848.3
  adv someday 839.12
some time ago 837.16
somewhat
  n some 244.3
  adv to a degree 245.7
  limited 248.10
somewhere 159.26
somewhere else
  adj abstracted 985.11
  adv away 222.18
somnambulism
  sleep 22.2
  trance 92.19
  nightwalking 177.9
somnolent sleepy 22.21
  languid 331.20
so much for that
  interj that's that! 407.15
  phrs that's all for 820.14
son male child 559.3
  offspring 561.1
  descendant 561.3
sonar 182.2
song melody 708.4
  vocal music 708.13
  types 708.14
  poetry 720.1
song and dance
  deception 356.9
  act 704.7
songbird bird 311.28
  singer 710.13
  singing bird 710.23

sonic 50.17
sonic boom sonics 50.6
  noise 53.3
  air speed 184.31
son-in-law 564.2
son of a bitch 660.5
sonogram 91.9
sonorous
  sounding 50.15
  loud 53.11
  resonant 54.10
  grandiloquent 545.8
  melodious 708.48
soon in the future 839.9
  presently 845.16
sooner than
  preferably 371.28
  instead of 862.12
soon to be 840.3
soot
  n blackness 38.4
  blacking 38.6
  dirt 80.6
  dregs 256.2
  combustion product 1020.16
  powder 1051.5
  v blacken 38.7
  dirty 80.15
soothe
  relieve 120.5
  quiet 173.8
  pacify 465.7
  calm 670.7
soothing
  n palliative 86.10
  relief 120.1
  pacification 465.1
  modulation 670.2
  adj palliative 86.40
  sedative 86.45
  relieving 120.9
  pacificatory 465.12
  tranquilizing 670.15
  lubricant 1056.10
soothsayer 962.4
sooty dingy 38.11
  dirty 80.22
sop
  n weakling 16.6
  bribe 378.2
  fool 924.1
  v soak 1065.13
sophisticated
  experienced 413.28
  elegant 496.9
  chic 578.13
  ungullible 956.5
  disillusioned 977.5
sophistry
  insincerity 354.5
  cunning 415.1
  misteaching 569.1
  reasoning 935.1
  illogicalness 936.1
  specious argument 936.3
  philosophy 952.1
sophomore
  undergraduate 572.6
  jockey 757.2
soporific
  n sleep-inducer 22.10

  adj sleepy 22.21
  sleep-inducing 22.23
  sedative 86.45
  apathetic 94.13
sopping wet 1065.17
soprano
  n high voice 58.6
  part 708.22
  voice 709.5
  adj high 58.13
  vocal 708.50
sorcerer
  Satanist 680.15
  necromancer 690.5
  illusoriness 976.2
  diviner 689.16
sorceress 690.8
sordid squalid 80.25
  greedy 100.27
  niggardly 484.8
  disreputable 661.10
  slovenly 810.15
  terrible 1000.9
sore
  n soreness 26.4
  symptom 85.9
  lesion 85.37
  pain 96.5
  adj raw 26.11
  distressing 98.20
  resentful 152.26
  angry 152.30
  hostile 589.10
  disastrous 1011.15
  straitened 1013.26
sorehead
  malcontent 108.4
  grouch 110.11
  complainer 115.9
sore point
  sore spot 24.4
  provocation 152.11
  bone of contention 456.7
sore throat 85.9
sorghum 66.2
sorority
  affiliation 450.2
  sisterhood 587.2
  club 617.3
sorrel
  n horse 311.11
  adj brown 40.3
sorrow
  n affliction 96.8
  grief 112.10
  regret 113.1
  lamentation 115.1
  v distress 98.14
  grieve 112.17
  aggrieve 112.19
  lament 115.10
sorry unhappy 112.21
  regretful 113.8
  low 497.15
  disgraceful 661.11
  paltry 998.21
sort
  n nature 767.4
  kind 809.3
  v size 257.15
  analyze 801.8

  arrange 808.11
  classify 809.6
  discriminate 944.4
sortie
  Air Force mission 184.11
  attack 459.1
sort of
  to a degree 245.7
  so to speak 784.19
SOS 400.1
so-so
  adj medium 246.3
  mediocre 1005.7
  adv mediocrely 1005.11
so thick you can cut it with a
  knife 319.10
so to speak
  figuratively 536.4
  in a manner of speaking
    784.19
sotto voce
  adv in an undertone 52.22
  secretly 345.17
  adj music 708.53
sou'wester 318.9
soufflé
  n foam 320.2
  adj light 298.10
  bubbly 320.6
sought-after
  desirable 100.30
  fashionable 578.11
  distinguished 662.16
soul passion 93.2
  heart 93.3
  content 196.5
  interior 207.2
  life force 306.3
  person 312.5
  theosophy 689.18
  entity 763.3
  essence 767.2
  inner nature 767.5
  particularity 865.1
  individual 872.4
  psyche 919.4
  genius 920.8
soul food 10.1
soulful 93.17
soul-searching 113.3
sound
  n noise 50.1
  sonance 50.1
  inlet 242.1
  feeler 942.4
  v appear to be 33.10
  make a noise 50.14
  blare 53.10
  reverberate 54.7
  ring 54.8
  fathom 275.9
  measure 300.10
  plunge 367.6
  say 524.22
  play music 708.42
  investigate 938.23
  sound out 942.9
  adj firm 15.18
  whole 83.11
  orthodox 687.7
  solvent 729.18

sturdy 763.7
stable 855.12
sensible 920.18
sane 925.4
logical 935.20
reliable 970.17
valid 973.14
realistic 987.6
good 999.12
intact 1002.7
unhazardous 1007.5
sound an alarm 517.22
sound asleep 22.22
sound barrier
  sonics 50.6
  speed of sound 174.2
  air speed 184.31
sound bite
  information 551.3
  news item 552.3
  excerpt 557.3
  piece 793.3
sound economy 731.7
sound effects 1034.18
sounding
  n sonation 50.4
  fathoming 275.5
  adj sonorous 50.15
  reverberating 54.12
  ringing 54.13
sound judgment 920.7
sound like
  appear to be 33.10
  resemble 784.7
sound mind 925.1
sound off
  vociferate 59.8
  affirm 334.5
  boast 502.7
  bluster 503.3
  speak 524.20
  speak up 524.21
sound out 942.9
soundproof
  v proof 15.14
  adj resistant 15.20
sound sleep 22.5
sound the alarm
  warn 399.5
  alarm 400.3
sound track 714.10
soup potage 10.10
  atmosphere 184.32
  thinness 270.7
  processing solution 714.13
  semiliquid 1062.5
soup's on! 8.35
soup up 251.5
soupy foggy 319.10
  viscous 1062.12
sour
  n tartness 67.1
  sour foods 67.2
  v turn sour 67.4
  acerbate 110.16
  aggravate 119.2
  adj dissonant 61.4
  flavored 62.9
  bitter 64.6
  tart 67.5
  pungent 68.6

unpleasant 98.17
discontented 108.7
sour-tempered 110.23
tainted 393.41
source
  headwaters 238.2
  motive 375.1
  source of supply 386.4
  informant 551.5
  origin 886.5
sour cream 67.2
sourdough food 67.2
  miner 1058.9
sour grapes 512.1
sour note 61.1
sourpuss
  malcontent 108.4
  melancholic 112.13
  complainer 115.9
  spoilsport 1012.9
souse
  n drunk 88.12
  submergence 367.2
  soaking 1065.7
  v intoxicate 88.23
  drink 88.25
  submerge 367.7
  soak 1065.13
south
  n points of the compass 161.3
  adj southern 161.14
  adv southward 161.16
  down 194.13
South America
  world region 231.6
  continent 235.1
Southeast Asia Treaty
  Organization 437.2
Southern Hemisphere 231.6
southern lights 1025.16
southpaw
  n left-hander 220.3
  baseball player 745.2
  adj left-handed 220.5
South Pole
  opposites 215.2
  remote region 261.4
  cold place 1023.4
southwestwardly 161.22
souvenir memory 989.1
  memento 989.7
sovereign
  n potentate 575.8
  coin 728.4
  adj omnipotent 18.13
  chief 249.14
  regal 417.17
  independent 430.22
  governing 612.18
  almighty 677.17
sovereign state 232.1
so very much 247.15
sow
  disperse 771.4
  plant 1069.18
sow
  female animal 77.10
  swine 311.9
  cast 1058.5
sow dissension 456.14
so what? who cares? 102.11

what does it matter? 998.26
so what else is new? 118.15
sow one's wild oats
  misbehave 322.4
  let oneself go 430.19
  be promiscuous 665.19
  dissipate 669.6
  make merry 743.24
spa bathing place 79.10
  fitness 84.1
  health resort 91.23
  resort 228.27
space
  n expanse 158.1
  extent 158.1
  atmosphere 184.32
  compartment 197.2
  interval 224.1
  region 231.1
  degree 245.1
  capacity 257.2
  distance 261.1
  opening 292.1
  latitude 430.4
  spacing 548.7
  musical staff 708.29
  time 821.1
  period 824.1
  opportunity 843.2
  outer space 1072.3
  v interspace 224.3
  dispose 808.9
  adj spatial 158.10
  extraterrestrial 1072.26
Space Age 824.6
space cadet 87.21
spacecraft 1075.2
spaced out
  unconscious 25.8
  interspaced 224.6
space observatory 1075.6
space rocket 1075.2
space satellite 1075.6
spaceship
  rocket plane 181.4
  spacecraft 1075.2
space shuttle
  aircraft 181.1
  spacecraft 1075.2
space station 1075.5
space suit 1075.11
space-time continuum 158.6
space travel
  space flight 1075.1
  astronautics 1075.1
spacious roomy 158.11
  large 247.7
  voluminous 257.17
  broad 269.6
spade
  n race 312.3
  v ladle 176.17
  excavate 284.15
  cultivate 1069.17
spaghetti 10.33
spaghetti junction 170.2
spam 1042.19
span
  n rig 179.5
  short distance 223.2
  distance 261.1

length 267.1
breadth 269.1
arch 279.4
bridge 383.9
period 824.1
short time 828.3
two 873.2
v extend 158.9
overlie 295.30
measure 300.10
put together 800.5
double 873.5
spandex 1048.3
spangled spotted 47.13
  ornamented 498.11
  illuminated 1025.39
spaniel 138.3
Spanish fly 75.6
spank
  n slap 902.8
  v reprove 510.17
  punish 604.13
  pound 902.16
  slap 902.19
spanking new 841.10
spar
  n mast 180.13
  beam 273.3
  boxing 457.9
  lever 906.4
  v quarrel 456.11
  contend 457.13
  fight 754.4
  argue 935.16
spare
  n bowling 750.2
  surplus 993.5
  v have pity 145.4
  forgive 148.3
  refrain 329.3
  not use 390.5
  preserve 397.8
  exempt 430.14
  relinquish 475.3
  give away 478.21
  afford 626.7
  abstain 668.7
  adj additional 253.10
  remaining 256.7
  lean 270.17
  reserved 386.15
  unused 390.12
  leisure 402.5
  plain-speaking 535.3
  economical 635.6
  simple 798.6
  occasional 848.3
  substitute 862.8
  meager 992.10
  superfluous 993.17
  surplus 993.18
spare no expense 485.3
spare part 386.3
spare room 158.3
spare the rod
  be easy on 427.5
  indulge 427.6
spare time 402.1
spare tire 2.19
spark
  n hint 248.4

inspiration 375.9
prompter 375.10
dandy 500.9
immediate cause 886.3
fire 1019.15
glitter 1025.7
v motivate 375.12
kindle 375.18
court 562.21
cause 886.10
be hot 1019.22
glitter 1025.24
sparkle
n bubbling 320.3
spirit 544.4
spark 1019.15
glitter 1025.7
v exude cheerfulness 109.6
bubble 320.4
joke 489.13
be brilliant 920.11
glitter 1025.24
sparkling water 10.49
spark plug
energizer 17.6
prompter 375.10
sparring partner 754.2
sparse dispersed 771.9
infrequent 848.2
scant 885.5
scarce 992.11
Spartan
n stoic 134.3
man of few words 344.5
adj patient 134.9
strict 425.6
inornate 499.9
plain-speaking 535.3
concise 537.6
abstinent 668.10
meager 992.10
spasm pang 26.2
seizure 85.6
symptom 85.9
pain 96.5
outburst 105.9
bustle 330.4
upheaval 671.5
revolution 860.1
convulsion 917.6
frenzy 926.7
spastic
n sick person 85.43
idiot 924.8
adj convulsive 671.23
irregular 851.3
jerky 917.19
unintelligent 922.17
mentally deficient 922.22
foolish 923.8
spat
n quarrel 456.5
offspring 561.2
v quarrel 456.11
spate flow 238.4
torrent 238.5
quantity 247.3
lot 247.4
rainstorm 316.2
outburst 671.6
throng 770.4

plenty 991.2
superabundance 993.2
spatter
n staccato 55.1
stain 1004.3
sprinkle 1065.5
v splatter 80.18
rain 316.10
sprinkle 771.6
spot 1004.5
moisten 1065.12
spatula
art equipment 712.18
sculpture tool 715.4
spawn
n egg 305.15
offspring 561.2
v reproduce 78.9
originate 892.12
spay 255.11
spaying 255.4
speak sound 50.14
hail a ship 182.52
affirm 334.5
communicate 343.6
command 420.8
signal 517.22
use language 523.18
talk 524.19
remark 524.24
address 524.26
make a speech 543.9
speakeasy 88.20
speaker
loudspeaker 50.8
talker 524.17
speechmaker 543.4
chairman 574.5
spokesman 576.5
Speaker of the House 610.3
speak for
be in front 216.7
represent 576.14
defend 600.10
speak in tongues
talk nonsense 520.5
be incomprehensible 522.10
speak too soon 844.4
speak up affirm 334.5
come out 348.6
brave 492.11
speak out 524.21
spear
n leaf 310.19
branch 310.20
stem 310.21
weapon 462.8
v perforate 292.15
stab 459.25
catch 480.17
spearhead
n vanguard 216.2
v lead 165.2
special
n train 179.14
commodity 735.2
feature 866.2
adj student 572.12
detailed 766.9
other 780.8
classificational 809.7

particular 865.12
notable 997.19
special delivery 553.4
special edition 555.2
special education student
572.4
special effects 706.5
Special Forces 461.15
special interest
pressure group 609.31
interest 983.2
specialist
n doctor 90.4
dentist 90.6
stockbroker 737.10
specializer 866.3
adj specialized 866.5
specialize in
practice 328.8
study to be 570.15
go in for 866.4
special police 1008.17
special privilege 430.8
specialty study 568.8
occupation 724.4
vocation 724.6
component 796.2
particularity 865.2
characteristic 865.4
object of special attention
866
speciality 866.1
science 928.10
specie money 728.1
hard money 728.4
species
nomenclature 527.1
race 559.4
kind 809.3
classifications 809.5
biology 1068.1
specific
n remedy 86.1
adj circumscribed 210.6
detailed 766.9
classificational 809.7
particular 865.12
specification
circumscription 210.1
description 349.2
indication 517.3
accusation 599.1
circumstantiation 766.5
differentiation 780.4
designation 865.6
qualification 959.1
condition 959.2
specific gravity
weight 297.5
density 1045.1
specify
circumscribe 210.4
designate 517.18
name 527.11
itemize 766.6
differentiate 780.6
specialize 865.11
focus on 937.3
call attention to 983.10
specimen sample 62.4
representative 349.7

model 786.3
specious
meretricious 354.27
pretexted 376.5
sophistical 936.10
illusory 976.9
speck
n spottiness 47.3
modicum 248.2
minute thing 258.7
mark 517.5
intruder 774.2
stain 1004.3
v variegate 47.7
mark 517.19
sprinkle 771.6
spot 1004.5
speckle
n spottiness 47.3
mark 517.5
stain 1004.3
v variegate 47.7
mark 517.19
sprinkle 771.6
spot 1004.5
spectacle sight 33.7
marvel 122.2
display 501.4
spectacles 29.3
spectacular
astonishing 122.12
gaudy 501.20
theatrical 501.24
dramatic 704.33
Spectacular Bid 311.15
spectator audience 48.6
attender 221.5
recipient 479.3
playgoer 704.27
gambler 759.21
observer 918.1
witness 957.6
specter apparition 33.5
frightener 127.9
spirit 678.5
phantom 976.4
ghost 988.1
spectrometer 29.1
spectroscope
optical instrument 29.1
astronomical instrument
1072.17
spectrum
color system 35.7
variegation 47.6
range 158.2
series 812.2
optical illusion 976.5
frequency 1034.12
spectrum analysis 35.10
speculate invest 729.17
trade 737.23
gamble 759.23
consider 931.12
theorize 951.9
predict 962.9
speculator
stock investor 737.11
gambler 759.21
theorist 951.7
philosopher 952.8

speech
  n communication 343.1
  language 523.1
  utterance 524
  talk 524.1
  diction 532.1
  conversation 541.3
  public speaking 543.2
  story teller 722.4
  adj communicational 343.9
  language 524.29
speech impediment 525.1
speechless mute 51.12
  taciturn 344.9
speechmaker 543.4
speech therapist 90.8
speech-writer 543.8
speed
  n amphetamines 87.4
  velocity 174.1
  hastiness 401.2
  v move 172.5
  go fast 174.8
  hasten 401.4
  be useful 449.17
  facilitate 1014.7
speedboat 180.4
speed bump
  bulge 283.3
  hindrance 1012.1
speed demon 174.5
speeder racer 174.5
  driver 178.10
speed of light 174.2
speed of sound
  sonics 50.6
  sonic speed 174.2
  air speed 184.31
speedometer 174.7
speed skating 760.7
speed up
  accelerate 174.10
  hasten 401.4
speedway 756.1
speedwriting 547.8
speedy fast 174.15
  quick 330.18
  hasty 401.9
  brief 828.8
  sudden 830.5
  prompt 845.9
spell
  n sorcery 690.1
  magic spell 691.1
  period 824.1
  term 824.3
  period of duty 825
  turn 825.2
  round 850.3
  superstition 954.3
  bad influence 1000.4
  v augur 133.12
  fascinate 377.7
  mean 518.8
  orthographize 546.7
  cast a spell 691.7
  take one's turn 825.5
  substitute for 862.5
spellbound
  wondering 122.9
  enchanted 691.12

gripped 983.18
  dreamy 986.25
speller 554.10
spelling bee 546.4
spell out
  explain 341.10
  simplify 499.5
  make clear 521.6
  spell 546.7
  itemize 766.6
  elaborate 861.6
  particularize 865.9
spend
  use up 387.13
  consume 388.3
  waste 486.4
  expend 626.5
  occupy 724.10
  experience 831.8
spending money 728.19
spendthrift
  n prodigal 486.2
  adj prodigal 486.8
spend time 821.6
spent weakened 16.18
  burnt-out 21.10
  used up 388.5
  worn-out 393.36
  wasted 486.9
  paid 624.22
sperm body fluid 13.2
  copulation 75.7
  spermatozoa 305.11
spermatozoa 305.11
spermicide 86.23
spew
  n jet 238.9
  outburst 671.6
  vomiting 909.8
  v salivate 13.6
  run out 190.13
  jet 238.20
  erupt 671.13
  disgorge 909.25
  vomit 909.26
sphere
  n space 158.1
  domain 231.2
  rank 245.2
  ball 282.2
  arena 463.1
  occupation 724.4
  science 928.10
  stars 1072.4
  v ball 282.7
spheres of influence 609.5
sphincter 280.2
spice
  n flavoring 63.3
  zest 68.2
  fragrance 70.1
  admixture 797.7
  v flavor 63.7
spick and span 79.26
spicy zestful 68.7
  fragrant 70.9
  risqué 666.7
  interesting 983.19
spider spinner 271.5
  insect 311.33
spider's web 271.1

spiel
  n sales talk 734.5
  v publicize 352.15
  speak 524.20
  declaim 543.10
spiff up 5.42
spiffy chic 578.13
  excellent 999.13
spigot valve 239.10
  stopper 293.4
spike
  n rig 179.5
  thorn 285.5
  stopper 293.4
  plant part 310.27
  ear of corn 310.29
  card 758.2
  v disable 19.9
  perforate 292.15
  stab 459.25
  adulterate 797.12
  thwart 1012.15
spill
  n tumble 194.3
  overturn 205.2
  overflow 238.6
  stopper 293.4
  lighter 1021.4
  v overflow 238.17
  betray 351.6
  confess 351.7
  waste 486.4
spill over
  overflow 238.17
  superabound 993.8
spill the beans
  disclose 351.4
  betray 351.6
  inform on 551.13
spillway 239.2
spin
  n aspect 33.3
  ride 177.7
  air maneuver 184.15
  perversion 265.2
  misrepresentation 350.1
  partiality 650.3
  tennis play 748.2
  tendency 896.1
  rotation 915.1
  whirl 915.2
  v turn round 163.9
  move 172.5
  maneuver aircraft 184.40
  eddy 238.21
  make threads 271.6
  rotate 915.9
  whirl 915.11
  adv at top speed 756.5
spin a long yarn 538.8
spindle 915.5
spindly
  unsteady 16.16
  lean 270.17
spin doctor publicist 352.9
  motive 375.1
  mediator 466.3
  informant 551.5
  spokesman 576.5
spine ridge 237.5
  bulge 283.3

thorn 285.5
  supporter 901.2
spineless weak 16.12
  weak-willed 362.12
  inconstant 854.7
spinning wheel 271.5
spin-off
  adjunct 254.1
  aftermath 817.3
  effect 887.1
  extract 893.3
spin one's wheels
  be impotent 19.7
  be useless 391.8
  miss 410.14
spin out
  v lengthen 267.6
  protract 538.8
  prolong 827.9
  postpone 846.9
  sustain 856.4
  adv at top speed 756.5
spinster woman 77.5
  spinner 271.5
  unmarried woman 565.4
spiny pointed 285.9
  difficult 1013.17
spiracle outlet 190.9
  air passage 239.13
spiral
  n air maneuvers 184.13
  coil 281.2
  circuitousness 914.1
  whirl 915.2
  galaxy 1072.6
  v maneuver aircraft 184.40
  ascend 193.8
  circle 914.5
  rotate 915.9
  adj curled 281.8
  circuitous 914.7
  rotary 915.15
spiraling up 193.1
spiral notebook 549.11
spiral staircase 193.3
spire
  n summit 198.2
  tower 272.6
  projection 285.4
  leaf 310.19
  stem 310.21
  v ascend 193.8
  take off 193.10
  tower 272.10
spirit
  n animation 17.4
  passion 93.2
  heart 93.3
  eagerness 101.1
  zeal 101.2
  gaiety 109.4
  extract 192.8
  content 196.5
  milieu 209.3
  life force 306.3
  liveliness 330.2
  enterprise 330.7
  pluck 359.3
  fortitude 492.6
  meaning 518.1
  eloquence 544.4

pagan diety 678.5
supernatural being 678.12
spiritualism 689.5
theosophy 689.18
intangible thing 764.3
essence 767.2
nature 767.4
inner nature 767.5
psyche 919.4
genius 920.8
mood 978.4
specter 988.1
v inspire 375.20
Spirit 677.6
spirit away 482.20
spirited energetic 17.13
eager 101.8
zealous 101.9
cheerful 109.14
active 330.17
resolute 492.18
eloquent 544.12
the Spirit of God 677.12
spirits liquor 88.13
gaiety 109.4
the gods 678.1
mood 978.4
spiritual sacred 685.7
psychic 689.24
godly 692.9
supernatural 870.15
mental 919.7
attitudinal 978.7
spectral 988.7
immaterial 1053.7
spiritual father 699.5
spiritual healer 90.9
spirituality 692.1
spirochete 85.42
spit
n body fluid 2.24
saliva 13.3
sibilation 57.1
jet 238.9
point of land 283.9
fire iron 1020.12
v salivate 13.6
snapping noise 56.7
sibilate 57.2
growl 60.4
show resentment 152.14
jet 238.20
perforate 292.15
rain 316.10
stab 459.25
spit and polish
meticulousness 339.3
pretext 376.1
strictness 425.1
fastidiousness 495.1
spite hate 103.1
spitefulness 144.6
hostility 589.3
grudge 589.5
spit it out 351.7
spitting 56.2
spitting image
image 349.5
the same 778.3
splash
n spottiness 47.3

ripple 52.5
lap 238.8
display 501.4
mark 517.5
stain 1004.3
sprinkle 1065.5
v ripple 52.11
spatter 80.18
lap 238.19
cut a dash 501.13
sprinkle 771.6
dramatize 997.16
spot 1004.5
moisten 1065.12
splashdown 1075.2
splashy showy 501.19
slimy 1062.14
watery 1065.16
splat
n explosive sound 56.1
wood 1054.3
v make explosive sound
56.6
splatter
n rain 316.1
stain 1004.3
sprinkle 1065.5
v drum 55.4
spatter 80.18
sprinkle 771.6
spot 1004.5
moisten 1065.12
splay
n expansion 259.1
dispersion 771.1
v diverge 171.5
lie 201.5
spread 259.6
open 292.11
disperse 771.4
adj sprawled 201.8
spread 259.11
spleen viscera 2.16
unpleasure 96.1
ill humor 110.1
melancholy 112.5
weariness 118.3
bitterness 152.3
splendid
grandiose 501.21
illustrious 662.19
good 999.12
superb 999.15
gorgeous 1016.21
bright 1025.32
splendor
grandeur 501.5
illustriousness 662.6
gorgeousness 1016.6
brightness 1025.4
splice
n joining 800.1
fastening 800.3
v join in marriage 563.14
weave 740.6
put together 800.5
bind 800.9
spline 271.4
splint
n medical dressing 86.33
v treat 91.24

splinter
n scrap 248.3
thinness 270.7
party 617.4
intruder 774.2
piece 793.3
break 802.4
v shatter 802.13
splinter group 617.4
split
n crack 224.2
opening 292.1
falling-out 456.4
stock 738.2
bowling 750.2
break 802.4
blemish 1004.1
v laugh 116.8
depart 188.7
leave 222.10
cleave 224.4
open 292.11
flee 368.11
be damaged 393.23
demolish 395.17
fall out 456.10
apportion 477.6
separate 802.8
sever 802.11
break off 802.12
divide up 802.18
disintegrate 806.3
blemish 1004.4
adj cleft 224.7
impaired 393.27
severed 802.23
halved 875.6
blemished 1004.8
split decision 754.3
split fifty fifty
v double 873.5
adj two 873.6
split hairs
differentiate 780.6
quibble 936.9
discriminate 944.4
split-level 228.5
split off
diverge 171.5
interspace 224.3
dissent 333.4
separate 802.8
split personality 92.20
split second 830.3
split the atom 1038.17
split the difference
average 246.2
compromise 468.2
share 476.6
split ticket 609.19
splotch
n spottiness 47.3
mark 517.5
stain 1004.3
v variegate 47.7
spatter 80.18
mark 517.19
spot 1004.5
splurge
n display 501.4
v cut a dash 501.13

spend 626.5
spoil
n gain 472.3
booty 482.11
v mar 393.10
decay 393.22
bungle 414.11
indulge 427.6
plunder 482.17
thwart 1012.15
offend 1015.5
spoilage decay 393.6
rot 393.7
spoiled brat 302.4
spoiler plunderer 483.6
automobile racing 756.1
spoil for 100.16
spoke radius 171.2
step 193.5
curb 1012.7
spoken
vernacular 523.20
speech 524.29
spoken for 421.10
spokesperson
mediator 466.3
informant 551.5
deputy 576.5
sponge
n washing 79.5
bath 79.8
drunk 88.12
parasite 138.5
absorption 187.6
porousness 292.8
lightness 298.2
marine animal 311.30
eradicator 395.9
pulp 1063.2
v wash 79.19
feed on 138.12
absorb 187.13
obliterate 395.16
freeload 634.4
moisten 1065.12
dry 1066.6
sponge medical 86.33
spongy
absorbent 187.17
porous 292.20
soft 1047.11
pulpy 1063.6
sponsor
n guarantor 438.6
supporter 616.9
financer 729.10
v secure 438.9
patronize 449.15
accept the responsibility
641.9
finance 729.16
spontaneous
voluntary 324.7
unpremeditated 365.11
instinctive 934.6
automated 1041.22
spontaneous combustion
1020.5
spontaneous generation 78.6
spoof
n hoax 356.7

v fool 356.15
spook
  n specter 988.1
  v frighten 127.15
  discompose 811.4
  haunt 988.6
spoon ladle 176.17
  make love 562.15
spoonerism
  wordplay 489.8
  word form 526.4
  grammatical error 975.7
spoon-feed 449.16
spoor odor 69.1
  track 517.8
  clue 517.9
  hint 551.4
sporadic
  not highly contagious 85.62
  dispersed 771.9
  nonuniform 782.3
  unordered 810.12
  intermittent 851.3
spore germ 85.42
  microspore 305.13
sport
  n hunting 382.2
  loser 412.5
  joke 489.6
  banter 490.1
  dandy 500.9
  fun 743.2
  toy 743.16
  athletics 744.1
  gambler 759.21
  misfit 789.4
  transformation 852.3
  v wear 5.44
  hunt 382.9
  flaunt 501.17
  play 743.23
  gamble 759.23
sporting
  n hunting 382.2
  gambling 759.1
  adj fair-minded 649.9
  sports 743.30
sporting goods
  dry goods 735.3
  hard goods 735.4
the sport of kings
  racing 457.11
  horse racing 757.1
sportscaster 1034.23
sportsman
  hunter 382.5
  athlete 743.19
  gambler 759.21
sportsmanship
  competition 457.2
  fairness 649.3
sportswear clothing 5.1
  dry goods 735.3
sporty
  casually dressed 5.47
  showy 501.19
spot
  n spottiness 47.3
  soil 80.5
  drink 88.7
  location 159.1

modicum 248.2
advertisement 352.6
mark 517.5
stigma 661.6
lights 704.18
bowling 750.1
state 765.1
intruder 774.2
crisis 843.4
stain 1004.3
predicament 1013.5
commercial 1034.20
radar signal 1036.11
  v see 27.12
variegate 47.7
soil 80.16
spatter 80.18
locate 159.11
mark 517.19
sprinkle 771.6
detect 941.5
recognize 989.12
bespot 1004.5
use radar 1036.17
spot check 938.6
spotless clean 79.25
  honest 644.13
  virtuous 653.7
  innocent 657.7
  chaste 664.4
  perfect 1002.6
spotlight
  n publicity 352.4
  lights 704.18
  v manifest 348.5
  emphasize 997.14
  illuminate 1025.28
spotter
  secret agent 576.9
  detective 576.11
  watchman 1008.10
spotty spotted 47.13
  discontinuous 813.4
  irregular 851.3
  sparse 885.5
  spotted 1004.9
spouse 563.6
spout
  n outlet 190.9
  ascent 193.1
  jet 238.9
  channel 239.8
  rainstorm 316.2
  disgorgement 909.7
  v run out 190.13
  jet 238.20
  pledge 438.10
  chatter 540.5
  declaim 543.10
  erupt 671.13
  overact 704.31
  disgorge 909.25
sprain 393.13
sprawl
  n tumble 194.3
  recumbency 201.2
  oversize 257.5
  v rest 20.6
  tumble 194.8
  lie 201.5
  spread 259.6

be long 267.5
spray
  n perfume 70.6
  jet 238.9
  branch 310.20
  bouquet 310.25
  foam 320.2
  volley 459.9
  member 793.4
  shot 904.4
  sprinkle 1065.5
  sprinkler 1065.8
  vaporizer 1067.6
  v jet 238.20
  moisten 1065.12
  vaporize 1067.8
spray can 1065.8
spread
  n meal 8.5
  food 10.1
  space 158.1
  divergence 171.1
  transferal 176.1
  increase 251.1
  size 257.1
  expansion 259.1
  breadth 269.1
  blanket 295.10
  publication 352.1
  advertisement 352.6
  stock option 737.21
  dispersion 771.1
  caption 937.2
  v extend 158.9
  diverge 171.5
  radiate 171.6
  transfer 176.10
  grow 251.6
  expand 259.6
  broaden 269.4
  open 292.11
  publish 352.10
  be published 352.16
  report 552.11
  disperse 771.4
  generalize 864.9
  adj recumbent 201.8
  increased 251.7
  spreading 259.11
  published 352.17
  dispersed 771.9
spread-eagle
  tumble 194.8
  fell 913.5
spread far and wide 352.10
spread it on thick
  exaggerate 355.3
  commend 509.11
spread like wildfire
  spread 259.6
  be published 352.16
spread oneself too thin
  overindulge 669.5
  strain 725.10
  overdo 993.10
spreadsheet
  arranger 808.5
  list 871.1
  systems program 1042.12
spree
  n drinking bout 88.5

revel 743.6
  v go on a spree 88.28
  make merry 743.24
sprig youngster 302.1
  sprout 302.11
  branch 310.20
  member 793.4
sprightly
  cheerful 109.14
  active 330.17
  agile 413.23
  witty 489.15
spring
  n progression 162.1
  ascent 193.1
  resort 228.27
  lake 241.1
  springtime 313.2
  leap 366.1
  motive 375.1
  source of supply 386.4
  group of teal 770.6
  fountainhead 886.6
  bedding 901.20
  recoil 903.2
  resilience 1048.1
  elastic object 1048.3
  v speed 174.8
  distort 265.5
  leap 366.5
  blow up 395.18
  exempt 430.14
  release 431.5
  recoil 903.6
  have resilience 1048.5
  adj seasonal 313.9
spring a leak 393.23
springboard 1048.3
springbok 311.5
spring fever 331.5
spring for
  subsidize 478.19
  pay for 624.18
spring from 887.5
spring up grow 14.2
  burst forth 33.9
  shoot up 193.9
  mature 259.7
  originate 818.13
  turn up 831.6
springy quick 330.18
  recoiling 903.10
  pliant 1047.9
  elastic 1048.7
sprinkle
  n rain 316.1
  spray 1065.5
  v variegate 47.7
  rain 316.10
  baptize 701.17
  spatter 771.6
  moisten 1065.12
sprinkler
  extinguisher 1022.3
  shower 1065.8
sprint
  n run 174.3
  v speed 174.8
sprinter 174.5
sprite fairy 678.8
  imp 680.7

refutation 958.2
v silence 51.8
sibilate 57.2
cover up 345.8
extinguish 395.15
suppress 428.8
refute 958.5
squib wit 489.1
burlesque 508.6
lampoon 512.5
squib kick 746.3
squid fish 10.24
snare 356.13
squint
n defective vision 28.5
obliquity 204.1
v look askance 27.18
squinch 28.9
squire
n beau 104.13
proprietor 470.2
attendant 577.5
nobleman 608.4
escort 769.5
v court 562.21
escort 769.8
squirm
n wiggle 917.7
v be excited 105.18
be impatient 135.4
wiggle 917.14
squirrel away
store 386.10
save up 386.11
not use 390.5
squirt
n jet 238.9
disgorgement 909.7
a nobody 998.7
v jet 238.20
disgorge 909.25
squish
n sibilation 57.1
v sibilate 57.2
shatter 802.13
Sr
n mister 76.7
senior 304.5
adj older 842.19
stab
n pang 26.2
trauma 85.38
attempt 403.3
thrust 459.3
guess 951.4
v pain 26.7
aggrieve 96.17
perforate 292.15
injure 393.13
attack 459.25
stability
strength 15.3
staunchness 359.2
perseverance 360.1
moderation 670.1
substantiality 763.1
uniformity 781.1
continuity 812.1
durability 827.1
perpetuity 829.1
permanence 853.1

firmness 855.1
reliability 970.4
stabilize calm 670.7
make uniform 781.4
make firm 855.7
stab in the back
n surprise attack 459.2
betrayal 645.8
v slander 512.11
stable
n sty 80.11
barn 228.20
company 770.3
farm 1070.5
v enclose 212.5
house 225.10
adj firm 15.18
persevering 360.8
faithful 644.20
restrained 670.11
sturdy 763.7
uniform 781.5
continuous 812.8
durable 827.10
permanent 853.7
substantial 855.12
reliable 970.17
unhazardous 1007.5
stableboy 1070.2
staccato
n repeated sounds 55.1
music 708.25
musical execution 708.30
note 709.14
constancy 847.2
pulsation 916.3
adj drumming 55.7
music 708.53
constant 847.5
pulsative 916.18
stack
n chimney 239.14
lot 247.4
store 386.1
storehouse 386.6
bookholder 554.17
pile 770.10
v load 159.15
tamper with 354.17
pile 770.19
stacked deck 965.2
stacks 197.6
stadium hall 197.4
arena 463.1
football 746.1
track 755.1
staff
n stave 273.2
scepter 417.9
council 423.1
faculty 571.9
personnel 577.11
insignia 647.1
pastoral staff 702.3
music 708.29
supporter 901.2
base 901.8
v equip 385.8
stag
n male animal 76.8
hoofed animal 311.5

jumper 366.4
speculator 737.11
v trade 737.23
stage
n setting 209.2
layer 296.1
arena 463.1
theater 704.16
period 824.1
scaffold 901.12
platform 901.13
v dramatize 704.28
staged 245.5
stage fright
fearfulness 127.3
nervousness 128.1
aphasia 525.6
stagehand 704.24
stage lighting 704.18
stage name 527.8
stagger
n gait 177.12
irregularity 851.1
flounder 917.8
v be drunk 88.27
agitate 105.14
astonish 122.6
frighten 127.15
startle 131.8
way of walking 177.28
tumble 194.8
zigzag 204.12
not know one's own mind 362.6
alternate 854.5
flounder 917.15
be unbelievable 955.7
staggering
astonishing 122.12
surprising 131.11
slow 175.10
irregular 851.3
stagnant inert 173.14
passive 329.6
languid 331.20
stagy affected 500.15
theatrical 501.24
dramatic 704.33
staid sedate 106.14
solemn 111.3
unimaginative 987.5
stain
n color 35.8
soil 80.5
mark 517.5
stigma 661.6
taint 1004.3
v color 35.14
soil 80.16
mark 517.19
stigmatize 661.9
bestain 1004.6
stained glass
picture 712.11
light filter 1028.4
stainless
clean 79.25
honest 644.13
innocent 657.7
chaste 664.4
perfect 1002.6

stair step 193.5
degree 245.1
staircase 193.3
stake
n region 231.5
shaft 273.6
collateral 438.3
estate 471.4
portion 477.5
execution 605.5
financing 729.2
bet 759.3
v pledge 438.10
finance 729.16
bet 759.25
stake a claim 421.6
stake out look 27.13
circumscribe 210.4
reconnoiter 938.28
stalactite 295.14
stalagmite 295.14
stale
n urine 12.5
v urinate 12.14
adj insipid 65.2
trite 117.9
tainted 393.41
fusty 842.14
stalemate
n the same 790.3
stop 857.2
impasse 1013.6
v put a stop to 857.11
Stalinist
n Communist 611.13
adj Communist 611.21
stalk
n journey 177.5
gait 177.12
shaft 273.1
stem 310.21
base 901.8
search 938.15
v way of walking 177.28
lurk 346.9
ambush 346.10
hunt 382.9
strut 501.15
trace 938.35
stall
n air 184.13
compartment 197.2
hut 228.9
barn 228.20
church seat 703.14
auditorium 704.15
booth 736.3
procrastination 846.5
v lose power 184.45
fail 410.16
procrastinate 846.11
come to a halt 857.7
hinder 1012.10
stop 1012.13
stallion
male animal 76.8
horse 311.10
jockey 757.2
stalwart
n strong man 15.6
brave person 492.8

staple
  n source of supply 386.4
  commodity 735.2
  marketplace 736.2
  materials 1054.1
  v fasten 800.8
  adj fixed 855.14
star
  n superior 249.4
  successful person 409.6
  skillful person 413.14
  decoration 646.5
  military insignia 647.5
  celebrity 662.9
  movie star 706.4
  lead 707.6
  chief 997.10
  first-rater 999.6
  heavenly body 1072.8
  v rule 249.11
  dramatize 704.28
  act 704.29
  matter 997.12
  emphasize 997.14
  feature 997.15
  adj chief 249.14
starboard
  n right side 219.1
  adj right 219.4
  adv rightward 219.7
starch
  n carbohydrate 7.5
  energy 17.3
  semiliquid 1062.5
  v stiffen 1046.9
  adj prim 580.9
stardom
  great success 409.3
  distinction 662.5
  notability 997.2
stare
  n gaze 27.5
  v gaze 27.15
  wonder 122.5
  be curious 981.3
stare down gaze 27.15
  defy 454.3
  outbrave 492.12
stargaze 985.9
stark
  adj downright 247.12
  mere 248.8
  inornate 499.9
  plain-speaking 535.3
  simple 798.6
  adv absolutely 794.15
stark-naked 6.14
stark-raving mad 926.30
starlet
  movie actress 706.4
  entertainer 707.4
starlight 1025.12
star of David 882.2
starring 704.10
starry-eyed
  happy 95.16
  visionary 986.24
Stars and Stripes 647.7
Star-Spangled Banner 647.7
start
  n shock 131.3

starting 188.2
  point of departure 188.5
  boundary 211.3
  advantage 249.2
  auto race 756.3
  horse race 757.3
  beginning 818.1
  jerk 905.3
  v startle 127.12
  be startled 131.5
  set out 188.8
  leap 366.5
  hunt 382.9
  break 393.23
  propose 439.5
  drive 756.4
  race 757.5
  come apart 802.9
  begin 818.7
  set in motion 904.13
start all over 856.6
starter
  baseball team 745.2
  light source 1026.1
the starting gun 188.2
starting line
  point of departure 188.5
  boundary 211.3
startle
  astonish 122.6
  start 127.12
  frighten 127.15
  be startled 131.5
  shock 131.8
  alarm 400.3
start the ball rolling
  begin 818.7
  inaugurate 818.11
  set in motion 904.13
start up
  burst forth 33.9
  shoot up 193.9
  protrude 283.10
  leap 366.5
  begin 818.7
  make a beginning 818.8
  inaugurate 818.11
  set in motion 904.13
starvation diet 515.2
starvation wages 992.5
starve hunger 100.19
  die 307.24
  kill 308.13
  stint 484.5
  be poor 619.5
Star Wars 460.2
starwatching 1072.19
star worship 697.1
stash
  n hiding place 346.4
  v secrete 346.7
  store 386.10
stasis inertness 173.4
  inaction 329.1
  permanence 853.1
stat
  n print 785.5
  v copy 785.8
state
  n region 231.5
  country 232.1

grandeur 501.5
  pomp 501.6
  mode 765.1
  v affirm 334.5
  announce 352.12
  declare 524.23
  phrase 532.4
  specify 865.11
  assert 953.12
  adj public 312.16
state assembly 613.1
stated
  circumscribed 210.6
  affirmed 334.9
  published 352.17
  fixed 855.14
  conditional 959.8
  assured 970.20
stately
  dignified 136.12
  grandiose 501.21
  lofty 544.14
  ceremonious 580.8
statement
  affirmation 334.1
  account 349.3
  announcement 352.2
  remark 524.3
  report 549.7
  information 551.1
  declaration 598.7
  bill 628.3
  passage 708.24
  list 871.5
  premise 935.7
  testimony 957.2
  summation 1017.11
state of affairs 831.4
state of emergency 843.4
state of grace 685.3
state of mind 978.4
state-of-the-art 841.14
state one's case 957.9
state park 397.7
state police 1008.17
state prison 429.8
stateroom cabin 197.9
  room on train 197.10
state secret 345.5
state's evidence 351.2
states' rights 609.4
stateside 232.3
statesman
  expert 413.11
  politician 610.2
state-wide 864.14
static
  n audio distortion 50.13
  meaninglessness 520.1
  pandemonium 810.5
  reception 1034.21
  adj motionless 173.13
  inert 173.14
  passive 329.6
  inactive 331.17
  permanent 853.7
  electric 1032.30
  biostatic 1039.8
station
  n status 159.2
  rank 245.2

class 607.1
  prestige 662.4
  position 724.5
  state 765.1
  category 809.2
  farm 1070.5
  v place 159.12
stationary
  motionless 173.13
  passive 329.6
  inactive 331.17
  permanent 853.7
  immovable 855.15
stationed 159.18
stationery
  handwriting style 547.4
  paper 1054.5
statistical
  probable 968.6
  numerative 1017.24
statistician
  calculator 1017.15
  mathematician 1017.16
statistics
  baseball 745.4
  football 746.4
  horse racing records 757.4
  mathematical probability 968.2
  figures 1017.14
statuary
  n sculptor 716.6
  adj sculptural 715.6
statue figure 349.6
  work of art 712.10
  sculpture 715.2
statuesque
  dignified 136.12
  giant 272.16
  sculptural 715.6
  comely 1016.19
stature height 272.1
  authority 417.4
  prestige 662.4
status station 159.2
  rank 245.2
  class 607.1
  prestige 662.4
  state 765.1
  category 809.2
status quo state 765.1
  circumstances 766.2
statute
  prohibition 444.1
  law 673.3
statutory
  preceptive 419.4
  legal 673.11
staunch solid 15.18
  close 293.12
  firm 359.12
  devoted 587.21
  faithful 644.20
  strict 687.8
  reliable 970.17
stave step 193.5
  staff 273.2
  musical staff 708.29
  poetry 720.9
  supporter 901.2
  wood 1054.3

volunteer 439.10
step in enter 189.7
  mediate 466.6
step into the breach
  be willing 324.3
  volunteer 439.10
  mediate 466.6
stepladder 193.4
step lively speed 174.9
  hustle 330.13
step off
  measure off 300.11
  die 307.20
step on it! 401.17
step on one's toes
  cause resentment 152.21
  offend 156.5
step out 743.24
step out of line
  disobey 327.6
  go wrong 654.9
  misbelieve 688.8
steppe open space 158.4
  horizontal 201.3
  plain 236.1
  grassland 310.8
stepped-up
  aggravated 119.4
  increased 251.7
step up
  n promotion 446.1
  v aggravate 119.2
  approach 167.3
  accelerate 174.10
  intensify 251.5
  make good 409.10
  electrify 1032.26
stereophonic system 50.11
stereoscopic
  optical 29.10
  spatial 158.10
stereotype
  n habit 373.3
  printing surface 548.8
  v autotype 548.15
  make uniform 781.4
  fix 855.9
  generalize 864.9
sterile ineffective 19.15
  sanitary 79.27
  dull 117.6
  fruitless 391.12
  unproductive 891.4
sterling
  n money 728.1
  adj honest 644.13
  monetary 728.30
  genuine 973.15
  superb 999.15
stern
  n rear 217.1
  buttocks 217.5
  heel 217.7
  adj harsh 144.24
  unyielding 361.9
  strict 425.6
steroid 7.7
stet 855.19
stethoscope 48.8
stevedore carrier 176.7
  longshoreman 183.9

stew
  n food 10.11
  drunk 88.12
  dither 105.6
  anxiety 126.1
  impatience 135.1
  dudgeon 152.7
  flight attendant 185.4
  bustle 330.4
  hostess 577.5
  brothel 665.9
  prostitute 665.16
  hodgepodge 797.6
  bewilderment 971.3
  confusion 985.3
  predicament 1013.5
  v cook 11.5
  intoxicate 88.23
  feel anxious 126.6
  be impatient 135.4
  show resentment 152.14
  be angry 152.15
  seethe 671.12
  be hot 1019.22
  boil 1020.20
steward
  n ship's crew 183.6
  flight attendant 185.4
  provider 385.6
  bailiff 574.4
  agent 576.3
  attendant 577.5
  major-domo 577.10
  treasurer 729.12
  jockey 757.2
  guardian 1008.6
  v treat 387.12
stewardess
  ship's crew 183.6
  flight attendant 185.4
  attendant 577.5
stew over 931.9
stick
  n marijuana cigarette 87.12
  spar 180.13
  slim 270.8
  pole 273.1
  staff 273.2
  punishment 605.2
  baton 711.22
  field hockey 749.4
  supporter 901.2
  wood 1054.3
  dryness 1066.2
  v endure 134.6
  place 159.12
  be still 173.7
  come to a point 285.6
  perforate 292.15
  deceive 356.19
  remain firm 359.9
  persevere 360.7
  injure 393.13
  stall 410.16
  resist 453.4
  stab 459.25
  overprice 632.7
  fasten 800.8
  cohere 803.6
  stabilize 855.7
  fix 855.10

stop 857.7
  stump 971.14
stick around 846.12
stick by 449.13
sticker thorn 285.5
  label 517.13
  enigma 522.8
  price 630.1
  adhesive 803.4
stick in
  insert 191.3
  interpose 213.6
stick in one's throat 98.11
stick-in-the-mud
  n slowpoke 175.5
  idler 331.8
  conservative 853.4
  adj untraveled 173.15
stick it out
  endure 134.6
  persevere 360.7
  resist 453.4
  keep up one's courage 492.15
  stand fast 855.11
  persist 856.5
stickler
  obstinate person 361.6
  perfectionist 495.6
  tyrant 575.14
stick like glue 803.8
stick one's foot in it
  bungle 414.12
  make a boner 975.15
stick one's head in the sand
  984.2
stick out like a sore thumb
  show 31.4
  be manifest 348.7
the sticks
  the country 233.1
  remote region 261.4
stick together
  put together 800.5
  cohere 803.6
  cement 803.9
  be true 973.8
stick to it
  persevere 360.7
  persist 856.5
stick to one's guns
  remain firm 359.9
  stay with it 360.4
  balk 361.7
  resist 453.4
  keep up one's courage 492.15
  stand fast 855.11
stick up rise 200.8
  protrude 283.10
  rob 482.16
  elevate 912.5
stick up for
  back 449.13
  defend 600.10
stick with it
  remain firm 359.9
  persevere 360.7
  be conservative 853.6
  persist 856.5
sticky sweaty 12.22
  sentimental 93.21
  adhesive 803.12

difficult 1013.17
  sultry 1019.28
  viscous 1062.12
  moist 1065.15
stiff
  n vagabond 178.3
  corpse 307.16
  horse 311.12
  bum 331.9
  proletarian 607.9
  wretch 660.2
  laborer 726.2
  blackjack 759.11
  v mistreat 389.6
  adj dull 117.6
  seaworthy 180.18
  stone-dead 307.31
  unyielding 361.9
  out of practice 414.18
  bungling 414.20
  strict 425.7
  stilted 534.3
  formal 580.9
  expensive 632.11
  excessive 993.16
  rigid 1046.11
  tough 1049.4
  adv firmly 425.9
stifle silence 51.8
  control feelings 106.8
  strangle 308.19
  cover up 345.8
  extinguish 395.15
  suppress 428.8
  moderate 670.6
  obstruct 1012.12
  be hot 1019.22
  fight fire 1022.7
stigma sore 85.37
  flower 310.28
  mark 517.5
  disrepute 661.6
  stain 1004.3
stigmatize
  variegate 47.7
  vilify 512.10
  designate 517.18
  mark 517.19
  brand 661.9
  stain 1004.6
stile stairs 193.3
  post 273.4
stiletto 459.25
still
  n silence 51.1
  distillery 88.21
  photograph 714.3
  vaporizer 1067.6
  v silence 51.8
  calm 670.7
  adj silent 51.10
  quiescent 173.12
  motionless 173.13
  dead 307.30
  adv quiescently 173.18
  notwithstanding
    338.8
  until now 838.4
stillborn born 1.4
  dead 307.30
  unsuccessful 410.18

still life
　work of art 712.10
　picture 712.11
still photograph 714.3
stilt 270.8
stimulant
　n energizer 17.6
　tonic 86.9
　drug 87.3
　adj provocative 375.27
stimulate refresh 9.2
　energize 17.10
　sensitize 24.7
　whet 105.13
　elicit 192.14
　motivate 375.12
　interest 983.12
stimulus energizer 17.6
　excitation 105.11
　incentive 375.7
　cause 886.1
sting
　n acrimony 17.5
　pain 26.3
　tingle 74.1
　point 285.3
　deception 356.9
　goad 375.8
　cheating 759.13
　stinger 1001.5
　v pain 26.7
　bite 68.5
　tingle 74.5
　affect 93.14
　aggressive 96.17
　offend 152.21
　be sharp 285.6
　deceive 356.19
　goad 375.15
　overprice 632.7
stingy illiberal 484.9
　ungenerous 651.6
　sparse 885.5
　meager 992.10
stink
　n odor 69.1
　stench 71.1
　v have an odor 69.6
　smell 71.4
stinker stinkard 71.3
　cigar 89.4
　bad person 660.5
stint
　n degree 245.1
　restriction 428.3
　task 724.2
　shift 825.3
　v limit 210.5
　restrict 428.9
　scrimp 484.5
stipend subsidy 478.8
　fee 624.5
stipple
　n spottiness 47.3
　engraving 713.2
　v color 35.14
　variegate 47.7
　engrave 713.9
stipulate fight for 421.7
　contract 437.5
　specify 865.11

　suppose 951.10
　make conditional 959.4
stir
　n excitement 105.4
　motion 172.1
　activity 330.1
　bustle 330.4
　jail 429.9
　commotion 810.4
　agitation 917.1
　v awake 23.4
　sensitize 24.7
　affect 93.14
　excite 105.12
　perturb 105.14
　move 172.5
　be active 330.11
　bustle 330.12
　rouse 375.19
　seethe 671.12
　be turbulent 915.12
　agitate 917.10
stir-fry 11.5
stirrup ear 2.10
　saddle parts 901.18
stir up excite 105.12
　provoke 152.24
　incite 375.17
　rouse 375.19
　mix 797.10
　agitate 917.10
stir up a hornet's nest
　1013.14
stitch
　n pang 26.2
　scrap 248.3
　piece 793.3
　joint 800.4
　v sew 741.4
　fasten 800.8
a stitch in time 845.1
stock
　n stem 310.21
　animal life 311.1
　humankind 312.1
　means 384.2
　store 386.1
　assets 471.7
　portion 477.5
　laughingstock 508.7
　race 559.4
　lineage 560.4
　show business 704.1
　repertoire 704.9
　merchandise 735.1
　shares 738.2
　source 886.5
　belief 953.1
　materials 1054.1
　paper 1054.5
　mineral deposit 1058.7
　v provide 385.7
　gather materials 1054.7
　adj trite 117.9
　customary 373.13
　usual 869.9
stockade 429.8
stockbroker
　broker 730.9
　sharebroker 737.10
stock dividend 738.7

stock exchange
　exchange 737.7
　workplace 739.1
stockholder 737.14
stockings 5.28
stock in trade
　means 384.2
　supply 386.2
stock market
　the market 737.1
　stock exchange 737.7
stockpile
　n store 386.1
　reserve 386.3
　accumulation 770.9
　v store up 386.11
stocks and bonds
　securities 738.1
　guarantee 438.1
stock up
　store up 386.11
　gather materials 1054.7
stocky
　corpulent 257.18
　stubby 268.10
stodgy dull 117.6
　old-fogyish 842.17
　viscous 1062.12
stogie 89.4
stoic
　n Spartan 134.3
　adj apathetic 94.13
　inexcitable 106.10
　patient 134.9
　quiescent 173.12
　stable 855.12
stoke ignite 1020.22
　fuel 1021.8
stolen 482.23
stolid
　inexcitable 106.10
　quiescent 173.12
　stable 855.12
　incurious 982.3
　unimaginative 987.5
stoma 292.1
stomach
　n digestive system 2.18
　taste 62.1
　appetite 100.7
　v endure 134.8
　permit 443.10
stomachache 26.5
stomp
　n stamp 902.10
　v way of walking 177.28
　stamp 902.22
stone
　n fruit seed 310.31
　pavement 383.6
　missile 462.18
　jewel 498.6
　monument 549.12
　lithographic plate 713.6
　hardness 1046.6
　building material 1054.2
　rock 1059.1
　v intoxicate 88.23
　cover face 295.23
　strike dead 308.18
　pelt 459.27

　execute 604.17
　adj rock 1059.11
stone-cold
　stone-dead 307.31
　cold 1023.14
stoned
　unconscious 25.8
　high 87.24
　drunk 88.33
stone's throw 223.2
stonewall be silent 51.6
　outwit 415.11
　delay 846.8
　hinder 1012.10
stony callous 94.12
　rugged 288.7
　without money 619.10
　hard 1046.10
　rocky 1059.12
stooge
　n flatterer 138.4
　follower 166.2
　dupe 358.1
　instrument 384.4
　loser 412.5
　figurehead 575.5
　retainer 577.1
　flunky 616.8
　actor 707.2
　v act 704.29
stool
　n defecation 12.2
　feces 12.4
　toilet 12.11
　v defecate 12.13
　betray 351.6
　inform on 551.13
stool pigeon shill 357.5
　informer 551.6
stoop
　n descent 194.1
　porch 197.21
　plunge 367.1
　crouch 913.3
　v humble oneself 137.8
　fawn 138.7
　condescend 141.8
　descend 194.5
　plunge 367.6
　bow down 433.10
　incur disgrace 661.7
　crouch 913.8
stop
　n standstill 173.3
　destination 186.5
　sojourn 225.5
　obstruction 293.3
　stopper 293.4
　speech sound 524.12
　punctuation 530.15
　delay 846.2
　stoppage 857.2
　prevention 1012.2
　curb 1012.7
　impasse 1013.6
　v muffle 51.9
　daunt 127.18
　quiet 173.8
　sojourn 225.8
　stop up 293.7
　be vigilant 339.8

disaccustom 374.2
break the habit 374.3
cease to use 390.4
fend off 460.10
swear off 668.8
end 820.5
delay 846.8
cease 857.6
come to a halt 857.7
put a stop to 857.11
stay 1012.13
stop at nothing 359.10
stopgap
  n stopper 293.4
  improvisation 365.5
  expedient 995.2
  adj extemporaneous 365.12
  substitute 862.8
  makeshift 995.5
stop in one's tracks
  daunt 127.18
  strike dead 308.18
  stop 857.7
  shoot 904.12
stop it! 857.13
stop light signal 517.15
  traffic light 1026.4
stopoff 225.5
stop over sojourn 225.8
  visit 582.19
stoppage seizure 85.6
  obstruction 293.3
  end 820.1
  delay 846.2
  cessation 857.2
  prevention 1012.2
stopped
  stopped up 293.11
  phonetic 524.30
  late 846.16
stopper
  n plug 293.4
  cover 295.5
  baseball team 745.2
  finishing stroke 820.4
  v stop up 293.7
  top 295.21
stop the clock 853.6
storage
  placement 159.6
  stowage 386.5
  storehouse 386.6
  fee 630.6
  computer memory 1042.7
store
  n provisions 10.5
  supply 386.2
  hoard 386.1
  storehouse 386.6
  preserve 397.7
  gain 472.3
  market 736.1
  workplace 739.1
  casino 759.19
  belief 953.1
  materials 1054.1
  v load 159.15
  provide 385.7
  stow 386.10
  put away 390.6
  gather materials 1054.7

store-bought
  tailored 5.48
  bought 733.11
storekeeper
  provider 385.6
  merchant 730.2
the stork 1.1
storm
  n frenzy 105.9
  fit of anger 152.9
  windstorm 318.12
  attack 459.6
  tempest 671.4
  v be excitable 105.16
  be angry 152.15
  blow 318.20
  raid 459.20
  bluster 503.3
  rage 671.11
  cause trouble 1013.14
storm cellar
  cellar 197.17
  shelter 1009.3
storm clouds
  omen 133.6
  danger 1006.1
storm troops
  elite troops 461.15
  army 461.23
storm watch or warning 317.7
stormy
  passionate 105.29
  tempestuous 318.23
  cloudy 319.8
  turbulent 671.18
  gloomy 1027.14
story
  n floor 197.23
  layer 296.1
  lie 354.11
  joke 489.6
  record 549.1
  news item 552.3
  gossip 552.7
  history 719.1
  tale 719.3
  work of fiction 722.3
  plot 722.4
  v lie 354.19
storybook
  n book 554.1
  adj visionary 986.24
storyteller
  liar 357.9
  author 547.15
  narrator 718.4
  yarn spinner 722.5
stout strong 15.15
  firm 15.18
  hale 83.12
  corpulent 257.18
  courageous 492.17
  sturdy 763.7
stouthearted 492.17
stove kiln 742.5
  heater 1020.10
stove in 292.14
stovepipe 239.14
stow load 159.15
  store 386.10
  put away 390.6

stowaway 774.4
stow away
  secrete 346.7
  store 386.10
straddle
  n stock option 737.21
  v extend 158.9
  way of walking 177.28
  rest on 901.22
  pass 910.8
  adv on 901.25
straddle the fence
  n be a timeserver 363.9
  v hesitate 362.7
  remain neutral 467.5
Stradivarius 711.5
strafe 459.22
straggle stray 164.4
  lag 166.4
  wander 177.23
  way of walking 177.28
  be behind 217.8
  be long 267.5
straggler 178.2
straight
  n heterosexual 75.13
  straight line 277.2
  adj directional 161.12
  straight-lined 277.6
  sober 516.3
  aboveboard 644.14
  candid 644.17
  trustworthy 644.19
  virtuous 653.6
  thorough 794.10
  unmixed 798.7
  continuous 812.8
  conformist 867.6
  unconditional 960.2
  accurate 973.16
  adv directly 161.23
  straightly 277.7
  accurately 973.20
  exactly 973.21
the straight and narrow 653.1
straight arrow 644.8
straightaway
  n straight line 277.2
  racetrack 756.3
  adj directional 161.12
  adv at once 830.8
  promptly 845.15
straightedge 277.3
straight face
  unfeeling 94.1
  solemnity 111.1
  unastonishment 123.1
  reticence 344.3
  unexpressiveness 522.5
straightforward
  adj directional 161.12
  natural 499.7
  clear 521.11
  elegant 533.6
  plain-speaking 535.3
  candid 644.17
  uncomplicated 798.8
  easy 1014.13
  adv directly 161.23
straight man 707.2

strain
  n fatigue 21.1
  anxiety 126.1
  tension 128.3
  humankind 312.1
  endeavor 403.1
  style 532.2
  race 559.4
  lineage 560.4
  enmity 589.1
  melody 708.4
  musical passage 708.24
  poetry 720.9
  exertion 725.2
  class 809.2
  kind 809.3
  pull 905.2
  disposition 978.3
  overdoing 993.6
  overextension 993.7
  stretching 1048.2
  v refine 79.22
  exude 190.15
  pervert 265.6
  demur 325.4
  falsify 354.16
  injure 393.13
  endeavor 403.5
  tax oneself 725.10
  overextend 993.13
strained anxious 126.7
  tense 128.13
  falsified 265.11
  unfriendly 589.9
  laborious 725.18
  farfetched 776.8
strainer refinery 79.13
  porousness 292.8
strain one's credulity
  be unbelievable 955.7
  be improbable 969.2
strait
  n inlet 242.1
  narrow place 270.3
  crisis 843.4
  danger 1006.1
  predicament 1013.4
  adj limited 210.7
  narrow 270.14
straitlaced 425.7
strand
  n shore 234.2
  filament 271.1
  v shipwreck 182.42
stranded stuck 855.16
  grounded 1013.27
strange
  wonderful 122.10
  extraneous 774.5
  unrelated 776.6
  novel 841.11
  odd 870.11
  insane 926.26
  eccentric 927.5
  unknown 930.17
stranger outsider 773.3
  alien 774.3
strangle disable 19.10
  contract 260.7
  close 293.6
  die 307.24

garrote 308.19
extinguish 395.15
suppress 428.8
execute 604.17
obstruct 1012.12
stranglehold
shackle 428.4
wrestling 474.3
hindrance 1012.1
strangler killer 308.11
executioner 604.8
strap
n strip 271.4
whip 605.1
stock option 737.21
v bandage 91.24
sharpen 285.7
restrain 428.10
whip 604.13
bind 800.9
straphanger 178.1
strapless 6.13
strapped limited 210.7
bound 428.16
poor 619.7
without money 619.10
strapping
n corporal punishment
604.4
adj strong 15.15
corpulent 257.18
stratagem trick 356.6
pretext 376.1
intrigue 381.5
artifice 415.3
expedient 995.2
strategic
planned 381.12
cunning 415.12
strategist
planner 381.6
tactician 415.7
politics 610.6
strategy plan 381.1
stratagem 415.3
war tactics 458.5
baseball game 745.3
football game 746.3
basketball game 747.3
tennis game 748.2
boxing 754.3
stratified
layered 296.6
classified 809.8
stratosphere 272.2
stratum layer 296.1
social status 607.1
class 809.2
straw
n feed 10.4
tube 239.6
remainder 256.1
lightness 298.2
stem 310.21
trifle 998.5
adj yellow 43.4
strawberry blond 35.9
strawberry fields 87.10
straw hat 704.1
straw man 500.7
straw poll 371.6

**straw that broke the camel's
back** 886.3
straw vote vote 371.6
feeler 942.4
stray
n vagabond 178.3
v go astray 164.4
wander 177.23
digress 538.9
go wrong 654.9
misbelieve 688.8
err 975.9
be inattentive 984.3
muse 985.9
adj deviative 164.7
abnormal 870.9
purposeless 972.16
streak
n stripe 47.5
swiftness 174.6
thinness 270.7
furrow 290.1
line 517.6
nature 767.4
disposition 978.3
ray 1025.5
v variegate 47.7
furrow 290.3
mark 517.19
streak of luck 1010.3
streaky 47.15
stream
n course 172.2
vapor trail 184.30
waterway 238.1
flow 238.4
channel 239.1
wind 318.1
procession 812.3
trend 896.2
plenty 991.2
ray 1025.5
v move 172.5
travel 177.18
flow 238.16
rain 316.10
come together 770.16
abound 991.5
stream bed
stream 238.1
watercourse 239.2
streamer
flag 647.7
caption 937.2
ray 1025.5
streamline
n straight line 277.2
v simplify 798.4
modernize 841.6
stream of consciousness
association 92.33
thoughts 931.4
street 383.5
streetcar 179.17
street fight 457.4
street person
homeless person 331.10
poor man 619.4
street-smart 928.16
street urchin 178.3
streetwalker 665.16

streetwise 928.16
strength
might 15.1
energy 17.1
power 18.1
pungency 68.3
haleness 83.3
quantity 244.1
greatness 247.1
will power 359.4
authoritativeness 417.2
vigor 544.3
substantiality 763.1
hardness 1046.1
toughness 1049.1
strengthen
nourish 7.17
invigorate 15.13
intensify 251.5
grow 251.6
add to 253.5
confirm 957.11
stiffen 1046.9
toughen 1049.3
strength of character 359.5
strenuous
energetic 17.13
industrious 330.22
laborious 725.18
difficult 1013.17
streptococcus 85.42
stress
n psychological stress 92.17
distress 96.5
anxiety 126.1
tension 128.3
urge 375.6
accent 524.10
meter 720.7
exertion 725.2
thrust 902.2
urgency 997.4
adversity 1011.1
v strain 725.10
thrust 902.12
emphasize 997.14
stress and strain
tension 128.3
strain 725.2
stressed out weakened 16.18
pained 26.9
stress pattern 524.10
stress test 91.12
stretch
n range 158.2
walk 177.10
distance 261.1
length 267.1
strain 725.2
exercise 725.6
racetrack 743.11
period 824.1
spell 825.1
term 825.4
overextension 993.7
elasticity 1048.1
extension 1048.2
v exercise 84.4
reach 158.9
expand 259.4
become larger 259.5

be long 267.5
lengthen 267.6
exaggerate 355.3
hang 604.18
strain 725.10
suffice 991.4
overextend 993.13
extend 1048.4
adj elastic 1048.7
stretcher 901.19
stretcher-bearer 176.7
stretch limo 179.13
stretch of the imagination
986.5
stretch one's luck 493.6
stretch the legs 177.29
stretch the truth
lie 354.19
exaggerate 355.3
stretchy sleepy 22.21
elastic 1048.7
strewn 771.9
striation stripe 47.5
furrow 290.1
line 517.6
stricken affected 93.23
wretched 96.26
overcome 112.29
unnerved 128.14
strict
meticulous 339.12
imperious 417.16
exacting 425.6
fastidious 495.9
conscientious 644.15
orthodox 687.8
precise 973.17
strict interpretation 687.5
strictly on the up-and-up
973.13
strictly speaking
truly 973.18
to be exact 973.22
stricture
contraction 260.1
narrowing 270.2
censure 510.3
criticism 510.4
hindrance 1012.1
stride
n velocity 172.4
step 177.11
gait 177.12
distance 261.1
jazz 708.9
v walk 177.27
way of walking 177.28
straddle 901.22
strident
acrimonious 17.14
stridulant 58.12
dissonant 61.4
strife quarrel 456.5
contention 457.1
strike
n revolt 327.4
objection 333.2
score 409.5
attack 459.1
walkout 727.5
baseball 745.3

bowling 750.2
stop 857.2
discovery 941.1
v impress 93.15
delete 255.12
revolt 327.7
object 333.5
attack 459.14
advance against 459.17
print 548.14
slap 604.12
go on strike 727.10
stop work 857.8
collide 902.13
hit 902.14
shoot 904.12
occur to 931.18
impress 931.19
discover 941.1
strike a balance
average 246.2
weigh 297.10
be neutral 467.6
compromise 468.2
pay in full 624.13
keep accounts 628.8
be moderate 670.5
equalize 790.6
strike a bargain
sign 437.7
compromise 468.2
make a deal 731.19
strike a blow 328.5
strike a pose 500.13
strike a sour note 61.3
strike back 506.4
strikebreaker
apostate 363.5
scab 727.8
strike dead
astonish 122.6
fell 308.18
strike down
put an end to 395.12
repeal 445.2
strike it rich
grow rich 618.10
be fortunate 1010.11
strike oil 1010.11
strike one as 33.10
strike one's colors 433.8
strike one's fancy
please 95.6
enamor 104.23
strikeout 745.3
strike out set out 188.8
delete 255.12
obliterate 395.16
fail 410.10
baseball 745.5
eliminate 773.5
originate 892.12
strike out at
lash out at 459.16
criticize 510.14
strike out for 161.9
strike terror into 127.17
strike the first blow 457.14
strike up 708.37
strike up a conversation 541.9
strike up a tune 708.37

strike up the band 708.37
strike while the iron is hot
843.8
striking
n deletion 255.5
coining 728.24
adj powerful 18.12
exciting 105.30
wonderful 122.10
remarkable 247.10
conspicuous 348.12
eloquent 544.11
notable 997.19
striking resemblance 784.4
string
n swimwear 5.29
step 193.5
line 267.3
cord 271.2
utterance 524.2
team 617.7
violin family 711.5
chord 711.20
bowling 750.2
company 770.3
part of writing 793.2
series 812.2
procession 812.3
condition 959.2
v tune 708.36
continue 812.4
string along
follow 166.3
deceive 356.14
flatter 511.6
stringent
acrimonious 17.14
harsh 144.24
strict 425.6
stringer 555.4
string musician 710.5
string out
lengthen 267.6
protract 538.8
align 812.5
postpone 846.9
sustain 856.4
strings
proviso 421.3
orchestra 710.12
stringed instrument 711.2
backstairs influence 894.3
string up 604.18
stringy
threadlike 271.7
tough 1049.4
viscous 1062.12
strip
n runway 184.23
a length 267.2
line 267.3
strap 271.4
stripe 517.6
stock option 737.21
horse racing 757.1
v divest 6.5
undress 6.7
peel 6.8
excise 255.10
strip clean 480.24
simplify 798.4

tear apart 802.14
dismiss 909.19
stripe
n streak 47.5
line 267.3
slash 517.6
corporal punishment 604.4
military insignia 647.5
nature 767.4
kind 809.3
slap 902.8
disposition 978.3
v variegate 47.7
mark 517.19
whip 604.13
striped streaked 47.15
netlike 170.11
strip mining 1058.8
stripper nudity 6.3
dancer 705.3
entertainer 707.1
separator 802.7
strip-search 6.5
strive endeavor 403.5
contend 457.13
struggle 725.11
strobe light 1025.7
stroke
n touch 73.1
seizure 85.6
paralysis 85.27
pain 96.5
act 328.3
attempt 403.2
stratagem 415.3
compliment 509.6
line 517.6
upheaval 671.5
work 725.4
tennis 748.2
hockey 749.6
golf swing 751.3
instant 830.3
hit 902.4
spasm 917.6
expedient 995.2
v pet 73.8
delight 95.11
encourage 375.21
exploit 387.16
flatter 511.6
rub 1044.6
stroke of luck 1010.3
stroll
n slow motion 175.2
walk 177.10
gait 177.12
v go slowly 175.6
wander 177.23
way of walking 177.28
stroller wanderer 178.2
baby carriage 179.6
actor 707.2
strong forceful 15.15
energetic 17.13
powerful 18.12
pungent 68.8
strong-smelling 69.10
malodorous 71.5
hale 83.12
alcoholic 88.37

great 247.6
tainted 393.41
accented 524.30
eloquent 544.11
sturdy 763.7
influential 894.13
tough 1049.4
strong-arm
v exert strength 15.12
coerce 424.8
adj coercive 424.12
strongbox
storehouse 386.6
treasury 729.13
stronghold
fortification 460.6
refuge 1009.1
strong language
cursing 513.3
vigor 544.3
strong-minded
strong-willed 359.15
intelligent 920.12
strong point
talent 413.4
stronghold 460.6
specialty 866.1
good reasoning 935.10
strop
n strip 271.4
v sharpen 285.7
struck down 445.3
structural
formal 266.6
semantic 518.12
linguistic 523.19
grammatical 530.17
organizational 808.15
constructional 892.15
structure
n house 228.5
form 262.1
arrangement 266.1
construction 266.1
building 266.2
texture 294.1
clearness 521.2
syntax 530.2
plot 722.4
composition 796.1
order 807.1
v construct 266.5
compose 796.3
order 807.4
structural engineering 1043.1
strudel 10.41
struggle
n endeavor 403.1
contention 457.1
fight 457.4
exertion 725.3
v endeavor 403.5
contend 457.13
strive 725.11
flounder 917.15
have difficulty 1013.11
strum 708.40
strut
n gait 177.12
swagger 501.8
v way of walking 177.28

show defiance 454.5
swagger 501.15
stub cigarette 89.5
tail 217.6
label 517.13
extremity 820.2
stubble beard 3.8
remainder 256.1
bristle 288.3
refuse 391.4
stubborn
persevering 360.8
obstinate 361.8
strict 425.7
tenacious 803.12
inflexible 1046.12
tough 1049.4
stubborn as a mule 361.8
stubby 268.10
stub one's toe 414.12
stucco 295.25
stuck fastened 800.14
cohesive 803.10
caught 855.16
baffled 971.26
at an impasse 1013.24
stranded 1013.27
stuck-up
conceited 140.11
arrogant 141.9
contemptuous 157.8
stuck with 643.8
stud
n sex object 75.4
man 76.5
male animal 76.8
beam 273.6
knob 283.3
horse 311.10
print 517.7
jockey 757.2
poker 759.10
v variegate 47.7
roughen 288.4
sprinkle 771.6
studded spotted 47.13
knobbed 283.17
gnarled 288.8
bristly 288.9
nappy 294.7
ornamented 498.11
sprinkled 771.10
teeming 884.9
illuminated 1025.39
student pupil 572.1
scholar 929.3
stud farm 1070.5
studied
intentional 380.8
affected 533.9
reasoned 935.21
studio library 197.6
atelier 712.17
workplace 739.1
radio station 1034.6
study
n diagnosis 91.12
library 197.6
intention 380.1
discussion 541.7
treatise 556.1

branch of learning 568.8
studying 570.3
work of art 712.10
drawing 712.13
office 739.7
science 928.10
consideration 931.2
thoughtfulness 931.3
examination 938.3
engrossment 983.3
abstractedness 985.2
retreat 1009.5
v endeavor 403.5
discuss 541.12
learn 570.12
consider 931.12
examine 938.24
pay attention 983.8
memorize 989.17
stuff
n fabric 4.1
essential content 196.5
equipment 385.4
game 745.3
substance 763.2
essence 767.2
matter 1052.2
materials 1054.1
v nourish 8.19
gorge 8.25
cram 196.7
clog 293.7
embalm 397.10
gluttonize 672.4
fill 794.7
overload 993.15
satiate 994.4
stuffed clogged 293.11
full 794.11
overfull 993.20
satiated 994.6
stuffed animal 743.16
stuffed shirt 501.9
stuffing
n food 10.27
padding 196.3
extra 254.4
blockage 293.5
embalming 397.3
adj gluttonous 672.6
stuffy malodorous 71.5
dull 117.6
airless 173.16
unyielding 361.9
perverse 361.11
prudish 500.19
pompous 501.22
old-fogyish 842.17
conformist 867.6
narrow-minded 980.10
unimaginative 987.5
sultry 1019.28
stultify suppress 428.8
neutralize 900.7
make a fool of 923.7
stumble
n tumble 194.3
collapse 410.3
bungle 414.5
flounder 917.8
slip 975.4

v tumble 194.8
not know one's own mind
362.6
bungle 414.11
stammer 525.8
flounder 917.15
err 975.9
stumblebum 414.9
stumble on
arrive at 186.7
come across 941.3
stumbling block 1012.4
stump
n remainder 256.1
public speaking 543.1
art equipment 712.18
piece 793.3
extremity 820.2
platform 901.13
v plod 175.7
way of walking 177.28
make a speech 543.9
electioneer 609.40
go into politics 610.13
boggle 971.14
thwart 1012.15
stumper enigma 522.8
campaigner 610.10
stumpy
deformed 265.12
stubby 268.10
low 274.7
stun deaden 25.4
deafen 49.5
din 53.7
numb 94.8
astonish 122.6
terrify 127.17
startle 131.8
stung 96.23
stun gun 462.10
stunning
deadening 25.9
astonishing 122.12
frightening 127.28
terrifying 127.29
surprising 131.11
excellent 999.13
beautiful 1016.22
stunt
n act 328.3
acting 704.8
v air maneuver
184.40
shorten 268.6
stunted dwarf 258.13
undeveloped 406.12
incomplete 795.4
meager 992.10
stunt man 185.1
stupefy deaden 25.4
numb 94.8
astonish 122.6
terrify 127.17
stupendous
wonderful 122.10
large 247.7
huge 257.20
extraordinary 870.14
stupid dumb 922.15
foolish 923.8

stupidity
stupidness 922.3
foolishness 923.1
folly 923.4
blunder 975.5
stupor sleep 22.6
unconsciousness 25.2
trance 92.19
apathy 94.4
languor 331.6
sturdy strong 15.15
firm 15.18
hale 83.12
stable 763.7
stutter
n stammering 525.3
v stammer 525.8
sty pigsty 80.11
eye disease 85.37
hovel 228.11
blemish 1004.1
style
n clothing 5.1
aspect 33.3
form 262.1
flower part 310.28
behavior 321.1
preference 371.5
manner 384.1
skill 413.1
motif 498.7
name 527.3
way of speaking 532.2
fashion 578.1
lines 712.8
engraving tool 713.8
race 753.3
fight 754.3
mode 765.4
kind 809.3
specialty 866.1
v name 527.11
phrase 532.4
stylish dressed up 5.46
skillful 413.22
modish 578.12
stylus 50.11
stymie
n golf 751.3
v stop 1012.13
styptic pencil 260.6
Styx
river of death 307.4
Hades 682.4
suave smooth 287.10
glib 504.18
sub
n submarine 180.9
baseball 745.2
football 746.2
substitute 862.2
adj inferior 250.6
subatomic particle
minute particle 258.8
elementary particle 1038.6
subclass 809.5
subcommittee
committee 423.2
delegation 576.13
subconscious
n psyche 92.28

inmost mind 919.3
adj unconscious 92.42
subconscious urge 934.2
subcutaneous
 n injection 91.17
 adj cutaneous 2.27
subdivide
 analyze 801.6
 apportion 802.18
 classify 809.6
 bisect 875.4
 discriminate 944.4
subdue muffle 51.9
 relieve 120.5
 conquer 412.10
 suppress 428.8
 master 432.9
 moderate 670.6
 calm 670.7
 soften 1047.6
subhead
 n caption 937.2
 v focus on 937.3
subhuman
 cruel 144.26
 animal 311.40
subject
 n citizen 227.4
 vassal 432.7
 syntax 530.2
 discipline 568.8
 field of study 570.3
 passage 708.24
 plot 722.4
 doer 726.1
 topic 937.1
 examinee 938.19
 experimental subject
  942.7
 v subjugate 432.8
 adj inferior 250.6
 dependent 432.13
subjection
 inferiority 250.1
 subjugation 432.1
 submission 433.1
subjective
 introverted 92.40
 intrinsic 767.7
 mental 919.7
subjectivism 1053.3
subject oneself 652.3
subject to
 v impose 643.4
 adj liable to 897.6
 contingent 959.9
 conj provided 959.12
subjugate
 conquer 412.10
 subject 432.8
 appropriate 480.19
 domineer 612.16
sublet
 v rent 615.15
 rent out 615.16
 adj employed 615.20
sublimate
 n dregs 256.2
 v refine 79.22
 suppress 106.8
 vaporize 1067.8

sublime
 v refine 79.22
 vaporize 1067.8
 adj blissful 97.9
 distinguished 247.9
 lofty 272.14
 eloquent 544.14
 magnanimous 652.6
 eminent 662.18
 raised 912.9
 gorgeous 1016.21
subliminal
 n psyche 92.28
 adj subconscious 92.42
 instinctive 934.6
submarine
 n sub 180.9
 diving equipment
  367.5
 adj underwater 275.13
submerge
 submarines 182.47
 sink 194.6
 overflow 238.17
 submerse 367.7
 flood 1065.14
submersible
 n submarine 180.9
 adj submergible 367.9
submission
 resignation 134.2
 obeisance 155.2
 obedience 326.1
 submittal 433.1
 offer 439.1
 consent 441.1
submissive
 resigned 134.10
 servile 138.13
 assenting 332.13
 compliant 433.12
 conformable 867.5
 pliant 1047.9
 obedient 326.3
 humblehearted 137.11
 obeisant 155.10
 downtrodden 432.16
 consenting 441.1
submit affirm 334.5
 nominate 371.19
 advise 422.5
 comply 433.6
 offer 439.4
 propose 439.5
 obey 326.2
 acquiesce 441.3
 yield 1047.7
subordinate
 n inferior 250.2
 junior 432.5
 retainer 577.1
 nonessential 768.2
 v subjugate 432.8
 arrange 808.11
 adj inferior 250.6
 subject 432.13
 unessential 768.4
suborn bribe 378.3
 induce 886.11
subpar 1000.9
subplot 722.4

subpoena
 n summons 598.2
 v summon 420.11
 summons 598.14
sub rosa 345.17
subscribe abet 449.14
 contribute 478.14
 belong 617.15
subscript 254.2
subscription
 ratification 332.4
 giving 478.1
 donation 478.6
 signature 527.10
subsequent
 succeeding 815.4
 after 835.4
subservient
 servile 138.13
 inferior 250.6
 instrumental 384.8
 subject 432.13
 submissive 433.12
 deferential 433.16
 helping 449.20
subset 793.1
subside quiet 173.8
 sink 194.6
 decrease 252.6
 descend 297.15
 decline 393.17
subsidiary
 n nonessential 768.2
 adj helping 449.20
 endowed 478.26
 unessential 768.4
subsidize provide 385.7
 support 449.12
 finance 478.19
 treat 624.19
 sponsor 729.16
 maintain 901.21
subsidy provision 385.1
 support 449.3
 grant 478.8
 treat 624.8
 financing 729.2
 upkeep 901.1
subsist remain 256.5
 live 306.9
 support oneself 385.12
 exist 761.8
 endure 827.6
 persist 853.5
subsistence
 n accommodations 385.3
 support 449.3
 existence 761.1
 adj meager 992.10
subsistence farming 1069.1
subsisting 761.13
subspecies
 humankind 312.1
 part 793.1
 classifications 809.5
substance
 content 196.5
 quantity 244.1
 meaning 518.1
 summary 557.2
 warrant 600.6

 wealth 618.1
 funds 728.14
 substantiality 763.1
 stuff 763.2
 essence 767.2
 major part 792.6
 topic 937.1
 salient point 997.6
 matter 1052.2
substance abuse 87.1
substandard
 vernacular 523.20
 below par 1005.10
substantiate
 itemize 766.6
 test 942.8
 confirm 957.11
 materialize 1052.9
substantive
 n noun 530.5
 adj grammatical 530.17
 substantial 763.6
 essential 767.9
 vital 997.23
substitute
 n surrogate 92.31
 deputy 576.1
 supporting actor 707.7
 baseball team 745.2
 football team 746.2
 successor 817.4
 replacement 862.2
 v exchange 862.4
 adj alternate 862.8
substitution
 defense mechanism 92.23
 compensation 338.1
 switch 862.1
 substitute 862.2
subterfuge
 secrecy 345.1
 concealment 346.1
 deception 356.1
 trick 356.6
 pretext 376.1
 stratagem 415.3
 quibbling 936.5
subterranean 275.12
subtext 519.2
subtile dainty 248.7
 tenuous 764.6
 shrewd 920.15
 discriminating 944.7
subtitle
 n book 554.12
 caption 937.2
 v focus on 937.3
subtle
 soft-colored 35.22
 dainty 248.7
 thin 270.16
 rare 299.4
 meticulous 339.12
 cunning 415.12
 nice 495.11
 elegant 496.9
 tenuous 764.6
 complex 799.4
 shrewd 920.15
 discriminating 944.7
 exact 973.17

subtle distinction
margin 780.2
distinction 944.3
subtotal 253.2
subtract deduct 255.9
separate 802.8
calculate 1017.18
subtropics zone 231.3
hot place 1019.11
suburb 230.1
suburban
surrounding 209.8
urban 230.11
upper-class 607.10
ordinary 1005.8
subversion
overturn 205.2
fall 395.3
indoctrination 858.5
revolution 860.1
refutation 958.2
subversionary 395.26
subversive
n rebel 327.5
saboteur 357.11
radical 611.12
revolutionist 860.3
adj rebellious 327.11
destructive 395.26
radical 611.20
changed 852.10
subway train 179.14
underground area
284.5
subzero 1023.14
succeed
accomplish 407.4
prevail 409.7
triumph 411.3
change hands 629.4
be a hit 704.28
be next 815.2
follow 817.5
come after 835.3
substitute for 862.5
prosper 1010.7
succession
authority 417.12
inheritance 479.2
lineage 560.4
offspring 561.1
devolution 629.2
series 812.2
sequence 815.1
subsequence 835.1
constancy 847.2
thoughts 931.4
successive
consecutive 812.9
succeeding 815.4
subsequent 835.4
successor
follower 166.2
survivor 256.3
heir 479.5
replacement 817.4
sequel 835.2
substitute 862.2
succession 862.1
success story 409.3
succinct short 268.8

concise 537.6
aphoristic 974.6
succor
n remedy 86.1
aid 449.1
v aid 449.11
benefit 592.3
succulent
n plant 310.4
adj edible 8.33
tasty 63.8
delectable 97.10
interesting 983.19
fluid 1061.4
pulpy 1063.6
succumb burn out 21.5
faint 25.5
die 307.19
perish 395.23
lose 412.12
submit 433.6
such 784.3
such as 784.12
suck
n sip 8.4
drink 88.7
drawing in 187.5
v sip 8.29
perform oral sex 75.22
draw in 187.12
draw off 192.12
suck dry exploit 387.16
consume 388.3
strip 480.24
sucked into 898.5
sucker
n sprout 302.11
branch 310.20
dupe 358.2
customer 733.4
cheater 759.22
trusting soul 954.4
v exploit 387.16
suck in drink 8.29
draw in 187.12
lure 377.5
suckle
breast-feed 8.19
drink 8.29
draw in 187.12
foster 449.16
suckling 302.9
suck up to
curry favor 138.9
cultivate 587.12
suction
drawing in 187.5
extraction 192.3
favor 894.2
sudatory secretory 13.7
cleanness 79.1
sudden
adj unexpected 131.10
impulsive 365.9
precipitate 401.10
abrupt 830.5
adv suddenly 830.9
sudden death
fatal disease 85.2
early death 307.5
sudden death overtime 749.3

sudden infant death syndrome
85.2
suddenly
unexpectedly 131.14
abruptly 268.13
suds
n beer 88.16
foam 320.2
v foam 320.5
sue petition 440.10
solicit 440.14
court 562.21
litigate 598.13
suet 10.14
suffer
feel pain 26.8
ail 85.46
hurt 96.19
endure 134.5
submit 433.6
countenance 443.10
be punished 604.20
experience 831.8
sufferer
sick person 85.43
victim 96.11
suffer the consequences
604.20
sufficient
satisfactory 107.11
valid 973.14
sufficing 991.6
tolerable 999.20
suffix
n addition 254.2
morphology 526.3
sequel 817.1
v add 253.4
place after 815.3
suffocate die 307.24
strangle 308.19
extinguish 395.15
suppress 428.8
obstruct 1012.12
be hot 1019.22
suffrage vote 371.6
participation 476.1
franchise 609.17
suffragette
suffrage 609.17
women's rightist 642.5
suffuse
pervade 221.7
imbue 797.11
suffused with light 1025.39
sugar
n carbohydrate 7.5
sweetening 66.2
LSD 87.10
loved one 104.11
endearment term 562.6
money 728.2
v sweeten 66.3
sugar daddy
beau 104.13
giver 478.11
suggest promise 133.13
advise 422.5
propose 439.5
signify 517.17
mean 518.8

imply 519.4
hint 551.10
resemble 784.7
evidence 957.8
remind 989.20
suggestion hint 248.4
advice 422.1
proposal 439.2
aspersion 512.4
indication 517.3
clue 517.9
implication 519.2
veiled reference 551.4
admixture 797.7
influence 894.1
supposition 951.5
suicidal
wretched 96.26
dejected 112.22
murderous 308.24
destructive 395.26
unwise 923.10
suicide 308.5
suit
n clothing 5.6
entreaty 440.2
solicitation 440.5
courtship 562.7
lawsuit 598.1
accusation 599.1
prayer 696.4
soccer 752.1
playing cards 758.2
bridge 758.3
set 770.12
important person 997.9
v outfit 5.41
please 95.6
be satisfactory 107.6
fit 405.8
agree 788.8
be timely 843.6
conform 867.3
suffice 991.4
suitable eligible 371.24
decorous 496.10
right 637.3
apt 788.10
timely 843.9
sufficient 991.6
expedient 995.5
suite apartment 228.13
furniture 229.1
attendance 769.6
set 770.12
suit oneself 430.20
suitor desirer 100.12
lover 104.12
petitioner 440.7
litigant 598.11
accuser 599.5
suit the occasion 995.3
suit up 5.43
sulfa drug 86.29
sulfate 1060.8
sulfuric 1058.15
sulk
n refusal 325.1
v mope 110.14
sulky
discontented 108.7

sullen 110.24
glum 112.25
unwilling 325.5
obstinate 361.8
perverse 361.11
sullen dark 38.9
sulky 110.24
glum 112.25
unwilling 325.5
obstinate 361.8
perverse 361.11
unsociable 583.5
sully soil 80.16
defile 80.17
vilify 512.10
corrupt 654.10
stigmatize 661.9
seduce 665.20
sultan 575.10
sultry
obscene 666.9
stifling 1019.28
sum
n quantity 244.1
amount 244.2
math terms 253.2
meaning 518.1
summary 557.2
amount of money 728.13
total 792.2
summation 1017.6
v compute 253.6
sum up 1017.19
summa cum laude 646.11
summarize
shorten 268.6
abridge 557.5
iterate 849.8
sum up 1017.19
summary
n shortening 268.3
résumé 557.2
iteration 849.2
summation 1017.11
adj short 268.8
concise 537.6
prompt 845.9
summary execution 604.7
summation
math terms 253.2
shortening 268.3
résumé 557.2
testimony 598.8
sum 1017.6
summary 1017.11
summer
n summertide 313.3
hot weather 1019.7
v vacation 313.8
spend time 821.6
adj seasonal 313.9
summer solstice 313.7
summery green 44.4
seasonal 313.9
warm 1019.24
summit top 198.2
mountain 237.6
supremacy 249.3
limit 794.5
acme of perfection 1002.3
summit conference 541.6

summon attract 377.6
call 420.11
invite 440.13
enlist 615.17
conjure 690.11
convene 770.17
summons
n bidding 420.5
invitation 440.4
call 517.16
subpoena 598.2
enlistment 615.7
v summon 420.11
issue a summons 598.14
sumo 457.10
sump
receptacle of filth 80.12
drain 239.5
lake 241.1
marsh 243.1
pit 284.4
sumptuous
grandiose 501.21
expensive 632.11
sum total 792.2
sum up
shorten 268.6
iterate 849.8
sum 1017.19
sun
n moment 824.2
light source 1026.1
orb of day 1072.13
v sunbathe 1020.19
dry 1066.6
sunbaked 1019.24
the Sunbelt 231.7
sunblind 1028.1
sun-block 1056.3
sunburn
n burn 1020.6
v brown 40.2
sundae 10.47
Sunday
n day of rest 20.5
holy day 701.12
v vacation 20.9
Sunday paper 555.2
Sunday school 567.8
sundown 315.2
sundry
diversified 783.4
several 884.7
sunglasses
spectacles 29.3
eyeshade 1028.2
sunk
concave 284.16
spoiled 393.29
depressed 913.12
sunless 1027.13
Sunni
n Muslim 675.23
adj Muslim 675.31
sunny
bright 97.11
cheerful 109.11
optimistic 124.12
warm 1019.24
luminous 1025.30
sunrise east 161.3

dawn 314.3
sunset
west 161.3
evening 315.2
sunshine 1072.13
sun worshiper 697.4
sup
n drink 8.4
sip 62.2
nip 88.7
hint 248.4
v dine 8.21
drink 8.29
taste 62.7
tipple 88.24
super
n volume 554.4
supporting actor or actress 707.7
adj superior 249.12
excellent 999.13
magnificent 999.15
superb
eminent 247.9
grandiose 501.21
super 999.15
superannuated 837.1
Super Bowl 746.1
supercharged 993.20
supercomputer 1042.2
superconductor 1032.14
supercooled 1023.14
superego psyche 92.28
conscience 636.5
self 865.5
supererogatory 253.1
superficial
apparent 33.11
dull 117.6
spatial 158.10
exterior 206.7
insignificant 248.6
shallow 276.5
hasty 401.9
formal 580.7
frivolous 922.20
half-learned 930.15
insufficient 992.9
trivial 998.19
superfluous
remaining 256.7
useless 391.9
unessential 768.4
redundant 993.17
superheated 1020.29
superhero
celebrity 662.9
ideal 786.4
superhuman
divine 677.16
supernatural 870.15
superimpose 295.19
superintendent
n supervisor 574.2
policeman 1008.15
adj supervising 573.13
superior
n boss 249.4
chief 575.3
adj arrogant 141.9
remarkable 247.10

greater 249.12
higher 272.19
authoritative 417.15
important 997.17
above par 999.14
superiority power 18.1
greatness 247.1
preeminence 249.1
dominance 417.6
precedence 814.1
abnormality 870.1
overrunning 910.1
importance 997.1
goodness 999.1
superiority complex 92.22
superlative
n exaggeration 355.1
the best 999.8
adj downright 247.12
supreme 249.13
high 272.14
exaggerated 355.4
superman 249.4
Superman 15.6
supermarket 736.1
supernatural
divine 677.16
occult 689.23
preternatural 870.15
spectral 988.7
immaterial 1053.7
supernova 1072.8
superpose add 253.4
cover 295.19
superpower 232.1
superscript 254.2
supersede 862.5
supersensitive 24.12
supersonic
acoustic 50.17
transsonic 174.16
superstar
n superior 249.4
successful person 409.6
skillful person 413.14
celebrity 662.9
lead 707.6
chief 997.10
first-rater 999.6
adj chief 249.14
superstitious 954.8
superstore 736.1
superstructure 266.2
supervise
wield authority 417.13
superintend 573.10
govern 612.12
supervisor
superintendent 574.2
public official 575.17
supine apathetic 94.13
recumbent 201.8
low 274.7
languid 331.20
submissive 433.12
supper 8.6
suppertime 315.2
supplant depose 447.4
substitute for 862.5
supple
v soften 1047.6

adj timeserving 363.10
versatile 413.25
cunning 415.12
changeable 854.6
pliant 1047.9
supplement
n adjunct 254.1
nonessential 768.2
sequel 817.1
v add to 253.5
supplementary
additional 253.10
unessential 768.4
supplicate
entreat 440.11
pray 696.13
supplier 385.6
supplies
provisions 10.5
merchandise 385.2
store 386.1
supply
n means 384.2
provision 385.1
hoard 386.1
fund 386.2
materials 1054.1
v provide 385.7
furnish 478.15
supply depot 386.6
supply line 385.1
supply side economics
731.11
support
n nutriment 10.3
consolation 121.4
assent 332.1
means 384.2
preservation 397.1
aid 449.1
maintenance 449.3
reinforcements 449.8
subsidy 478.8
supporter 616.9
treat 624.8
supporting actor 707.7
financing 729.2
backing 901.1
bearer 901.2
confirmation 957.4
v strengthen 15.13
comfort 121.6
give hope 124.10
endure 134.5
ratify 332.12
provide 385.7
preserve 397.8
help 449.12
subsidize 478.19
encourage 492.16
commend 509.11
benefit 592.3
defend 600.10
back politically 609.41
treat 624.19
afford 626.7
enact 704.30
finance 729.16
bear 901.21
confirm 957.11
care for 1008.19

supporter
follower 166.2
suspender 202.5
attender 221.5
defender 460.7
giver 478.11
friend 588.1
upholder 616.9
financer 729.10
support 901.2
support group 449.2
supporting actor
assistant 616.6
motion-picture studio 706.4
support 707.7
supporting evidence 957.4
suppose imply 519.4
judge 946.8
assume 951.10
think 953.11
presume 968.5
imagine 986.14
supposed implied 519.7
assumed 951.14
suppress repress 106.8
cover up 345.8
extinguish 395.15
conquer 412.10
restrain 428.8
subdue 432.9
prohibit 444.3
retain 474.5
domineer 612.16
moderate 670.6
cushion 670.8
hinder 1012.10
suppurate fester 12.15
decay 393.22
supranational 312.16
supranational government
612.7
supremacy primacy 249.3
dominance 417.6
influence 894.1
importance 997.1
superexcellence 999.2
supreme
omnipotent 18.13
top 198.10
superlative 249.13
authoritative 417.15
governing 612.18
almighty 677.17
paramount 997.24
best 999.16
surcease
n respite 20.2
release 120.2
cessation 857.1
v release 120.6
surcharge
n burden 297.7
overcharge 632.5
overfullness 993.3
v falsify accounts 628.10
overprice 632.7
overload 993.15
sure
adj expectant 130.11
secured 438.11
trustworthy 644.19

belief 953.21
evidential 957.16
inevitable 963.15
certain 970.13
reliable 970.17
confident 970.21
adv surely 970.24
interj yeah 332.19
sure as death and taxes
inevitable 963.15
dead sure 970.14
sure bet
sure success 409.2
lock 970.2
good chance 972.8
surefire
successful 409.14
reliable 970.17
Sûreté 1008.17
sure thing
n sure success 409.2
bet 759.3
dead certainty 970.2
good chance 972.8
adv surely 970.24
interj yeah 332.19
surety security 438.1
pledge 438.2
guarantor 438.6
belief 953.1
certainty 970.1
confidence 970.5
safety 1007.1
surf
n breaker 238.14
foam 320.2
wave 916.4
v navigate 182.13
surface
n space 158.1
top 198.1
exterior 206.2
shallowness 276.1
texture 294.1
tennis 748.1
v show 31.4
submarines 182.47
arrive 186.6
emerge 190.11
shoot up 193.9
cover 295.22
come out 348.6
be manifest 348.7
be revealed 351.8
adj apparent 33.11
spatial 158.10
exterior 206.7
shallow 276.5
formal 580.7
insufficient 992.9
surfboard 180.11
surfeit
n overfullness 993.3
satiety 994.1
v fill 794.7
overload 993.15
satiate 994.4
surfing 760.2
surge
n loudness 53.1
ascent 193.1

flow 238.4
billow 238.14
increase 251.1
whirl 915.2
wave 916.4
v din 53.7
run out 190.13
ascend 193.8
flow 238.16
jet 238.20
billow 238.22
come together 770.16
whirl 915.11
surgeon 90.5
surgery operation 90.2
surgical treatment 91.19
hospital room 197.25
severance 802.2
surgical strike 459.1
surly sullen 110.24
gruff 505.7
surmise
n supposition 951.3
guess 951.4
v suppose 951.10
think 953.11
surmount climb 193.11
top 198.9
rise above 272.11
defeat 411.5
overcome 412.7
surname 527.5
surpass excel 249.6
outdistance 249.10
exceed 993.9
do better 999.11
surplus
n difference 255.8
remainder 256.4
overrunning 910.1
excess 993.5
v dismiss 909.19
adj additional 253.10
remaining 256.7
excess 993.18
surprise
n wonder 122.1
astonishment 131.2
surprise attack 459.2
v astonish 122.6
take by surprise 131.7
attack 459.14
surreal odd 870.11
illusory 976.9
surrender
n abandonment 370.3
capitulation 433.2
compromise 468.1
relinquishment 475.1
giving 478.1
transfer 629.1
v weaken 16.9
yield 370.7
give up 433.8
compromise 468.2
relinquish 475.3
deliver 478.13
transfer 629.3
surreptitious
covert 345.12
in hiding 346.14

deceitful 356.22
surrogate
  psychological substitute
    92.31
  deputy 576.1
  replacement 862.2
surround
  n environment 209.1
  setting 209.2
  nearness 223.1
  circumstances 766.2
  frame 901.10
  v devour 8.22
  extend 158.9
  internalize 207.5
  envelop 209.6
  circumscribe 210.4
  bound 211.8
  enclose 212.5
  circle 280.10
  wrap 295.20
  besiege 459.19
  go around 914.5
surveillance
  vigilance 339.4
  ambush 346.3
  supervision 573.2
  shadowing 938.9
survey
  n scrutiny 27.6
  field of view 31.3
  measurement 300.1
  treatise 556.1
  abridgment 557.1
  assemblage 770.1
  examination 938.3
  canvass 938.14
  v scrutinize 27.14
  measure 300.10
  write upon 556.5
  examine 938.24
  canvass 938.29
surveyor
  measurer 300.9
  superintendent 574.2
survival of the fittest 861.4
survive remain 256.5
  keep alive 306.12
  support oneself 385.12
  recover 396.20
  endure 827.6
  outlast 827.8
  live on 839.7
  sustain 856.4
  persist 856.5
survivor 256.3
susceptible
  sensible 24.11
  sensitive 93.20
  teachable 570.18
  influenceable 894.15
  liable 897.5
  exposed 1006.15
  pliant 1047.9
sushi 10.24
suspect
  n accused 599.6
  v be jealous 153.3
  suppose 951.10
  think 953.11
  doubt 955.6

adj unbelievable 955.10
  doubted 955.12
  questionable 971.17
suspend release 120.6
  hang 202.8
  repeal 445.2
  depose 447.4
  postpone 846.9
  interrupt 857.10
  dismiss 909.19
suspenders 202.5
suspense anxiety 126.1
  expectancy 130.3
  inertness 173.4
  pendency 202.1
  uncertainty 971.1
suspension respite 20.2
  release 120.2
  pendency 202.1
  inactivity 331.1
  discontinuance 390.2
  repeal 445.1
  deposal 447.2
  harmonization 709.2
  elimination 773.2
  interruption 813.2
  delay 846.2
  pause 857.3
  dismissal 909.5
  solution 1064.3
suspicion
  suspiciousness 153.2
  hint 248.4
  small amount 258.7
  wariness 494.2
  leeriness 551.4
  admixture 797.7
  hunch 934.3
  suggestion 951.5
  doubt 955.2
  incredulity 956.1
suspicious
  jealous 153.5
  wary 494.9
  dishonest 645.16
  doubting 955.9
  unbelievable 955.10
  incredulous 956.4
  doubtful 971.17
sustain nourish 7.17
  feed 8.18
  strengthen 15.13
  tolerate 134.5
  buoy 298.8
  preserve 397.8
  maintain 449.12
  foster 449.16
  defend 600.10
  endure 827.6
  experience 831.8
  protract 856.4
  support 901.21
  confirm 957.11
sustenance food 10.1
  nutriment 10.3
  maintenance 449.3
  continuance 856.1
  support 901.1
suttee suicide 308.5
  oblation 696.7
  burning 1020.5

suture filament 271.1
  sewing 741.1
  joint 800.4
svelte 270.16
Svengali hypnotist 22.9
  influence 894.6
swab wash 79.19
  dry 1066.6
swaddle
  n children's wear 5.30
  v clothe 5.39
  wrap 295.20
  bind 800.9
swag
  n sinkage 194.2
  hang 202.2
  inclination 204.2
  curve 279.2
  booty 482.11
  swing 916.6
  v sink 194.6
  hang 202.6
  incline 204.10
  curve 279.6
  oscillate 916.10
  adj drooping 202.10
swagger
  n gait 177.12
  strut 501.8
  boasting 502.1
  bluster 503.1
  v way of walking 177.28
  strut 501.15
  boast 502.6
  bluster 503.3
swagger stick 273.2
swain
  n desirer 100.12
  beau 104.13
  escort 769.5
  v court 562.21
swale marsh 243.1
  lowland 274.3
  grassland 310.8
swallow
  n bite 8.2
  swiftness 174.6
  ingestion 187.4
  recant 363.8
  v devour 8.22
  endure 134.6
  disregard 148.6
  condone 148.4
  ingest 187.11
  consume 388.3
  believe 953.10
  kid oneself 954.6
swallow one's pride 137.7
swamp
  n receptacle of filth 80.12
  marsh 243.1
  predicament 1013.4
  v overflow 238.17
  overwhelm 395.21
  oversupply 993.14
  flood 1065.14
swan whiteness 37.2
  bird 311.28
swan dive 367.1
swanky
  grandiose 501.21

chic 578.13
swan song
  leave-taking 188.4
  death song 307.10
  theatrical performance
    704.12
  musical performance 708.33
  sequel 817.1
  end 820.1
swap
  n explosive sound 56.1
  bargain 731.5
  trading 863.2
  v make explosive sound
    56.6
  trade 731.15
  interchange 863.4
swarm
  n migration 177.4
  assemblage 770.6
  multitude 884.3
  infestation 910.2
  v migrate 177.22
  come together 770.16
  infest 910.6
  superabound 993.8
swarthy 38.9
swashbuckler
  combatant 461.1
  strutter 501.10
  blusterer 503.2
swastika cross 170.4
  insignia 647.1
  charm 691.5
swat
  n blow 902.5
  v strike 902.15
SWAT 1008.17
swatch 786.3
swath 812.2
sway
  n inclination 204.2
  supremacy 249.3
  authority 417.5
  dominance 417.6
  government 612.1
  influence 894.1
  swing 916.6
  flounder 917.8
  v pitch 182.55
  oblique 204.9
  incline 204.10
  induce 375.22
  persuade 375.23
  break down 393.24
  rule 612.14
  change 854.5
  influence 894.7
  oscillate 916.10
  flounder 917.15
  prejudice 980.9
sway-backed 265.12
swear affirm 334.6
  administer an oath
    334.7
  promise 436.4
  curse 513.6
  blaspheme 694.5
  state 953.12
  testify 957.9
swear by 953.16

swear in
administer an oath 334.7
call to witness 598.17
swear off
break the habit 374.3
relinquish 475.3
renounce 668.8
sweat
n body fluid 2.24
perspiration 12.7
trepidation 127.5
nervousness 128.2
impatience 135.1
bustle 330.4
work 725.4
confusion 985.3
v perspire 12.16
fear 127.10
await 130.8
be impatient 135.4
trickle 238.18
endeavor 403.5
work hard 725.13
overwork 725.16
be hot 1019.22
be damp 1065.11
sweater shirt 5.15
gambler 759.21
sweat it out
be strong 15.11
await 130.8
be impatient 135.4
wait impatiently 846.13
Swedish bath 79.8
sweep
n vision 27.1
view 33.6
sweeper 79.16
range 158.2
deviation 164.1
gliding 177.16
oar 180.15
bend 279.3
lottery 759.14
v touch lightly 73.7
clean 79.23
extend 158.9
speed 174.9
traverse 177.20
glide 177.35
overflow 238.17
curve 279.6
plunder 482.17
push 904.9
go easily 1014.10
receive 1036.17
sweeper 79.16
sweeping change 860.1
sweepings
remainder 256.1
refuse 391.4
sweep off one's feet
enamor 104.23
take one's breath away 122.7
fascinate 377.7
convince 858.16
sweepstakes
award 646.2
lottery 759.14
sweet
n food 10.40

sweetness 66.1
endearment term 562.6
adj soft-colored 35.22
flavored 62.9
sweetish 66.4
fragrant 70.9
clean 79.25
pleasant 97.6
endearing 104.25
good-natured 143.14
harmonious 533.8
melodious 708.48
sweetbread veal 10.15
organ meat 10.20
sweetener 478.5
sweetheart
n loved one 104.10
endearment term 562.6
good person 659.2
first-rate 999.7
v court 562.21
sweet nothings
flattery 511.1
endearment 562.5
sweets
confectionery 10.40
sweetening 66.2
loved one 104.11
endearment term 562.6
the sweet science 754.1
sweet sixteen 301.14
sweet tooth 66.1
swell
n loudness 53.1
hill 237.4
wave 238.14
distension 259.2
dandy 500.9
aristocrat 607.4
nobleman 608.4
notation 709.12
keyboard 711.17
v din 53.7
be excited 105.18
be vain 140.7
billow 238.22
grow 251.6
enlarge 259.4
increase 259.5
bulge 283.11
give oneself airs 501.14
overextend 993.13
adj grandiose 501.21
chic 578.13
excellent 999.13
swelled head 140.4
swelter
n sweat 12.7
sultriness 1019.6
v sweat 12.16
be hot 1019.22
swept 238.25
swept-back 217.12
swept up 983.17
swerve
n deviation 164.1
bias 204.3
angle 278.2
v deviate 164.3
change course 182.30
oblique 204.9

angle 278.5
dodge 368.8
be changed 852.6
pull back 903.7
swift
fast 174.15
quick 330.18
hasty 401.9
brief 828.8
sudden 830.5
prompt 845.9
swig
n drink 8.4
snort 88.7
v drink 8.29
booze 88.25
swill
n drink 8.4
feed 10.4
offal 80.9
snort 88.7
refuse 391.4
mud 1062.8
v drink 8.29
booze 88.25
ingest 187.11
swim
n aquatics 182.11
v bathe 182.56
conform 867.4
swim against the tide
dissent 333.4
not conform 868.4
counteract 900.6
swimming pool 743.12
swim suit 5.29
swindle
n fake 354.13
fraud 356.8
theft 482.1
v cheat 356.18
steal 482.13
overprice 632.7
swine
filthy person 80.13
pig 311.9
beast 660.6
sensualist 663.3
slob 810.7
swing
n room 158.3
gait 177.12
hang 202.2
latitude 430.4
thrust 459.3
supporting actor 707.7
jazz 708.9
rhythm 709.22
meter 720.7
playground apparatus 743.15
golf 751.3
trend 896.2
hit 902.4
swinging 916.6
oscillator 916.9
flounder 917.8
v turn round 163.9
way of walking 177.28
toss at sea 182.55
hang 202.6
do 328.6

angle 278.5
accomplish 407.4
manage 409.12
be hanged 604.19
afford 626.7
be promiscuous 665.19
syncopate 708.43
change 854.5
rotate 915.9
oscillate 916.10
wave 916.11
alternate 916.13
flounder 917.15
adj music 708.51
swinger
person of fashion 578.7
libertine 665.10
swing into action
behave 321.4
take action 328.5
undertake 404.3
begin 818.7
swing shift 825.3
swing vote 609.28
swipe
n criticism 510.4
hit 902.4
v rob 482.16
hit 902.14
swirl
n excitement 105.4
eddy 238.12
coil 281.2
bustle 330.4
whirl 915.2
agitation 917.1
v eddy 238.21
convolve 281.4
whirl 915.11
agitate 917.10
swish
n sibilation 57.1
v ripple 52.11
rustle 52.12
sibilate 57.2
basketball 747.4
Swiss cheese 284.6
switch
n false hair 3.13
surprise 131.2
branch 310.20
apostatize 363.7
whip 605.2
plot 722.4
member 793.4
change 852.1
conversion 858.1
substitution 862.1
trading 863.2
v avoid 164.6
transfer 176.10
whip 604.13
trade 731.15
convert 858.11
substitute 862.4
interchange 863.4
switchback
zigzag 204.8
race 756.3
switchboard
telephone 347.8
stage 704.16

switch hitter 745.2
switch over
  n apostatize 363.7
  v convert 858.11
swivel
  n axle 915.5
  v turn round 163.9
  rotate 915.9
swivet dither 105.6
  confusion 985.3
swollen
  diseased 85.60
  puffed up 136.10
  increased 251.7
  corpulent 257.18
  distended 259.13
  bulged 283.16
  pompous 501.22
  boastful 502.12
  bombastic 545.9
  full 794.11
  overfull 993.20
swoon
  n stupor 22.6
  unconsciousness 25.2
  v faint 25.5
swoop
  n descent 194.1
  plunge 367.1
  v descend 194.5
  plunge 367.6
sword
  n combatant 461.1
  blade 462.5
  cutlery 1040.2
  v stab 459.25
sword of Damocles
  threat 514.1
  dangerousness 1006.2
sworn affirmed 334.9
  promised 436.8
sworn enemy 589.6
sworn statement
  deposition 334.3
  certificate 549.6
  statement of principles 953.4
  testimony 957.2
sycophant toady 138.3
  flatterer 511.4
  follower 616.8
syllabic
  n letter 546.1
  adj phonetic 524.30
syllable
  n speech sound 524.12
  word 526.1
  poetry 720.9
  v syllabify 546.7
syllabus 557.1
syllogism reasoning 935.3
  prosyllogism 935.6
sylvan hinterland 233.9
  woodland 310.40
symbiotic
  cooperative 450.5
  agreeing 788.9
  concurrent 899.4
symbol
  n psychological symbol 92.30
  representation 349.1
  emblem 517.2

sign 518.6
letter 546.1
insignia 647.1
musical notation 709.12
example 786.2
substitute 862.2
number 1017.3
  v designate 517.18
symbolic indicative 517.23
  meaningful 518.10
  semantic 518.12
  figurative 519.10
symmetrical
  balanced 264.4
  harmonious 533.8
  orderly 807.6
symmetry
  balance 264.1
  harmony 533.2
  correlation 777.1
  agreement 788.1
  equality 790.1
  order 807.1
sympathetic
  sensitive 24.12
  responsive 93.20
  comforting 121.13
  kind 143.13
  pitying 145.7
  condoling 147.3
  in accord 455.3
  related 775.9
  attracting 907.5
  tolerant 979.11
sympathy
  sensitivity 24.3
  fellow feeling 93.5
  inclination 100.3
  consolation 121.4
  kindness 143.1
  pity 145.1
  condolence 147.1
  patronage 449.4
  accord 455.1
  good terms 587.3
  relation 775.1
  attraction 907.1
  tolerance 979.4
symphony accord 455.1
  harmony 708.3
symposium
  drinking 8.3
  spree 88.5
  forum 423.3
  discussion 541.7
  compilation 554.7
  assembly 770.2
symptom
  medical sign 91.13
  warning sign 399.3
  sign 517.1
  hint 551.4
  evidence 957.1
synagogue 703.2
synapse 2.14
sync
  n agreement 788.1
  v make agree 788.7
synchronicity 689.6
synchronized
  harmonious 708.49

accompanying
  769.9
agreeing 788.9
arranged 808.14
simultaneous 836.6
syncopation
  dance music 708.8
  tempo 709.24
syncope
  unconsciousness 25.2
  shortening 268.3
  abbreviation 537.4
  tempo 709.24
syndicate
  n council 423.1
  company 617.9
  v combine 805.3
the syndicate
  the underworld 660.10
  illicit business 732.1
syndication 805.1
syndrome 85.1
synergy
  cooperation 450.1
  concurrence 899.1
synod council 423.1
  ecclesiastical council 423.4
  diocese 698.8
  assembly 770.2
synonym word 526.1
  the same 778.3
synopsis
  shortening 268.3
  abridgment 557.1
syntax
  grammatical structure 530.2
  arrangement 808.1
synthesis
  identification 778.2
  composition 796.1
  combination 805.1
  reasoning 935.3
synthesize
  identify 778.5
  compose 796.3
  combine 805.3
  reason 935.15
synthesizer
  musical instrument 711.1
  reasoner 935.11
  theorist 951.7
synthetic
  n plastic 1054.6
  adj imitation 336.8
  spurious 354.26
  similar 784.10
  dialectic 935.22
synthetic fuels 1021.1
syringe
  n sprinkler 1065.8
  v wash 79.19
  moisten 1065.12
syrup
  sweetening 66.2
  medicine 86.4
  adhesive 803.4
  semiliquid 1062.5
system plan 381.1
  manner 384.1
  nature 767.4
  order 807.1

orderliness 807.3
outlook 978.2
universe 1072.1
systematic
  uniform 781.5
  orderly 807.6
  regular 850.6
systemic 1001.3
system of government 612.1
system of values 373.2
systems analysis 1041.2
syzygy
  juxtaposition 223.3
  meter 720.7
T 170.4
tab
  n bulge 283.3
  statement 628.3
  price 630.1
  scenery 704.20
  afterpart 817.2
  v label 517.20
  appoint 615.11
tabby
  n iridescence 47.2
  cat 311.21
  newsmonger 552.9
  v variegate 47.7
  adj striped 47.15
tabernacle 703.2
table
  n meal 8.5
  food 10.1
  horizontal 201.3
  furniture 229.1
  plain 236.1
  plateau 237.3
  steppe 272.4
  lamina 296.2
  diagram 381.3
  register 549.1
  record book 549.11
  outline 801.4
  code 808.4
  contents 871.2
  board 901.15
  summation 1017.11
  v put away 390.6
  legislate 613.10
  postpone 846.9
tableau spectacle 33.7
  picture 712.11
table manners 580.3
table of contents
  book 554.12
  outline 801.4
  table 871.2
table setting 498.1
tablespoon 8.12
tablet pill 86.7
  lamina 296.2
  record book 549.11
  monument 549.12
tabloid 555.2
taboo
  n prohibition 444.1
  exclusion 773.1
  v prohibit 444.3
  exclude 773.4
  adj prohibited 444.7
  jargonish 523.21

tabular
 horizontal 201.7
 classified 809.8
tabula rasa void 222.3
 revolution 860.1
 ignorance 930.1
 thoughtlessness 933.1
tabulate record 549.15
 classify 809.6
 list 871.8
tachometer 174.7
tachycardia
 symptom 85.9
 pulsation 916.3
tacit
 wordless 51.11
 implicit 519.8
taciturn
 untalkative 344.9
 concise 537.6
tack
 n direction 161.2
 deviation 164.1
 cordage 271.3
 manner 384.1
 harness 385.5
 horse racing 757.1
 inferiority 1005.3
 v deviate 164.3
 change course 182.30
 fasten 800.8
 be changed 852.6
tackle
 n rigging 180.12
 cordage 271.3
 equipment 385.4
 harness 385.5
 impedimenta 471.3
 linemen 746.2
 football game 746.3
 hockey game 749.6
 soccer game 752.3
 purchase 906.6
 lifter 912.3
 v practice 328.8
 treat 387.12
 attempt 403.7
 undertake 404.3
 set to work 725.15
 football 746.5
 hockey 749.7
 soccer 752.4
 reel in 906.9
tack on 253.4
tacky frail 16.14
 unpleasant 98.17
 shabby 393.32
 vulgar 497.10
 gaudy 501.20
 base 661.12
 adhesive 803.12
 slovenly 810.15
 inferior 1005.9
 viscous 1062.12
 moist 1065.15
tact sensitivity 24.3
 considerateness 143.3
 skill 413.1
 courtesy 504.1
 intuition 934.1
 discrimination 944.1

tactic stratagem 415.3
 expedient 995.2
tactical planned 381.12
 cunning 415.12
tactician planner 381.6
 strategist 415.7
tactile tactual 73.10
 touchable 73.11
tad 302.3
tadpole
 fledgling 302.10
 amphibian 311.27
tag
 n scrap 248.3
 label 517.13
 name 527.3
 rabble 606.3
 token 728.12
 sequel 817.1
 afterpart 817.2
 extremity 820.2
 v follow 166.3
 add 253.4
 allot 477.9
 label 517.20
 name 527.11
tag along 166.3
tag sale 734.3
taiga 243.1
tail
 n braid 3.7
 follower 166.2
 rear 217.1
 buttocks 217.5
 cauda 217.6
 added to writing 254.2
 book 554.12
 appendage 793.4
 afterpart 817.2
 extremity 820.2
 v look 27.13
 follow 166.3
 trace 938.35
 adj rear 217.9
 caudal 217.11
 final 820.11
tailback 746.2
tailgate 815.2
tail gunner 185.4
tail off weaken 16.9
 recede 168.2
 decrease 252.6
 cease to exist 762.6
tailor
 n garmentmaker 5.35
 sewer 741.2
 v outfit 5.41
 form 262.7
 sew 741.4
 make agree 788.7
tailored
 custom-made 5.48
 formative 262.9
 apt 788.10
tailpiece rear 217.1
 tail 217.6
 adjunct 254.1
 coda 708.24
 afterpart 817.2
tails
 formal dress 5.11

 opposite side 215.3
tailspin
 air maneuver 184.15
 collapse 410.3
tail wind
 atmosphere 184.32
 wind 318.1
 nautical 318.11
taint
 n infection 85.4
 stigma 661.6
 admixture 797.7
 characteristic 865.4
 fault 1003.2
 stain 1004.3
 v defile 80.17
 infect 85.51
 corrupt 393.12
 stigmatize 661.9
 blaspheme 694.5
 work evil 1000.6
 stain 1004.6
take
 n winnings 251.3
 explanation 341.4
 profit 472.3
 catch 480.10
 booty 482.11
 receipts 627.1
 shot 706.5
 motion picture 714.8
 change 852.1
 production 893.2
 answer 939.1
 v eat 8.20
 take sick 85.47
 pocket 134.8
 condone 148.4
 transport 176.12
 interpret 341.9
 succeed 409.7
 submit 433.6
 acquire 472.8
 receive 479.6
 possess 480.13
 possess sexually 480.15
 catch 480.17
 steal 482.13
 understand 521.7
 adopt 621.4
 entail 772.4
 combine 805.3
 suppose 951.10
 think 953.11
take aback
 dismay 127.19
 surprise 131.7
 startle 131.8
take a back seat
 efface oneself 139.7
 retreat 163.6
 retract 168.3
 be inferior 250.4
 depend on 432.12
take a break
 take a rest 20.8
 intervene 826.3
 pause 857.9
 interrupt 857.10
take a chance
 venture 759.24

 risk 972.12
 take chances 1006.7
take action 328.5
take a cut 328.5
take a dim view of
 shudder at 99.5
 disapprove 510.10
take a dive 356.18
take advantage of
 avail oneself of 387.15
 exploit 387.16
 impose on 643.7
 improve the occasion 843.8
take a flier
 trade 737.23
 chance 759.24
take after
 emulate 336.7
 resemble 784.7
take a hard line 425.5
take a header
 tumble 194.8
 plunge 367.6
take a hike! 909.32
take aim at
 intend 380.4
 pull the trigger 459.22
take a liking to 104.22
take a load off 121.8
take a look at 27.13
take a nap
 take a rest 20.8
 sleep 22.13
take an interest in
 love 104.19
 be curious 981.3
 attend to 983.5
take a nose dive
 decrease 252.6
 plunge 367.6
 decline 393.17
take apart
 demolish 395.17
 tear apart 802.14
 disassemble 802.15
take a peek 27.13
take a percentage 631.2
take a picture 714.14
take a powder
 depart 188.7
 flee 368.11
take a raincheck 329.2
take a reading 300.10
take a second look
 repeat 849.7
 re-examine 938.27
take a short cut 268.7
take a stab at 403.7
take a stand 348.6
take at one's word
 believe 953.10
 trust 953.17
take a turn for the better
 rally 392.8
 recuperate 396.19
take a turn for the worse
 worsen 119.3
 decline 393.17
take a walk
 go for a walk 177.29
 not interfere 430.17

take away
  remove 176.11
  subtract 255.9
take a whack at
  attempt 403.7
  enter 818.9
take back deny 335.4
  recant 363.8
  restore 481.4
  recover 481.6
  apologize 658.5
take by surprise 131.7
take by the hand 449.11
take care
  be careful 339.7
  beware 494.7
  pay attention 983.8
take care of
  kill 308.14
  perform 328.9
  look after 339.9
  bribe 378.3
  accomplish 407.4
  supervise 573.10
  serve 577.13
  punish 604.11
  operate 889.5
  care for 1008.19
take care of number one 651.4
take center stage 501.12
take charge
  be able 18.11
  take command 417.14
take comfort 121.7
take cover hide 346.8
  take refuge 1009.7
take credit 622.7
take down devour 8.22
  abase 137.5
  raze 395.19
  reprove 510.17
  record 549.15
  disassemble 802.15
  depress 913.4
  fell 913.5
take effect 889.7
take evasive action 368.8
take exception
  dissent 333.4
  find fault 510.15
take for suppose 951.10
  think 953.11
take for a ride
  kill 308.14
  deceive 356.19
take for granted
  accept 123.2
  expect 130.5
  neglect 340.6
  imply 519.4
  suppose 951.10
  believe 953.10
take heart
  cheer up 109.9
  be comforted 121.7
  be hopeful 124.8
  take courage 492.14
take heed
  be careful 339.7
  beware 494.7
  pay attention 983.8

take hold of
  seize 480.14
  cohere 803.6
  attend to 983.5
take-home pay
  pay 624.4
  standard of living 731.8
take in devour 8.22
  see 27.12
  hear 48.11
  extend 158.9
  let in 187.10
  absorb 187.13
  enter 189.7
  attend 221.8
  shorten 268.6
  deceive 356.14
  receive 479.6
  capture 480.18
  understand 521.7
  learn 570.7
  host 585.7
  include 772.3
  entail 772.4
  put together 800.5
  watch 918.5
take in stride
  accept 123.2
  patience 134.7
take in the sights 918.6
take into consideration
  include 772.3
  allow for 959.5
  take cognizance of 983.9
take into custody
  arrest 429.15
  capture 480.18
take issue with
  deny 335.4
  oppose 451.3
  dispute 457.21
take it be strong 15.11
  endure 134.6
  submit 433.6
  suppose 951.10
  think 953.11
  suffice 991.4
take it easy rest 20.6
  compose oneself 106.7
  take things as they come 331.15
  be cautious 494.5
  pause 857.9
  swim with the stream 1014.12
take it lying down
  take 134.8
  submit 433.6
take it on the chin
  be strong 15.11
  endure 134.6
  fail 410.10
take it or leave it
  be indifferent 102.5
  have no choice 963.11
take it out on 152.16
take it slow relax 20.7
  go slowly 175.6
  be cautious 494.5
take kindly to
  assent 332.8

  concur 332.9
  consent 441.2
  approve 509.9
take leave
  vacation 20.9
  depart 188.6
  bid farewell 188.16
  absent oneself 222.8
take leave of one's senses
  be foolish 923.6
  go mad 926.21
take legal action 673.9
take liberties
  have the audacity 142.7
  presume on 640.7
take notice 983.6
taken up with 983.17
taken with
  adj pleased 95.15
  fond of 104.30
  prep compared to 943.11
take odds 759.25
takeoff flight 184.8
  start 188.2
  embarkation 188.2
  point of departure 188.5
  ascent 193.1
  imitation 336.1
  burlesque 508.6
  similarity 784.1
take off remove 6.6
  become airborne 184.38
  depart 188.7
  leave the ground 193.10
  excise 255.10
  kill 308.13
  mimic 336.6
  impersonate 349.12
  improve 392.7
  put an end to 395.12
  gesture 517.21
  discount 631.2
  resemble 784.7
  detach 802.10
  begin 818.7
take offense 152.13
take off for 161.9
take office 615.13
take on
  grieve 112.17
  complain 115.16
  feel anxious 126.6
  be angry 152.15
  practice 328.8
  treat 387.12
  attempt 403.7
  undertake 404.3
  contend against 451.4
  engage 457.16
  receive 479.6
  employ 615.14
  adopt 621.4
  set to work 725.15
take one's leave
  depart 188.6
  separate 802.8
take one's life in one's hands
  brave 492.11
  risk one's neck 1006.7
take one's medicine
  submit 433.6

  take one's punishment 604.21
take one's own life 308.22
take one step at a time 494.5
take one's time
  dawdle 175.8
  idle 331.12
  dally 331.14
  take one's leisure 402.4
  wait 846.12
take one's word for
  believe 953.10
  rely on 953.16
take one up on
  assent 332.8
  acquiesce 441.3
  take a dare 454.6
  suppose 951.10
take orders obey 326.2
  be ordained 698.11
takeout 8.6
take out extract 192.10
  excise 255.10
  kill 308.14
  annihilate 762.7
  escort 769.8
  end 820.5
take out after
  follow 166.3
  pursue 382.8
  censure 510.13
takeover
  appropriation 480.4
  stock trading 737.19
  combination 805.1
take over
  take command 417.14
  take possession 472.10
  receive 479.6
  appropriate 480.19
  adopt 621.4
  usurp 640.8
  combine 805.3
  succeed 815.2
take pains
  be careful 339.7
  make a special effort 403.11
take part 476.5
take pity on 145.4
take place 831.5
take pleasure in 95.13
take possession
  appropriate 472.10
  take 480.13
take precautions
  take steps 494.6
  play safe 1007.3
take precedence
  rule 249.11
  precede 814.2
take pride 136.5
take prisoner
  arrest 429.15
  capture 480.18
take refuge 1009.7
take refuge in 376.4
take revenge
  get even with 506.7
  avenge 507.4
take risks 492.10
take shape
  be formed 262.8

form 807.5
take shelter 1009.7
take sides with
   back 449.13
   side with 450.4
take steps
   take action 328.5
   take precautions 494.6
take stock
   take account of 628.9
   check 1017.21
take the bait
   react 903.5
   kid oneself 954.6
take the bull by the horns
   be determined 359.8
   attempt 403.6
   undertake 404.3
   brave 492.11
   seize the opportunity 843.7
take the cake
   best 249.7
   triumph 411.3
take the edge off
   weaken 16.10
   blunt 286.2
   moderate 670.6
take the first step 818.10
take the floor
   speak up 524.21
   make a speech 543.9
   legislate 613.10
take the heat for
   be responsible for 641.6
   accept the responsibility
      641.9
take the law into one's own
   hands
   have one's will 323.3
   violate 435.4
   break the law 674.5
take the lead
   lead 165.2
   be in front 216.7
   take command 417.14
   direct 573.8
   dominate 612.15
   initiate 818.10
take the next step 817.5
take the offensive 459.14
take the opportunity 843.7
take the place of
   follow after 835.3
   substitute for 862.5
take the rap 604.21
take the stand
   depose 334.6
   call to witness 598.17
take the trouble 324.3
take the wind out of one's
   sails
   disable 19.10
   sadden 112.18
   humiliate 137.6
   becalm 173.11
   disincline 379.4
   refute 958.5
   thwart 1012.15
take the words out of one's
   mouth 845.6
take the wraps off 351.4

take the wrong way 342.2
take things as they come
   keep cool 106.9
   accept 134.7
   take it easy 331.15
take time
   spend time 821.6
   wait 846.12
take to desire 100.14
   fall in love 104.22
   practice 328.8
   become used to 373.11
   avail oneself of 387.14
take to heart
   respond 93.11
   take amiss 152.13
   internalize 207.5
   believe 953.10
take to mean 341.9
take to task
   reprove 510.17
   accuse 599.7
   punish 604.10
take to the cleaners
   best 249.7
   lose 473.4
   strip 480.24
take turns 825.5
take under consideration
   931.14
take under one's wing
   back 449.13
   benefit 592.3
   care for 1008.19
take up
   absorb 187.13
   practice 328.8
   adopt 371.15
   undertake 404.3
   patronize 449.15
   take possession 472.10
   collect 472.11
   appropriate 480.19
   espouse 509.13
   discuss 541.12
   write upon 556.5
   pay in full 624.13
   busy oneself with 724.11
   assemble 770.18
   include 772.3
   enter 818.9
   pick up 912.8
   engross 983.13
take up a collection 770.18
take up arms
   contend 457.13
   go to war 458.16
take upon oneself
   undertake 404.3
   presume 640.6
   accept the responsibility
      641.9
take up residence 159.17
take up the cause of 449.13
take up with
   confer 541.11
   associate with 582.18
   befriend 587.10
take with a grain of salt
   doubt 955.6
   allow for 959.5

talcum powder 1016.12
tale lie 354.11
   gossip 552.7
   story 719.3
   yarn 722.3
   tally 1017.6
talent ability 18.2
   flair 413.4
   talented person 413.12
   artistry 712.7
   smartness 920.2
   genius 920.8
talented gifted 413.29
   smart 920.14
talent scout 704.27
talisman 691.5
talk
   n language 523.1
   speech 524.1
   diction 532.1
   conversation 541.3
   oration 543.2
   report 552.6
   gossip 552.7
   lesson 568.7
   v communicate 343.6
   betray 351.6
   signify 517.17
   speak 523.18
   converse 524.19
   discuss 541.12
   make a speech 543.9
   gossip 552.12
talkative
   v loquacious 540.9
   adj communicative 343.10
   disclosive 351.10
   speaking 524.31
   wordy 538.12
talk back
   be insolent 142.8
   answer 939.4
talk dirty 513.6
talk down to
   condescend 137.8
   give oneself airs 141.8
talking-to 510.6
talk into 375.23
talk of the town
   report 552.6
   repute 662.1
talk on 540.5
talk out of 379.3
talk out of turn
   betray 351.6
   speak inopportunely 844.4
talk over
   persuade 375.23
   confer 541.11
   discuss 541.12
   convince 953.18
talk show 1034.18
talk-show host 1034.23
talk someone's ear off 524.20
talk to oneself 542.3
talk turkey 535.2
talk with 541.9
tall large 257.16
   long 267.7
   giant 272.16
   inflated 502.12

grandiloquent 545.8
   unbelievable 955.10
tall order 1013.2
tallow whiteness 37.2
   oil 1056.1
tall tale 354.11
tally
   n label 517.13
   report 549.7
   account 628.2
   likeness 784.3
   agreement 788.1
   list 871.1
   sum 1017.6
   v compute 253.6
   coincide 778.4
   agree 788.6
   list 871.8
   number 1017.17
   calculate 1017.18
tallyho! 382.13
Talmud scripture 683.5
   tradition 842.2
talons
   governance 417.5
   clutches 474.4
   control 612.2
tame
   v accustom 373.9
   domesticate 432.11
   moderate 670.6
   tend 1070.7
   adj inert 173.14
   domesticated 228.34
   meek 433.15
   moderate 670.10
tamp indent 284.14
   thrust 902.12
tamper with
   meddle 214.7
   manipulate 354.17
   bribe 378.3
   adulterate 797.12
tampon
   medical dressing
      86.33
   wadding 293.5
tan
   v brown 40.2
   embalm 397.10
   prepare 405.6
   punish 604.15
   adj brown 40.3
tandem
   n rig 179.5
   adv behind 217.13
tang taste 62.1
   zest 68.2
   characteristic 865.4
   sting 1001.5
tangent
   n convergence 169.1
   neighbor 223.6
   straight line 277.2
   adj converging 169.3
   in contact 223.17
tangerine 42.2
tangible
   touchable 73.11
   manifest 348.8
   substantial 763.6

tangle
n complex 799.2
v trap 356.20
catch 480.17
complicate 799.3
involve 898.2
hamper 1012.11
tangle with 457.17
tangy 68.7
tank
n reservoir 241.1
storehouse 386.6
prison 429.8
jail 429.9
v package 212.9
prearrange 965.5
tanker ship 1075.2
tank top 5.29
tanned brown 40.3
prepared 405.16
tannery 739.3
tantalizing
appetizing 63.10
delightful 97.7
desirable 100.30
exciting 105.30
disappointing 132.6
alluring 377.8
interesting 983.19
tantamount
reciprocal 777.10
equivalent 790.8
tantrum 152.8
Taoist 675.32
tap
n thud 52.3
explosive sound 56.1
touch 73.1
outlet 190.9
tube 239.6
valve 239.10
stopper 293.4
root 310.22
rap 902.7
v listen 48.10
thud 52.15
make explosive sound 56.6
touch 73.6
transport 176.14
draw off 192.12
open 292.11
perforate 292.15
take from 480.21
beat time 708.44
rap 902.18
tap-dance
dance 705.5
procrastinate 846.11
quibble 936.9
tape
n record 50.12
medical dressing 86.33
strip 271.4
recording media 549.10
boxing 754.1
end 820.1
v sound 50.14
record 549.15
put together 800.5
teleview 1035.15
tape cassette 50.12

tape measure 271.4
taper
n narrowing 270.2
lighter 1021.4
light source 1026.1
candle 1026.2
wick 1026.7
v converge 169.2
narrow 270.11
sharpen 285.7
adj tapered 270.15
tape recorder 50.11
tape recording 50.12
tapestry 712.11
tapeworm
appetite 100.7
worm 311.39
tap out fail 410.9
lose 473.4
go bankrupt 625.7
taps blare 53.5
funeral 309.5
night 315.4
call 517.16
end 820.1
tap water 10.49
tar
n blackness 38.4
opium 87.16
mariner 183.1
v cover 295.22
coat 295.24
tar and feather 604.16
tarantula 311.33
tardy retarded 175.12
anachronistic 833.3
late 846.16
tares 391.4
target
objective 380.2
laughingstock 508.7
fission 1038.8
target shooting 744.1
tariff 773.4
tarmac 383.6
tarnish
n stigma 661.6
stain 1004.3
v decolor 36.5
defile 80.17
vilify 512.10
stigmatize 661.9
stain 1004.6
tarot reading 962.2
tarry
v be still 173.7
dawdle 175.8
endure 827.6
linger on 827.7
wait 846.12
continue 856.3
adj black 38.8
tart
n pastry 10.41
strumpet 665.14
adj acrimonious 17.14
bitter 64.6
sour 67.5
caustic 144.23
tartan check 47.4
insignia 647.1

Tartar 110.11
Tarzan 15.6
task
n undertaking 404.1
lesson 568.7
commission 615.1
charge 643.3
job 724.2
work 725.4
v accuse 599.7
impose 643.4
work 725.16
task force
military unit 461.22
navy 461.27
taskmaster 574.2
taste
n bite 8.2
senses 24.5
gust 62.1
sample 62.4
liking 100.2
appetite 100.7
hint 248.4
preference 371.5
fastidiousness 495.1
tastefulness 496.1
elegance 533.1
specimen 786.3
characteristic 865.4
discrimination 944.1
v eat 8.20
sense 24.6
taste of 62.7
savor 63.5
experience 831.8
experiment 942.8
taste bud 62.5
tasteful
in good taste 496.8
elegant 533.6
artistic 712.20
tasteless
wishy-washy 16.17
insipid 65.2
dull 117.6
vulgar 497.10
inelegant 534.2
base 661.12
taste test 62.4
tasty good 63.8
delectable 97.10
tata 188.22
tater
vegetables 10.35
baseball 745.3
tatter
n scrap 248.3
piece 793.3
v wear 393.20
tattle
n gossip 552.7
v betray 351.6
inform on 551.12
gossip 552.12
tattletale
n informer 551.6
newsmonger 552.9
adj telltale 551.19
tattoo
n fanfare 53.5

staccato 55.1
mark 517.5
constancy 847.2
hit 902.4
shot 904.4
v variegate 47.7
rain 316.10
mark 517.19
taught 928.18
taunt
n indignity 156.2
gibe 508.2
v be insolent 142.7
offend 156.5
scoff 508.9
taupe gray 39.4
brown 40.3
taut tense 128.13
in suspense 130.12
shipshape 180.20
rigid 1046.11
tautology
wordiness 538.2
redundancy 849.3
superfluity 993.4
tavern
restaurant 8.17
bar 88.20
inn 228.15
entertainment 743.13
tawdry gaudy 501.20
paltry 998.21
tawny 40.3
tax
n demand 421.1
taxation 630.9
charge 643.3
overdoing 993.6
v burden 297.13
accuse 599.7
charge 630.12
impose 643.4
strain 725.10
task 725.16
taxable income
pay 624.4
tax 630.9
tax collector
taxer 630.10
collector 770.15
tax-deductible 630.16
tax evasion
shirking 368.2
tax 630.9
taxi
n public vehicle 179.13
v ride 177.33
take off 184.38
taxidermy 397.3
taxing
n burden 297.7
demand 421.1
accusation 599.1
imposition 643.1
strain 725.2
adj demanding 421.9
taxonomy
biological classification 305.3
nomenclature 527.1
classification 801.3
grouping 808.3

arrangement 809.1
taxpayer payer 624.9
  good or respectable citizen
   659.3
tax return 630.9
tea meal 8.6
  marijuana 87.11
  afternoon tea 582.13
teach 568.10
teacher preparer 405.5
  adviser 422.3
  tutor 568.1
  instructor 571.1
  master 575.1
  clergy 699.10
  professional 726.4
teacher's pet
  weakling 16.6
  favorite 104.16
teach one a lesson 604.10
team
  n rig 179.5
  outfit 617.7
  baseball team 745.2
  football team 746.2
  basketball team 747.2
  hockey team 749.2
  attack 749.5
  lawn bowling 750.3
  golfer 751.2
  squad 752.2
  company 770.3
  two 873.2
  v double 873.5
teamed 805.6
teammate
  companion 588.3
  co-worker 616.5
teamster
  coachman 178.9
  driver 178.10
team up
  cooperate 450.3
  befriend 587.11
  double 873.5
tear
  n humor 2.24
  weeping 115.2
  v secrete 13.5
tear
  n trauma 85.38
  drinking spree 88.6
  break 802.4
  v pain 26.7
  speed 174.8
  hurry 174.9
  open 292.11
  injure 393.13
  make haste 401.5
  rage 671.11
  sever 802.11
tear apart
  demolish 395.17
  find fault 510.15
  pull apart 802.14
tear down blacken 38.7
  raze 395.19
  find fault 510.15
  defame 512.9
  disassemble 802.15
teardrop tear 2.24

weeping 115.2
drop 282.3
tearful
  sorrowful 112.26
  teary 115.21
tearing
  n severance 802.2
  adj welling 2.33
tearjerker 93.8
tear limb from limb
  torture 604.16
  rip apart 802.14
tearoom 8.17
tear open open 292.11
  breach 292.14
tears
  secretion 13.2
  weeping 115.2
tease
  n tormentor 96.10
  disappointment 132.1
  deceiver 357.1
  v annoy 96.13
  disappoint 132.2
  attract 377.6
  importune 440.12
  banter 490.5
teaspoon 8.12
teatime 8.6
teats 283.6
technical
  skilled 413.26
  occupational 724.16
  specialized 866.5
  scientific 928.28
  insignificant 998.17
technicality
  technical term 526.5
  complexity 799.1
  specialty 866.1
  an insignificancy 998.6
technical knockout 754.3
technician
  expert 413.11
  skilled worker 726.6
  engineer 726.7
  specialist 866.3
  computer whiz 1042.17
technicolored 35.16
technique
  manner 384.1
  skill 413.1
  art 413.7
  artistic treatment 712.9
  skiing 753.3
  knowledge 928.1
technology art 413.7
  engineer 726.7
  science 928.10
technospeak 523.9
tectonics 266.1
teddy bear figure 349.6
  toy 743.16
tedious dull 117.6
  monotonous 118.9
  same 781.6
  repetitive 849.15
  mediocre 1005.7
tee 751.1
teed off 152.30
teed up 405.16

teeming
  n proliferation 890.2
  infestation 910.2
  adj pregnant 78.18
  permeated 221.15
  diffuse 538.11
  crowded 770.22
  swarming 884.9
  productive 890.9
  infested 910.11
  imaginative 986.18
  plentiful 991.7
  superabundant 993.19
teen-aged 301.14
teenager 302.1
tee off on
  attack 459.15
  criticize 510.14
teeter
  n alternation 916.5
  oscillator 916.9
  v be weak 16.8
  vacillate 362.8
  change 854.5
  alternate 916.13
teeth dentition 2.8
  acrimony 17.5
  clutches 474.4
  speech organ 524.18
sail in the teeth of the wind
  182.24
teetotaler 668.4
Teflon-coated 1008.23
telecast
  n television broadcast 1035.2
  v publish 352.10
  televise 1035.14
  adj published 352.17
telecommunication
  communications 343.5
  signaling 347.1
  radio 1034.1
telecommute 724.1
teleconference
  telephone call 347.13
  conference 541.6
telegram
  n telegraph 347.14
  message 552.4
  v telegraph 347.20
telegraph
  n telegraph recorder 347.2
  telegram 347.14
  v send a message 347.20
telekinesis 689.6
telemarketing 347.13
telemetry
  measurement 300.1
  semiautomatic control
   1041.4
  rocketry 1074.1
telepathic
  communicational 343.9
  psychic 689.24
telepathy
  communication 343.1
  mental telepathy 689.9
telephone
  n communication device
   347.4
  v phone 347.19

telephone book
  reference book 554.9
  directory 574.10
telephone number 347.12
telephone operator 347.9
telephoto 714.17
telescope
  n optical instrument 29.4
  observatory 1072.17
  v shorten 268.6
televise publish 352.10
  telecast 1035.14
television
  communications medium
   347.3
  informant 551.5
  news 552.1
  electronics 1033.1
  TV 1035.1
television personality 1035.2
television repairman 1035.13
television studio 1035.6
telex
  n telegraph 347.2
  telegram 347.14
  v telegraph 347.20
tell impress 93.15
  communicate 343.7
  divulge 351.5
  say 524.22
  inform 551.8
  report 552.11
  narrate 719.6
  spin a yarn 722.6
  have influence 894.10
  evidence 957.8
  recognize 989.12
  matter 997.12
  number 1017.17
teller
  informant 551.5
  banker 729.11
telling
  n informing 343.2
  fiction 722.1
  narration 722.2
  numeration 1017.9
  adj powerful 18.12
  exciting 105.30
  vigorous 544.11
  influential 894.13
  evidential 957.16
  notable 997.19
tell it like it is 644.12
tell off 510.18
tell on betray 351.6
  inform on 551.13
telltale
  n divulgence 351.2
  clue 517.9
  hint 551.4
  informer 551.6
  newsmonger 552.9
  adj tattletale 551.19
tell the truth
  confess 351.7
  speak true 644.11
  disillusion 977.2
temerity 493.1
temp worker 726.2
  temperature 1019.3

temper
  n firmness 15.3
  hot temper 110.4
  anger 152.6
  nature 767.4
  disposition 978.3
  mood 978.4
  tempering 1046.4
  v strengthen 15.13
  mature 303.9
  moderate 670.6
  imbue 797.11
  qualify 959.3
  harden 1046.7
  toughen 1049.3
temperament
  pitch 709.4
  nature 767.4
  disposition 978.3
temperance
  sedateness 106.4
  sobriety 516.1
  cardinal virtues 653.4
  temperateness 668.1
  restraint 670.1
temperate
  sedate 106.14
  sober 516.3
  moderate 668.9
  mild 670.10
  warm 1019.24
  cool 1023.12
temperature 1019.3
temper tantrum 152.8
tempest outburst 105.9
  windstorm 318.12
  storm 671.4
tempest in a teacup 998.3
tempest in a teapot 355.2
template 786.6
temple side 218.1
  religious building 703.2
tempo time 709.24
  pulsation 916.3
temporal
  unsacred 686.3
  secularist 695.16
  lay 700.3
  chronological 821.7
  transient 828.7
  timekeeping 832.15
  material 1052.10
temporary
  n worker 726.2
  adj interim 826.4
  transient 828.7
  substitute 862.8
  conditional 959.8
  unreliable 971.20
  makeshift 995.7
temporize
  n be a timeserver
    363.9
  v not face up to 368.13
  protract 827.9
  procrastinate 846.11
tempt seduce 104.23
  induce 375.22
  attract 377.6
tempt fate endeavor 403.1
  be foolish 923.6

temptress
  tempter 377.4
  seductress 665.15
tempus fugit 821.17
ten
  n card 758.2
  number 882.6
  beauty 1016.9
  v intervene 826.3
tenable
  acceptable 107.12
  defensible 460.15
  believable 953.24
tenacious
  resolute 359.11
  persevering 360.8
  obstinate 361.8
  retentive 474.8
  courageous 492.18
  adhesive 803.12
  tough 1049.4
  viscous 1062.12
tenant
  n inhabitant 227.2
  lodger 227.8
  occupant 470.4
  v inhabit 225.7
Ten Commandments
  ethics 636.1
  ten 882.6
tend
  take direction 161.7
  gravitate 297.15
  look after 339.9
  serve 577.13
  have a tendency 896.3
  heed 983.6
  care for 1008.19
  groom 1070.7
tendency
  direction 161.1
  preference 371.5
  aptitude 413.5
  nature 767.4
  inclination 896.1
  probability 968.1
  disposition 978.3
tender
  n attendant 577.5
  v offer 439.4
  give 478.12
  pay 624.10
  adj sensitive 24.12
  sore 26.11
  soft-colored 35.22
  sympathetic 93.20
  loving 104.27
  kind 143.13
  pitying 145.7
  seaworthy 180.18
  light 298.12
  immature 301.10
  careful 339.10
  lenient 427.7
  unbalanced 791.5
  soft 1047.8
tenderfoot
  recruit 461.18
  novice 572.9
  jockey 757.2
  newcomer 774.4

  beginner 818.2
  ignoramus 930.8
tenderize 1047.6
tenderloin
  city district 230.6
  brothel 665.9
tender loving care 449.2
tendon 271.2
tendril filament 271.1
  coil 281.2
  branch 310.20
  part 793.4
tenement sty 80.11
  apartment 228.13
  high rise 228.14
tenet rule 419.2
  a belief 953.2
tennis 748
tennis ball
  tennis 748.1
  elastic 1048.3
tennis court
  smoothness 287.3
  playing area 743.11
  tennis 748.1
tennis shoes 5.27
tenor
  n high voice 58.6
  direction 161.1
  meaning 518.1
  music part 708.22
  voice 709.5
  mode 765.4
  nature 767.4
  transcript 785.4
  trend 896.2
  adj high 58.13
  vocal 708.50
tenpins 750.1
tense
  n grammar 530.12
  time 821.1
  v strain 725.10
  stiffen 1046.9
  adj restless 105.27
  anxious 126.7
  nervous 128.13
  in suspense 130.12
  phonetic 524.30
  unfriendly 589.9
  rigid 1046.11
tension
  n anxiety 126.1
  tenseness 128.3
  disaccord 456.1
  enmity 589.1
  strain 725.2
  overextension 993.7
  urgency 997.4
  voltage 1032.12
  rigidity 1046.2
  stretching 1048.2
  v stiffen 1046.9
tent
  n medical apparatus 86.33
  canvas 295.8
  v camp 225.11
tentacles 474.4
tentative
  n attempt 403.2
  adj slow 175.10

  hesitant 362.11
  trial 403.16
  cautious 494.8
  interim 826.4
  substitute 862.8
  ignorant 930.12
  examining 938.37
  experimental 942.11
  unreliable 971.20
  makeshift 995.7
tenterhooks 126.1
tenth
  n fraction 882.14
  adj ordinal number 882.22
ten to one 968.8
tenuous dainty 248.7
  infinitesimal 258.14
  thin 270.16
  rare 299.4
  ethereal 764.6
  incoherent 804.4
tenure possession 469.1
  position 724.5
  term 824.3
  period of duty 825.4
tepee 228.10
tepid indifferent 102.6
  warm 1019.24
tergiversate 854.5
term
  n boundary 211.3
  sign 518.6
  word 526.1
  phrase 529.1
  end 820.1
  time 821.1
  moment 824.2
  duration 824.3
  tenure 825.4
  v name 527.11
terminal
  n destination 186.5
  railway 383.7
  speech component 524.9
  end 820.1
  stop 857.2
  output device 1042.9
  adj unhealthy 85.54
  past hope 125.15
  limital 210.10
  bordering 211.11
  dying 307.33
  deadly 308.23
  completing 407.9
  final 820.11
  disastrous 1011.15
terminal illness 85.2
terminate
  complete 407.6
  end 820.5
  cease 857.6
  result 887.4
terminology
  nomenclature 527.1
  dictionary 871.4
termite 311.34
term paper 556.1
terra land 234.1
  Earth 1072.10
terrace
  balcony 197.22

horizontal 201.3
platform 901.13
terra cotta 715.2
terra-cotta 40.4
terra firma
ground 199.3
land 234.1
foundation 901.6
terrain
open space 158.4
region 231.1
land 234.1
arena 463.1
terrapin 311.25
terrarium 228.24
terrestrial
terrene 234.4
secularist 695.16
celestial 1072.25
terrible
horrid 98.19
frightening 127.30
remarkable 247.11
wrong 638.3
dreadful 1000.9
hideous 1015.11
terrific
frightening 127.30
remarkable 247.11
superb 999.15
terrified 127.26
territorial 231.8
territory
open space 158.4
region 231.1
area 231.5
country 232.1
land 234.1
sphere of influence 894.4
terror
n fear 127.1
frightener 127.9
ruffian 593.4
violent person 671.10
adj terrifying 127.29
terrorism
terrorization 127.7
despotism 612.10
violence 671.1
revolutionism 860.2
terrorist
n alarmist 127.8
destroyer 395.8
violent person 671.9
revolutionist 860.3
adj revolutionist 860.6
terrorize
intimidate 127.20
threaten 514.2
domineer 612.16
rage 671.11
terror-stricken
terrified 127.26
panicky 127.27
terse taciturn 344.9
elegant 533.6
concise 537.6
aphoristic 974.6
tertiary
n color system 35.7
adj third 877.4

tessellation
mosaic 47.4
insertion 191.1
test
n diagnosis 91.12
shell 295.15
measure 300.2
contest 457.3
examination 938.2
trial 942.2
v interrogate 938.21
experiment 942.8
verify 970.12
adj experimental 942.11
testament 478.10
Testament 683.2
test case 942.2
testes 2.13
test flight flight 184.9
tryout 942.3
testicles 2.13
testify depose 334.6
signify 517.17
call to witness 598.17
attest 957.9
testify against 551.12
testimonial
n advertisement 352.6
celebration 487.1
recommendation 509.4
certificate 549.6
monument 549.12
testimony 957.2
adj documentary 549.18
testimony
deposition 334.3
evidence 598.8
attestation 957.2
test pilot aviator 185.1
experimenter 942.6
test run 942.3
test the waters
try one's hand 403.10
sound out 942.9
test tube 858.10
testy
irascible 110.19
argumentative 935.19
tetanus 85.6
tête-à-tête
n chat 541.4
adj intimate 582.24
both 873.7
adv conversationally 541.14
tether
n shackle 428.4
v bind 428.10
yoke 800.10
secure 855.8
tetrad
n four 879.1
adj four 879.4
tetrahedral 278.9
Texas Leaguer 745.3
Texas tea 87.11
text
rendering 341.2
representation 349.1
sign 518.6
writing 547.10
literature 547.12

printed matter 548.10
textbook 554.10
book contents 554.12
playbook 704.21
musical score 708.28
book 718.1
part of writing 793.2
topic 937.1
maxim 974.1
textbook book 554.1
text 554.10
textile
n material 4.1
adj woven 740.7
texture material 4.1
network 170.3
structure 266.1
surface texture 294.1
weaving 740.1
than
adv otherwise 780.11
prep compared to 943.11
thank 150.4
thankful 150.5
thankless
unpleasant 98.17
disliked 99.9
ungrateful 151.4
thanksgiving
thanks 150.2
prayer 696.4
thank-you 150.2
that
adj this 865.14
conj lest 897.7
that's the ticket
interj bravo! 509.22
phrs that's it 788.13
thatch
n head of hair 3.4
v cover 295.23
thaw
n melting 1020.3
v have pity 145.4
melt 1020.21
liquefy 1064.5
theater hall 197.4
setting 209.2
enclosed place 212.3
arena 463.1
battlefield 463.2
schoolroom 567.11
the entertainment industry 704.1
playhouse 704.14
theater of operations
war 458.1
battlefield 463.2
theater of the absurd 704.1
theatrical
n actor 707.2
adj emotionalistic 93.19
affected 500.15
stagy 501.24
dramatic 704.33
theatrics
emotionalism 93.9
display 501.4
dramatics 704.2
theft
taking 480.1

thievery 482.1
robbery 482.3
theism
monotheism 675.5
piety 692.1
them
the authorities 575.15
the others 865.5
thematic
recurrent 849.13
topical 937.4
theme
motif 498.7
identification 517.11
morphology 526.3
treatise 556.1
musical passage 708.24
plot 722.4
topic 937.1
theme park 743.14
theme song
identification 517.11
radio signature 1034.19
themselves 865.5
then
adj former 837.10
adv additionally 253.11
at that time 821.9
thereat 821.11
subsequently 835.6
formerly 837.13
hence 888.7
then and there 830.8
theocracy
government 612.4
hierarchy 698.7
theological
n theologian 676.3
adj religious 676.4
theologist 676.3
theology
religious doctrine 675.1
religion 676.1
theorem premise 935.7
axiom 974.2
theoretical
ideational 932.9
hypothetical 951.13
theorist 951.7
theory
harmonics 709.1
idea 932.1
hypothesis 951.1
theorization 951.1
explanation 951.2
opinion 953.6
theory of evolution 861.4
theory of relativity 158.6
therapeutic
remedial 86.39
helpful 449.21
therapist
health care professional 90.8
psychologist 92.10
therapy medicine 90.1
therapeutics 91.1
cure 396.7
aid 449.1
there
at that location 159.24
present 221.16

thereabouts
  there 159.24
  near 223.20
thereafter
  subsequently 835.6
  in future 839.10
thereby 384.12
therefore
  accordingly 766.11
  consequently 887.7
  hence 888.7
  all things considered 946.17
therein 207.10
thereof 188.20
thermal
  n hot air 1019.9
  adj warm 1019.24
thermal unit 1019.19
thermochemical
  pyrological 1019.32
  chemical 1060.9
thermodynamic 1019.32
thermometer 1019.20
thermonuclear 1038.19
thermonuclear power
  nuclear energy 18.4
  atomic energy 1038.15
thermonuclear reaction fission
  1038.8
  fusion 1038.9
thermonuclear weapons 462.1
thermostat 1019.20
thesaurus
  vocabulary 526.13
  reference book 554.9
  dictionary 871.4
these 865.14
thesis treatise 556.1
  accent 709.25
  meter 720.7
  beat 850.3
  premise 935.7
  supposition 951.3
thespian
  n actor 707.2
  adj dramatic 704.33
thew 15.2
they
  the authorities 575.15
  exclusiveness 773.3
  them 865.5
thick
  n middle 819.1
  v thicken 269.5
  density 1045.10
  adj raucous 58.15
  three-dimensional 269.8
  luxuriant 310.43
  inarticulate 525.12
  familiar 587.19
  teeming 884.9
  stupid 922.15
  unbelievable 955.10
  dense 1045.12
  viscous 1062.12
  adv densely 1045.15
thicken increase 251.4
  grow thick 269.5
  densify 1045.10
  solidify 1046.8
  emulsify 1062.10

thicket
  dense plant growth 310.15
  bunch 770.7
thick skin
  insensibility 25.1
  callousness 94.3
  shell 295.15
  armor 460.3
thief robber 483.1
  evildoer 593.1
  criminal 660.9
thigh body part 2.7
  fowl part 10.23
  leg 177.14
thimbleful 248.2
thin
  v dilute 16.11
  subtract 255.9
  shrink 260.9
  thin down 270.12
  rarefy 299.3
  dissipate 771.5
  liquefy 1064.5
  prune 1069.17
  adj shrill 58.14
  insipid 65.2
  dainty 248.7
  infinitesimal 258.14
  shrunk 260.13
  slender 270.16
  shallow 276.5
  rare 299.4
  tenuous 764.6
  sparse 885.5
  unbelievable 955.10
  meager 992.10
  transparent 1029.4
  adv thinly 270.23
thin air air 317.1
  spirit 764.3
thing love affair 104.6
  act 328.3
  preference 371.5
  occupation 724.1
  something 763.3
  mode 765.4
  particular 766.3
  affair 831.3
  specialty 866.1
  object 1052.4
things wardrobe 5.2
  equipment 385.4
  belongings 471.2
thingumajig 1052.5
thin ice 1006.1
think expect 130.5
  care 339.6
  intend 380.4
  cogitate 931.8
  suppose 951.10
  opine 953.11
think ahead
  anticipate 839.6
  foresee 961.5
think back 989.10
think better of
  repent 113.7
  reconsider 931.15
thinker wise man 921.1
  intellectual 929.1
  reasoner 935.11

  philosopher 952.8
think highly of
  respect 155.4
  value 997.13
think little of
  disdain 157.3
  not hesitate 359.10
  disapprove 510.10
  underestimate 950.2
  be inattentive 984.2
  attach little importance to
  998.12
think nothing of
  disdain 157.3
  not hesitate 359.10
  underestimate 950.2
  be inattentive 984.2
  attach little importance to
  998.12
  take it easy 1014.12
think out loud 542.3
think over 931.13
think tank 942.5
think the world of 104.21
think the worst of 125.9
think twice
  be cautious 494.5
  be unsure 971.10
thinner
  paint 35.8
  solvent 270.10
  diluting agent 1064.4
thinning
  n weakening 16.5
  shrinking 260.3
  rarefaction 299.2
  dispersion 771.1
  cultivation 1069.13
  adj solvent 1064.8
thin-skinned
  sensitive 24.12
  touchy 110.21
third
  n harmonic interval 709.20
  baseball 745.1
  fraction 878.2
  mediocre 1005.6
  v trisect 878.3
  adj tertiary 877.4
the third-degree 938.13
third-degree burn
  trauma 85.38
  burn 1020.6
the third dimension 269.2
the third estate 606.1
third person 530.7
third-rate 1005.9
third string
  n inferiority 250.1
  team 617.7
  substitute 862.2
  adj inferior 250.6
third world
  independents 430.12
  neutral 467.4
  the poor 619.3
thirst
  n craving 100.6
  appetite 100.7
  tendency 896.1
  dryness 1066.1

  v hunger 100.19
  drink up 1066.5
thirsty
  craving 100.24
  needing water 100.26
  absorbent 187.17
  dry 1066.7
thirteen 882.7
thirty-second note 709.14
thirty-two 882.7
this 865.14
this day
  n the present 838.1
  adv now 838.3
this instant 838.1
thistle thorn 285.5
  insignia 647.1
thistledown down 3.19
  lightness 298.2
  softness 1047.4
this way 766.10
thong
  swimwear 5.29
  strip 271.4
  whip 605.1
Thor thunder 56.5
  rain 316.6
  lightning 1025.17
thorax 283.6
thorn
  affliction 96.8
  bramble 285.5
  adhering thing 803.4
  bane 1001.1
thorny
  prickly 285.10
  difficult 1013.17
thorough
  downright 247.12
  painstaking 339.11
  meticulous 339.12
  confirmed 373.18
  complete 407.12
  cautious 494.8
  thoroughgoing 794.10
thoroughbred
  n aristocrat 607.4
  nobleman 608.4
  horse 757.2
  adj upper-class 607.10
  wellborn 608.11
those 865.14
though 338.8
thought
  n expectation 130.1
  considerateness 143.3
  swift thing 174.6
  hint 248.4
  advice 422.1
  remark 524.3
  admixture 797.7
  intellect 919.1
  act of thought 931
  idea 932.1
  opinion 953.6
  attention 983.1
  adj cognitive 931.21
thoughtful
  solemn 111.3
  considerate 143.16
  careful 339.10

be tedious 118.6
tired clothing 5.45
  fatigued 21.7
  weary 118.11
  worn-out 393.36
  aphoristic 974.6
tireless
  industrious 330.22
  persevering 360.8
tires 756.1
tiresome
  fatiguing 21.13
  annoying 98.22
  boring 118.10
  prosaic 721.5
tissue
  n material 4.1
  network 170.3
  structure 266.1
  organic matter 305.1
  weaving 740.1
  v weave 740.6
titan 257.13
titanic large 247.7
  huge 257.20
tit for tat offset 338.2
  retaliation 506.3
  reciprosity 777.3
  substitution 862.1
  interchange 863.1
tit-for-tat 777.10
tithe
  n donation 478.6
  tax 630.9
  tenth part 882.14
  v charge 630.12
  adj tenth 882.22
titillate tickle 74.6
  delight 95.10
  thrill 105.15
  attract 377.6
  amuse 743.21
  interest 983.12
title
  n possession 469.1
  ownership 469.2
  estate 471.4
  name 527.3
  book 554.1
  book part 554.12
  prerogative 642.1
  honorific 648.1
  golf 751.1
  class 809.2
  caption 937.2
  v name 527.11
  focus on 937.3
titled named 527.14
  noble 608.10
titleholder 470.2
title of respect or address 527.3
title page label 517.13
  book part 554.12
  caption 937.2
titrate 801.6
tits
  n bosom 283.7
  adj excellent 999.13
tizzy dither 105.6
  confusion 985.3

TKO 754.3
TLC carefulness 339.1
  support 449.3
to at 159.27
  toward 161.26
  into 189.14
  as far as 261.20
  for the purpose of 380.11
  until 821.15
toad sycophant 138.3
  amphibian 311.27
to a degree
  to some extent 245.7
  limited 248.10
  relatively 775.12
toad-stool 310.4
to advantage
  usefully 387.26
  helpfully 449.24
  profitably 472.17
  expediently 995.8
toady
  n sycophant 138.3
  assenter 332.6
  v fawn 138.7
to a fault 993.23
to a great extent 247.15
to all appearances
  apparently 33.12
  externally 206.10
to a man 332.17
to and fro
  reciprocally 777.12
  alternately 850.11
  changeably 854.8
  back and forth 916.21
toast
  n pledge 88.10
  celebration 487.1
  fine lady 500.10
  v drink 8.29
  cook 11.5
  drink to 88.29
  be hot 1019.22
  adj brown 40.3
  delightful 97.8
to a T
  to completion 407.14
  exactly 973.21
  to a nicety 973.23
  to perfection 1002.11
to a turn
  carefully 339.15
  to completion 407.14
  to a nicety 973.23
  to perfection 1002.11
tobacco
  n tabac 89.1
  adj tobaccoey 89.15
to beat the band
  swiftly 174.18
  utterly 794.16
  to perfection 1002.11
to be brief 537.8
to be desired
  desirable 100.30
  expedient 995.5
to be exact 973.22
to be expected
  adj as expected 130.14

  adv imminently 840.4
  normally 869.10
to be fair 649.12
to be reckoned with 894.13
to be seen
  visible 31.6
  manifest 348.8
to be specific 865.15
to be sure
  adv surely 970.24
  interj yes 332.18
toboggan 177.35
to boot 253.11
to come
  approaching 167.4
  future 839.8
  imminent 840.3
  scheduled 965.9
to completion 407.14
tocsin
  warning sign 399.3
  alarm 400.1
to date 838.4
today
  n the present 838.1
  adv now 838.3
toddler 302.9
to die for 100.3
to-do
  excitement 105.4
  bustle 330.4
  commotion 810.4
  agitation 917.1
toe base 199.2
  foot 199.5
toehold hold 474.2
  wrestling 474.3
  footing 901.5
  purchase 906.2
toe the mark
  obey 326.2
  follow the rule 867.4
toe-to-toe 779.6
to extremes
  intemperately 669.10
  in or to excess 993.23
tofu 10.48
together
  v assemble 770.18
  adj composed 106.13
  in accord 455.3
  sane 925.4
  adv unanimously 332.17
  cooperatively 450.6
  collectively 769.11
  jointly 800.18
  continuously 812.10
  simultaneously 836.7
  concurrently 899.5
togetherness
  accord 455.1
  accompaniment 769.1
toggle 800.8
to good use 387.26
togs clothing 5.1
  garment 5.3
toil
  n work 725.4
  v work 724.12
  drudge 725.14
  hamper 1012.11

toilet
  n latrine 12.10
  stool 12.11
  bathroom 197.26
  casino 759.19
  adj cursing 513.8
toiletries 735.6
to infinity 823.4
token
  n omen 133.3
  symbol 517.2
  password 517.12
  label 517.13
  sign 518.6
  record 549.1
  counter 728.12
  substitute 862.2
  characteristic 865.4
  evidence 957.1
  memento 989.7
  v augur 133.12
  manifest 348.5
  adj cheap 633.7
  substitute 862.8
token gesture 354.6
to leeward
  leeward 182.68
  windward 218.9
tolerable
  bearable 107.13
  satisfactory 999.20
  mediocre 1005.7
tolerance
  resistance 87.1
  patience 134.1
  forgiveness 148.1
  leniency 427.1
  latitude 430.4
  liberalism 430.10
  sufferance 443.2
  inclusion 772.1
  inaccuracy 975.2
  broad-mindedness 979.4
tolerate endure 134.5
  be easy on 427.5
  suffer 443.10
  keep an open mind 979.7
toll
  n ringing 54.3
  fee 630.6
  tax 630.9
  v ring 54.8
tollbooth 228.9
tomahawk 745.5
to make a long story short 537.8
tomato
  vegetables 10.35
  woman 77.6
  girl 302.7
tomb
  n sepulcher 309.16
  monument 549.12
  v inter 309.19
tomboy mannish female 76.9
  schoolgirl 302.8
tomcat
  male animal 76.8
  cat 311.21
tome book 554.1
  volume 554.4

tomorrow
  n the future 839.1
  adv in the future 839.9
tom-tom 55.1
ton quantity 247.3
  fashion 578.1
  popularity 578.2
tonal sounding 50.15
  phonetic 524.30
  harmonics 709.27
tone
  n muscularity 15.2
  color 35.1
  hue 35.6
  audio frequency 50.2
  fitness 84.1
  feeling 93.1
  milieu 209.3
  behavior 321.1
  manner 384.1
  intonation 524.6
  voice 524.7
  melody 708.2
  tonality 709.3
  pitch 709.4
  note 709.14
  interval 709.20
  artistic treatment 712.9
  plot 722.4
  nature 767.4
  trend 896.2
  mood 978.4
  elasticity 1048.1
  v color 35.14
  influence 894.7
tone-deaf 49.6
tone down decolor 36.5
  muffle 51.9
  moderate 670.6
  tune 708.36
  dull 1027.10
  soften 1047.6
toneless colorless 36.7
  monotone 50.15
tongs 1020.12
tongue
  n food 10.20
  bell 54.4
  taste 62.1
  taste bud 62.5
  shaft 273.1
  point of land 283.9
  language 523.1
  utterance 524.2
  speech organ 524.18
  v lick 73.9
  blow a horn 708.42
tongue-in-cheek 489.15
tongue-lashing 510.7
tongue-tied mute 51.12
  taciturn 344.9
tonic
  n refreshment 9.1
  beverage 10.49
  energizer 17.6
  medicine 86.8
  bracer 88.8
  harmonics 709.15
  adj refreshing 9.3
  energizing 17.15
  healthful 81.5

stimulating 86.44
restorative 396.22
phonetic 524.30
tonal 709.27
tonight 838.3
tonnage ships 180.10
  capacity 257.2
  weight 297.1
  fee 630.7
too additionally 253.11
  excessively 993.22
too bad
  disgraceful 661.11
  terrible 1000.9
too big 257.23
too big for one's britches
  conceited 140.11
  strutting 501.23
too close for comfort 1006.9
too close to call 790.7
too far 993.23
too few
  n a few 885.2
  adj insufficient 992.9
tool
  n sycophant 138.3
  means 384.4
  agent 576.3
  gambling device 759.16
  instrument 1040.1
  v speed 174.9
  engrave 713.9
  tool up 1040.13
too late 844.6
tooled 713.11
too little too late 992.1
tools of the trade 384.2
tool up
  prepare oneself 405.13
  equip with tools 1040.13
too many 993.2
too many cooks spoil the broth
  advice 422.9
  intrusion 214.10
too many irons in the fire 993.6
too much
  n intemperance 669.1
  excess 993.1
  superabundance 993.2
  adj insufferable 98.25
  extreme 247.13
  intemperate 669.7
  excessive 993.16
  adv inordinately 993.22
to one's credit 622.9
to one's face 348.15
to one side
  obliquely 204.21
  aside 218.10
  dismiss 984.4
to one's knowledge 928.30
to one's liking 97.6
to one's satisfaction 107.16
too quick on the draw 845.8
to order 420.15
too soon
  adj untimely 844.6
  premature 845.8
  adv too early 845.13

toot
  n blare 53.5
  cocaine 87.7
  drinking spree 88.6
  v blare 53.10
  snort cocaine 87.22
  blow a horn 708.42
tooth
  n mouth part 2.8
  taste 62.1
  point 285.3
  roughness 288.1
  v notch 289.4
  coarsen 294.4
toothache 26.5
tooth and nail
  resolutely 359.17
  savagely 671.27
  laboriously 725.19
  utterly 794.16
toothbrush 3.11
a tooth for a tooth 506.3
toothless 286.4
toothpaste
  cleanser 79.17
  dentifrice 86.22
toot one's own horn
  be vain 140.6
  boast 502.6
  brag 502.7
top
  n top side 198.1
  summit 198.2
  exterior 206.2
  cover 295.5
  roof 295.6
  tent 295.8
  toy 743.16
  limit 794.5
  rotator 915.4
  acme of perfection 1002.3
  v cap 198.9
  excel 249.6
  overshadow 249.8
  rise above 272.11
  cover 295.21
  golf 751.4
  exceed 993.9
  adj topmost 198.10
  superlative 249.13
  expensive 632.11
top billing 704.1
topcoat 5.13
top dog superior 249.4
  victor 411.2
  chief 575.4
  important person 997.11
top-drawer top 198.10
  first-rate 999.18
to perfection 1002.11
top-flight 198.10
top-heavy
  corpulent 257.18
  unbalanced 791.5
topic plot 722.4
  subject 937.1
  question 938.10
topical local 231.9
  current 838.2
  thematic 937.4
topless unclad 6.13

bare-breasted 6.16
headless 198.13
high 272.14
top-notch
  superlative 249.13
  first-rate 999.18
top off crown 198.9
  provision 385.9
  perfect 407.6
  complete 794.6
  fill 794.7
  fuel 1021.8
top of the line
  the best 249.5
  the ultimate 999.8
top of the world 198.2
topography map 159.5
  geography 159.8
toponym 527.3
topping
  n icing 198.3
  adj crowning 198.11
  superior 249.12
  high 272.14
  first-rate 999.18
  prep atop 198.16
topple tumble 194.8
  break down 393.24
  be destroyed 395.22
  fell 913.5
top priority 814.1
the tops 999.8
top secret 345.11
topside
  n top 198.1
  adv on board 182.62
  atop 198.15
topsoil land 234.1
  layer 296.1
top-spin 748.2
topsy-turvy
  v overturn 205.6
  adj inverted 205.7
  confused 810.16
  adv inversely 205.8
  contrarily 779.9
Torah 683.3
torch
  n blowtorch 1020.14
  lighter 1021.4
  light source 1026.1
  flame 1026.3
  v ignite 1020.22
torched 1020.30
toreador 461.4
torment
  n agony 26.6
  torture 96.7
  tormentor 96.10
  harshness 98.4
  worry 126.2
  punishment 604.2
  bane 1001.1
  v pain 26.7
  annoy 96.13
  torture 96.18
  desolate 98.12
  aggrieve 112.19
  make anxious 126.5
  bear malice 144.15
  persecute 389.7

work evil 1000.6
trouble 1013.13
torn affected 93.23
impaired 393.27
shabby 393.32
alienated 589.11
severed 802.23
tornado outburst 105.9
whirlwind 318.14
storm 671.4
torpedo
n killer 308.11
missile 462.18
ruffian 593.4
rocket 1074.3
v destroy 395.11
attack 459.22
shoot 904.12
torpor apathy 94.4
inertness 173.4
inaction 329.1
languor 331.6
permanence 853.1
torque circle 280.3
necklace 498.6
Torquemada 144.14
torrential flowing 238.24
rainy 316.11
torrid 1019.25
torsion deflection 164.2
distortion 265.1
convolution 281.1
torso 1052.3
tort misdeed 655.2
offense 674.4
tortilla 10.29
tortoise slowpoke 175.5
reptile 311.25
tortoise shell 47.6
tortoni 10.47
tortuous
distorted 265.10
curved 279.7
convolutional 281.6
grandiloquent 545.8
torture
n agony 26.6
torment 96.7
harshness 98.4
deflection 164.2
punishment 604.2
v pain 26.7
torment 96.18
agonize 98.12
bear malice 144.15
deflect 164.5
pervert 265.6
deform 265.7
misinterpret 342.2
put to the question
604.16
work evil 1000.6
Tory 611.9
to spare
remaining 256.7
unused 390.12
superfluous 993.17
toss
n gamble 759.2
throw 904.3
flounder 917.8

search 938.15
even chance 972.7
v be excited 105.18
place violently 159.13
pitch 182.55
billow 238.22
gamble 759.23
throw 904.10
oscillate 916.10
flounder 917.15
ransack 938.33
toss and turn
keep awake 23.3
be excited 105.18
flounder 917.15
toss-up election 609.15
uncertainty 759.2
stop 857.2
gamble 971.8
even chance 972.7
total
n amount 244.2
math terms 253.2
whole 792.2
sum 1017.6
v compute 253.6
spoil 393.11
demolish 395.17
amount to 792.8
sum up 1017.19
adj great 247.6
downright 247.12
unmitigated 671.17
cumulative 770.23
comprehensive 772.7
whole 792.9
complete 794.9
thorough 794.10
universal 864.14
unqualified 960.2
sound 1002.7
total assets assets 471.7
funds 728.14
total darkness 1027.1
total eclipse
darkness 1027.8
sun 1072.13
totaled high 87.24
spoiled 393.29
disintegrative 806.5
ended 820.9
totalitarian
authoritative 417.15
governmental 612.17
totality whole 792.1
wholeness 792.5
completeness 794.1
all 864.4
universe 1072.1
total lack 222.1
total loss
wreck 393.8
debacle 395.4
failure 410.2
loss 473.1
total recall 989.3
total victory 411.1
total war
death struggle 457.6
war 458.1
tote board 759.17

to tell the truth
truthfully 644.22
truly 973.18
totem symbol 517.2
race 559.4
familiar spirit 678.12
idol 697.3
totem pole
shaft 273.1
symbol 517.2
tote up compute 253.6
sum up 1017.19
to the contrary
adv contrarily 779.9
interj no 335.8
by no means 335.9
to the death
deathly 307.37
throughout 794.17
to the end to completion
407.14
throughout 794.17
to the bitter end 820.13
to the extreme 993.23
to the four winds
from everywhere 158.14
in every direction 161.25
to the good
helpfully 449.24
profitably 472.17
to one's account 622.9
to the heart of 207.13
to the hilt
completely 794.14
throughout 794.17
to the letter 973.21
to the limit
to completion 407.14
utterly 794.16
to the max
utterly 794.16
in excess 993.23
to the nth degree 794.16
to the point
adj concise 537.6
relevant 775.11
apt 788.10
adv plainly 535.4
to the second 845.14
to the side
adj side 218.6
adv aside 218.10
to the tune of
adv at a price 630.17
prep to the amount of 244.7
tots 302.2
totter
n gait 177.12
flounder 917.8
v be weak 16.8
way of walking 177.28
tumble 194.8
age 303.10
vacillate 362.8
break down 393.24
change 854.5
flounder 917.15
touch
n senses 24.5
sense of touch 73.1
contact 223.5

hint 248.4
communication 343.1
skill 413.1
knack 413.6
motif 498.7
signal 517.15
implication 519.2
execution 708.30
admixture 797.7
tap 902.7
v sense 24.6
feel 73.6
affect 93.14
move 145.5
contact 223.10
beg 440.15
signal 517.22
borrow 621.3
relate to 775.5
equal 790.5
tap 902.18
touch and go
gamble 759.2
uncertainty 971.8
even chance 972.7
touch a nerve 24.8
touchdown
landing 184.18
score 409.5
game 746.3
touché
adv right! 973.24
phrs that's it 788.13
touched affected 93.23
penitent 113.9
insane 926.26
touch off kindle 375.18
explode 671.14
ignite 1020.22
touch on
remark 524.24
evidence 957.8
call attention to 983.10
touch up 392.11
touchy sensitive 24.12
excitable 105.28
tetchy 110.21
partisan 456.17
precarious 1006.12
tough
n strong man 15.7
combatant 461.1
ruffian 593.4
violent person 671.10
adj firm 15.18
obdurate 361.10
strict 425.6
resolute 492.18
hard to understand 522.14
violent 671.16
laborious 725.18
sturdy 763.7
adhesive 803.12
durable 827.10
excellent 999.13
difficult 1013.17
hard 1046.10
resistant 1049.4
viscous 1062.12
tough act to follow
expert 413.11

series 812.2
procession 812.3
afterpart 817.2
v direct 161.5
accustom 373.9
drill 568.13
be taught 570.11
play 744.2
pull 905.4
tend 1070.7
trained
accustomed 373.15
skilled 413.26
informed 928.18
trainee recruit 461.18
student 572.1
beginner 818.2
traipse
n walk 177.10
v go slow 175.6
wander 177.23
walk 177.27
way of walking 177.28
trait culture 373.2
sign 517.1
characteristic 865.4
traitor rebel 327.5
treasonist 357.10
apostate 363.5
criminal 645.10
turncoat 660.9
convert 858.8
trajectory course 172.2
route 383.1
orbit 1072.16
rocket launching 1074.9
tram 179.17
tramp
n walk 177.10
vagabond 178.3
bum 331.9
beggar 440.8
wretch 660.2
transient 828.4
oddity 870.4
v plod 175.7
wander 177.23
march 177.30
trample stamp 902.22
run over 910.7
trampoline
exerciser 725.7
elastic 1048.3
trance
n stupor 22.6
hypnosis 22.7
daze 92.19
ecstasy 691.3
abstractedness 985.2
v put to sleep 22.20
cast a spell 691.7
tranquil calm 106.12
quiescent 173.12
pacific 464.9
equable 670.13
thoughtless 933.4
tranquilizer
anesthetic 25.3
sedative 86.12
moderator 670.3
transact perform 328.9

execute 437.9
transaction
performance 328.2
act 328.3
compact 437.1
execution 437.4
business transaction 731.4
affair 831.3
transatlantic 261.11
transcend
loom 247.5
excel 249.6
exceed 993.9
transcendental
n immaterialism 1053.3
adj superior 249.12
recondite 522.16
heavenly 681.12
supernatural 870.15
visionary 986.24
numeric 1017.23
extraterrestrial 1072.26
transcontinental 261.11
transcribe
translate 341.12
letter 546.6
write 547.19
compose 708.46
copy 785.8
transducer 858.10
transect 875.4
transept
crosspiece 170.5
church 703.9
transfer
n transferal 176.1
informing 343.2
transference 629.1
transcript 785.4
v transmit 176.10
communicate 343.7
deliver 478.13
commission 615.10
convey 629.3
transfigure
make better 392.9
transform 852.8
transfix
perforate 292.15
stab 459.25
stabilize 855.7
transform
make better 392.9
transfigure 852.8
convert 858.11
transfusion
blood transfusion 91.18
transferal 176.1
permeation 221.3
transgress
disobey 327.6
violate 435.4
do wrong 655.4
break the law 674.5
overstep 910.9
transgression 655.1
transiency 828.1
transient
n traveler 178.1
lodger 227.8
guest 828.4

adj vanishing 34.3
wandering 177.37
emerging 190.18
short 268.8
mortal 307.34
transitory 828.7
changeable 854.6
transistor 1033.12
transit
n crossing 170.1
transferal 176.1
travel 177.1
instrument 278.4
conversion 858.1
v traverse 177.20
transition
transferal 176.1
motion-picture editing 706.6
change 852.1
conversion 858.1
transitive
n verb 530.4
adj grammatical 530.17
transient 828.7
translate
transfer 176.10
render 341.12
transform 852.8
translation
transferal 176.1
transcription 341.3
removal to heaven 681.11
transformation 852.3
translucent
clear 521.11
light 1025.31
lucent 1030.5
transmigration
transferal 176.1
migration 177.4
transformation 852.3
materialization 1052.8
transmission
transferal 176.1
informing 343.2
information 551.1
conveyance 629.1
radio broadcasting 1034.16
gear 1040.9
transmit
change over 176.10
send 176.15
communicate 343.7
bequeath 478.18
transfer 629.3
broadcast 1034.25
send 1036.15
transmitter
telegraph 347.2
telephone 347.4
radio transmitter 1034.4
televisor 1035.8
transmogrification 852.3
transoceanic 261.11
transom
crosspiece 170.5
stern 217.7
air passage 239.13
transparency
clearness 521.2
photograph 714.3

print 714.5
nonopacity 1029
transparence 1029.1
transparent
clear 521.11
candid 644.17
light 1025.31
transpicuous 1029.4
transpire
exude 190.15
be revealed 351.8
occur 831.5
transplant
n insertion 191.1
plant 739.3
v treat 91.24
transfer 176.10
implant 191.8
set 1069.18
transport
n happiness 95.2
fury 105.8
transportation 176.3
trance 691.3
v delight 95.10
convey 176.12
fascinate 377.7
banish 909.17
transportation
transplacement 176.1
conveyance 176.3
banishment 909.4
transpose
transfer 176.10
invert 205.5
compose 708.46
reverse 779.5
interchange 863.4
transsexual 75.17
transverse
n crosspiece 170.5
diagonal 204.7
v cross 170.6
adj transversal 170.9
crosswise 204.19
adv crossways 170.13
transvestite
n sexual pervert 75.16
adj homosexual 75.30
trap
n mouth 292.4
ambush 346.3
gin 356.12
lure 377.3
basketball game 747.3
soccer 752.3
hidden danger 1006.5
v entrap 356.20
catch 480.17
play 752.4
trapeze 725.7
trapezoid 278.9
trapper 382.5
trappings
wardrobe 5.2
harness 385.5
belongings 471.2
finery 498.3
Trappist
n religious person 667.2
adj ascetic 667.4

trap shooting 744.1
trash
  n derelict 370.4
  rubbish 391.5
  nonsense 520.2
  rabble 606.3
  poker 759.10
  trivia 998.4
  v be disrespectful 156.6
  censure 510.13
trashy worthless 391.11
  nonsensical 520.7
  paltry 998.21
trauma shock 85.26
  wound 85.38
  psychological stress 92.17
traumatic 393.27
travail
  n birth 1.1
  work 725.4
  v give birth 1.3
  drudge 725.14
travel
  n progression 162.1
  course 172.2
  transportation 176.3
  journeying 177.1
  traveling 177.1
  v progress 162.2
  move 172.5
  go 177.18
  journey 177.21
travel agency 177.5
travels 177.2
traverse
  n crosspiece 170.5
  v cross 170.6
  travel 177.20
  navigate 182.13
  oppose 451.3
  contradict 451.6
  ski 753.4
  adj transverse 170.9
  adv crosswise 170.13
travesty
  n reproduction 336.3
  bad likeness 350.2
  exaggeration 355.1
  wit 489.1
  burlesque 508.6
  v misrepresent 350.3
  exaggerate 355.3
  burlesque 508.11
trawler 382.6
treacherous
  falsehearted 354.31
  deceitful 356.22
  perfidious 645.21
  unreliable 971.20
  unsafe 1006.11
treachery
  falseheartedness 354.4
  treacherousness 645.6
  unreliability 971.6
treacle sweetening 66.2
  semiliquid 1062.5
tread
  n velocity 172.4
  travel 177.11
  gait 177.12
  step 193.5

degree 245.1
  v walk 177.27
  stamp 902.22
treading water 182.11
treadmill
  n routine 373.5
  punishment 605.3
  work 725.4
  adj tedious 118.9
tread underfoot
  conquer 412.10
  subdue 432.9
  domineer 612.16
treason apostasy 363.2
  petty crime 645.7
  conversion 858.3
treasure
  n store 386.1
  wealth 618.1
  funds 728.14
  collection 770.11
  good thing 999.5
  v cherish 104.21
  store up 386.11
  hold 474.7
  keep in memory 989.13
  value 997.13
treasurer
  executive 574.3
  payer 624.9
  financial officer 729.12
treasury store 386.1
  bank 386.6
  funds 728.14
  cash 728.18
  treasure-house 729.13
  collection 770.11
treasury bill 728.11
treat
  n meal 8.5
  delicacy 10.8
  regalement 95.3
  payment 624.8
  v remedy 86.38
  practice medicine 90.14
  doctor 91.24
  use 321.6
  handle 387.12
  prepare 405.6
  discuss 541.12
  write upon 556.5
  pay for 624.19
  operate on 889.6
treatise tract 556
  piece 556.1
treatment
  medicine 90.1
  therapy 91.1
  medical attention 91.14
  usage 387.2
  preparation 405.1
  discussion 541.7
  treatise 556.1
  script 706.3
  technique 712.9
treaty 437.2
treble
  n stridency 58.6
  air 708.4
  part 708.22
  voice 709.5

  v triplicate 877.2
  adj high 58.13
  vocal 708.50
  triple 877.3
tree
  n cross 170.4
  spar 180.13
  timber 310.10
  genealogy 560.5
  execution 605.5
  v corner 1013.16
tree line 237.2
trek
  n migration 177.4
  journey 177.5
  v journey 177.21
  migrate 177.22
trellis
  n network 170.3
  v net 170.7
tremble
  n trepidation 105.5
  trill 709.19
  agitate 917.3
  v be weak 16.8
  be excited 105.18
  shake 127.14
  fidget 128.6
  quiver 917.11
  freeze 1023.9
tremendous
  terrible 127.30
  large 247.7
  huge 257.20
  superb 999.15
tremor thrill 105.2
  trepidation 105.5
  speech defect 525.1
  trill 709.19
  shake 917.3
tremulous
  fearful 127.23
  jittery 128.12
  inarticulate 525.12
  shaking 917.17
trench
  n crack 224.2
  channel 239.1
  ocean depths 275.4
  valley 284.9
  trough 290.2
  entrenchment 460.5
  shelter 1009.3
  v intrude 214.5
  cleave 224.4
  channel 239.15
  excavate 284.15
  furrow 290.3
trenchant
  energetic 17.13
  acrimonious 17.14
  pungent 68.6
  caustic 144.23
  vigorous 544.11
  sagacious 920.16
trencherman eater 8.16
  glutton 672.3
trench warfare 458.1
trend
  n direction 161.1
  course 172.2

flow 238.4
  fashion 578.1
  drift 896.2
  v take direction 161.7
  deviate 164.3
  flow 238.16
  tend 896.3
trendsetter 578.7
trendy
  fashionable 578.11
  faddish 578.15
  knowledgeable 928.17
trepidation
  trepidity 105.5
  fear 127.5
  nervousness 128.1
  agitation 917.1
trés bien 332.18
trés bon 999.12
trespass
  n intrusion 214.1
  violation 435.2
  usurpation 640.3
  misdeed 655.2
  lawbreaking 674.3
  overstepping 910.3
  v intrude 214.5
  violate 435.4
  usurp 640.8
  do wrong 655.4
  break the law 674.5
  overstep 910.9
tresses 3.4
trestle
  railway 383.7
  horse 901.16
trey card 758.2
  three 876.1
trial
  n annoyance 96.2
  tribulation 96.9
  attempt 403.2
  preparation 405.1
  contest 457.3
  number 530.8
  legal action 598.5
  experiment 942.1
  test 942.2
  adversity 1011.1
  adj tentative 403.16
  three 876.3
  experimental 942.11
trial and error
  attempt 403.2
  experiment 942.1
trial balloon
  question 938.10
  feeler 942.4
trial by jury 598.5
trials and tribulations 96.9
triangle bell 54.4
  love affair 104.6
  straightedge 277.3
  punishment 605.3
  three 876.1
triangulate
  v locate 159.11
  measure 300.10
  adj tripartite 878.4
triathlon sport 744.1
  track meet 755.2

tribe race 559.4
 company 770.3
 kind 809.3
 classifications 809.5
tribunal
 n council 423.1
 court 595.1
 forum 595.1
 platform 901.13
 adj judicial 595.7
tributary
 n feeder 238.3
 adj subject 432.13
tribute demand 421.1
 gift 478.4
 celebration 487.1
 praise 509.5
 fee 624.5
 tax 630.9
 citation 646.4
 acknowledgment 888.2
trick
 n act 328.3
 artifice 356.6
 habit 373.3
 pretext 376.1
 intrigue 381.5
 knack 413.6
 stratagem 415.3
 prank 489.10
 mannerism 500.2
 style 532.2
 bridge 758.3
 shift 825.3
 characteristic 865.4
 quirk 927.2
 goof 975.6
 illusion 976.1
 expedient 995.2
 v deceive 356.14
 fool 356.15
 live by one's wits 415.9
 play a practical joke 489.14
trickle
 n leakage 190.5
 tricklet 238.7
 a few 885.2
 v leak 190.14
 dribble 238.18
tricks of the trade 356.6
tricky deceptive 356.21
 deceitful 356.22
 cunning 415.12
 waggish 489.17
 dishonest 645.16
 improper 645.18
 treacherous 645.21
 difficult 1013.17
tricycle 179.8
trident
 n fork 171.4
 three 876.1
 adj tripartite 878.4
tried and true
 experienced 413.28
 devoted 587.21
 trustworthy 644.19
 traditional 842.12
 proven 942.12
trifle
 n hardly anything 248.5

thing of naught 764.2
 particular 766.3
 triviality 998.5
 v waste time 331.13
 leave undone 340.7
 make love 562.14
 be foolish 923.6
 dally 998.14
trifle with
 disrespect 156.4
 do carelessly 340.9
trifurcation 878.1
trigger
 n immediate cause 886.3
 v kindle 375.18
 explode 671.14
 cause 886.10
 receive 1036.17
trigger-happy
 jittery 128.12
 warlike 458.21
trigger man
 killer 308.11
 ruffian 593.4
triglyceride 7.7
trigonal
 triangular 278.8
 tripartite 878.4
trigonometry 278.3
trihedral sided 218.7
 tripartite 878.4
trilateral sided 218.7
 triangular 278.8
 tripartite 878.4
trill
 n trillo 709.19
 v ripple 52.11
 bird sound 60.5
 leak 190.14
 sing 708.38
trilogy 876.1
trim
 n ornamentation 498.1
 good condition 765.3
 v cut the hair 3.22
 trim ship 182.49
 border 211.10
 shorten 268.6
 prepare 405.6
 defeat 412.9
 remain neutral 467.5
 ornament 498.8
 disapprove 510.18
 punish 604.15
 cheapen 633.6
 fasten 800.7
 sever 802.11
 tidy 808.12
 reel in 906.9
 adj in trim 180.19
 shipshape 180.20
 shapely 264.5
 elegant 533.6
 chic 578.13
 tidy 807.8
trimester
 moment 824.2
 three 876.1
trim sail 182.20
trim size volume 554.4
 makeup 554.12

trinity three 876.1
 threeness 876.2
 Godhead 677.9
trinket gewgaw 498.4
 toy 743.16
 trifle 998.5
Trinkgeld 478.5
trinomial
 n three 876.1
 adj terminological 527.17
trio cooperation 450.1
 part music 708.18
 three 876.1
trip
 n journey 177.5
 flight 184.9
 tumble 194.3
 bungle 414.5
 misdeed 655.2
 group of animals 770.5
 slip 975.4
 illusion 976.1
 figment of the imagination 986.5
 v use 87.22
 speed 174.8
 way of walking 177.28
 tumble 194.8
 trap 356.20
 caper 366.6
 overcome 412.7
 bungle 414.11
 go wrong 654.9
 explode 671.14
 dance 705.5
 play 743.23
 fell 913.5
 err 975.9
 dream 986.17
tripartite 878.4
tripe food 10.20
 bull 520.3
triple
 n game 745.3
 v intensify 251.5
 play 745.5
 triplicate 877.2
 adj three 876.3
 triplicate 877.3
triple crown
 ecclesiastical insignia 647.4
 horse racing 757.1
 three 876.1
triple play 745.3
triplet note 709.14
 tempo 709.24
 poetry 720.9
 three 876.1
triplicate
 n reproduce 785.3
 triplication 877.1
 v copy 785.8
 triple 877.2
 adj triple 877.3
tripod three 876.1
 fire iron 1020.12
tripping
 n hallucination 976.7
 adj high 87.24
 harmonious 533.8
 fluent 544.9

trip up
 abase 137.5
 trap 356.20
 overcome 412.7
 discompose 811.4
 fell 913.5
 make a boner 975.15
 distract 985.6
tripwire 1006.5
trisect 878.3
trite corny 117.9
 habitual 373.14
 commonplace 864.16
 well-known 928.27
 aphoristic 974.6
 trivial 998.19
tritium 1038.5
Triton
 spirit of the sea 240.4
 water god 678.10
triumph
 n rejoicing 116.1
 great success 409.3
 victory 411.1
 celebration 487.1
 crowing 502.4
 v best 249.7
 win through 409.13
 prevail 411.3
 exult 502.9
triumphant
 successful 409.14
 victorious 411.7
 crowing 502.13
triumvirate
 cooperation 450.1
 government 612.4
 three 876.1
trivet
 three 876.1
 fire iron 1020.12
trivia 551.1
trivial
 insignificant 248.6
 inadequate 250.7
 shallow 276.5
 worthless 391.11
 quibbling 936.14
 trifling 998.19
troglodyte
 barbarian 497.7
 ancient 842.7
troika
 cooperation 450.1
 three 876.1
Trojan horse
 subversive 357.11
 language 1042.13
troll
 n round 708.19
 v fish 382.10
 sing 708.38
 push 904.9
 pull 905.4
 roll 915.10
trolley handcar 179.16
 streetcar 179.17
trollop reprobate 660.4
 strumpet 665.14
 slob 810.7
trombonist 710.4

troop
military unit 461.22
company 770.3
group of animals 770.5
trooper
cavalryman 461.12
war-horse 461.30
policeman 1008.15
trophy
desire 100.11
victory 411.1
monument 549.12
laurel 646.3
tennis 748.1
memento 989.7
good thing 999.5
tropical 1019.24
tropical fish 311.31
Tropic of Cancer 231.3
Tropic of Capricorn 231.3
tropics zone 231.3
hot place 1019.11
trot
n run 174.3
gait 177.12
old woman 304.3
translation 341.3
repetitiousness 849.4
v speed 174.8
go on horseback 177.34
depart 188.7
trot out 348.5
trotter foot 199.5
race horse 311.14
jockey 757.2
troubadour
wanderer 178.2
minstrel 710.14
poet 720.11
trouble
n annoyance 96.2
affliction 96.8
anxiety 126.1
imposition 643.1
exertion 725.1
commotion 810.4
inconvenience 996.3
adversity 1011.1
impediment 1012.6
the matter 1013.3
v distress 96.16
vex 98.15
excite 105.14
concern 126.4
presume upon 640.7
discompose 811.4
agitate 917.10
inconvenience 996.4
beset 1013.13
trouble-free
perfect 1002.6
unhazardous 1007.5
troublemaker
rebel 327.5
instigator 375.11
mischief-maker 593.2
troubleshooter 396.10
troubleshooting 466.1
trouble spot 458.1
trough
n atmosphere 184.32

wave 238.14
channel 239.1
gutter 239.3
cavity 284.2
valley 284.9
trench 290.2
oscillation 916.4
v excavate 284.15
furrow 290.3
trounce best 249.7
defeat 412.9
criticize 510.20
whip 604.13
troupe
n cast 707.11
company 770.3
v act 704.29
trousers 5.18
trousseau 5.2
trove find 472.6
discovery 941.1
trowel 1040.2
truant
n absentee 222.5
shirker 368.3
wretch 660.2
adj absent without leave
222.13
truce armistice 465.5
pause 857.3
truck
n lorry 179.12
communication 343.1
rubbish 391.5
impedimenta 471.3
commerce 731.1
groceries 735.7
relation 775.1
v haul 176.13
trade 731.15
truculent
cruel 144.26
warlike 458.21
gruff 505.7
trudge
n slow motion 175.2
walk 177.10
v plod 175.7
way of walking 177.28
true
v make agree 788.7
adj straight 277.6
firm 359.12
observant 434.4
devoted 587.21
honest 644.16
trustworthy 644.19
faithful 644.20
orthodox 687.7
real 761.15
certain 970.13
truthful 973.13
true believer
orthodox Christian 687.4
believer 953.9
true blue fidelity 644.7
person of honor 644.8
true course
direction 161.2
course 184.34
true meaning 518.1

true to form
typical 349.15
characteristic 865.13
true to life
descriptive 349.14
lifelike 784.16
genuine 973.15
truism
generalization 864.8
axiom 974.2
truly
adv really 761.16
certainly 970.23
interj yes 332.18
trump
n good person 659.2
bridge 758.3
expedient 995.2
v excel 249.6
trump card
opportunity 843.2
influence 894.1
trumped-up 354.28
trumpet
n blare 53.5
v blare 53.10
proclaim 352.13
flaunt 501.17
praise 509.12
speak 524.25
blow a horn 708.42
truncate excise 255.10
deform 265.7
shorten 268.6
truncheon
n scepter 417.9
v whip 604.13
trundle push 904.9
roll 915.10
trunk
cylinder 282.4
nose 283.8
stem 310.21
line 347.17
base 901.8
body 1052.3
trunk line 347.17
trunks 5.29
truss
n bundle 770.8
v bundle 770.20
bind 800.9
trust
n hope 124.1
estate 471.4
commission 615.1
association 617.9
credit 622.1
investment company
737.16
belief 953.1
confidence 970.5
v hope 124.7
commit 478.16
give credit 622.6
believe 953.10
confide in 953.17
trustee fiduciary 470.5
recipient 479.3
treasurer 729.12
trust fund 737.16

trustworthy
trusty 644.19
believable 953.24
reliable 970.17
unhazardous 1007.5
trusty
n prisoner 429.11
person of honor 644.8
adj trustworthy 644.19
dependable 953.22
believable 953.24
reliable 970.17
truth
honesty 644.3
reality 761.2
certainty 970.1
trueness 973.1
axiom 974.2
**the truth, the whole truth, and
nothing but the truth**
973.3
the truth of the matter
fact 761.3
existence 761.4
the real story 973.3
try
n attempt 403.3
test 942.2
v refine 79.22
attempt 403.6
try a case 598.18
experiment 942.8
sit in judgment 946.12
trying
n experiment 942.1
adj weakening 16.20
fatiguing 21.13
oppressive 98.24
examining 938.37
experimental 942.11
adverse 1011.13
troublesome 1013.18
tryout
audition 48.2
preparation 405.1
theatrical performance
704.12
workout 942.3
tryst 582.9
T-shirt 5.15
T square
instrument 200.6
straightedge 277.3
tsunami wave 238.14
upheaval 671.5
wave 916.4
tub
n bath 79.8
washbasin 79.12
car 179.10
ship 180.1
heavyweight 257.12
v wash 79.19
tubby corpulent 257.18
stubby 268.10
tube
n train 179.14
pipe 239.6
cylinder 282.4
wave 916.4
electronics 1033.10

v transport 176.14
tuber 310.22
tuberculosis
  epidemic 85.5
  white plague 85.17
tubing 239.6
tub-thumper 543.4
tubular tubate 239.16
  cylindric 282.11
tuck
  n food 10.2
  fold 291.1
  game 746.3
  race 753.3
  v fold 291.5
tuckered out 21.8
tuff 1059.1
tuft flock 3.6
  beard 3.8
  feather 3.16
  growth 310.2
  bunch 770.7
tug
  n strain 725.2
  pull 905.2
  attraction 907.1
  v strain 725.10
  pull 905.4
  attract 907.4
tug-of-war fight 457.4
  pulling 905.1
tuition 568.1
tumble
  n fall 194.3
  collapse 410.3
  jumble 810.3
  flounder 917.8
  v be excited 105.18
  pitch 182.55
  fall 194.8
  be destroyed 395.22
  lose 412.12
  confuse 811.3
  fell 913.5
  wallow 915.13
  flounder 917.15
  confound 945.3
tummy goozle 2.19
  middle 819.1
tummyache 26.5
tumor symptom 85.9
  growth 85.39
  swelling 283.4
tumult noise 53.3
  excitement 105.4
  bustle 330.4
  turbulence 671.2
  commotion 810.4
  agitation 917.1
tundra plain 236.1
  cold place 1023.4
tune
  n melody 708.2
  harmony 708.3
  air 708.4
  pitch 709.4
  v fit 405.8
  harmonize 708.35
  tune up 708.36
  make agree 788.7
  organize 808.10

rearrange 808.13
tune in
  listen in 1034.27
  receive 1036.17
tune out exclude 773.4
  be inattentive 984.2
  listen in 1034.27
tune up tune 708.36
  organize 808.10
  rearrange 808.13
  listen in 1034.27
tuning fork 711.22
tunnel
  n lair 228.26
  channel 239.1
  cave 284.5
  passageway 383.3
  entrenchment 460.5
  v deepen 275.8
  excavate 284.15
tunnel vision
  faulty eyesight 28.1
  narrow-mindedness 980.1
turbid
  disorderly 810.13
  opaque 1031.3
  fluid 1061.4
  slimy 1062.14
turbine 904.6
turbocharger 756.1
turbojet 181.3
turbulent
  noisy 53.13
  tumultuous 105.24
  stormy 318.23
  rebellious 327.11
  bustling 330.20
  violent 671.18
  disorderly 810.13
  agitated 917.16
turd feces 12.4
  bad person 660.5
turf abode 228.1
  sod 310.6
  arena 463.1
  occupation 724.4
  horse racing 757.1
  sphere of influence 894.4
turgid
  distended 259.13
  bulged 283.16
  pompous 501.22
  stiff 534.3
  bombastic 545.9
turkey
  poultry 311.29
  failure 410.2
  loser 410.8
  stage show 704.4
  game 750.2
Turkish bath 79.8
turmoil
  excitement 105.4
  anarchy 418.2
  turbulence 671.2
  jumble 810.3
  commotion 810.4
  agitation 917.1
turn
  n looks 33.4
  inclination 100.3

start 131.3
  act of kindness 143.7
  deviation 164.1
  journey 177.5
  walk 177.10
  bias 204.3
  form 262.1
  distortion 265.1
  bend 279.3
  act 328.3
  aptitude 413.5
  show business 704.7
  ornament 709.18
  transaction 731.4
  trading 737.19
  ski move 753.3
  race 756.3
  bout 825.2
  shift 825.3
  crisis 843.4
  round 850.3
  change 852.1
  reversion 859.1
  tendency 896.1
  circuitousness 914.1
  circuit 914.2
  whirl 915.2
  disposition 978.3
  v direct 161.5
  take direction 161.7
  turn round 163.9
  deviate 164.3
  change course 182.30
  oblique 204.9
  distort 265.5
  curve 279.6
  convolve 281.4
  blunt 286.2
  ski 753.4
  recur 850.5
  be changed 852.6
  change 854.5
  turn back 859.5
  tend 896.3
  go around 914.6
  rotate 915.9
turn a blind eye
  take 134.8
  exclude 773.4
  be inattentive 984.2
turnabout
  n regression 163.3
  reverse 363.1
  apostate 363.5
  change 852.1
  reversion 859.1
  v turn 163.9
turn a deaf ear
  be deaf 49.4
  show no mercy 146.2
  exclude 773.4
turn against
  act the traitor 645.15
  defect 858.13
turnaround
  n regression 163.3
  reverse 363.1
  v turn 163.9
turn aside
  deviate 164.3
  avoid 164.6

disincline 379.4
  fend off 460.10
  digress 538.9
  be changed 852.6
  pull back 903.7
  prevent 1012.14
turn away avoid 164.6
  reject 372.2
  disincline 379.4
turn back
  put back 163.8
  avoid 164.6
  change course 182.30
  repeat 849.11
  convert 858.11
  change back 859.5
  repulse 908.3
turn back the clock
  make young 301.8
  be conservative 853.6
turncoat
  n traitor 357.10
  apostate 363.5
  convert 858.8
  adj traitorous 645.22
turn down invert 205.5
  refuse 442.3
turn down the volume 670.6
turned 393.41
turn in go to bed 22.18
  invert 205.5
  betray 645.14
turn informer 551.12
turning point
  crisis 843.4
  crucial moment 843.5
  urgency 997.4
  salient point 997.6
turn in one's badge 448.2
turn inside out
  invert 205.5
  ransack 938.33
turn into
  translate 341.12
  become 761.12
  be changed 852.6
  convert 858.11
  be converted into 858.17
turnip 832.6
turn loose 431.5
turn of events 831.2
turn off offend 98.11
  disincline 379.4
  shut off 857.12
  dismiss 909.18
  stop 909.19
  electrify 1032.26
turn of phrase 529.1
turn of the screw 251.2
turn on excite 105.12
  rouse 375.19
  inaugurate 818.11
  result from 887.5
  depend 959.6
  electrify 1032.26
turn on a dime 163.9
turn one's back on
  quit 188.9
  slight 340.8
  defect 370.6
  reject 372.2

two-faced
falsehearted 354.31
deceitful 356.22
treacherous 645.21
two 873.6
twofold 874.5
two of a kind 784.5
two-party system 609.24
two-sided sided 218.7
ambiguous 539.4
two 873.6
two-timer cheat 357.3
criminal 660.9
two-way 777.11
tycoon ruler 575.9
businessman 730.1
personage 997.8
type
n omen 133.3
form 262.1
measure 300.2
representative 349.7
preference 371.5
symbol 517.2
sign 518.6
print 548.6
nature 767.4
model 786.1
example 786.2
kind 809.3
specialty 866.1
oddity 870.4
disposition 978.3
v write 547.19
classify 809.6
type A 2.25
type AB 2.25
Type A behavior 321.1
type B 2.25
Type B behavior 321.1
typeface 548.6
type O 2.25
typeset 548.19
typesetter 548.12
type size 548.6
typewritten 547.22
typhoon
windstorm 318.12
whirlwind 318.14
storm 671.4
typical typic 349.15
indicative 517.23
model 786.8
classificational 809.7
normal 869.8
typify augur 133.12
designate 517.18
typographer 548.12
typographical error 975.3
tyranny force 424.2
subjection 432.1
government 612.4
absolutism 612.9
despotism 612.10
tyrant 575.14
ubiquitous
omnipresent 221.13
almighty 677.17
thorough 794.10
recurrent 849.13
U-boat 180.9

udder 283.6
UFO 1075.3
ugly
unpleasant 98.17
irascible 110.20
dangerous 1006.9
unsightly 1015.6
ugly duckling
nonconformist 868.3
eyesore 1015.4
UHF 1034.12
UK 232.4
ulcer 85.37
ulterior
additional 253.10
thither 261.10
secret 345.11
extraneous 774.5
ultimate
n acme of perfection 1002.3
adj top 198.10
farthest 261.12
completing 407.9
mandatory 420.12
ending 820.10
final 820.11
eventual 831.11
future 839.8
ultimatum
warning 399.1
demand 421.1
last word 439.3
condition 959.2
ultra
n radical 611.12
adj extreme 247.13
ultraconservative
n political principles 611.9
conservative 853.4
adj conservative 611.17
radical 611.20
political 853.8
ultrahigh frequency 1034.12
ultramodern 841.13
ultrasonic
acoustic 50.17
supersonic 174.16
ultrasound sound 50.1
diagnosis 91.9
ultraviolet light 1025.1
ultra-violet radiation 1037.1
Ulysses 178.2
umber 40.3
umbilical 208.11
umbrage offense 152.2
foliage 310.18
shadow 1027.3
umbrella
parachute 181.13
Air Force mission 184.11
gamp 295.7
safeguard 1008.3
shade 1028.1
umlaut 524.13
umpire
n arbitrator 466.4
judge 596.1
game 745.3
referee 747.3
mediator 748.2
linesman 749.6

ruler 946.6
v mediate 466.6
play 745.5
sit in judgment 946.12
UN 614.1
unabashed
brazen 142.11
undaunted 492.21
immodest 666.6
unabated
unweakened 15.21
undiminished 247.14
unmitigated 671.17
unable incapable 19.14
incompetent 414.19
unabridged 792.12
unacceptable
inadmissible 108.10
unpraiseworthy 510.24
unwelcome 586.9
unaccompanied
separate 802.20
alone 872.8
unaccountable
lawless 418.5
exempt 430.30
inexplicable 522.18
inconstant 854.7
fantastic 870.12
uncertain 971.16
purposeless 972.16
unaccustomed 374.4
unadorned mere 248.8
natural 416.6
undecorated 499.8
elegant 533.6
plain-speaking 535.3
simple 798.6
unadulterated
clean 79.25
unadorned 499.8
unmixed 798.7
unqualified 960.2
genuine 973.15
perfect 1002.6
unaffected
unmoved 94.11
unyielding 361.9
natural 416.6
tasteful 496.8
plain 499.7
elegant 533.6
plain-speaking 535.3
informal 581.3
undeceptive 644.18
uninfluenced 895.5
genuine 973.15
unaffectionate
unfeeling 94.9
unkind 144.16
unafraid
unfearing 492.20
confident 970.21
unaided
adj alone 872.8
adv singly 872.13
unalterable
unyielding 361.9
unchangeable 855.17
inflexible 1046.12
unamazed 123.3

unambiguous
clear 521.11
certain 970.13
unambitious
undesirous 102.8
modest 139.9
unanimous
solid 332.15
agreeing 788.9
unannounced 131.10
unanswerable
exempt 430.30
obvious 970.15
unanticipated
unexpected 131.10
sudden 830.5
unappealing 98.17
unappeased 100.27
unappetizing
unsavory 64.5
unpleasant 98.17
unappreciated 99.9
unapprehended 930.17
unapproachable
peerless 249.15
out-of-the-way 261.9
reticent 344.10
aloof 583.6
inaccessible 967.9
unarguable 970.15
unarmed unfitted 406.9
unprotected 1006.14
unaroused 173.14
unashamed
unregretful 114.4
immodest 666.6
unaspiring
undesirous 102.8
modest 139.9
unimaginative 987.5
unassailable 15.19
unassisted 872.8
unassuming
modest 139.9
natural 416.6
plain 499.7
informal 581.3
undeceptive 644.18
genuine 973.15
unattached
free 430.21
separate 802.20
unattainable
impracticable 967.8
inaccessible 967.9
unattended
separate 802.20
alone 872.8
unprotected 1006.14
unattracted 102.8
unauthorized
prohibited 444.7
illegal 674.6
unavailable 967.9
unavailing
ineffective 19.15
useless 391.9
unavoidable 963.15
unaware
insensible 94.10
inexpectant 131.9

unconscious 930.13
unawed
unastonished 123.3
undaunted 492.21
unbalanced
eccentric 160.12
unjust 650.9
ill-balanced 791.5
insane 926.26
unbathed 80.20
unbearable
insufferable 98.25
downright 247.12
unbeatable
impregnable 15.19
peerless 249.15
unbeaten
unused 390.12
undefeated 411.8
new 841.7
unbecoming
vulgar 497.10
disgraceful 661.11
indecent 666.5
inappropriate 789.7
unbefitting
inappropriate 789.7
untimely 844.6
inexpedient 996.5
unbelievable
fantastic 870.12
incredible 955.10
unbend relax 20.7
straighten 277.5
moderate 670.9
yield 1047.7
unbiased
impartial 649.10
unprejudiced 979.12
unbidden
unwanted 99.11
voluntary 324.7
unwelcome 586.9
unblemished
clean 79.25
honest 644.13
spotless 657.7
chaste 664.4
perfect 1002.6
unblinking
unnervous 129.2
alert 339.14
undaunted 492.21
unblock unclose 292.12
facilitate 1014.7
unborn 762.10
unbound
unrestricted 430.27
untied 430.28
liberated 431.10
unfastened 802.22
unbowed
unweakened 15.21
straight 277.6
undefeated 411.8
unbreakable firm 15.18
nonbreakable 1049.5
unbreatheable 345.11
unbridled
lawless 418.5
unrestrained 430.24

profligate 665.25
intemperate 669.7
unruly 671.19
excessive 993.16
unbroken
directional 161.12
straight 277.6
smooth 287.10
unsubject 430.29
uniform 781.5
continuous 812.8
constant 847.5
undamaged 1002.8
unbuckle
loose 431.6
detach 802.10
unburden
relieve 120.7
lighten 298.6
unload 909.23
unbutton 802.10
uncage 431.6
uncalled-for
unwanted 99.11
impudent 142.10
voluntary 324.7
needless 391.10
superfluous 993.17
uncanny
awesome 122.11
creepy 127.31
deathly 307.29
weird 988.9
uncap 292.12
uncaring
n carelessness 340.2
incuriosity 982.1
adj apathetic 94.13
careless 340.11
unceasing
continuous 812.8
perpetual 829.7
constant 847.5
continuing 856.7
uncensored 430.28
unceremonious 581.3
uncertain
inconspicuous 32.6
irresolute 362.9
ambiguous 539.4
speculative 759.27
relative 775.7
irregular 851.3
inconstant 854.7
doubting 955.9
unsure 971.16
unsafe 1006.11
uncertified
unproved 958.8
unauthoritative 971.21
unchained
unbound 430.28
unfastened 802.22
unchallenged
unanimous 332.15
undoubted 970.16
unchangeable
unyielding 361.9
uniform 781.5
permanent 853.7
not to be changed 855.17

unchanging
almighty 677.17
uniform 781.5
constant 847.5
permanent 853.7
unchangeable 855.17
unchaperoned 340.14
uncharitable
unbenevolent 144.17
narrow-minded 980.10
uncharted 930.17
unchaste
unvirtuous 654.12
sensual 663.5
lascivious 665.23
obscene 666.9
unchecked
lawless 418.5
unrestrained 430.24
permitted 443.16
candid 644.17
permanent 853.7
unauthoritative 971.21
uncirculated 841.9
uncircumcised 688.10
uncivilized
cruel 144.26
unrefined 497.12
savage 671.21
unclad 6.13
unclasp release 475.4
detach 802.10
unclassified
open 348.10
unordered 810.12
unknown 930.17
uncle 559.3
unclean
unwashed 80.20
unvirtuous 654.12
unchaste 665.23
obscene 666.9
demoniac 680.17
terrible 1000.9
unclear
inconspicuous 32.6
faint 52.16
formless 263.4
obscure 522.15
illegible 522.19
vague 971.19
unclench 292.12
Uncle Sam
country 232.5
the government 612.3
unclog unclose 292.12
evacuate 909.22
facilitate 1014.7
unclothe 6.7
unclouded visible 31.6
unhidden 348.11
light 1025.31
transparent 1029.4
uncluttered 798.6
uncoded 521.12
uncoil disinvolve 798.5
unfold 861.7
uncollected accounts 628.1
uncolored
colorless 36.7
genuine 973.15

uncombed
unrefined 497.12
disheveled 810.14
uncomfortable
distressed 96.22
unpleasant 98.20
uncommitted
free 430.21
neutral 467.7
cautious 494.8
uncommon
remarkable 247.10
novel 841.11
infrequent 848.2
unusual 870.10
scarce 992.11
uncommunicative
silent 343.10
indisposed to communicate 344.8
secretive 345.15
cautious 494.8
inexpressive 522.20
unsociable 583.5
uncomplaining
content 107.7
resigned 134.10
submissive 433.12
uncompleted
unaccomplished 408.3
incomplete 795.4
uncomplexity
unadornment 499.3
facility 1014.1
uncomplicated
unadorned 499.8
uninvolved 798.8
easy 1014.13
uncomplimentary 510.21
uncomprehending
undiscerning 922.14
ignorant 930.12
uncompromising
unyielding 361.9
firm 425.7
unconcealed
visible 31.6
unhidden 348.11
unconcerned
insensible 25.6
apathetic 94.13
uninterested 102.7
nonchalant 106.15
incurious 982.3
uncondemned 148.7
unconditional
unrestricted 430.27
thorough 794.10
unqualified 960.2
unconducive 391.14
unconfined 430.27
unconfirmed
unproved 958.8
unauthoritative 971.21
unconnected
unintelligible 522.13
unrelated 776.6
separate 802.20
incoherent 804.4
discontinuous 813.4
illogical 936.11

unconquered
undefeated 411.8
unsubject 430.29
unconscionable
downright 247.12
overpriced 632.12
dishonest 645.16
unjustifiable 650.12
violent 671.16
excessive 993.16
unconscious
n psyche 92.28
adj asleep 22.22
senseless 25.8
subconscious 92.42
insensible 94.10
unpremeditated
365.11
unaware 930.13
instinctive 934.6
involuntary 963.14
unintentional 972.17
oblivious 984.7
abstracted 985.11
inanimate 1055.5
unconsidered
neglected 340.14
unheeded 340.15
unexamined 340.16
unpremeditated 365.11
unwise 923.10
unthought-of 933.5
unconstitutional 674.6
unconstrained
communicative 343.10
unrestrained 430.24
informal 581.3
candid 644.17
intemperate 669.7
unconsumed
remaining 256.7
unused 390.12
uncontaminated
natural 416.6
perfect 1002.6
uncontested
unanimous 332.15
believed 953.23
undoubted 970.16
uncontrollable
frenzied 105.25
ungovernable 361.12
rabid 926.30
inevitable 963.15
unconventional
informal 581.3
unorthodox 868.6
eccentric 927.5
unconvinced
unbelieving 955.8
uncertain 971.16
uncooked 406.10
uncooperative
inconsiderate 144.18
insubordinate 327.9
obstinate 361.8
unconsenting 442.6
oppositional 451.8
resistant 453.5
uncoordinated 414.20
uncork 292.12

uncorroborated
unproved 958.8
unauthoritative 971.21
uncounted
innumerable 884.10
undecided 971.18
uncouple 802.8
uncouth
countrified 233.7
bungling 414.20
unrefined 497.12
inelegant 534.2
vulgar 666.8
uncover divest 6.5
disinter 192.11
unclose 292.12
disclose 351.4
greet 585.10
unearth 941.4
uncritical
obedient 326.3
unmeticulous 340.13
uncriticizing 509.18
undiscriminating 945.5
credulous 954.8
unction balm 86.11
flattery 511.2
function of Holy Ghost
677.15
sanctimony 693.1
sacred unction 701.5
ointment 1056.3
lubrication 1056.6
uncultivated
countrified 233.7
undeveloped 406.12
fallow 406.14
unrefined 497.12
unproductive 891.4
unlearned 930.14
uncultured
countrified 233.7
undeveloped 406.12
unrefined 497.12
unlearned 930.14
uncurl 277.5
uncut unformed 263.5
undeveloped 406.12
undivided 792.11
complete 794.9
undamaged
preserved 397.13
intact 792.10
unharmed 1002.8
safe 1007.4
undaunted
persevering 360.8
undismayed 492.21
undecided
irresolute 362.9
undetermined 971.18
undecided issue 971.8
undeclared 519.9
undefeated 411.8
undefended 1006.14
undefined
inconspicuous 32.6
formless 263.4
anonymous 528.3
almighty 677.17
vague 971.19

undeflected 277.6
undeformed 1002.8
undemanding
unstrict 426.5
undiscriminating 945.5
undeniable
downright 247.12
real 761.15
obvious 970.15
undependable
fickle 364.6
untrustworthy 645.19
inconstant 854.7
unreliable 971.20
unsafe 1006.11
under
adj lower 274.8
adv below 274.10
prep below 274.11
beneath 432.17
underachiever 572.4
under a cloud
accused 599.15
in disrepute 661.13
unreliable 955.11
doubted 955.12
under advisement 938.38
underage
n deficiency 795.2
shortcoming 911.1
adj immature 301.10
under arrest 429.22
under a spell 691.12
under attack
adj accused 599.15
adv under fire 459.31
underbelly
digestive system 2.18
bottom 199.1
underbrush 310.17
undercarriage 901.6
the underclass
the underprivileged 607.8
the poor 619.3
unfortunate 1011.7
underclothes 5.22
undercoating
color 35.8
painting 35.12
under consideration 938.38
under construction
in preparation 405.22
in production 892.21
under control
adj restrained 428.13
adv in hand 612.20
undercooked
underdone 11.9
raw 406.10
under cost 631.3
undercover
adj covert 345.12
adv secretly 345.17
undercurrent
feeling 93.1
flow 238.4
wind 318.1
opposition 451.1
implication 519.2
counterforce 900.4
hidden danger 1006.5

undercut
sell 734.8
disprove 958.4
underdeveloped
undeveloped 406.12
incomplete 795.4
underdog 412.5
underdone
undercooked 11.9
raw 406.10
under duress 514.4
underestimate
n underestimation 950.1
v misestimate 950.2
under fire
adj accused 599.15
adv under attack 459.31
underfoot 274.10
under full steam 174.20
undergarments 5.22
undergo afford 626.7
experience 831.8
undergraduate
n undergrad 572.6
adj studentlike 572.12
underground
n train 179.14
dissent 333.1
secret passage 346.5
subversive 357.11
irregular 461.16
adj subterranean 275.12
dissenting 333.6
covert 345.12
concealed 346.11
adv beneath the sod 309.23
secretly 345.17
undergrowth 310.17
underhanded
covert 345.12
deceitful 356.22
dishonest 645.16
under handicap 1012.21
under house arrest
concealed 346.11
under arrest 429.22
under investigation 938.38
underlayer
bottom 199.1
layer 296.1
underlie base on 199.6
lie low 274.5
be latent 519.3
support 901.21
underline
n line 517.6
v mark 517.19
emphasize 997.14
underling
inferior 250.2
subordinate 432.5
retainer 577.1
under lock and key
jailed 429.21
in safety 1007.6
underlying
basic 199.8
latent 519.5
essential 767.9
undermine
weaken 16.10

sap 393.15
overthrow 395.20
refute 958.5
underneath
n bottom 199.1
prep below 274.11
under 432.17
under no circumstances
adv no way 248.11
interj by no means 335.9
undernourish 270.12
under oath
adj promissory 436.7
adv affirmatively 334.10
under one's nose
before 216.12
near 223.20
openly 348.15
under one's thumb
subjugated 432.14
influenceable 894.15
underpaid 625.12
underpass 383.3
underpinning 901.6
under power 182.63
under pressure 325.8
underprice 633.6
underprivileged
inferior 250.6
indigent 619.8
unfortunate 1011.14
under protest
adj protesting 333.7
adv reluctantly 325.9
underrated 950.3
under restraint
restrained 428.13
confined 429.19
under sail
under way 172.9
traveling 182.63
underscore
n line 517.6
v mark 517.19
emphasize 997.14
undersecretary 575.17
undersell 734.8
underside 199.1
under siege 459.31
the undersigned 332.7
undersized
dwarf 258.13
lean 270.17
understaffed 992.9
understand
interpret 341.9
comprehend 521.7
know 928.12
suppose 951.10
understanding
n unanimity 332.5
obligation 436.2
compact 437.1
accord 455.1
compromise 468.1
entente 788.2
intellect 919.1
intelligence 920.1
comprehension 928.3
adj patient 134.9
pitying 145.7

in accord 455.3
intelligent 920.12
sagacious 920.16
knowing 928.15
understated 496.8
understructure
understruction 266.3
foundation 901.6
understudy
n deputy 576.1
supporting actor 707.7
substitute 862.2
v represent 576.14
under surveillance 938.38
under suspicion
adj doubted 955.12
adv on trial 942.14
undertake
practice 328.8
attempt 403.6
assume 404.3
commit 436.5
contract 437.5
set to work 725.15
undertaker 309.8
under the circumstances
766.11
under-the-counter
covert 345.12
illegal 674.6
under the gun
obligatorily 424.15
under duress 514.4
under the impression 953.21
under the influence
intoxicated 87.23
inebriated 88.31
under the sun
adj existent 761.13
adv everywhere 158.13
on earth 234.9
under the surface
adj latent 519.5
adv internally 207.9
under the table
adj dead-drunk 88.32
adv surreptitiously 345.18
under the weather 85.56
under the wire 846.19
undertone
murmur 52.4
milieu 209.3
meaning 518.1
implication 519.2
undertow flow 238.4
opposition 451.1
hidden danger 1006.5
undervalue 950.2
underwater 275.13
underwater explorer 240.8
under way
adj undertaken 404.7
in preparation 405.22
happening 831.9
adv under sail 172.9
making way 182.63
underwear 5.22
underweight
n leanness 270.5
weight 297.1
adj lean 270.17

lightweight 298.13
underworld 275.3
under wraps
secret 345.11
concealed 346.11
underwrite
ratify 332.12
promise 436.4
secure 438.9
protect 1008.18
underwriter
endorser 332.7
guarantor 438.6
insurance 1008.4
undeserved
undue 640.9
unjust 650.9
undesirable
n outcast 586.4
bad person 660.1
adj unpleasant 98.17
unacceptable 108.10
unwelcome 586.9
inexpedient 996.5
undetached
partial 650.11
discriminatory 980.12
undetectable 32.5
undetermined
irresolute 362.9
unproved 958.8
undecided 971.18
vague 971.19
chance 972.15
undeveloped
immature 301.10
unfinished 406.12
inexperienced 414.17
incomplete 795.4
new 841.7
imperfect 1003.4
undeviating
directional 161.12
straight 277.6
uniform 781.5
unchangeable 855.17
exact 973.17
undifferentiated
identical 778.7
uniform 781.5
simple 798.6
continuous 812.8
general 864.11
indistinguishable
945.6
undigested 406.11
undignified
vulgar 497.10
inelegant 534.2
undiluted 798.7
undiminished
unweakened 15.21
unabated 247.14
undivided 792.11
complete 794.9
undiscernible 32.5
undisciplined
disobedient 327.8
lawless 418.5
intemperate 669.7
inconstant 854.7

undisclosed
invisible 32.5
secret 345.11
unrevealed 346.12
unknown 930.17
undiscovered
unrevealed 346.12
unknown 930.17
undisguised
visible 31.6
unhidden 348.11
undeceptive 644.18
genuine 973.15
undismayed 492.21
undisputed
believed 953.23
undoubted 970.16
undistorted
straight 277.6
genuine 973.15
undisturbed
unexcited 106.11
untroubled 107.8
quiescent 173.12
undivided uncut 792.11
joined 800.13
one 872.7
undo take off 6.6
unnerve 128.10
unclose 292.12
do for 395.11
abolish 395.13
demolish 395.17
defeat 412.6
detach 802.10
neutralize 900.7
solve 940.2
undoing
destruction 395.1
defeat 412.1
disassembly 802.6
neutralization 900.2
undoubted
believed 953.23
not to be doubted 970.16
true 973.13
undress
n dishabille 5.20
unadornment 499.3
v unclothe 6.7
undue
overpriced 632.12
wrong 638.3
unowed 640.9
unjust 650.9
excessive 993.16
undulate
v maneuver 184.40
billow 238.22
recur 850.5
wave 916.11
adj wavy 281.10
unduplicated 337.6
undying
immortal 829.9
indestructible 855.18
continuing 856.7
uneager 102.8
unearned 640.9
unearth extract 192.10
uncover 941.4

unearthly
deathly 307.29
heavenly 681.12
godly 692.9
extraneous 774.5
odd 870.11
supernatural 870.15
unbelievable 955.10
weird 988.9
immaterial 1053.7

unease
unpleasure 96.1
discontent 108.1
anxiety 126.1
agitation 917.1

uneasy
pleasureless 96.20
distressed 96.22
restless 105.27
discontented 108.7
anxious 126.7
nervous 128.11
impatient 135.6
agitated 917.16

uneconomical 406.15

uneducated
vernacular 523.20
unlearned 930.14

unembellished
natural 416.6
unadorned 499.8
prosaic 721.5

unemotional 94.9

unemployed
motionless 173.13
idle 331.18
unused 390.12

unencumbered
lightened 298.11
unhampered 430.26

unending
continuous 812.8
perpetual 829.7
continuing 856.7

unendurable 98.25

unenjoyable
unpleasant 98.17
uninteresting 117.7

unenlightened
blind 30.9
ignorant 930.12

unenvied 156.9

unequaled 249.15

unequipped
unfitted 406.9
incompetent 414.19

unequivocal
downright 247.12
unrestricted 430.27
clear 521.11
candid 644.17
unqualified 960.2
certain 970.13

unerring
uncorrupt 653.8
infallible 970.19
exact 973.17

unescorted 872.8

unessential
n nonessential 768.2
adj needless 391.10

circumstantial 766.7
extrinsic 768.4
irrelevant 776.7
superfluous 993.17
insignificant 998.17

unestablished
unplaced 160.10
unproved 958.8
undecided 971.18

unethical
dishonest 645.16
vice-prone 654.11

uneven
rough 288.6
unjust 650.9
nonuniform 782.3
unequal 791.4
irregular 851.3
imperfect 1003.4

uneventful
uninteresting 117.7
tedious 118.9

unexamined 340.16

unexceptional
normal 869.8
ordinary 1005.8

unexhausted
unwearied 9.5
unweakened 15.21

unexpected
unanticipated 131.10
sudden 830.5
unusual 870.10
fantastic 870.12
improbable 969.3
chance 972.15

unexplained
unrevealed 346.12
unknown 930.17

unexplored
unexamined 340.16
unrevealed 346.12
unknown 930.17

unexposed
unrevealed 346.12
unknown 930.17

unfabricated 973.15

unfaded
unweakened 15.21
undamaged 1002.8

unfailing
persevering 360.8
faithful 644.20
permanent 853.7
reliable 970.17

unfair 650.10

unfaithful
nonobservant 435.5
faithless 645.20

unfamiliar
novel 841.11
unusual 870.10
ignorant 930.12
unknown 930.17

unfashionable
old-fashioned 842.16
unconventional 868.6

unfastened 802.22

unfathomable
abysmal 275.11
unintelligible 522.13

infinite 823.3

unfavorable
ominous 133.17
oppositional 451.8
disapproving 510.21
untimely 844.6
disadvantageous 996.6
bad 1000.7
adverse 1011.13

unfed fasting 515.5
ill-provided 992.12

unfeeling
n insensibility 25.1
unfeelingness 94.1
heartlessness 144.10
adj insensible 25.6
unemotional 94.9
heartless 144.25
pitiless 146.3
inanimate 1055.5

unfelt 25.6

unfertile 891.4

unfettered
unbound 430.28
unfastened 802.22

unfilled hungry 100.25
available 222.15

unfinished
undeveloped 406.12
unaccomplished 408.3
unskilled 414.16
incomplete 795.4
imperfect 1003.4

unfit
v disable 19.9
adj unable 19.14
unserviceable 391.14
unfitted 406.9
incompetent 414.19
wrong 638.3
inappropriate 789.7
untimely 844.6
inexpedient 996.5

unflagging
unweakened 15.21
industrious 330.22
persevering 360.8

unflappable
inexcitable 106.10
firm 359.12
stable 855.12

unflattering
undeceptive 644.18
genuine 973.15

unflavored 65.2

unflinching
unnervous 129.2
unhesitating 359.13
persevering 360.8
undaunted 492.21
stable 855.12

unfold spread 259.6
unclose 292.12
explain 341.10
manifest 348.5
disclose 351.4
amplify 538.7
unroll 861.7
result 887.4

unforced
adj voluntary 324.7

unrestrained 430.24
adv at will 323.5

unforeseen
unexpected 131.10
sudden 830.5
chance 972.15

unforgettable
never to be forgotten 989.26
notable 997.19

unforgivable
unjustifiable 650.12
wicked 654.16

unforgotten 989.23

unfortified
unmixed 798.7
unprotected 1006.14

unfortunate
n unlucky person 1011.7
adj ominous 133.17
unsuccessful 410.18
untimely 844.6
inexpedient 996.5
unlucky 1011.14

unfounded false 354.25
unsubstantial 764.8
baseless 936.13
unproved 958.8
unauthentic 975.19
illusory 976.9

unfreeze 1020.21

unfriendly
unpleasant 98.17
averse 99.8
oppositional 451.8
warlike 458.21
unsociable 583.5
inhospitable 586.7
inimical 589.9

unfrozen 1019.24

unfulfilled
pleasureless 96.20
discontented 108.7
unaccomplished 408.3

unfurl disclose 351.4
unfold 861.7

ungainly
bungling 414.20
ungraceful 1015.9

unglued
unnerved 128.14
unfastened 802.22

ungodly
unvirtuous 654.12
godless 695.17
unbelievable 955.10
execrable 1000.10

ungracious
unkind 144.16
discourteous 505.4
inhospitable 586.7

ungrammatical 531.4

ungrateful 151.4

ungrounded
unsubstantial 764.8
baseless 936.13

unguarded
negligent 340.10
unthinking 365.10
artless 416.5
candid 644.17
unintentional 972.17

unalert 984.8
unprotected 1006.14
unguided
  unlearned 930.14
  unintentional 972.17
unhampered
  communicative 343.10
  untrammeled 430.26
  unqualified 960.2
unhand liberate 431.5
  release 475.4
unhappy
  pleasureless 96.20
  discontented 108.7
  uncheerful 112.21
  disapproving 510.21
  untimely 844.6
  inexpedient 996.5
  unfortunate 1011.14
unharmed
  undamaged 1002.8
  safe 1007.4
unharness 431.6
unhealthy
  unhealthful 82.5
  healthless 85.54
  unwholesome 85.55
  bad 1000.7
  unsafe 1006.11
unheard-of
  wonderful 122.10
  unrenowned 661.14
  novel 841.11
  unusual 870.10
  unknown 930.17
unheated 1023.13
unheeded 340.15
unheralded 131.10
unhesitant 359.13
unhidden visible 31.6
  open 292.17
  unconcealed 348.11
unhinged
  dislocated 160.9
  insane 926.26
unhitch 802.10
unholy unsacred 686.3
  ungodly 695.17
  execrable 1000.10
unhook 802.10
unhurried slow 175.10
  leisurely 402.6
unhurt
  undamaged 1002.8
  safe 1007.4
unicellular
  cellular 305.19
  unipartite 872.11
unicorn rig 179.5
  heraldry 647.2
unidentified
  anonymous 528.3
  unknown 930.17
unidentified flying object
  1075.3
unidirectional
  directional 161.12
  unipartite 872.11
uniform
  n livery 5.7
  insignia 647.1

  soccer 752.1
  v outfit 5.41
  adj symmetric 264.4
  smooth 287.10
  equable 781.5
  agreeing 788.9
  simple 798.6
  orderly 807.6
  continuous 812.8
  regular 850.6
  one 872.7
  indistinguishable 945.6
unify identify 778.5
  put together 800.5
  combine 805.3
  reduce to unity 872.5
unilateral
  sided 218.7
  unipartite 872.11
unimaginable
  wonderful 122.10
  fantastic 870.12
  unbelievable 955.10
  impossible 967.7
unimaginative
  dull 117.8
  plain-speaking 535.3
  prosaic 721.5
  unfanciful 987.5
unimpaired
  sound 83.11
  intact 792.10
  undamaged 1002.8
unimpeachable
  honest 644.13
  inculpable 657.8
  believable 953.24
  obvious 970.15
  accurate 973.16
unimpeded 430.26
unimportant
  insignificant 248.6
  of no importance 998.16
  humble 137.10
unimpressed
  unaffected 94.11
  unastonished 123.3
unimpressive 998.17
uninfected 79.27
uninfluenced
  voluntary 324.7
  impartial 649.10
  unmoved 895.5
  unprejudiced 979.12
uninformed
  inexpectant 131.9
  ignorant 930.12
uninhabitable 586.8
uninhibited
  unrestrained 430.24
  profligate 665.25
  intemperate 669.7
uninitiated
  unskilled 414.16
  ignorant 930.12
uninjured 1002.8
uninspired
  unaffected 94.11
  unimaginative 987.5
unintelligent
  unskillful 414.15

  unintellectual 922.13
  ignorant 930.12
unintelligible 522.13
unintended
  unpremeditated 365.11
  unintentional 972.17
uninterrupted
  directional 161.12
  omnipresent 221.13
  straight 277.6
  persevering 360.8
  consistent 803.11
  continuous 812.8
  perpetual 829.7
  constant 847.5
uninvited
  unwanted 99.11
  voluntary 324.7
  unwelcome 586.9
uninvolved
  free 430.21
  neutral 467.7
  uncomplicated 798.8
  incurious 982.3
union
  convergence 169.1
  juxtaposition 223.3
  affiliation 450.2
  accord 455.1
  marriage 563.1
  association 617.1
  relation 775.1
  identification 778.2
  agreement 788.1
  joining 800.1
  binding 800.4
  combination 805.1
  concurrence 899.1
unique
  wonderful 122.10
  peerless 249.15
  original 337.5
  other 780.8
  novel 841.11
  infrequent 848.2
  characteristic 865.13
  unusual 870.10
  one 872.7
  sole 872.9
unisex 872.11
unison
  n unanimity 332.5
  accord 455.1
  harmony 708.3
  agreement 788.1
  simultaneity 836.1
  adj simultaneous 836.5
unit
  military unit 461.22
  something 763.3
  one 872.3
  individual 872.4
unite converge 169.2
  cooperate 450.3
  wed 563.14
  come together 770.16
  identify 778.5
  form a whole 792.7
  put together 800.5
  join 800.11
  combine 805.3

unify 872.5
  concur 899.2
United Kingdom 232.4
United Nations
  supranational government
    612.7
  United Nations 614.1
  League of Nations 614.1
United Press International
  555.3
United States Government
  613.2
United States of America
  232.3
unit of measurement 1032.1
unity accord 455.1
  sameness 778.1
  uniformity 781.1
  whole 792.1
  totality 792.5
  completeness 794.1
  simplicity 798.1
  oneness 872.1
  indivisibility 1045.2
universal
  n philosophy 932.2
  immaterialism 1053.3
  adj comprehensive 772.7
  whole 792.9
  thorough 794.10
  infinite 823.3
  general 864.14
  usual 869.9
  cosmic 1072.24
universal law 869.4
universe
  completeness 794.1
  outlook 978.2
  world 1072.1
university
  n college 567.5
  adj scholastic 567.13
UNIX 1042.12
unjust 650.9
unkempt rough 288.6
  unrefined 497.12
  slovenly 810.15
unkind
  nasty 144.16
  bad 1000.7
unknowing
  n ignorance 930.1
  adj ignorant 930.12
  unaware 930.13
unknown
  concealed 346.11
  anonymous 528.3
  unrenowned 661.14
  unbeknown 930.17
unlaced 802.22
unlatch unclose 292.12
  loose 431.6
unlawful
  prohibited 444.7
  wrong 638.3
  unjust 650.9
  illegal 674.6
unleash liberate 431.6
  detach 802.10
  loosen 804.3
unleavened 798.7

unless 959.16
unlicensed 444.7
unlighted 1027.13
unlike different 780.7
  dissimilar 787.4
  incomparable 943.9
unlikely 969.3
unlimber 1046.12
unlimited
  omnipotent 18.13
  unrestricted 430.27
  intemperate 669.7
  almighty 677.17
  infinite 823.3
  unqualified 960.2
unlisted number 347.12
unlit 1027.13
unlivable 586.8
unload relieve 120.7
  lighten 298.6
  deal 734.8
  sell 737.24
  off-load 909.23
  disembarrass 1014.9
unlock
  unclose 292.12
  explain 341.10
  loose 431.6
  solve 940.2
unloved 99.10
unlucky
  ominous 133.17
  speculative 759.27
  untimely 844.6
  unfortunate 1011.14
unmade
  unprepared 406.8
  uncreated 762.10
unmanageable
  ungovernable 361.12
  unwieldy 1013.19
unmaneuverable 1013.19
unmanned
  impotent 19.19
  terrified 127.26
  unnerved 128.14
  available 222.15
  downtrodden 432.16
  cowardly 491.10
unmarked
  unheeded 340.15
  undamaged 1002.8
unmarried
  n celibate 565.2
  adj unwedded 565.7
unmask 351.4
unmatched
  peerless 249.15
  dissimilar 787.4
  best 999.16
  first-rate 999.17
unmentionable
  indescribable 122.13
  base 661.12
unmerciful
  heartless 144.25
  pitiless 146.3
unmet 256.7
unmindful
  unconcerned 102.7
  inconsiderate 144.18

ungrateful 151.4
  careless 340.11
  unaware 930.13
  incurious 982.3
  inattentive 984.6
  forgetful 990.9
unmistakable
  distinct 31.7
  manifest 348.8
  clear 521.11
  unqualified 960.2
  certain 970.13
unmitigated
  downright 247.12
  undiminished 247.14
  unsoftened 671.17
  thorough 794.10
  changed 852.10
  unqualified 960.2
unmixed
  unmitigated 671.17
  unmingled 798.7
  perfect 1002.6
unmolested 1007.4
unmotivated 972.16
unmoved
  unaffected 94.11
  unastonished 123.3
  quiescent 173.12
  motionless 173.13
  unyielding 361.9
  uninfluenced 895.5
unnamed 528.3
unnatural
  heartless 144.25
  spurious 354.26
  affected 500.15
  elegant 533.9
  abnormal 870.9
  eccentric 927.5
unnavigable 276.6
unnecessary
  needless 391.10
  unessential 768.4
  superfluous 993.17
unneighborly 586.7
unnerving
  weakening 16.20
  frightening 127.28
  nerve-racking 128.15
unnoticed
  invisible 32.5
  unheeded 340.15
  unrenowned 661.14
unnumbered
  infinite 823.3
  innumerable
    884.10
unobjectionable
  desirable 100.30
  acceptable 107.12
  justifiable 600.14
  inculpable 657.8
  tolerable 999.20
unobliging 144.18
unobscured
  unhidden 348.11
  light 1025.31
unobserved
  invisible 32.5
  unheeded 340.15

unobstructed
  open 292.17
  unhampered 430.26
unobtainable 967.9
unobtrusive
  modest 139.9
  covert 345.12
  tasteful 496.8
unoccupied
  available 222.15
  idle 331.18
  leisure 402.5
  thoughtless 933.4
unofficial
  informal 581.3
  illegal 674.6
  unauthoritative 971.21
unopen 293.9
unopposed 332.15
unordered
  formless 263.4
  orderless 810.12
unordinary 870.10
unorganized
  formless 263.4
  unprepared 406.8
  unordered 810.12
  inorganic 1055.4
unorthodox
  nonorthodox 688.9
  nonuniform 782.3
  nonconformist 789.9
  unconventional 868.6
  erroneous 975.16
unpack disclose 351.4
  unload 909.23
unpaid due 623.10
  unremunerated 625.12
unpalatable
  unsavory 64.5
  unpleasant 98.17
unparalleled
  peerless 249.15
  extraordinary 870.14
  best 999.16
unpardonable
  unjustifiable 650.12
  wicked 654.16
unpayable
  irredeemable 625.13
  expensive 632.11
unperceptive
  insensible 25.6
  undiscerning 922.14
unperformed 408.3
unperturbed
  unexcited 106.11
  untroubled 107.8
  quiescent 173.12
unplanned
  unprepared 406.8
  unintentional 972.17
unpleasant
  unsavory 64.5
  unpleasing 98.17
  unlikable 99.7
  bad 1000.7
unplug 292.12
unpolished
  countrified 233.7
  rough 288.6

undeveloped 406.12
unskilled 414.16
unrefined 497.12
inelegant 534.2
unpolluted 79.25
unpopular
  disliked 99.9
  unrenowned 661.14
unpopulated 222.15
unpracticed
  unaccustomed 374.4
  inexperienced 414.17
unprecedented
  wonderful 122.10
  original 337.5
  unimitated 337.6
  extraordinary 870.14
unprecise
  unmeticulous 340.13
  inaccurate 975.17
unpredictable
  unexpected 131.10
  fickle 364.6
  unessential 768.4
  inconstant 854.7
  improbable 969.3
  uncertain 971.16
  chance 972.15
  unsafe 1006.11
unprejudiced 979.12
unpremeditated
  unmeditated 365.11
  unprepared 406.8
  premature 845.8
  unintentional 972.17
unprepared
  inexpectant 131.9
  careless 340.11
  unready 406.8
  unskilled 414.16
  premature 845.8
  unalert 984.8
unprepossessing 1015.7
unpretentious
  humble 137.10
  modest 139.9
  natural 416.6
  plain 499.7
  unselfish 652.5
unprincipled 645.16
unprintable 666.9
unprocessed 406.12
unproductive
  fruitless 391.12
  nonproductive 891.4
unprofessional 414.16
unprofitable
  fruitless 391.12
  inexpedient 996.5
  disadvantageous 996.6
unpronounced
  silent 51.10
  unexpressed 519.9
unprotected
  helpless 19.18
  unshielded 1006.14
unprovable
  controvertible 958.9
  uncertain 971.16
unproved
  unsound 936.12

not proved 958.8
unauthoritative 971.21
erroneous 975.16
unprovoked 640.9
unpublished 519.9
unqualified
   unable 19.14
   downright 247.12
   unfitted 406.9
   incompetent 414.19
   unrestricted 430.27
   inappropriate 789.7
   thorough 794.10
   unconditional 960.2
   genuine 973.15
   insufficient 992.9
   sound 1002.7
unquenchable
   greedy 100.27
   indestructible 855.18
unquestionable
   downright 247.12
   intrinsic 767.7
   believable 953.24
   obvious 970.15
   true 973.13
unravel extract 192.10
   explain 341.10
   extricate 431.7
   disinvolve 798.5
   come apart 802.9
   loosen 804.3
   solve 940.2
unreachable 967.9
unread 930.14
unreadable 522.19
unready
   inexpectant 131.9
   careless 340.11
   unprepared 406.8
   untimely 844.6
   late 846.16
   unalert 984.8
unreal
   spurious 354.26
   unrealistic 762.9
   thin 764.6
   illusory 976.9
   imaginary 986.19
unrealistic
   unreal 762.9
   imaginary 986.19
   visionary 986.24
unrealized
   invisible 32.5 ·
   unaccomplished 408.3
unreasonable
   capricious 364.5
   overpriced 632.12
   unjustifiable 650.12
   unwise 923.10
   fanatic 926.32
   illogical 936.11
   excessive 993.16
unreceptive
   inhospitable 586.7
   uninfluenceable 895.4
unrecognizable 32.6
unreconstructed
   impenitent 114.5
   ungovernable 361.12

unsubject 430.29
conservative 611.17
permanent 853.8
unrecorded 519.9
unredeemable 654.18
unreduced
   undiminished 247.14
   undivided 792.11
unrefined
   countrified 233.7
   rough 288.6
   coarse 294.6
   undeveloped 406.12
   unpolished 497.12
   ill-bred 505.6
   inelegant 534.2
   unlearned 930.14
unregenerate
   obstinate 361.8
   irreclaimable 654.18
   unsacred 686.3
   unredeemed 695.18
unregretful 114.4
unregulated
   permitted 443.16
   illegal 674.6
unrehearsed 365.12
unrelated 776.6
unrelaxed tense 128.13
   rigid 1046.11
unrelenting
   persevering 360.8
   unyielding 361.9
   firm 425.7
   wordy 538.12
   constant 847.5
unreliable fickle 364.6
   untrustworthy 645.19
   inconstant 854.7
   under a cloud 955.11
   undependable 971.20
   inauthentic 975.19
   unsafe 1006.11
unrelieved
   vacant 222.14
   downright 247.12
   same 781.6
   continuous 812.8
unreligious 695.15
unremarkable 1005.8
unremitting
   industrious 330.22
   persevering 360.8
   continuous 812.8
   perpetual 829.7
   constant 847.5
   unchangeable 855.17
   continuing 856.7
unremorseful
   unregretful 114.4
   pitiless 146.3
unrepentant 114.5
unrequited
   unthanked 151.5
   unpaid 625.12
unreserved
   communicative 343.10
   artless 416.5
   unrestrained 430.24
   candid 644.17
   thorough 794.10

unqualified 960.2
unresisting
   resigned 134.10
   submissive 433.12
unresolved
   remaining 256.7
   irresolute 362.9
unresponsive
   unfeeling 94.9
   heartless 144.25
   uninfluenceable 895.4
unrest
   trepidation 105.5
   motion 172.1
   agitation 917.1
unrestored 21.7
unrestrained
   fervent 93.18
   communicative 343.10
   capricious 364.5
   lawless 418.5
   lax 426.4
   unconstrained 430.24
   candid 644.17
   incontinent 665.24
   intemperate 669.7
   inconstant 854.7
   excessive 993.16
unrestricted
   undiminished 247.14
   open 292.17
   communicative 343.10
   unconfined 430.27
   thorough 794.10
   unqualified 960.2
unrevealing 346.15
unrewarded
   unthanked 151.5
   unpaid 625.12
unripe sour 67.5
   immature 301.10
   unprepared 406.11
   inexperienced 414.17
   untimely 844.6
   premature 845.8
   ignorant 930.12
unrivaled 249.15
unrobed 6.13
unroll unclose 292.12
   disclose 351.4
   unfold 861.7
unruffled
   unaffected 94.11
   unexcited 106.11
   quiescent 173.12
   smooth 287.10
   uniform 781.5
unruly
   defiant 327.10
   ungovernable 361.12
   anarchic 418.6
   unrestrained 430.24
   disorderly 671.19
unsafe 1006.11
unsaid tacit 51.11
   unexpressed 519.9
unsalvageable 125.15
unsanctioned 444.7
unsanitary 82.5
unsatisfactory
   dissatisfactory 108.9

disappointing 132.6
insufficient 992.9
unsaturated fat 1056.1
unsavory
   unpalatable 64.5
   insipid 65.2
   unpleasant 98.17
   dishonest 645.16
   disreputable 661.10
unscathed
   undamaged 1002.8
   safe 1007.4
unscented 72.5
unschooled
   unskilled 414.16
   unlearned 930.14
unscientific 936.11
unscramble
   disinvolve 798.5
   solve 940.2
   disembarrass 1014.9
unscratched 1002.8
unscrew 802.10
unscrubbed 80.20
unscrupulous
   unmeticulous 340.13
   dishonest 645.16
unseal 292.12
unsearched 340.16
unseasonable
   inappropriate 789.7
   anachronous 833.3
   untimely 844.6
   inexpedient 996.5
unseat
   dislodge 160.6
   depose 447.4
   disjoint 802.16
unseeing blind 30.9
   unwise 923.10
   unaware 930.13
unseemly
   vulgar 497.10
   inelegant 534.2
   wrong 638.3
   indecent 666.5
   inappropriate
     789.7
   inexpedient 996.5
unseen invisible 32.5
   unheeded 340.15
   unrevealed 346.12
unselfish
   liberal 485.4
   impartial 649.10
   selfless 652.5
unserviceable 391.14
unsettle excite 105.14
   disorder 810.9
   discompose 811.4
   agitate 917.10
   confuse 985.7
unshaded 348.11
unshakeable 326.3
unshaken
   unweakened 15.21
   unnervous 129.2
   firm 359.12
unshaven 3.25
unsheathed 6.12
unshielded 1006.14

unsightly
slovenly 810.15
ugly 1015.6
unsimulated 973.15
unskilled 414.16
unskilled laborer 726.2
unsmiling
solemn 111.3
unhappy 112.21
unsnap 802.10
unsnarl
straighten 277.5
extricate 431.7
disinvolve 798.5
arrange 808.8
disembarrass 1014.9
unsociable
uncommunicative 344.8
insociable 583.5
unfriendly 589.9
misanthropic 590.3
unsoiled clean 79.25
spotless 657.7
chaste 664.4
unsold 734.15
unsolicited
voluntary 324.7
neglected 340.14
unsolid unsound 16.15
unsubstantial 764.5
unreliable 971.20
unsolved 346.12
unsophisticated
artless 416.5
unadorned 499.8
unmixed 798.7
gullible 954.9
unsound infirm 16.15
unhealthy 85.54
unwholesome 85.55
unorthodox 688.9
insolvent 729.19
fragile 764.7
unwise 923.10
insane 926.26
unsubstantial 936.12
unreliable 971.20
imperfect 1003.4
unsafe 1006.11
unsparing harsh 144.24
industrious 330.22
strict 425.6
liberal 485.4
unspeakable
horrid 98.19
indescribable 122.13
insulting 156.8
wicked 654.16
base 661.12
sacred 685.7
extraordinary 870.14
unspecified
anonymous 528.3
general 864.11
vague 971.19
unspectacular 1005.8
unspoiled
downright 247.12
preserved 397.13
natural 416.6
intact 792.10

unmixed 798.7
undamaged 1002.8
unspoken tacit 51.11
secret 345.11
unexpressed 519.9
unsportsmanlike 650.10
unspotted clean 79.25
honest 644.13
spotless 657.7
chaste 664.4
perfect 1002.6
unstable
unsound 16.15
nonuniform 782.3
unbalanced 791.5
transient 828.7
inconstant 854.7
unreliable 971.20
unsafe 1006.11
unstained clean 79.25
honest 644.13
chaste 664.4
unsteady shaky 16.16
nonuniform 782.3
unbalanced 791.5
irregular 851.3
inconstant 854.7
fluttering 917.18
unreliable 971.20
unsafe 1006.11
unstick detach 802.10
loosen 804.3
unstoppable 963.15
unstrap loose 431.6
detach 802.10
unstructured
unformed 263.5
diffuse 538.11
unstuck 802.22
unsturdy 16.15
unsubstantial
frail 16.14
weak 16.15
rare 299.4
unreal 762.9
insubstantial 764.5
unsound 936.12
unreliable 971.20
illusory 976.9
immaterial 1053.7
unsubstantiated 958.8
unsuccessful 410.18
unsuitable
unacceptable 108.10
unserviceable 391.14
vulgar 497.10
wrong 638.3
inappropriate 789.7
untimely 844.6
inexpedient 996.5
unsuited
unfitted 406.9
inappropriate 789.7
unsullied clean 79.25
natural 406.13
honest 644.13
spotless 657.7
chaste 664.4
unsung disliked 99.9
unexpressed 519.9
unrenowned 661.14

unsupportable
baseless 936.13
unprovable 958.9
unsuppressed
communicative 343.10
unrestrained 430.24
unsure
untrustworthy 645.19
ignorant 930.12
uncertain 971.16
unreliable 971.20
unconfident 971.23
unsafe 1006.11
unsurpassed
peerless 249.15
best 999.16
unsuspecting
inexpectant 131.9
unaware 930.13
trusting 953.22
credulous 954.8
unprotected 1006.14
unsustained
unsound 936.12
baseless 936.13
unproved 958.8
unswayed
impartial 649.10
uninfluenced 895.5
unprejudiced 979.12
unsweetened 67.5
unswept 80.20
unswerving
directional 161.12
straight 277.6
firm 359.12
persevering 360.8
faithful 644.20
unsymmetrical
distorted 265.10
unordered 810.12
unsympathetic
insensible 25.6
unfeeling 94.9
unkind 144.16
pitiless 146.3
unsynchronized 456.15
untactful
careless 340.11
undiscriminating 945.5
untainted clean 79.25
preserved 397.13
natural 416.6
spotless 657.7
chaste 664.4
perfect 1002.6
untalented
unable 19.14
unskilled 414.16
unintelligent 922.13
untamed defiant 327.10
unsubject 430.29
unrefined 497.12
savage 671.21
untangle
extricate 431.7
disinvolve 798.5
solve 940.2
untapped 390.12
untarnished
clean 79.25

honest 644.13
chaste 664.4
untaxed 634.5
unteachable 922.15
untenable
helpless 19.18
unacceptable 108.10
baseless 936.13
untended
available 222.15
neglected 340.14
untested 958.8
unthawed 1023.13
unthinkable
unbelievable 955.10
impossible 967.7
unthinking
inconsiderate 144.18
careless 340.11
unreasoning 365.10
unintelligent 922.13
unwise 923.10
thoughtless 933.4
credulous 954.8
involuntary 963.14
unintentional 972.17
unthoughtful
inconsiderate 144.18
unthinking 365.10
unwise 923.10
untidy dirty 80.22
slipshod 340.12
slovenly 810.15
untied adrift 182.61
unbound 430.28
liberated 431.10
unfastened 802.22
until 821.15
until we meet again!
188.22
untimely
inappropriate 789.7
unseasonable 844.6
premature 845.8
late 846.16
inexpedient 996.5
unto 821.15
untogether 810.12
untold secret 345.11
unexpressed 519.9
infinite 823.3
innumerable 884.10
undecided 971.18
untouchable
n outcast 586.4
adj unfeeling 94.9
disliked 99.9
out-of-the-way 261.9
prohibited 444.7
sacred 685.7
untouched
unaffected 94.11
impenitent 114.5
unused 390.12
natural 406.13
intact 792.10
unmixed 798.7
new 841.7
unknown 930.17
undamaged 1002.8
safe 1007.4

untoward
　ominous 133.17
　untimely 844.6
　bad 1000.7
　adverse 1011.13
untracked 346.12
untrained
　unaccustomed 374.4
　unskilled 414.16
untrammeled
　lawless 418.5
　lax 426.4
　unhampered 430.26
　profligate 665.25
untreated 406.12
untried
　inexperienced 414.17
　new 841.7
　unproved 958.8
untrimmed
　unadorned 499.8
　undeceptive 644.18
untroubled
　unexcited 106.11
　unbothered 107.8
　quiescent 173.12
　pacific 464.9
untrue
　adj false 354.25
　nonobservant 435.5
　unfaithful 645.20
　erroneous 975.16
　adv erroneously 975.20
untruthfulness 354.8
untwist
　disinvolve 798.5
　solve 940.2
untying 431.2
unusable 391.14
unused
　remaining 256.7
　unaccustomed 374.4
　unutilized 390.12
　new 841.7
　surplus 993.18
unusual novel 841.11
　infrequent 848.2
　nonconforming 868.5
　unordinary 870.10
unutterable
　indescribable 122.13
　secret 345.11
　sacred 685.7
unvarnished
　natural 416.6
　unadorned 499.8
　plain-speaking 535.3
　undeceptive 644.18
　genuine 973.15
unvarying
　tedious 118.9
　uniform 781.5
　constant 847.5
　permanent 853.7
　unchangeable 855.17
unveil divest 6.5
　unclose 292.12
　disclose 351.4
unventilated
　stuffy 173.16
　closed 293.9

unverified
　unproved 958.8
　unauthoritative 971.21
unwanted
　unwished 99.11
　unwelcome 586.9
unwarranted
　overpriced 632.12
　undue 640.9
　illegal 674.6
　baseless 936.13
　unauthoritative 971.21
unwary
　negligent 340.10
　artless 416.5
　rash 493.7
　unalert 984.8
unwashed 80.20
unwatched
　neglected 340.14
　unprotected 1006.14
unwavering
　unnervous 129.2
　persevering 360.8
　stable 855.12
　confident 970.21
unwed 565.7
unwelcome
　unpleasant 98.17
　unwanted 99.11
　inhospitable 586.9
unwieldy bulky 257.19
　onerous 297.17
　bungling 414.20
　stiff 534.3
　inconvenient 996.7
　unmanageable
　　1013.19
unwilling
　disinclined 325.5
　unconsenting 442.6
　involuntary 963.14
unwind relax 20.7
　compose oneself 106.7
　disinvolve 798.5
　unfold 861.7
unwise
　unintelligent 922.13
　injudicious 923.10
　inexpedient 996.5
unwitting
　unaware 930.13
　involuntary 963.14
　unintentional 972.17
unworkable
　unserviceable 391.14
　impracticable 967.8
　inexpedient 996.5
unworldly
　heavenly 681.12
　godly 692.9
　supernatural 870.15
　immaterial 1053.7
unworn
　unweakened 15.21
　undamaged 1002.8
unworthy
　n bad person 660.1
　adj undue 640.9
　wicked 654.16
　worthless 998.22

unwrap
　take off 6.6
　unclose 292.12
　disclose 351.4
unwritten
　unexpressed 519.9
　speech 524.29
　traditional 842.12
unyielding
　impregnable 15.19
　pitiless 146.3
　resolute 359.12
　unbending 361.9
　firm 425.7
　resistant 453.5
　sturdy 763.7
　immovable 855.15
　uninfluenceable 895.4
　inevitable 963.15
　inflexible 1046.12
unzipped 802.22
up
　n increase 251.1
　v ascend 193.8
　increase 251.4
　enlarge 259.4
　promote 446.2
　elevate 912.5
　adj awake 23.8
　adv upward 193.16
　vertically 200.13
　on high 272.21
　prep toward 161.26
up against
　adj contrapositive 215.5
　resistant 453.5
　prep near 223.25
up and about 83.10
up and at 'em! 459.32
up and down
　perpendicularly 200.14
　alternately 850.11
　to and fro 916.21
up-and-up 644.14
up a tree
　unfortunate 1011.14
　in trouble 1013.22
　cornered 1013.25
upbeat
　n improvement 392.1
　beat 709.26
　round 850.3
　adj optimistic 124.12
upbraid 510.17
upcoming
　n ascent 193.1
　adj approaching 167.4
　ascending 193.14
　imminent 840.3
update date 832.13
　modernize 841.6
updraft
　ascent 193.1
　wind 318.1
upended 200.11
up for grabs 971.18
up for sale 734.16
up front 818.18
upgrade
　n ascent 193.1
　acclivity 204.6

　improvement 392.1
　v make better 392.9
　promote 446.2
　adj ascending 193.14
　sloping upward 204.17
　adv slantingly 204.23
upheaval
　outburst 105.9
　fall 395.3
　convulsion 671.5
　revolution 852.2
　elevation 912.1
upheld 901.24
uphill
　n ascent 193.1
　acclivity 204.6
　adj ascending 193.14
　sloping upward 204.17
　laborious 725.18
　difficult 1013.17
　adv up 193.16
　slantingly 204.23
uphold buoy 298.8
　preserve 397.8
　aid 449.12
　approve 509.9
　defend 600.10
　support 901.21
　elevate 912.5
　confirm 957.11
upholstered 295.34
UPI 555.3
up in arms
　adj prepared 405.16
　resistant 453.5
　at odds 456.16
　adv in opposition 451.9
　at war 458.24
up in the air 971.18
upkeep
　n preservation 397.1
　aid 449.3
　support 901.1
　v aid 449.12
　support 901.21
upland area 237.1
uplift
　n ascent 193.1
　acclivity 204.6
　improvement 392.1
　elevation 912.1
　v elate 109.8
　erect 200.9
　buoy 298.8
　make better 392.9
　glorify 662.13
　elevate 912.5
upon
　adv after which 835.7
　prep toward 161.26
　atop 198.16
　against 223.25
　on 295.37
　relation to 775.13
up on skilled in 413.27
　informed 928.18
　versed in 928.19
up one's sleeve 345.17
upper
　n excitement 105.3
　adj superior 249.12

higher 272.19
upper case 548.6
upper class
  the best 249.5
  social status 607.2
  aristocracy 608.1
upperclassman 572.6
upper crust
  the best 249.5
  society 578.6
  upper class 607.2
  aristocracy 608.1
upper hand
  advantage 249.2
  dominance 417.6
  influence 894.1
upper middle class 607.5
uppermost top 198.10
  superlative 249.13
  higher 272.19
  paramount 997.24
uppers 87.4
uppity arrogant 141.9
  insolent 142.9
upraised
  vertical 200.11
  raised 912.9
upright
  n vertical 200.2
  post 273.4
  base 901.8
  v erect 200.9
  adj vertical 200.11
  straight 277.6
  honest 644.13
  virtuous 653.6
  raised 912.9
  adv vertically 200.13
uprising
  n ascent 193.1
  rising 200.5
  acclivity 204.6
  revolt 327.4
  adj ascending 193.14
  sloping upward 204.17
uproar
  noise 53.3
  outcry 59.4
  agitation 105.4
  turbulence 671.2
  commotion 810.4
uproot
  dislodge 160.6
  extract 192.10
  exterminate 395.14
upscale
  upper-class 607.10
  wealthy 618.15
  expensive 632.11
  prosperous 1010.12
upset
  n anxiety 126.1
  dislodgment 160.2
  overturn 205.2
  fall 395.3
  turbulence 671.2
  disorder 810.1
  revolution 860.1
  agitation 917.1
  refutation 958.2
  bewilderment 971.3

confusion 985.3
frustration 1012.3
v chagrin 96.15
distress 96.16
excite 105.14
concern 126.4
make anxious 126.5
unnerve 128.10
capsize 182.44
overturn 205.6
overthrow 395.20
overcome 412.7
unbalance 791.3
disorder 810.9
discompose 811.4
revolutionize 860.4
agitate 917.10
refute 958.5
bewilder 971.12
confuse 985.7
thwart 1012.15
adj distressed 96.22
excited 105.23
overwrought 105.26
unnerved 128.14
defeated 412.14
disorderly 810.13
agitated 917.16
disproved 958.7
bewildered 971.24
confused 985.12
upshoot
  n ascent 193.1
  v grow 14.2
  shoot up 193.9
  expand 259.7
upside-down
  inverted 205.7
  confused 810.16
upstage
  n stage 704.16
  v snub 157.5
  act 704.29
  adj arrogant 141.9
  adv on the stage 704.36
upstairs up 193.16
  on high 272.21
upstanding
  vertical 200.11
  honest 644.13
upstart
  n impudent person 142.5
  vulgarian 497.6
  parvenu 606.7
  modern 841.4
  v shoot up 193.9
  adj populational 606.8
upstream
  v ascend 193.8
  adv up 193.16
upsurge
  n ascent 193.1
  increase 251.1
  v ascend 193.8
upswing ascent 193.1
  increase 251.1
  improvement 392.1
uptake 939.1
up the creek
  unfortunate 1011.14
  in trouble 1013.22

uptight
  tense 128.13
  conformist 867.6
up to
  v be able 18.11
  adj able 18.14
  prepared for 405.18
  competent 413.24
  sufficient 991.6
  prep until 821.15
up-to-date
  fashionable 578.11
  present 838.2
  modern 841.13
  informed 928.18
up to no good
  dishonest 645.16
  wicked 654.16
up to snuff
  competent 413.24
  in order 807.7
  up to par 999.19
up-to-the-minute
  fashionable 578.11
  present 838.2
  modern 841.13
  state-of-the-art 841.14
uptown
  n city district 230.6
  adj urban 230.11
  adv up 193.16
upturn
  n uptrend 193.2
  overturn 205.2
  increase 251.1
  business cycle 731.10
  v turn up 193.13
  overturn 205.6
upward mobility
  improvement 392.1
  class 607.1
  change 852.1
  prosperity 1010.1
upwind
  land 184.43
  ascend 193.8
upwind
  leeward 182.68
  windward 218.9
uranium 1038.5
Uranus 1072.9
urban 230.11
urbane decorous 496.10
  courteous 504.14
  sociable 582.22
urban legend 678.14
urban renewal 396.4
urban sprawl 771.3
urchin vagabond 178.3
  brat 302.4
urea 12.5
urethra 2.23
urge
  n desire 100.1
  impulse 365.1
  urgency 375.6
  v press 375.14
  insist 421.8
  admonish 422.6
  importune 440.12
  hasten 401.4

urgent
  motivating 375.25
  hasty 401.9
  demanding 421.9
  importunate 440.18
  vehement 544.13
  necessary 963.12
  imperative 997.22
urinal latrine 12.10
  toilet 12.11
urinate 12.14
urine humor 2.24
  water 12.5
urn
  cinerary urn 309.12
  ceramic ware 742.2
USA 232.3
usable 387.23
USAF 461.29
usage custom 373.1
  habit 373.3
  use 387.1
  treatment 387.2
  acceptation 518.4
  language 523.1
  word 526.1
  phrase 529.1
  diction 532.1
US Air Force 461.29
US Cabinet 423.1
use
  n custom 373.1
  habit 373.3
  employment
    387.1
  utility 387.3
  benefit 387.4
  function 387.5
  wear 393.5
  estate 471.4
  expenditure 626.1
  v be on 87.22
  treat 321.6
  practice 328.8
  handle 384.5
  utilize 387.10
  treat 387.12
  exploit 387.16
  spend 626.5
  exert 725.8
used
  employed 387.24
  lost 473.7
  wasted 486.9
  secondhand 842.18
used to
  accustomed 373.15
  familiar with
    373.16
  habituated 373.17
use force 15.12
useful modal 384.8
  employable 387.18
  helpful 449.21
  expedient 995.5
  good 999.12
useless
  ineffective 19.15
  of no use 391.9
  unsuccessful 410.18
  disadvantageous 996.6

use one's head
  have all one's wits about one
    920.10
  think 931.8
user addict 87.21
  use 387.7
  employer 387.9
user-friendly 1014.15
use some elbow grease
  endeavor 403.5
  exert oneself 725.9
use up fatigue 21.4
  spend 387.13
  consume 388.3
  waste 486.4
usher
  n wedding party 563.4
  attendant 577.5
  theater man 704.23
  escort 769.5
  doorkeeper 1008.12
  v escort 769.8
usual medium 246.3
  typical 349.15
  customary 373.13
  same 781.6
  orderly 807.6
  frequent 847.4
  prevalent 864.12
  regular 869.9
  ordinary 1005.8
usurp
  take command 417.14
  appropriate 480.19
  arrogate 640.8
  overstep 910.9
usury lending 620.1
  interest 623.3
  illicit business 732.1
utensil container 195.1
  tool 1040.1
uterus genitals 2.13
  vital force 886.7
utilitarian
  useful 387.18
  occupied 724.15
utility
  n usefulness 387.3
  helpfulness 449.10
  machinery 1040.3
  adj substitute 862.8
utility man
  deputy 576.1
  actor 707.2
utility player
  baseball team 745.2
  substitute 862.2
utility pole 273.1
utilize manage 384.5
  use 387.10
  gather materials 1054.7
utmost
  n limit 794.5
  adj extreme 247.13
  superlative 249.13
  trial 403.16
Utopia 986.11
utopian
  n optimist 124.6
  reformer 392.6
  visionary 986.13

  adj optimistic 124.12
  emendatory 392.16
  ideal 986.23
utter
  v divulge 351.5
  say 524.22
  monetize 728.26
  coin 728.28
  disperse 771.4
  adj downright 247.12
  thorough 794.10
  unqualified 960.2
  sound 1002.7
U-turn reverse 163.3
  bend 279.3
  change of mind 363.1
V fork 171.4
  five 882.1
vacancy vacuity 222.2
  absence 222.2
  position 724.5
  nonexistence 762.1
  empty-headedness 922.6
  thoughtlessness 933.1
vacate quit 188.9
  abandon 370.5
  repeal 445.2
  resign 448.2
  relinquish 475.3
vacation
  n holiday 20.3
  absence 222.4
  repeal 445.1
  interim 826.1
  pause 857.3
  v get away from it all 20.9
  absent oneself 222.8
vacational 20.10
vaccine
  vaccination 86.28
  inoculation 91.16
vacillate waver 362.8
  blow hot and cold 364.4
  change 854.5
  oscillate 916.10
  hang in doubt 971.10
vacuous vacant 222.14
  nonexistent 762.8
  empty-headed 922.19
  ignorant 930.12
  thoughtless 933.4
  trivial 998.19
vacuum
  n void 222.3
  nonexistence 762.1
  deficiency 795.2
  empty-headedness 922.6
  v sweep 79.23
vacuum-packed 212.12
vacuum tube 1033.10
vagabond
  n displaced person 160.4
  vagrant 178.3
  wretch 660.2
  transient 828.4
  v wander 177.23
  adj wandering 177.37
vagary obliquity 204.1
  caprice 364.1
vagina genitals 2.13
  duct 2.23

vagrancy
  wandering 177.3
  indolence 331.5
vagrant
  n vagabond 178.3
  bum 331.9
  wretch 660.2
  adj deviative 164.7
  wandering 177.37
  capricious 364.5
  inconstant 854.7
vague
  inconspicuous 32.6
  formless 263.4
  thin 270.16
  obscure 522.15
  unordered 810.12
  general 864.11
  indefinite 971.19
  inaccurate 975.17
vain ineffective 19.15
  conceited 136.9
  vainglorious 140.8
  futile 391.13
  boastful 502.10
  baseless 936.13
  trivial 998.19
valedictorian 543.4
valedictory
  n leave-taking 188.4
  speech 543.2
  adj departing 188.18
valence electrons 1033.3
valentine 562.13
valet
  n man 577.4
  v serve 577.13
valetudinarianism 82.1
valiant
  n brave person 492.8
  adj courageous 492.17
valid powerful 18.12
  legal 673.11
  evidential 957.16
  sound 973.14
  good 999.12
validate ratify 332.12
  authorize 443.11
  legalize 673.9
  experiment 942.8
  confirm 957.11
  verify 970.12
valley crack 224.2
  vale 237.7
  pit 275.2
  concavity 284.9
valor 492.1
valuable
  of value 387.22
  precious 632.10
value
  n color quality 35.6
  measure 300.2
  benefit 387.4
  meaning 518.1
  worth 630.2
  preciousness 632.2
  importance 997.1
  goodness 999.1
  v respect 155.4
  measure 300.10

  price 630.11
  estimate 946.9
  esteem 997.13
value judgment 946.3
value system 952.2
valve gate 239.10
  stopper 293.4
  wind instrument 711.6
  electron tube 1033.10
  cutlery 1040.2
vamp
  n lover 104.12
  tempter 377.4
  flirt 562.11
  demimonde 665.15
  overture 708.26
  impromptu 708.27
  fire fighter 1022.4
  v enamor 104.23
  improvise 365.8
  fascinate 377.7
  perfect 392.11
vampire lover 104.12
  frightener 127.9
  tempter 377.4
  extortionist 480.12
  monster 593.6
  demimonde 665.15
  demon 680.6
  bewitcher 690.9
van leading 165.1
  wagon 179.2
  vanguard 216.2
  guard 1008.9
vandal destroyer 395.8
  savage 593.5
vandalism
  cruelty 144.11
  misbehavior 322.1
  destruction 395.1
  violence 671.1
vane 318.17
vanguard leading 165.1
  border 211.4
  van 216.2
  precursor 816.1
  novelty 841.2
  guard 1008.9
vanilla
  unadorned 499.8
  elegant 533.6
  simple 798.6
vanish disappear 34.2
  quit 188.9
  perish 395.23
  cease to exist 762.6
  flit 828.6
vanishing cream 1016.12
vanishing point
  disappearance 34.1
  convergence 169.1
  minute 258.7
  the distance 261.3
vanity pride 136.1
  self-admiration 140.1
  vainness 140.1
  futility 391.2
  boasting 502.1
  triviality 998.3
vanity press 554.2
vanquish 412.10

vantage viewpoint 27.7
  advantage 249.2
vantage point 272.2
vapid
  wishy-washy 16.17
  insipid 65.2
  dull 117.6
  prosaic 721.5
  empty-headed 922.19
  trivial 998.19
  mediocre 1005.7
vapor
  n fog 319.3
  spirit 764.3
  illusion 976.1
  figment of the imagination 986.5
  hot water 1019.10
  volatile 1067.1
  steam 1067.1
  v boast 502.6
  bluster 503.3
  talk nonsense 520.5
  talk big 545.6
  let out 909.24
vaporize
  strike dead 308.18
  destroy 395.10
  evaporate 1067.8
vaquero rider 178.8
  herder 1070.3
variable
  n process variable 1041.9
  adj relative 775.7
  nonuniform 782.3
  multiform 783.3
  irregular 851.3
  changeable 854.6
  inconstant 854.7
  uncertain 971.16
variable-rate mortgage 438.4
variance dissent 333.1
  permission 443.1
  disaccord 456.2
  relativity 775.2
  difference 780.1
  disagreement 789.1
variation
  deviation 164.1
  passage 708.24
  difference 780.1
  differentiation 780.4
  nonuniformity 782.1
  multiformity 783.1
  change 852.1
  inconstancy 854.2
  changing 854.3
varicose vein 2.23
varied different 780.7
  diversified 783.4
  mixed 797.14
variegated
  chromatic 35.16
  many-colored 47.9
  different 780.7
  nonuniform 782.3
variety sect 675.3
  show business 704.1
  miscellany 770.13
  difference 780.1
  nonuniformity 782.1

multiformity 783.1
kind 809.3
classifications 809.5
change 852.1
inconstancy 854.2
plurality 883.1
variety show 1035.2
various different 780.7
  nonuniform 782.3
  diversified 783.4
  plural 883.7
  several 884.7
varnish
  n blanket 295.12
  sham 354.3
  pretext 376.1
  extenuation 600.5
  art equipment 712.18
  v color 35.14
  pervert 265.6
  polish 287.7
  conceal 346.6
  falsify 354.16
  ornament 545.7
  extenuate 600.12
varsity 617.7
vary deviate 164.3
  vacillate 362.8
  differ 780.5
  differentiate 780.6
  diversify 782.2
  multiform 783.2
  disguise 787.3
  disagree 789.5
  intermit 851.2
  shift 852.6
  alternate 852.7
  change 854.5
vas 2.23
vascular 2.33
vase 742.2
Vaseline 1056.2
vassal
  n subject 432.7
  retainer 577.1
  adj subject 432.13
vast spacious 158.11
  large 247.7
  huge 257.20
vat 386.6
the Vatican 698.6
Vatican Library 558.1
vaudeville 704.1
vault
  n ascent 193.1
  compartment 197.2
  arch 279.4
  tomb 309.16
  leap 366.1
  storehouse 386.6
  treasury 729.13
  the heavens 1072.2
  v curve 279.6
  leap 366.5
vaulter 366.4
vaunt
  n display 501.4
  boasting 502.1
  v flaunt 501.17
  boast 502.6
VCR record 50.12

television receiver 1035.11
VD 85.18
veal 10.15
vector infection 85.4
  carrier 85.44
  direction 161.2
  course 184.34
  straight line 277.2
the Vedas 683.8
veep 574.3
veer
  n deviation 164.1
  bias 204.3
  angle 278.2
  v turn round 163.9
  deviate 164.3
  change course 182.30
  oblique 204.9
  go sideways 218.5
  angle 278.5
  be changed 852.6
vegan vegetarian 8.16
  diet 8.31
  temperance 668.1
vegetable
  n plant 310.3
  adj vegetal 310.36
  passive 329.6
  languid 331.20
  permanent 853.7
vegetarian
  n eater 8.16
  abstainer 668.4
  adj eating 8.31
  vegetable 310.36
  abstinent 668.10
vegetate develop 14.2
  stagnate 173.9
  grow 259.7
  sprout 310.34
  do nothing 329.2
  merely exist 761.10
vegetation
  physical development 14.1
  inertness 173.4
  growth 259.3
  plants 310.1
  life 310.32
  inaction 329.1
  mere existence 761.6
vehement
  acrimonious 17.14
  zealous 101.9
  passionate 105.29
  industrious 330.22
  emphatic 544.13
  violent 671.16
vehicle color 35.8
  means of transport 179
  conveyance 179.1
  instrument 384.4
  stage show 704.4
  film 714.10
veil
  n clothing 5.26
  cover 295.2
  veil of secrecy 345.3
  curtain 346.2
  pretext 376.1
  shade 1028.1
  v cover 295.19

keep secret 345.7
conceal 346.6
shade 1028.5
veiled covered 295.31
  latent 519.5
  vague 971.19
  shaded 1028.7
vein
  n duct 2.23
  thinness 270.7
  source of supply 386.4
  style 532.2
  mode 765.4
  nature 767.4
  disposition 978.3
  mood 978.4
  deposit 1058.7
  v variegate 47.7
veld the country 233.1
  plain 236.1
  grassland 310.8
velocity rate 172.4
  speed 174.1
  gait 177.12
velvet comfort 121.1
  smoothness 287.3
  texture 294.3
  prosperity 1010.1
  easy 1014.4
  softness 1047.4
vena cava 2.23
venal greedy 100.27
  bribable 378.4
  corruptible 645.23
vendetta quarrel 456.5
  revenge 507.1
  animosity 589.4
vending machine 736.4
vendor peddler 730.5
  vending machine 736.4
veneer
  n shallowness 276.1
  blanket 295.12
  lamina 296.2
  v face 295.23
venerable
  dignified 136.12
  reverend 155.12
  aged 303.16
  reputable 662.15
  sacred 685.7
  old 842.10
  traditional 842.12
venerate
  respect 155.4
  worship 696.11
venereal disease 85.18
vengeance
  revenge 507.1
  deserts 639.3
venial 600.14
venison 10.13
venom
  poisonousness 82.3
  rancor 144.7
  animosity 589.4
  violence 671.1
  evil 1000.3
  bane 1001.3
vent
  n parachute 181.13

emergence 190.1
outlet 190.9
air passage 239.13
escape 369.1
v divulge 351.5
evacuate 909.22
ventilate
deodorize 72.4
air 317.11
disclose 351.4
divulge 351.5
make public 352.11
discuss 541.12
refrigerate 1024.10
ventral 2.31
ventricular 2.31
ventriloquist 524.15
venture
n undertaking 404.1
investment 729.4
trading 737.19
gamble 759.2
v attempt 403.6
dare 492.10
presume 640.6
invest 729.17
trade 737.23
chance 759.24
venture capital
supply 386.2
capital 728.15
trading 737.19
venue 159.2
Venus Love 104.8
beauty 1016.10
stars 1072.4
planet 1072.9
Venus's flytrap 356.12
Venus de Milo 1016.10
veracity honesty 644.3
truth 973.1
veranda 197.21
verb 530.4
verbal
n verb 530.4
adj communicational 343.9
semantic 518.12
speech 524.29
vocabular 526.18
grammatical 530.17
genuine 973.15
verbalize 524.22
verbatim
adj genuine 973.15
adv exactly 973.21
verbiage diction 532.1
wordiness 538.2
verboten 444.7
verdant green 44.4
verdurous 310.42
verdict judgment 598.9
solution 940.1
decision 946.5
verge
n border 211.4
insignia 647.1
v take direction 161.7
border 211.10
tend 896.3
verify
experiment 942.8

collate 943.5
confirm 957.11
certify 970.12
check 1017.21
verisimilitude
probability 968.1
genuineness 973.7
veritable
straight 644.14
real 761.15
thorough 794.10
true 973.13
vérité 706.1
vermicelli 10.33
vermicide
vermifuge 86.24
poison 1001.3
vermiform coiled 281.7
wormlike 311.53
vermilion
v make red 41.4
adj red 41.6
vermin
creature 311.3
parasite 311.37
rabble 606.3
beast 660.6
vernacular
n dead language 523.2
mother tongue 523.3
nonformal speech 523.5
substandard language 523.6
jargon 523.9
plain speech 535.1
adj local 231.9
common 497.14
colloquial 523.20
usual 869.9
vernal green 44.4
immature 301.10
seasonal 313.9
new 841.7
vernal equinox
season 313.7
orbit 1072.16
versatile fickle 364.6
handy 387.20
ambidextrous 413.25
multiform 783.3
verse
n part 554.13
passage 708.24
poetry 720.1
poem 720.4
part of writing 793.2
curtain-raiser 816.2
maxim 974.1
v inform 551.8
poetize 720.13
versed in
skilled in 413.27
informed in 928.19
version
reproduction 336.3
rendering 341.2
writing 547.10
sect 675.3
score 708.28
story 722.3
verso left side 220.1
makeup 554.12

versus toward 161.26
against 215.7
opposed to 451.10
vertebrate
n creature 311.3
adj chordate 311.41
vertex summit 198.2
angle 278.2
vertical
n upright 200.2
adj top 198.10
upright 200.11
steep 204.18
straight 277.6
vertigo symptom 85.9
ear disease 85.15
dizziness 985.4
verve vim 17.2
passion 93.2
eagerness 101.1
gaiety 109.4
liveliness 330.2
spirit 544.4
lively imagination 986.4
very to a degree 245.7
exceedingly 247.18
vesicle bulge 283.3
bubble 320.1
blemish 1004.1
vespers 696.8
vessel duct 2.23
ship 180.1
container 195.1
vest
n waistcoat 5.14
v establish 159.16
endow 478.17
commission 615.10
vestal virgin 565.4
vested clothing 5.45
established 855.13
vested interest
estate 471.4
pressure group 609.31
prerogative 642.1
vestibule ear 2.10
entrance 189.5
portal 197.19
vestige
remainder 256.1
print 517.7
clue 517.9
record 549.1
admixture 797.7
antiquity 842.6
vestment
clothing 5.1
garment 5.3
cover 295.2
vest-pocket
insignificant 248.6
miniature 258.12
shortened 268.9
concise 537.6
vestry
ecclesiastical council 423.4
church 703.9
veteran
n old man 304.2
vet 413.16
combat participant 461.19

adj experienced 413.28
veterinarian 90.7
veto
n negative 444.2
executive privilege 613.7
v put one's veto upon 444.5
oppose 451.3
disapprove 510.10
legislate 613.10
vex annoy 96.13
irk 98.15
make anxious 126.5
provoke 152.24
trouble 1013.13
V formation 184.12
VHF 1034.12
via 161.27
viable energizing 17.15
acceptable 107.12
living 306.13
workable 889.10
practicable 966.7
of importance 997.18
viaduct crossing 170.2
bridge 383.9
vibrant energetic 17.13
resonant 54.10
vibrate resonate 54.6
be frequent 847.3
oscillate 916.10
shake 917.11
vibrato
n screech 58.4
trill 709.19
adj shrill 58.14
vicar deputy 576.1
substitute 862.2
vicarious 862.8
vice
n misbehavior 322.1
deputy 576.1
moral badness 654
viciousness 654.1
weakness 654.2
wrongdoing 655.1
substitute 862.2
prep instead of 862.12
vice-president
executive 574.3
vice-chairman 576.8
substitute 862.2
viceroy
governor 575.13
vice-president 576.8
vice versa
inversely 205.8
reciprocally 777.12
contrarily 779.9
vicinity
environment 209.1
nearness 223.1
region 231.1
vicious cruel 144.26
vice-prone 654.11
wicked 654.16
savage 671.21
bad 1000.7
harmful 1000.12
vicious circle
circle 280.2
futility 391.2

sophistry 936.1
vicissitudes 972.5
vicious cycle 391.2
vicissitude
 changing 854.3
 adversity 1011.1
victim
 sick person 85.43
 sufferer 96.11
 dupe 358.1
 quarry 382.7
 loser 412.5
 laughingstock 508.7
 cheater 759.22
 unfortunate 1011.7
victimize cheat 356.18
 persecute 389.7
 outwit 415.11
 overprice 632.7
victor
 successful person 409.6
 winner 411.2
Victorian
 n prude 500.11
 adj prudish 500.19
 antiquated 842.13
victorious 411.7
victory success 409.1
 triumph 411
 win 411.1
victuals food 10.2
 groceries 735.7
video
 n television 1035.1
 adj televisional 1035.16
video camera camera 714.11
 television 1035.1
video-cassette recorder
 record 50.12
 television receiver 1035.11
video game 743.9
videotape
 n recording media 549.10
 v record 549.15
vie compete 457.18
 be comparable 943.7
 excel 999.11
Vietcong
 n irregular 461.16
 revolutionist 860.3
 adj revolutionist 860.6
view
 n look 27.3
 field of view 31.3
 aspect 33.3
 appearance 33.6
 intention 380.1
 scene 712.12
 estimate 946.3
 opinion 953.6
 outlook 978.2
 v see 27.12
 look 27.13
 think of 931.17
 take the attitude 978.6
 heed 983.6
viewer
 optical instrument 29.1
 recipient 479.3
 spectator 918.1
 televiewer 1035.12

viewpoint
 standpoint 27.7
 field of view 31.3
 aspect 33.3
 station 159.2
 outlook 978.2
vigil wakefulness 23.1
 vigilance 339.4
vigilant wakeful 23.7
 wary 339.13
 prepared 405.16
 protective 1008.23
vignette
 description 349.2
 drawing 712.13
 print 713.5
vigor strength 15.1
 energy 17.1
 power 18.1
 haleness 83.3
 gaiety 109.4
 force 544.3
vigorish 793.1
viking mariner 183.1
 pirate 483.7
vile nasty 64.7
 malodorous 71.5
 filthy 80.23
 offensive 98.18
 low 497.15
 cursing 513.8
 knavish 645.17
 wicked 654.16
 base 661.12
 obscene 666.9
 paltry 998.21
 terrible 1000.9
vilify berate 510.19
 revile 512.10
 abuse 513.7
 stigmatize 661.9
 blaspheme 694.5
villa 228.7
village
 n hamlet 230.2
 region 231.5
 adj urban 230.11
villain evildoer 593.1
 rascal 660.3
 role 704.10
 actor 707.2
vim verve 17.2
 power 18.1
 gaiety 109.4
 liveliness 330.2
vinaigrette 70.6
vindicate justify 600.9
 acquit 601.4
vindictive 507.7
vine 310.4
vinegar sour 67.2
 preservative 397.4
vineyard 1069.10
vintage 472.5
violate disobey 327.6
 misuse 389.4
 corrupt 393.12
 break 435.4
 possess sexually 480.15
 seduce 665.20
 rage 671.11

 break the law 674.5
 work evil 1000.6
violence acrimony 17.5
 excitability 105.10
 cruelty 144.11
 rage 152.10
 mistreatment 389.2
 coercion 424.3
 vehement action 671
 agitation 671.1
violet
 n purpleness 46.1
 adj purple 46.3
violinist 710.5
VIP celebrity 662.9
 influence 894.6
 important person 997.9
viper serpent 311.26
 beast 660.6
virgin
 n schoolgirl 302.8
 single woman 565.4
 adj hinterland 233.9
 natural 406.13
 unmarried 565.7
 continent 664.6
 intact 792.10
 unmixed 798.7
 new 841.7
 unproductive 891.4
 unknown 930.17
 undamaged 1002.8
virgule diagonal 204.7
 line 517.6
virile potent 76.13
 courageous 492.17
virtual 519.5
virtue power 18.1
 courage 492.1
 morality 636.3
 probity 644.1
 moral goodness
  653
 virtuousness 653.1
 chastity 664.1
 goodness 999.1
virtuoso
 n superior 249.4
 master 413.13
 connoisseur 496.7
 musician 710.1
 first-rater 999.6
 adj skillful 413.22
 musical 708.47
virtuous honest 644.13
 good 653.6
 chaste 664.4
 pure 999.12
virulent
 acrimonious 17.14
 poisonous 82.7
 rancorous 144.22
 resentful 152.26
 deadly 308.23
 hostile 589.10
 violent 671.16
 harmful 1000.12
virus infection 85.4
 germ 85.42
 organism 305.2
 poison 1001.3

visa
 n ratification 332.4
 pass 443.7
 signature 527.10
 certificate 549.6
 v ratify 332.12
visage looks 33.4
 face 216.4
vis à vis 790.4
viscera vitals 2.16
 heart 93.3
 insides 207.4
viscount 608.4
viscous thick 269.8
 dense 1045.12
 viscid 1062.12
vise 260.6
visible visual 27.20
 clear 31.6
 apparent 33.11
 manifest 348.8
vision
 n sight 27.1
 optics 27.1
 apparition 33.5
 deception 356.1
 phantom 976.4
 figment of the imagination
  986.5
 visualization 986.6
 dream 986.9
 specter 988.1
 thing of beauty 1016.7
 v visualize 986.15
visit
 n chat 541.4
 social call 582.7
 v go to 177.25
 enter 189.7
 attend 221.8
 chat 541.10
 pay a visit 582.19
visitor traveler 178.1
 incomer 189.4
 attender 221.5
 superintendent 574.2
 guest 585.6
 examiner 938.17
visor cover 356.11
 eyeshade 1028.2
vista field of view 31.3
 view 33.6
visual eye 2.28
 ocular 27.20
 visible 31.6
visualize
 think of 931.17
 vision 986.15
vital
 powerful 18.12
 hale 83.12
 eager 101.8
 gay 109.14
 organic 305.17
 living 306.13
 vigorous 544.11
 durable 827.10
 requisite 963.13
 all-important 997.23
vitality
 strength 15.1

wadding lining 196.3
  stopping 293.5
waddle
  n slow motion 175.2
  gait 177.12
  v go slow 175.6
  way of walking 177.28
wade 182.56
wade into
  confront 216.8
  attack 459.15
  set to work 725.15
wading bird 311.28
wafer biscuit 10.30
  thinness 270.7
  lamina 296.2
  Eucharist 701.7
waffle
  n pancake 10.45
  bull 520.3
  v slight 340.8
  prevaricate 344.7
  vacillate 362.8
  remain neutral 467.5
  talk nonsense 520.5
  change 854.5
waft
  n transportation 176.3
  puff 318.4
  v transport 176.12
  buoy 298.8
  blow 318.20
wag
  n mischief-maker 322.3
  humorist 489.12
  swing 916.6
  wiggle 917.7
  v oscillate 916.10
  wave 916.11
  wiggle 917.14
wage
  n pay 624.4
  v practice 328.8
wager
  n bet 759.3
  gamble 971.8
  v chance 759.24
  bet 759.25
wagon vehicle 179.2
  police car 179.11
waif vagabond 178.3
  derelict 370.4
wail
  n screech 58.4
  lament 115.3
  v screech 58.8
  cry 60.2
  ululate 115.13
  sigh 318.21
  speak 524.25
wainscot
  n lining 196.3
  base 199.2
  v fill 196.7
waist shirt 5.15
  middle 819.1
waistband 5.19
waistcoat 5.14
waistline 819.1
wait
  n minstrel 710.14

delay 846.2
  v await 130.8
  be patient 134.4
  serve 577.13
  delay 846.12
waiter 577.7
waiting list 871.1
wait on await 130.8
  toady to 138.8
  extend courtesy 504.12
  serve 577.13
  accompany 769.7
  escort 769.8
waitress 577.7
wait up 846.12
waive give up 370.7
  reject 372.2
  cease to use 390.4
  not use 390.5
  permit 443.9
  repeal 445.2
  relinquish 475.3
  postpone 846.9
  allow for 959.5
waiver
  relinquishment 370.3
  discontinuance 390.2
  permission 443.1
  repeal 445.1
  quitclaim 475.2
  qualification 959.1
wake
  n wakefulness 23.1
  track 182.7
  wash 184.30
  last offices 309.4
  sign 517.8
  social gathering 582.10
  afterpart 817.2
  aftereffect 887.3
  v awake 23.4
  get up 23.5
  excite 105.12
wale
  sore 85.37
  bulge 283.3
  texture 294.1
  blemish 1004.1
walk
  n slow motion 175.2
  ramble 177.10
  gait 177.12
  sphere 231.2
  route 383.1
  path 383.2
  race 457.12
  arena 463.1
  occupation 724.4
  vocation 724.6
  game 745.3
  circuit 914.2
  v exercise 84.4
  go slow 175.6
  ambulate 177.27
  get off 369.7
  win hands down 411.4
  be free 430.18
  liberate 431.9
  strike 727.10
  play 745.5
walk all over 612.16

walk a tightrope 1013.11
walk away quit 188.9
  outdistance 249.10
  abandon 370.5
  dismiss 984.4
walker
  pedestrian 178.6
  baby carriage 179.6
walking papers 909.5
walk of life 765.1
walk-on role 704.10
  supporting actor 707.7
walk out exit 190.12
  strike 727.10
  stop work 857.8
walkover 411.1
walk-through 704.13
walkup 228.13
walkway 383.2
wall
  n precipice 200.3
  fence 212.4
  partition 213.5
  slope 237.2
  barrier 1012.5
  v fence 212.7
  fortify 460.9
walled-in
  enclosed 212.10
  covered 295.31
wallet 729.15
wall off partition 213.8
  quarantine 429.13
wallop
  n blow 902.5
  v punish 604.15
  strike 902.15
  beat 902.17
  flounder 917.15
wallow
  n marsh 243.1
  flounder 917.8
  v pitch 182.55
  be promiscuous 665.19
  bow 913.9
  welter 915.13
  flounder 917.15
wallpaper 295.23
Wall Street
  stock market 737.1
  stock exchange 737.7
  financial district 737.8
wall-to-wall
  adj comprehensive 772.7
  same 781.6
  thorough 794.10
  continuous 812.8
  adv continuously 812.10
wall-to-wall carpet 295.9
walnut 40.3
waltz
  n easy 1014.4
  v win hands down 411.4
  dance 705.5
wampum jewel 498.6
  money 728.2
  names for 728.3
wan
  v lose color 36.6
  adj tired-looking 21.9
  colorless 36.7

deathly 307.29
  languid 331.20
  lackluster 1027.17
wand fitness 84.1
  scepter 417.9
  insignia 647.1
  wish-bringer 691.6
  dowsing 962.3
wander deviate 164.4
  roam 177.23
  digress 538.9
  misbelieve 688.8
  be insane 926.20
  err 975.9
  stray 984.3
  muse 985.9
wanderer rover 178.2
  alien 774.3
  transient 828.4
  planet 1072.9
Wandering Jew
  displaced person 160.4
  wanderer 178.2
wanderlust 177.3
wane
  n standstill 173.3
  decline 252.2
  deterioration 393.3
  v disappear 34.2
  recede 168.2
  move 172.5
  quiet 173.8
  decrease 252.6
  age 303.10
  decline 393.17
wangle elicit 192.14
  persuade 375.23
  plot 381.9
  maneuver 415.10
wannabee
  desirer 100.12
  petitioner 440.7
  candidate 610.9
want
  n desire 100.1
  absence 222.1
  indigence 619.2
  deficiency 795.2
  requirement 963.2
  lack 992.4
  imperfection 1003.1
  v desire 100.14
  be inferior 250.4
  be poor 619.5
  necessitate 795.3
  fall short 911.2
  require 963.9
  lack 992.7
  be insufficient 992.8
wanted
  desired 100.29
  welcome 585.12
  requisite 963.13
want for lack 795.3
  fall short 911.2
  be insufficient 992.8
wanton
  n libertine 665.10
  strumpet 665.14
  v make love 562.14
  be promiscuous 665.19

dissipate 669.6
make merry 743.24
adj capricious 364.5
unrestrained 430.24
reckless 493.8
unvirtuous 654.12
wayward 665.26
inconstant 854.7
wapiti 311.5
war
  n disaccord 456.1
  contention 457.1
  warfare 458.1
  campaign 458.4
  military science 458.6
  v contend 457.13
  do battle 458.14
warble bird sound 60.5
  speak 524.25
  sing 708.38
war cry cry 59.1
  challenge 454.2
  call to arms 458.8
  signal 517.16
ward
  hospital room 197.25
  region 231.5
  custody 429.5
  dependent 432.6
  defense 460.1
  stronghold 460.6
  election district 609.16
  protectorship 1008.2
warden jailer 429.10
  executive 574.3
  public official 575.17
  guardian 1008.6
  doorkeeper 1008.12
ward heeler
  follower 166.2
  partisan 609.27
  henchman 610.8
ward off dodge 368.8
  fend off 460.10
  repulse 908.3
  prevent 1012.14
wardrobe
  furnishings 5.2
  closet 197.15
warehouse
  n storehouse 386.6
  market 736.1
  v load 159.15
  store 386.10
warehouse store 736.1
wares 735.1
warfare
  contention 457.1
  war 458.1
  battle 458.1
warhead charge 462.16
  rocket 1074.3
warlock 690.5
warlord 575.13
warm
  n man 76.5
  v energize 17.10
  make red 41.4
  excite 105.12
  heat 1020.17
  adj chromatic 35.16

red 41.6
fervent 93.18
zealous 101.9
heated 105.22
comfortable 121.11
kind 143.13
near 223.14
vehement 544.13
hospitable 585.11
cordial 587.16
wealthy 618.15
on the right scent 941.10
calid 1019.24
warm-blooded 1019.29
warmonger 461.5
warm over prose 117.5
  revive 396.16
  heat 1020.17
warn forebode 133.11
  dissuade 379.3
  caution 399.5
  alarm 400.3
  demand 421.5
  admonish 422.6
  threaten 514.2
warning
  n forewarning 133.4
  dissuasion 379.1
  caution 399.1
  preparation 405.1
  demand 421.1
  advice 422.1
  threat 514.1
  tip-off 551.3
  adj premonitory 133.16
  cautioning 399.7
  advisory 422.8
war of words quarrel 456.5
  contention 457.1
  argumentation 935.4
warp
  n deviation 164.1
  bias 204.3
  distortion 265.1
  woof 740.3
  tendency 896.1
  disposition 978.3
  blemish 1004.1
  v deflect 164.5
  ship activity 182.48
  distort 265.5
  misrepresent 350.3
  falsify 354.16
  corrupt 393.12
  be changed 852.6
  tend 896.3
  prejudice 980.9
  blemish 1004.4
  adj supersonic 174.16
war paint 1016.12
warpath 458.11
warrant
  n ratification 332.4
  oath 334.4
  security 438.1
  authorization 443.3
  permit 443.6
  certificate 549.6
  summons 598.2
  reason 600.6
  commission 615.1

acknowledgment 627.2
privilege 642.2
negotiable instrument
  728.11
v acknowledge 332.11
ratify 332.12
depose 334.6
promise 436.4
secure 438.9
authorize 443.11
justify 600.9
commission 615.10
state 953.12
testify 957.9
confirm 957.11
warrantee 438.7
warrant officer
  commissioned officer
    575.18
  naval officer 575.20
warrantor 438.6
warranty
  promise 436.1
  security 438.1
  authorization 443.3
  certificate 549.6
warren sty 80.11
  cave 284.5
  productiveness 890.6
warrior 461.6
wart growth 85.39
  runt 258.4
  bulge 283.3
  blemish 1004.1
warts and all 973.19
war whoop cry 59.1
  challenge 454.2
  call to arms 458.8
  call 517.16
wary
  vigilant 339.13
  cunning 415.12
  chary 494.9
  doubting 955.9
  incredulous 956.4
war zone 458.1
wash
  n color 35.8
  washing 79.5
  laundering 79.6
  trail 182.7
  wake 184.30
  lap 238.8
  marsh 243.1
  painting 712.14
  the same 790.3
  tie 836.3
  stop 857.2
  v color 35.14
  ripple 52.11
  bathe 79.19
  lap 238.19
  shuffle 758.5
  be true 973.8
  soak 1065.13
wash away wash 79.19
  recede 168.2
  subtract 255.9
  exterminate 395.14
  obliterate 395.16
washbasin 79.12

washboard
  roughness 288.2
  pavement 383.6
washed-out
  ineffective 19.15
  colorless 36.7
  weatherworn 393.34
washed up
  ruined 395.29
  completed 407.11
  ended 820.8
  finished 820.9
washer
  washbasin 79.12
  launderer 79.15
washing machine
  79.12
wash one's hands of
  give up 370.7
  refuse 442.3
  relinquish 475.3
  disapprove 510.10
washout washing 79.5
  airmanship 184.3
  overflow 238.6
  debacle 395.4
  scrub 410.2
  abortion 410.5
  failure 410.8
wash over 238.17
wasp
  sorehead 110.11
  bee 311.35
waste
  n excrement 12.3
  offal 80.9
  decrement 252.3
  remainder 256.1
  derelict 370.4
  consumption 388.1
  refuse 391.4
  wastage 393.4
  destruction 395.1
  loss 473.2
  prodigality 486.1
  disintegration 806.1
  wasteland 891.2
  extract 893.3
  v disappear 34.2
  fail 85.48
  decrease 252.6
  shrink 260.9
  kill 308.14
  be consumed 388.4
  impair 393.19
  destroy 395.10
  put an end to 395.12
  deplete 473.5
  consume 486.4
  annihilate 762.7
  end 820.5
  adj hinterland 233.9
  unproductive 891.4
wastebasket 391.7
waste disposal 390.3
wasteful
  destructive 395.26
  prodigal 486.8
wasteland
  hinterland 233.2
  waste 891.2

affect 500.12
endure 827.6
abrade 1044.7
wear and tear
decrement 252.3
impairment 393.5
disintegration 806.1
wear away
weaken 16.9
disappear 34.2
decrease 252.6
subtract 255.9
consume 388.3
wear 393.20
waste 473.5
disintegrate 806.3
come to an end 820.6
abrade 1044.7
wear down fatigue 21.4
persuade 375.23
wear 393.20
influence 894.7
wear off wear 393.20
come to an end 820.6
wear out
fatigue 21.4
oppress 98.16
wear 393.20
wear thin
weaken 16.9
fall flat 117.4
wear well
enjoy good health 83.6
endure 827.6
weary
v fatigue 21.4
burn out 21.5
oppress 98.16
be tedious 118.6
adj tired 21.7
gloomy 112.24
weariful 118.11
languid 331.20
weary-worn 21.7
weasel
n sharp vision 27.11
sled sleigh 179.20
wild animal 311.23
man of few words 344.5
recant 363.8
v prevaricate 344.7
equivocate 539.3
inform on 551.13
pull back 903.7
weather
n atmosphere 184.32
windward side 218.3
climate 317.3
air 317.3
v sail against the wind
  182.24
ride out the storm 182.40
wear 393.20
stand fast 855.11
be safe 1007.2
adj side 218.6
weather balloon 317.8
weather-beaten 393.34
weathered 393.34
weather eye
sharp eye 27.10

seamanship 182.3
vigilance 339.4
weather forecast 317.6
weather the storm
weather 182.40
recover 396.20
win through 409.13
stand fast 855.11
be safe 1007.2
weather vane
instrument 317.8
weathercock 318.17
changeableness 854.4
feeler 942.4
weave
n material 4.1
network 170.3
structure 266.1
texture 294.1
weaving 740.1
v loom 740.6
web
n material 4.1
network 170.3
structure 266.1
filament 271.1
presswork 548.9
weaving 740.1
v net 170.7
weave 740.6
web-footed 170.12
weblike 170.12
web of intrigue 381.5
web press 548.9
website 1042.19
Webster's 554.9
wed
v join in marriage 563.14
unite 563.15
relate 775.6
put together 800.5
combine 805.3
league 805.4
adj related 775.9
leagued 805.6
wedding
marriage 563.3
joining 800.1
combination 805.1
wedding anniversary 850.4
wedge
n phonetic symbol
  546.2
v hook 800.8
secure 855.8
get a purchase 906.8
wedlock 563.1
wee 258.11
wee bit 248.2
weed
n marijuana 87.11
plant 310.3
intruder 774.2
v subtract 255.9
cultivate 1069.17
weed out use 87.22
extract 192.10
eliminate 773.5
cultivate 1069.17
week moment 824.2
seven 882.3

weekend
n vacation 20.3
v vacation 20.9
spend time 821.6
weep
n exuding 190.6
v excrete 12.12
fester 12.15
secrete 13.5
grieve 112.17
sob 115.12
exude 190.15
hang 202.6
trickle 238.18
rain 316.10
be damp 1065.11
weepy tearful 115.21
exudative 190.20
weevil 311.37
weigh
weight 297.10
measure 300.10
classify 801.8
have influence 894.10
consider 931.12
compare 943.4
estimate 946.9
matter 997.12
weigh anchor
up-anchor 182.18
embark 188.15
detach 802.10
weigh heavy on
burden 297.13
domineer 612.16
go hard with 1011.8
weigh in
appear 33.8
enter 189.7
weigh 297.10
judge 946.8
weigh in the balance 297.10
weight
n power 18.1
fitness 84.1
affliction 96.8
heaviness 297.1
paperweight 297.6
extent 300.3
prestige 417.4
formality 580.1
charge 643.3
exerciser 725.7
boxer 754.2
influence 894.1
validity 973.6
importance 997.1
impediment 1012.6
v weigh 297.10
pull down 297.12
fill 794.7
weightless 764.5
weight training
exercise 84.2
sport 744.1
weight-watching 270.9
weird
n spell 691.1
fate 964.2
adj awesome 122.11
creepy 127.31

deathly 307.29
sorcerous 690.14
odd 870.11
absurd 923.11
eccentric 927.6
eerie 988.9
weirdo
oddity 870.4
lunatic 926.16
freak 927.4
welcome
n greetings 186.4
reception 187.1
receptivity 187.9
assent 332.1
liberality 485.1
hospitality 585.2
v receive 187.10
assent 332.8
be hospitable 585.9
incur 897.4
adj pleasant 97.6
hospitable 585.12
weld
n joint 800.4
v sculpture 715.5
relate 775.6
put together 800.5
stick together 803.9
burn 1020.24
welder
blowtorch 1020.14
machinery 1040.3
welfare
n kindness 143.5
subsidy 478.8
welfarism 611.7
good 999.4
prosperity 1010.1
adj benevolent 143.15
welfare state
welfare 143.5
relief 611.7
government 612.4
welfare worker 143.8
well
n lake 241.1
depth 275.2
pit 284.4
source of supply 386.4
fountainhead 886.6
v run out 190.13
jet 238.20
adj unailing 83.10
adv ably 18.16
kindly 143.18
successfully 409.15
skillfully 413.31
excellently 999.22
well-advised 920.19
well-balanced
composed 106.13
symmetric 264.4
stable 855.12
sensible 920.18
well-being health 83.1
pleasure 95.1
contentment 107.1
comfort 121.1
good 999.4
prosperity 1010.1

well-bred
highbred 504.17
upper-class 607.10
wellborn 608.11
well-built
able-bodied 15.16
sturdy 763.7
made 892.18
comely 1016.19
well-defined
distinct 31.7
clear 521.11
well-deserving 509.20
well-developed
grown 14.3
expanded 259.12
mature 303.13
well-disposed
well-meaning 143.17
willing 324.5
favorable 449.22
approving 509.17
friendly 587.15
well-educated 928.20
well-established
sturdy 763.7
established 855.13
obvious 970.15
well-fed 257.18
well-known trite 117.9
distinguished 662.16
real 761.15
well-kenned 928.27
well-made
shapely 264.5
sturdy 763.7
made 892.18
comely 1016.19
well-mannered
mannerly 504.16
ceremonious 580.8
well-meaning
well-meant 143.17
favorable 449.22
friendly 587.15
harmless 999.21
well-nigh 223.22
well-off 618.14
well-oiled 88.33
well-prepared 405.16
well-preserved
young 301.9
preserved 397.13
well-proportioned
shapely 264.5
comely 1016.19
well-put 533.7
well-rounded 413.25
well-suited
fitted 405.17
competent 413.24
well-thought-of
respected 155.11
approved 509.19
reputable 662.15
well-to-do 618.14
well-traveled 177.40
well-versed
skilled in 413.27
knowledgeable 928.18
well-informed 928.20

welsh
n recant 363.8
v shirk 368.9
repeal 445.2
not pay 625.6
welt
n sore 85.37
edging 211.7
bulge 283.3
blemish 1004.1
v punish 604.15
welterweight 297.3
wench woman 77.6
girl 302.6
maid 577.8
strumpet 665.14
werewolf
frightener 127.9
monster 593.6
evil spirit 680.12
west
n points of the compass 161.3
adj directional 161.14
adv W 161.18
Western Hemisphere 231.6
wet
n drink 88.7
rain 316.1
weather 316.4
liberal 611.11
moisture 1065.1
v urinate 12.14
moisten 1065.12
adj left 220.4
liberal 611.19
foolish 923.8
fluid 1061.4
moist 1065.15
wetback migrant 178.5
derogatory names 232.7
fugitive 368.5
wet behind the ears
untried 301.10
immature 406.11
inexperienced 414.17
wet blanket
killjoy 112.14
bore 118.4
deterrent 379.2
spoilsport 1012.9
extinguisher 1022.3
wetlands shore 234.2
shoal 276.2
wet-nurse nourish 8.19
foster 449.16
whack
n report 56.1
attempt 403.3
slap 604.3
turn 825.2
hit 902.4
v crack 56.6
slap 604.12
hit 902.14
whale
n largeness 257.11
heavyweight 257.12
behemoth 257.14
marine animal 311.30
v fish 382.10

whip 604.13
punish 604.15
wham
n report 56.1
v crack 56.6
strike 902.15
whammy
n gaze 27.5
malevolence 144.4
curse 513.1
spell 691.1
charm 691.5
bad influence 1000.4
v bring bad luck 1011.12
wharf 1009.6
what 864.6
whatever
n no matter what 864.6
adv any kind 809.9
what goes around comes around 887.9
what goes up must come down 887.9
what's what 761.4
wheat 10.4
wheedle urge 375.14
importune 440.12
flatter 511.5
wheel
n cycle 179.8
circle 280.2
change one's mind 363.6
helm 573.5
torture 605.4
potter's wheel 742.4
automobile racing 756.1
roulette 759.12
round 850.3
propeller 904.6
whirl 915.2
rotator 915.4
important person 997.9
v turn about 163.9
ride 177.33
recur 850.5
circle 914.5
rotate 915.9
whirl 915.11
wheel chair 179.7
wheeler-dealer
man of action 330.8
politics 610.6
influence 894.6
wheel of fortune
gambling wheel 759.16
changeableness 854.4
fate 964.2
Chance 972.2
wheeze
n breathing 2.21
sibilation 57.1
joke 489.6
v burn out 21.5
sibilate 57.2
whelp
n boy 302.5
fledgling 302.10
dog 311.17
beast 660.6
v give birth 1.3
whenever when 821.8

time 821.12
when hell freezes over 822.2
when least expected
unexpectedly 131.14
suddenly 830.9
where 159.21
whereabouts
n location 159.1
adv where 159.21
whereas
n condition 959.2
prep when 821.16
conj because 888.10
whereby 384.12
wherein 207.10
where it's at fact 761.3
state of affairs 765.2
essence 767.3
novelty 841.2
what's what 973.4
salient point 997.6
wherever 159.22
wherewithal
n means 384.2
funds 728.14
adv herewith 384.12
whet
n appetizer 10.9
incentive 375.7
v sensitize 24.7
stimulate 105.13
intensify 251.5
sharpen 285.7
incite 375.17
whew! 122.20
whey 1061.2
whichever
n whatever 864.6
adj every 864.15
while
n time 821.1
period 824.1
meantime 826.2
v spend 387.13
prep when 821.16
while away
spend 387.13
fritter away 486.5
whim caprice 364.1
quirk 927.2
figment of the imagination 986.5
whimper
n lament 115.3
v sigh 52.14
weep 115.12
whine 115.14
whimsical
capricious 364.5
humorous 488.4
witty 489.15
inconstant 854.7
eccentric 927.5
uncertain 971.16
fanciful 986.20
whine
n screech 58.4
lament 115.3
v sigh 52.14
screech 58.8
cry 60.2

whimper 115.14
speak 524.25
nasalize 525.10
whinny 60.2
whiny
discontented 108.7
plaintive 115.19
whip
n driver 178.9
goad 375.8
lash 605.1
legislator 610.3
merry-go-round 743.15
slap 902.8
v best 249.7
foam 320.5
goad 375.15
hasten 401.4
defeat 412.9
give a beating 604.13
pound 902.16
slap 902.19
agitate 917.10
emulsify 1062.10
drive 1070.8
whip into shape
complete 407.6
arrange 808.8
perfect 1002.5
whiplash trauma 85.38
goad 375.8
whip 605.1
whipped cream 10.40
whippersnapper
impudent person 142.5
brat 302.4
a nobody 998.7
whipping boy 862.3
whip up excite 105.12
improvise 365.8
incite 375.17
seize 480.14
agitate 917.10
whir
n rotation 915.1
v hum 52.13
whirl
n agitation 105.4
ride 177.7
eddy 238.12
coil 281.2
bustle 330.4
round of pleasure 743.7
wheel 915.2
v turn around 163.9
move 172.5
eddy 238.21
convolve 281.4
whirligig 915.11
Whirlaway 311.15
whirlpool
n eddy 238.12
whirl 915.2
v rotation 915.11
whirlwind
outburst 105.9
wind 318.14
whirl 915.2
whirlybird 181.5
whisk
n tap 902.7

agitator 917.9
v sweep 79.23
speed 174.9
transport 176.12
foam 320.5
tap 902.18
agitate 917.10
whisker
n bristle 288.3
v grow hair 3.20
whiskey 88.13
whisper
n murmur 52.4
touch 73.1
mumbling 525.4
tip-off 551.3
hint 551.4
report 552.6
v murmur 52.10
sigh 318.21
tell confidentially 345.9
publish 352.10
say 524.22
speak 524.25
mumble 525.9
tip 551.11
adj murmuring 52.18
whistle
n blare 53.5
noisemaker 53.6
sibilation 57.1
screech 58.4
alarm 400.1
call 517.16
v blare 53.10
sibilate 57.2
screech 58.8
bird sound 60.5
exude cheerfulness 109.6
rejoice 116.5
sigh 318.21
sing 708.38
blow a horn 708.42
whistle-stop campaign 609.13
whit 248.2
white
n whiteness 37.1
cocaine 87.7
egg 305.15
v whiten 37.5
whitewash 37.6
adj pure 37.7
clean 79.25
vacant 222.14
aged 303.16
spotless 657.7
chaste 664.4
white-bearded 303.16
whitecap
body of water 238.14
wave 916.4
white-collar crime 655.2
white-collar worker
bourgeois 607.6
worker 726.2
white corpuscle 2.25
white elephant 1012.6
white flag
peace offer 465.2
signal 517.15
race 756.3

white-hot zealous 101.9
fiery 671.22
hot 1019.25
White House 228.5
white knight 460.7
white lie 354.11
white lightning
liquor 88.14
bootleg 88.18
white meat 10.23
white out 35.14
white supremacist 103.4
whitewash
n appearance 33.2
whitening agent 37.4
cleanser 79.17
pretext 376.1
utter defeat 412.3
extenuation 600.5
v color 35.14
whiten 37.5
hide 37.6
scratch the surface 206.6
conceal 346.6
falsify 354.16
acquit 601.4
white water
rapids 238.10
foam 320.2
whittle
n cutlery 1040.2
v form 262.7
sever 802.11
whiz
n sibilation 57.1
skillful person 413.14
first-rate 999.7
v hum 52.13
sibilate 57.2
speed 174.9
whiz kid 413.12
Who's Who 549.9
whoa! 857.13
whoever 864.7
who knows? 930.19
whole
n contents 196.1
quantity 244.1
inclusion 772.1
totality 792.1
all 864.4
sum 1017.6
adj healthy 83.11
comprehensive 772.7
total 792.9
complete 794.9
one 872.7
unqualified 960.2
sound 1002.7
wholehearted 359.11
whole kit and caboodle 792.4
whole nine yards 792.4
whole note 709.14
whole rest 709.21
wholesale
n sale 734.1
v deal in 731.16
sell 734.8
adj commercial 731.22
sales 734.13
thorough 794.10

extensive 864.13
undiscriminating 945.5
plentiful 991.7
adv cheaply 633.10
wholesome
healthful 81.5
sound 83.11
sane 925.4
whomever 864.7
whomp
n report 56.1
slap 604.3
impact 902.3
v crack 56.6
defeat 412.9
slap 604.12
collide 902.13
whoop
n cry 59.1
v cry 59.6
whoop it up
be noisy 53.9
have a party 582.21
make merry 743.24
create disorder 810.11
whoops! 975.22
whoosh
n sibilation 57.1
v sibilate 57.2
whopper
largeness 257.11
monstrous lie 354.12
whore
n flirt 562.11
reprobate 660.4
strumpet 665.14
prostitute 665.16
card 758.2
v be promiscuous 665.19
whorehouse
disapproved place 228.28
brothel 665.9
whorl
n coil 281.2
v convolve 281.4
why
n enigma 522.8
adv whyever 888.8
wick
village 230.2
taper 1026.7
wicked
malicious 144.20
wrong 638.3
evil 654.16
wrongdoing 655.5
ungodly 695.17
bad 1000.7
difficult 1013.17
wicker 170.3
wide
adj spacious 158.11
voluminous 257.17
broad 269.6
phonetic 524.30
extensive 864.13
erroneous 975.16
broad-minded 979.8
adv far and wide 261.16
clear 261.19
wide-angle 269.7

wide-awake
  awake 23.8
  alert 339.14
  clear-witted 920.13
wide berth 430.4
widen grow 251.6
  enlarge 259.4
  expand 259.5
  spread 259.6
  broaden 269.4
  generalize 864.9
wide of the mark
  adj irrelevant 776.7
  erroneous 975.16
  adv wide 261.19
wide open 174.20
wide-ranging
  spacious 158.11
  broad 269.6
  extensive 864.13
  broad-minded 979.8
wide receiver 746.2
widespread
  spacious 158.11
  spread 259.11
  broad 269.6
  customary 373.13
  dispersed 771.9
  extensive 864.13
widget 1052.5
widow
  n survivor 256.3
  widow woman 566.4
  v bereave 307.28
  leave behind 566.6
widow's peak 3.6
widower survivor 256.3
  widow 566.4
width size 257.1
  breadth 269.1
wield touch 73.6
  use 387.10
  wave 916.11
wieldy 1014.15
wiener roast 8.6
Wiener Schnitzel 10.19
wife woman 77.5
  married woman 563.8
wig 3.14
wiggle
  n wriggle 917.7
  v be excited 105.18
  way of walking 177.28
  wriggle 917.14
wig out use 87.22
  get excited 105.17
  lose self-control 128.8
  fly into a rage 152.20
  go mad 926.22
wigwam 228.10
wild
  n wasteland 891.2
  adj overzealous 101.12
  frenzied 105.25
  passionate 105.29
  infuriated 152.32
  hinterland 233.9
  animal 311.40
  defiant 327.10
  ungovernable 361.12
  unrestrained 430.24

  reckless 493.8
  foolhardy 493.9
  unrefined 497.12
  profligate 665.25
  turbulent 671.18
  unruly 671.19
  boisterous 671.20
  savage 671.21
  absurd 923.11
  rabid 926.30
  distracted 985.10
  fanciful 986.20
wild about 101.11
wild animals 311.1
wildcat strike 727.5
wildebeest 311.5
wilderness
  n open space 158.4
  hinterland 233.2
  complex 799.2
  wasteland 891.2
  adj hinterland 233.9
wild-eyed
  frenzied 105.25
  turbulent 671.18
  fanatic 926.32
wildfire 1019.13
wildflower 310.24
wild-goose chase
  lost cause 125.8
  labor in vain 391.3
  abortion 410.5
wild guess 951.4
wildlife 311.1
wildlife preserve 397.7
wild man
  daredevil 493.4
  savage 593.5
wild West 233.2
wiles 415.1
will
  n desire 100.1
  volition 323.1
  resolution 359.1
  will power 359.4
  choice 371.1
  intention 380.1
  command 420.1
  bequest 478.10
  v see fit 323.2
  resolve 359.7
  bequeath 478.18
willful
  disobedient 327.8
  obstinate 361.8
  intentional 380.8
  lawless 418.5
willies 128.2
willing volitional 323.4
  willinghearted 324.5
  obedient 326.3
  trial 403.16
  consenting 441.4
  teachable 570.18
will-o'-the-wisp
  deception 356.1
  illusion 976.1
  mirage 976.6
  fire 1019.13
  luminescence 1025.13
willowy thin 270.16

  folded 291.7
  pliant 1047.9
will power will 323.1
  resolution 359.4
wilt sweat 12.16
  weaken 16.9
  fatigue 21.4
  burn out 21.5
  fail 85.48
  languish 393.18
wily deceitful 356.22
  cunning 415.12
  shrewd 920.15
wimp weakling 16.6
  impotent 19.6
  vacillator 362.5
  coward 491.5
wimpy weak 16.12
  impotent 19.13
  irresolute 362.12
  cowardly 491.10
  uninfluential 895.3
win
  n victory 411.1
  fight 754.3
  v best 249.7
  persuade 375.23
  triumph 411.3
  acquire 472.8
  race 757.5
win back 396.12
win by a nose 411.3
wince
  n retreat 903.3
  v suffer 26.8
  flinch 127.13
  retract 168.3
  demur 325.4
  pull back 903.7
winch
  n windlass 906.7
  v reel in 906.9
wind
  stray 164.4
  change course 182.30
  curve 279.6
  convolve 281.4
  trap 356.20
  prime 405.9
  rotate 915.9
wind
  n breathing 2.21
  swiftness 174.6
  current 318.1
  bull 520.3
  wind instrument 711.6
  belch 909.9
  fart 909.10
  v fatigue 21.4
  blare 53.10
  air 317.11
  blow a horn 708.42
windbag
  braggart 502.5
  chatterer 540.4
windblown 318.24
wind chill 318.8
wind down
  decrease 252.6
  cease to exist 762.6
  turn off 857.12

windfall find 472.6
  good thing 999.5
winding
  deviative 164.7
  convolutional 281.6
wind instrument 711.6
windjammer
  sailboat 180.3
  mariner 183.1
  braggart 502.5
  chatterer 540.4
windmill
  rotor plane 181.5
  automobile racing 756.1
window
  casement 292.7
  radar 1036.13
window dressing
  appearance 33.2
  front 216.1
  sham 354.3
  ornamentation 498.1
window frame
  structure 266.4
  opening 292.7
window of opportunity 843.2
windowpane
  window 292.7
  transparent substance 1029.2
window-shop 733.8
windpipe 2.22
wind power 1021.7
windshield 1008.3
wind sock
  flying and landing guides
    marker 184.19
  weather vane 318.17
windstorm
  high wind 318.12
  storm 671.4
windsurfing 182.11
wind tunnel 239.13
windup
  completion 407.2
  game 745.3
  end 820.1
wind up prime 405.9
  complete 407.6
  end 820.5
  turn off 857.12
  result 887.4
windward
  n windward side 218.3
  adj side 218.6
  adv clockwise 161.24
  leeward 182.68
  side 218.9
windy
  n braggart 502.5
  v talkative 540.9
  adj distended 259.13
  rare 299.4
  blowy 318.22
  inflated 502.12
  wordy 538.12
  bombastic 545.9
  thin 764.6
  trivial 998.19
wine
  n kinds of 88.17
  adj red 41.6

wine cellar
room 197.17
storehouse 386.6
wine cooler 1024.3
**win friends and influence
people** 894.7
wing
n fowl part 10.23
adjunct 254.3
air force 461.29
party 617.4
branch 617.10
scenery 704.20
company 770.3
member 793.4
protectorship 1008.2
v disable 19.9
transport 176.12
fly 184.36
cripple 393.14
make good 409.10
wing it improvise 365.8
do easily 1014.8
wingspan 257.1
win hands down 1014.11
wink
n nap 22.3
glance 27.4
signal 517.15
hint 551.4
instant 830.3
v blink 28.10
signal 517.22
the wink of an eye 828.3
wink of sleep 22.3
winner superior 249.4
man of action 330.8
sure success 409.2
successful person 409.6
victor 411.2
jockey 757.2
good thing 999.5
winning
n victory 411.1
acquisition 472.1
adj delightful 97.7
desirable 100.30
endearing 104.25
alluring 377.8
victorious 411.7
in the money 757.6
speculative 759.27
influential 894.13
winnings
increase 251.3
gain 472.3
winnow
n refinery 79.13
v refine 79.22
air 317.11
select 371.14
segregate 773.6
classify 801.8
discriminate 944.4
wino 88.12
win one's wings
succeed 409.7
triumph 411.3
win over
persuade 375.23
convert 858.16

convince 953.18
seem true 973.9
winsome
delightful 97.7
endearing 104.25
cheerful 109.11
alluring 377.8
Winston Churchill 543.6
winter
n wintertide 313.6
cold weather 1023.3
v summer 313.8
spend time 821.6
adj seasonal 313.9
winter solstice 313.7
wintry seasonal 313.9
cold 1023.14
wipe
n disappearance 34.1
v clean 79.18
dry 1066.6
wipe off the map 395.16
wipeout 34.1
wipe out clean 79.18
excise 255.10
kill 308.14
exterminate 395.14
obliterate 395.16
bankrupt 625.8
declare a moratorium 625.9
annihilate 762.7
end 820.5
wipe up the floor with 604.11
wire
n cord 271.2
telegram 347.14
automobile racing 756.1
end 820.1
electrical device 1032.21
v telegraph 347.20
bind 800.9
electrify 1032.26
wired high 87.24
assured 970.20
wireless
n communications 347.3
radiophone 347.5
radio 1034.1
radio receiver 1034.3
v broadcast 1034.25
adj communicational 347.21
radio 1034.28
wire-puller
schemer 381.7
strategist 415.7
politician 609.30
politics 610.6
influence 894.6
wire service
telegraph 347.2
news 552.1
the press 555.3
wiretap
n surveillance 938.9
v listen 48.10
wiry able-bodied 15.16
threadlike 271.7
tough 1049.4
wisdom
mental grasp 920.1
ripe wisdom 920.5

understanding 928.3
maxim 974.1
expedience 995.1
wisdom tooth 2.8
wise
n aspect 33.3
manner 384.1
adj sage 920.17
learned 928.21
ungullible 956.5
wisecrack
n witticism 489.7
v joke 489.13
wise guy
impudent person 142.6
wiseacre 921.6
wise man
intelligence 920.9
wise woman 921.1
intellectual 929.1
wise to 928.16
wise up 551.9
wish
n desire 100.1
will 323.1
request 440.1
v desire 100.14
request 440.9
wishbone
fowl part 10.23
fork 171.4
wish-bringer 691.6
wishful 100.23
wishful thinking
defense mechanism 92.23
wistfulness 100.4
deception 356.1
credulity 954.1
idealism 986.7
wishing well 691.6
wishy-washy
tasteless 16.17
insipid 65.2
inconstant 854.7
mediocre 1005.7
wisp runt 258.4
bunch 770.7
luminescence 1025.13
wispy frail 16.14
thin 270.16
wistful
wishful 100.23
melancholy 112.23
regretful 113.8
cognitive 931.21
wit
skill 413.1
cunning 415.1
pleasantry 489.1
humor 489.1
humorist 489.12
intelligence 920.1
witch
n bitch 110.12
frightener 127.9
old woman 304.3
hag 593.7
violent person 671.9
sorceress 690.8
eyesore 1015.4
v fascinate 377.7

bewitch 691.9
adj sorcerous 690.14
witchcraft 690.1
witch-hunt
persecution 389.3
investigation 938.4
the witching hour 315.6
with
adv in spite of 338.9
prep at 159.27
plus 253.12
by means of 384.13
in cooperation with 450.8
in company with 769.12
in agreement with 788.12
among 797.17
with abandon 430.32
with a grain of salt
unbelievingly 955.13
conditionally 959.11
with all haste
swiftly 174.17
hastily 401.12
with a straight face
unfeelingly 94.14
solemnly 111.4
with authority 417.18
with a vengeance
powerfully 18.15
extremely 247.22
violently 671.25
utterly 794.16
with bated breath
adj in suspense 130.12
adv in an undertone 52.22
fearfully 127.32
expectantly 130.15
humbly 137.16
secretly 345.17
with care
carefully 339.15
cautiously 494.12
with child 78.18
with difficulty
disadvantageously 996.9
difficultly 1013.28
with dignity
solemnly 111.4
dignifiedly 136.14
with dispatch
quickly 330.26
hastily 401.12
withdraw
n recant 363.8
v use 87.22
retreat 163.6
recede 168.2
retract 168.3
quit 188.9
extract 192.10
subtract 255.9
dissent 333.4
hesitate 362.7
abandon 370.5
repeal 445.2
separate 802.8
stand alone 872.6
withdrawal
substance abuse 87.1
defense mechanism 92.23
unfeeling 94.1

retreat 163.2
recession 168.1
departure 188.1
extraction 192.1
dissent 333.1
reticence 344.3
recantation 363.3
abandonment 370.1
repeal 445.1
resignation 448.1
seclusion 584.1
elimination 773.2
separation 802.1
aloneness 872.2
incuriosity 982.1
with ease 121.14
wither
fail 85.48
decrease 252.6
shrink 260.9
age 303.10
languish 393.18
dry 1066.6
with feeling 93.25
with finesse
skillfully 413.31
discriminatingly 944.9
with flying colors 501.25
with gusto
eagerly 101.13
gaily 109.18
actively 330.25
with haste 401.12
withhold
keep secret 345.7
reserve 386.12
restrain 428.7
deny 442.4
hold back 484.6
abstain 668.7
withholding 442.1
within
adv in 207.10
prep in 207.13
within easy reach 633.7
within range 223.20
within reach
adj present 221.12
cheap 633.7
accessible 966.8
adv near 223.20
within reason
moderately 670.17
reasonably 935.24
with intent 380.10
with interest 983.21
within the realm of possibility
966.6
with it
adj knowledgeable 928.17
adv in step 788.11
with love 104.32
with malice aforethought
malevolently 144.30
intentionally 380.10
with might and main
powerfully 18.15
by force 18.17
laboriously 725.19
with no strings attached
extremely 247.22

completely 794.14
with no time to spare 845.12
with one foot in the grave
stricken in years 303.18
dying 307.33
**with one hand tied behind
 one's back** 1014.16
with one voice
adj unanimous 332.15
adv unanimously 332.17
cooperatively 450.6
in step 788.11
simultaneously 836.7
concurrently 899.5
with open arms
eagerly 101.13
willingly 324.8
hospitably 585.13
amicably 587.22
without
adv externally 206.10
prep absent 222.19
off 255.14
excluding 773.10
minus 992.17
conj unless 959.16
without a break 812.10
without a clue 971.24
without a stitch 6.14
without charge
adj costless 634.5
adv gratuitously 634.6
without contradiction 332.17
without delay
at once 830.8
promptly 845.15
without difficulty 1014.16
without distinction
adj identical 778.7
indistinguishable 945.6
adv justly 649.11
equally 790.11
without doubt
positively 247.19
believingly 953.28
unquestionably 970.25
without end
adj long 267.7
infinite 823.3
perpetual 829.7
innumerable 884.10
adv infinitely 823.4
perpetually 829.10
without equal 249.15
without exception
adj comprehensive
 772.7
unqualified 960.2
adv regularly 781.8
always 829.11
universally 864.18
without fail 970.26
without foundation
unsubstantiated 764.8
baseless 936.13
without further ado
suddenly 830.9
promptly 845.15
without hesitation 324.9
without mercy 146.3
without merit 598.21

without question
willingly 324.8
believingly 953.28
unquestionably 970.25
truly 973.18
without rhyme or reason
adj meaningless 520.6
illogical 936.11
adv capriciously 364.7
without shame 645.16
without warning
adj unexpected 131.10
adv unexpectedly 131.14
suddenly 830.9
with permission 443.19
with pleasure 95.19
with pride 136.13
with purpose 380.10
with regard to 775.13
with relish
eagerly 101.13
willingly 324.8
with respect 443.20
with respect to 775.13
withstand oppose 451.3
resist 453.2
defend 453.3
with taste 496.11
with the exception of
prep off 255.14
excluding 773.10
with the understanding 959.12
with tongue in cheek 489.19
witless
unintelligent 922.13
foolish 923.8
unwise 923.10
insane 926.26
unaware 930.13
scatterbrained 985.16
witness
n certificate 549.6
informant 551.5
litigant 598.11
function of Holy Ghost
 677.15
spectator 918.1
examinee 938.19
testimony 957.2
eyewitness 957.6
v see 27.12
attend 221.8
depose 334.6
be pious 692.6
spectate 918.5
testify 957.9
witness stand 595.6
wits 919.2
witticism
pleasantry 489.7
maxim 974.1
witty humorous 488.4
amusing 489.15
wizard
n master 413.13
sorcerer 690.5
adj excellent 999.13
wizened dwarf 258.13
shrunk 260.13
haggard 270.20
stricken in years 303.18

wasted 393.35
dried 1066.9
wobble
n irregularity 851.1
shake 917.3
v way of walking 177.28
vacillate 362.8
change 854.5
oscillate 916.10
shake 917.11
woe wretchedness 96.6
affliction 96.8
distressfulness 98.5
sorrow 112.10
evil 1000.3
bane 1001.1
wolf
n discord 61.1
fox 311.20
philanderer 562.12
libertine 665.10
violent person 671.9
v gobble 8.23
gluttonize 672.4
wolf at the door 619.2
wolverine 311.23
woman
womankind 77.3
Eve 77.5
adult 304.1
person 312.5
wife 563.8
mistress 665.17
womanizer 665.10
woman of means 618.7
woman of substance 618.7
woman of the world 578.7
womb genitals 2.13
vital force 886.7
women's liberation
liberation 431.1
women's rights 642.4
wonder
n awe 122.1
wonderment 122.1
marvel 122.2
miracle 870.8
first-rater 999.6
v marvel 122.5
not know 930.11
be uncertain 971.9
wonder drug 86.4
wonderful
wondrous 122.10
remarkable 247.10
extraordinary 870.14
superb 999.15
wondrous
adj wonderful 122.10
miraculous 870.16
adv intensely 247.20
wont
n custom 373.1
habit 373.3
v accustom 373.9
be used to 373.11
adj accustomed 373.15
won ton 10.33
woo lure 377.5
solicit 440.14
court 562.21

feel anxious 126.6
trouble 1013.13
worrywart
pessimist 125.7
worrier 126.3
worse aggravated 119.4
impaired 393.27
changed 852.10
the worse for wear
stricken in years 303.18
worn 393.31
dilapidated 393.33
worsen irritate 96.14
aggravate 119.2
get worse 119.3
impair 393.9
deteriorate 393.16
be changed 852.6
change 852.7
worship
n love 104.1
respect 155.1
piety 692.1
reverence 696.1
worshiping 696.1
v cherish 104.21
respect 155.4
adore 696.11
Worship 648.2
worst
v best 249.7
defeat 412.6
adj terrible 1000.9
worst-case
depressing 112.30
hopeless 125.12
worth
n benefit 387.4
assets 471.7
value 630.2
preciousness 632.2
funds 728.14
importance 997.1
goodness 999.1
adj possessing 469.9
priced 630.14
worthless
valueless 391.11
disadvantageous 996.6
paltry 998.21
unworthy 998.22
terrible 1000.9
worthwhile
valuable 387.22
gainful 472.16
expedient 995.5
worthy
n good person 659.1
celebrity 662.9
personage 997.8
adj dignified 136.12
eligible 371.24
competent 413.24
praiseworthy 509.20
precious 632.10
warranted 639.9
honest 644.13
reputable 662.15
would-be
presumptuous 141.10
nominal 527.15

wound
n trauma 85.38
displease 96.5
v pain 26.7
hurt 96.17
offend 152.21
injure 393.13
work evil 1000.6
wound up
completed 407.11
ended 820.8
past 837.7
woven webbed 170.12
loomed 740.7
wow
n audio distortion 50.13
success 409.4
joke 489.6
first-rate 999.7
v delight 95.11
amuse 743.21
wracked 93.23
wraith phantom 976.4
specter 988.1
double 988.3
wrangle
n quarrel 456.5
v quarrel 456.11
argue 935.16
drive 1070.8
wrangler
oppositionist 452.3
combatant 461.1
student 572.7
arguer 935.12
herder 1070.3
wrap
n dishabille 5.20
wrapper 295.18
v clothe 5.39
surround 209.6
enclose 212.5
package 212.9
fold 291.5
enwrap 295.20
bundle 770.20
bind 800.9
end 820.5
wrapped up
completed 407.11
assembled 770.21
wrapped up in
fond of 104.30
involved in 898.5
engrossed 983.17
wrapper
dishabille 5.20
wrapping 295.18
bookbinding 554.14
wrath anger 152.5
revenge 507.1
wrath of God
revenge 507.1
deserts 639.3
wreak havoc
destroy 395.10
rage 671.11
wreath circle 280.2
bouquet 310.25
trophy 646.3
heraldry 647.2

braid 740.2
wreck
n nervousness 128.5
car 179.10
ruins 393.8
destruction 395.1
debacle 395.4
misfortune 1011.2
v disable 19.9
shipwreck 182.42
spoil 393.10
destroy 395.10
demolish 395.17
rage 671.11
wreckage 395.5
wrench
n pang 26.2
trauma 85.38
pain 96.5
extortion 192.6
distortion 265.1
jerk 905.3
tool 1040.1
v pain 26.7
distort 265.5
misinterpret 342.2
misrepresent 350.3
injure 393.13
wrest 480.22
jerk 905.5
wrest
n extortion 192.6
distortion 265.1
v extort 192.15
distort 265.5
wring 480.22
wrestle
n struggle 725.3
v contend 457.13
struggle 725.11
wrestler 461.3
wrestling match 457.10
wretch sufferer 96.11
miserable person 660.2
wretched squalid 80.25
miserable 96.26
distressing 98.20
unhappy 112.21
base 661.12
paltry 998.21
terrible 1000.9
adverse 1011.13
the wretched of the earth
the underprivileged
606.4
unfortunate 1011.7
wriggle
n wiggle 917.7
v be excited 105.18
wiggle 917.14
wring
n extortion 192.6
distortion 265.1
v pain 26.7
torture 96.18
extraction 192.16
distort 265.5
convolve 281.4
wrest 480.22
wringer 192.9
wring one's hands 115.11

wrinkle
n extra 254.4
furrow 290.1
corrugation 291.3
fad 578.5
v contract 260.7
ruffle 288.5
furrow 290.3
corrugate 291.6
age 303.10
languish 393.18
wrist member 2.7
joint 800.4
arm 906.5
wristband circle 280.3
jewel 498.6
writ document 549.5
summons 598.2
write represent 349.8
describe 349.9
pen 547.19
author 547.21
record 549.15
correspond 553.10
compose 708.46
create 718.6
produce 892.8
write-in vote 371.6
write off forget 148.5
excise 255.10
give up 370.7
discard 390.7
repeal 445.2
declare a moratorium 625.9
keep accounts 628.8
discount 631.2
write-off excision 255.3
repeal 445.1
moratorium 625.2
tax 630.9
discount 631.1
writer penman 547.13
recorder 547.15
correspondent 553.8
discourser 556.3
scribbler 718.3
author 718.4
narrator 722.5
writer's cramp 547.2
writhe
n wiggle 917.7
v pain 26.8
suffer 96.19
be excited 105.18
distort 265.5
wiggle 917.14
writing
representation 349.1
letter 546.1
composition 547.2
scrivening 547.1
authorship 547.2
document 549.5
book 554.1
elementary education
568.5
literature 718.2
the written word 547.10
wrong
impropriety 638.1
injustice 650.1

crime 650.4
iniquity 654.3
misdeed 655.2
offense 674.4
error 975.1
evil 1000.3
v do one an injustice 650.7
work evil 1000.6
adj wrongful 638.3
unjust 650.9
wicked 654.16
wrongdoing 655.5
untimely 844.6
erroneous 975.16
mistaken 975.18
inexpedient 996.5
bad 1000.7
adv wrongly 638.4
erroneously 975.20
badly 1000.13
wrongheaded
perverse 361.11
stupid 922.15
wrong number 660.4
wrought 407.10
wrung pained 26.9
tortured 96.25
wry 204.14
wunderkind 413.12
X cross 170.4
signature 527.10
motion pictures 706.1
ten 882.6
X chromosome
chromosome 305.8
heredity 560.6
xenophobia
exclusiveness 773.3
discrimination 980.4
Xerox
n print 714.5
copy 785.5
v copy 785.8
x marks the spot 159.29
X-rated 665.29
X ray diagnosis 91.9
shadowgraph 714.6
ray 1025.5
yacht
n sailboat 180.3
v navigate 182.13
yachtsman 183.1
yahoo vulgarian 497.6
stupid person 924.2
yak
n cattle 311.6
chatter 540.3
v speak 524.20
chatter 540.5
yakkety-yak
n speech 524.1
chatter 540.3
v speak 524.20
chatter 540.5
yank
n pulling 905.3
v jerk 905.5
Yank 461.7
Yankee
regional 227.11
dialect 523.7

revolutionist 860.3
yard
n enclosed place 212.3
money 728.7
plant 739.3
thousand 882.10
supporter 901.2
v enclose 212.5
yardage
length 267.1
game 746.3
yardarm 901.2
yardstick 300.2
yarn cord 271.2
lie 354.11
joke 489.6
tale 719.3
story 722.3
yaw
n deviation 164.1
v drift off course 182.29
change course 182.30
pitch 182.55
maneuver 184.40
yawn
n opening 292.1
gaping 292.2
v gape 292.16
Y chromosome
chromosome 305.8
heredity 560.6
yea
n affirmative 332.2
vote 371.6
consent 441.1
approval 509.1
side 935.14
adv chiefly 249.17
thus 766.10
interj yes 332.18
year class 572.11
moment 824.2
yearbook report 549.7
record book 549.11
periodical 555.1
year in year out
regularly 781.8
continuously 812.10
for a long time 827.14
constantly 847.7
repeatedly 849.16
yearling infant 302.9
cattle 311.6
jockey 757.2
yeast 852.5
yell
n cry 59.1
cheer 116.2
v cry 59.6
wail 115.13
cheer 116.6
speak 524.25
yellow
n color 43.1
LSD 87.10
egg 305.15
v turn yellow 43.3
adj jaundiced 43.4
sensational 105.32
jealous 153.5
cowardly 491.10

yellow-belly 491.5
yellow jacket 311.35
yellow journalism 93.9
Yellow Pages 574.10
yelp
n cry 59.1
v cry 59.6
wail 60.2
complain 115.15
speak 524.25
yen yearning 100.5
tendency 896.1
yeoman hand 183.6
retainer 577.1
attendant 577.5
bodyguard 1008.14
agriculturist 1069.5
yes
n affirmative 332.2
vote 371.6
side 935.14
v assent 332.8
adv consentingly 441.5
interj yea 332.18
yes-man flatterer 138.4
inferior 250.2
assenter 332.6
follower 616.8
conformist 867.2
yesterday
n the past 837.1
adv formerly 837.13
yet
additionally 253.11
notwithstanding
338.8
previously 834.6
until now 838.4
yield
n output 472.5
receipts 627.1
dividend 738.7
production 893.2
v weaken 16.9
acknowledge 332.11
hesitate 362.7
give up 370.7
provide 385.7
cede 433.7
compromise 468.2
relinquish 475.3
allow 478.12
bring in 627.4
conform 867.3
bear 892.13
soften 1047.7
stretch 1048.5
yield the floor 613.10
yo! hark! 48.16
greeting 585.16
hey! 983.23
yodel
n vocal music 708.13
v sing 708.38
yodeler 710.13
yoga occultism 689.1
exercise 725.6
yogi ascetic 667.2
occultist 689.11
clergy 699.13
yogurt 67.2

yoke
n shackle 428.4
two 873.2
v put together 800.5
hitch up 800.10
combine 805.3
league 805.4
double 873.5
tend 1070.7
yokel
n bungler 414.8
simple soul 416.3
vulgarian 497.6
peasant 606.6
oaf 924.5
adj not urbane 233.8
yolk 305.15
Yom Kippur
fast day 515.3
penance 658.3
yonder
adj thither 261.10
adv yon 261.13
yore 837.2
you 865.5
young
n young people 302.2
adj youngling 301.9
new 841.7
youngster
young person 302.1
adolescent 302.1
yourself 865.5
yours truly 865.5
youth early years 301.1
youthhead 301.1
youngster 302.1
young people 302.2
boy 302.5
origin 818.4
memory 837.4
yowl
n cry 59.1
lament 115.3
v cry 59.6
yelp 60.2
wail 115.13
yo-yo 924.3
Y-shaped forked 171.10
angular 278.6
yucca 285.5
yuck 116.4
yucky 99.7
the Yukon 1023.4
yummy tasty 63.8
delightful 97.8
yuppie 867.2
zany humorist 489.12
buffoon 707.10
fool 924.1
zap kill 308.14
do for 395.11
annihilate 762.7
end 820.5
zeal vim 17.2
passion 93.2
ardor 101.2
anxiety 126.1
willingness 324.1
turbulence 671.2
zealousness 692.3

cause 886.9
interest 983.2
zealot
enthusiast 101.4
believer 692.4
oddity 870.4
fanatic 926.18
zebra variegation 47.6
crossing 170.2
game 746.3
Zen Buddhism 675.14
zenith summit 198.2
supremacy 249.3
height 272.2
zephyr breeze 318.5
softness 1047.4
zeppelin 181.11
zero
roulette 759.12
nothing 762.2
thing of naught 764.2
temperature 1019.3
zero hour
time of attack 459.13

crucial moment 843.5
zero in 798.4
zero option
dilemma 371.3
restriction 428.3
choicelessness 963.6
zero-sum
compensating 338.6
equal 790.7
neutralizing 900.9
zest
animation 17.4
savor 63.2
zestfulness 68.2
pleasure 95.1
eagerness 101.1
gaiety 109.4
Zeus 316.6
zigzag
n deviation 164.1
zig 204.8
angle 278.2
avoidance 368.1
v deflect 164.5

zig 204.12
angle 278.5
alternate 916.13
adj deviative 164.7
crooked 204.20
angular 278.6
zilch 762.3
zip
n energy 17.3
sibilation 57.1
zest 68.2
gaiety 109.4
address 553.9
nothing 762.3
v sibilate 57.2
speed 174.9
zip code 553.9
zipper
close 293.6
hook 800.8
ziti 10.33
zodiac
circle 280.3
orbit 1072.16

astrology 1072.20
zombie 988.1
zone
n region 231.1
climate 231.3
circle 280.3
layer 296.1
address 553.9
middle 819.1
orbit 1072.16
v encircle 209.7
apportion 802.18
zoning law 444.1
zoo menagerie 228.19
collection 770.11
zoological
animal 311.40
biological 1068.4
zoologist 1068.2
zoom
n maneuvers 184.13
v speed 174.8
ascend 184.39
take off 193.10